POKÉMON SWORD

POKÉ... SHIELD

D0129380

The Official Galar Region Pokédex

Pokémon Lists

The list below includes all the species you must collect to complete the Galar Pokédex in *Pokémon Sword* or *Pokémon Shield*. They are listed here in Pokédex order, together with page references that will lead you to the Pokédex entry and move table pages for each Pokémon. If a species has multiple forms that can be caught or otherwise obtained in these games, they'll also be shown here. But don't worry about obtaining every last form for each Pokémon—just one will be enough to register that species in your Pokédex!

	Pokédex Number	Name	Pokédex Entry	Move Tables
✓	001	Grookey	p. 24	p. 189
✓	002	Thwackey	p. 24	p. 189
✓	003	Rillaboom	p. 24	p. 190
✓	004	Scorbunny	p. 25	p. 190
✓	005	Raboot	p. 25	p. 191
✓	006	Cinderace	p. 25	p. 191
✓	007	Sobble	p. 26	p. 192
✓	008	Drizzile	p. 26	p. 192
✓	009	Inteleon	p. 26	p. 193
✓	010	Blipbug	p. 27	p. 193
✓	011	Dottler	p. 27	p. 194
✓	012	Orbeetle	p. 27	p. 194
✓	013	Caterpie	p. 28	p. 195
✓	014	Metapod	p. 28	p. 195
✓	015	Butterfree	p. 28	p. 196
✓	016	Grubbin	p. 29	p. 196
✓	017	Charjabug	p. 29	p. 197
✓	018	Vikavolt	p. 29	p. 197
✓	019	Hoothoot	p. 30	p. 198
✓	020	Noctowl	p. 30	p. 198
✓	021	Rookidee	p. 31	p. 199
✓	022	Corvisquire	p. 31	p. 199
✓	023	Corviknight	p. 31	p. 200
✓	024	Skwovet	p. 32	p. 200
✓	025	Greedent	p. 32	p. 201
✓	026	Pidove	p. 33	p. 201
✓	027	Tranquill	p. 33	p. 202
✓	028	Unfezant	p. 33	p. 202
✓	029	Nickit	p. 34	p. 203
✓	030	Thievul	p. 34	p. 203
✓	031	Zigzagoon	p. 35	p. 204
✓	032	Linoone	p. 35	p. 204
✓	033	Obstagoon	p. 35	p. 205
✓	034	Wooloo	p. 36	p. 205
✓	035	Dubwool	p. 36	p. 206

	Pokédex Number	Name	Pokédex Entry	Move Tables
✓	036	Lotad	p. 37	p. 206
✓	037	Lombre	p. 37	p. 207
✓	038	Ludicolo	p. 37	p. 207
✓	039	Seedot	p. 38	p. 208
✓	040	Nuzleaf	p. 38	p. 208
✓	041	Shiftry	p. 38	p. 209
✓	042	Chewtle	p. 39	p. 209
✓	043	Drednaw	p. 39	p. 210
✓	044	Purrloin	p. 40	p. 210
✓	045	Liepard	p. 40	p. 211
✓	046	Yamper	p. 40	p. 211
✓	047	Boltund	p. 40	p. 212
✓	048	Bunnelby	p. 41	p. 212
✓	049	Diggersby	p. 41	p. 213
✓	050	Minccino	p. 41	p. 213
✓	051	Cinccino	p. 41	p. 214
✓	052	Bounsweet	p. 42	p. 214
✓	053	Steenee	p. 42	p. 215
✓	054	Tsareena	p. 42	p. 215
✓	055	Oddish	p. 43	p. 216
✓	056	Gloom	p. 43	p. 216
✓	057	Vileplume	p. 43	p. 217
✓	058	Bellossom	p. 43	p. 217
✓	059	Budew	p. 44	p. 218
✓	060	Roselia	p. 44	p. 218
✓	061	Roserade	p. 44	p. 219
✓	062	Wingull	p. 45	p. 219
✓	063	Pelipper	p. 45	p. 220
✓	064	Joltik	p. 46	p. 220
✓	065	Galvantula	p. 46	p. 221
✓	066	Electrike	p. 46	p. 221
✓	067	Manectric	p. 46	p. 222
✓	068	Vulpix	p. 47	p. 222
✓	069	Ninetales	p. 47	p. 223
✓	070	Growlithe	p. 47	p. 223

	Pokédex Number	Name	Pokédex Entry	Move Tables
✓	071	Arcanine	p. 47	p. 224
✓	072	Vanillite	p. 48	p. 224
✓	073	Vanillish	p. 48	p. 225
✓	074	Vanilluxe	p. 48	p. 225
✓	075	Swinub	p. 49	p. 226
✓	076	Piloswine	p. 49	p. 226
✓	077	Mamoswine	p. 49	p. 227
✓	078	Delibird	p. 50	p. 227
✓	079	Snorunt	p. 50	p. 228
✓	080	Glalie	p. 50	p. 228
✓	081	Froslass	p. 50	p. 229
✓	082	Baltoy	p. 51	p. 229
✓	083	Claydol	p. 51	p. 230
✓	084	Mudbray	p. 51	p. 230
✓	085	Mudsdale	p. 51	p. 231
✓	086	Dwebble	p. 52	p. 231
✓	087	Crustle	p. 52	p. 232
✓	088	Golett	p. 52	p. 232
✓	089	Golurk	p. 52	p. 233
✓	090	Munna	p. 53	p. 233
✓	091	Musharna	p. 53	p. 234
✓	092	Natu	p. 53	p. 234
✓	093	Xatu	p. 53	p. 235
✓	094	Stufful	p. 54	p. 235
✓	095	Bewear	p. 54	p. 236
✓	096	Snover	p. 55	p. 236
✓	097	Abomasnow	p. 55	p. 237
✓	098	Krabby	p. 56	p. 237
✓	099	Kingler	p. 56	p. 238
✓	100	Wooper	p. 56	p. 238
✓	101	Quagsire	p. 56	p. 239
✓	102	Corphish	p. 57	p. 239
✓	103	Crawdaunt	p. 57	p. 240
✓	104	Nincada	p. 58	p. 240
✓	105	Ninjask	p. 58	p. 241

	Pokédex Number	Name	Pokédex Entry	Move Tables
✓	106	Shedinja	p. 58	p. 241
✓	107	Tyrogue	p. 59	p. 242
✓	108	Hitmonlee	p. 59	p. 242
✓	109	Hitmonchan	p. 59	p. 243
✓	110	Hitmontop	p. 59	p. 243
✓	111	Pancham	p. 60	p. 244
✓	112	Pangoro	p. 60	p. 244
✓	113	Klink	p. 61	p. 245
✓	114	Klang	p. 61	p. 245
✓	115	Klinklang	p. 61	p. 246
✓	116	Combee	p. 62	p. 246
✓	117	Vespiquen	p. 62	p. 247
✓	118	Bronzor	p. 63	p. 247
✓	119	Bronzong	p. 63	p. 248
✓	120	Ralts	p. 64	p. 248
✓	121	Kirlia	p. 64	p. 249
✓	122	Gardevoir	p. 64	p. 249
✓	123	Gallade	p. 64	p. 250
✓	124	Drifloon	p. 65	p. 250
✓	125	Drifblim	p. 65	p. 251
✓	126	Gossifleur	p. 65	p. 251
✓	127	Eldegoss	p. 65	p. 252
✓	128	Cherubi	p. 66	p. 252
✓	129	Cherrim	p. 66	p. 253
✓	130	Stunky	p. 67	p. 253
✓	131	Skuntank	p. 67	p. 254
✓	132	Tympole	p. 68	p. 254
✓	133	Palpitoad	p. 68	p. 255
✓	134	Seismitoad	p. 68	p. 255
✓	135	Duskull	p. 69	p. 256
✓	136	Dusclops	p. 69	p. 256
✓	137	Dusknoir	p. 69	p. 257
✓	138	Machop	p. 70	p. 257
✓	139	Machoke	p. 70	p. 258
✓	140	Machamp	p. 70	p. 258
✓	141	Gastly	p. 71	p. 259
✓	142	Haunter	p. 71	p. 259
✓	143	Gengar	p. 71	p. 260
✓	144	Magikarp	p. 72	p. 260
✓	145	Gyarados	p. 72	p. 261
✓	146	Goldeen	p. 73	p. 261
✓	147	Seaking	p. 73	p. 262

	Pokédex Number	Name	Pokédex Entry	Move Tables
✓	148	Remoraid	p. 73	p. 262
✓	149	Octillery	p. 73	p. 263
✓	150	Shellder	p. 74	p. 263
✓	151	Cloyster	p. 74	p. 264
✓	152	Feebas	p. 75	p. 264
✓	153	Milotic	p. 75	p. 265
✓	154	Basculin	p. 75	p. 265–266
✓	155	Wishiwashi	p. 76	p. 266
✓	156	Pyukumuku	p. 76	p. 267
✓	157	Trubbish	p. 77	p. 267
✓	158	Garbodor	p. 77	p. 268
✓	159	Sizzlipede	p. 77	p. 268
✓	160	Centiskorch	p. 77	p. 269
✓	161	Rolycoly	p. 78	p. 269
✓	162	Carkol	p. 78	p. 270
✓	163	Coalossal	p. 78	p. 270
✓	164	Diglett	p. 79	p. 271
✓	165	Dugtrio	p. 79	p. 271
✓	166	Drilbur	p. 79	p. 272
✓	167	Excadrill	p. 79	p. 272
✓	168	Roggenrola	p. 80	p. 273
✓	169	Boldore	p. 80	p. 273
✓	170	Gigalith	p. 80	p. 274
✓	171	Timburr	p. 81	p. 274
✓	172	Gurdurr	p. 81	p. 275
✓	173	Conkeldurr	p. 81	p. 275
✓	174	Woobat	p. 82	p. 276
✓	175	Swoobat	p. 82	p. 276
✓	176	Noibat	p. 82	p. 277
✓	177	Noivern	p. 82	p. 277
✓	178	Onix	p. 83	p. 278
✓	179	Steelix	p. 83	p. 278
✓	180	Arrokuda	p. 84	p. 279
✓	181	Barraskewda	p. 84	p. 279
✓	182	Meowth	p. 85	p. 280
✓	183	Perrserker	p. 85	p. 281
✓	184	Persian	p. 85	p. 281
✓	185	Milcery	p. 86	p. 282
✓	186	Alcremie	p. 86	p. 282
✓	187	Cutiefly	p. 87	p. 283
✓	188	Ribombee	p. 87	p. 283

	Pokédex Number	Name	Pokédex Entry	Move Tables
✓	189	Ferroseed	p. 87	p. 284
✓	190	Ferrothorn	p. 87	p. 284
✓	191	Pumpkaboo	p. 88	p. 285
✓	192	Gourgeist	p. 88	p. 285
✓	193	Pichu	p. 89	p. 286
✓	194	Pikachu	p. 89	p. 286
✓	195	Raichu	p. 89	p. 287
✓	196	Eevee	p. 90	p. 287
✓	197	Vaporeon	p. 91	p. 288
✓	198	Jolteon	p. 91	p. 288
✓	199	Flareon	p. 91	p. 289
✓	200	Espeon	p. 91	p. 289
✓	201	Umbreon	p. 92	p. 290
✓	202	Leafeon	p. 92	p. 290
✓	203	Glaceon	p. 92	p. 291
✓	204	Sylveon	p. 92	p. 291
✓	205	Applin	p. 93	p. 292
✓	206	Flapple	p. 93	p. 292
✓	207	Appletun	p. 93	p. 293
✓	208	Espurr	p. 94	p. 293
✓	209	Meowstic	p. 94	p. 294
✓	210	Swirlix	p. 95	p. 295
✓	211	Slurpuff	p. 95	p. 295
✓	212	Spritzee	p. 95	p. 296
✓	213	Aromatisse	p. 95	p. 296
✓	214	Dewpider	p. 96	p. 297
✓	215	Araquanid	p. 96	p. 297
✓	216	Wynaut	p. 96	p. 298
✓	217	Wobbuffet	p. 96	p. 298
✓	218	Farfetch'd	p. 97	p. 299
✓	219	Sirfetch'd	p. 97	p. 299
✓	220	Chinchou	p. 97	p. 300
✓	221	Lanturn	p. 97	p. 300
✓	222	Croagunk	p. 98	p. 301
✓	223	Toxicroak	p. 98	p. 301
✓	224	Scraggy	p. 98	p. 302
✓	225	Scrafty	p. 98	p. 302
✓	226	Stunfisk	p. 99	p. 303
✓	227	Shuckle	p. 99	p. 303
✓	228	Barboach	p. 99	p. 304
✓	229	Whiscash	p. 99	p. 304
✓	230	Shellos	p. 100	p. 305

Pokédex Number	Name	Pokédex Entry	Move Tables
231	Gastrodon	p. 100	p. 305
232	Wimpod	p. 101	p. 306
233	Golisopod	p. 101	p. 306
234	Binacle	p. 102	p. 307
235	Barbaracle	p. 102	p. 307
236	Corsola	p. 102	p. 308
237	Cursola	p. 102	p. 308
238	Impidimp	p. 103	p. 309
239	Morgrem	p. 103	p. 309
240	Grimmsnarl	p. 103	p. 310
241	Hatenna	p. 104	p. 310
242	Hattrem	p. 104	p. 311
243	Hatterene	p. 104	p. 311
244	Salandit	p. 105	p. 312
245	Salazzle	p. 105	p. 312
246	Pawniard	p. 105	p. 313
247	Bisharp	p. 105	p. 313
248	Throh	p. 106	p. 314
249	Sawk	p. 106	p. 314
250	Koffing	p. 107	p. 315
251	Weezing	p. 107	p. 315
252	Bonsly	p. 107	p. 316
253	Sudowoodo	p. 107	p. 316
254	Cleffa	p. 108	p. 317
255	Clefairy	p. 108	p. 317
256	Clefable	p. 108	p. 318
257	Togepi	p. 109	p. 318
258	Togetic	p. 109	p. 319
259	Togekiss	p. 109	p. 319
260	Munchlax	p. 110	p. 320
261	Snorlax	p. 110	p. 320
262	Cottonee	p. 110	p. 321
263	Whimsicott	p. 110	p. 321
264	Rhyhorn	p. 111	p. 322
265	Rhydon	p. 111	p. 322
266	Rhyperior	p. 111	p. 323
267	Gothita	p. 112	p. 323
268	Gothorita	p. 112	p. 324
269	Gothitelle	p. 112	p. 324
270	Solosis	p. 113	p. 325
271	Duosion	p. 113	p. 325
272	Reuniclus	p. 113	p. 326

Pokédex Number	Name	Pokédex Entry	Move Tables
273	Karrablast	p. 114	p. 326
274	Escavalier	p. 114	p. 327
275	Shelmet	p. 114	p. 327
276	Accelgor	p. 114	p. 328
277	Elgyem	p. 115	p. 328
278	Beheeyem	p. 115	p. 329
279	Cubchoo	p. 115	p. 329
280	Beartic	p. 115	p. 330
281	Rufflet	p. 116	p. 330
282	Braviary	p. 116	p. 331
283	Vullaby	p. 116	p. 331
284	Mandibuzz	p. 116	p. 332
285	Skorupi	p. 117	p. 332
286	Drapion	p. 117	p. 333
287	Litwick	p. 118	p. 333
288	Lampent	p. 118	p. 334
289	Chandelure	p. 118	p. 334
290	Inkay	p. 119	p. 335
291	Malamar	p. 119	p. 335
292	Sneasel	p. 119	p. 336
293	Weavile	p. 119	p. 336
294	Sableye	p. 120	p. 337
295	Mawile	p. 120	p. 337
296	Maractus	p. 120	p. 338
297	Sigilyph	p. 121	p. 338
298	Riolu	p. 121	p. 339
299	Lucario	p. 121	p. 339
300	Torkoal	p. 122	p. 340
301	Mimikyu	p. 122	p. 340
302	Cufant	p. 123	p. 341
303	Copperajah	p. 123	p. 341
304	Qwilfish	p. 123	p. 342
305	Frillish	p. 124	p. 342
306	Jellicent	p. 124	p. 343
307	Mareanie	p. 125	p. 343
308	Toxapex	p. 125	p. 344
309	Cramorant	p. 125	p. 344
310	Toxel	p. 126	p. 345
311	Toxtricity	p. 126	p. 345 –346
312	Silicobra	p. 127	p. 346
313	Sandaconda	p. 127	p. 347
314	Hippopotas	p. 127	p. 347

Pokédex Number	Name	Pokédex Entry	Move Tables
315	Hippowdon	p. 127	p. 348
316	Durant	p. 128	p. 348
317	Heatmor	p. 128	p. 349
318	Helioptile	p. 128	p. 349
319	Heliolisk	p. 128	p. 350
320	Hawlucha	p. 129	p. 350
321	Trapinch	p. 129	p. 351
322	Vibrava	p. 129	p. 351
323	Flygon	p. 129	p. 352
324	Axew	p. 130	p. 352
325	Fraxure	p. 130	p. 353
326	Haxorus	p. 130	p. 353
327	Yamask	p. 131	p. 354
328	Runerigus	p. 131	p. 355
329	Cofagrigus	p. 131	p. 355
330	Honedge	p. 132	p. 356
331	Doublade	p. 132	p. 356
332	Aegislash	p. 132	p. 357
333	Ponyta	p. 133	p. 357
334	Rapidash	p. 133	p. 358
335	Sinistea	p. 134	p. 358
336	Polteageist	p. 134	p. 359
337	Indeedee	p. 135	p. 359 –360
338	Phantump	p. 136	p. 360
339	Trevenant	p. 136	p. 361
340	Morelull	p. 136	p. 361
341	Shiinotic	p. 136	p. 362
342	Oranguru	p. 137	p. 362
343	Passimian	p. 137	p. 363
344	Morpeko	p. 138	p. 363
345	Falinks	p. 138	p. 364
346	Drampa	p. 139	p. 364
347	Turtonator	p. 139	p. 365
348	Togedemaru	p. 139	p. 365
349	Snom	p. 140	p. 366
350	Frosmoth	p. 140	p. 366
351	Clobbopus	p. 140	p. 367
352	Grapploct	p. 140	p. 367
353	Pincurchin	p. 141	p. 368
354	Mantyke	p. 141	p. 368
355	Mantine	p. 141	p. 369
356	Wailmer	p. 142	p. 369

	Pokédex Number	Name	Pokédex Entry	Move Tables
✓	357	Wailord	p. 142	p. 370
✓	358	Bergmite	p. 143	p. 370
✓	359	Avalugg	p. 143	p. 371
✓	360	Dhelmise	p. 143	p. 371
✓	361	Lapras	p. 144	p. 372
✓	362	Lunatone	p. 144	p. 372
✓	363	Solrock	p. 144	p. 373
✓	364	Mime Jr.	p. 145	p. 373
✓	365	Mr. Mime	p. 145	p. 374
✓	366	Mr. Rime	p. 145	p. 375
✓	367	Darumaka	p. 146	p. 375
✓	368	Darmanitan	p. 146	p. 376
✓	369	Stonjourner	p. 147	p. 376
✓	370	Eiscue	p. 147	p. 377
✓	371	Duraludon	p. 148	p. 377

	Pokédex Number	Name	Pokédex Entry	Move Tables
✓	372	Rotom	p. 148	p. 378
✓	373	Ditto	p. 149	p. 378
✓	374	Dracozolt	p. 149	p. 379
✓	375	Arctozolt	p. 149	p. 379
✓	376	Dracovish	p. 150	p. 380
✓	377	Arctovish	p. 150	p. 380
✓	378	Charmander	p. 151	p. 381
✓	379	Charmeleon	p. 151	p. 381
✓	380	Charizard	p. 151	p. 382
✓	381	Type: Null	p. 152	p. 382
✓	382	Silvally	p. 152	p. 383
✓	383	Larvitar	p. 153	p. 383
✓	384	Pupitar	p. 153	p. 384
✓	385	Tyranitar	p. 153	p. 384

	Pokédex Number	Name	Pokédex Entry	Move Tables
✓	386	Deino	p. 154	p. 385
✓	387	Zweilous	p. 154	p. 385
✓	388	Hydreigon	p. 154	p. 386
✓	389	Goomy	p. 155	p. 386
✓	390	Sliggoo	p. 155	p. 387
✓	391	Goodra	p. 155	p. 387
✓	392	Jangmo-o	p. 156	p. 388
✓	393	Hakamo-o	p. 156	p. 388
✓	394	Kommo-o	p. 156	p. 389
✓	395	Dreepy	p. 157	p. 389
✓	396	Drakloak	p. 157	p. 390
✓	397	Dragapult	p. 157	p. 390
✓	398	Zacian	p. 158	p. 391
✓	399	Zamazenta	p. 159	p. 391
✓	400	Eternatus	p. 160	p. 392

Alphabetical List

Looking for a particular Pokémon by name? Here is an alphabetical list of the Pokémon in the Galar Pokédex so that you can zip right to the page you're looking for.

No.	Name	No.	Name	No.	Name	No.	Name	No.	Name	No.	Name	No.	Name
097	Abomasnow	010	Blipbug	256	Clefable	078	Delibird	137	Dusknoir	065	Galvantula	016	Grubbin
276	Accelgor	169	Boldore	255	Clefairy	214	Dewpider	135	Duskull	158	Garbodor	172	Gurdurr
332	Aegislash	047	Boltund	254	Cleffa	360	Dhelmise	086	Dwebble	122	Gardevoir	145	Gyarados
186	Alcremie	252	Bonsly	351	Clobbopus	049	Diggersby	196	Eevee	141	Gastly	393	Hakamo-o
207	Appletun	052	Bounsweet	151	Cloyster	164	Diglett	370	Eiscue	231	Gastrodon	241	Hatenna
205	Applin	282	Braviary	163	Coalossal	373	Ditto	127	Eldegoss	143	Gengar	243	Hatterene
215	Araquanid	119	Bronzong	329	Cofagrigus	011	Dottler	066	Electrike	170	Gigalith	242	Hattrem
071	Arcanine	118	Bronzor	116	Combee	331	Doublade	277	Elgyem	203	Glaceon	142	Haunter
377	Arctovish	059	Budew	173	Conkeldurr	376	Dracovish	274	Escavalier	080	Glalie	320	Hawlucha
375	Arctozolt	048	Bunnelby	303	Copperajah	374	Dracozolt	200	Espeon	056	Gloom	326	Haxorus
213	Aromatisse	015	Butterfree	102	Corphish	397	Dragapult	208	Espurr	146	Goldeen	317	Heatmor
180	Arrokuda	162	Carkol	236	Corsola	396	Drakloak	400	Eternatus	088	Golett	319	Heliolisk
359	Avalugg	013	Caterpie	023	Corviknight	346	Drampa	167	Excadrill	233	Golisopod	318	Helioptile
324	Axew	160	Centiskorch	022	Corvisquire	286	Drapion	345	Falinks	089	Golurk	314	Hippopotas
082	Baltoy	289	Chandelure	262	Cottonee	043	Drednaw	218	Farfetch'd	391	Goodra	315	Hippowdon
235	Barbaracle	380	Charizard	309	Cramorant	395	Dreepy	152	Feebas	389	Goomy	109	Hitmonchan
228	Barboach	017	Charjabug	103	Crawdaunt	286	Drapion	189	Ferroseed	126	Gossifleur	108	Hitmonlee
181	Barraskewda	378	Charmander	222	Croagunk	124	Drifloon	190	Ferrothorn	267	Gothita	110	Hitmontop
154	Basculin	379	Charmeleon	087	Crustle	166	Drilbur	206	Flapple	269	Gothitelle	330	Honedge
280	Beartic	129	Cherrim	279	Cubchoo	008	Drizzile	199	Flareon	268	Gothorita	019	Hoothoot
278	Beheeyem	128	Cherubi	302	Cufant	035	Dubwool	323	Flygon	192	Gourgeist	388	Hydreigon
058	Bellossom	042	Chewtle	237	Cursola	165	Dugtrio	325	Fraxure	352	Grapploct	238	Impidimp
358	Bergmite	220	Chinchou	187	Cutiefly	271	Duosion	305	Frillish	025	Greedent	337	Indeedee
095	Bewear	051	Cinccino	368	Darmanitan	371	Duraludon	081	Froslass	240	Grimmsnarl	290	Inkay
234	Binacle	006	Cinderace	367	Darumaka	316	Durant	350	Frosmoth	001	Grookey	009	Inteleon
247	Bisharp	083	Claydol	386	Deino	136	Dusclops	123	Gallade	070	Growlithe	392	Jangmo-o

No.	Name	No.	Name	No.	Name	No.	Name	No.	Name	No.	Name	No.	Name
306	Jellicent	067	Manectric	040	Nuzleaf	334	Rapidash	041	Shiftry	175	Swoobat	322	Vibrava
198	Jolteon	355	Mantine	033	Obstagoon	148	Remoraid	341	Shiinotic	204	Sylveon	018	Vikavolt
064	Joltik	354	Mantyke	149	Octillery	272	Reuniclus	227	Shuckle	030	Thievul	057	Vileplume
273	Karrablast	296	Maractus	055	Oddish	265	Rhydon	297	Sigilyph	248	Throh	283	Vullaby
099	Kingler	307	Mareanie	178	Onix	264	Rhyhorn	312	Silicobra	002	Thwackey	068	Vulpix
121	Kirlia	295	Mawile	342	Oranguru	266	Rhyperior	382	Silvally	171	Timburr	356	Wailmer
114	Klang	209	Meowstic	012	Orbeetle	188	Ribombee	335	Sinistea	348	Togedemaru	357	Wailord
113	Klink	182	Meowth	133	Palpitoad	003	Rillaboom	219	Sirfetch'd	259	Togekiss	293	Weavile
115	Klinklang	014	Metapod	111	Pancham	298	Riolu	159	Sizzlipede	257	Togepi	251	Weezing
250	Koffing	185	Milcery	112	Pangoro	168	Roggenrola	285	Skorupi	258	Togetic	263	Whimsicott
394	Kommo-o	153	Milotic	343	Passimian	161	Rolycoly	131	Skuntank	300	Torkoal	229	Whiscash
098	Krabby	364	Mime Jr.	246	Pawniard	021	Rookidee	024	Skwovet	308	Toxapex	232	Wimpod
288	Lampent	301	Mimikyu	063	Pelipper	060	Roselia	390	Sliggoo	310	Toxel	062	Wingull
221	Lanturn	050	Minccino	183	Perrserker	061	Roserade	211	Slurpuff	223	Toxicroak	155	Wishiwashi
361	Lapras	340	Morelull	184	Persian	372	Rotom	292	Sneasel	311	Toxtricity	217	Wobbuffet
383	Larvitar	239	Morgrem	338	Phantump	281	Rufflet	349	Snom	027	Tranquill	174	Woobat
202	Leafeon	344	Morpeko	193	Pichu	328	Runerigus	261	Snorlax	321	Trapinch	034	Wooloo
045	Liepard	365	Mr. Mime	026	Pidove	294	Sableye	079	Snorunt	339	Trevenant	100	Wooper
032	Linoone	366	Mr. Rime	194	Pikachu	244	Salandit	096	Snover	157	Trubbish	216	Wynaut
287	Litwick	084	Mudbray	076	Piloswine	245	Salazzle	007	Sobble	054	Tsareena	093	Xatu
037	Lombre	085	Mudsdale	353	Pincurchin	313	Sandaconda	270	Solosis	347	Turtonator	327	Yamask
036	Lotad	260	Munchlax	336	Polteageist	249	Sawk	363	Solrock	132	Tympole	046	Yamper
299	Lucario	090	Munna	333	Ponyta	004	Scorbunny	212	Spritzee	381	Type: Null	398	Zacian
038	Ludicolo	091	Musharna	191	Pumpkaboo	225	Scrafty	179	Steelix	385	Tyranitar	399	Zamazenta
362	Lunatone	092	Natu	384	Pupitar	224	Scraggy	053	Steenee	107	Tyrogue	031	Zigzagoon
140	Machamp	029	Nickit	044	Purrloin	147	Seaking	369	Stonjourner	201	Umbreon	387	Zweilous
139	Machoke	104	Nincada	156	Pyukumuku	039	Seedot	094	Stufful	028	Unfezant		
138	Machop	069	Ninetales	101	Quagsire	134	Seismitoad	226	Stunfisk	073	Vanillish		
144	Magikarp	105	Ninjask	304	Qwilfish	106	Shedinja	130	Stunky	072	Vanillite		
291	Malamar	020	Noctowl	005	Raboot	150	Shellder	253	Sudowoodo	074	Vanilluxe		
077	Mamoswine	176	Noibat	195	Raichu	230	Shellos	075	Swinub	197	Vaporeon		
284	Mandibuzz	177	Noivern	120	Ralts	275	Shelmet	210	Swirlix	117	Vespiquen		

Completing Your Pokédex

The pages before you are packed with details about all the Pokémon you can obtain to fill your Galar Pokédex. Obtaining all 400 species and completing your Pokédex in the game is a lofty goal that many Trainers dream of completing. If you're up to the challenge, this volume is here to help you!

> If you complete the Pokédex in your game, head to Circhester and talk to the game director in Hotel Ionia. You'll earn a special certificate celebrating your accomplishment, and you'll get a Shiny Charm to boot. A Shiny Charm increases your chances of running into super-rare Shiny Pokémon. Shiny Pokémon aren't necessarily any stronger than their regular counterparts, but it's always exciting to see familiar species with different looks!

Use the Pokédex in Your Game

Once you get the Pokédex added to your Rotom Phone, you'll be able to access it from the X menu (which is pulled up by pressing Ⓧ) when you're out on your adventure. It'll be a great aid in your goal of obtaining all 400 Pokémon. Not only does it track information on how many Pokémon you've already seen or obtained but also it helps provide daily recommendations of Pokémon you can catch and where they may appear.

Pokémon recommendations

Recommended Pokémon will be Pokémon that can be found near the area you're in when you first check your Pokédex that day. The first recommendations you'll see will be species that you've seen but not caught yet. Better yet, as long as they're listed in the recommendations, you'll be slightly more likely to run into them than usual! Recommendations will be refreshed at midnight (according to the settings on your Nintendo Switch) or when you've caught all the current recommendations.

Keep your eyes peeled for Pokémon that have a weather icon next to them, as they're particularly likely to appear in that weather. In fact some Pokémon only appear in certain weather conditions, especially in the Wild Area. You'll find relevant weather conditions mentioned in the recommendations for how to obtain each species in this book. Pay attention to the notifications on your X menu, since they'll alert you when there's unusual weather appearing in the Wild Area! You can also check the weather around the region by opening up your Town Map.

① This section will show the areas where recommended Pokémon will be easy to find!

② Here you'll see how many Pokémon you've obtained as well as how many you've seen.

③ Here's where you'll see the current recommendations of Pokémon to catch.

Pokémon habitats

When you view the detailed page in your in-game Pokédex for a species you've seen before, you'll be able to check its habitat by pressing Ⓧ. You can see which areas of the Galar region it appears in, as well as a variety of icons indicating the type of weather the Pokémon may be more likely to appear in or whether it needs to be fished up from a body of water.

These icons can give you a hint about special conditions for encountering a species.

Some Pokémon only appear in particular weather conditions.

Others have to be fished up from dark spots in the water where you see bubbles rising up.

> Once you make it to Circhester, go to the west wing of Hotel Ionia and head up in the lift. In one of the rooms, you'll find the game director, who will give you a Catching Charm. It increases your chances of getting a critical catch, which is when you catch a Pokémon after the Poké Ball shakes just once!

Trade Pokémon

You'll have to get certain Pokémon by trading with other players. Just as a Pokémon Trainer needs their team, they also need other Trainers. Working together is the key to reaching the greatest heights, whether it's battling against other strong Trainers or trading Pokémon to complete your Pokédex.

You can set up Pokémon trades using Y-Comm. Simply open Y-Comm by pressing ⓨ during your adventure and send out a stamp to tell others you're looking for a trade. Once another Trainer is found who wants to trade, you'll be automatically connected using either local wireless or your internet connection, depending on your settings.

❗ Online trades require a membership to Nintendo Switch Online, a paid service.* To learn more about it, visit Nintendo's official website.

A trade partner has been found! Time for a trade!

Pokémon HOME

Pokémon HOME is a new service scheduled for launch in 2020. It will provide a new home for Pokémon you've obtained in earlier games, including *Pokémon: Let's Go, Pikachu!* and *Pokémon: Let's Go, Eevee!* You can bring Pokémon from even older games into Pokémon HOME via *Pokémon Bank*, and many species can then be moved to *Pokémon Sword* and *Pokémon Shield*! You'll also be able to trade Pokémon directly between Pokémon HOME accounts, too, with easy settings to search out exactly the Pokémon you're looking for. For more information on Pokémon HOME, keep an eye on Pokémon's official website.

*Nintendo Switch Online membership (sold separately) and Nintendo Account required for online play. Not available in all countries. Internet access required for online features. Terms apply. Visit nintendo.com for details.

Evolve Your Pokémon

There are a number of Pokémon species that are difficult to encounter in the wild. If you want to get them for your team or to complete your Pokédex, you may want to catch a species that's earlier in the Evolutionary line and evolve it. A large number of Pokémon species evolve simply by leveling up to a high enough level, but there are some examples of Pokémon that evolve in much more unusual ways. Evolution methods are explained on each Pokémon's page in this book.

Pokémon that evolve when they're friendly

High friendship is another Evolution requirement you might see, sometimes paired with additional conditions. Pokémon become friendly with you naturally while they travel around with you in your party and take part in battles with you. But they'll grow much friendlier if you play with them at your Pokémon Camp! So visit your camp by selecting the Pokémon Camp option on your X menu and take the time to play and cook with your Pokémon! You'll be able to tell how friendly your Pokémon are becoming as you see more and more hearts around them when you talk to them at camp.

Eevee is eager to play.

Pokémon that evolve when they know certain moves

Some Pokémon must know a particular move in order to evolve. If that's the case, you'll find it listed on that species' page in the Pokédex Entries pages. The moves are generally ones the Pokémon would naturally learn by leveling up, but if your Pokémon have forgotten a move they need to know or you missed your chance for them to learn it, visit Jack. This jack-of-all-trades, found behind one of the counters in every Pokémon Center, can help you with many things, including helping Pokémon remember moves.

 Some Pokémon evolve when they're traded! If you see trading listed in the way to obtain a given species, use Y-Comm to trade Pokémon with a pal and try to get those Pokémon!

Some Pokémon need to have certain items used on them to evolve. If you don't have the item they need, turn to page 466 where the Items list begins.

Leveling Up Your Pokémon

If you've got some Pokémon you need to level up a lot in order to evolve them, there are a few methods you might try to maximize your results!

- Battle a lot and especially against high-level opponents! Put Pokémon you want to level up on your team as you complete the tournaments held at Wyndon Stadium after you become Champion, for example.
- Get your hands on Exp. Candies by swapping Watts for them with certain hikers you meet in the Wild Area—or by receiving them as rewards for completing tough Max Raid Battles against Dynamax Pokémon!
- Use Poké Jobs! Most jobs reward Exp. Points, and the higher-tiered jobs can award a great deal of Exp. Points to a lot of Pokémon at once—especially if you manage to do a great job by sending the right types of Pokémon for the job!
- Your Pokémon can even earn Exp. Points from the time they spend at camp with you! Play lots with them and cook up fantastic curries together, and you'll see that they get a little boost to their Exp. Points when you leave camp.

Hatch Pokémon Eggs

Pokémon Eggs can be found when you leave two compatible Pokémon at the Pokémon Nursery found on Route 5 or the one in the Wild Area, northeast of Motostoke. If you carry an Egg around with you in your party, eventually it will hatch into a Pokémon! The Pokémon that hatches will usually be the first species in the Evolutionary line of the female Pokémon you left at the Nursery, but there are some tricks to know.

Your quick guide to Eggs!

- Leave a male and female Pokémon at the Nursery
  > Or Ditto and another Pokémon of any gender!

- Check that they share at least one Egg Group
  > Unless one is Ditto!

- Be sure they aren't in the No Eggs Discovered group
  > Even with Ditto, you won't find an Egg!

- Find Pokémon Eggs after a while
  > An Oval Charm will sure help!

- Carry the Eggs in your party until they hatch
  > Use Abilities to speed up hatching!
  > Riding your bike speeds up hatching, too!

These are just the basics, but read on for all the details you need to know!

A few species will only hatch from a Pokémon Egg if one of the Pokémon you leave at the Pokémon Nursery is holding a particular incense. You can get incense from a seller in the port town of Hulbury, on the east coast of Galar. For the Pokémon that can only be found in this way, you'll find the incense they need listed in their Pokédex Entries section, starting on page 23.

Growl	NORMAL	40/40
Tackle	NORMAL	35/35
Tail Whip	NORMAL	30/30
Wish	NORMAL	10/10

Eevee Lv. 1

Category	
Power	—
Accuracy	—

One turn after this move is used, the user's or its replacement's HP is restored by half the user's max HP.

A Swap   X TMs   B Back

! Find each species' Egg Groups on their page in the Move Tables section, or search for species in the Egg Group tables starting on page 12.

Finally, finding and hatching Pokémon Eggs can do more than simply help you fill your Pokédex in your game. It can also help you get some great Pokémon by passing on competitive individual strengths, useful Abilities, advantageous Natures, and unusual Egg Moves from the two Pokémon you leave at the Pokémon Nursery.

Eggs can inherit moves from either Pokémon

Pokémon that hatch from Eggs automatically know some of the basic moves that their species can know at Lv. 1, but they may also know special moves inherited from the two Pokémon left at the Nursery. These can be moves that their species would normally learn at a later level, or they can be rare Egg Moves! Egg Moves are moves that can usually only be inherited by Pokémon that start as Eggs and cannot be learned by leveling up or from a TM. The Egg Moves each species can learn are listed in the Egg Moves tables on their page in the Move Tables section, starting on page 187. To pass on a move that Pokémon normally wouldn't learn until a much higher level, both Pokémon left at the Pokémon Nursery need to know it before that move can be inherited.

⚡ Brilliant Pokémon may also know Egg Moves! Flip to page 19 to find out more about these rare Pokémon.

Knows Bite   Knows Bite

Eggs inherit their Ability from the female

An Egg usually inherits its Ability from the female Pokémon of a pair, but it may also get one of the other regular Abilities that its species can have. An Egg can only have a Hidden Ability if the female left at the Nursery has one. Hidden Abilities are very rare Abilities—specimens caught as Dynamax Pokémon in Max Raid Battles sometimes have them. And it's also worth remembering that if you ever leave a male or gender-unknown Pokémon at a Nursery with a Ditto and there's no female at all, the Egg will inherit the Ability of the non-Ditto Pokémon.

♀ Healer   +   ♂ Iron Barbs   =   Healer

> The Ability Capsule item lets you switch between the two Abilities that a Pokémon species can normally have. Pick up this handy item in exchange for BP at the BP Shop in Wyndon's Battle Tower. But remember that an Ability Capsule won't let you switch from a regular Ability to a Hidden Ability, and it won't do anything if the species of the Pokémon you're trying to use it on normally has only one Ability.

Eggs can inherit their Nature from either Pokémon

Pokémon that hatch from Eggs typically have one of the 25 Natures at random. If you want to choose a specific Nature for your Egg, make sure that one of the Pokémon you leave at the Nursery has that Nature and give it an Everstone to hold. This will guarantee that your Egg will hatch into a Pokémon with the same Nature. Flip to page 465 for the full table of Natures and which stats they affect.

♀ Quiet Nature   +   ♂ Timid Nature   =   Timid Nature

> There are also special mints you can use to change how a Pokémon's stats will grow, much like their inherent Nature will. These can be bought with BP at the left BP Shop in Wyndon's Battle Tower or earned by winning battles there and climbing the Battle Tower ranks.

Eggs can inherit individual strengths from either Pokémon

The two Pokémon you leave at the Nursery will usually pass down a total of three individual strengths to any Eggs found. However, which ones are passed down (and from which Pokémon) is decided at random. But with the help of certain held items, you can control this process to some extent. Leave Pokémon with great individual strengths and the right items at the Nursery, and you'll greatly improve your chances of finding Eggs that are overflowing with potential! All of these items can be obtained in exchange for BP at the BP Shop in the central Pokémon Center in Hammerlocke.

	Item name	Individual strength passed down
	Power Weight	HP of the holder
	Power Bracer	Attack of the holder
	Power Belt	Defense of the holder
	Power Lens	Sp. Atk of the holder
	Power Band	Sp. Def of the holder
	Power Anklet	Speed of the holder
	Destiny Knot	Five individual strengths (rather than the usual three) randomly chosen from the two Pokémon left at the Nursery

Eggs can hatch into Pokémon with different forms

Eggs in Galar will usually hatch into a Pokémon's Galarian form (if it has one) regardless of the form of the Pokémon you left at the Nursery. For example, if you obtain a female Meowth from another region and it finds an Egg in Galar, that Egg will hatch into a Galarian Meowth. If you don't want this to happen, you would need to give that Meowth from another region an Everstone. If a Pokémon is holding an Everstone when you leave it at the Nursery, the Eggs you find will hatch into the same form as the Everstone-holding Pokémon!

Egg Group tables

On the following pages, you'll find tables listing the Egg Groups for all the Pokémon you'll meet in the Galar region. The first column shows their Galar Pokédex number, to help you track them down in this book and find out more about how to obtain each. The last column shows if you can find both male and female specimens, just one or the other, or if they are gender unknown.

Some Pokémon have multiple forms, which can arise from factors such as how they are evolved (like Alcremie) or what region they were caught in (like Meowth). These Pokémon typically have the same Egg Group, so they won't be listed separately. For example, you'll see just one entry for Meowth, even though it can have a different form when it's been brought to Galar from another region.

Amorphous Group

Amorphous Group Only

124	Drifloon	♂/♀
125	Drifblim	♂/♀
135	Duskull	♂/♀
136	Dusclops	♂/♀
137	Dusknoir	♂/♀
141	Gastly	♂/♀
142	Haunter	♂/♀
143	Gengar	♂/♀
191	Pumpkaboo	♂/♀
192	Gourgeist	♂/♀
217	Wobbuffet	♂/♀
250	Koffing	♂/♀
251	Weezing	♂/♀
270	Solosis	♂/♀
271	Duosion	♂/♀
272	Reuniclus	♂/♀
287	Litwick	♂/♀
288	Lampent	♂/♀
289	Chandelure	♂/♀
301	Mimikyu	♂/♀
305	Frillish	♂/♀
306	Jellicent	♂/♀
372	Rotom	Unknown

Amorphous Group and Dragon Group

395	Dreepy	♂/♀
396	Drakloak	♂/♀
397	Dragapult	♂/♀

Amorphous Group and Fairy Group

185	Milcery	♀ only
186	Alcremie	♀ only

Amorphous Group and Grass Group

338	Phantump	♂/♀
339	Trevenant	♂/♀

Amorphous Group and Humanlike Group

120	Ralts	♂/♀
121	Kirlia	♂/♀
122	Gardevoir	♂/♀
123	Gallade	♂ only

Amorphous Group and Mineral Group

327	Yamask	♂/♀
328	Runerigus	♂/♀
329	Cofagrigus	♂/♀
335	Sinistea	Unknown
336	Polteageist	Unknown

Amorphous Group and Water 1 Group

226	Stunfisk	♂/♀
230	Shellos	♂/♀
231	Gastrodon	♂/♀
353	Pincurchin	♂/♀

Bug Group

Bug Group Only

010	Blipbug	♂/♀
011	Dottler	♂/♀
012	Orbeetle	♂/♀
013	Caterpie	♂/♀
014	Metapod	♂/♀
015	Butterfree	♂/♀
016	Grubbin	♂/♀
017	Charjabug	♂/♀
018	Vikavolt	♂/♀
064	Joltik	♂/♀
065	Galvantula	♂/♀
104	Nincada	♂/♀
105	Ninjask	♂/♀
116	Combee	♂/♀
117	Vespiquen	♀ only
159	Sizzlipede	♂/♀

160	Centiskorch	♂/♀
227	Shuckle	♂/♀
273	Karrablast	♂/♀
274	Escavalier	♂/♀
275	Shelmet	♂/♀
276	Accelgor	♂/♀
316	Durant	♂/♀
349	Snom	♂/♀
350	Frosmoth	♂/♀

Bug Group and Dragon Group

321	Trapinch	♂/♀
322	Vibrava	♂/♀
323	Flygon	♂/♀

Bug Group and Fairy Group

187	Cutiefly	♂/♀
188	Ribombee	♂/♀

Bug Group and Mineral Group

086	Dwebble	♂/♀
087	Crustle	♂/♀

Bug Group and Water 1 Group

214	Dewpider	♂/♀
215	Araquanid	♂/♀

Bug Group and Water 3 Group

232	Wimpod	♂/♀
233	Golisopod	♂/♀
285	Skorupi	♂/♀
286	Drapion	♂/♀

Ditto Group

Ditto Group Only

373	Ditto	Unknown

Dragon Group

Dragon Group Only

386	Deino	♂/♀
387	Zweilous	♂/♀
388	Hydreigon	♂/♀

389	Goomy	♂/♀
390	Sliggoo	♂/♀
391	Goodra	♂/♀
392	Jangmo-o	♂/♀
393	Hakamo-o	♂/♀
394	Kommo-o	♂/♀

Dragon Group and Amorphous Group

395	Dreepy	♂/♀
396	Drakloak	♂/♀
397	Dragapult	♂/♀

Dragon Group and Bug Group

321	Trapinch	♂/♀
322	Vibrava	♂/♀
323	Flygon	♂/♀

Dragon Group and Field Group

224	Scraggy	♂/♀
225	Scrafty	♂/♀
312	Silicobra	♂/♀
313	Sandaconda	♂/♀

Dragon Group and Flying Group

176	Noibat	♂/♀
177	Noivern	♂/♀

Dragon Group and Grass Group

205	Applin	♂/♀
206	Flapple	♂/♀
207	Appletun	♂/♀

Dragon Group and Mineral Group

371	Duraludon	♂/♀

Dragon Group and Monster Group

244	Salandit	♂/♀
245	Salazzle	♀ only
318	Helioptile	♂/♀
319	Heliolisk	♂/♀
324	Axew	♂/♀
325	Fraxure	♂/♀

#	Pokémon	Gender
326	Haxorus	♂/♀
346	Drampa	♂/♀
347	Turtonator	♂/♀
378	Charmander	♂/♀
379	Charmeleon	♂/♀
380	Charizard	♂/♀

Dragon Group and Water 1 Group

#	Pokémon	Gender
152	Feebas	♂/♀
153	Milotic	♂/♀

Dragon Group and Water 2 Group

#	Pokémon	Gender
144	Magikarp	♂/♀
145	Gyarados	♂/♀

Fairy Group
Fairy Group Only

#	Pokémon	Gender
210	Swirlix	♂/♀
211	Slurpuff	♂/♀
212	Spritzee	♂/♀
213	Aromatisse	♂/♀
241	Hatenna	♀ only
242	Hattrem	♀ only
243	Hatterene	♀ only
255	Clefairy	♂/♀
256	Clefable	♂/♀
337	Indeedee	♂/♀

Fairy Group and Amorphous Group

#	Pokémon	Gender
185	Milcery	♀ only
186	Alcremie	♀ only

Fairy Group and Bug Group

#	Pokémon	Gender
187	Cutiefly	♂/♀
188	Ribombee	♂/♀

Fairy Group and Field Group

#	Pokémon	Gender
194	Pikachu	♂/♀
195	Raichu	♂/♀
295	Mawile	♂/♀
344	Morpeko	♂/♀
348	Togedemaru	♂/♀

Fairy Group and Flying Group

#	Pokémon	Gender
258	Togetic	♂/♀
259	Togekiss	♂/♀

Fairy Group and Grass Group

#	Pokémon	Gender
060	Roselia	♂/♀
061	Roserade	♂/♀
128	Cherubi	♂/♀
129	Cherrim	♂/♀
262	Cottonee	♂/♀
263	Whimsicott	♂/♀

Fairy Group and Humanlike Group

#	Pokémon	Gender
238	Impidimp	♂ only
239	Morgrem	♂ only
240	Grimmsnarl	♂ only

Fairy Group and Mineral Group

#	Pokémon	Gender
079	Snorunt	♂/♀
080	Glalie	♂/♀
081	Froslass	♀ only
345	Falinks	Unknown

Field Group
Field Group Only

#	Pokémon	Gender
024	Skwovet	♂/♀
025	Greedent	♂/♀
029	Nickit	♂/♀
030	Thievul	♂/♀
031	Zigzagoon	♂/♀
032	Linoone	♂/♀
033	Obstagoon	♂/♀
034	Wooloo	♂/♀
035	Dubwool	♂/♀
044	Purrloin	♂/♀
045	Liepard	♂/♀
046	Yamper	♂/♀
047	Boltund	♂/♀
048	Bunnelby	♂/♀
049	Diggersby	♂/♀
050	Minccino	♂/♀
051	Cinccino	♂/♀
066	Electrike	♂/♀
067	Manectric	♂/♀
068	Vulpix	♂/♀
069	Ninetales	♂/♀
070	Growlithe	♂/♀
071	Arcanine	♂/♀
075	Swinub	♂/♀
076	Piloswine	♂/♀
077	Mamoswine	♂/♀
084	Mudbray	♂/♀
085	Mudsdale	♂/♀
090	Munna	♂/♀
091	Musharna	♂/♀
094	Stufful	♂/♀
095	Bewear	♂/♀
130	Stunky	♂/♀
131	Skuntank	♂/♀
164	Diglett	♂/♀
165	Dugtrio	♂/♀
166	Drilbur	♂/♀
167	Excadrill	♂/♀
182	Meowth	♂/♀
183	Perrserker	♂/♀
184	Persian	♂/♀
196	Eevee	♂/♀
197	Vaporeon	♂/♀
198	Jolteon	♂/♀
199	Flareon	♂/♀
200	Espeon	♂/♀
201	Umbreon	♂/♀
202	Leafeon	♂/♀
203	Glaceon	♂/♀
204	Sylveon	♂/♀
208	Espurr	♂/♀
209	Meowstic	♂/♀
279	Cubchoo	♂/♀
280	Beartic	♂/♀
292	Sneasel	♂/♀
293	Weavile	♂/♀
300	Torkoal	♂/♀
314	Hippopotas	♂/♀
315	Hippowdon	♂/♀
317	Heatmor	♂/♀
333	Ponyta	♂/♀
334	Rapidash	♂/♀
342	Oranguru	♂/♀
343	Passimian	♂/♀
367	Darumaka	♂/♀
368	Darmanitan	♂/♀

Field Group and Dragon Group

#	Pokémon	Gender
224	Scraggy	♂/♀
225	Scrafty	♂/♀
312	Silicobra	♂/♀
313	Sandaconda	♂/♀

Field Group and Fairy Group

#	Pokémon	Gender
194	Pikachu	♂/♀
195	Raichu	♂/♀
295	Mawile	♂/♀
344	Morpeko	♂/♀
348	Togedemaru	♂/♀

Field Group and Flying Group

#	Pokémon	Gender
174	Woobat	♂/♀
175	Swoobat	♂/♀
218	Farfetch'd	♂/♀
219	Sirfetch'd	♂/♀

Field Group and Grass Group

#	Pokémon	Gender
001	Grookey	♂/♀
002	Thwackey	♂/♀
003	Rillaboom	♂/♀
039	Seedot	♂/♀
040	Nuzleaf	♂/♀
041	Shiftry	♂/♀

Field Group and Humanlike Group

#	Pokémon	Gender
004	Scorbunny	♂/♀
005	Raboot	♂/♀
006	Cinderace	♂/♀
111	Pancham	♂/♀
112	Pangoro	♂/♀
299	Lucario	♂/♀

Field Group and Mineral Group

#	Pokémon	Gender
302	Cufant	♂/♀
303	Copperajah	♂/♀

Field Group and Monster Group

#	Pokémon	Gender
264	Rhyhorn	♂/♀
265	Rhydon	♂/♀
266	Rhyperior	♂/♀

Field Group and Water 1 Group

#	Pokémon	Gender
007	Sobble	♂/♀
008	Drizzile	♂/♀
009	Inteleon	♂/♀
078	Delibird	♂/♀
100	Wooper	♂/♀
101	Quagsire	♂/♀
370	Eiscue	♂/♀

Field Group and Water 2 Group

#	Pokémon	Gender
356	Wailmer	♂/♀
357	Wailord	♂/♀

Flying Group
Flying Group Only

#	Pokémon	Gender
019	Hoothoot	♂/♀
020	Noctowl	♂/♀
021	Rookidee	♂/♀
022	Corvisquire	♂/♀
023	Corviknight	♂/♀
026	Pidove	♂/♀
027	Tranquill	♂/♀
028	Unfezant	♂/♀
092	Natu	♂/♀
093	Xatu	♂/♀
281	Rufflet	♂ only

282	Braviary	♂ only
283	Vullaby	♀ only
284	Mandibuzz	♀ only
297	Sigilyph	♂/♀

Flying Group and Dragon Group

| 176 | Noibat | ♂/♀ |
| 177 | Noivern | ♂/♀ |

Flying Group and Fairy Group

| 258 | Togetic | ♂/♀ |
| 259 | Togekiss | ♂/♀ |

Flying Group and Field Group

174	Woobat	♂/♀
175	Swoobat	♂/♀
218	Farfetch'd	♂/♀
219	Sirfetch'd	♂/♀

Flying Group and Humanlike Group

| 320 | Hawlucha | ♂/♀ |

Flying Group and Water 1 Group

062	Wingull	♂/♀
063	Pelipper	♂/♀
309	Cramorant	♂/♀

Grass Group

Grass Group Only

052	Bounsweet	♀ only
053	Steenee	♀ only
054	Tsareena	♀ only
055	Oddish	♂/♀
056	Gloom	♂/♀
057	Vileplume	♂/♀
058	Bellossom	♂/♀
126	Gossifleur	♂/♀
127	Eldegoss	♂/♀
296	Maractus	♂/♀
340	Morelull	♂/♀
341	Shiinotic	♂/♀

Grass Group and Amorphous Group

| 338 | Phantump | ♂/♀ |
| 339 | Trevenant | ♂/♀ |

Grass Group and Dragon Group

205	Applin	♂/♀
206	Flapple	♂/♀
207	Appletun	♂/♀

Grass Group and Fairy Group

060	Roselia	♂/♀
061	Roserade	♂/♀
128	Cherubi	♂/♀
129	Cherrim	♂/♀
262	Cottonee	♂/♀
263	Whimsicott	♂/♀

Grass Group and Field Group

001	Grookey	♂/♀
002	Thwackey	♂/♀
003	Rillaboom	♂/♀
039	Seedot	♂/♀
040	Nuzleaf	♂/♀
041	Shiftry	♂/♀

Grass Group and Mineral Group

| 189 | Ferroseed | ♂/♀ |
| 190 | Ferrothorn | ♂/♀ |

Grass Group and Monster Group

| 096 | Snover | ♂/♀ |
| 097 | Abomasnow | ♂/♀ |

Grass Group and Water 1 Group

036	Lotad	♂/♀
037	Lombre	♂/♀
038	Ludicolo	♂/♀

Humanlike Group

Humanlike Group Only

108	Hitmonlee	♂ only
109	Hitmonchan	♂ only
110	Hitmontop	♂ only
138	Machop	♂/♀
139	Machoke	♂/♀
140	Machamp	♂/♀
171	Timburr	♂/♀
172	Gurdurr	♂/♀
173	Conkeldurr	♂/♀
222	Croagunk	♂/♀
223	Toxicroak	♂/♀
246	Pawniard	♂/♀
247	Bisharp	♂/♀
248	Throh	♂ only
249	Sawk	♂ only
267	Gothita	♂/♀
268	Gothorita	♂/♀
269	Gothitelle	♂/♀

277	Elgyem	♂/♀
278	Beheeyem	♂/♀
294	Sableye	♂/♀
311	Toxtricity	♂/♀
365	Mr. Mime	♂/♀
366	Mr. Rime	♂/♀

Humanlike Group and Amorphous Group

120	Ralts	♂/♀
121	Kirlia	♂/♀
122	Gardevoir	♂/♀
123	Gallade	♂ only

Humanlike Group and Fairy Group

238	Impidimp	♂ only
239	Morgrem	♂ only
240	Grimmsnarl	♂ only

Humanlike Group and Field Group

004	Scorbunny	♂/♀
005	Raboot	♂/♀
006	Cinderace	♂/♀
111	Pancham	♂/♀
112	Pangoro	♂/♀
299	Lucario	♂/♀

Humanlike Group and Flying Group

| 320 | Hawlucha | ♂/♀ |

Humanlike Group and Water 1 Group

| 351 | Clobbopus | ♂/♀ |
| 352 | Grapploct | ♂/♀ |

Mineral Group

Mineral Group Only

072	Vanillite	♂/♀
073	Vanillish	♂/♀
074	Vanilluxe	♂/♀
082	Baltoy	Unknown
083	Claydol	Unknown
088	Golett	Unknown
089	Golurk	Unknown
106	Shedinja	Unknown
113	Klink	Unknown
114	Klang	Unknown
115	Klinklang	Unknown
118	Bronzor	Unknown
119	Bronzong	Unknown
157	Trubbish	♂/♀

158	Garbodor	♂/♀
161	Rolycoly	♂/♀
162	Carkol	♂/♀
163	Coalossal	♂/♀
168	Roggenrola	♂/♀
169	Boldore	♂/♀
170	Gigalith	♂/♀
178	Onix	♂/♀
179	Steelix	♂/♀
253	Sudowoodo	♂/♀
330	Honedge	♂/♀
331	Doublade	♂/♀
332	Aegislash	♂/♀
360	Dhelmise	Unknown
362	Lunatone	Unknown
363	Solrock	Unknown
369	Stonjourner	♂/♀

Mineral Group and Amorphous Group

327	Yamask	♂/♀
328	Runerigus	♂/♀
329	Cofagrigus	♂/♀
335	Sinistea	Unknown
336	Polteageist	Unknown

Mineral Group and Bug Group

| 086 | Dwebble | ♂/♀ |
| 087 | Crustle | ♂/♀ |

Mineral Group and Dragon Group

| 371 | Duraludon | ♂/♀ |

Mineral Group and Fairy Group

079	Snorunt	♂/♀
080	Glalie	♂/♀
081	Froslass	♀ only
345	Falinks	Unknown

Mineral Group and Field Group

| 302 | Cufant | ♂/♀ |
| 303 | Copperajah | ♂/♀ |

Mineral Group and Grass Group

| 189 | Ferroseed | ♂/♀ |
| 190 | Ferrothorn | ♂/♀ |

Mineral Group and Monster Group

| 358 | Bergmite | ♂/♀ |
| 359 | Avalugg | ♂/♀ |

Monster Group

Monster Group Only

261		Snorlax	♂/♀
383		Larvitar	♂/♀
384		Pupitar	♂/♀
385		Tyranitar	♂/♀

Monster Group and Dragon Group

244		Salandit	♂/♀
245		Salazzle	♀ only
318		Helioptile	♂/♀
319		Heliolisk	♂/♀
324		Axew	♂/♀
325		Fraxure	♂/♀
326		Haxorus	♂/♀
346		Drampa	♂/♀
347		Turtonator	♂/♀
378		Charmander	♂/♀
379		Charmeleon	♂/♀
380		Charizard	♂/♀

Monster Group and Field Group

264		Rhyhorn	♂/♀
265		Rhydon	♂/♀
266		Rhyperior	♂/♀

Monster Group and Grass Group

096		Snover	♂/♀
097		Abomasnow	♂/♀

Monster Group and Mineral Group

358		Bergmite	♂/♀
359		Avalugg	♂/♀

Monster Group and Water 1 Group

042		Chewtle	♂/♀
043		Drednaw	♂/♀
361		Lapras	♂/♀

Water 1 Group

Water 1 Group Only

132		Tympole	♂/♀
133		Palpitoad	♂/♀
134		Seismitoad	♂/♀
156		Pyukumuku	♂/♀
307		Mareanie	♂/♀
308		Toxapex	♂/♀
355		Mantine	♂/♀

Water 1 Group and Amorphous Group

226		Stunfisk	♂/♀
230		Shellos	♂/♀
231		Gastrodon	♂/♀
353		Pincurchin	♂/♀

Water 1 Group and Bug Group

214		Dewpider	♂/♀
215		Araquanid	♂/♀

Water 1 Group and Dragon Group

152		Feebas	♂/♀
153		Milotic	♂/♀

Water 1 Group and Field Group

007		Sobble	♂/♀
008		Drizzile	♂/♀
009		Inteleon	♂/♀
078		Delibird	♂/♀
100		Wooper	♂/♀
101		Quagsire	♂/♀
370		Eiscue	♂/♀

Water 1 Group and Flying Group

062		Wingull	♂/♀
063		Pelipper	♂/♀
309		Cramorant	♂/♀

Water 1 Group and Grass Group

036		Lotad	♂/♀
037		Lombre	♂/♀
038		Ludicolo	♂/♀

Water 1 Group and Humanlike Group

351		Clobbopus	♂/♀
352		Grapploct	♂/♀

Water 1 Group and Monster Group

042		Chewtle	♂/♀
043		Drednaw	♂/♀
361		Lapras	♂/♀

Water 1 Group and Water 2 Group

148		Remoraid	♂/♀
149		Octillery	♂/♀
290		Inkay	♂/♀
291		Malamar	♂/♀

Water 1 Group and Water 3 Group

102		Corphish	♂/♀
103		Crawdaunt	♂/♀
236		Corsola	♂/♀
237		Cursola	♂/♀

Water 2 Group

Water 2 Group Only

146		Goldeen	♂/♀
147		Seaking	♂/♀
154		Basculin	♂/♀
155		Wishiwashi	♂/♀
180		Arrokuda	♂/♀
181		Barraskewda	♂/♀
220		Chinchou	♂/♀
221		Lanturn	♂/♀
228		Barboach	♂/♀
229		Whiscash	♂/♀
304		Qwilfish	♂/♀

Water 2 Group and Dragon Group

144		Magikarp	♂/♀
145		Gyarados	♂/♀

Water 2 Group and Field Group

356		Wailmer	♂/♀
357		Wailord	♂/♀

Water 2 Group and Water 1 Group

148		Remoraid	♂/♀
149		Octillery	♂/♀
290		Inkay	♂/♀
291		Malamar	♂/♀

Water 3 Group

Water 3 Group Only

098		Krabby	♂/♀
099		Kingler	♂/♀
150		Shellder	♂/♀
151		Cloyster	♂/♀
234		Binacle	♂/♀
235		Barbaracle	♂/♀

Water 3 Group and Bug Group

232		Wimpod	♂/♀
233		Golisopod	♂/♀
285		Skorupi	♂/♀
286		Drapion	♂/♀

Water 3 Group and Water 1 Group

102		Corphish	♂/♀
103		Crawdaunt	♂/♀
236		Corsola	♂/♀
237		Cursola	♂/♀

No Eggs Discovered

059		Budew	♂/♀
107		Tyrogue	♂ only
193		Pichu	♂/♀
216		Wynaut	♂/♀
252		Bonsly	♂/♀
254		Cleffa	♂/♀
257		Togepi	♂/♀
260		Munchlax	♂/♀
298		Riolu	♂/♀
310		Toxel	♂/♀
354		Mantyke	♂/♀
364		Mime Jr.	♂/♀
374		Dracozolt	Unknown
375		Arctozolt	Unknown
376		Dracovish	Unknown
377		Arctovish	Unknown
381		Type: Null	Unknown
382		Silvally	Unknown
398		Zacian	Unknown
399		Zamazenta	Unknown
400		Eternatus	Unknown

Explore the Wild Area

If you're aiming to complete your Pokédex, then the Wild Area—the heart of the Galar region—is where you'll spend a great deal of your time! More species appear in the Wild Area than anywhere else in Galar—not least of all because this one area is simply the largest in the region! It's so large, in fact, that it's split up into 18 zones, each with its own name. Getting familiar with them will be a big help to finding your way around, and they're all labeled on the map on page 21.

In a place as wide as the Wild Area, you'll find all sorts of different microclimates. As you pass from one zone to the next, you may see the weather change. The weather will also change over time, even within the same zone. This weather will affect more than just how certain moves perform in battle. It will also change which Pokémon you encounter!

You'll find all kinds of environments in the vast Wild Area.

Not only does the landscape change—the weather does, too!

Explore all the zones of the Wild Area if you hope to encounter all the species they hold!

Baltoy is more likely to appear in sandstorms...

But Cufant appears in blizzards.

And you can find Mimikyu in the fog!

Weather	Pokémon types more likely to appear in the Wild Area	Effects on battles
☀ Clear	Normal, Grass, Flying	—
⛅ Cloudy	Fighting, Poison, Dark	—
🌧 Rain	Water, Bug	**Rain** Boosts the power of Water-type moves and reduces the power of Fire-type moves, among other effects
⛈ Thunderstorm	Water, Electric, Dragon	**Rain** Boosts the power of Water-type moves and reduces the power of Fire-type moves, among other effects **Electric Terrain** Boosts the power of Electric-type moves for Pokémon on the ground and prevents them from falling asleep
❄ Snow	Ice	**Hail** Damages all Pokémon that aren't Ice types, among other effects
❄ Blizzard	Ice, Steel	**Hail** Damages all Pokémon that aren't Ice types, among other effects
☀ Harsh sunlight	Fire, Ground	**Harsh sunlight** Boosts the power of Fire-type moves and reduces the power of Water-type moves, among other effects
Sandstorm	Ground, Rock	**Sandstorm** Damages all Pokémon that aren't Ground, Rock, or Steel types, among other effects
🌫 Fog	Psychic, Ghost, Fairy	**Misty Terrain** Halves the damage taken from Dragon-type moves for Pokémon on the ground and protects them from status conditions and confusion

Some of these weather patterns are particularly rare, and the Pokémon that appear in them can be even rarer. Luckily you're not entirely on your own when it comes to nabbing these rare chances. Every time you open your X menu in the game, you'll get little pop-ups. Sometimes they'll be reminding you of things like where you should go next, but you'll also get notifications if there are particularly rare types of weather occurring in the Wild Area.

Keep your eyes peeled for notifications, and go check the weather when you see them!

> ❗ The rarest weather conditions—which are the only ways to encounter a number of species for your Pokédex—are fog, sandstorms, blizzards, and thunderstorms. Feel like you're never seeing them? It might not just be your imagination, depending on how far you've made it through your game! You won't see blizzards or sandstorms until you've reached Hammerlocke for the first time, and you won't see the elusive fog that many Pokémon hide in until you've beaten the main game by becoming Champion!

What Are Watts?

Watts are a special currency that you can use for a variety of purposes in the Wild Area, such as trading for Poké Balls, TRs, and other items. There are lots of ways to earn Watts! Completing Rotom Rallies, checking out Pokémon Dens, and battling Brilliant Pokémon (p. 19) will net you more Watts.

> ❗ If you want to earn the most Watts, there are a few things you can do. First of all, be sure to check all the Pokémon Dens that have pillars of light coming out of them. Each one will reward you with 300 W, and you'll usually find several of these dens per day. You don't have to participate in a den's Max Raid Battle to get the Watts, either, so it's a quick and easy way to build up your savings.
>
> You'll also earn more Watts by completing longer Rotom Rally courses. Completing the longest course, which is the one between Hammerlocke and the Meetup Spot, can earn you over 400 W per run if you get used to it! Just keep doing that back and forth, and you'll rack up Watts in no time!

Advice for exploring the Wild Area

You'll spend a lot of time running back and forth and all around in the Wild Area, chasing after and being chased by wild Pokémon. This'll be great for filling out your Pokédex and helping your team train, but your party might need a bit of a pick-me-up after a while, too.

Use your Pokémon Camp to recover

Cooking up great curries at your camp can help the Pokémon in your party recover all their HP and PP, and they can even recover from status conditions or from fainting. One way to cook some of the best curries is to use rare ingredients and Berries. And you're in luck, because there are a ton of Berry trees right in the Wild Area that you can collect Berries from, plus Ingredients Sellers that offer a changing selection of ingredients each day. You can also find a number of ingredients on the ground, if you look for them, like the Pungent Roots found near the shore of Lake Axewell and the Lake of Outrage.

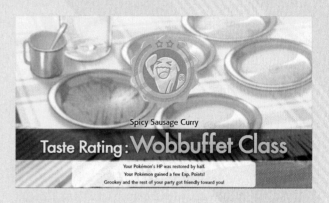

Spicy Sausage Curry

Taste Rating : Wobbuffet Class

Your Pokémon's HP was restored by half.
Your Pokémon gained a few Exp. Points!
Grookey and the rest of your party got friendly toward you!

Make the most of Max Raid Battles

Look out for pillars of light erupting from Pokémon Dens around the Wild Area. Inside, wild Dynamax Pokémon are waiting to be taken on in Max Raid Battles! These battles are more than just a fun challenge—they're also the only way to catch certain Pokémon species in the game or to try to get specimens with the Gigantamax Factor, which allows them to transform into Gigantamax Pokémon (p. 161)! Gigantamax Pokémon are incredibly rare and only appear in five-star Max Raid Battles, which won't appear until you reach the end of your game.

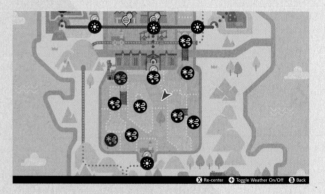

Check the weather each day

The weather in the various zones of the Wild Area changes daily. Check the weather on your Town Map each day to see if there are any unusual weather conditions cropping up. If there are, you may want to spend some time in one area over another in the hopes of tracking down a rare Pokémon.

Talk to the people in the Wild Area

If you're playing near other players or are connected to the internet, you'll see other Trainers like you camping and looking for adventure. But you'll also find some other familiar faces from the Galar region, like hikers, backpackers, fishers, and more. Many of these people will be willing to trade useful items for your Watts, including Exp. Candies to help you level up your team. There are also two brothers who call themselves the Digging Duo near the Pokémon Nursery in the middle of the Wild Area. They can dig up handy items, including the four Fossils you'll need if you want to complete your Galar Pokédex!

Find Brilliant Pokémon

There are some particularly brilliant specimens of Pokémon you can find in the wild, under the right conditions. These aren't Shiny Pokémon—though they can be. Rather, they're Pokémon that appear to be exuding a golden glow when you see them wandering around in the wild. This glow goes away after you catch them, but the rest of their benefits do not!

Benefits Brilliant Pokémon may have:

- Higher levels than most other Pokémon in the area
- At least two or three stats with max individual strengths, helping them grow into great specimens
- A rare Egg Move as one of their moves, which regular Pokémon never know when caught in the wild
- Watts given out when you catch them, which you can trade for items in the Wild Area

> ! Brilliant Pokémon don't appear in random encounters—that is, encounters where unseen Pokémon attack unexpectedly when you're walking through tall grass.

This all sounds pretty tempting, so how can you increase your chances of encountering Brilliant Pokémon? The answer lies in battling a Pokémon species over and over. The more times you catch or defeat a Pokémon species in battle, the more likely you'll be to encounter specimens with this special glow in the future.

Number of times you've battled a species	Effects on future encounters with that species
At least one time	• Becomes possible to encounter Brilliant Pokémon • Chance of encountering Shiny Pokémon doesn't change
At least 20 times	• About 1.3× the usual chance of encountering Brilliant Pokémon • Chance of encountering Shiny Pokémon doesn't change
At least 50 times	• About 1.6× the usual chance of encountering Brilliant Pokémon • 2× the usual chance of encountering Shiny Pokémon
At least 100 times	• 2× the usual chance of encountering Brilliant Pokémon • 3× the usual chance of encountering Shiny Pokémon
At least 200 times	• 2× the usual chance of encountering Brilliant Pokémon • 4× the usual chance of encountering Shiny Pokémon
At least 300 times	• 2× the usual chance of encountering Brilliant Pokémon • 5× the usual chance of encountering Shiny Pokémon
At least 500 times	• 2× the usual chance of encountering Brilliant Pokémon • 6× the usual chance of encountering Shiny Pokémon

Check Your Numbers!

Look at that nice Pokédex you've got on your Rotom Phone, and you can see how many times you've caught or defeated a species. The number is listed right there, beside the words "Number Battled."

ENG		
No. 046	Yamper	
	Puppy Pokémon	
Type	ELECTRIC	
Height	1'	
Weight	29.8 lbs.	
Number Battled	3	

This Pokémon is very popular as a herding dog in the Galar region. As it runs, it generates electricity from the base of its tail.

Ⓐ Motion/Cry Ⓧ Habitat Ⓡ Switch Languages Ⓑ Back

Fishing chains

When it comes to fishing up Brilliant Pokémon, it's not the times you've battled a particular species that matters most. Instead, the likelihood of reeling in such a Pokémon will be tied to the number of times you're successful in hooking a bite in a row—no matter what species you fish up.

If you can keep getting bites and defeating whatever you've hooked, you'll become more likely to fish up Brilliant Pokémon and get all the benefits that come along with them. But if you leave the area, turn off your game, or fail to reel anything in, then your chain will break. Catching the Pokémon, being defeated, or running from battle will also break a chain. You've got to defeat the Pokémon you fish up to reap these rewards!

Number of successful hooks in a row	Effects on future fishing encounters
0–2	Roughly the usual chance of encountering Brilliant Pokémon
3–6	About 1.3× the usual chance of encountering Brilliant Pokémon
7–14	About 3.3× the usual chance of encountering Brilliant Pokémon
15–24	About 6.6× the usual chance of encountering Brilliant Pokémon
25+	About 16.6× the usual chance of encountering Brilliant Pokémon

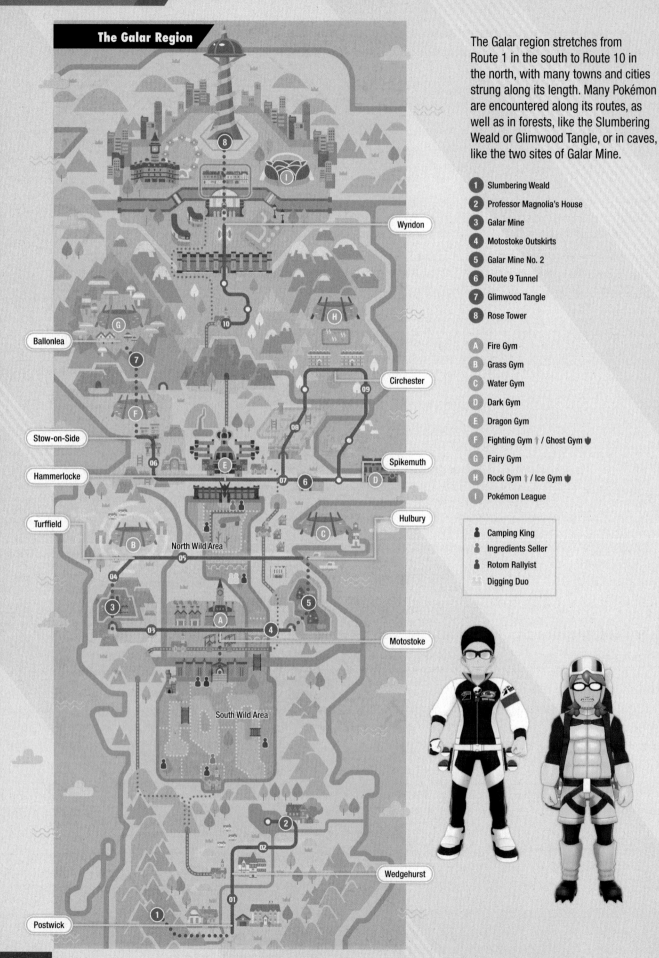

The Galar Region

Wyndon

Ballonlea

Circhester

Stow-on-Side

Hammerlocke

Spikemuth

Turffield

Hulbury

North Wild Area

Motostoke

South Wild Area

Wedgehurst

Postwick

The Galar region stretches from Route 1 in the south to Route 10 in the north, with many towns and cities strung along its length. Many Pokémon are encountered along its routes, as well as in forests, like the Slumbering Weald or Glimwood Tangle, or in caves, like the two sites of Galar Mine.

1. Slumbering Weald
2. Professor Magnolia's House
3. Galar Mine
4. Motostoke Outskirts
5. Galar Mine No. 2
6. Route 9 Tunnel
7. Glimwood Tangle
8. Rose Tower

A. Fire Gym
B. Grass Gym
C. Water Gym
D. Dark Gym
E. Dragon Gym
F. Fighting Gym ♂ / Ghost Gym ♀
G. Fairy Gym
H. Rock Gym ♂ / Ice Gym ♀
I. Pokémon League

- Camping King
- Ingredients Seller
- Rotom Rallyist
- Digging Duo

The Wild Area

In the heart of the Galar region is a vast wilderness called the Wild Area, which is where you'll find the greatest diversity of Pokémon species to battle and catch. If you're trying to fill your Pokédex, you'll definitely be spending a lot of time here. Use the map below to familiarize yourself with each of the Wild Area's 18 zones.

1 Meetup Spot
2 Dappled Grove
3 Rolling Fields
4 Giant's Seat
5 West Lake Axewell
6 Axew's Eye

7 South Lake Miloch
8 Watchtower Ruins
9 East Lake Axewell
10 North Lake Miloch
11 Motostoke Riverbank
12 Bridge Field

13 Stony Wilderness
14 Giant's Cap
15 Dusty Bowl
16 Giant's Mirror
17 Lake of Outrage
18 Hammerlocke Hills

How to Use This Book

The information for each species of Pokémon is split into two broad sections: Pokédex Entries and Move Tables. Check out the Pokédex Entries section for different species and forms to learn general info about them and how to obtain them. When you want to know about each species in more detail, turn to their page in the Move Tables section to see all the moves they can learn, how they'll take damage in battle, what Abilities they can have, and more info relevant for battle.

Pokédex Entries

1. You can see the artwork of each Pokémon here.

2. If genders look different, they'll be shown here.

3. Evolution conditions are summarized here.

4. Type icons here show the Pokémon's type or types.

5. Galar Pokédex number, category, and name are found here—followed by height, weight, and the page where you'll find the Pokémon in the Move Tables section.

6. Descriptions from both *Pokémon Sword* and *Pokémon Shield* are here to tell you more about this species, and there's also advice on how you can get the Pokémon for yourself. Some of the special terms used to describe where to find Pokémon are explained below.

   Appears in tall grass   This Pokémon will be visible moving about in tall patches of grass.

   Appears as a random encounter   This Pokémon will be lurking unseen in the tall grass. A ❗ will appear where you may run into them.

   Appears on the ground   This Pokémon will be visible on the ground in places like caves.

   Appears flying   This Pokémon will be visible floating or flying overhead.

   Appears on the water's surface   This Pokémon will be visible swimming on the surface of a body of water.

   Appears wandering   This Pokémon will be visible wandering in unusual ways or won't simply stick to the tall grass.

7. If Pokémon have form names for different appearances, they'll be on the side here.

8. Sometimes there is a special entry here when a Pokémon needs a bit more explanation.

9. Items that the Pokémon may be holding when you catch one in the wild are shown here.

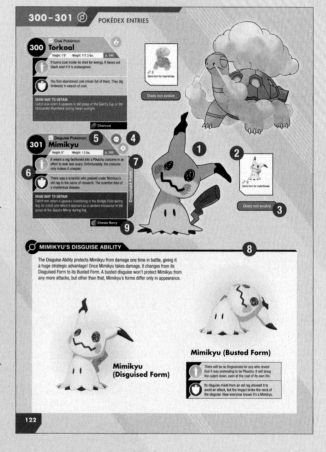

Move Tables

1. In the corner, you'll find an image of how the Pokémon appears in-game, beside its Galar Pokédex number and types.

2. Here is its name and what page it's on in the Pokédex Entries section, plus a form name if it has one.

3. Abilities and Hidden Abilities this species can have are found here.

4. Species strengths, which affect how quickly this species' stats tend to grow, are illustrated here.

5. See here how its types can affect how much damage it takes from moves of each type (and if any of its Abilities can affect these matchups, the affected matchups will be marked with a ❶).

6. Egg Groups are shown here, if you're hoping to find Pokémon Eggs.

7. And here are all the move tables themselves. For a breakdown of the different categories of move displayed in each table, see page 188.

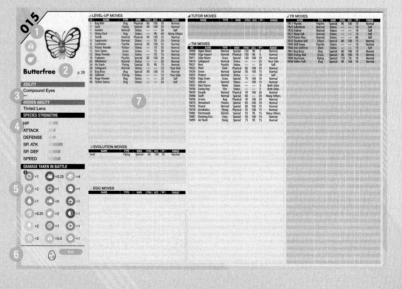

POKÉDEX ENTRIES

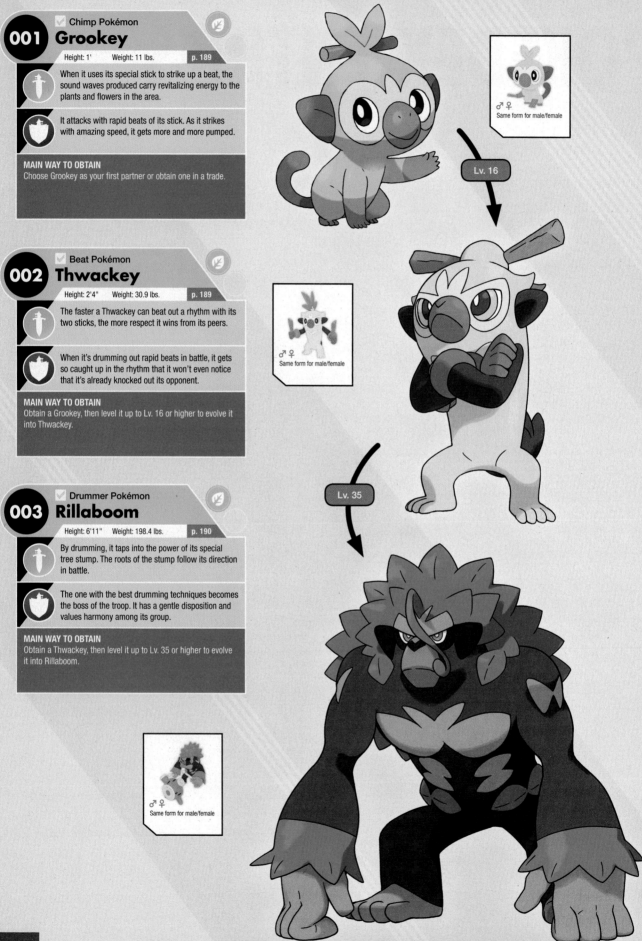

001 Grookey
Chimp Pokémon

Height: 1'   Weight: 11 lbs.   p. 189

When it uses its special stick to strike up a beat, the sound waves produced carry revitalizing energy to the plants and flowers in the area.

It attacks with rapid beats of its stick. As it strikes with amazing speed, it gets more and more pumped.

MAIN WAY TO OBTAIN
Choose Grookey as your first partner or obtain one in a trade.

Same form for male/female

Lv. 16

002 Thwackey
Beat Pokémon

Height: 2'4"   Weight: 30.9 lbs.   p. 189

The faster a Thwackey can beat out a rhythm with its two sticks, the more respect it wins from its peers.

When it's drumming out rapid beats in battle, it gets so caught up in the rhythm that it won't even notice that it's already knocked out its opponent.

MAIN WAY TO OBTAIN
Obtain a Grookey, then level it up to Lv. 16 or higher to evolve it into Thwackey.

Same form for male/female

Lv. 35

003 Rillaboom
Drummer Pokémon

Height: 6'11"   Weight: 198.4 lbs.   p. 190

By drumming, it taps into the power of its special tree stump. The roots of the stump follow its direction in battle.

The one with the best drumming techniques becomes the boss of the troop. It has a gentle disposition and values harmony among its group.

MAIN WAY TO OBTAIN
Obtain a Thwackey, then level it up to Lv. 35 or higher to evolve it into Rillaboom.

Same form for male/female

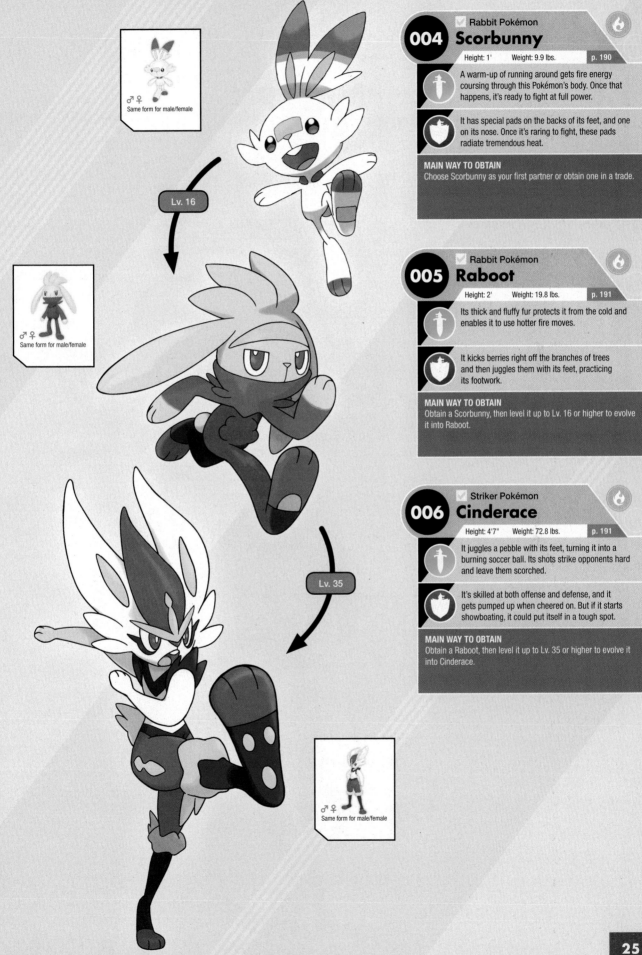

Same form for male/female

Lv. 16

Same form for male/female

Lv. 35

Same form for male/female

004 Scorbunny
☑ Rabbit Pokémon

Height: 1'   Weight: 9.9 lbs.   p. 190

A warm-up of running around gets fire energy coursing through this Pokémon's body. Once that happens, it's ready to fight at full power.

It has special pads on the backs of its feet, and one on its nose. Once it's raring to fight, these pads radiate tremendous heat.

MAIN WAY TO OBTAIN
Choose Scorbunny as your first partner or obtain one in a trade.

005 Raboot
☑ Rabbit Pokémon

Height: 2'   Weight: 19.8 lbs.   p. 191

Its thick and fluffy fur protects it from the cold and enables it to use hotter fire moves.

It kicks berries right off the branches of trees and then juggles them with its feet, practicing its footwork.

MAIN WAY TO OBTAIN
Obtain a Scorbunny, then level it up to Lv. 16 or higher to evolve it into Raboot.

006 Cinderace
☑ Striker Pokémon

Height: 4'7"   Weight: 72.8 lbs.   p. 191

It juggles a pebble with its feet, turning it into a burning soccer ball. Its shots strike opponents hard and leave them scorched.

It's skilled at both offense and defense, and it gets pumped up when cheered on. But if it starts showboating, it could put itself in a tough spot.

MAIN WAY TO OBTAIN
Obtain a Raboot, then level it up to Lv. 35 or higher to evolve it into Cinderace.

007 ☑ Water Lizard Pokémon
Sobble

| Height: 1' | Weight: 8.8 lbs. | p. 192 |

When scared, this Pokémon cries. Its tears pack the chemical punch of 100 onions, and attackers won't be able to resist weeping.

When it gets wet, its skin changes color, and this Pokémon becomes invisible as if it were camouflaged.

MAIN WAY TO OBTAIN
Choose Sobble as your first partner or obtain one in a trade.

♂ ♀
Same form for male/female

Lv. 16

008 ☑ Water Lizard Pokémon
Drizzile

| Height: 2'4" | Weight: 25.4 lbs. | p. 192 |

A clever combatant, this Pokémon battles using water balloons created with moisture secreted from its palms.

Highly intelligent but also very lazy, it keeps enemies out of its territory by laying traps everywhere.

MAIN WAY TO OBTAIN
Obtain a Sobble, then level it up to Lv. 16 or higher to evolve it into Drizzile.

♂ ♀
Same form for male/female

Lv. 35

009 ☑ Secret Agent Pokémon
Inteleon

| Height: 6'3" | Weight: 99.6 lbs. | p. 193 |

It has many hidden capabilities, such as fingertips that can shoot water and a membrane on its back that it can use to glide through the air.

Its nictitating membranes let it pick out foes' weak points so it can precisely blast them with water that shoots from its fingertips at Mach 3.

MAIN WAY TO OBTAIN
Obtain a Drizzile, then level it up to Lv. 35 or higher to evolve it into Inteleon.

♂ ♀
Same form for male/female

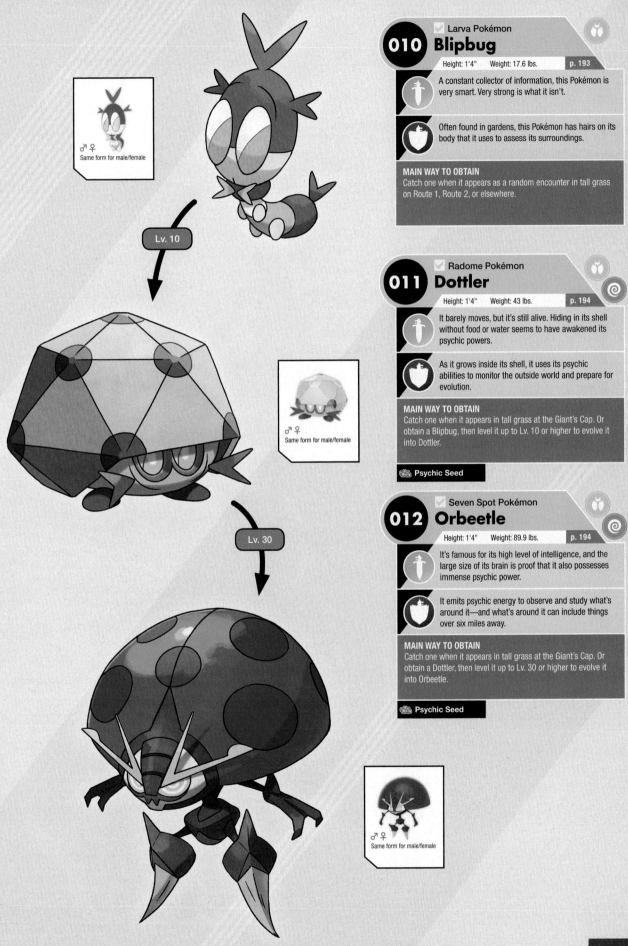

♂ ♀
Same form for male/female

Lv. 10

Lv. 30

♂ ♀
Same form for male/female

♂ ♀
Same form for male/female

010 Blipbug
☑ Larva Pokémon

| Height: 1'4" | Weight: 17.6 lbs. | p. 193 |

A constant collector of information, this Pokémon is very smart. Very strong is what it isn't.

Often found in gardens, this Pokémon has hairs on its body that it uses to assess its surroundings.

MAIN WAY TO OBTAIN
Catch one when it appears as a random encounter in tall grass on Route 1, Route 2, or elsewhere.

011 Dottler
☑ Radome Pokémon

| Height: 1'4" | Weight: 43 lbs. | p. 194 |

It barely moves, but it's still alive. Hiding in its shell without food or water seems to have awakened its psychic powers.

As it grows inside its shell, it uses its psychic abilities to monitor the outside world and prepare for evolution.

MAIN WAY TO OBTAIN
Catch one when it appears in tall grass at the Giant's Cap. Or obtain a Blipbug, then level it up to Lv. 10 or higher to evolve it into Dottler.

🌀 Psychic Seed

012 Orbeetle
☑ Seven Spot Pokémon

| Height: 1'4" | Weight: 89.9 lbs. | p. 194 |

It's famous for its high level of intelligence, and the large size of its brain is proof that it also possesses immense psychic power.

It emits psychic energy to observe and study what's around it—and what's around it can include things over six miles away.

MAIN WAY TO OBTAIN
Catch one when it appears in tall grass at the Giant's Cap. Or obtain a Dottler, then level it up to Lv. 30 or higher to evolve it into Orbeetle.

🌀 Psychic Seed

013 Caterpie
Worm Pokémon

| Height: 1' | Weight: 6.4 lbs. | p. 195 |

For protection, it releases a horrible stench from the antenna on its head to drive away enemies.

Its short feet are tipped with suction pads that enable it to tirelessly climb slopes and walls.

MAIN WAY TO OBTAIN
Catch one when it appears as a random encounter in tall grass on Route 1.

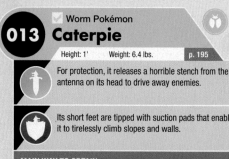

♂ ♀
Same form for male/female

014 Metapod
Cocoon Pokémon

| Height: 2'4" | Weight: 21.8 lbs. | p. 195 |

It is waiting for the moment to evolve. At this stage, it can only harden, so it remains motionless to avoid attack.

Even though it is encased in a sturdy shell, the body inside is tender. It can't withstand a harsh attack.

MAIN WAY TO OBTAIN
Catch one when it appears in tall grass in the Rolling Fields. Or obtain a Caterpie, then level it up to Lv. 7 or higher to evolve it into Metapod.

015 Butterfree
Butterfly Pokémon

| Height: 3'7" | Weight: 70.5 lbs. | p. 196 |

In battle, it flaps its wings at great speed to release highly toxic dust into the air.

It collects honey every day. It rubs honey onto the hairs on its legs to carry it back to its nest.

MAIN WAY TO OBTAIN
Catch one when it appears flying in the sky above the Rolling Fields. Or obtain a Metapod, then level it up to Lv. 10 or higher to evolve it into Butterfree.

◆ Silver Powder

♂   ♀
The male's lower wings are white at their center, where the female's lower wings are black.

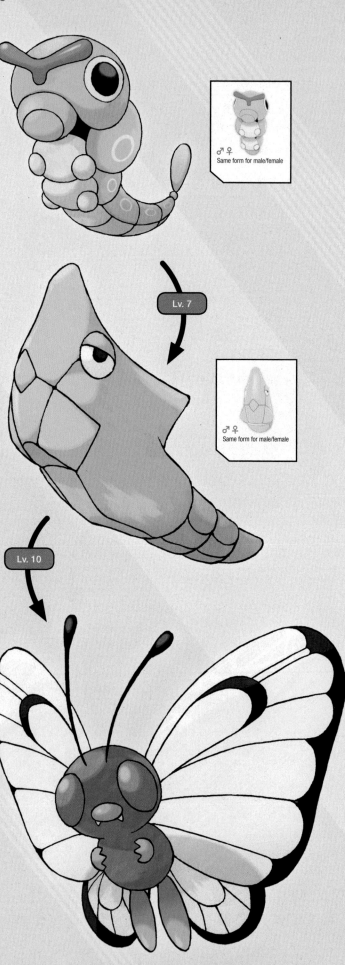

Lv. 7

♂ ♀
Same form for male/female

Lv. 10

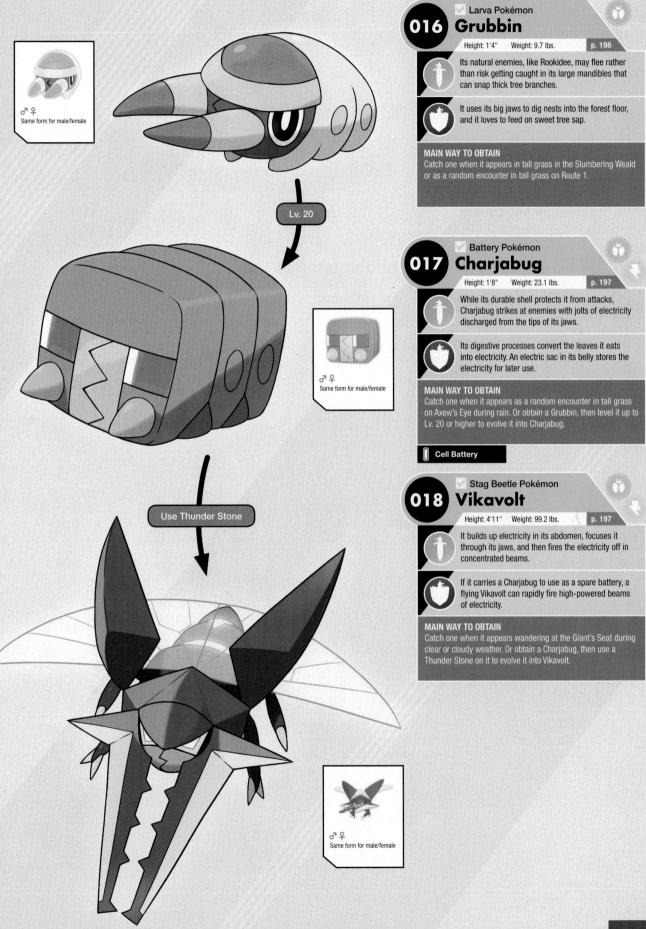

Same form for male/female

Lv. 20

Use Thunder Stone

016 Grubbin
☑ Larva Pokémon

Height: 1'4"   Weight: 9.7 lbs.   p. 196

Its natural enemies, like Rookidee, may flee rather than risk getting caught in its large mandibles that can snap thick tree branches.

It uses its big jaws to dig nests into the forest floor, and it loves to feed on sweet tree sap.

MAIN WAY TO OBTAIN
Catch one when it appears in tall grass in the Slumbering Weald or as a random encounter in tall grass on Route 1.

017 Charjabug
☑ Battery Pokémon

Height: 1'8"   Weight: 23.1 lbs.   p. 197

While its durable shell protects it from attacks, Charjabug strikes at enemies with jolts of electricity discharged from the tips of its jaws.

Its digestive processes convert the leaves it eats into electricity. An electric sac in its belly stores the electricity for later use.

MAIN WAY TO OBTAIN
Catch one when it appears as a random encounter in tall grass on Axew's Eye during rain. Or obtain a Grubbin, then level it up to Lv. 20 or higher to evolve it into Charjabug.

🔋 Cell Battery

018 Vikavolt
☑ Stag Beetle Pokémon

Height: 4'11"   Weight: 99.2 lbs.   p. 197

It builds up electricity in its abdomen, focuses it through its jaws, and then fires the electricity off in concentrated beams.

If it carries a Charjabug to use as a spare battery, a flying Vikavolt can rapidly fire high-powered beams of electricity.

MAIN WAY TO OBTAIN
Catch one when it appears wandering at the Giant's Seat during clear or cloudy weather. Or obtain a Charjabug, then use a Thunder Stone on it to evolve it into Vikavolt.

Same form for male/female

019 Hoothoot

☑ Owl Pokémon

Height: 2'4"   Weight: 46.7 lbs.   p. 198

It always stands on one foot. It changes feet so fast, the movement can rarely be seen.

It begins to hoot at the same time every day. Some Trainers use them in place of clocks.

MAIN WAY TO OBTAIN
Catch one when it appears as a random encounter in tall grass on Route 1 or Route 2.

020 Noctowl

☑ Owl Pokémon

Height: 5'3"   Weight: 89.9 lbs.   p. 198

Its eyes are specially developed to enable it to see clearly even in murky darkness and minimal light.

When it needs to think, it rotates its head 180 degrees to sharpen its intellectual power.

MAIN WAY TO OBTAIN
Catch one when it appears in tall grass in the Motostoke Outskirts. Or obtain a Hoothoot, then level it up to Lv. 20 or higher to evolve it into Noctowl.

♂ ♀
Same form for male/female

Lv. 20

♂ ♀
Same form for male/female

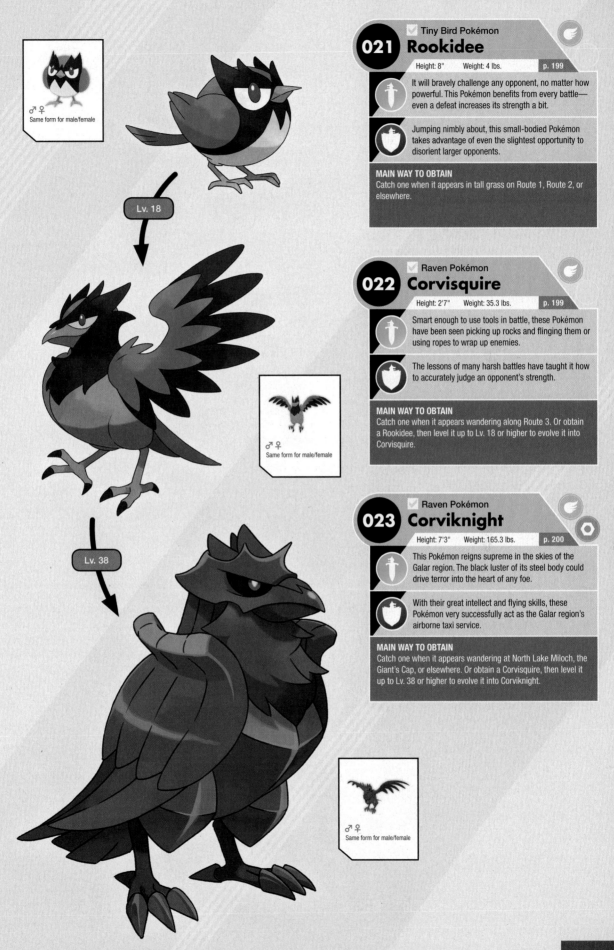

♂♀
Same form for male/female

Lv. 18

☑ Tiny Bird Pokémon

021 Rookidee

| Height: 8" | Weight: 4 lbs. | p. 199 |

It will bravely challenge any opponent, no matter how powerful. This Pokémon benefits from every battle—even a defeat increases its strength a bit.

Jumping nimbly about, this small-bodied Pokémon takes advantage of even the slightest opportunity to disorient larger opponents.

MAIN WAY TO OBTAIN
Catch one when it appears in tall grass on Route 1, Route 2, or elsewhere.

☑ Raven Pokémon

022 Corvisquire

| Height: 2'7" | Weight: 35.3 lbs. | p. 199 |

Smart enough to use tools in battle, these Pokémon have been seen picking up rocks and flinging them or using ropes to wrap up enemies.

The lessons of many harsh battles have taught it how to accurately judge an opponent's strength.

MAIN WAY TO OBTAIN
Catch one when it appears wandering along Route 3. Or obtain a Rookidee, then level it up to Lv. 18 or higher to evolve it into Corvisquire.

♂♀
Same form for male/female

Lv. 38

☑ Raven Pokémon

023 Corviknight

| Height: 7'3" | Weight: 165.3 lbs. | p. 200 |

This Pokémon reigns supreme in the skies of the Galar region. The black luster of its steel body could drive terror into the heart of any foe.

With their great intellect and flying skills, these Pokémon very successfully act as the Galar region's airborne taxi service.

MAIN WAY TO OBTAIN
Catch one when it appears wandering at North Lake Miloch, the Giant's Cap, or elsewhere. Or obtain a Corvisquire, then level it up to Lv. 38 or higher to evolve it into Corviknight.

♂♀
Same form for male/female

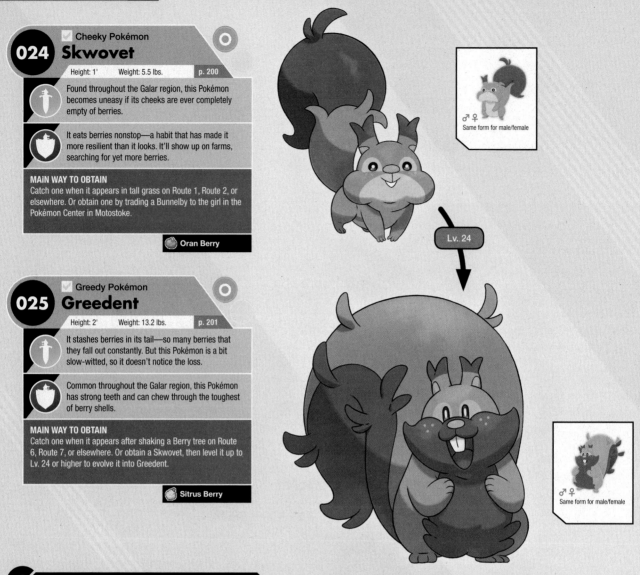

024 ☑ Cheeky Pokémon
Skwovet

| Height: 1' | Weight: 5.5 lbs. | p. 200 |

Found throughout the Galar region, this Pokémon becomes uneasy if its cheeks are ever completely empty of berries.

It eats berries nonstop—a habit that has made it more resilient than it looks. It'll show up on farms, searching for yet more berries.

MAIN WAY TO OBTAIN
Catch one when it appears in tall grass on Route 1, Route 2, or elsewhere. Or obtain one by trading a Bunnelby to the girl in the Pokémon Center in Motostoke.

⬤ Oran Berry

Same form for male/female

Lv. 24

025 ☑ Greedy Pokémon
Greedent

| Height: 2' | Weight: 13.2 lbs. | p. 201 |

It stashes berries in its tail—so many berries that they fall out constantly. But this Pokémon is a bit slow-witted, so it doesn't notice the loss.

Common throughout the Galar region, this Pokémon has strong teeth and can chew through the toughest of berry shells.

MAIN WAY TO OBTAIN
Catch one when it appears after shaking a Berry tree on Route 6, Route 7, or elsewhere. Or obtain a Skwovet, then level it up to Lv. 24 or higher to evolve it into Greedent.

⬤ Sitrus Berry

Same form for male/female

⊙ MALE AND FEMALE SPECIMENS

Unfezant is a Pokémon that can look radically different depending on its gender. It isn't the only one, though. A number of Pokémon can have different appearances for males and females. Sometimes these differences are very subtle and can be easily overlooked, but others can be like Unfezant here—so different in appearance that you might accidentally assume they were different Pokémon! For most Pokémon, these gender differences don't have any effect on the Pokémon's stats or anything else. When they do, each form will be covered separately in this book.

Male Unfezant   **Female Unfezant**

Same form for male/female

026 Pidove
Tiny Pigeon Pokémon

Height: 1' | Weight: 4.6 lbs. | p. 201

Where people go, these Pokémon follow. If you're scattering food for them, be careful—several hundred of them can gather at once.

It's forgetful and not very bright, but many Trainers love it anyway for its friendliness and sincerity.

MAIN WAY TO OBTAIN
Catch one when it appears flying in the sky above the Rolling Fields or East Lake Axewell.

Lv. 21

027 Tranquill
Wild Pigeon Pokémon

Height: 2' | Weight: 33.1 lbs. | p. 202

It can fly moderately quickly. No matter how far it travels, it can always find its way back to its master and its nest.

These bright Pokémon have acute memories. Apparently delivery workers often choose them as their partners.

MAIN WAY TO OBTAIN
Catch one when it appears flying in the sky above the Stony Wilderness. Or obtain a Pidove, then level it up to Lv. 21 or higher to evolve it into Tranquill.

Same form for male/female

Lv. 32

028 Unfezant
Proud Pokémon

Height: 3'11" | Weight: 63.9 lbs. | p. 202

Unfezant are exceptional fliers. The females are known for their stamina, while the males outclass them in terms of speed.

This Pokémon is intelligent and intensely proud. People will sit up and take notice if you become the Trainer of one.

MAIN WAY TO OBTAIN
Catch one when it appears flying in the sky above Hammerlocke Hills. Or obtain a Tranquill, then level it up to Lv. 32 or higher to evolve it into Unfezant.

♂ ♀
The male has masklike plumage and a green pattern on its belly, where the female has no plumage and a brown pattern on its belly.

029 ☑ Fox Pokémon
Nickit

Height: 2'   Weight: 19.6 lbs.   p. 203

Aided by the soft pads on its feet, it silently raids the food stores of other Pokémon. It survives off its ill-gotten gains.

Cunning and cautious, this Pokémon survives by stealing food from others. It erases its tracks with swipes of its tail as it makes off with its plunder.

MAIN WAY TO OBTAIN
Catch one when it appears in tall grass on Route 2.

030 ☑ Fox Pokémon
Thievul

Height: 3'11"   Weight: 43.9 lbs.   p. 203

It secretly marks potential targets with a scent. By following the scent, it stalks its targets and steals from them when they least expect it.

With a lithe body and sharp claws, it goes around stealing food and eggs. Boltund is its natural enemy.

MAIN WAY TO OBTAIN
Catch one when it appears in tall grass on Route 7. Or obtain a Nickit, then level it up to Lv. 18 or higher to evolve it into Thievul.

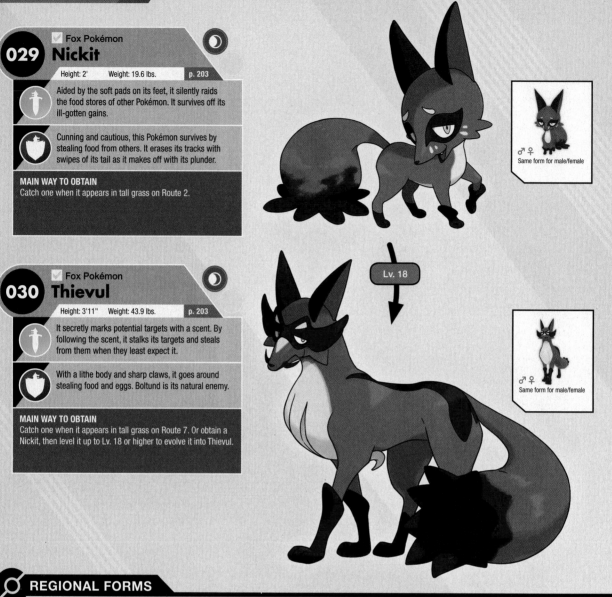

♂ ♀
Same form for male/female

Lv. 18

♂ ♀
Same form for male/female

⚙ REGIONAL FORMS

If you've played other Pokémon games in the past, you might remember Zigzagoon looking a bit different. The Galarian Zigzagoon is what's known as a regional form—a Pokémon adapted to thrive in a particular region. These Pokémon have different characteristics than those you might be familiar with, such as different types or Abilities when compared to the usual form of the same Pokémon species. There are a number of such Pokémon adapted to the Galar region in this way, so they have Galarian forms. You can also find Alolan forms in some games, which have adapted to the tropical climate in the Alola region!

Galarian Zigzagoon

Zigzagoon as it can sometimes be found in other regions

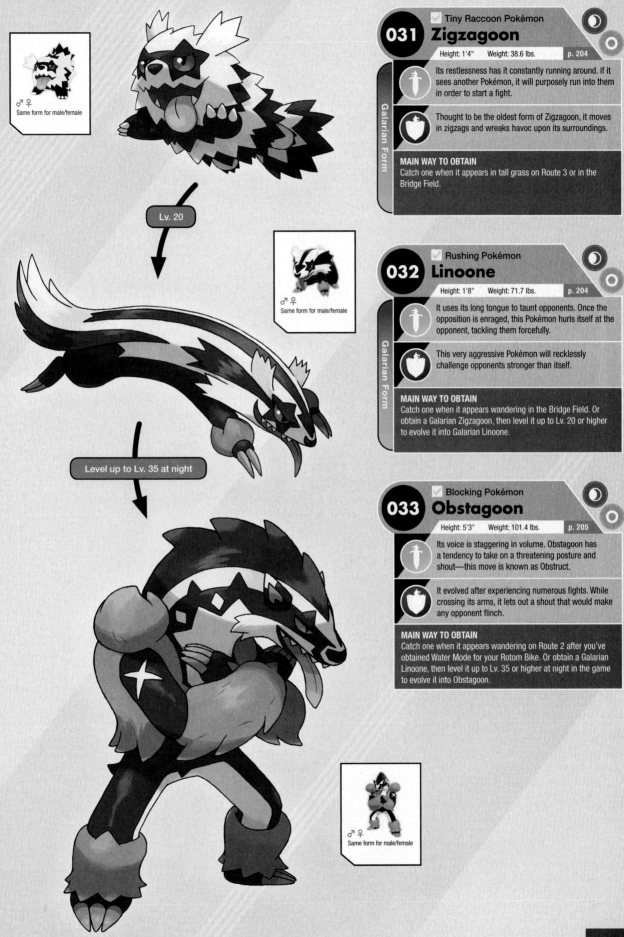

Same form for male/female

Lv. 20

Level up to Lv. 35 at night

Same form for male/female

Same form for male/female

031 Zigzagoon
Tiny Raccoon Pokémon

Height: 1'4" Weight: 38.6 lbs. p. 204

Galarian Form

Its restlessness has it constantly running around. If it sees another Pokémon, it will purposely run into them in order to start a fight.

Thought to be the oldest form of Zigzagoon, it moves in zigzags and wreaks havoc upon its surroundings.

MAIN WAY TO OBTAIN
Catch one when it appears in tall grass on Route 3 or in the Bridge Field.

032 Linoone
Rushing Pokémon

Height: 1'8" Weight: 71.7 lbs. p. 204

Galarian Form

It uses its long tongue to taunt opponents. Once the opposition is enraged, this Pokémon hurls itself at the opponent, tackling them forcefully.

This very aggressive Pokémon will recklessly challenge opponents stronger than itself.

MAIN WAY TO OBTAIN
Catch one when it appears wandering in the Bridge Field. Or obtain a Galarian Zigzagoon, then level it up to Lv. 20 or higher to evolve it into Galarian Linoone.

033 Obstagoon
Blocking Pokémon

Height: 5'3" Weight: 101.4 lbs. p. 205

Its voice is staggering in volume. Obstagoon has a tendency to take on a threatening posture and shout—this move is known as Obstruct.

It evolved after experiencing numerous fights. While crossing its arms, it lets out a shout that would make any opponent flinch.

MAIN WAY TO OBTAIN
Catch one when it appears wandering on Route 2 after you've obtained Water Mode for your Rotom Bike. Or obtain a Galarian Linoone, then level it up to Lv. 35 or higher at night in the game to evolve it into Obstagoon.

034 ☑ Sheep Pokémon
Wooloo

| Height: 2' | Weight: 13.2 lbs. | p. 205 |

Its curly fleece is such an effective cushion that this Pokémon could fall off a cliff and stand right back up at the bottom, unharmed.

If its fleece grows too long, Wooloo won't be able to move. Cloth made with the wool of this Pokémon is surprisingly strong.

MAIN WAY TO OBTAIN
Catch one when it appears in tall grass on Route 1 or more commonly as a random encounter in tall grass on Route 4.

035 ☑ Sheep Pokémon
Dubwool

| Height: 4'3" | Weight: 94.8 lbs. | p. 206 |

Weave a carpet from its springy wool, and you end up with something closer to a trampoline. You'll start to bounce the moment you set foot on it.

Its majestic horns are meant only to impress the opposite gender. They never see use in battle.

MAIN WAY TO OBTAIN
Catch one when it appears wandering in the Rolling Fields after you become Champion. Or obtain a Wooloo, then level it up to Lv. 24 or higher to evolve it into Dubwool.

♂ ♀
Same form for male/female

Lv. 24

♂ ♀
Same form for male/female

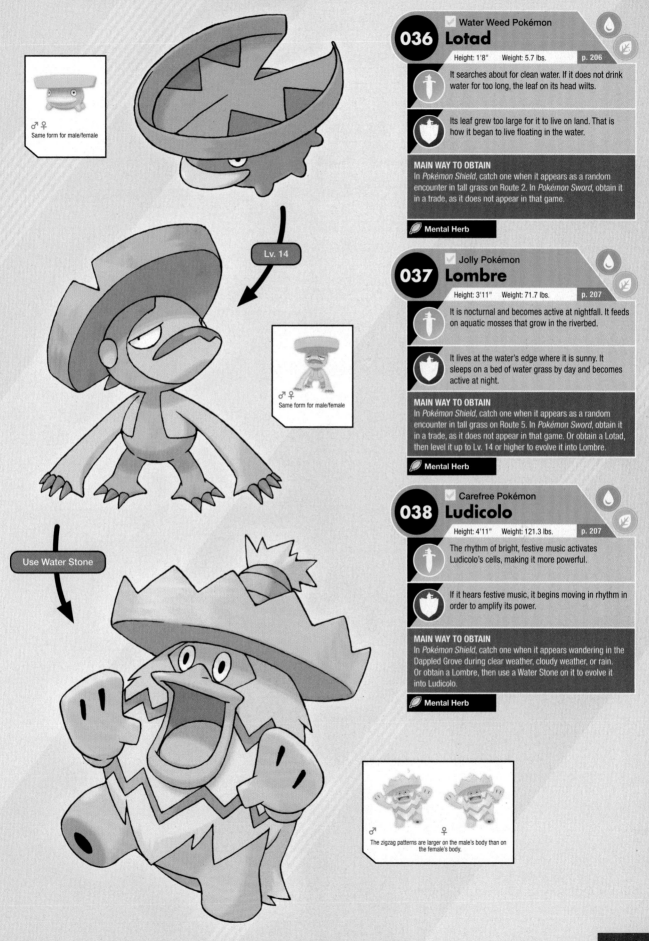

Same form for male/female

Lv. 14

Same form for male/female

Use Water Stone

036 Lotad

Water Weed Pokémon

Height: 1'8" Weight: 5.7 lbs. p. 206

It searches about for clean water. If it does not drink water for too long, the leaf on its head wilts.

Its leaf grew too large for it to live on land. That is how it began to live floating in the water.

MAIN WAY TO OBTAIN
In *Pokémon Shield*, catch one when it appears as a random encounter in tall grass on Route 2. In *Pokémon Sword*, obtain it in a trade, as it does not appear in that game.

Mental Herb

037 Lombre

Jolly Pokémon

Height: 3'11" Weight: 71.7 lbs. p. 207

It is nocturnal and becomes active at nightfall. It feeds on aquatic mosses that grow in the riverbed.

It lives at the water's edge where it is sunny. It sleeps on a bed of water grass by day and becomes active at night.

MAIN WAY TO OBTAIN
In *Pokémon Shield*, catch one when it appears as a random encounter in tall grass on Route 5. In *Pokémon Sword*, obtain it in a trade, as it does not appear in that game. Or obtain a Lotad, then level it up to Lv. 14 or higher to evolve it into Lombre.

Mental Herb

038 Ludicolo

Carefree Pokémon

Height: 4'11" Weight: 121.3 lbs. p. 207

The rhythm of bright, festive music activates Ludicolo's cells, making it more powerful.

If it hears festive music, it begins moving in rhythm in order to amplify its power.

MAIN WAY TO OBTAIN
In *Pokémon Shield*, catch one when it appears wandering in the Dappled Grove during clear weather, cloudy weather, or rain. Or obtain a Lombre, then use a Water Stone on it to evolve it into Ludicolo.

Mental Herb

♂ ♀
The zigzag patterns are larger on the male's body than on the female's body.

039 Seedot

☑ Acorn Pokémon

Height: 1'8"   Weight: 8.8 lbs.   p. 208

If it remains still, it looks just like a real nut. It delights in surprising foraging Pokémon.

It attaches itself to a tree branch using the top of its head. Strong winds can sometimes make it fall.

MAIN WAY TO OBTAIN
In *Pokémon Sword*, catch one when it appears as a random encounter in tall grass on Route 2. In *Pokémon Shield*, obtain it in a trade, as it does not appear in that game.

🍃 Power Herb

040 Nuzleaf

☑ Wily Pokémon

Height: 3'3"   Weight: 61.7 lbs.   p. 208

It lives deep in forests. With the leaf on its head, it makes a flute whose song makes listeners uneasy.

They live in holes bored in large trees. The sound of Nuzleaf's grass flute fills listeners with dread.

MAIN WAY TO OBTAIN
In *Pokémon Sword*, catch one when it appears as a random encounter in tall grass on Route 5. In *Pokémon Shield*, obtain it in a trade, as it does not appear in that game. Or obtain a Seedot, then level it up to Lv. 14 or higher to evolve it into Nuzleaf.

🍃 Power Herb

041 Shiftry

☑ Wicked Pokémon

Height: 4'3"   Weight: 131.4 lbs.   p. 209

A Pokémon that was feared as a forest guardian. It can read the foe's mind and take preemptive action.

It lives quietly in the deep forest. It is said to create chilly winter winds with the fans it holds.

MAIN WAY TO OBTAIN
In *Pokémon Sword*, catch one when it appears wandering in the Dappled Grove during clear weather, cloudy weather, or rain. Or obtain a Nuzleaf, then use a Leaf Stone on it to evolve it into Shiftry.

🍃 Power Herb

♂ ♀
Same form for male/female

Lv. 14

♂   ♀
The male has a larger leaf on its head than the female.

Use Leaf Stone

♂   ♀
The male has larger leaves on its hands than the female.

♂♀
Same form for male/female

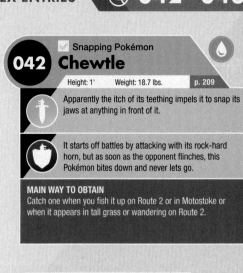

☑ Snapping Pokémon
042 Chewtle

| Height: 1' | Weight: 18.7 lbs. | p. 209 |

Apparently the itch of its teething impels it to snap its jaws at anything in front of it.

It starts off battles by attacking with its rock-hard horn, but as soon as the opponent flinches, this Pokémon bites down and never lets go.

MAIN WAY TO OBTAIN
Catch one when you fish it up on Route 2 or in Motostoke or when it appears in tall grass or wandering on Route 2.

☑ Bite Pokémon
043 Drednaw

| Height: 3'3" | Weight: 254.6 lbs. | p. 210 |

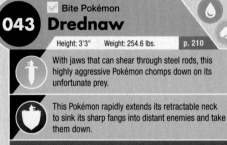

With jaws that can shear through steel rods, this highly aggressive Pokémon chomps down on its unfortunate prey.

This Pokémon rapidly extends its retractable neck to sink its sharp fangs into distant enemies and take them down.

MAIN WAY TO OBTAIN
Catch one when you fish it up in the Bridge Field or at the Giant's Mirror, or when it appears wandering at the Giant's Cap. Or obtain a Chewtle, then level it up to Lv. 22 or higher to evolve it into Drednaw.

Lv. 22

♂♀
Same form for male/female

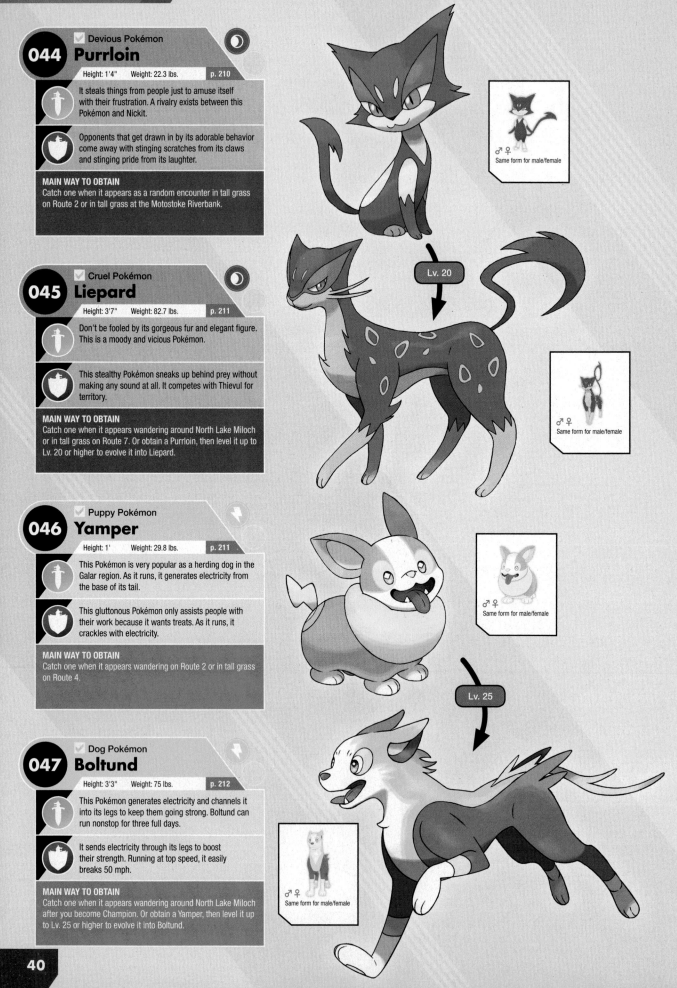

044 Purrloin
☑ Devious Pokémon 🌙

Height: 1'4" Weight: 22.3 lbs. p. 210

⚔ It steals things from people just to amuse itself with their frustration. A rivalry exists between this Pokémon and Nickit.

🛡 Opponents that get drawn in by its adorable behavior come away with stinging scratches from its claws and stinging pride from its laughter.

MAIN WAY TO OBTAIN
Catch one when it appears as a random encounter in tall grass on Route 2 or in tall grass at the Motostoke Riverbank.

Same form for male/female ♂ ♀

045 Liepard
☑ Cruel Pokémon 🌙

Height: 3'7" Weight: 82.7 lbs. p. 211

⚔ Don't be fooled by its gorgeous fur and elegant figure. This is a moody and vicious Pokémon.

🛡 This stealthy Pokémon sneaks up behind prey without making any sound at all. It competes with Thievul for territory.

MAIN WAY TO OBTAIN
Catch one when it appears wandering around North Lake Miloch or in tall grass on Route 7. Or obtain a Purrloin, then level it up to Lv. 20 or higher to evolve it into Liepard.

Lv. 20

Same form for male/female ♂ ♀

046 Yamper
☑ Puppy Pokémon ⚡

Height: 1' Weight: 29.8 lbs. p. 211

⚔ This Pokémon is very popular as a herding dog in the Galar region. As it runs, it generates electricity from the base of its tail.

🛡 This gluttonous Pokémon only assists people with their work because it wants treats. As it runs, it crackles with electricity.

MAIN WAY TO OBTAIN
Catch one when it appears wandering on Route 2 or in tall grass on Route 4.

Same form for male/female ♂ ♀

Lv. 25

047 Boltund
☑ Dog Pokémon ⚡

Height: 3'3" Weight: 75 lbs. p. 212

⚔ This Pokémon generates electricity and channels it into its legs to keep them going strong. Boltund can run nonstop for three full days.

🛡 It sends electricity through its legs to boost their strength. Running at top speed, it easily breaks 50 mph.

MAIN WAY TO OBTAIN
Catch one when it appears wandering around North Lake Miloch after you become Champion. Or obtain a Yamper, then level it up to Lv. 25 or higher to evolve it into Boltund.

Same form for male/female ♂ ♀

Same form for male/female

Lv. 20

Same form for male/female

Same form for male/female

Use Shiny Stone

Same form for male/female

048 Bunnelby
Digging Pokémon

Height: 1'4" Weight: 11 lbs. p. 212

It excels at digging holes. Using its ears, it can dig a nest 33 feet deep in one night.

It's very sensitive to danger. The sound of Corviknight's flapping will have Bunnelby digging a hole to hide underground in moments.

MAIN WAY TO OBTAIN
Catch one when it appears in tall grass or as a random encounter in tall grass in the Rolling Fields.

049 Diggersby
Digging Pokémon

Height: 3'3" Weight: 93.5 lbs. p. 213

With power equal to an excavator, it can dig through dense bedrock. It's a huge help during tunnel construction.

The fur on its belly retains heat exceptionally well. People used to make heavy winter clothing from fur shed by this Pokémon.

MAIN WAY TO OBTAIN
Catch one when it appears wandering in the Rolling Fields. Or obtain a Bunnelby, then level it up to Lv. 20 or higher to evolve it into Diggersby.

050 Minccino
Chinchilla Pokémon

Height: 1'4" Weight: 12.8 lbs. p. 213

The way it brushes away grime with its tail can be helpful when cleaning. But its focus on spotlessness can make cleaning more of a hassle.

They pet each other with their tails as a form of greeting. Of the two, the one whose tail is fluffier is a bit more boastful.

MAIN WAY TO OBTAIN
Catch one when it appears in tall grass on Route 5.

051 Cinccino
Scarf Pokémon

Height: 1'8" Weight: 16.5 lbs. p. 214

Its body secretes oil that this Pokémon spreads over its nest as a coating to protect it from dust. Cinccino won't tolerate even a speck of the stuff.

A special oil that seeps through their fur helps them avoid attacks. The oil fetches a high price at market.

MAIN WAY TO OBTAIN
Catch one when it appears wandering at the Giant's Cap during clear or cloudy weather. Or obtain a Minccino, then use a Shiny Stone on it to evolve it into Cinccino.

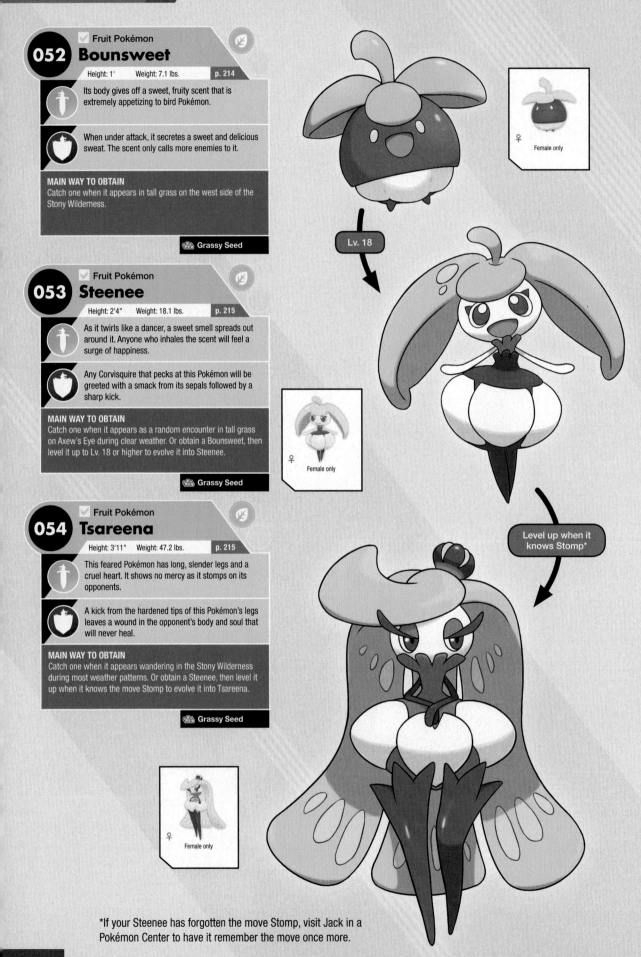

052 Bounsweet
☑ Fruit Pokémon

Height: 1'   Weight: 7.1 lbs.   p. 214

Its body gives off a sweet, fruity scent that is extremely appetizing to bird Pokémon.

When under attack, it secretes a sweet and delicious sweat. The scent only calls more enemies to it.

MAIN WAY TO OBTAIN
Catch one when it appears in tall grass on the west side of the Stony Wilderness.

🌱 Grassy Seed

♀ Female only

Lv. 18

053 Steenee
☑ Fruit Pokémon

Height: 2'4"   Weight: 18.1 lbs.   p. 215

As it twirls like a dancer, a sweet smell spreads out around it. Anyone who inhales the scent will feel a surge of happiness.

Any Corvisquire that pecks at this Pokémon will be greeted with a smack from its sepals followed by a sharp kick.

MAIN WAY TO OBTAIN
Catch one when it appears as a random encounter in tall grass on Axew's Eye during clear weather. Or obtain a Bounsweet, then level it up to Lv. 18 or higher to evolve it into Steenee.

🌱 Grassy Seed

♀ Female only

Level up when it knows Stomp*

054 Tsareena
☑ Fruit Pokémon

Height: 3'11"   Weight: 47.2 lbs.   p. 215

This feared Pokémon has long, slender legs and a cruel heart. It shows no mercy as it stomps on its opponents.

A kick from the hardened tips of this Pokémon's legs leaves a wound in the opponent's body and soul that will never heal.

MAIN WAY TO OBTAIN
Catch one when it appears wandering in the Stony Wilderness during most weather patterns. Or obtain a Steenee, then level it up when it knows the move Stomp to evolve it into Tsareena.

🌱 Grassy Seed

♀ Female only

*If your Steenee has forgotten the move Stomp, visit Jack in a Pokémon Center to have it remember the move once more.

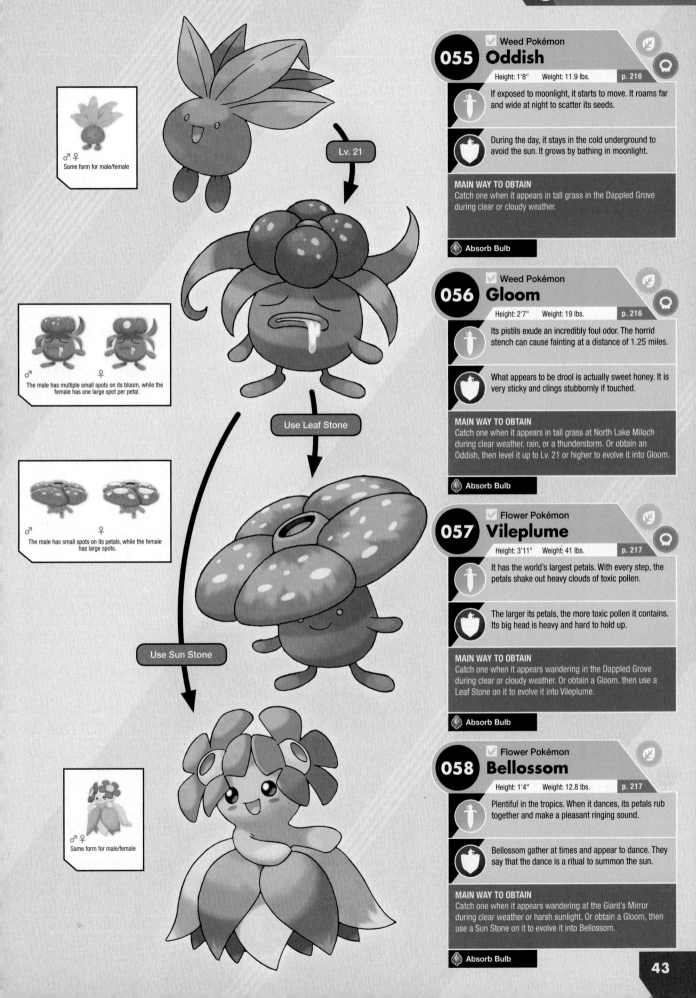

Same form for male/female

Lv. 21

The male has multiple small spots on its bloom, while the female has one large spot per petal.

Use Leaf Stone

The male has small spots on its petals, while the female has large spots.

Use Sun Stone

Same form for male/female

055 Oddish
Weed Pokémon

Height: 1'8" Weight: 11.9 lbs. p. 216

If exposed to moonlight, it starts to move. It roams far and wide at night to scatter its seeds.

During the day, it stays in the cold underground to avoid the sun. It grows by bathing in moonlight.

MAIN WAY TO OBTAIN
Catch one when it appears in tall grass in the Dappled Grove during clear or cloudy weather.

Absorb Bulb

056 Gloom
Weed Pokémon

Height: 2'7" Weight: 19 lbs. p. 216

Its pistils exude an incredibly foul odor. The horrid stench can cause fainting at a distance of 1.25 miles.

What appears to be drool is actually sweet honey. It is very sticky and clings stubbornly if touched.

MAIN WAY TO OBTAIN
Catch one when it appears in tall grass at North Lake Miloch during clear weather, rain, or a thunderstorm. Or obtain an Oddish, then level it up to Lv. 21 or higher to evolve it into Gloom.

Absorb Bulb

057 Vileplume
Flower Pokémon

Height: 3'11" Weight: 41 lbs. p. 217

It has the world's largest petals. With every step, the petals shake out heavy clouds of toxic pollen.

The larger its petals, the more toxic pollen it contains. Its big head is heavy and hard to hold up.

MAIN WAY TO OBTAIN
Catch one when it appears wandering in the Dappled Grove during clear or cloudy weather. Or obtain a Gloom, then use a Leaf Stone on it to evolve it into Vileplume.

Absorb Bulb

058 Bellossom
Flower Pokémon

Height: 1'4" Weight: 12.8 lbs. p. 217

Plentiful in the tropics. When it dances, its petals rub together and make a pleasant ringing sound.

Bellossom gather at times and appear to dance. They say that the dance is a ritual to summon the sun.

MAIN WAY TO OBTAIN
Catch one when it appears wandering at the Giant's Mirror during clear weather or harsh sunlight. Or obtain a Gloom, then use a Sun Stone on it to evolve it into Bellossom.

Absorb Bulb

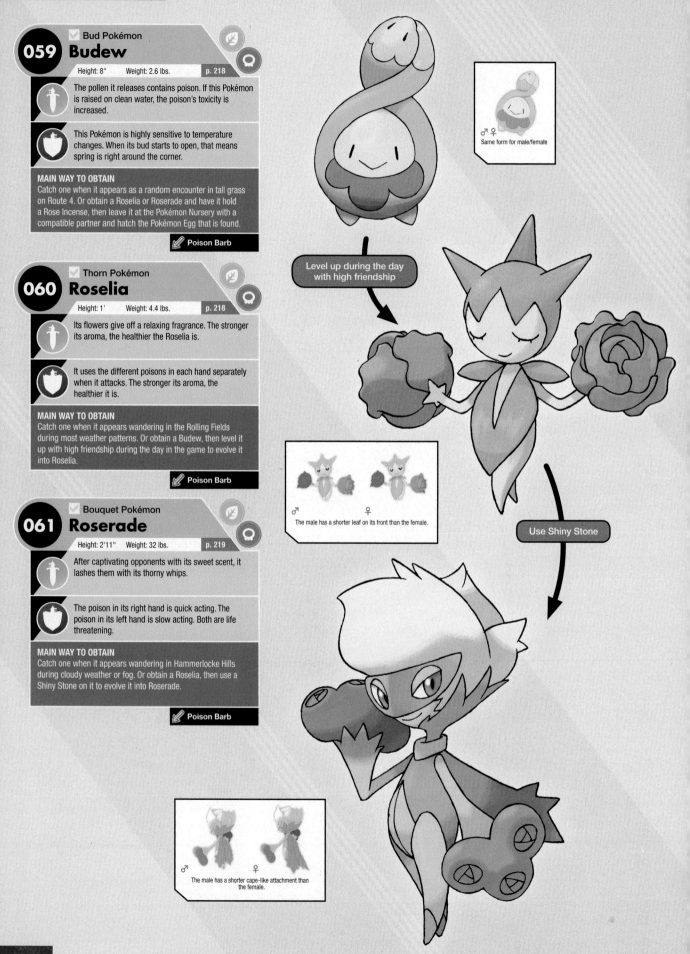

059 Budew

☑ Bud Pokémon

Height: 8"   Weight: 2.6 lbs.   p. 218

The pollen it releases contains poison. If this Pokémon is raised on clean water, the poison's toxicity is increased.

This Pokémon is highly sensitive to temperature changes. When its bud starts to open, that means spring is right around the corner.

MAIN WAY TO OBTAIN
Catch one when it appears as a random encounter in tall grass on Route 4. Or obtain a Roselia or Roserade and have it hold a Rose Incense, then leave it at the Pokémon Nursery with a compatible partner and hatch the Pokémon Egg that is found.

✎ Poison Barb

060 Roselia

☑ Thorn Pokémon

Height: 1'   Weight: 4.4 lbs.   p. 218

Its flowers give off a relaxing fragrance. The stronger its aroma, the healthier the Roselia is.

It uses the different poisons in each hand separately when it attacks. The stronger its aroma, the healthier it is.

MAIN WAY TO OBTAIN
Catch one when it appears wandering in the Rolling Fields during most weather patterns. Or obtain a Budew, then level it up with high friendship during the day in the game to evolve it into Roselia.

✎ Poison Barb

061 Roserade

☑ Bouquet Pokémon

Height: 2'11"   Weight: 32 lbs.   p. 219

After captivating opponents with its sweet scent, it lashes them with its thorny whips.

The poison in its right hand is quick acting. The poison in its left hand is slow acting. Both are life threatening.

MAIN WAY TO OBTAIN
Catch one when it appears wandering in Hammerlocke Hills during cloudy weather or fog. Or obtain a Roselia, then use a Shiny Stone on it to evolve it into Roserade.

✎ Poison Barb

♂ ♀
Same form for male/female

Level up during the day with high friendship

♂   ♀
The male has a shorter leaf on its front than the female.

Use Shiny Stone

♂   ♀
The male has a shorter cape-like attachment than the female.

♂ ♀
Same form for male/female

Lv. 25

♂ ♀
Same form for male/female

062 Wingull
☑ Seagull Pokémon

| Height: 2' | Weight: 20.9 lbs. | p. 219 |

It makes its nest on sheer cliffs. Riding the sea breeze, it glides up into the expansive skies.

It soars on updrafts without flapping its wings. It makes a nest on sheer cliffs at the sea's edge.

MAIN WAY TO OBTAIN
Catch one when it appears flying over the water's surface at South Lake Miloch or East Lake Axewell.

🖌 Pretty Feather

063 Pelipper
☑ Water Bird Pokémon

| Height: 3'11" | Weight: 61.7 lbs. | p. 220 |

It is a messenger of the skies, carrying small Pokémon and eggs to safety in its bill.

Skimming the water's surface, it dips its large bill in the sea, scoops up food and water, and carries it.

MAIN WAY TO OBTAIN
Catch one when it appears in tall grass on the north end of Route 9. Or obtain a Wingull, then level it up to Lv. 25 or higher to evolve it into Pelipper.

🖌 Pretty Feather

SPLIT EVOLUTIONS

Most Pokémon that can evolve do so in a straight line, with no branching options. But it's not so simple for all Pokémon! Some have split Evolutions, in which a species can evolve into two or more different species next, depending on the conditions at the time it evolves. Gloom here can evolve into Vileplume when a Leaf Stone is used on it, which may not seem out of the ordinary. But use a Sun Stone on a Gloom, and you might be surprised to find it blossom into the sunny Bellossom!

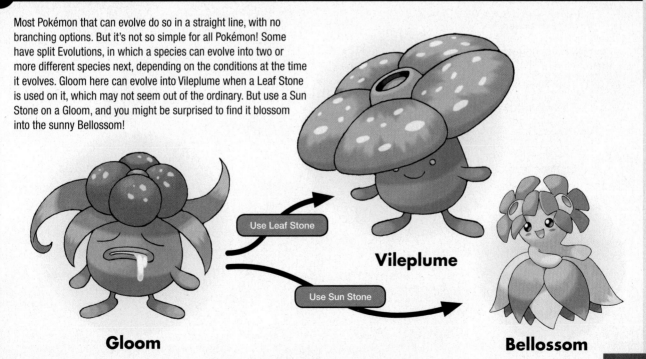

Use Leaf Stone

Use Sun Stone

Gloom

Vileplume

Bellossom

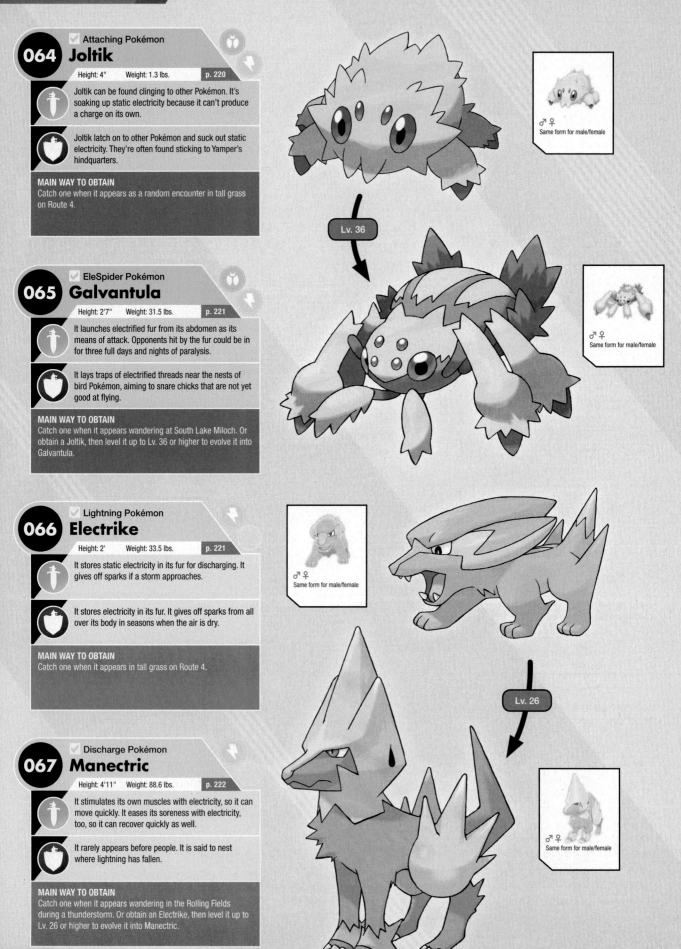

064 Joltik
☑ Attaching Pokémon

Height: 4" Weight: 1.3 lbs. p. 220

Joltik can be found clinging to other Pokémon. It's soaking up static electricity because it can't produce a charge on its own.

Joltik latch on to other Pokémon and suck out static electricity. They're often found sticking to Yamper's hindquarters.

MAIN WAY TO OBTAIN
Catch one when it appears as a random encounter in tall grass on Route 4.

♂ ♀
Same form for male/female

Lv. 36

065 Galvantula
☑ EleSpider Pokémon

Height: 2'7" Weight: 31.5 lbs. p. 221

It launches electrified fur from its abdomen as its means of attack. Opponents hit by the fur could be in for three full days and nights of paralysis.

It lays traps of electrified threads near the nests of bird Pokémon, aiming to snare chicks that are not yet good at flying.

MAIN WAY TO OBTAIN
Catch one when it appears wandering at South Lake Miloch. Or obtain a Joltik, then level it up to Lv. 36 or higher to evolve it into Galvantula.

♂ ♀
Same form for male/female

066 Electrike
☑ Lightning Pokémon

Height: 2' Weight: 33.5 lbs. p. 221

It stores static electricity in its fur for discharging. It gives off sparks if a storm approaches.

It stores electricity in its fur. It gives off sparks from all over its body in seasons when the air is dry.

MAIN WAY TO OBTAIN
Catch one when it appears in tall grass on Route 4.

♂ ♀
Same form for male/female

Lv. 26

067 Manectric
☑ Discharge Pokémon

Height: 4'11" Weight: 88.6 lbs. p. 222

It stimulates its own muscles with electricity, so it can move quickly. It eases its soreness with electricity, too, so it can recover quickly as well.

It rarely appears before people. It is said to nest where lightning has fallen.

MAIN WAY TO OBTAIN
Catch one when it appears wandering in the Rolling Fields during a thunderstorm. Or obtain an Electrike, then level it up to Lv. 26 or higher to evolve it into Manectric.

♂ ♀
Same form for male/female

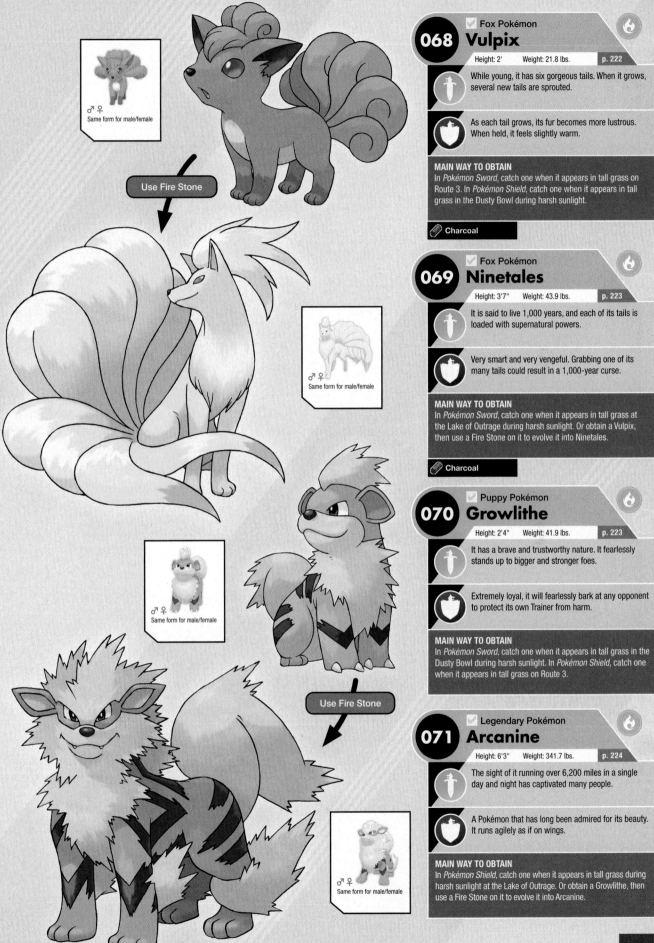

Same form for male/female ♂ ♀

Use Fire Stone

Same form for male/female ♂ ♀

Same form for male/female ♂ ♀

Use Fire Stone

Same form for male/female ♂ ♀

068 Vulpix

Fox Pokémon

Height: 2'   Weight: 21.8 lbs.   p. 222

While young, it has six gorgeous tails. When it grows, several new tails are sprouted.

As each tail grows, its fur becomes more lustrous. When held, it feels slightly warm.

MAIN WAY TO OBTAIN
In *Pokémon Sword*, catch one when it appears in tall grass on Route 3. In *Pokémon Shield*, catch one when it appears in tall grass in the Dusty Bowl during harsh sunlight.

Charcoal

069 Ninetales

Fox Pokémon

Height: 3'7"   Weight: 43.9 lbs.   p. 223

It is said to live 1,000 years, and each of its tails is loaded with supernatural powers.

Very smart and very vengeful. Grabbing one of its many tails could result in a 1,000-year curse.

MAIN WAY TO OBTAIN
In *Pokémon Sword*, catch one when it appears in tall grass at the Lake of Outrage during harsh sunlight. Or obtain a Vulpix, then use a Fire Stone on it to evolve it into Ninetales.

Charcoal

070 Growlithe

Puppy Pokémon

Height: 2'4"   Weight: 41.9 lbs.   p. 223

It has a brave and trustworthy nature. It fearlessly stands up to bigger and stronger foes.

Extremely loyal, it will fearlessly bark at any opponent to protect its own Trainer from harm.

MAIN WAY TO OBTAIN
In *Pokémon Sword*, catch one when it appears in tall grass in the Dusty Bowl during harsh sunlight. In *Pokémon Shield*, catch one when it appears in tall grass on Route 3.

071 Arcanine

Legendary Pokémon

Height: 6'3"   Weight: 341.7 lbs.   p. 224

The sight of it running over 6,200 miles in a single day and night has captivated many people.

A Pokémon that has long been admired for its beauty. It runs agilely as if on wings.

MAIN WAY TO OBTAIN
In *Pokémon Shield*, catch one when it appears in tall grass during harsh sunlight at the Lake of Outrage. Or obtain a Growlithe, then use a Fire Stone on it to evolve it into Arcanine.

072 Vanillite

Fresh Snow Pokémon

Height: 1'4" Weight: 12.6 lbs. p. 224

Unable to survive in hot areas, it makes itself comfortable by breathing out air cold enough to cause snow. It burrows into the snow to sleep.

Supposedly, this Pokémon was born from an icicle. It spews out freezing air at −58 degrees Fahrenheit to make itself more comfortable.

MAIN WAY TO OBTAIN
Catch one when it appears in tall grass in the Rolling Fields, or on the water's surface at East Lake Axewell, West Lake Axewell, or elsewhere during snow or a blizzard.

Never-Melt Ice

073 Vanillish

Icy Snow Pokémon

Height: 3'7" Weight: 90.4 lbs. p. 225

By drinking pure water, it grows its icy body. This Pokémon can be hard to find on days with warm, sunny weather.

It blasts enemies with cold air reaching −148 degrees Fahrenheit, freezing them solid. But it spares their lives afterward—it's a kind Pokémon.

MAIN WAY TO OBTAIN
Catch one when it appears wandering in the Dappled Grove or North Lake Miloch during snow or a blizzard. Or obtain a Vanillite, then level it up to Lv. 35 or higher to evolve it into Vanillish.

Never-Melt Ice

074 Vanilluxe

Snowstorm Pokémon

Height: 4'3" Weight: 126.8 lbs. p. 225

When its anger reaches a breaking point, this Pokémon unleashes a fierce blizzard that freezes every creature around it, be they friend or foe.

People believe this Pokémon formed when two Vanillish stuck together. Its body temperature is roughly 21 degrees Fahrenheit.

MAIN WAY TO OBTAIN
Catch one when it appears on the water's surface at East Lake Axewell, West Lake Axewell, or elsewhere during snow or a blizzard. Or obtain a Vanillish, then level it up to Lv. 47 or higher to evolve it into Vanilluxe.

Never-Melt Ice

Same form for male/female

Lv. 35

Same form for male/female

Lv. 47

Same form for male/female

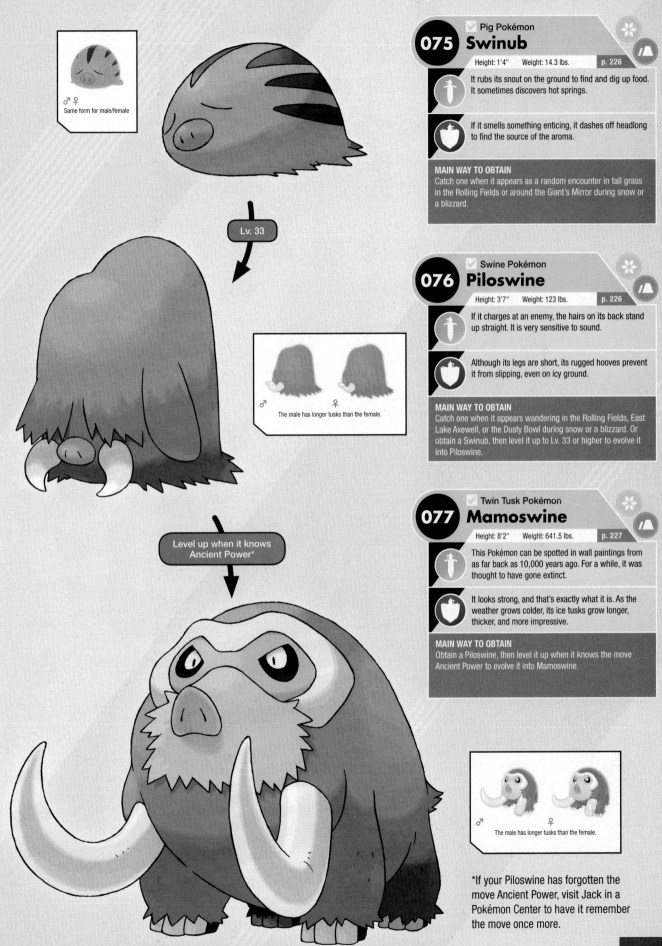

♂♀
Same form for male/female

Lv. 33

Level up when it knows Ancient Power*

The male has longer tusks than the female.

♂ ♀

The male has longer tusks than the female.

♂ ♀

☑ Pig Pokémon

075 Swinub

| Height: 1'4" | Weight: 14.3 lbs. | p. 226 |

It rubs its snout on the ground to find and dig up food. It sometimes discovers hot springs.

If it smells something enticing, it dashes off headlong to find the source of the aroma.

MAIN WAY TO OBTAIN
Catch one when it appears as a random encounter in tall grass in the Rolling Fields or around the Giant's Mirror during snow or a blizzard.

☑ Swine Pokémon

076 Piloswine

| Height: 3'7" | Weight: 123 lbs. | p. 226 |

If it charges at an enemy, the hairs on its back stand up straight. It is very sensitive to sound.

Although its legs are short, its rugged hooves prevent it from slipping, even on icy ground.

MAIN WAY TO OBTAIN
Catch one when it appears wandering in the Rolling Fields, East Lake Axewell, or the Dusty Bowl during snow or a blizzard. Or obtain a Swinub, then level it up to Lv. 33 or higher to evolve it into Piloswine.

☑ Twin Tusk Pokémon

077 Mamoswine

| Height: 8'2" | Weight: 641.5 lbs. | p. 227 |

This Pokémon can be spotted in wall paintings from as far back as 10,000 years ago. For a while, it was thought to have gone extinct.

It looks strong, and that's exactly what it is. As the weather grows colder, its ice tusks grow longer, thicker, and more impressive.

MAIN WAY TO OBTAIN
Obtain a Piloswine, then level it up when it knows the move Ancient Power to evolve it into Mamoswine.

*If your Piloswine has forgotten the move Ancient Power, visit Jack in a Pokémon Center to have it remember the move once more.

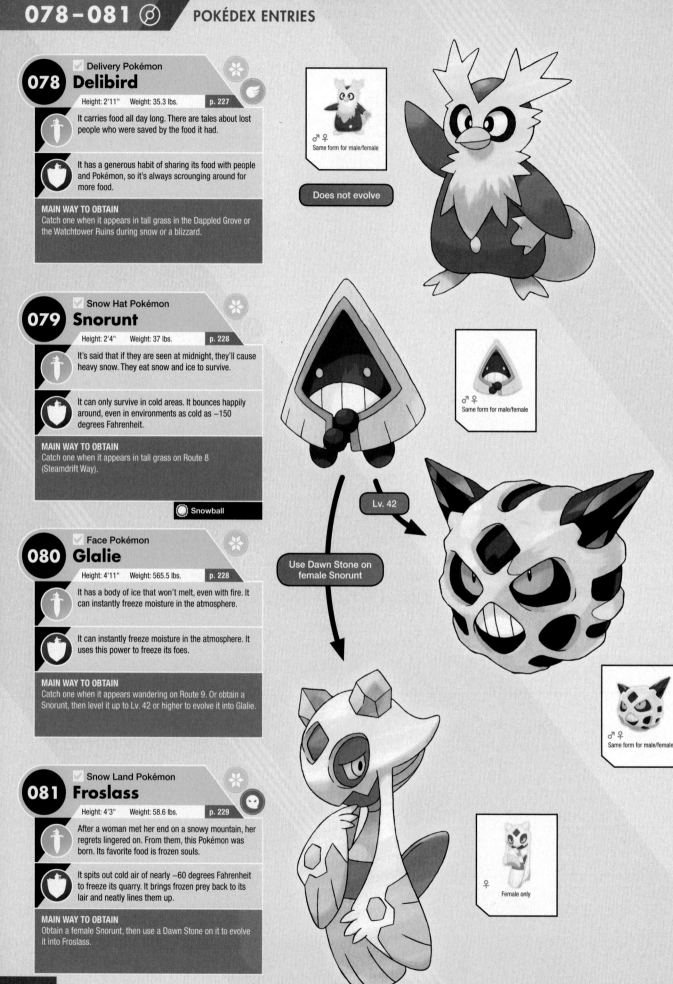

078 Delibird
☑ Delivery Pokémon

Height: 2'11"   Weight: 35.3 lbs.   p. 227

⚔ It carries food all day long. There are tales about lost people who were saved by the food it had.

🛡 It has a generous habit of sharing its food with people and Pokémon, so it's always scrounging around for more food.

MAIN WAY TO OBTAIN
Catch one when it appears in tall grass in the Dappled Grove or the Watchtower Ruins during snow or a blizzard.

♂ ♀ Same form for male/female

Does not evolve

079 Snorunt
☑ Snow Hat Pokémon

Height: 2'4"   Weight: 37 lbs.   p. 228

⚔ It's said that if they are seen at midnight, they'll cause heavy snow. They eat snow and ice to survive.

🛡 It can only survive in cold areas. It bounces happily around, even in environments as cold as –150 degrees Fahrenheit.

MAIN WAY TO OBTAIN
Catch one when it appears in tall grass on Route 8 (Steamdrift Way).

⦿ Snowball

♂ ♀ Same form for male/female

080 Glalie
☑ Face Pokémon

Height: 4'11"   Weight: 565.5 lbs.   p. 228

⚔ It has a body of ice that won't melt, even with fire. It can instantly freeze moisture in the atmosphere.

🛡 It can instantly freeze moisture in the atmosphere. It uses this power to freeze its foes.

MAIN WAY TO OBTAIN
Catch one when it appears wandering on Route 9. Or obtain a Snorunt, then level it up to Lv. 42 or higher to evolve it into Glalie.

Lv. 42

Use Dawn Stone on female Snorunt

♂ ♀ Same form for male/female

081 Froslass
☑ Snow Land Pokémon

Height: 4'3"   Weight: 58.6 lbs.   p. 229

⚔ After a woman met her end on a snowy mountain, her regrets lingered on. From them, this Pokémon was born. Its favorite food is frozen souls.

🛡 It spits out cold air of nearly –60 degrees Fahrenheit to freeze its quarry. It brings frozen prey back to its lair and neatly lines them up.

MAIN WAY TO OBTAIN
Obtain a female Snorunt, then use a Dawn Stone on it to evolve it into Froslass.

♀ Female only

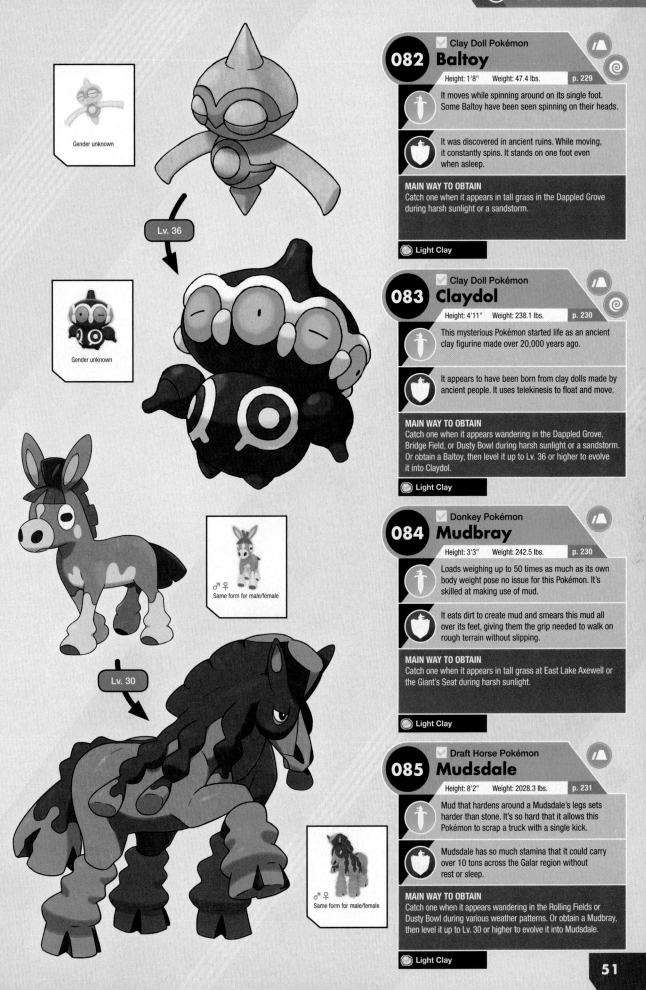

Gender unknown

Lv. 36

Gender unknown

Lv. 30

♂ ♀
Same form for male/female

♂ ♀
Same form for male/female

☑ Clay Doll Pokémon
082 Baltoy
Height: 1'8" Weight: 47.4 lbs. p. 229

It moves while spinning around on its single foot. Some Baltoy have been seen spinning on its heads.

It was discovered in ancient ruins. While moving, it constantly spins. It stands on one foot even when asleep.

MAIN WAY TO OBTAIN
Catch one when it appears in tall grass in the Dappled Grove during harsh sunlight or a sandstorm.

◉ Light Clay

☑ Clay Doll Pokémon
083 Claydol
Height: 4'11" Weight: 238.1 lbs. p. 230

This mysterious Pokémon started life as an ancient clay figurine made over 20,000 years ago.

It appears to have been born from clay dolls made by ancient people. It uses telekinesis to float and move.

MAIN WAY TO OBTAIN
Catch one when it appears wandering in the Dappled Grove, Bridge Field, or Dusty Bowl during harsh sunlight or a sandstorm. Or obtain a Baltoy, then level it up to Lv. 36 or higher to evolve it into Claydol.

◉ Light Clay

☑ Donkey Pokémon
084 Mudbray
Height: 3'3" Weight: 242.5 lbs. p. 230

Loads weighing up to 50 times as much as its own body weight pose no issue for this Pokémon. It's skilled at making use of mud.

It eats dirt to create mud and smears this mud all over its feet, giving them the grip needed to walk on rough terrain without slipping.

MAIN WAY TO OBTAIN
Catch one when it appears in tall grass at East Lake Axewell or the Giant's Seat during harsh sunlight.

◉ Light Clay

☑ Draft Horse Pokémon
085 Mudsdale
Height: 8'2" Weight: 2028.3 lbs. p. 231

Mud that hardens around a Mudsdale's legs sets harder than stone. It's so hard that it allows this Pokémon to scrap a truck with a single kick.

Mudsdale has so much stamina that it could carry over 10 tons across the Galar region without rest or sleep.

MAIN WAY TO OBTAIN
Catch one when it appears wandering in the Rolling Fields or Dusty Bowl during various weather patterns. Or obtain a Mudbray, then level it up to Lv. 30 or higher to evolve it into Mudsdale.

◉ Light Clay

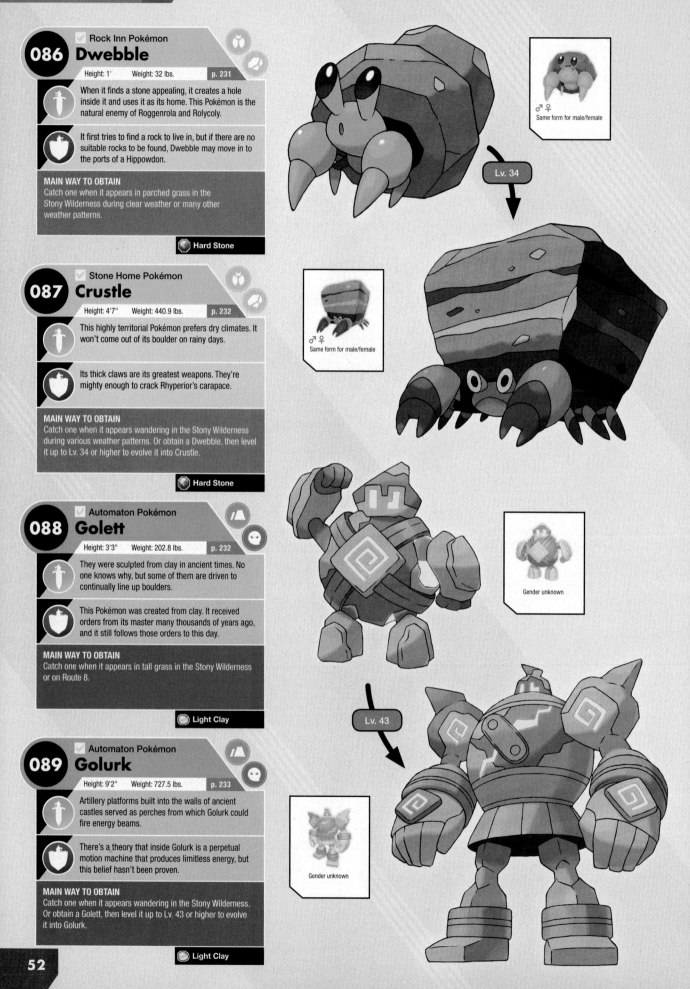

086 Dwebble
☑ Rock Inn Pokémon

| Height: 1' | Weight: 32 lbs. | p. 231 |

When it finds a stone appealing, it creates a hole inside it and uses it as its home. This Pokémon is the natural enemy of Roggenrola and Rolycoly.

It first tries to find a rock to live in, but if there are no suitable rocks to be found, Dwebble may move in to the ports of a Hippowdon.

MAIN WAY TO OBTAIN
Catch one when it appears in parched grass in the Stony Wilderness during clear weather or many other weather patterns.

🔘 Hard Stone

♂ ♀
Same form for male/female

Lv. 34

087 Crustle
☑ Stone Home Pokémon

| Height: 4'7" | Weight: 440.9 lbs. | p. 232 |

This highly territorial Pokémon prefers dry climates. It won't come out of its boulder on rainy days.

Its thick claws are its greatest weapons. They're mighty enough to crack Rhyperior's carapace.

MAIN WAY TO OBTAIN
Catch one when it appears wandering in the Stony Wilderness during various weather patterns. Or obtain a Dwebble, then level it up to Lv. 34 or higher to evolve it into Crustle.

🔘 Hard Stone

♂ ♀
Same form for male/female

088 Golett
☑ Automaton Pokémon

| Height: 3'3" | Weight: 202.8 lbs. | p. 232 |

They were sculpted from clay in ancient times. No one knows why, but some of them are driven to continually line up boulders.

This Pokémon was created from clay. It received orders from its master many thousands of years ago, and it still follows those orders to this day.

MAIN WAY TO OBTAIN
Catch one when it appears in tall grass in the Stony Wilderness or on Route 8.

🔘 Light Clay

Gender unknown

Lv. 43

089 Golurk
☑ Automaton Pokémon

| Height: 9'2" | Weight: 727.5 lbs. | p. 233 |

Artillery platforms built into the walls of ancient castles served as perches from which Golurk could fire energy beams.

There's a theory that inside Golurk is a perpetual motion machine that produces limitless energy, but this belief hasn't been proven.

MAIN WAY TO OBTAIN
Catch one when it appears wandering in the Stony Wilderness. Or obtain a Golett, then level it up to Lv. 43 or higher to evolve it into Golurk.

Gender unknown

🔘 Light Clay

Same form for male/female

Use Moon Stone

Same form for male/female

Lv. 25

Same form for male/female

♂ ♀

The male has three lines on its body, where the female has two.

090 Munna
Dream Eater Pokémon

Height: 2' Weight: 51.4 lbs. p. 233

Late at night, it appears beside people's pillows. As it feeds on dreams, the patterns on its body give off a faint glow.

It eats dreams and releases mist. The mist is pink when it's eating a good dream, and black when it's eating a nightmare.

MAIN WAY TO OBTAIN
Catch one when it appears in tall grass on the west side of the Slumbering Weald.

091 Musharna
Drowsing Pokémon

Height: 3'7" Weight: 133.4 lbs. p. 234

When dark mists emanate from its body, don't get too near. If you do, your nightmares will become reality.

It drowses and dreams all the time. It's best to leave it be if it's just woken up, as it's a terrible grump when freshly roused from sleep.

MAIN WAY TO OBTAIN
Catch one when it appears wandering in the Bridge Field or at the Giant's Seat during fog. Or obtain a Munna, then use a Moon Stone on it to evolve it into Musharna.

092 Natu
Tiny Bird Pokémon

Height: 8" Weight: 4.4 lbs. p. 234

It is extremely good at climbing tree trunks and likes to eat the new sprouts on the trees.

Because its wings aren't yet fully grown, it has to hop to get around. It is always staring at something.

MAIN WAY TO OBTAIN
Catch one when it appears in tall grass at the Giant's Mirror during various weather patterns or as a random encounter in tall grass in West Lake Axewell, South Lake Miloch, or North Lake Miloch during fog.

093 Xatu
Mystic Pokémon

Height: 4'11" Weight: 33.1 lbs. p. 235

They say that it stays still and quiet because it is seeing both the past and future at the same time.

This odd Pokémon can see both the past and the future. It eyes the sun's movement all day.

MAIN WAY TO OBTAIN
Catch one when it appears wandering at East Lake Axewell or the Giant's Mirror during various weather patterns. Or obtain a Natu, then level it up to Lv. 25 or higher to evolve it into Xatu.

094 Stufful

☑ Flailing Pokémon

Height: 1'8" Weight: 15 lbs. p. 235

Its fluffy fur is a delight to pet, but carelessly reaching out to touch this Pokémon could result in painful retaliation.

The way it protects itself by flailing its arms may be an adorable sight, but stay well away. This is flailing that can snap thick tree trunks.

MAIN WAY TO OBTAIN
Catch one when it appears in tall grass at East Lake Axewell or on Route 5.

095 Bewear

☑ Strong Arm Pokémon

Height: 6'11" Weight: 297.6 lbs. p. 236

Once it accepts you as a friend, it tries to show its affection with a hug. Letting it do that is dangerous— it could easily shatter your bones.

The moves it uses to take down its prey would make a martial artist jealous. It tucks subdued prey under its arms to carry them to its nest.

MAIN WAY TO OBTAIN
Catch one when it appears wandering in the Dappled Grove or Bridge Field during various weather patterns. Or obtain a Stufful, then level it up to Lv. 27 or higher to evolve it into Bewear.

♂ ♀
Same form for male/female

Lv. 27

♂ ♀
Same form for male/female

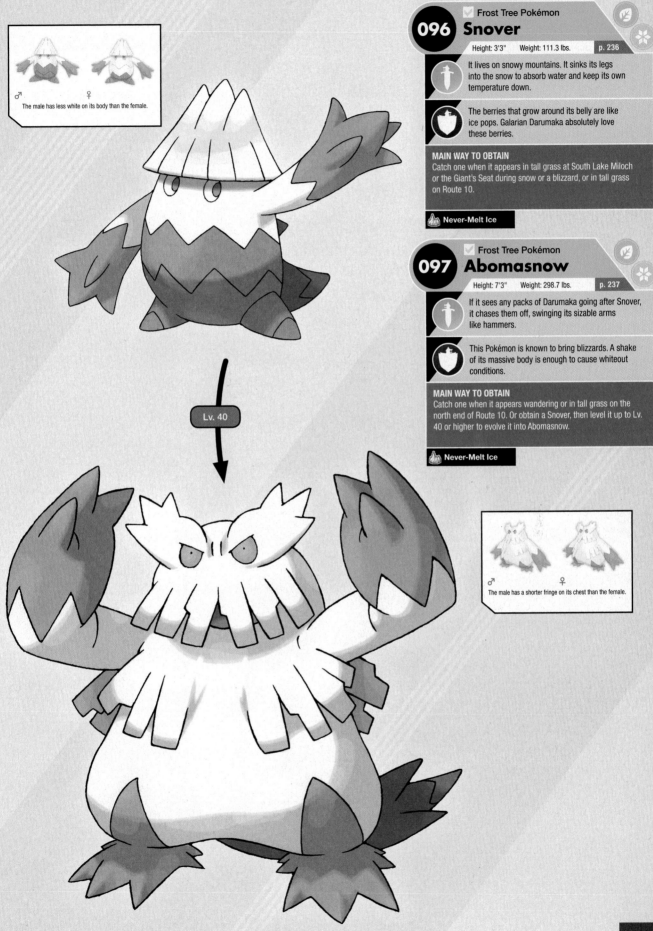

The male has less white on its body than the female.

096 Snover

☑ Frost Tree Pokémon

Height: 3'3"   Weight: 111.3 lbs.   p. 236

It lives on snowy mountains. It sinks its legs into the snow to absorb water and keep its own temperature down.

The berries that grow around its belly are like ice pops. Galarian Darumaka absolutely love these berries.

MAIN WAY TO OBTAIN
Catch one when it appears in tall grass at South Lake Miloch or the Giant's Seat during snow or a blizzard, or in tall grass on Route 10.

🔺 Never-Melt Ice

097 Abomasnow

☑ Frost Tree Pokémon

Height: 7'3"   Weight: 298.7 lbs.   p. 237

If it sees any packs of Darumaka going after Snover, it chases them off, swinging its sizable arms like hammers.

This Pokémon is known to bring blizzards. A shake of its massive body is enough to cause whiteout conditions.

MAIN WAY TO OBTAIN
Catch one when it appears wandering or in tall grass on the north end of Route 10. Or obtain a Snover, then level it up to Lv. 40 or higher to evolve it into Abomasnow.

🔺 Never-Melt Ice

Lv. 40

The male has a shorter fringe on its chest than the female.

098 Krabby

☑ River Crab Pokémon

Height: 1'4" Weight: 14.3 lbs. p. 237

It can be found near the sea. The large pincers grow back if they are torn out of their sockets.

If it senses danger approaching, it cloaks itself with bubbles from its mouth so it will look bigger.

MAIN WAY TO OBTAIN
Catch one when it appears as a random encounter in tall grass at West Lake Axewell during most weather patterns, or when you fish it up at the Giant's Cap.

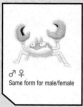
♂ ♀
Same form for male/female

Lv. 28

099 Kingler

☑ Pincer Pokémon

Height: 4'3" Weight: 132.3 lbs. p. 238

Its large and hard pincer has 10,000-horsepower strength. However, being so big, it is unwieldy to move.

Its oversized claw is very powerful, but when it's not in battle, the claw just gets in the way.

MAIN WAY TO OBTAIN
Catch one when it appears as a random encounter in tall grass on the north end of Route 9. Or obtain a Krabby, then level it up to Lv. 28 or higher to evolve it into Kingler.

♂ ♀
Same form for male/female

100 Wooper

☑ Water Fish Pokémon

Height: 1'4" Weight: 18.7 lbs. p. 238

This Pokémon lives in cold water. It will leave the water to search for food when it gets cold outside.

When walking on land, it covers its body with a poisonous film that keeps its skin from dehydrating.

MAIN WAY TO OBTAIN
Catch one when it appears in tall grass at West Lake Axewell during clear weather, rain, or a thunderstorm.

♂   ♀
The male has more frills on its head than the female.

Lv. 20

101 Quagsire

☑ Water Fish Pokémon

Height: 4'7" Weight: 165.3 lbs. p. 239

It has an easygoing nature. It doesn't care if it bumps its head on boats and boulders while swimming.

Its body is always slimy. It often bangs its head on the river bottom as it swims but seems not to care.

MAIN WAY TO OBTAIN
Catch one when it appears wandering at West Lake Axewell during various weather patterns. Or obtain a Wooper, then level it up to Lv. 20 or higher to evolve it into Quagsire.

♂   ♀
The male has larger fins on its back than the female.

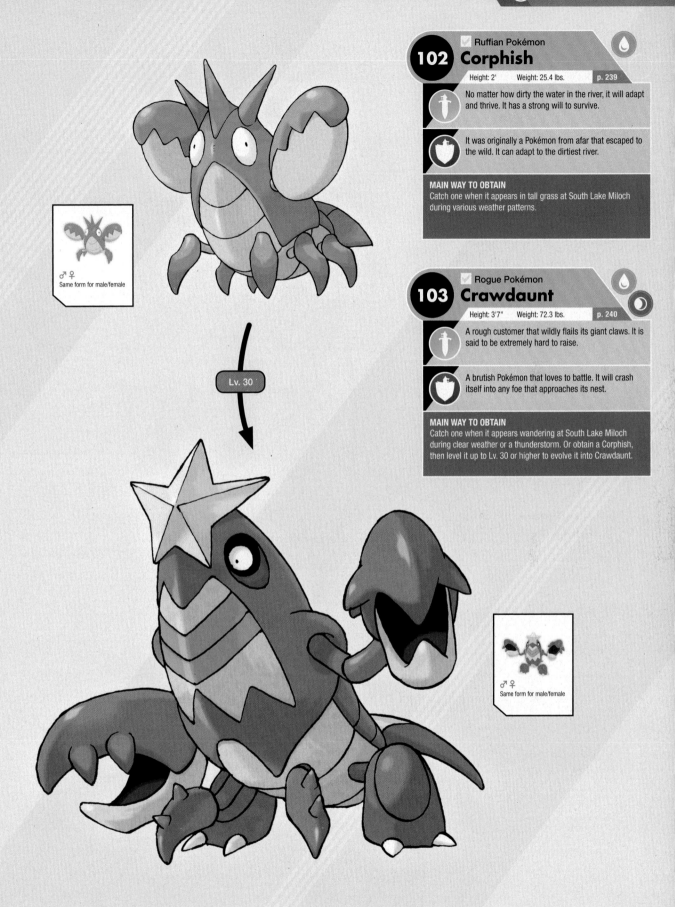

102 Corphish
Ruffian Pokémon

Height: 2'   Weight: 25.4 lbs.   p. 239

No matter how dirty the water in the river, it will adapt and thrive. It has a strong will to survive.

It was originally a Pokémon from afar that escaped to the wild. It can adapt to the dirtiest river.

MAIN WAY TO OBTAIN
Catch one when it appears in tall grass at South Lake Miloch during various weather patterns.

Same form for male/female

Lv. 30

103 Crawdaunt
Rogue Pokémon

Height: 3'7"   Weight: 72.3 lbs.   p. 240

A rough customer that wildly flails its giant claws. It is said to be extremely hard to raise.

A brutish Pokémon that loves to battle. It will crash itself into any foe that approaches its nest.

MAIN WAY TO OBTAIN
Catch one when it appears wandering at South Lake Miloch during clear weather or a thunderstorm. Or obtain a Corphish, then level it up to Lv. 30 or higher to evolve it into Crawdaunt.

Same form for male/female

104 Nincada
☑ Trainee Pokémon

| Height: 1'8" | Weight: 12.1 lbs. | p. 240 |

Because it lived almost entirely underground, it is nearly blind. It uses its antennae instead.

It can sometimes live underground for more than 10 years. It absorbs nutrients from the roots of trees.

MAIN WAY TO OBTAIN
Catch one when it appears as a random encounter in tall grass at South Lake Miloch during harsh sunlight or a sandstorm.

🜄 Soft Sand

105 Ninjask
☑ Ninja Pokémon

| Height: 2'7" | Weight: 26.5 lbs. | p. 241 |

Its cry leaves a lasting headache if heard for too long. It moves so quickly that it is almost invisible.

This Pokémon is so quick, it is said to be able to avoid any attack. It loves to feed on tree sap.

MAIN WAY TO OBTAIN
Catch one when it appears wandering in the Rolling Fields. Or obtain a Nincada, then level it up to Lv. 20 or higher to evolve it into Ninjask.

106 Shedinja
☑ Shed Pokémon

| Height: 2'7" | Weight: 2.6 lbs. | p. 241 |

A most peculiar Pokémon that somehow appears in a Poké Ball when a Nincada evolves.

A strange Pokémon—it flies without moving its wings, has a hollow shell for a body, and does not breathe.

MAIN WAY TO OBTAIN
Obtain a Nincada, then level it up to Lv. 20 or higher. Allow it to evolve into Ninjask while you have an empty space in your party and a spare Poké Ball in your Bag to obtain Shedinja.

♂ ♀
Same form for male/female

Lv. 20

♂ ♀
Same form for male/female

Level up Nincada to Lv. 20 with an empty space in your party and a spare Poké Ball

Gender unknown

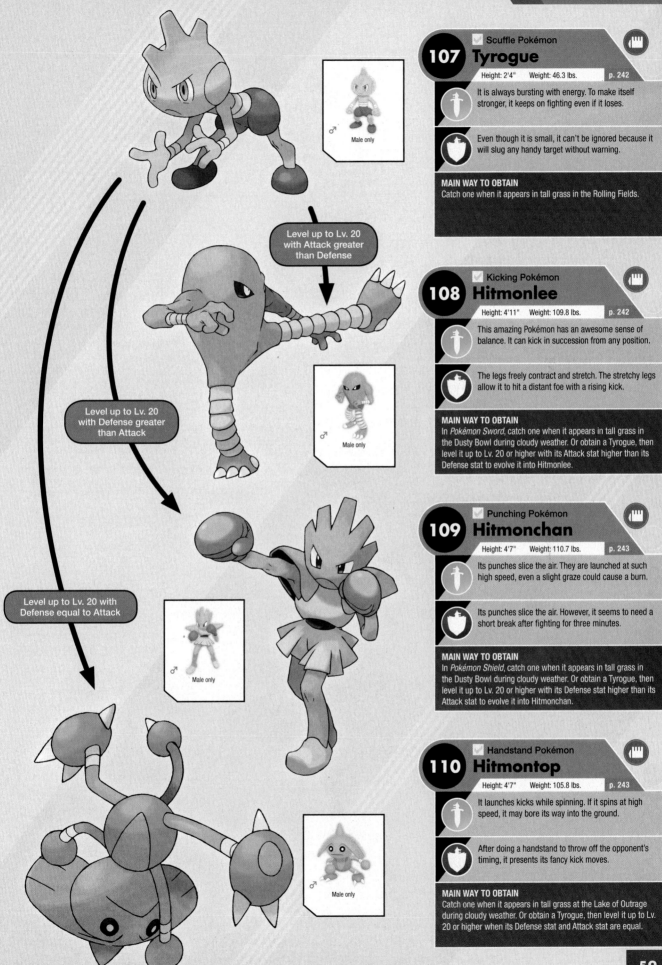

Male only

107 Tyrogue
Scuffle Pokémon

Height: 2'4" Weight: 46.3 lbs. p. 242

It is always bursting with energy. To make itself stronger, it keeps on fighting even if it loses.

Even though it is small, it can't be ignored because it will slug any handy target without warning.

MAIN WAY TO OBTAIN
Catch one when it appears in tall grass in the Rolling Fields.

Level up to Lv. 20 with Attack greater than Defense

108 Hitmonlee
Kicking Pokémon

Height: 4'11" Weight: 109.8 lbs. p. 242

This amazing Pokémon has an awesome sense of balance. It can kick in succession from any position.

The legs freely contract and stretch. The stretchy legs allow it to hit a distant foe with a rising kick.

MAIN WAY TO OBTAIN
In *Pokémon Sword*, catch one when it appears in tall grass in the Dusty Bowl during cloudy weather. Or obtain a Tyrogue, then level it up to Lv. 20 or higher with its Attack stat higher than its Defense stat to evolve it into Hitmonlee.

Male only

Level up to Lv. 20 with Defense greater than Attack

109 Hitmonchan
Punching Pokémon

Height: 4'7" Weight: 110.7 lbs. p. 243

Its punches slice the air. They are launched at such high speed, even a slight graze could cause a burn.

Its punches slice the air. However, it seems to need a short break after fighting for three minutes.

MAIN WAY TO OBTAIN
In *Pokémon Shield*, catch one when it appears in tall grass in the Dusty Bowl during cloudy weather. Or obtain a Tyrogue, then level it up to Lv. 20 or higher with its Defense stat higher than its Attack stat to evolve it into Hitmonchan.

Male only

Level up to Lv. 20 with Defense equal to Attack

110 Hitmontop
Handstand Pokémon

Height: 4'7" Weight: 105.8 lbs. p. 243

It launches kicks while spinning. If it spins at high speed, it may bore its way into the ground.

After doing a handstand to throw off the opponent's timing, it presents its fancy kick moves.

MAIN WAY TO OBTAIN
Catch one when it appears in tall grass at the Lake of Outrage during cloudy weather. Or obtain a Tyrogue, then level it up to Lv. 20 or higher when its Defense stat and Attack stat are equal.

Male only

111 Pancham

☑ Playful Pokémon

Height: 2'   Weight: 17.6 lbs.   p. 244

It chooses a Pangoro as its master and then imitates its master's actions. This is how it learns to battle and hunt for prey.

Wanting to make sure it's taken seriously, Pancham's always giving others a glare. But if it's not focusing, it ends up smiling.

MAIN WAY TO OBTAIN
Catch one when it appears in tall grass in the west part of the Rolling Fields.

🍃 Mental Herb

♂ ♀
Same form for male/female

112 Pangoro

☑ Daunting Pokémon

Height: 6'11"   Weight: 299.8 lbs.   p. 244

This Pokémon is quick to anger, and it has no problem using its prodigious strength to get its way. It lives for duels against Obstagoon.

Using its leaf, Pangoro can predict the moves of its opponents. It strikes with punches that can turn a dump truck into scrap with just one hit.

MAIN WAY TO OBTAIN
Catch one when it appears wandering in the Rolling Fields, Dappled Grove, or the Bridge Field during various weather patterns. Or obtain a Pancham, then level it up to Lv. 32 or higher with a Dark-type Pokémon in your party.

🍃 Mental Herb

Level up to Lv. 32 with a Dark-type Pokémon in your party

♂ ♀
Same form for male/female

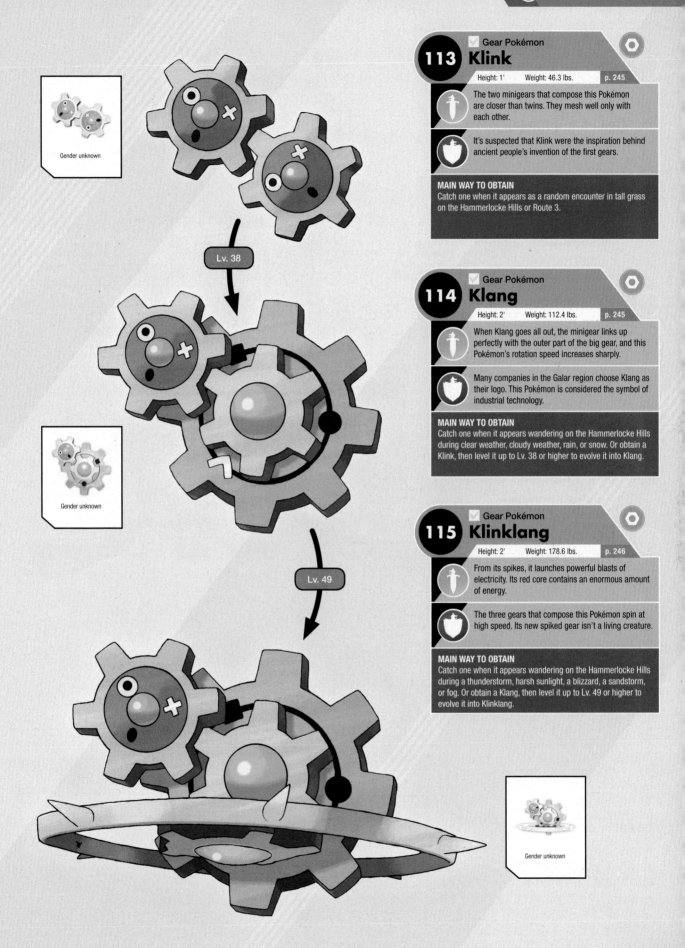

Gender unknown

Lv. 38

Gender unknown

Lv. 49

Gender unknown

Gear Pokémon

113 Klink

| Height: 1' | Weight: 46.3 lbs. | p. 245 |

The two minigears that compose this Pokémon are closer than twins. They mesh well only with each other.

It's suspected that Klink were the inspiration behind ancient people's invention of the first gears.

MAIN WAY TO OBTAIN
Catch one when it appears as a random encounter in tall grass on the Hammerlocke Hills or Route 3.

Gear Pokémon

114 Klang

| Height: 2' | Weight: 112.4 lbs. | p. 245 |

When Klang goes all out, the minigear links up perfectly with the outer part of the big gear, and this Pokémon's rotation speed increases sharply.

Many companies in the Galar region choose Klang as their logo. This Pokémon is considered the symbol of industrial technology.

MAIN WAY TO OBTAIN
Catch one when it appears wandering on the Hammerlocke Hills during clear weather, cloudy weather, rain, or snow. Or obtain a Klink, then level it up to Lv. 38 or higher to evolve it into Klang.

Gear Pokémon

115 Klinklang

| Height: 2' | Weight: 178.6 lbs. | p. 246 |

From its spikes, it launches powerful blasts of electricity. Its red core contains an enormous amount of energy.

The three gears that compose this Pokémon spin at high speed. Its new spiked gear isn't a living creature.

MAIN WAY TO OBTAIN
Catch one when it appears wandering on the Hammerlocke Hills during a thunderstorm, harsh sunlight, a blizzard, a sandstorm, or fog. Or obtain a Klang, then level it up to Lv. 49 or higher to evolve it into Klinklang.

116 Combee

Tiny Bee Pokémon

Height: 1' Weight: 12.1 lbs. p. 246

The members of the trio spend all their time together. Each one has a slightly different taste in nectar.

It ceaselessly gathers nectar from sunrise to sundown, all for the sake of Vespiquen and the swarm.

MAIN WAY TO OBTAIN
Catch one when it appears in tall grass in the Rolling Fields during clear weather.

🍯 Honey

117 Vespiquen

Beehive Pokémon

Height: 3'11" Weight: 84.9 lbs. p. 247

It skillfully commands its grubs in battles with its enemies. The grubs are willing to risk their lives to defend Vespiquen.

Vespiquen that give off more pheromones have larger swarms of Combee attendants.

MAIN WAY TO OBTAIN
Catch one when it appears wandering in the Rolling Fields during clear weather. Or obtain a female Combee, then level it up to Lv. 21 or higher to evolve it into Vespiquen.

✏️ Poison Barb

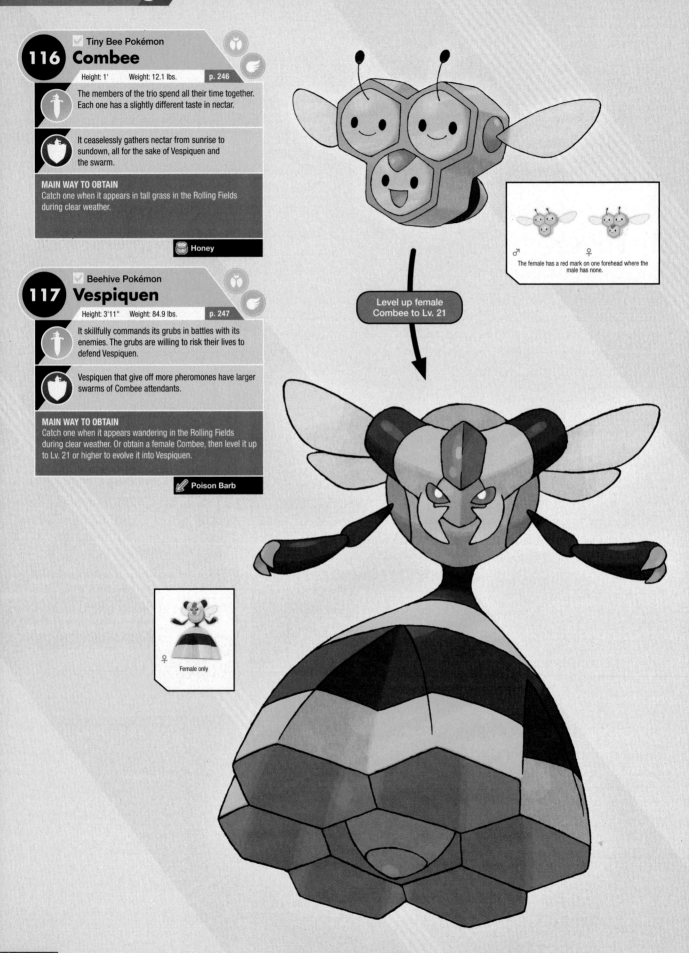

♂ ♀
The female has a red mark on one forehead where the male has none.

Level up female
Combee to Lv. 21

♀
Female only

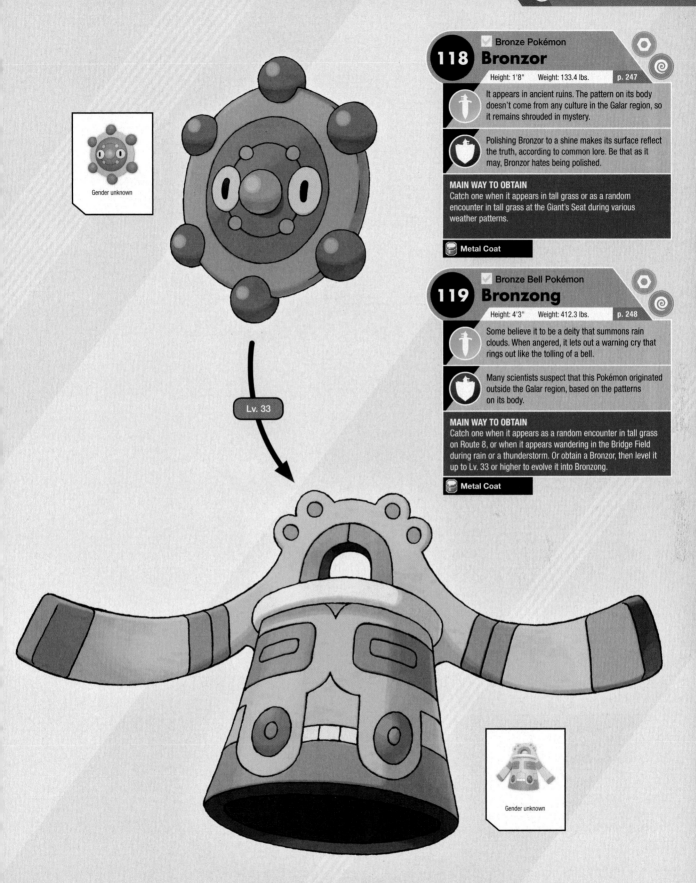

Gender unknown

Lv. 33

Gender unknown

118 Bronzor

☑ Bronze Pokémon

Height: 1'8"   Weight: 133.4 lbs.   p. 247

It appears in ancient ruins. The pattern on its body doesn't come from any culture in the Galar region, so it remains shrouded in mystery.

Polishing Bronzor to a shine makes its surface reflect the truth, according to common lore. Be that as it may, Bronzor hates being polished.

MAIN WAY TO OBTAIN
Catch one when it appears in tall grass or as a random encounter in tall grass at the Giant's Seat during various weather patterns.

Metal Coat

119 Bronzong

☑ Bronze Bell Pokémon

Height: 4'3"   Weight: 412.3 lbs.   p. 248

Some believe it to be a deity that summons rain clouds. When angered, it lets out a warning cry that rings out like the tolling of a bell.

Many scientists suspect that this Pokémon originated outside the Galar region, based on the patterns on its body.

MAIN WAY TO OBTAIN
Catch one when it appears as a random encounter in tall grass on Route 8, or when it appears wandering in the Bridge Field during rain or a thunderstorm. Or obtain a Bronzor, then level it up to Lv. 33 or higher to evolve it into Bronzong.

Metal Coat

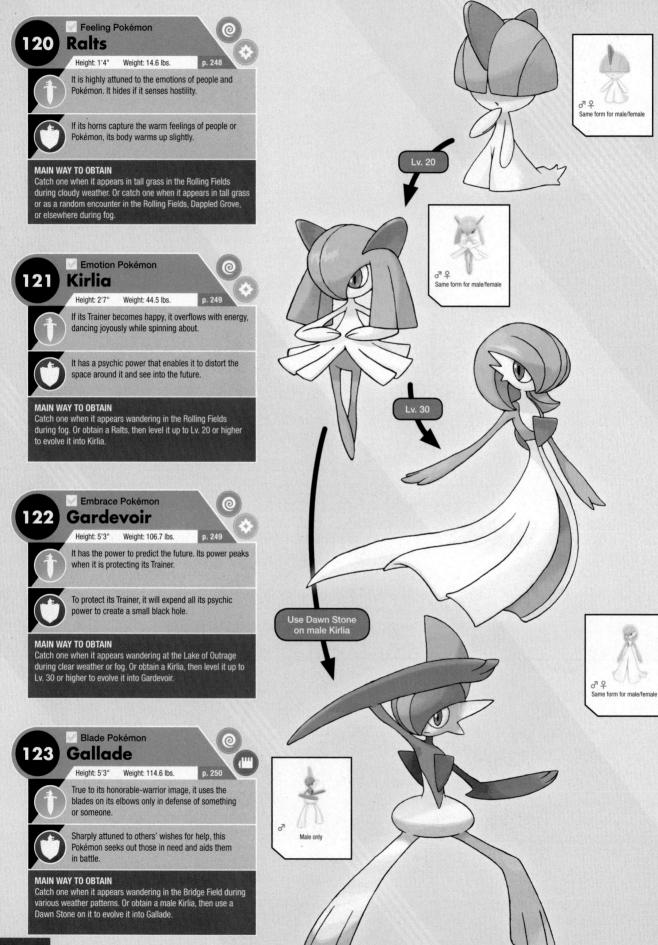

☑ Feeling Pokémon

120 Ralts

| Height: 1'4" | Weight: 14.6 lbs. | p. 248 |

It is highly attuned to the emotions of people and Pokémon. It hides if it senses hostility.

If its horns capture the warm feelings of people or Pokémon, its body warms up slightly.

MAIN WAY TO OBTAIN
Catch one when it appears in tall grass in the Rolling Fields during cloudy weather. Or catch one when it appears in tall grass or as a random encounter in the Rolling Fields, Dappled Grove, or elsewhere during fog.

☑ Emotion Pokémon

121 Kirlia

| Height: 2'7" | Weight: 44.5 lbs. | p. 249 |

If its Trainer becomes happy, it overflows with energy, dancing joyously while spinning about.

It has a psychic power that enables it to distort the space around it and see into the future.

MAIN WAY TO OBTAIN
Catch one when it appears wandering in the Rolling Fields during fog. Or obtain a Ralts, then level it up to Lv. 20 or higher to evolve it into Kirlia.

☑ Embrace Pokémon

122 Gardevoir

| Height: 5'3" | Weight: 106.7 lbs. | p. 249 |

It has the power to predict the future. Its power peaks when it is protecting its Trainer.

To protect its Trainer, it will expend all its psychic power to create a small black hole.

MAIN WAY TO OBTAIN
Catch one when it appears wandering at the Lake of Outrage during clear weather or fog. Or obtain a Kirlia, then level it up to Lv. 30 or higher to evolve it into Gardevoir.

☑ Blade Pokémon

123 Gallade

| Height: 5'3" | Weight: 114.6 lbs. | p. 250 |

True to its honorable-warrior image, it uses the blades on its elbows only in defense of something or someone.

Sharply attuned to others' wishes for help, this Pokémon seeks out those in need and aids them in battle.

MAIN WAY TO OBTAIN
Catch one when it appears wandering in the Bridge Field during various weather patterns. Or obtain a male Kirlia, then use a Dawn Stone on it to evolve it into Gallade.

Same form for male/female

Lv. 20

♂ ♀ Same form for male/female

Lv. 30

Use Dawn Stone on male Kirlia

♂ ♀ Same form for male/female

♂ Male only

Same form for male/female

Lv. 28

♂ ♀
Same form for male/female

♂ ♀
Same form for male/female

Lv. 20

♂ ♀
Same form for male/female

☑ Balloon Pokémon
124 Drifloon

Height: 1'4"   Weight: 2.6 lbs.   p. 250

Perhaps seeking company, it approaches children. However, it often quickly runs away again when the children play too roughly with it.

The gathering of many souls gave rise to this Pokémon. During humid seasons, they seem to appear in abundance.

MAIN WAY TO OBTAIN
Catch one when it appears in tall grass or as a random encounter in tall grass at the Watchtower Ruins during various weather patterns.

☑ Blimp Pokémon
125 Drifblim

Height: 3'11"   Weight: 33.1 lbs.   p. 251

Some say this Pokémon is a collection of souls burdened with regrets, silently drifting through the dusk.

It grabs people and Pokémon and carries them off somewhere. Where do they go? Nobody knows.

MAIN WAY TO OBTAIN
Catch one when it appears wandering at the Watchtower Ruins during clear weather, harsh sunlight, or snow. Or obtain a Drifloon, then level it up to Lv. 28 or higher to evolve it into Drifblim.

☑ Flowering Pokémon
126 Gossifleur

Height: 1'4"   Weight: 4.9 lbs.   p. 251

It anchors itself in the ground with its single leg, then basks in the sun. After absorbing enough sunlight, its petals spread as it blooms brilliantly.

It whirls around in the wind while singing a joyous song. This delightful display has charmed many into raising this Pokémon.

MAIN WAY TO OBTAIN
Catch one when it appears in tall grass on Route 3 or the Motostoke Riverbank during clear weather.

☑ Cotton Bloom Pokémon
127 Eldegoss

Height: 1'8"   Weight: 5.5 lbs.   p. 252

The seeds attached to its cotton fluff are full of nutrients. It spreads them on the wind so that plants and other Pokémon can benefit from them.

The cotton on the head of this Pokémon can be spun into a glossy, gorgeous yarn—a Galar regional specialty.

MAIN WAY TO OBTAIN
Catch one when it appears wandering on Route 5. Or obtain a Gossifleur, then level it up to Lv. 20 or higher to evolve it into Eldegoss.

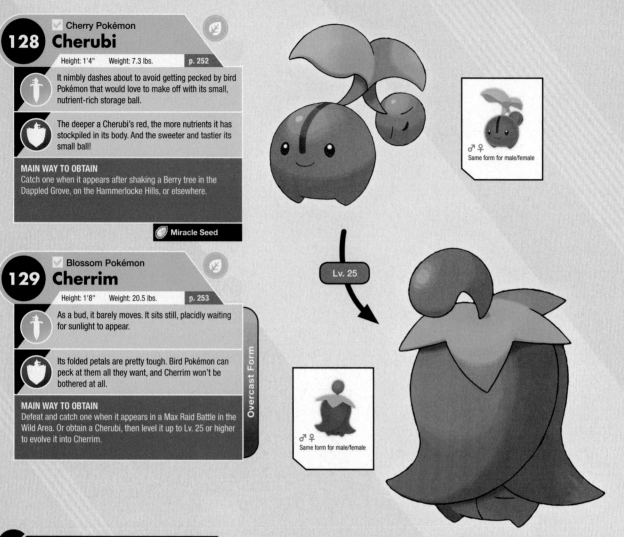

128 Cherubi
Cherry Pokémon

Height: 1'4" Weight: 7.3 lbs. p. 252

It nimbly dashes about to avoid getting pecked by bird Pokémon that would love to make off with its small, nutrient-rich storage ball.

The deeper a Cherubi's red, the more nutrients it has stockpiled in its body. And the sweeter and tastier its small ball!

MAIN WAY TO OBTAIN
Catch one when it appears after shaking a Berry tree in the Dappled Grove, on the Hammerlocke Hills, or elsewhere.

Miracle Seed

♂ ♀
Same form for male/female

Lv. 25

129 Cherrim
Blossom Pokémon

Height: 1'8" Weight: 20.5 lbs. p. 253

As a bud, it barely moves. It sits still, placidly waiting for sunlight to appear.

Its folded petals are pretty tough. Bird Pokémon can peck at them all they want, and Cherrim won't be bothered at all.

MAIN WAY TO OBTAIN
Defeat and catch one when it appears in a Max Raid Battle in the Wild Area. Or obtain a Cherubi, then level it up to Lv. 25 or higher to evolve it into Cherrim.

Overcast Form

♂ ♀
Same form for male/female

FORM CHANGES IN BATTLE

Cherrim is one of a number of Pokémon that can change form under the right conditions in battle. In the rain, hail, sandstorm, or clear weather conditions, Cherrim appears in its Overcast Form. But in harsh sunlight, it will bloom into its smiley Sunshine Form thanks to its Ability, Flower Gift! This Ability also boosts the Attack and Sp. Def of Cherrim and its allies on the battlefield by 150% while the harsh sunlight lasts. As you'll see throughout the Pokédex, form changes tie in to Pokémon stats, Abilities, and battle strategies in a variety of different ways!

Cherrim (Overcast Form)

Cherrim (Sunshine Form)

After absorbing plenty of sunlight, Cherrim takes this form. It's full of energy while it's like this, and its liveliness will go on until sundown.

The faint scent that emanates from its full blossom entices bug Pokémon to it.

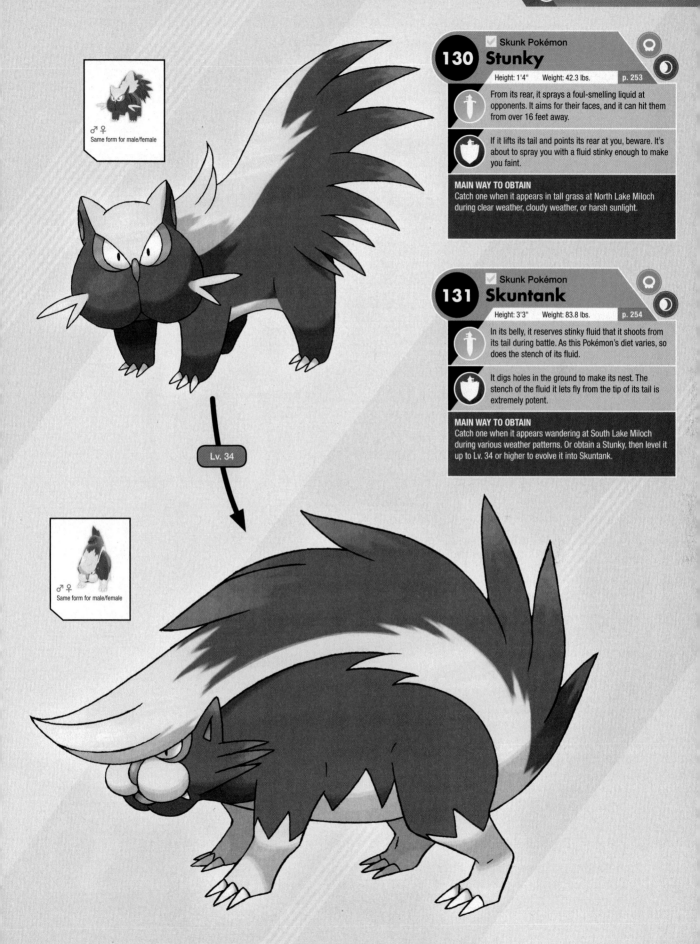

Same form for male/female

130 Stunky

☑ Skunk Pokémon

Height: 1'4"   Weight: 42.3 lbs.   p. 253

From its rear, it sprays a foul-smelling liquid at opponents. It aims for their faces, and it can hit them from over 16 feet away.

If it lifts its tail and points its rear at you, beware. It's about to spray you with a fluid stinky enough to make you faint.

MAIN WAY TO OBTAIN
Catch one when it appears in tall grass at North Lake Miloch during clear weather, cloudy weather, or harsh sunlight.

131 Skuntank

☑ Skunk Pokémon

Height: 3'3"   Weight: 83.8 lbs.   p. 254

In its belly, it reserves stinky fluid that it shoots from its tail during battle. As this Pokémon's diet varies, so does the stench of its fluid.

It digs holes in the ground to make its nest. The stench of the fluid it lets fly from the tip of its tail is extremely potent.

MAIN WAY TO OBTAIN
Catch one when it appears wandering at South Lake Miloch during various weather patterns. Or obtain a Stunky, then level it up to Lv. 34 or higher to evolve it into Skuntank.

Lv. 34

Same form for male/female

132 Tympole
☑ Tadpole Pokémon

Height: 1'8" Weight: 9.9 lbs. p. 254

Graceful ripples running across the water's surface are a sure sign that Tympole are singing in high-pitched voices below.

It uses sound waves to communicate with others of its kind. People and other Pokémon species can't hear its cries of warning.

MAIN WAY TO OBTAIN
Catch one when it appears in tall grass or as a random encounter in tall grass in the Dappled Grove, at North Lake Miloch, or elsewhere during rain.

133 Palpitoad
☑ Vibration Pokémon

Height: 2'7" Weight: 37.5 lbs. p. 255

It weakens its prey with sound waves intense enough to cause headaches, then entangles them with its sticky tongue.

On occasion, their cries are sublimely pleasing to the ear. Palpitoad with larger lumps on their bodies can sing with a wider range of sounds.

MAIN WAY TO OBTAIN
Catch one when it appears in tall grass at North Lake Miloch, on the Hammerlocke Hills, or elsewhere during rain or a thunderstorm. Or obtain a Tympole, then level it up to Lv. 25 or higher to evolve it into Palpitoad.

134 Seismitoad
☑ Vibration Pokémon

Height: 4'11" Weight: 136.7 lbs. p. 255

The vibrating of the bumps all over its body causes earthquake-like tremors. Seismitoad and Croagunk are similar species.

This Pokémon is popular among the elderly, who say the vibrations of its lumps are great for massages.

MAIN WAY TO OBTAIN
Catch one when it appears wandering in the Dappled Grove, the Bridge Field, or the Dusty Bowl during rain or a thunderstorm. Or obtain a Palpitoad, then level it up to Lv. 36 or higher to evolve it into Seismitoad.

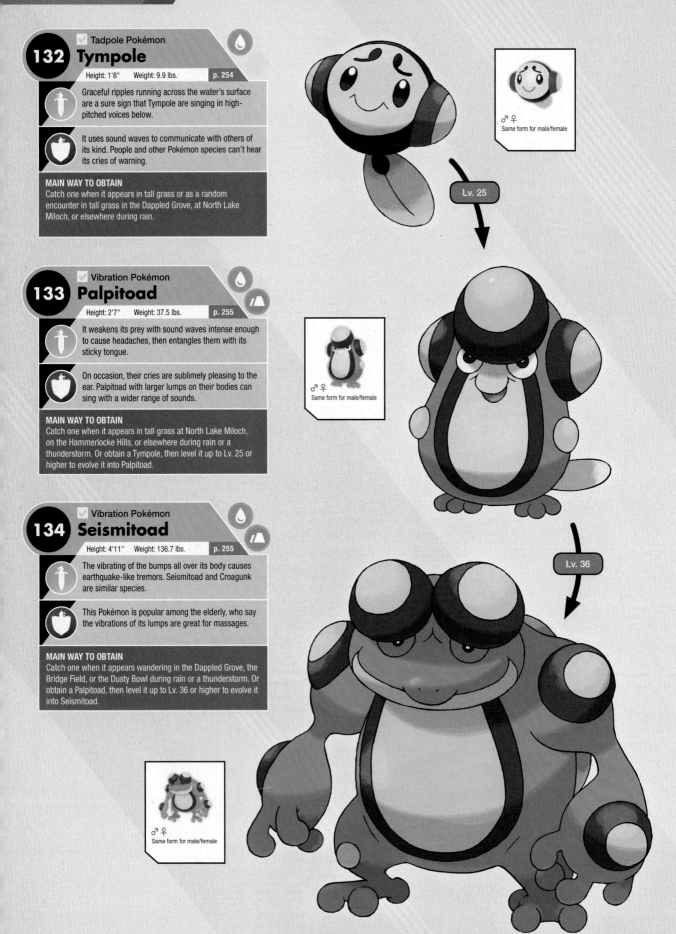

Same form for male/female

Lv. 25

Same form for male/female

Lv. 36

Same form for male/female

Same form for male/female

Lv. 37

Same form for male/female

Trade while holding
Reaper Cloth

Same form for male/female

135 Duskull
Requiem Pokémon

Height: 2'7"   Weight: 33.1 lbs.   p. 256

If it finds bad children who won't listen to their parents, it will spirit them away—or so it's said.

Making itself invisible, it silently sneaks up to prey. It has the ability to slip through thick walls.

MAIN WAY TO OBTAIN
Catch one when it appears in tall grass or as a random encounter in tall grass at the Watchtower Ruins during various weather patterns.

Spell Tag

136 Dusclops
Beckon Pokémon

Height: 5'3"   Weight: 67.5 lbs.   p. 256

Its body is entirely hollow. When it opens its mouth, it sucks everything in as if it were a black hole.

It seeks drifting will-o'-the-wisps and sucks them into its empty body. What happens inside is a mystery.

MAIN WAY TO OBTAIN
Catch one when it appears wandering at the Watchtower Ruins during cloudy weather, rain, a thunderstorm, or fog. Or obtain a Duskull, then level it up to Lv. 37 or higher to evolve it into Dusclops.

Spell Tag

137 Dusknoir
Gripper Pokémon

Height: 7'3"   Weight: 235 lbs.   p. 257

At the bidding of transmissions from the spirit world, it steals people and Pokémon away. No one knows whether it has a will of its own.

With the mouth on its belly, Dusknoir swallows its target whole. The soul is the only thing eaten— Dusknoir disgorges the body before departing.

MAIN WAY TO OBTAIN
Catch one when it appears wandering in the Stony Wilderness. Or receive a Dusclops holding a Reaper Cloth in a trade, and it will immediately evolve into Dusknoir.

Spell Tag

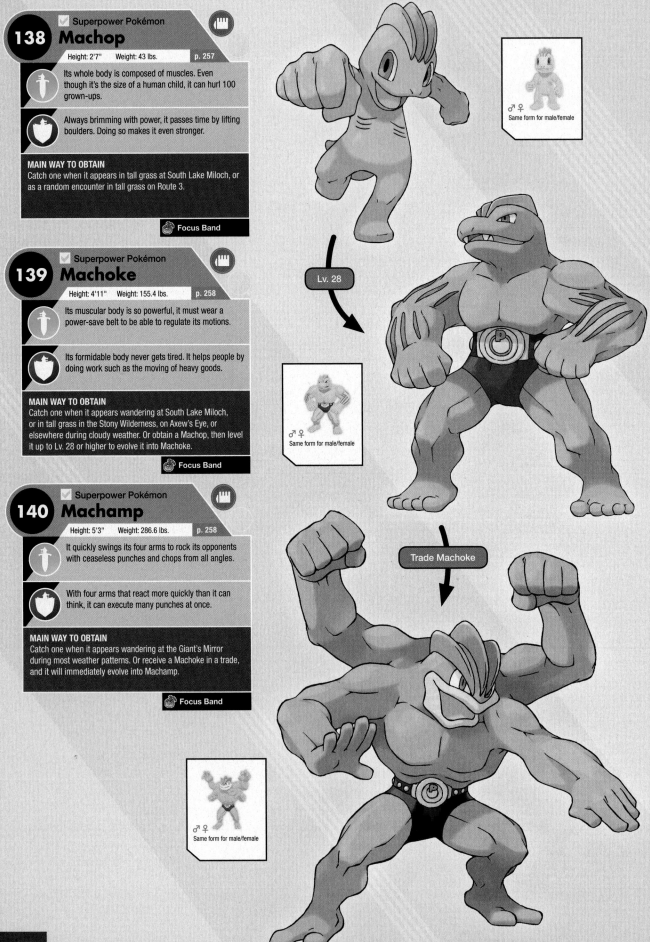

138 Machop

Superpower Pokémon

Height: 2'7"   Weight: 43 lbs.   p. 257

Its whole body is composed of muscles. Even though it's the size of a human child, it can hurl 100 grown-ups.

Always brimming with power, it passes time by lifting boulders. Doing so makes it even stronger.

MAIN WAY TO OBTAIN
Catch one when it appears in tall grass at South Lake Miloch, or as a random encounter in tall grass on Route 3.

🍶 Focus Band

139 Machoke

Superpower Pokémon

Height: 4'11"   Weight: 155.4 lbs.   p. 258

Its muscular body is so powerful, it must wear a power-save belt to be able to regulate its motions.

Its formidable body never gets tired. It helps people by doing work such as the moving of heavy goods.

MAIN WAY TO OBTAIN
Catch one when it appears wandering at South Lake Miloch, or in tall grass in the Stony Wilderness, on Axew's Eye, or elsewhere during cloudy weather. Or obtain a Machop, then level it up to Lv. 28 or higher to evolve it into Machoke.

🍶 Focus Band

140 Machamp

Superpower Pokémon

Height: 5'3"   Weight: 286.6 lbs.   p. 258

It quickly swings its four arms to rock its opponents with ceaseless punches and chops from all angles.

With four arms that react more quickly than it can think, it can execute many punches at once.

MAIN WAY TO OBTAIN
Catch one when it appears wandering at the Giant's Mirror during most weather patterns. Or receive a Machoke in a trade, and it will immediately evolve into Machamp.

🍶 Focus Band

Same form for male/female

Lv. 28

Trade Machoke

Same form for male/female

Same form for male/female

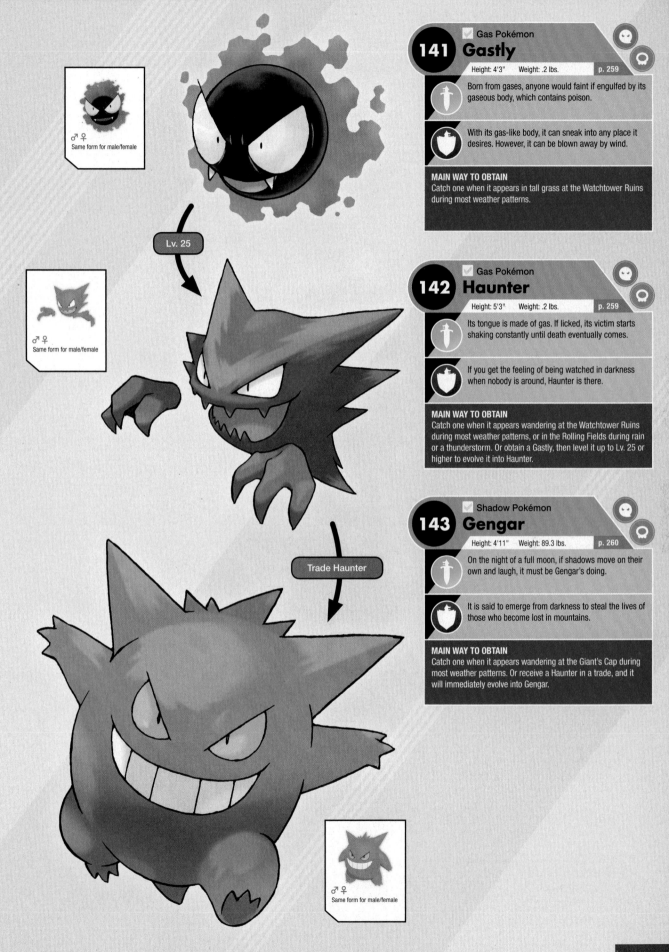

Same form for male/female

Lv. 25

Same form for male/female

Trade Haunter

Same form for male/female

141 Gastly

☑ Gas Pokémon

Height: 4'3"   Weight: .2 lbs.   p. 259

Born from gases, anyone would faint if engulfed by its gaseous body, which contains poison.

With its gas-like body, it can sneak into any place it desires. However, it can be blown away by wind.

MAIN WAY TO OBTAIN
Catch one when it appears in tall grass at the Watchtower Ruins during most weather patterns.

142 Haunter

☑ Gas Pokémon

Height: 5'3"   Weight: .2 lbs.   p. 259

Its tongue is made of gas. If licked, its victim starts shaking constantly until death eventually comes.

If you get the feeling of being watched in darkness when nobody is around, Haunter is there.

MAIN WAY TO OBTAIN
Catch one when it appears wandering at the Watchtower Ruins during most weather patterns, or in the Rolling Fields during rain or a thunderstorm. Or obtain a Gastly, then level it up to Lv. 25 or higher to evolve it into Haunter.

143 Gengar

☑ Shadow Pokémon

Height: 4'11"   Weight: 89.3 lbs.   p. 260

On the night of a full moon, if shadows move on their own and laugh, it must be Gengar's doing.

It is said to emerge from darkness to steal the lives of those who become lost in mountains.

MAIN WAY TO OBTAIN
Catch one when it appears wandering at the Giant's Cap during most weather patterns. Or receive a Haunter in a trade, and it will immediately evolve into Gengar.

144 Magikarp

☑ Fish Pokémon

Height: 2'11" Weight: 22 lbs. p. 260

It is virtually worthless in terms of both power and speed. It is the most weak and pathetic Pokémon in the world.

This weak and pathetic Pokémon gets easily pushed along rivers when there are strong currents.

MAIN WAY TO OBTAIN
Catch one when you fish it up on Route 2, Route 4, or elsewhere.

The male has yellow whiskers where the female has white whiskers.

145 Gyarados

☑ Atrocious Pokémon

Height: 21'4" Weight: 518.1 lbs. p. 261

It has an extremely aggressive nature. The Hyper Beam it shoots from its mouth totally incinerates all targets.

Once it begins to rampage, a Gyarados will burn everything down, even in a harsh storm.

MAIN WAY TO OBTAIN
Catch one when it appears on the water's surface at East Lake Axewell, South Lake Miloch, or elsewhere during most weather patterns. Or obtain a Magikarp, then level it up to Lv. 20 or higher to evolve it into Gyarados.

Lv. 20

The male has blue whiskers where the female has white whiskers.

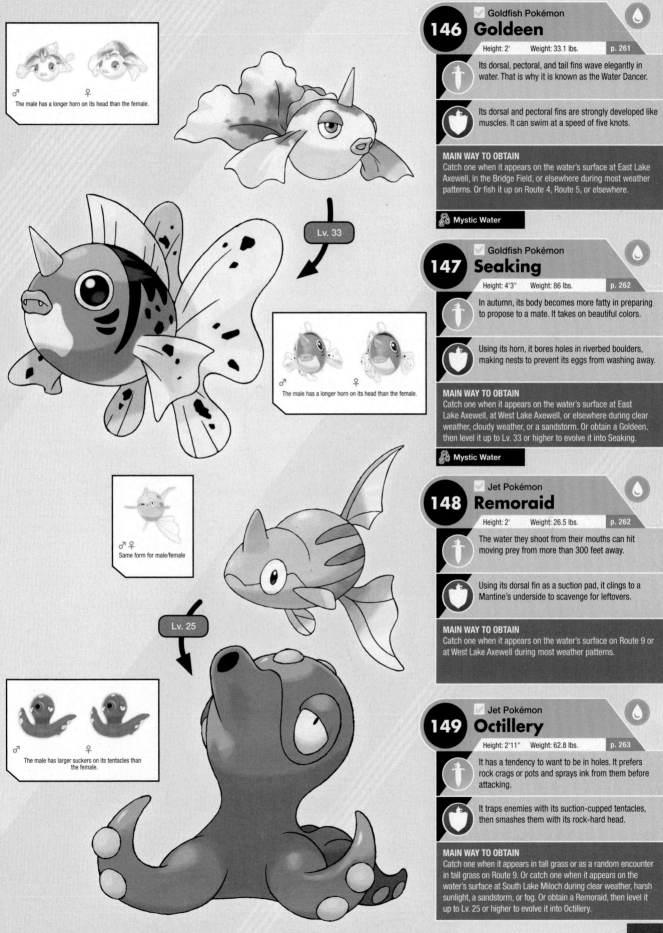

The male has a longer horn on its head than the female.
♂ ♀

Lv. 33

The male has a longer horn on its head than the female.
♂ ♀

Same form for male/female
♂ ♀

Lv. 25

The male has larger suckers on its tentacles than the female.
♂ ♀

146 Goldeen

Goldfish Pokémon

Height: 2'   Weight: 33.1 lbs.   p. 261

Its dorsal, pectoral, and tail fins wave elegantly in water. That is why it is known as the Water Dancer.

Its dorsal and pectoral fins are strongly developed like muscles. It can swim at a speed of five knots.

MAIN WAY TO OBTAIN
Catch one when it appears on the water's surface at East Lake Axewell, in the Bridge Field, or elsewhere during most weather patterns. Or fish it up on Route 4, Route 5, or elsewhere.

Mystic Water

147 Seaking

Goldfish Pokémon

Height: 4'3"   Weight: 86 lbs.   p. 262

In autumn, its body becomes more fatty in preparing to propose to a mate. It takes on beautiful colors.

Using its horn, it bores holes in riverbed boulders, making nests to prevent its eggs from washing away.

MAIN WAY TO OBTAIN
Catch one when it appears on the water's surface at East Lake Axewell, at West Lake Axewell, or elsewhere during clear weather, cloudy weather, or a sandstorm. Or obtain a Goldeen, then level it up to Lv. 33 or higher to evolve it into Seaking.

Mystic Water

148 Remoraid

Jet Pokémon

Height: 2'   Weight: 26.5 lbs.   p. 262

The water they shoot from their mouths can hit moving prey from more than 300 feet away.

Using its dorsal fin as a suction pad, it clings to a Mantine's underside to scavenge for leftovers.

MAIN WAY TO OBTAIN
Catch one when it appears on the water's surface on Route 9 or at West Lake Axewell during most weather patterns.

149 Octillery

Jet Pokémon

Height: 2'11"   Weight: 62.8 lbs.   p. 263

It has a tendency to want to be in holes. It prefers rock crags or pots and sprays ink from them before attacking.

It traps enemies with its suction-cupped tentacles, then smashes them with its rock-hard head.

MAIN WAY TO OBTAIN
Catch one when it appears in tall grass or as a random encounter in tall grass on Route 9. Or catch one when it appears on the water's surface at South Lake Miloch during clear weather, harsh sunlight, a sandstorm, or fog. Or obtain a Remoraid, then level it up to Lv. 25 or higher to evolve it into Octillery.

150 Shellder

☑ Bivalve Pokémon

Height: 1'   Weight: 8.8 lbs.   p. 263

It swims facing backward by opening and closing its two-piece shell. It is surprisingly fast.

Its hard shell repels any kind of attack. It is vulnerable only when its shell is open.

MAIN WAY TO OBTAIN
Catch one when it appears on the water's surface at East Lake Axewell during all weather patterns, or at West Lake Axewell during snow. Or fish it up at East Lake Axewell or the Giant's Seat during clear weather.

◉ Pearl   ◉ Big Pearl

151 Cloyster

☑ Bivalve Pokémon

Height: 4'11"   Weight: 292.1 lbs.   p. 264

Its shell is extremely hard. It cannot be shattered, even with a bomb. The shell opens only when it is attacking.

Once it slams its shell shut, it is impossible to open, even by those with superior strength.

MAIN WAY TO OBTAIN
Catch one when it appears on the water's surface at East Lake Axewell or West Lake Axewell during clear weather or fog. Or obtain a Shellder, then use a Water Stone on it to evolve it into Cloyster.

◉ Pearl   ◉ Big Pearl

♂ ♀
Same form for male/female

Use Water Stone

♂ ♀
Same form for male/female

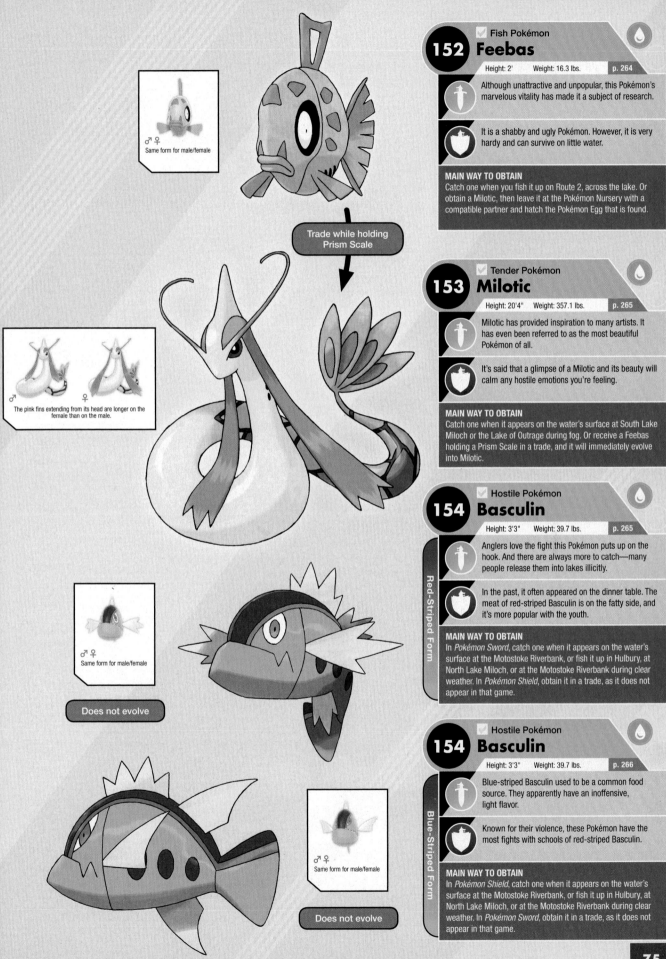

Same form for male/female

The pink fins extending from its head are longer on the female than on the male.

Trade while holding Prism Scale

Same form for male/female

Does not evolve

Does not evolve

152 Feebas

Fish Pokémon

Height: 2'   Weight: 16.3 lbs.   p. 264

Although unattractive and unpopular, this Pokémon's marvelous vitality has made it a subject of research.

It is a shabby and ugly Pokémon. However, it is very hardy and can survive on little water.

MAIN WAY TO OBTAIN
Catch one when you fish it up on Route 2, across the lake. Or obtain a Milotic, then leave it at the Pokémon Nursery with a compatible partner and hatch the Pokémon Egg that is found.

153 Milotic

Tender Pokémon

Height: 20'4"   Weight: 357.1 lbs.   p. 265

Milotic has provided inspiration to many artists. It has even been referred to as the most beautiful Pokémon of all.

It's said that a glimpse of a Milotic and its beauty will calm any hostile emotions you're feeling.

MAIN WAY TO OBTAIN
Catch one when it appears on the water's surface at South Lake Miloch or the Lake of Outrage during fog. Or receive a Feebas holding a Prism Scale in a trade, and it will immediately evolve into Milotic.

154 Basculin

Hostile Pokémon

Height: 3'3"   Weight: 39.7 lbs.   p. 265

Anglers love the fight this Pokémon puts up on the hook. And there are always more to catch—many people release them into lakes illicitly.

In the past, it often appeared on the dinner table. The meat of red-striped Basculin is on the fatty side, and it's more popular with the youth.

MAIN WAY TO OBTAIN
In *Pokémon Sword*, catch one when it appears on the water's surface at the Motostoke Riverbank, or fish it up in Hulbury, at North Lake Miloch, or at the Motostoke Riverbank during clear weather. In *Pokémon Shield*, obtain it in a trade, as it does not appear in that game.

Red-Striped Form

154 Basculin

Hostile Pokémon

Height: 3'3"   Weight: 39.7 lbs.   p. 266

Blue-striped Basculin used to be a common food source. They apparently have an inoffensive, light flavor.

Known for their violence, these Pokémon have the most fights with schools of red-striped Basculin.

MAIN WAY TO OBTAIN
In *Pokémon Shield*, catch one when it appears on the water's surface at the Motostoke Riverbank, or fish it up in Hulbury, at North Lake Miloch, or at the Motostoke Riverbank during clear weather. In *Pokémon Sword*, obtain it in a trade, as it does not appear in that game.

Blue-Striped Form

155 Wishiwashi

☑ Small Fry Pokémon

Height: 8" Weight: .7 lbs. p. 266

Individually, they're incredibly weak. It's by gathering up into schools that they're able to confront opponents.

When it senses danger, its eyes tear up. The sparkle of its tears signals other Wishiwashi to gather.

MAIN WAY TO OBTAIN
Catch one when you fish it up at West Lake Axewell, at East Lake Axewell, or elsewhere during clear weather.

Solo Form

♂♀
Same form for male/female

Does not evolve

156 Pyukumuku

☑ Sea Cucumber Pokémon

Height: 1' Weight: 2.6 lbs. p. 267

It lives in warm, shallow waters. If it encounters a foe, it will spit out its internal organs as a means to punch them.

It's covered in a slime that keeps its skin moist, allowing it to stay on land for days without drying up.

MAIN WAY TO OBTAIN
Catch one when you fish it up at the Giant's Seat, on Route 9, or at South Lake Miloch during clear weather. Or catch one when it appears in tall grass at South Lake Miloch during a thunderstorm.

♂♀
Same form for male/female

Does not evolve

⊘ WISHIWASHI'S SCHOOL FORM

Wishiwashi is another Pokémon that can change form during battle if the conditions are right. In Wishiwashi's case, any Wishiwashi that is at least Lv. 20 can change form thanks to its Schooling Ability. When its HP is above 25% of its maximum, it will change into its impressive School Form. It returns to its Solo Form whenever its HP drops to 25% of its max or below, though. This form change affects Wishiwashi's height, weight, and species strengths, but since the form is only a temporary one that appears in battle, it does not affect its Ability, moves, or other parameters.

SPECIES STRENGTHS

	Solo Form		School Form
HP	▦▦▦	HP	▦▦▦
ATTACK	▦▦	ATTACK	▦▦▦▦▦▦▦▦▦
DEFENSE	▦▦	DEFENSE	▦▦▦▦▦▦▦▦
SP. ATK	▦▦	SP. ATK	▦▦▦▦▦▦▦▦▦
SP. DEF	▦▦	SP. DEF	▦▦▦▦▦▦▦▦
SPEED	▦▦▦▦	SPEED	▦▦

School Form Wishiwashi has far higher Attack, Defense, Sp. Atk, and Sp. Def stats than a Solo Form Wishiwashi has!

⬤ Wishiwashi (School Form)

Height: 26'11" Weight: 173.3 lbs.

On their own, they're very weak. But when Wishiwashi pool their power together in a school, they become a demon of the sea.

When facing tough opponents, they get into formation. But if they get wounded in battle, they'll scatter and become solitary again.

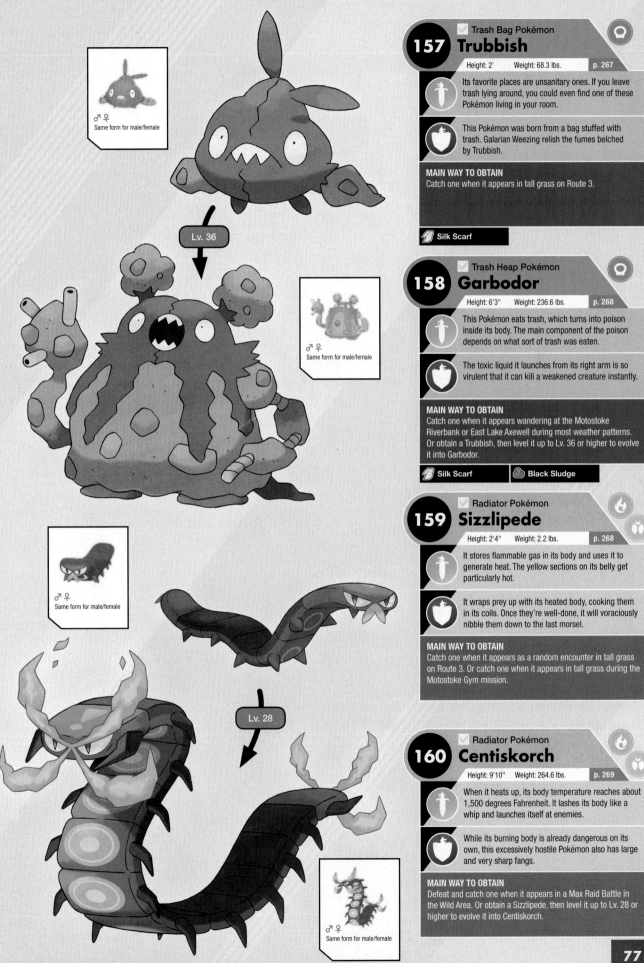

♂♀
Same form for male/female

Lv. 36

♂♀
Same form for male/female

♂♀
Same form for male/female

Lv. 28

♂♀
Same form for male/female

157 Trubbish
Trash Bag Pokémon

| Height: 2' | Weight: 68.3 lbs. | p. 267 |

Its favorite places are unsanitary ones. If you leave trash lying around, you could even find one of these Pokémon living in your room.

This Pokémon was born from a bag stuffed with trash. Galarian Weezing relish the fumes belched by Trubbish.

MAIN WAY TO OBTAIN
Catch one when it appears in tall grass on Route 3.

Silk Scarf

158 Garbodor
Trash Heap Pokémon

| Height: 6'3" | Weight: 236.6 lbs. | p. 268 |

This Pokémon eats trash, which turns into poison inside its body. The main component of the poison depends on what sort of trash was eaten.

The toxic liquid it launches from its right arm is so virulent that it can kill a weakened creature instantly.

MAIN WAY TO OBTAIN
Catch one when it appears wandering at the Motostoke Riverbank or East Lake Axewell during most weather patterns. Or obtain a Trubbish, then level it up to Lv. 36 or higher to evolve it into Garbodor.

Silk Scarf   Black Sludge

159 Sizzlipede
Radiator Pokémon

| Height: 2'4" | Weight: 2.2 lbs. | p. 268 |

It stores flammable gas in its body and uses it to generate heat. The yellow sections on its belly get particularly hot.

It wraps prey up with its heated body, cooking them in its coils. Once they're well-done, it will voraciously nibble them down to the last morsel.

MAIN WAY TO OBTAIN
Catch one when it appears as a random encounter in tall grass on Route 3. Or catch one when it appears in tall grass during the Motostoke Gym mission.

160 Centiskorch
Radiator Pokémon

| Height: 9'10" | Weight: 264.6 lbs. | p. 269 |

When it heats up, its body temperature reaches about 1,500 degrees Fahrenheit. It lashes its body like a whip and launches itself at enemies.

While its burning body is already dangerous on its own, this excessively hostile Pokémon also has large and very sharp fangs.

MAIN WAY TO OBTAIN
Defeat and catch one when it appears in a Max Raid Battle in the Wild Area. Or obtain a Sizzlipede, then level it up to Lv. 28 or higher to evolve it into Centiskorch.

161 Rolycoly

☑ Coal Pokémon

Height: 1' Weight: 26.5 lbs. p. 269

Most of its body has the same composition as coal. Fittingly, this Pokémon was first discovered in coal mines about 400 years ago.

It can race around like a unicycle, even on rough, rocky terrain. Burning coal sustains it.

MAIN WAY TO OBTAIN
Catch one when it appears in tall grass on Route 3 or on the ground in Galar Mine. Or catch one when it appears on the ground at the Giant's Cap.

♂ ♀
Same form for male/female

Lv. 18

162 Carkol

☑ Coal Pokémon

Height: 3'7" Weight: 172 lbs. p. 270

It forms coal inside its body. Coal dropped by this Pokémon once helped fuel the lives of people in the Galar region.

By rapidly rolling its legs, it can travel at over 18 mph. The temperature of the flames it breathes exceeds 1,800 degrees Fahrenheit.

MAIN WAY TO OBTAIN
Catch one when it appears wandering in Galar Mine. Or catch one when it appears in tall grass at the Giant's Cap during harsh sunlight or a sandstorm. Or obtain a Rolycoly, then level it up to Lv. 18 or higher to evolve it into Carkol.

♂ ♀
Same form for male/female

163 Coalossal

☑ Coal Pokémon

Height: 9'2" Weight: 684.5 lbs. p. 270

It's usually peaceful, but the vandalism of mines enrages it. Offenders will be incinerated with flames that reach 2,700 degrees Fahrenheit.

While it's engaged in battle, its mountain of coal will burn bright red, sending off sparks that scorch the surrounding area.

MAIN WAY TO OBTAIN
Catch one when it appears as a random encounter in tall grass in the Dusty Bowl or at the Lake of Outrage during harsh sunlight. Or catch one when it appears wandering at the Giant's Cap after you become Champion. Or obtain a Carkol, then level it up to Lv. 34 or higher to evolve it into Coalossal.

Lv. 34

♂ ♀
Same form for male/female

Same form for male/female

♂ ♀
Same form for male/female

Lv. 26

♂ ♀
Same form for male/female

Same form for male/female

Lv. 31

♂ ♀
Same form for male/female

☑ Mole Pokémon
164 Diglett

| Height: 8" | Weight: 1.8 lbs. | p. 271 |

If a Diglett digs through a field, it leaves the soil perfectly tilled and ideal for planting crops.

It burrows through the ground at a shallow depth. It leaves raised earth in its wake, making it easy to spot.

MAIN WAY TO OBTAIN
Catch one when it appears on the ground in the Rolling Fields or Galar Mine.

💥 Soft Sand

☑ Mole Pokémon
165 Dugtrio

| Height: 2'4" | Weight: 73.4 lbs. | p. 271 |

A team of Diglett triplets. It triggers huge earthquakes by burrowing 60 miles underground.

These Diglett triplets dig over 60 miles below sea level. No one knows what it's like underground.

MAIN WAY TO OBTAIN
Catch one when it appears on the ground at the Giant's Mirror. Or catch one when it appears in tall grass on Route 6. Or obtain a Diglett, then level it up to Lv. 26 or higher to evolve it into Dugtrio.

💥 Soft Sand

☑ Mole Pokémon
166 Drilbur

| Height: 1' | Weight: 18.7 lbs. | p. 272 |

It brings its claws together and whirls around at high speed before rushing toward its prey.

It's a digger, using its claws to burrow through the ground. It causes damage to vegetable crops, so many farmers have little love for it.

MAIN WAY TO OBTAIN
Catch one when it appears on the ground in Galar Mine. Or catch one when it appears as a random encounter on the Hammerlocke Hills, at the Giant's Cap, or in the Stony Wilderness during a sandstorm.

☑ Subterrene Pokémon
167 Excadrill

| Height: 2'4" | Weight: 89.1 lbs. | p. 272 |

It's not uncommon for tunnels that appear to have formed naturally to actually be a result of Excadrill's rampant digging.

Known as the Drill King, this Pokémon can tunnel through the terrain at speeds of over 90 mph.

MAIN WAY TO OBTAIN
Catch one when it appears on the ground at the Giant's Mirror. Or obtain a Drilbur, then level it up to Lv. 31 or higher to evolve it into Excadrill.

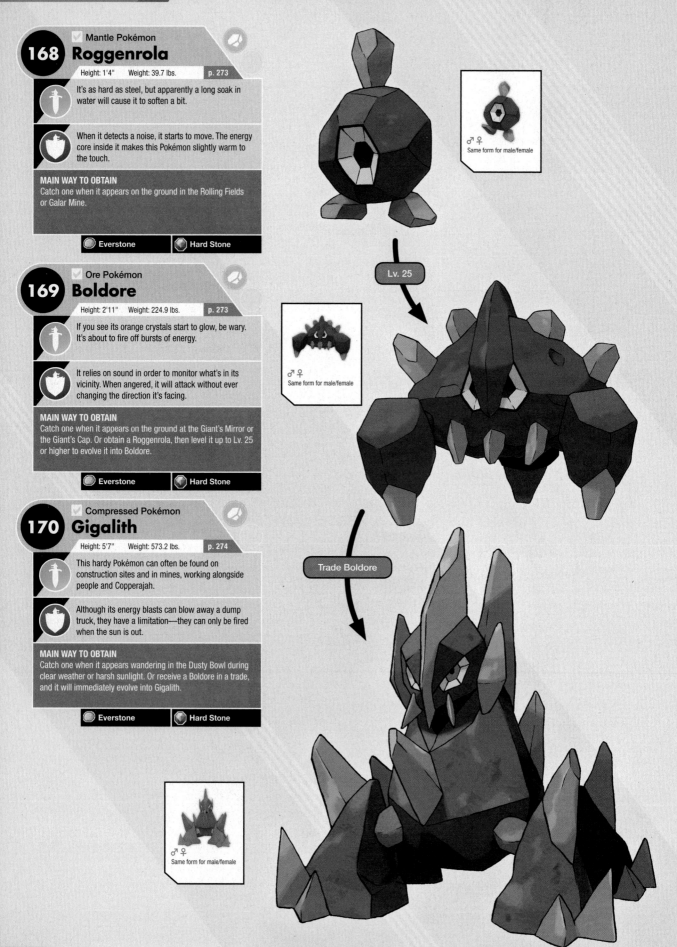

☑ Mantle Pokémon
168 Roggenrola

Height: 1'4" Weight: 39.7 lbs. p. 273

It's as hard as steel, but apparently a long soak in water will cause it to soften a bit.

When it detects a noise, it starts to move. The energy core inside it makes this Pokémon slightly warm to the touch.

MAIN WAY TO OBTAIN
Catch one when it appears on the ground in the Rolling Fields or Galar Mine.

◉ Everstone | ◈ Hard Stone

♂ ♀
Same form for male/female

Lv. 25

☑ Ore Pokémon
169 Boldore

Height: 2'11" Weight: 224.9 lbs. p. 273

If you see its orange crystals start to glow, be wary. It's about to fire off bursts of energy.

It relies on sound in order to monitor what's in its vicinity. When angered, it will attack without ever changing the direction it's facing.

MAIN WAY TO OBTAIN
Catch one when it appears on the ground at the Giant's Mirror or the Giant's Cap. Or obtain a Roggenrola, then level it up to Lv. 25 or higher to evolve it into Boldore.

◉ Everstone | ◈ Hard Stone

♂ ♀
Same form for male/female

Trade Boldore

☑ Compressed Pokémon
170 Gigalith

Height: 5'7" Weight: 573.2 lbs. p. 274

This hardy Pokémon can often be found on construction sites and in mines, working alongside people and Copperajah.

Although its energy blasts can blow away a dump truck, they have a limitation—they can only be fired when the sun is out.

MAIN WAY TO OBTAIN
Catch one when it appears wandering in the Dusty Bowl during clear weather or harsh sunlight. Or receive a Boldore in a trade, and it will immediately evolve into Gigalith.

◉ Everstone | ◈ Hard Stone

♂ ♀
Same form for male/female

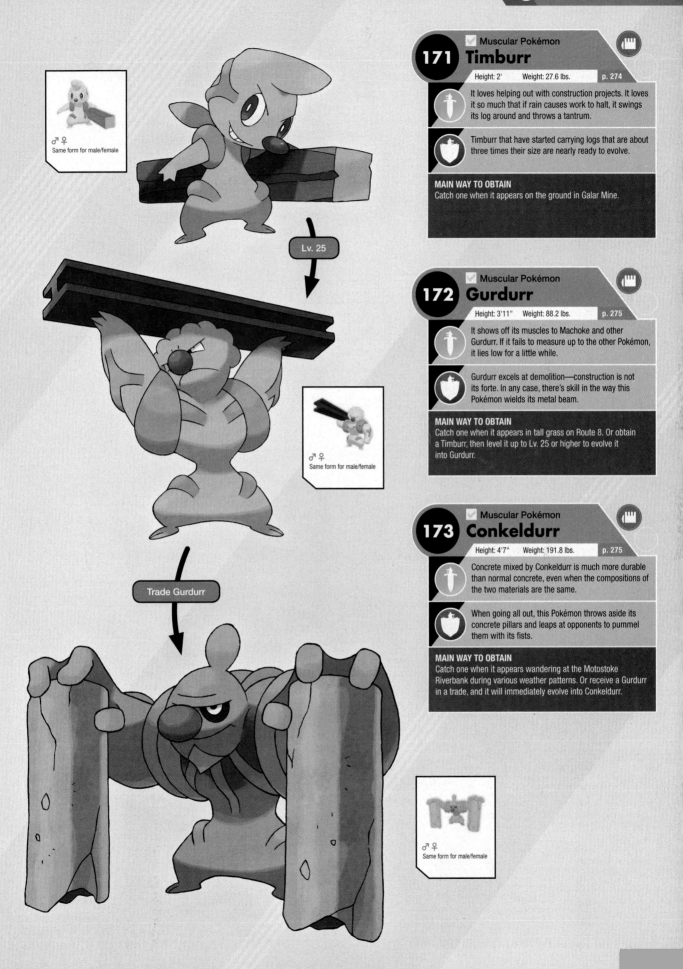

Same form for male/female

171 ☑ Muscular Pokémon
Timburr

Height: 2'   Weight: 27.6 lbs.   p. 274

It loves helping out with construction projects. It loves it so much that if rain causes work to halt, it swings its log around and throws a tantrum.

Timburr that have started carrying logs that are about three times their size are nearly ready to evolve.

MAIN WAY TO OBTAIN
Catch one when it appears on the ground in Galar Mine.

Lv. 25

172 ☑ Muscular Pokémon
Gurdurr

Height: 3'11"   Weight: 88.2 lbs.   p. 275

It shows off its muscles to Machoke and other Gurdurr. If it fails to measure up to the other Pokémon, it lies low for a little while.

Gurdurr excels at demolition—construction is not its forte. In any case, there's skill in the way this Pokémon wields its metal beam.

MAIN WAY TO OBTAIN
Catch one when it appears in tall grass on Route 8. Or obtain a Timburr, then level it up to Lv. 25 or higher to evolve it into Gurdurr.

Same form for male/female

Trade Gurdurr

173 ☑ Muscular Pokémon
Conkeldurr

Height: 4'7"   Weight: 191.8 lbs.   p. 275

Concrete mixed by Conkeldurr is much more durable than normal concrete, even when the compositions of the two materials are the same.

When going all out, this Pokémon throws aside its concrete pillars and leaps at opponents to pummel them with its fists.

MAIN WAY TO OBTAIN
Catch one when it appears wandering at the Motostoke Riverbank during various weather patterns. Or receive a Gurdurr in a trade, and it will immediately evolve into Conkeldurr.

Same form for male/female

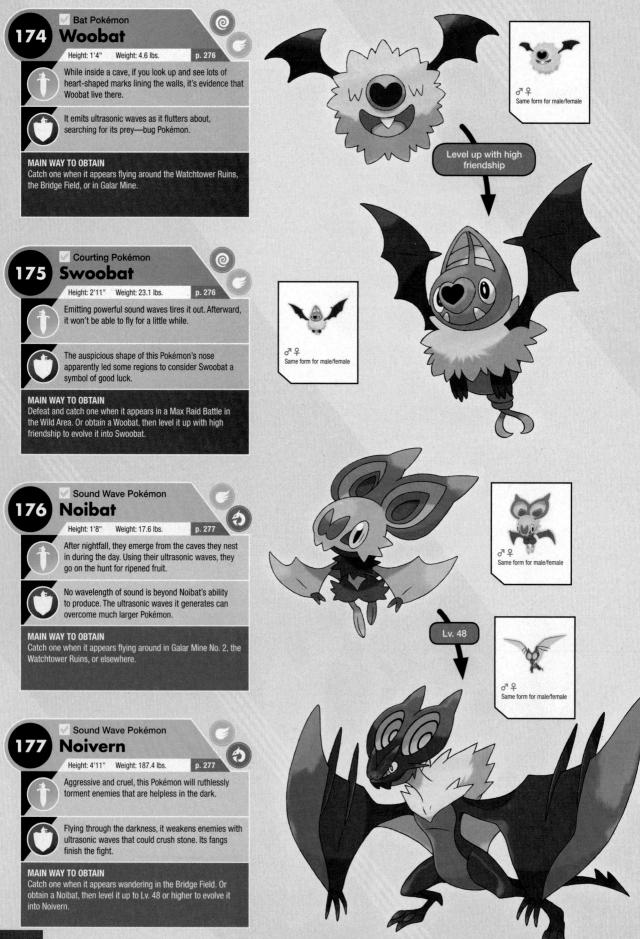

174 Woobat
Bat Pokémon

Height: 1'4" Weight: 4.6 lbs. p. 276

While inside a cave, if you look up and see lots of heart-shaped marks lining the walls, it's evidence that Woobat live there.

It emits ultrasonic waves as it flutters about, searching for its prey—bug Pokémon.

MAIN WAY TO OBTAIN
Catch one when it appears flying around the Watchtower Ruins, the Bridge Field, or in Galar Mine.

Same form for male/female

Level up with high friendship

175 Swoobat
Courting Pokémon

Height: 2'11" Weight: 23.1 lbs. p. 276

Emitting powerful sound waves tires it out. Afterward, it won't be able to fly for a little while.

The auspicious shape of this Pokémon's nose apparently led some regions to consider Swoobat a symbol of good luck.

MAIN WAY TO OBTAIN
Defeat and catch one when it appears in a Max Raid Battle in the Wild Area. Or obtain a Woobat, then level it up with high friendship to evolve it into Swoobat.

Same form for male/female

176 Noibat
Sound Wave Pokémon

Height: 1'8" Weight: 17.6 lbs. p. 277

After nightfall, they emerge from the caves they nest in during the day. Using their ultrasonic waves, they go on the hunt for ripened fruit.

No wavelength of sound is beyond Noibat's ability to produce. The ultrasonic waves it generates can overcome much larger Pokémon.

MAIN WAY TO OBTAIN
Catch one when it appears flying around in Galar Mine No. 2, the Watchtower Ruins, or elsewhere.

Same form for male/female

Lv. 48

Same form for male/female

177 Noivern
Sound Wave Pokémon

Height: 4'11" Weight: 187.4 lbs. p. 277

Aggressive and cruel, this Pokémon will ruthlessly torment enemies that are helpless in the dark.

Flying through the darkness, it weakens enemies with ultrasonic waves that could crush stone. Its fangs finish the fight.

MAIN WAY TO OBTAIN
Catch one when it appears wandering in the Bridge Field. Or obtain a Noibat, then level it up to Lv. 48 or higher to evolve it into Noivern.

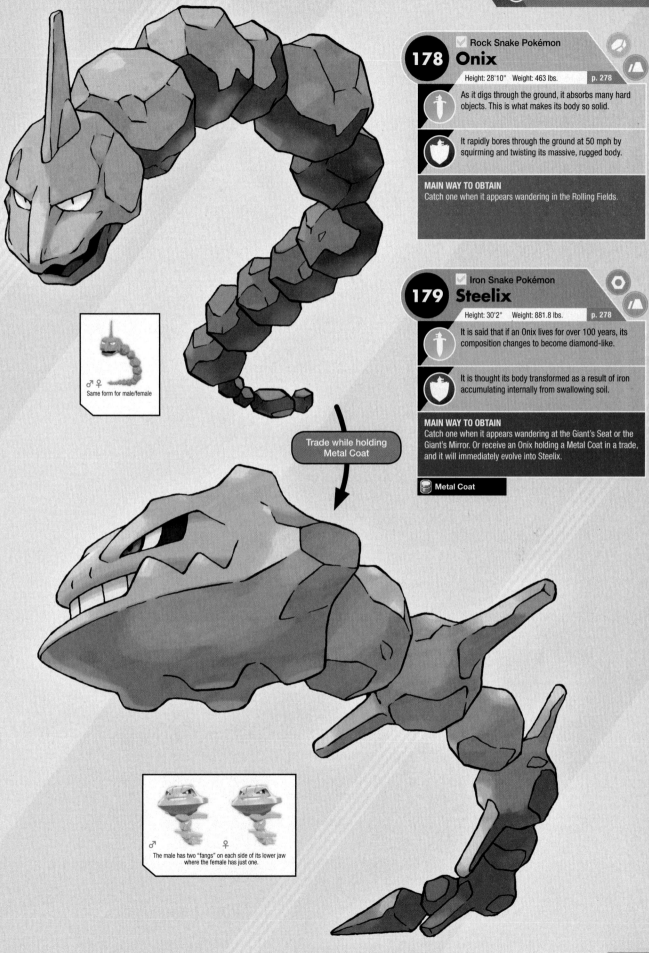

178 Onix

✓ Rock Snake Pokémon

Height: 28'10" Weight: 463 lbs. p. 278

As it digs through the ground, it absorbs many hard objects. This is what makes its body so solid.

It rapidly bores through the ground at 50 mph by squirming and twisting its massive, rugged body.

MAIN WAY TO OBTAIN
Catch one when it appears wandering in the Rolling Fields.

179 Steelix

✓ Iron Snake Pokémon

Height: 30'2" Weight: 881.8 lbs. p. 278

It is said that if an Onix lives for over 100 years, its composition changes to become diamond-like.

It is thought its body transformed as a result of iron accumulating internally from swallowing soil.

MAIN WAY TO OBTAIN
Catch one when it appears wandering at the Giant's Seat or the Giant's Mirror. Or receive an Onix holding a Metal Coat in a trade, and it will immediately evolve into Steelix.

Metal Coat

Trade while holding Metal Coat

♂ ♀ Same form for male/female

♂ ♀
The male has two "fangs" on each side of its lower jaw where the female has just one.

83

180 Arrokuda

☑ Rush Pokémon

Height: 1'8"   Weight: 2.2 lbs.   p. 279

If it sees any movement around it, this Pokémon charges for it straightaway, leading with its sharply pointed jaw. It's very proud of that jaw.

After it's eaten its fill, its movements become extremely sluggish. That's when Cramorant swallows it up.

MAIN WAY TO OBTAIN

Catch one when you fish it up in Hulbury, at the Motostoke Riverbank, or on Route 2. Or catch it when it appears on the water's surface at the Motostoke Riverbank.

181 Barraskewda

☑ Skewer Pokémon

Height: 4'3"   Weight: 66.1 lbs.   p. 279

This Pokémon has a jaw that's as sharp as a spear and as strong as steel. Apparently Barraskewda's flesh is surprisingly tasty, too.

It spins its tail fins to propel itself, surging forward at speeds of over 100 knots before ramming prey and spearing into them.

MAIN WAY TO OBTAIN

Catch one when you fish it up in the Dusty Bowl, at the Lake of Outrage, or at the Motostoke Riverbank. Or obtain an Arrokuda, then level it up to Lv. 26 or higher to evolve it into Barraskewda.

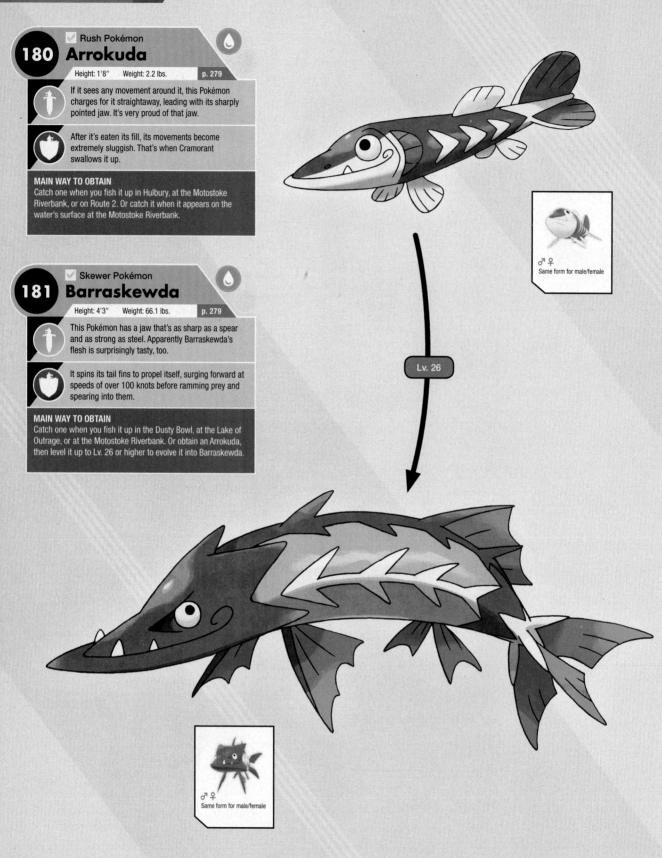

♂ ♀
Same form for male/female

Lv. 26

♂ ♀
Same form for male/female

Same form for male/female

182 Meowth
Scratch Cat Pokémon

Height: 1'4" Weight: 9.3 lbs. p. 280

It loves to collect shiny things. If it's in a good mood, it might even let its Trainer have a look at its hoard of treasures.

It washes its face regularly to keep the coin on its forehead spotless. It doesn't get along with Galarian Meowth.

MAIN WAY TO OBTAIN
Obtain one by trading a Galarian Meowth to the boy in Turffield Stadium.

182 Meowth
Scratch Cat Pokémon

Height: 1'4" Weight: 16.5 lbs. p. 280

Galarian Form

Living with a savage, seafaring people has toughened this Pokémon's body so much that parts of it have turned to iron.

These daring Pokémon have coins on their foreheads. Darker coins are harder, and harder coins garner more respect among Meowth.

MAIN WAY TO OBTAIN
Catch one when it appears in tall grass or as a random encounter in tall grass on Route 4.

183 Perrserker
Viking Pokémon

Height: 2'7" Weight: 61.7 lbs. p. 281

What appears to be an iron helmet is actually hardened hair. This Pokémon lives for the thrill of battle.

After many battles, it evolved dangerous claws that come together to form daggers when extended.

MAIN WAY TO OBTAIN
Catch one when it appears in tall grass on Route 7. Or catch one when it appears wandering at the Giant's Mirror after you become Champion. Or obtain a Galarian Meowth, then level it up to Lv. 28 or higher to evolve it into Perrserker.

184 Persian
Classy Cat Pokémon

Height: 3'3" Weight: 70.5 lbs. p. 281

Getting this prideful Pokémon to warm up to you takes a lot of effort, and it will claw at you the moment it gets annoyed.

Its elegant and refined behavior clashes with that of the barbaric Perrserker. The relationship between the two is one of mutual disdain.

MAIN WAY TO OBTAIN
Obtain a Meowth from another region, then level it up to Lv. 28 or higher to evolve it into Persian.

Lv. 28

Lv. 28

Same form for male/female

Same form for male/female

Same form for male/female

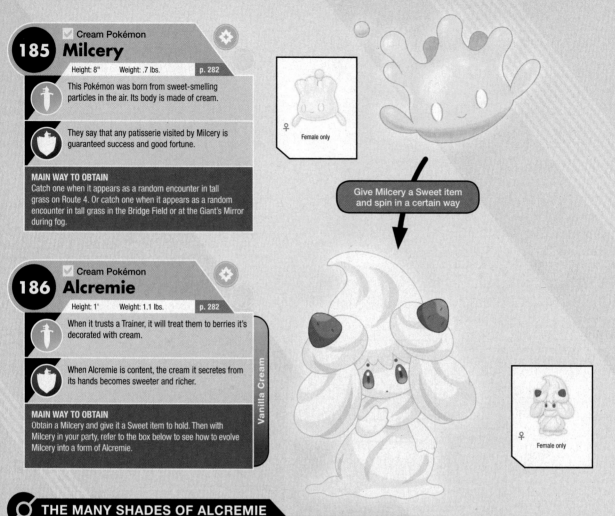

185 ☑ Cream Pokémon
Milcery

| Height: 8" | Weight: .7 lbs. | p. 282 |

This Pokémon was born from sweet-smelling particles in the air. Its body is made of cream.

They say that any patisserie visited by Milcery is guaranteed success and good fortune.

MAIN WAY TO OBTAIN
Catch one when it appears as a random encounter in tall grass on Route 4. Or catch one when it appears as a random encounter in tall grass in the Bridge Field or at the Giant's Mirror during fog.

♀ Female only

Give Milcery a Sweet item and spin in a certain way

186 ☑ Cream Pokémon
Alcremie

| Height: 1' | Weight: 1.1 lbs. | p. 282 |

When it trusts a Trainer, it will treat them to berries it's decorated with cream.

When Alcremie is content, the cream it secretes from its hands becomes sweeter and richer.

MAIN WAY TO OBTAIN
Obtain a Milcery and give it a Sweet item to hold. Then with Milcery in your party, refer to the box below to see how to evolve Milcery into a form of Alcremie.

Vanilla Cream

♀ Female only

⚙ THE MANY SHADES OF ALCREMIE

Milcery can evolve into many different forms of Alcremie, if you only know the magic trick! Just like following a recipe, there are a number of steps involved. The first is to give your Milcery a special Sweet item to hold. That Sweet will decide the decorations you see on Alcremie's head when it evolves, as well as its eye color, as you can see in the table below. Once Milcery is holding one of these items, put it in your party and spin your character according to the instructions below to try to evolve Milcery into that form of Alcremie!

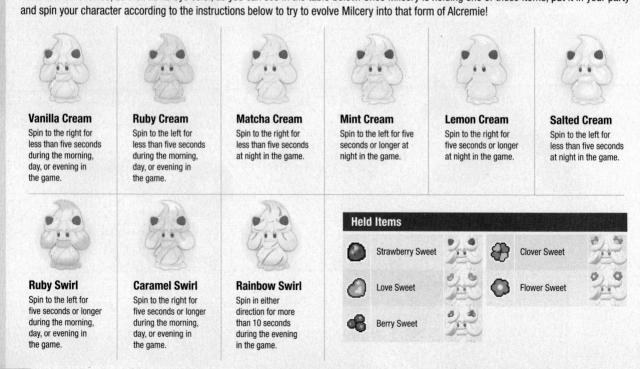

Vanilla Cream
Spin to the right for less than five seconds during the morning, day, or evening in the game.

Ruby Cream
Spin to the left for less than five seconds during the morning, day, or evening in the game.

Matcha Cream
Spin to the right for less than five seconds at night in the game.

Mint Cream
Spin to the left for five seconds or longer at night in the game.

Lemon Cream
Spin to the right for five seconds or longer at night in the game.

Salted Cream
Spin to the left for less than five seconds at night in the game.

Ruby Swirl
Spin to the left for five seconds or longer during the morning, day, or evening in the game.

Caramel Swirl
Spin to the right for five seconds or longer during the morning, day, or evening in the game.

Rainbow Swirl
Spin in either direction for more than 10 seconds during the evening in the game.

Held Items

Strawberry Sweet

Love Sweet

Berry Sweet

Clover Sweet

Flower Sweet

Same form for male/female

Lv. 25

Same form for male/female

Same form for male/female

Lv. 40

Same form for male/female

187 Cutiefly
Bee Fly Pokémon

Height: 4"   Weight: .4 lbs.   p. 283

Nectar and pollen are its favorite fare. You can find Cutiefly hovering around Gossifleur, trying to get some of Gossifleur's pollen.

An opponent's aura can tell Cutiefly what that opponent's next move will be. Then Cutiefly can glide around the attack and strike back.

MAIN WAY TO OBTAIN
Catch one when it appears in tall grass at the Motostoke Riverbank, in the Bridge Field, or at the Giant's Mirror during various weather patterns.

Honey

188 Ribombee
Bee Fly Pokémon

Height: 8"   Weight: 1.1 lbs.   p. 283

It makes pollen puffs from pollen and nectar. The puffs' effects depend on the type of ingredients and how much of each one is used.

Ribombee absolutely hate getting wet or rained on. In the cloudy Galar region, they are very seldom seen.

MAIN WAY TO OBTAIN
Catch one when it appears wandering at the Motostoke Riverbank or in the Bridge Field during various weather patterns. Or obtain a Cutiefly, then level it up to Lv. 25 or higher to evolve it into Ribombee.

Honey

189 Ferroseed
Thorn Seed Pokémon

Height: 2'   Weight: 41.4 lbs.   p. 284

It defends itself by launching spikes, but its aim isn't very good at first. Only after a lot of practice will it improve.

Mossy caves are their preferred dwellings. Enzymes contained in mosses help Ferroseed's spikes grow big and strong.

MAIN WAY TO OBTAIN
Catch one when it appears in tall grass in the Stony Wilderness during a blizzard. Or catch one when it appears as a random encounter in tall grass in the Bridge Field.

Sticky Barb

190 Ferrothorn
Thorn Pod Pokémon

Height: 3'3"   Weight: 242.5 lbs.   p. 284

This Pokémon scrapes its spikes across rocks, and then uses the tips of its feelers to absorb the nutrients it finds within the stone.

Its spikes are harder than steel. This Pokémon crawls across rock walls by stabbing the spikes on its feelers into the stone.

MAIN WAY TO OBTAIN
Catch one when it appears wandering in the Bridge Field. Or obtain a Ferroseed, then level it up to Lv. 40 or higher to evolve it into Ferrothorn.

Sticky Barb

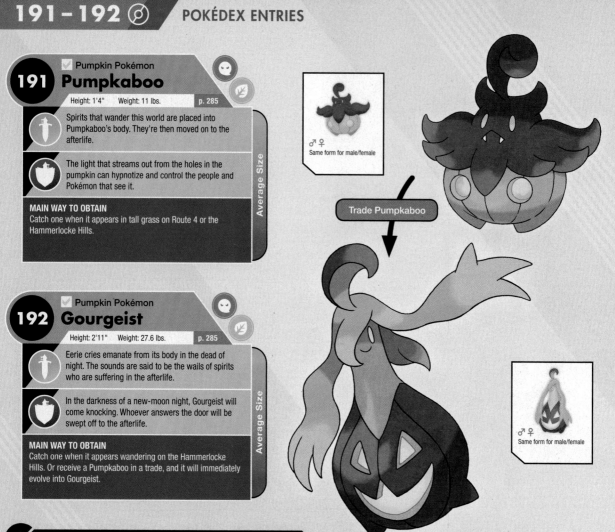

191 ☑ Pumpkin Pokémon
Pumpkaboo
Height: 1'4"   Weight: 11 lbs.   **p. 285**

Spirits that wander this world are placed into Pumpkaboo's body. They're then moved on to the afterlife.

The light that streams out from the holes in the pumpkin can hypnotize and control the people and Pokémon that see it.

MAIN WAY TO OBTAIN
Catch one when it appears in tall grass on Route 4 or the Hammerlocke Hills.

Average Size

♂ ♀
Same form for male/female

Trade Pumpkaboo

192 ☑ Pumpkin Pokémon
Gourgeist
Height: 2'11"   Weight: 27.6 lbs.   **p. 285**

Eerie cries emanate from its body in the dead of night. The sounds are said to be the wails of spirits who are suffering in the afterlife.

In the darkness of a new-moon night, Gourgeist will come knocking. Whoever answers the door will be swept off to the afterlife.

MAIN WAY TO OBTAIN
Catch one when it appears wandering on the Hammerlocke Hills. Or receive a Pumpkaboo in a trade, and it will immediately evolve into Gourgeist.

Average Size

♂ ♀
Same form for male/female

PUMPKABOO AND GOURGEIST'S SIZES

At first glance, all the Pumpkaboo you encounter might look the same, but they actually come in four different sizes. These sizes affect their heights and weights, of course, but that's not all. Their size also affects their species strengths! The larger sizes tend to have lower Speed, but they have higher HP and Attack. If your Pumpkaboo evolves into Gourgeist, then that Gourgeist will inherit the same size!

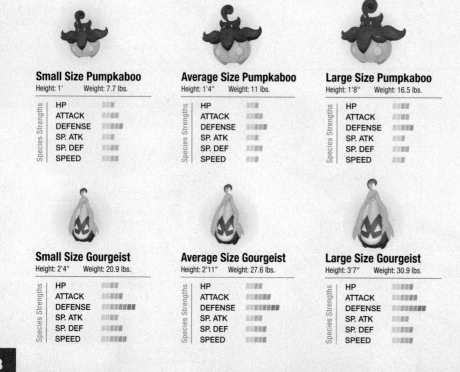

Miracle Seed

Small Size Pumpkaboo
Height: 1'   Weight: 7.7 lbs.

Species Strengths
- HP
- ATTACK
- DEFENSE
- SP. ATK
- SP. DEF
- SPEED

Average Size Pumpkaboo
Height: 1'4"   Weight: 11 lbs.

Species Strengths
- HP
- ATTACK
- DEFENSE
- SP. ATK
- SP. DEF
- SPEED

Large Size Pumpkaboo
Height: 1'8"   Weight: 16.5 lbs.

Species Strengths
- HP
- ATTACK
- DEFENSE
- SP. ATK
- SP. DEF
- SPEED

Super Size Pumpkaboo
Height: 2'7"   Weight: 33.1 lbs.

Species Strengths
- HP
- ATTACK
- DEFENSE
- SP. ATK
- SP. DEF
- SPEED

Small Size Gourgeist
Height: 2'4"   Weight: 20.9 lbs.

Species Strengths
- HP
- ATTACK
- DEFENSE
- SP. ATK
- SP. DEF
- SPEED

Average Size Gourgeist
Height: 2'11"   Weight: 27.6 lbs.

Species Strengths
- HP
- ATTACK
- DEFENSE
- SP. ATK
- SP. DEF
- SPEED

Large Size Gourgeist
Height: 3'7"   Weight: 30.9 lbs.

Species Strengths
- HP
- ATTACK
- DEFENSE
- SP. ATK
- SP. DEF
- SPEED

Super Size Gourgeist
Height: 5'7"   Weight: 86 lbs.

Species Strengths
- HP
- ATTACK
- DEFENSE
- SP. ATK
- SP. DEF
- SPEED

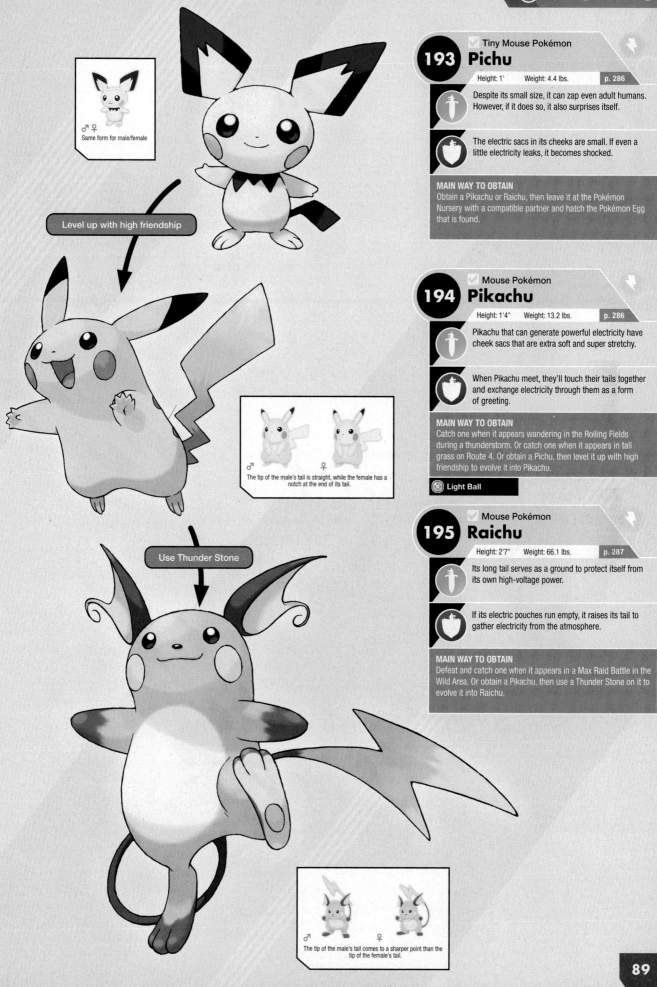

Same form for male/female ♂♀

Level up with high friendship

The tip of the male's tail is straight, while the female has a notch at the end of its tail. ♂ ♀

Use Thunder Stone

The tip of the male's tail comes to a sharper point than the tip of the female's tail. ♂ ♀

Tiny Mouse Pokémon
193 Pichu

| Height: 1' | Weight: 4.4 lbs. | p. 286 |

Despite its small size, it can zap even adult humans. However, if it does so, it also surprises itself.

The electric sacs in its cheeks are small. If even a little electricity leaks, it becomes shocked.

MAIN WAY TO OBTAIN
Obtain a Pikachu or Raichu, then leave it at the Pokémon Nursery with a compatible partner and hatch the Pokémon Egg that is found.

Mouse Pokémon
194 Pikachu

| Height: 1'4" | Weight: 13.2 lbs. | p. 286 |

Pikachu that can generate powerful electricity have cheek sacs that are extra soft and super stretchy.

When Pikachu meet, they'll touch their tails together and exchange electricity through them as a form of greeting.

MAIN WAY TO OBTAIN
Catch one when it appears wandering in the Rolling Fields during a thunderstorm. Or catch one when it appears in tall grass on Route 4. Or obtain a Pichu, then level it up with high friendship to evolve it into Pikachu.

⊗ Light Ball

Mouse Pokémon
195 Raichu

| Height: 2'7" | Weight: 66.1 lbs. | p. 287 |

Its long tail serves as a ground to protect itself from its own high-voltage power.

If its electric pouches run empty, it raises its tail to gather electricity from the atmosphere.

MAIN WAY TO OBTAIN
Defeat and catch one when it appears in a Max Raid Battle in the Wild Area. Or obtain a Pikachu, then use a Thunder Stone on it to evolve it into Raichu.

196 Eevee

☑ Evolution Pokémon

Height: 1'   Weight: 14.3 lbs.   **p. 287**

It has the ability to alter the composition of its body to suit its surrounding environment.

Thanks to its unstable genetic makeup, this special Pokémon conceals many different possible evolutions.

MAIN WAY TO OBTAIN
Catch one when it appears in tall grass on Route 4.

♂   ♀

The white tip of the female's tail has larger, rounder scallops than the male's tail

EEVEE'S EVOLUTIONS

Vaporeon

Leafeon

Flareon

Use Water Stone

Use Leaf Stone

Use Fire Stone

Level up at night with high friend-ship

Umbreon

Use Thunder Stone

Jolteon

Level up with high friendship when it knows a Fairy-type move

Level up during the day with high friendship

Use Ice Stone

Sylveon

Glaceon

Espeon

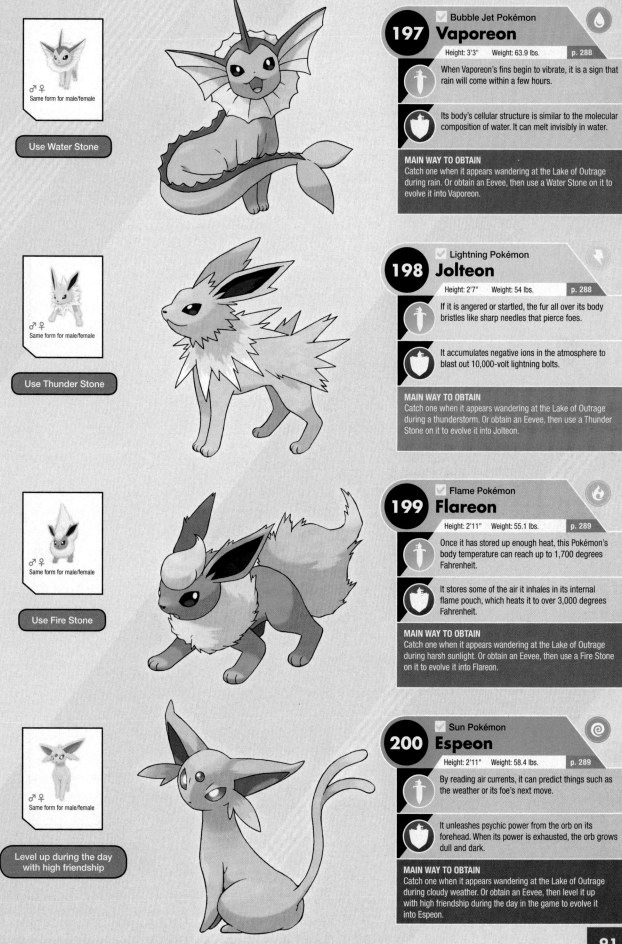

Same form for male/female

Use Water Stone

197 Vaporeon
☑ Bubble Jet Pokémon

Height: 3'3" Weight: 63.9 lbs. p. 288

When Vaporeon's fins begin to vibrate, it is a sign that rain will come within a few hours.

Its body's cellular structure is similar to the molecular composition of water. It can melt invisibly in water.

MAIN WAY TO OBTAIN
Catch one when it appears wandering at the Lake of Outrage during rain. Or obtain an Eevee, then use a Water Stone on it to evolve it into Vaporeon.

Same form for male/female

Use Thunder Stone

198 Jolteon
☑ Lightning Pokémon

Height: 2'7" Weight: 54 lbs. p. 288

If it is angered or startled, the fur all over its body bristles like sharp needles that pierce foes.

It accumulates negative ions in the atmosphere to blast out 10,000-volt lightning bolts.

MAIN WAY TO OBTAIN
Catch one when it appears wandering at the Lake of Outrage during a thunderstorm. Or obtain an Eevee, then use a Thunder Stone on it to evolve it into Jolteon.

Same form for male/female

Use Fire Stone

199 Flareon
☑ Flame Pokémon

Height: 2'11" Weight: 55.1 lbs. p. 289

Once it has stored up enough heat, this Pokémon's body temperature can reach up to 1,700 degrees Fahrenheit.

It stores some of the air it inhales in its internal flame pouch, which heats it to over 3,000 degrees Fahrenheit.

MAIN WAY TO OBTAIN
Catch one when it appears wandering at the Lake of Outrage during harsh sunlight. Or obtain an Eevee, then use a Fire Stone on it to evolve it into Flareon.

Same form for male/female

Level up during the day with high friendship

200 Espeon
☑ Sun Pokémon

Height: 2'11" Weight: 58.4 lbs. p. 289

By reading air currents, it can predict things such as the weather or its foe's next move.

It unleashes psychic power from the orb on its forehead. When its power is exhausted, the orb grows dull and dark.

MAIN WAY TO OBTAIN
Catch one when it appears wandering at the Lake of Outrage during cloudy weather. Or obtain an Eevee, then level it up with high friendship during the day in the game to evolve it into Espeon.

201 Umbreon

Moonlight Pokémon

Height: 3'3"   Weight: 59.5 lbs.   p. 290

When this Pokémon becomes angry, its pores secrete a poisonous sweat, which it sprays at its opponent's eyes.

On the night of a full moon, or when it gets excited, the ring patterns on its body glow yellow.

MAIN WAY TO OBTAIN
Catch one when it appears wandering at the Lake of Outrage during a sandstorm. Or obtain an Eevee, then level it up with high friendship during the night in the game to evolve it into Umbreon.

Same form for male/female

Level up at night with high friendship

202 Leafeon

Verdant Pokémon

Height: 3'3"   Weight: 56.2 lbs.   p. 290

Galarians favor the distinctive aroma that drifts from this Pokémon's leaves. There's a popular perfume made using that scent.

This Pokémon's tail is blade sharp, with a fantastic cutting edge that can slice right though large trees.

MAIN WAY TO OBTAIN
Catch one when it appears wandering at the Lake of Outrage during clear weather. Or obtain an Eevee, then use a Leaf Stone on it to evolve it into Leafeon.

Same form for male/female

Use Leaf Stone

203 Glaceon

Fresh Snow Pokémon

Height: 2'7"   Weight: 57.1 lbs.   p. 291

Any who become captivated by the beauty of the snowfall that Glaceon creates will be frozen before they know it.

The coldness emanating from Glaceon causes powdery snow to form, making it quite a popular Pokémon at ski resorts.

MAIN WAY TO OBTAIN
Catch one when it appears wandering at the Lake of Outrage during snow or a blizzard. Or obtain an Eevee, then use an Ice Stone on it to evolve it into Glaceon.

Same form for male/female

Use Ice Stone

204 Sylveon

Intertwining Pokémon

Height: 3'3"   Weight: 51.8 lbs.   p. 291

By releasing enmity-erasing waves from its ribbonlike feelers, Sylveon stops any conflict.

There's a Galarian fairy tale that describes a beautiful Sylveon vanquishing a dreadful dragon Pokémon.

MAIN WAY TO OBTAIN
Catch one when it appears wandering at the Lake of Outrage during fog. Or obtain an Eevee, then level it up with high friendship when it knows at least one Fairy-type move.

Same form for male/female

Level up with high friendship when it knows a Fairy-type move*

*If your Eevee has forgotten all of its Fairy-type moves, use a TM to teach it one or visit Jack in a Pokémon Center to have it remember the move once more.

205 Apple Core Pokémon
Applin

Height: 8" Weight: 1.1 lbs. p. 292

It spends its entire life inside an apple. It hides from its natural enemies, bird Pokémon, by pretending it's just an apple and nothing more.

As soon as it's born, it burrows into an apple. Not only does the apple serve as its food source, but the flavor of the fruit determines its evolution.

MAIN WAY TO OBTAIN
Catch one when it appears as a random encounter in tall grass on Route 5 or in the Dusty Bowl during clear weather, or at the Giant's Mirror or in the Stony Wilderness during a thunderstorm.

♂♀
Same form for male/female

Use Tart Apple

206 Apple Wing Pokémon
Flapple

Height: 1' Weight: 2.2 lbs. p. 292

It ate a sour apple, and that induced its evolution. In its cheeks, it stores an acid capable of causing chemical burns.

It flies on wings of apple skin and spits a powerful acid. It can also change its shape into that of an apple.

MAIN WAY TO OBTAIN
Obtain an Applin, then use a Tart Apple on it to evolve it into Flapple.

♂♀
Same form for male/female

Use Sweet Apple

207 Apple Nectar Pokémon
Appletun

Height: 1'4" Weight: 28.7 lbs. p. 293

Eating a sweet apple caused its evolution. A nectarous scent wafts from its body, luring in the bug Pokémon it preys on.

Its body is covered in sweet nectar, and the skin on its back is especially yummy. Children used to have it as a snack.

MAIN WAY TO OBTAIN
Obtain an Applin, then use a Sweet Apple on it to evolve it into Appletun.

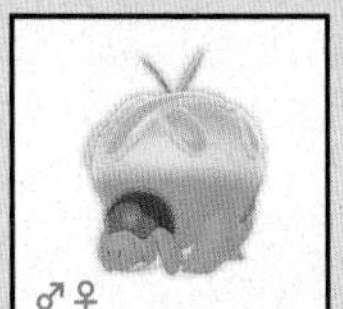

♂♀
Same form for male/female

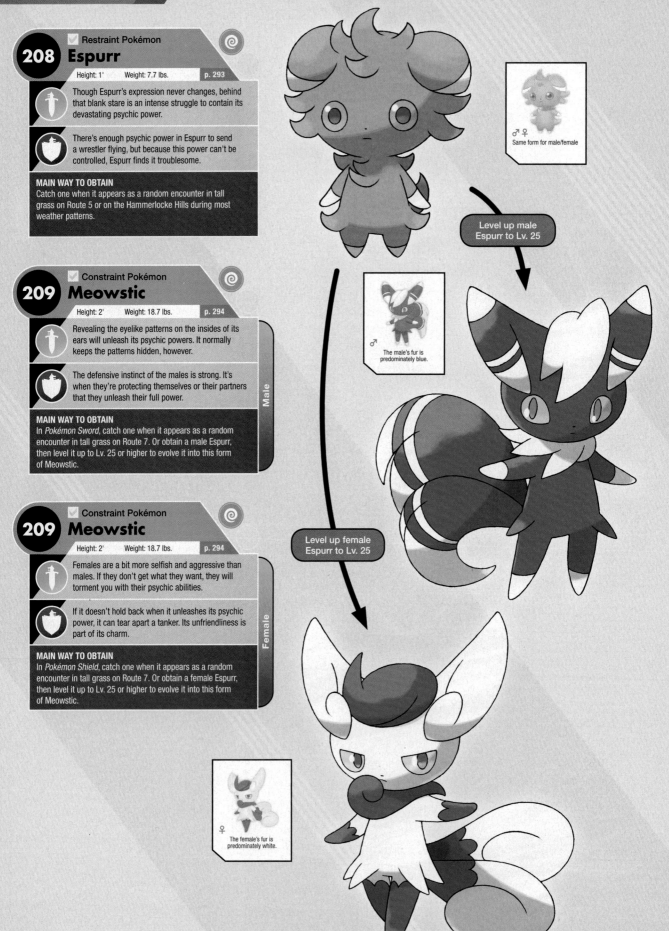

208 Espurr
☑ Restraint Pokémon

Height: 1'　　Weight: 7.7 lbs.　　p. 293

Though Espurr's expression never changes, behind that blank stare is an intense struggle to contain its devastating psychic power.

There's enough psychic power in Espurr to send a wrestler flying, but because this power can't be controlled, Espurr finds it troublesome.

MAIN WAY TO OBTAIN
Catch one when it appears as a random encounter in tall grass on Route 5 or on the Hammerlocke Hills during most weather patterns.

♂ ♀
Same form for male/female

Level up male Espurr to Lv. 25

The male's fur is predominately blue. ♂

209 Meowstic
☑ Constraint Pokémon

Height: 2'　　Weight: 18.7 lbs.　　p. 294

Revealing the eyelike patterns on the insides of its ears will unleash its psychic powers. It normally keeps the patterns hidden, however.

The defensive instinct of the males is strong. It's when they're protecting themselves or their partners that they unleash their full power.

MAIN WAY TO OBTAIN
In *Pokémon Sword*, catch one when it appears as a random encounter in tall grass on Route 7. Or obtain a male Espurr, then level it up to Lv. 25 or higher to evolve it into this form of Meowstic.

Male

209 Meowstic
☑ Constraint Pokémon

Height: 2'　　Weight: 18.7 lbs.　　p. 294

Females are a bit more selfish and aggressive than males. If they don't get what they want, they will torment you with their psychic abilities.

If it doesn't hold back when it unleashes its psychic power, it can tear apart a tanker. Its unfriendliness is part of its charm.

MAIN WAY TO OBTAIN
In *Pokémon Shield*, catch one when it appears as a random encounter in tall grass on Route 7. Or obtain a female Espurr, then level it up to Lv. 25 or higher to evolve it into this form of Meowstic.

Female

Level up female Espurr to Lv. 25

The female's fur is predominately white. ♀

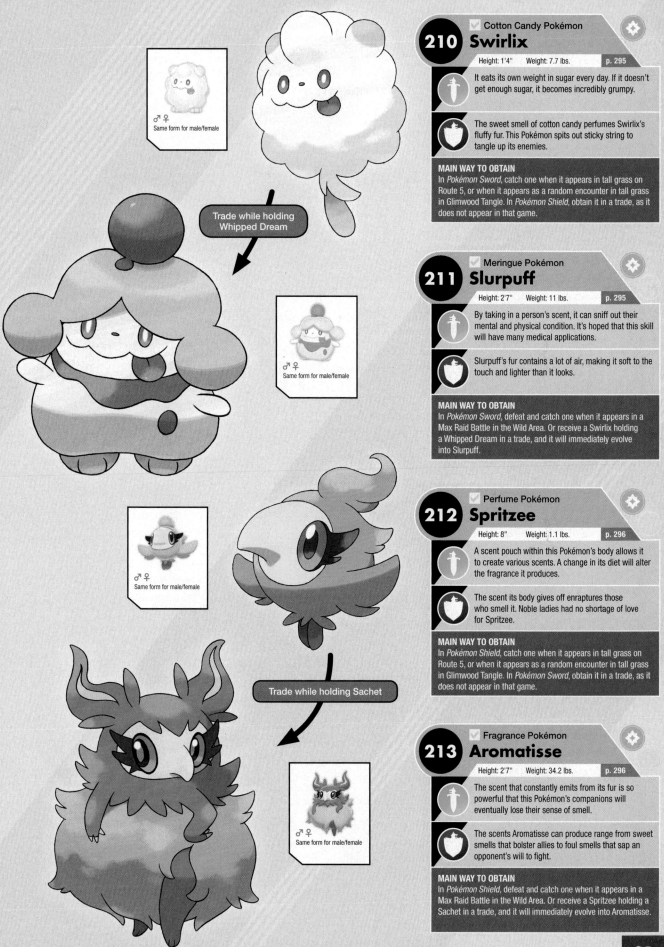

Same form for male/female

♂ ♀
Same form for male/female

Trade while holding
Whipped Dream

♂ ♀
Same form for male/female

Trade while holding Sachet

♂ ♀
Same form for male/female

210 Swirlix
☑ Cotton Candy Pokémon

Height: 1'4"   Weight: 7.7 lbs.   p. 295

It eats its own weight in sugar every day. If it doesn't get enough sugar, it becomes incredibly grumpy.

The sweet smell of cotton candy perfumes Swirlix's fluffy fur. This Pokémon spits out sticky string to tangle up its enemies.

MAIN WAY TO OBTAIN
In *Pokémon Sword*, catch one when it appears in tall grass on Route 5, or when it appears as a random encounter in tall grass in Glimwood Tangle. In *Pokémon Shield*, obtain it in a trade, as it does not appear in that game.

211 Slurpuff
☑ Meringue Pokémon

Height: 2'7"   Weight: 11 lbs.   p. 295

By taking in a person's scent, it can sniff out their mental and physical condition. It's hoped that this skill will have many medical applications.

Slurpuff's fur contains a lot of air, making it soft to the touch and lighter than it looks.

MAIN WAY TO OBTAIN
In *Pokémon Sword*, defeat and catch one when it appears in a Max Raid Battle in the Wild Area. Or receive a Swirlix holding a Whipped Dream in a trade, and it will immediately evolve into Slurpuff.

212 Spritzee
☑ Perfume Pokémon

Height: 8"   Weight: 1.1 lbs.   p. 296

A scent pouch within this Pokémon's body allows it to create various scents. A change in its diet will alter the fragrance it produces.

The scent its body gives off enraptures those who smell it. Noble ladies had no shortage of love for Spritzee.

MAIN WAY TO OBTAIN
In *Pokémon Shield*, catch one when it appears in tall grass on Route 5, or when it appears as a random encounter in tall grass in Glimwood Tangle. In *Pokémon Sword*, obtain it in a trade, as it does not appear in that game.

213 Aromatisse
☑ Fragrance Pokémon

Height: 2'7"   Weight: 34.2 lbs.   p. 296

The scent that constantly emits from its fur is so powerful that this Pokémon's companions will eventually lose their sense of smell.

The scents Aromatisse can produce range from sweet smells that bolster allies to foul smells that sap an opponent's will to fight.

MAIN WAY TO OBTAIN
In *Pokémon Shield*, defeat and catch one when it appears in a Max Raid Battle in the Wild Area. Or receive a Spritzee holding a Sachet in a trade, and it will immediately evolve into Aromatisse.

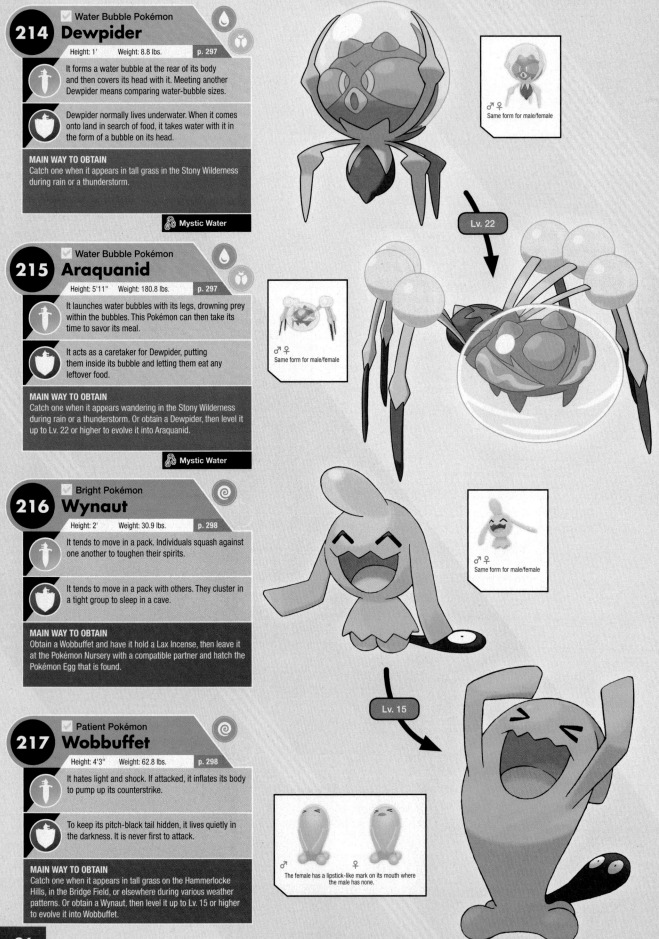

Water Bubble Pokémon
214 Dewpider

Height: 1'   Weight: 8.8 lbs.   p. 297

It forms a water bubble at the rear of its body and then covers its head with it. Meeting another Dewpider means comparing water-bubble sizes.

Dewpider normally lives underwater. When it comes onto land in search of food, it takes water with it in the form of a bubble on its head.

MAIN WAY TO OBTAIN
Catch one when it appears in tall grass in the Stony Wilderness during rain or a thunderstorm.

Mystic Water

Same form for male/female

Lv. 22

Water Bubble Pokémon
215 Araquanid

Height: 5'11"   Weight: 180.8 lbs.   p. 297

It launches water bubbles with its legs, drowning prey within the bubbles. This Pokémon can then take its time to savor its meal.

It acts as a caretaker for Dewpider, putting them inside its bubble and letting them eat any leftover food.

MAIN WAY TO OBTAIN
Catch one when it appears wandering in the Stony Wilderness during rain or a thunderstorm. Or obtain a Dewpider, then level it up to Lv. 22 or higher to evolve it into Araquanid.

Mystic Water

Same form for male/female

Bright Pokémon
216 Wynaut

Height: 2'   Weight: 30.9 lbs.   p. 298

It tends to move in a pack. Individuals squash against one another to toughen their spirits.

It tends to move in a pack with others. They cluster in a tight group to sleep in a cave.

MAIN WAY TO OBTAIN
Obtain a Wobbuffet and have it hold a Lax Incense, then leave it at the Pokémon Nursery with a compatible partner and hatch the Pokémon Egg that is found.

Same form for male/female

Lv. 15

Patient Pokémon
217 Wobbuffet

Height: 4'3"   Weight: 62.8 lbs.   p. 298

It hates light and shock. If attacked, it inflates its body to pump up its counterstrike.

To keep its pitch-black tail hidden, it lives quietly in the darkness. It is never first to attack.

MAIN WAY TO OBTAIN
Catch one when it appears in tall grass on the Hammerlocke Hills, in the Bridge Field, or elsewhere during various weather patterns. Or obtain a Wynaut, then level it up to Lv. 15 or higher to evolve it into Wobbuffet.

The female has a lipstick-like mark on its mouth where the male has none.

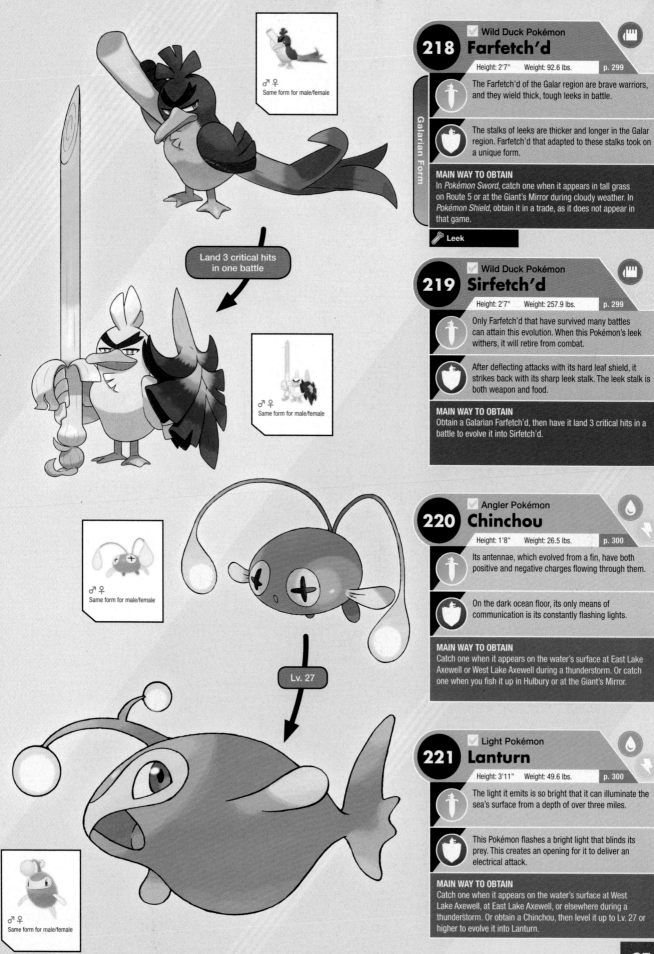

Same form for male/female ♂ ♀

Land 3 critical hits in one battle

Same form for male/female ♂ ♀

Same form for male/female ♂ ♀

Lv. 27

Same form for male/female ♂ ♀

Galarian Form

218 Farfetch'd
Wild Duck Pokémon

Height: 2'7"   Weight: 92.6 lbs.   p. 299

The Farfetch'd of the Galar region are brave warriors, and they wield thick, tough leeks in battle.

The stalks of leeks are thicker and longer in the Galar region. Farfetch'd that adapted to these stalks took on a unique form.

MAIN WAY TO OBTAIN
In *Pokémon Sword*, catch one when it appears in tall grass on Route 5 or at the Giant's Mirror during cloudy weather. In *Pokémon Shield*, obtain it in a trade, as it does not appear in that game.

Leek

219 Sirfetch'd
Wild Duck Pokémon

Height: 2'7"   Weight: 257.9 lbs.   p. 299

Only Farfetch'd that have survived many battles can attain this evolution. When this Pokémon's leek withers, it will retire from combat.

After deflecting attacks with its hard leaf shield, it strikes back with its sharp leek stalk. The leek stalk is both weapon and food.

MAIN WAY TO OBTAIN
Obtain a Galarian Farfetch'd, then have it land 3 critical hits in a battle to evolve it into Sirfetch'd.

220 Chinchou
Angler Pokémon

Height: 1'8"   Weight: 26.5 lbs.   p. 300

Its antennae, which evolved from a fin, have both positive and negative charges flowing through them.

On the dark ocean floor, its only means of communication is its constantly flashing lights.

MAIN WAY TO OBTAIN
Catch one when it appears on the water's surface at East Lake Axewell or West Lake Axewell during a thunderstorm. Or catch one when you fish it up in Hulbury or at the Giant's Mirror.

221 Lanturn
Light Pokémon

Height: 3'11"   Weight: 49.6 lbs.   p. 300

The light it emits is so bright that it can illuminate the sea's surface from a depth of over three miles.

This Pokémon flashes a bright light that blinds its prey. This creates an opening for it to deliver an electrical attack.

MAIN WAY TO OBTAIN
Catch one when it appears on the water's surface at West Lake Axewell, at East Lake Axewell, or elsewhere during a thunderstorm. Or obtain a Chinchou, then level it up to Lv. 27 or higher to evolve it into Lanturn.

222 Croagunk
☑ Toxic Mouth Pokémon

Height: 2'4"   Weight: 50.7 lbs.   **p. 301**

It makes frightening noises with its poison-filled cheek sacs. When opponents flinch, Croagunk hits them with a poison jab.

Once diluted, its poison becomes medicinal. This Pokémon came into popularity after a pharmaceutical company chose it as a mascot.

MAIN WAY TO OBTAIN
In *Pokémon Shield*, catch one when it appears in tall grass in the Bridge Field, the Stony Wilderness, or elsewhere during cloudy weather. In *Pokémon Sword*, obtain it in a trade, as it does not appear in that game.

● Black Sludge

The stripes on the male's abdomen are located lower than the stripes on the female's abdomen.

Lv. 37

223 Toxicroak
☑ Toxic Mouth Pokémon

Height: 4'3"   Weight: 97.9 lbs.   **p. 301**

It bounces toward opponents and gouges them with poisonous claws. No more than a scratch is needed to knock out its adversaries.

It booms out a victory croak when its prey goes down in defeat. This Pokémon and Seismitoad are related species.

MAIN WAY TO OBTAIN
In *Pokémon Shield*, catch one when it appears in tall grass in the Stony Wilderness during cloudy weather. Or obtain a Croagunk, then level it up to Lv. 37 or higher to evolve it into Toxicroak.

● Black Sludge

The male has a larger throat sac than the female.

224 Scraggy
☑ Shedding Pokémon

Height: 2'   Weight: 26 lbs.   **p. 302**

If it locks eyes with you, watch out! Nothing and no one is safe from the reckless headbutts of this troublesome Pokémon.

It protects itself with its durable skin. It's thought that this Pokémon will evolve once its skin has completely stretched out.

MAIN WAY TO OBTAIN
In *Pokémon Sword*, catch one when it appears in tall grass in the Bridge Field, the Stony Wilderness, or elsewhere during cloudy weather. In *Pokémon Shield*, obtain it in a trade, as it does not appear in that game.

● Shed Shell

Same form for male/female

225 Scrafty
☑ Hoodlum Pokémon

Height: 3'7"   Weight: 66.1 lbs.   **p. 302**

As halfhearted as this Pokémon's kicks may seem, they pack enough power to shatter Conkeldurr's concrete pillars.

While mostly known for having the temperament of an aggressive ruffian, this Pokémon takes very good care of its family, friends, and territory.

MAIN WAY TO OBTAIN
In *Pokémon Sword*, defeat and catch one when it appears in a Max Raid Battle in the Wild Area. Or obtain a Scraggy, then level it up to Lv. 39 or higher to evolve it into Scrafty.

Lv. 39

Same form for male/female

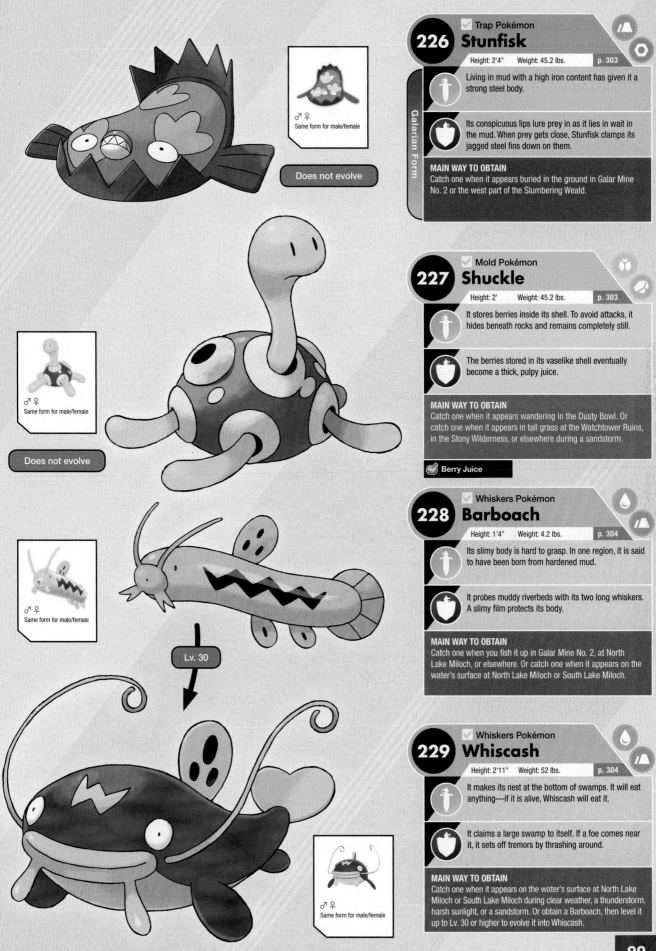

Same form for male/female

Does not evolve

226 Stunfisk
Trap Pokémon

Height: 2'4"   Weight: 45.2 lbs.   p. 303

Galarian Form

Living in mud with a high iron content has given it a strong steel body.

Its conspicuous lips lure prey in as it lies in wait in the mud. When prey gets close, Stunfisk clamps its jagged steel fins down on them.

MAIN WAY TO OBTAIN
Catch one when it appears buried in the ground in Galar Mine No. 2 or the west part of the Slumbering Weald.

Same form for male/female

Does not evolve

227 Shuckle
Mold Pokémon

Height: 2'   Weight: 45.2 lbs.   p. 303

It stores berries inside its shell. To avoid attacks, it hides beneath rocks and remains completely still.

The berries stored in its vaselike shell eventually become a thick, pulpy juice.

MAIN WAY TO OBTAIN
Catch one when it appears wandering in the Dusty Bowl. Or catch one when it appears in tall grass at the Watchtower Ruins, in the Stony Wilderness, or elsewhere during a sandstorm.

🍶 Berry Juice

Same form for male/female

Lv. 30

228 Barboach
Whiskers Pokémon

Height: 1'4"   Weight: 4.2 lbs.   p. 304

Its slimy body is hard to grasp. In one region, it is said to have been born from hardened mud.

It probes muddy riverbeds with its two long whiskers. A slimy film protects its body.

MAIN WAY TO OBTAIN
Catch one when you fish it up in Galar Mine No. 2, at North Lake Miloch, or elsewhere. Or catch one when it appears on the water's surface at North Lake Miloch or South Lake Miloch.

---

229 Whiscash
Whiskers Pokémon

Height: 2'11"   Weight: 52 lbs.   p. 304

It makes its nest at the bottom of swamps. It will eat anything—if it is alive, Whiscash will eat it.

It claims a large swamp to itself. If a foe comes near it, it sets off tremors by thrashing around.

MAIN WAY TO OBTAIN
Catch one when it appears on the water's surface at North Lake Miloch or South Lake Miloch during clear weather, a thunderstorm, harsh sunlight, or a sandstorm. Or obtain a Barboach, then level it up to Lv. 30 or higher to evolve it into Whiscash.

Same form for male/female

230 Shellos
Sea Slug Pokémon

Height: 1'   Weight: 13.9 lbs.   p. 305

There's speculation that its appearance is determined by what it eats, but the truth remains elusive.

Its appearance changes depending on the environment. One theory suggests that living in cold seas causes Shellos to take on this form.

MAIN WAY TO OBTAIN
Catch one when it appears in Galar Mine No. 2. Or catch one when it appears on the water's surface in the Dusty Bowl.

East Sea

♂♀
Same form for male/female

Lv. 30

♂♀
Same form for male/female

231 Gastrodon
Sea Slug Pokémon

Height: 2'11"   Weight: 65.9 lbs.   p. 305

It secretes a purple fluid to deter enemies. This fluid isn't poisonous—instead, it's super sticky, and once it sticks, it's very hard to unstick.

Its body is covered in a sticky slime. It's very susceptible to dehydration, so it can't spend too much time on land.

MAIN WAY TO OBTAIN
Catch one when it appears on the water's surface at the Giant's Mirror or in the Dusty Bowl. Or obtain an East Sea Shellos, then level it up to Lv. 30 or higher to evolve it into East Sea Gastrodon.

East Sea

SHELLOS OF ANOTHER SHADE

Reports have it that Shellos have been spotted in some other regions with a rather different look! That goes for Shellos's Evolution, Gastrodon, too. These differing appearances aren't regional forms, though. Shellos and Gastrodon both have a West Sea form and an East Sea form. But for some reason, it seems that Trainers have only ever found the East Sea Shellos and Gastrodon in the Galar region.

West Sea Shellos   West Sea Gastrodon

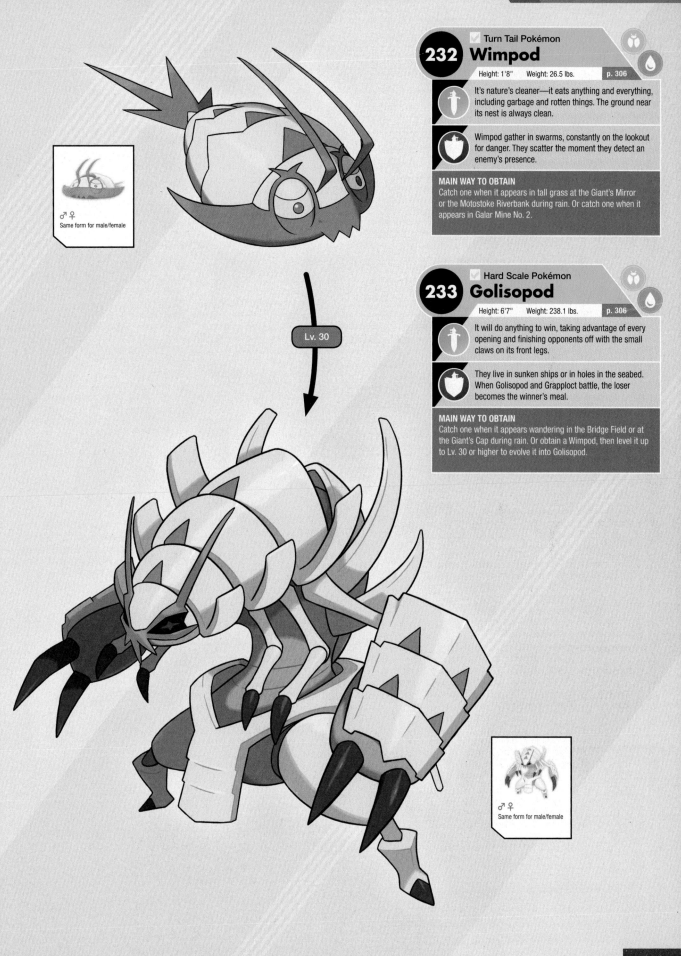

☑ Turn Tail Pokémon

232 Wimpod

| Height: 1'8" | Weight: 26.5 lbs. | p. 306 |

It's nature's cleaner—it eats anything and everything, including garbage and rotten things. The ground near its nest is always clean.

Wimpod gather in swarms, constantly on the lookout for danger. They scatter the moment they detect an enemy's presence.

MAIN WAY TO OBTAIN
Catch one when it appears in tall grass at the Giant's Mirror or the Motostoke Riverbank during rain. Or catch one when it appears in Galar Mine No. 2.

♂ ♀
Same form for male/female

☑ Hard Scale Pokémon

233 Golisopod

| Height: 6'7" | Weight: 238.1 lbs. | p. 306 |

It will do anything to win, taking advantage of every opening and finishing opponents off with the small claws on its front legs.

They live in sunken ships or in holes in the seabed. When Golisopod and Grapploct battle, the loser becomes the winner's meal.

MAIN WAY TO OBTAIN
Catch one when it appears wandering in the Bridge Field or at the Giant's Cap during rain. Or obtain a Wimpod, then level it up to Lv. 30 or higher to evolve it into Golisopod.

Lv. 30

♂ ♀
Same form for male/female

234 Binacle
Two-Handed Pokémon

Height: 1'8"   Weight: 68.3 lbs.   p. 307

After two Binacle find a suitably sized rock, they adhere themselves to it and live together. They cooperate to gather food during high tide.

If the two don't work well together, both their offense and defense fall apart. Without good teamwork, they won't survive.

MAIN WAY TO OBTAIN
Catch one when it appears in Galar Mine No. 2. Or catch one when it appears as a random encounter in tall grass at the Motostoke Riverbank or in the Bridge Field during rain.

♂♀
Same form for male/female

Lv. 39

235 Barbaracle
Collective Pokémon

Height: 4'3"   Weight: 211.6 lbs.   p. 307

Seven Binacle come together to form one Barbaracle. The Binacle that serves as the head gives orders to those serving as the limbs.

Having an eye on each palm allows it to keep watch in all directions. In a pinch, its limbs start to act on their own to ensure the enemy's defeat.

MAIN WAY TO OBTAIN
Catch one when it appears wandering in the Dusty Bowl during cloudy weather, rain, or a thunderstorm. Or obtain a Binacle, then level it up to Lv. 39 or higher to evolve it into Barbaracle.

♂♀
Same form for male/female

236 Corsola
Coral Pokémon

Height: 2'   Weight: 1.1 lbs.   p. 308

Watch your step when wandering areas oceans once covered. What looks like a stone could be this Pokémon, and it will curse you if you kick it.

Sudden climate change wiped out this ancient kind of Corsola. This Pokémon absorbs others' life-force through its branches.

MAIN WAY TO OBTAIN
In *Pokémon Shield*, catch one when it appears in tall grass at the Giant's Mirror during cloudy weather. In *Pokémon Sword*, obtain it in a trade, as it does not appear in that game.

Galarian Form

♂♀
Same form for male/female

Lv. 38

237 Cursola
Coral Pokémon

Height: 3'3"   Weight: .9 lbs.   p. 308

Its shell is overflowing with its heightened otherworldly energy. The ectoplasm serves as protection for this Pokémon's core spirit.

Be cautious of the ectoplasmic body surrounding its soul. You'll become stiff as stone if you touch it.

MAIN WAY TO OBTAIN
In *Pokémon Shield*, defeat and catch one when it appears in a Max Raid Battle. Or obtain a Galarian Corsola, then level it up to Lv. 38 or higher to evolve it into Cursola.

♂♀
Same form for male/female

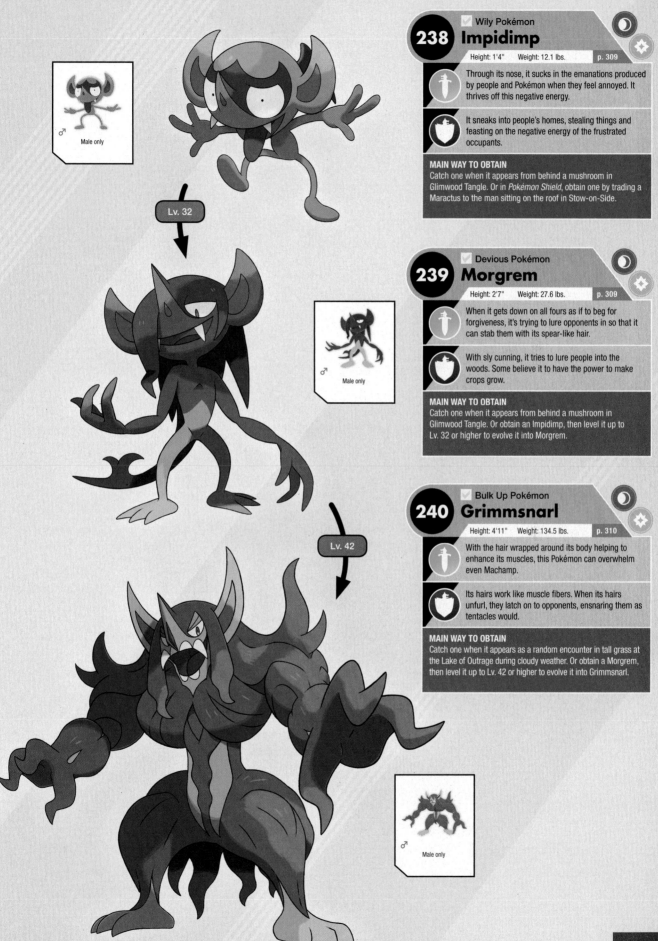

238 Impidimp

☑ Wily Pokémon

Height: 1'4"   Weight: 12.1 lbs.   p. 309

Through its nose, it sucks in the emanations produced by people and Pokémon when they feel annoyed. It thrives off this negative energy.

It sneaks into people's homes, stealing things and feasting on the negative energy of the frustrated occupants.

MAIN WAY TO OBTAIN
Catch one when it appears from behind a mushroom in Glimwood Tangle. Or in *Pokémon Shield*, obtain one by trading a Maractus to the man sitting on the roof in Stow-on-Side.

Male only

Lv. 32

239 Morgrem

☑ Devious Pokémon

Height: 2'7"   Weight: 27.6 lbs.   p. 309

When it gets down on all fours as if to beg for forgiveness, it's trying to lure opponents in so that it can stab them with its spear-like hair.

With sly cunning, it tries to lure people into the woods. Some believe it to have the power to make crops grow.

MAIN WAY TO OBTAIN
Catch one when it appears from behind a mushroom in Glimwood Tangle. Or obtain an Impidimp, then level it up to Lv. 32 or higher to evolve it into Morgrem.

Male only

Lv. 42

240 Grimmsnarl

☑ Bulk Up Pokémon

Height: 4'11"   Weight: 134.5 lbs.   p. 310

With the hair wrapped around its body helping to enhance its muscles, this Pokémon can overwhelm even Machamp.

Its hairs work like muscle fibers. When its hairs unfurl, they latch on to opponents, ensnaring them as tentacles would.

MAIN WAY TO OBTAIN
Catch one when it appears as a random encounter in tall grass at the Lake of Outrage during cloudy weather. Or obtain a Morgrem, then level it up to Lv. 42 or higher to evolve it into Grimmsnarl.

Male only

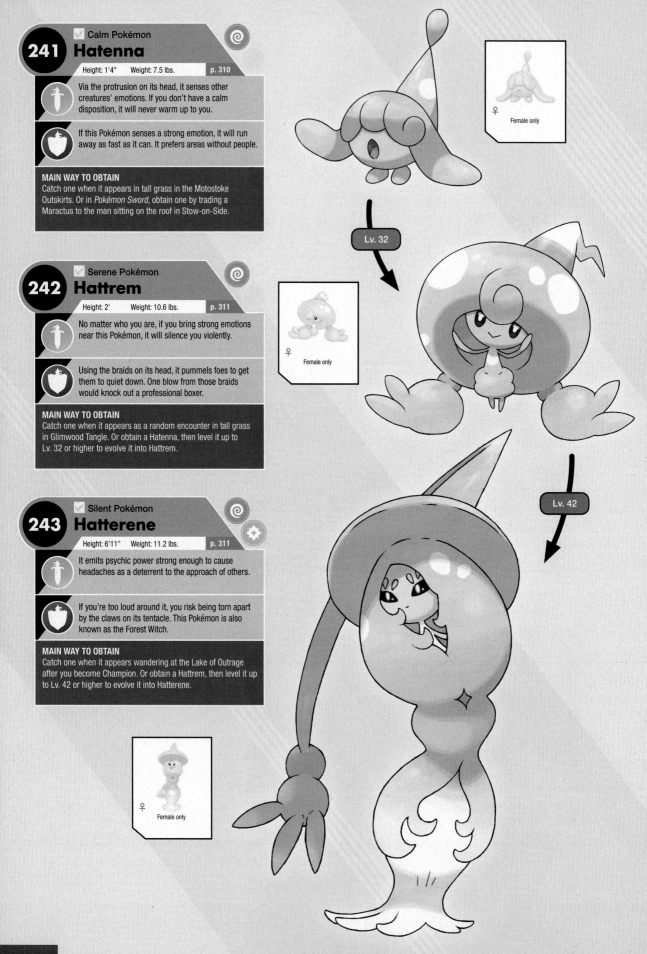

241 Hatenna

☑ Calm Pokémon

Height: 1'4"   Weight: 7.5 lbs.   p. 310

Via the protrusion on its head, it senses other creatures' emotions. If you don't have a calm disposition, it will never warm up to you.

If this Pokémon senses a strong emotion, it will run away as fast as it can. It prefers areas without people.

MAIN WAY TO OBTAIN
Catch one when it appears in tall grass in the Motostoke Outskirts. Or in *Pokémon Sword*, obtain one by trading a Maractus to the man sitting on the roof in Stow-on-Side.

♀ Female only

Lv. 32

242 Hattrem

☑ Serene Pokémon

Height: 2'   Weight: 10.6 lbs.   p. 311

No matter who you are, if you bring strong emotions near this Pokémon, it will silence you violently.

Using the braids on its head, it pummels foes to get them to quiet down. One blow from those braids would knock out a professional boxer.

MAIN WAY TO OBTAIN
Catch one when it appears as a random encounter in tall grass in Glimwood Tangle. Or obtain a Hatenna, then level it up to Lv. 32 or higher to evolve it into Hattrem.

♀ Female only

Lv. 42

243 Hatterene

☑ Silent Pokémon

Height: 6'11"   Weight: 11.2 lbs.   p. 311

It emits psychic power strong enough to cause headaches as a deterrent to the approach of others.

If you're too loud around it, you risk being torn apart by the claws on its tentacle. This Pokémon is also known as the Forest Witch.

MAIN WAY TO OBTAIN
Catch one when it appears wandering at the Lake of Outrage after you become Champion. Or obtain a Hattrem, then level it up to Lv. 42 or higher to evolve it into Hatterene.

♀ Female only

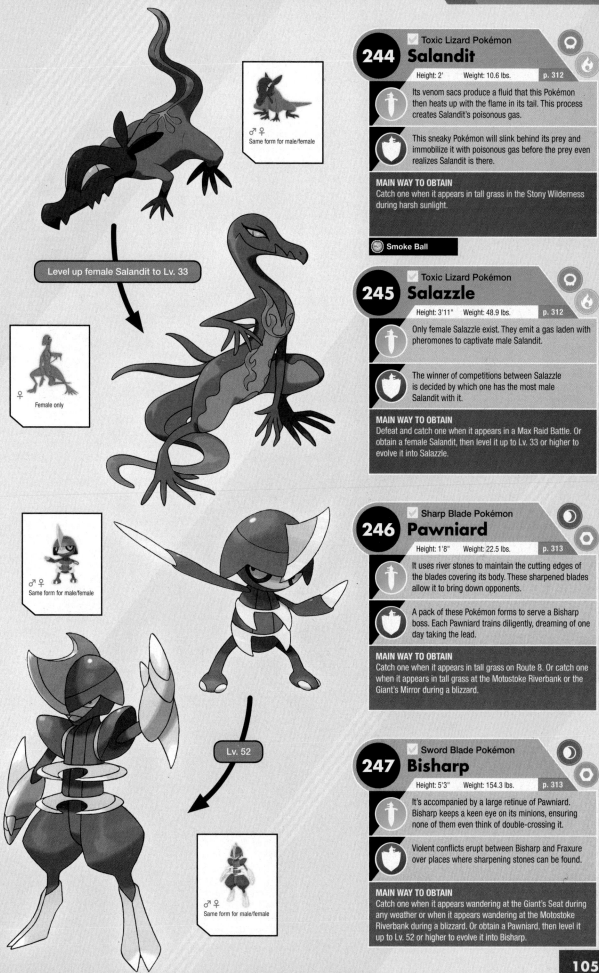

Same form for male/female

Level up female Salandit to Lv. 33

Female only

Same form for male/female

Lv. 52

Same form for male/female

244 Salandit
Toxic Lizard Pokémon

Height: 2' | Weight: 10.6 lbs. | p. 312

Its venom sacs produce a fluid that this Pokémon then heats up with the flame in its tail. This process creates Salandit's poisonous gas.

This sneaky Pokémon will slink behind its prey and immobilize it with poisonous gas before the prey even realizes Salandit is there.

MAIN WAY TO OBTAIN
Catch one when it appears in tall grass in the Stony Wilderness during harsh sunlight.

Smoke Ball

245 Salazzle
Toxic Lizard Pokémon

Height: 3'11" | Weight: 48.9 lbs. | p. 312

Only female Salazzle exist. They emit a gas laden with pheromones to captivate male Salandit.

The winner of competitions between Salazzle is decided by which one has the most male Salandit with it.

MAIN WAY TO OBTAIN
Defeat and catch one when it appears in a Max Raid Battle. Or obtain a female Salandit, then level it up to Lv. 33 or higher to evolve it into Salazzle.

246 Pawniard
Sharp Blade Pokémon

Height: 1'8" | Weight: 22.5 lbs. | p. 313

It uses river stones to maintain the cutting edges of the blades covering its body. These sharpened blades allow it to bring down opponents.

A pack of these Pokémon forms to serve a Bisharp boss. Each Pawniard trains diligently, dreaming of one day taking the lead.

MAIN WAY TO OBTAIN
Catch one when it appears in tall grass on Route 8. Or catch one when it appears in tall grass at the Motostoke Riverbank or the Giant's Mirror during a blizzard.

247 Bisharp
Sword Blade Pokémon

Height: 5'3" | Weight: 154.3 lbs. | p. 313

It's accompanied by a large retinue of Pawniard. Bisharp keeps a keen eye on its minions, ensuring none of them even think of double-crossing it.

Violent conflicts erupt between Bisharp and Fraxure over places where sharpening stones can be found.

MAIN WAY TO OBTAIN
Catch one when it appears wandering at the Giant's Seat during any weather or when it appears wandering at the Motostoke Riverbank during a blizzard. Or obtain a Pawniard, then level it up to Lv. 52 or higher to evolve it into Bisharp.

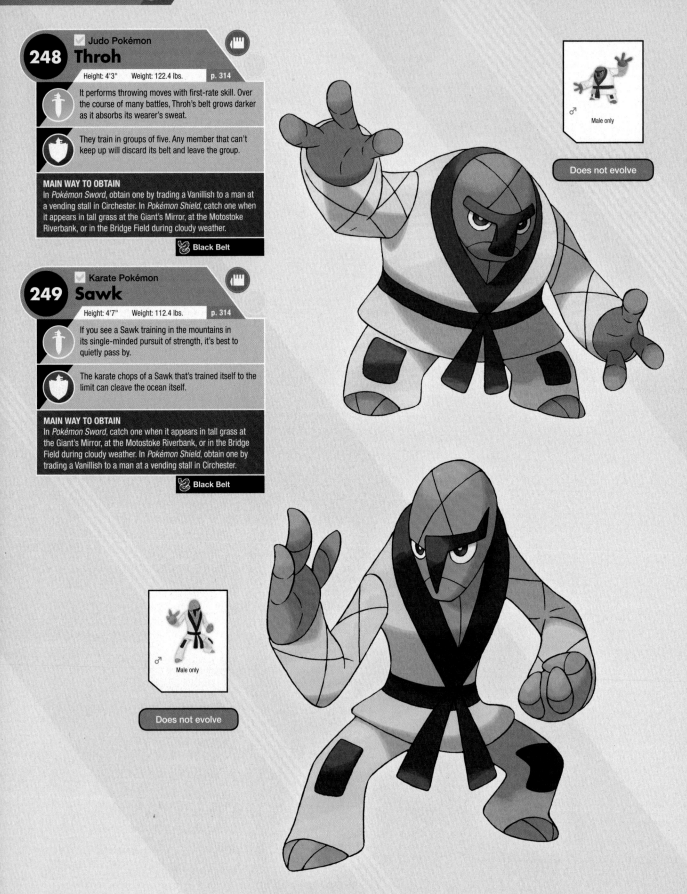

248 Throh
☑ Judo Pokémon

Height: 4'3"   Weight: 122.4 lbs.   p. 314

It performs throwing moves with first-rate skill. Over the course of many battles, Throh's belt grows darker as it absorbs its wearer's sweat.

They train in groups of five. Any member that can't keep up will discard its belt and leave the group.

MAIN WAY TO OBTAIN
In *Pokémon Sword*, obtain one by trading a Vanillish to a man at a vending stall in Circhester. In *Pokémon Shield*, catch one when it appears in tall grass at the Giant's Mirror, at the Motostoke Riverbank, or in the Bridge Field during cloudy weather.

Black Belt

♂ Male only

Does not evolve

249 Sawk
☑ Karate Pokémon

Height: 4'7"   Weight: 112.4 lbs.   p. 314

If you see a Sawk training in the mountains in its single-minded pursuit of strength, it's best to quietly pass by.

The karate chops of a Sawk that's trained itself to the limit can cleave the ocean itself.

MAIN WAY TO OBTAIN
In *Pokémon Sword*, catch one when it appears in tall grass at the Giant's Mirror, at the Motostoke Riverbank, or in the Bridge Field during cloudy weather. In *Pokémon Shield*, obtain one by trading a Vanillish to a man at a vending stall in Circhester.

Black Belt

♂ Male only

Does not evolve

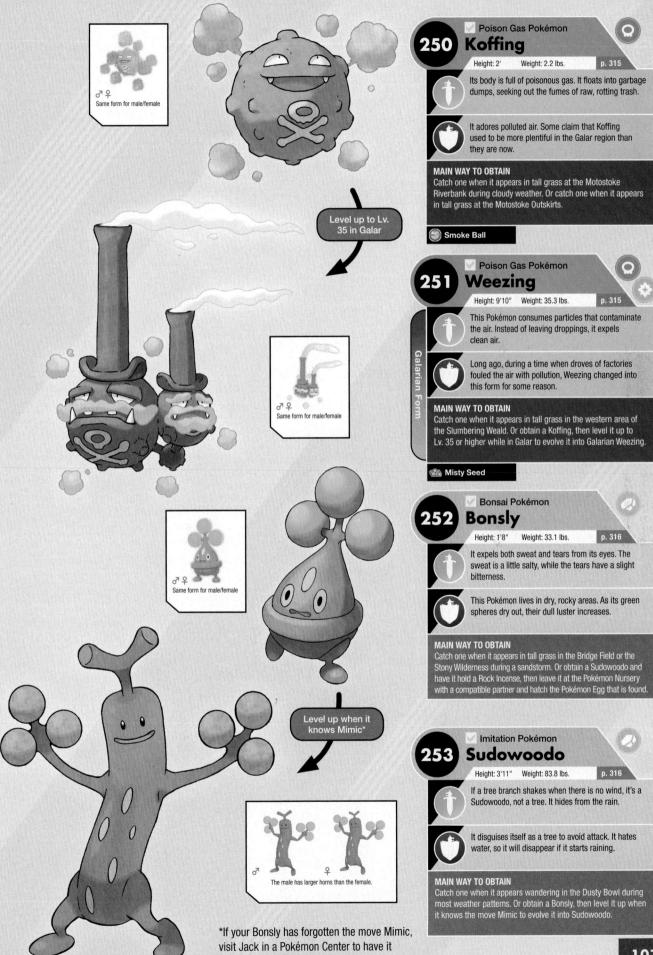

♂♀
Same form for male/female

Level up to Lv. 35 in Galar

Galarian Form

Same form for male/female

♂♀
Same form for male/female

Level up when it knows Mimic*

♂   ♀
The male has larger horns than the female.

*If your Bonsly has forgotten the move Mimic, visit Jack in a Pokémon Center to have it remember the move once more.

☑ Poison Gas Pokémon
250 Koffing

| Height: 2' | Weight: 2.2 lbs. | p. 315 |

Its body is full of poisonous gas. It floats into garbage dumps, seeking out the fumes of raw, rotting trash.

It adores polluted air. Some claim that Koffing used to be more plentiful in the Galar region than they are now.

MAIN WAY TO OBTAIN
Catch one when it appears in tall grass at the Motostoke Riverbank during cloudy weather. Or catch one when it appears in tall grass at the Motostoke Outskirts.

⬡ Smoke Ball

☑ Poison Gas Pokémon
251 Weezing

| Height: 9'10" | Weight: 35.3 lbs. | p. 315 |

This Pokémon consumes particles that contaminate the air. Instead of leaving droppings, it expels clean air.

Long ago, during a time when droves of factories fouled the air with pollution, Weezing changed into this form for some reason.

MAIN WAY TO OBTAIN
Catch one when it appears in tall grass in the western area of the Slumbering Weald. Or obtain a Koffing, then level it up to Lv. 35 or higher while in Galar to evolve it into Galarian Weezing.

⬡ Misty Seed

☑ Bonsai Pokémon
252 Bonsly

| Height: 1'8" | Weight: 33.1 lbs. | p. 316 |

It expels both sweat and tears from its eyes. The sweat is a little salty, while the tears have a slight bitterness.

This Pokémon lives in dry, rocky areas. As its green spheres dry out, their dull luster increases.

MAIN WAY TO OBTAIN
Catch one when it appears in tall grass in the Bridge Field or the Stony Wilderness during a sandstorm. Or obtain a Sudowoodo and have it hold a Rock Incense, then leave it at the Pokémon Nursery with a compatible partner and hatch the Pokémon Egg that is found.

☑ Imitation Pokémon
253 Sudowoodo

| Height: 3'11" | Weight: 83.8 lbs. | p. 316 |

If a tree branch shakes when there is no wind, it's a Sudowoodo, not a tree. It hides from the rain.

It disguises itself as a tree to avoid attack. It hates water, so it will disappear if it starts raining.

MAIN WAY TO OBTAIN
Catch one when it appears wandering in the Dusty Bowl during most weather patterns. Or obtain a Bonsly, then level it up when it knows the move Mimic to evolve it into Sudowoodo.

254 Cleffa

☑ Star Shape Pokémon

Height: 1' Weight: 6.6 lbs. p. 317

According to local rumors, Cleffa are often seen in places where shooting stars have fallen.

Because of its unusual, starlike silhouette, people believe that it came here on a meteor.

MAIN WAY TO OBTAIN
Defeat and catch one when it appears in a Max Raid Battle in the Wild Area. Or obtain a Clefairy or Clefable, then leave it at the Pokémon Nursery with a compatible partner and hatch the Pokémon Egg that is found.

♂ ♀
Same form for male/female

Level up with high friendship

255 Clefairy

☑ Fairy Pokémon

Height: 2' Weight: 16.5 lbs. p. 317

It is said that happiness will come to those who see a gathering of Clefairy dancing under a full moon.

Its adorable behavior and cry make it highly popular. However, this cute Pokémon is rarely found.

MAIN WAY TO OBTAIN
Catch one when it appears in tall grass at the Giant's Cap or the Motostoke Riverbank during fog. Or obtain a Cleffa, then level it up with high friendship to evolve it into Clefairy.

🌑 Moon Stone

♂ ♀
Same form for male/female

Use Moon Stone

256 Clefable

☑ Fairy Pokémon

Height: 4'3" Weight: 88.2 lbs. p. 318

A timid fairy Pokémon that is rarely seen, it will run and hide the moment it senses people.

Their ears are sensitive enough to hear a pin drop from over a mile away, so they're usually found in quiet places.

MAIN WAY TO OBTAIN
Catch one when it appears wandering at the Motostoke Riverbank during fog. Or obtain a Clefairy, then use a Moon Stone on it to evolve it into Clefable.

🌑 Moon Stone

♂ ♀
Same form for male/female

♂ ♀
Same form for male/female

Level up with high friendship

♂ ♀
Same form for male/female

Use Shiny Stone

♂ ♀
Same form for male/female

257 Togepi
Spike Ball Pokémon

Height: 1'   Weight: 3.3 lbs.   p. 318

The shell seems to be filled with joy. It is said that it will share good luck when treated kindly.

It is considered to be a symbol of good luck. Its shell is said to be filled with happiness.

MAIN WAY TO OBTAIN
Catch one when it appears as a random encounter in tall grass in the Bridge Field during clear weather, cloudy weather, or fog. Or obtain one by trading a Toxel to the woman in the park in the west part of Hammerlocke.

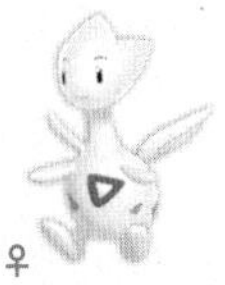

258 Togetic
Happiness Pokémon

Height: 2'   Weight: 7.1 lbs.   p. 319

They say that it will appear before kindhearted, caring people and shower them with happiness.

It grows dispirited if it is not with kind people. It can float in midair without moving its wings.

MAIN WAY TO OBTAIN
Catch one when it appears as a random encounter in tall grass in the Stony Wilderness during fog. Or obtain a Togepi, then level it up with high friendship to evolve it into Togetic.

259 Togekiss
Jubilee Pokémon

Height: 4'11"   Weight: 83.8 lbs.   p. 319

These Pokémon are never seen anywhere near conflict or turmoil. In recent times, they've hardly been seen at all.

Known as a bringer of blessings, it's been depicted on good-luck charms since ancient times.

MAIN WAY TO OBTAIN
Catch one when it appears flying around in the Dusty Bowl during fog. Or obtain a Togetic, then use a Shiny Stone on it to evolve it into Togekiss.

260 ☑ Big Eater Pokémon
Munchlax

Height: 2'   Weight: 231.5 lbs.   p. 320

Stuffing itself with vast amounts of food is its only concern. Whether the food is rotten or fresh, yummy or tasteless—it does not care.

It stores food beneath its fur. It might share just one bite, but only if it really trusts you.

MAIN WAY TO OBTAIN
Catch one when it appears in tall grass at the Motostoke Riverbank during clear weather. Or obtain a Snorlax and have it hold a Full Incense, then leave it at the Pokémon Nursery with a compatible partner and hatch the Pokémon Egg that is found.

🏵 Leftovers

261 ☑ Sleeping Pokémon
Snorlax

Height: 6'11"   Weight: 1014.1 lbs.   p. 320

It is not satisfied unless it eats over 880 pounds of food every day. When it is done eating, it goes promptly to sleep.

This Pokémon's stomach is so strong, even eating moldy or rotten food will not affect it.

MAIN WAY TO OBTAIN
Catch one when it appears wandering at the Motostoke Riverbank during most weather patterns. Or obtain a Munchlax, then level it up with high friendship to evolve it into Snorlax.

🏵 Leftovers

262 ☑ Cotton Puff Pokémon
Cottonee

Height: 1'   Weight: 1.3 lbs.   p. 321

It shoots cotton from its body to protect itself. If it gets caught up in hurricane-strength winds, it can get sent to the other side of the Earth.

Weaving together the cotton of both Cottonee and Eldegoss produces exquisite cloth that's highly prized by many luxury brands.

MAIN WAY TO OBTAIN
Catch one when it appears as a random encounter in tall grass in the Stony Wilderness during cloudy weather.

◈ Absorb Bulb

263 ☑ Windveiled Pokémon
Whimsicott

Height: 2'4"   Weight: 14.6 lbs.   p. 321

It scatters cotton all over the place as a prank. If it gets wet, it'll become too heavy to move and have no choice but to answer for its mischief.

As long as this Pokémon bathes in sunlight, its cotton keeps growing. If too much cotton fluff builds up, Whimsicott tears it off and scatters it.

MAIN WAY TO OBTAIN
Defeat and catch one when it appears in a Max Raid Battle in the Wild Area. Or obtain a Cottonee, then use a Sun Stone on it to evolve it into Whimsicott.

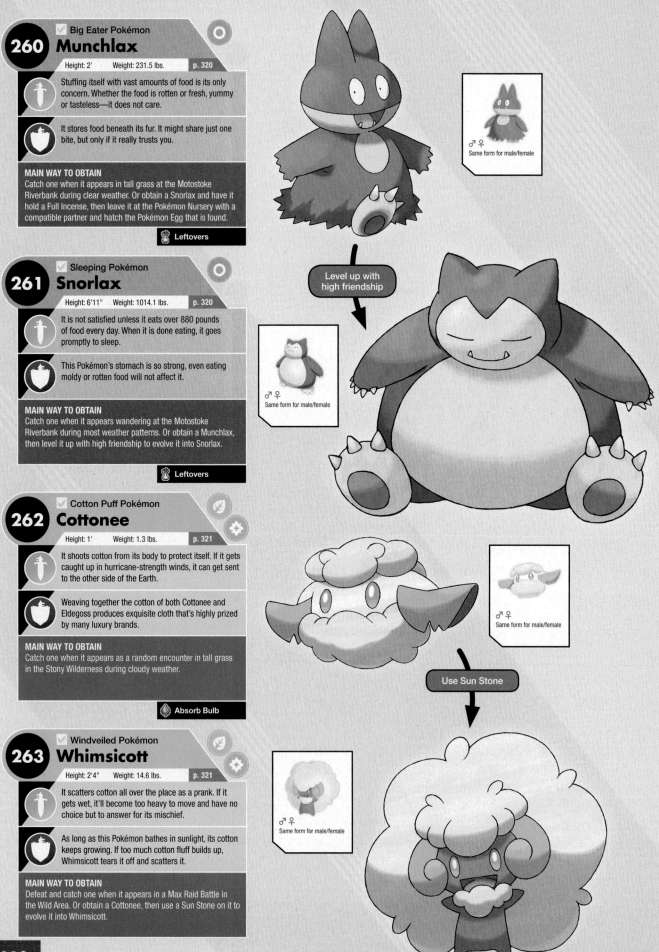

♂ ♀
Same form for male/female

Level up with high friendship

♂ ♀
Same form for male/female

♂ ♀
Same form for male/female

Use Sun Stone

♂ ♀
Same form for male/female

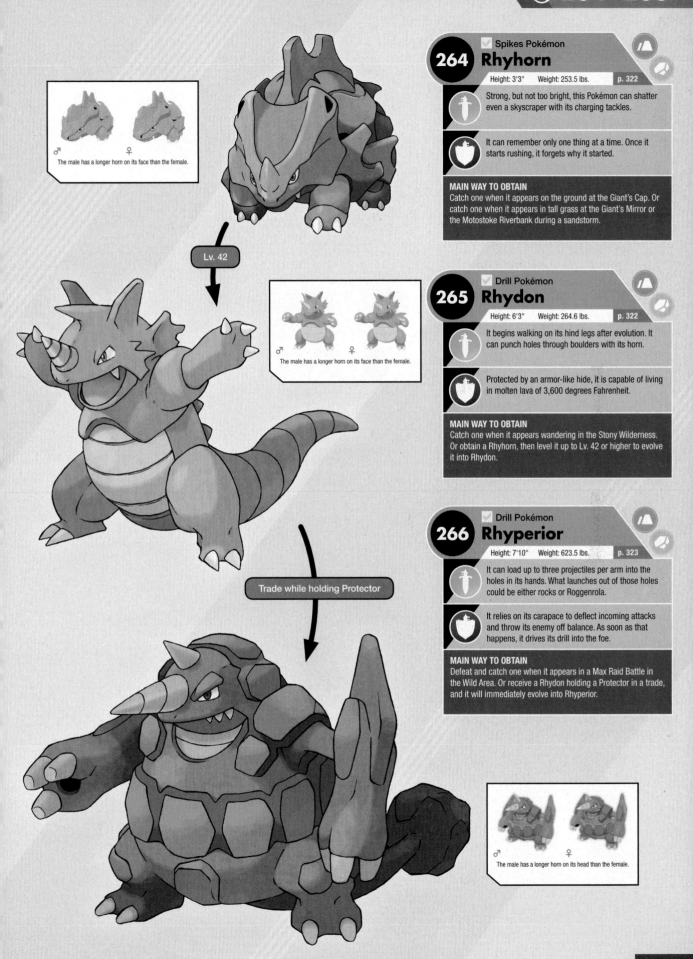

The male has a longer horn on its face than the female.

♂   ♀

Lv. 42

The male has a longer horn on its face than the female.

♂   ♀

Trade while holding Protector

The male has a longer horn on its head than the female.

♂   ♀

---

264 Rhyhorn
Spikes Pokémon

Height: 3'3"   Weight: 253.5 lbs.   p. 322

Strong, but not too bright, this Pokémon can shatter even a skyscraper with its charging tackles.

It can remember only one thing at a time. Once it starts rushing, it forgets why it started.

MAIN WAY TO OBTAIN
Catch one when it appears on the ground at the Giant's Cap. Or catch one when it appears in tall grass at the Giant's Mirror or the Motostoke Riverbank during a sandstorm.

---

265 Rhydon
Drill Pokémon

Height: 6'3"   Weight: 264.6 lbs.   p. 322

It begins walking on its hind legs after evolution. It can punch holes through boulders with its horn.

Protected by an armor-like hide, it is capable of living in molten lava of 3,600 degrees Fahrenheit.

MAIN WAY TO OBTAIN
Catch one when it appears wandering in the Stony Wilderness. Or obtain a Rhyhorn, then level it up to Lv. 42 or higher to evolve it into Rhydon.

---

266 Rhyperior
Drill Pokémon

Height: 7'10"   Weight: 623.5 lbs.   p. 323

It can load up to three projectiles per arm into the holes in its hands. What launches out of those holes could be either rocks or Roggenrola.

It relies on its carapace to deflect incoming attacks and throw its enemy off balance. As soon as that happens, it drives its drill into the foe.

MAIN WAY TO OBTAIN
Defeat and catch one when it appears in a Max Raid Battle in the Wild Area. Or receive a Rhydon holding a Protector in a trade, and it will immediately evolve into Rhyperior.

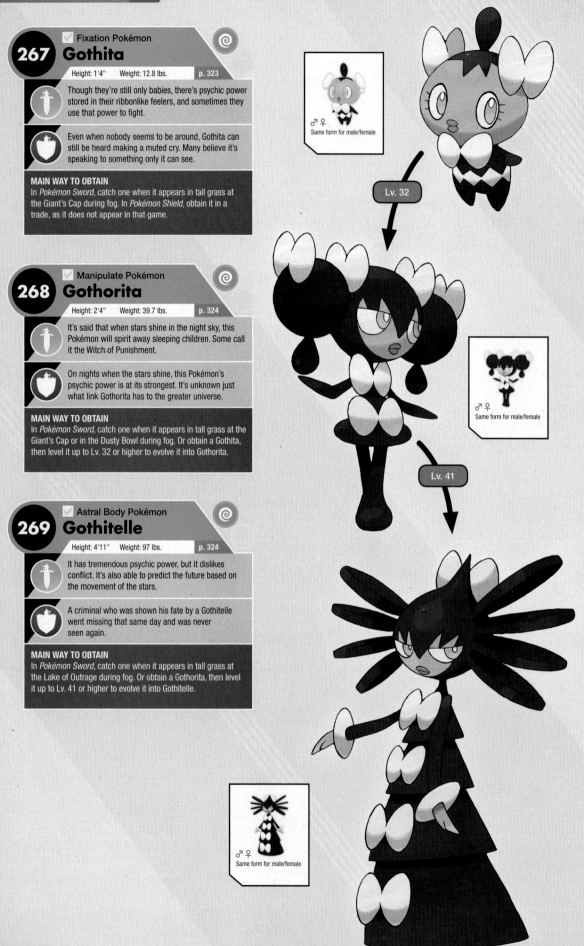

☑ Fixation Pokémon

267 Gothita

Height: 1'4"   Weight: 12.8 lbs.   p. 323

Though they're still only babies, there's psychic power stored in their ribbonlike feelers, and sometimes they use that power to fight.

Even when nobody seems to be around, Gothita can still be heard making a muted cry. Many believe it's speaking to something only it can see.

MAIN WAY TO OBTAIN
In *Pokémon Sword*, catch one when it appears in tall grass at the Giant's Cap during fog. In *Pokémon Shield*, obtain it in a trade, as it does not appear in that game.

♂♀
Same form for male/female

Lv. 32

☑ Manipulate Pokémon

268 Gothorita

Height: 2'4"   Weight: 39.7 lbs.   p. 324

It's said that when stars shine in the night sky, this Pokémon will spirit away sleeping children. Some call it the Witch of Punishment.

On nights when the stars shine, this Pokémon's psychic power is at its strongest. It's unknown just what link Gothorita has to the greater universe.

MAIN WAY TO OBTAIN
In *Pokémon Sword*, catch one when it appears in tall grass at the Giant's Cap or in the Dusty Bowl during fog. Or obtain a Gothita, then level it up to Lv. 32 or higher to evolve it into Gothorita.

♂♀
Same form for male/female

Lv. 41

☑ Astral Body Pokémon

269 Gothitelle

Height: 4'11"   Weight: 97 lbs.   p. 324

It has tremendous psychic power, but it dislikes conflict. It's also able to predict the future based on the movement of the stars.

A criminal who was shown his fate by a Gothitelle went missing that same day and was never seen again.

MAIN WAY TO OBTAIN
In *Pokémon Sword*, catch one when it appears in tall grass at the Lake of Outrage during fog. Or obtain a Gothorita, then level it up to Lv. 41 or higher to evolve it into Gothitelle.

♂♀
Same form for male/female

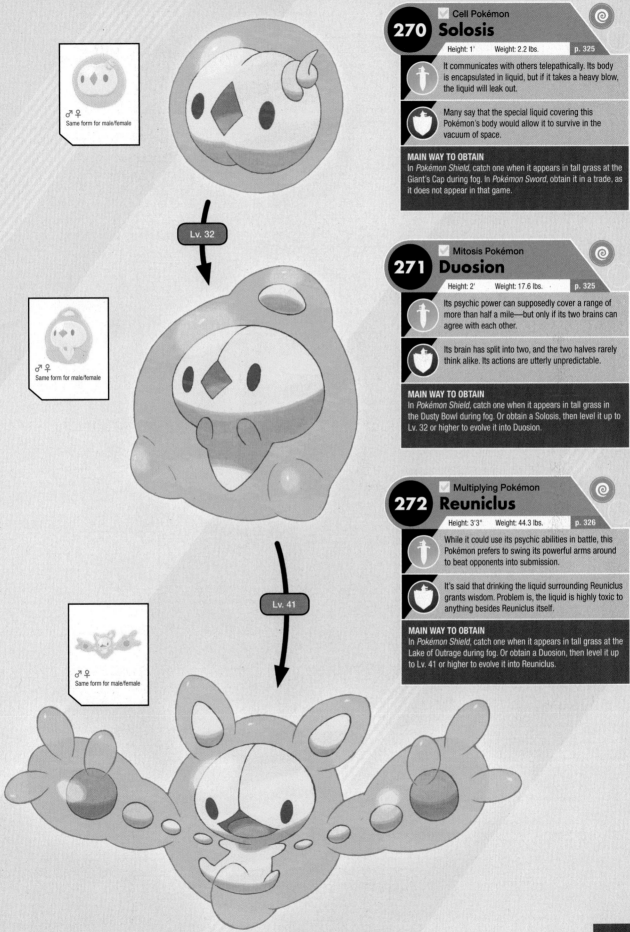

Same form for male/female

Lv. 32

Same form for male/female

Lv. 41

Same form for male/female

Cell Pokémon
270 Solosis

| Height: 1' | Weight: 2.2 lbs. | p. 325 |

It communicates with others telepathically. Its body is encapsulated in liquid, but if it takes a heavy blow, the liquid will leak out.

Many say that the special liquid covering this Pokémon's body would allow it to survive in the vacuum of space.

MAIN WAY TO OBTAIN

In *Pokémon Shield*, catch one when it appears in tall grass at the Giant's Cap during fog. In *Pokémon Sword*, obtain it in a trade, as it does not appear in that game.

Mitosis Pokémon
271 Duosion

| Height: 2' | Weight: 17.6 lbs. | p. 325 |

Its psychic power can supposedly cover a range of more than half a mile—but only if its two brains can agree with each other.

Its brain has split into two, and the two halves rarely think alike. Its actions are utterly unpredictable.

MAIN WAY TO OBTAIN

In *Pokémon Shield*, catch one when it appears in tall grass in the Dusty Bowl during fog. Or obtain a Solosis, then level it up to Lv. 32 or higher to evolve it into Duosion.

Multiplying Pokémon
272 Reuniclus

| Height: 3'3" | Weight: 44.3 lbs. | p. 326 |

While it could use its psychic abilities in battle, this Pokémon prefers to swing its powerful arms around to beat opponents into submission.

It's said that drinking the liquid surrounding Reuniclus grants wisdom. Problem is, the liquid is highly toxic to anything besides Reuniclus itself.

MAIN WAY TO OBTAIN

In *Pokémon Shield*, catch one when it appears in tall grass at the Lake of Outrage during fog. Or obtain a Duosion, then level it up to Lv. 41 or higher to evolve it into Reuniclus.

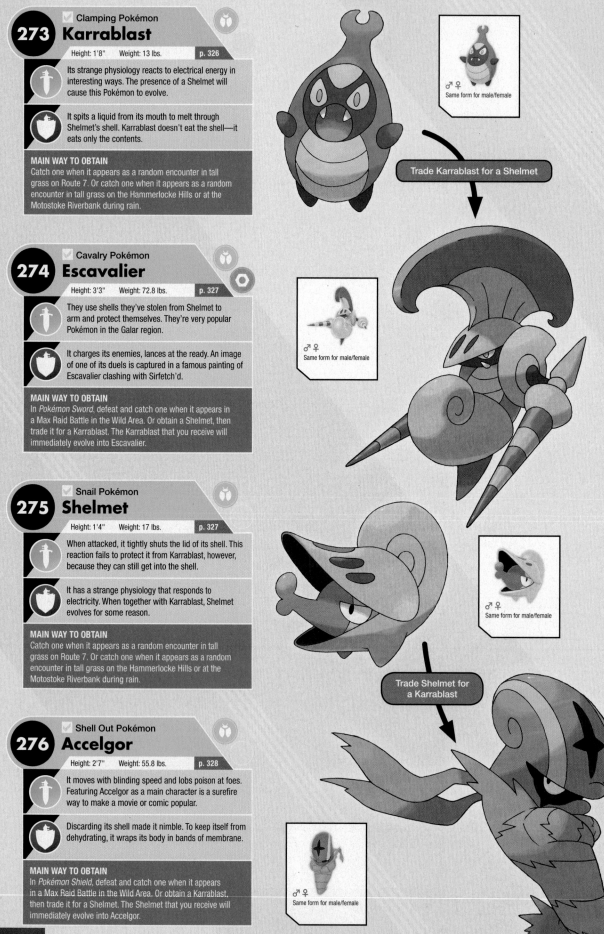

273 Karrablast

☑ Clamping Pokémon

Height: 1'8" Weight: 13 lbs.   p. 326

Its strange physiology reacts to electrical energy in interesting ways. The presence of a Shelmet will cause this Pokémon to evolve.

It spits a liquid from its mouth to melt through Shelmet's shell. Karrablast doesn't eat the shell—it eats only the contents.

MAIN WAY TO OBTAIN
Catch one when it appears as a random encounter in tall grass on Route 7. Or catch one when it appears as a random encounter in tall grass on the Hammerlocke Hills or at the Motostoke Riverbank during rain.

♂ ♀
Same form for male/female

Trade Karrablast for a Shelmet

274 Escavalier

☑ Cavalry Pokémon

Height: 3'3" Weight: 72.8 lbs.   p. 327

They use shells they've stolen from Shelmet to arm and protect themselves. They're very popular Pokémon in the Galar region.

It charges its enemies, lances at the ready. An image of one of its duels is captured in a famous painting of Escavalier clashing with Sirfetch'd.

MAIN WAY TO OBTAIN
In *Pokémon Sword*, defeat and catch one when it appears in a Max Raid Battle in the Wild Area. Or obtain a Shelmet, then trade it for a Karrablast. The Karrablast that you receive will immediately evolve into Escavalier.

♂ ♀
Same form for male/female

275 Shelmet

☑ Snail Pokémon

Height: 1'4" Weight: 17 lbs.   p. 327

When attacked, it tightly shuts the lid of its shell. This reaction fails to protect it from Karrablast, however, because they can still get into the shell.

It has a strange physiology that responds to electricity. When together with Karrablast, Shelmet evolves for some reason.

MAIN WAY TO OBTAIN
Catch one when it appears as a random encounter in tall grass on Route 7. Or catch one when it appears as a random encounter in tall grass on the Hammerlocke Hills or at the Motostoke Riverbank during rain.

♂ ♀
Same form for male/female

Trade Shelmet for a Karrablast

276 Accelgor

☑ Shell Out Pokémon

Height: 2'7" Weight: 55.8 lbs.   p. 328

It moves with blinding speed and lobs poison at foes. Featuring Accelgor as a main character is a surefire way to make a movie or comic popular.

Discarding its shell made it nimble. To keep itself from dehydrating, it wraps its body in bands of membrane.

MAIN WAY TO OBTAIN
In *Pokémon Shield*, defeat and catch one when it appears in a Max Raid Battle in the Wild Area. Or obtain a Karrablast, then trade it for a Shelmet. The Shelmet that you receive will immediately evolve into Accelgor.

♂ ♀
Same form for male/female

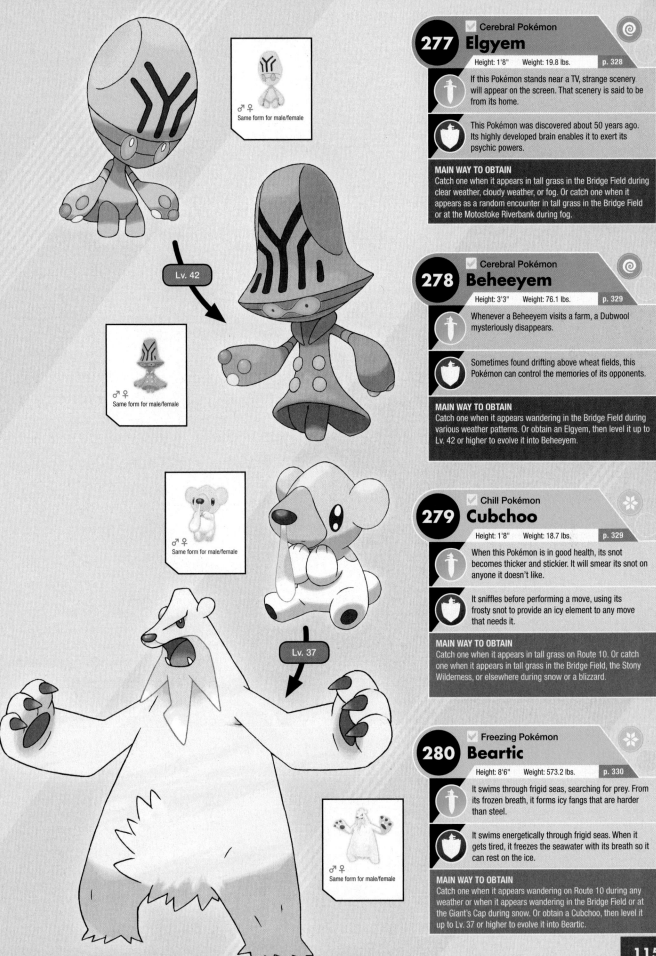

♂ ♀
Same form for male/female

Lv. 42

♂ ♀
Same form for male/female

♂ ♀
Same form for male/female

Lv. 37

♂ ♀
Same form for male/female

277 Elgyem
Cerebral Pokémon

Height: 1'8"   Weight: 19.8 lbs.   p. 328

If this Pokémon stands near a TV, strange scenery will appear on the screen. That scenery is said to be from its home.

This Pokémon was discovered about 50 years ago. Its highly developed brain enables it to exert its psychic powers.

MAIN WAY TO OBTAIN
Catch one when it appears in tall grass in the Bridge Field during clear weather, cloudy weather, or fog. Or catch one when it appears as a random encounter in tall grass in the Bridge Field or at the Motostoke Riverbank during fog.

278 Beheeyem
Cerebral Pokémon

Height: 3'3"   Weight: 76.1 lbs.   p. 329

Whenever a Beheeyem visits a farm, a Dubwool mysteriously disappears.

Sometimes found drifting above wheat fields, this Pokémon can control the memories of its opponents.

MAIN WAY TO OBTAIN
Catch one when it appears wandering in the Bridge Field during various weather patterns. Or obtain an Elgyem, then level it up to Lv. 42 or higher to evolve it into Beheeyem.

279 Cubchoo
Chill Pokémon

Height: 1'8"   Weight: 18.7 lbs.   p. 329

When this Pokémon is in good health, its snot becomes thicker and stickier. It will smear its snot on anyone it doesn't like.

It sniffles before performing a move, using its frosty snot to provide an icy element to any move that needs it.

MAIN WAY TO OBTAIN
Catch one when it appears in tall grass on Route 10. Or catch one when it appears in tall grass in the Bridge Field, the Stony Wilderness, or elsewhere during snow or a blizzard.

280 Beartic
Freezing Pokémon

Height: 8'6"   Weight: 573.2 lbs.   p. 330

It swims through frigid seas, searching for prey. From its frozen breath, it forms icy fangs that are harder than steel.

It swims energetically through frigid seas. When it gets tired, it freezes the seawater with its breath so it can rest on the ice.

MAIN WAY TO OBTAIN
Catch one when it appears wandering on Route 10 during any weather or when it appears wandering in the Bridge Field or at the Giant's Cap during snow. Or obtain a Cubchoo, then level it up to Lv. 37 or higher to evolve it into Beartic.

281 Rufflet

Eaglet Pokémon

Height: 1'8"   Weight: 23.1 lbs.   p. 330

If it spies a strong Pokémon, Rufflet can't resist challenging it to a battle. But if Rufflet loses, it starts bawling.

A combative Pokémon, it's ready to pick a fight with anyone. It has talons that can crush hard berries.

MAIN WAY TO OBTAIN
In *Pokémon Sword*, catch one when it appears in tall grass on Route 8 or in the Stony Wilderness. In *Pokémon Shield*, obtain it in a trade, as it does not appear in that game.

♂ Male only

282 Braviary

Valiant Pokémon

Height: 4'11"   Weight: 90.4 lbs.   p. 331

Known for its bravery and pride, this majestic Pokémon is often seen as a motif for various kinds of emblems.

Because this Pokémon is hotheaded and belligerent, it's Corviknight that's taken the role of transportation in Galar.

MAIN WAY TO OBTAIN
In *Pokémon Sword*, catch one when it appears flying around in the Dusty Bowl. Or obtain a Rufflet, then level it up to Lv. 54 or higher to evolve it into Braviary.

Lv. 54

♂ Male only

283 Vullaby

Diapered Pokémon

Height: 1'8"   Weight: 19.8 lbs.   p. 331

It wears a bone to protect its rear. It often squabbles with others of its kind over particularly comfy bones.

Vullaby grow quickly. Bones that have gotten too small for older Vullaby to wear often get passed down to younger ones in the nest.

MAIN WAY TO OBTAIN
In *Pokémon Shield*, catch one when it appears in tall grass on Route 8 or in the Stony Wilderness. In *Pokémon Sword*, obtain it in a trade, as it does not appear in that game.

♀ Female only

284 Mandibuzz

Bone Vulture Pokémon

Height: 3'11"   Weight: 87.1 lbs.   p. 332

Although it's a bit of a ruffian, this Pokémon will take lost Vullaby under its wing and care for them till they're ready to leave the nest.

They adorn themselves with bones. There seem to be fashion trends among them, as different bones come into and fall out of popularity.

MAIN WAY TO OBTAIN
In *Pokémon Shield*, catch one when it appears flying around in the Dusty Bowl. Or obtain a Vullaby, then level it up to Lv. 54 or higher to evolve it into Mandibuzz.

Lv. 54

♀ Female only

Same form for male/female

285 Skorupi

Scorpion Pokémon

Height: 2'7" Weight: 26.5 lbs. p. 332

After burrowing into the sand, it waits patiently for prey to come near. This Pokémon and Sizzlipede share common descent.

It attacks using the claws on its tail. Once locked in its grip, its prey is unable to move as this Pokémon's poison seeps in.

MAIN WAY TO OBTAIN
Catch one when it appears in tall grass at the Motostoke Riverbank during clear weather, rain, a thunderstorm, harsh sunlight, or a sandstorm. Or catch one when it appears as a random encounter in tall grass on Route 6.

Poison Barb

286 Drapion

Ogre Scorpion Pokémon

Height: 4'3" Weight: 135.6 lbs. p. 333

Its poison is potent, but it rarely sees use. This Pokémon prefers to use physical force instead, going on rampages with its car-crushing strength.

It's so vicious that it's called the Sand Demon. Yet when confronted by Hippowdon, Drapion keeps a low profile and will never pick a fight.

MAIN WAY TO OBTAIN
Catch one when it appears wandering at the Motostoke Riverbank during clear weather, rain, a thunderstorm, harsh sunlight, or a sandstorm. Or obtain a Skorupi, then level it up to Lv. 40 or higher to evolve it into Drapion.

Poison Barb

Lv. 40

Same form for male/female

287 Litwick

☑ Candle Pokémon

Height: 1' Weight: 6.8 lbs. p. 333

The flame on its head keeps its body slightly warm. This Pokémon takes lost children by the hand to guide them to the spirit world.

The younger the life this Pokémon absorbs, the brighter and eerier the flame on its head burns.

MAIN WAY TO OBTAIN
Catch one when it appears as a random encounter in tall grass at the Motostoke Riverbank or in the Bridge Field during harsh sunlight. Or catch one when it appears in tall grass during the Motostoke Gym mission.

♂ ♀
Same form for male/female

288 Lampent

☑ Lamp Pokémon

Height: 2' Weight: 28.7 lbs. p. 334

This Pokémon appears just before someone passes away, so it's feared as an emissary of death.

It lurks in cities, pretending to be a lamp. Once it finds someone whose death is near, it will trail quietly after them.

MAIN WAY TO OBTAIN
Catch one when it appears in tall grass at the Lake of Outrage during harsh sunlight. Or obtain a Litwick, then level it up to Lv. 41 or higher to evolve it into Lampent.

Lv. 41

♂ ♀
Same form for male/female

289 Chandelure

☑ Luring Pokémon

Height: 3'3" Weight: 75.6 lbs. p. 334

This Pokémon haunts dilapidated mansions. It sways its arms to hypnotize opponents with the ominous dancing of its flames.

In homes illuminated by Chandelure instead of lights, funerals were a constant occurrence—or so it's said.

MAIN WAY TO OBTAIN
Catch one when it appears wandering at the Lake of Outrage during harsh sunlight. Or obtain a Lampent, then use a Dusk Stone on it to evolve it into Chandelure.

Use Dusk Stone

♂ ♀
Same form for male/female

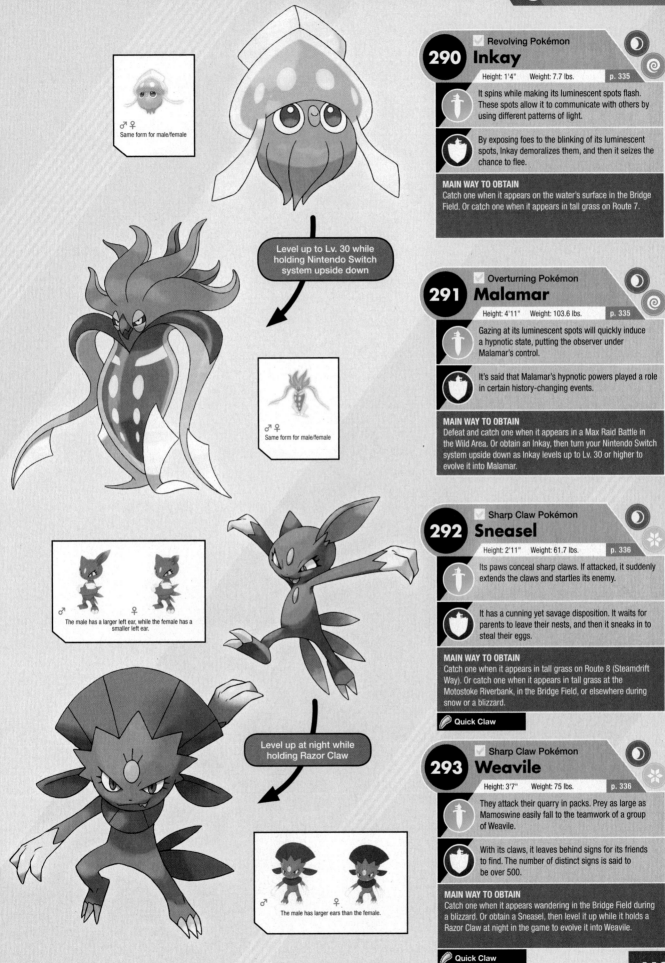

Same form for male/female

Level up to Lv. 30 while holding Nintendo Switch system upside down

Same form for male/female

♂ ♀
The male has a larger left ear, while the female has a smaller left ear.

Level up at night while holding Razor Claw

♂   ♀
The male has larger ears than the female.

290 Inkay
Revolving Pokémon

Height: 1'4"   Weight: 7.7 lbs.   p. 335

It spins while making its luminescent spots flash. These spots allow it to communicate with others by using different patterns of light.

By exposing foes to the blinking of its luminescent spots, Inkay demoralizes them, and then it seizes the chance to flee.

MAIN WAY TO OBTAIN
Catch one when it appears on the water's surface in the Bridge Field. Or catch one when it appears in tall grass on Route 7.

291 Malamar
Overturning Pokémon

Height: 4'11"   Weight: 103.6 lbs.   p. 335

Gazing at its luminescent spots will quickly induce a hypnotic state, putting the observer under Malamar's control.

It's said that Malamar's hypnotic powers played a role in certain history-changing events.

MAIN WAY TO OBTAIN
Defeat and catch one when it appears in a Max Raid Battle in the Wild Area. Or obtain an Inkay, then turn your Nintendo Switch system upside down as Inkay levels up to Lv. 30 or higher to evolve it into Malamar.

292 Sneasel
Sharp Claw Pokémon

Height: 2'11"   Weight: 61.7 lbs.   p. 336

Its paws conceal sharp claws. If attacked, it suddenly extends the claws and startles its enemy.

It has a cunning yet savage disposition. It waits for parents to leave their nests, and then it sneaks in to steal their eggs.

MAIN WAY TO OBTAIN
Catch one when it appears in tall grass on Route 8 (Steamdrift Way). Or catch one when it appears in tall grass at the Motostoke Riverbank, in the Bridge Field, or elsewhere during snow or a blizzard.

Quick Claw

293 Weavile
Sharp Claw Pokémon

Height: 3'7"   Weight: 75 lbs.   p. 336

They attack their quarry in packs. Prey as large as Mamoswine easily fall to the teamwork of a group of Weavile.

With its claws, it leaves behind signs for its friends to find. The number of distinct signs is said to be over 500.

MAIN WAY TO OBTAIN
Catch one when it appears wandering in the Bridge Field during a blizzard. Or obtain a Sneasel, then level it up while it holds a Razor Claw at night in the game to evolve it into Weavile.

Quick Claw

294 Sableye

Darkness Pokémon

Height: 1'8" Weight: 24.3 lbs. p. 337

This Pokémon is feared. When its gemstone eyes begin to glow with a sinister shine, it's believed that Sableye will steal people's spirits away.

It feeds on gemstone crystals. In darkness, its eyes sparkle with the glitter of jewels.

MAIN WAY TO OBTAIN
In *Pokémon Shield*, catch one when it appears in tall grass in the Dusty Bowl during fog. In *Pokémon Sword*, obtain it in a trade, as it does not appear in that game.

Wide Lens

♂ ♀ Same form for male/female

Does not evolve

295 Mawile

Deceiver Pokémon

Height: 2' Weight: 25.4 lbs. p. 337

It uses its docile-looking face to lull foes into complacency, then bites with its huge, relentless jaws.

It chomps with its gaping mouth. Its huge jaws are actually steel horns that have been transformed.

MAIN WAY TO OBTAIN
In *Pokémon Sword*, catch one when it appears in tall grass in the Dusty Bowl during a blizzard. In *Pokémon Shield*, obtain it in a trade, as it does not appear in that game.

Iron Ball

♂ ♀ Same form for male/female

Does not evolve

296 Maractus

Cactus Pokémon

Height: 3'3" Weight: 61.7 lbs. p. 338

With noises that could be mistaken for the rattles of maracas, it creates an upbeat rhythm, startling bird Pokémon and making them fly off in a hurry.

Once each year, this Pokémon scatters its seeds. They're jam-packed with nutrients, making them a precious food source out in the desert.

MAIN WAY TO OBTAIN
Catch one when it appears in tall grass on Route 6. Or catch one when it appears in tall grass in the Bridge Field, the Stony Wilderness, or elsewhere during harsh sunlight.

Miracle Seed

♂ ♀ Same form for male/female

Does not evolve

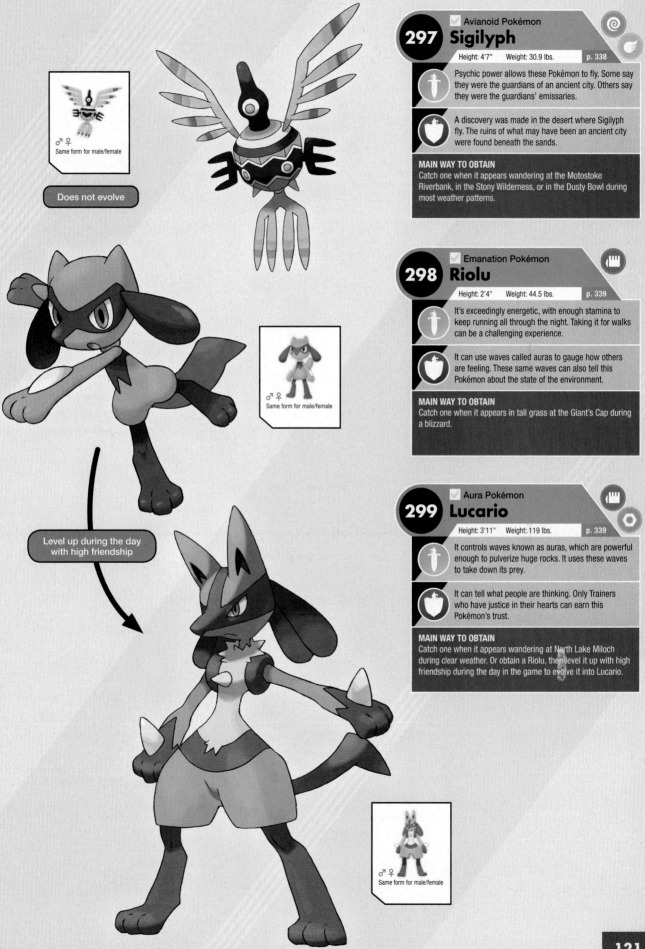

Same form for male/female

Does not evolve

Level up during the day
with high friendship

297 Sigilyph

☑ Avianoid Pokémon

Height: 4'7"   Weight: 30.9 lbs.   p. 338

Psychic power allows these Pokémon to fly. Some say they were the guardians of an ancient city. Others say they were the guardians' emissaries.

A discovery was made in the desert where Sigilyph fly. The ruins of what may have been an ancient city were found beneath the sands.

MAIN WAY TO OBTAIN
Catch one when it appears wandering at the Motostoke Riverbank, in the Stony Wilderness, or in the Dusty Bowl during most weather patterns.

298 Riolu

☑ Emanation Pokémon

Height: 2'4"   Weight: 44.5 lbs.   p. 339

It's exceedingly energetic, with enough stamina to keep running all through the night. Taking it for walks can be a challenging experience.

It can use waves called auras to gauge how others are feeling. These same waves can also tell this Pokémon about the state of the environment.

MAIN WAY TO OBTAIN
Catch one when it appears in tall grass at the Giant's Cap during a blizzard.

Same form for male/female

299 Lucario

☑ Aura Pokémon

Height: 3'11"   Weight: 119 lbs.   p. 339

It controls waves known as auras, which are powerful enough to pulverize huge rocks. It uses these waves to take down its prey.

It can tell what people are thinking. Only Trainers who have justice in their hearts can earn this Pokémon's trust.

MAIN WAY TO OBTAIN
Catch one when it appears wandering at North Lake Miloch during clear weather. Or obtain a Riolu, then level it up with high friendship during the day in the game to evolve it into Lucario.

Same form for male/female

300 Coal Pokémon
Torkoal

Height: 1'8" Weight: 177.3 lbs. p. 340

It burns coal inside its shell for energy. It blows out black soot if it is endangered.

You find abandoned coal mines full of them. They dig tirelessly in search of coal.

MAIN WAY TO OBTAIN
Catch one when it appears in tall grass at the Giant's Cap or the Motostoke Riverbank during harsh sunlight.

Charcoal

♂ ♀
Same form for male/female

Does not evolve

301 Disguise Pokémon
Mimikyu

Height: 8" Weight: 1.5 lbs. p. 340

It wears a rag fashioned into a Pikachu costume in an effort to look less scary. Unfortunately, the costume only makes it creepier.

There was a scientist who peeked under Mimikyu's old rag in the name of research. The scientist died of a mysterious disease.

MAIN WAY TO OBTAIN
Catch one when it appears wandering in the Bridge Field during fog. Or catch one when it appears as a random encounter in tall grass at the Giant's Mirror during fog.

Disguised Form

Chesto Berry

♂ ♀
Same form for male/female

Does not evolve

MIMIKYU'S DISGUISE ABILITY

The Disguise Ability protects Mimikyu from most damage one time in battle, giving it a huge strategic advantage! The first time Mimikyu is hit with a damage-dealing move, it takes only a small amount of damage and changes to its Busted Form. A busted disguise won't protect Mimikyu from any more attacks, but other than that, Mimikyu's forms differ only in appearance.

Mimikyu (Disguised Form)

Mimikyu (Busted Form)

There will be no forgiveness for any who reveal that it was pretending to be Pikachu. It will bring the culprit down, even at the cost of its own life.

Its disguise made from an old rag allowed it to avoid an attack, but the impact broke the neck of the disguise. Now everyone knows it's a Mimikyu.

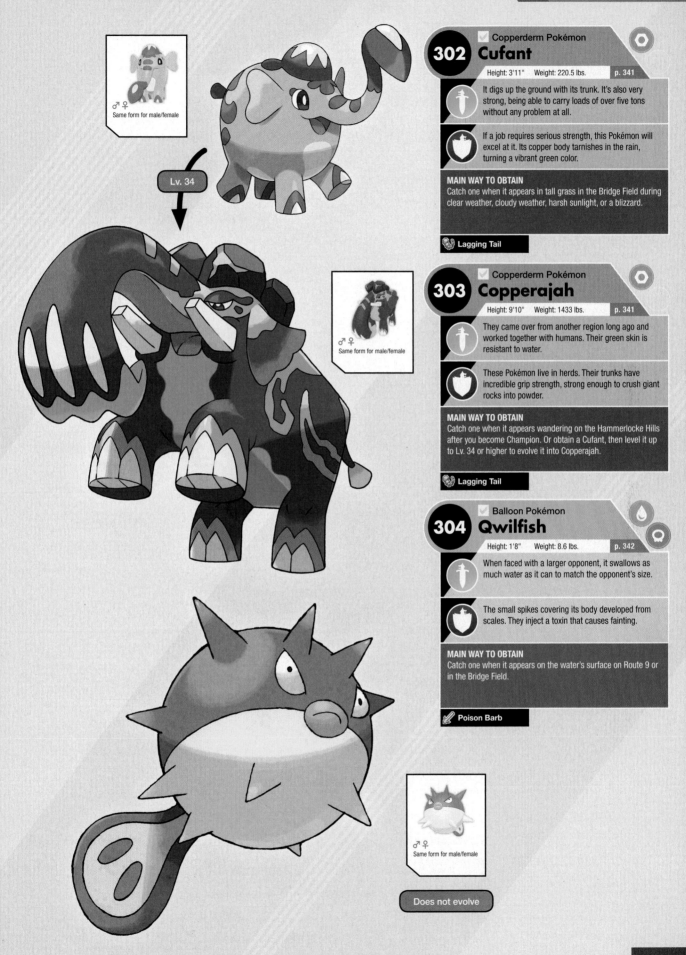

Same form for male/female

Lv. 34

Same form for male/female

Same form for male/female

302 Cufant
Copperderm Pokémon

Height: 3'11" Weight: 220.5 lbs. p. 341

It digs up the ground with its trunk. It's also very strong, being able to carry loads of over five tons without any problem at all.

If a job requires serious strength, this Pokémon will excel at it. Its copper body tarnishes in the rain, turning a vibrant green color.

MAIN WAY TO OBTAIN
Catch one when it appears in tall grass in the Bridge Field during clear weather, cloudy weather, harsh sunlight, or a blizzard.

Lagging Tail

303 Copperajah
Copperderm Pokémon

Height: 9'10" Weight: 1433 lbs. p. 341

They came over from another region long ago and worked together with humans. Their green skin is resistant to water.

These Pokémon live in herds. Their trunks have incredible grip strength, strong enough to crush giant rocks into powder.

MAIN WAY TO OBTAIN
Catch one when it appears wandering on the Hammerlocke Hills after you become Champion. Or obtain a Cufant, then level it up to Lv. 34 or higher to evolve it into Copperajah.

Lagging Tail

304 Qwilfish
Balloon Pokémon

Height: 1'8" Weight: 8.6 lbs. p. 342

When faced with a larger opponent, it swallows as much water as it can to match the opponent's size.

The small spikes covering its body developed from scales. They inject a toxin that causes fainting.

MAIN WAY TO OBTAIN
Catch one when it appears on the water's surface on Route 9 or in the Bridge Field.

Poison Barb

Does not evolve

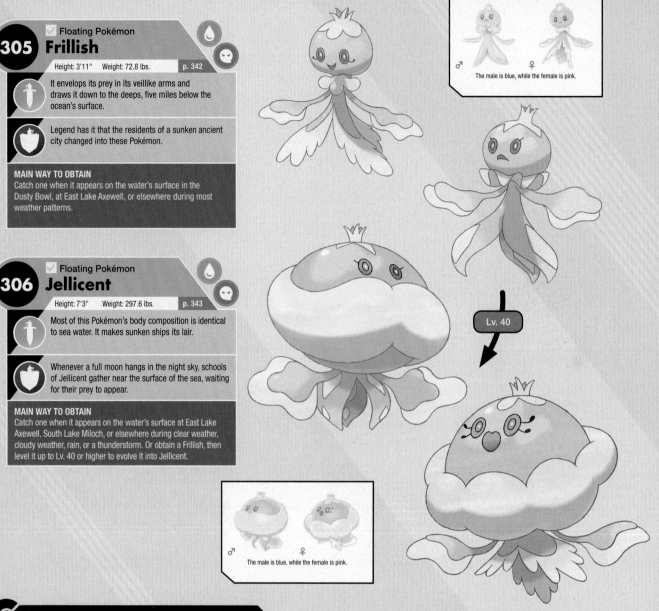

305 Frillish

☑ Floating Pokémon

Height: 3'11"　Weight: 72.8 lbs.　p. 342

It envelops its prey in its veillike arms and draws it down to the deeps, five miles below the ocean's surface.

Legend has it that the residents of a sunken ancient city changed into these Pokémon.

MAIN WAY TO OBTAIN
Catch one when it appears on the water's surface in the Dusty Bowl, at East Lake Axewell, or elsewhere during most weather patterns.

306 Jellicent

☑ Floating Pokémon

Height: 7'3"　Weight: 297.6 lbs.　p. 343

Most of this Pokémon's body composition is identical to sea water. It makes sunken ships its lair.

Whenever a full moon hangs in the night sky, schools of Jellicent gather near the surface of the sea, waiting for their prey to appear.

MAIN WAY TO OBTAIN
Catch one when it appears on the water's surface at East Lake Axewell, South Lake Miloch, or elsewhere during clear weather, cloudy weather, rain, or a thunderstorm. Or obtain a Frillish, then level it up to Lv. 40 or higher to evolve it into Jellicent.

♂　♀
The male is blue, while the female is pink.

Lv. 40

♂　♀
The male is blue, while the female is pink.

CRAMORANT'S DIFFERENT FORMS

If a Cramorant uses the move Surf or Dive during battle, it will come back with a little surprise! If its HP is above half its max, Cramorant will change form to its Gulping Form. Once in this form, it will spit out an Arrokuda it's caught when hit by an opponent's damage-dealing move, lowering that opponent's Defense and dealing it some damage in return. If the Cramorant's HP is at or below half of its max when it uses Surf or Dive, it will fish up a Pikachu and change to its Gorging Form! Launching a Pikachu at its opponent will deal some damage and inflict paralysis, too!

Cramorant (Gulping Form)

Cramorant's gluttony led it to try to swallow an Arrokuda whole, which in turn led to Cramorant getting an Arrokuda stuck in its throat.

The slightest shock is sometimes enough to get this Pokémon to spit out the Arrokuda lodged in its throat.

Cramorant (Gorging Form)

This Cramorant has accidentally gotten a Pikachu lodged in its gullet. Cramorant is choking a little, but it isn't really bothered.

The half-swallowed Pikachu is so startled that it isn't struggling yet, but it's still looking for a chance to strike back.

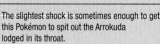

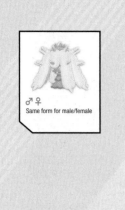

♂ ♀
Same form for male/female

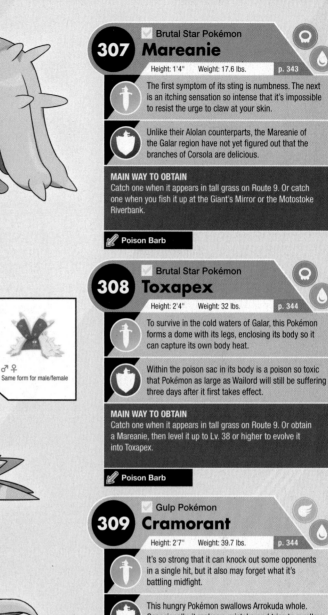

Lv. 38

♂ ♀
Same form for male/female

♂ ♀
Same form for male/female

Does not evolve

307 Mareanie

☑ Brutal Star Pokémon

Height: 1'4"   Weight: 17.6 lbs.   p. 343

The first symptom of its sting is numbness. The next is an itching sensation so intense that it's impossible to resist the urge to claw at your skin.

Unlike their Alolan counterparts, the Mareanie of the Galar region have not yet figured out that the branches of Corsola are delicious.

MAIN WAY TO OBTAIN
Catch one when it appears in tall grass on Route 9. Or catch one when you fish it up at the Giant's Mirror or the Motostoke Riverbank.

✎ Poison Barb

308 Toxapex

☑ Brutal Star Pokémon

Height: 2'4"   Weight: 32 lbs.   p. 344

To survive in the cold waters of Galar, this Pokémon forms a dome with its legs, enclosing its body so it can capture its own body heat.

Within the poison sac in its body is a poison so toxic that Pokémon as large as Wailord will still be suffering three days after it first takes effect.

MAIN WAY TO OBTAIN
Catch one when it appears in tall grass on Route 9. Or obtain a Mareanie, then level it up to Lv. 38 or higher to evolve it into Toxapex.

✎ Poison Barb

309 Cramorant

☑ Gulp Pokémon

Height: 2'7"   Weight: 39.7 lbs.   p. 344

It's so strong that it can knock out some opponents in a single hit, but it also may forget what it's battling midfight.

This hungry Pokémon swallows Arrokuda whole. Occasionally, it makes a mistake and tries to swallow a Pokémon other than its preferred prey.

MAIN WAY TO OBTAIN
Catch one when it appears as a random encounter in tall grass on Route 9. Or catch one when it appears wandering on Axew's Eye after you become Champion.

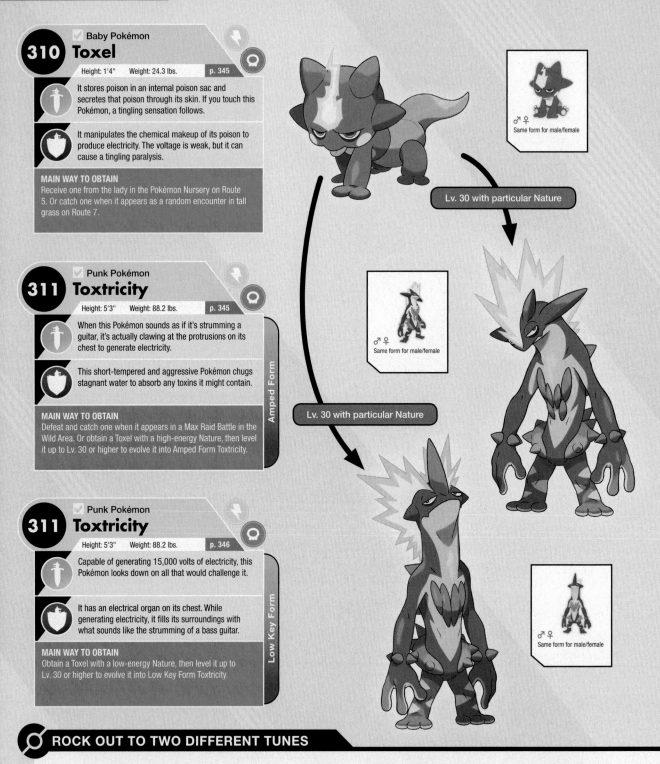

☑ Baby Pokémon

310 Toxel

Height: 1'4" Weight: 24.3 lbs. p. 345

It stores poison in an internal poison sac and secretes that poison through its skin. If you touch this Pokémon, a tingling sensation follows.

It manipulates the chemical makeup of its poison to produce electricity. The voltage is weak, but it can cause a tingling paralysis.

MAIN WAY TO OBTAIN
Receive one from the lady in the Pokémon Nursery on Route 5. Or catch one when it appears as a random encounter in tall grass on Route 7.

Same form for male/female

Lv. 30 with particular Nature

☑ Punk Pokémon

311 Toxtricity

Height: 5'3" Weight: 88.2 lbs. p. 345

When this Pokémon sounds as if it's strumming a guitar, it's actually clawing at the protrusions on its chest to generate electricity.

This short-tempered and aggressive Pokémon chugs stagnant water to absorb any toxins it might contain.

MAIN WAY TO OBTAIN
Defeat and catch one when it appears in a Max Raid Battle in the Wild Area. Or obtain a Toxel with a high-energy Nature, then level it up to Lv. 30 or higher to evolve it into Amped Form Toxtricity.

Amped Form

Same form for male/female

Lv. 30 with particular Nature

☑ Punk Pokémon

311 Toxtricity

Height: 5'3" Weight: 88.2 lbs. p. 346

Capable of generating 15,000 volts of electricity, this Pokémon looks down on all that would challenge it.

It has an electrical organ on its chest. While generating electricity, it fills its surroundings with what sounds like the strumming of a bass guitar.

MAIN WAY TO OBTAIN
Obtain a Toxel with a low-energy Nature, then level it up to Lv. 30 or higher to evolve it into Low Key Form Toxtricity.

Low Key Form

Same form for male/female

☮ ROCK OUT TO TWO DIFFERENT TUNES

Toxtricity is one of those Pokémon that has two forms, but in Toxtricity's case, the form it becomes depends on the Nature it had when it was a Toxel! Check the table below to see which form of Toxtricity your Toxel will evolve into!

Toxtricity (Amped Form)

Adamant, Brave, Docile, Hardy, Hasty, Impish, Jolly, Lax, Naive, Naughty, Quirky, Rash, Sassy

Toxtricity (Low Key Form)

Bashful, Bold, Calm, Careful, Gentle, Lonely, Mild, Modest, Quiet, Relaxed, Serious, Timid

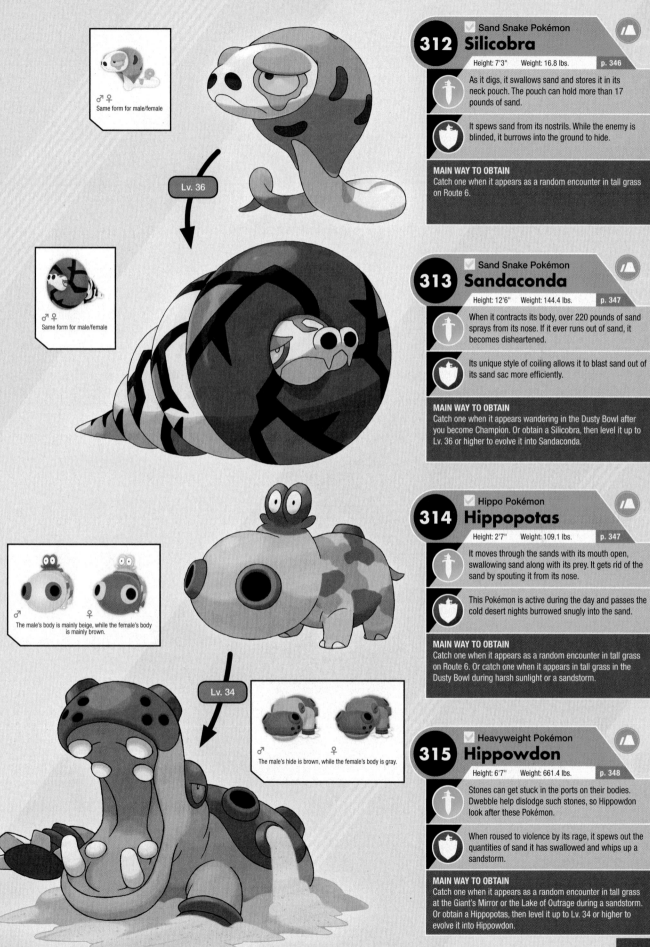

Same form for male/female

Lv. 36

Same form for male/female

312 Silicobra
Sand Snake Pokémon

Height: 7'3" Weight: 16.8 lbs. p. 346

As it digs, it swallows sand and stores it in its neck pouch. The pouch can hold more than 17 pounds of sand.

It spews sand from its nostrils. While the enemy is blinded, it burrows into the ground to hide.

MAIN WAY TO OBTAIN
Catch one when it appears as a random encounter in tall grass on Route 6.

313 Sandaconda
Sand Snake Pokémon

Height: 12'6" Weight: 144.4 lbs. p. 347

When it contracts its body, over 220 pounds of sand sprays from its nose. If it ever runs out of sand, it becomes disheartened.

Its unique style of coiling allows it to blast sand out of its sand sac more efficiently.

MAIN WAY TO OBTAIN
Catch one when it appears wandering in the Dusty Bowl after you become Champion. Or obtain a Silicobra, then level it up to Lv. 36 or higher to evolve it into Sandaconda.

314 Hippopotas
Hippo Pokémon

Height: 2'7" Weight: 109.1 lbs. p. 347

It moves through the sands with its mouth open, swallowing sand along with its prey. It gets rid of the sand by spouting it from its nose.

This Pokémon is active during the day and passes the cold desert nights burrowed snugly into the sand.

MAIN WAY TO OBTAIN
Catch one when it appears as a random encounter in tall grass on Route 6. Or catch one when it appears in tall grass in the Dusty Bowl during harsh sunlight or a sandstorm.

The male's body is mainly beige, while the female's body is mainly brown.

Lv. 34

The male's hide is brown, while the female's body is gray.

315 Hippowdon
Heavyweight Pokémon

Height: 6'7" Weight: 661.4 lbs. p. 348

Stones can get stuck in the ports on their bodies. Dwebble help dislodge such stones, so Hippowdon look after these Pokémon.

When roused to violence by its rage, it spews out the quantities of sand it has swallowed and whips up a sandstorm.

MAIN WAY TO OBTAIN
Catch one when it appears as a random encounter in tall grass at the Giant's Mirror or the Lake of Outrage during a sandstorm. Or obtain a Hippopotas, then level it up to Lv. 34 or higher to evolve it into Hippowdon.

316　Durant

☑ Iron Ant Pokémon

Height: 1'　　Weight: 72.8 lbs.　　p. 348

They lay their eggs deep inside their nests. When attacked by Heatmor, they retaliate using their massive mandibles.

With their large mandibles, these Pokémon can crunch their way through rock. They work together to protect their eggs from Sandaconda.

MAIN WAY TO OBTAIN
Catch one when it appears as a random encounter in tall grass on Route 6. Or catch one when it appears in tall grass at the Giant's Mirror or the Lake of Outrage during harsh sunlight.

♂ ♀
Same form for male/female

Does not evolve

317　Heatmor

☑ Anteater Pokémon

Height: 4'7"　　Weight: 127.9 lbs.　　p. 349

There's a hole in its tail that allows it to draw in the air it needs to keep its fire burning. If the hole gets blocked, this Pokémon will fall ill.

A flame serves as its tongue, melting through the hard shell of Durant so that Heatmor can devour their insides.

MAIN WAY TO OBTAIN
Catch one when it appears as a random encounter in tall grass on Route 6. Or catch one when it appears in tall grass at the Giant's Mirror or the Lake of Outrage during harsh sunlight.

♂ ♀
Same form for male/female

Does not evolve

318　Helioptile

☑ Generator Pokémon

Height: 1'8"　　Weight: 13.2 lbs.　　p. 349

When spread, the frills on its head act like solar panels, generating the power behind this Pokémon's electric moves.

The sun powers this Pokémon's electricity generation. Interruption of that process stresses Helioptile to the point of weakness.

MAIN WAY TO OBTAIN
Catch one when it appears in tall grass on Route 6. Or catch one when it appears in tall grass at the Giant's Mirror during a thunderstorm.

♂ ♀
Same form for male/female

Use Sun Stone

319　Heliolisk

☑ Generator Pokémon

Height: 3'3"　　Weight: 46.3 lbs.　　p. 350

A now-vanished desert culture treasured these Pokémon. Appropriately, when Heliolisk came to the Galar region, treasure came with them.

One Heliolisk basking in the sun with its frill outspread is all it would take to produce enough electricity to power a city.

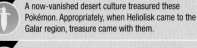

♂ ♀
Same form for male/female

♂ ♀
Same form for male/female

Does not evolve

♂ ♀
Same form for male/female

Lv. 35

♂ ♀
Same form for male/female

Lv. 45

♂ ♀
Same form for male/female

320 Hawlucha
☑ Wrestling Pokémon

Height: 2'7" Weight: 47.4 lbs. p. 350

It drives its opponents to exhaustion with its agile maneuvers, then ends the fight with a flashy finishing move.

It always strikes a pose before going for its finishing move. Sometimes opponents take advantage of that time to counterattack.

MAIN WAY TO OBTAIN
Catch one when it appears wandering on the Hammerlocke Hills.

King's Rock

321 Trapinch
☑ Ant Pit Pokémon

Height: 2'4" Weight: 33.1 lbs. p. 351

Its nest is a sloped, bowl-like pit in the desert. Once something has fallen in, there is no escape.

It makes an inescapable conical pit and lies in wait at the bottom for prey to come tumbling down.

MAIN WAY TO OBTAIN
Catch one when it appears in tall grass on Route 6.

Soft Sand

322 Vibrava
☑ Vibration Pokémon

Height: 3'7" Weight: 33.7 lbs. p. 351

The ultrasonic waves it generates by rubbing its two wings together cause severe headaches.

To help make its wings grow, it dissolves quantities of prey in its digestive juices and guzzles them down every day.

MAIN WAY TO OBTAIN
Obtain a Trapinch, then level it up to Lv. 35 or higher to evolve it into Vibrava.

323 Flygon
☑ Mystic Pokémon

Height: 6'7" Weight: 180.8 lbs. p. 352

This Pokémon hides in the heart of sandstorms it creates and seldom appears where people can see it.

It is nicknamed the Desert Spirit because the flapping of its wings sounds like a woman singing.

MAIN WAY TO OBTAIN
Catch one when it appears wandering in the Dusty Bowl during clear weather or a sandstorm. Or obtain a Vibrava, then level it up to Lv. 45 or higher to evolve it into Flygon.

324 Axew

☑ Tusk Pokémon

Height: 2' Weight: 39.7 lbs. p. 352

These Pokémon nest in the ground and use their tusks to crush hard berries. Crushing berries is also how they test each other's strength.

They play with each other by knocking their large tusks together. Their tusks break sometimes, but they grow back so quickly that it isn't a concern.

MAIN WAY TO OBTAIN
Catch one when it appears in tall grass on Route 6. Or catch one when it appears in tall grass on Axew's Eye during clear weather, cloudy weather, rain, or fog.

325 Fraxure

☑ Axe Jaw Pokémon

Height: 3'3" Weight: 79.4 lbs. p. 353

After battle, this Pokémon carefully sharpens its tusks on river rocks. It needs to take care of its tusks—if one breaks, it will never grow back.

Its skin is as hard as a suit of armor. Fraxure's favorite strategy is to tackle its opponents, stabbing them with its tusks at the same time.

MAIN WAY TO OBTAIN
Obtain an Axew, then level it up to Lv. 38 or higher to evolve it into Fraxure.

326 Haxorus

☑ Axe Jaw Pokémon

Height: 5'11" Weight: 232.6 lbs. p. 353

Its resilient tusks are its pride and joy. It licks up dirt to take in the minerals it needs to keep its tusks in top condition.

While usually kindhearted, it can be terrifying if angered. Tusks that can slice through steel beams are how Haxorus deals with its adversaries.

MAIN WAY TO OBTAIN
Catch one when it appears wandering on Axew's Eye during most weather patterns. Or obtain a Fraxure, then level it up to Lv. 48 or higher to evolve it into Haxorus.

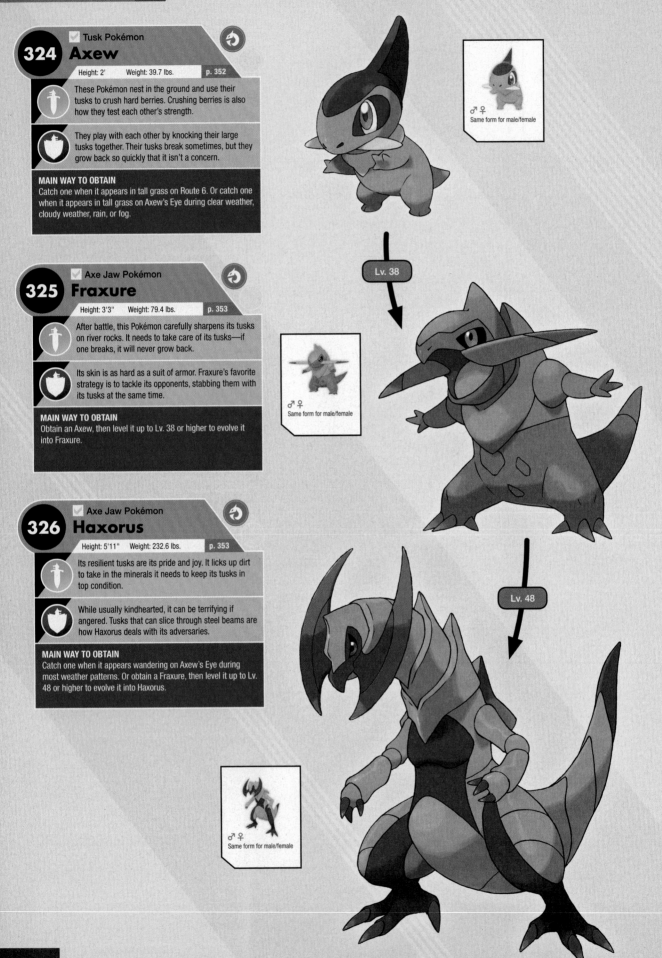

♂ ♀ Same form for male/female

Lv. 38

Lv. 48

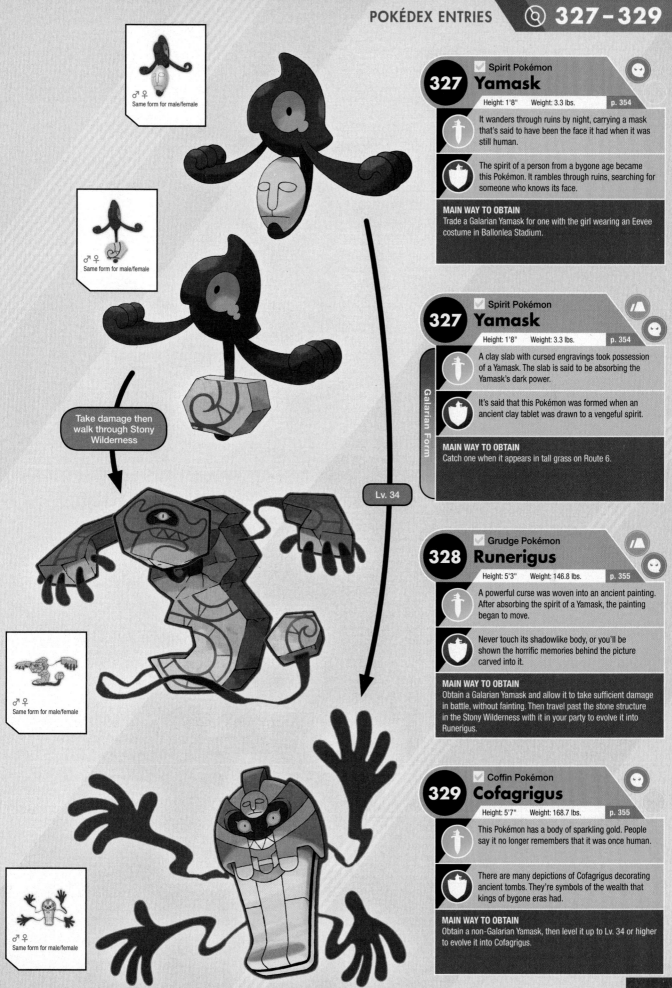

☑ Spirit Pokémon

327 Yamask

Height: 1'8" Weight: 3.3 lbs. p. 354

It wanders through ruins by night, carrying a mask that's said to have been the face it had when it was still human.

The spirit of a person from a bygone age became this Pokémon. It rambles through ruins, searching for someone who knows its face.

MAIN WAY TO OBTAIN
Trade a Galarian Yamask for one with the girl wearing an Eevee costume in Ballonlea Stadium.

☑ Spirit Pokémon

327 Yamask

Height: 1'8" Weight: 3.3 lbs. p. 354

Galarian Form

A clay slab with cursed engravings took possession of a Yamask. The slab is said to be absorbing the Yamask's dark power.

It's said that this Pokémon was formed when an ancient clay tablet was drawn to a vengeful spirit.

MAIN WAY TO OBTAIN
Catch one when it appears in tall grass on Route 6.

Same form for male/female

Same form for male/female

Take damage then walk through Stony Wilderness

Lv. 34

☑ Grudge Pokémon

328 Runerigus

Height: 5'3" Weight: 146.8 lbs. p. 355

A powerful curse was woven into an ancient painting. After absorbing the spirit of a Yamask, the painting began to move.

Never touch its shadowlike body, or you'll be shown the horrific memories behind the picture carved into it.

MAIN WAY TO OBTAIN
Obtain a Galarian Yamask and allow it to take sufficient damage in battle, without fainting. Then travel past the stone structure in the Stony Wilderness with it in your party to evolve it into Runerigus.

Same form for male/female

☑ Coffin Pokémon

329 Cofagrigus

Height: 5'7" Weight: 168.7 lbs. p. 355

This Pokémon has a body of sparkling gold. People say it no longer remembers that it was once human.

There are many depictions of Cofagrigus decorating ancient tombs. They're symbols of the wealth that kings of bygone eras had.

MAIN WAY TO OBTAIN
Obtain a non-Galarian Yamask, then level it up to Lv. 34 or higher to evolve it into Cofagrigus.

Same form for male/female

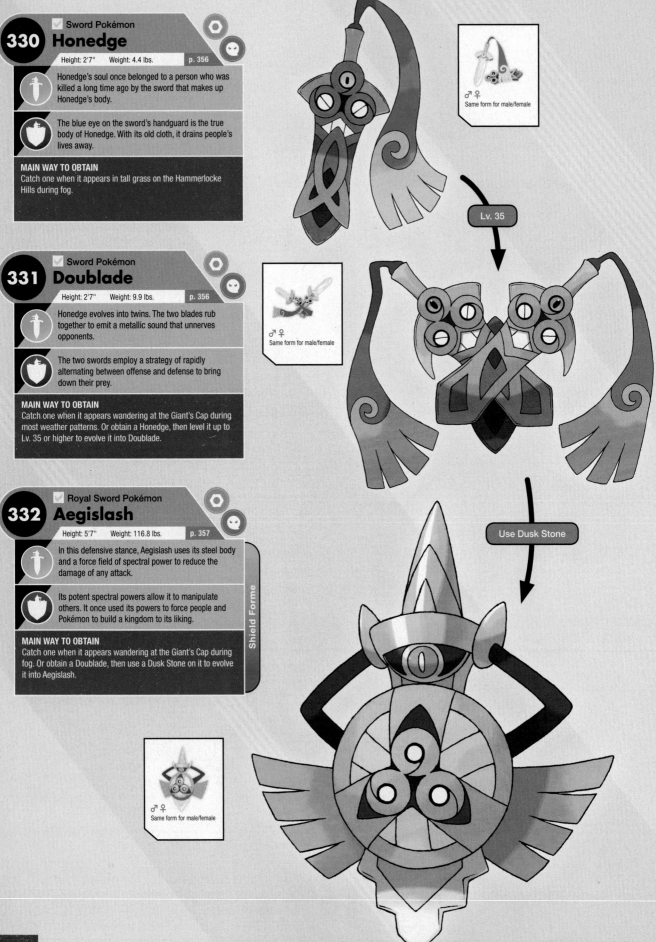

330 Honedge
☑ Sword Pokémon

Height: 2'7" Weight: 4.4 lbs. p. 356

Honedge's soul once belonged to a person who was killed a long time ago by the sword that makes up Honedge's body.

The blue eye on the sword's handguard is the true body of Honedge. With its old cloth, it drains people's lives away.

MAIN WAY TO OBTAIN
Catch one when it appears in tall grass on the Hammerlocke Hills during fog.

♂ ♀
Same form for male/female

Lv. 35

331 Doublade
☑ Sword Pokémon

Height: 2'7" Weight: 9.9 lbs. p. 356

Honedge evolves into twins. The two blades rub together to emit a metallic sound that unnerves opponents.

The two swords employ a strategy of rapidly alternating between offense and defense to bring down their prey.

MAIN WAY TO OBTAIN
Catch one when it appears wandering at the Giant's Cap during most weather patterns. Or obtain a Honedge, then level it up to Lv. 35 or higher to evolve it into Doublade.

♂ ♀
Same form for male/female

Use Dusk Stone

332 Aegislash
☑ Royal Sword Pokémon

Height: 5'7" Weight: 116.8 lbs. p. 357

In this defensive stance, Aegislash uses its steel body and a force field of spectral power to reduce the damage of any attack.

Its potent spectral powers allow it to manipulate others. It once used its powers to force people and Pokémon to build a kingdom to its liking.

MAIN WAY TO OBTAIN
Catch one when it appears wandering at the Giant's Cap during fog. Or obtain a Doublade, then use a Dusk Stone on it to evolve it into Aegislash.

Shield Forme

♂ ♀
Same form for male/female

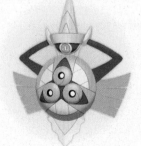

♂♀
Same form for male/female

Lv. 40

♂♀
Same form for male/female

333 Ponyta

☑ Unique Horn Pokémon

Height: 2'7"   Weight: 52.9 lbs.   p. 357

Galarian Form

Its small horn hides a healing power. With a few rubs from this Pokémon's horn, any slight wound you have will be healed.

This Pokémon will look into your eyes and read the contents of your heart. If it finds evil there, it promptly hides away.

MAIN WAY TO OBTAIN
In *Pokémon Shield*, catch one when it appears as a random encounter in tall grass in Glimwood Tangle. In *Pokémon Sword*, obtain it in a trade, as it does not appear in that game.

334 Rapidash

☑ Unique Horn Pokémon

Height: 5'7"   Weight: 176.4 lbs.   p. 358

Galarian Form

Little can stand up to its psycho cut. Unleashed from this Pokémon's horn, the move will punch a hole right through a thick metal sheet.

Brave and prideful, this Pokémon dashes airily through the forest, its steps aided by the psychic power stored in the fur on its fetlocks.

MAIN WAY TO OBTAIN
Obtain a Galarian Ponyta, then level it up to Lv. 40 or higher to evolve it into Galarian Rapidash.

UNSHEATHE THE BLADE!

You'll typically see Aegislash in its Shield Forme, which has good Defense and Sp. Defense stats but lower Attack and Sp. Atk. But did you know that Aegislash actually has a different form more geared toward offense? Just have it use a damage-dealing move in battle, and its Stance Change Ability will trigger, causing it to change into its Blade Forme! While in this form, Aegislash will have higher Attack and Sp. Atk, allowing it to deal extra damage. If you want to switch it back to Shield Forme, just use the move King's Shield!

Aegislash (Blade Forme)

SPECIES STRENGTHS

HP	▪▪▪▪
ATTACK	▪▪▪▪▪▪▪▪▪▪
DEFENSE	▪▪▪
SP. ATK	▪▪▪▪▪▪▪▪▪▪
SP. DEF	▪▪▪
SPEED	▪▪▪▪▪

This stance is dedicated to offense. It can cleave any opponent with the strength and weight of its steel blade.

Once upon a time, a king with an Aegislash reigned over the land. His Pokémon eventually drained him of life, and his kingdom fell with him.

Aegislash (Shield Forme)

SPECIES STRENGTHS

HP	▪▪▪▪
ATTACK	▪▪▪
DEFENSE	▪▪▪▪▪▪▪▪▪▪
SP. ATK	▪▪▪
SP. DEF	▪▪▪▪▪▪▪
SPEED	▪▪▪▪

335 Sinistea

☑ Black Tea Pokémon

Height: 4"   Weight: .4 lbs.   p. 358

This Pokémon is said to have been born when a lonely spirit possessed a cold, leftover cup of tea.

The teacup in which this Pokémon makes its home is a famous piece of antique tableware. Many forgeries are in circulation.

MAIN WAY TO OBTAIN
Catch one when it appears as a random encounter in tall grass in Glimwood Tangle.

Phony Form

♂ ♀
Same form for male/female

Use Cracked Pot

336 Polteageist

☑ Black Tea Pokémon

Height: 8"   Weight: .9 lbs.   p. 359

This species lives in antique teapots. Most pots are forgeries, but on rare occasions, an authentic work is found.

Leaving leftover black tea unattended is asking for this Pokémon to come along and pour itself into it, turning the tea into a new Polteageist.

MAIN WAY TO OBTAIN
Obtain a Phony Form Sinistea, then use a Cracked Pot on it to evolve it into Phony Form Polteageist.

Phony Form

♂ ♀
Same form for male/female

TIME FOR AN AUTHENTICITY CHECK

You might have caught a Sinistea in the wild, and maybe you've even used an item to evolve it into a Polteageist. But did you know both Pokémon actually have two forms? Sinistea can be caught in either its Phony Form or its Antique Form, and it will evolve into a Polteageist of the same form if the correct item is used. One form requires a Cracked Pot to evolve Sinistea into Polteageist, and the other requires a Chipped Pot. But what is different about these forms? Neither is any stronger than the other. It seems like there must be a difference somewhere, if only someone could find it...

Antique Form Sinistea

The swirl pattern in this Pokémon's body is its weakness. If it gets stirred, the swirl loses its shape, and Sinistea gets dizzy.

It absorbs the life force of those who drink it. It waits patiently, but opportunities are fleeting—it tastes so bad that it gets spat out immediately.

Antique Form Polteageist

Trainers Polteageist trusts will be allowed to experience its distinctive flavor and aroma firsthand by sampling just a tiny bit of its tea.

When angered, it launches tea from its body at the offender's mouth. The tea causes strong chills if swallowed.

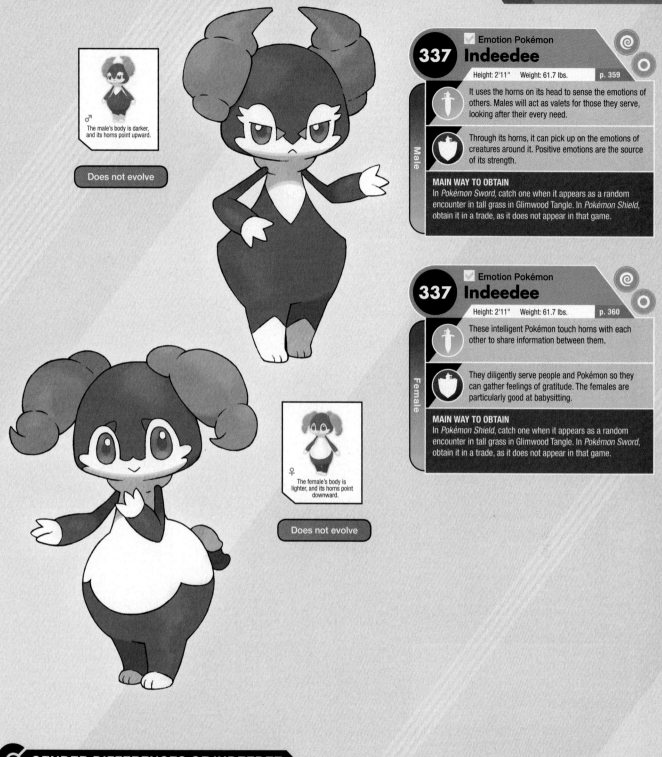

The male's body is darker, and its horns point upward.

Does not evolve

337 Indeedee
Emotion Pokémon

Height: 2'11"   Weight: 61.7 lbs.   p. 359

Male

It uses the horns on its head to sense the emotions of others. Males will act as valets for those they serve, looking after their every need.

Through its horns, it can pick up on the emotions of creatures around it. Positive emotions are the source of its strength.

MAIN WAY TO OBTAIN
In *Pokémon Sword*, catch one when it appears as a random encounter in tall grass in Glimwood Tangle. In *Pokémon Shield*, obtain it in a trade, as it does not appear in that game.

337 Indeedee
Emotion Pokémon

Height: 2'11"   Weight: 61.7 lbs.   p. 360

Female

These intelligent Pokémon touch horns with each other to share information between them.

They diligently serve people and Pokémon so they can gather feelings of gratitude. The females are particularly good at babysitting.

MAIN WAY TO OBTAIN
In *Pokémon Shield*, catch one when it appears as a random encounter in tall grass in Glimwood Tangle. In *Pokémon Sword*, obtain it in a trade, as it does not appear in that game.

The female's body is lighter, and its horns point downward.

Does not evolve

GENDER DIFFERENCES OF INDEEDEE

You may have already noticed that some Pokémon have different appearances based on their gender, and Indeedee is another example of this. Male Indeedee have a darker coloration and upward-pointing horns, while female Indeedee have a lighter coloration and horns that point downward. You can only catch male Indeedee in *Pokémon Sword*, while female Indeedee are exclusive to *Pokémon Shield*. If you want to get both, you'll have to trade with a friend!

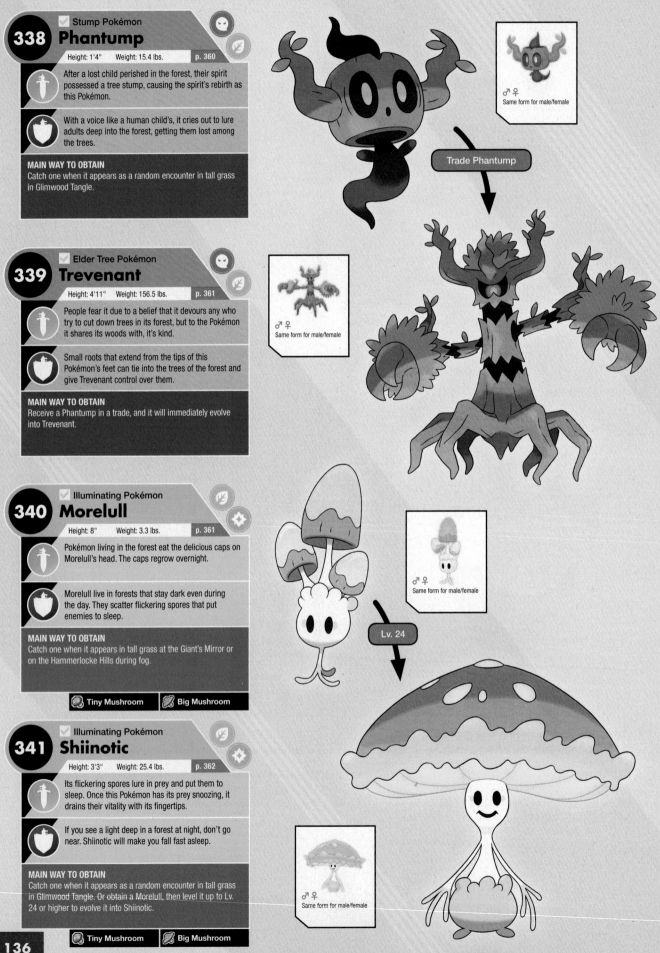

338 Phantump
☑ Stump Pokémon

Height: 1'4" Weight: 15.4 lbs. p. 360

After a lost child perished in the forest, their spirit possessed a tree stump, causing the spirit's rebirth as this Pokémon.

With a voice like a human child's, it cries out to lure adults deep into the forest, getting them lost among the trees.

MAIN WAY TO OBTAIN
Catch one when it appears as a random encounter in tall grass in Glimwood Tangle.

♂ ♀
Same form for male/female

Trade Phantump

339 Trevenant
☑ Elder Tree Pokémon

Height: 4'11" Weight: 156.5 lbs. p. 361

People fear it due to a belief that it devours any who try to cut down trees in its forest, but to the Pokémon it shares its woods with, it's kind.

Small roots that extend from the tips of this Pokémon's feet can tie into the trees of the forest and give Trevenant control over them.

MAIN WAY TO OBTAIN
Receive a Phantump in a trade, and it will immediately evolve into Trevenant.

♂ ♀
Same form for male/female

340 Morelull
☑ Illuminating Pokémon

Height: 8" Weight: 3.3 lbs. p. 361

Pokémon living in the forest eat the delicious caps on Morelull's head. The caps regrow overnight.

Morelull live in forests that stay dark even during the day. They scatter flickering spores that put enemies to sleep.

MAIN WAY TO OBTAIN
Catch one when it appears in tall grass at the Giant's Mirror or on the Hammerlocke Hills during fog.

🍄 Tiny Mushroom 🍄 Big Mushroom

♂ ♀
Same form for male/female

Lv. 24

341 Shiinotic
☑ Illuminating Pokémon

Height: 3'3" Weight: 25.4 lbs. p. 362

Its flickering spores lure in prey and put them to sleep. Once this Pokémon has its prey snoozing, it drains their vitality with its fingertips.

If you see a light deep in a forest at night, don't go near. Shiinotic will make you fall fast asleep.

MAIN WAY TO OBTAIN
Catch one when it appears as a random encounter in tall grass in Glimwood Tangle. Or obtain a Morelull, then level it up to Lv. 24 or higher to evolve it into Shiinotic.

🍄 Tiny Mushroom 🍄 Big Mushroom

♂ ♀
Same form for male/female

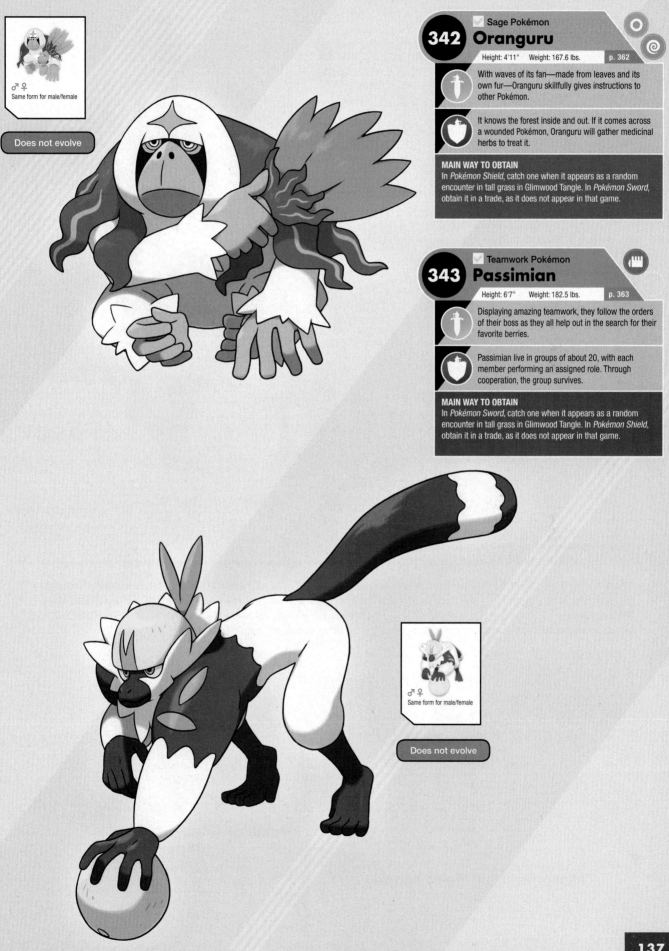

Same form for male/female ♂ ♀

Does not evolve

342 Oranguru
☑ Sage Pokémon

Height: 4'11" Weight: 167.6 lbs. p. 362

With waves of its fan—made from leaves and its own fur—Oranguru skillfully gives instructions to other Pokémon.

It knows the forest inside and out. If it comes across a wounded Pokémon, Oranguru will gather medicinal herbs to treat it.

MAIN WAY TO OBTAIN
In *Pokémon Shield*, catch one when it appears as a random encounter in tall grass in Glimwood Tangle. In *Pokémon Sword*, obtain it in a trade, as it does not appear in that game.

343 Passimian
☑ Teamwork Pokémon

Height: 6'7" Weight: 182.5 lbs. p. 363

Displaying amazing teamwork, they follow the orders of their boss as they all help out in the search for their favorite berries.

Passimian live in groups of about 20, with each member performing an assigned role. Through cooperation, the group survives.

MAIN WAY TO OBTAIN
In *Pokémon Sword*, catch one when it appears as a random encounter in tall grass in Glimwood Tangle. In *Pokémon Shield*, obtain it in a trade, as it does not appear in that game.

Same form for male/female ♂ ♀

Does not evolve

137

344 Morpeko

☑ Two-Sided Pokémon

Height: 1'   Weight: 6.6 lbs.   p. 363

As it eats the seeds stored up in its pocket-like pouches, this Pokémon is not just satisfying its constant hunger. It's also generating electricity.

It carries electrically roasted seeds with it as if they're precious treasures. No matter how much it eats, it always gets hungry again in short order.

MAIN WAY TO OBTAIN
Catch one when it appears in tall grass on Route 7 or when it appears as a random encounter in tall grass on Route 9 (Outer Spikemuth).

Full Belly Mode

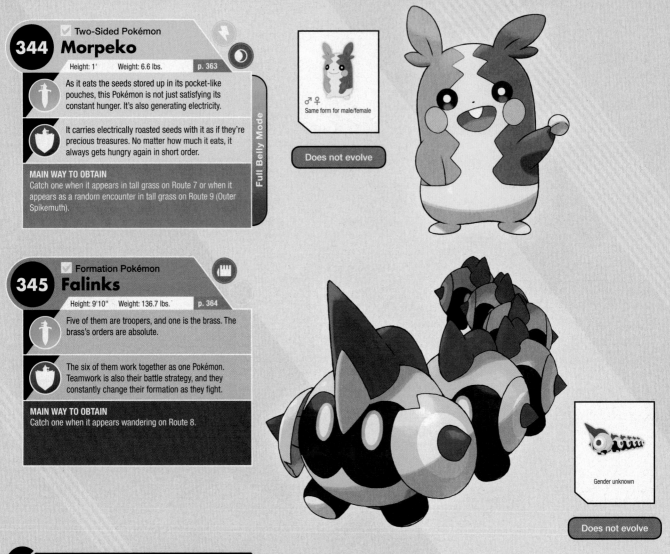

♂ ♀
Same form for male/female

Does not evolve

345 Falinks

☑ Formation Pokémon

Height: 9'10"   Weight: 136.7 lbs.   p. 364

Five of them are troopers, and one is the brass. The brass's orders are absolute.

The six of them work together as one Pokémon. Teamwork is also their battle strategy, and they constantly change their formation as they fight.

MAIN WAY TO OBTAIN
Catch one when it appears wandering on Route 8.

Gender unknown

Does not evolve

FORM CHANGING EVERY TURN

Morpeko is another example of a Pokémon with different forms, but unlike with most other examples, you're likely to see Morpeko change forms multiple times during battle—every turn, to be exact! Thanks to its Hunger Switch Ability, Morpeko will shift from its Full Belly Mode to Hangry Mode at the end of one turn, and then it'll shift the other way at the end of the next, and so on. The change in form doesn't impact Morpeko's type or stats, but it does change the type of its signature move, Aura Wheel, from Electric to Dark!

Morpeko (Full Belly Mode)

Morpeko (Hangry Mode)

Intense hunger drives it to extremes of violence, and the electricity in its cheek sacs has converted into a Dark-type energy.

Hunger hormones affect its temperament. Until its hunger is appeased, it gets up to all manner of evil deeds.

Same form for male/female

Does not evolve

Same form for male/female

Does not evolve

Same form for male/female

Does not evolve

☑ Placid Pokémon
346 Drampa

Height: 9'10"   Weight: 407.9 lbs.   p. 364

The mountains it calls home are nearly two miles in height. On rare occasions, it descends to play with the children living in the towns below.

Drampa is a kind and friendly Pokémon—up until it's angered. When that happens, it stirs up a gale and flattens everything around.

MAIN WAY TO OBTAIN
In *Pokémon Shield*, catch one when it appears as a random encounter in tall grass at the Lake of Outrage during a thunderstorm. In *Pokémon Sword*, obtain it in a trade, as it does not appear in that game.

🍈 Persim Berry

☑ Blast Turtle Pokémon
347 Turtonator

Height: 6'7"   Weight: 467.4 lbs.   p. 365

Explosive substances coat the shell on its back. Enemies that dare attack it will be blown away by an immense detonation.

Eating sulfur in its volcanic habitat is what causes explosive compounds to develop in its shell. Its droppings are also dangerously explosive.

MAIN WAY TO OBTAIN
In *Pokémon Sword*, catch one when it appears as a random encounter in tall grass at the Lake of Outrage during harsh sunlight. In *Pokémon Shield*, obtain it in a trade, as it does not appear in that game.

▬ Charcoal

☑ Roly-Poly Pokémon
348 Togedemaru

Height: 1'   Weight: 7.3 lbs.   p. 365

With the long hairs on its back, this Pokémon takes in electricity from other electric Pokémon. It stores what it absorbs in an electric sac.

When it's in trouble, it curls up into a ball, makes its fur spikes stand on end, and then discharges electricity indiscriminately.

MAIN WAY TO OBTAIN
Catch one when it appears in tall grass on Route 8. Or catch one when it appears as a random encounter in tall grass at the Lake of Outrage during a blizzard.

🌰 Electric Seed

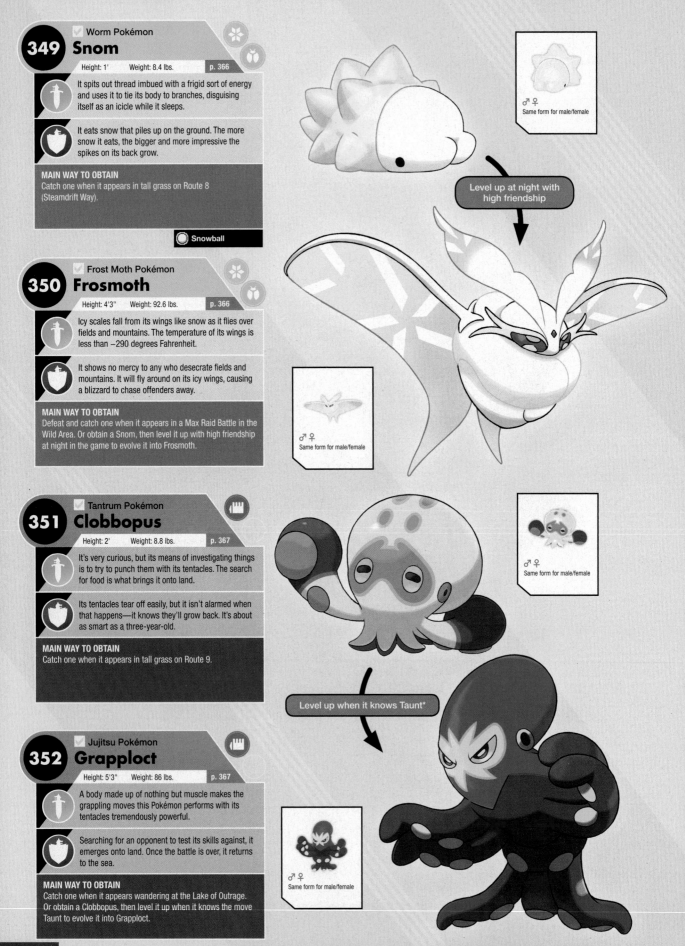

349 Snom
☑ Worm Pokémon

| Height: 1' | Weight: 8.4 lbs. | p. 366 |

It spits out thread imbued with a frigid sort of energy and uses it to tie its body to branches, disguising itself as an icicle while it sleeps.

It eats snow that piles up on the ground. The more snow it eats, the bigger and more impressive the spikes on its back grow.

MAIN WAY TO OBTAIN
Catch one when it appears in tall grass on Route 8 (Steamdrift Way).

◯ Snowball

♂ ♀
Same form for male/female

Level up at night with high friendship

350 Frosmoth
☑ Frost Moth Pokémon

| Height: 4'3" | Weight: 92.6 lbs. | p. 366 |

Icy scales fall from its wings like snow as it flies over fields and mountains. The temperature of its wings is less than −290 degrees Fahrenheit.

It shows no mercy to any who desecrate fields and mountains. It will fly around on its icy wings, causing a blizzard to chase offenders away.

MAIN WAY TO OBTAIN
Defeat and catch one when it appears in a Max Raid Battle in the Wild Area. Or obtain a Snom, then level it up with high friendship at night in the game to evolve it into Frosmoth.

♂ ♀
Same form for male/female

351 Clobbopus
☑ Tantrum Pokémon

| Height: 2' | Weight: 8.8 lbs. | p. 367 |

It's very curious, but its means of investigating things is to try to punch them with its tentacles. The search for food is what brings it onto land.

Its tentacles tear off easily, but it isn't alarmed when that happens—it knows they'll grow back. It's about as smart as a three-year-old.

MAIN WAY TO OBTAIN
Catch one when it appears in tall grass on Route 9.

♂ ♀
Same form for male/female

Level up when it knows Taunt*

352 Grapploct
☑ Jujitsu Pokémon

| Height: 5'3" | Weight: 86 lbs. | p. 367 |

A body made up of nothing but muscle makes the grappling moves this Pokémon performs with its tentacles tremendously powerful.

Searching for an opponent to test its skills against, it emerges onto land. Once the battle is over, it returns to the sea.

MAIN WAY TO OBTAIN
Catch one when it appears wandering at the Lake of Outrage. Or obtain a Clobbopus, then level it up when it knows the move Taunt to evolve it into Grapploct.

♂ ♀
Same form for male/female

*If your Clobbopus has forgotten the move Taunt, visit Jack in a Pokémon Center to have it remember the move once more.

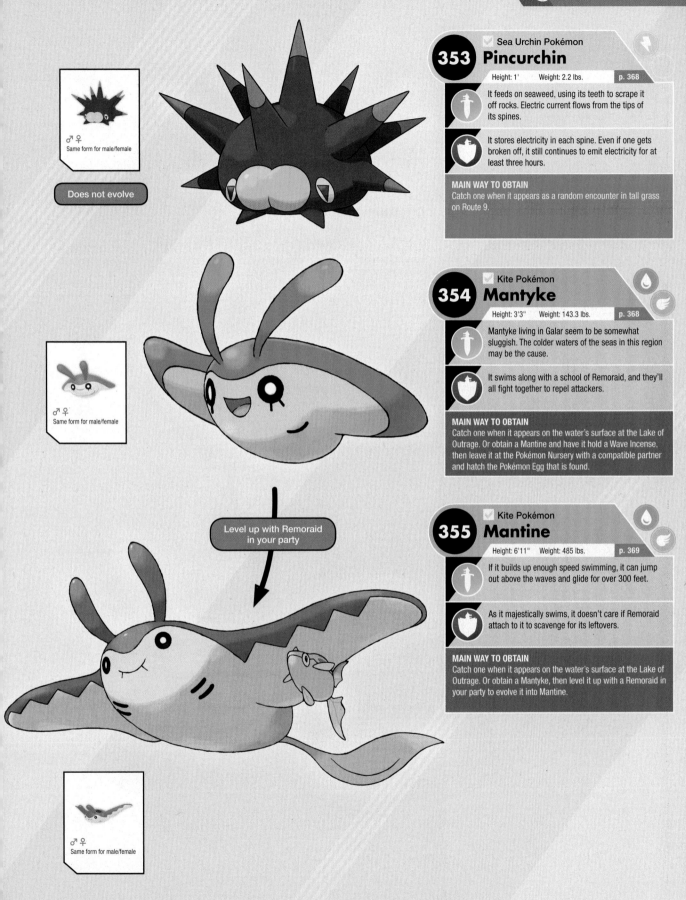

Same form for male/female

Does not evolve

353 Pincurchin
Sea Urchin Pokémon

Height: 1'   Weight: 2.2 lbs.   p. 368

It feeds on seaweed, using its teeth to scrape it off rocks. Electric current flows from the tips of its spines.

It stores electricity in each spine. Even if one gets broken off, it still continues to emit electricity for at least three hours.

MAIN WAY TO OBTAIN
Catch one when it appears as a random encounter in tall grass on Route 9.

Same form for male/female

Level up with Remoraid in your party

354 Mantyke
Kite Pokémon

Height: 3'3"   Weight: 143.3 lbs.   p. 368

Mantyke living in Galar seem to be somewhat sluggish. The colder waters of the seas in this region may be the cause.

It swims along with a school of Remoraid, and they'll all fight together to repel attackers.

MAIN WAY TO OBTAIN
Catch one when it appears on the water's surface at the Lake of Outrage. Or obtain a Mantine and have it hold a Wave Incense, then leave it at the Pokémon Nursery with a compatible partner and hatch the Pokémon Egg that is found.

355 Mantine
Kite Pokémon

Height: 6'11"   Weight: 485 lbs.   p. 369

If it builds up enough speed swimming, it can jump out above the waves and glide for over 300 feet.

As it majestically swims, it doesn't care if Remoraid attach to it to scavenge for its leftovers.

MAIN WAY TO OBTAIN
Catch one when it appears on the water's surface at the Lake of Outrage. Or obtain a Mantyke, then level it up with a Remoraid in your party to evolve it into Mantine.

Same form for male/female

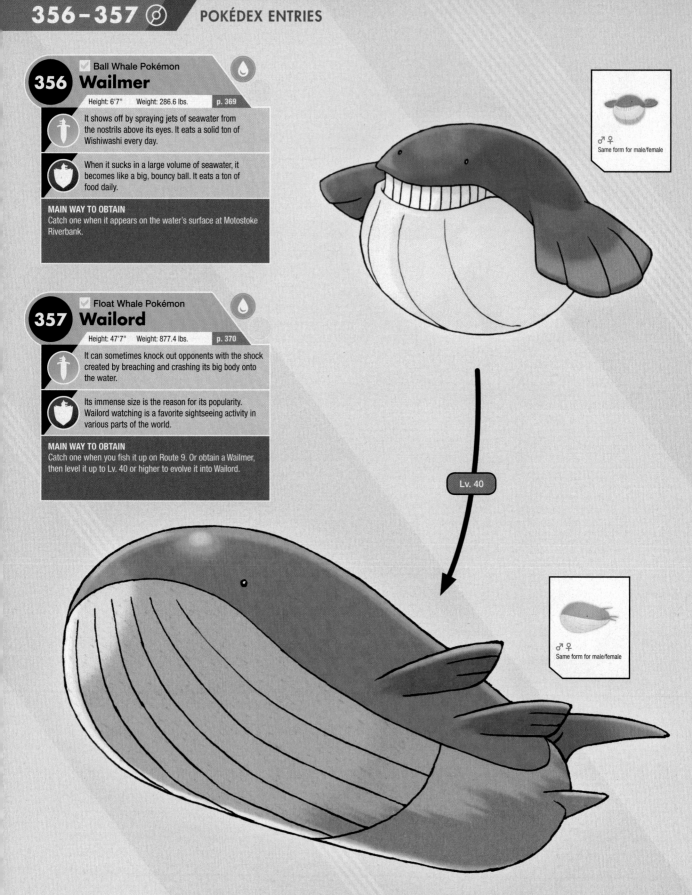

☑ Ball Whale Pokémon

356 Wailmer

| Height: 6'7" | Weight: 286.6 lbs. | p. 369 |

It shows off by spraying jets of seawater from the nostrils above its eyes. It eats a solid ton of Wishiwashi every day.

When it sucks in a large volume of seawater, it becomes like a big, bouncy ball. It eats a ton of food daily.

MAIN WAY TO OBTAIN
Catch one when it appears on the water's surface at Motostoke Riverbank.

♂ ♀
Same form for male/female

☑ Float Whale Pokémon

357 Wailord

| Height: 47'7" | Weight: 877.4 lbs. | p. 370 |

It can sometimes knock out opponents with the shock created by breaching and crashing its big body onto the water.

Its immense size is the reason for its popularity. Wailord watching is a favorite sightseeing activity in various parts of the world.

MAIN WAY TO OBTAIN
Catch one when you fish it up on Route 9. Or obtain a Wailmer, then level it up to Lv. 40 or higher to evolve it into Wailord.

Lv. 40

♂ ♀
Same form for male/female

♂ ♀
Same form for male/female

Lv. 37

♂ ♀
Same form for male/female

Gender unknown

Does not evolve

358 Bergmite
Ice Chunk Pokémon

Height: 3'3" Weight: 219.4 lbs. p. 370

They chill the air around them to −150 degrees Fahrenheit, freezing the water in the air into ice that they use as armor.

This Pokémon lives in areas of frigid cold. It secures itself to the back of an Avalugg by freezing its feet in place.

MAIN WAY TO OBTAIN
Catch one when it appears in tall grass on Route 9.

359 Avalugg
Iceberg Pokémon

Height: 6'7" Weight: 1113.3 lbs. p. 371

At high latitudes, this Pokémon can be found with clusters of Bergmite on its back as it swims among the icebergs.

As Avalugg moves about during the day, the cracks in its body deepen. The Pokémon's body returns to a pristine state overnight.

MAIN WAY TO OBTAIN
Catch one when it appears wandering at the Lake of Outrage during snow or a blizzard. Or obtain a Bergmite, then level it up to Lv. 37 or higher to evolve it into Avalugg.

360 Dhelmise
Sea Creeper Pokémon

Height: 12'10" Weight: 463 lbs. p. 371

After a piece of seaweed merged with debris from a sunken ship, it was reborn as this ghost Pokémon.

After lowering its anchor, it waits for its prey. It catches large Wailord and drains their life-force.

MAIN WAY TO OBTAIN
Catch one when it appears in tall grass on Route 9.

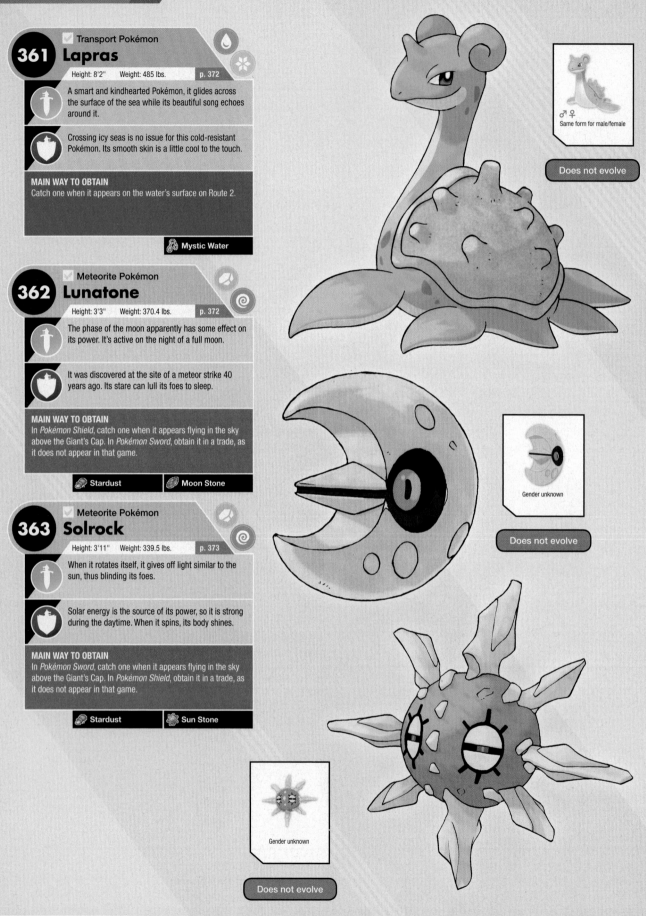

361 Lapras

☑ Transport Pokémon

Height: 8'2"   Weight: 485 lbs.   p. 372

A smart and kindhearted Pokémon, it glides across the surface of the sea while its beautiful song echoes around it.

Crossing icy seas is no issue for this cold-resistant Pokémon. Its smooth skin is a little cool to the touch.

MAIN WAY TO OBTAIN
Catch one when it appears on the water's surface on Route 2.

Mystic Water

♂ ♀
Same form for male/female

Does not evolve

362 Lunatone

☑ Meteorite Pokémon

Height: 3'3"   Weight: 370.4 lbs.   p. 372

The phase of the moon apparently has some effect on its power. It's active on the night of a full moon.

It was discovered at the site of a meteor strike 40 years ago. Its stare can lull its foes to sleep.

MAIN WAY TO OBTAIN
In *Pokémon Shield*, catch one when it appears flying in the sky above the Giant's Cap. In *Pokémon Sword*, obtain it in a trade, as it does not appear in that game.

Stardust   Moon Stone

Gender unknown

Does not evolve

363 Solrock

☑ Meteorite Pokémon

Height: 3'11"   Weight: 339.5 lbs.   p. 373

When it rotates itself, it gives off light similar to the sun, thus blinding its foes.

Solar energy is the source of its power, so it is strong during the daytime. When it spins, its body shines.

MAIN WAY TO OBTAIN
In *Pokémon Sword*, catch one when it appears flying in the sky above the Giant's Cap. In *Pokémon Shield*, obtain it in a trade, as it does not appear in that game.

Stardust   Sun Stone

Gender unknown

Does not evolve

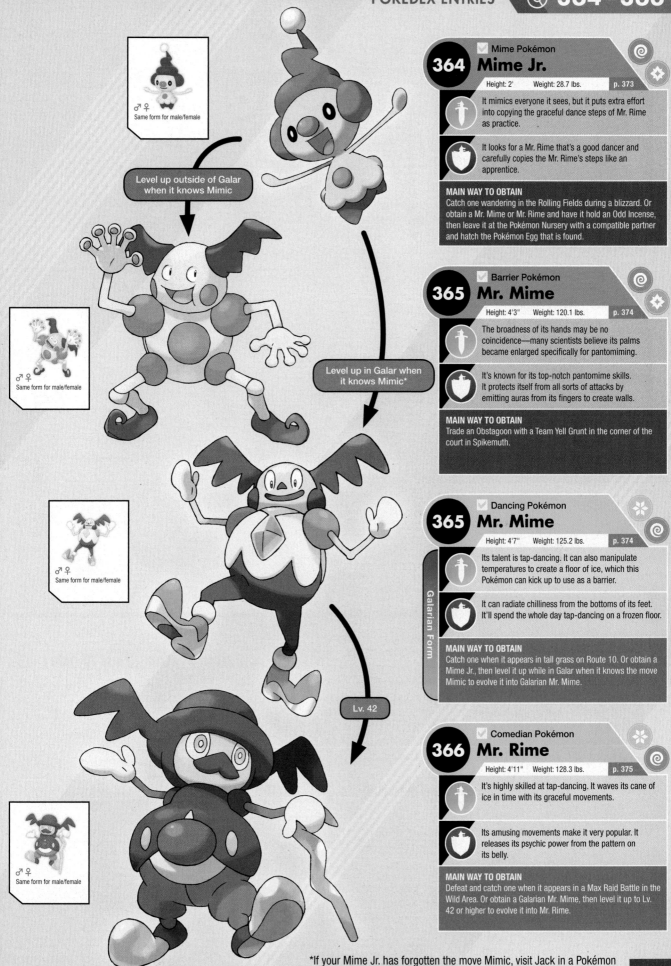

Same form for male/female ♂♀

Level up outside of Galar
when it knows Mimic

Same form for male/female ♂♀

Level up in Galar when
it knows Mimic*

Same form for male/female ♂♀

Lv. 42

Same form for male/female ♂♀

Galarian Form

364 Mime Pokémon
Mime Jr.

| Height: 2' | Weight: 28.7 lbs. | p. 373 |

It mimics everyone it sees, but it puts extra effort into copying the graceful dance steps of Mr. Rime as practice.

It looks for a Mr. Rime that's a good dancer and carefully copies the Mr. Rime's steps like an apprentice.

MAIN WAY TO OBTAIN
Catch one wandering in the Rolling Fields during a blizzard. Or obtain a Mr. Mime or Mr. Rime and have it hold an Odd Incense, then leave it at the Pokémon Nursery with a compatible partner and hatch the Pokémon Egg that is found.

365 Barrier Pokémon
Mr. Mime

| Height: 4'3" | Weight: 120.1 lbs. | p. 374 |

The broadness of its hands may be no coincidence—many scientists believe its palms became enlarged specifically for pantomiming.

It's known for its top-notch pantomime skills. It protects itself from all sorts of attacks by emitting auras from its fingers to create walls.

MAIN WAY TO OBTAIN
Trade an Obstagoon with a Team Yell Grunt in the corner of the court in Spikemuth.

365 Dancing Pokémon
Mr. Mime

| Height: 4'7" | Weight: 125.2 lbs. | p. 374 |

Its talent is tap-dancing. It can also manipulate temperatures to create a floor of ice, which this Pokémon can kick up to use as a barrier.

It can radiate chilliness from the bottoms of its feet. It'll spend the whole day tap-dancing on a frozen floor.

MAIN WAY TO OBTAIN
Catch one when it appears in tall grass on Route 10. Or obtain a Mime Jr., then level it up while in Galar when it knows the move Mimic to evolve it into Galarian Mr. Mime.

366 Comedian Pokémon
Mr. Rime

| Height: 4'11" | Weight: 128.3 lbs. | p. 375 |

It's highly skilled at tap-dancing. It waves its cane of ice in time with its graceful movements.

Its amusing movements make it very popular. It releases its psychic power from the pattern on its belly.

MAIN WAY TO OBTAIN
Defeat and catch one when it appears in a Max Raid Battle in the Wild Area. Or obtain a Galarian Mr. Mime, then level it up to Lv. 42 or higher to evolve it into Mr. Rime.

*If your Mime Jr. has forgotten the move Mimic, visit Jack in a Pokémon Center to have it remember the move once more.

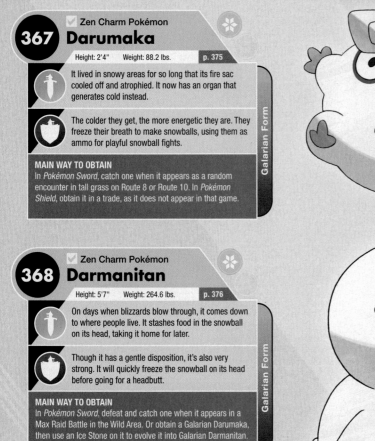

367 Darumaka

☑ Zen Charm Pokémon

Height: 2'4"   Weight: 88.2 lbs.   p. 375

It lived in snowy areas for so long that its fire sac cooled off and atrophied. It now has an organ that generates cold instead.

The colder they get, the more energetic they are. They freeze their breath to make snowballs, using them as ammo for playful snowball fights.

MAIN WAY TO OBTAIN
In *Pokémon Sword*, catch one when it appears as a random encounter in tall grass on Route 8 or Route 10. In *Pokémon Shield*, obtain it in a trade, as it does not appear in that game.

Galarian Form

Same form for male/female ♂♀

Use Ice Stone

368 Darmanitan

☑ Zen Charm Pokémon

Height: 5'7"   Weight: 264.6 lbs.   p. 376

On days when blizzards blow through, it comes down to where people live. It stashes food in the snowball on its head, taking it home for later.

Though it has a gentle disposition, it's also very strong. It will quickly freeze the snowball on its head before going for a headbutt.

MAIN WAY TO OBTAIN
In *Pokémon Sword*, defeat and catch one when it appears in a Max Raid Battle in the Wild Area. Or obtain a Galarian Darumaka, then use an Ice Stone on it to evolve it into Galarian Darmanitan.

Galarian Form

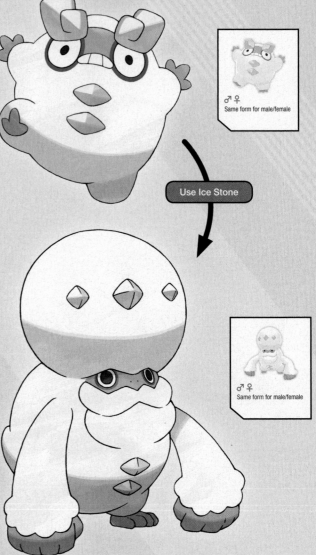

Same form for male/female ♂♀

DARMANITAN'S MODE CHANGE

Darmanitan is a Pokémon that evolves from Darumaka. The Darmanitan you find in the Galar region is the Galarian Form—but Galarian Form Darmanitan can also change modes during battle to reveal yet another form! As long as your Darmanitan has the Zen Mode Hidden Ability, it will change into its Zen Mode once its HP gets reduced to half or less during battle. In its Zen Mode, Darmanitan will get a significant boost to its Attack and a huge Speed boost, too! It will also become a dual-type Pokémon, gaining the Fire type in addition to the Ice type of its Standard Mode. Take advantage of this sudden type change to catch your opponents off guard!

Darmanitan (Zen Mode)

SPECIES STRENGTHS

HP	▊▊▊▊▊▊▊
ATTACK	▊▊▊▊▊▊▊▊▊▊▊
DEFENSE	▊▊▊▊
SP. ATK	▊▊
SP. DEF	▊▊▊▊
SPEED	▊▊▊▊▊▊▊▊▊

Anger has reignited its atrophied flame sac. This Pokémon spews fire everywhere as it rampages indiscriminately.

Darmanitan takes this form when enraged. It won't stop spewing flames until its rage has settled, even if its body starts to melt.

Darmanitan (Standard Mode)

SPECIES STRENGTHS

HP	▊▊▊▊▊▊▊
ATTACK	▊▊▊▊▊▊▊▊▊
DEFENSE	▊▊▊▊
SP. ATK	▊▊
SP. DEF	▊▊▊▊
SPEED	▊▊▊▊▊▊▊

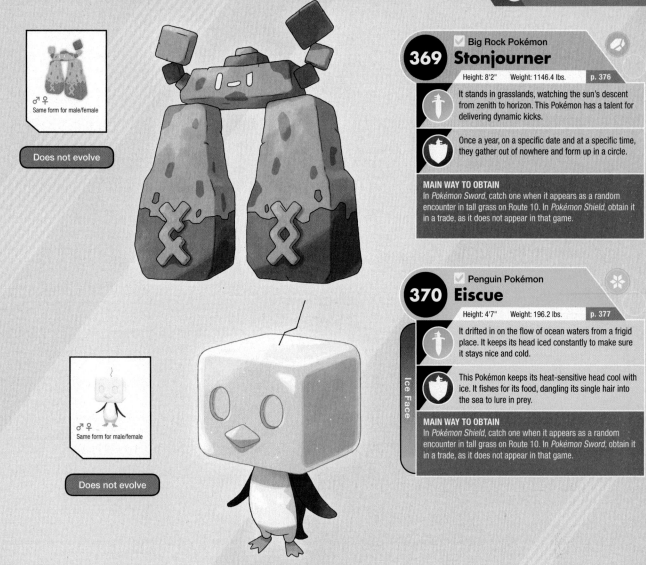

Same form for male/female

Does not evolve

Big Rock Pokémon

369 Stonjourner

Height: 8'2"   Weight: 1146.4 lbs.   p. 376

It stands in grasslands, watching the sun's descent from zenith to horizon. This Pokémon has a talent for delivering dynamic kicks.

Once a year, on a specific date and at a specific time, they gather out of nowhere and form up in a circle.

MAIN WAY TO OBTAIN
In *Pokémon Sword*, catch one when it appears as a random encounter in tall grass on Route 10. In *Pokémon Shield*, obtain it in a trade, as it does not appear in that game.

Penguin Pokémon

370 Eiscue

Height: 4'7"   Weight: 196.2 lbs.   p. 377

Ice Face

It drifted in on the flow of ocean waters from a frigid place. It keeps its head iced constantly to make sure it stays nice and cold.

This Pokémon keeps its heat-sensitive head cool with ice. It fishes for its food, dangling its single hair into the sea to lure in prey.

MAIN WAY TO OBTAIN
In *Pokémon Shield*, catch one when it appears as a random encounter in tall grass on Route 10. In *Pokémon Sword*, obtain it in a trade, as it does not appear in that game.

Same form for male/female

Does not evolve

ICE OR NOICE?

Eiscue is one of those Pokémon that has an Ability that allows it to change form. When it enters battle, it will be rocking its supercool Ice Face. Once it's hit with a physical move, though, its Ice Face shatters, revealing its Noice Face while negating any damage it might take from the move. Now it's stuck with its Noice Face—unless you're able to change the weather to hail. If hail is falling, it will help Eiscue switch back to its Ice Face! Each of these forms also comes with its own stat changes, shown below.

Eiscue (Noice Face)

SPECIES STRENGTHS

HP
ATTACK
DEFENSE
SP. ATK
SP. DEF
SPEED

The ice covering this Pokémon's face has shattered, revealing a slightly worried expression that many people are enamored with.

The hair on its head connects to the surface of its brain. When this Pokémon has something on its mind, its hair chills the air around it.

Eiscue (Ice Face)

SPECIES STRENGTHS

HP
ATTACK
DEFENSE
SP. ATK
SP. DEF
SPEED

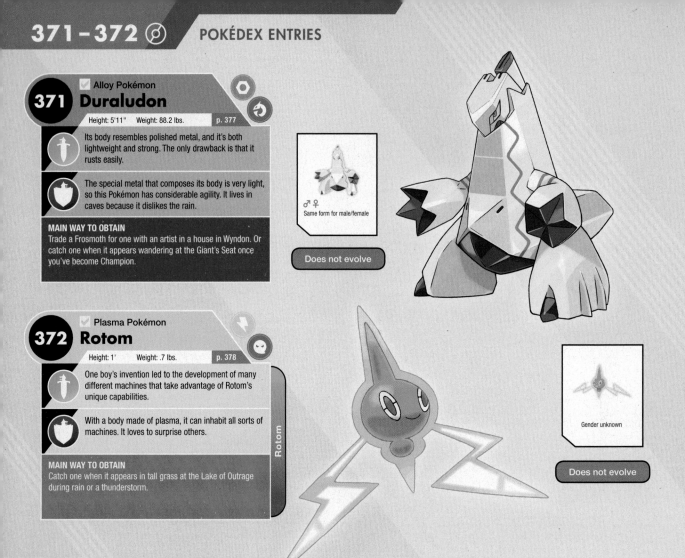

371 ☑ Alloy Pokémon
Duraludon

Height: 5'11"   Weight: 88.2 lbs.   p. 377

Its body resembles polished metal, and it's both lightweight and strong. The only drawback is that it rusts easily.

The special metal that composes its body is very light, so this Pokémon has considerable agility. It lives in caves because it dislikes the rain.

MAIN WAY TO OBTAIN
Trade a Frosmoth for one with an artist in a house in Wyndon. Or catch one when it appears wandering at the Giant's Seat once you've become Champion.

♂ ♀
Same form for male/female

Does not evolve

372 ☑ Plasma Pokémon
Rotom

Height: 1'   Weight: .7 lbs.   p. 378

One boy's invention led to the development of many different machines that take advantage of Rotom's unique capabilities.

With a body made of plasma, it can inhabit all sorts of machines. It loves to surprise others.

MAIN WAY TO OBTAIN
Catch one when it appears in tall grass at the Lake of Outrage during rain or a thunderstorm.

Rotom

Gender unknown

Does not evolve

⊘ ROTOM'S MANY FORMS

Rotom can take up residence in more than just your Rotom Phone—if you get the Rotom Catalog item in Wyndon, you can use it from your Bag to have a Rotom you've obtained possess all kinds of other machines as well! These form changes will give it a small boost to its Attack and Sp. Atk stats and a bigger boost to its Defense and Sp. Def. It will even gain a new type and a new move to boot.

SPECIES STRENGTHS

HP		SP. ATK
ATTACK		SP. DEF
DEFENSE		SPEED

Heat Rotom
Use the Rotom Catalog and have Rotom possess a microwave oven.

Learns Overheat

Wash Rotom
Use the Rotom Catalog and have Rotom possess a washing machine.

Learns Hydro Pump

Frost Rotom
Use the Rotom Catalog and have Rotom possess a refrigerator.

Learns Blizzard

Fan Rotom
Use the Rotom Catalog and have Rotom possess an electric fan.

Learns Air Slash

Mow Rotom
Use the Rotom Catalog and have Rotom possess a lawn mower.

Learns Leaf Storm

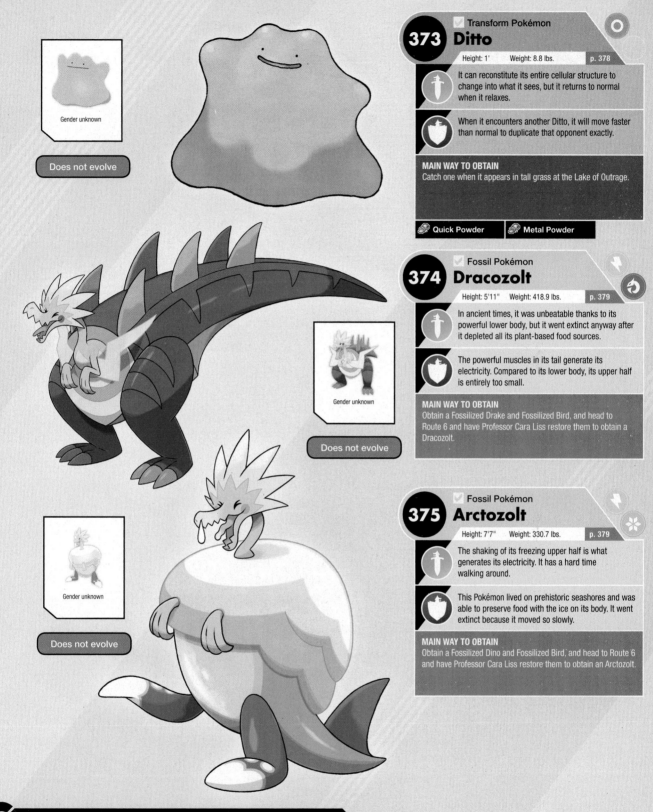

Gender unknown

Does not evolve

373 Ditto
☑ Transform Pokémon

| Height: 1' | Weight: 8.8 lbs. | p. 378 |

It can reconstitute its entire cellular structure to change into what it sees, but it returns to normal when it relaxes.

When it encounters another Ditto, it will move faster than normal to duplicate that opponent exactly.

MAIN WAY TO OBTAIN
Catch one when it appears in tall grass at the Lake of Outrage.

🔩 Quick Powder   🔩 Metal Powder

374 Dracozolt
☑ Fossil Pokémon

| Height: 5'11" | Weight: 418.9 lbs. | p. 379 |

In ancient times, it was unbeatable thanks to its powerful lower body, but it went extinct anyway after it depleted all its plant-based food sources.

The powerful muscles in its tail generate its electricity. Compared to its lower body, its upper half is entirely too small.

MAIN WAY TO OBTAIN
Obtain a Fossilized Drake and Fossilized Bird, and head to Route 6 and have Professor Cara Liss restore them to obtain a Dracozolt.

Gender unknown

Does not evolve

375 Arctozolt
☑ Fossil Pokémon

| Height: 7'7" | Weight: 330.7 lbs. | p. 379 |

The shaking of its freezing upper half is what generates its electricity. It has a hard time walking around.

This Pokémon lived on prehistoric seashores and was able to preserve food with the ice on its body. It went extinct because it moved so slowly.

MAIN WAY TO OBTAIN
Obtain a Fossilized Dino and Fossilized Bird, and head to Route 6 and have Professor Cara Liss restore them to obtain an Arctozolt.

Gender unknown

Does not evolve

YOUR BEST FRIEND WHEN LOOKING FOR EGGS

Ditto is an unassuming Pokémon by any standard, with low stats and only one move it can learn. But there's more to this wobbly little fellow—it can pair up with any other Pokémon to find Eggs, so long as that Pokémon isn't in the Egg Group titled No Eggs Discovered. Any Egg it finds will always hatch into the non-Ditto Pokémon while being able to inherit its individual strengths from Ditto. So if you have a Ditto with great individual strengths, then it's time to try to find some Eggs at the Pokémon Nurseries!

376 Dracovish

☑ Fossil Pokémon

Height: 7'7" Weight: 474 lbs. p. 380

Powerful legs and jaws made it the apex predator of its time. Its own overhunting of its prey was what drove it to extinction.

Its mighty legs are capable of running at speeds exceeding 40 mph, but this Pokémon can't breathe unless it's underwater.

MAIN WAY TO OBTAIN
Obtain a Fossilized Drake and Fossilized Fish, and head to Route 6 and have Professor Cara Liss restore them to obtain a Dracovish.

Gender unknown

Does not evolve

377 Arctovish

☑ Fossil Pokémon

Height: 6'7" Weight: 385.8 lbs. p. 380

Though it's able to capture prey by freezing its surroundings, it has trouble eating the prey afterward because its mouth is on top of its head.

The skin on its face is impervious to attack, but breathing difficulties made this Pokémon go extinct anyway.

MAIN WAY TO OBTAIN
Obtain a Fossilized Dino and Fossilized Fish, and head to Route 6 and have Professor Cara Liss restore them to obtain an Arctovish.

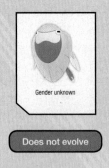

Gender unknown

Does not evolve

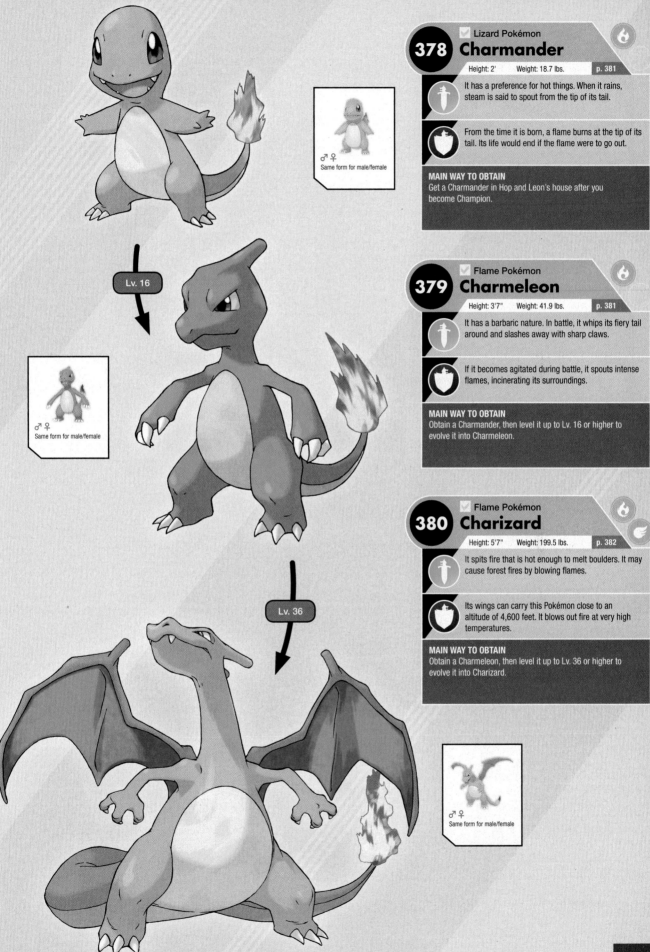

♂ ♀
Same form for male/female

378 ☑ Lizard Pokémon
Charmander
| Height: 2' | Weight: 18.7 lbs. | p. 381 |

It has a preference for hot things. When it rains, steam is said to spout from the tip of its tail.

From the time it is born, a flame burns at the tip of its tail. Its life would end if the flame were to go out.

MAIN WAY TO OBTAIN
Get a Charmander in Hop and Leon's house after you become Champion.

Lv. 16

♂ ♀
Same form for male/female

379 ☑ Flame Pokémon
Charmeleon
| Height: 3'7" | Weight: 41.9 lbs. | p. 381 |

It has a barbaric nature. In battle, it whips its fiery tail around and slashes away with sharp claws.

If it becomes agitated during battle, it spouts intense flames, incinerating its surroundings.

MAIN WAY TO OBTAIN
Obtain a Charmander, then level it up to Lv. 16 or higher to evolve it into Charmeleon.

Lv. 36

380 ☑ Flame Pokémon
Charizard
| Height: 5'7" | Weight: 199.5 lbs. | p. 382 |

It spits fire that is hot enough to melt boulders. It may cause forest fires by blowing flames.

Its wings can carry this Pokémon close to an altitude of 4,600 feet. It blows out fire at very high temperatures.

MAIN WAY TO OBTAIN
Obtain a Charmeleon, then level it up to Lv. 36 or higher to evolve it into Charizard.

♂ ♀
Same form for male/female

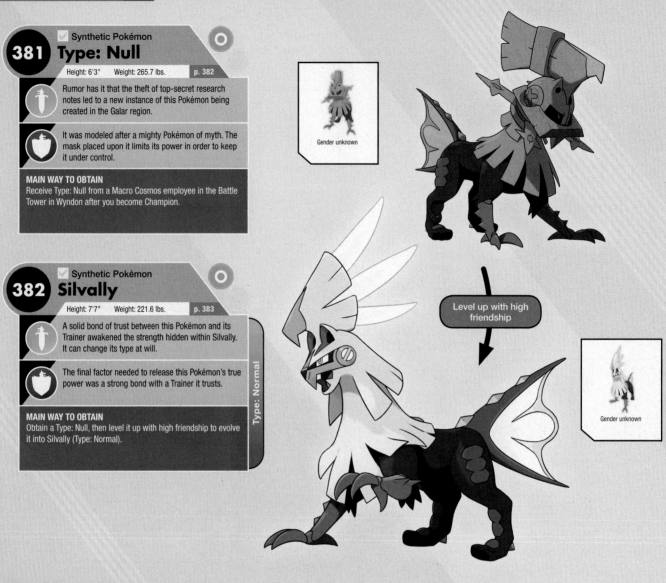

381 ☑ Synthetic Pokémon
Type: Null

Height: 6'3"   Weight: 265.7 lbs.   p. 382

Rumor has it that the theft of top-secret research notes led to a new instance of this Pokémon being created in the Galar region.

It was modeled after a mighty Pokémon of myth. The mask placed upon it limits its power in order to keep it under control.

MAIN WAY TO OBTAIN
Receive Type: Null from a Macro Cosmos employee in the Battle Tower in Wyndon after you become Champion.

Gender unknown

382 ☑ Synthetic Pokémon
Silvally

Height: 7'7"   Weight: 221.6 lbs.   p. 383

A solid bond of trust between this Pokémon and its Trainer awakened the strength hidden within Silvally. It can change its type at will.

The final factor needed to release this Pokémon's true power was a strong bond with a Trainer it trusts.

MAIN WAY TO OBTAIN
Obtain a Type: Null, then level it up with high friendship to evolve it into Silvally (Type: Normal).

Type: Normal

Level up with high friendship

Gender unknown

⊘ CHANGING SILVALLY'S TYPE

Silvally has the unique Ability RKS System, which allows it to change its type depending on the memory disc you give it to hold. This will also change the type of its signature move, Multi-Attack. There is a total of 17 memory discs, one for each type other than Normal, but you don't need to find them individually—you'll get all of them together when you receive Type: Null. If Silvally isn't holding a memory disc, its type will be Normal and Multi-Attack will be a Normal-type move.

Silvally (Type: Normal)   **Silvally (Type: Fire)**   **Silvally (Type: Grass)**

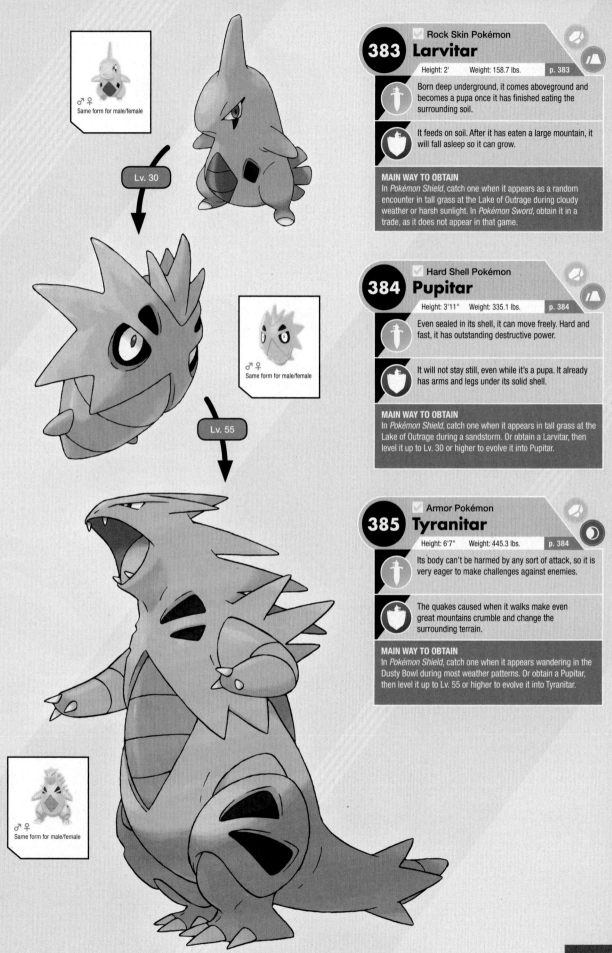

Same form for male/female

Lv. 30

Same form for male/female

Lv. 55

Same form for male/female

Rock Skin Pokémon
383 Larvitar

Height: 2'   Weight: 158.7 lbs.   p. 383

Born deep underground, it comes aboveground and becomes a pupa once it has finished eating the surrounding soil.

It feeds on soil. After it has eaten a large mountain, it will fall asleep so it can grow.

MAIN WAY TO OBTAIN
In *Pokémon Shield*, catch one when it appears as a random encounter in tall grass at the Lake of Outrage during cloudy weather or harsh sunlight. In *Pokémon Sword*, obtain it in a trade, as it does not appear in that game.

Hard Shell Pokémon
384 Pupitar

Height: 3'11"   Weight: 335.1 lbs.   p. 384

Even sealed in its shell, it can move freely. Hard and fast, it has outstanding destructive power.

It will not stay still, even while it's a pupa. It already has arms and legs under its solid shell.

MAIN WAY TO OBTAIN
In *Pokémon Shield*, catch one when it appears in tall grass at the Lake of Outrage during a sandstorm. Or obtain a Larvitar, then level it up to Lv. 30 or higher to evolve it into Pupitar.

Armor Pokémon
385 Tyranitar

Height: 6'7"   Weight: 445.3 lbs.   p. 384

Its body can't be harmed by any sort of attack, so it is very eager to make challenges against enemies.

The quakes caused when it walks make even great mountains crumble and change the surrounding terrain.

MAIN WAY TO OBTAIN
In *Pokémon Shield*, catch one when it appears wandering in the Dusty Bowl during most weather patterns. Or obtain a Pupitar, then level it up to Lv. 55 or higher to evolve it into Tyranitar.

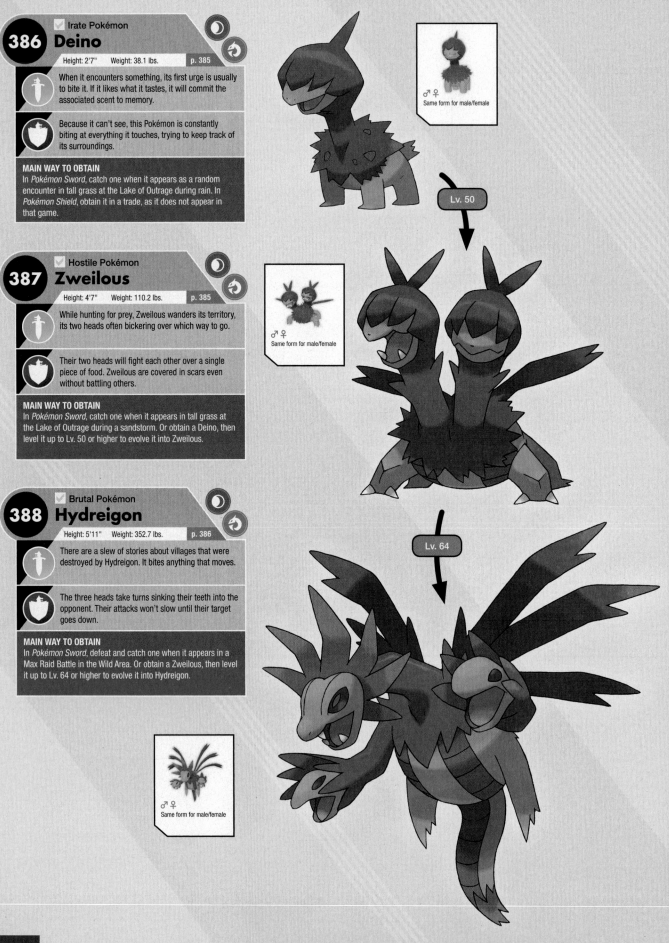

386 Deino

☑ Irate Pokémon

Height: 2'7" Weight: 38.1 lbs. p. 385

When it encounters something, its first urge is usually to bite it. If it likes what it tastes, it will commit the associated scent to memory.

Because it can't see, this Pokémon is constantly biting at everything it touches, trying to keep track of its surroundings.

MAIN WAY TO OBTAIN
In *Pokémon Sword*, catch one when it appears as a random encounter in tall grass at the Lake of Outrage during rain. In *Pokémon Shield*, obtain it in a trade, as it does not appear in that game.

♂ ♀
Same form for male/female

Lv. 50

387 Zweilous

☑ Hostile Pokémon

Height: 4'7" Weight: 110.2 lbs. p. 385

While hunting for prey, Zweilous wanders its territory, its two heads often bickering over which way to go.

Their two heads will fight each other over a single piece of food. Zweilous are covered in scars even without battling others.

MAIN WAY TO OBTAIN
In *Pokémon Sword*, catch one when it appears in tall grass at the Lake of Outrage during a sandstorm. Or obtain a Deino, then level it up to Lv. 50 or higher to evolve it into Zweilous.

♂ ♀
Same form for male/female

Lv. 64

388 Hydreigon

☑ Brutal Pokémon

Height: 5'11" Weight: 352.7 lbs. p. 386

There are a slew of stories about villages that were destroyed by Hydreigon. It bites anything that moves.

The three heads take turns sinking their teeth into the opponent. Their attacks won't slow until their target goes down.

MAIN WAY TO OBTAIN
In *Pokémon Sword*, defeat and catch one when it appears in a Max Raid Battle in the Wild Area. Or obtain a Zweilous, then level it up to Lv. 64 or higher to evolve it into Hydreigon.

♂ ♀
Same form for male/female

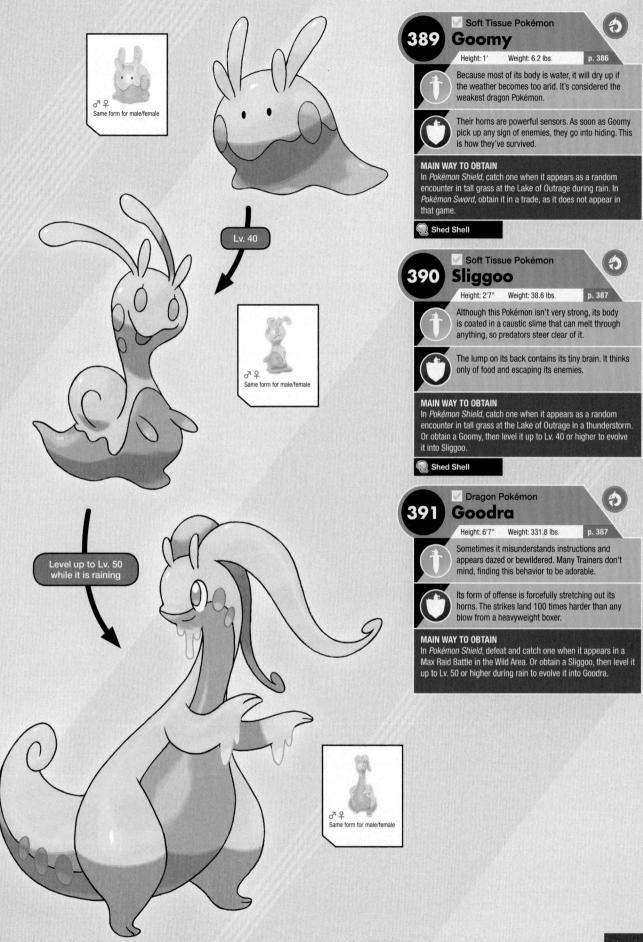

Same form for male/female

Lv. 40

Same form for male/female

Level up to Lv. 50
while it is raining

Same form for male/female

389 Goomy
☑ Soft Tissue Pokémon

Height: 1' Weight: 6.2 lbs. p. 386

Because most of its body is water, it will dry up if the weather becomes too arid. It's considered the weakest dragon Pokémon.

Their horns are powerful sensors. As soon as Goomy pick up any sign of enemies, they go into hiding. This is how they've survived.

MAIN WAY TO OBTAIN
In *Pokémon Shield*, catch one when it appears as a random encounter in tall grass at the Lake of Outrage during rain. In *Pokémon Sword*, obtain it in a trade, as it does not appear in that game.

Shed Shell

390 Sliggoo
☑ Soft Tissue Pokémon

Height: 2'7" Weight: 38.6 lbs. p. 387

Although this Pokémon isn't very strong, its body is coated in a caustic slime that can melt through anything, so predators steer clear of it.

The lump on its back contains its tiny brain. It thinks only of food and escaping its enemies.

MAIN WAY TO OBTAIN
In *Pokémon Shield*, catch one when it appears as a random encounter in tall grass at the Lake of Outrage in a thunderstorm. Or obtain a Goomy, then level it up to Lv. 40 or higher to evolve it into Sliggoo.

Shed Shell

391 Goodra
☑ Dragon Pokémon

Height: 6'7" Weight: 331.8 lbs. p. 387

Sometimes it misunderstands instructions and appears dazed or bewildered. Many Trainers don't mind, finding this behavior to be adorable.

Its form of offense is forcefully stretching out its horns. The strikes land 100 times harder than any blow from a heavyweight boxer.

MAIN WAY TO OBTAIN
In *Pokémon Shield*, defeat and catch one when it appears in a Max Raid Battle in the Wild Area. Or obtain a Sliggoo, then level it up to Lv. 50 or higher during rain to evolve it into Goodra.

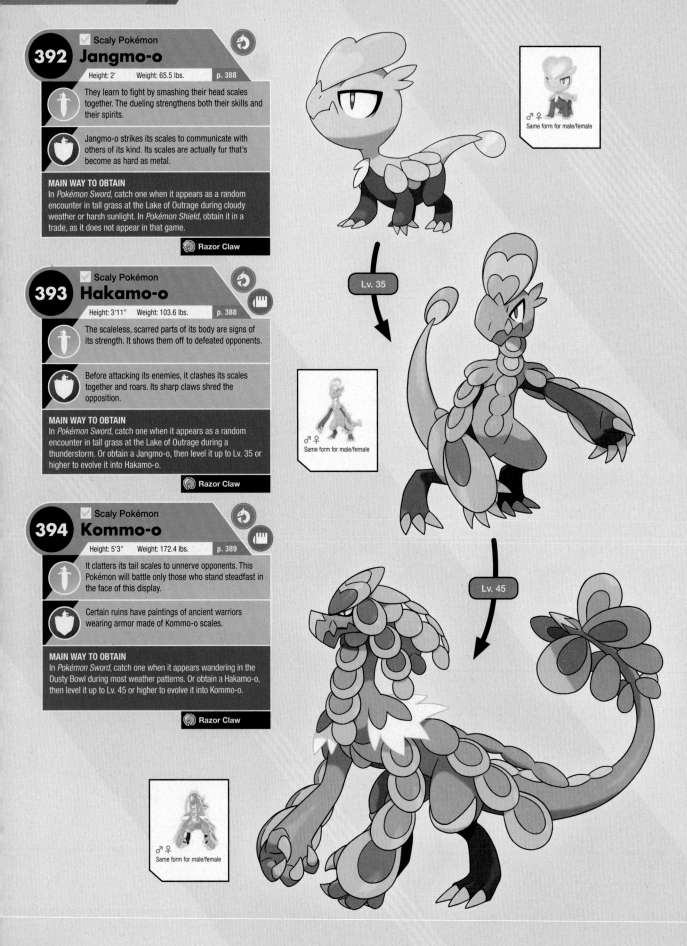

392 Jangmo-o

☑ Scaly Pokémon

Height: 2'   Weight: 65.5 lbs.   p. 388

They learn to fight by smashing their head scales together. The dueling strengthens both their skills and their spirits.

Jangmo-o strikes its scales to communicate with others of its kind. Its scales are actually fur that's become as hard as metal.

MAIN WAY TO OBTAIN
In *Pokémon Sword*, catch one when it appears as a random encounter in tall grass at the Lake of Outrage during cloudy weather or harsh sunlight. In *Pokémon Shield*, obtain it in a trade, as it does not appear in that game.

🔘 Razor Claw

Same form for male/female

Lv. 35

393 Hakamo-o

☑ Scaly Pokémon

Height: 3'11"   Weight: 103.6 lbs.   p. 388

The scaleless, scarred parts of its body are signs of its strength. It shows them off to defeated opponents.

Before attacking its enemies, it clashes its scales together and roars. Its sharp claws shred the opposition.

MAIN WAY TO OBTAIN
In *Pokémon Sword*, catch one when it appears as a random encounter in tall grass at the Lake of Outrage during a thunderstorm. Or obtain a Jangmo-o, then level it up to Lv. 35 or higher to evolve it into Hakamo-o.

🔘 Razor Claw

Same form for male/female

Lv. 45

394 Kommo-o

☑ Scaly Pokémon

Height: 5'3"   Weight: 172.4 lbs.   p. 389

It clatters its tail scales to unnerve opponents. This Pokémon will battle only those who stand steadfast in the face of this display.

Certain ruins have paintings of ancient warriors wearing armor made of Kommo-o scales.

MAIN WAY TO OBTAIN
In *Pokémon Sword*, catch one when it appears wandering in the Dusty Bowl during most weather patterns. Or obtain a Hakamo-o, then level it up to Lv. 45 or higher to evolve it into Kommo-o.

🔘 Razor Claw

Same form for male/female

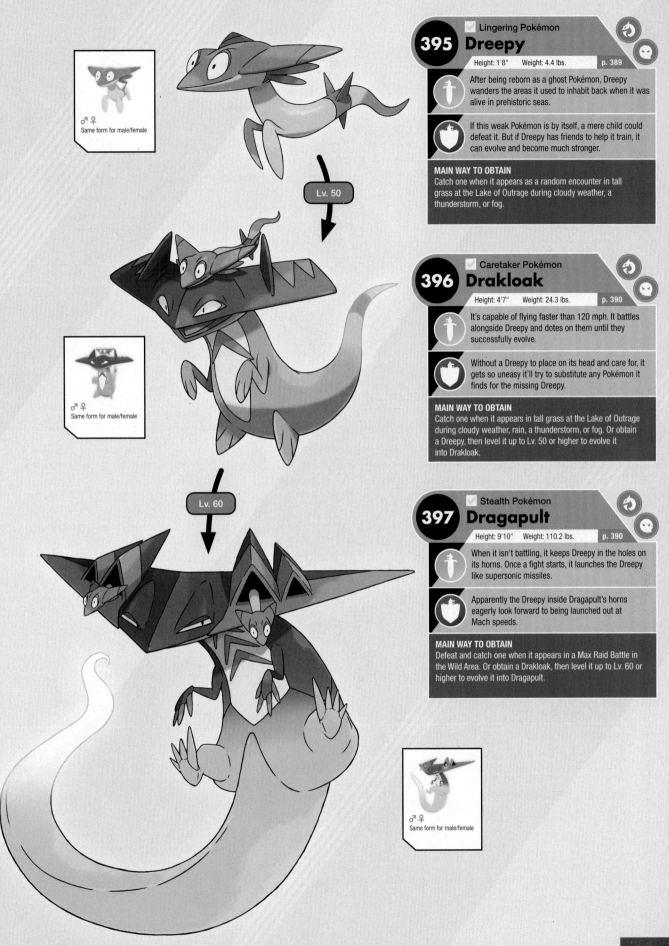

Same form for male/female

395 Dreepy
☑ Lingering Pokémon

Height: 1'8" Weight: 4.4 lbs. p. 389

After being reborn as a ghost Pokémon, Dreepy wanders the areas it used to inhabit back when it was alive in prehistoric seas.

If this weak Pokémon is by itself, a mere child could defeat it. But if Dreepy has friends to help it train, it can evolve and become much stronger.

MAIN WAY TO OBTAIN
Catch one when it appears as a random encounter in tall grass at the Lake of Outrage during cloudy weather, a thunderstorm, or fog.

Lv. 50

Same form for male/female

396 Drakloak
☑ Caretaker Pokémon

Height: 4'7" Weight: 24.3 lbs. p. 390

It's capable of flying faster than 120 mph. It battles alongside Dreepy and dotes on them until they successfully evolve.

Without a Dreepy to place on its head and care for, it gets so uneasy it'll try to substitute any Pokémon it finds for the missing Dreepy.

MAIN WAY TO OBTAIN
Catch one when it appears in tall grass at the Lake of Outrage during cloudy weather, rain, a thunderstorm, or fog. Or obtain a Dreepy, then level it up to Lv. 50 or higher to evolve it into Drakloak.

Lv. 60

397 Dragapult
☑ Stealth Pokémon

Height: 9'10" Weight: 110.2 lbs. p. 390

When it isn't battling, it keeps Dreepy in the holes on its horns. Once a fight starts, it launches the Dreepy like supersonic missiles.

Apparently the Dreepy inside Dragapult's horns eagerly look forward to being launched out at Mach speeds.

MAIN WAY TO OBTAIN
Defeat and catch one when it appears in a Max Raid Battle in the Wild Area. Or obtain a Drakloak, then level it up to Lv. 60 or higher to evolve it into Dragapult.

Same form for male/female

398 Zacian

☑ Warrior Pokémon

Height: 9'2" Weight: 242.5 lbs. p. 391

Known as a legendary hero, this Pokémon absorbs metal particles, transforming them into a weapon it uses to battle.

This Pokémon has slumbered for many years. Some say it's Zamazenta's elder sister—others say the two Pokémon are rivals.

MAIN WAY TO OBTAIN

In *Pokémon Sword*, complete the events involving Sordward and Shielbert after you become Champion for your chance to catch this Pokémon. In *Pokémon Shield*, obtain it in a trade, as it does not appear in that game.

Hero of Many Battles

Gender unknown

Does not evolve

CROWNED SWORD ZACIAN

Zacian changes to its Crowned Sword form when it enters battle if it is holding the Rusted Sword. When Zacian is in this form its Attack gets a boost. Plus, if it knows the move Iron Head, that move will be replaced with the Behemoth Blade move for the length of the battle. But once Zacian is knocked out or withdrawn, it will revert to its normal form and Behemoth Blade will revert to Iron Head.

SPECIES STRENGTHS

Hero of Many Battles		Crowned Sword	
HP	▨▨▨▨▨	HP	▨▨▨▨▨
ATTACK	▨▨▨▨▨▨▨▨	ATTACK	▨▨▨▨▨▨▨▨▨
DEFENSE	▨▨▨▨▨▨	DEFENSE	▨▨▨▨▨▨
SP. ATK	▨▨▨▨▨	SP. ATK	▨▨▨▨▨
SP. DEF	▨▨▨▨▨▨	SP. DEF	▨▨▨▨▨▨
SPEED	▨▨▨▨▨▨▨▨	SPEED	▨▨▨▨▨▨▨▨

Crowned Sword Zacian

Height: 9'2"
Weight: 782.6 lbs.

Now armed with a weapon it used in ancient times, this Pokémon needs only a single strike to fell even Gigantamax Pokémon.

Able to cut down anything with a single strike, it became known as the Fairy King's Sword, and it inspired awe in friend and foe alike.

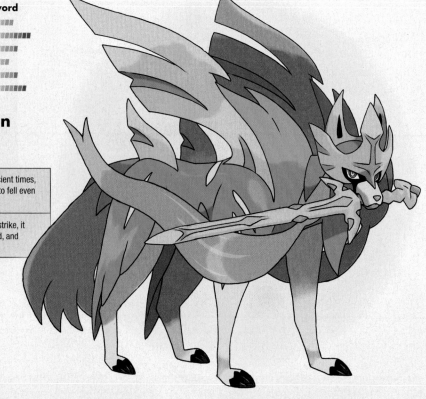

DAMAGE TAKEN IN BATTLE

◎ ×0.5	✳ ×0.5	◎ ×0.5	◐ ×0.5
◉ ×2	▥ ×1	♈ ×0.25	◉ ×1
◉ ×1	◉ ×0	◉ ×0.5	◉ ×0.5
◉ ×0.5	◭ ×2	◉ ×1	
◈ ×1	◉ ×0.5	◉ ×0	

☑ Warrior Pokémon

399 Zamazenta

Height: 9'6" Weight: 463 lbs. p. 391

Hero of Many Battles

In times past, it worked together with a king of the people to save the Galar region. It absorbs metal that it then uses in battle.

This Pokémon slept for aeons while in the form of a statue. It was asleep for so long, people forgot that it ever existed.

MAIN WAY TO OBTAIN
In *Pokémon Shield*, complete the events involving Sordward and Shielbert after you become Champion for your chance to catch this Pokémon. In *Pokémon Sword*, obtain it in a trade, as it does not appear in that game.

Gender unknown

Does not evolve

CROWNED SHIELD ZAMAZENTA

Zamazenta changes to its Crowned Shield form when it enters battle if it is holding the Rusted Shield. When Zamazenta is in this form its Defense and Sp. Def get a boost. Plus, if it knows the move Iron Head, that move will be replaced with the Behemoth Bash move for the length of the battle. But once Zamazenta is knocked out or withdrawn, it will revert to its normal form and Behemoth Bash will revert to Iron Head.

SPECIES STRENGTHS

Hero of Many Battles		Crowned Shield	
HP	▮▮▮▮▮▮	HP	▮▮▮▮▮▮
ATTACK	▮▮▮▮▮▮▮▮	ATTACK	▮▮▮▮▮▮▮
DEFENSE	▮▮▮▮▮▮	DEFENSE	▮▮▮▮▮▮▮▮
SP. ATK	▮▮▮▮	SP. ATK	▮▮▮▮
SP. DEF	▮▮▮▮▮▮	SP. DEF	▮▮▮▮▮▮▮▮
SPEED	▮▮▮▮▮▮▮	SPEED	▮▮▮▮▮▮▮

Crowned Shield Zamazenta

Height: 9'6"
Weight: 1730.6 lbs.

Its ability to deflect any attack led to it being known as the Fighting Master's Shield. It was feared and respected by all.

Now that it's equipped with its shield, it can shrug off impressive blows, including the attacks of Dynamax Pokémon.

DAMAGE TAKEN IN BATTLE

×0.5	×0.5	×1	×0.5
×2	×2	×0.25	×0.5
×1	×0	×0.25	×1
×0.5	×2	×1	
×1	×1	×0.5	

Gigantic Pokémon

400 Eternatus

Height: 65'7"　Weight: 2094.4 lbs.　p. 392

The core on its chest absorbs energy emanating from the lands of the Galar region. This energy is what allows Eternatus to stay active.

It was inside a meteorite that fell 20,000 years ago. There seems to be a connection between this Pokémon and the Dynamax phenomenon.

MAIN WAY TO OBTAIN
Catch it when you face this Pokémon at the climax of your adventure.

Gender unknown

Does not evolve

ETERNAMAX ETERNATUS

During your adventure, you will see Eternatus take on this fearsome form. As awesome as it may appear, it's not a form that Eternatus can regularly take on. If you manage to catch Eternatus yourself, you'll only be able to see this form when Eternatus uses Eternabeam. Just be glad you made it through your battle against it!

Eternamax Eternatus

Height: 328'1"
Weight: ????.? lbs.

As a result of Rose's meddling, Eternatus absorbed all the energy in the Galar region. It's now in a state of power overload.

Infinite amounts of energy pour from this Pokémon's enlarged core, warping the surrounding space-time.

GIGANTAMAX POKÉMON

Gigantamax Pokémon

During your adventures across the Galar region, you may have noticed that some Pokémon don't just get bigger when they Dynamax—their appearance changes, too! These are called Gigantamax Pokémon. While extremely rare, they're definitely worth catching, because each has access to a special G-Max Move that has unique different effects than the regular Max Move it's based on!

Pokémon must have a special quality called the Gigantamax Factor in order to Gigantamax—and not every specimen of a given species does. In other words, a Charizard you catch in the Galar region will only transform into Gigantamax Charizard if it has the Gigantamax Factor. Otherwise, your Charizard will transform into the more common Dynamax Charizard when you Dynamax it.

The Gigantamax Factor can't be passed on to Eggs, either. If you leave a Pokémon with the Gigantamax Factor at the Nursery with another Pokémon, you'll only find Eggs for Pokémon that turn into their Dynamax form. The following pages feature the Pokémon species known to date that can sometimes be found with the Gigantamax Factor. Still, this phenomenon is shrouded in mystery, so who knows? There might just be other Pokémon out there that can Gigantamax, too...

> **!** While Gigantamax Pokémon will have their own entries in your Pokédex, they don't count toward completing it. If you're focusing on that, you don't need to hunt down each and every Gigantamax Pokémon!

Finding Gigantamax Pokémon

You can find Gigantamax Pokémon by participating in Max Raid Battles in the Wild Area, but searching blindly won't be much help! Make sure you know the following things so you can maximize your chances of encountering these rare Pokémon.

1. Gigantamax Pokémon will only appear in five-star Max Raid Battles. You can trigger five-star Max Raid Battles once you obtain a Dragon Badge in Hammerlocke, so hold off on searching for wild Gigantamax Pokémon until then!

2. Keep your eyes open for pillars of light that seem more purple in hue, wreathed in swirling energy. Dens emitting this kind of light are more likely to have rare Pokémon hiding in them, including Gigantamax Pokémon!

3. Use your Wishing Pieces! Throwing a Wishing Piece into a dormant Pokémon Den will attract a wild Dynamax Pokémon, and it can even attract wild Gigantamax Pokémon if you're incredibly lucky! You can use as many Wishing Pieces as you want in a day, but you can only use Wishing Pieces to lure one Pokémon at a time. If you use another Wishing Piece on a different den before battling the Pokémon lured by the first Wishing Piece, the first Pokémon will go away and you'll lose your chance to battle it!

4. Each day, aim to beat every den that has a pillar of light erupting from it! Every day, different dens light up in the Wild Area. If you manage to defeat the Dynamax Pokémon in each one, a new set of dens will light up. When they do, at least one will contain a rare Pokémon—guaranteed!

Get the Wild Area news

Stay up-to-date on what's happening in the Wild Area! Select Mystery Gift from your X menu, and choose to get the latest Wild Area news. If you do, you may find that different kinds of Pokémon appear the next time new Pokémon Dens light up in the Wild Area (whether that happens because a new day has begun or because you've conquered every lit-up den you had available to you). After that, you can continue to use Wishing Pieces and the other methods already mentioned to try to encounter more of these unusual Pokémon.

Get rare Dynamax Crystals

News isn't all you can get from the Mystery Gift menu! You may also sometimes receive special items known as Dynamax Crystals! These items can be used at the broken watchtower in the Watchtower Ruins area. Dynamax Crystals will cause the Watchtower Lair beneath the tower to light up, and you'll have a chance to battle and try to catch the Dynamax Pokémon that appears! The tower will stay lit until the day ends (when the time set on your Nintendo Switch reaches midnight) or until you catch the wild Pokémon that appeared in the Watchtower Lair.

012 ☑ Seven Spot Pokémon

Orbeetle

Height: 45'11"+   Weight: ?????.? lbs.

Its brain has grown to a gargantuan size, as has the rest of its body. This Pokémon's intellect and psychic abilities are overpowering.

If it were to utilize every last bit of its power, it could control the minds of every living being in its vicinity.

Gigantamax

MAIN WAY TO OBTAIN
Defeat and catch a Gigantamax Orbeetle when one appears in a Max Raid Battle in the Wild Area.

⊚ GIGANTAMAX EFFECTS

Gigantamax Orbeetle can use G-Max Gravitas. In addition to dealing Psychic-type damage on the turn it is used, it grounds airborne Pokémon so Ground-type moves will hit Pokémon normally-immune to them. It also prevents the use of Bounce, Fly, Flying Press, High Jump Kick, Magnet Rise, and Splash, and it raises the accuracy of all Pokémon in battle. These effects last 5 turns.

GIGANTAMAX EFFECTS

Gigantamax Butterfree can use G-Max Befuddle. In addition to dealing Bug-type damage on the turn it is used, it inflicts the poison, paralysis, or asleep status condition on all opposing Pokémon.

☑ Butterfly Pokémon

015 Butterfree

Height: 55'9"+   Weight: ????.? lbs.

Crystallized Gigantamax energy makes up this Pokémon's blindingly bright and highly toxic scales.

Once it has opponents trapped in a tornado that could blow away a 10-ton truck, it finishes them off with its poisonous scales.

MAIN WAY TO OBTAIN
Defeat and catch a Gigantamax Butterfree when one appears in a Max Raid Battle in the Wild Area.

Gigantamax

☑ Raven Pokémon

023 **Corviknight**

Height: 45'11"+ Weight: ????.? lbs.

Imbued with Gigantamax energy, its wings can whip up winds more forceful than any a hurricane could muster. The gusts blow everything away.

The eight feathers on its back are called blade birds, and they can launch off its body to attack foes independently.

MAIN WAY TO OBTAIN

Defeat and catch a Gigantamax Corviknight when one appears in a Max Raid Battle in the Wild Area.

Gigantamax

🅟 **GIGANTAMAX EFFECTS**

Gigantamax Corviknight can use G-Max Wind Rage. In addition to dealing Flying-type damage on the turn it is used, it nullifies Aurora Veil, Light Screen, Mist, Reflect, and Safeguard on the opponents' side. Nullifies Spikes, Stealth Rock, Sticky Web, and Toxic Spikes on both sides.

GIGANTAMAX EFFECTS

Gigantamax Drednaw can use G-Max Stonesurge. In addition to dealing Water-type damage on the turn it is used, it damages Pokémon as they are sent out to the opposing side. This damage is Rock type and subject to type matchups.

☑ Bite Pokémon

043 **Drednaw**

Height: 78'9"+   Weight: ????.? lbs.

Gigantamax

It responded to Gigantamax energy by becoming bipedal. First it comes crashing down on foes, and then it finishes them off with its massive jaws.

In the Galar region, there's a tale about this Pokémon chewing up a mountain and using the rubble to stop a flood.

MAIN WAY TO OBTAIN
Defeat and catch a Gigantamax Drednaw when one appears in a Max Raid Battle in the Wild Area.

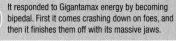

Pincer Pokémon

099 Kingler

Height: 62'4"+   Weight: ????.? lbs.

The flow of Gigantamax energy has spurred this Pokémon's left pincer to grow to an enormous size. That claw can pulverize anything.

The bubbles it spews out are strongly alkaline. Any opponents hit by them will have their bodies quickly melted away.

MAIN WAY TO OBTAIN
Defeat and catch a Gigantamax Kingler when one appears in a Max Raid Battle in the Wild Area.

Gigantamax

GIGANTAMAX EFFECTS

Gigantamax Kingler can use G-Max Foam Burst. In addition to dealing Water-type damage on the turn it is used, it decreases the Speed stats of all opposing Pokémon by 2 stages.

GIGANTAMAX EFFECTS

Gigantamax Machamp can use G-Max Chi Strike. In addition to dealing Fighting-type damage on the turn it is used, it increases critical hit rates of all ally Pokémon by 2 stages.

Superpower Pokémon

140 Machamp

Height: 82'+   Weight: ????.? lbs.

The Gigantamax energy coursing through its arms makes its punches hit as hard as bomb blasts.

One of these Pokémon once used its immeasurable strength to lift a large ship that was in trouble. It then carried the ship to port.

MAIN WAY TO OBTAIN
In *Pokémon Sword*, defeat and catch a Gigantamax Machamp when one appears in a Max Raid Battle in the Wild Area. In *Pokémon Shield*, obtain it in a trade, as it does not appear in that game.

Gigantamax

☑ Shadow Pokémon

143 Gengar

Height: 65'7"+   Weight: ????.? lbs.

Rumor has it that its gigantic mouth leads not into its body, filled with cursed energy, but instead directly to the afterlife.

It lays traps, hoping to steal the lives of those it catches. If you stand in front of its mouth, you'll hear your loved ones' voices calling out to you.

MAIN WAY TO OBTAIN
In *Pokémon Shield*, defeat and catch a Gigantamax Gengar when one appears in a Max Raid Battle in the Wild Area. In *Pokémon Sword*, obtain it in a trade, as it does not appear in that game.

Gigantamax

GIGANTAMAX EFFECTS

Gigantamax Gengar can use G-Max Terror. In addition to dealing Ghost-type damage on the turn it is used, it prevents all opposing Pokémon from fleeing or being switched out while this Pokémon is in battle.

GIGANTAMAX EFFECTS

Gigantamax Garbodor can use G-Max Malodor. In addition to dealing Poison-type damage on the turn it is used, it inflicts the poison status condition on all opposing Pokémon.

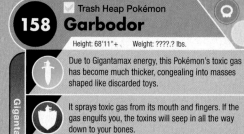

Trash Heap Pokémon

158 Garbodor

Height: 68'11"+   Weight: ????.? lbs.

Due to Gigantamax energy, this Pokémon's toxic gas has become much thicker, congealing into masses shaped like discarded toys.

It sprays toxic gas from its mouth and fingers. If the gas engulfs you, the toxins will seep in all the way down to your bones.

MAIN WAY TO OBTAIN
Defeat and catch a Gigantamax Garbodor when one appears in a Max Raid Battle in the Wild Area.

Gigantamax

☑ Radiator Pokémon

160 **Centiskorch**

Height: 246'1"+   Weight: ????.? lbs.

Gigantamax energy has evoked a rise in its body temperature, now reaching over 1,800 degrees Fahrenheit. Its heat waves incinerate its enemies.

The heat that comes off a Gigantamax Centiskorch may destabilize air currents. Sometimes it can even cause storms.

MAIN WAY TO OBTAIN
Defeat and catch a Gigantamax Centiskorch when one appears in a Max Raid Battle in the Wild Area.

Gigantamax

GIGANTAMAX EFFECTS

Gigantamax Centiskorch can use G-Max Centiferno. In addition to dealing Fire-type damage on the turn it is used, it inflicts damage equal to 1/8 of max HP to all opponents at the end of each turn for 4 to 5 turns. Opponents cannot flee or be switched out of battle during that time.

GIGANTAMAX EFFECTS

Gigantamax Coalossal can use G-Max Volcalith. In addition to dealing Rock-type damage on the turn it is used, it inflicts damage equal to 1/6 of max HP to all non-Rock-type opponents for 4 turns.

☑ Coal Pokémon

163 Coalossal

Height: 137'10"+   Weight: ????.? lbs.

Its body is a colossal stove. With Gigantamax energy stoking the fire, this Pokémon's flame burns hotter than 3,600 degrees Fahrenheit.

When Galar was hit by a harsh cold wave, this Pokémon served as a giant heating stove and saved many lives.

Gigantamax

MAIN WAY TO OBTAIN

In *Pokémon Sword*, defeat and catch a Gigantamax Coalossal when one appears in a Max Raid Battle in the Wild Area. In *Pokémon Shield*, obtain it in a trade, as it does not appear in that game.

182 Meowth

☑ Scratch Cat Pokémon

Height: 108'3"+   Weight: ????.? lbs.

The pattern that has appeared on its giant coin is thought to be the key to unlocking the secrets of the Dynamax phenomenon.

Its body has grown incredibly long and the coin on its forehead has grown incredibly large—all thanks to Gigantamax power.

MAIN WAY TO OBTAIN
A Meowth with the Gigantamax Factor was available as a special gift for early purchasers. If you missed your chance, watch the official website for future announcements.

Gigantamax

GIGANTAMAX EFFECTS

Gigantamax Meowth can use G-Max Gold Rush. In addition to dealing Normal-type damage on the turn it is used, it confuses all opposing Pokémon and pays out money after the battle. (First use: ₽100 × user's level. Second use: ₽300 × user's level. Third use: ₽600 × user's level.)

GIGANTAMAX EFFECTS

Gigantamax Alcremie can use G-Max Finale. In addition to dealing Fairy-type damage on the turn it is used, it restores 1/6 of all ally Pokémon's max HP.

☑ Cream Pokémon
186 Alcremie

Height: 98'5"+   Weight: ????.? lbs.

Gigantamax

Cream pours endlessly from this Pokémon's body. The cream stiffens when compressed by an impact. A harder impact results in harder cream.

It launches swarms of missiles, each made of cream and loaded with 100,000 kilocalories. Get hit by one of these, and your head will swim.

MAIN WAY TO OBTAIN
Defeat and catch a Gigantamax Alcremie when one appears in a Max Raid Battle in the Wild Area.

194 Pikachu
Mouse Pokémon

Height: 68'11"+   Weight: ????.? lbs.

Its Gigantamax power expanded, forming its supersized body and towering tail.

When it smashes its opponents with its bolt-shaped tail, it delivers a surge of electricity equivalent to a lightning strike.

MAIN WAY TO OBTAIN
Receive a Pikachu with the Gigantamax Factor from a girl in the Wild Area Station if you have save data from *Pokémon: Let's Go, Pikachu!* on your system.

Gigantamax

GIGANTAMAX EFFECTS

Gigantamax Pikachu can use G-Max Volt Crash. In addition to dealing Electric-type damage on the turn it is used, it inflicts the paralysis status condition on all opposing Pokémon.

GIGANTAMAX EFFECTS

Gigantamax Eevee can use G-Max Cuddle. In addition to dealing Normal-type damage on the turn it is used, it makes all opposing Pokémon become infatuated, which causes moves to fail 50% of the time.

☑ Evolution Pokémon

196 Eevee

Height: 59'1"+   Weight: ????.? lbs.

Gigantamax energy upped the fluffiness of the fur around Eevee's neck. The fur will envelop a foe, capturing its body and captivating its mind.

Having gotten even friendlier and more innocent, Eevee tries to play with anyone around, only to end up crushing them with its immense body.

MAIN WAY TO OBTAIN
Receive an Eevee with the Gigantamax Factor from a boy in the Wild Area Station if you have save data from *Pokémon: Let's Go, Eevee!* on your system.

Gigantamax

206   Flapple
☑ Apple Wing Pokémon

Height: 78'9"+   Weight: ????.? lbs.

Under the influence of Gigantamax energy, it produces much more sweet nectar, and its shape has changed to resemble a giant apple.

If it stretches its neck, the strong aroma of its nectar pours out. The scent is so sickeningly sweet that one whiff makes other Pokémon faint.

MAIN WAY TO OBTAIN

In *Pokémon Sword*, defeat and catch a Gigantamax Flapple when one appears in a Max Raid Battle in the Wild Area. In *Pokémon Shield*, obtain it in a trade, as it does not appear in that game.

Gigantamax

🔴 GIGANTAMAX EFFECTS

Gigantamax Flapple can use G-Max Tartness. In addition to dealing Grass-type damage on the turn it is used, it decreases the evasiveness of all opposing Pokémon by 1 stage.

207   Appletun
☑ Apple Nectar Pokémon

Height: 78'9"+   Weight: ????.? lbs.

It blasts its opponents with massive amounts of sweet, sticky nectar, drowning them under the deluge.

Due to Gigantamax energy, this Pokémon's nectar has thickened. The increased viscosity lets the nectar absorb more damage than before.

MAIN WAY TO OBTAIN

In *Pokémon Shield*, defeat and catch a Gigantamax Appletun when one appears in a Max Raid Battle in the Wild Area. In *Pokémon Sword*, obtain it in a trade, as it does not appear in that game.

Gigantamax

🔴 GIGANTAMAX EFFECTS

Gigantamax Appletun can use G-Max Sweetness. In addition to dealing Grass-type damage on the turn it is used, it heals the status conditions of all ally Pokémon in battle.

GIGANTAMAX EFFECTS

Gigantamax Grimmsnarl can use G-Max Snooze. In addition to dealing Dark-type damage on the turn it is used, it inflicts the asleep status condition on the target at the end of the next turn unless the target switches out.

Bulk Up Pokémon

240 Grimmsnarl

Height: 105'+   Weight: ????.? lbs.

Gigantamax

By transforming its leg hair, this Pokémon delivers power-packed drill kicks that can bore huge holes in Galar's terrain.

Gigantamax energy has caused more hair to sprout all over its body. With the added strength, it can jump over the world's tallest building.

MAIN WAY TO OBTAIN
Defeat and catch a Gigantamax Grimmsnarl when one appears in a Max Raid Battle in the Wild Area.

243 Hatterene

☐ Silent Pokémon

Height: 85'4"+   Weight: ????.? lbs.

This Pokémon can read the emotions of creatures over 30 miles away. The minute it senses hostility, it goes on the attack.

Beams like lightning shoot down from its tentacles. It's known to some as the Raging Goddess.

MAIN WAY TO OBTAIN
Defeat and catch a Gigantamax Hatterene when one appears in a Max Raid Battle in the Wild Area.

Gigantamax

GIGANTAMAX EFFECTS

Gigantamax Hatterene can use G-Max Smite. In addition to dealing Fairy-type damage on the turn it is used, it makes all opposing Pokémon confused.

GIGANTAMAX EFFECTS

Gigantamax Snorlax can use G-Max Replenish. In addition to dealing Normal-type damage on the turn it is used, it recycles the Berries held by all ally Pokémon.

☑ Sleeping Pokémon

261 Snorlax

Height: 114'10"+   Weight: ????.? lbs.

Gigantamax energy has affected stray seeds and even pebbles that got stuck to Snorlax, making them grow to a huge size.

Terrifyingly strong, this Pokémon is the size of a mountain—and moves about as much as one as well.

Gigantamax

MAIN WAY TO OBTAIN
Defeat and catch a Gigantamax Snorlax when one appears in a Max Raid Battle in the Wild Area. It may only appear during select periods, so get the latest Wild Area news regularly from the Mystery Gift menu.

☑ Copperderm Pokémon

303 Copperajah

Height: 75'6"+   Weight: ????.? lbs.

So much power is packed within its trunk that if it were to unleash that power, the resulting blast could level mountains and change the landscape.

After this Pokémon has Gigantamaxed, its massive nose can utterly demolish large structures with a single smashing blow.

MAIN WAY TO OBTAIN
Defeat and catch a Gigantamax Copperajah when one appears in a Max Raid Battle in the Wild Area.

Gigantamax

GIGANTAMAX EFFECTS

Gigantamax Copperajah can use G-Max Steelsurge. In addition to dealing Steel-type damage on the turn it is used, it damages Pokémon as they are sent out to the opposing side. This damage is Steel type and subject to type matchups.

GIGANTAMAX EFFECTS

Gigantamax Sandaconda can use G-Max Sandblast. In addition to dealing Ground-type damage on the turn it is used, it inflicts damage equal to 1/8 of max HP to all opponents at the end of each turn for 4 to 5 turns. Opponents cannot flee or be switched out of battle during that time.

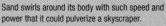

☐ Sand Snake Pokémon

313 Sandaconda

Height: 72'2"+   Weight: ????.? lbs.

Its sand pouch has grown to tremendous proportions. More than 1,000,000 tons of sand now swirl around its body.

Sand swirls around its body with such speed and power that it could pulverize a skyscraper.

MAIN WAY TO OBTAIN
Defeat and catch a Gigantamax Sandaconda when one appears in a Max Raid Battle in the Wild Area.

Gigantamax

361 Lapras

☑ Transport Pokémon

Height: 78'9"+   Weight: ????.? lbs.

Over 5,000 people can ride on its shell at once. And it's a very comfortable ride, without the slightest shaking or swaying.

It surrounds itself with a huge ring of gathered ice particles. It uses the ring to smash any icebergs that might impede its graceful swimming.

MAIN WAY TO OBTAIN

In *Pokémon Shield*, defeat and catch one when it appears in a Max Raid Battle in the Wild Area. In *Pokémon Sword*, obtain it in a trade, as it does not appear in that game.

Gigantamax

GIGANTAMAX EFFECTS

Gigantamax Lapras can use G-Max Resonance. In addition to dealing Ice-type damage on the turn it is used, it reduces damage from physical and special moves for 5 turns.

GIGANTAMAX EFFECTS

Gigantamax Duraludon can use G-Max Depletion. In addition to dealing Dragon-type damage on the turn it is used, it reduces the PP of the moves used by all opposing Pokémon by 2.

☑ Alloy Pokémon

371 Duraludon

Height: 141'1"+   Weight: ????.? lbs.

It's grown to resemble a skyscraper. Parts of its towering body glow due to a profusion of energy.

The hardness of its cells is exceptional, even among Steel types. It also has a body structure that's resistant to earthquakes.

MAIN WAY TO OBTAIN
Defeat and catch one when it appears in a Max Raid Battle in the Wild Area.

Gigantamax

☑ Flame Pokémon

380 Charizard

Height: 91'10"+   Weight: ????.? lbs.

This colossal, flame-winged figure of a Charizard was brought about by Gigantamax energy.

The flame inside its body burns hotter than 3,600 degrees Fahrenheit. When Charizard roars, that temperature climbs even higher.

MAIN WAY TO OBTAIN
Get a special Charmander with the Gigantamax Factor in Hop and Leon's house after you become Champion. It can be evolved into a Charizard capable of Gigantamaxing.

Gigantamax

GIGANTAMAX EFFECTS

Gigantamax Charizard can use G-Max Wildfire. In addition to dealing Fire-type damage on the turn it is used, it inflicts damage equal to 1/6 of max HP to all non-Fire-type opponents for 4 turns.

MOVE TABLES

Move Tables

The following pages help you check all the moves that each Pokémon species can learn in *Pokémon Sword* and *Pokémon Shield*. There are many different ways that Pokémon can learn moves, and they're broken down below. Each move will be listed in these move tables together with its type, category, power, accuracy, base PP, and range. If you're not sure what any of these mean, turn to page 394, where these qualities are all broken down in a handy key!

> You'll also see which Abilities each species can have, but remember that you can't "teach" your Pokémon an Ability. Each specimen will have the Ability it has. Pokémon can change their current Ability to another common Ability using an item called an Ability Capsule (p. 470). But if you want to get a Pokémon with a Hidden Ability, you'll have to be lucky enough to catch one in a Max Raid Battle!

Level-Up Moves

These moves include those that your Pokémon can learn as it levels up. The level that the move can be learned at is shown in the first column. Some moves say they're learned at Lv. 1—those are moves that the Pokémon might know when it first hatches from an Egg or is first caught in the wild.

> What happens if you chose not to learn a move when your Pokémon leveled up? Is it lost forever? Not at all! You can talk to Jack, the fellow behind the left-hand counter in any Pokémon Center, to have your Pokémon remember level-up moves they've forgotten or that they chose not to learn when they had the chance. He can also remind your Pokémon of moves learned at Lv. 1. Keep an eye out especially for fully evolved Pokémon with Lv. 1 moves they wouldn't normally be able to learn without Jack's help!

Evolution Moves

These are moves that a Pokémon can learn when it evolves into a given species. If you see Octolock listed as an Evolution move for Grapploct, that means that a Clobbopus evolving into Grapploct will have the chance to learn that move. If you catch a Grapploct in the wild or you get one in a trade that doesn't know that move, don't fret—Jack at the Pokémon Center can help Pokémon remember Evolution moves they missed, too!

TM Moves and TR Moves

Both of these tables show moves that a Pokémon can learn from certain items. TMs are items that can be used over and over to teach countless Pokémon the moves they contain. You can buy some of them at Poké Marts in Pokémon Centers, and many others can be found in the field in containers that look like yellow Poké Balls. Check out the list starting on page 413 to see where to get them all.

TRs are similar to TMs, but they can only be used one time each. If you want to teach the move in a TR to more than one Pokémon, then you'll need more than one of that TR! You can get TRs from Rotom Rallyists in the Wild Area, who will sell you TRs in exchange for Watts, and you can also get them as rewards for winning Max Raid Battles.

> Don't know about Pokémon Nurseries or how to find Pokémon Eggs? Turn back to page 10, where these topics are introduced!

Egg Moves

Egg Moves are moves that a Pokémon won't learn by leveling up. As the name "Egg Move" implies, if you want your Pokémon to know an Egg Move, you ought to visit a Pokémon Nursery. The usual way a Pokémon learns an Egg Move at a Nursery is by hatching from an Egg found while at least one of the Pokémon that were left at the Nursery knows the Egg Move in question. Another more curious way is to leave a Pokémon at the Nursery together with another Pokémon of the same species that knows one of the first Pokémon's Egg Moves. The first Pokémon might end up learning that move from its playmate at the Nursery, as long as it has an empty move slot. This process takes about the same time as it might take to find an Egg!

Tutor Moves

Finally, a few moves can be taught to some Pokémon by specialized Move Tutors. These Move Tutors can be found around the region. Find more details about where to find each one on page 412!

001

LEVEL-UP MOVES

LV.	NAME	TYPE	KIND	POW.	ACC.	PP	RANGE
1	Growl	Normal	Status	—	100	40	Many Others
1	Scratch	Normal	Physical	40	100	35	Normal
6	Branch Poke	Grass	Physical	40	100	40	Normal
8	Taunt	Dark	Status	—	100	20	Normal
12	Razor Leaf	Grass	Physical	55	95	25	Many Others
17	Screech	Normal	Status	—	85	40	Normal
20	Knock Off	Dark	Physical	65	100	20	Normal
24	Slam	Normal	Physical	80	75	20	Normal
28	Uproar	Normal	Special	90	100	10	1 Random
32	Wood Hammer	Grass	Physical	120	100	15	Normal
36	Endeavor	Normal	Physical	—	100	5	Normal

EVOLUTION MOVES

NAME	TYPE	KIND	POW.	ACC.	PP	RANGE

EGG MOVES

NAME	TYPE	KIND	POW.	ACC.	PP	RANGE
Fake Out	Normal	Physical	40	100	10	Normal
Growth	Normal	Status	—	—	20	Self
Hammer Arm	Fighting	Physical	100	90	10	Normal
Leech Seed	Grass	Status	—	90	10	Normal
Nature Power	Normal	Status	—	—	20	Normal
Strength	Normal	Physical	80	100	15	Normal
Worry Seed	Grass	Status	—	100	10	Normal

TUTOR MOVES

NAME	TYPE	KIND	POW.	ACC.	PP	RANGE
Grass Pledge	Grass	Special	80	100	10	Normal

TM MOVES

NO.	NAME	TYPE	KIND	POW.	ACC.	PP	RANGE
TM00	Mega Punch	Normal	Physical	80	85	20	Normal
TM01	Mega Kick	Normal	Physical	120	75	5	Normal
TM10	Magical Leaf	Grass	Special	60	—	20	Normal
TM11	Solar Beam	Grass	Special	120	100	10	Normal
TM12	Solar Blade	Grass	Physical	125	100	10	Normal
TM16	Screech	Normal	Status	—	85	40	Normal
TM21	Rest	Psychic	Status	—	—	10	Self
TM24	Snore	Normal	Special	50	100	15	Normal
TM25	Protect	Normal	Status	—	—	10	Self
TM28	Giga Drain	Grass	Special	75	100	10	Normal
TM31	Attract	Normal	Status	—	100	15	Normal
TM34	Sunny Day	Fire	Status	—	—	5	Both Sides
TM39	Facade	Normal	Physical	70	100	20	Normal
TM40	Swift	Normal	Special	60	—	20	Many Others
TM56	U-turn	Bug	Physical	70	100	20	Normal
TM58	Assurance	Dark	Physical	60	100	10	Normal
TM59	Fling	Dark	Physical	—	100	10	Normal
TM63	Drain Punch	Fighting	Physical	75	100	10	Normal
TM76	Round	Normal	Special	60	100	15	Normal
TM78	Acrobatics	Flying	Physical	55	100	15	Normal
TM94	False Swipe	Normal	Physical	40	100	40	Normal

TR MOVES

NO.	NAME	TYPE	KIND	POW.	ACC.	PP	RANGE
TR00	Swords Dance	Normal	Status	—	—	20	Self
TR07	Low Kick	Fighting	Physical	—	100	20	Normal
TR13	Focus Energy	Normal	Status	—	—	30	Self
TR20	Substitute	Normal	Status	—	—	10	Self
TR26	Endure	Normal	Status	—	—	10	Self
TR27	Sleep Talk	Normal	Status	—	—	10	Self
TR35	Uproar	Normal	Special	90	100	10	1 Random
TR37	Taunt	Dark	Status	—	100	20	Normal
TR65	Energy Ball	Grass	Special	90	100	10	Normal
TR77	Grass Knot	Grass	Special	—	100	20	Normal
TR85	Work Up	Normal	Status	—	—	30	Self

Grookey
p. 24

ABILITY
Overgrow
—

HIDDEN ABILITY
—

SPECIES STRENGTHS
HP
ATTACK
DEFENSE
SP. ATK
SP. DEF
SPEED

DAMAGE TAKEN IN BATTLE
×1 ×1 ×1
×2 ×2 ×1
×0.5 ×0.5 ×1
×0.5 ×2 ×1
×0.5 ×1 ×1
×2 ×2 ×1

FIELD
GRASS

002

LEVEL-UP MOVES

LV.	NAME	TYPE	KIND	POW.	ACC.	PP	RANGE
1	Branch Poke	Grass	Physical	40	100	40	Normal
1	Double Hit	Normal	Physical	35	90	10	Normal
1	Growl	Normal	Status	—	100	40	Many Others
1	Scratch	Normal	Physical	40	100	35	Normal
1	Taunt	Dark	Status	—	100	20	Normal
12	Razor Leaf	Grass	Physical	55	95	25	Many Others
17	Screech	Normal	Status	—	85	40	Normal
24	Knock Off	Dark	Physical	65	100	20	Normal
30	Slam	Normal	Physical	80	75	20	Normal
36	Uproar	Normal	Special	90	100	10	1 Random
42	Wood Hammer	Grass	Physical	120	100	15	Normal
48	Endeavor	Normal	Physical	—	100	5	Normal

EVOLUTION MOVES

NAME	TYPE	KIND	POW.	ACC.	PP	RANGE
Double Hit	Normal	Physical	35	90	10	Normal

EGG MOVES

NAME	TYPE	KIND	POW.	ACC.	PP	RANGE

TUTOR MOVES

NAME	TYPE	KIND	POW.	ACC.	PP	RANGE
Grass Pledge	Grass	Special	80	100	10	Normal

TM MOVES

NO.	NAME	TYPE	KIND	POW.	ACC.	PP	RANGE
TM00	Mega Punch	Normal	Physical	80	85	20	Normal
TM01	Mega Kick	Normal	Physical	120	75	5	Normal
TM10	Magical Leaf	Grass	Special	60	—	20	Normal
TM11	Solar Beam	Grass	Special	120	100	10	Normal
TM12	Solar Blade	Grass	Physical	125	100	10	Normal
TM16	Screech	Normal	Status	—	85	40	Normal
TM21	Rest	Psychic	Status	—	—	10	Self
TM24	Snore	Normal	Special	50	100	15	Normal
TM25	Protect	Normal	Status	—	—	10	Self
TM28	Giga Drain	Grass	Special	75	100	10	Normal
TM31	Attract	Normal	Status	—	100	15	Normal
TM34	Sunny Day	Fire	Status	—	—	5	Both Sides
TM39	Facade	Normal	Physical	70	100	20	Normal
TM40	Swift	Normal	Special	60	—	20	Many Others
TM56	U-turn	Bug	Physical	70	100	20	Normal
TM58	Assurance	Dark	Physical	60	100	10	Normal
TM59	Fling	Dark	Physical	—	100	10	Normal
TM63	Drain Punch	Fighting	Physical	75	100	10	Normal
TM76	Round	Normal	Special	60	100	15	Normal
TM78	Acrobatics	Flying	Physical	55	100	15	Normal
TM94	False Swipe	Normal	Physical	40	100	40	Normal

TR MOVES

NO.	NAME	TYPE	KIND	POW.	ACC.	PP	RANGE
TR00	Swords Dance	Normal	Status	—	—	20	Self
TR07	Low Kick	Fighting	Physical	—	100	20	Normal
TR13	Focus Energy	Normal	Status	—	—	30	Self
TR20	Substitute	Normal	Status	—	—	10	Self
TR26	Endure	Normal	Status	—	—	10	Self
TR27	Sleep Talk	Normal	Status	—	—	10	Self
TR35	Uproar	Normal	Special	90	100	10	1 Random
TR37	Taunt	Dark	Status	—	100	20	Normal
TR65	Energy Ball	Grass	Special	90	100	10	Normal
TR77	Grass Knot	Grass	Special	—	100	20	Normal
TR85	Work Up	Normal	Status	—	—	30	Self

Thwackey
p. 24

ABILITY
Overgrow
—

HIDDEN ABILITY
—

SPECIES STRENGTHS
HP
ATTACK
DEFENSE
SP. ATK
SP. DEF
SPEED

DAMAGE TAKEN IN BATTLE
×1 ×1 ×1
×2 ×2 ×1
×0.5 ×0.5 ×1
×0.5 ×2 ×1
×0.5 ×1 ×1
×2 ×1 ×1

FIELD
GRASS

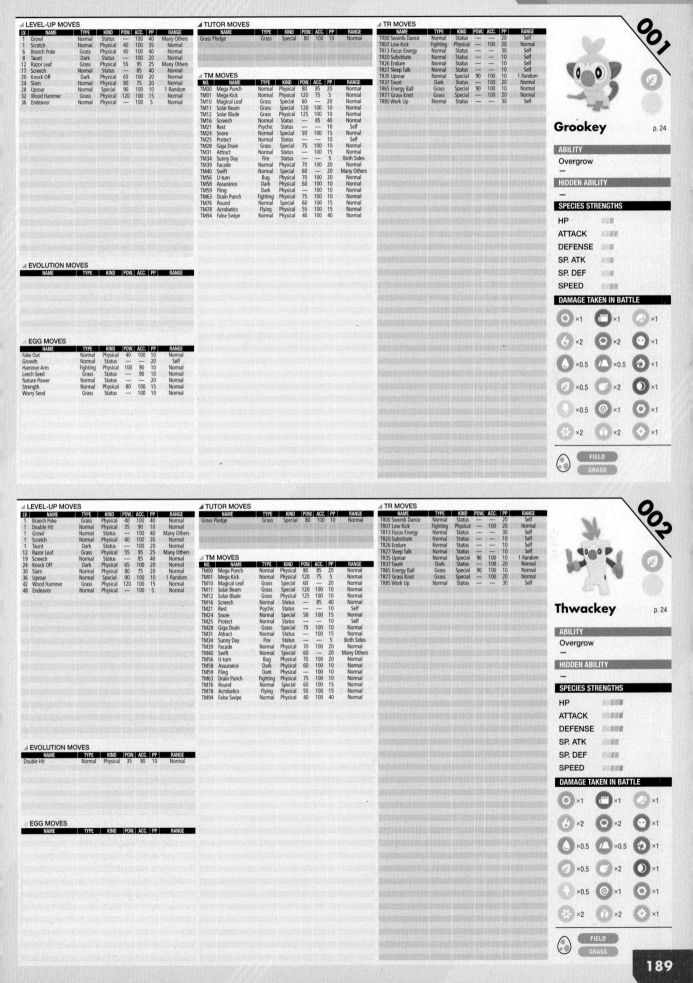

003 Rillaboom
p. 24

ABILITY
Overgrow
—

HIDDEN ABILITY
—

SPECIES STRENGTHS

HP	▉▉▉▉▉
ATTACK	▉▉▉▉▉▉▉
DEFENSE	▉▉▉▉
SP. ATK	▉▉▉
SP. DEF	▉▉▉
SPEED	▉▉▉▉

DAMAGE TAKEN IN BATTLE

×1	×1	×1
×2	×2	×1
×0.5	×0.5	×1
×0.5	×2	×1
×0.5	×1	×1
×2	×2	×1

FIELD / GRASS

LEVEL-UP MOVES

LV.	NAME	TYPE	KIND	POW.	ACC.	PP	RANGE
1	Branch Poke	Grass	Physical	40	100	40	Normal
1	Double Hit	Normal	Physical	35	90	10	Normal
1	Drum Beating	Grass	Physical	80	100	10	Normal
1	Grassy Terrain	Grass	Status	—	—	10	Both Sides
1	Growl	Normal	Status	—	100	40	Many Others
1	Noble Roar	Normal	Status	—	100	30	Normal
1	Scratch	Normal	Physical	40	100	35	Normal
1	Taunt	Dark	Status	—	100	20	Normal
12	Razor Leaf	Grass	Physical	55	95	25	Many Others
19	Screech	Normal	Status	—	85	40	Normal
24	Knock Off	Dark	Physical	65	100	20	Normal
30	Slam	Normal	Physical	80	75	20	Normal
38	Uproar	Normal	Special	90	100	10	1 Random
46	Wood Hammer	Grass	Physical	120	100	15	Normal
54	Endeavor	Normal	Physical	—	100	5	Normal
62	Boomburst	Normal	Special	140	100	10	All Others

EVOLUTION MOVES

NAME	TYPE	KIND	POW.	ACC.	PP	RANGE
Drum Beating	Grass	Physical	80	100	10	Normal

EGG MOVES

NAME	TYPE	KIND	POW.	ACC.	PP	RANGE

TUTOR MOVES

NAME	TYPE	KIND	POW.	ACC.	PP	RANGE
Frenzy Plant	Grass	Special	150	90	5	Normal
Grass Pledge	Grass	Special	80	100	10	Normal

TM MOVES

NO.	NAME	TYPE	KIND	POW.	ACC.	PP	RANGE
TM00	Mega Punch	Normal	Physical	80	85	20	Normal
TM01	Mega Kick	Normal	Physical	120	75	5	Normal
TM08	Hyper Beam	Normal	Physical	150	90	5	Normal
TM09	Giga Impact	Normal	Physical	150	90	5	Normal
TM10	Magical Leaf	Grass	Special	60	—	20	Normal
TM11	Solar Beam	Grass	Special	120	100	10	Normal
TM12	Solar Blade	Grass	Physical	125	100	10	Normal
TM16	Screech	Normal	Status	—	85	40	Normal
TM21	Rest	Psychic	Status	—	—	10	Self
TM24	Snore	Normal	Special	50	100	15	Normal
TM25	Protect	Normal	Status	—	—	10	Self
TM26	Scary Face	Normal	Status	—	100	10	Normal
TM28	Giga Drain	Grass	Special	75	100	10	Normal
TM31	Attract	Normal	Status	—	100	15	Normal
TM34	Sunny Day	Fire	Status	—	—	5	Both Sides
TM39	Facade	Normal	Physical	70	100	20	Normal
TM40	Swift	Normal	Special	60	—	20	Many Others
TM43	Brick Break	Fighting	Physical	75	100	15	Normal
TM50	Bullet Seed	Grass	Physical	25	100	30	Normal
TM53	Mud Shot	Ground	Special	55	95	15	Normal
TM56	U-turn	Bug	Physical	70	100	20	Normal
TM58	Assurance	Dark	Physical	60	100	10	Normal
TM59	Fling	Dark	Physical	—	100	10	Normal
TM63	Drain Punch	Fighting	Physical	75	100	10	Normal
TM76	Round	Normal	Special	60	100	15	Normal
TM78	Acrobatics	Flying	Physical	55	100	15	Normal
TM81	Bulldoze	Ground	Physical	60	100	20	All Others
TM85	Snarl	Dark	Special	55	95	15	Many Others
TM88	Grassy Terrain	Grass	Status	—	—	10	Both Sides
TM94	False Swipe	Normal	Physical	40	100	40	Normal
TM97	Brutal Swing	Dark	Physical	60	100	20	All Others
TM98	Stomping Tantrum	Ground	Physical	75	100	10	Normal

TR MOVES

NO.	NAME	TYPE	KIND	POW.	ACC.	PP	RANGE
TR00	Swords Dance	Normal	Status	—	—	20	Self
TR01	Body Slam	Normal	Physical	85	100	15	Normal
TR07	Low Kick	Fighting	Physical	—	100	20	Normal
TR10	Earthquake	Ground	Physical	100	100	10	All Others
TR13	Focus Energy	Normal	Status	—	—	30	Self
TR20	Substitute	Normal	Status	—	—	10	Self
TR26	Endure	Normal	Status	—	—	10	Self
TR27	Sleep Talk	Normal	Status	—	—	10	Self
TR35	Uproar	Normal	Special	90	100	10	1 Random
TR37	Taunt	Dark	Status	—	100	20	Normal
TR39	Superpower	Fighting	Physical	120	100	5	Normal
TR42	Hyper Voice	Normal	Special	90	100	10	Many Others
TR48	Bulk Up	Fighting	Status	—	—	20	Self
TR64	Focus Blast	Fighting	Special	120	70	5	Normal
TR65	Energy Ball	Grass	Special	90	100	10	Normal
TR67	Earth Power	Ground	Special	90	100	10	Normal
TR71	Leaf Storm	Grass	Special	130	90	5	Normal
TR77	Grass Knot	Grass	Special	—	100	20	Normal
TR85	Work Up	Normal	Status	—	—	30	Self
TR93	Darkest Lariat	Dark	Physical	85	100	10	Normal
TR94	High Horsepower	Ground	Physical	95	95	10	Normal
TR99	Body Press	Fighting	Physical	80	100	10	Normal

004 Scorbunny
p. 25

ABILITY
Blaze
—

HIDDEN ABILITY
—

SPECIES STRENGTHS

HP	▉▉▉
ATTACK	▉▉▉▉
DEFENSE	▉▉▉
SP. ATK	▉▉▉
SP. DEF	▉▉▉
SPEED	▉▉▉▉▉

DAMAGE TAKEN IN BATTLE

×1	×1	×2
×0.5	×1	×1
×2	×2	×1
×0.5	×1	×1
×1	×1	×0.5
×0.5	×0.5	×0.5

FIELD / HUMANLIKE

LEVEL-UP MOVES

LV.	NAME	TYPE	KIND	POW.	ACC.	PP	RANGE
1	Growl	Normal	Status	—	100	40	Many Others
1	Tackle	Normal	Physical	40	100	35	Normal
6	Ember	Fire	Special	40	100	25	Normal
8	Quick Attack	Normal	Physical	40	100	30	Normal
12	Double Kick	Fighting	Physical	30	100	30	Normal
17	Flame Charge	Fire	Physical	50	100	20	Normal
20	Agility	Psychic	Status	—	—	30	Self
24	Headbutt	Normal	Physical	70	100	15	Normal
28	Counter	Fighting	Physical	—	100	20	Varies
32	Bounce	Flying	Physical	85	85	5	Normal
36	Double-Edge	Normal	Physical	120	100	15	Normal

EVOLUTION MOVES

NAME	TYPE	KIND	POW.	ACC.	PP	RANGE

EGG MOVES

NAME	TYPE	KIND	POW.	ACC.	PP	RANGE
High Jump Kick	Fighting	Physical	130	90	10	Normal
Sand Attack	Ground	Status	—	100	15	Normal
Sucker Punch	Dark	Physical	70	100	5	Normal
Super Fang	Normal	Physical	—	90	10	Normal

TUTOR MOVES

NAME	TYPE	KIND	POW.	ACC.	PP	RANGE
Fire Pledge	Fire	Special	80	100	10	Normal

TM MOVES

NO.	NAME	TYPE	KIND	POW.	ACC.	PP	RANGE
TM01	Mega Kick	Normal	Physical	120	75	5	Normal
TM21	Rest	Psychic	Status	—	—	10	Self
TM24	Snore	Normal	Special	50	100	15	Normal
TM25	Protect	Normal	Status	—	—	10	Self
TM31	Attract	Normal	Status	—	100	15	Normal
TM34	Sunny Day	Fire	Status	—	—	5	Both Sides
TM39	Facade	Normal	Physical	70	100	20	Normal
TM40	Swift	Normal	Special	60	—	20	Many Others
TM52	Bounce	Flying	Physical	85	85	5	Normal
TM53	Mud Shot	Ground	Special	55	95	15	Normal
TM56	U-turn	Bug	Physical	70	100	20	Normal
TM58	Assurance	Dark	Physical	60	100	10	Normal
TM68	Fire Fang	Fire	Physical	65	95	15	Normal
TM75	Low Sweep	Fighting	Physical	65	100	20	Normal
TM76	Round	Normal	Special	60	100	15	Normal
TM78	Acrobatics	Flying	Physical	55	100	15	Normal

TR MOVES

NO.	NAME	TYPE	KIND	POW.	ACC.	PP	RANGE
TR02	Flamethrower	Fire	Special	90	100	15	Normal
TR07	Low Kick	Fighting	Physical	—	100	20	Normal
TR12	Agility	Psychic	Status	—	—	30	Self
TR13	Focus Energy	Normal	Status	—	—	30	Self
TR15	Fire Blast	Fire	Special	110	85	5	Normal
TR20	Substitute	Normal	Status	—	—	10	Self
TR21	Reversal	Fighting	Physical	—	100	15	Normal
TR26	Endure	Normal	Status	—	—	10	Self
TR27	Sleep Talk	Normal	Status	—	—	10	Self
TR29	Baton Pass	Normal	Status	—	—	40	Self
TR36	Heat Wave	Fire	Special	95	90	10	Many Others
TR37	Taunt	Dark	Status	—	100	20	Normal
TR41	Blaze Kick	Fire	Physical	85	90	10	Normal
TR43	Overheat	Fire	Special	130	90	5	Normal
TR73	Gunk Shot	Poison	Physical	120	80	5	Normal
TR80	Electro Ball	Electric	Special	—	100	10	Normal
TR83	Ally Switch	Psychic	Status	—	—	15	Self
TR85	Work Up	Normal	Status	—	—	30	Self

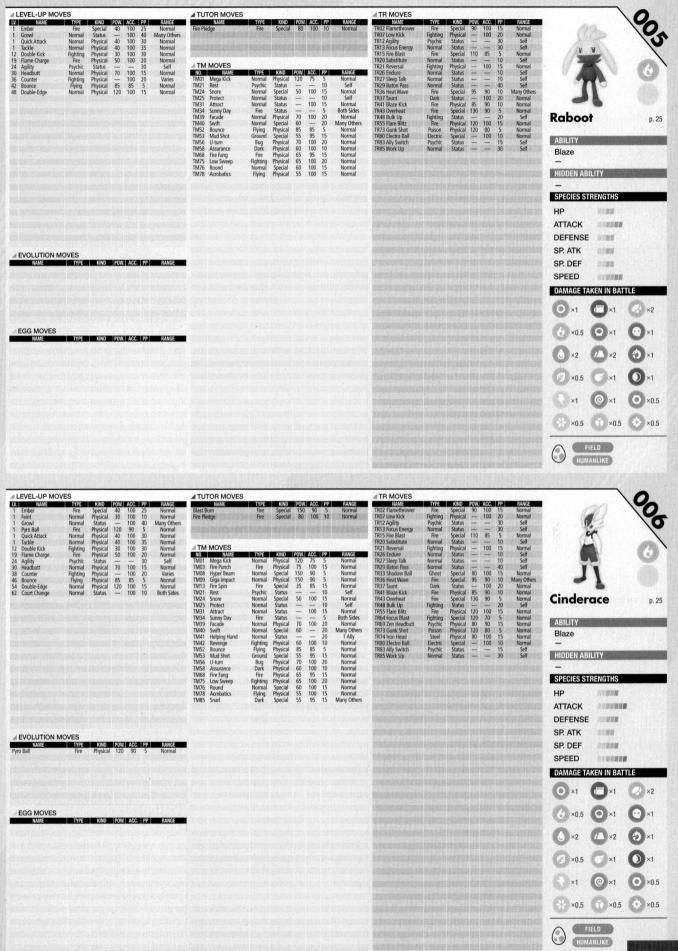

005 Raboot — p. 25

LEVEL-UP MOVES

LV.	NAME	TYPE	KIND	POW.	ACC.	PP	RANGE
1	Ember	Fire	Special	40	100	25	Normal
1	Growl	Normal	Status	—	100	40	Many Others
1	Quick Attack	Normal	Physical	40	100	30	Normal
1	Tackle	Normal	Physical	40	100	35	Normal
12	Double Kick	Fighting	Physical	30	100	30	Normal
19	Flame Charge	Fire	Physical	50	100	20	Normal
24	Agility	Psychic	Status	—	—	30	Self
30	Headbutt	Normal	Physical	70	100	15	Normal
36	Counter	Fighting	Physical	—	100	20	Varies
42	Bounce	Flying	Physical	85	85	5	Normal
48	Double-Edge	Normal	Physical	120	100	15	Normal

EVOLUTION MOVES

NAME	TYPE	KIND	POW.	ACC.	PP	RANGE

EGG MOVES

NAME	TYPE	KIND	POW.	ACC.	PP	RANGE

TUTOR MOVES

NAME	TYPE	KIND	POW.	ACC.	PP	RANGE
Fire Pledge	Fire	Special	80	100	10	Normal

TM MOVES

NO.	NAME	TYPE	KIND	POW.	ACC.	PP	RANGE
TM01	Mega Kick	Normal	Physical	120	75	5	Normal
TM21	Rest	Psychic	Status	—	—	10	Self
TM24	Snore	Normal	Special	50	100	15	Normal
TM25	Protect	Normal	Status	—	—	10	Self
TM31	Attract	Normal	Status	—	100	15	Normal
TM34	Sunny Day	Fire	Status	—	—	5	Both Sides
TM39	Facade	Normal	Physical	70	100	20	Normal
TM40	Swift	Normal	Special	60	—	20	Many Others
TM52	Bounce	Flying	Physical	85	85	5	Normal
TM53	Mud Shot	Ground	Special	55	95	15	Normal
TM56	U-turn	Bug	Physical	70	100	20	Normal
TM58	Assurance	Dark	Physical	60	100	10	Normal
TM68	Fire Fang	Fire	Physical	65	95	15	Normal
TM75	Low Sweep	Fighting	Physical	65	100	20	Normal
TM76	Round	Normal	Special	60	100	15	Normal
TM78	Acrobatics	Flying	Physical	55	100	15	Normal

TR MOVES

NO.	NAME	TYPE	KIND	POW.	ACC.	PP	RANGE
TR02	Flamethrower	Fire	Special	90	100	15	Normal
TR07	Low Kick	Fighting	Physical	—	100	20	Normal
TR12	Agility	Psychic	Status	—	—	30	Self
TR13	Focus Energy	Normal	Status	—	—	30	Self
TR15	Fire Blast	Fire	Special	110	85	5	Normal
TR20	Substitute	Normal	Status	—	—	10	Self
TR21	Reversal	Fighting	Physical	—	100	15	Normal
TR26	Endure	Normal	Status	—	—	10	Self
TR27	Sleep Talk	Normal	Status	—	—	10	Self
TR29	Baton Pass	Normal	Status	—	—	40	Self
TR36	Heat Wave	Fire	Special	95	90	10	Many Others
TR37	Taunt	Dark	Status	—	100	20	Normal
TR41	Blaze Kick	Fire	Physical	85	90	10	Normal
TR43	Overheat	Fire	Special	130	90	5	Normal
TR48	Bulk Up	Fighting	Status	—	—	20	Self
TR55	Flare Blitz	Fire	Physical	120	100	15	Normal
TR73	Gunk Shot	Poison	Physical	120	80	5	Normal
TR80	Electro Ball	Electric	Special	—	100	10	Normal
TR83	Ally Switch	Psychic	Status	—	—	15	Self
TR85	Work Up	Normal	Status	—	—	30	Self

ABILITY
Blaze
—

HIDDEN ABILITY
—

SPECIES STRENGTHS
HP
ATTACK
DEFENSE
SP. ATK
SP. DEF
SPEED

DAMAGE TAKEN IN BATTLE
×1 | ×1 | ×2
×0.5 | ×1 | ×1
×2 | ×2 | ×1
×0.5 | ×1 | ×1
×1 | ×1 | ×0.5
×0.5 | ×0.5 | ×0.5

FIELD / HUMANLIKE

---

006 Cinderace — p. 25

LEVEL-UP MOVES

LV.	NAME	TYPE	KIND	POW.	ACC.	PP	RANGE
1	Ember	Fire	Special	40	100	25	Normal
1	Feint	Normal	Physical	30	100	10	Normal
1	Growl	Normal	Status	—	100	40	Many Others
1	Pyro Ball	Fire	Physical	120	90	5	Normal
1	Quick Attack	Normal	Physical	40	100	30	Normal
1	Tackle	Normal	Physical	40	100	35	Normal
12	Double Kick	Fighting	Physical	30	100	30	Normal
19	Flame Charge	Fire	Physical	50	100	20	Normal
24	Agility	Psychic	Status	—	—	30	Self
30	Headbutt	Normal	Physical	70	100	15	Normal
38	Counter	Fighting	Physical	—	100	20	Varies
46	Bounce	Flying	Physical	85	85	5	Normal
54	Double-Edge	Normal	Physical	120	100	15	Normal
62	Court Change	Normal	Status	—	100	10	Both Sides

EVOLUTION MOVES

NAME	TYPE	KIND	POW.	ACC.	PP	RANGE
Pyro Ball	Fire	Physical	120	90	5	Normal

EGG MOVES

NAME	TYPE	KIND	POW.	ACC.	PP	RANGE

TUTOR MOVES

NAME	TYPE	KIND	POW.	ACC.	PP	RANGE
Blast Burn	Fire	Special	150	90	5	Normal
Fire Pledge	Fire	Special	80	100	10	Normal

TM MOVES

NO.	NAME	TYPE	KIND	POW.	ACC.	PP	RANGE
TM01	Mega Kick	Normal	Physical	120	75	5	Normal
TM03	Fire Punch	Fire	Physical	75	100	15	Normal
TM08	Hyper Beam	Normal	Special	150	90	5	Normal
TM09	Giga Impact	Normal	Physical	150	90	5	Normal
TM13	Fire Spin	Fire	Special	35	85	15	Normal
TM21	Rest	Psychic	Status	—	—	10	Self
TM24	Snore	Normal	Special	50	100	15	Normal
TM25	Protect	Normal	Status	—	—	10	Self
TM31	Attract	Normal	Status	—	100	15	Normal
TM34	Sunny Day	Fire	Status	—	—	5	Both Sides
TM39	Facade	Normal	Physical	70	100	20	Normal
TM40	Swift	Normal	Special	60	—	20	Many Others
TM41	Helping Hand	Normal	Status	—	—	20	1 Ally
TM42	Revenge	Fighting	Physical	60	100	10	Normal
TM52	Bounce	Flying	Physical	85	85	5	Normal
TM53	Mud Shot	Ground	Special	55	95	15	Normal
TM56	U-turn	Bug	Physical	70	100	20	Normal
TM58	Assurance	Dark	Physical	60	100	10	Normal
TM68	Fire Fang	Fire	Physical	65	95	15	Normal
TM75	Low Sweep	Fighting	Physical	65	100	20	Normal
TM76	Round	Normal	Special	60	100	15	Normal
TM78	Acrobatics	Flying	Physical	55	100	15	Normal
TM85	Snarl	Dark	Special	55	95	15	Many Others

TR MOVES

NO.	NAME	TYPE	KIND	POW.	ACC.	PP	RANGE
TR02	Flamethrower	Fire	Special	90	100	15	Normal
TR07	Low Kick	Fighting	Physical	—	100	20	Normal
TR12	Agility	Psychic	Status	—	—	30	Self
TR13	Focus Energy	Normal	Status	—	—	30	Self
TR15	Fire Blast	Fire	Special	110	85	5	Normal
TR20	Substitute	Normal	Status	—	—	10	Self
TR21	Reversal	Fighting	Physical	—	100	15	Normal
TR26	Endure	Normal	Status	—	—	10	Self
TR27	Sleep Talk	Normal	Status	—	—	10	Self
TR29	Baton Pass	Normal	Status	—	—	40	Self
TR33	Shadow Ball	Ghost	Special	80	100	15	Normal
TR36	Heat Wave	Fire	Special	95	90	10	Many Others
TR37	Taunt	Dark	Status	—	100	20	Normal
TR41	Blaze Kick	Fire	Physical	85	90	10	Normal
TR43	Overheat	Fire	Special	130	90	5	Normal
TR48	Bulk Up	Fighting	Status	—	—	20	Self
TR55	Flare Blitz	Fire	Physical	120	100	15	Normal
TR64	Focus Blast	Fighting	Special	120	70	5	Normal
TR69	Zen Headbutt	Psychic	Physical	80	90	15	Normal
TR73	Gunk Shot	Poison	Physical	120	80	5	Normal
TR74	Iron Head	Steel	Physical	80	100	15	Normal
TR80	Electro Ball	Electric	Special	—	100	10	Normal
TR83	Ally Switch	Psychic	Status	—	—	15	Self
TR85	Work Up	Normal	Status	—	—	30	Self

ABILITY
Blaze
—

HIDDEN ABILITY
—

SPECIES STRENGTHS
HP
ATTACK
DEFENSE
SP. ATK
SP. DEF
SPEED

DAMAGE TAKEN IN BATTLE
×1 | ×1 | ×2
×0.5 | ×1 | ×1
×2 | ×2 | ×1
×0.5 | ×1 | ×1
×1 | ×1 | ×0.5
×0.5 | ×0.5 | ×0.5

FIELD / HUMANLIKE

007

Sobble
p. 26

ABILITY

Torrent
—

HIDDEN ABILITY

—

SPECIES STRENGTHS

HP	
ATTACK	
DEFENSE	
SP. ATK	
SP. DEF	
SPEED	

DAMAGE TAKEN IN BATTLE

×1		×1		×1	
×0.5		×1		×1	
×0.5		×1		×1	
×2		×1		×1	
×2		×1		×0.5	
×0.5		×1		×1	

WATER 1
FIELD

LEVEL-UP MOVES

LV.	NAME	TYPE	KIND	POW.	ACC.	PP	RANGE
1	Growl	Normal	Status	—	100	40	Many Others
1	Pound	Normal	Physical	40	100	35	Normal
6	Water Gun	Water	Special	40	100	25	Normal
8	Bind	Normal	Physical	15	85	20	Normal
12	Water Pulse	Water	Special	60	100	20	Normal
17	Tearful Look	Normal	Status	—	—	20	Normal
20	Sucker Punch	Dark	Physical	70	100	5	Normal
24	U-turn	Bug	Physical	70	100	20	Normal
28	Liquidation	Water	Physical	85	100	10	Normal
32	Soak	Water	Status	—	100	20	Normal
36	Rain Dance	Water	Status	—	—	5	Both Sides

EVOLUTION MOVES

NAME	TYPE	KIND	POW.	ACC.	PP	RANGE

EGG MOVES

NAME	TYPE	KIND	POW.	ACC.	PP	RANGE
Aqua Jet	Water	Physical	40	100	20	Normal
Aqua Ring	Water	Status	—	—	20	Self
Double Team	Normal	Status	—	—	15	Self
Fell Stinger	Bug	Physical	50	100	25	Normal
Haze	Ice	Status	—	—	30	Both Sides
Ice Shard	Ice	Physical	40	100	30	Normal
Mist	Ice	Status	—	—	30	Your Side

TUTOR MOVES

NAME	TYPE	KIND	POW.	ACC.	PP	RANGE
Water Pledge	Water	Special	80	100	10	Normal

TM MOVES

NO.	NAME	TYPE	KIND	POW.	ACC.	PP	RANGE
TM17	Light Screen	Psychic	Status	—	—	30	Your Side
TM18	Reflect	Psychic	Status	—	—	20	Your Side
TM19	Safeguard	Normal	Status	—	—	25	Your Side
TM21	Rest	Psychic	Status	—	—	10	Self
TM24	Snore	Normal	Special	50	100	15	Normal
TM25	Protect	Normal	Status	—	—	10	Self
TM31	Attract	Normal	Status	—	100	15	Normal
TM33	Rain Dance	Water	Status	—	—	5	Both Sides
TM36	Whirlpool	Water	Special	35	85	15	Normal
TM39	Facade	Normal	Physical	70	100	20	Normal
TM40	Swift	Normal	Special	60	—	20	Many Others
TM45	Dive	Water	Physical	80	100	10	Normal
TM46	Weather Ball*	Normal	Special	50	100	10	Normal
TM52	Bounce	Flying	Physical	85	85	5	Normal
TM53	Mud Shot	Ground	Special	55	95	15	Normal
TM56	U-turn	Bug	Physical	70	100	15	Normal
TM76	Round	Normal	Special	60	100	15	Normal

TR MOVES

NO.	NAME	TYPE	KIND	POW.	ACC.	PP	RANGE
TR04	Surf	Water	Special	90	100	15	All Others
TR20	Substitute	Normal	Status	—	—	10	Self
TR26	Endure	Normal	Status	—	—	10	Self
TR27	Sleep Talk	Normal	Status	—	—	10	Self
TR29	Baton Pass	Normal	Status	—	—	40	Self
TR45	Muddy Water	Water	Special	90	85	10	Many Others
TR85	Work Up	Normal	Status	—	—	30	Self
TR98	Liquidation	Water	Physical	85	100	10	Normal

008

Drizzile
p. 26

ABILITY

Torrent
—

HIDDEN ABILITY

—

SPECIES STRENGTHS

HP	
ATTACK	
DEFENSE	
SP. ATK	
SP. DEF	
SPEED	

DAMAGE TAKEN IN BATTLE

×1		×1		×1	
×0.5		×1		×1	
×0.5		×1		×1	
×2		×1		×1	
×2		×1		×0.5	
×0.5		×1		×1	

WATER 1
FIELD

LEVEL-UP MOVES

LV.	NAME	TYPE	KIND	POW.	ACC.	PP	RANGE
1	Bind	Normal	Physical	15	85	20	Normal
1	Growl	Normal	Status	—	100	40	Many Others
1	Pound	Normal	Physical	40	100	35	Normal
1	Water Gun	Water	Special	40	100	25	Normal
12	Water Pulse	Water	Special	60	100	20	Normal
19	Tearful Look	Normal	Status	—	—	20	Normal
24	Sucker Punch	Dark	Physical	70	100	5	Normal
30	U-turn	Bug	Physical	70	100	20	Normal
36	Liquidation	Water	Physical	85	100	10	Normal
42	Soak	Water	Status	—	100	20	Normal
48	Rain Dance	Water	Status	—	—	5	Both Sides

EVOLUTION MOVES

NAME	TYPE	KIND	POW.	ACC.	PP	RANGE

EGG MOVES

NAME	TYPE	KIND	POW.	ACC.	PP	RANGE

TUTOR MOVES

NAME	TYPE	KIND	POW.	ACC.	PP	RANGE
Water Pledge	Water	Special	80	100	10	Normal

TM MOVES

NO.	NAME	TYPE	KIND	POW.	ACC.	PP	RANGE
TM17	Light Screen	Psychic	Status	—	—	30	Your Side
TM18	Reflect	Psychic	Status	—	—	20	Your Side
TM19	Safeguard	Normal	Status	—	—	25	Your Side
TM21	Rest	Psychic	Status	—	—	10	Self
TM24	Snore	Normal	Special	50	100	15	Normal
TM25	Protect	Normal	Status	—	—	10	Self
TM31	Attract	Normal	Status	—	100	15	Normal
TM33	Rain Dance	Water	Status	—	—	5	Both Sides
TM36	Whirlpool	Water	Special	35	85	15	Normal
TM39	Facade	Normal	Physical	70	100	20	Normal
TM40	Swift	Normal	Special	60	—	20	Many Others
TM45	Dive	Water	Physical	80	100	10	Normal
TM46	Weather Ball*	Normal	Special	50	100	10	Normal
TM52	Bounce	Flying	Physical	85	85	5	Normal
TM53	Mud Shot	Ground	Special	55	95	15	Normal
TM56	U-turn	Bug	Physical	70	100	20	Normal
TM59	Fling	Dark	Physical	—	100	10	Normal
TM76	Round	Normal	Special	60	100	15	Normal

TR MOVES

NO.	NAME	TYPE	KIND	POW.	ACC.	PP	RANGE
TR04	Surf	Water	Special	90	100	15	All Others
TR20	Substitute	Normal	Status	—	—	10	Self
TR26	Endure	Normal	Status	—	—	10	Self
TR27	Sleep Talk	Normal	Status	—	—	10	Self
TR29	Baton Pass	Normal	Status	—	—	40	Self
TR45	Muddy Water	Water	Special	90	85	10	Many Others
TR85	Work Up	Normal	Status	—	—	30	Self
TR98	Liquidation	Water	Physical	85	100	10	Normal

009 Inteleon — p.26

LEVEL-UP MOVES

LV.	NAME	TYPE	KIND	POW.	ACC.	PP	RANGE
1	Acrobatics	Flying	Physical	55	100	15	Normal
1	Bind	Normal	Physical	15	85	20	Normal
1	Growl	Normal	Status	—	100	40	Many Others
1	Pound	Normal	Physical	40	100	35	Normal
1	Snipe Shot	Water	Special	80	100	15	Normal
1	Water Gun	Water	Special	40	100	25	Normal
12	Water Pulse	Water	Special	60	100	20	Normal
19	Tearful Look	Normal	Status	—	—	20	Normal
24	Sucker Punch	Dark	Physical	70	100	5	Normal
30	U-turn	Bug	Physical	70	100	20	Normal
38	Liquidation	Water	Physical	85	100	10	Normal
46	Soak	Water	Status	—	100	20	Normal
54	Rain Dance	Water	Status	—	—	5	Both Sides
62	Hydro Pump	Water	Special	110	80	5	Normal

EVOLUTION MOVES

NAME	TYPE	KIND	POW.	ACC.	PP	RANGE
Snipe Shot	Water	Special	80	100	15	Normal

EGG MOVES

NAME	TYPE	KIND	POW.	ACC.	PP	RANGE

TUTOR MOVES

NAME	TYPE	KIND	POW.	ACC.	PP	RANGE
Hydro Cannon	Water	Special	150	90	5	Normal
Water Pledge	Water	Special	80	100	10	Normal

TM MOVES

NO.	NAME	TYPE	KIND	POW.	ACC.	PP	RANGE
TM08	Hyper Beam	Normal	Special	150	90	5	Normal
TM09	Giga Impact	Normal	Physical	150	90	5	Normal
TM17	Light Screen	Psychic	Status	—	—	30	Your Side
TM18	Reflect	Psychic	Status	—	—	20	Your Side
TM19	Safeguard	Normal	Status	—	—	25	Your Side
TM21	Rest	Psychic	Status	—	—	10	Self
TM24	Snore	Normal	Special	50	100	15	Normal
TM25	Protect	Normal	Status	—	—	10	Self
TM27	Icy Wind	Ice	Special	55	95	15	Many Others
TM31	Attract	Normal	Status	—	100	15	Normal
TM33	Rain Dance	Water	Status	—	—	5	Both Sides
TM36	Whirlpool	Water	Special	35	85	15	Normal
TM39	Facade	Normal	Physical	70	100	20	Normal
TM40	Swift	Normal	Special	60	—	20	Many Others
TM45	Dive	Water	Physical	80	100	10	Normal
TM46	Weather Ball*	Normal	Special	50	100	10	Normal
TM51	Icicle Spear	Ice	Physical	25	100	30	Normal
TM52	Bounce	Flying	Physical	85	85	5	Normal
TM53	Mud Shot	Ground	Special	55	95	15	Normal
TM56	U-turn	Bug	Physical	70	100	20	Normal
TM59	Fling	Dark	Physical	—	100	10	Normal
TM76	Round	Normal	Special	60	100	15	Normal
TM78	Acrobatics	Flying	Physical	55	100	15	Normal
TM95	Air Slash	Flying	Special	75	95	15	Normal
TM99	Breaking Swipe	Dragon	Physical	60	100	15	Many Others

TR MOVES

NAME	TYPE	KIND	POW.	ACC.	PP	RANGE
TR00 Swords Dance	Normal	Status	—	—	20	Self
TR03 Hydro Pump	Water	Special	110	80	5	Normal
TR04 Surf	Water	Special	90	100	15	All Others
TR05 Ice Beam	Ice	Special	90	100	10	Normal
TR06 Blizzard	Ice	Special	110	70	5	Many Others
TR12 Agility	Psychic	Status	—	—	30	Self
TR13 Focus Energy	Normal	Status	—	—	30	Self
TR14 Metronome	Normal	Status	—	—	10	Self
TR16 Waterfall	Water	Physical	80	100	15	Normal
TR20 Substitute	Normal	Status	—	—	10	Self
TR26 Endure	Normal	Status	—	—	10	Self
TR27 Sleep Talk	Normal	Status	—	—	10	Self
TR29 Baton Pass	Normal	Status	—	—	40	Self
TR33 Shadow Ball	Ghost	Special	80	100	15	Normal
TR45 Muddy Water	Water	Special	90	85	10	Many Others
TR58 Dark Pulse	Dark	Special	80	100	15	Normal
TR84 Scald	Water	Special	80	100	15	Normal
TR85 Work Up	Normal	Status	—	—	30	Self
TR98 Liquidation	Water	Physical	85	100	10	Normal

ABILITY
Torrent
—

HIDDEN ABILITY
—

SPECIES STRENGTHS
HP
ATTACK
DEFENSE
SP. ATK
SP. DEF
SPEED

DAMAGE TAKEN IN BATTLE
×1 ×1 ×1
×0.5 ×1 ×1
×0.5 ×1 ×1
×2 ×1 ×1
×2 ×1 ×0.5
×0.5 ×1 ×1

WATER 1 / FIELD

*Weather Ball changes type depending on weather condition. (Harsh sunlight: Fire type. Rain: Water type. Hail: Ice type. Sandstorm: Rock type.)

---

010 Blipbug — p.27

LEVEL-UP MOVES

LV.	NAME	TYPE	KIND	POW.	ACC.	PP	RANGE
1	Struggle Bug	Bug	Special	50	100	20	Many Others

EVOLUTION MOVES

NAME	TYPE	KIND	POW.	ACC.	PP	RANGE

EGG MOVES

NAME	TYPE	KIND	POW.	ACC.	PP	RANGE
Infestation	Bug	Special	20	100	20	Normal
Recover	Normal	Status	—	—	10	Self
Sticky Web	Bug	Status	—	—	20	Other Side
Supersonic	Normal	Status	—	55	20	Normal

TUTOR MOVES

NAME	TYPE	KIND	POW.	ACC.	PP	RANGE

TM MOVES

NO.	NAME	TYPE	KIND	POW.	ACC.	PP	RANGE

TR MOVES

NAME	TYPE	KIND	POW.	ACC.	PP	RANGE

ABILITY
Swarm
Compound Eyes

HIDDEN ABILITY
Telepathy

SPECIES STRENGTHS
HP
ATTACK
DEFENSE
SP. ATK
SP. DEF
SPEED

DAMAGE TAKEN IN BATTLE
×1 ×0.5 ×2
×2 ×1 ×1
×1 ×0.5 ×1
×0.5 ×2 ×1
×1 ×1 ×1
×1 ×1 ×1

BUG

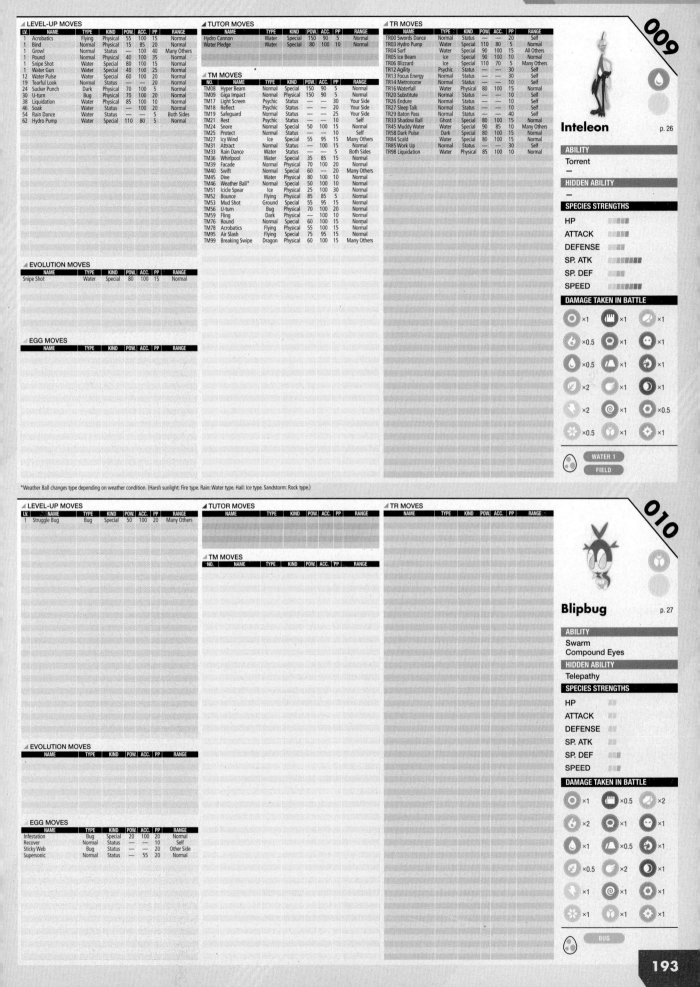

011

Dottler p. 27

LEVEL-UP MOVES

LV.	NAME	TYPE	KIND	POW.	ACC.	PP	RANGE
1	Confusion	Psychic	Special	50	100	25	Normal
1	Light Screen	Psychic	Status	—	—	30	Your Side
1	Reflect	Psychic	Status	—	—	20	Your Side
1	Struggle Bug	Bug	Special	50	100	20	Many Others

TUTOR MOVES

NAME	TYPE	KIND	POW.	ACC.	PP	RANGE

TM MOVES

NO.	NAME	TYPE	KIND	POW.	ACC.	PP	RANGE
TM11	Solar Beam	Grass	Special	120	100	10	Normal
TM17	Light Screen	Psychic	Status	—	—	30	Your Side
TM18	Reflect	Psychic	Status	—	—	20	Your Side
TM19	Safeguard	Normal	Status	—	—	25	Your Side
TM21	Rest	Psychic	Status	—	—	10	Self
TM24	Snore	Normal	Special	50	100	15	Normal
TM25	Protect	Normal	Status	—	—	10	Self
TM31	Attract	Normal	Status	—	100	15	Normal
TM39	Facade	Normal	Physical	70	100	20	Normal
TM41	Helping Hand	Normal	Status	—	—	20	1 Ally
TM44	Imprison	Psychic	Status	—	—	10	Self
TM57	Payback	Dark	Physical	50	100	10	Normal
TM60	Power Swap	Psychic	Status	—	—	10	Normal
TM61	Guard Swap	Psychic	Status	—	—	10	Normal
TM70	Trick Room	Psychic	Status	—	—	5	Both Sides
TM71	Wonder Room	Psychic	Status	—	—	10	Both Sides
TM72	Magic Room	Psychic	Status	—	—	10	Both Sides
TM76	Round	Normal	Special	60	100	15	Normal
TM91	Psychic Terrain	Psychic	Status	—	—	10	Both Sides

TR MOVES

NO.	NAME	TYPE	KIND	POW.	ACC.	PP	RANGE
TR11	Psychic	Psychic	Special	90	100	10	Normal
TR18	Leech Life	Bug	Physical	80	100	10	Normal
TR20	Substitute	Normal	Status	—	—	10	Self
TR25	Psyshock	Psychic	Special	80	100	10	Normal
TR26	Endure	Normal	Status	—	—	10	Self
TR27	Sleep Talk	Normal	Status	—	—	10	Self
TR33	Shadow Ball	Ghost	Special	80	100	15	Normal
TR34	Future Sight	Psychic	Special	120	100	10	Normal
TR38	Trick	Psychic	Status	—	100	10	Normal
TR40	Skill Swap	Psychic	Status	—	—	10	Normal
TR46	Iron Defense	Steel	Status	—	—	15	Self
TR49	Calm Mind	Psychic	Status	—	—	20	Self
TR61	Bug Buzz	Bug	Special	90	100	10	Normal
TR65	Energy Ball	Grass	Special	90	100	10	Normal
TR69	Zen Headbutt	Psychic	Physical	80	90	15	Normal
TR82	Stored Power	Psychic	Special	20	100	10	Normal
TR83	Ally Switch	Psychic	Status	—	—	15	Self
TR99	Body Press	Fighting	Physical	80	100	10	Normal

EVOLUTION MOVES

NAME	TYPE	KIND	POW.	ACC.	PP	RANGE
Confusion	Psychic	Special	50	100	25	Normal
Light Screen	Psychic	Status	—	—	30	Your Side
Reflect	Psychic	Status	—	—	20	Your Side

EGG MOVES

NAME	TYPE	KIND	POW.	ACC.	PP	RANGE

ABILITY

Swarm
Compound Eyes

HIDDEN ABILITY

Telepathy

SPECIES STRENGTHS

HP
ATTACK
DEFENSE
SP. ATK
SP. DEF
SPEED

DAMAGE TAKEN IN BATTLE

×1	×0.25	×2
×2	×1	×2
×1	×0.5	×1
×0.5	×2	×2
×1	×0.5	×1
×1	×2	×1

BUG

012

Orbeetle p. 27

LEVEL-UP MOVES

LV.	NAME	TYPE	KIND	POW.	ACC.	PP	RANGE
1	Confusion	Psychic	Special	50	100	25	Normal
1	Light Screen	Psychic	Status	—	—	30	Your Side
1	Reflect	Psychic	Status	—	—	20	Your Side
1	Struggle Bug	Bug	Special	50	100	20	Many Others
4	Confuse Ray	Ghost	Status	—	100	10	Normal
8	Magic Coat	Psychic	Status	—	—	15	Self
12	Agility	Psychic	Status	—	—	30	Self
16	Psybeam	Psychic	Special	65	100	20	Normal
20	Hypnosis	Psychic	Status	—	60	20	Normal
24	Ally Switch	Psychic	Status	—	—	15	Self
28	Bug Buzz	Bug	Special	90	100	10	Normal
32	Mirror Coat	Psychic	Special	—	100	20	Varies
36	Psychic	Psychic	Special	90	100	10	Normal
40	After You	Normal	Status	—	—	15	Normal
44	Calm Mind	Psychic	Status	—	—	20	Self
48	Psychic Terrain	Psychic	Status	—	—	10	Both Sides

TUTOR MOVES

NAME	TYPE	KIND	POW.	ACC.	PP	RANGE

TM MOVES

NO.	NAME	TYPE	KIND	POW.	ACC.	PP	RANGE
TM08	Hyper Beam	Normal	Special	150	90	5	Normal
TM09	Giga Impact	Normal	Physical	150	90	5	Normal
TM11	Solar Beam	Grass	Special	120	100	10	Normal
TM17	Light Screen	Psychic	Status	—	—	30	Your Side
TM18	Reflect	Psychic	Status	—	—	20	Your Side
TM19	Safeguard	Normal	Status	—	—	25	Your Side
TM21	Rest	Psychic	Status	—	—	10	Self
TM24	Snore	Normal	Special	50	100	15	Normal
TM25	Protect	Normal	Status	—	—	10	Self
TM28	Giga Drain	Grass	Special	75	100	10	Normal
TM31	Attract	Normal	Status	—	100	15	Normal
TM39	Facade	Normal	Physical	70	100	20	Normal
TM41	Helping Hand	Normal	Status	—	—	20	1 Ally
TM44	Imprison	Psychic	Status	—	—	10	Self
TM56	U-turn	Bug	Physical	70	100	20	Normal
TM57	Payback	Dark	Physical	50	100	10	Normal
TM60	Power Swap	Psychic	Status	—	—	10	Normal
TM61	Guard Swap	Psychic	Status	—	—	10	Normal
TM69	Psycho Cut	Psychic	Physical	70	100	20	Normal
TM70	Trick Room	Psychic	Status	—	—	5	Both Sides
TM71	Wonder Room	Psychic	Status	—	—	10	Both Sides
TM72	Magic Room	Psychic	Status	—	—	10	Both Sides
TM76	Round	Normal	Special	60	100	15	Normal
TM91	Psychic Terrain	Psychic	Status	—	—	10	Both Sides

TR MOVES

NO.	NAME	TYPE	KIND	POW.	ACC.	PP	RANGE
TR11	Psychic	Psychic	Special	90	100	10	Normal
TR12	Agility	Psychic	Status	—	—	30	Self
TR18	Leech Life	Bug	Physical	80	100	10	Normal
TR20	Substitute	Normal	Status	—	—	10	Self
TR25	Psyshock	Psychic	Special	80	100	10	Normal
TR26	Endure	Normal	Status	—	—	10	Self
TR27	Sleep Talk	Normal	Status	—	—	10	Self
TR29	Baton Pass	Normal	Status	—	—	40	Self
TR33	Shadow Ball	Ghost	Special	80	100	15	Normal
TR34	Future Sight	Psychic	Special	120	100	10	Normal
TR38	Trick	Psychic	Status	—	100	10	Normal
TR40	Skill Swap	Psychic	Status	—	—	10	Normal
TR46	Iron Defense	Steel	Status	—	—	15	Self
TR49	Calm Mind	Psychic	Status	—	—	20	Self
TR61	Bug Buzz	Bug	Special	90	100	10	Normal
TR65	Energy Ball	Grass	Special	90	100	10	Normal
TR69	Zen Headbutt	Psychic	Physical	80	90	15	Normal
TR82	Stored Power	Psychic	Special	20	100	10	Normal
TR83	Ally Switch	Psychic	Status	—	—	15	Self
TR99	Body Press	Fighting	Physical	80	100	10	Normal

EVOLUTION MOVES

NAME	TYPE	KIND	POW.	ACC.	PP	RANGE

EGG MOVES

NAME	TYPE	KIND	POW.	ACC.	PP	RANGE

ABILITY

Swarm
Frisk

HIDDEN ABILITY

Telepathy

SPECIES STRENGTHS

HP
ATTACK
DEFENSE
SP. ATK
SP. DEF
SPEED

DAMAGE TAKEN IN BATTLE

×1	×0.25	×2
×2	×1	×2
×1	×0.5	×1
×0.5	×2	×2
×1	×0.5	×1
×1	×2	×1

BUG

013

LEVEL-UP MOVES

LV.	NAME	TYPE	KIND	POW.	ACC.	PP	RANGE
1	String Shot	Bug	Status	—	95	40	Many Others
1	Tackle	Normal	Physical	40	100	35	Normal
9	Bug Bite	Bug	Physical	60	100	20	Normal

EVOLUTION MOVES

NAME	TYPE	KIND	POW.	ACC.	PP	RANGE

EGG MOVES

NAME	TYPE	KIND	POW.	ACC.	PP	RANGE

TUTOR MOVES

NAME	TYPE	KIND	POW.	ACC.	PP	RANGE

TM MOVES

NO.	NAME	TYPE	KIND	POW.	ACC.	PP	RANGE
TM82	Electroweb	Electric	Special	55	95	15	Many Others

TR MOVES

NAME	TYPE	KIND	POW.	ACC.	PP	RANGE

Caterpie
p. 28

ABILITY
Shield Dust
—

HIDDEN ABILITY
Run Away

SPECIES STRENGTHS
HP
ATTACK
DEFENSE
SP. ATK
SP. DEF
SPEED

DAMAGE TAKEN IN BATTLE
×1 ×0.5 ×2
×2 ×1 ×1
×1 ×0.5 ×1
×0.5 ×2 ×1
×1 ×1 ×1
×1 ×1 ×1

BUG

014

LEVEL-UP MOVES

LV.	NAME	TYPE	KIND	POW.	ACC.	PP	RANGE
1	Harden	Normal	Status	—	—	30	Self

EVOLUTION MOVES

NAME	TYPE	KIND	POW.	ACC.	PP	RANGE
Harden	Normal	Status	—	—	30	Self

EGG MOVES

NAME	TYPE	KIND	POW.	ACC.	PP	RANGE

TUTOR MOVES

NAME	TYPE	KIND	POW.	ACC.	PP	RANGE

TM MOVES

NO.	NAME	TYPE	KIND	POW.	ACC.	PP	RANGE
TM82	Electroweb	Electric	Special	55	95	15	Many Others

TR MOVES

NO.	NAME	TYPE	KIND	POW.	ACC.	PP	RANGE
TR46	Iron Defense	Steel	Status	—	—	15	Self

Metapod
p. 28

ABILITY
Shed Skin
—

HIDDEN ABILITY
—

SPECIES STRENGTHS
HP
ATTACK
DEFENSE
SP. ATK
SP. DEF
SPEED

DAMAGE TAKEN IN BATTLE
×1 ×0.5 ×2
×2 ×1 ×1
×1 ×0.5 ×1
×0.5 ×2 ×1
×1 ×1 ×1
×1 ×1 ×1

BUG

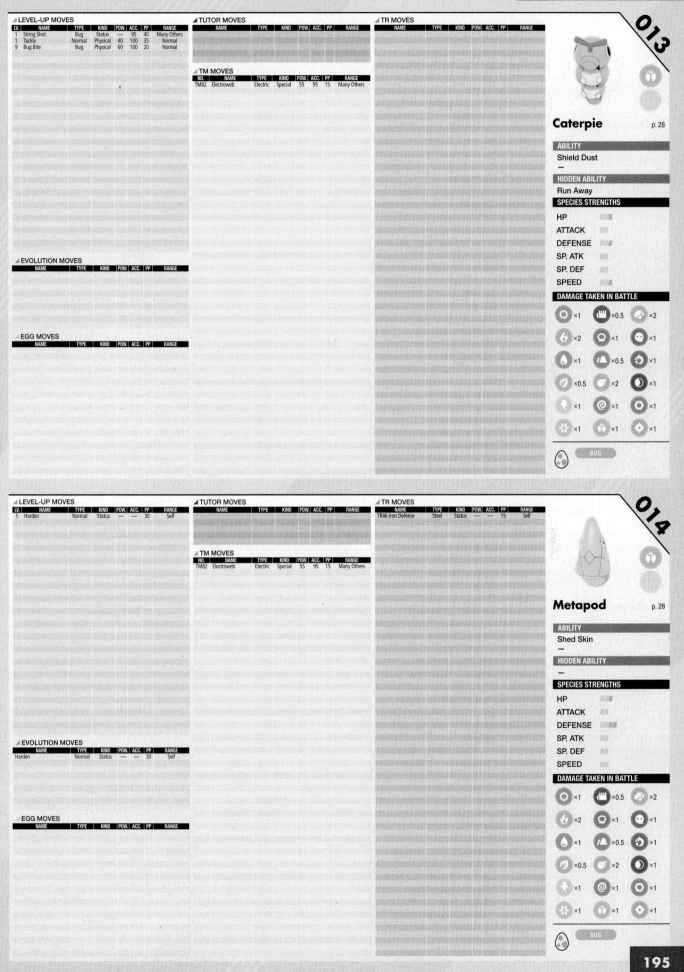

015 Butterfree

p. 28

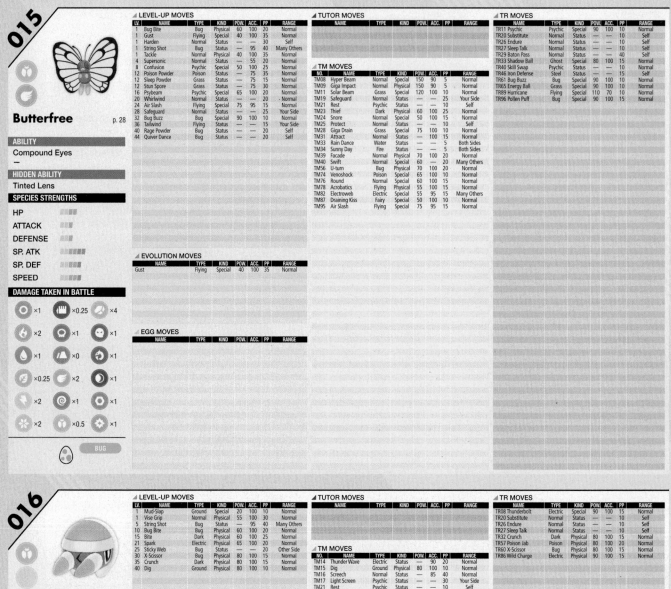

ABILITY
Compound Eyes
—

HIDDEN ABILITY
Tinted Lens

SPECIES STRENGTHS
HP
ATTACK
DEFENSE
SP. ATK
SP. DEF
SPEED

DAMAGE TAKEN IN BATTLE

×1	×0.25	×4
×2	×1	×1
×1	×0	×1
×0.25	×2	×1
×2	×1	×1
×2	×0.5	×1

BUG

LEVEL-UP MOVES

LV.	NAME	TYPE	KIND	POW.	ACC.	PP	RANGE
1	Bug Bite	Bug	Physical	60	100	20	Normal
1	Gust	Flying	Special	40	100	35	Normal
1	Harden	Normal	Status	—	—	30	Self
1	String Shot	Bug	Status	—	95	40	Many Others
1	Tackle	Normal	Physical	40	100	35	Normal
4	Supersonic	Normal	Status	—	55	20	Normal
8	Confusion	Psychic	Special	50	100	25	Normal
12	Poison Powder	Poison	Status	—	75	35	Normal
12	Sleep Powder	Grass	Status	—	75	15	Normal
12	Stun Spore	Grass	Status	—	75	30	Normal
16	Psybeam	Psychic	Special	65	100	20	Normal
20	Whirlwind	Normal	Status	—	—	20	Normal
24	Air Slash	Flying	Special	75	95	15	Normal
28	Safeguard	Normal	Status	—	—	25	Your Side
32	Bug Buzz	Bug	Special	90	100	10	Normal
36	Tailwind	Flying	Status	—	—	15	Your Side
40	Rage Powder	Bug	Status	—	—	20	Self
44	Quiver Dance	Bug	Status	—	—	20	Self

EVOLUTION MOVES

NAME	TYPE	KIND	POW.	ACC.	PP	RANGE
Gust	Flying	Special	40	100	35	Normal

EGG MOVES

NAME	TYPE	KIND	POW.	ACC.	PP	RANGE

TUTOR MOVES

NAME	TYPE	KIND	POW.	ACC.	PP	RANGE

TM MOVES

NO.	NAME	TYPE	KIND	POW.	ACC.	PP	RANGE
TM08	Hyper Beam	Normal	Special	150	90	5	Normal
TM09	Giga Impact	Normal	Physical	150	90	5	Normal
TM11	Solar Beam	Grass	Special	120	100	10	Normal
TM19	Safeguard	Normal	Status	—	—	25	Your Side
TM21	Rest	Psychic	Status	—	—	10	Self
TM23	Thief	Dark	Physical	60	100	25	Normal
TM24	Snore	Normal	Special	50	100	15	Normal
TM25	Protect	Normal	Status	—	—	10	Self
TM28	Giga Drain	Grass	Special	75	100	10	Normal
TM31	Attract	Normal	Status	—	100	15	Normal
TM33	Rain Dance	Water	Status	—	—	5	Both Sides
TM34	Sunny Day	Fire	Status	—	—	5	Both Sides
TM39	Facade	Normal	Physical	70	100	20	Normal
TM40	Swift	Normal	Special	60	—	20	Many Others
TM56	U-turn	Bug	Physical	70	100	20	Normal
TM74	Venoshock	Poison	Special	65	100	10	Normal
TM76	Round	Normal	Special	60	100	15	Normal
TM78	Acrobatics	Flying	Physical	55	100	15	Normal
TM82	Electroweb	Electric	Special	55	95	15	Many Others
TM87	Draining Kiss	Fairy	Special	50	100	10	Normal
TM95	Air Slash	Flying	Special	75	95	15	Normal

TR MOVES

NAME	TYPE	KIND	POW.	ACC.	PP	RANGE
TR11 Psychic	Psychic	Special	90	100	10	Normal
TR20 Substitute	Normal	Status	—	—	10	Self
TR26 Endure	Normal	Status	—	—	10	Self
TR27 Sleep Talk	Normal	Status	—	—	10	Self
TR29 Baton Pass	Normal	Status	—	—	40	Self
TR33 Shadow Ball	Ghost	Special	80	100	15	Normal
TR40 Skill Swap	Psychic	Status	—	—	10	Normal
TR46 Iron Defense	Steel	Status	—	—	15	Self
TR61 Bug Buzz	Bug	Special	90	100	10	Normal
TR65 Energy Ball	Grass	Special	90	100	10	Normal
TR89 Hurricane	Flying	Special	110	70	10	Normal
TR96 Pollen Puff	Bug	Special	90	100	15	Normal

---

016 Grubbin

p. 29

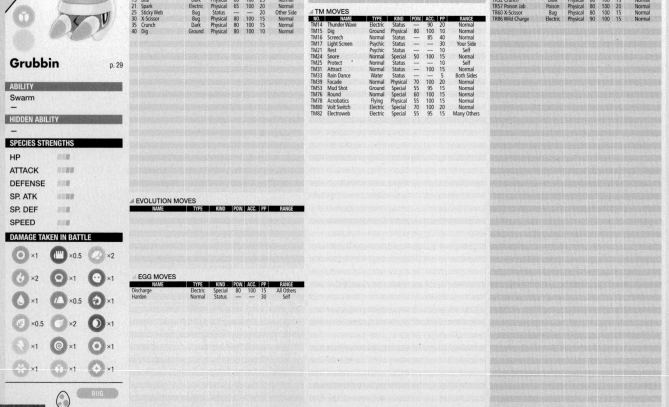

ABILITY
Swarm
—

HIDDEN ABILITY
—

SPECIES STRENGTHS
HP
ATTACK
DEFENSE
SP. ATK
SP. DEF
SPEED

DAMAGE TAKEN IN BATTLE

×1	×0.5	×2
×2	×1	×1
×1	×0.5	×1
×0.5	×2	×1
×1	×1	×1
×1	×1	×1

BUG

LEVEL-UP MOVES

LV.	NAME	TYPE	KIND	POW.	ACC.	PP	RANGE
1	Mud-Slap	Ground	Special	20	100	10	Normal
1	Vise Grip	Normal	Physical	55	100	30	Normal
5	String Shot	Bug	Status	—	95	40	Many Others
10	Bug Bite	Bug	Physical	60	100	20	Normal
15	Bite	Dark	Physical	60	100	25	Normal
21	Spark	Electric	Physical	65	100	20	Normal
25	Sticky Web	Bug	Status	—	—	20	Other Side
30	X-Scissor	Bug	Physical	80	100	15	Normal
35	Crunch	Dark	Physical	80	100	15	Normal
40	Dig	Ground	Physical	80	100	10	Normal

EVOLUTION MOVES

NAME	TYPE	KIND	POW.	ACC.	PP	RANGE

EGG MOVES

NAME	TYPE	KIND	POW.	ACC.	PP	RANGE
Discharge	Electric	Special	80	100	15	All Others
Harden	Normal	Status	—	—	30	Self

TUTOR MOVES

NAME	TYPE	KIND	POW.	ACC.	PP	RANGE

TM MOVES

NO.	NAME	TYPE	KIND	POW.	ACC.	PP	RANGE
TM14	Thunder Wave	Electric	Status	—	90	20	Normal
TM15	Dig	Ground	Physical	80	100	10	Normal
TM16	Screech	Normal	Status	—	85	40	Normal
TM17	Light Screen	Psychic	Status	—	—	30	Your Side
TM21	Rest	Psychic	Status	—	—	10	Self
TM24	Snore	Normal	Special	50	100	15	Normal
TM25	Protect	Normal	Status	—	—	10	Self
TM31	Attract	Normal	Status	—	100	15	Normal
TM33	Rain Dance	Water	Status	—	—	5	Both Sides
TM39	Facade	Normal	Physical	70	100	20	Normal
TM53	Mud Shot	Ground	Special	55	95	15	Normal
TM76	Round	Normal	Special	60	100	15	Normal
TM78	Acrobatics	Flying	Physical	55	100	15	Normal
TM80	Volt Switch	Electric	Special	70	100	20	Normal
TM82	Electroweb	Electric	Special	55	95	15	Many Others

TR MOVES

NAME	TYPE	KIND	POW.	ACC.	PP	RANGE
TR08 Thunderbolt	Electric	Special	90	100	15	Normal
TR20 Substitute	Normal	Status	—	—	10	Self
TR26 Endure	Normal	Status	—	—	10	Self
TR27 Sleep Talk	Normal	Status	—	—	10	Self
TR32 Crunch	Dark	Physical	80	100	15	Normal
TR57 Poison Jab	Poison	Physical	80	100	20	Normal
TR60 X-Scissor	Bug	Physical	80	100	15	Normal
TR86 Wild Charge	Electric	Physical	90	100	15	Normal

017

LEVEL-UP MOVES

LV.	NAME	TYPE	KIND	POW.	ACC.	PP	RANGE
1	Bug Bite	Bug	Physical	60	100	20	Normal
1	Charge	Electric	Status	—	—	20	Self
1	Mud-Slap	Ground	Special	20	100	10	Normal
1	String Shot	Bug	Status	—	95	40	Many Others
1	Vise Grip	Normal	Physical	55	100	30	Normal
15	Bite	Dark	Physical	60	100	25	Normal
23	Spark	Electric	Physical	65	100	20	Normal
29	Sticky Web	Bug	Status	—	—	20	Other Side
36	X-Scissor	Bug	Physical	80	100	15	Normal
43	Crunch	Dark	Physical	80	100	15	Normal
50	Dig	Ground	Physical	80	100	10	Normal
57	Iron Defense	Steel	Status	—	—	15	Self
64	Discharge	Electric	Special	80	100	15	All Others

EVOLUTION MOVES

NAME	TYPE	KIND	POW.	ACC.	PP	RANGE
Charge	Electric	Status	—	—	20	Self

EGG MOVES

NAME	TYPE	KIND	POW.	ACC.	PP	RANGE

TUTOR MOVES

NAME	TYPE	KIND	POW.	ACC.	PP	RANGE

TM MOVES

NO.	NAME	TYPE	KIND	POW.	ACC.	PP	RANGE
TM14	Thunder Wave	Electric	Status	—	90	20	Normal
TM15	Dig	Ground	Physical	80	100	10	Normal
TM16	Screech	Normal	Status	—	85	40	Normal
TM17	Light Screen	Psychic	Status	—	—	30	Your Side
TM21	Rest	Psychic	Status	—	—	10	Self
TM24	Snore	Normal	Special	50	100	15	Normal
TM25	Protect	Normal	Status	—	—	10	Self
TM31	Attract	Normal	Status	—	100	15	Normal
TM33	Rain Dance	Water	Status	—	—	5	Both Sides
TM39	Facade	Normal	Physical	70	100	20	Normal
TM53	Mud Shot	Ground	Special	55	95	15	Normal
TM76	Round	Normal	Special	60	100	15	Normal
TM78	Acrobatics	Flying	Physical	55	100	15	Normal
TM80	Volt Switch	Electric	Special	70	100	20	Normal
TM82	Electroweb	Electric	Special	55	95	15	Many Others
TM93	Eerie Impulse	Electric	Status	—	100	15	Normal

TR MOVES

NAME	TYPE	KIND	POW.	ACC.	PP	RANGE
TR08 Thunderbolt	Electric	Special	90	100	15	Normal
TR20 Substitute	Normal	Status	—	—	10	Self
TR26 Endure	Normal	Status	—	—	10	Self
TR27 Sleep Talk	Normal	Status	—	—	10	Self
TR32 Crunch	Dark	Physical	80	100	15	Normal
TR46 Iron Defense	Steel	Status	—	—	15	Self
TR57 Poison Jab	Poison	Physical	80	100	20	Normal
TR60 X-Scissor	Bug	Physical	80	100	15	Normal
TR80 Electro Ball	Electric	Special	—	100	10	Normal
TR86 Wild Charge	Electric	Physical	90	100	15	Normal

Charjabug p. 29

ABILITY
Battery
—

HIDDEN ABILITY
—

SPECIES STRENGTHS

HP	
ATTACK	
DEFENSE	
SP. ATK	
SP. DEF	
SPEED	

DAMAGE TAKEN IN BATTLE

×1 ×0.5 ×2
×2 ×1 ×1
×1 ×1 ×1
×0.5 ×1 ×1
×0.5 ×1 ×0.5
×1 ×1 ×1

BUG

018

LEVEL-UP MOVES

LV.	NAME	TYPE	KIND	POW.	ACC.	PP	RANGE
1	Bug Bite	Bug	Physical	60	100	20	Normal
1	Charge	Electric	Status	—	—	20	Self
1	Crunch	Dark	Physical	80	100	15	Normal
1	Dig	Ground	Physical	80	100	10	Normal
1	Discharge	Electric	Special	80	100	15	All Others
1	Iron Defense	Steel	Status	—	—	15	Self
1	Mud-Slap	Ground	Special	20	100	10	Normal
1	String Shot	Bug	Status	—	95	40	Many Others
1	Thunderbolt	Electric	Special	90	100	15	Normal
1	Vise Grip	Normal	Physical	55	100	30	Normal
1	X-Scissor	Bug	Physical	80	100	15	Normal
15	Bite	Dark	Physical	60	100	25	Normal
23	Spark	Electric	Physical	65	100	20	Normal
29	Sticky Web	Bug	Status	—	—	20	Other Side
36	Bug Buzz	Bug	Special	90	100	10	Normal
43	Guillotine	Normal	Physical	—	30	5	Normal
50	Fly	Flying	Physical	90	95	15	Normal
57	Agility	Psychic	Status	—	—	30	Self
64	Zap Cannon	Electric	Special	120	50	5	Normal

EVOLUTION MOVES

NAME	TYPE	KIND	POW.	ACC.	PP	RANGE
Thunderbolt	Electric	Special	90	100	15	Normal

EGG MOVES

NAME	TYPE	KIND	POW.	ACC.	PP	RANGE

TUTOR MOVES

NAME	TYPE	KIND	POW.	ACC.	PP	RANGE

TM MOVES

NO.	NAME	TYPE	KIND	POW.	ACC.	PP	RANGE
TM06	Fly	Flying	Physical	90	95	15	Normal
TM08	Hyper Beam	Normal	Special	150	90	5	Normal
TM09	Giga Impact	Normal	Physical	150	90	5	Normal
TM11	Solar Beam	Grass	Special	120	100	10	Normal
TM14	Thunder Wave	Electric	Status	—	90	20	Normal
TM15	Dig	Ground	Physical	80	100	10	Normal
TM16	Screech	Normal	Status	—	85	40	Normal
TM17	Light Screen	Psychic	Status	—	—	30	Your Side
TM21	Rest	Psychic	Status	—	—	10	Self
TM24	Snore	Normal	Special	50	100	15	Normal
TM25	Protect	Normal	Status	—	—	10	Self
TM31	Attract	Normal	Status	—	100	15	Normal
TM33	Rain Dance	Water	Status	—	—	5	Both Sides
TM39	Facade	Normal	Physical	70	100	20	Normal
TM53	Mud Shot	Ground	Special	55	95	15	Normal
TM76	Round	Normal	Special	60	100	15	Normal
TM78	Acrobatics	Flying	Physical	55	100	15	Normal
TM80	Volt Switch	Electric	Special	70	100	20	Normal
TM82	Electroweb	Electric	Special	55	95	15	Many Others
TM93	Eerie Impulse	Electric	Status	—	100	15	Normal
TM95	Air Slash	Flying	Special	75	95	15	Normal

TR MOVES

NAME	TYPE	KIND	POW.	ACC.	PP	RANGE
TR08 Thunderbolt	Electric	Special	90	100	15	Normal
TR09 Thunder	Electric	Special	110	70	10	Normal
TR12 Agility	Psychic	Status	—	—	30	Self
TR20 Substitute	Normal	Status	—	—	10	Self
TR26 Endure	Normal	Status	—	—	10	Self
TR27 Sleep Talk	Normal	Status	—	—	10	Self
TR32 Crunch	Dark	Physical	80	100	15	Normal
TR46 Iron Defense	Steel	Status	—	—	15	Self
TR57 Poison Jab	Poison	Physical	80	100	20	Normal
TR60 X-Scissor	Bug	Physical	80	100	15	Normal
TR61 Bug Buzz	Bug	Special	90	100	10	Normal
TR65 Energy Ball	Grass	Special	90	100	10	Normal
TR70 Flash Cannon	Steel	Special	80	100	10	Normal
TR80 Electro Ball	Electric	Special	—	100	10	Normal
TR86 Wild Charge	Electric	Physical	90	100	15	Normal

Vikavolt p. 29

ABILITY
Levitate
—

HIDDEN ABILITY
—

SPECIES STRENGTHS

HP	
ATTACK	
DEFENSE	
SP. ATK	
SP. DEF	
SPEED	

DAMAGE TAKEN IN BATTLE

×1 ×0.5 ×2
×2 ×1 ×1
×1 ×1 ×1
×0.5 ×1 ×1
×0.5 ×1 ×0.5
×1 ×1 ×1

BUG

019

Hoothoot
p. 30

ABILITY
Insomnia
Keen Eye

HIDDEN ABILITY
Tinted Lens

SPECIES STRENGTHS
HP
ATTACK
DEFENSE
SP. ATK
SP. DEF
SPEED

LEVEL-UP MOVES

LV.	NAME	TYPE	KIND	POW.	ACC.	PP	RANGE
1	Growl	Normal	Status	—	100	40	Many Others
1	Peck	Flying	Physical	35	100	35	Normal
3	Tackle	Normal	Physical	40	100	35	Normal
6	Echoed Voice	Normal	Special	40	100	15	Normal
9	Confusion	Psychic	Special	50	100	25	Normal
12	Reflect	Psychic	Status	—	—	20	Your Side
15	Psycho Shift	Psychic	Status	—	100	10	Normal
18	Air Slash	Flying	Special	75	95	15	Normal
21	Extrasensory	Psychic	Special	80	100	20	Normal
24	Take Down	Normal	Physical	90	85	20	Normal
27	Uproar	Normal	Special	90	100	10	1 Random
30	Roost	Flying	Status	—	—	10	Self
33	Moonblast	Fairy	Special	95	100	15	Normal
36	Hypnosis	Psychic	Status	—	60	20	Normal
39	Dream Eater	Psychic	Special	100	100	15	Normal

EVOLUTION MOVES

NAME	TYPE	KIND	POW.	ACC.	PP	RANGE

EGG MOVES

NAME	TYPE	KIND	POW.	ACC.	PP	RANGE
Defog	Flying	Status	—	—	15	Normal
Feather Dance	Flying	Status	—	100	15	Normal
Night Shade	Ghost	Special	—	100	15	Normal
Supersonic	Normal	Status	—	55	20	Normal
Whirlwind	Normal	Status	—	—	20	Normal
Wing Attack	Flying	Physical	60	100	35	Normal

TUTOR MOVES

NAME	TYPE	KIND	POW.	ACC.	PP	RANGE

TM MOVES

NO.	NAME	TYPE	KIND	POW.	ACC.	PP	RANGE
TM06	Fly	Flying	Physical	90	95	15	Normal
TM16	Screech	Normal	Status	—	85	40	Normal
TM18	Reflect	Psychic	Status	—	—	20	Your Side
TM21	Rest	Psychic	Status	—	—	10	Self
TM23	Thief	Dark	Physical	60	100	25	Normal
TM24	Snore	Normal	Special	50	100	15	Normal
TM25	Protect	Normal	Status	—	—	10	Self
TM30	Steel Wing	Steel	Physical	70	90	25	Normal
TM31	Attract	Normal	Status	—	100	15	Normal
TM33	Rain Dance	Water	Status	—	—	5	Both Sides
TM34	Sunny Day	Fire	Status	—	—	5	Both Sides
TM39	Facade	Normal	Physical	70	100	20	Normal
TM40	Swift	Normal	Special	60	—	20	Many Others
TM44	Imprison	Psychic	Status	—	—	10	Self
TM76	Round	Normal	Special	60	100	15	Normal
TM95	Air Slash	Flying	Special	75	95	15	Normal

TR MOVES

NAME	TYPE	KIND	POW.	ACC.	PP	RANGE
TR11 Psychic	Psychic	Special	90	100	10	Normal
TR12 Agility	Psychic	Status	—	—	30	Self
TR17 Amnesia	Psychic	Status	—	—	20	Self
TR20 Substitute	Normal	Status	—	—	10	Self
TR26 Endure	Normal	Status	—	—	10	Self
TR27 Sleep Talk	Normal	Status	—	—	10	Self
TR33 Shadow Ball	Ghost	Special	80	100	15	Normal
TR35 Uproar	Normal	Special	90	100	10	1 Random
TR36 Heat Wave	Fire	Special	95	90	10	Many Others
TR42 Hyper Voice	Normal	Special	90	100	10	Many Others
TR49 Calm Mind	Psychic	Status	—	—	20	Self
TR68 Nasty Plot	Dark	Status	—	—	20	Self
TR69 Zen Headbutt	Psychic	Physical	80	90	15	Normal
TR82 Stored Power	Psychic	Special	20	100	10	Normal
TR85 Work Up	Normal	Status	—	—	30	Self
TR89 Hurricane	Flying	Special	110	70	10	Normal

DAMAGE TAKEN IN BATTLE

×1 ×1 ×2
×1 ×1 ×0
×1 ×0 ×1
×0.5 ×1 ×1
×2 ×1 ×1
×2 ×0.5 ×1

FLYING

020

Noctowl
p. 30

ABILITY
Insomnia
Keen Eye

HIDDEN ABILITY
Tinted Lens

SPECIES STRENGTHS
HP
ATTACK
DEFENSE
SP. ATK
SP. DEF
SPEED

LEVEL-UP MOVES

LV.	NAME	TYPE	KIND	POW.	ACC.	PP	RANGE
1	Echoed Voice	Normal	Special	40	100	15	Normal
1	Growl	Normal	Status	—	100	40	Many Others
1	Peck	Flying	Physical	35	100	35	Normal
1	Sky Attack	Flying	Physical	140	90	5	Normal
3	Tackle	Normal	Physical	40	100	35	Normal
9	Confusion	Psychic	Special	50	100	25	Normal
12	Reflect	Psychic	Status	—	—	20	Your Side
15	Psycho Shift	Psychic	Status	—	100	10	Normal
18	Air Slash	Flying	Special	75	95	15	Normal
23	Extrasensory	Psychic	Special	80	100	20	Normal
28	Take Down	Normal	Physical	90	85	20	Normal
33	Uproar	Normal	Special	90	100	10	1 Random
38	Roost	Flying	Status	—	—	10	Self
43	Moonblast	Fairy	Special	95	100	15	Normal
48	Hypnosis	Psychic	Status	—	60	20	Normal
53	Dream Eater	Psychic	Special	100	100	15	Normal

EVOLUTION MOVES

NAME	TYPE	KIND	POW.	ACC.	PP	RANGE

EGG MOVES

NAME	TYPE	KIND	POW.	ACC.	PP	RANGE

TUTOR MOVES

NAME	TYPE	KIND	POW.	ACC.	PP	RANGE

TM MOVES

NO.	NAME	TYPE	KIND	POW.	ACC.	PP	RANGE
TM06	Fly	Flying	Physical	90	95	15	Normal
TM08	Hyper Beam	Normal	Special	150	90	5	Normal
TM09	Giga Impact	Normal	Physical	150	90	5	Normal
TM16	Screech	Normal	Status	—	85	40	Normal
TM18	Reflect	Psychic	Status	—	—	20	Your Side
TM21	Rest	Psychic	Status	—	—	10	Self
TM23	Thief	Dark	Physical	60	100	25	Normal
TM24	Snore	Normal	Special	50	100	15	Normal
TM25	Protect	Normal	Status	—	—	10	Self
TM30	Steel Wing	Steel	Physical	70	90	25	Normal
TM31	Attract	Normal	Status	—	100	15	Normal
TM33	Rain Dance	Water	Status	—	—	5	Both Sides
TM34	Sunny Day	Fire	Status	—	—	5	Both Sides
TM39	Facade	Normal	Physical	70	100	20	Normal
TM40	Swift	Normal	Special	60	—	20	Many Others
TM44	Imprison	Psychic	Status	—	—	10	Self
TM76	Round	Normal	Special	60	100	15	Normal
TM95	Air Slash	Flying	Special	75	95	15	Normal

TR MOVES

NAME	TYPE	KIND	POW.	ACC.	PP	RANGE
TR11 Psychic	Psychic	Special	90	100	10	Normal
TR12 Agility	Psychic	Status	—	—	30	Self
TR17 Amnesia	Psychic	Status	—	—	20	Self
TR20 Substitute	Normal	Status	—	—	10	Self
TR26 Endure	Normal	Status	—	—	10	Self
TR27 Sleep Talk	Normal	Status	—	—	10	Self
TR33 Shadow Ball	Ghost	Special	80	100	15	Normal
TR34 Future Sight	Psychic	Special	120	100	10	Normal
TR35 Uproar	Normal	Special	90	100	10	1 Random
TR36 Heat Wave	Fire	Special	95	90	10	Many Others
TR42 Hyper Voice	Normal	Special	90	100	10	Many Others
TR49 Calm Mind	Psychic	Status	—	—	20	Self
TR68 Nasty Plot	Dark	Status	—	—	20	Self
TR69 Zen Headbutt	Psychic	Physical	80	90	15	Normal
TR82 Stored Power	Psychic	Special	20	100	10	Normal
TR85 Work Up	Normal	Status	—	—	30	Self
TR89 Hurricane	Flying	Special	110	70	10	Normal

DAMAGE TAKEN IN BATTLE

×1 ×1 ×2
×1 ×1 ×0
×1 ×0 ×1
×0.5 ×1 ×1
×2 ×1 ×1
×2 ×0.5 ×1

FLYING

021 Rookidee

LEVEL-UP MOVES

LV.	NAME	TYPE	KIND	POW.	ACC.	PP	RANGE
1	Leer	Normal	Status	—	100	30	Many Others
1	Peck	Flying	Physical	35	100	35	Normal
4	Power Trip	Dark	Physical	20	100	10	Normal
8	Hone Claws	Dark	Status	—	—	15	Self
12	Fury Attack	Normal	Physical	15	85	20	Normal
16	Pluck	Flying	Physical	60	100	20	Normal
20	Taunt	Dark	Status	—	100	20	Normal
24	Scary Face	Normal	Status	—	100	10	Normal
28	Drill Peck	Flying	Physical	80	100	20	Normal
32	Swagger	Normal	Status	—	85	15	Normal
36	Brave Bird	Flying	Physical	120	100	15	Normal

EVOLUTION MOVES

NAME	TYPE	KIND	POW.	ACC.	PP	RANGE

EGG MOVES

NAME	TYPE	KIND	POW.	ACC.	PP	RANGE
Defog	Flying	Status	—	—	15	Normal
Rock Smash	Fighting	Physical	40	100	15	Normal
Roost	Flying	Status	—	—	10	Self
Sand Attack	Ground	Status	—	100	15	Normal
Sky Attack	Flying	Physical	140	90	5	Normal
Spite	Ghost	Status	—	100	10	Normal
Tailwind	Flying	Status	—	—	15	Your Side

TUTOR MOVES

NAME	TYPE	KIND	POW.	ACC.	PP	RANGE

TM MOVES

NO.	NAME	TYPE	KIND	POW.	ACC.	PP	RANGE
TM06	Fly	Flying	Physical	90	95	15	Normal
TM21	Rest	Psychic	Status	—	—	10	Self
TM23	Thief	Dark	Physical	60	100	25	Normal
TM24	Snore	Normal	Special	50	100	15	Normal
TM25	Protect	Normal	Status	—	—	10	Self
TM26	Scary Face	Normal	Status	—	100	10	Normal
TM31	Attract	Normal	Status	—	100	15	Normal
TM39	Facade	Normal	Physical	70	100	20	Normal
TM40	Swift	Normal	Special	60	—	20	Many Others
TM42	Revenge	Fighting	Physical	60	100	10	Normal
TM47	Fake Tears	Dark	Status	—	100	20	Normal
TM56	U-turn	Bug	Physical	70	100	20	Normal
TM57	Payback	Dark	Physical	50	100	10	Normal
TM58	Assurance	Dark	Physical	60	100	10	Normal
TM76	Round	Normal	Special	60	100	15	Normal
TM79	Retaliate	Normal	Physical	70	100	5	Normal
TM95	Air Slash	Flying	Special	75	95	15	Normal

TR MOVES

NO.	NAME	TYPE	KIND	POW.	ACC.	PP	RANGE
TR12	Agility	Psychic	Status	—	—	30	Self
TR13	Focus Energy	Normal	Status	—	—	30	Self
TR20	Substitute	Normal	Status	—	—	10	Self
TR21	Reversal	Fighting	Physical	—	100	15	Normal
TR26	Endure	Normal	Status	—	—	10	Self
TR27	Sleep Talk	Normal	Status	—	—	10	Self
TR37	Taunt	Dark	Status	—	100	20	Normal
TR66	Brave Bird	Flying	Physical	120	100	15	Normal
TR68	Nasty Plot	Dark	Status	—	—	20	Self
TR85	Work Up	Normal	Status	—	—	30	Self

Rookidee p. 31

ABILITY
Keen Eye
Unnerve

HIDDEN ABILITY
Big Pecks

SPECIES STRENGTHS

HP
ATTACK
DEFENSE
SP. ATK
SP. DEF
SPEED

DAMAGE TAKEN IN BATTLE

×1 ×0.5 ×2 ×1 ×1 ×1 ×1 ×0 ×1 ×0.5 ×1 ×1 ×2 ×1 ×1 ×2 ×0.5 ×1

FLYING

---

022 Corvisquire

LEVEL-UP MOVES

LV.	NAME	TYPE	KIND	POW.	ACC.	PP	RANGE
1	Hone Claws	Dark	Status	—	—	15	Self
1	Leer	Normal	Status	—	100	30	Many Others
1	Peck	Flying	Physical	35	100	35	Normal
1	Power Trip	Dark	Physical	20	100	10	Normal
12	Fury Attack	Normal	Physical	15	85	20	Normal
16	Pluck	Flying	Physical	60	100	20	Normal
22	Taunt	Dark	Status	—	100	20	Normal
28	Scary Face	Normal	Status	—	100	10	Normal
34	Drill Peck	Flying	Physical	80	100	20	Normal
40	Swagger	Normal	Status	—	85	15	Normal
46	Brave Bird	Flying	Physical	120	100	15	Normal

EVOLUTION MOVES

NAME	TYPE	KIND	POW.	ACC.	PP	RANGE

EGG MOVES

NAME	TYPE	KIND	POW.	ACC.	PP	RANGE

TUTOR MOVES

NAME	TYPE	KIND	POW.	ACC.	PP	RANGE

TM MOVES

NO.	NAME	TYPE	KIND	POW.	ACC.	PP	RANGE
TM06	Fly	Flying	Physical	90	95	15	Normal
TM21	Rest	Psychic	Status	—	—	10	Self
TM23	Thief	Dark	Physical	60	100	25	Normal
TM24	Snore	Normal	Special	50	100	15	Normal
TM25	Protect	Normal	Status	—	—	10	Self
TM26	Scary Face	Normal	Status	—	100	10	Normal
TM31	Attract	Normal	Status	—	100	15	Normal
TM39	Facade	Normal	Physical	70	100	20	Normal
TM40	Swift	Normal	Special	60	—	20	Many Others
TM42	Revenge	Fighting	Physical	60	100	10	Normal
TM47	Fake Tears	Dark	Status	—	100	20	Normal
TM56	U-turn	Bug	Physical	70	100	20	Normal
TM57	Payback	Dark	Physical	50	100	10	Normal
TM58	Assurance	Dark	Physical	60	100	10	Normal
TM76	Round	Normal	Special	60	100	15	Normal
TM79	Retaliate	Normal	Physical	70	100	5	Normal
TM95	Air Slash	Flying	Special	75	95	15	Normal

TR MOVES

NO.	NAME	TYPE	KIND	POW.	ACC.	PP	RANGE
TR12	Agility	Psychic	Status	—	—	30	Self
TR13	Focus Energy	Normal	Status	—	—	30	Self
TR20	Substitute	Normal	Status	—	—	10	Self
TR21	Reversal	Fighting	Physical	—	100	15	Normal
TR26	Endure	Normal	Status	—	—	10	Self
TR27	Sleep Talk	Normal	Status	—	—	10	Self
TR37	Taunt	Dark	Status	—	100	20	Normal
TR66	Brave Bird	Flying	Physical	120	100	15	Normal
TR68	Nasty Plot	Dark	Status	—	—	20	Self
TR85	Work Up	Normal	Status	—	—	30	Self

Corvisquire p. 31

ABILITY
Keen Eye
Unnerve

HIDDEN ABILITY
Big Pecks

SPECIES STRENGTHS

HP
ATTACK
DEFENSE
SP. ATK
SP. DEF
SPEED

DAMAGE TAKEN IN BATTLE

×1 ×0.5 ×2 ×1 ×1 ×1 ×1 ×0 ×1 ×0.5 ×1 ×1 ×2 ×1 ×1 ×2 ×0.5 ×1

FLYING

023

Corviknight   p. 31

ABILITY
Pressure
Unnerve

HIDDEN ABILITY
Mirror Armor

SPECIES STRENGTHS

HP	▰▰▰▱▱▱
ATTACK	▰▰▰▰▱▱
DEFENSE	▰▰▰▰▰▱
SP. ATK	▰▰▱▱▱▱
SP. DEF	▰▰▰▱▱▱
SPEED	▰▰▰▱▱▱

DAMAGE TAKEN IN BATTLE

×0.5	×1	×1
×2	×0	×1
×1	×0	×0.5
×0.25	×0.5	×1
×2	×0.5	×0.5
×1	×0.25	×0.5

FLYING

LEVEL-UP MOVES

LV.	NAME	TYPE	KIND	POW.	ACC.	PP	RANGE
1	Hone Claws	Dark	Status	—	—	15	Self
1	Iron Defense	Steel	Status	—	—	15	Self
1	Leer	Normal	Status	—	100	30	Many Others
1	Metal Sound	Steel	Status	—	85	40	Normal
1	Peck	Flying	Physical	35	100	35	Normal
1	Power Trip	Dark	Physical	20	100	10	Normal
1	Steel Wing	Steel	Physical	70	90	25	Normal
12	Fury Attack	Normal	Physical	15	85	20	Normal
16	Pluck	Flying	Physical	60	100	20	Normal
22	Taunt	Dark	Status	—	100	20	Normal
28	Scary Face	Normal	Status	—	100	10	Normal
34	Drill Peck	Flying	Physical	80	100	20	Normal
42	Swagger	Normal	Status	—	85	15	Normal
50	Brave Bird	Flying	Physical	120	100	15	Normal

EVOLUTION MOVES

NAME	TYPE	KIND	POW.	ACC.	PP	RANGE
Steel Wing	Steel	Physical	70	90	25	Normal

EGG MOVES

NAME	TYPE	KIND	POW.	ACC.	PP	RANGE

TUTOR MOVES

NAME	TYPE	KIND	POW.	ACC.	PP	RANGE
Steel Beam	Steel	Special	140	95	5	Normal

TM MOVES

NO.	NAME	TYPE	KIND	POW.	ACC.	PP	RANGE
TM06	Fly	Flying	Physical	90	95	15	Normal
TM08	Hyper Beam	Normal	Special	150	90	5	Normal
TM09	Giga Impact	Normal	Physical	150	90	5	Normal
TM16	Screech	Normal	Status	—	85	40	Normal
TM17	Light Screen	Psychic	Status	—	—	30	Your Side
TM18	Reflect	Psychic	Status	—	—	20	Your Side
TM21	Rest	Psychic	Status	—	—	10	Self
TM23	Thief	Dark	Physical	60	100	25	Normal
TM24	Snore	Normal	Special	50	100	15	Normal
TM25	Protect	Normal	Status	—	—	10	Self
TM26	Scary Face	Normal	Status	—	100	10	Normal
TM30	Steel Wing	Steel	Physical	70	90	25	Normal
TM31	Attract	Normal	Status	—	100	15	Normal
TM39	Facade	Normal	Physical	70	100	20	Normal
TM40	Swift	Normal	Special	60	—	20	Many Others
TM42	Revenge	Fighting	Physical	60	100	10	Normal
TM47	Fake Tears	Dark	Status	—	100	20	Normal
TM56	U-turn	Bug	Physical	70	100	20	Normal
TM57	Payback	Dark	Physical	50	100	10	Normal
TM58	Assurance	Dark	Physical	60	100	10	Normal
TM76	Round	Normal	Special	60	100	15	Normal
TM79	Retaliate	Normal	Physical	70	100	5	Normal
TM95	Air Slash	Flying	Special	75	95	15	Normal

TR MOVES

NO.	NAME	TYPE	KIND	POW.	ACC.	PP	RANGE
TR01	Body Slam	Normal	Physical	85	100	15	Normal
TR12	Agility	Psychic	Status	—	—	30	Self
TR13	Focus Energy	Normal	Status	—	—	30	Self
TR20	Substitute	Normal	Status	—	—	10	Self
TR21	Reversal	Fighting	Physical	—	100	15	Normal
TR26	Endure	Normal	Status	—	—	10	Self
TR27	Sleep Talk	Normal	Status	—	—	10	Self
TR37	Taunt	Dark	Status	—	100	20	Normal
TR46	Iron Defense	Steel	Status	—	—	15	Self
TR48	Bulk Up	Fighting	Status	—	—	20	Self
TR66	Brave Bird	Flying	Physical	120	100	15	Normal
TR68	Nasty Plot	Dark	Status	—	—	20	Self
TR70	Flash Cannon	Steel	Special	80	100	10	Normal
TR74	Iron Head	Steel	Physical	80	100	15	Normal
TR79	Heavy Slam	Steel	Physical	—	100	10	Normal
TR85	Work Up	Normal	Status	—	—	30	Self
TR89	Hurricane	Flying	Special	110	70	10	Normal
TR99	Body Press	Fighting	Physical	80	100	10	Normal

024

Skwovet   p. 32

ABILITY
Cheek Pouch
—

HIDDEN ABILITY
—

SPECIES STRENGTHS

HP	▰▰▰▱▱▱
ATTACK	▰▰▱▱▱▱
DEFENSE	▰▰▱▱▱▱
SP. ATK	▰▱▱▱▱▱
SP. DEF	▰▱▱▱▱▱
SPEED	▰▱▱▱▱▱

DAMAGE TAKEN IN BATTLE

×1	×2	×1
×1	×1	×0
×1	×1	×1
×1	×1	×1
×1	×1	×1
×1	×1	×1

FIELD

LEVEL-UP MOVES

LV.	NAME	TYPE	KIND	POW.	ACC.	PP	RANGE
1	Tackle	Normal	Physical	40	100	35	Normal
1	Tail Whip	Normal	Status	—	100	30	Many Others
5	Bite	Dark	Physical	60	100	25	Normal
10	Stuff Cheeks	Normal	Status	—	—	10	Self
15	Spit Up	Normal	Special	—	100	10	Normal
15	Stockpile	Normal	Status	—	—	20	Self
15	Swallow	Normal	Status	—	—	10	Self
20	Body Slam	Normal	Physical	85	100	15	Normal
25	Rest	Psychic	Status	—	—	10	Self
30	Counter	Fighting	Physical	—	100	20	Varies
35	Bullet Seed	Grass	Physical	25	100	30	Normal
40	Super Fang	Normal	Physical	—	90	10	Normal
45	Belch	Poison	Special	120	90	10	Normal

EVOLUTION MOVES

NAME	TYPE	KIND	POW.	ACC.	PP	RANGE

EGG MOVES

NAME	TYPE	KIND	POW.	ACC.	PP	RANGE
Belly Drum	Normal	Status	—	—	10	Self
Defense Curl	Normal	Status	—	—	40	Self
Last Resort	Normal	Physical	140	100	5	Normal
Rollout	Rock	Physical	30	90	20	Normal

TUTOR MOVES

NAME	TYPE	KIND	POW.	ACC.	PP	RANGE

TM MOVES

NO.	NAME	TYPE	KIND	POW.	ACC.	PP	RANGE
TM15	Dig	Ground	Physical	80	100	10	Normal
TM21	Rest	Psychic	Status	—	—	10	Self
TM23	Thief	Dark	Physical	60	100	25	Normal
TM24	Snore	Normal	Special	50	100	15	Normal
TM25	Protect	Normal	Status	—	—	10	Self
TM31	Attract	Normal	Status	—	100	15	Normal
TM39	Facade	Normal	Physical	70	100	20	Normal
TM50	Bullet Seed	Grass	Physical	25	100	30	Normal
TM53	Mud Shot	Ground	Special	55	95	15	Normal
TM57	Payback	Dark	Physical	50	100	10	Normal
TM58	Assurance	Dark	Physical	60	100	10	Normal
TM59	Fling	Dark	Physical	—	100	10	Normal
TM76	Round	Normal	Special	60	100	15	Normal
TM84	Tail Slap	Normal	Physical	25	85	10	Normal
TM97	Brutal Swing	Dark	Physical	60	100	20	All Others

TR MOVES

NO.	NAME	TYPE	KIND	POW.	ACC.	PP	RANGE
TR01	Body Slam	Normal	Physical	85	100	15	Normal
TR12	Amnesia	Psychic	Status	—	—	20	Self
TR20	Substitute	Normal	Status	—	—	10	Self
TR26	Endure	Normal	Status	—	—	10	Self
TR27	Sleep Talk	Normal	Status	—	—	10	Self
TR31	Iron Tail	Steel	Physical	100	75	15	Normal
TR32	Crunch	Dark	Physical	80	100	15	Normal
TR35	Uproar	Normal	Special	90	100	10	1 Random
TR42	Hyper Voice	Normal	Special	90	100	10	Many Others
TR52	Gyro Ball	Steel	Physical	—	100	5	Normal
TR59	Seed Bomb	Grass	Physical	80	100	15	Normal

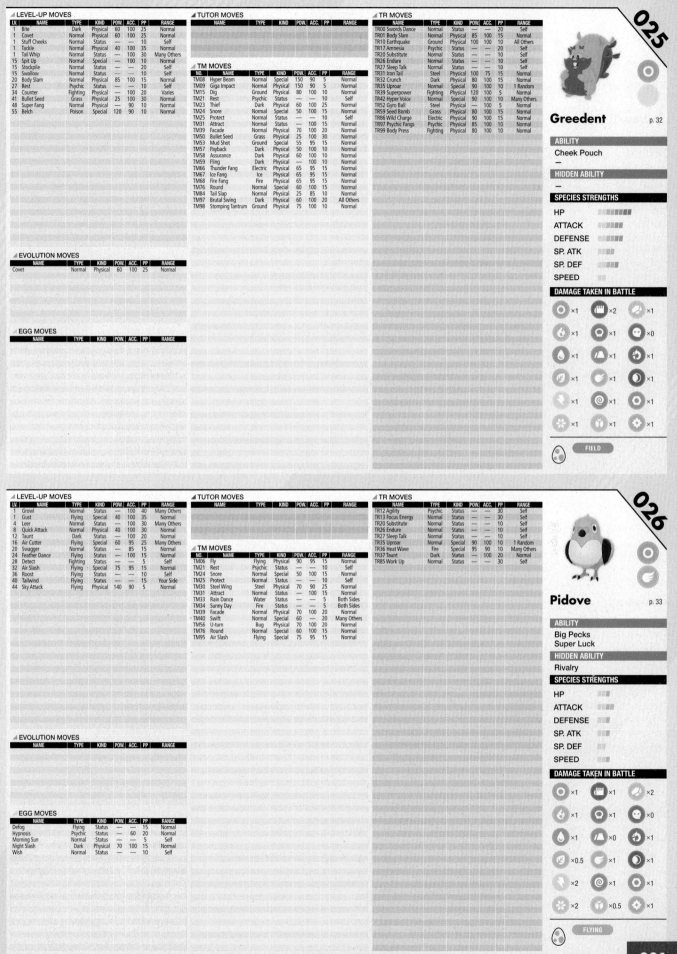

025

Greedent

p. 32

LEVEL-UP MOVES

LV.	NAME	TYPE	KIND	POW.	ACC.	PP	RANGE
1	Bite	Dark	Physical	60	100	25	Normal
1	Covet	Normal	Physical	60	100	25	Normal
1	Stuff Cheeks	Normal	Status	—	—	10	Self
1	Tackle	Normal	Physical	40	100	35	Normal
1	Tail Whip	Normal	Status	—	100	30	Many Others
15	Spit Up	Normal	Special	—	100	10	Normal
15	Stockpile	Normal	Status	—	—	20	Self
15	Swallow	Normal	Status	—	—	10	Self
20	Body Slam	Normal	Physical	85	100	15	Normal
27	Rest	Psychic	Status	—	—	10	Self
34	Counter	Fighting	Physical	—	100	20	Varies
41	Bullet Seed	Grass	Physical	25	100	30	Normal
48	Super Fang	Normal	Physical	—	90	10	Normal
55	Belch	Poison	Special	120	90	10	Normal

EVOLUTION MOVES

NAME	TYPE	KIND	POW.	ACC.	PP	RANGE
Covet	Normal	Physical	60	100	25	Normal

EGG MOVES

NAME	TYPE	KIND	POW.	ACC.	PP	RANGE

TUTOR MOVES

NAME	TYPE	KIND	POW.	ACC.	PP	RANGE

TM MOVES

NO.	NAME	TYPE	KIND	POW.	ACC.	PP	RANGE
TM08	Hyper Beam	Normal	Special	150	90	5	Normal
TM09	Giga Impact	Normal	Physical	150	90	5	Normal
TM15	Dig	Ground	Physical	80	100	10	Normal
TM21	Rest	Psychic	Status	—	—	10	Self
TM23	Thief	Dark	Physical	60	100	25	Normal
TM24	Snore	Normal	Special	50	100	15	Normal
TM25	Protect	Normal	Status	—	—	10	Self
TM31	Attract	Normal	Status	—	100	15	Normal
TM39	Facade	Normal	Physical	70	100	20	Normal
TM50	Bullet Seed	Grass	Physical	25	100	30	Normal
TM53	Mud Shot	Ground	Special	55	95	15	Normal
TM57	Payback	Dark	Physical	50	100	10	Normal
TM58	Assurance	Dark	Physical	60	100	10	Normal
TM59	Fling	Dark	Physical	—	100	10	Normal
TM66	Thunder Fang	Electric	Physical	65	95	15	Normal
TM67	Ice Fang	Ice	Physical	65	95	15	Normal
TM68	Fire Fang	Fire	Physical	65	95	15	Normal
TM76	Round	Normal	Special	60	100	15	Normal
TM84	Tail Slap	Normal	Physical	25	85	10	Normal
TM97	Brutal Swing	Dark	Physical	60	100	20	All Others
TM98	Stomping Tantrum	Ground	Physical	75	100	10	Normal

TR MOVES

NAME	TYPE	KIND	POW.	ACC.	PP	RANGE
TR00 Swords Dance	Normal	Status	—	—	20	Self
TR01 Body Slam	Normal	Physical	85	100	15	Normal
TR10 Earthquake	Ground	Physical	100	100	10	All Others
TR17 Amnesia	Psychic	Status	—	—	20	Self
TR20 Substitute	Normal	Status	—	—	10	Self
TR26 Endure	Normal	Status	—	—	10	Self
TR27 Sleep Talk	Normal	Status	—	—	10	Self
TR31 Iron Tail	Steel	Physical	100	75	15	Normal
TR32 Crunch	Dark	Physical	80	100	15	Normal
TR35 Uproar	Normal	Special	90	100	10	1 Random
TR39 Superpower	Fighting	Physical	120	100	5	Normal
TR42 Hyper Voice	Normal	Special	90	100	10	Many Others
TR52 Gyro Ball	Steel	Physical	—	100	5	Normal
TR59 Seed Bomb	Grass	Physical	80	100	15	Normal
TR86 Wild Charge	Electric	Physical	90	100	15	Normal
TR97 Psychic Fangs	Psychic	Physical	85	100	10	Normal
TR99 Body Press	Fighting	Physical	80	100	10	Normal

ABILITY

Cheek Pouch

HIDDEN ABILITY

—

SPECIES STRENGTHS

HP

ATTACK

DEFENSE

SP. ATK

SP. DEF

SPEED

DAMAGE TAKEN IN BATTLE

×1 ×2 ×1
×1 ×1 ×0
×1 ×1 ×1
×1 ×1 ×1
×1 ×1 ×1
×1 ×1 ×1

FIELD

026

Pidove

p. 33

LEVEL-UP MOVES

LV.	NAME	TYPE	KIND	POW.	ACC.	PP	RANGE
1	Growl	Normal	Status	—	100	40	Many Others
1	Gust	Flying	Special	40	100	35	Normal
4	Leer	Normal	Status	—	100	30	Many Others
8	Quick Attack	Normal	Physical	40	100	30	Normal
12	Taunt	Dark	Status	—	100	20	Normal
16	Air Cutter	Flying	Special	60	95	25	Many Others
20	Swagger	Normal	Status	—	85	15	Normal
24	Feather Dance	Flying	Status	—	100	15	Normal
28	Detect	Fighting	Status	—	—	5	Self
32	Air Slash	Flying	Special	75	95	15	Normal
36	Roost	Flying	Status	—	—	10	Self
40	Tailwind	Flying	Status	—	—	15	Your Side
44	Sky Attack	Flying	Physical	140	90	5	Normal

EVOLUTION MOVES

NAME	TYPE	KIND	POW.	ACC.	PP	RANGE

EGG MOVES

NAME	TYPE	KIND	POW.	ACC.	PP	RANGE
Defog	Flying	Status	—	—	15	Normal
Hypnosis	Psychic	Status	—	60	20	Normal
Morning Sun	Normal	Status	—	—	5	Self
Night Slash	Dark	Physical	70	100	15	Normal
Wish	Normal	Status	—	—	10	Self

TUTOR MOVES

NAME	TYPE	KIND	POW.	ACC.	PP	RANGE

TM MOVES

NO.	NAME	TYPE	KIND	POW.	ACC.	PP	RANGE
TM06	Fly	Flying	Physical	90	95	15	Normal
TM21	Rest	Psychic	Status	—	—	10	Self
TM24	Snore	Normal	Special	50	100	15	Normal
TM25	Protect	Normal	Status	—	—	10	Self
TM30	Steel Wing	Steel	Physical	70	90	25	Normal
TM31	Attract	Normal	Status	—	100	15	Normal
TM33	Rain Dance	Water	Status	—	—	5	Both Sides
TM34	Sunny Day	Fire	Status	—	—	5	Both Sides
TM39	Facade	Normal	Physical	70	100	20	Normal
TM40	Swift	Normal	Special	60	—	20	Many Others
TM56	U-turn	Bug	Physical	70	100	20	Normal
TM76	Round	Normal	Special	60	100	15	Normal
TM95	Air Slash	Flying	Special	75	95	15	Normal

TR MOVES

NAME	TYPE	KIND	POW.	ACC.	PP	RANGE
TR12 Agility	Psychic	Status	—	—	30	Self
TR13 Focus Energy	Normal	Status	—	—	30	Self
TR20 Substitute	Normal	Status	—	—	10	Self
TR26 Endure	Normal	Status	—	—	10	Self
TR27 Sleep Talk	Normal	Status	—	—	10	Self
TR35 Uproar	Normal	Special	90	100	10	1 Random
TR36 Heat Wave	Fire	Special	95	90	10	Many Others
TR37 Taunt	Dark	Status	—	100	20	Normal
TR85 Work Up	Normal	Status	—	—	30	Self

ABILITY

Big Pecks
Super Luck

HIDDEN ABILITY

Rivalry

SPECIES STRENGTHS

HP

ATTACK

DEFENSE

SP. ATK

SP. DEF

SPEED

DAMAGE TAKEN IN BATTLE

×1 ×1 ×2
×1 ×1 ×0
×1 ×0 ×1
×0.5 ×1 ×1
×2 ×1 ×1
×2 ×0.5 ×1

FLYING

027 Tranquill

p. 33

ABILITY
Big Pecks
Super Luck

HIDDEN ABILITY
Rivalry

SPECIES STRENGTHS
HP
ATTACK
DEFENSE
SP. ATK
SP. DEF
SPEED

DAMAGE TAKEN IN BATTLE
×1 ×1 ×2
×1 ×1 ×0
×1 ×0 ×1
×0.5 ×1 ×1
×2 ×1 ×1
×2 ×0.5 ×1

FLYING

LEVEL-UP MOVES

LV.	NAME	TYPE	KIND	POW.	ACC.	PP	RANGE
1	Growl	Normal	Status	—	100	40	Many Others
1	Gust	Flying	Special	40	100	35	Normal
1	Leer	Normal	Status	—	100	30	Many Others
1	Quick Attack	Normal	Physical	40	100	30	Normal
12	Taunt	Dark	Status	—	100	20	Normal
16	Air Cutter	Flying	Special	60	95	25	Many Others
20	Swagger	Normal	Status	—	85	15	Normal
26	Feather Dance	Flying	Status	—	100	15	Normal
34	Detect	Fighting	Status	—	—	5	Self
38	Air Slash	Flying	Special	75	95	15	Normal
44	Roost	Flying	Status	—	—	10	Self
50	Tailwind	Flying	Status	—	—	15	Your Side
56	Sky Attack	Flying	Physical	140	90	5	Normal

EVOLUTION MOVES

NAME	TYPE	KIND	POW.	ACC.	PP	RANGE

EGG MOVES

NAME	TYPE	KIND	POW.	ACC.	PP	RANGE

TUTOR MOVES

NAME	TYPE	KIND	POW.	ACC.	PP	RANGE

TM MOVES

NO.	NAME	TYPE	KIND	POW.	ACC.	PP	RANGE
TM06	Fly	Flying	Physical	90	95	15	Normal
TM21	Rest	Psychic	Status	—	—	10	Self
TM24	Snore	Normal	Special	50	100	15	Normal
TM25	Protect	Normal	Status	—	—	10	Self
TM30	Steel Wing	Steel	Physical	70	90	25	Normal
TM31	Attract	Normal	Status	—	100	15	Normal
TM33	Rain Dance	Water	Status	—	—	5	Both Sides
TM34	Sunny Day	Fire	Status	—	—	5	Both Sides
TM39	Facade	Normal	Physical	70	100	20	Normal
TM40	Swift	Normal	Special	60	—	20	Many Others
TM56	U-turn	Bug	Physical	70	100	20	Normal
TM76	Round	Normal	Special	60	100	15	Normal
TM95	Air Slash	Flying	Special	75	95	15	Normal

TR MOVES

NAME	TYPE	KIND	POW.	ACC.	PP	RANGE
TR12 Agility	Psychic	Status	—	—	30	Self
TR13 Focus Energy	Normal	Status	—	—	30	Self
TR20 Substitute	Normal	Status	—	—	10	Self
TR26 Endure	Normal	Status	—	—	10	Self
TR27 Sleep Talk	Normal	Status	—	—	10	Self
TR35 Uproar	Normal	Special	90	100	10	1 Random
TR36 Heat Wave	Fire	Special	95	90	10	Many Others
TR37 Taunt	Dark	Status	—	100	20	Normal
TR85 Work Up	Normal	Status	—	—	30	Self

028 Unfezant

p. 33

ABILITY
Big Pecks
Super Luck

HIDDEN ABILITY
Rivalry

SPECIES STRENGTHS
HP
ATTACK
DEFENSE
SP. ATK
SP. DEF
SPEED

DAMAGE TAKEN IN BATTLE
×1 ×1 ×2
×1 ×1 ×0
×1 ×0 ×1
×0.5 ×1 ×1
×2 ×1 ×1
×2 ×0.5 ×1

FLYING

LEVEL-UP MOVES

LV.	NAME	TYPE	KIND	POW.	ACC.	PP	RANGE
1	Growl	Normal	Status	—	100	40	Many Others
1	Gust	Flying	Special	40	100	35	Normal
1	Leer	Normal	Status	—	100	30	Many Others
1	Quick Attack	Normal	Physical	40	100	30	Normal
12	Taunt	Dark	Status	—	100	20	Normal
16	Air Cutter	Flying	Special	60	95	25	Many Others
20	Swagger	Normal	Status	—	85	15	Normal
26	Feather Dance	Flying	Status	—	100	15	Normal
36	Detect	Fighting	Status	—	—	5	Self
42	Air Slash	Flying	Special	75	95	15	Normal
50	Roost	Flying	Status	—	—	10	Self
58	Tailwind	Flying	Status	—	—	15	Your Side
66	Sky Attack	Flying	Physical	140	90	5	Normal

EVOLUTION MOVES

NAME	TYPE	KIND	POW.	ACC.	PP	RANGE

EGG MOVES

NAME	TYPE	KIND	POW.	ACC.	PP	RANGE

TUTOR MOVES

NAME	TYPE	KIND	POW.	ACC.	PP	RANGE

TM MOVES

NO.	NAME	TYPE	KIND	POW.	ACC.	PP	RANGE
TM06	Fly	Flying	Physical	90	95	15	Normal
TM08	Hyper Beam	Normal	Special	150	90	5	Normal
TM09	Giga Impact	Normal	Physical	150	90	5	Normal
TM21	Rest	Psychic	Status	—	—	10	Self
TM24	Snore	Normal	Special	50	100	15	Normal
TM25	Protect	Normal	Status	—	—	10	Self
TM30	Steel Wing	Steel	Physical	70	90	25	Normal
TM31	Attract	Normal	Status	—	100	15	Normal
TM33	Rain Dance	Water	Status	—	—	5	Both Sides
TM34	Sunny Day	Fire	Status	—	—	5	Both Sides
TM39	Facade	Normal	Physical	70	100	20	Normal
TM40	Swift	Normal	Special	60	—	20	Many Others
TM56	U-turn	Bug	Physical	70	100	20	Normal
TM76	Round	Normal	Special	60	100	15	Normal
TM95	Air Slash	Flying	Special	75	95	15	Normal

TR MOVES

NAME	TYPE	KIND	POW.	ACC.	PP	RANGE
TR12 Agility	Psychic	Status	—	—	30	Self
TR13 Focus Energy	Normal	Status	—	—	30	Self
TR20 Substitute	Normal	Status	—	—	10	Self
TR26 Endure	Normal	Status	—	—	10	Self
TR27 Sleep Talk	Normal	Status	—	—	10	Self
TR35 Uproar	Normal	Special	90	100	10	1 Random
TR36 Heat Wave	Fire	Special	95	90	10	Many Others
TR66 Brave Bird	Flying	Physical	120	100	15	Normal
TR85 Work Up	Normal	Status	—	—	30	Self
TR89 Hurricane	Flying	Special	110	70	10	Normal

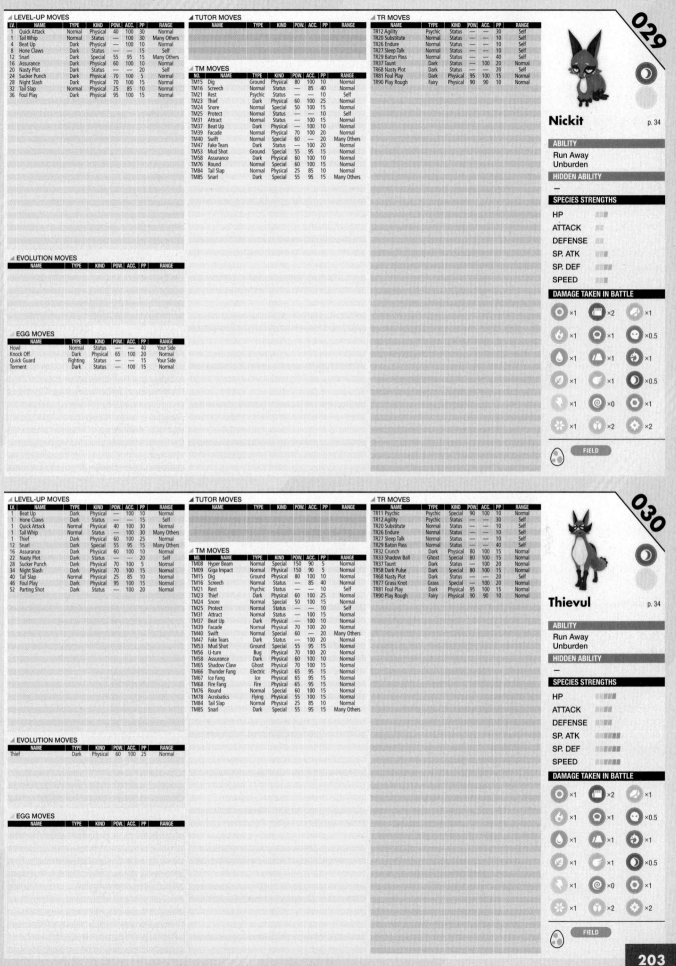

029 — Nickit

LEVEL-UP MOVES

LV.	NAME	TYPE	KIND	POW.	ACC.	PP	RANGE
1	Quick Attack	Normal	Physical	40	100	30	Normal
1	Tail Whip	Normal	Status	—	100	30	Many Others
4	Beat Up	Dark	Physical	—	100	10	Normal
8	Hone Claws	Dark	Status	—	—	15	Self
12	Snarl	Dark	Special	55	95	15	Many Others
16	Assurance	Dark	Physical	60	100	10	Normal
20	Nasty Plot	Dark	Status	—	—	20	Self
24	Sucker Punch	Dark	Physical	70	100	5	Normal
28	Night Slash	Dark	Physical	70	100	15	Normal
32	Tail Slap	Normal	Physical	25	85	10	Normal
36	Foul Play	Dark	Physical	95	100	15	Normal

EVOLUTION MOVES

NAME	TYPE	KIND	POW.	ACC.	PP	RANGE

EGG MOVES

NAME	TYPE	KIND	POW.	ACC.	PP	RANGE
Howl	Normal	Status	—	—	40	Your Side
Knock Off	Dark	Physical	65	100	20	Normal
Quick Guard	Fighting	Status	—	—	15	Your Side
Torment	Dark	Status	—	100	15	Normal

TUTOR MOVES

NAME	TYPE	KIND	POW.	ACC.	PP	RANGE

TM MOVES

NO.	NAME	TYPE	KIND	POW.	ACC.	PP	RANGE
TM15	Dig	Ground	Physical	80	100	10	Normal
TM16	Screech	Normal	Status	—	85	40	Normal
TM21	Rest	Psychic	Status	—	—	10	Self
TM23	Thief	Dark	Physical	60	100	25	Normal
TM24	Snore	Normal	Special	50	100	15	Normal
TM25	Protect	Normal	Status	—	—	10	Self
TM31	Attract	Normal	Status	—	100	15	Normal
TM37	Beat Up	Dark	Physical	—	100	10	Normal
TM39	Facade	Normal	Physical	70	100	20	Normal
TM40	Swift	Normal	Special	60	—	20	Many Others
TM47	Fake Tears	Dark	Status	—	100	20	Normal
TM53	Mud Shot	Ground	Special	55	95	15	Normal
TM58	Assurance	Dark	Physical	60	100	15	Normal
TM76	Round	Normal	Special	60	100	15	Normal
TM84	Tail Slap	Normal	Physical	25	85	10	Normal
TM85	Snarl	Dark	Special	55	95	15	Many Others

TR MOVES

NAME	TYPE	KIND	POW.	ACC.	PP	RANGE
TR12 Agility	Psychic	Status	—	—	30	Self
TR20 Substitute	Normal	Status	—	—	10	Self
TR26 Endure	Normal	Status	—	—	10	Self
TR27 Sleep Talk	Normal	Status	—	—	10	Self
TR29 Baton Pass	Normal	Status	—	—	40	Self
TR37 Taunt	Dark	Status	—	100	20	Normal
TR68 Nasty Plot	Dark	Status	—	—	20	Self
TR81 Foul Play	Dark	Physical	95	100	15	Normal
TR90 Play Rough	Fairy	Physical	90	90	10	Normal

Nickit — p. 34

ABILITY
Run Away
Unburden

HIDDEN ABILITY
—

SPECIES STRENGTHS
HP
ATTACK
DEFENSE
SP. ATK
SP. DEF
SPEED

DAMAGE TAKEN IN BATTLE
×1 ×2 ×1 ×1 ×1 ×0.5 ×1 ×1 ×1 ×1 ×1 ×0.5 ×1 ×0 ×1 ×1 ×2 ×2

FIELD

---

030 — Thievul

LEVEL-UP MOVES

LV.	NAME	TYPE	KIND	POW.	ACC.	PP	RANGE
1	Beat Up	Dark	Physical	—	100	15	Normal
1	Hone Claws	Dark	Status	—	—	15	Self
1	Quick Attack	Normal	Physical	40	100	30	Normal
1	Tail Whip	Normal	Status	—	100	30	Many Others
1	Thief	Dark	Physical	60	100	25	Normal
12	Snarl	Dark	Special	55	95	15	Many Others
16	Assurance	Dark	Physical	60	100	10	Normal
22	Nasty Plot	Dark	Status	—	—	20	Self
28	Sucker Punch	Dark	Physical	70	100	5	Normal
34	Night Slash	Dark	Physical	70	100	15	Normal
40	Tail Slap	Normal	Physical	25	85	10	Normal
46	Foul Play	Dark	Physical	95	100	15	Normal
52	Parting Shot	Dark	Status	—	100	20	Normal

EVOLUTION MOVES

NAME	TYPE	KIND	POW.	ACC.	PP	RANGE
Thief	Dark	Physical	60	100	25	Normal

EGG MOVES

NAME	TYPE	KIND	POW.	ACC.	PP	RANGE

TUTOR MOVES

NAME	TYPE	KIND	POW.	ACC.	PP	RANGE

TM MOVES

NO.	NAME	TYPE	KIND	POW.	ACC.	PP	RANGE
TM08	Hyper Beam	Normal	Special	150	90	5	Normal
TM09	Giga Impact	Normal	Physical	150	90	5	Normal
TM15	Dig	Ground	Physical	80	100	10	Normal
TM16	Screech	Normal	Status	—	85	40	Normal
TM21	Rest	Psychic	Status	—	—	10	Self
TM23	Thief	Dark	Physical	60	100	25	Normal
TM24	Snore	Normal	Special	50	100	15	Normal
TM25	Protect	Normal	Status	—	—	10	Self
TM31	Attract	Normal	Status	—	100	15	Normal
TM37	Beat Up	Dark	Physical	—	100	10	Normal
TM39	Facade	Normal	Physical	70	100	20	Normal
TM40	Swift	Normal	Special	60	—	20	Many Others
TM47	Fake Tears	Dark	Status	—	100	20	Normal
TM53	Mud Shot	Ground	Special	55	95	15	Normal
TM56	U-turn	Bug	Physical	70	100	20	Normal
TM58	Assurance	Dark	Physical	60	100	15	Normal
TM65	Shadow Claw	Ghost	Physical	70	100	15	Normal
TM66	Thunder Fang	Electric	Physical	65	95	15	Normal
TM67	Ice Fang	Ice	Physical	65	95	15	Normal
TM68	Fire Fang	Fire	Physical	65	95	15	Normal
TM76	Round	Normal	Special	60	100	15	Normal
TM78	Acrobatics	Flying	Physical	55	100	15	Normal
TM84	Tail Slap	Normal	Physical	25	85	10	Normal
TM85	Snarl	Dark	Special	55	95	15	Many Others

TR MOVES

NAME	TYPE	KIND	POW.	ACC.	PP	RANGE
TR11 Psychic	Psychic	Special	90	100	10	Normal
TR12 Agility	Psychic	Status	—	—	30	Self
TR20 Substitute	Normal	Status	—	—	10	Self
TR26 Endure	Normal	Status	—	—	10	Self
TR27 Sleep Talk	Normal	Status	—	—	10	Self
TR29 Baton Pass	Normal	Status	—	—	40	Self
TR32 Crunch	Dark	Physical	80	100	15	Normal
TR33 Shadow Ball	Ghost	Special	80	100	15	Normal
TR37 Taunt	Dark	Status	—	100	20	Normal
TR58 Dark Pulse	Dark	Special	80	100	15	Normal
TR68 Nasty Plot	Dark	Status	—	—	20	Self
TR77 Grass Knot	Grass	Special	—	100	20	Normal
TR81 Foul Play	Dark	Physical	95	100	15	Normal
TR90 Play Rough	Fairy	Physical	90	90	10	Normal

Thievul — p. 34

ABILITY
Run Away
Unburden

HIDDEN ABILITY
—

SPECIES STRENGTHS
HP
ATTACK
DEFENSE
SP. ATK
SP. DEF
SPEED

DAMAGE TAKEN IN BATTLE
×1 ×2 ×1 ×1 ×1 ×0.5 ×1 ×1 ×1 ×1 ×1 ×0.5 ×1 ×0 ×1 ×1 ×2 ×2

FIELD

031

Zigzagoon
p. 35
Galarian Form

ABILITY
Pickup
Gluttony

HIDDEN ABILITY
Quick Feet

SPECIES STRENGTHS
HP
ATTACK
DEFENSE
SP. ATK
SP. DEF
SPEED

DAMAGE TAKEN IN BATTLE

◉ ×1	⛊ ×4	⟋ ×1
🔥 ×1	◍ ×1	◕ ×0
💧 ×1	⛰ ×1	↻ ×1
⚡ ×1	🍃 ×1	◑ ×0.5
❄ ×1	◎ ×0	◓ ×1
✳ ×1	👊 ×2	✦ ×2

FIELD

LEVEL-UP MOVES

LV.	NAME	TYPE	KIND	POW.	ACC.	PP	RANGE
1	Leer	Normal	Status	—	100	30	Many Others
1	Tackle	Normal	Physical	40	100	35	Normal
3	Sand Attack	Ground	Status	—	100	15	Normal
6	Lick	Ghost	Physical	30	100	30	Normal
9	Snarl	Dark	Special	55	95	15	Many Others
12	Headbutt	Normal	Physical	70	100	15	Normal
15	Baby-Doll Eyes	Fairy	Status	—	100	30	Normal
18	Pin Missile	Bug	Physical	25	95	20	Normal
21	Rest	Psychic	Status	—	—	10	Self
24	Take Down	Normal	Physical	90	85	20	Normal
27	Scary Face	Normal	Status	—	100	10	Normal
30	Counter	Fighting	Physical	—	100	20	Varies
33	Taunt	Dark	Status	—	100	20	Normal
36	Double-Edge	Normal	Physical	120	100	15	Normal

EVOLUTION MOVES

NAME	TYPE	KIND	POW.	ACC.	PP	RANGE

EGG MOVES

NAME	TYPE	KIND	POW.	ACC.	PP	RANGE
Knock Off	Dark	Physical	65	100	20	Normal
Parting Shot	Dark	Status	—	100	20	Normal
Quick Guard	Fighting	Status	—	—	15	Your Side

TUTOR MOVES

NAME	TYPE	KIND	POW.	ACC.	PP	RANGE

TM MOVES

NO.	NAME	TYPE	KIND	POW.	ACC.	PP	RANGE
TM07	Pin Missile	Bug	Physical	25	95	20	Normal
TM14	Thunder Wave	Electric	Status	—	90	20	Normal
TM15	Dig	Ground	Physical	80	100	10	Normal
TM16	Screech	Normal	Status	—	85	40	Normal
TM21	Rest	Psychic	Status	—	—	10	Self
TM23	Thief	Dark	Physical	60	100	25	Normal
TM24	Snore	Normal	Special	50	100	15	Normal
TM25	Protect	Normal	Status	—	—	10	Self
TM26	Scary Face	Normal	Status	—	100	10	Normal
TM27	Icy Wind	Ice	Special	55	95	15	Many Others
TM31	Attract	Normal	Status	—	100	15	Normal
TM33	Rain Dance	Water	Status	—	—	5	Both Sides
TM34	Sunny Day	Fire	Status	—	—	5	Both Sides
TM36	Whirlpool	Water	Special	35	85	15	Normal
TM39	Facade	Normal	Physical	70	100	20	Normal
TM40	Swift	Normal	Special	60	—	20	Many Others
TM41	Helping Hand	Normal	Status	—	—	20	1 Ally
TM47	Fake Tears	Dark	Status	—	100	20	Normal
TM53	Mud Shot	Ground	Special	55	95	15	Normal
TM57	Payback	Dark	Physical	50	100	10	Normal
TM58	Assurance	Dark	Physical	60	100	10	Normal
TM59	Fling	Dark	Physical	—	100	10	Normal
TM76	Round	Normal	Special	60	100	15	Normal
TM79	Retaliate	Normal	Physical	70	100	5	Normal
TM85	Snarl	Dark	Special	55	95	15	Many Others

TR MOVES

NO.	NAME	TYPE	KIND	POW.	ACC.	PP	RANGE
TR01	Body Slam	Normal	Physical	85	100	15	Normal
TR04	Surf	Water	Special	90	100	15	All Others
TR05	Ice Beam	Ice	Special	90	100	10	Normal
TR06	Blizzard	Ice	Special	110	70	5	Many Others
TR08	Thunderbolt	Electric	Special	90	100	15	Normal
TR09	Thunder	Electric	Special	110	70	10	Normal
TR20	Substitute	Normal	Status	—	—	10	Self
TR26	Endure	Normal	Status	—	—	10	Self
TR27	Sleep Talk	Normal	Status	—	—	10	Self
TR31	Iron Tail	Steel	Physical	100	75	15	Normal
TR33	Shadow Ball	Ghost	Special	80	100	15	Normal
TR37	Taunt	Dark	Status	—	100	20	Normal
TR38	Trick	Psychic	Status	—	100	10	Normal
TR42	Hyper Voice	Normal	Special	90	100	10	Many Others
TR59	Seed Bomb	Grass	Physical	80	100	15	Normal
TR73	Gunk Shot	Poison	Physical	120	80	5	Normal
TR77	Grass Knot	Grass	Special	—	100	20	Normal
TR85	Work Up	Normal	Status	—	—	30	Self

032

Linoone
p. 35
Galarian Form

ABILITY
Pickup
Gluttony

HIDDEN ABILITY
Quick Feet

SPECIES STRENGTHS
HP
ATTACK
DEFENSE
SP. ATK
SP. DEF
SPEED

DAMAGE TAKEN IN BATTLE

◉ ×1	⛊ ×4	⟋ ×1
🔥 ×1	◍ ×1	◕ ×0
💧 ×1	⛰ ×1	↻ ×1
⚡ ×1	🍃 ×1	◑ ×0.5
❄ ×1	◎ ×0	◓ ×1
✳ ×1	👊 ×2	✦ ×2

FIELD

LEVEL-UP MOVES

LV.	NAME	TYPE	KIND	POW.	ACC.	PP	RANGE
1	Baby-Doll Eyes	Fairy	Status	—	100	30	Normal
1	Leer	Normal	Status	—	100	30	Many Others
1	Lick	Ghost	Physical	30	100	30	Normal
1	Night Slash	Dark	Physical	70	100	15	Normal
1	Pin Missile	Bug	Physical	25	95	20	Normal
1	Sand Attack	Ground	Status	—	100	15	Normal
1	Switcheroo	Dark	Status	—	100	10	Normal
1	Tackle	Normal	Physical	40	100	35	Normal
9	Snarl	Dark	Special	55	95	15	Many Others
12	Headbutt	Normal	Physical	70	100	15	Normal
15	Hone Claws	Dark	Status	—	—	15	Self
18	Fury Swipes	Normal	Physical	18	80	15	Normal
23	Rest	Psychic	Status	—	—	10	Self
28	Take Down	Normal	Physical	90	85	20	Normal
33	Scary Face	Normal	Status	—	100	10	Normal
38	Counter	Fighting	Physical	—	100	20	Varies
43	Taunt	Dark	Status	—	100	20	Normal
48	Double-Edge	Normal	Physical	120	100	15	Normal

EVOLUTION MOVES

NAME	TYPE	KIND	POW.	ACC.	PP	RANGE
Night Slash	Dark	Physical	70	100	15	Normal

EGG MOVES

NAME	TYPE	KIND	POW.	ACC.	PP	RANGE

TUTOR MOVES

NAME	TYPE	KIND	POW.	ACC.	PP	RANGE

TM MOVES

NO.	NAME	TYPE	KIND	POW.	ACC.	PP	RANGE
TM07	Pin Missile	Bug	Physical	25	95	20	Normal
TM08	Hyper Beam	Normal	Special	150	90	5	Normal
TM09	Giga Impact	Normal	Physical	150	90	5	Normal
TM14	Thunder Wave	Electric	Status	—	90	20	Normal
TM15	Dig	Ground	Physical	80	100	10	Normal
TM16	Screech	Normal	Status	—	85	40	Normal
TM21	Rest	Psychic	Status	—	—	10	Self
TM23	Thief	Dark	Physical	60	100	25	Normal
TM24	Snore	Normal	Special	50	100	15	Normal
TM25	Protect	Normal	Status	—	—	10	Self
TM26	Scary Face	Normal	Status	—	100	10	Normal
TM27	Icy Wind	Ice	Special	55	95	15	Many Others
TM31	Attract	Normal	Status	—	100	15	Normal
TM33	Rain Dance	Water	Status	—	—	5	Both Sides
TM34	Sunny Day	Fire	Status	—	—	5	Both Sides
TM36	Whirlpool	Water	Special	35	85	15	Normal
TM39	Facade	Normal	Physical	70	100	20	Normal
TM40	Swift	Normal	Special	60	—	20	Many Others
TM41	Helping Hand	Normal	Status	—	—	20	1 Ally
TM47	Fake Tears	Dark	Status	—	100	20	Normal
TM53	Mud Shot	Ground	Special	55	95	15	Normal
TM57	Payback	Dark	Physical	50	100	10	Normal
TM58	Assurance	Dark	Physical	60	100	10	Normal
TM59	Fling	Dark	Physical	—	100	10	Normal
TM65	Shadow Claw	Ghost	Physical	70	100	15	Normal
TM76	Round	Normal	Special	60	100	15	Normal
TM79	Retaliate	Normal	Physical	70	100	5	Normal
TM85	Snarl	Dark	Special	55	95	15	Many Others
TM98	Stomping Tantrum	Ground	Physical	75	100	10	Normal

TR MOVES

NO.	NAME	TYPE	KIND	POW.	ACC.	PP	RANGE
TR01	Body Slam	Normal	Physical	85	100	15	Normal
TR04	Surf	Water	Special	90	100	15	All Others
TR05	Ice Beam	Ice	Special	90	100	10	Normal
TR06	Blizzard	Ice	Special	110	70	5	Many Others
TR08	Thunderbolt	Electric	Special	90	100	15	Normal
TR09	Thunder	Electric	Special	110	70	10	Normal
TR20	Substitute	Normal	Status	—	—	10	Self
TR26	Endure	Normal	Status	—	—	10	Self
TR27	Sleep Talk	Normal	Status	—	—	10	Self
TR31	Iron Tail	Steel	Physical	100	75	15	Normal
TR33	Shadow Ball	Ghost	Special	80	100	15	Normal
TR37	Taunt	Dark	Status	—	100	20	Normal
TR38	Trick	Psychic	Status	—	100	10	Normal
TR42	Hyper Voice	Normal	Special	90	100	10	Many Others
TR59	Seed Bomb	Grass	Physical	80	100	15	Normal
TR73	Gunk Shot	Poison	Physical	120	80	5	Normal
TR77	Grass Knot	Grass	Special	—	100	20	Normal
TR85	Work Up	Normal	Status	—	—	30	Self
TR95	Throat Chop	Dark	Physical	80	100	15	Normal
TR99	Body Press	Fighting	Physical	80	100	10	Normal

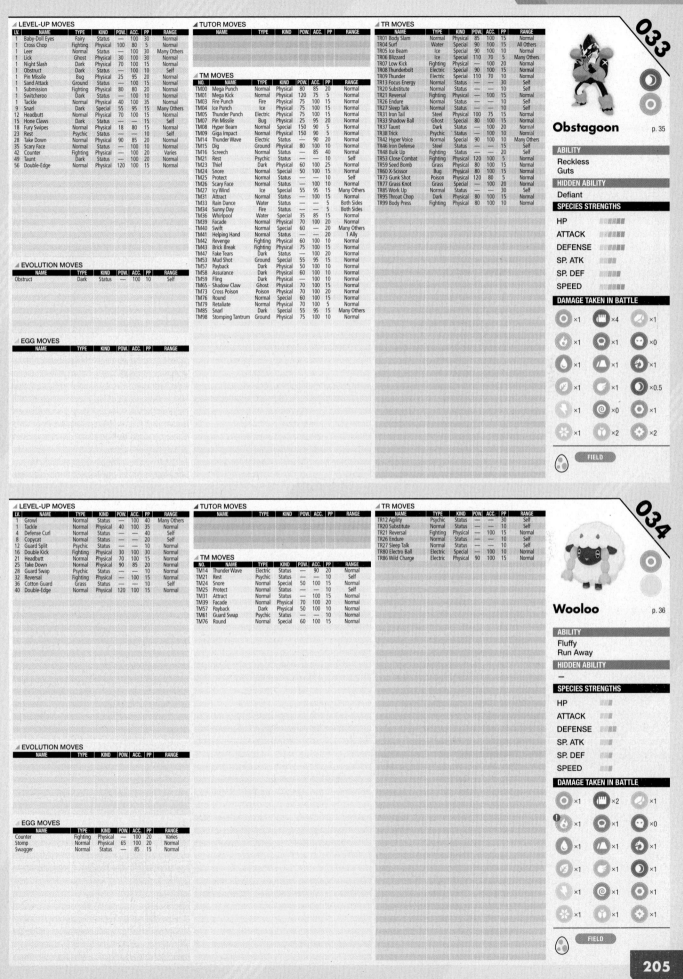

033 Obstagoon (p. 35)

LEVEL-UP MOVES

LV.	NAME	TYPE	KIND	POW.	ACC.	PP	RANGE
1	Baby-Doll Eyes	Fairy	Status	—	100	30	Normal
1	Cross Chop	Fighting	Physical	100	80	5	Normal
1	Leer	Normal	Status	—	100	30	Many Others
1	Lick	Ghost	Physical	30	100	30	Normal
1	Night Slash	Dark	Physical	70	100	15	Normal
1	Obstruct	Dark	Status	—	100	10	Self
1	Pin Missile	Bug	Physical	25	95	20	Normal
1	Sand Attack	Ground	Status	—	100	15	Normal
1	Submission	Fighting	Physical	80	80	20	Normal
1	Switcheroo	Dark	Status	—	100	10	Normal
1	Tackle	Normal	Physical	40	100	35	Normal
9	Snarl	Dark	Special	55	95	15	Many Others
12	Headbutt	Normal	Physical	70	100	15	Normal
15	Hone Claws	Dark	Status	—	—	15	Self
18	Fury Swipes	Normal	Physical	18	80	15	Normal
23	Rest	Psychic	Status	—	—	10	Self
28	Take Down	Normal	Physical	90	85	20	Normal
35	Scary Face	Normal	Status	—	100	10	Normal
42	Counter	Fighting	Physical	—	100	20	Varies
49	Taunt	Dark	Status	—	100	20	Normal
56	Double-Edge	Normal	Physical	120	100	15	Normal

EVOLUTION MOVES

NAME	TYPE	KIND	POW.	ACC.	PP	RANGE
Obstruct	Dark	Status	—	100	10	Self

EGG MOVES

NAME	TYPE	KIND	POW.	ACC.	PP	RANGE

TUTOR MOVES

NAME	TYPE	KIND	POW.	ACC.	PP	RANGE

TM MOVES

NO.	NAME	TYPE	KIND	POW.	ACC.	PP	RANGE
TM00	Mega Punch	Normal	Physical	80	85	20	Normal
TM01	Mega Kick	Normal	Physical	120	75	5	Normal
TM03	Fire Punch	Fire	Physical	75	100	15	Normal
TM04	Ice Punch	Ice	Physical	75	100	15	Normal
TM05	Thunder Punch	Electric	Physical	75	100	15	Normal
TM07	Pin Missile	Bug	Physical	25	95	20	Normal
TM08	Hyper Beam	Normal	Special	150	90	5	Normal
TM09	Giga Impact	Normal	Physical	150	90	5	Normal
TM14	Thunder Wave	Electric	Status	—	90	20	Normal
TM15	Dig	Ground	Physical	80	100	10	Normal
TM16	Screech	Normal	Status	—	85	40	Normal
TM21	Rest	Psychic	Status	—	—	10	Self
TM23	Thief	Dark	Physical	60	100	25	Normal
TM24	Snore	Normal	Special	50	100	15	Normal
TM25	Protect	Normal	Status	—	—	10	Self
TM26	Scary Face	Normal	Status	—	100	10	Many Others
TM27	Icy Wind	Ice	Special	55	95	15	Many Others
TM31	Attract	Normal	Status	—	100	15	Normal
TM33	Rain Dance	Water	Status	—	—	5	Both Sides
TM34	Sunny Day	Fire	Status	—	—	5	Both Sides
TM36	Whirlpool	Water	Special	35	85	15	Normal
TM39	Facade	Normal	Physical	70	100	20	Normal
TM40	Swift	Normal	Special	60	—	20	Many Others
TM41	Helping Hand	Normal	Status	—	—	20	1 Ally
TM42	Revenge	Fighting	Physical	60	100	10	Normal
TM43	Brick Break	Fighting	Physical	75	100	15	Normal
TM47	Fake Tears	Dark	Status	—	100	20	Normal
TM53	Mud Shot	Ground	Special	55	95	15	Normal
TM57	Payback	Dark	Physical	50	100	10	Normal
TM58	Assurance	Dark	Physical	60	100	10	Normal
TM59	Fling	Dark	Physical	—	100	10	Normal
TM65	Shadow Claw	Ghost	Physical	70	100	15	Normal
TM73	Cross Poison	Poison	Physical	70	100	20	Normal
TM76	Round	Normal	Special	60	100	15	Normal
TM79	Retaliate	Normal	Physical	70	100	5	Normal
TM85	Snarl	Dark	Special	55	95	15	Many Others
TM98	Stomping Tantrum	Ground	Physical	75	100	10	Normal

TR MOVES

NAME	TYPE	KIND	POW.	ACC.	PP	RANGE
TR01 Body Slam	Normal	Physical	85	100	15	Normal
TR04 Surf	Water	Special	90	100	15	All Others
TR05 Ice Beam	Ice	Special	90	100	10	Normal
TR06 Blizzard	Ice	Special	110	70	5	Many Others
TR07 Low Kick	Fighting	Physical	—	100	20	Normal
TR08 Thunderbolt	Electric	Special	90	100	15	Normal
TR08 Thunder	Electric	Special	110	70	10	Normal
TR13 Focus Energy	Normal	Status	—	—	30	Self
TR20 Substitute	Normal	Status	—	—	10	Self
TR21 Reversal	Fighting	Physical	—	100	15	Normal
TR26 Endure	Normal	Status	—	—	10	Self
TR27 Sleep Talk	Normal	Status	—	—	10	Self
TR31 Iron Tail	Steel	Physical	100	75	15	Normal
TR33 Shadow Ball	Ghost	Special	80	100	15	Normal
TR37 Taunt	Dark	Status	—	100	20	Normal
TR38 Trick	Psychic	Status	—	100	10	Normal
TR42 Hyper Voice	Normal	Special	90	100	10	Many Others
TR46 Iron Defense	Steel	Status	—	—	15	Self
TR48 Bulk Up	Fighting	Status	—	—	20	Self
TR53 Close Combat	Fighting	Physical	120	100	5	Normal
TR59 Seed Bomb	Grass	Physical	80	100	15	Normal
TR60 X-Scissor	Bug	Physical	80	100	15	Normal
TR73 Gunk Shot	Poison	Physical	120	80	5	Normal
TR77 Grass Knot	Grass	Special	—	100	20	Normal
TR85 Work Up	Normal	Status	—	—	30	Self
TR95 Throat Chop	Dark	Physical	80	100	15	Normal
TR99 Body Press	Fighting	Physical	80	100	10	Normal

ABILITY: Reckless / Guts
HIDDEN ABILITY: Defiant

SPECIES STRENGTHS: HP, ATTACK, DEFENSE, SP. ATK, SP. DEF, SPEED

DAMAGE TAKEN IN BATTLE: ×1, ×4, ×1, ×1, ×1, ×0, ×1, ×1, ×1, ×1, ×1, ×0.5, ×0, ×1, ×2, ×2

FIELD

---

034 Wooloo (p. 36)

LEVEL-UP MOVES

LV.	NAME	TYPE	KIND	POW.	ACC.	PP	RANGE
1	Growl	Normal	Status	—	100	40	Many Others
1	Tackle	Normal	Physical	40	100	35	Normal
4	Defense Curl	Normal	Status	—	—	40	Self
4	Copycat	Normal	Status	—	—	20	Self
12	Guard Split	Psychic	Status	—	—	10	Normal
12	Double Kick	Fighting	Physical	30	100	30	Normal
21	Headbutt	Normal	Physical	70	100	15	Normal
25	Take Down	Normal	Physical	90	85	20	Normal
28	Guard Swap	Psychic	Status	—	—	10	Normal
32	Reversal	Fighting	Physical	—	100	15	Normal
36	Cotton Guard	Grass	Status	—	—	10	Self
40	Double-Edge	Normal	Physical	120	100	15	Normal

EVOLUTION MOVES

NAME	TYPE	KIND	POW.	ACC.	PP	RANGE

EGG MOVES

NAME	TYPE	KIND	POW.	ACC.	PP	RANGE
Counter	Fighting	Physical	—	100	20	Varies
Stomp	Normal	Physical	65	100	20	Normal
Swagger	Normal	Status	—	85	15	Normal

TUTOR MOVES

NAME	TYPE	KIND	POW.	ACC.	PP	RANGE

TM MOVES

NO.	NAME	TYPE	KIND	POW.	ACC.	PP	RANGE
TM14	Thunder Wave	Electric	Status	—	90	20	Normal
TM21	Rest	Psychic	Status	—	—	10	Self
TM24	Snore	Normal	Special	50	100	15	Normal
TM25	Protect	Normal	Status	—	—	10	Self
TM31	Attract	Normal	Status	—	100	15	Normal
TM39	Facade	Normal	Physical	70	100	20	Normal
TM57	Payback	Dark	Physical	50	100	10	Normal
TM61	Guard Swap	Psychic	Status	—	—	10	Normal
TM76	Round	Normal	Special	60	100	15	Normal

TR MOVES

NAME	TYPE	KIND	POW.	ACC.	PP	RANGE
TR12 Agility	Psychic	Status	—	—	30	Self
TR20 Substitute	Normal	Status	—	—	10	Self
TR21 Reversal	Fighting	Physical	—	100	15	Normal
TR26 Endure	Normal	Status	—	—	10	Self
TR27 Sleep Talk	Normal	Status	—	—	10	Self
TR80 Electro Ball	Electric	Special	—	100	10	Normal
TR86 Wild Charge	Electric	Physical	90	100	15	Normal

ABILITY: Fluffy / Run Away
HIDDEN ABILITY: —

SPECIES STRENGTHS: HP, ATTACK, DEFENSE, SP. ATK, SP. DEF, SPEED

DAMAGE TAKEN IN BATTLE: ×1, ×2, ×1, ×1, ×1, ×0, ×1, ×1, ×1, ×1, ×1, ×1

FIELD

035 Dubwool

p. 36

ABILITY
Fluffy
Steadfast

HIDDEN ABILITY
—

SPECIES STRENGTHS

HP	
ATTACK	
DEFENSE	
SP. ATK	
SP. DEF	
SPEED	

DAMAGE TAKEN IN BATTLE

◎ ×1	🏢 ×2	🗡 ×1
🔥 ×1	💧 ×1	×0
💧 ×1	🔺 ×1	↻ ×1
🌀 ×1	🪶 ×1	🌙 ×1
✊ ×1	◎ ×1	◎ ×1
❄ ×1	🦠 ×1	✦ ×1

🥚 FIELD

LEVEL-UP MOVES

LV.	NAME	TYPE	KIND	POW.	ACC.	PP	RANGE
1	Copycat	Normal	Status	—	—	20	Self
1	Defense Curl	Normal	Status	—	—	40	Self
1	Growl	Normal	Status	—	100	40	Many Others
1	Tackle	Normal	Physical	40	100	35	Normal
12	Guard Split	Psychic	Status	—	—	10	Normal
16	Double Kick	Fighting	Physical	30	100	30	Normal
21	Headbutt	Normal	Physical	70	100	15	Normal
27	Take Down	Normal	Physical	90	85	20	Normal
32	Guard Swap	Psychic	Status	—	—	10	Normal
38	Reversal	Fighting	Physical	—	100	15	Normal
44	Cotton Guard	Grass	Status	—	—	10	Self
50	Double-Edge	Normal	Physical	120	100	15	Normal
56	Last Resort	Normal	Physical	140	100	5	Normal

EVOLUTION MOVES

NAME	TYPE	KIND	POW.	ACC.	PP	RANGE

EGG MOVES

NAME	TYPE	KIND	POW.	ACC.	PP	RANGE

TUTOR MOVES

NAME	TYPE	KIND	POW.	ACC.	PP	RANGE

TM MOVES

NO.	NAME	TYPE	KIND	POW.	ACC.	PP	RANGE
TM01	Mega Kick	Normal	Physical	120	75	5	Normal
TM08	Hyper Beam	Normal	Special	150	90	5	Normal
TM09	Giga Impact	Normal	Physical	150	90	5	Normal
TM14	Thunder Wave	Electric	Status	—	90	20	Normal
TM21	Rest	Psychic	Status	—	—	10	Self
TM24	Snore	Normal	Special	50	100	15	Normal
TM25	Protect	Normal	Status	—	—	10	Self
TM31	Attract	Normal	Status	—	100	15	Normal
TM39	Facade	Normal	Physical	70	100	20	Normal
TM52	Bounce	Flying	Physical	85	85	5	Normal
TM57	Payback	Dark	Physical	50	100	10	Normal
TM61	Guard Swap	Psychic	Status	—	—	10	Normal
TM76	Round	Normal	Special	60	100	15	Normal
TM79	Retaliate	Normal	Physical	70	100	5	Normal

TR MOVES

NO.	NAME	TYPE	KIND	POW.	ACC.	PP	RANGE
TR00	Swords Dance	Normal	Status	—	—	20	Self
TR01	Body Slam	Normal	Physical	85	100	15	Normal
TR12	Agility	Psychic	Status	—	—	30	Self
TR20	Substitute	Normal	Status	—	—	10	Self
TR21	Reversal	Fighting	Physical	—	100	15	Normal
TR26	Endure	Normal	Status	—	—	10	Self
TR27	Sleep Talk	Normal	Status	—	—	10	Self
TR29	Baton Pass	Normal	Status	—	—	40	Self
TR69	Zen Headbutt	Psychic	Physical	80	90	15	Normal
TR80	Electro Ball	Electric	Special	—	100	10	Normal
TR86	Wild Charge	Electric	Physical	90	100	15	Normal
TR99	Body Press	Fighting	Physical	80	100	10	Normal

036 Lotad

p. 37

ABILITY
Swift Swim
Rain Dish

HIDDEN ABILITY
Own Tempo

SPECIES STRENGTHS

HP	
ATTACK	
DEFENSE	
SP. ATK	
SP. DEF	
SPEED	

DAMAGE TAKEN IN BATTLE

◎ ×1	🏢 ×1	🗡 ×1
🔥 ×1	💧 ×2	×1
💧 ×0.25	🔺 ×0.5	↻ ×1
🌀 ×1	🪶 ×2	🌙 ×1
✊ ×1	◎ ×1	◎ ×0.5
❄ ×1	🦠 ×2	✦ ×1

🥚 WATER 1 / GRASS

LEVEL-UP MOVES

LV.	NAME	TYPE	KIND	POW.	ACC.	PP	RANGE
1	Astonish	Ghost	Physical	30	100	15	Normal
1	Growl	Normal	Status	—	100	40	Many Others
3	Absorb	Grass	Special	20	100	25	Normal
6	Water Gun	Water	Special	40	100	25	Normal
9	Mist	Ice	Status	—	—	30	Your Side
12	Mega Drain	Grass	Special	40	100	15	Normal
16	Hail	Normal	Physical	—	100	15	Normal
20	Bubble Beam	Water	Special	65	100	20	Normal
24	Nature Power	Normal	Status	—	—	20	Normal
28	Giga Drain	Grass	Special	75	100	10	Normal
33	Rain Dance	Water	Status	—	—	5	Both Sides
38	Zen Headbutt	Psychic	Physical	80	90	15	Normal
43	Energy Ball	Grass	Special	90	100	10	Normal

EVOLUTION MOVES

NAME	TYPE	KIND	POW.	ACC.	PP	RANGE

EGG MOVES

NAME	TYPE	KIND	POW.	ACC.	PP	RANGE
Counter	Fighting	Physical	—	100	20	Varies
Leech Seed	Grass	Status	—	90	10	Normal
Razor Leaf	Grass	Physical	55	95	25	Many Others
Sweet Scent	Normal	Status	—	100	20	Many Others
Synthesis	Grass	Status	—	—	5	Self
Teeter Dance	Normal	Status	—	100	20	All Others
Tickle	Normal	Status	—	100	20	Normal

TUTOR MOVES

NAME	TYPE	KIND	POW.	ACC.	PP	RANGE

TM MOVES

NO.	NAME	TYPE	KIND	POW.	ACC.	PP	RANGE
TM11	Solar Beam	Grass	Special	120	100	10	Normal
TM21	Rest	Psychic	Status	—	—	10	Self
TM23	Thief	Dark	Physical	60	100	25	Normal
TM24	Snore	Normal	Special	50	100	15	Normal
TM25	Protect	Normal	Status	—	—	10	Self
TM27	Icy Wind	Ice	Special	55	95	15	Many Others
TM28	Giga Drain	Grass	Special	75	100	10	Normal
TM31	Attract	Normal	Status	—	100	15	Normal
TM33	Rain Dance	Water	Status	—	—	5	Both Sides
TM34	Sunny Day	Fire	Status	—	—	5	Both Sides
TM35	Hail	Ice	Status	—	—	10	Both Sides
TM36	Whirlpool	Water	Special	35	85	15	Normal
TM39	Facade	Normal	Physical	70	100	20	Normal
TM50	Bullet Seed	Grass	Physical	25	100	30	Normal
TM76	Round	Normal	Special	60	100	15	Normal

TR MOVES

NO.	NAME	TYPE	KIND	POW.	ACC.	PP	RANGE
TR00	Swords Dance	Normal	Status	—	—	20	Self
TR01	Body Slam	Normal	Physical	85	100	15	Normal
TR04	Surf	Water	Special	90	100	15	All Others
TR05	Ice Beam	Ice	Special	90	100	10	Normal
TR06	Blizzard	Ice	Special	110	70	5	Many Others
TR20	Substitute	Normal	Status	—	—	10	Self
TR26	Endure	Normal	Status	—	—	10	Self
TR27	Sleep Talk	Normal	Status	—	—	10	Self
TR35	Uproar	Normal	Special	90	100	10	1 Random
TR59	Seed Bomb	Grass	Physical	80	100	15	Normal
TR65	Energy Ball	Grass	Special	90	100	10	Normal
TR69	Zen Headbutt	Psychic	Physical	80	90	15	Normal
TR77	Grass Knot	Grass	Special	—	100	20	Normal
TR84	Scald	Water	Special	80	100	15	Normal

037 Lombre

p. 37

LEVEL-UP MOVES

LV.	NAME	TYPE	KIND	POW.	ACC.	PP	RANGE
1	Absorb	Grass	Special	20	100	25	Normal
1	Astonish	Ghost	Physical	30	100	15	Normal
1	Fake Out	Normal	Physical	40	100	10	Normal
1	Flail	Normal	Physical	—	100	15	Normal
1	Growl	Normal	Status	—	100	40	Many Others
1	Knock Off	Dark	Physical	65	100	20	Normal
1	Teeter Dance	Normal	Status	—	100	20	All Others
1	Water Gun	Water	Special	40	100	25	Normal
9	Mist	Ice	Status	—	—	30	Your Side
12	Mega Drain	Grass	Special	40	100	15	Normal
18	Fury Swipes	Normal	Physical	18	80	15	Normal
24	Bubble Beam	Water	Special	65	100	20	Normal
30	Nature Power	Normal	Status	—	—	20	Normal
36	Giga Drain	Grass	Special	75	100	10	Normal
43	Rain Dance	Water	Status	—	—	5	Both Sides
50	Zen Headbutt	Psychic	Physical	80	90	15	Normal
57	Energy Ball	Grass	Special	90	100	10	Normal
64	Hydro Pump	Water	Special	110	80	5	Normal

EVOLUTION MOVES

NAME	TYPE	KIND	POW.	ACC.	PP	RANGE

EGG MOVES

NAME	TYPE	KIND	POW.	ACC.	PP	RANGE

TUTOR MOVES

NAME	TYPE	KIND	POW.	ACC.	PP	RANGE

TM MOVES

NO.	NAME	TYPE	KIND	POW.	ACC.	PP	RANGE
TM00	Mega Punch	Normal	Physical	80	85	20	Normal
TM01	Mega Kick	Normal	Physical	120	75	5	Normal
TM03	Fire Punch	Fire	Physical	75	100	15	Normal
TM04	Ice Punch	Ice	Physical	75	100	15	Normal
TM05	Thunder Punch	Electric	Physical	75	100	15	Normal
TM11	Solar Beam	Grass	Special	120	100	10	Normal
TM21	Rest	Psychic	Status	—	—	10	Self
TM23	Thief	Dark	Physical	60	100	25	Normal
TM24	Snore	Normal	Special	50	100	15	Normal
TM25	Protect	Normal	Status	—	—	10	Self
TM27	Icy Wind	Ice	Special	55	95	15	Many Others
TM28	Giga Drain	Grass	Special	75	100	10	Normal
TM31	Attract	Normal	Status	—	100	15	Normal
TM33	Rain Dance	Water	Status	—	—	5	Both Sides
TM34	Sunny Day	Fire	Status	—	—	5	Both Sides
TM35	Hail	Ice	Status	—	—	10	Both Sides
TM36	Whirlpool	Water	Special	35	85	15	Normal
TM39	Facade	Normal	Physical	70	100	20	Normal
TM43	Brick Break	Fighting	Physical	75	100	15	Normal
TM45	Dive	Water	Physical	80	100	10	Normal
TM50	Bullet Seed	Grass	Physical	25	100	30	Normal
TM53	Mud Shot	Ground	Special	55	95	15	Normal
TM59	Fling	Dark	Physical	—	100	10	Normal
TM63	Drain Punch	Fighting	Physical	75	100	10	Normal
TM76	Round	Normal	Special	60	100	15	Normal

TR MOVES

NO.	NAME	TYPE	KIND	POW.	ACC.	PP	RANGE
TR00	Swords Dance	Normal	Status	—	—	20	Self
TR01	Body Slam	Normal	Physical	85	100	15	Normal
TR03	Hydro Pump	Water	Special	110	80	5	Normal
TR04	Surf	Water	Special	90	100	15	All Others
TR05	Ice Beam	Ice	Special	90	100	10	Normal
TR06	Blizzard	Ice	Special	110	70	5	Many Others
TR16	Waterfall	Water	Physical	80	100	15	Normal
TR20	Substitute	Normal	Status	—	—	10	Self
TR26	Endure	Normal	Status	—	—	10	Self
TR27	Sleep Talk	Normal	Status	—	—	10	Self
TR30	Encore	Normal	Status	—	100	5	Normal
TR35	Uproar	Normal	Special	90	100	10	1 Random
TR42	Hyper Voice	Normal	Special	90	100	10	Many Others
TR45	Muddy Water	Water	Special	90	85	10	Many Others
TR59	Seed Bomb	Grass	Physical	80	100	15	Normal
TR65	Energy Ball	Grass	Special	90	100	10	Normal
TR69	Zen Headbutt	Psychic	Physical	80	90	15	Normal
TR77	Grass Knot	Grass	Special	—	100	20	Normal
TR84	Scald	Water	Special	80	100	15	Normal

ABILITY
Swift Swim
Rain Dish

HIDDEN ABILITY
Own Tempo

SPECIES STRENGTHS
HP
ATTACK
DEFENSE
SP. ATK
SP. DEF
SPEED

DAMAGE TAKEN IN BATTLE

×1	×1	×1	×1	×2	×1
×0.25	×0.5	×1	×1	×2	×1
×1	×1	×0.5	×1	×2	×1

WATER 1
GRASS

---

038 Ludicolo

p. 37

LEVEL-UP MOVES

LV.	NAME	TYPE	KIND	POW.	ACC.	PP	RANGE
1	Absorb	Grass	Special	20	100	25	Normal
1	Astonish	Ghost	Physical	30	100	15	Normal
1	Bubble Beam	Water	Special	65	100	20	Normal
1	Energy Ball	Grass	Special	90	100	10	Normal
1	Fake Out	Normal	Physical	40	100	10	Normal
1	Flail	Normal	Physical	—	100	15	Normal
1	Fury Swipes	Normal	Physical	18	80	15	Normal
1	Giga Drain	Grass	Special	75	100	10	Normal
1	Growl	Normal	Status	—	100	40	Many Others
1	Hydro Pump	Water	Special	110	80	5	Normal
1	Knock Off	Dark	Physical	65	100	20	Normal
1	Mega Drain	Grass	Special	40	100	15	Normal
1	Mist	Ice	Status	—	—	30	Your Side
1	Nature Power	Normal	Status	—	—	20	Normal
1	Rain Dance	Water	Status	—	—	5	Both Sides
1	Teeter Dance	Normal	Status	—	100	20	All Others
1	Water Gun	Water	Special	40	100	25	Normal
1	Zen Headbutt	Psychic	Physical	80	90	15	Normal

EVOLUTION MOVES

NAME	TYPE	KIND	POW.	ACC.	PP	RANGE

EGG MOVES

NAME	TYPE	KIND	POW.	ACC.	PP	RANGE

TUTOR MOVES

NAME	TYPE	KIND	POW.	ACC.	PP	RANGE

TM MOVES

NO.	NAME	TYPE	KIND	POW.	ACC.	PP	RANGE
TM00	Mega Punch	Normal	Physical	80	85	20	Normal
TM01	Mega Kick	Normal	Physical	120	75	5	Normal
TM03	Fire Punch	Fire	Physical	75	100	15	Normal
TM04	Ice Punch	Ice	Physical	75	100	15	Normal
TM05	Thunder Punch	Electric	Physical	75	100	15	Normal
TM08	Hyper Beam	Normal	Special	150	90	5	Normal
TM09	Giga Impact	Normal	Physical	150	90	5	Normal
TM11	Solar Beam	Grass	Special	120	100	10	Normal
TM21	Rest	Psychic	Status	—	—	10	Self
TM23	Thief	Dark	Physical	60	100	25	Normal
TM24	Snore	Normal	Special	50	100	15	Normal
TM25	Protect	Normal	Status	—	—	10	Self
TM27	Icy Wind	Ice	Special	55	95	15	Many Others
TM28	Giga Drain	Grass	Special	75	100	10	Normal
TM31	Attract	Normal	Status	—	100	15	Normal
TM33	Rain Dance	Water	Status	—	—	5	Both Sides
TM34	Sunny Day	Fire	Status	—	—	5	Both Sides
TM35	Hail	Ice	Status	—	—	10	Both Sides
TM36	Whirlpool	Water	Special	35	85	15	Normal
TM39	Facade	Normal	Physical	70	100	20	Normal
TM43	Brick Break	Fighting	Physical	75	100	15	Normal
TM45	Dive	Water	Physical	80	100	10	Normal
TM46	Weather Ball*	Normal	Special	50	100	10	Normal
TM50	Bullet Seed	Grass	Physical	25	100	30	Normal
TM53	Mud Shot	Ground	Special	55	95	15	Normal
TM59	Fling	Dark	Physical	—	100	10	Normal
TM63	Drain Punch	Fighting	Physical	75	100	10	Normal
TM76	Round	Normal	Special	60	100	15	Normal

TR MOVES

NO.	NAME	TYPE	KIND	POW.	ACC.	PP	RANGE
TR00	Swords Dance	Normal	Status	—	—	20	Self
TR01	Body Slam	Normal	Physical	85	100	15	Normal
TR03	Hydro Pump	Water	Special	110	80	5	Normal
TR04	Surf	Water	Special	90	100	15	All Others
TR05	Ice Beam	Ice	Special	90	100	10	Normal
TR06	Blizzard	Ice	Special	110	70	5	Many Others
TR14	Metronome	Normal	Status	—	—	10	Self
TR16	Waterfall	Water	Physical	80	100	15	Normal
TR17	Amnesia	Psychic	Status	—	—	20	Self
TR20	Substitute	Normal	Status	—	—	10	Self
TR26	Endure	Normal	Status	—	—	10	Self
TR27	Sleep Talk	Normal	Status	—	—	10	Self
TR30	Encore	Normal	Status	—	100	5	Normal
TR35	Uproar	Normal	Special	90	100	10	1 Random
TR42	Hyper Voice	Normal	Special	90	100	10	Many Others
TR45	Muddy Water	Water	Special	90	85	10	Many Others
TR59	Seed Bomb	Grass	Physical	80	100	15	Normal
TR64	Focus Blast	Fighting	Special	120	70	5	Normal
TR65	Energy Ball	Grass	Special	90	100	10	Normal
TR69	Zen Headbutt	Psychic	Physical	80	90	15	Normal
TR71	Leaf Storm	Grass	Special	130	90	5	Normal
TR77	Grass Knot	Grass	Special	—	100	20	Normal
TR84	Scald	Water	Special	80	100	15	Normal

ABILITY
Swift Swim
Rain Dish

HIDDEN ABILITY
Own Tempo

SPECIES STRENGTHS
HP
ATTACK
DEFENSE
SP. ATK
SP. DEF
SPEED

DAMAGE TAKEN IN BATTLE

×1	×1	×1	×1	×2	×1
×0.25	×0.5	×1	×1	×2	×1
×1	×1	×0.5	×1	×2	×1

WATER 1
GRASS

*Weather Ball changes type depending on weather condition. (Harsh sunlight: Fire type. Rain: Water type. Hail: Ice type. Sandstorm: Rock type.)

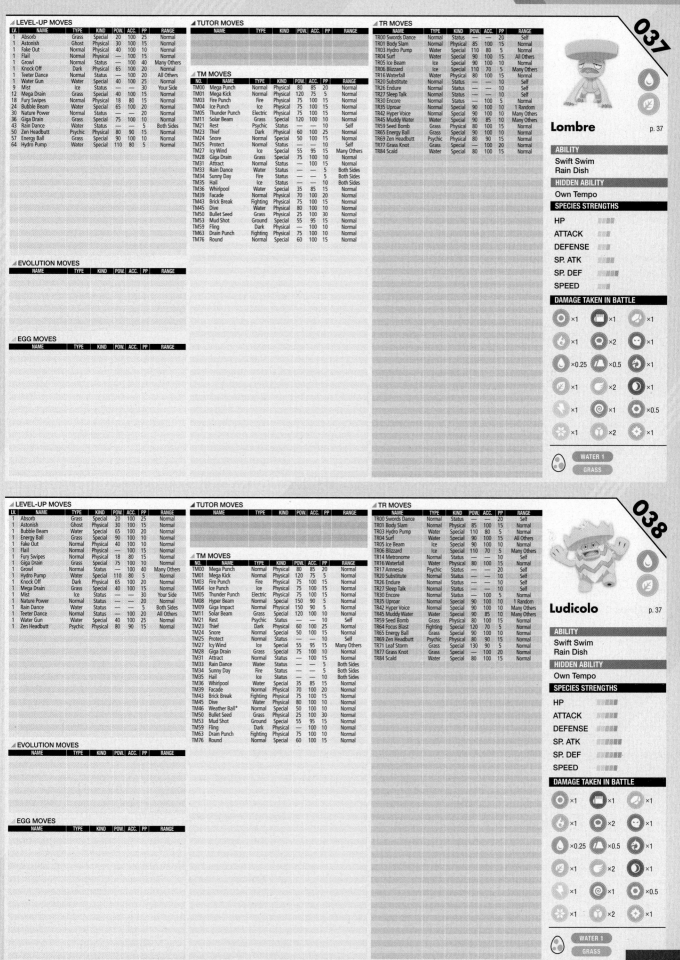

039 Seedot

p. 38

ABILITY
Chlorophyll
Early Bird

HIDDEN ABILITY
Pickpocket

SPECIES STRENGTHS

HP
ATTACK
DEFENSE
SP. ATK
SP. DEF
SPEED

DAMAGE TAKEN IN BATTLE

×1 ×1 ×1
×2 ×2 ×1
×0.5 ×0.5 ×1
×0.5 ×2 ×1
×0.5 ×1 ×1
×2 ×2 ×1

FIELD
GRASS

LEVEL-UP MOVES

LV.	NAME	TYPE	KIND	POW.	ACC.	PP	RANGE
1	Harden	Normal	Status	—	—	30	Self
1	Tackle	Normal	Physical	40	100	35	Normal
3	Absorb	Grass	Special	20	100	25	Normal
6	Astonish	Ghost	Physical	30	100	15	Normal
9	Growth	Normal	Status	—	—	20	Self
12	Rollout	Rock	Physical	30	90	20	Normal
15	Mega Drain	Grass	Special	40	100	15	Normal
18	Payback	Dark	Physical	50	100	10	Normal
21	Nature Power	Normal	Status	—	—	20	Normal
24	Sunny Day	Fire	Status	—	—	5	Both Sides
27	Synthesis	Grass	Status	—	—	5	Self
30	Sucker Punch	Dark	Physical	70	100	5	Normal
33	Explosion	Normal	Physical	250	100	5	All Others

EVOLUTION MOVES

NAME	TYPE	KIND	POW.	ACC.	PP	RANGE

EGG MOVES

NAME	TYPE	KIND	POW.	ACC.	PP	RANGE
Defog	Flying	Status	—	—	15	Normal
Leech Seed	Grass	Status	—	90	10	Normal
Night Slash	Dark	Physical	70	100	15	Normal
Quick Attack	Normal	Physical	40	100	30	Normal
Take Down	Normal	Physical	90	85	20	Normal
Worry Seed	Grass	Status	—	100	10	Normal

TUTOR MOVES

NAME	TYPE	KIND	POW.	ACC.	PP	RANGE

TM MOVES

NO.	NAME	TYPE	KIND	POW.	ACC.	PP	RANGE
TM11	Solar Beam	Grass	Special	120	100	10	Normal
TM15	Dig	Ground	Physical	80	100	10	Normal
TM20	Self-Destruct	Normal	Physical	200	100	5	All Others
TM21	Rest	Psychic	Status	—	—	10	Self
TM24	Snore	Normal	Special	50	100	15	Normal
TM25	Protect	Normal	Status	—	—	10	Self
TM28	Giga Drain	Grass	Special	75	100	10	Normal
TM31	Attract	Normal	Status	—	100	15	Normal
TM34	Sunny Day	Fire	Status	—	—	5	Both Sides
TM37	Beat Up	Dark	Physical	—	100	10	Normal
TM39	Facade	Normal	Physical	70	100	20	Normal
TM50	Bullet Seed	Grass	Physical	25	100	30	Normal
TM57	Payback	Dark	Physical	50	100	10	Normal
TM60	Power Swap	Psychic	Status	—	—	10	Normal
TM76	Round	Normal	Special	60	100	15	Normal
TM79	Retaliate	Normal	Physical	70	100	5	Normal
TM88	Grassy Terrain	Grass	Status	—	—	10	Both Sides
TM94	False Swipe	Normal	Physical	40	100	40	Normal

TR MOVES

NAME	TYPE	KIND	POW.	ACC.	PP	RANGE
TR00 Swords Dance	Normal	Status	—	—	20	Self
TR01 Body Slam	Normal	Physical	85	100	15	Normal
TR17 Amnesia	Psychic	Status	—	—	10	Self
TR20 Substitute	Normal	Status	—	—	10	Self
TR26 Endure	Normal	Status	—	—	10	Self
TR27 Sleep Talk	Normal	Status	—	—	10	Self
TR33 Shadow Ball	Ghost	Special	80	100	15	Normal
TR59 Seed Bomb	Grass	Physical	80	100	15	Normal
TR65 Energy Ball	Grass	Special	90	100	10	Normal
TR68 Nasty Plot	Dark	Status	—	—	20	Self
TR77 Grass Knot	Grass	Special	—	100	20	Normal
TR81 Foul Play	Dark	Physical	95	100	15	Normal

040 Nuzleaf

p. 38

ABILITY
Chlorophyll
Early Bird

HIDDEN ABILITY
Pickpocket

SPECIES STRENGTHS

HP
ATTACK
DEFENSE
SP. ATK
SP. DEF
SPEED

DAMAGE TAKEN IN BATTLE

×1 ×2 ×1
×2 ×2 ×0.5
×0.5 ×0.5 ×1
×0.5 ×2 ×0.5
×0.5 ×0 ×1
×2 ×4 ×2

FIELD
GRASS

LEVEL-UP MOVES

LV.	NAME	TYPE	KIND	POW.	ACC.	PP	RANGE
1	Absorb	Grass	Special	20	100	25	Normal
1	Air Cutter	Flying	Special	60	95	25	Many Others
1	Astonish	Ghost	Physical	30	100	15	Normal
1	Explosion	Normal	Physical	250	100	5	All Others
1	Fake Out	Normal	Physical	40	100	10	Normal
1	Harden	Normal	Status	—	—	30	Self
1	Razor Leaf	Grass	Physical	55	95	25	Many Others
1	Swagger	Normal	Status	—	85	15	Normal
1	Synthesis	Grass	Status	—	—	5	Self
1	Tackle	Normal	Physical	40	100	35	Normal
1	Torment	Dark	Status	—	100	15	Normal
9	Growth	Normal	Status	—	—	20	Self
12	Rollout	Rock	Physical	30	90	20	Normal
15	Mega Drain	Grass	Special	40	100	15	Normal
18	Payback	Dark	Physical	50	100	10	Normal
30	Nature Power	Normal	Status	—	—	20	Normal
36	Sunny Day	Fire	Status	—	—	5	Both Sides
43	Extrasensory	Psychic	Special	80	100	20	Normal
50	Sucker Punch	Dark	Physical	70	100	5	Normal
57	Leaf Blade	Grass	Physical	90	100	15	Normal

EVOLUTION MOVES

NAME	TYPE	KIND	POW.	ACC.	PP	RANGE
Razor Leaf	Grass	Physical	55	95	25	Many Others

EGG MOVES

NAME	TYPE	KIND	POW.	ACC.	PP	RANGE

TUTOR MOVES

NAME	TYPE	KIND	POW.	ACC.	PP	RANGE

TM MOVES

NO.	NAME	TYPE	KIND	POW.	ACC.	PP	RANGE
TM01	Mega Kick	Normal	Physical	120	75	5	Normal
TM08	Hyper Beam	Normal	Special	150	90	5	Normal
TM11	Solar Beam	Grass	Special	120	100	10	Normal
TM12	Solar Blade	Grass	Physical	125	100	10	Normal
TM15	Dig	Ground	Physical	80	100	10	Normal
TM20	Self-Destruct	Normal	Physical	200	100	5	All Others
TM21	Rest	Psychic	Status	—	—	10	Self
TM22	Rock Slide	Rock	Physical	75	90	10	Many Others
TM23	Thief	Dark	Physical	60	100	25	Normal
TM24	Snore	Normal	Special	50	100	15	Normal
TM25	Protect	Normal	Status	—	—	10	Self
TM28	Giga Drain	Grass	Special	75	100	10	Normal
TM31	Attract	Normal	Status	—	100	15	Normal
TM34	Sunny Day	Fire	Status	—	—	5	Both Sides
TM37	Beat Up	Dark	Physical	—	100	10	Normal
TM39	Facade	Normal	Physical	70	100	20	Normal
TM40	Swift	Normal	Special	60	—	20	Many Others
TM43	Brick Break	Fighting	Physical	75	100	15	Normal
TM48	Rock Tomb	Rock	Physical	60	95	15	Normal
TM50	Bullet Seed	Grass	Physical	25	100	30	Normal
TM57	Payback	Dark	Physical	50	100	10	Normal
TM58	Assurance	Dark	Physical	60	100	10	Normal
TM59	Fling	Dark	Physical	—	100	10	Normal
TM60	Power Swap	Psychic	Status	—	—	10	Normal
TM75	Low Sweep	Fighting	Physical	65	100	20	Normal
TM76	Round	Normal	Special	60	100	15	Normal
TM79	Retaliate	Normal	Physical	70	100	5	Normal
TM85	Snarl	Dark	Special	55	95	15	Many Others
TM88	Grassy Terrain	Grass	Status	—	—	10	Both Sides
TM94	False Swipe	Normal	Physical	40	100	40	Normal

TR MOVES

NAME	TYPE	KIND	POW.	ACC.	PP	RANGE
TR00 Swords Dance	Normal	Status	—	—	20	Self
TR01 Body Slam	Normal	Physical	85	100	15	Normal
TR07 Low Kick	Fighting	Physical	—	100	20	Normal
TR17 Amnesia	Psychic	Status	—	—	20	Self
TR20 Substitute	Normal	Status	—	—	10	Self
TR26 Endure	Normal	Status	—	—	10	Self
TR27 Sleep Talk	Normal	Status	—	—	10	Self
TR33 Shadow Ball	Ghost	Special	80	100	15	Normal
TR50 Leaf Blade	Grass	Physical	90	100	15	Normal
TR58 Dark Pulse	Dark	Special	80	100	15	Normal
TR59 Seed Bomb	Grass	Physical	80	100	15	Normal
TR65 Energy Ball	Grass	Special	90	100	10	Normal
TR68 Nasty Plot	Dark	Status	—	—	20	Self
TR77 Grass Knot	Grass	Special	—	100	20	Normal
TR81 Foul Play	Dark	Physical	95	100	15	Normal

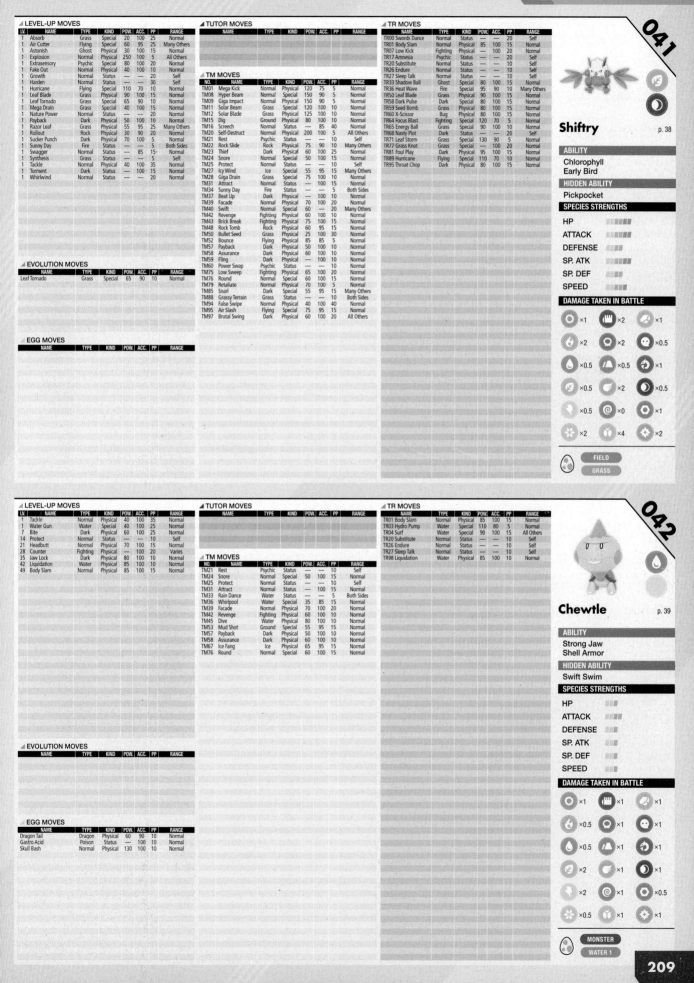

041

Shiftry
p. 38

ABILITY
Chlorophyll
Early Bird

HIDDEN ABILITY
Pickpocket

SPECIES STRENGTHS
- HP
- ATTACK
- DEFENSE
- SP. ATK
- SP. DEF
- SPEED

DAMAGE TAKEN IN BATTLE

×1 | ×2 | ×1
×2 | ×2 | ×0.5
×0.5 | ×0.5 | ×1
×0.5 | ×2 | ×0.5
×0.5 | ×0 | ×1
×1 | ×4 | ×2

FIELD / GRASS

LEVEL-UP MOVES

LV.	NAME	TYPE	KIND	POW.	ACC.	PP	RANGE
1	Absorb	Grass	Special	20	100	25	Normal
1	Air Cutter	Flying	Special	60	95	25	Many Others
1	Astonish	Ghost	Physical	30	100	15	Normal
1	Explosion	Normal	Physical	250	100	5	All Others
1	Extrasensory	Psychic	Special	80	100	20	Normal
1	Fake Out	Normal	Physical	40	100	10	Normal
1	Growth	Normal	Status	—	—	20	Self
1	Harden	Normal	Status	—	—	30	Self
1	Hurricane	Flying	Special	110	70	10	Normal
1	Leaf Blade	Grass	Physical	90	100	15	Normal
1	Leaf Tornado	Grass	Special	65	90	10	Normal
1	Mega Drain	Grass	Special	40	100	15	Normal
1	Nature Power	Normal	Status	—	—	20	Normal
1	Payback	Dark	Physical	50	100	10	Normal
1	Razor Leaf	Grass	Physical	55	95	25	Many Others
1	Rollout	Rock	Physical	30	90	20	Normal
1	Sucker Punch	Dark	Physical	70	100	5	Normal
1	Sunny Day	Fire	Status	—	—	5	Both Sides
1	Swagger	Normal	Status	—	85	15	Normal
1	Synthesis	Grass	Status	—	—	5	Self
1	Tackle	Normal	Physical	40	100	35	Normal
1	Torment	Dark	Status	—	100	15	Normal
1	Whirlwind	Normal	Status	—	—	20	Normal

EVOLUTION MOVES

NAME	TYPE	KIND	POW.	ACC.	PP	RANGE
Leaf Tornado	Grass	Special	65	90	10	Normal

EGG MOVES

NAME	TYPE	KIND	POW.	ACC.	PP	RANGE

TUTOR MOVES

NAME	TYPE	KIND	POW.	ACC.	PP	RANGE

TM MOVES

NO.	NAME	TYPE	KIND	POW.	ACC.	PP	RANGE
TM01	Mega Kick	Normal	Physical	120	75	5	Normal
TM08	Hyper Beam	Normal	Special	150	90	5	Normal
TM09	Giga Impact	Normal	Physical	150	90	5	Normal
TM11	Solar Beam	Grass	Special	120	100	10	Normal
TM12	Solar Blade	Grass	Physical	125	100	10	Normal
TM15	Dig	Ground	Physical	80	100	10	Normal
TM16	Screech	Normal	Status	—	85	40	Normal
TM20	Self-Destruct	Normal	Physical	200	100	5	All Others
TM21	Rest	Psychic	Status	—	—	10	Self
TM22	Rock Slide	Rock	Physical	75	90	10	Many Others
TM23	Thief	Dark	Physical	60	100	25	Normal
TM24	Snore	Normal	Special	50	100	15	Normal
TM25	Protect	Normal	Status	—	—	10	Self
TM27	Icy Wind	Ice	Special	55	95	15	Many Others
TM28	Giga Drain	Grass	Special	75	100	10	Normal
TM31	Attract	Normal	Status	—	100	15	Normal
TM34	Sunny Day	Fire	Status	—	—	5	Both Sides
TM37	Beat Up	Dark	Physical	—	100	10	Normal
TM39	Facade	Normal	Physical	70	100	20	Normal
TM40	Swift	Normal	Special	60	—	20	Many Others
TM42	Revenge	Fighting	Physical	60	100	10	Normal
TM43	Brick Break	Fighting	Physical	75	100	15	Normal
TM48	Rock Tomb	Rock	Physical	60	95	15	Normal
TM50	Bullet Seed	Grass	Physical	25	100	30	Normal
TM52	Bounce	Flying	Physical	85	85	5	Normal
TM57	Payback	Dark	Physical	50	100	10	Normal
TM58	Assurance	Dark	Physical	60	100	10	Normal
TM59	Fling	Dark	Physical	—	100	10	Normal
TM60	Power Swap	Psychic	Status	—	—	10	Normal
TM75	Low Sweep	Fighting	Physical	65	100	20	Normal
TM76	Round	Normal	Special	60	100	15	Normal
TM79	Retaliate	Normal	Physical	70	100	5	Normal
TM85	Snarl	Dark	Special	55	95	15	Many Others
TM88	Grassy Terrain	Grass	Status	—	—	10	Both Sides
TM94	False Swipe	Normal	Physical	40	100	40	Normal
TM95	Air Slash	Flying	Special	75	95	15	Normal
TM97	Brutal Swing	Dark	Physical	60	100	20	All Others

TR MOVES

NAME	TYPE	KIND	POW.	ACC.	PP	RANGE
TR00 Swords Dance	Normal	Status	—	—	20	Self
TR01 Body Slam	Normal	Physical	85	100	15	Normal
TR07 Low Kick	Fighting	Physical	—	100	20	Normal
TR17 Amnesia	Psychic	Status	—	—	20	Self
TR20 Substitute	Normal	Status	—	—	10	Self
TR27 Sleep Talk	Normal	Status	—	—	10	Self
TR33 Shadow Ball	Ghost	Special	80	100	15	Normal
TR36 Heat Wave	Fire	Special	95	90	10	Many Others
TR50 Leaf Blade	Grass	Physical	90	100	15	Normal
TR58 Dark Pulse	Dark	Special	80	100	15	Normal
TR59 Seed Bomb	Grass	Physical	80	100	15	Normal
TR60 X-Scissor	Bug	Physical	80	100	15	Normal
TR64 Focus Blast	Fighting	Special	120	70	5	Normal
TR65 Energy Ball	Grass	Special	90	100	10	Normal
TR68 Nasty Plot	Dark	Status	—	—	20	Self
TR71 Leaf Storm	Grass	Special	130	90	5	Normal
TR77 Grass Knot	Grass	Special	—	100	20	Normal
TR81 Foul Play	Dark	Physical	95	100	15	Normal
TR89 Hurricane	Flying	Special	110	70	10	Normal
TR95 Throat Chop	Dark	Physical	80	100	15	Normal

042

Chewtle
p. 39

ABILITY
Strong Jaw
Shell Armor

HIDDEN ABILITY
Swift Swim

SPECIES STRENGTHS
- HP
- ATTACK
- DEFENSE
- SP. ATK
- SP. DEF
- SPEED

DAMAGE TAKEN IN BATTLE

×1 | ×1 | ×1
×0.5 | ×1 | ×1
×0.5 | ×1 | ×1
×1 | ×1 | ×1
×2 | ×1 | ×0.5
×0.5 | ×1 | ×1

MONSTER / WATER 1

LEVEL-UP MOVES

LV.	NAME	TYPE	KIND	POW.	ACC.	PP	RANGE
1	Tackle	Normal	Physical	40	100	35	Normal
1	Water Gun	Water	Special	40	100	25	Normal
7	Bite	Dark	Physical	60	100	25	Normal
14	Protect	Normal	Status	—	—	10	Self
21	Headbutt	Normal	Physical	70	100	15	Normal
28	Counter	Fighting	Physical	—	100	20	Varies
35	Jaw Lock	Dark	Physical	80	100	10	Normal
42	Liquidation	Water	Physical	85	100	10	Normal
49	Body Slam	Normal	Physical	85	100	15	Normal

EVOLUTION MOVES

NAME	TYPE	KIND	POW.	ACC.	PP	RANGE

EGG MOVES

NAME	TYPE	KIND	POW.	ACC.	PP	RANGE
Dragon Tail	Dragon	Physical	60	90	10	Normal
Gastro Acid	Poison	Status	—	100	10	Normal
Skull Bash	Normal	Physical	130	100	10	Normal

TUTOR MOVES

NAME	TYPE	KIND	POW.	ACC.	PP	RANGE

TM MOVES

NO.	NAME	TYPE	KIND	POW.	ACC.	PP	RANGE
TM21	Rest	Psychic	Status	—	—	10	Self
TM24	Snore	Normal	Special	50	100	15	Normal
TM25	Protect	Normal	Status	—	—	10	Self
TM31	Attract	Normal	Status	—	100	15	Normal
TM33	Rain Dance	Water	Status	—	—	5	Both Sides
TM36	Whirlpool	Water	Special	35	85	15	Normal
TM39	Facade	Normal	Physical	70	100	20	Normal
TM42	Revenge	Fighting	Physical	60	100	10	Normal
TM45	Dive	Water	Physical	80	100	10	Normal
TM53	Mud Shot	Ground	Special	55	95	15	Normal
TM57	Payback	Dark	Physical	50	100	10	Normal
TM58	Assurance	Dark	Physical	60	100	10	Normal
TM67	Ice Fang	Ice	Physical	65	95	15	Normal
TM76	Round	Normal	Special	60	100	15	Normal

TR MOVES

NAME	TYPE	KIND	POW.	ACC.	PP	RANGE
TR01 Body Slam	Normal	Physical	85	100	15	Normal
TR03 Hydro Pump	Water	Special	110	80	5	Normal
TR04 Surf	Water	Special	90	100	15	All Others
TR20 Substitute	Normal	Status	—	—	10	Self
TR26 Endure	Normal	Status	—	—	10	Self
TR27 Sleep Talk	Normal	Status	—	—	10	Self
TR98 Liquidation	Water	Physical	85	100	10	Normal

043

Drednaw p. 39

ABILITY
Strong Jaw
Shell Armor

HIDDEN ABILITY
Swift Swim

SPECIES STRENGTHS

HP	
ATTACK	
DEFENSE	
SP. ATK	
SP. DEF	
SPEED	

DAMAGE TAKEN IN BATTLE

- ×0.5
- ×2
- ×1
- ×0.25
- ×0.5
- ×1
- ×1
- ×2
- ×1
- ×4
- ×0.5
- ×1
- ×2
- ×1
- ×1
- ×0.5
- ×1
- ×1

MONSTER
WATER 1

LEVEL-UP MOVES

LV.	NAME	TYPE	KIND	POW.	ACC.	PP	RANGE
1	Bite	Dark	Physical	60	100	25	Normal
1	Crunch	Dark	Physical	80	100	15	Normal
1	Protect	Normal	Status	—	—	10	Self
1	Razor Shell	Water	Physical	75	95	10	Normal
1	Rock Polish	Rock	Status	—	—	20	Self
1	Rock Tomb	Rock	Physical	60	95	15	Normal
1	Tackle	Normal	Physical	40	100	35	Normal
1	Water Gun	Water	Special	40	100	25	Normal
21	Headbutt	Normal	Physical	70	100	15	Normal
30	Counter	Fighting	Physical	—	100	20	Varies
39	Jaw Lock	Dark	Physical	80	100	10	Normal
48	Liquidation	Water	Physical	85	100	10	Normal
57	Body Slam	Normal	Physical	85	100	15	Normal
66	Head Smash	Rock	Physical	150	80	5	Normal

EVOLUTION MOVES

NAME	TYPE	KIND	POW.	ACC.	PP	RANGE
Rock Tomb	Rock	Physical	60	95	15	Normal

EGG MOVES

NAME	TYPE	KIND	POW.	ACC.	PP	RANGE

TUTOR MOVES

NAME	TYPE	KIND	POW.	ACC.	PP	RANGE

TM MOVES

NO.	NAME	TYPE	KIND	POW.	ACC.	PP	RANGE
TM08	Hyper Beam	Normal	Special	150	90	5	Normal
TM09	Giga Impact	Normal	Physical	150	90	5	Normal
TM15	Dig	Ground	Physical	80	100	10	Normal
TM21	Rest	Psychic	Status	—	—	10	Self
TM22	Rock Slide	Rock	Physical	75	90	10	Many Others
TM24	Snore	Normal	Special	50	100	15	Normal
TM25	Protect	Normal	Status	—	—	10	Self
TM26	Scary Face	Normal	Status	—	100	10	Normal
TM31	Attract	Normal	Status	—	100	15	Normal
TM32	Sandstorm	Rock	Status	—	—	10	Both Sides
TM33	Rain Dance	Water	Status	—	—	5	Both Sides
TM36	Whirlpool	Water	Special	35	85	15	Normal
TM39	Facade	Normal	Physical	70	100	20	Normal
TM42	Revenge	Fighting	Physical	60	100	10	Normal
TM45	Dive	Water	Physical	80	100	10	Normal
TM48	Rock Tomb	Rock	Physical	60	95	15	Normal
TM49	Sand Tomb	Ground	Physical	35	85	15	Normal
TM53	Mud Shot	Ground	Special	55	95	15	Normal
TM54	Rock Blast	Rock	Physical	25	90	10	Normal
TM57	Payback	Dark	Physical	50	100	10	Normal
TM58	Assurance	Dark	Physical	60	100	10	Normal
TM67	Ice Fang	Ice	Physical	65	95	15	Normal
TM76	Round	Normal	Special	60	100	15	Normal
TM81	Bulldoze	Ground	Physical	60	100	20	All Others
TM83	Razor Shell	Water	Physical	75	95	10	Normal
TM94	False Swipe	Normal	Physical	40	100	40	Normal
TM96	Smart Strike	Steel	Physical	70	—	10	Normal
TM98	Stomping Tantrum	Ground	Physical	75	100	10	Normal

TR MOVES

NO.	NAME	TYPE	KIND	POW.	ACC.	PP	RANGE
TR00	Swords Dance	Normal	Status	—	—	20	Self
TR01	Body Slam	Normal	Physical	85	100	15	Normal
TR03	Hydro Pump	Water	Special	110	80	5	Normal
TR04	Surf	Water	Special	90	100	15	All Others
TR05	Ice Beam	Ice	Special	90	100	10	Normal
TR06	Blizzard	Ice	Special	110	70	5	Many Others
TR10	Earthquake	Ground	Physical	100	100	10	All Others
TR16	Waterfall	Water	Physical	80	100	15	Normal
TR20	Substitute	Normal	Status	—	—	10	Self
TR26	Endure	Normal	Status	—	—	10	Self
TR27	Sleep Talk	Normal	Status	—	—	10	Self
TR28	Megahorn	Bug	Physical	120	85	10	Normal
TR31	Iron Tail	Steel	Physical	100	75	15	Normal
TR32	Crunch	Dark	Physical	80	100	15	Normal
TR39	Superpower	Fighting	Physical	120	100	5	Normal
TR45	Muddy Water	Water	Special	90	85	10	Many Others
TR46	Iron Defense	Steel	Status	—	—	15	Self
TR57	Poison Jab	Poison	Physical	80	100	20	Normal
TR67	Earth Power	Ground	Special	90	100	10	Normal
TR75	Stone Edge	Rock	Physical	100	80	5	Normal
TR76	Stealth Rock	Rock	Status	—	—	20	Other Side
TR84	Scald	Water	Special	80	100	15	Normal
TR94	High Horsepower	Ground	Physical	95	95	10	Normal
TR95	Throat Chop	Dark	Physical	80	100	15	Normal
TR98	Liquidation	Water	Physical	85	100	10	Normal
TR99	Body Press	Fighting	Physical	80	100	10	Normal

044

Purrloin p. 40

ABILITY
Limber
Unburden

HIDDEN ABILITY
Prankster

SPECIES STRENGTHS

HP	
ATTACK	
DEFENSE	
SP. ATK	
SP. DEF	
SPEED	

DAMAGE TAKEN IN BATTLE

- ×1
- ×2
- ×1
- ×1
- ×1
- ×0.5
- ×1
- ×1
- ×1
- ×1
- ×1
- ×0.5
- ×1
- ×0
- ×1
- ×1
- ×2
- ×2

FIELD

LEVEL-UP MOVES

LV.	NAME	TYPE	KIND	POW.	ACC.	PP	RANGE
1	Growl	Normal	Status	—	100	40	Many Others
1	Scratch	Normal	Physical	40	100	35	Normal
4	Sand Attack	Ground	Status	—	100	15	Normal
5	Fake Out	Normal	Physical	40	100	10	Normal
12	Fury Swipes	Normal	Physical	18	80	15	Normal
16	Torment	Dark	Status	—	100	15	Normal
21	Assurance	Dark	Physical	60	100	10	Normal
24	Hone Claws	Dark	Status	—	—	15	Self
28	Sucker Punch	Dark	Physical	70	100	5	Normal
32	Nasty Plot	Dark	Status	—	—	20	Self
36	Night Slash	Dark	Physical	70	100	15	Normal
40	Play Rough	Fairy	Physical	90	90	10	Normal

EVOLUTION MOVES

NAME	TYPE	KIND	POW.	ACC.	PP	RANGE

EGG MOVES

NAME	TYPE	KIND	POW.	ACC.	PP	RANGE
Copycat	Normal	Status	—	—	20	Self
Covet	Normal	Physical	60	100	25	Normal
Double Team	Normal	Status	—	—	15	Self
Quick Attack	Normal	Physical	40	100	30	Normal
Slash	Normal	Physical	70	100	20	Normal
Yawn	Normal	Status	—	—	10	Normal

TUTOR MOVES

NAME	TYPE	KIND	POW.	ACC.	PP	RANGE

TM MOVES

NO.	NAME	TYPE	KIND	POW.	ACC.	PP	RANGE
TM02	Pay Day	Normal	Physical	40	100	20	Normal
TM14	Thunder Wave	Electric	Status	—	90	20	Normal
TM16	Screech	Normal	Status	—	85	40	Normal
TM21	Rest	Psychic	Status	—	—	10	Self
TM23	Thief	Dark	Physical	60	100	25	Normal
TM24	Snore	Normal	Special	50	100	15	Normal
TM25	Protect	Normal	Status	—	—	10	Self
TM29	Charm	Fairy	Status	—	100	20	Normal
TM31	Attract	Normal	Status	—	100	15	Normal
TM33	Rain Dance	Water	Status	—	—	5	Both Sides
TM34	Sunny Day	Fire	Status	—	—	5	Both Sides
TM39	Facade	Normal	Physical	70	100	20	Normal
TM40	Swift	Normal	Special	60	—	20	Many Others
TM47	Fake Tears	Dark	Status	—	100	20	Normal
TM56	U-turn	Bug	Physical	70	100	20	Normal
TM57	Payback	Dark	Physical	50	100	10	Normal
TM58	Assurance	Dark	Physical	60	100	10	Normal
TM65	Shadow Claw	Ghost	Physical	70	100	15	Normal
TM76	Round	Normal	Special	60	100	15	Normal
TM85	Snarl	Dark	Special	55	95	15	Many Others

TR MOVES

NO.	NAME	TYPE	KIND	POW.	ACC.	PP	RANGE
TR20	Substitute	Normal	Status	—	—	10	Self
TR26	Endure	Normal	Status	—	—	10	Self
TR27	Sleep Talk	Normal	Status	—	—	10	Self
TR29	Baton Pass	Normal	Status	—	—	40	Self
TR30	Encore	Normal	Status	—	100	5	Normal
TR31	Iron Tail	Steel	Physical	100	75	15	Normal
TR33	Shadow Ball	Ghost	Special	80	100	15	Normal
TR37	Taunt	Dark	Status	—	100	20	Normal
TR38	Trick	Psychic	Status	—	100	10	Normal
TR42	Hyper Voice	Normal	Special	90	100	10	Many Others
TR58	Dark Pulse	Dark	Special	80	100	15	Normal
TR59	Seed Bomb	Grass	Physical	80	100	15	Normal
TR68	Nasty Plot	Dark	Status	—	—	20	Self
TR73	Gunk Shot	Poison	Physical	120	80	5	Normal
TR77	Grass Knot	Grass	Special	—	100	20	Normal
TR81	Foul Play	Dark	Physical	95	100	15	Normal
TR90	Play Rough	Fairy	Physical	90	90	10	Normal

045 Liepard p. 40

LEVEL-UP MOVES

LV.	NAME	TYPE	KIND	POW.	ACC.	PP	RANGE
1	Fake Out	Normal	Physical	40	100	10	Normal
1	Growl	Normal	Status	—	100	40	Many Others
1	Sand Attack	Ground	Status	—	100	15	Normal
1	Scratch	Normal	Physical	40	100	35	Normal
12	Fury Swipes	Normal	Physical	18	80	15	Normal
16	Torment	Dark	Status	—	100	15	Normal
23	Assurance	Dark	Physical	60	100	10	Normal
26	Hone Claws	Dark	Status	—	—	15	Self
34	Sucker Punch	Dark	Physical	70	100	5	Normal
40	Nasty Plot	Dark	Status	—	—	20	Self
46	Night Slash	Dark	Physical	70	100	15	Normal
52	Play Rough	Fairy	Physical	90	90	10	Normal

EVOLUTION MOVES

NAME	TYPE	KIND	POW.	ACC.	PP	RANGE

EGG MOVES

NAME	TYPE	KIND	POW.	ACC.	PP	RANGE

TUTOR MOVES

NAME	TYPE	KIND	POW.	ACC.	PP	RANGE

TM MOVES

NO.	NAME	TYPE	KIND	POW.	ACC.	PP	RANGE
TM02	Pay Day	Normal	Physical	40	100	20	Normal
TM08	Hyper Beam	Normal	Special	150	90	5	Normal
TM09	Giga Impact	Normal	Physical	150	90	5	Normal
TM14	Thunder Wave	Electric	Status	—	90	20	Normal
TM16	Screech	Normal	Status	—	85	40	Normal
TM21	Rest	Psychic	Status	—	—	10	Self
TM23	Thief	Dark	Physical	60	100	25	Normal
TM24	Snore	Normal	Special	50	100	15	Normal
TM25	Protect	Normal	Status	—	—	10	Self
TM29	Charm	Fairy	Status	—	100	20	Normal
TM31	Attract	Normal	Status	—	100	15	Normal
TM33	Rain Dance	Water	Status	—	—	5	Both Sides
TM34	Sunny Day	Fire	Status	—	—	5	Both Sides
TM39	Facade	Normal	Physical	70	100	20	Normal
TM40	Swift	Normal	Special	60	—	20	Many Others
TM47	Fake Tears	Dark	Status	—	100	20	Normal
TM56	U-turn	Bug	Physical	70	100	20	Normal
TM57	Payback	Dark	Physical	50	100	10	Normal
TM58	Assurance	Dark	Physical	60	100	10	Normal
TM65	Shadow Claw	Ghost	Physical	70	100	15	Normal
TM69	Psycho Cut	Psychic	Physical	70	100	20	Normal
TM76	Round	Normal	Special	60	100	15	Normal
TM85	Snarl	Dark	Special	55	95	15	Many Others

TR MOVES

NO.	NAME	TYPE	KIND	POW.	ACC.	PP	RANGE
TR20	Substitute	Normal	Status	—	—	10	Self
TR26	Endure	Normal	Status	—	—	10	Self
TR27	Sleep Talk	Normal	Status	—	—	10	Self
TR29	Baton Pass	Normal	Status	—	—	40	Self
TR30	Encore	Normal	Status	—	100	5	Normal
TR31	Iron Tail	Steel	Physical	100	75	15	Normal
TR33	Shadow Ball	Ghost	Special	80	100	15	Normal
TR37	Taunt	Dark	Status	—	100	20	Normal
TR38	Trick	Psychic	Status	—	100	10	Normal
TR42	Hyper Voice	Normal	Special	90	100	10	Many Others
TR58	Dark Pulse	Dark	Special	80	100	15	Normal
TR59	Seed Bomb	Grass	Physical	80	100	15	Normal
TR68	Nasty Plot	Dark	Status	—	—	20	Self
TR73	Gunk Shot	Poison	Physical	120	80	5	Normal
TR77	Grass Knot	Grass	Special	—	100	20	Normal
TR81	Foul Play	Dark	Physical	95	100	15	Normal
TR90	Play Rough	Fairy	Physical	90	90	10	Normal
TR95	Throat Chop	Dark	Physical	80	100	15	Normal

ABILITY
Limber
Unburden

HIDDEN ABILITY
Prankster

SPECIES STRENGTHS
HP
ATTACK
DEFENSE
SP. ATK
SP. DEF
SPEED

DAMAGE TAKEN IN BATTLE
×1 ×2 ×1
×1 ×1 ×0.5
×1 ×1 ×1
×1 ×1 ×0.5
×1 ×0 ×1
×2 ×2 ×2

FIELD

---

046 Yamper p. 40

LEVEL-UP MOVES

LV.	NAME	TYPE	KIND	POW.	ACC.	PP	RANGE
1	Tackle	Normal	Physical	40	100	35	Normal
1	Tail Whip	Normal	Status	—	100	30	Many Others
5	Nuzzle	Electric	Physical	20	100	20	Normal
10	Bite	Dark	Physical	60	100	25	Normal
15	Roar	Normal	Status	—	—	20	Normal
20	Spark	Electric	Physical	65	100	20	Normal
26	Charm	Fairy	Status	—	100	20	Normal
30	Crunch	Dark	Physical	80	100	15	Normal
35	Charge	Electric	Status	—	—	20	Self
40	Wild Charge	Electric	Physical	90	100	15	Normal
45	Play Rough	Fairy	Physical	90	90	10	Normal

EVOLUTION MOVES

NAME	TYPE	KIND	POW.	ACC.	PP	RANGE

EGG MOVES

NAME	TYPE	KIND	POW.	ACC.	PP	RANGE
Discharge	Electric	Special	80	100	15	All Others
Double-Edge	Normal	Physical	120	100	15	Normal
Flame Charge	Fire	Physical	50	100	20	Normal
Howl	Normal	Status	—	—	40	Your Side
Sand Attack	Ground	Status	—	100	15	Normal

TUTOR MOVES

NAME	TYPE	KIND	POW.	ACC.	PP	RANGE

TM MOVES

NO.	NAME	TYPE	KIND	POW.	ACC.	PP	RANGE
TM14	Thunder Wave	Electric	Status	—	90	20	Normal
TM15	Dig	Ground	Physical	80	100	10	Normal
TM21	Rest	Psychic	Status	—	—	10	Self
TM24	Snore	Normal	Special	50	100	15	Normal
TM25	Protect	Normal	Status	—	—	10	Self
TM29	Charm	Fairy	Status	—	100	20	Normal
TM31	Attract	Normal	Status	—	100	15	Normal
TM39	Facade	Normal	Physical	70	100	20	Normal
TM40	Swift	Normal	Special	60	—	20	Many Others
TM41	Helping Hand	Normal	Status	—	—	20	1 Ally
TM66	Thunder Fang	Electric	Physical	65	95	15	Normal
TM68	Fire Fang	Fire	Physical	65	95	15	Normal
TM76	Round	Normal	Special	60	100	15	Normal
TM80	Volt Switch	Electric	Special	70	100	20	Normal
TM85	Snarl	Dark	Special	55	95	15	Many Others

TR MOVES

NO.	NAME	TYPE	KIND	POW.	ACC.	PP	RANGE
TR08	Thunderbolt	Electric	Special	90	100	15	Normal
TR09	Thunder	Electric	Special	110	70	10	Normal
TR20	Substitute	Normal	Status	—	—	10	Self
TR26	Endure	Normal	Status	—	—	10	Self
TR27	Sleep Talk	Normal	Status	—	—	10	Self
TR32	Crunch	Dark	Physical	80	100	15	Normal
TR35	Uproar	Normal	Special	90	100	10	1 Random
TR80	Electro Ball	Electric	Special	—	100	10	Normal
TR86	Wild Charge	Electric	Physical	90	100	15	Normal
TR90	Play Rough	Fairy	Physical	90	90	10	Normal

ABILITY
Ball Fetch
—

HIDDEN ABILITY
—

SPECIES STRENGTHS
HP
ATTACK
DEFENSE
SP. ATK
SP. DEF
SPEED

DAMAGE TAKEN IN BATTLE
×1 ×1 ×1
×1 ×1 ×1
×1 ×2 ×1
×1 ×0.5 ×1
×0.5 ×1 ×0.5
×1 ×1 ×1

FIELD

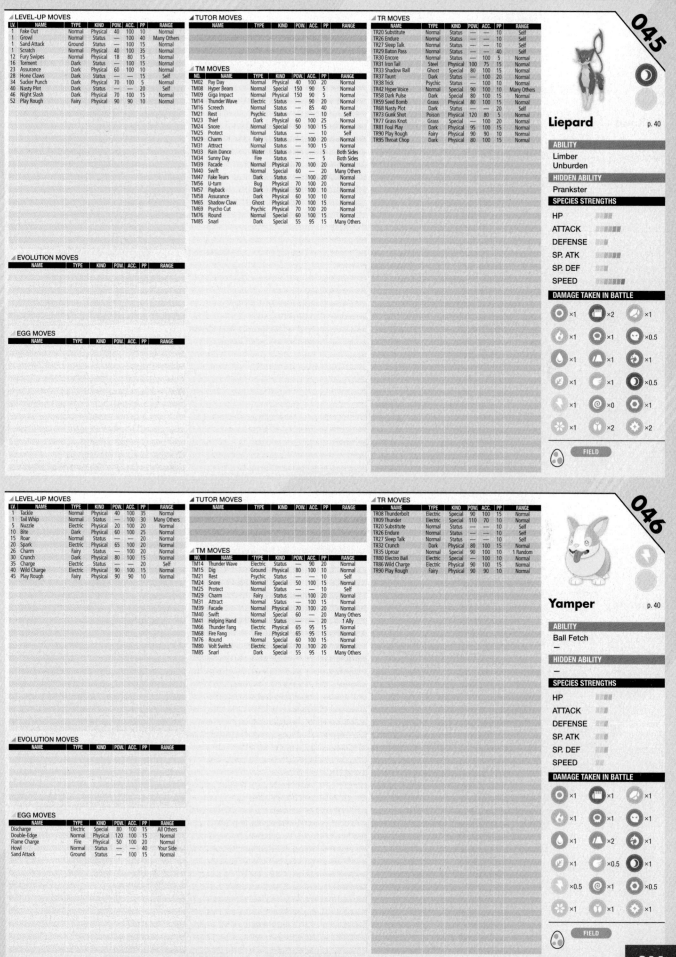

047

Boltund   p. 40

ABILITY
Strong Jaw
—

HIDDEN ABILITY
—

SPECIES STRENGTHS

HP
ATTACK
DEFENSE
SP. ATK
SP. DEF
SPEED

DAMAGE TAKEN IN BATTLE

×1   ×1   ×1
×1   ×1   ×1
×1   ×2   ×1
×1   ×0.5   ×1
×0.5   ×1   ×0.5
×1   ×1   ×1

FIELD

LEVEL-UP MOVES

LV.	NAME	TYPE	KIND	POW.	ACC.	PP	RANGE
1	Bite	Dark	Physical	60	100	25	Normal
1	Electrify	Electric	Status	—	—	20	Normal
1	Nuzzle	Electric	Physical	20	100	20	Normal
1	Tackle	Normal	Physical	40	100	35	Normal
1	Tail Whip	Normal	Status	—	100	30	Many Others
15	Roar	Normal	Status	—	—	20	Normal
20	Spark	Electric	Physical	65	100	20	Normal
28	Charm	Fairy	Status	—	100	20	Normal
34	Crunch	Dark	Physical	80	100	15	Normal
41	Charge	Electric	Status	—	—	20	Self
48	Wild Charge	Electric	Physical	90	100	15	Normal
55	Play Rough	Fairy	Physical	90	90	10	Normal
62	Electric Terrain	Electric	Status	—	—	10	Both Sides

EVOLUTION MOVES

NAME	TYPE	KIND	POW.	ACC.	PP	RANGE

EGG MOVES

NAME	TYPE	KIND	POW.	ACC.	PP	RANGE

TUTOR MOVES

NAME	TYPE	KIND	POW.	ACC.	PP	RANGE

TM MOVES

NO.	NAME	TYPE	KIND	POW.	ACC.	PP	RANGE
TM08	Hyper Beam	Normal	Special	150	90	5	Normal
TM09	Giga Impact	Normal	Physical	150	90	5	Normal
TM14	Thunder Wave	Electric	Status	—	90	20	Normal
TM15	Dig	Ground	Physical	80	100	10	Normal
TM21	Rest	Psychic	Status	—	—	10	Self
TM24	Snore	Normal	Special	50	100	15	Normal
TM25	Protect	Normal	Status	—	—	10	Self
TM29	Charm	Fairy	Status	—	100	20	Normal
TM31	Attract	Normal	Status	—	100	15	Normal
TM39	Facade	Normal	Physical	70	100	20	Normal
TM40	Swift	Normal	Special	60	—	20	Many Others
TM41	Helping Hand	Normal	Status	—	—	20	1 Ally
TM66	Thunder Fang	Electric	Physical	65	95	15	Normal
TM68	Fire Fang	Fire	Physical	65	95	15	Normal
TM76	Round	Normal	Special	60	100	15	Normal
TM80	Volt Switch	Electric	Special	70	100	20	Normal
TM85	Snarl	Dark	Special	55	95	15	Many Others
TM90	Electric Terrain	Electric	Status	—	—	10	Both Sides
TM93	Eerie Impulse	Electric	Status	—	100	15	Normal

TR MOVES

NO.	NAME	TYPE	KIND	POW.	ACC.	PP	RANGE
TR08	Thunderbolt	Electric	Special	90	100	15	Normal
TR09	Thunder	Electric	Special	110	70	10	Normal
TR12	Agility	Psychic	Status	—	—	30	Self
TR13	Focus Energy	Normal	Status	—	—	30	Self
TR20	Substitute	Normal	Status	—	—	10	Self
TR26	Endure	Normal	Status	—	—	10	Self
TR27	Sleep Talk	Normal	Status	—	—	10	Self
TR32	Crunch	Dark	Physical	80	100	15	Normal
TR35	Uproar	Normal	Special	90	100	10	1 Random
TR42	Hyper Voice	Normal	Special	90	100	10	Many Others
TR48	Bulk Up	Fighting	Status	—	—	20	Self
TR80	Electro Ball	Electric	Special	—	100	10	Normal
TR86	Wild Charge	Electric	Physical	90	100	15	Normal
TR90	Play Rough	Fairy	Physical	90	90	10	Normal
TR97	Psychic Fangs	Psychic	Physical	85	100	10	Normal

048

Bunnelby   p. 41

ABILITY
Pickup
Cheek Pouch

HIDDEN ABILITY
Huge Power

SPECIES STRENGTHS

HP
ATTACK
DEFENSE
SP. ATK
SP. DEF
SPEED

DAMAGE TAKEN IN BATTLE

×1   ×2   ×1
×1   ×1   ×0
×1   ×1   ×1
×1   ×1   ×1
×1   ×1   ×1
×1   ×1   ×1

FIELD

LEVEL-UP MOVES

LV.	NAME	TYPE	KIND	POW.	ACC.	PP	RANGE
1	Leer	Normal	Status	—	100	30	Many Others
1	Mud-Slap	Ground	Special	20	100	10	Normal
3	Tackle	Normal	Physical	40	100	35	Normal
6	Laser Focus	Normal	Status	—	—	30	Self
9	Quick Attack	Normal	Physical	40	100	30	Normal
12	Mud Shot	Ground	Special	55	95	15	Normal
15	Flail	Normal	Physical	—	100	15	Normal
18	Double Kick	Fighting	Physical	30	100	30	Normal
21	Bulldoze	Ground	Physical	60	100	20	All Others
24	Dig	Ground	Physical	80	100	10	Normal
27	Bounce	Flying	Physical	85	85	5	Normal
30	Take Down	Normal	Physical	90	85	20	Normal
33	Swords Dance	Normal	Status	—	—	20	Self
36	Earthquake	Ground	Physical	100	100	10	All Others
39	Super Fang	Normal	Physical	—	90	10	Normal

EVOLUTION MOVES

NAME	TYPE	KIND	POW.	ACC.	PP	RANGE

EGG MOVES

NAME	TYPE	KIND	POW.	ACC.	PP	RANGE
Defense Curl	Normal	Status	—	—	40	Self
Rollout	Rock	Physical	30	90	20	Normal

TUTOR MOVES

NAME	TYPE	KIND	POW.	ACC.	PP	RANGE

TM MOVES

NO.	NAME	TYPE	KIND	POW.	ACC.	PP	RANGE
TM15	Dig	Ground	Physical	80	100	10	Normal
TM21	Rest	Psychic	Status	—	—	10	Self
TM22	Rock Slide	Rock	Physical	75	90	10	Many Others
TM23	Thief	Dark	Physical	60	100	25	Normal
TM24	Snore	Normal	Special	50	100	15	Normal
TM25	Protect	Normal	Status	—	—	10	Self
TM31	Attract	Normal	Status	—	100	15	Normal
TM32	Sandstorm	Rock	Status	—	—	10	Both Sides
TM39	Facade	Normal	Physical	70	100	20	Normal
TM43	Brick Break	Fighting	Physical	75	100	15	Normal
TM48	Rock Tomb	Rock	Physical	60	95	15	Normal
TM52	Bounce	Flying	Physical	85	85	5	Normal
TM53	Mud Shot	Ground	Special	55	95	15	Normal
TM56	U-turn	Bug	Physical	70	100	20	Normal
TM57	Payback	Dark	Physical	50	100	10	Normal
TM59	Fling	Dark	Physical	—	100	10	Normal
TM76	Round	Normal	Special	60	100	15	Normal
TM81	Bulldoze	Ground	Physical	60	100	20	All Others

TR MOVES

NO.	NAME	TYPE	KIND	POW.	ACC.	PP	RANGE
TR00	Swords Dance	Normal	Status	—	—	20	Self
TR04	Surf	Water	Special	90	100	15	All Others
TR10	Earthquake	Ground	Physical	100	100	10	All Others
TR12	Agility	Psychic	Status	—	—	30	Self
TR20	Substitute	Normal	Status	—	—	10	Self
TR22	Sludge Bomb	Poison	Special	90	100	10	Normal
TR23	Spikes	Ground	Status	—	—	20	Other Side
TR26	Endure	Normal	Status	—	—	10	Self
TR27	Sleep Talk	Normal	Status	—	—	10	Self
TR31	Iron Tail	Steel	Physical	100	75	15	Normal
TR48	Bulk Up	Fighting	Status	—	—	20	Self
TR74	Iron Head	Steel	Physical	80	100	15	Normal
TR75	Stone Edge	Rock	Physical	100	80	5	Normal
TR77	Grass Knot	Grass	Special	—	100	20	Normal
TR85	Work Up	Normal	Status	—	—	30	Self
TR86	Wild Charge	Electric	Physical	90	100	15	Normal

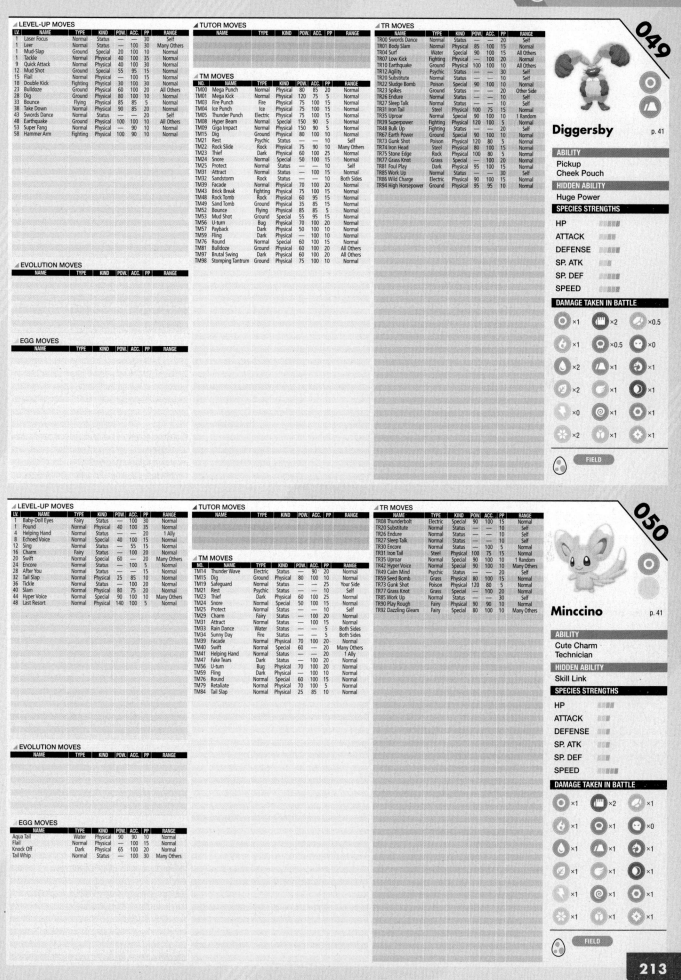

049 — Diggersby

ABILITY: Pickup / Cheek Pouch
HIDDEN ABILITY: Huge Power
Diggersby — p. 41

LEVEL-UP MOVES

LV.	NAME	TYPE	KIND	POW.	ACC.	PP	RANGE
1	Laser Focus	Normal	Status	—	—	30	Self
1	Leer	Normal	Status	—	100	30	Many Others
1	Mud-Slap	Ground	Special	20	100	10	Normal
4	Tackle	Normal	Physical	40	100	35	Normal
9	Quick Attack	Normal	Physical	40	100	30	Normal
12	Mud Shot	Ground	Special	55	95	15	Normal
15	Flail	Normal	Physical	—	100	15	Normal
18	Double Kick	Fighting	Physical	30	100	30	Normal
23	Bulldoze	Ground	Physical	60	100	20	All Others
28	Dig	Ground	Physical	80	100	10	Normal
33	Bounce	Flying	Physical	85	85	5	Normal
38	Take Down	Normal	Physical	90	85	20	Normal
43	Swords Dance	Normal	Status	—	—	20	Self
48	Earthquake	Ground	Physical	100	100	10	All Others
53	Super Fang	Normal	Physical	—	90	10	Normal
58	Hammer Arm	Fighting	Physical	100	90	10	Normal

EVOLUTION MOVES
NAME	TYPE	KIND	POW.	ACC.	PP	RANGE

EGG MOVES
NAME	TYPE	KIND	POW.	ACC.	PP	RANGE

TUTOR MOVES
NAME	TYPE	KIND	POW.	ACC.	PP	RANGE

TM MOVES

NO.	NAME	TYPE	KIND	POW.	ACC.	PP	RANGE
TM00	Mega Punch	Normal	Physical	80	85	20	Normal
TM01	Mega Kick	Normal	Physical	120	75	5	Normal
TM03	Fire Punch	Fire	Physical	75	100	15	Normal
TM04	Ice Punch	Ice	Physical	75	100	15	Normal
TM05	Thunder Punch	Electric	Physical	75	100	15	Normal
TM08	Hyper Beam	Normal	Special	150	90	5	Normal
TM09	Giga Impact	Normal	Physical	150	90	5	Normal
TM15	Dig	Ground	Physical	80	100	10	Normal
TM21	Rest	Psychic	Status	—	—	10	Self
TM22	Rock Slide	Rock	Physical	75	90	10	Many Others
TM23	Thief	Dark	Physical	60	100	25	Normal
TM24	Snore	Normal	Physical	50	100	15	Normal
TM25	Protect	Normal	Status	—	—	10	Self
TM31	Attract	Normal	Status	—	100	15	Normal
TM32	Sandstorm	Rock	Status	—	—	10	Both Sides
TM39	Facade	Normal	Physical	70	100	20	Normal
TM43	Brick Break	Fighting	Physical	75	100	15	Normal
TM48	Rock Tomb	Rock	Physical	60	95	15	Normal
TM49	Sand Tomb	Ground	Physical	35	85	15	Normal
TM52	Bounce	Flying	Physical	85	85	5	Normal
TM53	Mud Shot	Ground	Special	55	95	15	Normal
TM56	U-turn	Bug	Physical	70	100	20	Normal
TM57	Payback	Dark	Physical	50	100	10	Normal
TM59	Fling	Dark	Physical	—	100	10	Normal
TM76	Round	Normal	Special	60	100	15	Normal
TM81	Bulldoze	Ground	Physical	60	100	20	All Others
TM97	Brutal Swing	Dark	Physical	60	100	20	All Others
TM98	Stomping Tantrum	Ground	Physical	75	100	10	Normal

TR MOVES

NO.	NAME	TYPE	KIND	POW.	ACC.	PP	RANGE
TR00	Swords Dance	Normal	Status	—	—	20	Self
TR01	Body Slam	Normal	Physical	85	100	15	Normal
TR04	Surf	Water	Special	90	100	15	All Others
TR07	Low Kick	Fighting	Physical	—	100	20	Normal
TR10	Earthquake	Ground	Physical	100	100	10	All Others
TR12	Agility	Psychic	Status	—	—	30	Self
TR20	Substitute	Normal	Status	—	—	10	Self
TR22	Sludge Bomb	Poison	Special	90	100	10	Normal
TR23	Spikes	Ground	Status	—	—	20	Other Side
TR26	Endure	Normal	Status	—	—	10	Self
TR27	Sleep Talk	Normal	Status	—	—	10	Self
TR31	Iron Tail	Steel	Physical	100	75	15	Normal
TR35	Uproar	Normal	Special	90	100	10	1 Random
TR39	Superpower	Fighting	Physical	120	100	5	Normal
TR48	Bulk Up	Fighting	Status	—	—	20	Self
TR67	Earth Power	Ground	Special	90	100	10	Normal
TR74	Iron Head	Steel	Physical	80	100	15	Normal
TR75	Stone Edge	Rock	Physical	100	80	5	Normal
TR77	Grass Knot	Grass	Special	—	100	20	Normal
TR81	Foul Play	Dark	Physical	95	100	15	Normal
TR85	Work Up	Normal	Status	—	—	30	Self
TR86	Wild Charge	Electric	Physical	90	100	15	Normal
TR94	High Horsepower	Ground	Physical	95	95	10	Normal

SPECIES STRENGTHS: HP / ATTACK / DEFENSE / SP. ATK / SP. DEF / SPEED

DAMAGE TAKEN IN BATTLE:
- Normal ×1 · Fighting ×2 · Flying ×0.5
- Poison ×1 · Ground ×0.5 · Rock ×0
- Bug ×2 · Ghost ×1 · Steel ×1
- Fire ×2 · Water ×1 · Grass ×1
- Electric ×0 · Psychic ×1 · Ice ×1
- Dragon ×2 · Dark ×1 · Fairy ×1

FIELD

---

050 — Minccino

ABILITY: Cute Charm / Technician
HIDDEN ABILITY: Skill Link
Minccino — p. 41

LEVEL-UP MOVES

LV.	NAME	TYPE	KIND	POW.	ACC.	PP	RANGE
1	Baby-Doll Eyes	Fairy	Status	—	100	30	Normal
1	Pound	Normal	Physical	40	100	35	Normal
4	Helping Hand	Normal	Status	—	—	20	1 Ally
8	Echoed Voice	Normal	Special	40	100	15	Normal
12	Sing	Normal	Status	—	55	15	Normal
16	Charm	Fairy	Status	—	100	20	Normal
20	Swift	Normal	Special	60	—	20	Many Others
24	Encore	Normal	Status	—	100	5	Normal
28	After You	Normal	Status	—	—	15	Normal
32	Tail Slap	Normal	Physical	25	85	10	Normal
36	Tickle	Normal	Status	—	100	20	Normal
40	Slam	Normal	Physical	80	75	20	Normal
44	Hyper Voice	Normal	Special	90	100	10	Many Others
48	Last Resort	Normal	Physical	140	100	5	Normal

EVOLUTION MOVES
NAME	TYPE	KIND	POW.	ACC.	PP	RANGE

EGG MOVES

NAME	TYPE	KIND	POW.	ACC.	PP	RANGE
Aqua Tail	Water	Physical	90	90	10	Normal
Flail	Normal	Physical	—	100	15	Normal
Knock Off	Dark	Physical	65	100	20	Normal
Tail Whip	Normal	Status	—	100	30	Many Others

TUTOR MOVES
NAME	TYPE	KIND	POW.	ACC.	PP	RANGE

TM MOVES

NO.	NAME	TYPE	KIND	POW.	ACC.	PP	RANGE
TM14	Thunder Wave	Electric	Status	—	90	20	Normal
TM15	Dig	Ground	Physical	80	100	10	Normal
TM19	Safeguard	Normal	Status	—	—	25	Your Side
TM21	Rest	Psychic	Status	—	—	10	Self
TM23	Thief	Dark	Physical	60	100	25	Normal
TM24	Snore	Normal	Physical	50	100	15	Normal
TM25	Protect	Normal	Status	—	—	10	Self
TM29	Charm	Fairy	Status	—	100	20	Normal
TM31	Attract	Normal	Status	—	100	15	Normal
TM33	Rain Dance	Water	Status	—	—	5	Both Sides
TM34	Sunny Day	Fire	Status	—	—	5	Both Sides
TM39	Facade	Normal	Physical	70	100	20	Normal
TM40	Swift	Normal	Special	60	—	20	Many Others
TM41	Helping Hand	Normal	Status	—	—	20	1 Ally
TM47	Fake Tears	Dark	Status	—	100	20	Normal
TM56	U-turn	Bug	Physical	70	100	20	Normal
TM59	Fling	Dark	Physical	—	100	10	Normal
TM76	Round	Normal	Special	60	100	15	Normal
TM79	Retaliate	Normal	Physical	70	100	5	Normal
TM84	Tail Slap	Normal	Physical	25	85	10	Normal

TR MOVES

NO.	NAME	TYPE	KIND	POW.	ACC.	PP	RANGE
TR08	Thunderbolt	Electric	Special	90	100	15	Normal
TR20	Substitute	Normal	Status	—	—	10	Self
TR26	Endure	Normal	Status	—	—	10	Self
TR27	Sleep Talk	Normal	Status	—	—	10	Self
TR32	Encore	Normal	Status	—	100	5	Normal
TR31	Iron Tail	Steel	Physical	100	75	15	Normal
TR35	Uproar	Normal	Special	90	100	10	1 Random
TR42	Hyper Voice	Normal	Special	90	100	10	Many Others
TR49	Calm Mind	Psychic	Status	—	—	20	Self
TR59	Seed Bomb	Grass	Physical	80	100	15	Normal
TR73	Gunk Shot	Poison	Physical	120	80	5	Normal
TR77	Grass Knot	Grass	Special	—	100	20	Normal
TR85	Work Up	Normal	Status	—	—	30	Self
TR90	Play Rough	Fairy	Physical	90	90	10	Normal
TR92	Dazzling Gleam	Fairy	Special	80	100	10	Many Others

SPECIES STRENGTHS: HP / ATTACK / DEFENSE / SP. ATK / SP. DEF / SPEED

DAMAGE TAKEN IN BATTLE:
- Normal ×1 · Fighting ×2 · Flying ×1
- Poison ×1 · Ground ×1 · Rock ×0
- Bug ×1 · Ghost ×1 · Steel ×1
- Fire ×1 · Water ×1 · Grass ×1
- Electric ×1 · Psychic ×1 · Ice ×1
- Dragon ×1 · Dark ×1 · Fairy ×1

FIELD

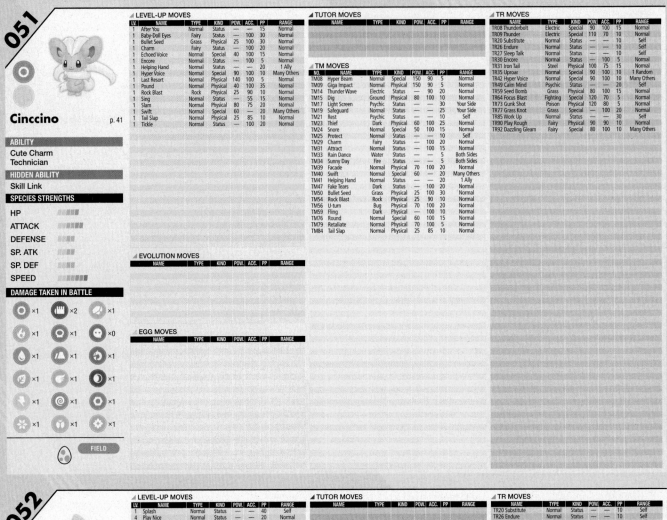

051

Cinccino
p. 41

ABILITY
Cute Charm
Technician

HIDDEN ABILITY
Skill Link

SPECIES STRENGTHS
HP
ATTACK
DEFENSE
SP. ATK
SP. DEF
SPEED

DAMAGE TAKEN IN BATTLE

×1	×2	×1	×1	×1	×0
×1	×1	×1	×1	×1	×1
×1	×1	×1	×1	×1	×1

FIELD

LEVEL-UP MOVES

LV.	NAME	TYPE	KIND	POW.	ACC.	PP	RANGE
1	After You	Normal	Status	—	—	15	Normal
1	Baby-Doll Eyes	Fairy	Status	—	100	30	Normal
1	Bullet Seed	Grass	Physical	25	100	30	Normal
1	Charm	Fairy	Status	—	100	20	Normal
1	Echoed Voice	Normal	Special	40	100	15	Normal
1	Encore	Normal	Status	—	100	5	Normal
1	Helping Hand	Normal	Status	—	—	20	1 Ally
1	Hyper Voice	Normal	Special	90	100	10	Many Others
1	Last Resort	Normal	Physical	140	100	5	Normal
1	Pound	Normal	Physical	40	100	35	Normal
1	Rock Blast	Rock	Physical	25	90	10	Normal
1	Sing	Normal	Status	—	55	15	Normal
1	Slam	Normal	Physical	80	75	20	Normal
1	Swift	Normal	Special	60	—	20	Many Others
1	Tail Slap	Normal	Physical	25	85	10	Normal
1	Tickle	Normal	Status	—	100	20	Normal

EVOLUTION MOVES

NAME	TYPE	KIND	POW.	ACC.	PP	RANGE

EGG MOVES

NAME	TYPE	KIND	POW.	ACC.	PP	RANGE

TUTOR MOVES

NAME	TYPE	KIND	POW.	ACC.	PP	RANGE

TM MOVES

NO.	NAME	TYPE	KIND	POW.	ACC.	PP	RANGE
TM08	Hyper Beam	Normal	Special	150	90	5	Normal
TM09	Giga Impact	Normal	Physical	150	90	5	Normal
TM14	Thunder Wave	Electric	Status	—	90	20	Normal
TM15	Dig	Ground	Physical	80	100	10	Normal
TM17	Light Screen	Psychic	Status	—	—	30	Your Side
TM19	Safeguard	Normal	Status	—	—	25	Your Side
TM21	Rest	Psychic	Status	—	—	10	Self
TM23	Thief	Dark	Physical	60	100	25	Normal
TM24	Snore	Normal	Special	50	100	15	Normal
TM25	Protect	Normal	Status	—	—	10	Self
TM29	Charm	Fairy	Status	—	100	20	Normal
TM31	Attract	Normal	Status	—	100	15	Normal
TM33	Rain Dance	Water	Status	—	—	5	Both Sides
TM34	Sunny Day	Fire	Status	—	—	5	Both Sides
TM39	Facade	Normal	Physical	70	100	20	Normal
TM40	Swift	Normal	Special	60	—	20	Many Others
TM41	Helping Hand	Normal	Status	—	—	20	1 Ally
TM47	Fake Tears	Dark	Status	—	100	20	Normal
TM50	Bullet Seed	Grass	Physical	25	100	30	Normal
TM54	Rock Blast	Rock	Physical	25	90	10	Normal
TM56	U-turn	Bug	Physical	70	100	20	Normal
TM59	Fling	Dark	Physical	—	100	10	Normal
TM76	Round	Normal	Special	60	100	15	Normal
TM79	Retaliate	Normal	Physical	70	100	5	Normal
TM84	Tail Slap	Normal	Physical	25	85	10	Normal

TR MOVES

NO.	NAME	TYPE	KIND	POW.	ACC.	PP	RANGE
TR08	Thunderbolt	Electric	Special	90	100	15	Normal
TR09	Thunder	Electric	Special	110	70	10	Normal
TR20	Substitute	Normal	Status	—	—	10	Self
TR26	Endure	Normal	Status	—	—	10	Self
TR27	Sleep Talk	Normal	Status	—	—	10	Self
TR30	Encore	Normal	Status	—	100	5	Normal
TR31	Iron Tail	Steel	Physical	100	75	15	Normal
TR35	Uproar	Normal	Special	90	100	10	1 Random
TR42	Hyper Voice	Normal	Special	90	100	10	Many Others
TR49	Calm Mind	Psychic	Status	—	—	20	Self
TR59	Seed Bomb	Grass	Physical	80	100	15	Normal
TR64	Focus Blast	Fighting	Special	120	70	5	Normal
TR73	Gunk Shot	Poison	Physical	120	80	5	Normal
TR77	Grass Knot	Grass	Special	—	100	20	Normal
TR85	Work Up	Normal	Status	—	—	30	Self
TR90	Play Rough	Fairy	Physical	90	90	10	Normal
TR92	Dazzling Gleam	Fairy	Special	80	100	10	Many Others

052

Bounsweet
p. 42

ABILITY
Leaf Guard
Oblivious

HIDDEN ABILITY
Sweet Veil

SPECIES STRENGTHS
HP
ATTACK
DEFENSE
SP. ATK
SP. DEF
SPEED

DAMAGE TAKEN IN BATTLE

×1	×1	×1	×2	×2	×1
×0.5	×0.5	×1	×0.5	×1	×1
×0.5	×1	×1	×2	×2	×1

GRASS

LEVEL-UP MOVES

LV.	NAME	TYPE	KIND	POW.	ACC.	PP	RANGE
1	Splash	Normal	Status	—	—	40	Self
4	Play Nice	Normal	Status	—	—	20	Normal
8	Rapid Spin	Normal	Physical	50	100	40	Normal
12	Razor Leaf	Grass	Physical	55	95	25	Many Others
16	Sweet Scent	Normal	Status	—	100	20	Many Others
20	Magical Leaf	Grass	Special	60	—	20	Normal
24	Flail	Normal	Physical	—	100	15	Normal
28	Teeter Dance	Normal	Status	—	100	20	All Others
32	Aromatic Mist	Fairy	Status	—	—	20	1 Ally
36	Aromatherapy	Grass	Status	—	—	5	Your Party

EVOLUTION MOVES

NAME	TYPE	KIND	POW.	ACC.	PP	RANGE

EGG MOVES

NAME	TYPE	KIND	POW.	ACC.	PP	RANGE
Acupressure	Normal	Status	—	—	30	Self/Ally
Endeavor	Normal	Physical	—	100	5	Normal
Synthesis	Grass	Status	—	—	5	Self

TUTOR MOVES

NAME	TYPE	KIND	POW.	ACC.	PP	RANGE

TM MOVES

NO.	NAME	TYPE	KIND	POW.	ACC.	PP	RANGE
TM10	Magical Leaf	Grass	Special	60	—	20	Normal
TM11	Solar Beam	Grass	Special	120	100	10	Normal
TM17	Light Screen	Psychic	Status	—	—	30	Your Side
TM18	Reflect	Psychic	Status	—	—	20	Your Side
TM19	Safeguard	Normal	Status	—	—	25	Your Side
TM21	Rest	Psychic	Status	—	—	10	Self
TM24	Snore	Normal	Special	50	100	15	Normal
TM25	Protect	Normal	Status	—	—	10	Self
TM28	Giga Drain	Grass	Special	75	100	10	Normal
TM29	Charm	Fairy	Status	—	100	20	Normal
TM31	Attract	Normal	Status	—	100	15	Normal
TM34	Sunny Day	Fire	Status	—	—	5	Both Sides
TM39	Facade	Normal	Physical	70	100	20	Normal
TM41	Helping Hand	Normal	Status	—	—	20	1 Ally
TM52	Bounce	Flying	Physical	85	85	5	Normal
TM76	Round	Normal	Special	60	100	15	Normal
TM87	Draining Kiss	Fairy	Special	50	100	10	Normal

TR MOVES

NO.	NAME	TYPE	KIND	POW.	ACC.	PP	RANGE
TR20	Substitute	Normal	Status	—	—	10	Self
TR26	Endure	Normal	Status	—	—	10	Self
TR27	Sleep Talk	Normal	Status	—	—	10	Self
TR59	Seed Bomb	Grass	Physical	80	100	15	Normal
TR65	Energy Ball	Grass	Special	90	100	10	Normal
TR69	Zen Headbutt	Psychic	Physical	80	90	15	Normal
TR77	Grass Knot	Grass	Special	—	100	20	Normal
TR90	Play Rough	Fairy	Physical	90	90	10	Normal
TR92	Dazzling Gleam	Fairy	Special	80	100	10	Many Others

053 Steenee

LEVEL-UP MOVES

LV.	NAME	TYPE	KIND	POW.	ACC.	PP	RANGE
1	Flail	Normal	Physical	—	100	15	Normal
1	Play Nice	Normal	Status	—	—	20	Normal
1	Rapid Spin	Normal	Physical	50	100	40	Normal
1	Razor Leaf	Grass	Physical	55	95	25	Many Others
1	Splash	Normal	Status	—	—	40	Self
16	Sweet Scent	Normal	Status	—	100	20	Many Others
22	Magical Leaf	Grass	Special	60	—	20	Normal
28	Stomp	Normal	Physical	65	100	20	Normal
34	Teeter Dance	Normal	Status	—	100	20	All Others
40	Aromatic Mist	Fairy	Status	—	—	20	1 Ally
46	Aromatherapy	Grass	Status	—	—	5	Your Party
52	Leaf Storm	Grass	Special	130	90	5	Normal

EVOLUTION MOVES

NAME	TYPE	KIND	POW.	ACC.	PP	RANGE

EGG MOVES

NAME	TYPE	KIND	POW.	ACC.	PP	RANGE

TUTOR MOVES

NAME	TYPE	KIND	POW.	ACC.	PP	RANGE

TM MOVES

NO.	NAME	TYPE	KIND	POW.	ACC.	PP	RANGE
TM10	Magical Leaf	Grass	Special	60	—	20	Normal
TM11	Solar Beam	Grass	Special	120	100	10	Normal
TM17	Light Screen	Psychic	Status	—	—	30	Your Side
TM18	Reflect	Psychic	Status	—	—	20	Your Side
TM19	Safeguard	Normal	Status	—	—	25	Your Side
TM21	Rest	Psychic	Status	—	—	10	Self
TM24	Snore	Normal	Special	50	100	15	Normal
TM25	Protect	Normal	Status	—	—	10	Self
TM28	Giga Drain	Grass	Special	75	100	10	Normal
TM29	Charm	Fairy	Status	—	100	20	Normal
TM31	Attract	Normal	Status	—	100	15	Normal
TM34	Sunny Day	Fire	Status	—	—	5	Both Sides
TM39	Facade	Normal	Physical	70	100	20	Normal
TM41	Helping Hand	Normal	Status	—	—	20	1 Ally
TM52	Bounce	Flying	Physical	85	85	5	Normal
TM57	Payback	Dark	Physical	50	100	10	Normal
TM59	Fling	Dark	Physical	—	100	10	Normal
TM75	Low Sweep	Fighting	Physical	65	100	20	Normal
TM76	Round	Normal	Special	60	100	15	Normal
TM87	Draining Kiss	Fairy	Special	50	100	10	Normal

TR MOVES

NAME	TYPE	KIND	POW.	ACC.	PP	RANGE
TR20 Substitute	Normal	Status	—	—	10	Self
TR26 Endure	Normal	Status	—	—	10	Self
TR27 Sleep Talk	Normal	Status	—	—	10	Self
TR59 Seed Bomb	Grass	Physical	80	100	15	Normal
TR65 Energy Ball	Grass	Special	90	100	10	Normal
TR69 Zen Headbutt	Psychic	Physical	80	90	15	Normal
TR71 Leaf Storm	Grass	Special	130	90	5	Normal
TR77 Grass Knot	Grass	Special	—	100	20	Normal
TR90 Play Rough	Fairy	Physical	90	90	10	Normal
TR92 Dazzling Gleam	Fairy	Special	80	100	10	Many Others

Steenee p. 42

ABILITY
Leaf Guard
Oblivious

HIDDEN ABILITY
Sweet Veil

SPECIES STRENGTHS
HP
ATTACK
DEFENSE
SP. ATK
SP. DEF
SPEED

DAMAGE TAKEN IN BATTLE
×1 ×1 ×1
×2 ×2 ×1
×0.5 ×0.5 ×1
×0.5 ×2 ×1
×0.5 ×1 ×1
×2 ×2 ×1

GRASS

---

054 Tsareena

LEVEL-UP MOVES

LV.	NAME	TYPE	KIND	POW.	ACC.	PP	RANGE
1	Flail	Normal	Physical	—	100	15	Normal
1	Play Nice	Normal	Status	—	—	20	Normal
1	Power Whip	Grass	Physical	120	85	10	Normal
1	Rapid Spin	Normal	Physical	50	100	40	Normal
1	Razor Leaf	Grass	Physical	55	95	25	Many Others
1	Splash	Normal	Status	—	—	40	Self
1	Swagger	Normal	Status	—	85	15	Normal
1	Trop Kick	Grass	Physical	70	100	15	Normal
16	Sweet Scent	Normal	Status	—	100	20	Many Others
22	Magical Leaf	Grass	Special	60	—	20	Normal
28	Stomp	Normal	Physical	65	100	20	Normal
34	Teeter Dance	Normal	Status	—	100	20	All Others
40	Aromatic Mist	Fairy	Status	—	—	20	1 Ally
46	Aromatherapy	Grass	Status	—	—	5	Your Party
52	Leaf Storm	Grass	Special	130	90	5	Normal
58	High Jump Kick	Fighting	Physical	130	90	10	Normal

EVOLUTION MOVES

NAME	TYPE	KIND	POW.	ACC.	PP	RANGE
Trop Kick	Grass	Physical	70	100	15	Normal

EGG MOVES

NAME	TYPE	KIND	POW.	ACC.	PP	RANGE

TUTOR MOVES

NAME	TYPE	KIND	POW.	ACC.	PP	RANGE

TM MOVES

NO.	NAME	TYPE	KIND	POW.	ACC.	PP	RANGE
TM01	Mega Kick	Normal	Physical	120	75	5	Normal
TM08	Hyper Beam	Normal	Special	150	90	5	Normal
TM09	Giga Impact	Normal	Physical	150	90	5	Normal
TM10	Magical Leaf	Grass	Special	60	—	20	Normal
TM11	Solar Beam	Grass	Special	120	100	10	Normal
TM12	Solar Blade	Grass	Physical	125	100	10	Normal
TM17	Light Screen	Psychic	Status	—	—	30	Your Side
TM18	Reflect	Psychic	Status	—	—	20	Your Side
TM19	Safeguard	Normal	Status	—	—	25	Your Side
TM21	Rest	Psychic	Status	—	—	10	Self
TM24	Snore	Normal	Special	50	100	15	Normal
TM25	Protect	Normal	Status	—	—	10	Self
TM28	Giga Drain	Grass	Special	75	100	10	Normal
TM29	Charm	Fairy	Status	—	100	20	Normal
TM31	Attract	Normal	Status	—	100	15	Normal
TM34	Sunny Day	Fire	Status	—	—	5	Both Sides
TM39	Facade	Normal	Physical	70	100	20	Normal
TM41	Helping Hand	Normal	Status	—	—	20	1 Ally
TM52	Bounce	Flying	Physical	85	85	5	Normal
TM56	U-turn	Bug	Physical	70	100	20	Normal
TM57	Payback	Dark	Physical	50	100	10	Normal
TM59	Fling	Dark	Physical	—	100	10	Normal
TM75	Low Sweep	Fighting	Physical	65	100	20	Normal
TM76	Round	Normal	Special	60	100	15	Normal
TM78	Acrobatics	Flying	Physical	55	100	15	Normal
TM87	Draining Kiss	Fairy	Special	50	100	10	Normal

TR MOVES

NAME	TYPE	KIND	POW.	ACC.	PP	RANGE
TR07 Low Kick	Fighting	Physical	—	100	20	Normal
TR20 Substitute	Normal	Status	—	—	10	Self
TR26 Endure	Normal	Status	—	—	10	Self
TR27 Sleep Talk	Normal	Status	—	—	10	Self
TR37 Taunt	Dark	Status	—	100	20	Normal
TR59 Seed Bomb	Grass	Physical	80	100	15	Normal
TR65 Energy Ball	Grass	Special	90	100	10	Normal
TR69 Zen Headbutt	Psychic	Physical	80	90	15	Normal
TR71 Leaf Storm	Grass	Special	130	90	5	Normal
TR72 Power Whip	Grass	Physical	120	85	10	Normal
TR77 Grass Knot	Grass	Special	—	100	20	Normal
TR90 Play Rough	Fairy	Physical	90	90	10	Normal
TR92 Dazzling Gleam	Fairy	Special	80	100	10	Many Others

Tsareena p. 42

ABILITY
Leaf Guard
Queenly Majesty

HIDDEN ABILITY
Sweet Veil

SPECIES STRENGTHS
HP
ATTACK
DEFENSE
SP. ATK
SP. DEF
SPEED

DAMAGE TAKEN IN BATTLE
×1 ×1 ×1
×2 ×2 ×1
×0.5 ×0.5 ×1
×0.5 ×2 ×1
×0.5 ×1 ×1
×2 ×2 ×1

GRASS

055

Oddish
p. 43

ABILITY
Chlorophyll
—

HIDDEN ABILITY
Run Away

SPECIES STRENGTHS

HP	
ATTACK	
DEFENSE	
SP. ATK	
SP. DEF	
SPEED	

DAMAGE TAKEN IN BATTLE

×1	×0.5	×1
×2	×1	×1
×0.5	×1	×1
×0.25	×2	×1
×0.5	×2	×1
×2	×1	×0.5

GRASS

LEVEL-UP MOVES

LV.	NAME	TYPE	KIND	POW.	ACC.	PP	RANGE
1	Absorb	Grass	Special	20	100	25	Normal
1	Growth	Normal	Status	—	—	20	Self
4	Acid	Poison	Special	40	100	30	Many Others
8	Sweet Scent	Normal	Status	—	100	20	Many Others
12	Mega Drain	Grass	Special	40	100	15	Normal
14	Poison Powder	Poison	Status	—	75	35	Normal
16	Stun Spore	Grass	Status	—	75	30	Normal
18	Sleep Powder	Grass	Status	—	75	15	Normal
20	Giga Drain	Grass	Special	75	100	10	Normal
24	Toxic	Poison	Status	—	90	10	Normal
28	Moonblast	Fairy	Special	95	100	15	Normal
32	Grassy Terrain	Grass	Status	—	—	10	Both Sides
36	Moonlight	Fairy	Status	—	—	5	Self
40	Petal Dance	Grass	Special	120	100	10	1 Random

EVOLUTION MOVES

NAME	TYPE	KIND	POW.	ACC.	PP	RANGE

EGG MOVES

NAME	TYPE	KIND	POW.	ACC.	PP	RANGE
After You	Normal	Status	—	—	15	Normal
Flail	Normal	Physical	—	100	15	Normal
Ingrain	Grass	Status	—	—	20	Self
Leech Seed	Grass	Status	—	90	10	Normal
Nature Power	Normal	Status	—	—	20	Many Others
Razor Leaf	Grass	Physical	55	95	25	Many Others
Strength Sap	Grass	Status	—	100	10	Normal
Synthesis	Grass	Status	—	—	5	Self
Teeter Dance	Normal	Status	—	100	20	All Others
Tickle	Normal	Status	—	100	20	Normal

TUTOR MOVES

NAME	TYPE	KIND	POW.	ACC.	PP	RANGE

TM MOVES

NO.	NAME	TYPE	KIND	POW.	ACC.	PP	RANGE
TM11	Solar Beam	Grass	Special	120	100	10	Normal
TM21	Rest	Psychic	Status	—	—	10	Self
TM24	Snore	Normal	Special	50	100	15	Normal
TM25	Protect	Normal	Status	—	—	10	Self
TM28	Giga Drain	Grass	Special	75	100	10	Normal
TM29	Charm	Fairy	Status	—	100	20	Normal
TM31	Attract	Normal	Status	—	100	15	Normal
TM34	Sunny Day	Fire	Status	—	—	5	Both Sides
TM39	Facade	Normal	Physical	70	100	20	Normal
TM50	Bullet Seed	Grass	Physical	25	100	30	Normal
TM74	Venoshock	Poison	Special	65	100	10	Normal
TM76	Round	Normal	Special	60	100	15	Normal
TM88	Grassy Terrain	Grass	Status	—	—	10	Both Sides

TR MOVES

NAME	TYPE	KIND	POW.	ACC.	PP	RANGE
TR00 Swords Dance	Normal	Status	—	—	20	Self
TR20 Substitute	Normal	Status	—	—	10	Self
TR22 Sludge Bomb	Poison	Special	90	100	10	Normal
TR26 Endure	Normal	Status	—	—	10	Self
TR27 Sleep Talk	Normal	Status	—	—	10	Self
TR59 Seed Bomb	Grass	Physical	80	100	15	Normal
TR65 Energy Ball	Grass	Special	90	100	10	Normal
TR77 Grass Knot	Grass	Special	—	100	20	Normal
TR92 Dazzling Gleam	Fairy	Special	80	100	10	Many Others

056

Gloom
p. 43

ABILITY
Chlorophyll
—

HIDDEN ABILITY
Stench

SPECIES STRENGTHS

HP	
ATTACK	
DEFENSE	
SP. ATK	
SP. DEF	
SPEED	

DAMAGE TAKEN IN BATTLE

×1	×0.5	×1
×2	×1	×1
×0.5	×1	×1
×0.25	×2	×1
×0.5	×2	×1
×2	×1	×0.5

GRASS

LEVEL-UP MOVES

LV.	NAME	TYPE	KIND	POW.	ACC.	PP	RANGE
1	Absorb	Grass	Special	20	100	25	Normal
1	Acid	Poison	Special	40	100	30	Many Others
1	Growth	Normal	Status	—	—	20	Self
1	Sweet Scent	Normal	Status	—	100	20	Many Others
12	Mega Drain	Grass	Special	40	100	15	Normal
14	Poison Powder	Poison	Status	—	75	35	Normal
16	Stun Spore	Grass	Status	—	75	30	Normal
18	Sleep Powder	Grass	Status	—	75	15	Normal
20	Giga Drain	Grass	Special	75	100	10	Normal
26	Toxic	Poison	Status	—	90	10	Normal
32	Moonblast	Fairy	Special	95	100	15	Normal
38	Grassy Terrain	Grass	Status	—	—	10	Both Sides
44	Moonlight	Fairy	Status	—	—	5	Self
50	Petal Dance	Grass	Special	120	100	10	1 Random

EVOLUTION MOVES

NAME	TYPE	KIND	POW.	ACC.	PP	RANGE

EGG MOVES

NAME	TYPE	KIND	POW.	ACC.	PP	RANGE

TUTOR MOVES

NAME	TYPE	KIND	POW.	ACC.	PP	RANGE

TM MOVES

NO.	NAME	TYPE	KIND	POW.	ACC.	PP	RANGE
TM11	Solar Beam	Grass	Special	120	100	10	Normal
TM21	Rest	Psychic	Status	—	—	10	Self
TM24	Snore	Normal	Special	50	100	15	Normal
TM25	Protect	Normal	Status	—	—	10	Self
TM28	Giga Drain	Grass	Special	75	100	10	Normal
TM29	Charm	Fairy	Status	—	100	20	Normal
TM31	Attract	Normal	Status	—	100	15	Normal
TM34	Sunny Day	Fire	Status	—	—	5	Both Sides
TM39	Facade	Normal	Physical	70	100	20	Normal
TM50	Bullet Seed	Grass	Physical	25	100	30	Normal
TM59	Fling	Dark	Physical	—	100	10	Normal
TM63	Drain Punch	Fighting	Physical	75	100	10	Normal
TM74	Venoshock	Poison	Special	65	100	10	Normal
TM76	Round	Normal	Special	60	100	15	Normal
TM88	Grassy Terrain	Grass	Status	—	—	10	Both Sides

TR MOVES

NAME	TYPE	KIND	POW.	ACC.	PP	RANGE
TR00 Swords Dance	Normal	Status	—	—	20	Self
TR20 Substitute	Normal	Status	—	—	10	Self
TR22 Sludge Bomb	Poison	Special	90	100	10	Normal
TR26 Endure	Normal	Status	—	—	10	Self
TR27 Sleep Talk	Normal	Status	—	—	10	Self
TR59 Seed Bomb	Grass	Physical	80	100	15	Normal
TR65 Energy Ball	Grass	Special	90	100	10	Normal
TR77 Grass Knot	Grass	Special	—	100	20	Normal
TR92 Dazzling Gleam	Fairy	Special	80	100	10	Many Others

057 Vileplume

p. 43

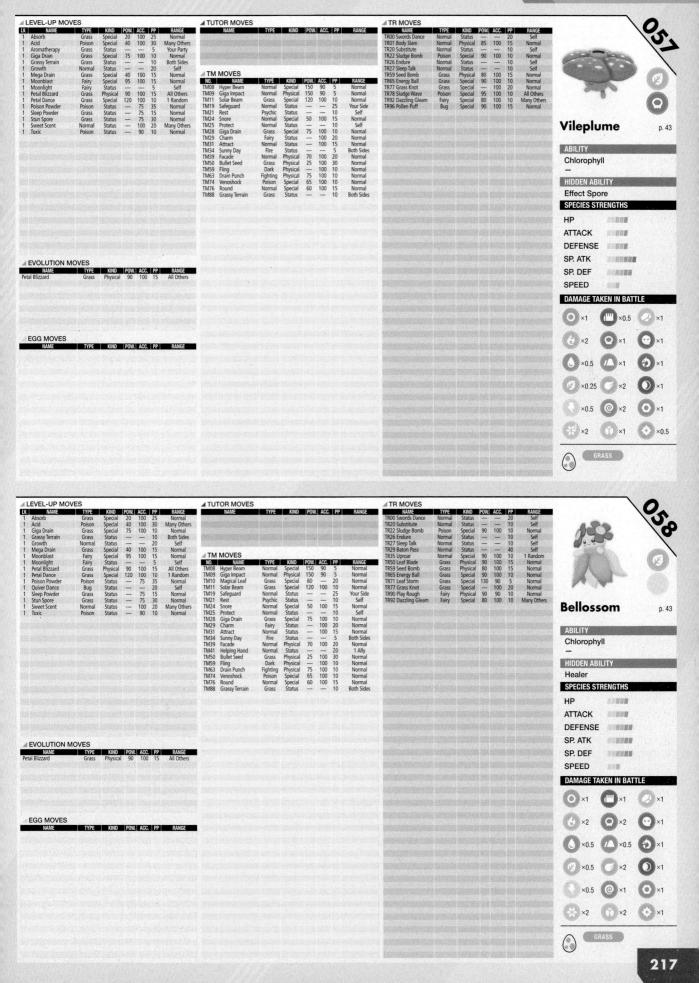

LEVEL-UP MOVES

LV.	NAME	TYPE	KIND	POW.	ACC.	PP	RANGE
1	Absorb	Grass	Special	20	100	25	Normal
1	Acid	Poison	Special	40	100	30	Many Others
1	Aromatherapy	Grass	Status	—	—	5	Your Party
1	Giga Drain	Grass	Special	75	100	10	Normal
1	Grassy Terrain	Grass	Status	—	—	10	Both Sides
1	Growth	Normal	Status	—	—	20	Self
1	Mega Drain	Grass	Special	40	100	15	Normal
1	Moonblast	Fairy	Special	95	100	15	Normal
1	Moonlight	Fairy	Status	—	—	5	Self
1	Petal Blizzard	Grass	Physical	90	100	15	All Others
1	Petal Dance	Grass	Special	120	100	10	1 Random
1	Poison Powder	Poison	Status	—	75	35	Normal
1	Sleep Powder	Grass	Status	—	75	15	Normal
1	Stun Spore	Grass	Status	—	75	30	Normal
1	Sweet Scent	Normal	Status	—	100	20	Many Others
1	Toxic	Poison	Status	—	90	10	Normal

EVOLUTION MOVES

NAME	TYPE	KIND	POW.	ACC.	PP	RANGE
Petal Blizzard	Grass	Physical	90	100	15	All Others

EGG MOVES

NAME	TYPE	KIND	POW.	ACC.	PP	RANGE

TUTOR MOVES

NAME	TYPE	KIND	POW.	ACC.	PP	RANGE

TM MOVES

NO.	NAME	TYPE	KIND	POW.	ACC.	PP	RANGE
TM08	Hyper Beam	Normal	Special	150	90	5	Normal
TM09	Giga Impact	Normal	Physical	150	90	5	Normal
TM11	Solar Beam	Grass	Special	120	100	10	Normal
TM19	Safeguard	Normal	Status	—	—	25	Your Side
TM21	Rest	Psychic	Status	—	—	10	Self
TM24	Snore	Normal	Special	50	100	15	Normal
TM25	Protect	Normal	Status	—	—	10	Self
TM28	Giga Drain	Grass	Special	75	100	10	Normal
TM29	Charm	Fairy	Status	—	100	20	Normal
TM31	Attract	Normal	Status	—	100	15	Normal
TM34	Sunny Day	Fire	Status	—	—	5	Both Sides
TM39	Facade	Normal	Physical	70	100	20	Normal
TM50	Bullet Seed	Grass	Physical	25	100	30	Normal
TM59	Fling	Dark	Physical	—	100	10	Normal
TM63	Drain Punch	Fighting	Physical	75	100	10	Normal
TM74	Venoshock	Poison	Special	65	100	10	Normal
TM76	Round	Normal	Special	60	100	15	Normal
TM88	Grassy Terrain	Grass	Status	—	—	10	Both Sides

TR MOVES

NO.	NAME	TYPE	KIND	POW.	ACC.	PP	RANGE
TR00	Swords Dance	Normal	Status	—	—	20	Self
TR01	Body Slam	Normal	Physical	85	100	15	Normal
TR20	Substitute	Normal	Status	—	—	10	Self
TR22	Sludge Bomb	Poison	Special	90	100	10	Normal
TR26	Endure	Normal	Status	—	—	10	Self
TR27	Sleep Talk	Normal	Status	—	—	10	Self
TR59	Seed Bomb	Grass	Physical	80	100	15	Normal
TR65	Energy Ball	Grass	Special	90	100	10	Normal
TR77	Grass Knot	Grass	Special	—	100	20	Normal
TR78	Sludge Wave	Poison	Special	95	100	10	All Others
TR92	Dazzling Gleam	Fairy	Special	80	100	10	Many Others
TR96	Pollen Puff	Bug	Special	90	100	15	Normal

ABILITY
Chlorophyll
—

HIDDEN ABILITY
Effect Spore

SPECIES STRENGTHS
HP
ATTACK
DEFENSE
SP. ATK
SP. DEF
SPEED

DAMAGE TAKEN IN BATTLE
×1 ×0.5 ×1
×2 ×1 ×1
×0.5 ×1 ×1
×0.25 ×2 ×1
×0.5 ×2 ×1
×2 ×1 ×0.5

GRASS

---

058 Bellossom

p. 43

LEVEL-UP MOVES

LV.	NAME	TYPE	KIND	POW.	ACC.	PP	RANGE
1	Absorb	Grass	Special	20	100	25	Normal
1	Acid	Poison	Special	40	100	30	Many Others
1	Giga Drain	Grass	Special	75	100	10	Normal
1	Grassy Terrain	Grass	Status	—	—	10	Both Sides
1	Growth	Normal	Status	—	—	20	Self
1	Mega Drain	Grass	Special	40	100	15	Normal
1	Moonblast	Fairy	Special	95	100	15	Normal
1	Moonlight	Fairy	Status	—	—	5	Self
1	Petal Blizzard	Grass	Physical	90	100	15	All Others
1	Petal Dance	Grass	Special	120	100	10	1 Random
1	Poison Powder	Poison	Status	—	75	35	Normal
1	Quiver Dance	Bug	Status	—	—	20	Self
1	Sleep Powder	Grass	Status	—	75	15	Normal
1	Stun Spore	Grass	Status	—	75	30	Normal
1	Sweet Scent	Normal	Status	—	100	20	Many Others
1	Toxic	Poison	Status	—	90	10	Normal

EVOLUTION MOVES

NAME	TYPE	KIND	POW.	ACC.	PP	RANGE
Petal Blizzard	Grass	Physical	90	100	15	All Others

EGG MOVES

NAME	TYPE	KIND	POW.	ACC.	PP	RANGE

TUTOR MOVES

NAME	TYPE	KIND	POW.	ACC.	PP	RANGE

TM MOVES

NO.	NAME	TYPE	KIND	POW.	ACC.	PP	RANGE
TM08	Hyper Beam	Normal	Special	150	90	5	Normal
TM09	Giga Impact	Normal	Physical	150	90	5	Normal
TM10	Magical Leaf	Grass	Special	60	—	20	Normal
TM11	Solar Beam	Grass	Special	120	100	10	Normal
TM19	Safeguard	Normal	Status	—	—	25	Your Side
TM21	Rest	Psychic	Status	—	—	10	Self
TM24	Snore	Normal	Special	50	100	15	Normal
TM25	Protect	Normal	Status	—	—	10	Self
TM28	Giga Drain	Grass	Special	75	100	10	Normal
TM29	Charm	Fairy	Status	—	100	20	Normal
TM31	Attract	Normal	Status	—	100	15	Normal
TM34	Sunny Day	Fire	Status	—	—	5	Both Sides
TM39	Facade	Normal	Physical	70	100	20	Normal
TM41	Helping Hand	Normal	Status	—	—	20	1 Ally
TM50	Bullet Seed	Grass	Physical	25	100	30	Normal
TM59	Fling	Dark	Physical	—	100	10	Normal
TM63	Drain Punch	Fighting	Physical	75	100	10	Normal
TM74	Venoshock	Poison	Special	65	100	10	Normal
TM76	Round	Normal	Special	60	100	15	Normal
TM88	Grassy Terrain	Grass	Status	—	—	10	Both Sides

TR MOVES

NO.	NAME	TYPE	KIND	POW.	ACC.	PP	RANGE
TR00	Swords Dance	Normal	Status	—	—	20	Self
TR20	Substitute	Normal	Status	—	—	10	Self
TR22	Sludge Bomb	Poison	Special	90	100	10	Normal
TR26	Endure	Normal	Status	—	—	10	Self
TR27	Sleep Talk	Normal	Status	—	—	10	Self
TR29	Baton Pass	Normal	Status	—	—	40	Self
TR35	Uproar	Normal	Special	90	100	10	1 Random
TR50	Leaf Blade	Grass	Physical	90	100	15	Normal
TR59	Seed Bomb	Grass	Physical	80	100	15	Normal
TR65	Energy Ball	Grass	Special	90	100	10	Normal
TR71	Leaf Storm	Grass	Special	130	90	5	Normal
TR77	Grass Knot	Grass	Special	—	100	20	Normal
TR90	Play Rough	Fairy	Physical	90	90	10	Normal
TR92	Dazzling Gleam	Fairy	Special	80	100	10	Many Others

ABILITY
Chlorophyll
—

HIDDEN ABILITY
Healer

SPECIES STRENGTHS
HP
ATTACK
DEFENSE
SP. ATK
SP. DEF
SPEED

DAMAGE TAKEN IN BATTLE
×1 ×1 ×1
×2 ×2 ×1
×0.5 ×0.5 ×1
×0.5 ×2 ×1
×0.5 ×1 ×1
×2 ×2 ×1

GRASS

059 Budew

p. 44

ABILITY
Natural Cure
Poison Point

HIDDEN ABILITY
Leaf Guard

SPECIES STRENGTHS

HP
ATTACK
DEFENSE
SP. ATK
SP. DEF
SPEED

DAMAGE TAKEN IN BATTLE

⊙ ×1	▦ ×0.5	⊘ ×1			
⊙ ×2	⊙ ×1	⊙ ×1			
⊙ ×0.5	⊿ ×1	↻ ×1			
⊘ ×0.25	⊿ ×2	⊙ ×1			
⊙ ×0.5	◎ ×2	⊙ ×1			
✳ ×2	⊙ ×1	◈ ×0.5			

NO EGGS

LEVEL-UP MOVES

LV.	NAME	TYPE	KIND	POW.	ACC.	PP	RANGE
1	Absorb	Grass	Special	20	100	25	Normal
1	Growth	Normal	Status	—	—	20	Self
1	Stun Spore	Grass	Status	—	75	30	Normal
1	Worry Seed	Grass	Status	—	100	10	Normal

EVOLUTION MOVES

NAME	TYPE	KIND	POW.	ACC.	PP	RANGE

EGG MOVES

NAME	TYPE	KIND	POW.	ACC.	PP	RANGE
Cotton Spore	Grass	Status	—	100	40	Many Others
Extrasensory	Psychic	Special	80	100	20	Normal
Life Dew	Water	Status	—	—	10	Your Side
Razor Leaf	Grass	Physical	55	95	25	Many Others
Sleep Powder	Grass	Status	—	75	15	Normal
Synthesis	Grass	Status	—	—	5	Self

TUTOR MOVES

NAME	TYPE	KIND	POW.	ACC.	PP	RANGE

TM MOVES

NO.	NAME	TYPE	KIND	POW.	ACC.	PP	RANGE
TM07	Pin Missile	Bug	Physical	25	95	20	Normal
TM11	Solar Beam	Grass	Special	120	100	10	Normal
TM21	Rest	Psychic	Status	—	—	10	Self
TM24	Snore	Normal	Special	50	100	15	Normal
TM25	Protect	Normal	Status	—	—	10	Self
TM28	Giga Drain	Grass	Special	75	100	10	Normal
TM31	Attract	Normal	Status	—	100	15	Normal
TM33	Rain Dance	Water	Status	—	—	5	Both Sides
TM34	Sunny Day	Fire	Status	—	—	5	Both Sides
TM39	Facade	Normal	Physical	70	100	20	Normal
TM40	Swift	Normal	Special	60	—	20	Many Others
TM46	Weather Ball*	Normal	Special	50	100	10	Normal
TM50	Bullet Seed	Grass	Physical	25	100	30	Normal
TM74	Venoshock	Poison	Special	65	100	10	Normal
TM76	Round	Normal	Special	60	100	15	Normal

TR MOVES

NO.	NAME	TYPE	KIND	POW.	ACC.	PP	RANGE
TR00	Swords Dance	Normal	Status	—	—	20	Self
TR20	Substitute	Normal	Status	—	—	10	Self
TR22	Sludge Bomb	Poison	Special	90	100	10	Normal
TR23	Spikes	Ground	Status	—	—	20	Other Side
TR26	Endure	Normal	Status	—	—	10	Self
TR27	Sleep Talk	Normal	Status	—	—	10	Self
TR33	Shadow Ball	Ghost	Special	80	100	15	Normal
TR35	Uproar	Normal	Special	90	100	10	1 Random
TR59	Seed Bomb	Grass	Physical	80	100	15	Normal
TR65	Energy Ball	Grass	Special	90	100	10	Normal
TR71	Leaf Storm	Grass	Special	130	90	5	Normal
TR77	Grass Knot	Grass	Special	—	100	20	Normal
TR92	Dazzling Gleam	Fairy	Special	80	100	10	Many Others

---

060 Roselia

p. 44

ABILITY
Natural Cure
Poison Point

HIDDEN ABILITY
Leaf Guard

SPECIES STRENGTHS

HP
ATTACK
DEFENSE
SP. ATK
SP. DEF
SPEED

DAMAGE TAKEN IN BATTLE

⊙ ×1	▦ ×0.5	⊘ ×1			
⊙ ×2	⊙ ×1	⊙ ×1			
⊙ ×0.5	⊿ ×1	↻ ×1			
⊘ ×0.25	⊿ ×2	⊙ ×1			
⊙ ×0.5	◎ ×2	⊙ ×1			
✳ ×2	⊙ ×1	◈ ×0.5			

FAIRY
GRASS

LEVEL-UP MOVES

LV.	NAME	TYPE	KIND	POW.	ACC.	PP	RANGE
1	Absorb	Grass	Special	20	100	25	Normal
1	Growth	Normal	Status	—	—	20	Self
1	Poison Sting	Poison	Physical	15	100	35	Normal
1	Stun Spore	Grass	Status	—	75	30	Normal
1	Worry Seed	Grass	Status	—	100	10	Normal
5	Mega Drain	Grass	Special	40	100	15	Normal
10	Leech Seed	Grass	Status	—	90	10	Normal
15	Magical Leaf	Grass	Special	60	—	20	Normal
20	Toxic Spikes	Poison	Status	—	—	20	Other Side
25	Sweet Scent	Normal	Status	—	100	20	Many Others
30	Giga Drain	Grass	Special	75	100	10	Normal
35	Synthesis	Grass	Status	—	—	5	Self
40	Toxic	Poison	Status	—	90	10	Normal
45	Petal Blizzard	Grass	Physical	90	100	15	All Others
50	Aromatherapy	Grass	Status	—	—	5	Your Party
55	Ingrain	Grass	Status	—	—	20	Self
60	Petal Dance	Grass	Special	120	100	10	1 Random

EVOLUTION MOVES

NAME	TYPE	KIND	POW.	ACC.	PP	RANGE
Poison Sting	Poison	Physical	15	100	35	Normal

EGG MOVES

NAME	TYPE	KIND	POW.	ACC.	PP	RANGE
Cotton Spore	Grass	Status	—	100	40	Many Others
Extrasensory	Psychic	Special	80	100	20	Normal
Life Dew	Water	Status	—	—	10	Your Side
Razor Leaf	Grass	Physical	55	95	25	Many Others
Sleep Powder	Grass	Status	—	75	15	Normal

TUTOR MOVES

NAME	TYPE	KIND	POW.	ACC.	PP	RANGE

TM MOVES

NO.	NAME	TYPE	KIND	POW.	ACC.	PP	RANGE
TM07	Pin Missile	Bug	Physical	25	95	20	Normal
TM10	Magical Leaf	Grass	Special	60	—	20	Normal
TM11	Solar Beam	Grass	Special	120	100	10	Normal
TM21	Rest	Psychic	Status	—	—	10	Self
TM24	Snore	Normal	Special	50	100	15	Normal
TM25	Protect	Normal	Status	—	—	10	Self
TM28	Giga Drain	Grass	Special	75	100	10	Normal
TM31	Attract	Normal	Status	—	100	15	Normal
TM33	Rain Dance	Water	Status	—	—	5	Both Sides
TM34	Sunny Day	Fire	Status	—	—	5	Both Sides
TM39	Facade	Normal	Physical	70	100	20	Normal
TM40	Swift	Normal	Special	60	—	20	Many Others
TM46	Weather Ball*	Normal	Special	50	100	10	Normal
TM50	Bullet Seed	Grass	Physical	25	100	30	Normal
TM74	Venoshock	Poison	Special	65	100	10	Normal
TM76	Round	Normal	Special	60	100	15	Normal

TR MOVES

NO.	NAME	TYPE	KIND	POW.	ACC.	PP	RANGE
TR00	Swords Dance	Normal	Status	—	—	20	Self
TR01	Body Slam	Normal	Physical	85	100	15	Normal
TR20	Substitute	Normal	Status	—	—	10	Self
TR22	Sludge Bomb	Poison	Special	90	100	10	Normal
TR23	Spikes	Ground	Status	—	—	20	Other Side
TR26	Endure	Normal	Status	—	—	10	Self
TR27	Sleep Talk	Normal	Status	—	—	10	Self
TR33	Shadow Ball	Ghost	Special	80	100	15	Normal
TR35	Uproar	Normal	Special	90	100	10	1 Random
TR54	Toxic Spikes	Poison	Status	—	—	20	Other Side
TR57	Poison Jab	Poison	Physical	80	100	20	Normal
TR59	Seed Bomb	Grass	Physical	80	100	15	Normal
TR65	Energy Ball	Grass	Special	90	100	10	Normal
TR71	Leaf Storm	Grass	Special	130	90	5	Normal
TR72	Power Whip	Grass	Physical	120	85	10	Normal
TR77	Grass Knot	Grass	Special	—	100	20	Normal
TR92	Dazzling Gleam	Fairy	Special	80	100	10	Many Others

061

LEVEL-UP MOVES

LV.	NAME	TYPE	KIND	POW.	ACC.	PP	RANGE
1	Absorb	Grass	Special	20	100	25	Normal
1	Aromatherapy	Grass	Status	—	—	5	Your Party
1	Giga Drain	Grass	Special	75	100	10	Normal
1	Grassy Terrain	Grass	Status	—	—	10	Both Sides
1	Growth	Normal	Status	—	—	20	Self
1	Ingrain	Grass	Status	—	—	20	Self
1	Leech Seed	Grass	Status	—	90	10	Normal
1	Magical Leaf	Grass	Special	60	—	20	Normal
1	Mega Drain	Grass	Special	40	100	15	Normal
1	Petal Blizzard	Grass	Physical	90	100	15	All Others
1	Petal Dance	Grass	Special	120	100	10	1 Random
1	Poison Sting	Poison	Physical	15	100	35	Normal
1	Stun Spore	Grass	Status	—	75	30	Normal
1	Sweet Scent	Normal	Status	—	100	20	Many Others
1	Synthesis	Grass	Status	—	—	5	Self
1	Toxic	Poison	Status	—	90	10	Normal
1	Toxic Spikes	Poison	Status	—	—	20	Other Side
1	Venom Drench	Poison	Status	—	100	20	Many Others
1	Worry Seed	Grass	Status	—	100	10	Normal

EVOLUTION MOVES

NAME	TYPE	KIND	POW.	ACC.	PP	RANGE

EGG MOVES

NAME	TYPE	KIND	POW.	ACC.	PP	RANGE

TUTOR MOVES

NAME	TYPE	KIND	POW.	ACC.	PP	RANGE

TM MOVES

NO.	NAME	TYPE	KIND	POW.	ACC.	PP	RANGE
TM07	Pin Missile	Bug	Physical	25	95	20	Normal
TM08	Hyper Beam	Normal	Special	150	90	5	Normal
TM09	Giga Impact	Normal	Physical	150	90	5	Normal
TM10	Magical Leaf	Grass	Special	60	—	20	Normal
TM11	Solar Beam	Grass	Special	120	100	10	Normal
TM21	Rest	Psychic	Status	—	—	10	Self
TM24	Snore	Normal	Special	50	100	15	Normal
TM25	Protect	Normal	Status	—	—	10	Self
TM28	Giga Drain	Grass	Special	75	100	10	Normal
TM31	Attract	Normal	Status	—	100	15	Normal
TM33	Rain Dance	Water	Status	—	—	5	Both Sides
TM34	Sunny Day	Fire	Status	—	—	5	Both Sides
TM39	Facade	Normal	Physical	70	100	20	Normal
TM40	Swift	Normal	Special	60	—	20	Many Others
TM46	Weather Ball*	Normal	Special	50	100	10	Normal
TM50	Bullet Seed	Grass	Physical	25	100	30	Normal
TM74	Venoshock	Poison	Special	65	100	10	Normal
TM76	Round	Normal	Special	60	100	15	Normal
TM88	Grassy Terrain	Grass	Status	—	—	10	Both Sides

TR MOVES

NO.	NAME	TYPE	KIND	POW.	ACC.	PP	RANGE
TR00	Swords Dance	Normal	Status	—	—	20	Self
TR01	Body Slam	Normal	Physical	85	100	15	Normal
TR20	Substitute	Normal	Status	—	—	10	Self
TR22	Sludge Bomb	Poison	Special	90	100	10	Normal
TR23	Spikes	Ground	Status	—	—	20	Other Side
TR26	Endure	Normal	Status	—	—	10	Self
TR27	Sleep Talk	Normal	Status	—	—	10	Self
TR33	Shadow Ball	Ghost	Special	80	100	15	Normal
TR35	Uproar	Normal	Special	90	100	10	1 Random
TR54	Toxic Spikes	Poison	Status	—	—	20	Other Side
TR57	Poison Jab	Poison	Physical	80	100	20	Normal
TR59	Seed Bomb	Grass	Physical	80	100	15	Normal
TR65	Energy Ball	Grass	Special	90	100	10	Normal
TR71	Leaf Storm	Grass	Special	130	90	5	Normal
TR72	Power Whip	Grass	Physical	120	85	10	Normal
TR77	Grass Knot	Grass	Special	—	100	20	Normal
TR91	Venom Drench	Poison	Status	—	100	20	Many Others
TR92	Dazzling Gleam	Fairy	Special	80	100	10	Many Others

Roserade
p. 44

ABILITY
Natural Cure
Poison Point

HIDDEN ABILITY
Technician

SPECIES STRENGTHS

HP	▮▮▮
ATTACK	▮▮▮▮
DEFENSE	▮▮▮
SP. ATK	▮▮▮▮▮▮▮
SP. DEF	▮▮▮▮▮
SPEED	▮▮▮▮▮

DAMAGE TAKEN IN BATTLE

×1	×0.5	×1
×2	×1	×1
×0.5	×1	×1
×0.25	×2	×1
×0.5	×2	×1
×2	×1	×0.5

Egg Groups: FAIRY / GRASS

*Weather Ball changes type depending on weather condition. (Harsh sunlight: Fire type. Rain: Water type. Hail: Ice type. Sandstorm: Rock type.)

062

LEVEL-UP MOVES

LV.	NAME	TYPE	KIND	POW.	ACC.	PP	RANGE
1	Growl	Normal	Status	—	100	40	Many Others
1	Water Gun	Water	Special	40	100	25	Normal
5	Quick Attack	Normal	Physical	40	100	30	Normal
10	Supersonic	Normal	Status	—	55	20	Normal
15	Wing Attack	Flying	Physical	60	100	35	Normal
20	Water Pulse	Water	Special	60	100	20	Normal
26	Agility	Psychic	Status	—	—	30	Self
30	Air Slash	Flying	Special	75	95	15	Normal
35	Mist	Ice	Status	—	—	30	Your Side
40	Roost	Flying	Status	—	—	10	Self
45	Hurricane	Flying	Special	110	70	10	Normal

EVOLUTION MOVES

NAME	TYPE	KIND	POW.	ACC.	PP	RANGE

EGG MOVES

NAME	TYPE	KIND	POW.	ACC.	PP	RANGE
Aerial Ace	Flying	Physical	60	—	20	Normal
Air Cutter	Flying	Special	60	95	25	Many Others
Aqua Ring	Water	Status	—	—	20	Self
Gust	Flying	Special	40	100	35	Normal
Knock Off	Dark	Physical	65	100	20	Normal
Soak	Water	Status	—	100	20	Normal
Twister	Dragon	Special	40	100	20	Many Others
Wide Guard	Rock	Status	—	—	10	Your Side

TUTOR MOVES

NAME	TYPE	KIND	POW.	ACC.	PP	RANGE

TM MOVES

NO.	NAME	TYPE	KIND	POW.	ACC.	PP	RANGE
TM06	Fly	Flying	Physical	90	95	15	Normal
TM21	Rest	Psychic	Status	—	—	10	Self
TM23	Thief	Dark	Physical	60	100	25	Normal
TM24	Snore	Normal	Special	50	100	15	Normal
TM25	Protect	Normal	Status	—	—	10	Self
TM27	Icy Wind	Ice	Special	55	95	15	Many Others
TM30	Steel Wing	Steel	Physical	70	90	25	Normal
TM31	Attract	Normal	Status	—	100	15	Normal
TM33	Rain Dance	Water	Status	—	—	5	Both Sides
TM35	Hail	Ice	Status	—	—	10	Both Sides
TM39	Facade	Normal	Physical	70	100	20	Normal
TM40	Swift	Normal	Special	60	—	20	Many Others
TM55	Brine	Water	Special	65	100	10	Normal
TM56	U-turn	Bug	Physical	70	100	20	Normal
TM76	Round	Normal	Special	60	100	15	Normal
TM95	Air Slash	Flying	Special	75	95	15	Normal

TR MOVES

NO.	NAME	TYPE	KIND	POW.	ACC.	PP	RANGE
TR05	Ice Beam	Ice	Special	90	100	10	Normal
TR06	Blizzard	Ice	Special	110	70	5	Many Others
TR12	Agility	Psychic	Status	—	—	30	Self
TR20	Substitute	Normal	Status	—	—	10	Self
TR26	Endure	Normal	Status	—	—	10	Self
TR27	Sleep Talk	Normal	Status	—	—	10	Self
TR35	Uproar	Normal	Special	90	100	10	1 Random
TR84	Scald	Water	Special	80	100	15	Normal
TR89	Hurricane	Flying	Special	110	70	10	Normal
TR98	Liquidation	Water	Physical	85	100	10	Normal

Wingull
p. 45

ABILITY
Keen Eye
Hydration

HIDDEN ABILITY
Rain Dish

SPECIES STRENGTHS

HP	▮▮
ATTACK	▮
DEFENSE	▮
SP. ATK	▮▮
SP. DEF	▮▮
SPEED	▮▮▮

DAMAGE TAKEN IN BATTLE

×1	×0.5	×2
×0.5	×1	×1
×0.5	×0	×1
×1	×1	×1
×4	×1	×0.5
×1	×0.5	×1

Egg Groups: WATER 1 / FLYING

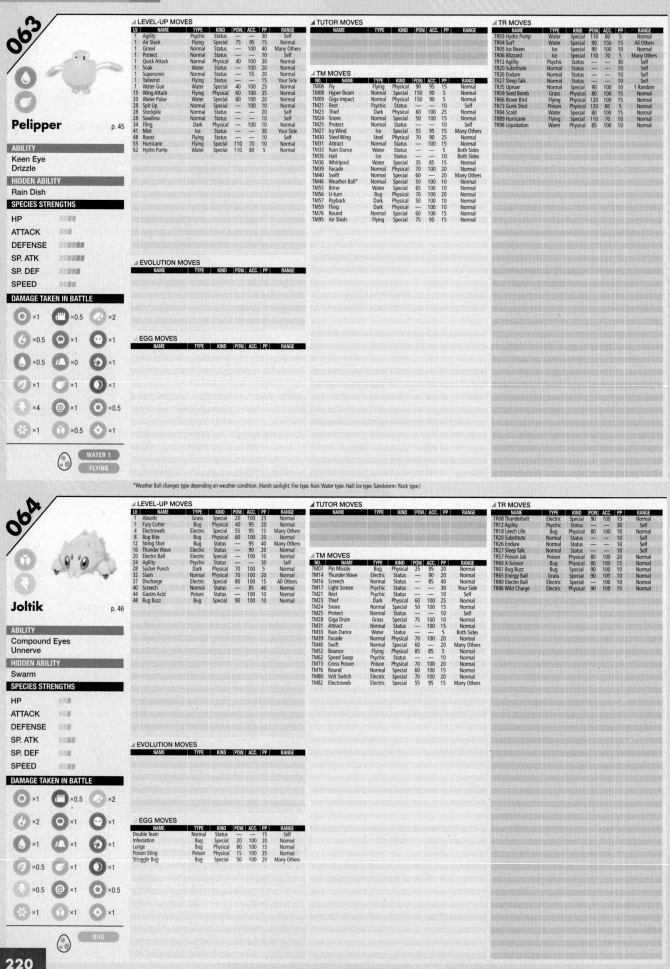

063 Pelipper p. 45

ABILITY
Keen Eye
Drizzle

HIDDEN ABILITY
Rain Dish

SPECIES STRENGTHS

HP	
ATTACK	
DEFENSE	
SP. ATK	
SP. DEF	
SPEED	

DAMAGE TAKEN IN BATTLE

×1	×0.5	×2			
×0.5	×1	×1			
×0.5	×0	×1			
×1	×1	×1			
×4	×1	×0.5			
×1	×0.5	×1			

WATER 1 / FLYING

LEVEL-UP MOVES

LV.	NAME	TYPE	KIND	POW.	ACC.	PP	RANGE
1	Agility	Psychic	Status	—	—	30	Self
1	Air Slash	Flying	Special	75	95	15	Normal
1	Growl	Normal	Status	—	100	40	Many Others
1	Protect	Normal	Status	—	—	10	Self
1	Quick Attack	Normal	Physical	40	100	30	Normal
1	Soak	Water	Status	—	100	20	Normal
1	Supersonic	Normal	Status	—	55	20	Normal
1	Tailwind	Flying	Status	—	—	15	Your Side
1	Water Gun	Water	Special	40	100	25	Normal
15	Wing Attack	Flying	Physical	60	100	35	Normal
20	Water Pulse	Water	Special	60	100	10	Normal
28	Spit Up	Normal	Special	—	100	10	Normal
28	Stockpile	Normal	Status	—	—	20	Self
28	Swallow	Normal	Status	—	—	10	Self
34	Fling	Dark	Physical	—	100	10	Normal
41	Mist	Ice	Status	—	—	30	Your Side
48	Roost	Flying	Status	—	—	10	Self
55	Hurricane	Flying	Special	110	70	10	Normal
62	Hydro Pump	Water	Special	110	80	5	Normal

EVOLUTION MOVES

NAME	TYPE	KIND	POW.	ACC.	PP	RANGE

EGG MOVES

NAME	TYPE	KIND	POW.	ACC.	PP	RANGE

TUTOR MOVES

NAME	TYPE	KIND	POW.	ACC.	PP	RANGE

TM MOVES

NO.	NAME	TYPE	KIND	POW.	ACC.	PP	RANGE
TM06	Fly	Flying	Physical	90	95	15	Normal
TM08	Hyper Beam	Normal	Special	150	90	5	Normal
TM09	Giga Impact	Normal	Physical	150	90	5	Normal
TM21	Rest	Psychic	Status	—	—	10	Self
TM23	Thief	Dark	Physical	60	100	25	Normal
TM24	Snore	Normal	Special	50	100	15	Normal
TM25	Protect	Normal	Status	—	—	10	Self
TM27	Icy Wind	Ice	Special	55	95	15	Many Others
TM30	Steel Wing	Steel	Physical	70	90	25	Normal
TM31	Attract	Normal	Status	—	100	15	Normal
TM33	Rain Dance	Water	Status	—	—	5	Both Sides
TM35	Hail	Ice	Status	—	—	10	Both Sides
TM36	Whirlpool	Water	Special	35	85	15	Normal
TM39	Facade	Normal	Physical	70	100	20	Normal
TM40	Swift	Normal	Special	60	—	20	Many Others
TM46	Weather Ball*	Normal	Special	50	100	10	Normal
TM55	Brine	Water	Special	65	100	10	Normal
TM56	U-turn	Bug	Physical	70	100	20	Normal
TM57	Payback	Dark	Physical	50	100	10	Normal
TM59	Fling	Dark	Physical	—	100	10	Normal
TM76	Round	Normal	Special	60	100	15	Normal
TM95	Air Slash	Flying	Special	75	95	15	Normal

TR MOVES

NAME	TYPE	KIND	POW.	ACC.	PP	RANGE
TR03 Hydro Pump	Water	Special	110	80	5	Normal
TR04 Surf	Water	Special	90	100	15	All Others
TR05 Ice Beam	Ice	Special	90	100	10	Normal
TR06 Blizzard	Ice	Special	110	70	5	Many Others
TR12 Agility	Psychic	Status	—	—	30	Self
TR20 Substitute	Normal	Status	—	—	10	Self
TR26 Endure	Normal	Status	—	—	10	Self
TR27 Sleep Talk	Normal	Status	—	—	10	Self
TR35 Uproar	Normal	Special	90	100	10	1 Random
TR59 Seed Bomb	Grass	Physical	80	100	15	Normal
TR66 Brave Bird	Flying	Physical	120	100	15	Normal
TR73 Gunk Shot	Poison	Physical	120	80	5	Normal
TR84 Scald	Water	Special	80	100	15	Normal
TR89 Hurricane	Flying	Special	110	70	10	Normal
TR98 Liquidation	Water	Physical	85	100	10	Normal

*Weather Ball changes type depending on weather condition. (Harsh sunlight: Fire type. Rain: Water type. Hail: Ice type. Sandstorm: Rock type.)

064 Joltik p. 46

ABILITY
Compound Eyes
Unnerve

HIDDEN ABILITY
Swarm

SPECIES STRENGTHS

HP	
ATTACK	
DEFENSE	
SP. ATK	
SP. DEF	
SPEED	

DAMAGE TAKEN IN BATTLE

×1	×0.5	×2			
×2	×1	×1			
×1	×1	×1			
×0.5	×1	×1			
×0.5	×1	×0.5			
×1	×1	×1			

BUG

LEVEL-UP MOVES

LV.	NAME	TYPE	KIND	POW.	ACC.	PP	RANGE
1	Absorb	Grass	Special	20	100	25	Normal
1	Fury Cutter	Bug	Physical	40	95	20	Normal
4	Electroweb	Electric	Special	55	95	15	Many Others
8	Bug Bite	Bug	Physical	60	100	20	Normal
12	String Shot	Bug	Status	—	95	40	Many Others
16	Thunder Wave	Electric	Status	—	90	20	Normal
20	Electro Ball	Electric	Special	—	100	10	Normal
24	Agility	Psychic	Status	—	—	30	Self
28	Sucker Punch	Dark	Physical	70	100	5	Normal
32	Slash	Normal	Physical	70	100	20	Normal
37	Discharge	Electric	Special	80	100	15	All Others
40	Screech	Normal	Status	—	85	40	Normal
44	Gastro Acid	Poison	Status	—	100	10	Normal
48	Bug Buzz	Bug	Special	90	100	10	Normal

EVOLUTION MOVES

NAME	TYPE	KIND	POW.	ACC.	PP	RANGE

EGG MOVES

NAME	TYPE	KIND	POW.	ACC.	PP	RANGE
Double Team	Normal	Status	—	—	15	Self
Infestation	Bug	Special	20	100	20	Normal
Lunge	Bug	Physical	80	100	15	Normal
Poison Sting	Poison	Physical	15	100	35	Normal
Struggle Bug	Bug	Special	50	100	20	Many Others

TUTOR MOVES

NAME	TYPE	KIND	POW.	ACC.	PP	RANGE

TM MOVES

NO.	NAME	TYPE	KIND	POW.	ACC.	PP	RANGE
TM07	Pin Missile	Bug	Physical	25	95	20	Normal
TM14	Thunder Wave	Electric	Status	—	90	20	Normal
TM16	Screech	Normal	Status	—	85	40	Normal
TM17	Light Screen	Psychic	Status	—	—	30	Your Side
TM21	Rest	Psychic	Status	—	—	10	Self
TM23	Thief	Dark	Physical	60	100	25	Normal
TM24	Snore	Normal	Special	50	100	15	Normal
TM25	Protect	Normal	Status	—	—	10	Self
TM28	Giga Drain	Grass	Special	75	100	10	Normal
TM31	Attract	Normal	Status	—	100	15	Normal
TM33	Rain Dance	Water	Status	—	—	5	Both Sides
TM39	Facade	Normal	Physical	70	100	20	Normal
TM40	Swift	Normal	Special	60	—	20	Many Others
TM52	Bounce	Flying	Physical	85	85	5	Normal
TM62	Speed Swap	Psychic	Status	—	—	10	Normal
TM73	Cross Poison	Poison	Physical	70	100	20	Normal
TM76	Round	Normal	Special	60	100	15	Normal
TM80	Volt Switch	Electric	Special	70	100	20	Normal
TM82	Electroweb	Electric	Special	55	95	15	Many Others

TR MOVES

NAME	TYPE	KIND	POW.	ACC.	PP	RANGE
TR08 Thunderbolt	Electric	Special	90	100	15	Normal
TR12 Agility	Psychic	Status	—	—	30	Self
TR18 Leech Life	Bug	Physical	80	100	10	Normal
TR20 Substitute	Normal	Status	—	—	10	Self
TR26 Endure	Normal	Status	—	—	10	Self
TR57 Poison Jab	Poison	Physical	80	100	20	Normal
TR60 X-Scissor	Bug	Physical	80	100	15	Normal
TR61 Bug Buzz	Bug	Special	90	100	10	Normal
TR65 Energy Ball	Grass	Special	90	100	10	Normal
TR80 Electro Ball	Electric	Special	—	100	10	Normal
TR86 Wild Charge	Electric	Physical	90	100	15	Normal

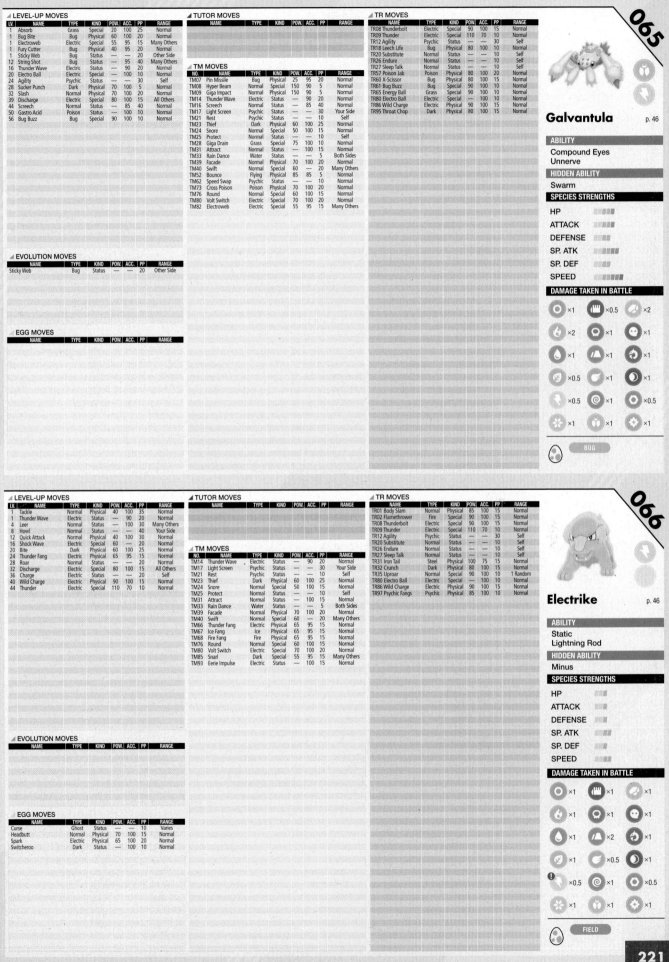

065 — Galvantula

LEVEL-UP MOVES

LV.	NAME	TYPE	KIND	POW.	ACC.	PP	RANGE
1	Absorb	Grass	Special	20	100	25	Normal
1	Bug Bite	Bug	Physical	60	100	20	Normal
1	Electroweb	Electric	Special	55	95	15	Many Others
1	Fury Cutter	Bug	Physical	40	95	20	Normal
1	Sticky Web	Bug	Status	—	—	20	Other Side
5	String Shot	Bug	Status	—	95	40	Many Others
12	Thunder Wave	Electric	Status	—	90	20	Normal
16	Electro Ball	Electric	Special	—	100	10	Normal
20	Agility	Psychic	Status	—	—	30	Self
24	Sucker Punch	Dark	Physical	70	100	5	Normal
28	Slash	Normal	Physical	70	100	20	Normal
32	Discharge	Electric	Special	80	100	15	All Others
39	Screech	Normal	Status	—	85	40	Normal
44	Gastro Acid	Poison	Status	—	100	10	Normal
50	Bug Buzz	Bug	Special	90	100	10	Normal

EVOLUTION MOVES

NAME	TYPE	KIND	POW.	ACC.	PP	RANGE
Sticky Web	Bug	Status	—	—	20	Other Side

EGG MOVES

NAME	TYPE	KIND	POW.	ACC.	PP	RANGE

TUTOR MOVES

NAME	TYPE	KIND	POW.	ACC.	PP	RANGE

TM MOVES

NO.	NAME	TYPE	KIND	POW.	ACC.	PP	RANGE
TM07	Pin Missile	Bug	Physical	25	95	20	Normal
TM08	Hyper Beam	Normal	Special	150	90	5	Normal
TM09	Giga Impact	Normal	Physical	150	90	5	Normal
TM14	Thunder Wave	Electric	Status	—	90	20	Normal
TM16	Screech	Normal	Status	—	85	40	Normal
TM17	Light Screen	Psychic	Status	—	—	30	Your Side
TM21	Rest	Psychic	Status	—	—	10	Self
TM23	Thief	Dark	Physical	60	100	25	Normal
TM24	Snore	Normal	Special	50	100	15	Normal
TM25	Protect	Normal	Status	—	—	10	Self
TM28	Giga Drain	Grass	Special	75	100	10	Normal
TM31	Attract	Normal	Status	—	100	15	Normal
TM33	Rain Dance	Water	Status	—	—	5	Both Sides
TM39	Facade	Normal	Physical	70	100	20	Normal
TM40	Swift	Normal	Special	60	—	20	Many Others
TM52	Bounce	Flying	Physical	85	85	5	Normal
TM62	Speed Swap	Psychic	Status	—	—	10	Normal
TM73	Cross Poison	Poison	Physical	70	100	20	Normal
TM76	Round	Normal	Special	60	100	15	Normal
TM80	Volt Switch	Electric	Special	70	100	20	Normal
TM82	Electroweb	Electric	Special	55	95	15	Many Others

TR MOVES

NO.	NAME	TYPE	KIND	POW.	ACC.	PP	RANGE
TR08	Thunderbolt	Electric	Special	90	100	15	Normal
TR09	Thunder	Electric	Special	110	70	10	Normal
TR12	Agility	Psychic	Status	—	—	30	Self
TR18	Leech Life	Bug	Physical	80	100	10	Normal
TR20	Substitute	Normal	Status	—	—	10	Self
TR26	Endure	Normal	Status	—	—	10	Self
TR27	Sleep Talk	Normal	Status	—	—	10	Self
TR57	Poison Jab	Poison	Physical	80	100	20	Normal
TR60	X-Scissor	Bug	Physical	80	100	15	Normal
TR61	Bug Buzz	Bug	Special	90	100	10	Normal
TR65	Energy Ball	Grass	Special	90	100	10	Normal
TR80	Electro Ball	Electric	Special	—	100	10	Normal
TR86	Wild Charge	Electric	Physical	90	100	15	Normal
TR95	Throat Chop	Dark	Physical	80	100	15	Normal

Galvantula — p. 46

ABILITY
Compound Eyes
Unnerve

HIDDEN ABILITY
Swarm

SPECIES STRENGTHS
HP, ATTACK, DEFENSE, SP. ATK, SP. DEF, SPEED

DAMAGE TAKEN IN BATTLE
×1, ×0.5, ×2 / ×2, ×1, ×1 / ×1, ×1, ×1 / ×0.5, ×1, ×1 / ×0.5, ×1, ×0.5 / ×1, ×1, ×1

BUG

---

066 — Electrike

LEVEL-UP MOVES

LV.	NAME	TYPE	KIND	POW.	ACC.	PP	RANGE
1	Tackle	Normal	Physical	40	100	35	Normal
1	Thunder Wave	Electric	Status	—	90	20	Normal
4	Leer	Normal	Status	—	100	30	Many Others
8	Howl	Normal	Status	—	—	40	Your Side
12	Quick Attack	Normal	Physical	40	100	30	Normal
16	Shock Wave	Electric	Special	60	—	20	Normal
20	Bite	Dark	Physical	60	100	25	Normal
24	Thunder Fang	Electric	Physical	65	95	15	Normal
28	Roar	Normal	Status	—	—	20	Normal
32	Discharge	Electric	Special	80	100	15	All Others
36	Charge	Electric	Status	—	—	20	Self
40	Wild Charge	Electric	Physical	90	100	15	Normal
44	Thunder	Electric	Special	110	70	10	Normal

EVOLUTION MOVES

NAME	TYPE	KIND	POW.	ACC.	PP	RANGE

EGG MOVES

NAME	TYPE	KIND	POW.	ACC.	PP	RANGE
Curse	Ghost	Status	—	—	10	Varies
Headbutt	Normal	Physical	70	100	15	Normal
Spark	Electric	Physical	65	100	20	Normal
Switcheroo	Dark	Status	—	100	10	Normal

TUTOR MOVES

NAME	TYPE	KIND	POW.	ACC.	PP	RANGE

TM MOVES

NO.	NAME	TYPE	KIND	POW.	ACC.	PP	RANGE
TM14	Thunder Wave	Electric	Status	—	90	20	Normal
TM17	Light Screen	Psychic	Status	—	—	30	Your Side
TM21	Rest	Psychic	Status	—	—	10	Self
TM23	Thief	Dark	Physical	60	100	25	Normal
TM24	Snore	Normal	Special	50	100	15	Normal
TM25	Protect	Normal	Status	—	—	10	Self
TM31	Attract	Normal	Status	—	100	15	Normal
TM33	Rain Dance	Water	Status	—	—	5	Both Sides
TM39	Facade	Normal	Physical	70	100	20	Normal
TM40	Swift	Normal	Special	60	—	20	Many Others
TM66	Thunder Fang	Electric	Physical	65	95	15	Normal
TM67	Ice Fang	Ice	Physical	65	95	15	Normal
TM68	Fire Fang	Fire	Physical	65	95	15	Normal
TM76	Round	Normal	Special	60	100	15	Normal
TM80	Volt Switch	Electric	Special	70	100	20	Normal
TM85	Snarl	Dark	Special	55	95	15	Many Others
TM93	Eerie Impulse	Electric	Status	—	100	15	Normal

TR MOVES

NO.	NAME	TYPE	KIND	POW.	ACC.	PP	RANGE
TR01	Body Slam	Normal	Physical	85	100	15	Normal
TR02	Flamethrower	Fire	Special	90	100	15	Normal
TR08	Thunderbolt	Electric	Special	90	100	15	Normal
TR09	Thunder	Electric	Special	110	70	10	Normal
TR12	Agility	Psychic	Status	—	—	30	Self
TR20	Substitute	Normal	Status	—	—	10	Self
TR26	Endure	Normal	Status	—	—	10	Self
TR27	Sleep Talk	Normal	Status	—	—	10	Self
TR31	Iron Tail	Steel	Physical	100	75	15	Normal
TR32	Crunch	Dark	Physical	80	100	15	Normal
TR35	Uproar	Normal	Special	90	100	10	1 Random
TR80	Electro Ball	Electric	Special	—	100	10	Normal
TR86	Wild Charge	Electric	Physical	90	100	15	Normal
TR97	Psychic Fangs	Psychic	Physical	85	100	10	Normal

Electrike — p. 46

ABILITY
Static
Lightning Rod

HIDDEN ABILITY
Minus

SPECIES STRENGTHS
HP, ATTACK, DEFENSE, SP. ATK, SP. DEF, SPEED

DAMAGE TAKEN IN BATTLE
×1, ×1, ×1 / ×1, ×1, ×1 / ×1, ×2, ×1 / ×1, ×0.5, ×1 / ×0.5, ×1, ×0.5 / ×1, ×1, ×1

FIELD

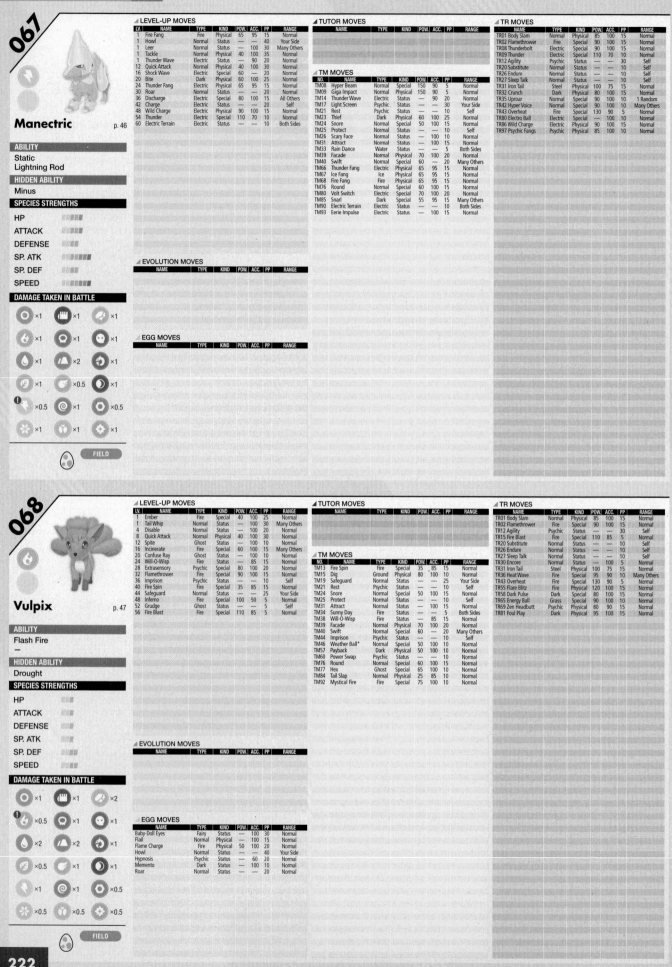

067 Manectric p. 46

ABILITY
Static
Lightning Rod

HIDDEN ABILITY
Minus

SPECIES STRENGTHS
HP
ATTACK
DEFENSE
SP. ATK
SP. DEF
SPEED

DAMAGE TAKEN IN BATTLE
×1 ×1 ×1
×1 ×1 ×1
×1 ×2 ×1
×1 ×0.5 ×1
×0.5 ×1 ×0.5
×1 ×1 ×1

FIELD

LEVEL-UP MOVES
LV.	NAME	TYPE	KIND	POW.	ACC.	PP	RANGE
1	Fire Fang	Fire	Physical	65	95	15	Normal
1	Howl	Normal	Status	—	—	40	Your Side
1	Leer	Normal	Status	—	100	30	Many Others
1	Tackle	Normal	Physical	40	100	35	Normal
1	Thunder Wave	Electric	Status	—	90	20	Normal
12	Quick Attack	Normal	Physical	40	100	30	Normal
16	Shock Wave	Electric	Special	60	—	20	Normal
20	Bite	Dark	Physical	60	100	25	Normal
24	Thunder Fang	Electric	Physical	65	95	15	Normal
30	Roar	Normal	Status	—	—	20	Normal
36	Discharge	Electric	Special	80	100	15	All Others
42	Charge	Electric	Status	—	—	20	Self
48	Wild Charge	Electric	Physical	90	100	15	Normal
54	Thunder	Electric	Special	110	70	10	Normal
60	Electric Terrain	Electric	Status	—	—	10	Both Sides

TUTOR MOVES
NAME	TYPE	KIND	POW.	ACC.	PP	RANGE

TM MOVES
NO.	NAME	TYPE	KIND	POW.	ACC.	PP	RANGE
TM08	Hyper Beam	Normal	Special	150	90	5	Normal
TM09	Giga Impact	Normal	Physical	150	90	5	Normal
TM14	Thunder Wave	Electric	Status	—	90	20	Normal
TM17	Light Screen	Psychic	Status	—	—	30	Your Side
TM21	Rest	Psychic	Status	—	—	10	Self
TM23	Thief	Dark	Physical	60	100	25	Normal
TM24	Snore	Normal	Special	50	100	15	Normal
TM25	Protect	Normal	Status	—	—	10	Self
TM26	Scary Face	Normal	Status	—	100	10	Normal
TM31	Attract	Normal	Status	—	100	15	Normal
TM33	Rain Dance	Water	Status	—	—	5	Both Sides
TM39	Facade	Normal	Physical	70	100	20	Normal
TM40	Swift	Normal	Special	60	—	20	Many Others
TM66	Thunder Fang	Electric	Physical	65	95	15	Normal
TM67	Ice Fang	Ice	Physical	65	95	15	Normal
TM68	Fire Fang	Fire	Physical	65	95	15	Normal
TM76	Round	Normal	Special	60	100	15	Normal
TM80	Volt Switch	Electric	Special	70	100	20	Normal
TM85	Snarl	Dark	Special	55	95	15	Many Others
TM90	Electric Terrain	Electric	Status	—	—	10	Both Sides
TM93	Eerie Impulse	Electric	Status	—	100	15	Normal

TR MOVES
NO.	NAME	TYPE	KIND	POW.	ACC.	PP	RANGE
TR01	Body Slam	Normal	Physical	85	100	15	Normal
TR02	Flamethrower	Fire	Special	90	100	15	Normal
TR08	Thunderbolt	Electric	Special	90	100	15	Normal
TR09	Thunder	Electric	Special	110	70	10	Normal
TR12	Agility	Psychic	Status	—	—	30	Self
TR20	Substitute	Normal	Status	—	—	10	Self
TR26	Endure	Normal	Status	—	—	10	Self
TR27	Sleep Talk	Normal	Status	—	—	10	Self
TR31	Iron Tail	Steel	Physical	100	75	15	Normal
TR32	Crunch	Dark	Physical	80	100	15	Normal
TR35	Uproar	Normal	Special	90	100	10	1 Random
TR42	Hyper Voice	Normal	Special	90	100	10	Many Others
TR43	Overheat	Fire	Special	130	90	5	Normal
TR80	Electro Ball	Electric	Special	—	100	10	Normal
TR86	Wild Charge	Electric	Physical	90	100	15	Normal
TR97	Psychic Fangs	Psychic	Physical	85	100	10	Normal

EVOLUTION MOVES
NAME	TYPE	KIND	POW.	ACC.	PP	RANGE

EGG MOVES
NAME	TYPE	KIND	POW.	ACC.	PP	RANGE

---

068 Vulpix p. 47

ABILITY
Flash Fire
—

HIDDEN ABILITY
Drought

SPECIES STRENGTHS
HP
ATTACK
DEFENSE
SP. ATK
SP. DEF
SPEED

DAMAGE TAKEN IN BATTLE
×1 ×1 ×2
×0.5 ×1 ×1
×2 ×2 ×1
×0.5 ×1 ×1
×1 ×1 ×0.5
×0.5 ×0.5 ×0.5

FIELD

LEVEL-UP MOVES
LV.	NAME	TYPE	KIND	POW.	ACC.	PP	RANGE
1	Ember	Fire	Special	40	100	25	Normal
1	Tail Whip	Normal	Status	—	100	30	Many Others
4	Disable	Normal	Status	—	100	20	Normal
8	Quick Attack	Normal	Physical	40	100	30	Normal
12	Spite	Ghost	Status	—	100	10	Normal
16	Incinerate	Fire	Special	60	100	15	Many Others
20	Confuse Ray	Ghost	Status	—	100	10	Normal
24	Will-O-Wisp	Fire	Status	—	85	15	Normal
28	Extrasensory	Psychic	Special	80	100	20	Normal
32	Flamethrower	Fire	Special	90	100	15	Normal
36	Imprison	Psychic	Status	—	—	10	Self
40	Fire Spin	Fire	Special	35	85	15	Normal
44	Safeguard	Normal	Status	—	—	25	Your Side
48	Inferno	Fire	Special	100	50	5	Normal
52	Grudge	Ghost	Status	—	—	5	Self
56	Fire Blast	Fire	Special	110	85	5	Normal

TUTOR MOVES
NAME	TYPE	KIND	POW.	ACC.	PP	RANGE

TM MOVES
NO.	NAME	TYPE	KIND	POW.	ACC.	PP	RANGE
TM13	Fire Spin	Fire	Special	35	85	15	Normal
TM15	Dig	Ground	Physical	80	100	10	Normal
TM19	Safeguard	Normal	Status	—	—	25	Your Side
TM21	Rest	Psychic	Status	—	—	10	Self
TM24	Snore	Normal	Special	50	100	15	Normal
TM25	Protect	Normal	Status	—	—	10	Self
TM31	Attract	Normal	Status	—	100	15	Normal
TM34	Sunny Day	Fire	Status	—	—	5	Both Sides
TM38	Will-O-Wisp	Fire	Status	—	85	15	Normal
TM39	Facade	Normal	Physical	70	100	20	Normal
TM40	Swift	Normal	Special	60	—	20	Many Others
TM44	Imprison	Psychic	Status	—	—	10	Self
TM46	Weather Ball*	Normal	Special	50	100	10	Normal
TM57	Payback	Dark	Physical	50	100	10	Normal
TM60	Power Swap	Psychic	Status	—	—	10	Normal
TM76	Round	Normal	Special	60	100	15	Normal
TM77	Hex	Ghost	Special	65	100	10	Normal
TM84	Tail Slap	Normal	Physical	25	85	10	Normal
TM92	Mystical Fire	Fire	Special	75	100	10	Normal

TR MOVES
NO.	NAME	TYPE	KIND	POW.	ACC.	PP	RANGE
TR01	Body Slam	Normal	Physical	85	100	15	Normal
TR02	Flamethrower	Fire	Special	90	100	15	Normal
TR12	Agility	Psychic	Status	—	—	30	Self
TR15	Fire Blast	Fire	Special	110	85	5	Normal
TR20	Substitute	Normal	Status	—	—	10	Self
TR26	Endure	Normal	Status	—	—	10	Self
TR27	Sleep Talk	Normal	Status	—	—	10	Self
TR30	Encore	Normal	Status	—	100	5	Normal
TR31	Iron Tail	Steel	Physical	100	75	15	Normal
TR36	Heat Wave	Fire	Special	95	90	10	Many Others
TR43	Overheat	Fire	Special	130	90	5	Normal
TR55	Flare Blitz	Fire	Physical	120	100	15	Normal
TR58	Dark Pulse	Dark	Special	80	100	15	Normal
TR65	Energy Ball	Grass	Special	90	100	10	Normal
TR69	Zen Headbutt	Psychic	Physical	80	90	15	Normal
TR81	Foul Play	Dark	Physical	95	100	15	Normal

EVOLUTION MOVES
NAME	TYPE	KIND	POW.	ACC.	PP	RANGE

EGG MOVES
NAME	TYPE	KIND	POW.	ACC.	PP	RANGE
Baby-Doll Eyes	Fairy	Status	—	100	30	Normal
Flail	Normal	Physical	—	100	15	Normal
Flame Charge	Fire	Physical	50	100	20	Normal
Howl	Normal	Status	—	—	40	Your Side
Hypnosis	Psychic	Status	—	60	20	Normal
Memento	Dark	Status	—	100	10	Normal
Roar	Normal	Status	—	—	20	Normal

069 Ninetales

p. 47

LEVEL-UP MOVES

LV.	NAME	TYPE	KIND	POW.	ACC.	PP	RANGE
1	Confuse Ray	Ghost	Status	—	100	10	Normal
1	Disable	Normal	Status	—	100	20	Normal
1	Ember	Fire	Special	40	100	25	Normal
1	Extrasensory	Psychic	Special	80	100	20	Normal
1	Fire Blast	Fire	Special	110	85	5	Normal
1	Fire Spin	Fire	Special	35	85	15	Normal
1	Flamethrower	Fire	Special	90	100	15	Normal
1	Grudge	Ghost	Status	—	—	5	Self
1	Imprison	Psychic	Status	—	—	10	Self
1	Incinerate	Fire	Special	60	100	15	Many Others
1	Inferno	Fire	Special	100	50	5	Normal
1	Nasty Plot	Dark	Status	—	—	20	Self
1	Quick Attack	Normal	Physical	40	100	30	Normal
1	Safeguard	Normal	Status	—	—	25	Your Side
1	Spite	Ghost	Status	—	100	10	Normal
1	Tail Whip	Normal	Status	—	100	30	Many Others
1	Will-O-Wisp	Fire	Status	—	85	15	Normal

EVOLUTION MOVES

NAME	TYPE	KIND	POW.	ACC.	PP	RANGE

EGG MOVES

NAME	TYPE	KIND	POW.	ACC.	PP	RANGE

TUTOR MOVES

NAME	TYPE	KIND	POW.	ACC.	PP	RANGE

TM MOVES

NO.	NAME	TYPE	KIND	POW.	ACC.	PP	RANGE
TM08	Hyper Beam	Normal	Special	150	90	5	Normal
TM09	Giga Impact	Normal	Physical	150	90	5	Normal
TM11	Solar Beam	Grass	Special	120	100	10	Normal
TM13	Fire Spin	Fire	Special	35	85	15	Normal
TM15	Dig	Ground	Physical	80	100	10	Normal
TM19	Safeguard	Normal	Status	—	—	25	Your Side
TM21	Rest	Psychic	Status	—	—	10	Self
TM24	Snore	Normal	Special	50	100	15	Normal
TM25	Protect	Normal	Status	—	—	10	Self
TM31	Attract	Normal	Status	—	100	15	Normal
TM34	Sunny Day	Fire	Status	—	—	5	Both Sides
TM38	Will-O-Wisp	Fire	Status	—	85	15	Normal
TM39	Facade	Normal	Physical	70	100	20	Normal
TM40	Swift	Normal	Special	60	—	20	Many Others
TM44	Imprison	Psychic	Status	—	—	10	Self
TM46	Weather Ball*	Normal	Special	50	100	10	Normal
TM47	Fake Tears	Dark	Status	—	100	20	Normal
TM57	Payback	Dark	Physical	50	100	10	Normal
TM60	Power Swap	Psychic	Status	—	—	10	Normal
TM76	Round	Normal	Special	60	100	15	Normal
TM77	Hex	Ghost	Special	65	100	10	Normal
TM84	Tail Slap	Normal	Physical	25	85	10	Normal
TM92	Mystical Fire	Fire	Special	75	100	10	Normal

TR MOVES

NO.	NAME	TYPE	KIND	POW.	ACC.	PP	RANGE
TR01	Body Slam	Normal	Physical	85	100	15	Normal
TR02	Flamethrower	Fire	Special	90	100	15	Normal
TR12	Agility	Psychic	Status	—	—	30	Self
TR15	Fire Blast	Fire	Special	110	85	5	Normal
TR20	Substitute	Normal	Status	—	—	10	Self
TR25	Psyshock	Psychic	Special	80	100	10	Normal
TR26	Endure	Normal	Status	—	—	10	Self
TR27	Sleep Talk	Normal	Status	—	—	10	Self
TR30	Encore	Normal	Status	—	100	5	Normal
TR31	Iron Tail	Steel	Physical	100	75	15	Normal
TR33	Shadow Ball	Ghost	Special	80	100	15	Normal
TR36	Heat Wave	Fire	Special	95	90	10	Many Others
TR43	Overheat	Fire	Special	130	90	5	Normal
TR49	Calm Mind	Psychic	Status	—	—	20	Self
TR55	Flare Blitz	Fire	Physical	120	100	15	Normal
TR58	Dark Pulse	Dark	Special	80	100	15	Normal
TR65	Energy Ball	Grass	Special	90	100	10	Normal
TR68	Nasty Plot	Dark	Status	—	—	20	Self
TR69	Zen Headbutt	Psychic	Physical	80	90	15	Normal
TR81	Foul Play	Dark	Physical	95	100	15	Normal
TR82	Stored Power	Psychic	Special	20	100	10	Normal

ABILITY

Flash Fire
—

HIDDEN ABILITY

Drought

SPECIES STRENGTHS

- HP
- ATTACK
- DEFENSE
- SP. ATK
- SP. DEF
- SPEED

DAMAGE TAKEN IN BATTLE

×1 ×1 ×2
×0.5 ×1 ×1
×2 ×2 ×1
×0.5 ×1 ×1
×1 ×1 ×0.5
×0.5 ×0.5 ×0.5

FIELD

*Weather Ball changes type depending on weather condition. (Harsh sunlight: Fire type. Rain: Water type. Hail: Ice type. Sandstorm: Rock type.)

070 Growlithe

p. 47

LEVEL-UP MOVES

LV.	NAME	TYPE	KIND	POW.	ACC.	PP	RANGE
1	Ember	Fire	Special	40	100	25	Normal
1	Leer	Normal	Status	—	100	30	Many Others
4	Howl	Normal	Status	—	—	40	Your Side
8	Bite	Dark	Physical	60	100	25	Normal
12	Flame Wheel	Fire	Physical	60	100	25	Normal
16	Helping Hand	Normal	Status	—	—	20	1 Ally
20	Agility	Psychic	Status	—	—	30	Self
24	Fire Fang	Fire	Physical	65	95	15	Normal
28	Retaliate	Normal	Physical	70	100	5	Normal
32	Crunch	Dark	Physical	80	100	15	Normal
36	Take Down	Normal	Physical	90	85	20	Normal
40	Flamethrower	Fire	Special	90	100	15	Normal
44	Roar	Normal	Status	—	—	20	Normal
48	Play Rough	Fairy	Physical	90	90	10	Normal
52	Reversal	Fighting	Physical	—	100	15	Normal
56	Flare Blitz	Fire	Physical	120	100	15	Normal

EVOLUTION MOVES

NAME	TYPE	KIND	POW.	ACC.	PP	RANGE

EGG MOVES

NAME	TYPE	KIND	POW.	ACC.	PP	RANGE
Covet	Normal	Physical	60	100	25	Normal
Double Kick	Fighting	Physical	30	100	30	Normal
Double-Edge	Normal	Physical	120	100	15	Normal
Morning Sun	Normal	Status	—	—	5	Self
Thrash	Normal	Physical	120	100	10	1 Random

TUTOR MOVES

NAME	TYPE	KIND	POW.	ACC.	PP	RANGE

TM MOVES

NO.	NAME	TYPE	KIND	POW.	ACC.	PP	RANGE
TM13	Fire Spin	Fire	Special	35	85	15	Normal
TM15	Dig	Ground	Physical	80	100	10	Normal
TM19	Safeguard	Normal	Status	—	—	25	Your Side
TM21	Rest	Psychic	Status	—	—	10	Self
TM23	Thief	Dark	Physical	60	100	25	Normal
TM24	Snore	Normal	Special	50	100	15	Normal
TM25	Protect	Normal	Status	—	—	10	Self
TM31	Attract	Normal	Status	—	100	15	Normal
TM34	Sunny Day	Fire	Status	—	—	5	Both Sides
TM38	Will-O-Wisp	Fire	Status	—	85	15	Normal
TM39	Facade	Normal	Physical	70	100	20	Normal
TM40	Swift	Normal	Special	60	—	20	Many Others
TM41	Helping Hand	Normal	Status	—	—	20	1 Ally
TM68	Fire Fang	Fire	Physical	65	95	15	Normal
TM76	Round	Normal	Special	60	100	15	Normal
TM79	Retaliate	Normal	Physical	70	100	5	Normal
TM85	Snarl	Dark	Special	55	95	15	Many Others

TR MOVES

NO.	NAME	TYPE	KIND	POW.	ACC.	PP	RANGE
TR01	Body Slam	Normal	Physical	85	100	15	Normal
TR02	Flamethrower	Fire	Special	90	100	15	Normal
TR12	Agility	Psychic	Status	—	—	30	Self
TR15	Fire Blast	Fire	Special	110	85	5	Normal
TR20	Substitute	Normal	Status	—	—	10	Self
TR21	Reversal	Fighting	Physical	—	100	15	Normal
TR24	Outrage	Dragon	Physical	120	100	10	1 Random
TR26	Endure	Normal	Status	—	—	10	Self
TR27	Sleep Talk	Normal	Status	—	—	10	Self
TR31	Iron Tail	Steel	Physical	100	75	15	Normal
TR32	Crunch	Dark	Physical	80	100	15	Normal
TR36	Heat Wave	Fire	Special	95	90	10	Many Others
TR43	Overheat	Fire	Special	130	90	5	Normal
TR53	Close Combat	Fighting	Physical	120	100	5	Normal
TR55	Flare Blitz	Fire	Physical	120	100	15	Normal
TR86	Wild Charge	Electric	Physical	90	100	15	Normal
TR90	Play Rough	Fairy	Physical	90	90	10	Normal
TR97	Psychic Fangs	Psychic	Physical	85	100	10	Normal

ABILITY

Intimidate
Flash Fire

HIDDEN ABILITY

Justified

SPECIES STRENGTHS

- HP
- ATTACK
- DEFENSE
- SP. ATK
- SP. DEF
- SPEED

DAMAGE TAKEN IN BATTLE

×1 ×1 ×2
×0.5 ×1 ×1
×2 ×2 ×1
×0.5 ×1 ×1
×1 ×1 ×0.5
×0.5 ×0.5 ×0.5

FIELD

071

Arcanine
p. 47

ABILITY
Intimidate
Flash Fire

HIDDEN ABILITY
Justified

SPECIES STRENGTHS

HP	
ATTACK	
DEFENSE	
SP. ATK	
SP. DEF	
SPEED	

DAMAGE TAKEN IN BATTLE

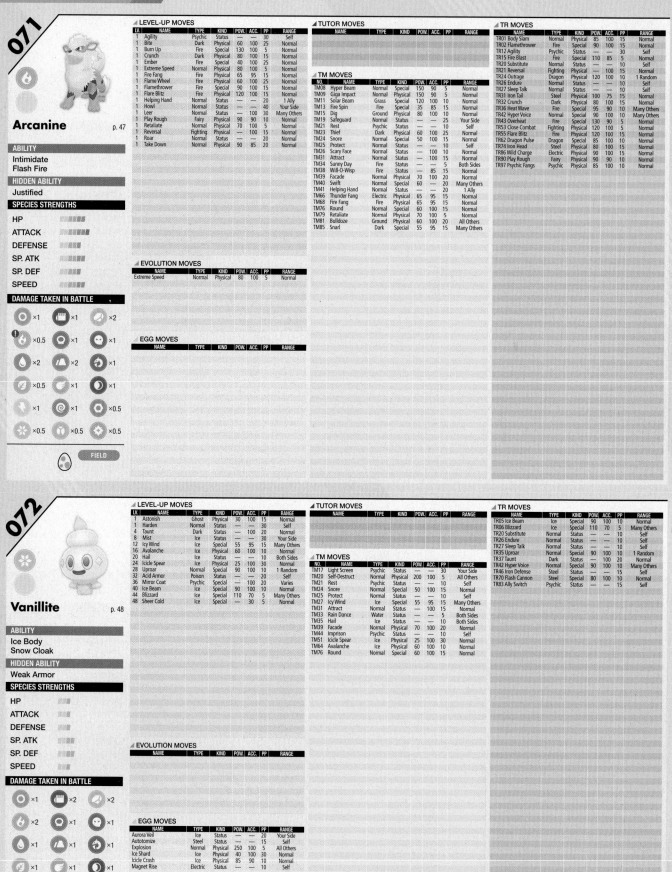

×1 ×1 ×2
×0.5 ×1 ×1
×2 ×2 ×1
×0.5 ×1 ×1
×1 ×1 ×0.5
×0.5 ×0.5 ×0.5

FIELD

LEVEL-UP MOVES

LV.	NAME	TYPE	KIND	POW.	ACC.	PP	RANGE
1	Agility	Psychic	Status	—	—	30	Self
1	Bite	Dark	Physical	60	100	25	Normal
1	Burn Up	Fire	Special	130	100	5	Normal
1	Crunch	Dark	Physical	80	100	15	Normal
1	Ember	Fire	Special	40	100	25	Normal
1	Extreme Speed	Normal	Physical	80	95	5	Normal
1	Fire Fang	Fire	Physical	65	95	15	Normal
1	Flame Wheel	Fire	Physical	60	100	25	Normal
1	Flamethrower	Fire	Special	90	100	15	Normal
1	Flare Blitz	Fire	Physical	120	100	15	Normal
1	Helping Hand	Normal	Status	—	—	20	1 Ally
1	Howl	Normal	Status	—	—	40	Your Side
1	Leer	Normal	Status	—	100	30	Many Others
1	Play Rough	Fairy	Physical	90	90	10	Normal
1	Retaliate	Normal	Physical	70	100	5	Normal
1	Reversal	Fighting	Physical	—	100	15	Normal
1	Roar	Normal	Status	—	—	20	Normal
1	Take Down	Normal	Physical	90	85	20	Normal

EVOLUTION MOVES

NAME	TYPE	KIND	POW.	ACC.	PP	RANGE
Extreme Speed	Normal	Physical	80	100	5	Normal

EGG MOVES

NAME	TYPE	KIND	POW.	ACC.	PP	RANGE

TUTOR MOVES

NAME	TYPE	KIND	POW.	ACC.	PP	RANGE

TM MOVES

NO.	NAME	TYPE	KIND	POW.	ACC.	PP	RANGE
TM08	Hyper Beam	Normal	Special	150	90	5	Normal
TM09	Giga Impact	Normal	Physical	150	90	5	Normal
TM11	Solar Beam	Grass	Special	120	100	10	Normal
TM13	Fire Spin	Fire	Special	35	85	15	Normal
TM15	Dig	Ground	Physical	80	100	10	Normal
TM19	Safeguard	Normal	Status	—	—	25	Your Side
TM21	Rest	Psychic	Status	—	—	10	Self
TM23	Thief	Dark	Physical	60	100	25	Normal
TM24	Snore	Normal	Special	50	100	15	Normal
TM25	Protect	Normal	Status	—	—	10	Self
TM26	Scary Face	Normal	Status	—	100	10	Normal
TM31	Attract	Normal	Status	—	100	15	Normal
TM34	Sunny Day	Fire	Status	—	—	5	Both Sides
TM38	Will-O-Wisp	Fire	Status	—	85	15	Normal
TM39	Facade	Normal	Physical	70	100	20	Normal
TM40	Swift	Normal	Special	60	—	20	Many Others
TM41	Helping Hand	Normal	Status	—	—	20	1 Ally
TM66	Thunder Fang	Electric	Physical	65	95	15	Normal
TM68	Fire Fang	Fire	Physical	65	95	15	Normal
TM76	Round	Normal	Special	60	100	15	Normal
TM79	Retaliate	Normal	Physical	70	100	5	Normal
TM81	Bulldoze	Ground	Physical	60	100	20	All Others
TM85	Snarl	Dark	Special	55	95	15	Many Others

TR MOVES

NAME	TYPE	KIND	POW.	ACC.	PP	RANGE
TR01 Body Slam	Normal	Physical	85	100	15	Normal
TR02 Flamethrower	Fire	Special	90	100	15	Normal
TR12 Agility	Psychic	Status	—	—	30	Self
TR15 Fire Blast	Fire	Special	110	85	5	Normal
TR20 Substitute	Normal	Status	—	—	10	Self
TR21 Reversal	Fighting	Physical	—	100	15	Normal
TR24 Outrage	Dragon	Physical	120	100	10	1 Random
TR26 Endure	Normal	Status	—	—	10	Self
TR27 Sleep Talk	Normal	Status	—	—	10	Self
TR31 Iron Tail	Steel	Physical	100	75	15	Normal
TR32 Crunch	Dark	Physical	80	100	15	Normal
TR36 Heat Wave	Fire	Special	95	90	10	Many Others
TR42 Hyper Voice	Normal	Special	90	100	10	Many Others
TR43 Overheat	Fire	Special	130	90	5	Normal
TR53 Close Combat	Fighting	Physical	120	100	5	Normal
TR55 Flare Blitz	Fire	Physical	120	100	15	Normal
TR62 Dragon Pulse	Dragon	Special	85	100	10	Normal
TR74 Iron Head	Steel	Physical	80	100	15	Normal
TR86 Wild Charge	Electric	Physical	90	100	15	Normal
TR90 Play Rough	Fairy	Physical	90	90	10	Normal
TR97 Psychic Fangs	Psychic	Physical	85	100	10	Normal

072

Vanillite
p. 48

ABILITY
Ice Body
Snow Cloak

HIDDEN ABILITY
Weak Armor

SPECIES STRENGTHS

HP	
ATTACK	
DEFENSE	
SP. ATK	
SP. DEF	
SPEED	

DAMAGE TAKEN IN BATTLE

×1 ×2 ×2
×2 ×1 ×1
×1 ×1 ×1
×1 ×1 ×2
×1 ×1 ×2
×0.5 ×1 ×1

MINERAL

LEVEL-UP MOVES

LV.	NAME	TYPE	KIND	POW.	ACC.	PP	RANGE
1	Astonish	Ghost	Physical	30	100	15	Normal
1	Harden	Normal	Status	—	—	30	Self
4	Taunt	Dark	Status	—	100	20	Normal
8	Mist	Ice	Status	—	—	30	Your Side
12	Icy Wind	Ice	Special	55	95	15	Many Others
16	Avalanche	Ice	Physical	60	100	10	Normal
20	Hail	Ice	Status	—	—	10	Both Sides
24	Icicle Spear	Ice	Physical	25	100	30	Normal
28	Uproar	Normal	Special	90	100	10	1 Random
32	Acid Armor	Poison	Status	—	—	20	Self
36	Mirror Coat	Psychic	Special	—	100	20	Varies
40	Ice Beam	Ice	Special	90	100	10	Normal
44	Blizzard	Ice	Special	110	70	5	Many Others
48	Sheer Cold	Ice	Special	—	30	5	Normal

EVOLUTION MOVES

NAME	TYPE	KIND	POW.	ACC.	PP	RANGE

EGG MOVES

NAME	TYPE	KIND	POW.	ACC.	PP	RANGE
Aurora Veil	Ice	Status	—	—	20	Your Side
Autotomize	Steel	Status	—	—	15	Self
Explosion	Normal	Physical	250	100	5	All Others
Ice Shard	Ice	Physical	40	100	30	Normal
Icicle Crash	Ice	Physical	85	90	10	Normal
Magnet Rise	Electric	Status	—	—	10	Self

TUTOR MOVES

NAME	TYPE	KIND	POW.	ACC.	PP	RANGE

TM MOVES

NO.	NAME	TYPE	KIND	POW.	ACC.	PP	RANGE
TM17	Light Screen	Psychic	Status	—	—	30	Your Side
TM20	Self-Destruct	Normal	Physical	200	100	5	All Others
TM21	Rest	Psychic	Status	—	—	10	Self
TM24	Snore	Normal	Special	50	100	15	Normal
TM25	Protect	Normal	Status	—	—	10	Self
TM27	Icy Wind	Ice	Special	55	95	15	Many Others
TM31	Attract	Normal	Status	—	100	15	Normal
TM33	Rain Dance	Water	Status	—	—	5	Both Sides
TM35	Hail	Ice	Status	—	—	10	Both Sides
TM39	Facade	Normal	Physical	70	100	20	Normal
TM44	Imprison	Psychic	Status	—	—	10	Self
TM51	Icicle Spear	Ice	Physical	25	100	30	Normal
TM64	Avalanche	Ice	Physical	60	100	10	Normal
TM76	Round	Normal	Special	60	100	15	Normal

TR MOVES

NAME	TYPE	KIND	POW.	ACC.	PP	RANGE
TR05 Ice Beam	Ice	Special	90	100	10	Normal
TR06 Blizzard	Ice	Special	110	70	5	Many Others
TR20 Substitute	Normal	Status	—	—	10	Self
TR26 Endure	Normal	Status	—	—	10	Self
TR27 Sleep Talk	Normal	Status	—	—	10	Self
TR35 Uproar	Normal	Special	90	100	10	1 Random
TR37 Taunt	Dark	Status	—	100	20	Normal
TR42 Hyper Voice	Normal	Special	90	100	10	Many Others
TR46 Iron Defense	Steel	Status	—	—	15	Self
TR70 Flash Cannon	Steel	Special	80	100	10	Normal
TR83 Ally Switch	Psychic	Status	—	—	15	Self

073 — Vanillish

LEVEL-UP MOVES

LV.	NAME	TYPE	KIND	POW.	ACC.	PP	RANGE
1	Astonish	Ghost	Physical	30	100	15	Normal
1	Harden	Normal	Status	—	—	30	Self
1	Mist	Ice	Status	—	—	30	Your Side
1	Taunt	Dark	Status	—	100	20	Normal
12	Icy Wind	Ice	Special	55	95	15	Many Others
16	Avalanche	Ice	Physical	60	100	10	Normal
20	Hail	Ice	Status	—	—	10	Both Sides
24	Icicle Spear	Ice	Physical	25	100	30	Normal
28	Uproar	Normal	Special	90	100	10	1 Random
32	Acid Armor	Poison	Status	—	—	20	Self
38	Mirror Coat	Psychic	Status	—	100	20	Varies
44	Ice Beam	Ice	Special	90	100	10	Normal
50	Blizzard	Ice	Special	110	70	5	Many Others
56	Sheer Cold	Ice	Special	—	30	5	Normal

TUTOR MOVES

NAME	TYPE	KIND	POW.	ACC.	PP	RANGE

TM MOVES

NO.	NAME	TYPE	KIND	POW.	ACC.	PP	RANGE
TM17	Light Screen	Psychic	Status	—	—	30	Your Side
TM20	Self-Destruct	Normal	Physical	200	100	5	All Others
TM21	Rest	Psychic	Status	—	—	10	Self
TM24	Snore	Normal	Special	50	100	15	Normal
TM25	Protect	Normal	Status	—	—	10	Self
TM27	Icy Wind	Ice	Special	55	95	15	Many Others
TM31	Attract	Normal	Status	—	100	15	Normal
TM33	Rain Dance	Water	Status	—	—	5	Both Sides
TM35	Hail	Ice	Status	—	—	10	Both Sides
TM39	Facade	Normal	Physical	70	100	20	Normal
TM44	Imprison	Psychic	Status	—	—	10	Self
TM51	Icicle Spear	Ice	Physical	25	100	30	Normal
TM64	Avalanche	Ice	Physical	60	100	10	Normal
TM76	Round	Normal	Special	60	100	15	Normal

TR MOVES

NO.	NAME	TYPE	KIND	POW.	ACC.	PP	RANGE
TR05	Ice Beam	Ice	Special	90	100	10	Normal
TR06	Blizzard	Ice	Special	110	70	5	Many Others
TR20	Substitute	Normal	Status	—	—	10	Self
TR26	Endure	Normal	Status	—	—	10	Self
TR27	Sleep Talk	Normal	Status	—	—	10	Self
TR35	Uproar	Normal	Special	90	100	10	1 Random
TR37	Taunt	Dark	Status	—	100	20	Normal
TR42	Hyper Voice	Normal	Special	90	100	10	Many Others
TR46	Iron Defense	Steel	Status	—	—	15	Self
TR70	Flash Cannon	Steel	Special	80	100	10	Normal
TR83	Ally Switch	Psychic	Status	—	—	15	Self

EVOLUTION MOVES

NAME	TYPE	KIND	POW.	ACC.	PP	RANGE

EGG MOVES

NAME	TYPE	KIND	POW.	ACC.	PP	RANGE

Vanillish p. 48

ABILITY
Ice Body
Snow Cloak

HIDDEN ABILITY
Weak Armor

SPECIES STRENGTHS
HP
ATTACK
DEFENSE
SP. ATK
SP. DEF
SPEED

DAMAGE TAKEN IN BATTLE
×1 / ×2 / ×2
×2 / ×1 / ×1
×1 / ×1 / ×1
×1 / ×1 / ×2
×0.5 / ×1 / ×1

MINERAL

---

074 — Vanilluxe

LEVEL-UP MOVES

LV.	NAME	TYPE	KIND	POW.	ACC.	PP	RANGE
1	Astonish	Ghost	Physical	30	100	15	Normal
1	Freeze-Dry	Ice	Special	70	100	20	Normal
1	Harden	Normal	Status	—	—	30	Self
1	Icicle Crash	Ice	Physical	85	90	10	Normal
1	Mist	Ice	Status	—	—	30	Your Side
1	Taunt	Dark	Status	—	100	20	Normal
1	Weather Ball*	Normal	Special	50	100	10	Normal
12	Icy Wind	Ice	Special	55	95	15	Many Others
16	Avalanche	Ice	Physical	60	100	10	Normal
20	Hail	Ice	Status	—	—	10	Both Sides
24	Icicle Spear	Ice	Physical	25	100	30	Normal
28	Uproar	Normal	Special	90	100	10	1 Random
32	Acid Armor	Poison	Status	—	—	20	Self
38	Mirror Coat	Psychic	Status	—	100	20	Varies
44	Ice Beam	Ice	Special	90	100	10	Normal
52	Blizzard	Ice	Special	110	70	5	Many Others
60	Sheer Cold	Ice	Special	—	30	5	Normal

TUTOR MOVES

NAME	TYPE	KIND	POW.	ACC.	PP	RANGE

TM MOVES

NO.	NAME	TYPE	KIND	POW.	ACC.	PP	RANGE
TM08	Hyper Beam	Normal	Special	150	90	5	Normal
TM09	Giga Impact	Normal	Physical	150	90	5	Normal
TM17	Light Screen	Psychic	Status	—	—	30	Your Side
TM20	Self-Destruct	Normal	Physical	200	100	5	All Others
TM21	Rest	Psychic	Status	—	—	10	Self
TM24	Snore	Normal	Special	50	100	15	Normal
TM25	Protect	Normal	Status	—	—	10	Self
TM27	Icy Wind	Ice	Special	55	95	15	Many Others
TM31	Attract	Normal	Status	—	100	15	Normal
TM33	Rain Dance	Water	Status	—	—	5	Both Sides
TM35	Hail	Ice	Status	—	—	10	Both Sides
TM37	Beat Up	Dark	Physical	—	100	10	Normal
TM39	Facade	Normal	Physical	70	100	20	Normal
TM44	Imprison	Psychic	Status	—	—	10	Self
TM46	Weather Ball*	Normal	Special	50	100	10	Normal
TM51	Icicle Spear	Ice	Physical	25	100	30	Normal
TM64	Avalanche	Ice	Physical	60	100	10	Normal
TM76	Round	Normal	Special	60	100	15	Normal

TR MOVES

NO.	NAME	TYPE	KIND	POW.	ACC.	PP	RANGE
TR05	Ice Beam	Ice	Special	90	100	10	Normal
TR06	Blizzard	Ice	Special	110	70	5	Many Others
TR20	Substitute	Normal	Status	—	—	10	Self
TR26	Endure	Normal	Status	—	—	10	Self
TR27	Sleep Talk	Normal	Status	—	—	10	Self
TR35	Uproar	Normal	Special	90	100	10	1 Random
TR37	Taunt	Dark	Status	—	100	20	Normal
TR42	Hyper Voice	Normal	Special	90	100	10	Many Others
TR46	Iron Defense	Steel	Status	—	—	15	Self
TR70	Flash Cannon	Steel	Special	80	100	10	Normal
TR83	Ally Switch	Psychic	Status	—	—	15	Self

EVOLUTION MOVES

NAME	TYPE	KIND	POW.	ACC.	PP	RANGE

EGG MOVES

NAME	TYPE	KIND	POW.	ACC.	PP	RANGE

Vanilluxe p. 48

ABILITY
Ice Body
Snow Warning

HIDDEN ABILITY
Weak Armor

SPECIES STRENGTHS
HP
ATTACK
DEFENSE
SP. ATK
SP. DEF
SPEED

DAMAGE TAKEN IN BATTLE
×1 / ×2 / ×2
×2 / ×1 / ×1
×1 / ×1 / ×1
×1 / ×1 / ×2
×0.5 / ×1 / ×1

MINERAL

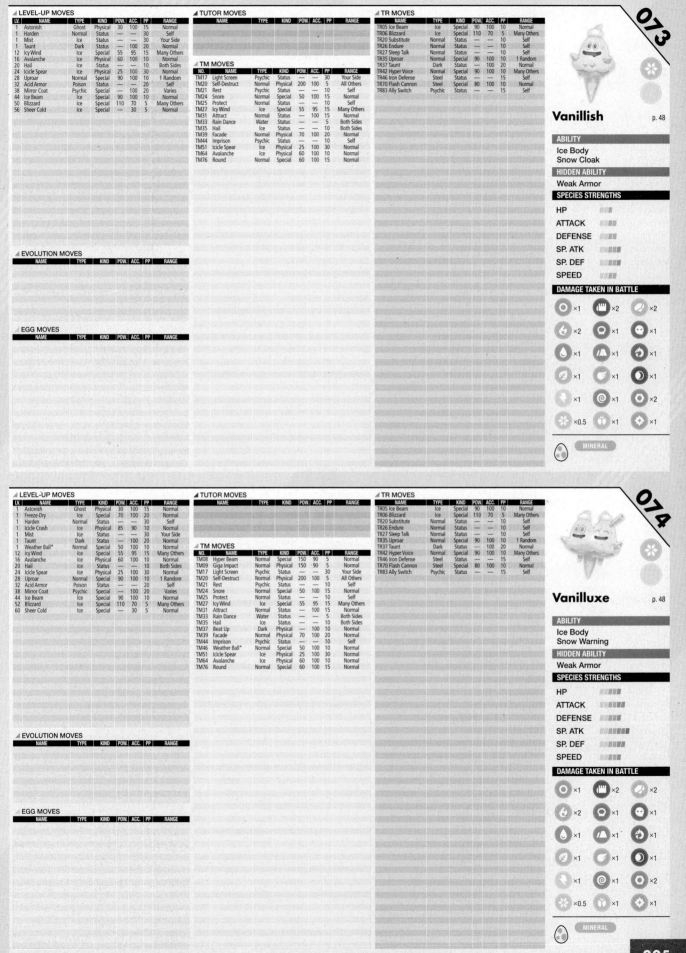

*Weather Ball changes type depending on weather condition. (Harsh sunlight: Fire type. Rain: Water type. Hail: Ice type. Sandstorm: Rock type.)

075

Swinub
p. 49

ABILITY
Oblivious
Snow Cloak

HIDDEN ABILITY
Thick Fat

SPECIES STRENGTHS

HP
ATTACK
DEFENSE
SP. ATK
SP. DEF
SPEED

DAMAGE TAKEN IN BATTLE

●×1	▦×2	◆×1
●×2	●×0.5	●×1
●×2	▲×1	●×1
●×2	●×1	●×2
●×0	●×1	●×2
●×1	●×1	●×1

FIELD

LEVEL-UP MOVES

LV.	NAME	TYPE	KIND	POW.	ACC.	PP	RANGE
1	Mud-Slap	Ground	Special	20	100	10	Normal
1	Tackle	Normal	Physical	40	100	35	Normal
5	Powder Snow	Ice	Special	40	100	25	Many Others
10	Flail	Normal	Physical	—	100	15	Normal
15	Ice Shard	Ice	Physical	40	100	30	Normal
20	Mist	Ice	Status	—	—	30	Your Side
25	Endure	Normal	Status	—	—	10	Self
30	Icy Wind	Ice	Special	55	95	15	Many Others
35	Amnesia	Psychic	Status	—	—	20	Self
40	Take Down	Normal	Physical	90	85	20	Normal
45	Earthquake	Ground	Physical	100	100	10	All Others
50	Blizzard	Ice	Special	110	70	5	Many Others

EVOLUTION MOVES

NAME	TYPE	KIND	POW.	ACC.	PP	RANGE

EGG MOVES

NAME	TYPE	KIND	POW.	ACC.	PP	RANGE
Ancient Power	Rock	Special	60	100	5	Normal
Bite	Dark	Physical	60	100	25	Normal
Curse	Ghost	Status	—	—	10	Varies
Double-Edge	Normal	Physical	120	100	15	Normal
Fissure	Ground	Physical	—	30	5	Normal
Freeze-Dry	Ice	Special	70	100	20	Normal
Icicle Crash	Ice	Physical	85	90	10	Normal

TUTOR MOVES

NAME	TYPE	KIND	POW.	ACC.	PP	RANGE

TM MOVES

NO.	NAME	TYPE	KIND	POW.	ACC.	PP	RANGE
TM15	Dig	Ground	Physical	80	100	10	Normal
TM17	Light Screen	Psychic	Status	—	—	30	Your Side
TM18	Reflect	Psychic	Status	—	—	20	Your Side
TM21	Rest	Psychic	Status	—	—	10	Self
TM22	Rock Slide	Rock	Physical	75	90	10	Many Others
TM24	Snore	Normal	Special	50	100	15	Normal
TM25	Protect	Normal	Status	—	—	10	Self
TM26	Scary Face	Normal	Status	—	100	10	Normal
TM27	Icy Wind	Ice	Special	55	95	15	Many Others
TM31	Attract	Normal	Status	—	100	15	Normal
TM32	Sandstorm	Rock	Status	—	—	10	Both Sides
TM33	Rain Dance	Water	Status	—	—	5	Both Sides
TM35	Hail	Ice	Status	—	—	10	Both Sides
TM39	Facade	Normal	Physical	70	100	20	Normal
TM48	Rock Tomb	Rock	Physical	60	95	15	Normal
TM49	Sand Tomb	Ground	Physical	35	85	15	Normal
TM51	Icicle Spear	Ice	Physical	25	100	30	Normal
TM53	Mud Shot	Ground	Special	55	95	15	Normal
TM64	Avalanche	Ice	Physical	60	100	10	Normal
TM76	Round	Normal	Special	60	100	15	Normal
TM81	Bulldoze	Ground	Physical	60	100	20	All Others

TR MOVES

NAME	TYPE	KIND	POW.	ACC.	PP	RANGE
TR01 Body Slam	Normal	Physical	85	100	15	Normal
TR05 Ice Beam	Ice	Special	90	100	10	Normal
TR06 Blizzard	Ice	Special	110	70	5	Many Others
TR10 Earthquake	Ground	Physical	100	100	10	All Others
TR17 Amnesia	Psychic	Status	—	—	20	Self
TR20 Substitute	Normal	Status	—	—	10	Self
TR26 Endure	Normal	Status	—	—	10	Self
TR27 Sleep Talk	Normal	Status	—	—	10	Self
TR39 Superpower	Fighting	Physical	120	100	5	Normal
TR67 Earth Power	Ground	Special	90	100	10	Normal
TR76 Stealth Rock	Rock	Status	—	—	20	Other Side

076

Piloswine
p. 49

ABILITY
Oblivious
Snow Cloak

HIDDEN ABILITY
Thick Fat

SPECIES STRENGTHS

HP
ATTACK
DEFENSE
SP. ATK
SP. DEF
SPEED

DAMAGE TAKEN IN BATTLE

●×1	▦×2	◆×1
●×2	●×0.5	●×1
●×2	▲×1	●×1
●×2	●×1	●×1
●×0	●×1	●×2
●×1	●×1	●×1

FIELD

LEVEL-UP MOVES

LV.	NAME	TYPE	KIND	POW.	ACC.	PP	RANGE
1	Ancient Power	Rock	Special	60	100	5	Normal
1	Flail	Normal	Physical	—	100	15	Normal
1	Ice Fang	Ice	Physical	65	95	15	Normal
1	Mud-Slap	Ground	Special	20	100	10	Normal
1	Powder Snow	Ice	Special	40	100	25	Many Others
1	Tackle	Normal	Physical	40	100	35	Normal
15	Ice Shard	Ice	Physical	40	100	30	Normal
20	Mist	Ice	Status	—	—	30	Your Side
25	Endure	Normal	Status	—	—	10	Self
30	Icy Wind	Ice	Special	55	95	15	Many Others
37	Amnesia	Psychic	Status	—	—	20	Self
44	Take Down	Normal	Physical	90	85	20	Normal
51	Earthquake	Ground	Physical	100	100	10	All Others
58	Blizzard	Ice	Special	110	70	5	Many Others
65	Thrash	Normal	Physical	120	100	10	1 Random

EVOLUTION MOVES

NAME	TYPE	KIND	POW.	ACC.	PP	RANGE
Ice Fang	Ice	Physical	65	95	15	Normal

EGG MOVES

NAME	TYPE	KIND	POW.	ACC.	PP	RANGE

TUTOR MOVES

NAME	TYPE	KIND	POW.	ACC.	PP	RANGE

TM MOVES

NO.	NAME	TYPE	KIND	POW.	ACC.	PP	RANGE
TM08	Hyper Beam	Normal	Special	150	90	5	Normal
TM09	Giga Impact	Normal	Physical	150	90	5	Normal
TM15	Dig	Ground	Physical	80	100	10	Normal
TM17	Light Screen	Psychic	Status	—	—	30	Your Side
TM18	Reflect	Psychic	Status	—	—	20	Your Side
TM21	Rest	Psychic	Status	—	—	10	Self
TM22	Rock Slide	Rock	Physical	75	90	10	Many Others
TM24	Snore	Normal	Special	50	100	15	Normal
TM25	Protect	Normal	Status	—	—	10	Self
TM26	Scary Face	Normal	Status	—	100	10	Normal
TM27	Icy Wind	Ice	Special	55	95	15	Many Others
TM31	Attract	Normal	Status	—	100	15	Normal
TM32	Sandstorm	Rock	Status	—	—	10	Both Sides
TM33	Rain Dance	Water	Status	—	—	5	Both Sides
TM35	Hail	Ice	Status	—	—	10	Both Sides
TM39	Facade	Normal	Physical	70	100	20	Normal
TM48	Rock Tomb	Rock	Physical	60	95	15	Normal
TM49	Sand Tomb	Ground	Physical	35	85	15	Normal
TM51	Icicle Spear	Ice	Physical	25	100	30	Normal
TM53	Mud Shot	Ground	Special	55	95	15	Normal
TM64	Avalanche	Ice	Physical	60	100	10	Normal
TM67	Ice Fang	Ice	Physical	65	95	15	Normal
TM76	Round	Normal	Special	60	100	15	Normal
TM81	Bulldoze	Ground	Physical	60	100	20	All Others
TM98	Stomping Tantrum	Ground	Physical	75	100	10	Normal

TR MOVES

NAME	TYPE	KIND	POW.	ACC.	PP	RANGE
TR01 Body Slam	Normal	Physical	85	100	15	Normal
TR05 Ice Beam	Ice	Special	90	100	10	Normal
TR06 Blizzard	Ice	Special	110	70	5	Many Others
TR10 Earthquake	Ground	Physical	100	100	10	All Others
TR17 Amnesia	Psychic	Status	—	—	20	Self
TR20 Substitute	Normal	Status	—	—	10	Self
TR26 Endure	Normal	Status	—	—	10	Self
TR27 Sleep Talk	Normal	Status	—	—	10	Self
TR39 Superpower	Fighting	Physical	120	100	5	Normal
TR67 Earth Power	Ground	Special	90	100	10	Normal
TR76 Stone Edge	Rock	Physical	100	80	5	Normal
TR76 Stealth Rock	Rock	Status	—	—	20	Other Side
TR94 High Horsepower	Ground	Physical	95	95	10	Normal

077 — Mamoswine

p. 49

LEVEL-UP MOVES

LV.	NAME	TYPE	KIND	POW.	ACC.	PP	RANGE
1	Ancient Power	Rock	Special	60	100	5	Normal
1	Double Hit	Normal	Physical	35	90	10	Normal
1	Flail	Normal	Physical	—	100	15	Normal
1	Ice Fang	Ice	Physical	65	95	15	Normal
1	Mud-Slap	Ground	Special	20	100	10	Normal
1	Powder Snow	Ice	Special	40	100	25	Many Others
1	Tackle	Normal	Physical	40	100	35	Normal
15	Ice Shard	Ice	Physical	40	100	30	Normal
20	Mist	Ice	Status	—	—	30	Your Side
25	Endure	Normal	Status	—	—	10	Self
30	Icy Wind	Ice	Special	55	95	15	Many Others
37	Amnesia	Psychic	Status	—	—	20	Self
44	Take Down	Normal	Physical	90	85	20	Normal
51	Earthquake	Ground	Physical	100	100	10	All Others
58	Blizzard	Ice	Special	110	70	5	Many Others
65	Thrash	Normal	Physical	120	100	10	1 Random

EVOLUTION MOVES

NAME	TYPE	KIND	POW.	ACC.	PP	RANGE
Double Hit	Normal	Physical	35	90	10	Normal

EGG MOVES

NAME	TYPE	KIND	POW.	ACC.	PP	RANGE

TUTOR MOVES

NAME	TYPE	KIND	POW.	ACC.	PP	RANGE

TM MOVES

NO.	NAME	TYPE	KIND	POW.	ACC.	PP	RANGE
TM08	Hyper Beam	Normal	Special	150	90	5	Normal
TM09	Giga Impact	Normal	Physical	150	90	5	Normal
TM15	Dig	Ground	Physical	80	100	10	Normal
TM17	Light Screen	Psychic	Status	—	—	30	Your Side
TM18	Reflect	Psychic	Status	—	—	20	Your Side
TM21	Rest	Psychic	Status	—	—	10	Self
TM22	Rock Slide	Rock	Physical	75	90	10	Many Others
TM24	Snore	Normal	Special	50	100	15	Normal
TM25	Protect	Normal	Status	—	—	10	Self
TM26	Scary Face	Normal	Status	—	100	10	Normal
TM27	Icy Wind	Ice	Special	55	95	15	Many Others
TM31	Attract	Normal	Status	—	100	15	Normal
TM32	Sandstorm	Rock	Status	—	—	10	Both Sides
TM33	Rain Dance	Water	Status	—	—	5	Both Sides
TM35	Hail	Ice	Status	—	—	10	Both Sides
TM39	Facade	Normal	Physical	70	100	20	Normal
TM48	Rock Tomb	Rock	Physical	60	95	15	Normal
TM49	Sand Tomb	Ground	Physical	35	85	15	Normal
TM51	Icicle Spear	Ice	Physical	25	100	30	Normal
TM53	Mud Shot	Ground	Special	55	95	15	Normal
TM54	Rock Blast	Rock	Physical	25	90	10	Normal
TM64	Avalanche	Ice	Physical	60	100	10	Normal
TM67	Ice Fang	Ice	Physical	65	95	15	Normal
TM76	Round	Normal	Special	60	100	15	Normal
TM81	Bulldoze	Ground	Physical	60	100	20	All Others
TM98	Stomping Tantrum	Ground	Physical	75	100	10	Normal

TR MOVES

NO.	NAME	TYPE	KIND	POW.	ACC.	PP	RANGE
TR01	Body Slam	Normal	Physical	85	100	15	Normal
TR05	Ice Beam	Ice	Special	90	100	10	Normal
TR06	Blizzard	Ice	Special	110	70	5	Many Others
TR10	Earthquake	Ground	Physical	100	100	10	All Others
TR17	Amnesia	Psychic	Status	—	—	20	Self
TR20	Substitute	Normal	Status	—	—	10	Self
TR26	Endure	Normal	Status	—	—	10	Self
TR27	Sleep Talk	Normal	Status	—	—	10	Self
TR39	Superpower	Fighting	Physical	120	100	5	Normal
TR67	Earth Power	Ground	Special	90	100	10	Normal
TR74	Iron Head	Steel	Physical	80	100	15	Normal
TR75	Stone Edge	Rock	Physical	100	80	5	Normal
TR76	Stealth Rock	Rock	Status	—	—	20	Other Side
TR79	Heavy Slam	Steel	Physical	—	100	10	Normal
TR94	High Horsepower	Ground	Physical	95	95	10	Normal
TR99	Body Press	Fighting	Physical	80	100	10	Normal

ABILITY
Oblivious
Snow Cloak

HIDDEN ABILITY
Thick Fat

SPECIES STRENGTHS

HP
ATTACK
DEFENSE
SP. ATK
SP. DEF
SPEED

DAMAGE TAKEN IN BATTLE

×1 ×2 ×1
×2 ×0.5 ×1
×1 ×1 ×1
×2 ×1 ×1
×0 ×1 ×2
×1 ×1 ×1

FIELD

078 — Delibird

p. 50

LEVEL-UP MOVES

LV.	NAME	TYPE	KIND	POW.	ACC.	PP	RANGE
1	Present	Normal	Physical	—	90	15	Normal
25	Drill Peck	Flying	Physical	80	100	20	Normal

EVOLUTION MOVES

NAME	TYPE	KIND	POW.	ACC.	PP	RANGE

EGG MOVES

NAME	TYPE	KIND	POW.	ACC.	PP	RANGE
Aurora Beam	Ice	Special	65	100	20	Normal
Aurora Veil	Ice	Status	—	—	20	Your Side
Counter	Fighting	Physical	—	100	20	Varies
Destiny Bond	Ghost	Status	—	—	5	Self
Fake Out	Normal	Physical	40	100	10	Normal
Freeze-Dry	Ice	Special	70	100	20	Normal
Ice Shard	Ice	Physical	40	100	30	Normal
Memento	Dark	Status	—	100	10	Normal
Quick Attack	Normal	Physical	40	100	30	Normal
Rapid Spin	Normal	Physical	50	100	40	Normal
Splash	Normal	Status	—	—	40	Self

TUTOR MOVES

NAME	TYPE	KIND	POW.	ACC.	PP	RANGE

TM MOVES

NO.	NAME	TYPE	KIND	POW.	ACC.	PP	RANGE
TM00	Mega Punch	Normal	Physical	80	85	20	Normal
TM01	Mega Kick	Normal	Physical	120	75	5	Normal
TM04	Ice Punch	Ice	Physical	75	100	15	Normal
TM06	Fly	Flying	Physical	90	95	15	Normal
TM21	Rest	Psychic	Status	—	—	10	Self
TM23	Thief	Dark	Physical	60	100	25	Normal
TM24	Snore	Normal	Special	50	100	15	Normal
TM25	Protect	Normal	Status	—	—	10	Self
TM27	Icy Wind	Ice	Special	55	95	15	Many Others
TM30	Steel Wing	Steel	Physical	70	90	25	Normal
TM31	Attract	Normal	Status	—	100	15	Normal
TM33	Rain Dance	Water	Status	—	—	5	Both Sides
TM35	Hail	Ice	Status	—	—	10	Both Sides
TM39	Facade	Normal	Physical	70	100	20	Normal
TM40	Swift	Normal	Special	60	—	20	Many Others
TM41	Helping Hand	Normal	Status	—	—	20	1 Ally
TM43	Brick Break	Fighting	Physical	75	100	15	Normal
TM46	Weather Ball*	Normal	Special	50	100	10	Normal
TM51	Icicle Spear	Ice	Physical	25	100	30	Normal
TM52	Bounce	Flying	Physical	85	85	5	Normal
TM58	Assurance	Dark	Physical	60	100	10	Normal
TM59	Fling	Dark	Physical	—	100	10	Normal
TM64	Avalanche	Ice	Physical	60	100	10	Normal
TM76	Round	Normal	Special	60	100	15	Normal
TM97	Brutal Swing	Dark	Physical	60	100	20	All Others

TR MOVES

NO.	NAME	TYPE	KIND	POW.	ACC.	PP	RANGE
TR01	Body Slam	Normal	Physical	85	100	15	Normal
TR05	Ice Beam	Ice	Special	90	100	10	Normal
TR06	Blizzard	Ice	Special	110	70	5	Many Others
TR12	Agility	Psychic	Status	—	—	30	Self
TR20	Substitute	Normal	Status	—	—	10	Self
TR23	Spikes	Ground	Status	—	—	20	Other Side
TR26	Endure	Normal	Status	—	—	10	Self
TR27	Sleep Talk	Normal	Status	—	—	10	Self
TR29	Baton Pass	Normal	Status	—	—	40	Self
TR34	Future Sight	Psychic	Special	120	100	10	Normal
TR59	Seed Bomb	Grass	Physical	80	100	15	Normal
TR66	Brave Bird	Flying	Physical	120	100	15	Normal
TR73	Gunk Shot	Poison	Physical	120	80	5	Normal
TR87	Drill Run	Ground	Physical	80	95	10	Normal

ABILITY
Vital Spirit
Hustle

HIDDEN ABILITY
Insomnia

SPECIES STRENGTHS

HP
ATTACK
DEFENSE
SP. ATK
SP. DEF
SPEED

DAMAGE TAKEN IN BATTLE

×1 ×1 ×4
×2 ×1 ×1
×1 ×0 ×1
×0.5 ×1 ×1
×2 ×1 ×2
×1 ×0.5 ×1

WATER 1
FIELD

*Weather Ball changes type depending on weather condition. (Harsh sunlight: Fire type. Rain: Water type. Hail: Ice type. Sandstorm: Rock type.)

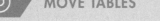
079 Snorunt   p. 50

ABILITY
Inner Focus
Ice Body

HIDDEN ABILITY
Moody

SPECIES STRENGTHS

HP	▮▮▯
ATTACK	▮▮▯
DEFENSE	▮▮▯
SP. ATK	▮▮▯
SP. DEF	▮▮▯
SPEED	▮▮▯

DAMAGE TAKEN IN BATTLE

×1	×2	×2
×2	×1	×1
×1	×1	×1
×1	×1	×1
×1	×1	×2
×0.5	×1	×1

FAIRY / MINERAL

LEVEL-UP MOVES

LV.	NAME	TYPE	KIND	POW.	ACC.	PP	RANGE
1	Astonish	Ghost	Physical	30	100	15	Normal
1	Powder Snow	Ice	Special	40	100	25	Many Others
5	Leer	Normal	Status	—	100	30	Many Others
10	Double Team	Normal	Status	—	—	15	Self
15	Ice Shard	Ice	Physical	40	100	30	Normal
20	Protect	Normal	Status	—	—	10	Self
25	Icy Wind	Ice	Special	55	95	15	Many Others
30	Frost Breath	Ice	Special	60	90	10	Normal
35	Bite	Dark	Physical	60	100	25	Normal
40	Ice Fang	Ice	Physical	65	95	15	Normal
45	Hail	Ice	Status	—	—	10	Both Sides
50	Headbutt	Normal	Physical	70	100	15	Normal
55	Crunch	Dark	Physical	80	100	15	Normal
60	Blizzard	Ice	Special	110	70	5	Many Others

EVOLUTION MOVES

NAME	TYPE	KIND	POW.	ACC.	PP	RANGE

EGG MOVES

NAME	TYPE	KIND	POW.	ACC.	PP	RANGE
Block	Normal	Status	—	—	5	Normal
Disable	Normal	Status	—	100	20	Normal
Icicle Crash	Ice	Physical	85	90	10	Normal
Rollout	Rock	Physical	30	90	20	Normal
Switcheroo	Dark	Status	—	100	10	Normal

TUTOR MOVES

NAME	TYPE	KIND	POW.	ACC.	PP	RANGE

TM MOVES

NO.	NAME	TYPE	KIND	POW.	ACC.	PP	RANGE
TM17	Light Screen	Psychic	Status	—	—	30	Your Side
TM19	Safeguard	Normal	Status	—	—	25	Your Side
TM21	Rest	Psychic	Status	—	—	10	Self
TM24	Snore	Normal	Special	50	100	15	Normal
TM25	Protect	Normal	Status	—	—	10	Self
TM27	Icy Wind	Ice	Special	55	95	15	Many Others
TM31	Attract	Normal	Status	—	100	15	Normal
TM33	Rain Dance	Water	Status	—	—	5	Both Sides
TM35	Hail	Ice	Status	—	—	10	Both Sides
TM39	Facade	Normal	Physical	70	100	20	Normal
TM46	Weather Ball*	Normal	Special	50	100	10	Normal
TM47	Fake Tears	Dark	Status	—	100	20	Normal
TM64	Avalanche	Ice	Physical	60	100	10	Normal
TM67	Ice Fang	Ice	Physical	65	95	15	Normal
TM76	Round	Normal	Special	60	100	15	Normal
TM77	Hex	Ghost	Special	65	100	10	Normal

TR MOVES

NAME	TYPE	KIND	POW.	ACC.	PP	RANGE
TR01 Body Slam	Normal	Physical	85	100	15	Normal
TR05 Ice Beam	Ice	Special	90	100	10	Normal
TR06 Blizzard	Ice	Special	110	70	5	Many Others
TR20 Substitute	Normal	Status	—	—	10	Self
TR23 Spikes	Ground	Status	—	—	20	Other Side
TR26 Endure	Normal	Status	—	—	10	Self
TR27 Sleep Talk	Normal	Status	—	—	10	Self
TR32 Crunch	Dark	Physical	80	100	15	Normal
TR33 Shadow Ball	Ghost	Special	80	100	15	Normal

---

080 Glalie   p. 50

ABILITY
Inner Focus
Ice Body

HIDDEN ABILITY
Moody

SPECIES STRENGTHS

HP	▮▮▮▮▯
ATTACK	▮▮▮▮▯
DEFENSE	▮▮▮▮▯
SP. ATK	▮▮▮▮▯
SP. DEF	▮▮▮▮▯
SPEED	▮▮▮▮▯

DAMAGE TAKEN IN BATTLE

×1	×2	×2
×2	×1	×1
×1	×1	×1
×1	×1	×1
×1	×1	×2
×0.5	×1	×1

FAIRY / MINERAL

LEVEL-UP MOVES

LV.	NAME	TYPE	KIND	POW.	ACC.	PP	RANGE
1	Astonish	Ghost	Physical	30	100	15	Normal
1	Double Team	Normal	Status	—	—	15	Self
1	Freeze-Dry	Ice	Special	70	100	20	Normal
1	Leer	Normal	Status	—	100	30	Many Others
1	Powder Snow	Ice	Special	40	100	25	Many Others
1	Sheer Cold	Ice	Special	—	30	5	Normal
15	Ice Shard	Ice	Physical	40	100	30	Normal
20	Protect	Normal	Status	—	—	10	Self
25	Icy Wind	Ice	Special	55	95	15	Many Others
30	Frost Breath	Ice	Special	60	90	10	Normal
35	Bite	Dark	Physical	60	100	25	Normal
40	Ice Fang	Ice	Physical	65	95	15	Normal
47	Hail	Ice	Status	—	—	10	Both Sides
54	Headbutt	Normal	Physical	70	100	15	Normal
61	Crunch	Dark	Physical	80	100	15	Normal
68	Blizzard	Ice	Special	110	70	5	Many Others

EVOLUTION MOVES

NAME	TYPE	KIND	POW.	ACC.	PP	RANGE
Freeze-Dry	Ice	Special	70	100	20	Normal

EGG MOVES

NAME	TYPE	KIND	POW.	ACC.	PP	RANGE

TUTOR MOVES

NAME	TYPE	KIND	POW.	ACC.	PP	RANGE

TM MOVES

NO.	NAME	TYPE	KIND	POW.	ACC.	PP	RANGE
TM08	Hyper Beam	Normal	Special	150	90	5	Normal
TM09	Giga Impact	Normal	Physical	150	90	5	Normal
TM17	Light Screen	Psychic	Status	—	—	30	Your Side
TM19	Safeguard	Normal	Status	—	—	25	Your Side
TM20	Self-Destruct	Normal	Physical	200	100	5	All Others
TM21	Rest	Psychic	Status	—	—	10	Self
TM24	Snore	Normal	Special	50	100	15	Normal
TM25	Protect	Normal	Status	—	—	10	Self
TM26	Scary Face	Normal	Status	—	100	10	Normal
TM27	Icy Wind	Ice	Special	55	95	15	Many Others
TM31	Attract	Normal	Status	—	100	15	Normal
TM33	Rain Dance	Water	Status	—	—	5	Both Sides
TM35	Hail	Ice	Status	—	—	10	Both Sides
TM39	Facade	Normal	Physical	70	100	20	Normal
TM46	Weather Ball*	Normal	Special	50	100	10	Normal
TM47	Fake Tears	Dark	Status	—	100	20	Normal
TM51	Icicle Spear	Ice	Physical	25	100	30	Normal
TM57	Payback	Dark	Physical	50	100	10	Normal
TM64	Avalanche	Ice	Physical	60	100	10	Normal
TM67	Ice Fang	Ice	Physical	65	95	15	Normal
TM76	Round	Normal	Special	60	100	15	Normal
TM77	Hex	Ghost	Special	65	100	10	Normal
TM81	Bulldoze	Ground	Physical	60	100	20	All Others

TR MOVES

NAME	TYPE	KIND	POW.	ACC.	PP	RANGE
TR01 Body Slam	Normal	Physical	85	100	15	Normal
TR05 Ice Beam	Ice	Special	90	100	10	Normal
TR06 Blizzard	Ice	Special	110	70	5	Many Others
TR10 Earthquake	Ground	Physical	100	100	10	All Others
TR20 Substitute	Normal	Status	—	—	10	Self
TR23 Spikes	Ground	Status	—	—	20	Other Side
TR26 Endure	Normal	Status	—	—	10	Self
TR27 Sleep Talk	Normal	Status	—	—	10	Self
TR32 Crunch	Dark	Physical	80	100	15	Normal
TR33 Shadow Ball	Ghost	Special	80	100	15	Normal
TR37 Taunt	Dark	Status	—	100	20	Normal
TR52 Gyro Ball	Steel	Physical	—	100	5	Normal
TR58 Dark Pulse	Dark	Special	80	100	15	Normal
TR74 Iron Head	Steel	Physical	80	100	15	Normal

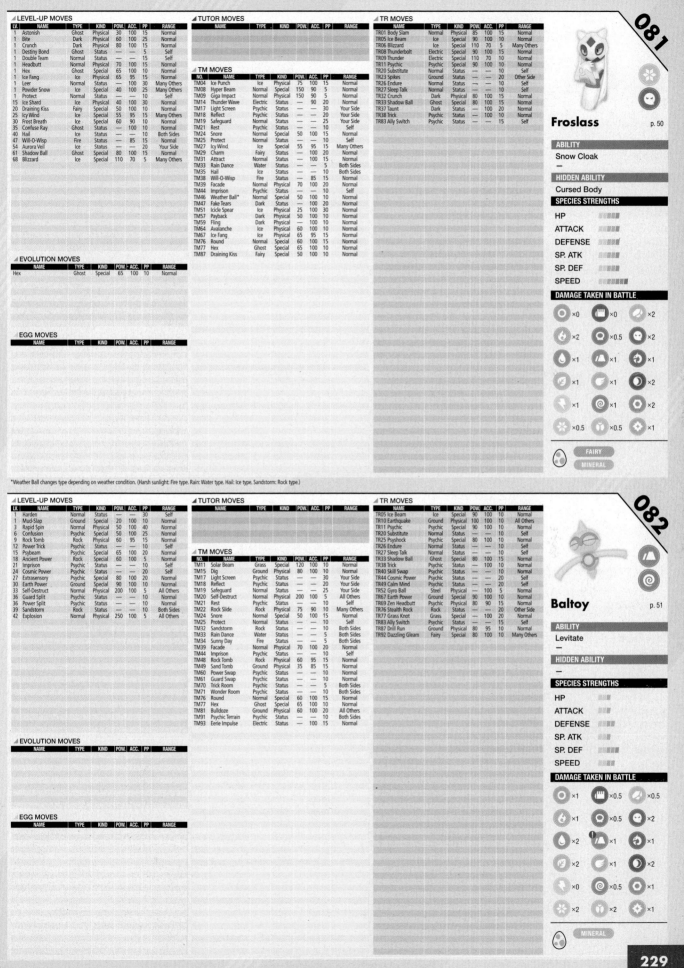

081 Froslass — p. 50

LEVEL-UP MOVES

LV.	NAME	TYPE	KIND	POW.	ACC.	PP	RANGE
1	Astonish	Ghost	Physical	30	100	15	Normal
1	Bite	Dark	Physical	60	100	25	Normal
1	Crunch	Dark	Physical	80	100	15	Normal
1	Destiny Bond	Ghost	Status	—	—	5	Self
1	Double Team	Normal	Status	—	—	15	Self
1	Headbutt	Normal	Physical	70	100	15	Normal
1	Hex	Ghost	Special	65	100	10	Normal
1	Ice Fang	Ice	Physical	65	95	15	Normal
1	Leer	Normal	Status	—	100	30	Many Others
1	Powder Snow	Ice	Special	40	100	25	Many Others
1	Protect	Normal	Status	—	—	10	Self
15	Ice Shard	Ice	Physical	40	100	30	Normal
20	Draining Kiss	Fairy	Special	50	100	10	Normal
25	Icy Wind	Ice	Special	55	95	15	Many Others
30	Frost Breath	Ice	Special	60	90	10	Normal
35	Confuse Ray	Ghost	Status	—	100	10	Normal
40	Hail	Ice	Status	—	—	10	Both Sides
47	Will-O-Wisp	Fire	Status	—	85	15	Normal
54	Aurora Veil	Ice	Status	—	—	20	Your Side
61	Shadow Ball	Ghost	Special	80	100	15	Normal
68	Blizzard	Ice	Special	110	70	5	Many Others

TUTOR MOVES

NAME	TYPE	KIND	POW.	ACC.	PP	RANGE

TM MOVES

NO.	NAME	TYPE	KIND	POW.	ACC.	PP	RANGE
TM04	Ice Punch	Ice	Physical	75	100	15	Normal
TM08	Hyper Beam	Normal	Special	150	90	5	Normal
TM09	Giga Impact	Normal	Physical	150	90	5	Normal
TM14	Thunder Wave	Electric	Status	—	90	20	Normal
TM17	Light Screen	Psychic	Status	—	—	30	Your Side
TM18	Reflect	Psychic	Status	—	—	20	Your Side
TM19	Safeguard	Normal	Status	—	—	25	Your Side
TM21	Rest	Psychic	Status	—	—	10	Self
TM24	Snore	Normal	Special	50	100	15	Normal
TM25	Protect	Normal	Status	—	—	10	Self
TM27	Icy Wind	Ice	Special	55	95	15	Many Others
TM29	Charm	Fairy	Status	—	100	20	Normal
TM31	Attract	Normal	Status	—	100	15	Normal
TM33	Rain Dance	Water	Status	—	—	5	Both Sides
TM35	Hail	Ice	Status	—	—	10	Both Sides
TM38	Will-O-Wisp	Fire	Status	—	85	15	Normal
TM39	Facade	Normal	Physical	70	100	20	Normal
TM44	Imprison	Psychic	Status	—	—	10	Self
TM46	Weather Ball*	Normal	Special	50	100	10	Normal
TM47	Fake Tears	Dark	Status	—	100	20	Normal
TM51	Icicle Spear	Ice	Physical	25	100	30	Normal
TM57	Payback	Dark	Physical	50	100	10	Normal
TM59	Fling	Dark	Physical	—	100	10	Normal
TM64	Avalanche	Ice	Physical	60	100	10	Normal
TM67	Ice Fang	Ice	Physical	65	95	15	Normal
TM76	Round	Normal	Special	60	100	15	Normal
TM77	Hex	Ghost	Special	65	100	10	Normal
TM87	Draining Kiss	Fairy	Special	50	100	10	Normal

TR MOVES

NO.	NAME	TYPE	KIND	POW.	ACC.	PP	RANGE
TR01	Body Slam	Normal	Physical	85	100	15	Normal
TR05	Ice Beam	Ice	Special	90	100	10	Normal
TR06	Blizzard	Ice	Special	110	70	5	Many Others
TR08	Thunderbolt	Electric	Special	90	100	15	Normal
TR09	Thunder	Electric	Special	110	70	10	Normal
TR11	Psychic	Psychic	Special	90	100	10	Normal
TR20	Substitute	Normal	Status	—	—	10	Self
TR23	Spikes	Ground	Status	—	—	20	Other Side
TR26	Endure	Normal	Status	—	—	10	Self
TR27	Sleep Talk	Normal	Status	—	—	10	Self
TR32	Crunch	Dark	Physical	80	100	15	Normal
TR33	Shadow Ball	Ghost	Special	80	100	15	Normal
TR37	Taunt	Dark	Status	—	100	20	Normal
TR38	Trick	Psychic	Status	—	100	10	Normal
TR83	Ally Switch	Psychic	Status	—	—	15	Self

EVOLUTION MOVES

NAME	TYPE	KIND	POW.	ACC.	PP	RANGE
Hex	Ghost	Special	65	100	10	Normal

EGG MOVES

NAME	TYPE	KIND	POW.	ACC.	PP	RANGE

ABILITY

Snow Cloak

—

HIDDEN ABILITY

Cursed Body

SPECIES STRENGTHS

HP

ATTACK

DEFENSE

SP. ATK

SP. DEF

SPEED

DAMAGE TAKEN IN BATTLE

×0 / ×0 / ×2 / ×2 / ×0.5 / ×2 / ×1 / ×1 / ×1 / ×1 / ×1 / ×1 / ×1 / ×1 / ×2 / ×0.5 / ×0.5 / ×1

FAIRY
MINERAL

*Weather Ball changes type depending on weather condition. (Harsh sunlight: Fire type. Rain: Water type. Hail: Ice type. Sandstorm: Rock type.)

---

082 Baltoy — p. 51

LEVEL-UP MOVES

LV.	NAME	TYPE	KIND	POW.	ACC.	PP	RANGE
1	Harden	Normal	Status	—	—	30	Self
1	Mud-Slap	Ground	Special	20	100	10	Normal
3	Rapid Spin	Normal	Physical	50	100	40	Normal
6	Confusion	Psychic	Special	50	100	25	Normal
9	Rock Tomb	Rock	Physical	60	95	15	Normal
12	Power Trick	Psychic	Status	—	—	10	Self
15	Psybeam	Psychic	Special	65	100	20	Normal
18	Ancient Power	Rock	Special	60	100	5	Normal
21	Imprison	Psychic	Status	—	—	10	Self
24	Cosmic Power	Psychic	Status	—	—	20	Self
27	Extrasensory	Psychic	Special	80	100	20	Normal
30	Earth Power	Ground	Special	90	100	10	Normal
33	Self-Destruct	Normal	Physical	200	100	5	All Others
36	Guard Split	Psychic	Status	—	—	10	Normal
36	Power Split	Psychic	Status	—	—	10	Normal
39	Sandstorm	Rock	Status	—	—	10	Both Sides
42	Explosion	Normal	Physical	250	100	5	All Others

TUTOR MOVES

NAME	TYPE	KIND	POW.	ACC.	PP	RANGE

TM MOVES

NO.	NAME	TYPE	KIND	POW.	ACC.	PP	RANGE
TM11	Solar Beam	Grass	Special	120	100	10	Normal
TM15	Dig	Ground	Physical	80	100	10	Normal
TM17	Light Screen	Psychic	Status	—	—	30	Your Side
TM18	Reflect	Psychic	Status	—	—	20	Your Side
TM19	Safeguard	Normal	Status	—	—	25	Your Side
TM20	Self-Destruct	Normal	Physical	200	100	5	All Others
TM21	Rest	Psychic	Status	—	—	10	Self
TM22	Rock Slide	Rock	Physical	75	90	10	Many Others
TM24	Snore	Normal	Special	50	100	15	Normal
TM25	Protect	Normal	Status	—	—	10	Self
TM32	Sandstorm	Rock	Status	—	—	10	Both Sides
TM33	Rain Dance	Water	Status	—	—	5	Both Sides
TM34	Sunny Day	Fire	Status	—	—	5	Both Sides
TM39	Facade	Normal	Physical	70	100	20	Normal
TM44	Imprison	Psychic	Status	—	—	10	Self
TM48	Rock Tomb	Rock	Physical	60	95	15	Normal
TM49	Sand Tomb	Ground	Physical	35	85	15	Normal
TM60	Power Swap	Psychic	Status	—	—	10	Normal
TM61	Guard Swap	Psychic	Status	—	—	10	Normal
TM70	Trick Room	Psychic	Status	—	—	5	Both Sides
TM71	Wonder Room	Psychic	Status	—	—	10	Both Sides
TM76	Round	Normal	Special	60	100	15	Normal
TM77	Hex	Ghost	Special	65	100	10	Normal
TM81	Bulldoze	Ground	Physical	60	100	20	All Others
TM91	Psychic Terrain	Psychic	Status	—	—	10	Both Sides
TM93	Eerie Impulse	Electric	Status	—	100	15	Normal

TR MOVES

NO.	NAME	TYPE	KIND	POW.	ACC.	PP	RANGE
TR05	Ice Beam	Ice	Special	90	100	10	Normal
TR10	Earthquake	Ground	Physical	100	100	10	All Others
TR11	Psychic	Psychic	Special	90	100	10	Normal
TR20	Substitute	Normal	Status	—	—	10	Self
TR25	Psyshock	Psychic	Special	80	100	10	Normal
TR26	Endure	Normal	Status	—	—	10	Self
TR27	Sleep Talk	Normal	Status	—	—	10	Self
TR33	Shadow Ball	Ghost	Special	80	100	15	Normal
TR38	Trick	Psychic	Status	—	100	10	Normal
TR40	Skill Swap	Psychic	Status	—	—	10	Normal
TR44	Cosmic Power	Psychic	Status	—	—	20	Self
TR49	Calm Mind	Psychic	Status	—	—	20	Self
TR52	Gyro Ball	Steel	Physical	—	100	5	Normal
TR67	Earth Power	Ground	Special	90	100	10	Normal
TR69	Zen Headbutt	Psychic	Physical	80	90	15	Normal
TR76	Stealth Rock	Rock	Status	—	—	20	Other Side
TR77	Grass Knot	Grass	Special	—	100	20	Normal
TR83	Ally Switch	Psychic	Status	—	—	15	Self
TR87	Drill Run	Ground	Physical	80	95	10	Normal
TR92	Dazzling Gleam	Fairy	Special	80	100	10	Many Others

EVOLUTION MOVES

NAME	TYPE	KIND	POW.	ACC.	PP	RANGE

EGG MOVES

NAME	TYPE	KIND	POW.	ACC.	PP	RANGE

ABILITY

Levitate

—

HIDDEN ABILITY

SPECIES STRENGTHS

HP

ATTACK

DEFENSE

SP. ATK

SP. DEF

SPEED

DAMAGE TAKEN IN BATTLE

×1 / ×0.5 / ×0.5 / ×1 / ×0.5 / ×2 / ×2 / ×1 / ×1 / ×2 / ×1 / ×2 / ×0 / ×0.5 / ×1 / ×2 / ×2 / ×1

MINERAL

083 Claydol (p. 51)

ABILITY
Levitate
—

HIDDEN ABILITY
—

SPECIES STRENGTHS
HP
ATTACK
DEFENSE
SP. ATK
SP. DEF
SPEED

DAMAGE TAKEN IN BATTLE
×1 ×0.5 ×0.5
×1 ×0.5 ×2
×2 ×1 ×1
×2 ×1 ×2
×0 ×0.5 ×1
×2 ×2 ×1

MINERAL

LEVEL-UP MOVES

LV.	NAME	TYPE	KIND	POW.	ACC.	PP	RANGE
1	Confusion	Psychic	Special	50	100	25	Normal
1	Harden	Normal	Status	—	—	30	Self
1	Hyper Beam	Normal	Special	150	90	5	Normal
1	Mud-Slap	Ground	Special	20	100	10	Normal
1	Rapid Spin	Normal	Physical	50	100	40	Normal
1	Teleport	Psychic	Status	—	—	20	Self
9	Rock Tomb	Rock	Physical	60	95	15	Normal
12	Power Trick	Psychic	Status	—	—	10	Self
15	Psybeam	Psychic	Special	65	100	20	Normal
18	Ancient Power	Rock	Special	60	100	5	Normal
21	Imprison	Psychic	Status	—	—	10	Self
24	Cosmic Power	Psychic	Status	—	—	20	Self
27	Extrasensory	Psychic	Special	80	100	20	Normal
30	Earth Power	Ground	Special	90	100	10	Normal
33	Self-Destruct	Normal	Physical	200	100	5	All Others
38	Guard Split	Psychic	Status	—	—	10	Normal
38	Power Split	Psychic	Status	—	—	10	Normal
43	Sandstorm	Rock	Status	—	—	10	Both Sides
48	Explosion	Normal	Physical	250	100	5	All Others

EVOLUTION MOVES

NAME	TYPE	KIND	POW.	ACC.	PP	RANGE
Hyper Beam	Normal	Special	150	90	5	Normal

EGG MOVES

NAME	TYPE	KIND	POW.	ACC.	PP	RANGE

TUTOR MOVES

NAME	TYPE	KIND	POW.	ACC.	PP	RANGE

TM MOVES

NO.	NAME	TYPE	KIND	POW.	ACC.	PP	RANGE
TM08	Hyper Beam	Normal	Special	150	90	5	Normal
TM09	Giga Impact	Normal	Physical	150	90	5	Normal
TM11	Solar Beam	Grass	Special	120	100	10	Normal
TM15	Dig	Ground	Physical	80	100	10	Normal
TM17	Light Screen	Psychic	Status	—	—	30	Your Side
TM18	Reflect	Psychic	Status	—	—	20	Your Side
TM19	Safeguard	Normal	Status	—	—	25	Your Side
TM20	Self-Destruct	Normal	Physical	200	100	5	All Others
TM21	Rest	Psychic	Status	—	—	10	Self
TM22	Rock Slide	Rock	Physical	75	90	10	Many Others
TM24	Snore	Normal	Special	50	100	15	Normal
TM25	Protect	Normal	Status	—	—	10	Self
TM32	Sandstorm	Rock	Status	—	—	10	Both Sides
TM33	Rain Dance	Water	Status	—	—	5	Both Sides
TM34	Sunny Day	Fire	Status	—	—	5	Both Sides
TM39	Facade	Normal	Physical	70	100	20	Normal
TM44	Imprison	Psychic	Status	—	—	10	Self
TM48	Rock Tomb	Rock	Physical	60	95	15	Normal
TM49	Sand Tomb	Ground	Physical	35	85	15	Normal
TM60	Power Swap	Psychic	Status	—	—	10	Normal
TM61	Guard Swap	Psychic	Status	—	—	10	Normal
TM70	Trick Room	Psychic	Status	—	—	5	Both Sides
TM71	Wonder Room	Psychic	Status	—	—	10	Both Sides
TM76	Round	Normal	Special	60	100	15	Normal
TM77	Hex	Ghost	Special	65	100	10	Normal
TM81	Bulldoze	Ground	Physical	60	100	20	All Others
TM91	Psychic Terrain	Psychic	Status	—	—	10	Both Sides
TM93	Eerie Impulse	Electric	Status	—	100	15	Normal

TR MOVES

NAME	TYPE	KIND	POW.	ACC.	PP	RANGE
TR05 Ice Beam	Ice	Special	90	100	10	Normal
TR10 Earthquake	Ground	Physical	100	100	10	All Others
TR11 Psychic	Psychic	Special	90	100	10	Normal
TR20 Substitute	Normal	Status	—	—	10	Self
TR25 Psyshock	Psychic	Special	80	100	10	Normal
TR26 Endure	Normal	Status	—	—	10	Self
TR27 Sleep Talk	Normal	Status	—	—	10	Self
TR33 Shadow Ball	Ghost	Special	80	100	15	Normal
TR34 Future Sight	Psychic	Special	120	100	10	Normal
TR38 Trick	Psychic	Status	—	100	10	Normal
TR40 Skill Swap	Psychic	Status	—	—	10	Normal
TR44 Cosmic Power	Psychic	Status	—	—	20	Self
TR46 Iron Defense	Steel	Status	—	—	15	Self
TR49 Calm Mind	Psychic	Status	—	—	20	Self
TR52 Gyro Ball	Steel	Physical	—	100	5	Normal
TR67 Earth Power	Ground	Special	90	100	10	Normal
TR68 Nasty Plot	Dark	Status	—	—	20	Self
TR69 Zen Headbutt	Psychic	Physical	80	90	15	Normal
TR75 Stone Edge	Rock	Physical	100	80	5	Normal
TR76 Stealth Rock	Rock	Status	—	—	20	Other Side
TR77 Grass Knot	Grass	Special	—	100	20	Normal
TR82 Stored Power	Psychic	Special	20	100	10	Normal
TR83 Ally Switch	Psychic	Status	—	—	15	Self
TR87 Drill Run	Ground	Physical	80	95	10	Normal
TR92 Dazzling Gleam	Fairy	Special	80	100	10	Many Others
TR99 Body Press	Fighting	Physical	80	100	10	Normal

084 Mudbray (p. 51)

ABILITY
Own Tempo
Stamina

HIDDEN ABILITY
Inner Focus

SPECIES STRENGTHS
HP
ATTACK
DEFENSE
SP. ATK
SP. DEF
SPEED

DAMAGE TAKEN IN BATTLE
×1 ×1 ×0.5
×1 ×0.5 ×1
×2 ×1 ×1
×2 ×1 ×1
×0 ×1 ×1
×2 ×1 ×1

FIELD

LEVEL-UP MOVES

LV.	NAME	TYPE	KIND	POW.	ACC.	PP	RANGE
1	Mud-Slap	Ground	Special	20	100	10	Normal
1	Rock Smash	Fighting	Physical	40	100	15	Normal
4	Iron Defense	Steel	Status	—	—	15	Self
8	Double Kick	Fighting	Physical	30	100	30	Normal
12	Bulldoze	Ground	Physical	60	100	20	All Others
16	Stomp	Normal	Physical	65	100	20	Normal
20	Strength	Normal	Physical	80	100	15	Normal
24	Counter	Fighting	Physical	—	100	20	Varies
28	High Horsepower	Ground	Physical	95	95	10	Normal
32	Heavy Slam	Steel	Physical	—	100	10	Normal
36	Earthquake	Ground	Physical	100	100	10	All Others
40	Mega Kick	Normal	Physical	120	75	5	Normal
44	Superpower	Fighting	Physical	120	100	5	Normal

EVOLUTION MOVES

NAME	TYPE	KIND	POW.	ACC.	PP	RANGE

EGG MOVES

NAME	TYPE	KIND	POW.	ACC.	PP	RANGE
Double-Edge	Normal	Physical	120	100	15	Normal
Fissure	Ground	Physical	—	30	5	Normal
Roar	Normal	Status	—	—	20	Normal
Smack Down	Rock	Physical	50	100	15	Normal

TUTOR MOVES

NAME	TYPE	KIND	POW.	ACC.	PP	RANGE

TM MOVES

NO.	NAME	TYPE	KIND	POW.	ACC.	PP	RANGE
TM01	Mega Kick	Normal	Physical	120	75	5	Normal
TM21	Rest	Psychic	Status	—	—	10	Self
TM22	Rock Slide	Rock	Physical	75	90	10	Many Others
TM24	Snore	Normal	Special	50	100	15	Normal
TM25	Protect	Normal	Status	—	—	10	Self
TM31	Attract	Normal	Status	—	100	15	Normal
TM32	Sandstorm	Rock	Status	—	—	10	Both Sides
TM39	Facade	Normal	Physical	70	100	20	Normal
TM48	Rock Tomb	Rock	Physical	60	95	15	Normal
TM49	Sand Tomb	Ground	Physical	35	85	15	Normal
TM57	Payback	Dark	Physical	50	100	10	Normal
TM75	Low Sweep	Fighting	Physical	65	100	20	Normal
TM76	Round	Normal	Special	60	100	15	Normal
TM81	Bulldoze	Ground	Physical	60	100	20	All Others
TM98	Stomping Tantrum	Ground	Physical	75	100	10	Normal

TR MOVES

NAME	TYPE	KIND	POW.	ACC.	PP	RANGE
TR01 Body Slam	Normal	Physical	85	100	15	Normal
TR07 Low Kick	Fighting	Physical	—	100	20	Normal
TR10 Earthquake	Ground	Physical	100	100	10	All Others
TR20 Substitute	Normal	Status	—	—	10	Self
TR26 Endure	Normal	Status	—	—	10	Self
TR27 Sleep Talk	Normal	Status	—	—	10	Self
TR39 Superpower	Fighting	Physical	120	100	5	Normal
TR46 Iron Defense	Steel	Status	—	—	15	Self
TR53 Close Combat	Fighting	Physical	120	100	5	Normal
TR67 Earth Power	Ground	Special	90	100	10	Normal
TR74 Iron Head	Steel	Physical	80	100	15	Normal
TR76 Stealth Rock	Rock	Status	—	—	20	Other Side
TR79 Heavy Slam	Steel	Physical	—	100	10	Normal
TR94 High Horsepower	Ground	Physical	95	95	10	Normal

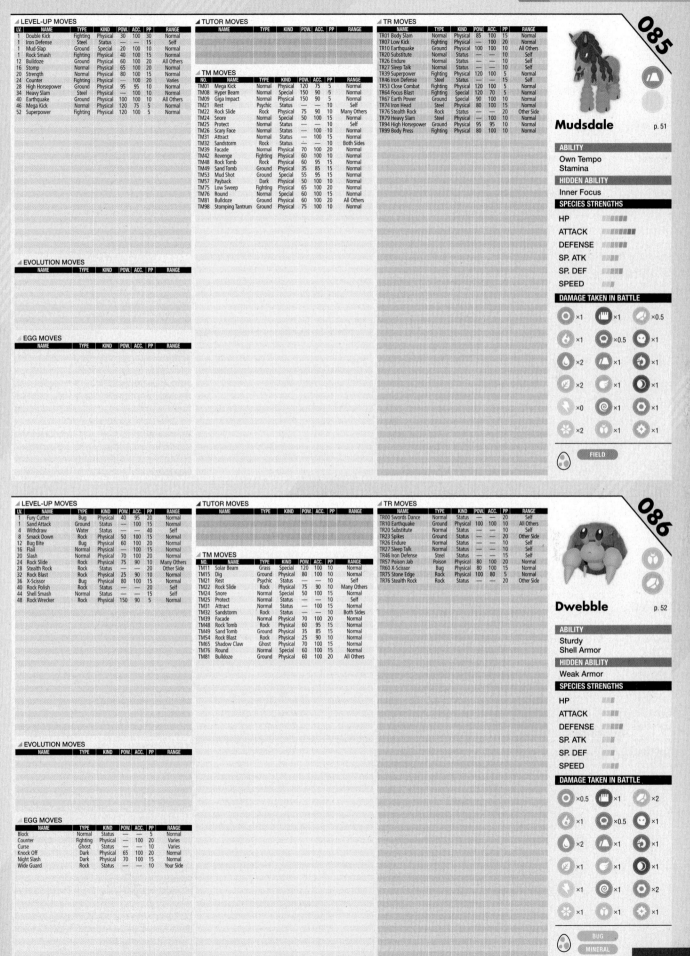

085 — Mudsdale

LEVEL-UP MOVES

LV.	NAME	TYPE	KIND	POW.	ACC.	PP	RANGE
1	Double Kick	Fighting	Physical	30	100	30	Normal
1	Iron Defense	Steel	Status	—	—	15	Self
1	Mud-Slap	Ground	Special	20	100	10	Normal
1	Rock Smash	Fighting	Physical	40	100	15	Normal
12	Bulldoze	Ground	Physical	60	100	20	All Others
16	Stomp	Normal	Physical	65	100	20	Normal
20	Strength	Normal	Physical	80	100	15	Normal
24	Counter	Fighting	Physical	—	100	20	Varies
28	High Horsepower	Ground	Physical	95	95	10	Normal
34	Heavy Slam	Steel	Physical	—	100	10	Normal
40	Earthquake	Ground	Physical	100	100	10	All Others
46	Mega Kick	Normal	Physical	120	75	5	Normal
52	Superpower	Fighting	Physical	120	100	5	Normal

EVOLUTION MOVES

NAME	TYPE	KIND	POW.	ACC.	PP	RANGE

EGG MOVES

NAME	TYPE	KIND	POW.	ACC.	PP	RANGE

TUTOR MOVES

NAME	TYPE	KIND	POW.	ACC.	PP	RANGE

TM MOVES

NO.	NAME	TYPE	KIND	POW.	ACC.	PP	RANGE
TM01	Mega Kick	Normal	Physical	120	75	5	Normal
TM08	Hyper Beam	Normal	Special	150	90	5	Normal
TM09	Giga Impact	Normal	Physical	150	90	5	Normal
TM21	Rest	Psychic	Status	—	—	10	Self
TM22	Rock Slide	Rock	Physical	75	90	10	Many Others
TM24	Snore	Normal	Special	50	100	15	Normal
TM25	Protect	Normal	Status	—	—	10	Self
TM26	Scary Face	Normal	Status	—	100	10	Normal
TM31	Attract	Normal	Status	—	100	15	Normal
TM32	Sandstorm	Rock	Status	—	—	10	Both Sides
TM39	Facade	Normal	Physical	70	100	20	Normal
TM42	Revenge	Fighting	Physical	60	100	10	Normal
TM48	Rock Tomb	Rock	Physical	60	95	15	Normal
TM49	Sand Tomb	Ground	Physical	35	85	15	Normal
TM53	Mud Shot	Ground	Special	55	95	15	Normal
TM57	Payback	Dark	Physical	50	100	10	Normal
TM75	Low Sweep	Fighting	Physical	65	100	20	Normal
TM76	Round	Normal	Special	60	100	15	Normal
TM81	Bulldoze	Ground	Physical	60	100	20	All Others
TM98	Stomping Tantrum	Ground	Physical	75	100	10	Normal

TR MOVES

NO.	NAME	TYPE	KIND	POW.	ACC.	PP	RANGE
TR01	Body Slam	Normal	Physical	85	100	15	Normal
TR07	Low Kick	Fighting	Physical	—	100	20	Normal
TR10	Earthquake	Ground	Physical	100	100	10	All Others
TR20	Substitute	Normal	Status	—	—	10	Self
TR26	Endure	Normal	Status	—	—	10	Self
TR27	Sleep Talk	Normal	Status	—	—	10	Self
TR39	Superpower	Fighting	Physical	120	100	5	Normal
TR46	Iron Defense	Steel	Status	—	—	15	Self
TR53	Close Combat	Fighting	Physical	120	100	5	Normal
TR64	Focus Blast	Fighting	Special	120	70	5	Normal
TR67	Earth Power	Ground	Special	90	100	10	Normal
TR74	Iron Head	Steel	Physical	80	100	15	Normal
TR76	Stealth Rock	Rock	Status	—	—	20	Other Side
TR79	Heavy Slam	Steel	Physical	—	100	10	Normal
TR94	High Horsepower	Ground	Physical	95	95	10	Normal
TR99	Body Press	Fighting	Physical	80	100	10	Normal

Mudsdale — p. 51

ABILITY
Own Tempo
Stamina

HIDDEN ABILITY
Inner Focus

SPECIES STRENGTHS
HP
ATTACK
DEFENSE
SP. ATK
SP. DEF
SPEED

DAMAGE TAKEN IN BATTLE

×1 ×1 ×0.5
×1 ×0.5 ×1
×2 ×1 ×1
×1 ×1 ×1
×0 ×1 ×1
×2 ×1 ×1

FIELD

086 — Dwebble

LEVEL-UP MOVES

LV.	NAME	TYPE	KIND	POW.	ACC.	PP	RANGE
1	Fury Cutter	Bug	Physical	40	95	20	Normal
1	Sand Attack	Ground	Status	—	100	15	Normal
4	Withdraw	Water	Status	—	—	40	Self
8	Smack Down	Rock	Physical	50	100	15	Normal
12	Bug Bite	Bug	Physical	60	100	20	Normal
16	Flail	Normal	Physical	—	100	15	Normal
20	Slash	Normal	Physical	70	100	20	Normal
24	Rock Slide	Rock	Physical	75	90	10	Many Others
28	Stealth Rock	Rock	Status	—	—	20	Other Side
32	Rock Blast	Rock	Physical	25	90	10	Normal
36	X-Scissor	Bug	Physical	80	100	15	Normal
40	Rock Polish	Rock	Status	—	—	20	Self
44	Shell Smash	Normal	Status	—	—	15	Self
48	Rock Wrecker	Rock	Physical	150	90	5	Normal

EVOLUTION MOVES

NAME	TYPE	KIND	POW.	ACC.	PP	RANGE

EGG MOVES

NAME	TYPE	KIND	POW.	ACC.	PP	RANGE
Block	Normal	Status	—	—	5	Normal
Counter	Fighting	Physical	—	100	20	Varies
Curse	Ghost	Status	—	—	10	Varies
Knock Off	Dark	Physical	65	100	20	Normal
Night Slash	Dark	Physical	70	100	15	Normal
Wide Guard	Rock	Status	—	—	10	Your Side

TUTOR MOVES

NAME	TYPE	KIND	POW.	ACC.	PP	RANGE

TM MOVES

NO.	NAME	TYPE	KIND	POW.	ACC.	PP	RANGE
TM11	Solar Beam	Grass	Special	120	100	10	Normal
TM15	Dig	Ground	Physical	80	100	10	Normal
TM21	Rest	Psychic	Status	—	—	10	Self
TM22	Rock Slide	Rock	Physical	75	90	10	Many Others
TM24	Snore	Normal	Special	50	100	15	Normal
TM25	Protect	Normal	Status	—	—	10	Self
TM31	Attract	Normal	Status	—	100	15	Normal
TM32	Sandstorm	Rock	Status	—	—	10	Both Sides
TM39	Facade	Normal	Physical	70	100	20	Normal
TM48	Rock Tomb	Rock	Physical	60	95	15	Normal
TM49	Sand Tomb	Ground	Physical	35	85	15	Normal
TM54	Rock Blast	Rock	Physical	25	90	10	Normal
TM65	Shadow Claw	Ghost	Physical	70	100	15	Normal
TM76	Round	Normal	Special	60	100	15	Normal
TM81	Bulldoze	Ground	Physical	60	100	20	All Others

TR MOVES

NO.	NAME	TYPE	KIND	POW.	ACC.	PP	RANGE
TR00	Swords Dance	Normal	Status	—	—	20	Self
TR10	Earthquake	Ground	Physical	100	100	10	All Others
TR20	Substitute	Normal	Status	—	—	10	Self
TR23	Spikes	Ground	Status	—	—	20	Other Side
TR26	Endure	Normal	Status	—	—	10	Self
TR27	Sleep Talk	Normal	Status	—	—	10	Self
TR46	Iron Defense	Steel	Status	—	—	15	Self
TR57	Poison Jab	Poison	Physical	80	100	20	Normal
TR60	X-Scissor	Bug	Physical	80	100	15	Normal
TR75	Stone Edge	Rock	Physical	100	80	5	Normal
TR76	Stealth Rock	Rock	Status	—	—	20	Other Side

Dwebble — p. 52

ABILITY
Sturdy
Shell Armor

HIDDEN ABILITY
Weak Armor

SPECIES STRENGTHS
HP
ATTACK
DEFENSE
SP. ATK
SP. DEF
SPEED

DAMAGE TAKEN IN BATTLE

×0.5 ×1 ×2
×1 ×0.5 ×1
×2 ×1 ×1
×1 ×1 ×1
×1 ×1 ×2
×1 ×1 ×1

BUG
MINERAL

087 Crustle

p. 52

ABILITY
Sturdy
Shell Armor

HIDDEN ABILITY
Weak Armor

SPECIES STRENGTHS
HP
ATTACK
DEFENSE
SP. ATK
SP. DEF
SPEED

DAMAGE TAKEN IN BATTLE

◎ ×0.5	▦ ×1	✎ ×2
◔ ×1	◉ ×0.5	✺ ×1
◐ ×2	◭ ×1	⟳ ×1
◢ ×1	◔ ×1	☾ ×1
⚡ ×1	◎ ×1	◉ ×2
✳ ×1	⬡ ×1	◈ ×1

BUG
MINERAL

LEVEL-UP MOVES

LV.	NAME	TYPE	KIND	POW.	ACC.	PP	RANGE
1	Fury Cutter	Bug	Physical	40	95	20	Normal
1	Sand Attack	Ground	Status	—	100	15	Normal
1	Smack Down	Rock	Physical	50	100	15	Normal
1	Withdraw	Water	Status	—	—	40	Self
12	Bug Bite	Bug	Physical	60	100	20	Normal
16	Flail	Normal	Physical	—	100	15	Normal
20	Slash	Normal	Physical	70	100	20	Normal
24	Rock Slide	Rock	Physical	75	90	10	Many Others
28	Stealth Rock	Rock	Status	—	—	20	Other Side
32	Rock Blast	Rock	Physical	25	90	10	Normal
38	X-Scissor	Bug	Physical	80	100	15	Normal
44	Rock Polish	Rock	Status	—	—	20	Self
50	Shell Smash	Normal	Status	—	—	15	Self
56	Rock Wrecker	Rock	Physical	150	90	5	Normal

TUTOR MOVES

NAME	TYPE	KIND	POW.	ACC.	PP	RANGE

TM MOVES

NO.	NAME	TYPE	KIND	POW.	ACC.	PP	RANGE
TM08	Hyper Beam	Normal	Special	150	90	5	Normal
TM09	Giga Impact	Normal	Physical	150	90	5	Normal
TM11	Solar Beam	Grass	Special	120	100	10	Normal
TM12	Solar Blade	Grass	Physical	125	100	10	Normal
TM15	Dig	Ground	Physical	80	100	10	Normal
TM21	Rest	Psychic	Status	—	—	10	Self
TM22	Rock Slide	Rock	Physical	75	90	10	Many Others
TM24	Snore	Normal	Special	50	100	15	Normal
TM25	Protect	Normal	Status	—	—	10	Self
TM31	Attract	Normal	Status	—	100	15	Normal
TM32	Sandstorm	Rock	Status	—	—	10	Both Sides
TM39	Facade	Normal	Physical	70	100	20	Normal
TM48	Rock Tomb	Rock	Physical	60	95	15	Normal
TM49	Sand Tomb	Ground	Physical	35	85	15	Normal
TM54	Rock Blast	Rock	Physical	25	90	10	Normal
TM65	Shadow Claw	Ghost	Physical	70	100	15	Normal
TM76	Round	Normal	Special	60	100	15	Normal
TM81	Bulldoze	Ground	Physical	60	100	20	All Others
TM98	Stomping Tantrum	Ground	Physical	75	100	10	Normal

TR MOVES

NO.	NAME	TYPE	KIND	POW.	ACC.	PP	RANGE
TR00	Swords Dance	Normal	Status	—	—	20	Self
TR10	Earthquake	Ground	Physical	100	100	10	All Others
TR20	Substitute	Normal	Status	—	—	10	Self
TR23	Spikes	Ground	Status	—	—	20	Other Side
TR26	Endure	Normal	Status	—	—	10	Self
TR27	Sleep Talk	Normal	Status	—	—	10	Self
TR57	Poison Jab	Poison	Physical	80	100	20	Normal
TR60	X-Scissor	Bug	Physical	80	100	15	Normal
TR75	Stone Edge	Rock	Physical	100	80	5	Normal
TR76	Stealth Rock	Rock	Status	—	—	20	Other Side
TR79	Heavy Slam	Steel	Physical	—	100	10	Normal
TR99	Body Press	Fighting	Physical	80	100	10	Normal

EVOLUTION MOVES

NAME	TYPE	KIND	POW.	ACC.	PP	RANGE

EGG MOVES

NAME	TYPE	KIND	POW.	ACC.	PP	RANGE

---

088 Golett

p. 52

ABILITY
Iron Fist
Klutz

HIDDEN ABILITY
No Guard

SPECIES STRENGTHS
HP
ATTACK
DEFENSE
SP. ATK
SP. DEF
SPEED

DAMAGE TAKEN IN BATTLE

◎ ×0	▦ ×0	✎ ×0.5
◔ ×1	◉ ×0.25	✺ ×2
◐ ×2	◭ ×1	⟳ ×1
◢ ×2	◔ ×1	☾ ×2
⚡ ×0	◎ ×1	◉ ×2
✳ ×1	⬡ ×0.5	◈ ×1

MINERAL

LEVEL-UP MOVES

LV.	NAME	TYPE	KIND	POW.	ACC.	PP	RANGE
1	Astonish	Ghost	Physical	30	100	15	Normal
1	Mud-Slap	Ground	Special	20	100	10	Normal
4	Defense Curl	Normal	Status	—	—	40	Self
8	Pound	Normal	Physical	40	100	35	Normal
12	Shadow Punch	Ghost	Physical	60	—	20	Normal
16	Curse	Ghost	Status	—	—	10	Varies
20	Night Shade	Ghost	Special	—	100	15	Normal
24	Stomping Tantrum	Ground	Physical	75	100	10	Normal
28	Iron Defense	Steel	Status	—	—	15	Self
32	Mega Punch	Normal	Physical	80	85	20	Normal
36	Shadow Ball	Ghost	Special	80	100	15	Normal
40	Heavy Slam	Steel	Physical	—	100	10	Normal
44	Phantom Force	Ghost	Physical	90	100	10	Normal
48	Hammer Arm	Fighting	Physical	100	90	10	Normal
52	Earthquake	Ground	Physical	100	100	10	All Others
56	Dynamic Punch	Fighting	Physical	100	50	5	Normal

TUTOR MOVES

NAME	TYPE	KIND	POW.	ACC.	PP	RANGE

TM MOVES

NO.	NAME	TYPE	KIND	POW.	ACC.	PP	RANGE
TM00	Mega Punch	Normal	Physical	80	85	20	Normal
TM01	Mega Kick	Normal	Physical	120	75	5	Normal
TM03	Fire Punch	Fire	Physical	75	100	15	Normal
TM04	Ice Punch	Ice	Physical	75	100	15	Normal
TM05	Thunder Punch	Electric	Physical	75	100	15	Normal
TM15	Dig	Ground	Physical	80	100	10	Normal
TM19	Safeguard	Normal	Status	—	—	25	Your Side
TM20	Self-Destruct	Normal	Physical	200	100	5	All Others
TM21	Rest	Psychic	Status	—	—	10	Self
TM22	Rock Slide	Rock	Physical	75	90	10	Many Others
TM23	Thief	Dark	Physical	60	100	25	Normal
TM24	Snore	Normal	Special	50	100	15	Normal
TM25	Protect	Normal	Status	—	—	10	Self
TM27	Icy Wind	Ice	Special	55	95	15	Many Others
TM33	Rain Dance	Water	Status	—	—	5	Both Sides
TM39	Facade	Normal	Physical	70	100	20	Normal
TM41	Helping Hand	Normal	Status	—	—	20	1 Ally
TM43	Brick Break	Fighting	Physical	75	100	15	Normal
TM44	Imprison	Psychic	Status	—	—	10	Self
TM48	Rock Tomb	Rock	Physical	60	95	15	Normal
TM59	Fling	Dark	Physical	—	100	10	Normal
TM63	Drain Punch	Fighting	Physical	75	100	10	Normal
TM75	Low Sweep	Fighting	Physical	65	100	20	Normal
TM76	Round	Normal	Special	60	100	15	Normal
TM81	Bulldoze	Ground	Physical	60	100	20	All Others
TM86	Phantom Force	Ghost	Physical	90	100	10	Normal
TM98	Stomping Tantrum	Ground	Physical	75	100	10	Normal

TR MOVES

NO.	NAME	TYPE	KIND	POW.	ACC.	PP	RANGE
TR05	Ice Beam	Ice	Special	90	100	10	Normal
TR07	Low Kick	Fighting	Physical	—	100	20	Normal
TR10	Earthquake	Ground	Physical	100	100	10	All Others
TR11	Psychic	Psychic	Special	90	100	10	Normal
TR20	Substitute	Normal	Status	—	—	10	Self
TR26	Endure	Normal	Status	—	—	10	Self
TR27	Sleep Talk	Normal	Status	—	—	10	Self
TR33	Shadow Ball	Ghost	Special	80	100	15	Normal
TR39	Superpower	Fighting	Physical	120	100	5	Normal
TR46	Iron Defense	Steel	Status	—	—	15	Self
TR52	Gyro Ball	Steel	Physical	—	100	5	Normal
TR64	Focus Blast	Fighting	Special	120	70	5	Normal
TR67	Earth Power	Ground	Special	90	100	10	Normal
TR76	Stealth Rock	Rock	Status	—	—	20	Other Side
TR77	Grass Knot	Grass	Special	—	100	20	Normal
TR79	Heavy Slam	Steel	Physical	—	100	10	Normal
TR83	Ally Switch	Psychic	Status	—	—	15	Self

EVOLUTION MOVES

NAME	TYPE	KIND	POW.	ACC.	PP	RANGE

EGG MOVES

NAME	TYPE	KIND	POW.	ACC.	PP	RANGE

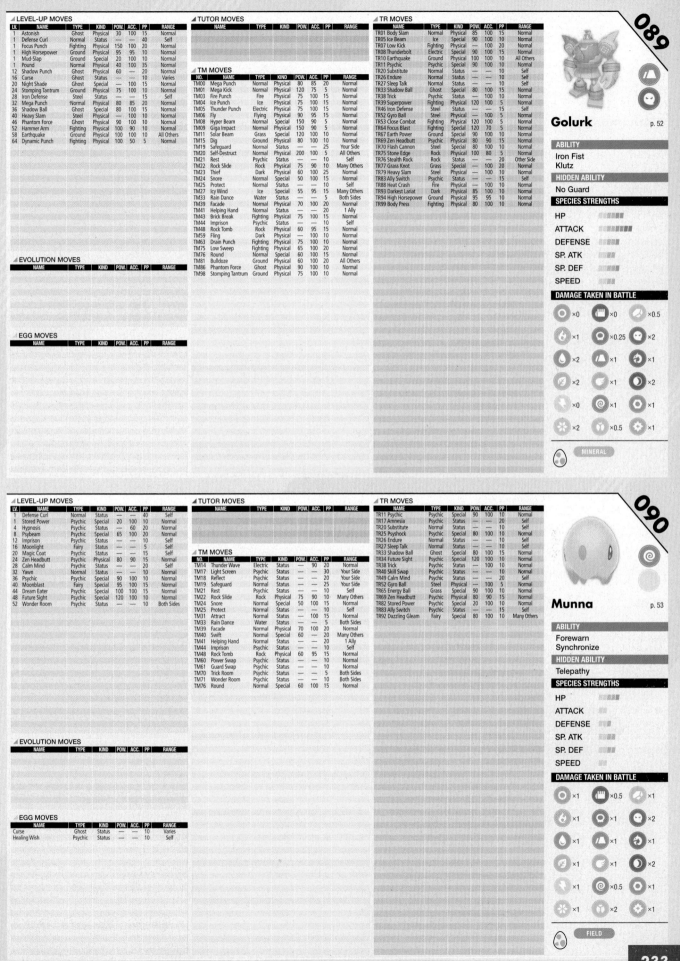

089 — Golurk (p. 52)

ABILITY: Iron Fist, Klutz
HIDDEN ABILITY: No Guard

LEVEL-UP MOVES

LV.	NAME	TYPE	KIND	POW.	ACC.	PP	RANGE
1	Astonish	Ghost	Physical	30	100	15	Normal
1	Defense Curl	Normal	Status	—	—	40	Normal
1	Focus Punch	Fighting	Physical	150	100	20	Normal
1	High Horsepower	Ground	Physical	95	95	10	Normal
1	Mud-Slap	Ground	Special	20	100	10	Normal
1	Pound	Normal	Physical	40	100	35	Normal
12	Shadow Punch	Ghost	Physical	60	—	20	Normal
16	Curse	Ghost	Status	—	—	10	Varies
20	Night Shade	Ghost	Special	—	100	15	Normal
24	Stomping Tantrum	Ground	Physical	75	100	10	Normal
28	Iron Defense	Steel	Status	—	—	15	Self
32	Mega Punch	Normal	Physical	80	85	20	Normal
36	Shadow Ball	Ghost	Special	80	100	15	Normal
40	Heavy Slam	Steel	Physical	—	100	10	Normal
46	Phantom Force	Ghost	Physical	90	100	10	Normal
52	Hammer Arm	Fighting	Physical	100	90	10	Normal
58	Earthquake	Ground	Physical	100	100	10	All Others
64	Dynamic Punch	Fighting	Physical	100	50	5	Normal

EVOLUTION MOVES

(none)

EGG MOVES

(none)

TUTOR MOVES

(none)

TM MOVES

NO.	NAME	TYPE	KIND	POW.	ACC.	PP	RANGE
TM00	Mega Punch	Normal	Physical	80	85	20	Normal
TM01	Mega Kick	Normal	Physical	120	75	5	Normal
TM03	Fire Punch	Fire	Physical	75	100	15	Normal
TM04	Ice Punch	Ice	Physical	75	100	15	Normal
TM05	Thunder Punch	Electric	Physical	75	100	15	Normal
TM06	Fly	Flying	Physical	90	95	15	Normal
TM08	Hyper Beam	Normal	Special	150	90	5	Normal
TM09	Giga Impact	Normal	Physical	150	90	5	Normal
TM11	Solar Beam	Grass	Special	120	100	10	Normal
TM15	Dig	Ground	Physical	80	100	10	Normal
TM19	Safeguard	Normal	Status	—	—	25	Your Side
TM20	Self-Destruct	Normal	Physical	200	100	5	All Others
TM21	Rest	Psychic	Status	—	—	10	Self
TM22	Rock Slide	Rock	Physical	75	90	10	Many Others
TM23	Thief	Dark	Physical	60	100	25	Normal
TM24	Snore	Normal	Special	50	100	15	Normal
TM25	Protect	Normal	Status	—	—	10	Self
TM27	Icy Wind	Ice	Special	55	95	15	Many Others
TM33	Rain Dance	Water	Status	—	—	5	Both Sides
TM39	Facade	Normal	Physical	70	100	20	Normal
TM41	Helping Hand	Normal	Status	—	—	20	1 Ally
TM43	Brick Break	Fighting	Physical	75	100	15	Normal
TM44	Imprison	Psychic	Status	—	—	10	Self
TM48	Rock Tomb	Rock	Physical	60	95	15	Normal
TM59	Fling	Dark	Physical	—	100	10	Normal
TM63	Drain Punch	Fighting	Physical	75	100	10	Normal
TM75	Low Sweep	Fighting	Physical	65	100	20	Normal
TM76	Round	Normal	Special	60	100	15	Normal
TM81	Bulldoze	Ground	Physical	60	100	20	All Others
TM86	Phantom Force	Ghost	Physical	90	100	10	Normal
TM98	Stomping Tantrum	Ground	Physical	75	100	10	Normal

TR MOVES

NO.	NAME	TYPE	KIND	POW.	ACC.	PP	RANGE
TR01	Body Slam	Normal	Physical	85	100	15	Normal
TR05	Ice Beam	Ice	Special	90	100	10	Normal
TR08	Thunderbolt	Electric	Special	90	100	15	Normal
TR10	Earthquake	Ground	Physical	100	100	10	All Others
TR11	Psychic	Psychic	Special	90	100	10	Normal
TR20	Substitute	Normal	Status	—	—	10	Self
TR26	Endure	Normal	Status	—	—	10	Self
TR27	Sleep Talk	Normal	Status	—	—	10	Self
TR33	Shadow Ball	Ghost	Special	80	100	15	Normal
TR38	Trick	Psychic	Status	—	100	10	Normal
TR39	Superpower	Fighting	Physical	120	100	5	Normal
TR46	Iron Defense	Steel	Status	—	—	15	Self
TR52	Gyro Ball	Steel	Physical	—	100	5	Normal
TR53	Close Combat	Fighting	Physical	120	100	5	Normal
TR64	Focus Blast	Fighting	Special	120	70	5	Normal
TR67	Earth Power	Ground	Special	90	100	10	Normal
TR69	Zen Headbutt	Psychic	Physical	80	90	15	Normal
TR70	Flash Cannon	Steel	Special	80	100	10	Normal
TR75	Stone Edge	Rock	Physical	100	80	5	Normal
TR76	Stealth Rock	Rock	Status	—	—	20	Other Side
TR77	Grass Knot	Grass	Special	—	100	20	Normal
TR79	Heavy Slam	Steel	Physical	—	100	10	Normal
TR83	Ally Switch	Psychic	Status	—	—	15	Self
TR88	Heat Crash	Fire	Physical	—	100	10	Normal
TR93	Darkest Lariat	Dark	Physical	85	100	10	Normal
TR94	High Horsepower	Ground	Physical	95	95	10	Normal
TR99	Body Press	Fighting	Physical	80	100	10	Normal

SPECIES STRENGTHS: HP, ATTACK, DEFENSE, SP. ATK, SP. DEF, SPEED

DAMAGE TAKEN IN BATTLE: ×0, ×0, ×0.5, ×2, ×0.25, ×2, ×2, ×1, ×1, ×2, ×1, ×1, ×0, ×1, ×1, ×2, ×0.5, ×1

Egg group: MINERAL

---

090 — Munna (p. 53)

ABILITY: Forewarn, Synchronize
HIDDEN ABILITY: Telepathy

LEVEL-UP MOVES

LV.	NAME	TYPE	KIND	POW.	ACC.	PP	RANGE
1	Defense Curl	Normal	Status	—	—	40	Self
1	Stored Power	Psychic	Special	20	100	10	Normal
4	Hypnosis	Psychic	Status	—	60	20	Normal
8	Psybeam	Psychic	Special	65	100	10	Normal
12	Imprison	Psychic	Status	—	—	10	Self
16	Moonlight	Fairy	Status	—	—	5	Self
20	Magic Coat	Psychic	Status	—	—	15	Self
24	Zen Headbutt	Psychic	Physical	80	90	15	Normal
28	Calm Mind	Psychic	Status	—	—	20	Self
32	Yawn	Normal	Status	—	—	10	Normal
36	Psychic	Psychic	Special	90	100	10	Normal
40	Moonblast	Fairy	Special	95	100	15	Normal
44	Dream Eater	Psychic	Special	100	100	15	Normal
48	Future Sight	Psychic	Special	120	100	10	Normal
52	Wonder Room	Psychic	Status	—	—	10	Both Sides

EVOLUTION MOVES

(none)

EGG MOVES

NAME	TYPE	KIND	POW.	ACC.	PP	RANGE
Curse	Ghost	Status	—	—	10	Varies
Healing Wish	Psychic	Status	—	—	10	Self

TUTOR MOVES

(none)

TM MOVES

NO.	NAME	TYPE	KIND	POW.	ACC.	PP	RANGE
TM14	Thunder Wave	Electric	Status	—	90	20	Normal
TM17	Light Screen	Psychic	Status	—	—	30	Your Side
TM18	Reflect	Psychic	Status	—	—	20	Your Side
TM19	Safeguard	Normal	Status	—	—	25	Your Side
TM21	Rest	Psychic	Status	—	—	10	Self
TM22	Rock Slide	Rock	Physical	75	90	10	Many Others
TM24	Snore	Normal	Special	50	100	15	Normal
TM25	Protect	Normal	Status	—	—	10	Self
TM31	Attract	Normal	Status	—	100	15	Normal
TM33	Rain Dance	Water	Status	—	—	5	Both Sides
TM39	Facade	Normal	Physical	70	100	20	Normal
TM40	Swift	Normal	Special	60	—	20	Many Others
TM41	Helping Hand	Normal	Status	—	—	20	1 Ally
TM44	Imprison	Psychic	Status	—	—	10	Self
TM48	Rock Tomb	Rock	Physical	60	95	15	Normal
TM60	Power Swap	Psychic	Status	—	—	10	Normal
TM61	Guard Swap	Psychic	Status	—	—	10	Normal
TM70	Trick Room	Psychic	Status	—	—	5	Both Sides
TM71	Wonder Room	Psychic	Status	—	—	10	Both Sides
TM76	Round	Normal	Special	60	100	15	Normal

TR MOVES

NO.	NAME	TYPE	KIND	POW.	ACC.	PP	RANGE
TR11	Psychic	Psychic	Special	90	100	10	Normal
TR17	Amnesia	Psychic	Status	—	—	10	Self
TR20	Substitute	Normal	Status	—	—	10	Self
TR25	Psyshock	Psychic	Special	80	100	10	Normal
TR26	Endure	Normal	Status	—	—	10	Self
TR27	Sleep Talk	Normal	Status	—	—	10	Self
TR33	Shadow Ball	Ghost	Special	80	100	15	Normal
TR34	Future Sight	Psychic	Special	120	100	10	Normal
TR38	Trick	Psychic	Status	—	100	10	Normal
TR40	Skill Swap	Psychic	Status	—	—	10	Normal
TR49	Calm Mind	Psychic	Status	—	—	20	Self
TR52	Gyro Ball	Steel	Physical	—	100	5	Normal
TR69	Zen Headbutt	Psychic	Physical	80	90	15	Normal
TR82	Stored Power	Psychic	Physical	20	100	10	Normal
TR83	Ally Switch	Psychic	Status	—	—	15	Self
TR92	Dazzling Gleam	Fairy	Special	80	100	10	Many Others

SPECIES STRENGTHS: HP, ATTACK, DEFENSE, SP. ATK, SP. DEF, SPEED

DAMAGE TAKEN IN BATTLE: ×1, ×0.5, ×1, ×1, ×1, ×2, ×1, ×1, ×1, ×1, ×1, ×2, ×1, ×0.5, ×1, ×2, ×2, ×1

Egg group: FIELD

091

Musharna p. 53

ABILITY
Forewarn
Synchronize

HIDDEN ABILITY
Telepathy

SPECIES STRENGTHS
HP
ATTACK
DEFENSE
SP. ATK
SP. DEF
SPEED

DAMAGE TAKEN IN BATTLE
×1　×0.5　×1
×1　×1　×2
×1　×1　×1
×1　×1　×2
×1　×0.5　×1
×1　×2　×1

FIELD

LEVEL-UP MOVES

LV.	NAME	TYPE	KIND	POW.	ACC.	PP	RANGE
1	Calm Mind	Psychic	Status	—	—	20	Self
1	Defense Curl	Normal	Status	—	—	40	Self
1	Dream Eater	Psychic	Special	100	100	15	Normal
1	Future Sight	Psychic	Special	120	100	10	Normal
1	Hypnosis	Psychic	Status	—	60	20	Normal
1	Imprison	Psychic	Status	—	—	10	Self
1	Magic Coat	Psychic	Status	—	—	15	Self
1	Moonblast	Fairy	Special	95	100	15	Normal
1	Moonlight	Fairy	Status	—	—	5	Self
1	Psybeam	Psychic	Special	65	100	20	Normal
1	Psychic	Psychic	Special	90	100	10	Normal
1	Psychic Terrain	Psychic	Status	—	—	10	Both Sides
1	Stored Power	Psychic	Special	20	100	10	Normal
1	Wonder Room	Psychic	Status	—	—	10	Both Sides
1	Yawn	Normal	Status	—	—	10	Normal
1	Zen Headbutt	Psychic	Physical	80	90	15	Normal

TUTOR MOVES

NAME	TYPE	KIND	POW.	ACC.	PP	RANGE

TM MOVES

NO.	NAME	TYPE	KIND	POW.	ACC.	PP	RANGE
TM08	Hyper Beam	Normal	Special	150	90	5	Normal
TM09	Giga Impact	Normal	Physical	150	90	5	Normal
TM14	Thunder Wave	Electric	Status	—	90	20	Normal
TM17	Light Screen	Psychic	Status	—	—	30	Your Side
TM18	Reflect	Psychic	Status	—	—	20	Your Side
TM19	Safeguard	Normal	Status	—	—	25	Your Side
TM21	Rest	Psychic	Status	—	—	10	Self
TM22	Rock Slide	Rock	Physical	75	90	10	Many Others
TM24	Snore	Normal	Special	50	100	15	Normal
TM25	Protect	Normal	Status	—	—	10	Self
TM31	Attract	Normal	Status	—	100	15	Normal
TM33	Rain Dance	Water	Status	—	—	5	Both Sides
TM39	Facade	Normal	Physical	70	100	20	Normal
TM40	Swift	Normal	Special	60	—	20	Many Others
TM41	Helping Hand	Normal	Status	—	—	20	1 Ally
TM44	Imprison	Psychic	Status	—	—	10	Self
TM48	Rock Tomb	Rock	Physical	60	95	15	Normal
TM60	Power Swap	Psychic	Status	—	—	10	Normal
TM61	Guard Swap	Psychic	Status	—	—	10	Normal
TM70	Trick Room	Psychic	Status	—	—	5	Both Sides
TM71	Wonder Room	Psychic	Status	—	—	10	Both Sides
TM76	Round	Normal	Special	60	100	15	Normal
TM91	Psychic Terrain	Psychic	Status	—	—	10	Both Sides

TR MOVES

NAME	TYPE	KIND	POW.	ACC.	PP	RANGE
TR11 Psychic	Psychic	Special	90	100	10	Normal
TR17 Amnesia	Psychic	Status	—	—	20	Self
TR20 Substitute	Normal	Status	—	—	10	Self
TR25 Psyshock	Psychic	Special	80	100	10	Normal
TR26 Endure	Normal	Status	—	—	10	Self
TR27 Sleep Talk	Normal	Status	—	—	10	Self
TR33 Shadow Ball	Ghost	Special	80	100	15	Normal
TR34 Future Sight	Psychic	Special	120	100	10	Normal
TR38 Trick	Psychic	Status	—	100	10	Normal
TR40 Skill Swap	Psychic	Status	—	—	10	Normal
TR49 Calm Mind	Psychic	Status	—	—	20	Self
TR52 Gyro Ball	Steel	Physical	—	100	5	Normal
TR65 Energy Ball	Grass	Special	90	100	10	Normal
TR69 Zen Headbutt	Psychic	Physical	80	90	15	Normal
TR82 Stored Power	Psychic	Special	20	100	10	Normal
TR83 Ally Switch	Psychic	Status	—	—	15	Self
TR92 Dazzling Gleam	Fairy	Special	80	100	10	Many Others

EVOLUTION MOVES

NAME	TYPE	KIND	POW.	ACC.	PP	RANGE

EGG MOVES

NAME	TYPE	KIND	POW.	ACC.	PP	RANGE

092

Natu p. 53

ABILITY
Synchronize
Early Bird

HIDDEN ABILITY
Magic Bounce

SPECIES STRENGTHS
HP
ATTACK
DEFENSE
SP. ATK
SP. DEF
SPEED

DAMAGE TAKEN IN BATTLE
×1　×0.25　×2
×1　×1　×2
×1　×0　×1
×0.5　×1　×2
×2　×0.5　×1
×2　×1　×1

FLYING

LEVEL-UP MOVES

LV.	NAME	TYPE	KIND	POW.	ACC.	PP	RANGE
1	Leer	Normal	Status	—	100	30	Many Others
1	Peck	Flying	Physical	35	100	35	Normal
5	Stored Power	Psychic	Special	20	100	10	Normal
10	Teleport	Psychic	Status	—	—	20	Self
15	Confuse Ray	Ghost	Status	—	100	10	Normal
20	Night Shade	Ghost	Special	—	100	15	Normal
26	Psycho Shift	Psychic	Status	—	100	10	Normal
30	Power Swap	Psychic	Status	—	—	10	Normal
35	Guard Swap	Psychic	Status	—	—	10	Normal
35	Psychic	Psychic	Special	90	100	10	Normal
40	Wish	Normal	Status	—	—	10	Self
45	Future Sight	Psychic	Special	120	100	10	Normal

TUTOR MOVES

NAME	TYPE	KIND	POW.	ACC.	PP	RANGE

TM MOVES

NO.	NAME	TYPE	KIND	POW.	ACC.	PP	RANGE
TM11	Solar Beam	Grass	Special	120	100	10	Normal
TM14	Thunder Wave	Electric	Status	—	90	20	Normal
TM17	Light Screen	Psychic	Status	—	—	30	Your Side
TM18	Reflect	Psychic	Status	—	—	20	Your Side
TM21	Rest	Psychic	Status	—	—	10	Self
TM23	Thief	Dark	Physical	60	100	25	Normal
TM24	Snore	Normal	Special	50	100	15	Normal
TM25	Protect	Normal	Status	—	—	10	Self
TM28	Giga Drain	Grass	Special	75	100	10	Normal
TM30	Steel Wing	Steel	Physical	70	90	25	Normal
TM31	Attract	Normal	Status	—	100	15	Normal
TM33	Rain Dance	Water	Status	—	—	5	Both Sides
TM34	Sunny Day	Fire	Status	—	—	5	Both Sides
TM39	Facade	Normal	Physical	70	100	20	Normal
TM40	Swift	Normal	Special	60	—	20	Many Others
TM44	Imprison	Psychic	Status	—	—	10	Self
TM56	U-turn	Bug	Physical	70	100	20	Normal
TM60	Power Swap	Psychic	Status	—	—	10	Normal
TM61	Guard Swap	Psychic	Status	—	—	10	Normal
TM70	Trick Room	Psychic	Status	—	—	5	Both Sides
TM72	Magic Room	Psychic	Status	—	—	10	Both Sides
TM76	Round	Normal	Special	60	100	15	Normal
TM95	Air Slash	Flying	Special	75	95	15	Normal

TR MOVES

NAME	TYPE	KIND	POW.	ACC.	PP	RANGE
TR11 Psychic	Psychic	Special	90	100	10	Normal
TR20 Substitute	Normal	Status	—	—	10	Self
TR25 Psyshock	Psychic	Special	80	100	10	Normal
TR26 Endure	Normal	Status	—	—	10	Self
TR27 Sleep Talk	Normal	Status	—	—	10	Self
TR29 Baton Pass	Normal	Status	—	—	40	Self
TR33 Shadow Ball	Ghost	Special	80	100	15	Normal
TR34 Future Sight	Psychic	Special	120	100	10	Normal
TR36 Heat Wave	Fire	Special	95	90	10	Many Others
TR38 Trick	Psychic	Status	—	100	10	Normal
TR40 Skill Swap	Psychic	Status	—	—	10	Normal
TR44 Cosmic Power	Psychic	Status	—	—	20	Self
TR49 Calm Mind	Psychic	Status	—	—	20	Self
TR69 Zen Headbutt	Psychic	Physical	80	90	15	Normal
TR77 Grass Knot	Grass	Special	—	100	20	Normal
TR82 Stored Power	Psychic	Special	20	100	10	Normal
TR83 Ally Switch	Psychic	Status	—	—	15	Self
TR92 Dazzling Gleam	Fairy	Special	80	100	10	Many Others

EVOLUTION MOVES

NAME	TYPE	KIND	POW.	ACC.	PP	RANGE

EGG MOVES

NAME	TYPE	KIND	POW.	ACC.	PP	RANGE
Drill Peck	Flying	Physical	80	100	20	Normal
Feather Dance	Flying	Status	—	100	15	Normal
Quick Attack	Normal	Physical	40	100	30	Normal
Roost	Flying	Status	—	—	10	Self
Simple Beam	Normal	Status	—	100	15	Normal
Sucker Punch	Dark	Physical	70	100	5	Normal

093 — Xatu

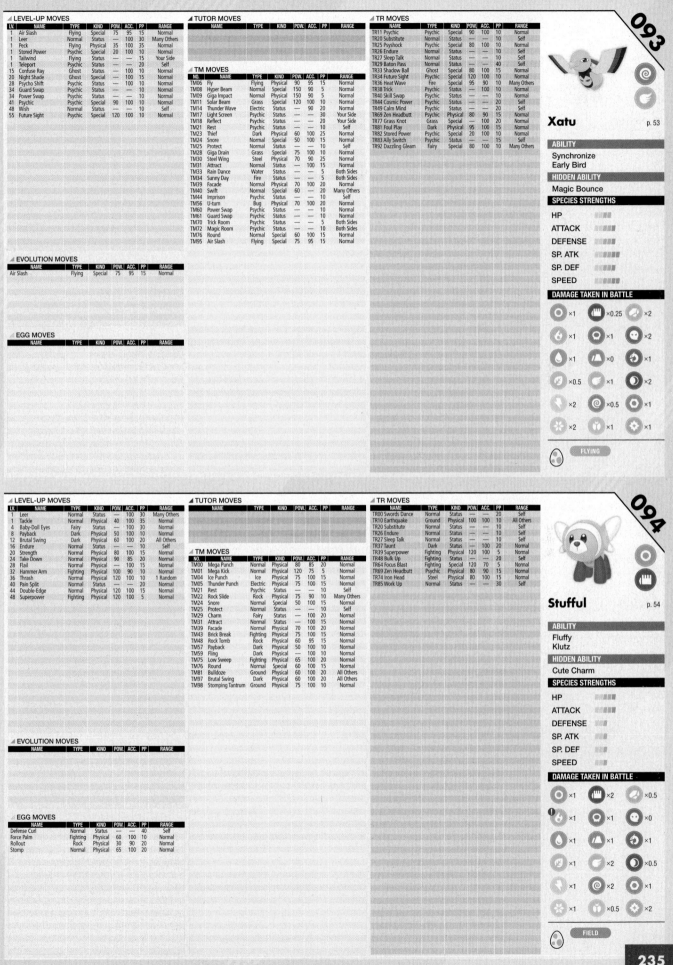

LEVEL-UP MOVES

LV.	NAME	TYPE	KIND	POW.	ACC.	PP	RANGE
1	Air Slash	Flying	Special	75	95	15	Normal
1	Leer	Normal	Status	—	100	30	Many Others
1	Peck	Flying	Physical	35	100	35	Normal
1	Stored Power	Psychic	Special	20	100	10	Normal
1	Tailwind	Flying	Status	—	—	15	Your Side
1	Teleport	Psychic	Status	—	—	20	Self
15	Confuse Ray	Ghost	Status	—	100	10	Normal
20	Night Shade	Ghost	Special	—	100	15	Normal
28	Psycho Shift	Psychic	Status	—	100	10	Normal
34	Guard Swap	Psychic	Status	—	—	10	Normal
34	Power Swap	Psychic	Status	—	—	10	Normal
41	Psychic	Psychic	Special	90	100	10	Normal
48	Wish	Normal	Status	—	—	10	Self
55	Future Sight	Psychic	Special	120	100	10	Normal

EVOLUTION MOVES

NAME	TYPE	KIND	POW.	ACC.	PP	RANGE
Air Slash	Flying	Special	75	95	15	Normal

EGG MOVES

NAME	TYPE	KIND	POW.	ACC.	PP	RANGE

TUTOR MOVES

NAME	TYPE	KIND	POW.	ACC.	PP	RANGE

TM MOVES

NO.	NAME	TYPE	KIND	POW.	ACC.	PP	RANGE
TM06	Fly	Flying	Physical	90	95	15	Normal
TM08	Hyper Beam	Normal	Special	150	90	5	Normal
TM09	Giga Impact	Normal	Physical	150	90	5	Normal
TM11	Solar Beam	Grass	Special	120	100	10	Normal
TM14	Thunder Wave	Electric	Status	—	90	20	Normal
TM17	Light Screen	Psychic	Status	—	—	30	Your Side
TM18	Reflect	Psychic	Status	—	—	20	Your Side
TM21	Rest	Psychic	Status	—	—	10	Self
TM23	Thief	Dark	Physical	60	100	25	Normal
TM24	Snore	Normal	Special	50	100	15	Normal
TM25	Protect	Normal	Status	—	—	10	Self
TM28	Giga Drain	Grass	Special	75	100	10	Normal
TM30	Steel Wing	Steel	Physical	70	90	25	Normal
TM31	Attract	Normal	Status	—	100	15	Normal
TM33	Rain Dance	Water	Status	—	—	5	Both Sides
TM34	Sunny Day	Fire	Status	—	—	5	Both Sides
TM39	Facade	Normal	Physical	70	100	20	Normal
TM40	Swift	Normal	Special	60	—	20	Many Others
TM44	Imprison	Psychic	Status	—	—	10	Self
TM56	U-turn	Bug	Physical	70	100	20	Normal
TM60	Power Swap	Psychic	Status	—	—	10	Normal
TM61	Guard Swap	Psychic	Status	—	—	10	Normal
TM70	Trick Room	Psychic	Status	—	—	5	Both Sides
TM72	Magic Room	Psychic	Status	—	—	10	Both Sides
TM76	Round	Normal	Special	60	100	15	Normal
TM95	Air Slash	Flying	Special	75	95	15	Normal

TR MOVES

NAME	TYPE	KIND	POW.	ACC.	PP	RANGE
TR11 Psychic	Psychic	Special	90	100	10	Normal
TR20 Substitute	Normal	Status	—	—	10	Self
TR25 Psyshock	Psychic	Special	80	100	10	Normal
TR26 Endure	Normal	Status	—	—	10	Self
TR27 Sleep Talk	Normal	Status	—	—	10	Self
TR29 Baton Pass	Normal	Status	—	—	40	Self
TR33 Shadow Ball	Ghost	Special	80	100	15	Normal
TR34 Future Sight	Psychic	Special	120	100	10	Normal
TR36 Heat Wave	Fire	Special	95	90	10	Many Others
TR38 Trick	Psychic	Status	—	100	10	Normal
TR40 Skill Swap	Psychic	Status	—	—	10	Normal
TR44 Cosmic Power	Psychic	Status	—	—	20	Self
TR49 Calm Mind	Psychic	Status	—	—	20	Self
TR69 Zen Headbutt	Psychic	Physical	80	90	15	Normal
TR77 Grass Knot	Grass	Special	—	100	20	Normal
TR81 Foul Play	Dark	Physical	95	100	15	Normal
TR82 Stored Power	Psychic	Special	20	100	10	Normal
TR83 Ally Switch	Psychic	Status	—	—	15	Self
TR92 Dazzling Gleam	Fairy	Special	80	100	10	Many Others

Xatu p. 53

ABILITY
Synchronize
Early Bird

HIDDEN ABILITY
Magic Bounce

SPECIES STRENGTHS
HP
ATTACK
DEFENSE
SP. ATK
SP. DEF
SPEED

DAMAGE TAKEN IN BATTLE

×1	×0.25	×2
×1	×1	×2
×1	×0	×1
×0.5	×1	×2
×2	×0.5	×1
×2	×1	×1

FLYING

---

094 — Stuffu l

LEVEL-UP MOVES

LV.	NAME	TYPE	KIND	POW.	ACC.	PP	RANGE
1	Leer	Normal	Status	—	100	30	Many Others
1	Tackle	Normal	Physical	40	100	35	Normal
4	Baby-Doll Eyes	Fairy	Status	—	100	30	Normal
8	Payback	Dark	Physical	50	100	10	Normal
12	Brutal Swing	Dark	Physical	60	100	20	All Others
16	Endure	Normal	Status	—	—	10	Self
20	Strength	Normal	Physical	80	100	15	Normal
24	Take Down	Normal	Physical	90	85	20	Normal
28	Flail	Normal	Physical	—	100	15	Normal
32	Hammer Arm	Fighting	Physical	100	90	10	Normal
36	Thrash	Normal	Physical	120	100	10	1 Random
40	Pain Split	Normal	Status	—	—	20	Normal
44	Double-Edge	Normal	Physical	120	100	15	Normal
48	Superpower	Fighting	Physical	120	100	5	Normal

EVOLUTION MOVES

NAME	TYPE	KIND	POW.	ACC.	PP	RANGE

EGG MOVES

NAME	TYPE	KIND	POW.	ACC.	PP	RANGE
Defense Curl	Normal	Status	—	—	40	Self
Force Palm	Fighting	Physical	60	100	10	Normal
Rollout	Rock	Physical	30	90	20	Normal
Stomp	Normal	Physical	65	100	20	Normal

TUTOR MOVES

NAME	TYPE	KIND	POW.	ACC.	PP	RANGE

TM MOVES

NO.	NAME	TYPE	KIND	POW.	ACC.	PP	RANGE
TM00	Mega Punch	Normal	Physical	80	85	20	Normal
TM01	Mega Kick	Normal	Physical	120	75	5	Normal
TM04	Ice Punch	Ice	Physical	75	100	15	Normal
TM05	Thunder Punch	Electric	Physical	75	100	15	Normal
TM21	Rest	Psychic	Status	—	—	10	Self
TM22	Rock Slide	Rock	Physical	75	90	10	Many Others
TM24	Snore	Normal	Special	50	100	15	Normal
TM25	Protect	Normal	Status	—	—	10	Self
TM29	Charm	Fairy	Status	—	100	20	Normal
TM31	Attract	Normal	Status	—	100	15	Normal
TM39	Facade	Normal	Physical	70	100	20	Normal
TM43	Brick Break	Fighting	Physical	75	100	15	Normal
TM48	Rock Tomb	Rock	Physical	60	95	15	Normal
TM57	Payback	Dark	Physical	50	100	10	Normal
TM59	Fling	Dark	Physical	—	100	10	Normal
TM75	Low Sweep	Fighting	Physical	65	100	20	Normal
TM76	Round	Normal	Special	60	100	15	Normal
TM81	Bulldoze	Ground	Physical	60	100	20	All Others
TM97	Brutal Swing	Dark	Physical	60	100	20	All Others
TM98	Stomping Tantrum	Ground	Physical	75	100	10	Normal

TR MOVES

NAME	TYPE	KIND	POW.	ACC.	PP	RANGE
TR00 Swords Dance	Normal	Status	—	—	20	Self
TR10 Earthquake	Ground	Physical	100	100	10	All Others
TR20 Substitute	Normal	Status	—	—	10	Self
TR26 Endure	Normal	Status	—	—	10	Self
TR27 Sleep Talk	Normal	Status	—	—	10	Self
TR37 Taunt	Dark	Status	—	100	20	Normal
TR39 Superpower	Fighting	Physical	120	100	5	Normal
TR48 Bulk Up	Fighting	Status	—	—	20	Self
TR64 Focus Blast	Fighting	Special	120	70	5	Normal
TR69 Zen Headbutt	Psychic	Physical	80	90	15	Normal
TR74 Iron Head	Steel	Physical	80	100	15	Normal
TR85 Work Up	Normal	Status	—	—	30	Self

Stuffu l p. 54

ABILITY
Fluffy
Klutz

HIDDEN ABILITY
Cute Charm

SPECIES STRENGTHS
HP
ATTACK
DEFENSE
SP. ATK
SP. DEF
SPEED

DAMAGE TAKEN IN BATTLE

×1	×2	×0.5
×1	×1	×0
×1	×1	×1
×1	×2	×0.5
×1	×2	×1
×0.5	×0.5	×2

FIELD

095 Bewear

p. 54

ABILITY
Fluffy
Klutz

HIDDEN ABILITY
Unnerve

SPECIES STRENGTHS

HP	
ATTACK	
DEFENSE	
SP. ATK	
SP. DEF	
SPEED	

DAMAGE TAKEN IN BATTLE

⊙ ×1	⊞ ×2	✎ ×0.5
❗ ×1	◉ ×1	×0
◐ ×1	◔ ×1	◓ ×1
◍ ×1	✦ ×2	◉ ×0.5
◊ ×1	◉ ×2	◯ ×1
✤ ×1	◍ ×0.5	✿ ×2

FIELD

LEVEL-UP MOVES

LV.	NAME	TYPE	KIND	POW.	ACC.	PP	RANGE
1	Baby-Doll Eyes	Fairy	Status	—	100	30	Normal
1	Bind	Normal	Physical	15	85	20	Normal
1	Leer	Normal	Status	—	100	30	Many Others
1	Payback	Dark	Physical	50	100	10	Normal
1	Tackle	Normal	Physical	40	100	35	Normal
12	Brutal Swing	Dark	Physical	60	100	20	All Others
16	Endure	Normal	Status	—	—	10	Self
20	Strength	Normal	Physical	80	100	15	Normal
24	Take Down	Normal	Physical	90	85	20	Normal
30	Flail	Normal	Physical	—	100	15	Normal
36	Hammer Arm	Fighting	Physical	100	90	10	Normal
42	Thrash	Normal	Physical	120	100	10	1 Random
48	Pain Split	Normal	Status	—	—	20	Normal
54	Double-Edge	Normal	Physical	120	100	15	Normal
60	Superpower	Fighting	Physical	120	100	5	Normal

EVOLUTION MOVES

NAME	TYPE	KIND	POW.	ACC.	PP	RANGE
Bind	Normal	Physical	15	85	20	Normal

EGG MOVES

NAME	TYPE	KIND	POW.	ACC.	PP	RANGE

TUTOR MOVES

NAME	TYPE	KIND	POW.	ACC.	PP	RANGE

TM MOVES

NO.	NAME	TYPE	KIND	POW.	ACC.	PP	RANGE
TM00	Mega Punch	Normal	Physical	80	85	20	Normal
TM01	Mega Kick	Normal	Physical	120	75	5	Normal
TM04	Ice Punch	Ice	Physical	75	100	15	Normal
TM05	Thunder Punch	Electric	Physical	75	100	15	Normal
TM08	Hyper Beam	Normal	Special	150	90	5	Normal
TM09	Giga Impact	Normal	Physical	150	90	5	Normal
TM21	Rest	Psychic	Status	—	—	10	Self
TM22	Rock Slide	Rock	Physical	75	90	10	Many Others
TM24	Snore	Normal	Special	50	100	15	Normal
TM25	Protect	Normal	Status	—	—	10	Self
TM29	Charm	Fairy	Status	—	100	20	Normal
TM31	Attract	Normal	Status	—	100	15	Normal
TM39	Facade	Normal	Physical	70	100	20	Normal
TM42	Revenge	Fighting	Physical	60	100	10	Normal
TM43	Brick Break	Fighting	Physical	75	100	15	Normal
TM48	Rock Tomb	Rock	Physical	60	95	15	Normal
TM57	Payback	Dark	Physical	50	100	10	Normal
TM59	Fling	Dark	Physical	—	100	10	Normal
TM63	Drain Punch	Fighting	Physical	75	100	10	Normal
TM65	Shadow Claw	Ghost	Physical	70	100	15	Normal
TM75	Low Sweep	Fighting	Physical	65	100	20	Normal
TM76	Round	Normal	Special	60	100	15	Normal
TM81	Bulldoze	Ground	Physical	60	100	20	All Others
TM97	Brutal Swing	Dark	Physical	60	100	20	All Others
TM98	Stomping Tantrum	Ground	Physical	75	100	10	Normal

TR MOVES

NAME	TYPE	KIND	POW.	ACC.	PP	RANGE
TR00 Swords Dance	Normal	Status	—	—	20	Self
TR01 Body Slam	Normal	Physical	85	100	15	Normal
TR07 Low Kick	Fighting	Physical	—	100	20	Normal
TR10 Earthquake	Ground	Physical	100	100	10	All Others
TR20 Substitute	Normal	Status	—	—	10	Self
TR21 Reversal	Fighting	Physical	—	100	15	Normal
TR26 Endure	Normal	Status	—	—	10	Self
TR27 Sleep Talk	Normal	Status	—	—	10	Self
TR37 Taunt	Dark	Status	—	100	20	Normal
TR39 Superpower	Fighting	Physical	120	100	5	Normal
TR47 Dragon Claw	Dragon	Physical	80	100	15	Normal
TR48 Bulk Up	Fighting	Status	—	—	20	Self
TR53 Close Combat	Fighting	Physical	120	100	5	Normal
TR64 Focus Blast	Fighting	Special	120	70	5	Normal
TR69 Zen Headbutt	Psychic	Physical	80	90	15	Normal
TR74 Iron Head	Steel	Physical	80	100	15	Normal
TR85 Work Up	Normal	Status	—	—	30	Self
TR93 Darkest Lariat	Dark	Physical	85	100	10	Normal
TR94 High Horsepower	Ground	Physical	95	95	10	Normal
TR99 Body Press	Fighting	Physical	80	100	10	Normal

---

096 Snover

p. 55

ABILITY
Snow Warning
—

HIDDEN ABILITY
Soundproof

SPECIES STRENGTHS

HP	
ATTACK	
DEFENSE	
SP. ATK	
SP. DEF	
SPEED	

DAMAGE TAKEN IN BATTLE

⊙ ×1	⊞ ×2	✎ ×2
❗ ×4	◉ ×2	×1
◐ ×0.5	◔ ×0.5	◓ ×1
◍ ×0.5	✦ ×2	◉ ×1
◊ ×0.5	◉ ×1	◯ ×2
✤ ×1	◍ ×2	✿ ×1

MONSTER
GRASS

LEVEL-UP MOVES

LV.	NAME	TYPE	KIND	POW.	ACC.	PP	RANGE
1	Leer	Normal	Status	—	100	30	Many Others
1	Powder Snow	Ice	Special	40	100	25	Many Others
5	Leafage	Grass	Physical	40	100	40	Normal
10	Mist	Ice	Status	—	—	30	Your Side
15	Ice Shard	Ice	Physical	40	100	30	Normal
20	Razor Leaf	Grass	Physical	55	95	25	Many Others
25	Icy Wind	Ice	Special	55	95	15	Many Others
30	Swagger	Normal	Status	—	85	15	Normal
35	Ingrain	Grass	Status	—	—	20	Self
41	Wood Hammer	Grass	Physical	120	100	15	Normal
45	Blizzard	Ice	Special	110	70	5	Many Others
50	Sheer Cold	Ice	Special	—	30	5	Normal

EVOLUTION MOVES

NAME	TYPE	KIND	POW.	ACC.	PP	RANGE

EGG MOVES

NAME	TYPE	KIND	POW.	ACC.	PP	RANGE
Double-Edge	Normal	Physical	120	100	15	Normal
Growth	Normal	Status	—	—	20	Self
Leech Seed	Grass	Status	—	90	10	Normal
Skull Bash	Normal	Physical	130	100	10	Normal
Stomp	Normal	Physical	65	100	20	Normal

TUTOR MOVES

NAME	TYPE	KIND	POW.	ACC.	PP	RANGE

TM MOVES

NO.	NAME	TYPE	KIND	POW.	ACC.	PP	RANGE
TM00	Mega Punch	Normal	Physical	80	85	20	Normal
TM04	Ice Punch	Ice	Physical	75	100	15	Normal
TM10	Magical Leaf	Grass	Special	60	—	20	Normal
TM11	Solar Beam	Grass	Special	120	100	10	Normal
TM17	Light Screen	Psychic	Status	—	—	30	Your Side
TM19	Safeguard	Normal	Status	—	—	25	Your Side
TM21	Rest	Psychic	Status	—	—	10	Self
TM24	Snore	Normal	Special	50	100	15	Normal
TM25	Protect	Normal	Status	—	—	10	Self
TM27	Icy Wind	Ice	Special	55	95	15	Many Others
TM28	Giga Drain	Grass	Special	75	100	10	Normal
TM31	Attract	Normal	Status	—	100	15	Normal
TM33	Rain Dance	Water	Status	—	—	5	Both Sides
TM35	Hail	Ice	Status	—	—	10	Both Sides
TM39	Facade	Normal	Physical	70	100	20	Normal
TM46	Weather Ball*	Normal	Special	50	100	10	Normal
TM50	Bullet Seed	Grass	Physical	25	100	30	Normal
TM64	Avalanche	Ice	Physical	60	100	10	Normal
TM76	Round	Normal	Special	60	100	15	Normal

TR MOVES

NAME	TYPE	KIND	POW.	ACC.	PP	RANGE
TR00 Swords Dance	Normal	Status	—	—	20	Self
TR05 Ice Beam	Ice	Special	90	100	10	Normal
TR06 Blizzard	Ice	Special	110	70	5	Many Others
TR20 Substitute	Normal	Status	—	—	10	Self
TR26 Endure	Normal	Status	—	—	10	Self
TR27 Sleep Talk	Normal	Status	—	—	10	Self
TR31 Iron Tail	Steel	Physical	100	75	15	Normal
TR33 Shadow Ball	Ghost	Special	80	100	15	Normal
TR59 Seed Bomb	Grass	Physical	80	100	15	Normal
TR65 Energy Ball	Grass	Special	90	100	10	Normal
TR77 Grass Knot	Grass	Special	—	100	20	Normal

097

Abomasnow p. 55

LEVEL-UP MOVES

LV.	NAME	TYPE	KIND	POW.	ACC.	PP	RANGE
1	Aurora Veil	Ice	Status	—	—	20	Your Side
1	Ice Punch	Ice	Physical	75	100	15	Normal
1	Leafage	Grass	Physical	40	100	40	Normal
1	Leer	Normal	Status	—	100	30	Many Others
1	Mist	Ice	Status	—	—	30	Your Side
1	Powder Snow	Ice	Special	40	100	25	Many Others
15	Ice Shard	Ice	Physical	40	100	30	Normal
20	Razor Leaf	Grass	Physical	55	95	25	Many Others
25	Icy Wind	Ice	Special	55	95	15	Many Others
30	Swagger	Normal	Status	—	85	15	Normal
35	Ingrain	Grass	Status	—	—	20	Self
43	Wood Hammer	Grass	Physical	120	100	15	Normal
49	Blizzard	Ice	Special	110	70	5	Many Others
56	Sheer Cold	Ice	Special	—	30	5	Normal

EVOLUTION MOVES

NAME	TYPE	KIND	POW.	ACC.	PP	RANGE
Ice Punch	Ice	Physical	75	100	15	Normal

EGG MOVES

NAME	TYPE	KIND	POW.	ACC.	PP	RANGE

TUTOR MOVES

NAME	TYPE	KIND	POW.	ACC.	PP	RANGE

TM MOVES

NO.	NAME	TYPE	KIND	POW.	ACC.	PP	RANGE
TM00	Mega Punch	Normal	Physical	80	85	20	Normal
TM01	Mega Kick	Normal	Physical	120	75	5	Normal
TM04	Ice Punch	Ice	Physical	75	100	15	Normal
TM08	Hyper Beam	Normal	Special	150	90	5	Normal
TM09	Giga Impact	Normal	Physical	150	90	5	Normal
TM10	Magical Leaf	Grass	Special	60	—	20	Normal
TM11	Solar Beam	Grass	Special	120	100	10	Normal
TM17	Light Screen	Psychic	Status	—	—	30	Your Side
TM19	Safeguard	Normal	Status	—	—	25	Your Side
TM21	Rest	Psychic	Status	—	—	10	Self
TM22	Rock Slide	Rock	Physical	75	90	10	Many Others
TM24	Snore	Normal	Special	50	100	15	Normal
TM25	Protect	Normal	Status	—	—	10	Self
TM27	Icy Wind	Ice	Special	55	95	15	Many Others
TM28	Giga Drain	Grass	Special	75	100	10	Normal
TM31	Attract	Normal	Status	—	100	15	Normal
TM33	Rain Dance	Water	Status	—	—	5	Both Sides
TM35	Hail	Ice	Status	—	—	10	Both Sides
TM39	Facade	Normal	Physical	70	100	20	Normal
TM43	Brick Break	Fighting	Physical	75	100	15	Normal
TM46	Weather Ball*	Normal	Special	50	100	10	Normal
TM48	Rock Tomb	Rock	Physical	60	95	15	Normal
TM50	Bullet Seed	Grass	Physical	25	100	30	Normal
TM51	Icicle Spear	Ice	Physical	25	100	30	Normal
TM59	Fling	Dark	Physical	—	100	10	Normal
TM64	Avalanche	Ice	Physical	60	100	10	Normal
TM76	Round	Normal	Special	60	100	15	Normal
TM81	Bulldoze	Ground	Physical	60	100	20	All Others
TM98	Stomping Tantrum	Ground	Physical	75	100	10	Normal

TR MOVES

NAME	TYPE	KIND	POW.	ACC.	PP	RANGE
TR00 Swords Dance	Normal	Status	—	—	20	Self
TR05 Ice Beam	Ice	Special	90	100	10	Normal
TR06 Blizzard	Ice	Special	110	70	5	Many Others
TR10 Earthquake	Ground	Physical	100	100	10	All Others
TR20 Substitute	Normal	Status	—	—	10	Self
TR24 Outrage	Dragon	Physical	120	100	10	1 Random
TR26 Endure	Normal	Status	—	—	10	Self
TR27 Sleep Talk	Normal	Status	—	—	10	Self
TR31 Iron Tail	Steel	Physical	100	75	15	Normal
TR33 Shadow Ball	Ghost	Special	80	100	15	Normal
TR59 Seed Bomb	Grass	Physical	80	100	15	Normal
TR64 Focus Blast	Fighting	Special	120	70	5	Normal
TR65 Energy Ball	Grass	Special	90	100	10	Normal
TR67 Earth Power	Ground	Special	90	100	10	Normal
TR71 Leaf Storm	Grass	Special	130	90	5	Normal
TR77 Grass Knot	Grass	Special	—	100	20	Normal

ABILITY

Snow Warning
—

HIDDEN ABILITY

Soundproof

SPECIES STRENGTHS

HP
ATTACK
DEFENSE
SP. ATK
SP. DEF
SPEED

DAMAGE TAKEN IN BATTLE

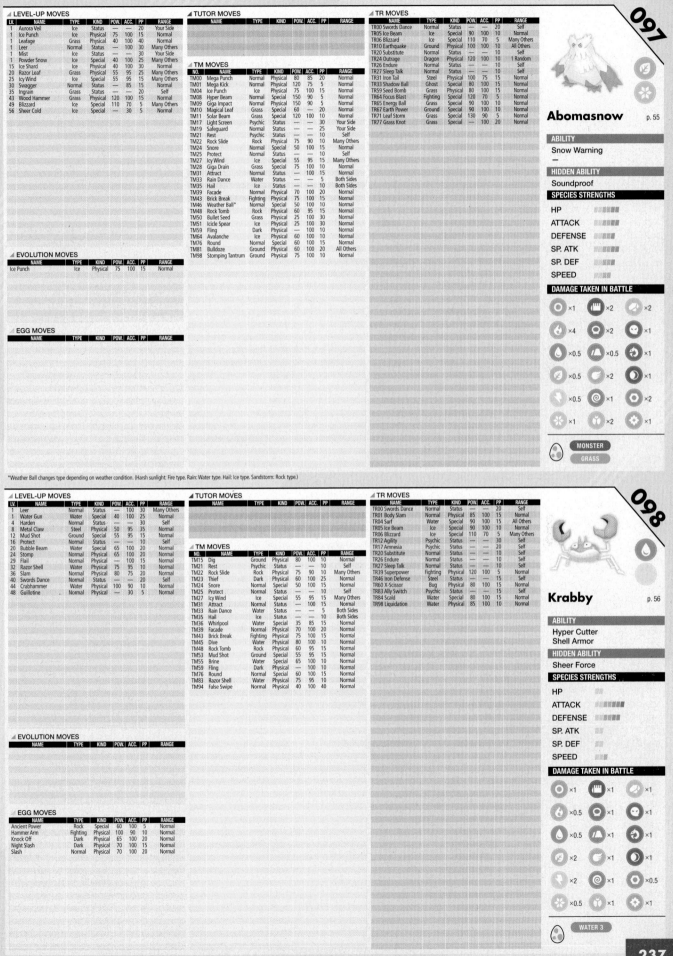

×1 | ×2 | ×2
×4 | ×2 | ×1
×0.5 | ×0.5 | ×1
×0.5 | ×2 | ×1
×0.5 | ×1 | ×2
×1 | ×2 | ×1

MONSTER
GRASS

*Weather Ball changes type depending on weather condition. (Harsh sunlight: Fire type. Rain: Water type. Hail: Ice type. Sandstorm: Rock type.)

098

Krabby p. 56

LEVEL-UP MOVES

LV.	NAME	TYPE	KIND	POW.	ACC.	PP	RANGE
1	Leer	Normal	Status	—	100	30	Many Others
1	Water Gun	Water	Special	40	100	25	Normal
4	Harden	Normal	Status	—	—	30	Self
8	Metal Claw	Steel	Physical	50	95	35	Normal
12	Mud Shot	Ground	Special	55	95	15	Normal
16	Protect	Normal	Status	—	—	10	Self
20	Bubble Beam	Water	Special	65	100	20	Normal
24	Stomp	Normal	Physical	65	100	20	Normal
29	Flail	Normal	Physical	—	100	15	Normal
32	Razor Shell	Water	Physical	75	95	10	Normal
36	Slam	Normal	Physical	80	75	20	Normal
40	Swords Dance	Normal	Status	—	—	20	Self
44	Crabhammer	Water	Physical	100	90	10	Normal
48	Guillotine	Normal	Physical	—	30	5	Normal

EVOLUTION MOVES

NAME	TYPE	KIND	POW.	ACC.	PP	RANGE

EGG MOVES

NAME	TYPE	KIND	POW.	ACC.	PP	RANGE
Ancient Power	Rock	Special	60	100	5	Normal
Hammer Arm	Fighting	Physical	100	90	10	Normal
Knock Off	Dark	Physical	65	100	20	Normal
Night Slash	Dark	Physical	70	100	15	Normal
Slash	Normal	Physical	70	100	20	Normal

TUTOR MOVES

NAME	TYPE	KIND	POW.	ACC.	PP	RANGE

TM MOVES

NO.	NAME	TYPE	KIND	POW.	ACC.	PP	RANGE
TM15	Dig	Ground	Physical	80	100	10	Normal
TM21	Rest	Psychic	Status	—	—	10	Self
TM22	Rock Slide	Rock	Physical	75	90	10	Many Others
TM23	Thief	Dark	Physical	60	100	25	Normal
TM24	Snore	Normal	Special	50	100	15	Normal
TM25	Protect	Normal	Status	—	—	10	Self
TM27	Icy Wind	Ice	Special	55	95	15	Many Others
TM31	Attract	Normal	Status	—	100	15	Normal
TM33	Rain Dance	Water	Status	—	—	5	Both Sides
TM35	Hail	Ice	Status	—	—	10	Both Sides
TM36	Whirlpool	Water	Special	35	85	15	Normal
TM39	Facade	Normal	Physical	70	100	20	Normal
TM43	Brick Break	Fighting	Physical	75	100	15	Normal
TM45	Dive	Water	Physical	80	100	10	Normal
TM48	Rock Tomb	Rock	Physical	60	95	15	Normal
TM53	Mud Shot	Ground	Special	55	95	15	Normal
TM55	Brine	Water	Special	65	100	10	Normal
TM59	Fling	Dark	Physical	—	100	10	Normal
TM76	Round	Normal	Special	60	100	15	Normal
TM83	Razor Shell	Water	Physical	75	95	10	Normal
TM94	False Swipe	Normal	Physical	40	100	40	Normal

TR MOVES

NAME	TYPE	KIND	POW.	ACC.	PP	RANGE
TR00 Swords Dance	Normal	Status	—	—	20	Self
TR01 Body Slam	Normal	Physical	85	100	15	Normal
TR04 Surf	Water	Special	90	100	15	All Others
TR05 Ice Beam	Ice	Special	90	100	10	Normal
TR06 Blizzard	Ice	Special	110	70	5	Many Others
TR12 Agility	Psychic	Status	—	—	30	Self
TR17 Amnesia	Psychic	Status	—	—	20	Self
TR20 Substitute	Normal	Status	—	—	10	Self
TR26 Endure	Normal	Status	—	—	10	Self
TR27 Sleep Talk	Normal	Status	—	—	10	Self
TR39 Superpower	Fighting	Physical	120	100	5	Normal
TR46 Iron Defense	Steel	Status	—	—	15	Self
TR60 X-Scissor	Bug	Physical	80	100	15	Normal
TR83 Ally Switch	Psychic	Status	—	—	15	Self
TR84 Scald	Water	Special	80	100	15	Normal
TR98 Liquidation	Water	Physical	85	100	10	Normal

ABILITY

Hyper Cutter
Shell Armor

HIDDEN ABILITY

Sheer Force

SPECIES STRENGTHS

HP
ATTACK
DEFENSE
SP. ATK
SP. DEF
SPEED

DAMAGE TAKEN IN BATTLE

×1 | ×1 | ×1
×0.5 | ×1 | ×1
×0.5 | ×1 | ×1
×2 | ×1 | ×1
×2 | ×1 | ×0.5
×0.5 | ×1 | ×1

WATER 3

099 Kingler p. 56

ABILITY
Hyper Cutter
Shell Armor

HIDDEN ABILITY
Sheer Force

SPECIES STRENGTHS

HP	▰▰▰
ATTACK	▰▰▰▰▰▰▰
DEFENSE	▰▰▰▰▰▰
SP. ATK	▰▰▰
SP. DEF	▰▰▰
SPEED	▰▰▰▰

DAMAGE TAKEN IN BATTLE

●×1	▥×1	×1			
×0.5	×1	×1			
×0.5	×1	×1			
×2	×1	×1			
×2	×1	×0.5			
×0.5	×1	×1			

🥚 WATER 3

LEVEL-UP MOVES

LV.	NAME	TYPE	KIND	POW.	ACC.	PP	RANGE
1	Hammer Arm	Fighting	Physical	100	90	10	Normal
1	Harden	Normal	Status	—	—	30	Self
1	Leer	Normal	Status	—	100	30	Many Others
1	Metal Claw	Steel	Physical	50	95	35	Normal
1	Water Gun	Water	Special	40	100	25	Normal
1	Wide Guard	Rock	Status	—	—	10	Your Side
12	Mud Shot	Ground	Special	55	95	15	Normal
16	Protect	Normal	Status	—	—	10	Self
20	Bubble Beam	Water	Special	65	100	20	Normal
24	Stomp	Normal	Physical	65	100	20	Normal
31	Flail	Normal	Physical	—	100	15	Normal
36	Razor Shell	Water	Physical	75	95	10	Normal
42	Slam	Normal	Physical	80	75	20	Normal
48	Swords Dance	Normal	Status	—	—	20	Self
54	Crabhammer	Water	Physical	100	90	10	Normal
60	Guillotine	Normal	Physical	—	30	5	Normal

EVOLUTION MOVES

NAME	TYPE	KIND	POW.	ACC.	PP	RANGE

EGG MOVES

NAME	TYPE	KIND	POW.	ACC.	PP	RANGE

TUTOR MOVES

NAME	TYPE	KIND	POW.	ACC.	PP	RANGE

TM MOVES

NO.	NAME	TYPE	KIND	POW.	ACC.	PP	RANGE
TM08	Hyper Beam	Normal	Special	150	90	5	Normal
TM09	Giga Impact	Normal	Physical	150	90	5	Normal
TM15	Dig	Ground	Physical	80	100	10	Normal
TM21	Rest	Psychic	Status	—	—	10	Self
TM22	Rock Slide	Rock	Physical	75	90	10	Many Others
TM23	Thief	Dark	Physical	60	100	25	Normal
TM24	Snore	Normal	Special	50	100	15	Normal
TM25	Protect	Normal	Status	—	—	10	Self
TM27	Icy Wind	Ice	Special	55	95	15	Many Others
TM31	Attract	Normal	Status	—	100	15	Normal
TM33	Rain Dance	Water	Status	—	—	5	Both Sides
TM35	Hail	Ice	Status	—	—	10	Both Sides
TM36	Whirlpool	Water	Special	35	85	15	Normal
TM39	Facade	Normal	Physical	70	100	20	Normal
TM43	Brick Break	Fighting	Physical	75	100	15	Normal
TM45	Dive	Water	Physical	80	100	10	Normal
TM48	Rock Tomb	Rock	Physical	60	95	15	Normal
TM53	Mud Shot	Ground	Special	55	95	15	Normal
TM55	Brine	Water	Special	65	100	10	Normal
TM59	Fling	Dark	Physical	—	100	10	Normal
TM76	Round	Normal	Special	60	100	15	Normal
TM83	Razor Shell	Water	Physical	75	95	10	Normal
TM94	False Swipe	Normal	Physical	40	100	40	Normal
TM97	Brutal Swing	Dark	Physical	60	100	20	All Others
TM98	Stomping Tantrum	Ground	Physical	75	100	10	Normal

TR MOVES

NO.	NAME	TYPE	KIND	POW.	ACC.	PP	RANGE
TR00	Swords Dance	Normal	Status	—	—	20	Self
TR01	Body Slam	Normal	Physical	85	100	15	Normal
TR03	Hydro Pump	Water	Special	110	80	5	Normal
TR04	Surf	Water	Special	90	100	15	All Others
TR05	Ice Beam	Ice	Special	90	100	10	Normal
TR06	Blizzard	Ice	Special	110	70	5	Many Others
TR12	Agility	Psychic	Status	—	—	30	Self
TR17	Amnesia	Psychic	Status	—	—	20	Self
TR20	Substitute	Normal	Status	—	—	10	Self
TR26	Endure	Normal	Status	—	—	10	Self
TR27	Sleep Talk	Normal	Status	—	—	10	Self
TR39	Superpower	Fighting	Physical	120	100	5	Normal
TR46	Iron Defense	Steel	Status	—	—	15	Self
TR60	X-Scissor	Bug	Physical	80	100	15	Normal
TR83	Ally Switch	Psychic	Status	—	—	15	Self
TR84	Scald	Water	Special	80	100	15	Normal
TR94	High Horsepower	Ground	Physical	95	95	10	Normal
TR98	Liquidation	Water	Physical	85	100	10	Normal

---

100 Wooper p. 56

ABILITY
Damp
Water Absorb

HIDDEN ABILITY
Unaware

SPECIES STRENGTHS

HP	▰▰▰
ATTACK	▰▰▰
DEFENSE	▰▰
SP. ATK	▰▰
SP. DEF	▰▰
SPEED	▰

DAMAGE TAKEN IN BATTLE

●×1	▥×1	×0.5			
×0.5	×0.5	×1			
×1	×1	×1			
×4	×1	×1			
×0	×1	×0.5			
×1	×1	×1			

🥚 WATER 1
FIELD

LEVEL-UP MOVES

LV.	NAME	TYPE	KIND	POW.	ACC.	PP	RANGE
1	Tail Whip	Normal	Status	—	100	30	Many Others
1	Water Gun	Water	Special	40	100	25	Normal
4	Rain Dance	Water	Status	—	—	5	Both Sides
8	Mud Shot	Ground	Special	55	95	15	Normal
12	Haze	Ice	Status	—	—	30	Both Sides
12	Mist	Ice	Status	—	—	30	Your Side
16	Slam	Normal	Physical	80	75	20	Normal
21	Yawn	Normal	Status	—	—	10	Normal
24	Aqua Tail	Water	Physical	90	90	10	Normal
28	Muddy Water	Water	Special	90	85	10	Many Others
32	Amnesia	Psychic	Status	—	—	20	Self
36	Toxic	Poison	Status	—	90	10	Normal
40	Earthquake	Ground	Physical	100	100	10	All Others

EVOLUTION MOVES

NAME	TYPE	KIND	POW.	ACC.	PP	RANGE

EGG MOVES

NAME	TYPE	KIND	POW.	ACC.	PP	RANGE
Acid Spray	Poison	Special	40	100	20	Normal
After You	Normal	Status	—	—	15	Normal
Ancient Power	Rock	Special	60	100	5	Normal
Counter	Fighting	Physical	—	100	20	Varies
Curse	Ghost	Status	—	—	10	Varies
Double Kick	Fighting	Physical	30	100	30	Normal
Power-Up Punch	Fighting	Physical	40	100	20	Normal
Recover	Normal	Status	—	—	10	Self
Spit Up	Normal	Special	—	100	10	Normal
Stockpile	Normal	Status	—	—	20	Self
Swallow	Normal	Status	—	—	10	Self

TUTOR MOVES

NAME	TYPE	KIND	POW.	ACC.	PP	RANGE

TM MOVES

NO.	NAME	TYPE	KIND	POW.	ACC.	PP	RANGE
TM04	Ice Punch	Ice	Physical	75	100	15	Normal
TM15	Dig	Ground	Physical	80	100	10	Normal
TM19	Safeguard	Normal	Status	—	—	25	Your Side
TM21	Rest	Psychic	Status	—	—	10	Self
TM24	Snore	Normal	Special	50	100	15	Normal
TM25	Protect	Normal	Status	—	—	10	Self
TM27	Icy Wind	Ice	Special	55	95	15	Many Others
TM31	Attract	Normal	Status	—	100	15	Normal
TM32	Sandstorm	Rock	Status	—	—	10	Both Sides
TM33	Rain Dance	Water	Status	—	—	5	Both Sides
TM35	Hail	Ice	Status	—	—	10	Both Sides
TM36	Whirlpool	Water	Special	35	85	15	Normal
TM39	Facade	Normal	Physical	70	100	20	Normal
TM45	Dive	Water	Physical	80	100	10	Normal
TM53	Mud Shot	Ground	Special	55	95	15	Normal
TM61	Guard Swap	Psychic	Status	—	—	10	Normal
TM76	Round	Normal	Special	60	100	15	Normal
TM81	Bulldoze	Ground	Physical	60	100	20	All Others
TM93	Eerie Impulse	Electric	Status	—	100	15	Normal
TM98	Stomping Tantrum	Ground	Physical	75	100	10	Normal

TR MOVES

NO.	NAME	TYPE	KIND	POW.	ACC.	PP	RANGE
TR01	Body Slam	Normal	Physical	85	100	15	Normal
TR03	Hydro Pump	Water	Special	110	80	5	Normal
TR04	Surf	Water	Special	90	100	15	All Others
TR05	Ice Beam	Ice	Special	90	100	10	Normal
TR06	Blizzard	Ice	Special	110	70	5	Many Others
TR10	Earthquake	Ground	Physical	100	100	10	All Others
TR16	Waterfall	Water	Physical	80	100	15	Normal
TR17	Amnesia	Psychic	Status	—	—	20	Self
TR20	Substitute	Normal	Status	—	—	10	Self
TR22	Sludge Bomb	Poison	Special	90	100	10	Normal
TR26	Endure	Normal	Status	—	—	10	Self
TR27	Sleep Talk	Normal	Status	—	—	10	Self
TR30	Encore	Normal	Status	—	100	5	Normal
TR31	Iron Tail	Steel	Physical	100	75	15	Normal
TR45	Muddy Water	Water	Special	90	85	10	Many Others
TR67	Earth Power	Ground	Special	90	100	10	Normal
TR78	Sludge Wave	Poison	Special	95	100	10	All Others
TR84	Scald	Water	Special	80	100	15	Normal

101 Quagsire

p. 56

LEVEL-UP MOVES

LV.	NAME	TYPE	KIND	POW.	ACC.	PP	RANGE
1	Mud Shot	Ground	Special	55	95	15	Normal
1	Rain Dance	Water	Status	—	—	5	Both Sides
1	Tail Whip	Normal	Status	—	100	30	Many Others
1	Water Gun	Water	Special	40	100	25	Normal
12	Haze	Ice	Status	—	—	30	Both Sides
12	Mist	Ice	Status	—	—	30	Your Side
16	Slam	Normal	Physical	80	75	20	Normal
23	Yawn	Normal	Status	—	—	10	Normal
28	Aqua Tail	Water	Physical	90	90	10	Normal
34	Muddy Water	Water	Special	90	85	10	Many Others
40	Amnesia	Psychic	Status	—	—	20	Self
46	Toxic	Poison	Status	—	90	10	Normal
52	Earthquake	Ground	Physical	100	100	10	All Others

EVOLUTION MOVES

NAME	TYPE	KIND	POW.	ACC.	PP	RANGE

EGG MOVES

NAME	TYPE	KIND	POW.	ACC.	PP	RANGE

TUTOR MOVES

NAME	TYPE	KIND	POW.	ACC.	PP	RANGE

TM MOVES

NO.	NAME	TYPE	KIND	POW.	ACC.	PP	RANGE
TM00	Mega Punch	Normal	Physical	80	85	20	Normal
TM01	Mega Kick	Normal	Physical	120	75	5	Normal
TM04	Ice Punch	Ice	Physical	75	100	15	Normal
TM08	Hyper Beam	Normal	Special	150	90	5	Normal
TM09	Giga Impact	Normal	Physical	150	90	5	Normal
TM15	Dig	Ground	Physical	80	100	10	Normal
TM19	Safeguard	Normal	Status	—	—	25	Your Side
TM21	Rest	Psychic	Status	—	—	10	Self
TM22	Rock Slide	Rock	Physical	75	90	5	Many Others
TM23	Thief	Dark	Physical	60	100	25	Normal
TM24	Snore	Normal	Special	50	100	15	Normal
TM25	Protect	Normal	Status	—	—	10	Self
TM27	Icy Wind	Ice	Special	55	95	15	Many Others
TM31	Attract	Normal	Status	—	100	15	Normal
TM32	Sandstorm	Rock	Status	—	—	10	Both Sides
TM33	Rain Dance	Water	Status	—	—	5	Both Sides
TM35	Hail	Ice	Status	—	—	10	Both Sides
TM36	Whirlpool	Water	Special	35	85	15	Normal
TM39	Facade	Normal	Physical	70	100	20	Normal
TM43	Brick Break	Fighting	Physical	75	100	15	Normal
TM45	Dive	Water	Physical	80	100	10	Normal
TM48	Rock Tomb	Rock	Physical	60	95	15	Normal
TM53	Mud Shot	Ground	Special	55	95	15	Normal
TM59	Fling	Dark	Physical	—	100	10	Normal
TM61	Guard Swap	Psychic	Status	—	—	10	Normal
TM76	Round	Normal	Special	60	100	15	Normal
TM81	Bulldoze	Ground	Physical	60	100	20	All Others
TM93	Eerie Impulse	Electric	Status	—	100	15	Normal
TM98	Stomping Tantrum	Ground	Physical	75	100	10	Normal

TR MOVES

NO.	NAME	TYPE	KIND	POW.	ACC.	PP	RANGE
TR01	Body Slam	Normal	Physical	85	100	15	Normal
TR03	Hydro Pump	Water	Special	110	80	5	Normal
TR04	Surf	Water	Special	90	100	15	All Others
TR05	Ice Beam	Ice	Special	90	100	10	Normal
TR06	Blizzard	Ice	Special	110	70	5	Many Others
TR10	Earthquake	Ground	Physical	100	100	10	All Others
TR16	Waterfall	Water	Physical	80	100	15	Normal
TR17	Amnesia	Psychic	Status	—	—	20	Self
TR20	Substitute	Normal	Status	—	—	10	Self
TR22	Sludge Bomb	Poison	Special	90	100	10	Normal
TR26	Endure	Normal	Status	—	—	10	Self
TR27	Sleep Talk	Normal	Status	—	—	10	Self
TR30	Encore	Normal	Status	—	100	5	Normal
TR31	Iron Tail	Steel	Physical	100	75	15	Normal
TR45	Muddy Water	Water	Special	90	85	10	Many Others
TR64	Focus Blast	Fighting	Special	120	70	5	Normal
TR67	Earth Power	Ground	Special	90	100	10	Normal
TR75	Stone Edge	Rock	Physical	100	80	5	Normal
TR78	Sludge Wave	Poison	Special	95	100	10	All Others
TR84	Scald	Water	Special	80	100	15	Normal
TR94	High Horsepower	Ground	Physical	95	95	10	Normal
TR98	Liquidation	Water	Physical	85	100	10	Normal

ABILITY
Damp
Water Absorb

HIDDEN ABILITY
Unaware

SPECIES STRENGTHS

HP
ATTACK
DEFENSE
SP. ATK
SP. DEF
SPEED

DAMAGE TAKEN IN BATTLE

×1 ×1 ×0.5
×0.5 ×0.5 ×1
×1 ×1 ×1
×4 ×1 ×1
×0 ×1 ×0.5
×1 ×1 ×1

WATER 1
FIELD

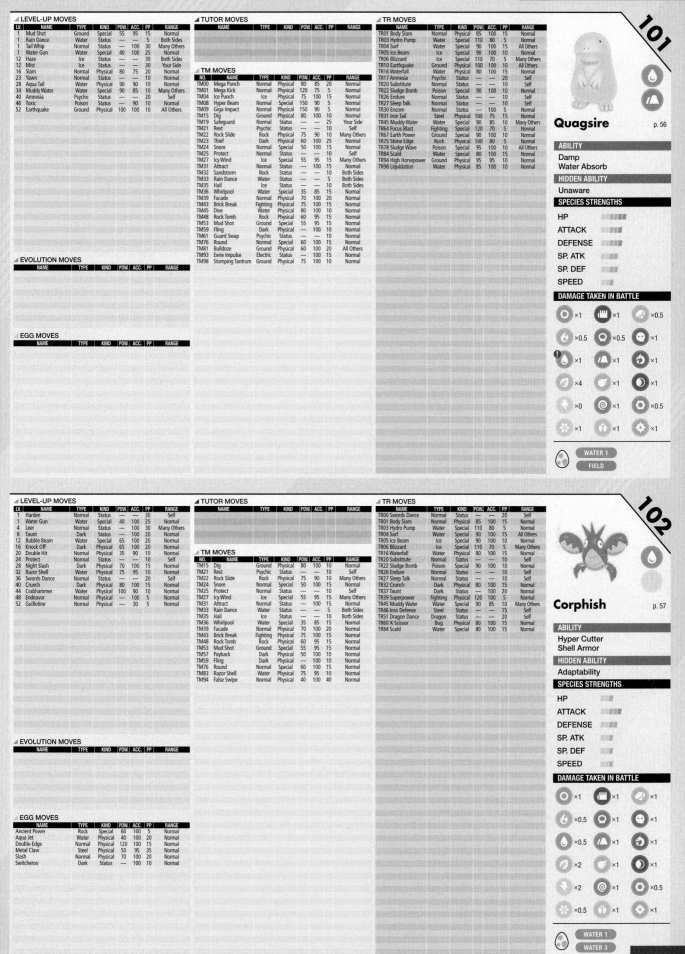

102 Corphish

p. 57

LEVEL-UP MOVES

LV.	NAME	TYPE	KIND	POW.	ACC.	PP	RANGE
1	Harden	Normal	Status	—	—	30	Self
1	Water Gun	Water	Special	40	100	25	Normal
4	Leer	Normal	Status	—	100	30	Many Others
8	Taunt	Dark	Status	—	100	20	Normal
12	Bubble Beam	Water	Special	65	100	20	Normal
16	Knock Off	Dark	Physical	65	100	20	Normal
20	Double Hit	Normal	Physical	35	90	10	Normal
24	Protect	Normal	Status	—	—	10	Self
28	Night Slash	Dark	Physical	70	100	15	Normal
32	Razor Shell	Water	Physical	75	95	10	Normal
36	Swords Dance	Normal	Status	—	—	20	Self
40	Crunch	Dark	Physical	80	100	15	Normal
44	Crabhammer	Water	Physical	100	90	10	Normal
48	Endeavor	Normal	Physical	—	100	5	Normal
52	Guillotine	Normal	Physical	—	30	5	Normal

EVOLUTION MOVES

NAME	TYPE	KIND	POW.	ACC.	PP	RANGE

EGG MOVES

NAME	TYPE	KIND	POW.	ACC.	PP	RANGE
Ancient Power	Rock	Special	60	100	5	Normal
Aqua Jet	Water	Physical	40	100	20	Normal
Double-Edge	Normal	Physical	120	100	15	Normal
Metal Claw	Steel	Physical	50	95	35	Normal
Slash	Normal	Physical	70	100	20	Normal
Switcheroo	Dark	Status	—	100	10	Normal

TUTOR MOVES

NAME	TYPE	KIND	POW.	ACC.	PP	RANGE

TM MOVES

NO.	NAME	TYPE	KIND	POW.	ACC.	PP	RANGE
TM15	Dig	Ground	Physical	80	100	10	Normal
TM21	Rest	Psychic	Status	—	—	10	Self
TM22	Rock Slide	Rock	Physical	75	90	5	Many Others
TM24	Snore	Normal	Special	50	100	15	Normal
TM25	Protect	Normal	Status	—	—	10	Self
TM27	Icy Wind	Ice	Special	55	95	15	Many Others
TM31	Attract	Normal	Status	—	100	15	Normal
TM33	Rain Dance	Water	Status	—	—	5	Both Sides
TM35	Hail	Ice	Status	—	—	10	Both Sides
TM36	Whirlpool	Water	Special	35	85	15	Normal
TM39	Facade	Normal	Physical	70	100	20	Normal
TM43	Brick Break	Fighting	Physical	75	100	15	Normal
TM48	Rock Tomb	Rock	Physical	60	95	15	Normal
TM53	Mud Shot	Ground	Special	55	95	15	Normal
TM57	Payback	Dark	Physical	50	100	10	Normal
TM59	Fling	Dark	Physical	—	100	10	Normal
TM76	Round	Normal	Special	60	100	15	Normal
TM83	Razor Shell	Water	Physical	75	95	10	Normal
TM94	False Swipe	Normal	Physical	40	100	40	Normal

TR MOVES

NO.	NAME	TYPE	KIND	POW.	ACC.	PP	RANGE
TR00	Swords Dance	Normal	Status	—	—	20	Self
TR01	Body Slam	Normal	Physical	85	100	15	Normal
TR03	Hydro Pump	Water	Special	110	80	5	Normal
TR04	Surf	Water	Special	90	100	15	All Others
TR05	Ice Beam	Ice	Special	90	100	10	Normal
TR06	Blizzard	Ice	Special	110	70	5	Many Others
TR16	Waterfall	Water	Physical	80	100	15	Normal
TR20	Substitute	Normal	Status	—	—	10	Self
TR22	Sludge Bomb	Poison	Special	90	100	10	Normal
TR26	Endure	Normal	Status	—	—	10	Self
TR27	Sleep Talk	Normal	Status	—	—	10	Self
TR32	Crunch	Dark	Physical	80	100	15	Normal
TR37	Taunt	Dark	Status	—	100	20	Normal
TR39	Superpower	Fighting	Physical	120	100	5	Normal
TR45	Muddy Water	Water	Special	90	85	10	Many Others
TR46	Iron Defense	Steel	Status	—	—	15	Self
TR51	Dragon Dance	Dragon	Status	—	—	20	Self
TR60	X-Scissor	Bug	Physical	80	100	15	Normal
TR84	Scald	Water	Special	80	100	15	Normal

ABILITY
Hyper Cutter
Shell Armor

HIDDEN ABILITY
Adaptability

SPECIES STRENGTHS

HP
ATTACK
DEFENSE
SP. ATK
SP. DEF
SPEED

DAMAGE TAKEN IN BATTLE

×1 ×1 ×1
×0.5 ×1 ×1
×0.5 ×1 ×1
×2 ×1 ×1
×2 ×1 ×0.5
×0.5 ×1 ×1

WATER 1
WATER 3

103

Crawdaunt   p. 57

ABILITY
Hyper Cutter
Shell Armor

HIDDEN ABILITY
Adaptability

SPECIES STRENGTHS

HP	▮▮▮
ATTACK	▮▮▮▮▮▮▮
DEFENSE	▮▮▮▮
SP. ATK	▮▮▮▮▮
SP. DEF	▮▮▮
SPEED	▮▮▮

DAMAGE TAKEN IN BATTLE

◉ ×1	▥ ×2	✦ ×1
🔥 ×0.5	◉ ×1	✦ ×0.5
💧 ×0.5	△ ×1	✦ ×1
◍ ×2	✦ ×1	◐ ×0.5
⚡ ×2	◉ ×0	◉ ×0.5
❋ ×0.5	◉ ×2	✦ ×2

WATER 1
WATER 3

LEVEL-UP MOVES

LV.	NAME	TYPE	KIND	POW.	ACC.	PP	RANGE
1	Harden	Normal	Status	—	—	30	Self
1	Leer	Normal	Status	—	100	30	Many Others
1	Swift	Normal	Special	60	—	20	Many Others
1	Taunt	Dark	Status	—	100	20	Normal
1	Water Gun	Water	Special	40	100	25	Normal
12	Bubble Beam	Water	Special	65	100	20	Normal
16	Knock Off	Dark	Physical	65	100	20	Normal
20	Double Hit	Normal	Physical	35	90	10	Normal
24	Protect	Normal	Status	—	—	10	Self
28	Night Slash	Dark	Physical	70	100	15	Normal
34	Razor Shell	Water	Physical	75	95	10	Normal
40	Swords Dance	Normal	Status	—	—	20	Self
46	Crunch	Dark	Physical	80	100	15	Normal
52	Crabhammer	Water	Physical	100	90	10	Normal
58	Endeavor	Normal	Physical	—	100	5	Normal
64	Guillotine	Normal	Physical	—	30	5	Normal

EVOLUTION MOVES

NAME	TYPE	KIND	POW.	ACC.	PP	RANGE
Swift	Normal	Special	60	—	20	Many Others

EGG MOVES

NAME	TYPE	KIND	POW.	ACC.	PP	RANGE

TUTOR MOVES

NAME	TYPE	KIND	POW.	ACC.	PP	RANGE

TM MOVES

NO.	NAME	TYPE	KIND	POW.	ACC.	PP	RANGE
TM08	Hyper Beam	Normal	Special	150	90	5	Normal
TM09	Giga Impact	Normal	Physical	150	90	5	Normal
TM15	Dig	Ground	Physical	80	100	10	Normal
TM21	Rest	Psychic	Status	—	—	10	Self
TM22	Rock Slide	Rock	Physical	75	90	10	Many Others
TM24	Snore	Normal	Special	50	100	15	Normal
TM25	Protect	Normal	Status	—	—	10	Self
TM27	Icy Wind	Ice	Special	55	95	15	Many Others
TM31	Attract	Normal	Status	—	100	15	Normal
TM33	Rain Dance	Water	Status	—	—	5	Both Sides
TM35	Hail	Ice	Status	—	—	10	Both Sides
TM36	Whirlpool	Water	Special	35	85	15	Normal
TM39	Facade	Normal	Physical	70	100	20	Normal
TM40	Swift	Normal	Special	60	—	20	Many Others
TM42	Revenge	Fighting	Physical	60	100	10	Normal
TM43	Brick Break	Fighting	Physical	75	100	15	Normal
TM45	Dive	Water	Physical	80	100	10	Normal
TM48	Rock Tomb	Rock	Physical	60	95	15	Normal
TM53	Mud Shot	Ground	Special	55	95	15	Normal
TM57	Payback	Dark	Physical	50	100	10	Normal
TM59	Fling	Dark	Physical	—	100	10	Normal
TM64	Avalanche	Ice	Physical	60	100	10	Normal
TM76	Round	Normal	Special	60	100	15	Normal
TM79	Retaliate	Normal	Physical	70	100	5	Normal
TM83	Razor Shell	Water	Physical	75	95	10	Normal
TM85	Snarl	Dark	Special	55	95	15	Many Others
TM94	False Swipe	Normal	Physical	40	100	40	Normal

TR MOVES

NO.	NAME	TYPE	KIND	POW.	ACC.	PP	RANGE
TR00	Swords Dance	Normal	Status	—	—	20	Self
TR01	Body Slam	Normal	Physical	85	100	15	Normal
TR03	Hydro Pump	Water	Special	110	80	5	Normal
TR04	Surf	Water	Special	90	100	15	All Others
TR05	Ice Beam	Ice	Special	90	100	10	Normal
TR06	Blizzard	Ice	Special	110	70	5	Many Others
TR16	Waterfall	Water	Physical	80	100	15	Normal
TR20	Substitute	Normal	Status	—	—	10	Self
TR22	Sludge Bomb	Poison	Special	90	100	10	Normal
TR26	Endure	Normal	Status	—	—	10	Self
TR27	Sleep Talk	Normal	Status	—	—	10	Self
TR32	Crunch	Dark	Physical	80	100	15	Normal
TR37	Taunt	Dark	Status	—	100	20	Normal
TR39	Superpower	Fighting	Physical	120	100	5	Normal
TR45	Muddy Water	Water	Special	90	85	10	Many Others
TR46	Iron Defense	Steel	Status	—	—	15	Self
TR51	Dragon Dance	Dragon	Status	—	—	20	Self
TR53	Close Combat	Fighting	Physical	120	100	5	Normal
TR58	Dark Pulse	Dark	Special	80	100	15	Normal
TR68	X-Scissor	Bug	Physical	80	100	15	Normal
TR68	Nasty Plot	Dark	Status	—	—	20	Self
TR78	Sludge Wave	Poison	Special	95	100	10	All Others
TR84	Scald	Water	Special	80	100	15	Normal
TR98	Liquidation	Water	Physical	85	100	10	Normal

104

Nincada   p. 58

ABILITY
Compound Eyes
—

HIDDEN ABILITY
Run Away

SPECIES STRENGTHS

HP	▮▮
ATTACK	▮▮▮
DEFENSE	▮▮▮▮▮
SP. ATK	▮▮
SP. DEF	▮▮
SPEED	▮▮▮

DAMAGE TAKEN IN BATTLE

◉ ×1	▥ ×0.5	✦ ×1
🔥 ×2	◉ ×0.5	✦ ×1
💧 ×2	△ ×0.5	✦ ×1
◍ ×1	✦ ×2	◐ ×1
⚡ ×0	◉ ×1	◉ ×1
❋ ×2	◉ ×1	✦ ×1

BUG

LEVEL-UP MOVES

LV.	NAME	TYPE	KIND	POW.	ACC.	PP	RANGE
1	Sand Attack	Ground	Status	—	100	15	Normal
1	Scratch	Normal	Physical	40	100	35	Normal
5	Harden	Normal	Status	—	—	30	Self
10	False Swipe	Normal	Physical	40	100	40	Normal
15	Mud-Slap	Ground	Special	20	100	10	Normal
21	Absorb	Grass	Special	20	100	25	Normal
25	Metal Claw	Steel	Physical	50	95	35	Normal
30	Fury Swipes	Normal	Physical	18	80	15	Normal
35	Mind Reader	Normal	Status	—	—	5	Normal
40	Dig	Ground	Physical	80	100	10	Normal

EVOLUTION MOVES

NAME	TYPE	KIND	POW.	ACC.	PP	RANGE

EGG MOVES

NAME	TYPE	KIND	POW.	ACC.	PP	RANGE
Bug Bite	Bug	Physical	60	100	20	Normal
Final Gambit	Fighting	Special	—	100	5	Normal
Flail	Normal	Physical	—	100	15	Normal
Gust	Flying	Special	40	100	35	Normal
Night Slash	Dark	Physical	70	100	15	Normal

TUTOR MOVES

NAME	TYPE	KIND	POW.	ACC.	PP	RANGE

TM MOVES

NO.	NAME	TYPE	KIND	POW.	ACC.	PP	RANGE
TM11	Solar Beam	Grass	Special	120	100	10	Normal
TM15	Dig	Ground	Physical	80	100	10	Normal
TM21	Rest	Psychic	Status	—	—	10	Self
TM24	Snore	Normal	Special	50	100	15	Normal
TM25	Protect	Normal	Status	—	—	10	Self
TM28	Giga Drain	Grass	Special	75	100	10	Normal
TM32	Sandstorm	Rock	Status	—	—	10	Both Sides
TM34	Sunny Day	Fire	Status	—	—	5	Both Sides
TM39	Facade	Normal	Physical	70	100	20	Normal
TM76	Round	Normal	Special	60	100	15	Normal
TM94	False Swipe	Normal	Physical	40	100	40	Normal

TR MOVES

NO.	NAME	TYPE	KIND	POW.	ACC.	PP	RANGE
TR18	Leech Life	Bug	Physical	80	100	10	Normal
TR20	Substitute	Normal	Status	—	—	10	Self
TR26	Endure	Normal	Status	—	—	10	Self
TR27	Sleep Talk	Normal	Status	—	—	10	Self
TR33	Shadow Ball	Ghost	Special	80	100	15	Normal
TR60	X-Scissor	Bug	Physical	80	100	15	Normal
TR61	Bug Buzz	Bug	Special	90	100	10	Normal

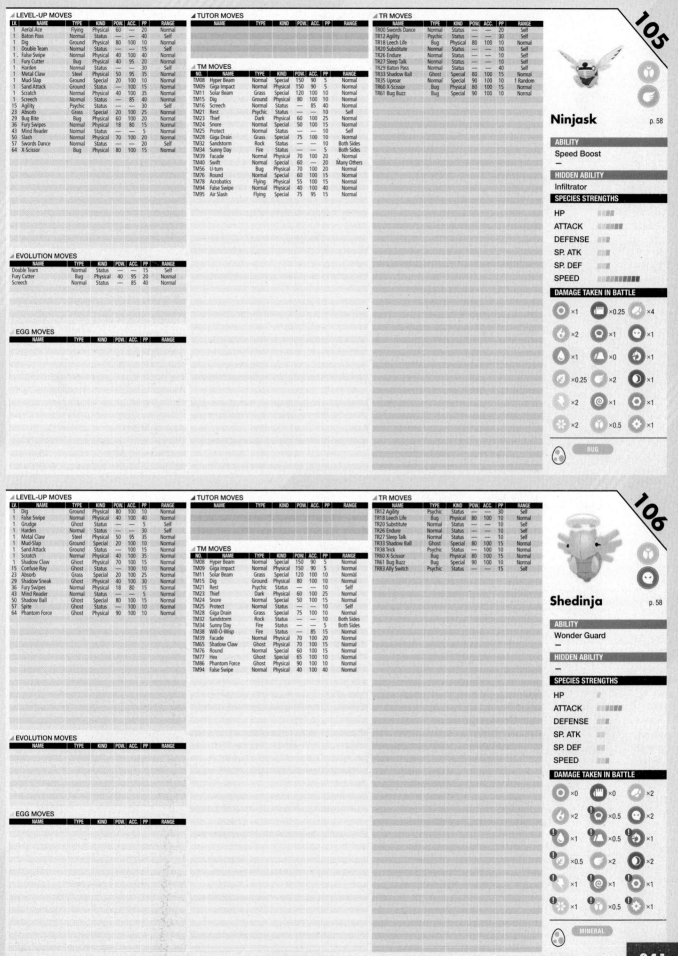

105 — Ninjask

LEVEL-UP MOVES

LV.	NAME	TYPE	KIND	POW.	ACC.	PP	RANGE
1	Aerial Ace	Flying	Physical	60	—	20	Normal
1	Baton Pass	Normal	Status	—	—	40	Self
1	Dig	Ground	Physical	80	100	10	Normal
1	Double Team	Normal	Status	—	—	15	Self
1	False Swipe	Normal	Physical	40	100	40	Normal
1	Fury Cutter	Bug	Physical	40	95	20	Normal
1	Harden	Normal	Status	—	—	30	Self
1	Metal Claw	Steel	Physical	50	95	35	Normal
1	Mud-Slap	Ground	Special	20	100	10	Normal
1	Sand Attack	Ground	Status	—	100	15	Normal
1	Scratch	Normal	Physical	40	100	35	Normal
1	Screech	Normal	Status	—	85	40	Normal
15	Agility	Psychic	Status	—	—	30	Self
23	Absorb	Grass	Special	20	100	25	Normal
29	Bug Bite	Bug	Physical	60	100	20	Normal
36	Fury Swipes	Normal	Physical	18	80	15	Normal
43	Mind Reader	Normal	Status	—	—	5	Normal
50	Slash	Normal	Physical	70	100	20	Normal
57	Swords Dance	Normal	Status	—	—	20	Self
64	X-Scissor	Bug	Physical	80	100	15	Normal

EVOLUTION MOVES

NAME	TYPE	KIND	POW.	ACC.	PP	RANGE
Double Team	Normal	Status	—	—	15	Self
Fury Cutter	Bug	Physical	40	95	20	Normal
Screech	Normal	Status	—	85	40	Normal

EGG MOVES

NAME	TYPE	KIND	POW.	ACC.	PP	RANGE

TUTOR MOVES

NAME	TYPE	KIND	POW.	ACC.	PP	RANGE

TM MOVES

NO.	NAME	TYPE	KIND	POW.	ACC.	PP	RANGE
TM08	Hyper Beam	Normal	Special	150	90	5	Normal
TM09	Giga Impact	Normal	Physical	150	90	5	Normal
TM11	Solar Beam	Grass	Special	120	100	10	Normal
TM15	Dig	Ground	Physical	80	100	10	Normal
TM16	Screech	Normal	Status	—	85	40	Normal
TM21	Rest	Psychic	Status	—	—	10	Self
TM23	Thief	Dark	Physical	60	100	25	Normal
TM24	Snore	Normal	Special	50	100	15	Normal
TM25	Protect	Normal	Status	—	—	10	Self
TM28	Giga Drain	Grass	Special	75	100	10	Normal
TM32	Sandstorm	Rock	Status	—	—	10	Both Sides
TM34	Sunny Day	Fire	Status	—	—	5	Both Sides
TM39	Facade	Normal	Physical	70	100	20	Normal
TM40	Swift	Normal	Special	60	—	20	Many Others
TM56	U-turn	Bug	Physical	70	100	20	Normal
TM76	Round	Normal	Special	60	100	15	Normal
TM78	Acrobatics	Flying	Physical	55	100	15	Normal
TM94	False Swipe	Normal	Physical	40	100	40	Normal
TM95	Air Slash	Flying	Special	75	95	15	Normal

TR MOVES

NAME	TYPE	KIND	POW.	ACC.	PP	RANGE
TR00 Swords Dance	Normal	Status	—	—	20	Self
TR12 Agility	Psychic	Status	—	—	30	Self
TR18 Leech Life	Bug	Physical	80	100	10	Normal
TR20 Substitute	Normal	Status	—	—	10	Self
TR26 Endure	Normal	Status	—	—	10	Self
TR29 Baton Pass	Normal	Status	—	—	40	Self
TR33 Shadow Ball	Ghost	Special	80	100	15	Normal
TR35 Uproar	Normal	Special	90	100	10	1 Random
TR60 X-Scissor	Bug	Physical	80	100	15	Normal
TR61 Bug Buzz	Bug	Special	90	100	10	Normal

Ninjask — p. 58

ABILITY
Speed Boost
—

HIDDEN ABILITY
Infiltrator

SPECIES STRENGTHS
- HP
- ATTACK
- DEFENSE
- SP. ATK
- SP. DEF
- SPEED

DAMAGE TAKEN IN BATTLE
×1, ×0.25, ×4
×2, ×1, ×1
×1, ×0, ×1
×0.25, ×2, ×1
×2, ×1, ×1
×2, ×0.5, ×1

BUG

---

106 — Shedinja

LEVEL-UP MOVES

LV.	NAME	TYPE	KIND	POW.	ACC.	PP	RANGE
1	Dig	Ground	Physical	80	100	10	Normal
1	False Swipe	Normal	Physical	40	100	40	Normal
1	Grudge	Ghost	Status	—	—	5	Self
1	Harden	Normal	Status	—	—	30	Self
1	Metal Claw	Steel	Physical	50	95	35	Normal
1	Mud-Slap	Ground	Special	20	100	10	Normal
1	Scratch	Normal	Physical	40	100	35	Normal
1	Shadow Claw	Ghost	Physical	70	100	15	Normal
15	Confuse Ray	Ghost	Status	—	100	10	Normal
23	Absorb	Grass	Special	20	100	25	Normal
29	Shadow Sneak	Ghost	Physical	40	100	30	Normal
36	Fury Swipes	Normal	Physical	18	80	15	Normal
43	Mind Reader	Normal	Status	—	—	5	Normal
50	Shadow Ball	Ghost	Special	80	100	15	Normal
57	Spite	Ghost	Status	—	—	10	Normal
64	Phantom Force	Ghost	Physical	90	100	10	Normal

EVOLUTION MOVES

NAME	TYPE	KIND	POW.	ACC.	PP	RANGE

EGG MOVES

NAME	TYPE	KIND	POW.	ACC.	PP	RANGE

TUTOR MOVES

NAME	TYPE	KIND	POW.	ACC.	PP	RANGE

TM MOVES

NO.	NAME	TYPE	KIND	POW.	ACC.	PP	RANGE
TM08	Hyper Beam	Normal	Special	150	90	5	Normal
TM09	Giga Impact	Normal	Physical	150	90	5	Normal
TM11	Solar Beam	Grass	Special	120	100	10	Normal
TM15	Dig	Ground	Physical	80	100	10	Normal
TM21	Rest	Psychic	Status	—	—	10	Self
TM23	Thief	Dark	Physical	60	100	25	Normal
TM24	Snore	Normal	Special	50	100	15	Normal
TM25	Protect	Normal	Status	—	—	10	Self
TM28	Giga Drain	Grass	Special	75	100	10	Normal
TM32	Sandstorm	Rock	Status	—	—	10	Both Sides
TM34	Sunny Day	Fire	Status	—	—	5	Both Sides
TM38	Will-O-Wisp	Fire	Status	—	85	15	Normal
TM39	Facade	Normal	Physical	70	100	20	Normal
TM65	Shadow Claw	Ghost	Physical	70	100	15	Normal
TM76	Round	Normal	Special	60	100	15	Normal
TM77	Hex	Ghost	Special	65	100	10	Normal
TM86	Phantom Force	Ghost	Physical	90	100	10	Normal
TM94	False Swipe	Normal	Physical	40	100	40	Normal

TR MOVES

NAME	TYPE	KIND	POW.	ACC.	PP	RANGE
TR12 Agility	Psychic	Status	—	—	30	Self
TR18 Leech Life	Bug	Physical	80	100	10	Normal
TR20 Substitute	Normal	Status	—	—	10	Self
TR26 Endure	Normal	Status	—	—	10	Self
TR27 Sleep Talk	Normal	Status	—	—	10	Self
TR33 Shadow Ball	Ghost	Special	80	100	15	Normal
TR38 Trick	Psychic	Status	—	—	10	Normal
TR60 X-Scissor	Bug	Physical	80	100	15	Normal
TR61 Bug Buzz	Bug	Special	90	100	10	Normal
TR83 Ally Switch	Psychic	Status	—	—	15	Self

Shedinja — p. 58

ABILITY
Wonder Guard
—

HIDDEN ABILITY
—

SPECIES STRENGTHS
- HP
- ATTACK
- DEFENSE
- SP. ATK
- SP. DEF
- SPEED

DAMAGE TAKEN IN BATTLE
×0, ×0, ×2
×2, ×0.5, ×2
×1, ×0.5, ×1
×0.5, ×2, ×2
×1, ×1, ×1
×1, ×0.5, ×1

MINERAL

107 Tyrogue — p. 59

ABILITY
Guts
Steadfast

HIDDEN ABILITY
Vital Spirit

SPECIES STRENGTHS

HP	
ATTACK	
DEFENSE	
SP. ATK	
SP. DEF	
SPEED	

DAMAGE TAKEN IN BATTLE

×1 ×1 ×0.5
×1 ×1 ×1
×1 ×1 ×1
×1 ×2 ×0.5
×1 ×2 ×1
×1 ×0.5 ×2

NO EGGS

LEVEL-UP MOVES

LV.	NAME	TYPE	KIND	POW.	ACC.	PP	RANGE
1	Fake Out	Normal	Physical	40	100	10	Normal
1	Focus Energy	Normal	Status	—	—	30	Self
1	Helping Hand	Normal	Status	—	—	20	1 Ally
1	Tackle	Normal	Physical	40	100	35	Normal

EVOLUTION MOVES

NAME	TYPE	KIND	POW.	ACC.	PP	RANGE

EGG MOVES

NAME	TYPE	KIND	POW.	ACC.	PP	RANGE
Bullet Punch	Steel	Physical	40	100	30	Normal
Counter	Fighting	Physical	—	100	20	Varies
Feint	Normal	Physical	30	100	10	Normal
High Jump Kick	Fighting	Physical	130	90	10	Normal
Mach Punch	Fighting	Physical	40	100	30	Normal
Mind Reader	Normal	Status	—	—	5	Normal
Rapid Spin	Normal	Physical	50	100	40	Normal
Vacuum Wave	Fighting	Special	40	100	30	Normal

TUTOR MOVES

NAME	TYPE	KIND	POW.	ACC.	PP	RANGE

TM MOVES

NO.	NAME	TYPE	KIND	POW.	ACC.	PP	RANGE
TM00	Mega Punch	Normal	Physical	80	85	20	Normal
TM01	Mega Kick	Normal	Physical	120	75	5	Normal
TM21	Rest	Psychic	Status	—	—	10	Self
TM22	Rock Slide	Rock	Physical	75	90	10	Many Others
TM23	Thief	Dark	Physical	60	100	25	Normal
TM24	Snore	Normal	Special	50	100	15	Normal
TM25	Protect	Normal	Status	—	—	10	Self
TM31	Attract	Normal	Status	—	100	15	Normal
TM33	Rain Dance	Water	Status	—	—	5	Both Sides
TM34	Sunny Day	Fire	Status	—	—	5	Both Sides
TM39	Facade	Normal	Physical	70	100	20	Normal
TM40	Swift	Normal	Special	60	—	20	Many Others
TM41	Helping Hand	Normal	Status	—	—	20	1 Ally
TM43	Brick Break	Fighting	Physical	75	100	15	Normal
TM75	Low Sweep	Fighting	Physical	65	100	20	Normal
TM76	Round	Normal	Special	60	100	15	Normal
TM79	Retaliate	Normal	Physical	70	100	5	Normal
TM81	Bulldoze	Ground	Physical	60	100	20	All Others

TR MOVES

NO.	NAME	TYPE	KIND	POW.	ACC.	PP	RANGE
TR01	Body Slam	Normal	Physical	85	100	15	Normal
TR07	Low Kick	Fighting	Physical	—	100	20	Normal
TR10	Earthquake	Ground	Physical	100	100	10	All Others
TR13	Focus Energy	Normal	Status	—	—	30	Self
TR20	Substitute	Normal	Status	—	—	10	Self
TR26	Endure	Normal	Status	—	—	10	Self
TR27	Sleep Talk	Normal	Status	—	—	10	Self
TR35	Uproar	Normal	Special	90	100	10	1 Random
TR48	Bulk Up	Fighting	Status	—	—	20	Self
TR85	Work Up	Normal	Status	—	—	30	Self

---

108 Hitmonlee — p. 59

ABILITY
Limber
Reckless

HIDDEN ABILITY
Unburden

SPECIES STRENGTHS

HP	
ATTACK	
DEFENSE	
SP. ATK	
SP. DEF	
SPEED	

DAMAGE TAKEN IN BATTLE

×1 ×1 ×0.5
×1 ×1 ×1
×1 ×1 ×1
×2 ×0.5
×1 ×2 ×1
×1 ×0.5 ×2

HUMANLIKE

LEVEL-UP MOVES

LV.	NAME	TYPE	KIND	POW.	ACC.	PP	RANGE
1	Brick Break	Fighting	Physical	75	100	15	Normal
1	Fake Out	Normal	Physical	40	100	10	Normal
1	Feint	Normal	Physical	30	100	10	Normal
1	Focus Energy	Normal	Status	—	—	30	Self
1	Helping Hand	Normal	Status	—	—	20	1 Ally
1	Low Sweep	Fighting	Physical	65	100	20	Normal
1	Tackle	Normal	Physical	40	100	35	Normal
4	Double Kick	Fighting	Physical	30	100	30	Normal
8	Low Kick	Fighting	Physical	—	100	20	Normal
12	Endure	Normal	Status	—	—	10	Self
16	Revenge	Fighting	Physical	60	100	10	Normal
20	Wide Guard	Rock	Status	—	—	10	Your Side
24	Blaze Kick	Fire	Physical	85	90	10	Normal
28	Mind Reader	Normal	Status	—	—	5	Normal
32	Mega Kick	Normal	Physical	120	75	5	Normal
36	Close Combat	Fighting	Physical	120	100	5	Normal
40	Reversal	Fighting	Physical	—	100	15	Normal
44	High Jump Kick	Fighting	Physical	130	90	10	Normal

EVOLUTION MOVES

NAME	TYPE	KIND	POW.	ACC.	PP	RANGE
Brick Break	Fighting	Physical	75	100	15	Normal

EGG MOVES

NAME	TYPE	KIND	POW.	ACC.	PP	RANGE

TUTOR MOVES

NAME	TYPE	KIND	POW.	ACC.	PP	RANGE

TM MOVES

NO.	NAME	TYPE	KIND	POW.	ACC.	PP	RANGE
TM00	Mega Punch	Normal	Physical	80	85	20	Normal
TM01	Mega Kick	Normal	Physical	120	75	5	Normal
TM21	Rest	Psychic	Status	—	—	10	Self
TM22	Rock Slide	Rock	Physical	75	90	10	Many Others
TM23	Thief	Dark	Physical	60	100	25	Normal
TM24	Snore	Normal	Special	50	100	15	Normal
TM25	Protect	Normal	Status	—	—	10	Self
TM31	Attract	Normal	Status	—	100	15	Normal
TM33	Rain Dance	Water	Status	—	—	5	Both Sides
TM34	Sunny Day	Fire	Status	—	—	5	Both Sides
TM39	Facade	Normal	Physical	70	100	20	Normal
TM40	Swift	Normal	Special	60	—	20	Many Others
TM41	Helping Hand	Normal	Status	—	—	20	1 Ally
TM42	Revenge	Fighting	Physical	60	100	10	Normal
TM43	Brick Break	Fighting	Physical	75	100	15	Normal
TM48	Rock Tomb	Rock	Physical	60	95	15	Normal
TM52	Bounce	Flying	Physical	85	85	5	Normal
TM59	Fling	Dark	Physical	—	100	10	Normal
TM75	Low Sweep	Fighting	Physical	65	100	20	Normal
TM76	Round	Normal	Special	60	100	15	Normal
TM79	Retaliate	Normal	Physical	70	100	5	Normal
TM81	Bulldoze	Ground	Physical	60	100	20	All Others
TM98	Stomping Tantrum	Ground	Physical	75	100	10	Normal

TR MOVES

NO.	NAME	TYPE	KIND	POW.	ACC.	PP	RANGE
TR01	Body Slam	Normal	Physical	85	100	15	Normal
TR07	Low Kick	Fighting	Physical	—	100	20	Normal
TR10	Earthquake	Ground	Physical	100	100	10	All Others
TR13	Focus Energy	Normal	Status	—	—	30	Self
TR14	Metronome	Normal	Status	—	—	10	Self
TR20	Substitute	Normal	Status	—	—	10	Self
TR21	Reversal	Fighting	Physical	—	100	15	Normal
TR26	Endure	Normal	Status	—	—	10	Self
TR27	Sleep Talk	Normal	Status	—	—	10	Self
TR35	Uproar	Normal	Special	90	100	10	1 Random
TR39	Superpower	Fighting	Physical	120	100	5	Normal
TR41	Blaze Kick	Fire	Physical	85	90	10	Normal
TR48	Bulk Up	Fighting	Status	—	—	20	Self
TR53	Close Combat	Fighting	Physical	120	100	5	Normal
TR56	Aura Sphere	Fighting	Special	80	—	20	Normal
TR57	Poison Jab	Poison	Physical	80	100	20	Normal
TR64	Focus Blast	Fighting	Special	120	70	5	Normal
TR75	Stone Edge	Rock	Physical	100	80	5	Normal
TR85	Work Up	Normal	Status	—	—	30	Self
TR95	Throat Chop	Dark	Physical	80	100	15	Normal

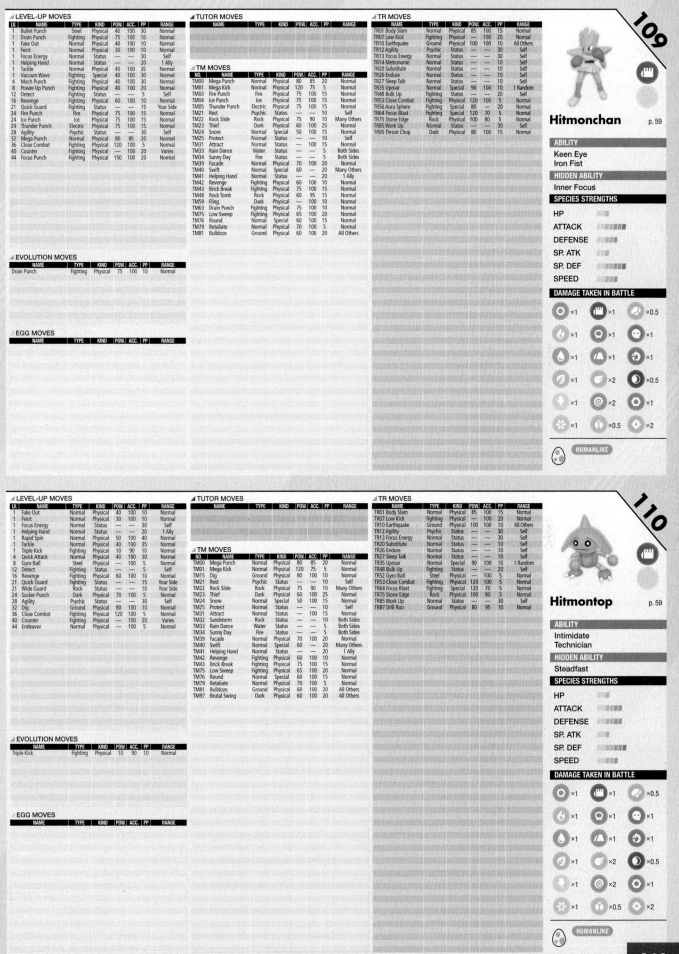

109

Hitmonchan — p. 59

LEVEL-UP MOVES

LV.	NAME	TYPE	KIND	POW.	ACC.	PP	RANGE
1	Bullet Punch	Steel	Physical	40	100	30	Normal
1	Drain Punch	Fighting	Physical	75	100	10	Normal
1	Fake Out	Normal	Physical	40	100	10	Normal
1	Feint	Normal	Physical	30	100	10	Normal
1	Focus Energy	Normal	Status	—	—	30	Self
1	Helping Hand	Normal	Status	—	—	20	1 Ally
1	Tackle	Normal	Physical	40	100	35	Normal
1	Vacuum Wave	Fighting	Special	40	100	30	Normal
4	Mach Punch	Fighting	Physical	40	100	30	Normal
8	Power-Up Punch	Fighting	Physical	40	100	20	Normal
12	Detect	Fighting	Status	—	—	5	Self
16	Revenge	Fighting	Physical	60	100	10	Normal
21	Quick Guard	Fighting	Status	—	—	15	Your Side
24	Fire Punch	Fire	Physical	75	100	15	Normal
24	Ice Punch	Ice	Physical	75	100	15	Normal
24	Thunder Punch	Electric	Physical	75	100	15	Normal
28	Agility	Psychic	Status	—	—	30	Self
32	Mega Punch	Normal	Physical	80	85	20	Normal
36	Close Combat	Fighting	Physical	120	100	5	Normal
40	Counter	Fighting	Physical	—	100	20	Varies
44	Focus Punch	Fighting	Physical	150	100	20	Normal

EVOLUTION MOVES

NAME	TYPE	KIND	POW.	ACC.	PP	RANGE
Drain Punch	Fighting	Physical	75	100	10	Normal

EGG MOVES

NAME	TYPE	KIND	POW.	ACC.	PP	RANGE

TUTOR MOVES

NAME	TYPE	KIND	POW.	ACC.	PP	RANGE

TM MOVES

NO.	NAME	TYPE	KIND	POW.	ACC.	PP	RANGE
TM00	Mega Punch	Normal	Physical	80	85	20	Normal
TM01	Mega Kick	Normal	Physical	120	75	5	Normal
TM03	Fire Punch	Fire	Physical	75	100	15	Normal
TM04	Ice Punch	Ice	Physical	75	100	15	Normal
TM05	Thunder Punch	Electric	Physical	75	100	15	Normal
TM21	Rest	Psychic	Status	—	—	10	Self
TM22	Rock Slide	Rock	Physical	75	90	10	Many Others
TM23	Thief	Dark	Physical	60	100	25	Normal
TM24	Snore	Normal	Special	50	100	15	Normal
TM25	Protect	Normal	Status	—	—	10	Self
TM31	Attract	Normal	Status	—	100	15	Normal
TM33	Rain Dance	Water	Status	—	—	5	Both Sides
TM34	Sunny Day	Fire	Status	—	—	5	Both Sides
TM39	Facade	Normal	Physical	70	100	20	Normal
TM40	Swift	Normal	Special	60	—	20	Many Others
TM41	Helping Hand	Normal	Status	—	—	20	1 Ally
TM42	Revenge	Fighting	Physical	60	100	10	Normal
TM43	Brick Break	Fighting	Physical	75	100	15	Normal
TM48	Rock Tomb	Rock	Physical	60	95	15	Normal
TM59	Fling	Dark	Physical	—	100	10	Normal
TM63	Drain Punch	Fighting	Physical	75	100	10	Normal
TM75	Low Sweep	Fighting	Physical	65	100	20	Normal
TM76	Round	Normal	Special	60	100	15	Normal
TM79	Retaliate	Normal	Physical	70	100	5	Normal
TM81	Bulldoze	Ground	Physical	60	100	20	All Others

TR MOVES

NAME	TYPE	KIND	POW.	ACC.	PP	RANGE
TR01	Body Slam	Normal	Physical	85	100	15	Normal
TR07	Low Kick	Fighting	Physical	—	100	20	Normal
TR10	Earthquake	Ground	Physical	100	100	10	All Others
TR12	Agility	Psychic	Status	—	—	30	Self
TR13	Focus Energy	Normal	Status	—	—	30	Self
TR14	Metronome	Normal	Status	—	—	10	Self
TR20	Substitute	Normal	Status	—	—	10	Self
TR26	Endure	Normal	Status	—	—	10	Self
TR27	Sleep Talk	Normal	Status	—	—	10	Self
TR35	Uproar	Normal	Special	90	100	10	1 Random
TR48	Bulk Up	Fighting	Status	—	—	20	Self
TR53	Close Combat	Fighting	Physical	120	100	5	Normal
TR56	Aura Sphere	Fighting	Special	80	—	20	Normal
TR64	Focus Blast	Fighting	Special	120	70	5	Normal
TR75	Stone Edge	Rock	Physical	100	80	5	Normal
TR85	Work Up	Normal	Status	—	—	30	Self
TR95	Throat Chop	Dark	Physical	80	100	15	Normal

ABILITY
Keen Eye
Iron Fist

HIDDEN ABILITY
Inner Focus

SPECIES STRENGTHS
- HP
- ATTACK
- DEFENSE
- SP. ATK
- SP. DEF
- SPEED

DAMAGE TAKEN IN BATTLE

×1	×1	×0.5
×1	×1	×1
×1	×1	×1
×1	×2	×0.5
×1	×2	×1
×1	×0.5	×2

HUMANLIKE

110

Hitmontop — p. 59

LEVEL-UP MOVES

LV.	NAME	TYPE	KIND	POW.	ACC.	PP	RANGE
1	Fake Out	Normal	Physical	40	100	10	Normal
1	Feint	Normal	Physical	30	100	10	Normal
1	Focus Energy	Normal	Status	—	—	30	Self
1	Helping Hand	Normal	Status	—	—	20	1 Ally
1	Rapid Spin	Normal	Physical	50	100	40	Normal
1	Tackle	Normal	Physical	40	100	35	Normal
1	Triple Kick	Fighting	Physical	10	90	10	Normal
4	Quick Attack	Normal	Physical	40	100	30	Normal
8	Gyro Ball	Steel	Physical	—	100	5	Normal
12	Detect	Fighting	Status	—	—	5	Self
16	Revenge	Fighting	Physical	60	100	10	Normal
21	Quick Guard	Fighting	Status	—	—	15	Your Side
21	Wide Guard	Rock	Status	—	—	10	Your Side
24	Sucker Punch	Dark	Physical	70	100	5	Normal
28	Agility	Psychic	Status	—	—	30	Self
32	Dig	Ground	Physical	80	100	10	Normal
36	Close Combat	Fighting	Physical	120	100	5	Normal
40	Counter	Fighting	Physical	—	100	20	Varies
44	Endeavor	Normal	Physical	—	100	5	Normal

EVOLUTION MOVES

NAME	TYPE	KIND	POW.	ACC.	PP	RANGE
Triple Kick	Fighting	Physical	10	90	10	Normal

EGG MOVES

NAME	TYPE	KIND	POW.	ACC.	PP	RANGE

TUTOR MOVES

NAME	TYPE	KIND	POW.	ACC.	PP	RANGE

TM MOVES

NO.	NAME	TYPE	KIND	POW.	ACC.	PP	RANGE
TM00	Mega Punch	Normal	Physical	80	85	20	Normal
TM01	Mega Kick	Normal	Physical	120	75	5	Normal
TM15	Dig	Ground	Physical	80	100	10	Normal
TM21	Rest	Psychic	Status	—	—	10	Self
TM22	Rock Slide	Rock	Physical	75	90	10	Many Others
TM23	Thief	Dark	Physical	60	100	25	Normal
TM24	Snore	Normal	Special	50	100	15	Normal
TM25	Protect	Normal	Status	—	—	10	Self
TM31	Attract	Normal	Status	—	100	15	Normal
TM32	Sandstorm	Rock	Status	—	—	10	Both Sides
TM33	Rain Dance	Water	Status	—	—	5	Both Sides
TM34	Sunny Day	Fire	Status	—	—	5	Both Sides
TM39	Facade	Normal	Physical	70	100	20	Normal
TM40	Swift	Normal	Special	60	—	20	Many Others
TM41	Helping Hand	Normal	Status	—	—	20	1 Ally
TM42	Revenge	Fighting	Physical	60	100	10	Normal
TM43	Brick Break	Fighting	Physical	75	100	15	Normal
TM75	Low Sweep	Fighting	Physical	65	100	20	Normal
TM76	Round	Normal	Special	60	100	15	Normal
TM79	Retaliate	Normal	Physical	70	100	5	Normal
TM81	Bulldoze	Ground	Physical	60	100	20	All Others
TM97	Brutal Swing	Dark	Physical	60	100	20	All Others

TR MOVES

NAME	TYPE	KIND	POW.	ACC.	PP	RANGE
TR01	Body Slam	Normal	Physical	85	100	15	Normal
TR07	Low Kick	Fighting	Physical	—	100	20	Normal
TR10	Earthquake	Ground	Physical	100	100	10	All Others
TR12	Agility	Psychic	Status	—	—	30	Self
TR13	Focus Energy	Normal	Status	—	—	30	Self
TR20	Substitute	Normal	Status	—	—	10	Self
TR26	Endure	Normal	Status	—	—	10	Self
TR27	Sleep Talk	Normal	Status	—	—	10	Self
TR35	Uproar	Normal	Special	90	100	10	1 Random
TR48	Bulk Up	Fighting	Status	—	—	20	Self
TR52	Gyro Ball	Steel	Physical	—	100	5	Normal
TR53	Close Combat	Fighting	Physical	120	100	5	Normal
TR64	Focus Blast	Fighting	Special	120	70	5	Normal
TR75	Stone Edge	Rock	Physical	100	80	5	Normal
TR85	Work Up	Normal	Status	—	—	30	Self
TR87	Drill Run	Ground	Physical	80	95	10	Normal

ABILITY
Intimidate
Technician

HIDDEN ABILITY
Steadfast

SPECIES STRENGTHS
- HP
- ATTACK
- DEFENSE
- SP. ATK
- SP. DEF
- SPEED

DAMAGE TAKEN IN BATTLE

×1	×1	×0.5
×1	×1	×1
×1	×1	×1
×1	×2	×0.5
×1	×2	×1
×1	×0.5	×2

HUMANLIKE

111 Pancham p. 60

ABILITY
Iron Fist
Mold Breaker

HIDDEN ABILITY
Scrappy

SPECIES STRENGTHS
HP
ATTACK
DEFENSE
SP. ATK
SP. DEF
SPEED

DAMAGE TAKEN IN BATTLE

×1	×1	×0.5
×1	×1	×1
×1	×1	×1
×2		×0.5
×1	×2	×1
×1	×0.5	×2

FIELD / HUMANLIKE

LEVEL-UP MOVES

LV.	NAME	TYPE	KIND	POW.	ACC.	PP	RANGE
1	Leer	Normal	Status	—	100	30	Many Others
1	Tackle	Normal	Physical	40	100	35	Normal
4	Arm Thrust	Fighting	Physical	15	100	20	Normal
8	Taunt	Dark	Status	—	100	30	Normal
12	Circle Throw	Fighting	Physical	60	90	10	Normal
16	Low Sweep	Fighting	Physical	65	100	20	Normal
20	Work Up	Normal	Status	—	—	30	Self
24	Slash	Normal	Physical	70	100	20	Normal
28	Vital Throw	Fighting	Physical	70	—	10	Normal
33	Crunch	Dark	Physical	80	100	15	Normal
36	Body Slam	Normal	Physical	85	100	15	Normal
40	Parting Shot	Dark	Status	—	100	20	Normal
44	Entrainment	Normal	Status	—	100	15	Normal

EVOLUTION MOVES

NAME	TYPE	KIND	POW.	ACC.	PP	RANGE

EGG MOVES

NAME	TYPE	KIND	POW.	ACC.	PP	RANGE
Power Trip	Dark	Physical	20	100	10	Normal
Quash	Dark	Status	—	100	15	Normal
Quick Guard	Fighting	Status	—	—	15	Your Side
Seismic Toss	Fighting	Physical	—	100	20	Normal
Storm Throw	Fighting	Physical	60	100	10	Normal

TUTOR MOVES

NAME	TYPE	KIND	POW.	ACC.	PP	RANGE

TM MOVES

NO.	NAME	TYPE	KIND	POW.	ACC.	PP	RANGE
TM00	Mega Punch	Normal	Physical	80	85	20	Normal
TM01	Mega Kick	Normal	Physical	120	75	5	Normal
TM03	Fire Punch	Fire	Physical	75	100	15	Normal
TM04	Ice Punch	Ice	Physical	75	100	15	Normal
TM05	Thunder Punch	Electric	Physical	75	100	15	Normal
TM15	Dig	Ground	Physical	80	100	10	Normal
TM21	Rest	Psychic	Status	—	—	10	Self
TM22	Rock Slide	Rock	Physical	75	90	10	Many Others
TM24	Snore	Normal	Special	50	100	15	Normal
TM25	Protect	Normal	Status	—	—	10	Self
TM31	Attract	Normal	Status	—	100	15	Normal
TM33	Rain Dance	Water	Status	—	—	5	Both Sides
TM34	Sunny Day	Fire	Status	—	—	5	Both Sides
TM39	Facade	Normal	Physical	70	100	20	Normal
TM41	Helping Hand	Normal	Status	—	—	20	1 Ally
TM43	Brick Break	Fighting	Physical	75	100	15	Normal
TM48	Rock Tomb	Rock	Physical	60	95	15	Normal
TM57	Payback	Dark	Physical	50	100	10	Normal
TM59	Fling	Dark	Physical	—	100	10	Normal
TM63	Drain Punch	Fighting	Physical	75	100	10	Normal
TM65	Shadow Claw	Ghost	Physical	70	100	15	Normal
TM75	Low Sweep	Fighting	Physical	65	100	20	Normal
TM76	Round	Normal	Special	60	100	15	Normal
TM79	Retaliate	Normal	Physical	70	100	5	Normal
TM81	Bulldoze	Ground	Physical	60	100	20	All Others
TM94	False Swipe	Normal	Physical	40	100	40	Normal

TR MOVES

NO.	NAME	TYPE	KIND	POW.	ACC.	PP	RANGE
TR00	Swords Dance	Normal	Status	—	—	20	Self
TR01	Body Slam	Normal	Physical	85	100	15	Normal
TR04	Surf	Water	Special	90	100	15	All Others
TR07	Low Kick	Fighting	Physical	—	100	20	Normal
TR20	Substitute	Normal	Status	—	—	10	Self
TR22	Sludge Bomb	Poison	Special	90	100	10	Normal
TR26	Endure	Normal	Status	—	—	10	Self
TR27	Sleep Talk	Normal	Status	—	—	10	Self
TR32	Crunch	Dark	Physical	80	100	15	Normal
TR35	Uproar	Normal	Special	90	100	10	1 Random
TR37	Taunt	Dark	Status	—	100	20	Normal
TR39	Superpower	Fighting	Physical	120	100	5	Normal
TR42	Hyper Voice	Normal	Special	90	100	10	Many Others
TR48	Bulk Up	Fighting	Status	—	—	20	Self
TR58	Dark Pulse	Dark	Special	80	100	15	Normal
TR69	Zen Headbutt	Psychic	Physical	80	90	15	Normal
TR73	Gunk Shot	Poison	Physical	120	80	5	Normal
TR74	Iron Head	Steel	Physical	80	100	15	Normal
TR77	Stone Edge	Rock	Physical	100	80	5	Normal
TR81	Foul Play	Dark	Physical	95	100	15	Normal
TR85	Work Up	Normal	Status	—	—	30	Self

112 Pangoro p. 60

ABILITY
Iron Fist
Mold Breaker

HIDDEN ABILITY
Scrappy

SPECIES STRENGTHS
HP
ATTACK
DEFENSE
SP. ATK
SP. DEF
SPEED

DAMAGE TAKEN IN BATTLE

×1	×2	×0.5
×1	×1	×0.5
×1	×1	×1
×1	×2	×0.25
×1	×0	×1
×1	×1	×4

FIELD / HUMANLIKE

LEVEL-UP MOVES

LV.	NAME	TYPE	KIND	POW.	ACC.	PP	RANGE
1	Arm Thrust	Fighting	Physical	15	100	20	Normal
1	Bullet Punch	Steel	Physical	40	100	30	Normal
1	Leer	Normal	Status	—	100	30	Many Others
1	Night Slash	Dark	Physical	70	100	15	Normal
1	Tackle	Normal	Physical	40	100	35	Normal
1	Taunt	Dark	Status	—	100	20	Normal
12	Circle Throw	Fighting	Physical	60	90	10	Normal
16	Low Sweep	Fighting	Physical	65	100	20	Normal
20	Work Up	Normal	Status	—	—	30	Self
24	Slash	Normal	Physical	70	100	20	Normal
28	Vital Throw	Fighting	Physical	70	—	10	Normal
35	Crunch	Dark	Physical	80	100	15	Normal
40	Body Slam	Normal	Physical	85	100	15	Normal
46	Parting Shot	Dark	Status	—	100	20	Normal
52	Entrainment	Normal	Status	—	100	15	Normal
58	Hammer Arm	Fighting	Physical	100	90	10	Normal

EVOLUTION MOVES

NAME	TYPE	KIND	POW.	ACC.	PP	RANGE
Night Slash	Dark	Physical	70	100	15	Normal

EGG MOVES

NAME	TYPE	KIND	POW.	ACC.	PP	RANGE

TUTOR MOVES

NAME	TYPE	KIND	POW.	ACC.	PP	RANGE

TM MOVES

NO.	NAME	TYPE	KIND	POW.	ACC.	PP	RANGE
TM00	Mega Punch	Normal	Physical	80	85	20	Normal
TM01	Mega Kick	Normal	Physical	120	75	5	Normal
TM03	Fire Punch	Fire	Physical	75	100	15	Normal
TM04	Ice Punch	Ice	Physical	75	100	15	Normal
TM05	Thunder Punch	Electric	Physical	75	100	15	Normal
TM08	Hyper Beam	Normal	Special	150	90	5	Normal
TM09	Giga Impact	Normal	Physical	150	90	5	Normal
TM15	Dig	Ground	Physical	80	100	10	Normal
TM21	Rest	Psychic	Status	—	—	10	Self
TM22	Rock Slide	Rock	Physical	75	90	10	Many Others
TM23	Thief	Dark	Physical	60	100	25	Normal
TM24	Snore	Normal	Special	50	100	15	Normal
TM25	Protect	Normal	Status	—	—	10	Self
TM26	Scary Face	Normal	Status	—	100	10	Normal
TM31	Attract	Normal	Status	—	100	15	Normal
TM33	Rain Dance	Water	Status	—	—	5	Both Sides
TM34	Sunny Day	Fire	Status	—	—	5	Both Sides
TM37	Beat Up	Dark	Physical	—	100	10	Normal
TM39	Facade	Normal	Physical	70	100	20	Normal
TM41	Helping Hand	Normal	Status	—	—	20	1 Ally
TM42	Revenge	Fighting	Physical	60	100	10	Normal
TM43	Brick Break	Fighting	Physical	75	100	15	Normal
TM48	Rock Tomb	Rock	Physical	60	95	15	Normal
TM57	Payback	Dark	Physical	50	100	10	Normal
TM59	Fling	Dark	Physical	—	100	10	Normal
TM63	Drain Punch	Fighting	Physical	75	100	10	Normal
TM65	Shadow Claw	Ghost	Physical	70	100	15	Normal
TM75	Low Sweep	Fighting	Physical	65	100	20	Normal
TM76	Round	Normal	Special	60	100	15	Normal
TM79	Retaliate	Normal	Physical	70	100	5	Normal
TM81	Bulldoze	Ground	Physical	60	100	20	All Others
TM85	Snarl	Dark	Special	55	95	15	Many Others
TM94	False Swipe	Normal	Physical	40	100	40	Normal
TM98	Stomping Tantrum	Ground	Physical	75	100	10	Normal

TR MOVES

NO.	NAME	TYPE	KIND	POW.	ACC.	PP	RANGE
TR00	Swords Dance	Normal	Status	—	—	20	Self
TR01	Body Slam	Normal	Physical	85	100	15	Normal
TR04	Surf	Water	Special	90	100	15	All Others
TR07	Low Kick	Fighting	Physical	—	100	20	Normal
TR10	Earthquake	Ground	Physical	100	100	10	All Others
TR13	Focus Energy	Normal	Status	—	—	30	Self
TR20	Substitute	Normal	Status	—	—	10	Self
TR21	Reversal	Fighting	Physical	—	100	15	Normal
TR22	Sludge Bomb	Poison	Special	90	100	10	Normal
TR24	Outrage	Dragon	Physical	120	100	10	1 Random
TR26	Endure	Normal	Status	—	—	10	Self
TR27	Sleep Talk	Normal	Status	—	—	10	Self
TR32	Crunch	Dark	Physical	80	100	15	Normal
TR35	Uproar	Normal	Special	90	100	10	1 Random
TR37	Taunt	Dark	Status	—	100	20	Normal
TR39	Superpower	Fighting	Physical	120	100	5	Normal
TR42	Hyper Voice	Normal	Special	90	100	10	Many Others
TR47	Dragon Claw	Dragon	Physical	80	100	15	Normal
TR48	Bulk Up	Fighting	Status	—	—	20	Self
TR53	Close Combat	Fighting	Physical	120	100	5	Normal
TR57	Poison Jab	Poison	Physical	80	100	15	Normal
TR58	Dark Pulse	Dark	Special	80	100	15	Normal
TR60	X-Scissor	Bug	Physical	80	100	15	Normal
TR64	Focus Blast	Fighting	Special	120	70	5	Normal
TR69	Zen Headbutt	Psychic	Physical	80	90	15	Normal
TR73	Gunk Shot	Poison	Physical	120	80	5	Normal
TR74	Iron Head	Steel	Physical	80	100	15	Normal
TR75	Stone Edge	Rock	Physical	100	80	5	Normal
TR77	Grass Knot	Grass	Special	—	100	20	Normal
TR81	Foul Play	Dark	Physical	95	100	15	Normal
TR85	Work Up	Normal	Status	—	—	30	Self
TR93	Darkest Lariat	Dark	Physical	85	100	10	Normal
TR95	Throat Chop	Dark	Physical	80	100	15	Normal

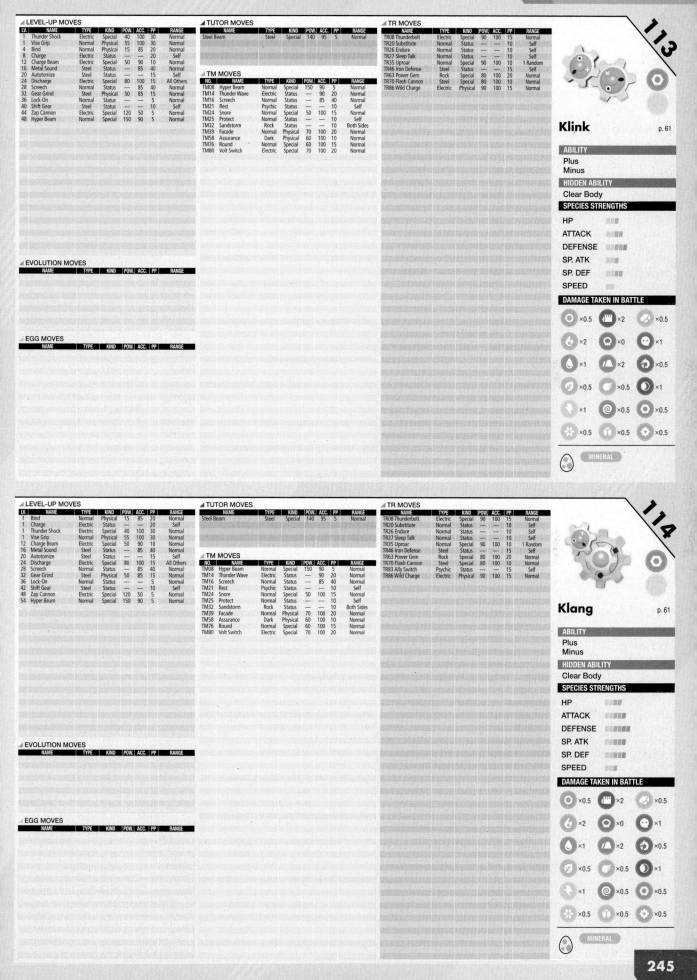

113 Klink p. 61

LEVEL-UP MOVES

LV.	NAME	TYPE	KIND	POW.	ACC.	PP	RANGE
1	Thunder Shock	Electric	Special	40	100	30	Normal
1	Vise Grip	Normal	Physical	55	100	30	Normal
4	Bind	Normal	Physical	15	85	20	Normal
8	Charge	Electric	Status	—	—	20	Self
12	Charge Beam	Electric	Special	50	90	10	Normal
16	Metal Sound	Steel	Status	—	85	40	Normal
20	Autotomize	Steel	Status	—	—	15	Self
24	Discharge	Electric	Special	80	100	15	All Others
28	Screech	Normal	Status	—	85	40	Normal
32	Gear Grind	Steel	Physical	50	85	15	Normal
36	Lock-On	Normal	Status	—	—	5	Normal
40	Shift Gear	Steel	Status	—	—	10	Self
44	Zap Cannon	Electric	Special	120	50	5	Normal
48	Hyper Beam	Normal	Special	150	90	5	Normal

TUTOR MOVES

NAME	TYPE	KIND	POW.	ACC.	PP	RANGE
Steel Beam	Steel	Special	140	95	5	Normal

TM MOVES

NO.	NAME	TYPE	KIND	POW.	ACC.	PP	RANGE
TM08	Hyper Beam	Normal	Special	150	90	5	Normal
TM14	Thunder Wave	Electric	Status	—	90	20	Normal
TM16	Screech	Normal	Status	—	85	40	Normal
TM21	Rest	Psychic	Status	—	—	10	Self
TM24	Snore	Normal	Special	50	100	15	Normal
TM25	Protect	Normal	Status	—	—	10	Self
TM32	Sandstorm	Rock	Status	—	—	10	Both Sides
TM39	Facade	Normal	Physical	70	100	20	Normal
TM58	Assurance	Dark	Physical	60	100	10	Normal
TM76	Round	Normal	Special	60	100	15	Normal
TM80	Volt Switch	Electric	Special	70	100	20	Normal

TR MOVES

NO.	NAME	TYPE	KIND	POW.	ACC.	PP	RANGE
TR08	Thunderbolt	Electric	Special	90	100	15	Normal
TR20	Substitute	Normal	Status	—	—	10	Self
TR26	Endure	Normal	Status	—	—	10	Self
TR27	Sleep Talk	Normal	Status	—	—	10	Self
TR35	Uproar	Normal	Special	90	100	10	1 Random
TR46	Iron Defense	Steel	Status	—	—	15	Self
TR63	Power Gem	Rock	Special	80	100	20	Normal
TR70	Flash Cannon	Steel	Special	80	100	10	Normal
TR86	Wild Charge	Electric	Physical	90	100	15	Normal

EVOLUTION MOVES

NAME	TYPE	KIND	POW.	ACC.	PP	RANGE

EGG MOVES

NAME	TYPE	KIND	POW.	ACC.	PP	RANGE

ABILITY
Plus
Minus

HIDDEN ABILITY
Clear Body

SPECIES STRENGTHS
HP
ATTACK
DEFENSE
SP. ATK
SP. DEF
SPEED

DAMAGE TAKEN IN BATTLE
×0.5 ×2 ×0.5
×2 ×0 ×1
×1 ×2 ×0.5
×0.5 ×0.5 ×1
×1 ×0.5 ×0.5
×0.5 ×0.5 ×0.5

MINERAL

114 Klang p. 61

LEVEL-UP MOVES

LV.	NAME	TYPE	KIND	POW.	ACC.	PP	RANGE
1	Bind	Normal	Physical	15	85	20	Normal
1	Charge	Electric	Status	—	—	20	Self
1	Thunder Shock	Electric	Special	40	100	30	Normal
1	Vise Grip	Normal	Physical	55	100	30	Normal
12	Charge Beam	Electric	Special	50	90	10	Normal
16	Metal Sound	Steel	Status	—	85	40	Normal
20	Autotomize	Steel	Status	—	—	15	Self
24	Discharge	Electric	Special	80	100	15	All Others
28	Screech	Normal	Status	—	85	40	Normal
32	Gear Grind	Steel	Physical	50	85	15	Normal
36	Lock-On	Normal	Status	—	—	5	Normal
42	Shift Gear	Steel	Status	—	—	10	Self
48	Zap Cannon	Electric	Special	120	50	5	Normal
54	Hyper Beam	Normal	Special	150	90	5	Normal

TUTOR MOVES

NAME	TYPE	KIND	POW.	ACC.	PP	RANGE
Steel Beam	Steel	Special	140	95	5	Normal

TM MOVES

NO.	NAME	TYPE	KIND	POW.	ACC.	PP	RANGE
TM08	Hyper Beam	Normal	Special	150	90	5	Normal
TM14	Thunder Wave	Electric	Status	—	90	20	Normal
TM16	Screech	Normal	Status	—	85	40	Normal
TM21	Rest	Psychic	Status	—	—	10	Self
TM24	Snore	Normal	Special	50	100	15	Normal
TM25	Protect	Normal	Status	—	—	10	Self
TM32	Sandstorm	Rock	Status	—	—	10	Both Sides
TM39	Facade	Normal	Physical	70	100	20	Normal
TM58	Assurance	Dark	Physical	60	100	10	Normal
TM76	Round	Normal	Special	60	100	15	Normal
TM80	Volt Switch	Electric	Special	70	100	20	Normal

TR MOVES

NO.	NAME	TYPE	KIND	POW.	ACC.	PP	RANGE
TR08	Thunderbolt	Electric	Special	90	100	15	Normal
TR20	Substitute	Normal	Status	—	—	10	Self
TR26	Endure	Normal	Status	—	—	10	Self
TR27	Sleep Talk	Normal	Status	—	—	10	Self
TR35	Uproar	Normal	Special	90	100	10	1 Random
TR46	Iron Defense	Steel	Status	—	—	15	Self
TR63	Power Gem	Rock	Special	80	100	20	Normal
TR70	Flash Cannon	Steel	Special	80	100	10	Normal
TR83	Ally Switch	Psychic	Status	—	—	15	Self
TR86	Wild Charge	Electric	Physical	90	100	15	Normal

EVOLUTION MOVES

NAME	TYPE	KIND	POW.	ACC.	PP	RANGE

EGG MOVES

NAME	TYPE	KIND	POW.	ACC.	PP	RANGE

ABILITY
Plus
Minus

HIDDEN ABILITY
Clear Body

SPECIES STRENGTHS
HP
ATTACK
DEFENSE
SP. ATK
SP. DEF
SPEED

DAMAGE TAKEN IN BATTLE
×0.5 ×2 ×0.5
×2 ×0 ×1
×1 ×2 ×0.5
×0.5 ×0.5 ×1
×1 ×0.5 ×0.5
×0.5 ×0.5 ×0.5

MINERAL

115

Klinklang p. 61

ABILITY
Plus
Minus

HIDDEN ABILITY
Clear Body

SPECIES STRENGTHS
HP
ATTACK
DEFENSE
SP. ATK
SP. DEF
SPEED

DAMAGE TAKEN IN BATTLE

×0.5	×2	×0.5
×2	×0	×1
×1	×2	×0.5
×0.5	×0.5	×1
×1	×0.5	×0.5
×0.5	×0.5	×0.5

MINERAL

LEVEL-UP MOVES

LV.	NAME	TYPE	KIND	POW.	ACC.	PP	RANGE
1	Bind	Normal	Physical	15	85	20	Normal
1	Charge	Electric	Status	—	—	20	Self
1	Gear Up	Steel	Status	—	—	20	Your Side
1	Magnetic Flux	Electric	Status	—	—	20	Your Side
1	Thunder Shock	Electric	Special	40	100	30	Normal
1	Vise Grip	Normal	Physical	55	100	30	Normal
12	Charge Beam	Electric	Special	50	90	10	Normal
16	Metal Sound	Steel	Status	—	85	40	Normal
20	Autotomize	Steel	Status	—	—	15	Self
24	Discharge	Electric	Special	80	100	15	All Others
28	Screech	Normal	Status	—	85	40	Normal
32	Gear Grind	Steel	Physical	50	85	15	Normal
36	Lock-On	Normal	Status	—	—	5	Normal
42	Shift Gear	Steel	Status	—	—	10	Self
48	Zap Cannon	Electric	Special	120	50	5	Normal
56	Hyper Beam	Normal	Special	150	90	5	Normal
64	Electric Terrain	Electric	Status	—	—	10	Both Sides

EVOLUTION MOVES

NAME	TYPE	KIND	POW.	ACC.	PP	RANGE

EGG MOVES

NAME	TYPE	KIND	POW.	ACC.	PP	RANGE

TUTOR MOVES

NAME	TYPE	KIND	POW.	ACC.	PP	RANGE
Steel Beam	Steel	Special	140	95	5	Normal

TM MOVES

NO.	NAME	TYPE	KIND	POW.	ACC.	PP	RANGE
TM08	Hyper Beam	Normal	Special	150	90	5	Normal
TM09	Giga Impact	Normal	Physical	150	90	5	Normal
TM14	Thunder Wave	Electric	Status	—	90	20	Normal
TM16	Screech	Normal	Status	—	85	40	Normal
TM21	Rest	Psychic	Status	—	—	10	Self
TM24	Snore	Normal	Special	50	100	15	Normal
TM25	Protect	Normal	Status	—	—	10	Self
TM32	Sandstorm	Rock	Status	—	—	10	Both Sides
TM39	Facade	Normal	Physical	70	100	20	Normal
TM58	Assurance	Dark	Physical	60	100	10	Normal
TM70	Trick Room	Psychic	Status	—	—	5	Both Sides
TM76	Round	Normal	Special	60	100	15	Normal
TM80	Volt Switch	Electric	Special	70	100	20	Normal
TM90	Electric Terrain	Electric	Status	—	—	10	Both Sides

TR MOVES

NAME	TYPE	KIND	POW.	ACC.	PP	RANGE
TR08 Thunderbolt	Electric	Special	90	100	15	Normal
TR09 Thunder	Electric	Special	110	70	10	Normal
TR20 Substitute	Normal	Status	—	—	10	Self
TR26 Endure	Normal	Status	—	—	10	Self
TR27 Sleep Talk	Normal	Status	—	—	10	Self
TR35 Uproar	Normal	Special	90	100	10	1 Random
TR46 Iron Defense	Steel	Status	—	—	15	Self
TR63 Power Gem	Rock	Special	80	100	20	Normal
TR70 Flash Cannon	Steel	Special	80	100	10	Normal
TR83 Ally Switch	Psychic	Status	—	—	15	Self
TR86 Wild Charge	Electric	Physical	90	100	15	Normal

116

Combee p. 62

ABILITY
Honey Gather
—

HIDDEN ABILITY
Hustle

SPECIES STRENGTHS
HP
ATTACK
DEFENSE
SP. ATK
SP. DEF
SPEED

DAMAGE TAKEN IN BATTLE

×1	×0.25	×4
×2	×1	×1
×1	×0	×1
×0.25	×2	×1
×2	×1	×1
×2	×0.5	×1

BUG

LEVEL-UP MOVES

LV.	NAME	TYPE	KIND	POW.	ACC.	PP	RANGE
1	Bug Bite	Bug	Physical	60	100	20	Normal
1	Gust	Flying	Special	40	100	35	Normal
1	Struggle Bug	Bug	Special	50	100	20	Many Others
1	Sweet Scent	Normal	Status	—	100	20	Many Others

EVOLUTION MOVES

NAME	TYPE	KIND	POW.	ACC.	PP	RANGE

EGG MOVES

NAME	TYPE	KIND	POW.	ACC.	PP	RANGE

TUTOR MOVES

NAME	TYPE	KIND	POW.	ACC.	PP	RANGE

TM MOVES

NO.	NAME	TYPE	KIND	POW.	ACC.	PP	RANGE
TM24	Snore	Normal	Special	50	100	15	Normal

TR MOVES

NAME	TYPE	KIND	POW.	ACC.	PP	RANGE
TR61 Bug Buzz	Bug	Special	90	100	10	Normal

117 — Vespiquen (p. 62)

LEVEL-UP MOVES

LV	NAME	TYPE	KIND	POW.	ACC.	PP	RANGE
1	Bug Bite	Bug	Physical	60	100	20	Normal
1	Confuse Ray	Ghost	Status	—	100	10	Normal
1	Gust	Flying	Special	40	100	35	Normal
1	Poison Sting	Poison	Physical	15	100	35	Normal
1	Slash	Normal	Physical	70	100	20	Normal
1	Struggle Bug	Bug	Special	50	100	20	Many Others
1	Sweet Scent	Normal	Status	—	100	20	Many Others
4	Fury Cutter	Bug	Physical	40	95	20	Normal
8	Aromatic Mist	Fairy	Status	—	—	20	1 Ally
12	Fell Stinger	Bug	Physical	50	100	25	Normal
16	Fury Swipes	Normal	Physical	18	80	15	Normal
20	Swagger	Normal	Status	—	85	15	Normal
24	Aromatherapy	Grass	Status	—	—	5	Your Party
28	Air Slash	Flying	Special	75	95	15	Normal
32	Power Gem	Rock	Special	80	100	20	Normal
36	Toxic	Poison	Status	—	90	10	Normal
40	Attack Order	Bug	Physical	90	100	15	Normal
40	Defend Order	Bug	Status	—	—	10	Self
44	Destiny Bond	Ghost	Status	—	—	5	Self

EVOLUTION MOVES

NAME	TYPE	KIND	POW.	ACC.	PP	RANGE
Slash	Normal	Physical	70	100	20	Normal

EGG MOVES

NAME	TYPE	KIND	POW.	ACC.	PP	RANGE

TUTOR MOVES

NAME	TYPE	KIND	POW.	ACC.	PP	RANGE

TM MOVES

NO.	NAME	TYPE	KIND	POW.	ACC.	PP	RANGE
TM07	Pin Missile	Bug	Physical	25	95	20	Normal
TM08	Hyper Beam	Normal	Special	150	90	5	Normal
TM09	Giga Impact	Normal	Physical	150	90	5	Normal
TM16	Screech	Normal	Status	—	85	40	Normal
TM21	Rest	Psychic	Status	—	—	10	Self
TM23	Thief	Dark	Physical	60	100	25	Normal
TM24	Snore	Normal	Special	50	100	15	Normal
TM25	Protect	Normal	Status	—	—	10	Self
TM31	Attract	Normal	Status	—	100	15	Normal
TM33	Rain Dance	Water	Status	—	—	5	Both Sides
TM34	Sunny Day	Fire	Status	—	—	5	Both Sides
TM37	Beat Up	Dark	Physical	—	100	10	Normal
TM39	Facade	Normal	Physical	70	100	20	Normal
TM40	Swift	Normal	Special	60	—	20	Many Others
TM42	Revenge	Fighting	Physical	60	100	10	Normal
TM56	U-turn	Bug	Physical	70	100	20	Normal
TM58	Assurance	Dark	Physical	60	100	10	Normal
TM59	Fling	Dark	Physical	—	100	10	Normal
TM73	Cross Poison	Poison	Physical	70	100	20	Normal
TM74	Venoshock	Poison	Special	65	100	10	Normal
TM76	Round	Normal	Special	60	100	15	Normal
TM77	Hex	Ghost	Special	65	100	10	Normal
TM78	Acrobatics	Flying	Physical	55	100	15	Normal
TM95	Air Slash	Flying	Special	75	95	15	Normal

TR MOVES

NO.	NAME	TYPE	KIND	POW.	ACC.	PP	RANGE
TR20	Substitute	Normal	Status	—	—	10	Self
TR21	Reversal	Fighting	Physical	—	100	15	Normal
TR22	Sludge Bomb	Poison	Special	90	100	10	Normal
TR26	Endure	Normal	Status	—	—	10	Self
TR27	Sleep Talk	Normal	Status	—	—	10	Self
TR35	Uproar	Normal	Special	90	100	10	1 Random
TR54	Toxic Spikes	Poison	Status	—	—	20	Other Side
TR60	X-Scissor	Bug	Physical	80	100	15	Normal
TR61	Bug Buzz	Bug	Special	90	100	10	Normal
TR63	Power Gem	Rock	Special	80	100	20	Normal

Vespiquen p. 62

ABILITY
Pressure
—

HIDDEN ABILITY
Unnerve

SPECIES STRENGTHS
- HP
- ATTACK
- DEFENSE
- SP. ATK
- SP. DEF
- SPEED

DAMAGE TAKEN IN BATTLE
×1 · ×0.25 · ×4
×2 · ×1 · ×1
×1 · ×0 · ×1
×0.25 · ×2 · ×1
×2 · ×1 · ×1
×2 · ×0.5 · ×1

BUG

---

118 — Bronzor (p. 63)

LEVEL-UP MOVES

LV	NAME	TYPE	KIND	POW.	ACC.	PP	RANGE
1	Confusion	Psychic	Special	50	100	25	Normal
1	Tackle	Normal	Physical	40	100	35	Normal
4	Confuse Ray	Ghost	Status	—	100	10	Normal
8	Payback	Dark	Physical	50	100	10	Normal
12	Imprison	Psychic	Status	—	—	10	Self
16	Gyro Ball	Steel	Physical	—	100	5	Normal
20	Hypnosis	Psychic	Status	—	60	20	Normal
24	Safeguard	Normal	Status	—	—	25	Your Side
28	Extrasensory	Psychic	Special	80	100	20	Normal
32	Heavy Slam	Steel	Physical	—	100	10	Normal
36	Iron Defense	Steel	Status	—	—	15	Self
40	Metal Sound	Steel	Status	—	85	40	Normal
44	Future Sight	Psychic	Special	120	100	10	Normal

EVOLUTION MOVES

NAME	TYPE	KIND	POW.	ACC.	PP	RANGE

EGG MOVES

NAME	TYPE	KIND	POW.	ACC.	PP	RANGE

TUTOR MOVES

NAME	TYPE	KIND	POW.	ACC.	PP	RANGE
Steel Beam	Steel	Special	140	95	5	Normal

TM MOVES

NO.	NAME	TYPE	KIND	POW.	ACC.	PP	RANGE
TM11	Solar Beam	Grass	Special	120	100	10	Normal
TM17	Light Screen	Psychic	Status	—	—	30	Your Side
TM18	Reflect	Psychic	Status	—	—	20	Your Side
TM19	Safeguard	Normal	Status	—	—	25	Your Side
TM21	Rest	Psychic	Status	—	—	10	Self
TM22	Rock Slide	Rock	Physical	75	90	10	Many Others
TM24	Snore	Normal	Special	50	100	15	Normal
TM25	Protect	Normal	Status	—	—	10	Self
TM32	Sandstorm	Rock	Status	—	—	10	Both Sides
TM33	Rain Dance	Water	Status	—	—	5	Both Sides
TM34	Sunny Day	Fire	Status	—	—	5	Both Sides
TM39	Facade	Normal	Physical	70	100	20	Normal
TM44	Imprison	Psychic	Status	—	—	10	Self
TM48	Rock Tomb	Rock	Physical	60	95	15	Normal
TM57	Payback	Dark	Physical	50	100	10	Normal
TM60	Power Swap	Psychic	Status	—	—	10	Normal
TM61	Guard Swap	Psychic	Status	—	—	10	Normal
TM62	Speed Swap	Psychic	Status	—	—	10	Normal
TM70	Trick Room	Psychic	Status	—	—	5	Both Sides
TM71	Wonder Room	Psychic	Status	—	—	10	Both Sides
TM76	Round	Normal	Special	60	100	15	Normal
TM77	Hex	Ghost	Special	65	100	10	Normal
TM81	Bulldoze	Ground	Physical	60	100	20	All Others

TR MOVES

NO.	NAME	TYPE	KIND	POW.	ACC.	PP	RANGE
TR10	Earthquake	Ground	Physical	100	100	10	All Others
TR11	Psychic	Psychic	Special	90	100	10	Normal
TR20	Substitute	Normal	Status	—	—	10	Self
TR25	Psyshock	Psychic	Special	80	100	10	Normal
TR26	Endure	Normal	Status	—	—	10	Self
TR27	Sleep Talk	Normal	Status	—	—	10	Self
TR33	Shadow Ball	Ghost	Special	80	100	15	Normal
TR34	Future Sight	Psychic	Special	120	100	10	Normal
TR38	Trick	Psychic	Status	—	100	10	Normal
TR40	Skill Swap	Psychic	Status	—	—	15	Normal
TR46	Iron Defense	Steel	Status	—	—	15	Self
TR49	Calm Mind	Psychic	Status	—	—	20	Self
TR52	Gyro Ball	Steel	Physical	—	100	5	Normal
TR70	Flash Cannon	Steel	Special	80	100	10	Normal
TR76	Stealth Rock	Rock	Status	—	—	20	Other Side
TR77	Grass Knot	Grass	Special	—	100	20	Normal
TR79	Heavy Slam	Steel	Physical	—	100	10	Normal
TR83	Ally Switch	Psychic	Status	—	—	15	Self

Bronzor p. 63

ABILITY
Levitate
Heatproof

HIDDEN ABILITY
Heavy Metal

SPECIES STRENGTHS
- HP
- ATTACK
- DEFENSE
- SP. ATK
- SP. DEF
- SPEED

DAMAGE TAKEN IN BATTLE
×0.5 · ×1 · ×0.5
×2 · ×0 · ×2
×1 · ×2 · ×0.5
×0.5 · ×0.5 · ×2
×1 · ×0.25 · ×0.5
×0.5 · ×1 · ×0.5

MINERAL

119

Bronzong p. 63

ABILITY
Levitate
Heatproof

HIDDEN ABILITY
Heavy Metal

SPECIES STRENGTHS
HP
ATTACK
DEFENSE
SP. ATK
SP. DEF
SPEED

DAMAGE TAKEN IN BATTLE

⊙ ×0.5	×1	×0.5			
×2	×0	×2			
×1	×2	×0.5			
×0.5	×0.5	×2			
×1	×0.25	×0.5			
×0.5	×1	×0.5			

MINERAL

LEVEL-UP MOVES

LV.	NAME	TYPE	KIND	POW.	ACC.	PP	RANGE
1	Block	Normal	Status	—	—	5	Normal
1	Confuse Ray	Ghost	Status	—	100	10	Normal
1	Confusion	Psychic	Special	50	100	25	Normal
1	Payback	Dark	Physical	50	100	10	Normal
1	Sunny Day	Fire	Status	—	—	5	Both Sides
1	Tackle	Normal	Physical	40	100	35	Normal
1	Weather Ball*	Normal	Special	50	100	10	Normal
12	Imprison	Psychic	Status	—	—	10	Self
16	Gyro Ball	Steel	Physical	—	100	5	Normal
20	Hypnosis	Psychic	Status	—	60	20	Normal
24	Safeguard	Normal	Status	—	—	25	Your Side
28	Extrasensory	Psychic	Special	80	100	20	Normal
32	Heavy Slam	Steel	Physical	—	100	10	Normal
38	Iron Defense	Steel	Status	—	—	15	Self
44	Metal Sound	Steel	Status	—	85	40	Normal
50	Future Sight	Psychic	Special	120	100	10	Normal
56	Rain Dance	Water	Status	—	—	5	Both Sides

EVOLUTION MOVES

NAME	TYPE	KIND	POW.	ACC.	PP	RANGE
Block	Normal	Status	—	—	5	Normal

EGG MOVES

NAME	TYPE	KIND	POW.	ACC.	PP	RANGE

TUTOR MOVES

NAME	TYPE	KIND	POW.	ACC.	PP	RANGE
Steel Beam	Steel	Special	140	95	5	Normal

TM MOVES

NO.	NAME	TYPE	KIND	POW.	ACC.	PP	RANGE
TM08	Hyper Beam	Normal	Special	150	90	5	Normal
TM09	Giga Impact	Normal	Physical	150	90	5	Normal
TM11	Solar Beam	Grass	Special	120	100	10	Normal
TM17	Light Screen	Psychic	Status	—	—	30	Your Side
TM18	Reflect	Psychic	Status	—	—	20	Your Side
TM19	Safeguard	Normal	Status	—	—	25	Your Side
TM21	Rest	Psychic	Status	—	—	10	Self
TM22	Rock Slide	Rock	Physical	75	90	10	Many Others
TM24	Snore	Normal	Special	50	100	15	Normal
TM25	Protect	Normal	Status	—	—	10	Self
TM32	Sandstorm	Rock	Status	—	—	10	Both Sides
TM33	Rain Dance	Water	Status	—	—	5	Both Sides
TM34	Sunny Day	Fire	Status	—	—	5	Both Sides
TM39	Facade	Normal	Physical	70	100	20	Normal
TM44	Imprison	Psychic	Status	—	—	10	Self
TM46	Weather Ball*	Normal	Special	50	100	10	Normal
TM48	Rock Tomb	Rock	Physical	60	95	15	Normal
TM57	Payback	Dark	Physical	50	100	10	Normal
TM60	Power Swap	Psychic	Status	—	—	10	Normal
TM61	Guard Swap	Psychic	Status	—	—	10	Normal
TM62	Speed Swap	Psychic	Status	—	—	10	Normal
TM70	Trick Room	Psychic	Status	—	—	5	Both Sides
TM71	Wonder Room	Psychic	Status	—	—	10	Both Sides
TM76	Round	Normal	Special	60	100	15	Normal
TM77	Hex	Ghost	Special	65	100	10	Normal
TM81	Bulldoze	Ground	Physical	60	100	20	All Others
TM91	Psychic Terrain	Psychic	Status	—	—	10	Both Sides

TR MOVES

NO.	NAME	TYPE	KIND	POW.	ACC.	PP	RANGE
TR10	Earthquake	Ground	Physical	100	100	10	All Others
TR11	Psychic	Psychic	Special	90	100	10	Normal
TR20	Substitute	Normal	Status	—	—	10	Self
TR25	Psyshock	Psychic	Special	80	100	10	Normal
TR26	Endure	Normal	Status	—	—	10	Self
TR27	Sleep Talk	Normal	Status	—	—	10	Self
TR33	Shadow Ball	Ghost	Special	80	100	15	Normal
TR34	Future Sight	Psychic	Special	120	100	10	Normal
TR38	Trick	Psychic	Status	—	100	10	Normal
TR40	Skill Swap	Psychic	Status	—	—	10	Normal
TR46	Iron Defense	Steel	Status	—	—	15	Self
TR49	Calm Mind	Psychic	Status	—	—	20	Self
TR52	Gyro Ball	Steel	Physical	—	100	5	Normal
TR69	Zen Headbutt	Psychic	Physical	80	90	15	Normal
TR70	Flash Cannon	Steel	Special	80	100	10	Normal
TR76	Stealth Rock	Rock	Status	—	—	20	Other Side
TR77	Grass Knot	Grass	Special	—	100	20	Normal
TR79	Heavy Slam	Steel	Physical	—	100	10	Normal
TR83	Ally Switch	Psychic	Status	—	—	15	Self
TR99	Body Press	Fighting	Physical	80	100	10	Normal

*Weather Ball changes type depending on weather condition. (Harsh sunlight: Fire type. Rain: Water type. Hail: Ice type. Sandstorm: Rock type.)

120

Ralts p. 64

ABILITY
Synchronize
Trace

HIDDEN ABILITY
Telepathy

SPECIES STRENGTHS
HP
ATTACK
DEFENSE
SP. ATK
SP. DEF
SPEED

DAMAGE TAKEN IN BATTLE

⊙ ×1	×0.25	×1			
×1	×2	×2			
×1	×1	×0			
×1	×1	×1			
×1	×0.5	×2			
×1	×1	×1			

HUMANLIKE
AMORPHOUS

LEVEL-UP MOVES

LV.	NAME	TYPE	KIND	POW.	ACC.	PP	RANGE
1	Disarming Voice	Fairy	Special	40	—	15	Many Others
1	Growl	Normal	Status	—	100	40	Many Others
3	Double Team	Normal	Status	—	—	15	Self
6	Confusion	Psychic	Special	50	100	25	Normal
9	Hypnosis	Psychic	Status	—	60	20	Normal
12	Draining Kiss	Fairy	Special	50	100	10	Normal
15	Teleport	Psychic	Status	—	—	20	Self
18	Psybeam	Psychic	Special	65	100	20	Normal
21	Life Dew	Water	Status	—	—	10	Your Side
24	Charm	Fairy	Status	—	100	20	Normal
27	Calm Mind	Psychic	Status	—	—	20	Self
30	Psychic	Psychic	Special	90	100	10	Normal
33	Heal Pulse	Psychic	Status	—	—	10	Normal
36	Dream Eater	Psychic	Special	100	100	15	Normal
39	Future Sight	Psychic	Special	120	100	10	Normal

EVOLUTION MOVES

NAME	TYPE	KIND	POW.	ACC.	PP	RANGE

EGG MOVES

NAME	TYPE	KIND	POW.	ACC.	PP	RANGE
Confuse Ray	Ghost	Status	—	100	10	Normal
Destiny Bond	Ghost	Status	—	—	5	Self
Disable	Normal	Status	—	100	20	Normal
Grudge	Ghost	Status	—	—	5	Self
Knock Off	Dark	Physical	65	100	20	Normal
Mean Look	Normal	Status	—	—	5	Normal
Memento	Dark	Status	—	100	10	Normal
Shadow Sneak	Ghost	Physical	40	100	30	Normal

TUTOR MOVES

NAME	TYPE	KIND	POW.	ACC.	PP	RANGE

TM MOVES

NO.	NAME	TYPE	KIND	POW.	ACC.	PP	RANGE
TM00	Mega Punch	Normal	Physical	80	85	20	Normal
TM01	Mega Kick	Normal	Physical	120	75	5	Normal
TM02	Fire Punch	Fire	Physical	75	100	15	Normal
TM03	Ice Punch	Ice	Physical	75	100	15	Normal
TM04	Thunder Punch	Electric	Physical	75	100	15	Normal
TM05	Thunder Wave	Electric	Status	—	90	20	Normal
TM10	Magical Leaf	Grass	Special	60	—	20	Normal
TM14	Thunder Wave	Electric	Status	—	90	20	Normal
TM17	Light Screen	Psychic	Status	—	—	30	Your Side
TM18	Reflect	Psychic	Status	—	—	20	Your Side
TM19	Safeguard	Normal	Status	—	—	25	Your Side
TM21	Rest	Psychic	Status	—	—	10	Self
TM23	Thief	Dark	Physical	60	100	25	Normal
TM24	Snore	Normal	Special	50	100	15	Normal
TM25	Protect	Normal	Status	—	—	10	Self
TM27	Icy Wind	Ice	Special	55	95	15	Many Others
TM29	Charm	Fairy	Status	—	100	20	Normal
TM31	Attract	Normal	Status	—	100	15	Normal
TM33	Rain Dance	Water	Status	—	—	5	Both Sides
TM34	Sunny Day	Fire	Status	—	—	5	Both Sides
TM38	Will-O-Wisp	Fire	Status	—	85	15	Normal
TM39	Facade	Normal	Physical	70	100	20	Normal
TM40	Swift	Normal	Special	60	—	20	Many Others
TM41	Helping Hand	Normal	Status	—	—	20	1 Ally
TM44	Imprison	Psychic	Status	—	—	10	Self
TM59	Fling	Dark	Physical	—	100	10	Normal
TM70	Trick Room	Psychic	Status	—	—	5	Both Sides
TM71	Wonder Room	Psychic	Status	—	—	10	Both Sides
TM72	Magic Room	Psychic	Status	—	—	10	Both Sides
TM76	Round	Normal	Special	60	100	15	Normal
TM87	Draining Kiss	Fairy	Special	50	100	10	Normal
TM89	Misty Terrain	Fairy	Status	—	—	10	Both Sides

TR MOVES

NO.	NAME	TYPE	KIND	POW.	ACC.	PP	RANGE
TR01	Body Slam	Normal	Physical	85	100	15	Normal
TR08	Thunderbolt	Electric	Special	90	100	15	Normal
TR11	Psychic	Psychic	Special	90	100	10	Normal
TR20	Substitute	Normal	Status	—	—	10	Self
TR25	Psyshock	Psychic	Special	80	100	10	Normal
TR26	Endure	Normal	Status	—	—	10	Self
TR27	Sleep Talk	Normal	Status	—	—	10	Self
TR30	Encore	Normal	Status	—	100	5	Normal
TR33	Shadow Ball	Ghost	Special	80	100	15	Normal
TR34	Future Sight	Psychic	Special	120	100	10	Normal
TR37	Taunt	Dark	Status	—	100	20	Normal
TR38	Trick	Psychic	Status	—	100	10	Normal
TR40	Skill Swap	Psychic	Status	—	—	10	Normal
TR42	Hyper Voice	Normal	Special	90	100	10	Many Others
TR49	Calm Mind	Psychic	Status	—	—	20	Self
TR69	Zen Headbutt	Psychic	Physical	80	90	15	Normal
TR77	Grass Knot	Grass	Special	—	100	20	Normal
TR82	Stored Power	Psychic	Special	20	100	10	Normal
TR83	Ally Switch	Psychic	Status	—	—	15	Self
TR92	Dazzling Gleam	Fairy	Special	80	100	10	Many Others

121 Kirlia

p. 64

LEVEL-UP MOVES

LV.	NAME	TYPE	KIND	POW.	ACC.	PP	RANGE
1	Confusion	Psychic	Special	50	100	25	Normal
1	Disarming Voice	Fairy	Special	40	—	15	Many Others
1	Double Team	Normal	Status	—	—	15	Self
1	Growl	Normal	Status	—	100	40	Many Others
6	Hypnosis	Psychic	Status	—	60	20	Normal
12	Draining Kiss	Fairy	Special	50	100	10	Normal
15	Teleport	Psychic	Status	—	—	20	Self
18	Psybeam	Psychic	Special	65	100	20	Normal
23	Life Dew	Water	Status	—	—	10	Your Side
28	Charm	Fairy	Status	—	100	20	Normal
33	Calm Mind	Psychic	Status	—	—	20	Self
38	Psychic	Psychic	Special	90	100	10	Normal
43	Heal Pulse	Psychic	Status	—	—	10	Normal
48	Dream Eater	Psychic	Special	100	100	15	Normal
53	Future Sight	Psychic	Special	120	100	10	Normal

EVOLUTION MOVES

NAME	TYPE	KIND	POW.	ACC.	PP	RANGE

EGG MOVES

NAME	TYPE	KIND	POW.	ACC.	PP	RANGE

TUTOR MOVES

NAME	TYPE	KIND	POW.	ACC.	PP	RANGE

TM MOVES

NO.	NAME	TYPE	KIND	POW.	ACC.	PP	RANGE
TM00	Mega Punch	Normal	Physical	80	85	20	Normal
TM01	Mega Kick	Normal	Physical	120	75	5	Normal
TM03	Fire Punch	Fire	Physical	75	100	15	Normal
TM04	Ice Punch	Ice	Physical	75	100	15	Normal
TM05	Thunder Punch	Electric	Physical	75	100	15	Normal
TM10	Magical Leaf	Grass	Special	60	—	20	Normal
TM14	Thunder Wave	Electric	Status	—	90	20	Normal
TM17	Light Screen	Psychic	Status	—	—	30	Your Side
TM18	Reflect	Psychic	Status	—	—	20	Your Side
TM19	Safeguard	Normal	Status	—	—	25	Your Side
TM21	Rest	Psychic	Status	—	—	10	Self
TM23	Thief	Dark	Physical	60	100	25	Normal
TM24	Snore	Normal	Special	50	100	15	Normal
TM25	Protect	Normal	Status	—	—	10	Self
TM27	Icy Wind	Ice	Special	55	95	15	Many Others
TM29	Charm	Fairy	Status	—	100	20	Normal
TM31	Attract	Normal	Status	—	100	15	Normal
TM33	Rain Dance	Water	Status	—	—	5	Both Sides
TM34	Sunny Day	Fire	Status	—	—	5	Both Sides
TM38	Will-O-Wisp	Fire	Status	—	85	15	Normal
TM39	Facade	Normal	Physical	70	100	20	Normal
TM40	Swift	Normal	Special	60	—	20	Many Others
TM41	Helping Hand	Normal	Status	—	—	20	1 Ally
TM44	Imprison	Psychic	Status	—	—	10	Self
TM59	Fling	Dark	Physical	—	100	10	Normal
TM70	Trick Room	Psychic	Status	—	—	5	Both Sides
TM71	Wonder Room	Psychic	Status	—	—	10	Both Sides
TM72	Magic Room	Psychic	Status	—	—	10	Both Sides
TM76	Round	Normal	Special	60	100	15	Normal
TM87	Draining Kiss	Fairy	Special	50	100	10	Normal
TM89	Misty Terrain	Fairy	Status	—	—	10	Both Sides

TR MOVES

NAME	TYPE	KIND	POW.	ACC.	PP	RANGE
TR01 Body Slam	Normal	Physical	85	100	15	Normal
TR08 Thunderbolt	Electric	Special	90	100	15	Normal
TR11 Psychic	Psychic	Special	90	100	10	Normal
TR20 Substitute	Normal	Status	—	—	10	Self
TR25 Psyshock	Psychic	Special	80	100	10	Normal
TR26 Endure	Normal	Status	—	—	10	Self
TR27 Sleep Talk	Normal	Status	—	—	10	Self
TR30 Encore	Normal	Status	—	100	5	Normal
TR33 Shadow Ball	Ghost	Special	80	100	15	Normal
TR34 Future Sight	Psychic	Special	120	100	10	Normal
TR37 Taunt	Dark	Status	—	100	20	Normal
TR38 Trick	Psychic	Status	—	100	10	Normal
TR40 Skill Swap	Psychic	Status	—	—	10	Normal
TR42 Hyper Voice	Normal	Special	90	100	10	Many Others
TR49 Calm Mind	Psychic	Status	—	—	20	Self
TR69 Zen Headbutt	Psychic	Physical	80	90	15	Normal
TR77 Grass Knot	Grass	Special	—	100	20	Normal
TR82 Stored Power	Psychic	Special	20	100	10	Normal
TR83 Ally Switch	Psychic	Status	—	—	15	Self
TR92 Dazzling Gleam	Fairy	Special	80	100	10	Many Others

ABILITY
Synchronize
Trace

HIDDEN ABILITY
Telepathy

SPECIES STRENGTHS
HP
ATTACK
DEFENSE
SP. ATK
SP. DEF
SPEED

DAMAGE TAKEN IN BATTLE

×1　×0.25　×1
×2　×2
×1　×1　×0
×1　×1　×1
×1　×0.5　×2
×1　×1　×1

HUMANLIKE
AMORPHOUS

---

122 Gardevoir

p. 64

LEVEL-UP MOVES

LV.	NAME	TYPE	KIND	POW.	ACC.	PP	RANGE
1	Charm	Fairy	Status	—	100	20	Normal
1	Confusion	Psychic	Special	50	100	25	Normal
1	Dazzling Gleam	Fairy	Special	80	100	10	Many Others
1	Disarming Voice	Fairy	Special	40	—	15	Many Others
1	Double Team	Normal	Status	—	—	15	Self
1	Growl	Normal	Status	—	100	40	Many Others
1	Healing Wish	Psychic	Status	—	—	10	Self
1	Misty Terrain	Fairy	Status	—	—	10	Both Sides
1	Moonblast	Fairy	Special	95	100	15	Normal
6	Hypnosis	Psychic	Status	—	60	20	Normal
12	Draining Kiss	Fairy	Special	50	100	10	Normal
15	Teleport	Psychic	Status	—	—	20	Self
18	Psybeam	Psychic	Special	65	100	20	Normal
23	Life Dew	Water	Status	—	—	10	Your Side
28	Wish	Normal	Status	—	—	10	Self
35	Calm Mind	Psychic	Status	—	—	20	Self
42	Psychic	Psychic	Special	90	100	10	Normal
49	Heal Pulse	Psychic	Status	—	—	10	Normal
56	Dream Eater	Psychic	Special	100	100	15	Normal
63	Future Sight	Psychic	Special	120	100	10	Normal

EVOLUTION MOVES

NAME	TYPE	KIND	POW.	ACC.	PP	RANGE
Dazzling Gleam	Fairy	Special	80	100	10	Many Others

EGG MOVES

NAME	TYPE	KIND	POW.	ACC.	PP	RANGE

TUTOR MOVES

NAME	TYPE	KIND	POW.	ACC.	PP	RANGE

TM MOVES

NO.	NAME	TYPE	KIND	POW.	ACC.	PP	RANGE
TM00	Mega Punch	Normal	Physical	80	85	20	Normal
TM01	Mega Kick	Normal	Physical	120	75	5	Normal
TM03	Fire Punch	Fire	Physical	75	100	15	Normal
TM04	Ice Punch	Ice	Physical	75	100	15	Normal
TM05	Thunder Punch	Electric	Physical	75	100	15	Normal
TM08	Hyper Beam	Normal	Special	150	90	5	Normal
TM09	Giga Impact	Normal	Physical	150	90	5	Normal
TM10	Magical Leaf	Grass	Special	60	—	20	Normal
TM14	Thunder Wave	Electric	Status	—	90	20	Normal
TM17	Light Screen	Psychic	Status	—	—	30	Your Side
TM18	Reflect	Psychic	Status	—	—	20	Your Side
TM19	Safeguard	Normal	Status	—	—	25	Your Side
TM21	Rest	Psychic	Status	—	—	10	Self
TM23	Thief	Dark	Physical	60	100	25	Normal
TM24	Snore	Normal	Special	50	100	15	Normal
TM25	Protect	Normal	Status	—	—	10	Self
TM27	Icy Wind	Ice	Special	55	95	15	Many Others
TM29	Charm	Fairy	Status	—	100	20	Normal
TM31	Attract	Normal	Status	—	100	15	Normal
TM33	Rain Dance	Water	Status	—	—	5	Both Sides
TM34	Sunny Day	Fire	Status	—	—	5	Both Sides
TM38	Will-O-Wisp	Fire	Status	—	85	15	Normal
TM39	Facade	Normal	Physical	70	100	20	Normal
TM40	Swift	Normal	Special	60	—	20	Many Others
TM41	Helping Hand	Normal	Status	—	—	20	1 Ally
TM44	Imprison	Psychic.	Status	—	—	10	Self
TM59	Fling	Dark	Physical	—	100	10	Normal
TM60	Power Swap	Psychic	Status	—	—	10	Normal
TM61	Guard Swap	Psychic	Status	—	—	10	Normal
TM70	Trick Room	Psychic	Status	—	—	5	Both Sides
TM71	Wonder Room	Psychic	Status	—	—	10	Both Sides
TM72	Magic Room	Psychic	Status	—	—	10	Both Sides
TM76	Round	Normal	Special	60	100	15	Normal
TM87	Draining Kiss	Fairy	Special	50	100	10	Normal
TM89	Misty Terrain	Fairy	Status	—	—	10	Both Sides
TM91	Psychic Terrain	Psychic	Status	—	—	10	Both Sides
TM92	Mystical Fire	Fire	Special	75	100	10	Normal

TR MOVES

NAME	TYPE	KIND	POW.	ACC.	PP	RANGE
TR01 Body Slam	Normal	Physical	85	100	15	Normal
TR08 Thunderbolt	Electric	Special	90	100	15	Normal
TR11 Psychic	Psychic	Special	90	100	10	Normal
TR20 Substitute	Normal	Status	—	—	10	Self
TR25 Psyshock	Psychic	Special	80	100	10	Normal
TR26 Endure	Normal	Status	—	—	10	Self
TR27 Sleep Talk	Normal	Status	—	—	10	Self
TR30 Encore	Normal	Status	—	100	5	Normal
TR33 Shadow Ball	Ghost	Special	80	100	15	Normal
TR34 Future Sight	Psychic	Special	120	100	10	Normal
TR37 Taunt	Dark	Status	—	100	20	Normal
TR38 Trick	Psychic	Status	—	100	10	Normal
TR40 Skill Swap	Psychic	Status	—	—	10	Normal
TR42 Hyper Voice	Normal	Special	90	100	10	Many Others
TR49 Calm Mind	Psychic	Status	—	—	20	Self
TR64 Focus Blast	Fighting	Special	120	70	5	Normal
TR65 Energy Ball	Grass	Special	90	100	10	Normal
TR69 Zen Headbutt	Psychic	Physical	80	90	15	Normal
TR77 Grass Knot	Grass	Special	—	100	20	Normal
TR82 Stored Power	Psychic	Special	20	100	10	Normal
TR83 Ally Switch	Psychic	Status	—	—	15	Self
TR92 Dazzling Gleam	Fairy	Special	80	100	10	Many Others

ABILITY
Synchronize
Trace

HIDDEN ABILITY
Telepathy

SPECIES STRENGTHS
HP
ATTACK
DEFENSE
SP. ATK
SP. DEF
SPEED

DAMAGE TAKEN IN BATTLE

×1　×0.25　×1
×1　×2　×2
×1　×1　×0
×1　×1　×1
×1　×0.5　×2
×1　×1　×1

HUMANLIKE
AMORPHOUS

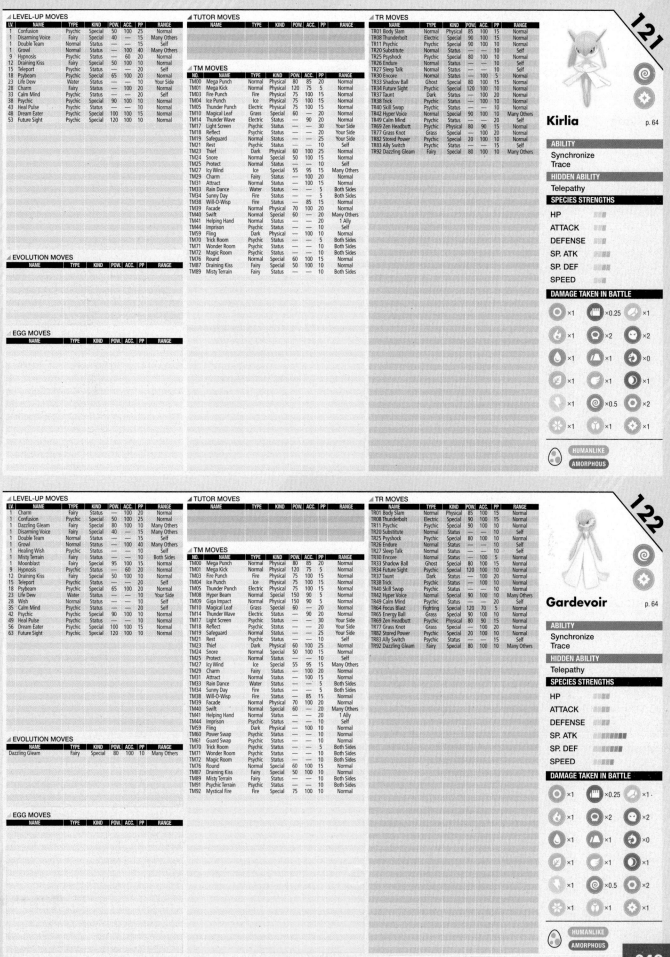

123

Gallade

p. 64

ABILITY
Steadfast
—

HIDDEN ABILITY
Justified

SPECIES STRENGTHS
HP
ATTACK
DEFENSE
SP. ATK
SP. DEF
SPEED

DAMAGE TAKEN IN BATTLE

×1 ×0.5 ×0.5
×1 ×1 ×2
×1 ×1 ×1
×1 ×2 ×1
×1 ×1 ×1
×1 ×1 ×2

HUMANLIKE
AMORPHOUS

LEVEL-UP MOVES

LV.	NAME	TYPE	KIND	POW.	ACC.	PP	RANGE
1	Calm Mind	Psychic	Status	—	—	20	Self
1	Charm	Fairy	Status	—	100	20	Normal
1	Confusion	Psychic	Special	50	100	25	Normal
1	Disarming Voice	Fairy	Special	40	—	15	Many Others
1	Double Team	Normal	Status	—	—	15	Self
1	Draining Kiss	Fairy	Special	50	100	10	Normal
1	Dream Eater	Psychic	Special	100	100	15	Normal
1	Fury Cutter	Bug	Physical	40	95	20	Normal
1	Future Sight	Psychic	Special	120	100	10	Normal
1	Growl	Normal	Status	—	100	40	Many Others
1	Hypnosis	Psychic	Status	—	60	20	Normal
1	Imprison	Psychic	Status	—	—	10	Self
1	Leer	Normal	Status	—	100	30	Many Others
1	Life Dew	Water	Status	—	—	10	Your Side
1	Night Slash	Dark	Physical	70	100	15	Normal
1	Psybeam	Psychic	Special	65	100	20	Normal
1	Psychic	Psychic	Special	90	100	10	Normal
1	Slash	Normal	Physical	70	100	20	Normal
9	Helping Hand	Normal	Status	—	—	20	1 Ally
12	Feint	Normal	Physical	30	100	10	Normal
15	Teleport	Psychic	Status	—	—	20	Self
18	Aerial Ace	Flying	Physical	60	—	20	Normal
23	False Swipe	Normal	Physical	40	100	40	Normal
28	Protect	Normal	Status	—	—	10	Self
35	Swords Dance	Normal	Status	—	—	20	Self
42	Psycho Cut	Psychic	Physical	70	100	20	Normal
49	Heal Pulse	Psychic	Status	—	—	10	Normal
56	Quick Guard	Fighting	Status	—	—	15	Your Side
56	Wide Guard	Rock	Status	—	—	10	Your Side
63	Close Combat	Fighting	Physical	120	100	5	Normal

EVOLUTION MOVES

NAME	TYPE	KIND	POW.	ACC.	PP	RANGE
Slash	Normal	Physical	70	100	20	Normal

EGG MOVES

NAME	TYPE	KIND	POW.	ACC.	PP	RANGE

TUTOR MOVES

NAME	TYPE	KIND	POW.	ACC.	PP	RANGE

TM MOVES

NO.	NAME	TYPE	KIND	POW.	ACC.	PP	RANGE
TM00	Mega Punch	Normal	Physical	80	85	20	Normal
TM01	Mega Kick	Normal	Physical	120	75	5	Normal
TM03	Fire Punch	Fire	Physical	75	100	15	Normal
TM04	Ice Punch	Ice	Physical	75	100	15	Normal
TM05	Thunder Punch	Electric	Physical	75	100	15	Normal
TM08	Hyper Beam	Normal	Special	150	90	5	Normal
TM09	Giga Impact	Normal	Physical	150	90	5	Normal
TM10	Magical Leaf	Grass	Special	60	—	20	Normal
TM12	Solar Blade	Grass	Physical	125	100	10	Normal
TM14	Thunder Wave	Electric	Status	—	90	20	Normal
TM17	Light Screen	Psychic	Status	—	—	30	Your Side
TM18	Reflect	Psychic	Status	—	—	20	Your Side
TM19	Safeguard	Normal	Status	—	—	25	Your Side
TM21	Rest	Psychic	Status	—	—	10	Self
TM22	Rock Slide	Rock	Physical	75	90	10	Many Others
TM23	Thief	Dark	Physical	60	100	25	Normal
TM24	Snore	Normal	Special	50	100	15	Normal
TM25	Protect	Normal	Status	—	—	10	Self
TM27	Icy Wind	Ice	Special	55	95	15	Many Others
TM29	Charm	Fairy	Status	—	100	20	Normal
TM31	Attract	Normal	Status	—	100	15	Normal
TM33	Rain Dance	Water	Status	—	—	5	Both Sides
TM34	Sunny Day	Fire	Status	—	—	5	Both Sides
TM38	Will-O-Wisp	Fire	Status	—	85	15	Normal
TM39	Facade	Normal	Physical	70	100	20	Normal
TM40	Swift	Normal	Special	60	—	20	Many Others
TM41	Helping Hand	Normal	Status	—	—	20	1 Ally
TM42	Revenge	Fighting	Physical	60	100	10	Normal
TM43	Brick Break	Fighting	Physical	75	100	15	Normal
TM44	Imprison	Psychic	Status	—	—	10	Self
TM48	Rock Tomb	Rock	Physical	60	95	15	Normal
TM59	Fling	Dark	Physical	—	100	10	Normal
TM63	Drain Punch	Fighting	Physical	75	100	10	Normal
TM69	Psycho Cut	Psychic	Physical	70	100	20	Normal
TM70	Trick Room	Psychic	Status	—	—	5	Both Sides
TM71	Wonder Room	Psychic	Status	—	—	10	Both Sides
TM72	Magic Room	Psychic	Status	—	—	10	Both Sides
TM75	Low Sweep	Fighting	Physical	65	100	20	Normal
TM76	Round	Normal	Special	60	100	15	Normal
TM79	Retaliate	Normal	Physical	70	100	5	Normal
TM81	Bulldoze	Ground	Physical	60	100	20	All Others
TM87	Draining Kiss	Fairy	Special	50	100	10	Normal
TM89	Misty Terrain	Fairy	Status	—	—	10	Both Sides
TM94	False Swipe	Normal	Physical	40	100	40	Normal
TM95	Air Slash	Flying	Special	75	95	15	Normal

TR MOVES

NAME	TYPE	KIND	POW.	ACC.	PP	RANGE
TR00 Swords Dance	Normal	Status	—	—	20	Self
TR01 Body Slam	Normal	Physical	85	100	15	Normal
TR07 Low Kick	Fighting	Physical	—	100	20	Normal
TR08 Thunderbolt	Electric	Special	90	100	15	Normal
TR10 Earthquake	Ground	Physical	100	100	10	All Others
TR11 Psychic	Psychic	Special	90	100	10	Normal
TR20 Substitute	Normal	Status	—	—	10	Self
TR21 Reversal	Fighting	Physical	—	100	15	Normal
TR25 Psyshock	Psychic	Special	80	100	10	Normal
TR26 Endure	Normal	Status	—	—	10	Self
TR27 Sleep Talk	Normal	Status	—	—	10	Self
TR30 Encore	Normal	Status	—	100	5	Normal
TR33 Shadow Ball	Ghost	Special	80	100	15	Normal
TR34 Future Sight	Psychic	Special	120	100	10	Normal
TR37 Taunt	Dark	Status	—	100	20	Normal
TR38 Trick	Psychic	Status	—	100	10	Normal
TR40 Skill Swap	Psychic	Status	—	—	10	Normal
TR42 Hyper Voice	Normal	Special	90	100	10	Many Others
TR48 Bulk Up	Fighting	Status	—	—	20	Self
TR49 Calm Mind	Psychic	Status	—	—	20	Self
TR50 Leaf Blade	Grass	Physical	90	100	15	Normal
TR53 Close Combat	Fighting	Physical	120	100	5	Normal
TR56 Aura Sphere	Fighting	Special	80	—	20	Normal
TR57 Poison Jab	Poison	Physical	80	100	20	Normal
TR60 X-Scissor	Bug	Physical	80	100	15	Normal
TR64 Focus Blast	Fighting	Special	120	70	5	Normal
TR65 Energy Ball	Grass	Special	90	100	10	Normal
TR69 Zen Headbutt	Psychic	Physical	80	90	15	Normal
TR75 Stone Edge	Rock	Physical	100	80	5	Normal
TR77 Grass Knot	Grass	Special	—	100	20	Normal
TR82 Stored Power	Psychic	Special	20	100	10	Normal
TR83 Ally Switch	Psychic	Status	—	—	15	Self
TR85 Work Up	Normal	Status	—	—	30	Self
TR92 Dazzling Gleam	Fairy	Special	80	100	10	Many Others
TR95 Throat Chop	Dark	Physical	80	100	15	Normal

124

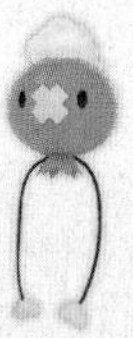

Drifloon

p. 65

ABILITY
Aftermath
Unburden

HIDDEN ABILITY
Flare Boost

SPECIES STRENGTHS
HP
ATTACK
DEFENSE
SP. ATK
SP. DEF
SPEED

DAMAGE TAKEN IN BATTLE

×0 ×0 ×2
×1 ×0.5 ×2
×1 ×0 ×1
×0.5 ×1 ×2
×2 ×1 ×1
×2 ×0.25 ×1

AMORPHOUS

LEVEL-UP MOVES

LV.	NAME	TYPE	KIND	POW.	ACC.	PP	RANGE
1	Astonish	Ghost	Physical	30	100	15	Normal
1	Minimize	Normal	Status	—	—	10	Self
4	Gust	Flying	Special	40	100	35	Normal
8	Focus Energy	Normal	Status	—	—	30	Self
12	Payback	Dark	Physical	50	100	10	Normal
16	Hex	Ghost	Special	65	100	10	Normal
20	Shadow Ball	Ghost	Special	80	100	15	Normal
24	Spit Up	Normal	Special	—	100	10	Normal
24	Stockpile	Normal	Status	—	—	20	Self
24	Swallow	Normal	Status	—	—	10	Self
29	Self-Destruct	Normal	Physical	200	100	5	All Others
32	Destiny Bond	Ghost	Status	—	—	5	Self
36	Baton Pass	Normal	Status	—	—	40	Self
40	Tailwind	Flying	Status	—	—	15	Your Side
44	Explosion	Normal	Physical	250	100	5	All Others

EVOLUTION MOVES

NAME	TYPE	KIND	POW.	ACC.	PP	RANGE

EGG MOVES

NAME	TYPE	KIND	POW.	ACC.	PP	RANGE
Clear Smog	Poison	Special	50	—	15	Normal
Defog	Flying	Status	—	—	15	Normal
Disable	Normal	Status	—	100	20	Normal
Haze	Ice	Status	—	—	30	Both Sides
Hypnosis	Psychic	Status	—	60	20	Normal
Memento	Dark	Status	—	100	10	Normal

TUTOR MOVES

NAME	TYPE	KIND	POW.	ACC.	PP	RANGE

TM MOVES

NO.	NAME	TYPE	KIND	POW.	ACC.	PP	RANGE
TM14	Thunder Wave	Electric	Status	—	90	20	Normal
TM20	Self-Destruct	Normal	Physical	200	100	5	All Others
TM21	Rest	Psychic	Status	—	—	10	Self
TM23	Thief	Dark	Physical	60	100	25	Normal
TM24	Snore	Normal	Special	50	100	15	Normal
TM25	Protect	Normal	Status	—	—	10	Self
TM27	Icy Wind	Ice	Special	55	95	15	Many Others
TM31	Attract	Normal	Status	—	100	15	Normal
TM33	Rain Dance	Water	Status	—	—	5	Both Sides
TM34	Sunny Day	Fire	Status	—	—	5	Both Sides
TM38	Will-O-Wisp	Fire	Status	—	85	15	Normal
TM39	Facade	Normal	Physical	70	100	20	Normal
TM40	Swift	Normal	Special	60	—	20	Many Others
TM46	Weather Ball*	Normal	Special	50	100	10	Normal
TM57	Payback	Dark	Physical	50	100	10	Normal
TM76	Round	Normal	Special	60	100	15	Normal
TM77	Hex	Ghost	Special	65	100	10	Normal
TM78	Acrobatics	Flying	Physical	55	100	15	Normal
TM97	Brutal Swing	Dark	Physical	60	100	20	All Others

TR MOVES

NAME	TYPE	KIND	POW.	ACC.	PP	RANGE
TR01 Body Slam	Normal	Physical	85	100	15	Normal
TR08 Thunderbolt	Electric	Special	90	100	15	Normal
TR09 Thunder	Electric	Special	110	70	10	Normal
TR11 Psychic	Psychic	Special	90	100	10	Normal
TR13 Focus Energy	Normal	Status	—	—	30	Self
TR17 Amnesia	Psychic	Status	—	—	20	Self
TR20 Substitute	Normal	Status	—	—	10	Self
TR26 Endure	Normal	Status	—	—	10	Self
TR27 Sleep Talk	Normal	Status	—	—	10	Self
TR29 Baton Pass	Normal	Status	—	—	40	Self
TR33 Shadow Ball	Ghost	Special	80	100	15	Normal
TR38 Trick	Psychic	Status	—	100	10	Normal
TR40 Skill Swap	Psychic	Status	—	—	10	Normal
TR49 Calm Mind	Psychic	Status	—	—	20	Self
TR52 Gyro Ball	Steel	Physical	—	100	5	Normal
TR83 Ally Switch	Psychic	Status	—	—	15	Self

125 — Drifblim

LEVEL-UP MOVES

LV.	NAME	TYPE	KIND	POW.	ACC.	PP	RANGE
1	Astonish	Ghost	Physical	30	100	15	Normal
1	Focus Energy	Normal	Status	—	—	30	Self
1	Gust	Flying	Special	40	100	35	Normal
1	Minimize	Normal	Status	—	—	10	Self
1	Phantom Force	Ghost	Physical	90	100	10	Normal
1	Strength Sap	Grass	Status	—	100	10	Normal
12	Payback	Dark	Physical	50	100	10	Normal
16	Hex	Ghost	Special	65	100	10	Normal
20	Shadow Ball	Ghost	Special	80	100	15	Normal
24	Spit Up	Normal	Special	—	100	10	Normal
24	Stockpile	Normal	Status	—	—	20	Self
24	Swallow	Normal	Status	—	—	10	Self
31	Self-Destruct	Normal	Physical	200	100	5	All Others
36	Destiny Bond	Ghost	Status	—	—	5	Self
42	Baton Pass	Normal	Status	—	—	40	Self
48	Tailwind	Flying	Status	—	—	15	Your Side
54	Explosion	Normal	Physical	250	100	5	All Others

EVOLUTION MOVES

NAME	TYPE	KIND	POW.	ACC.	PP	RANGE
Phantom Force	Ghost	Physical	90	100	10	Normal

EGG MOVES

NAME	TYPE	KIND	POW.	ACC.	PP	RANGE

TUTOR MOVES

NAME	TYPE	KIND	POW.	ACC.	PP	RANGE

TM MOVES

NO.	NAME	TYPE	KIND	POW.	ACC.	PP	RANGE
TM06	Fly	Flying	Physical	90	95	15	Normal
TM08	Hyper Beam	Normal	Special	150	90	5	Normal
TM09	Giga Impact	Normal	Physical	150	90	5	Normal
TM14	Thunder Wave	Electric	Status	—	90	20	Normal
TM20	Self-Destruct	Normal	Physical	200	100	5	All Others
TM21	Rest	Psychic	Status	—	—	10	Self
TM23	Thief	Dark	Physical	60	100	25	Normal
TM24	Snore	Normal	Special	50	100	15	Normal
TM25	Protect	Normal	Status	—	—	10	Self
TM27	Icy Wind	Ice	Special	55	95	15	Many Others
TM31	Attract	Normal	Status	—	100	15	Normal
TM33	Rain Dance	Water	Status	—	—	5	Both Sides
TM34	Sunny Day	Fire	Status	—	—	5	Both Sides
TM38	Will-O-Wisp	Fire	Status	—	85	15	Normal
TM39	Facade	Normal	Physical	70	100	20	Normal
TM40	Swift	Normal	Special	60	—	20	Many Others
TM44	Imprison	Psychic	Status	—	—	10	Self
TM46	Weather Ball*	Normal	Special	50	100	10	Normal
TM57	Payback	Dark	Physical	50	100	10	Normal
TM76	Round	Normal	Special	60	100	15	Normal
TM77	Hex	Ghost	Special	65	100	10	Normal
TM78	Acrobatics	Flying	Physical	55	100	15	Normal
TM86	Phantom Force	Ghost	Physical	90	100	10	Normal
TM97	Brutal Swing	Dark	Physical	60	100	20	All Others

TR MOVES

NO.	NAME	TYPE	KIND	POW.	ACC.	PP	RANGE
TR01	Body Slam	Normal	Physical	85	100	15	Normal
TR08	Thunderbolt	Electric	Special	90	100	15	Normal
TR09	Thunder	Electric	Special	110	70	10	Normal
TR11	Psychic	Psychic	Special	90	100	10	Normal
TR13	Focus Energy	Normal	Status	—	—	30	Self
TR17	Amnesia	Psychic	Status	—	—	20	Self
TR20	Substitute	Normal	Status	—	—	10	Self
TR26	Endure	Normal	Status	—	—	10	Self
TR27	Sleep Talk	Normal	Status	—	—	10	Self
TR29	Baton Pass	Normal	Status	—	—	40	Self
TR33	Shadow Ball	Ghost	Special	80	100	15	Normal
TR38	Trick	Psychic	Status	—	100	10	Normal
TR40	Skill Swap	Psychic	Status	—	—	10	Normal
TR49	Calm Mind	Psychic	Status	—	—	20	Self
TR52	Gyro Ball	Steel	Physical	—	100	5	Normal
TR83	Ally Switch	Psychic	Status	—	—	15	Self

Drifblim p. 65

ABILITY
Aftermath
Unburden

HIDDEN ABILITY
Flare Boost

SPECIES STRENGTHS
HP
ATTACK
DEFENSE
SP. ATK
SP. DEF
SPEED

DAMAGE TAKEN IN BATTLE

×0 ×0 ×2
×1 ×0.5 ×2
×1 ×0 ×1
×0.5 ×1 ×2
×2 ×1 ×1
×2 ×0.25 ×1

AMORPHOUS

*Weather Ball changes type depending on weather condition. (Harsh sunlight: Fire type. Rain: Water type. Hail: Ice type. Sandstorm: Rock type.)

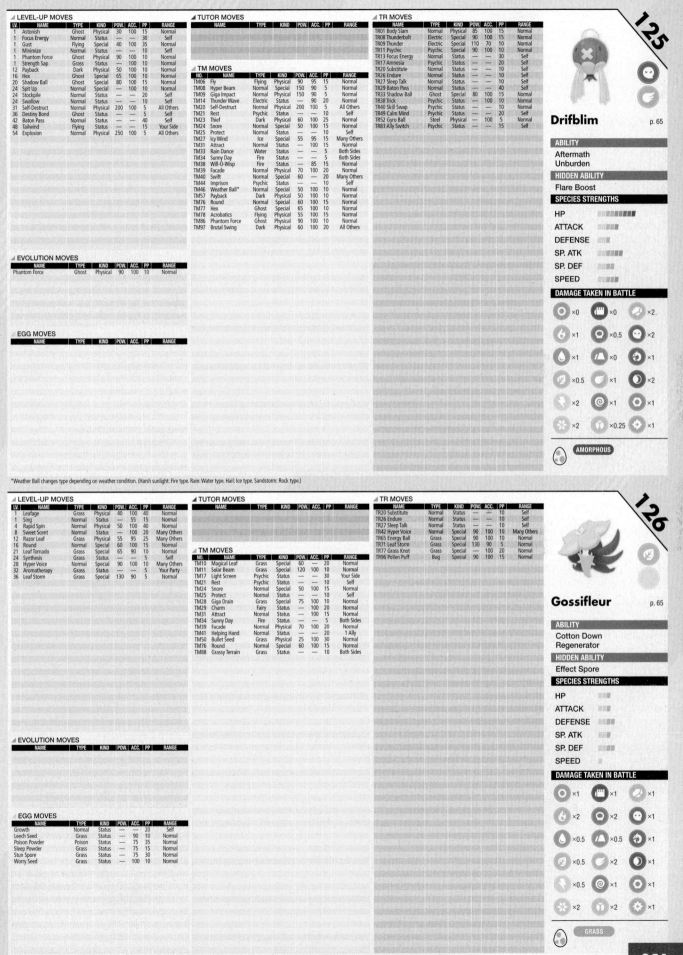

126 — Gossifleur

LEVEL-UP MOVES

LV.	NAME	TYPE	KIND	POW.	ACC.	PP	RANGE
1	Leafage	Grass	Physical	40	100	40	Normal
1	Sing	Normal	Status	—	55	15	Normal
4	Rapid Spin	Normal	Physical	50	100	40	Normal
8	Sweet Scent	Normal	Status	—	100	20	Many Others
12	Razor Leaf	Grass	Physical	55	95	25	Many Others
16	Round	Normal	Special	60	100	15	Normal
21	Leaf Tornado	Grass	Special	65	90	10	Normal
24	Synthesis	Grass	Status	—	—	5	Self
28	Hyper Voice	Normal	Special	90	100	10	Many Others
32	Aromatherapy	Grass	Status	—	—	5	Your Party
36	Leaf Storm	Grass	Special	130	90	5	Normal

EVOLUTION MOVES

NAME	TYPE	KIND	POW.	ACC.	PP	RANGE

EGG MOVES

NAME	TYPE	KIND	POW.	ACC.	PP	RANGE
Growth	Normal	Status	—	—	20	Self
Leech Seed	Grass	Status	—	90	10	Normal
Poison Powder	Poison	Status	—	75	35	Normal
Sleep Powder	Grass	Status	—	75	15	Normal
Stun Spore	Grass	Status	—	75	30	Normal
Worry Seed	Grass	Status	—	100	10	Normal

TUTOR MOVES

NAME	TYPE	KIND	POW.	ACC.	PP	RANGE

TM MOVES

NO.	NAME	TYPE	KIND	POW.	ACC.	PP	RANGE
TM10	Magical Leaf	Grass	Special	60	—	20	Normal
TM11	Solar Beam	Grass	Special	120	100	10	Normal
TM17	Light Screen	Psychic	Status	—	—	30	Your Side
TM21	Rest	Psychic	Status	—	—	10	Self
TM24	Snore	Normal	Special	50	100	15	Normal
TM25	Protect	Normal	Status	—	—	10	Self
TM28	Giga Drain	Grass	Special	75	100	10	Normal
TM29	Charm	Fairy	Status	—	100	20	Normal
TM31	Attract	Normal	Status	—	100	15	Normal
TM34	Sunny Day	Fire	Status	—	—	5	Both Sides
TM39	Facade	Normal	Physical	70	100	20	Normal
TM41	Helping Hand	Normal	Status	—	—	20	1 Ally
TM50	Bullet Seed	Grass	Physical	25	100	30	Normal
TM76	Round	Normal	Special	60	100	15	Normal
TM88	Grassy Terrain	Grass	Status	—	—	10	Both Sides

TR MOVES

NO.	NAME	TYPE	KIND	POW.	ACC.	PP	RANGE
TR20	Substitute	Normal	Status	—	—	10	Self
TR26	Endure	Normal	Status	—	—	10	Self
TR27	Sleep Talk	Normal	Status	—	—	10	Self
TR42	Hyper Voice	Normal	Special	90	100	10	Many Others
TR65	Energy Ball	Grass	Special	90	100	10	Normal
TR71	Leaf Storm	Grass	Special	130	90	5	Normal
TR77	Grass Knot	Grass	Special	—	100	20	Normal
TR96	Pollen Puff	Bug	Special	90	100	15	Normal

Gossifleur p. 65

ABILITY
Cotton Down
Regenerator

HIDDEN ABILITY
Effect Spore

SPECIES STRENGTHS
HP
ATTACK
DEFENSE
SP. ATK
SP. DEF
SPEED

DAMAGE TAKEN IN BATTLE

×1 ×1 ×1
×2 ×2 ×1
×0.5 ×0.5 ×1
×0.5 ×2 ×1
×0.5 ×1 ×1
×2 ×1 ×1

GRASS

127 Eldegoss — p. 65

LEVEL-UP MOVES

LV.	NAME	TYPE	KIND	POW.	ACC.	PP	RANGE
1	Cotton Spore	Grass	Status	—	100	40	Many Others
1	Leafage	Grass	Physical	40	100	40	Normal
1	Rapid Spin	Normal	Physical	50	100	40	Normal
1	Sing	Normal	Status	—	55	15	Normal
1	Sweet Scent	Normal	Status	—	100	20	Many Others
12	Razor Leaf	Grass	Physical	55	95	25	Many Others
16	Round	Normal	Special	60	100	15	Normal
23	Leaf Tornado	Grass	Special	65	90	10	Normal
28	Synthesis	Grass	Status	—	—	5	Self
34	Hyper Voice	Normal	Special	90	100	10	Many Others
40	Aromatherapy	Grass	Status	—	—	5	Your Party
46	Leaf Storm	Grass	Special	130	90	5	Normal
52	Cotton Guard	Grass	Status	—	—	10	Self

EVOLUTION MOVES

NAME	TYPE	KIND	POW.	ACC.	PP	RANGE
Cotton Spore	Grass	Status	—	100	40	Many Others

EGG MOVES

NAME	TYPE	KIND	POW.	ACC.	PP	RANGE

TUTOR MOVES

NAME	TYPE	KIND	POW.	ACC.	PP	RANGE

TM MOVES

NO.	NAME	TYPE	KIND	POW.	ACC.	PP	RANGE
TM08	Hyper Beam	Normal	Special	150	90	5	Normal
TM09	Giga Impact	Normal	Physical	150	90	5	Normal
TM10	Magical Leaf	Grass	Special	60	—	20	Normal
TM11	Solar Beam	Grass	Special	120	100	10	Normal
TM17	Light Screen	Psychic	Status	—	—	30	Your Side
TM21	Rest	Psychic	Status	—	—	10	Self
TM24	Snore	Normal	Special	50	100	15	Normal
TM25	Protect	Normal	Status	—	—	10	Self
TM28	Giga Drain	Grass	Special	75	100	10	Normal
TM29	Charm	Fairy	Status	—	100	20	Normal
TM31	Attract	Normal	Status	—	100	15	Normal
TM34	Sunny Day	Fire	Status	—	—	5	Both Sides
TM39	Facade	Normal	Physical	70	100	20	Normal
TM41	Helping Hand	Normal	Status	—	—	20	1 Ally
TM46	Weather Ball*	Normal	Special	50	100	10	Normal
TM50	Bullet Seed	Grass	Physical	25	100	30	Normal
TM76	Round	Normal	Special	60	100	15	Normal
TM88	Grassy Terrain	Grass	Status	—	—	10	Both Sides

TR MOVES

NO.	NAME	TYPE	KIND	POW.	ACC.	PP	RANGE
TR20	Substitute	Normal	Status	—	—	10	Self
TR26	Endure	Normal	Status	—	—	10	Self
TR27	Sleep Talk	Normal	Status	—	—	10	Self
TR42	Hyper Voice	Normal	Special	90	100	10	Many Others
TR59	Seed Bomb	Grass	Physical	80	100	15	Normal
TR65	Energy Ball	Grass	Special	90	100	10	Normal
TR71	Leaf Storm	Grass	Special	130	90	5	Normal
TR77	Grass Knot	Grass	Special	—	100	20	Normal
TR96	Pollen Puff	Bug	Special	90	100	15	Normal

ABILITY
Cotton Down
Regenerator

HIDDEN ABILITY
Effect Spore

SPECIES STRENGTHS
HP
ATTACK
DEFENSE
SP. ATK
SP. DEF
SPEED

DAMAGE TAKEN IN BATTLE

×1 ×1 ×1
×2 ×2 ×1
×0.5 ×0.5 ×1
×0.5 ×2 ×1
×0.5 ×1 ×1
×2 ×2 ×1

GRASS

---

128 Cherubi — p. 66

LEVEL-UP MOVES

LV.	NAME	TYPE	KIND	POW.	ACC.	PP	RANGE
1	Morning Sun	Normal	Status	—	—	5	Self
1	Tackle	Normal	Physical	40	100	35	Normal
5	Leafage	Grass	Physical	40	100	40	Normal
10	Growth	Normal	Status	—	—	20	Self
15	Helping Hand	Normal	Status	—	—	20	1 Ally
20	Magical Leaf	Grass	Special	60	—	20	Normal
26	Leech Seed	Grass	Status	—	90	10	Normal
30	Take Down	Normal	Physical	90	85	20	Normal
35	Petal Blizzard	Grass	Physical	90	100	15	All Others
40	Worry Seed	Grass	Status	—	100	10	Normal
45	Solar Beam	Grass	Special	120	100	10	Normal

EVOLUTION MOVES

NAME	TYPE	KIND	POW.	ACC.	PP	RANGE

EGG MOVES

NAME	TYPE	KIND	POW.	ACC.	PP	RANGE
Aromatherapy	Grass	Status	—	—	5	Your Party
Defense Curl	Normal	Status	—	—	40	Self
Flower Shield	Fairy	Status	—	—	10	All
Heal Pulse	Psychic	Status	—	—	10	Normal
Healing Wish	Psychic	Status	—	—	10	Self
Nature Power	Normal	Status	—	—	20	Normal
Razor Leaf	Grass	Physical	55	95	25	Many Others
Rollout	Rock	Physical	30	90	20	Normal
Sweet Scent	Normal	Status	—	100	20	Many Others
Tickle	Normal	Status	—	100	20	Normal

TUTOR MOVES

NAME	TYPE	KIND	POW.	ACC.	PP	RANGE

TM MOVES

NO.	NAME	TYPE	KIND	POW.	ACC.	PP	RANGE
TM10	Magical Leaf	Grass	Special	60	—	20	Normal
TM11	Solar Beam	Grass	Special	120	100	10	Normal
TM19	Safeguard	Normal	Status	—	—	25	Your Side
TM21	Rest	Psychic	Status	—	—	10	Self
TM24	Snore	Normal	Special	50	100	15	Normal
TM25	Protect	Normal	Status	—	—	10	Self
TM28	Giga Drain	Grass	Special	75	100	10	Normal
TM31	Attract	Normal	Status	—	100	15	Normal
TM34	Sunny Day	Fire	Status	—	—	5	Both Sides
TM39	Facade	Normal	Physical	70	100	20	Normal
TM41	Helping Hand	Normal	Status	—	—	20	1 Ally
TM46	Weather Ball*	Normal	Special	50	100	10	Normal
TM50	Bullet Seed	Grass	Physical	25	100	30	Normal
TM76	Round	Normal	Special	60	100	15	Normal
TM87	Draining Kiss	Fairy	Special	50	100	10	Normal
TM88	Grassy Terrain	Grass	Status	—	—	10	Both Sides

TR MOVES

NO.	NAME	TYPE	KIND	POW.	ACC.	PP	RANGE
TR00	Swords Dance	Normal	Status	—	—	20	Self
TR20	Substitute	Normal	Status	—	—	10	Self
TR26	Endure	Normal	Status	—	—	10	Self
TR27	Sleep Talk	Normal	Status	—	—	10	Self
TR59	Seed Bomb	Grass	Physical	80	100	15	Normal
TR65	Energy Ball	Grass	Special	90	100	10	Normal
TR77	Grass Knot	Grass	Special	—	100	20	Normal
TR92	Dazzling Gleam	Fairy	Special	80	100	10	Many Others
TR96	Pollen Puff	Bug	Special	90	100	15	Normal

ABILITY
Chlorophyll
—

HIDDEN ABILITY
—

SPECIES STRENGTHS
HP
ATTACK
DEFENSE
SP. ATK
SP. DEF
SPEED

DAMAGE TAKEN IN BATTLE

×1 ×1 ×1
×2 ×2 ×1
×0.5 ×0.5 ×1
×0.5 ×2 ×1
×0.5 ×1 ×1
×2 ×1 ×1

FAIRY
GRASS

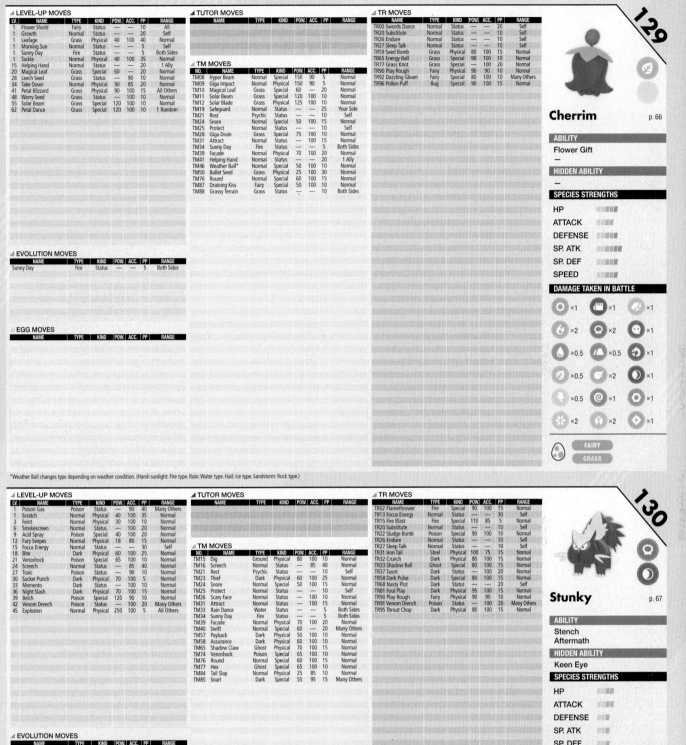

129

LEVEL-UP MOVES

LV.	NAME	TYPE	KIND	POW.	ACC.	PP	RANGE
1	Flower Shield	Fairy	Status	—	—	10	All
1	Growth	Normal	Status	—	—	20	Self
1	Leafage	Grass	Physical	40	100	40	Normal
1	Morning Sun	Normal	Status	—	—	5	Self
1	Sunny Day	Fire	Status	—	—	5	Both Sides
1	Tackle	Normal	Physical	40	100	35	Normal
15	Helping Hand	Normal	Status	—	—	20	1 Ally
20	Magical Leaf	Grass	Special	60	—	20	Normal
28	Take Down	Normal	Physical	90	85	20	Normal
34	Leech Seed	Grass	Status	—	90	10	Normal
41	Petal Blizzard	Grass	Physical	90	100	15	All Others
48	Worry Seed	Grass	Status	—	100	10	Normal
55	Solar Beam	Grass	Special	120	100	10	Normal
62	Petal Dance	Grass	Special	120	100	10	1 Random

EVOLUTION MOVES

NAME	TYPE	KIND	POW.	ACC.	PP	RANGE
Sunny Day	Fire	Status	—	—	5	Both Sides

EGG MOVES

NAME	TYPE	KIND	POW.	ACC.	PP	RANGE

TUTOR MOVES

NAME	TYPE	KIND	POW.	ACC.	PP	RANGE

TM MOVES

NO.	NAME	TYPE	KIND	POW.	ACC.	PP	RANGE
TM08	Hyper Beam	Normal	Special	150	90	5	Normal
TM09	Giga Impact	Normal	Physical	150	90	5	Normal
TM10	Magical Leaf	Grass	Special	60	—	20	Normal
TM11	Solar Beam	Grass	Special	120	100	10	Normal
TM12	Solar Blade	Grass	Physical	125	100	10	Normal
TM19	Safeguard	Normal	Status	—	—	25	Your Side
TM21	Rest	Psychic	Status	—	—	10	Self
TM24	Snore	Normal	Special	50	100	15	Normal
TM25	Protect	Normal	Status	—	—	10	Self
TM28	Giga Drain	Grass	Special	75	100	10	Normal
TM31	Attract	Normal	Status	—	100	15	Normal
TM34	Sunny Day	Fire	Status	—	—	5	Both Sides
TM39	Facade	Normal	Physical	70	100	20	Normal
TM41	Helping Hand	Normal	Status	—	—	20	1 Ally
TM46	Weather Ball*	Normal	Special	50	100	10	Normal
TM50	Bullet Seed	Grass	Physical	25	100	30	Normal
TM76	Round	Normal	Special	60	100	15	Normal
TM87	Draining Kiss	Fairy	Special	50	100	10	Normal
TM88	Grassy Terrain	Grass	Status	—	—	10	Both Sides

TR MOVES

NO.	NAME	TYPE	KIND	POW.	ACC.	PP	RANGE
TR00	Swords Dance	Normal	Status	—	—	20	Self
TR20	Substitute	Normal	Status	—	—	10	Self
TR26	Endure	Normal	Status	—	—	10	Self
TR27	Sleep Talk	Normal	Status	—	—	10	Self
TR59	Seed Bomb	Grass	Physical	80	100	15	Normal
TR65	Energy Ball	Grass	Special	90	100	10	Normal
TR77	Grass Knot	Grass	Special	—	100	20	Normal
TR90	Play Rough	Fairy	Physical	90	90	10	Normal
TR92	Dazzling Gleam	Fairy	Special	80	100	10	Many Others
TR96	Pollen Puff	Bug	Special	90	100	15	Normal

Cherrim
p. 66

ABILITY
Flower Gift
—

HIDDEN ABILITY
—

SPECIES STRENGTHS
HP
ATTACK
DEFENSE
SP. ATK
SP. DEF
SPEED

DAMAGE TAKEN IN BATTLE

×1	×1	×1
×2	×2	×1
×0.5	×0.5	×1
×0.5	×2	×1
×0.5	×1	×1
×2	×2	×1

FAIRY
GRASS

*Weather Ball changes type depending on weather condition. (Harsh sunlight: Fire type. Rain: Water type. Hail: Ice type. Sandstorm: Rock type.)

130

LEVEL-UP MOVES

LV.	NAME	TYPE	KIND	POW.	ACC.	PP	RANGE
1	Poison Gas	Poison	Status	—	90	40	Many Others
1	Scratch	Normal	Physical	40	100	35	Normal
3	Feint	Normal	Physical	30	100	10	Normal
6	Smokescreen	Normal	Status	—	100	20	Normal
9	Acid Spray	Poison	Special	40	100	20	Normal
12	Fury Swipes	Normal	Physical	18	80	15	Normal
15	Focus Energy	Normal	Status	—	—	30	Self
18	Bite	Dark	Physical	60	100	25	Normal
21	Venoshock	Poison	Special	65	100	10	Normal
24	Screech	Normal	Status	—	85	40	Normal
27	Toxic	Poison	Status	—	90	10	Normal
30	Sucker Punch	Dark	Physical	70	100	5	Normal
33	Memento	Dark	Status	—	100	10	Normal
36	Night Slash	Dark	Physical	70	100	15	Normal
39	Belch	Poison	Special	120	90	10	Normal
42	Venom Drench	Poison	Status	—	100	20	Many Others
45	Explosion	Normal	Physical	250	100	5	All Others

EVOLUTION MOVES

NAME	TYPE	KIND	POW.	ACC.	PP	RANGE

EGG MOVES

NAME	TYPE	KIND	POW.	ACC.	PP	RANGE
Astonish	Ghost	Physical	30	100	15	Normal
Double-Edge	Normal	Physical	120	100	15	Normal
Haze	Ice	Status	—	—	30	Both Sides
Leer	Normal	Status	—	100	30	Many Others
Slash	Normal	Physical	70	100	20	Normal
Smog	Poison	Special	30	70	20	Normal

TUTOR MOVES

NAME	TYPE	KIND	POW.	ACC.	PP	RANGE

TM MOVES

NO.	NAME	TYPE	KIND	POW.	ACC.	PP	RANGE
TM15	Dig	Ground	Physical	80	100	10	Normal
TM16	Screech	Normal	Status	—	85	40	Normal
TM21	Rest	Psychic	Status	—	—	10	Self
TM23	Thief	Dark	Physical	60	100	25	Normal
TM24	Snore	Normal	Special	50	100	15	Normal
TM25	Protect	Normal	Status	—	—	10	Self
TM26	Scary Face	Normal	Status	—	100	10	Normal
TM31	Attract	Normal	Status	—	100	15	Normal
TM33	Rain Dance	Water	Status	—	—	5	Both Sides
TM34	Sunny Day	Fire	Status	—	—	5	Both Sides
TM39	Facade	Normal	Physical	70	100	20	Normal
TM40	Swift	Normal	Special	60	—	20	Many Others
TM57	Payback	Dark	Physical	50	100	10	Normal
TM58	Assurance	Dark	Physical	60	100	10	Normal
TM65	Shadow Claw	Ghost	Physical	70	100	15	Normal
TM74	Venoshock	Poison	Special	65	100	10	Normal
TM76	Round	Normal	Special	60	100	15	Normal
TM77	Hex	Ghost	Special	65	100	10	Normal
TM84	Tail Slap	Normal	Physical	25	85	10	Normal
TM85	Snarl	Dark	Special	55	95	15	Many Others

TR MOVES

NO.	NAME	TYPE	KIND	POW.	ACC.	PP	RANGE
TR02	Flamethrower	Fire	Special	90	100	15	Normal
TR13	Focus Energy	Normal	Status	—	—	30	Self
TR15	Fire Blast	Fire	Special	110	85	5	Normal
TR20	Substitute	Normal	Status	—	—	10	Self
TR22	Sludge Bomb	Poison	Special	90	100	10	Normal
TR26	Endure	Normal	Status	—	—	10	Self
TR27	Sleep Talk	Normal	Status	—	—	10	Self
TR31	Iron Tail	Steel	Physical	100	75	15	Normal
TR32	Crunch	Dark	Physical	80	100	15	Normal
TR33	Shadow Ball	Ghost	Special	80	100	15	Normal
TR37	Taunt	Dark	Status	—	100	20	Normal
TR58	Dark Pulse	Dark	Special	80	100	15	Normal
TR68	Nasty Plot	Dark	Status	—	—	20	Self
TR81	Foul Play	Dark	Physical	95	100	15	Normal
TR90	Play Rough	Fairy	Physical	90	90	10	Normal
TR91	Venom Drench	Poison	Status	—	100	20	Many Others
TR95	Throat Chop	Dark	Physical	80	100	15	Normal

Stunky
p. 67

ABILITY
Stench
Aftermath

HIDDEN ABILITY
Keen Eye

SPECIES STRENGTHS
HP
ATTACK
DEFENSE
SP. ATK
SP. DEF
SPEED

DAMAGE TAKEN IN BATTLE

×1	×1	×1
×1	×0.5	×0.5
×1	×2	×1
×0.5	×1	×0.5
×1	×0	×1
×1	×1	×1

FIELD

131

Skuntank
p. 67

ABILITY
Stench
Aftermath

HIDDEN ABILITY
Keen Eye

SPECIES STRENGTHS
HP
ATTACK
DEFENSE
SP. ATK
SP. DEF
SPEED

DAMAGE TAKEN IN BATTLE

●×1	▦×1	◢×1
●×1	●×0.5	●×0.5
●×1	◢×2	↻×1
●×0.5	●×1	●×0.5
●×1	◎×0	●×1
✱×1	♈×1	✦×1

FIELD

LEVEL-UP MOVES

LV.	NAME	TYPE	KIND	POW.	ACC.	PP	RANGE
1	Feint	Normal	Physical	30	100	10	Normal
1	Flamethrower	Fire	Special	90	100	15	Normal
1	Poison Gas	Poison	Status	—	90	40	Many Others
1	Scratch	Normal	Physical	40	100	35	Normal
1	Smokescreen	Normal	Status	—	100	20	Normal
9	Acid Spray	Poison	Special	40	100	20	Normal
12	Fury Swipes	Normal	Physical	18	80	15	Normal
15	Focus Energy	Normal	Status	—	—	30	Self
18	Bite	Dark	Physical	60	100	25	Normal
21	Venoshock	Poison	Special	65	100	10	Normal
24	Screech	Normal	Status	—	85	40	Normal
27	Toxic	Poison	Status	—	90	10	Normal
30	Sucker Punch	Dark	Physical	70	100	5	Normal
33	Memento	Dark	Status	—	100	10	Normal
38	Night Slash	Dark	Physical	70	100	15	Normal
43	Belch	Poison	Special	120	90	10	Normal
48	Venom Drench	Poison	Status	—	100	20	Many Others
53	Explosion	Normal	Physical	250	100	5	All Others

EVOLUTION MOVES

NAME	TYPE	KIND	POW.	ACC.	PP	RANGE
Flamethrower	Fire	Special	90	100	15	Normal

EGG MOVES

NAME	TYPE	KIND	POW.	ACC.	PP	RANGE

TUTOR MOVES

NAME	TYPE	KIND	POW.	ACC.	PP	RANGE

TM MOVES

NO.	NAME	TYPE	KIND	POW.	ACC.	PP	RANGE
TM08	Hyper Beam	Normal	Special	150	90	5	Normal
TM09	Giga Impact	Normal	Physical	150	90	5	Normal
TM13	Fire Spin	Fire	Special	35	85	15	Normal
TM15	Dig	Ground	Physical	80	100	10	Normal
TM16	Screech	Normal	Status	—	85	40	Normal
TM21	Rest	Psychic	Status	—	—	10	Self
TM23	Thief	Dark	Physical	60	100	25	Normal
TM24	Snore	Normal	Special	50	100	15	Normal
TM25	Protect	Normal	Status	—	—	10	Self
TM26	Scary Face	Normal	Status	—	100	10	Normal
TM31	Attract	Normal	Status	—	100	15	Normal
TM33	Rain Dance	Water	Status	—	—	5	Both Sides
TM34	Sunny Day	Fire	Status	—	—	5	Both Sides
TM39	Facade	Normal	Physical	70	100	20	Normal
TM40	Swift	Normal	Special	60	—	20	Many Others
TM57	Payback	Dark	Physical	50	100	10	Normal
TM58	Assurance	Dark	Physical	60	100	10	Normal
TM65	Shadow Claw	Ghost	Physical	70	100	15	Normal
TM74	Venoshock	Poison	Special	65	100	10	Normal
TM76	Round	Normal	Special	60	100	15	Normal
TM77	Hex	Ghost	Special	65	100	10	Normal
TM84	Tail Slap	Normal	Physical	25	85	10	Normal
TM85	Snarl	Dark	Special	55	95	15	Many Others

TR MOVES

NO.	NAME	TYPE	KIND	POW.	ACC.	PP	RANGE
TR02	Flamethrower	Fire	Special	90	100	15	Normal
TR13	Focus Energy	Normal	Status	—	—	30	Self
TR15	Fire Blast	Fire	Special	110	85	5	Normal
TR20	Substitute	Normal	Status	—	—	10	Self
TR22	Sludge Bomb	Poison	Special	90	100	10	Normal
TR26	Endure	Normal	Status	—	—	10	Self
TR27	Sleep Talk	Normal	Status	—	—	10	Self
TR31	Iron Tail	Steel	Physical	100	75	15	Normal
TR32	Crunch	Dark	Physical	80	100	15	Normal
TR33	Shadow Ball	Ghost	Special	80	100	15	Normal
TR37	Taunt	Dark	Status	—	100	20	Normal
TR57	Poison Jab	Poison	Physical	80	100	20	Normal
TR58	Dark Pulse	Dark	Special	80	100	15	Normal
TR68	Nasty Plot	Dark	Status	—	—	20	Self
TR81	Foul Play	Dark	Physical	95	100	15	Normal
TR90	Play Rough	Fairy	Physical	90	90	10	Normal
TR91	Venom Drench	Poison	Status	—	100	20	Many Others
TR95	Throat Chop	Dark	Physical	80	100	15	Normal

132

Tympole
p. 68

ABILITY
Swift Swim
Hydration

HIDDEN ABILITY
Water Absorb

SPECIES STRENGTHS
HP
ATTACK
DEFENSE
SP. ATK
SP. DEF
SPEED

DAMAGE TAKEN IN BATTLE

●×1	▦×1	◢×1
●×0.5	●×1	●×1
●×0.5	◢×1	↻×1
●×2	●×1	●×0.5
●×2	◎×1	●×0.5
✱×0.5	♈×1	✦×1

WATER 1

LEVEL-UP MOVES

LV.	NAME	TYPE	KIND	POW.	ACC.	PP	RANGE
1	Echoed Voice	Normal	Special	40	100	15	Normal
1	Growl	Normal	Status	—	100	40	Many Others
4	Acid	Poison	Special	40	100	30	Many Others
8	Supersonic	Normal	Status	—	55	20	Normal
12	Mud Shot	Ground	Special	55	95	15	Normal
16	Round	Normal	Special	60	100	15	Normal
20	Bubble Beam	Water	Special	65	100	10	Normal
24	Flail	Normal	Physical	—	100	15	Normal
28	Uproar	Normal	Special	90	100	10	1 Random
32	Aqua Ring	Water	Status	—	—	20	Self
36	Hyper Voice	Normal	Special	90	100	10	Many Others
40	Muddy Water	Water	Special	90	85	10	Many Others
44	Rain Dance	Water	Status	—	—	5	Both Sides
48	Hydro Pump	Water	Special	110	80	5	Normal

EVOLUTION MOVES

NAME	TYPE	KIND	POW.	ACC.	PP	RANGE

EGG MOVES

NAME	TYPE	KIND	POW.	ACC.	PP	RANGE
Mist	Ice	Status	—	—	30	Your Side
Mud-Slap	Ground	Special	20	100	10	Normal
Toxic	Poison	Status	—	90	10	Normal
Water Pulse	Water	Special	60	100	20	Normal

TUTOR MOVES

NAME	TYPE	KIND	POW.	ACC.	PP	RANGE

TM MOVES

NO.	NAME	TYPE	KIND	POW.	ACC.	PP	RANGE
TM16	Screech	Normal	Status	—	85	40	Normal
TM21	Rest	Psychic	Status	—	—	10	Self
TM24	Snore	Normal	Special	50	100	15	Normal
TM25	Protect	Normal	Status	—	—	10	Self
TM27	Icy Wind	Ice	Special	55	95	15	Many Others
TM31	Attract	Normal	Status	—	100	15	Normal
TM33	Rain Dance	Water	Status	—	—	5	Both Sides
TM35	Hail	Ice	Status	—	—	10	Both Sides
TM39	Facade	Normal	Physical	70	100	20	Normal
TM46	Weather Ball*	Normal	Special	50	100	10	Normal
TM52	Bounce	Flying	Physical	85	85	5	Normal
TM53	Mud Shot	Ground	Special	55	95	15	Normal
TM76	Round	Normal	Special	60	100	15	Normal

TR MOVES

NO.	NAME	TYPE	KIND	POW.	ACC.	PP	RANGE
TR03	Hydro Pump	Water	Special	110	80	5	Normal
TR04	Surf	Water	Special	90	100	15	All Others
TR20	Substitute	Normal	Status	—	—	10	Self
TR22	Sludge Bomb	Poison	Special	90	100	10	Normal
TR26	Endure	Normal	Status	—	—	10	Self
TR27	Sleep Talk	Normal	Status	—	—	10	Self
TR35	Uproar	Normal	Special	90	100	10	1 Random
TR42	Hyper Voice	Normal	Special	90	100	10	Many Others
TR45	Muddy Water	Water	Special	90	85	10	Many Others
TR67	Earth Power	Ground	Special	90	100	10	Normal
TR78	Sludge Wave	Poison	Special	95	100	10	All Others
TR84	Scald	Water	Special	80	100	15	Normal
TR91	Venom Drench	Poison	Status	—	100	20	Many Others

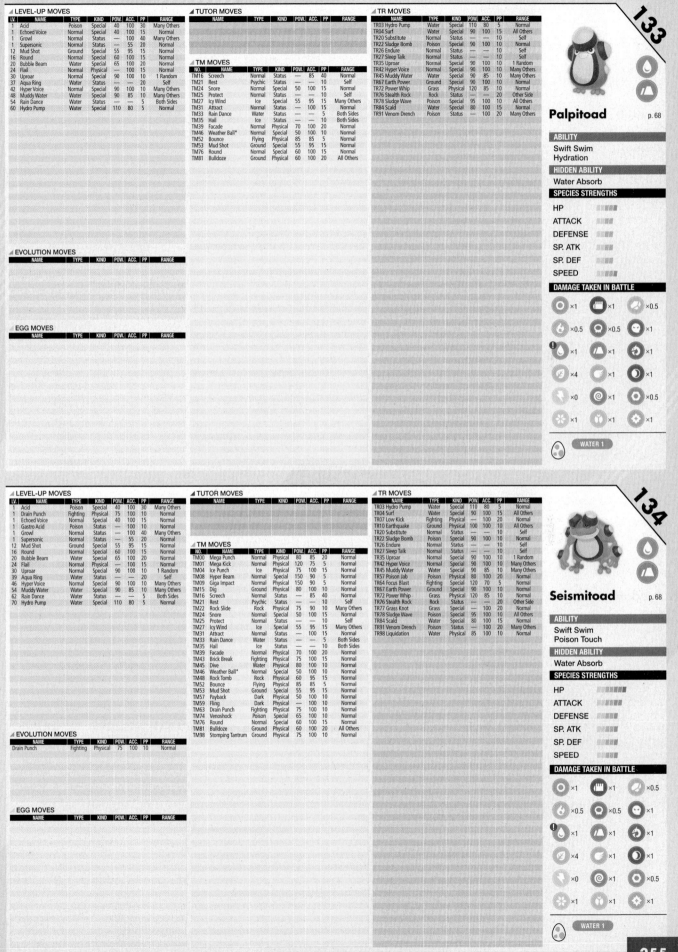

133 — Palpitoad

LEVEL-UP MOVES

LV.	NAME	TYPE	KIND	POW.	ACC.	PP	RANGE
1	Acid	Poison	Special	40	100	30	Many Others
1	Echoed Voice	Normal	Special	40	100	15	Normal
1	Growl	Normal	Status	—	100	40	Many Others
1	Supersonic	Normal	Status	—	55	20	Normal
12	Mud Shot	Ground	Special	55	95	15	Normal
16	Round	Normal	Special	60	100	15	Normal
20	Bubble Beam	Water	Special	65	100	20	Normal
24	Flail	Normal	Physical	—	100	15	Normal
30	Uproar	Normal	Special	90	100	10	1 Random
37	Aqua Ring	Water	Status	—	—	20	Self
42	Hyper Voice	Normal	Special	90	100	10	Many Others
48	Muddy Water	Water	Special	90	85	10	Many Others
54	Rain Dance	Water	Status	—	—	5	Both Sides
60	Hydro Pump	Water	Special	110	80	5	Normal

EVOLUTION MOVES

NAME	TYPE	KIND	POW.	ACC.	PP	RANGE

EGG MOVES

NAME	TYPE	KIND	POW.	ACC.	PP	RANGE

TUTOR MOVES

NAME	TYPE	KIND	POW.	ACC.	PP	RANGE

TM MOVES

NO.	NAME	TYPE	KIND	POW.	ACC.	PP	RANGE
TM16	Screech	Normal	Status	—	85	40	Normal
TM21	Rest	Psychic	Status	—	—	10	Self
TM24	Snore	Normal	Special	50	100	15	Normal
TM25	Protect	Normal	Status	—	—	10	Self
TM27	Icy Wind	Ice	Special	55	95	15	Many Others
TM31	Attract	Normal	Status	—	100	15	Normal
TM33	Rain Dance	Water	Status	—	—	5	Both Sides
TM35	Hail	Ice	Status	—	—	10	Both Sides
TM39	Facade	Normal	Physical	70	100	20	Normal
TM46	Weather Ball*	Normal	Special	50	100	10	Normal
TM52	Bounce	Flying	Physical	85	85	5	Normal
TM53	Mud Shot	Ground	Special	55	95	15	Normal
TM76	Round	Normal	Special	60	100	15	Normal
TM81	Bulldoze	Ground	Physical	60	100	20	All Others

TR MOVES

NO.	NAME	TYPE	KIND	POW.	ACC.	PP	RANGE
TR03	Hydro Pump	Water	Special	110	80	5	Normal
TR04	Surf	Water	Special	90	100	15	All Others
TR20	Substitute	Normal	Status	—	—	10	Self
TR22	Sludge Bomb	Poison	Special	90	100	10	Normal
TR26	Endure	Normal	Status	—	—	10	Self
TR27	Sleep Talk	Normal	Status	—	—	10	Self
TR35	Uproar	Normal	Special	90	100	10	1 Random
TR42	Hyper Voice	Normal	Special	90	100	10	Many Others
TR45	Muddy Water	Water	Special	90	85	10	Many Others
TR67	Earth Power	Ground	Special	90	100	10	Normal
TR72	Power Whip	Grass	Physical	120	85	10	Normal
TR76	Stealth Rock	Rock	Status	—	—	20	Other Side
TR78	Sludge Wave	Poison	Special	95	100	10	All Sides
TR84	Scald	Water	Special	80	100	15	Normal
TR91	Venom Drench	Poison	Status	—	100	20	Many Others

Palpitoad p. 68

ABILITY
Swift Swim
Hydration

HIDDEN ABILITY
Water Absorb

SPECIES STRENGTHS
HP
ATTACK
DEFENSE
SP. ATK
SP. DEF
SPEED

DAMAGE TAKEN IN BATTLE
×1 ×1 ×0.5
×0.5 ×0.5 ×1
×1 ×1 ×1
×4 ×1 ×1
×0 ×1 ×0.5
×1 ×1 ×1

WATER 1

---

134 — Seismitoad

LEVEL-UP MOVES

LV.	NAME	TYPE	KIND	POW.	ACC.	PP	RANGE
1	Acid	Poison	Special	40	100	30	Many Others
1	Drain Punch	Fighting	Physical	75	100	10	Normal
1	Echoed Voice	Normal	Special	40	100	15	Normal
1	Gastro Acid	Poison	Status	—	100	10	Normal
1	Growl	Normal	Status	—	100	40	Many Others
1	Supersonic	Normal	Status	—	55	20	Normal
12	Mud Shot	Ground	Special	55	95	15	Normal
16	Round	Normal	Special	60	100	15	Normal
20	Bubble Beam	Water	Special	65	100	20	Normal
24	Flail	Normal	Physical	—	100	15	Normal
30	Uproar	Normal	Special	90	100	10	1 Random
39	Aqua Ring	Water	Status	—	—	20	Self
46	Hyper Voice	Normal	Special	90	100	10	Many Others
54	Muddy Water	Water	Special	90	85	10	Many Others
62	Rain Dance	Water	Status	—	—	5	Both Sides
70	Hydro Pump	Water	Special	110	80	5	Normal

EVOLUTION MOVES

NAME	TYPE	KIND	POW.	ACC.	PP	RANGE
Drain Punch	Fighting	Physical	75	100	10	Normal

EGG MOVES

NAME	TYPE	KIND	POW.	ACC.	PP	RANGE

TUTOR MOVES

NAME	TYPE	KIND	POW.	ACC.	PP	RANGE

TM MOVES

NO.	NAME	TYPE	KIND	POW.	ACC.	PP	RANGE
TM00	Mega Punch	Normal	Physical	80	85	20	Normal
TM01	Mega Kick	Normal	Physical	120	75	5	Normal
TM04	Ice Punch	Ice	Physical	75	100	15	Normal
TM08	Hyper Beam	Normal	Special	150	90	5	Normal
TM09	Giga Impact	Normal	Physical	150	90	5	Normal
TM15	Dig	Ground	Physical	80	100	10	Normal
TM16	Screech	Normal	Status	—	85	40	Normal
TM21	Rest	Psychic	Status	—	—	10	Self
TM22	Rock Slide	Rock	Physical	75	90	10	Many Others
TM24	Snore	Normal	Special	50	100	15	Normal
TM25	Protect	Normal	Status	—	—	10	Self
TM27	Icy Wind	Ice	Special	55	95	15	Many Others
TM31	Attract	Normal	Status	—	100	15	Normal
TM33	Rain Dance	Water	Status	—	—	5	Both Sides
TM35	Hail	Ice	Status	—	—	10	Both Sides
TM39	Facade	Normal	Physical	70	100	20	Normal
TM43	Brick Break	Fighting	Physical	75	100	15	Normal
TM45	Dive	Water	Physical	80	100	10	Normal
TM46	Weather Ball*	Normal	Special	50	100	10	Normal
TM48	Rock Tomb	Rock	Physical	60	95	15	Normal
TM52	Bounce	Flying	Physical	85	85	5	Normal
TM53	Mud Shot	Ground	Special	55	95	15	Normal
TM57	Payback	Dark	Physical	50	100	10	Normal
TM59	Fling	Dark	Physical	—	100	10	Normal
TM63	Drain Punch	Fighting	Physical	75	100	10	Normal
TM74	Venoshock	Poison	Special	65	100	10	Normal
TM76	Round	Normal	Special	60	100	15	Normal
TM81	Bulldoze	Ground	Physical	60	100	20	All Others
TM98	Stomping Tantrum	Ground	Physical	75	100	10	Normal

TR MOVES

NO.	NAME	TYPE	KIND	POW.	ACC.	PP	RANGE
TR03	Hydro Pump	Water	Special	110	80	5	Normal
TR04	Surf	Water	Special	90	100	15	All Others
TR07	Low Kick	Fighting	Physical	—	100	20	Normal
TR10	Earthquake	Ground	Physical	100	100	10	All Others
TR20	Substitute	Normal	Status	—	—	10	Self
TR22	Sludge Bomb	Poison	Special	90	100	10	Normal
TR26	Endure	Normal	Status	—	—	10	Self
TR27	Sleep Talk	Normal	Status	—	—	10	Self
TR35	Uproar	Normal	Special	90	100	10	1 Random
TR42	Hyper Voice	Normal	Special	90	100	10	Many Others
TR45	Muddy Water	Water	Special	90	85	10	Many Others
TR57	Poison Jab	Poison	Physical	80	100	20	Normal
TR64	Focus Blast	Fighting	Special	120	70	5	Normal
TR67	Earth Power	Ground	Special	90	100	10	Normal
TR72	Power Whip	Grass	Physical	120	85	10	Normal
TR76	Stealth Rock	Rock	Status	—	—	20	Other Side
TR77	Grass Knot	Grass	Special	—	100	20	Normal
TR78	Sludge Wave	Poison	Special	95	100	10	All Others
TR84	Scald	Water	Special	80	100	15	Normal
TR91	Venom Drench	Poison	Status	—	100	20	Many Others
TR98	Liquidation	Water	Physical	85	100	10	Normal

Seismitoad p. 68

ABILITY
Swift Swim
Poison Touch

HIDDEN ABILITY
Water Absorb

SPECIES STRENGTHS
HP
ATTACK
DEFENSE
SP. ATK
SP. DEF
SPEED

DAMAGE TAKEN IN BATTLE
×1 ×1 ×0.5
×0.5 ×0.5 ×1
×1 ×1 ×1
×4 ×1 ×1
×0 ×1 ×0.5
×1 ×1 ×1

WATER 1

*Weather Ball changes type depending on weather condition. (Harsh sunlight: Fire type. Rain: Water type. Hail: Ice type. Sandstorm: Rock type.)

135 Duskull — p. 69

ABILITY: Levitate / —
HIDDEN ABILITY: Frisk

SPECIES STRENGTHS: HP / ATTACK / DEFENSE / SP. ATK / SP. DEF / SPEED

AMORPHOUS

LEVEL-UP MOVES

LV.	NAME	TYPE	KIND	POW.	ACC.	PP	RANGE
1	Astonish	Ghost	Physical	30	100	15	Normal
1	Leer	Normal	Status	—	100	30	Many Others
4	Disable	Normal	Status	—	100	20	Normal
8	Shadow Sneak	Ghost	Physical	40	100	30	Normal
12	Confuse Ray	Ghost	Status	—	100	10	Normal
16	Night Shade	Ghost	Special	—	100	15	Normal
20	Payback	Dark	Physical	50	100	10	Normal
24	Will-O-Wisp	Fire	Status	—	85	15	Normal
28	Mean Look	Normal	Status	—	—	5	Normal
32	Hex	Ghost	Special	65	100	10	Normal
36	Curse	Ghost	Status	—	—	10	Varies
40	Shadow Ball	Ghost	Special	80	100	15	Normal
44	Future Sight	Psychic	Special	120	100	10	Normal

TM MOVES

NO.	NAME	TYPE	KIND	POW.	ACC.	PP	RANGE
TM21	Rest	Psychic	Status	—	—	10	Self
TM23	Thief	Dark	Physical	60	100	25	Normal
TM24	Snore	Normal	Special	50	100	15	Normal
TM25	Protect	Normal	Status	—	—	10	Self
TM27	Icy Wind	Ice	Special	55	95	15	Many Others
TM31	Attract	Normal	Status	—	100	15	Normal
TM33	Rain Dance	Water	Status	—	—	5	Both Sides
TM34	Sunny Day	Fire	Status	—	—	5	Both Sides
TM38	Will-O-Wisp	Fire	Status	—	85	15	Normal
TM39	Facade	Normal	Physical	70	100	20	Normal
TM41	Helping Hand	Normal	Status	—	—	20	1 Ally
TM42	Revenge	Fighting	Physical	60	100	10	Normal
TM44	Imprison	Psychic	Status	—	—	10	Self
TM57	Payback	Dark	Physical	50	100	10	Normal
TM59	Fling	Dark	Physical	—	100	10	Normal
TM70	Trick Room	Psychic	Status	—	—	5	Both Sides
TM71	Wonder Room	Psychic	Status	—	—	10	Both Sides
TM76	Round	Normal	Special	60	100	15	Normal
TM77	Hex	Ghost	Special	65	100	10	Normal

TR MOVES

NAME	TYPE	KIND	POW.	ACC.	PP	RANGE
TR01 Body Slam	Normal	Physical	85	100	15	Normal
TR05 Ice Beam	Ice	Special	90	100	10	Normal
TR06 Blizzard	Ice	Special	110	70	5	Many Others
TR11 Psychic	Psychic	Special	90	100	10	Normal
TR20 Substitute	Normal	Status	—	—	10	Self
TR26 Endure	Normal	Status	—	—	10	Self
TR27 Sleep Talk	Normal	Status	—	—	10	Self
TR33 Shadow Ball	Ghost	Special	80	100	15	Normal
TR34 Future Sight	Psychic	Special	120	100	10	Normal
TR37 Taunt	Dark	Status	—	100	20	Normal
TR38 Trick	Psychic	Status	—	100	10	Normal
TR40 Skill Swap	Psychic	Status	—	—	10	Normal
TR49 Calm Mind	Psychic	Status	—	—	20	Self
TR58 Dark Pulse	Dark	Special	80	100	15	Normal
TR83 Ally Switch	Psychic	Status	—	—	15	Self

EVOLUTION MOVES

NAME	TYPE	KIND	POW.	ACC.	PP	RANGE

EGG MOVES

NAME	TYPE	KIND	POW.	ACC.	PP	RANGE
Grudge	Ghost	Status	—	—	5	Self
Haze	Ice	Status	—	—	30	Both Sides
Memento	Dark	Status	—	100	10	Normal
Pain Split	Normal	Status	—	—	20	Normal

---

136 Dusclops — p. 69

ABILITY: Pressure / —
HIDDEN ABILITY: Frisk

SPECIES STRENGTHS: HP / ATTACK / DEFENSE / SP. ATK / SP. DEF / SPEED

AMORPHOUS

LEVEL-UP MOVES

LV.	NAME	TYPE	KIND	POW.	ACC.	PP	RANGE
1	Astonish	Ghost	Physical	30	100	15	Normal
1	Bind	Normal	Physical	15	85	20	Normal
1	Disable	Normal	Status	—	100	20	Normal
1	Fire Punch	Fire	Physical	75	100	15	Normal
1	Gravity	Psychic	Status	—	—	5	Both Sides
1	Ice Punch	Ice	Physical	75	100	15	Normal
1	Leer	Normal	Status	—	100	30	Many Others
1	Shadow Punch	Ghost	Physical	60	—	20	Normal
8	Shadow Sneak	Ghost	Physical	40	100	30	Normal
1	Thunder Punch	Electric	Physical	75	100	15	Normal
12	Confuse Ray	Ghost	Status	—	100	10	Normal
16	Night Shade	Ghost	Special	—	100	15	Normal
20	Payback	Dark	Physical	50	100	10	Normal
24	Will-O-Wisp	Fire	Status	—	85	15	Normal
28	Mean Look	Normal	Status	—	—	5	Normal
32	Hex	Ghost	Special	65	100	10	Normal
36	Curse	Ghost	Status	—	—	10	Varies
42	Shadow Ball	Ghost	Special	80	100	15	Normal
48	Future Sight	Psychic	Special	120	100	10	Normal

TM MOVES

NO.	NAME	TYPE	KIND	POW.	ACC.	PP	RANGE
TM00	Mega Punch	Normal	Physical	80	85	20	Normal
TM01	Mega Kick	Normal	Physical	120	75	5	Normal
TM03	Fire Punch	Fire	Physical	75	100	15	Normal
TM04	Ice Punch	Ice	Physical	75	100	15	Normal
TM05	Thunder Punch	Electric	Physical	75	100	15	Normal
TM08	Hyper Beam	Normal	Special	150	90	5	Normal
TM09	Giga Impact	Normal	Physical	150	90	5	Normal
TM21	Rest	Psychic	Status	—	—	10	Self
TM22	Rock Slide	Rock	Physical	75	90	10	Many Others
TM23	Thief	Dark	Physical	60	100	25	Normal
TM24	Snore	Normal	Special	50	100	15	Normal
TM25	Protect	Normal	Status	—	—	10	Self
TM27	Icy Wind	Ice	Special	55	95	15	Many Others
TM31	Attract	Normal	Status	—	100	15	Normal
TM33	Rain Dance	Water	Status	—	—	5	Both Sides
TM34	Sunny Day	Fire	Status	—	—	5	Both Sides
TM38	Will-O-Wisp	Fire	Status	—	85	15	Normal
TM39	Facade	Normal	Physical	70	100	20	Normal
TM41	Helping Hand	Normal	Status	—	—	20	1 Ally
TM42	Revenge	Fighting	Physical	60	100	10	Normal
TM43	Brick Break	Fighting	Physical	75	100	15	Normal
TM44	Imprison	Psychic	Status	—	—	10	Self
TM48	Rock Tomb	Rock	Physical	60	95	15	Normal
TM57	Payback	Dark	Physical	50	100	10	Normal
TM59	Fling	Dark	Physical	—	100	10	Normal
TM70	Trick Room	Psychic	Status	—	—	5	Both Sides
TM71	Wonder Room	Psychic	Status	—	—	10	Both Sides
TM76	Round	Normal	Special	60	100	15	Normal
TM77	Hex	Ghost	Special	65	100	10	Normal
TM81	Bulldoze	Ground	Physical	60	100	20	All Others

TR MOVES

NAME	TYPE	KIND	POW.	ACC.	PP	RANGE
TR01 Body Slam	Normal	Physical	85	100	15	Normal
TR05 Ice Beam	Ice	Special	90	100	10	Normal
TR06 Blizzard	Ice	Special	110	70	5	Many Others
TR10 Earthquake	Ground	Physical	100	100	10	All Others
TR11 Psychic	Psychic	Special	90	100	10	Normal
TR14 Metronome	Normal	Status	—	—	10	Self
TR20 Substitute	Normal	Status	—	—	10	Self
TR26 Endure	Normal	Status	—	—	10	Self
TR27 Sleep Talk	Normal	Status	—	—	10	Self
TR33 Shadow Ball	Ghost	Special	80	100	15	Normal
TR34 Future Sight	Psychic	Special	120	100	10	Normal
TR37 Taunt	Dark	Status	—	100	20	Normal
TR38 Trick	Psychic	Status	—	100	10	Normal
TR40 Skill Swap	Psychic	Status	—	—	10	Normal
TR49 Calm Mind	Psychic	Status	—	—	20	Self
TR58 Dark Pulse	Dark	Special	80	100	15	Normal
TR83 Ally Switch	Psychic	Status	—	—	15	Self

EVOLUTION MOVES

NAME	TYPE	KIND	POW.	ACC.	PP	RANGE
Shadow Punch	Ghost	Physical	60	—	20	Normal

EGG MOVES

NAME	TYPE	KIND	POW.	ACC.	PP	RANGE

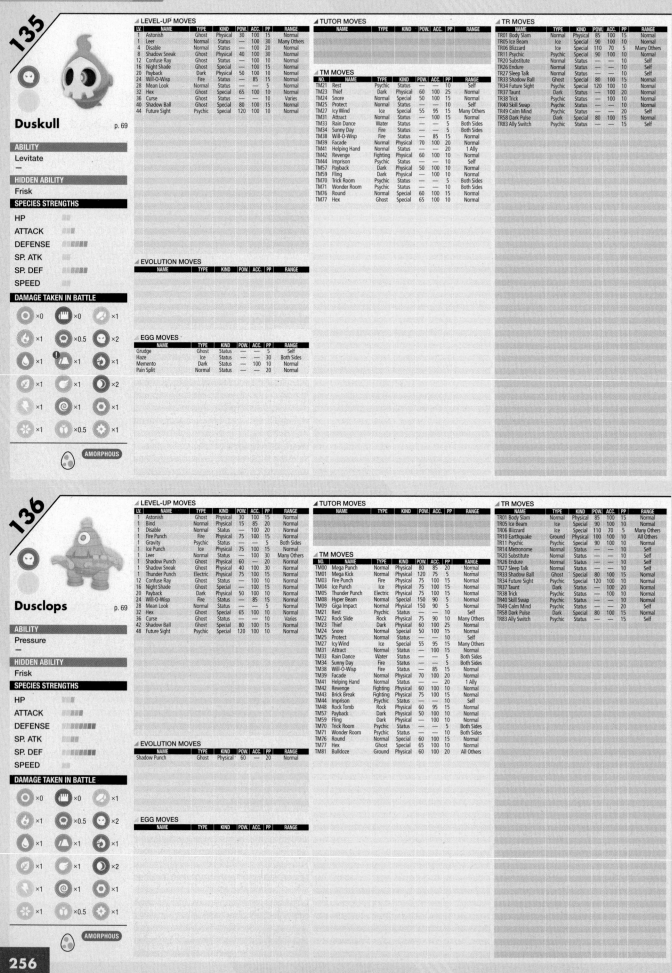

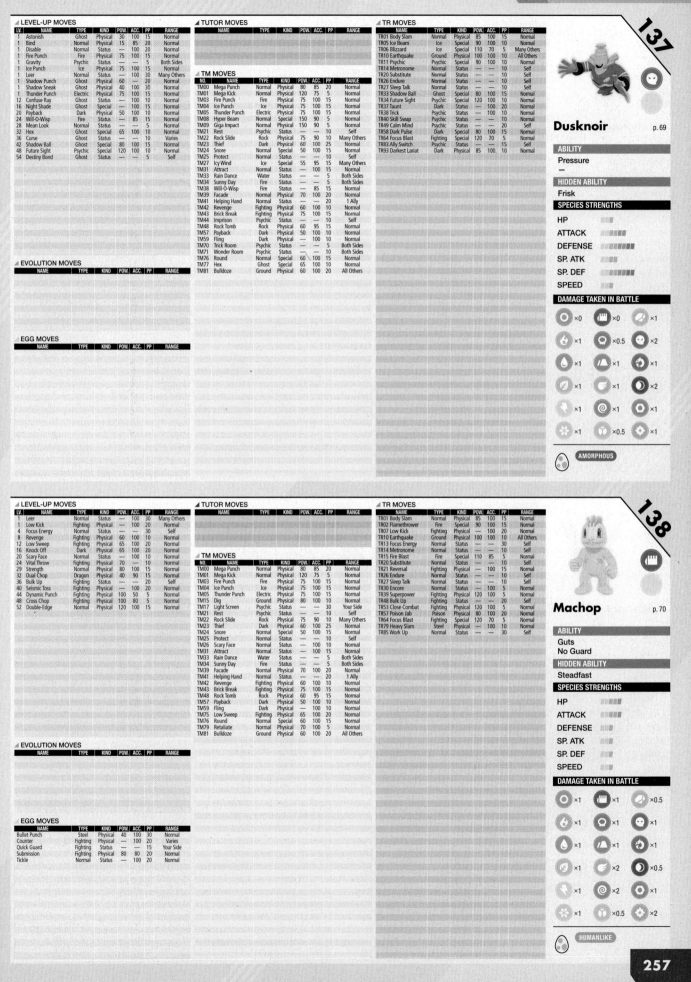

137 Dusknoir

LEVEL-UP MOVES

LV.	NAME	TYPE	KIND	POW.	ACC.	PP	RANGE
1	Astonish	Ghost	Physical	30	100	15	Normal
1	Bind	Normal	Physical	15	85	20	Normal
1	Disable	Normal	Status	—	100	20	Normal
1	Fire Punch	Fire	Physical	75	100	15	Normal
1	Gravity	Psychic	Status	—	—	5	Both Sides
1	Ice Punch	Ice	Physical	75	100	15	Normal
1	Leer	Normal	Status	—	100	30	Many Others
1	Shadow Punch	Ghost	Physical	60	—	20	Normal
1	Shadow Sneak	Ghost	Physical	40	100	30	Normal
1	Thunder Punch	Electric	Physical	75	100	15	Normal
12	Confuse Ray	Ghost	Status	—	100	10	Normal
16	Night Shade	Ghost	Special	—	100	15	Normal
20	Payback	Dark	Physical	50	100	10	Normal
24	Will-O-Wisp	Fire	Status	—	85	15	Normal
28	Mean Look	Normal	Status	—	—	5	Normal
32	Hex	Ghost	Special	65	100	10	Normal
36	Curse	Ghost	Status	—	—	10	Varies
42	Shadow Ball	Ghost	Special	80	100	15	Normal
48	Future Sight	Psychic	Special	120	100	10	Normal
54	Destiny Bond	Ghost	Status	—	—	5	Self

EVOLUTION MOVES

NAME	TYPE	KIND	POW.	ACC.	PP	RANGE

EGG MOVES

NAME	TYPE	KIND	POW.	ACC.	PP	RANGE

TUTOR MOVES

NAME	TYPE	KIND	POW.	ACC.	PP	RANGE

TM MOVES

NO.	NAME	TYPE	KIND	POW.	ACC.	PP	RANGE
TM00	Mega Punch	Normal	Physical	80	85	20	Normal
TM01	Mega Kick	Normal	Physical	120	75	5	Normal
TM03	Fire Punch	Fire	Physical	75	100	15	Normal
TM04	Ice Punch	Ice	Physical	75	100	15	Normal
TM05	Thunder Punch	Electric	Physical	75	100	15	Normal
TM08	Hyper Beam	Normal	Special	150	90	5	Normal
TM09	Giga Impact	Normal	Physical	150	90	5	Normal
TM21	Rest	Psychic	Status	—	—	10	Self
TM22	Rock Slide	Rock	Physical	75	90	10	Many Others
TM23	Thief	Dark	Physical	60	100	25	Normal
TM24	Snore	Normal	Special	50	100	15	Normal
TM25	Protect	Normal	Status	—	—	10	Self
TM27	Icy Wind	Ice	Special	55	95	15	Many Others
TM31	Attract	Normal	Status	—	100	15	Normal
TM33	Rain Dance	Water	Status	—	—	5	Both Sides
TM34	Sunny Day	Fire	Status	—	—	5	Both Sides
TM38	Will-O-Wisp	Fire	Status	—	85	15	Normal
TM39	Facade	Normal	Physical	70	100	20	Normal
TM41	Helping Hand	Normal	Status	—	—	20	1 Ally
TM42	Revenge	Fighting	Physical	60	100	10	Normal
TM43	Brick Break	Fighting	Physical	75	100	15	Normal
TM44	Imprison	Psychic	Status	—	—	10	Self
TM48	Rock Tomb	Rock	Physical	60	95	15	Normal
TM57	Payback	Dark	Physical	50	100	10	Normal
TM59	Fling	Dark	Physical	—	100	10	Normal
TM70	Trick Room	Psychic	Status	—	—	5	Both Sides
TM71	Wonder Room	Psychic	Status	—	—	10	Both Sides
TM76	Round	Normal	Special	60	100	15	Normal
TM77	Hex	Ghost	Special	65	100	10	Normal
TM81	Bulldoze	Ground	Physical	60	100	20	All Others

TR MOVES

NO.	NAME	TYPE	KIND	POW.	ACC.	PP	RANGE
TR01	Body Slam	Normal	Physical	85	100	15	Normal
TR05	Ice Beam	Ice	Special	90	100	10	Normal
TR06	Blizzard	Ice	Special	110	70	5	Many Others
TR10	Earthquake	Ground	Physical	100	100	10	All Others
TR11	Psychic	Psychic	Special	90	100	10	Normal
TR14	Metronome	Normal	Status	—	—	10	Self
TR20	Substitute	Normal	Status	—	—	10	Self
TR26	Endure	Normal	Status	—	—	10	Self
TR27	Sleep Talk	Normal	Status	—	—	10	Self
TR33	Shadow Ball	Ghost	Special	80	100	15	Normal
TR34	Future Sight	Psychic	Special	120	100	10	Normal
TR37	Taunt	Dark	Status	—	100	20	Normal
TR38	Trick	Psychic	Status	—	100	10	Normal
TR40	Skill Swap	Psychic	Status	—	—	10	Normal
TR49	Calm Mind	Psychic	Status	—	—	20	Self
TR58	Dark Pulse	Dark	Special	80	100	15	Normal
TR64	Focus Blast	Fighting	Special	120	70	5	Normal
TR83	Ally Switch	Psychic	Status	—	—	15	Self
TR93	Darkest Lariat	Dark	Physical	85	100	10	Normal

Dusknoir p. 69

ABILITY
Pressure
—

HIDDEN ABILITY
Frisk

SPECIES STRENGTHS
HP
ATTACK
DEFENSE
SP. ATK
SP. DEF
SPEED

DAMAGE TAKEN IN BATTLE
×0 ×0 ×1
×1 ×0.5 ×2
×1 ×1 ×1
×1 ×1 ×2
×1 ×1 ×1
×1 ×0.5 ×1

AMORPHOUS

---

138 Machop

LEVEL-UP MOVES

LV.	NAME	TYPE	KIND	POW.	ACC.	PP	RANGE
1	Leer	Normal	Status	—	100	30	Many Others
1	Low Kick	Fighting	Physical	—	100	20	Normal
4	Focus Energy	Normal	Status	—	—	30	Self
8	Revenge	Fighting	Physical	60	100	10	Normal
12	Low Sweep	Fighting	Physical	65	100	20	Normal
16	Knock Off	Dark	Physical	65	100	20	Normal
20	Scary Face	Normal	Status	—	100	10	Normal
24	Vital Throw	Fighting	Physical	70	—	10	Normal
29	Strength	Normal	Physical	80	100	15	Normal
32	Dual Chop	Dragon	Physical	40	90	15	Normal
36	Bulk Up	Fighting	Status	—	—	20	Self
40	Seismic Toss	Fighting	Physical	—	100	20	Normal
44	Dynamic Punch	Fighting	Physical	100	50	5	Normal
48	Cross Chop	Fighting	Physical	100	80	5	Normal
52	Double-Edge	Normal	Physical	120	100	15	Normal

EVOLUTION MOVES

NAME	TYPE	KIND	POW.	ACC.	PP	RANGE

EGG MOVES

NAME	TYPE	KIND	POW.	ACC.	PP	RANGE
Bullet Punch	Steel	Physical	40	100	30	Normal
Counter	Fighting	Physical	—	100	20	Varies
Quick Guard	Fighting	Status	—	—	15	Your Side
Submission	Fighting	Physical	80	80	20	Normal
Tickle	Normal	Status	—	100	20	Normal

TUTOR MOVES

NAME	TYPE	KIND	POW.	ACC.	PP	RANGE

TM MOVES

NO.	NAME	TYPE	KIND	POW.	ACC.	PP	RANGE
TM00	Mega Punch	Normal	Physical	80	85	20	Normal
TM01	Mega Kick	Normal	Physical	120	75	5	Normal
TM03	Fire Punch	Fire	Physical	75	100	15	Normal
TM04	Ice Punch	Ice	Physical	75	100	15	Normal
TM05	Thunder Punch	Electric	Physical	75	100	15	Normal
TM15	Dig	Ground	Physical	80	100	10	Normal
TM17	Light Screen	Psychic	Status	—	—	30	Your Side
TM21	Rest	Psychic	Status	—	—	10	Self
TM22	Rock Slide	Rock	Physical	75	90	10	Many Others
TM23	Thief	Dark	Physical	60	100	25	Normal
TM24	Snore	Normal	Special	50	100	15	Normal
TM25	Protect	Normal	Status	—	—	10	Self
TM26	Scary Face	Normal	Status	—	100	10	Normal
TM31	Attract	Normal	Status	—	100	15	Normal
TM33	Rain Dance	Water	Status	—	—	5	Both Sides
TM34	Sunny Day	Fire	Status	—	—	5	Both Sides
TM39	Facade	Normal	Physical	70	100	20	Normal
TM41	Helping Hand	Normal	Status	—	—	20	1 Ally
TM42	Revenge	Fighting	Physical	60	100	10	Normal
TM43	Brick Break	Fighting	Physical	75	100	15	Normal
TM48	Rock Tomb	Rock	Physical	60	95	15	Normal
TM57	Payback	Dark	Physical	50	100	10	Normal
TM59	Fling	Dark	Physical	—	100	10	Normal
TM75	Low Sweep	Fighting	Physical	65	100	20	Normal
TM76	Round	Normal	Special	60	100	15	Normal
TM79	Retaliate	Normal	Physical	70	100	5	Normal
TM81	Bulldoze	Ground	Physical	60	100	20	All Others

TR MOVES

NO.	NAME	TYPE	KIND	POW.	ACC.	PP	RANGE
TR01	Body Slam	Normal	Physical	85	100	15	Normal
TR02	Flamethrower	Fire	Special	90	100	15	Normal
TR07	Low Kick	Fighting	Physical	—	100	20	Normal
TR10	Earthquake	Ground	Physical	100	100	10	All Others
TR13	Focus Energy	Normal	Status	—	—	30	Self
TR14	Metronome	Normal	Status	—	—	10	Self
TR15	Fire Blast	Fire	Special	110	85	5	Normal
TR20	Substitute	Normal	Status	—	—	10	Self
TR21	Reversal	Fighting	Physical	—	100	15	Normal
TR26	Endure	Normal	Status	—	—	10	Self
TR27	Sleep Talk	Normal	Status	—	—	10	Self
TR30	Encore	Normal	Status	—	100	5	Normal
TR39	Superpower	Fighting	Physical	120	100	5	Normal
TR48	Bulk Up	Fighting	Status	—	—	20	Self
TR53	Close Combat	Fighting	Physical	120	100	5	Normal
TR57	Poison Jab	Poison	Physical	80	100	20	Normal
TR64	Focus Blast	Fighting	Special	120	70	5	Normal
TR79	Heavy Slam	Steel	Physical	—	100	10	Normal
TR85	Work Up	Normal	Status	—	—	30	Self

Machop p. 70

ABILITY
Guts
No Guard

HIDDEN ABILITY
Steadfast

SPECIES STRENGTHS
HP
ATTACK
DEFENSE
SP. ATK
SP. DEF
SPEED

DAMAGE TAKEN IN BATTLE
×1 ×1 ×0.5
×1 ×1 ×1
×1 ×1 ×1
×1 ×2 ×0.5
×1 ×2 ×1
×0.5 ×0.5 ×2

HUMANLIKE

139 Machoke p. 70

ABILITY
Guts
No Guard

HIDDEN ABILITY
Steadfast

SPECIES STRENGTHS
- HP
- ATTACK
- DEFENSE
- SP. ATK
- SP. DEF
- SPEED

DAMAGE TAKEN IN BATTLE

×1	×1	×0.5
×1	×1	×1
×1	×1	×1
×1	×2	×0.5
×1	×2	×1
×1	×0.5	×2

HUMANLIKE

LEVEL-UP MOVES

LV.	NAME	TYPE	KIND	POW.	ACC.	PP	RANGE
1	Focus Energy	Normal	Status	—	—	30	Self
1	Leer	Normal	Status	—	100	30	Many Others
1	Low Kick	Fighting	Physical	—	100	20	Normal
1	Revenge	Fighting	Physical	60	100	10	Normal
12	Low Sweep	Fighting	Physical	65	100	20	Normal
16	Knock Off	Dark	Physical	65	100	20	Normal
20	Scary Face	Normal	Status	—	100	10	Normal
24	Vital Throw	Fighting	Physical	70	—	10	Normal
31	Strength	Normal	Physical	80	100	15	Normal
36	Dual Chop	Dragon	Physical	40	90	15	Normal
42	Bulk Up	Fighting	Status	—	—	20	Self
48	Seismic Toss	Fighting	Physical	—	100	20	Normal
54	Dynamic Punch	Fighting	Physical	100	50	5	Normal
60	Cross Chop	Fighting	Physical	100	80	5	Normal
66	Double-Edge	Normal	Physical	120	100	15	Normal

EVOLUTION MOVES

NAME	TYPE	KIND	POW.	ACC.	PP	RANGE

EGG MOVES

NAME	TYPE	KIND	POW.	ACC.	PP	RANGE

TUTOR MOVES

NAME	TYPE	KIND	POW.	ACC.	PP	RANGE

TM MOVES

NO.	NAME	TYPE	KIND	POW.	ACC.	PP	RANGE
TM00	Mega Punch	Normal	Physical	80	85	20	Normal
TM01	Mega Kick	Normal	Physical	120	75	5	Normal
TM03	Fire Punch	Fire	Physical	75	100	15	Normal
TM04	Ice Punch	Ice	Physical	75	100	15	Normal
TM05	Thunder Punch	Electric	Physical	75	100	15	Normal
TM15	Dig	Ground	Physical	80	100	10	Normal
TM17	Light Screen	Psychic	Status	—	—	30	Your Side
TM21	Rest	Psychic	Status	—	—	10	Self
TM22	Rock Slide	Rock	Physical	75	90	10	Many Others
TM23	Thief	Dark	Physical	60	100	25	Normal
TM24	Snore	Normal	Special	50	100	15	Normal
TM25	Protect	Normal	Status	—	—	10	Self
TM26	Scary Face	Normal	Status	—	100	10	Normal
TM31	Attract	Normal	Status	—	100	15	Normal
TM33	Rain Dance	Water	Status	—	—	5	Both Sides
TM34	Sunny Day	Fire	Status	—	—	5	Both Sides
TM39	Facade	Normal	Physical	70	100	20	Normal
TM41	Helping Hand	Normal	Status	—	—	20	1 Ally
TM42	Revenge	Fighting	Physical	60	100	10	Normal
TM43	Brick Break	Fighting	Physical	75	100	15	Normal
TM48	Rock Tomb	Rock	Physical	60	95	15	Normal
TM57	Payback	Dark	Physical	50	100	10	Normal
TM59	Fling	Dark	Physical	—	100	10	Normal
TM75	Low Sweep	Fighting	Physical	65	100	20	Normal
TM76	Round	Normal	Special	60	100	15	Normal
TM79	Retaliate	Normal	Physical	70	100	5	Normal
TM81	Bulldoze	Ground	Physical	60	100	20	All Others
TM98	Stomping Tantrum	Ground	Physical	75	100	10	Normal

TR MOVES

NAME	TYPE	KIND	POW.	ACC.	PP	RANGE
TR01 Body Slam	Normal	Physical	85	100	15	Normal
TR02 Flamethrower	Fire	Special	90	100	15	Normal
TR07 Low Kick	Fighting	Physical	—	100	20	Normal
TR10 Earthquake	Ground	Physical	100	100	10	All Others
TR13 Focus Energy	Normal	Status	—	—	30	Self
TR14 Metronome	Normal	Status	—	—	10	Self
TR15 Fire Blast	Fire	Special	110	85	5	Normal
TR20 Substitute	Normal	Status	—	—	10	Self
TR21 Reversal	Fighting	Physical	—	100	15	Normal
TR26 Endure	Normal	Status	—	—	10	Self
TR27 Sleep Talk	Normal	Status	—	—	10	Self
TR30 Encore	Normal	Status	—	100	5	Normal
TR39 Superpower	Fighting	Physical	120	100	5	Normal
TR48 Bulk Up	Fighting	Status	—	—	20	Self
TR53 Close Combat	Fighting	Physical	120	100	5	Normal
TR57 Poison Jab	Poison	Physical	80	100	20	Normal
TR64 Focus Blast	Fighting	Special	120	70	5	Normal
TR79 Heavy Slam	Steel	Physical	—	100	10	Normal
TR85 Work Up	Normal	Status	—	—	30	Self

---

140 Machamp p. 70

ABILITY
Guts
No Guard

HIDDEN ABILITY
Steadfast

SPECIES STRENGTHS
- HP
- ATTACK
- DEFENSE
- SP. ATK
- SP. DEF
- SPEED

DAMAGE TAKEN IN BATTLE

×1	×1	×0.5
×1	×1	×1
×1	×1	×1
×1	×1	×0.5
×1	×2	×1
×1	×0.5	×2

HUMANLIKE

LEVEL-UP MOVES

LV.	NAME	TYPE	KIND	POW.	ACC.	PP	RANGE
1	Focus Energy	Normal	Status	—	—	30	Self
1	Leer	Normal	Status	—	100	30	Many Others
1	Low Kick	Fighting	Physical	—	100	20	Normal
1	Revenge	Fighting	Physical	60	100	10	Normal
1	Wide Guard	Rock	Status	—	—	10	Your Side
12	Low Sweep	Fighting	Physical	65	100	20	Normal
16	Knock Off	Dark	Physical	65	100	20	Normal
20	Scary Face	Normal	Status	—	100	10	Normal
24	Vital Throw	Fighting	Physical	70	—	10	Normal
31	Strength	Normal	Physical	80	100	15	Normal
36	Dual Chop	Dragon	Physical	40	90	15	Normal
42	Bulk Up	Fighting	Status	—	—	20	Self
48	Seismic Toss	Fighting	Physical	—	100	20	Normal
54	Dynamic Punch	Fighting	Physical	100	50	5	Normal
60	Cross Chop	Fighting	Physical	100	80	5	Normal
66	Double-Edge	Normal	Physical	120	100	15	Normal

EVOLUTION MOVES

NAME	TYPE	KIND	POW.	ACC.	PP	RANGE

EGG MOVES

NAME	TYPE	KIND	POW.	ACC.	PP	RANGE

TUTOR MOVES

NAME	TYPE	KIND	POW.	ACC.	PP	RANGE

TM MOVES

NO.	NAME	TYPE	KIND	POW.	ACC.	PP	RANGE
TM00	Mega Punch	Normal	Physical	80	85	20	Normal
TM01	Mega Kick	Normal	Physical	120	75	5	Normal
TM03	Fire Punch	Fire	Physical	75	100	15	Normal
TM04	Ice Punch	Ice	Physical	75	100	15	Normal
TM05	Thunder Punch	Electric	Physical	75	100	15	Normal
TM08	Hyper Beam	Normal	Special	150	90	5	Normal
TM09	Giga Impact	Normal	Physical	150	90	5	Normal
TM15	Dig	Ground	Physical	80	100	10	Normal
TM17	Light Screen	Psychic	Status	—	—	30	Your Side
TM21	Rest	Psychic	Status	—	—	10	Self
TM22	Rock Slide	Rock	Physical	75	90	10	Many Others
TM23	Thief	Dark	Physical	60	100	25	Normal
TM24	Snore	Normal	Special	50	100	15	Normal
TM25	Protect	Normal	Status	—	—	10	Self
TM26	Scary Face	Normal	Status	—	100	10	Normal
TM31	Attract	Normal	Status	—	100	15	Normal
TM33	Rain Dance	Water	Status	—	—	5	Both Sides
TM34	Sunny Day	Fire	Status	—	—	5	Both Sides
TM39	Facade	Normal	Physical	70	100	20	Normal
TM41	Helping Hand	Normal	Status	—	—	20	1 Ally
TM42	Revenge	Fighting	Physical	60	100	10	Normal
TM43	Brick Break	Fighting	Physical	75	100	15	Normal
TM48	Rock Tomb	Rock	Physical	60	95	15	Normal
TM54	Rock Blast	Rock	Physical	25	90	10	Normal
TM57	Payback	Dark	Physical	50	100	10	Normal
TM58	Assurance	Dark	Physical	60	100	10	Normal
TM59	Fling	Dark	Physical	—	100	10	Normal
TM73	Cross Poison	Poison	Physical	70	100	20	Normal
TM75	Low Sweep	Fighting	Physical	65	100	20	Normal
TM76	Round	Normal	Special	60	100	15	Normal
TM79	Retaliate	Normal	Physical	70	100	5	Normal
TM81	Bulldoze	Ground	Physical	60	100	20	All Others
TM98	Stomping Tantrum	Ground	Physical	75	100	10	Normal

TR MOVES

NAME	TYPE	KIND	POW.	ACC.	PP	RANGE
TR01 Body Slam	Normal	Physical	85	100	15	Normal
TR02 Flamethrower	Fire	Special	90	100	15	Normal
TR07 Low Kick	Fighting	Physical	—	100	20	Normal
TR10 Earthquake	Ground	Physical	100	100	10	All Others
TR13 Focus Energy	Normal	Status	—	—	30	Self
TR14 Metronome	Normal	Status	—	—	10	Self
TR15 Fire Blast	Fire	Special	110	85	5	Normal
TR20 Substitute	Normal	Status	—	—	10	Self
TR21 Reversal	Fighting	Physical	—	100	15	Normal
TR26 Endure	Normal	Status	—	—	10	Self
TR27 Sleep Talk	Normal	Status	—	—	10	Self
TR30 Encore	Normal	Status	—	100	5	Normal
TR39 Superpower	Fighting	Physical	120	100	5	Normal
TR48 Bulk Up	Fighting	Status	—	—	20	Self
TR53 Close Combat	Fighting	Physical	120	100	5	Normal
TR57 Poison Jab	Poison	Physical	80	100	20	Normal
TR64 Focus Blast	Fighting	Special	120	70	5	Normal
TR75 Stone Edge	Rock	Physical	100	80	5	Normal
TR79 Heavy Slam	Steel	Physical	—	100	10	Normal
TR85 Work Up	Normal	Status	—	—	30	Self
TR93 Darkest Lariat	Dark	Physical	85	100	10	Normal
TR94 High Horsepower	Ground	Physical	95	95	10	Normal
TR95 Throat Chop	Dark	Physical	80	100	15	Normal

141 Gastly

p. 71

▲ LEVEL-UP MOVES

LV.	NAME	TYPE	KIND	POW.	ACC.	PP	RANGE
1	Confuse Ray	Ghost	Status	—	100	10	Normal
1	Lick	Ghost	Physical	30	100	30	Normal
4	Hypnosis	Psychic	Status	—	60	20	Normal
8	Mean Look	Normal	Status	—	—	5	Normal
12	Payback	Dark	Physical	50	100	10	Normal
16	Spite	Ghost	Status	—	100	10	Normal
20	Curse	Ghost	Status	—	—	10	Varies
24	Hex	Ghost	Special	65	100	10	Normal
28	Night Shade	Ghost	Special	—	100	15	Normal
32	Sucker Punch	Dark	Physical	70	100	5	Normal
36	Dark Pulse	Dark	Special	80	100	15	Normal
40	Shadow Ball	Ghost	Special	80	100	15	Normal
44	Destiny Bond	Ghost	Status	—	—	5	Self
48	Dream Eater	Psychic	Special	100	100	15	Normal

▲ EVOLUTION MOVES

NAME	TYPE	KIND	POW.	ACC.	PP	RANGE

▲ EGG MOVES

NAME	TYPE	KIND	POW.	ACC.	PP	RANGE
Astonish	Ghost	Physical	30	100	15	Normal
Clear Smog	Poison	Special	50	—	15	Normal
Disable	Normal	Status	—	100	20	Normal
Grudge	Ghost	Status	—	—	5	Self
Haze	Ice	Status	—	—	30	Both Sides
Perish Song	Normal	Status	—	—	5	All
Reflect Type	Normal	Status	—	—	15	Normal
Smog	Poison	Special	30	70	20	Normal
Toxic	Poison	Status	—	90	10	Normal

▲ TUTOR MOVES

NAME	TYPE	KIND	POW.	ACC.	PP	RANGE

▲ TM MOVES

NO.	NAME	TYPE	KIND	POW.	ACC.	PP	RANGE
TM03	Fire Punch	Fire	Physical	75	100	15	Normal
TM04	Ice Punch	Ice	Physical	75	100	15	Normal
TM05	Thunder Punch	Electric	Physical	75	100	15	Normal
TM20	Self-Destruct	Normal	Physical	200	100	5	All Others
TM21	Rest	Psychic	Status	—	—	10	Self
TM23	Thief	Dark	Physical	60	100	25	Normal
TM24	Snore	Normal	Special	50	100	15	Normal
TM25	Protect	Normal	Status	—	—	10	Self
TM26	Scary Face	Normal	Status	—	100	10	Normal
TM27	Icy Wind	Ice	Special	55	95	15	Many Others
TM28	Giga Drain	Grass	Special	75	100	10	Normal
TM31	Attract	Normal	Status	—	100	15	Normal
TM33	Rain Dance	Water	Status	—	—	5	Both Sides
TM34	Sunny Day	Fire	Status	—	—	5	Both Sides
TM38	Will-O-Wisp	Fire	Status	—	85	15	Normal
TM39	Facade	Normal	Physical	70	100	20	Normal
TM57	Payback	Dark	Physical	50	100	10	Normal
TM70	Trick Room	Psychic	Status	—	—	5	Both Sides
TM71	Wonder Room	Psychic	Status	—	—	10	Both Sides
TM74	Venoshock	Poison	Special	65	100	10	Normal
TM76	Round	Normal	Special	60	100	15	Normal
TM77	Hex	Ghost	Special	65	100	10	Normal

▲ TR MOVES

NO.	NAME	TYPE	KIND	POW.	ACC.	PP	RANGE
TR08	Thunderbolt	Electric	Special	90	100	15	Normal
TR11	Psychic	Psychic	Special	90	100	10	Normal
TR20	Substitute	Normal	Status	—	—	10	Self
TR22	Sludge Bomb	Poison	Special	90	100	10	Normal
TR26	Endure	Normal	Status	—	—	10	Self
TR27	Sleep Talk	Normal	Status	—	—	10	Self
TR33	Shadow Ball	Ghost	Special	80	100	15	Normal
TR35	Uproar	Normal	Special	90	100	10	1 Random
TR37	Taunt	Dark	Status	—	100	20	Normal
TR38	Trick	Psychic	Status	—	100	10	Normal
TR40	Skill Swap	Psychic	Status	—	—	10	Normal
TR57	Poison Jab	Poison	Physical	80	100	20	Normal
TR58	Dark Pulse	Dark	Special	80	100	15	Normal
TR65	Energy Ball	Grass	Special	90	100	10	Normal
TR78	Sludge Wave	Poison	Special	95	100	10	All Others
TR81	Foul Play	Dark	Physical	95	100	15	Normal
TR83	Ally Switch	Psychic	Status	—	—	15	Self
TR92	Dazzling Gleam	Fairy	Special	80	100	10	Many Others

ABILITY
Levitate
—

HIDDEN ABILITY

SPECIES STRENGTHS
HP
ATTACK
DEFENSE
SP. ATK
SP. DEF
SPEED

DAMAGE TAKEN IN BATTLE
×0 · ×0 · ×1 · ×1 · ×0.25 · ×2 · ×1 · ×2 · ×1 · ×0.5 · ×1 · ×2 · ×1 · ×2 · ×1 · ×1 · ×0.25 · ×0.5

AMORPHOUS

---

142 Haunter

p. 71

▲ LEVEL-UP MOVES

LV.	NAME	TYPE	KIND	POW.	ACC.	PP	RANGE
1	Confuse Ray	Ghost	Status	—	100	10	Normal
1	Hypnosis	Psychic	Status	—	60	20	Normal
1	Lick	Ghost	Physical	30	100	30	Normal
1	Mean Look	Normal	Status	—	—	5	Normal
1	Shadow Punch	Ghost	Physical	60	—	20	Normal
12	Payback	Dark	Physical	50	100	10	Normal
16	Spite	Ghost	Status	—	100	10	Normal
20	Curse	Ghost	Status	—	—	10	Varies
24	Hex	Ghost	Special	65	100	10	Normal
30	Night Shade	Ghost	Special	—	100	15	Normal
36	Sucker Punch	Dark	Physical	70	100	5	Normal
42	Dark Pulse	Dark	Special	80	100	15	Normal
48	Shadow Ball	Ghost	Special	80	100	15	Normal
54	Destiny Bond	Ghost	Status	—	—	5	Self
60	Dream Eater	Psychic	Special	100	100	15	Normal

▲ EVOLUTION MOVES

NAME	TYPE	KIND	POW.	ACC.	PP	RANGE
Shadow Punch	Ghost	Physical	60	—	20	Normal

▲ EGG MOVES

NAME	TYPE	KIND	POW.	ACC.	PP	RANGE

▲ TUTOR MOVES

NAME	TYPE	KIND	POW.	ACC.	PP	RANGE

▲ TM MOVES

NO.	NAME	TYPE	KIND	POW.	ACC.	PP	RANGE
TM03	Fire Punch	Fire	Physical	75	100	15	Normal
TM04	Ice Punch	Ice	Physical	75	100	15	Normal
TM05	Thunder Punch	Electric	Physical	75	100	15	Normal
TM20	Self-Destruct	Normal	Physical	200	100	5	All Others
TM21	Rest	Psychic	Status	—	—	10	Self
TM23	Thief	Dark	Physical	60	100	25	Normal
TM24	Snore	Normal	Special	50	100	15	Normal
TM25	Protect	Normal	Status	—	—	10	Self
TM26	Scary Face	Normal	Status	—	100	10	Normal
TM27	Icy Wind	Ice	Special	55	95	15	Many Others
TM28	Giga Drain	Grass	Special	75	100	10	Normal
TM31	Attract	Normal	Status	—	100	15	Normal
TM33	Rain Dance	Water	Status	—	—	5	Both Sides
TM34	Sunny Day	Fire	Status	—	—	5	Both Sides
TM38	Will-O-Wisp	Fire	Status	—	85	15	Normal
TM39	Facade	Normal	Physical	70	100	20	Normal
TM57	Payback	Dark	Physical	50	100	10	Normal
TM59	Fling	Dark	Physical	—	100	10	Normal
TM65	Shadow Claw	Ghost	Physical	70	100	15	Normal
TM70	Trick Room	Psychic	Status	—	—	5	Both Sides
TM71	Wonder Room	Psychic	Status	—	—	10	Both Sides
TM74	Venoshock	Poison	Special	65	100	10	Normal
TM76	Round	Normal	Special	60	100	15	Normal
TM77	Hex	Ghost	Special	65	100	10	Normal

▲ TR MOVES

NO.	NAME	TYPE	KIND	POW.	ACC.	PP	RANGE
TR08	Thunderbolt	Electric	Special	90	100	15	Normal
TR11	Psychic	Psychic	Special	90	100	10	Normal
TR20	Substitute	Normal	Status	—	—	10	Self
TR22	Sludge Bomb	Poison	Special	90	100	10	Normal
TR26	Endure	Normal	Status	—	—	10	Self
TR27	Sleep Talk	Normal	Status	—	—	10	Self
TR30	Encore	Normal	Status	—	100	5	Normal
TR33	Shadow Ball	Ghost	Special	80	100	15	Normal
TR35	Uproar	Normal	Special	90	100	10	1 Random
TR37	Taunt	Dark	Status	—	100	20	Normal
TR38	Trick	Psychic	Status	—	100	10	Normal
TR40	Skill Swap	Psychic	Status	—	—	10	Normal
TR57	Poison Jab	Poison	Physical	80	100	20	Normal
TR58	Dark Pulse	Dark	Special	80	100	15	Normal
TR65	Energy Ball	Grass	Special	90	100	10	Normal
TR78	Sludge Wave	Poison	Special	95	100	10	All Others
TR81	Foul Play	Dark	Physical	95	100	15	Normal
TR83	Ally Switch	Psychic	Status	—	—	15	Self
TR92	Dazzling Gleam	Fairy	Special	80	100	10	Many Others

ABILITY
Levitate
—

HIDDEN ABILITY

SPECIES STRENGTHS
HP
ATTACK
DEFENSE
SP. ATK
SP. DEF
SPEED

DAMAGE TAKEN IN BATTLE
×0 · ×0 · ×1 · ×1 · ×0.25 · ×2 · ×1 · ×2 · ×1 · ×0.5 · ×1 · ×2 · ×1 · ×2 · ×1 · ×1 · ×0.25 · ×0.5

AMORPHOUS

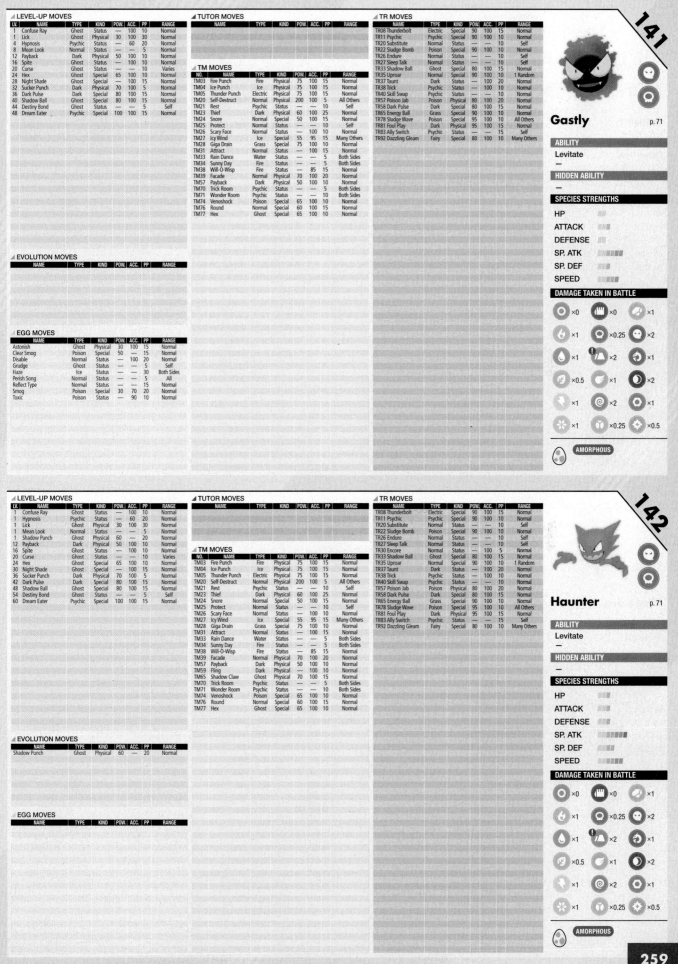

143

Gengar
p. 71

ABILITY
Cursed Body
—

HIDDEN ABILITY
—

SPECIES STRENGTHS

HP
ATTACK
DEFENSE
SP. ATK
SP. DEF
SPEED

DAMAGE TAKEN IN BATTLE

×0	×0	×1
×1	×0.25	×2
×1	×2	×1
×0.5	×1	×2
×1	×2	×1
×1	×0.25	×0.5

AMORPHOUS

LEVEL-UP MOVES

LV.	NAME	TYPE	KIND	POW.	ACC.	PP	RANGE
1	Confuse Ray	Ghost	Status	—	100	10	Normal
1	Hypnosis	Psychic	Status	—	60	20	Normal
1	Lick	Ghost	Physical	30	100	30	Normal
1	Mean Look	Normal	Status	—	—	5	Normal
1	Perish Song	Normal	Status	—	—	5	All
1	Reflect Type	Normal	Status	—	—	15	Normal
12	Shadow Punch	Ghost	Physical	60	—	20	Normal
12	Payback	Dark	Physical	50	100	10	Normal
16	Spite	Ghost	Status	—	100	10	Normal
20	Curse	Ghost	Status	—	—	10	Varies
24	Hex	Ghost	Special	65	100	10	Normal
30	Night Shade	Ghost	Special	—	100	15	Normal
36	Sucker Punch	Dark	Physical	70	100	5	Normal
42	Dark Pulse	Dark	Special	80	100	15	Normal
48	Shadow Ball	Ghost	Special	80	100	15	Normal
54	Destiny Bond	Ghost	Status	—	—	5	Self
60	Dream Eater	Psychic	Special	100	100	15	Normal

EVOLUTION MOVES

NAME	TYPE	KIND	POW.	ACC.	PP	RANGE

EGG MOVES

NAME	TYPE	KIND	POW.	ACC.	PP	RANGE

TUTOR MOVES

NAME	TYPE	KIND	POW.	ACC.	PP	RANGE

TM MOVES

NO.	NAME	TYPE	KIND	POW.	ACC.	PP	RANGE
TM00	Mega Punch	Normal	Physical	80	85	20	Normal
TM01	Mega Kick	Normal	Physical	120	75	5	Normal
TM03	Fire Punch	Fire	Physical	75	100	15	Normal
TM04	Ice Punch	Ice	Physical	75	100	15	Normal
TM05	Thunder Punch	Electric	Physical	75	100	15	Normal
TM08	Hyper Beam	Normal	Special	150	90	5	Normal
TM09	Giga Impact	Normal	Physical	150	90	5	Normal
TM20	Self-Destruct	Normal	Physical	200	100	5	All Others
TM21	Rest	Psychic	Status	—	—	10	Self
TM23	Thief	Dark	Physical	60	100	25	Normal
TM24	Snore	Normal	Special	50	100	15	Normal
TM25	Protect	Normal	Status	—	—	10	Self
TM26	Scary Face	Normal	Status	—	100	10	Normal
TM27	Icy Wind	Ice	Special	55	95	15	Many Others
TM28	Giga Drain	Grass	Special	75	100	10	Normal
TM31	Attract	Normal	Status	—	100	15	Normal
TM33	Rain Dance	Water	Status	—	—	5	Both Sides
TM34	Sunny Day	Fire	Status	—	—	5	Both Sides
TM38	Will-O-Wisp	Fire	Status	—	85	15	Normal
TM39	Facade	Normal	Physical	70	100	20	Normal
TM43	Brick Break	Fighting	Physical	75	100	15	Normal
TM44	Imprison	Psychic	Status	—	—	10	Self
TM57	Payback	Dark	Physical	50	100	10	Normal
TM59	Fling	Dark	Physical	—	100	10	Normal
TM63	Drain Punch	Fighting	Physical	75	100	10	Normal
TM65	Shadow Claw	Ghost	Physical	70	100	15	Normal
TM70	Trick Room	Psychic	Status	—	—	5	Both Sides
TM71	Wonder Room	Psychic	Status	—	—	10	Both Sides
TM74	Venoshock	Poison	Special	65	100	10	Normal
TM76	Round	Normal	Special	60	100	15	Normal
TM77	Hex	Ghost	Special	65	100	10	Normal
TM86	Phantom Force	Ghost	Physical	90	100	10	Normal

TR MOVES

NO.	NAME	TYPE	KIND	POW.	ACC.	PP	RANGE
TR01	Body Slam	Normal	Physical	85	100	15	Normal
TR08	Thunderbolt	Electric	Special	90	100	15	Normal
TR09	Thunder	Electric	Special	110	70	10	Normal
TR11	Psychic	Psychic	Special	90	100	10	Normal
TR14	Metronome	Normal	Status	—	—	10	Self
TR22	Sludge Bomb	Poison	Special	90	100	10	Normal
TR26	Endure	Normal	Status	—	—	10	Self
TR27	Sleep Talk	Normal	Status	—	—	10	Self
TR30	Encore	Normal	Status	—	100	5	Normal
TR33	Shadow Ball	Ghost	Special	80	100	15	Normal
TR35	Uproar	Normal	Special	90	100	10	1 Random
TR37	Taunt	Dark	Status	—	100	20	Normal
TR38	Trick	Psychic	Status	—	100	10	Normal
TR57	Poison Jab	Poison	Physical	80	100	20	Normal
TR58	Dark Pulse	Dark	Special	80	100	15	Normal
TR64	Focus Blast	Fighting	Special	120	70	5	Normal
TR65	Energy Ball	Grass	Special	90	100	10	Normal
TR68	Nasty Plot	Dark	Status	—	—	20	Self
TR78	Sludge Wave	Poison	Special	95	100	10	All Others
TR81	Foul Play	Dark	Physical	95	100	15	Normal
TR83	Ally Switch	Psychic	Status	—	—	15	Self
TR92	Dazzling Gleam	Fairy	Special	80	100	10	Many Others

144

Magikarp
p. 72

ABILITY
Swift Swim
—

HIDDEN ABILITY
Rattled

SPECIES STRENGTHS

HP
ATTACK
DEFENSE
SP. ATK
SP. DEF
SPEED

DAMAGE TAKEN IN BATTLE

×1	×1	×1
×0.5	×1	×1
×0.5	×1	×1
×2	×1	×1
×2	×1	×0.5
×0.5	×1	×1

WATER 2
DRAGON

LEVEL-UP MOVES

LV.	NAME	TYPE	KIND	POW.	ACC.	PP	RANGE
1	Splash	Normal	Status	—	—	40	Self
15	Tackle	Normal	Physical	40	100	35	Normal
25	Flail	Normal	Physical	—	100	15	Normal

EVOLUTION MOVES

NAME	TYPE	KIND	POW.	ACC.	PP	RANGE

EGG MOVES

NAME	TYPE	KIND	POW.	ACC.	PP	RANGE

TUTOR MOVES

NAME	TYPE	KIND	POW.	ACC.	PP	RANGE

TM MOVES

NO.	NAME	TYPE	KIND	POW.	ACC.	PP	RANGE
TM52	Bounce	Flying	Physical	85	85	5	Normal

TR MOVES

NO.	NAME	TYPE	KIND	POW.	ACC.	PP	RANGE
TR03	Hydro Pump	Water	Special	110	80	5	Normal

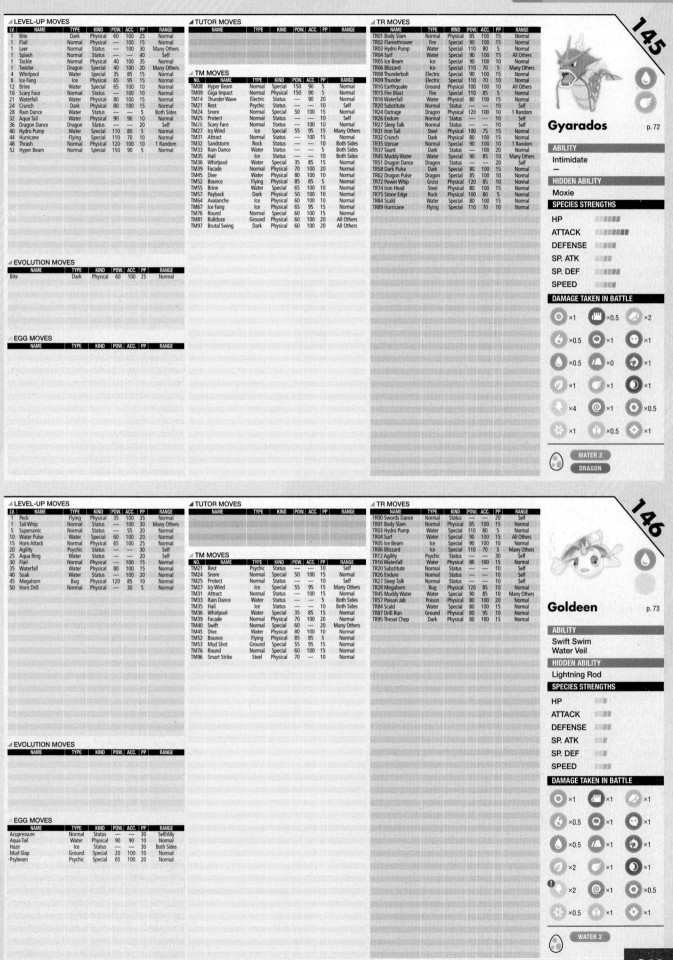

145 — Gyarados (p. 72)

LEVEL-UP MOVES

LV.	NAME	TYPE	KIND	POW.	ACC.	PP	RANGE
1	Bite	Dark	Physical	60	100	25	Normal
1	Flail	Normal	Physical	—	100	15	Normal
1	Leer	Normal	Status	—	100	30	Many Others
1	Splash	Normal	Status	—	—	40	Self
1	Tackle	Normal	Physical	40	100	35	Normal
1	Twister	Dragon	Special	40	100	20	Many Others
4	Whirlpool	Water	Special	35	85	15	Normal
8	Ice Fang	Ice	Physical	65	95	15	Normal
12	Brine	Water	Special	65	100	10	Normal
16	Scary Face	Normal	Status	—	100	10	Normal
21	Waterfall	Water	Physical	80	100	15	Normal
24	Crunch	Dark	Physical	80	100	15	Normal
28	Rain Dance	Water	Status	—	—	5	Both Sides
32	Aqua Tail	Water	Physical	90	90	10	Normal
36	Dragon Dance	Dragon	Status	—	—	20	Self
40	Hydro Pump	Water	Special	110	80	5	Normal
44	Hurricane	Flying	Special	110	70	10	Normal
48	Thrash	Normal	Physical	120	100	10	1 Random
52	Hyper Beam	Normal	Special	150	90	5	Normal

EVOLUTION MOVES

NAME	TYPE	KIND	POW.	ACC.	PP	RANGE
Bite	Dark	Physical	60	100	25	Normal

EGG MOVES

NAME	TYPE	KIND	POW.	ACC.	PP	RANGE

TUTOR MOVES

NAME	TYPE	KIND	POW.	ACC.	PP	RANGE

TM MOVES

NO.	NAME	TYPE	KIND	POW.	ACC.	PP	RANGE
TM08	Hyper Beam	Normal	Special	150	90	5	Normal
TM09	Giga Impact	Normal	Physical	150	90	5	Normal
TM14	Thunder Wave	Electric	Status	—	90	20	Normal
TM21	Rest	Psychic	Status	—	—	10	Self
TM24	Snore	Normal	Special	50	100	15	Normal
TM25	Protect	Normal	Status	—	—	10	Self
TM26	Scary Face	Normal	Status	—	100	10	Normal
TM27	Icy Wind	Ice	Special	55	95	15	Many Others
TM31	Attract	Normal	Status	—	100	15	Normal
TM32	Sandstorm	Rock	Status	—	—	10	Both Sides
TM33	Rain Dance	Water	Status	—	—	5	Both Sides
TM35	Hail	Ice	Status	—	—	10	Both Sides
TM36	Whirlpool	Water	Special	35	85	15	Normal
TM39	Facade	Normal	Physical	70	100	20	Normal
TM45	Dive	Water	Physical	80	100	10	Normal
TM52	Bounce	Flying	Physical	85	85	5	Normal
TM55	Brine	Water	Special	65	100	10	Normal
TM57	Payback	Dark	Physical	50	100	10	Normal
TM64	Avalanche	Ice	Physical	60	100	10	Normal
TM67	Ice Fang	Ice	Physical	65	95	15	Normal
TM76	Round	Normal	Special	60	100	15	Normal
TM81	Bulldoze	Ground	Physical	60	100	20	All Others
TM97	Brutal Swing	Dark	Physical	60	100	20	All Others

TR MOVES

NO.	NAME	TYPE	KIND	POW.	ACC.	PP	RANGE
TR01	Body Slam	Normal	Physical	85	100	15	Normal
TR02	Flamethrower	Fire	Special	90	100	15	Normal
TR03	Hydro Pump	Water	Special	110	80	5	Normal
TR04	Surf	Water	Special	90	100	15	All Others
TR05	Ice Beam	Ice	Special	90	100	10	Normal
TR06	Blizzard	Ice	Special	110	70	5	Many Others
TR08	Thunderbolt	Electric	Special	90	100	15	Normal
TR09	Thunder	Electric	Special	110	70	10	Normal
TR10	Earthquake	Ground	Physical	100	100	10	All Others
TR15	Fire Blast	Fire	Special	110	85	5	Normal
TR16	Waterfall	Water	Physical	80	100	15	Normal
TR20	Substitute	Normal	Status	—	—	10	Self
TR24	Outrage	Dragon	Physical	120	100	10	1 Random
TR26	Endure	Normal	Status	—	—	10	Self
TR27	Sleep Talk	Normal	Status	—	—	10	Self
TR31	Iron Tail	Steel	Physical	100	75	15	Normal
TR32	Crunch	Dark	Physical	80	100	15	Normal
TR35	Uproar	Normal	Special	90	100	10	1 Random
TR37	Taunt	Dark	Status	—	100	20	Normal
TR51	Dragon Dance	Dragon	Status	—	—	20	Self
TR58	Dark Pulse	Dark	Special	80	100	15	Normal
TR62	Dragon Pulse	Dragon	Special	85	100	10	Normal
TR72	Power Whip	Grass	Physical	120	85	10	Normal
TR75	Stone Edge	Rock	Physical	100	80	5	Normal
TR84	Scald	Water	Special	80	100	15	Normal
TR89	Hurricane	Flying	Special	110	70	10	Normal

Gyarados p. 72

ABILITY
Intimidate
—

HIDDEN ABILITY
Moxie

SPECIES STRENGTHS
HP
ATTACK
DEFENSE
SP. ATK
SP. DEF
SPEED

DAMAGE TAKEN IN BATTLE
×1 ×0.5 ×2
×0.5 ×1 ×1
×0.5 ×0 ×1
×1 ×1 ×1
×4 ×1 ×0.5
×1 ×0.5 ×1

WATER 2 / DRAGON

---

146 — Goldeen (p. 73)

LEVEL-UP MOVES

LV.	NAME	TYPE	KIND	POW.	ACC.	PP	RANGE
1	Peck	Flying	Physical	35	100	35	Normal
1	Tail Whip	Normal	Status	—	100	30	Many Others
5	Supersonic	Normal	Status	—	55	20	Normal
10	Water Pulse	Water	Special	60	100	20	Normal
15	Horn Attack	Normal	Physical	65	100	25	Normal
20	Agility	Psychic	Status	—	—	30	Self
25	Aqua Ring	Water	Status	—	—	20	Self
30	Flail	Normal	Physical	—	100	15	Normal
35	Waterfall	Water	Physical	80	100	15	Normal
40	Soak	Water	Status	—	100	20	Normal
45	Megahorn	Bug	Physical	120	85	10	Normal
50	Horn Drill	Normal	Physical	—	30	5	Normal

EVOLUTION MOVES

NAME	TYPE	KIND	POW.	ACC.	PP	RANGE

EGG MOVES

NAME	TYPE	KIND	POW.	ACC.	PP	RANGE
Acupressure	Normal	Status	—	—	30	Self/Ally
Aqua Tail	Water	Physical	90	90	10	Normal
Haze	Ice	Status	—	—	30	Both Sides
Mud-Slap	Ground	Special	20	100	10	Normal
Psybeam	Psychic	Special	65	100	20	Normal

TUTOR MOVES

NAME	TYPE	KIND	POW.	ACC.	PP	RANGE

TM MOVES

NO.	NAME	TYPE	KIND	POW.	ACC.	PP	RANGE
TM21	Rest	Psychic	Status	—	—	10	Self
TM24	Snore	Normal	Special	50	100	15	Normal
TM25	Protect	Normal	Status	—	—	10	Self
TM27	Icy Wind	Ice	Special	55	95	15	Many Others
TM31	Attract	Normal	Status	—	100	15	Normal
TM33	Rain Dance	Water	Status	—	—	5	Both Sides
TM35	Hail	Ice	Status	—	—	10	Both Sides
TM36	Whirlpool	Water	Special	35	85	15	Normal
TM39	Facade	Normal	Physical	70	100	20	Normal
TM40	Swift	Normal	Special	60	—	20	Many Others
TM45	Dive	Water	Physical	80	100	10	Normal
TM52	Bounce	Flying	Physical	85	85	5	Normal
TM53	Mud Shot	Ground	Special	55	95	15	Normal
TM76	Round	Normal	Special	60	100	15	Normal
TM96	Smart Strike	Steel	Physical	70	—	10	Normal

TR MOVES

NO.	NAME	TYPE	KIND	POW.	ACC.	PP	RANGE
TR00	Swords Dance	Normal	Status	—	—	20	Self
TR01	Body Slam	Normal	Physical	85	100	15	Normal
TR03	Hydro Pump	Water	Special	110	80	5	Normal
TR04	Surf	Water	Special	90	100	15	All Others
TR05	Ice Beam	Ice	Special	90	100	10	Normal
TR06	Blizzard	Ice	Special	110	70	5	Many Others
TR12	Agility	Psychic	Status	—	—	30	Self
TR16	Waterfall	Water	Physical	80	100	15	Normal
TR20	Substitute	Normal	Status	—	—	10	Self
TR26	Endure	Normal	Status	—	—	10	Self
TR27	Sleep Talk	Normal	Status	—	—	10	Self
TR28	Megahorn	Bug	Physical	120	85	10	Normal
TR45	Muddy Water	Water	Special	90	85	10	Many Others
TR57	Poison Jab	Poison	Physical	80	100	20	Normal
TR84	Scald	Water	Special	80	100	15	Normal
TR87	Drill Run	Ground	Physical	80	95	10	Normal
TR95	Throat Chop	Dark	Physical	80	100	15	Normal

Goldeen p. 73

ABILITY
Swift Swim
Water Veil

HIDDEN ABILITY
Lightning Rod

SPECIES STRENGTHS
HP
ATTACK
DEFENSE
SP. ATK
SP. DEF
SPEED

DAMAGE TAKEN IN BATTLE
×1 ×1 ×1
×0.5 ×1 ×1
×0.5 ×1 ×1
×2 ×1 ×1
×2 ×1 ×0.5
×0.5 ×1 ×1

WATER 2

147

Seaking
p. 73

ABILITY
Swift Swim
Water Veil

HIDDEN ABILITY
Lightning Rod

SPECIES STRENGTHS

HP	
ATTACK	
DEFENSE	
SP. ATK	
SP. DEF	
SPEED	

DAMAGE TAKEN IN BATTLE

×1	×1	×1			
×0.5	×1	×1			
×0.5	×1	×1			
×2	×1	×1			
×2	×1	×0.5			
×0.5	×1	×1			

WATER 2

LEVEL-UP MOVES

LV.	NAME	TYPE	KIND	POW.	ACC.	PP	RANGE
1	Peck	Flying	Physical	35	100	35	Normal
1	Supersonic	Normal	Status	—	55	20	Normal
1	Tail Whip	Normal	Status	—	100	30	Many Others
1	Water Pulse	Water	Special	60	100	20	Normal
15	Horn Attack	Normal	Physical	65	100	25	Normal
20	Agility	Psychic	Status	—	—	30	Self
25	Aqua Ring	Water	Status	—	—	20	Self
30	Flail	Normal	Physical	—	100	15	Normal
37	Waterfall	Water	Physical	80	100	15	Normal
44	Soak	Water	Status	—	100	20	Normal
51	Megahorn	Bug	Physical	120	85	10	Normal
58	Horn Drill	Normal	Physical	—	30	5	Normal

TUTOR MOVES

NAME	TYPE	KIND	POW.	ACC.	PP	RANGE

TM MOVES

NO.	NAME	TYPE	KIND	POW.	ACC.	PP	RANGE
TM08	Hyper Beam	Normal	Special	150	90	5	Normal
TM09	Giga Impact	Normal	Physical	150	90	5	Normal
TM21	Rest	Psychic	Status	—	—	10	Self
TM24	Snore	Normal	Special	50	100	15	Normal
TM25	Protect	Normal	Status	—	—	10	Self
TM27	Icy Wind	Ice	Special	55	95	15	Many Others
TM31	Attract	Normal	Status	—	100	15	Normal
TM33	Rain Dance	Water	Status	—	—	5	Both Sides
TM35	Hail	Ice	Status	—	—	10	Both Sides
TM36	Whirlpool	Water	Special	35	85	15	Normal
TM39	Facade	Normal	Physical	70	100	20	Normal
TM40	Swift	Normal	Special	60	—	20	Many Others
TM45	Dive	Water	Physical	80	100	10	Normal
TM52	Bounce	Flying	Physical	85	85	5	Normal
TM53	Mud Shot	Ground	Special	55	95	15	Normal
TM76	Round	Normal	Special	60	100	15	Normal
TM96	Smart Strike	Steel	Physical	70	—	10	Normal

TR MOVES

NAME	TYPE	KIND	POW.	ACC.	PP	RANGE
TR00 Swords Dance	Normal	Status	—	—	20	Self
TR01 Body Slam	Normal	Physical	85	100	15	Normal
TR03 Hydro Pump	Water	Special	110	80	5	Normal
TR04 Surf	Water	Special	90	100	15	All Others
TR05 Ice Beam	Ice	Special	90	100	10	Normal
TR06 Blizzard	Ice	Special	110	70	5	Many Others
TR12 Agility	Psychic	Status	—	—	30	Self
TR16 Waterfall	Water	Physical	80	100	15	Normal
TR20 Substitute	Normal	Status	—	—	10	Self
TR26 Endure	Normal	Status	—	—	10	Self
TR27 Sleep Talk	Normal	Status	—	—	10	Self
TR28 Megahorn	Bug	Physical	120	85	10	Normal
TR45 Muddy Water	Water	Special	90	85	10	Many Others
TR57 Poison Jab	Poison	Physical	80	100	20	Normal
TR84 Scald	Water	Special	80	100	15	Normal
TR87 Drill Run	Ground	Physical	80	95	10	Normal
TR95 Throat Chop	Dark	Physical	80	100	15	Normal

EVOLUTION MOVES

NAME	TYPE	KIND	POW.	ACC.	PP	RANGE

EGG MOVES

NAME	TYPE	KIND	POW.	ACC.	PP	RANGE

148

Remoraid
p. 73

ABILITY
Hustle
Sniper

HIDDEN ABILITY
Moody

SPECIES STRENGTHS

HP	
ATTACK	
DEFENSE	
SP. ATK	
SP. DEF	
SPEED	

DAMAGE TAKEN IN BATTLE

×1	×1	×1			
×0.5	×1	×1			
×0.5	×1	×1			
×2	×1	×1			
×2	×1	×0.5			
×0.5	×1	×1			

WATER 1
WATER 2

LEVEL-UP MOVES

LV.	NAME	TYPE	KIND	POW.	ACC.	PP	RANGE
1	Helping Hand	Normal	Status	—	—	20	1 Ally
1	Water Gun	Water	Special	40	100	25	Normal
4	Water Pulse	Water	Special	60	100	20	Normal
8	Focus Energy	Normal	Status	—	—	30	Self
12	Psybeam	Psychic	Special	65	100	20	Normal
16	Aurora Beam	Ice	Special	65	100	20	Normal
20	Bubble Beam	Water	Special	65	100	20	Normal
24	Lock-On	Normal	Status	—	—	5	Normal
28	Bullet Seed	Grass	Physical	25	100	30	Normal
32	Ice Beam	Ice	Special	90	100	10	Normal
36	Hydro Pump	Water	Special	110	80	5	Normal
40	Soak	Water	Status	—	100	20	Normal
44	Hyper Beam	Normal	Special	150	90	5	Normal

TUTOR MOVES

NAME	TYPE	KIND	POW.	ACC.	PP	RANGE

TM MOVES

NO.	NAME	TYPE	KIND	POW.	ACC.	PP	RANGE
TM08	Hyper Beam	Normal	Special	150	90	5	Normal
TM14	Thunder Wave	Electric	Status	—	90	20	Normal
TM16	Screech	Normal	Status	—	85	40	Normal
TM21	Rest	Psychic	Status	—	—	10	Self
TM23	Thief	Dark	Physical	60	100	25	Normal
TM24	Snore	Normal	Special	50	100	15	Normal
TM25	Protect	Normal	Status	—	—	10	Self
TM27	Icy Wind	Ice	Special	55	95	15	Many Others
TM31	Attract	Normal	Status	—	100	15	Normal
TM33	Rain Dance	Water	Status	—	—	5	Both Sides
TM34	Sunny Day	Fire	Status	—	—	5	Both Sides
TM36	Whirlpool	Water	Special	35	85	15	Normal
TM39	Facade	Normal	Physical	70	100	20	Normal
TM40	Swift	Normal	Special	60	—	20	Many Others
TM41	Helping Hand	Normal	Status	—	—	20	1 Ally
TM45	Dive	Water	Physical	80	100	10	Normal
TM50	Bullet Seed	Grass	Physical	25	100	30	Normal
TM52	Bounce	Flying	Physical	85	85	5	Normal
TM53	Mud Shot	Ground	Special	55	95	15	Normal
TM54	Rock Blast	Rock	Physical	25	90	10	Normal
TM55	Brine	Water	Special	65	100	10	Normal
TM58	Assurance	Dark	Physical	60	100	10	Normal
TM76	Round	Normal	Special	60	100	15	Normal

TR MOVES

NAME	TYPE	KIND	POW.	ACC.	PP	RANGE
TR02 Flamethrower	Fire	Special	90	100	15	Normal
TR03 Hydro Pump	Water	Special	110	80	5	Normal
TR04 Surf	Water	Special	90	100	15	All Others
TR05 Ice Beam	Ice	Special	90	100	10	Normal
TR06 Blizzard	Ice	Special	110	70	5	Many Others
TR11 Psychic	Psychic	Special	90	100	10	Normal
TR13 Focus Energy	Normal	Status	—	—	30	Self
TR15 Fire Blast	Fire	Special	110	85	5	Normal
TR16 Waterfall	Water	Physical	80	100	15	Normal
TR20 Substitute	Normal	Status	—	—	10	Self
TR26 Endure	Normal	Status	—	—	10	Self
TR27 Sleep Talk	Normal	Status	—	—	10	Self
TR59 Seed Bomb	Grass	Physical	80	100	15	Normal
TR73 Gunk Shot	Poison	Physical	120	80	5	Normal
TR84 Scald	Water	Special	80	100	15	Normal

EVOLUTION MOVES

NAME	TYPE	KIND	POW.	ACC.	PP	RANGE

EGG MOVES

NAME	TYPE	KIND	POW.	ACC.	PP	RANGE
Acid Spray	Poison	Special	40	100	20	Normal
Flail	Normal	Physical	—	100	15	Normal
Haze	Ice	Status	—	—	30	Both Sides
Octazooka	Water	Special	65	85	10	Normal
Supersonic	Normal	Status	—	55	20	Normal
Water Spout	Water	Special	150	100	5	Many Others

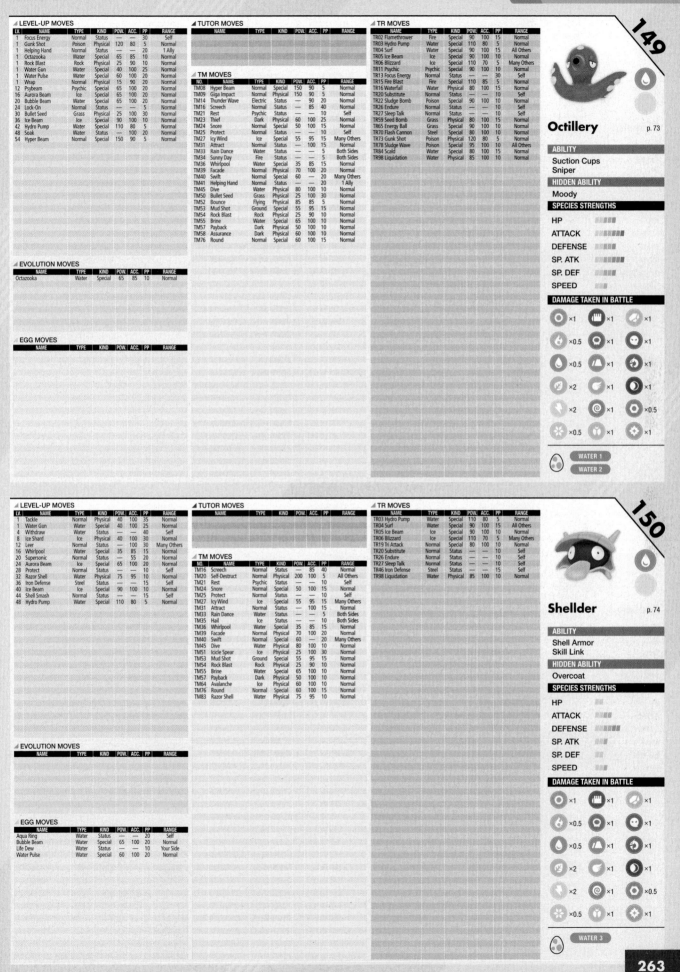

149

LEVEL-UP MOVES

LV.	NAME	TYPE	KIND	POW.	ACC.	PP	RANGE
1	Focus Energy	Normal	Status	—	—	30	Self
1	Gunk Shot	Poison	Physical	120	80	5	Normal
1	Helping Hand	Normal	Status	—	—	20	1 Ally
1	Octazooka	Water	Special	65	85	10	Normal
1	Rock Blast	Rock	Physical	25	90	10	Normal
1	Water Gun	Water	Special	40	100	25	Normal
1	Water Pulse	Water	Special	60	100	20	Normal
1	Wrap	Normal	Physical	15	90	20	Normal
12	Psybeam	Psychic	Special	65	100	20	Normal
16	Aurora Beam	Ice	Special	65	100	20	Normal
20	Bubble Beam	Water	Special	65	100	20	Normal
24	Lock-On	Normal	Status	—	—	5	Normal
30	Bullet Seed	Grass	Physical	25	100	30	Normal
36	Ice Beam	Ice	Special	90	100	10	Normal
42	Hydro Pump	Water	Special	110	80	5	Normal
48	Soak	Water	Status	—	100	20	Normal
54	Hyper Beam	Normal	Special	150	90	5	Normal

EVOLUTION MOVES

NAME	TYPE	KIND	POW.	ACC.	PP	RANGE
Octazooka	Water	Special	65	85	10	Normal

EGG MOVES

NAME	TYPE	KIND	POW.	ACC.	PP	RANGE

TUTOR MOVES

NAME	TYPE	KIND	POW.	ACC.	PP	RANGE

TM MOVES

NO.	NAME	TYPE	KIND	POW.	ACC.	PP	RANGE
TM08	Hyper Beam	Normal	Special	150	90	5	Normal
TM09	Giga Impact	Normal	Physical	150	90	5	Normal
TM14	Thunder Wave	Electric	Status	—	90	20	Normal
TM16	Screech	Normal	Status	—	85	40	Normal
TM21	Rest	Psychic	Status	—	—	10	Self
TM23	Thief	Dark	Physical	60	100	25	Normal
TM24	Snore	Normal	Special	50	100	15	Normal
TM25	Protect	Normal	Status	—	—	10	Self
TM27	Icy Wind	Ice	Special	55	95	15	Many Others
TM31	Attract	Normal	Status	—	100	15	Normal
TM33	Rain Dance	Water	Status	—	—	5	Both Sides
TM34	Sunny Day	Fire	Status	—	—	5	Both Sides
TM36	Whirlpool	Water	Special	35	85	15	Normal
TM39	Facade	Normal	Physical	70	100	20	Normal
TM40	Swift	Normal	Special	60	—	20	Many Others
TM41	Helping Hand	Normal	Status	—	—	20	1 Ally
TM45	Dive	Water	Physical	80	100	10	Normal
TM50	Bullet Seed	Grass	Physical	25	100	30	Normal
TM52	Bounce	Flying	Physical	85	85	5	Normal
TM53	Mud Shot	Ground	Special	55	95	15	Normal
TM54	Rock Blast	Rock	Physical	25	90	10	Normal
TM55	Brine	Water	Special	65	100	10	Normal
TM57	Payback	Dark	Physical	50	100	10	Normal
TM58	Assurance	Dark	Physical	60	100	10	Normal
TM76	Round	Normal	Special	60	100	15	Normal

TR MOVES

NO.	NAME	TYPE	KIND	POW.	ACC.	PP	RANGE
TR02	Flamethrower	Fire	Special	90	100	15	Normal
TR03	Hydro Pump	Water	Special	110	80	5	Normal
TR04	Surf	Water	Special	90	100	15	All Others
TR05	Ice Beam	Ice	Special	90	100	10	Normal
TR06	Blizzard	Ice	Special	110	70	5	Many Others
TR11	Psychic	Psychic	Special	90	100	10	Normal
TR13	Focus Energy	Normal	Status	—	—	30	Self
TR15	Fire Blast	Fire	Special	110	85	5	Normal
TR16	Waterfall	Water	Physical	80	100	15	Normal
TR20	Substitute	Normal	Status	—	—	10	Self
TR22	Sludge Bomb	Poison	Special	90	100	10	Normal
TR26	Endure	Normal	Status	—	—	10	Self
TR27	Sleep Talk	Normal	Status	—	—	10	Self
TR59	Seed Bomb	Grass	Physical	80	100	15	Normal
TR65	Energy Ball	Grass	Special	90	100	10	Normal
TR70	Flash Cannon	Steel	Special	80	100	10	Normal
TR73	Gunk Shot	Poison	Physical	120	80	5	Normal
TR78	Sludge Wave	Poison	Special	95	100	10	All Others
TR84	Scald	Water	Special	80	100	15	Normal
TR98	Liquidation	Water	Physical	85	100	10	Normal

Octillery
p. 73

ABILITY
Suction Cups
Sniper

HIDDEN ABILITY
Moody

SPECIES STRENGTHS
- HP
- ATTACK
- DEFENSE
- SP. ATK
- SP. DEF
- SPEED

DAMAGE TAKEN IN BATTLE
×1 ×1 ×1 ×0.5 ×1 ×1 ×0.5 ×1 ×1 ×2 ×1 ×1 ×2 ×1 ×0.5 ×0.5 ×1 ×1

WATER 1
WATER 2

150

LEVEL-UP MOVES

LV.	NAME	TYPE	KIND	POW.	ACC.	PP	RANGE
1	Tackle	Normal	Physical	40	100	35	Normal
1	Water Gun	Water	Special	40	100	25	Normal
4	Withdraw	Water	Status	—	—	40	Self
8	Ice Shard	Ice	Physical	40	100	30	Normal
12	Leer	Normal	Status	—	100	30	Many Others
16	Whirlpool	Water	Special	35	85	15	Normal
20	Supersonic	Normal	Status	—	55	20	Normal
24	Aurora Beam	Ice	Special	65	100	20	Normal
28	Protect	Normal	Status	—	—	10	Self
32	Razor Shell	Water	Physical	75	95	10	Normal
36	Iron Defense	Steel	Status	—	—	15	Self
40	Ice Beam	Ice	Special	90	100	10	Normal
44	Shell Smash	Normal	Status	—	—	15	Self
48	Hydro Pump	Water	Special	110	80	5	Normal

EVOLUTION MOVES

NAME	TYPE	KIND	POW.	ACC.	PP	RANGE

EGG MOVES

NAME	TYPE	KIND	POW.	ACC.	PP	RANGE
Aqua Ring	Water	Status	—	—	20	Self
Bubble Beam	Water	Special	65	100	20	Normal
Life Dew	Water	Status	—	—	10	Your Side
Water Pulse	Water	Special	60	100	20	Normal

TUTOR MOVES

NAME	TYPE	KIND	POW.	ACC.	PP	RANGE

TM MOVES

NO.	NAME	TYPE	KIND	POW.	ACC.	PP	RANGE
TM16	Screech	Normal	Status	—	85	40	Normal
TM20	Self-Destruct	Normal	Physical	200	100	5	All Others
TM21	Rest	Psychic	Status	—	—	10	Self
TM24	Snore	Normal	Special	50	100	15	Normal
TM25	Protect	Normal	Status	—	—	10	Self
TM27	Icy Wind	Ice	Special	55	95	15	Many Others
TM31	Attract	Normal	Status	—	100	15	Normal
TM33	Rain Dance	Water	Status	—	—	5	Both Sides
TM35	Hail	Ice	Status	—	—	10	Both Sides
TM36	Whirlpool	Water	Special	35	85	15	Normal
TM39	Facade	Normal	Physical	70	100	20	Normal
TM40	Swift	Normal	Special	60	—	20	Many Others
TM45	Dive	Water	Physical	80	100	10	Normal
TM51	Icicle Spear	Ice	Physical	25	100	30	Normal
TM53	Mud Shot	Ground	Special	55	95	15	Normal
TM54	Rock Blast	Rock	Physical	25	90	10	Normal
TM55	Brine	Water	Special	65	100	10	Normal
TM57	Payback	Dark	Physical	50	100	10	Normal
TM64	Avalanche	Ice	Physical	60	100	10	Normal
TM76	Round	Normal	Special	60	100	15	Normal
TM83	Razor Shell	Water	Physical	75	95	10	Normal

TR MOVES

NO.	NAME	TYPE	KIND	POW.	ACC.	PP	RANGE
TR03	Hydro Pump	Water	Special	110	80	5	Normal
TR04	Surf	Water	Special	90	100	15	All Others
TR05	Ice Beam	Ice	Special	90	100	10	Normal
TR06	Blizzard	Ice	Special	110	70	5	Many Others
TR19	Tri Attack	Normal	Special	80	100	10	Normal
TR20	Substitute	Normal	Status	—	—	10	Self
TR26	Endure	Normal	Status	—	—	10	Self
TR27	Sleep Talk	Normal	Status	—	—	10	Self
TR46	Iron Defense	Steel	Status	—	—	15	Self
TR98	Liquidation	Water	Physical	85	100	10	Normal

Shellder
p. 74

ABILITY
Shell Armor
Skill Link

HIDDEN ABILITY
Overcoat

SPECIES STRENGTHS
- HP
- ATTACK
- DEFENSE
- SP. ATK
- SP. DEF
- SPEED

DAMAGE TAKEN IN BATTLE
×1 ×1 ×1 ×0.5 ×1 ×1 ×0.5 ×1 ×1 ×2 ×1 ×1 ×2 ×1 ×0.5 ×0.5 ×1 ×1

WATER 3

151 Cloyster p. 74

ABILITY
Shell Armor
Skill Link

HIDDEN ABILITY
Overcoat

SPECIES STRENGTHS

HP	
ATTACK	
DEFENSE	
SP. ATK	
SP. DEF	
SPEED	

DAMAGE TAKEN IN BATTLE

×1	×2	×2			
×1	×1	×1			
×0.5	×1	×1			
×2	×1	×1			
×2	×1	×1			
×0.25	×1	×1			

WATER 3

LEVEL-UP MOVES

LV.	NAME	TYPE	KIND	POW.	ACC.	PP	RANGE
1	Aurora Beam	Ice	Special	65	100	20	Normal
1	Hydro Pump	Water	Special	110	80	5	Normal
1	Ice Beam	Ice	Special	90	100	10	Normal
1	Ice Shard	Ice	Physical	40	100	30	Normal
1	Icicle Crash	Ice	Physical	85	90	10	Normal
1	Icicle Spear	Ice	Physical	25	100	30	Normal
1	Iron Defense	Steel	Status	—	—	15	Self
1	Leer	Normal	Status	—	100	30	Many Others
1	Protect	Normal	Status	—	—	10	Self
1	Razor Shell	Water	Physical	75	95	10	Normal
1	Shell Smash	Normal	Status	—	—	15	Self
1	Spikes	Ground	Status	—	—	20	Other Side
1	Supersonic	Normal	Status	—	55	20	Normal
1	Tackle	Normal	Physical	40	100	35	Normal
1	Toxic Spikes	Poison	Status	—	—	20	Other Side
1	Water Gun	Water	Special	40	100	25	Normal
1	Whirlpool	Water	Special	35	85	15	Normal
1	Withdraw	Water	Status	—	—	40	Self

EVOLUTION MOVES

NAME	TYPE	KIND	POW.	ACC.	PP	RANGE
Icicle Spear	Ice	Physical	25	100	30	Normal

EGG MOVES

NAME	TYPE	KIND	POW.	ACC.	PP	RANGE

TUTOR MOVES

NAME	TYPE	KIND	POW.	ACC.	PP	RANGE

TM MOVES

NO.	NAME	TYPE	KIND	POW.	ACC.	PP	RANGE
TM07	Pin Missile	Bug	Physical	25	95	20	Normal
TM08	Hyper Beam	Normal	Special	150	90	5	Normal
TM09	Giga Impact	Normal	Physical	150	90	5	Normal
TM16	Screech	Normal	Status	—	85	40	Normal
TM17	Light Screen	Psychic	Status	—	—	30	Your Side
TM20	Self-Destruct	Normal	Physical	200	100	5	All Others
TM21	Rest	Psychic	Status	—	—	10	Self
TM24	Snore	Normal	Special	50	100	15	Normal
TM25	Protect	Normal	Status	—	—	10	Self
TM27	Icy Wind	Ice	Special	55	95	15	Many Others
TM31	Attract	Normal	Status	—	100	15	Normal
TM33	Rain Dance	Water	Status	—	—	5	Both Sides
TM35	Hail	Ice	Status	—	—	10	Both Sides
TM36	Whirlpool	Water	Special	35	85	15	Normal
TM39	Facade	Normal	Physical	70	100	20	Normal
TM40	Swift	Normal	Special	60	—	20	Many Others
TM45	Dive	Water	Physical	80	100	10	Normal
TM46	Weather Ball*	Normal	Special	50	100	10	Normal
TM51	Icicle Spear	Ice	Physical	25	100	30	Normal
TM53	Mud Shot	Ground	Special	55	95	15	Normal
TM54	Rock Blast	Rock	Physical	25	90	10	Normal
TM55	Brine	Water	Special	65	100	10	Normal
TM57	Payback	Dark	Physical	50	100	10	Normal
TM64	Avalanche	Ice	Physical	60	100	10	Normal
TM76	Round	Normal	Special	60	100	15	Normal
TM83	Razor Shell	Water	Physical	75	95	10	Normal
TM96	Smart Strike	Steel	Physical	70	—	10	Normal

TR MOVES

NO.	NAME	TYPE	KIND	POW.	ACC.	PP	RANGE
TR03	Hydro Pump	Water	Special	110	80	5	Normal
TR04	Surf	Water	Special	90	100	15	All Others
TR05	Ice Beam	Ice	Special	90	100	10	Normal
TR06	Blizzard	Ice	Special	110	70	5	Many Others
TR19	Tri Attack	Normal	Special	80	100	10	Normal
TR20	Substitute	Normal	Status	—	—	10	Self
TR23	Spikes	Ground	Status	—	—	20	Other Side
TR26	Endure	Normal	Status	—	—	10	Self
TR27	Sleep Talk	Normal	Status	—	—	10	Self
TR46	Iron Defense	Steel	Status	—	—	15	Self
TR54	Toxic Spikes	Poison	Status	—	—	20	Other Side
TR57	Poison Jab	Poison	Physical	80	100	20	Normal
TR98	Liquidation	Water	Physical	85	100	10	Normal

---

152 Feebas p. 75

ABILITY
Swift Swim
Oblivious

HIDDEN ABILITY
Adaptability

SPECIES STRENGTHS

HP	
ATTACK	
DEFENSE	
SP. ATK	
SP. DEF	
SPEED	

DAMAGE TAKEN IN BATTLE

×1	×1	×1			
×0.5	×1	×1			
×0.5	×1	×1			
×2	×1	×1			
×2	×1	×0.5			
×0.5	×1	×1			

WATER 1
DRAGON

LEVEL-UP MOVES

LV.	NAME	TYPE	KIND	POW.	ACC.	PP	RANGE
1	Splash	Normal	Status	—	—	40	Self
15	Tackle	Normal	Physical	40	100	35	Normal
25	Flail	Normal	Physical	—	100	15	Normal

EVOLUTION MOVES

NAME	TYPE	KIND	POW.	ACC.	PP	RANGE

EGG MOVES

NAME	TYPE	KIND	POW.	ACC.	PP	RANGE
Confuse Ray	Ghost	Status	—	100	10	Normal
Dragon Breath	Dragon	Special	60	100	20	Normal
Haze	Ice	Status	—	—	30	Both Sides
Hypnosis	Psychic	Status	—	60	20	Normal
Mirror Coat	Psychic	Special	—	100	20	Varies
Mist	Ice	Status	—	—	30	Your Side
Tickle	Normal	Status	—	100	20	Normal

TUTOR MOVES

NAME	TYPE	KIND	POW.	ACC.	PP	RANGE

TM MOVES

NO.	NAME	TYPE	KIND	POW.	ACC.	PP	RANGE
TM17	Light Screen	Psychic	Status	—	—	30	Your Side
TM21	Rest	Psychic	Status	—	—	10	Self
TM24	Snore	Normal	Special	50	100	15	Normal
TM25	Protect	Normal	Status	—	—	10	Self
TM27	Icy Wind	Ice	Special	55	95	15	Many Others
TM31	Attract	Normal	Status	—	100	15	Normal
TM33	Rain Dance	Water	Status	—	—	5	Both Sides
TM35	Hail	Ice	Status	—	—	10	Both Sides
TM36	Whirlpool	Water	Special	35	85	15	Normal
TM39	Facade	Normal	Physical	70	100	20	Normal
TM40	Swift	Normal	Special	60	—	20	Many Others
TM45	Dive	Water	Physical	80	100	10	Normal
TM53	Mud Shot	Ground	Special	55	95	15	Normal
TM55	Brine	Water	Special	65	100	10	Normal
TM76	Round	Normal	Special	60	100	15	Normal

TR MOVES

NO.	NAME	TYPE	KIND	POW.	ACC.	PP	RANGE
TR04	Surf	Water	Special	90	100	15	All Others
TR05	Ice Beam	Ice	Special	90	100	10	Normal
TR06	Blizzard	Ice	Special	110	70	5	Many Others
TR16	Waterfall	Water	Physical	80	100	15	Normal
TR20	Substitute	Normal	Status	—	—	10	Self
TR26	Endure	Normal	Status	—	—	10	Self
TR27	Sleep Talk	Normal	Status	—	—	10	Self
TR31	Iron Tail	Steel	Physical	100	75	15	Normal
TR45	Muddy Water	Water	Special	90	85	10	Many Others
TR62	Dragon Pulse	Dragon	Special	85	100	10	Normal
TR84	Scald	Water	Special	80	100	15	Normal

153

LEVEL-UP MOVES

LV.	NAME	TYPE	KIND	POW.	ACC.	PP	RANGE
1	Flail	Normal	Physical	—	100	15	Normal
1	Splash	Normal	Status	—	—	40	Self
1	Tackle	Normal	Physical	40	100	35	Normal
1	Water Gun	Water	Special	40	100	25	Normal
1	Water Pulse	Water	Special	60	100	20	Normal
1	Wrap	Normal	Physical	15	90	20	Normal
4	Disarming Voice	Fairy	Special	40	—	15	Many Others
8	Twister	Dragon	Special	40	100	20	Many Others
12	Aqua Ring	Water	Status	—	—	20	Self
16	Attract	Normal	Status	—	100	15	Normal
20	Life Dew	Water	Status	—	—	10	Your Side
24	Dragon Tail	Dragon	Physical	60	90	10	Normal
28	Recover	Normal	Status	—	—	10	Self
32	Aqua Tail	Water	Physical	90	90	10	Normal
36	Safeguard	Normal	Status	—	—	25	Your Side
40	Surf	Water	Special	90	100	15	All Others
44	Rain Dance	Water	Status	—	—	5	Both Sides
48	Coil	Poison	Status	—	—	20	Self
52	Hydro Pump	Water	Special	110	80	5	Normal

EVOLUTION MOVES

NAME	TYPE	KIND	POW.	ACC.	PP	RANGE
Water Pulse	Water	Special	60	100	20	Normal

EGG MOVES

NAME	TYPE	KIND	POW.	ACC.	PP	RANGE

TUTOR MOVES

NAME	TYPE	KIND	POW.	ACC.	PP	RANGE

TM MOVES

NO.	NAME	TYPE	KIND	POW.	ACC.	PP	RANGE
TM08	Hyper Beam	Normal	Special	150	90	5	Normal
TM09	Giga Impact	Normal	Physical	150	90	5	Normal
TM17	Light Screen	Psychic	Status	—	—	30	Your Side
TM19	Safeguard	Normal	Status	—	—	25	Your Side
TM21	Rest	Psychic	Status	—	—	10	Self
TM24	Snore	Normal	Special	50	100	15	Normal
TM25	Protect	Normal	Status	—	—	10	Self
TM27	Icy Wind	Ice	Special	55	95	15	Many Others
TM31	Attract	Normal	Status	—	100	15	Normal
TM33	Rain Dance	Water	Status	—	—	5	Both Sides
TM35	Hail	Ice	Status	—	—	10	Both Sides
TM36	Whirlpool	Water	Special	35	85	15	Normal
TM39	Facade	Normal	Physical	70	100	20	Normal
TM40	Swift	Normal	Special	60	—	20	Many Others
TM41	Helping Hand	Normal	Status	—	—	20	1 Ally
TM44	Imprison	Psychic	Status	—	—	10	Self
TM45	Dive	Water	Physical	80	100	10	Normal
TM46	Weather Ball*	Normal	Special	50	100	10	Normal
TM53	Mud Shot	Ground	Special	55	95	15	Normal
TM55	Brine	Water	Special	65	100	10	Normal
TM64	Avalanche	Ice	Physical	60	100	10	Normal
TM76	Round	Normal	Special	60	100	15	Normal
TM81	Bulldoze	Ground	Physical	60	100	20	All Others
TM97	Brutal Swing	Dark	Physical	60	100	20	All Others
TM99	Breaking Swipe	Dragon	Physical	60	100	15	Many Others

TR MOVES

NO.	NAME	TYPE	KIND	POW.	ACC.	PP	RANGE
TR01	Body Slam	Normal	Physical	85	100	15	Normal
TR03	Hydro Pump	Water	Special	110	80	5	Normal
TR04	Surf	Water	Special	90	100	15	All Others
TR05	Ice Beam	Ice	Special	90	100	10	Normal
TR06	Blizzard	Ice	Special	110	70	5	Many Others
TR16	Waterfall	Water	Physical	80	100	15	Normal
TR20	Substitute	Normal	Status	—	—	10	Self
TR26	Endure	Normal	Status	—	—	10	Self
TR27	Sleep Talk	Normal	Status	—	—	10	Self
TR31	Iron Tail	Steel	Physical	100	75	15	Normal
TR45	Muddy Water	Water	Special	90	85	10	Many Others
TR51	Dragon Dance	Dragon	Status	—	—	20	Self
TR62	Dragon Pulse	Dragon	Special	85	100	10	Normal
TR74	Iron Head	Steel	Physical	80	100	15	Normal
TR84	Scald	Water	Special	80	100	15	Normal

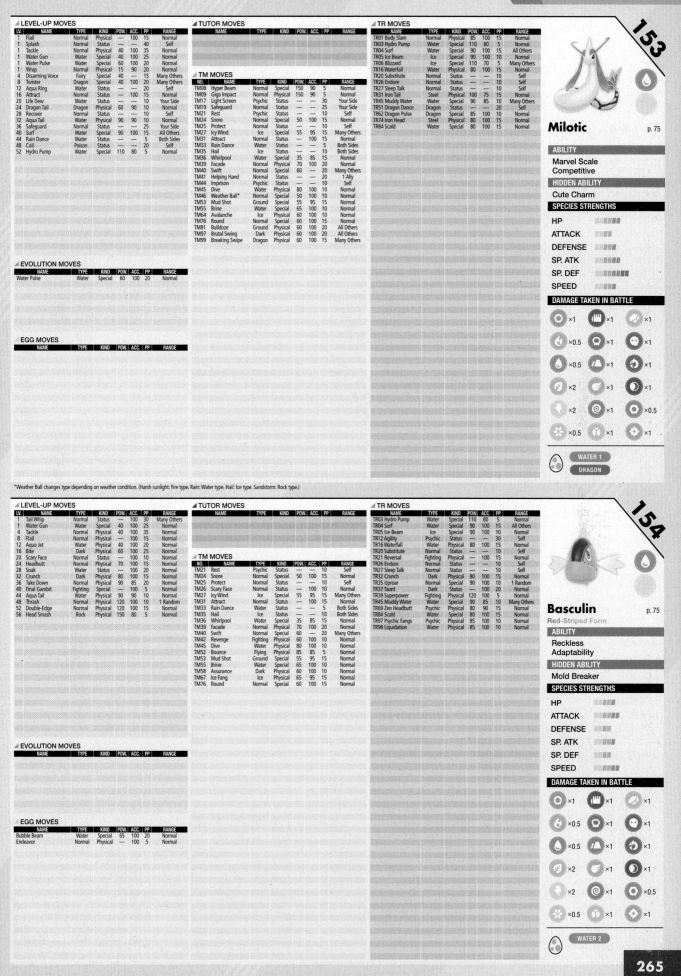

Milotic
p. 75

ABILITY
Marvel Scale
Competitive

HIDDEN ABILITY
Cute Charm

SPECIES STRENGTHS

HP	
ATTACK	
DEFENSE	
SP. ATK	
SP. DEF	
SPEED	

DAMAGE TAKEN IN BATTLE

×1 | ×1 | ×1
×0.5 | ×1 | ×1
×0.5 | ×1 | ×1
×2 | | ×1
×2 | ×1 | ×0.5
×0.5 | ×1 | ×1

WATER 1
DRAGON

*Weather Ball changes type depending on weather condition. (Harsh sunlight: Fire type. Rain: Water type. Hail: Ice type. Sandstorm: Rock type.)

154

LEVEL-UP MOVES

LV.	NAME	TYPE	KIND	POW.	ACC.	PP	RANGE
1	Tail Whip	Normal	Status	—	100	30	Many Others
1	Water Gun	Water	Special	40	100	25	Normal
4	Tackle	Normal	Physical	40	100	35	Normal
8	Flail	Normal	Physical	—	100	15	Normal
12	Aqua Jet	Water	Physical	40	100	20	Normal
16	Bite	Dark	Physical	60	100	25	Normal
20	Scary Face	Normal	Status	—	100	10	Normal
24	Headbutt	Normal	Physical	70	100	15	Normal
28	Soak	Water	Status	—	100	20	Normal
32	Crunch	Dark	Physical	80	100	15	Normal
36	Take Down	Normal	Physical	90	85	20	Normal
40	Final Gambit	Fighting	Special	—	100	5	Normal
44	Aqua Tail	Water	Physical	90	90	10	Normal
48	Thrash	Normal	Physical	120	100	10	1 Random
52	Double-Edge	Normal	Physical	120	100	15	Normal
56	Head Smash	Rock	Physical	150	80	5	Normal

EVOLUTION MOVES

NAME	TYPE	KIND	POW.	ACC.	PP	RANGE

EGG MOVES

NAME	TYPE	KIND	POW.	ACC.	PP	RANGE
Bubble Beam	Water	Special	65	100	20	Normal
Endeavor	Normal	Physical	—	100	5	Normal

TUTOR MOVES

NAME	TYPE	KIND	POW.	ACC.	PP	RANGE

TM MOVES

NO.	NAME	TYPE	KIND	POW.	ACC.	PP	RANGE
TM21	Rest	Psychic	Status	—	—	10	Self
TM24	Snore	Normal	Special	50	100	15	Normal
TM25	Protect	Normal	Status	—	—	10	Self
TM26	Scary Face	Normal	Status	—	100	10	Normal
TM27	Icy Wind	Ice	Special	55	95	15	Many Others
TM31	Attract	Normal	Status	—	100	15	Normal
TM33	Rain Dance	Water	Status	—	—	5	Both Sides
TM35	Hail	Ice	Status	—	—	10	Both Sides
TM36	Whirlpool	Water	Special	35	85	15	Normal
TM39	Facade	Normal	Physical	70	100	20	Normal
TM40	Swift	Normal	Special	60	—	20	Many Others
TM42	Revenge	Fighting	Physical	60	100	10	Normal
TM45	Dive	Water	Physical	80	100	10	Normal
TM52	Bounce	Flying	Physical	85	85	5	Normal
TM53	Mud Shot	Ground	Special	55	95	15	Normal
TM55	Brine	Water	Special	65	100	10	Normal
TM58	Assurance	Dark	Physical	60	100	10	Normal
TM67	Ice Fang	Ice	Physical	65	95	15	Normal
TM76	Round	Normal	Special	60	100	15	Normal

TR MOVES

NO.	NAME	TYPE	KIND	POW.	ACC.	PP	RANGE
TR03	Hydro Pump	Water	Special	110	80	5	Normal
TR04	Surf	Water	Special	90	100	10	All Others
TR05	Ice Beam	Ice	Special	90	100	10	Normal
TR12	Agility	Psychic	Status	—	—	30	Self
TR16	Waterfall	Water	Physical	80	100	15	Normal
TR20	Substitute	Normal	Status	—	—	10	Self
TR21	Reversal	Fighting	Physical	—	100	15	Normal
TR26	Endure	Normal	Status	—	—	10	Self
TR27	Sleep Talk	Normal	Status	—	—	10	Self
TR32	Crunch	Dark	Physical	80	100	15	Normal
TR35	Uproar	Normal	Special	90	100	10	1 Random
TR37	Taunt	Dark	Status	—	100	20	Normal
TR39	Superpower	Fighting	Physical	120	100	5	Normal
TR45	Muddy Water	Water	Special	90	85	10	Many Others
TR69	Zen Headbutt	Psychic	Physical	80	90	15	Normal
TR84	Scald	Water	Special	80	100	15	Normal
TR97	Psychic Fangs	Psychic	Physical	85	100	10	Normal
TR98	Liquidation	Water	Physical	85	100	10	Normal

Basculin
p. 75
Red-Striped Form

ABILITY
Reckless
Adaptability

HIDDEN ABILITY
Mold Breaker

SPECIES STRENGTHS

HP	
ATTACK	
DEFENSE	
SP. ATK	
SP. DEF	
SPEED	

DAMAGE TAKEN IN BATTLE

×1 | ×1 | ×1
×0.5 | ×1 | ×1
×0.5 | ×1 | ×1
×2 | | ×1
×2 | ×1 | ×0.5
×0.5 | ×1 | ×1

WATER 2

154 Basculin

Blue-Striped Form — p. 75

ABILITY
Rock Head
Adaptability

HIDDEN ABILITY
Mold Breaker

SPECIES STRENGTHS
- HP
- ATTACK
- DEFENSE
- SP. ATK
- SP. DEF
- SPEED

LEVEL-UP MOVES

LV.	NAME	TYPE	KIND	POW.	ACC.	PP	RANGE
1	Tail Whip	Normal	Status	—	100	30	Many Others
1	Water Gun	Water	Special	40	100	25	Normal
4	Tackle	Normal	Physical	40	100	35	Normal
8	Flail	Normal	Physical	—	100	15	Normal
12	Aqua Jet	Water	Physical	40	100	20	Normal
16	Bite	Dark	Physical	60	100	25	Normal
20	Scary Face	Normal	Status	—	100	10	Normal
24	Headbutt	Normal	Physical	70	100	15	Normal
28	Soak	Water	Status	—	100	20	Normal
32	Crunch	Dark	Physical	80	100	15	Normal
36	Take Down	Normal	Physical	90	85	20	Normal
40	Final Gambit	Fighting	Special	—	100	5	Normal
44	Aqua Tail	Water	Physical	90	90	10	Normal
48	Thrash	Normal	Physical	120	100	10	1 Random
52	Double-Edge	Normal	Physical	120	100	15	Normal
56	Head Smash	Rock	Physical	150	80	5	Normal

TM MOVES

NO.	NAME	TYPE	KIND	POW.	ACC.	PP	RANGE
TM21	Rest	Psychic	Status	—	—	10	Self
TM24	Snore	Normal	Special	50	100	15	Normal
TM25	Protect	Normal	Status	—	—	10	Self
TM26	Scary Face	Normal	Status	—	100	10	Normal
TM27	Icy Wind	Ice	Special	55	95	15	Many Others
TM31	Attract	Normal	Status	—	100	15	Normal
TM33	Rain Dance	Water	Status	—	—	5	Both Sides
TM35	Hail	Ice	Status	—	—	10	Both Sides
TM36	Whirlpool	Water	Special	35	85	15	Normal
TM39	Facade	Normal	Physical	70	100	20	Normal
TM40	Swift	Normal	Special	60	—	20	Many Others
TM42	Revenge	Fighting	Physical	60	100	10	Normal
TM45	Dive	Water	Physical	80	100	10	Normal
TM52	Bounce	Flying	Physical	85	85	5	Normal
TM53	Mud Shot	Ground	Special	55	95	15	Normal
TM55	Brine	Water	Special	65	100	10	Normal
TM58	Assurance	Dark	Physical	60	100	10	Normal
TM67	Ice Fang	Ice	Physical	65	95	15	Normal
TM76	Round	Normal	Special	60	100	15	Normal

TUTOR MOVES

(none)

TR MOVES

NO.	NAME	TYPE	KIND	POW.	ACC.	PP	RANGE
TR03	Hydro Pump	Water	Special	110	80	5	Normal
TR04	Surf	Water	Special	90	100	15	All Others
TR05	Ice Beam	Ice	Special	90	100	10	Normal
TR12	Agility	Psychic	Status	—	—	30	Self
TR16	Waterfall	Water	Physical	80	100	15	Normal
TR20	Substitute	Normal	Status	—	—	10	Self
TR21	Reversal	Fighting	Physical	—	100	15	Normal
TR26	Endure	Normal	Status	—	—	10	Self
TR27	Sleep Talk	Normal	Status	—	—	10	Self
TR32	Crunch	Dark	Physical	80	100	15	Normal
TR35	Uproar	Normal	Special	90	100	10	1 Random
TR37	Taunt	Dark	Status	—	100	20	Normal
TR39	Superpower	Fighting	Physical	120	100	5	Normal
TR45	Muddy Water	Water	Special	90	85	10	Many Others
TR69	Zen Headbutt	Psychic	Physical	80	90	15	Normal
TR84	Scald	Water	Special	80	100	15	Normal
TR97	Psychic Fangs	Psychic	Physical	85	100	10	Normal
TR98	Liquidation	Water	Physical	85	100	10	Normal

EVOLUTION MOVES

(none)

EGG MOVES

(none)

DAMAGE TAKEN IN BATTLE: ×1, ×1, ×1, ×0.5, ×1, ×1, ×0.5, ×1, ×1, ×2, ×1, ×1, ×2, ×1, ×0.5, ×0.5, ×1, ×1

WATER 2

---

155 Wishiwashi

p. 76

ABILITY
Schooling
—

HIDDEN ABILITY
—

SPECIES STRENGTHS
- HP
- ATTACK
- DEFENSE
- SP. ATK
- SP. DEF
- SPEED

LEVEL-UP MOVES

LV.	NAME	TYPE	KIND	POW.	ACC.	PP	RANGE
1	Growl	Normal	Status	—	100	40	Many Others
1	Water Gun	Water	Special	40	100	25	Normal
4	Helping Hand	Normal	Status	—	—	20	1 Ally
8	Beat Up	Dark	Physical	—	100	10	Normal
12	Brine	Water	Special	65	100	10	Normal
16	Tearful Look	Normal	Status	—	—	20	Normal
20	Dive	Water	Physical	80	100	10	Normal
24	Soak	Water	Status	—	100	20	Normal
28	Uproar	Normal	Special	90	100	10	1 Random
32	Aqua Tail	Water	Physical	90	90	10	Normal
36	Aqua Ring	Water	Status	—	—	20	Self
40	Endeavor	Normal	Physical	—	100	5	Normal
44	Hydro Pump	Water	Special	110	80	5	Normal
48	Double-Edge	Normal	Physical	120	100	15	Normal

TM MOVES

NO.	NAME	TYPE	KIND	POW.	ACC.	PP	RANGE
TM21	Rest	Psychic	Status	—	—	10	Self
TM24	Snore	Normal	Special	50	100	15	Normal
TM25	Protect	Normal	Status	—	—	10	Self
TM31	Attract	Normal	Status	—	100	15	Normal
TM33	Rain Dance	Water	Status	—	—	5	Both Sides
TM35	Hail	Ice	Status	—	—	10	Both Sides
TM36	Whirlpool	Water	Special	35	85	15	Normal
TM37	Beat Up	Dark	Physical	—	100	10	Normal
TM39	Facade	Normal	Physical	70	100	20	Normal
TM41	Helping Hand	Normal	Status	—	—	20	1 Ally
TM45	Dive	Water	Physical	80	100	10	Normal
TM53	Mud Shot	Ground	Special	55	95	15	Normal
TM55	Brine	Water	Special	65	100	10	Normal
TM56	U-turn	Bug	Physical	70	100	20	Normal
TM76	Round	Normal	Special	60	100	15	Normal
TM81	Bulldoze	Ground	Physical	60	100	20	All Others

TUTOR MOVES

(none)

TR MOVES

NO.	NAME	TYPE	KIND	POW.	ACC.	PP	RANGE
TR03	Hydro Pump	Water	Special	110	80	5	Normal
TR04	Surf	Water	Special	90	100	15	All Others
TR05	Ice Beam	Ice	Special	90	100	10	Normal
TR10	Earthquake	Ground	Physical	100	100	10	All Others
TR16	Waterfall	Water	Physical	80	100	15	Normal
TR20	Substitute	Normal	Status	—	—	10	Self
TR26	Endure	Normal	Status	—	—	10	Self
TR27	Sleep Talk	Normal	Status	—	—	10	Self
TR31	Iron Tail	Steel	Physical	100	75	15	Normal
TR35	Uproar	Normal	Special	90	100	10	1 Random
TR45	Muddy Water	Water	Special	90	85	10	Many Others
TR84	Scald	Water	Special	80	100	15	Normal
TR98	Liquidation	Water	Physical	85	100	10	Normal

EVOLUTION MOVES

(none)

EGG MOVES

NAME	TYPE	KIND	POW.	ACC.	PP	RANGE
Mist	Ice	Status	—	—	30	Your Side
Take Down	Normal	Physical	90	85	20	Normal
Water Pulse	Water	Special	60	100	20	Normal

DAMAGE TAKEN IN BATTLE: ×1, ×1, ×1, ×0.5, ×1, ×1, ×0.5, ×1, ×1, ×2, ×1, ×1, ×2, ×1, ×0.5, ×0.5, ×1, ×1

WATER 2

156

Pyukumuku p. 76

LEVEL-UP MOVES

LV.	NAME	TYPE	KIND	POW.	ACC.	PP	RANGE
1	Baton Pass	Normal	Status	—	—	40	Self
1	Harden	Normal	Status	—	—	30	Self
5	Helping Hand	Normal	Status	—	—	20	1 Ally
10	Taunt	Dark	Status	—	100	20	Normal
15	Safeguard	Normal	Status	—	—	25	Your Side
20	Counter	Fighting	Physical	—	100	20	Varies
25	Purify	Poison	Status	—	—	20	Normal
30	Curse	Ghost	Status	—	—	10	Varies
35	Gastro Acid	Poison	Status	—	100	10	Normal
40	Pain Split	Normal	Status	—	—	20	Normal
45	Recover	Normal	Status	—	—	10	Self
50	Soak	Water	Status	—	100	20	Normal
55	Toxic	Poison	Status	—	90	10	Normal
60	Memento	Dark	Status	—	100	10	Normal

EVOLUTION MOVES

NAME	TYPE	KIND	POW.	ACC.	PP	RANGE

EGG MOVES

NAME	TYPE	KIND	POW.	ACC.	PP	RANGE
Mirror Coat	Psychic	Special	—	100	20	Varies
Spite	Ghost	Status	—	100	10	Normal
Swagger	Normal	Status	—	85	15	Normal
Tickle	Normal	Status	—	100	20	Normal

TUTOR MOVES

NAME	TYPE	KIND	POW.	ACC.	PP	RANGE

TM MOVES

NO.	NAME	TYPE	KIND	POW.	ACC.	PP	RANGE
TM16	Screech	Normal	Status	—	85	40	Normal
TM17	Light Screen	Psychic	Status	—	—	30	Your Side
TM18	Reflect	Psychic	Status	—	—	20	Your Side
TM19	Safeguard	Normal	Status	—	—	25	Your Side
TM21	Rest	Psychic	Status	—	—	10	Self
TM25	Protect	Normal	Status	—	—	10	Self
TM31	Attract	Normal	Status	—	100	15	Normal
TM33	Rain Dance	Water	Status	—	—	5	Both Sides
TM35	Hail	Ice	Status	—	—	10	Both Sides
TM41	Helping Hand	Normal	Status	—	—	20	1 Ally

TR MOVES

NAME	TYPE	KIND	POW.	ACC.	PP	RANGE
TR20 Substitute	Normal	Status	—	—	10	Self
TR26 Endure	Normal	Status	—	—	10	Self
TR27 Sleep Talk	Normal	Status	—	—	10	Self
TR29 Baton Pass	Normal	Status	—	—	40	Self
TR37 Taunt	Dark	Status	—	100	20	Normal
TR91 Venom Drench	Poison	Status	—	100	20	Many Others

ABILITY
Innards Out
—

HIDDEN ABILITY
Unaware

SPECIES STRENGTHS
HP
ATTACK
DEFENSE
SP. ATK
SP. DEF
SPEED

DAMAGE TAKEN IN BATTLE

WATER 1

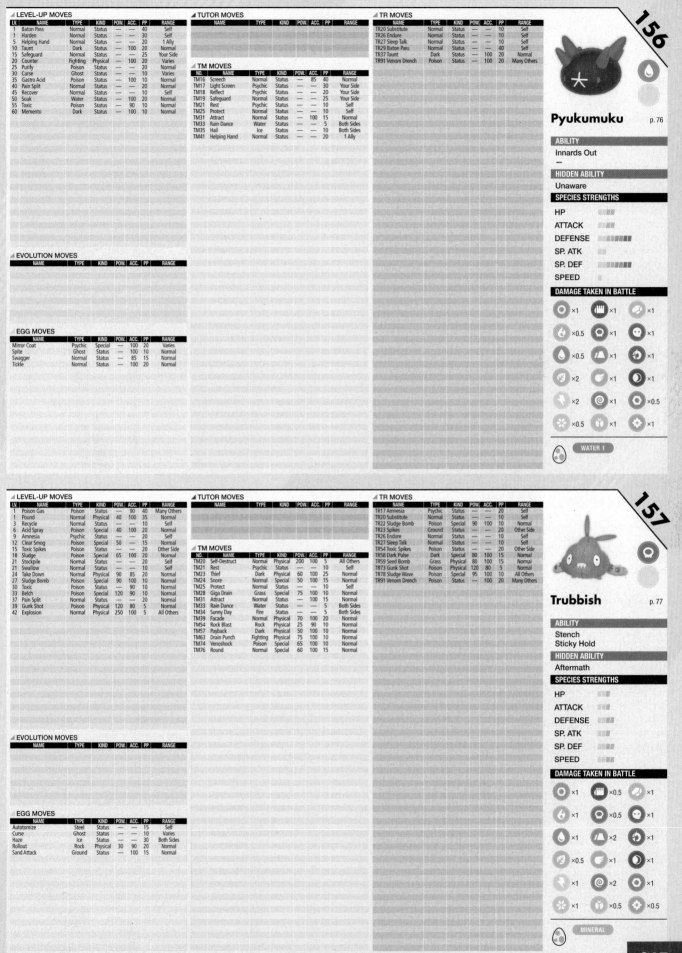

157

Trubbish p. 77

LEVEL-UP MOVES

LV.	NAME	TYPE	KIND	POW.	ACC.	PP	RANGE
1	Poison Gas	Poison	Status	—	90	40	Many Others
1	Pound	Normal	Physical	40	100	35	Normal
3	Recycle	Normal	Status	—	—	10	Self
6	Acid Spray	Poison	Special	40	100	20	Normal
9	Amnesia	Psychic	Status	—	—	20	Self
12	Clear Smog	Poison	Special	50	—	15	Normal
15	Toxic Spikes	Poison	Status	—	—	20	Other Side
18	Sludge	Poison	Special	65	100	20	Normal
21	Stockpile	Normal	Status	—	—	20	Self
21	Swallow	Normal	Status	—	—	10	Self
24	Take Down	Normal	Physical	90	85	20	Normal
27	Sludge Bomb	Poison	Special	90	100	10	Normal
30	Toxic	Poison	Status	—	90	10	Normal
33	Belch	Poison	Special	120	90	10	Normal
36	Pain Split	Normal	Status	—	—	20	Normal
39	Gunk Shot	Poison	Physical	120	80	5	Normal
42	Explosion	Normal	Physical	250	100	5	All Others

EVOLUTION MOVES

NAME	TYPE	KIND	POW.	ACC.	PP	RANGE

EGG MOVES

NAME	TYPE	KIND	POW.	ACC.	PP	RANGE
Autotomize	Steel	Status	—	—	15	Self
Curse	Ghost	Status	—	—	10	Varies
Haze	Ice	Status	—	—	30	Both Sides
Rollout	Rock	Physical	30	90	20	Normal
Sand Attack	Ground	Status	—	100	15	Normal

TUTOR MOVES

NAME	TYPE	KIND	POW.	ACC.	PP	RANGE

TM MOVES

NO.	NAME	TYPE	KIND	POW.	ACC.	PP	RANGE
TM20	Self-Destruct	Normal	Physical	200	100	5	All Others
TM21	Rest	Psychic	Status	—	—	10	Self
TM23	Thief	Dark	Physical	60	100	25	Normal
TM24	Snore	Normal	Special	50	100	15	Normal
TM25	Protect	Normal	Status	—	—	10	Self
TM28	Giga Drain	Grass	Special	75	100	10	Normal
TM31	Attract	Normal	Status	—	100	15	Normal
TM33	Rain Dance	Water	Status	—	—	5	Both Sides
TM34	Sunny Day	Fire	Status	—	—	5	Both Sides
TM39	Facade	Normal	Physical	70	100	20	Normal
TM54	Rock Blast	Rock	Physical	25	90	10	Normal
TM57	Payback	Dark	Physical	50	100	10	Normal
TM63	Drain Punch	Fighting	Physical	75	100	10	Normal
TM74	Venoshock	Poison	Special	65	100	10	Normal
TM76	Round	Normal	Special	60	100	15	Normal

TR MOVES

NAME	TYPE	KIND	POW.	ACC.	PP	RANGE
TR17 Amnesia	Psychic	Status	—	—	20	Self
TR20 Substitute	Normal	Status	—	—	10	Self
TR22 Sludge Bomb	Poison	Special	90	100	10	Normal
TR23 Spikes	Ground	Status	—	—	20	Other Side
TR26 Endure	Normal	Status	—	—	10	Self
TR27 Sleep Talk	Normal	Status	—	—	10	Self
TR54 Toxic Spikes	Poison	Status	—	—	20	Other Side
TR58 Dark Pulse	Dark	Special	80	100	15	Normal
TR59 Seed Bomb	Grass	Physical	80	100	15	Normal
TR73 Gunk Shot	Poison	Physical	120	80	5	Normal
TR78 Sludge Wave	Poison	Special	95	100	10	All Others
TR91 Venom Drench	Poison	Status	—	100	20	Many Others

ABILITY
Stench
Sticky Hold

HIDDEN ABILITY
Aftermath

SPECIES STRENGTHS
HP
ATTACK
DEFENSE
SP. ATK
SP. DEF
SPEED

DAMAGE TAKEN IN BATTLE

MINERAL

158 Garbodor — p. 77

ABILITY
Stench
Weak Armor

HIDDEN ABILITY
Aftermath

SPECIES STRENGTHS
HP
ATTACK
DEFENSE
SP. ATK
SP. DEF
SPEED

LEVEL-UP MOVES

LV.	NAME	TYPE	KIND	POW.	ACC.	PP	RANGE
1	Acid Spray	Poison	Special	40	100	20	Normal
1	Metal Claw	Steel	Physical	50	95	35	Normal
1	Poison Gas	Poison	Status	—	90	40	Many Others
1	Pound	Normal	Physical	40	100	35	Normal
1	Recycle	Normal	Status	—	—	10	Self
1	Take Down	Normal	Physical	90	85	20	Normal
9	Amnesia	Psychic	Status	—	—	20	Self
12	Clear Smog	Poison	Special	50	—	15	Normal
15	Toxic Spikes	Poison	Status	—	—	20	Other Side
18	Sludge	Poison	Special	65	100	20	Normal
21	Stockpile	Normal	Status	—	—	20	Self
21	Swallow	Normal	Status	—	—	10	Self
24	Body Slam	Normal	Physical	85	100	15	Normal
27	Sludge Bomb	Poison	Special	90	100	10	Normal
30	Toxic	Poison	Status	—	90	10	Normal
33	Belch	Poison	Special	120	90	10	Normal
39	Pain Split	Normal	Status	—	—	20	Normal
43	Gunk Shot	Poison	Physical	120	80	5	Normal
48	Explosion	Normal	Physical	250	100	5	All Others

TM MOVES

NO.	NAME	TYPE	KIND	POW.	ACC.	PP	RANGE
TM08	Hyper Beam	Normal	Special	150	90	5	Normal
TM09	Giga Impact	Normal	Physical	150	90	5	Normal
TM11	Solar Beam	Grass	Special	120	100	10	Normal
TM16	Screech	Normal	Status	—	85	40	Normal
TM20	Self-Destruct	Normal	Physical	200	100	5	All Others
TM21	Rest	Psychic	Status	—	—	10	Self
TM23	Thief	Dark	Physical	60	100	25	Normal
TM24	Snore	Normal	Special	50	100	15	Normal
TM25	Protect	Normal	Status	—	—	10	Self
TM28	Giga Drain	Grass	Special	75	100	10	Normal
TM31	Attract	Normal	Status	—	100	15	Normal
TM33	Rain Dance	Water	Status	—	—	5	Both Sides
TM34	Sunny Day	Fire	Status	—	—	5	Both Sides
TM39	Facade	Normal	Physical	70	100	20	Normal
TM54	Rock Blast	Rock	Physical	25	90	10	Normal
TM57	Payback	Dark	Physical	50	100	10	Normal
TM59	Fling	Dark	Physical	—	100	10	Normal
TM63	Drain Punch	Fighting	Physical	75	100	10	Normal
TM73	Cross Poison	Poison	Physical	70	100	20	Normal
TM74	Venoshock	Poison	Special	65	100	10	Normal
TM76	Round	Normal	Special	60	100	15	Normal
TM98	Stomping Tantrum	Ground	Physical	75	100	10	Normal

TR MOVES

NAME	TYPE	KIND	POW.	ACC.	PP	RANGE
TR01 Body Slam	Normal	Physical	85	100	15	Normal
TR08 Thunderbolt	Electric	Special	90	100	15	Normal
TR11 Psychic	Psychic	Special	90	100	10	Normal
TR17 Amnesia	Psychic	Status	—	—	20	Self
TR22 Sludge Bomb	Poison	Special	90	100	10	Normal
TR23 Spikes	Ground	Status	—	—	20	Other Side
TR26 Endure	Normal	Status	—	—	10	Self
TR27 Sleep Talk	Normal	Status	—	—	10	Self
TR54 Toxic Spikes	Poison	Status	—	—	20	Other Side
TR58 Dark Pulse	Dark	Special	80	100	15	Normal
TR59 Seed Bomb	Grass	Physical	80	100	15	Normal
TR64 Focus Blast	Fighting	Special	120	70	5	Normal
TR73 Gunk Shot	Poison	Physical	120	80	5	Normal
TR78 Sludge Wave	Poison	Special	95	100	10	All Others
TR91 Venom Drench	Poison	Status	—	100	20	Many Others
TR99 Body Press	Fighting	Physical	80	100	10	Normal

EVOLUTION MOVES — (none)
EGG MOVES — (none)
Egg group: MINERAL

DAMAGE TAKEN IN BATTLE: ×1, ×0.5, ×1, ×1, ×0.5, ×1, ×1, ×2, ×1, ×0.5, ×1, ×1, ×1, ×2, ×1, ×1, ×0.5, ×0.5

---

159 Sizzlipede — p. 77

ABILITY
Flash Fire
White Smoke

HIDDEN ABILITY
Flame Body

SPECIES STRENGTHS
HP
ATTACK
DEFENSE
SP. ATK
SP. DEF
SPEED

LEVEL-UP MOVES

LV.	NAME	TYPE	KIND	POW.	ACC.	PP	RANGE
1	Ember	Fire	Special	40	100	25	Normal
1	Smokescreen	Normal	Status	—	100	20	Normal
5	Wrap	Normal	Physical	15	90	20	Normal
10	Bite	Dark	Physical	60	100	25	Normal
15	Flame Wheel	Fire	Physical	60	100	25	Normal
20	Bug Bite	Bug	Physical	60	100	20	Normal
25	Coil	Poison	Status	—	—	20	Self
30	Slam	Normal	Physical	80	75	20	Normal
35	Fire Spin	Fire	Special	35	85	15	Normal
40	Crunch	Dark	Physical	80	100	15	Normal
45	Fire Lash	Fire	Physical	80	100	15	Normal
50	Lunge	Bug	Physical	80	100	15	Normal
55	Burn Up	Fire	Special	130	100	5	Normal

TM MOVES

NO.	NAME	TYPE	KIND	POW.	ACC.	PP	RANGE
TM13	Fire Spin	Fire	Special	35	85	15	Normal
TM21	Rest	Psychic	Status	—	—	10	Self
TM24	Snore	Normal	Special	50	100	15	Normal
TM25	Protect	Normal	Status	—	—	10	Self
TM31	Attract	Normal	Status	—	100	15	Normal
TM34	Sunny Day	Fire	Status	—	—	5	Both Sides
TM39	Facade	Normal	Physical	70	100	20	Normal
TM74	Venoshock	Poison	Special	65	100	10	Normal
TM76	Round	Normal	Special	60	100	15	Normal
TM97	Brutal Swing	Dark	Physical	60	100	20	All Others

TR MOVES

NAME	TYPE	KIND	POW.	ACC.	PP	RANGE
TR18 Leech Life	Bug	Physical	80	100	10	Normal
TR20 Substitute	Normal	Status	—	—	10	Self
TR26 Endure	Normal	Status	—	—	10	Self
TR27 Sleep Talk	Normal	Status	—	—	10	Self
TR32 Crunch	Dark	Physical	80	100	15	Normal
TR36 Heat Wave	Fire	Special	95	90	10	Many Others
TR61 Bug Buzz	Bug	Special	90	100	10	Normal
TR72 Power Whip	Grass	Physical	120	85	10	Normal
TR84 Scald	Water	Special	80	100	15	Normal
TR88 Heat Crash	Fire	Physical	—	100	10	Normal

EGG MOVES

NAME	TYPE	KIND	POW.	ACC.	PP	RANGE
Defense Curl	Normal	Status	—	—	40	Self
Knock Off	Dark	Physical	65	100	20	Normal
Rollout	Rock	Physical	30	90	20	Normal
Struggle Bug	Bug	Special	50	100	20	Many Others

Egg group: BUG

DAMAGE TAKEN IN BATTLE: ×1, ×0.5, ×4, ×1, ×1, ×1, ×2, ×1, ×1, ×0.25, ×2, ×1, ×1, ×1, ×0.5, ×0.5, ×0.5, ×0.5

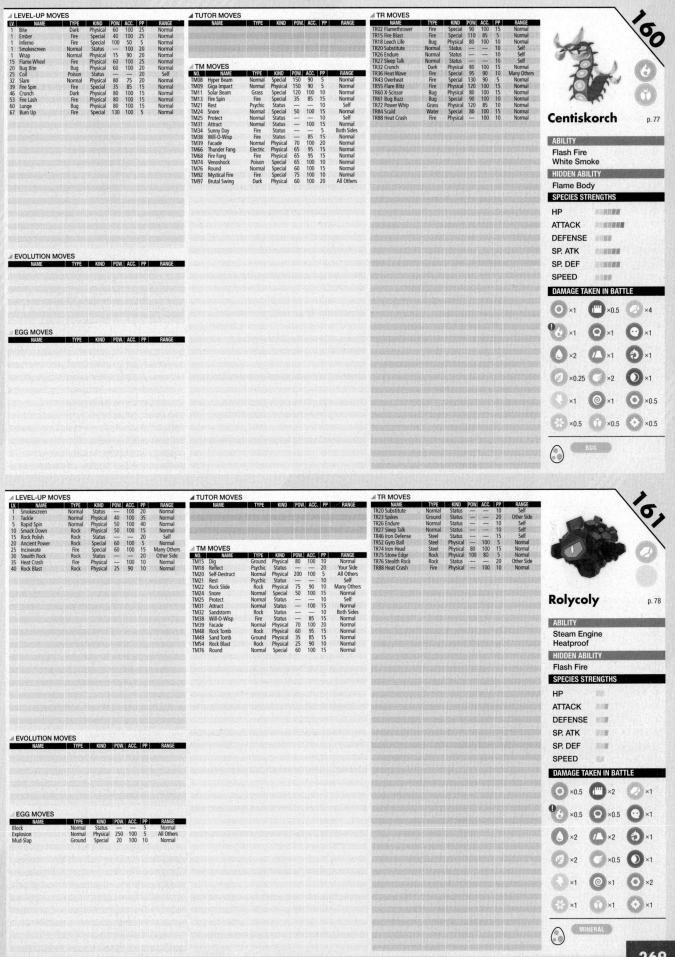

160 — Centiskorch

LEVEL-UP MOVES

LV.	NAME	TYPE	KIND	POW.	ACC.	PP	RANGE
1	Bite	Dark	Physical	60	100	25	Normal
1	Ember	Fire	Special	40	100	25	Normal
1	Inferno	Fire	Special	100	50	5	Normal
1	Smokescreen	Normal	Status	—	100	20	Normal
1	Wrap	Normal	Physical	15	90	20	Normal
15	Flame Wheel	Fire	Physical	60	100	25	Normal
20	Bug Bite	Bug	Physical	60	100	20	Normal
25	Coil	Poison	Status	—	—	20	Self
32	Slam	Normal	Physical	80	75	20	Normal
39	Fire Spin	Fire	Special	35	85	15	Normal
46	Crunch	Dark	Physical	80	100	15	Normal
53	Fire Lash	Fire	Physical	80	100	15	Normal
60	Lunge	Bug	Physical	80	100	15	Normal
67	Burn Up	Fire	Special	130	100	5	Normal

EVOLUTION MOVES

NAME	TYPE	KIND	POW.	ACC.	PP	RANGE

EGG MOVES

NAME	TYPE	KIND	POW.	ACC.	PP	RANGE

TUTOR MOVES

NAME	TYPE	KIND	POW.	ACC.	PP	RANGE

TM MOVES

NO.	NAME	TYPE	KIND	POW.	ACC.	PP	RANGE
TM08	Hyper Beam	Normal	Special	150	90	5	Normal
TM09	Giga Impact	Normal	Physical	150	90	5	Normal
TM11	Solar Beam	Grass	Special	120	100	10	Normal
TM13	Fire Spin	Fire	Special	35	85	15	Normal
TM21	Rest	Psychic	Status	—	—	10	Self
TM24	Snore	Normal	Special	50	100	15	Normal
TM25	Protect	Normal	Status	—	—	10	Self
TM31	Attract	Normal	Status	—	100	15	Normal
TM34	Sunny Day	Fire	Status	—	—	5	Both Sides
TM38	Will-O-Wisp	Fire	Status	—	85	15	Normal
TM39	Facade	Normal	Physical	70	100	20	Normal
TM66	Thunder Fang	Electric	Physical	65	95	15	Normal
TM68	Fire Fang	Fire	Physical	65	95	15	Normal
TM74	Venoshock	Poison	Special	65	100	10	Normal
TM76	Round	Normal	Special	60	100	15	Normal
TM92	Mystical Fire	Fire	Special	75	100	10	Normal
TM97	Brutal Swing	Dark	Physical	60	100	20	All Others

TR MOVES

NO.	NAME	TYPE	KIND	POW.	ACC.	PP	RANGE
TR02	Flamethrower	Fire	Special	90	100	15	Normal
TR15	Fire Blast	Fire	Special	110	85	5	Normal
TR18	Leech Life	Bug	Physical	80	100	10	Normal
TR20	Substitute	Normal	Status	—	—	10	Self
TR26	Endure	Normal	Status	—	—	10	Self
TR27	Sleep Talk	Normal	Status	—	—	10	Self
TR32	Crunch	Dark	Physical	80	100	15	Normal
TR36	Heat Wave	Fire	Special	95	90	10	Many Others
TR43	Overheat	Fire	Special	130	90	5	Normal
TR55	Flare Blitz	Fire	Physical	120	100	15	Normal
TR60	X-Scissor	Bug	Physical	80	100	15	Normal
TR61	Bug Buzz	Bug	Special	90	100	10	Normal
TR72	Power Whip	Grass	Physical	120	85	10	Normal
TR84	Scald	Water	Special	80	100	15	Normal
TR88	Heat Crash	Fire	Physical	—	100	10	Normal

Centiskorch p. 77

ABILITY
Flash Fire
White Smoke

HIDDEN ABILITY
Flame Body

SPECIES STRENGTHS
HP
ATTACK
DEFENSE
SP. ATK
SP. DEF
SPEED

DAMAGE TAKEN IN BATTLE
×1 ×0.5 ×4
×1 ×1 ×1
×2 ×1 ×1
×0.25 ×2 ×1
×1 ×0.5
×0.5 ×0.5 ×0.5

BUG

---

161 — Rolycoly

LEVEL-UP MOVES

LV.	NAME	TYPE	KIND	POW.	ACC.	PP	RANGE
1	Smokescreen	Normal	Status	—	100	20	Normal
1	Tackle	Normal	Physical	40	100	35	Normal
5	Rapid Spin	Normal	Physical	50	100	40	Normal
10	Smack Down	Rock	Physical	50	100	15	Normal
15	Rock Polish	Rock	Status	—	—	20	Self
20	Ancient Power	Rock	Special	60	100	5	Normal
25	Incinerate	Fire	Special	60	100	15	Many Others
30	Stealth Rock	Rock	Status	—	—	20	Other Side
35	Heat Crash	Fire	Physical	—	100	10	Normal
40	Rock Blast	Rock	Physical	25	90	10	Normal

EVOLUTION MOVES

NAME	TYPE	KIND	POW.	ACC.	PP	RANGE

EGG MOVES

NAME	TYPE	KIND	POW.	ACC.	PP	RANGE
Block	Normal	Status	—	—	5	Normal
Explosion	Normal	Physical	250	100	5	All Others
Mud-Slap	Ground	Special	20	100	10	Normal

TUTOR MOVES

NAME	TYPE	KIND	POW.	ACC.	PP	RANGE

TM MOVES

NO.	NAME	TYPE	KIND	POW.	ACC.	PP	RANGE
TM15	Dig	Ground	Physical	80	100	10	Normal
TM18	Reflect	Psychic	Status	—	—	20	Your Side
TM20	Self-Destruct	Normal	Physical	200	100	5	All Others
TM21	Rest	Psychic	Status	—	—	10	Self
TM22	Rock Slide	Rock	Physical	75	90	10	Many Others
TM24	Snore	Normal	Special	50	100	15	Normal
TM25	Protect	Normal	Status	—	—	10	Self
TM31	Attract	Normal	Status	—	100	15	Normal
TM32	Sandstorm	Rock	Status	—	—	10	Both Sides
TM38	Will-O-Wisp	Fire	Status	—	85	15	Normal
TM39	Facade	Normal	Physical	70	100	20	Normal
TM48	Rock Tomb	Rock	Physical	60	95	15	Normal
TM49	Sand Tomb	Ground	Physical	35	85	15	Normal
TM54	Rock Blast	Rock	Physical	25	90	10	Normal
TM76	Round	Normal	Special	60	100	15	Normal

TR MOVES

NO.	NAME	TYPE	KIND	POW.	ACC.	PP	RANGE
TR20	Substitute	Normal	Status	—	—	10	Self
TR23	Spikes	Ground	Status	—	—	20	Other Side
TR26	Endure	Normal	Status	—	—	10	Self
TR27	Sleep Talk	Normal	Status	—	—	10	Self
TR46	Iron Defense	Steel	Status	—	—	15	Self
TR52	Gyro Ball	Steel	Physical	—	100	5	Normal
TR74	Iron Head	Steel	Physical	80	100	15	Normal
TR75	Stone Edge	Rock	Physical	100	80	5	Normal
TR76	Stealth Rock	Rock	Status	—	—	20	Other Side
TR88	Heat Crash	Fire	Physical	—	100	10	Normal

Rolycoly p. 78

ABILITY
Steam Engine
Heatproof

HIDDEN ABILITY
Flash Fire

SPECIES STRENGTHS
HP
ATTACK
DEFENSE
SP. ATK
SP. DEF
SPEED

DAMAGE TAKEN IN BATTLE
×0.5 ×2 ×1
×0.5 ×0.5 ×1
×2 ×2 ×1
×2 ×0.5 ×1
×1 ×1 ×2
×1 ×1 ×1

MINERAL

162 Carkol
p. 78

ABILITY
Steam Engine
Flame Body

HIDDEN ABILITY
Flash Fire

SPECIES STRENGTHS
HP
ATTACK
DEFENSE
SP. ATK
SP. DEF
SPEED

DAMAGE TAKEN IN BATTLE

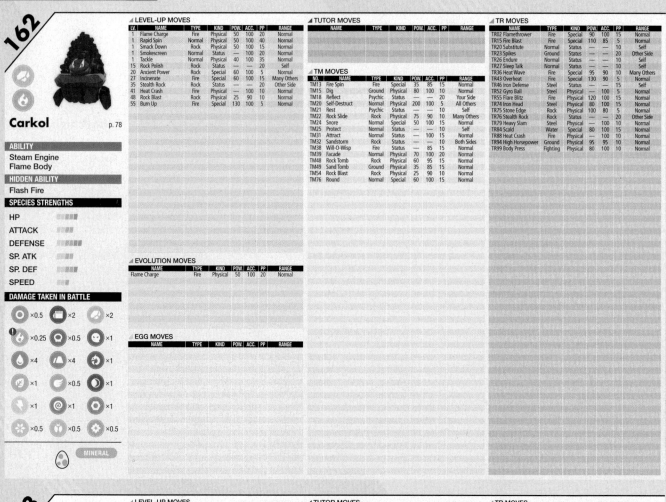

×0.5 ×2 ×2
×0.25 ×0.5 ×1
×4 ×4 ×1
×1 ×0.5 ×1
×1 ×1 ×1
×0.5 ×0.5 ×0.5

MINERAL

LEVEL-UP MOVES

LV.	NAME	TYPE	KIND	POW.	ACC.	PP	RANGE
1	Flame Charge	Fire	Physical	50	100	20	Normal
1	Rapid Spin	Normal	Physical	50	100	40	Normal
1	Smack Down	Rock	Physical	50	100	15	Normal
1	Smokescreen	Normal	Status	—	100	20	Normal
1	Tackle	Normal	Physical	40	100	35	Normal
15	Rock Polish	Rock	Status	—	—	20	Self
20	Ancient Power	Rock	Special	60	100	5	Normal
27	Incinerate	Fire	Special	60	100	15	Many Others
35	Stealth Rock	Rock	Status	—	—	20	Other Side
41	Heat Crash	Fire	Physical	—	100	10	Normal
48	Rock Blast	Rock	Physical	25	90	10	Normal
55	Burn Up	Fire	Special	130	100	5	Normal

EVOLUTION MOVES

NAME	TYPE	KIND	POW.	ACC.	PP	RANGE
Flame Charge	Fire	Physical	50	100	20	Normal

EGG MOVES

NAME	TYPE	KIND	POW.	ACC.	PP	RANGE

TUTOR MOVES

NAME	TYPE	KIND	POW.	ACC.	PP	RANGE

TM MOVES

NO.	NAME	TYPE	KIND	POW.	ACC.	PP	RANGE
TM13	Fire Spin	Fire	Special	35	85	15	Normal
TM15	Dig	Ground	Physical	80	100	10	Normal
TM18	Reflect	Psychic	Status	—	—	20	Your Side
TM20	Self-Destruct	Normal	Physical	200	100	5	All Others
TM21	Rest	Psychic	Status	—	—	10	Self
TM22	Rock Slide	Rock	Physical	75	90	10	Many Others
TM24	Snore	Normal	Special	50	100	15	Normal
TM25	Protect	Normal	Status	—	—	10	Self
TM31	Attract	Normal	Status	—	100	15	Normal
TM32	Sandstorm	Rock	Status	—	—	10	Both Sides
TM38	Will-O-Wisp	Fire	Status	—	85	15	Normal
TM39	Facade	Normal	Physical	70	100	20	Normal
TM48	Rock Tomb	Rock	Physical	60	95	15	Normal
TM49	Sand Tomb	Ground	Physical	35	85	15	Normal
TM54	Rock Blast	Rock	Physical	25	90	10	Normal
TM76	Round	Normal	Special	60	100	15	Normal

TR MOVES

NO.	NAME	TYPE	KIND	POW.	ACC.	PP	RANGE
TR02	Flamethrower	Fire	Special	90	100	15	Normal
TR15	Fire Blast	Fire	Special	110	85	5	Normal
TR20	Substitute	Normal	Status	—	—	10	Self
TR23	Spikes	Ground	Status	—	—	20	Other Side
TR26	Endure	Normal	Status	—	—	10	Self
TR27	Sleep Talk	Normal	Status	—	—	10	Self
TR43	Heat Wave	Fire	Special	95	90	10	Many Others
TR43	Overheat	Fire	Special	130	90	5	Normal
TR52	Gyro Ball	Steel	Physical	—	100	5	Normal
TR55	Flare Blitz	Fire	Physical	120	100	15	Normal
TR74	Iron Head	Steel	Physical	80	100	15	Normal
TR75	Stone Edge	Rock	Physical	100	80	5	Normal
TR76	Stealth Rock	Rock	Status	—	—	20	Other Side
TR79	Heavy Slam	Steel	Physical	—	100	10	Normal
TR84	Scald	Water	Special	80	100	15	Normal
TR88	Heat Crash	Fire	Physical	—	100	10	Normal
TR94	High Horsepower	Ground	Physical	95	95	10	Normal
TR99	Body Press	Fighting	Physical	80	100	10	Normal

163 Coalossal
p. 78

ABILITY
Steam Engine
Flame Body

HIDDEN ABILITY
Flash Fire

SPECIES STRENGTHS
HP
ATTACK
DEFENSE
SP. ATK
SP. DEF
SPEED

DAMAGE TAKEN IN BATTLE

×0.5 ×2 ×2
×0.25 ×0.5 ×1
×4 ×4 ×1
×1 ×0.5 ×1
×1 ×1 ×1
×0.5 ×0.5 ×0.5

MINERAL

LEVEL-UP MOVES

LV.	NAME	TYPE	KIND	POW.	ACC.	PP	RANGE
1	Flame Charge	Fire	Physical	50	100	20	Normal
1	Rapid Spin	Normal	Physical	50	100	40	Normal
1	Smack Down	Rock	Physical	50	100	15	Normal
1	Smokescreen	Normal	Status	—	100	20	Normal
1	Tackle	Normal	Physical	40	100	35	Normal
1	Tar Shot	Rock	Status	—	100	15	Normal
15	Rock Polish	Rock	Status	—	—	20	Self
20	Ancient Power	Rock	Special	60	100	5	Normal
27	Incinerate	Fire	Special	60	100	15	Many Others
37	Stealth Rock	Rock	Status	—	—	20	Other Side
45	Heat Crash	Fire	Physical	—	100	10	Normal
54	Rock Blast	Rock	Physical	25	90	10	Normal
63	Burn Up	Fire	Special	130	100	5	Normal

EVOLUTION MOVES

NAME	TYPE	KIND	POW.	ACC.	PP	RANGE
Tar Shot	Rock	Status	—	100	15	Normal

EGG MOVES

NAME	TYPE	KIND	POW.	ACC.	PP	RANGE

TUTOR MOVES

NAME	TYPE	KIND	POW.	ACC.	PP	RANGE

TM MOVES

NO.	NAME	TYPE	KIND	POW.	ACC.	PP	RANGE
TM00	Mega Punch	Normal	Physical	80	85	20	Normal
TM01	Mega Kick	Normal	Physical	120	75	5	Normal
TM03	Fire Punch	Fire	Physical	75	100	15	Normal
TM08	Hyper Beam	Normal	Special	150	90	5	Normal
TM09	Giga Impact	Normal	Physical	150	90	5	Normal
TM11	Solar Beam	Grass	Special	120	100	10	Normal
TM13	Fire Spin	Fire	Special	35	85	15	Normal
TM15	Dig	Ground	Physical	80	100	10	Normal
TM18	Reflect	Psychic	Status	—	—	20	Your Side
TM20	Self-Destruct	Normal	Physical	200	100	5	All Others
TM21	Rest	Psychic	Status	—	—	10	Self
TM22	Rock Slide	Rock	Physical	75	90	10	Many Others
TM24	Snore	Normal	Special	50	100	15	Normal
TM25	Protect	Normal	Status	—	—	10	Self
TM31	Attract	Normal	Status	—	100	15	Normal
TM32	Sandstorm	Rock	Status	—	—	10	Both Sides
TM38	Will-O-Wisp	Fire	Status	—	85	15	Normal
TM39	Facade	Normal	Physical	70	100	20	Normal
TM48	Rock Tomb	Rock	Physical	60	95	15	Normal
TM49	Sand Tomb	Ground	Physical	35	85	15	Normal
TM54	Rock Blast	Rock	Physical	25	90	10	Normal
TM76	Round	Normal	Special	60	100	15	Normal
TM81	Bulldoze	Ground	Physical	60	100	20	All Others

TR MOVES

NO.	NAME	TYPE	KIND	POW.	ACC.	PP	RANGE
TR01	Body Slam	Normal	Physical	85	100	15	Normal
TR02	Flamethrower	Fire	Special	90	100	15	Normal
TR10	Earthquake	Ground	Physical	100	100	10	All Others
TR15	Fire Blast	Fire	Special	110	85	5	Normal
TR20	Substitute	Normal	Status	—	—	10	Self
TR23	Spikes	Ground	Status	—	—	20	Other Side
TR26	Endure	Normal	Status	—	—	10	Self
TR27	Sleep Talk	Normal	Status	—	—	10	Self
TR36	Heat Wave	Fire	Special	95	90	10	Many Others
TR43	Overheat	Fire	Special	130	90	5	Normal
TR46	Iron Defense	Steel	Status	—	—	15	Self
TR52	Gyro Ball	Steel	Physical	—	100	5	Normal
TR55	Flare Blitz	Fire	Physical	120	100	15	Normal
TR67	Earth Power	Ground	Special	90	100	10	Normal
TR74	Iron Head	Steel	Physical	80	100	15	Normal
TR75	Stone Edge	Rock	Physical	100	80	5	Normal
TR76	Stealth Rock	Rock	Status	—	—	20	Other Side
TR79	Heavy Slam	Steel	Physical	—	100	10	Normal
TR84	Scald	Water	Special	80	100	15	Normal
TR88	Heat Crash	Fire	Physical	—	100	10	Normal
TR94	High Horsepower	Ground	Physical	95	95	10	Normal
TR99	Body Press	Fighting	Physical	80	100	10	Normal

164

Diglett — p. 79

LEVEL-UP MOVES

LV.	NAME	TYPE	KIND	POW.	ACC.	PP	RANGE
1	Sand Attack	Ground	Status	—	100	15	Normal
1	Scratch	Normal	Physical	40	100	35	Normal
4	Growl	Normal	Status	—	100	40	Many Others
8	Astonish	Ghost	Physical	30	100	15	Normal
12	Mud-Slap	Ground	Special	20	100	10	Normal
16	Bulldoze	Ground	Physical	60	100	20	All Others
20	Sucker Punch	Dark	Physical	70	100	5	Normal
24	Slash	Normal	Physical	70	100	20	Normal
28	Sandstorm	Rock	Status	—	—	10	Both Sides
32	Dig	Ground	Physical	80	100	10	Normal
36	Earth Power	Ground	Special	90	100	10	Normal
40	Earthquake	Ground	Physical	100	100	10	All Others
44	Fissure	Ground	Physical	—	30	5	Normal

EVOLUTION MOVES

NAME	TYPE	KIND	POW.	ACC.	PP	RANGE

EGG MOVES

NAME	TYPE	KIND	POW.	ACC.	PP	RANGE
Ancient Power	Rock	Special	60	100	5	Normal
Final Gambit	Fighting	Special	—	100	5	Normal
Headbutt	Normal	Physical	70	100	15	Normal
Hone Claws	Dark	Status	—	—	15	Self
Memento	Dark	Status	—	100	10	Normal

TUTOR MOVES

NAME	TYPE	KIND	POW.	ACC.	PP	RANGE

TM MOVES

NO.	NAME	TYPE	KIND	POW.	ACC.	PP	RANGE
TM15	Dig	Ground	Physical	80	100	10	Normal
TM16	Screech	Normal	Status	—	85	40	Normal
TM21	Rest	Psychic	Status	—	—	10	Self
TM22	Rock Slide	Rock	Physical	75	90	10	Many Others
TM23	Thief	Dark	Physical	60	100	25	Normal
TM24	Snore	Normal	Special	50	100	15	Normal
TM25	Protect	Normal	Status	—	—	10	Self
TM31	Attract	Normal	Status	—	100	15	Normal
TM32	Sandstorm	Rock	Status	—	—	10	Both Sides
TM34	Sunny Day	Fire	Status	—	—	5	Both Sides
TM37	Beat Up	Dark	Physical	—	100	10	Normal
TM39	Facade	Normal	Physical	70	100	20	Normal
TM48	Rock Tomb	Rock	Physical	60	95	15	Normal
TM58	Assurance	Dark	Physical	60	100	10	Normal
TM65	Shadow Claw	Ghost	Physical	70	100	15	Normal
TM76	Round	Normal	Special	60	100	15	Normal
TM81	Bulldoze	Ground	Physical	60	100	20	All Others
TM98	Stomping Tantrum	Ground	Physical	75	100	10	Normal

TR MOVES

NAME	TYPE	KIND	POW.	ACC.	PP	RANGE
TR01 Body Slam	Normal	Physical	85	100	15	Normal
TR10 Earthquake	Ground	Physical	100	100	10	All Others
TR12 Agility	Psychic	Status	—	—	30	Self
TR20 Substitute	Normal	Status	—	—	10	Self
TR21 Reversal	Fighting	Physical	—	100	15	Normal
TR22 Sludge Bomb	Poison	Special	90	100	10	Normal
TR26 Endure	Normal	Status	—	—	10	Self
TR27 Sleep Talk	Normal	Status	—	—	10	Self
TR35 Uproar	Normal	Special	90	100	10	1 Random
TR67 Earth Power	Ground	Special	90	100	10	Normal
TR76 Stealth Rock	Rock	Status	—	—	20	Other Side
TR83 Ally Switch	Psychic	Status	—	—	15	Self
TR85 Work Up	Normal	Status	—	—	30	Self

ABILITY: Sand Veil / Arena Trap
HIDDEN ABILITY: Sand Force

SPECIES STRENGTHS: HP, ATTACK, DEFENSE, SP. ATK, SP. DEF, SPEED

DAMAGE TAKEN IN BATTLE: ×1, ×1, ×0.5, ×1, ×0.5, ×1, ×2, ×1, ×1, ×2, ×1, ×1, ×0, ×1, ×1, ×2, ×1, ×1

FIELD

165

Dugtrio — p. 79

LEVEL-UP MOVES

LV.	NAME	TYPE	KIND	POW.	ACC.	PP	RANGE
1	Astonish	Ghost	Physical	30	100	15	Normal
1	Growl	Normal	Status	—	100	40	Many Others
1	Night Slash	Dark	Physical	70	100	15	Normal
1	Sand Attack	Ground	Status	—	100	15	Normal
1	Sand Tomb	Ground	Physical	35	85	15	Normal
1	Scratch	Normal	Physical	40	100	35	Normal
1	Tri Attack	Normal	Special	80	100	10	Normal
12	Mud-Slap	Ground	Special	20	100	10	Normal
16	Bulldoze	Ground	Physical	60	100	20	All Others
20	Sucker Punch	Dark	Physical	70	100	5	Normal
24	Slash	Normal	Physical	70	100	20	Normal
30	Sandstorm	Rock	Status	—	—	10	Both Sides
36	Dig	Ground	Physical	80	100	10	Normal
42	Earth Power	Ground	Special	90	100	10	Normal
48	Earthquake	Ground	Physical	100	100	10	All Others
54	Fissure	Ground	Physical	—	30	5	Normal

EVOLUTION MOVES

NAME	TYPE	KIND	POW.	ACC.	PP	RANGE
Sand Tomb	Ground	Physical	35	85	15	Normal

EGG MOVES

NAME	TYPE	KIND	POW.	ACC.	PP	RANGE

TUTOR MOVES

NAME	TYPE	KIND	POW.	ACC.	PP	RANGE

TM MOVES

NO.	NAME	TYPE	KIND	POW.	ACC.	PP	RANGE
TM08	Hyper Beam	Normal	Special	150	90	5	Normal
TM09	Giga Impact	Normal	Physical	150	90	5	Normal
TM15	Dig	Ground	Physical	80	100	10	Normal
TM16	Screech	Normal	Status	—	85	40	Normal
TM21	Rest	Psychic	Status	—	—	10	Self
TM22	Rock Slide	Rock	Physical	75	90	10	Many Others
TM23	Thief	Dark	Physical	60	100	25	Normal
TM24	Snore	Normal	Special	50	100	15	Normal
TM25	Protect	Normal	Status	—	—	10	Self
TM31	Attract	Normal	Status	—	100	15	Normal
TM32	Sandstorm	Rock	Status	—	—	10	Both Sides
TM34	Sunny Day	Fire	Status	—	—	5	Both Sides
TM37	Beat Up	Dark	Physical	—	100	10	Normal
TM39	Facade	Normal	Physical	70	100	20	Normal
TM48	Rock Tomb	Rock	Physical	60	95	15	Normal
TM49	Sand Tomb	Ground	Physical	35	85	15	Normal
TM58	Assurance	Dark	Physical	60	100	10	Normal
TM65	Shadow Claw	Ghost	Physical	70	100	15	Normal
TM76	Round	Normal	Special	60	100	15	Normal
TM81	Bulldoze	Ground	Physical	60	100	20	All Others
TM98	Stomping Tantrum	Ground	Physical	75	100	10	Normal

TR MOVES

NAME	TYPE	KIND	POW.	ACC.	PP	RANGE
TR01 Body Slam	Normal	Physical	85	100	15	Normal
TR10 Earthquake	Ground	Physical	100	100	10	All Others
TR12 Agility	Psychic	Status	—	—	30	Self
TR19 Tri Attack	Normal	Special	80	100	10	Normal
TR20 Substitute	Normal	Status	—	—	10	Self
TR21 Reversal	Fighting	Physical	—	100	15	Normal
TR22 Sludge Bomb	Poison	Special	90	100	10	Normal
TR26 Endure	Normal	Status	—	—	10	Self
TR27 Sleep Talk	Normal	Status	—	—	10	Self
TR35 Uproar	Normal	Special	90	100	10	1 Random
TR67 Earth Power	Ground	Special	90	100	10	Normal
TR75 Stone Edge	Rock	Physical	100	80	5	Normal
TR76 Stealth Rock	Rock	Status	—	—	20	Other Side
TR83 Ally Switch	Psychic	Status	—	—	15	Self
TR85 Work Up	Normal	Status	—	—	30	Self
TR94 High Horsepower	Ground	Physical	95	95	10	Normal

ABILITY: Sand Veil / Arena Trap
HIDDEN ABILITY: Sand Force

SPECIES STRENGTHS: HP, ATTACK, DEFENSE, SP. ATK, SP. DEF, SPEED

DAMAGE TAKEN IN BATTLE: ×1, ×1, ×0.5, ×1, ×0.5, ×1, ×2, ×1, ×1, ×2, ×1, ×1, ×0, ×1, ×1, ×2, ×1, ×1

FIELD

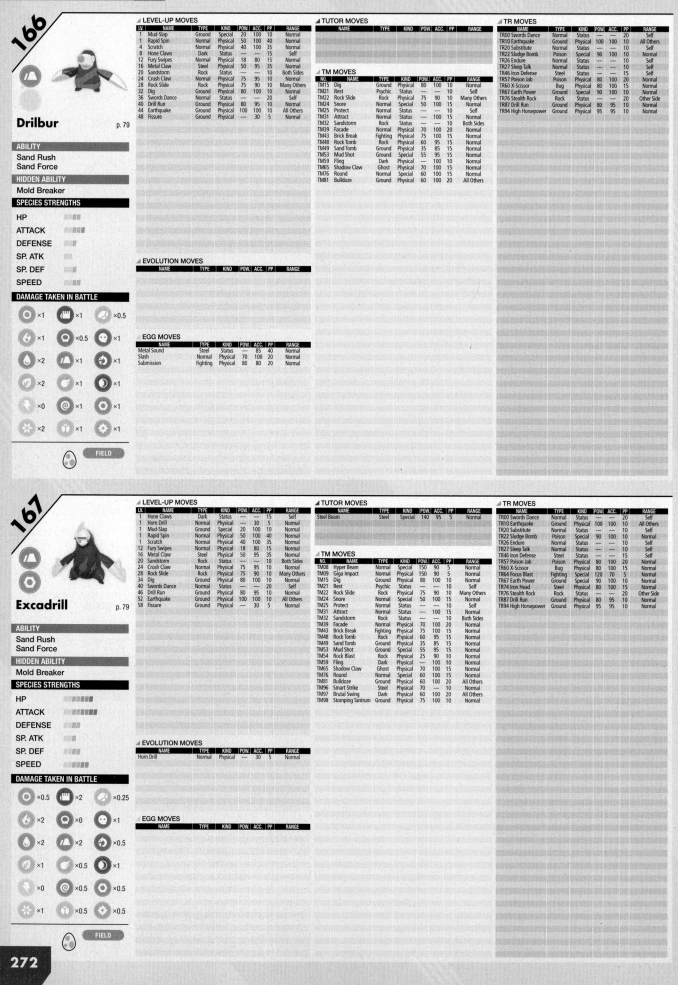

166

Drilbur
p. 79

ABILITY
Sand Rush
Sand Force

HIDDEN ABILITY
Mold Breaker

SPECIES STRENGTHS

HP
ATTACK
DEFENSE
SP. ATK
SP. DEF
SPEED

DAMAGE TAKEN IN BATTLE

×1	×1	×0.5
×1	×0.5	×1
×2	×1	×1
×2	×1	×1
×0	×1	×1
×2	×1	×1

FIELD

LEVEL-UP MOVES

LV.	NAME	TYPE	KIND	POW.	ACC.	PP	RANGE
1	Mud-Slap	Ground	Special	20	100	10	Normal
1	Rapid Spin	Normal	Physical	50	100	40	Normal
4	Scratch	Normal	Physical	40	100	35	Normal
8	Hone Claws	Dark	Status	—	—	15	Self
12	Fury Swipes	Normal	Physical	18	80	15	Normal
16	Metal Claw	Steel	Physical	50	95	35	Normal
20	Sandstorm	Rock	Status	—	—	10	Both Sides
24	Crush Claw	Normal	Physical	75	95	10	Normal
28	Rock Slide	Rock	Physical	75	90	10	Many Others
32	Dig	Ground	Physical	80	100	10	Normal
36	Swords Dance	Normal	Status	—	—	20	Self
40	Drill Run	Ground	Physical	80	95	10	Normal
44	Earthquake	Ground	Physical	100	100	10	All Others
48	Fissure	Ground	Physical	—	30	5	Normal

EVOLUTION MOVES

NAME	TYPE	KIND	POW.	ACC.	PP	RANGE

EGG MOVES

NAME	TYPE	KIND	POW.	ACC.	PP	RANGE
Metal Sound	Steel	Status	—	85	40	Normal
Slash	Normal	Physical	70	100	20	Normal
Submission	Fighting	Physical	80	80	20	Normal

TUTOR MOVES

NAME	TYPE	KIND	POW.	ACC.	PP	RANGE

TM MOVES

NO.	NAME	TYPE	KIND	POW.	ACC.	PP	RANGE
TM15	Dig	Ground	Physical	80	100	10	Normal
TM21	Rest	Psychic	Status	—	—	10	Self
TM22	Rock Slide	Rock	Physical	75	90	10	Many Others
TM24	Snore	Normal	Special	50	100	15	Normal
TM25	Protect	Normal	Status	—	—	10	Self
TM31	Attract	Normal	Status	—	100	15	Normal
TM32	Sandstorm	Rock	Status	—	—	10	Both Sides
TM39	Facade	Normal	Physical	70	100	20	Normal
TM43	Brick Break	Fighting	Physical	75	100	15	Normal
TM48	Rock Tomb	Rock	Physical	60	95	15	Normal
TM49	Sand Tomb	Ground	Physical	35	85	15	Normal
TM53	Mud Shot	Ground	Special	55	95	15	Normal
TM59	Fling	Dark	Physical	—	100	10	Normal
TM65	Shadow Claw	Ghost	Physical	70	100	15	Normal
TM76	Round	Normal	Special	60	100	15	Normal
TM81	Bulldoze	Ground	Physical	60	100	20	All Others

TR MOVES

NO.	NAME	TYPE	KIND	POW.	ACC.	PP	RANGE
TR00	Swords Dance	Normal	Status	—	—	20	Self
TR10	Earthquake	Ground	Physical	100	100	10	All Others
TR20	Substitute	Normal	Status	—	—	10	Self
TR22	Sludge Bomb	Poison	Special	90	100	10	Normal
TR26	Endure	Normal	Status	—	—	10	Self
TR27	Sleep Talk	Normal	Status	—	—	10	Self
TR46	Iron Defense	Steel	Status	—	—	15	Self
TR57	Poison Jab	Poison	Physical	80	100	20	Normal
TR60	X-Scissor	Bug	Physical	80	100	15	Normal
TR67	Earth Power	Ground	Special	90	100	10	Normal
TR76	Stealth Rock	Rock	Status	—	—	20	Other Side
TR87	Drill Run	Ground	Physical	80	95	10	Normal
TR94	High Horsepower	Ground	Physical	95	95	10	Normal

167

Excadrill
p. 79

ABILITY
Sand Rush
Sand Force

HIDDEN ABILITY
Mold Breaker

SPECIES STRENGTHS

HP
ATTACK
DEFENSE
SP. ATK
SP. DEF
SPEED

DAMAGE TAKEN IN BATTLE

×0.5	×2	×0.25
×2	×0	×1
×2	×2	×0.5
×1	×0.5	×1
×0	×0.5	×0.5
×0.5	×0.5	×0.5

FIELD

LEVEL-UP MOVES

LV.	NAME	TYPE	KIND	POW.	ACC.	PP	RANGE
1	Hone Claws	Dark	Status	—	—	15	Self
1	Horn Drill	Normal	Physical	—	30	5	Normal
1	Mud-Slap	Ground	Special	20	100	10	Normal
1	Rapid Spin	Normal	Physical	50	100	40	Normal
1	Scratch	Normal	Physical	40	100	35	Normal
1	Fury Swipes	Normal	Physical	18	80	15	Normal
16	Metal Claw	Steel	Physical	50	95	35	Normal
20	Sandstorm	Rock	Status	—	—	10	Both Sides
24	Crush Claw	Normal	Physical	75	95	10	Normal
28	Rock Slide	Rock	Physical	75	90	10	Many Others
34	Dig	Ground	Physical	80	100	10	Normal
40	Swords Dance	Normal	Status	—	—	20	Self
46	Drill Run	Ground	Physical	80	95	10	Normal
52	Earthquake	Ground	Physical	100	100	10	All Others
58	Fissure	Ground	Physical	—	30	5	Normal

EVOLUTION MOVES

NAME	TYPE	KIND	POW.	ACC.	PP	RANGE
Horn Drill	Normal	Physical	—	30	5	Normal

EGG MOVES

NAME	TYPE	KIND	POW.	ACC.	PP	RANGE

TUTOR MOVES

NAME	TYPE	KIND	POW.	ACC.	PP	RANGE
Steel Beam	Steel	Special	140	95	5	Normal

TM MOVES

NO.	NAME	TYPE	KIND	POW.	ACC.	PP	RANGE
TM08	Hyper Beam	Normal	Special	150	90	5	Normal
TM09	Giga Impact	Normal	Physical	150	90	5	Normal
TM15	Dig	Ground	Physical	80	100	10	Normal
TM21	Rest	Psychic	Status	—	—	10	Self
TM22	Rock Slide	Rock	Physical	75	90	10	Many Others
TM24	Snore	Normal	Special	50	100	15	Normal
TM25	Protect	Normal	Status	—	—	10	Self
TM31	Attract	Normal	Status	—	100	15	Normal
TM32	Sandstorm	Rock	Status	—	—	10	Both Sides
TM39	Facade	Normal	Physical	70	100	20	Normal
TM43	Brick Break	Fighting	Physical	75	100	15	Normal
TM48	Rock Tomb	Rock	Physical	60	95	15	Normal
TM49	Sand Tomb	Ground	Physical	35	85	15	Normal
TM53	Mud Shot	Ground	Special	55	95	15	Normal
TM54	Rock Blast	Rock	Physical	25	90	10	Normal
TM59	Fling	Dark	Physical	—	100	10	Normal
TM65	Shadow Claw	Ghost	Physical	70	100	15	Normal
TM76	Round	Normal	Special	60	100	15	Normal
TM81	Bulldoze	Ground	Physical	60	100	20	All Others
TM96	Smart Strike	Steel	Physical	70	—	10	Normal
TM97	Brutal Swing	Dark	Physical	60	100	20	All Others
TM98	Stomping Tantrum	Ground	Physical	75	100	10	Normal

TR MOVES

NO.	NAME	TYPE	KIND	POW.	ACC.	PP	RANGE
TR00	Swords Dance	Normal	Status	—	—	20	Self
TR10	Earthquake	Ground	Physical	100	100	10	All Others
TR20	Substitute	Normal	Status	—	—	10	Self
TR22	Sludge Bomb	Poison	Special	90	100	10	Normal
TR26	Endure	Normal	Status	—	—	10	Self
TR46	Iron Defense	Steel	Status	—	—	15	Self
TR57	Poison Jab	Poison	Physical	80	100	20	Normal
TR60	X-Scissor	Bug	Physical	80	100	15	Normal
TR64	Focus Blast	Fighting	Special	120	70	5	Normal
TR67	Earth Power	Ground	Special	90	100	10	Normal
TR74	Iron Head	Steel	Physical	80	100	15	Normal
TR76	Stealth Rock	Rock	Status	—	—	20	Other Side
TR87	Drill Run	Ground	Physical	80	95	10	Normal
TR94	High Horsepower	Ground	Physical	95	95	10	Normal

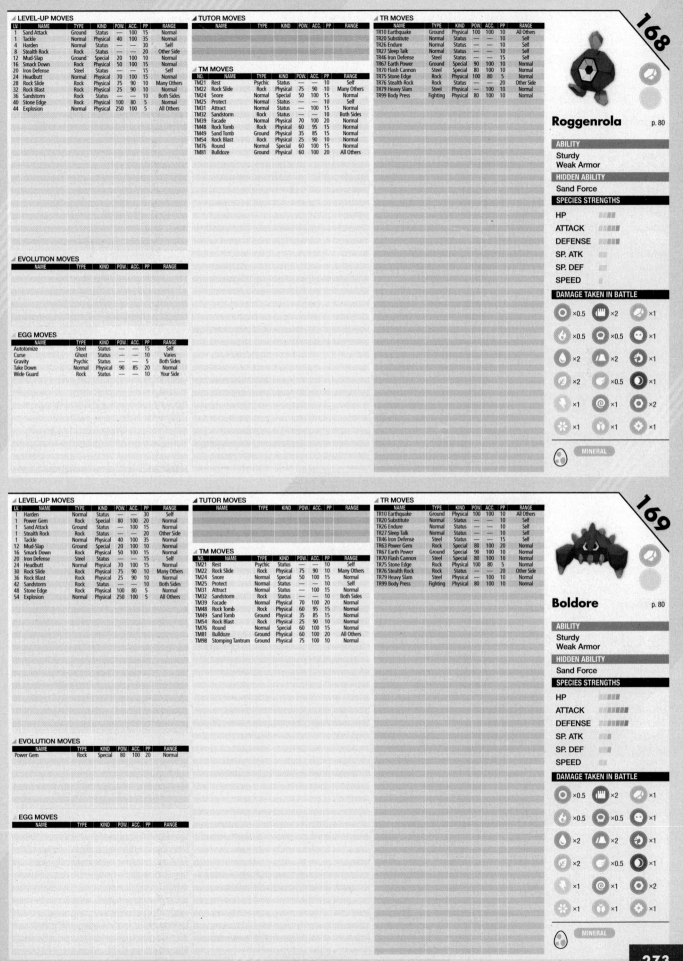

168 — Roggenrola (p. 80)

LEVEL-UP MOVES

LV.	NAME	TYPE	KIND	POW.	ACC.	PP	RANGE
1	Sand Attack	Ground	Status	—	100	15	Normal
1	Tackle	Normal	Physical	40	100	35	Normal
4	Harden	Normal	Status	—	—	30	Self
8	Stealth Rock	Rock	Status	—	—	20	Other Side
12	Mud-Slap	Ground	Special	20	100	10	Normal
16	Smack Down	Rock	Physical	50	100	15	Normal
20	Iron Defense	Steel	Status	—	—	15	Self
24	Headbutt	Normal	Physical	70	100	15	Normal
28	Rock Slide	Rock	Physical	75	90	10	Many Others
32	Rock Blast	Rock	Physical	25	90	10	Normal
36	Sandstorm	Rock	Status	—	—	10	Both Sides
40	Stone Edge	Rock	Physical	100	80	5	Normal
44	Explosion	Normal	Physical	250	100	5	All Others

EVOLUTION MOVES

EGG MOVES

NAME	TYPE	KIND	POW.	ACC.	PP	RANGE
Autotomize	Steel	Status	—	—	15	Self
Curse	Ghost	Status	—	—	10	Varies
Gravity	Psychic	Status	—	—	5	Both Sides
Take Down	Normal	Physical	90	85	20	Normal
Wide Guard	Rock	Status	—	—	10	Your Side

TUTOR MOVES

TM MOVES

NO.	NAME	TYPE	KIND	POW.	ACC.	PP	RANGE
TM21	Rest	Psychic	Status	—	—	10	Self
TM22	Rock Slide	Rock	Physical	75	90	10	Many Others
TM24	Snore	Normal	Special	50	100	15	Normal
TM25	Protect	Normal	Status	—	—	10	Self
TM31	Attract	Normal	Status	—	100	15	Normal
TM32	Sandstorm	Rock	Status	—	—	10	Both Sides
TM39	Facade	Normal	Physical	70	100	20	Normal
TM48	Rock Tomb	Rock	Physical	60	95	15	Normal
TM49	Sand Tomb	Ground	Physical	35	85	15	Normal
TM54	Rock Blast	Rock	Physical	25	90	10	Normal
TM76	Round	Normal	Special	60	100	15	Normal
TM81	Bulldoze	Ground	Physical	60	100	20	All Others

TR MOVES

NO.	NAME	TYPE	KIND	POW.	ACC.	PP	RANGE
TR10	Earthquake	Ground	Physical	100	100	10	All Others
TR20	Substitute	Normal	Status	—	—	10	Self
TR26	Endure	Normal	Status	—	—	10	Self
TR27	Sleep Talk	Normal	Status	—	—	10	Self
TR46	Iron Defense	Steel	Status	—	—	15	Self
TR67	Earth Power	Ground	Special	90	100	10	Normal
TR70	Flash Cannon	Steel	Special	80	100	10	Normal
TR75	Stone Edge	Rock	Physical	100	80	5	Normal
TR76	Stealth Rock	Rock	Status	—	—	20	Other Side
TR79	Heavy Slam	Steel	Physical	—	100	10	Normal
TR99	Body Press	Fighting	Physical	80	100	10	Normal

Roggenrola p. 80

ABILITY
Sturdy
Weak Armor

HIDDEN ABILITY
Sand Force

SPECIES STRENGTHS
- HP
- ATTACK
- DEFENSE
- SP. ATK
- SP. DEF
- SPEED

DAMAGE TAKEN IN BATTLE
×0.5 | ×2 | ×1
×0.5 | ×0.5 | ×1
×2 | ×2 | ×1
×2 | ×0.5 | ×1
×1 | ×1 | ×2
×1 | ×1 | ×1

MINERAL

---

169 — Boldore (p. 80)

LEVEL-UP MOVES

LV.	NAME	TYPE	KIND	POW.	ACC.	PP	RANGE
1	Harden	Normal	Status	—	—	30	Self
1	Power Gem	Rock	Special	80	100	20	Normal
1	Sand Attack	Ground	Status	—	100	15	Normal
1	Stealth Rock	Rock	Status	—	—	20	Other Side
1	Tackle	Normal	Physical	40	100	35	Normal
12	Mud-Slap	Ground	Special	20	100	10	Normal
16	Smack Down	Rock	Physical	50	100	15	Normal
20	Iron Defense	Steel	Status	—	—	15	Self
24	Headbutt	Normal	Physical	70	100	15	Normal
30	Rock Slide	Rock	Physical	75	90	10	Many Others
36	Rock Blast	Rock	Physical	25	90	10	Normal
42	Sandstorm	Rock	Status	—	—	10	Both Sides
48	Stone Edge	Rock	Physical	100	80	5	Normal
54	Explosion	Normal	Physical	250	100	5	All Others

EVOLUTION MOVES

NAME	TYPE	KIND	POW.	ACC.	PP	RANGE
Power Gem	Rock	Special	80	100	20	Normal

EGG MOVES

TUTOR MOVES

TM MOVES

NO.	NAME	TYPE	KIND	POW.	ACC.	PP	RANGE
TM21	Rest	Psychic	Status	—	—	10	Self
TM22	Rock Slide	Rock	Physical	75	90	10	Many Others
TM24	Snore	Normal	Special	50	100	15	Normal
TM25	Protect	Normal	Status	—	—	10	Self
TM31	Attract	Normal	Status	—	100	15	Normal
TM32	Sandstorm	Rock	Status	—	—	10	Both Sides
TM39	Facade	Normal	Physical	70	100	20	Normal
TM48	Rock Tomb	Rock	Physical	60	95	15	Normal
TM49	Sand Tomb	Ground	Physical	35	85	15	Normal
TM54	Rock Blast	Rock	Physical	25	90	10	Normal
TM76	Round	Normal	Special	60	100	15	Normal
TM81	Bulldoze	Ground	Physical	60	100	20	All Others
TM98	Stomping Tantrum	Ground	Physical	75	100	10	Normal

TR MOVES

NO.	NAME	TYPE	KIND	POW.	ACC.	PP	RANGE
TR10	Earthquake	Ground	Physical	100	100	10	All Others
TR20	Substitute	Normal	Status	—	—	10	Self
TR26	Endure	Normal	Status	—	—	10	Self
TR27	Sleep Talk	Normal	Status	—	—	10	Self
TR46	Iron Defense	Steel	Status	—	—	15	Self
TR63	Power Gem	Rock	Special	80	100	20	Normal
TR67	Earth Power	Ground	Special	90	100	10	Normal
TR70	Flash Cannon	Steel	Special	80	100	10	Normal
TR75	Stone Edge	Rock	Physical	100	80	5	Normal
TR76	Stealth Rock	Rock	Status	—	—	20	Other Side
TR79	Heavy Slam	Steel	Physical	—	100	10	Normal
TR99	Body Press	Fighting	Physical	80	100	10	Normal

Boldore p. 80

ABILITY
Sturdy
Weak Armor

HIDDEN ABILITY
Sand Force

SPECIES STRENGTHS
- HP
- ATTACK
- DEFENSE
- SP. ATK
- SP. DEF
- SPEED

DAMAGE TAKEN IN BATTLE
×0.5 | ×2 | ×1
×0.5 | ×0.5 | ×1
×2 | ×2 | ×1
×2 | ×0.5 | ×1
×1 | ×1 | ×2
×1 | ×1 | ×1

MINERAL

170

Gigalith
p. 80

ABILITY
Sturdy
Sand Stream

HIDDEN ABILITY
Sand Force

SPECIES STRENGTHS

HP	
ATTACK	
DEFENSE	
SP. ATK	
SP. DEF	
SPEED	

DAMAGE TAKEN IN BATTLE

×0.5 | ×2 | ×1
×0.5 | ×0.5 | ×1
×2 | ×2 | ×1
×2 | ×0.5 | ×1
×1 | ×1 | ×2
×1 | ×1 | ×1

MINERAL

LEVEL-UP MOVES

LV.	NAME	TYPE	KIND	POW.	ACC.	PP	RANGE
1	Harden	Normal	Status	—	—	30	Self
1	Power Gem	Rock	Special	80	100	20	Normal
1	Sand Attack	Ground	Status	—	100	15	Normal
1	Stealth Rock	Rock	Status	—	—	20	Other Side
1	Tackle	Normal	Physical	40	100	35	Normal
12	Mud-Slap	Ground	Special	20	100	10	Normal
16	Smack Down	Rock	Physical	50	100	15	Normal
20	Iron Defense	Steel	Status	—	—	15	Self
24	Headbutt	Normal	Physical	70	100	15	Normal
30	Rock Slide	Rock	Physical	75	90	10	Many Others
36	Rock Blast	Rock	Physical	25	90	10	Normal
42	Sandstorm	Rock	Status	—	—	10	Both Sides
48	Stone Edge	Rock	Physical	100	80	5	Normal
54	Explosion	Normal	Physical	250	100	5	All Others

EVOLUTION MOVES

NAME	TYPE	KIND	POW.	ACC.	PP	RANGE

EGG MOVES

NAME	TYPE	KIND	POW.	ACC.	PP	RANGE

TUTOR MOVES

NAME	TYPE	KIND	POW.	ACC.	PP	RANGE

TM MOVES

NO.	NAME	TYPE	KIND	POW.	ACC.	PP	RANGE
TM08	Hyper Beam	Normal	Special	150	90	5	Normal
TM09	Giga Impact	Normal	Physical	150	90	5	Normal
TM11	Solar Beam	Grass	Special	120	100	10	Normal
TM20	Self-Destruct	Normal	Physical	200	100	5	All Others
TM21	Rest	Psychic	Status	—	—	10	Self
TM22	Rock Slide	Rock	Physical	75	90	10	Many Others
TM24	Snore	Normal	Special	50	100	15	Normal
TM25	Protect	Normal	Status	—	—	10	Self
TM31	Attract	Normal	Status	—	100	15	Normal
TM32	Sandstorm	Rock	Status	—	—	10	Both Sides
TM39	Facade	Normal	Physical	70	100	20	Normal
TM46	Weather Ball*	Normal	Special	50	100	10	Normal
TM48	Rock Tomb	Rock	Physical	60	95	15	Normal
TM49	Sand Tomb	Ground	Physical	35	85	15	Normal
TM54	Rock Blast	Rock	Physical	25	90	10	Normal
TM76	Round	Normal	Special	60	100	15	Normal
TM81	Bulldoze	Ground	Physical	60	100	20	All Others
TM98	Stomping Tantrum	Ground	Physical	75	100	10	Normal

TR MOVES

NAME	TYPE	KIND	POW.	ACC.	PP	RANGE
TR10 Earthquake	Ground	Physical	100	100	10	All Others
TR20 Substitute	Normal	Status	—	—	10	Self
TR26 Endure	Normal	Status	—	—	10	Self
TR27 Sleep Talk	Normal	Status	—	—	10	Self
TR39 Superpower	Fighting	Physical	120	100	5	Normal
TR46 Iron Defense	Steel	Status	—	—	15	Self
TR63 Power Gem	Rock	Special	80	100	20	Normal
TR67 Earth Power	Ground	Special	90	100	10	Normal
TR70 Flash Cannon	Steel	Special	80	100	10	Normal
TR74 Iron Head	Steel	Physical	80	100	15	Normal
TR75 Stone Edge	Rock	Physical	100	80	5	Normal
TR76 Stealth Rock	Rock	Status	—	—	20	Other Side
TR79 Heavy Slam	Steel	Physical	—	100	10	Normal
TR95 Throat Chop	Dark	Physical	80	100	15	Normal
TR99 Body Press	Fighting	Physical	80	100	10	Normal

*Weather Ball changes type depending on weather condition. (Harsh sunlight: Fire type. Rain: Water type. Hail: Ice type. Sandstorm: Rock type.)

171

Timburr
p. 81

ABILITY
Guts
Sheer Force

HIDDEN ABILITY
Iron Fist

SPECIES STRENGTHS

HP	
ATTACK	
DEFENSE	
SP. ATK	
SP. DEF	
SPEED	

DAMAGE TAKEN IN BATTLE

×1 | ×1 | ×0.5
×1 | ×1 | ×1
×1 | ×1 | ×1
×1 | ×2 | ×0.5
×1 | ×2 | ×1
×1 | ×0.5 | ×2

HUMANLIKE

LEVEL-UP MOVES

LV.	NAME	TYPE	KIND	POW.	ACC.	PP	RANGE
1	Leer	Normal	Status	—	100	30	Many Others
1	Pound	Normal	Physical	40	100	35	Normal
4	Low Kick	Fighting	Physical	—	100	20	Normal
8	Rock Throw	Rock	Physical	50	90	15	Normal
12	Focus Energy	Normal	Status	—	—	30	Self
16	Bulk Up	Fighting	Status	—	—	20	Self
20	Rock Slide	Rock	Physical	75	90	10	Many Others
24	Slam	Normal	Physical	80	75	20	Normal
28	Scary Face	Normal	Status	—	100	10	Normal
32	Dynamic Punch	Fighting	Physical	100	50	5	Normal
36	Hammer Arm	Fighting	Physical	100	90	10	Normal
40	Stone Edge	Rock	Physical	100	80	5	Normal
44	Superpower	Fighting	Physical	120	100	5	Normal
48	Focus Punch	Fighting	Physical	150	100	20	Normal

EVOLUTION MOVES

NAME	TYPE	KIND	POW.	ACC.	PP	RANGE

EGG MOVES

NAME	TYPE	KIND	POW.	ACC.	PP	RANGE
Counter	Fighting	Physical	—	100	20	Varies
Defog	Flying	Status	—	—	15	Normal
Detect	Fighting	Status	—	—	5	Self
Mach Punch	Fighting	Physical	40	100	30	Normal
Power-Up Punch	Fighting	Physical	40	100	20	Normal
Wide Guard	Rock	Status	—	—	10	Your Side

TUTOR MOVES

NAME	TYPE	KIND	POW.	ACC.	PP	RANGE

TM MOVES

NO.	NAME	TYPE	KIND	POW.	ACC.	PP	RANGE
TM00	Mega Punch	Normal	Physical	80	85	20	Normal
TM01	Mega Kick	Normal	Physical	120	75	5	Normal
TM02	Fire Punch	Fire	Physical	75	100	15	Normal
TM04	Ice Punch	Ice	Physical	75	100	15	Normal
TM05	Thunder Punch	Electric	Physical	75	100	15	Normal
TM15	Dig	Ground	Physical	80	100	10	Normal
TM21	Rest	Psychic	Status	—	—	10	Self
TM22	Rock Slide	Rock	Physical	75	90	10	Many Others
TM24	Snore	Normal	Special	50	100	15	Normal
TM25	Protect	Normal	Status	—	—	10	Self
TM26	Scary Face	Normal	Status	—	100	10	Normal
TM31	Attract	Normal	Status	—	100	15	Normal
TM33	Rain Dance	Water	Status	—	—	5	Both Sides
TM34	Sunny Day	Fire	Status	—	—	5	Both Sides
TM39	Facade	Normal	Physical	70	100	20	Normal
TM41	Helping Hand	Normal	Status	—	—	20	1 Ally
TM42	Revenge	Fighting	Physical	60	100	10	Normal
TM43	Brick Break	Fighting	Physical	75	100	15	Normal
TM48	Rock Tomb	Rock	Physical	60	95	15	Normal
TM57	Payback	Dark	Physical	50	100	10	Normal
TM59	Fling	Dark	Physical	—	100	10	Normal
TM63	Drain Punch	Fighting	Physical	75	100	10	Normal
TM75	Low Sweep	Fighting	Physical	65	100	20	Normal
TM76	Round	Normal	Special	60	100	15	Normal
TM79	Retaliate	Normal	Physical	70	100	5	Normal
TM97	Brutal Swing	Dark	Physical	60	100	20	All Others

TR MOVES

NAME	TYPE	KIND	POW.	ACC.	PP	RANGE
TR07 Low Kick	Fighting	Physical	—	100	20	Normal
TR13 Focus Energy	Normal	Status	—	—	30	Self
TR20 Substitute	Normal	Status	—	—	10	Self
TR21 Reversal	Fighting	Physical	—	100	15	Normal
TR26 Endure	Normal	Status	—	—	10	Self
TR27 Sleep Talk	Normal	Status	—	—	10	Self
TR37 Taunt	Dark	Status	—	100	20	Normal
TR39 Superpower	Fighting	Physical	120	100	5	Normal
TR48 Bulk Up	Fighting	Status	—	—	20	Self
TR57 Poison Jab	Poison	Physical	80	100	20	Normal
TR64 Focus Blast	Fighting	Special	120	70	5	Normal
TR75 Stone Edge	Rock	Physical	100	80	5	Normal
TR77 Grass Knot	Grass	Special	—	100	20	Normal
TR85 Work Up	Normal	Status	—	—	30	Self

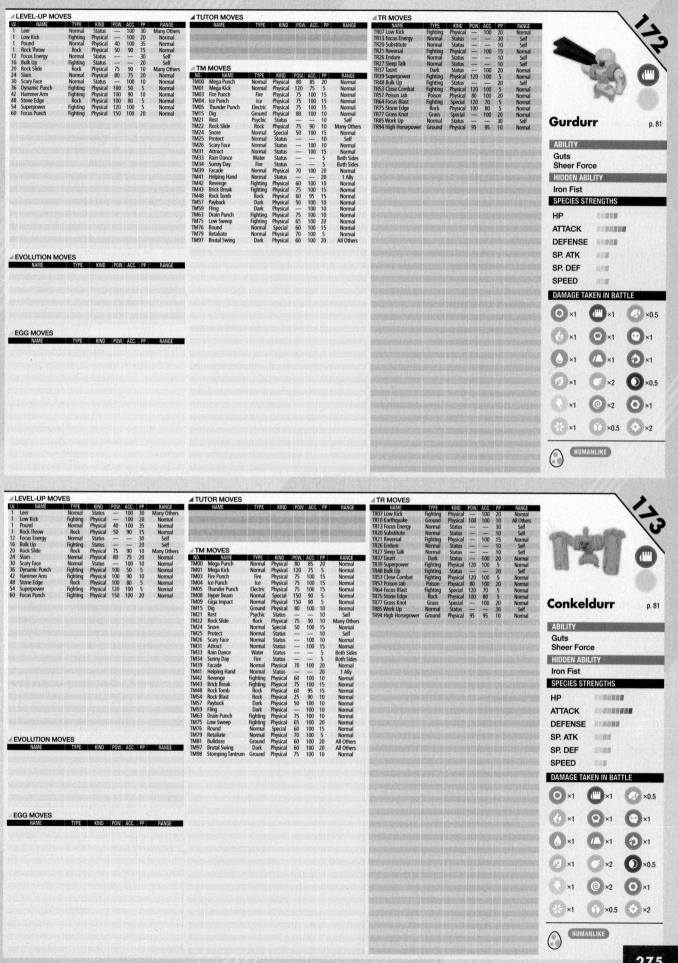

172 Gurdurr — p. 81

LEVEL-UP MOVES

LV.	NAME	TYPE	KIND	POW.	ACC.	PP	RANGE
1	Leer	Normal	Status	—	100	30	Many Others
1	Low Kick	Fighting	Physical	—	100	20	Normal
1	Pound	Normal	Physical	40	100	35	Normal
1	Rock Throw	Rock	Physical	50	90	15	Normal
12	Focus Energy	Normal	Status	—	—	30	Self
16	Bulk Up	Fighting	Status	—	—	20	Self
20	Rock Slide	Rock	Physical	75	90	10	Many Others
24	Slam	Normal	Physical	80	75	20	Normal
30	Scary Face	Normal	Status	—	100	10	Normal
36	Dynamic Punch	Fighting	Physical	100	50	5	Normal
42	Hammer Arm	Fighting	Physical	100	90	10	Normal
48	Stone Edge	Rock	Physical	100	80	5	Normal
54	Superpower	Fighting	Physical	120	100	5	Normal
60	Focus Punch	Fighting	Physical	150	100	20	Normal

EVOLUTION MOVES

NAME	TYPE	KIND	POW.	ACC.	PP	RANGE

EGG MOVES

NAME	TYPE	KIND	POW.	ACC.	PP	RANGE

TUTOR MOVES

NAME	TYPE	KIND	POW.	ACC.	PP	RANGE

TM MOVES

NO.	NAME	TYPE	KIND	POW.	ACC.	PP	RANGE
TM00	Mega Punch	Normal	Physical	80	85	20	Normal
TM01	Mega Kick	Normal	Physical	120	75	5	Normal
TM03	Fire Punch	Fire	Physical	75	100	15	Normal
TM04	Ice Punch	Ice	Physical	75	100	15	Normal
TM05	Thunder Punch	Electric	Physical	75	100	15	Normal
TM15	Dig	Ground	Physical	80	100	10	Normal
TM21	Rest	Psychic	Status	—	—	10	Self
TM22	Rock Slide	Rock	Physical	75	90	10	Many Others
TM24	Snore	Normal	Special	50	100	15	Normal
TM25	Protect	Normal	Status	—	—	10	Self
TM26	Scary Face	Normal	Status	—	100	10	Normal
TM31	Attract	Normal	Status	—	100	15	Normal
TM33	Rain Dance	Water	Status	—	—	5	Both Sides
TM34	Sunny Day	Fire	Status	—	—	5	Both Sides
TM39	Facade	Normal	Physical	70	100	20	Normal
TM41	Helping Hand	Normal	Status	—	—	20	1 Ally
TM42	Revenge	Fighting	Physical	60	100	10	Normal
TM43	Brick Break	Fighting	Physical	75	100	15	Normal
TM48	Rock Tomb	Rock	Physical	60	95	15	Normal
TM57	Payback	Dark	Physical	50	100	10	Normal
TM59	Fling	Dark	Physical	—	100	10	Normal
TM63	Drain Punch	Fighting	Physical	75	100	10	Normal
TM75	Low Sweep	Fighting	Physical	65	100	20	Normal
TM76	Round	Normal	Special	60	100	15	Normal
TM79	Retaliate	Normal	Physical	70	100	5	Normal
TM97	Brutal Swing	Dark	Physical	60	100	20	All Others

TR MOVES

NAME	TYPE	KIND	POW.	ACC.	PP	RANGE
TR07 Low Kick	Fighting	Physical	—	100	20	Normal
TR13 Focus Energy	Normal	Status	—	—	30	Self
TR20 Substitute	Normal	Status	—	—	10	Self
TR21 Reversal	Fighting	Physical	—	100	15	Normal
TR26 Endure	Normal	Status	—	—	10	Self
TR27 Sleep Talk	Normal	Status	—	—	10	Self
TR37 Taunt	Dark	Status	—	100	20	Normal
TR39 Superpower	Fighting	Physical	120	100	5	Normal
TR48 Bulk Up	Fighting	Status	—	—	20	Self
TR53 Close Combat	Fighting	Physical	120	100	5	Normal
TR57 Poison Jab	Poison	Physical	80	100	20	Normal
TR64 Focus Blast	Fighting	Special	120	70	5	Normal
TR75 Stone Edge	Rock	Physical	100	80	5	Normal
TR77 Grass Knot	Grass	Special	—	100	20	Normal
TR94 High Horsepower	Ground	Physical	95	95	10	Normal

ABILITY: Guts / Sheer Force
HIDDEN ABILITY: Iron Fist

SPECIES STRENGTHS
HP / ATTACK / DEFENSE / SP. ATK / SP. DEF / SPEED

DAMAGE TAKEN IN BATTLE
×1 ×1 ×0.5
×1 ×1 ×1
×1 ×1 ×1
×1 ×2 ×0.5
×1 ×2 ×1
×0.5 ×0.5 ×2

HUMANLIKE

---

173 Conkeldurr — p. 81

LEVEL-UP MOVES

LV.	NAME	TYPE	KIND	POW.	ACC.	PP	RANGE
1	Leer	Normal	Status	—	100	30	Many Others
1	Low Kick	Fighting	Physical	—	100	20	Normal
1	Pound	Normal	Physical	40	100	35	Normal
1	Rock Throw	Rock	Physical	50	90	15	Normal
12	Focus Energy	Normal	Status	—	—	30	Self
16	Bulk Up	Fighting	Status	—	—	20	Self
20	Rock Slide	Rock	Physical	75	90	10	Many Others
24	Slam	Normal	Physical	80	75	20	Normal
30	Scary Face	Normal	Status	—	100	10	Normal
36	Dynamic Punch	Fighting	Physical	100	50	5	Normal
42	Hammer Arm	Fighting	Physical	100	90	10	Normal
48	Stone Edge	Rock	Physical	100	80	5	Normal
54	Superpower	Fighting	Physical	120	100	5	Normal
60	Focus Punch	Fighting	Physical	150	100	20	Normal

EVOLUTION MOVES

NAME	TYPE	KIND	POW.	ACC.	PP	RANGE

EGG MOVES

NAME	TYPE	KIND	POW.	ACC.	PP	RANGE

TUTOR MOVES

NAME	TYPE	KIND	POW.	ACC.	PP	RANGE

TM MOVES

NO.	NAME	TYPE	KIND	POW.	ACC.	PP	RANGE
TM00	Mega Punch	Normal	Physical	80	85	20	Normal
TM01	Mega Kick	Normal	Physical	120	75	5	Normal
TM03	Fire Punch	Fire	Physical	75	100	15	Normal
TM04	Ice Punch	Ice	Physical	75	100	15	Normal
TM05	Thunder Punch	Electric	Physical	75	100	15	Normal
TM08	Hyper Beam	Normal	Special	150	90	5	Normal
TM09	Giga Impact	Normal	Physical	150	90	5	Normal
TM15	Dig	Ground	Physical	80	100	10	Normal
TM21	Rest	Psychic	Status	—	—	10	Self
TM22	Rock Slide	Rock	Physical	75	90	10	Many Others
TM24	Snore	Normal	Special	50	100	15	Normal
TM25	Protect	Normal	Status	—	—	10	Self
TM26	Scary Face	Normal	Status	—	100	10	Normal
TM31	Attract	Normal	Status	—	100	15	Normal
TM33	Rain Dance	Water	Status	—	—	5	Both Sides
TM34	Sunny Day	Fire	Status	—	—	5	Both Sides
TM39	Facade	Normal	Physical	70	100	20	Normal
TM41	Helping Hand	Normal	Status	—	—	20	1 Ally
TM42	Revenge	Fighting	Physical	60	100	10	Normal
TM43	Brick Break	Fighting	Physical	75	100	15	Normal
TM48	Rock Tomb	Rock	Physical	60	95	15	Normal
TM54	Rock Blast	Rock	Physical	25	90	10	Normal
TM57	Payback	Dark	Physical	50	100	10	Normal
TM59	Fling	Dark	Physical	—	100	10	Normal
TM63	Drain Punch	Fighting	Physical	75	100	10	Normal
TM75	Low Sweep	Fighting	Physical	65	100	20	Normal
TM76	Round	Normal	Special	60	100	15	Normal
TM79	Retaliate	Normal	Physical	70	100	5	Normal
TM81	Bulldoze	Ground	Physical	60	100	20	All Others
TM97	Brutal Swing	Dark	Physical	60	100	20	All Others
TM98	Stomping Tantrum	Ground	Physical	75	100	10	Normal

TR MOVES

NAME	TYPE	KIND	POW.	ACC.	PP	RANGE
TR07 Low Kick	Fighting	Physical	—	100	20	Normal
TR10 Earthquake	Ground	Physical	100	100	10	All Others
TR13 Focus Energy	Normal	Status	—	—	30	Self
TR20 Substitute	Normal	Status	—	—	10	Self
TR21 Reversal	Fighting	Physical	—	100	15	Normal
TR26 Endure	Normal	Status	—	—	10	Self
TR27 Sleep Talk	Normal	Status	—	—	10	Self
TR37 Taunt	Dark	Status	—	100	20	Normal
TR39 Superpower	Fighting	Physical	120	100	5	Normal
TR48 Bulk Up	Fighting	Status	—	—	20	Self
TR53 Close Combat	Fighting	Physical	120	100	5	Normal
TR57 Poison Jab	Poison	Physical	80	100	20	Normal
TR64 Focus Blast	Fighting	Special	120	70	5	Normal
TR75 Stone Edge	Rock	Physical	100	80	5	Normal
TR77 Grass Knot	Grass	Special	—	100	20	Normal
TR85 Work Up	Normal	Status	—	—	30	Self
TR94 High Horsepower	Ground	Physical	95	95	10	Normal

ABILITY: Guts / Sheer Force
HIDDEN ABILITY: Iron Fist

SPECIES STRENGTHS
HP / ATTACK / DEFENSE / SP. ATK / SP. DEF / SPEED

DAMAGE TAKEN IN BATTLE
×1 ×1 ×0.5
×1 ×1 ×1
×1 ×1 ×1
×1 ×2 ×0.5
×1 ×2 ×1
×0.5 ×0.5 ×2

HUMANLIKE

174 Woobat p. 82

ABILITY
Unaware
Klutz

HIDDEN ABILITY
Simple

SPECIES STRENGTHS

HP	▦▦
ATTACK	▦▦
DEFENSE	▦▦
SP. ATK	▦▦▦
SP. DEF	▦▦
SPEED	▦▦▦▦

DAMAGE TAKEN IN BATTLE

◎ ×1	🖐 ×0.25	✈ ×2			
🔥 ×1	👊 ×1	👻 ×2			
💧 ×1	⛰ ×0	🔄 ×1			
🌿 ×0.5	☾ ×1	☽ ×1			
⚡ ×2	◉ ×0.5	⚙ ×1			
❄ ×2	✦ ×1	✧ ×1			

FIELD / FLYING

LEVEL-UP MOVES

LV.	NAME	TYPE	KIND	POW.	ACC.	PP	RANGE
1	Attract	Normal	Status	—	100	15	Normal
1	Gust	Flying	Special	40	100	35	Normal
5	Confusion	Psychic	Special	50	100	25	Normal
10	Endeavor	Normal	Physical	—	100	5	Normal
15	Air Cutter	Flying	Special	60	95	25	Many Others
20	Imprison	Psychic	Status	—	—	10	Self
25	Assurance	Dark	Physical	60	100	10	Normal
30	Amnesia	Psychic	Status	—	—	20	Self
35	Air Slash	Flying	Special	75	95	15	Normal
40	Psychic	Psychic	Special	90	100	10	Normal
45	Calm Mind	Psychic	Status	—	—	20	Self
50	Future Sight	Psychic	Special	120	100	10	Normal
55	Simple Beam	Normal	Status	—	100	15	Normal

EVOLUTION MOVES

NAME	TYPE	KIND	POW.	ACC.	PP	RANGE

EGG MOVES

NAME	TYPE	KIND	POW.	ACC.	PP	RANGE
Flatter	Dark	Status	—	100	15	Normal
Knock Off	Dark	Physical	65	100	20	Normal
Psycho Shift	Psychic	Status	—	100	10	Normal
Roost	Flying	Status	—	—	10	Self
Supersonic	Normal	Status	—	55	20	Normal

TUTOR MOVES

NAME	TYPE	KIND	POW.	ACC.	PP	RANGE

TM MOVES

NO.	NAME	TYPE	KIND	POW.	ACC.	PP	RANGE
TM06	Fly	Flying	Physical	90	95	15	Normal
TM14	Thunder Wave	Electric	Status	—	90	20	Normal
TM17	Light Screen	Psychic	Status	—	—	30	Your Side
TM18	Reflect	Psychic	Status	—	—	20	Your Side
TM19	Safeguard	Normal	Status	—	—	25	Your Side
TM21	Rest	Psychic	Status	—	—	10	Self
TM23	Thief	Dark	Physical	60	100	25	Normal
TM24	Snore	Normal	Special	50	100	15	Normal
TM25	Protect	Normal	Status	—	—	10	Self
TM28	Giga Drain	Grass	Special	75	100	10	Normal
TM29	Charm	Fairy	Status	—	100	20	Normal
TM30	Steel Wing	Steel	Physical	70	90	25	Normal
TM31	Attract	Normal	Status	—	100	15	Normal
TM33	Rain Dance	Water	Status	—	—	5	Both Sides
TM39	Facade	Normal	Physical	70	100	20	Normal
TM40	Swift	Normal	Special	60	—	20	Many Others
TM41	Helping Hand	Normal	Status	—	—	20	1 Ally
TM44	Imprison	Psychic	Status	—	—	10	Self
TM47	Fake Tears	Dark	Status	—	100	20	Normal
TM56	U-turn	Bug	Physical	70	100	20	Normal
TM58	Assurance	Dark	Physical	60	100	10	Normal
TM62	Speed Swap	Psychic	Status	—	—	10	Normal
TM69	Psycho Cut	Psychic	Physical	70	100	20	Normal
TM70	Trick Room	Psychic	Status	—	—	5	Both Sides
TM76	Round	Normal	Special	60	100	15	Normal
TM78	Acrobatics	Flying	Physical	55	100	15	Normal
TM95	Air Slash	Flying	Special	75	95	15	Normal

TR MOVES

NAME	TYPE	KIND	POW.	ACC.	PP	RANGE
TR11 Psychic	Psychic	Special	90	100	10	Normal
TR17 Amnesia	Psychic	Status	—	—	20	Self
TR20 Substitute	Normal	Status	—	—	10	Self
TR25 Psyshock	Psychic	Special	80	100	10	Normal
TR26 Endure	Normal	Status	—	—	10	Self
TR27 Sleep Talk	Normal	Status	—	—	10	Self
TR29 Baton Pass	Normal	Status	—	—	40	Self
TR33 Shadow Ball	Ghost	Special	80	100	15	Normal
TR34 Future Sight	Psychic	Special	120	100	10	Normal
TR35 Uproar	Normal	Special	90	100	10	1 Random
TR36 Heat Wave	Fire	Special	95	90	10	Many Others
TR37 Taunt	Dark	Status	—	100	20	Normal
TR38 Trick	Psychic	Status	—	100	10	Normal
TR40 Skill Swap	Psychic	Status	—	—	10	Normal
TR49 Calm Mind	Psychic	Status	—	—	20	Self
TR52 Gyro Ball	Steel	Physical	—	100	5	Normal
TR65 Energy Ball	Grass	Special	90	100	10	Normal
TR68 Nasty Plot	Dark	Status	—	—	20	Self
TR69 Zen Headbutt	Psychic	Physical	80	90	15	Normal
TR82 Stored Power	Psychic	Special	20	100	10	Normal
TR83 Ally Switch	Psychic	Status	—	—	15	Self
TR91 Venom Drench	Poison	Status	—	100	20	Many Others

---

175 Swoobat p. 82

ABILITY
Unaware
Klutz

HIDDEN ABILITY
Simple

SPECIES STRENGTHS

HP	▦▦▦
ATTACK	▦▦▦
DEFENSE	▦▦▦
SP. ATK	▦▦▦▦
SP. DEF	▦▦▦
SPEED	▦▦▦▦▦

DAMAGE TAKEN IN BATTLE

◎ ×1	🖐 ×0.25	✈ ×2			
🔥 ×1	👊 ×1	👻 ×2			
💧 ×1	⛰ ×0	🔄 ×1			
🌿 ×0.5	☾ ×1	☽ ×2			
⚡ ×2	◉ ×0.5	⚙ ×1			
❄ ×2	✦ ×1	✧ ×1			

FIELD / FLYING

LEVEL-UP MOVES

LV.	NAME	TYPE	KIND	POW.	ACC.	PP	RANGE
1	Attract	Normal	Status	—	100	15	Normal
1	Confusion	Psychic	Special	50	100	25	Normal
1	Endeavor	Normal	Physical	—	100	5	Normal
1	Gust	Flying	Special	40	100	35	Normal
15	Air Cutter	Flying	Special	60	95	25	Many Others
20	Imprison	Psychic	Status	—	—	10	Self
25	Assurance	Dark	Physical	60	100	10	Normal
30	Amnesia	Psychic	Status	—	—	20	Self
35	Air Slash	Flying	Special	75	95	15	Normal
40	Psychic	Psychic	Special	90	100	10	Normal
45	Calm Mind	Psychic	Status	—	—	20	Self
50	Future Sight	Psychic	Special	120	100	10	Normal
55	Simple Beam	Normal	Status	—	100	15	Normal

EVOLUTION MOVES

NAME	TYPE	KIND	POW.	ACC.	PP	RANGE

EGG MOVES

NAME	TYPE	KIND	POW.	ACC.	PP	RANGE

TUTOR MOVES

NAME	TYPE	KIND	POW.	ACC.	PP	RANGE

TM MOVES

NO.	NAME	TYPE	KIND	POW.	ACC.	PP	RANGE
TM06	Fly	Flying	Physical	90	95	15	Normal
TM08	Hyper Beam	Normal	Special	150	90	5	Normal
TM09	Giga Impact	Normal	Physical	150	90	5	Normal
TM14	Thunder Wave	Electric	Status	—	90	20	Normal
TM17	Light Screen	Psychic	Status	—	—	30	Your Side
TM18	Reflect	Psychic	Status	—	—	20	Your Side
TM19	Safeguard	Normal	Status	—	—	25	Your Side
TM21	Rest	Psychic	Status	—	—	10	Self
TM23	Thief	Dark	Physical	60	100	25	Normal
TM24	Snore	Normal	Special	50	100	15	Normal
TM25	Protect	Normal	Status	—	—	10	Self
TM28	Giga Drain	Grass	Special	75	100	10	Normal
TM29	Charm	Fairy	Status	—	100	20	Normal
TM30	Steel Wing	Steel	Physical	70	90	25	Normal
TM31	Attract	Normal	Status	—	100	15	Normal
TM33	Rain Dance	Water	Status	—	—	5	Both Sides
TM39	Facade	Normal	Physical	70	100	20	Normal
TM40	Swift	Normal	Special	60	—	20	Many Others
TM41	Helping Hand	Normal	Status	—	—	20	1 Ally
TM44	Imprison	Psychic	Status	—	—	10	Self
TM47	Fake Tears	Dark	Status	—	100	20	Normal
TM56	U-turn	Bug	Physical	70	100	20	Normal
TM58	Assurance	Dark	Physical	60	100	10	Normal
TM62	Speed Swap	Psychic	Status	—	—	10	Normal
TM69	Psycho Cut	Psychic	Physical	70	100	20	Normal
TM70	Trick Room	Psychic	Status	—	—	5	Both Sides
TM76	Round	Normal	Special	60	100	15	Normal
TM78	Acrobatics	Flying	Physical	55	100	15	Normal
TM95	Air Slash	Flying	Special	75	95	15	Normal

TR MOVES

NAME	TYPE	KIND	POW.	ACC.	PP	RANGE
TR11 Psychic	Psychic	Special	90	100	10	Normal
TR17 Amnesia	Psychic	Status	—	—	20	Self
TR20 Substitute	Normal	Status	—	—	10	Self
TR25 Psyshock	Psychic	Special	80	100	10	Normal
TR26 Endure	Normal	Status	—	—	10	Self
TR27 Sleep Talk	Normal	Status	—	—	10	Self
TR29 Baton Pass	Normal	Status	—	—	40	Self
TR33 Shadow Ball	Ghost	Special	80	100	15	Normal
TR34 Future Sight	Psychic	Special	120	100	10	Normal
TR35 Uproar	Normal	Special	90	100	10	1 Random
TR36 Heat Wave	Fire	Special	95	90	10	Many Others
TR37 Taunt	Dark	Status	—	100	20	Normal
TR38 Trick	Psychic	Status	—	100	10	Normal
TR40 Skill Swap	Psychic	Status	—	—	10	Normal
TR49 Calm Mind	Psychic	Status	—	—	20	Self
TR52 Gyro Ball	Steel	Physical	—	100	5	Normal
TR65 Energy Ball	Grass	Special	90	100	10	Normal
TR68 Nasty Plot	Dark	Status	—	—	20	Self
TR69 Zen Headbutt	Psychic	Physical	80	90	15	Normal
TR82 Stored Power	Psychic	Special	20	100	10	Normal
TR83 Ally Switch	Psychic	Status	—	—	15	Self
TR91 Venom Drench	Poison	Status	—	100	20	Many Others
TR97 Psychic Fangs	Psychic	Physical	85	100	10	Normal

176 — Noibat

LEVEL-UP MOVES

LV.	NAME	TYPE	KIND	POW.	ACC.	PP	RANGE
1	Absorb	Grass	Special	20	100	25	Normal
1	Tackle	Normal	Physical	40	100	35	Normal
1	Gust	Flying	Special	40	100	35	Normal
8	Supersonic	Normal	Status	—	55	20	Normal
12	Double Team	Normal	Status	—	—	15	Self
16	Wing Attack	Flying	Physical	60	100	35	Normal
20	Bite	Dark	Physical	60	100	25	Normal
24	Air Cutter	Flying	Special	60	95	25	Many Others
28	Whirlwind	Normal	Status	—	—	20	Normal
32	Super Fang	Normal	Physical	—	90	10	Normal
36	Air Slash	Flying	Special	75	95	15	Normal
40	Screech	Normal	Status	—	85	40	Normal
44	Roost	Flying	Status	—	—	10	Self
49	Tailwind	Flying	Status	—	—	15	Your Side
52	Hurricane	Flying	Special	110	70	10	Normal

EVOLUTION MOVES

NAME	TYPE	KIND	POW.	ACC.	PP	RANGE

EGG MOVES

NAME	TYPE	KIND	POW.	ACC.	PP	RANGE
Defog	Flying	Status	—	—	15	Normal
Dragon Rush	Dragon	Physical	100	75	10	Normal

TUTOR MOVES

NAME	TYPE	KIND	POW.	ACC.	PP	RANGE
Draco Meteor	Dragon	Special	130	90	5	Normal

TM MOVES

NO.	NAME	TYPE	KIND	POW.	ACC.	PP	RANGE
TM06	Fly	Flying	Physical	90	95	15	Normal
TM11	Solar Beam	Grass	Special	120	100	10	Normal
TM16	Screech	Normal	Status	—	85	40	Normal
TM21	Rest	Psychic	Status	—	—	10	Self
TM23	Thief	Dark	Physical	60	100	25	Normal
TM24	Snore	Normal	Special	50	100	15	Normal
TM25	Protect	Normal	Status	—	—	10	Self
TM30	Steel Wing	Steel	Physical	70	90	25	Normal
TM31	Attract	Normal	Status	—	100	15	Normal
TM34	Sunny Day	Fire	Status	—	—	5	Both Sides
TM39	Facade	Normal	Physical	70	100	20	Normal
TM40	Swift	Normal	Special	60	—	20	Many Others
TM43	Brick Break	Fighting	Physical	75	100	15	Normal
TM56	U-turn	Bug	Physical	70	100	20	Normal
TM65	Shadow Claw	Ghost	Physical	70	100	15	Normal
TM76	Round	Normal	Special	60	100	15	Normal
TM78	Acrobatics	Flying	Physical	55	100	15	Normal
TM95	Air Slash	Flying	Special	75	95	15	Normal

TR MOVES

NO.	NAME	TYPE	KIND	POW.	ACC.	PP	RANGE
TR11	Psychic	Psychic	Special	90	100	10	Normal
TR12	Agility	Psychic	Status	—	—	30	Self
TR18	Leech Life	Bug	Physical	80	100	10	Normal
TR20	Substitute	Normal	Status	—	—	10	Self
TR24	Outrage	Dragon	Physical	120	100	10	1 Random
TR26	Endure	Normal	Status	—	—	10	Self
TR27	Sleep Talk	Normal	Status	—	—	10	Self
TR31	Iron Tail	Steel	Physical	100	75	15	Normal
TR33	Shadow Ball	Ghost	Special	80	100	15	Normal
TR35	Uproar	Normal	Special	90	100	10	1 Random
TR36	Heat Wave	Fire	Special	95	90	10	Many Others
TR37	Taunt	Dark	Status	—	100	20	Normal
TR42	Hyper Voice	Normal	Special	90	100	10	Many Others
TR58	Dark Pulse	Dark	Special	80	100	15	Normal
TR60	X-Scissor	Bug	Physical	80	100	15	Normal
TR62	Dragon Pulse	Dragon	Special	85	100	10	Normal
TR86	Wild Charge	Electric	Physical	90	100	15	Normal
TR89	Hurricane	Flying	Special	110	70	10	Normal

Noibat p. 82

ABILITY
Frisk
Infiltrator

HIDDEN ABILITY
Telepathy

SPECIES STRENGTHS
HP
ATTACK
DEFENSE
SP. ATK
SP. DEF
SPEED

DAMAGE TAKEN IN BATTLE
×1 ×0.5 ×2
×0.5 ×1 ×1
×0.5 ×0 ×2
×0.25 ×1 ×1
×1 ×1 ×1
×4 ×0.5 ×1

FLYING
DRAGON

177 — Noivern

LEVEL-UP MOVES

LV.	NAME	TYPE	KIND	POW.	ACC.	PP	RANGE
1	Absorb	Grass	Special	20	100	25	Normal
1	Dragon Pulse	Dragon	Special	85	100	10	Normal
1	Gust	Flying	Special	40	100	35	Normal
1	Moonlight	Fairy	Status	—	—	5	Self
1	Supersonic	Normal	Status	—	55	20	Normal
1	Tackle	Normal	Physical	40	100	35	Normal
12	Double Team	Normal	Status	—	—	15	Self
16	Wing Attack	Flying	Physical	60	100	35	Normal
20	Bite	Dark	Physical	60	100	25	Normal
24	Air Cutter	Flying	Special	60	95	25	Many Others
28	Whirlwind	Normal	Status	—	—	20	Normal
32	Super Fang	Normal	Physical	—	90	10	Normal
36	Air Slash	Flying	Special	75	95	15	Normal
40	Screech	Normal	Status	—	85	40	Normal
44	Roost	Flying	Status	—	—	10	Self
51	Tailwind	Flying	Status	—	—	15	Your Side
56	Hurricane	Flying	Special	110	70	10	Normal
62	Boomburst	Normal	Special	140	100	10	All Others

EVOLUTION MOVES

NAME	TYPE	KIND	POW.	ACC.	PP	RANGE
Dragon Pulse	Dragon	Special	85	100	10	Normal

EGG MOVES

NAME	TYPE	KIND	POW.	ACC.	PP	RANGE

TUTOR MOVES

NAME	TYPE	KIND	POW.	ACC.	PP	RANGE
Draco Meteor	Dragon	Special	130	90	5	Normal

TM MOVES

NO.	NAME	TYPE	KIND	POW.	ACC.	PP	RANGE
TM06	Fly	Flying	Physical	90	95	15	Normal
TM08	Hyper Beam	Normal	Special	150	90	5	Normal
TM09	Giga Impact	Normal	Physical	150	90	5	Normal
TM11	Solar Beam	Grass	Special	120	100	10	Normal
TM16	Screech	Normal	Status	—	85	40	Normal
TM21	Rest	Psychic	Status	—	—	10	Self
TM23	Thief	Dark	Physical	60	100	25	Normal
TM24	Snore	Normal	Special	50	100	15	Normal
TM25	Protect	Normal	Status	—	—	10	Self
TM30	Steel Wing	Steel	Physical	70	90	25	Normal
TM31	Attract	Normal	Status	—	100	15	Normal
TM34	Sunny Day	Fire	Status	—	—	5	Both Sides
TM39	Facade	Normal	Physical	70	100	20	Normal
TM40	Swift	Normal	Special	60	—	20	Many Others
TM43	Brick Break	Fighting	Physical	75	100	15	Normal
TM56	U-turn	Bug	Physical	70	100	20	Normal
TM65	Shadow Claw	Ghost	Physical	70	100	15	Normal
TM76	Round	Normal	Special	60	100	15	Normal
TM78	Acrobatics	Flying	Physical	55	100	15	Normal
TM95	Air Slash	Flying	Special	75	95	15	Normal

TR MOVES

NO.	NAME	TYPE	KIND	POW.	ACC.	PP	RANGE
TR02	Flamethrower	Fire	Special	90	100	15	Normal
TR11	Psychic	Psychic	Special	90	100	10	Normal
TR12	Agility	Psychic	Status	—	—	30	Self
TR18	Leech Life	Bug	Physical	80	100	10	Normal
TR20	Substitute	Normal	Status	—	—	10	Self
TR24	Outrage	Dragon	Physical	120	100	10	1 Random
TR26	Endure	Normal	Status	—	—	10	Self
TR27	Sleep Talk	Normal	Status	—	—	10	Self
TR31	Iron Tail	Steel	Physical	100	75	15	Normal
TR33	Shadow Ball	Ghost	Special	80	100	15	Normal
TR35	Uproar	Normal	Special	90	100	10	1 Random
TR36	Heat Wave	Fire	Special	95	90	10	Many Others
TR37	Taunt	Dark	Status	—	100	20	Normal
TR42	Hyper Voice	Normal	Special	90	100	10	Many Others
TR47	Dragon Claw	Dragon	Physical	80	100	15	Normal
TR51	Dragon Dance	Dragon	Status	—	—	20	Self
TR58	Dark Pulse	Dark	Special	80	100	15	Normal
TR60	X-Scissor	Bug	Physical	80	100	15	Normal
TR62	Dragon Pulse	Dragon	Special	85	100	10	Normal
TR64	Focus Blast	Fighting	Special	120	70	5	Normal
TR86	Wild Charge	Electric	Physical	90	100	15	Normal
TR89	Hurricane	Flying	Special	110	70	10	Normal

Noivern p. 82

ABILITY
Frisk
Infiltrator

HIDDEN ABILITY
Telepathy

SPECIES STRENGTHS
HP
ATTACK
DEFENSE
SP. ATK
SP. DEF
SPEED

DAMAGE TAKEN IN BATTLE
×1 ×0.5 ×2
×0.5 ×1 ×1
×0.5 ×0 ×2
×0.25 ×1 ×1
×1 ×1 ×1
×4 ×0.5 ×2

FLYING
DRAGON

178 Onix — p. 83

ABILITY: Rock Head / Sturdy
HIDDEN ABILITY: Weak Armor

SPECIES STRENGTHS
- HP
- ATTACK
- DEFENSE
- SP. ATK
- SP. DEF
- SPEED

DAMAGE TAKEN IN BATTLE
×0.5, ×2, ×0.5, ×0.5, ×0.25, ×1, ×4, ×2, ×1, ×4, ×0.5, ×1, ×0, ×2, ×2, ×2, ×1, ×1

MINERAL

LEVEL-UP MOVES

LV.	NAME	TYPE	KIND	POW.	ACC.	PP	RANGE
1	Bind	Normal	Physical	15	85	20	Normal
1	Harden	Normal	Status	—	—	30	Self
1	Rock Throw	Rock	Physical	50	90	15	Normal
1	Tackle	Normal	Physical	40	100	35	Normal
4	Smack Down	Rock	Physical	50	100	15	Normal
8	Rock Polish	Rock	Status	—	—	20	Self
12	Dragon Breath	Dragon	Special	60	100	20	Normal
16	Curse	Ghost	Status	—	—	10	Varies
20	Rock Slide	Rock	Physical	75	90	10	Many Others
24	Screech	Normal	Status	—	85	40	Normal
28	Sand Tomb	Ground	Physical	35	85	15	Normal
32	Stealth Rock	Rock	Status	—	—	20	Other Side
36	Slam	Normal	Physical	80	75	20	Normal
40	Sandstorm	Rock	Status	—	—	10	Both Sides
44	Dig	Ground	Physical	80	100	10	Normal
48	Iron Tail	Steel	Physical	100	75	15	Normal
52	Stone Edge	Rock	Physical	100	80	5	Normal
56	Double-Edge	Normal	Physical	120	100	15	Normal

EVOLUTION MOVES

NAME	TYPE	KIND	POW.	ACC.	PP	RANGE

EGG MOVES

NAME	TYPE	KIND	POW.	ACC.	PP	RANGE
Block	Normal	Status	—	—	5	Normal
Defense Curl	Normal	Status	—	—	40	Self
Dragon Tail	Dragon	Physical	60	90	10	Normal
Flail	Normal	Physical	—	100	15	Normal
Head Smash	Rock	Physical	150	80	5	Normal
Rollout	Rock	Physical	30	90	20	Normal
Wide Guard	Rock	Status	—	—	10	Your Side

TUTOR MOVES

NAME	TYPE	KIND	POW.	ACC.	PP	RANGE

TM MOVES

NO.	NAME	TYPE	KIND	POW.	ACC.	PP	RANGE
TM15	Dig	Ground	Physical	80	100	10	Normal
TM16	Screech	Normal	Status	—	85	40	Normal
TM20	Self-Destruct	Normal	Physical	200	100	5	All Others
TM21	Rest	Psychic	Status	—	—	10	Self
TM22	Rock Slide	Rock	Physical	75	90	10	Many Others
TM24	Snore	Normal	Special	50	100	15	Normal
TM25	Protect	Normal	Status	—	—	10	Self
TM26	Scary Face	Normal	Status	—	100	10	Normal
TM31	Attract	Normal	Status	—	100	15	Normal
TM32	Sandstorm	Rock	Status	—	—	10	Both Sides
TM34	Sunny Day	Fire	Status	—	—	10	Both Sides
TM39	Facade	Normal	Physical	70	100	20	Normal
TM48	Rock Tomb	Rock	Physical	60	95	15	Normal
TM49	Sand Tomb	Ground	Physical	35	85	15	Normal
TM54	Rock Blast	Rock	Physical	25	90	10	Normal
TM57	Payback	Dark	Physical	50	100	10	Normal
TM76	Round	Normal	Special	60	100	15	Normal
TM81	Bulldoze	Ground	Physical	60	100	20	All Others
TM97	Brutal Swing	Dark	Physical	60	100	20	All Others
TM98	Stomping Tantrum	Ground	Physical	75	100	10	Normal
TM99	Breaking Swipe	Dragon	Physical	60	100	15	Many Others

TR MOVES

NO.	NAME	TYPE	KIND	POW.	ACC.	PP	RANGE
TR01	Body Slam	Normal	Physical	85	100	15	Normal
TR10	Earthquake	Ground	Physical	100	100	10	All Others
TR20	Substitute	Normal	Status	—	—	10	Self
TR26	Endure	Normal	Status	—	—	10	Self
TR27	Sleep Talk	Normal	Status	—	—	10	Self
TR31	Iron Tail	Steel	Physical	100	75	15	Normal
TR37	Taunt	Dark	Status	—	100	20	Normal
TR51	Dragon Dance	Dragon	Status	—	—	20	Self
TR52	Gyro Ball	Steel	Physical	—	100	5	Normal
TR62	Dragon Pulse	Dragon	Special	85	100	10	Normal
TR67	Earth Power	Ground	Special	90	100	10	Normal
TR70	Flash Cannon	Steel	Special	80	100	10	Normal
TR74	Iron Head	Steel	Physical	80	100	15	Normal
TR75	Stone Edge	Rock	Physical	100	80	5	Normal
TR76	Stealth Rock	Rock	Status	—	—	20	Other Side
TR79	Heavy Slam	Steel	Physical	—	100	10	Normal
TR87	Drill Run	Ground	Physical	80	95	10	Normal
TR94	High Horsepower	Ground	Physical	95	95	10	Normal
TR99	Body Press	Fighting	Physical	80	100	10	Normal

179 Steelix — p. 83

ABILITY: Rock Head / Sturdy
HIDDEN ABILITY: Sheer Force

SPECIES STRENGTHS
- HP
- ATTACK
- DEFENSE
- SP. ATK
- SP. DEF
- SPEED

DAMAGE TAKEN IN BATTLE
×0.5, ×2, ×0.25, ×2, ×0, ×1, ×2, ×2, ×0.5, ×1, ×0.5, ×1, ×0, ×0.5, ×0.5, ×0.5, ×0.5, ×0.5

MINERAL

LEVEL-UP MOVES

LV.	NAME	TYPE	KIND	POW.	ACC.	PP	RANGE
1	Bind	Normal	Physical	15	85	20	Normal
1	Crunch	Dark	Physical	80	100	15	Normal
1	Fire Fang	Fire	Physical	65	95	15	Normal
1	Harden	Normal	Status	—	—	30	Self
1	Ice Fang	Ice	Physical	65	95	15	Normal
1	Rock Polish	Rock	Status	—	—	20	Self
1	Rock Throw	Rock	Physical	50	90	15	Normal
1	Tackle	Normal	Physical	40	100	35	Normal
1	Thunder Fang	Electric	Physical	65	95	15	Normal
4	Smack Down	Rock	Physical	50	100	15	Normal
8	Autotomize	Steel	Status	—	—	15	Self
12	Dragon Breath	Dragon	Special	60	100	20	Normal
16	Curse	Ghost	Status	—	—	10	Varies
20	Rock Slide	Rock	Physical	75	90	10	Many Others
24	Screech	Normal	Status	—	85	40	Normal
28	Sand Tomb	Ground	Physical	35	85	15	Normal
32	Stealth Rock	Rock	Status	—	—	20	Other Side
36	Slam	Normal	Physical	80	75	20	Normal
40	Sandstorm	Rock	Status	—	—	10	Both Sides
44	Dig	Ground	Physical	80	100	10	Normal
48	Iron Tail	Steel	Physical	100	75	15	Normal
52	Stone Edge	Rock	Physical	100	80	5	Normal
56	Double-Edge	Normal	Physical	120	100	15	Normal
60	Magnet Rise	Electric	Status	—	—	10	Self

EVOLUTION MOVES

NAME	TYPE	KIND	POW.	ACC.	PP	RANGE

EGG MOVES

NAME	TYPE	KIND	POW.	ACC.	PP	RANGE

TUTOR MOVES

NAME	TYPE	KIND	POW.	ACC.	PP	RANGE
Steel Beam	Steel	Special	140	95	5	Normal

TM MOVES

NO.	NAME	TYPE	KIND	POW.	ACC.	PP	RANGE
TM08	Hyper Beam	Normal	Special	150	90	5	Normal
TM09	Giga Impact	Normal	Physical	150	90	5	Normal
TM15	Dig	Ground	Physical	80	100	10	Normal
TM16	Screech	Normal	Status	—	85	40	Normal
TM20	Self-Destruct	Normal	Physical	200	100	5	All Others
TM21	Rest	Psychic	Status	—	—	10	Self
TM22	Rock Slide	Rock	Physical	75	90	10	Many Others
TM24	Snore	Normal	Special	50	100	15	Normal
TM25	Protect	Normal	Status	—	—	10	Self
TM26	Scary Face	Normal	Status	—	100	10	Normal
TM31	Attract	Normal	Status	—	100	15	Normal
TM32	Sandstorm	Rock	Status	—	—	10	Both Sides
TM34	Sunny Day	Fire	Status	—	—	5	Both Sides
TM39	Facade	Normal	Physical	70	100	20	Normal
TM48	Rock Tomb	Rock	Physical	60	95	15	Normal
TM49	Sand Tomb	Ground	Physical	35	85	15	Normal
TM54	Rock Blast	Rock	Physical	25	90	10	Normal
TM57	Payback	Dark	Physical	50	100	10	Normal
TM66	Thunder Fang	Electric	Physical	65	95	15	Normal
TM67	Ice Fang	Ice	Physical	65	95	15	Normal
TM68	Fire Fang	Fire	Physical	65	95	15	Normal
TM76	Round	Normal	Special	60	100	15	Normal
TM81	Bulldoze	Ground	Physical	60	100	20	All Others
TM97	Brutal Swing	Dark	Physical	60	100	20	All Others
TM98	Stomping Tantrum	Ground	Physical	75	100	10	Normal
TM99	Breaking Swipe	Dragon	Physical	60	100	15	Many Others

TR MOVES

NO.	NAME	TYPE	KIND	POW.	ACC.	PP	RANGE
TR01	Body Slam	Normal	Physical	85	100	15	Normal
TR10	Earthquake	Ground	Physical	100	100	10	All Others
TR20	Substitute	Normal	Status	—	—	10	Self
TR26	Endure	Normal	Status	—	—	10	Self
TR27	Sleep Talk	Normal	Status	—	—	10	Self
TR31	Iron Tail	Steel	Physical	100	75	15	Normal
TR32	Crunch	Dark	Physical	80	100	15	Normal
TR37	Taunt	Dark	Status	—	100	20	Normal
TR46	Iron Defense	Steel	Status	—	—	15	Self
TR51	Dragon Dance	Dragon	Status	—	—	20	Self
TR52	Gyro Ball	Steel	Physical	—	100	5	Normal
TR58	Dark Pulse	Dark	Special	80	100	15	Normal
TR62	Dragon Pulse	Dragon	Special	85	100	10	Normal
TR67	Earth Power	Ground	Special	90	100	10	Normal
TR70	Flash Cannon	Steel	Special	80	100	10	Normal
TR74	Iron Head	Steel	Physical	80	100	15	Normal
TR75	Stone Edge	Rock	Physical	100	80	5	Normal
TR76	Stealth Rock	Rock	Status	—	—	20	Other Side
TR79	Heavy Slam	Steel	Physical	—	100	10	Normal
TR87	Drill Run	Ground	Physical	80	95	10	Normal
TR94	High Horsepower	Ground	Physical	95	95	10	Normal
TR97	Psychic Fangs	Psychic	Physical	85	100	10	Normal
TR99	Body Press	Fighting	Physical	80	100	10	Normal

180 — Arrokuda

LEVEL-UP MOVES

LV.	NAME	TYPE	KIND	POW.	ACC.	PP	RANGE
1	Aqua Jet	Water	Physical	40	100	20	Normal
1	Peck	Flying	Physical	35	100	35	Normal
6	Fury Attack	Normal	Physical	15	85	20	Normal
12	Bite	Dark	Physical	60	100	25	Normal
18	Agility	Psychic	Status	—	—	30	Self
24	Dive	Water	Physical	80	100	10	Normal
30	Laser Focus	Normal	Status	—	—	30	Self
36	Crunch	Dark	Physical	80	100	15	Normal
42	Liquidation	Water	Physical	85	100	10	Normal
48	Double-Edge	Normal	Physical	120	100	15	Normal

TUTOR MOVES

NAME	TYPE	KIND	POW.	ACC.	PP	RANGE

TM MOVES

NO.	NAME	TYPE	KIND	POW.	ACC.	PP	RANGE
TM21	Rest	Psychic	Status	—	—	10	Self
TM24	Snore	Normal	Special	50	100	15	Normal
TM25	Protect	Normal	Status	—	—	10	Self
TM31	Attract	Normal	Status	—	100	15	Normal
TM33	Rain Dance	Water	Status	—	—	5	Both Sides
TM36	Whirlpool	Water	Special	35	85	15	Normal
TM39	Facade	Normal	Physical	70	100	20	Normal
TM40	Swift	Normal	Special	60	—	20	Many Others
TM43	Brick Break	Fighting	Physical	75	100	15	Normal
TM45	Dive	Water	Physical	80	100	10	Normal
TM52	Bounce	Flying	Physical	85	85	5	Normal
TM58	Assurance	Dark	Physical	60	100	10	Normal
TM67	Ice Fang	Ice	Physical	65	95	15	Normal
TM76	Round	Normal	Special	60	100	15	Normal

TR MOVES

NO.	NAME	TYPE	KIND	POW.	ACC.	PP	RANGE
TR12	Agility	Psychic	Status	—	—	30	Self
TR13	Focus Energy	Normal	Status	—	—	30	Self
TR16	Waterfall	Water	Physical	80	100	15	Self
TR20	Substitute	Normal	Status	—	—	10	Self
TR26	Endure	Normal	Status	—	—	10	Self
TR27	Sleep Talk	Normal	Status	—	—	10	Self
TR32	Crunch	Dark	Physical	80	100	15	Normal
TR53	Close Combat	Fighting	Physical	120	100	5	Normal
TR57	Poison Jab	Poison	Physical	80	100	20	Normal
TR84	Scald	Water	Special	80	100	15	Normal
TR87	Drill Run	Ground	Physical	80	95	10	Normal
TR95	Throat Chop	Dark	Physical	80	100	15	Normal
TR97	Psychic Fangs	Psychic	Physical	85	100	10	Normal
TR98	Liquidation	Water	Physical	85	100	10	Normal

EVOLUTION MOVES

NAME	TYPE	KIND	POW.	ACC.	PP	RANGE

EGG MOVES

NAME	TYPE	KIND	POW.	ACC.	PP	RANGE
Acupressure	Normal	Status	—	—	30	Self/Ally
Night Slash	Dark	Physical	70	100	15	Normal
Slash	Normal	Physical	70	100	20	Normal
Thrash	Normal	Physical	120	100	10	1 Random

Arrokuda p. 84

ABILITY
Swift Swim

HIDDEN ABILITY
Propeller Tail

SPECIES STRENGTHS

HP	
ATTACK	
DEFENSE	
SP. ATK	
SP. DEF	
SPEED	

DAMAGE TAKEN IN BATTLE

×1	×1	×1
×0.5	×1	×1
×0.5	×1	×1
×2	×1	×1
×2	×1	×0.5
×0.5	×1	×1

WATER 2

181 — Barraskewda

LEVEL-UP MOVES

LV.	NAME	TYPE	KIND	POW.	ACC.	PP	RANGE
1	Aqua Jet	Water	Physical	40	100	20	Normal
1	Bite	Dark	Physical	60	100	25	Normal
1	Fury Attack	Normal	Physical	15	85	20	Normal
1	Peck	Flying	Physical	35	100	35	Normal
1	Throat Chop	Dark	Physical	80	100	15	Normal
18	Agility	Psychic	Status	—	—	30	Self
24	Dive	Water	Physical	80	100	10	Normal
32	Laser Focus	Normal	Status	—	—	30	Self
40	Crunch	Dark	Physical	80	100	15	Normal
48	Liquidation	Water	Physical	85	100	10	Normal
56	Double-Edge	Normal	Physical	120	100	15	Normal

TUTOR MOVES

NAME	TYPE	KIND	POW.	ACC.	PP	RANGE

TM MOVES

NO.	NAME	TYPE	KIND	POW.	ACC.	PP	RANGE
TM08	Hyper Beam	Normal	Special	150	90	5	Normal
TM09	Giga Impact	Normal	Physical	150	90	5	Normal
TM21	Rest	Psychic	Status	—	—	10	Self
TM24	Snore	Normal	Special	50	100	15	Normal
TM25	Protect	Normal	Status	—	—	10	Self
TM26	Scary Face	Normal	Status	—	100	10	Normal
TM31	Attract	Normal	Status	—	100	15	Normal
TM33	Rain Dance	Water	Status	—	—	5	Both Sides
TM36	Whirlpool	Water	Special	35	85	15	Normal
TM39	Facade	Normal	Physical	70	100	20	Normal
TM40	Swift	Normal	Special	60	—	20	Many Others
TM43	Brick Break	Fighting	Physical	75	100	15	Normal
TM45	Dive	Water	Physical	80	100	10	Normal
TM52	Bounce	Flying	Physical	85	85	5	Normal
TM58	Assurance	Dark	Physical	60	100	10	Normal
TM67	Ice Fang	Ice	Physical	65	95	15	Normal
TM76	Round	Normal	Special	60	100	15	Normal

TR MOVES

NO.	NAME	TYPE	KIND	POW.	ACC.	PP	RANGE
TR03	Hydro Pump	Water	Special	110	80	5	Normal
TR04	Surf	Water	Special	90	100	15	All Others
TR12	Agility	Psychic	Status	—	—	30	Self
TR13	Focus Energy	Normal	Status	—	—	30	Self
TR16	Waterfall	Water	Physical	80	100	15	Normal
TR20	Substitute	Normal	Status	—	—	10	Self
TR26	Endure	Normal	Status	—	—	10	Self
TR27	Sleep Talk	Normal	Status	—	—	10	Self
TR32	Crunch	Dark	Physical	80	100	15	Normal
TR53	Close Combat	Fighting	Physical	120	100	5	Normal
TR57	Poison Jab	Poison	Physical	80	100	20	Normal
TR84	Scald	Water	Special	80	100	15	Normal
TR87	Drill Run	Ground	Physical	80	95	10	Normal
TR95	Throat Chop	Dark	Physical	80	100	15	Normal
TR97	Psychic Fangs	Psychic	Physical	85	100	10	Normal
TR98	Liquidation	Water	Physical	85	100	10	Normal

EVOLUTION MOVES

NAME	TYPE	KIND	POW.	ACC.	PP	RANGE

EGG MOVES

NAME	TYPE	KIND	POW.	ACC.	PP	RANGE

Barraskewda p. 84

ABILITY
Swift Swim
—

HIDDEN ABILITY
Propeller Tail

SPECIES STRENGTHS

HP	
ATTACK	
DEFENSE	
SP. ATK	
SP. DEF	
SPEED	

DAMAGE TAKEN IN BATTLE

×1	×1	×1
×0.5	×1	×1
×0.5	×1	×1
×2	×1	×1
×2	×1	×0.5
×0.5	×1	×1

WATER 2

182 — Meowth (p. 85)

ABILITY: Pickup, Technician
HIDDEN ABILITY: Unnerve

SPECIES STRENGTHS
HP · ATTACK · DEFENSE · SP. ATK · SP. DEF · SPEED

LEVEL-UP MOVES

LV.	NAME	TYPE	KIND	POW.	ACC.	PP	RANGE
1	Fake Out	Normal	Physical	40	100	10	Normal
1	Growl	Normal	Status	—	100	40	Many Others
4	Feint	Normal	Physical	30	100	10	Normal
8	Scratch	Normal	Physical	40	100	35	Normal
12	Pay Day	Normal	Physical	40	100	20	Normal
16	Bite	Dark	Physical	60	100	25	Normal
20	Taunt	Dark	Status	—	100	20	Normal
24	Assurance	Dark	Physical	60	100	10	Normal
29	Fury Swipes	Normal	Physical	18	80	15	Normal
32	Screech	Normal	Status	—	85	40	Normal
36	Slash	Normal	Physical	70	100	20	Normal
40	Nasty Plot	Dark	Status	—	—	20	Self
44	Play Rough	Fairy	Physical	90	90	10	Normal

EVOLUTION MOVES

NAME	TYPE	KIND	POW.	ACC.	PP	RANGE

EGG MOVES

NAME	TYPE	KIND	POW.	ACC.	PP	RANGE
Covet	Normal	Physical	60	100	25	Normal
Flail	Normal	Physical	—	100	15	Normal
Hypnosis	Psychic	Status	—	60	20	Normal
Last Resort	Normal	Physical	140	100	5	Normal
Spite	Ghost	Status	—	100	10	Normal
Tail Whip	Normal	Status	—	100	30	Many Others

TUTOR MOVES

NAME	TYPE	KIND	POW.	ACC.	PP	RANGE

TM MOVES

NO.	NAME	TYPE	KIND	POW.	ACC.	PP	RANGE
TM02	Pay Day	Normal	Physical	40	100	20	Normal
TM15	Dig	Ground	Physical	80	100	10	Normal
TM16	Screech	Normal	Status	—	85	40	Normal
TM21	Rest	Psychic	Status	—	—	10	Self
TM23	Thief	Dark	Physical	60	100	25	Normal
TM24	Snore	Normal	Special	50	100	15	Normal
TM25	Protect	Normal	Status	—	—	10	Self
TM27	Icy Wind	Ice	Special	55	95	15	Many Others
TM29	Charm	Fairy	Status	—	100	20	Normal
TM31	Attract	Normal	Status	—	100	15	Normal
TM33	Rain Dance	Water	Status	—	—	5	Both Sides
TM34	Sunny Day	Fire	Status	—	—	5	Both Sides
TM39	Facade	Normal	Physical	70	100	20	Normal
TM40	Swift	Normal	Special	60	—	20	Many Others
TM56	U-turn	Bug	Physical	70	100	20	Normal
TM57	Payback	Dark	Physical	50	100	10	Normal
TM58	Assurance	Dark	Physical	60	100	10	Normal
TM65	Shadow Claw	Ghost	Physical	70	100	15	Normal
TM76	Round	Normal	Special	60	100	15	Normal
TM79	Retaliate	Normal	Physical	70	100	5	Normal

TR MOVES

NO.	NAME	TYPE	KIND	POW.	ACC.	PP	RANGE
TR01	Body Slam	Normal	Physical	85	100	15	Normal
TR08	Thunderbolt	Electric	Special	90	100	15	Normal
TR09	Thunder	Electric	Special	110	70	10	Normal
TR17	Amnesia	Psychic	Status	—	—	20	Self
TR20	Substitute	Normal	Status	—	—	10	Self
TR26	Endure	Normal	Status	—	—	10	Self
TR27	Sleep Talk	Normal	Status	—	—	10	Self
TR31	Iron Tail	Steel	Physical	100	75	15	Normal
TR33	Shadow Ball	Ghost	Special	80	100	15	Normal
TR35	Uproar	Normal	Special	90	100	10	1 Random
TR37	Taunt	Dark	Status	—	100	20	Normal
TR42	Hyper Voice	Normal	Special	90	100	10	Many Others
TR58	Dark Pulse	Dark	Special	80	100	15	Normal
TR59	Seed Bomb	Grass	Physical	80	100	15	Normal
TR68	Nasty Plot	Dark	Status	—	—	20	Self
TR73	Gunk Shot	Poison	Physical	120	80	5	Normal
TR81	Foul Play	Dark	Physical	95	100	15	Normal
TR85	Work Up	Normal	Status	—	—	30	Self
TR90	Play Rough	Fairy	Physical	90	90	10	Normal
TR95	Throat Chop	Dark	Physical	80	100	15	Normal

DAMAGE TAKEN IN BATTLE
×1 · ×2 · ×1 · ×1 · ×1 · ×0 · ×1 · ×1 · ×1 · ×1 · ×1 · ×1 · ×1 · ×1 · ×1 · ×1 · ×1 · ×1

FIELD

---

182 — Meowth (Galarian Form) (p. 85)

ABILITY: Pickup, Tough Claws
HIDDEN ABILITY: Unnerve

SPECIES STRENGTHS
HP · ATTACK · DEFENSE · SP. ATK · SP. DEF · SPEED

LEVEL-UP MOVES

LV.	NAME	TYPE	KIND	POW.	ACC.	PP	RANGE
1	Fake Out	Normal	Physical	40	100	10	Normal
1	Growl	Normal	Status	—	100	40	Many Others
4	Hone Claws	Dark	Status	—	—	15	Self
8	Scratch	Normal	Physical	40	100	35	Normal
12	Pay Day	Normal	Physical	40	100	20	Normal
16	Metal Claw	Steel	Physical	50	95	35	Normal
20	Taunt	Dark	Status	—	100	20	Normal
24	Swagger	Normal	Status	—	85	15	Normal
29	Fury Swipes	Normal	Physical	18	80	15	Normal
32	Screech	Normal	Status	—	85	40	Normal
36	Slash	Normal	Physical	70	100	20	Normal
40	Metal Sound	Steel	Status	—	85	40	Normal
44	Thrash	Normal	Physical	120	100	10	1 Random

EVOLUTION MOVES

NAME	TYPE	KIND	POW.	ACC.	PP	RANGE

EGG MOVES

NAME	TYPE	KIND	POW.	ACC.	PP	RANGE
Covet	Normal	Physical	60	100	25	Normal
Curse	Ghost	Status	—	—	10	Varies
Double-Edge	Normal	Physical	120	100	15	Normal
Flail	Normal	Physical	—	100	15	Normal
Night Slash	Dark	Physical	70	100	15	Normal
Spite	Ghost	Status	—	100	10	Normal

TUTOR MOVES

NAME	TYPE	KIND	POW.	ACC.	PP	RANGE
Steel Beam	Steel	Special	140	95	5	Normal

TM MOVES

NO.	NAME	TYPE	KIND	POW.	ACC.	PP	RANGE
TM02	Pay Day	Normal	Physical	40	100	20	Normal
TM15	Dig	Ground	Physical	80	100	10	Normal
TM16	Screech	Normal	Status	—	85	40	Normal
TM21	Rest	Psychic	Status	—	—	10	Self
TM23	Thief	Dark	Physical	60	100	25	Normal
TM24	Snore	Normal	Special	50	100	15	Normal
TM25	Protect	Normal	Status	—	—	10	Self
TM31	Attract	Normal	Status	—	100	15	Normal
TM33	Rain Dance	Water	Status	—	—	5	Both Sides
TM34	Sunny Day	Fire	Status	—	—	5	Both Sides
TM39	Facade	Normal	Physical	70	100	20	Normal
TM56	U-turn	Bug	Physical	70	100	20	Normal
TM57	Payback	Dark	Physical	50	100	10	Normal
TM58	Assurance	Dark	Physical	60	100	10	Normal
TM65	Shadow Claw	Ghost	Physical	70	100	15	Normal
TM76	Round	Normal	Special	60	100	15	Normal
TM79	Retaliate	Normal	Physical	70	100	5	Normal

TR MOVES

NO.	NAME	TYPE	KIND	POW.	ACC.	PP	RANGE
TR00	Swords Dance	Normal	Status	—	—	20	Self
TR01	Body Slam	Normal	Physical	85	100	15	Normal
TR08	Thunderbolt	Electric	Special	90	100	15	Normal
TR09	Thunder	Electric	Special	110	70	10	Normal
TR17	Amnesia	Psychic	Status	—	—	20	Self
TR20	Substitute	Normal	Status	—	—	10	Self
TR26	Endure	Normal	Status	—	—	10	Self
TR27	Sleep Talk	Normal	Status	—	—	10	Self
TR31	Iron Tail	Steel	Physical	100	75	15	Normal
TR32	Crunch	Dark	Physical	80	100	15	Normal
TR33	Shadow Ball	Ghost	Special	80	100	15	Normal
TR35	Uproar	Normal	Special	90	100	10	1 Random
TR37	Taunt	Dark	Status	—	100	20	Normal
TR42	Hyper Voice	Normal	Special	90	100	10	Many Others
TR46	Iron Defense	Steel	Status	—	—	15	Self
TR52	Gyro Ball	Steel	Physical	—	100	5	Normal
TR58	Dark Pulse	Dark	Special	80	100	15	Normal
TR59	Seed Bomb	Grass	Physical	80	100	15	Normal
TR68	Nasty Plot	Dark	Status	—	—	20	Self
TR73	Gunk Shot	Poison	Physical	120	80	5	Normal
TR74	Iron Head	Steel	Physical	80	100	15	Normal
TR81	Foul Play	Dark	Physical	95	100	15	Normal
TR85	Work Up	Normal	Status	—	—	30	Self
TR90	Play Rough	Fairy	Physical	90	90	10	Normal
TR95	Throat Chop	Dark	Physical	80	100	15	Normal

DAMAGE TAKEN IN BATTLE
×0.5 · ×2 · ×0.5 · ×2 · ×0 · ×1 · ×1 · ×2 · ×0.5 · ×0.5 · ×0.5 · ×1 · ×1 · ×0.5 · ×0.5 · ×0.5 · ×0.5 · ×0.5

FIELD

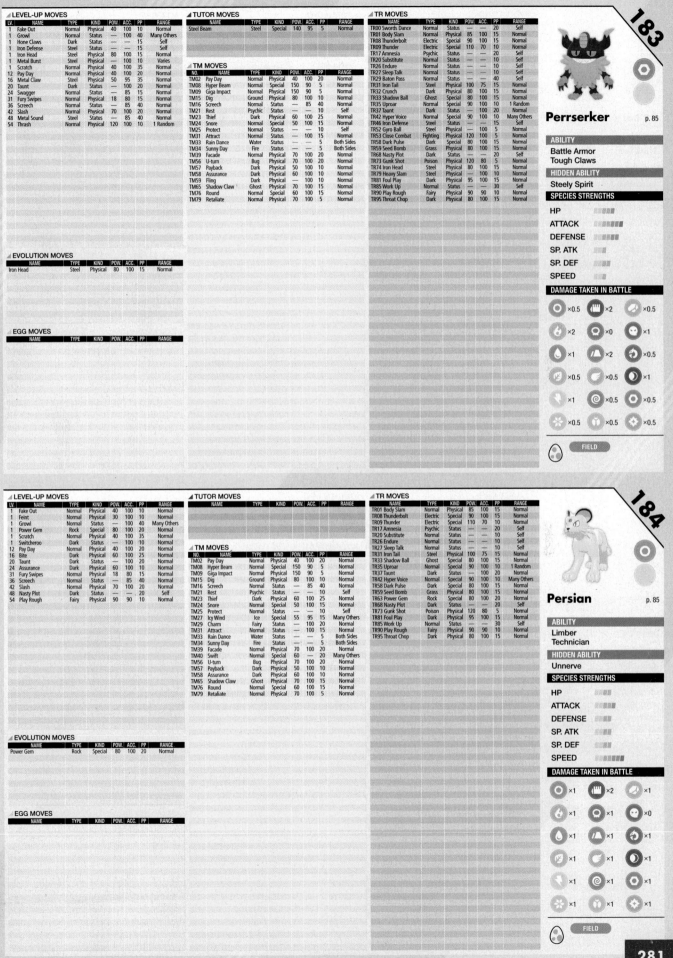

183 Perrserker

LEVEL-UP MOVES

LV.	NAME	TYPE	KIND	POW.	ACC.	PP	RANGE
1	Fake Out	Normal	Physical	40	100	10	Normal
1	Growl	Normal	Status	—	100	40	Many Others
1	Hone Claws	Dark	Status	—	—	15	Self
1	Iron Defense	Steel	Status	—	—	15	Self
1	Iron Head	Steel	Physical	80	100	15	Normal
1	Metal Burst	Steel	Physical	—	100	10	Varies
1	Scratch	Normal	Physical	40	100	35	Normal
12	Pay Day	Normal	Physical	40	100	20	Normal
16	Metal Claw	Steel	Physical	50	95	35	Normal
20	Taunt	Dark	Status	—	100	20	Normal
24	Swagger	Normal	Status	—	85	15	Normal
31	Fury Swipes	Normal	Physical	18	80	15	Normal
36	Screech	Normal	Status	—	85	40	Normal
42	Slash	Normal	Physical	70	100	20	Normal
48	Metal Sound	Steel	Status	—	85	40	Normal
54	Thrash	Normal	Physical	120	100	10	1 Random

EVOLUTION MOVES

NAME	TYPE	KIND	POW.	ACC.	PP	RANGE
Iron Head	Steel	Physical	80	100	15	Normal

EGG MOVES

NAME	TYPE	KIND	POW.	ACC.	PP	RANGE

TUTOR MOVES

NAME	TYPE	KIND	POW.	ACC.	PP	RANGE
Steel Beam	Steel	Special	140	95	5	Normal

TM MOVES

NO.	NAME	TYPE	KIND	POW.	ACC.	PP	RANGE
TM02	Pay Day	Normal	Physical	40	100	20	Normal
TM08	Hyper Beam	Normal	Special	150	90	5	Normal
TM09	Giga Impact	Normal	Physical	150	90	5	Normal
TM15	Dig	Ground	Physical	80	100	10	Normal
TM16	Screech	Normal	Status	—	85	40	Normal
TM21	Rest	Psychic	Status	—	—	10	Self
TM23	Thief	Dark	Physical	60	100	25	Normal
TM24	Snore	Normal	Special	50	100	15	Normal
TM25	Protect	Normal	Status	—	—	10	Self
TM31	Attract	Normal	Status	—	100	15	Normal
TM33	Rain Dance	Water	Status	—	—	5	Both Sides
TM34	Sunny Day	Fire	Status	—	—	5	Both Sides
TM39	Facade	Normal	Physical	70	100	20	Normal
TM56	U-turn	Bug	Physical	70	100	20	Normal
TM57	Payback	Dark	Physical	50	100	10	Normal
TM58	Assurance	Dark	Physical	60	100	10	Normal
TM59	Fling	Dark	Physical	—	100	10	Normal
TM65	Shadow Claw	Ghost	Physical	70	100	15	Normal
TM76	Round	Normal	Special	60	100	15	Normal
TM79	Retaliate	Normal	Physical	70	100	5	Normal

TR MOVES

NO.	NAME	TYPE	KIND	POW.	ACC.	PP	RANGE
TR00	Swords Dance	Normal	Status	—	—	20	Self
TR01	Body Slam	Normal	Physical	85	100	15	Normal
TR08	Thunderbolt	Electric	Special	90	100	15	Normal
TR09	Thunder	Electric	Special	110	70	10	Normal
TR17	Amnesia	Psychic	Status	—	—	20	Self
TR20	Substitute	Normal	Status	—	—	10	Self
TR26	Endure	Normal	Status	—	—	10	Self
TR27	Sleep Talk	Normal	Status	—	—	10	Self
TR29	Baton Pass	Normal	Status	—	—	40	Self
TR31	Iron Tail	Steel	Physical	100	75	15	Normal
TR32	Crunch	Dark	Physical	80	100	15	Normal
TR33	Shadow Ball	Ghost	Special	80	100	15	Normal
TR35	Uproar	Normal	Special	90	100	10	1 Random
TR37	Taunt	Dark	Status	—	100	15	Normal
TR42	Hyper Voice	Normal	Special	90	100	10	Many Others
TR46	Iron Defense	Steel	Status	—	—	15	Self
TR52	Gyro Ball	Steel	Physical	—	100	5	Normal
TR53	Close Combat	Fighting	Physical	120	100	5	Normal
TR58	Dark Pulse	Dark	Special	80	100	15	Normal
TR59	Seed Bomb	Grass	Physical	80	100	15	Normal
TR68	Nasty Plot	Dark	Status	—	—	20	Self
TR73	Gunk Shot	Poison	Physical	120	80	5	Normal
TR74	Iron Head	Steel	Physical	80	100	15	Normal
TR79	Heavy Slam	Steel	Physical	—	100	10	Normal
TR81	Foul Play	Dark	Physical	95	100	15	Normal
TR85	Work Up	Normal	Status	—	—	30	Self
TR90	Play Rough	Fairy	Physical	90	90	10	Normal
TR95	Throat Chop	Dark	Physical	80	100	15	Normal

Perrserker p. 85

ABILITY
Battle Armor
Tough Claws

HIDDEN ABILITY
Steely Spirit

SPECIES STRENGTHS

HP	
ATTACK	
DEFENSE	
SP. ATK	
SP. DEF	
SPEED	

DAMAGE TAKEN IN BATTLE

×0.5 ×2 ×0.5
×2 ×0 ×1
×1 ×2 ×0.5
×0.5 ×0.5 ×1
×1 ×0.5 ×0.5
×0.5 ×0.5 ×0.5

FIELD

---

184 Persian

LEVEL-UP MOVES

LV.	NAME	TYPE	KIND	POW.	ACC.	PP	RANGE
1	Fake Out	Normal	Physical	40	100	10	Normal
1	Feint	Normal	Physical	30	100	10	Normal
1	Growl	Normal	Status	—	100	40	Many Others
1	Power Gem	Rock	Special	80	100	20	Normal
1	Scratch	Normal	Physical	40	100	35	Normal
1	Switcheroo	Dark	Status	—	100	10	Normal
12	Pay Day	Normal	Physical	40	100	20	Normal
16	Bite	Dark	Physical	60	100	25	Normal
20	Taunt	Dark	Status	—	100	20	Normal
24	Assurance	Dark	Physical	60	100	10	Normal
31	Fury Swipes	Normal	Physical	18	80	15	Normal
36	Screech	Normal	Status	—	85	40	Normal
42	Slash	Normal	Physical	70	100	20	Normal
48	Nasty Plot	Dark	Status	—	—	20	Self
54	Play Rough	Fairy	Physical	90	90	10	Normal

EVOLUTION MOVES

NAME	TYPE	KIND	POW.	ACC.	PP	RANGE
Power Gem	Rock	Special	80	100	20	Normal

EGG MOVES

NAME	TYPE	KIND	POW.	ACC.	PP	RANGE

TUTOR MOVES

NAME	TYPE	KIND	POW.	ACC.	PP	RANGE

TM MOVES

NO.	NAME	TYPE	KIND	POW.	ACC.	PP	RANGE
TM02	Pay Day	Normal	Physical	40	100	20	Normal
TM08	Hyper Beam	Normal	Special	150	90	5	Normal
TM09	Giga Impact	Normal	Physical	150	90	5	Normal
TM15	Dig	Ground	Physical	80	100	10	Normal
TM16	Screech	Normal	Status	—	85	40	Normal
TM21	Rest	Psychic	Status	—	—	10	Self
TM23	Thief	Dark	Physical	60	100	25	Normal
TM24	Snore	Normal	Special	50	100	15	Normal
TM25	Protect	Normal	Status	—	—	10	Self
TM27	Icy Wind	Ice	Special	55	95	15	Many Others
TM29	Charm	Fairy	Status	—	100	20	Normal
TM31	Attract	Normal	Status	—	100	15	Normal
TM33	Rain Dance	Water	Status	—	—	5	Both Sides
TM34	Sunny Day	Fire	Status	—	—	5	Both Sides
TM39	Facade	Normal	Physical	70	100	20	Normal
TM40	Swift	Normal	Special	60	—	20	Many Others
TM56	U-turn	Bug	Physical	70	100	20	Normal
TM57	Payback	Dark	Physical	50	100	10	Normal
TM58	Assurance	Dark	Physical	60	100	10	Normal
TM65	Shadow Claw	Ghost	Physical	70	100	15	Normal
TM76	Round	Normal	Special	60	100	15	Normal
TM79	Retaliate	Normal	Physical	70	100	5	Normal

TR MOVES

NO.	NAME	TYPE	KIND	POW.	ACC.	PP	RANGE
TR01	Body Slam	Normal	Physical	85	100	15	Normal
TR08	Thunderbolt	Electric	Special	90	100	15	Normal
TR09	Thunder	Electric	Special	110	70	10	Normal
TR17	Amnesia	Psychic	Status	—	—	20	Self
TR20	Substitute	Normal	Status	—	—	10	Self
TR26	Endure	Normal	Status	—	—	10	Self
TR27	Sleep Talk	Normal	Status	—	—	10	Self
TR31	Iron Tail	Steel	Physical	100	75	15	Normal
TR33	Shadow Ball	Ghost	Special	80	100	15	Normal
TR35	Uproar	Normal	Special	90	100	10	1 Random
TR37	Taunt	Dark	Status	—	100	15	Normal
TR42	Hyper Voice	Normal	Special	90	100	10	Many Others
TR58	Dark Pulse	Dark	Special	80	100	15	Normal
TR59	Seed Bomb	Grass	Physical	80	100	15	Normal
TR63	Power Gem	Rock	Special	80	100	20	Normal
TR68	Nasty Plot	Dark	Status	—	—	20	Self
TR73	Gunk Shot	Poison	Physical	120	80	5	Normal
TR81	Foul Play	Dark	Physical	95	100	15	Normal
TR85	Work Up	Normal	Status	—	—	30	Self
TR90	Play Rough	Fairy	Physical	90	90	10	Normal
TR95	Throat Chop	Dark	Physical	80	100	15	Normal

Persian p. 85

ABILITY
Limber
Technician

HIDDEN ABILITY
Unnerve

SPECIES STRENGTHS

HP	
ATTACK	
DEFENSE	
SP. ATK	
SP. DEF	
SPEED	

DAMAGE TAKEN IN BATTLE

×1 ×2 ×1
×1 ×1 ×0
×1 ×1 ×1
×1 ×1 ×1
×1 ×1 ×1
×1 ×1 ×1

FIELD

185 Milcery
p. 86

ABILITY
Sweet Veil
—

HIDDEN ABILITY
Aroma Veil

SPECIES STRENGTHS

HP	▮▮
ATTACK	▮▮▮
DEFENSE	▮▮▮
SP. ATK	▮▮▮
SP. DEF	▮▮▮▮
SPEED	▮▮

DAMAGE TAKEN IN BATTLE

◎ ×1	▦ ×0.5	🍃 ×1
🔥 ×1	⊙ ×2	☀ ×1
💧 ×1	⛰ ×1	↻ ×0
⚡ ×1	◉ ×1	☾ ×0.5
🗡 ×1	⊚ ×1	◯ ×2
❄ ×1	🜨 ×0.5	◈ ×1

FAIRY
AMORPHOUS

LEVEL-UP MOVES

LV.	NAME	TYPE	KIND	POW.	ACC.	PP	RANGE
1	Aromatic Mist	Fairy	Status	—	—	20	1 Ally
1	Tackle	Normal	Physical	40	100	35	Normal
5	Sweet Kiss	Fairy	Status	—	75	10	Normal
10	Sweet Scent	Normal	Status	—	100	20	Many Others
15	Draining Kiss	Fairy	Special	50	100	10	Normal
20	Aromatherapy	Grass	Status	—	—	5	Your Party
25	Attract	Normal	Status	—	100	15	Normal
30	Acid Armor	Poison	Status	—	—	20	Self
35	Dazzling Gleam	Fairy	Special	80	100	10	Many Others
40	Recover	Normal	Status	—	—	10	Self
45	Misty Terrain	Fairy	Status	—	—	10	Both Sides
50	Entrainment	Normal	Status	—	100	15	Normal

EVOLUTION MOVES

NAME	TYPE	KIND	POW.	ACC.	PP	RANGE

EGG MOVES

NAME	TYPE	KIND	POW.	ACC.	PP	RANGE
Baby-Doll Eyes	Fairy	Status	—	100	30	Normal
Last Resort	Normal	Physical	140	100	5	Normal

TUTOR MOVES

NAME	TYPE	KIND	POW.	ACC.	PP	RANGE

TM MOVES

NO.	NAME	TYPE	KIND	POW.	ACC.	PP	RANGE
TM21	Rest	Psychic	Status	—	—	10	Self
TM24	Snore	Normal	Special	50	100	15	Normal
TM25	Protect	Normal	Status	—	—	10	Self
TM29	Charm	Fairy	Status	—	100	20	Normal
TM31	Attract	Normal	Status	—	100	15	Normal
TM39	Facade	Normal	Physical	70	100	20	Normal
TM41	Helping Hand	Normal	Status	—	—	20	1 Ally
TM59	Fling	Dark	Physical	—	100	10	Normal
TM76	Round	Normal	Special	60	100	15	Normal
TM87	Draining Kiss	Fairy	Special	50	100	10	Normal
TM89	Misty Terrain	Fairy	Status	—	—	10	Both Sides

TR MOVES

NO.	NAME	TYPE	KIND	POW.	ACC.	PP	RANGE
TR20	Substitute	Normal	Status	—	—	10	Self
TR26	Endure	Normal	Status	—	—	10	Self
TR27	Sleep Talk	Normal	Status	—	—	10	Self
TR82	Stored Power	Psychic	Special	20	100	10	Normal
TR92	Dazzling Gleam	Fairy	Special	80	100	10	Many Others

---

186 Alcremie
p. 86

ABILITY
Sweet Veil
—

HIDDEN ABILITY
Aroma Veil

SPECIES STRENGTHS

HP	▮▮▮▮
ATTACK	▮▮▮
DEFENSE	▮▮▮▮
SP. ATK	▮▮▮▮▮▮
SP. DEF	▮▮▮▮▮▮▮
SPEED	▮▮▮

DAMAGE TAKEN IN BATTLE

◎ ×1	▦ ×0.5	🍃 ×1
🔥 ×1	⊙ ×2	☀ ×1
💧 ×1	⛰ ×1	↻ ×0
⚡ ×1	◉ ×1	☾ ×0.5
🗡 ×1	⊚ ×1	◯ ×1
❄ ×1	🜨 ×0.5	◈ ×1

FAIRY
AMORPHOUS

LEVEL-UP MOVES

LV.	NAME	TYPE	KIND	POW.	ACC.	PP	RANGE
1	Aromatic Mist	Fairy	Status	—	—	20	1 Ally
1	Decorate	Fairy	Status	—	—	15	Normal
1	Sweet Kiss	Fairy	Status	—	75	10	Normal
1	Sweet Scent	Normal	Status	—	100	20	Many Others
1	Tackle	Normal	Physical	40	100	35	Normal
15	Draining Kiss	Fairy	Special	50	100	10	Normal
20	Aromatherapy	Grass	Status	—	—	5	Your Party
25	Attract	Normal	Status	—	100	15	Normal
30	Acid Armor	Poison	Status	—	—	20	Self
35	Dazzling Gleam	Fairy	Special	80	100	10	Many Others
40	Recover	Normal	Status	—	—	10	Self
45	Misty Terrain	Fairy	Status	—	—	10	Both Sides
50	Entrainment	Normal	Status	—	100	15	Normal

EVOLUTION MOVES

NAME	TYPE	KIND	POW.	ACC.	PP	RANGE
Decorate	Fairy	Status	—	—	15	Normal

EGG MOVES

NAME	TYPE	KIND	POW.	ACC.	PP	RANGE

TUTOR MOVES

NAME	TYPE	KIND	POW.	ACC.	PP	RANGE

TM MOVES

NO.	NAME	TYPE	KIND	POW.	ACC.	PP	RANGE
TM08	Hyper Beam	Normal	Special	150	90	5	Normal
TM09	Giga Impact	Normal	Physical	150	90	5	Normal
TM10	Magical Leaf	Grass	Special	60	—	20	Normal
TM11	Solar Beam	Grass	Special	120	100	10	Normal
TM17	Light Screen	Psychic	Status	—	—	30	Your Side
TM19	Safeguard	Normal	Status	—	—	25	Your Side
TM21	Rest	Psychic	Status	—	—	10	Self
TM24	Snore	Normal	Special	50	100	15	Normal
TM25	Protect	Normal	Status	—	—	10	Self
TM28	Giga Drain	Grass	Special	75	100	10	Normal
TM29	Charm	Fairy	Status	—	100	20	Normal
TM31	Attract	Normal	Status	—	100	15	Normal
TM39	Facade	Normal	Physical	70	100	20	Normal
TM41	Helping Hand	Normal	Status	—	—	20	1 Ally
TM44	Imprison	Psychic	Status	—	—	10	Self
TM47	Fake Tears	Dark	Status	—	100	20	Normal
TM59	Fling	Dark	Physical	—	100	10	Normal
TM63	Drain Punch	Fighting	Physical	75	100	10	Normal
TM71	Wonder Room	Psychic	Status	—	—	10	Both Sides
TM72	Magic Room	Psychic	Status	—	—	10	Both Sides
TM76	Round	Normal	Special	60	100	15	Normal
TM87	Draining Kiss	Fairy	Special	50	100	10	Normal
TM89	Misty Terrain	Fairy	Status	—	—	10	Both Sides
TM92	Mystical Fire	Fire	Special	75	100	10	Normal

TR MOVES

NO.	NAME	TYPE	KIND	POW.	ACC.	PP	RANGE
TR11	Psychic	Psychic	Special	90	100	10	Normal
TR14	Metronome	Normal	Status	—	—	10	Self
TR19	Tri Attack	Normal	Special	80	100	10	Normal
TR20	Substitute	Normal	Status	—	—	10	Self
TR25	Psyshock	Psychic	Special	80	100	10	Normal
TR26	Endure	Normal	Status	—	—	10	Self
TR27	Sleep Talk	Normal	Status	—	—	10	Self
TR30	Encore	Normal	Status	—	100	5	Normal
TR49	Calm Mind	Psychic	Status	—	—	20	Self
TR65	Energy Ball	Grass	Special	90	100	10	Normal
TR82	Stored Power	Psychic	Special	20	100	10	Normal
TR90	Play Rough	Fairy	Physical	90	90	10	Normal
TR92	Dazzling Gleam	Fairy	Special	80	100	10	Many Others

187

Cutiefly — p. 87

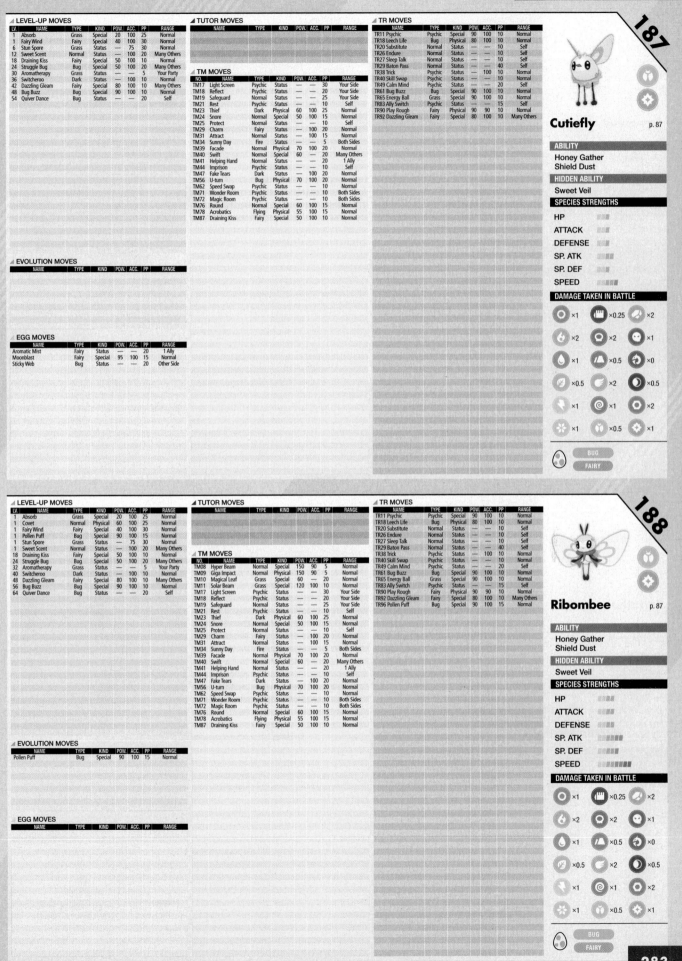

LEVEL-UP MOVES

LV.	NAME	TYPE	KIND	POW.	ACC.	PP	RANGE
1	Absorb	Grass	Special	20	100	25	Normal
1	Fairy Wind	Fairy	Special	40	100	30	Normal
6	Stun Spore	Grass	Status	—	75	30	Normal
12	Sweet Scent	Normal	Status	—	100	20	Many Others
18	Draining Kiss	Fairy	Special	50	100	10	Normal
24	Struggle Bug	Bug	Special	50	100	20	Many Others
30	Aromatherapy	Grass	Status	—	—	5	Your Party
36	Switcheroo	Dark	Status	—	100	10	Normal
42	Dazzling Gleam	Fairy	Special	80	100	10	Many Others
48	Bug Buzz	Bug	Special	90	100	10	Normal
54	Quiver Dance	Bug	Status	—	—	20	Self

EVOLUTION MOVES

NAME	TYPE	KIND	POW.	ACC.	PP	RANGE

EGG MOVES

NAME	TYPE	KIND	POW.	ACC.	PP	RANGE
Aromatic Mist	Fairy	Status	—	—	20	1 Ally
Moonblast	Fairy	Special	95	100	15	Normal
Sticky Web	Bug	Status	—	—	20	Other Side

TUTOR MOVES

NAME	TYPE	KIND	POW.	ACC.	PP	RANGE

TM MOVES

NO.	NAME	TYPE	KIND	POW.	ACC.	PP	RANGE
TM17	Light Screen	Psychic	Status	—	—	30	Your Side
TM18	Reflect	Psychic	Status	—	—	20	Your Side
TM19	Safeguard	Normal	Status	—	—	25	Your Side
TM21	Rest	Psychic	Status	—	—	10	Self
TM23	Thief	Dark	Physical	60	100	25	Normal
TM24	Snore	Normal	Special	50	100	15	Normal
TM25	Protect	Normal	Status	—	—	10	Self
TM29	Charm	Fairy	Status	—	100	20	Normal
TM31	Attract	Normal	Status	—	100	15	Normal
TM34	Sunny Day	Fire	Status	—	—	5	Both Sides
TM39	Facade	Normal	Physical	70	100	20	Normal
TM40	Swift	Normal	Special	60	—	20	Many Others
TM41	Helping Hand	Normal	Status	—	—	20	1 Ally
TM44	Imprison	Psychic	Status	—	—	10	Self
TM47	Fake Tears	Dark	Status	—	100	20	Normal
TM56	U-turn	Bug	Physical	70	100	20	Normal
TM62	Speed Swap	Psychic	Status	—	—	10	Normal
TM71	Wonder Room	Psychic	Status	—	—	10	Both Sides
TM72	Magic Room	Psychic	Status	—	—	10	Both Sides
TM76	Round	Normal	Special	60	100	15	Normal
TM78	Acrobatics	Flying	Physical	55	100	15	Normal
TM87	Draining Kiss	Fairy	Special	50	100	10	Normal

TR MOVES

NO.	NAME	TYPE	KIND	POW.	ACC.	PP	RANGE
TR11	Psychic	Psychic	Special	90	100	10	Normal
TR18	Leech Life	Bug	Physical	80	100	10	Normal
TR20	Substitute	Normal	Status	—	—	10	Self
TR26	Endure	Normal	Status	—	—	10	Self
TR27	Sleep Talk	Normal	Status	—	—	10	Self
TR29	Baton Pass	Normal	Status	—	—	40	Self
TR38	Trick	Psychic	Status	—	100	10	Normal
TR40	Skill Swap	Psychic	Status	—	—	10	Normal
TR61	Bug Buzz	Bug	Special	90	100	10	Normal
TR65	Energy Ball	Grass	Special	90	100	10	Normal
TR83	Ally Switch	Psychic	Status	—	—	15	Self
TR90	Play Rough	Fairy	Physical	90	90	10	Normal
TR92	Dazzling Gleam	Fairy	Special	80	100	10	Many Others

ABILITY
Honey Gather
Shield Dust

HIDDEN ABILITY
Sweet Veil

SPECIES STRENGTHS

HP
ATTACK
DEFENSE
SP. ATK
SP. DEF
SPEED

DAMAGE TAKEN IN BATTLE

×1 | ×0.25 | ×2
×2 | ×2 | ×1
×1 | ×0.5 | ×0
×0.5 | ×2 | ×0.5
×1 | ×1 | ×2
×1 | ×0.5 | ×1

BUG
FAIRY

188

Ribombee — p. 87

LEVEL-UP MOVES

LV.	NAME	TYPE	KIND	POW.	ACC.	PP	RANGE
1	Absorb	Grass	Special	20	100	25	Normal
1	Covet	Normal	Physical	60	100	25	Normal
1	Fairy Wind	Fairy	Special	40	100	30	Normal
1	Pollen Puff	Bug	Special	90	100	15	Normal
1	Stun Spore	Grass	Status	—	75	30	Normal
1	Sweet Scent	Normal	Status	—	100	20	Many Others
18	Draining Kiss	Fairy	Special	50	100	10	Normal
24	Struggle Bug	Bug	Special	50	100	20	Many Others
32	Aromatherapy	Grass	Status	—	—	5	Your Party
40	Switcheroo	Dark	Status	—	100	10	Normal
48	Dazzling Gleam	Fairy	Special	80	100	10	Many Others
56	Bug Buzz	Bug	Special	90	100	10	Normal
64	Quiver Dance	Bug	Status	—	—	20	Self

EVOLUTION MOVES

NAME	TYPE	KIND	POW.	ACC.	PP	RANGE
Pollen Puff	Bug	Special	90	100	15	Normal

EGG MOVES

NAME	TYPE	KIND	POW.	ACC.	PP	RANGE

TUTOR MOVES

NAME	TYPE	KIND	POW.	ACC.	PP	RANGE

TM MOVES

NO.	NAME	TYPE	KIND	POW.	ACC.	PP	RANGE
TM08	Hyper Beam	Normal	Special	150	90	5	Normal
TM09	Giga Impact	Normal	Physical	150	90	5	Normal
TM10	Magical Leaf	Grass	Special	60	—	20	Normal
TM11	Solar Beam	Grass	Special	120	100	10	Normal
TM17	Light Screen	Psychic	Status	—	—	30	Your Side
TM18	Reflect	Psychic	Status	—	—	20	Your Side
TM19	Safeguard	Normal	Status	—	—	25	Your Side
TM21	Rest	Psychic	Status	—	—	10	Self
TM23	Thief	Dark	Physical	60	100	25	Normal
TM24	Snore	Normal	Special	50	100	15	Normal
TM25	Protect	Normal	Status	—	—	10	Self
TM29	Charm	Fairy	Status	—	100	20	Normal
TM31	Attract	Normal	Status	—	100	15	Normal
TM34	Sunny Day	Fire	Status	—	—	5	Both Sides
TM39	Facade	Normal	Physical	70	100	20	Normal
TM40	Swift	Normal	Special	60	—	20	Many Others
TM41	Helping Hand	Normal	Status	—	—	20	1 Ally
TM44	Imprison	Psychic	Status	—	—	10	Self
TM47	Fake Tears	Dark	Status	—	100	20	Normal
TM56	U-turn	Bug	Physical	70	100	20	Normal
TM62	Speed Swap	Psychic	Status	—	—	10	Normal
TM71	Wonder Room	Psychic	Status	—	—	10	Both Sides
TM72	Magic Room	Psychic	Status	—	—	10	Both Sides
TM76	Round	Normal	Special	60	100	15	Normal
TM78	Acrobatics	Flying	Physical	55	100	15	Normal
TM87	Draining Kiss	Fairy	Special	50	100	10	Normal

TR MOVES

NO.	NAME	TYPE	KIND	POW.	ACC.	PP	RANGE
TR11	Psychic	Psychic	Special	90	100	10	Normal
TR18	Leech Life	Bug	Physical	80	100	10	Normal
TR20	Substitute	Normal	Status	—	—	10	Self
TR26	Endure	Normal	Status	—	—	10	Self
TR27	Sleep Talk	Normal	Status	—	—	10	Self
TR29	Baton Pass	Normal	Status	—	—	40	Self
TR38	Trick	Psychic	Status	—	100	10	Normal
TR40	Skill Swap	Psychic	Status	—	—	10	Normal
TR49	Calm Mind	Psychic	Status	—	—	20	Self
TR61	Bug Buzz	Bug	Special	90	100	10	Normal
TR65	Energy Ball	Grass	Special	90	100	10	Normal
TR83	Ally Switch	Psychic	Status	—	—	15	Self
TR90	Play Rough	Fairy	Physical	90	90	10	Normal
TR92	Dazzling Gleam	Fairy	Special	80	100	10	Many Others
TR96	Pollen Puff	Bug	Special	90	100	15	Normal

ABILITY
Honey Gather
Shield Dust

HIDDEN ABILITY
Sweet Veil

SPECIES STRENGTHS

HP
ATTACK
DEFENSE
SP. ATK
SP. DEF
SPEED

DAMAGE TAKEN IN BATTLE

×1 | ×0.25 | ×2
×2 | ×2 | ×1
×1 | ×0.5 | ×0
×0.5 | ×2 | ×0.5
×1 | ×1 | ×2
×1 | ×0.5 | ×1

BUG
FAIRY

189 Ferroseed (p. 87)

ABILITY: Iron Barbs / —

HIDDEN ABILITY: —

SPECIES STRENGTHS: HP, ATTACK, DEFENSE, SP. ATK, SP. DEF, SPEED

Egg Groups: GRASS, MINERAL

LEVEL-UP MOVES

LV.	NAME	TYPE	KIND	POW.	ACC.	PP	RANGE
1	Harden	Normal	Status	—	—	30	Self
1	Tackle	Normal	Physical	40	100	35	Normal
5	Metal Claw	Steel	Physical	50	95	35	Normal
10	Pin Missile	Bug	Physical	25	95	20	Normal
15	Ingrain	Grass	Status	—	—	20	Self
20	Flash Cannon	Steel	Special	80	100	10	Normal
25	Iron Head	Steel	Physical	80	100	15	Normal
30	Self-Destruct	Normal	Physical	200	100	5	All Others
35	Iron Defense	Steel	Status	—	—	15	Self
41	Curse	Ghost	Status	—	—	10	Varies
45	Gyro Ball	Steel	Physical	—	100	5	Normal
50	Explosion	Normal	Physical	250	100	5	All Others

TUTOR MOVES

NAME	TYPE	KIND	POW.	ACC.	PP	RANGE
Steel Beam	Steel	Special	140	95	5	Normal

TM MOVES

NO.	NAME	TYPE	KIND	POW.	ACC.	PP	RANGE
TM07	Pin Missile	Bug	Physical	25	95	20	Normal
TM11	Solar Beam	Grass	Special	120	100	10	Normal
TM14	Thunder Wave	Electric	Status	—	90	20	Normal
TM20	Self-Destruct	Normal	Physical	200	100	5	All Others
TM21	Rest	Psychic	Status	—	—	10	Self
TM24	Snore	Normal	Special	50	100	15	Normal
TM25	Protect	Normal	Status	—	—	10	Self
TM28	Giga Drain	Grass	Special	75	100	10	Normal
TM31	Attract	Normal	Status	—	100	15	Normal
TM34	Sunny Day	Fire	Status	—	—	5	Both Sides
TM39	Facade	Normal	Physical	70	100	20	Normal
TM42	Revenge	Fighting	Physical	60	100	10	Normal
TM50	Bullet Seed	Grass	Physical	25	100	30	Normal
TM57	Payback	Dark	Physical	50	100	10	Normal
TM58	Assurance	Dark	Physical	60	100	10	Normal
TM76	Round	Normal	Special	60	100	15	Normal

TR MOVES

NO.	NAME	TYPE	KIND	POW.	ACC.	PP	RANGE
TR08	Thunderbolt	Electric	Special	90	100	15	Normal
TR20	Substitute	Normal	Status	—	—	10	Self
TR23	Spikes	Ground	Status	—	—	20	Other Side
TR26	Endure	Normal	Status	—	—	10	Self
TR27	Sleep Talk	Normal	Status	—	—	10	Self
TR46	Iron Defense	Steel	Status	—	—	15	Self
TR57	Poison Jab	Poison	Physical	80	100	20	Normal
TR59	Seed Bomb	Grass	Physical	80	100	15	Normal
TR65	Energy Ball	Grass	Special	90	100	10	Normal
TR70	Flash Cannon	Steel	Special	80	100	10	Normal
TR74	Iron Head	Steel	Physical	80	100	15	Normal
TR76	Stealth Rock	Rock	Status	—	—	20	Other Side

EVOLUTION MOVES

NAME	TYPE	KIND	POW.	ACC.	PP	RANGE

EGG MOVES

NAME	TYPE	KIND	POW.	ACC.	PP	RANGE
Acid Spray	Poison	Special	40	100	20	Normal
Gravity	Psychic	Status	—	—	5	Both Sides
Knock Off	Dark	Physical	65	100	20	Normal
Leech Seed	Grass	Status	—	90	10	Normal
Toxic	Poison	Status	—	90	10	Normal

190 Ferrothorn (p. 87)

ABILITY: Iron Barbs / —

HIDDEN ABILITY: Anticipation

SPECIES STRENGTHS: HP, ATTACK, DEFENSE, SP. ATK, SP. DEF, SPEED

Egg Groups: GRASS, MINERAL

LEVEL-UP MOVES

LV.	NAME	TYPE	KIND	POW.	ACC.	PP	RANGE
1	Harden	Normal	Status	—	—	30	Self
1	Metal Claw	Steel	Physical	50	95	35	Normal
1	Pin Missile	Bug	Physical	25	95	20	Normal
1	Power Whip	Grass	Physical	120	85	10	Normal
1	Tackle	Normal	Physical	40	100	35	Normal
15	Ingrain	Grass	Status	—	—	20	Self
20	Flash Cannon	Steel	Special	80	100	10	Normal
25	Iron Head	Steel	Physical	80	100	15	Normal
30	Self-Destruct	Normal	Physical	200	100	5	All Others
35	Iron Defense	Steel	Status	—	—	15	Self
43	Curse	Ghost	Status	—	—	10	Varies
49	Gyro Ball	Steel	Physical	—	100	5	Normal
56	Explosion	Normal	Physical	250	100	5	All Others

TUTOR MOVES

NAME	TYPE	KIND	POW.	ACC.	PP	RANGE
Steel Beam	Steel	Special	140	95	5	Normal

TM MOVES

NO.	NAME	TYPE	KIND	POW.	ACC.	PP	RANGE
TM07	Pin Missile	Bug	Physical	25	95	20	Normal
TM08	Hyper Beam	Normal	Special	150	90	5	Normal
TM09	Giga Impact	Normal	Physical	150	90	5	Normal
TM11	Solar Beam	Grass	Special	120	100	10	Normal
TM14	Thunder Wave	Electric	Status	—	90	20	Normal
TM20	Self-Destruct	Normal	Physical	200	100	5	All Others
TM21	Rest	Psychic	Status	—	—	10	Self
TM24	Snore	Normal	Special	50	100	15	Normal
TM25	Protect	Normal	Status	—	—	10	Self
TM28	Giga Drain	Grass	Special	75	100	10	Normal
TM31	Attract	Normal	Status	—	100	15	Normal
TM32	Sandstorm	Rock	Status	—	—	10	Both Sides
TM34	Sunny Day	Fire	Status	—	—	5	Both Sides
TM39	Facade	Normal	Physical	70	100	20	Normal
TM42	Revenge	Fighting	Physical	60	100	10	Normal
TM50	Bullet Seed	Grass	Physical	25	100	30	Normal
TM57	Payback	Dark	Physical	50	100	10	Normal
TM58	Assurance	Dark	Physical	60	100	10	Normal
TM65	Shadow Claw	Ghost	Physical	70	100	15	Normal
TM76	Round	Normal	Special	60	100	15	Normal
TM81	Bulldoze	Ground	Physical	60	100	20	All Others
TM97	Brutal Swing	Dark	Physical	60	100	20	All Others

TR MOVES

NO.	NAME	TYPE	KIND	POW.	ACC.	PP	RANGE
TR00	Swords Dance	Normal	Status	—	—	20	Self
TR08	Thunderbolt	Electric	Special	90	100	15	Normal
TR09	Thunder	Electric	Special	110	70	10	Normal
TR20	Substitute	Normal	Status	—	—	10	Self
TR23	Spikes	Ground	Status	—	—	20	Other Side
TR26	Endure	Normal	Status	—	—	10	Self
TR27	Sleep Talk	Normal	Status	—	—	10	Self
TR46	Iron Defense	Steel	Status	—	—	15	Self
TR52	Gyro Ball	Steel	Physical	—	100	5	Normal
TR57	Poison Jab	Poison	Physical	80	100	20	Normal
TR59	Seed Bomb	Grass	Physical	80	100	15	Normal
TR65	Energy Ball	Grass	Special	90	100	10	Normal
TR70	Flash Cannon	Steel	Special	80	100	10	Normal
TR72	Power Whip	Grass	Physical	120	85	10	Normal
TR74	Iron Head	Steel	Physical	80	100	15	Normal
TR76	Stealth Rock	Rock	Status	—	—	20	Other Side
TR77	Grass Knot	Grass	Special	—	100	20	Normal
TR79	Heavy Slam	Steel	Physical	—	100	10	Normal
TR99	Body Press	Fighting	Physical	80	100	10	Normal

EVOLUTION MOVES

NAME	TYPE	KIND	POW.	ACC.	PP	RANGE
Power Whip	Grass	Physical	120	85	10	Normal

EGG MOVES

NAME	TYPE	KIND	POW.	ACC.	PP	RANGE

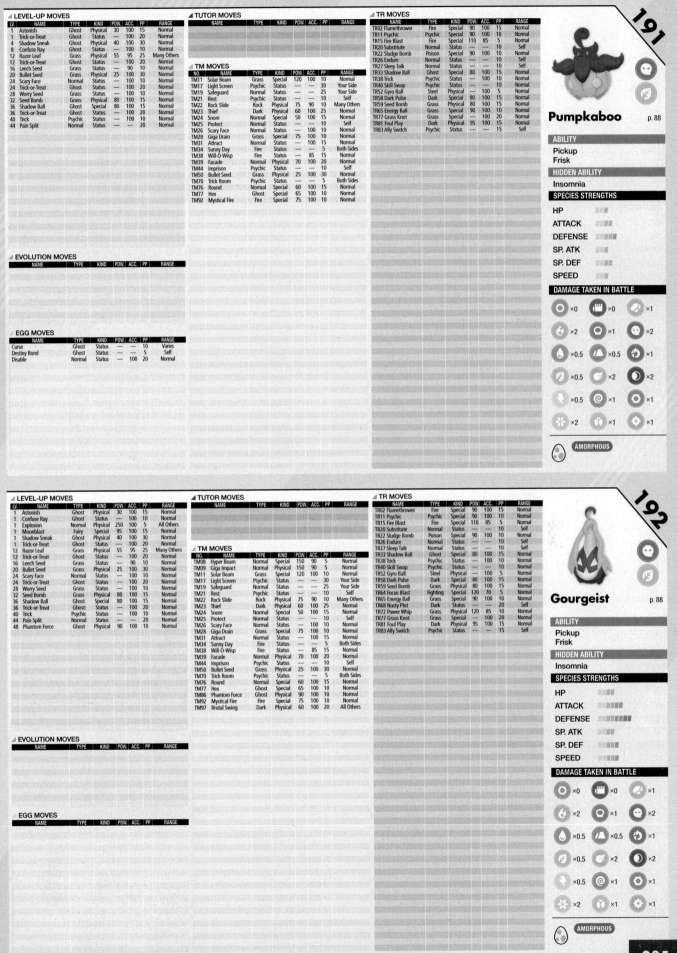

191

Pumpkaboo — p. 88

LEVEL-UP MOVES

LV.	NAME	TYPE	KIND	POW.	ACC.	PP	RANGE
1	Astonish	Ghost	Physical	30	100	15	Normal
1	Trick-or-Treat	Ghost	Status	—	100	20	Normal
4	Shadow Sneak	Ghost	Physical	40	100	30	Normal
8	Confuse Ray	Ghost	Status	—	100	10	Normal
12	Razor Leaf	Grass	Physical	55	95	25	Many Others
12	Trick-or-Treat	Ghost	Status	—	100	20	Normal
16	Leech Seed	Grass	Status	—	90	10	Normal
20	Bullet Seed	Grass	Physical	25	100	30	Normal
24	Scary Face	Normal	Status	—	100	10	Normal
24	Trick-or-Treat	Ghost	Status	—	100	20	Normal
28	Worry Seed	Grass	Status	—	100	10	Normal
32	Seed Bomb	Grass	Physical	80	100	15	Normal
36	Shadow Ball	Ghost	Special	80	100	15	Normal
36	Trick-or-Treat	Ghost	Status	—	100	20	Normal
40	Trick	Psychic	Status	—	100	10	Normal
44	Pain Split	Normal	Status	—	—	20	Normal

EVOLUTION MOVES

NAME	TYPE	KIND	POW.	ACC.	PP	RANGE

EGG MOVES

NAME	TYPE	KIND	POW.	ACC.	PP	RANGE
Curse	Ghost	Status	—	—	10	Varies
Destiny Bond	Ghost	Status	—	—	5	Self
Disable	Normal	Status	—	100	20	Normal

TUTOR MOVES

NAME	TYPE	KIND	POW.	ACC.	PP	RANGE

TM MOVES

NO.	NAME	TYPE	KIND	POW.	ACC.	PP	RANGE
TM11	Solar Beam	Grass	Special	120	100	10	Normal
TM17	Light Screen	Psychic	Status	—	—	30	Your Side
TM19	Safeguard	Normal	Status	—	—	25	Your Side
TM21	Rest	Psychic	Status	—	—	10	Self
TM22	Rock Slide	Rock	Physical	75	90	10	Many Others
TM23	Thief	Dark	Physical	60	100	15	Normal
TM24	Snore	Normal	Special	50	100	15	Normal
TM25	Protect	Normal	Status	—	—	10	Self
TM26	Scary Face	Normal	Status	—	100	10	Normal
TM28	Giga Drain	Grass	Special	75	100	10	Normal
TM31	Attract	Normal	Status	—	100	15	Normal
TM34	Sunny Day	Fire	Status	—	—	5	Both Sides
TM38	Will-O-Wisp	Fire	Status	—	85	15	Normal
TM39	Facade	Normal	Physical	70	100	20	Normal
TM44	Imprison	Psychic	Status	—	—	10	Self
TM50	Bullet Seed	Grass	Physical	25	100	30	Normal
TM70	Trick Room	Psychic	Status	—	—	5	Both Sides
TM76	Round	Normal	Special	60	100	15	Normal
TM77	Hex	Ghost	Special	65	100	10	Normal
TM92	Mystical Fire	Fire	Special	75	100	10	Normal

TR MOVES

NO.	NAME	TYPE	KIND	POW.	ACC.	PP	RANGE
TR02	Flamethrower	Fire	Special	90	100	15	Normal
TR11	Psychic	Psychic	Special	90	100	10	Normal
TR15	Fire Blast	Fire	Special	110	85	5	Normal
TR20	Substitute	Normal	Status	—	—	10	Self
TR22	Sludge Bomb	Poison	Special	90	100	10	Normal
TR26	Endure	Normal	Status	—	—	10	Self
TR27	Sleep Talk	Normal	Status	—	—	10	Self
TR33	Shadow Ball	Ghost	Special	80	100	15	Normal
TR38	Trick	Psychic	Status	—	100	10	Normal
TR40	Skill Swap	Psychic	Status	—	—	10	Normal
TR52	Gyro Ball	Steel	Physical	—	100	5	Normal
TR58	Dark Pulse	Dark	Special	80	100	15	Normal
TR59	Seed Bomb	Grass	Physical	80	100	15	Normal
TR65	Energy Ball	Grass	Special	90	100	10	Normal
TR77	Grass Knot	Grass	Special	—	100	20	Normal
TR81	Foul Play	Dark	Physical	95	100	15	Normal
TR83	Ally Switch	Psychic	Status	—	—	15	Self

ABILITY

Pickup
Frisk

HIDDEN ABILITY

Insomnia

SPECIES STRENGTHS

HP
ATTACK
DEFENSE
SP. ATK
SP. DEF
SPEED

DAMAGE TAKEN IN BATTLE

×0 ×0 ×1
×2 ×1 ×2
×0.5 ×0.5 ×1
×0.5 ×2 ×2
×0.5 ×1 ×1
×2 ×1 ×1

AMORPHOUS

192

Gourgeist — p. 88

LEVEL-UP MOVES

LV.	NAME	TYPE	KIND	POW.	ACC.	PP	RANGE
1	Astonish	Ghost	Physical	30	100	15	Normal
1	Confuse Ray	Ghost	Status	—	100	10	Normal
1	Explosion	Normal	Physical	250	100	5	All Others
1	Moonblast	Fairy	Special	95	100	15	Normal
1	Shadow Sneak	Ghost	Physical	40	100	30	Normal
1	Trick-or-Treat	Ghost	Status	—	100	20	Normal
1	Razor Leaf	Grass	Physical	55	95	25	Many Others
12	Trick-or-Treat	Ghost	Status	—	100	20	Normal
12	Leech Seed	Grass	Status	—	90	10	Normal
20	Bullet Seed	Grass	Physical	25	100	30	Normal
24	Scary Face	Normal	Status	—	100	10	Normal
24	Trick-or-Treat	Ghost	Status	—	100	20	Normal
28	Worry Seed	Grass	Status	—	100	10	Normal
32	Seed Bomb	Grass	Physical	80	100	15	Normal
36	Shadow Ball	Ghost	Special	80	100	15	Normal
36	Trick-or-Treat	Ghost	Status	—	100	20	Normal
40	Trick	Psychic	Status	—	100	10	Normal
44	Pain Split	Normal	Status	—	—	20	Normal
48	Phantom Force	Ghost	Physical	90	100	10	Normal

EVOLUTION MOVES

NAME	TYPE	KIND	POW.	ACC.	PP	RANGE

EGG MOVES

NAME	TYPE	KIND	POW.	ACC.	PP	RANGE

TUTOR MOVES

NAME	TYPE	KIND	POW.	ACC.	PP	RANGE

TM MOVES

NO.	NAME	TYPE	KIND	POW.	ACC.	PP	RANGE
TM08	Hyper Beam	Normal	Special	150	90	5	Normal
TM09	Giga Impact	Normal	Physical	150	90	5	Normal
TM11	Solar Beam	Grass	Special	120	100	10	Normal
TM17	Light Screen	Psychic	Status	—	—	30	Your Side
TM19	Safeguard	Normal	Status	—	—	25	Your Side
TM21	Rest	Psychic	Status	—	—	10	Self
TM22	Rock Slide	Rock	Physical	75	90	10	Many Others
TM23	Thief	Dark	Physical	60	100	25	Normal
TM24	Snore	Normal	Special	50	100	15	Normal
TM25	Protect	Normal	Status	—	—	10	Self
TM26	Scary Face	Normal	Status	—	100	10	Normal
TM28	Giga Drain	Grass	Special	75	100	10	Normal
TM31	Attract	Normal	Status	—	100	15	Normal
TM34	Sunny Day	Fire	Status	—	—	5	Both Sides
TM38	Will-O-Wisp	Fire	Status	—	85	15	Normal
TM39	Facade	Normal	Physical	70	100	20	Normal
TM44	Imprison	Psychic	Status	—	—	10	Self
TM50	Bullet Seed	Grass	Physical	25	100	30	Normal
TM70	Trick Room	Psychic	Status	—	—	5	Both Sides
TM76	Round	Normal	Special	60	100	15	Normal
TM77	Hex	Ghost	Special	65	100	10	Normal
TM86	Phantom Force	Ghost	Physical	90	100	10	Normal
TM92	Mystical Fire	Fire	Special	75	100	10	Normal
TM97	Brutal Swing	Dark	Physical	60	100	20	All Others

TR MOVES

NO.	NAME	TYPE	KIND	POW.	ACC.	PP	RANGE
TR02	Flamethrower	Fire	Special	90	100	15	Normal
TR11	Psychic	Psychic	Special	90	100	10	Normal
TR15	Fire Blast	Fire	Special	110	85	5	Normal
TR20	Substitute	Normal	Status	—	—	10	Self
TR22	Sludge Bomb	Poison	Special	90	100	10	Normal
TR26	Endure	Normal	Status	—	—	10	Self
TR27	Sleep Talk	Normal	Status	—	—	10	Self
TR33	Shadow Ball	Ghost	Special	80	100	15	Normal
TR38	Trick	Psychic	Status	—	100	10	Normal
TR40	Skill Swap	Psychic	Status	—	—	10	Normal
TR52	Gyro Ball	Steel	Physical	—	100	5	Normal
TR58	Dark Pulse	Dark	Special	80	100	15	Normal
TR59	Seed Bomb	Grass	Physical	80	100	15	Normal
TR65	Energy Ball	Grass	Special	90	100	10	Normal
TR68	Nasty Plot	Dark	Status	—	—	20	Self
TR72	Power Whip	Grass	Physical	120	85	10	Normal
TR77	Grass Knot	Grass	Special	—	100	20	Normal
TR81	Foul Play	Dark	Physical	95	100	15	Normal
TR83	Ally Switch	Psychic	Status	—	—	15	Self

ABILITY

Pickup
Frisk

HIDDEN ABILITY

Insomnia

SPECIES STRENGTHS

HP
ATTACK
DEFENSE
SP. ATK
SP. DEF
SPEED

DAMAGE TAKEN IN BATTLE

×0 ×0 ×1
×2 ×1 ×2
×0.5 ×0.5 ×1
×0.5 ×2 ×2
×0.5 ×1 ×1
×2 ×1 ×1

AMORPHOUS

193

Pichu
p. 89

ABILITY
Static
—

HIDDEN ABILITY
Lightning Rod

SPECIES STRENGTHS

HP
ATTACK
DEFENSE
SP. ATK
SP. DEF
SPEED

DAMAGE TAKEN IN BATTLE

×1 ×1 ×1
×1 ×1 ×1
×1 ×2 ×1
×1 ×0.5 ×1
×0.5 ×1 ×0.5
×1 ×1 ×1

NO EGGS

LEVEL-UP MOVES

LV.	NAME	TYPE	KIND	POW.	ACC.	PP	RANGE
1	Tail Whip	Normal	Status	—	100	30	Many Others
1	Thunder Shock	Electric	Special	40	100	30	Normal
4	Play Nice	Normal	Status	—	—	20	Normal
8	Sweet Kiss	Fairy	Status	—	75	10	Normal
12	Nuzzle	Electric	Physical	20	100	20	Normal
16	Nasty Plot	Dark	Status	—	—	20	Self
20	Charm	Fairy	Status	—	100	20	Normal

EVOLUTION MOVES

NAME	TYPE	KIND	POW.	ACC.	PP	RANGE

EGG MOVES

NAME	TYPE	KIND	POW.	ACC.	PP	RANGE
Charge	Electric	Status	—	—	20	Self
Disarming Voice	Fairy	Special	40	—	15	Many Others
Fake Out	Normal	Physical	40	100	10	Normal
Flail	Normal	Physical	—	100	15	Normal
Present	Normal	Physical	—	90	15	Normal
Tickle	Normal	Status	—	100	20	Normal
Volt Tackle*	Electric	Physical	120	100	15	Normal
Wish	Normal	Status	—	—	10	Self

TUTOR MOVES

NAME	TYPE	KIND	POW.	ACC.	PP	RANGE

TM MOVES

NO.	NAME	TYPE	KIND	POW.	ACC.	PP	RANGE
TM00	Mega Punch	Normal	Physical	80	85	20	Normal
TM01	Mega Kick	Normal	Physical	120	75	5	Normal
TM05	Thunder Punch	Electric	Physical	75	100	15	Normal
TM14	Thunder Wave	Electric	Status	—	90	20	Normal
TM17	Light Screen	Psychic	Status	—	—	30	Your Side
TM18	Reflect	Psychic	Status	—	—	20	Your Side
TM21	Rest	Psychic	Status	—	—	10	Self
TM24	Snore	Normal	Special	50	100	15	Normal
TM25	Protect	Normal	Status	—	—	10	Self
TM29	Charm	Fairy	Status	—	100	20	Normal
TM31	Attract	Normal	Status	—	100	15	Normal
TM33	Rain Dance	Water	Status	—	—	5	Both Sides
TM39	Facade	Normal	Physical	70	100	20	Normal
TM40	Swift	Normal	Special	60	—	20	Many Others
TM41	Helping Hand	Normal	Status	—	—	20	1 Ally
TM59	Fling	Dark	Physical	—	100	10	Normal
TM76	Round	Normal	Special	60	100	15	Normal
TM80	Volt Switch	Electric	Special	70	100	20	Normal
TM82	Electroweb	Electric	Special	55	95	15	Many Others
TM90	Electric Terrain	Electric	Status	—	—	10	Both Sides

TR MOVES

NO.	NAME	TYPE	KIND	POW.	ACC.	PP	RANGE
TR01	Body Slam	Normal	Physical	85	100	15	Normal
TR04	Surf	Water	Special	90	100	15	All Others
TR08	Thunderbolt	Electric	Special	90	100	15	Normal
TR09	Thunder	Electric	Special	110	70	10	Normal
TR20	Substitute	Normal	Status	—	—	10	Self
TR21	Reversal	Fighting	Physical	—	100	15	Normal
TR26	Endure	Normal	Status	—	—	10	Self
TR27	Sleep Talk	Normal	Status	—	—	10	Self
TR30	Encore	Normal	Status	—	100	5	Normal
TR31	Iron Tail	Steel	Physical	100	75	15	Normal
TR35	Uproar	Normal	Special	90	100	10	1 Random
TR68	Nasty Plot	Dark	Status	—	—	20	Self
TR77	Grass Knot	Grass	Special	—	100	20	Normal
TR86	Wild Charge	Electric	Physical	90	100	15	Normal
TR90	Play Rough	Fairy	Physical	90	90	10	Normal

*Leave Pikachu or Raichu at the Pokémon Nursery with a compatible partner. One of the two Pokémon must be holding a Light Ball if you hope to find an Egg that will hatch into a Pichu that knows Volt Tackle.

194

Pikachu
p. 89

ABILITY
Static
—

HIDDEN ABILITY
Lightning Rod

SPECIES STRENGTHS

HP
ATTACK
DEFENSE
SP. ATK
SP. DEF
SPEED

DAMAGE TAKEN IN BATTLE

×1 ×1 ×1
×1 ×1 ×1
×1 ×2 ×1
×1 ×0.5 ×1
×0.5 ×1 ×0.5
×1 ×1 ×1

FIELD
FAIRY

LEVEL-UP MOVES

LV.	NAME	TYPE	KIND	POW.	ACC.	PP	RANGE
1	Charm	Fairy	Status	—	100	20	Normal
1	Growl	Normal	Status	—	100	40	Many Others
1	Nasty Plot	Dark	Status	—	—	20	Self
1	Nuzzle	Electric	Physical	20	100	20	Normal
1	Play Nice	Normal	Status	—	—	20	Normal
1	Quick Attack	Normal	Physical	40	100	30	Normal
1	Sweet Kiss	Fairy	Status	—	75	10	Normal
1	Tail Whip	Normal	Status	—	100	30	Many Others
1	Thunder Shock	Electric	Special	40	100	30	Normal
4	Thunder Wave	Electric	Status	—	90	20	Normal
8	Double Team	Normal	Status	—	—	15	Self
12	Electro Ball	Electric	Special	—	100	10	Normal
16	Feint	Normal	Physical	30	100	10	Normal
20	Spark	Electric	Physical	65	100	20	Normal
24	Agility	Psychic	Status	—	—	30	Self
28	Slam	Normal	Physical	80	75	20	Normal
32	Discharge	Electric	Special	80	100	15	All Others
36	Thunderbolt	Electric	Special	90	100	15	Normal
40	Light Screen	Psychic	Status	—	—	30	Your Side
44	Thunder	Electric	Special	110	70	10	Normal

EVOLUTION MOVES

NAME	TYPE	KIND	POW.	ACC.	PP	RANGE

EGG MOVES

NAME	TYPE	KIND	POW.	ACC.	PP	RANGE

TUTOR MOVES

NAME	TYPE	KIND	POW.	ACC.	PP	RANGE

TM MOVES

NO.	NAME	TYPE	KIND	POW.	ACC.	PP	RANGE
TM00	Mega Punch	Normal	Physical	80	85	20	Normal
TM01	Mega Kick	Normal	Physical	120	75	5	Normal
TM02	Pay Day	Normal	Physical	40	100	20	Normal
TM05	Thunder Punch	Electric	Physical	75	100	15	Normal
TM14	Thunder Wave	Electric	Status	—	90	20	Normal
TM15	Dig	Ground	Physical	80	100	10	Normal
TM17	Light Screen	Psychic	Status	—	—	30	Your Side
TM18	Reflect	Psychic	Status	—	—	20	Your Side
TM21	Rest	Psychic	Status	—	—	10	Self
TM23	Thief	Dark	Special	60	100	25	Normal
TM24	Snore	Normal	Special	50	100	15	Normal
TM25	Protect	Normal	Status	—	—	10	Self
TM29	Charm	Fairy	Status	—	100	20	Normal
TM31	Attract	Normal	Status	—	100	15	Normal
TM33	Rain Dance	Water	Status	—	—	5	Both Sides
TM39	Facade	Normal	Physical	70	100	20	Normal
TM40	Swift	Normal	Special	60	—	20	Many Others
TM41	Helping Hand	Normal	Status	—	—	20	1 Ally
TM43	Brick Break	Fighting	Physical	75	100	15	Normal
TM59	Fling	Dark	Physical	—	100	10	Normal
TM76	Round	Normal	Special	60	100	15	Normal
TM80	Volt Switch	Electric	Special	70	100	20	Normal
TM82	Electroweb	Electric	Special	55	95	15	Many Others
TM87	Draining Kiss	Fairy	Special	50	100	10	Normal
TM90	Electric Terrain	Electric	Status	—	—	10	Both Sides

TR MOVES

NO.	NAME	TYPE	KIND	POW.	ACC.	PP	RANGE
TR01	Body Slam	Normal	Physical	85	100	15	Normal
TR04	Surf	Water	Special	90	100	15	All Others
TR08	Thunderbolt	Electric	Special	90	100	15	Normal
TR09	Thunder	Electric	Special	110	70	10	Normal
TR12	Agility	Psychic	Status	—	—	30	Self
TR20	Substitute	Normal	Status	—	—	10	Self
TR21	Reversal	Fighting	Physical	—	100	15	Normal
TR27	Sleep Talk	Normal	Status	—	—	10	Self
TR30	Encore	Normal	Status	—	100	5	Normal
TR31	Iron Tail	Steel	Physical	100	75	15	Normal
TR35	Uproar	Normal	Special	90	100	10	1 Random
TR68	Nasty Plot	Dark	Status	—	—	20	Self
TR77	Grass Knot	Grass	Special	—	100	20	Normal
TR80	Electro Ball	Electric	Special	—	100	10	Normal
TR86	Wild Charge	Electric	Physical	90	100	15	Normal
TR90	Play Rough	Fairy	Physical	90	90	10	Normal

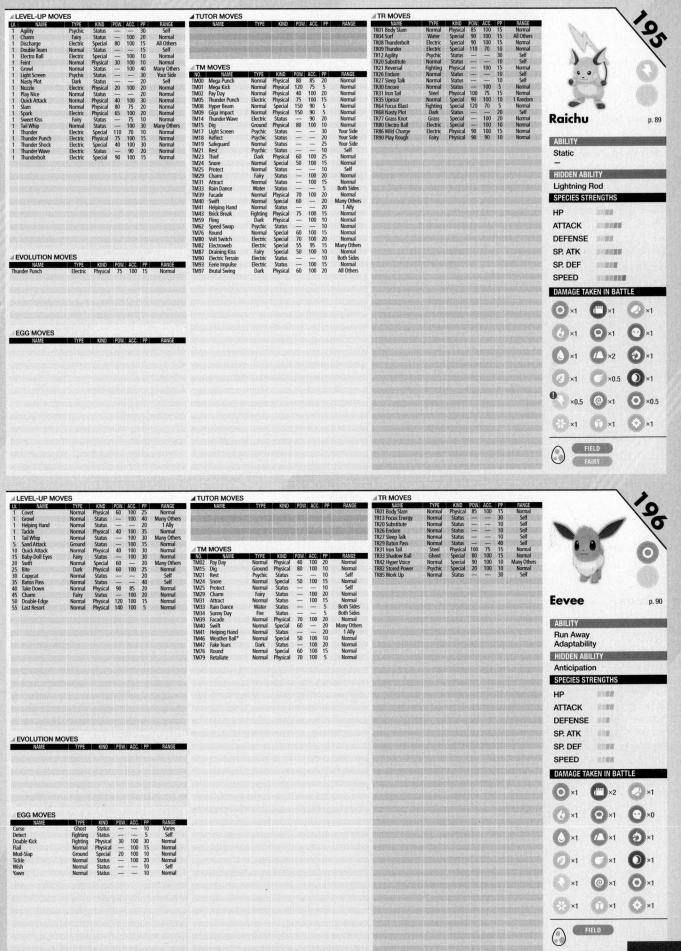

195 — Raichu (p. 89)

LEVEL-UP MOVES

LV.	NAME	TYPE	KIND	POW.	ACC.	PP	RANGE
1	Agility	Psychic	Status	—	—	30	Self
1	Charm	Fairy	Status	—	100	20	Normal
1	Discharge	Electric	Special	80	100	15	All Others
1	Double Team	Normal	Status	—	—	15	Self
1	Electro Ball	Electric	Special	—	100	10	Normal
1	Feint	Normal	Physical	30	100	10	Normal
1	Growl	Normal	Status	—	100	40	Many Others
1	Light Screen	Psychic	Status	—	—	30	Your Side
1	Nasty Plot	Dark	Status	—	—	20	Self
1	Nuzzle	Electric	Physical	20	100	20	Normal
1	Play Nice	Normal	Status	—	—	20	Normal
1	Quick Attack	Normal	Physical	40	100	30	Normal
1	Slam	Normal	Physical	80	75	20	Normal
1	Spark	Electric	Physical	65	100	20	Normal
1	Sweet Kiss	Fairy	Status	—	75	10	Normal
1	Tail Whip	Normal	Status	—	100	30	Many Others
1	Thunder	Electric	Special	110	70	10	Normal
1	Thunder Punch	Electric	Physical	75	100	15	Normal
1	Thunder Shock	Electric	Special	40	100	30	Normal
1	Thunder Wave	Electric	Status	—	90	20	Normal
1	Thunderbolt	Electric	Special	90	100	15	Normal

EVOLUTION MOVES

NAME	TYPE	KIND	POW.	ACC.	PP	RANGE
Thunder Punch	Electric	Physical	75	100	15	Normal

EGG MOVES

NAME	TYPE	KIND	POW.	ACC.	PP	RANGE

TUTOR MOVES

NAME	TYPE	KIND	POW.	ACC.	PP	RANGE

TM MOVES

NO.	NAME	TYPE	KIND	POW.	ACC.	PP	RANGE
TM00	Mega Punch	Normal	Physical	80	85	20	Normal
TM01	Mega Kick	Normal	Physical	120	75	5	Normal
TM02	Pay Day	Normal	Physical	40	100	20	Normal
TM05	Thunder Punch	Electric	Physical	75	100	15	Normal
TM08	Hyper Beam	Normal	Special	150	90	5	Normal
TM09	Giga Impact	Normal	Physical	150	90	5	Normal
TM14	Thunder Wave	Electric	Status	—	90	20	Normal
TM15	Dig	Ground	Physical	80	100	10	Normal
TM17	Light Screen	Psychic	Status	—	—	30	Your Side
TM18	Reflect	Psychic	Status	—	—	20	Your Side
TM19	Safeguard	Normal	Status	—	—	25	Your Side
TM21	Rest	Psychic	Status	—	—	10	Self
TM23	Thief	Dark	Physical	60	100	25	Normal
TM24	Snore	Normal	Special	50	100	15	Normal
TM25	Protect	Normal	Status	—	—	10	Self
TM29	Charm	Fairy	Status	—	100	20	Normal
TM31	Attract	Normal	Status	—	100	15	Normal
TM33	Rain Dance	Water	Status	—	—	5	Both Sides
TM39	Facade	Normal	Physical	70	100	20	Normal
TM40	Swift	Normal	Special	60	—	20	Many Others
TM41	Helping Hand	Normal	Status	—	—	20	1 Ally
TM43	Brick Break	Fighting	Physical	75	100	15	Normal
TM59	Fling	Dark	Physical	—	100	10	Normal
TM62	Speed Swap	Psychic	Status	—	—	10	Normal
TM76	Round	Normal	Special	60	100	15	Normal
TM80	Volt Switch	Electric	Special	70	100	20	Normal
TM82	Electroweb	Electric	Special	55	95	15	Many Others
TM87	Draining Kiss	Fairy	Special	50	100	10	Normal
TM90	Electric Terrain	Electric	Status	—	—	10	Both Sides
TM93	Eerie Impulse	Electric	Status	—	100	15	Normal
TM97	Brutal Swing	Dark	Physical	60	100	20	All Others

TR MOVES

NO.	NAME	TYPE	KIND	POW.	ACC.	PP	RANGE
TR01	Body Slam	Normal	Physical	85	100	15	Normal
TR04	Surf	Water	Special	90	100	15	All Others
TR08	Thunderbolt	Electric	Special	90	100	15	Normal
TR09	Thunder	Electric	Special	110	70	10	Normal
TR12	Agility	Psychic	Status	—	—	30	Self
TR20	Substitute	Normal	Status	—	—	10	Self
TR21	Reversal	Fighting	Physical	—	100	15	Normal
TR26	Endure	Normal	Status	—	—	10	Self
TR27	Sleep Talk	Normal	Status	—	—	10	Self
TR30	Encore	Normal	Status	—	100	5	Normal
TR31	Iron Tail	Steel	Physical	100	75	15	Normal
TR35	Uproar	Normal	Special	90	100	10	1 Random
TR64	Focus Blast	Fighting	Special	120	70	5	Normal
TR68	Nasty Plot	Dark	Status	—	—	20	Self
TR77	Grass Knot	Grass	Special	—	100	20	Normal
TR80	Electro Ball	Electric	Special	—	100	10	Normal
TR86	Wild Charge	Electric	Physical	90	100	15	Normal
TR90	Play Rough	Fairy	Physical	90	90	10	Normal

ABILITY
Static
—

HIDDEN ABILITY
Lightning Rod

SPECIES STRENGTHS
HP
ATTACK
DEFENSE
SP. ATK
SP. DEF
SPEED

DAMAGE TAKEN IN BATTLE
×1 ×1 ×1
×1 ×1 ×1
×1 ×2 ×1
×1 ×0.5 ×1
×0.5 ×1 ×0.5
×1 ×1 ×1

FIELD · FAIRY

196 — Eevee (p. 90)

LEVEL-UP MOVES

LV.	NAME	TYPE	KIND	POW.	ACC.	PP	RANGE
1	Covet	Normal	Physical	60	100	25	Normal
1	Growl	Normal	Status	—	100	40	Many Others
1	Helping Hand	Normal	Status	—	—	20	1 Ally
1	Tackle	Normal	Physical	40	100	35	Normal
1	Tail Whip	Normal	Status	—	100	30	Many Others
5	Sand Attack	Ground	Status	—	100	15	Normal
10	Quick Attack	Normal	Physical	40	100	30	Normal
15	Baby-Doll Eyes	Fairy	Status	—	100	30	Normal
20	Swift	Normal	Special	60	—	20	Many Others
25	Bite	Dark	Physical	60	100	25	Normal
30	Copycat	Normal	Status	—	—	20	Self
35	Baton Pass	Normal	Status	—	—	40	Self
40	Take Down	Normal	Physical	90	85	20	Normal
45	Charm	Fairy	Status	—	100	20	Normal
50	Double-Edge	Normal	Physical	120	100	15	Normal
55	Last Resort	Normal	Physical	140	100	5	Normal

EVOLUTION MOVES

NAME	TYPE	KIND	POW.	ACC.	PP	RANGE

EGG MOVES

NAME	TYPE	KIND	POW.	ACC.	PP	RANGE
Curse	Ghost	Status	—	—	10	Varies
Detect	Fighting	Status	—	—	5	Self
Double Kick	Fighting	Physical	30	100	30	Normal
Flail	Normal	Physical	—	100	15	Normal
Mud-Slap	Ground	Special	20	100	10	Normal
Tickle	Normal	Status	—	100	20	Normal
Wish	Normal	Status	—	—	10	Self
Yawn	Normal	Status	—	—	10	Normal

TUTOR MOVES

NAME	TYPE	KIND	POW.	ACC.	PP	RANGE

TM MOVES

NO.	NAME	TYPE	KIND	POW.	ACC.	PP	RANGE
TM02	Pay Day	Normal	Physical	40	100	20	Normal
TM15	Dig	Ground	Physical	80	100	10	Normal
TM21	Rest	Psychic	Status	—	—	10	Self
TM24	Snore	Normal	Special	50	100	15	Normal
TM25	Protect	Normal	Status	—	—	10	Self
TM29	Charm	Fairy	Status	—	100	20	Normal
TM31	Attract	Normal	Status	—	100	15	Normal
TM33	Rain Dance	Water	Status	—	—	5	Both Sides
TM34	Sunny Day	Fire	Status	—	—	5	Both Sides
TM39	Facade	Normal	Physical	70	100	20	Normal
TM40	Swift	Normal	Special	60	—	20	Many Others
TM41	Helping Hand	Normal	Status	—	—	20	1 Ally
TM46	Weather Ball*	Normal	Special	50	100	10	Normal
TM47	Fake Tears	Dark	Status	—	100	20	Normal
TM76	Round	Normal	Special	60	100	15	Normal
TM79	Retaliate	Normal	Physical	70	100	5	Normal

TR MOVES

NO.	NAME	TYPE	KIND	POW.	ACC.	PP	RANGE
TR01	Body Slam	Normal	Physical	85	100	15	Normal
TR13	Focus Energy	Normal	Status	—	—	30	Self
TR20	Substitute	Normal	Status	—	—	10	Self
TR26	Endure	Normal	Status	—	—	10	Self
TR27	Sleep Talk	Normal	Status	—	—	10	Self
TR29	Baton Pass	Normal	Status	—	—	40	Self
TR31	Iron Tail	Steel	Physical	100	75	15	Normal
TR33	Shadow Ball	Ghost	Special	80	100	15	Normal
TR42	Hyper Voice	Normal	Special	90	100	10	Many Others
TR82	Stored Power	Psychic	Special	20	100	10	Normal
TR85	Work Up	Normal	Status	—	—	30	Self

ABILITY
Run Away
Adaptability

HIDDEN ABILITY
Anticipation

SPECIES STRENGTHS
HP
ATTACK
DEFENSE
SP. ATK
SP. DEF
SPEED

DAMAGE TAKEN IN BATTLE
×1 ×2 ×1
×1 ×1 ×0
×1 ×1 ×1
×1 ×1 ×1
×1 ×1 ×1
×1 ×1 ×1

FIELD

*Weather Ball changes type depending on weather condition. (Harsh sunlight: Fire type. Rain: Water type. Hail: Ice type. Sandstorm: Rock type.)

197 Vaporeon
p. 91

ABILITY
Water Absorb
—

HIDDEN ABILITY
Hydration

SPECIES STRENGTHS

HP	▓▓▓▓▓▓
ATTACK	▓▓▓
DEFENSE	▓▓▓
SP. ATK	▓▓▓▓▓
SP. DEF	▓▓▓▓
SPEED	▓▓▓

DAMAGE TAKEN IN BATTLE

×1	×1	×1
×0.5	×1	×1
×0.5	×1	×1
×2	×1	×1
×2	×1	×0.5
×0.5	×1	×1

FIELD

LEVEL-UP MOVES

LV	NAME	TYPE	KIND	POW.	ACC.	PP	RANGE
1	Baton Pass	Normal	Status	—	—	40	Self
1	Bite	Dark	Physical	60	100	25	Normal
1	Charm	Fairy	Status	—	100	20	Normal
1	Copycat	Normal	Status	—	—	20	Self
1	Covet	Normal	Physical	60	100	25	Normal
1	Double-Edge	Normal	Physical	120	100	15	Normal
1	Growl	Normal	Status	—	100	40	Many Others
1	Helping Hand	Normal	Status	—	—	20	1 Ally
1	Swift	Normal	Special	60	—	20	Many Others
1	Tackle	Normal	Physical	40	100	35	Normal
1	Tail Whip	Normal	Status	—	100	30	Many Others
1	Take Down	Normal	Physical	90	85	20	Normal
1	Water Gun	Water	Special	40	100	25	Normal
5	Sand Attack	Ground	Status	—	100	15	Normal
10	Quick Attack	Normal	Physical	40	100	30	Normal
15	Baby-Doll Eyes	Fairy	Status	—	100	30	Normal
20	Haze	Ice	Status	—	—	30	Both Sides
25	Water Pulse	Water	Special	60	100	20	Normal
30	Aurora Beam	Ice	Special	65	100	20	Normal
35	Aqua Ring	Water	Status	—	—	20	Self
40	Muddy Water	Water	Special	90	85	10	Many Others
45	Acid Armor	Poison	Status	—	—	20	Self
50	Hydro Pump	Water	Special	110	80	5	Normal
55	Last Resort	Normal	Physical	140	100	5	Normal

EVOLUTION MOVES

NAME	TYPE	KIND	POW.	ACC.	PP	RANGE
Water Gun	Water	Special	40	100	25	Normal

EGG MOVES

NAME	TYPE	KIND	POW.	ACC.	PP	RANGE

TUTOR MOVES

NAME	TYPE	KIND	POW.	ACC.	PP	RANGE

TM MOVES

NO.	NAME	TYPE	KIND	POW.	ACC.	PP	RANGE
TM02	Pay Day	Normal	Physical	40	100	20	Normal
TM08	Hyper Beam	Normal	Special	150	90	5	Normal
TM09	Giga Impact	Normal	Physical	150	90	5	Normal
TM15	Dig	Ground	Physical	80	100	10	Normal
TM21	Rest	Psychic	Status	—	—	10	Self
TM24	Snore	Normal	Special	50	100	15	Normal
TM25	Protect	Normal	Status	—	—	10	Self
TM27	Icy Wind	Ice	Special	55	95	15	Many Others
TM29	Charm	Fairy	Status	—	100	20	Normal
TM31	Attract	Normal	Status	—	100	15	Normal
TM33	Rain Dance	Water	Status	—	—	5	Both Sides
TM34	Sunny Day	Fire	Status	—	—	5	Both Sides
TM35	Hail	Ice	Status	—	—	10	Both Sides
TM36	Whirlpool	Water	Special	35	85	15	Normal
TM39	Facade	Normal	Physical	70	100	20	Normal
TM40	Swift	Normal	Special	60	—	20	Many Others
TM41	Helping Hand	Normal	Status	—	—	20	1 Ally
TM45	Dive	Water	Physical	80	100	10	Normal
TM46	Weather Ball*	Normal	Special	50	100	10	Normal
TM47	Fake Tears	Dark	Status	—	100	20	Normal
TM55	Brine	Water	Special	65	100	10	Normal
TM76	Round	Normal	Special	60	100	15	Normal
TM79	Retaliate	Normal	Physical	70	100	5	Normal

TR MOVES

NO.	NAME	TYPE	KIND	POW.	ACC.	PP	RANGE
TR01	Body Slam	Normal	Physical	85	100	15	Normal
TR03	Hydro Pump	Water	Special	110	80	5	Normal
TR04	Surf	Water	Special	90	100	15	All Others
TR05	Ice Beam	Ice	Special	90	100	10	Normal
TR06	Blizzard	Ice	Special	110	70	5	Many Others
TR13	Focus Energy	Normal	Status	—	—	30	Self
TR16	Waterfall	Water	Physical	80	100	15	Normal
TR20	Substitute	Normal	Status	—	—	10	Self
TR26	Endure	Normal	Status	—	—	10	Self
TR27	Sleep Talk	Normal	Status	—	—	10	Self
TR29	Baton Pass	Normal	Status	—	—	40	Self
TR31	Iron Tail	Steel	Physical	100	75	15	Normal
TR33	Shadow Ball	Ghost	Special	80	100	15	Normal
TR42	Hyper Voice	Normal	Special	90	100	10	Many Others
TR45	Muddy Water	Water	Special	90	85	10	Many Others
TR82	Stored Power	Psychic	Special	20	100	10	Normal
TR84	Scald	Water	Special	80	100	15	Normal
TR85	Work Up	Normal	Status	—	—	30	Self
TR98	Liquidation	Water	Physical	85	100	10	Normal

---

198 Jolteon
p. 91

ABILITY
Volt Absorb
—

HIDDEN ABILITY
Quick Feet

SPECIES STRENGTHS

HP	▓▓▓
ATTACK	▓▓▓
DEFENSE	▓▓▓
SP. ATK	▓▓▓▓▓▓
SP. DEF	▓▓▓▓▓
SPEED	▓▓▓▓▓▓▓

DAMAGE TAKEN IN BATTLE

×1	×1	×1
×1	×1	×1
×1	×2	×1
×1	×0.5	×1
×0.5	×1	×0.5
×1	×1	×1

FIELD

LEVEL-UP MOVES

LV	NAME	TYPE	KIND	POW.	ACC.	PP	RANGE
1	Baton Pass	Normal	Status	—	—	40	Self
1	Bite	Dark	Physical	60	100	25	Normal
1	Charm	Fairy	Status	—	100	20	Normal
1	Copycat	Normal	Status	—	—	20	Self
1	Covet	Normal	Physical	60	100	25	Normal
1	Double-Edge	Normal	Physical	120	100	15	Normal
1	Growl	Normal	Status	—	100	40	Many Others
1	Helping Hand	Normal	Status	—	—	20	1 Ally
1	Swift	Normal	Special	60	—	20	Many Others
1	Tackle	Normal	Physical	40	100	35	Normal
1	Tail Whip	Normal	Status	—	100	30	Many Others
1	Take Down	Normal	Physical	90	85	20	Normal
1	Thunder Shock	Electric	Special	40	100	30	Normal
5	Sand Attack	Ground	Status	—	100	15	Normal
10	Quick Attack	Normal	Physical	40	100	30	Normal
15	Baby-Doll Eyes	Fairy	Status	—	100	30	Normal
20	Thunder Wave	Electric	Status	—	90	20	Normal
25	Double Kick	Fighting	Physical	30	100	30	Normal
30	Thunder Fang	Electric	Physical	65	95	15	Normal
35	Pin Missile	Bug	Physical	25	95	20	Normal
40	Discharge	Electric	Special	80	100	15	All Others
45	Agility	Psychic	Status	—	—	30	Self
50	Thunder	Electric	Special	110	70	10	Normal
55	Last Resort	Normal	Physical	140	100	5	Normal

EVOLUTION MOVES

NAME	TYPE	KIND	POW.	ACC.	PP	RANGE
Thunder Shock	Electric	Special	40	100	30	Normal

EGG MOVES

NAME	TYPE	KIND	POW.	ACC.	PP	RANGE

TUTOR MOVES

NAME	TYPE	KIND	POW.	ACC.	PP	RANGE

TM MOVES

NO.	NAME	TYPE	KIND	POW.	ACC.	PP	RANGE
TM02	Pay Day	Normal	Physical	40	100	20	Normal
TM07	Pin Missile	Bug	Physical	25	95	20	Normal
TM08	Hyper Beam	Normal	Special	150	90	5	Normal
TM09	Giga Impact	Normal	Physical	150	90	5	Normal
TM14	Thunder Wave	Electric	Status	—	90	20	Normal
TM15	Dig	Ground	Physical	80	100	10	Normal
TM17	Light Screen	Psychic	Status	—	—	30	Your Side
TM21	Rest	Psychic	Status	—	—	10	Self
TM24	Snore	Normal	Special	50	100	15	Normal
TM25	Protect	Normal	Status	—	—	10	Self
TM29	Charm	Fairy	Status	—	100	20	Normal
TM31	Attract	Normal	Status	—	100	15	Normal
TM33	Rain Dance	Water	Status	—	—	5	Both Sides
TM34	Sunny Day	Fire	Status	—	—	5	Both Sides
TM39	Facade	Normal	Physical	70	100	20	Normal
TM40	Swift	Normal	Special	60	—	20	Many Others
TM41	Helping Hand	Normal	Status	—	—	20	1 Ally
TM46	Weather Ball*	Normal	Special	50	100	10	Normal
TM47	Fake Tears	Dark	Status	—	100	20	Normal
TM66	Thunder Fang	Electric	Physical	65	95	15	Normal
TM76	Round	Normal	Special	60	100	15	Normal
TM79	Retaliate	Normal	Physical	70	100	5	Normal
TM80	Volt Switch	Electric	Special	70	100	20	Normal

TR MOVES

NO.	NAME	TYPE	KIND	POW.	ACC.	PP	RANGE
TR01	Body Slam	Normal	Physical	85	100	15	Normal
TR08	Thunderbolt	Electric	Special	90	100	15	Normal
TR09	Thunder	Electric	Special	110	70	10	Normal
TR12	Agility	Psychic	Status	—	—	30	Self
TR13	Focus Energy	Normal	Status	—	—	30	Self
TR20	Substitute	Normal	Status	—	—	10	Self
TR26	Endure	Normal	Status	—	—	10	Self
TR27	Sleep Talk	Normal	Status	—	—	10	Self
TR29	Baton Pass	Normal	Status	—	—	40	Self
TR31	Iron Tail	Steel	Physical	100	75	15	Normal
TR33	Shadow Ball	Ghost	Special	80	100	15	Normal
TR42	Hyper Voice	Normal	Special	90	100	10	Many Others
TR80	Electro Ball	Electric	Special	—	100	10	Normal
TR82	Stored Power	Psychic	Special	20	100	10	Normal
TR85	Work Up	Normal	Status	—	—	30	Self
TR86	Wild Charge	Electric	Physical	90	100	15	Normal

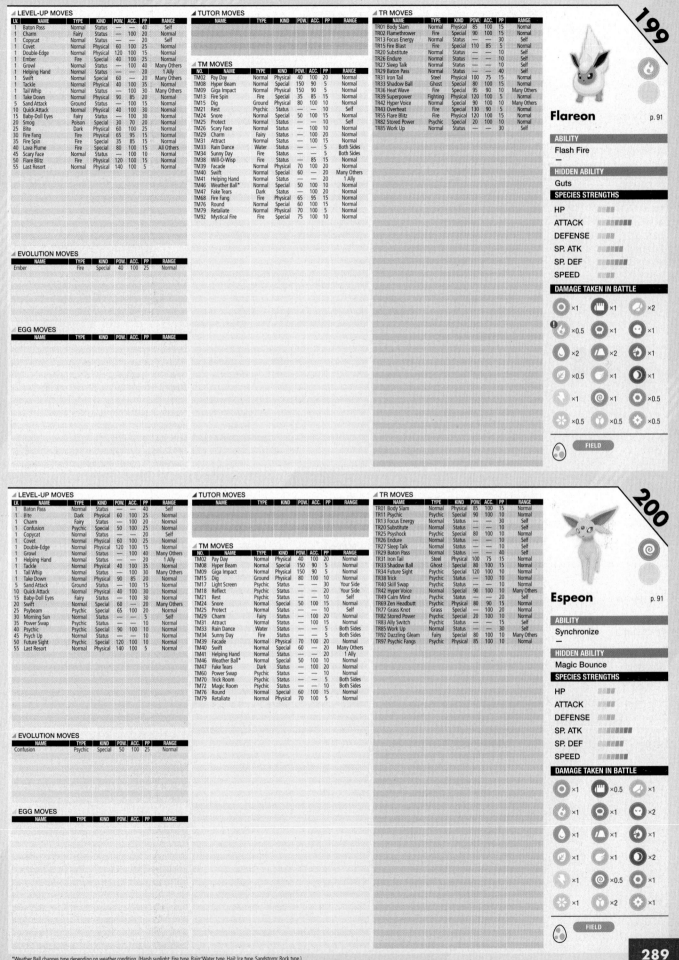

199 — Flareon (p. 91)

LEVEL-UP MOVES
LV.	NAME	TYPE	KIND	POW.	ACC.	PP	RANGE
1	Baton Pass	Normal	Status	—	—	40	Self
1	Charm	Fairy	Status	—	100	20	Normal
1	Copycat	Normal	Status	—	—	20	Self
1	Covet	Normal	Physical	60	100	25	Normal
1	Double-Edge	Normal	Physical	120	100	15	Normal
1	Ember	Fire	Special	40	100	25	Normal
1	Growl	Normal	Status	—	100	40	Many Others
1	Helping Hand	Normal	Status	—	—	20	1 Ally
1	Swift	Normal	Special	60	—	20	Many Others
1	Tackle	Normal	Physical	40	100	35	Normal
1	Tail Whip	Normal	Status	—	100	30	Many Others
1	Take Down	Normal	Physical	90	85	20	Normal
5	Sand Attack	Ground	Status	—	100	15	Normal
10	Quick Attack	Normal	Physical	40	100	30	Normal
15	Baby-Doll Eyes	Fairy	Status	—	100	30	Normal
20	Smog	Poison	Special	30	70	20	Normal
25	Bite	Dark	Physical	60	100	25	Normal
30	Fire Fang	Fire	Physical	65	95	15	Normal
35	Fire Spin	Fire	Special	35	85	15	Normal
40	Lava Plume	Fire	Special	80	100	15	All Others
45	Scary Face	Normal	Status	—	100	10	Normal
50	Flare Blitz	Fire	Physical	120	100	15	Normal
55	Last Resort	Normal	Physical	140	100	5	Normal

EVOLUTION MOVES
NAME	TYPE	KIND	POW.	ACC.	PP	RANGE
Ember	Fire	Special	40	100	25	Normal

EGG MOVES
NAME	TYPE	KIND	POW.	ACC.	PP	RANGE

TUTOR MOVES
NAME	TYPE	KIND	POW.	ACC.	PP	RANGE

TM MOVES
NO.	NAME	TYPE	KIND	POW.	ACC.	PP	RANGE
TM02	Pay Day	Normal	Physical	40	100	20	Normal
TM08	Hyper Beam	Normal	Special	150	90	5	Normal
TM09	Giga Impact	Normal	Physical	150	90	5	Normal
TM13	Fire Spin	Fire	Special	35	85	15	Normal
TM15	Dig	Ground	Physical	80	100	10	Normal
TM21	Rest	Psychic	Status	—	—	10	Self
TM24	Snore	Normal	Special	50	100	15	Normal
TM25	Protect	Normal	Status	—	—	10	Self
TM26	Scary Face	Normal	Status	—	100	10	Normal
TM29	Charm	Fairy	Status	—	100	20	Normal
TM31	Attract	Normal	Status	—	100	15	Normal
TM33	Rain Dance	Water	Status	—	—	5	Both Sides
TM34	Sunny Day	Fire	Status	—	—	5	Both Sides
TM38	Will-O-Wisp	Fire	Status	—	85	15	Normal
TM39	Facade	Normal	Physical	70	100	20	Normal
TM40	Swift	Normal	Special	60	—	20	Many Others
TM41	Helping Hand	Normal	Status	—	—	20	1 Ally
TM46	Weather Ball*	Normal	Special	50	100	10	Normal
TM47	Fake Tears	Dark	Status	—	100	20	Normal
TM68	Fire Fang	Fire	Physical	65	95	15	Normal
TM76	Round	Normal	Special	60	100	15	Normal
TM79	Retaliate	Normal	Physical	70	100	5	Normal
TM92	Mystical Fire	Fire	Special	75	100	10	Normal

TR MOVES
NO.	NAME	TYPE	KIND	POW.	ACC.	PP	RANGE
TR01	Body Slam	Normal	Physical	85	100	15	Normal
TR02	Flamethrower	Fire	Special	90	100	15	Normal
TR13	Focus Energy	Normal	Status	—	—	30	Self
TR15	Fire Blast	Fire	Special	110	85	5	Normal
TR20	Substitute	Normal	Status	—	—	10	Self
TR26	Endure	Normal	Status	—	—	10	Self
TR27	Sleep Talk	Normal	Status	—	—	10	Self
TR29	Baton Pass	Normal	Status	—	—	40	Self
TR31	Iron Tail	Steel	Physical	100	75	15	Normal
TR33	Shadow Ball	Ghost	Special	80	100	15	Normal
TR36	Heat Wave	Fire	Special	95	90	10	Many Others
TR39	Superpower	Fighting	Physical	120	100	5	Normal
TR42	Hyper Voice	Normal	Special	90	100	10	Many Others
TR43	Overheat	Fire	Special	130	90	5	Normal
TR55	Flare Blitz	Fire	Physical	120	100	15	Normal
TR82	Stored Power	Psychic	Special	20	100	10	Normal
TR85	Work Up	Normal	Status	—	—	30	Self

Flareon — p. 91

ABILITY: Flash Fire

HIDDEN ABILITY: Guts

SPECIES STRENGTHS: HP / ATTACK / DEFENSE / SP. ATK / SP. DEF / SPEED

DAMAGE TAKEN IN BATTLE: ×1, ×1, ×2, ×0.5, ×1, ×1, ×2, ×2, ×1, ×0.5, ×1, ×1, ×0.5, ×0.5, ×0.5

---

200 — Espeon (p. 91)

LEVEL-UP MOVES
LV.	NAME	TYPE	KIND	POW.	ACC.	PP	RANGE
1	Baton Pass	Normal	Status	—	—	40	Self
1	Bite	Dark	Physical	60	100	25	Normal
1	Charm	Fairy	Status	—	100	20	Normal
1	Confusion	Psychic	Special	50	100	25	Normal
1	Copycat	Normal	Status	—	—	20	Self
1	Covet	Normal	Physical	60	100	25	Normal
1	Double-Edge	Normal	Physical	120	100	15	Normal
1	Growl	Normal	Status	—	100	40	Many Others
1	Helping Hand	Normal	Status	—	—	20	1 Ally
1	Tackle	Normal	Physical	40	100	35	Normal
1	Tail Whip	Normal	Status	—	100	30	Many Others
1	Take Down	Normal	Physical	90	85	20	Normal
5	Sand Attack	Ground	Status	—	100	15	Normal
10	Quick Attack	Normal	Physical	40	100	30	Normal
15	Baby-Doll Eyes	Fairy	Status	—	100	30	Normal
20	Swift	Normal	Special	60	—	20	Many Others
25	Psybeam	Psychic	Special	65	100	20	Normal
30	Morning Sun	Normal	Status	—	—	5	Self
35	Power Swap	Psychic	Status	—	—	10	Normal
40	Psychic	Psychic	Special	90	100	10	Normal
45	Psych Up	Normal	Status	—	—	10	Normal
50	Future Sight	Psychic	Special	120	100	10	Normal
55	Last Resort	Normal	Physical	140	100	5	Normal

EVOLUTION MOVES
NAME	TYPE	KIND	POW.	ACC.	PP	RANGE
Confusion	Psychic	Special	50	100	25	Normal

EGG MOVES
NAME	TYPE	KIND	POW.	ACC.	PP	RANGE

TUTOR MOVES
NAME	TYPE	KIND	POW.	ACC.	PP	RANGE

TM MOVES
NO.	NAME	TYPE	KIND	POW.	ACC.	PP	RANGE
TM02	Pay Day	Normal	Physical	40	100	20	Normal
TM08	Hyper Beam	Normal	Special	150	90	5	Normal
TM09	Giga Impact	Normal	Physical	150	90	5	Normal
TM15	Dig	Ground	Physical	80	100	10	Normal
TM17	Light Screen	Psychic	Status	—	—	30	Your Side
TM18	Reflect	Psychic	Status	—	—	20	Your Side
TM21	Rest	Psychic	Status	—	—	10	Self
TM24	Snore	Normal	Special	50	100	15	Normal
TM25	Protect	Normal	Status	—	—	10	Self
TM29	Charm	Fairy	Status	—	100	20	Normal
TM31	Attract	Normal	Status	—	100	15	Normal
TM33	Rain Dance	Water	Status	—	—	5	Both Sides
TM34	Sunny Day	Fire	Status	—	—	5	Both Sides
TM39	Facade	Normal	Physical	70	100	20	Normal
TM40	Swift	Normal	Special	60	—	20	Many Others
TM41	Helping Hand	Normal	Status	—	—	20	1 Ally
TM46	Weather Ball*	Normal	Special	50	100	10	Normal
TM47	Fake Tears	Dark	Status	—	100	20	Normal
TM60	Power Swap	Psychic	Status	—	—	10	Normal
TM70	Trick Room	Psychic	Status	—	—	5	Both Sides
TM72	Magic Room	Psychic	Status	—	—	10	Both Sides
TM76	Round	Normal	Special	60	100	15	Normal
TM79	Retaliate	Normal	Physical	70	100	5	Normal

TR MOVES
NO.	NAME	TYPE	KIND	POW.	ACC.	PP	RANGE
TR01	Body Slam	Normal	Physical	85	100	15	Normal
TR11	Psychic	Psychic	Special	90	100	10	Normal
TR13	Focus Energy	Normal	Status	—	—	30	Self
TR20	Substitute	Normal	Status	—	—	10	Self
TR25	Psyshock	Psychic	Special	80	100	10	Normal
TR26	Endure	Normal	Status	—	—	10	Self
TR27	Sleep Talk	Normal	Status	—	—	10	Self
TR29	Baton Pass	Normal	Status	—	—	40	Self
TR31	Iron Tail	Steel	Physical	100	75	15	Normal
TR33	Shadow Ball	Ghost	Special	80	100	15	Normal
TR34	Future Sight	Psychic	Special	120	100	10	Normal
TR38	Trick	Psychic	Status	—	100	10	Normal
TR40	Skill Swap	Psychic	Status	—	—	10	Normal
TR42	Hyper Voice	Normal	Special	90	100	10	Many Others
TR49	Calm Mind	Psychic	Status	—	—	20	Self
TR69	Zen Headbutt	Psychic	Physical	80	90	15	Normal
TR77	Grass Knot	Grass	Special	—	100	20	Normal
TR82	Stored Power	Psychic	Special	20	100	10	Normal
TR83	Ally Switch	Psychic	Status	—	—	15	Self
TR85	Work Up	Normal	Status	—	—	30	Self
TR92	Dazzling Gleam	Fairy	Special	80	100	10	Many Others
TR97	Psychic Fangs	Psychic	Physical	85	100	10	Normal

Espeon — p. 91

ABILITY: Synchronize

HIDDEN ABILITY: Magic Bounce

SPECIES STRENGTHS: HP / ATTACK / DEFENSE / SP. ATK / SP. DEF / SPEED

DAMAGE TAKEN IN BATTLE: ×1, ×0.5, ×1, ×1, ×1, ×2, ×1, ×1, ×1, ×1, ×2, ×1, ×0.5, ×2, ×2, ×1

---

*Weather Ball changes type depending on weather condition. (Harsh sunlight: Fire type. Rain: Water type. Hail: Ice type. Sandstorm: Rock type.)

201 Umbreon — p. 92

ABILITY
Synchronize
—

HIDDEN ABILITY
Inner Focus

SPECIES STRENGTHS

HP	
ATTACK	
DEFENSE	
SP. ATK	
SP. DEF	
SPEED	

DAMAGE TAKEN IN BATTLE

×1	×2	×1	×1	×1	×0.5
×1	×1	×1	×1	×1	×0.5
×1	×0	×1	×1	×2	×2

FIELD

LEVEL-UP MOVES

LV.	NAME	TYPE	KIND	POW.	ACC.	PP	RANGE
1	Baton Pass	Normal	Status	—	—	40	Self
1	Bite	Dark	Physical	60	100	25	Normal
1	Charm	Fairy	Status	—	100	20	Normal
1	Copycat	Normal	Status	—	—	20	Self
1	Covet	Normal	Physical	60	100	25	Normal
1	Double-Edge	Normal	Physical	120	100	15	Normal
1	Growl	Normal	Status	—	100	40	Many Others
1	Helping Hand	Normal	Status	—	—	20	1 Ally
1	Snarl	Dark	Special	55	95	15	Many Others
1	Swift	Normal	Special	60	—	20	Many Others
1	Tackle	Normal	Physical	40	100	35	Normal
1	Tail Whip	Normal	Status	—	100	30	Many Others
1	Take Down	Normal	Physical	90	85	20	Normal
5	Sand Attack	Ground	Status	—	100	15	Normal
10	Quick Attack	Normal	Physical	40	100	30	Normal
15	Baby-Doll Eyes	Fairy	Status	—	100	30	Normal
20	Confuse Ray	Ghost	Status	—	100	10	Normal
25	Assurance	Dark	Physical	60	100	10	Normal
30	Moonlight	Fairy	Status	—	—	5	Self
30	Guard Swap	Psychic	Status	—	—	10	Normal
40	Dark Pulse	Dark	Special	80	100	15	Normal
45	Screech	Normal	Status	—	85	40	Normal
50	Mean Look	Normal	Status	—	—	5	Normal
55	Last Resort	Normal	Physical	140	100	5	Normal

EVOLUTION MOVES

NAME	TYPE	KIND	POW.	ACC.	PP	RANGE
Snarl	Dark	Special	55	95	15	Many Others

EGG MOVES

NAME	TYPE	KIND	POW.	ACC.	PP	RANGE

TUTOR MOVES

NAME	TYPE	KIND	POW.	ACC.	PP	RANGE

TM MOVES

NO.	NAME	TYPE	KIND	POW.	ACC.	PP	RANGE
TM02	Pay Day	Normal	Physical	40	100	20	Normal
TM08	Hyper Beam	Normal	Special	150	90	5	Normal
TM09	Giga Impact	Normal	Physical	150	90	5	Normal
TM15	Dig	Ground	Physical	80	100	10	Normal
TM16	Screech	Normal	Status	—	85	40	Normal
TM21	Rest	Psychic	Status	—	—	10	Self
TM23	Thief	Dark	Physical	60	100	25	Normal
TM24	Snore	Normal	Special	50	100	15	Normal
TM25	Protect	Normal	Status	—	—	10	Self
TM29	Charm	Fairy	Status	—	100	20	Normal
TM31	Attract	Normal	Status	—	100	15	Normal
TM33	Rain Dance	Water	Status	—	—	5	Both Sides
TM34	Sunny Day	Fire	Status	—	—	5	Both Sides
TM39	Facade	Normal	Physical	70	100	20	Normal
TM40	Swift	Normal	Special	60	—	20	Many Others
TM41	Helping Hand	Normal	Status	—	—	20	1 Ally
TM46	Weather Ball*	Normal	Special	50	100	10	Normal
TM47	Fake Tears	Dark	Status	—	100	20	Normal
TM57	Payback	Dark	Physical	50	100	10	Normal
TM58	Assurance	Dark	Physical	60	100	10	Normal
TM61	Guard Swap	Psychic	Status	—	—	10	Normal
TM71	Wonder Room	Psychic	Status	—	—	10	Both Sides
TM76	Round	Normal	Special	60	100	15	Normal
TM79	Retaliate	Normal	Physical	70	100	5	Normal
TM85	Snarl	Dark	Special	55	95	15	Many Others

TR MOVES

NAME	TYPE	KIND	POW.	ACC.	PP	RANGE
TR01 Body Slam	Normal	Physical	85	100	15	Normal
TR11 Psychic	Psychic	Special	90	100	10	Normal
TR13 Focus Energy	Normal	Status	—	—	30	Self
TR20 Substitute	Normal	Status	—	—	10	Self
TR26 Endure	Normal	Status	—	—	10	Self
TR27 Sleep Talk	Normal	Status	—	—	10	Self
TR29 Baton Pass	Normal	Status	—	—	40	Self
TR31 Iron Tail	Steel	Physical	100	75	15	Normal
TR32 Crunch	Dark	Physical	80	100	15	Normal
TR33 Shadow Ball	Ghost	Special	80	100	15	Normal
TR37 Taunt	Dark	Status	—	100	20	Normal
TR42 Hyper Voice	Normal	Special	90	100	10	Many Others
TR58 Dark Pulse	Dark	Special	80	100	15	Normal
TR81 Foul Play	Dark	Physical	95	100	15	Normal
TR82 Stored Power	Psychic	Special	20	100	10	Normal
TR85 Work Up	Normal	Status	—	—	30	Self
TR95 Throat Chop	Dark	Physical	80	100	15	Normal

202 Leafeon — p. 92

ABILITY
Leaf Guard
—

HIDDEN ABILITY
Chlorophyll

SPECIES STRENGTHS

HP	
ATTACK	
DEFENSE	
SP. ATK	
SP. DEF	
SPEED	

DAMAGE TAKEN IN BATTLE

×1	×1	×1	×2	×2	×1
×0.5	×0.5	×1	×0.5	×2	×1
×0.5	×1	×1	×2	×2	×1

FIELD

LEVEL-UP MOVES

LV.	NAME	TYPE	KIND	POW.	ACC.	PP	RANGE
1	Baton Pass	Normal	Status	—	—	40	Self
1	Bite	Dark	Physical	60	100	25	Normal
1	Charm	Fairy	Status	—	100	20	Normal
1	Copycat	Normal	Status	—	—	20	Self
1	Covet	Normal	Physical	60	100	25	Normal
1	Double-Edge	Normal	Physical	120	100	15	Normal
1	Growl	Normal	Status	—	100	40	Many Others
1	Helping Hand	Normal	Status	—	—	20	1 Ally
1	Razor Leaf	Grass	Physical	55	95	25	Many Others
1	Swift	Normal	Special	60	—	20	Many Others
1	Tackle	Normal	Physical	40	100	35	Normal
1	Tail Whip	Normal	Status	—	100	30	Many Others
1	Take Down	Normal	Physical	90	85	20	Normal
5	Sand Attack	Ground	Status	—	100	15	Normal
10	Quick Attack	Normal	Physical	40	100	30	Normal
15	Baby-Doll Eyes	Fairy	Status	—	100	30	Normal
20	Leech Seed	Grass	Status	—	90	10	Normal
25	Magical Leaf	Grass	Special	60	—	20	Normal
30	Synthesis	Grass	Status	—	—	5	Self
35	Sunny Day	Fire	Status	—	—	5	Both Sides
40	Giga Drain	Grass	Special	75	100	10	Normal
45	Swords Dance	Normal	Status	—	—	20	Self
50	Leaf Blade	Grass	Physical	90	100	15	Normal
55	Last Resort	Normal	Physical	140	100	5	Normal

EVOLUTION MOVES

NAME	TYPE	KIND	POW.	ACC.	PP	RANGE
Razor Leaf	Grass	Physical	55	95	25	Many Others

EGG MOVES

NAME	TYPE	KIND	POW.	ACC.	PP	RANGE

TUTOR MOVES

NAME	TYPE	KIND	POW.	ACC.	PP	RANGE

TM MOVES

NO.	NAME	TYPE	KIND	POW.	ACC.	PP	RANGE
TM02	Pay Day	Normal	Physical	40	100	20	Normal
TM08	Hyper Beam	Normal	Special	150	90	5	Normal
TM09	Giga Impact	Normal	Physical	150	90	5	Normal
TM10	Magical Leaf	Grass	Special	60	—	20	Normal
TM11	Solar Beam	Grass	Special	120	100	10	Normal
TM12	Solar Blade	Grass	Physical	125	100	10	Normal
TM15	Dig	Ground	Physical	80	100	10	Normal
TM21	Rest	Psychic	Status	—	—	10	Self
TM24	Snore	Normal	Special	50	100	15	Normal
TM25	Protect	Normal	Status	—	—	10	Self
TM28	Giga Drain	Grass	Special	75	100	10	Normal
TM29	Charm	Fairy	Status	—	100	20	Normal
TM31	Attract	Normal	Status	—	100	15	Normal
TM33	Rain Dance	Water	Status	—	—	5	Both Sides
TM34	Sunny Day	Fire	Status	—	—	5	Both Sides
TM39	Facade	Normal	Physical	70	100	20	Normal
TM40	Swift	Normal	Special	60	—	20	Many Others
TM41	Helping Hand	Normal	Status	—	—	20	1 Ally
TM46	Weather Ball*	Normal	Special	50	100	10	Normal
TM47	Fake Tears	Dark	Status	—	100	20	Normal
TM50	Bullet Seed	Grass	Physical	25	100	30	Normal
TM76	Round	Normal	Special	60	100	15	Normal
TM79	Retaliate	Normal	Physical	70	100	5	Normal

TR MOVES

NAME	TYPE	KIND	POW.	ACC.	PP	RANGE
TR00 Swords Dance	Normal	Status	—	—	20	Self
TR01 Body Slam	Normal	Physical	85	100	15	Normal
TR13 Focus Energy	Normal	Status	—	—	30	Self
TR20 Substitute	Normal	Status	—	—	10	Self
TR26 Endure	Normal	Status	—	—	10	Self
TR27 Sleep Talk	Normal	Status	—	—	10	Self
TR29 Baton Pass	Normal	Status	—	—	40	Self
TR31 Iron Tail	Steel	Physical	100	75	15	Normal
TR33 Shadow Ball	Ghost	Special	80	100	15	Normal
TR42 Hyper Voice	Normal	Special	90	100	10	Many Others
TR50 Leaf Blade	Grass	Physical	90	100	15	Normal
TR59 Seed Bomb	Grass	Physical	80	100	15	Normal
TR60 X-Scissor	Bug	Physical	80	100	15	Normal
TR65 Energy Ball	Grass	Special	90	100	10	Normal
TR71 Leaf Storm	Grass	Special	130	90	5	Normal
TR77 Grass Knot	Grass	Special	—	100	20	Normal
TR82 Stored Power	Psychic	Special	20	100	10	Normal
TR85 Work Up	Normal	Status	—	—	30	Self

203 — Glaceon

LEVEL-UP MOVES

LV.	NAME	TYPE	KIND	POW.	ACC.	PP	RANGE
1	Baton Pass	Normal	Status	—	—	40	Self
1	Charm	Fairy	Status	—	100	20	Normal
1	Copycat	Normal	Status	—	—	20	Self
1	Covet	Normal	Physical	60	100	25	Normal
1	Double-Edge	Normal	Physical	120	100	15	Normal
1	Growl	Normal	Status	—	100	40	Many Others
1	Helping Hand	Normal	Status	—	—	20	1 Ally
1	Icy Wind	Ice	Special	55	95	15	Many Others
1	Swift	Normal	Special	60	—	20	Many Others
1	Tackle	Normal	Physical	40	100	35	Normal
1	Tail Whip	Normal	Status	—	100	30	Many Others
1	Take Down	Normal	Physical	90	85	20	Normal
5	Sand Attack	Ground	Status	—	100	15	Normal
10	Quick Attack	Normal	Physical	40	100	30	Normal
15	Baby-Doll Eyes	Fairy	Status	—	100	30	Normal
20	Ice Shard	Ice	Physical	40	100	30	Normal
25	Bite	Dark	Physical	60	100	25	Normal
30	Ice Fang	Ice	Physical	65	95	15	Normal
35	Hail	Ice	Status	—	—	10	Both Sides
40	Freeze-Dry	Ice	Special	70	100	20	Normal
45	Mirror Coat	Psychic	Special	—	100	20	Varies
50	Blizzard	Ice	Special	110	70	5	Many Others
55	Last Resort	Normal	Physical	140	100	5	Normal

EVOLUTION MOVES

NAME	TYPE	KIND	POW.	ACC.	PP	RANGE
Icy Wind	Ice	Special	55	95	15	Many Others

EGG MOVES

NAME	TYPE	KIND	POW.	ACC.	PP	RANGE

TUTOR MOVES

NAME	TYPE	KIND	POW.	ACC.	PP	RANGE

TM MOVES

NO.	NAME	TYPE	KIND	POW.	ACC.	PP	RANGE
TM02	Pay Day	Normal	Physical	40	100	20	Normal
TM08	Hyper Beam	Normal	Special	150	90	5	Normal
TM09	Giga Impact	Normal	Physical	150	90	5	Normal
TM15	Dig	Ground	Physical	80	100	10	Normal
TM21	Rest	Psychic	Status	—	—	10	Self
TM24	Snore	Normal	Special	50	100	15	Normal
TM25	Protect	Normal	Status	—	—	10	Self
TM27	Icy Wind	Ice	Special	55	95	15	Many Others
TM29	Charm	Fairy	Status	—	100	20	Normal
TM31	Attract	Normal	Status	—	100	15	Normal
TM33	Rain Dance	Water	Status	—	—	5	Both Sides
TM34	Sunny Day	Fire	Status	—	—	5	Both Sides
TM35	Hail	Ice	Status	—	—	10	Both Sides
TM39	Facade	Normal	Physical	70	100	20	Normal
TM40	Swift	Normal	Special	60	—	20	Many Others
TM41	Helping Hand	Normal	Status	—	—	20	1 Ally
TM46	Weather Ball*	Normal	Special	50	100	10	Normal
TM47	Fake Tears	Dark	Status	—	100	20	Normal
TM51	Icicle Spear	Ice	Physical	25	100	30	Normal
TM64	Avalanche	Ice	Physical	60	100	10	Normal
TM67	Ice Fang	Ice	Physical	65	95	15	Normal
TM76	Round	Normal	Special	60	100	15	Normal
TM79	Retaliate	Normal	Physical	70	100	5	Normal

TR MOVES

NO.	NAME	TYPE	KIND	POW.	ACC.	PP	RANGE
TR01	Body Slam	Normal	Physical	85	100	15	Normal
TR05	Ice Beam	Ice	Special	90	100	10	Normal
TR06	Blizzard	Ice	Special	110	70	5	Many Others
TR13	Focus Energy	Normal	Status	—	—	30	Self
TR20	Substitute	Normal	Status	—	—	10	Self
TR26	Endure	Normal	Status	—	—	10	Self
TR27	Sleep Talk	Normal	Status	—	—	10	Self
TR29	Baton Pass	Normal	Status	—	—	40	Self
TR31	Iron Tail	Steel	Physical	100	75	15	Normal
TR33	Shadow Ball	Ghost	Special	80	100	15	Normal
TR42	Hyper Voice	Normal	Special	90	100	10	Many Others
TR82	Stored Power	Psychic	Special	20	100	10	Normal
TR85	Work Up	Normal	Status	—	—	30	Self

Glaceon p. 92

ABILITY
Snow Cloak
—

HIDDEN ABILITY
Ice Body

SPECIES STRENGTHS

- HP
- ATTACK
- DEFENSE
- SP. ATK
- SP. DEF
- SPEED

DAMAGE TAKEN IN BATTLE
×1 ×2 ×2 ×2 ×1 ×1 ×1 ×1 ×1 ×1 ×1 ×1 ×0.5 ×1 ×1

FIELD

---

204 — Sylveon

LEVEL-UP MOVES

LV.	NAME	TYPE	KIND	POW.	ACC.	PP	RANGE
1	Baton Pass	Normal	Status	—	—	40	Self
1	Bite	Dark	Physical	60	100	25	Normal
1	Charm	Fairy	Status	—	100	20	Normal
1	Copycat	Normal	Status	—	—	20	Self
1	Covet	Normal	Physical	60	100	25	Normal
1	Disarming Voice	Fairy	Special	40	—	15	Many Others
1	Double-Edge	Normal	Physical	120	100	15	Normal
1	Growl	Normal	Status	—	100	40	Many Others
1	Helping Hand	Normal	Status	—	—	20	1 Ally
1	Tackle	Normal	Physical	40	100	35	Normal
1	Tail Whip	Normal	Status	—	100	30	Many Others
1	Take Down	Normal	Physical	90	85	20	Normal
5	Sand Attack	Ground	Status	—	100	15	Normal
10	Quick Attack	Normal	Physical	40	100	30	Normal
15	Baby-Doll Eyes	Fairy	Status	—	100	30	Normal
20	Swift	Normal	Special	60	—	20	Many Others
25	Light Screen	Psychic	Status	—	—	30	Your Side
30	Draining Kiss	Fairy	Special	50	100	10	Normal
35	Misty Terrain	Fairy	Status	—	—	10	Both Sides
40	Skill Swap	Psychic	Status	—	—	10	Normal
45	Psych Up	Normal	Status	—	—	10	Normal
50	Moonblast	Fairy	Special	95	100	15	Normal
55	Last Resort	Normal	Physical	140	100	5	Normal

EVOLUTION MOVES

NAME	TYPE	KIND	POW.	ACC.	PP	RANGE
Disarming Voice	Fairy	Special	40	—	15	Many Others

EGG MOVES

NAME	TYPE	KIND	POW.	ACC.	PP	RANGE

TUTOR MOVES

NAME	TYPE	KIND	POW.	ACC.	PP	RANGE

TM MOVES

NO.	NAME	TYPE	KIND	POW.	ACC.	PP	RANGE
TM02	Pay Day	Normal	Physical	40	100	20	Normal
TM08	Hyper Beam	Normal	Special	150	90	5	Normal
TM09	Giga Impact	Normal	Physical	150	90	5	Normal
TM10	Magical Leaf	Grass	Special	60	—	20	Normal
TM15	Dig	Ground	Physical	80	100	10	Normal
TM17	Light Screen	Psychic	Status	—	—	30	Your Side
TM18	Reflect	Psychic	Status	—	—	20	Your Side
TM19	Safeguard	Normal	Status	—	—	25	Your Side
TM21	Rest	Psychic	Status	—	—	10	Self
TM24	Snore	Normal	Special	50	100	15	Normal
TM25	Protect	Normal	Status	—	—	10	Self
TM29	Charm	Fairy	Status	—	100	20	Normal
TM31	Attract	Normal	Status	—	100	15	Normal
TM33	Rain Dance	Water	Status	—	—	5	Both Sides
TM34	Sunny Day	Fire	Status	—	—	5	Both Sides
TM39	Facade	Normal	Physical	70	100	20	Normal
TM40	Swift	Normal	Special	60	—	20	Many Others
TM41	Helping Hand	Normal	Status	—	—	20	1 Ally
TM46	Weather Ball*	Normal	Special	50	100	10	Normal
TM47	Fake Tears	Dark	Status	—	100	20	Normal
TM76	Round	Normal	Special	60	100	15	Normal
TM79	Retaliate	Normal	Physical	70	100	5	Normal
TM87	Draining Kiss	Fairy	Special	50	100	10	Normal
TM89	Misty Terrain	Fairy	Status	—	—	10	Both Sides
TM92	Mystical Fire	Fire	Special	75	100	10	Normal

TR MOVES

NO.	NAME	TYPE	KIND	POW.	ACC.	PP	RANGE
TR01	Body Slam	Normal	Physical	85	100	15	Normal
TR13	Focus Energy	Normal	Status	—	—	30	Self
TR20	Substitute	Normal	Status	—	—	10	Self
TR25	Psyshock	Psychic	Special	80	100	10	Normal
TR26	Endure	Normal	Status	—	—	10	Self
TR27	Sleep Talk	Normal	Status	—	—	10	Self
TR29	Baton Pass	Normal	Status	—	—	40	Self
TR31	Iron Tail	Steel	Physical	100	75	15	Normal
TR33	Shadow Ball	Ghost	Special	80	100	15	Normal
TR40	Skill Swap	Psychic	Status	—	—	10	Normal
TR42	Hyper Voice	Normal	Special	90	100	10	Many Others
TR49	Calm Mind	Psychic	Status	—	—	20	Self
TR82	Stored Power	Psychic	Special	20	100	10	Normal
TR85	Work Up	Normal	Status	—	—	30	Self
TR90	Play Rough	Fairy	Physical	90	90	10	Normal
TR92	Dazzling Gleam	Fairy	Special	80	100	10	Many Others

Sylveon p. 92

ABILITY
Cute Charm
—

HIDDEN ABILITY
Pixilate

SPECIES STRENGTHS

- HP
- ATTACK
- DEFENSE
- SP. ATK
- SP. DEF
- SPEED

DAMAGE TAKEN IN BATTLE
×1 ×0.5 ×1 ×1 ×2 ×1 ×1 ×1 ×0 ×1 ×1 ×0.5 ×1 ×1 ×2 ×0.5 ×1

FIELD

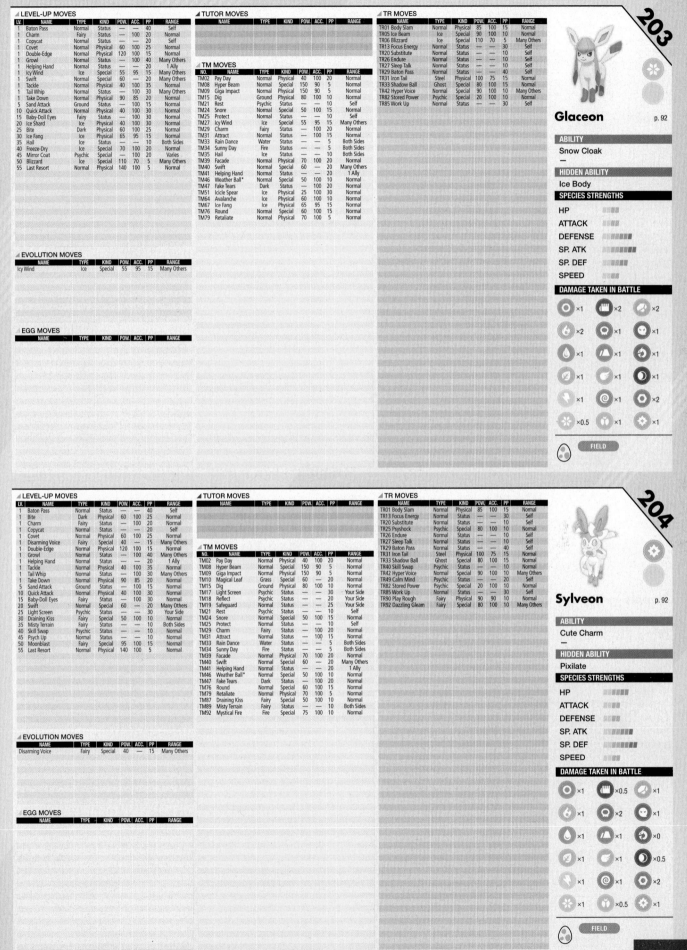

*Weather Ball changes type depending on weather condition. (Harsh sunlight: Fire type. Rain: Water type. Hail: Ice type. Sandstorm: Rock type.)

205 Applin

p. 93

ABILITY
Ripen
Gluttony

HIDDEN ABILITY
Bulletproof

SPECIES STRENGTHS
HP
ATTACK
DEFENSE
SP. ATK
SP. DEF
SPEED

DAMAGE TAKEN IN BATTLE

×1 ×1 ×1
×1 ×2 ×1
×0.25 ×0.5 ×2
×0.25 ×2 ×1
×0.25 ×1 ×1
×4 ×2 ×2

GRASS
DRAGON

LEVEL-UP MOVES

LV.	NAME	TYPE	KIND	POW.	ACC.	PP	RANGE
1	Astonish	Ghost	Physical	30	100	15	Normal
1	Withdraw	Water	Status	—	—	40	Self

EVOLUTION MOVES

NAME	TYPE	KIND	POW.	ACC.	PP	RANGE

EGG MOVES

NAME	TYPE	KIND	POW.	ACC.	PP	RANGE
Defense Curl	Normal	Status	—	—	40	Self
Recycle	Normal	Status	—	—	10	Self
Rollout	Rock	Physical	30	90	20	Normal
Sucker Punch	Dark	Physical	70	100	5	Normal

TUTOR MOVES

NAME	TYPE	KIND	POW.	ACC.	PP	RANGE
Draco Meteor	Dragon	Special	130	90	5	Normal

TM MOVES

NO.	NAME	TYPE	KIND	POW.	ACC.	PP	RANGE
TM31	Attract	Normal	Status	—	100	15	Normal

TR MOVES

NAME	TYPE	KIND	POW.	ACC.	PP	RANGE

---

206 Flapple

p. 93

ABILITY
Ripen
Gluttony

HIDDEN ABILITY
Hustle

SPECIES STRENGTHS
HP
ATTACK
DEFENSE
SP. ATK
SP. DEF
SPEED

DAMAGE TAKEN IN BATTLE

×1 ×1 ×1
×1 ×2 ×1
×0.25 ×0.5 ×2
×0.25 ×1 ×1
×0.25 ×1 ×1
×4 ×2 ×2

GRASS
DRAGON

LEVEL-UP MOVES

LV.	NAME	TYPE	KIND	POW.	ACC.	PP	RANGE
1	Astonish	Ghost	Physical	30	100	15	Normal
1	Growth	Normal	Status	—	—	20	Self
1	Recycle	Normal	Status	—	—	10	Self
1	Twister	Dragon	Special	40	100	20	Many Others
1	Wing Attack	Flying	Physical	60	100	35	Normal
1	Withdraw	Water	Status	—	—	40	Self
4	Acid Spray	Poison	Special	40	100	20	Normal
8	Acrobatics	Flying	Physical	55	100	15	Normal
12	Leech Seed	Grass	Status	—	90	10	Normal
16	Protect	Normal	Status	—	—	10	Self
20	Dragon Breath	Dragon	Special	60	100	20	Normal
24	Dragon Dance	Dragon	Status	—	—	20	Self
28	Dragon Pulse	Dragon	Special	85	100	10	Normal
32	Grav Apple	Grass	Physical	80	100	10	Normal
36	Iron Defense	Steel	Status	—	—	15	Self
40	Fly	Flying	Physical	90	95	15	Normal
44	Dragon Rush	Dragon	Physical	100	75	10	Normal

EVOLUTION MOVES

NAME	TYPE	KIND	POW.	ACC.	PP	RANGE
Wing Attack	Flying	Physical	60	100	35	Normal

EGG MOVES

NAME	TYPE	KIND	POW.	ACC.	PP	RANGE

TUTOR MOVES

NAME	TYPE	KIND	POW.	ACC.	PP	RANGE
Draco Meteor	Dragon	Special	130	90	5	Normal

TM MOVES

NO.	NAME	TYPE	KIND	POW.	ACC.	PP	RANGE
TM06	Fly	Flying	Physical	90	95	15	Normal
TM08	Hyper Beam	Normal	Special	150	90	5	Normal
TM09	Giga Impact	Normal	Physical	150	90	5	Normal
TM11	Solar Beam	Grass	Special	120	100	10	Normal
TM21	Rest	Psychic	Status	—	—	10	Self
TM24	Snore	Normal	Special	50	100	15	Normal
TM25	Protect	Normal	Status	—	—	10	Self
TM26	Scary Face	Normal	Status	—	100	10	Normal
TM28	Giga Drain	Grass	Special	75	100	10	Normal
TM31	Attract	Normal	Status	—	100	15	Normal
TM34	Sunny Day	Fire	Status	—	—	5	Both Sides
TM39	Facade	Normal	Physical	70	100	20	Normal
TM50	Bullet Seed	Grass	Physical	25	100	30	Normal
TM56	U-turn	Bug	Physical	70	100	20	Normal
TM76	Round	Normal	Special	60	100	15	Normal
TM78	Acrobatics	Flying	Physical	55	100	15	Normal
TM95	Air Slash	Flying	Special	75	95	15	Normal

TR MOVES

NAME	TYPE	KIND	POW.	ACC.	PP	RANGE
TR13 Focus Energy	Normal	Status	—	—	30	Self
TR20 Substitute	Normal	Status	—	—	10	Self
TR24 Outrage	Dragon	Physical	120	100	10	1 Random
TR26 Endure	Normal	Status	—	—	10	Self
TR27 Sleep Talk	Normal	Status	—	—	10	Self
TR46 Iron Defense	Steel	Status	—	—	15	Self
TR51 Dragon Dance	Dragon	Status	—	—	20	Self
TR59 Seed Bomb	Grass	Physical	80	100	15	Normal
TR62 Dragon Pulse	Dragon	Special	85	100	10	Normal
TR65 Energy Ball	Grass	Special	90	100	10	Normal
TR77 Grass Knot	Grass	Special	—	100	20	Normal
TR79 Heavy Slam	Steel	Physical	—	100	10	Normal

207 — Appletun

LEVEL-UP MOVES

LV	NAME	TYPE	KIND	POW.	ACC.	PP	RANGE
1	Astonish	Ghost	Physical	30	100	15	Normal
1	Growth	Normal	Status	—	—	20	Self
1	Headbutt	Normal	Physical	70	100	15	Normal
1	Recycle	Normal	Status	—	—	10	Self
1	Sweet Scent	Normal	Status	—	100	20	Many Others
1	Withdraw	Water	Status	—	—	40	Self
4	Curse	Ghost	Status	—	—	10	Varies
8	Stomp	Normal	Physical	65	100	20	Normal
12	Leech Seed	Grass	Status	—	90	10	Normal
16	Protect	Normal	Status	—	—	10	Self
20	Bullet Seed	Grass	Physical	25	100	30	Normal
24	Recover	Normal	Status	—	—	10	Self
28	Apple Acid	Grass	Special	80	100	10	Normal
32	Body Slam	Normal	Physical	85	100	15	Normal
36	Iron Defense	Steel	Status	—	—	15	Self
40	Dragon Pulse	Dragon	Special	85	100	10	Normal
44	Energy Ball	Grass	Special	90	100	10	Normal

EVOLUTION MOVES

NAME	TYPE	KIND	POW.	ACC.	PP	RANGE
Headbutt	Normal	Physical	70	100	15	Normal

EGG MOVES

NAME	TYPE	KIND	POW.	ACC.	PP	RANGE

TUTOR MOVES

NAME	TYPE	KIND	POW.	ACC.	PP	RANGE
Draco Meteor	Dragon	Special	130	90	5	Normal

TM MOVES

NO.	NAME	TYPE	KIND	POW.	ACC.	PP	RANGE
TM08	Hyper Beam	Normal	Special	150	90	5	Normal
TM09	Giga Impact	Normal	Physical	150	90	5	Normal
TM11	Solar Beam	Grass	Special	120	100	10	Normal
TM17	Light Screen	Psychic	Status	—	—	30	Your Side
TM18	Reflect	Psychic	Status	—	—	20	Your Side
TM19	Safeguard	Normal	Status	—	—	25	Your Side
TM21	Rest	Psychic	Status	—	—	10	Self
TM24	Snore	Normal	Physical	50	100	15	Normal
TM25	Protect	Normal	Status	—	—	10	Self
TM28	Giga Drain	Grass	Special	75	100	10	Normal
TM31	Attract	Normal	Status	—	100	15	Normal
TM34	Sunny Day	Fire	Status	—	—	5	Both Sides
TM39	Facade	Normal	Physical	70	100	20	Normal
TM50	Bullet Seed	Grass	Physical	25	100	30	Normal
TM57	Payback	Dark	Physical	50	100	10	Normal
TM76	Round	Normal	Special	60	100	15	Normal
TM81	Bulldoze	Ground	Physical	60	100	20	All Others

TR MOVES

NO.	NAME	TYPE	KIND	POW.	ACC.	PP	RANGE
TR01	Body Slam	Normal	Physical	85	100	15	Normal
TR10	Earthquake	Ground	Physical	100	100	10	All Others
TR17	Amnesia	Psychic	Status	—	—	20	Self
TR20	Substitute	Normal	Status	—	—	10	Self
TR24	Outrage	Dragon	Physical	120	100	10	1 Random
TR26	Endure	Normal	Status	—	—	10	Self
TR27	Sleep Talk	Normal	Status	—	—	10	Self
TR39	Superpower	Fighting	Physical	120	100	5	Normal
TR46	Iron Defense	Steel	Status	—	—	15	Self
TR52	Gyro Ball	Steel	Physical	—	100	5	Normal
TR59	Seed Bomb	Grass	Physical	80	100	15	Normal
TR62	Dragon Pulse	Dragon	Special	85	100	10	Normal
TR65	Energy Ball	Grass	Special	90	100	10	Normal
TR77	Grass Knot	Grass	Special	—	100	20	Normal
TR79	Heavy Slam	Steel	Physical	—	100	10	Normal
TR94	High Horsepower	Ground	Physical	95	95	10	Normal
TR99	Body Press	Fighting	Physical	80	100	10	Normal

Appletun p. 93

ABILITY
Ripen
Gluttony

HIDDEN ABILITY
Thick Fat

SPECIES STRENGTHS
HP
ATTACK
DEFENSE
SP. ATK
SP. DEF
SPEED

DAMAGE TAKEN IN BATTLE
×1, ×1, ×1
×1, ×2, ×1
×0.25, ×0.5, ×2
×0.25, ×2, ×1
×0.25, ×1, ×1
×4, ×2, ×2

Egg groups: GRASS, DRAGON

---

208 — Espurr

LEVEL-UP MOVES

LV	NAME	TYPE	KIND	POW.	ACC.	PP	RANGE
1	Leer	Normal	Status	—	100	30	Many Others
1	Scratch	Normal	Physical	40	100	35	Normal
3	Fake Out	Normal	Physical	40	100	10	Normal
4	Disarming Voice	Fairy	Special	40	—	15	Many Others
9	Confusion	Psychic	Special	50	100	25	Normal
18	Covet	Normal	Physical	60	100	25	Normal
21	Psybeam	Psychic	Special	65	100	20	Normal
30	Light Screen	Psychic	Status	—	—	30	Your Side
30	Reflect	Psychic	Status	—	—	20	Your Side
33	Psyshock	Psychic	Special	80	100	10	Normal

EVOLUTION MOVES

NAME	TYPE	KIND	POW.	ACC.	PP	RANGE

EGG MOVES

NAME	TYPE	KIND	POW.	ACC.	PP	RANGE
Tickle	Normal	Status	—	100	20	Normal
Yawn	Normal	Status	—	—	10	Normal

TUTOR MOVES

NAME	TYPE	KIND	POW.	ACC.	PP	RANGE

TM MOVES

NO.	NAME	TYPE	KIND	POW.	ACC.	PP	RANGE
TM02	Pay Day	Normal	Physical	40	100	20	Normal
TM14	Thunder Wave	Electric	Status	—	90	20	Normal
TM17	Light Screen	Psychic	Status	—	—	30	Your Side
TM18	Reflect	Psychic	Status	—	—	20	Your Side
TM19	Safeguard	Normal	Status	—	—	25	Your Side
TM21	Rest	Psychic	Status	—	—	10	Self
TM24	Snore	Normal	Physical	50	100	15	Normal
TM25	Protect	Normal	Status	—	—	10	Self
TM31	Attract	Normal	Status	—	100	15	Normal
TM33	Rain Dance	Water	Status	—	—	5	Both Sides
TM34	Sunny Day	Fire	Status	—	—	5	Both Sides
TM39	Facade	Normal	Physical	70	100	20	Normal
TM40	Swift	Normal	Special	60	—	20	Many Others
TM41	Helping Hand	Normal	Status	—	—	20	1 Ally
TM47	Fake Tears	Dark	Status	—	100	20	Normal
TM57	Payback	Dark	Physical	50	100	10	Normal
TM70	Trick Room	Psychic	Status	—	—	5	Both Sides
TM71	Wonder Room	Psychic	Status	—	—	10	Both Sides
TM72	Magic Room	Psychic	Status	—	—	10	Both Sides
TM76	Round	Normal	Special	60	100	15	Normal

TR MOVES

NO.	NAME	TYPE	KIND	POW.	ACC.	PP	RANGE
TR08	Thunderbolt	Electric	Special	90	100	15	Normal
TR11	Psychic	Psychic	Special	90	100	10	Normal
TR20	Substitute	Normal	Status	—	—	10	Self
TR25	Psyshock	Psychic	Special	80	100	10	Normal
TR26	Endure	Normal	Status	—	—	10	Self
TR27	Sleep Talk	Normal	Status	—	—	10	Self
TR31	Iron Tail	Steel	Physical	100	75	15	Normal
TR38	Trick	Psychic	Status	—	100	10	Normal
TR40	Skill Swap	Psychic	Status	—	—	10	Normal
TR49	Calm Mind	Psychic	Status	—	—	20	Self
TR58	Dark Pulse	Dark	Special	80	100	15	Normal
TR65	Energy Ball	Grass	Special	90	100	10	Normal
TR68	Nasty Plot	Dark	Status	—	—	20	Self
TR69	Zen Headbutt	Psychic	Physical	80	90	15	Normal
TR83	Ally Switch	Psychic	Status	—	—	15	Self
TR85	Work Up	Normal	Status	—	—	30	Self
TR90	Play Rough	Fairy	Physical	90	90	10	Normal

Espurr p. 94

ABILITY
Keen Eye
Infiltrator

HIDDEN ABILITY
Own Tempo

SPECIES STRENGTHS
HP
ATTACK
DEFENSE
SP. ATK
SP. DEF
SPEED

DAMAGE TAKEN IN BATTLE
×1, ×0.5, ×1
×1, ×1, ×2
×1, ×1, ×1
×1, ×1, ×2
×1, ×0.5, ×1
×1, ×2, ×1

Egg group: FIELD

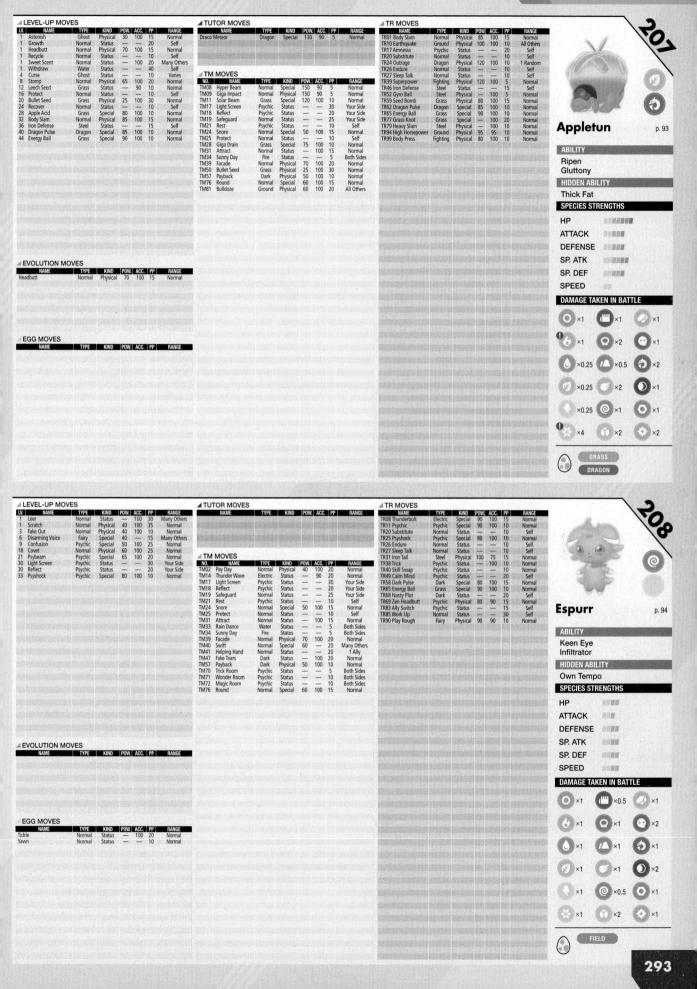

209

Meowstic
Male p. 94

ABILITY
Keen Eye
Infiltrator

HIDDEN ABILITY
Prankster

SPECIES STRENGTHS

HP	
ATTACK	
DEFENSE	
SP. ATK	
SP. DEF	
SPEED	

DAMAGE TAKEN IN BATTLE

⊙ ×1	🥊 ×0.5	🪶 ×1			
🔥 ×1	💀 ×1	👁 ×2			
💧 ×1	⛰ ×1	🔆 ×1			
🌿 ×1	🌀 ×1	🌙 ×2			
⚡ ×0.5	🔮 ×1				
❄ ×1	👊 ×2	◆ ×1			

FIELD

LEVEL-UP MOVES

LV.	NAME	TYPE	KIND	POW.	ACC.	PP	RANGE
1	Disarming Voice	Fairy	Special	40	—	15	Many Others
1	Fake Out	Normal	Physical	40	100	10	Normal
1	Leer	Normal	Status	—	100	30	Many Others
1	Mean Look	Normal	Status	—	—	5	Normal
1	Scratch	Normal	Physical	40	100	35	Normal
9	Confusion	Psychic	Special	50	100	25	Normal
12	Helping Hand	Normal	Status	—	—	20	1 Ally
15	Charm	Fairy	Status	—	100	20	Normal
18	Covet	Normal	Physical	60	100	25	Normal
21	Psybeam	Psychic	Special	65	100	20	Normal
24	Sucker Punch	Dark	Physical	70	100	5	Normal
29	Role Play	Psychic	Status	—	—	10	Normal
34	Light Screen	Psychic	Status	—	—	30	Your Side
34	Reflect	Psychic	Status	—	—	20	Your Side
39	Psyshock	Psychic	Special	80	100	10	Normal
44	Imprison	Psychic	Status	—	—	10	Self
49	Quick Guard	Fighting	Status	—	—	15	Your Side
54	Psychic	Psychic	Special	90	100	10	Normal
59	Misty Terrain	Fairy	Status	—	—	10	Both Sides

EVOLUTION MOVES

NAME	TYPE	KIND	POW.	ACC.	PP	RANGE

EGG MOVES

NAME	TYPE	KIND	POW.	ACC.	PP	RANGE

TUTOR MOVES

NAME	TYPE	KIND	POW.	ACC.	PP	RANGE

TM MOVES

NO.	NAME	TYPE	KIND	POW.	ACC.	PP	RANGE
TM02	Pay Day	Normal	Physical	40	100	20	Normal
TM08	Hyper Beam	Normal	Special	150	90	5	Normal
TM09	Giga Impact	Normal	Physical	150	90	5	Normal
TM14	Thunder Wave	Electric	Status	—	90	20	Normal
TM15	Dig	Ground	Physical	80	100	10	Normal
TM17	Light Screen	Psychic	Status	—	—	30	Your Side
TM18	Reflect	Psychic	Status	—	—	20	Your Side
TM19	Safeguard	Normal	Status	—	—	25	Your Side
TM21	Rest	Psychic	Status	—	—	10	Self
TM24	Snore	Normal	Special	50	100	15	Normal
TM25	Protect	Normal	Status	—	—	10	Self
TM29	Charm	Fairy	Status	—	100	20	Normal
TM31	Attract	Normal	Status	—	100	15	Normal
TM33	Rain Dance	Water	Status	—	—	5	Both Sides
TM34	Sunny Day	Fire	Status	—	—	5	Both Sides
TM39	Facade	Normal	Physical	70	100	20	Normal
TM40	Swift	Normal	Special	60	—	20	Many Others
TM41	Helping Hand	Normal	Status	—	—	20	1 Ally
TM44	Imprison	Psychic	Status	—	—	10	Self
TM47	Fake Tears	Dark	Status	—	100	20	Normal
TM57	Payback	Dark	Physical	50	100	10	Normal
TM70	Trick Room	Psychic	Status	—	—	5	Both Sides
TM71	Wonder Room	Psychic	Status	—	—	10	Both Sides
TM72	Magic Room	Psychic	Status	—	—	10	Both Sides
TM76	Round	Normal	Special	60	100	15	Normal
TM84	Tail Slap	Normal	Physical	25	85	10	Normal
TM89	Misty Terrain	Fairy	Status	—	—	10	Both Sides
TM91	Psychic Terrain	Psychic	Status	—	—	10	Both Sides

TR MOVES

NAME	TYPE	KIND	POW.	ACC.	PP	RANGE
TR08 Thunderbolt	Electric	Special	90	100	15	Normal
TR11 Psychic	Psychic	Special	90	100	10	Normal
TR20 Substitute	Normal	Status	—	—	10	Self
TR25 Psyshock	Psychic	Special	80	100	10	Normal
TR26 Endure	Normal	Status	—	—	10	Self
TR27 Sleep Talk	Normal	Status	—	—	10	Self
TR31 Iron Tail	Steel	Physical	100	75	15	Normal
TR33 Shadow Ball	Ghost	Special	80	100	15	Normal
TR38 Trick	Psychic	Status	—	100	10	Normal
TR40 Skill Swap	Psychic	Status	—	—	10	Normal
TR49 Calm Mind	Psychic	Status	—	—	10	Self
TR58 Dark Pulse	Dark	Special	80	100	15	Normal
TR65 Energy Ball	Grass	Special	90	100	10	Normal
TR68 Nasty Plot	Dark	Status	—	—	20	Self
TR69 Zen Headbutt	Psychic	Physical	80	90	15	Normal
TR83 Ally Switch	Psychic	Status	—	—	15	Self
TR85 Work Up	Normal	Status	—	—	30	Self
TR90 Play Rough	Fairy	Physical	90	90	10	Normal

209

Meowstic
Female p. 94

ABILITY
Keen Eye
Infiltrator

HIDDEN ABILITY
Competitive

SPECIES STRENGTHS

HP	
ATTACK	
DEFENSE	
SP. ATK	
SP. DEF	
SPEED	

DAMAGE TAKEN IN BATTLE

⊙ ×1	🥊 ×0.5	🪶 ×1			
🔥 ×1	💀 ×1	👁 ×2			
💧 ×1	⛰ ×1	🔆 ×1			
🌿 ×1	🌀 ×1	🌙 ×2			
⚡ ×1	🔮 ×0.5				
❄ ×1	👊 ×2	◆ ×1			

FIELD

LEVEL-UP MOVES

LV.	NAME	TYPE	KIND	POW.	ACC.	PP	RANGE
1	Disarming Voice	Fairy	Special	40	—	15	Many Others
1	Fake Out	Normal	Physical	40	100	10	Normal
1	Leer	Normal	Status	—	100	30	Many Others
1	Magical Leaf	Grass	Special	60	—	20	Normal
1	Scratch	Normal	Physical	40	100	35	Normal
9	Confusion	Psychic	Special	50	100	25	Normal
12	Stored Power	Psychic	Special	20	100	10	Normal
15	Charge Beam	Electric	Special	50	90	10	Normal
18	Covet	Normal	Physical	60	100	25	Normal
21	Psybeam	Psychic	Special	65	100	20	Normal
24	Sucker Punch	Dark	Physical	70	100	5	Normal
29	Role Play	Psychic	Status	—	—	10	Normal
34	Light Screen	Psychic	Status	—	—	30	Your Side
34	Reflect	Psychic	Status	—	—	20	Your Side
39	Psyshock	Psychic	Special	80	100	10	Normal
44	Extrasensory	Psychic	Special	80	100	20	Normal
49	Shadow Ball	Ghost	Special	80	100	15	Normal
54	Psychic	Psychic	Special	90	100	10	Normal
59	Future Sight	Psychic	Special	120	100	10	Normal

EVOLUTION MOVES

NAME	TYPE	KIND	POW.	ACC.	PP	RANGE

EGG MOVES

NAME	TYPE	KIND	POW.	ACC.	PP	RANGE

TUTOR MOVES

NAME	TYPE	KIND	POW.	ACC.	PP	RANGE

TM MOVES

NO.	NAME	TYPE	KIND	POW.	ACC.	PP	RANGE
TM02	Pay Day	Normal	Physical	40	100	20	Normal
TM08	Hyper Beam	Normal	Special	150	90	5	Normal
TM09	Giga Impact	Normal	Physical	150	90	5	Normal
TM10	Magical Leaf	Grass	Special	60	—	20	Normal
TM14	Thunder Wave	Electric	Status	—	90	20	Normal
TM15	Dig	Ground	Physical	80	100	10	Normal
TM17	Light Screen	Psychic	Status	—	—	30	Your Side
TM18	Reflect	Psychic	Status	—	—	20	Your Side
TM19	Safeguard	Normal	Status	—	—	25	Your Side
TM21	Rest	Psychic	Status	—	—	10	Self
TM24	Snore	Normal	Special	50	100	15	Normal
TM25	Protect	Normal	Status	—	—	10	Self
TM29	Charm	Fairy	Status	—	100	20	Normal
TM31	Attract	Normal	Status	—	100	15	Normal
TM33	Rain Dance	Water	Status	—	—	5	Both Sides
TM34	Sunny Day	Fire	Status	—	—	5	Both Sides
TM39	Facade	Normal	Physical	70	100	20	Normal
TM40	Swift	Normal	Special	60	—	20	Many Others
TM41	Helping Hand	Normal	Status	—	—	20	1 Ally
TM47	Fake Tears	Dark	Status	—	100	20	Normal
TM57	Payback	Dark	Physical	50	100	10	Normal
TM70	Trick Room	Psychic	Status	—	—	5	Both Sides
TM71	Wonder Room	Psychic	Status	—	—	10	Both Sides
TM72	Magic Room	Psychic	Status	—	—	10	Both Sides
TM76	Round	Normal	Special	60	100	15	Normal
TM84	Tail Slap	Normal	Physical	25	85	10	Normal
TM91	Psychic Terrain	Psychic	Status	—	—	10	Both Sides

TR MOVES

NAME	TYPE	KIND	POW.	ACC.	PP	RANGE
TR08 Thunderbolt	Electric	Special	90	100	10	Normal
TR11 Psychic	Psychic	Special	90	100	10	Normal
TR20 Substitute	Normal	Status	—	—	10	Self
TR25 Psyshock	Psychic	Special	80	100	10	Normal
TR26 Endure	Normal	Status	—	—	10	Self
TR27 Sleep Talk	Normal	Status	—	—	10	Self
TR31 Iron Tail	Steel	Physical	100	75	15	Normal
TR33 Shadow Ball	Ghost	Special	80	100	15	Normal
TR34 Future Sight	Psychic	Special	120	100	10	Normal
TR38 Trick	Psychic	Status	—	100	10	Normal
TR40 Skill Swap	Psychic	Status	—	—	10	Normal
TR49 Calm Mind	Psychic	Status	—	—	20	Self
TR58 Dark Pulse	Dark	Special	80	100	15	Normal
TR65 Energy Ball	Grass	Special	90	100	10	Normal
TR68 Nasty Plot	Dark	Status	—	—	20	Self
TR69 Zen Headbutt	Psychic	Physical	80	90	15	Normal
TR82 Stored Power	Psychic	Special	20	100	10	Normal
TR83 Ally Switch	Psychic	Status	—	—	15	Self
TR85 Work Up	Normal	Status	—	—	30	Self
TR90 Play Rough	Fairy	Physical	90	90	10	Normal

210

Swirlix — p. 95

LEVEL-UP MOVES

LV.	NAME	TYPE	KIND	POW.	ACC.	PP	RANGE
1	Sweet Scent	Normal	Status	—	100	20	Many Others
1	Tackle	Normal	Physical	40	100	35	Normal
3	Play Nice	Normal	Status	—	—	20	Normal
6	Fairy Wind	Fairy	Special	40	100	30	Normal
9	Aromatherapy	Grass	Status	—	—	5	Your Party
12	Draining Kiss	Fairy	Special	50	100	10	Normal
15	Fake Tears	Dark	Status	—	100	20	Normal
18	Round	Normal	Special	60	100	15	Normal
21	String Shot	Bug	Status	—	95	40	Many Others
24	Cotton Spore	Grass	Status	—	100	40	Many Others
27	Energy Ball	Grass	Special	90	100	10	Normal
30	Wish	Normal	Status	—	—	10	Self
33	Play Rough	Fairy	Physical	90	90	10	Normal
36	Cotton Guard	Grass	Status	—	—	10	Self
39	Endeavor	Normal	Physical	—	100	5	Normal

EVOLUTION MOVES

NAME	TYPE	KIND	POW.	ACC.	PP	RANGE

EGG MOVES

NAME	TYPE	KIND	POW.	ACC.	PP	RANGE
After You	Normal	Status	—	—	15	Normal
Copycat	Normal	Status	—	—	20	Self
Sticky Web	Bug	Status	—	—	20	Other Side
Yawn	Normal	Status	—	—	10	Normal

TUTOR MOVES

NAME	TYPE	KIND	POW.	ACC.	PP	RANGE

TM MOVES

NO.	NAME	TYPE	KIND	POW.	ACC.	PP	RANGE
TM17	Light Screen	Psychic	Status	—	—	30	Your Side
TM19	Safeguard	Normal	Status	—	—	25	Your Side
TM21	Rest	Psychic	Status	—	—	10	Self
TM23	Thief	Dark	Physical	60	100	25	Normal
TM24	Snore	Normal	Special	50	100	15	Normal
TM25	Protect	Normal	Status	—	—	10	Self
TM29	Charm	Fairy	Status	—	100	20	Normal
TM31	Attract	Normal	Status	—	100	15	Normal
TM33	Rain Dance	Water	Status	—	—	5	Both Sides
TM34	Sunny Day	Fire	Status	—	—	5	Both Sides
TM39	Facade	Normal	Physical	70	100	20	Normal
TM41	Helping Hand	Normal	Status	—	—	20	1 Ally
TM47	Fake Tears	Dark	Status	—	100	20	Normal
TM76	Round	Normal	Special	60	100	15	Normal
TM87	Draining Kiss	Fairy	Special	50	100	10	Normal

TR MOVES

NO.	NAME	TYPE	KIND	POW.	ACC.	PP	RANGE
TR02	Flamethrower	Fire	Special	90	100	15	Normal
TR04	Surf	Water	Special	90	100	15	All Others
TR08	Thunderbolt	Electric	Special	90	100	15	Normal
TR11	Psychic	Psychic	Special	90	100	10	Normal
TR17	Amnesia	Psychic	Status	—	—	20	Self
TR20	Substitute	Normal	Status	—	—	10	Self
TR26	Endure	Normal	Status	—	—	10	Self
TR27	Sleep Talk	Normal	Status	—	—	10	Self
TR49	Calm Mind	Psychic	Status	—	—	20	Self
TR65	Energy Ball	Grass	Special	90	100	10	Normal
TR90	Play Rough	Fairy	Physical	90	90	10	Normal
TR92	Dazzling Gleam	Fairy	Special	80	100	10	Many Others

ABILITY
Sweet Veil

HIDDEN ABILITY
Unburden

SPECIES STRENGTHS

- HP
- ATTACK
- DEFENSE
- SP. ATK
- SP. DEF
- SPEED

DAMAGE TAKEN IN BATTLE

×1, ×0.5, ×1
×1, ×2, ×1
×1, ×1, ×0
×1, ×1, ×0.5
×1, ×1, ×2
×1, ×0.5, ×1

FAIRY

211

Slurpuff — p. 95

LEVEL-UP MOVES

LV.	NAME	TYPE	KIND	POW.	ACC.	PP	RANGE
1	Fairy Wind	Fairy	Special	40	100	30	Normal
1	Play Nice	Normal	Status	—	—	20	Normal
1	Sweet Scent	Normal	Status	—	100	20	Many Others
1	Tackle	Normal	Physical	40	100	35	Normal
9	Aromatherapy	Grass	Status	—	—	5	Your Party
12	Draining Kiss	Fairy	Special	50	100	10	Normal
15	Fake Tears	Dark	Status	—	100	20	Normal
18	Round	Normal	Special	60	100	15	Normal
21	String Shot	Bug	Status	—	95	40	Many Others
24	Cotton Spore	Grass	Status	—	100	40	Many Others
27	Energy Ball	Grass	Special	90	100	10	Normal
30	Wish	Normal	Status	—	—	10	Self
33	Play Rough	Fairy	Physical	90	90	10	Normal
36	Cotton Guard	Grass	Status	—	—	10	Self
39	Endeavor	Normal	Physical	—	100	5	Normal
42	Sticky Web	Bug	Status	—	—	20	Other Side

EVOLUTION MOVES

NAME	TYPE	KIND	POW.	ACC.	PP	RANGE

EGG MOVES

NAME	TYPE	KIND	POW.	ACC.	PP	RANGE

TUTOR MOVES

NAME	TYPE	KIND	POW.	ACC.	PP	RANGE

TM MOVES

NO.	NAME	TYPE	KIND	POW.	ACC.	PP	RANGE
TM08	Hyper Beam	Normal	Special	150	90	5	Normal
TM09	Giga Impact	Normal	Physical	150	90	5	Normal
TM17	Light Screen	Psychic	Status	—	—	30	Your Side
TM19	Safeguard	Normal	Status	—	—	25	Your Side
TM21	Rest	Psychic	Status	—	—	10	Self
TM23	Thief	Dark	Physical	60	100	25	Normal
TM24	Snore	Normal	Special	50	100	15	Normal
TM25	Protect	Normal	Status	—	—	10	Self
TM29	Charm	Fairy	Status	—	100	20	Normal
TM31	Attract	Normal	Status	—	100	15	Normal
TM33	Rain Dance	Water	Status	—	—	5	Both Sides
TM34	Sunny Day	Fire	Status	—	—	5	Both Sides
TM39	Facade	Normal	Physical	70	100	20	Normal
TM41	Helping Hand	Normal	Status	—	—	20	1 Ally
TM47	Fake Tears	Dark	Status	—	100	20	Normal
TM63	Drain Punch	Fighting	Physical	75	100	10	Normal
TM76	Round	Normal	Special	60	100	15	Normal
TM87	Draining Kiss	Fairy	Special	50	100	10	Normal

TR MOVES

NO.	NAME	TYPE	KIND	POW.	ACC.	PP	RANGE
TR02	Flamethrower	Fire	Special	90	100	15	Normal
TR04	Surf	Water	Special	90	100	15	All Others
TR08	Thunderbolt	Electric	Special	90	100	15	Normal
TR09	Thunder	Electric	Special	110	70	10	Normal
TR11	Psychic	Psychic	Special	90	100	10	Normal
TR14	Metronome	Normal	Status	—	—	10	Self
TR17	Amnesia	Psychic	Status	—	—	20	Self
TR20	Substitute	Normal	Status	—	—	10	Self
TR26	Endure	Normal	Status	—	—	10	Self
TR27	Sleep Talk	Normal	Status	—	—	10	Self
TR49	Calm Mind	Psychic	Status	—	—	20	Self
TR65	Energy Ball	Grass	Special	90	100	10	Normal
TR90	Play Rough	Fairy	Physical	90	90	10	Normal
TR92	Dazzling Gleam	Fairy	Special	80	100	10	Many Others

ABILITY
Sweet Veil
—

HIDDEN ABILITY
Unburden

SPECIES STRENGTHS

- HP
- ATTACK
- DEFENSE
- SP. ATK
- SP. DEF
- SPEED

DAMAGE TAKEN IN BATTLE

×1, ×0.5, ×1
×1, ×2, ×1
×1, ×1, ×0
×1, ×1, ×0.5
×1, ×1, ×2
×1, ×0.5, ×1

FAIRY

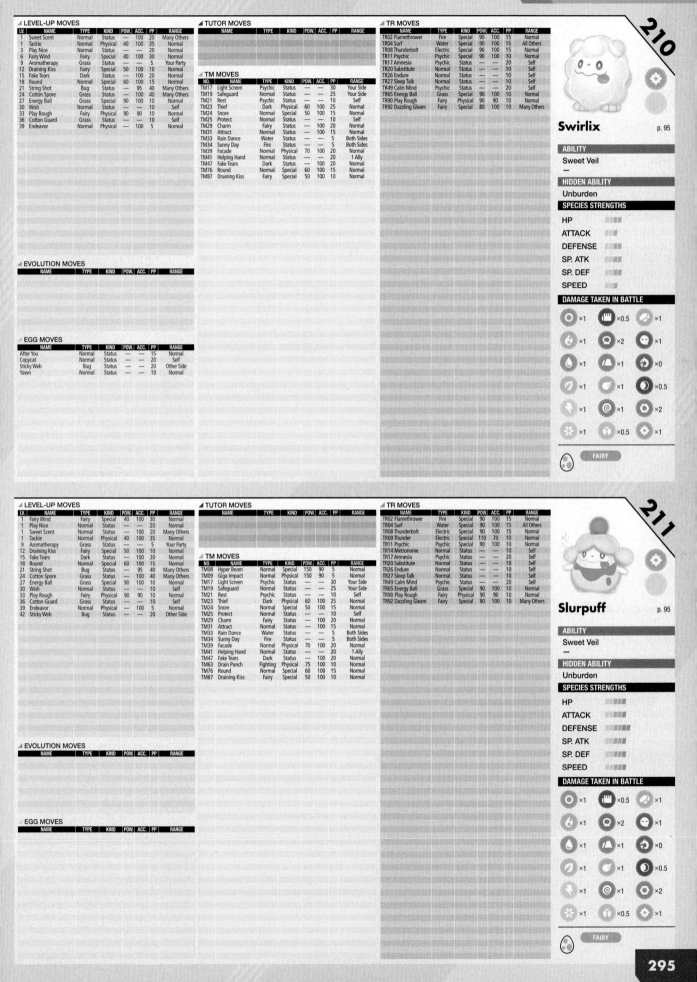

212 Spritzee

p. 95

ABILITY
Healer
—

HIDDEN ABILITY
Aroma Veil

SPECIES STRENGTHS

HP	
ATTACK	
DEFENSE	
SP. ATK	
SP. DEF	
SPEED	

DAMAGE TAKEN IN BATTLE

◎ ×1	⊞ ×0.5	🪶 ×1
🔥 ×1	☁ ×2	×1
💧 ×1	⛰ ×1	×0
⚡ ×1	🪽 ×1	🌙 ×0.5
🌿 ×1	◎ ×1	◉ ×2
❄ ×1	⦿ ×0.5	✦ ×1

FAIRY

LEVEL-UP MOVES

LV.	NAME	TYPE	KIND	POW.	ACC.	PP	RANGE
1	Fairy Wind	Fairy	Special	40	100	30	Normal
1	Sweet Scent	Normal	Status	—	100	20	Many Others
3	Sweet Kiss	Fairy	Status	—	75	10	Normal
6	Echoed Voice	Normal	Special	40	100	15	Normal
9	Draining Kiss	Fairy	Special	50	100	10	Normal
12	Aromatherapy	Grass	Status	—	—	5	Your Party
15	Draining Kiss	Fairy	Special	50	100	10	Normal
18	Attract	Normal	Status	—	100	15	Normal
21	Flail	Normal	Physical	—	100	15	Normal
24	Misty Terrain	Fairy	Status	—	—	10	Both Sides
27	Psychic	Psychic	Special	90	100	10	Normal
30	Charm	Fairy	Status	—	100	20	Normal
33	Calm Mind	Psychic	Status	—	—	20	Self
36	Moonblast	Fairy	Special	95	100	15	Normal
39	Skill Swap	Psychic	Status	—	—	10	Normal

TUTOR MOVES

NAME	TYPE	KIND	POW.	ACC.	PP	RANGE

TM MOVES

NO.	NAME	TYPE	KIND	POW.	ACC.	PP	RANGE
TM17	Light Screen	Psychic	Status	—	—	30	Your Side
TM18	Reflect	Psychic	Status	—	—	20	Your Side
TM21	Rest	Psychic	Status	—	—	10	Self
TM24	Snore	Normal	Special	50	100	15	Normal
TM25	Protect	Normal	Status	—	—	10	Self
TM29	Charm	Fairy	Status	—	100	20	Normal
TM31	Attract	Normal	Status	—	100	15	Normal
TM33	Rain Dance	Water	Status	—	—	5	Both Sides
TM34	Sunny Day	Fire	Status	—	—	5	Both Sides
TM39	Facade	Normal	Physical	70	100	20	Normal
TM41	Helping Hand	Normal	Status	—	—	20	1 Ally
TM47	Fake Tears	Dark	Status	—	100	20	Normal
TM70	Trick Room	Psychic	Status	—	—	5	Both Sides
TM76	Round	Normal	Special	60	100	15	Normal
TM87	Draining Kiss	Fairy	Special	50	100	10	Normal
TM89	Misty Terrain	Fairy	Status	—	—	10	Both Sides

TR MOVES

NAME	TYPE	KIND	POW.	ACC.	PP	RANGE
TR08 Thunderbolt	Electric	Special	90	100	15	Normal
TR11 Psychic	Psychic	Special	90	100	10	Normal
TR20 Substitute	Normal	Status	—	—	10	Self
TR26 Endure	Normal	Status	—	—	10	Self
TR27 Sleep Talk	Normal	Status	—	—	10	Self
TR30 Encore	Normal	Status	—	100	5	Normal
TR40 Skill Swap	Psychic	Status	—	—	10	Normal
TR49 Calm Mind	Psychic	Status	—	—	20	Self
TR52 Gyro Ball	Steel	Physical	—	100	5	Normal
TR65 Energy Ball	Grass	Special	90	100	10	Normal
TR68 Nasty Plot	Dark	Status	—	—	20	Self
TR70 Flash Cannon	Steel	Special	80	100	10	Normal
TR83 Ally Switch	Psychic	Status	—	—	15	Self
TR92 Dazzling Gleam	Fairy	Special	80	100	10	Many Others

EVOLUTION MOVES

NAME	TYPE	KIND	POW.	ACC.	PP	RANGE

EGG MOVES

NAME	TYPE	KIND	POW.	ACC.	PP	RANGE
After You	Normal	Status	—	—	15	Normal
Disable	Normal	Status	—	100	20	Normal
Wish	Normal	Status	—	—	10	Self

---

213 Aromatisse

p. 95

ABILITY
Healer
—

HIDDEN ABILITY
Aroma Veil

SPECIES STRENGTHS

HP	
ATTACK	
DEFENSE	
SP. ATK	
SP. DEF	
SPEED	

DAMAGE TAKEN IN BATTLE

◎ ×1	⊞ ×0.5	🪶 ×1
🔥 ×1	☁ ×2	×1
💧 ×1	⛰ ×1	×0
⚡ ×1	🪽 ×1	🌙 ×0.5
🌿 ×1	◎ ×1	◉ ×2
❄ ×1	⦿ ×0.5	✦ ×1

FAIRY

LEVEL-UP MOVES

LV.	NAME	TYPE	KIND	POW.	ACC.	PP	RANGE
1	Aromatic Mist	Fairy	Status	—	—	20	1 Ally
1	Echoed Voice	Normal	Special	40	100	15	Normal
1	Fairy Wind	Fairy	Special	40	100	30	Normal
1	Heal Pulse	Psychic	Status	—	—	10	Normal
1	Sweet Kiss	Fairy	Status	—	75	10	Normal
1	Sweet Scent	Normal	Status	—	100	20	Many Others
9	Disarming Voice	Fairy	Special	40	—	15	Many Others
12	Aromatherapy	Grass	Status	—	—	5	Your Party
15	Draining Kiss	Fairy	Special	50	100	10	Normal
18	Attract	Normal	Status	—	100	15	Normal
21	Flail	Normal	Physical	—	100	15	Normal
24	Misty Terrain	Fairy	Status	—	—	10	Both Sides
27	Psychic	Psychic	Special	90	100	10	Normal
30	Charm	Fairy	Status	—	100	20	Normal
33	Calm Mind	Psychic	Status	—	—	20	Self
36	Moonblast	Fairy	Special	95	100	15	Normal
39	Skill Swap	Psychic	Status	—	—	10	Normal
42	Psych Up	Normal	Status	—	—	10	Normal

TUTOR MOVES

NAME	TYPE	KIND	POW.	ACC.	PP	RANGE

TM MOVES

NO.	NAME	TYPE	KIND	POW.	ACC.	PP	RANGE
TM08	Hyper Beam	Normal	Special	150	90	5	Normal
TM09	Giga Impact	Normal	Physical	150	90	5	Normal
TM17	Light Screen	Psychic	Status	—	—	30	Your Side
TM18	Reflect	Psychic	Status	—	—	20	Your Side
TM21	Rest	Psychic	Status	—	—	10	Self
TM24	Snore	Normal	Special	50	100	15	Normal
TM25	Protect	Normal	Status	—	—	10	Self
TM29	Charm	Fairy	Status	—	100	20	Normal
TM31	Attract	Normal	Status	—	100	15	Normal
TM33	Rain Dance	Water	Status	—	—	5	Both Sides
TM34	Sunny Day	Fire	Status	—	—	5	Both Sides
TM39	Facade	Normal	Physical	70	100	20	Normal
TM41	Helping Hand	Normal	Status	—	—	20	1 Ally
TM47	Fake Tears	Dark	Status	—	100	20	Normal
TM63	Drain Punch	Fighting	Physical	75	100	10	Normal
TM70	Trick Room	Psychic	Status	—	—	5	Both Sides
TM76	Round	Normal	Special	60	100	15	Normal
TM87	Draining Kiss	Fairy	Special	50	100	10	Normal
TM89	Misty Terrain	Fairy	Status	—	—	10	Both Sides

TR MOVES

NAME	TYPE	KIND	POW.	ACC.	PP	RANGE
TR08 Thunderbolt	Electric	Special	90	100	15	Normal
TR09 Thunder	Electric	Special	110	70	10	Normal
TR11 Psychic	Psychic	Special	90	100	10	Normal
TR14 Metronome	Normal	Status	—	—	10	Self
TR20 Substitute	Normal	Status	—	—	10	Self
TR25 Psyshock	Psychic	Special	80	100	10	Normal
TR26 Endure	Normal	Status	—	—	10	Self
TR27 Sleep Talk	Normal	Status	—	—	10	Self
TR30 Encore	Normal	Status	—	100	5	Normal
TR40 Skill Swap	Psychic	Status	—	—	10	Normal
TR49 Calm Mind	Psychic	Status	—	—	20	Self
TR52 Gyro Ball	Steel	Physical	—	100	5	Normal
TR65 Energy Ball	Grass	Special	90	100	10	Normal
TR68 Nasty Plot	Dark	Status	—	—	20	Self
TR70 Flash Cannon	Steel	Special	80	100	10	Normal
TR83 Ally Switch	Psychic	Status	—	—	15	Self
TR92 Dazzling Gleam	Fairy	Special	80	100	10	Many Others

EVOLUTION MOVES

NAME	TYPE	KIND	POW.	ACC.	PP	RANGE

EGG MOVES

NAME	TYPE	KIND	POW.	ACC.	PP	RANGE

214 Dewpider

LEVEL-UP MOVES

LV.	NAME	TYPE	KIND	POW.	ACC.	PP	RANGE
1	Infestation	Bug	Special	20	100	20	Normal
1	Water Gun	Water	Special	40	100	25	Normal
4	Bug Bite	Bug	Physical	60	100	20	Normal
8	Bite	Dark	Physical	60	100	25	Normal
12	Bubble Beam	Water	Special	65	100	20	Normal
16	Aqua Ring	Water	Status	—	—	20	Self
20	Headbutt	Normal	Physical	70	100	15	Normal
24	Crunch	Dark	Physical	80	100	15	Normal
28	Soak	Water	Status	—	100	20	Normal
32	Entrainment	Normal	Status	—	100	15	Normal
36	Lunge	Bug	Physical	80	100	15	Normal
40	Liquidation	Water	Physical	85	100	10	Normal
44	Leech Life	Bug	Physical	80	100	10	Normal
48	Mirror Coat	Psychic	Special	—	100	20	Varies

EVOLUTION MOVES

NAME	TYPE	KIND	POW.	ACC.	PP	RANGE

EGG MOVES

NAME	TYPE	KIND	POW.	ACC.	PP	RANGE
Power Split	Psychic	Status	—	—	10	Normal
Spit Up	Normal	Special	—	100	10	Normal
Sticky Web	Bug	Status	—	—	20	Other Side
Stockpile	Normal	Status	—	—	20	Self

TUTOR MOVES

NAME	TYPE	KIND	POW.	ACC.	PP	RANGE

TM MOVES

NO.	NAME	TYPE	KIND	POW.	ACC.	PP	RANGE
TM21	Rest	Psychic	Status	—	—	10	Self
TM24	Snore	Normal	Special	50	100	15	Normal
TM25	Protect	Normal	Status	—	—	10	Self
TM27	Icy Wind	Ice	Special	55	95	15	Many Others
TM28	Giga Drain	Grass	Special	75	100	10	Normal
TM31	Attract	Normal	Status	—	100	15	Normal
TM33	Rain Dance	Water	Status	—	—	5	Both Sides
TM39	Facade	Normal	Physical	70	100	20	Normal
TM71	Wonder Room	Psychic	Status	—	—	10	Both Sides
TM72	Magic Room	Psychic	Status	—	—	10	Both Sides
TM76	Round	Normal	Special	60	100	15	Normal

TR MOVES

NO.	NAME	TYPE	KIND	POW.	ACC.	PP	RANGE
TR04	Surf	Water	Special	90	100	15	All Others
TR05	Ice Beam	Ice	Special	90	100	10	Normal
TR06	Blizzard	Ice	Special	110	70	5	Many Others
TR16	Waterfall	Water	Physical	80	100	15	Normal
TR18	Leech Life	Bug	Physical	80	100	10	Normal
TR20	Substitute	Normal	Status	—	—	10	Self
TR26	Endure	Normal	Status	—	—	10	Self
TR27	Sleep Talk	Normal	Status	—	—	10	Self
TR32	Crunch	Dark	Physical	80	100	15	Normal
TR46	Iron Defense	Steel	Status	—	—	15	Self
TR57	Poison Jab	Poison	Physical	80	100	20	Normal
TR60	X-Scissor	Bug	Physical	80	100	15	Normal
TR61	Bug Buzz	Bug	Special	90	100	10	Normal
TR84	Scald	Water	Special	80	100	15	Normal
TR98	Liquidation	Water	Physical	85	100	10	Normal

Dewpider p. 96

ABILITY
Water Bubble
—

HIDDEN ABILITY
Water Absorb

SPECIES STRENGTHS
- HP
- ATTACK
- DEFENSE
- SP. ATK
- SP. DEF
- SPEED

DAMAGE TAKEN IN BATTLE

×1 | ×0.5 | ×2
×1 | ×1 | ×1
×0.5 | ×0.5 | ×1
×1 | ×2 | ×1
×2 | ×1 | ×0.5
×0.5 | ×1 | ×1

WATER 1
BUG

---

215 Araquanid

LEVEL-UP MOVES

LV.	NAME	TYPE	KIND	POW.	ACC.	PP	RANGE
1	Bite	Dark	Physical	60	100	25	Normal
1	Bug Bite	Bug	Physical	60	100	20	Normal
1	Infestation	Bug	Special	20	100	20	Normal
1	Water Gun	Water	Special	40	100	25	Normal
1	Wide Guard	Rock	Status	—	—	10	Your Side
12	Bubble Beam	Water	Special	65	100	20	Normal
16	Aqua Ring	Water	Status	—	—	20	Self
20	Headbutt	Normal	Physical	70	100	15	Normal
26	Crunch	Dark	Physical	80	100	15	Normal
32	Soak	Water	Status	—	100	20	Normal
38	Entrainment	Normal	Status	—	100	15	Normal
44	Lunge	Bug	Physical	80	100	15	Normal
50	Liquidation	Water	Physical	85	100	10	Normal
56	Leech Life	Bug	Physical	80	100	10	Normal
62	Mirror Coat	Psychic	Special	—	100	20	Varies

EVOLUTION MOVES

NAME	TYPE	KIND	POW.	ACC.	PP	RANGE

EGG MOVES

NAME	TYPE	KIND	POW.	ACC.	PP	RANGE

TUTOR MOVES

NAME	TYPE	KIND	POW.	ACC.	PP	RANGE

TM MOVES

NO.	NAME	TYPE	KIND	POW.	ACC.	PP	RANGE
TM18	Reflect	Psychic	Status	—	—	20	Your Side
TM19	Safeguard	Normal	Status	—	—	25	Your Side
TM21	Rest	Psychic	Status	—	—	10	Self
TM24	Snore	Normal	Special	50	100	15	Normal
TM25	Protect	Normal	Status	—	—	10	Self
TM27	Icy Wind	Ice	Special	55	95	15	Many Others
TM28	Giga Drain	Grass	Special	75	100	10	Normal
TM31	Attract	Normal	Status	—	100	15	Normal
TM33	Rain Dance	Water	Status	—	—	5	Both Sides
TM39	Facade	Normal	Physical	70	100	20	Normal
TM45	Dive	Water	Physical	80	100	10	Normal
TM71	Wonder Room	Psychic	Status	—	—	10	Both Sides
TM72	Magic Room	Psychic	Status	—	—	10	Both Sides
TM76	Round	Normal	Special	60	100	15	Normal

TR MOVES

NO.	NAME	TYPE	KIND	POW.	ACC.	PP	RANGE
TR03	Hydro Pump	Water	Special	110	80	5	Normal
TR04	Surf	Water	Special	90	100	15	All Others
TR05	Ice Beam	Ice	Special	90	100	10	Normal
TR06	Blizzard	Ice	Special	110	70	5	Many Others
TR16	Waterfall	Water	Physical	80	100	15	Normal
TR18	Leech Life	Bug	Physical	80	100	10	Normal
TR20	Substitute	Normal	Status	—	—	10	Self
TR26	Endure	Normal	Status	—	—	10	Self
TR27	Sleep Talk	Normal	Status	—	—	10	Self
TR32	Crunch	Dark	Physical	80	100	15	Normal
TR46	Iron Defense	Steel	Status	—	—	15	Self
TR57	Poison Jab	Poison	Physical	80	100	20	Normal
TR60	X-Scissor	Bug	Physical	80	100	15	Normal
TR61	Bug Buzz	Bug	Special	90	100	10	Normal
TR84	Scald	Water	Special	80	100	15	Normal
TR98	Liquidation	Water	Physical	85	100	10	Normal

Araquanid p. 96

ABILITY
Water Bubble
—

HIDDEN ABILITY
Water Absorb

SPECIES STRENGTHS
- HP
- ATTACK
- DEFENSE
- SP. ATK
- SP. DEF
- SPEED

DAMAGE TAKEN IN BATTLE

×1 | ×0.5 | ×2
×1 | ×1 | ×1
×0.5 | ×0.5 | ×1
×1 | ×2 | ×1
×2 | ×1 | ×0.5
×0.5 | ×1 | ×1

WATER 1
BUG

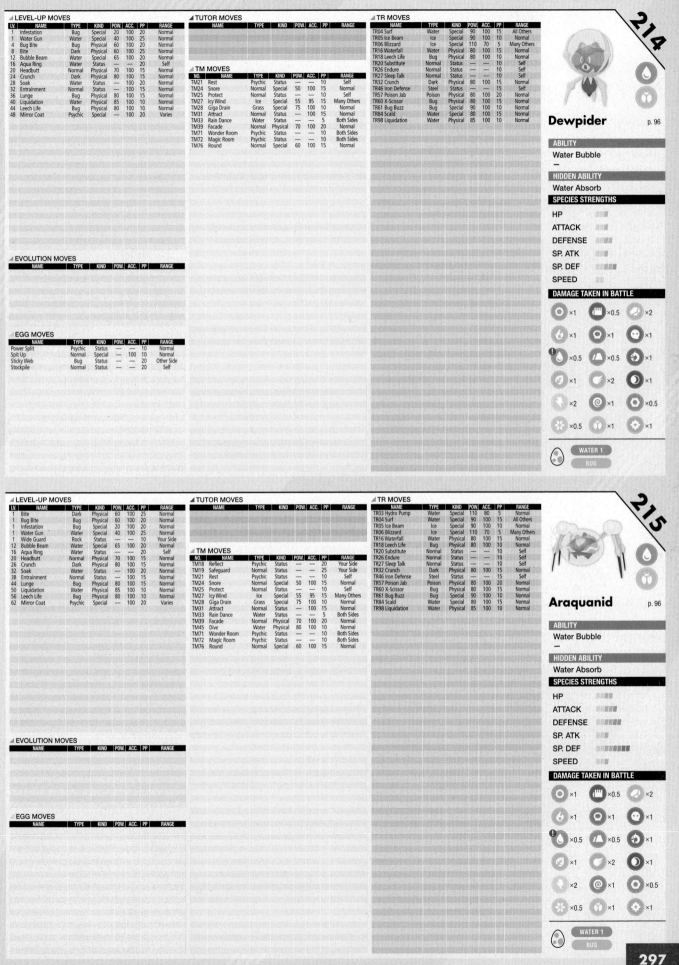

216

Wynaut
p. 96

ABILITY
Shadow Tag
—

HIDDEN ABILITY
Telepathy

SPECIES STRENGTHS

HP	
ATTACK	
DEFENSE	
SP. ATK	
SP. DEF	
SPEED	

DAMAGE TAKEN IN BATTLE

×1	×0.5	×1			
×1	×1	×2			
×1	×1	×1			
×1	×1	×2			
×1	×0.5	×1			
×1	×2	×1			

NO EGGS

LEVEL-UP MOVES

LV.	NAME	TYPE	KIND	POW.	ACC.	PP	RANGE
1	Amnesia	Psychic	Status	—	—	20	Self
1	Charm	Fairy	Status	—	100	20	Normal
1	Counter	Fighting	Physical	—	100	20	Varies
1	Destiny Bond	Ghost	Status	—	—	5	Self
1	Encore	Normal	Status	—	100	5	Normal
1	Mirror Coat	Psychic	Special	—	100	20	Varies
1	Safeguard	Normal	Status	—	—	25	Your Side
1	Splash	Normal	Status	—	—	40	Self

EVOLUTION MOVES

NAME	TYPE	KIND	POW.	ACC.	PP	RANGE

EGG MOVES

NAME	TYPE	KIND	POW.	ACC.	PP	RANGE

TUTOR MOVES

NAME	TYPE	KIND	POW.	ACC.	PP	RANGE

TM MOVES

NO.	NAME	TYPE	KIND	POW.	ACC.	PP	RANGE
TM19	Safeguard	Normal	Status	—	—	25	Your Side
TM29	Charm	Fairy	Status	—	100	20	Normal

TR MOVES

NAME	TYPE	KIND	POW.	ACC.	PP	RANGE
TR17 Amnesia	Psychic	Status	—	—	20	Self
TR30 Encore	Normal	Status	—	100	5	Normal

217

Wobbuffet
p. 96

ABILITY
Shadow Tag
—

HIDDEN ABILITY
Telepathy

SPECIES STRENGTHS

HP	
ATTACK	
DEFENSE	
SP. ATK	
SP. DEF	
SPEED	

DAMAGE TAKEN IN BATTLE

×1	×0.5	×1			
×1	×1	×2			
×1	×1	×1			
×1	×1	×2			
×1	×0.5	×1			
×1	×2	×1			

AMORPHOUS

LEVEL-UP MOVES

LV.	NAME	TYPE	KIND	POW.	ACC.	PP	RANGE
1	Amnesia	Psychic	Status	—	—	20	Self
1	Charm	Fairy	Status	—	100	20	Normal
1	Counter	Fighting	Physical	—	100	20	Varies
1	Destiny Bond	Ghost	Status	—	—	5	Self
1	Encore	Normal	Status	—	100	5	Normal
1	Mirror Coat	Psychic	Special	—	100	20	Varies
1	Safeguard	Normal	Status	—	—	25	Your Side
1	Splash	Normal	Status	—	—	40	Self

EVOLUTION MOVES

NAME	TYPE	KIND	POW.	ACC.	PP	RANGE
Counter	Fighting	Physical	—	100	20	Varies
Destiny Bond	Ghost	Status	—	—	5	Self
Mirror Coat	Psychic	Special	—	100	20	Varies
Safeguard	Normal	Status	—	—	25	Your Side

EGG MOVES

NAME	TYPE	KIND	POW.	ACC.	PP	RANGE

TUTOR MOVES

NAME	TYPE	KIND	POW.	ACC.	PP	RANGE

TM MOVES

NO.	NAME	TYPE	KIND	POW.	ACC.	PP	RANGE
TM19	Safeguard	Normal	Status	—	—	25	Your Side
TM29	Charm	Fairy	Status	—	100	20	Normal

TR MOVES

NAME	TYPE	KIND	POW.	ACC.	PP	RANGE
TR17 Amnesia	Psychic	Status	—	—	20	Self
TR30 Encore	Normal	Status	—	100	5	Normal

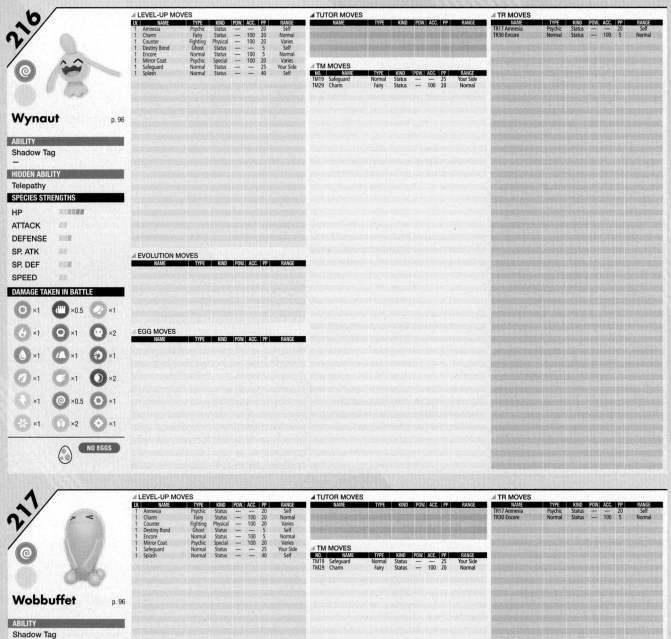

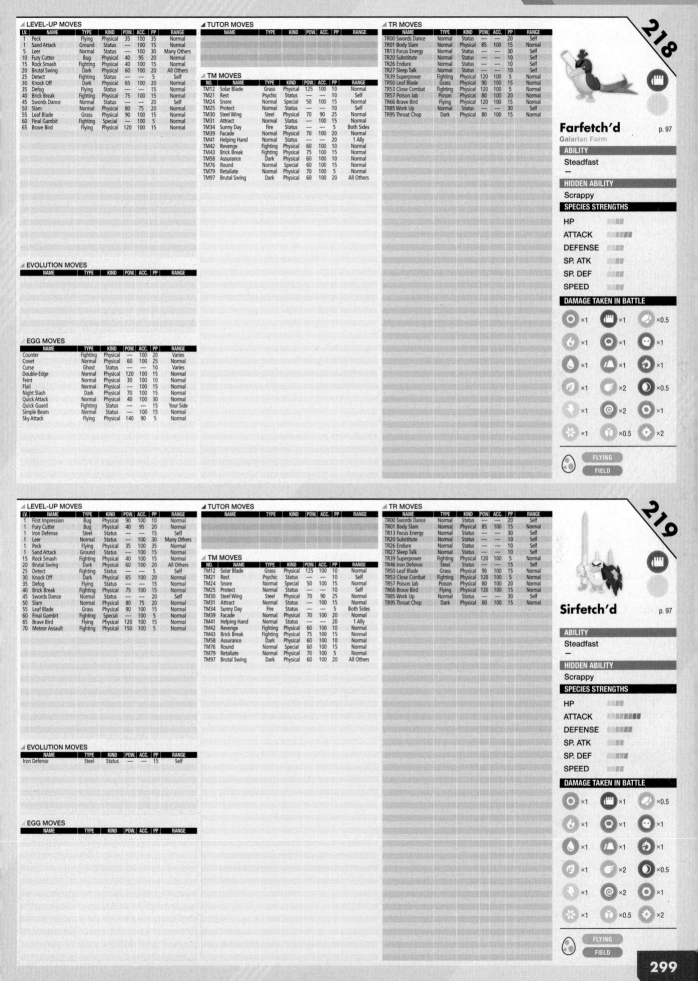

218

Farfetch'd
Galarian Form
p. 97

ABILITY
Steadfast
—

HIDDEN ABILITY
Scrappy

LEVEL-UP MOVES

LV.	NAME	TYPE	KIND	POW.	ACC.	PP	RANGE
1	Peck	Flying	Physical	35	100	35	Normal
1	Sand Attack	Ground	Status	—	100	15	Normal
5	Leer	Normal	Status	—	100	30	Many Others
10	Fury Cutter	Bug	Physical	40	95	20	Normal
15	Rock Smash	Fighting	Physical	40	100	15	Normal
20	Brutal Swing	Dark	Physical	60	100	20	All Others
25	Detect	Fighting	Status	—	—	5	Self
30	Knock Off	Dark	Physical	65	100	20	Normal
35	Defog	Flying	Status	—	—	15	Normal
40	Brick Break	Fighting	Physical	75	100	15	Normal
45	Swords Dance	Normal	Status	—	—	20	Self
50	Slam	Normal	Physical	80	75	20	Normal
55	Leaf Blade	Grass	Physical	90	100	15	Normal
60	Final Gambit	Fighting	Special	—	100	5	Normal
65	Brave Bird	Flying	Physical	120	100	15	Normal

EVOLUTION MOVES

NAME	TYPE	KIND	POW.	ACC.	PP	RANGE

EGG MOVES

NAME	TYPE	KIND	POW.	ACC.	PP	RANGE
Counter	Fighting	Physical	—	100	20	Varies
Covet	Normal	Physical	60	100	25	Normal
Curse	Ghost	Status	—	—	10	Varies
Double-Edge	Normal	Physical	120	100	15	Normal
Feint	Normal	Physical	30	100	10	Normal
Flail	Normal	Physical	—	100	15	Normal
Night Slash	Dark	Physical	70	100	15	Normal
Quick Attack	Normal	Physical	40	100	30	Normal
Quick Guard	Fighting	Status	—	—	15	Your Side
Simple Beam	Normal	Status	—	100	15	Normal
Sky Attack	Flying	Physical	140	90	5	Normal

TUTOR MOVES

NAME	TYPE	KIND	POW.	ACC.	PP	RANGE

TM MOVES

NO.	NAME	TYPE	KIND	POW.	ACC.	PP	RANGE
TM12	Solar Blade	Grass	Physical	125	100	10	Normal
TM21	Rest	Psychic	Status	—	—	10	Self
TM24	Snore	Normal	Special	50	100	15	Normal
TM25	Protect	Normal	Status	—	—	10	Self
TM30	Steel Wing	Steel	Physical	70	90	25	Normal
TM31	Attract	Normal	Status	—	100	15	Normal
TM34	Sunny Day	Fire	Status	—	—	5	Both Sides
TM39	Facade	Normal	Physical	70	100	20	Normal
TM41	Helping Hand	Normal	Status	—	—	20	1 Ally
TM42	Revenge	Fighting	Physical	60	100	10	Normal
TM43	Brick Break	Fighting	Physical	75	100	15	Normal
TM58	Assurance	Dark	Physical	60	100	10	Normal
TM76	Round	Normal	Special	60	100	15	Normal
TM79	Retaliate	Normal	Physical	70	100	5	Normal
TM97	Brutal Swing	Dark	Physical	60	100	20	All Others

TR MOVES

NO.	NAME	TYPE	KIND	POW.	ACC.	PP	RANGE
TR00	Swords Dance	Normal	Status	—	—	20	Self
TR01	Body Slam	Normal	Physical	85	100	15	Normal
TR13	Focus Energy	Normal	Status	—	—	30	Self
TR20	Substitute	Normal	Status	—	—	10	Self
TR26	Endure	Normal	Status	—	—	10	Self
TR27	Sleep Talk	Normal	Status	—	—	10	Self
TR39	Superpower	Fighting	Physical	120	100	5	Normal
TR50	Leaf Blade	Grass	Physical	90	100	15	Normal
TR57	Poison Jab	Poison	Physical	80	100	20	Normal
TR66	Brave Bird	Flying	Physical	120	100	15	Normal
TR85	Work Up	Normal	Status	—	—	30	Self
TR95	Throat Chop	Dark	Physical	80	100	15	Normal

SPECIES STRENGTHS
- HP
- ATTACK
- DEFENSE
- SP. ATK
- SP. DEF
- SPEED

DAMAGE TAKEN IN BATTLE

×1	×1	×0.5
×1	×1	×1
×1	×1	×1
×1	×2	×0.5
×1	×2	×2
×1	×0.5	×2

FLYING · FIELD

219

Sirfetch'd
p. 97

ABILITY
Steadfast
—

HIDDEN ABILITY
Scrappy

LEVEL-UP MOVES

LV.	NAME	TYPE	KIND	POW.	ACC.	PP	RANGE
1	First Impression	Bug	Physical	90	100	10	Normal
1	Fury Cutter	Bug	Physical	40	95	20	Normal
1	Iron Defense	Steel	Status	—	—	15	Self
1	Leer	Normal	Status	—	100	30	Many Others
1	Peck	Flying	Physical	35	100	35	Normal
1	Sand Attack	Ground	Status	—	100	15	Normal
15	Rock Smash	Fighting	Physical	40	100	15	Normal
20	Brutal Swing	Dark	Physical	60	100	20	All Others
25	Detect	Fighting	Status	—	—	5	Self
30	Knock Off	Dark	Physical	65	100	20	Normal
35	Defog	Flying	Status	—	—	15	Normal
40	Brick Break	Fighting	Physical	75	100	15	Normal
45	Swords Dance	Normal	Status	—	—	20	Self
50	Slam	Normal	Physical	80	75	20	Normal
55	Leaf Blade	Grass	Physical	90	100	15	Normal
60	Final Gambit	Fighting	Special	—	100	5	Normal
65	Brave Bird	Flying	Physical	120	100	15	Normal
70	Meteor Assault	Fighting	Physical	150	100	5	Normal

EVOLUTION MOVES

NAME	TYPE	KIND	POW.	ACC.	PP	RANGE
Iron Defense	Steel	Status	—	—	15	Self

EGG MOVES

NAME	TYPE	KIND	POW.	ACC.	PP	RANGE

TUTOR MOVES

NAME	TYPE	KIND	POW.	ACC.	PP	RANGE

TM MOVES

NO.	NAME	TYPE	KIND	POW.	ACC.	PP	RANGE
TM12	Solar Blade	Grass	Physical	125	100	10	Normal
TM21	Rest	Psychic	Status	—	—	10	Self
TM24	Snore	Normal	Special	50	100	15	Normal
TM25	Protect	Normal	Status	—	—	10	Self
TM30	Steel Wing	Steel	Physical	70	90	25	Normal
TM31	Attract	Normal	Status	—	100	15	Normal
TM34	Sunny Day	Fire	Status	—	—	5	Both Sides
TM39	Facade	Normal	Physical	70	100	20	Normal
TM41	Helping Hand	Normal	Status	—	—	20	1 Ally
TM42	Revenge	Fighting	Physical	60	100	10	Normal
TM43	Brick Break	Fighting	Physical	75	100	15	Normal
TM58	Assurance	Dark	Physical	60	100	10	Normal
TM76	Round	Normal	Special	60	100	15	Normal
TM79	Retaliate	Normal	Physical	70	100	5	Normal
TM97	Brutal Swing	Dark	Physical	60	100	20	All Others

TR MOVES

NO.	NAME	TYPE	KIND	POW.	ACC.	PP	RANGE
TR00	Swords Dance	Normal	Status	—	—	20	Self
TR01	Body Slam	Normal	Physical	85	100	15	Normal
TR13	Focus Energy	Normal	Status	—	—	30	Self
TR20	Substitute	Normal	Status	—	—	10	Self
TR26	Endure	Normal	Status	—	—	10	Self
TR27	Sleep Talk	Normal	Status	—	—	10	Self
TR39	Superpower	Fighting	Physical	120	100	5	Normal
TR46	Iron Defense	Steel	Status	—	—	15	Self
TR50	Leaf Blade	Grass	Physical	90	100	15	Normal
TR53	Close Combat	Fighting	Physical	120	100	5	Normal
TR57	Poison Jab	Poison	Physical	80	100	20	Normal
TR66	Brave Bird	Flying	Physical	120	100	15	Normal
TR85	Work Up	Normal	Status	—	—	30	Self
TR95	Throat Chop	Dark	Physical	80	100	15	Normal

SPECIES STRENGTHS
- HP
- ATTACK
- DEFENSE
- SP. ATK
- SP. DEF
- SPEED

DAMAGE TAKEN IN BATTLE

×1	×1	×0.5
×1	×1	×1
×1	×1	×1
×1	×2	×0.5
×1	×2	×2
×1	×0.5	×2

FLYING · FIELD

220

Chinchou
p. 97

ABILITY
Volt Absorb
Illuminate

HIDDEN ABILITY
Water Absorb

SPECIES STRENGTHS

HP
ATTACK
DEFENSE
SP. ATK
SP. DEF
SPEED

DAMAGE TAKEN IN BATTLE

×1	×1	×1
×0.5	×1	×1
×0.5	×2	×1
×2	×0.5	×1
×1	×1	×0.25
×0.5	×1	×1

WATER 2

LEVEL-UP MOVES

LV.	NAME	TYPE	KIND	POW.	ACC.	PP	RANGE
1	Supersonic	Normal	Status	—	55	20	Normal
1	Water Gun	Water	Special	40	100	25	Normal
4	Electro Ball	Electric	Special	—	100	10	Normal
8	Thunder Wave	Electric	Status	—	90	20	Normal
12	Bubble Beam	Water	Special	65	100	20	Normal
16	Confuse Ray	Ghost	Status	—	100	10	Normal
20	Spark	Electric	Physical	65	100	20	Normal
24	Charge	Electric	Status	—	—	20	Self
28	Discharge	Electric	Special	80	100	15	All Others
32	Aqua Ring	Water	Status	—	—	20	Self
36	Flail	Normal	Physical	—	100	15	Normal
40	Take Down	Normal	Physical	90	85	20	Normal
44	Hydro Pump	Water	Special	110	80	5	Normal

EVOLUTION MOVES

NAME	TYPE	KIND	POW.	ACC.	PP	RANGE

EGG MOVES

NAME	TYPE	KIND	POW.	ACC.	PP	RANGE
Mist	Ice	Status	—	—	30	Your Side
Psybeam	Psychic	Special	65	100	20	Normal
Soak	Water	Status	—	100	20	Normal
Water Pulse	Water	Special	60	100	20	Normal

TUTOR MOVES

NAME	TYPE	KIND	POW.	ACC.	PP	RANGE

TM MOVES

NO.	NAME	TYPE	KIND	POW.	ACC.	PP	RANGE
TM14	Thunder Wave	Electric	Status	—	90	20	Normal
TM16	Screech	Normal	Status	—	85	40	Normal
TM21	Rest	Psychic	Status	—	—	10	Self
TM24	Snore	Normal	Special	50	100	15	Normal
TM25	Protect	Normal	Status	—	—	10	Self
TM27	Icy Wind	Ice	Special	55	95	15	Many Others
TM31	Attract	Normal	Status	—	100	15	Normal
TM33	Rain Dance	Water	Status	—	—	5	Both Sides
TM35	Hail	Ice	Status	—	—	10	Both Sides
TM36	Whirlpool	Water	Special	35	85	15	Normal
TM39	Facade	Normal	Physical	70	100	20	Normal
TM45	Dive	Water	Physical	80	100	10	Normal
TM52	Bounce	Flying	Physical	85	85	5	Normal
TM55	Brine	Water	Special	65	100	10	Normal
TM76	Round	Normal	Special	60	100	15	Normal
TM80	Volt Switch	Electric	Special	70	100	20	Normal

TR MOVES

NO.	NAME	TYPE	KIND	POW.	ACC.	PP	RANGE
TR03	Hydro Pump	Water	Special	110	80	5	Normal
TR04	Surf	Water	Special	90	100	15	All Others
TR05	Ice Beam	Ice	Special	90	100	10	Normal
TR06	Blizzard	Ice	Special	110	70	5	Many Others
TR08	Thunderbolt	Electric	Special	90	100	15	Normal
TR09	Thunder	Electric	Special	110	70	10	Normal
TR12	Agility	Psychic	Status	—	—	30	Self
TR16	Waterfall	Water	Physical	80	100	15	Normal
TR17	Amnesia	Psychic	Status	—	—	20	Self
TR20	Substitute	Normal	Status	—	—	10	Self
TR26	Endure	Normal	Status	—	—	10	Self
TR27	Sleep Talk	Normal	Status	—	—	10	Self
TR80	Electro Ball	Electric	Special	—	100	10	Normal
TR84	Scald	Water	Special	80	100	15	Normal
TR86	Wild Charge	Electric	Physical	90	100	15	Normal
TR92	Dazzling Gleam	Fairy	Special	80	100	10	Many Others

221

Lanturn
p. 97

ABILITY
Volt Absorb
Illuminate

HIDDEN ABILITY
Water Absorb

SPECIES STRENGTHS

HP
ATTACK
DEFENSE
SP. ATK
SP. DEF
SPEED

DAMAGE TAKEN IN BATTLE

×1	×1	×1
×0.5	×1	×1
×0.5	×2	×1
×2	×0.5	×1
×1	×1	×0.25
×0.5	×1	×1

WATER 2

LEVEL-UP MOVES

LV.	NAME	TYPE	KIND	POW.	ACC.	PP	RANGE
1	Eerie Impulse	Electric	Status	—	100	15	Normal
1	Electro Ball	Electric	Special	—	100	10	Normal
1	Spit Up	Normal	Special	—	—	10	Normal
1	Stockpile	Normal	Status	—	—	20	Self
1	Supersonic	Normal	Status	—	55	20	Normal
1	Swallow	Normal	Status	—	—	10	Self
1	Thunder Wave	Electric	Status	—	90	20	Normal
1	Water Gun	Water	Special	40	100	25	Normal
12	Bubble Beam	Water	Special	65	100	20	Normal
16	Confuse Ray	Ghost	Status	—	100	10	Normal
20	Spark	Electric	Physical	65	100	20	Normal
24	Charge	Electric	Status	—	—	20	Self
30	Discharge	Electric	Special	80	100	15	All Others
36	Aqua Ring	Water	Status	—	—	20	Self
42	Flail	Normal	Physical	—	100	15	Normal
48	Take Down	Normal	Physical	90	85	20	Normal
54	Hydro Pump	Water	Special	110	80	5	Normal

EVOLUTION MOVES

NAME	TYPE	KIND	POW.	ACC.	PP	RANGE
Spit Up	Normal	Special	—	100	10	Normal
Stockpile	Normal	Status	—	—	20	Self
Swallow	Normal	Status	—	—	10	Self

EGG MOVES

NAME	TYPE	KIND	POW.	ACC.	PP	RANGE

TUTOR MOVES

NAME	TYPE	KIND	POW.	ACC.	PP	RANGE

TM MOVES

NO.	NAME	TYPE	KIND	POW.	ACC.	PP	RANGE
TM08	Hyper Beam	Normal	Special	150	90	5	Normal
TM09	Giga Impact	Normal	Physical	150	90	5	Normal
TM14	Thunder Wave	Electric	Status	—	90	20	Normal
TM16	Screech	Normal	Status	—	85	40	Normal
TM21	Rest	Psychic	Status	—	—	10	Self
TM24	Snore	Normal	Special	50	100	15	Normal
TM25	Protect	Normal	Status	—	—	10	Self
TM27	Icy Wind	Ice	Special	55	95	15	Many Others
TM31	Attract	Normal	Status	—	100	15	Normal
TM33	Rain Dance	Water	Status	—	—	5	Both Sides
TM35	Hail	Ice	Status	—	—	10	Both Sides
TM36	Whirlpool	Water	Special	35	85	15	Normal
TM39	Facade	Normal	Physical	70	100	20	Normal
TM45	Dive	Water	Physical	80	100	10	Normal
TM52	Bounce	Flying	Physical	85	85	5	Normal
TM55	Brine	Water	Special	65	100	10	Normal
TM76	Round	Normal	Special	60	100	15	Normal
TM80	Volt Switch	Electric	Special	70	100	20	Normal
TM93	Eerie Impulse	Electric	Status	—	100	15	Normal

TR MOVES

NO.	NAME	TYPE	KIND	POW.	ACC.	PP	RANGE
TR03	Hydro Pump	Water	Special	110	80	5	Normal
TR04	Surf	Water	Special	90	100	15	All Others
TR05	Ice Beam	Ice	Special	90	100	10	Normal
TR06	Blizzard	Ice	Special	110	70	5	Many Others
TR08	Thunderbolt	Electric	Special	90	100	15	Normal
TR09	Thunder	Electric	Special	110	70	10	Normal
TR12	Agility	Psychic	Status	—	—	30	Self
TR16	Waterfall	Water	Physical	80	100	15	Normal
TR17	Amnesia	Psychic	Status	—	—	20	Self
TR20	Substitute	Normal	Status	—	—	10	Self
TR26	Endure	Normal	Status	—	—	10	Self
TR27	Sleep Talk	Normal	Status	—	—	10	Self
TR80	Electro Ball	Electric	Special	—	100	10	Normal
TR84	Scald	Water	Special	80	100	15	Normal
TR86	Wild Charge	Electric	Physical	90	100	15	Normal
TR92	Dazzling Gleam	Fairy	Special	80	100	10	Many Others

222 — Croagunk

LEVEL-UP MOVES

LV.	NAME	TYPE	KIND	POW.	ACC.	PP	RANGE
1	Mud-Slap	Ground	Special	20	100	10	Normal
1	Poison Sting	Poison	Physical	15	100	35	Normal
4	Astonish	Ghost	Physical	30	100	15	Normal
8	Taunt	Dark	Status	—	100	20	Normal
12	Flatter	Dark	Status	—	100	15	Normal
16	Revenge	Fighting	Physical	60	100	10	Normal
20	Venoshock	Poison	Special	65	100	10	Normal
24	Sucker Punch	Dark	Physical	70	100	5	Normal
28	Swagger	Normal	Status	—	85	15	Normal
32	Poison Jab	Poison	Physical	80	100	20	Normal
36	Toxic	Poison	Status	—	90	10	Normal
40	Nasty Plot	Dark	Status	—	—	20	Self
44	Sludge Bomb	Poison	Special	90	100	10	Normal
48	Belch	Poison	Special	120	90	10	Normal

EVOLUTION MOVES

NAME	TYPE	KIND	POW.	ACC.	PP	RANGE

EGG MOVES

NAME	TYPE	KIND	POW.	ACC.	PP	RANGE
Bullet Punch	Steel	Physical	40	100	30	Normal
Counter	Fighting	Physical	—	100	20	Varies
Cross Chop	Fighting	Physical	100	80	5	Normal
Dynamic Punch	Fighting	Physical	100	50	5	Normal
Fake Out	Normal	Physical	40	100	10	Normal
Feint	Normal	Physical	30	100	10	Normal
Headbutt	Normal	Physical	70	100	15	Normal
Quick Guard	Fighting	Status	—	—	15	Your Side
Vacuum Wave	Fighting	Special	40	100	30	Normal

TUTOR MOVES

NAME	TYPE	KIND	POW.	ACC.	PP	RANGE

TM MOVES

NO.	NAME	TYPE	KIND	POW.	ACC.	PP	RANGE
TM00	Mega Punch	Normal	Physical	80	85	20	Normal
TM01	Mega Kick	Normal	Physical	120	75	5	Normal
TM04	Ice Punch	Ice	Physical	75	100	15	Normal
TM05	Thunder Punch	Electric	Physical	75	100	15	Normal
TM15	Dig	Ground	Physical	80	100	10	Normal
TM16	Screech	Normal	Status	—	85	40	Normal
TM21	Rest	Psychic	Status	—	—	10	Self
TM22	Rock Slide	Rock	Physical	75	90	10	Many Others
TM23	Thief	Dark	Physical	60	100	25	Normal
TM24	Snore	Normal	Special	50	100	15	Normal
TM25	Protect	Normal	Status	—	—	10	Self
TM27	Icy Wind	Ice	Special	55	95	15	Many Others
TM31	Attract	Normal	Status	—	100	15	Normal
TM33	Rain Dance	Water	Status	—	—	5	Both Sides
TM34	Sunny Day	Fire	Status	—	—	5	Both Sides
TM39	Facade	Normal	Physical	70	100	20	Normal
TM41	Helping Hand	Normal	Status	—	—	20	1 Ally
TM42	Revenge	Fighting	Physical	60	100	10	Normal
TM43	Brick Break	Fighting	Physical	75	100	15	Normal
TM48	Rock Tomb	Rock	Physical	60	95	15	Normal
TM52	Bounce	Flying	Physical	85	85	5	Normal
TM57	Payback	Dark	Physical	50	100	10	Normal
TM58	Assurance	Dark	Physical	60	100	10	Normal
TM59	Fling	Dark	Physical	—	100	10	Normal
TM63	Drain Punch	Fighting	Physical	75	100	10	Normal
TM74	Venoshock	Poison	Special	65	100	10	Normal
TM75	Low Sweep	Fighting	Physical	65	100	20	Normal
TM76	Round	Normal	Special	60	100	15	Normal
TM79	Retaliate	Normal	Physical	70	100	5	Normal
TM81	Bulldoze	Ground	Physical	60	100	20	All Others

TR MOVES

NO.	NAME	TYPE	KIND	POW.	ACC.	PP	RANGE
TR07	Low Kick	Fighting	Physical	—	100	20	Normal
TR10	Earthquake	Ground	Physical	100	100	10	All Others
TR20	Substitute	Normal	Status	—	—	10	Self
TR22	Sludge Bomb	Poison	Special	90	100	10	Normal
TR26	Endure	Normal	Status	—	—	10	Self
TR27	Sleep Talk	Normal	Status	—	—	10	Self
TR29	Baton Pass	Normal	Status	—	—	5	Self
TR30	Encore	Normal	Status	—	100	5	Normal
TR33	Shadow Ball	Ghost	Special	80	100	15	Normal
TR37	Taunt	Dark	Status	—	100	20	Normal
TR48	Bulk Up	Fighting	Status	—	—	20	Self
TR57	Poison Jab	Poison	Physical	80	100	20	Normal
TR58	Dark Pulse	Dark	Special	80	100	15	Normal
TR60	X-Scissor	Bug	Physical	80	100	15	Normal
TR68	Nasty Plot	Dark	Status	—	—	20	Self
TR73	Gunk Shot	Poison	Physical	120	80	5	Normal
TR78	Sludge Wave	Poison	Special	95	100	10	All Others
TR81	Foul Play	Dark	Physical	95	100	15	Normal
TR85	Work Up	Normal	Status	—	—	30	Self
TR91	Venom Drench	Poison	Status	—	100	20	Many Others

Croagunk p. 98

ABILITY: Anticipation / Dry Skin
HIDDEN ABILITY: Poison Touch

SPECIES STRENGTHS: HP · ATTACK · DEFENSE · SP. ATK · SP. DEF · SPEED

DAMAGE TAKEN IN BATTLE:
×1, ×0.5, ×0.5, ×1, ×0.5, ×1, ×1, ×2, ×1, ×0.5, ×2, ×0.5, ×1, ×4, ×1, ×1, ×0.25, ×1

HUMANLIKE

---

223 — Toxicroak

LEVEL-UP MOVES

LV.	NAME	TYPE	KIND	POW.	ACC.	PP	RANGE
1	Astonish	Ghost	Physical	30	100	15	Normal
1	Mud-Slap	Ground	Special	20	100	10	Normal
1	Poison Sting	Poison	Physical	15	100	35	Normal
1	Taunt	Dark	Status	—	100	20	Normal
12	Flatter	Dark	Status	—	100	15	Normal
16	Revenge	Fighting	Physical	60	100	10	Normal
20	Venoshock	Poison	Special	65	100	10	Normal
24	Sucker Punch	Dark	Physical	70	100	5	Normal
28	Swagger	Normal	Status	—	85	15	Normal
32	Poison Jab	Poison	Physical	80	100	20	Normal
36	Toxic	Poison	Status	—	90	10	Normal
42	Nasty Plot	Dark	Status	—	—	20	Self
48	Sludge Bomb	Poison	Special	90	100	10	Normal
54	Belch	Poison	Special	120	90	10	Normal

EVOLUTION MOVES

NAME	TYPE	KIND	POW.	ACC.	PP	RANGE

EGG MOVES

NAME	TYPE	KIND	POW.	ACC.	PP	RANGE

TUTOR MOVES

NAME	TYPE	KIND	POW.	ACC.	PP	RANGE

TM MOVES

NO.	NAME	TYPE	KIND	POW.	ACC.	PP	RANGE
TM00	Mega Punch	Normal	Physical	80	85	20	Normal
TM01	Mega Kick	Normal	Physical	120	75	5	Normal
TM04	Ice Punch	Ice	Physical	75	100	15	Normal
TM05	Thunder Punch	Electric	Physical	75	100	15	Normal
TM08	Hyper Beam	Normal	Special	150	90	5	Normal
TM09	Giga Impact	Normal	Physical	150	90	5	Normal
TM15	Dig	Ground	Physical	80	100	10	Normal
TM16	Screech	Normal	Status	—	85	40	Normal
TM21	Rest	Psychic	Status	—	—	10	Self
TM22	Rock Slide	Rock	Physical	75	90	10	Many Others
TM23	Thief	Dark	Physical	60	100	25	Normal
TM24	Snore	Normal	Special	50	100	15	Normal
TM25	Protect	Normal	Status	—	—	10	Self
TM27	Icy Wind	Ice	Special	55	95	15	Many Others
TM31	Attract	Normal	Status	—	100	15	Normal
TM33	Rain Dance	Water	Status	—	—	5	Both Sides
TM34	Sunny Day	Fire	Status	—	—	5	Both Sides
TM39	Facade	Normal	Physical	70	100	20	Normal
TM41	Helping Hand	Normal	Status	—	—	20	1 Ally
TM42	Revenge	Fighting	Physical	60	100	10	Normal
TM43	Brick Break	Fighting	Physical	75	100	15	Normal
TM48	Rock Tomb	Rock	Physical	60	95	15	Normal
TM52	Bounce	Flying	Physical	85	85	5	Normal
TM57	Payback	Dark	Physical	50	100	10	Normal
TM58	Assurance	Dark	Physical	60	100	10	Normal
TM59	Fling	Dark	Physical	—	100	10	Normal
TM63	Drain Punch	Fighting	Physical	75	100	10	Normal
TM73	Cross Poison	Poison	Physical	70	100	20	Normal
TM74	Venoshock	Poison	Special	65	100	10	Normal
TM75	Low Sweep	Fighting	Physical	65	100	20	Normal
TM76	Round	Normal	Special	60	100	15	Normal
TM79	Retaliate	Normal	Physical	70	100	5	Normal
TM81	Bulldoze	Ground	Physical	60	100	20	All Others

TR MOVES

NO.	NAME	TYPE	KIND	POW.	ACC.	PP	RANGE
TR00	Swords Dance	Normal	Status	—	—	20	Self
TR07	Low Kick	Fighting	Physical	—	100	20	Normal
TR10	Earthquake	Ground	Physical	100	100	10	All Others
TR20	Substitute	Normal	Status	—	—	10	Self
TR26	Endure	Normal	Status	—	—	10	Self
TR27	Sleep Talk	Normal	Status	—	—	10	Self
TR29	Baton Pass	Normal	Status	—	—	40	Self
TR30	Encore	Normal	Status	—	100	5	Normal
TR33	Shadow Ball	Ghost	Special	80	100	15	Normal
TR37	Taunt	Dark	Status	—	100	20	Normal
TR48	Bulk Up	Fighting	Status	—	—	20	Self
TR57	Poison Jab	Poison	Physical	80	100	20	Normal
TR58	Dark Pulse	Dark	Special	80	100	15	Normal
TR60	X-Scissor	Bug	Physical	80	100	15	Normal
TR64	Focus Blast	Fighting	Special	120	70	5	Normal
TR68	Nasty Plot	Dark	Status	—	—	20	Self
TR73	Gunk Shot	Poison	Physical	120	80	5	Normal
TR75	Stone Edge	Rock	Physical	100	80	5	Normal
TR78	Sludge Wave	Poison	Special	95	100	10	All Others
TR81	Foul Play	Dark	Physical	95	100	15	Normal
TR85	Work Up	Normal	Status	—	—	30	Self
TR91	Venom Drench	Poison	Status	—	100	20	Many Others
TR95	Throat Chop	Dark	Physical	80	100	15	Normal

Toxicroak p. 98

ABILITY: Anticipation / Dry Skin
HIDDEN ABILITY: Poison Touch

SPECIES STRENGTHS: HP · ATTACK · DEFENSE · SP. ATK · SP. DEF · SPEED

DAMAGE TAKEN IN BATTLE:
×1, ×0.5, ×0.5, ×1, ×0.5, ×1, ×1, ×2, ×1, ×0.5, ×2, ×0.5, ×1, ×4, ×1, ×1, ×0.25, ×1

HUMANLIKE

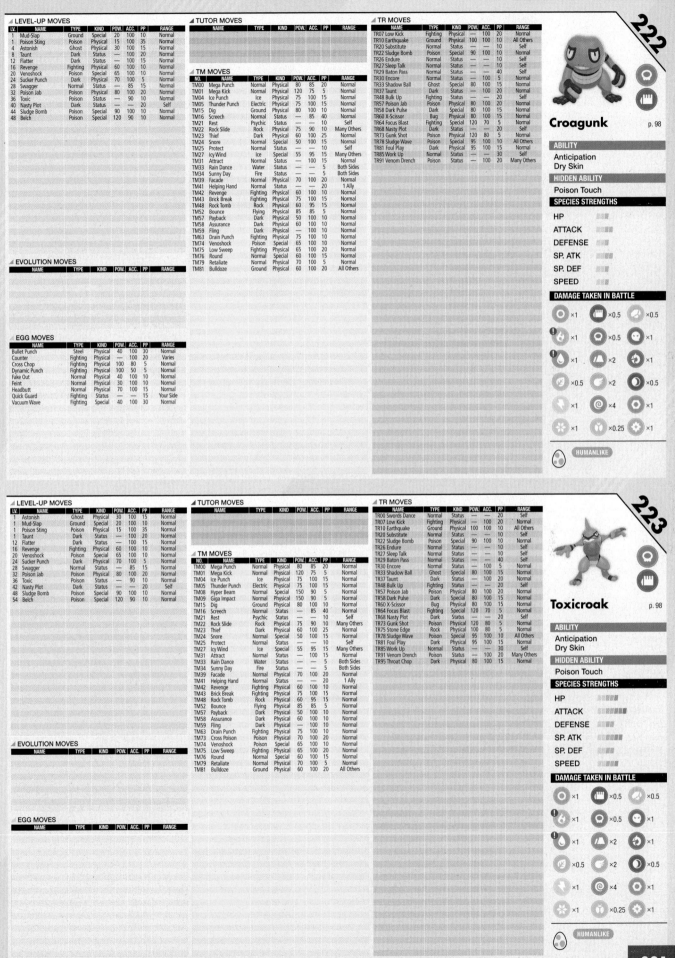

224

Scraggy　p. 98

ABILITY
Shed Skin
Moxie

HIDDEN ABILITY
Intimidate

SPECIES STRENGTHS

Stat	
HP	
ATTACK	
DEFENSE	
SP. ATK	
SP. DEF	
SPEED	

DAMAGE TAKEN IN BATTLE

×1	×2	×0.5			
×1	×1	×0.5			
×1	×1	×1			
×1	×2	×0.25			
×1	×0	×1			
×1	×1	×4			

FIELD
DRAGON

LEVEL-UP MOVES

LV.	NAME	TYPE	KIND	POW.	ACC.	PP	RANGE
1	Leer	Normal	Status	—	100	30	Many Others
1	Low Kick	Fighting	Physical	—	100	20	Normal
4	Payback	Dark	Physical	50	100	10	Normal
8	Headbutt	Normal	Physical	70	100	15	Normal
12	Sand Attack	Ground	Status	—	100	15	Normal
16	Facade	Normal	Physical	70	100	20	Normal
20	Protect	Normal	Status	—	—	10	Self
24	Beat Up	Dark	Physical	—	100	10	Normal
28	Scary Face	Normal	Status	—	100	10	Normal
32	Brick Break	Fighting	Physical	75	100	15	Normal
36	Swagger	Normal	Status	—	85	15	Normal
40	Crunch	Dark	Physical	80	100	15	Normal
44	High Jump Kick	Fighting	Physical	130	90	10	Normal
48	Focus Punch	Fighting	Physical	150	100	20	Normal
52	Head Smash	Rock	Physical	150	80	5	Normal

EVOLUTION MOVES

NAME	TYPE	KIND	POW.	ACC.	PP	RANGE

EGG MOVES

NAME	TYPE	KIND	POW.	ACC.	PP	RANGE
Acid Spray	Poison	Special	40	100	20	Normal
Counter	Fighting	Physical	—	100	20	Varies
Detect	Fighting	Status	—	—	5	Self
Fake Out	Normal	Physical	40	100	10	Normal
Power-Up Punch	Fighting	Physical	40	100	20	Normal
Quick Guard	Fighting	Status	—	—	15	Your Side

TUTOR MOVES

NAME	TYPE	KIND	POW.	ACC.	PP	RANGE

TM MOVES

NO.	NAME	TYPE	KIND	POW.	ACC.	PP	RANGE
TM00	Mega Punch	Normal	Physical	80	85	20	Normal
TM01	Mega Kick	Normal	Physical	120	75	5	Normal
TM03	Fire Punch	Fire	Physical	75	100	15	Normal
TM04	Ice Punch	Ice	Physical	75	100	15	Normal
TM05	Thunder Punch	Electric	Physical	75	100	15	Normal
TM15	Dig	Ground	Physical	80	100	10	Normal
TM21	Rest	Psychic	Status	—	—	10	Self
TM22	Rock Slide	Rock	Physical	75	90	10	Many Others
TM23	Thief	Dark	Physical	60	100	25	Normal
TM24	Snore	Normal	Special	50	100	15	Normal
TM25	Protect	Normal	Status	—	—	10	Self
TM26	Scary Face	Normal	Status	—	100	10	Normal
TM31	Attract	Normal	Status	—	100	15	Normal
TM33	Rain Dance	Water	Status	—	—	5	Both Sides
TM34	Sunny Day	Fire	Status	—	—	5	Both Sides
TM37	Beat Up	Dark	Physical	—	100	10	Normal
TM39	Facade	Normal	Physical	70	100	20	Normal
TM42	Revenge	Fighting	Physical	60	100	10	Normal
TM43	Brick Break	Fighting	Physical	75	100	15	Normal
TM47	Fake Tears	Dark	Status	—	100	20	Normal
TM48	Rock Tomb	Rock	Physical	60	95	15	Normal
TM57	Payback	Dark	Physical	50	100	10	Normal
TM58	Assurance	Dark	Physical	60	100	10	Normal
TM59	Fling	Dark	Physical	—	100	10	Normal
TM63	Drain Punch	Fighting	Physical	75	100	10	Normal
TM75	Low Sweep	Fighting	Physical	65	100	20	Normal
TM76	Round	Normal	Special	60	100	15	Normal
TM79	Retaliate	Normal	Physical	70	100	5	Normal
TM85	Snarl	Dark	Special	55	95	15	Many Others

TR MOVES

NO.	NAME	TYPE	KIND	POW.	ACC.	PP	RANGE
TR07	Low Kick	Fighting	Physical	—	100	20	Normal
TR17	Amnesia	Psychic	Status	—	—	20	Self
TR20	Substitute	Normal	Status	—	—	10	Self
TR22	Sludge Bomb	Poison	Special	90	100	10	Normal
TR26	Endure	Normal	Status	—	—	10	Self
TR27	Sleep Talk	Normal	Status	—	—	10	Self
TR31	Iron Tail	Steel	Physical	100	75	15	Normal
TR32	Crunch	Dark	Physical	80	100	15	Normal
TR37	Taunt	Dark	Status	—	100	20	Normal
TR46	Iron Defense	Steel	Status	—	—	15	Self
TR47	Dragon Claw	Dragon	Physical	80	100	15	Normal
TR48	Bulk Up	Fighting	Status	—	—	20	Self
TR51	Dragon Dance	Dragon	Status	—	—	20	Self
TR57	Poison Jab	Poison	Physical	80	100	20	Normal
TR58	Dark Pulse	Dark	Special	80	100	15	Normal
TR62	Dragon Pulse	Dragon	Special	85	100	10	Normal
TR64	Focus Blast	Fighting	Special	120	70	5	Normal
TR69	Zen Headbutt	Psychic	Physical	80	90	15	Normal
TR74	Iron Head	Steel	Physical	80	100	15	Normal
TR75	Stone Edge	Rock	Physical	100	80	5	Normal
TR77	Grass Knot	Grass	Special	—	100	20	Normal
TR81	Foul Play	Dark	Physical	95	100	15	Normal
TR85	Work Up	Normal	Status	—	—	30	Self

225

Scrafty　p. 98

ABILITY
Shed Skin
Moxie

HIDDEN ABILITY
Intimidate

SPECIES STRENGTHS

Stat	
HP	
ATTACK	
DEFENSE	
SP. ATK	
SP. DEF	
SPEED	

DAMAGE TAKEN IN BATTLE

×1	×2	×0.5			
×1	×1	×0.5			
×1	×1	×1			
×1	×2	×0.25			
×1	×0	×1			
×1	×1	×4			

FIELD
DRAGON

LEVEL-UP MOVES

LV.	NAME	TYPE	KIND	POW.	ACC.	PP	RANGE
1	Headbutt	Normal	Physical	70	100	15	Normal
1	Leer	Normal	Status	—	100	30	Many Others
1	Low Kick	Fighting	Physical	—	100	20	Normal
1	Payback	Dark	Physical	50	100	10	Normal
12	Sand Attack	Ground	Status	—	100	15	Normal
16	Facade	Normal	Physical	70	100	20	Normal
20	Protect	Normal	Status	—	—	10	Self
24	Beat Up	Dark	Physical	—	100	10	Normal
28	Scary Face	Normal	Status	—	100	10	Normal
32	Brick Break	Fighting	Physical	75	100	15	Normal
36	Swagger	Normal	Status	—	85	15	Normal
42	Crunch	Dark	Physical	80	100	15	Normal
48	High Jump Kick	Fighting	Physical	130	90	10	Normal
54	Focus Punch	Fighting	Physical	150	100	20	Normal
60	Head Smash	Rock	Physical	150	80	5	Normal

EVOLUTION MOVES

NAME	TYPE	KIND	POW.	ACC.	PP	RANGE

EGG MOVES

NAME	TYPE	KIND	POW.	ACC.	PP	RANGE

TUTOR MOVES

NAME	TYPE	KIND	POW.	ACC.	PP	RANGE

TM MOVES

NO.	NAME	TYPE	KIND	POW.	ACC.	PP	RANGE
TM00	Mega Punch	Normal	Physical	80	85	20	Normal
TM01	Mega Kick	Normal	Physical	120	75	5	Normal
TM03	Fire Punch	Fire	Physical	75	100	15	Normal
TM04	Ice Punch	Ice	Physical	75	100	15	Normal
TM05	Thunder Punch	Electric	Physical	75	100	15	Normal
TM08	Hyper Beam	Normal	Special	150	90	5	Normal
TM09	Giga Impact	Normal	Physical	150	90	5	Normal
TM15	Dig	Ground	Physical	80	100	10	Normal
TM21	Rest	Psychic	Status	—	—	10	Self
TM22	Rock Slide	Rock	Physical	75	90	10	Many Others
TM23	Thief	Dark	Physical	60	100	25	Normal
TM24	Snore	Normal	Special	50	100	15	Normal
TM25	Protect	Normal	Status	—	—	10	Self
TM26	Scary Face	Normal	Status	—	100	10	Normal
TM31	Attract	Normal	Status	—	100	15	Normal
TM33	Rain Dance	Water	Status	—	—	5	Both Sides
TM34	Sunny Day	Fire	Status	—	—	5	Both Sides
TM37	Beat Up	Dark	Physical	—	100	10	Normal
TM39	Facade	Normal	Physical	70	100	20	Normal
TM42	Revenge	Fighting	Physical	60	100	10	Normal
TM43	Brick Break	Fighting	Physical	75	100	15	Normal
TM47	Fake Tears	Dark	Status	—	100	20	Normal
TM48	Rock Tomb	Rock	Physical	60	95	15	Normal
TM57	Payback	Dark	Physical	50	100	10	Normal
TM58	Assurance	Dark	Physical	60	100	10	Normal
TM59	Fling	Dark	Physical	—	100	10	Normal
TM63	Drain Punch	Fighting	Physical	75	100	10	Normal
TM75	Low Sweep	Fighting	Physical	65	100	20	Normal
TM76	Round	Normal	Special	60	100	15	Normal
TM79	Retaliate	Normal	Physical	70	100	5	Normal
TM85	Snarl	Dark	Special	55	95	15	Many Others

TR MOVES

NO.	NAME	TYPE	KIND	POW.	ACC.	PP	RANGE
TR07	Low Kick	Fighting	Physical	—	100	20	Normal
TR17	Amnesia	Psychic	Status	—	—	20	Self
TR20	Substitute	Normal	Status	—	—	10	Self
TR22	Sludge Bomb	Poison	Special	90	100	10	Normal
TR24	Outrage	Dragon	Physical	120	100	10	1 Random
TR26	Endure	Normal	Status	—	—	10	Self
TR27	Sleep Talk	Normal	Status	—	—	10	Self
TR31	Iron Tail	Steel	Physical	100	75	15	Normal
TR32	Crunch	Dark	Physical	80	100	15	Normal
TR37	Taunt	Dark	Status	—	100	20	Normal
TR46	Iron Defense	Steel	Status	—	—	15	Self
TR47	Dragon Claw	Dragon	Physical	80	100	15	Normal
TR48	Bulk Up	Fighting	Status	—	—	20	Self
TR51	Dragon Dance	Dragon	Status	—	—	20	Self
TR53	Close Combat	Fighting	Physical	120	100	5	Normal
TR57	Poison Jab	Poison	Physical	80	100	20	Normal
TR58	Dark Pulse	Dark	Special	80	100	15	Normal
TR62	Dragon Pulse	Dragon	Special	85	100	10	Normal
TR64	Focus Blast	Fighting	Special	120	70	5	Normal
TR69	Zen Headbutt	Psychic	Physical	80	90	15	Normal
TR74	Iron Head	Steel	Physical	80	100	15	Normal
TR75	Stone Edge	Rock	Physical	100	80	5	Normal
TR77	Grass Knot	Grass	Special	—	100	20	Normal
TR81	Foul Play	Dark	Physical	95	100	15	Normal
TR85	Work Up	Normal	Status	—	—	30	Self
TR95	Throat Chop	Dark	Physical	80	100	15	Normal

226 — Stunfisk (Galarian Form)

LEVEL-UP MOVES

LV.	NAME	TYPE	KIND	POW.	ACC.	PP	RANGE
1	Metal Claw	Steel	Physical	50	95	35	Normal
1	Mud-Slap	Ground	Special	20	100	10	Normal
1	Tackle	Normal	Physical	40	100	35	Normal
1	Water Gun	Water	Special	40	100	25	Normal
5	Endure	Normal	Status	—	—	10	Self
10	Mud Shot	Ground	Special	55	95	15	Normal
15	Revenge	Fighting	Physical	60	100	10	Normal
20	Metal Sound	Steel	Status	—	85	40	Normal
25	Sucker Punch	Dark	Physical	70	100	5	Normal
30	Iron Defense	Steel	Status	—	—	15	Self
35	Bounce	Flying	Physical	85	85	5	Normal
40	Muddy Water	Water	Special	90	85	10	Many Others
45	Snap Trap	Grass	Physical	35	100	15	Normal
50	Flail	Normal	Physical	—	100	15	Normal
55	Fissure	Ground	Physical	—	30	5	Normal

EVOLUTION MOVES

NAME	TYPE	KIND	POW.	ACC.	PP	RANGE

EGG MOVES

NAME	TYPE	KIND	POW.	ACC.	PP	RANGE
Astonish	Ghost	Physical	30	100	15	Normal
Bind	Normal	Physical	15	85	20	Normal
Counter	Fighting	Physical	—	100	20	Varies
Curse	Ghost	Status	—	—	10	Varies
Pain Split	Normal	Status	—	—	20	Normal
Reflect Type	Normal	Status	—	—	15	Normal
Spite	Ghost	Status	—	100	10	Normal
Yawn	Normal	Status	—	—	10	Normal

TUTOR MOVES

NAME	TYPE	KIND	POW.	ACC.	PP	RANGE
Steel Beam	Steel	Special	140	95	5	Normal

TM MOVES

NO.	NAME	TYPE	KIND	POW.	ACC.	PP	RANGE
TM14	Thunder Wave	Electric	Status	—	90	20	Normal
TM15	Dig	Ground	Physical	80	100	10	Normal
TM16	Screech	Normal	Status	—	85	40	Normal
TM21	Rest	Psychic	Status	—	—	10	Self
TM22	Rock Slide	Rock	Physical	75	90	10	Many Others
TM24	Snore	Normal	Special	50	100	15	Normal
TM25	Protect	Normal	Status	—	—	10	Self
TM31	Attract	Normal	Status	—	100	15	Normal
TM32	Sandstorm	Rock	Status	—	—	10	Both Sides
TM33	Rain Dance	Water	Status	—	—	5	Both Sides
TM39	Facade	Normal	Physical	70	100	20	Normal
TM42	Revenge	Fighting	Physical	60	100	10	Normal
TM48	Rock Tomb	Rock	Physical	60	95	15	Normal
TM52	Bounce	Flying	Physical	85	85	5	Normal
TM53	Mud Shot	Ground	Special	55	95	15	Normal
TM57	Payback	Dark	Physical	50	100	10	Normal
TM67	Ice Fang	Ice	Physical	65	95	15	Normal
TM76	Round	Normal	Special	60	100	15	Normal
TM81	Bulldoze	Ground	Physical	60	100	20	All Others
TM98	Stomping Tantrum	Ground	Physical	75	100	10	Normal

TR MOVES

NO.	NAME	TYPE	KIND	POW.	ACC.	PP	RANGE
TR04	Surf	Water	Special	90	100	15	All Others
TR10	Earthquake	Ground	Physical	100	100	10	All Others
TR20	Substitute	Normal	Status	—	—	10	Self
TR22	Sludge Bomb	Poison	Special	90	100	10	Normal
TR26	Endure	Normal	Status	—	—	10	Self
TR27	Sleep Talk	Normal	Status	—	—	10	Self
TR32	Crunch	Dark	Physical	80	100	15	Normal
TR35	Uproar	Normal	Special	90	100	10	1 Random
TR45	Muddy Water	Water	Special	90	85	10	Many Others
TR46	Iron Defense	Steel	Status	—	—	15	Self
TR67	Earth Power	Ground	Special	90	100	10	Normal
TR70	Flash Cannon	Steel	Special	80	100	10	Normal
TR75	Stone Edge	Rock	Physical	100	80	5	Normal
TR76	Stealth Rock	Rock	Status	—	—	20	Other Side
TR78	Sludge Wave	Poison	Special	95	100	10	All Others
TR81	Foul Play	Dark	Physical	95	100	15	Normal
TR84	Scald	Water	Special	80	100	15	Normal

Stunfisk p. 99
Galarian Form

ABILITY
Mimicry
—

HIDDEN ABILITY
—

SPECIES STRENGTHS
- HP
- ATTACK
- DEFENSE
- SP. ATK
- SP. DEF
- SPEED

DAMAGE TAKEN IN BATTLE
×0.5, ×2, ×0.25, ×2, ×0, ×1, ×2, ×2, ×0.5, ×1, ×0.5, ×1, ×0, ×0.5, ×0.5, ×1, ×0.5, ×0.5

Egg Groups: WATER 1, AMORPHOUS

---

227 — Shuckle

LEVEL-UP MOVES

LV.	NAME	TYPE	KIND	POW.	ACC.	PP	RANGE
1	Withdraw	Water	Status	—	—	40	Self
1	Wrap	Normal	Physical	15	90	20	Normal
5	Rollout	Rock	Physical	30	90	20	Normal
10	Struggle Bug	Bug	Special	50	100	20	Many Others
15	Rock Throw	Rock	Physical	50	90	15	Normal
20	Safeguard	Normal	Status	—	—	25	Your Side
25	Rest	Psychic	Status	—	—	10	Self
30	Bug Bite	Bug	Physical	60	100	20	Normal
35	Guard Split	Psychic	Status	—	—	10	Normal
35	Power Split	Psychic	Status	—	—	10	Normal
40	Rock Slide	Rock	Physical	75	90	10	Many Others
45	Gastro Acid	Poison	Status	—	100	10	Normal
50	Sticky Web	Bug	Status	—	—	20	Other Side
55	Power Trick	Psychic	Status	—	—	10	Self
60	Stone Edge	Rock	Physical	100	80	5	Normal
65	Shell Smash	Normal	Status	—	—	15	Self

EVOLUTION MOVES

NAME	TYPE	KIND	POW.	ACC.	PP	RANGE

EGG MOVES

NAME	TYPE	KIND	POW.	ACC.	PP	RANGE
Acid	Poison	Special	40	100	30	Many Others
Acupressure	Normal	Status	—	—	30	Self/Ally
Covet	Normal	Physical	60	100	25	Normal
Defense Curl	Normal	Status	—	—	40	Self
Final Gambit	Fighting	Special	—	100	5	Normal
Infestation	Bug	Special	20	100	20	Normal
Knock Off	Dark	Physical	65	100	20	Normal
Sweet Scent	Normal	Status	—	100	20	Many Others
Toxic	Poison	Status	—	90	10	Normal

TUTOR MOVES

NAME	TYPE	KIND	POW.	ACC.	PP	RANGE

TM MOVES

NO.	NAME	TYPE	KIND	POW.	ACC.	PP	RANGE
TM15	Dig	Ground	Physical	80	100	10	Normal
TM19	Safeguard	Normal	Status	—	—	25	Your Side
TM21	Rest	Psychic	Status	—	—	10	Self
TM22	Rock Slide	Rock	Physical	75	90	10	Many Others
TM24	Snore	Normal	Special	50	100	15	Normal
TM25	Protect	Normal	Status	—	—	10	Self
TM31	Attract	Normal	Status	—	100	15	Normal
TM32	Sandstorm	Rock	Status	—	—	10	Both Sides
TM34	Sunny Day	Fire	Status	—	—	5	Both Sides
TM39	Facade	Normal	Physical	70	100	20	Normal
TM41	Helping Hand	Normal	Status	—	—	20	1 Ally
TM48	Rock Tomb	Rock	Physical	60	95	15	Normal
TM49	Sand Tomb	Ground	Physical	35	85	15	Normal
TM53	Mud Shot	Ground	Special	55	95	15	Normal
TM54	Rock Blast	Rock	Physical	25	90	10	Normal
TM74	Venoshock	Poison	Special	65	100	10	Normal
TM76	Round	Normal	Special	60	100	15	Normal
TM81	Bulldoze	Ground	Physical	60	100	20	All Others

TR MOVES

NO.	NAME	TYPE	KIND	POW.	ACC.	PP	RANGE
TR01	Body Slam	Normal	Physical	85	100	15	Normal
TR10	Earthquake	Ground	Physical	100	100	10	All Others
TR20	Substitute	Normal	Status	—	—	10	Self
TR21	Reversal	Fighting	Physical	—	100	15	Normal
TR22	Sludge Bomb	Poison	Special	90	100	10	Normal
TR26	Endure	Normal	Status	—	—	10	Self
TR27	Sleep Talk	Normal	Status	—	—	10	Self
TR30	Encore	Normal	Status	—	100	5	Normal
TR46	Iron Defense	Steel	Status	—	—	15	Self
TR52	Gyro Ball	Steel	Physical	—	100	5	Normal
TR67	Earth Power	Ground	Special	90	100	10	Normal
TR75	Stone Edge	Rock	Physical	100	80	5	Normal
TR76	Stealth Rock	Rock	Status	—	—	20	Other Side
TR78	Sludge Wave	Poison	Special	95	100	10	All Others

Shuckle p. 99

ABILITY
Sturdy
Gluttony

HIDDEN ABILITY
Contrary

SPECIES STRENGTHS
- HP
- ATTACK
- DEFENSE
- SP. ATK
- SP. DEF
- SPEED

DAMAGE TAKEN IN BATTLE
×0.5, ×1, ×2, ×1, ×0.5, ×1, ×2, ×1, ×1, ×1, ×1, ×1, ×1, ×1, ×2, ×1, ×1, ×1

Egg Group: BUG

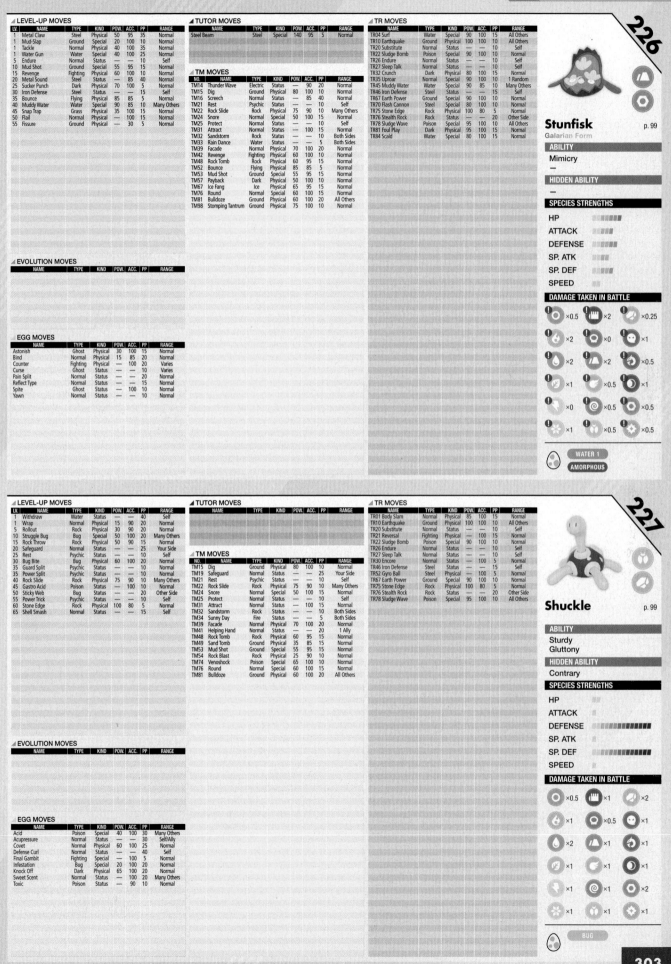

228 Barboach p. 99

ABILITY: Oblivious / Anticipation
HIDDEN ABILITY: Hydration

SPECIES STRENGTHS
- HP
- ATTACK
- DEFENSE
- SP. ATK
- SP. DEF
- SPEED

DAMAGE TAKEN IN BATTLE
×1	×1	×0.5
×0.5	×0.5	×1
×1	×1	×1
×4	×1	×1
×0	×1	×0.5
×1	×1	×1

WATER 2

LEVEL-UP MOVES
LV.	NAME	TYPE	KIND	POW.	ACC.	PP	RANGE
1	Mud-Slap	Ground	Special	20	100	10	Normal
1	Water Gun	Water	Special	40	100	25	Normal
6	Rest	Psychic	Status	—	—	10	Self
6	Snore	Normal	Special	50	100	15	Normal
12	Water Pulse	Water	Special	60	100	20	Normal
18	Amnesia	Psychic	Status	—	—	20	Self
24	Aqua Tail	Water	Physical	90	90	10	Normal
31	Muddy Water	Water	Special	90	85	10	Many Others
36	Earthquake	Ground	Physical	100	100	10	All Others
42	Future Sight	Psychic	Special	120	100	10	Normal
48	Fissure	Ground	Physical	—	30	5	Normal

EVOLUTION MOVES
NAME	TYPE	KIND	POW.	ACC.	PP	RANGE

EGG MOVES
NAME	TYPE	KIND	POW.	ACC.	PP	RANGE
Flail	Normal	Physical	—	100	15	Normal
Spark	Electric	Physical	65	100	20	Normal
Take Down	Normal	Physical	90	85	20	Normal
Thrash	Normal	Physical	120	100	10	1 Random

TUTOR MOVES
NAME	TYPE	KIND	POW.	ACC.	PP	RANGE

TM MOVES
NO.	NAME	TYPE	KIND	POW.	ACC.	PP	RANGE
TM21	Rest	Psychic	Status	—	—	10	Self
TM24	Snore	Normal	Special	50	100	15	Normal
TM25	Protect	Normal	Status	—	—	10	Self
TM27	Icy Wind	Ice	Special	55	95	15	Many Others
TM31	Attract	Normal	Status	—	100	15	Normal
TM32	Sandstorm	Rock	Status	—	—	10	Both Sides
TM33	Rain Dance	Water	Status	—	—	5	Both Sides
TM35	Hail	Ice	Status	—	—	10	Both Sides
TM36	Whirlpool	Water	Special	35	85	15	Normal
TM39	Facade	Normal	Physical	70	100	20	Normal
TM45	Dive	Water	Physical	80	100	10	Normal
TM48	Rock Tomb	Rock	Physical	60	95	15	Normal
TM52	Bounce	Flying	Physical	85	85	5	Normal
TM53	Mud Shot	Ground	Special	55	95	15	Normal
TM76	Round	Normal	Special	60	100	15	Normal
TM81	Bulldoze	Ground	Physical	60	100	20	All Others

TR MOVES
NO.	NAME	TYPE	KIND	POW.	ACC.	PP	RANGE
TR03	Hydro Pump	Water	Special	110	80	5	Normal
TR04	Surf	Water	Special	90	100	15	All Others
TR05	Ice Beam	Ice	Special	90	100	10	Normal
TR06	Blizzard	Ice	Special	110	70	5	Many Others
TR10	Earthquake	Ground	Physical	100	100	10	All Others
TR16	Waterfall	Water	Physical	80	100	15	Normal
TR17	Amnesia	Psychic	Status	—	—	20	Self
TR20	Substitute	Normal	Status	—	—	10	Self
TR26	Endure	Normal	Status	—	—	10	Self
TR27	Sleep Talk	Normal	Status	—	—	10	Self
TR34	Future Sight	Psychic	Special	120	100	10	Normal
TR45	Muddy Water	Water	Special	90	85	10	Many Others
TR51	Dragon Dance	Dragon	Status	—	—	20	Self
TR67	Earth Power	Ground	Special	90	100	10	Normal
TR84	Scald	Water	Special	80	100	15	Normal

229 Whiscash p. 99

ABILITY: Oblivious / Anticipation
HIDDEN ABILITY: Hydration

SPECIES STRENGTHS
- HP
- ATTACK
- DEFENSE
- SP. ATK
- SP. DEF
- SPEED

DAMAGE TAKEN IN BATTLE
×1	×1	×0.5
×0.5	×0.5	×1
×1	×1	×1
×4	×1	×1
×0	×1	×0.5
×1	×1	×1

WATER 2

LEVEL-UP MOVES
LV.	NAME	TYPE	KIND	POW.	ACC.	PP	RANGE
1	Belch	Poison	Special	120	90	10	Normal
1	Mud-Slap	Ground	Special	20	100	10	Normal
1	Rest	Psychic	Status	—	—	10	Self
1	Snore	Normal	Special	50	100	15	Normal
1	Thrash	Normal	Physical	120	100	10	1 Random
1	Tickle	Normal	Status	—	100	20	Normal
1	Water Gun	Water	Special	40	100	25	Normal
1	Zen Headbutt	Psychic	Physical	80	90	15	Normal
12	Water Pulse	Water	Special	60	100	20	Normal
18	Amnesia	Psychic	Status	—	—	20	Self
24	Aqua Tail	Water	Physical	90	90	10	Normal
33	Muddy Water	Water	Special	90	85	10	Many Others
40	Earthquake	Ground	Physical	100	100	10	All Others
48	Future Sight	Psychic	Special	120	100	10	Normal
56	Fissure	Ground	Physical	—	30	5	Normal

EVOLUTION MOVES
NAME	TYPE	KIND	POW.	ACC.	PP	RANGE
Thrash	Normal	Physical	120	100	10	1 Random

EGG MOVES
NAME	TYPE	KIND	POW.	ACC.	PP	RANGE

TUTOR MOVES
NAME	TYPE	KIND	POW.	ACC.	PP	RANGE

TM MOVES
NO.	NAME	TYPE	KIND	POW.	ACC.	PP	RANGE
TM08	Hyper Beam	Normal	Special	150	90	5	Normal
TM09	Giga Impact	Normal	Physical	150	90	5	Normal
TM21	Rest	Psychic	Status	—	—	10	Self
TM22	Rock Slide	Rock	Physical	75	90	10	Many Others
TM24	Snore	Normal	Special	50	100	15	Normal
TM25	Protect	Normal	Status	—	—	10	Self
TM27	Icy Wind	Ice	Special	55	95	15	Many Others
TM31	Attract	Normal	Status	—	100	15	Normal
TM32	Sandstorm	Rock	Status	—	—	10	Both Sides
TM33	Rain Dance	Water	Status	—	—	5	Both Sides
TM35	Hail	Ice	Status	—	—	10	Both Sides
TM36	Whirlpool	Water	Special	35	85	15	Normal
TM39	Facade	Normal	Physical	70	100	20	Normal
TM45	Dive	Water	Physical	80	100	10	Normal
TM46	Weather Ball*	Normal	Special	50	100	10	Normal
TM48	Rock Tomb	Rock	Physical	60	95	15	Normal
TM49	Sand Tomb	Ground	Physical	35	85	15	Normal
TM52	Bounce	Flying	Physical	85	85	5	Normal
TM53	Mud Shot	Ground	Special	55	95	15	Normal
TM76	Round	Normal	Special	60	100	15	Normal
TM81	Bulldoze	Ground	Physical	60	100	20	All Others
TM98	Stomping Tantrum	Ground	Physical	75	100	10	Normal

TR MOVES
NO.	NAME	TYPE	KIND	POW.	ACC.	PP	RANGE
TR03	Hydro Pump	Water	Special	110	80	5	Normal
TR04	Surf	Water	Special	90	100	15	All Others
TR05	Ice Beam	Ice	Special	90	100	10	Normal
TR06	Blizzard	Ice	Special	110	70	5	Many Others
TR10	Earthquake	Ground	Physical	100	100	10	All Others
TR16	Waterfall	Water	Physical	80	100	15	Normal
TR17	Amnesia	Psychic	Status	—	—	20	Self
TR20	Substitute	Normal	Status	—	—	10	Self
TR26	Endure	Normal	Status	—	—	10	Self
TR27	Sleep Talk	Normal	Status	—	—	10	Self
TR34	Future Sight	Psychic	Special	120	100	10	Normal
TR35	Uproar	Normal	Special	90	100	10	1 Random
TR45	Muddy Water	Water	Special	90	85	10	Many Others
TR51	Dragon Dance	Dragon	Status	—	—	20	Self
TR67	Earth Power	Ground	Special	90	100	10	Normal
TR69	Zen Headbutt	Psychic	Physical	80	90	15	Normal
TR75	Stone Edge	Rock	Physical	100	80	5	Normal
TR84	Scald	Water	Special	80	100	15	Normal
TR98	Liquidation	Water	Physical	85	100	10	Normal

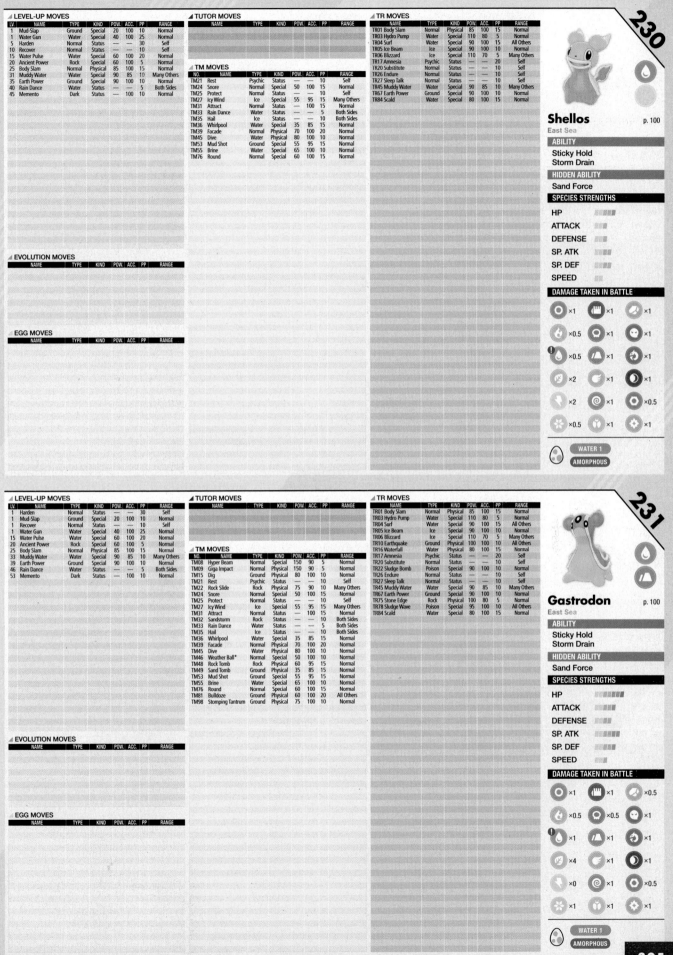

230 — Shellos (East Sea) — p. 100

LEVEL-UP MOVES

LV.	NAME	TYPE	KIND	POW.	ACC.	PP	RANGE
1	Mud-Slap	Ground	Special	20	100	10	Normal
1	Water Gun	Water	Special	40	100	25	Normal
5	Harden	Normal	Status	—	—	30	Self
10	Recover	Normal	Status	—	—	10	Self
15	Water Pulse	Water	Special	60	100	20	Normal
20	Ancient Power	Rock	Special	60	100	5	Normal
25	Body Slam	Normal	Physical	85	100	15	Normal
31	Muddy Water	Water	Special	90	85	10	Many Others
35	Earth Power	Ground	Special	90	100	10	Normal
40	Rain Dance	Water	Status	—	—	5	Both Sides
45	Memento	Dark	Status	—	100	10	Normal

EVOLUTION MOVES

NAME	TYPE	KIND	POW.	ACC.	PP	RANGE

EGG MOVES

NAME	TYPE	KIND	POW.	ACC.	PP	RANGE

TUTOR MOVES

NAME	TYPE	KIND	POW.	ACC.	PP	RANGE

TM MOVES

NO.	NAME	TYPE	KIND	POW.	ACC.	PP	RANGE
TM21	Rest	Psychic	Status	—	—	10	Self
TM24	Snore	Normal	Special	50	100	15	Normal
TM25	Protect	Normal	Status	—	—	10	Self
TM27	Icy Wind	Ice	Special	55	95	15	Many Others
TM31	Attract	Normal	Status	—	100	15	Normal
TM33	Rain Dance	Water	Status	—	—	5	Both Sides
TM35	Hail	Ice	Status	—	—	10	Both Sides
TM36	Whirlpool	Water	Special	35	85	15	Normal
TM39	Facade	Normal	Physical	70	100	20	Normal
TM45	Dive	Water	Physical	80	100	10	Normal
TM53	Mud Shot	Ground	Special	55	95	15	Normal
TM55	Brine	Water	Special	65	100	10	Normal
TM76	Round	Normal	Special	60	100	15	Normal

TR MOVES

NO.	NAME	TYPE	KIND	POW.	ACC.	PP	RANGE
TR01	Body Slam	Normal	Physical	85	100	15	Normal
TR03	Hydro Pump	Water	Special	110	80	5	Normal
TR04	Surf	Water	Special	90	100	15	All Others
TR05	Ice Beam	Ice	Special	90	100	10	Normal
TR06	Blizzard	Ice	Special	110	70	5	Many Others
TR17	Amnesia	Psychic	Status	—	—	20	Self
TR20	Substitute	Normal	Status	—	—	10	Self
TR26	Endure	Normal	Status	—	—	10	Self
TR27	Sleep Talk	Normal	Status	—	—	10	Self
TR45	Muddy Water	Water	Special	90	85	10	Many Others
TR67	Earth Power	Ground	Special	90	100	10	Normal
TR84	Scald	Water	Special	80	100	15	Normal

Shellos — East Sea — p. 100

ABILITY: Sticky Hold / Storm Drain
HIDDEN ABILITY: Sand Force

SPECIES STRENGTHS: HP, ATTACK, DEFENSE, SP. ATK, SP. DEF, SPEED

DAMAGE TAKEN IN BATTLE:

×1	×1	×1
×0.5	×1	×1
×0.5	×1	×1
×2	×1	×1
×2	×1	×0.5
×0.5	×1	×1

Egg Groups: WATER 1 / AMORPHOUS

---

231 — Gastrodon (East Sea) — p. 100

LEVEL-UP MOVES

LV.	NAME	TYPE	KIND	POW.	ACC.	PP	RANGE
1	Harden	Normal	Status	—	—	30	Self
1	Mud-Slap	Ground	Special	20	100	10	Normal
1	Recover	Normal	Status	—	—	10	Self
1	Water Gun	Water	Special	40	100	25	Normal
15	Water Pulse	Water	Special	60	100	20	Normal
20	Ancient Power	Rock	Special	60	100	5	Normal
25	Body Slam	Normal	Physical	85	100	15	Normal
33	Muddy Water	Water	Special	90	85	10	Many Others
39	Earth Power	Ground	Special	90	100	10	Normal
46	Rain Dance	Water	Status	—	—	5	Both Sides
53	Memento	Dark	Status	—	100	10	Normal

EVOLUTION MOVES

NAME	TYPE	KIND	POW.	ACC.	PP	RANGE

EGG MOVES

NAME	TYPE	KIND	POW.	ACC.	PP	RANGE

TUTOR MOVES

NAME	TYPE	KIND	POW.	ACC.	PP	RANGE

TM MOVES

NO.	NAME	TYPE	KIND	POW.	ACC.	PP	RANGE
TM08	Hyper Beam	Normal	Special	150	90	5	Normal
TM09	Giga Impact	Normal	Physical	150	90	5	Normal
TM15	Dig	Ground	Physical	80	100	10	Normal
TM21	Rest	Psychic	Status	—	—	10	Self
TM22	Rock Slide	Rock	Physical	75	90	10	Many Others
TM24	Snore	Normal	Special	50	100	15	Normal
TM25	Protect	Normal	Status	—	—	10	Self
TM27	Icy Wind	Ice	Special	55	95	15	Many Others
TM31	Attract	Normal	Status	—	100	15	Normal
TM32	Sandstorm	Rock	Status	—	—	10	Both Sides
TM33	Rain Dance	Water	Status	—	—	5	Both Sides
TM35	Hail	Ice	Status	—	—	10	Both Sides
TM36	Whirlpool	Water	Special	35	85	15	Normal
TM39	Facade	Normal	Physical	70	100	20	Normal
TM45	Dive	Water	Physical	80	100	10	Normal
TM46	Weather Ball*	Normal	Special	50	100	10	Normal
TM48	Rock Tomb	Rock	Physical	60	95	15	Normal
TM49	Sand Tomb	Ground	Physical	35	85	15	Normal
TM53	Mud Shot	Ground	Special	55	95	15	Normal
TM55	Brine	Water	Special	65	100	10	Normal
TM76	Round	Normal	Special	60	100	15	Normal
TM81	Bulldoze	Ground	Physical	60	100	20	All Others
TM98	Stomping Tantrum	Ground	Physical	75	100	10	Normal

TR MOVES

NO.	NAME	TYPE	KIND	POW.	ACC.	PP	RANGE
TR01	Body Slam	Normal	Physical	85	100	15	Normal
TR03	Hydro Pump	Water	Special	110	80	5	Normal
TR04	Surf	Water	Special	90	100	15	All Others
TR05	Ice Beam	Ice	Special	90	100	10	Normal
TR06	Blizzard	Ice	Special	110	70	5	Many Others
TR10	Earthquake	Ground	Physical	100	100	10	All Others
TR16	Waterfall	Water	Physical	80	100	15	Normal
TR17	Amnesia	Psychic	Status	—	—	20	Self
TR20	Substitute	Normal	Status	—	—	10	Self
TR22	Sludge Bomb	Poison	Special	90	100	10	Normal
TR26	Endure	Normal	Status	—	—	10	Self
TR27	Sleep Talk	Normal	Status	—	—	10	Self
TR45	Muddy Water	Water	Special	90	85	10	Many Others
TR67	Earth Power	Ground	Special	90	100	10	Normal
TR75	Stone Edge	Rock	Physical	100	80	5	Normal
TR78	Sludge Wave	Poison	Special	95	100	10	All Others
TR84	Scald	Water	Special	80	100	15	Normal

Gastrodon — East Sea — p. 100

ABILITY: Sticky Hold / Storm Drain
HIDDEN ABILITY: Sand Force

SPECIES STRENGTHS: HP, ATTACK, DEFENSE, SP. ATK, SP. DEF, SPEED

DAMAGE TAKEN IN BATTLE:

×1	×1	×0.5
×0.5	×0.5	×1
×1	×1	×1
×4	×1	×1
×0	×1	×0.5
×1	×1	×1

Egg Groups: WATER 1 / AMORPHOUS

*Weather Ball changes type depending on weather condition. (Harsh sunlight: Fire type. Rain: Water type. Hail: Ice type. Sandstorm: Rock type.)

232 — Wimpod (p. 101)

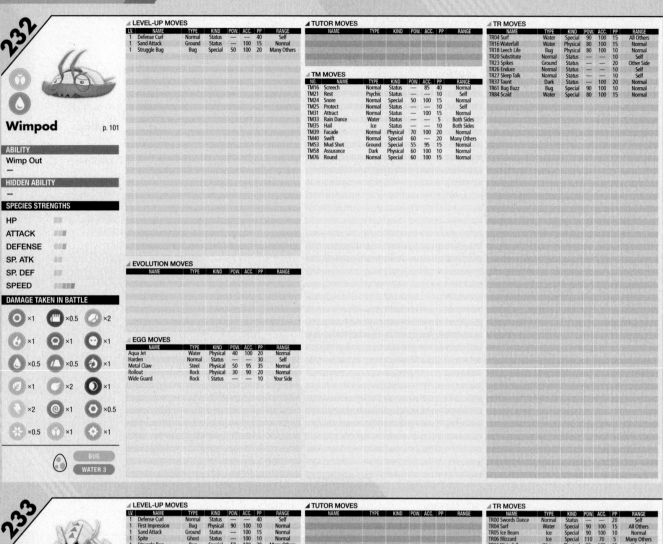

LEVEL-UP MOVES

LV.	NAME	TYPE	KIND	POW.	ACC.	PP	RANGE
1	Defense Curl	Normal	Status	—	—	40	Self
1	Sand Attack	Ground	Status	—	100	15	Normal
1	Struggle Bug	Bug	Special	50	100	20	Many Others

TUTOR MOVES

NAME	TYPE	KIND	POW.	ACC.	PP	RANGE

TM MOVES

NO.	NAME	TYPE	KIND	POW.	ACC.	PP	RANGE
TM16	Screech	Normal	Status	—	85	40	Normal
TM21	Rest	Psychic	Status	—	—	10	Self
TM24	Snore	Normal	Special	50	100	15	Normal
TM25	Protect	Normal	Status	—	—	10	Self
TM31	Attract	Normal	Status	—	100	15	Normal
TM33	Rain Dance	Water	Status	—	—	5	Both Sides
TM35	Hail	Ice	Status	—	—	10	Both Sides
TM39	Facade	Normal	Physical	70	100	20	Normal
TM40	Swift	Normal	Special	60	—	20	Many Others
TM53	Mud Shot	Ground	Special	55	95	15	Normal
TM58	Assurance	Dark	Physical	60	100	10	Normal
TM76	Round	Normal	Special	60	100	15	Normal

TR MOVES

NO.	NAME	TYPE	KIND	POW.	ACC.	PP	RANGE
TR04	Surf	Water	Special	90	100	15	All Others
TR16	Waterfall	Water	Physical	80	100	15	Normal
TR18	Leech Life	Bug	Physical	80	100	10	Normal
TR20	Substitute	Normal	Status	—	—	10	Self
TR23	Spikes	Ground	Status	—	—	20	Other Side
TR26	Endure	Normal	Status	—	—	10	Self
TR27	Sleep Talk	Normal	Status	—	—	10	Self
TR37	Taunt	Dark	Status	—	100	20	Normal
TR61	Bug Buzz	Bug	Special	90	100	10	Normal
TR84	Scald	Water	Special	80	100	15	Normal

EVOLUTION MOVES

NAME	TYPE	KIND	POW.	ACC.	PP	RANGE

EGG MOVES

NAME	TYPE	KIND	POW.	ACC.	PP	RANGE
Aqua Jet	Water	Physical	40	100	20	Normal
Harden	Normal	Status	—	—	30	Self
Metal Claw	Steel	Physical	50	95	35	Normal
Rollout	Rock	Physical	30	90	20	Normal
Wide Guard	Rock	Status	—	—	10	Your Side

ABILITY
Wimp Out
—

HIDDEN ABILITY
—

SPECIES STRENGTHS
HP, ATTACK, DEFENSE, SP. ATK, SP. DEF, SPEED

DAMAGE TAKEN IN BATTLE
×1, ×0.5, ×2, ×1, ×1, ×1, ×0.5, ×0.5, ×1, ×1, ×2, ×0.5, ×2, ×1, ×0.5, ×0.5, ×1, ×1

Egg groups: BUG / WATER 3

---

233 — Golisopod (p. 101)

LEVEL-UP MOVES

LV.	NAME	TYPE	KIND	POW.	ACC.	PP	RANGE
1	Defense Curl	Normal	Status	—	—	40	Self
1	First Impression	Bug	Physical	90	100	10	Normal
1	Sand Attack	Ground	Status	—	100	15	Normal
1	Spite	Ghost	Status	—	100	10	Normal
1	Struggle Bug	Bug	Special	50	100	20	Many Others
4	Rock Smash	Fighting	Physical	40	100	15	Normal
8	Fury Cutter	Bug	Physical	40	95	20	Normal
12	Mud Shot	Ground	Special	55	95	15	Normal
16	Bug Bite	Bug	Physical	60	100	20	Normal
20	Iron Defense	Steel	Status	—	—	15	Self
24	Sucker Punch	Dark	Physical	70	100	5	Normal
28	Slash	Normal	Physical	70	100	20	Normal
32	Razor Shell	Water	Physical	75	95	10	Normal
36	Pin Missile	Bug	Physical	25	95	20	Normal
40	Swords Dance	Normal	Status	—	—	20	Self
44	Liquidation	Water	Physical	85	100	10	Normal

TUTOR MOVES

NAME	TYPE	KIND	POW.	ACC.	PP	RANGE

TM MOVES

NO.	NAME	TYPE	KIND	POW.	ACC.	PP	RANGE
TM07	Pin Missile	Bug	Physical	25	95	20	Normal
TM08	Hyper Beam	Normal	Special	150	90	5	Normal
TM09	Giga Impact	Normal	Physical	150	90	5	Normal
TM16	Screech	Normal	Status	—	85	40	Normal
TM21	Rest	Psychic	Status	—	—	10	Self
TM22	Rock Slide	Rock	Physical	75	90	10	Many Others
TM24	Snore	Normal	Special	50	100	15	Normal
TM25	Protect	Normal	Status	—	—	10	Self
TM27	Icy Wind	Ice	Special	55	95	15	Many Others
TM31	Attract	Normal	Status	—	100	15	Normal
TM33	Rain Dance	Water	Status	—	—	5	Both Sides
TM35	Hail	Ice	Status	—	—	10	Both Sides
TM39	Facade	Normal	Physical	70	100	20	Normal
TM40	Swift	Normal	Special	60	—	20	Many Others
TM43	Brick Break	Fighting	Physical	75	100	15	Normal
TM45	Dive	Water	Physical	80	100	10	Normal
TM48	Rock Tomb	Rock	Physical	60	95	15	Normal
TM53	Mud Shot	Ground	Special	55	95	15	Normal
TM57	Payback	Dark	Physical	50	100	10	Normal
TM58	Assurance	Dark	Physical	60	100	10	Normal
TM59	Fling	Dark	Physical	—	100	10	Normal
TM65	Shadow Claw	Ghost	Physical	70	100	15	Normal
TM74	Venoshock	Poison	Special	65	100	10	Normal
TM76	Round	Normal	Special	60	100	15	Normal
TM83	Razor Shell	Water	Physical	75	95	10	Normal
TM85	Snarl	Dark	Special	55	95	15	Many Others
TM94	False Swipe	Normal	Physical	40	100	40	Normal

TR MOVES

NO.	NAME	TYPE	KIND	POW.	ACC.	PP	RANGE
TR00	Swords Dance	Normal	Status	—	—	20	Self
TR04	Surf	Water	Special	90	100	15	All Others
TR05	Ice Beam	Ice	Special	90	100	10	Normal
TR06	Blizzard	Ice	Special	110	70	5	Many Others
TR16	Waterfall	Water	Physical	80	100	15	Normal
TR18	Leech Life	Bug	Physical	80	100	10	Normal
TR20	Substitute	Normal	Status	—	—	10	Self
TR22	Sludge Bomb	Poison	Special	90	100	10	Normal
TR23	Spikes	Ground	Status	—	—	20	Other Side
TR26	Endure	Normal	Status	—	—	10	Self
TR27	Sleep Talk	Normal	Status	—	—	10	Self
TR37	Taunt	Dark	Status	—	100	20	Normal
TR45	Muddy Water	Water	Special	90	85	10	Many Others
TR46	Iron Defense	Steel	Status	—	—	15	Self
TR48	Bulk Up	Fighting	Status	—	—	20	Self
TR53	Close Combat	Fighting	Physical	120	100	5	Normal
TR57	Poison Jab	Poison	Physical	80	100	20	Normal
TR58	Dark Pulse	Dark	Special	80	100	15	Normal
TR60	X-Scissor	Bug	Physical	80	100	15	Normal
TR61	Bug Buzz	Bug	Special	90	100	10	Normal
TR64	Focus Blast	Fighting	Special	120	70	5	Normal
TR74	Iron Head	Steel	Physical	80	100	15	Normal
TR78	Sludge Wave	Poison	Special	95	100	10	All Others
TR84	Scald	Water	Special	80	100	15	Normal
TR87	Drill Run	Ground	Physical	80	95	10	Normal
TR95	Throat Chop	Dark	Physical	80	100	15	Normal
TR98	Liquidation	Water	Physical	85	100	10	Normal

EVOLUTION MOVES

NAME	TYPE	KIND	POW.	ACC.	PP	RANGE
First Impression	Bug	Physical	90	100	10	Normal

EGG MOVES

NAME	TYPE	KIND	POW.	ACC.	PP	RANGE

ABILITY
Emergency Exit
—

HIDDEN ABILITY
—

SPECIES STRENGTHS
HP, ATTACK, DEFENSE, SP. ATK, SP. DEF, SPEED

DAMAGE TAKEN IN BATTLE
×1, ×0.5, ×2, ×1, ×1, ×1, ×0.5, ×0.5, ×1, ×1, ×2, ×1, ×2, ×1, ×0.5, ×0.5, ×1, ×1

Egg groups: BUG / WATER 3

234 Binacle — p. 102

LEVEL-UP MOVES

LV	NAME	TYPE	KIND	POW.	ACC.	PP	RANGE
1	Mud-Slap	Ground	Special	20	100	10	Normal
1	Scratch	Normal	Physical	40	100	35	Normal
4	Withdraw	Water	Status	—	—	40	Self
8	Water Gun	Water	Special	40	100	25	Normal
12	Fury Cutter	Bug	Physical	40	95	20	Normal
16	Fury Swipes	Normal	Physical	18	80	15	Normal
20	Ancient Power	Rock	Special	60	100	5	Normal
24	Rock Polish	Rock	Status	—	—	20	Self
28	Slash	Normal	Physical	70	100	20	Normal
32	Hone Claws	Dark	Status	—	—	15	Self
36	Razor Shell	Water	Physical	75	95	10	Normal
40	Shell Smash	Normal	Status	—	—	15	Self
44	Cross Chop	Fighting	Physical	100	80	5	Normal

EVOLUTION MOVES

NAME	TYPE	KIND	POW.	ACC.	PP	RANGE

EGG MOVES

NAME	TYPE	KIND	POW.	ACC.	PP	RANGE
Night Slash	Dark	Physical	70	100	15	Normal
Sand Attack	Ground	Status	—	100	15	Normal
Switcheroo	Dark	Status	—	100	10	Normal

TUTOR MOVES

NAME	TYPE	KIND	POW.	ACC.	PP	RANGE

TM MOVES

NO.	NAME	TYPE	KIND	POW.	ACC.	PP	RANGE
TM15	Dig	Ground	Physical	80	100	10	Normal
TM16	Screech	Normal	Status	—	85	40	Normal
TM19	Safeguard	Normal	Status	—	—	25	Your Side
TM21	Rest	Psychic	Status	—	—	10	Self
TM22	Rock Slide	Rock	Physical	75	90	10	Many Others
TM23	Thief	Dark	Physical	60	100	25	Normal
TM24	Snore	Normal	Special	50	100	15	Normal
TM25	Protect	Normal	Status	—	—	10	Self
TM27	Icy Wind	Ice	Special	55	95	15	Many Others
TM31	Attract	Normal	Status	—	100	15	Normal
TM32	Sandstorm	Rock	Status	—	—	10	Both Sides
TM33	Rain Dance	Water	Status	—	—	5	Both Sides
TM37	Beat Up	Dark	Physical	—	100	10	Normal
TM39	Facade	Normal	Physical	70	100	20	Normal
TM41	Helping Hand	Normal	Status	—	—	20	1 Ally
TM43	Brick Break	Fighting	Physical	75	100	15	Normal
TM48	Rock Tomb	Rock	Physical	60	95	15	Normal
TM53	Mud Shot	Ground	Special	55	95	15	Normal
TM54	Rock Blast	Rock	Physical	25	90	10	Normal
TM57	Payback	Dark	Physical	50	100	10	Normal
TM58	Assurance	Dark	Physical	60	100	10	Normal
TM59	Fling	Dark	Physical	—	100	10	Normal
TM65	Shadow Claw	Ghost	Physical	70	100	15	Normal
TM76	Round	Normal	Special	60	100	15	Normal
TM81	Bulldoze	Ground	Physical	60	100	20	All Others
TM83	Razor Shell	Water	Physical	75	95	10	Normal
TM94	False Swipe	Normal	Physical	40	100	40	Normal

TR MOVES

NAME	TYPE	KIND	POW.	ACC.	PP	RANGE
TR00 Swords Dance	Normal	Status	—	—	20	Self
TR04 Surf	Water	Special	90	100	15	All Others
TR05 Ice Beam	Ice	Special	90	100	10	Normal
TR06 Blizzard	Ice	Special	110	70	5	Many Others
TR10 Earthquake	Ground	Physical	100	100	10	All Others
TR20 Substitute	Normal	Status	—	—	10	Self
TR22 Sludge Bomb	Poison	Special	90	100	10	Normal
TR26 Endure	Normal	Status	—	—	10	Self
TR27 Sleep Talk	Normal	Status	—	—	10	Self
TR35 Uproar	Normal	Special	90	100	10	1 Random
TR37 Taunt	Dark	Status	—	100	20	Normal
TR46 Iron Defense	Steel	Status	—	—	15	Self
TR57 Poison Jab	Poison	Physical	80	100	20	Normal
TR60 X-Scissor	Bug	Physical	80	100	15	Normal
TR75 Stone Edge	Rock	Physical	100	80	5	Normal
TR76 Stealth Rock	Rock	Status	—	—	20	Other Side
TR77 Grass Knot	Grass	Special	—	100	20	Normal
TR78 Sludge Wave	Poison	Special	95	100	10	All Others
TR84 Scald	Water	Special	80	100	15	Normal
TR98 Liquidation	Water	Physical	85	100	10	Normal

ABILITY
Tough Claws
Sniper

HIDDEN ABILITY
Pickpocket

SPECIES STRENGTHS
HP
ATTACK
DEFENSE
SP. ATK
SP. DEF
SPEED

DAMAGE TAKEN IN BATTLE
×0.5 | ×2 | ×1
×0.25 | ×0.5 | ×1
×1 | ×2 | ×1
×4 | ×0.5 | ×1
×2 | ×1 | ×1
×0.5 | ×1 | ×1

WATER 3

---

235 Barbaracle — p. 102

LEVEL-UP MOVES

LV	NAME	TYPE	KIND	POW.	ACC.	PP	RANGE
1	Mud-Slap	Ground	Special	20	100	10	Normal
1	Scratch	Normal	Physical	40	100	35	Normal
1	Skull Bash	Normal	Physical	130	100	10	Normal
1	Water Gun	Water	Special	40	100	25	Normal
	Withdraw	Water	Status	—	—	40	Self
12	Fury Cutter	Bug	Physical	40	95	20	Normal
16	Fury Swipes	Normal	Physical	18	80	15	Normal
20	Ancient Power	Rock	Special	60	100	5	Normal
24	Rock Polish	Rock	Status	—	—	20	Self
28	Slash	Normal	Physical	70	100	20	Normal
32	Hone Claws	Dark	Status	—	—	15	Self
36	Razor Shell	Water	Physical	75	95	10	Normal
42	Shell Smash	Normal	Status	—	—	15	Self
48	Cross Chop	Fighting	Physical	100	80	5	Normal
54	Stone Edge	Rock	Physical	100	80	5	Normal

EVOLUTION MOVES

NAME	TYPE	KIND	POW.	ACC.	PP	RANGE

EGG MOVES

NAME	TYPE	KIND	POW.	ACC.	PP	RANGE

TUTOR MOVES

NAME	TYPE	KIND	POW.	ACC.	PP	RANGE

TM MOVES

NO.	NAME	TYPE	KIND	POW.	ACC.	PP	RANGE
TM08	Hyper Beam	Normal	Special	150	90	5	Normal
TM09	Giga Impact	Normal	Physical	150	90	5	Normal
TM15	Dig	Ground	Physical	80	100	10	Normal
TM16	Screech	Normal	Status	—	85	40	Normal
TM19	Safeguard	Normal	Status	—	—	25	Your Side
TM21	Rest	Psychic	Status	—	—	10	Self
TM22	Rock Slide	Rock	Physical	75	90	10	Many Others
TM23	Thief	Dark	Physical	60	100	25	Normal
TM24	Snore	Normal	Special	50	100	15	Normal
TM25	Protect	Normal	Status	—	—	10	Self
TM27	Icy Wind	Ice	Special	55	95	15	Many Others
TM31	Attract	Normal	Status	—	100	15	Normal
TM32	Sandstorm	Rock	Status	—	—	10	Both Sides
TM33	Rain Dance	Water	Status	—	—	5	Both Sides
TM36	Whirlpool	Water	Special	35	85	15	Normal
TM37	Beat Up	Dark	Physical	—	100	10	Normal
TM39	Facade	Normal	Physical	70	100	20	Normal
TM41	Helping Hand	Normal	Status	—	—	20	1 Ally
TM43	Brick Break	Fighting	Physical	75	100	15	Normal
TM45	Dive	Water	Physical	80	100	10	Normal
TM48	Rock Tomb	Rock	Physical	60	95	15	Normal
TM53	Mud Shot	Ground	Special	55	95	15	Normal
TM54	Rock Blast	Rock	Physical	25	90	10	Normal
TM57	Payback	Dark	Physical	50	100	10	Normal
TM58	Assurance	Dark	Physical	60	100	10	Normal
TM59	Fling	Dark	Physical	—	100	10	Normal
TM65	Shadow Claw	Ghost	Physical	70	100	15	Normal
TM76	Round	Normal	Special	60	100	15	Normal
TM81	Bulldoze	Ground	Physical	60	100	20	All Others
TM83	Razor Shell	Water	Physical	75	95	10	Normal
TM94	False Swipe	Normal	Physical	40	100	40	Normal
TM97	Brutal Swing	Dark	Physical	60	100	20	All Others

TR MOVES

NAME	TYPE	KIND	POW.	ACC.	PP	RANGE
TR00 Swords Dance	Normal	Status	—	—	20	Self
TR04 Surf	Water	Special	90	100	15	All Others
TR05 Ice Beam	Ice	Special	90	100	15	Normal
TR06 Blizzard	Ice	Special	110	70	5	Many Others
TR07 Low Kick	Fighting	Physical	—	100	20	Normal
TR10 Earthquake	Ground	Physical	100	100	10	All Others
TR20 Substitute	Normal	Status	—	—	10	Self
TR22 Sludge Bomb	Poison	Special	90	100	10	Normal
TR26 Endure	Normal	Status	—	—	10	Self
TR27 Sleep Talk	Normal	Status	—	—	10	Self
TR35 Uproar	Normal	Special	90	100	10	1 Random
TR37 Taunt	Dark	Status	—	100	20	Normal
TR39 Superpower	Fighting	Physical	120	100	5	Normal
TR45 Muddy Water	Water	Special	90	85	10	Many Others
TR46 Iron Defense	Steel	Status	—	—	15	Self
TR47 Dragon Claw	Dragon	Physical	80	100	15	Normal
TR48 Bulk Up	Fighting	Status	—	—	20	Self
TR57 Poison Jab	Poison	Physical	80	100	20	Normal
TR60 X-Scissor	Bug	Physical	80	100	15	Normal
TR64 Focus Blast	Fighting	Special	120	70	5	Normal
TR67 Earth Power	Ground	Special	90	100	10	Normal
TR75 Stone Edge	Rock	Physical	100	80	5	Normal
TR76 Stealth Rock	Rock	Status	—	—	20	Other Side
TR77 Grass Knot	Grass	Special	—	100	20	Normal
TR78 Sludge Wave	Poison	Special	95	100	10	All Others
TR84 Scald	Water	Special	80	100	15	Normal
TR98 Liquidation	Water	Physical	85	100	10	Normal

ABILITY
Tough Claws
Sniper

HIDDEN ABILITY
Pickpocket

SPECIES STRENGTHS
HP
ATTACK
DEFENSE
SP. ATK
SP. DEF
SPEED

DAMAGE TAKEN IN BATTLE
×0.5 | ×2 | ×1
×0.25 | ×0.5 | ×1
×1 | ×2 | ×1
×4 | ×0.5 | ×1
×2 | ×1 | ×1
×0.5 | ×1 | ×1

WATER 3

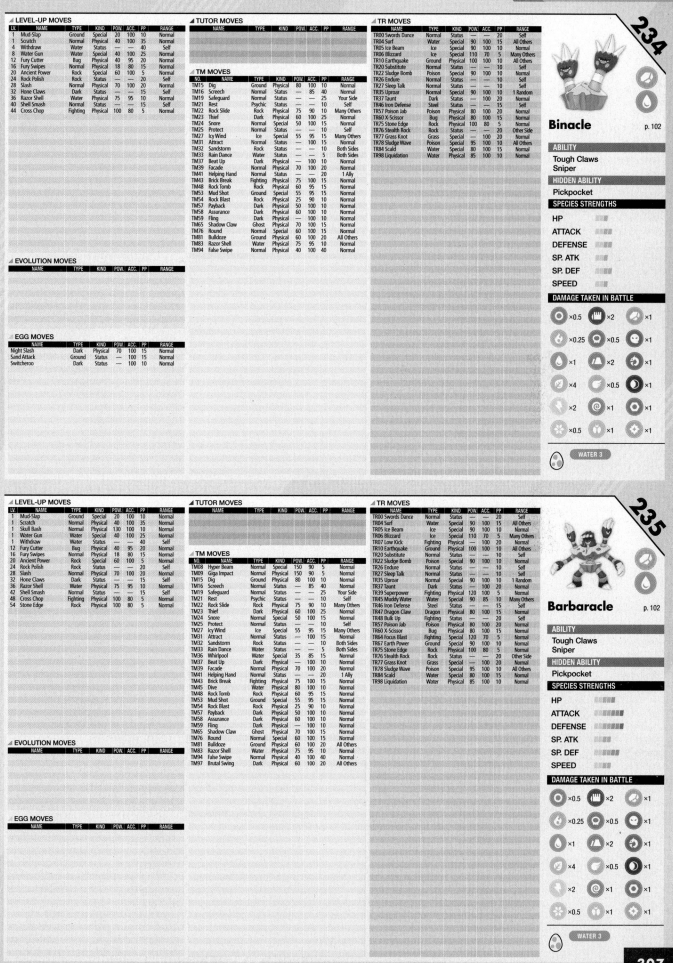

236

Corsola
Galarian Form p. 102

ABILITY
Weak Armor
—

HIDDEN ABILITY
Cursed Body

SPECIES STRENGTHS

HP	
ATTACK	
DEFENSE	
SP. ATK	
SP. DEF	
SPEED	

DAMAGE TAKEN IN BATTLE

×0	×0	×1
×1	×0.5	×2
×1	×1	×1
×1	×1	×1
×1	×1	×1
×1	×0.5	×1

WATER 1
WATER 3

LEVEL-UP MOVES

LV.	NAME	TYPE	KIND	POW.	ACC.	PP	RANGE
1	Harden	Normal	Status	—	—	30	Self
1	Tackle	Normal	Physical	40	100	35	Normal
5	Astonish	Ghost	Physical	30	100	15	Normal
10	Disable	Normal	Status	—	100	20	Normal
15	Spite	Ghost	Status	—	100	10	Normal
20	Ancient Power	Rock	Special	60	100	5	Normal
25	Hex	Ghost	Special	65	100	10	Normal
30	Curse	Ghost	Status	—	—	10	Varies
35	Strength Sap	Grass	Status	—	100	10	Normal
40	Power Gem	Rock	Special	80	100	20	Normal
45	Night Shade	Ghost	Special	—	100	15	Normal
50	Grudge	Ghost	Status	—	—	5	Self
55	Mirror Coat	Psychic	Special	—	100	20	Varies

EVOLUTION MOVES

NAME	TYPE	KIND	POW.	ACC.	PP	RANGE

EGG MOVES

NAME	TYPE	KIND	POW.	ACC.	PP	RANGE
Confuse Ray	Ghost	Status	—	100	10	Normal
Destiny Bond	Ghost	Status	—	—	5	Self
Haze	Ice	Status	—	—	30	Both Sides
Head Smash	Rock	Physical	150	80	5	Normal
Nature Power	Normal	Status	—	—	20	Normal
Water Pulse	Water	Special	60	100	20	Normal

TUTOR MOVES

NAME	TYPE	KIND	POW.	ACC.	PP	RANGE

TM MOVES

NO.	NAME	TYPE	KIND	POW.	ACC.	PP	RANGE
TM15	Dig	Ground	Physical	80	100	10	Normal
TM16	Screech	Normal	Status	—	85	40	Normal
TM17	Light Screen	Psychic	Status	—	—	30	Your Side
TM18	Reflect	Psychic	Status	—	—	20	Your Side
TM19	Safeguard	Normal	Status	—	—	25	Your Side
TM20	Self-Destruct	Normal	Physical	200	100	5	All Others
TM21	Rest	Psychic	Status	—	—	10	Self
TM22	Rock Slide	Rock	Physical	75	90	10	Many Others
TM24	Snore	Normal	Special	50	100	15	Normal
TM25	Protect	Normal	Status	—	—	10	Self
TM27	Icy Wind	Ice	Special	55	95	15	Many Others
TM28	Giga Drain	Grass	Special	75	100	10	Normal
TM31	Attract	Normal	Status	—	100	15	Normal
TM32	Sandstorm	Rock	Status	—	—	10	Both Sides
TM33	Rain Dance	Water	Status	—	—	5	Both Sides
TM34	Sunny Day	Fire	Status	—	—	5	Both Sides
TM35	Hail	Ice	Status	—	—	10	Both Sides
TM36	Whirlpool	Water	Special	35	85	15	Normal
TM38	Will-O-Wisp	Fire	Status	—	85	15	Normal
TM39	Facade	Normal	Physical	70	100	20	Normal
TM48	Rock Tomb	Rock	Physical	60	95	15	Normal
TM51	Icicle Spear	Ice	Physical	25	100	30	Normal
TM54	Rock Blast	Rock	Physical	25	90	10	Normal
TM55	Brine	Water	Special	65	100	10	Normal
TM76	Round	Normal	Special	60	100	15	Normal
TM77	Hex	Ghost	Special	65	100	10	Normal
TM81	Bulldoze	Ground	Physical	60	100	20	All Others
TM98	Stomping Tantrum	Ground	Physical	75	100	10	Normal

TR MOVES

NO.	NAME	TYPE	KIND	POW.	ACC.	PP	RANGE
TR01	Body Slam	Normal	Physical	85	100	15	Normal
TR03	Hydro Pump	Water	Special	110	80	5	Normal
TR04	Surf	Water	Special	90	100	15	All Others
TR05	Ice Beam	Ice	Special	90	100	10	Normal
TR06	Blizzard	Ice	Special	110	70	5	Many Others
TR10	Earthquake	Ground	Physical	100	100	10	All Others
TR11	Psychic	Psychic	Special	90	100	10	Normal
TR17	Amnesia	Psychic	Status	—	—	20	Self
TR20	Substitute	Normal	Status	—	—	10	Self
TR26	Endure	Normal	Status	—	—	10	Self
TR27	Sleep Talk	Normal	Status	—	—	10	Self
TR33	Shadow Ball	Ghost	Special	80	100	15	Normal
TR46	Iron Defense	Steel	Status	—	—	15	Self
TR49	Calm Mind	Psychic	Status	—	—	20	Self
TR63	Power Gem	Rock	Special	80	100	20	Normal
TR67	Earth Power	Ground	Special	90	100	10	Normal
TR75	Stone Edge	Rock	Physical	100	80	5	Normal
TR76	Stealth Rock	Rock	Status	—	—	20	Other Side
TR84	Scald	Water	Special	80	100	15	Normal
TR95	Throat Chop	Dark	Physical	80	100	15	Normal
TR98	Liquidation	Water	Physical	85	100	10	Normal

237

Cursola
p. 102

ABILITY
Weak Armor
—

HIDDEN ABILITY
Perish Body

SPECIES STRENGTHS

HP	
ATTACK	
DEFENSE	
SP. ATK	
SP. DEF	
SPEED	

DAMAGE TAKEN IN BATTLE

×0	×0	×1
×1	×0.5	×2
×1	×1	×1
×1	×1	×2
×1	×1	×1
×1	×0.5	×1

WATER 1
WATER 3

LEVEL-UP MOVES

LV.	NAME	TYPE	KIND	POW.	ACC.	PP	RANGE
1	Astonish	Ghost	Physical	30	100	15	Normal
1	Disable	Normal	Status	—	100	20	Normal
1	Harden	Normal	Status	—	—	30	Self
1	Perish Song	Normal	Status	—	—	5	All
1	Tackle	Normal	Physical	40	100	35	Normal
15	Spite	Ghost	Status	—	100	10	Normal
20	Ancient Power	Rock	Special	60	100	5	Normal
25	Hex	Ghost	Special	65	100	10	Normal
30	Curse	Ghost	Status	—	—	10	Varies
35	Strength Sap	Grass	Status	—	100	10	Normal
40	Power Gem	Rock	Special	80	100	20	Normal
45	Night Shade	Ghost	Special	—	100	15	Normal
50	Grudge	Ghost	Status	—	—	5	Self
55	Mirror Coat	Psychic	Special	—	100	20	Varies

EVOLUTION MOVES

NAME	TYPE	KIND	POW.	ACC.	PP	RANGE

EGG MOVES

NAME	TYPE	KIND	POW.	ACC.	PP	RANGE

TUTOR MOVES

NAME	TYPE	KIND	POW.	ACC.	PP	RANGE

TM MOVES

NO.	NAME	TYPE	KIND	POW.	ACC.	PP	RANGE
TM07	Pin Missile	Bug	Physical	25	95	20	Normal
TM08	Hyper Beam	Normal	Special	150	90	5	Normal
TM09	Giga Impact	Normal	Physical	150	90	5	Normal
TM15	Dig	Ground	Physical	80	100	10	Normal
TM16	Screech	Normal	Status	—	85	40	Normal
TM17	Light Screen	Psychic	Status	—	—	30	Your Side
TM18	Reflect	Psychic	Status	—	—	20	Your Side
TM19	Safeguard	Normal	Status	—	—	25	Your Side
TM20	Self-Destruct	Normal	Physical	200	100	5	All Others
TM21	Rest	Psychic	Status	—	—	10	Self
TM22	Rock Slide	Rock	Physical	75	90	10	Many Others
TM24	Snore	Normal	Special	50	100	15	Normal
TM25	Protect	Normal	Status	—	—	10	Self
TM27	Icy Wind	Ice	Special	55	95	15	Many Others
TM28	Giga Drain	Grass	Special	75	100	10	Normal
TM31	Attract	Normal	Status	—	100	15	Normal
TM32	Sandstorm	Rock	Status	—	—	10	Both Sides
TM33	Rain Dance	Water	Status	—	—	5	Both Sides
TM34	Sunny Day	Fire	Status	—	—	5	Both Sides
TM35	Hail	Ice	Status	—	—	10	Both Sides
TM36	Whirlpool	Water	Special	35	85	15	Normal
TM38	Will-O-Wisp	Fire	Status	—	85	15	Normal
TM39	Facade	Normal	Physical	70	100	20	Normal
TM42	Revenge	Fighting	Physical	60	100	10	Normal
TM48	Rock Tomb	Rock	Physical	60	95	15	Normal
TM51	Icicle Spear	Ice	Physical	25	100	30	Normal
TM54	Rock Blast	Rock	Physical	25	90	10	Normal
TM55	Brine	Water	Special	65	100	10	Normal
TM76	Round	Normal	Special	60	100	15	Normal
TM77	Hex	Ghost	Special	65	100	10	Normal
TM81	Bulldoze	Ground	Physical	60	100	20	All Others
TM98	Stomping Tantrum	Ground	Physical	75	100	10	Normal

TR MOVES

NO.	NAME	TYPE	KIND	POW.	ACC.	PP	RANGE
TR01	Body Slam	Normal	Physical	85	100	15	Normal
TR03	Hydro Pump	Water	Special	110	80	5	Normal
TR04	Surf	Water	Special	90	100	15	All Others
TR05	Ice Beam	Ice	Special	90	100	10	Normal
TR06	Blizzard	Ice	Special	110	70	5	Many Others
TR10	Earthquake	Ground	Physical	100	100	10	All Others
TR11	Psychic	Psychic	Special	90	100	10	Normal
TR17	Amnesia	Psychic	Status	—	—	20	Self
TR18	Leech Life	Bug	Physical	80	100	10	Normal
TR20	Substitute	Normal	Status	—	—	10	Self
TR26	Endure	Normal	Status	—	—	10	Self
TR27	Sleep Talk	Normal	Status	—	—	10	Self
TR33	Shadow Ball	Ghost	Special	80	100	15	Normal
TR49	Calm Mind	Psychic	Status	—	—	20	Self
TR63	Power Gem	Rock	Special	80	100	20	Normal
TR67	Earth Power	Ground	Special	90	100	10	Normal
TR75	Stone Edge	Rock	Physical	100	80	5	Normal
TR76	Stealth Rock	Rock	Status	—	—	20	Other Side
TR84	Scald	Water	Special	80	100	15	Normal
TR95	Throat Chop	Dark	Physical	80	100	15	Normal
TR98	Liquidation	Water	Physical	85	100	10	Normal

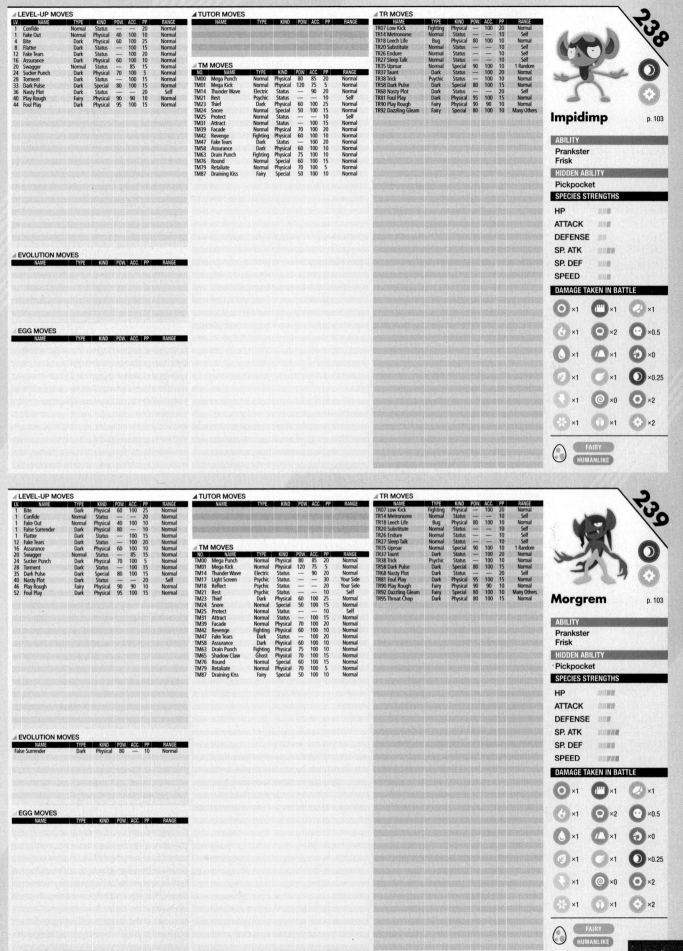

238 Impidimp — p. 103

LEVEL-UP MOVES

LV.	NAME	TYPE	KIND	POW.	ACC.	PP	RANGE
1	Confide	Normal	Status	—	—	20	Normal
1	Fake Out	Normal	Physical	40	100	10	Normal
4	Bite	Dark	Physical	60	100	25	Normal
8	Flatter	Dark	Status	—	100	15	Normal
12	Fake Tears	Dark	Status	—	100	20	Normal
16	Assurance	Dark	Physical	60	100	10	Normal
20	Swagger	Normal	Status	—	85	15	Normal
24	Sucker Punch	Dark	Physical	70	100	5	Normal
28	Torment	Dark	Status	—	100	15	Normal
33	Dark Pulse	Dark	Special	80	100	15	Normal
36	Nasty Plot	Dark	Status	—	—	20	Self
40	Play Rough	Fairy	Physical	90	90	10	Normal
44	Foul Play	Dark	Physical	95	100	15	Normal

EVOLUTION MOVES

NAME	TYPE	KIND	POW.	ACC.	PP	RANGE

EGG MOVES

NAME	TYPE	KIND	POW.	ACC.	PP	RANGE

TUTOR MOVES

NAME	TYPE	KIND	POW.	ACC.	PP	RANGE

TM MOVES

NO.	NAME	TYPE	KIND	POW.	ACC.	PP	RANGE
TM00	Mega Punch	Normal	Physical	80	85	20	Normal
TM01	Mega Kick	Normal	Physical	120	75	5	Normal
TM14	Thunder Wave	Electric	Status	—	90	20	Normal
TM21	Rest	Psychic	Status	—	—	10	Self
TM23	Thief	Dark	Physical	60	100	25	Normal
TM24	Snore	Normal	Special	50	100	15	Normal
TM25	Protect	Normal	Status	—	—	10	Self
TM31	Attract	Normal	Status	—	100	15	Normal
TM39	Facade	Normal	Physical	70	100	20	Normal
TM42	Revenge	Fighting	Physical	60	100	10	Normal
TM47	Fake Tears	Dark	Status	—	100	20	Normal
TM58	Assurance	Dark	Physical	60	100	10	Normal
TM63	Drain Punch	Fighting	Physical	75	100	10	Normal
TM76	Round	Normal	Special	60	100	15	Normal
TM79	Retaliate	Normal	Physical	70	100	5	Normal
TM87	Draining Kiss	Fairy	Special	50	100	10	Normal

TR MOVES

NO.	NAME	TYPE	KIND	POW.	ACC.	PP	RANGE
TR07	Low Kick	Fighting	Physical	—	100	20	Normal
TR14	Metronome	Normal	Status	—	—	10	Self
TR18	Leech Life	Bug	Physical	80	100	10	Normal
TR20	Substitute	Normal	Status	—	—	10	Self
TR26	Endure	Normal	Status	—	—	10	Self
TR27	Sleep Talk	Normal	Status	—	—	10	Self
TR35	Uproar	Normal	Special	90	100	10	1 Random
TR37	Taunt	Dark	Status	—	100	20	Normal
TR38	Trick	Psychic	Status	—	100	10	Normal
TR58	Dark Pulse	Dark	Special	80	100	15	Normal
TR68	Nasty Plot	Dark	Status	—	—	20	Self
TR81	Foul Play	Dark	Physical	95	100	15	Normal
TR90	Play Rough	Fairy	Physical	90	90	10	Normal
TR92	Dazzling Gleam	Fairy	Special	80	100	10	Many Others

ABILITY
Prankster
Frisk

HIDDEN ABILITY
Pickpocket

SPECIES STRENGTHS
HP
ATTACK
DEFENSE
SP. ATK
SP. DEF
SPEED

DAMAGE TAKEN IN BATTLE
×1 ×1 ×1
×1 ×2 ×0.5
×1 ×1 ×0
×1 ×1 ×0.25
×1 ×0 ×2
×1 ×1 ×2

FAIRY
HUMANLIKE

239 Morgrem — p. 103

LEVEL-UP MOVES

LV.	NAME	TYPE	KIND	POW.	ACC.	PP	RANGE
1	Bite	Dark	Physical	60	100	25	Normal
1	Confide	Normal	Status	—	—	20	Normal
1	Fake Out	Normal	Physical	40	100	10	Normal
1	False Surrender	Dark	Physical	80	—	10	Normal
1	Flatter	Dark	Status	—	100	15	Normal
12	Fake Tears	Dark	Status	—	100	20	Normal
16	Assurance	Dark	Physical	60	100	10	Normal
20	Swagger	Normal	Status	—	85	15	Normal
24	Sucker Punch	Dark	Physical	70	100	5	Normal
27	Torment	Dark	Status	—	100	15	Normal
35	Dark Pulse	Dark	Special	80	100	15	Normal
40	Nasty Plot	Dark	Status	—	—	20	Self
46	Play Rough	Fairy	Physical	90	90	10	Normal
52	Foul Play	Dark	Physical	95	100	15	Normal

EVOLUTION MOVES

NAME	TYPE	KIND	POW.	ACC.	PP	RANGE
False Surrender	Dark	Physical	80	—	10	Normal

EGG MOVES

NAME	TYPE	KIND	POW.	ACC.	PP	RANGE

TUTOR MOVES

NAME	TYPE	KIND	POW.	ACC.	PP	RANGE

TM MOVES

NO.	NAME	TYPE	KIND	POW.	ACC.	PP	RANGE
TM00	Mega Punch	Normal	Physical	80	85	20	Normal
TM01	Mega Kick	Normal	Physical	120	75	5	Normal
TM14	Thunder Wave	Electric	Status	—	90	20	Normal
TM17	Light Screen	Psychic	Status	—	—	20	Your Side
TM18	Reflect	Psychic	Status	—	—	20	Your Side
TM21	Rest	Psychic	Status	—	—	10	Self
TM23	Thief	Dark	Physical	60	100	25	Normal
TM24	Snore	Normal	Special	50	100	15	Normal
TM25	Protect	Normal	Status	—	—	10	Self
TM31	Attract	Normal	Status	—	100	15	Normal
TM39	Facade	Normal	Physical	70	100	20	Normal
TM42	Revenge	Fighting	Physical	60	100	10	Normal
TM47	Fake Tears	Dark	Status	—	100	20	Normal
TM58	Assurance	Dark	Physical	60	100	10	Normal
TM63	Drain Punch	Fighting	Physical	75	100	10	Normal
TM65	Shadow Claw	Ghost	Physical	70	100	15	Normal
TM76	Round	Normal	Special	60	100	15	Normal
TM79	Retaliate	Normal	Physical	70	100	5	Normal
TM87	Draining Kiss	Fairy	Special	50	100	10	Normal

TR MOVES

NO.	NAME	TYPE	KIND	POW.	ACC.	PP	RANGE
TR07	Low Kick	Fighting	Physical	—	100	20	Normal
TR14	Metronome	Normal	Status	—	—	10	Self
TR18	Leech Life	Bug	Physical	80	100	10	Normal
TR20	Substitute	Normal	Status	—	—	10	Self
TR26	Endure	Normal	Status	—	—	10	Self
TR27	Sleep Talk	Normal	Status	—	—	10	Self
TR35	Uproar	Normal	Special	90	100	10	1 Random
TR37	Taunt	Dark	Status	—	100	20	Normal
TR38	Trick	Psychic	Status	—	100	10	Normal
TR58	Dark Pulse	Dark	Special	80	100	15	Normal
TR68	Nasty Plot	Dark	Status	—	—	20	Self
TR81	Foul Play	Dark	Physical	95	100	15	Normal
TR90	Play Rough	Fairy	Physical	90	90	10	Normal
TR92	Dazzling Gleam	Fairy	Special	80	100	10	Many Others
TR95	Throat Chop	Dark	Physical	80	100	15	Normal

ABILITY
Prankster
Frisk

HIDDEN ABILITY
Pickpocket

SPECIES STRENGTHS
HP
ATTACK
DEFENSE
SP. ATK
SP. DEF
SPEED

DAMAGE TAKEN IN BATTLE
×1 ×1 ×1
×1 ×2 ×0.5
×1 ×1 ×0
×1 ×1 ×0.25
×1 ×0 ×2
×1 ×1 ×2

FAIRY
HUMANLIKE

240 Grimmsnarl

p. 103

ABILITY
Prankster
Frisk

HIDDEN ABILITY
Pickpocket

SPECIES STRENGTHS

HP	▮▮▮▯▯
ATTACK	▮▮▮▮▮▮▯
DEFENSE	▮▮▯▯
SP. ATK	▮▮▮▮▯
SP. DEF	▮▮▮▯
SPEED	▮▮▮▯

DAMAGE TAKEN IN BATTLE

◉ ×1	▥ ×1	▨ ×1
◔ ×1	◉ ×2	◉ ×0.5
◉ ×1	◭ ×1	↻ ×0
◹ ×1	◌ ×1	◐ ×0.25
◥ ×0	◎ ×2	◉ ×1
✳ ×1	⍟ ×1	✦ ×2

Egg groups: FAIRY, HUMANLIKE

LEVEL-UP MOVES

LV.	NAME	TYPE	KIND	POW.	ACC.	PP	RANGE
1	Bite	Dark	Physical	60	100	25	Normal
1	Bulk Up	Fighting	Status	—	—	20	Self
1	Confide	Normal	Status	—	—	20	Normal
1	Fake Out	Normal	Physical	40	100	10	Normal
1	Fake Surrender	Dark	Physical	80	100	10	Normal
1	Flatter	Dark	Status	—	100	15	Normal
1	Power-Up Punch	Fighting	Physical	40	100	20	Normal
1	Spirit Break	Fairy	Physical	75	100	15	Normal
12	Fake Tears	Dark	Status	—	100	20	Normal
16	Assurance	Dark	Physical	60	100	10	Normal
20	Swagger	Normal	Status	—	85	15	Normal
24	Sucker Punch	Dark	Physical	70	100	5	Normal
28	Torment	Dark	Status	—	100	15	Normal
35	Dark Pulse	Dark	Special	80	100	15	Normal
40	Nasty Plot	Dark	Status	—	—	20	Self
48	Play Rough	Fairy	Physical	90	90	10	Normal
56	Foul Play	Dark	Physical	95	100	15	Normal
64	Hammer Arm	Fighting	Physical	100	90	10	Normal

EVOLUTION MOVES

NAME	TYPE	KIND	POW.	ACC.	PP	RANGE
Spirit Break	Fairy	Physical	75	100	15	Normal

EGG MOVES

NAME	TYPE	KIND	POW.	ACC.	PP	RANGE

TUTOR MOVES

NAME	TYPE	KIND	POW.	ACC.	PP	RANGE

TM MOVES

NO.	NAME	TYPE	KIND	POW.	ACC.	PP	RANGE
TM00	Mega Punch	Normal	Physical	80	85	20	Normal
TM01	Mega Kick	Normal	Physical	120	75	5	Normal
TM03	Fire Punch	Fire	Physical	75	100	15	Normal
TM04	Ice Punch	Ice	Physical	75	100	15	Normal
TM05	Thunder Punch	Electric	Physical	75	100	15	Normal
TM08	Hyper Beam	Normal	Special	150	90	5	Normal
TM09	Giga Impact	Normal	Physical	150	90	5	Normal
TM14	Thunder Wave	Electric	Status	—	90	20	Normal
TM17	Light Screen	Psychic	Status	—	—	30	Your Side
TM18	Reflect	Psychic	Status	—	—	20	Your Side
TM21	Rest	Psychic	Status	—	—	10	Self
TM23	Thief	Dark	Physical	60	100	25	Normal
TM24	Snore	Normal	Special	50	100	15	Normal
TM25	Protect	Normal	Status	—	—	10	Self
TM26	Scary Face	Normal	Status	—	100	10	Normal
TM31	Attract	Normal	Status	—	100	15	Normal
TM39	Facade	Normal	Physical	70	100	20	Normal
TM42	Revenge	Fighting	Physical	60	100	10	Normal
TM43	Brick Break	Fighting	Physical	75	100	15	Normal
TM47	Fake Tears	Dark	Status	—	100	20	Normal
TM58	Assurance	Dark	Physical	60	100	10	Normal
TM60	Power Swap	Psychic	Status	—	—	10	Normal
TM63	Drain Punch	Fighting	Physical	75	100	10	Normal
TM65	Shadow Claw	Ghost	Physical	70	100	15	Normal
TM71	Wonder Room	Psychic	Status	—	—	10	Both Sides
TM75	Low Sweep	Fighting	Physical	65	100	20	Normal
TM76	Round	Normal	Special	60	100	15	Normal
TM79	Retaliate	Normal	Physical	70	100	5	Normal
TM87	Draining Kiss	Fairy	Special	50	100	10	Normal
TM98	Stomping Tantrum	Ground	Physical	75	100	10	Normal

TR MOVES

NO.	NAME	TYPE	KIND	POW.	ACC.	PP	RANGE
TR01	Body Slam	Normal	Physical	85	100	15	Normal
TR07	Low Kick	Fighting	Physical	—	100	20	Normal
TR13	Focus Energy	Normal	Status	—	—	30	Self
TR14	Metronome	Normal	Status	—	—	10	Self
TR18	Leech Life	Bug	Physical	80	100	10	Normal
TR20	Substitute	Normal	Status	—	—	10	Self
TR26	Endure	Normal	Status	—	—	10	Self
TR27	Sleep Talk	Normal	Status	—	—	10	Self
TR32	Crunch	Dark	Physical	80	100	15	Normal
TR35	Uproar	Normal	Special	90	100	10	1 Random
TR37	Taunt	Dark	Status	—	100	20	Normal
TR38	Trick	Psychic	Status	—	100	10	Normal
TR39	Superpower	Fighting	Physical	120	100	5	Normal
TR48	Bulk Up	Fighting	Status	—	—	20	Self
TR58	Dark Pulse	Dark	Special	80	100	15	Normal
TR64	Focus Blast	Fighting	Special	120	70	5	Normal
TR68	Nasty Plot	Dark	Status	—	—	20	Self
TR72	Power Whip	Grass	Physical	120	85	10	Normal
TR81	Foul Play	Dark	Physical	95	100	15	Normal
TR90	Play Rough	Fairy	Physical	90	90	10	Normal
TR92	Dazzling Gleam	Fairy	Special	80	100	10	Many Others
TR93	Darkest Lariat	Dark	Physical	85	100	10	Normal
TR95	Throat Chop	Dark	Physical	80	100	15	Normal
TR99	Body Press	Fighting	Physical	80	100	10	Normal

241 Hatenna

p. 104

ABILITY
Healer
Anticipation

HIDDEN ABILITY
Magic Bounce

SPECIES STRENGTHS

HP	▮▮
ATTACK	▮▮
DEFENSE	▮▮
SP. ATK	▮▮▮
SP. DEF	▮▮▮
SPEED	▮▮

DAMAGE TAKEN IN BATTLE

◉ ×1	▥ ×0.5	▨ ×1
◔ ×1	◉ ×1	◉ ×2
◉ ×1	◭ ×1	↻ ×1
◹ ×1	◌ ×1	◐ ×2
◥ ×1	◎ ×0.5	◉ ×1
✳ ×1	⍟ ×2	✦ ×1

Egg group: FAIRY

LEVEL-UP MOVES

LV.	NAME	TYPE	KIND	POW.	ACC.	PP	RANGE
1	Confusion	Psychic	Special	50	100	25	Normal
1	Play Nice	Normal	Status	—	—	20	Normal
5	Life Dew	Water	Status	—	—	10	Your Side
10	Disarming Voice	Fairy	Special	40	—	15	Many Others
15	Aromatherapy	Grass	Status	—	—	5	Your Party
20	Psybeam	Psychic	Special	65	100	20	Normal
25	Heal Pulse	Psychic	Status	—	—	10	Normal
30	Dazzling Gleam	Fairy	Special	80	100	10	Many Others
35	Calm Mind	Psychic	Status	—	—	20	Self
40	Psychic	Psychic	Special	90	100	10	Normal
45	Healing Wish	Psychic	Status	—	—	10	Self

EVOLUTION MOVES

NAME	TYPE	KIND	POW.	ACC.	PP	RANGE

EGG MOVES

NAME	TYPE	KIND	POW.	ACC.	PP	RANGE
After You	Normal	Status	—	—	15	Normal
Aromatic Mist	Fairy	Status	—	—	20	1 Ally
Nuzzle	Electric	Physical	20	100	20	Normal
Quash	Dark	Status	—	100	15	Normal

TUTOR MOVES

NAME	TYPE	KIND	POW.	ACC.	PP	RANGE

TM MOVES

NO.	NAME	TYPE	KIND	POW.	ACC.	PP	RANGE
TM10	Magical Leaf	Grass	Special	60	—	20	Normal
TM14	Thunder Wave	Electric	Status	—	90	20	Normal
TM17	Light Screen	Psychic	Status	—	—	30	Your Side
TM19	Safeguard	Normal	Status	—	—	25	Your Side
TM21	Rest	Psychic	Status	—	—	10	Self
TM24	Snore	Normal	Special	50	100	15	Normal
TM25	Protect	Normal	Status	—	—	10	Self
TM28	Giga Drain	Grass	Special	75	100	10	Normal
TM29	Charm	Fairy	Status	—	100	20	Normal
TM31	Attract	Normal	Status	—	100	15	Normal
TM39	Facade	Normal	Physical	70	100	20	Normal
TM41	Helping Hand	Normal	Status	—	—	20	1 Ally
TM44	Imprison	Psychic	Status	—	—	10	Self
TM76	Round	Normal	Special	60	100	15	Normal
TM87	Draining Kiss	Fairy	Special	50	100	10	Normal
TM92	Mystical Fire	Fire	Special	75	100	10	Normal

TR MOVES

NO.	NAME	TYPE	KIND	POW.	ACC.	PP	RANGE
TR11	Psychic	Psychic	Special	90	100	10	Normal
TR20	Substitute	Normal	Status	—	—	10	Self
TR25	Psyshock	Psychic	Special	80	100	10	Normal
TR26	Endure	Normal	Status	—	—	10	Self
TR27	Sleep Talk	Normal	Status	—	—	10	Self
TR29	Baton Pass	Normal	Status	—	—	40	Self
TR40	Skill Swap	Psychic	Status	—	—	10	Normal
TR49	Calm Mind	Psychic	Status	—	—	20	Self
TR58	Dark Pulse	Dark	Special	80	100	15	Normal
TR82	Stored Power	Psychic	Special	20	100	10	Normal
TR90	Play Rough	Fairy	Physical	90	90	10	Normal
TR92	Dazzling Gleam	Fairy	Special	80	100	10	Many Others

242

LEVEL-UP MOVES

LV.	NAME	TYPE	KIND	POW.	ACC.	PP	RANGE
1	Brutal Swing	Dark	Physical	60	100	20	All Others
1	Confusion	Psychic	Special	50	100	25	Normal
1	Disarming Voice	Fairy	Special	40	—	15	Many Others
1	Life Dew	Water	Status	—	—	10	Your Side
1	Play Nice	Normal	Status	—	—	20	Normal
15	Aromatherapy	Grass	Status	—	—	5	Your Party
20	Psybeam	Psychic	Special	65	100	20	Normal
25	Heal Pulse	Psychic	Status	—	—	10	Normal
30	Dazzling Gleam	Fairy	Special	80	100	10	Many Others
37	Calm Mind	Psychic	Status	—	—	20	Self
44	Psychic	Psychic	Special	90	100	10	Normal
51	Healing Wish	Psychic	Status	—	—	10	Self

EVOLUTION MOVES

NAME	TYPE	KIND	POW.	ACC.	PP	RANGE
Brutal Swing	Dark	Physical	60	100	20	All Others

EGG MOVES

NAME	TYPE	KIND	POW.	ACC.	PP	RANGE

TUTOR MOVES

NAME	TYPE	KIND	POW.	ACC.	PP	RANGE

TM MOVES

NO.	NAME	TYPE	KIND	POW.	ACC.	PP	RANGE
TM10	Magical Leaf	Grass	Special	60	—	20	Normal
TM14	Thunder Wave	Electric	Status	—	90	20	Normal
TM17	Light Screen	Psychic	Status	—	—	30	Your Side
TM19	Safeguard	Normal	Status	—	—	25	Your Side
TM21	Rest	Psychic	Status	—	—	10	Self
TM24	Snore	Normal	Special	50	100	15	Normal
TM25	Protect	Normal	Status	—	—	10	Self
TM28	Giga Drain	Grass	Special	75	100	10	Normal
TM29	Charm	Fairy	Status	—	100	20	Normal
TM31	Attract	Normal	Status	—	100	15	Normal
TM39	Facade	Normal	Physical	70	100	20	Normal
TM41	Helping Hand	Normal	Status	—	—	20	1 Ally
TM44	Imprison	Psychic	Status	—	—	10	Self
TM76	Round	Normal	Special	60	100	15	Normal
TM87	Draining Kiss	Fairy	Special	50	100	10	Normal
TM92	Mystical Fire	Fire	Special	75	100	10	Normal
TM97	Brutal Swing	Dark	Physical	60	100	20	All Others

TR MOVES

NAME	TYPE	KIND	POW.	ACC.	PP	RANGE
TR11 Psychic	Psychic	Special	90	100	10	Normal
TR20 Substitute	Normal	Status	—	—	10	Self
TR25 Psyshock	Psychic	Special	80	100	10	Normal
TR26 Endure	Normal	Status	—	—	10	Self
TR27 Sleep Talk	Normal	Status	—	—	10	Self
TR29 Baton Pass	Normal	Status	—	—	40	Self
TR40 Skill Swap	Psychic	Status	—	—	10	Normal
TR49 Calm Mind	Psychic	Status	—	—	20	Self
TR58 Dark Pulse	Dark	Special	80	100	15	Normal
TR82 Stored Power	Psychic	Special	20	100	10	Normal
TR90 Play Rough	Fairy	Physical	90	90	10	Normal
TR92 Dazzling Gleam	Fairy	Special	80	100	10	Many Others

Hattrem — p. 104

ABILITY
Healer
Anticipation

HIDDEN ABILITY
Magic Bounce

SPECIES STRENGTHS
HP
ATTACK
DEFENSE
SP. ATK
SP. DEF
SPEED

DAMAGE TAKEN IN BATTLE

FAIRY

243

LEVEL-UP MOVES

LV.	NAME	TYPE	KIND	POW.	ACC.	PP	RANGE
1	Brutal Swing	Dark	Physical	60	100	20	All Others
1	Confusion	Psychic	Special	50	100	25	Normal
1	Disarming Voice	Fairy	Special	40	—	15	Many Others
1	Life Dew	Water	Status	—	—	10	Your Side
1	Play Nice	Normal	Status	—	—	20	Normal
1	Psycho Cut	Psychic	Physical	70	100	20	Normal
15	Aromatherapy	Grass	Status	—	—	5	Your Party
20	Psybeam	Psychic	Special	65	100	20	Normal
25	Heal Pulse	Psychic	Status	—	—	10	Normal
30	Dazzling Gleam	Fairy	Special	80	100	10	Many Others
37	Calm Mind	Psychic	Status	—	—	20	Self
46	Psychic	Psychic	Special	90	100	10	Normal
55	Healing Wish	Psychic	Status	—	—	10	Self
64	Magic Powder	Psychic	Status	—	100	20	Normal

EVOLUTION MOVES

NAME	TYPE	KIND	POW.	ACC.	PP	RANGE
Psycho Cut	Psychic	Physical	70	100	20	Normal

EGG MOVES

NAME	TYPE	KIND	POW.	ACC.	PP	RANGE

TUTOR MOVES

NAME	TYPE	KIND	POW.	ACC.	PP	RANGE

TM MOVES

NO.	NAME	TYPE	KIND	POW.	ACC.	PP	RANGE
TM08	Hyper Beam	Normal	Special	150	90	5	Normal
TM09	Giga Impact	Normal	Physical	150	90	5	Normal
TM10	Magical Leaf	Grass	Special	60	—	20	Normal
TM14	Thunder Wave	Electric	Status	—	90	20	Normal
TM17	Light Screen	Psychic	Status	—	—	30	Your Side
TM19	Safeguard	Normal	Status	—	—	25	Your Side
TM21	Rest	Psychic	Status	—	—	10	Self
TM24	Snore	Normal	Special	50	100	15	Normal
TM25	Protect	Normal	Status	—	—	10	Self
TM28	Giga Drain	Grass	Special	75	100	10	Normal
TM29	Charm	Fairy	Status	—	100	20	Normal
TM31	Attract	Normal	Status	—	100	15	Normal
TM39	Facade	Normal	Physical	70	100	20	Normal
TM41	Helping Hand	Normal	Status	—	—	20	1 Ally
TM44	Imprison	Psychic	Status	—	—	10	Self
TM60	Power Swap	Psychic	Status	—	—	10	Normal
TM61	Guard Swap	Psychic	Status	—	—	10	Normal
TM65	Shadow Claw	Ghost	Physical	70	100	15	Normal
TM69	Psycho Cut	Psychic	Physical	70	100	20	Normal
TM70	Trick Room	Psychic	Status	—	—	5	Both Sides
TM71	Wonder Room	Psychic	Status	—	—	10	Both Sides
TM72	Magic Room	Psychic	Status	—	—	10	Both Sides
TM76	Round	Normal	Special	60	100	15	Normal
TM87	Draining Kiss	Fairy	Special	50	100	10	Normal
TM92	Mystical Fire	Fire	Special	75	100	10	Normal
TM97	Brutal Swing	Dark	Physical	60	100	20	All Others

TR MOVES

NAME	TYPE	KIND	POW.	ACC.	PP	RANGE
TR00 Swords Dance	Normal	Status	—	—	20	Self
TR11 Psychic	Psychic	Special	90	100	10	Normal
TR20 Substitute	Normal	Status	—	—	10	Self
TR25 Psyshock	Psychic	Special	80	100	10	Normal
TR26 Endure	Normal	Status	—	—	10	Self
TR27 Sleep Talk	Normal	Status	—	—	10	Self
TR29 Baton Pass	Normal	Status	—	—	40	Self
TR33 Shadow Ball	Ghost	Special	80	100	15	Normal
TR34 Future Sight	Psychic	Special	120	100	10	Normal
TR40 Skill Swap	Psychic	Status	—	—	10	Normal
TR49 Calm Mind	Psychic	Status	—	—	20	Self
TR58 Dark Pulse	Dark	Special	80	100	15	Normal
TR72 Power Whip	Grass	Physical	120	85	10	Normal
TR82 Stored Power	Psychic	Special	20	100	10	Normal
TR90 Play Rough	Fairy	Physical	90	90	10	Normal
TR92 Dazzling Gleam	Fairy	Special	80	100	10	Many Others

Hatterene — p. 104

ABILITY
Healer
Anticipation

HIDDEN ABILITY
Magic Bounce

SPECIES STRENGTHS
HP
ATTACK
DEFENSE
SP. ATK
SP. DEF
SPEED

DAMAGE TAKEN IN BATTLE

FAIRY

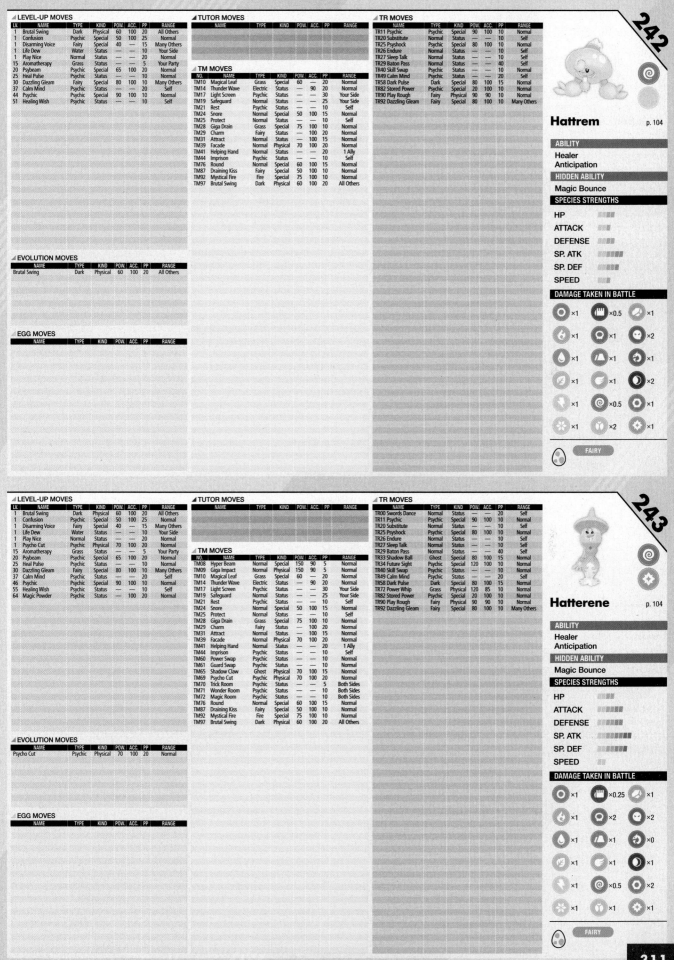

244

Salandit
p. 105

ABILITY
Corrosion
—

HIDDEN ABILITY
Oblivious

SPECIES STRENGTHS
- HP
- ATTACK
- DEFENSE
- SP. ATK
- SP. DEF
- SPEED

DAMAGE TAKEN IN BATTLE

⊙ ×1	×0.5	×2
×0.5	×0.5	×1
×2	×4	×1
×0.25	×1	×1
×1	×2	×0.5
×0.5	×0.25	×0.25

MONSTER
DRAGON

LEVEL-UP MOVES

LV.	NAME	TYPE	KIND	POW.	ACC.	PP	RANGE
1	Poison Gas	Poison	Status	—	90	40	Many Others
1	Scratch	Normal	Physical	40	100	35	Normal
5	Smog	Poison	Special	30	70	20	Normal
10	Ember	Fire	Special	40	100	25	Normal
15	Poison Fang	Poison	Physical	50	100	15	Normal
20	Sweet Scent	Normal	Status	—	100	20	Many Others
25	Nasty Plot	Dark	Status	—	—	20	Self
30	Incinerate	Fire	Special	60	100	15	Many Others
35	Venoshock	Poison	Special	65	100	10	Normal
40	Dragon Pulse	Dragon	Special	85	100	10	Normal
45	Venom Drench	Poison	Status	—	100	20	Many Others
50	Flamethrower	Fire	Special	90	100	15	Normal
55	Toxic	Poison	Status	—	90	10	Normal
60	Endeavor	Normal	Physical	—	100	5	Normal

EVOLUTION MOVES

NAME	TYPE	KIND	POW.	ACC.	PP	RANGE

EGG MOVES

NAME	TYPE	KIND	POW.	ACC.	PP	RANGE
Belch	Poison	Special	120	90	10	Normal
Fake Out	Normal	Physical	40	100	10	Normal
Mud-Slap	Ground	Special	20	100	10	Normal
Sand Attack	Ground	Status	—	100	15	Normal

TUTOR MOVES

NAME	TYPE	KIND	POW.	ACC.	PP	RANGE

TM MOVES

NO.	NAME	TYPE	KIND	POW.	ACC.	PP	RANGE
TM14	Thunder Wave	Electric	Status	—	90	20	Normal
TM21	Rest	Psychic	Status	—	—	10	Self
TM23	Thief	Dark	Physical	60	100	25	Normal
TM24	Snore	Normal	Special	50	100	15	Normal
TM25	Protect	Normal	Status	—	—	10	Self
TM31	Attract	Normal	Status	—	100	15	Normal
TM37	Beat Up	Dark	Physical	—	100	10	Normal
TM38	Will-O-Wisp	Fire	Status	—	85	15	Normal
TM39	Facade	Normal	Physical	70	100	20	Normal
TM40	Swift	Normal	Special	60	—	20	Many Others
TM41	Helping Hand	Normal	Status	—	—	20	1 Ally
TM57	Payback	Dark	Physical	50	100	10	Normal
TM59	Fling	Dark	Physical	—	100	10	Normal
TM65	Shadow Claw	Ghost	Physical	70	100	15	Normal
TM74	Venoshock	Poison	Special	65	100	10	Normal
TM76	Round	Normal	Special	60	100	15	Normal

TR MOVES

NO.	NAME	TYPE	KIND	POW.	ACC.	PP	RANGE
TR02	Flamethrower	Fire	Special	90	100	15	Normal
TR15	Fire Blast	Fire	Special	110	85	5	Normal
TR18	Leech Life	Bug	Physical	80	100	10	Normal
TR20	Substitute	Normal	Status	—	—	10	Self
TR22	Sludge Bomb	Poison	Special	90	100	10	Normal
TR26	Endure	Normal	Status	—	—	10	Self
TR27	Sleep Talk	Normal	Status	—	—	10	Self
TR31	Iron Tail	Steel	Physical	100	75	15	Normal
TR36	Heat Wave	Fire	Special	95	90	10	Many Others
TR37	Taunt	Dark	Status	—	100	20	Normal
TR43	Overheat	Fire	Special	130	90	5	Normal
TR47	Dragon Claw	Dragon	Physical	80	100	15	Normal
TR57	Poison Jab	Poison	Physical	80	100	20	Normal
TR62	Dragon Pulse	Dragon	Special	85	100	10	Normal
TR68	Nasty Plot	Dark	Status	—	—	20	Self
TR73	Gunk Shot	Poison	Physical	120	80	5	Normal
TR78	Sludge Wave	Poison	Special	95	100	10	All Others
TR81	Foul Play	Dark	Physical	95	100	15	Normal
TR91	Venom Drench	Poison	Status	—	100	20	Many Others

245

Salazzle
p. 105

ABILITY
Corrosion
—

HIDDEN ABILITY
Oblivious

SPECIES STRENGTHS
- HP
- ATTACK
- DEFENSE
- SP. ATK
- SP. DEF
- SPEED

DAMAGE TAKEN IN BATTLE

⊙ ×1	×0.5	×2
×0.5	×0.5	×1
×2	×4	×1
×0.25	×1	×1
×1	×2	×0.5
×0.5	×0.25	×0.25

MONSTER
DRAGON

LEVEL-UP MOVES

LV.	NAME	TYPE	KIND	POW.	ACC.	PP	RANGE
1	Disable	Normal	Status	—	100	20	Normal
1	Ember	Fire	Special	40	100	25	Normal
1	Encore	Normal	Status	—	100	5	Normal
1	Endeavor	Normal	Physical	—	100	5	Normal
1	Fire Lash	Fire	Physical	80	100	15	Normal
1	Knock Off	Dark	Physical	65	100	20	Normal
1	Poison Gas	Poison	Status	—	90	40	Many Others
1	Pound	Normal	Physical	40	100	35	Normal
1	Scratch	Normal	Physical	40	100	35	Normal
1	Smog	Poison	Special	30	70	20	Normal
1	Swagger	Normal	Status	—	85	15	Normal
1	Torment	Dark	Status	—	100	15	Normal
15	Poison Fang	Poison	Physical	50	100	15	Normal
20	Sweet Scent	Normal	Status	—	100	20	Many Others
25	Nasty Plot	Dark	Status	—	—	20	Self
30	Incinerate	Fire	Special	60	100	15	Many Others
37	Venoshock	Poison	Special	65	100	10	Normal
44	Dragon Pulse	Dragon	Special	85	100	10	Normal
51	Venom Drench	Poison	Status	—	100	20	Many Others
58	Flamethrower	Fire	Special	90	100	15	Normal
65	Toxic	Poison	Status	—	90	10	Normal

EVOLUTION MOVES

NAME	TYPE	KIND	POW.	ACC.	PP	RANGE
Fire Lash	Fire	Physical	80	100	15	Normal

EGG MOVES

NAME	TYPE	KIND	POW.	ACC.	PP	RANGE

TUTOR MOVES

NAME	TYPE	KIND	POW.	ACC.	PP	RANGE

TM MOVES

NO.	NAME	TYPE	KIND	POW.	ACC.	PP	RANGE
TM14	Thunder Wave	Electric	Status	—	90	20	Normal
TM21	Rest	Psychic	Status	—	—	10	Self
TM23	Thief	Dark	Physical	60	100	25	Normal
TM24	Snore	Normal	Special	50	100	15	Normal
TM25	Protect	Normal	Status	—	—	10	Self
TM31	Attract	Normal	Status	—	100	15	Normal
TM37	Beat Up	Dark	Physical	—	100	10	Normal
TM38	Will-O-Wisp	Fire	Status	—	85	15	Normal
TM39	Facade	Normal	Physical	70	100	20	Normal
TM40	Swift	Normal	Special	60	—	20	Many Others
TM41	Helping Hand	Normal	Status	—	—	20	1 Ally
TM47	Fake Tears	Dark	Status	—	100	20	Normal
TM57	Payback	Dark	Physical	50	100	10	Normal
TM59	Fling	Dark	Physical	—	100	10	Normal
TM65	Shadow Claw	Ghost	Physical	70	100	15	Normal
TM73	Cross Poison	Poison	Physical	70	100	20	Normal
TM74	Venoshock	Poison	Special	65	100	10	Normal
TM76	Round	Normal	Special	60	100	15	Normal
TM78	Acrobatics	Flying	Physical	55	100	15	Normal
TM99	Breaking Swipe	Dragon	Physical	60	100	15	Many Others

TR MOVES

NO.	NAME	TYPE	KIND	POW.	ACC.	PP	RANGE
TR02	Flamethrower	Fire	Special	90	100	15	Normal
TR15	Fire Blast	Fire	Special	110	85	5	Normal
TR18	Leech Life	Bug	Physical	80	100	10	Normal
TR20	Substitute	Normal	Status	—	—	10	Self
TR22	Sludge Bomb	Poison	Special	90	100	10	Normal
TR26	Endure	Normal	Status	—	—	10	Self
TR27	Sleep Talk	Normal	Status	—	—	10	Self
TR30	Encore	Normal	Status	—	100	5	Normal
TR31	Iron Tail	Steel	Physical	100	75	15	Normal
TR36	Heat Wave	Fire	Special	95	90	10	Many Others
TR37	Taunt	Dark	Status	—	100	20	Normal
TR43	Overheat	Fire	Special	130	90	5	Normal
TR47	Dragon Claw	Dragon	Physical	80	100	15	Normal
TR51	Dragon Dance	Dragon	Status	—	—	20	Self
TR55	Flare Blitz	Fire	Physical	120	100	15	Normal
TR57	Poison Jab	Poison	Physical	80	100	20	Normal
TR62	Dragon Pulse	Dragon	Special	85	100	10	Normal
TR68	Nasty Plot	Dark	Status	—	—	20	Self
TR73	Gunk Shot	Poison	Physical	120	80	5	Normal
TR78	Sludge Wave	Poison	Special	95	100	10	All Others
TR81	Foul Play	Dark	Physical	95	100	15	Normal
TR91	Venom Drench	Poison	Status	—	100	20	Many Others

246 — Pawniard

LEVEL-UP MOVES

LV.	NAME	TYPE	KIND	POW.	ACC.	PP	RANGE
1	Leer	Normal	Status	—	100	30	Many Others
1	Scratch	Normal	Physical	40	100	35	Normal
5	Fury Cutter	Bug	Physical	40	95	20	Normal
10	Metal Claw	Steel	Physical	50	95	35	Normal
15	Torment	Dark	Status	—	100	15	Normal
20	Scary Face	Normal	Status	—	100	10	Normal
25	Assurance	Dark	Physical	60	100	10	Normal
30	Metal Sound	Steel	Status	—	85	40	Normal
35	Slash	Normal	Physical	70	100	20	Normal
40	Night Slash	Dark	Physical	70	100	15	Normal
45	Iron Defense	Steel	Status	—	—	15	Self
50	Laser Focus	Normal	Status	—	—	30	Self
55	Iron Head	Steel	Physical	80	100	15	Normal
60	Swords Dance	Normal	Status	—	—	20	Self
65	Guillotine	Normal	Physical	—	30	5	Normal

EVOLUTION MOVES

NAME	TYPE	KIND	POW.	ACC.	PP	RANGE

EGG MOVES

NAME	TYPE	KIND	POW.	ACC.	PP	RANGE
Headbutt	Normal	Physical	70	100	15	Normal
Mean Look	Normal	Status	—	—	5	Normal
Quick Guard	Fighting	Status	—	—	15	Your Side
Sucker Punch	Dark	Physical	70	100	5	Normal

TUTOR MOVES

NAME	TYPE	KIND	POW.	ACC.	PP	RANGE
Steel Beam	Steel	Special	140	95	5	Normal

TM MOVES

NO.	NAME	TYPE	KIND	POW.	ACC.	PP	RANGE
TM14	Thunder Wave	Electric	Status	—	90	20	Normal
TM15	Dig	Ground	Physical	80	100	10	Normal
TM16	Screech	Normal	Status	—	85	40	Normal
TM21	Rest	Psychic	Status	—	—	10	Self
TM23	Thief	Dark	Physical	60	100	25	Normal
TM24	Snore	Normal	Special	50	100	15	Normal
TM25	Protect	Normal	Status	—	—	10	Self
TM26	Scary Face	Normal	Status	—	100	10	Normal
TM31	Attract	Normal	Status	—	100	15	Normal
TM32	Sandstorm	Rock	Status	—	—	10	Both Sides
TM33	Rain Dance	Water	Status	—	—	5	Both Sides
TM37	Beat Up	Dark	Physical	—	100	10	Normal
TM39	Facade	Normal	Physical	70	100	20	Normal
TM42	Revenge	Fighting	Physical	60	100	10	Normal
TM43	Brick Break	Fighting	Physical	75	100	15	Normal
TM48	Rock Tomb	Rock	Physical	60	95	15	Normal
TM57	Payback	Dark	Physical	50	100	10	Normal
TM58	Assurance	Dark	Physical	60	100	10	Normal
TM59	Fling	Dark	Physical	—	100	10	Normal
TM65	Shadow Claw	Ghost	Physical	70	100	15	Normal
TM69	Psycho Cut	Psychic	Physical	70	100	20	Normal
TM75	Low Sweep	Fighting	Physical	65	100	20	Normal
TM76	Round	Normal	Special	60	100	15	Normal
TM79	Retaliate	Normal	Physical	70	100	5	Normal
TM85	Snarl	Dark	Special	55	95	15	Many Others
TM94	False Swipe	Normal	Physical	40	100	40	Normal

TR MOVES

NO.	NAME	TYPE	KIND	POW.	ACC.	PP	RANGE
TR00	Swords Dance	Normal	Status	—	—	20	Self
TR07	Low Kick	Fighting	Physical	—	100	20	Normal
TR20	Substitute	Normal	Status	—	—	10	Self
TR26	Endure	Normal	Status	—	—	10	Self
TR27	Sleep Talk	Normal	Status	—	—	10	Self
TR37	Taunt	Dark	Status	—	100	20	Normal
TR46	Iron Defense	Steel	Status	—	—	15	Self
TR57	Poison Jab	Poison	Physical	80	100	20	Normal
TR58	Dark Pulse	Dark	Special	80	100	15	Normal
TR60	X-Scissor	Bug	Physical	80	100	15	Normal
TR74	Iron Head	Steel	Physical	80	100	15	Normal
TR76	Stealth Rock	Rock	Status	—	—	20	Other Side
TR77	Grass Knot	Grass	Special	—	100	20	Normal
TR81	Foul Play	Dark	Physical	95	100	15	Normal

Pawniard p. 105

ABILITY: Defiant / Inner Focus
HIDDEN ABILITY: Pressure

SPECIES STRENGTHS
- HP
- ATTACK
- DEFENSE
- SP. ATK
- SP. DEF
- SPEED

DAMAGE TAKEN IN BATTLE
- Normal ×0.5, Fighting ×4, Flying ×0.5
- Poison ×2, Ground ×0, Rock ×0.5
- Water ×1, Grass ×2, Electric ×0.5
- Fire ×0.5, Ice ×0.5, Psychic ×0.5
- Bug ×1, Ghost ×0, Dark ×0.5
- Dragon ×0.5, Steel ×1, Fairy ×1

HUMANLIKE

---

247 — Bisharp

LEVEL-UP MOVES

LV.	NAME	TYPE	KIND	POW.	ACC.	PP	RANGE
1	Fury Cutter	Bug	Physical	40	95	20	Normal
1	Leer	Normal	Status	—	100	30	Many Others
1	Metal Burst	Steel	Physical	—	100	10	Varies
1	Metal Claw	Steel	Physical	50	95	35	Normal
1	Scratch	Normal	Physical	40	100	35	Normal
15	Torment	Dark	Status	—	100	15	Normal
20	Scary Face	Normal	Status	—	100	10	Normal
25	Assurance	Dark	Physical	60	100	10	Normal
30	Metal Sound	Steel	Status	—	85	40	Normal
35	Slash	Normal	Physical	70	100	20	Normal
40	Night Slash	Dark	Physical	70	100	15	Normal
45	Iron Defense	Steel	Status	—	—	15	Self
50	Laser Focus	Normal	Status	—	—	30	Self
57	Iron Head	Steel	Physical	80	100	15	Normal
64	Swords Dance	Normal	Status	—	—	20	Self
71	Guillotine	Normal	Physical	—	30	5	Normal

EVOLUTION MOVES

NAME	TYPE	KIND	POW.	ACC.	PP	RANGE

EGG MOVES

NAME	TYPE	KIND	POW.	ACC.	PP	RANGE

TUTOR MOVES

NAME	TYPE	KIND	POW.	ACC.	PP	RANGE
Steel Beam	Steel	Special	140	95	5	Normal

TM MOVES

NO.	NAME	TYPE	KIND	POW.	ACC.	PP	RANGE
TM08	Hyper Beam	Normal	Special	150	90	5	Normal
TM09	Giga Impact	Normal	Physical	150	90	5	Normal
TM14	Thunder Wave	Electric	Status	—	90	20	Normal
TM15	Dig	Ground	Physical	80	100	10	Normal
TM16	Screech	Normal	Status	—	85	40	Normal
TM21	Rest	Psychic	Status	—	—	10	Self
TM23	Thief	Dark	Physical	60	100	25	Normal
TM24	Snore	Normal	Special	50	100	15	Normal
TM25	Protect	Normal	Status	—	—	10	Self
TM26	Scary Face	Normal	Status	—	100	10	Normal
TM31	Attract	Normal	Status	—	100	15	Normal
TM32	Sandstorm	Rock	Status	—	—	10	Both Sides
TM33	Rain Dance	Water	Status	—	—	5	Both Sides
TM37	Beat Up	Dark	Physical	—	100	10	Normal
TM39	Facade	Normal	Physical	70	100	20	Normal
TM42	Revenge	Fighting	Physical	60	100	10	Normal
TM43	Brick Break	Fighting	Physical	75	100	15	Normal
TM48	Rock Tomb	Rock	Physical	60	95	15	Normal
TM57	Payback	Dark	Physical	50	100	10	Normal
TM58	Assurance	Dark	Physical	60	100	10	Normal
TM59	Fling	Dark	Physical	—	100	10	Normal
TM65	Shadow Claw	Ghost	Physical	70	100	15	Normal
TM69	Psycho Cut	Psychic	Physical	70	100	20	Normal
TM75	Low Sweep	Fighting	Physical	65	100	20	Normal
TM76	Round	Normal	Special	60	100	15	Normal
TM79	Retaliate	Normal	Physical	70	100	5	Normal
TM85	Snarl	Dark	Special	55	95	15	Many Others
TM94	False Swipe	Normal	Physical	40	100	40	Normal
TM95	Air Slash	Flying	Special	75	95	15	Normal

TR MOVES

NO.	NAME	TYPE	KIND	POW.	ACC.	PP	RANGE
TR00	Swords Dance	Normal	Status	—	—	20	Self
TR07	Low Kick	Fighting	Physical	—	100	20	Normal
TR20	Substitute	Normal	Status	—	—	10	Self
TR26	Endure	Normal	Status	—	—	10	Self
TR27	Sleep Talk	Normal	Status	—	—	10	Self
TR37	Taunt	Dark	Status	—	100	20	Normal
TR46	Iron Defense	Steel	Status	—	—	15	Self
TR57	Poison Jab	Poison	Physical	80	100	20	Normal
TR58	Dark Pulse	Dark	Special	80	100	15	Normal
TR60	X-Scissor	Bug	Physical	80	100	15	Normal
TR64	Focus Blast	Fighting	Special	120	70	5	Normal
TR74	Iron Head	Steel	Physical	80	100	15	Normal
TR75	Stone Edge	Rock	Physical	100	80	5	Normal
TR76	Stealth Rock	Rock	Status	—	—	20	Other Side
TR77	Grass Knot	Grass	Special	—	100	20	Normal
TR81	Foul Play	Dark	Physical	95	100	15	Normal
TR95	Throat Chop	Dark	Physical	80	100	15	Normal

Bisharp p. 105

ABILITY: Defiant / Inner Focus
HIDDEN ABILITY: Pressure

SPECIES STRENGTHS
- HP
- ATTACK
- DEFENSE
- SP. ATK
- SP. DEF
- SPEED

DAMAGE TAKEN IN BATTLE
- Normal ×0.5, Fighting ×4, Flying ×0.5
- Poison ×2, Ground ×0, Rock ×0.5
- Water ×1, Grass ×2, Electric ×0.5
- Fire ×0.5, Ice ×0.5, Psychic ×0.5
- Bug ×1, Ghost ×0, Dark ×0.5
- Dragon ×0.5, Steel ×1, Fairy ×1

HUMANLIKE

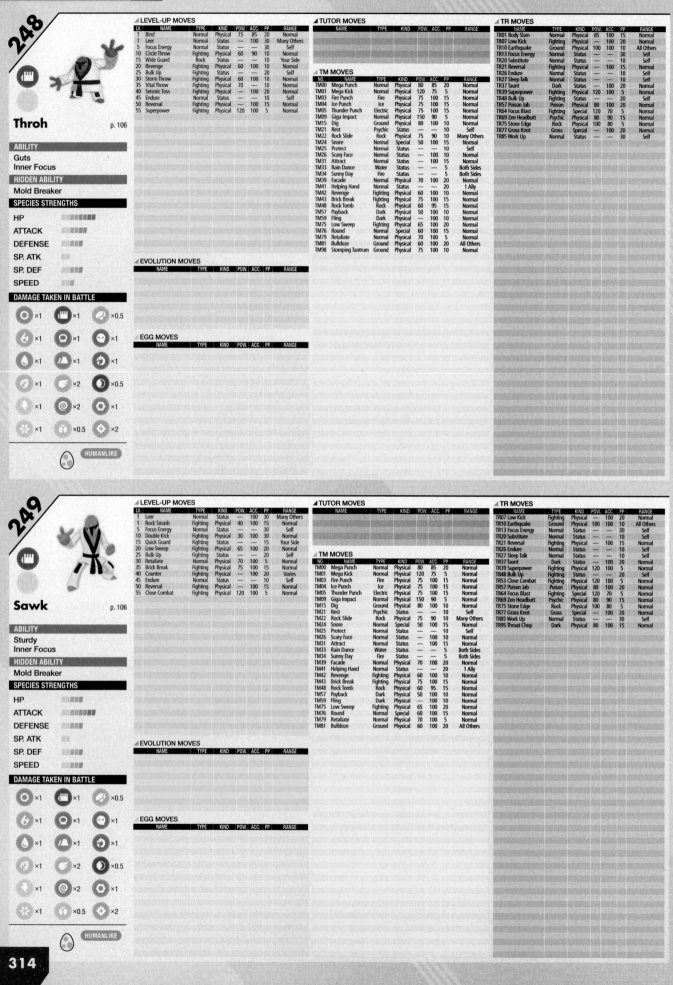

248 Throh

p. 106

ABILITY
Guts
Inner Focus

HIDDEN ABILITY
Mold Breaker

SPECIES STRENGTHS
- HP
- ATTACK
- DEFENSE
- SP. ATK
- SP. DEF
- SPEED

DAMAGE TAKEN IN BATTLE
×1 ×1 ×0.5
×1 ×1 ×1
×1 ×1 ×1
×1 ×2 ×0.5
×1 ×2 ×1
×1 ×0.5 ×2

HUMANLIKE

LEVEL-UP MOVES

LV.	NAME	TYPE	KIND	POW.	ACC.	PP	RANGE
1	Bind	Normal	Physical	15	85	20	Normal
1	Leer	Normal	Status	—	100	30	Many Others
5	Focus Energy	Normal	Status	—	—	30	Self
10	Circle Throw	Fighting	Physical	60	90	10	Normal
15	Wide Guard	Rock	Status	—	—	10	Your Side
20	Revenge	Fighting	Physical	60	100	10	Normal
20	Bulk Up	Fighting	Status	—	—	20	Self
30	Storm Throw	Fighting	Physical	60	100	10	Normal
35	Vital Throw	Fighting	Physical	70	—	10	Normal
40	Seismic Toss	Fighting	Physical	—	100	20	Normal
45	Endure	Normal	Status	—	—	10	Self
50	Reversal	Fighting	Physical	—	100	15	Normal
55	Superpower	Fighting	Physical	120	100	5	Normal

EVOLUTION MOVES

NAME	TYPE	KIND	POW.	ACC.	PP	RANGE

EGG MOVES

NAME	TYPE	KIND	POW.	ACC.	PP	RANGE

TUTOR MOVES

NAME	TYPE	KIND	POW.	ACC.	PP	RANGE

TM MOVES

NO.	NAME	TYPE	KIND	POW.	ACC.	PP	RANGE
TM00	Mega Punch	Normal	Physical	80	85	20	Normal
TM01	Mega Kick	Normal	Physical	120	75	5	Normal
TM03	Fire Punch	Fire	Physical	75	100	15	Normal
TM04	Ice Punch	Ice	Physical	75	100	15	Normal
TM05	Thunder Punch	Electric	Physical	75	100	15	Normal
TM09	Giga Impact	Normal	Physical	150	90	5	Normal
TM15	Dig	Ground	Physical	80	100	10	Normal
TM21	Rest	Psychic	Status	—	—	10	Self
TM22	Rock Slide	Rock	Physical	75	90	10	Many Others
TM24	Snore	Normal	Special	50	100	15	Normal
TM25	Protect	Normal	Status	—	—	10	Self
TM26	Scary Face	Normal	Status	—	100	10	Normal
TM31	Attract	Normal	Status	—	100	15	Normal
TM33	Rain Dance	Water	Status	—	—	5	Both Sides
TM34	Sunny Day	Fire	Status	—	—	5	Both Sides
TM39	Facade	Normal	Physical	70	100	20	Normal
TM41	Helping Hand	Normal	Status	—	—	20	1 Ally
TM42	Revenge	Fighting	Physical	60	100	10	Normal
TM43	Brick Break	Fighting	Physical	75	100	15	Normal
TM48	Rock Tomb	Rock	Physical	60	95	15	Normal
TM57	Payback	Dark	Physical	50	100	10	Normal
TM59	Fling	Dark	Physical	—	100	10	Normal
TM75	Low Sweep	Fighting	Physical	65	100	20	Normal
TM76	Round	Normal	Special	60	100	15	Normal
TM79	Retaliate	Normal	Physical	70	100	5	Normal
TM81	Bulldoze	Ground	Physical	60	100	20	All Others
TM98	Stomping Tantrum	Ground	Physical	75	100	10	Normal

TR MOVES

NO.	NAME	TYPE	KIND	POW.	ACC.	PP	RANGE
TR01	Body Slam	Normal	Physical	85	100	15	Normal
TR07	Low Kick	Fighting	Physical	—	100	20	Normal
TR10	Earthquake	Ground	Physical	100	100	10	All Others
TR13	Focus Energy	Normal	Status	—	—	30	Self
TR20	Substitute	Normal	Status	—	—	10	Self
TR21	Reversal	Fighting	Physical	—	100	15	Normal
TR26	Endure	Normal	Status	—	—	10	Self
TR27	Sleep Talk	Normal	Status	—	—	10	Self
TR37	Taunt	Dark	Status	—	100	20	Normal
TR39	Superpower	Fighting	Physical	120	100	5	Normal
TR48	Bulk Up	Fighting	Status	—	—	20	Self
TR57	Poison Jab	Poison	Physical	80	100	20	Normal
TR64	Focus Blast	Fighting	Special	120	70	5	Normal
TR69	Zen Headbutt	Psychic	Physical	80	90	15	Normal
TR75	Stone Edge	Rock	Physical	100	80	5	Normal
TR77	Grass Knot	Grass	Special	—	100	20	Normal
TR85	Work Up	Normal	Status	—	—	30	Self

249 Sawk

p. 106

ABILITY
Sturdy
Inner Focus

HIDDEN ABILITY
Mold Breaker

SPECIES STRENGTHS
- HP
- ATTACK
- DEFENSE
- SP. ATK
- SP. DEF
- SPEED

DAMAGE TAKEN IN BATTLE
×1 ×1 ×0.5
×1 ×1 ×1
×1 ×1 ×1
×1 ×2 ×0.5
×1 ×2 ×1
×1 ×0.5 ×2

HUMANLIKE

LEVEL-UP MOVES

LV.	NAME	TYPE	KIND	POW.	ACC.	PP	RANGE
1	Leer	Normal	Status	—	100	30	Many Others
1	Rock Smash	Fighting	Physical	40	100	15	Normal
5	Focus Energy	Normal	Status	—	—	30	Self
10	Double Kick	Fighting	Physical	30	100	30	Normal
15	Quick Guard	Fighting	Status	—	—	15	Your Side
20	Low Sweep	Fighting	Physical	65	100	20	Normal
25	Bulk Up	Fighting	Status	—	—	20	Self
30	Retaliate	Normal	Physical	70	100	5	Normal
35	Brick Break	Fighting	Physical	75	100	15	Normal
40	Counter	Fighting	Physical	—	100	20	Varies
45	Endure	Normal	Status	—	—	10	Self
50	Reversal	Fighting	Physical	—	100	15	Normal
55	Close Combat	Fighting	Physical	120	100	5	Normal

EVOLUTION MOVES

NAME	TYPE	KIND	POW.	ACC.	PP	RANGE

EGG MOVES

NAME	TYPE	KIND	POW.	ACC.	PP	RANGE

TUTOR MOVES

NAME	TYPE	KIND	POW.	ACC.	PP	RANGE

TM MOVES

NO.	NAME	TYPE	KIND	POW.	ACC.	PP	RANGE
TM00	Mega Punch	Normal	Physical	80	85	20	Normal
TM01	Mega Kick	Normal	Physical	120	75	5	Normal
TM03	Fire Punch	Fire	Physical	75	100	15	Normal
TM04	Ice Punch	Ice	Physical	75	100	15	Normal
TM05	Thunder Punch	Electric	Physical	75	100	15	Normal
TM09	Giga Impact	Normal	Physical	150	90	5	Normal
TM15	Dig	Ground	Physical	80	100	10	Normal
TM21	Rest	Psychic	Status	—	—	10	Self
TM22	Rock Slide	Rock	Physical	75	90	10	Many Others
TM24	Snore	Normal	Special	50	100	15	Normal
TM25	Protect	Normal	Status	—	—	10	Self
TM26	Scary Face	Normal	Status	—	100	10	Normal
TM31	Attract	Normal	Status	—	100	15	Normal
TM33	Rain Dance	Water	Status	—	—	5	Both Sides
TM34	Sunny Day	Fire	Status	—	—	5	Both Sides
TM39	Facade	Normal	Physical	70	100	20	Normal
TM41	Helping Hand	Normal	Status	—	—	20	1 Ally
TM42	Revenge	Fighting	Physical	60	100	10	Normal
TM43	Brick Break	Fighting	Physical	75	100	15	Normal
TM48	Rock Tomb	Rock	Physical	60	95	15	Normal
TM57	Payback	Dark	Physical	50	100	10	Normal
TM59	Fling	Dark	Physical	—	100	10	Normal
TM75	Low Sweep	Fighting	Physical	65	100	20	Normal
TM76	Round	Normal	Special	60	100	15	Normal
TM79	Retaliate	Normal	Physical	70	100	5	Normal
TM81	Bulldoze	Ground	Physical	60	100	20	All Others

TR MOVES

NO.	NAME	TYPE	KIND	POW.	ACC.	PP	RANGE
TR07	Low Kick	Fighting	Physical	—	100	20	Normal
TR10	Earthquake	Ground	Physical	100	100	10	All Others
TR13	Focus Energy	Normal	Status	—	—	30	Self
TR20	Substitute	Normal	Status	—	—	10	Self
TR21	Reversal	Fighting	Physical	—	100	15	Normal
TR26	Endure	Normal	Status	—	—	10	Self
TR27	Sleep Talk	Normal	Status	—	—	10	Self
TR37	Taunt	Dark	Status	—	100	20	Normal
TR39	Superpower	Fighting	Physical	120	100	5	Normal
TR48	Bulk Up	Fighting	Status	—	—	20	Self
TR53	Close Combat	Fighting	Physical	120	100	5	Normal
TR57	Poison Jab	Poison	Physical	80	100	20	Normal
TR64	Focus Blast	Fighting	Special	120	70	5	Normal
TR69	Zen Headbutt	Psychic	Physical	80	90	15	Normal
TR75	Stone Edge	Rock	Physical	100	80	5	Normal
TR77	Grass Knot	Grass	Special	—	100	20	Normal
TR85	Work Up	Normal	Status	—	—	30	Self
TR95	Throat Chop	Dark	Physical	80	100	15	Normal

250

Koffing
p. 107

LEVEL-UP MOVES

LV	NAME	TYPE	KIND	POW.	ACC.	PP	RANGE
1	Poison Gas	Poison	Status	—	90	40	Many Others
1	Tackle	Normal	Physical	40	100	35	Normal
4	Smog	Poison	Special	30	70	20	Normal
8	Smokescreen	Normal	Status	—	100	20	Normal
12	Clear Smog	Poison	Special	50	—	15	Normal
16	Assurance	Dark	Physical	60	100	10	Normal
20	Sludge	Poison	Special	65	100	20	Normal
24	Haze	Ice	Status	—	—	30	Both Sides
28	Self-Destruct	Normal	Physical	200	100	5	All Others
32	Sludge Bomb	Poison	Special	90	100	10	Normal
36	Toxic	Poison	Status	—	90	10	Normal
40	Belch	Poison	Special	120	90	10	Normal
44	Explosion	Normal	Physical	250	100	5	All Others
48	Memento	Dark	Status	—	100	10	Normal
52	Destiny Bond	Ghost	Status	—	—	5	Self

EVOLUTION MOVES

NAME	TYPE	KIND	POW.	ACC.	PP	RANGE

EGG MOVES

NAME	TYPE	KIND	POW.	ACC.	PP	RANGE
Curse	Ghost	Status	—	—	10	Varies
Grudge	Ghost	Status	—	—	5	Self
Pain Split	Normal	Status	—	—	20	Normal
Psybeam	Psychic	Special	65	100	20	Normal
Spit Up	Normal	Special	—	100	10	Normal
Spite	Ghost	Status	—	100	10	Normal
Stockpile	Normal	Status	—	—	20	Self
Swallow	Normal	Status	—	—	10	Self

TUTOR MOVES

NAME	TYPE	KIND	POW.	ACC.	PP	RANGE

TM MOVES

NO.	NAME	TYPE	KIND	POW.	ACC.	PP	RANGE
TM16	Screech	Normal	Status	—	85	40	Normal
TM20	Self-Destruct	Normal	Physical	200	100	5	All Others
TM21	Rest	Psychic	Status	—	—	10	Self
TM23	Thief	Dark	Physical	60	100	25	Normal
TM24	Snore	Normal	Special	50	100	15	Normal
TM25	Protect	Normal	Status	—	—	10	Self
TM31	Attract	Normal	Status	—	100	15	Normal
TM33	Rain Dance	Water	Status	—	—	5	Both Sides
TM34	Sunny Day	Fire	Status	—	—	5	Both Sides
TM38	Will-O-Wisp	Fire	Status	—	85	15	Normal
TM39	Facade	Normal	Physical	70	100	20	Normal
TM57	Payback	Dark	Physical	50	100	10	Normal
TM58	Assurance	Dark	Physical	60	100	10	Normal
TM74	Venoshock	Poison	Special	65	100	10	Normal
TM76	Round	Normal	Special	60	100	15	Normal

TR MOVES

NO.	NAME	TYPE	KIND	POW.	ACC.	PP	RANGE
TR02	Flamethrower	Fire	Special	90	100	15	Normal
TR08	Thunderbolt	Electric	Special	90	100	15	Normal
TR09	Thunder	Electric	Special	110	70	10	Normal
TR15	Fire Blast	Fire	Special	110	85	5	Normal
TR20	Substitute	Normal	Status	—	—	10	Self
TR22	Sludge Bomb	Poison	Special	90	100	10	Normal
TR26	Endure	Normal	Status	—	—	10	Self
TR27	Sleep Talk	Normal	Status	—	—	10	Self
TR33	Shadow Ball	Ghost	Special	80	100	15	Normal
TR35	Uproar	Normal	Special	90	100	10	1 Random
TR37	Taunt	Dark	Status	—	100	20	Normal
TR52	Gyro Ball	Steel	Physical	—	100	5	Normal
TR54	Toxic Spikes	Poison	Status	—	—	20	Other Side
TR58	Dark Pulse	Dark	Special	80	100	15	Normal
TR78	Sludge Wave	Poison	Special	95	100	10	All Others
TR91	Venom Drench	Poison	Status	—	100	20	Many Others

ABILITY
Levitate
Neutralizing Gas

HIDDEN ABILITY
Stench

SPECIES STRENGTHS
HP
ATTACK
DEFENSE
SP. ATK
SP. DEF
SPEED

DAMAGE TAKEN IN BATTLE

×1	×0.5	×1	
×1	×0.5	×1	
×1	×2	×1	
×0.5	×1	×1	
×1	×2	×1	
×1	×0.5	×0.5	

AMORPHOUS

251

Weezing
Galarian Form
p. 107

LEVEL-UP MOVES

LV	NAME	TYPE	KIND	POW.	ACC.	PP	RANGE
1	Aromatic Mist	Fairy	Status	—	—	20	1 Ally
1	Defog	Flying	Status	—	—	15	Normal
1	Double Hit	Normal	Physical	35	90	10	Normal
1	Fairy Wind	Fairy	Special	40	100	30	Normal
1	Haze	Ice	Status	—	—	30	Both Sides
1	Heat Wave	Fire	Special	95	90	10	Many Others
1	Poison Gas	Poison	Status	—	90	40	Many Others
1	Smog	Poison	Special	30	70	20	Normal
1	Smokescreen	Normal	Status	—	100	20	Normal
1	Strange Steam	Fairy	Special	90	95	10	Normal
1	Tackle	Normal	Physical	40	100	35	Normal
12	Clear Smog	Poison	Special	50	—	15	Normal
16	Assurance	Dark	Physical	60	100	10	Normal
20	Sludge	Poison	Special	65	100	20	Normal
24	Aromatherapy	Grass	Status	—	—	5	Your Party
28	Self-Destruct	Normal	Physical	200	100	5	All Others
32	Sludge Bomb	Poison	Special	90	100	10	Normal
38	Toxic	Poison	Status	—	90	10	Normal
44	Belch	Poison	Special	120	90	10	Normal
50	Explosion	Normal	Physical	250	100	5	All Others
56	Memento	Dark	Status	—	100	10	Normal
62	Destiny Bond	Ghost	Status	—	—	5	Self
68	Misty Terrain	Fairy	Status	—	—	10	Both Sides

EVOLUTION MOVES

NAME	TYPE	KIND	POW.	ACC.	PP	RANGE
Double Hit	Normal	Physical	35	90	10	Normal

EGG MOVES

NAME	TYPE	KIND	POW.	ACC.	PP	RANGE

TUTOR MOVES

NAME	TYPE	KIND	POW.	ACC.	PP	RANGE

TM MOVES

NO.	NAME	TYPE	KIND	POW.	ACC.	PP	RANGE
TM08	Hyper Beam	Normal	Special	150	90	5	Normal
TM09	Giga Impact	Normal	Physical	150	90	5	Normal
TM16	Screech	Normal	Status	—	85	40	Normal
TM20	Self-Destruct	Normal	Physical	200	100	5	All Others
TM21	Rest	Psychic	Status	—	—	10	Self
TM23	Thief	Dark	Physical	60	100	25	Normal
TM24	Snore	Normal	Special	50	100	15	Normal
TM25	Protect	Normal	Status	—	—	10	Self
TM31	Attract	Normal	Status	—	100	15	Normal
TM33	Rain Dance	Water	Status	—	—	5	Both Sides
TM34	Sunny Day	Fire	Status	—	—	5	Both Sides
TM38	Will-O-Wisp	Fire	Status	—	85	15	Normal
TM39	Facade	Normal	Physical	70	100	20	Normal
TM57	Payback	Dark	Physical	50	100	10	Normal
TM58	Assurance	Dark	Physical	60	100	10	Normal
TM71	Wonder Room	Psychic	Status	—	—	10	Both Sides
TM74	Venoshock	Poison	Special	65	100	10	Normal
TM76	Round	Normal	Special	60	100	15	Normal
TM89	Misty Terrain	Fairy	Status	—	—	10	Both Sides
TM97	Brutal Swing	Dark	Physical	60	100	20	All Others

TR MOVES

NO.	NAME	TYPE	KIND	POW.	ACC.	PP	RANGE
TR02	Flamethrower	Fire	Special	90	100	15	Normal
TR08	Thunderbolt	Electric	Special	90	100	15	Normal
TR09	Thunder	Electric	Special	110	70	10	Normal
TR15	Fire Blast	Fire	Special	110	85	5	Normal
TR20	Substitute	Normal	Status	—	—	10	Self
TR22	Sludge Bomb	Poison	Special	90	100	10	Normal
TR26	Endure	Normal	Status	—	—	10	Self
TR27	Sleep Talk	Normal	Status	—	—	10	Self
TR33	Shadow Ball	Ghost	Special	80	100	15	Normal
TR35	Uproar	Normal	Special	90	100	10	1 Random
TR36	Heat Wave	Fire	Special	95	90	10	Many Others
TR37	Taunt	Dark	Status	—	100	20	Normal
TR43	Overheat	Fire	Special	130	90	5	Normal
TR52	Gyro Ball	Steel	Physical	—	100	5	Normal
TR54	Toxic Spikes	Poison	Status	—	—	20	Other Side
TR58	Dark Pulse	Dark	Special	80	100	15	Normal
TR78	Sludge Wave	Poison	Special	95	100	10	All Others
TR90	Play Rough	Fairy	Physical	90	90	10	Normal
TR91	Venom Drench	Poison	Status	—	100	20	Many Others
TR92	Dazzling Gleam	Fairy	Special	80	100	10	Many Others

ABILITY
Levitate
Neutralizing Gas

HIDDEN ABILITY
Misty Surge

SPECIES STRENGTHS
HP
ATTACK
DEFENSE
SP. ATK
SP. DEF
SPEED

DAMAGE TAKEN IN BATTLE

×1	×0.25	×1	
×1	×1	×1	
×1	×2	×0	
×0.5	×1	×0.5	
×1	×2	×2	
×0.25	×0.25	×0.5	

AMORPHOUS

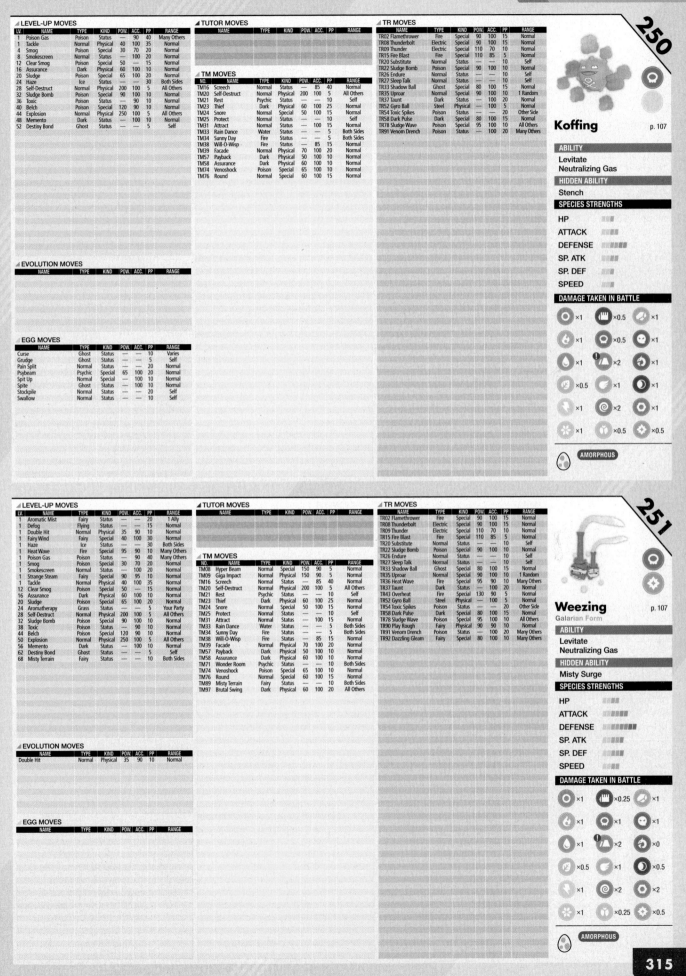

252 Bonsly

p. 107

ABILITY
Sturdy
Rock Head

HIDDEN ABILITY
Rattled

SPECIES STRENGTHS

HP
ATTACK
DEFENSE
SP. ATK
SP. DEF
SPEED

DAMAGE TAKEN IN BATTLE

○ ×0.5 | ×2 | ×1
○ ×0.5 | ○ ×0.5 | ×1
○ ×2 | ×2 | ×1
○ ×2 | ×0.5 | ○ ×2
○ ×1 | ○ ×1 | ○ ×2
○ ×1 | ×1 | ×1

NO EGGS

LEVEL-UP MOVES

LV.	NAME	TYPE	KIND	POW.	ACC.	PP	RANGE
1	Copycat	Normal	Status	—	—	20	Self
1	Fake Tears	Dark	Status	—	100	20	Normal
4	Flail	Normal	Physical	—	100	15	Normal
8	Rock Throw	Rock	Physical	50	90	15	Normal
12	Block	Normal	Status	—	—	5	Normal
16	Mimic	Normal	Status	—	—	10	Normal
20	Rock Tomb	Rock	Physical	60	95	15	Normal
24	Tearful Look	Normal	Status	—	—	20	Normal
28	Sucker Punch	Dark	Physical	70	100	5	Normal
32	Rock Slide	Rock	Physical	75	90	10	Many Others
36	Low Kick	Fighting	Physical	—	100	20	Normal
40	Counter	Fighting	Physical	—	100	20	Varies
44	Double-Edge	Normal	Physical	120	100	15	Normal

TUTOR MOVES

NAME	TYPE	KIND	POW.	ACC.	PP	RANGE

TM MOVES

NO.	NAME	TYPE	KIND	POW.	ACC.	PP	RANGE
TM15	Dig	Ground	Physical	80	100	10	Normal
TM20	Self-Destruct	Normal	Physical	200	100	5	All Others
TM21	Rest	Psychic	Status	—	—	10	Self
TM22	Rock Slide	Rock	Physical	75	90	10	Many Others
TM23	Thief	Dark	Physical	60	100	25	Normal
TM24	Snore	Normal	Special	50	100	15	Normal
TM25	Protect	Normal	Status	—	—	10	Self
TM31	Attract	Normal	Status	—	100	15	Normal
TM32	Sandstorm	Rock	Status	—	—	10	Both Sides
TM34	Sunny Day	Fire	Status	—	—	5	Both Sides
TM39	Facade	Normal	Physical	70	100	20	Normal
TM41	Helping Hand	Normal	Status	—	—	20	1 Ally
TM43	Brick Break	Fighting	Physical	75	100	15	Normal
TM47	Fake Tears	Dark	Status	—	100	20	Normal
TM48	Rock Tomb	Rock	Physical	60	95	15	Normal
TM49	Sand Tomb	Ground	Physical	35	85	15	Normal
TM76	Round	Normal	Special	60	100	15	Normal
TM98	Stomping Tantrum	Ground	Physical	75	100	10	Normal

TR MOVES

NAME	TYPE	KIND	POW.	ACC.	PP	RANGE
TR07 Low Kick	Fighting	Physical	—	100	20	Normal
TR20 Substitute	Normal	Status	—	—	10	Self
TR26 Endure	Normal	Status	—	—	10	Self
TR27 Sleep Talk	Normal	Status	—	—	10	Self
TR35 Uproar	Normal	Special	90	100	10	1 Random
TR49 Calm Mind	Psychic	Status	—	—	20	Self
TR67 Earth Power	Ground	Special	90	100	10	Normal
TR76 Stealth Rock	Rock	Status	—	—	20	Other Side
TR81 Foul Play	Dark	Physical	95	100	15	Normal

EVOLUTION MOVES

NAME	TYPE	KIND	POW.	ACC.	PP	RANGE

EGG MOVES

NAME	TYPE	KIND	POW.	ACC.	PP	RANGE
Curse	Ghost	Status	—	—	10	Varies
Defense Curl	Normal	Status	—	—	40	Self
Harden	Normal	Status	—	—	30	Self
Headbutt	Normal	Physical	70	100	15	Normal
Rock Polish	Rock	Status	—	—	20	Self
Rollout	Rock	Physical	30	90	20	Normal

---

253 Sudowoodo

p. 107

ABILITY
Sturdy
Rock Head

HIDDEN ABILITY
Rattled

SPECIES STRENGTHS

HP
ATTACK
DEFENSE
SP. ATK
SP. DEF
SPEED

DAMAGE TAKEN IN BATTLE

○ ×0.5 | ×2 | ×1
○ ×0.5 | ○ ×0.5 | ×1
○ ×2 | ×2 | ×1
○ ×2 | ×0.5 | ○ ×1
○ ×1 | ○ ×1 | ○ ×1
○ ×1 | ×1 | ×1

MINERAL

LEVEL-UP MOVES

LV.	NAME	TYPE	KIND	POW.	ACC.	PP	RANGE
1	Copycat	Normal	Status	—	—	20	Self
1	Fake Tears	Dark	Status	—	100	20	Normal
1	Flail	Normal	Physical	—	100	15	Normal
1	Hammer Arm	Fighting	Physical	100	90	10	Normal
1	Rock Throw	Rock	Physical	50	90	15	Normal
1	Slam	Normal	Physical	80	75	20	Normal
1	Stone Edge	Rock	Physical	100	80	5	Normal
1	Wood Hammer	Grass	Physical	120	100	15	Normal
12	Block	Normal	Status	—	—	5	Normal
16	Mimic	Normal	Status	—	—	10	Normal
20	Rock Tomb	Rock	Physical	60	95	15	Normal
24	Tearful Look	Normal	Status	—	—	20	Normal
28	Sucker Punch	Dark	Physical	70	100	5	Normal
32	Rock Slide	Rock	Physical	75	90	10	Many Others
36	Low Kick	Fighting	Physical	—	100	20	Normal
40	Counter	Fighting	Physical	—	100	20	Varies
44	Double-Edge	Normal	Physical	120	100	15	Normal
48	Head Smash	Rock	Physical	150	80	5	Normal

TUTOR MOVES

NAME	TYPE	KIND	POW.	ACC.	PP	RANGE

TM MOVES

NO.	NAME	TYPE	KIND	POW.	ACC.	PP	RANGE
TM00	Mega Punch	Normal	Physical	80	85	20	Normal
TM01	Mega Kick	Normal	Physical	120	75	5	Normal
TM03	Fire Punch	Fire	Physical	75	100	15	Normal
TM04	Ice Punch	Ice	Physical	75	100	15	Normal
TM05	Thunder Punch	Electric	Physical	75	100	15	Normal
TM15	Dig	Ground	Physical	80	100	10	Normal
TM20	Self-Destruct	Normal	Physical	200	100	5	All Others
TM21	Rest	Psychic	Status	—	—	10	Self
TM22	Rock Slide	Rock	Physical	75	90	10	Many Others
TM23	Thief	Dark	Physical	60	100	25	Normal
TM24	Snore	Normal	Special	50	100	15	Normal
TM25	Protect	Normal	Status	—	—	10	Self
TM31	Attract	Normal	Status	—	100	15	Normal
TM32	Sandstorm	Rock	Status	—	—	10	Both Sides
TM34	Sunny Day	Fire	Status	—	—	5	Both Sides
TM39	Facade	Normal	Physical	70	100	20	Normal
TM41	Helping Hand	Normal	Status	—	—	20	1 Ally
TM43	Brick Break	Fighting	Physical	75	100	15	Normal
TM47	Fake Tears	Dark	Status	—	100	20	Normal
TM48	Rock Tomb	Rock	Physical	60	95	15	Normal
TM49	Sand Tomb	Ground	Physical	35	85	15	Normal
TM54	Rock Blast	Rock	Physical	25	90	10	Normal
TM59	Fling	Dark	Physical	—	100	10	Normal
TM76	Round	Normal	Special	60	100	15	Normal
TM81	Bulldoze	Ground	Physical	60	100	20	All Others
TM98	Stomping Tantrum	Ground	Physical	75	100	10	Normal

TR MOVES

NAME	TYPE	KIND	POW.	ACC.	PP	RANGE
TR01 Body Slam	Normal	Physical	85	100	15	Normal
TR07 Low Kick	Fighting	Physical	—	100	20	Normal
TR10 Earthquake	Ground	Physical	100	100	10	All Others
TR20 Substitute	Normal	Status	—	—	10	Self
TR26 Endure	Normal	Status	—	—	10	Self
TR27 Sleep Talk	Normal	Status	—	—	10	Self
TR35 Uproar	Normal	Special	90	100	10	1 Random
TR37 Taunt	Dark	Status	—	100	20	Normal
TR46 Iron Defense	Steel	Status	—	—	15	Self
TR49 Calm Mind	Psychic	Status	—	—	20	Self
TR67 Earth Power	Ground	Special	90	100	10	Normal
TR75 Stone Edge	Rock	Physical	100	80	5	Normal
TR76 Stealth Rock	Rock	Status	—	—	20	Other Side
TR81 Foul Play	Dark	Physical	95	100	15	Normal
TR99 Body Press	Fighting	Physical	80	100	10	Normal

EVOLUTION MOVES

NAME	TYPE	KIND	POW.	ACC.	PP	RANGE
Slam	Normal	Physical	80	75	20	Normal

EGG MOVES

NAME	TYPE	KIND	POW.	ACC.	PP	RANGE
Curse	Ghost	Status	—	—	10	Varies
Defense Curl	Normal	Status	—	—	40	Self
Harden	Normal	Status	—	—	30	Self
Headbutt	Normal	Physical	70	100	15	Normal
Rock Polish	Rock	Status	—	—	20	Self
Rollout	Rock	Physical	30	90	20	Normal

254 Cleffa — p. 108

LEVEL-UP MOVES

LV	NAME	TYPE	KIND	POW.	ACC.	PP	RANGE
1	Copycat	Normal	Status	—	—	20	Self
1	Pound	Normal	Physical	40	100	35	Normal
1	Splash	Normal	Status	—	—	40	Self
4	Sing	Normal	Status	—	55	15	Normal
8	Sweet Kiss	Fairy	Status	—	75	10	Normal
12	Disarming Voice	Fairy	Special	40	—	15	Many Others
16	Encore	Normal	Status	—	100	5	Normal
20	Charm	Fairy	Status	—	100	20	Normal

EVOLUTION MOVES

NAME	TYPE	KIND	POW.	ACC.	PP	RANGE

EGG MOVES

NAME	TYPE	KIND	POW.	ACC.	PP	RANGE
Aromatherapy	Grass	Status	—	—	5	Your Party
Heal Pulse	Psychic	Status	—	—	10	Normal
Present	Normal	Physical	—	90	15	Normal
Tickle	Normal	Status	—	100	20	Normal
Wish	Normal	Status	—	—	10	Self

TUTOR MOVES

NAME	TYPE	KIND	POW.	ACC.	PP	RANGE

TM MOVES

NO.	NAME	TYPE	KIND	POW.	ACC.	PP	RANGE
TM00	Mega Punch	Normal	Physical	80	85	20	Normal
TM01	Mega Kick	Normal	Physical	120	75	5	Normal
TM10	Magical Leaf	Grass	Special	60	—	20	Normal
TM11	Solar Beam	Grass	Special	120	100	10	Normal
TM14	Thunder Wave	Electric	Status	—	90	20	Normal
TM15	Dig	Ground	Physical	80	100	10	Normal
TM17	Light Screen	Psychic	Status	—	—	30	Your Side
TM18	Reflect	Psychic	Status	—	—	20	Your Side
TM19	Safeguard	Normal	Status	—	—	25	Your Side
TM21	Rest	Psychic	Status	—	—	10	Self
TM24	Snore	Normal	Special	50	100	15	Normal
TM25	Protect	Normal	Status	—	—	10	Self
TM27	Icy Wind	Ice	Special	55	95	15	Many Others
TM29	Charm	Fairy	Status	—	100	20	Normal
TM31	Attract	Normal	Status	—	100	15	Normal
TM33	Rain Dance	Water	Status	—	—	5	Both Sides
TM34	Sunny Day	Fire	Status	—	—	5	Both Sides
TM39	Facade	Normal	Physical	70	100	20	Normal
TM41	Helping Hand	Normal	Status	—	—	20	1 Ally
TM47	Fake Tears	Dark	Status	—	100	20	Normal
TM59	Fling	Dark	Physical	—	100	10	Normal
TM71	Wonder Room	Psychic	Status	—	—	10	Both Sides
TM76	Round	Normal	Special	60	100	15	Normal
TM87	Draining Kiss	Fairy	Special	50	100	10	Normal
TM89	Misty Terrain	Fairy	Status	—	—	10	Both Sides

TR MOVES

NO.	NAME	TYPE	KIND	POW.	ACC.	PP	RANGE
TR01	Body Slam	Normal	Physical	85	100	15	Normal
TR02	Flamethrower	Fire	Special	90	100	15	Normal
TR11	Psychic	Psychic	Special	90	100	10	Normal
TR14	Metronome	Normal	Status	—	—	10	Self
TR15	Fire Blast	Fire	Special	110	85	5	Normal
TR17	Amnesia	Psychic	Status	—	—	20	Self
TR20	Substitute	Normal	Status	—	—	10	Self
TR25	Psyshock	Psychic	Special	80	100	10	Normal
TR26	Endure	Normal	Status	—	—	10	Self
TR27	Sleep Talk	Normal	Status	—	—	10	Self
TR30	Encore	Normal	Status	—	100	5	Normal
TR31	Iron Tail	Steel	Physical	100	75	15	Normal
TR33	Shadow Ball	Ghost	Special	80	100	15	Normal
TR35	Uproar	Normal	Special	90	100	10	1 Random
TR38	Trick	Psychic	Status	—	100	10	Normal
TR42	Hyper Voice	Normal	Special	90	100	10	Many Others
TR69	Zen Headbutt	Psychic	Physical	80	90	15	Normal
TR77	Grass Knot	Grass	Special	—	100	20	Normal
TR82	Stored Power	Psychic	Special	20	100	10	Normal
TR85	Work Up	Normal	Status	—	—	30	Self
TR90	Play Rough	Fairy	Physical	90	90	10	Normal

ABILITY: Cute Charm / Magic Guard
HIDDEN ABILITY: Friend Guard

SPECIES STRENGTHS: HP, ATTACK, DEFENSE, SP. ATK, SP. DEF, SPEED

DAMAGE TAKEN IN BATTLE: ×1, ×0.5, ×1, ×1, ×2, ×1, ×1, ×1, ×0, ×1, ×1, ×0.5, ×1, ×1, ×2, ×1, ×0.5, ×1

NO EGGS

255 Clefairy — p. 108

LEVEL-UP MOVES

LV	NAME	TYPE	KIND	POW.	ACC.	PP	RANGE
1	Charm	Fairy	Status	—	100	20	Normal
1	Copycat	Normal	Status	—	—	20	Self
1	Defense Curl	Normal	Status	—	—	40	Self
1	Disarming Voice	Fairy	Special	40	—	15	Many Others
1	Encore	Normal	Status	—	100	5	Normal
1	Growl	Normal	Status	—	100	40	Many Others
1	Pound	Normal	Physical	40	100	35	Normal
1	Sing	Normal	Status	—	55	15	Normal
1	Splash	Normal	Status	—	—	40	Self
1	Sweet Kiss	Fairy	Status	—	75	10	Normal
4	Stored Power	Psychic	Special	20	100	10	Normal
8	Minimize	Normal	Status	—	—	10	Self
12	After You	Normal	Status	—	—	15	Normal
16	Life Dew	Water	Status	—	—	10	Your Side
20	Metronome	Normal	Status	—	—	10	Self
24	Moonlight	Fairy	Status	—	—	5	Self
28	Gravity	Psychic	Status	—	—	5	Both Sides
32	Meteor Mash	Steel	Physical	90	90	10	Normal
36	Follow Me	Normal	Status	—	—	20	Self
40	Cosmic Power	Psychic	Status	—	—	20	Self
44	Moonblast	Fairy	Special	95	100	15	Normal
48	Healing Wish	Psychic	Status	—	—	10	Self

EVOLUTION MOVES

NAME	TYPE	KIND	POW.	ACC.	PP	RANGE

EGG MOVES

NAME	TYPE	KIND	POW.	ACC.	PP	RANGE

TUTOR MOVES

NAME	TYPE	KIND	POW.	ACC.	PP	RANGE

TM MOVES

NO.	NAME	TYPE	KIND	POW.	ACC.	PP	RANGE
TM00	Mega Punch	Normal	Physical	80	85	20	Normal
TM01	Mega Kick	Normal	Physical	120	75	5	Normal
TM03	Fire Punch	Fire	Physical	75	100	15	Normal
TM04	Ice Punch	Ice	Physical	75	100	15	Normal
TM05	Thunder Punch	Electric	Physical	75	100	15	Normal
TM10	Magical Leaf	Grass	Special	60	—	20	Normal
TM11	Solar Beam	Grass	Special	120	100	10	Normal
TM14	Thunder Wave	Electric	Status	—	90	20	Normal
TM15	Dig	Ground	Physical	80	100	10	Normal
TM17	Light Screen	Psychic	Status	—	—	30	Your Side
TM18	Reflect	Psychic	Status	—	—	20	Your Side
TM19	Safeguard	Normal	Status	—	—	25	Your Side
TM21	Rest	Psychic	Status	—	—	10	Self
TM24	Snore	Normal	Special	50	100	15	Normal
TM25	Protect	Normal	Status	—	—	10	Self
TM27	Icy Wind	Ice	Special	55	95	15	Many Others
TM29	Charm	Fairy	Status	—	100	20	Normal
TM31	Attract	Normal	Status	—	100	15	Normal
TM33	Rain Dance	Water	Status	—	—	5	Both Sides
TM34	Sunny Day	Fire	Status	—	—	5	Both Sides
TM39	Facade	Normal	Physical	70	100	20	Normal
TM41	Helping Hand	Normal	Status	—	—	20	1 Ally
TM43	Brick Break	Fighting	Physical	75	100	15	Normal
TM44	Imprison	Psychic	Status	—	—	10	Self
TM47	Fake Tears	Dark	Status	—	100	20	Normal
TM52	Bounce	Flying	Physical	85	85	5	Normal
TM59	Fling	Dark	Physical	—	100	10	Normal
TM63	Drain Punch	Fighting	Physical	75	100	10	Normal
TM71	Wonder Room	Psychic	Status	—	—	10	Both Sides
TM76	Round	Normal	Special	60	100	15	Normal
TM79	Retaliate	Normal	Physical	70	100	5	Normal
TM87	Draining Kiss	Fairy	Special	50	100	10	Normal
TM89	Misty Terrain	Fairy	Status	—	—	10	Both Sides
TM92	Mystical Fire	Fire	Special	75	100	10	Normal

TR MOVES

NO.	NAME	TYPE	KIND	POW.	ACC.	PP	RANGE
TR01	Body Slam	Normal	Physical	85	100	15	Normal
TR02	Flamethrower	Fire	Special	90	100	15	Normal
TR05	Ice Beam	Ice	Special	90	100	10	Normal
TR06	Blizzard	Ice	Special	110	70	5	Many Others
TR08	Thunderbolt	Electric	Special	90	100	15	Normal
TR09	Thunder	Electric	Special	110	70	10	Normal
TR11	Psychic	Psychic	Special	90	100	10	Normal
TR14	Metronome	Normal	Status	—	—	10	Self
TR15	Fire Blast	Fire	Special	110	85	5	Normal
TR17	Amnesia	Psychic	Status	—	—	20	Self
TR19	Tri Attack	Normal	Special	80	100	10	Normal
TR20	Substitute	Normal	Status	—	—	10	Self
TR25	Psyshock	Psychic	Special	80	100	10	Normal
TR26	Endure	Normal	Status	—	—	10	Self
TR27	Sleep Talk	Normal	Status	—	—	10	Self
TR29	Baton Pass	Normal	Status	—	—	40	Self
TR30	Encore	Normal	Status	—	100	5	Normal
TR31	Iron Tail	Steel	Physical	100	75	15	Normal
TR33	Shadow Ball	Ghost	Special	80	100	15	Normal
TR35	Uproar	Normal	Special	90	100	10	1 Random
TR38	Trick	Psychic	Status	—	100	10	Normal
TR42	Hyper Voice	Normal	Special	90	100	10	Many Others
TR44	Cosmic Power	Psychic	Status	—	—	20	Self
TR49	Calm Mind	Psychic	Status	—	—	20	Self
TR69	Zen Headbutt	Psychic	Physical	80	90	15	Normal
TR76	Stealth Rock	Rock	Status	—	—	20	Other Side
TR77	Grass Knot	Grass	Special	—	100	20	Normal
TR82	Stored Power	Psychic	Special	20	100	10	Normal
TR83	Ally Switch	Psychic	Status	—	—	15	Self
TR85	Work Up	Normal	Status	—	—	30	Self
TR90	Play Rough	Fairy	Physical	90	90	10	Normal
TR92	Dazzling Gleam	Fairy	Special	80	100	10	Many Others

ABILITY: Cute Charm / Magic Guard
HIDDEN ABILITY: Friend Guard

SPECIES STRENGTHS: HP, ATTACK, DEFENSE, SP. ATK, SP. DEF, SPEED

DAMAGE TAKEN IN BATTLE: ×1, ×0.5, ×1, ×1, ×2, ×1, ×1, ×1, ×0, ×1, ×1, ×0.5, ×1, ×1, ×2, ×1, ×0.5, ×1

FAIRY

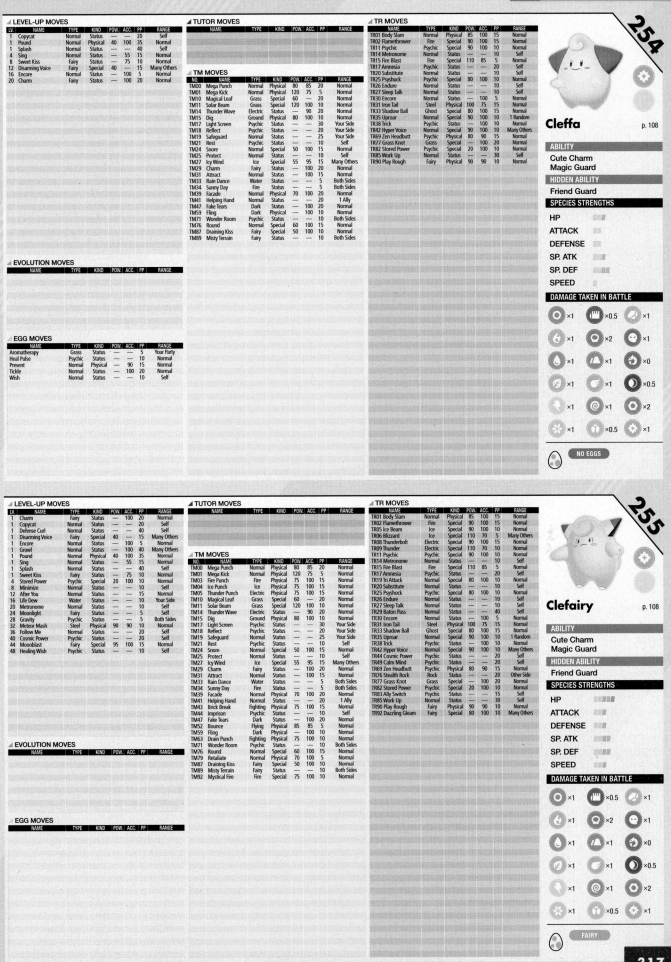

256

Clefable p. 108

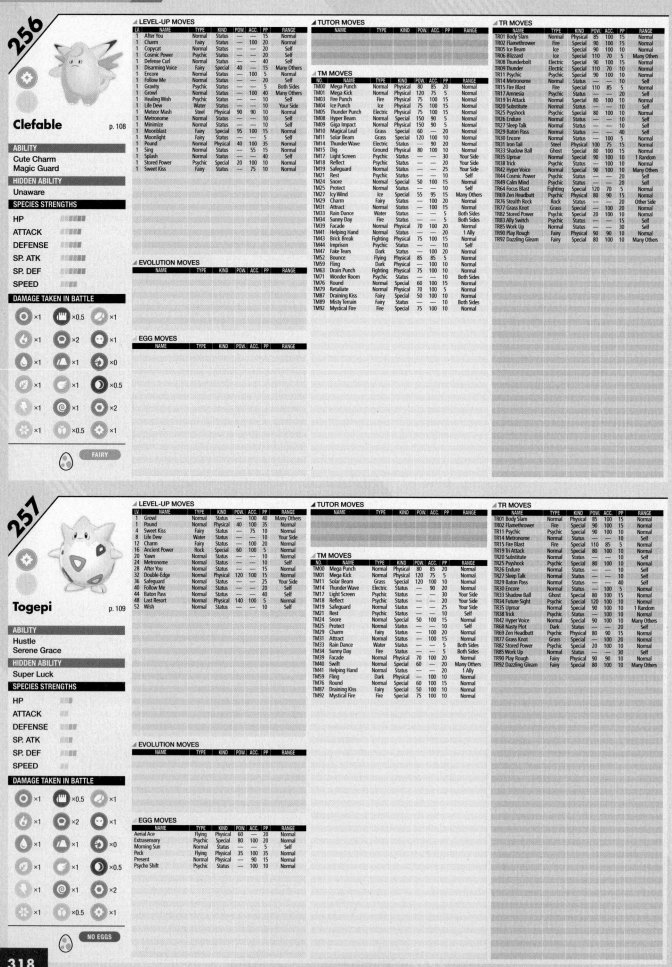

ABILITY
Cute Charm
Magic Guard

HIDDEN ABILITY
Unaware

SPECIES STRENGTHS

HP
ATTACK
DEFENSE
SP. ATK
SP. DEF
SPEED

DAMAGE TAKEN IN BATTLE

×1 ×0.5 ×1
×1 ×2 ×1
×1 ×1 ×0
×1 ×1 ×0.5
×1 ×1 ×2
×1 ×0.5 ×1

FAIRY

LEVEL-UP MOVES

LV.	NAME	TYPE	KIND	POW.	ACC.	PP	RANGE
1	After You	Normal	Status	—	—	15	Normal
1	Charm	Fairy	Status	—	100	20	Normal
1	Copycat	Normal	Status	—	—	20	Self
1	Cosmic Power	Psychic	Status	—	—	20	Self
1	Defense Curl	Normal	Status	—	—	40	Self
1	Disarming Voice	Fairy	Special	40	—	15	Many Others
1	Encore	Normal	Status	—	100	5	Normal
1	Follow Me	Normal	Status	—	—	20	Self
1	Gravity	Psychic	Status	—	—	5	Both Sides
1	Growl	Normal	Status	—	100	40	Many Others
1	Healing Wish	Psychic	Status	—	—	10	Self
1	Life Dew	Water	Status	—	—	10	Your Side
1	Meteor Mash	Steel	Physical	90	90	10	Normal
1	Metronome	Normal	Status	—	—	10	Self
1	Minimize	Normal	Status	—	—	10	Self
1	Moonblast	Fairy	Special	95	100	15	Normal
1	Moonlight	Fairy	Status	—	—	5	Self
1	Pound	Normal	Physical	40	100	35	Normal
1	Sing	Normal	Status	—	55	15	Normal
1	Splash	Normal	Status	—	—	40	Self
1	Stored Power	Psychic	Special	20	100	10	Normal
1	Sweet Kiss	Fairy	Status	—	75	10	Normal

EVOLUTION MOVES

NAME	TYPE	KIND	POW.	ACC.	PP	RANGE

EGG MOVES

NAME	TYPE	KIND	POW.	ACC.	PP	RANGE

TUTOR MOVES

NAME	TYPE	KIND	POW.	ACC.	PP	RANGE

TM MOVES

NO.	NAME	TYPE	KIND	POW.	ACC.	PP	RANGE
TM00	Mega Punch	Normal	Physical	80	85	20	Normal
TM01	Mega Kick	Normal	Physical	120	75	5	Normal
TM03	Fire Punch	Fire	Physical	75	100	15	Normal
TM04	Ice Punch	Ice	Physical	75	100	15	Normal
TM05	Thunder Punch	Electric	Physical	75	100	15	Normal
TM08	Hyper Beam	Normal	Special	150	90	5	Normal
TM09	Giga Impact	Normal	Physical	150	90	5	Normal
TM10	Magical Leaf	Grass	Special	60	—	20	Normal
TM11	Solar Beam	Grass	Special	120	100	10	Normal
TM14	Thunder Wave	Electric	Status	—	90	20	Normal
TM15	Dig	Ground	Physical	80	100	10	Normal
TM17	Light Screen	Psychic	Status	—	—	30	Your Side
TM18	Reflect	Psychic	Status	—	—	20	Your Side
TM19	Safeguard	Normal	Status	—	—	25	Your Side
TM21	Rest	Psychic	Status	—	—	10	Self
TM24	Snore	Normal	Special	50	100	15	Normal
TM25	Protect	Normal	Status	—	—	10	Self
TM27	Icy Wind	Ice	Special	55	95	15	Many Others
TM29	Charm	Fairy	Status	—	100	20	Normal
TM31	Attract	Normal	Status	—	100	15	Normal
TM33	Rain Dance	Water	Status	—	—	5	Both Sides
TM34	Sunny Day	Fire	Status	—	—	5	Both Sides
TM39	Facade	Normal	Physical	70	100	20	Normal
TM41	Helping Hand	Normal	Status	—	—	20	1 Ally
TM43	Brick Break	Fighting	Physical	75	100	15	Normal
TM44	Imprison	Psychic	Status	—	—	10	Self
TM47	Fake Tears	Dark	Status	—	100	20	Normal
TM52	Bounce	Flying	Physical	85	85	5	Normal
TM59	Fling	Dark	Physical	—	100	10	Normal
TM63	Drain Punch	Fighting	Physical	75	100	10	Normal
TM71	Wonder Room	Psychic	Status	—	—	10	Both Sides
TM76	Round	Normal	Special	60	100	15	Normal
TM79	Retaliate	Normal	Physical	70	100	5	Normal
TM87	Draining Kiss	Fairy	Special	50	100	10	Normal
TM89	Misty Terrain	Fairy	Status	—	—	10	Both Sides
TM92	Mystical Fire	Fire	Special	75	100	10	Normal

TR MOVES

NO.	NAME	TYPE	KIND	POW.	ACC.	PP	RANGE
TR01	Body Slam	Normal	Physical	85	100	15	Normal
TR02	Flamethrower	Fire	Special	90	100	15	Normal
TR05	Ice Beam	Ice	Special	90	100	10	Normal
TR06	Blizzard	Ice	Special	110	70	5	Many Others
TR08	Thunderbolt	Electric	Special	90	100	15	Normal
TR09	Thunder	Electric	Special	110	70	10	Normal
TR11	Psychic	Psychic	Special	90	100	10	Normal
TR14	Metronome	Normal	Status	—	—	10	Self
TR15	Fire Blast	Fire	Special	110	85	5	Normal
TR17	Amnesia	Psychic	Status	—	—	20	Self
TR19	Tri Attack	Normal	Special	80	100	10	Normal
TR20	Substitute	Normal	Status	—	—	10	Self
TR25	Psyshock	Psychic	Special	80	100	10	Normal
TR26	Endure	Normal	Status	—	—	10	Self
TR27	Sleep Talk	Normal	Status	—	—	10	Self
TR29	Baton Pass	Normal	Status	—	—	40	Self
TR30	Encore	Normal	Status	—	100	5	Normal
TR31	Iron Tail	Steel	Physical	100	75	15	Normal
TR33	Shadow Ball	Ghost	Special	80	100	15	Normal
TR35	Uproar	Normal	Special	90	100	10	1 Random
TR38	Trick	Psychic	Status	—	100	10	Normal
TR42	Hyper Voice	Normal	Special	90	100	10	Many Others
TR44	Cosmic Power	Psychic	Status	—	—	20	Self
TR49	Calm Mind	Psychic	Status	—	—	20	Self
TR64	Focus Blast	Fighting	Special	120	70	5	Normal
TR69	Zen Headbutt	Psychic	Physical	80	90	15	Normal
TR76	Stealth Rock	Rock	Status	—	—	20	Other Side
TR77	Grass Knot	Grass	Special	—	100	20	Normal
TR82	Stored Power	Psychic	Special	20	100	10	Normal
TR83	Ally Switch	Psychic	Status	—	—	15	Self
TR85	Work Up	Normal	Status	—	—	30	Self
TR90	Play Rough	Fairy	Physical	90	90	10	Normal
TR92	Dazzling Gleam	Fairy	Special	80	100	10	Many Others

257

Togepi p. 109

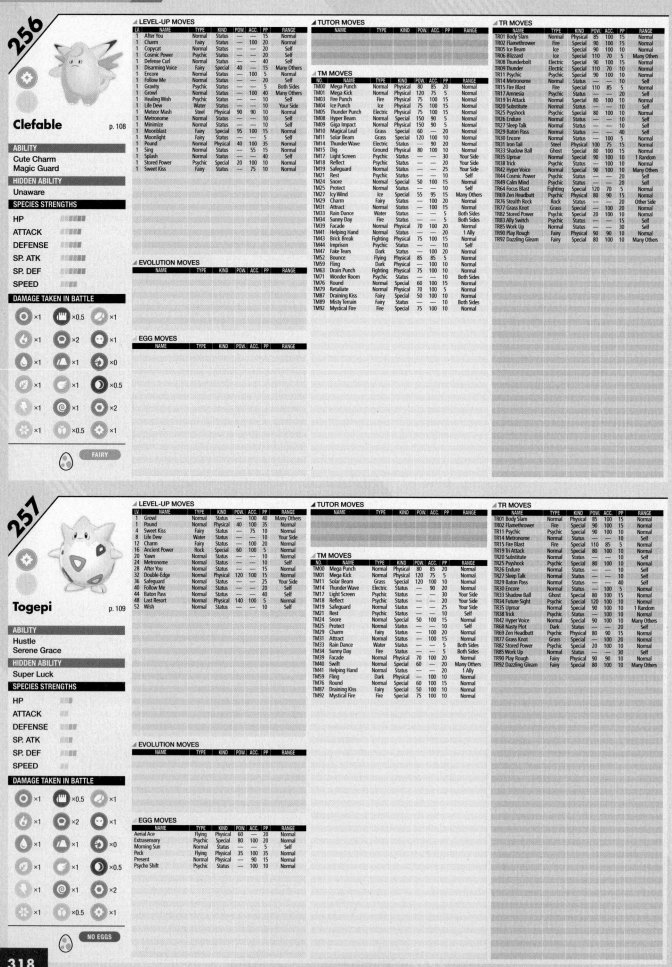

ABILITY
Hustle
Serene Grace

HIDDEN ABILITY
Super Luck

SPECIES STRENGTHS

HP
ATTACK
DEFENSE
SP. ATK
SP. DEF
SPEED

DAMAGE TAKEN IN BATTLE

×1 ×0.5 ×1
×1 ×2 ×1
×1 ×1 ×0
×1 ×1 ×0.5
×1 ×1 ×2
×1 ×0.5 ×1

NO EGGS

LEVEL-UP MOVES

LV.	NAME	TYPE	KIND	POW.	ACC.	PP	RANGE
1	Growl	Normal	Status	—	100	40	Many Others
1	Pound	Normal	Physical	40	100	35	Normal
4	Sweet Kiss	Fairy	Status	—	75	10	Normal
8	Life Dew	Water	Status	—	—	10	Your Side
12	Charm	Fairy	Status	—	100	20	Normal
16	Ancient Power	Rock	Special	60	100	5	Normal
20	Yawn	Normal	Status	—	—	10	Normal
24	Metronome	Normal	Status	—	—	10	Self
28	After You	Normal	Status	—	—	15	Normal
32	Double-Edge	Normal	Physical	120	100	15	Normal
36	Safeguard	Normal	Status	—	—	25	Your Side
40	Follow Me	Normal	Status	—	—	20	Self
44	Baton Pass	Normal	Status	—	—	40	Self
48	Last Resort	Normal	Physical	140	100	5	Normal
52	Wish	Normal	Status	—	—	10	Self

EVOLUTION MOVES

NAME	TYPE	KIND	POW.	ACC.	PP	RANGE

EGG MOVES

NAME	TYPE	KIND	POW.	ACC.	PP	RANGE
Aerial Ace	Flying	Physical	60	—	20	Normal
Extrasensory	Psychic	Special	80	100	20	Normal
Morning Sun	Normal	Status	—	—	5	Self
Peck	Flying	Physical	35	100	35	Normal
Present	Normal	Physical	—	90	15	Normal
Psycho Shift	Psychic	Status	—	100	10	Normal

TUTOR MOVES

NAME	TYPE	KIND	POW.	ACC.	PP	RANGE

TM MOVES

NO.	NAME	TYPE	KIND	POW.	ACC.	PP	RANGE
TM00	Mega Punch	Normal	Physical	80	85	20	Normal
TM01	Mega Kick	Normal	Physical	120	75	5	Normal
TM11	Solar Beam	Grass	Special	120	100	10	Normal
TM14	Thunder Wave	Electric	Status	—	90	20	Normal
TM17	Light Screen	Psychic	Status	—	—	30	Your Side
TM18	Reflect	Psychic	Status	—	—	20	Your Side
TM19	Safeguard	Normal	Status	—	—	25	Your Side
TM21	Rest	Psychic	Status	—	—	10	Self
TM24	Snore	Normal	Special	50	100	15	Normal
TM25	Protect	Normal	Status	—	—	10	Self
TM29	Charm	Fairy	Status	—	100	20	Normal
TM31	Attract	Normal	Status	—	100	15	Normal
TM33	Rain Dance	Water	Status	—	—	5	Both Sides
TM34	Sunny Day	Fire	Status	—	—	5	Both Sides
TM39	Facade	Normal	Physical	70	100	20	Normal
TM40	Swift	Normal	Special	60	—	20	Many Others
TM41	Helping Hand	Normal	Status	—	—	20	1 Ally
TM59	Fling	Dark	Physical	—	100	10	Normal
TM76	Round	Normal	Special	60	100	15	Normal
TM87	Draining Kiss	Fairy	Special	50	100	10	Normal
TM92	Mystical Fire	Fire	Special	75	100	10	Normal

TR MOVES

NO.	NAME	TYPE	KIND	POW.	ACC.	PP	RANGE
TR01	Body Slam	Normal	Physical	85	100	15	Normal
TR02	Flamethrower	Fire	Special	90	100	15	Normal
TR11	Psychic	Psychic	Special	90	100	10	Normal
TR14	Metronome	Normal	Status	—	—	10	Self
TR15	Fire Blast	Fire	Special	110	85	5	Normal
TR19	Tri Attack	Normal	Special	80	100	10	Normal
TR20	Substitute	Normal	Status	—	—	10	Self
TR25	Psyshock	Psychic	Special	80	100	10	Normal
TR26	Endure	Normal	Status	—	—	10	Self
TR27	Sleep Talk	Normal	Status	—	—	10	Self
TR29	Baton Pass	Normal	Status	—	—	40	Self
TR30	Encore	Normal	Status	—	100	5	Normal
TR33	Shadow Ball	Ghost	Special	80	100	15	Normal
TR34	Future Sight	Psychic	Special	120	100	10	Normal
TR35	Uproar	Normal	Special	90	100	10	1 Random
TR38	Trick	Psychic	Status	—	100	10	Normal
TR42	Hyper Voice	Normal	Special	90	100	10	Many Others
TR68	Nasty Plot	Dark	Status	—	—	20	Self
TR69	Zen Headbutt	Psychic	Physical	80	90	15	Normal
TR77	Grass Knot	Grass	Special	—	100	20	Normal
TR82	Stored Power	Psychic	Special	20	100	10	Normal
TR85	Work Up	Normal	Status	—	—	30	Self
TR90	Play Rough	Fairy	Physical	90	90	10	Normal
TR92	Dazzling Gleam	Fairy	Special	80	100	10	Many Others

258 — Togetic

LEVEL-UP MOVES

LV.	NAME	TYPE	KIND	POW.	ACC.	PP	RANGE
1	Fairy Wind	Fairy	Special	40	100	30	Normal
1	Growl	Normal	Status	—	100	40	Many Others
1	Life Dew	Water	Status	—	—	10	Your Side
1	Pound	Normal	Physical	40	100	35	Normal
1	Sweet Kiss	Fairy	Status	—	75	10	Normal
12	Charm	Fairy	Status	—	100	20	Normal
16	Ancient Power	Rock	Special	60	100	5	Normal
20	Yawn	Normal	Status	—	—	10	Normal
24	Metronome	Normal	Status	—	—	10	Self
28	After You	Normal	Status	—	—	15	Normal
32	Double-Edge	Normal	Physical	120	100	15	Normal
36	Safeguard	Normal	Status	—	—	25	Your Side
40	Follow Me	Normal	Status	—	—	20	Self
44	Baton Pass	Normal	Status	—	—	40	Self
48	Last Resort	Normal	Physical	140	100	5	Normal
52	Wish	Normal	Status	—	—	10	Self

EVOLUTION MOVES

NAME	TYPE	KIND	POW.	ACC.	PP	RANGE
Fairy Wind	Fairy	Special	40	100	30	Normal

EGG MOVES

NAME	TYPE	KIND	POW.	ACC.	PP	RANGE

TUTOR MOVES

NAME	TYPE	KIND	POW.	ACC.	PP	RANGE

TM MOVES

NO.	NAME	TYPE	KIND	POW.	ACC.	PP	RANGE
TM00	Mega Punch	Normal	Physical	80	85	20	Normal
TM01	Mega Kick	Normal	Physical	120	75	5	Normal
TM06	Fly	Flying	Physical	90	95	15	Normal
TM08	Hyper Beam	Normal	Special	150	90	5	Normal
TM09	Giga Impact	Normal	Physical	150	90	5	Normal
TM10	Magical Leaf	Grass	Special	60	—	20	Normal
TM11	Solar Beam	Grass	Special	120	100	10	Normal
TM14	Thunder Wave	Electric	Status	—	90	20	Normal
TM17	Light Screen	Psychic	Status	—	—	30	Your Side
TM18	Reflect	Psychic	Status	—	—	20	Your Side
TM19	Safeguard	Normal	Status	—	—	25	Your Side
TM21	Rest	Psychic	Status	—	—	10	Self
TM24	Snore	Normal	Special	50	100	15	Normal
TM25	Protect	Normal	Status	—	—	10	Self
TM29	Charm	Fairy	Status	—	100	20	Normal
TM30	Steel Wing	Steel	Physical	70	90	25	Normal
TM31	Attract	Normal	Status	—	100	15	Normal
TM33	Rain Dance	Water	Status	—	—	5	Both Sides
TM34	Sunny Day	Fire	Status	—	—	5	Both Sides
TM39	Facade	Normal	Physical	70	100	20	Normal
TM40	Swift	Normal	Special	60	—	20	Many Others
TM41	Helping Hand	Normal	Status	—	—	20	1 Ally
TM43	Brick Break	Fighting	Physical	75	100	15	Normal
TM44	Imprison	Psychic	Status	—	—	10	Self
TM59	Fling	Dark	Physical	—	100	10	Normal
TM63	Drain Punch	Fighting	Physical	75	100	10	Normal
TM76	Round	Normal	Special	60	100	15	Normal
TM79	Retaliate	Normal	Physical	70	100	5	Normal
TM87	Draining Kiss	Fairy	Special	50	100	10	Normal
TM92	Mystical Fire	Fire	Special	75	100	10	Normal
TM96	Smart Strike	Steel	Physical	70	—	10	Normal

TR MOVES

NO.	NAME	TYPE	KIND	POW.	ACC.	PP	RANGE
TR01	Body Slam	Normal	Physical	85	100	15	Normal
TR02	Flamethrower	Fire	Special	90	100	15	Normal
TR11	Psychic	Psychic	Special	90	100	10	Normal
TR14	Metronome	Normal	Status	—	—	10	Self
TR15	Fire Blast	Fire	Special	110	85	5	Normal
TR19	Tri Attack	Normal	Special	80	100	10	Normal
TR20	Substitute	Normal	Status	—	—	10	Self
TR25	Psyshock	Psychic	Special	80	100	10	Normal
TR26	Endure	Normal	Status	—	—	10	Self
TR27	Sleep Talk	Normal	Status	—	—	10	Self
TR29	Baton Pass	Normal	Status	—	—	40	Self
TR30	Encore	Normal	Status	—	100	5	Normal
TR33	Shadow Ball	Ghost	Special	80	100	15	Normal
TR34	Future Sight	Psychic	Special	120	100	10	Normal
TR35	Uproar	Normal	Special	90	100	10	1 Random
TR36	Heat Wave	Fire	Special	95	90	10	Many Others
TR38	Trick	Psychic	Status	—	100	10	Normal
TR42	Hyper Voice	Normal	Special	90	100	10	Many Others
TR68	Nasty Plot	Dark	Status	—	—	20	Self
TR69	Zen Headbutt	Psychic	Physical	80	90	15	Normal
TR77	Grass Knot	Grass	Special	—	100	20	Normal
TR82	Stored Power	Psychic	Special	20	100	10	Normal
TR85	Work Up	Normal	Status	—	—	30	Self
TR90	Play Rough	Fairy	Physical	90	90	10	Normal
TR92	Dazzling Gleam	Fairy	Special	80	100	10	Many Others

Togetic — p. 109

ABILITY
Hustle
Serene Grace

HIDDEN ABILITY
Super Luck

SPECIES STRENGTHS
- HP
- ATTACK
- DEFENSE
- SP. ATK
- SP. DEF
- SPEED

DAMAGE TAKEN IN BATTLE

×1	×0.25	×2
×1	×2	×1
×1	×0	×0
×0.5	×1	×0.5
×2	×1	×2
×2	×0.25	×1

Egg Groups: FLYING, FAIRY

---

259 — Togekiss

LEVEL-UP MOVES

LV.	NAME	TYPE	KIND	POW.	ACC.	PP	RANGE
1	After You	Normal	Status	—	—	15	Normal
1	Air Slash	Flying	Special	75	95	15	Normal
1	Ancient Power	Rock	Special	60	100	5	Normal
1	Aura Sphere	Fighting	Special	80	—	20	Normal
1	Baton Pass	Normal	Status	—	—	40	Self
1	Charm	Fairy	Status	—	100	20	Normal
1	Double-Edge	Normal	Physical	120	100	15	Normal
1	Extreme Speed	Normal	Physical	80	100	5	Normal
1	Fairy Wind	Fairy	Special	40	100	30	Normal
1	Follow Me	Normal	Status	—	—	20	Normal
1	Growl	Normal	Status	—	100	40	Many Others
1	Last Resort	Normal	Physical	140	100	5	Normal
1	Life Dew	Water	Status	—	—	10	Your Side
1	Metronome	Normal	Status	—	—	10	Self
1	Pound	Normal	Physical	40	100	35	Normal
1	Safeguard	Normal	Status	—	—	25	Your Side
1	Sky Attack	Flying	Physical	140	90	5	Normal
1	Sweet Kiss	Fairy	Status	—	75	10	Normal
1	Tri Attack	Normal	Special	80	100	10	Normal
1	Wish	Normal	Status	—	—	10	Self
1	Yawn	Normal	Status	—	—	10	Normal

EVOLUTION MOVES

NAME	TYPE	KIND	POW.	ACC.	PP	RANGE
Air Slash	Flying	Special	75	95	15	Normal

EGG MOVES

NAME	TYPE	KIND	POW.	ACC.	PP	RANGE

TUTOR MOVES

NAME	TYPE	KIND	POW.	ACC.	PP	RANGE

TM MOVES

NO.	NAME	TYPE	KIND	POW.	ACC.	PP	RANGE
TM00	Mega Punch	Normal	Physical	80	85	20	Normal
TM01	Mega Kick	Normal	Physical	120	75	5	Normal
TM06	Fly	Flying	Physical	90	95	15	Normal
TM08	Hyper Beam	Normal	Special	150	90	5	Normal
TM09	Giga Impact	Normal	Physical	150	90	5	Normal
TM10	Magical Leaf	Grass	Special	60	—	20	Normal
TM11	Solar Beam	Grass	Special	120	100	10	Normal
TM17	Light Screen	Psychic	Status	—	—	30	Your Side
TM18	Reflect	Psychic	Status	—	—	20	Your Side
TM19	Safeguard	Normal	Status	—	—	25	Your Side
TM21	Rest	Psychic	Status	—	—	10	Self
TM24	Snore	Normal	Special	50	100	15	Normal
TM25	Protect	Normal	Status	—	—	10	Self
TM29	Charm	Fairy	Status	—	100	20	Normal
TM30	Steel Wing	Steel	Physical	70	90	25	Normal
TM31	Attract	Normal	Status	—	100	15	Normal
TM33	Rain Dance	Water	Status	—	—	5	Both Sides
TM34	Sunny Day	Fire	Status	—	—	5	Both Sides
TM39	Facade	Normal	Physical	70	100	20	Normal
TM40	Swift	Normal	Special	60	—	20	Many Others
TM41	Helping Hand	Normal	Status	—	—	20	1 Ally
TM43	Brick Break	Fighting	Physical	75	100	15	Normal
TM44	Imprison	Psychic	Status	—	—	10	Self
TM59	Fling	Dark	Physical	—	100	10	Normal
TM63	Drain Punch	Fighting	Physical	75	100	10	Normal
TM76	Round	Normal	Special	60	100	15	Normal
TM79	Retaliate	Normal	Physical	70	100	5	Normal
TM87	Draining Kiss	Fairy	Special	50	100	10	Normal
TM92	Mystical Fire	Fire	Special	75	100	10	Normal
TM95	Air Slash	Flying	Special	75	95	15	Normal
TM96	Smart Strike	Steel	Physical	70	—	10	Normal

TR MOVES

NO.	NAME	TYPE	KIND	POW.	ACC.	PP	RANGE
TR01	Body Slam	Normal	Physical	85	100	15	Normal
TR02	Flamethrower	Fire	Special	90	100	15	Normal
TR11	Psychic	Psychic	Special	90	100	10	Normal
TR14	Metronome	Normal	Status	—	—	10	Self
TR15	Fire Blast	Fire	Special	110	85	5	Normal
TR17	Amnesia	Psychic	Status	—	—	20	Self
TR19	Tri Attack	Normal	Special	80	100	10	Normal
TR20	Substitute	Normal	Status	—	—	10	Self
TR25	Psyshock	Psychic	Special	80	100	10	Normal
TR26	Endure	Normal	Status	—	—	10	Self
TR27	Sleep Talk	Normal	Status	—	—	10	Self
TR29	Baton Pass	Normal	Status	—	—	40	Self
TR30	Encore	Normal	Status	—	100	5	Normal
TR33	Shadow Ball	Ghost	Special	80	100	15	Normal
TR34	Future Sight	Psychic	Special	120	100	10	Normal
TR35	Uproar	Normal	Special	90	100	10	1 Random
TR36	Heat Wave	Fire	Special	95	90	10	Many Others
TR38	Trick	Psychic	Status	—	100	10	Normal
TR42	Hyper Voice	Normal	Special	90	100	10	Many Others
TR56	Aura Sphere	Fighting	Special	80	—	20	Normal
TR68	Nasty Plot	Dark	Status	—	—	20	Self
TR69	Zen Headbutt	Psychic	Physical	80	90	15	Normal
TR77	Grass Knot	Grass	Special	—	100	20	Normal
TR82	Stored Power	Psychic	Special	20	100	10	Normal
TR83	Ally Switch	Psychic	Status	—	—	15	Self
TR85	Work Up	Normal	Status	—	—	30	Self
TR90	Play Rough	Fairy	Physical	90	90	10	Normal
TR92	Dazzling Gleam	Fairy	Special	80	100	10	Many Others

Togekiss — p. 109

ABILITY
Hustle
Serene Grace

HIDDEN ABILITY
Super Luck

SPECIES STRENGTHS
- HP
- ATTACK
- DEFENSE
- SP. ATK
- SP. DEF
- SPEED

DAMAGE TAKEN IN BATTLE

×1	×0.25	×2
×1	×2	×1
×1	×0	×0
×0.5	×1	×0.5
×2	×1	×2
×2	×0.25	×1

Egg Groups: FLYING, FAIRY

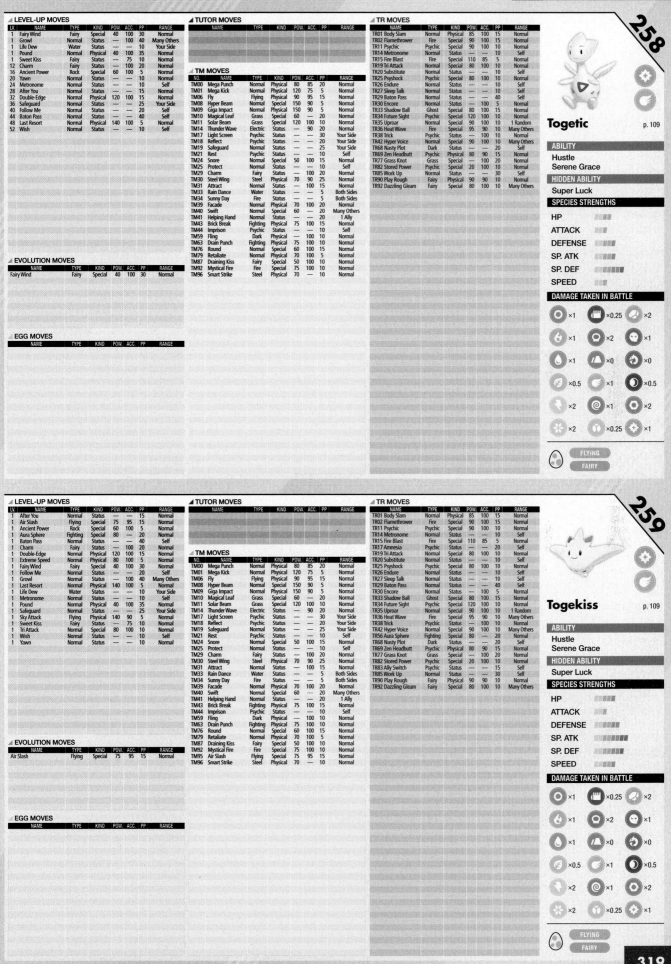

260 Munchlax

p. 110

ABILITY
Pickup
Thick Fat

HIDDEN ABILITY
Gluttony

SPECIES STRENGTHS
HP ▮▮▮▮▮▮▮
ATTACK ▮▮▮▮
DEFENSE ▮▮
SP. ATK ▮▮▮
SP. DEF ▮▮▮▮▮
SPEED ▮

DAMAGE TAKEN IN BATTLE

⊙ ×1	▥ ×2	◐ ×1
❗ ×1	◑ ×1	◉ ×0
◊ ×1	◭ ×1	◖ ×1
◿ ×1	❀ ×1	◗ ×1
×1	◉ ×1	◎ ×1
❗ ×1	◉ ×1	✦ ×1

NO EGGS

LEVEL-UP MOVES

LV.	NAME	TYPE	KIND	POW.	ACC.	PP	RANGE
1	Lick	Ghost	Physical	30	100	30	Normal
1	Tackle	Normal	Physical	40	100	35	Normal
4	Defense Curl	Normal	Status	—	—	40	Self
8	Recycle	Normal	Status	—	—	10	Self
12	Covet	Normal	Physical	60	100	25	Normal
16	Bite	Dark	Physical	60	100	25	Normal
20	Stockpile	Normal	Status	—	—	20	Self
20	Swallow	Normal	Status	—	—	10	Self
24	Screech	Normal	Status	—	85	40	Normal
28	Body Slam	Normal	Physical	85	100	15	Normal
32	Fling	Dark	Physical	—	100	10	Normal
36	Amnesia	Psychic	Status	—	—	20	Self
40	Metronome	Normal	Status	—	—	10	Self
44	Flail	Normal	Physical	—	100	15	Normal
48	Belly Drum	Normal	Status	—	—	10	Self
52	Last Resort	Normal	Physical	140	100	5	Normal

EVOLUTION MOVES

NAME	TYPE	KIND	POW.	ACC.	PP	RANGE

EGG MOVES

NAME	TYPE	KIND	POW.	ACC.	PP	RANGE
Belch	Poison	Special	120	90	10	Normal
Counter	Fighting	Physical	—	100	20	Varies
Curse	Ghost	Status	—	—	10	Varies
Double-Edge	Normal	Physical	120	100	15	Normal
Fissure	Ground	Physical	—	30	5	Normal

TUTOR MOVES

NAME	TYPE	KIND	POW.	ACC.	PP	RANGE

TM MOVES

NO.	NAME	TYPE	KIND	POW.	ACC.	PP	RANGE
TM00	Mega Punch	Normal	Physical	80	85	20	Normal
TM01	Mega Kick	Normal	Physical	120	75	5	Normal
TM02	Pay Day	Normal	Physical	40	100	20	Normal
TM03	Fire Punch	Fire	Physical	75	100	15	Normal
TM04	Ice Punch	Ice	Physical	75	100	15	Normal
TM05	Thunder Punch	Electric	Physical	75	100	15	Normal
TM11	Solar Beam	Grass	Special	120	100	10	Normal
TM16	Screech	Normal	Status	—	85	40	Normal
TM20	Self-Destruct	Normal	Physical	200	100	5	All Others
TM21	Rest	Psychic	Status	—	—	10	Self
TM22	Rock Slide	Rock	Physical	75	90	10	Many Others
TM24	Snore	Normal	Special	50	100	15	Normal
TM25	Protect	Normal	Status	—	—	10	Self
TM27	Icy Wind	Ice	Special	55	95	15	Many Others
TM29	Charm	Fairy	Status	—	100	20	Normal
TM31	Attract	Normal	Status	—	100	15	Normal
TM32	Sandstorm	Rock	Status	—	—	10	Both Sides
TM33	Rain Dance	Water	Status	—	—	5	Both Sides
TM34	Sunny Day	Fire	Status	—	—	5	Both Sides
TM36	Whirlpool	Water	Special	35	85	15	Normal
TM39	Facade	Normal	Physical	70	100	20	Normal
TM43	Brick Break	Fighting	Physical	75	100	15	Normal
TM48	Rock Tomb	Rock	Physical	60	95	15	Normal
TM59	Fling	Dark	Physical	—	100	10	Normal
TM76	Round	Normal	Special	60	100	15	Normal
TM79	Retaliate	Normal	Physical	70	100	5	Normal
TM81	Bulldoze	Ground	Physical	60	100	20	All Others
TM98	Stomping Tantrum	Ground	Physical	75	100	10	Normal

TR MOVES

NO.	NAME	TYPE	KIND	POW.	ACC.	PP	RANGE
TR01	Body Slam	Normal	Physical	85	100	15	Normal
TR02	Flamethrower	Fire	Special	90	100	15	Normal
TR03	Hydro Pump	Water	Special	110	80	5	Normal
TR04	Surf	Water	Special	90	100	15	All Others
TR05	Ice Beam	Ice	Special	90	100	10	Normal
TR06	Blizzard	Ice	Special	110	70	5	Many Others
TR08	Thunderbolt	Electric	Special	90	100	15	Normal
TR09	Thunder	Electric	Special	110	70	10	Normal
TR10	Earthquake	Ground	Physical	100	100	10	All Others
TR11	Psychic	Psychic	Special	90	100	10	Normal
TR14	Metronome	Normal	Status	—	—	10	Self
TR15	Fire Blast	Fire	Special	110	85	5	Normal
TR17	Amnesia	Psychic	Status	—	—	20	Self
TR20	Substitute	Normal	Status	—	—	10	Self
TR26	Endure	Normal	Status	—	—	10	Self
TR27	Sleep Talk	Normal	Status	—	—	10	Self
TR30	Encore	Normal	Status	—	100	5	Normal
TR33	Shadow Ball	Ghost	Special	80	100	15	Normal
TR35	Uproar	Normal	Special	90	100	10	1 Random
TR39	Superpower	Fighting	Physical	120	100	5	Normal
TR42	Hyper Voice	Normal	Special	90	100	10	Many Others
TR59	Seed Bomb	Grass	Physical	80	100	15	Normal
TR69	Zen Headbutt	Psychic	Physical	80	90	15	Normal
TR73	Gunk Shot	Poison	Physical	120	80	5	Normal
TR85	Work Up	Normal	Status	—	—	30	Self

---

261 Snorlax

p. 110

ABILITY
Immunity
Thick Fat

HIDDEN ABILITY
Gluttony

SPECIES STRENGTHS
HP ▮▮▮▮▮▮▮▮▮▮
ATTACK ▮▮▮▮▮▮▮
DEFENSE ▮▮▮
SP. ATK ▮▮▮▮
SP. DEF ▮▮▮▮▮▮▮
SPEED ▮▮

DAMAGE TAKEN IN BATTLE

⊙ ×1	▥ ×2	◐ ×1
❗ ×1	◑ ×1	◉ ×0
◊ ×1	◭ ×1	◖ ×1
◿ ×1	❀ ×1	◗ ×1
×1	◉ ×1	◎ ×1
❗ ×1	◉ ×1	✦ ×1

MONSTER

LEVEL-UP MOVES

LV.	NAME	TYPE	KIND	POW.	ACC.	PP	RANGE
1	Block	Normal	Status	—	—	5	Normal
1	Covet	Normal	Physical	60	100	25	Normal
1	Defense Curl	Normal	Status	—	—	40	Self
1	Flail	Normal	Physical	—	100	15	Normal
1	Fling	Dark	Physical	—	100	10	Normal
1	Last Resort	Normal	Physical	140	100	5	Normal
1	Lick	Ghost	Physical	30	100	30	Normal
1	Metronome	Normal	Status	—	—	10	Self
1	Recycle	Normal	Status	—	—	10	Self
1	Screech	Normal	Status	—	85	40	Normal
1	Stockpile	Normal	Status	—	—	20	Self
1	Swallow	Normal	Status	—	—	10	Self
1	Tackle	Normal	Physical	40	100	35	Normal
12	Yawn	Normal	Status	—	—	10	Normal
16	Bite	Dark	Physical	60	100	25	Normal
20	Rest	Psychic	Status	—	—	10	Self
20	Sleep Talk	Normal	Status	—	—	10	Self
20	Snore	Normal	Special	50	100	15	Normal
24	Crunch	Dark	Physical	80	100	15	Normal
28	Body Slam	Normal	Physical	85	100	15	Normal
32	Heavy Slam	Steel	Physical	—	100	10	Normal
36	Amnesia	Psychic	Status	—	—	20	Self
40	High Horsepower	Ground	Physical	95	95	10	Normal
44	Hammer Arm	Fighting	Physical	100	90	10	Normal
48	Belly Drum	Normal	Status	—	—	10	Self
52	Belch	Poison	Special	120	90	10	Normal
56	Giga Impact	Normal	Physical	150	90	5	Normal

EVOLUTION MOVES

NAME	TYPE	KIND	POW.	ACC.	PP	RANGE

EGG MOVES

NAME	TYPE	KIND	POW.	ACC.	PP	RANGE
Counter	Fighting	Physical	—	100	20	Varies
Curse	Ghost	Status	—	—	10	Varies
Double-Edge	Normal	Physical	120	100	15	Normal
Fissure	Ground	Physical	—	30	5	Normal
Gastro Acid	Poison	Status	—	100	10	Normal

TUTOR MOVES

NAME	TYPE	KIND	POW.	ACC.	PP	RANGE

TM MOVES

NO.	NAME	TYPE	KIND	POW.	ACC.	PP	RANGE
TM00	Mega Punch	Normal	Physical	80	85	20	Normal
TM01	Mega Kick	Normal	Physical	120	75	5	Normal
TM02	Pay Day	Normal	Physical	40	100	20	Normal
TM03	Fire Punch	Fire	Physical	75	100	15	Normal
TM04	Ice Punch	Ice	Physical	75	100	15	Normal
TM05	Thunder Punch	Electric	Physical	75	100	15	Normal
TM08	Hyper Beam	Normal	Special	150	90	5	Normal
TM09	Giga Impact	Normal	Physical	150	90	5	Normal
TM11	Solar Beam	Grass	Special	120	100	10	Normal
TM16	Screech	Normal	Status	—	85	40	Normal
TM20	Self-Destruct	Normal	Physical	200	—	5	All Others
TM21	Rest	Psychic	Status	—	—	10	Self
TM22	Rock Slide	Rock	Physical	75	90	10	Many Others
TM24	Snore	Normal	Special	50	100	15	Normal
TM25	Protect	Normal	Status	—	—	10	Self
TM27	Icy Wind	Ice	Special	55	95	15	Many Others
TM29	Charm	Fairy	Status	—	100	20	Normal
TM31	Attract	Normal	Status	—	100	15	Normal
TM32	Sandstorm	Rock	Status	—	—	10	Both Sides
TM33	Rain Dance	Water	Status	—	—	5	Both Sides
TM34	Sunny Day	Fire	Status	—	—	5	Both Sides
TM36	Whirlpool	Water	Special	35	85	15	Normal
TM39	Facade	Normal	Physical	70	100	20	Normal
TM43	Brick Break	Fighting	Physical	75	100	15	Normal
TM48	Rock Tomb	Rock	Physical	60	95	15	Normal
TM59	Fling	Dark	Physical	—	100	10	Normal
TM76	Round	Normal	Special	60	100	15	Normal
TM79	Retaliate	Normal	Physical	70	100	5	Normal
TM81	Bulldoze	Ground	Physical	60	100	20	All Others
TM98	Stomping Tantrum	Ground	Physical	75	100	10	Normal

TR MOVES

NO.	NAME	TYPE	KIND	POW.	ACC.	PP	RANGE
TR01	Body Slam	Normal	Physical	85	100	15	Normal
TR02	Flamethrower	Fire	Special	90	100	15	Normal
TR03	Hydro Pump	Water	Special	110	80	5	Normal
TR04	Surf	Water	Special	90	100	15	All Others
TR05	Ice Beam	Ice	Special	90	100	10	Normal
TR06	Blizzard	Ice	Special	110	70	5	Many Others
TR08	Thunderbolt	Electric	Special	90	100	15	Normal
TR09	Thunder	Electric	Special	110	70	10	Normal
TR10	Earthquake	Ground	Physical	100	100	10	All Others
TR11	Psychic	Psychic	Special	90	100	10	Normal
TR14	Metronome	Normal	Status	—	—	10	Self
TR15	Fire Blast	Fire	Special	110	85	5	Normal
TR17	Amnesia	Psychic	Status	—	—	20	Self
TR20	Substitute	Normal	Status	—	—	10	Self
TR24	Outrage	Dragon	Physical	120	100	10	1 Random
TR26	Endure	Normal	Status	—	—	10	Self
TR27	Sleep Talk	Normal	Status	—	—	10	Self
TR30	Encore	Normal	Status	—	100	5	Normal
TR32	Crunch	Dark	Physical	80	100	15	Normal
TR33	Shadow Ball	Ghost	Special	80	100	15	Normal
TR35	Uproar	Normal	Special	90	100	10	1 Random
TR39	Superpower	Fighting	Physical	120	100	5	Normal
TR42	Hyper Voice	Normal	Special	90	100	10	Many Others
TR59	Seed Bomb	Grass	Physical	80	100	15	Normal
TR64	Focus Blast	Fighting	Special	120	70	5	Normal
TR69	Zen Headbutt	Psychic	Physical	80	90	15	Normal
TR73	Gunk Shot	Poison	Physical	120	80	5	Normal
TR74	Iron Head	Steel	Physical	80	100	15	Normal
TR79	Heavy Slam	Steel	Physical	—	100	10	Normal
TR85	Work Up	Normal	Status	—	—	30	Self
TR86	Wild Charge	Electric	Physical	90	100	15	Normal
TR88	Heat Crash	Fire	Physical	—	100	10	Normal
TR93	Darkest Lariat	Dark	Physical	85	100	10	Normal
TR94	High Horsepower	Ground	Physical	95	95	10	Normal
TR99	Body Press	Fighting	Physical	80	100	10	Normal

262

Cottonee p. 110

LEVEL-UP MOVES

LV.	NAME	TYPE	KIND	POW.	ACC.	PP	RANGE
1	Absorb	Grass	Special	20	100	25	Normal
1	Helping Hand	Normal	Status	—	—	20	1 Ally
3	Fairy Wind	Fairy	Special	40	100	30	Normal
6	Stun Spore	Grass	Status	—	75	30	Normal
12	Mega Drain	Grass	Special	40	100	15	Normal
15	Razor Leaf	Grass	Physical	55	95	25	Many Others
18	Growth	Normal	Status	—	—	20	Self
21	Poison Powder	Poison	Status	—	75	35	Normal
24	Giga Drain	Grass	Special	75	100	10	Normal
27	Charm	Fairy	Status	—	100	20	Normal
30	Leech Seed	Grass	Status	—	90	10	Normal
33	Cotton Spore	Grass	Status	—	100	40	Many Others
36	Energy Ball	Grass	Special	90	100	10	Normal
39	Sunny Day	Fire	Status	—	—	5	Both Sides
42	Endeavor	Normal	Physical	—	100	5	Normal
45	Cotton Guard	Grass	Status	—	—	10	Self
48	Solar Beam	Grass	Special	120	100	10	Normal

EVOLUTION MOVES

NAME	TYPE	KIND	POW.	ACC.	PP	RANGE

EGG MOVES

NAME	TYPE	KIND	POW.	ACC.	PP	RANGE
Memento	Dark	Status	—	100	10	Normal
Nature Power	Normal	Status	—	—	20	Normal
Switcheroo	Dark	Status	—	100	10	Normal
Tickle	Normal	Status	—	100	20	Normal
Worry Seed	Grass	Status	—	100	10	Normal

TUTOR MOVES

NAME	TYPE	KIND	POW.	ACC.	PP	RANGE

TM MOVES

NO.	NAME	TYPE	KIND	POW.	ACC.	PP	RANGE
TM11	Solar Beam	Grass	Special	120	100	10	Normal
TM19	Safeguard	Normal	Status	—	—	25	Your Side
TM21	Rest	Psychic	Status	—	—	10	Self
TM24	Snore	Normal	Special	50	100	15	Normal
TM25	Protect	Normal	Status	—	—	10	Self
TM28	Giga Drain	Grass	Special	75	100	10	Normal
TM29	Charm	Fairy	Status	—	100	20	Normal
TM31	Attract	Normal	Status	—	100	15	Normal
TM34	Sunny Day	Fire	Status	—	—	5	Both Sides
TM37	Beat Up	Dark	Physical	—	100	10	Normal
TM39	Facade	Normal	Physical	70	100	20	Normal
TM40	Swift	Normal	Special	60	—	20	Many Others
TM41	Helping Hand	Normal	Status	—	—	20	1 Ally
TM47	Fake Tears	Dark	Status	—	100	20	Normal
TM76	Round	Normal	Special	60	100	15	Normal
TM88	Grassy Terrain	Grass	Status	—	—	10	Both Sides
TM89	Misty Terrain	Fairy	Status	—	—	10	Both Sides

TR MOVES

NAME	TYPE	KIND	POW.	ACC.	PP	RANGE
TR20 Substitute	Normal	Status	—	—	10	Self
TR26 Endure	Normal	Status	—	—	10	Self
TR27 Sleep Talk	Normal	Status	—	—	10	Self
TR30 Encore	Normal	Status	—	100	5	Normal
TR37 Taunt	Dark	Status	—	100	20	Normal
TR59 Seed Bomb	Grass	Physical	80	100	15	Normal
TR65 Energy Ball	Grass	Special	90	100	10	Normal
TR77 Grass Knot	Grass	Special	—	100	20	Normal
TR92 Dazzling Gleam	Fairy	Special	80	100	10	Many Others

ABILITY
Prankster
Infiltrator

HIDDEN ABILITY
Chlorophyll

SPECIES STRENGTHS
- HP
- ATTACK
- DEFENSE
- SP. ATK
- SP. DEF
- SPEED

DAMAGE TAKEN IN BATTLE

×1 · ×0.5 · ×1
×2 · ×4 · ×2
×0.5 · ×0.5 · ×0
×0.5 · ×2 · ×0.5
×0.5 · ×1 · ×2
×2 · ×1 · ×1

GRASS
FAIRY

263

Whimsicott p. 110

LEVEL-UP MOVES

LV.	NAME	TYPE	KIND	POW.	ACC.	PP	RANGE
1	Absorb	Grass	Special	20	100	25	Normal
1	Charm	Fairy	Status	—	100	20	Normal
1	Cotton Guard	Grass	Status	—	—	10	Self
1	Cotton Spore	Grass	Status	—	100	40	Many Others
1	Endeavor	Normal	Physical	—	100	5	Normal
1	Energy Ball	Grass	Special	90	100	10	Normal
1	Fairy Wind	Fairy	Special	40	100	30	Normal
1	Giga Drain	Grass	Special	75	100	10	Normal
1	Growth	Normal	Status	—	—	20	Self
1	Gust	Flying	Special	40	100	35	Normal
1	Helping Hand	Normal	Status	—	—	20	1 Ally
1	Hurricane	Flying	Special	110	70	10	Normal
1	Leech Seed	Grass	Status	—	90	10	Normal
1	Mega Drain	Grass	Special	40	100	15	Normal
1	Memento	Dark	Status	—	100	10	Normal
1	Moonblast	Fairy	Special	95	100	15	Normal
1	Poison Powder	Poison	Status	—	75	35	Normal
1	Razor Leaf	Grass	Physical	55	95	25	Many Others
1	Solar Beam	Grass	Special	120	100	10	Normal
1	Stun Spore	Grass	Status	—	75	30	Normal
1	Sunny Day	Fire	Status	—	—	5	Both Sides
1	Tailwind	Flying	Status	—	—	15	Your Side

EVOLUTION MOVES

NAME	TYPE	KIND	POW.	ACC.	PP	RANGE

EGG MOVES

NAME	TYPE	KIND	POW.	ACC.	PP	RANGE

TUTOR MOVES

NAME	TYPE	KIND	POW.	ACC.	PP	RANGE

TM MOVES

NO.	NAME	TYPE	KIND	POW.	ACC.	PP	RANGE
TM08	Hyper Beam	Normal	Special	150	90	5	Normal
TM09	Giga Impact	Normal	Physical	150	90	5	Normal
TM11	Solar Beam	Grass	Special	120	100	10	Normal
TM17	Light Screen	Psychic	Status	—	—	30	Your Side
TM19	Safeguard	Normal	Status	—	—	25	Your Side
TM21	Rest	Psychic	Status	—	—	10	Self
TM23	Thief	Dark	Physical	60	100	25	Normal
TM24	Snore	Normal	Special	50	100	15	Normal
TM25	Protect	Normal	Status	—	—	10	Self
TM28	Giga Drain	Grass	Special	75	100	10	Normal
TM29	Charm	Fairy	Status	—	100	20	Normal
TM31	Attract	Normal	Status	—	100	15	Normal
TM34	Sunny Day	Fire	Status	—	—	5	Both Sides
TM37	Beat Up	Dark	Physical	—	100	10	Normal
TM39	Facade	Normal	Physical	70	100	20	Normal
TM40	Swift	Normal	Special	60	—	20	Many Others
TM41	Helping Hand	Normal	Status	—	—	20	1 Ally
TM47	Fake Tears	Dark	Status	—	100	20	Normal
TM56	U-turn	Bug	Physical	70	100	20	Normal
TM59	Fling	Dark	Physical	—	100	10	Normal
TM70	Trick Room	Psychic	Status	—	—	5	Both Sides
TM76	Round	Normal	Special	60	100	15	Normal
TM88	Grassy Terrain	Grass	Status	—	—	10	Both Sides
TM89	Misty Terrain	Fairy	Status	—	—	10	Both Sides

TR MOVES

NAME	TYPE	KIND	POW.	ACC.	PP	RANGE
TR11 Psychic	Psychic	Special	90	100	10	Normal
TR20 Substitute	Normal	Status	—	—	10	Self
TR26 Endure	Normal	Status	—	—	10	Self
TR27 Sleep Talk	Normal	Status	—	—	10	Self
TR30 Encore	Normal	Status	—	100	5	Normal
TR33 Shadow Ball	Ghost	Special	80	100	15	Normal
TR37 Taunt	Dark	Status	—	100	20	Normal
TR59 Seed Bomb	Grass	Physical	80	100	15	Normal
TR65 Energy Ball	Grass	Special	90	100	10	Normal
TR77 Grass Knot	Grass	Special	—	100	20	Normal
TR89 Hurricane	Flying	Special	110	70	10	Normal
TR90 Play Rough	Fairy	Physical	90	90	10	Normal
TR92 Dazzling Gleam	Fairy	Special	80	100	10	Many Others

ABILITY
Prankster
Infiltrator

HIDDEN ABILITY
Chlorophyll

SPECIES STRENGTHS
- HP
- ATTACK
- DEFENSE
- SP. ATK
- SP. DEF
- SPEED

DAMAGE TAKEN IN BATTLE

×1 · ×0.5 · ×1
×2 · ×4 · ×2
×0.5 · ×0.5 · ×0
×0.5 · ×2 · ×0.5
×0.5 · ×1 · ×2
×2 · ×1 · ×1

GRASS
FAIRY

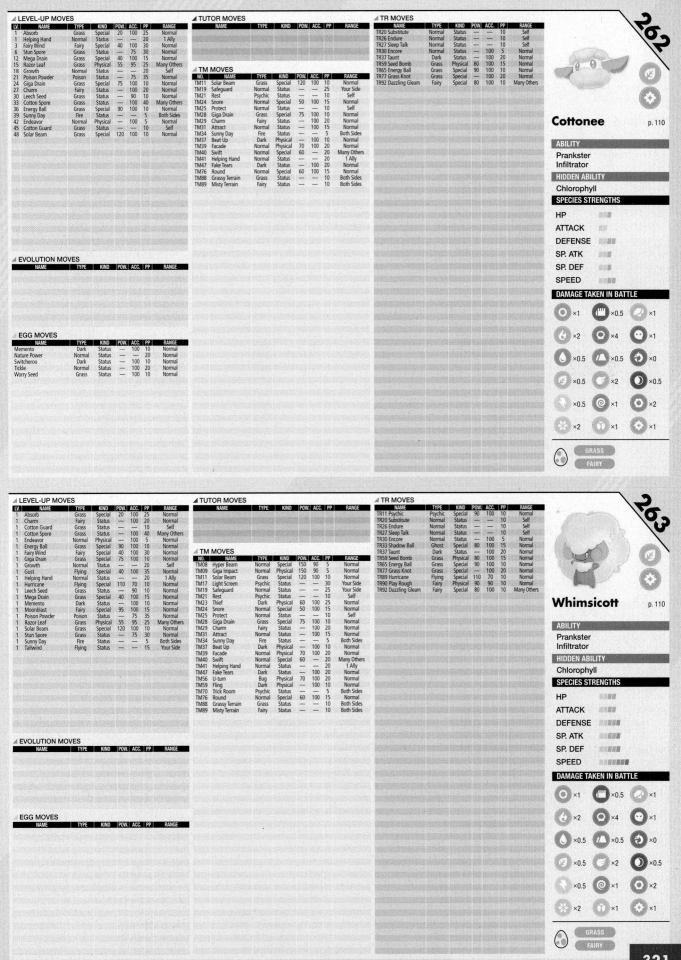

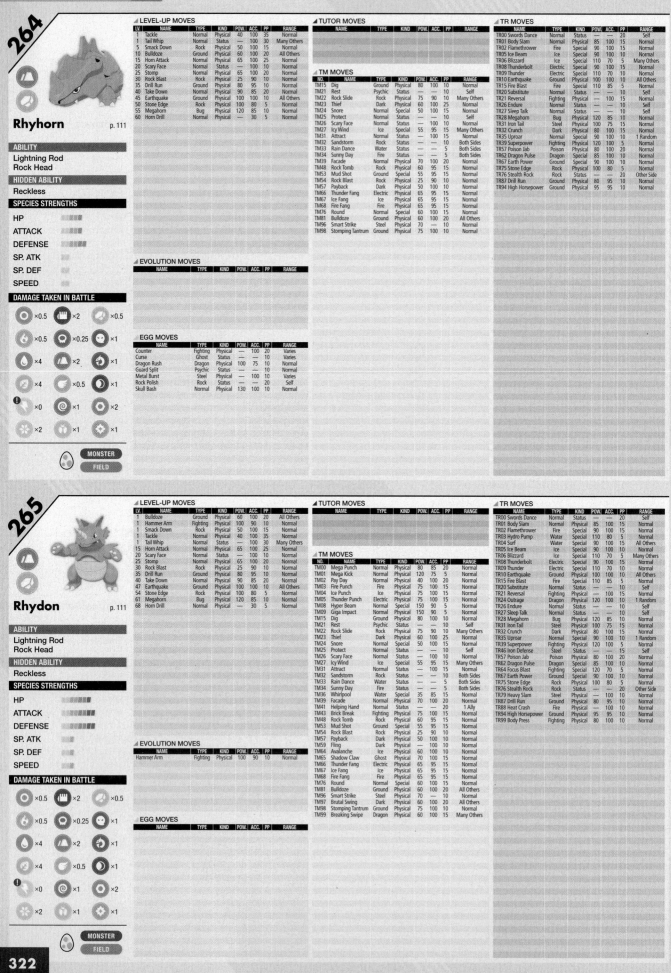

264

Rhyhorn p. 111

ABILITY

Lightning Rod
Rock Head

HIDDEN ABILITY

Reckless

SPECIES STRENGTHS

HP
ATTACK
DEFENSE
SP. ATK
SP. DEF
SPEED

DAMAGE TAKEN IN BATTLE

×0.5 ×2 ×0.5
×0.5 ×0.25 ×1
×4 ×2 ×1
×4 ×0.5 ×1
×0 ×1 ×2
×2 ×1 ×1

MONSTER
FIELD

LEVEL-UP MOVES

LV.	NAME	TYPE	KIND	POW.	ACC.	PP	RANGE
1	Tackle	Normal	Physical	40	100	35	Normal
1	Tail Whip	Normal	Status	—	100	30	Many Others
5	Smack Down	Rock	Physical	50	100	15	Normal
10	Bulldoze	Ground	Physical	60	100	20	All Others
15	Horn Attack	Normal	Physical	65	100	25	Normal
20	Scary Face	Normal	Status	—	100	10	Normal
25	Stomp	Normal	Physical	65	100	20	Normal
30	Rock Blast	Rock	Physical	25	90	10	Normal
35	Drill Run	Ground	Physical	80	95	10	Normal
40	Take Down	Normal	Physical	90	85	20	Normal
45	Earthquake	Ground	Physical	100	100	10	All Others
50	Stone Edge	Rock	Physical	100	80	5	Normal
55	Megahorn	Bug	Physical	120	85	10	Normal
60	Horn Drill	Normal	Physical	—	30	5	Normal

EVOLUTION MOVES

NAME	TYPE	KIND	POW.	ACC.	PP	RANGE

EGG MOVES

NAME	TYPE	KIND	POW.	ACC.	PP	RANGE
Counter	Fighting	Physical	—	100	20	Varies
Curse	Ghost	Status	—	—	10	Varies
Dragon Rush	Dragon	Physical	100	75	10	Normal
Guard Split	Psychic	Status	—	—	10	Normal
Metal Burst	Steel	Physical	—	100	10	Varies
Rock Polish	Rock	Status	—	—	20	Self
Skull Bash	Normal	Physical	130	100	10	Normal

TUTOR MOVES

NAME	TYPE	KIND	POW.	ACC.	PP	RANGE

TM MOVES

NO.	NAME	TYPE	KIND	POW.	ACC.	PP	RANGE
TM15	Dig	Ground	Physical	80	100	10	Normal
TM21	Rest	Psychic	Status	—	—	10	Self
TM22	Rock Slide	Rock	Physical	75	90	10	Many Others
TM23	Thief	Dark	Physical	60	100	25	Normal
TM24	Snore	Normal	Special	50	100	15	Normal
TM25	Protect	Normal	Status	—	—	10	Self
TM26	Scary Face	Normal	Status	—	100	10	Normal
TM27	Icy Wind	Ice	Special	55	95	15	Many Others
TM31	Attract	Normal	Status	—	100	15	Normal
TM32	Sandstorm	Rock	Status	—	—	10	Both Sides
TM33	Rain Dance	Water	Status	—	—	5	Both Sides
TM34	Sunny Day	Fire	Status	—	—	5	Both Sides
TM39	Facade	Normal	Physical	70	100	20	Normal
TM48	Rock Tomb	Rock	Physical	60	95	15	Normal
TM53	Mud Shot	Ground	Special	55	95	15	Normal
TM54	Rock Blast	Rock	Physical	25	90	10	Normal
TM57	Payback	Dark	Physical	50	100	10	Normal
TM66	Thunder Fang	Electric	Physical	65	95	15	Normal
TM67	Ice Fang	Ice	Physical	65	95	15	Normal
TM68	Fire Fang	Fire	Physical	65	95	15	Normal
TM76	Round	Normal	Special	60	100	15	Normal
TM81	Bulldoze	Ground	Physical	60	100	20	All Others
TM96	Smart Strike	Steel	Physical	70	—	10	Normal
TM98	Stomping Tantrum	Ground	Physical	75	100	10	Normal

TR MOVES

NAME	TYPE	KIND	POW.	ACC.	PP	RANGE
TR00 Swords Dance	Normal	Status	—	—	20	Self
TR01 Body Slam	Normal	Physical	85	100	15	Normal
TR02 Flamethrower	Fire	Special	90	100	15	Normal
TR05 Ice Beam	Ice	Special	90	100	10	Normal
TR06 Blizzard	Ice	Special	110	70	5	Many Others
TR08 Thunderbolt	Electric	Special	90	100	15	Normal
TR09 Thunder	Electric	Special	110	70	10	Normal
TR10 Earthquake	Ground	Physical	100	100	10	All Others
TR15 Fire Blast	Fire	Special	110	85	5	Normal
TR20 Substitute	Normal	Status	—	—	10	Self
TR21 Reversal	Fighting	Physical	—	100	15	Normal
TR26 Endure	Normal	Status	—	—	10	Self
TR27 Sleep Talk	Normal	Status	—	—	10	Self
TR28 Megahorn	Bug	Physical	120	85	10	Normal
TR31 Iron Tail	Steel	Physical	100	75	15	Normal
TR32 Crunch	Dark	Physical	80	100	15	Normal
TR35 Uproar	Normal	Special	90	100	10	1 Random
TR39 Superpower	Fighting	Physical	120	100	5	Normal
TR57 Poison Jab	Poison	Physical	80	100	20	Normal
TR62 Dragon Pulse	Dragon	Special	85	100	10	Normal
TR67 Earth Power	Ground	Special	90	100	10	Normal
TR75 Stone Edge	Rock	Physical	100	80	5	Normal
TR76 Stealth Rock	Rock	Status	—	—	20	Other Side
TR87 Drill Run	Ground	Physical	80	95	10	Normal
TR94 High Horsepower	Ground	Physical	95	95	10	Normal

265

Rhydon p. 111

ABILITY

Lightning Rod
Rock Head

HIDDEN ABILITY

Reckless

SPECIES STRENGTHS

HP
ATTACK
DEFENSE
SP. ATK
SP. DEF
SPEED

DAMAGE TAKEN IN BATTLE

×0.5 ×2 ×0.5
×0.5 ×0.25 ×1
×4 ×2 ×1
×4 ×0.5 ×1
×0 ×1 ×2
×2 ×1 ×1

MONSTER
FIELD

LEVEL-UP MOVES

LV.	NAME	TYPE	KIND	POW.	ACC.	PP	RANGE
1	Bulldoze	Ground	Physical	60	100	20	All Others
1	Hammer Arm	Fighting	Physical	100	90	10	Normal
1	Smack Down	Rock	Physical	50	100	15	Normal
1	Tackle	Normal	Physical	40	100	35	Normal
1	Tail Whip	Normal	Status	—	100	30	Many Others
15	Horn Attack	Normal	Physical	65	100	25	Normal
20	Scary Face	Normal	Status	—	100	10	Normal
25	Stomp	Normal	Physical	65	100	20	Normal
30	Rock Blast	Rock	Physical	25	90	10	Normal
35	Drill Run	Ground	Physical	80	95	10	Normal
40	Take Down	Normal	Physical	90	85	20	Normal
47	Earthquake	Ground	Physical	100	100	10	All Others
54	Stone Edge	Rock	Physical	100	80	5	Normal
61	Megahorn	Bug	Physical	120	85	10	Normal
68	Horn Drill	Normal	Physical	—	30	5	Normal

EVOLUTION MOVES

NAME	TYPE	KIND	POW.	ACC.	PP	RANGE
Hammer Arm	Fighting	Physical	100	90	10	Normal

EGG MOVES

NAME	TYPE	KIND	POW.	ACC.	PP	RANGE

TUTOR MOVES

NAME	TYPE	KIND	POW.	ACC.	PP	RANGE

TM MOVES

NO.	NAME	TYPE	KIND	POW.	ACC.	PP	RANGE
TM00	Mega Punch	Normal	Physical	80	85	20	Normal
TM01	Mega Kick	Normal	Physical	120	75	5	Normal
TM02	Pay Day	Normal	Physical	40	100	20	Normal
TM03	Fire Punch	Fire	Physical	75	100	15	Normal
TM04	Ice Punch	Ice	Physical	75	100	15	Normal
TM05	Thunder Punch	Electric	Physical	75	100	15	Normal
TM08	Hyper Beam	Normal	Special	150	90	5	Normal
TM09	Giga Impact	Normal	Physical	150	90	5	Normal
TM15	Dig	Ground	Physical	80	100	10	Normal
TM21	Rest	Psychic	Status	—	—	10	Self
TM22	Rock Slide	Rock	Physical	75	90	10	Many Others
TM23	Thief	Dark	Physical	60	100	25	Normal
TM24	Snore	Normal	Special	50	100	15	Normal
TM25	Protect	Normal	Status	—	—	10	Self
TM26	Scary Face	Normal	Status	—	100	10	Normal
TM27	Icy Wind	Ice	Special	55	95	15	Many Others
TM31	Attract	Normal	Status	—	100	15	Normal
TM32	Sandstorm	Rock	Status	—	—	10	Both Sides
TM33	Rain Dance	Water	Status	—	—	5	Both Sides
TM34	Sunny Day	Fire	Status	—	—	5	Both Sides
TM36	Whirlpool	Water	Special	35	85	15	Normal
TM39	Facade	Normal	Physical	70	100	20	Normal
TM41	Helping Hand	Normal	Status	—	—	20	1 Ally
TM43	Brick Break	Fighting	Physical	75	100	15	Normal
TM48	Rock Tomb	Rock	Physical	60	95	15	Normal
TM53	Mud Shot	Ground	Special	55	95	15	Normal
TM54	Rock Blast	Rock	Physical	25	90	10	Normal
TM57	Payback	Dark	Physical	50	100	10	Normal
TM59	Fling	Dark	Physical	—	100	10	Normal
TM64	Avalanche	Ice	Physical	60	100	10	Normal
TM65	Shadow Claw	Ghost	Physical	70	100	15	Normal
TM66	Thunder Fang	Electric	Physical	65	95	15	Normal
TM67	Ice Fang	Ice	Physical	65	95	15	Normal
TM68	Fire Fang	Fire	Physical	65	95	15	Normal
TM76	Round	Normal	Special	60	100	15	Normal
TM81	Bulldoze	Ground	Physical	60	100	20	All Others
TM96	Smart Strike	Steel	Physical	70	—	10	Normal
TM97	Brutal Swing	Dark	Physical	60	100	20	All Others
TM98	Stomping Tantrum	Ground	Physical	75	100	10	Normal
TM99	Breaking Swipe	Dragon	Physical	60	100	15	Many Others

TR MOVES

NAME	TYPE	KIND	POW.	ACC.	PP	RANGE
TR00 Swords Dance	Normal	Status	—	—	20	Self
TR01 Body Slam	Normal	Physical	85	100	15	Normal
TR02 Flamethrower	Fire	Special	90	100	15	Normal
TR03 Hydro Pump	Water	Special	110	80	5	Normal
TR04 Surf	Water	Special	90	100	15	All Others
TR05 Ice Beam	Ice	Special	90	100	10	Normal
TR06 Blizzard	Ice	Special	110	70	5	Many Others
TR08 Thunderbolt	Electric	Special	90	100	15	Normal
TR09 Thunder	Electric	Special	110	70	10	Normal
TR10 Earthquake	Ground	Physical	100	100	10	All Others
TR15 Fire Blast	Fire	Special	110	85	5	Normal
TR20 Substitute	Normal	Status	—	—	10	Self
TR21 Reversal	Fighting	Physical	—	100	15	Normal
TR24 Outrage	Dragon	Physical	120	100	10	1 Random
TR26 Endure	Normal	Status	—	—	10	Self
TR27 Sleep Talk	Normal	Status	—	—	10	Self
TR28 Megahorn	Bug	Physical	120	85	10	Normal
TR31 Iron Tail	Steel	Physical	100	75	15	Normal
TR32 Crunch	Dark	Physical	80	100	15	Normal
TR35 Uproar	Normal	Special	90	100	10	1 Random
TR39 Superpower	Fighting	Physical	120	100	5	Normal
TR46 Iron Defense	Steel	Status	—	—	15	Self
TR57 Poison Jab	Poison	Physical	80	100	20	Normal
TR62 Dragon Pulse	Dragon	Special	85	100	10	Normal
TR64 Focus Blast	Fighting	Special	120	70	5	Normal
TR67 Earth Power	Ground	Special	90	100	10	Normal
TR75 Stone Edge	Rock	Physical	100	80	5	Normal
TR76 Stealth Rock	Rock	Status	—	—	20	Other Side
TR79 Heavy Slam	Steel	Physical	—	100	10	Normal
TR87 Drill Run	Ground	Physical	80	95	10	Normal
TR88 Heat Crash	Fire	Physical	—	100	10	Normal
TR94 High Horsepower	Ground	Physical	95	95	10	Normal
TR99 Body Press	Fighting	Physical	80	100	10	Normal

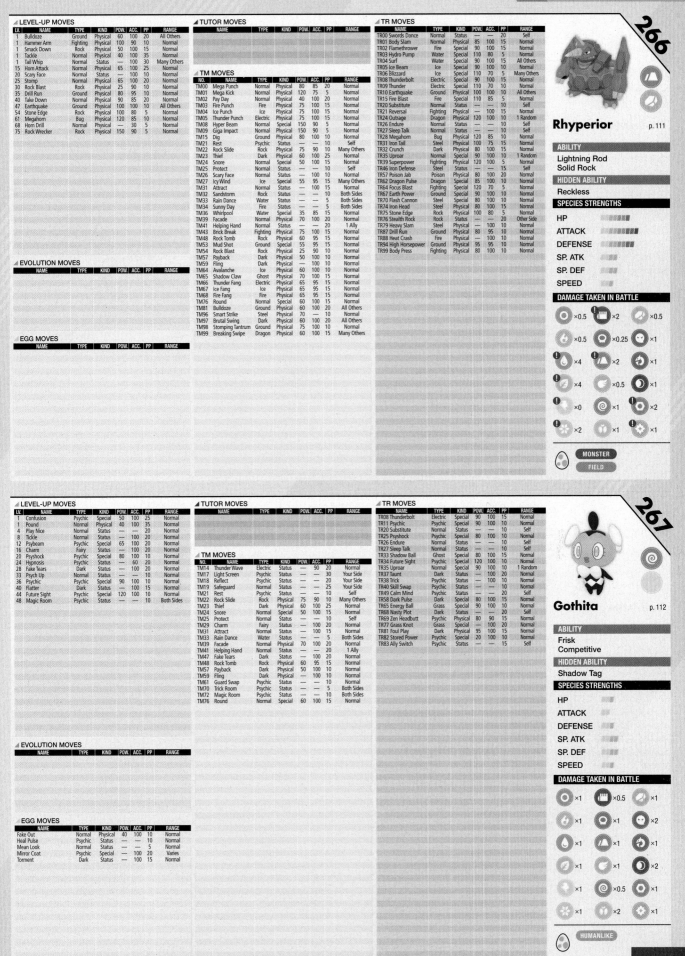

266 — Rhyperior — p. 111

LEVEL-UP MOVES

LV.	NAME	TYPE	KIND	POW.	ACC.	PP	RANGE
1	Bulldoze	Ground	Physical	60	100	20	All Others
1	Hammer Arm	Fighting	Physical	100	90	10	Normal
1	Smack Down	Rock	Physical	50	100	15	Normal
1	Tackle	Normal	Physical	40	100	35	Normal
1	Tail Whip	Normal	Status	—	100	30	Many Others
15	Horn Attack	Normal	Physical	65	100	25	Normal
20	Scary Face	Normal	Status	—	100	10	Normal
25	Stomp	Normal	Physical	65	100	20	Normal
30	Rock Blast	Rock	Physical	25	90	10	Normal
35	Drill Run	Ground	Physical	80	95	10	Normal
40	Take Down	Normal	Physical	90	85	20	Normal
47	Earthquake	Ground	Physical	100	100	10	All Others
54	Stone Edge	Rock	Physical	100	80	5	Normal
61	Megahorn	Bug	Physical	120	85	10	Normal
68	Horn Drill	Normal	Physical	—	30	5	Normal
75	Rock Wrecker	Rock	Physical	150	90	5	Normal

EVOLUTION MOVES

NAME	TYPE	KIND	POW.	ACC.	PP	RANGE

EGG MOVES

NAME	TYPE	KIND	POW.	ACC.	PP	RANGE

TUTOR MOVES

NAME	TYPE	KIND	POW.	ACC.	PP	RANGE

TM MOVES

NO.	NAME	TYPE	KIND	POW.	ACC.	PP	RANGE
TM00	Mega Punch	Normal	Physical	80	85	20	Normal
TM01	Mega Kick	Normal	Physical	120	75	5	Normal
TM02	Pay Day	Normal	Physical	40	100	20	Normal
TM03	Fire Punch	Fire	Physical	75	100	15	Normal
TM04	Ice Punch	Ice	Physical	75	100	15	Normal
TM05	Thunder Punch	Electric	Physical	75	100	15	Normal
TM08	Hyper Beam	Normal	Special	150	90	5	Normal
TM09	Giga Impact	Normal	Physical	150	90	5	Normal
TM15	Dig	Ground	Physical	80	100	10	Normal
TM21	Rest	Psychic	Status	—	—	10	Self
TM22	Rock Slide	Rock	Physical	75	90	10	Many Others
TM23	Thief	Dark	Physical	60	100	25	Normal
TM24	Snore	Normal	Special	50	100	15	Normal
TM25	Protect	Normal	Status	—	—	10	Self
TM26	Scary Face	Normal	Status	—	100	10	Many Others
TM27	Icy Wind	Ice	Special	55	95	15	Many Others
TM31	Attract	Normal	Status	—	100	15	Normal
TM32	Sandstorm	Rock	Status	—	—	10	Both Sides
TM33	Rain Dance	Water	Status	—	—	5	Both Sides
TM34	Sunny Day	Fire	Status	—	—	5	Both Sides
TM36	Whirlpool	Water	Special	35	85	15	Normal
TM39	Facade	Normal	Physical	70	100	20	Normal
TM41	Helping Hand	Normal	Status	—	—	20	1 Ally
TM43	Brick Break	Fighting	Physical	75	100	15	Normal
TM48	Rock Tomb	Rock	Physical	60	95	15	Normal
TM53	Mud Shot	Ground	Special	55	95	15	Normal
TM54	Rock Blast	Rock	Physical	25	90	10	Normal
TM57	Payback	Dark	Physical	50	100	10	Normal
TM59	Fling	Dark	Physical	—	100	10	Normal
TM64	Avalanche	Ice	Physical	60	100	10	Normal
TM65	Shadow Claw	Ghost	Physical	70	100	15	Normal
TM66	Thunder Fang	Electric	Physical	65	95	15	Normal
TM67	Ice Fang	Ice	Physical	65	95	15	Normal
TM68	Fire Fang	Fire	Physical	65	95	15	Normal
TM76	Round	Normal	Special	60	100	15	Normal
TM81	Bulldoze	Ground	Physical	60	100	20	All Others
TM96	Smart Strike	Steel	Physical	70	—	10	Normal
TM97	Brutal Swing	Dark	Physical	60	100	20	All Others
TM98	Stomping Tantrum	Ground	Physical	75	100	10	Normal
TM99	Breaking Swipe	Dragon	Physical	60	100	15	Many Others

TR MOVES

NO.	NAME	TYPE	KIND	POW.	ACC.	PP	RANGE
TR00	Swords Dance	Normal	Status	—	—	20	Self
TR01	Body Slam	Normal	Physical	85	100	15	Normal
TR02	Flamethrower	Fire	Special	90	100	15	Normal
TR03	Hydro Pump	Water	Special	110	80	5	Normal
TR04	Surf	Water	Special	90	100	15	All Others
TR05	Ice Beam	Ice	Special	90	100	10	Normal
TR06	Blizzard	Ice	Special	110	70	5	Many Others
TR08	Thunderbolt	Electric	Special	90	100	15	Normal
TR09	Thunder	Electric	Special	110	70	10	Normal
TR10	Earthquake	Ground	Physical	100	100	10	All Others
TR15	Fire Blast	Fire	Special	110	85	5	Normal
TR20	Substitute	Normal	Status	—	—	10	Self
TR21	Reversal	Fighting	Physical	—	100	15	Normal
TR24	Outrage	Dragon	Physical	120	100	10	1 Random
TR26	Endure	Normal	Status	—	—	10	Self
TR27	Sleep Talk	Normal	Status	—	—	10	Self
TR28	Megahorn	Bug	Physical	120	85	10	Normal
TR31	Iron Tail	Steel	Physical	100	75	15	Normal
TR32	Crunch	Dark	Physical	80	100	15	Normal
TR35	Uproar	Normal	Special	90	100	10	1 Random
TR39	Superpower	Fighting	Physical	120	100	5	Normal
TR46	Iron Defense	Steel	Status	—	—	15	Self
TR57	Poison Jab	Poison	Physical	80	100	20	Normal
TR62	Dragon Pulse	Dragon	Special	85	100	10	Normal
TR64	Focus Blast	Fighting	Special	120	70	5	Normal
TR70	Flash Cannon	Steel	Special	80	100	10	Normal
TR74	Iron Head	Steel	Physical	80	100	15	Normal
TR75	Stone Edge	Rock	Physical	100	80	5	Normal
TR76	Stealth Rock	Rock	Status	—	—	20	Other Side
TR79	Heavy Slam	Steel	Physical	—	100	10	Normal
TR87	Drill Run	Ground	Physical	80	95	10	Normal
TR88	Heat Crash	Fire	Physical	—	100	10	Normal
TR94	High Horsepower	Ground	Physical	95	95	10	Normal
TR99	Body Press	Fighting	Physical	80	100	10	Normal

ABILITY
Lightning Rod
Solid Rock

HIDDEN ABILITY
Reckless

SPECIES STRENGTHS

HP	
ATTACK	
DEFENSE	
SP. ATK	
SP. DEF	
SPEED	

DAMAGE TAKEN IN BATTLE

×0.5 ×2 ×0.5
×0.5 ×0.25 ×1
×4 ×2 ×1
×4 ×0.5 ×1
×0 ×1 ×2
×2 ×1 ×1

MONSTER
FIELD

267 — Gothita — p. 112

LEVEL-UP MOVES

LV.	NAME	TYPE	KIND	POW.	ACC.	PP	RANGE
1	Confusion	Psychic	Special	50	100	25	Normal
1	Pound	Normal	Physical	40	100	35	Normal
4	Play Nice	Normal	Status	—	—	20	Normal
8	Tickle	Normal	Status	—	100	20	Normal
12	Psybeam	Psychic	Special	65	100	20	Normal
16	Charm	Fairy	Status	—	100	20	Normal
20	Psyshock	Psychic	Special	80	100	10	Normal
24	Hypnosis	Psychic	Status	—	60	20	Normal
28	Fake Tears	Dark	Status	—	100	20	Normal
33	Psych Up	Normal	Status	—	—	10	Normal
36	Psychic	Psychic	Special	90	100	10	Normal
40	Flatter	Dark	Status	—	100	15	Normal
44	Future Sight	Psychic	Special	120	100	10	Normal
48	Magic Room	Psychic	Status	—	—	10	Both Sides

EVOLUTION MOVES

NAME	TYPE	KIND	POW.	ACC.	PP	RANGE

EGG MOVES

NAME	TYPE	KIND	POW.	ACC.	PP	RANGE
Fake Out	Normal	Physical	40	100	10	Normal
Heal Pulse	Psychic	Status	—	—	10	Normal
Mean Look	Normal	Status	—	—	5	Normal
Mirror Coat	Psychic	Special	—	100	20	Varies
Torment	Dark	Status	—	100	15	Normal

TUTOR MOVES

NAME	TYPE	KIND	POW.	ACC.	PP	RANGE

TM MOVES

NO.	NAME	TYPE	KIND	POW.	ACC.	PP	RANGE
TM14	Thunder Wave	Electric	Status	—	90	20	Normal
TM17	Light Screen	Psychic	Status	—	—	30	Your Side
TM18	Reflect	Psychic	Status	—	—	20	Your Side
TM19	Safeguard	Normal	Status	—	—	25	Your Side
TM21	Rest	Psychic	Status	—	—	10	Self
TM22	Rock Slide	Rock	Physical	75	90	10	Many Others
TM23	Thief	Dark	Physical	60	100	25	Normal
TM24	Snore	Normal	Special	50	100	15	Normal
TM25	Protect	Normal	Status	—	—	10	Self
TM29	Charm	Fairy	Status	—	100	20	Normal
TM31	Attract	Normal	Status	—	100	15	Normal
TM33	Rain Dance	Water	Status	—	—	5	Both Sides
TM39	Facade	Normal	Physical	70	100	20	Normal
TM41	Helping Hand	Normal	Status	—	—	20	1 Ally
TM47	Fake Tears	Dark	Status	—	100	20	Normal
TM48	Rock Tomb	Rock	Physical	60	95	15	Normal
TM57	Payback	Dark	Physical	50	100	10	Normal
TM59	Fling	Dark	Physical	—	100	10	Normal
TM61	Guard Swap	Psychic	Status	—	—	10	Normal
TM70	Trick Room	Psychic	Status	—	—	5	Both Sides
TM72	Magic Room	Psychic	Status	—	—	10	Both Sides
TM76	Round	Normal	Special	60	100	15	Normal

TR MOVES

NO.	NAME	TYPE	KIND	POW.	ACC.	PP	RANGE
TR08	Thunderbolt	Electric	Special	90	100	15	Normal
TR11	Psychic	Psychic	Special	90	100	10	Normal
TR20	Substitute	Normal	Status	—	—	10	Self
TR25	Psyshock	Psychic	Special	80	100	10	Normal
TR26	Endure	Normal	Status	—	—	10	Self
TR27	Sleep Talk	Normal	Status	—	—	10	Self
TR33	Shadow Ball	Ghost	Special	80	100	15	Normal
TR34	Future Sight	Psychic	Special	120	100	10	Normal
TR35	Uproar	Normal	Special	90	100	10	1 Random
TR37	Taunt	Dark	Status	—	100	10	Normal
TR38	Trick	Psychic	Status	—	100	10	Normal
TR40	Skill Swap	Psychic	Status	—	—	10	Normal
TR49	Calm Mind	Psychic	Status	—	—	20	Self
TR58	Dark Pulse	Dark	Special	80	100	15	Normal
TR65	Energy Ball	Grass	Special	90	100	10	Normal
TR68	Nasty Plot	Dark	Status	—	—	20	Self
TR69	Zen Headbutt	Psychic	Physical	80	90	15	Normal
TR77	Grass Knot	Grass	Special	—	100	20	Normal
TR81	Foul Play	Dark	Physical	95	100	15	Normal
TR82	Stored Power	Psychic	Special	20	100	10	Normal
TR83	Ally Switch	Psychic	Status	—	—	15	Self

ABILITY
Frisk
Competitive

HIDDEN ABILITY
Shadow Tag

SPECIES STRENGTHS

HP	
ATTACK	
DEFENSE	
SP. ATK	
SP. DEF	
SPEED	

DAMAGE TAKEN IN BATTLE

×1 ×0.5 ×1
×1 ×1 ×2
×1 ×1 ×1
×1 ×1 ×2
×1 ×0.5 ×1
×2 ×1 ×1

HUMANLIKE

268

Gothorita   p. 112

ABILITY
Frisk
Competitive

HIDDEN ABILITY
Shadow Tag

SPECIES STRENGTHS

HP	▮▮▮
ATTACK	▮▮▮
DEFENSE	▮▮▮▮
SP. ATK	▮▮▮▮
SP. DEF	▮▮▮▮
SPEED	▮▮▮

DAMAGE TAKEN IN BATTLE

◉ ×1	▥ ×0.5	◢ ×1			
◈ ×1	◉ ×1	◉ ×2			
◉ ×1	◮ ×1	◉ ×1			
◉ ×1	◈ ×1	◖ ×2			
◤ ×1	◉ ×0.5	◉ ×1			
✳ ×1	◉ ×2	◈ ×1			

HUMANLIKE

▲ LEVEL-UP MOVES

LV.	NAME	TYPE	KIND	POW.	ACC.	PP	RANGE
1	Confusion	Psychic	Special	50	100	25	Normal
1	Play Nice	Normal	Status	—	—	20	Normal
1	Pound	Normal	Physical	40	100	35	Normal
1	Tickle	Normal	Status	—	100	20	Normal
12	Psybeam	Psychic	Special	65	100	20	Normal
16	Charm	Fairy	Status	—	100	20	Normal
20	Psyshock	Psychic	Special	80	100	10	Normal
24	Hypnosis	Psychic	Status	—	60	20	Normal
28	Fake Tears	Dark	Status	—	100	20	Normal
35	Psych Up	Normal	Status	—	—	10	Normal
40	Psychic	Psychic	Special	90	100	10	Normal
46	Flatter	Dark	Status	—	100	15	Normal
52	Future Sight	Psychic	Special	120	100	10	Normal
58	Magic Room	Psychic	Status	—	—	10	Both Sides

▶ TUTOR MOVES

NAME	TYPE	KIND	POW.	ACC.	PP	RANGE

▶ TM MOVES

NO.	NAME	TYPE	KIND	POW.	ACC.	PP	RANGE
TM14	Thunder Wave	Electric	Status	—	90	20	Normal
TM17	Light Screen	Psychic	Status	—	—	30	Your Side
TM18	Reflect	Psychic	Status	—	—	20	Your Side
TM19	Safeguard	Normal	Status	—	—	25	Your Side
TM21	Rest	Psychic	Status	—	—	10	Self
TM22	Rock Slide	Rock	Physical	75	90	10	Many Others
TM23	Thief	Dark	Physical	60	100	25	Normal
TM24	Snore	Normal	Special	50	100	15	Normal
TM25	Protect	Normal	Status	—	—	10	Self
TM29	Charm	Fairy	Status	—	100	20	Normal
TM31	Attract	Normal	Status	—	100	15	Normal
TM33	Rain Dance	Water	Status	—	—	5	Both Sides
TM39	Facade	Normal	Physical	70	100	20	Normal
TM41	Helping Hand	Normal	Status	—	—	20	1 Ally
TM47	Fake Tears	Dark	Status	—	100	20	Normal
TM48	Rock Tomb	Rock	Physical	60	95	15	Normal
TM57	Payback	Dark	Physical	50	100	10	Normal
TM59	Fling	Dark	Physical	—	100	10	Normal
TM61	Guard Swap	Psychic	Status	—	—	10	Normal
TM70	Trick Room	Psychic	Status	—	—	5	Both Sides
TM72	Magic Room	Psychic	Status	—	—	10	Both Sides
TM76	Round	Normal	Special	60	100	15	Normal

▲ EVOLUTION MOVES

NAME	TYPE	KIND	POW.	ACC.	PP	RANGE

EGG MOVES

NAME	TYPE	KIND	POW.	ACC.	PP	RANGE

▶ TR MOVES

NAME	TYPE	KIND	POW.	ACC.	PP	RANGE
TR08 Thunderbolt	Electric	Special	90	100	15	Normal
TR11 Psychic	Psychic	Special	90	100	10	Normal
TR20 Substitute	Normal	Status	—	—	10	Self
TR25 Psyshock	Psychic	Special	80	100	10	Normal
TR26 Endure	Normal	Status	—	—	10	Self
TR27 Sleep Talk	Normal	Status	—	—	10	Self
TR33 Shadow Ball	Ghost	Special	80	100	15	Normal
TR34 Future Sight	Psychic	Special	120	100	10	Normal
TR35 Uproar	Normal	Special	90	100	10	1 Random
TR37 Taunt	Dark	Status	—	100	20	Normal
TR38 Trick	Psychic	Status	—	100	10	Normal
TR40 Skill Swap	Psychic	Status	—	—	10	Normal
TR49 Calm Mind	Psychic	Status	—	—	20	Self
TR58 Dark Pulse	Dark	Special	80	100	15	Normal
TR65 Energy Ball	Grass	Special	90	100	10	Normal
TR68 Nasty Plot	Dark	Status	—	—	20	Self
TR69 Zen Headbutt	Psychic	Physical	80	90	15	Normal
TR77 Grass Knot	Grass	Special	—	100	20	Normal
TR81 Foul Play	Dark	Physical	95	100	15	Normal
TR82 Stored Power	Psychic	Special	20	100	10	Normal
TR83 Ally Switch	Psychic	Status	—	—	15	Self

269

Gothitelle   p. 112

ABILITY
Frisk
Competitive

HIDDEN ABILITY
Shadow Tag

SPECIES STRENGTHS

HP	▮▮▮▮
ATTACK	▮▮▮
DEFENSE	▮▮▮▮▮
SP. ATK	▮▮▮▮▮
SP. DEF	▮▮▮▮▮▮
SPEED	▮▮▮

DAMAGE TAKEN IN BATTLE

◉ ×1	▥ ×0.5	◢ ×1			
◈ ×1	◉ ×1	◉ ×2			
◉ ×1	◮ ×1	◉ ×1			
◉ ×1	◈ ×1	◖ ×2			
◤ ×1	◉ ×0.5	◉ ×1			
✳ ×1	◉ ×2	◈ ×1			

HUMANLIKE

▲ LEVEL-UP MOVES

LV.	NAME	TYPE	KIND	POW.	ACC.	PP	RANGE
1	Confusion	Psychic	Special	50	100	25	Normal
1	Play Nice	Normal	Status	—	—	20	Normal
1	Pound	Normal	Physical	40	100	35	Normal
1	Tickle	Normal	Status	—	100	20	Normal
12	Psybeam	Psychic	Special	65	100	20	Normal
16	Charm	Fairy	Status	—	100	20	Normal
20	Psyshock	Psychic	Special	80	100	10	Normal
24	Hypnosis	Psychic	Status	—	60	20	Normal
28	Fake Tears	Dark	Status	—	100	20	Normal
35	Psych Up	Normal	Status	—	—	10	Normal
40	Psychic	Psychic	Special	90	100	10	Normal
48	Flatter	Dark	Status	—	100	15	Normal
56	Future Sight	Psychic	Special	120	100	10	Normal
64	Magic Room	Psychic	Status	—	—	10	Both Sides

▶ TUTOR MOVES

NAME	TYPE	KIND	POW.	ACC.	PP	RANGE

▶ TM MOVES

NO.	NAME	TYPE	KIND	POW.	ACC.	PP	RANGE
TM08	Hyper Beam	Normal	Special	150	90	5	Normal
TM09	Giga Impact	Normal	Physical	150	90	5	Normal
TM14	Thunder Wave	Electric	Status	—	90	20	Normal
TM17	Light Screen	Psychic	Status	—	—	30	Your Side
TM18	Reflect	Psychic	Status	—	—	20	Your Side
TM19	Safeguard	Normal	Status	—	—	25	Your Side
TM21	Rest	Psychic	Status	—	—	10	Self
TM22	Rock Slide	Rock	Physical	75	90	10	Many Others
TM23	Thief	Dark	Physical	60	100	25	Normal
TM24	Snore	Normal	Special	50	100	15	Normal
TM25	Protect	Normal	Status	—	—	10	Self
TM29	Charm	Fairy	Status	—	100	20	Normal
TM31	Attract	Normal	Status	—	100	15	Normal
TM33	Rain Dance	Water	Status	—	—	5	Both Sides
TM39	Facade	Normal	Physical	70	100	20	Normal
TM41	Helping Hand	Normal	Status	—	—	20	1 Ally
TM43	Brick Break	Fighting	Physical	75	100	15	Normal
TM44	Imprison	Psychic	Status	—	—	10	Self
TM47	Fake Tears	Dark	Status	—	100	20	Normal
TM48	Rock Tomb	Rock	Physical	60	95	15	Normal
TM57	Payback	Dark	Physical	50	100	10	Normal
TM59	Fling	Dark	Physical	—	100	10	Normal
TM61	Guard Swap	Psychic	Status	—	—	10	Normal
TM70	Trick Room	Psychic	Status	—	—	5	Both Sides
TM72	Magic Room	Psychic	Status	—	—	10	Both Sides
TM75	Low Sweep	Fighting	Physical	65	100	20	Normal
TM76	Round	Normal	Special	60	100	15	Normal

▲ EVOLUTION MOVES

NAME	TYPE	KIND	POW.	ACC.	PP	RANGE

EGG MOVES

NAME	TYPE	KIND	POW.	ACC.	PP	RANGE

▶ TR MOVES

NAME	TYPE	KIND	POW.	ACC.	PP	RANGE
TR08 Thunderbolt	Electric	Special	90	100	15	Normal
TR11 Psychic	Psychic	Special	90	100	10	Normal
TR20 Substitute	Normal	Status	—	—	10	Self
TR25 Psyshock	Psychic	Special	80	100	10	Normal
TR26 Endure	Normal	Status	—	—	10	Self
TR27 Sleep Talk	Normal	Status	—	—	10	Self
TR33 Shadow Ball	Ghost	Special	80	100	15	Normal
TR34 Future Sight	Psychic	Special	120	100	10	Normal
TR35 Uproar	Normal	Special	90	100	10	1 Random
TR37 Taunt	Dark	Status	—	100	20	Normal
TR38 Trick	Psychic	Status	—	100	10	Normal
TR40 Skill Swap	Psychic	Status	—	—	10	Normal
TR44 Cosmic Power	Psychic	Status	—	—	20	Self
TR49 Calm Mind	Psychic	Status	—	—	20	Self
TR58 Dark Pulse	Dark	Special	80	100	15	Normal
TR65 Energy Ball	Grass	Special	90	100	10	Normal
TR68 Nasty Plot	Dark	Status	—	—	20	Self
TR69 Zen Headbutt	Psychic	Physical	80	90	15	Normal
TR77 Grass Knot	Grass	Special	—	100	20	Normal
TR81 Foul Play	Dark	Physical	95	100	15	Normal
TR82 Stored Power	Psychic	Special	20	100	10	Normal
TR83 Ally Switch	Psychic	Status	—	—	15	Self

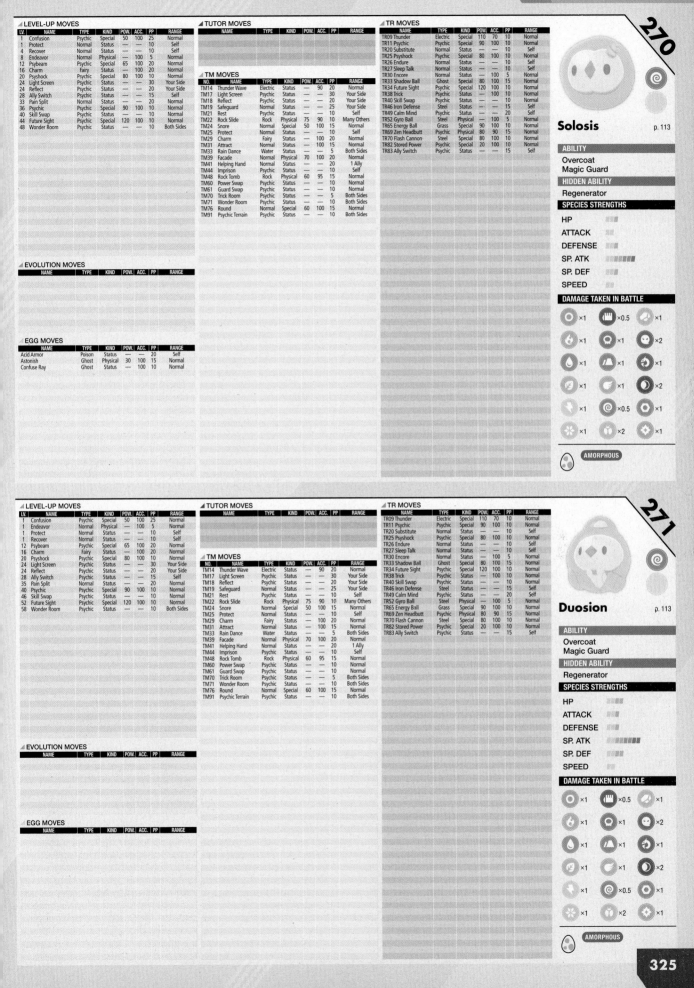

270

LEVEL-UP MOVES

LV.	NAME	TYPE	KIND	POW.	ACC.	PP	RANGE
1	Confusion	Psychic	Special	50	100	25	Normal
1	Protect	Normal	Status	—	—	10	Self
4	Recover	Normal	Status	—	—	10	Self
8	Endeavor	Normal	Physical	—	100	5	Normal
12	Psybeam	Psychic	Special	65	100	20	Normal
16	Charm	Fairy	Status	—	100	20	Normal
20	Psyshock	Psychic	Special	80	100	10	Normal
24	Light Screen	Psychic	Status	—	—	30	Your Side
24	Reflect	Psychic	Status	—	—	20	Your Side
28	Ally Switch	Psychic	Status	—	—	15	Self
33	Pain Split	Normal	Status	—	—	20	Normal
36	Psychic	Psychic	Special	90	100	10	Normal
40	Skill Swap	Psychic	Status	—	—	10	Normal
44	Future Sight	Psychic	Special	120	100	10	Normal
48	Wonder Room	Psychic	Status	—	—	10	Both Sides

EVOLUTION MOVES

NAME	TYPE	KIND	POW.	ACC.	PP	RANGE

EGG MOVES

NAME	TYPE	KIND	POW.	ACC.	PP	RANGE
Acid Armor	Poison	Status	—	—	20	Self
Astonish	Ghost	Physical	30	100	15	Normal
Confuse Ray	Ghost	Status	—	100	10	Normal

TUTOR MOVES

NAME	TYPE	KIND	POW.	ACC.	PP	RANGE

TM MOVES

NO.	NAME	TYPE	KIND	POW.	ACC.	PP	RANGE
TM14	Thunder Wave	Electric	Status	—	90	20	Normal
TM17	Light Screen	Psychic	Status	—	—	30	Your Side
TM18	Reflect	Psychic	Status	—	—	20	Your Side
TM19	Safeguard	Normal	Status	—	—	25	Your Side
TM21	Rest	Psychic	Status	—	—	10	Self
TM22	Rock Slide	Rock	Physical	75	90	10	Many Others
TM24	Snore	Normal	Special	50	100	15	Normal
TM25	Protect	Normal	Status	—	—	10	Self
TM29	Charm	Fairy	Status	—	100	20	Normal
TM31	Attract	Normal	Status	—	100	15	Normal
TM33	Rain Dance	Water	Status	—	—	5	Both Sides
TM39	Facade	Normal	Physical	70	100	20	Normal
TM41	Helping Hand	Normal	Status	—	—	20	1 Ally
TM44	Imprison	Psychic	Status	—	—	10	Self
TM48	Rock Tomb	Rock	Physical	60	95	15	Normal
TM60	Power Swap	Psychic	Status	—	—	10	Normal
TM61	Guard Swap	Psychic	Status	—	—	10	Normal
TM70	Trick Room	Psychic	Status	—	—	5	Both Sides
TM71	Wonder Room	Psychic	Status	—	—	10	Both Sides
TM76	Round	Normal	Special	60	100	15	Normal
TM91	Psychic Terrain	Psychic	Status	—	—	10	Both Sides

TR MOVES

NO.	NAME	TYPE	KIND	POW.	ACC.	PP	RANGE
TR09	Thunder	Electric	Special	110	70	10	Normal
TR11	Psychic	Psychic	Special	90	100	10	Normal
TR20	Substitute	Normal	Status	—	—	10	Self
TR25	Psyshock	Psychic	Special	80	100	10	Normal
TR26	Endure	Normal	Status	—	—	10	Self
TR27	Sleep Talk	Normal	Status	—	—	10	Self
TR30	Encore	Normal	Status	—	100	5	Normal
TR33	Shadow Ball	Ghost	Special	80	100	15	Normal
TR34	Future Sight	Psychic	Special	120	100	10	Normal
TR38	Trick	Psychic	Status	—	100	10	Normal
TR40	Skill Swap	Psychic	Status	—	—	10	Normal
TR46	Iron Defense	Steel	Status	—	—	15	Self
TR49	Calm Mind	Psychic	Status	—	—	20	Self
TR52	Gyro Ball	Steel	Physical	—	100	5	Normal
TR65	Energy Ball	Grass	Special	90	100	10	Normal
TR69	Zen Headbutt	Psychic	Physical	80	90	15	Normal
TR70	Flash Cannon	Steel	Special	80	100	10	Normal
TR82	Stored Power	Psychic	Special	20	100	10	Normal
TR83	Ally Switch	Psychic	Status	—	—	15	Self

Solosis p. 113

ABILITY
Overcoat
Magic Guard

HIDDEN ABILITY
Regenerator

SPECIES STRENGTHS
- HP
- ATTACK
- DEFENSE
- SP. ATK
- SP. DEF
- SPEED

DAMAGE TAKEN IN BATTLE

AMORPHOUS

271

LEVEL-UP MOVES

LV.	NAME	TYPE	KIND	POW.	ACC.	PP	RANGE
1	Confusion	Psychic	Special	50	100	25	Normal
1	Endeavor	Normal	Physical	—	100	5	Normal
1	Protect	Normal	Status	—	—	10	Self
1	Recover	Normal	Status	—	—	10	Self
12	Psybeam	Psychic	Special	65	100	20	Normal
16	Charm	Fairy	Status	—	100	20	Normal
20	Psyshock	Psychic	Special	80	100	10	Normal
24	Light Screen	Psychic	Status	—	—	30	Your Side
24	Reflect	Psychic	Status	—	—	20	Your Side
28	Ally Switch	Psychic	Status	—	—	15	Self
35	Pain Split	Normal	Status	—	—	20	Normal
40	Psychic	Psychic	Special	90	100	10	Normal
46	Skill Swap	Psychic	Status	—	—	10	Normal
52	Future Sight	Psychic	Special	120	100	10	Normal
58	Wonder Room	Psychic	Status	—	—	10	Both Sides

EVOLUTION MOVES

NAME	TYPE	KIND	POW.	ACC.	PP	RANGE

EGG MOVES

NAME	TYPE	KIND	POW.	ACC.	PP	RANGE

TUTOR MOVES

NAME	TYPE	KIND	POW.	ACC.	PP	RANGE

TM MOVES

NO.	NAME	TYPE	KIND	POW.	ACC.	PP	RANGE
TM14	Thunder Wave	Electric	Status	—	90	20	Normal
TM17	Light Screen	Psychic	Status	—	—	30	Your Side
TM18	Reflect	Psychic	Status	—	—	20	Your Side
TM19	Safeguard	Normal	Status	—	—	25	Your Side
TM21	Rest	Psychic	Status	—	—	10	Self
TM22	Rock Slide	Rock	Physical	75	90	10	Many Others
TM24	Snore	Normal	Special	50	100	15	Normal
TM25	Protect	Normal	Status	—	—	10	Self
TM29	Charm	Fairy	Status	—	100	20	Normal
TM31	Attract	Normal	Status	—	100	15	Normal
TM33	Rain Dance	Water	Status	—	—	5	Both Sides
TM39	Facade	Normal	Physical	70	100	20	Normal
TM41	Helping Hand	Normal	Status	—	—	20	1 Ally
TM44	Imprison	Psychic	Status	—	—	10	Self
TM48	Rock Tomb	Rock	Physical	60	95	15	Normal
TM60	Power Swap	Psychic	Status	—	—	10	Normal
TM61	Guard Swap	Psychic	Status	—	—	10	Normal
TM70	Trick Room	Psychic	Status	—	—	5	Both Sides
TM71	Wonder Room	Psychic	Status	—	—	10	Both Sides
TM76	Round	Normal	Special	60	100	15	Normal
TM91	Psychic Terrain	Psychic	Status	—	—	10	Both Sides

TR MOVES

NO.	NAME	TYPE	KIND	POW.	ACC.	PP	RANGE
TR09	Thunder	Electric	Special	110	70	10	Normal
TR11	Psychic	Psychic	Special	90	100	10	Normal
TR20	Substitute	Normal	Status	—	—	10	Self
TR25	Psyshock	Psychic	Special	80	100	10	Normal
TR26	Endure	Normal	Status	—	—	10	Self
TR27	Sleep Talk	Normal	Status	—	—	10	Self
TR30	Encore	Normal	Status	—	100	5	Normal
TR33	Shadow Ball	Ghost	Special	80	100	15	Normal
TR34	Future Sight	Psychic	Special	120	100	10	Normal
TR38	Trick	Psychic	Status	—	100	10	Normal
TR40	Skill Swap	Psychic	Status	—	—	10	Normal
TR46	Iron Defense	Steel	Status	—	—	15	Self
TR49	Calm Mind	Psychic	Status	—	—	20	Self
TR52	Gyro Ball	Steel	Physical	—	100	5	Normal
TR65	Energy Ball	Grass	Special	90	100	10	Normal
TR69	Zen Headbutt	Psychic	Physical	80	90	15	Normal
TR70	Flash Cannon	Steel	Special	80	100	10	Normal
TR82	Stored Power	Psychic	Special	20	100	10	Normal
TR83	Ally Switch	Psychic	Status	—	—	15	Self

Duosion p. 113

ABILITY
Overcoat
Magic Guard

HIDDEN ABILITY
Regenerator

SPECIES STRENGTHS
- HP
- ATTACK
- DEFENSE
- SP. ATK
- SP. DEF
- SPEED

DAMAGE TAKEN IN BATTLE

AMORPHOUS

272

Reuniclus
p. 113

ABILITY
Overcoat
Magic Guard

HIDDEN ABILITY
Regenerator

SPECIES STRENGTHS
HP
ATTACK
DEFENSE
SP. ATK
SP. DEF
SPEED

DAMAGE TAKEN IN BATTLE

×1	×0.5	×1			
×1	×1	×2			
×1	×1	×1			
×1	×1	×2			
×1	×0.5	×1			
×1	×2	×1			

AMORPHOUS

LEVEL-UP MOVES

LV.	NAME	TYPE	KIND	POW.	ACC.	PP	RANGE
1	Confusion	Psychic	Special	50	100	25	Normal
1	Endeavor	Normal	Physical	—	100	5	Normal
1	Hammer Arm	Fighting	Physical	100	90	10	Normal
1	Protect	Normal	Status	—	—	10	Self
1	Recover	Normal	Status	—	—	10	Self
12	Psybeam	Psychic	Special	65	100	20	Normal
16	Charm	Fairy	Status	—	100	10	Normal
20	Psyshock	Psychic	Special	80	100	10	Normal
24	Light Screen	Psychic	Status	—	—	30	Your Side
24	Reflect	Psychic	Status	—	—	20	Your Side
28	Ally Switch	Psychic	Status	—	—	15	Self
35	Pain Split	Normal	Status	—	—	20	Normal
40	Psychic	Psychic	Special	90	100	10	Normal
48	Skill Swap	Psychic	Status	—	—	10	Normal
56	Future Sight	Psychic	Special	120	100	10	Normal
64	Wonder Room	Psychic	Status	—	—	10	Both Sides

EVOLUTION MOVES

NAME	TYPE	KIND	POW.	ACC.	PP	RANGE
Hammer Arm	Fighting	Physical	100	90	10	Normal

EGG MOVES

NAME	TYPE	KIND	POW.	ACC.	PP	RANGE

TUTOR MOVES

NAME	TYPE	KIND	POW.	ACC.	PP	RANGE

TM MOVES

NO.	NAME	TYPE	KIND	POW.	ACC.	PP	RANGE
TM00	Mega Punch	Normal	Physical	80	85	20	Normal
TM03	Fire Punch	Fire	Physical	75	100	15	Normal
TM04	Ice Punch	Ice	Physical	75	100	15	Normal
TM05	Thunder Punch	Electric	Physical	75	100	15	Normal
TM08	Hyper Beam	Normal	Special	150	90	5	Normal
TM09	Giga Impact	Normal	Physical	150	90	5	Normal
TM14	Thunder Wave	Electric	Status	—	90	20	Normal
TM17	Light Screen	Psychic	Status	—	—	30	Your Side
TM18	Reflect	Psychic	Status	—	—	20	Your Side
TM19	Safeguard	Normal	Status	—	—	25	Your Side
TM21	Rest	Psychic	Status	—	—	10	Self
TM22	Rock Slide	Rock	Physical	75	90	10	Many Others
TM24	Snore	Normal	Special	50	100	15	Normal
TM25	Protect	Normal	Status	—	—	10	Self
TM29	Charm	Fairy	Status	—	100	20	Normal
TM31	Attract	Normal	Status	—	100	15	Normal
TM33	Rain Dance	Water	Status	—	—	5	Both Sides
TM39	Facade	Normal	Physical	70	100	20	Normal
TM41	Helping Hand	Normal	Status	—	—	20	1 Ally
TM44	Imprison	Psychic	Status	—	—	10	Self
TM48	Rock Tomb	Rock	Physical	60	95	15	Normal
TM59	Fling	Dark	Physical	—	100	10	Normal
TM60	Power Swap	Psychic	Status	—	—	10	Normal
TM61	Guard Swap	Psychic	Status	—	—	10	Normal
TM63	Drain Punch	Fighting	Physical	75	100	10	Normal
TM70	Trick Room	Psychic	Status	—	—	5	Both Sides
TM71	Wonder Room	Psychic	Status	—	—	10	Both Sides
TM76	Round	Normal	Special	60	100	15	Normal
TM91	Psychic Terrain	Psychic	Status	—	—	10	Both Sides

TR MOVES

NO.	NAME	TYPE	KIND	POW.	ACC.	PP	RANGE
TR09	Thunder	Electric	Special	110	70	10	Normal
TR11	Psychic	Psychic	Special	90	100	10	Normal
TR20	Substitute	Normal	Status	—	—	10	Self
TR25	Psyshock	Psychic	Special	80	100	10	Normal
TR26	Endure	Normal	Status	—	—	10	Self
TR27	Sleep Talk	Normal	Status	—	—	10	Self
TR33	Shadow Ball	Ghost	Special	80	100	15	Normal
TR34	Future Sight	Psychic	Special	120	100	10	Normal
TR38	Trick	Psychic	Status	—	100	10	Normal
TR39	Superpower	Fighting	Physical	120	100	5	Normal
TR40	Skill Swap	Psychic	Status	—	—	10	Normal
TR46	Iron Defense	Steel	Status	—	—	15	Self
TR49	Calm Mind	Psychic	Status	—	—	20	Self
TR52	Gyro Ball	Steel	Physical	—	100	5	Normal
TR64	Focus Blast	Fighting	Special	120	70	5	Normal
TR65	Energy Ball	Grass	Special	90	100	10	Normal
TR69	Zen Headbutt	Psychic	Physical	80	90	15	Normal
TR70	Flash Cannon	Steel	Special	80	100	10	Normal
TR77	Grass Knot	Grass	Special	—	100	20	Normal
TR82	Stored Power	Psychic	Special	20	100	10	Normal
TR83	Ally Switch	Psychic	Status	—	—	15	Self

273

Karrablast
p. 114

ABILITY
Swarm
Shed Skin

HIDDEN ABILITY
No Guard

SPECIES STRENGTHS
HP
ATTACK
DEFENSE
SP. ATK
SP. DEF
SPEED

DAMAGE TAKEN IN BATTLE

×1	×0.5	×2			
×2	×1	×1			
×1	×0.5	×1			
×0.5	×2	×1			
×1	×1	×1			
×1	×1	×1			

BUG

LEVEL-UP MOVES

LV.	NAME	TYPE	KIND	POW.	ACC.	PP	RANGE
1	Leer	Normal	Status	—	100	30	Many Others
1	Peck	Flying	Physical	35	100	35	Normal
4	Fury Cutter	Bug	Physical	40	95	20	Normal
8	Endure	Normal	Status	—	—	10	Self
12	False Swipe	Normal	Physical	40	100	40	Normal
16	Acid Spray	Poison	Special	40	100	20	Normal
20	Headbutt	Normal	Physical	70	100	15	Normal
24	Flail	Normal	Physical	—	100	15	Normal
28	Scary Face	Normal	Status	—	100	10	Normal
32	X-Scissor	Bug	Physical	80	100	15	Normal
36	Swords Dance	Normal	Status	—	—	20	Self
40	Take Down	Normal	Physical	90	85	20	Normal
44	Bug Buzz	Bug	Special	90	100	10	Normal
48	Double-Edge	Normal	Physical	120	100	15	Normal

EVOLUTION MOVES

NAME	TYPE	KIND	POW.	ACC.	PP	RANGE

EGG MOVES

NAME	TYPE	KIND	POW.	ACC.	PP	RANGE
Bug Bite	Bug	Physical	60	100	20	Normal
Counter	Fighting	Physical	—	100	20	Varies
Knock Off	Dark	Physical	65	100	20	Normal
Night Slash	Dark	Physical	70	100	15	Normal
Slash	Normal	Physical	70	100	20	Normal

TUTOR MOVES

NAME	TYPE	KIND	POW.	ACC.	PP	RANGE

TM MOVES

NO.	NAME	TYPE	KIND	POW.	ACC.	PP	RANGE
TM16	Screech	Normal	Status	—	85	40	Normal
TM21	Rest	Psychic	Status	—	—	10	Self
TM24	Snore	Normal	Special	50	100	15	Normal
TM25	Protect	Normal	Status	—	—	10	Self
TM26	Scary Face	Normal	Status	—	100	10	Normal
TM28	Giga Drain	Grass	Special	75	100	10	Normal
TM31	Attract	Normal	Status	—	100	15	Normal
TM33	Rain Dance	Water	Status	—	—	5	Both Sides
TM39	Facade	Normal	Physical	70	100	20	Normal
TM76	Round	Normal	Special	60	100	15	Normal
TM94	False Swipe	Normal	Physical	40	100	40	Normal

TR MOVES

NO.	NAME	TYPE	KIND	POW.	ACC.	PP	RANGE
TR00	Swords Dance	Normal	Status	—	—	20	Self
TR20	Substitute	Normal	Status	—	—	10	Self
TR26	Endure	Normal	Status	—	—	10	Self
TR27	Sleep Talk	Normal	Status	—	—	10	Self
TR28	Megahorn	Bug	Physical	120	85	10	Normal
TR30	Encore	Normal	Status	—	100	5	Normal
TR46	Iron Defense	Steel	Status	—	—	15	Self
TR57	Poison Jab	Poison	Physical	80	100	20	Normal
TR60	X-Scissor	Bug	Physical	80	100	15	Normal
TR61	Bug Buzz	Bug	Special	90	100	10	Normal
TR65	Energy Ball	Grass	Special	90	100	10	Normal
TR87	Drill Run	Ground	Physical	80	95	10	Normal

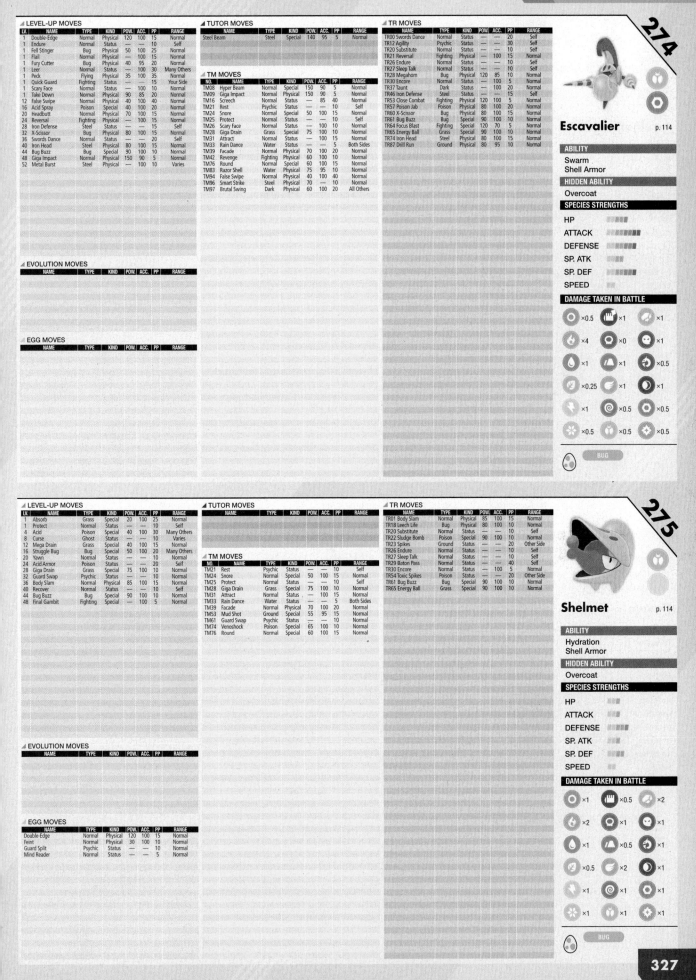

274

Escavalier — p. 114

LEVEL-UP MOVES

LV	NAME	TYPE	KIND	POW.	ACC.	PP	RANGE
1	Double-Edge	Normal	Physical	120	100	15	Normal
1	Endure	Normal	Status	—	—	10	Self
1	Fell Stinger	Bug	Physical	50	100	25	Normal
1	Flail	Normal	Physical	—	100	15	Normal
1	Fury Cutter	Bug	Physical	40	95	20	Normal
1	Leer	Normal	Status	—	100	30	Many Others
1	Peck	Flying	Physical	35	100	35	Normal
1	Quick Guard	Fighting	Status	—	—	15	Your Side
1	Scary Face	Normal	Status	—	100	10	Normal
1	Take Down	Normal	Physical	90	85	20	Normal
12	False Swipe	Normal	Physical	40	100	40	Normal
16	Acid Spray	Poison	Special	40	100	20	Normal
20	Headbutt	Normal	Physical	70	100	15	Normal
24	Reversal	Fighting	Physical	—	100	15	Normal
28	Iron Defense	Steel	Status	—	—	15	Self
32	X-Scissor	Bug	Physical	80	100	15	Normal
36	Swords Dance	Normal	Status	—	—	20	Self
40	Iron Head	Steel	Physical	80	100	15	Normal
44	Bug Buzz	Bug	Special	90	100	10	Normal
48	Giga Impact	Normal	Physical	150	90	5	Normal
52	Metal Burst	Steel	Physical	—	100	10	Varies

EVOLUTION MOVES

NAME	TYPE	KIND	POW.	ACC.	PP	RANGE

EGG MOVES

NAME	TYPE	KIND	POW.	ACC.	PP	RANGE

TUTOR MOVES

NAME	TYPE	KIND	POW.	ACC.	PP	RANGE
Steel Beam	Steel	Special	140	95	5	Normal

TM MOVES

NO.	NAME	TYPE	KIND	POW.	ACC.	PP	RANGE
TM08	Hyper Beam	Normal	Special	150	90	5	Normal
TM09	Giga Impact	Normal	Physical	150	90	5	Normal
TM16	Screech	Normal	Status	—	85	40	Normal
TM21	Rest	Psychic	Status	—	—	10	Self
TM24	Snore	Normal	Special	50	100	15	Normal
TM25	Protect	Normal	Status	—	—	10	Self
TM26	Scary Face	Normal	Status	—	100	10	Normal
TM28	Giga Drain	Grass	Special	75	100	10	Normal
TM31	Attract	Normal	Status	—	100	15	Normal
TM33	Rain Dance	Water	Status	—	—	5	Both Sides
TM39	Facade	Normal	Physical	70	100	20	Normal
TM42	Revenge	Fighting	Physical	60	100	10	Normal
TM76	Round	Normal	Special	60	100	15	Normal
TM83	Razor Shell	Water	Physical	75	95	10	Normal
TM94	False Swipe	Normal	Physical	40	100	40	Normal
TM96	Smart Strike	Steel	Physical	70	—	10	Normal
TM97	Brutal Swing	Dark	Physical	60	100	20	All Others

TR MOVES

NO.	NAME	TYPE	KIND	POW.	ACC.	PP	RANGE
TR00	Swords Dance	Normal	Status	—	—	20	Self
TR12	Agility	Psychic	Status	—	—	30	Self
TR20	Substitute	Normal	Status	—	—	10	Self
TR21	Reversal	Fighting	Physical	—	100	15	Normal
TR26	Endure	Normal	Status	—	—	10	Self
TR27	Sleep Talk	Normal	Status	—	—	10	Self
TR28	Megahorn	Bug	Physical	120	85	10	Normal
TR30	Encore	Normal	Status	—	100	5	Normal
TR37	Taunt	Dark	Status	—	100	20	Normal
TR46	Iron Defense	Steel	Status	—	—	15	Self
TR53	Close Combat	Fighting	Physical	120	100	5	Normal
TR57	Poison Jab	Poison	Physical	80	100	20	Normal
TR60	X-Scissor	Bug	Physical	80	100	15	Normal
TR64	Focus Blast	Fighting	Special	120	70	5	Normal
TR65	Energy Ball	Grass	Special	90	100	10	Normal
TR74	Iron Head	Steel	Physical	80	100	15	Normal
TR87	Drill Run	Ground	Physical	80	95	10	Normal

ABILITY
Swarm
Shell Armor

HIDDEN ABILITY
Overcoat

SPECIES STRENGTHS

- HP
- ATTACK
- DEFENSE
- SP. ATK
- SP. DEF
- SPEED

DAMAGE TAKEN IN BATTLE

×0.5	×1	×1
×4	×0	×1
×1	×1	×0.5
×0.25	×1	×1
×1	×0.5	×0.5
×0.5	×0.5	×0.5

BUG

275

Shelmet — p. 114

LEVEL-UP MOVES

LV	NAME	TYPE	KIND	POW.	ACC.	PP	RANGE
1	Absorb	Grass	Special	20	100	25	Normal
1	Protect	Normal	Status	—	—	10	Self
4	Acid	Poison	Special	40	100	30	Many Others
8	Curse	Ghost	Status	—	—	10	Varies
12	Mega Drain	Grass	Special	40	100	15	Normal
16	Struggle Bug	Bug	Special	50	100	20	Many Others
20	Yawn	Normal	Status	—	—	10	Normal
24	Acid Armor	Poison	Status	—	—	20	Self
28	Giga Drain	Grass	Special	75	100	10	Normal
32	Guard Swap	Psychic	Status	—	—	10	Normal
36	Body Slam	Normal	Physical	85	100	15	Normal
40	Recover	Normal	Status	—	—	10	Self
44	Bug Buzz	Bug	Special	90	100	10	Normal
48	Final Gambit	Fighting	Special	—	100	5	Normal

EVOLUTION MOVES

NAME	TYPE	KIND	POW.	ACC.	PP	RANGE

EGG MOVES

NAME	TYPE	KIND	POW.	ACC.	PP	RANGE
Double-Edge	Normal	Physical	120	100	15	Normal
Feint	Normal	Physical	30	100	10	Normal
Guard Split	Psychic	Status	—	—	10	Normal
Mind Reader	Normal	Status	—	—	5	Normal

TUTOR MOVES

NAME	TYPE	KIND	POW.	ACC.	PP	RANGE

TM MOVES

NO.	NAME	TYPE	KIND	POW.	ACC.	PP	RANGE
TM21	Rest	Psychic	Status	—	—	10	Self
TM24	Snore	Normal	Special	50	100	15	Normal
TM25	Protect	Normal	Status	—	—	10	Self
TM28	Giga Drain	Grass	Special	75	100	10	Normal
TM31	Attract	Normal	Status	—	100	15	Normal
TM33	Rain Dance	Water	Status	—	—	5	Both Sides
TM39	Facade	Normal	Physical	70	100	20	Normal
TM53	Mud Shot	Ground	Special	55	95	15	Normal
TM61	Guard Swap	Psychic	Status	—	—	10	Normal
TM74	Venoshock	Poison	Special	65	100	10	Normal
TM76	Round	Normal	Special	60	100	15	Normal

TR MOVES

NO.	NAME	TYPE	KIND	POW.	ACC.	PP	RANGE
TR01	Body Slam	Normal	Physical	85	100	15	Normal
TR18	Leech Life	Bug	Physical	80	100	10	Normal
TR20	Substitute	Normal	Status	—	—	10	Self
TR22	Sludge Bomb	Poison	Special	90	100	10	Normal
TR23	Spikes	Ground	Status	—	—	20	Other Side
TR26	Endure	Normal	Status	—	—	10	Self
TR27	Sleep Talk	Normal	Status	—	—	10	Self
TR28	Baton Pass	Normal	Status	—	—	40	Self
TR30	Encore	Normal	Status	—	100	5	Normal
TR54	Toxic Spikes	Poison	Status	—	—	20	Other Side
TR61	Bug Buzz	Bug	Special	90	100	10	Normal
TR65	Energy Ball	Grass	Special	90	100	10	Normal

ABILITY
Hydration
Shell Armor

HIDDEN ABILITY
Overcoat

SPECIES STRENGTHS

- HP
- ATTACK
- DEFENSE
- SP. ATK
- SP. DEF
- SPEED

DAMAGE TAKEN IN BATTLE

×1	×0.5	×2
×2	×1	×1
×1	×0.5	×1
×0.5	×2	×1
×1	×1	×1
×1	×1	×1

BUG

276 Accelgor p. 114

ABILITY
Hydration
Sticky Hold

HIDDEN ABILITY
Unburden

SPECIES STRENGTHS
HP
ATTACK
DEFENSE
SP. ATK
SP. DEF
SPEED

DAMAGE TAKEN IN BATTLE

×1	×0.5	×2
×2	×1	×1
×1	×0.5	×1
×0.5	×2	×1
×1	×1	×1
×1	×1	×1

BUG

LEVEL-UP MOVES

LV.	NAME	TYPE	KIND	POW.	ACC.	PP	RANGE
1	Absorb	Grass	Special	20	100	25	Normal
1	Acid	Poison	Special	40	100	30	Many Others
1	Acid Armor	Poison	Status	—	—	20	Self
1	Acid Spray	Poison	Special	40	100	20	Normal
1	Body Slam	Normal	Physical	85	100	15	Normal
1	Curse	Ghost	Status	—	—	10	Varies
1	Double Team	Normal	Status	—	—	15	Self
1	Guard Swap	Psychic	Status	—	—	10	Normal
1	Quick Attack	Normal	Physical	40	100	30	Normal
1	Water Shuriken	Water	Special	15	100	20	Normal
1	Yawn	Normal	Status	—	—	10	Normal
12	Mega Drain	Grass	Special	40	100	15	Normal
16	Struggle Bug	Bug	Special	50	100	20	Many Others
20	Swift	Normal	Special	60	—	20	Many Others
24	Agility	Psychic	Status	—	—	30	Self
28	Giga Drain	Grass	Special	75	100	10	Normal
32	Power Swap	Psychic	Status	—	—	10	Normal
36	U-turn	Bug	Physical	70	100	20	Normal
40	Recover	Normal	Status	—	—	10	Self
44	Bug Buzz	Bug	Special	90	100	10	Normal
48	Final Gambit	Fighting	Special	—	100	5	Normal
52	Toxic	Poison	Status	—	90	10	Normal

TUTOR MOVES

NAME	TYPE	KIND	POW.	ACC.	PP	RANGE

TM MOVES

NO.	NAME	TYPE	KIND	POW.	ACC.	PP	RANGE
TM08	Hyper Beam	Normal	Special	150	90	5	Normal
TM09	Giga Impact	Normal	Physical	150	90	5	Normal
TM21	Rest	Psychic	Status	—	—	10	Self
TM24	Snore	Normal	Special	50	100	15	Normal
TM25	Protect	Normal	Status	—	—	10	Self
TM28	Giga Drain	Grass	Special	75	100	10	Normal
TM31	Attract	Normal	Status	—	100	15	Normal
TM32	Sandstorm	Rock	Status	—	—	10	Both Sides
TM33	Rain Dance	Water	Status	—	—	5	Both Sides
TM39	Facade	Normal	Physical	70	100	20	Normal
TM40	Swift	Normal	Special	60	—	20	Many Others
TM53	Mud Shot	Ground	Special	55	95	15	Normal
TM56	U-turn	Bug	Physical	70	100	20	Normal
TM60	Power Swap	Psychic	Status	—	—	10	Normal
TM61	Guard Swap	Psychic	Status	—	—	10	Normal
TM63	Drain Punch	Fighting	Physical	75	100	10	Normal
TM74	Venoshock	Poison	Special	65	100	10	Normal
TM76	Round	Normal	Special	60	100	15	Normal

EVOLUTION MOVES

NAME	TYPE	KIND	POW.	ACC.	PP	RANGE

EGG MOVES

NAME	TYPE	KIND	POW.	ACC.	PP	RANGE

TR MOVES

NAME	TYPE	KIND	POW.	ACC.	PP	RANGE
TR01 Body Slam	Normal	Physical	85	100	15	Normal
TR12 Agility	Psychic	Status	—	—	30	Self
TR18 Leech Life	Bug	Physical	80	100	10	Normal
TR20 Substitute	Normal	Status	—	—	10	Self
TR21 Reversal	Fighting	Physical	—	100	15	Normal
TR22 Sludge Bomb	Poison	Special	90	100	10	Normal
TR23 Spikes	Ground	Status	—	—	20	Other Side
TR26 Endure	Normal	Status	—	—	10	Self
TR27 Sleep Talk	Normal	Status	—	—	10	Self
TR29 Baton Pass	Normal	Status	—	—	40	Self
TR30 Encore	Normal	Status	—	100	5	Normal
TR54 Toxic Spikes	Poison	Status	—	—	20	Other Side
TR61 Bug Buzz	Bug	Special	90	100	10	Normal
TR64 Focus Blast	Fighting	Special	120	70	5	Normal
TR65 Energy Ball	Grass	Special	90	100	10	Normal
TR91 Venom Drench	Poison	Status	—	100	20	Many Others

---

277 Elgyem p. 115

ABILITY
Telepathy
Synchronize

HIDDEN ABILITY
Analytic

SPECIES STRENGTHS
HP
ATTACK
DEFENSE
SP. ATK
SP. DEF
SPEED

DAMAGE TAKEN IN BATTLE

×1	×0.5	×1
×1	×1	×2
×1	×1	×1
×1	×1	×1
×1	×0.5	×1
×1	×2	×1

HUMANLIKE

LEVEL-UP MOVES

LV.	NAME	TYPE	KIND	POW.	ACC.	PP	RANGE
1	Confusion	Psychic	Special	50	100	25	Normal
1	Growl	Normal	Status	—	100	40	Many Others
6	Imprison	Psychic	Status	—	—	10	Self
12	Teleport	Psychic	Status	—	—	20	Self
18	Psybeam	Psychic	Special	65	100	20	Normal
24	Guard Split	Psychic	Status	—	—	10	Normal
24	Power Split	Psychic	Status	—	—	10	Normal
30	Headbutt	Normal	Physical	70	100	15	Normal
36	Zen Headbutt	Psychic	Physical	80	90	15	Normal
43	Recover	Normal	Status	—	—	10	Self
48	Calm Mind	Psychic	Status	—	—	20	Self
54	Wonder Room	Psychic	Status	—	—	10	Both Sides
60	Psychic	Psychic	Special	90	100	10	Normal

TUTOR MOVES

NAME	TYPE	KIND	POW.	ACC.	PP	RANGE

TM MOVES

NO.	NAME	TYPE	KIND	POW.	ACC.	PP	RANGE
TM14	Thunder Wave	Electric	Status	—	90	20	Normal
TM16	Screech	Normal	Status	—	85	40	Normal
TM17	Light Screen	Psychic	Status	—	—	30	Your Side
TM18	Reflect	Psychic	Status	—	—	20	Your Side
TM19	Safeguard	Normal	Status	—	—	25	Your Side
TM21	Rest	Psychic	Status	—	—	10	Self
TM22	Rock Slide	Rock	Physical	75	90	10	Many Others
TM23	Thief	Dark	Physical	60	100	25	Normal
TM24	Snore	Normal	Special	50	100	15	Normal
TM25	Protect	Normal	Status	—	—	10	Self
TM30	Steel Wing	Steel	Physical	70	90	25	Normal
TM31	Attract	Normal	Status	—	100	15	Normal
TM33	Rain Dance	Water	Status	—	—	5	Both Sides
TM39	Facade	Normal	Physical	70	100	20	Normal
TM44	Imprison	Psychic	Status	—	—	10	Self
TM48	Rock Tomb	Rock	Physical	60	95	15	Normal
TM60	Power Swap	Psychic	Status	—	—	10	Normal
TM61	Guard Swap	Psychic	Status	—	—	10	Normal
TM70	Trick Room	Psychic	Status	—	—	5	Both Sides
TM71	Wonder Room	Psychic	Status	—	—	10	Both Sides
TM76	Round	Normal	Special	60	100	15	Normal

EVOLUTION MOVES

NAME	TYPE	KIND	POW.	ACC.	PP	RANGE

EGG MOVES

NAME	TYPE	KIND	POW.	ACC.	PP	RANGE
Astonish	Ghost	Physical	30	100	15	Normal
Destiny Bond	Ghost	Status	—	—	5	Self
Disable	Normal	Status	—	100	20	Normal
Psych Up	Normal	Status	—	—	10	Normal

TR MOVES

NAME	TYPE	KIND	POW.	ACC.	PP	RANGE
TR08 Thunderbolt	Electric	Special	90	100	15	Normal
TR11 Psychic	Psychic	Special	90	100	10	Normal
TR12 Agility	Psychic	Status	—	—	30	Self
TR20 Substitute	Normal	Status	—	—	10	Self
TR25 Psyshock	Psychic	Special	80	100	10	Normal
TR26 Endure	Normal	Status	—	—	10	Self
TR27 Sleep Talk	Normal	Status	—	—	10	Self
TR33 Shadow Ball	Ghost	Special	80	100	15	Normal
TR35 Uproar	Normal	Special	90	100	10	1 Random
TR38 Trick	Psychic	Status	—	100	10	Normal
TR40 Skill Swap	Psychic	Status	—	—	10	Normal
TR44 Cosmic Power	Psychic	Status	—	—	20	Self
TR49 Calm Mind	Psychic	Status	—	—	20	Self
TR58 Dark Pulse	Dark	Special	80	100	15	Normal
TR65 Energy Ball	Grass	Special	90	100	10	Normal
TR68 Nasty Plot	Dark	Status	—	—	20	Self
TR69 Zen Headbutt	Psychic	Physical	80	90	15	Normal
TR82 Stored Power	Psychic	Special	20	100	10	Normal
TR83 Ally Switch	Psychic	Status	—	—	15	Self

278 — Beheeyem

LEVEL-UP MOVES

LV	NAME	TYPE	KIND	POW	ACC	PP	RANGE
1	Confusion	Psychic	Special	50	100	25	Normal
1	Growl	Normal	Status	—	100	40	Many Others
1	Imprison	Psychic	Status	—	—	10	Self
1	Psychic Terrain	Psychic	Status	—	—	10	Both Sides
1	Teleport	Psychic	Status	—	—	20	Self
18	Psybeam	Psychic	Special	65	100	20	Normal
24	Guard Split	Psychic	Status	—	—	10	Normal
24	Power Split	Psychic	Status	—	—	10	Normal
30	Headbutt	Normal	Physical	70	100	15	Normal
36	Zen Headbutt	Psychic	Physical	80	90	15	Normal
45	Recover	Normal	Status	—	—	10	Self
52	Calm Mind	Psychic	Status	—	—	20	Self
60	Wonder Room	Psychic	Status	—	—	10	Both Sides
68	Psychic	Psychic	Special	90	100	10	Normal

EVOLUTION MOVES

NAME	TYPE	KIND	POW.	ACC.	PP	RANGE

EGG MOVES

NAME	TYPE	KIND	POW.	ACC.	PP	RANGE

TUTOR MOVES

NAME	TYPE	KIND	POW.	ACC.	PP	RANGE

TM MOVES

NO.	NAME	TYPE	KIND	POW.	ACC.	PP	RANGE
TM08	Hyper Beam	Normal	Special	150	90	5	Normal
TM09	Giga Impact	Normal	Physical	150	90	5	Normal
TM14	Thunder Wave	Electric	Status	—	90	20	Normal
TM16	Screech	Normal	Status	—	85	40	Normal
TM17	Light Screen	Psychic	Status	—	—	30	Your Side
TM18	Reflect	Psychic	Status	—	—	20	Your Side
TM19	Safeguard	Normal	Status	—	—	25	Your Side
TM21	Rest	Psychic	Status	—	—	10	Self
TM22	Rock Slide	Rock	Physical	75	90	10	Many Others
TM23	Thief	Dark	Physical	60	100	25	Normal
TM24	Snore	Normal	Special	50	100	15	Normal
TM25	Protect	Normal	Status	—	—	10	Self
TM30	Steel Wing	Steel	Physical	70	90	25	Normal
TM31	Attract	Normal	Status	—	100	15	Normal
TM33	Rain Dance	Water	Status	—	—	5	Both Sides
TM39	Facade	Normal	Physical	70	100	20	Normal
TM44	Imprison	Psychic	Status	—	—	10	Self
TM48	Rock Tomb	Rock	Physical	60	95	15	Normal
TM60	Power Swap	Psychic	Status	—	—	10	Normal
TM61	Guard Swap	Psychic	Status	—	—	10	Normal
TM70	Trick Room	Psychic	Status	—	—	5	Both Sides
TM71	Wonder Room	Psychic	Status	—	—	10	Both Sides
TM76	Round	Normal	Special	60	100	15	Normal
TM91	Psychic Terrain	Psychic	Status	—	—	10	Both Sides

TR MOVES

NAME	TYPE	KIND	POW.	ACC.	PP	RANGE
TR08 Thunderbolt	Electric	Special	90	100	15	Normal
TR11 Psychic	Psychic	Special	90	100	10	Normal
TR12 Agility	Psychic	Status	—	—	30	Self
TR19 Tri Attack	Normal	Special	80	100	10	Normal
TR20 Substitute	Normal	Status	—	—	10	Self
TR25 Psyshock	Psychic	Special	80	100	10	Normal
TR26 Endure	Normal	Status	—	—	10	Self
TR27 Sleep Talk	Normal	Status	—	—	10	Self
TR33 Shadow Ball	Ghost	Special	80	100	15	Normal
TR34 Future Sight	Psychic	Special	120	100	10	Normal
TR35 Uproar	Normal	Special	90	100	10	1 Random
TR38 Trick	Psychic	Status	—	100	10	Normal
TR40 Skill Swap	Psychic	Status	—	—	10	Normal
TR44 Cosmic Power	Psychic	Status	—	—	20	Self
TR49 Calm Mind	Psychic	Status	—	—	20	Self
TR58 Dark Pulse	Dark	Special	80	100	15	Normal
TR65 Energy Ball	Grass	Special	90	100	10	Normal
TR68 Nasty Plot	Dark	Status	—	—	20	Self
TR69 Zen Headbutt	Psychic	Physical	80	90	15	Normal
TR70 Flash Cannon	Steel	Special	80	100	10	Normal
TR82 Stored Power	Psychic	Special	20	100	10	Normal
TR83 Ally Switch	Psychic	Status	—	—	15	Self

Beheeyem p. 115

ABILITY
Telepathy
Synchronize

HIDDEN ABILITY
Analytic

SPECIES STRENGTHS

HP · ATTACK · DEFENSE · SP. ATK · SP. DEF · SPEED

DAMAGE TAKEN IN BATTLE

×1 · ×0.5 · ×1 · ×1 · ×1 · ×2 · ×1 · ×1 · ×1 · ×1 · ×1 · ×2 · ×1 · ×0.5 · ×1 · ×1 · ×2 · ×1

HUMANLIKE

---

279 — Cubchoo

LEVEL-UP MOVES

LV	NAME	TYPE	KIND	POW.	ACC.	PP	RANGE
1	Growl	Normal	Status	—	100	40	Many Others
1	Powder Snow	Ice	Special	40	100	25	Many Others
3	Endure	Normal	Status	—	—	10	Self
6	Fury Swipes	Normal	Physical	18	80	15	Normal
9	Icy Wind	Ice	Special	55	95	15	Many Others
12	Play Nice	Normal	Status	—	—	20	Normal
15	Brine	Water	Special	65	100	10	Normal
18	Frost Breath	Ice	Special	60	90	10	Normal
21	Slash	Normal	Physical	70	100	20	Normal
24	Flail	Normal	Physical	—	100	15	Normal
27	Charm	Fairy	Status	—	100	20	Normal
30	Hail	Ice	Status	—	—	10	Both Sides
33	Thrash	Normal	Physical	120	100	10	1 Random
36	Rest	Psychic	Status	—	—	10	Self
39	Blizzard	Ice	Special	110	70	5	Many Others
42	Sheer Cold	Ice	Special	—	30	5	Normal

EVOLUTION MOVES

NAME	TYPE	KIND	POW.	ACC.	PP	RANGE

EGG MOVES

NAME	TYPE	KIND	POW.	ACC.	PP	RANGE
Focus Punch	Fighting	Physical	150	100	20	Normal
Night Slash	Dark	Physical	70	100	15	Normal
Yawn	Normal	Status	—	—	10	Normal

TUTOR MOVES

NAME	TYPE	KIND	POW.	ACC.	PP	RANGE

TM MOVES

NO.	NAME	TYPE	KIND	POW.	ACC.	PP	RANGE
TM00	Mega Punch	Normal	Physical	80	85	20	Normal
TM01	Mega Kick	Normal	Physical	120	75	5	Normal
TM04	Ice Punch	Ice	Physical	75	100	15	Normal
TM15	Dig	Ground	Physical	80	100	10	Normal
TM21	Rest	Psychic	Status	—	—	10	Self
TM24	Snore	Normal	Special	50	100	15	Normal
TM25	Protect	Normal	Status	—	—	10	Self
TM27	Icy Wind	Ice	Special	55	95	15	Many Others
TM29	Charm	Fairy	Status	—	100	20	Normal
TM31	Attract	Normal	Status	—	100	15	Normal
TM33	Rain Dance	Water	Status	—	—	5	Both Sides
TM35	Hail	Ice	Status	—	—	10	Both Sides
TM39	Facade	Normal	Physical	70	100	20	Normal
TM48	Rock Tomb	Rock	Physical	60	95	15	Normal
TM55	Brine	Water	Special	65	100	10	Normal
TM58	Assurance	Dark	Physical	60	100	10	Normal
TM59	Fling	Dark	Physical	—	100	10	Normal
TM64	Avalanche	Ice	Physical	60	100	10	Normal
TM65	Shadow Claw	Ghost	Physical	70	100	15	Normal
TM67	Ice Fang	Ice	Physical	65	95	15	Normal
TM76	Round	Normal	Special	60	100	15	Normal

TR MOVES

NAME	TYPE	KIND	POW.	ACC.	PP	RANGE
TR04 Surf	Water	Special	90	100	15	All Others
TR05 Ice Beam	Ice	Special	90	100	10	Normal
TR06 Blizzard	Ice	Special	110	70	5	Many Others
TR07 Low Kick	Fighting	Physical	—	100	20	Normal
TR20 Substitute	Normal	Status	—	—	10	Self
TR26 Endure	Normal	Status	—	—	10	Self
TR27 Sleep Talk	Normal	Status	—	—	10	Self
TR30 Encore	Normal	Status	—	100	5	Normal
TR39 Superpower	Fighting	Physical	120	100	5	Normal
TR77 Grass Knot	Grass	Special	—	100	20	Normal
TR90 Play Rough	Fairy	Physical	90	90	10	Normal

Cubchoo p. 115

ABILITY
Snow Cloak
Slush Rush

HIDDEN ABILITY
Rattled

SPECIES STRENGTHS

HP · ATTACK · DEFENSE · SP. ATK · SP. DEF · SPEED

DAMAGE TAKEN IN BATTLE

×1 · ×2 · ×2 · ×2 · ×1 · ×1 · ×1 · ×1 · ×1 · ×1 · ×1 · ×1 · ×1 · ×2 · ×0.5 · ×1 · ×1

FIELD

280

Beartic
p. 115

ABILITY
Snow Cloak
Slush Rush

HIDDEN ABILITY
Swift Swim

SPECIES STRENGTHS

HP	
ATTACK	
DEFENSE	
SP. ATK	
SP. DEF	
SPEED	

DAMAGE TAKEN IN BATTLE

×1 ×2 ×2
×2 ×1 ×1
×1 ×1 ×1
×1 ×1 ×1
×1 ×1 ×2
×0.5 ×1 ×1

FIELD

LEVEL-UP MOVES

LV.	NAME	TYPE	KIND	POW.	ACC.	PP	RANGE
1	Aqua Jet	Water	Physical	40	100	20	Normal
1	Charm	Fairy	Status	—	100	20	Normal
1	Endure	Normal	Status	—	—	10	Self
1	Fury Swipes	Normal	Physical	18	80	15	Normal
1	Growl	Normal	Status	—	100	40	Many Others
1	Icicle Crash	Ice	Physical	85	90	10	Normal
1	Powder Snow	Ice	Special	40	100	25	Many Others
9	Icy Wind	Ice	Special	55	95	15	Many Others
12	Play Nice	Normal	Status	—	—	20	Normal
15	Brine	Water	Special	65	100	10	Normal
18	Frost Breath	Ice	Special	60	90	10	Normal
21	Slash	Normal	Physical	70	100	20	Normal
24	Flail	Normal	Physical	—	100	15	Normal
27	Swagger	Normal	Status	—	85	15	Normal
30	Hail	Ice	Status	—	—	10	Both Sides
33	Thrash	Normal	Physical	120	100	10	1 Random
36	Rest	Psychic	Status	—	—	10	Self
41	Blizzard	Ice	Special	110	70	5	Many Others
46	Sheer Cold	Ice	Special	—	30	5	Normal
51	Superpower	Fighting	Physical	120	100	5	Normal

EVOLUTION MOVES

NAME	TYPE	KIND	POW.	ACC.	PP	RANGE
Icicle Crash	Ice	Physical	85	90	10	Normal

EGG MOVES

NAME	TYPE	KIND	POW.	ACC.	PP	RANGE

TUTOR MOVES

NAME	TYPE	KIND	POW.	ACC.	PP	RANGE

TM MOVES

NO.	NAME	TYPE	KIND	POW.	ACC.	PP	RANGE
TM00	Mega Punch	Normal	Physical	80	85	20	Normal
TM01	Mega Kick	Normal	Physical	120	75	5	Normal
TM04	Ice Punch	Ice	Physical	75	100	15	Normal
TM08	Hyper Beam	Normal	Special	150	90	5	Normal
TM09	Giga Impact	Normal	Physical	150	90	5	Normal
TM15	Dig	Ground	Physical	80	100	10	Normal
TM21	Rest	Psychic	Status	—	—	10	Self
TM22	Rock Slide	Rock	Physical	75	90	10	Many Others
TM24	Snore	Normal	Special	50	100	15	Normal
TM25	Protect	Normal	Status	—	—	10	Self
TM26	Scary Face	Normal	Status	—	100	10	Normal
TM27	Icy Wind	Ice	Special	55	95	15	Many Others
TM29	Charm	Fairy	Status	—	100	20	Normal
TM31	Attract	Normal	Status	—	100	15	Normal
TM33	Rain Dance	Water	Status	—	—	5	Both Sides
TM35	Hail	Ice	Status	—	—	10	Both Sides
TM39	Facade	Normal	Physical	70	100	20	Normal
TM43	Brick Break	Fighting	Physical	75	100	15	Normal
TM45	Dive	Water	Physical	80	100	10	Normal
TM48	Rock Tomb	Rock	Physical	60	95	15	Normal
TM51	Icicle Spear	Ice	Physical	25	100	30	Normal
TM55	Brine	Water	Special	65	100	10	Normal
TM58	Assurance	Dark	Physical	60	100	10	Normal
TM59	Fling	Dark	Physical	—	100	10	Normal
TM64	Avalanche	Ice	Physical	60	100	10	Normal
TM65	Shadow Claw	Ghost	Physical	70	100	15	Normal
TM67	Ice Fang	Ice	Physical	65	95	15	Normal
TM76	Round	Normal	Special	60	100	15	Normal
TM81	Bulldoze	Ground	Physical	60	100	20	All Others

TR MOVES

NAME	TYPE	KIND	POW.	ACC.	PP	RANGE
TR00 Swords Dance	Normal	Status	—	—	20	Self
TR04 Surf	Water	Special	90	100	15	All Others
TR05 Ice Beam	Ice	Special	90	100	10	Normal
TR06 Blizzard	Ice	Special	110	70	5	Many Others
TR07 Low Kick	Fighting	Physical	—	100	20	Normal
TR20 Substitute	Normal	Status	—	—	10	Self
TR26 Endure	Normal	Status	—	—	10	Self
TR27 Sleep Talk	Normal	Status	—	—	10	Self
TR30 Encore	Normal	Status	—	100	5	Normal
TR37 Taunt	Dark	Status	—	100	20	Normal
TR39 Superpower	Fighting	Physical	120	100	5	Normal
TR48 Bulk Up	Fighting	Status	—	—	20	Self
TR64 Focus Blast	Fighting	Special	120	70	5	Normal
TR75 Stone Edge	Rock	Physical	100	80	5	Normal
TR77 Grass Knot	Grass	Special	—	100	20	Normal
TR79 Heavy Slam	Steel	Physical	—	100	10	Normal
TR90 Play Rough	Fairy	Physical	90	90	10	Normal
TR95 Throat Chop	Dark	Physical	80	100	15	Normal
TR98 Liquidation	Water	Physical	85	100	10	Normal
TR99 Body Press	Fighting	Physical	80	100	10	Normal

281

Rufflet
p. 116

ABILITY
Keen Eye
Sheer Force

HIDDEN ABILITY
Hustle

SPECIES STRENGTHS

HP	
ATTACK	
DEFENSE	
SP. ATK	
SP. DEF	
SPEED	

DAMAGE TAKEN IN BATTLE

×1 ×1 ×2
×1 ×1 ×0
×1 ×0 ×1
×0.5 ×1 ×1
×2 ×1 ×1
×2 ×0.5 ×1

FLYING

LEVEL-UP MOVES

LV.	NAME	TYPE	KIND	POW.	ACC.	PP	RANGE
1	Leer	Normal	Status	—	100	30	Many Others
1	Peck	Flying	Physical	35	100	35	Normal
6	Hone Claws	Dark	Status	—	—	15	Self
12	Wing Attack	Flying	Physical	60	100	35	Normal
18	Tailwind	Flying	Status	—	—	15	Your Side
24	Scary Face	Normal	Status	—	100	10	Normal
30	Aerial Ace	Flying	Physical	60	—	20	Normal
36	Slash	Normal	Physical	70	100	20	Normal
42	Whirlwind	Normal	Status	—	—	20	Normal
48	Crush Claw	Normal	Physical	75	95	10	Normal
55	Air Slash	Flying	Special	75	95	15	Normal
60	Defog	Flying	Status	—	—	15	Normal
66	Thrash	Normal	Physical	120	100	10	1 Random
72	Brave Bird	Flying	Physical	120	100	15	Normal

EVOLUTION MOVES

NAME	TYPE	KIND	POW.	ACC.	PP	RANGE

EGG MOVES

NAME	TYPE	KIND	POW.	ACC.	PP	RANGE

TUTOR MOVES

NAME	TYPE	KIND	POW.	ACC.	PP	RANGE

TM MOVES

NO.	NAME	TYPE	KIND	POW.	ACC.	PP	RANGE
TM06	Fly	Flying	Physical	90	95	15	Normal
TM21	Rest	Psychic	Status	—	—	10	Self
TM22	Rock Slide	Rock	Physical	75	90	10	Many Others
TM24	Snore	Normal	Special	50	100	15	Normal
TM25	Protect	Normal	Status	—	—	10	Self
TM26	Scary Face	Normal	Status	—	100	10	Normal
TM30	Steel Wing	Steel	Physical	70	90	25	Normal
TM31	Attract	Normal	Status	—	100	15	Normal
TM33	Rain Dance	Water	Status	—	—	5	Both Sides
TM34	Sunny Day	Fire	Status	—	—	5	Both Sides
TM39	Facade	Normal	Physical	70	100	20	Normal
TM40	Swift	Normal	Special	60	—	20	Many Others
TM48	Rock Tomb	Rock	Physical	60	95	15	Normal
TM56	U-turn	Bug	Physical	70	100	20	Normal
TM58	Assurance	Dark	Physical	60	100	10	Normal
TM65	Shadow Claw	Ghost	Physical	70	100	15	Normal
TM76	Round	Normal	Special	60	100	15	Normal
TM79	Retaliate	Normal	Physical	70	100	5	Normal
TM95	Air Slash	Flying	Special	75	95	15	Normal

TR MOVES

NAME	TYPE	KIND	POW.	ACC.	PP	RANGE
TR12 Agility	Psychic	Status	—	—	30	Self
TR20 Substitute	Normal	Status	—	—	10	Self
TR26 Endure	Normal	Status	—	—	10	Self
TR27 Sleep Talk	Normal	Status	—	—	10	Self
TR36 Heat Wave	Fire	Special	95	90	10	Many Others
TR39 Superpower	Fighting	Physical	120	100	5	Normal
TR48 Bulk Up	Fighting	Status	—	—	20	Self
TR53 Close Combat	Fighting	Physical	120	100	5	Normal
TR66 Brave Bird	Flying	Physical	120	100	15	Normal
TR69 Zen Headbutt	Psychic	Physical	80	90	15	Normal
TR85 Work Up	Normal	Status	—	—	30	Self
TR89 Hurricane	Flying	Special	110	70	10	Normal

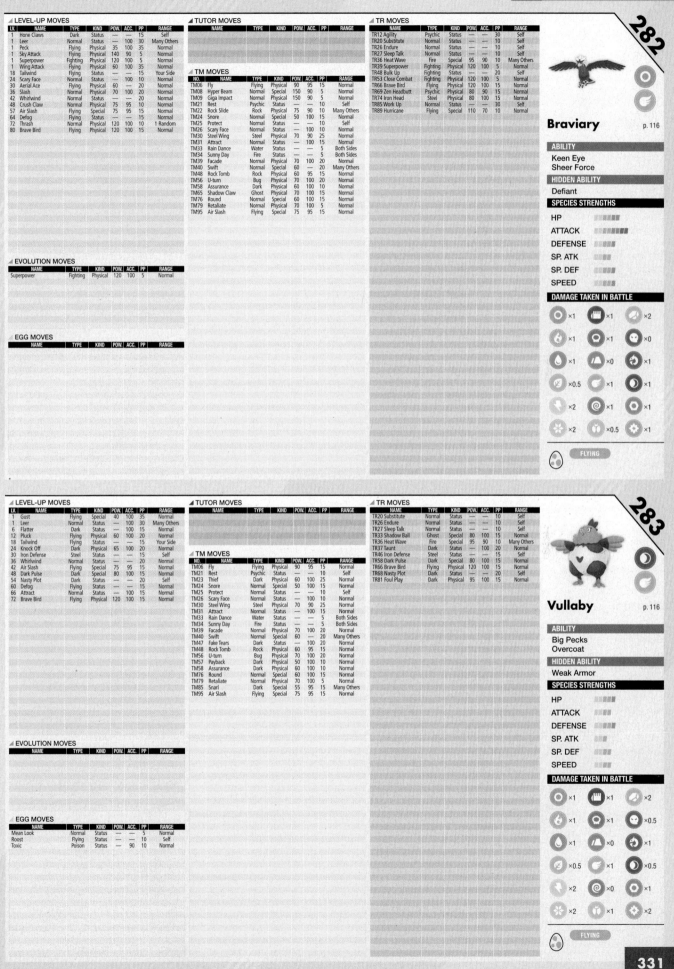

282

LEVEL-UP MOVES

LV.	NAME	TYPE	KIND	POW.	ACC.	PP	RANGE
1	Hone Claws	Dark	Status	—	—	15	Self
1	Leer	Normal	Status	—	100	30	Many Others
1	Peck	Flying	Physical	35	100	35	Normal
1	Sky Attack	Flying	Physical	140	90	5	Normal
1	Superpower	Fighting	Physical	120	100	5	Normal
1	Wing Attack	Flying	Physical	60	100	35	Normal
18	Tailwind	Flying	Status	—	—	15	Your Side
24	Scary Face	Normal	Status	—	100	10	Normal
30	Aerial Ace	Flying	Physical	60	—	20	Normal
36	Slash	Normal	Physical	70	100	20	Normal
42	Whirlwind	Normal	Status	—	—	20	Normal
48	Crush Claw	Normal	Physical	75	95	10	Normal
57	Air Slash	Flying	Special	75	95	15	Normal
64	Defog	Flying	Status	—	—	15	Normal
72	Thrash	Normal	Physical	120	100	10	1 Random
80	Brave Bird	Flying	Physical	120	100	15	Normal

EVOLUTION MOVES

NAME	TYPE	KIND	POW.	ACC.	PP	RANGE
Superpower	Fighting	Physical	120	100	5	Normal

EGG MOVES

NAME	TYPE	KIND	POW.	ACC.	PP	RANGE

TUTOR MOVES

NAME	TYPE	KIND	POW.	ACC.	PP	RANGE

TM MOVES

NO.	NAME	TYPE	KIND	POW.	ACC.	PP	RANGE
TM06	Fly	Flying	Physical	90	95	15	Normal
TM08	Hyper Beam	Normal	Special	150	90	5	Normal
TM09	Giga Impact	Normal	Physical	150	90	5	Normal
TM21	Rest	Psychic	Status	—	—	10	Self
TM22	Rock Slide	Rock	Physical	75	90	10	Many Others
TM24	Snore	Normal	Special	50	100	15	Normal
TM25	Protect	Normal	Status	—	—	10	Self
TM26	Scary Face	Normal	Status	—	100	10	Normal
TM30	Steel Wing	Steel	Physical	70	90	25	Normal
TM31	Attract	Normal	Status	—	100	15	Normal
TM33	Rain Dance	Water	Status	—	—	5	Both Sides
TM34	Sunny Day	Fire	Status	—	—	5	Both Sides
TM39	Facade	Normal	Physical	70	100	20	Normal
TM40	Swift	Normal	Special	60	—	20	Many Others
TM48	Rock Tomb	Rock	Physical	60	95	15	Normal
TM56	U-turn	Bug	Physical	70	100	20	Normal
TM58	Assurance	Dark	Physical	60	100	10	Normal
TM65	Shadow Claw	Ghost	Physical	70	100	15	Normal
TM76	Round	Normal	Special	60	100	15	Normal
TM79	Retaliate	Normal	Physical	70	100	5	Normal
TM95	Air Slash	Flying	Special	75	95	15	Normal

TR MOVES

NO.	NAME	TYPE	KIND	POW.	ACC.	PP	RANGE
TR12	Agility	Psychic	Status	—	—	30	Self
TR20	Substitute	Normal	Status	—	—	10	Self
TR26	Endure	Normal	Status	—	—	10	Self
TR27	Sleep Talk	Normal	Status	—	—	10	Self
TR36	Heat Wave	Fire	Special	95	90	10	Many Others
TR39	Superpower	Fighting	Physical	120	100	5	Normal
TR48	Bulk Up	Fighting	Status	—	—	20	Self
TR53	Close Combat	Fighting	Physical	120	100	5	Normal
TR66	Brave Bird	Flying	Physical	120	100	15	Normal
TR69	Zen Headbutt	Psychic	Physical	80	90	15	Normal
TR74	Iron Head	Steel	Physical	80	100	15	Normal
TR85	Work Up	Normal	Status	—	—	30	Self
TR89	Hurricane	Flying	Special	110	70	10	Normal

Braviary
p. 116

ABILITY
Keen Eye
Sheer Force

HIDDEN ABILITY
Defiant

SPECIES STRENGTHS
HP
ATTACK
DEFENSE
SP. ATK
SP. DEF
SPEED

DAMAGE TAKEN IN BATTLE
×1 ×1 ×2
×1 ×1 ×0
×1 ×0 ×1
×0.5 ×1 ×1
×2 ×1 ×1
×2 ×0.5 ×1

FLYING

283

LEVEL-UP MOVES

LV.	NAME	TYPE	KIND	POW.	ACC.	PP	RANGE
1	Gust	Flying	Special	40	100	35	Normal
1	Leer	Normal	Status	—	100	30	Many Others
6	Flatter	Dark	Status	—	100	15	Normal
12	Pluck	Flying	Physical	60	100	20	Normal
18	Tailwind	Flying	Status	—	—	15	Your Side
24	Knock Off	Dark	Physical	65	100	20	Normal
30	Iron Defense	Steel	Status	—	—	15	Self
36	Whirlwind	Normal	Status	—	—	20	Normal
42	Air Slash	Flying	Special	75	95	15	Normal
48	Dark Pulse	Dark	Special	80	100	15	Normal
54	Nasty Plot	Dark	Status	—	—	20	Self
60	Defog	Flying	Status	—	—	15	Normal
66	Attract	Normal	Status	—	100	15	Normal
72	Brave Bird	Flying	Physical	120	100	15	Normal

EVOLUTION MOVES

NAME	TYPE	KIND	POW.	ACC.	PP	RANGE

EGG MOVES

NAME	TYPE	KIND	POW.	ACC.	PP	RANGE
Mean Look	Normal	Status	—	—	5	Normal
Roost	Flying	Status	—	—	10	Self
Toxic	Poison	Status	—	90	10	Normal

TUTOR MOVES

NAME	TYPE	KIND	POW.	ACC.	PP	RANGE

TM MOVES

NO.	NAME	TYPE	KIND	POW.	ACC.	PP	RANGE
TM06	Fly	Flying	Physical	90	95	15	Normal
TM21	Rest	Psychic	Status	—	—	10	Self
TM23	Thief	Dark	Physical	60	100	25	Normal
TM24	Snore	Normal	Special	50	100	15	Normal
TM25	Protect	Normal	Status	—	—	10	Self
TM26	Scary Face	Normal	Status	—	100	10	Normal
TM30	Steel Wing	Steel	Physical	70	90	25	Normal
TM31	Attract	Normal	Status	—	100	15	Normal
TM33	Rain Dance	Water	Status	—	—	5	Both Sides
TM34	Sunny Day	Fire	Status	—	—	5	Both Sides
TM39	Facade	Normal	Physical	70	100	20	Normal
TM40	Swift	Normal	Special	60	—	20	Many Others
TM47	Fake Tears	Dark	Status	—	100	20	Normal
TM48	Rock Tomb	Rock	Physical	60	95	15	Normal
TM56	U-turn	Bug	Physical	70	100	20	Normal
TM57	Payback	Dark	Physical	50	100	10	Normal
TM58	Assurance	Dark	Physical	60	100	10	Normal
TM76	Round	Normal	Special	60	100	15	Normal
TM79	Retaliate	Normal	Physical	70	100	5	Normal
TM85	Snarl	Dark	Special	55	95	15	Many Others
TM95	Air Slash	Flying	Special	75	95	15	Normal

TR MOVES

NO.	NAME	TYPE	KIND	POW.	ACC.	PP	RANGE
TR20	Substitute	Normal	Status	—	—	10	Self
TR26	Endure	Normal	Status	—	—	10	Self
TR27	Sleep Talk	Normal	Status	—	—	10	Self
TR33	Shadow Ball	Ghost	Special	80	100	15	Normal
TR36	Heat Wave	Fire	Special	95	90	10	Many Others
TR37	Taunt	Dark	Status	—	100	20	Normal
TR46	Iron Defense	Steel	Status	—	—	15	Self
TR58	Dark Pulse	Dark	Special	80	100	15	Normal
TR66	Brave Bird	Flying	Physical	120	100	15	Normal
TR68	Nasty Plot	Dark	Status	—	—	20	Self
TR81	Foul Play	Dark	Physical	95	100	15	Normal

Vullaby
p. 116

ABILITY
Big Pecks
Overcoat

HIDDEN ABILITY
Weak Armor

SPECIES STRENGTHS
HP
ATTACK
DEFENSE
SP. ATK
SP. DEF
SPEED

DAMAGE TAKEN IN BATTLE
×1 ×1 ×2
×1 ×1 ×0.5
×1 ×0 ×1
×0.5 ×1 ×0.5
×2 ×0 ×1
×1 ×1 ×2

FLYING

284

Mandibuzz p. 116

ABILITY
Big Pecks
Overcoat

HIDDEN ABILITY
Weak Armor

SPECIES STRENGTHS

HP	
ATTACK	
DEFENSE	
SP. ATK	
SP. DEF	
SPEED	

DAMAGE TAKEN IN BATTLE

×1	×1	×2
×1	×1	×0.5
×1	×0	×1
×0.5	×1	×0.5
×2	×0	×1
×2	×1	×2

FLYING

LEVEL-UP MOVES

LV.	NAME	TYPE	KIND	POW.	ACC.	PP	RANGE
1	Bone Rush	Ground	Physical	25	90	10	Normal
1	Flatter	Dark	Status	—	100	15	Normal
1	Gust	Flying	Special	40	100	35	Normal
1	Leer	Normal	Status	—	100	30	Many Others
1	Pluck	Flying	Physical	60	100	20	Normal
1	Sky Attack	Flying	Physical	140	90	5	Normal
1	Toxic	Poison	Status	—	90	10	Normal
18	Tailwind	Flying	Status	—	—	15	Your Side
24	Knock Off	Dark	Physical	65	100	20	Normal
30	Iron Defense	Steel	Status	—	—	15	Self
36	Whirlwind	Normal	Status	—	—	20	Normal
42	Air Slash	Flying	Special	75	95	15	Normal
48	Dark Pulse	Dark	Special	80	100	15	Normal
57	Nasty Plot	Dark	Status	—	—	20	Self
64	Defog	Flying	Status	—	—	15	Normal
72	Attract	Normal	Status	—	100	15	Normal
80	Brave Bird	Flying	Physical	120	100	15	Normal

EVOLUTION MOVES

NAME	TYPE	KIND	POW.	ACC.	PP	RANGE
Bone Rush	Ground	Physical	25	90	10	Normal

EGG MOVES

NAME	TYPE	KIND	POW.	ACC.	PP	RANGE

TUTOR MOVES

NAME	TYPE	KIND	POW.	ACC.	PP	RANGE

TM MOVES

NO.	NAME	TYPE	KIND	POW.	ACC.	PP	RANGE
TM06	Fly	Flying	Physical	90	95	15	Normal
TM08	Hyper Beam	Normal	Special	150	90	5	Normal
TM09	Giga Impact	Normal	Physical	150	90	5	Normal
TM21	Rest	Psychic	Status	—	—	10	Self
TM23	Thief	Dark	Physical	60	100	25	Normal
TM24	Snore	Normal	Special	50	100	15	Normal
TM25	Protect	Normal	Status	—	—	10	Self
TM26	Scary Face	Normal	Status	—	100	10	Normal
TM30	Steel Wing	Steel	Physical	70	90	25	Normal
TM31	Attract	Normal	Status	—	100	15	Normal
TM33	Rain Dance	Water	Status	—	—	5	Both Sides
TM34	Sunny Day	Fire	Status	—	—	5	Both Sides
TM39	Facade	Normal	Physical	70	100	20	Normal
TM40	Swift	Normal	Special	60	—	20	Many Others
TM47	Fake Tears	Dark	Status	—	100	20	Normal
TM48	Rock Tomb	Rock	Physical	60	95	15	Normal
TM56	U-turn	Bug	Physical	70	100	20	Normal
TM57	Payback	Dark	Physical	50	100	10	Normal
TM58	Assurance	Dark	Physical	60	100	10	Normal
TM76	Round	Normal	Special	60	100	15	Normal
TM79	Retaliate	Normal	Physical	70	100	5	Normal
TM85	Snarl	Dark	Special	55	95	15	Many Others
TM95	Air Slash	Flying	Special	75	95	15	Normal

TR MOVES

NAME	TYPE	KIND	POW.	ACC.	PP	RANGE
TR20 Substitute	Normal	Status	—	—	10	Self
TR26 Endure	Normal	Status	—	—	10	Self
TR27 Sleep Talk	Normal	Status	—	—	10	Self
TR33 Shadow Ball	Ghost	Special	80	100	15	Normal
TR36 Heat Wave	Fire	Special	95	90	10	Many Others
TR37 Taunt	Dark	Status	—	100	20	Normal
TR46 Iron Defense	Steel	Status	—	—	15	Self
TR58 Dark Pulse	Dark	Special	80	100	15	Normal
TR66 Brave Bird	Flying	Physical	120	100	15	Normal
TR68 Nasty Plot	Dark	Status	—	—	20	Self
TR81 Foul Play	Dark	Physical	95	100	15	Normal

285

Skorupi p. 117

ABILITY
Battle Armor
Sniper

HIDDEN ABILITY
Keen Eye

SPECIES STRENGTHS

HP	
ATTACK	
DEFENSE	
SP. ATK	
SP. DEF	
SPEED	

DAMAGE TAKEN IN BATTLE

×1	×0.25	×2
×2	×0.5	×1
×1	×1	×1
×0.25	×2	×1
×1	×2	×1
×1	×0.5	×0.5

BUG
WATER 3

LEVEL-UP MOVES

LV.	NAME	TYPE	KIND	POW.	ACC.	PP	RANGE
1	Leer	Normal	Status	—	100	30	Many Others
1	Poison Sting	Poison	Physical	15	100	35	Normal
3	Hone Claws	Dark	Status	—	—	15	Self
6	Fell Stinger	Bug	Physical	50	100	25	Normal
9	Poison Fang	Poison	Physical	50	100	15	Normal
12	Bite	Dark	Physical	60	100	25	Normal
15	Toxic Spikes	Poison	Status	—	—	20	Other Side
18	Bug Bite	Bug	Physical	60	100	20	Normal
21	Venoshock	Poison	Special	65	100	10	Normal
24	Knock Off	Dark	Physical	65	100	20	Normal
27	Scary Face	Normal	Status	—	100	10	Normal
30	Pin Missile	Bug	Physical	25	95	20	Normal
33	Toxic	Poison	Status	—	90	10	Normal
36	Night Slash	Dark	Physical	70	100	15	Normal
39	Cross Poison	Poison	Physical	70	100	20	Normal
42	X-Scissor	Bug	Physical	80	100	15	Normal
45	Acupressure	Normal	Status	—	—	30	Self/Ally
48	Crunch	Dark	Physical	80	100	15	Normal

EVOLUTION MOVES

NAME	TYPE	KIND	POW.	ACC.	PP	RANGE

EGG MOVES

NAME	TYPE	KIND	POW.	ACC.	PP	RANGE
Confuse Ray	Ghost	Status	—	100	10	Normal
Sand Attack	Ground	Status	—	100	15	Normal
Slash	Normal	Physical	70	100	20	Normal
Whirlwind	Normal	Status	—	—	20	Normal

TUTOR MOVES

NAME	TYPE	KIND	POW.	ACC.	PP	RANGE

TM MOVES

NO.	NAME	TYPE	KIND	POW.	ACC.	PP	RANGE
TM07	Pin Missile	Bug	Physical	25	95	20	Normal
TM15	Dig	Ground	Physical	80	100	10	Normal
TM16	Screech	Normal	Status	—	85	40	Normal
TM21	Rest	Psychic	Status	—	—	10	Self
TM23	Thief	Dark	Physical	60	100	25	Normal
TM24	Snore	Normal	Special	50	100	15	Normal
TM25	Protect	Normal	Status	—	—	10	Self
TM26	Scary Face	Normal	Status	—	100	10	Normal
TM31	Attract	Normal	Status	—	100	15	Normal
TM33	Rain Dance	Water	Status	—	—	5	Both Sides
TM34	Sunny Day	Fire	Status	—	—	5	Both Sides
TM39	Facade	Normal	Physical	70	100	20	Normal
TM43	Brick Break	Fighting	Physical	75	100	15	Normal
TM48	Rock Tomb	Rock	Physical	60	95	15	Normal
TM57	Payback	Dark	Physical	50	100	10	Normal
TM58	Assurance	Dark	Physical	60	100	10	Normal
TM59	Fling	Dark	Physical	—	100	10	Normal
TM73	Cross Poison	Poison	Physical	70	100	20	Normal
TM74	Venoshock	Poison	Special	65	100	10	Normal
TM76	Round	Normal	Special	60	100	15	Normal
TM94	False Swipe	Normal	Physical	40	100	40	Normal

TR MOVES

NAME	TYPE	KIND	POW.	ACC.	PP	RANGE
TR00 Swords Dance	Normal	Status	—	—	20	Self
TR12 Agility	Psychic	Status	—	—	30	Self
TR20 Substitute	Normal	Status	—	—	10	Self
TR22 Sludge Bomb	Poison	Special	90	100	10	Normal
TR26 Endure	Normal	Status	—	—	10	Self
TR27 Sleep Talk	Normal	Status	—	—	10	Self
TR31 Iron Tail	Steel	Physical	100	75	15	Normal
TR32 Crunch	Dark	Physical	80	100	15	Normal
TR33 Shadow Ball	Ghost	Special	80	100	15	Normal
TR37 Taunt	Dark	Status	—	100	20	Normal
TR54 Toxic Spikes	Poison	Status	—	—	20	Other Side
TR57 Poison Jab	Poison	Physical	80	100	20	Normal
TR58 Dark Pulse	Dark	Special	80	100	15	Normal
TR60 X-Scissor	Bug	Physical	80	100	15	Normal
TR61 Bug Buzz	Bug	Special	90	100	10	Normal

286

Drapion — p. 117

LEVEL-UP MOVES

LV.	NAME	TYPE	KIND	POW.	ACC.	PP	RANGE
1	Fell Stinger	Bug	Physical	50	100	25	Normal
1	Fire Fang	Fire	Physical	65	95	15	Normal
1	Hone Claws	Dark	Status	—	—	15	Self
1	Ice Fang	Ice	Physical	65	95	15	Normal
1	Leer	Normal	Status	—	100	30	Many Others
1	Poison Sting	Poison	Physical	15	100	35	Normal
1	Thunder Fang	Electric	Physical	65	95	15	Normal
9	Poison Fang	Poison	Physical	50	100	15	Normal
15	Bite	Dark	Physical	60	100	25	Normal
15	Toxic Spikes	Poison	Status	—	—	20	Other Side
18	Bug Bite	Bug	Physical	60	100	20	Normal
21	Venoshock	Poison	Special	65	100	10	Normal
24	Knock Off	Dark	Physical	65	100	20	Normal
27	Scary Face	Normal	Status	—	100	10	Normal
30	Pin Missile	Bug	Physical	25	95	20	Normal
33	Toxic	Poison	Status	—	90	10	Normal
36	Night Slash	Dark	Physical	70	100	15	Normal
39	Cross Poison	Poison	Physical	70	100	20	Normal
44	X-Scissor	Bug	Physical	80	100	15	Normal
49	Acupressure	Normal	Status	—	—	30	Self/Ally
54	Crunch	Dark	Physical	80	100	15	Normal

EVOLUTION MOVES

NAME	TYPE	KIND	POW.	ACC.	PP	RANGE

EGG MOVES

NAME	TYPE	KIND	POW.	ACC.	PP	RANGE

TUTOR MOVES

NAME	TYPE	KIND	POW.	ACC.	PP	RANGE

TM MOVES

NO.	NAME	TYPE	KIND	POW.	ACC.	PP	RANGE
TM07	Pin Missile	Bug	Physical	25	95	20	Normal
TM08	Hyper Beam	Normal	Special	150	90	5	Normal
TM09	Giga Impact	Normal	Physical	150	90	5	Normal
TM15	Dig	Ground	Physical	80	100	10	Normal
TM16	Screech	Normal	Status	—	85	40	Normal
TM21	Rest	Psychic	Status	—	—	10	Self
TM22	Rock Slide	Rock	Physical	75	90	10	Many Others
TM23	Thief	Dark	Physical	60	100	25	Normal
TM24	Snore	Normal	Special	50	100	15	Normal
TM25	Protect	Normal	Status	—	—	10	Self
TM26	Scary Face	Normal	Status	—	100	10	Normal
TM31	Attract	Normal	Status	—	100	15	Normal
TM33	Rain Dance	Water	Status	—	—	5	Both Sides
TM34	Sunny Day	Fire	Status	—	—	5	Both Sides
TM39	Facade	Normal	Physical	70	100	20	Normal
TM43	Brick Break	Fighting	Physical	75	100	15	Normal
TM48	Rock Tomb	Rock	Physical	60	95	15	Normal
TM49	Sand Tomb	Ground	Physical	35	85	15	Normal
TM57	Payback	Dark	Physical	50	100	10	Normal
TM58	Assurance	Dark	Physical	60	100	10	Normal
TM59	Fling	Dark	Physical	—	100	10	Normal
TM66	Thunder Fang	Electric	Physical	65	95	15	Normal
TM67	Ice Fang	Ice	Physical	65	95	15	Normal
TM68	Fire Fang	Fire	Physical	65	95	15	Normal
TM73	Cross Poison	Poison	Physical	70	100	20	Normal
TM74	Venoshock	Poison	Special	65	100	10	Normal
TM76	Round	Normal	Special	60	100	15	Normal
TM79	Retaliate	Normal	Physical	70	100	5	Normal
TM81	Bulldoze	Ground	Physical	60	100	20	All Others
TM85	Snarl	Dark	Special	55	95	15	Many Others
TM94	False Swipe	Normal	Physical	40	100	40	Normal
TM97	Brutal Swing	Dark	Physical	60	100	20	All Others
TM98	Stomping Tantrum	Ground	Physical	75	100	10	Normal

TR MOVES

NO.	NAME	TYPE	KIND	POW.	ACC.	PP	RANGE
TR00	Swords Dance	Normal	Status	—	—	20	Self
TR10	Earthquake	Ground	Physical	100	100	10	All Others
TR12	Agility	Psychic	Status	—	—	30	Self
TR18	Leech Life	Bug	Physical	80	100	10	Normal
TR20	Substitute	Normal	Status	—	—	10	Self
TR22	Sludge Bomb	Poison	Special	90	100	10	Normal
TR26	Endure	Normal	Status	—	—	10	Self
TR27	Sleep Talk	Normal	Status	—	—	10	Self
TR31	Iron Tail	Steel	Physical	100	75	15	Normal
TR32	Crunch	Dark	Physical	80	100	15	Normal
TR33	Shadow Ball	Ghost	Special	80	100	15	Normal
TR37	Taunt	Dark	Status	—	100	20	Normal
TR46	Iron Defense	Steel	Status	—	—	15	Self
TR54	Toxic Spikes	Poison	Status	—	—	20	Other Side
TR57	Poison Jab	Poison	Physical	80	100	20	Normal
TR58	Dark Pulse	Dark	Special	80	100	15	Normal
TR60	X-Scissor	Bug	Physical	80	100	15	Normal
TR61	Bug Buzz	Bug	Special	90	100	10	Normal
TR91	Venom Drench	Poison	Status	—	100	20	Many Others
TR95	Throat Chop	Dark	Physical	80	100	15	Normal

ABILITY
Battle Armor
Sniper

HIDDEN ABILITY
Keen Eye

SPECIES STRENGTHS
HP
ATTACK
DEFENSE
SP. ATK
SP. DEF
SPEED

DAMAGE TAKEN IN BATTLE
×1, ×1, ×1, ×1, ×0.5, ×0.5, ×1, ×2, ×1, ×0.5, ×1, ×0.5, ×1, ×0, ×1, ×1, ×1, ×1

Egg Groups: BUG / WATER 3

287

Litwick — p. 118

LEVEL-UP MOVES

LV.	NAME	TYPE	KIND	POW.	ACC.	PP	RANGE
1	Astonish	Ghost	Physical	30	100	15	Normal
1	Smog	Poison	Special	30	70	10	Normal
4	Ember	Fire	Special	40	100	25	Normal
8	Minimize	Normal	Status	—	—	10	Self
12	Confuse Ray	Ghost	Status	—	100	10	Normal
16	Hex	Ghost	Special	65	100	10	Normal
20	Will-O-Wisp	Fire	Status	—	85	15	Normal
24	Fire Spin	Fire	Special	35	85	15	Normal
28	Night Shade	Ghost	Special	—	100	15	Normal
32	Curse	Ghost	Status	—	—	10	Varies
36	Shadow Ball	Ghost	Special	80	100	15	Normal
40	Inferno	Fire	Special	100	50	5	Normal
44	Imprison	Psychic	Status	—	—	10	Self
48	Pain Split	Normal	Status	—	—	20	Normal
52	Overheat	Fire	Special	130	90	5	Normal
56	Memento	Dark	Status	—	100	10	Normal

EVOLUTION MOVES

NAME	TYPE	KIND	POW.	ACC.	PP	RANGE

EGG MOVES

NAME	TYPE	KIND	POW.	ACC.	PP	RANGE
Acid Armor	Poison	Status	—	—	20	Self
Clear Smog	Poison	Special	50	—	15	Normal
Haze	Ice	Status	—	—	30	Both Sides
Power Split	Psychic	Status	—	—	10	Normal

TUTOR MOVES

NAME	TYPE	KIND	POW.	ACC.	PP	RANGE

TM MOVES

NO.	NAME	TYPE	KIND	POW.	ACC.	PP	RANGE
TM11	Solar Beam	Grass	Special	120	100	10	Normal
TM13	Fire Spin	Fire	Special	35	85	15	Normal
TM19	Safeguard	Normal	Status	—	—	25	Your Side
TM21	Rest	Psychic	Status	—	—	10	Self
TM23	Thief	Dark	Physical	60	100	25	Normal
TM24	Snore	Normal	Special	50	100	15	Normal
TM25	Protect	Normal	Status	—	—	10	Self
TM31	Attract	Normal	Status	—	100	15	Normal
TM34	Sunny Day	Fire	Status	—	—	5	Both Sides
TM38	Will-O-Wisp	Fire	Status	—	85	15	Normal
TM39	Facade	Normal	Physical	70	100	20	Normal
TM44	Imprison	Psychic	Status	—	—	10	Self
TM57	Payback	Dark	Physical	50	100	10	Normal
TM70	Trick Room	Psychic	Status	—	—	5	Both Sides
TM76	Round	Normal	Special	60	100	15	Normal
TM77	Hex	Ghost	Special	65	100	10	Normal
TM92	Mystical Fire	Fire	Special	75	100	10	Normal

TR MOVES

NO.	NAME	TYPE	KIND	POW.	ACC.	PP	RANGE
TR02	Flamethrower	Fire	Special	90	100	15	Normal
TR11	Psychic	Psychic	Special	90	100	10	Normal
TR15	Fire Blast	Fire	Special	110	85	5	Normal
TR20	Substitute	Normal	Status	—	—	10	Self
TR26	Endure	Normal	Status	—	—	10	Self
TR27	Sleep Talk	Normal	Status	—	—	10	Self
TR33	Shadow Ball	Ghost	Special	80	100	15	Normal
TR36	Heat Wave	Fire	Special	95	90	10	Many Others
TR37	Taunt	Dark	Status	—	100	20	Normal
TR38	Trick	Psychic	Status	—	100	10	Normal
TR43	Overheat	Fire	Special	130	90	5	Normal
TR49	Calm Mind	Psychic	Status	—	—	20	Self
TR58	Dark Pulse	Dark	Special	80	100	15	Normal
TR65	Energy Ball	Grass	Special	90	100	10	Normal
TR83	Ally Switch	Psychic	Status	—	—	15	Self

ABILITY
Flash Fire
Flame Body

HIDDEN ABILITY
Infiltrator

SPECIES STRENGTHS
HP
ATTACK
DEFENSE
SP. ATK
SP. DEF
SPEED

DAMAGE TAKEN IN BATTLE
×0, ×0, ×2, ×0.5, ×0.5, ×2, ×2, ×2, ×1, ×0.5, ×1, ×2, ×1, ×1, ×0.5, ×0.5, ×0.25, ×0.5

Egg Group: AMORPHOUS

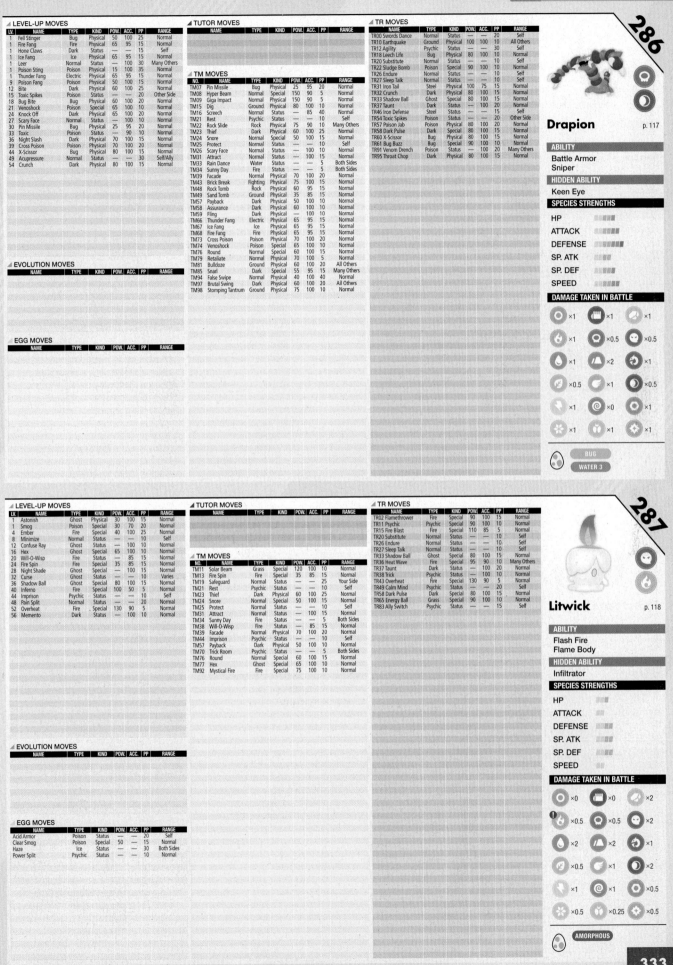

288

Lampent
p. 118

ABILITY
Flash Fire
Flame Body

HIDDEN ABILITY
Infiltrator

SPECIES STRENGTHS

HP	
ATTACK	
DEFENSE	
SP. ATK	
SP. DEF	
SPEED	

DAMAGE TAKEN IN BATTLE

×0	×0	×2
×0.5	×0.5	×2
×2	×2	×1
×0.5	×1	×2
×1	×1	×0.5
×0.5	×0.25	×0.5

AMORPHOUS

LEVEL-UP MOVES

LV.	NAME	TYPE	KIND	POW.	ACC.	PP	RANGE
1	Astonish	Ghost	Physical	30	100	15	Normal
1	Ember	Fire	Special	40	100	25	Normal
1	Minimize	Normal	Status	—	—	10	Self
1	Smog	Poison	Special	30	70	20	Normal
12	Confuse Ray	Ghost	Status	—	100	10	Normal
16	Hex	Ghost	Special	65	100	10	Normal
20	Will-O-Wisp	Fire	Status	—	85	15	Normal
24	Fire Spin	Fire	Special	35	85	15	Normal
28	Night Shade	Ghost	Special	—	100	15	Normal
32	Curse	Ghost	Status	—	—	10	Varies
36	Shadow Ball	Ghost	Special	80	100	15	Normal
40	Inferno	Fire	Special	100	50	5	Normal
46	Imprison	Psychic	Status	—	—	10	Self
52	Pain Split	Normal	Status	—	—	20	Normal
58	Overheat	Fire	Special	130	90	5	Normal
64	Memento	Dark	Status	—	100	10	Normal

TUTOR MOVES

NAME	TYPE	KIND	POW.	ACC.	PP	RANGE

TM MOVES

NO.	NAME	TYPE	KIND	POW.	ACC.	PP	RANGE
TM11	Solar Beam	Grass	Special	120	100	10	Normal
TM13	Fire Spin	Fire	Special	35	85	15	Normal
TM19	Safeguard	Normal	Status	—	—	25	Your Side
TM21	Rest	Psychic	Status	—	—	10	Self
TM23	Thief	Dark	Physical	60	100	25	Normal
TM24	Snore	Normal	Special	50	100	15	Normal
TM25	Protect	Normal	Status	—	—	10	Self
TM31	Attract	Normal	Status	—	100	15	Normal
TM34	Sunny Day	Fire	Status	—	—	5	Both Sides
TM38	Will-O-Wisp	Fire	Status	—	85	15	Normal
TM39	Facade	Normal	Physical	70	100	20	Normal
TM44	Imprison	Psychic	Status	—	—	10	Self
TM57	Payback	Dark	Physical	50	100	10	Normal
TM70	Trick Room	Psychic	Status	—	—	5	Both Sides
TM76	Round	Normal	Special	60	100	15	Normal
TM77	Hex	Ghost	Special	65	100	10	Normal
TM92	Mystical Fire	Fire	Special	75	100	10	Normal

EVOLUTION MOVES

NAME	TYPE	KIND	POW.	ACC.	PP	RANGE

EGG MOVES

NAME	TYPE	KIND	POW.	ACC.	PP	RANGE

TR MOVES

NO.	NAME	TYPE	KIND	POW.	ACC.	PP	RANGE
TR02	Flamethrower	Fire	Special	90	100	15	Normal
TR11	Psychic	Psychic	Special	90	100	10	Normal
TR15	Fire Blast	Fire	Special	110	85	5	Normal
TR20	Substitute	Normal	Status	—	—	10	Self
TR26	Endure	Normal	Status	—	—	10	Self
TR27	Sleep Talk	Normal	Status	—	—	10	Self
TR33	Shadow Ball	Ghost	Special	80	100	15	Normal
TR36	Heat Wave	Fire	Special	95	90	10	Many Others
TR37	Taunt	Dark	Status	—	100	20	Normal
TR38	Trick	Psychic	Status	—	100	10	Normal
TR43	Overheat	Fire	Special	130	90	5	Normal
TR49	Calm Mind	Psychic	Status	—	—	20	Self
TR58	Dark Pulse	Dark	Special	80	100	15	Normal
TR65	Energy Ball	Grass	Special	90	100	10	Normal
TR83	Ally Switch	Psychic	Status	—	—	15	Self

289

Chandelure
p. 118

ABILITY
Flash Fire
Flame Body

HIDDEN ABILITY
Infiltrator

SPECIES STRENGTHS

HP	
ATTACK	
DEFENSE	
SP. ATK	
SP. DEF	
SPEED	

DAMAGE TAKEN IN BATTLE

×0	×0	×2
×0.5	×0.5	×2
×2	×2	×1
×0.5	×1	×2
×1	×1	×0.5
×0.5	×0.25	×0.5

AMORPHOUS

LEVEL-UP MOVES

LV.	NAME	TYPE	KIND	POW.	ACC.	PP	RANGE
1	Astonish	Ghost	Physical	30	100	15	Normal
1	Confuse Ray	Ghost	Status	—	100	10	Normal
1	Curse	Ghost	Status	—	—	10	Varies
1	Ember	Fire	Special	40	100	25	Normal
1	Fire Spin	Fire	Special	35	85	15	Normal
1	Hex	Ghost	Special	65	100	10	Normal
1	Imprison	Psychic	Status	—	—	10	Self
1	Inferno	Fire	Special	100	50	5	Normal
1	Memento	Dark	Status	—	100	10	Normal
1	Minimize	Normal	Status	—	—	10	Self
1	Night Shade	Ghost	Special	—	100	15	Normal
1	Overheat	Fire	Special	130	90	5	Normal
1	Pain Split	Normal	Status	—	—	20	Normal
1	Shadow Ball	Ghost	Special	80	100	15	Normal
1	Smog	Poison	Special	30	70	20	Normal
1	Will-O-Wisp	Fire	Status	—	85	15	Normal

TUTOR MOVES

NAME	TYPE	KIND	POW.	ACC.	PP	RANGE

TM MOVES

NO.	NAME	TYPE	KIND	POW.	ACC.	PP	RANGE
TM08	Hyper Beam	Normal	Special	150	90	5	Normal
TM09	Giga Impact	Normal	Physical	150	90	5	Normal
TM11	Solar Beam	Grass	Special	120	100	10	Normal
TM13	Fire Spin	Fire	Special	35	85	15	Normal
TM19	Safeguard	Normal	Status	—	—	25	Your Side
TM21	Rest	Psychic	Status	—	—	10	Self
TM23	Thief	Dark	Physical	60	100	25	Normal
TM24	Snore	Normal	Special	50	100	15	Normal
TM25	Protect	Normal	Status	—	—	10	Self
TM31	Attract	Normal	Status	—	100	15	Normal
TM34	Sunny Day	Fire	Status	—	—	5	Both Sides
TM38	Will-O-Wisp	Fire	Status	—	85	15	Normal
TM39	Facade	Normal	Physical	70	100	20	Normal
TM44	Imprison	Psychic	Status	—	—	10	Self
TM57	Payback	Dark	Physical	50	100	10	Normal
TM70	Trick Room	Psychic	Status	—	—	5	Both Sides
TM76	Round	Normal	Special	60	100	15	Normal
TM77	Hex	Ghost	Special	65	100	10	Normal
TM92	Mystical Fire	Fire	Special	75	100	10	Normal

EVOLUTION MOVES

NAME	TYPE	KIND	POW.	ACC.	PP	RANGE

EGG MOVES

NAME	TYPE	KIND	POW.	ACC.	PP	RANGE

TR MOVES

NO.	NAME	TYPE	KIND	POW.	ACC.	PP	RANGE
TR02	Flamethrower	Fire	Special	90	100	15	Normal
TR11	Psychic	Psychic	Special	90	100	10	Normal
TR15	Fire Blast	Fire	Special	110	85	5	Normal
TR20	Substitute	Normal	Status	—	—	10	Self
TR26	Endure	Normal	Status	—	—	10	Self
TR27	Sleep Talk	Normal	Status	—	—	10	Self
TR33	Shadow Ball	Ghost	Special	80	100	15	Normal
TR36	Heat Wave	Fire	Special	95	90	10	Many Others
TR37	Taunt	Dark	Status	—	100	20	Normal
TR38	Trick	Psychic	Status	—	100	10	Normal
TR43	Overheat	Fire	Special	130	90	5	Normal
TR49	Calm Mind	Psychic	Status	—	—	20	Self
TR58	Dark Pulse	Dark	Special	80	100	15	Normal
TR65	Energy Ball	Grass	Special	90	100	10	Normal
TR83	Ally Switch	Psychic	Status	—	—	15	Self

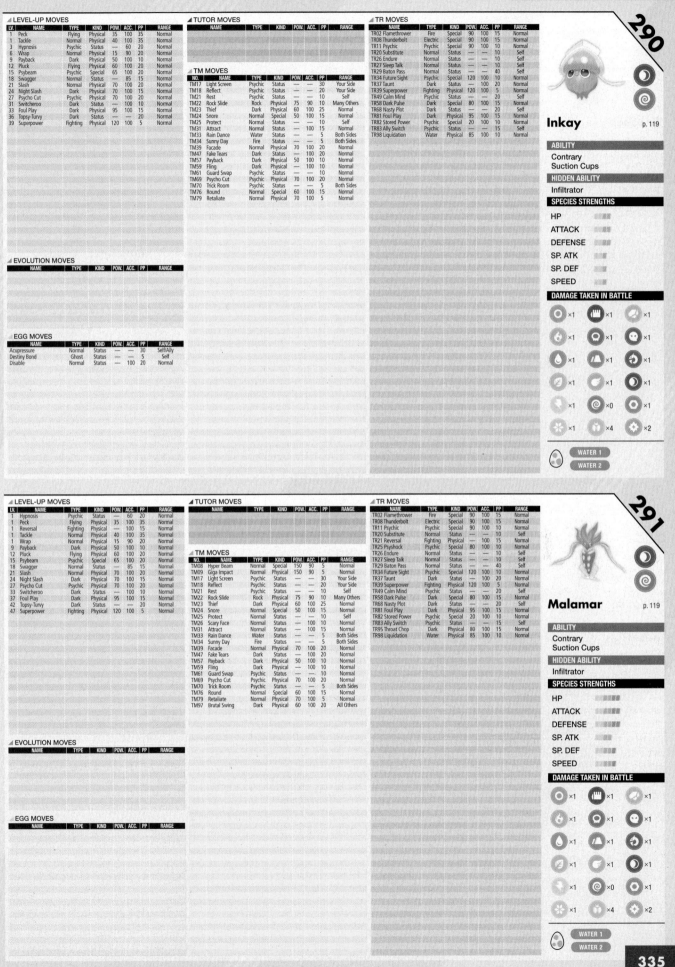

290 — Inkay

LEVEL-UP MOVES

LV	NAME	TYPE	KIND	POW.	ACC.	PP	RANGE
1	Peck	Flying	Physical	35	100	35	Normal
1	Tackle	Normal	Physical	40	100	35	Normal
3	Hypnosis	Psychic	Status	—	60	20	Normal
6	Wrap	Normal	Physical	15	90	20	Normal
9	Payback	Dark	Physical	50	100	10	Normal
12	Pluck	Flying	Physical	60	100	20	Normal
15	Psybeam	Psychic	Special	65	100	20	Normal
18	Swagger	Normal	Status	—	85	15	Normal
21	Slash	Normal	Physical	70	100	20	Normal
24	Night Slash	Dark	Physical	70	100	15	Normal
27	Psycho Cut	Psychic	Physical	70	100	20	Normal
31	Switcheroo	Dark	Status	—	100	10	Normal
33	Foul Play	Dark	Physical	95	100	15	Normal
36	Topsy-Turvy	Dark	Status	—	—	20	Normal
39	Superpower	Fighting	Physical	120	100	5	Normal

EVOLUTION MOVES

NAME	TYPE	KIND	POW.	ACC.	PP	RANGE

EGG MOVES

NAME	TYPE	KIND	POW.	ACC.	PP	RANGE
Acupressure	Normal	Status	—	—	30	Self/Ally
Destiny Bond	Ghost	Status	—	—	5	Self
Disable	Normal	Status	—	100	20	Normal

TUTOR MOVES

NAME	TYPE	KIND	POW.	ACC.	PP	RANGE

TM MOVES

NO.	NAME	TYPE	KIND	POW.	ACC.	PP	RANGE
TM17	Light Screen	Psychic	Status	—	—	30	Your Side
TM18	Reflect	Psychic	Status	—	—	20	Your Side
TM21	Rest	Psychic	Status	—	—	10	Self
TM22	Rock Slide	Rock	Physical	75	90	10	Many Others
TM23	Thief	Dark	Physical	60	100	25	Normal
TM24	Snore	Normal	Special	50	100	15	Normal
TM25	Protect	Normal	Status	—	—	10	Self
TM31	Attract	Normal	Status	—	100	15	Normal
TM33	Rain Dance	Water	Status	—	—	5	Both Sides
TM34	Sunny Day	Fire	Status	—	—	5	Both Sides
TM39	Facade	Normal	Physical	70	100	20	Normal
TM47	Fake Tears	Dark	Status	—	100	20	Normal
TM57	Payback	Dark	Physical	50	100	10	Normal
TM59	Fling	Dark	Physical	—	100	10	Normal
TM61	Guard Swap	Psychic	Status	—	—	10	Normal
TM69	Psycho Cut	Psychic	Physical	70	100	20	Normal
TM70	Trick Room	Psychic	Status	—	—	5	Both Sides
TM76	Round	Normal	Special	60	100	15	Normal
TM79	Retaliate	Normal	Physical	70	100	5	Normal

TR MOVES

NO.	NAME	TYPE	KIND	POW.	ACC.	PP	RANGE
TR02	Flamethrower	Fire	Special	90	100	15	Normal
TR08	Thunderbolt	Electric	Special	90	100	15	Normal
TR11	Psychic	Psychic	Special	90	100	10	Normal
TR20	Substitute	Normal	Status	—	—	10	Self
TR26	Endure	Normal	Status	—	—	10	Self
TR27	Sleep Talk	Normal	Status	—	—	10	Self
TR29	Baton Pass	Normal	Status	—	—	40	Self
TR34	Future Sight	Psychic	Special	120	100	10	Normal
TR37	Taunt	Dark	Status	—	100	20	Normal
TR39	Superpower	Fighting	Physical	120	100	5	Normal
TR49	Calm Mind	Psychic	Status	—	—	20	Self
TR58	Dark Pulse	Dark	Special	80	100	15	Normal
TR68	Nasty Plot	Dark	Status	—	—	20	Self
TR81	Foul Play	Dark	Physical	95	100	15	Normal
TR82	Stored Power	Psychic	Special	20	100	10	Normal
TR83	Ally Switch	Psychic	Status	—	—	15	Self
TR98	Liquidation	Water	Physical	85	100	10	Normal

Inkay p. 119

ABILITY
Contrary
Suction Cups

HIDDEN ABILITY
Infiltrator

SPECIES STRENGTHS
- HP
- ATTACK
- DEFENSE
- SP. ATK
- SP. DEF
- SPEED

DAMAGE TAKEN IN BATTLE

×1 ×1 ×1 ×1 ×1 ×1 ×1 ×1 ×1 ×1 ×1 ×1 ×1 ×0 ×1 ×1 ×4 ×2

WATER 1
WATER 2

291 — Malamar

LEVEL-UP MOVES

LV	NAME	TYPE	KIND	POW.	ACC.	PP	RANGE
1	Hypnosis	Psychic	Status	—	60	20	Normal
1	Peck	Flying	Physical	35	100	35	Normal
1	Reversal	Fighting	Physical	—	100	15	Normal
1	Tackle	Normal	Physical	40	100	35	Normal
1	Wrap	Normal	Physical	15	90	20	Normal
9	Payback	Dark	Physical	50	100	10	Normal
12	Pluck	Flying	Physical	60	100	20	Normal
15	Psybeam	Psychic	Special	65	100	20	Normal
18	Swagger	Normal	Status	—	85	15	Normal
21	Slash	Normal	Physical	70	100	20	Normal
24	Night Slash	Dark	Physical	70	100	15	Normal
27	Psycho Cut	Psychic	Physical	70	100	20	Normal
33	Switcheroo	Dark	Status	—	100	10	Normal
37	Foul Play	Dark	Physical	95	100	15	Normal
42	Topsy-Turvy	Dark	Status	—	—	20	Normal
47	Superpower	Fighting	Physical	120	100	5	Normal

EVOLUTION MOVES

NAME	TYPE	KIND	POW.	ACC.	PP	RANGE

EGG MOVES

NAME	TYPE	KIND	POW.	ACC.	PP	RANGE

TUTOR MOVES

NAME	TYPE	KIND	POW.	ACC.	PP	RANGE

TM MOVES

NO.	NAME	TYPE	KIND	POW.	ACC.	PP	RANGE
TM08	Hyper Beam	Normal	Special	150	90	5	Normal
TM09	Giga Impact	Normal	Physical	150	90	5	Normal
TM17	Light Screen	Psychic	Status	—	—	30	Your Side
TM18	Reflect	Psychic	Status	—	—	20	Your Side
TM21	Rest	Psychic	Status	—	—	10	Self
TM22	Rock Slide	Rock	Physical	75	90	10	Many Others
TM23	Thief	Dark	Physical	60	100	25	Normal
TM24	Snore	Normal	Special	50	100	15	Normal
TM25	Protect	Normal	Status	—	—	10	Self
TM26	Scary Face	Normal	Status	—	100	10	Normal
TM31	Attract	Normal	Status	—	100	15	Normal
TM33	Rain Dance	Water	Status	—	—	5	Both Sides
TM34	Sunny Day	Fire	Status	—	—	5	Both Sides
TM39	Facade	Normal	Physical	70	100	20	Normal
TM47	Fake Tears	Dark	Status	—	100	20	Normal
TM57	Payback	Dark	Physical	50	100	10	Normal
TM59	Fling	Dark	Physical	—	100	10	Normal
TM61	Guard Swap	Psychic	Status	—	—	10	Normal
TM69	Psycho Cut	Psychic	Physical	70	100	20	Normal
TM70	Trick Room	Psychic	Status	—	—	5	Both Sides
TM76	Round	Normal	Special	60	100	15	Normal
TM79	Retaliate	Normal	Physical	70	100	5	Normal
TM97	Brutal Swing	Dark	Physical	60	100	20	All Others

TR MOVES

NO.	NAME	TYPE	KIND	POW.	ACC.	PP	RANGE
TR02	Flamethrower	Fire	Special	90	100	15	Normal
TR08	Thunderbolt	Electric	Special	90	100	15	Normal
TR11	Psychic	Psychic	Special	90	100	10	Normal
TR20	Substitute	Normal	Status	—	—	10	Self
TR21	Reversal	Fighting	Physical	—	100	15	Normal
TR25	Psyshock	Psychic	Special	80	100	10	Normal
TR26	Endure	Normal	Status	—	—	10	Self
TR27	Sleep Talk	Normal	Status	—	—	10	Self
TR29	Baton Pass	Normal	Status	—	—	40	Self
TR34	Future Sight	Psychic	Special	120	100	10	Normal
TR37	Taunt	Dark	Status	—	100	20	Normal
TR39	Superpower	Fighting	Physical	120	100	5	Normal
TR49	Calm Mind	Psychic	Status	—	—	20	Self
TR58	Dark Pulse	Dark	Special	80	100	15	Normal
TR68	Nasty Plot	Dark	Status	—	—	20	Self
TR81	Foul Play	Dark	Physical	95	100	15	Normal
TR82	Stored Power	Psychic	Special	20	100	10	Normal
TR83	Ally Switch	Psychic	Status	—	—	15	Self
TR95	Throat Chop	Dark	Physical	80	100	15	Normal
TR98	Liquidation	Water	Physical	85	100	10	Normal

Malamar p. 119

ABILITY
Contrary
Suction Cups

HIDDEN ABILITY
Infiltrator

SPECIES STRENGTHS
- HP
- ATTACK
- DEFENSE
- SP. ATK
- SP. DEF
- SPEED

DAMAGE TAKEN IN BATTLE

×1 ×1 ×1 ×1 ×1 ×1 ×1 ×1 ×1 ×1 ×1 ×1 ×1 ×0 ×1 ×1 ×4 ×2

WATER 1
WATER 2

292 Sneasel

p. 119

ABILITY
Inner Focus
Keen Eye

HIDDEN ABILITY
Pickpocket

SPECIES STRENGTHS
HP
ATTACK
DEFENSE
SP. ATK
SP. DEF
SPEED

DAMAGE TAKEN IN BATTLE

×1	×4	×2			
×2	×1	×0.5			
×1	×1	×1			
×1	×1	×0.5			
×1	×0	×2			
×0.5	×2	×2			

FIELD

LEVEL-UP MOVES

LV.	NAME	TYPE	KIND	POW.	ACC.	PP	RANGE
1	Leer	Normal	Status	—	100	30	Many Others
1	Scratch	Normal	Physical	40	100	35	Normal
6	Taunt	Dark	Status	—	100	20	Normal
12	Quick Attack	Normal	Physical	40	100	30	Normal
18	Metal Claw	Steel	Physical	50	95	35	Normal
24	Icy Wind	Ice	Special	55	95	15	Many Others
30	Fury Swipes	Normal	Physical	18	80	15	Normal
36	Hone Claws	Dark	Status	—	—	15	Self
42	Beat Up	Dark	Physical	—	100	10	Normal
48	Agility	Psychic	Status	—	—	30	Self
54	Screech	Normal	Status	—	85	40	Normal
60	Slash	Normal	Physical	70	100	20	Normal

EVOLUTION MOVES

NAME	TYPE	KIND	POW.	ACC.	PP	RANGE

EGG MOVES

NAME	TYPE	KIND	POW.	ACC.	PP	RANGE
Bite	Dark	Physical	60	100	25	Normal
Counter	Fighting	Physical	—	100	20	Varies
Double Hit	Normal	Physical	35	90	10	Normal
Fake Out	Normal	Physical	40	100	10	Normal
Feint	Normal	Physical	30	100	10	Normal
Ice Shard	Ice	Physical	40	100	30	Normal
Icicle Crash	Ice	Physical	85	90	10	Normal
Spite	Ghost	Status	—	100	10	Normal

TUTOR MOVES

NAME	TYPE	KIND	POW.	ACC.	PP	RANGE

TM MOVES

NO.	NAME	TYPE	KIND	POW.	ACC.	PP	RANGE
TM00	Mega Punch	Normal	Physical	80	85	20	Normal
TM01	Mega Kick	Normal	Physical	120	75	5	Normal
TM04	Ice Punch	Ice	Physical	75	100	15	Normal
TM15	Dig	Ground	Physical	80	100	10	Normal
TM16	Screech	Normal	Status	—	85	40	Normal
TM18	Reflect	Psychic	Status	—	—	20	Your Side
TM21	Rest	Psychic	Status	—	—	10	Self
TM23	Thief	Dark	Physical	60	100	25	Normal
TM24	Snore	Normal	Special	50	100	15	Normal
TM25	Protect	Normal	Status	—	—	10	Self
TM27	Icy Wind	Ice	Special	55	95	15	Many Others
TM31	Attract	Normal	Status	—	100	15	Normal
TM33	Rain Dance	Water	Status	—	—	5	Both Sides
TM34	Sunny Day	Fire	Status	—	—	5	Both Sides
TM35	Hail	Ice	Status	—	—	10	Both Sides
TM36	Whirlpool	Water	Special	35	85	15	Normal
TM37	Beat Up	Dark	Physical	—	100	10	Normal
TM39	Facade	Normal	Physical	70	100	20	Normal
TM40	Swift	Normal	Special	60	—	20	Many Others
TM43	Brick Break	Fighting	Physical	75	100	15	Normal
TM47	Fake Tears	Dark	Status	—	100	20	Normal
TM57	Payback	Dark	Physical	50	100	10	Normal
TM59	Fling	Dark	Physical	—	100	10	Normal
TM64	Avalanche	Ice	Physical	60	100	10	Normal
TM65	Shadow Claw	Ghost	Physical	70	100	15	Normal
TM69	Psycho Cut	Psychic	Physical	70	100	20	Normal
TM75	Low Sweep	Fighting	Physical	65	100	20	Normal
TM76	Round	Normal	Special	60	100	15	Normal
TM79	Retaliate	Normal	Physical	70	100	5	Normal
TM85	Snarl	Dark	Special	55	95	15	Many Others
TM94	False Swipe	Normal	Physical	40	100	40	Normal

TR MOVES

NO.	NAME	TYPE	KIND	POW.	ACC.	PP	RANGE
TR00	Swords Dance	Normal	Status	—	—	20	Self
TR04	Surf	Water	Special	90	100	15	All Others
TR05	Ice Beam	Ice	Special	90	100	10	Normal
TR06	Blizzard	Ice	Special	110	70	5	Many Others
TR07	Low Kick	Fighting	Physical	—	100	20	Normal
TR12	Agility	Psychic	Status	—	—	30	Self
TR20	Substitute	Normal	Status	—	—	10	Self
TR26	Endure	Normal	Status	—	—	10	Self
TR27	Sleep Talk	Normal	Status	—	—	10	Self
TR31	Iron Tail	Steel	Physical	100	75	15	Normal
TR33	Shadow Ball	Ghost	Special	80	100	15	Normal
TR37	Taunt	Dark	Status	—	100	20	Normal
TR49	Calm Mind	Psychic	Status	—	—	20	Self
TR57	Poison Jab	Poison	Physical	80	100	20	Normal
TR58	Dark Pulse	Dark	Special	80	100	15	Normal
TR60	X-Scissor	Bug	Physical	80	100	15	Normal
TR81	Foul Play	Dark	Physical	95	100	15	Normal
TR95	Throat Chop	Dark	Physical	80	100	15	Normal

---

293 Weavile

p. 119

ABILITY
Pressure
—

HIDDEN ABILITY
Pickpocket

SPECIES STRENGTHS
HP
ATTACK
DEFENSE
SP. ATK
SP. DEF
SPEED

DAMAGE TAKEN IN BATTLE

×1	×4	×2			
×2	×1	×0.5			
×1	×1	×1			
×1	×1	×0.5			
×1	×0	×2			
×0.5	×2	×2			

FIELD

LEVEL-UP MOVES

LV.	NAME	TYPE	KIND	POW.	ACC.	PP	RANGE
1	Agility	Psychic	Status	—	—	30	Self
1	Assurance	Dark	Physical	60	100	10	Normal
1	Beat Up	Dark	Physical	—	100	10	Normal
1	Ice Shard	Ice	Physical	40	100	30	Normal
1	Leer	Normal	Status	—	100	30	Many Others
1	Quick Attack	Normal	Physical	40	100	30	Normal
1	Revenge	Fighting	Physical	60	100	10	Normal
1	Scratch	Normal	Physical	40	100	35	Normal
1	Slash	Normal	Physical	70	100	20	Normal
1	Taunt	Dark	Status	—	100	20	Normal
18	Metal Claw	Steel	Physical	50	95	35	Normal
24	Icy Wind	Ice	Special	55	95	15	Many Others
36	Hone Claws	Dark	Status	—	—	15	Self
42	Fling	Dark	Physical	—	100	10	Normal
48	Nasty Plot	Dark	Status	—	—	20	Self
54	Screech	Normal	Status	—	85	40	Normal
60	Night Slash	Dark	Physical	70	100	15	Normal
66	Dark Pulse	Dark	Special	80	100	15	Normal

EVOLUTION MOVES

NAME	TYPE	KIND	POW.	ACC.	PP	RANGE

EGG MOVES

NAME	TYPE	KIND	POW.	ACC.	PP	RANGE

TUTOR MOVES

NAME	TYPE	KIND	POW.	ACC.	PP	RANGE

TM MOVES

NO.	NAME	TYPE	KIND	POW.	ACC.	PP	RANGE
TM00	Mega Punch	Normal	Physical	80	85	20	Normal
TM01	Mega Kick	Normal	Physical	120	75	5	Normal
TM04	Ice Punch	Ice	Physical	75	100	15	Normal
TM08	Hyper Beam	Normal	Special	150	90	5	Normal
TM09	Giga Impact	Normal	Physical	150	90	5	Normal
TM15	Dig	Ground	Physical	80	100	10	Normal
TM16	Screech	Normal	Status	—	85	40	Normal
TM18	Reflect	Psychic	Status	—	—	20	Your Side
TM21	Rest	Psychic	Status	—	—	10	Self
TM23	Thief	Dark	Physical	60	100	25	Normal
TM24	Snore	Normal	Special	50	100	15	Normal
TM25	Protect	Normal	Status	—	—	10	Self
TM27	Icy Wind	Ice	Special	55	95	15	Many Others
TM31	Attract	Normal	Status	—	100	15	Normal
TM33	Rain Dance	Water	Status	—	—	5	Both Sides
TM34	Sunny Day	Fire	Status	—	—	5	Both Sides
TM35	Hail	Ice	Status	—	—	10	Both Sides
TM36	Whirlpool	Water	Special	35	85	15	Normal
TM37	Beat Up	Dark	Physical	—	100	10	Normal
TM39	Facade	Normal	Physical	70	100	20	Normal
TM40	Swift	Normal	Special	60	—	20	Many Others
TM42	Revenge	Fighting	Physical	60	100	10	Normal
TM43	Brick Break	Fighting	Physical	75	100	15	Normal
TM47	Fake Tears	Dark	Status	—	100	20	Normal
TM51	Icicle Spear	Ice	Physical	25	100	30	Normal
TM57	Payback	Dark	Physical	50	100	10	Normal
TM58	Assurance	Dark	Physical	60	100	10	Normal
TM59	Fling	Dark	Physical	—	100	10	Normal
TM64	Avalanche	Ice	Physical	60	100	10	Normal
TM65	Shadow Claw	Ghost	Physical	70	100	15	Normal
TM69	Psycho Cut	Psychic	Physical	70	100	20	Normal
TM75	Low Sweep	Fighting	Physical	65	100	20	Normal
TM76	Round	Normal	Special	60	100	15	Normal
TM79	Retaliate	Normal	Physical	70	100	5	Normal
TM85	Snarl	Dark	Special	55	95	15	Many Others
TM94	False Swipe	Normal	Physical	40	100	40	Normal

TR MOVES

NO.	NAME	TYPE	KIND	POW.	ACC.	PP	RANGE
TR00	Swords Dance	Normal	Status	—	—	20	Self
TR04	Surf	Water	Special	90	100	15	All Others
TR05	Ice Beam	Ice	Special	90	100	10	Normal
TR06	Blizzard	Ice	Special	110	70	5	Many Others
TR07	Low Kick	Fighting	Physical	—	100	20	Normal
TR12	Agility	Psychic	Status	—	—	30	Self
TR20	Substitute	Normal	Status	—	—	10	Self
TR26	Endure	Normal	Status	—	—	10	Self
TR27	Sleep Talk	Normal	Status	—	—	10	Self
TR31	Iron Tail	Steel	Physical	100	75	15	Normal
TR33	Shadow Ball	Ghost	Special	80	100	15	Normal
TR37	Taunt	Dark	Status	—	100	20	Normal
TR49	Calm Mind	Psychic	Status	—	—	20	Self
TR57	Poison Jab	Poison	Physical	80	100	20	Normal
TR58	Dark Pulse	Dark	Special	80	100	15	Normal
TR60	X-Scissor	Bug	Physical	80	100	15	Normal
TR64	Focus Blast	Fighting	Special	120	70	5	Normal
TR68	Nasty Plot	Dark	Status	—	—	20	Self
TR81	Foul Play	Dark	Physical	95	100	15	Normal
TR95	Throat Chop	Dark	Physical	80	100	15	Normal

294

Sableye
p. 120

LEVEL-UP MOVES

LV.	NAME	TYPE	KIND	POW.	ACC.	PP	RANGE
1	Leer	Normal	Status	—	100	30	Many Others
1	Scratch	Normal	Physical	40	100	35	Normal
3	Astonish	Ghost	Physical	30	100	15	Normal
6	Confuse Ray	Ghost	Status	—	100	10	Normal
9	Shadow Sneak	Ghost	Physical	40	100	30	Normal
12	Fake Out	Normal	Physical	40	100	10	Normal
15	Disable	Normal	Status	—	100	20	Normal
18	Detect	Fighting	Status	—	—	5	Self
21	Night Shade	Ghost	Special	—	100	15	Normal
24	Fury Swipes	Normal	Physical	18	80	15	Normal
27	Knock Off	Dark	Physical	65	100	20	Normal
30	Quash	Dark	Status	—	100	15	Normal
33	Shadow Claw	Ghost	Physical	70	100	15	Normal
36	Mean Look	Normal	Status	—	—	5	Normal
39	Power Gem	Rock	Special	80	100	20	Normal
42	Zen Headbutt	Psychic	Physical	80	90	15	Normal
45	Shadow Ball	Ghost	Special	80	100	15	Normal
48	Foul Play	Dark	Physical	95	100	15	Normal

EVOLUTION MOVES

NAME	TYPE	KIND	POW.	ACC.	PP	RANGE

EGG MOVES

NAME	TYPE	KIND	POW.	ACC.	PP	RANGE
Feint	Normal	Physical	30	100	10	Normal
Flatter	Dark	Status	—	100	15	Normal
Metal Burst	Steel	Physical	—	100	10	Varies
Recover	Normal	Status	—	—	10	Self
Sucker Punch	Dark	Physical	70	100	5	Normal
Torment	Dark	Status	—	100	15	Normal

TUTOR MOVES

NAME	TYPE	KIND	POW.	ACC.	PP	RANGE

TM MOVES

NO.	NAME	TYPE	KIND	POW.	ACC.	PP	RANGE
TM00	Mega Punch	Normal	Physical	80	85	20	Normal
TM01	Mega Kick	Normal	Physical	120	75	5	Normal
TM03	Fire Punch	Fire	Physical	75	100	15	Normal
TM04	Ice Punch	Ice	Physical	75	100	15	Normal
TM05	Thunder Punch	Electric	Physical	75	100	15	Normal
TM15	Dig	Ground	Physical	80	100	10	Normal
TM21	Rest	Psychic	Status	—	—	10	Self
TM23	Thief	Dark	Physical	60	100	25	Normal
TM24	Snore	Normal	Special	50	100	15	Normal
TM25	Protect	Normal	Status	—	—	10	Self
TM27	Icy Wind	Ice	Special	55	95	15	Many Others
TM31	Attract	Normal	Status	—	100	15	Normal
TM33	Rain Dance	Water	Status	—	—	5	Both Sides
TM34	Sunny Day	Fire	Status	—	—	5	Both Sides
TM38	Will-O-Wisp	Fire	Status	—	85	15	Normal
TM39	Facade	Normal	Physical	70	100	20	Normal
TM41	Helping Hand	Normal	Status	—	—	20	1 Ally
TM43	Brick Break	Fighting	Physical	75	100	15	Normal
TM44	Imprison	Psychic	Status	—	—	10	Self
TM48	Rock Tomb	Rock	Physical	60	95	15	Normal
TM57	Payback	Dark	Physical	50	100	10	Normal
TM59	Fling	Dark	Physical	—	100	10	Normal
TM63	Drain Punch	Fighting	Physical	75	100	10	Normal
TM65	Shadow Claw	Ghost	Physical	70	100	15	Normal
TM71	Wonder Room	Psychic	Status	—	—	10	Both Sides
TM75	Low Sweep	Fighting	Physical	65	100	20	Normal
TM76	Round	Normal	Special	60	100	15	Normal
TM77	Hex	Ghost	Special	65	100	10	Normal
TM79	Retaliate	Normal	Physical	70	100	5	Normal
TM85	Snarl	Dark	Special	55	95	15	Many Others

TR MOVES

NAME	TYPE	KIND	POW.	ACC.	PP	RANGE
TR01	Body Slam	Normal	Physical	85	100	15	Normal
TR07	Low Kick	Fighting	Physical	—	100	20	Normal
TR11	Psychic	Psychic	Special	90	100	10	Normal
TR14	Metronome	Normal	Status	—	—	10	Self
TR20	Substitute	Normal	Status	—	—	10	Self
TR26	Endure	Normal	Status	—	—	10	Self
TR27	Sleep Talk	Normal	Status	—	—	10	Self
TR30	Encore	Normal	Status	—	100	5	Normal
TR33	Shadow Ball	Ghost	Special	80	100	15	Normal
TR37	Taunt	Dark	Status	—	100	20	Normal
TR38	Trick	Psychic	Status	—	100	10	Normal
TR49	Calm Mind	Psychic	Status	—	—	20	Self
TR52	Gyro Ball	Steel	Physical	—	100	5	Normal
TR57	Poison Jab	Poison	Physical	80	100	20	Normal
TR58	Dark Pulse	Dark	Special	80	100	15	Normal
TR63	Power Gem	Rock	Special	80	100	20	Normal
TR68	Nasty Plot	Dark	Status	—	—	20	Self
TR69	Zen Headbutt	Psychic	Physical	80	90	15	Normal
TR81	Foul Play	Dark	Physical	95	100	15	Normal
TR83	Ally Switch	Psychic	Status	—	—	15	Self
TR92	Dazzling Gleam	Fairy	Special	80	100	10	Many Others

ABILITY
Keen Eye
Stall

HIDDEN ABILITY
Prankster

SPECIES STRENGTHS
HP
ATTACK
DEFENSE
SP. ATK
SP. DEF
SPEED

DAMAGE TAKEN IN BATTLE
×0 | ×0 | ×1
×1 | ×0.5 | ×1
×1 | ×1 | ×1
×1 | ×1 | ×1
×1 | ×0 | ×1
×1 | ×1 | ×2

HUMANLIKE

295

Mawile
p. 120

LEVEL-UP MOVES

LV.	NAME	TYPE	KIND	POW.	ACC.	PP	RANGE
1	Astonish	Ghost	Physical	30	100	15	Normal
1	Growl	Normal	Status	—	100	40	Many Others
4	Fairy Wind	Fairy	Special	40	100	30	Normal
8	Baton Pass	Normal	Status	—	—	40	Self
12	Bite	Dark	Physical	60	100	25	Normal
16	Spit Up	Normal	Special	—	100	10	Normal
16	Stockpile	Normal	Status	—	—	20	Self
16	Swallow	Normal	Status	—	—	10	Self
20	Sucker Punch	Dark	Physical	70	100	5	Normal
24	Iron Defense	Steel	Status	—	—	15	Self
28	Crunch	Dark	Physical	80	100	15	Normal
32	Sweet Scent	Normal	Status	—	100	20	Many Others
36	Iron Head	Steel	Physical	80	100	15	Normal
40	Taunt	Dark	Status	—	100	20	Normal
44	Fake Tears	Dark	Status	—	100	20	Normal
48	Play Rough	Fairy	Physical	90	90	10	Normal

EVOLUTION MOVES

NAME	TYPE	KIND	POW.	ACC.	PP	RANGE

EGG MOVES

NAME	TYPE	KIND	POW.	ACC.	PP	RANGE
Ancient Power	Rock	Special	60	100	5	Normal
Power-Up Punch	Fighting	Physical	40	100	20	Normal
Seismic Toss	Fighting	Physical	—	100	20	Normal
Slam	Normal	Physical	80	75	20	Normal
Tickle	Normal	Status	—	100	20	Normal

TUTOR MOVES

NAME	TYPE	KIND	POW.	ACC.	PP	RANGE
Steel Beam	Steel	Special	140	95	5	Normal

TM MOVES

NO.	NAME	TYPE	KIND	POW.	ACC.	PP	RANGE
TM00	Mega Punch	Normal	Physical	80	85	20	Normal
TM01	Mega Kick	Normal	Physical	120	75	5	Normal
TM04	Ice Punch	Ice	Physical	75	100	15	Normal
TM05	Thunder Punch	Electric	Physical	75	100	15	Normal
TM08	Hyper Beam	Normal	Special	150	90	5	Normal
TM09	Giga Impact	Normal	Physical	150	90	5	Normal
TM11	Solar Beam	Grass	Special	120	100	10	Normal
TM21	Rest	Psychic	Status	—	—	10	Self
TM22	Rock Slide	Rock	Physical	75	90	10	Many Others
TM24	Snore	Normal	Special	50	100	15	Normal
TM25	Protect	Normal	Status	—	—	10	Self
TM27	Icy Wind	Ice	Special	55	95	15	Many Others
TM31	Attract	Normal	Status	—	100	15	Normal
TM32	Sandstorm	Rock	Status	—	—	10	Both Sides
TM33	Rain Dance	Water	Status	—	—	5	Both Sides
TM34	Sunny Day	Fire	Status	—	—	5	Both Sides
TM39	Facade	Normal	Physical	70	100	20	Normal
TM41	Helping Hand	Normal	Status	—	—	20	1 Ally
TM43	Brick Break	Fighting	Physical	75	100	15	Normal
TM47	Fake Tears	Dark	Status	—	100	20	Normal
TM48	Rock Tomb	Rock	Physical	60	95	15	Normal
TM57	Payback	Dark	Physical	50	100	10	Normal
TM58	Assurance	Dark	Physical	60	100	10	Normal
TM59	Fling	Dark	Physical	—	100	10	Normal
TM61	Guard Swap	Psychic	Status	—	—	10	Normal
TM66	Thunder Fang	Electric	Physical	65	95	15	Normal
TM67	Ice Fang	Ice	Physical	65	95	15	Normal
TM68	Fire Fang	Fire	Physical	65	95	15	Normal
TM76	Round	Normal	Special	60	100	15	Normal
TM87	Draining Kiss	Fairy	Special	50	100	10	Normal
TM89	Misty Terrain	Fairy	Status	—	—	10	Both Sides
TM94	False Swipe	Normal	Physical	40	100	40	Normal
TM97	Brutal Swing	Dark	Physical	60	100	20	All Others

TR MOVES

NAME	TYPE	KIND	POW.	ACC.	PP	RANGE
TR00	Swords Dance	Normal	Status	—	—	20	Self
TR01	Body Slam	Normal	Physical	85	100	15	Normal
TR02	Flamethrower	Fire	Special	90	100	15	Normal
TR05	Ice Beam	Ice	Special	90	100	10	Normal
TR15	Fire Blast	Fire	Special	110	85	5	Normal
TR20	Substitute	Normal	Status	—	—	10	Self
TR22	Sludge Bomb	Poison	Special	90	100	10	Normal
TR26	Endure	Normal	Status	—	—	10	Self
TR27	Sleep Talk	Normal	Status	—	—	10	Self
TR29	Baton Pass	Normal	Status	—	—	40	Self
TR32	Crunch	Dark	Physical	80	100	15	Normal
TR33	Shadow Ball	Ghost	Special	80	100	15	Normal
TR37	Taunt	Dark	Status	—	100	20	Normal
TR46	Iron Defense	Steel	Status	—	—	15	Self
TR58	Dark Pulse	Dark	Special	80	100	15	Normal
TR64	Focus Blast	Fighting	Special	120	70	5	Normal
TR70	Flash Cannon	Steel	Special	80	100	10	Normal
TR74	Iron Head	Steel	Physical	80	100	15	Normal
TR75	Stone Edge	Rock	Physical	100	80	5	Normal
TR76	Stealth Rock	Rock	Status	—	—	20	Other Side
TR77	Grass Knot	Grass	Special	—	100	20	Normal
TR81	Foul Play	Dark	Physical	95	100	15	Normal
TR90	Play Rough	Fairy	Physical	90	90	10	Normal
TR97	Psychic Fangs	Psychic	Physical	85	100	10	Normal

ABILITY
Hyper Cutter
Intimidate

HIDDEN ABILITY
Sheer Force

SPECIES STRENGTHS
HP
ATTACK
DEFENSE
SP. ATK
SP. DEF
SPEED

DAMAGE TAKEN IN BATTLE
×0.5 | ×1 | ×0.5
×2 | ×0 | ×1
×1 | ×2 | ×0
×0.5 | ×0.5 | ×0.5
×1 | ×0.5 | ×1
×0.5 | ×0.25 | ×0.5

FIELD
FAIRY

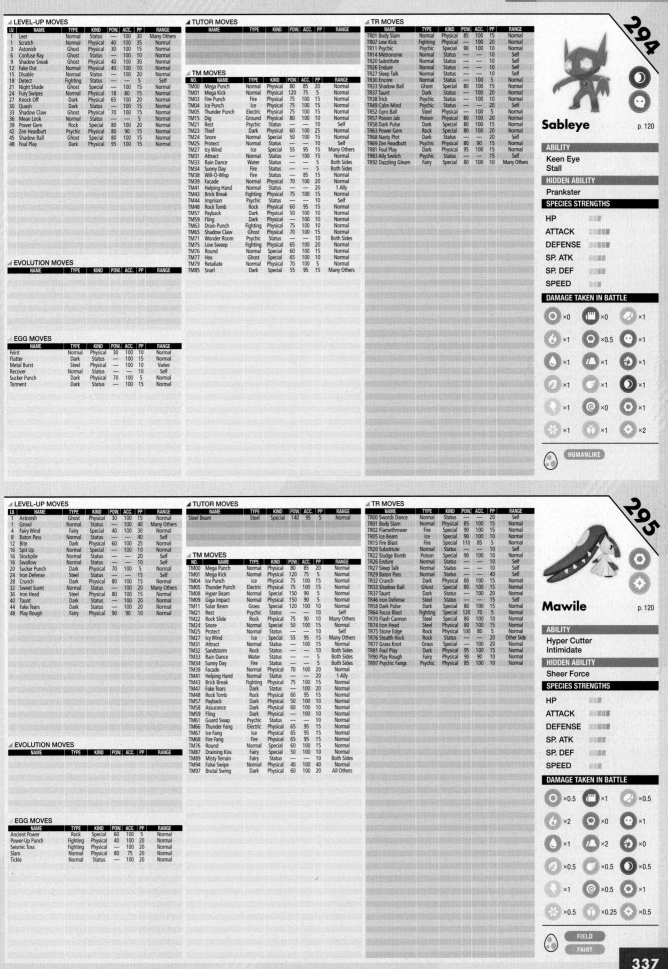

296 Maractus p. 120

ABILITY
Water Absorb
Chlorophyll

HIDDEN ABILITY
Storm Drain

SPECIES STRENGTHS

HP	▪▪▪▫▫
ATTACK	▪▪▪▪▫
DEFENSE	▪▪▫▫▫
SP. ATK	▪▪▪▪▫
SP. DEF	▪▪▫▫▫
SPEED	▪▫▫▫▫

DAMAGE TAKEN IN BATTLE

×1	×1	×1
×2	×2	×1
×0.5	×0.5	×1
×0.5	×2	×1
×0.5	×1	×1
×2	×2	×1

GRASS

LEVEL-UP MOVES

LV.	NAME	TYPE	KIND	POW.	ACC.	PP	RANGE
1	Absorb	Grass	Special	20	100	25	Normal
1	After You	Normal	Status	—	—	15	Normal
1	Ingrain	Grass	Status	—	—	20	Self
1	Peck	Flying	Physical	35	100	35	Normal
1	Spiky Shield	Grass	Status	—	—	10	Self
4	Growth	Normal	Status	—	—	20	Self
8	Mega Drain	Grass	Special	40	100	15	Normal
12	Leech Seed	Grass	Status	—	90	10	Normal
16	Sucker Punch	Dark	Physical	70	100	5	Normal
20	Pin Missile	Bug	Physical	25	95	20	Normal
24	Giga Drain	Grass	Special	75	100	10	Normal
28	Sweet Scent	Normal	Status	—	100	20	Many Others
32	Synthesis	Grass	Status	—	—	5	Self
36	Petal Blizzard	Grass	Physical	90	100	15	All Others
40	Cotton Spore	Grass	Status	—	100	40	Many Others
44	Sunny Day	Fire	Status	—	—	5	Both Sides
48	Solar Beam	Grass	Special	120	100	10	Normal
52	Acupressure	Normal	Status	—	—	30	Self/Ally
56	Petal Dance	Grass	Special	120	100	10	1 Random
60	Cotton Guard	Grass	Status	—	—	10	Self

EVOLUTION MOVES

NAME	TYPE	KIND	POW.	ACC.	PP	RANGE

EGG MOVES

NAME	TYPE	KIND	POW.	ACC.	PP	RANGE
Wood Hammer	Grass	Physical	120	100	15	Normal
Worry Seed	Grass	Status	—	100	10	Normal

TUTOR MOVES

NAME	TYPE	KIND	POW.	ACC.	PP	RANGE

TM MOVES

NO.	NAME	TYPE	KIND	POW.	ACC.	PP	RANGE
TM07	Pin Missile	Bug	Physical	25	95	20	Normal
TM11	Solar Beam	Grass	Special	120	100	10	Normal
TM16	Screech	Normal	Status	—	85	40	Normal
TM19	Safeguard	Normal	Status	—	—	25	Your Side
TM21	Rest	Psychic	Status	—	—	10	Self
TM24	Snore	Normal	Special	50	100	15	Normal
TM25	Protect	Normal	Status	—	—	10	Self
TM28	Giga Drain	Grass	Special	75	100	10	Normal
TM31	Attract	Normal	Status	—	100	15	Normal
TM33	Rain Dance	Water	Status	—	—	5	Both Sides
TM34	Sunny Day	Fire	Status	—	—	5	Both Sides
TM39	Facade	Normal	Physical	70	100	20	Normal
TM41	Helping Hand	Normal	Status	—	—	20	1 Ally
TM46	Weather Ball*	Normal	Special	50	100	10	Normal
TM50	Bullet Seed	Grass	Physical	25	100	30	Normal
TM52	Bounce	Flying	Physical	85	85	5	Normal
TM58	Assurance	Dark	Physical	60	100	10	Normal
TM63	Drain Punch	Fighting	Physical	75	100	10	Normal
TM76	Round	Normal	Special	60	100	15	Normal
TM88	Grassy Terrain	Grass	Status	—	—	10	Both Sides

TR MOVES

NO.	NAME	TYPE	KIND	POW.	ACC.	PP	RANGE
TR20	Substitute	Normal	Status	—	—	10	Self
TR23	Spikes	Ground	Status	—	—	20	Other Side
TR26	Endure	Normal	Status	—	—	10	Self
TR27	Sleep Talk	Normal	Status	—	—	10	Self
TR35	Uproar	Normal	Special	90	100	10	1 Random
TR42	Hyper Voice	Normal	Special	90	100	10	Many Others
TR57	Poison Jab	Poison	Physical	80	100	20	Normal
TR59	Seed Bomb	Grass	Physical	80	100	15	Normal
TR65	Energy Ball	Grass	Special	90	100	10	Normal
TR71	Leaf Storm	Grass	Special	130	90	5	Normal
TR77	Grass Knot	Grass	Special	—	100	20	Normal
TR95	Throat Chop	Dark	Physical	80	100	15	Normal

*Weather Ball changes type depending on weather condition. (Harsh sunlight: Fire type. Rain: Water type. Hail: Ice type. Sandstorm: Rock type.)

---

297 Sigilyph p. 121

ABILITY
Wonder Skin
Magic Guard

HIDDEN ABILITY
Tinted Lens

SPECIES STRENGTHS

HP	▪▪▪▫▫
ATTACK	▪▪▪▫▫
DEFENSE	▪▪▪▫▫
SP. ATK	▪▪▪▪▪
SP. DEF	▪▪▪▫▫
SPEED	▪▪▪▪▫

DAMAGE TAKEN IN BATTLE

×1	×0.25	×2
×1	×1	×2
×1	×0	×1
×0.5	×1	×2
×2	×0.5	×1
×2	×1	×1

FLYING

LEVEL-UP MOVES

LV.	NAME	TYPE	KIND	POW.	ACC.	PP	RANGE
1	Confusion	Psychic	Special	50	100	25	Normal
1	Gust	Flying	Special	40	100	35	Normal
5	Gravity	Psychic	Status	—	—	5	Both Sides
10	Hypnosis	Psychic	Status	—	60	20	Normal
15	Air Cutter	Flying	Special	60	95	25	Many Others
20	Psybeam	Psychic	Special	65	100	20	Normal
25	Whirlwind	Normal	Status	—	—	20	Normal
30	Cosmic Power	Psychic	Status	—	—	20	Self
35	Air Slash	Flying	Special	75	95	15	Normal
40	Psychic	Psychic	Special	90	100	10	Normal
45	Tailwind	Flying	Status	—	—	15	Your Side
50	Light Screen	Psychic	Status	—	—	30	Your Side
50	Reflect	Psychic	Status	—	—	20	Your Side
55	Sky Attack	Flying	Physical	140	90	5	Normal
60	Skill Swap	Psychic	Status	—	—	10	Normal

EVOLUTION MOVES

NAME	TYPE	KIND	POW.	ACC.	PP	RANGE

EGG MOVES

NAME	TYPE	KIND	POW.	ACC.	PP	RANGE
Ancient Power	Rock	Special	60	100	5	Normal
Psycho Shift	Psychic	Status	—	100	10	Normal
Roost	Flying	Status	—	—	10	Self

TUTOR MOVES

NAME	TYPE	KIND	POW.	ACC.	PP	RANGE

TM MOVES

NO.	NAME	TYPE	KIND	POW.	ACC.	PP	RANGE
TM06	Fly	Flying	Physical	90	95	15	Normal
TM08	Hyper Beam	Normal	Special	150	90	5	Normal
TM09	Giga Impact	Normal	Physical	150	90	5	Normal
TM11	Solar Beam	Grass	Special	120	100	10	Normal
TM14	Thunder Wave	Electric	Status	—	90	20	Normal
TM17	Light Screen	Psychic	Status	—	—	30	Your Side
TM18	Reflect	Psychic	Status	—	—	20	Your Side
TM19	Safeguard	Normal	Status	—	—	25	Your Side
TM21	Rest	Psychic	Status	—	—	10	Self
TM23	Thief	Dark	Physical	60	100	25	Normal
TM24	Snore	Normal	Special	50	100	15	Normal
TM25	Protect	Normal	Status	—	—	10	Self
TM27	Icy Wind	Ice	Special	55	95	15	Many Others
TM30	Steel Wing	Steel	Physical	70	90	25	Normal
TM31	Attract	Normal	Status	—	100	15	Normal
TM33	Rain Dance	Water	Status	—	—	5	Both Sides
TM39	Facade	Normal	Physical	70	100	20	Normal
TM40	Swift	Normal	Special	60	—	20	Many Others
TM44	Imprison	Psychic	Status	—	—	10	Self
TM60	Power Swap	Psychic	Status	—	—	10	Normal
TM62	Speed Swap	Psychic	Status	—	—	10	Normal
TM69	Psycho Cut	Psychic	Physical	70	100	20	Normal
TM70	Trick Room	Psychic	Status	—	—	5	Both Sides
TM72	Magic Room	Psychic	Status	—	—	10	Both Sides
TM76	Round	Normal	Special	60	100	15	Normal
TM95	Air Slash	Flying	Special	75	95	15	Normal

TR MOVES

NO.	NAME	TYPE	KIND	POW.	ACC.	PP	RANGE
TR05	Ice Beam	Ice	Special	90	100	10	Normal
TR11	Psychic	Psychic	Special	90	100	10	Normal
TR20	Substitute	Normal	Status	—	—	10	Self
TR25	Psyshock	Psychic	Special	80	100	10	Normal
TR26	Endure	Normal	Status	—	—	10	Self
TR27	Sleep Talk	Normal	Status	—	—	10	Self
TR33	Shadow Ball	Ghost	Special	80	100	15	Normal
TR34	Future Sight	Psychic	Special	120	100	10	Normal
TR36	Heat Wave	Fire	Special	95	90	10	Many Others
TR38	Trick	Psychic	Status	—	100	10	Normal
TR40	Skill Swap	Psychic	Status	—	—	10	Normal
TR44	Cosmic Power	Psychic	Status	—	—	20	Self
TR49	Calm Mind	Psychic	Status	—	—	20	Self
TR58	Dark Pulse	Dark	Special	80	100	15	Normal
TR65	Energy Ball	Grass	Special	90	100	10	Normal
TR69	Zen Headbutt	Psychic	Physical	80	90	15	Normal
TR70	Flash Cannon	Steel	Special	80	100	10	Normal
TR82	Stored Power	Psychic	Special	20	100	10	Normal
TR92	Dazzling Gleam	Fairy	Special	80	100	10	Many Others

298 — Riolu

LEVEL-UP MOVES

LV.	NAME	TYPE	KIND	POW.	ACC.	PP	RANGE
1	Endure	Normal	Status	—	—	10	Self
1	Quick Attack	Normal	Physical	40	100	30	Normal
4	Feint	Normal	Physical	30	100	10	Normal
8	Metal Claw	Steel	Physical	50	95	35	Normal
12	Counter	Fighting	Physical	—	100	20	Varies
16	Work Up	Normal	Status	—	—	30	Self
20	Rock Smash	Fighting	Physical	40	100	15	Normal
24	Nasty Plot	Dark	Status	—	—	20	Self
28	Screech	Normal	Status	—	85	40	Normal
32	Quick Guard	Fighting	Status	—	—	15	Your Side
36	Force Palm	Fighting	Physical	60	100	10	Normal
40	Swords Dance	Normal	Status	—	—	20	Self
44	Helping Hand	Normal	Status	—	—	20	1 Ally
48	Copycat	Normal	Status	—	—	20	Self
52	Final Gambit	Fighting	Special	—	100	5	Normal
56	Reversal	Fighting	Physical	—	100	15	Normal

EVOLUTION MOVES

NAME	TYPE	KIND	POW.	ACC.	PP	RANGE

EGG MOVES

NAME	TYPE	KIND	POW.	ACC.	PP	RANGE
Bite	Dark	Physical	60	100	25	Normal
Bullet Punch	Steel	Physical	40	100	30	Normal
Circle Throw	Fighting	Physical	60	-90	10	Normal
Cross Chop	Fighting	Physical	100	80	5	Normal
Detect	Fighting	Status	—	—	5	Self
High Jump Kick	Fighting	Physical	130	90	10	Normal
Howl	Normal	Status	—	—	40	Your Side
Mind Reader	Normal	Status	—	—	5	Normal
Vacuum Wave	Fighting	Special	40	100	30	Normal

TUTOR MOVES

NAME	TYPE	KIND	POW.	ACC.	PP	RANGE

TM MOVES

NO.	NAME	TYPE	KIND	POW.	ACC.	PP	RANGE
TM00	Mega Punch	Normal	Physical	80	85	20	Normal
TM01	Mega Kick	Normal	Physical	120	75	5	Normal
TM04	Ice Punch	Ice	Physical	75	100	15	Normal
TM05	Thunder Punch	Electric	Physical	75	100	15	Normal
TM15	Dig	Ground	Physical	80	100	10	Normal
TM16	Screech	Normal	Status	—	85	40	Normal
TM21	Rest	Psychic	Status	—	—	10	Self
TM22	Rock Slide	Rock	Physical	75	90	10	Many Others
TM24	Snore	Normal	Special	50	100	15	Normal
TM25	Protect	Normal	Status	—	—	10	Self
TM31	Attract	Normal	Status	—	100	15	Normal
TM33	Rain Dance	Water	Status	—	—	5	Both Sides
TM34	Sunny Day	Fire	Status	—	—	5	Both Sides
TM39	Facade	Normal	Physical	70	100	20	Normal
TM40	Swift	Normal	Special	60	—	20	Many Others
TM41	Helping Hand	Normal	Status	—	—	20	1 Ally
TM42	Revenge	Fighting	Physical	60	100	10	Normal
TM43	Brick Break	Fighting	Physical	75	100	15	Normal
TM48	Rock Tomb	Rock	Physical	60	95	15	Normal
TM57	Payback	Dark	Physical	50	100	10	Normal
TM59	Fling	Dark	Physical	—	100	10	Normal
TM63	Drain Punch	Fighting	Physical	75	100	10	Normal
TM65	Shadow Claw	Ghost	Physical	70	100	15	Normal
TM75	Low Sweep	Fighting	Physical	65	100	20	Normal
TM76	Round	Normal	Special	60	100	15	Normal
TM79	Retaliate	Normal	Physical	70	100	5	Normal
TM81	Bulldoze	Ground	Physical	60	100	20	All Others

TR MOVES

NO.	NAME	TYPE	KIND	POW.	ACC.	PP	RANGE
TR00	Swords Dance	Normal	Status	—	—	20	Self
TR07	Low Kick	Fighting	Physical	—	100	20	Normal
TR10	Earthquake	Ground	Physical	100	100	10	All Others
TR12	Agility	Psychic	Status	—	—	30	Self
TR20	Substitute	Normal	Status	—	—	10	Self
TR21	Reversal	Fighting	Physical	—	100	15	Normal
TR26	Endure	Normal	Status	—	—	10	Self
TR27	Sleep Talk	Normal	Status	—	—	10	Self
TR31	Iron Tail	Steel	Physical	100	75	15	Normal
TR32	Crunch	Dark	Physical	80	100	15	Normal
TR41	Blaze Kick	Fire	Physical	85	90	10	Normal
TR46	Iron Defense	Steel	Status	—	—	15	Self
TR48	Bulk Up	Fighting	Status	—	—	20	Self
TR57	Poison Jab	Poison	Physical	80	100	20	Normal
TR64	Focus Blast	Fighting	Special	120	70	5	Normal
TR68	Nasty Plot	Dark	Status	—	—	20	Self
TR69	Zen Headbutt	Psychic	Physical	80	90	15	Normal
TR85	Work Up	Normal	Status	—	—	30	Self

Riolu p. 121

ABILITY
Steadfast
Inner Focus

HIDDEN ABILITY
Prankster

SPECIES STRENGTHS

HP
ATTACK
DEFENSE
SP. ATK
SP. DEF
SPEED

DAMAGE TAKEN IN BATTLE

×1	×1	×0.5
×1	×1	×1
×1	×1	×1
×1	×2	×0.5
×1	×2	×1
×1	×0.5	×2

NO EGGS

---

299 — Lucario

LEVEL-UP MOVES

LV.	NAME	TYPE	KIND	POW.	ACC.	PP	RANGE
1	Aura Sphere	Fighting	Special	80	—	20	Normal
1	Copycat	Normal	Status	—	—	20	Self
1	Detect	Fighting	Status	—	—	5	Self
1	Feint	Normal	Physical	30	100	10	Normal
1	Final Gambit	Fighting	Special	—	100	5	Normal
1	Force Palm	Fighting	Physical	60	100	10	Normal
1	Helping Hand	Normal	Status	—	—	20	1 Ally
1	Life Dew	Water	Status	—	—	10	Your Side
1	Metal Claw	Steel	Physical	50	95	35	Normal
1	Nasty Plot	Dark	Status	—	—	20	Self
1	Quick Attack	Normal	Physical	40	100	30	Normal
1	Reversal	Fighting	Physical	—	100	15	Normal
1	Rock Smash	Fighting	Physical	40	100	15	Normal
1	Screech	Normal	Status	—	85	40	Normal
1	Work Up	Normal	Status	—	—	30	Self
12	Counter	Fighting	Physical	—	100	20	Varies
16	Laser Focus	Normal	Status	—	—	30	Self
20	Power-Up Punch	Fighting	Physical	40	100	20	Normal
24	Calm Mind	Psychic	Status	—	—	20	Self
28	Metal Sound	Steel	Status	—	85	40	Normal
32	Quick Guard	Fighting	Status	—	—	15	Your Side
36	Bone Rush	Ground	Physical	25	90	10	Normal
40	Swords Dance	Normal	Status	—	—	20	Self
44	Heal Pulse	Psychic	Status	—	—	10	Normal
48	Meteor Mash	Steel	Physical	90	90	10	Normal
52	Dragon Pulse	Dragon	Special	85	100	10	Normal
56	Extreme Speed	Normal	Physical	80	100	5	Normal
60	Close Combat	Fighting	Physical	120	100	5	Normal

EVOLUTION MOVES

NAME	TYPE	KIND	POW.	ACC.	PP	RANGE
Aura Sphere	Fighting	Special	80	—	20	Normal

EGG MOVES

NAME	TYPE	KIND	POW.	ACC.	PP	RANGE

TUTOR MOVES

NAME	TYPE	KIND	POW.	ACC.	PP	RANGE
Steel Beam	Steel	Special	140	95	5	Normal

TM MOVES

NO.	NAME	TYPE	KIND	POW.	ACC.	PP	RANGE
TM00	Mega Punch	Normal	Physical	80	85	20	Normal
TM01	Mega Kick	Normal	Physical	120	75	5	Normal
TM04	Ice Punch	Ice	Physical	75	100	15	Normal
TM05	Thunder Punch	Electric	Physical	75	100	15	Normal
TM08	Hyper Beam	Normal	Special	150	90	5	Normal
TM09	Giga Impact	Normal	Physical	150	90	5	Normal
TM15	Dig	Ground	Physical	80	100	10	Normal
TM16	Screech	Normal	Status	—	85	40	Normal
TM21	Rest	Psychic	Status	—	—	10	Self
TM22	Rock Slide	Rock	Physical	75	90	10	Many Others
TM24	Snore	Normal	Special	50	100	15	Normal
TM25	Protect	Normal	Status	—	—	10	Self
TM26	Scary Face	Normal	Status	—	100	10	Normal
TM31	Attract	Normal	Status	—	100	15	Normal
TM33	Rain Dance	Water	Status	—	—	5	Both Sides
TM34	Sunny Day	Fire	Status	—	—	5	Both Sides
TM39	Facade	Normal	Physical	70	100	20	Normal
TM40	Swift	Normal	Special	60	—	20	Many Others
TM41	Helping Hand	Normal	Status	—	—	20	1 Ally
TM42	Revenge	Fighting	Physical	60	100	10	Normal
TM43	Brick Break	Fighting	Physical	75	100	15	Normal
TM48	Rock Tomb	Rock	Physical	60	95	15	Normal
TM57	Payback	Dark	Physical	50	100	10	Normal
TM59	Fling	Dark	Physical	—	100	10	Normal
TM63	Drain Punch	Fighting	Physical	75	100	10	Normal
TM65	Shadow Claw	Ghost	Physical	70	100	15	Normal
TM75	Low Sweep	Fighting	Physical	65	100	20	Normal
TM76	Round	Normal	Special	60	100	15	Normal
TM79	Retaliate	Normal	Physical	70	100	5	Normal
TM81	Bulldoze	Ground	Physical	60	100	20	All Others

TR MOVES

NO.	NAME	TYPE	KIND	POW.	ACC.	PP	RANGE
TR00	Swords Dance	Normal	Status	—	—	20	Self
TR07	Low Kick	Fighting	Physical	—	100	20	Normal
TR10	Earthquake	Ground	Physical	100	100	10	All Others
TR11	Psychic	Psychic	Special	90	100	10	Normal
TR12	Agility	Psychic	Status	—	—	30	Self
TR13	Focus Energy	Normal	Status	—	—	30	Self
TR20	Substitute	Normal	Status	—	—	10	Self
TR21	Reversal	Fighting	Physical	—	100	15	Normal
TR26	Endure	Normal	Status	—	—	10	Self
TR27	Sleep Talk	Normal	Status	—	—	10	Self
TR31	Iron Tail	Steel	Physical	100	75	15	Normal
TR32	Crunch	Dark	Physical	80	100	15	Normal
TR33	Shadow Ball	Ghost	Special	80	100	15	Normal
TR41	Blaze Kick	Fire	Physical	85	90	10	Normal
TR46	Iron Defense	Steel	Status	—	—	15	Self
TR48	Bulk Up	Fighting	Status	—	—	20	Self
TR49	Calm Mind	Psychic	Status	—	—	20	Self
TR53	Close Combat	Fighting	Physical	120	100	5	Normal
TR56	Aura Sphere	Fighting	Special	80	—	20	Normal
TR57	Poison Jab	Poison	Physical	80	100	20	Normal
TR58	Dark Pulse	Dark	Special	80	100	15	Normal
TR62	Dragon Pulse	Dragon	Special	85	100	10	Normal
TR64	Focus Blast	Fighting	Special	120	70	5	Normal
TR68	Nasty Plot	Dark	Status	—	—	20	Self
TR69	Zen Headbutt	Psychic	Physical	80	90	15	Normal
TR74	Iron Head	Steel	Physical	80	100	15	Normal
TR75	Stone Edge	Rock	Physical	100	80	5	Normal
TR85	Work Up	Normal	Status	—	—	30	Self

Lucario p. 121

ABILITY
Steadfast
Inner Focus

HIDDEN ABILITY
Justified

SPECIES STRENGTHS

HP
ATTACK
DEFENSE
SP. ATK
SP. DEF
SPEED

DAMAGE TAKEN IN BATTLE

×0.5	×2	×0.25
×2	×0	×1
×1	×2	×0.5
×0.5	×1	×0.5
×1	×1	×0.5
×0.5	×0.25	×1

FIELD
HUMANLIKE

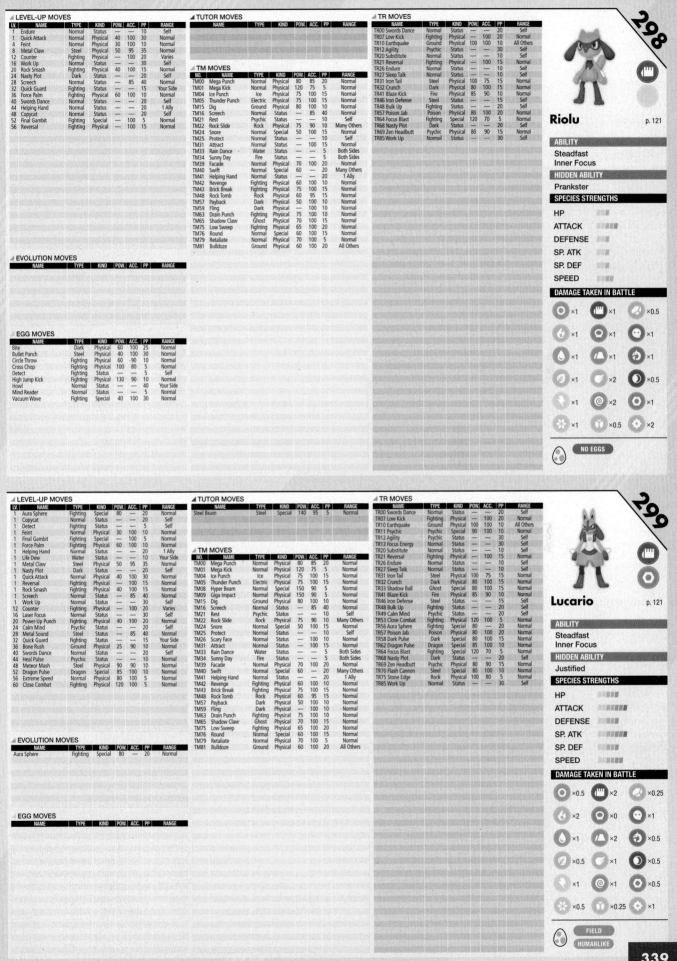

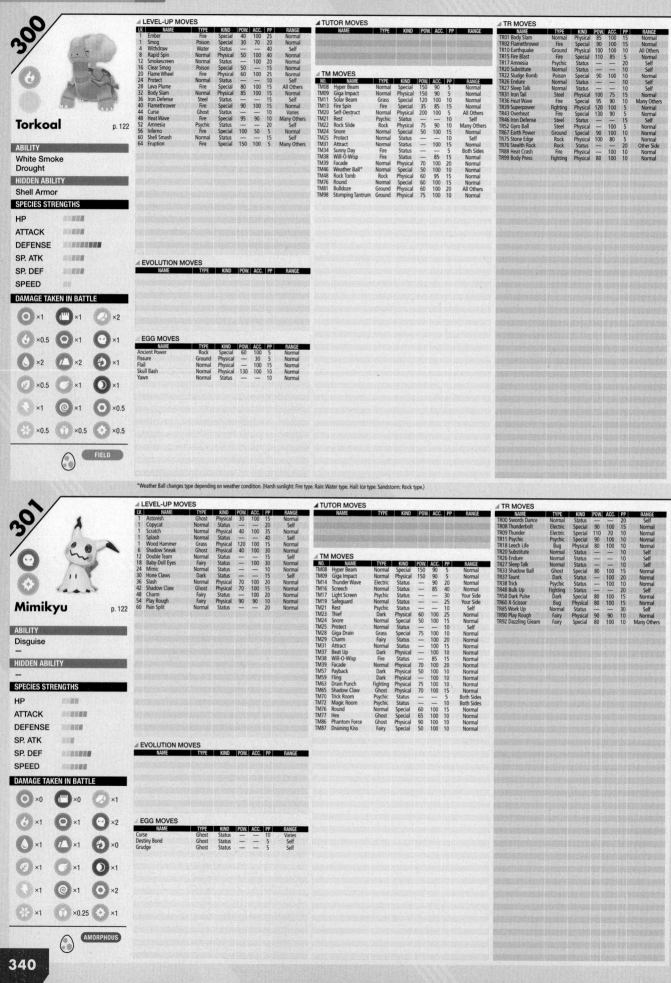

300 Torkoal

p. 122

ABILITY
White Smoke
Drought

HIDDEN ABILITY
Shell Armor

SPECIES STRENGTHS

HP	
ATTACK	
DEFENSE	
SP. ATK	
SP. DEF	
SPEED	

DAMAGE TAKEN IN BATTLE

×1	×1	×2			
×0.5	×1	×1			
×2	×2	×1			
×0.5	×1	×1			
×1	×1	×0.5			
×0.5	×0.5	×0.5			

FIELD

LEVEL-UP MOVES

LV.	NAME	TYPE	KIND	POW.	ACC.	PP	RANGE
1	Ember	Fire	Special	40	100	25	Normal
1	Smog	Poison	Special	30	70	20	Normal
4	Withdraw	Water	Status	—	—	40	Self
8	Rapid Spin	Normal	Physical	50	100	40	Normal
12	Smokescreen	Normal	Status	—	100	20	Normal
16	Clear Smog	Poison	Special	50	—	15	Normal
20	Flame Wheel	Fire	Physical	60	100	25	Normal
24	Protect	Normal	Status	—	—	10	Self
28	Lava Plume	Fire	Special	80	100	15	All Others
32	Body Slam	Normal	Physical	85	100	15	Normal
36	Iron Defense	Steel	Status	—	—	15	Self
40	Flamethrower	Fire	Special	90	100	15	Normal
44	Curse	Ghost	Status	—	—	10	Varies
48	Heat Wave	Fire	Special	95	90	10	Many Others
52	Amnesia	Psychic	Status	—	—	20	Self
56	Inferno	Fire	Special	100	50	5	Normal
60	Shell Smash	Normal	Status	—	—	15	Self
64	Eruption	Fire	Special	150	100	5	Many Others

EVOLUTION MOVES

NAME	TYPE	KIND	POW.	ACC.	PP	RANGE

EGG MOVES

NAME	TYPE	KIND	POW.	ACC.	PP	RANGE
Ancient Power	Rock	Special	60	100	5	Normal
Fissure	Ground	Physical	—	30	5	Normal
Flail	Normal	Physical	—	100	15	Normal
Skull Bash	Normal	Physical	130	100	10	Normal
Yawn	Normal	Status	—	—	10	Normal

TUTOR MOVES

NAME	TYPE	KIND	POW.	ACC.	PP	RANGE

TM MOVES

NO.	NAME	TYPE	KIND	POW.	ACC.	PP	RANGE
TM08	Hyper Beam	Normal	Special	150	90	5	Normal
TM09	Giga Impact	Normal	Physical	150	90	5	Normal
TM11	Solar Beam	Grass	Special	120	100	10	Normal
TM13	Fire Spin	Fire	Special	35	85	15	Normal
TM20	Self-Destruct	Normal	Physical	200	100	5	All Others
TM21	Rest	Psychic	Status	—	—	10	Self
TM22	Rock Slide	Rock	Physical	75	90	10	Many Others
TM24	Snore	Normal	Special	50	100	15	Normal
TM25	Protect	Normal	Status	—	—	10	Self
TM31	Attract	Normal	Status	—	100	15	Normal
TM34	Sunny Day	Fire	Status	—	—	5	Both Sides
TM38	Will-O-Wisp	Fire	Status	—	85	15	Normal
TM39	Facade	Normal	Physical	70	100	20	Normal
TM46	Weather Ball*	Normal	Special	50	100	10	Normal
TM48	Rock Tomb	Rock	Physical	60	95	15	Normal
TM76	Round	Normal	Special	60	100	15	Normal
TM81	Bulldoze	Ground	Physical	60	100	20	All Others
TM98	Stomping Tantrum	Ground	Physical	75	100	10	Normal

TR MOVES

NO.	NAME	TYPE	KIND	POW.	ACC.	PP	RANGE
TR01	Body Slam	Normal	Physical	85	100	15	Normal
TR02	Flamethrower	Fire	Special	90	100	15	Normal
TR10	Earthquake	Ground	Physical	100	100	10	All Others
TR15	Fire Blast	Fire	Special	110	85	5	Normal
TR17	Amnesia	Psychic	Status	—	—	20	Self
TR20	Substitute	Normal	Status	—	—	10	Self
TR22	Sludge Bomb	Poison	Special	90	100	10	Normal
TR26	Endure	Normal	Status	—	—	10	Self
TR27	Sleep Talk	Normal	Status	—	—	10	Self
TR31	Iron Tail	Steel	Physical	100	75	15	Normal
TR36	Heat Wave	Fire	Special	95	90	10	Many Others
TR39	Superpower	Fighting	Physical	120	100	5	Normal
TR43	Overheat	Fire	Special	130	90	5	Normal
TR46	Iron Defense	Steel	Status	—	—	15	Self
TR52	Gyro Ball	Steel	Physical	—	100	5	Normal
TR67	Earth Power	Ground	Special	90	100	10	Normal
TR75	Stone Edge	Rock	Physical	100	80	5	Normal
TR76	Stealth Rock	Rock	Status	—	—	20	Other Side
TR88	Heat Crash	Fire	Physical	—	100	10	Normal
TR99	Body Press	Fighting	Physical	80	100	10	Normal

*Weather Ball changes type depending on weather condition. (Harsh sunlight: Fire type. Rain: Water type. Hail: Ice type. Sandstorm: Rock type.)

301 Mimikyu

p. 122

ABILITY
Disguise
—

HIDDEN ABILITY
—

SPECIES STRENGTHS

HP	
ATTACK	
DEFENSE	
SP. ATK	
SP. DEF	
SPEED	

DAMAGE TAKEN IN BATTLE

×0	×0	×1			
×1	×1	×2			
×1	×1	×0			
×1	×1	×1			
×1	×1	×2			
×1	×0.25	×1			

AMORPHOUS

LEVEL-UP MOVES

LV.	NAME	TYPE	KIND	POW.	ACC.	PP	RANGE
1	Astonish	Ghost	Physical	30	100	15	Normal
1	Copycat	Normal	Status	—	—	20	Self
1	Scratch	Normal	Physical	40	100	35	Normal
1	Splash	Normal	Status	—	—	40	Self
6	Wood Hammer	Grass	Physical	120	100	15	Normal
9	Shadow Sneak	Ghost	Physical	40	100	30	Normal
12	Double Team	Normal	Status	—	—	15	Self
18	Baby-Doll Eyes	Fairy	Status	—	100	30	Normal
24	Mimic	Normal	Status	—	—	10	Normal
30	Hone Claws	Dark	Status	—	—	15	Self
36	Slash	Normal	Physical	70	100	20	Normal
42	Shadow Claw	Ghost	Physical	70	100	15	Normal
48	Charm	Fairy	Status	—	100	20	Normal
54	Play Rough	Fairy	Physical	90	90	10	Normal
60	Pain Split	Normal	Status	—	—	20	Normal

EVOLUTION MOVES

NAME	TYPE	KIND	POW.	ACC.	PP	RANGE

EGG MOVES

NAME	TYPE	KIND	POW.	ACC.	PP	RANGE
Curse	Ghost	Status	—	—	10	Varies
Destiny Bond	Ghost	Status	—	—	5	Self
Grudge	Ghost	Status	—	—	5	Self

TUTOR MOVES

NAME	TYPE	KIND	POW.	ACC.	PP	RANGE

TM MOVES

NO.	NAME	TYPE	KIND	POW.	ACC.	PP	RANGE
TM08	Hyper Beam	Normal	Special	150	90	5	Normal
TM09	Giga Impact	Normal	Physical	150	90	5	Normal
TM14	Thunder Wave	Electric	Status	—	90	20	Normal
TM16	Screech	Normal	Status	—	85	40	Normal
TM17	Light Screen	Psychic	Status	—	—	30	Your Side
TM19	Safeguard	Normal	Status	—	—	25	Your Side
TM21	Rest	Psychic	Status	—	—	10	Self
TM23	Thief	Dark	Physical	60	100	25	Normal
TM24	Snore	Normal	Special	50	100	15	Normal
TM25	Protect	Normal	Status	—	—	10	Self
TM28	Giga Drain	Grass	Special	75	100	10	Normal
TM29	Charm	Fairy	Status	—	100	20	Normal
TM31	Attract	Normal	Status	—	100	15	Normal
TM37	Beat Up	Dark	Physical	—	100	10	Normal
TM38	Will-O-Wisp	Fire	Status	—	85	15	Normal
TM39	Facade	Normal	Physical	70	100	20	Normal
TM57	Payback	Dark	Physical	50	100	10	Normal
TM59	Fling	Dark	Physical	—	100	10	Normal
TM63	Drain Punch	Fighting	Physical	75	100	10	Normal
TM65	Shadow Claw	Ghost	Physical	70	100	15	Normal
TM70	Trick Room	Psychic	Status	—	—	5	Both Sides
TM72	Magic Room	Psychic	Status	—	—	10	Both Sides
TM76	Round	Normal	Special	60	100	15	Normal
TM77	Hex	Ghost	Special	65	100	10	Normal
TM86	Phantom Force	Ghost	Physical	90	100	10	Normal
TM87	Draining Kiss	Fairy	Special	50	100	10	Normal

TR MOVES

NO.	NAME	TYPE	KIND	POW.	ACC.	PP	RANGE
TR00	Swords Dance	Normal	Status	—	—	20	Self
TR08	Thunderbolt	Electric	Special	90	100	15	Normal
TR09	Thunder	Electric	Special	110	70	10	Normal
TR11	Psychic	Psychic	Special	90	100	10	Normal
TR18	Leech Life	Bug	Physical	80	100	10	Normal
TR20	Substitute	Normal	Status	—	—	10	Self
TR26	Endure	Normal	Status	—	—	10	Self
TR27	Sleep Talk	Normal	Status	—	—	10	Self
TR33	Shadow Ball	Ghost	Special	80	100	15	Normal
TR37	Taunt	Dark	Status	—	100	20	Normal
TR38	Trick	Psychic	Status	—	100	10	Normal
TR58	Dark Pulse	Dark	Special	80	100	15	Normal
TR60	X-Scissor	Bug	Physical	80	100	15	Normal
TR85	Work Up	Normal	Status	—	—	30	Self
TR90	Play Rough	Fairy	Physical	90	90	10	Normal
TR92	Dazzling Gleam	Fairy	Special	80	100	10	Many Others

302 Cufant

p. 123

LEVEL-UP MOVES

LV.	NAME	TYPE	KIND	POW.	ACC.	PP	RANGE
1	Growl	Normal	Status	—	100	40	Many Others
1	Tackle	Normal	Physical	40	100	35	Normal
5	Rollout	Rock	Physical	30	90	20	Normal
10	Rock Smash	Fighting	Physical	40	100	15	Normal
15	Bulldoze	Ground	Physical	60	100	20	All Others
20	Stomp	Normal	Physical	65	100	20	Normal
25	Iron Defense	Steel	Status	—	—	15	Self
30	Dig	Ground	Physical	80	100	10	Normal
35	Strength	Normal	Physical	80	100	15	Normal
40	Iron Head	Steel	Physical	80	100	15	Normal
45	Play Rough	Fairy	Physical	90	90	10	Normal
50	High Horsepower	Ground	Physical	95	95	10	Normal
55	Superpower	Fighting	Physical	120	100	5	Normal

EVOLUTION MOVES

NAME	TYPE	KIND	POW.	ACC.	PP	RANGE

EGG MOVES

NAME	TYPE	KIND	POW.	ACC.	PP	RANGE
Belch	Poison	Special	120	90	10	Normal
Curse	Ghost	Status	—	—	10	Varies
Defense Curl	Normal	Status	—	—	40	Self
Double-Edge	Normal	Physical	120	100	15	Normal
Fissure	Ground	Physical	—	30	5	Normal
Slam	Normal	Physical	80	75	20	Normal
Swagger	Normal	Status	—	85	15	Normal
Whirlwind	Normal	Status	—	—	20	Normal

TUTOR MOVES

NAME	TYPE	KIND	POW.	ACC.	PP	RANGE
Steel Beam	Steel	Special	140	95	5	Normal

TM MOVES

NO.	NAME	TYPE	KIND	POW.	ACC.	PP	RANGE
TM01	Mega Kick	Normal	Physical	120	75	5	Normal
TM15	Dig	Ground	Physical	80	100	10	Normal
TM16	Screech	Normal	Status	—	85	40	Normal
TM21	Rest	Psychic	Status	—	—	10	Self
TM22	Rock Slide	Rock	Physical	75	90	10	Many Others
TM24	Snore	Normal	Special	50	100	15	Normal
TM25	Protect	Normal	Status	—	—	10	Self
TM31	Attract	Normal	Status	—	100	15	Normal
TM39	Facade	Normal	Physical	70	100	20	Normal
TM43	Brick Break	Fighting	Physical	75	100	15	Normal
TM48	Rock Tomb	Rock	Physical	60	95	15	Normal
TM53	Mud Shot	Ground	Special	55	95	15	Normal
TM54	Rock Blast	Rock	Physical	25	90	10	Normal
TM59	Fling	Dark	Physical	—	100	10	Normal
TM76	Round	Normal	Special	60	100	15	Normal
TM81	Bulldoze	Ground	Physical	60	100	20	All Others
TM97	Brutal Swing	Dark	Physical	60	100	20	All Others
TM98	Stomping Tantrum	Ground	Physical	75	100	10	Normal

TR MOVES

NO.	NAME	TYPE	KIND	POW.	ACC.	PP	RANGE
TR01	Body Slam	Normal	Physical	85	100	15	Normal
TR20	Substitute	Normal	Status	—	—	10	Self
TR26	Endure	Normal	Status	—	—	10	Self
TR27	Sleep Talk	Normal	Status	—	—	10	Self
TR39	Superpower	Fighting	Physical	120	100	5	Normal
TR46	Iron Defense	Steel	Status	—	—	15	Self
TR67	Earth Power	Ground	Special	90	100	10	Normal
TR69	Zen Headbutt	Psychic	Physical	80	90	15	Normal
TR72	Power Whip	Grass	Physical	120	85	10	Normal
TR74	Iron Head	Steel	Physical	80	100	15	Normal
TR76	Stealth Rock	Rock	Status	—	—	20	Other Side
TR85	Work Up	Normal	Status	—	—	30	Self
TR90	Play Rough	Fairy	Physical	90	90	10	Normal
TR94	High Horsepower	Ground	Physical	95	95	10	Normal
TR99	Body Press	Fighting	Physical	80	100	10	Normal

ABILITY
Sheer Force
—

HIDDEN ABILITY
Heavy Metal

SPECIES STRENGTHS
HP
ATTACK
DEFENSE
SP. ATK
SP. DEF
SPEED

DAMAGE TAKEN IN BATTLE
×0.5 ×2 ×0.5
×2 ×0 ×1
×1 ×2 ×0.5
×0.5 ×0.5 ×1
×1 ×0.5 ×0.5
×0.5 ×0.5 ×0.5

FIELD
MINERAL

303 Copperajah

p. 123

LEVEL-UP MOVES

LV.	NAME	TYPE	KIND	POW.	ACC.	PP	RANGE
1	Growl	Normal	Status	—	100	40	Many Others
1	Heavy Slam	Steel	Physical	—	100	10	Normal
1	Rock Smash	Fighting	Physical	40	100	15	Normal
1	Rollout	Rock	Physical	30	90	20	Normal
1	Tackle	Normal	Physical	40	100	35	Normal
15	Bulldoze	Ground	Physical	60	100	20	All Others
20	Stomp	Normal	Physical	65	100	20	Normal
25	Iron Defense	Steel	Status	—	—	15	Self
30	Dig	Ground	Physical	80	100	10	Normal
37	Strength	Normal	Physical	80	100	15	Normal
44	Iron Head	Steel	Physical	80	100	15	Normal
51	Play Rough	Fairy	Physical	90	90	10	Normal
58	High Horsepower	Ground	Physical	95	95	10	Normal
65	Superpower	Fighting	Physical	120	100	5	Normal

EVOLUTION MOVES

NAME	TYPE	KIND	POW.	ACC.	PP	RANGE
Heavy Slam	Steel	Physical	—	100	10	Normal

EGG MOVES

NAME	TYPE	KIND	POW.	ACC.	PP	RANGE

TUTOR MOVES

NAME	TYPE	KIND	POW.	ACC.	PP	RANGE
Steel Beam	Steel	Special	140	95	5	Normal

TM MOVES

NO.	NAME	TYPE	KIND	POW.	ACC.	PP	RANGE
TM01	Mega Kick	Normal	Physical	120	75	5	Normal
TM08	Hyper Beam	Normal	Special	150	90	5	Normal
TM09	Giga Impact	Normal	Physical	150	90	5	Normal
TM15	Dig	Ground	Physical	80	100	10	Normal
TM16	Screech	Normal	Status	—	85	40	Normal
TM21	Rest	Psychic	Status	—	—	10	Self
TM22	Rock Slide	Rock	Physical	75	90	10	Many Others
TM24	Snore	Normal	Special	50	100	15	Normal
TM25	Protect	Normal	Status	—	—	10	Self
TM26	Scary Face	Normal	Status	—	100	10	Normal
TM31	Attract	Normal	Status	—	100	15	Normal
TM39	Facade	Normal	Physical	70	100	20	Normal
TM42	Revenge	Fighting	Physical	60	100	10	Normal
TM43	Brick Break	Fighting	Physical	75	100	15	Normal
TM48	Rock Tomb	Rock	Physical	60	95	15	Normal
TM53	Mud Shot	Ground	Special	55	95	15	Normal
TM54	Rock Blast	Rock	Physical	25	90	10	Normal
TM57	Payback	Dark	Physical	50	100	10	Normal
TM59	Fling	Dark	Physical	—	100	10	Normal
TM76	Round	Normal	Special	60	100	15	Normal
TM81	Bulldoze	Ground	Physical	60	100	20	All Others
TM85	Snarl	Dark	Special	55	95	15	Many Others
TM97	Brutal Swing	Dark	Physical	60	100	20	All Others
TM98	Stomping Tantrum	Ground	Physical	75	100	10	Normal

TR MOVES

NO.	NAME	TYPE	KIND	POW.	ACC.	PP	RANGE
TR01	Body Slam	Normal	Physical	85	100	15	Normal
TR10	Earthquake	Ground	Physical	100	100	10	All Others
TR20	Substitute	Normal	Status	—	—	10	Self
TR24	Outrage	Dragon	Physical	120	100	10	1 Random
TR26	Endure	Normal	Status	—	—	10	Self
TR27	Sleep Talk	Normal	Status	—	—	10	Self
TR37	Taunt	Dark	Status	—	100	20	Normal
TR39	Superpower	Fighting	Physical	120	100	5	Normal
TR46	Iron Defense	Steel	Status	—	—	15	Self
TR67	Earth Power	Ground	Special	90	100	10	Normal
TR69	Zen Headbutt	Psychic	Physical	80	90	15	Normal
TR70	Flash Cannon	Steel	Special	80	100	10	Normal
TR72	Power Whip	Grass	Physical	120	85	10	Normal
TR74	Iron Head	Steel	Physical	80	100	15	Normal
TR75	Stone Edge	Rock	Physical	100	80	5	Normal
TR76	Stealth Rock	Rock	Status	—	—	20	Other Side
TR79	Heavy Slam	Steel	Physical	—	100	10	Normal
TR85	Work Up	Normal	Status	—	—	30	Self
TR88	Heat Crash	Fire	Physical	—	100	10	Normal
TR90	Play Rough	Fairy	Physical	90	90	10	Normal
TR94	High Horsepower	Ground	Physical	95	95	10	Normal
TR99	Body Press	Fighting	Physical	80	100	10	Normal

ABILITY
Sheer Force
—

HIDDEN ABILITY
Heavy Metal

SPECIES STRENGTHS
HP
ATTACK
DEFENSE
SP. ATK
SP. DEF
SPEED

DAMAGE TAKEN IN BATTLE
×0.5 ×2 ×0.5
×2 ×0 ×1
×1 ×2 ×0.5
×0.5 ×0.5 ×1
×1 ×0.5 ×0.5
×0.5 ×0.5 ×0.5

FIELD
MINERAL

304 Qwilfish

p. 123

ABILITY
Poison Point
Swift Swim

HIDDEN ABILITY
Intimidate

SPECIES STRENGTHS

HP	
ATTACK	
DEFENSE	
SP. ATK	
SP. DEF	
SPEED	

DAMAGE TAKEN IN BATTLE

×1	×0.5	×1			
×0.5	×0.5	×1			
×0.5	×2	×1			
×1	×1	×1			
×2	×2	×0.5			
×0.5	×0.5	×0.5			

WATER 2

LEVEL-UP MOVES

LV.	NAME	TYPE	KIND	POW.	ACC.	PP	RANGE
1	Poison Sting	Poison	Physical	15	100	35	Normal
1	Tackle	Normal	Physical	40	100	35	Normal
4	Harden	Normal	Status	—	—	30	Self
8	Water Gun	Water	Special	40	100	25	Normal
12	Fell Stinger	Bug	Physical	50	100	25	Normal
16	Minimize	Normal	Status	—	—	10	Self
20	Spikes	Ground	Status	—	—	20	Other Side
24	Brine	Water	Special	65	100	10	Normal
28	Revenge	Fighting	Physical	60	100	10	Normal
32	Pin Missile	Bug	Physical	25	95	20	Normal
36	Toxic Spikes	Poison	Status	—	—	20	Other Side
40	Poison Jab	Poison	Physical	80	100	20	Normal
44	Spit Up	Normal	Special	—	100	10	Normal
44	Stockpile	Normal	Status	—	—	20	Self
48	Take Down	Normal	Physical	90	85	20	Normal
52	Toxic	Poison	Status	—	90	10	Normal
56	Aqua Tail	Water	Physical	90	90	10	Normal
60	Acupressure	Normal	Status	—	—	30	Self/Ally
66	Destiny Bond	Ghost	Status	—	—	5	Self

TUTOR MOVES

NAME	TYPE	KIND	POW.	ACC.	PP	RANGE

TM MOVES

NO.	NAME	TYPE	KIND	POW.	ACC.	PP	RANGE
TM07	Pin Missile	Bug	Physical	25	95	20	Normal
TM14	Thunder Wave	Electric	Status	—	90	20	Normal
TM20	Self-Destruct	Normal	Physical	200	100	5	All Others
TM21	Rest	Psychic	Status	—	—	10	Self
TM24	Snore	Normal	Special	50	100	15	Normal
TM25	Protect	Normal	Status	—	—	10	Self
TM26	Scary Face	Normal	Status	—	100	10	Normal
TM27	Icy Wind	Ice	Special	55	95	15	Many Others
TM31	Attract	Normal	Status	—	100	15	Normal
TM33	Rain Dance	Water	Status	—	—	5	Both Sides
TM35	Hail	Ice	Status	—	—	10	Both Sides
TM36	Whirlpool	Water	Special	35	85	15	Normal
TM39	Facade	Normal	Physical	70	100	20	Normal
TM40	Swift	Normal	Special	60	—	20	Many Others
TM42	Revenge	Fighting	Physical	60	100	10	Normal
TM45	Dive	Water	Physical	80	100	10	Normal
TM52	Bounce	Flying	Physical	85	85	5	Normal
TM55	Brine	Water	Special	65	100	10	Normal
TM57	Payback	Dark	Physical	50	100	10	Normal
TM58	Assurance	Dark	Physical	60	100	10	Normal
TM74	Venoshock	Poison	Special	65	100	10	Normal
TM76	Round	Normal	Special	60	100	15	Normal
TM77	Hex	Ghost	Special	65	100	10	Normal

TR MOVES

NO.	NAME	TYPE	KIND	POW.	ACC.	PP	RANGE
TR00	Swords Dance	Normal	Status	—	—	20	Self
TR03	Hydro Pump	Water	Special	110	80	5	Normal
TR04	Surf	Water	Special	90	100	15	All Others
TR05	Ice Beam	Ice	Special	90	100	10	Normal
TR06	Blizzard	Ice	Special	110	70	5	Many Others
TR16	Waterfall	Water	Physical	80	100	15	Normal
TR20	Substitute	Normal	Status	—	—	10	Self
TR21	Reversal	Fighting	Physical	—	100	15	Normal
TR22	Sludge Bomb	Poison	Special	90	100	10	Normal
TR23	Spikes	Ground	Status	—	—	20	Other Side
TR26	Endure	Normal	Status	—	—	10	Self
TR27	Sleep Talk	Normal	Status	—	—	10	Self
TR33	Shadow Ball	Ghost	Special	80	100	15	Normal
TR37	Taunt	Dark	Status	—	100	20	Normal
TR52	Gyro Ball	Steel	Physical	—	100	5	Normal
TR54	Toxic Spikes	Poison	Status	—	—	20	Other Side
TR57	Poison Jab	Poison	Physical	80	100	20	Normal
TR78	Sludge Wave	Poison	Special	95	100	10	All Others
TR84	Scald	Water	Special	80	100	15	Normal
TR91	Venom Drench	Poison	Status	—	100	20	Many Others
TR95	Throat Chop	Dark	Physical	80	100	15	Normal
TR98	Liquidation	Water	Physical	85	100	10	Normal

EVOLUTION MOVES

NAME	TYPE	KIND	POW.	ACC.	PP	RANGE

EGG MOVES

NAME	TYPE	KIND	POW.	ACC.	PP	RANGE
Acid Spray	Poison	Special	40	100	20	Normal
Aqua Jet	Water	Physical	40	100	20	Normal
Astonish	Ghost	Physical	30	100	15	Normal
Bubble Beam	Water	Special	65	100	20	Normal
Flail	Normal	Physical	—	100	15	Normal
Haze	Ice	Status	—	—	30	Both Sides
Supersonic	Normal	Status	—	55	20	Normal
Water Pulse	Water	Special	60	100	20	Normal

---

305 Frillish

p. 124

ABILITY
Water Absorb
Cursed Body

HIDDEN ABILITY
Damp

SPECIES STRENGTHS

HP	
ATTACK	
DEFENSE	
SP. ATK	
SP. DEF	
SPEED	

DAMAGE TAKEN IN BATTLE

×0	×0	×1			
×0.5	×0.5	×2			
×0.5	×1	×1			
×2	×1	×2			
×2	×1	×0.5			
×0.5	×0.5	×1			

AMORPHOUS

LEVEL-UP MOVES

LV.	NAME	TYPE	KIND	POW.	ACC.	PP	RANGE
1	Absorb	Grass	Special	20	100	25	Normal
1	Water Gun	Water	Special	40	100	25	Normal
4	Poison Sting	Poison	Physical	15	100	35	Normal
8	Night Shade	Ghost	Special	—	100	15	Normal
12	Water Pulse	Water	Special	60	100	20	Normal
16	Rain Dance	Water	Status	—	—	5	Both Sides
20	Hex	Ghost	Special	65	100	10	Normal
24	Brine	Water	Special	65	100	10	Normal
28	Recover	Normal	Status	—	—	10	Self
32	Shadow Ball	Ghost	Special	80	100	15	Normal
36	Whirlpool	Water	Special	35	85	15	Normal
41	Hydro Pump	Water	Special	110	80	5	Normal
44	Destiny Bond	Ghost	Status	—	—	5	Self
48	Water Spout	Water	Special	150	100	5	Many Others

TUTOR MOVES

NAME	TYPE	KIND	POW.	ACC.	PP	RANGE

TM MOVES

NO.	NAME	TYPE	KIND	POW.	ACC.	PP	RANGE
TM19	Safeguard	Normal	Status	—	—	25	Your Side
TM21	Rest	Psychic	Status	—	—	10	Self
TM24	Snore	Normal	Special	50	100	15	Normal
TM25	Protect	Normal	Status	—	—	10	Self
TM27	Icy Wind	Ice	Special	55	95	15	Many Others
TM28	Giga Drain	Grass	Special	75	100	10	Normal
TM31	Attract	Normal	Status	—	100	15	Normal
TM33	Rain Dance	Water	Status	—	—	5	Both Sides
TM35	Hail	Ice	Status	—	—	10	Both Sides
TM36	Whirlpool	Water	Special	35	85	15	Normal
TM38	Will-O-Wisp	Fire	Status	—	85	15	Normal
TM39	Facade	Normal	Physical	70	100	20	Normal
TM44	Imprison	Psychic	Status	—	—	10	Self
TM45	Dive	Water	Physical	80	100	10	Normal
TM55	Brine	Water	Special	65	100	10	Normal
TM70	Trick Room	Psychic	Status	—	—	5	Both Sides
TM76	Round	Normal	Special	60	100	15	Normal
TM77	Hex	Ghost	Special	65	100	10	Normal

TR MOVES

NO.	NAME	TYPE	KIND	POW.	ACC.	PP	RANGE
TR03	Hydro Pump	Water	Special	110	80	5	Normal
TR04	Surf	Water	Special	90	100	15	All Others
TR05	Ice Beam	Ice	Special	90	100	10	Normal
TR06	Blizzard	Ice	Special	110	70	5	Many Others
TR11	Psychic	Psychic	Special	90	100	10	Normal
TR16	Waterfall	Water	Physical	80	100	15	Normal
TR20	Substitute	Normal	Status	—	—	10	Self
TR26	Endure	Normal	Status	—	—	10	Self
TR27	Sleep Talk	Normal	Status	—	—	10	Self
TR33	Shadow Ball	Ghost	Special	80	100	15	Normal
TR37	Taunt	Dark	Status	—	100	20	Normal
TR38	Trick	Psychic	Status	—	100	10	Normal
TR58	Dark Pulse	Dark	Special	80	100	15	Normal
TR65	Energy Ball	Grass	Special	90	100	10	Normal
TR78	Sludge Wave	Poison	Special	95	100	10	All Others
TR84	Scald	Water	Special	80	100	15	Normal
TR92	Dazzling Gleam	Fairy	Special	80	100	10	Many Others

EVOLUTION MOVES

NAME	TYPE	KIND	POW.	ACC.	PP	RANGE

EGG MOVES

NAME	TYPE	KIND	POW.	ACC.	PP	RANGE
Acid Armor	Poison	Status	—	—	20	Self
Bubble Beam	Water	Special	65	100	20	Normal
Confuse Ray	Ghost	Status	—	100	10	Normal
Mist	Ice	Status	—	—	30	Your Side
Pain Split	Normal	Status	—	—	20	Normal
Strength Sap	Grass	Status	—	100	10	Normal

306

LEVEL-UP MOVES

LV.	NAME	TYPE	KIND	POW.	ACC.	PP	RANGE
1	Absorb	Grass	Special	20	100	25	Normal
1	Acid Armor	Poison	Status	—	—	20	Self
1	Night Shade	Ghost	Special	—	100	15	Normal
1	Poison Sting	Poison	Physical	15	100	35	Normal
5	Water Gun	Water	Special	40	100	25	Normal
12	Water Pulse	Water	Special	60	100	20	Normal
16	Rain Dance	Water	Status	—	—	5	Both Sides
20	Hex	Ghost	Special	65	100	10	Normal
24	Brine	Water	Special	65	100	10	Normal
28	Recover	Normal	Status	—	—	10	Self
32	Shadow Ball	Ghost	Special	80	100	15	Normal
36	Whirlpool	Water	Special	35	85	15	Normal
43	Hydro Pump	Water	Special	110	80	5	Normal
48	Destiny Bond	Ghost	Status	—	—	5	Self
54	Water Spout	Water	Special	150	100	5	Many Others

EVOLUTION MOVES

NAME	TYPE	KIND	POW.	ACC.	PP	RANGE

EGG MOVES

NAME	TYPE	KIND	POW.	ACC.	PP	RANGE

TUTOR MOVES

NAME	TYPE	KIND	POW.	ACC.	PP	RANGE

TM MOVES

NO.	NAME	TYPE	KIND	POW.	ACC.	PP	RANGE
TM08	Hyper Beam	Normal	Special	150	90	5	Normal
TM09	Giga Impact	Normal	Physical	150	90	5	Normal
TM19	Safeguard	Normal	Status	—	—	25	Your Side
TM21	Rest	Psychic	Status	—	—	10	Self
TM24	Snore	Normal	Special	50	100	15	Normal
TM25	Protect	Normal	Status	—	—	10	Self
TM27	Icy Wind	Ice	Special	55	95	15	Many Others
TM28	Giga Drain	Grass	Special	75	100	10	Normal
TM31	Attract	Normal	Status	—	100	15	Normal
TM33	Rain Dance	Water	Status	—	—	5	Both Sides
TM35	Hail	Ice	Status	—	—	10	Both Sides
TM36	Whirlpool	Water	Special	35	85	15	Normal
TM38	Will-O-Wisp	Fire	Status	—	85	15	Normal
TM39	Facade	Normal	Physical	70	100	20	Normal
TM44	Imprison	Psychic	Status	—	—	10	Self
TM45	Dive	Water	Physical	80	100	10	Normal
TM55	Brine	Water	Special	65	100	10	Normal
TM70	Trick Room	Psychic	Status	—	—	5	Both Sides
TM76	Round	Normal	Special	60	100	15	Normal
TM77	Hex	Ghost	Special	65	100	10	Normal

TR MOVES

NO.	NAME	TYPE	KIND	POW.	ACC.	PP	RANGE
TR03	Hydro Pump	Water	Special	110	80	5	Normal
TR04	Surf	Water	Special	90	100	15	All Others
TR05	Ice Beam	Ice	Special	90	100	10	Normal
TR06	Blizzard	Ice	Special	110	70	5	Many Others
TR11	Psychic	Psychic	Special	90	100	10	Normal
TR16	Waterfall	Water	Physical	80	100	15	Normal
TR20	Substitute	Normal	Status	—	—	10	Self
TR22	Sludge Bomb	Poison	Special	90	100	10	Normal
TR26	Endure	Normal	Status	—	—	10	Self
TR27	Sleep Talk	Normal	Status	—	—	10	Self
TR33	Shadow Ball	Ghost	Special	80	100	15	Normal
TR37	Taunt	Dark	Status	—	100	20	Normal
TR38	Trick	Psychic	Status	—	100	10	Normal
TR45	Muddy Water	Water	Special	90	85	10	Many Others
TR58	Dark Pulse	Dark	Special	80	100	15	Normal
TR65	Energy Ball	Grass	Special	90	100	10	Normal
TR78	Sludge Wave	Poison	Special	95	100	10	All Others
TR84	Scald	Water	Special	80	100	15	Normal
TR92	Dazzling Gleam	Fairy	Special	80	100	10	Many Others

Jellicent
p. 124

ABILITY
Water Absorb
Cursed Body

HIDDEN ABILITY
Damp

SPECIES STRENGTHS
HP
ATTACK
DEFENSE
SP. ATK
SP. DEF
SPEED

DAMAGE TAKEN IN BATTLE

×0 ×0 ×1
×0.5 ×0.5 ×2
×0.5 ×1 ×1
×2 ×1 ×2
×1 ×1 ×0.5
×0.5 ×0.5 ×1

AMORPHOUS

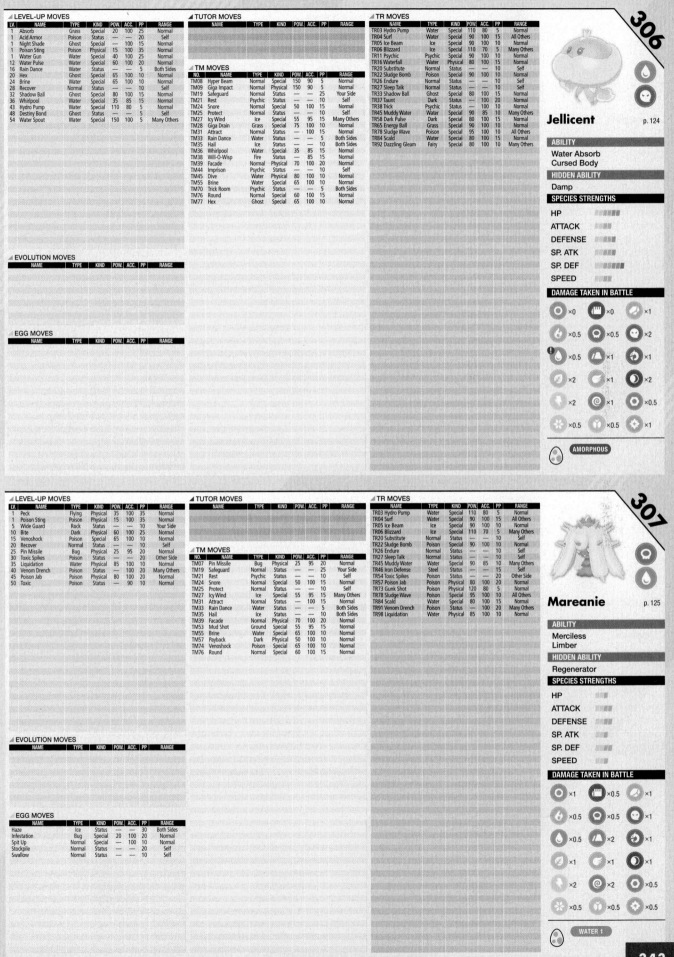

307

LEVEL-UP MOVES

LV.	NAME	TYPE	KIND	POW.	ACC.	PP	RANGE
1	Peck	Flying	Physical	35	100	35	Normal
1	Poison Sting	Poison	Physical	15	100	35	Normal
5	Wide Guard	Rock	Status	—	—	10	Your Side
10	Bite	Dark	Physical	60	100	25	Normal
15	Venoshock	Poison	Special	65	100	10	Normal
20	Recover	Normal	Status	—	—	10	Self
25	Pin Missile	Bug	Physical	25	95	20	Normal
30	Toxic Spikes	Poison	Status	—	—	20	Other Side
35	Liquidation	Water	Physical	85	100	10	Normal
40	Venom Drench	Poison	Status	—	100	20	Many Others
45	Poison Jab	Poison	Physical	80	100	20	Normal
50	Toxic	Poison	Status	—	90	10	Normal

EVOLUTION MOVES

NAME	TYPE	KIND	POW.	ACC.	PP	RANGE

EGG MOVES

NAME	TYPE	KIND	POW.	ACC.	PP	RANGE
Haze	Ice	Status	—	—	30	Both Sides
Infestation	Bug	Special	20	100	20	Normal
Spit Up	Normal	Special	—	100	10	Normal
Stockpile	Normal	Status	—	—	20	Self
Swallow	Normal	Status	—	—	10	Self

TUTOR MOVES

NAME	TYPE	KIND	POW.	ACC.	PP	RANGE

TM MOVES

NO.	NAME	TYPE	KIND	POW.	ACC.	PP	RANGE
TM07	Pin Missile	Bug	Physical	25	95	20	Normal
TM19	Safeguard	Normal	Status	—	—	25	Your Side
TM21	Rest	Psychic	Status	—	—	10	Self
TM24	Snore	Normal	Special	50	100	15	Normal
TM25	Protect	Normal	Status	—	—	10	Self
TM27	Icy Wind	Ice	Special	55	95	15	Many Others
TM31	Attract	Normal	Status	—	100	15	Normal
TM33	Rain Dance	Water	Status	—	—	5	Both Sides
TM35	Hail	Ice	Status	—	—	10	Both Sides
TM39	Facade	Normal	Physical	70	100	20	Normal
TM53	Mud Shot	Ground	Special	55	95	15	Normal
TM55	Brine	Water	Special	65	100	10	Normal
TM57	Payback	Dark	Physical	50	100	10	Normal
TM74	Venoshock	Poison	Special	65	100	10	Normal
TM76	Round	Normal	Special	60	100	15	Normal

TR MOVES

NO.	NAME	TYPE	KIND	POW.	ACC.	PP	RANGE
TR03	Hydro Pump	Water	Special	110	80	5	Normal
TR04	Surf	Water	Special	90	100	15	All Others
TR05	Ice Beam	Ice	Special	90	100	10	Normal
TR06	Blizzard	Ice	Special	110	70	5	Many Others
TR20	Substitute	Normal	Status	—	—	10	Self
TR22	Sludge Bomb	Poison	Special	90	100	10	Normal
TR26	Endure	Normal	Status	—	—	10	Self
TR27	Sleep Talk	Normal	Status	—	—	10	Self
TR45	Muddy Water	Water	Special	90	85	10	Many Others
TR46	Iron Defense	Steel	Status	—	—	15	Self
TR54	Toxic Spikes	Poison	Status	—	—	20	Other Side
TR57	Poison Jab	Poison	Physical	80	100	20	Normal
TR73	Gunk Shot	Poison	Physical	120	80	5	Normal
TR78	Sludge Wave	Poison	Special	95	100	10	All Others
TR84	Scald	Water	Special	80	100	15	Normal
TR91	Venom Drench	Poison	Status	—	100	20	Many Others
TR98	Liquidation	Water	Physical	85	100	10	Normal

Mareanie
p. 125

ABILITY
Merciless
Limber

HIDDEN ABILITY
Regenerator

SPECIES STRENGTHS
HP
ATTACK
DEFENSE
SP. ATK
SP. DEF
SPEED

DAMAGE TAKEN IN BATTLE

×1 ×0.5 ×1
×0.5 ×0.5 ×1
×0.5 ×2 ×1
×1 ×1 ×1
×2 ×2 ×0.5
×0.5 ×0.5 ×0.5

WATER 1

308

Toxapex
p. 125

ABILITY
Merciless
Limber

HIDDEN ABILITY
Regenerator

SPECIES STRENGTHS

HP
ATTACK
DEFENSE
SP. ATK
SP. DEF
SPEED

DAMAGE TAKEN IN BATTLE

×1 ×0.5 ×1
×0.5 ×0.5 ×1
×0.5 ×2 ×1
×1 ×1 ×1
×2 ×2 ×0.5
×0.5 ×0.5 ×0.5

WATER 1

LEVEL-UP MOVES

LV.	NAME	TYPE	KIND	POW.	ACC.	PP	RANGE
1	Baneful Bunker	Poison	Status	—	—	10	Self
1	Bite	Dark	Physical	60	100	25	Normal
1	Peck	Flying	Physical	35	100	35	Normal
1	Poison Sting	Poison	Physical	15	100	35	Normal
1	Wide Guard	Rock	Status	—	—	10	Your Side
15	Venoshock	Poison	Special	65	100	10	Normal
20	Recover	Normal	Status	—	—	10	Self
25	Pin Missile	Bug	Physical	25	95	20	Normal
30	Toxic Spikes	Poison	Status	—	—	20	Other Side
35	Liquidation	Water	Physical	85	100	10	Normal
42	Venom Drench	Poison	Status	—	100	20	Many Others
49	Poison Jab	Poison	Physical	80	100	20	Normal
56	Toxic	Poison	Status	—	90	10	Normal

TUTOR MOVES

NAME	TYPE	KIND	POW.	ACC.	PP	RANGE

TM MOVES

NO.	NAME	TYPE	KIND	POW.	ACC.	PP	RANGE
TM07	Pin Missile	Bug	Physical	25	95	20	Normal
TM17	Light Screen	Psychic	Status	—	—	30	Your Side
TM19	Safeguard	Normal	Status	—	—	25	Your Side
TM21	Rest	Psychic	Status	—	—	10	Self
TM24	Snore	Normal	Special	50	100	15	Normal
TM25	Protect	Normal	Status	—	—	10	Self
TM27	Icy Wind	Ice	Special	55	95	15	Many Others
TM31	Attract	Normal	Status	—	100	15	Normal
TM33	Rain Dance	Water	Status	—	—	5	Both Sides
TM35	Hail	Ice	Status	—	—	10	Both Sides
TM39	Facade	Normal	Physical	70	100	20	Normal
TM53	Mud Shot	Ground	Special	55	95	15	Normal
TM55	Brine	Water	Special	65	100	10	Normal
TM57	Payback	Dark	Physical	50	100	10	Normal
TM73	Cross Poison	Poison	Physical	70	100	20	Normal
TM74	Venoshock	Poison	Special	65	100	10	Normal
TM76	Round	Normal	Special	60	100	15	Normal
TM77	Hex	Ghost	Special	65	100	10	Normal

TR MOVES

NO.	NAME	TYPE	KIND	POW.	ACC.	PP	RANGE
TR03	Hydro Pump	Water	Special	110	80	5	Normal
TR04	Surf	Water	Special	90	100	10	All Others
TR05	Ice Beam	Ice	Special	90	100	10	Normal
TR06	Blizzard	Ice	Special	110	70	5	Many Others
TR20	Substitute	Normal	Status	—	—	10	Self
TR22	Sludge Bomb	Poison	Special	90	100	10	Normal
TR26	Endure	Normal	Status	—	—	10	Self
TR27	Sleep Talk	Normal	Status	—	—	10	Self
TR45	Muddy Water	Water	Special	90	85	10	Many Others
TR46	Iron Defense	Steel	Status	—	—	15	Self
TR54	Toxic Spikes	Poison	Status	—	—	20	Other Side
TR57	Poison Jab	Poison	Physical	80	100	20	Normal
TR73	Gunk Shot	Poison	Physical	120	80	5	Normal
TR78	Sludge Wave	Poison	Special	95	100	10	All Others
TR84	Scald	Water	Special	80	100	15	Normal
TR91	Venom Drench	Poison	Status	—	100	20	Many Others
TR98	Liquidation	Water	Physical	85	100	10	Normal

EVOLUTION MOVES

NAME	TYPE	KIND	POW.	ACC.	PP	RANGE
Baneful Bunker	Poison	Status	—	—	10	Self

EGG MOVES

NAME	TYPE	KIND	POW.	ACC.	PP	RANGE

309

Cramorant
p. 125

ABILITY
Gulp Missile
—

HIDDEN ABILITY
—

SPECIES STRENGTHS

HP
ATTACK
DEFENSE
SP. ATK
SP. DEF
SPEED

DAMAGE TAKEN IN BATTLE

×1 ×0.5 ×2
×0.5 ×1 ×1
×0.5 ×0 ×1
×1 ×1 ×1
×4 ×1 ×0.5
×0.5 ×0.5 ×1

WATER 1
FLYING

LEVEL-UP MOVES

LV.	NAME	TYPE	KIND	POW.	ACC.	PP	RANGE
1	Belch	Poison	Special	120	90	10	Normal
1	Peck	Flying	Physical	35	100	35	Normal
1	Spit Up	Normal	Special	—	100	10	Normal
1	Stockpile	Normal	Status	—	—	20	Self
1	Swallow	Normal	Status	—	—	10	Self
7	Water Gun	Water	Special	40	100	25	Normal
14	Fury Attack	Normal	Physical	15	85	20	Normal
21	Pluck	Flying	Physical	60	100	20	Normal
28	Dive	Water	Physical	80	100	10	Normal
35	Drill Peck	Flying	Physical	80	100	20	Normal
42	Amnesia	Psychic	Status	—	—	20	Self
49	Thrash	Normal	Physical	120	100	10	1 Random
56	Hydro Pump	Water	Special	110	80	5	Normal

TUTOR MOVES

NAME	TYPE	KIND	POW.	ACC.	PP	RANGE

TM MOVES

NO.	NAME	TYPE	KIND	POW.	ACC.	PP	RANGE
TM06	Fly	Flying	Physical	90	95	15	Normal
TM08	Hyper Beam	Normal	Special	150	90	5	Normal
TM09	Giga Impact	Normal	Physical	150	90	5	Normal
TM21	Rest	Psychic	Status	—	—	10	Self
TM23	Thief	Dark	Physical	60	100	25	Normal
TM24	Snore	Normal	Special	50	100	15	Normal
TM25	Protect	Normal	Status	—	—	10	Self
TM27	Icy Wind	Ice	Special	55	95	15	Many Others
TM30	Steel Wing	Steel	Physical	70	90	25	Normal
TM31	Attract	Normal	Status	—	100	15	Normal
TM33	Rain Dance	Water	Status	—	—	5	Both Sides
TM36	Whirlpool	Water	Special	35	85	15	Normal
TM39	Facade	Normal	Physical	70	100	20	Normal
TM45	Dive	Water	Physical	80	100	10	Normal
TM46	Weather Ball*	Normal	Special	50	100	10	Normal
TM58	Assurance	Dark	Physical	60	100	10	Normal
TM76	Round	Normal	Special	60	100	15	Normal
TM95	Air Slash	Flying	Special	75	95	15	Normal

TR MOVES

NO.	NAME	TYPE	KIND	POW.	ACC.	PP	RANGE
TR03	Hydro Pump	Water	Special	110	80	5	Normal
TR04	Surf	Water	Special	90	100	15	All Others
TR05	Ice Beam	Ice	Special	90	100	10	Normal
TR06	Blizzard	Ice	Special	110	70	5	Many Others
TR12	Agility	Psychic	Status	—	—	30	Self
TR17	Amnesia	Psychic	Status	—	—	20	Self
TR20	Substitute	Normal	Status	—	—	10	Self
TR21	Reversal	Fighting	Physical	—	100	15	Normal
TR26	Endure	Normal	Status	—	—	10	Self
TR27	Sleep Talk	Normal	Status	—	—	10	Self
TR35	Uproar	Normal	Special	90	100	10	1 Random
TR39	Superpower	Fighting	Physical	120	100	5	Normal
TR66	Brave Bird	Flying	Physical	120	100	15	Normal
TR84	Scald	Water	Special	80	100	15	Normal
TR89	Hurricane	Flying	Special	110	70	10	Normal
TR95	Throat Chop	Dark	Physical	80	100	15	Normal
TR98	Liquidation	Water	Physical	85	100	10	Normal

EVOLUTION MOVES

NAME	TYPE	KIND	POW.	ACC.	PP	RANGE

EGG MOVES

NAME	TYPE	KIND	POW.	ACC.	PP	RANGE
Aerial Ace	Flying	Physical	60	—	20	Normal
Aqua Ring	Water	Status	—	—	20	Self
Defog	Flying	Status	—	—	15	Normal
Feather Dance	Flying	Status	—	100	15	Normal
Roost	Flying	Status	—	—	10	Self

*Weather Ball changes type depending on weather condition. (Harsh sunlight: Fire type. Rain: Water type. Hail: Ice type. Sandstorm: Rock type.)

310

Toxel — p. 126

LEVEL-UP MOVES

LV.	NAME	TYPE	KIND	POW.	ACC.	PP	RANGE
1	Acid	Poison	Special	40	100	30	Many Others
1	Belch	Poison	Special	120	90	10	Normal
1	Flail	Normal	Physical	—	100	15	Normal
1	Growl	Normal	Status	—	100	40	Many Others
1	Nuzzle	Electric	Physical	20	100	20	Normal
1	Tearful Look	Normal	Status	—	—	20	Normal

TUTOR MOVES

NAME	TYPE	KIND	POW.	ACC.	PP	RANGE

TM MOVES

NO.	NAME	TYPE	KIND	POW.	ACC.	PP	RANGE
TM21	Rest	Psychic	Status	—	—	10	Self
TM24	Snore	Normal	Special	50	100	15	Normal
TM25	Protect	Normal	Status	—	—	10	Self
TM31	Attract	Normal	Status	—	100	15	Normal
TM39	Facade	Normal	Physical	70	100	20	Normal
TM76	Round	Normal	Special	60	100	15	Normal

TR MOVES

NAME	TYPE	KIND	POW.	ACC.	PP	RANGE
TR20 Substitute	Normal	Status	—	—	10	Self
TR26 Endure	Normal	Status	—	—	10	Self
TR27 Sleep Talk	Normal	Status	—	—	10	Self
TR30 Encore	Normal	Status	—	100	5	Normal

EVOLUTION MOVES

NAME	TYPE	KIND	POW.	ACC.	PP	RANGE

EGG MOVES

NAME	TYPE	KIND	POW.	ACC.	PP	RANGE
Endeavor	Normal	Physical	—	100	5	Normal
Metal Sound	Steel	Status	—	85	40	Normal
Power-Up Punch	Fighting	Physical	40	100	20	Normal

ABILITY
Rattled
Static

HIDDEN ABILITY
Klutz

SPECIES STRENGTHS
HP
ATTACK
DEFENSE
SP. ATK
SP. DEF
SPEED

DAMAGE TAKEN IN BATTLE

×1 ×0.5 ×1
×1 ×0.5 ×1
×1 ×4 ×1
×0.5 ×0.5 ×1
×0.5 ×2 ×0.5
×1 ×0.5 ×0.5

NO EGGS

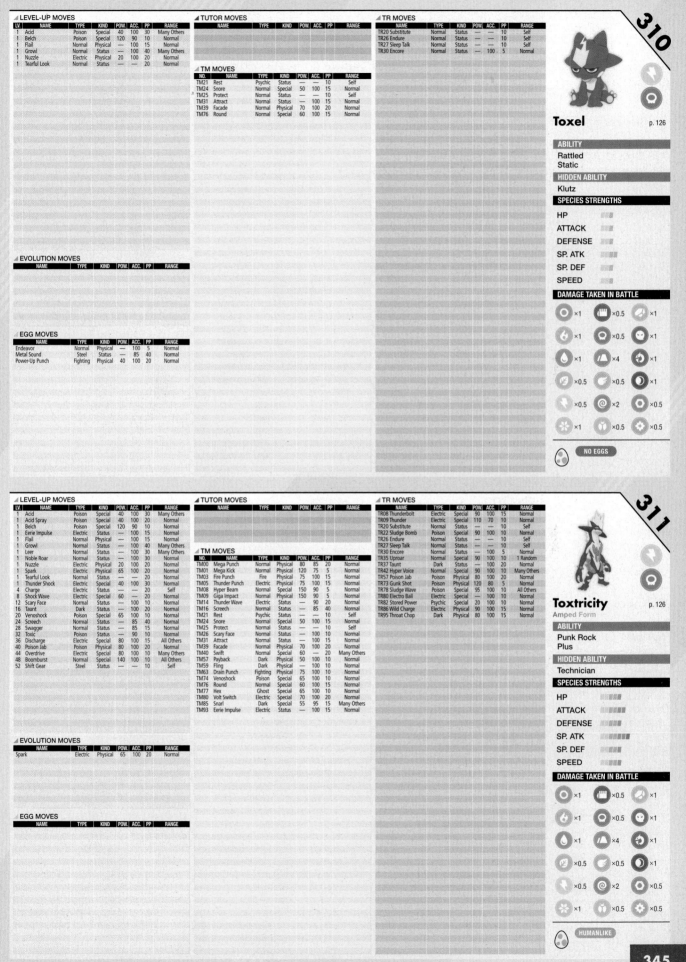

311

Toxtricity — p. 126
Amped Form

LEVEL-UP MOVES

LV.	NAME	TYPE	KIND	POW.	ACC.	PP	RANGE
1	Acid	Poison	Special	40	100	30	Many Others
1	Acid Spray	Poison	Special	40	100	20	Normal
1	Belch	Poison	Special	120	90	10	Normal
1	Eerie Impulse	Electric	Status	—	100	15	Normal
1	Flail	Normal	Physical	—	100	15	Normal
1	Growl	Normal	Status	—	100	40	Many Others
1	Leer	Normal	Status	—	100	30	Many Others
1	Noble Roar	Normal	Status	—	100	30	Normal
1	Nuzzle	Electric	Physical	20	100	20	Normal
1	Spark	Electric	Physical	65	100	20	Normal
1	Tearful Look	Normal	Status	—	—	20	Normal
1	Thunder Shock	Electric	Special	40	100	30	Normal
4	Charge	Electric	Status	—	—	20	Self
8	Shock Wave	Electric	Special	60	—	20	Normal
12	Scary Face	Normal	Status	—	100	10	Normal
16	Taunt	Dark	Status	—	100	20	Normal
20	Venoshock	Poison	Special	65	100	10	Normal
24	Screech	Normal	Status	—	85	40	Normal
28	Swagger	Normal	Status	—	85	15	Normal
32	Toxic	Poison	Status	—	90	10	Normal
36	Discharge	Electric	Special	80	100	15	All Others
40	Poison Jab	Poison	Physical	80	100	20	Normal
44	Overdrive	Electric	Special	80	100	10	Many Others
48	Boomburst	Normal	Special	140	100	10	All Others
52	Shift Gear	Steel	Status	—	—	10	Self

TUTOR MOVES

NAME	TYPE	KIND	POW.	ACC.	PP	RANGE

TM MOVES

NO.	NAME	TYPE	KIND	POW.	ACC.	PP	RANGE
TM00	Mega Punch	Normal	Physical	80	85	20	Normal
TM01	Mega Kick	Normal	Physical	120	75	5	Normal
TM03	Fire Punch	Fire	Physical	75	100	15	Normal
TM05	Thunder Punch	Electric	Physical	75	100	15	Normal
TM08	Hyper Beam	Normal	Special	150	90	5	Normal
TM09	Giga Impact	Normal	Physical	150	90	5	Normal
TM14	Thunder Wave	Electric	Status	—	90	20	Normal
TM16	Screech	Normal	Status	—	85	40	Normal
TM21	Rest	Psychic	Status	—	—	10	Self
TM24	Snore	Normal	Special	50	100	15	Normal
TM25	Protect	Normal	Status	—	—	10	Self
TM26	Scary Face	Normal	Status	—	100	10	Normal
TM31	Attract	Normal	Status	—	100	15	Normal
TM39	Facade	Normal	Physical	70	100	20	Normal
TM40	Swift	Normal	Special	60	—	20	Many Others
TM57	Payback	Dark	Physical	50	100	10	Normal
TM59	Fling	Dark	Physical	—	100	10	Normal
TM63	Drain Punch	Fighting	Physical	75	100	10	Normal
TM74	Venoshock	Poison	Special	65	100	10	Normal
TM76	Round	Normal	Special	60	100	15	Normal
TM77	Hex	Ghost	Special	65	100	10	Normal
TM80	Volt Switch	Electric	Special	70	100	20	Normal
TM85	Snarl	Dark	Special	55	95	15	Many Others
TM93	Eerie Impulse	Electric	Status	—	100	15	Normal

TR MOVES

NAME	TYPE	KIND	POW.	ACC.	PP	RANGE
TR08 Thunderbolt	Electric	Special	90	100	15	Normal
TR09 Thunder	Electric	Special	110	70	10	Normal
TR20 Substitute	Normal	Status	—	—	10	Self
TR22 Sludge Bomb	Poison	Special	90	100	10	Normal
TR26 Endure	Normal	Status	—	—	10	Self
TR27 Sleep Talk	Normal	Status	—	—	10	Self
TR30 Encore	Normal	Status	—	100	5	Normal
TR35 Uproar	Normal	Special	90	100	10	1 Random
TR37 Taunt	Dark	Status	—	100	20	Normal
TR42 Hyper Voice	Normal	Special	90	100	10	Many Others
TR57 Poison Jab	Poison	Physical	80	100	20	Normal
TR73 Gunk Shot	Poison	Physical	120	80	5	Normal
TR78 Sludge Wave	Poison	Special	95	100	10	All Others
TR80 Electro Ball	Electric	Special	—	100	10	Normal
TR82 Stored Power	Psychic	Special	20	100	10	Normal
TR86 Wild Charge	Electric	Physical	90	100	15	Normal
TR95 Throat Chop	Dark	Physical	80	100	15	Normal

EVOLUTION MOVES

NAME	TYPE	KIND	POW.	ACC.	PP	RANGE
Spark	Electric	Physical	65	100	20	Normal

EGG MOVES

NAME	TYPE	KIND	POW.	ACC.	PP	RANGE

ABILITY
Punk Rock
Plus

HIDDEN ABILITY
Technician

SPECIES STRENGTHS
HP
ATTACK
DEFENSE
SP. ATK
SP. DEF
SPEED

DAMAGE TAKEN IN BATTLE

×1 ×0.5 ×1
×1 ×0.5 ×1
×1 ×4 ×1
×0.5 ×0.5 ×1
×0.5 ×2 ×0.5
×1 ×0.5 ×0.5

HUMANLIKE

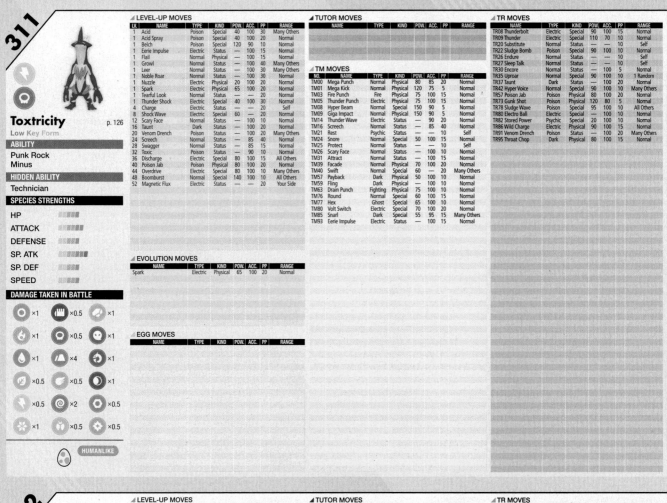

311

Toxtricity
Low Key Form　p. 126

ABILITY
Punk Rock
Minus

HIDDEN ABILITY
Technician

SPECIES STRENGTHS
HP
ATTACK
DEFENSE
SP. ATK
SP. DEF
SPEED

DAMAGE TAKEN IN BATTLE
×1 ×0.5 ×1
×1 ×0.5 ×1
×1 ×4 ×1
×0.5 ×0.5 ×1
×0.5 ×2 ×0.5
×1 ×0.5 ×0.5

HUMANLIKE

LEVEL-UP MOVES

LV.	NAME	TYPE	KIND	POW.	ACC.	PP	RANGE
1	Acid	Poison	Special	40	100	30	Many Others
1	Acid Spray	Poison	Special	40	100	20	Normal
1	Belch	Poison	Special	120	90	10	Normal
1	Eerie Impulse	Electric	Status	—	100	15	Normal
1	Flail	Normal	Physical	—	100	15	Normal
1	Growl	Normal	Status	—	100	40	Many Others
1	Leer	Normal	Status	—	100	30	Many Others
1	Noble Roar	Normal	Status	—	100	30	Normal
1	Nuzzle	Electric	Physical	20	100	20	Normal
1	Spark	Electric	Physical	65	100	20	Normal
1	Tearful Look	Normal	Status	—	—	20	Normal
1	Thunder Shock	Electric	Special	40	100	30	Normal
4	Charge	Electric	Status	—	—	20	Self
8	Shock Wave	Electric	Special	60	—	20	Normal
12	Scary Face	Normal	Status	—	100	10	Normal
16	Taunt	Dark	Status	—	100	20	Normal
20	Venom Drench	Poison	Status	—	100	20	Many Others
24	Screech	Normal	Status	—	85	40	Normal
28	Swagger	Normal	Status	—	85	15	Normal
32	Toxic	Poison	Status	—	90	10	Normal
36	Discharge	Electric	Special	80	100	15	All Others
40	Poison Jab	Poison	Physical	80	100	20	Normal
44	Overdrive	Electric	Special	80	100	10	Many Others
48	Boomburst	Normal	Special	140	100	10	All Others
52	Magnetic Flux	Electric	Status	—	—	20	Your Side

EVOLUTION MOVES

NAME	TYPE	KIND	POW.	ACC.	PP	RANGE
Spark	Electric	Physical	65	100	20	Normal

EGG MOVES

NAME	TYPE	KIND	POW.	ACC.	PP	RANGE

TUTOR MOVES

NAME	TYPE	KIND	POW.	ACC.	PP	RANGE

TM MOVES

NO.	NAME	TYPE	KIND	POW.	ACC.	PP	RANGE
TM00	Mega Punch	Normal	Physical	80	85	20	Normal
TM01	Mega Kick	Normal	Physical	120	75	5	Normal
TM03	Fire Punch	Fire	Physical	75	100	15	Normal
TM05	Thunder Punch	Electric	Physical	75	100	15	Normal
TM08	Hyper Beam	Normal	Special	150	90	5	Normal
TM09	Giga Impact	Normal	Physical	150	90	5	Normal
TM14	Thunder Wave	Electric	Status	—	90	20	Normal
TM16	Screech	Normal	Status	—	85	40	Normal
TM21	Rest	Psychic	Status	—	—	10	Self
TM24	Snore	Normal	Special	50	100	15	Normal
TM25	Protect	Normal	Status	—	—	10	Self
TM26	Scary Face	Normal	Status	—	100	10	Normal
TM31	Attract	Normal	Status	—	100	15	Normal
TM39	Facade	Normal	Physical	70	100	20	Normal
TM40	Swift	Normal	Special	60	—	20	Many Others
TM57	Payback	Dark	Physical	50	100	10	Normal
TM59	Fling	Dark	Physical	—	100	10	Normal
TM63	Drain Punch	Fighting	Physical	75	100	10	Normal
TM76	Round	Normal	Special	60	100	15	Normal
TM77	Hex	Ghost	Special	65	100	10	Normal
TM80	Volt Switch	Electric	Special	70	100	20	Normal
TM85	Snarl	Dark	Special	55	95	15	Many Others
TM93	Eerie Impulse	Electric	Status	—	100	15	Normal

TR MOVES

NO.	NAME	TYPE	KIND	POW.	ACC.	PP	RANGE
TR08	Thunderbolt	Electric	Special	90	100	15	Normal
TR09	Thunder	Electric	Special	110	70	10	Normal
TR20	Substitute	Normal	Status	—	—	10	Self
TR22	Sludge Bomb	Poison	Special	90	100	10	Normal
TR26	Endure	Normal	Status	—	—	10	Self
TR27	Sleep Talk	Normal	Status	—	—	10	Self
TR30	Encore	Normal	Status	—	100	5	Normal
TR35	Uproar	Normal	Special	90	100	10	1 Random
TR37	Taunt	Dark	Status	—	100	20	Normal
TR42	Hyper Voice	Normal	Special	90	100	10	Many Others
TR57	Poison Jab	Poison	Physical	80	100	20	Normal
TR73	Gunk Shot	Poison	Physical	120	80	5	Normal
TR78	Sludge Wave	Poison	Special	95	100	10	All Others
TR80	Electro Ball	Electric	Special	—	100	10	Normal
TR82	Stored Power	Psychic	Special	20	100	10	Normal
TR86	Wild Charge	Electric	Physical	90	100	15	Normal
TR91	Venom Drench	Poison	Status	—	100	20	Many Others
TR95	Throat Chop	Dark	Physical	80	100	15	Normal

312

Silicobra
p. 127

ABILITY
Sand Spit
Shed Skin

HIDDEN ABILITY
Sand Veil

SPECIES STRENGTHS
HP
ATTACK
DEFENSE
SP. ATK
SP. DEF
SPEED

DAMAGE TAKEN IN BATTLE
×1 ×1 ×0.5
×1 ×0.5 ×1
×2 ×1 ×1
×2 ×1 ×1
×0 ×1 ×1
×2 ×1 ×1

FIELD
DRAGON

LEVEL-UP MOVES

LV.	NAME	TYPE	KIND	POW.	ACC.	PP	RANGE
1	Sand Attack	Ground	Status	—	100	15	Normal
1	Wrap	Normal	Physical	15	90	20	Normal
5	Minimize	Normal	Status	—	—	10	Self
10	Brutal Swing	Dark	Physical	60	100	20	All Others
15	Bulldoze	Ground	Physical	60	100	20	All Others
20	Headbutt	Normal	Physical	70	100	15	Normal
25	Glare	Normal	Status	—	100	30	Normal
30	Dig	Ground	Physical	80	100	10	Normal
35	Sandstorm	Rock	Status	—	—	10	Both Sides
40	Slam	Normal	Physical	80	75	20	Normal
45	Coil	Poison	Status	—	—	20	Self
50	Sand Tomb	Ground	Physical	35	85	15	Normal

EVOLUTION MOVES

NAME	TYPE	KIND	POW.	ACC.	PP	RANGE

EGG MOVES

NAME	TYPE	KIND	POW.	ACC.	PP	RANGE
Belch	Poison	Special	120	90	10	Normal
Dragon Rush	Dragon	Physical	100	75	10	Normal
Last Resort	Normal	Physical	140	100	5	Normal
Mud-Slap	Ground	Special	20	100	10	Normal
Poison Tail	Poison	Physical	50	100	25	Normal

TUTOR MOVES

NAME	TYPE	KIND	POW.	ACC.	PP	RANGE

TM MOVES

NO.	NAME	TYPE	KIND	POW.	ACC.	PP	RANGE
TM15	Dig	Ground	Physical	80	100	10	Normal
TM16	Screech	Normal	Status	—	85	40	Normal
TM21	Rest	Psychic	Status	—	—	10	Self
TM24	Snore	Normal	Special	50	100	15	Normal
TM25	Protect	Normal	Status	—	—	10	Self
TM31	Attract	Normal	Status	—	100	15	Normal
TM32	Sandstorm	Rock	Status	—	—	10	Both Sides
TM39	Facade	Normal	Physical	70	100	20	Normal
TM49	Sand Tomb	Ground	Physical	35	85	15	Normal
TM53	Mud Shot	Ground	Special	55	95	15	Normal
TM76	Round	Normal	Special	60	100	15	Normal
TM81	Bulldoze	Ground	Physical	60	100	20	All Others
TM97	Brutal Swing	Dark	Physical	60	100	20	All Others

TR MOVES

NO.	NAME	TYPE	KIND	POW.	ACC.	PP	RANGE
TR10	Earthquake	Ground	Physical	100	100	10	All Others
TR20	Substitute	Normal	Status	—	—	10	Self
TR26	Endure	Normal	Status	—	—	10	Self
TR27	Sleep Talk	Normal	Status	—	—	10	Self
TR67	Earth Power	Ground	Special	90	100	10	Normal
TR87	Drill Run	Ground	Physical	80	95	10	Normal

313 Sandaconda — p. 127

LEVEL-UP MOVES

LV	NAME	TYPE	KIND	POW.	ACC.	PP	RANGE
1	Brutal Swing	Dark	Physical	60	100	20	All Others
1	Minimize	Normal	Status	—	—	10	Self
1	Sand Attack	Ground	Status	—	100	15	Normal
1	Skull Bash	Normal	Physical	130	100	10	Normal
1	Wrap	Normal	Physical	15	90	20	Normal
15	Bulldoze	Ground	Physical	60	100	20	All Others
20	Headbutt	Normal	Physical	70	100	15	Normal
25	Glare	Normal	Status	—	100	30	Normal
30	Dig	Ground	Physical	80	100	10	Normal
35	Sandstorm	Rock	Status	—	—	10	Both Sides
42	Slam	Normal	Physical	80	75	20	Normal
49	Coil	Poison	Status	—	—	20	Self
51	Sand Tomb	Ground	Physical	35	85	15	Normal

EVOLUTION MOVES

NAME	TYPE	KIND	POW.	ACC.	PP	RANGE

EGG MOVES

NAME	TYPE	KIND	POW.	ACC.	PP	RANGE

TUTOR MOVES

NAME	TYPE	KIND	POW.	ACC.	PP	RANGE

TM MOVES

NO.	NAME	TYPE	KIND	POW.	ACC.	PP	RANGE
TM08	Hyper Beam	Normal	Special	150	90	5	Normal
TM09	Giga Impact	Normal	Physical	150	90	5	Normal
TM15	Dig	Ground	Physical	80	100	10	Normal
TM16	Screech	Normal	Status	—	85	40	Normal
TM21	Rest	Psychic	Status	—	—	10	Self
TM22	Rock Slide	Rock	Physical	75	90	10	Many Others
TM24	Snore	Normal	Special	50	100	15	Normal
TM25	Protect	Normal	Status	—	—	10	Self
TM31	Attract	Normal	Status	—	100	15	Normal
TM32	Sandstorm	Rock	Status	—	—	10	Both Sides
TM39	Facade	Normal	Physical	70	100	20	Normal
TM48	Rock Tomb	Rock	Physical	60	95	15	Normal
TM49	Sand Tomb	Ground	Physical	35	85	15	Normal
TM53	Mud Shot	Ground	Special	55	95	15	Normal
TM54	Rock Blast	Rock	Physical	25	90	10	Normal
TM68	Fire Fang	Fire	Physical	65	95	15	Normal
TM76	Round	Normal	Special	60	100	15	Normal
TM81	Bulldoze	Ground	Physical	60	100	20	All Others
TM97	Brutal Swing	Dark	Physical	60	100	20	All Others

TR MOVES

NAME	TYPE	KIND	POW.	ACC.	PP	RANGE
TR10 Earthquake	Ground	Physical	100	100	10	All Others
TR20 Substitute	Normal	Status	—	—	10	Self
TR24 Outrage	Dragon	Physical	120	100	10	1 Random
TR26 Endure	Normal	Status	—	—	10	Self
TR27 Sleep Talk	Normal	Status	—	—	10	Self
TR46 Iron Defense	Steel	Status	—	—	15	Self
TR67 Earth Power	Ground	Special	90	100	10	Normal
TR69 Zen Headbutt	Psychic	Physical	80	90	15	Normal
TR74 Iron Head	Steel	Physical	80	100	15	Normal
TR75 Stone Edge	Rock	Physical	100	80	5	Normal
TR76 Stealth Rock	Rock	Status	—	—	20	Other Side
TR87 Drill Run	Ground	Physical	80	95	10	Normal
TR89 Hurricane	Flying	Special	110	70	10	Normal
TR94 High Horsepower	Ground	Physical	95	95	10	Normal
TR99 Body Press	Fighting	Physical	80	100	10	Normal

ABILITY: Sand Spit / Shed Skin
HIDDEN ABILITY: Sand Veil

SPECIES STRENGTHS: HP / ATTACK / DEFENSE / SP. ATK / SP. DEF / SPEED

DAMAGE TAKEN IN BATTLE: ×1, ×1, ×0.5, ×1, ×0.5, ×1, ×2, ×1, ×1, ×1, ×1, ×1, ×0, ×1, ×1, ×2, ×1, ×1

Egg Groups: FIELD / DRAGON

---

314 Hippopotas — p. 127

LEVEL-UP MOVES

LV	NAME	TYPE	KIND	POW.	ACC.	PP	RANGE
1	Sand Attack	Ground	Status	—	100	15	Normal
1	Tackle	Normal	Physical	40	100	35	Normal
4	Bite	Dark	Physical	60	100	25	Normal
8	Yawn	Normal	Status	—	—	10	Normal
12	Sand Tomb	Ground	Physical	35	85	15	Normal
16	Dig	Ground	Physical	80	100	10	Normal
20	Crunch	Dark	Physical	80	100	15	Normal
24	Sandstorm	Rock	Status	—	—	10	Both Sides
28	Take Down	Normal	Physical	90	85	20	Normal
32	Roar	Normal	Status	—	—	20	Normal
36	Rest	Psychic	Status	—	—	10	Self
40	Earthquake	Ground	Physical	100	100	10	All Others
44	Double-Edge	Normal	Physical	120	100	15	Normal
48	Fissure	Ground	Physical	—	30	5	Normal
52	Slack Off	Normal	Status	—	—	10	Self

EVOLUTION MOVES

NAME	TYPE	KIND	POW.	ACC.	PP	RANGE

EGG MOVES

NAME	TYPE	KIND	POW.	ACC.	PP	RANGE
Curse	Ghost	Status	—	—	10	Varies
Spit Up	Normal	Special	—	100	10	Normal
Stockpile	Normal	Status	—	—	20	Self
Swallow	Normal	Status	—	—	10	Self
Whirlwind	Normal	Status	—	—	20	Normal

TUTOR MOVES

NAME	TYPE	KIND	POW.	ACC.	PP	RANGE

TM MOVES

NO.	NAME	TYPE	KIND	POW.	ACC.	PP	RANGE
TM15	Dig	Ground	Physical	80	100	10	Normal
TM21	Rest	Psychic	Status	—	—	10	Self
TM22	Rock Slide	Rock	Physical	75	90	10	Many Others
TM24	Snore	Normal	Special	50	100	15	Normal
TM25	Protect	Normal	Status	—	—	10	Self
TM31	Attract	Normal	Status	—	100	15	Normal
TM32	Sandstorm	Rock	Status	—	—	10	Both Sides
TM34	Sunny Day	Fire	Status	—	—	5	Both Sides
TM39	Facade	Normal	Physical	70	100	20	Normal
TM42	Revenge	Fighting	Physical	60	100	10	Normal
TM46	Weather Ball*	Normal	Special	50	100	10	Normal
TM48	Rock Tomb	Rock	Physical	60	95	15	Normal
TM49	Sand Tomb	Ground	Physical	35	85	15	Normal
TM53	Mud Shot	Ground	Special	55	95	15	Normal
TM76	Round	Normal	Special	60	100	15	Normal
TM81	Bulldoze	Ground	Physical	60	100	20	All Others
TM98	Stomping Tantrum	Ground	Physical	75	100	10	Normal

TR MOVES

NAME	TYPE	KIND	POW.	ACC.	PP	RANGE
TR01 Body Slam	Normal	Physical	85	100	15	Normal
TR10 Earthquake	Ground	Physical	100	100	10	All Others
TR17 Amnesia	Psychic	Status	—	—	20	Self
TR20 Substitute	Normal	Status	—	—	10	Self
TR26 Endure	Normal	Status	—	—	10	Self
TR27 Sleep Talk	Normal	Status	—	—	10	Self
TR31 Iron Tail	Steel	Physical	100	75	15	Normal
TR32 Crunch	Dark	Physical	80	100	15	Normal
TR39 Superpower	Fighting	Physical	120	100	5	Normal
TR45 Muddy Water	Water	Special	90	85	10	Many Others
TR67 Earth Power	Ground	Special	90	100	10	Normal
TR76 Stealth Rock	Rock	Status	—	—	20	Other Side
TR94 High Horsepower	Ground	Physical	95	95	10	Normal

ABILITY: Sand Stream / —
HIDDEN ABILITY: Sand Force

SPECIES STRENGTHS: HP / ATTACK / DEFENSE / SP. ATK / SP. DEF / SPEED

DAMAGE TAKEN IN BATTLE: ×1, ×1, ×0.5, ×1, ×0.5, ×1, ×2, ×1, ×1, ×1, ×1, ×1, ×0, ×1, ×1, ×2, ×1, ×1

Egg Groups: FIELD

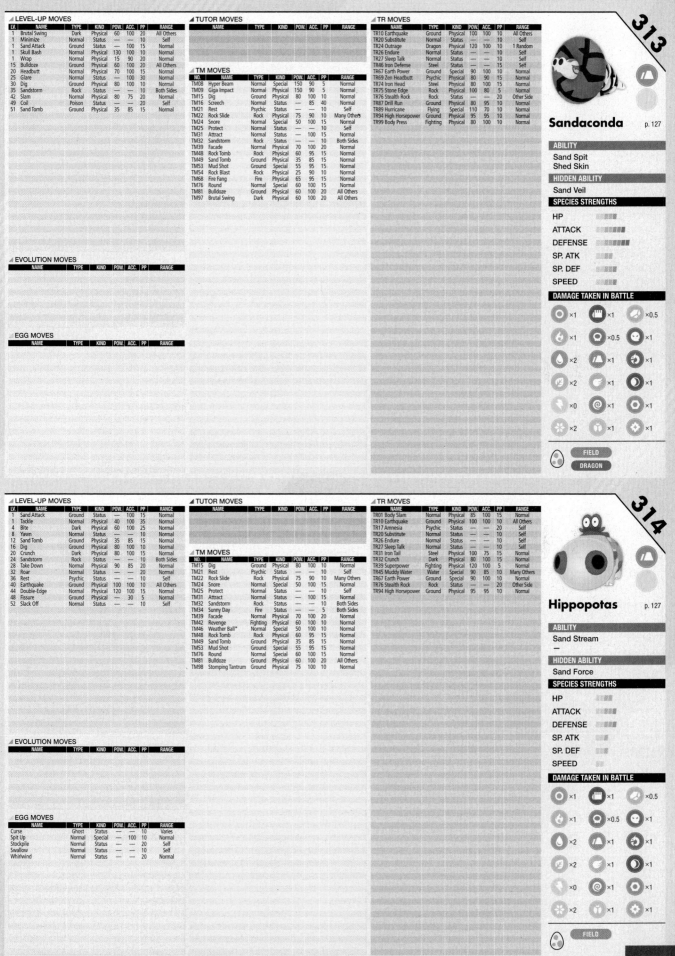

*Weather Ball changes type depending on weather condition. (Harsh sunlight: Fire type. Rain: Water type. Hail: Ice type. Sandstorm: Rock type.)

315

Hippowdon
p. 127

ABILITY

Sand Stream
—

HIDDEN ABILITY

Sand Force

SPECIES STRENGTHS

HP
ATTACK
DEFENSE
SP. ATK
SP. DEF
SPEED

DAMAGE TAKEN IN BATTLE

×1	×1	×0.5
×1	×0.5	×1
×2	×1	×1
×2	×1	×1
×0	×1	×1
×2	×1	×1

FIELD

LEVEL-UP MOVES

LV.	NAME	TYPE	KIND	POW.	ACC.	PP	RANGE
1	Bite	Dark	Physical	60	100	25	Normal
1	Fire Fang	Fire	Physical	65	95	15	Normal
1	Ice Fang	Ice	Physical	65	95	15	Normal
1	Sand Attack	Ground	Status	—	100	15	Normal
1	Tackle	Normal	Physical	40	100	35	Normal
1	Thunder Fang	Electric	Physical	65	95	15	Normal
1	Yawn	Normal	Status	—	—	10	Normal
12	Sand Tomb	Ground	Physical	35	85	15	Normal
16	Dig	Ground	Physical	80	100	10	Normal
20	Crunch	Dark	Physical	80	100	15	Normal
24	Sandstorm	Rock	Status	—	—	10	Both Sides
28	Take Down	Normal	Physical	90	85	20	Normal
32	Roar	Normal	Status	—	—	20	Normal
38	Rest	Psychic	Status	—	—	10	Self
44	Earthquake	Ground	Physical	100	100	10	All Others
50	Double-Edge	Normal	Physical	120	100	15	Normal
56	Fissure	Ground	Physical	—	30	5	Normal
62	Slack Off	Normal	Status	—	—	10	Self

EVOLUTION MOVES

NAME	TYPE	KIND	POW.	ACC.	PP	RANGE

EGG MOVES

NAME	TYPE	KIND	POW.	ACC.	PP	RANGE

TUTOR MOVES

NAME	TYPE	KIND	POW.	ACC.	PP	RANGE

TM MOVES

NO.	NAME	TYPE	KIND	POW.	ACC.	PP	RANGE
TM08	Hyper Beam	Normal	Special	150	90	5	Normal
TM09	Giga Impact	Normal	Physical	150	90	5	Normal
TM15	Dig	Ground	Physical	80	100	10	Normal
TM21	Rest	Psychic	Status	—	—	10	Self
TM22	Rock Slide	Rock	Physical	75	90	10	Many Others
TM24	Snore	Normal	Special	50	100	15	Normal
TM25	Protect	Normal	Status	—	—	10	Self
TM31	Attract	Normal	Status	—	100	15	Normal
TM32	Sandstorm	Rock	Status	—	—	10	Both Sides
TM34	Sunny Day	Fire	Status	—	—	5	Both Sides
TM39	Facade	Normal	Physical	70	100	20	Normal
TM42	Revenge	Fighting	Physical	60	100	10	Normal
TM46	Weather Ball*	Normal	Special	50	100	10	Normal
TM48	Rock Tomb	Rock	Physical	60	95	15	Normal
TM49	Sand Tomb	Ground	Physical	35	85	15	Normal
TM53	Mud Shot	Ground	Special	55	95	15	Normal
TM66	Thunder Fang	Electric	Physical	65	95	15	Normal
TM67	Ice Fang	Ice	Physical	65	95	15	Normal
TM68	Fire Fang	Fire	Physical	65	95	15	Normal
TM76	Round	Normal	Special	60	100	15	Normal
TM81	Bulldoze	Ground	Physical	60	100	20	All Others
TM98	Stomping Tantrum	Ground	Physical	75	100	10	Normal

TR MOVES

NO.	NAME	TYPE	KIND	POW.	ACC.	PP	RANGE
TR01	Body Slam	Normal	Physical	85	100	15	Normal
TR10	Earthquake	Ground	Physical	100	100	10	All Others
TR17	Amnesia	Psychic	Status	—	—	20	Self
TR20	Substitute	Normal	Status	—	—	10	Self
TR26	Endure	Normal	Status	—	—	10	Self
TR27	Sleep Talk	Normal	Status	—	—	10	Self
TR31	Iron Tail	Steel	Physical	100	75	15	Normal
TR32	Crunch	Dark	Physical	80	100	15	Normal
TR39	Superpower	Fighting	Physical	120	100	5	Normal
TR45	Muddy Water	Water	Special	90	85	10	Many Others
TR67	Earth Power	Ground	Special	90	100	10	Normal
TR74	Iron Head	Steel	Physical	80	100	15	Normal
TR76	Stealth Rock	Rock	Status	—	—	20	Other Side
TR79	Heavy Slam	Steel	Physical	—	100	10	Normal
TR94	High Horsepower	Ground	Physical	95	95	10	Normal
TR99	Body Press	Fighting	Physical	80	100	10	Normal

*Weather Ball changes type depending on weather condition. (Harsh sunlight: Fire type. Rain: Water type. Hail: Ice type. Sandstorm: Rock type.)

316

Durant
p. 128

ABILITY

Swarm
Hustle

HIDDEN ABILITY

Truant

SPECIES STRENGTHS

HP
ATTACK
DEFENSE
SP. ATK
SP. DEF
SPEED

DAMAGE TAKEN IN BATTLE

×0.5	×1	×1
×4	×0	×1
×1	×1	×0.5
×0.25	×1	×1
×1	×0.5	×0.5
×0.5	×0.5	×0.5

BUG

LEVEL-UP MOVES

LV.	NAME	TYPE	KIND	POW.	ACC.	PP	RANGE
1	Fury Cutter	Bug	Physical	40	95	20	Normal
1	Sand Attack	Ground	Status	—	100	15	Normal
4	Vise Grip	Normal	Physical	55	100	30	Normal
8	Metal Claw	Steel	Physical	50	95	35	Normal
12	Beat Up	Dark	Physical	—	100	10	Normal
16	Bug Bite	Bug	Physical	60	100	20	Normal
20	Bite	Dark	Physical	60	100	25	Normal
24	Agility	Psychic	Status	—	—	30	Self
28	Dig	Ground	Physical	80	100	10	Normal
32	X-Scissor	Bug	Physical	80	100	15	Normal
36	Crunch	Dark	Physical	80	100	15	Normal
40	Metal Sound	Steel	Status	—	85	40	Normal
44	Iron Head	Steel	Physical	80	100	15	Normal
48	Entrainment	Normal	Status	—	100	15	Normal
52	Iron Defense	Steel	Status	—	—	15	Self
56	Guillotine	Normal	Physical	—	30	5	Normal

EVOLUTION MOVES

NAME	TYPE	KIND	POW.	ACC.	PP	RANGE

EGG MOVES

NAME	TYPE	KIND	POW.	ACC.	PP	RANGE
First Impression	Bug	Physical	90	100	10	Normal
Flail	Normal	Physical	—	100	15	Normal
Infestation	Bug	Special	20	100	20	Normal
Metal Burst	Steel	Physical	—	100	10	Varies
Struggle Bug	Bug	Special	50	100	20	Many Others

TUTOR MOVES

NAME	TYPE	KIND	POW.	ACC.	PP	RANGE
Steel Beam	Steel	Special	140	95	5	Normal

TM MOVES

NO.	NAME	TYPE	KIND	POW.	ACC.	PP	RANGE
TM09	Giga Impact	Normal	Physical	150	90	5	Normal
TM14	Thunder Wave	Electric	Status	—	90	20	Normal
TM15	Dig	Ground	Physical	80	100	10	Normal
TM16	Screech	Normal	Status	—	85	40	Normal
TM21	Rest	Psychic	Status	—	—	10	Self
TM22	Rock Slide	Rock	Physical	75	90	10	Many Others
TM24	Snore	Normal	Special	50	100	15	Normal
TM25	Protect	Normal	Status	—	—	10	Self
TM31	Attract	Normal	Status	—	100	15	Normal
TM32	Sandstorm	Rock	Status	—	—	10	Both Sides
TM37	Beat Up	Dark	Physical	—	100	10	Normal
TM39	Facade	Normal	Physical	70	100	20	Normal
TM41	Helping Hand	Normal	Status	—	—	20	1 Ally
TM48	Rock Tomb	Rock	Physical	60	95	15	Normal
TM65	Shadow Claw	Ghost	Physical	70	100	15	Normal
TM66	Thunder Fang	Electric	Physical	65	95	15	Normal
TM76	Round	Normal	Special	60	100	15	Normal
TM79	Retaliate	Normal	Physical	70	100	5	Normal
TM98	Stomping Tantrum	Ground	Physical	75	100	10	Normal

TR MOVES

NO.	NAME	TYPE	KIND	POW.	ACC.	PP	RANGE
TR12	Agility	Psychic	Status	—	—	30	Self
TR20	Substitute	Normal	Status	—	—	10	Self
TR26	Endure	Normal	Status	—	—	10	Self
TR27	Sleep Talk	Normal	Status	—	—	10	Self
TR29	Baton Pass	Normal	Status	—	—	40	Self
TR32	Crunch	Dark	Physical	80	100	15	Normal
TR39	Superpower	Fighting	Physical	120	100	5	Normal
TR46	Iron Defense	Steel	Status	—	—	15	Self
TR60	X-Scissor	Bug	Physical	80	100	15	Normal
TR65	Energy Ball	Grass	Special	90	100	10	Normal
TR70	Flash Cannon	Steel	Special	80	100	10	Normal
TR74	Iron Head	Steel	Physical	80	100	15	Normal
TR75	Stone Edge	Rock	Physical	100	80	5	Normal

317

Heatmor — p. 128

LEVEL-UP MOVES

LV.	NAME	TYPE	KIND	POW.	ACC.	PP	RANGE
1	Lick	Ghost	Physical	30	100	30	Normal
1	Tackle	Normal	Physical	40	100	35	Normal
5	Fury Swipes	Normal	Physical	18	80	15	Normal
10	Incinerate	Fire	Special	60	100	15	Many Others
15	Bug Bite	Bug	Physical	60	100	20	Normal
20	Spit Up	Normal	Special	—	100	10	Normal
20	Stockpile	Normal	Status	—	—	20	Self
20	Swallow	Normal	Status	—	—	10	Self
25	Slash	Normal	Physical	70	100	20	Normal
30	Bind	Normal	Physical	15	85	20	Normal
35	Fire Lash	Fire	Physical	80	100	15	Normal
40	Hone Claws	Dark	Status	—	—	15	Self
45	Amnesia	Psychic	Status	—	—	20	Self
50	Fire Spin	Fire	Special	35	85	15	Normal
55	Inferno	Fire	Special	100	50	5	Normal
60	Flare Blitz	Fire	Physical	120	100	15	Normal

EVOLUTION MOVES

NAME	TYPE	KIND	POW.	ACC.	PP	RANGE

EGG MOVES

NAME	TYPE	KIND	POW.	ACC.	PP	RANGE
Belch	Poison	Special	120	90	10	Normal
Curse	Ghost	Status	—	—	10	Varies
Night Slash	Dark	Physical	70	100	15	Normal
Sucker Punch	Dark	Physical	70	100	5	Normal
Tickle	Normal	Status	—	100	20	Normal

TUTOR MOVES

NAME	TYPE	KIND	POW.	ACC.	PP	RANGE

TM MOVES

NO.	NAME	TYPE	KIND	POW.	ACC.	PP	RANGE
TM03	Fire Punch	Fire	Physical	75	100	15	Normal
TM05	Thunder Punch	Electric	Physical	75	100	15	Normal
TM09	Giga Impact	Normal	Physical	150	90	5	Normal
TM11	Solar Beam	Grass	Special	120	100	10	Normal
TM13	Fire Spin	Fire	Special	35	85	15	Normal
TM15	Dig	Ground	Physical	80	100	10	Normal
TM21	Rest	Psychic	Status	—	—	10	Self
TM23	Thief	Dark	Physical	60	100	25	Normal
TM24	Snore	Normal	Special	50	100	15	Normal
TM25	Protect	Normal	Status	—	—	10	Self
TM28	Giga Drain	Grass	Special	75	100	10	Normal
TM31	Attract	Normal	Status	—	100	15	Normal
TM33	Rain Dance	Water	Status	—	—	5	Both Sides
TM34	Sunny Day	Fire	Status	—	—	5	Both Sides
TM38	Will-O-Wisp	Fire	Status	—	85	15	Normal
TM39	Facade	Normal	Physical	70	100	20	Normal
TM48	Rock Tomb	Rock	Physical	60	95	15	Normal
TM59	Fling	Dark	Physical	—	100	10	Normal
TM63	Drain Punch	Fighting	Physical	75	100	10	Normal
TM65	Shadow Claw	Ghost	Physical	70	100	15	Normal
TM76	Round	Normal	Special	60	100	15	Normal
TM97	Brutal Swing	Dark	Physical	60	100	20	All Others
TM98	Stomping Tantrum	Ground	Physical	75	100	10	Normal

TR MOVES

NO.	NAME	TYPE	KIND	POW.	ACC.	PP	RANGE
TR01	Body Slam	Normal	Physical	85	100	15	Normal
TR02	Flamethrower	Fire	Special	90	100	15	Normal
TR07	Low Kick	Fighting	Physical	—	100	20	Normal
TR15	Fire Blast	Fire	Special	110	85	5	Normal
TR17	Amnesia	Psychic	Status	—	—	20	Self
TR20	Substitute	Normal	Status	—	—	10	Self
TR26	Endure	Normal	Status	—	—	10	Self
TR27	Sleep Talk	Normal	Status	—	—	10	Self
TR36	Heat Wave	Fire	Special	95	90	10	Many Others
TR37	Taunt	Dark	Status	—	100	20	Normal
TR39	Superpower	Fighting	Physical	120	100	5	Normal
TR43	Overheat	Fire	Special	130	90	5	Normal
TR55	Flare Blitz	Fire	Physical	120	100	15	Normal
TR64	Focus Blast	Fighting	Special	120	70	5	Normal
TR95	Throat Chop	Dark	Physical	80	100	15	Normal

ABILITY
Gluttony
Flash Fire

HIDDEN ABILITY
White Smoke

SPECIES STRENGTHS
- HP
- ATTACK
- DEFENSE
- SP. ATK
- SP. DEF
- SPEED

DAMAGE TAKEN IN BATTLE

×1	×1	×2
×0.5	×1	×1
×2	×2	×1
×0.5	×1	×1
	×1	×0.5
×0.5	×0.5	×0.5

FIELD

318

Helioptile — p. 128

LEVEL-UP MOVES

LV.	NAME	TYPE	KIND	POW.	ACC.	PP	RANGE
1	Mud-Slap	Ground	Special	20	100	10	Normal
1	Tail Whip	Normal	Status	—	100	30	Many Others
4	Pound	Normal	Physical	40	100	35	Normal
8	Thunder Shock	Electric	Special	40	100	30	Normal
12	Quick Attack	Normal	Physical	40	100	30	Normal
16	Charge	Electric	Status	—	—	20	Self
20	Bulldoze	Ground	Physical	60	100	20	All Others
24	Volt Switch	Electric	Special	70	100	20	Normal
28	Parabolic Charge	Electric	Special	65	100	20	All Others
32	Thunder Wave	Electric	Status	—	90	20	Normal
36	Thunderbolt	Electric	Special	90	100	15	Normal
40	Electrify	Electric	Status	—	—	20	Normal
44	Thunder	Electric	Special	110	70	10	Normal

EVOLUTION MOVES

NAME	TYPE	KIND	POW.	ACC.	PP	RANGE

EGG MOVES

NAME	TYPE	KIND	POW.	ACC.	PP	RANGE
Dragon Rush	Dragon	Physical	100	75	10	Normal
Dragon Tail	Dragon	Physical	60	90	10	Normal
Glare	Normal	Status	—	100	30	Normal

TUTOR MOVES

NAME	TYPE	KIND	POW.	ACC.	PP	RANGE

TM MOVES

NO.	NAME	TYPE	KIND	POW.	ACC.	PP	RANGE
TM14	Thunder Wave	Electric	Status	—	90	20	Normal
TM15	Dig	Ground	Physical	80	100	10	Normal
TM17	Light Screen	Psychic	Status	—	—	30	Your Side
TM21	Rest	Psychic	Status	—	—	10	Self
TM22	Rock Slide	Rock	Physical	75	90	10	Many Others
TM24	Snore	Normal	Special	50	100	15	Normal
TM25	Protect	Normal	Status	—	—	10	Self
TM31	Attract	Normal	Status	—	100	15	Normal
TM32	Sandstorm	Rock	Status	—	—	10	Both Sides
TM33	Rain Dance	Water	Status	—	—	5	Both Sides
TM39	Facade	Normal	Physical	70	100	20	Normal
TM40	Swift	Normal	Special	60	—	20	Many Others
TM48	Rock Tomb	Rock	Physical	60	95	15	Normal
TM56	U-turn	Bug	Physical	70	100	20	Normal
TM75	Low Sweep	Fighting	Physical	65	100	20	Normal
TM76	Round	Normal	Special	60	100	15	Normal
TM80	Volt Switch	Electric	Special	70	100	20	Normal
TM81	Bulldoze	Ground	Physical	60	100	20	All Others
TM82	Electroweb	Electric	Special	55	95	15	Many Others
TM90	Electric Terrain	Electric	Status	—	—	10	Both Sides

TR MOVES

NAME	TYPE	KIND	POW.	ACC.	PP	RANGE
TR04	Surf	Water	Special	90	100	15	All Others
TR08	Thunderbolt	Electric	Special	90	100	15	Normal
TR09	Thunder	Electric	Special	110	70	10	Normal
TR12	Agility	Psychic	Status	—	—	30	Self
TR20	Substitute	Normal	Status	—	—	10	Self
TR26	Endure	Normal	Status	—	—	10	Self
TR27	Sleep Talk	Normal	Status	—	—	10	Self
TR31	Iron Tail	Steel	Physical	100	75	15	Normal
TR58	Dark Pulse	Dark	Special	80	100	15	Normal
TR77	Grass Knot	Grass	Special	—	100	20	Normal
TR80	Electro Ball	Electric	Special	—	100	10	Normal
TR83	Ally Switch	Psychic	Status	—	—	15	Self
TR86	Wild Charge	Electric	Physical	90	100	15	Normal

ABILITY
Dry Skin
Sand Veil

HIDDEN ABILITY
Solar Power

SPECIES STRENGTHS
- HP
- ATTACK
- DEFENSE
- SP. ATK
- SP. DEF
- SPEED

DAMAGE TAKEN IN BATTLE

×1	×2	×1
×1	×1	×0
×1	×2	×1
×1	×0.5	×1
×0.5	×1	×0.5
×1	×1	×1

MONSTER
DRAGON

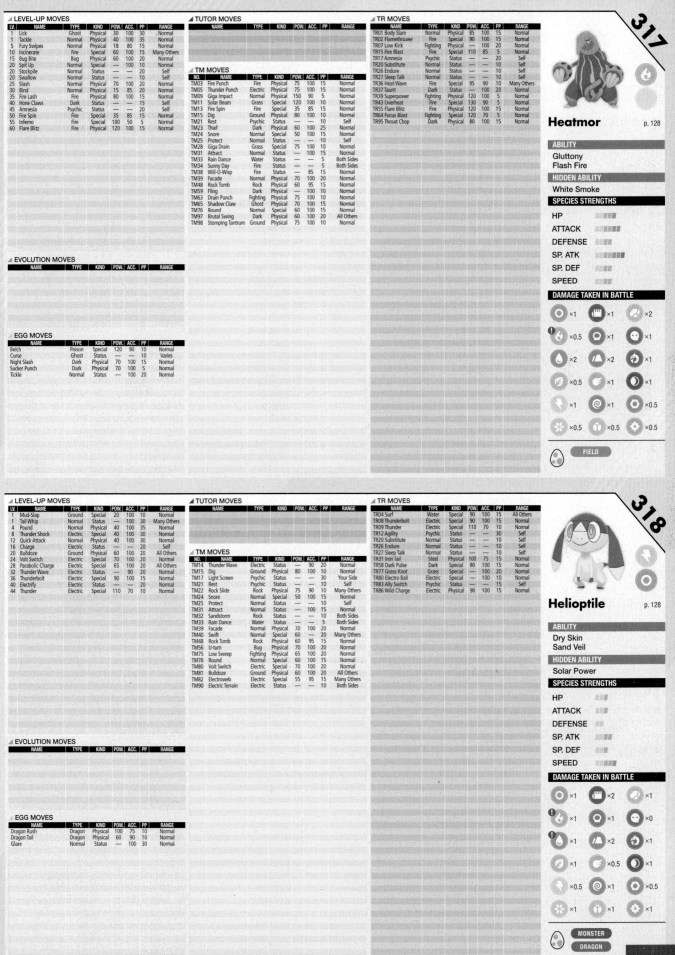

319 Heliolisk — p. 128

LEVEL-UP MOVES

LV.	NAME	TYPE	KIND	POW.	ACC.	PP	RANGE
1	Bulldoze	Ground	Physical	60	100	20	All Others
1	Charge	Electric	Status	—	—	20	Self
1	Discharge	Electric	Special	80	100	15	All Others
1	Eerie Impulse	Electric	Status	—	100	15	Normal
1	Electrify	Electric	Status	—	—	20	Normal
1	Mud-Slap	Ground	Special	20	100	10	Normal
1	Parabolic Charge	Electric	Special	65	100	20	All Others
1	Pound	Normal	Physical	40	100	35	Normal
1	Quick Attack	Normal	Physical	40	100	30	Normal
1	Tail Whip	Normal	Status	—	100	30	Many Others
1	Thunder	Electric	Special	110	70	10	Normal
1	Thunder Shock	Electric	Special	40	100	30	Normal
1	Thunder Wave	Electric	Status	—	90	20	Normal
1	Thunderbolt	Electric	Special	90	100	15	Normal
1	Volt Switch	Electric	Special	70	100	20	Normal

TUTOR MOVES

(none)

TM MOVES

NO.	NAME	TYPE	KIND	POW.	ACC.	PP	RANGE
TM00	Mega Punch	Normal	Physical	80	85	20	Normal
TM01	Mega Kick	Normal	Physical	120	75	5	Normal
TM03	Fire Punch	Fire	Physical	75	100	15	Normal
TM05	Thunder Punch	Electric	Physical	75	100	15	Normal
TM08	Hyper Beam	Normal	Special	150	90	5	Normal
TM09	Giga Impact	Normal	Physical	150	90	5	Normal
TM11	Solar Beam	Grass	Special	120	100	10	Normal
TM14	Thunder Wave	Electric	Status	—	90	20	Normal
TM15	Dig	Ground	Physical	80	100	10	Normal
TM17	Light Screen	Psychic	Status	—	—	30	Your Side
TM21	Rest	Psychic	Status	—	—	10	Self
TM22	Rock Slide	Rock	Physical	75	90	10	Many Others
TM24	Snore	Normal	Special	50	100	15	Normal
TM25	Protect	Normal	Status	—	—	10	Self
TM31	Attract	Normal	Status	—	100	15	Normal
TM32	Sandstorm	Rock	Status	—	—	10	Both Sides
TM33	Rain Dance	Water	Status	—	—	5	Both Sides
TM34	Sunny Day	Fire	Status	—	—	5	Both Sides
TM39	Facade	Normal	Physical	70	100	20	Normal
TM40	Swift	Normal	Special	60	—	20	Many Others
TM46	Weather Ball*	Normal	Special	50	100	10	Normal
TM48	Rock Tomb	Rock	Physical	60	95	15	Normal
TM56	U-turn	Bug	Physical	70	100	20	Normal
TM75	Low Sweep	Fighting	Physical	65	100	20	Normal
TM76	Round	Normal	Special	60	100	15	Normal
TM80	Volt Switch	Electric	Special	70	100	20	Normal
TM81	Bulldoze	Ground	Physical	60	100	20	All Others
TM82	Electroweb	Electric	Special	55	95	15	Many Others
TM90	Electric Terrain	Electric	Status	—	—	10	Both Sides
TM93	Eerie Impulse	Electric	Status	—	100	15	Normal
TM97	Brutal Swing	Dark	Physical	60	100	20	All Others
TM99	Breaking Swipe	Dragon	Physical	60	100	15	Many Others

TR MOVES

NO.	NAME	TYPE	KIND	POW.	ACC.	PP	RANGE
TR04	Surf	Water	Special	90	100	15	All Others
TR07	Low Kick	Fighting	Physical	—	100	20	Normal
TR08	Thunderbolt	Electric	Special	90	100	15	Normal
TR09	Thunder	Electric	Special	110	70	10	Normal
TR12	Agility	Psychic	Status	—	—	30	Self
TR20	Substitute	Normal	Status	—	—	10	Self
TR26	Endure	Normal	Status	—	—	10	Self
TR27	Sleep Talk	Normal	Status	—	—	10	Self
TR31	Iron Tail	Steel	Physical	100	75	15	Normal
TR42	Hyper Voice	Normal	Special	90	100	10	Many Others
TR58	Dark Pulse	Dark	Special	80	100	15	Normal
TR62	Dragon Pulse	Dragon	Special	85	100	10	Normal
TR64	Focus Blast	Fighting	Special	120	70	5	Normal
TR77	Grass Knot	Grass	Special	—	100	20	Normal
TR80	Electro Ball	Electric	Special	—	100	10	Normal
TR83	Ally Switch	Psychic	Status	—	—	15	Self
TR86	Wild Charge	Electric	Physical	90	100	15	Normal

EVOLUTION MOVES

(none)

EGG MOVES

(none)

ABILITY
Dry Skin
Sand Veil

HIDDEN ABILITY
Solar Power

SPECIES STRENGTHS
HP, ATTACK, DEFENSE, SP. ATK, SP. DEF, SPEED

DAMAGE TAKEN IN BATTLE

Normal	Fighting	Flying	Poison	Ground	Rock	Bug	Ghost	Steel	Fire	Water	Grass	Electric	Psychic	Ice	Dragon	Dark	Fairy
×1	×2	×0.5	×1	×2	×1	×1	×0	×0.5	×1	×1	×1	×0.5	×1	×1	×1	×1	×1

Egg Groups: MONSTER, DRAGON

*Weather Ball changes type depending on weather condition. (Harsh sunlight: Fire type. Rain: Water type. Hail: Ice type. Sandstorm: Rock type.)

---

320 Hawlucha — p. 129

LEVEL-UP MOVES

LV.	NAME	TYPE	KIND	POW.	ACC.	PP	RANGE
1	Hone Claws	Dark	Status	—	—	15	Self
1	Tackle	Normal	Physical	40	100	35	Normal
4	Wing Attack	Flying	Physical	60	100	35	Normal
8	Detect	Fighting	Status	—	—	5	Self
12	Aerial Ace	Flying	Physical	60	—	20	Normal
16	Encore	Normal	Status	—	100	5	Normal
20	Feather Dance	Flying	Status	—	100	15	Normal
24	Submission	Fighting	Physical	80	80	20	Normal
28	Bounce	Flying	Physical	85	85	5	Normal
32	Taunt	Dark	Status	—	100	20	Normal
36	Roost	Flying	Status	—	—	10	Self
40	Swords Dance	Normal	Status	—	—	20	Self
44	Flying Press*	Fighting	Physical	100	95	10	Normal
48	High Jump Kick	Fighting	Physical	130	90	10	Normal
52	Endeavor	Normal	Physical	—	100	5	Normal
56	Sky Attack	Flying	Physical	140	90	5	Normal

TUTOR MOVES

(none)

TM MOVES

NO.	NAME	TYPE	KIND	POW.	ACC.	PP	RANGE
TM00	Mega Punch	Normal	Physical	80	85	20	Normal
TM01	Mega Kick	Normal	Physical	120	75	5	Normal
TM03	Fire Punch	Fire	Physical	75	100	15	Normal
TM05	Thunder Punch	Electric	Physical	75	100	15	Normal
TM06	Fly	Flying	Physical	90	95	15	Normal
TM09	Giga Impact	Normal	Physical	150	90	5	Normal
TM15	Dig	Ground	Physical	80	100	10	Normal
TM21	Rest	Psychic	Status	—	—	10	Self
TM22	Rock Slide	Rock	Physical	75	90	10	Many Others
TM24	Snore	Normal	Special	50	100	15	Normal
TM25	Protect	Normal	Status	—	—	10	Self
TM30	Steel Wing	Steel	Physical	70	90	25	Normal
TM31	Attract	Normal	Status	—	100	15	Normal
TM33	Rain Dance	Water	Status	—	—	5	Both Sides
TM34	Sunny Day	Fire	Status	—	—	5	Both Sides
TM39	Facade	Normal	Physical	70	100	20	Normal
TM40	Swift	Normal	Special	60	—	20	Many Others
TM41	Helping Hand	Normal	Status	—	—	20	1 Ally
TM42	Revenge	Fighting	Physical	60	100	10	Normal
TM43	Brick Break	Fighting	Physical	75	100	15	Normal
TM48	Rock Tomb	Rock	Physical	60	95	15	Normal
TM52	Bounce	Flying	Physical	85	85	5	Normal
TM56	U-turn	Bug	Physical	70	100	20	Normal
TM57	Payback	Dark	Physical	50	100	10	Normal
TM58	Assurance	Dark	Physical	60	100	10	Normal
TM59	Fling	Dark	Physical	—	100	10	Normal
TM63	Drain Punch	Fighting	Physical	75	100	10	Normal
TM75	Low Sweep	Fighting	Physical	65	100	20	Normal
TM76	Round	Normal	Special	60	100	15	Normal
TM78	Acrobatics	Flying	Physical	55	100	15	Normal
TM79	Retaliate	Normal	Physical	70	100	5	Normal
TM94	False Swipe	Normal	Physical	40	100	40	Normal

TR MOVES

NO.	NAME	TYPE	KIND	POW.	ACC.	PP	RANGE
TR00	Swords Dance	Normal	Status	—	—	20	Self
TR07	Low Kick	Fighting	Physical	—	100	20	Normal
TR12	Agility	Psychic	Status	—	—	30	Self
TR20	Substitute	Normal	Status	—	—	10	Self
TR21	Reversal	Fighting	Physical	—	100	15	Normal
TR26	Endure	Normal	Status	—	—	10	Self
TR27	Sleep Talk	Normal	Status	—	—	10	Self
TR29	Baton Pass	Normal	Status	—	—	40	Self
TR30	Encore	Normal	Status	—	100	5	Normal
TR37	Taunt	Dark	Status	—	100	20	Normal
TR39	Superpower	Fighting	Physical	120	100	5	Normal
TR48	Bulk Up	Fighting	Status	—	—	20	Self
TR53	Close Combat	Fighting	Physical	120	100	5	Normal
TR57	Poison Jab	Poison	Physical	80	100	20	Normal
TR60	X-Scissor	Bug	Physical	80	100	15	Normal
TR64	Focus Blast	Fighting	Special	120	70	5	Normal
TR66	Brave Bird	Flying	Physical	120	100	15	Normal
TR69	Zen Headbutt	Psychic	Physical	80	90	15	Normal
TR74	Iron Head	Steel	Physical	80	100	15	Normal
TR75	Stone Edge	Rock	Physical	100	80	5	Normal
TR77	Grass Knot	Grass	Special	—	100	20	Normal
TR83	Ally Switch	Psychic	Status	—	—	15	Self
TR85	Work Up	Normal	Status	—	—	30	Self
TR95	Throat Chop	Dark	Physical	80	100	15	Normal
TR99	Body Press	Fighting	Physical	80	100	10	Normal

EVOLUTION MOVES

(none)

EGG MOVES

NAME	TYPE	KIND	POW.	ACC.	PP	RANGE
Cross Chop	Fighting	Physical	100	80	5	Normal
Defog	Flying	Status	—	—	15	Normal
Entrainment	Normal	Status	—	100	15	Normal
Feint	Normal	Physical	30	100	10	Normal
Mean Look	Normal	Status	—	—	5	Normal
Quick Guard	Fighting	Status	—	—	15	Your Side

ABILITY
Limber
Unburden

HIDDEN ABILITY
Mold Breaker

SPECIES STRENGTHS
HP, ATTACK, DEFENSE, SP. ATK, SP. DEF, SPEED

DAMAGE TAKEN IN BATTLE

Normal	Fighting	Flying	Poison	Ground	Rock	Bug	Ghost	Steel	Fire	Water	Grass	Electric	Psychic	Ice	Dragon	Dark	Fairy
×1	×0.5	×2	×1	×0	×1	×0.25	×1	×1	×1	×1	×0.5	×2	×2	×2	×1	×0.5	×2

Egg Groups: FLYING, HUMANLIKE

*Flying Press deals Flying-type damage as well as Fighting-type damage.

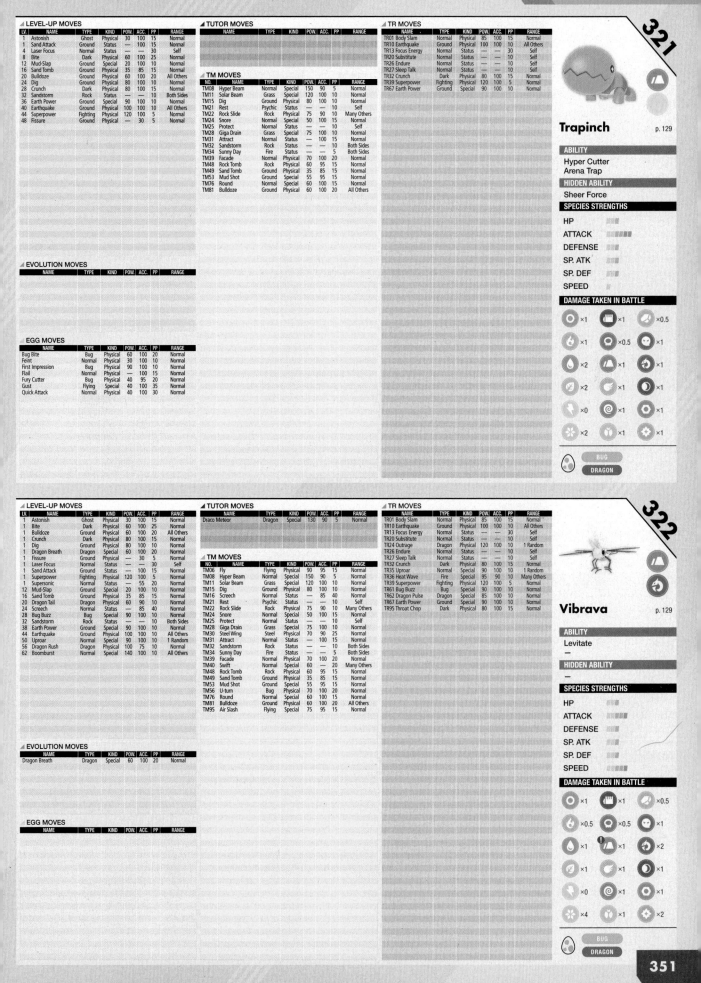

321

Trapinch
p. 129

LEVEL-UP MOVES

LV.	NAME	TYPE	KIND	POW.	ACC.	PP	RANGE
1	Astonish	Ghost	Physical	30	100	15	Normal
1	Sand Attack	Ground	Status	—	100	15	Normal
4	Laser Focus	Normal	Status	—	—	30	Self
8	Bite	Dark	Physical	60	100	25	Normal
12	Mud-Slap	Ground	Special	20	100	10	Normal
16	Sand Tomb	Ground	Special	35	85	15	Normal
20	Bulldoze	Ground	Physical	60	100	20	All Others
24	Dig	Ground	Physical	80	100	10	Normal
28	Crunch	Dark	Physical	80	100	15	Normal
32	Sandstorm	Rock	Status	—	—	10	Both Sides
36	Earth Power	Ground	Special	90	100	10	Normal
40	Earthquake	Ground	Physical	100	100	10	All Others
44	Superpower	Fighting	Physical	120	100	5	Normal
48	Fissure	Ground	Physical	—	30	5	Normal

EVOLUTION MOVES

NAME	TYPE	KIND	POW.	ACC.	PP	RANGE

EGG MOVES

NAME	TYPE	KIND	POW.	ACC.	PP	RANGE
Bug Bite	Bug	Physical	60	100	20	Normal
Feint	Normal	Physical	30	100	10	Normal
First Impression	Bug	Physical	90	100	10	Normal
Flail	Normal	Physical	—	100	15	Normal
Fury Cutter	Bug	Physical	40	95	20	Normal
Gust	Flying	Special	40	100	35	Normal
Quick Attack	Normal	Physical	40	100	30	Normal

TUTOR MOVES

NAME	TYPE	KIND	POW.	ACC.	PP	RANGE

TM MOVES

NO.	NAME	TYPE	KIND	POW.	ACC.	PP	RANGE
TM08	Hyper Beam	Normal	Special	150	90	5	Normal
TM11	Solar Beam	Grass	Special	120	100	10	Normal
TM15	Dig	Ground	Physical	80	100	10	Normal
TM21	Rest	Psychic	Status	—	—	10	Self
TM22	Rock Slide	Rock	Physical	75	90	10	Many Others
TM24	Snore	Normal	Special	50	100	15	Normal
TM25	Protect	Normal	Status	—	—	10	Self
TM28	Giga Drain	Grass	Special	75	100	10	Normal
TM31	Attract	Normal	Status	—	100	15	Normal
TM32	Sandstorm	Rock	Status	—	—	10	Both Sides
TM34	Sunny Day	Fire	Status	—	—	5	Both Sides
TM39	Facade	Normal	Physical	70	100	20	Normal
TM48	Rock Tomb	Rock	Physical	60	95	15	Normal
TM49	Sand Tomb	Ground	Special	35	85	15	Normal
TM53	Mud Shot	Ground	Special	55	95	15	Normal
TM76	Round	Normal	Special	60	100	15	Normal
TM81	Bulldoze	Ground	Physical	60	100	20	All Others

TR MOVES

NAME	TYPE	KIND	POW.	ACC.	PP	RANGE
TR01 Body Slam	Normal	Physical	85	100	15	Normal
TR10 Earthquake	Ground	Physical	100	100	10	All Others
TR13 Focus Energy	Normal	Status	—	—	30	Self
TR20 Substitute	Normal	Status	—	—	10	Self
TR26 Endure	Normal	Status	—	—	10	Self
TR27 Sleep Talk	Normal	Status	—	—	10	Self
TR32 Crunch	Dark	Physical	80	100	15	Normal
TR39 Superpower	Fighting	Physical	120	100	5	Normal
TR67 Earth Power	Ground	Special	90	100	10	Normal

ABILITY

Hyper Cutter
Arena Trap

HIDDEN ABILITY

Sheer Force

SPECIES STRENGTHS

HP
ATTACK
DEFENSE
SP. ATK
SP. DEF
SPEED

DAMAGE TAKEN IN BATTLE

×1	×1	×0.5
×1	×0.5	×1
×2	×1	×1
×2	×1	×1
×0	×1	×1
×2	×1	×1

BUG
DRAGON

322

Vibrava
p. 129

LEVEL-UP MOVES

LV.	NAME	TYPE	KIND	POW.	ACC.	PP	RANGE
1	Astonish	Ghost	Physical	30	100	15	Normal
1	Bite	Dark	Physical	60	100	25	Normal
1	Bulldoze	Ground	Physical	60	100	20	All Others
1	Crunch	Dark	Physical	80	100	15	Normal
1	Dig	Ground	Physical	80	100	10	Normal
1	Dragon Breath	Dragon	Special	60	100	20	Normal
1	Fissure	Ground	Physical	—	30	5	Normal
1	Laser Focus	Normal	Status	—	—	30	Self
1	Sand Attack	Ground	Status	—	100	15	Normal
1	Superpower	Fighting	Physical	120	100	5	Normal
1	Supersonic	Normal	Status	—	55	20	Normal
12	Mud-Slap	Ground	Special	20	100	10	Normal
16	Sand Tomb	Ground	Special	35	85	15	Normal
20	Dragon Tail	Dragon	Physical	60	90	10	Normal
24	Screech	Normal	Status	—	85	40	Normal
28	Bug Buzz	Bug	Special	90	100	10	Normal
32	Sandstorm	Rock	Status	—	—	10	Both Sides
38	Earth Power	Ground	Special	90	100	10	Normal
44	Earthquake	Ground	Physical	100	100	10	All Others
50	Uproar	Normal	Special	90	100	10	1 Random
56	Dragon Rush	Dragon	Physical	100	75	10	Normal
62	Boomburst	Normal	Special	140	100	10	All Others

EVOLUTION MOVES

NAME	TYPE	KIND	POW.	ACC.	PP	RANGE
Dragon Breath	Dragon	Special	60	100	20	Normal

EGG MOVES

NAME	TYPE	KIND	POW.	ACC.	PP	RANGE

TUTOR MOVES

NAME	TYPE	KIND	POW.	ACC.	PP	RANGE
Draco Meteor	Dragon	Special	130	90	5	Normal

TM MOVES

NO.	NAME	TYPE	KIND	POW.	ACC.	PP	RANGE
TM06	Fly	Flying	Physical	90	95	15	Normal
TM08	Hyper Beam	Normal	Special	150	90	5	Normal
TM11	Solar Beam	Grass	Special	120	100	10	Normal
TM15	Dig	Ground	Physical	80	100	10	Normal
TM16	Screech	Normal	Status	—	85	40	Normal
TM21	Rest	Psychic	Status	—	—	10	Self
TM22	Rock Slide	Rock	Physical	75	90	10	Many Others
TM24	Snore	Normal	Special	50	100	15	Normal
TM25	Protect	Normal	Status	—	—	10	Self
TM28	Giga Drain	Grass	Special	75	100	10	Normal
TM30	Steel Wing	Steel	Physical	70	90	25	Normal
TM31	Attract	Normal	Status	—	100	15	Normal
TM32	Sandstorm	Rock	Status	—	—	10	Both Sides
TM34	Sunny Day	Fire	Status	—	—	5	Both Sides
TM39	Facade	Normal	Physical	70	100	20	Normal
TM40	Swift	Normal	Special	60	—	20	Many Others
TM48	Rock Tomb	Rock	Physical	60	95	15	Normal
TM49	Sand Tomb	Ground	Special	35	85	15	Normal
TM53	Mud Shot	Ground	Special	55	95	15	Normal
TM56	U-turn	Bug	Physical	70	100	20	Normal
TM76	Round	Normal	Special	60	100	15	Normal
TM81	Bulldoze	Ground	Physical	60	100	20	All Others
TM95	Air Slash	Flying	Special	75	95	15	Normal

TR MOVES

NAME	TYPE	KIND	POW.	ACC.	PP	RANGE
TR01 Body Slam	Normal	Physical	85	100	15	Normal
TR10 Earthquake	Ground	Physical	100	100	10	All Others
TR13 Focus Energy	Normal	Status	—	—	30	Self
TR20 Substitute	Normal	Status	—	—	10	Self
TR24 Outrage	Dragon	Physical	120	100	10	1 Random
TR26 Endure	Normal	Status	—	—	10	Self
TR27 Sleep Talk	Normal	Status	—	—	10	Self
TR32 Crunch	Dark	Physical	80	100	15	Normal
TR35 Uproar	Normal	Special	90	100	10	1 Random
TR36 Heat Wave	Fire	Special	95	90	10	Many Others
TR39 Superpower	Fighting	Physical	120	100	5	Normal
TR61 Bug Buzz	Bug	Special	90	100	10	Normal
TR62 Dragon Pulse	Dragon	Special	85	100	10	Normal
TR67 Earth Power	Ground	Special	90	100	10	Normal
TR95 Throat Chop	Dark	Physical	80	100	15	Normal

ABILITY

Levitate
—

HIDDEN ABILITY

—

SPECIES STRENGTHS

HP
ATTACK
DEFENSE
SP. ATK
SP. DEF
SPEED

DAMAGE TAKEN IN BATTLE

×1	×1	×0.5
×0.5	×0.5	×1
×1	×1	×2
×1	×1	×1
×0	×1	×1
×4	×1	×2

BUG
DRAGON

323 Flygon — p. 129

ABILITY
Levitate
—

HIDDEN ABILITY
—

SPECIES STRENGTHS
- HP
- ATTACK
- DEFENSE
- SP. ATK
- SP. DEF
- SPEED

DAMAGE TAKEN IN BATTLE

×1	×1	×0.5
×0.5	×0.5	×1
×1	×1	×2
×1	×1	×1
×0	×1	×1
×4	×1	×2

Egg Groups: BUG, DRAGON

LEVEL-UP MOVES

LV.	NAME	TYPE	KIND	POW.	ACC.	PP	RANGE
1	Astonish	Ghost	Physical	30	100	15	Normal
1	Bite	Dark	Physical	60	100	25	Normal
1	Bulldoze	Ground	Physical	60	100	20	All Others
1	Crunch	Dark	Physical	80	100	15	Normal
1	Dig	Ground	Physical	80	100	10	Normal
1	Dragon Breath	Dragon	Special	60	100	20	Normal
1	Dragon Claw	Dragon	Physical	80	100	15	Normal
1	Dragon Dance	Dragon	Status	—	—	20	Self
1	Feint	Normal	Physical	30	100	10	Normal
1	Fissure	Ground	Physical	—	30	5	Normal
1	Laser Focus	Normal	Status	—	—	30	Self
1	Sand Attack	Ground	Status	—	100	15	Normal
1	Superpower	Fighting	Physical	120	100	5	Normal
1	Supersonic	Normal	Status	—	55	20	Normal
12	Mud-Slap	Ground	Special	20	100	10	Normal
16	Sand Tomb	Ground	Physical	35	85	15	Normal
20	Dragon Tail	Dragon	Physical	60	90	10	Normal
24	Screech	Normal	Status	—	85	40	Normal
28	Bug Buzz	Bug	Special	90	100	10	Normal
32	Sandstorm	Rock	Status	—	—	10	Both Sides
38	Earth Power	Ground	Special	90	100	10	Normal
44	Earthquake	Ground	Physical	100	100	10	All Others
52	Uproar	Normal	Special	90	100	10	1 Random
60	Dragon Rush	Dragon	Physical	100	75	10	Normal
68	Boomburst	Normal	Special	140	100	10	All Others

EVOLUTION MOVES

NAME	TYPE	KIND	POW.	ACC.	PP	RANGE
Dragon Claw	Dragon	Physical	80	100	15	Normal

EGG MOVES

NAME	TYPE	KIND	POW.	ACC.	PP	RANGE

TUTOR MOVES

NAME	TYPE	KIND	POW.	ACC.	PP	RANGE
Draco Meteor	Dragon	Special	130	90	5	Normal

TM MOVES

NO.	NAME	TYPE	KIND	POW.	ACC.	PP	RANGE
TM00	Mega Punch	Normal	Physical	80	85	20	Normal
TM01	Mega Kick	Normal	Physical	120	75	5	Normal
TM03	Fire Punch	Fire	Physical	75	100	15	Normal
TM05	Thunder Punch	Electric	Physical	75	100	15	Normal
TM06	Fly	Flying	Physical	90	95	15	Normal
TM08	Hyper Beam	Normal	Special	150	90	5	Normal
TM09	Giga Impact	Normal	Physical	150	90	5	Normal
TM11	Solar Beam	Grass	Special	120	100	10	Normal
TM13	Fire Spin	Fire	Special	35	85	15	Normal
TM15	Dig	Ground	Physical	80	100	10	Normal
TM16	Screech	Normal	Status	—	85	40	Normal
TM21	Rest	Psychic	Status	—	—	10	Self
TM22	Rock Slide	Rock	Physical	75	90	10	Many Others
TM24	Snore	Normal	Special	50	100	15	Normal
TM25	Protect	Normal	Status	—	—	10	Self
TM28	Giga Drain	Grass	Special	75	100	10	Normal
TM30	Steel Wing	Steel	Physical	70	90	25	Normal
TM31	Attract	Normal	Status	—	100	15	Normal
TM32	Sandstorm	Rock	Status	—	—	10	Both Sides
TM34	Sunny Day	Fire	Status	—	—	5	Both Sides
TM39	Facade	Normal	Physical	70	100	20	Normal
TM40	Swift	Normal	Special	60	—	20	Many Others
TM48	Rock Tomb	Rock	Physical	60	95	15	Normal
TM49	Sand Tomb	Ground	Physical	35	85	15	Normal
TM53	Mud Shot	Ground	Special	55	95	15	Normal
TM56	U-turn	Bug	Physical	70	100	20	Normal
TM76	Round	Normal	Special	60	100	15	Normal
TM81	Bulldoze	Ground	Physical	60	100	20	All Others
TM95	Air Slash	Flying	Special	75	95	15	Normal
TM97	Brutal Swing	Dark	Physical	60	100	20	All Others
TM99	Breaking Swipe	Dragon	Physical	60	100	15	Many Others

TR MOVES

NO.	NAME	TYPE	KIND	POW.	ACC.	PP	RANGE
TR01	Body Slam	Normal	Physical	85	100	15	Normal
TR02	Flamethrower	Fire	Special	90	100	15	Normal
TR10	Earthquake	Ground	Physical	100	100	10	All Others
TR13	Focus Energy	Normal	Status	—	—	30	Self
TR15	Fire Blast	Fire	Special	110	85	5	Normal
TR20	Substitute	Normal	Status	—	—	10	Self
TR24	Outrage	Dragon	Physical	120	100	10	1 Random
TR26	Endure	Normal	Status	—	—	10	Self
TR27	Sleep Talk	Normal	Status	—	—	10	Self
TR31	Iron Tail	Steel	Physical	100	75	15	Normal
TR32	Crunch	Dark	Physical	80	100	15	Normal
TR35	Uproar	Normal	Special	90	100	10	1 Random
TR36	Heat Wave	Fire	Special	95	90	10	Many Others
TR39	Superpower	Fighting	Physical	120	100	5	Normal
TR47	Dragon Claw	Dragon	Physical	80	100	15	Normal
TR51	Dragon Dance	Dragon	Status	—	—	20	Self
TR61	Bug Buzz	Bug	Special	90	100	10	Normal
TR62	Dragon Pulse	Dragon	Special	85	100	10	Normal
TR67	Earth Power	Ground	Special	90	100	10	Normal
TR75	Stone Edge	Rock	Physical	100	80	5	Normal
TR95	Throat Chop	Dark	Physical	80	100	15	Normal

324 Axew — p. 130

ABILITY
Rivalry
Mold Breaker

HIDDEN ABILITY
Unnerve

SPECIES STRENGTHS
- HP
- ATTACK
- DEFENSE
- SP. ATK
- SP. DEF
- SPEED

DAMAGE TAKEN IN BATTLE

×1	×1	×1
×0.5	×1	×1
×0.5	×1	×2
×0.5	×1	×1
×0.5	×1	×1
×1	×1	×2

Egg Groups: MONSTER, DRAGON

LEVEL-UP MOVES

LV.	NAME	TYPE	KIND	POW.	ACC.	PP	RANGE
1	Leer	Normal	Status	—	100	30	Many Others
1	Scratch	Normal	Physical	40	100	35	Normal
3	Bite	Dark	Physical	60	100	25	Normal
6	False Swipe	Normal	Physical	40	100	40	Normal
9	Assurance	Dark	Physical	60	100	10	Normal
12	Taunt	Dark	Status	—	100	20	Normal
15	Slash	Normal	Physical	70	100	20	Normal
18	Dragon Claw	Dragon	Physical	80	100	15	Normal
21	Scary Face	Normal	Status	—	100	10	Normal
24	Crunch	Dark	Physical	80	100	15	Normal
27	Dragon Dance	Dragon	Status	—	—	20	Self
30	Dual Chop	Dragon	Physical	40	90	15	Normal
33	Laser Focus	Normal	Status	—	—	30	Self
36	Dragon Pulse	Dragon	Special	85	100	10	Normal
39	Swords Dance	Normal	Status	—	—	20	Self
42	Outrage	Dragon	Physical	120	100	10	1 Random
45	Guillotine	Normal	Physical	—	30	5	Normal
48	Giga Impact	Normal	Physical	150	90	5	Normal

EVOLUTION MOVES

NAME	TYPE	KIND	POW.	ACC.	PP	RANGE

EGG MOVES

NAME	TYPE	KIND	POW.	ACC.	PP	RANGE
Counter	Fighting	Physical	—	100	20	Varies
Endeavor	Normal	Physical	—	100	5	Normal
First Impression	Bug	Physical	90	100	10	Normal
Harden	Normal	Status	—	—	30	Self
Night Slash	Dark	Physical	70	100	15	Normal

TUTOR MOVES

NAME	TYPE	KIND	POW.	ACC.	PP	RANGE
Draco Meteor	Dragon	Special	130	90	5	Normal

TM MOVES

NO.	NAME	TYPE	KIND	POW.	ACC.	PP	RANGE
TM09	Giga Impact	Normal	Physical	150	90	5	Normal
TM15	Dig	Ground	Physical	80	100	10	Normal
TM21	Rest	Psychic	Status	—	—	10	Self
TM24	Snore	Normal	Special	50	100	15	Normal
TM25	Protect	Normal	Status	—	—	10	Self
TM26	Scary Face	Normal	Status	—	100	10	Normal
TM32	Attract	Normal	Status	—	100	15	Normal
TM33	Rain Dance	Water	Status	—	—	5	Both Sides
TM34	Sunny Day	Fire	Status	—	—	5	Both Sides
TM39	Facade	Normal	Physical	70	100	20	Normal
TM40	Swift	Normal	Special	60	—	20	Many Others
TM48	Rock Tomb	Rock	Physical	60	95	15	Normal
TM57	Payback	Dark	Physical	50	100	10	Normal
TM58	Assurance	Dark	Physical	60	100	10	Normal
TM59	Fling	Dark	Physical	—	100	10	Normal
TM76	Round	Normal	Special	60	100	15	Normal
TM94	False Swipe	Normal	Physical	40	100	40	Normal
TM99	Breaking Swipe	Dragon	Physical	60	100	15	Many Others

TR MOVES

NO.	NAME	TYPE	KIND	POW.	ACC.	PP	RANGE
TR00	Swords Dance	Normal	Status	—	—	20	Self
TR13	Focus Energy	Normal	Status	—	—	30	Self
TR20	Substitute	Normal	Status	—	—	10	Self
TR21	Reversal	Fighting	Physical	—	100	15	Normal
TR24	Outrage	Dragon	Physical	120	100	10	1 Random
TR26	Endure	Normal	Status	—	—	10	Self
TR27	Sleep Talk	Normal	Status	—	—	10	Self
TR31	Iron Tail	Steel	Physical	100	75	15	Normal
TR32	Crunch	Dark	Physical	80	100	15	Normal
TR37	Taunt	Dark	Status	—	100	20	Normal
TR39	Superpower	Fighting	Physical	120	100	5	Normal
TR47	Dragon Claw	Dragon	Physical	80	100	15	Normal
TR51	Dragon Dance	Dragon	Status	—	—	20	Self
TR58	Poison Jab	Poison	Physical	80	100	20	Normal
TR60	X-Scissor	Bug	Physical	80	100	15	Normal
TR62	Dragon Pulse	Dragon	Special	85	100	10	Normal

325

LEVEL-UP MOVES

LV.	NAME	TYPE	KIND	POW.	ACC.	PP	RANGE
1	Bite	Dark	Physical	60	100	25	Normal
1	False Swipe	Normal	Physical	40	100	40	Normal
1	Leer	Normal	Status	—	100	30	Many Others
1	Scratch	Normal	Physical	40	100	35	Normal
9	Assurance	Dark	Physical	60	100	10	Normal
12	Taunt	Dark	Status	—	100	20	Normal
15	Slash	Normal	Physical	70	100	20	Normal
18	Dragon Claw	Dragon	Physical	80	100	15	Normal
21	Scary Face	Normal	Status	—	100	10	Normal
24	Crunch	Dark	Physical	80	100	15	Normal
27	Dragon Dance	Dragon	Status	—	—	20	Self
30	Dual Chop	Dragon	Physical	40	90	15	Normal
33	Laser Focus	Normal	Status	—	—	30	Self
36	Dragon Pulse	Dragon	Special	85	100	10	Normal
41	Swords Dance	Normal	Status	—	—	20	Self
46	Outrage	Dragon	Physical	120	100	10	1 Random
51	Guillotine	Normal	Physical	—	30	5	Normal
56	Giga Impact	Normal	Physical	150	90	5	Normal

EVOLUTION MOVES

NAME	TYPE	KIND	POW.	ACC.	PP	RANGE

EGG MOVES

NAME	TYPE	KIND	POW.	ACC.	PP	RANGE

TUTOR MOVES

NAME	TYPE	KIND	POW.	ACC.	PP	RANGE
Draco Meteor	Dragon	Special	130	90	5	Normal

TM MOVES

NO.	NAME	TYPE	KIND	POW.	ACC.	PP	RANGE
TM09	Giga Impact	Normal	Physical	150	90	5	Normal
TM15	Dig	Ground	Physical	80	100	10	Normal
TM21	Rest	Psychic	Status	—	—	10	Self
TM24	Snore	Normal	Special	50	100	15	Normal
TM25	Protect	Normal	Status	—	—	10	Self
TM26	Scary Face	Normal	Status	—	100	10	Normal
TM31	Attract	Normal	Status	—	100	15	Normal
TM33	Rain Dance	Water	Status	—	—	5	Both Sides
TM34	Sunny Day	Fire	Status	—	—	5	Both Sides
TM39	Facade	Normal	Physical	70	100	20	Normal
TM40	Swift	Normal	Special	60	—	20	Many Others
TM48	Rock Tomb	Rock	Physical	60	95	15	Normal
TM57	Payback	Dark	Physical	50	100	10	Normal
TM58	Assurance	Dark	Physical	60	100	10	Normal
TM59	Fling	Dark	Physical	—	100	10	Normal
TM65	Shadow Claw	Ghost	Physical	70	100	15	Normal
TM76	Round	Normal	Special	60	100	15	Normal
TM94	False Swipe	Normal	Physical	40	100	40	Normal
TM98	Stomping Tantrum	Ground	Physical	75	100	10	Normal
TM99	Breaking Swipe	Dragon	Physical	60	100	15	Many Others

TR MOVES

NAME	TYPE	KIND	POW.	ACC.	PP	RANGE
TR00 Swords Dance	Normal	Status	—	—	20	Self
TR07 Low Kick	Fighting	Physical	—	100	20	Normal
TR13 Focus Energy	Normal	Status	—	—	30	Self
TR20 Substitute	Normal	Status	—	—	10	Self
TR24 Outrage	Dragon	Physical	120	100	10	1 Random
TR26 Endure	Normal	Status	—	—	10	Self
TR27 Sleep Talk	Normal	Status	—	—	10	Self
TR31 Iron Tail	Steel	Physical	100	75	15	Normal
TR32 Crunch	Dark	Physical	80	100	15	Normal
TR37 Taunt	Dark	Status	—	100	20	Normal
TR39 Superpower	Fighting	Physical	120	100	5	Normal
TR47 Dragon Claw	Dragon	Physical	80	100	15	Normal
TR51 Dragon Dance	Dragon	Status	—	—	20	Self
TR57 Poison Jab	Poison	Physical	80	100	20	Normal
TR60 X-Scissor	Bug	Physical	80	100	15	Normal
TR62 Dragon Pulse	Dragon	Special	85	100	10	Normal

Fraxure p. 130

ABILITY
Rivalry
Mold Breaker

HIDDEN ABILITY
Unnerve

SPECIES STRENGTHS
HP
ATTACK
DEFENSE
SP. ATK
SP. DEF
SPEED

DAMAGE TAKEN IN BATTLE
×1 ×1 ×1
×0.5 ×1 ×1
×0.5 ×1 ×2
×0.5 ×1 ×1
×1 ×1 ×1
×2 ×1 ×2

MONSTER
DRAGON

326

LEVEL-UP MOVES

LV.	NAME	TYPE	KIND	POW.	ACC.	PP	RANGE
1	Bite	Dark	Physical	60	100	25	Normal
1	False Swipe	Normal	Physical	40	100	40	Normal
1	Leer	Normal	Status	—	100	30	Many Others
1	Scratch	Normal	Physical	40	100	35	Normal
9	Assurance	Dark	Physical	60	100	10	Normal
12	Taunt	Dark	Status	—	100	20	Normal
15	Slash	Normal	Physical	70	100	20	Normal
18	Dragon Claw	Dragon	Physical	80	100	15	Normal
21	Scary Face	Normal	Status	—	100	10	Normal
24	Crunch	Dark	Physical	80	100	15	Normal
27	Dragon Dance	Dragon	Status	—	—	20	Self
30	Dual Chop	Dragon	Physical	40	90	15	Normal
33	Laser Focus	Normal	Status	—	—	30	Self
36	Dragon Pulse	Dragon	Special	85	100	10	Normal
41	Swords Dance	Normal	Status	—	—	20	Self
46	Outrage	Dragon	Physical	120	100	10	1 Random
53	Guillotine	Normal	Physical	—	30	5	Normal
60	Giga Impact	Normal	Physical	150	90	5	Normal

EVOLUTION MOVES

NAME	TYPE	KIND	POW.	ACC.	PP	RANGE

EGG MOVES

NAME	TYPE	KIND	POW.	ACC.	PP	RANGE

TUTOR MOVES

NAME	TYPE	KIND	POW.	ACC.	PP	RANGE
Draco Meteor	Dragon	Special	130	90	5	Normal

TM MOVES

NO.	NAME	TYPE	KIND	POW.	ACC.	PP	RANGE
TM08	Hyper Beam	Normal	Special	150	90	5	Normal
TM09	Giga Impact	Normal	Physical	150	90	5	Normal
TM15	Dig	Ground	Physical	80	100	10	Normal
TM21	Rest	Psychic	Status	—	—	10	Self
TM22	Rock Slide	Rock	Physical	75	90	10	Many Others
TM24	Snore	Normal	Special	50	100	15	Normal
TM25	Protect	Normal	Status	—	—	10	Self
TM26	Scary Face	Normal	Status	—	100	10	Normal
TM31	Attract	Normal	Status	—	100	15	Normal
TM33	Rain Dance	Water	Status	—	—	5	Both Sides
TM34	Sunny Day	Fire	Status	—	—	5	Both Sides
TM39	Facade	Normal	Physical	70	100	20	Normal
TM40	Swift	Normal	Special	60	—	20	Many Others
TM43	Brick Break	Fighting	Physical	75	100	15	Normal
TM48	Rock Tomb	Rock	Physical	60	95	15	Normal
TM57	Payback	Dark	Physical	50	100	10	Normal
TM58	Assurance	Dark	Physical	60	100	10	Normal
TM59	Fling	Dark	Physical	—	100	10	Normal
TM65	Shadow Claw	Ghost	Physical	70	100	15	Normal
TM69	Psycho Cut	Psychic	Physical	70	100	20	Normal
TM76	Round	Normal	Special	60	100	15	Normal
TM81	Bulldoze	Ground	Physical	60	100	20	All Others
TM85	Snarl	Dark	Special	55	95	15	Many Others
TM94	False Swipe	Normal	Physical	40	100	40	Normal
TM97	Brutal Swing	Dark	Physical	60	100	20	All Others
TM98	Stomping Tantrum	Ground	Physical	75	100	10	Normal
TM99	Breaking Swipe	Dragon	Physical	60	100	15	Many Others

TR MOVES

NAME	TYPE	KIND	POW.	ACC.	PP	RANGE
TR00 Swords Dance	Normal	Status	—	—	20	Self
TR04 Surf	Water	Special	90	100	15	All Others
TR07 Low Kick	Fighting	Physical	—	100	20	Normal
TR10 Earthquake	Ground	Physical	100	100	10	All Others
TR13 Focus Energy	Normal	Status	—	—	30	Self
TR20 Substitute	Normal	Status	—	—	10	Self
TR21 Reversal	Fighting	Physical	—	100	15	Normal
TR24 Outrage	Dragon	Physical	120	100	10	1 Random
TR26 Endure	Normal	Status	—	—	10	Self
TR27 Sleep Talk	Normal	Status	—	—	10	Self
TR31 Iron Tail	Steel	Physical	100	75	15	Normal
TR32 Crunch	Dark	Physical	80	100	15	Normal
TR37 Taunt	Dark	Status	—	100	20	Normal
TR39 Superpower	Fighting	Physical	120	100	5	Normal
TR47 Dragon Claw	Dragon	Physical	80	100	15	Normal
TR51 Dragon Dance	Dragon	Status	—	—	20	Self
TR53 Close Combat	Fighting	Physical	120	100	5	Normal
TR57 Poison Jab	Poison	Physical	80	100	20	Normal
TR60 X-Scissor	Bug	Physical	80	100	15	Normal
TR62 Dragon Pulse	Dragon	Special	85	100	10	Normal
TR64 Focus Blast	Fighting	Special	120	70	5	Normal
TR77 Grass Knot	Grass	Special	—	100	20	Normal

Haxorus p. 130

ABILITY
Rivalry
Mold Breaker

HIDDEN ABILITY
Unnerve

SPECIES STRENGTHS
HP
ATTACK
DEFENSE
SP. ATK
SP. DEF
SPEED

DAMAGE TAKEN IN BATTLE
×1 ×1 ×1
×0.5 ×1 ×1
×0.5 ×1 ×2
×0.5 ×1 ×1
×0.5 ×1 ×1
×2 ×1 ×2

MONSTER
DRAGON

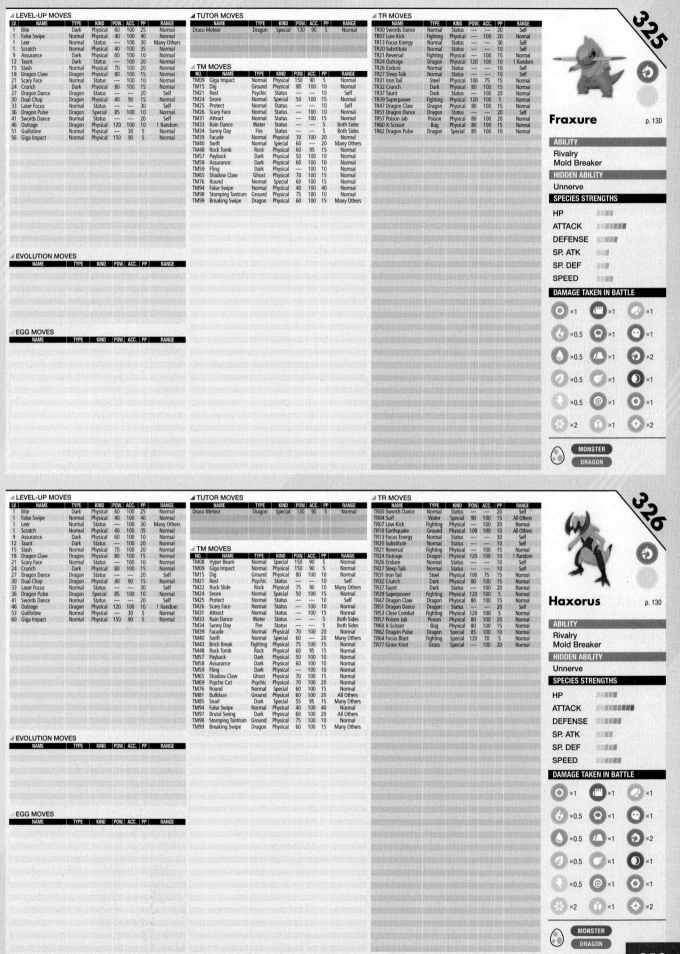

327

Yamask — p. 131

ABILITY
Mummy
—

HIDDEN ABILITY
—

SPECIES STRENGTHS
- HP
- ATTACK
- DEFENSE
- SP. ATK
- SP. DEF
- SPEED

LEVEL-UP MOVES

LV.	NAME	TYPE	KIND	POW.	ACC.	PP	RANGE
1	Astonish	Ghost	Physical	30	100	15	Normal
1	Protect	Normal	Status	—	—	10	Self
4	Haze	Ice	Status	—	—	30	Both Sides
8	Night Shade	Ghost	Special	—	100	15	Normal
12	Disable	Normal	Status	—	100	20	Normal
16	Will-O-Wisp	Fire	Status	—	85	15	Normal
20	Crafty Shield	Fairy	Status	—	—	10	Your Side
24	Hex	Ghost	Special	65	100	10	Normal
28	Mean Look	Normal	Status	—	—	5	Normal
32	Grudge	Ghost	Status	—	—	5	Self
36	Curse	Ghost	Status	—	—	10	Varies
40	Shadow Ball	Ghost	Special	80	100	15	Normal
44	Dark Pulse	Dark	Special	80	100	15	Normal
48	Guard Split	Psychic	Status	—	—	10	Normal
48	Power Split	Psychic	Status	—	—	10	Normal
52	Destiny Bond	Ghost	Status	—	—	5	Self

TUTOR MOVES

NAME	TYPE	KIND	POW.	ACC.	PP	RANGE

TM MOVES

NO.	NAME	TYPE	KIND	POW.	ACC.	PP	RANGE
TM19	Safeguard	Normal	Status	—	—	25	Your Side
TM21	Rest	Psychic	Status	—	—	10	Self
TM23	Thief	Dark	Physical	60	100	25	Normal
TM24	Snore	Normal	Special	50	100	15	Normal
TM25	Protect	Normal	Status	—	—	10	Self
TM31	Attract	Normal	Status	—	100	15	Normal
TM33	Rain Dance	Water	Status	—	—	5	Both Sides
TM38	Will-O-Wisp	Fire	Status	—	85	15	Normal
TM39	Facade	Normal	Physical	70	100	20	Normal
TM44	Imprison	Psychic	Status	—	—	10	Self
TM47	Fake Tears	Dark	Status	—	100	20	Normal
TM57	Payback	Dark	Physical	50	100	10	Normal
TM70	Trick Room	Psychic	Status	—	—	5	Both Sides
TM71	Wonder Room	Psychic	Status	—	—	10	Both Sides
TM76	Round	Normal	Special	60	100	15	Normal
TM77	Hex	Ghost	Special	65	100	10	Normal

TR MOVES

NAME	TYPE	KIND	POW.	ACC.	PP	RANGE
TR11 Psychic	Psychic	Special	90	100	10	Normal
TR20 Substitute	Normal	Status	—	—	10	Self
TR26 Endure	Normal	Status	—	—	10	Self
TR27 Sleep Talk	Normal	Status	—	—	10	Self
TR33 Shadow Ball	Ghost	Special	80	100	15	Normal
TR38 Trick	Psychic	Status	—	100	10	Normal
TR40 Skill Swap	Psychic	Status	—	—	10	Normal
TR46 Iron Defense	Steel	Status	—	—	15	Self
TR49 Calm Mind	Psychic	Status	—	—	20	Self
TR54 Toxic Spikes	Poison	Status	—	—	20	Other Side
TR58 Dark Pulse	Dark	Special	80	100	15	Normal
TR65 Energy Ball	Grass	Special	90	100	10	Normal
TR68 Nasty Plot	Dark	Status	—	—	20	Self
TR69 Zen Headbutt	Psychic	Physical	80	90	15	Normal
TR83 Ally Switch	Psychic	Status	—	—	15	Self

EVOLUTION MOVES

NAME	TYPE	KIND	POW.	ACC.	PP	RANGE

EGG MOVES

NAME	TYPE	KIND	POW.	ACC.	PP	RANGE
Memento	Dark	Status	—	100	10	Normal

DAMAGE TAKEN IN BATTLE
×0 ×0 ×1 ×1 ×0.5 ×2 ×1 ×1 ×1 ×1 ×1 ×2 ×1 ×0.5 ×1

MINERAL
AMORPHOUS

327

Yamask — p. 131
Galarian Form

ABILITY
Wandering Spirit
—

HIDDEN ABILITY
—

SPECIES STRENGTHS
- HP
- ATTACK
- DEFENSE
- SP. ATK
- SP. DEF
- SPEED

LEVEL-UP MOVES

LV.	NAME	TYPE	KIND	POW.	ACC.	PP	RANGE
1	Astonish	Ghost	Physical	30	100	15	Normal
1	Protect	Normal	Status	—	—	10	Self
4	Haze	Ice	Status	—	—	30	Both Sides
8	Night Shade	Ghost	Special	—	100	15	Normal
12	Disable	Normal	Status	—	100	20	Normal
16	Brutal Swing	Dark	Physical	60	100	20	All Others
20	Crafty Shield	Fairy	Status	—	—	10	Your Side
24	Hex	Ghost	Special	65	100	10	Normal
28	Mean Look	Normal	Status	—	—	5	Normal
32	Slam	Normal	Physical	80	75	20	Normal
36	Curse	Ghost	Status	—	—	10	Varies
40	Shadow Ball	Ghost	Special	80	100	15	Normal
44	Earthquake	Ground	Physical	100	100	10	All Others
48	Guard Split	Psychic	Status	—	—	10	Normal
48	Power Split	Psychic	Status	—	—	10	Normal
52	Destiny Bond	Ghost	Status	—	—	5	Self

TUTOR MOVES

NAME	TYPE	KIND	POW.	ACC.	PP	RANGE

TM MOVES

NO.	NAME	TYPE	KIND	POW.	ACC.	PP	RANGE
TM19	Safeguard	Normal	Status	—	—	25	Your Side
TM21	Rest	Psychic	Status	—	—	10	Self
TM22	Rock Slide	Rock	Physical	75	90	10	Many Others
TM23	Thief	Dark	Physical	60	100	25	Normal
TM24	Snore	Normal	Special	50	100	15	Normal
TM25	Protect	Normal	Status	—	—	10	Self
TM31	Attract	Normal	Status	—	100	15	Normal
TM32	Sandstorm	Rock	Status	—	—	10	Both Sides
TM33	Rain Dance	Water	Status	—	—	5	Both Sides
TM38	Will-O-Wisp	Fire	Status	—	85	15	Normal
TM39	Facade	Normal	Physical	70	100	20	Normal
TM44	Imprison	Psychic	Status	—	—	10	Self
TM47	Fake Tears	Dark	Status	—	100	20	Normal
TM48	Rock Tomb	Rock	Physical	60	95	15	Normal
TM57	Payback	Dark	Physical	50	100	10	Normal
TM70	Trick Room	Psychic	Status	—	—	5	Both Sides
TM71	Wonder Room	Psychic	Status	—	—	10	Both Sides
TM76	Round	Normal	Special	60	100	15	Normal
TM77	Hex	Ghost	Special	65	100	10	Normal
TM97	Brutal Swing	Dark	Physical	60	100	20	All Others

TR MOVES

NAME	TYPE	KIND	POW.	ACC.	PP	RANGE
TR10 Earthquake	Ground	Physical	100	100	10	All Others
TR11 Psychic	Psychic	Special	90	100	10	Normal
TR20 Substitute	Normal	Status	—	—	10	Self
TR26 Endure	Normal	Status	—	—	10	Self
TR27 Sleep Talk	Normal	Status	—	—	10	Self
TR33 Shadow Ball	Ghost	Special	80	100	15	Normal
TR38 Trick	Psychic	Status	—	100	10	Normal
TR40 Skill Swap	Psychic	Status	—	—	10	Normal
TR46 Iron Defense	Steel	Status	—	—	15	Self
TR49 Calm Mind	Psychic	Status	—	—	20	Self
TR54 Toxic Spikes	Poison	Status	—	—	20	Other Side
TR58 Dark Pulse	Dark	Special	80	100	15	Normal
TR65 Energy Ball	Grass	Special	90	100	10	Normal
TR67 Earth Power	Ground	Special	90	100	10	Normal
TR68 Nasty Plot	Dark	Status	—	—	20	Self
TR69 Zen Headbutt	Psychic	Physical	80	90	15	Normal
TR83 Ally Switch	Psychic	Status	—	—	15	Self

EVOLUTION MOVES

NAME	TYPE	KIND	POW.	ACC.	PP	RANGE

EGG MOVES

NAME	TYPE	KIND	POW.	ACC.	PP	RANGE
Memento	Dark	Status	—	100	10	Normal

DAMAGE TAKEN IN BATTLE
×0 ×0 ×0.5 ×1 ×0.25 ×2 ×2 ×1 ×1 ×2 ×1 ×2 ×0 ×1 ×1 ×2 ×0.5 ×1

MINERAL
AMORPHOUS

328

LEVEL-UP MOVES

LV.	NAME	TYPE	KIND	POW.	ACC.	PP	RANGE
1	Astonish	Ghost	Physical	30	100	15	Normal
1	Haze	Ice	Status	—	—	30	Both Sides
1	Night Shade	Ghost	Special	—	100	15	Normal
1	Protect	Normal	Status	—	—	10	Self
1	Scary Face	Normal	Status	—	100	10	Normal
1	Shadow Claw	Ghost	Physical	70	100	15	Normal
12	Disable	Normal	Status	—	100	20	Normal
16	Brutal Swing	Dark	Physical	60	100	20	All Others
20	Crafty Shield	Fairy	Status	—	—	10	Your Side
24	Hex	Ghost	Special	65	100	10	Normal
28	Mean Look	Normal	Status	—	—	5	Normal
32	Slam	Normal	Physical	80	75	20	Normal
38	Curse	Ghost	Status	—	—	10	Varies
44	Shadow Ball	Ghost	Special	80	100	15	Normal
50	Earthquake	Ground	Physical	100	100	10	All Others
56	Guard Split	Psychic	Status	—	—	10	Normal
56	Power Split	Psychic	Status	—	—	10	Normal
62	Destiny Bond	Ghost	Status	—	—	5	Self

EVOLUTION MOVES

NAME	TYPE	KIND	POW.	ACC.	PP	RANGE
Shadow Claw	Ghost	Physical	70	100	15	Normal

EGG MOVES

NAME	TYPE	KIND	POW.	ACC.	PP	RANGE

TUTOR MOVES

NAME	TYPE	KIND	POW.	ACC.	PP	RANGE

TM MOVES

NO.	NAME	TYPE	KIND	POW.	ACC.	PP	RANGE
TM08	Hyper Beam	Normal	Special	150	90	5	Normal
TM09	Giga Impact	Normal	Physical	150	90	5	Normal
TM19	Safeguard	Normal	Status	—	—	25	Your Side
TM21	Rest	Psychic	Status	—	—	10	Self
TM22	Rock Slide	Rock	Physical	75	90	10	Many Others
TM23	Thief	Dark	Physical	60	100	25	Normal
TM24	Snore	Normal	Special	50	100	15	Normal
TM25	Protect	Normal	Status	—	—	10	Self
TM26	Scary Face	Normal	Status	—	100	10	Normal
TM31	Attract	Normal	Status	—	100	15	Normal
TM32	Sandstorm	Rock	Status	—	—	10	Both Sides
TM33	Rain Dance	Water	Status	—	—	5	Both Sides
TM38	Will-O-Wisp	Fire	Status	—	85	15	Normal
TM39	Facade	Normal	Physical	70	100	20	Normal
TM42	Revenge	Fighting	Physical	60	100	10	Normal
TM44	Imprison	Psychic	Status	—	—	10	Self
TM47	Fake Tears	Dark	Status	—	100	20	Normal
TM48	Rock Tomb	Rock	Physical	60	95	15	Normal
TM49	Sand Tomb	Ground	Physical	35	85	15	Normal
TM54	Rock Blast	Rock	Physical	25	90	10	Normal
TM57	Payback	Dark	Physical	50	100	10	Normal
TM60	Power Swap	Psychic	Status	—	—	10	Normal
TM61	Guard Swap	Psychic	Status	—	—	10	Normal
TM65	Shadow Claw	Ghost	Physical	70	100	15	Normal
TM70	Trick Room	Psychic	Status	—	—	5	Both Sides
TM71	Wonder Room	Psychic	Status	—	—	10	Both Sides
TM76	Round	Normal	Special	60	100	15	Normal
TM77	Hex	Ghost	Special	65	100	10	Normal
TM81	Bulldoze	Ground	Physical	60	100	20	All Others
TM86	Phantom Force	Ghost	Physical	90	100	10	Normal
TM97	Brutal Swing	Dark	Physical	60	100	20	All Others

TR MOVES

NO.	NAME	TYPE	KIND	POW.	ACC.	PP	RANGE
TR10	Earthquake	Ground	Physical	100	100	10	All Others
TR11	Psychic	Psychic	Special	90	100	10	Normal
TR17	Amnesia	Psychic	Status	—	—	20	Self
TR20	Substitute	Normal	Status	—	—	10	Self
TR26	Endure	Normal	Status	—	—	10	Self
TR27	Sleep Talk	Normal	Status	—	—	10	Self
TR33	Shadow Ball	Ghost	Special	80	100	15	Normal
TR37	Taunt	Dark	Status	—	100	20	Normal
TR38	Trick	Psychic	Status	—	100	10	Normal
TR40	Skill Swap	Psychic	Status	—	—	10	Normal
TR46	Iron Defense	Steel	Status	—	—	15	Self
TR49	Calm Mind	Psychic	Status	—	—	20	Self
TR54	Toxic Spikes	Poison	Status	—	—	20	Other Side
TR58	Dark Pulse	Dark	Special	80	100	15	Normal
TR62	Dragon Pulse	Dragon	Special	85	100	10	Normal
TR65	Energy Ball	Grass	Special	90	100	10	Normal
TR67	Earth Power	Ground	Special	90	100	10	Normal
TR68	Nasty Plot	Dark	Status	—	—	20	Self
TR69	Zen Headbutt	Psychic	Physical	80	90	15	Normal
TR75	Stone Edge	Rock	Physical	100	80	5	Normal
TR76	Stealth Rock	Rock	Status	—	—	20	Other Side
TR77	Grass Knot	Grass	Special	—	100	20	Normal
TR83	Ally Switch	Psychic	Status	—	—	15	Self
TR99	Body Press	Fighting	Physical	80	100	10	Normal

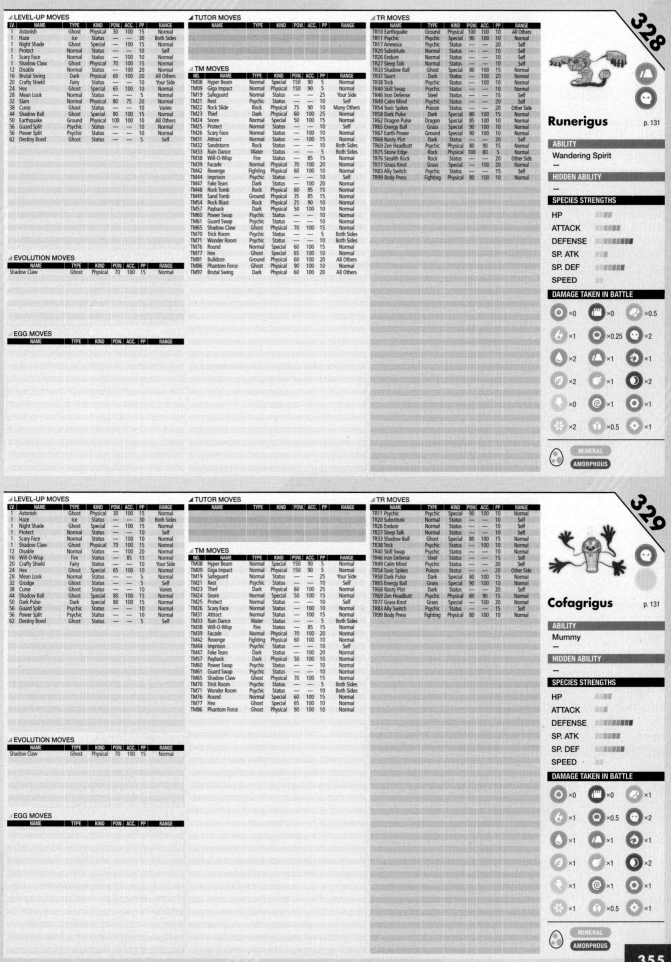

Runerigus p. 131

ABILITY
Wandering Spirit

HIDDEN ABILITY
—

SPECIES STRENGTHS
- HP
- ATTACK
- DEFENSE
- SP. ATK
- SP. DEF
- SPEED

DAMAGE TAKEN IN BATTLE
×0, ×0, ×0.5, ×1, ×0.25, ×2, ×1, ×1, ×1, ×2, ×1, ×2, ×0, ×1, ×1, ×2, ×0.5, ×1

MINERAL
AMORPHOUS

329

LEVEL-UP MOVES

LV.	NAME	TYPE	KIND	POW.	ACC.	PP	RANGE
1	Astonish	Ghost	Physical	30	100	15	Normal
1	Haze	Ice	Status	—	—	30	Both Sides
1	Night Shade	Ghost	Special	—	100	15	Normal
1	Protect	Normal	Status	—	—	10	Self
1	Scary Face	Normal	Status	—	100	10	Normal
1	Shadow Claw	Ghost	Physical	70	100	15	Normal
12	Disable	Normal	Status	—	100	20	Normal
6	Will-O-Wisp	Fire	Status	—	85	15	Normal
20	Crafty Shield	Fairy	Status	—	—	10	Your Side
24	Hex	Ghost	Special	65	100	10	Normal
28	Mean Look	Normal	Status	—	—	5	Normal
32	Grudge	Ghost	Status	—	—	5	Self
38	Curse	Ghost	Status	—	—	10	Varies
44	Shadow Ball	Ghost	Special	80	100	15	Normal
50	Dark Pulse	Dark	Special	80	100	15	Normal
56	Guard Split	Psychic	Status	—	—	10	Normal
56	Power Split	Psychic	Status	—	—	10	Normal
62	Destiny Bond	Ghost	Status	—	—	5	Self

EVOLUTION MOVES

NAME	TYPE	KIND	POW.	ACC.	PP	RANGE
Shadow Claw	Ghost	Physical	70	100	15	Normal

EGG MOVES

NAME	TYPE	KIND	POW.	ACC.	PP	RANGE

TUTOR MOVES

NAME	TYPE	KIND	POW.	ACC.	PP	RANGE

TM MOVES

NO.	NAME	TYPE	KIND	POW.	ACC.	PP	RANGE
TM08	Hyper Beam	Normal	Special	150	90	5	Normal
TM09	Giga Impact	Normal	Physical	150	90	5	Normal
TM19	Safeguard	Normal	Status	—	—	25	Your Side
TM21	Rest	Psychic	Status	—	—	10	Self
TM23	Thief	Dark	Physical	60	100	25	Normal
TM24	Snore	Normal	Special	50	100	15	Normal
TM25	Protect	Normal	Status	—	—	10	Self
TM26	Scary Face	Normal	Status	—	100	10	Normal
TM31	Attract	Normal	Status	—	100	15	Normal
TM33	Rain Dance	Water	Status	—	—	5	Both Sides
TM38	Will-O-Wisp	Fire	Status	—	85	15	Normal
TM39	Facade	Normal	Physical	70	100	20	Normal
TM42	Revenge	Fighting	Physical	60	100	10	Normal
TM44	Imprison	Psychic	Status	—	—	10	Self
TM47	Fake Tears	Dark	Status	—	100	20	Normal
TM57	Payback	Dark	Physical	50	100	10	Normal
TM60	Power Swap	Psychic	Status	—	—	10	Normal
TM61	Guard Swap	Psychic	Status	—	—	10	Normal
TM65	Shadow Claw	Ghost	Physical	70	100	15	Normal
TM70	Trick Room	Psychic	Status	—	—	5	Both Sides
TM71	Wonder Room	Psychic	Status	—	—	10	Both Sides
TM76	Round	Normal	Special	60	100	15	Normal
TM77	Hex	Ghost	Special	65	100	10	Normal
TM86	Phantom Force	Ghost	Physical	90	100	10	Normal

TR MOVES

NO.	NAME	TYPE	KIND	POW.	ACC.	PP	RANGE
TR11	Psychic	Psychic	Special	90	100	10	Normal
TR20	Substitute	Normal	Status	—	—	10	Self
TR26	Endure	Normal	Status	—	—	10	Self
TR27	Sleep Talk	Normal	Status	—	—	10	Self
TR33	Shadow Ball	Ghost	Special	80	100	15	Normal
TR38	Trick	Psychic	Status	—	100	10	Normal
TR40	Skill Swap	Psychic	Status	—	—	10	Normal
TR46	Iron Defense	Steel	Status	—	—	15	Self
TR49	Calm Mind	Psychic	Status	—	—	20	Self
TR54	Toxic Spikes	Poison	Status	—	—	20	Other Side
TR58	Dark Pulse	Dark	Special	80	100	15	Normal
TR65	Energy Ball	Grass	Special	90	100	10	Normal
TR68	Nasty Plot	Dark	Status	—	—	20	Self
TR69	Zen Headbutt	Psychic	Physical	80	90	15	Normal
TR77	Grass Knot	Grass	Special	—	100	20	Normal
TR83	Ally Switch	Psychic	Status	—	—	15	Self
TR99	Body Press	Fighting	Physical	80	100	10	Normal

Cofagrigus p. 131

ABILITY
Mummy

—

HIDDEN ABILITY
—

SPECIES STRENGTHS
- HP
- ATTACK
- DEFENSE
- SP. ATK
- SP. DEF
- SPEED

DAMAGE TAKEN IN BATTLE
×0, ×0, ×1, ×1, ×0.5, ×2, ×1, ×1, ×1, ×1, ×1, ×2, ×1, ×1, ×1, ×1, ×0.5, ×1

MINERAL
AMORPHOUS

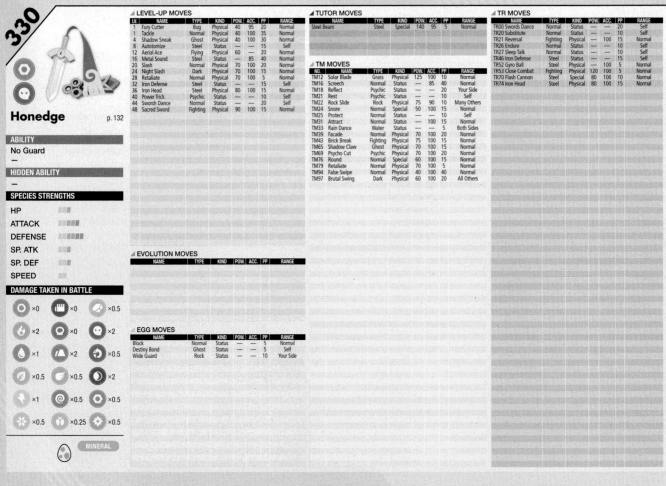

330 Honedge — p. 132

ABILITY
No Guard
—

HIDDEN ABILITY
—

SPECIES STRENGTHS
HP
ATTACK
DEFENSE
SP. ATK
SP. DEF
SPEED

DAMAGE TAKEN IN BATTLE

MINERAL

LEVEL-UP MOVES

LV.	NAME	TYPE	KIND	POW.	ACC.	PP	RANGE
1	Fury Cutter	Bug	Physical	40	95	20	Normal
1	Tackle	Normal	Physical	40	100	35	Normal
4	Shadow Sneak	Ghost	Physical	40	100	30	Normal
8	Autotomize	Steel	Status	—	—	15	Self
12	Aerial Ace	Flying	Physical	60	—	20	Normal
16	Metal Sound	Steel	Status	—	85	40	Normal
20	Slash	Normal	Physical	70	100	20	Normal
24	Night Slash	Dark	Physical	70	100	15	Normal
28	Retaliate	Normal	Physical	70	100	5	Normal
32	Iron Defense	Steel	Status	—	—	15	Self
36	Iron Head	Steel	Physical	80	100	15	Normal
40	Power Trick	Psychic	Status	—	—	10	Self
44	Swords Dance	Normal	Status	—	—	20	Self
48	Sacred Sword	Fighting	Physical	90	100	15	Normal

TUTOR MOVES

NAME	TYPE	KIND	POW.	ACC.	PP	RANGE
Steel Beam	Steel	Special	140	95	5	Normal

TM MOVES

NO.	NAME	TYPE	KIND	POW.	ACC.	PP	RANGE
TM12	Solar Blade	Grass	Physical	125	100	10	Normal
TM16	Screech	Normal	Status	—	85	40	Normal
TM18	Reflect	Psychic	Status	—	—	20	Your Side
TM21	Rest	Psychic	Status	—	—	10	Self
TM22	Rock Slide	Rock	Physical	75	90	10	Many Others
TM24	Snore	Normal	Special	50	100	15	Normal
TM25	Protect	Normal	Status	—	—	10	Self
TM31	Attract	Normal	Status	—	100	15	Normal
TM33	Rain Dance	Water	Status	—	—	5	Both Sides
TM39	Facade	Normal	Physical	70	100	20	Normal
TM43	Brick Break	Fighting	Physical	75	100	15	Normal
TM65	Shadow Claw	Ghost	Physical	70	100	15	Normal
TM69	Psycho Cut	Psychic	Physical	70	100	20	Normal
TM76	Round	Normal	Special	60	100	15	Normal
TM79	Retaliate	Normal	Physical	70	100	5	Normal
TM94	False Swipe	Normal	Physical	40	100	40	Normal
TM97	Brutal Swing	Dark	Physical	60	100	20	All Others

TR MOVES

NAME	TYPE	KIND	POW.	ACC.	PP	RANGE
TR00 Swords Dance	Normal	Status	—	—	20	Self
TR20 Substitute	Normal	Status	—	—	10	Self
TR21 Reversal	Fighting	Physical	—	100	15	Normal
TR26 Endure	Normal	Status	—	—	10	Self
TR27 Sleep Talk	Normal	Status	—	—	10	Self
TR46 Iron Defense	Steel	Status	—	—	15	Self
TR52 Gyro Ball	Steel	Physical	—	100	5	Normal
TR53 Close Combat	Fighting	Physical	120	100	5	Normal
TR70 Flash Cannon	Steel	Special	80	100	10	Normal
TR74 Iron Head	Steel	Physical	80	100	15	Normal

EVOLUTION MOVES

NAME	TYPE	KIND	POW.	ACC.	PP	RANGE

EGG MOVES

NAME	TYPE	KIND	POW.	ACC.	PP	RANGE
Block	Normal	Status	—	—	5	Normal
Destiny Bond	Ghost	Status	—	—	5	Self
Wide Guard	Rock	Status	—	—	10	Your Side

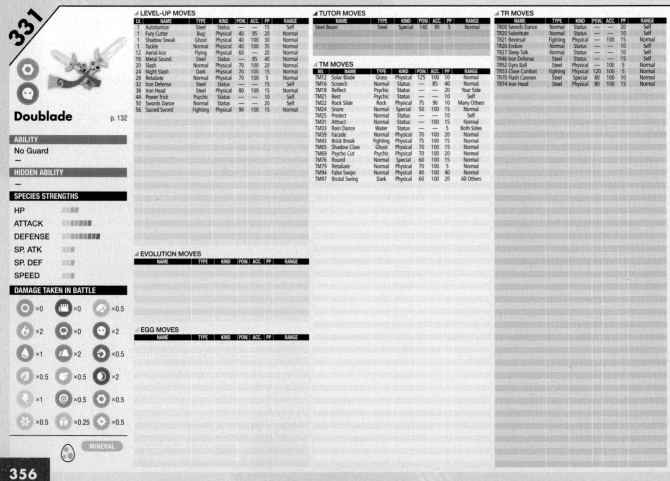

331 Doublade — p. 132

ABILITY
No Guard
—

HIDDEN ABILITY
—

SPECIES STRENGTHS
HP
ATTACK
DEFENSE
SP. ATK
SP. DEF
SPEED

DAMAGE TAKEN IN BATTLE

MINERAL

LEVEL-UP MOVES

LV.	NAME	TYPE	KIND	POW.	ACC.	PP	RANGE
1	Autotomize	Steel	Status	—	—	15	Self
1	Fury Cutter	Bug	Physical	40	95	20	Normal
1	Shadow Sneak	Ghost	Physical	40	100	30	Normal
1	Tackle	Normal	Physical	40	100	35	Normal
12	Aerial Ace	Flying	Physical	60	—	20	Normal
16	Metal Sound	Steel	Status	—	85	40	Normal
20	Slash	Normal	Physical	70	100	20	Normal
24	Night Slash	Dark	Physical	70	100	15	Normal
28	Retaliate	Normal	Physical	70	100	5	Normal
32	Iron Defense	Steel	Status	—	—	15	Self
38	Iron Head	Steel	Physical	80	100	15	Normal
44	Power Trick	Psychic	Status	—	—	10	Self
50	Swords Dance	Normal	Status	—	—	20	Self
56	Sacred Sword	Fighting	Physical	90	100	15	Normal

TUTOR MOVES

NAME	TYPE	KIND	POW.	ACC.	PP	RANGE
Steel Beam	Steel	Special	140	95	5	Normal

TM MOVES

NO.	NAME	TYPE	KIND	POW.	ACC.	PP	RANGE
TM12	Solar Blade	Grass	Physical	125	100	10	Normal
TM16	Screech	Normal	Status	—	85	40	Normal
TM18	Reflect	Psychic	Status	—	—	20	Your Side
TM21	Rest	Psychic	Status	—	—	10	Self
TM22	Rock Slide	Rock	Physical	75	90	10	Many Others
TM24	Snore	Normal	Special	50	100	15	Normal
TM25	Protect	Normal	Status	—	—	10	Self
TM31	Attract	Normal	Status	—	100	15	Normal
TM33	Rain Dance	Water	Status	—	—	5	Both Sides
TM39	Facade	Normal	Physical	70	100	20	Normal
TM43	Brick Break	Fighting	Physical	75	100	15	Normal
TM65	Shadow Claw	Ghost	Physical	70	100	15	Normal
TM69	Psycho Cut	Psychic	Physical	70	100	20	Normal
TM76	Round	Normal	Special	60	100	15	Normal
TM79	Retaliate	Normal	Physical	70	100	5	Normal
TM94	False Swipe	Normal	Physical	40	100	40	Normal
TM97	Brutal Swing	Dark	Physical	60	100	20	All Others

TR MOVES

NAME	TYPE	KIND	POW.	ACC.	PP	RANGE
TR00 Swords Dance	Normal	Status	—	—	20	Self
TR20 Substitute	Normal	Status	—	—	10	Self
TR21 Reversal	Fighting	Physical	—	100	15	Normal
TR26 Endure	Normal	Status	—	—	10	Self
TR27 Sleep Talk	Normal	Status	—	—	10	Self
TR46 Iron Defense	Steel	Status	—	—	15	Self
TR52 Gyro Ball	Steel	Physical	—	100	5	Normal
TR53 Close Combat	Fighting	Physical	120	100	5	Normal
TR70 Flash Cannon	Steel	Special	80	100	10	Normal
TR74 Iron Head	Steel	Physical	80	100	15	Normal

EVOLUTION MOVES

NAME	TYPE	KIND	POW.	ACC.	PP	RANGE

EGG MOVES

NAME	TYPE	KIND	POW.	ACC.	PP	RANGE

332

Aegislash — p. 132

LEVEL-UP MOVES

LV.	NAME	TYPE	KIND	POW.	ACC.	PP	RANGE
1	Aerial Ace	Flying	Physical	60	—	20	Normal
1	Autotomize	Steel	Status	—	—	15	Self
1	Fury Cutter	Bug	Physical	40	95	20	Normal
1	Head Smash	Rock	Physical	150	80	5	Normal
1	Iron Defense	Steel	Status	—	—	15	Self
1	Iron Head	Steel	Physical	80	100	15	Normal
1	King's Shield	Steel	Status	—	—	10	Self
1	Metal Sound	Steel	Status	—	85	40	Normal
1	Night Slash	Dark	Physical	70	100	15	Normal
1	Power Trick	Psychic	Status	—	—	10	Self
1	Retaliate	Normal	Physical	70	100	5	Normal
1	Sacred Sword	Fighting	Physical	90	100	15	Normal
1	Shadow Sneak	Ghost	Physical	40	100	30	Normal
1	Slash	Normal	Physical	70	100	20	Normal
1	Swords Dance	Normal	Status	—	—	20	Self
1	Tackle	Normal	Physical	40	100	35	Normal

EVOLUTION MOVES

NAME	TYPE	KIND	POW.	ACC.	PP	RANGE
King's Shield	Steel	Status	—	—	10	Self

EGG MOVES

NAME	TYPE	KIND	POW.	ACC.	PP	RANGE

TUTOR MOVES

NAME	TYPE	KIND	POW.	ACC.	PP	RANGE
Steel Beam	Steel	Special	140	95	5	Normal

TM MOVES

NO.	NAME	TYPE	KIND	POW.	ACC.	PP	RANGE
TM08	Hyper Beam	Normal	Special	150	90	5	Normal
TM09	Giga Impact	Normal	Physical	150	90	5	Normal
TM12	Solar Blade	Grass	Physical	125	100	10	Normal
TM16	Screech	Normal	Status	—	85	40	Normal
TM18	Reflect	Psychic	Status	—	—	20	Your Side
TM21	Rest	Psychic	Status	—	—	10	Self
TM22	Rock Slide	Rock	Physical	75	90	10	Many Others
TM24	Snore	Normal	Special	50	100	15	Normal
TM25	Protect	Normal	Status	—	—	10	Self
TM31	Attract	Normal	Status	—	100	15	Normal
TM33	Rain Dance	Water	Status	—	—	5	Both Sides
TM34	Sunny Day	Fire	Status	—	—	5	Both Sides
TM39	Facade	Normal	Physical	70	100	20	Normal
TM43	Brick Break	Fighting	Physical	75	100	15	Normal
TM65	Shadow Claw	Ghost	Physical	70	100	15	Normal
TM69	Psycho Cut	Psychic	Physical	70	100	20	Normal
TM76	Round	Normal	Special	60	100	15	Normal
TM79	Retaliate	Normal	Physical	70	100	5	Normal
TM94	False Swipe	Normal	Physical	40	100	40	Normal
TM95	Air Slash	Flying	Special	75	95	15	Normal
TM97	Brutal Swing	Dark	Physical	60	100	20	All Others

TR MOVES

NO.	NAME	TYPE	KIND	POW.	ACC.	PP	RANGE
TR00	Swords Dance	Normal	Status	—	—	20	Self
TR20	Substitute	Normal	Status	—	—	10	Self
TR21	Reversal	Fighting	Physical	—	100	15	Normal
TR26	Endure	Normal	Status	—	—	10	Self
TR27	Sleep Talk	Normal	Status	—	—	10	Self
TR33	Shadow Ball	Ghost	Special	80	100	15	Normal
TR46	Iron Defense	Steel	Status	—	—	15	Self
TR52	Gyro Ball	Steel	Physical	—	100	5	Normal
TR53	Close Combat	Fighting	Physical	120	100	5	Normal
TR70	Flash Cannon	Steel	Special	80	100	10	Normal
TR74	Iron Head	Steel	Physical	80	100	15	Normal

ABILITY
Stance Change
—

HIDDEN ABILITY
—

SPECIES STRENGTHS
- HP
- ATTACK
- DEFENSE
- SP. ATK
- SP. DEF
- SPEED

DAMAGE TAKEN IN BATTLE

×0	×0	×0.5
×2	×0	×2
×1	×2	×0.5
×0.5	×0.5	×2
×1	×0.5	×0.5
×0.5	×0.25	×0.5

MINERAL

333

Ponyta — p. 133
Galarian Form

LEVEL-UP MOVES

LV.	NAME	TYPE	KIND	POW.	ACC.	PP	RANGE
1	Growl	Normal	Status	—	100	40	Many Others
1	Tackle	Normal	Physical	40	100	35	Normal
5	Tail Whip	Normal	Status	—	100	30	Many Others
10	Confusion	Psychic	Special	50	100	25	Normal
15	Fairy Wind	Fairy	Special	40	100	30	Normal
20	Agility	Psychic	Status	—	—	30	Self
25	Psybeam	Psychic	Special	65	100	20	Normal
30	Stomp	Normal	Physical	65	100	20	Normal
35	Heal Pulse	Psychic	Status	—	—	10	Normal
41	Take Down	Normal	Physical	90	85	20	Normal
45	Dazzling Gleam	Fairy	Special	80	100	10	Many Others
50	Psychic	Psychic	Special	90	100	10	Normal
55	Healing Wish	Psychic	Status	—	—	10	Self

EVOLUTION MOVES

NAME	TYPE	KIND	POW.	ACC.	PP	RANGE

EGG MOVES

NAME	TYPE	KIND	POW.	ACC.	PP	RANGE
Double Kick	Fighting	Physical	30	100	30	Normal
Double-Edge	Normal	Physical	120	100	15	Normal
Horn Drill	Normal	Physical	—	30	5	Normal
Hypnosis	Psychic	Status	—	60	20	Normal
Morning Sun	Normal	Status	—	—	5	Self
Thrash	Normal	Physical	120	100	10	1 Random

TUTOR MOVES

NAME	TYPE	KIND	POW.	ACC.	PP	RANGE

TM MOVES

NO.	NAME	TYPE	KIND	POW.	ACC.	PP	RANGE
TM21	Rest	Psychic	Status	—	—	10	Self
TM24	Snore	Normal	Special	50	100	15	Normal
TM25	Protect	Normal	Status	—	—	10	Self
TM29	Charm	Fairy	Status	—	100	20	Normal
TM31	Attract	Normal	Status	—	100	15	Normal
TM39	Facade	Normal	Physical	70	100	20	Normal
TM40	Swift	Normal	Special	60	—	20	Many Others
TM44	Imprison	Psychic	Status	—	—	10	Self
TM52	Bounce	Flying	Physical	85	85	5	Normal
TM76	Round	Normal	Special	60	100	15	Normal
TM92	Mystical Fire	Fire	Special	75	100	10	Normal

TR MOVES

NO.	NAME	TYPE	KIND	POW.	ACC.	PP	RANGE
TR01	Body Slam	Normal	Physical	85	100	15	Normal
TR07	Low Kick	Fighting	Physical	—	100	20	Normal
TR11	Psychic	Psychic	Special	90	100	10	Normal
TR12	Agility	Psychic	Status	—	—	30	Self
TR20	Substitute	Normal	Status	—	—	10	Self
TR26	Endure	Normal	Status	—	—	10	Self
TR27	Sleep Talk	Normal	Status	—	—	10	Self
TR31	Iron Tail	Steel	Physical	100	75	15	Normal
TR34	Future Sight	Psychic	Special	120	100	10	Normal
TR49	Calm Mind	Psychic	Status	—	—	20	Self
TR69	Zen Headbutt	Psychic	Physical	80	90	15	Normal
TR82	Stored Power	Psychic	Special	20	100	10	Normal
TR83	Ally Switch	Psychic	Status	—	—	15	Self
TR86	Wild Charge	Electric	Physical	90	100	15	Normal
TR90	Play Rough	Fairy	Physical	90	90	10	Normal
TR92	Dazzling Gleam	Fairy	Special	80	100	10	Many Others
TR94	High Horsepower	Ground	Physical	95	95	10	Normal

ABILITY
Run Away
Pastel Veil

HIDDEN ABILITY
Anticipation

SPECIES STRENGTHS
- HP
- ATTACK
- DEFENSE
- SP. ATK
- SP. DEF
- SPEED

DAMAGE TAKEN IN BATTLE

×1	×0.5	×1
×1	×1	×2
×1	×1	×1
×1	×1	×2
×1	×0.5	×1
×2	×2	×1

FIELD

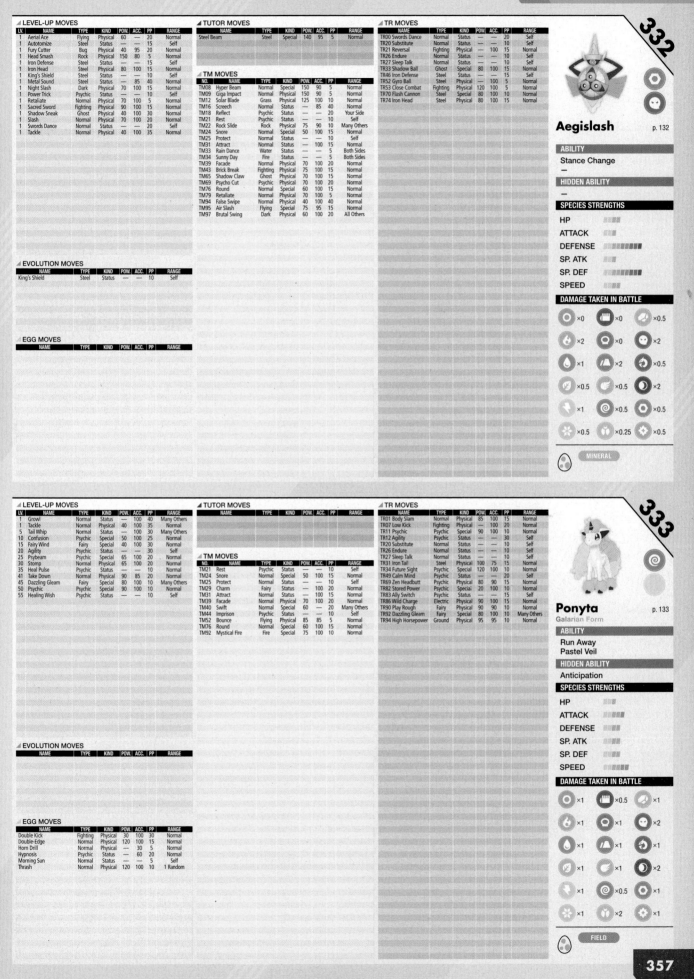

334 Rapidash
Galarian Form — p. 133

ABILITY
Run Away
Pastel Veil

HIDDEN ABILITY
Anticipation

SPECIES STRENGTHS

HP	
ATTACK	
DEFENSE	
SP. ATK	
SP. DEF	
SPEED	

DAMAGE TAKEN IN BATTLE

×1 ×0.25 ×1
×1 ×2 ×2
×1 ×1 ×0
×1 ×1 ×1
×0.5 ×2
×1 ×1 ×1

FIELD

LEVEL-UP MOVES

LV.	NAME	TYPE	KIND	POW.	ACC.	PP	RANGE
1	Confusion	Psychic	Special	50	100	25	Normal
1	Growl	Normal	Status	—	100	40	Many Others
1	Megahorn	Bug	Physical	120	85	10	Normal
1	Psycho Cut	Psychic	Physical	70	100	20	Normal
1	Quick Attack	Normal	Physical	40	100	30	Normal
1	Tackle	Normal	Physical	40	100	35	Normal
1	Tail Whip	Normal	Status	—	100	30	Many Others
15	Fairy Wind	Fairy	Special	40	100	30	Normal
20	Agility	Psychic	Status	—	—	30	Self
25	Psybeam	Psychic	Special	65	100	20	Normal
30	Stomp	Normal	Physical	65	100	20	Normal
35	Heal Pulse	Psychic	Status	—	—	10	Normal
43	Take Down	Normal	Physical	90	85	20	Normal
49	Dazzling Gleam	Fairy	Special	80	100	10	Many Others
56	Psychic	Psychic	Special	90	100	10	Normal
63	Healing Wish	Psychic	Status	—	—	10	Self

EVOLUTION MOVES

NAME	TYPE	KIND	POW.	ACC.	PP	RANGE
Psycho Cut	Psychic	Physical	70	100	20	Normal

EGG MOVES

NAME	TYPE	KIND	POW.	ACC.	PP	RANGE

TUTOR MOVES

NAME	TYPE	KIND	POW.	ACC.	PP	RANGE

TM MOVES

NO.	NAME	TYPE	KIND	POW.	ACC.	PP	RANGE
TM02	Pay Day	Normal	Physical	40	100	20	Normal
TM08	Hyper Beam	Normal	Special	150	90	5	Normal
TM09	Giga Impact	Normal	Physical	150	90	5	Normal
TM21	Rest	Psychic	Status	—	—	10	Self
TM24	Snore	Normal	Special	50	100	15	Normal
TM25	Protect	Normal	Status	—	—	10	Self
TM29	Charm	Fairy	Status	—	100	20	Normal
TM31	Attract	Normal	Status	—	100	15	Normal
TM39	Facade	Normal	Physical	70	100	20	Normal
TM40	Swift	Normal	Special	60	—	20	Many Others
TM44	Imprison	Psychic	Status	—	—	10	Self
TM52	Bounce	Flying	Physical	85	85	5	Normal
TM69	Psycho Cut	Psychic	Physical	70	100	20	Normal
TM70	Trick Room	Psychic	Status	—	—	5	Both Sides
TM71	Wonder Room	Psychic	Status	—	—	10	Both Sides
TM72	Magic Room	Psychic	Status	—	—	10	Both Sides
TM76	Round	Normal	Special	60	100	15	Normal
TM89	Misty Terrain	Fairy	Status	—	—	10	Both Sides
TM91	Psychic Terrain	Psychic	Status	—	—	10	Both Sides
TM92	Mystical Fire	Fire	Special	75	100	10	Normal
TM96	Smart Strike	Steel	Physical	70	—	10	Normal

TR MOVES

NO.	NAME	TYPE	KIND	POW.	ACC.	PP	RANGE
TR00	Swords Dance	Normal	Status	—	—	20	Self
TR01	Body Slam	Normal	Physical	85	100	15	Normal
TR07	Low Kick	Fighting	Physical	—	100	20	Normal
TR11	Psychic	Psychic	Special	90	100	10	Normal
TR12	Agility	Psychic	Status	—	—	30	Self
TR20	Substitute	Normal	Status	—	—	10	Self
TR26	Endure	Normal	Status	—	—	10	Self
TR27	Sleep Talk	Normal	Status	—	—	10	Self
TR28	Megahorn	Bug	Physical	120	85	10	Normal
TR29	Baton Pass	Normal	Status	—	—	40	Self
TR31	Iron Tail	Steel	Physical	100	75	15	Normal
TR34	Future Sight	Psychic	Special	120	100	10	Normal
TR49	Calm Mind	Psychic	Status	—	—	20	Self
TR69	Zen Headbutt	Psychic	Physical	80	90	15	Normal
TR82	Stored Power	Psychic	Special	20	100	10	Normal
TR83	Ally Switch	Psychic	Status	—	—	15	Self
TR86	Wild Charge	Electric	Physical	90	100	15	Normal
TR87	Drill Run	Ground	Physical	80	95	10	Normal
TR90	Play Rough	Fairy	Physical	90	90	10	Normal
TR92	Dazzling Gleam	Fairy	Special	80	100	10	Many Others
TR94	High Horsepower	Ground	Physical	95	95	10	Normal
TR95	Throat Chop	Dark	Physical	80	100	15	Normal

335 Sinistea
p. 134

ABILITY
Weak Armor
—

HIDDEN ABILITY
Cursed Body

SPECIES STRENGTHS

HP	
ATTACK	
DEFENSE	
SP. ATK	
SP. DEF	
SPEED	

DAMAGE TAKEN IN BATTLE

×0 ×0 ×1
×1 ×0.5 ×2
×1 ×1 ×1
×1 ×1 ×2
×1 ×1 ×1
×0.5 ×1

MINERAL
AMORPHOUS

LEVEL-UP MOVES

LV.	NAME	TYPE	KIND	POW.	ACC.	PP	RANGE
1	Astonish	Ghost	Physical	30	100	15	Normal
1	Withdraw	Water	Status	—	—	40	Self
6	Aromatic Mist	Fairy	Status	—	—	20	1 Ally
12	Mega Drain	Grass	Special	40	100	15	Normal
18	Protect	Normal	Status	—	—	10	Self
24	Sucker Punch	Dark	Physical	70	100	5	Normal
30	Aromatherapy	Grass	Status	—	—	5	Your Party
36	Giga Drain	Grass	Special	75	100	10	Normal
42	Nasty Plot	Dark	Status	—	—	20	Self
48	Shadow Ball	Ghost	Special	80	100	15	Normal
54	Memento	Dark	Status	—	100	10	Normal
60	Shell Smash	Normal	Status	—	—	15	Self

EVOLUTION MOVES

NAME	TYPE	KIND	POW.	ACC.	PP	RANGE

EGG MOVES

NAME	TYPE	KIND	POW.	ACC.	PP	RANGE

TUTOR MOVES

NAME	TYPE	KIND	POW.	ACC.	PP	RANGE

TM MOVES

NO.	NAME	TYPE	KIND	POW.	ACC.	PP	RANGE
TM21	Rest	Psychic	Status	—	—	10	Self
TM24	Snore	Normal	Special	50	100	15	Normal
TM25	Protect	Normal	Status	—	—	10	Self
TM28	Giga Drain	Grass	Special	75	100	10	Normal
TM38	Will-O-Wisp	Fire	Status	—	85	15	Normal
TM39	Facade	Normal	Physical	70	100	20	Normal
TM44	Imprison	Psychic	Status	—	—	10	Self
TM57	Payback	Dark	Physical	50	100	10	Normal
TM71	Wonder Room	Psychic	Status	—	—	10	Both Sides
TM76	Round	Normal	Special	60	100	15	Normal
TM77	Hex	Ghost	Special	65	100	10	Normal
TM86	Phantom Force	Ghost	Physical	90	100	10	Normal

TR MOVES

NO.	NAME	TYPE	KIND	POW.	ACC.	PP	RANGE
TR11	Psychic	Psychic	Special	90	100	10	Normal
TR14	Metronome	Normal	Status	—	—	10	Self
TR20	Substitute	Normal	Status	—	—	10	Self
TR25	Psyshock	Psychic	Special	80	100	10	Normal
TR26	Endure	Normal	Status	—	—	10	Self
TR27	Sleep Talk	Normal	Status	—	—	10	Self
TR29	Baton Pass	Normal	Status	—	—	40	Self
TR33	Shadow Ball	Ghost	Special	80	100	15	Normal
TR38	Trick	Psychic	Status	—	100	10	Normal
TR58	Dark Pulse	Dark	Special	80	100	15	Normal
TR68	Nasty Plot	Dark	Status	—	—	20	Self
TR81	Foul Play	Dark	Physical	95	100	15	Normal
TR82	Stored Power	Psychic	Special	20	100	10	Normal
TR83	Ally Switch	Psychic	Status	—	—	15	Self

336 Polteageist

LEVEL-UP MOVES

LV.	NAME	TYPE	KIND	POW.	ACC.	PP	RANGE
1	Aromatic Mist	Fairy	Status	—	—	20	1 Ally
1	Astonish	Ghost	Physical	30	100	15	Normal
1	Mega Drain	Grass	Special	40	100	15	Normal
1	Strength Sap	Grass	Status	—	100	10	Normal
1	Teatime	Normal	Status	—	—	10	All
1	Withdraw	Water	Status	—	—	40	Self
18	Protect	Normal	Status	—	—	10	Self
24	Sucker Punch	Dark	Physical	70	100	5	Normal
30	Aromatherapy	Grass	Status	—	—	5	Your Party
36	Giga Drain	Grass	Special	75	100	10	Normal
42	Nasty Plot	Dark	Status	—	—	20	Self
48	Shadow Ball	Ghost	Special	80	100	15	Normal
54	Memento	Dark	Status	—	100	10	Normal
60	Shell Smash	Normal	Status	—	—	15	Self
66	Curse	Ghost	Status	—	—	10	Varies

EVOLUTION MOVES

NAME	TYPE	KIND	POW.	ACC.	PP	RANGE
Teatime	Normal	Status	—	—	10	All

EGG MOVES

NAME	TYPE	KIND	POW.	ACC.	PP	RANGE

TUTOR MOVES

NAME	TYPE	KIND	POW.	ACC.	PP	RANGE

TM MOVES

NO.	NAME	TYPE	KIND	POW.	ACC.	PP	RANGE
TM08	Hyper Beam	Normal	Special	150	90	5	Normal
TM09	Giga Impact	Normal	Physical	150	90	5	Normal
TM17	Light Screen	Psychic	Status	—	—	30	Your Side
TM18	Reflect	Psychic	Status	—	—	20	Your Side
TM20	Self-Destruct	Normal	Physical	200	100	5	All Others
TM21	Rest	Psychic	Status	—	—	10	Self
TM24	Snore	Normal	Special	50	100	15	Normal
TM25	Protect	Normal	Status	—	—	10	Self
TM28	Giga Drain	Grass	Special	75	100	10	Normal
TM38	Will-O-Wisp	Fire	Status	—	85	15	Normal
TM39	Facade	Normal	Physical	70	100	20	Normal
TM44	Imprison	Psychic	Status	—	—	10	Self
TM57	Payback	Dark	Physical	50	100	10	Normal
TM71	Wonder Room	Psychic	Status	—	—	10	Both Sides
TM76	Round	Normal	Special	60	100	15	Normal
TM77	Hex	Ghost	Special	65	100	10	Normal
TM86	Phantom Force	Ghost	Physical	90	100	10	Normal

TR MOVES

NO.	NAME	TYPE	KIND	POW.	ACC.	PP	RANGE
TR11	Psychic	Psychic	Special	90	100	10	Normal
TR14	Metronome	Normal	Status	—	—	10	Self
TR20	Substitute	Normal	Status	—	—	10	Self
TR25	Psyshock	Psychic	Special	80	100	10	Normal
TR26	Endure	Normal	Status	—	—	10	Self
TR27	Sleep Talk	Normal	Status	—	—	10	Self
TR29	Baton Pass	Normal	Status	—	—	40	Self
TR33	Shadow Ball	Ghost	Special	80	100	15	Normal
TR38	Trick	Psychic	Status	—	100	10	Normal
TR58	Dark Pulse	Dark	Special	80	100	15	Normal
TR68	Nasty Plot	Dark	Status	—	—	20	Self
TR81	Foul Play	Dark	Physical	95	100	15	Normal
TR82	Stored Power	Psychic	Special	20	100	10	Normal
TR83	Ally Switch	Psychic	Status	—	—	15	Self

Polteageist p. 134

ABILITY
Weak Armor
—

HIDDEN ABILITY
Cursed Body

SPECIES STRENGTHS
HP
ATTACK
DEFENSE
SP. ATK
SP. DEF
SPEED

DAMAGE TAKEN IN BATTLE
×0 · ×0 · ×1
×1 · ×0.5 · ×2
×1 · ×1 · ×1
×1 · ×1 · ×2
×1 · ×1 · ×1
×1 · ×0.5 · ×1

MINERAL · AMORPHOUS

---

337 Indeedee

LEVEL-UP MOVES

LV.	NAME	TYPE	KIND	POW.	ACC.	PP	RANGE
1	Play Nice	Normal	Status	—	—	20	Normal
1	Stored Power	Psychic	Special	20	100	10	Normal
5	Encore	Normal	Status	—	100	5	Normal
10	Disarming Voice	Fairy	Special	40	—	15	Many Others
15	Psybeam	Psychic	Special	65	100	20	Normal
20	Helping Hand	Normal	Status	—	—	20	1 Ally
25	After You	Normal	Status	—	—	15	Normal
30	Aromatherapy	Grass	Status	—	—	5	Your Party
35	Psychic	Psychic	Special	90	100	10	Normal
40	Calm Mind	Psychic	Status	—	—	20	Self
45	Power Split	Psychic	Status	—	—	10	Normal
50	Psychic Terrain	Psychic	Status	—	—	10	Both Sides
55	Last Resort	Normal	Physical	140	100	5	Normal

EVOLUTION MOVES

NAME	TYPE	KIND	POW.	ACC.	PP	RANGE

EGG MOVES

NAME	TYPE	KIND	POW.	ACC.	PP	RANGE
Extrasensory	Psychic	Special	80	100	20	Normal
Fake Out	Normal	Physical	40	100	10	Normal
Psych Up	Normal	Status	—	—	10	Normal

TUTOR MOVES

NAME	TYPE	KIND	POW.	ACC.	PP	RANGE

TM MOVES

NO.	NAME	TYPE	KIND	POW.	ACC.	PP	RANGE
TM02	Pay Day	Normal	Physical	40	100	20	Normal
TM10	Magical Leaf	Grass	Special	60	—	20	Normal
TM21	Rest	Psychic	Status	—	—	10	Self
TM24	Snore	Normal	Special	50	100	15	Normal
TM25	Protect	Normal	Status	—	—	10	Self
TM31	Attract	Normal	Status	—	100	15	Normal
TM39	Facade	Normal	Physical	70	100	20	Normal
TM40	Swift	Normal	Special	60	—	20	Many Others
TM41	Helping Hand	Normal	Status	—	—	20	1 Ally
TM44	Imprison	Psychic	Status	—	—	10	Self
TM60	Power Swap	Psychic	Status	—	—	10	Normal
TM63	Drain Punch	Fighting	Physical	75	100	10	Normal
TM70	Trick Room	Psychic	Status	—	—	5	Both Sides
TM71	Wonder Room	Psychic	Status	—	—	10	Both Sides
TM72	Magic Room	Psychic	Status	—	—	10	Both Sides
TM76	Round	Normal	Special	60	100	15	Normal
TM87	Draining Kiss	Fairy	Special	50	100	10	Normal
TM91	Psychic Terrain	Psychic	Status	—	—	10	Both Sides
TM92	Mystical Fire	Fire	Special	75	100	10	Normal

TR MOVES

NO.	NAME	TYPE	KIND	POW.	ACC.	PP	RANGE
TR11	Psychic	Psychic	Special	90	100	10	Normal
TR14	Metronome	Normal	Status	—	—	10	Normal
TR19	Tri Attack	Normal	Special	80	100	10	Normal
TR20	Substitute	Normal	Status	—	—	10	Self
TR25	Psyshock	Psychic	Special	80	100	10	Normal
TR26	Endure	Normal	Status	—	—	10	Self
TR27	Sleep Talk	Normal	Status	—	—	10	Self
TR30	Encore	Normal	Status	—	100	5	Normal
TR33	Shadow Ball	Ghost	Special	80	100	15	Normal
TR34	Future Sight	Psychic	Special	120	100	10	Normal
TR38	Trick	Psychic	Status	—	100	10	Normal
TR42	Hyper Voice	Normal	Special	90	100	10	Many Others
TR49	Calm Mind	Psychic	Status	—	—	20	Self
TR65	Energy Ball	Grass	Special	90	100	10	Normal
TR69	Zen Headbutt	Psychic	Physical	80	90	15	Normal
TR82	Stored Power	Psychic	Special	20	100	10	Normal
TR83	Ally Switch	Psychic	Status	—	—	15	Self
TR90	Play Rough	Fairy	Physical	90	90	10	Normal
TR92	Dazzling Gleam	Fairy	Special	80	100	10	Many Others

Indeedee p. 135
Male

ABILITY
Inner Focus
Synchronize

HIDDEN ABILITY
Psychic Surge

SPECIES STRENGTHS
HP
ATTACK
DEFENSE
SP. ATK
SP. DEF
SPEED

DAMAGE TAKEN IN BATTLE
×1 · ×1 · ×1
×1 · ×1 · ×0
×1 · ×1 · ×1
×1 · ×1 · ×2
×1 · ×0.5 · ×1
×1 · ×2 · ×1

FAIRY

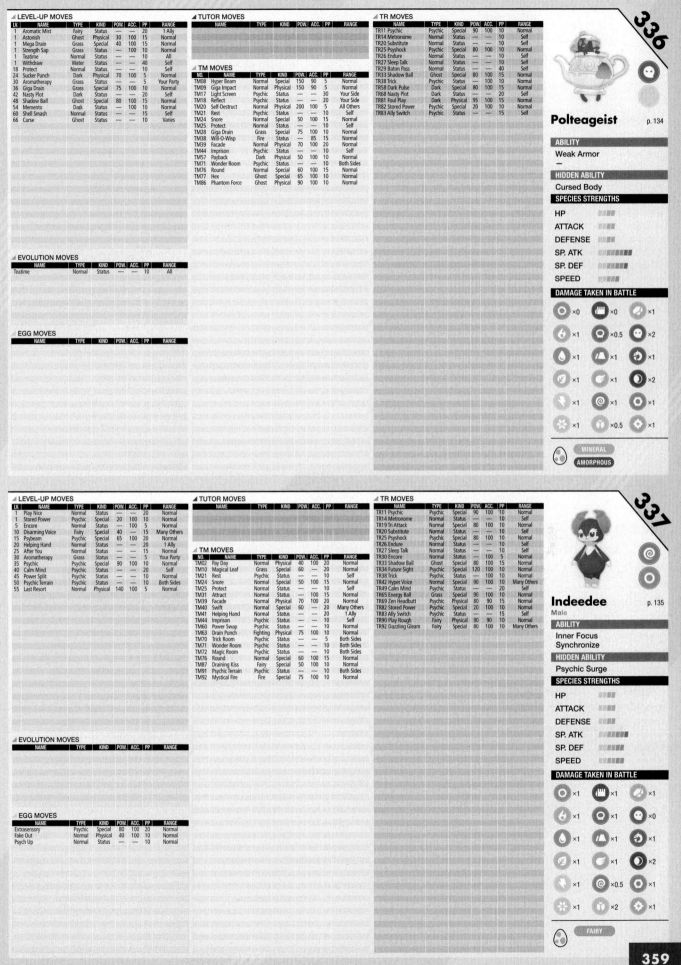

337 Indeedee

p. 135

Female

ABILITY

Own Tempo
Synchronize

HIDDEN ABILITY

Psychic Surge

SPECIES STRENGTHS

HP
ATTACK
DEFENSE
SP. ATK
SP. DEF
SPEED

DAMAGE TAKEN IN BATTLE

×1	×1	×1
×1	×1	×0
×1	×1	×1
×1	×1	×2
×1	×0.5	×1
×1	×2	×1

FAIRY

LEVEL-UP MOVES

LV.	NAME	TYPE	KIND	POW.	ACC.	PP	RANGE
1	Play Nice	Normal	Status	—	—	20	Normal
1	Stored Power	Psychic	Special	20	100	10	Normal
5	Baton Pass	Normal	Status	—	—	40	Self
10	Disarming Voice	Fairy	Special	40	—	15	Many Others
15	Psybeam	Psychic	Special	65	100	20	Normal
20	Helping Hand	Normal	Status	—	—	20	1 Ally
25	Follow Me	Normal	Status	—	—	20	Self
30	Aromatherapy	Grass	Status	—	—	5	Your Party
35	Psychic	Psychic	Special	90	100	10	Normal
40	Calm Mind	Psychic	Status	—	—	20	Self
45	Guard Split	Psychic	Status	—	—	10	Normal
50	Psychic Terrain	Psychic	Status	—	—	10	Both Sides
55	Healing Wish	Psychic	Status	—	—	10	Self

EVOLUTION MOVES

NAME	TYPE	KIND	POW.	ACC.	PP	RANGE

EGG MOVES

NAME	TYPE	KIND	POW.	ACC.	PP	RANGE
Fake Out	Normal	Physical	40	100	10	Normal
Heal Pulse	Psychic	Status	—	—	10	Normal
Psych Up	Normal	Status	—	—	10	Normal
Psycho Shift	Psychic	Status	—	100	10	Normal

TUTOR MOVES

NAME	TYPE	KIND	POW.	ACC.	PP	RANGE

TM MOVES

NO.	NAME	TYPE	KIND	POW.	ACC.	PP	RANGE
TM02	Pay Day	Normal	Physical	40	100	20	Normal
TM10	Magical Leaf	Grass	Special	60	—	20	Normal
TM17	Light Screen	Psychic	Status	—	—	30	Your Side
TM18	Reflect	Psychic	Status	—	—	20	Your Side
TM19	Safeguard	Normal	Status	—	—	25	Your Side
TM21	Rest	Psychic	Status	—	—	10	Self
TM24	Snore	Normal	Special	50	100	15	Normal
TM25	Protect	Normal	Status	—	—	10	Self
TM31	Attract	Normal	Status	—	100	15	Normal
TM39	Facade	Normal	Physical	70	100	20	Normal
TM40	Swift	Normal	Special	60	—	20	Many Others
TM41	Helping Hand	Normal	Status	—	—	20	1 Ally
TM44	Imprison	Psychic	Status	—	—	10	Self
TM61	Guard Swap	Psychic	Status	—	—	10	Normal
TM63	Drain Punch	Fighting	Physical	75	100	10	Normal
TM76	Round	Normal	Special	60	100	15	Normal
TM87	Draining Kiss	Fairy	Special	50	100	10	Normal
TM91	Psychic Terrain	Psychic	Status	—	—	10	Both Sides
TM92	Mystical Fire	Fire	Special	75	100	10	Normal

TR MOVES

NAME	TYPE	KIND	POW.	ACC.	PP	RANGE
TR11 Psychic	Psychic	Special	90	100	10	Normal
TR14 Metronome	Normal	Status	—	—	10	Self
TR20 Substitute	Normal	Status	—	—	10	Self
TR25 Psyshock	Psychic	Special	80	100	10	Normal
TR26 Endure	Normal	Status	—	—	10	Self
TR27 Sleep Talk	Normal	Status	—	—	10	Self
TR29 Baton Pass	Normal	Status	—	—	40	Self
TR33 Shadow Ball	Ghost	Special	80	100	15	Normal
TR34 Future Sight	Psychic	Special	120	100	10	Normal
TR38 Trick	Psychic	Status	—	100	10	Normal
TR42 Hyper Voice	Normal	Special	90	100	10	Many Others
TR49 Calm Mind	Psychic	Status	—	—	20	Self
TR69 Zen Headbutt	Psychic	Physical	80	90	15	Normal
TR82 Stored Power	Psychic	Special	20	100	10	Normal
TR83 Ally Switch	Psychic	Status	—	—	15	Self
TR90 Play Rough	Fairy	Physical	90	90	10	Normal
TR92 Dazzling Gleam	Fairy	Special	80	100	10	Many Others

338 Phantump

p. 136

ABILITY

Natural Cure
Frisk

HIDDEN ABILITY

Harvest

SPECIES STRENGTHS

HP
ATTACK
DEFENSE
SP. ATK
SP. DEF
SPEED

DAMAGE TAKEN IN BATTLE

×0	×0	×1
×2	×1	×2
×0.5	×0.5	×1
×0.5	×2	×2
×0.5	×1	×1
×2	×1	×1

GRASS
AMORPHOUS

LEVEL-UP MOVES

LV.	NAME	TYPE	KIND	POW.	ACC.	PP	RANGE
1	Astonish	Ghost	Physical	30	100	15	Normal
1	Tackle	Normal	Physical	40	100	35	Normal
4	Branch Poke	Grass	Physical	40	100	40	Normal
8	Leech Seed	Grass	Status	—	90	10	Normal
12	Confuse Ray	Ghost	Status	—	100	10	Normal
16	Will-O-Wisp	Fire	Status	—	85	15	Normal
20	Hex	Ghost	Special	65	100	10	Normal
24	Growth	Normal	Status	—	—	20	Self
28	Horn Leech	Grass	Physical	75	100	10	Normal
32	Curse	Ghost	Status	—	—	10	Varies
36	Phantom Force	Ghost	Physical	90	100	10	Normal
40	Ingrain	Grass	Status	—	—	20	Self
44	Wood Hammer	Grass	Physical	120	100	15	Normal
48	Destiny Bond	Ghost	Status	—	—	5	Self
52	Forest's Curse	Grass	Status	—	100	20	Normal

EVOLUTION MOVES

NAME	TYPE	KIND	POW.	ACC.	PP	RANGE

EGG MOVES

NAME	TYPE	KIND	POW.	ACC.	PP	RANGE
Disable	Normal	Status	—	100	20	Normal
Grudge	Ghost	Status	—	—	5	Self
Sucker Punch	Dark	Physical	70	100	5	Normal

TUTOR MOVES

NAME	TYPE	KIND	POW.	ACC.	PP	RANGE

TM MOVES

NO.	NAME	TYPE	KIND	POW.	ACC.	PP	RANGE
TM10	Magical Leaf	Grass	Special	60	—	20	Normal
TM11	Solar Beam	Grass	Special	120	100	10	Normal
TM15	Dig	Ground	Physical	80	100	10	Normal
TM18	Reflect	Psychic	Status	—	—	20	Your Side
TM19	Safeguard	Normal	Status	—	—	25	Your Side
TM21	Rest	Psychic	Status	—	—	10	Self
TM22	Rock Slide	Rock	Physical	75	90	10	Many Others
TM23	Thief	Dark	Physical	60	100	25	Normal
TM24	Snore	Normal	Special	50	100	15	Normal
TM25	Protect	Normal	Status	—	—	10	Self
TM28	Giga Drain	Grass	Special	75	100	10	Normal
TM31	Attract	Normal	Status	—	100	15	Normal
TM34	Sunny Day	Fire	Status	—	—	5	Both Sides
TM38	Will-O-Wisp	Fire	Status	—	85	15	Normal
TM39	Facade	Normal	Physical	70	100	20	Normal
TM44	Imprison	Psychic	Status	—	—	10	Self
TM65	Shadow Claw	Ghost	Physical	70	100	15	Normal
TM70	Trick Room	Psychic	Status	—	—	5	Both Sides
TM76	Round	Normal	Special	60	100	15	Normal
TM77	Hex	Ghost	Special	65	100	10	Normal
TM81	Bulldoze	Ground	Physical	60	100	20	All Others
TM86	Phantom Force	Ghost	Physical	90	100	10	Normal

TR MOVES

NAME	TYPE	KIND	POW.	ACC.	PP	RANGE
TR11 Psychic	Psychic	Special	90	100	10	Normal
TR20 Substitute	Normal	Status	—	—	10	Self
TR26 Endure	Normal	Status	—	—	10	Self
TR27 Sleep Talk	Normal	Status	—	—	10	Self
TR33 Shadow Ball	Ghost	Special	80	100	15	Normal
TR38 Trick	Psychic	Status	—	100	10	Normal
TR40 Skill Swap	Psychic	Status	—	—	10	Normal
TR57 Poison Jab	Poison	Physical	80	100	20	Normal
TR58 Dark Pulse	Dark	Special	80	100	15	Normal
TR59 Seed Bomb	Grass	Physical	80	100	15	Normal
TR65 Energy Ball	Grass	Special	90	100	10	Normal
TR77 Grass Knot	Grass	Special	—	100	20	Normal
TR81 Foul Play	Dark	Physical	95	100	15	Normal
TR83 Ally Switch	Psychic	Status	—	—	15	Self
TR91 Venom Drench	Poison	Status	—	100	20	Many Others

339 — Trevenant

LEVEL-UP MOVES

LV.	NAME	TYPE	KIND	POW.	ACC.	PP	RANGE
1	Astonish	Ghost	Physical	30	100	15	Normal
1	Branch Poke	Grass	Physical	40	100	40	Normal
1	Leech Seed	Grass	Status	—	90	10	Normal
1	Shadow Claw	Ghost	Physical	70	100	15	Normal
1	Tackle	Normal	Physical	40	100	35	Normal
12	Confuse Ray	Ghost	Status	—	100	10	Normal
16	Will-O-Wisp	Fire	Status	—	85	15	Normal
20	Hex	Ghost	Special	65	100	10	Normal
24	Growth	Normal	Status	—	—	20	Self
28	Horn Leech	Grass	Physical	75	100	10	Normal
32	Curse	Ghost	Status	—	—	10	Varies
36	Phantom Force	Ghost	Physical	90	100	10	Normal
40	Ingrain	Grass	Status	—	—	20	Self
44	Wood Hammer	Grass	Physical	120	100	15	Normal
48	Destiny Bond	Ghost	Status	—	—	5	Self
52	Forest's Curse	Grass	Status	—	100	20	Normal

EVOLUTION MOVES

NAME	TYPE	KIND	POW.	ACC.	PP	RANGE
Shadow Claw	Ghost	Physical	70	100	15	Normal

EGG MOVES

NAME	TYPE	KIND	POW.	ACC.	PP	RANGE

TUTOR MOVES

NAME	TYPE	KIND	POW.	ACC.	PP	RANGE

TM MOVES

NO.	NAME	TYPE	KIND	POW.	ACC.	PP	RANGE
TM08	Hyper Beam	Normal	Special	150	90	5	Normal
TM09	Giga Impact	Normal	Physical	150	90	5	Normal
TM10	Magical Leaf	Grass	Special	60	—	20	Normal
TM11	Solar Beam	Grass	Special	120	100	10	Normal
TM15	Dig	Ground	Physical	80	100	10	Normal
TM18	Reflect	Psychic	Status	—	—	20	Your Side
TM19	Safeguard	Normal	Status	—	—	25	Your Side
TM21	Rest	Psychic	Status	—	—	10	Self
TM22	Rock Slide	Rock	Physical	75	90	10	Many Others
TM23	Thief	Dark	Physical	60	100	25	Normal
TM24	Snore	Normal	Special	50	100	15	Normal
TM25	Protect	Normal	Status	—	—	10	Self
TM28	Giga Drain	Grass	Special	75	100	10	Normal
TM31	Attract	Normal	Status	—	100	15	Normal
TM34	Sunny Day	Fire	Status	—	—	5	Both Sides
TM38	Will-O-Wisp	Fire	Status	—	85	15	Normal
TM39	Facade	Normal	Physical	70	100	20	Normal
TM44	Imprison	Psychic	Status	—	—	10	Self
TM63	Drain Punch	Fighting	Physical	75	100	10	Normal
TM65	Shadow Claw	Ghost	Physical	70	100	15	Normal
TM70	Trick Room	Psychic	Status	—	—	5	Both Sides
TM76	Round	Normal	Special	60	100	15	Normal
TM77	Hex	Ghost	Special	65	100	10	Normal
TM81	Bulldoze	Ground	Physical	60	100	20	All Others
TM86	Phantom Force	Ghost	Physical	90	100	10	Normal
TM97	Brutal Swing	Dark	Physical	60	100	20	All Others

TR MOVES

NAME	TYPE	KIND	POW.	ACC.	PP	RANGE
TR10 Earthquake	Ground	Physical	100	100	10	All Others
TR11 Psychic	Psychic	Special	90	100	10	Normal
TR20 Substitute	Normal	Status	—	—	10	Self
TR26 Endure	Normal	Status	—	—	10	Self
TR27 Sleep Talk	Normal	Status	—	—	10	Self
TR33 Shadow Ball	Ghost	Special	80	100	15	Normal
TR38 Trick	Psychic	Status	—	100	10	Normal
TR40 Skill Swap	Psychic	Status	—	—	10	Normal
TR49 Calm Mind	Psychic	Status	—	—	20	Self
TR57 Poison Jab	Poison	Physical	80	100	20	Normal
TR58 Dark Pulse	Dark	Special	80	100	15	Normal
TR59 Seed Bomb	Grass	Physical	80	100	15	Normal
TR60 X-Scissor	Bug	Physical	80	100	15	Normal
TR64 Focus Blast	Fighting	Special	120	70	5	Normal
TR65 Energy Ball	Grass	Special	90	100	10	Normal
TR71 Leaf Storm	Grass	Special	130	90	5	Normal
TR77 Grass Knot	Grass	Special	—	100	20	Normal
TR81 Foul Play	Dark	Physical	95	100	15	Normal
TR83 Ally Switch	Psychic	Status	—	—	15	Self
TR91 Venom Drench	Poison	Status	—	100	20	Many Others

Trevenant p. 136

ABILITY
Natural Cure
Frisk

HIDDEN ABILITY
Harvest

SPECIES STRENGTHS
- HP
- ATTACK
- DEFENSE
- SP. ATK
- SP. DEF
- SPEED

DAMAGE TAKEN IN BATTLE
×0 ×0 ×1
×2 ×1 ×2
×0.5 ×0.5 ×1
×0.5 ×2 ×2
×2 ×1 ×1

GRASS
AMORPHOUS

---

340 — Morelull

LEVEL-UP MOVES

LV.	NAME	TYPE	KIND	POW.	ACC.	PP	RANGE
1	Absorb	Grass	Special	20	100	25	Normal
1	Astonish	Ghost	Physical	30	100	15	Normal
4	Confuse Ray	Ghost	Status	—	100	10	Normal
8	Ingrain	Grass	Status	—	—	20	Self
12	Mega Drain	Grass	Special	40	100	15	Normal
16	Sleep Powder	Grass	Status	—	75	15	Normal
20	Moonlight	Fairy	Status	—	—	5	Self
24	Strength Sap	Grass	Status	—	100	10	Normal
28	Giga Drain	Grass	Special	75	100	10	Normal
32	Dazzling Gleam	Fairy	Special	80	100	10	Many Others
36	Spore	Grass	Status	—	100	15	Normal
40	Moonblast	Fairy	Special	95	100	15	Normal
44	Dream Eater	Psychic	Special	100	100	15	Normal

EVOLUTION MOVES

NAME	TYPE	KIND	POW.	ACC.	PP	RANGE

EGG MOVES

NAME	TYPE	KIND	POW.	ACC.	PP	RANGE
Growth	Normal	Status	—	—	20	Self
Leech Seed	Grass	Status	—	90	10	Normal
Poison Powder	Poison	Status	—	75	35	Normal
Stun Spore	Grass	Status	—	75	30	Normal

TUTOR MOVES

NAME	TYPE	KIND	POW.	ACC.	PP	RANGE

TM MOVES

NO.	NAME	TYPE	KIND	POW.	ACC.	PP	RANGE
TM11	Solar Beam	Grass	Special	120	100	10	Normal
TM14	Thunder Wave	Electric	Status	—	90	20	Normal
TM17	Light Screen	Psychic	Status	—	—	30	Your Side
TM19	Safeguard	Normal	Status	—	—	25	Your Side
TM21	Rest	Psychic	Status	—	—	10	Self
TM24	Snore	Normal	Special	50	100	15	Normal
TM25	Protect	Normal	Status	—	—	10	Self
TM28	Giga Drain	Grass	Special	75	100	10	Normal
TM31	Attract	Normal	Status	—	100	15	Normal
TM34	Sunny Day	Fire	Status	—	—	5	Both Sides
TM39	Facade	Normal	Physical	70	100	20	Normal
TM71	Wonder Room	Psychic	Status	—	—	10	Both Sides
TM72	Magic Room	Psychic	Status	—	—	10	Both Sides
TM76	Round	Normal	Special	60	100	15	Normal
TM87	Draining Kiss	Fairy	Special	50	100	10	Normal

TR MOVES

NAME	TYPE	KIND	POW.	ACC.	PP	RANGE
TR17 Amnesia	Psychic	Status	—	—	20	Self
TR20 Substitute	Normal	Status	—	—	10	Self
TR22 Sludge Bomb	Poison	Special	90	100	10	Normal
TR26 Endure	Normal	Status	—	—	10	Self
TR27 Sleep Talk	Normal	Status	—	—	10	Self
TR59 Seed Bomb	Grass	Physical	80	100	15	Normal
TR65 Energy Ball	Grass	Special	90	100	10	Normal
TR77 Grass Knot	Grass	Special	—	100	20	Normal
TR92 Dazzling Gleam	Fairy	Special	80	100	10	Many Others
TR96 Pollen Puff	Bug	Special	90	100	15	Normal

Morelull p. 136

ABILITY
Illuminate
Effect Spore

HIDDEN ABILITY
Rain Dish

SPECIES STRENGTHS
- HP
- ATTACK
- DEFENSE
- SP. ATK
- SP. DEF
- SPEED

DAMAGE TAKEN IN BATTLE
×1 ×0.5 ×1
×2 ×4 ×1
×0.5 ×0.5 ×0
×0.5 ×2 ×0.5
×0.5 ×1 ×2
×2 ×1 ×1

GRASS

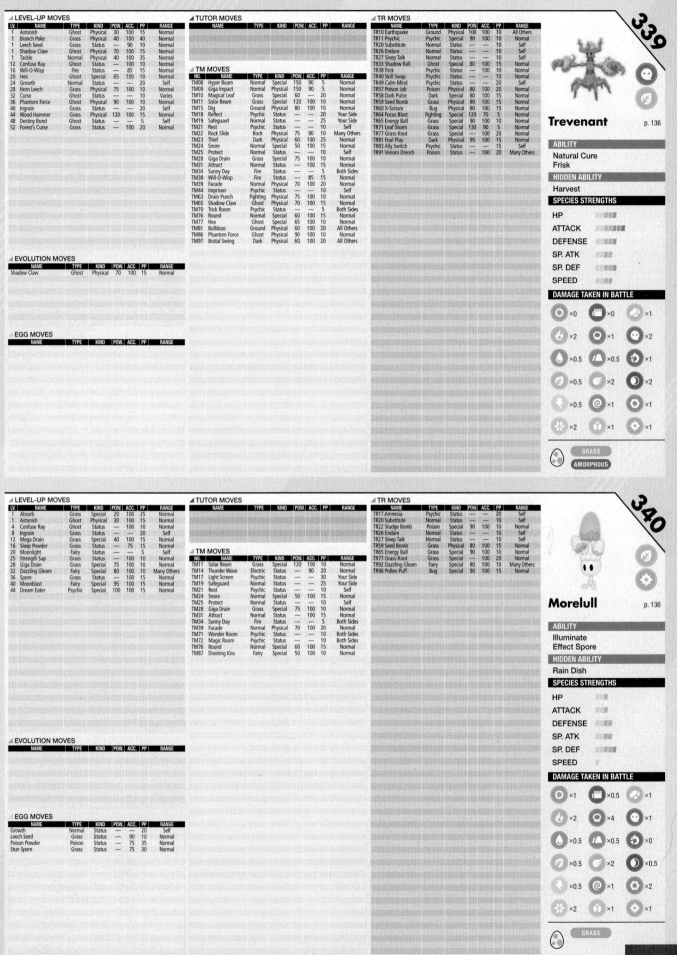

341 Shiinotic

p. 136

ABILITY
Illuminate
Effect Spore

HIDDEN ABILITY
Rain Dish

SPECIES STRENGTHS
HP
ATTACK
DEFENSE
SP. ATK
SP. DEF
SPEED

DAMAGE TAKEN IN BATTLE

×1	×0.5	×1
×2	×4	×1
×0.5	×0.5	×0
×0.5	×2	×0.5
×0.5	×1	×2
×2	×1	×1

GRASS

LEVEL-UP MOVES

LV.	NAME	TYPE	KIND	POW.	ACC.	PP	RANGE
1	Absorb	Grass	Special	20	100	25	Normal
1	Astonish	Ghost	Physical	30	100	15	Normal
1	Confuse Ray	Ghost	Status	—	100	10	Normal
1	Ingrain	Grass	Status	—	—	20	Self
12	Mega Drain	Grass	Special	40	100	15	Normal
16	Sleep Powder	Grass	Status	—	75	15	Normal
20	Moonlight	Fairy	Status	—	—	5	Self
27	Strength Sap	Grass	Status	—	100	10	Normal
32	Giga Drain	Grass	Special	75	100	10	Normal
38	Dazzling Gleam	Fairy	Special	80	100	10	Many Others
44	Spore	Grass	Status	—	100	15	Normal
50	Moonblast	Fairy	Special	95	100	15	Normal
56	Dream Eater	Psychic	Special	100	100	15	Normal

TUTOR MOVES

NAME	TYPE	KIND	POW.	ACC.	PP	RANGE

TM MOVES

NO.	NAME	TYPE	KIND	POW.	ACC.	PP	RANGE
TM08	Hyper Beam	Normal	Special	150	90	5	Normal
TM09	Giga Impact	Normal	Physical	150	90	5	Normal
TM11	Solar Beam	Grass	Special	120	100	10	Normal
TM14	Thunder Wave	Electric	Status	—	90	20	Normal
TM17	Light Screen	Psychic	Status	—	—	30	Your Side
TM19	Safeguard	Normal	Status	—	—	25	Your Side
TM21	Rest	Psychic	Status	—	—	10	Self
TM24	Snore	Normal	Special	50	100	15	Normal
TM25	Protect	Normal	Status	—	—	10	Self
TM28	Giga Drain	Grass	Special	75	100	10	Normal
TM31	Attract	Normal	Status	—	100	15	Normal
TM33	Rain Dance	Water	Status	—	—	5	Both Sides
TM34	Sunny Day	Fire	Status	—	—	5	Both Sides
TM39	Facade	Normal	Physical	70	100	20	Normal
TM46	Weather Ball*	Normal	Special	50	100	10	Normal
TM63	Drain Punch	Fighting	Physical	75	100	10	Normal
TM71	Wonder Room	Psychic	Status	—	—	10	Both Sides
TM72	Magic Room	Psychic	Status	—	—	10	Both Sides
TM76	Round	Normal	Special	60	100	15	Normal
TM87	Draining Kiss	Fairy	Special	50	100	10	Normal

TR MOVES

NAME	TYPE	KIND	POW.	ACC.	PP	RANGE
TR17 Amnesia	Psychic	Status	—	—	20	Self
TR20 Substitute	Normal	Status	—	—	10	Self
TR22 Sludge Bomb	Poison	Special	90	100	10	Normal
TR26 Endure	Normal	Status	—	—	10	Self
TR27 Sleep Talk	Normal	Status	—	—	10	Self
TR59 Seed Bomb	Grass	Physical	80	100	15	Normal
TR65 Energy Ball	Grass	Special	90	100	10	Normal
TR77 Grass Knot	Grass	Special	—	100	20	Normal
TR92 Dazzling Gleam	Fairy	Special	80	100	10	Many Others
TR96 Pollen Puff	Bug	Special	90	100	15	Normal

EVOLUTION MOVES

NAME	TYPE	KIND	POW.	ACC.	PP	RANGE

EGG MOVES

NAME	TYPE	KIND	POW.	ACC.	PP	RANGE

*Weather Ball changes type depending on weather condition. (Harsh sunlight: Fire type. Rain: Water type. Hail: Ice type. Sandstorm: Rock type.)

342 Oranguru

p. 137

ABILITY
Inner Focus
Telepathy

HIDDEN ABILITY
Symbiosis

SPECIES STRENGTHS
HP
ATTACK
DEFENSE
SP. ATK
SP. DEF
SPEED

DAMAGE TAKEN IN BATTLE

×1	×1	×1
×1	×1	×0
×1	×1	×1
×1	×1	×2
×1	×0.5	×1
×1	×2	×1

FIELD

LEVEL-UP MOVES

LV.	NAME	TYPE	KIND	POW.	ACC.	PP	RANGE
1	Confusion	Psychic	Special	50	100	25	Normal
1	Taunt	Dark	Status	—	100	20	Normal
5	After You	Normal	Status	—	—	15	Normal
10	Calm Mind	Psychic	Status	—	—	20	Self
15	Stored Power	Psychic	Special	20	100	10	Normal
20	Psych Up	Normal	Status	—	—	10	Normal
25	Quash	Dark	Status	—	100	15	Normal
30	Nasty Plot	Dark	Status	—	—	20	Self
35	Zen Headbutt	Psychic	Physical	80	90	15	Normal
40	Trick Room	Psychic	Status	—	—	5	Both Sides
45	Psychic	Psychic	Special	90	100	10	Normal
50	Instruct	Psychic	Status	—	—	15	Normal
55	Foul Play	Dark	Physical	95	100	15	Normal
60	Future Sight	Psychic	Special	120	100	10	Normal

TUTOR MOVES

NAME	TYPE	KIND	POW.	ACC.	PP	RANGE

TM MOVES

NO.	NAME	TYPE	KIND	POW.	ACC.	PP	RANGE
TM00	Mega Punch	Normal	Physical	80	85	20	Normal
TM01	Mega Kick	Normal	Physical	120	75	5	Normal
TM08	Hyper Beam	Normal	Special	150	90	5	Normal
TM09	Giga Impact	Normal	Physical	150	90	5	Normal
TM17	Light Screen	Psychic	Status	—	—	30	Your Side
TM18	Reflect	Psychic	Status	—	—	20	Your Side
TM19	Safeguard	Normal	Status	—	—	25	Your Side
TM21	Rest	Psychic	Status	—	—	10	Self
TM22	Rock Slide	Rock	Physical	75	90	10	Many Others
TM24	Snore	Normal	Special	50	100	15	Normal
TM25	Protect	Normal	Status	—	—	10	Self
TM31	Attract	Normal	Status	—	100	15	Normal
TM33	Rain Dance	Water	Status	—	—	5	Both Sides
TM34	Sunny Day	Fire	Status	—	—	5	Both Sides
TM39	Facade	Normal	Physical	70	100	20	Normal
TM43	Brick Break	Fighting	Physical	75	100	15	Normal
TM44	Imprison	Psychic	Status	—	—	10	Self
TM57	Payback	Dark	Physical	50	100	10	Normal
TM59	Fling	Dark	Physical	—	100	10	Normal
TM70	Trick Room	Psychic	Status	—	—	5	Both Sides
TM71	Wonder Room	Psychic	Status	—	—	10	Both Sides
TM72	Magic Room	Psychic	Status	—	—	10	Both Sides
TM76	Round	Normal	Special	60	100	15	Normal
TM81	Bulldoze	Ground	Physical	60	100	20	All Others
TM91	Psychic Terrain	Psychic	Status	—	—	10	Both Sides
TM97	Brutal Swing	Dark	Physical	60	100	20	All Others

TR MOVES

NAME	TYPE	KIND	POW.	ACC.	PP	RANGE
TR08 Thunderbolt	Electric	Special	90	100	15	Normal
TR09 Thunder	Electric	Special	110	70	10	Normal
TR10 Earthquake	Ground	Physical	100	100	10	All Others
TR11 Psychic	Psychic	Special	90	100	10	Normal
TR20 Substitute	Normal	Status	—	—	10	Self
TR25 Psyshock	Psychic	Special	80	100	10	Normal
TR26 Endure	Normal	Status	—	—	10	Self
TR27 Sleep Talk	Normal	Status	—	—	10	Self
TR30 Encore	Normal	Status	—	100	5	Normal
TR33 Shadow Ball	Ghost	Special	80	100	15	Normal
TR34 Future Sight	Psychic	Special	120	100	10	Normal
TR37 Taunt	Dark	Status	—	100	20	Normal
TR38 Trick	Psychic	Status	—	100	10	Normal
TR49 Calm Mind	Psychic	Status	—	—	20	Self
TR64 Focus Blast	Fighting	Special	120	70	5	Normal
TR65 Energy Ball	Grass	Special	90	100	10	Normal
TR68 Nasty Plot	Dark	Status	—	—	20	Self
TR69 Zen Headbutt	Psychic	Physical	80	90	15	Normal
TR81 Foul Play	Dark	Physical	95	100	15	Normal
TR82 Stored Power	Psychic	Special	20	100	10	Normal
TR83 Ally Switch	Psychic	Status	—	—	15	Self
TR85 Work Up	Normal	Status	—	—	30	Self

EVOLUTION MOVES

NAME	TYPE	KIND	POW.	ACC.	PP	RANGE

EGG MOVES

NAME	TYPE	KIND	POW.	ACC.	PP	RANGE
Dream Eater	Psychic	Special	100	100	15	Normal
Extrasensory	Psychic	Special	80	100	20	Normal
Last Resort	Normal	Physical	140	100	5	Normal
Yawn	Normal	Status	—	—	10	Normal

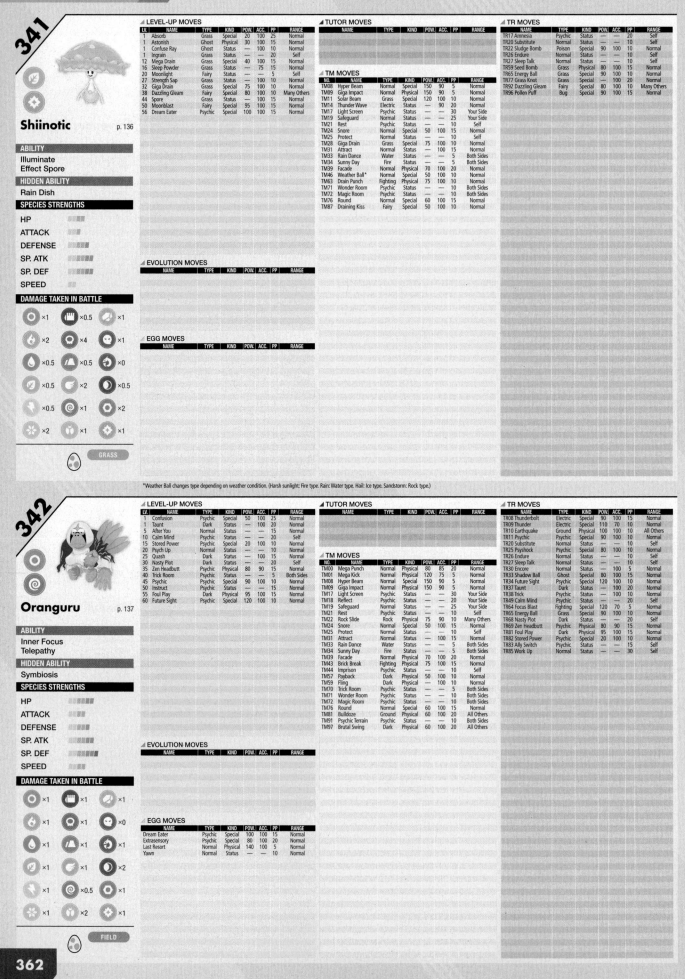

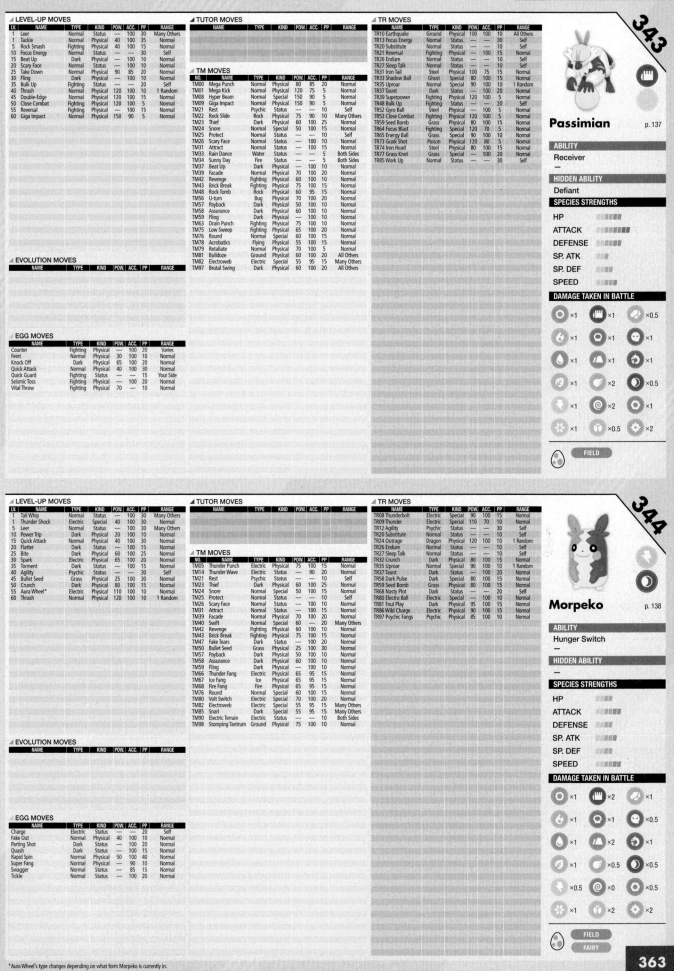

343 — Passimian

LEVEL-UP MOVES

LV.	NAME	TYPE	KIND	POW.	ACC.	PP	RANGE
1	Leer	Normal	Status	—	100	30	Many Others
1	Tackle	Normal	Physical	40	100	35	Normal
5	Rock Smash	Fighting	Physical	40	100	15	Normal
10	Focus Energy	Normal	Status	—	—	30	Self
15	Beat Up	Dark	Physical	—	100	10	Normal
20	Scary Face	Normal	Status	—	100	10	Normal
25	Take Down	Normal	Physical	90	85	20	Normal
30	Fling	Dark	Physical	—	100	10	Normal
35	Bulk Up	Fighting	Status	—	—	20	Self
40	Thrash	Normal	Physical	120	100	10	1 Random
45	Double-Edge	Normal	Physical	120	100	15	Normal
50	Close Combat	Fighting	Physical	120	100	5	Normal
55	Reversal	Fighting	Physical	—	100	15	Normal
60	Giga Impact	Normal	Physical	150	90	5	Normal

EVOLUTION MOVES

NAME	TYPE	KIND	POW.	ACC.	PP	RANGE

EGG MOVES

NAME	TYPE	KIND	POW.	ACC.	PP	RANGE
Counter	Fighting	Physical	—	100	20	Varies
Feint	Normal	Physical	30	100	10	Normal
Knock Off	Dark	Physical	65	100	20	Normal
Quick Attack	Normal	Physical	40	100	30	Normal
Quick Guard	Fighting	Status	—	—	15	Your Side
Seismic Toss	Fighting	Physical	—	100	20	Normal
Vital Throw	Fighting	Physical	70	—	10	Normal

TUTOR MOVES

NAME	TYPE	KIND	POW.	ACC.	PP	RANGE

TM MOVES

NO.	NAME	TYPE	KIND	POW.	ACC.	PP	RANGE
TM00	Mega Punch	Normal	Physical	80	85	20	Normal
TM01	Mega Kick	Normal	Physical	120	75	5	Normal
TM08	Hyper Beam	Normal	Special	150	90	5	Normal
TM09	Giga Impact	Normal	Physical	150	90	5	Normal
TM21	Rest	Psychic	Status	—	—	10	Self
TM22	Rock Slide	Rock	Physical	75	90	10	Many Others
TM23	Thief	Dark	Physical	60	100	25	Normal
TM24	Snore	Normal	Special	50	100	15	Normal
TM25	Protect	Normal	Status	—	—	10	Self
TM26	Scary Face	Normal	Status	—	100	10	Normal
TM31	Attract	Normal	Status	—	100	15	Normal
TM33	Rain Dance	Water	Status	—	—	5	Both Sides
TM34	Sunny Day	Fire	Status	—	—	5	Both Sides
TM37	Beat Up	Dark	Physical	—	100	10	Normal
TM39	Facade	Normal	Physical	70	100	20	Normal
TM42	Revenge	Fighting	Physical	60	100	10	Normal
TM43	Brick Break	Fighting	Physical	75	100	15	Normal
TM48	Rock Tomb	Rock	Physical	60	95	15	Normal
TM56	U-turn	Bug	Physical	70	100	20	Normal
TM57	Payback	Dark	Physical	50	100	10	Normal
TM58	Assurance	Dark	Physical	60	100	10	Normal
TM59	Fling	Dark	Physical	—	100	10	Normal
TM63	Drain Punch	Fighting	Physical	75	100	10	Normal
TM75	Low Sweep	Fighting	Physical	65	100	20	Normal
TM76	Round	Normal	Special	60	100	15	Normal
TM78	Acrobatics	Flying	Physical	55	100	15	Normal
TM79	Retaliate	Normal	Physical	70	100	5	Normal
TM81	Bulldoze	Ground	Physical	60	100	20	All Others
TM82	Electroweb	Electric	Special	55	95	15	Many Others
TM97	Brutal Swing	Dark	Physical	60	100	20	All Others

TR MOVES

NO.	NAME	TYPE	KIND	POW.	ACC.	PP	RANGE
TR10	Earthquake	Ground	Physical	100	100	10	All Others
TR13	Focus Energy	Normal	Status	—	—	30	Self
TR20	Substitute	Normal	Status	—	—	10	Self
TR21	Reversal	Fighting	Physical	—	100	15	Normal
TR26	Endure	Normal	Status	—	—	10	Self
TR27	Sleep Talk	Normal	Status	—	—	10	Self
TR31	Iron Tail	Steel	Physical	100	75	15	Normal
TR33	Shadow Ball	Ghost	Special	80	100	15	Normal
TR35	Uproar	Normal	Special	90	100	10	1 Random
TR37	Taunt	Dark	Status	—	100	20	Normal
TR39	Superpower	Fighting	Physical	120	100	5	Normal
TR48	Bulk Up	Fighting	Status	—	—	20	Self
TR52	Gyro Ball	Steel	Physical	—	100	5	Normal
TR53	Close Combat	Fighting	Physical	120	100	5	Normal
TR59	Seed Bomb	Grass	Physical	80	100	15	Normal
TR64	Focus Blast	Fighting	Special	120	70	5	Normal
TR65	Energy Ball	Grass	Special	90	100	10	Normal
TR73	Gunk Shot	Poison	Physical	120	80	5	Normal
TR74	Iron Head	Steel	Physical	80	100	15	Normal
TR77	Grass Knot	Grass	Special	—	100	20	Normal
TR85	Work Up	Normal	Status	—	—	30	Self

Passimian p. 137

ABILITY
Receiver
—

HIDDEN ABILITY
Defiant

SPECIES STRENGTHS
HP
ATTACK
DEFENSE
SP. ATK
SP. DEF
SPEED

DAMAGE TAKEN IN BATTLE

×1 | ×1 | ×0.5
×1 | ×1 | ×1
×1 | ×1 | ×1
×1 | ×2 | ×0.5
×1 | ×2 | ×1
×1 | ×0.5 | ×2

FIELD

---

344 — Morpeko

LEVEL-UP MOVES

LV.	NAME	TYPE	KIND	POW.	ACC.	PP	RANGE
1	Tail Whip	Normal	Status	—	100	30	Many Others
1	Thunder Shock	Electric	Special	40	100	30	Normal
5	Leer	Normal	Status	—	100	30	Many Others
10	Power Trip	Dark	Physical	20	100	10	Normal
15	Quick Attack	Normal	Physical	40	100	30	Normal
20	Flatter	Dark	Status	—	100	15	Normal
25	Bite	Dark	Physical	60	100	25	Normal
30	Spark	Electric	Physical	65	100	20	Normal
35	Torment	Dark	Status	—	100	15	Normal
40	Agility	Psychic	Status	—	—	30	Self
45	Bullet Seed	Grass	Physical	25	100	30	Normal
50	Crunch	Dark	Physical	80	100	15	Normal
55	Aura Wheel*	Electric	Physical	110	100	10	Normal
60	Thrash	Normal	Physical	120	100	10	1 Random

EVOLUTION MOVES

NAME	TYPE	KIND	POW.	ACC.	PP	RANGE

EGG MOVES

NAME	TYPE	KIND	POW.	ACC.	PP	RANGE
Charge	Electric	Status	—	—	20	Self
Fake Out	Normal	Physical	40	100	10	Normal
Parting Shot	Dark	Status	—	100	20	Normal
Quash	Dark	Status	—	100	15	Normal
Rapid Spin	Normal	Physical	50	100	40	Normal
Super Fang	Normal	Physical	—	90	10	Normal
Swagger	Normal	Status	—	85	15	Normal
Tickle	Normal	Status	—	100	20	Normal

TUTOR MOVES

NAME	TYPE	KIND	POW.	ACC.	PP	RANGE

TM MOVES

NO.	NAME	TYPE	KIND	POW.	ACC.	PP	RANGE
TM05	Thunder Punch	Electric	Physical	75	100	15	Normal
TM14	Thunder Wave	Electric	Status	—	90	20	Normal
TM21	Rest	Psychic	Status	—	—	10	Self
TM23	Thief	Dark	Physical	60	100	25	Normal
TM24	Snore	Normal	Special	50	100	15	Normal
TM25	Protect	Normal	Status	—	—	10	Self
TM26	Scary Face	Normal	Status	—	100	10	Normal
TM31	Attract	Normal	Status	—	100	15	Normal
TM39	Facade	Normal	Physical	70	100	20	Normal
TM40	Swift	Normal	Special	60	—	20	Many Others
TM42	Revenge	Fighting	Physical	60	100	10	Normal
TM43	Brick Break	Fighting	Physical	75	100	15	Normal
TM47	Fake Tears	Dark	Status	—	100	20	Normal
TM50	Bullet Seed	Grass	Physical	25	100	30	Normal
TM57	Payback	Dark	Physical	50	100	10	Normal
TM58	Assurance	Dark	Physical	60	100	10	Normal
TM59	Fling	Dark	Physical	—	100	10	Normal
TM66	Thunder Fang	Electric	Physical	65	95	15	Normal
TM67	Ice Fang	Ice	Physical	65	95	15	Normal
TM68	Fire Fang	Fire	Physical	65	95	15	Normal
TM76	Round	Normal	Special	60	100	15	Normal
TM80	Volt Switch	Electric	Special	70	100	20	Normal
TM82	Electroweb	Electric	Special	55	95	15	Many Others
TM85	Snarl	Dark	Special	55	95	15	Many Others
TM90	Electric Terrain	Electric	Status	—	—	10	Both Sides
TM98	Stomping Tantrum	Ground	Physical	75	100	10	Normal

TR MOVES

NO.	NAME	TYPE	KIND	POW.	ACC.	PP	RANGE
TR08	Thunderbolt	Electric	Special	90	100	15	Normal
TR09	Thunder	Electric	Special	110	70	10	Normal
TR12	Agility	Psychic	Status	—	—	30	Self
TR20	Substitute	Normal	Status	—	—	10	Self
TR24	Outrage	Dragon	Physical	120	100	10	1 Random
TR26	Endure	Normal	Status	—	—	10	Self
TR27	Sleep Talk	Normal	Status	—	—	10	Self
TR32	Crunch	Dark	Physical	80	100	15	Normal
TR35	Uproar	Normal	Special	90	100	10	1 Random
TR37	Taunt	Dark	Status	—	100	20	Normal
TR58	Dark Pulse	Dark	Special	80	100	15	Normal
TR68	Nasty Plot	Dark	Status	—	—	20	Self
TR80	Electro Ball	Electric	Special	—	100	10	Normal
TR81	Foul Play	Dark	Physical	95	100	15	Normal
TR86	Wild Charge	Electric	Physical	90	100	15	Normal
TR97	Psychic Fangs	Psychic	Physical	85	100	10	Normal

Morpeko p. 138

ABILITY
Hunger Switch
—

HIDDEN ABILITY
—

SPECIES STRENGTHS
HP
ATTACK
DEFENSE
SP. ATK
SP. DEF
SPEED

DAMAGE TAKEN IN BATTLE

×1 | ×2 | ×1
×1 | ×1 | ×0.5
×1 | ×2 | ×1
×0.5 | ×0.5 | ×0.5
×0.5 | ×0 | ×0.5
×1 | ×2 | ×2

FIELD
FAIRY

*Aura Wheel's type changes depending on what form Morpeko is currently in.

345

Falinks p. 138

ABILITY
Battle Armor
—

HIDDEN ABILITY
Defiant

SPECIES STRENGTHS
- HP
- ATTACK
- DEFENSE
- SP. ATK
- SP. DEF
- SPEED

DAMAGE TAKEN IN BATTLE
×1	×1	×0.5
×1	×1	×1
×1	×1	×1
×1	×2	×0.5
×1	×2	×1
×1	×0.5	×2

FAIRY
MINERAL

LEVEL-UP MOVES
LV.	NAME	TYPE	KIND	POW.	ACC.	PP	RANGE
1	Protect	Normal	Status	—	—	10	Self
1	Tackle	Normal	Physical	40	100	35	Normal
5	Rock Smash	Fighting	Physical	40	100	15	Normal
10	Focus Energy	Normal	Status	—	—	30	Self
15	Headbutt	Normal	Physical	70	100	15	Normal
20	Bulk Up	Fighting	Status	—	—	20	Self
25	Endure	Normal	Status	—	—	10	Self
30	Reversal	Fighting	Physical	—	100	15	Normal
35	First Impression	Bug	Physical	90	100	10	Normal
40	No Retreat	Fighting	Status	—	—	5	Self
45	Iron Defense	Steel	Status	—	—	15	Self
50	Close Combat	Fighting	Physical	120	100	5	Normal
55	Megahorn	Bug	Physical	120	85	10	Normal
60	Counter	Fighting	Physical	—	100	20	Varies

TUTOR MOVES
NAME	TYPE	KIND	POW.	ACC.	PP	RANGE

TM MOVES
NO.	NAME	TYPE	KIND	POW.	ACC.	PP	RANGE
TM08	Hyper Beam	Normal	Special	150	90	5	Normal
TM09	Giga Impact	Normal	Physical	150	90	5	Normal
TM16	Screech	Normal	Status	—	85	40	Normal
TM21	Rest	Psychic	Status	—	—	10	Self
TM22	Rock Slide	Rock	Physical	75	90	10	Many Others
TM24	Snore	Normal	Special	50	100	15	Normal
TM25	Protect	Normal	Status	—	—	10	Self
TM37	Beat Up	Dark	Special	—	100	10	Normal
TM39	Facade	Normal	Physical	70	100	20	Normal
TM41	Helping Hand	Normal	Status	—	—	20	1 Ally
TM42	Revenge	Fighting	Physical	60	100	10	Normal
TM43	Brick Break	Fighting	Physical	75	100	15	Normal
TM48	Rock Tomb	Rock	Physical	60	95	15	Normal
TM57	Payback	Dark	Physical	50	100	10	Normal
TM58	Assurance	Dark	Physical	60	100	10	Normal
TM76	Round	Normal	Special	60	100	15	Normal
TM79	Retaliate	Normal	Physical	70	100	5	Normal
TM94	False Swipe	Normal	Physical	40	100	40	Normal
TM96	Smart Strike	Steel	Physical	70	—	10	Normal

EVOLUTION MOVES
NAME	TYPE	KIND	POW.	ACC.	PP	RANGE

EGG MOVES
NAME	TYPE	KIND	POW.	ACC.	PP	RANGE

TR MOVES
NAME	TYPE	KIND	POW.	ACC.	PP	RANGE
TR00 Swords Dance	Normal	Status	—	—	20	Self
TR12 Agility	Psychic	Status	—	—	30	Self
TR13 Focus Energy	Normal	Status	—	—	30	Self
TR20 Substitute	Normal	Status	—	—	10	Self
TR21 Reversal	Fighting	Physical	—	100	15	Normal
TR26 Endure	Normal	Status	—	—	10	Self
TR27 Sleep Talk	Normal	Status	—	—	10	Self
TR28 Megahorn	Bug	Physical	120	85	10	Normal
TR39 Superpower	Fighting	Physical	120	100	5	Normal
TR46 Iron Defense	Steel	Status	—	—	15	Self
TR48 Bulk Up	Fighting	Status	—	—	20	Self
TR53 Close Combat	Fighting	Physical	120	100	5	Normal
TR57 Poison Jab	Poison	Physical	80	100	20	Normal
TR64 Focus Blast	Fighting	Special	120	70	5	Normal
TR69 Zen Headbutt	Psychic	Physical	80	90	15	Normal
TR74 Iron Head	Steel	Physical	80	100	15	Normal
TR95 Throat Chop	Dark	Physical	80	100	15	Normal

346

Drampa p. 139

ABILITY
Berserk
Sap Sipper

HIDDEN ABILITY
Cloud Nine

SPECIES STRENGTHS
- HP
- ATTACK
- DEFENSE
- SP. ATK
- SP. DEF
- SPEED

DAMAGE TAKEN IN BATTLE
×1	×2	×1
×0.5	×1	×0
×0.5	×1	×2
×0.5	×1	×1
×0.5	×1	×1
×2	×1	×2

MONSTER
DRAGON

LEVEL-UP MOVES
LV.	NAME	TYPE	KIND	POW.	ACC.	PP	RANGE
1	Echoed Voice	Normal	Special	40	100	15	Normal
1	Play Nice	Normal	Status	—	—	20	Normal
5	Twister	Dragon	Special	40	100	20	Many Others
7	Protect	Normal	Status	—	—	10	Self
15	Glare	Normal	Status	—	100	30	Normal
20	Safeguard	Normal	Status	—	—	25	Your Side
25	Dragon Breath	Dragon	Special	60	100	20	Normal
30	Extrasensory	Psychic	Special	80	100	20	Normal
35	Dragon Pulse	Dragon	Special	85	100	10	Normal
40	Light Screen	Psychic	Status	—	—	30	Your Side
45	Fly	Flying	Physical	90	95	15	Normal
50	Hyper Voice	Normal	Special	90	100	10	Many Others
55	Outrage	Dragon	Physical	120	100	10	1 Random

TUTOR MOVES
NAME	TYPE	KIND	POW.	ACC.	PP	RANGE
Draco Meteor	Dragon	Special	130	90	5	Normal

TM MOVES
NO.	NAME	TYPE	KIND	POW.	ACC.	PP	RANGE
TM06	Fly	Flying	Physical	90	95	15	Normal
TM08	Hyper Beam	Normal	Special	150	90	5	Normal
TM09	Giga Impact	Normal	Physical	150	90	5	Normal
TM11	Solar Beam	Grass	Special	120	100	10	Normal
TM14	Thunder Wave	Electric	Status	—	90	20	Normal
TM17	Light Screen	Psychic	Status	—	—	30	Your Side
TM19	Safeguard	Normal	Status	—	—	25	Your Side
TM21	Rest	Psychic	Status	—	—	10	Self
TM22	Rock Slide	Rock	Physical	75	90	10	Many Others
TM24	Snore	Normal	Special	50	100	15	Normal
TM25	Protect	Normal	Status	—	—	10	Self
TM27	Icy Wind	Ice	Special	55	95	15	Many Others
TM30	Steel Wing	Steel	Physical	70	90	25	Normal
TM31	Attract	Normal	Status	—	100	15	Normal
TM33	Rain Dance	Water	Status	—	—	5	Both Sides
TM34	Sunny Day	Fire	Status	—	—	5	Both Sides
TM39	Facade	Normal	Physical	70	100	20	Normal
TM40	Swift	Normal	Special	60	—	20	Many Others
TM41	Helping Hand	Normal	Status	—	—	20	1 Ally
TM59	Fling	Dark	Physical	—	100	10	Normal
TM65	Shadow Claw	Ghost	Physical	70	100	15	Normal
TM76	Round	Normal	Special	60	100	15	Normal
TM81	Bulldoze	Ground	Physical	60	100	20	All Others
TM85	Snarl	Dark	Special	55	95	15	Many Others
TM98	Stomping Tantrum	Ground	Physical	75	100	10	Normal
TM99	Breaking Swipe	Dragon	Physical	60	100	15	Many Others

EVOLUTION MOVES
NAME	TYPE	KIND	POW.	ACC.	PP	RANGE

EGG MOVES
NAME	TYPE	KIND	POW.	ACC.	PP	RANGE
Dragon Rush	Dragon	Physical	100	75	10	Normal
Mist	Ice	Status	—	—	30	Your Side
Tickle	Normal	Status	—	100	20	Normal

TR MOVES
NAME	TYPE	KIND	POW.	ACC.	PP	RANGE
TR02 Flamethrower	Fire	Special	90	100	15	Normal
TR03 Hydro Pump	Water	Special	110	80	5	Normal
TR04 Surf	Water	Special	90	100	15	All Others
TR05 Ice Beam	Ice	Special	90	100	10	Normal
TR06 Blizzard	Ice	Special	110	70	5	Many Others
TR08 Thunderbolt	Electric	Special	90	100	15	Normal
TR09 Thunder	Electric	Special	110	70	10	Normal
TR10 Earthquake	Ground	Physical	100	100	10	All Others
TR15 Fire Blast	Fire	Special	110	85	5	Normal
TR17 Amnesia	Psychic	Status	—	—	20	Self
TR20 Substitute	Normal	Status	—	—	10	Self
TR24 Outrage	Dragon	Physical	120	100	10	1 Random
TR26 Endure	Normal	Status	—	—	10	Self
TR27 Sleep Talk	Normal	Status	—	—	10	Self
TR33 Shadow Ball	Ghost	Special	80	100	15	Normal
TR35 Uproar	Normal	Special	90	100	10	1 Random
TR36 Heat Wave	Fire	Special	95	90	10	Many Others
TR39 Superpower	Fighting	Physical	120	100	5	Normal
TR42 Hyper Voice	Normal	Special	90	100	10	Many Others
TR47 Dragon Claw	Dragon	Physical	80	100	15	Normal
TR49 Calm Mind	Psychic	Status	—	—	20	Self
TR51 Dragon Dance	Dragon	Status	—	—	20	Self
TR62 Dragon Pulse	Dragon	Special	85	100	10	Normal
TR64 Focus Blast	Fighting	Special	120	70	5	Normal
TR65 Energy Ball	Grass	Special	90	100	10	Normal
TR77 Grass Knot	Grass	Special	—	100	20	Normal
TR85 Work Up	Normal	Status	—	—	30	Self
TR89 Hurricane	Flying	Special	110	70	10	Normal
TR90 Play Rough	Fairy	Physical	90	90	10	Normal

347 — Turtonator (p. 139)

LEVEL-UP MOVES

LV.	NAME	TYPE	KIND	POW.	ACC.	PP	RANGE
1	Smog	Poison	Special	30	70	20	Normal
1	Tackle	Normal	Physical	40	100	35	Normal
4	Ember	Fire	Special	40	100	25	Normal
8	Protect	Normal	Status	—	—	10	Self
12	Endure	Normal	Status	—	—	10	Self
16	Flail	Normal	Physical	—	100	15	Normal
20	Incinerate	Fire	Special	60	100	15	Many Others
24	Iron Defense	Steel	Status	—	—	15	Self
28	Dragon Pulse	Dragon	Special	85	100	10	Normal
32	Body Slam	Normal	Physical	85	100	15	Normal
36	Flamethrower	Fire	Special	90	100	15	Normal
40	Shell Trap	Fire	Special	150	100	5	Many Others
44	Shell Smash	Normal	Status	—	—	15	Self
48	Overheat	Fire	Special	130	90	5	Normal
52	Explosion	Normal	Physical	250	100	5	All Others

EVOLUTION MOVES

NAME	TYPE	KIND	POW.	ACC.	PP	RANGE

EGG MOVES

NAME	TYPE	KIND	POW.	ACC.	PP	RANGE
Curse	Ghost	Status	—	—	10	Varies
Head Smash	Rock	Physical	150	80	5	Normal
Rapid Spin	Normal	Physical	50	100	40	Normal
Wide Guard	Rock	Status	—	—	10	Your Side

TUTOR MOVES

NAME	TYPE	KIND	POW.	ACC.	PP	RANGE
Draco Meteor	Dragon	Special	130	90	5	Normal

TM MOVES

NO.	NAME	TYPE	KIND	POW.	ACC.	PP	RANGE
TM00	Mega Punch	Normal	Physical	80	85	20	Normal
TM01	Mega Kick	Normal	Physical	120	75	5	Normal
TM08	Hyper Beam	Normal	Special	150	90	5	Normal
TM09	Giga Impact	Normal	Physical	150	90	5	Normal
TM11	Solar Beam	Grass	Special	120	100	10	Normal
TM13	Fire Spin	Fire	Special	35	85	15	Normal
TM21	Rest	Psychic	Status	—	—	10	Self
TM24	Snore	Normal	Special	50	100	15	Normal
TM25	Protect	Normal	Status	—	—	10	Self
TM31	Attract	Normal	Status	—	100	15	Normal
TM34	Sunny Day	Fire	Status	—	—	5	Both Sides
TM38	Will-O-Wisp	Fire	Status	—	85	15	Normal
TM39	Facade	Normal	Physical	70	100	20	Normal
TM42	Revenge	Fighting	Physical	60	100	10	Normal
TM48	Rock Tomb	Rock	Physical	60	95	15	Normal
TM57	Payback	Dark	Physical	50	100	10	Normal
TM59	Fling	Dark	Physical	—	100	10	Normal
TM74	Venoshock	Poison	Special	65	100	10	Normal
TM76	Round	Normal	Special	60	100	15	Normal
TM81	Bulldoze	Ground	Physical	60	100	20	All Others
TM97	Brutal Swing	Dark	Physical	60	100	20	All Others
TM98	Stomping Tantrum	Ground	Physical	75	100	10	Normal

TR MOVES

NO.	NAME	TYPE	KIND	POW.	ACC.	PP	RANGE
TR01	Body Slam	Normal	Physical	85	100	15	Normal
TR02	Flamethrower	Fire	Special	90	100	15	Normal
TR10	Earthquake	Ground	Physical	100	100	10	All Others
TR15	Fire Blast	Fire	Special	110	85	5	Normal
TR20	Substitute	Normal	Status	—	—	10	Self
TR24	Outrage	Dragon	Physical	120	100	10	1 Random
TR26	Endure	Normal	Status	—	—	10	Self
TR27	Sleep Talk	Normal	Status	—	—	10	Self
TR31	Iron Tail	Steel	Physical	100	75	15	Normal
TR35	Uproar	Normal	Special	90	100	10	1 Random
TR36	Heat Wave	Fire	Special	95	90	10	Many Others
TR37	Taunt	Dark	Status	—	100	20	Normal
TR42	Overheat	Fire	Special	130	90	5	Normal
TR46	Iron Defense	Steel	Status	—	—	15	Self
TR47	Dragon Claw	Dragon	Physical	80	100	15	Normal
TR48	Bulk Up	Fighting	Status	—	—	20	Self
TR62	Dragon Pulse	Dragon	Special	85	100	10	Normal
TR64	Focus Blast	Fighting	Special	120	70	5	Normal
TR70	Flash Cannon	Steel	Special	80	100	10	Normal
TR74	Iron Head	Steel	Physical	80	100	15	Normal
TR75	Stone Edge	Rock	Physical	100	80	5	Normal
TR79	Heavy Slam	Steel	Physical	—	100	10	Normal
TR85	Work Up	Normal	Status	—	—	30	Self
TR88	Heat Crash	Fire	Physical	—	100	10	Normal
TR99	Body Press	Fighting	Physical	80	100	10	Normal

Turtonator p. 139

ABILITY
Shell Armor
—

HIDDEN ABILITY
—

SPECIES STRENGTHS
- HP
- ATTACK
- DEFENSE
- SP. ATK
- SP. DEF
- SPEED

DAMAGE TAKEN IN BATTLE

×1	×1	×2
×0.25	×1	×1
×1	×2	×2
×0.25	×1	×1
×0.5		×0.5
×1	×0.5	×1

Egg Groups: MONSTER / DRAGON

---

348 — Togedemaru (p. 139)

LEVEL-UP MOVES

LV.	NAME	TYPE	KIND	POW.	ACC.	PP	RANGE
1	Nuzzle	Electric	Physical	20	100	20	Normal
1	Tackle	Normal	Physical	40	100	35	Normal
5	Defense Curl	Normal	Status	—	—	40	Self
10	Charge	Electric	Status	—	—	20	Self
15	Thunder Shock	Electric	Special	40	100	30	Normal
20	Fell Stinger	Bug	Physical	50	100	25	Normal
25	Spark	Electric	Physical	65	100	20	Normal
30	Pin Missile	Bug	Physical	25	95	20	Normal
35	Magnet Rise	Electric	Status	—	—	10	Self
40	Zing Zap	Electric	Physical	80	100	10	Normal
45	Discharge	Electric	Special	80	100	15	All Others
50	Electric Terrain	Electric	Status	—	—	10	Both Sides
55	Wild Charge	Electric	Physical	90	100	15	Normal
60	Spiky Shield	Grass	Status	—	—	10	Self

EVOLUTION MOVES

NAME	TYPE	KIND	POW.	ACC.	PP	RANGE

EGG MOVES

NAME	TYPE	KIND	POW.	ACC.	PP	RANGE
Disarming Voice	Fairy	Special	40	—	15	Many Others
Fake Out	Normal	Physical	40	100	10	Normal
Flail	Normal	Physical	—	100	15	Normal
Present	Normal	Physical	—	90	15	Normal
Tickle	Normal	Status	—	100	20	Normal
Wish	Normal	Status	—	—	10	Self

TUTOR MOVES

NAME	TYPE	KIND	POW.	ACC.	PP	RANGE
Steel Beam	Steel	Special	140	95	5	Normal

TM MOVES

NO.	NAME	TYPE	KIND	POW.	ACC.	PP	RANGE
TM07	Pin Missile	Bug	Physical	25	95	20	Normal
TM08	Hyper Beam	Normal	Special	150	90	5	Normal
TM09	Giga Impact	Normal	Physical	150	90	5	Normal
TM14	Thunder Wave	Electric	Status	—	90	20	Normal
TM18	Reflect	Psychic	Status	—	—	20	Your Side
TM21	Rest	Psychic	Status	—	—	10	Self
TM23	Thief	Dark	Physical	60	100	25	Normal
TM24	Snore	Normal	Special	50	100	15	Normal
TM25	Protect	Normal	Status	—	—	10	Self
TM31	Attract	Normal	Status	—	100	15	Normal
TM39	Facade	Normal	Physical	70	100	20	Normal
TM40	Swift	Normal	Special	60	—	20	Many Others
TM41	Helping Hand	Normal	Status	—	—	20	1 Ally
TM52	Bounce	Flying	Physical	85	85	5	Normal
TM56	U-turn	Bug	Physical	70	100	20	Normal
TM57	Payback	Dark	Physical	50	100	10	Normal
TM58	Assurance	Dark	Physical	60	100	10	Normal
TM59	Fling	Dark	Physical	—	100	10	Normal
TM76	Round	Normal	Special	60	100	15	Normal
TM80	Volt Switch	Electric	Special	70	100	20	Normal
TM82	Electroweb	Electric	Special	55	95	15	Many Others
TM90	Electric Terrain	Electric	Status	—	—	10	Both Sides
TM93	Eerie Impulse	Electric	Status	—	100	15	Normal

TR MOVES

NO.	NAME	TYPE	KIND	POW.	ACC.	PP	RANGE
TR08	Thunderbolt	Electric	Special	90	100	15	Normal
TR09	Thunder	Electric	Special	110	70	10	Normal
TR12	Agility	Psychic	Status	—	—	30	Self
TR20	Substitute	Normal	Status	—	—	10	Self
TR21	Reversal	Fighting	Physical	—	100	15	Normal
TR26	Endure	Normal	Status	—	—	10	Self
TR27	Sleep Talk	Normal	Status	—	—	10	Self
TR30	Encore	Normal	Status	—	100	5	Normal
TR31	Iron Tail	Steel	Physical	100	75	15	Normal
TR52	Gyro Ball	Steel	Physical	—	100	5	Normal
TR57	Poison Jab	Poison	Physical	80	100	20	Normal
TR69	Zen Headbutt	Psychic	Physical	80	90	15	Normal
TR74	Iron Head	Steel	Physical	80	100	15	Normal
TR77	Grass Knot	Grass	Special	—	100	20	Normal
TR80	Electro Ball	Electric	Special	—	100	10	Normal
TR85	Work Up	Normal	Status	—	—	30	Self
TR86	Wild Charge	Electric	Physical	90	100	15	Normal

Togedemaru p. 139

ABILITY
Iron Barbs
Lightning Rod

HIDDEN ABILITY
Sturdy

SPECIES STRENGTHS
- HP
- ATTACK
- DEFENSE
- SP. ATK
- SP. DEF
- SPEED

DAMAGE TAKEN IN BATTLE

×0.5	×2	×0.5
×2	×0	×1
×1	×4	×0.5
×0.5	×0.25	×1
×0.5	×0.5	×0.25
×0.5	×0.5	×0.5

Egg Groups: FIELD / FAIRY

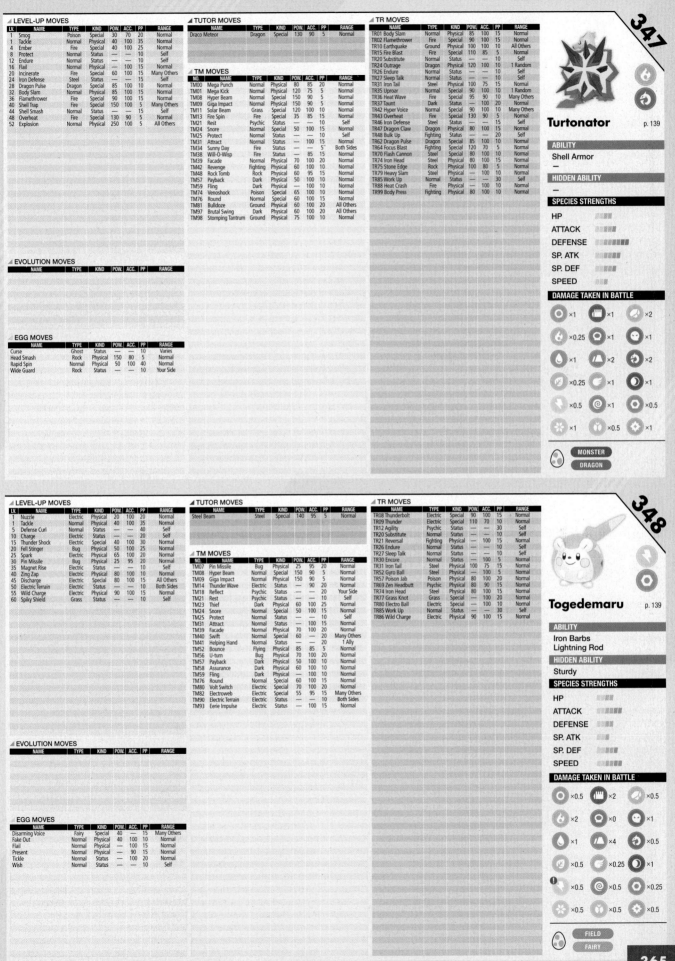

349 Snom — p. 140

ABILITY
Shield Dust
—

HIDDEN ABILITY
Ice Scales

SPECIES STRENGTHS
HP	■■
ATTACK	■■
DEFENSE	■■■
SP. ATK	■■■
SP. DEF	■■
SPEED	■

DAMAGE TAKEN IN BATTLE

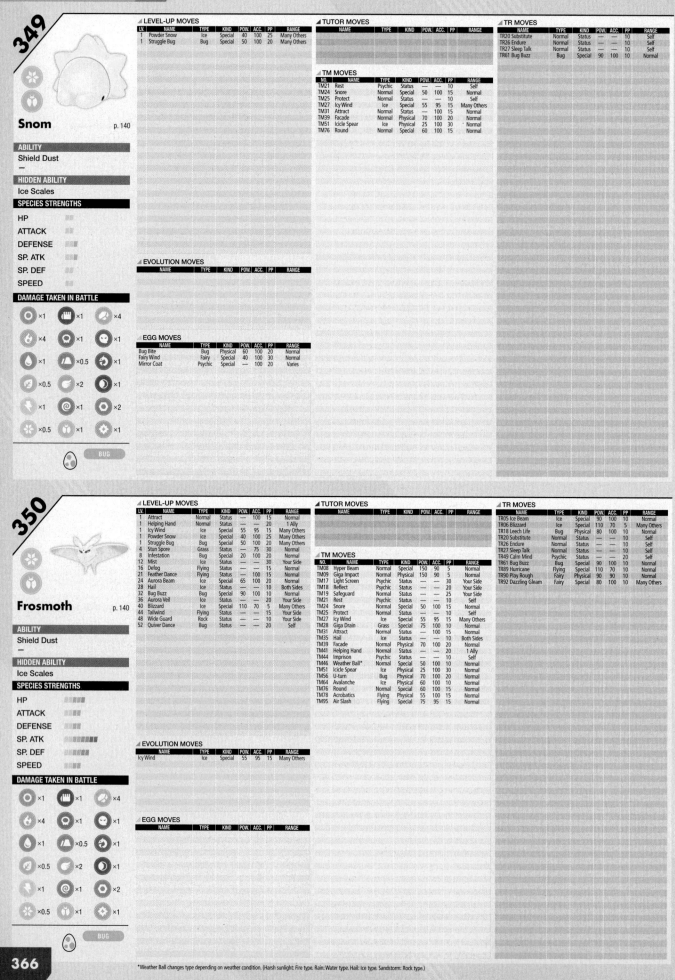

○ ×1	✊ ×1	◢ ×4	◇ ×4	○ ×1	◉ ×1
◇ ×1	⛨ ×0.5	↻ ×1	☇ ×0.5	✋ ×2	◐ ×1
❦ ×1	◎ ×1	◉ ×2	❄ ×0.5	◉ ×1	✦ ×1

BUG

LEVEL-UP MOVES

LV.	NAME	TYPE	KIND	POW.	ACC.	PP	RANGE
1	Powder Snow	Ice	Special	40	100	25	Many Others
1	Struggle Bug	Bug	Special	50	100	20	Many Others

EVOLUTION MOVES

NAME	TYPE	KIND	POW.	ACC.	PP	RANGE

EGG MOVES

NAME	TYPE	KIND	POW.	ACC.	PP	RANGE
Bug Bite	Bug	Physical	60	100	20	Normal
Fairy Wind	Fairy	Special	40	100	30	Normal
Mirror Coat	Psychic	Special	—	100	20	Varies

TUTOR MOVES

NAME	TYPE	KIND	POW.	ACC.	PP	RANGE

TM MOVES

NO.	NAME	TYPE	KIND	POW.	ACC.	PP	RANGE
TM21	Rest	Psychic	Status	—	—	10	Self
TM24	Snore	Normal	Special	50	100	15	Normal
TM25	Protect	Normal	Status	—	—	10	Self
TM27	Icy Wind	Ice	Special	55	95	15	Many Others
TM31	Attract	Normal	Status	—	100	15	Normal
TM39	Facade	Normal	Physical	70	100	20	Normal
TM51	Icicle Spear	Ice	Physical	25	100	30	Normal
TM76	Round	Normal	Special	60	100	15	Normal

TR MOVES

NAME	TYPE	KIND	POW.	ACC.	PP	RANGE
TR20 Substitute	Normal	Status	—	—	10	Self
TR26 Endure	Normal	Status	—	—	10	Self
TR27 Sleep Talk	Normal	Status	—	—	10	Self
TR61 Bug Buzz	Bug	Special	90	100	10	Normal

---

350 Frosmoth — p. 140

ABILITY
Shield Dust
—

HIDDEN ABILITY
Ice Scales

SPECIES STRENGTHS
HP	■■■
ATTACK	■■■
DEFENSE	■■■
SP. ATK	■■■■■■
SP. DEF	■■■
SPEED	■■■

DAMAGE TAKEN IN BATTLE

○ ×1	✊ ×1	◢ ×4	◇ ×4	○ ×1	◉ ×1
◇ ×1	⛨ ×0.5	↻ ×1	☇ ×0.5	✋ ×2	◐ ×1
❦ ×1	◎ ×1	◉ ×2	❄ ×0.5	◉ ×1	✦ ×1

BUG

LEVEL-UP MOVES

LV.	NAME	TYPE	KIND	POW.	ACC.	PP	RANGE
1	Attract	Normal	Status	—	100	15	Normal
1	Helping Hand	Normal	Status	—	—	20	1 Ally
1	Icy Wind	Ice	Special	55	95	15	Many Others
1	Powder Snow	Ice	Special	40	100	25	Many Others
1	Struggle Bug	Bug	Special	50	100	20	Many Others
5	Stun Spore	Grass	Status	—	75	30	Normal
8	Infestation	Bug	Special	20	100	20	Normal
12	Mist	Ice	Status	—	—	30	Your Side
16	Defog	Flying	Status	—	—	15	Normal
21	Feather Dance	Flying	Status	—	100	15	Normal
24	Aurora Beam	Ice	Special	65	100	20	Normal
28	Hail	Ice	Status	—	—	10	Both Sides
32	Bug Buzz	Bug	Special	90	100	10	Normal
36	Aurora Veil	Ice	Status	—	—	20	Your Side
40	Blizzard	Ice	Special	110	70	5	Many Others
44	Tailwind	Flying	Status	—	—	15	Your Side
48	Wide Guard	Rock	Status	—	—	10	Your Side
52	Quiver Dance	Bug	Status	—	—	20	Self

EVOLUTION MOVES

NAME	TYPE	KIND	POW.	ACC.	PP	RANGE
Icy Wind	Ice	Special	55	95	15	Many Others

EGG MOVES

NAME	TYPE	KIND	POW.	ACC.	PP	RANGE

TUTOR MOVES

NAME	TYPE	KIND	POW.	ACC.	PP	RANGE

TM MOVES

NO.	NAME	TYPE	KIND	POW.	ACC.	PP	RANGE
TM08	Hyper Beam	Normal	Special	150	90	5	Normal
TM09	Giga Impact	Normal	Physical	150	90	5	Normal
TM17	Light Screen	Psychic	Status	—	—	30	Your Side
TM18	Reflect	Psychic	Status	—	—	20	Your Side
TM19	Safeguard	Normal	Status	—	—	25	Your Side
TM21	Rest	Psychic	Status	—	—	10	Self
TM24	Snore	Normal	Special	50	100	15	Normal
TM25	Protect	Normal	Status	—	—	10	Self
TM27	Icy Wind	Ice	Special	55	95	15	Many Others
TM28	Giga Drain	Grass	Special	75	100	10	Normal
TM31	Attract	Normal	Status	—	100	15	Normal
TM35	Hail	Ice	Status	—	—	10	Both Sides
TM39	Facade	Normal	Physical	70	100	20	Normal
TM41	Helping Hand	Normal	Status	—	—	20	1 Ally
TM46	Weather Ball*	Normal	Special	50	100	10	Normal
TM51	Icicle Spear	Ice	Physical	25	100	30	Normal
TM56	U-turn	Bug	Physical	70	100	20	Normal
TM64	Avalanche	Ice	Physical	60	100	10	Normal
TM76	Round	Normal	Special	60	100	15	Normal
TM78	Acrobatics	Flying	Physical	55	100	15	Normal
TM95	Air Slash	Flying	Special	75	95	15	Normal

TR MOVES

NAME	TYPE	KIND	POW.	ACC.	PP	RANGE
TR05 Ice Beam	Ice	Special	90	100	10	Normal
TR06 Blizzard	Ice	Special	110	70	5	Many Others
TR18 Leech Life	Bug	Physical	80	100	10	Normal
TR20 Substitute	Normal	Status	—	—	10	Self
TR26 Endure	Normal	Status	—	—	10	Self
TR27 Sleep Talk	Normal	Status	—	—	10	Self
TR49 Calm Mind	Psychic	Status	—	—	20	Self
TR61 Bug Buzz	Bug	Special	90	100	10	Normal
TR89 Hurricane	Flying	Special	110	70	10	Normal
TR90 Play Rough	Fairy	Physical	90	90	10	Normal
TR92 Dazzling Gleam	Fairy	Special	80	100	10	Many Others

*Weather Ball changes type depending on weather condition. (Harsh sunlight: Fire type. Rain: Water type. Hail: Ice type. Sandstorm: Rock type.)

351

LEVEL-UP MOVES

LV.	NAME	TYPE	KIND	POW.	ACC.	PP	RANGE
1	Leer	Normal	Status	—	100	30	Many Others
1	Rock Smash	Fighting	Physical	40	100	15	Normal
5	Feint	Normal	Physical	30	100	10	Normal
10	Bind	Normal	Physical	15	85	20	Normal
15	Detect	Fighting	Status	—	—	5	Self
20	Brick Break	Fighting	Physical	75	100	15	Normal
25	Bulk Up	Fighting	Status	—	—	20	Self
30	Submission	Fighting	Physical	80	80	20	Normal
35	Taunt	Dark	Status	—	100	20	Normal
40	Reversal	Fighting	Physical	—	100	15	Normal
45	Superpower	Fighting	Physical	120	100	5	Normal

EVOLUTION MOVES

NAME	TYPE	KIND	POW.	ACC.	PP	RANGE

EGG MOVES

NAME	TYPE	KIND	POW.	ACC.	PP	RANGE
Circle Throw	Fighting	Physical	60	90	10	Normal
Pain Split	Normal	Status	—	—	20	Normal
Power-Up Punch	Fighting	Physical	40	100	20	Normal
Seismic Toss	Fighting	Physical	—	100	20	Normal
Soak	Water	Status	—	100	20	Normal
Sucker Punch	Dark	Physical	70	100	5	Normal

TUTOR MOVES

NAME	TYPE	KIND	POW.	ACC.	PP	RANGE

TM MOVES

NO.	NAME	TYPE	KIND	POW.	ACC.	PP	RANGE
TM00	Mega Punch	Normal	Physical	80	85	20	Normal
TM04	Ice Punch	Ice	Physical	75	100	15	Normal
TM21	Rest	Psychic	Status	—	—	10	Self
TM24	Snore	Normal	Special	50	100	15	Normal
TM25	Protect	Normal	Status	—	—	10	Self
TM31	Attract	Normal	Status	—	100	15	Normal
TM39	Facade	Normal	Physical	70	100	20	Normal
TM42	Revenge	Fighting	Physical	60	100	10	Normal
TM43	Brick Break	Fighting	Physical	75	100	15	Normal
TM45	Dive	Water	Physical	80	100	10	Normal
TM53	Mud Shot	Ground	Special	55	95	15	Normal
TM55	Brine	Water	Special	65	100	10	Normal
TM57	Payback	Dark	Physical	50	100	10	Normal
TM76	Round	Normal	Special	60	100	15	Normal
TM79	Retaliate	Normal	Physical	70	100	5	Normal

TR MOVES

NAME	TYPE	KIND	POW.	ACC.	PP	RANGE
TR01 Body Slam	Normal	Physical	85	100	15	Normal
TR16 Waterfall	Water	Physical	80	100	15	Normal
TR20 Substitute	Normal	Status	—	—	10	Self
TR21 Reversal	Fighting	Physical	—	100	15	Normal
TR26 Endure	Normal	Status	—	—	10	Self
TR27 Sleep Talk	Normal	Status	—	—	10	Self
TR37 Taunt	Dark	Status	—	100	20	Normal
TR39 Superpower	Fighting	Physical	120	100	5	Normal
TR45 Muddy Water	Water	Special	90	85	10	Many Others
TR48 Bulk Up	Fighting	Status	—	—	20	Self
TR53 Close Combat	Fighting	Physical	120	100	5	Normal
TR64 Focus Blast	Fighting	Special	120	70	5	Normal
TR85 Work Up	Normal	Status	—	—	30	Self
TR98 Liquidation	Water	Physical	85	100	10	Normal

Clobbopus p. 140

ABILITY
Limber
—

HIDDEN ABILITY
Technician

SPECIES STRENGTHS
HP
ATTACK
DEFENSE
SP. ATK
SP. DEF
SPEED

DAMAGE TAKEN IN BATTLE
×1 ×1 ×0.5
×1 ×1 ×1
×1 ×1 ×1
×1 ×2 ×0.5
×1 ×2 ×1
×1 ×0.5 ×2

WATER 1
HUMANLIKE

352

LEVEL-UP MOVES

LV.	NAME	TYPE	KIND	POW.	ACC.	PP	RANGE
1	Bind	Normal	Physical	15	85	20	Normal
1	Feint	Normal	Physical	30	100	10	Normal
1	Leer	Normal	Status	—	100	30	Many Others
1	Octazooka	Water	Special	65	85	10	Normal
1	Octolock	Fighting	Status	—	100	15	Normal
1	Rock Smash	Fighting	Physical	40	100	15	Normal
15	Detect	Fighting	Status	—	—	5	Self
20	Brick Break	Fighting	Physical	75	100	15	Normal
25	Bulk Up	Fighting	Status	—	—	20	Self
30	Submission	Fighting	Physical	80	80	20	Normal
35	Taunt	Dark	Status	—	100	20	Normal
40	Reversal	Fighting	Physical	—	100	15	Normal
45	Superpower	Fighting	Physical	120	100	5	Normal
50	Topsy-Turvy	Dark	Status	—	—	20	Normal

EVOLUTION MOVES

NAME	TYPE	KIND	POW.	ACC.	PP	RANGE
Octolock	Fighting	Status	—	100	15	Normal

EGG MOVES

NAME	TYPE	KIND	POW.	ACC.	PP	RANGE

TUTOR MOVES

NAME	TYPE	KIND	POW.	ACC.	PP	RANGE

TM MOVES

NO.	NAME	TYPE	KIND	POW.	ACC.	PP	RANGE
TM00	Mega Punch	Normal	Physical	80	85	20	Normal
TM04	Ice Punch	Ice	Physical	75	100	15	Normal
TM08	Hyper Beam	Normal	Special	150	90	5	Normal
TM09	Giga Impact	Normal	Physical	150	90	5	Normal
TM15	Dig	Ground	Physical	80	100	10	Normal
TM21	Rest	Psychic	Status	—	—	10	Self
TM24	Snore	Normal	Special	50	100	15	Normal
TM25	Protect	Normal	Status	—	—	10	Self
TM26	Scary Face	Normal	Status	—	100	10	Normal
TM31	Attract	Normal	Status	—	100	15	Normal
TM36	Whirlpool	Water	Special	35	85	15	Normal
TM39	Facade	Normal	Physical	70	100	20	Normal
TM42	Revenge	Fighting	Physical	60	100	10	Normal
TM43	Brick Break	Fighting	Physical	75	100	15	Normal
TM45	Dive	Water	Physical	80	100	10	Normal
TM53	Mud Shot	Ground	Special	55	95	15	Normal
TM55	Brine	Water	Special	65	100	10	Normal
TM57	Payback	Dark	Physical	50	100	10	Normal
TM63	Drain Punch	Fighting	Physical	75	100	10	Normal
TM76	Round	Normal	Special	60	100	15	Normal
TM79	Retaliate	Normal	Physical	70	100	5	Normal
TM97	Brutal Swing	Dark	Physical	60	100	20	All Others
TM98	Stomping Tantrum	Ground	Physical	75	100	10	Normal

TR MOVES

NAME	TYPE	KIND	POW.	ACC.	PP	RANGE
TR01 Body Slam	Normal	Physical	85	100	15	Normal
TR03 Hydro Pump	Water	Special	110	80	5	Normal
TR04 Surf	Water	Special	90	100	15	All Others
TR16 Waterfall	Water	Physical	80	100	15	Normal
TR20 Substitute	Normal	Status	—	—	10	Self
TR21 Reversal	Fighting	Physical	—	100	15	Normal
TR26 Endure	Normal	Status	—	—	10	Self
TR27 Sleep Talk	Normal	Status	—	—	10	Self
TR37 Taunt	Dark	Status	—	100	20	Normal
TR39 Superpower	Fighting	Physical	120	100	5	Normal
TR45 Muddy Water	Water	Special	90	85	10	Many Others
TR48 Bulk Up	Fighting	Status	—	—	20	Self
TR53 Close Combat	Fighting	Physical	120	100	5	Normal
TR64 Focus Blast	Fighting	Special	120	70	5	Normal
TR85 Work Up	Normal	Status	—	—	30	Self
TR98 Liquidation	Water	Physical	85	100	10	Normal

Grapploct p. 140

ABILITY
Limber
—

HIDDEN ABILITY
Technician

SPECIES STRENGTHS
HP
ATTACK
DEFENSE
SP. ATK
SP. DEF
SPEED

DAMAGE TAKEN IN BATTLE
×1 ×1 ×0.5
×1 ×1 ×1
×1 ×1 ×1
×1 ×2 ×0.5
×1 ×2 ×1
×1 ×0.5 ×2

WATER 1
HUMANLIKE

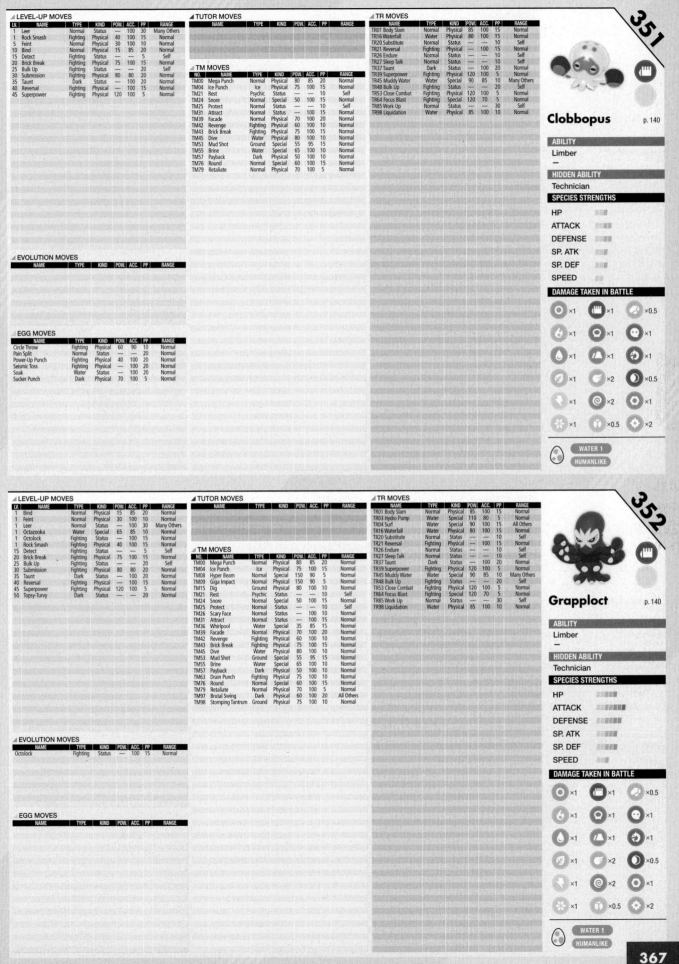

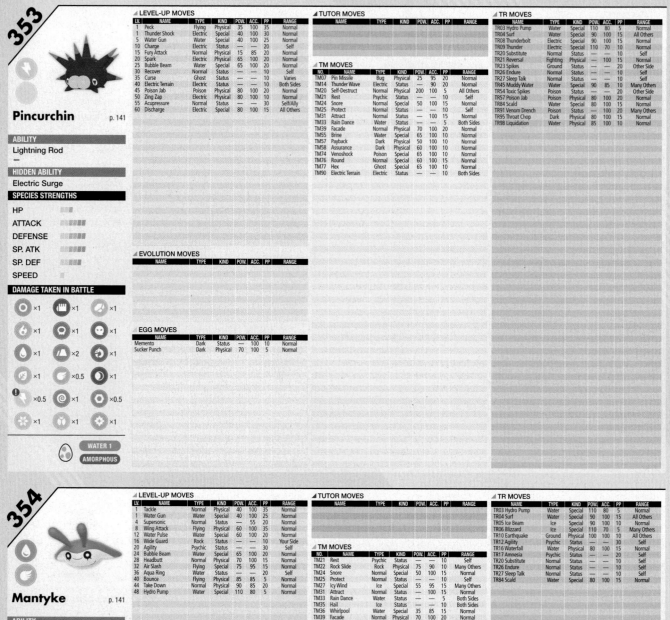

353 Pincurchin p. 141

ABILITY
Lightning Rod
—

HIDDEN ABILITY
Electric Surge

SPECIES STRENGTHS
- HP
- ATTACK
- DEFENSE
- SP. ATK
- SP. DEF
- SPEED

DAMAGE TAKEN IN BATTLE
×1 ×1 ×1
×1 ×1 ×1
×1 ×2 ×1
×1 ×0.5 ×1
×0.5 ×1 ×0.5
×1 ×1 ×1

WATER 1
AMORPHOUS

LEVEL-UP MOVES

LV.	NAME	TYPE	KIND	POW.	ACC.	PP	RANGE
1	Peck	Flying	Physical	35	100	35	Normal
1	Thunder Shock	Electric	Special	40	100	30	Normal
5	Water Gun	Water	Special	40	100	25	Normal
10	Charge	Electric	Status	—	—	20	Self
15	Fury Attack	Normal	Physical	15	85	20	Normal
20	Spark	Electric	Physical	65	100	20	Normal
25	Bubble Beam	Water	Special	65	100	20	Normal
30	Recover	Normal	Status	—	—	10	Self
35	Curse	Ghost	Status	—	—	10	Varies
40	Electric Terrain	Electric	Status	—	—	10	Both Sides
45	Poison Jab	Poison	Physical	80	100	20	Normal
50	Zing Zap	Electric	Physical	80	100	10	Normal
55	Acupressure	Normal	Status	—	—	30	Self/Ally
60	Discharge	Electric	Special	80	100	15	All Others

EVOLUTION MOVES

NAME	TYPE	KIND	POW.	ACC.	PP	RANGE

EGG MOVES

NAME	TYPE	KIND	POW.	ACC.	PP	RANGE
Memento	Dark	Status	—	100	10	Normal
Sucker Punch	Dark	Physical	70	100	5	Normal

TUTOR MOVES

NAME	TYPE	KIND	POW.	ACC.	PP	RANGE

TM MOVES

NO.	NAME	TYPE	KIND	POW.	ACC.	PP	RANGE
TM07	Pin Missile	Bug	Physical	25	95	20	Normal
TM14	Thunder Wave	Electric	Status	—	90	20	Normal
TM20	Self-Destruct	Normal	Physical	200	100	5	All Others
TM21	Rest	Psychic	Status	—	—	10	Self
TM24	Snore	Normal	Special	50	100	15	Normal
TM25	Protect	Normal	Status	—	—	10	Self
TM31	Attract	Normal	Status	—	100	15	Normal
TM33	Rain Dance	Water	Status	—	—	5	Both Sides
TM39	Facade	Normal	Physical	70	100	20	Normal
TM55	Brine	Water	Special	65	100	10	Normal
TM57	Payback	Dark	Physical	50	100	10	Normal
TM58	Assurance	Dark	Physical	60	100	10	Normal
TM74	Venoshock	Poison	Special	65	100	10	Normal
TM76	Round	Normal	Special	60	100	15	Normal
TM77	Hex	Ghost	Special	65	100	10	Normal
TM90	Electric Terrain	Electric	Status	—	—	10	Both Sides

TR MOVES

NAME	TYPE	KIND	POW.	ACC.	PP	RANGE
TR03 Hydro Pump	Water	Special	110	80	5	Normal
TR04 Surf	Water	Special	90	100	15	All Others
TR08 Thunderbolt	Electric	Special	90	100	15	Normal
TR09 Thunder	Electric	Special	110	70	10	Normal
TR20 Substitute	Normal	Status	—	—	10	Self
TR21 Reversal	Fighting	Physical	—	100	15	Normal
TR23 Spikes	Ground	Status	—	—	20	Other Side
TR26 Endure	Normal	Status	—	—	10	Self
TR27 Sleep Talk	Normal	Status	—	—	10	Self
TR45 Muddy Water	Water	Special	90	85	10	Many Others
TR54 Toxic Spikes	Poison	Status	—	—	20	Other Side
TR57 Poison Jab	Poison	Physical	80	100	20	Normal
TR84 Scald	Water	Special	80	100	15	Normal
TR91 Venom Drench	Poison	Status	—	100	20	Many Others
TR95 Throat Chop	Dark	Physical	80	100	15	Normal
TR98 Liquidation	Water	Physical	85	100	10	Normal

354 Mantyke p. 141

ABILITY
Swift Swim
Water Absorb

HIDDEN ABILITY
Water Veil

SPECIES STRENGTHS
- HP
- ATTACK
- DEFENSE
- SP. ATK
- SP. DEF
- SPEED

DAMAGE TAKEN IN BATTLE
×1 ×0.5 ×2
×0.5 ×1 ×1
×0.5 ×0 ×1
×1 ×1 ×1
×4 ×1 ×0.5
×1 ×0.5 ×1

NO EGGS

LEVEL-UP MOVES

LV.	NAME	TYPE	KIND	POW.	ACC.	PP	RANGE
1	Tackle	Normal	Physical	40	100	35	Normal
1	Water Gun	Water	Special	40	100	25	Normal
4	Supersonic	Normal	Status	—	55	20	Normal
8	Wing Attack	Flying	Physical	60	100	35	Normal
12	Water Pulse	Water	Special	60	100	20	Normal
16	Wide Guard	Rock	Status	—	—	10	Your Side
20	Agility	Psychic	Status	—	—	30	Self
24	Bubble Beam	Water	Special	65	100	20	Normal
28	Headbutt	Normal	Physical	70	100	15	Normal
32	Air Slash	Flying	Special	75	95	15	Normal
36	Aqua Ring	Water	Status	—	—	20	Self
40	Bounce	Flying	Physical	85	85	5	Normal
44	Take Down	Normal	Physical	90	85	20	Normal
48	Hydro Pump	Water	Special	110	80	5	Normal

EVOLUTION MOVES

NAME	TYPE	KIND	POW.	ACC.	PP	RANGE

EGG MOVES

NAME	TYPE	KIND	POW.	ACC.	PP	RANGE
Confuse Ray	Ghost	Status	—	100	10	Normal
Haze	Ice	Status	—	—	30	Both Sides
Mirror Coat	Psychic	Special	—	100	20	Varies
Slam	Normal	Physical	80	75	20	Normal
Splash	Normal	Status	—	—	40	Self
Tailwind	Flying	Status	—	—	15	Your Side
Twister	Dragon	Special	40	100	20	Many Others

TUTOR MOVES

NAME	TYPE	KIND	POW.	ACC.	PP	RANGE

TM MOVES

NO.	NAME	TYPE	KIND	POW.	ACC.	PP	RANGE
TM21	Rest	Psychic	Status	—	—	10	Self
TM22	Rock Slide	Rock	Physical	75	90	10	Many Others
TM24	Snore	Normal	Special	50	100	15	Normal
TM25	Protect	Normal	Status	—	—	10	Self
TM27	Icy Wind	Ice	Special	55	95	15	Many Others
TM31	Attract	Normal	Status	—	100	15	Normal
TM33	Rain Dance	Water	Status	—	—	5	Both Sides
TM35	Hail	Ice	Status	—	—	10	Both Sides
TM36	Whirlpool	Water	Special	35	85	15	Normal
TM39	Facade	Normal	Physical	70	100	20	Normal
TM40	Swift	Normal	Special	60	—	20	Many Others
TM41	Helping Hand	Normal	Status	—	—	20	1 Ally
TM45	Dive	Water	Physical	80	100	10	Normal
TM52	Bounce	Flying	Physical	85	85	5	Normal
TM76	Round	Normal	Special	60	100	15	Normal
TM78	Acrobatics	Flying	Physical	55	100	15	Normal
TM81	Bulldoze	Ground	Physical	60	100	20	All Others
TM95	Air Slash	Flying	Special	75	95	15	Normal

TR MOVES

NAME	TYPE	KIND	POW.	ACC.	PP	RANGE
TR03 Hydro Pump	Water	Special	110	80	5	Normal
TR04 Surf	Water	Special	90	100	15	All Others
TR05 Ice Beam	Ice	Special	90	100	10	Normal
TR06 Blizzard	Ice	Special	110	70	5	Many Others
TR10 Earthquake	Ground	Physical	100	100	10	All Others
TR12 Agility	Psychic	Status	—	—	30	Self
TR16 Waterfall	Water	Physical	80	100	15	Normal
TR17 Amnesia	Psychic	Status	—	—	20	Self
TR20 Substitute	Normal	Status	—	—	10	Self
TR26 Endure	Normal	Status	—	—	10	Self
TR27 Sleep Talk	Normal	Status	—	—	10	Self
TR84 Scald	Water	Special	80	100	15	Normal

355

LEVEL-UP MOVES

LV.	NAME	TYPE	KIND	POW.	ACC.	PP	RANGE
1	Bullet Seed	Grass	Physical	25	100	30	Normal
1	Psybeam	Psychic	Special	65	100	20	Normal
1	Roost	Flying	Status	—	—	10	Self
1	Supersonic	Normal	Status	—	55	20	Normal
1	Tackle	Normal	Physical	40	100	35	Normal
1	Water Gun	Water	Special	40	100	25	Normal
8	Wing Attack	Flying	Physical	60	100	35	Normal
12	Water Pulse	Water	Special	60	100	20	Normal
16	Wide Guard	Rock	Status	—	—	10	Your Side
20	Agility	Psychic	Status	—	—	30	Self
24	Bubble Beam	Water	Special	65	100	20	Normal
28	Headbutt	Normal	Physical	70	100	15	Normal
32	Air Slash	Flying	Special	75	95	15	Normal
36	Aqua Ring	Water	Status	—	—	20	Self
40	Bounce	Flying	Physical	85	85	5	Normal
44	Take Down	Normal	Physical	90	85	20	Normal
48	Hydro Pump	Water	Special	110	80	5	Normal

EVOLUTION MOVES

NAME	TYPE	KIND	POW.	ACC.	PP	RANGE

EGG MOVES

NAME	TYPE	KIND	POW.	ACC.	PP	RANGE
Confuse Ray	Ghost	Status	—	100	10	Normal
Haze	Ice	Status	—	—	30	Both Sides
Mirror Coat	Psychic	Special	—	100	20	Varies
Slam	Normal	Physical	80	75	20	Normal
Splash	Normal	Status	—	—	40	Self
Tailwind	Flying	Status	—	—	15	Your Side
Twister	Dragon	Special	40	100	20	Many Others

TUTOR MOVES

NAME	TYPE	KIND	POW.	ACC.	PP	RANGE

TM MOVES

NO.	NAME	TYPE	KIND	POW.	ACC.	PP	RANGE
TM08	Hyper Beam	Normal	Special	150	90	5	Normal
TM09	Giga Impact	Normal	Physical	150	90	5	Normal
TM21	Rest	Psychic	Status	—	—	10	Self
TM22	Rock Slide	Rock	Physical	75	90	10	Many Others
TM24	Snore	Normal	Special	50	100	15	Normal
TM25	Protect	Normal	Status	—	—	10	Self
TM27	Icy Wind	Ice	Special	55	95	15	Many Others
TM31	Attract	Normal	Status	—	100	15	Normal
TM33	Rain Dance	Water	Status	—	—	5	Both Sides
TM35	Hail	Ice	Status	—	—	10	Both Sides
TM36	Whirlpool	Water	Special	35	85	15	Normal
TM39	Facade	Normal	Physical	70	100	20	Normal
TM40	Swift	Normal	Special	60	—	20	Many Others
TM41	Helping Hand	Normal	Status	—	—	20	1 Ally
TM45	Dive	Water	Physical	80	100	10	Normal
TM48	Rock Tomb	Rock	Physical	60	95	15	Normal
TM50	Bullet Seed	Grass	Physical	25	100	30	Normal
TM52	Bounce	Flying	Physical	85	85	5	Normal
TM54	Rock Blast	Rock	Physical	25	90	10	Normal
TM55	Brine	Water	Special	65	100	10	Normal
TM58	Assurance	Dark	Physical	60	100	10	Normal
TM76	Round	Normal	Special	60	100	15	Normal
TM78	Acrobatics	Flying	Physical	55	100	15	Normal
TM81	Bulldoze	Ground	Physical	60	100	20	All Others
TM95	Air Slash	Flying	Special	75	95	15	Normal

TR MOVES

NO.	NAME	TYPE	KIND	POW.	ACC.	PP	RANGE
TR01	Body Slam	Normal	Physical	85	100	15	Normal
TR03	Hydro Pump	Water	Special	110	80	5	Normal
TR04	Surf	Water	Special	90	100	15	All Others
TR05	Ice Beam	Ice	Special	90	100	10	Normal
TR06	Blizzard	Ice	Special	110	70	5	Many Others
TR10	Earthquake	Ground	Physical	100	100	10	All Others
TR12	Agility	Psychic	Status	—	—	30	Self
TR16	Waterfall	Water	Physical	80	100	15	Normal
TR17	Amnesia	Psychic	Status	—	—	20	Self
TR20	Substitute	Normal	Status	—	—	10	Self
TR26	Endure	Normal	Status	—	—	10	Self
TR27	Sleep Talk	Normal	Status	—	—	10	Self
TR59	Seed Bomb	Grass	Physical	80	100	15	Normal
TR73	Gunk Shot	Poison	Physical	120	80	5	Normal
TR74	Iron Head	Steel	Physical	80	100	15	Normal
TR84	Scald	Water	Special	80	100	15	Normal
TR89	Hurricane	Flying	Special	110	70	10	Normal
TR98	Liquidation	Water	Physical	85	100	10	Normal
TR99	Body Press	Fighting	Physical	80	100	10	Normal

Mantine p. 141

ABILITY
Swift Swim
Water Absorb

HIDDEN ABILITY
Water Veil

SPECIES STRENGTHS
HP
ATTACK
DEFENSE
SP. ATK
SP. DEF
SPEED

DAMAGE TAKEN IN BATTLE

×1 ×0.5 ×2
×0.5 ×1 ×1
×0.5 ×0 ×1
×1 ×1 ×1
×4 ×1 ×0.5
×1 ×0.5 ×1

WATER 1

356

LEVEL-UP MOVES

LV.	NAME	TYPE	KIND	POW.	ACC.	PP	RANGE
1	Splash	Normal	Status	—	—	40	Self
3	Growl	Normal	Status	—	100	40	Many Others
6	Astonish	Ghost	Physical	30	100	15	Normal
12	Water Gun	Water	Special	40	100	25	Normal
15	Mist	Ice	Status	—	—	30	Your Side
18	Water Pulse	Water	Special	60	100	20	Normal
21	Heavy Slam	Steel	Physical	—	100	10	Normal
24	Brine	Water	Special	65	100	10	Normal
27	Whirlpool	Water	Special	35	85	15	Normal
30	Dive	Water	Physical	80	100	10	Normal
33	Bounce	Flying	Physical	85	85	5	Normal
36	Body Slam	Normal	Physical	85	100	15	Normal
39	Rest	Psychic	Status	—	—	10	Self
42	Amnesia	Psychic	Status	—	—	20	Self
45	Hydro Pump	Water	Special	110	80	5	Normal
48	Water Spout	Water	Special	150	100	5	Many Others

EVOLUTION MOVES

NAME	TYPE	KIND	POW.	ACC.	PP	RANGE

EGG MOVES

NAME	TYPE	KIND	POW.	ACC.	PP	RANGE
Aqua Ring	Water	Status	—	—	20	Self
Curse	Ghost	Status	—	—	10	Varies
Defense Curl	Normal	Status	—	—	40	Self
Double-Edge	Normal	Physical	120	100	15	Normal
Fissure	Ground	Physical	—	30	5	Normal
Rollout	Rock	Physical	30	90	20	Normal
Soak	Water	Status	—	100	20	Normal
Thrash	Normal	Physical	120	100	10	1 Random
Tickle	Normal	Status	—	100	20	Normal

TUTOR MOVES

NAME	TYPE	KIND	POW.	ACC.	PP	RANGE

TM MOVES

NO.	NAME	TYPE	KIND	POW.	ACC.	PP	RANGE
TM20	Self-Destruct	Normal	Physical	200	100	5	All Others
TM21	Rest	Psychic	Status	—	—	10	Self
TM24	Snore	Normal	Special	50	100	15	Normal
TM25	Protect	Normal	Status	—	—	10	Self
TM27	Icy Wind	Ice	Special	55	95	15	Many Others
TM31	Attract	Normal	Status	—	100	15	Normal
TM33	Rain Dance	Water	Status	—	—	5	Both Sides
TM35	Hail	Ice	Status	—	—	10	Both Sides
TM36	Whirlpool	Water	Special	35	85	15	Normal
TM39	Facade	Normal	Physical	70	100	20	Normal
TM45	Dive	Water	Physical	80	100	10	Normal
TM46	Weather Ball*	Normal	Special	50	100	10	Normal
TM48	Rock Tomb	Rock	Physical	60	95	15	Normal
TM52	Bounce	Flying	Physical	85	85	5	Normal
TM55	Brine	Water	Special	65	100	10	Normal
TM64	Avalanche	Ice	Physical	60	100	10	Normal
TM76	Round	Normal	Special	60	100	15	Normal
TM81	Bulldoze	Ground	Physical	60	100	20	All Others

TR MOVES

NO.	NAME	TYPE	KIND	POW.	ACC.	PP	RANGE
TR01	Body Slam	Normal	Physical	85	100	15	Normal
TR03	Hydro Pump	Water	Special	110	80	5	Normal
TR04	Surf	Water	Special	90	100	15	All Others
TR05	Ice Beam	Ice	Special	90	100	10	Normal
TR06	Blizzard	Ice	Special	110	70	5	Many Others
TR10	Earthquake	Ground	Physical	100	100	10	All Others
TR16	Waterfall	Water	Physical	80	100	15	Normal
TR17	Amnesia	Psychic	Status	—	—	20	Self
TR20	Substitute	Normal	Status	—	—	10	Self
TR26	Endure	Normal	Status	—	—	10	Self
TR27	Sleep Talk	Normal	Status	—	—	10	Self
TR42	Hyper Voice	Normal	Special	90	100	10	Many Others
TR69	Zen Headbutt	Psychic	Physical	80	90	15	Normal
TR79	Heavy Slam	Steel	Physical	—	100	10	Normal
TR84	Scald	Water	Special	80	100	15	Normal
TR99	Body Press	Fighting	Physical	80	100	10	Normal

Wailmer p. 142

ABILITY
Water Veil
Oblivious

HIDDEN ABILITY
Pressure

SPECIES STRENGTHS
HP
ATTACK
DEFENSE
SP. ATK
SP. DEF
SPEED

DAMAGE TAKEN IN BATTLE

×1 ×1 ×1
×0.5 ×1 ×1
×0.5 ×1 ×1
×2 ×1 ×1
×2 ×1 ×0.5
×0.5 ×1 ×1

FIELD
WATER 2

*Weather Ball changes type depending on weather condition. (Harsh sunlight: Fire type. Rain: Water type. Hail: Ice type. Sandstorm: Rock type.)

357

Wailord
p. 142

ABILITY
Water Veil
Oblivious

HIDDEN ABILITY
Pressure

SPECIES STRENGTHS

HP	▮▮▮▮▮▮▮▮
ATTACK	▮▮▮▮
DEFENSE	▮▮
SP. ATK	▮▮▮▮▮
SP. DEF	▮▮▮
SPEED	▮▮▮

DAMAGE TAKEN IN BATTLE

×1	×1	×1
×0.5	×1	×1
×0.5	×1	×1
×2	×1	×1
×2	×1	×0.5
×0.5	×1	×1

FIELD
WATER 2

LEVEL-UP MOVES

LV.	NAME	TYPE	KIND	POW.	ACC.	PP	RANGE
1	Astonish	Ghost	Physical	30	100	15	Normal
1	Growl	Normal	Status	—	100	40	Many Others
1	Noble Roar	Normal	Status	—	100	30	Normal
1	Soak	Water	Status	—	100	20	Normal
1	Splash	Normal	Status	—	—	40	Self
15	Water Gun	Water	Special	40	100	25	Normal
15	Mist	Ice	Status	—	—	30	Your Side
18	Water Pulse	Water	Special	60	100	20	Normal
21	Heavy Slam	Steel	Physical	—	100	10	Normal
24	Brine	Water	Special	65	100	10	Normal
27	Whirlpool	Water	Special	35	85	15	Normal
30	Dive	Water	Physical	80	100	10	Normal
33	Bounce	Flying	Physical	85	85	5	Normal
36	Body Slam	Normal	Physical	85	100	15	Normal
39	Rest	Psychic	Status	—	—	10	Self
44	Amnesia	Psychic	Status	—	—	20	Self
49	Hydro Pump	Water	Special	110	80	5	Normal
54	Water Spout	Water	Special	150	100	5	Many Others

EVOLUTION MOVES

NAME	TYPE	KIND	POW.	ACC.	PP	RANGE

EGG MOVES

NAME	TYPE	KIND	POW.	ACC.	PP	RANGE

TUTOR MOVES

NAME	TYPE	KIND	POW.	ACC.	PP	RANGE

TM MOVES

NO.	NAME	TYPE	KIND	POW.	ACC.	PP	RANGE
TM08	Hyper Beam	Normal	Special	150	90	5	Normal
TM09	Giga Impact	Normal	Physical	150	90	5	Normal
TM20	Self-Destruct	Normal	Physical	200	100	5	All Others
TM21	Rest	Psychic	Status	—	—	10	Self
TM24	Snore	Normal	Special	50	100	15	Normal
TM25	Protect	Normal	Status	—	—	10	Self
TM27	Icy Wind	Ice	Special	55	95	15	Many Others
TM31	Attract	Normal	Status	—	100	15	Normal
TM33	Rain Dance	Water	Status	—	—	5	Both Sides
TM35	Hail	Ice	Status	—	—	10	Both Sides
TM36	Whirlpool	Water	Special	35	85	15	Normal
TM39	Facade	Normal	Physical	70	100	20	Normal
TM45	Dive	Water	Physical	80	100	10	Normal
TM46	Weather Ball*	Normal	Special	50	100	10	Normal
TM48	Rock Tomb	Rock	Physical	60	95	15	Normal
TM52	Bounce	Flying	Physical	85	85	5	Normal
TM55	Brine	Water	Special	65	100	10	Normal
TM64	Avalanche	Ice	Physical	60	100	10	Normal
TM76	Round	Normal	Special	60	100	15	Normal
TM81	Bulldoze	Ground	Physical	60	100	20	All Others

TR MOVES

NAME	TYPE	KIND	POW.	ACC.	PP	RANGE
TR01 Body Slam	Normal	Physical	85	100	15	Normal
TR03 Hydro Pump	Water	Special	110	80	5	Normal
TR04 Surf	Water	Special	90	100	15	All Others
TR05 Ice Beam	Ice	Special	90	100	10	Normal
TR06 Blizzard	Ice	Special	110	70	5	Many Others
TR10 Earthquake	Ground	Physical	100	100	10	All Others
TR16 Waterfall	Water	Physical	80	100	15	Normal
TR17 Amnesia	Psychic	Status	—	—	20	Self
TR20 Substitute	Normal	Status	—	—	10	Self
TR26 Endure	Normal	Status	—	—	10	Self
TR27 Sleep Talk	Normal	Status	—	—	10	Self
TR42 Hyper Voice	Normal	Special	90	100	10	Many Others
TR69 Zen Headbutt	Psychic	Physical	80	90	15	Normal
TR74 Iron Head	Steel	Physical	80	100	15	Normal
TR79 Heavy Slam	Steel	Physical	—	100	10	Normal
TR84 Scald	Water	Special	80	100	15	Normal
TR98 Liquidation	Water	Physical	85	100	10	Normal
TR99 Body Press	Fighting	Physical	80	100	10	Normal

*Weather Ball changes type depending on weather condition. (Harsh sunlight: Fire type. Rain: Water type. Hail: Ice type. Sandstorm: Rock type.)

358

Bergmite
p. 143

ABILITY
Own Tempo
Ice Body

HIDDEN ABILITY
Sturdy

SPECIES STRENGTHS

HP	▮▮▮
ATTACK	▮▮▮▮
DEFENSE	▮▮▮▮▮
SP. ATK	▮▮
SP. DEF	▮▮▮
SPEED	▮▮

DAMAGE TAKEN IN BATTLE

×1	×2	×2
×2	×1	×1
×1	×1	×1
×1	×1	×1
×1	×1	×2
×0.5	×1	×1

MONSTER
MINERAL

LEVEL-UP MOVES

LV.	NAME	TYPE	KIND	POW.	ACC.	PP	RANGE
1	Harden	Normal	Status	—	—	30	Self
1	Rapid Spin	Normal	Physical	50	100	40	Normal
3	Tackle	Normal	Physical	40	100	35	Normal
6	Powder Snow	Ice	Special	40	100	25	Many Others
9	Curse	Ghost	Status	—	—	10	Varies
12	Icy Wind	Ice	Special	55	95	15	Many Others
15	Protect	Normal	Status	—	—	10	Self
18	Avalanche	Ice	Physical	60	100	10	Normal
21	Bite	Dark	Physical	60	100	25	Normal
24	Ice Fang	Ice	Physical	65	95	15	Normal
27	Iron Defense	Steel	Status	—	—	15	Self
30	Recover	Normal	Status	—	—	10	Self
33	Crunch	Dark	Physical	80	100	15	Normal
36	Take Down	Normal	Physical	90	85	20	Normal
39	Blizzard	Ice	Special	110	70	5	Many Others
42	Double-Edge	Normal	Physical	120	100	15	Normal

EVOLUTION MOVES

NAME	TYPE	KIND	POW.	ACC.	PP	RANGE

EGG MOVES

NAME	TYPE	KIND	POW.	ACC.	PP	RANGE
Aurora Veil	Ice	Status	—	—	20	Your Side
Mirror Coat	Psychic	Special	—	100	20	Varies
Mist	Ice	Status	—	—	30	Your Side

TUTOR MOVES

NAME	TYPE	KIND	POW.	ACC.	PP	RANGE

TM MOVES

NO.	NAME	TYPE	KIND	POW.	ACC.	PP	RANGE
TM19	Safeguard	Normal	Status	—	—	25	Your Side
TM21	Rest	Psychic	Status	—	—	10	Self
TM22	Rock Slide	Rock	Physical	75	90	10	Many Others
TM24	Snore	Normal	Special	50	100	15	Normal
TM25	Protect	Normal	Status	—	—	10	Self
TM27	Icy Wind	Ice	Special	55	95	15	Many Others
TM31	Attract	Normal	Status	—	100	15	Normal
TM33	Rain Dance	Water	Status	—	—	5	Both Sides
TM35	Hail	Ice	Status	—	—	10	Both Sides
TM39	Facade	Normal	Physical	70	100	20	Normal
TM48	Rock Tomb	Rock	Physical	60	95	15	Normal
TM51	Icicle Spear	Ice	Physical	25	100	30	Normal
TM64	Avalanche	Ice	Physical	60	100	10	Normal
TM67	Ice Fang	Ice	Physical	65	95	15	Normal
TM76	Round	Normal	Special	60	100	15	Normal

TR MOVES

NAME	TYPE	KIND	POW.	ACC.	PP	RANGE
TR04 Surf	Water	Special	90	100	15	All Others
TR05 Ice Beam	Ice	Special	90	100	10	Normal
TR06 Blizzard	Ice	Special	110	70	5	Many Others
TR20 Substitute	Normal	Status	—	—	10	Self
TR26 Endure	Normal	Status	—	—	10	Self
TR27 Sleep Talk	Normal	Status	—	—	10	Self
TR32 Crunch	Dark	Physical	80	100	15	Normal
TR46 Iron Defense	Steel	Status	—	—	15	Self
TR52 Gyro Ball	Steel	Physical	—	100	5	Normal
TR70 Flash Cannon	Steel	Special	80	100	10	Normal
TR75 Stone Edge	Rock	Physical	100	80	5	Normal

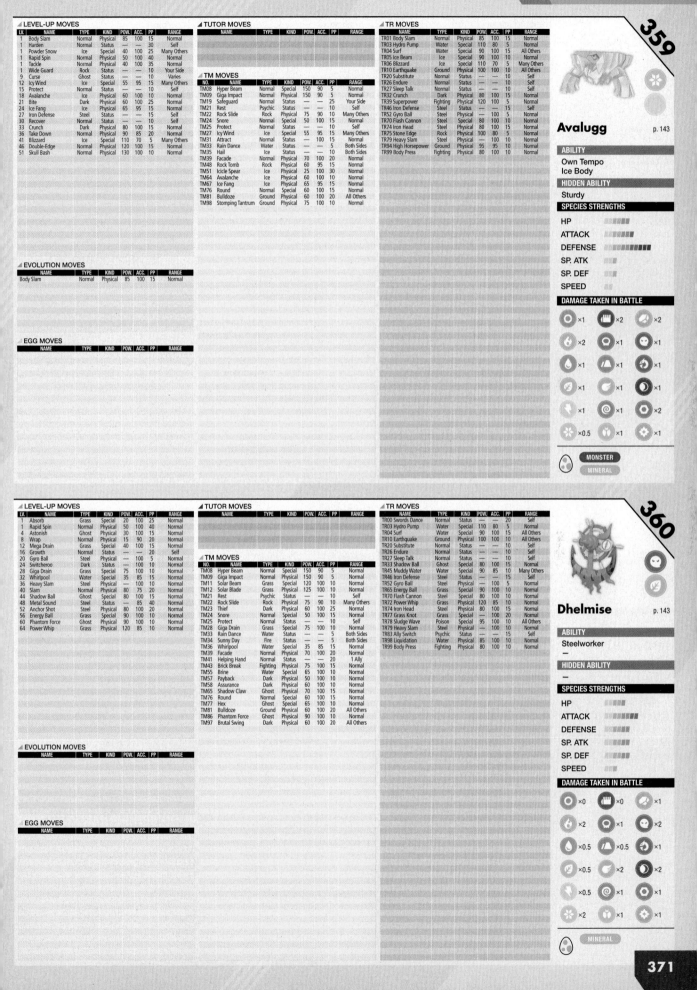

359

Avalugg — p. 143

LEVEL-UP MOVES

LV.	NAME	TYPE	KIND	POW.	ACC.	PP	RANGE
1	Body Slam	Normal	Physical	85	100	15	Normal
1	Harden	Normal	Status	—	—	30	Self
1	Powder Snow	Ice	Special	40	100	25	Many Others
1	Rapid Spin	Normal	Physical	50	100	40	Normal
1	Tackle	Normal	Physical	40	100	35	Normal
6	Wide Guard	Rock	Status	—	—	10	Your Side
9	Curse	Ghost	Status	—	—	10	Varies
12	Icy Wind	Ice	Special	55	95	15	Many Others
15	Protect	Normal	Status	—	—	10	Self
18	Avalanche	Ice	Physical	60	100	10	Normal
21	Bite	Dark	Physical	60	100	25	Normal
24	Ice Fang	Ice	Physical	65	95	15	Normal
27	Iron Defense	Steel	Status	—	—	15	Self
30	Recover	Normal	Status	—	—	10	Self
33	Crunch	Dark	Physical	80	100	15	Normal
36	Take Down	Normal	Physical	90	85	20	Normal
41	Blizzard	Ice	Special	110	70	5	Many Others
46	Double-Edge	Normal	Physical	120	100	15	Normal
51	Skull Bash	Normal	Physical	130	100	10	Normal

EVOLUTION MOVES

NAME	TYPE	KIND	POW.	ACC.	PP	RANGE
Body Slam	Normal	Physical	85	100	15	Normal

EGG MOVES

NAME	TYPE	KIND	POW.	ACC.	PP	RANGE

TUTOR MOVES

NAME	TYPE	KIND	POW.	ACC.	PP	RANGE

TM MOVES

NO.	NAME	TYPE	KIND	POW.	ACC.	PP	RANGE
TM08	Hyper Beam	Normal	Special	150	90	5	Normal
TM09	Giga Impact	Normal	Physical	150	90	5	Normal
TM19	Safeguard	Normal	Status	—	—	25	Your Side
TM21	Rest	Psychic	Status	—	—	10	Self
TM22	Rock Slide	Rock	Physical	75	90	10	Many Others
TM24	Snore	Normal	Special	50	100	15	Normal
TM25	Protect	Normal	Status	—	—	10	Self
TM27	Icy Wind	Ice	Special	55	95	15	Many Others
TM31	Attract	Normal	Status	—	100	15	Normal
TM33	Rain Dance	Water	Status	—	—	5	Both Sides
TM35	Hail	Ice	Status	—	—	10	Both Sides
TM39	Facade	Normal	Physical	70	100	20	Normal
TM48	Rock Tomb	Rock	Physical	60	95	15	Normal
TM51	Icicle Spear	Ice	Physical	25	100	30	Normal
TM64	Avalanche	Ice	Physical	60	100	10	Normal
TM67	Ice Fang	Ice	Physical	65	95	15	Normal
TM76	Round	Normal	Special	60	100	15	Normal
TM81	Bulldoze	Ground	Physical	60	100	20	All Others
TM98	Stomping Tantrum	Ground	Physical	75	100	10	Normal

TR MOVES

NO.	NAME	TYPE	KIND	POW.	ACC.	PP	RANGE
TR01	Body Slam	Normal	Physical	85	100	15	Normal
TR03	Hydro Pump	Water	Special	110	80	5	Normal
TR04	Surf	Water	Special	90	100	15	All Others
TR05	Ice Beam	Ice	Special	90	100	10	Normal
TR06	Blizzard	Ice	Special	110	70	5	Many Others
TR10	Earthquake	Ground	Physical	100	100	10	All Others
TR20	Substitute	Normal	Status	—	—	10	Self
TR26	Endure	Normal	Status	—	—	10	Self
TR27	Sleep Talk	Normal	Status	—	—	10	Self
TR32	Crunch	Dark	Physical	80	100	15	Normal
TR39	Superpower	Fighting	Physical	120	100	5	Normal
TR46	Iron Defense	Steel	Status	—	—	15	Self
TR52	Gyro Ball	Steel	Physical	—	100	5	Normal
TR70	Flash Cannon	Steel	Special	80	100	10	Normal
TR74	Iron Head	Steel	Physical	80	100	15	Normal
TR75	Stone Edge	Rock	Physical	100	80	5	Normal
TR79	Heavy Slam	Steel	Physical	—	100	10	Normal
TR94	High Horsepower	Ground	Physical	95	95	10	Normal
TR99	Body Press	Fighting	Physical	80	100	10	Normal

ABILITY
Own Tempo
Ice Body

HIDDEN ABILITY
Sturdy

SPECIES STRENGTHS
- HP
- ATTACK
- DEFENSE
- SP. ATK
- SP. DEF
- SPEED

DAMAGE TAKEN IN BATTLE
×1 ×2 ×2
×2 ×1 ×1
×1 ×1 ×1
×1 ×1 ×2
×0.5 ×1 ×1

Egg Groups: MONSTER / MINERAL

360

Dhelmise — p. 143

LEVEL-UP MOVES

LV.	NAME	TYPE	KIND	POW.	ACC.	PP	RANGE
1	Absorb	Grass	Special	20	100	25	Normal
1	Rapid Spin	Normal	Physical	50	100	40	Normal
1	Astonish	Ghost	Physical	30	100	15	Normal
8	Wrap	Normal	Physical	15	90	20	Normal
12	Mega Drain	Grass	Special	40	100	15	Normal
16	Growth	Normal	Status	—	—	20	Self
20	Gyro Ball	Steel	Physical	—	100	5	Normal
24	Switcheroo	Dark	Status	—	100	10	Normal
28	Giga Drain	Grass	Special	75	100	10	Normal
32	Whirlpool	Water	Special	35	85	15	Normal
36	Heavy Slam	Steel	Physical	—	100	10	Normal
40	Slam	Normal	Physical	80	75	20	Normal
44	Shadow Ball	Ghost	Special	80	100	15	Normal
48	Metal Sound	Steel	Status	—	85	40	Normal
52	Anchor Shot	Steel	Physical	80	100	20	Normal
56	Energy Ball	Grass	Special	90	100	10	Normal
60	Phantom Force	Ghost	Physical	90	100	10	Normal
64	Power Whip	Grass	Physical	120	85	10	Normal

EVOLUTION MOVES

NAME	TYPE	KIND	POW.	ACC.	PP	RANGE

EGG MOVES

NAME	TYPE	KIND	POW.	ACC.	PP	RANGE

TUTOR MOVES

NAME	TYPE	KIND	POW.	ACC.	PP	RANGE

TM MOVES

NO.	NAME	TYPE	KIND	POW.	ACC.	PP	RANGE
TM08	Hyper Beam	Normal	Special	150	90	5	Normal
TM09	Giga Impact	Normal	Physical	150	90	5	Normal
TM11	Solar Beam	Grass	Special	120	100	10	Normal
TM12	Solar Blade	Grass	Physical	125	100	10	Normal
TM21	Rest	Psychic	Status	—	—	10	Self
TM22	Rock Slide	Rock	Physical	75	90	10	Many Others
TM23	Thief	Dark	Physical	60	100	25	Normal
TM24	Snore	Normal	Special	50	100	15	Normal
TM25	Protect	Normal	Status	—	—	10	Self
TM28	Giga Drain	Grass	Special	75	100	10	Normal
TM33	Rain Dance	Water	Status	—	—	5	Both Sides
TM34	Sunny Day	Fire	Status	—	—	5	Both Sides
TM36	Whirlpool	Water	Special	35	85	15	Normal
TM39	Facade	Normal	Physical	70	100	20	Normal
TM41	Helping Hand	Normal	Status	—	—	20	1 Ally
TM43	Brick Break	Fighting	Physical	75	100	15	Normal
TM55	Brine	Water	Special	65	100	10	Normal
TM57	Payback	Dark	Physical	50	100	10	Normal
TM58	Assurance	Dark	Physical	60	100	10	Normal
TM65	Shadow Claw	Ghost	Physical	70	100	15	Normal
TM76	Round	Normal	Special	60	100	15	Normal
TM77	Hex	Ghost	Special	65	100	10	Normal
TM81	Bulldoze	Ground	Physical	60	100	20	All Others
TM86	Phantom Force	Ghost	Physical	90	100	10	Normal
TM97	Brutal Swing	Dark	Physical	60	100	20	All Others

TR MOVES

NO.	NAME	TYPE	KIND	POW.	ACC.	PP	RANGE
TR00	Swords Dance	Normal	Status	—	—	20	Self
TR03	Hydro Pump	Water	Special	110	80	5	Normal
TR04	Surf	Water	Special	90	100	15	All Others
TR10	Earthquake	Ground	Physical	100	100	10	All Others
TR20	Substitute	Normal	Status	—	—	10	Self
TR26	Endure	Normal	Status	—	—	10	Self
TR27	Sleep Talk	Normal	Status	—	—	10	Self
TR33	Shadow Ball	Ghost	Special	80	100	15	Normal
TR45	Muddy Water	Water	Special	90	85	10	Many Others
TR46	Iron Defense	Steel	Status	—	—	15	Self
TR52	Gyro Ball	Steel	Physical	—	100	5	Normal
TR65	Energy Ball	Grass	Special	90	100	10	Normal
TR70	Flash Cannon	Steel	Special	80	100	10	Normal
TR72	Power Whip	Grass	Physical	120	85	10	Normal
TR74	Iron Head	Steel	Physical	80	100	15	Normal
TR77	Grass Knot	Grass	Special	—	100	20	Normal
TR78	Sludge Wave	Poison	Special	95	100	10	All Others
TR79	Heavy Slam	Steel	Physical	—	100	10	Normal
TR83	Ally Switch	Psychic	Status	—	—	15	Self
TR98	Liquidation	Water	Physical	85	100	10	Normal
TR99	Body Press	Fighting	Physical	80	100	10	Normal

ABILITY
Steelworker
—

HIDDEN ABILITY
—

SPECIES STRENGTHS
- HP
- ATTACK
- DEFENSE
- SP. ATK
- SP. DEF
- SPEED

DAMAGE TAKEN IN BATTLE
×0 ×0 ×1
×2 ×1 ×2
×0.5 ×0.5 ×1
×0.5 ×2 ×1
×0.5 ×1 ×1
×2 ×1 ×1

Egg Groups: MINERAL

361 Lapras

p. 144

ABILITY
Water Absorb
Shell Armor

HIDDEN ABILITY
Hydration

SPECIES STRENGTHS

HP	
ATTACK	
DEFENSE	
SP. ATK	
SP. DEF	
SPEED	

DAMAGE TAKEN IN BATTLE

×1	×2	×2	×1	×1	×1
×0.5	×1	×1	×2	×1	×1
×2	×1	×1	×0.25	×1	×1

Egg Groups: MONSTER / WATER 1

LEVEL-UP MOVES

LV.	NAME	TYPE	KIND	POW.	ACC.	PP	RANGE
1	Growl	Normal	Status	—	100	40	Many Others
1	Water Gun	Water	Special	40	100	25	Normal
5	Sing	Normal	Status	—	55	15	Normal
10	Mist	Ice	Status	—	—	30	Your Side
15	Life Dew	Water	Status	—	—	10	Your Side
20	Ice Shard	Ice	Physical	40	100	30	Normal
25	Confuse Ray	Ghost	Status	—	100	10	Normal
30	Water Pulse	Water	Special	60	100	20	Normal
35	Brine	Water	Special	65	100	10	Normal
40	Body Slam	Normal	Physical	85	100	15	Normal
45	Ice Beam	Ice	Special	90	100	10	Normal
50	Rain Dance	Water	Status	—	—	5	Both Sides
55	Hydro Pump	Water	Special	110	80	5	Normal
60	Perish Song	Normal	Status	—	—	5	All
65	Sheer Cold	Ice	Special	—	30	5	Normal

EVOLUTION MOVES

NAME	TYPE	KIND	POW.	ACC.	PP	RANGE

EGG MOVES

NAME	TYPE	KIND	POW.	ACC.	PP	RANGE
Ancient Power	Rock	Special	60	100	5	Normal
Curse	Ghost	Status	—	—	10	Varies
Fissure	Ground	Physical	—	30	5	Normal
Freeze-Dry	Ice	Special	70	100	20	Normal
Horn Drill	Normal	Physical	—	30	5	Normal
Sparkling Aria	Water	Special	90	100	10	All Others
Tickle	Normal	Status	—	100	20	Normal

TUTOR MOVES

NAME	TYPE	KIND	POW.	ACC.	PP	RANGE

TM MOVES

NO.	NAME	TYPE	KIND	POW.	ACC.	PP	RANGE
TM08	Hyper Beam	Normal	Special	150	90	5	Normal
TM09	Giga Impact	Normal	Physical	150	90	5	Normal
TM19	Safeguard	Normal	Status	—	—	25	Your Side
TM21	Rest	Psychic	Status	—	—	10	Self
TM24	Snore	Normal	Special	50	100	15	Normal
TM25	Protect	Normal	Status	—	—	10	Self
TM27	Icy Wind	Ice	Special	55	95	15	Many Others
TM29	Charm	Fairy	Status	—	100	20	Normal
TM31	Attract	Normal	Status	—	100	15	Normal
TM33	Rain Dance	Water	Status	—	—	5	Both Sides
TM35	Hail	Ice	Status	—	—	10	Both Sides
TM36	Whirlpool	Water	Special	35	85	15	Normal
TM39	Facade	Normal	Physical	70	100	20	Normal
TM41	Helping Hand	Normal	Status	—	—	20	1 Ally
TM45	Dive	Water	Physical	80	100	10	Normal
TM46	Weather Ball*	Normal	Special	50	100	10	Normal
TM55	Brine	Water	Special	65	100	10	Normal
TM64	Avalanche	Ice	Physical	60	100	10	Normal
TM76	Round	Normal	Special	60	100	15	Normal
TM81	Bulldoze	Ground	Physical	60	100	20	All Others
TM96	Smart Strike	Steel	Physical	70	—	10	Normal

TR MOVES

NO.	NAME	TYPE	KIND	POW.	ACC.	PP	RANGE
TR01	Body Slam	Normal	Physical	85	100	15	Normal
TR03	Hydro Pump	Water	Special	110	80	5	Normal
TR04	Surf	Water	Special	90	100	15	All Others
TR05	Ice Beam	Ice	Special	90	100	10	Normal
TR06	Blizzard	Ice	Special	110	70	5	Many Others
TR08	Thunderbolt	Electric	Special	90	100	15	Normal
TR09	Thunder	Electric	Special	110	70	10	Normal
TR11	Psychic	Psychic	Special	90	100	10	Normal
TR16	Waterfall	Water	Physical	80	100	15	Normal
TR20	Substitute	Normal	Status	—	—	10	Self
TR24	Outrage	Dragon	Physical	120	100	10	1 Random
TR26	Endure	Normal	Status	—	—	10	Self
TR27	Sleep Talk	Normal	Status	—	—	10	Self
TR28	Megahorn	Bug	Physical	120	85	10	Normal
TR31	Iron Tail	Steel	Physical	100	75	15	Normal
TR34	Future Sight	Psychic	Special	120	100	10	Normal
TR42	Hyper Voice	Normal	Special	90	100	10	Many Others
TR51	Dragon Dance	Dragon	Status	—	—	20	Self
TR62	Dragon Pulse	Dragon	Special	85	100	10	Normal
TR69	Zen Headbutt	Psychic	Physical	80	90	15	Normal
TR74	Iron Head	Steel	Physical	80	100	15	Normal
TR87	Drill Run	Ground	Physical	80	95	10	Normal
TR98	Liquidation	Water	Physical	85	100	10	Normal
TR99	Body Press	Fighting	Physical	80	100	10	Normal

---

362 Lunatone

p. 144

ABILITY
Levitate
—

HIDDEN ABILITY
—

SPECIES STRENGTHS

HP	
ATTACK	
DEFENSE	
SP. ATK	
SP. DEF	
SPEED	

DAMAGE TAKEN IN BATTLE

×0.5	×1	×1	×0.5	×0.5	×2
×2	×2	×1	×2	×0.5	×2
×1	×0.5	×2	×2	×2	×1

Egg Group: MINERAL

LEVEL-UP MOVES

LV.	NAME	TYPE	KIND	POW.	ACC.	PP	RANGE
1	Confusion	Psychic	Special	50	100	25	Normal
1	Harden	Normal	Status	—	—	30	Self
1	Moonblast	Fairy	Special	95	100	15	Normal
1	Moonlight	Fairy	Status	—	—	5	Self
1	Rock Throw	Rock	Physical	50	90	15	Normal
1	Tackle	Normal	Physical	40	100	35	Normal
5	Hypnosis	Psychic	Status	—	60	20	Normal
10	Rock Polish	Rock	Status	—	—	20	Self
15	Rock Slide	Rock	Physical	75	90	10	Many Others
20	Psyshock	Psychic	Special	80	100	10	Normal
25	Cosmic Power	Psychic	Status	—	—	20	Self
30	Psychic	Psychic	Special	90	100	10	Normal
35	Stone Edge	Rock	Physical	100	80	5	Normal
40	Future Sight	Psychic	Special	120	100	10	Normal
45	Magic Room	Psychic	Status	—	—	10	Both Sides
50	Explosion	Normal	Physical	250	100	5	All Others

EVOLUTION MOVES

NAME	TYPE	KIND	POW.	ACC.	PP	RANGE

EGG MOVES

NAME	TYPE	KIND	POW.	ACC.	PP	RANGE

TUTOR MOVES

NAME	TYPE	KIND	POW.	ACC.	PP	RANGE

TM MOVES

NO.	NAME	TYPE	KIND	POW.	ACC.	PP	RANGE
TM08	Hyper Beam	Normal	Special	150	90	5	Normal
TM09	Giga Impact	Normal	Physical	150	90	5	Normal
TM17	Light Screen	Psychic	Status	—	—	30	Your Side
TM18	Reflect	Psychic	Status	—	—	20	Your Side
TM19	Safeguard	Normal	Status	—	—	25	Your Side
TM20	Self-Destruct	Normal	Physical	200	100	5	All Others
TM21	Rest	Psychic	Status	—	—	10	Self
TM22	Rock Slide	Rock	Physical	75	90	10	Many Others
TM24	Snore	Normal	Special	50	100	15	Normal
TM25	Protect	Normal	Status	—	—	10	Self
TM27	Icy Wind	Ice	Special	55	95	15	Many Others
TM32	Sandstorm	Rock	Status	—	—	10	Both Sides
TM33	Rain Dance	Water	Status	—	—	5	Both Sides
TM35	Hail	Ice	Status	—	—	10	Both Sides
TM39	Facade	Normal	Physical	70	100	20	Normal
TM40	Swift	Normal	Special	60	—	20	Many Others
TM41	Helping Hand	Normal	Status	—	—	20	1 Ally
TM46	Weather Ball*	Normal	Special	50	100	10	Normal
TM48	Rock Tomb	Rock	Physical	60	95	15	Normal
TM49	Sand Tomb	Ground	Physical	35	85	15	Normal
TM54	Rock Blast	Rock	Physical	25	90	10	Normal
TM60	Power Swap	Psychic	Status	—	—	10	Normal
TM70	Trick Room	Psychic	Status	—	—	5	Both Sides
TM72	Magic Room	Psychic	Status	—	—	10	Both Sides
TM76	Round	Normal	Special	60	100	15	Normal
TM78	Acrobatics	Flying	Physical	55	100	15	Normal
TM81	Bulldoze	Ground	Physical	60	100	20	All Others
TM91	Psychic Terrain	Psychic	Status	—	—	10	Both Sides
TM98	Stomping Tantrum	Ground	Physical	75	100	10	Normal

TR MOVES

NO.	NAME	TYPE	KIND	POW.	ACC.	PP	RANGE
TR01	Body Slam	Normal	Physical	85	100	15	Normal
TR05	Ice Beam	Ice	Special	90	100	10	Normal
TR06	Blizzard	Ice	Special	110	70	5	Many Others
TR10	Earthquake	Ground	Physical	100	100	10	All Others
TR11	Psychic	Psychic	Special	90	100	10	Normal
TR20	Substitute	Normal	Status	—	—	10	Self
TR25	Psyshock	Psychic	Special	80	100	10	Normal
TR26	Endure	Normal	Status	—	—	10	Self
TR27	Sleep Talk	Normal	Status	—	—	10	Self
TR29	Baton Pass	Normal	Status	—	—	40	Self
TR33	Shadow Ball	Ghost	Special	80	100	15	Normal
TR34	Future Sight	Psychic	Special	120	100	10	Normal
TR40	Skill Swap	Psychic	Status	—	—	10	Normal
TR44	Cosmic Power	Psychic	Status	—	—	20	Self
TR49	Calm Mind	Psychic	Status	—	—	20	Self
TR52	Gyro Ball	Steel	Physical	—	100	5	Normal
TR63	Power Gem	Rock	Special	80	100	20	Normal
TR67	Earth Power	Ground	Special	90	100	10	Normal
TR68	Nasty Plot	Dark	Status	—	—	20	Self
TR69	Zen Headbutt	Psychic	Physical	80	90	15	Normal
TR74	Iron Head	Steel	Physical	80	100	15	Normal
TR75	Stone Edge	Rock	Physical	100	80	5	Normal
TR76	Stealth Rock	Rock	Status	—	—	20	Other Side
TR77	Grass Knot	Grass	Special	—	100	20	Normal
TR82	Stored Power	Psychic	Special	20	100	10	Normal
TR83	Ally Switch	Psychic	Status	—	—	15	Self

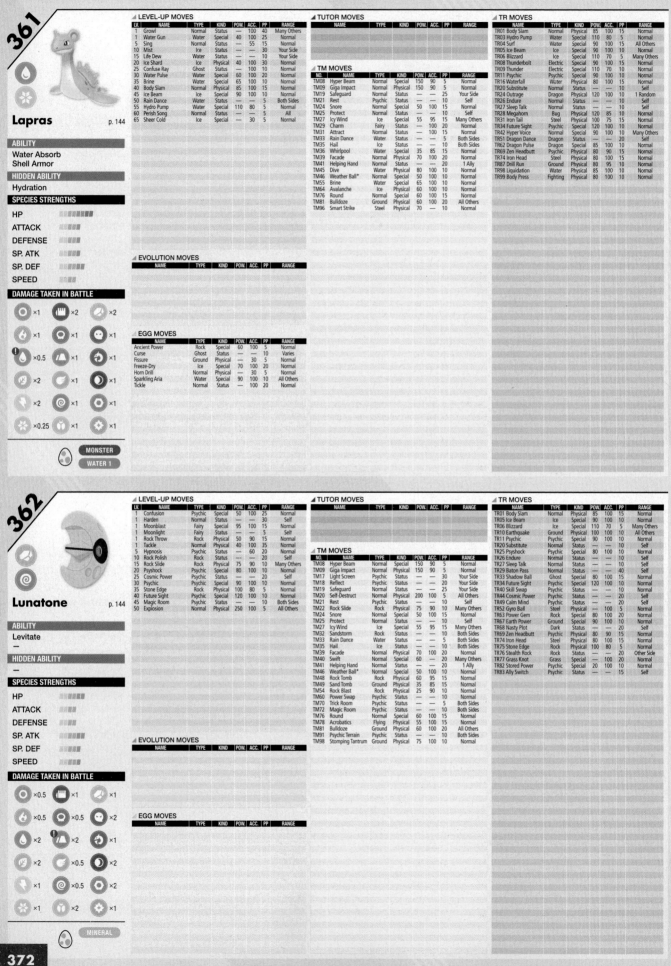

Solrock — p. 144

LEVEL-UP MOVES

LV.	NAME	TYPE	KIND	POW.	ACC.	PP	RANGE
1	Confusion	Psychic	Special	50	100	25	Normal
1	Flare Blitz	Fire	Physical	120	100	15	Normal
1	Harden	Normal	Status	—	—	30	Self
1	Morning Sun	Normal	Status	—	—	5	Self
1	Rock Throw	Rock	Physical	50	90	15	Normal
1	Tackle	Normal	Physical	40	100	35	Normal
5	Hypnosis	Psychic	Status	—	60	20	Normal
10	Rock Polish	Rock	Status	—	—	20	Self
15	Rock Slide	Rock	Physical	75	90	10	Many Others
20	Zen Headbutt	Psychic	Physical	80	90	15	Normal
25	Cosmic Power	Psychic	Status	—	—	20	Self
30	Psychic	Psychic	Special	90	100	10	Normal
35	Stone Edge	Rock	Physical	100	80	5	Normal
40	Solar Beam	Grass	Special	120	100	10	Normal
45	Wonder Room	Psychic	Status	—	—	10	Both Sides
50	Explosion	Normal	Physical	250	100	5	All Others

EVOLUTION MOVES

NAME	TYPE	KIND	POW.	ACC.	PP	RANGE

EGG MOVES

NAME	TYPE	KIND	POW.	ACC.	PP	RANGE

TUTOR MOVES

NAME	TYPE	KIND	POW.	ACC.	PP	RANGE

TM MOVES

NO.	NAME	TYPE	KIND	POW.	ACC.	PP	RANGE
TM08	Hyper Beam	Normal	Special	150	90	5	Normal
TM09	Giga Impact	Normal	Physical	150	90	5	Normal
TM11	Solar Beam	Grass	Special	120	100	10	Normal
TM13	Fire Spin	Fire	Special	35	85	15	Normal
TM17	Light Screen	Psychic	Status	—	—	30	Your Side
TM18	Reflect	Psychic	Status	—	—	20	Your Side
TM19	Safeguard	Normal	Status	—	—	25	Your Side
TM20	Self-Destruct	Normal	Physical	200	100	5	All Others
TM21	Rest	Psychic	Status	—	—	10	Self
TM22	Rock Slide	Rock	Physical	75	90	10	Many Others
TM24	Snore	Normal	Special	50	100	15	Normal
TM25	Protect	Normal	Status	—	—	10	Self
TM32	Sandstorm	Rock	Status	—	—	10	Both Sides
TM33	Rain Dance	Water	Status	—	—	5	Both Sides
TM34	Sunny Day	Fire	Status	—	—	5	Both Sides
TM38	Will-O-Wisp	Fire	Status	—	85	15	Normal
TM39	Facade	Normal	Physical	70	100	20	Normal
TM40	Swift	Normal	Special	60	—	20	Many Others
TM41	Helping Hand	Normal	Status	—	—	20	1 Ally
TM46	Weather Ball*	Normal	Special	50	100	10	Normal
TM48	Rock Tomb	Rock	Physical	60	95	15	Normal
TM49	Sand Tomb	Ground	Physical	35	85	15	Normal
TM54	Rock Blast	Rock	Physical	25	90	10	Normal
TM60	Power Swap	Psychic	Status	—	—	10	Normal
TM70	Trick Room	Psychic	Status	—	—	5	Both Sides
TM71	Wonder Room	Psychic	Status	—	—	10	Both Sides
TM76	Round	Normal	Special	60	100	15	Normal
TM78	Acrobatics	Flying	Physical	55	100	15	Normal
TM81	Bulldoze	Ground	Physical	60	100	20	All Others
TM91	Psychic Terrain	Psychic	Status	—	—	10	Both Sides
TM98	Stomping Tantrum	Ground	Physical	75	100	10	Normal

TR MOVES

NAME	TYPE	KIND	POW.	ACC.	PP	RANGE
TR00 Swords Dance	Normal	Status	—	—	20	Self
TR01 Body Slam	Normal	Physical	85	100	15	Normal
TR02 Flamethrower	Fire	Special	90	100	15	Normal
TR10 Earthquake	Ground	Physical	100	100	10	All Others
TR11 Psychic	Psychic	Special	90	100	10	Normal
TR15 Fire Blast	Fire	Special	110	85	5	Normal
TR25 Psyshock	Psychic	Special	80	100	10	Normal
TR26 Endure	Normal	Status	—	—	10	Self
TR27 Sleep Talk	Normal	Status	—	—	10	Self
TR29 Baton Pass	Normal	Status	—	—	40	Self
TR33 Shadow Ball	Ghost	Special	80	100	15	Normal
TR36 Heat Wave	Fire	Special	95	90	10	Many Others
TR40 Skill Swap	Psychic	Status	—	—	10	Normal
TR43 Overheat	Fire	Special	130	90	5	Normal
TR44 Cosmic Power	Psychic	Status	—	—	20	Self
TR46 Iron Defense	Steel	Status	—	—	15	Self
TR49 Calm Mind	Psychic	Status	—	—	20	Self
TR52 Gyro Ball	Steel	Physical	—	100	5	Normal
TR55 Flare Blitz	Fire	Physical	120	100	15	Normal
TR67 Earth Power	Ground	Special	90	100	10	Normal
TR69 Zen Headbutt	Psychic	Physical	80	90	15	Normal
TR74 Iron Head	Steel	Physical	80	100	15	Normal
TR75 Stone Edge	Rock	Physical	100	80	5	Normal
TR76 Stealth Rock	Rock	Status	—	—	20	Other Side
TR77 Grass Knot	Grass	Special	—	100	20	Normal
TR82 Stored Power	Psychic	Special	20	100	10	Normal
TR83 Ally Switch	Psychic	Status	—	—	15	Self

ABILITY
Levitate
—

HIDDEN ABILITY
—

SPECIES STRENGTHS

HP	
ATTACK	
DEFENSE	
SP. ATK	
SP. DEF	
SPEED	

DAMAGE TAKEN IN BATTLE

×0.5	×1	×1
×0.5	×0.5	×2
×2	×2	×1
×2	×0.5	×1
×1	×0.5	×1
×1	×2	×1

MINERAL

*Weather Ball changes type depending on weather condition. (Harsh sunlight: Fire type. Rain: Water type. Hail: Ice type. Sandstorm: Rock type.)

Mime Jr. — p. 145

LEVEL-UP MOVES

LV.	NAME	TYPE	KIND	POW.	ACC.	PP	RANGE
1	Copycat	Normal	Status	—	—	20	Self
1	Pound	Normal	Physical	40	100	35	Normal
4	Baton Pass	Normal	Status	—	—	40	Self
8	Encore	Normal	Status	—	100	5	Normal
12	Confusion	Psychic	Special	50	100	25	Normal
16	Role Play	Psychic	Status	—	—	10	Normal
20	Protect	Normal	Status	—	—	10	Self
24	Recycle	Normal	Status	—	—	10	Self
28	Psybeam	Psychic	Special	65	100	20	Normal
32	Mimic	Normal	Status	—	—	10	Normal
36	Light Screen	Psychic	Status	—	—	30	Your Side
36	Reflect	Psychic	Status	—	—	20	Your Side
36	Safeguard	Normal	Status	—	—	25	Your Side
40	Sucker Punch	Dark	Physical	70	100	5	Normal
44	Dazzling Gleam	Fairy	Special	80	100	10	Many Others
48	Psychic	Psychic	Special	90	100	10	Normal
52	Teeter Dance	Normal	Status	—	100	20	All Others

EVOLUTION MOVES

NAME	TYPE	KIND	POW.	ACC.	PP	RANGE

EGG MOVES

NAME	TYPE	KIND	POW.	ACC.	PP	RANGE
Confuse Ray	Ghost	Status	—	100	10	Normal
Fake Out	Normal	Physical	40	100	10	Normal
Hypnosis	Psychic	Status	—	60	20	Normal
Power Split	Psychic	Status	—	—	10	Normal
Tickle	Normal	Status	—	100	20	Normal

TUTOR MOVES

NAME	TYPE	KIND	POW.	ACC.	PP	RANGE

TM MOVES

NO.	NAME	TYPE	KIND	POW.	ACC.	PP	RANGE
TM11	Solar Beam	Grass	Special	120	100	10	Normal
TM14	Thunder Wave	Electric	Status	—	90	20	Normal
TM17	Light Screen	Psychic	Status	—	—	30	Your Side
TM18	Reflect	Psychic	Status	—	—	20	Your Side
TM19	Safeguard	Normal	Status	—	—	25	Your Side
TM21	Rest	Psychic	Status	—	—	10	Self
TM23	Thief	Dark	Physical	60	100	25	Normal
TM24	Snore	Normal	Special	50	100	15	Normal
TM25	Protect	Normal	Status	—	—	10	Self
TM27	Icy Wind	Ice	Special	55	95	15	Many Others
TM29	Charm	Fairy	Status	—	100	20	Normal
TM31	Attract	Normal	Status	—	100	15	Normal
TM33	Rain Dance	Water	Status	—	—	5	Both Sides
TM34	Sunny Day	Fire	Status	—	—	5	Both Sides
TM39	Facade	Normal	Physical	70	100	20	Normal
TM41	Helping Hand	Normal	Status	—	—	20	1 Ally
TM43	Brick Break	Fighting	Physical	75	100	15	Normal
TM59	Fling	Dark	Physical	—	100	10	Normal
TM63	Drain Punch	Fighting	Physical	75	100	10	Normal
TM70	Trick Room	Psychic	Status	—	—	5	Both Sides
TM71	Wonder Room	Psychic	Status	—	—	10	Both Sides
TM72	Magic Room	Psychic	Status	—	—	10	Both Sides
TM76	Round	Normal	Special	60	100	15	Normal
TM89	Misty Terrain	Fairy	Status	—	—	10	Both Sides
TM91	Psychic Terrain	Psychic	Status	—	—	10	Both Sides

TR MOVES

NAME	TYPE	KIND	POW.	ACC.	PP	RANGE
TR08 Thunderbolt	Electric	Special	90	100	15	Normal
TR09 Thunder	Electric	Special	110	70	10	Normal
TR11 Psychic	Psychic	Special	90	100	10	Normal
TR20 Substitute	Normal	Status	—	—	10	Self
TR25 Psyshock	Psychic	Special	80	100	10	Normal
TR26 Endure	Normal	Status	—	—	10	Self
TR27 Sleep Talk	Normal	Status	—	—	10	Self
TR29 Baton Pass	Normal	Status	—	—	40	Self
TR30 Encore	Normal	Status	—	100	5	Normal
TR33 Shadow Ball	Ghost	Special	80	100	15	Normal
TR34 Future Sight	Psychic	Special	120	100	10	Normal
TR35 Uproar	Normal	Special	90	100	10	1 Random
TR37 Taunt	Dark	Status	—	100	20	Normal
TR38 Trick	Psychic	Status	—	100	10	Normal
TR40 Skill Swap	Psychic	Status	—	—	10	Normal
TR49 Calm Mind	Psychic	Status	—	—	20	Self
TR68 Nasty Plot	Dark	Status	—	—	20	Self
TR77 Grass Knot	Grass	Special	—	100	20	Normal
TR82 Stored Power	Psychic	Special	20	100	10	Normal
TR83 Ally Switch	Psychic	Status	—	—	15	Self
TR92 Dazzling Gleam	Fairy	Special	80	100	10	Many Others

ABILITY
Soundproof
Filter

HIDDEN ABILITY
Technician

SPECIES STRENGTHS

HP	
ATTACK	
DEFENSE	
SP. ATK	
SP. DEF	
SPEED	

DAMAGE TAKEN IN BATTLE

×1	×0.25	×1
×1	×2	×2
×1	×1	×0
×1	×1	×1
×1	×0.5	×2
×1	×1	×1

NO EGGS

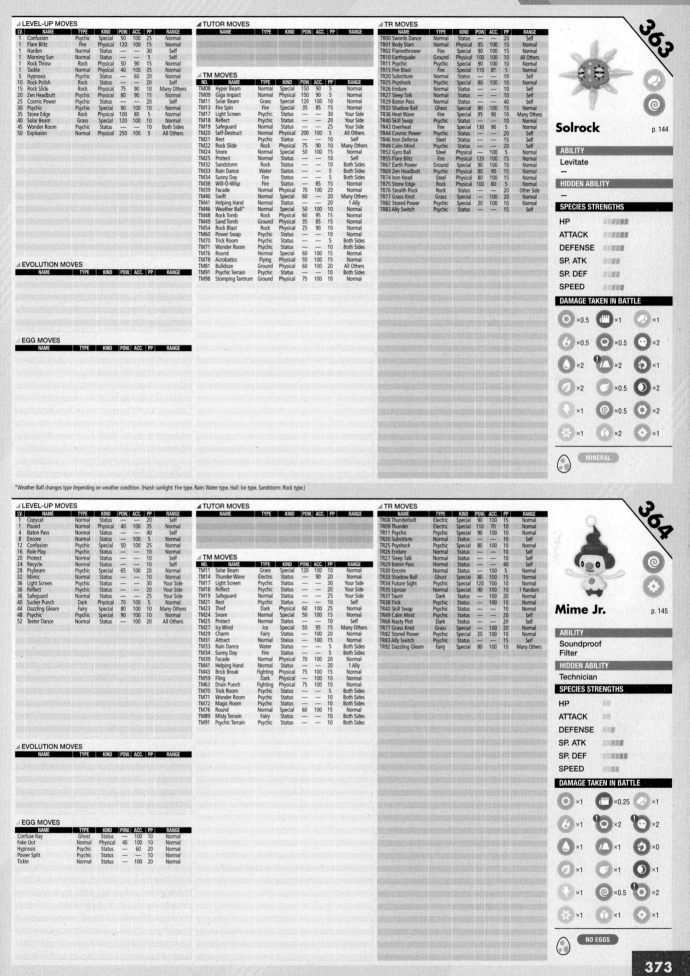

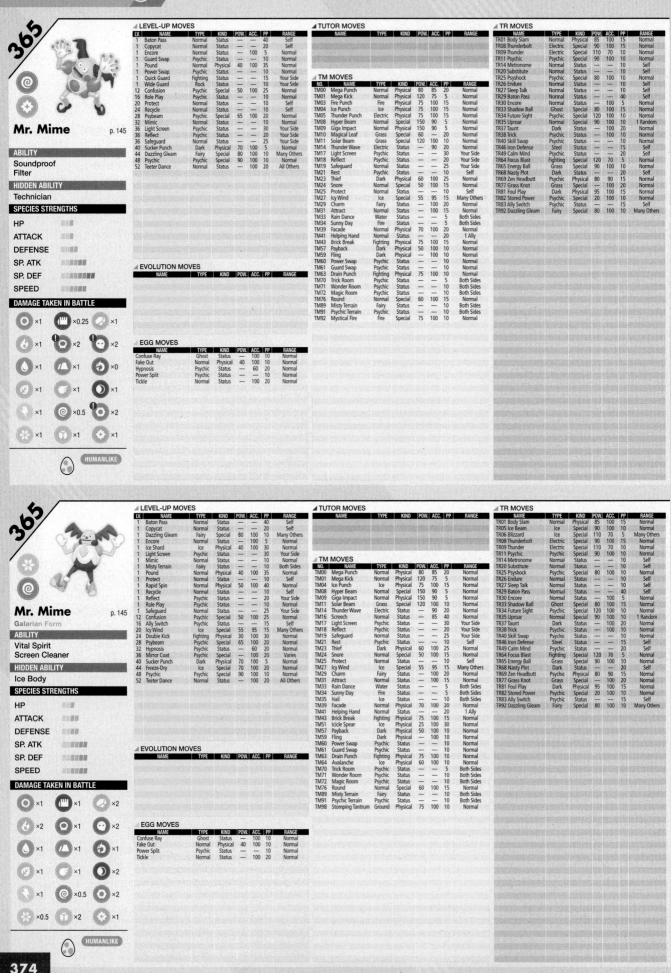

365

Mr. Mime

p. 145

ABILITY

Soundproof
Filter

HIDDEN ABILITY

Technician

SPECIES STRENGTHS

HP
ATTACK
DEFENSE
SP. ATK
SP. DEF
SPEED

DAMAGE TAKEN IN BATTLE

×1	×0.25	×1
×1	×2	×2
×1	×1	×0
×1	×1	×1
×1	×0.5	×2
×1	×1	×1

HUMANLIKE

LEVEL-UP MOVES

LV.	NAME	TYPE	KIND	POW.	ACC.	PP	RANGE
1	Baton Pass	Normal	Status	—	—	40	Self
1	Copycat	Normal	Status	—	—	20	Self
1	Encore	Normal	Status	—	100	5	Normal
1	Guard Swap	Psychic	Status	—	—	10	Normal
1	Pound	Normal	Physical	40	100	35	Normal
1	Power Swap	Psychic	Status	—	—	10	Normal
1	Quick Guard	Fighting	Status	—	—	15	Your Side
1	Wide Guard	Rock	Status	—	—	10	Your Side
12	Confusion	Psychic	Special	50	100	25	Normal
16	Role Play	Psychic	Status	—	—	10	Normal
20	Protect	Normal	Status	—	—	10	Self
24	Recycle	Normal	Status	—	—	10	Self
28	Psybeam	Psychic	Special	65	100	20	Normal
32	Mimic	Normal	Status	—	—	10	Normal
36	Light Screen	Psychic	Status	—	—	30	Your Side
36	Reflect	Psychic	Status	—	—	20	Your Side
36	Safeguard	Normal	Status	—	—	25	Your Side
40	Sucker Punch	Dark	Physical	70	100	5	Normal
44	Dazzling Gleam	Fairy	Special	80	100	10	Many Others
48	Psychic	Psychic	Special	90	100	10	Normal
52	Teeter Dance	Normal	Status	—	100	20	All Others

EVOLUTION MOVES

NAME	TYPE	KIND	POW.	ACC.	PP	RANGE

EGG MOVES

NAME	TYPE	KIND	POW.	ACC.	PP	RANGE
Confuse Ray	Ghost	Status	—	100	10	Normal
Fake Out	Normal	Physical	40	100	10	Normal
Hypnosis	Psychic	Status	—	60	20	Normal
Power Split	Psychic	Status	—	—	10	Normal
Tickle	Normal	Status	—	100	20	Normal

TUTOR MOVES

NAME	TYPE	KIND	POW.	ACC.	PP	RANGE

TM MOVES

NO.	NAME	TYPE	KIND	POW.	ACC.	PP	RANGE
TM00	Mega Punch	Normal	Physical	80	85	20	Normal
TM01	Mega Kick	Normal	Physical	120	75	5	Normal
TM03	Fire Punch	Fire	Physical	75	100	15	Normal
TM04	Ice Punch	Ice	Physical	75	100	15	Normal
TM05	Thunder Punch	Electric	Physical	75	100	15	Normal
TM08	Hyper Beam	Normal	Special	150	90	5	Normal
TM09	Giga Impact	Normal	Physical	150	90	5	Normal
TM10	Magical Leaf	Grass	Special	60	—	20	Normal
TM11	Solar Beam	Grass	Special	120	100	10	Normal
TM14	Thunder Wave	Electric	Status	—	90	20	Normal
TM17	Light Screen	Psychic	Status	—	—	30	Your Side
TM18	Reflect	Psychic	Status	—	—	20	Your Side
TM19	Safeguard	Normal	Status	—	—	25	Your Side
TM21	Rest	Psychic	Status	—	—	10	Self
TM23	Thief	Dark	Physical	60	100	25	Normal
TM24	Snore	Normal	Special	50	100	15	Normal
TM25	Protect	Normal	Status	—	—	10	Self
TM27	Icy Wind	Ice	Special	55	95	15	Many Others
TM29	Charm	Fairy	Status	—	100	20	Normal
TM31	Attract	Normal	Status	—	100	15	Normal
TM33	Rain Dance	Water	Status	—	—	5	Both Sides
TM34	Sunny Day	Fire	Status	—	—	5	Both Sides
TM39	Facade	Normal	Physical	70	100	20	Normal
TM41	Helping Hand	Normal	Status	—	—	20	1 Ally
TM43	Brick Break	Fighting	Physical	75	100	15	Normal
TM57	Payback	Dark	Physical	50	100	10	Normal
TM59	Fling	Dark	Physical	—	100	10	Normal
TM60	Power Swap	Psychic	Status	—	—	10	Normal
TM61	Guard Swap	Psychic	Status	—	—	10	Normal
TM63	Drain Punch	Fighting	Physical	75	100	10	Normal
TM70	Trick Room	Psychic	Status	—	—	5	Both Sides
TM71	Wonder Room	Psychic	Status	—	—	10	Both Sides
TM72	Magic Room	Psychic	Status	—	—	10	Both Sides
TM76	Round	Normal	Special	60	100	15	Normal
TM89	Misty Terrain	Fairy	Status	—	—	10	Both Sides
TM91	Psychic Terrain	Psychic	Status	—	—	10	Both Sides
TM92	Mystical Fire	Fire	Special	75	100	10	Normal

TR MOVES

NAME	TYPE	KIND	POW.	ACC.	PP	RANGE
TR01 Body Slam	Normal	Physical	85	100	15	Normal
TR08 Thunderbolt	Electric	Special	90	100	15	Normal
TR09 Thunder	Electric	Special	110	70	10	Normal
TR11 Psychic	Psychic	Special	90	100	10	Normal
TR14 Metronome	Normal	Status	—	—	10	Self
TR20 Substitute	Normal	Status	—	—	10	Self
TR25 Psyshock	Psychic	Special	80	100	10	Normal
TR26 Endure	Normal	Status	—	—	10	Self
TR27 Sleep Talk	Normal	Status	—	—	10	Self
TR29 Baton Pass	Normal	Status	—	—	40	Self
TR30 Encore	Normal	Status	—	100	5	Normal
TR33 Shadow Ball	Ghost	Special	80	100	15	Normal
TR34 Future Sight	Psychic	Special	120	100	10	Normal
TR35 Uproar	Normal	Special	90	100	10	1 Random
TR37 Taunt	Dark	Status	—	100	20	Normal
TR38 Trick	Psychic	Status	—	100	10	Normal
TR40 Skill Swap	Psychic	Status	—	—	10	Normal
TR46 Iron Defense	Steel	Status	—	—	15	Self
TR49 Calm Mind	Psychic	Status	—	—	20	Self
TR64 Focus Blast	Fighting	Special	120	70	5	Normal
TR65 Energy Ball	Grass	Special	90	100	10	Normal
TR68 Nasty Plot	Dark	Status	—	—	20	Self
TR69 Zen Headbutt	Psychic	Physical	80	90	15	Normal
TR77 Grass Knot	Grass	Special	—	100	20	Normal
TR81 Foul Play	Dark	Physical	95	100	15	Normal
TR82 Stored Power	Psychic	Special	20	100	10	Normal
TR83 Ally Switch	Psychic	Status	—	—	15	Self
TR92 Dazzling Gleam	Fairy	Special	80	100	10	Many Others

365

Mr. Mime

p. 145

Galarian Form

ABILITY

Vital Spirit
Screen Cleaner

HIDDEN ABILITY

Ice Body

SPECIES STRENGTHS

HP
ATTACK
DEFENSE
SP. ATK
SP. DEF
SPEED

DAMAGE TAKEN IN BATTLE

×1	×1	×2
×2	×1	×2
×1	×1	×1
×1	×1	×2
×1	×0.5	×2
×0.5	×2	×1

HUMANLIKE

LEVEL-UP MOVES

LV.	NAME	TYPE	KIND	POW.	ACC.	PP	RANGE
1	Baton Pass	Normal	Status	—	—	40	Self
1	Copycat	Normal	Status	—	—	20	Self
1	Dazzling Gleam	Fairy	Special	80	100	10	Many Others
1	Encore	Normal	Status	—	100	5	Normal
1	Ice Shard	Ice	Physical	40	100	30	Normal
1	Light Screen	Psychic	Status	—	—	30	Your Side
1	Mimic	Normal	Status	—	—	10	Normal
1	Misty Terrain	Fairy	Status	—	—	10	Both Sides
1	Pound	Normal	Physical	40	100	35	Normal
1	Protect	Normal	Status	—	—	10	Self
1	Rapid Spin	Normal	Physical	50	100	40	Normal
1	Recycle	Normal	Status	—	—	10	Self
1	Reflect	Psychic	Status	—	—	20	Your Side
1	Role Play	Psychic	Status	—	—	10	Normal
1	Safeguard	Normal	Status	—	—	25	Your Side
12	Confusion	Psychic	Special	50	100	25	Normal
16	Ally Switch	Psychic	Status	—	—	15	Self
20	Icy Wind	Ice	Special	55	95	15	Many Others
24	Double Kick	Fighting	Physical	30	100	30	Normal
28	Psybeam	Psychic	Special	65	100	20	Normal
32	Hypnosis	Psychic	Status	—	60	20	Normal
36	Mirror Coat	Psychic	Special	—	100	20	Varies
40	Sucker Punch	Dark	Physical	70	100	5	Normal
44	Freeze-Dry	Ice	Special	70	100	20	Normal
48	Psychic	Psychic	Special	90	100	10	Normal
52	Teeter Dance	Normal	Status	—	100	20	All Others

EVOLUTION MOVES

NAME	TYPE	KIND	POW.	ACC.	PP	RANGE

EGG MOVES

NAME	TYPE	KIND	POW.	ACC.	PP	RANGE
Confuse Ray	Ghost	Status	—	100	10	Normal
Fake Out	Normal	Physical	40	100	10	Normal
Power Split	Psychic	Status	—	—	10	Normal
Tickle	Normal	Status	—	100	20	Normal

TUTOR MOVES

NAME	TYPE	KIND	POW.	ACC.	PP	RANGE

TM MOVES

NO.	NAME	TYPE	KIND	POW.	ACC.	PP	RANGE
TM00	Mega Punch	Normal	Physical	80	85	20	Normal
TM01	Mega Kick	Normal	Physical	120	75	5	Normal
TM04	Ice Punch	Ice	Physical	75	100	15	Normal
TM08	Hyper Beam	Normal	Special	150	90	5	Normal
TM09	Giga Impact	Normal	Physical	150	90	5	Normal
TM11	Solar Beam	Grass	Special	120	100	10	Normal
TM14	Thunder Wave	Electric	Status	—	90	20	Normal
TM16	Screech	Normal	Status	—	85	40	Normal
TM17	Light Screen	Psychic	Status	—	—	30	Your Side
TM18	Reflect	Psychic	Status	—	—	20	Your Side
TM19	Safeguard	Normal	Status	—	—	25	Your Side
TM21	Rest	Psychic	Status	—	—	10	Self
TM23	Thief	Dark	Physical	60	100	25	Normal
TM24	Snore	Normal	Special	50	100	15	Normal
TM25	Protect	Normal	Status	—	—	10	Self
TM27	Icy Wind	Ice	Special	55	95	15	Many Others
TM29	Charm	Fairy	Status	—	100	20	Normal
TM31	Attract	Normal	Status	—	100	15	Normal
TM33	Rain Dance	Water	Status	—	—	5	Both Sides
TM34	Sunny Day	Fire	Status	—	—	5	Both Sides
TM35	Hail	Ice	Status	—	—	10	Both Sides
TM39	Facade	Normal	Physical	70	100	20	Normal
TM41	Helping Hand	Normal	Status	—	—	20	1 Ally
TM43	Brick Break	Fighting	Physical	75	100	15	Normal
TM51	Icicle Spear	Ice	Physical	25	100	30	Normal
TM57	Payback	Dark	Physical	50	100	10	Normal
TM59	Fling	Dark	Physical	—	100	10	Normal
TM60	Power Swap	Psychic	Status	—	—	10	Normal
TM61	Guard Swap	Psychic	Status	—	—	10	Normal
TM63	Drain Punch	Fighting	Physical	75	100	10	Normal
TM64	Avalanche	Ice	Physical	60	100	10	Normal
TM70	Trick Room	Psychic	Status	—	—	5	Both Sides
TM71	Wonder Room	Psychic	Status	—	—	10	Both Sides
TM72	Magic Room	Psychic	Status	—	—	10	Both Sides
TM76	Round	Normal	Special	60	100	15	Normal
TM89	Misty Terrain	Fairy	Status	—	—	10	Both Sides
TM91	Psychic Terrain	Psychic	Status	—	—	10	Both Sides
TM98	Stomping Tantrum	Ground	Physical	75	100	10	Normal

TR MOVES

NAME	TYPE	KIND	POW.	ACC.	PP	RANGE
TR01 Body Slam	Normal	Physical	85	100	15	Normal
TR05 Ice Beam	Ice	Special	90	100	10	Normal
TR06 Blizzard	Ice	Special	110	70	5	Many Others
TR08 Thunderbolt	Electric	Special	90	100	15	Normal
TR09 Thunder	Electric	Special	110	70	10	Normal
TR11 Psychic	Psychic	Special	90	100	10	Normal
TR14 Metronome	Normal	Status	—	—	10	Self
TR20 Substitute	Normal	Status	—	—	10	Self
TR25 Psyshock	Psychic	Special	80	100	10	Normal
TR26 Endure	Normal	Status	—	—	10	Self
TR27 Sleep Talk	Normal	Status	—	—	10	Self
TR29 Baton Pass	Normal	Status	—	—	40	Self
TR30 Encore	Normal	Status	—	100	5	Normal
TR33 Shadow Ball	Ghost	Special	80	100	15	Normal
TR34 Future Sight	Psychic	Special	120	100	10	Normal
TR35 Uproar	Normal	Special	90	100	10	1 Random
TR37 Taunt	Dark	Status	—	100	20	Normal
TR38 Trick	Psychic	Status	—	100	10	Normal
TR40 Skill Swap	Psychic	Status	—	—	10	Normal
TR46 Iron Defense	Steel	Status	—	—	15	Self
TR49 Calm Mind	Psychic	Status	—	—	20	Self
TR64 Focus Blast	Fighting	Special	120	70	5	Normal
TR65 Energy Ball	Grass	Special	90	100	10	Normal
TR68 Nasty Plot	Dark	Status	—	—	20	Self
TR69 Zen Headbutt	Psychic	Physical	80	90	15	Normal
TR77 Grass Knot	Grass	Special	—	100	20	Normal
TR81 Foul Play	Dark	Physical	95	100	15	Normal
TR82 Stored Power	Psychic	Special	20	100	10	Normal
TR83 Ally Switch	Psychic	Status	—	—	15	Self
TR92 Dazzling Gleam	Fairy	Special	80	100	10	Many Others

366

Mr. Rime

p. 145

LEVEL-UP MOVES

LV.	NAME	TYPE	KIND	POW.	ACC.	PP	RANGE
1	After You	Normal	Status	—	—	15	Normal
1	Baton Pass	Normal	Status	—	—	40	Self
1	Block	Normal	Status	—	—	5	Normal
1	Copycat	Normal	Status	—	—	20	Self
1	Dazzling Gleam	Fairy	Special	80	100	10	Many Others
1	Encore	Normal	Status	—	100	5	Normal
1	Fake Tears	Dark	Status	—	100	20	Normal
1	Ice Shard	Ice	Physical	40	100	30	Normal
1	Light Screen	Psychic	Status	—	—	30	Your Side
1	Mimic	Normal	Status	—	—	10	Normal
1	Misty Terrain	Fairy	Status	—	—	10	Both Sides
1	Pound	Normal	Physical	40	100	35	Normal
1	Protect	Normal	Status	—	—	10	Self
1	Rapid Spin	Normal	Physical	50	100	40	Normal
1	Recycle	Normal	Status	—	—	10	Self
1	Reflect	Psychic	Status	—	—	20	Your Side
1	Role Play	Psychic	Status	—	—	10	Normal
1	Safeguard	Normal	Status	—	—	25	Your Side
1	Slack Off	Normal	Status	—	—	10	Self
12	Confusion	Psychic	Special	50	100	25	Normal
16	Ally Switch	Psychic	Status	—	—	15	Self
20	Icy Wind	Ice	Special	55	95	15	Many Others
24	Double Kick	Fighting	Physical	30	100	30	Normal
28	Psybeam	Psychic	Special	65	100	20	Normal
32	Hypnosis	Psychic	Status	—	60	20	Normal
36	Mirror Coat	Psychic	Special	—	100	20	Varies
40	Sucker Punch	Dark	Physical	70	100	5	Normal
44	Freeze-Dry	Ice	Special	70	100	20	Normal
48	Psychic	Psychic	Special	90	100	10	Normal
52	Teeter Dance	Normal	Status	—	100	20	All Others

EVOLUTION MOVES

NAME	TYPE	KIND	POW.	ACC.	PP	RANGE

EGG MOVES

NAME	TYPE	KIND	POW.	ACC.	PP	RANGE

TUTOR MOVES

NAME	TYPE	KIND	POW.	ACC.	PP	RANGE

TM MOVES

NO.	NAME	TYPE	KIND	POW.	ACC.	PP	RANGE
TM00	Mega Punch	Normal	Physical	80	85	20	Normal
TM01	Mega Kick	Normal	Physical	120	75	5	Normal
TM04	Ice Punch	Ice	Physical	75	100	15	Normal
TM08	Hyper Beam	Normal	Special	150	90	5	Normal
TM09	Giga Impact	Normal	Physical	150	90	5	Normal
TM11	Solar Beam	Grass	Special	120	100	10	Normal
TM14	Thunder Wave	Electric	Status	—	90	20	Normal
TM16	Screech	Normal	Status	—	85	40	Normal
TM17	Light Screen	Psychic	Status	—	—	30	Your Side
TM18	Reflect	Psychic	Status	—	—	20	Your Side
TM19	Safeguard	Normal	Status	—	—	25	Your Side
TM21	Rest	Psychic	Status	—	—	10	Self
TM23	Thief	Dark	Physical	60	100	25	Normal
TM24	Snore	Normal	Special	50	100	15	Normal
TM25	Protect	Normal	Status	—	—	10	Self
TM27	Icy Wind	Ice	Special	55	95	15	Many Others
TM29	Charm	Fairy	Status	—	100	20	Normal
TM31	Attract	Normal	Status	—	100	15	Normal
TM33	Rain Dance	Water	Status	—	—	5	Both Sides
TM34	Sunny Day	Fire	Status	—	—	5	Both Sides
TM35	Hail	Ice	Status	—	—	10	Both Sides
TM39	Facade	Normal	Physical	70	100	20	Normal
TM41	Helping Hand	Normal	Status	—	—	20	1 Ally
TM43	Brick Break	Fighting	Physical	75	100	15	Normal
TM47	Fake Tears	Dark	Status	—	100	20	Normal
TM51	Icicle Spear	Ice	Physical	25	100	30	Normal
TM57	Payback	Dark	Physical	50	100	10	Normal
TM59	Fling	Dark	Physical	—	100	10	Normal
TM60	Power Swap	Psychic	Status	—	—	10	Normal
TM61	Guard Swap	Psychic	Status	—	—	10	Normal
TM63	Drain Punch	Fighting	Physical	75	100	10	Normal
TM64	Avalanche	Ice	Physical	60	100	10	Normal
TM70	Trick Room	Psychic	Status	—	—	5	Both Sides
TM71	Wonder Room	Psychic	Status	—	—	10	Both Sides
TM72	Magic Room	Psychic	Status	—	—	10	Both Sides
TM76	Round	Normal	Special	60	100	15	Normal
TM89	Misty Terrain	Fairy	Status	—	—	10	Both Sides
TM91	Psychic Terrain	Psychic	Status	—	—	10	Both Sides
TM98	Stomping Tantrum	Ground	Physical	75	100	10	Normal

TR MOVES

NAME	TYPE	KIND	POW.	ACC.	PP	RANGE
TR01 Body Slam	Normal	Physical	85	100	15	Normal
TR05 Ice Beam	Ice	Special	90	100	10	Normal
TR06 Blizzard	Ice	Special	110	70	5	Many Others
TR08 Thunderbolt	Electric	Special	90	100	15	Normal
TR09 Thunder	Electric	Special	110	70	10	Normal
TR11 Psychic	Psychic	Special	90	100	10	Normal
TR14 Metronome	Normal	Status	—	—	10	Self
TR20 Substitute	Normal	Status	—	—	10	Self
TR25 Psyshock	Psychic	Special	80	100	10	Normal
TR26 Endure	Normal	Status	—	—	10	Self
TR27 Sleep Talk	Normal	Status	—	—	10	Self
TR29 Baton Pass	Normal	Status	—	—	40	Self
TR30 Encore	Normal	Status	—	100	5	Normal
TR33 Shadow Ball	Ghost	Special	80	100	15	Normal
TR34 Future Sight	Psychic	Special	120	100	10	Normal
TR35 Uproar	Normal	Special	90	100	10	1 Random
TR37 Taunt	Dark	Status	—	100	20	Normal
TR38 Trick	Psychic	Status	—	100	10	Normal
TR40 Skill Swap	Psychic	Status	—	—	10	Normal
TR46 Iron Defense	Steel	Status	—	—	15	Self
TR49 Calm Mind	Psychic	Status	—	—	20	Self
TR64 Focus Blast	Fighting	Special	120	70	5	Normal
TR65 Energy Ball	Grass	Special	90	100	10	Normal
TR68 Nasty Plot	Dark	Status	—	—	20	Self
TR69 Zen Headbutt	Psychic	Physical	80	90	15	Normal
TR77 Grass Knot	Grass	Special	—	100	20	Normal
TR81 Foul Play	Dark	Physical	95	100	15	Normal
TR82 Stored Power	Psychic	Special	20	100	10	Normal
TR83 Ally Switch	Psychic	Status	—	—	15	Self
TR92 Dazzling Gleam	Fairy	Special	80	100	10	Many Others

ABILITY

Tangled Feet
Screen Cleaner

HIDDEN ABILITY

Ice Body

SPECIES STRENGTHS

HP
ATTACK
DEFENSE
SP. ATK
SP. DEF
SPEED

DAMAGE TAKEN IN BATTLE

×1	×1	×2
×2	×1	×2
×1	×1	×1
×1	×1	×2
×1	×0.5	×2
×0.5	×2	×1

HUMANLIKE

367

Darumaka

Galarian Form

p. 146

LEVEL-UP MOVES

LV.	NAME	TYPE	KIND	POW.	ACC.	PP	RANGE
1	Powder Snow	Ice	Special	40	100	25	Many Others
1	Tackle	Normal	Physical	40	100	35	Normal
4	Taunt	Dark	Status	—	100	20	Normal
8	Bite	Dark	Physical	60	100	25	Normal
12	Avalanche	Ice	Physical	60	100	10	Normal
16	Work Up	Normal	Status	—	—	30	Self
20	Ice Fang	Ice	Physical	65	95	15	Normal
24	Headbutt	Normal	Physical	70	100	15	Normal
28	Ice Punch	Ice	Physical	75	100	15	Normal
32	Uproar	Normal	Special	90	100	10	1 Random
36	Belly Drum	Normal	Status	—	—	10	Self
40	Blizzard	Ice	Special	110	70	5	Many Others
44	Thrash	Normal	Physical	120	100	10	1 Random
48	Superpower	Fighting	Physical	120	100	5	Normal

EVOLUTION MOVES

NAME	TYPE	KIND	POW.	ACC.	PP	RANGE

EGG MOVES

NAME	TYPE	KIND	POW.	ACC.	PP	RANGE
Flame Wheel	Fire	Physical	60	100	25	Normal
Focus Punch	Fighting	Physical	150	100	20	Normal
Freeze-Dry	Ice	Special	70	100	20	Normal
Hammer Arm	Fighting	Physical	100	90	10	Normal
Incinerate	Fire	Special	60	100	15	Many Others
Power-Up Punch	Fighting	Physical	40	100	20	Normal
Take Down	Normal	Physical	90	85	20	Normal
Yawn	Normal	Status	—	—	10	Normal

TUTOR MOVES

NAME	TYPE	KIND	POW.	ACC.	PP	RANGE

TM MOVES

NO.	NAME	TYPE	KIND	POW.	ACC.	PP	RANGE
TM00	Mega Punch	Normal	Physical	80	85	20	Normal
TM01	Mega Kick	Normal	Physical	120	75	5	Normal
TM03	Fire Punch	Fire	Physical	75	100	15	Normal
TM04	Ice Punch	Ice	Physical	75	100	15	Normal
TM11	Solar Beam	Grass	Special	120	100	10	Normal
TM13	Fire Spin	Fire	Special	35	85	15	Normal
TM15	Dig	Ground	Physical	80	100	10	Normal
TM21	Rest	Psychic	Status	—	—	10	Self
TM22	Rock Slide	Rock	Physical	75	90	10	Many Others
TM23	Thief	Dark	Physical	60	100	25	Normal
TM24	Snore	Normal	Special	50	100	15	Normal
TM25	Protect	Normal	Status	—	—	10	Self
TM31	Attract	Normal	Status	—	100	15	Normal
TM34	Sunny Day	Fire	Status	—	—	5	Both Sides
TM38	Will-O-Wisp	Fire	Status	—	85	15	Normal
TM39	Facade	Normal	Physical	70	100	20	Normal
TM43	Brick Break	Fighting	Physical	75	100	15	Normal
TM48	Rock Tomb	Rock	Physical	60	95	15	Normal
TM56	U-turn	Bug	Physical	70	100	20	Normal
TM59	Fling	Dark	Physical	—	100	10	Normal
TM64	Avalanche	Ice	Physical	60	100	10	Normal
TM67	Ice Fang	Ice	Physical	65	95	15	Normal
TM68	Fire Fang	Fire	Physical	65	95	15	Normal
TM76	Round	Normal	Special	60	100	15	Normal

TR MOVES

NAME	TYPE	KIND	POW.	ACC.	PP	RANGE
TR02 Flamethrower	Fire	Special	90	100	15	Normal
TR05 Ice Beam	Ice	Special	90	100	10	Normal
TR06 Blizzard	Ice	Special	110	70	5	Many Others
TR13 Focus Energy	Normal	Status	—	—	30	Self
TR15 Fire Blast	Fire	Special	110	85	5	Normal
TR20 Substitute	Normal	Status	—	—	10	Self
TR26 Endure	Normal	Status	—	—	10	Self
TR27 Sleep Talk	Normal	Status	—	—	10	Self
TR30 Encore	Normal	Status	—	100	5	Normal
TR35 Uproar	Normal	Special	90	100	10	1 Random
TR36 Heat Wave	Fire	Special	95	90	10	Many Others
TR37 Taunt	Dark	Status	—	100	20	Normal
TR39 Superpower	Fighting	Physical	120	100	5	Normal
TR43 Overheat	Fire	Special	130	90	5	Normal
TR52 Gyro Ball	Steel	Physical	—	100	5	Normal
TR55 Flare Blitz	Fire	Physical	120	100	15	Normal
TR69 Zen Headbutt	Psychic	Physical	80	90	15	Normal
TR77 Grass Knot	Grass	Special	—	100	20	Normal
TR85 Work Up	Normal	Status	—	—	30	Self

ABILITY

Hustle
—

HIDDEN ABILITY

Inner Focus

SPECIES STRENGTHS

HP
ATTACK
DEFENSE
SP. ATK
SP. DEF
SPEED

DAMAGE TAKEN IN BATTLE

×1	×2	×2
×2	×1	×1
×1	×1	×1
×1	×1	×1
×1	×1	×2
×0.5	×1	×1

FIELD

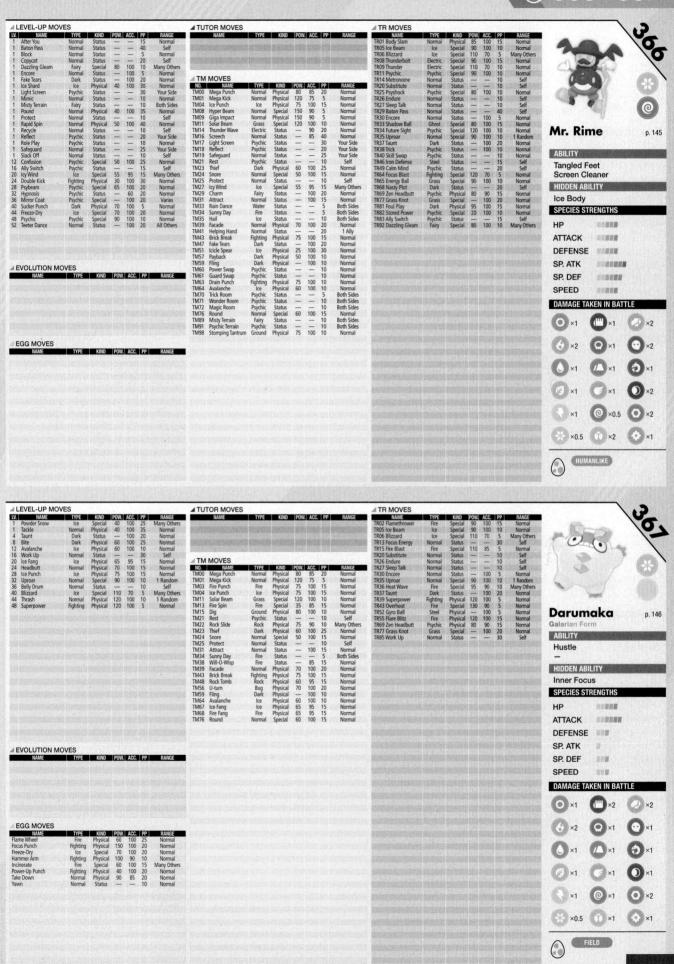

368 Darmanitan — Galarian Form — p. 146

ABILITY
Gorilla Tactics
—

HIDDEN ABILITY
Zen Mode

SPECIES STRENGTHS

HP	
ATTACK	
DEFENSE	
SP. ATK	
SP. DEF	
SPEED	

LEVEL-UP MOVES

LV.	NAME	TYPE	KIND	POW.	ACC.	PP	RANGE
1	Bite	Dark	Physical	60	100	25	Normal
1	Icicle Crash	Ice	Physical	85	90	10	Normal
1	Powder Snow	Ice	Special	40	100	25	Many Others
1	Tackle	Normal	Physical	40	100	35	Normal
1	Taunt	Dark	Status	—	100	20	Normal
12	Avalanche	Ice	Physical	60	100	10	Normal
16	Work Up	Normal	Status	—	—	30	Self
20	Ice Fang	Ice	Physical	65	95	15	Normal
24	Headbutt	Normal	Physical	70	100	15	Normal
28	Ice Punch	Ice	Physical	75	100	15	Normal
32	Uproar	Normal	Special	90	100	10	1 Random
38	Belly Drum	Normal	Status	—	—	10	Self
44	Blizzard	Ice	Special	110	70	5	Many Others
50	Thrash	Normal	Physical	120	100	10	1 Random
56	Superpower	Fighting	Physical	120	100	5	Normal

TUTOR MOVES

NAME	TYPE	KIND	POW.	ACC.	PP	RANGE

TM MOVES

NO.	NAME	TYPE	KIND	POW.	ACC.	PP	RANGE
TM00	Mega Punch	Normal	Physical	80	85	20	Normal
TM01	Mega Kick	Normal	Physical	120	75	5	Normal
TM03	Fire Punch	Fire	Physical	75	100	15	Normal
TM04	Ice Punch	Ice	Physical	75	100	15	Normal
TM08	Hyper Beam	Normal	Special	150	90	5	Normal
TM09	Giga Impact	Normal	Physical	150	90	5	Normal
TM11	Solar Beam	Grass	Special	120	100	10	Normal
TM13	Fire Spin	Fire	Special	35	85	15	Normal
TM15	Dig	Ground	Physical	80	100	10	Normal
TM21	Rest	Psychic	Status	—	—	10	Self
TM22	Rock Slide	Rock	Physical	75	90	10	Many Others
TM23	Thief	Dark	Physical	60	100	25	Normal
TM24	Snore	Normal	Special	50	100	15	Normal
TM25	Protect	Normal	Status	—	100	10	Self
TM31	Attract	Normal	Status	—	100	15	Normal
TM34	Sunny Day	Fire	Status	—	—	5	Both Sides
TM38	Will-O-Wisp	Fire	Status	—	85	15	Normal
TM39	Facade	Normal	Physical	70	100	20	Normal
TM43	Brick Break	Fighting	Physical	75	100	15	Normal
TM48	Rock Tomb	Rock	Physical	60	95	15	Normal
TM56	U-turn	Bug	Physical	70	100	20	Normal
TM57	Payback	Dark	Physical	50	100	10	Normal
TM59	Fling	Dark	Physical	—	100	10	Normal
TM64	Avalanche	Ice	Physical	60	100	10	Normal
TM67	Ice Fang	Ice	Physical	65	95	15	Normal
TM68	Fire Fang	Fire	Physical	65	95	15	Normal
TM76	Round	Normal	Special	60	100	15	Normal
TM81	Bulldoze	Ground	Physical	60	100	20	All Others

TR MOVES

NAME	TYPE	KIND	POW.	ACC.	PP	RANGE
TR01 Body Slam	Normal	Physical	85	100	15	Normal
TR02 Flamethrower	Fire	Special	90	100	15	Normal
TR05 Ice Beam	Ice	Special	90	100	10	Normal
TR06 Blizzard	Ice	Special	110	70	5	Many Others
TR10 Earthquake	Ground	Physical	100	100	10	All Others
TR11 Psychic	Psychic	Special	90	100	10	Normal
TR13 Focus Energy	Normal	Status	—	—	30	Self
TR15 Fire Blast	Fire	Special	110	85	5	Normal
TR20 Substitute	Normal	Status	—	—	10	Self
TR21 Reversal	Fighting	Physical	—	100	15	Normal
TR26 Endure	Normal	Status	—	—	10	Self
TR27 Sleep Talk	Normal	Status	—	—	10	Self
TR30 Encore	Normal	Status	—	100	5	Normal
TR35 Uproar	Normal	Special	90	100	10	1 Random
TR36 Heat Wave	Fire	Special	95	90	10	Many Others
TR37 Taunt	Dark	Status	—	100	20	Normal
TR39 Superpower	Fighting	Physical	120	100	5	Normal
TR43 Overheat	Fire	Special	130	90	5	Normal
TR46 Iron Defense	Steel	Status	—	—	15	Self
TR48 Bulk Up	Fighting	Status	—	—	20	Self
TR52 Gyro Ball	Steel	Physical	—	100	5	Normal
TR55 Flare Blitz	Fire	Physical	120	100	15	Normal
TR64 Focus Blast	Fighting	Special	120	70	5	Normal
TR69 Zen Headbutt	Psychic	Physical	80	90	15	Normal
TR74 Iron Head	Steel	Physical	80	100	15	Normal
TR75 Stone Edge	Rock	Physical	100	80	5	Normal
TR77 Grass Knot	Grass	Special	—	100	20	Normal
TR85 Work Up	Normal	Status	—	—	30	Self
TR99 Body Press	Fighting	Physical	80	100	10	Normal

EVOLUTION MOVES

NAME	TYPE	KIND	POW.	ACC.	PP	RANGE
Icicle Crash	Ice	Physical	85	90	10	Normal

EGG MOVES

NAME	TYPE	KIND	POW.	ACC.	PP	RANGE

DAMAGE TAKEN IN BATTLE

×1 | ×2 | ×2 | ×2 | ×1 | ×1 | ×1 | ×1 | ×1 | ×1 | ×1 | ×1 | ×2 | ×0.5 | ×1 | ×1

FIELD

---

369 Stonjourner — p. 147

ABILITY
Power Spot
—

HIDDEN ABILITY
—

SPECIES STRENGTHS

HP	
ATTACK	
DEFENSE	
SP. ATK	
SP. DEF	
SPEED	

LEVEL-UP MOVES

LV.	NAME	TYPE	KIND	POW.	ACC.	PP	RANGE
1	Block	Normal	Status	—	—	5	Normal
1	Rock Throw	Rock	Physical	50	90	15	Normal
6	Rock Polish	Rock	Status	—	—	20	Self
12	Rock Tomb	Rock	Physical	60	95	15	Normal
18	Gravity	Psychic	Status	—	—	5	Both Sides
24	Stomp	Normal	Physical	65	100	20	Normal
30	Stealth Rock	Rock	Status	—	—	20	Other Side
36	Rock Slide	Rock	Physical	75	90	10	Many Others
42	Body Slam	Normal	Physical	85	100	15	Normal
48	Wide Guard	Rock	Status	—	—	10	Your Side
54	Heavy Slam	Steel	Physical	—	100	10	Normal
60	Stone Edge	Rock	Physical	100	80	5	Normal
66	Mega Kick	Normal	Physical	120	75	5	Normal

TUTOR MOVES

NAME	TYPE	KIND	POW.	ACC.	PP	RANGE

TM MOVES

NO.	NAME	TYPE	KIND	POW.	ACC.	PP	RANGE
TM01	Mega Kick	Normal	Physical	120	75	5	Normal
TM08	Hyper Beam	Normal	Special	150	90	5	Normal
TM09	Giga Impact	Normal	Physical	150	90	5	Normal
TM19	Safeguard	Normal	Status	—	—	25	Your Side
TM20	Self-Destruct	Normal	Physical	200	100	5	All Others
TM21	Rest	Psychic	Status	—	—	10	Self
TM22	Rock Slide	Rock	Physical	75	90	10	Many Others
TM24	Snore	Normal	Special	50	100	15	Normal
TM25	Protect	Normal	Status	—	—	10	Self
TM31	Attract	Normal	Status	—	100	15	Normal
TM32	Sandstorm	Rock	Status	—	—	10	Both Sides
TM39	Facade	Normal	Physical	70	100	20	Normal
TM44	Imprison	Psychic	Status	—	—	10	Self
TM48	Rock Tomb	Rock	Physical	60	95	15	Normal
TM49	Sand Tomb	Ground	Physical	35	85	15	Normal
TM54	Rock Blast	Rock	Physical	25	90	10	Normal
TM58	Assurance	Dark	Physical	60	100	10	Normal
TM71	Wonder Room	Psychic	Status	—	—	10	Both Sides
TM76	Round	Normal	Special	60	100	15	Normal
TM81	Bulldoze	Ground	Physical	60	100	20	All Others
TM97	Brutal Swing	Dark	Physical	60	100	20	All Others
TM98	Stomping Tantrum	Ground	Physical	75	100	10	Normal

TR MOVES

NAME	TYPE	KIND	POW.	ACC.	PP	RANGE
TR01 Body Slam	Normal	Physical	85	100	15	Normal
TR10 Earthquake	Ground	Physical	100	100	10	All Others
TR20 Substitute	Normal	Status	—	—	10	Self
TR26 Endure	Normal	Status	—	—	10	Self
TR27 Sleep Talk	Normal	Status	—	—	10	Self
TR39 Superpower	Fighting	Physical	120	100	5	Normal
TR46 Iron Defense	Steel	Status	—	—	15	Self
TR67 Earth Power	Ground	Special	90	100	10	Normal
TR75 Stone Edge	Rock	Physical	100	80	5	Normal
TR76 Stealth Rock	Rock	Status	—	—	20	Other Side
TR79 Heavy Slam	Steel	Physical	—	100	10	Normal
TR88 Heat Crash	Fire	Physical	—	100	10	Normal
TR99 Body Press	Fighting	Physical	80	100	10	Normal

EVOLUTION MOVES

NAME	TYPE	KIND	POW.	ACC.	PP	RANGE

EGG MOVES

NAME	TYPE	KIND	POW.	ACC.	PP	RANGE
Ancient Power	Rock	Special	60	100	5	Normal
Curse	Ghost	Status	—	—	10	Varies

DAMAGE TAKEN IN BATTLE

×0.5 | ×2 | ×1 | ×0.5 | ×0.5 | ×1 | ×2 | ×2 | ×1 | ×2 | ×0.5 | ×1 | ×1 | ×1 | ×2

MINERAL

370

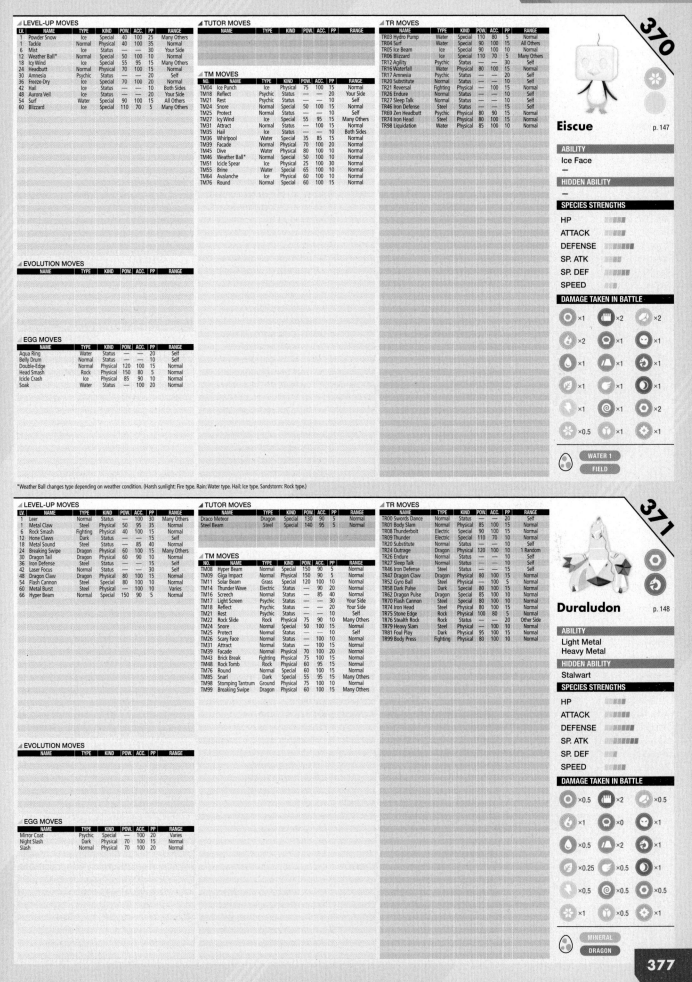

LEVEL-UP MOVES

LV.	NAME	TYPE	KIND	POW.	ACC.	PP	RANGE
1	Powder Snow	Ice	Special	40	100	25	Many Others
1	Tackle	Normal	Physical	40	100	35	Normal
6	Mist	Ice	Status	—	—	30	Your Side
12	Weather Ball*	Normal	Special	50	100	10	Normal
18	Icy Wind	Ice	Special	55	95	15	Many Others
24	Headbutt	Normal	Physical	70	100	15	Normal
30	Amnesia	Psychic	Status	—	—	20	Self
36	Freeze-Dry	Ice	Special	70	100	20	Normal
42	Hail	Ice	Status	—	—	10	Both Sides
48	Aurora Veil	Ice	Status	—	—	20	Your Side
54	Surf	Water	Special	90	100	15	All Others
60	Blizzard	Ice	Special	110	70	5	Many Others

EVOLUTION MOVES

NAME	TYPE	KIND	POW.	ACC.	PP	RANGE

EGG MOVES

NAME	TYPE	KIND	POW.	ACC.	PP	RANGE
Aqua Ring	Water	Status	—	—	20	Self
Belly Drum	Normal	Status	—	—	10	Self
Double-Edge	Normal	Physical	120	100	15	Normal
Head Smash	Rock	Physical	150	80	5	Normal
Icicle Crash	Ice	Physical	85	90	10	Normal
Soak	Water	Status	—	100	20	Normal

TUTOR MOVES

NAME	TYPE	KIND	POW.	ACC.	PP	RANGE

TM MOVES

NO.	NAME	TYPE	KIND	POW.	ACC.	PP	RANGE
TM04	Ice Punch	Ice	Physical	75	100	15	Normal
TM18	Reflect	Psychic	Status	—	—	20	Your Side
TM21	Rest	Psychic	Status	—	—	10	Self
TM24	Snore	Normal	Special	50	100	15	Normal
TM25	Protect	Normal	Status	—	—	10	Self
TM27	Icy Wind	Ice	Special	55	95	15	Many Others
TM31	Attract	Normal	Status	—	100	15	Normal
TM35	Hail	Ice	Status	—	—	10	Both Sides
TM36	Whirlpool	Water	Special	35	85	15	Normal
TM39	Facade	Normal	Physical	70	100	20	Normal
TM45	Dive	Water	Physical	80	100	10	Normal
TM46	Weather Ball*	Normal	Special	50	100	10	Normal
TM51	Icicle Spear	Ice	Physical	25	100	30	Normal
TM55	Brine	Water	Special	65	100	10	Normal
TM64	Avalanche	Ice	Physical	60	100	10	Normal
TM76	Round	Normal	Special	60	100	15	Normal

TR MOVES

NO.	NAME	TYPE	KIND	POW.	ACC.	PP	RANGE
TR03	Hydro Pump	Water	Special	110	80	5	Normal
TR04	Surf	Water	Special	90	100	15	All Others
TR05	Ice Beam	Ice	Special	90	100	10	Normal
TR06	Blizzard	Ice	Special	110	70	5	Many Others
TR12	Agility	Psychic	Status	—	—	30	Self
TR16	Waterfall	Water	Physical	80	100	15	Normal
TR17	Amnesia	Psychic	Status	—	—	20	Self
TR20	Substitute	Normal	Status	—	—	10	Self
TR21	Reversal	Fighting	Physical	—	100	15	Normal
TR26	Endure	Normal	Status	—	—	10	Self
TR27	Sleep Talk	Normal	Status	—	—	10	Self
TR46	Iron Defense	Steel	Status	—	—	15	Self
TR69	Zen Headbutt	Psychic	Physical	80	90	15	Normal
TR74	Iron Head	Steel	Physical	80	100	15	Normal
TR98	Liquidation	Water	Physical	85	100	10	Normal

Eiscue
p. 147

ABILITY
Ice Face

HIDDEN ABILITY
—

SPECIES STRENGTHS

HP	
ATTACK	
DEFENSE	
SP. ATK	
SP. DEF	
SPEED	

DAMAGE TAKEN IN BATTLE

×1 | ×2 | ×2
×2 | ×1 | ×1
×1 | ×1 | ×1
×1 | ×1 | ×1
 | ×2
×0.5 | ×1 | ×1

WATER 1
FIELD

*Weather Ball changes type depending on weather condition. (Harsh sunlight: Fire type. Rain: Water type. Hail: Ice type. Sandstorm: Rock type.)

371

LEVEL-UP MOVES

LV.	NAME	TYPE	KIND	POW.	ACC.	PP	RANGE
1	Leer	Normal	Status	—	100	30	Many Others
1	Metal Claw	Steel	Physical	50	95	35	Normal
6	Rock Smash	Fighting	Physical	40	100	15	Normal
12	Hone Claws	Dark	Status	—	—	15	Self
18	Metal Sound	Steel	Status	—	85	40	Normal
24	Breaking Swipe	Dragon	Physical	60	100	15	Many Others
30	Dragon Tail	Dragon	Physical	60	90	10	Normal
36	Iron Defense	Steel	Status	—	—	15	Self
42	Laser Focus	Normal	Status	—	—	30	Self
48	Dragon Claw	Dragon	Physical	80	100	15	Normal
54	Flash Cannon	Steel	Special	80	100	10	Normal
60	Metal Burst	Steel	Physical	—	100	10	Varies
66	Hyper Beam	Normal	Special	150	90	5	Normal

EVOLUTION MOVES

NAME	TYPE	KIND	POW.	ACC.	PP	RANGE

EGG MOVES

NAME	TYPE	KIND	POW.	ACC.	PP	RANGE
Mirror Coat	Psychic	Special	—	100	20	Varies
Night Slash	Dark	Physical	70	100	15	Normal
Slash	Normal	Physical	70	100	20	Normal

TUTOR MOVES

NAME	TYPE	KIND	POW.	ACC.	PP	RANGE
Draco Meteor	Dragon	Special	130	90	5	Normal
Steel Beam	Steel	Special	140	95	5	Normal

TM MOVES

NO.	NAME	TYPE	KIND	POW.	ACC.	PP	RANGE
TM08	Hyper Beam	Normal	Special	150	90	5	Normal
TM09	Giga Impact	Normal	Physical	150	90	5	Normal
TM11	Solar Beam	Grass	Special	120	100	10	Normal
TM14	Thunder Wave	Electric	Status	—	90	20	Normal
TM16	Screech	Normal	Status	—	85	40	Normal
TM17	Light Screen	Psychic	Status	—	—	30	Your Side
TM18	Reflect	Psychic	Status	—	—	20	Your Side
TM21	Rest	Psychic	Status	—	—	10	Self
TM22	Rock Slide	Rock	Physical	75	90	10	Many Others
TM24	Snore	Normal	Special	50	100	15	Normal
TM25	Protect	Normal	Status	—	—	10	Self
TM26	Scary Face	Normal	Status	—	100	10	Normal
TM31	Attract	Normal	Status	—	100	15	Normal
TM39	Facade	Normal	Physical	70	100	20	Normal
TM43	Brick Break	Fighting	Physical	75	100	15	Normal
TM48	Rock Tomb	Rock	Physical	60	95	15	Normal
TM76	Round	Normal	Special	60	100	15	Normal
TM85	Snarl	Dark	Special	55	95	15	Many Others
TM98	Stomping Tantrum	Ground	Physical	75	100	10	Normal
TM99	Breaking Swipe	Dragon	Physical	60	100	15	Many Others

TR MOVES

NO.	NAME	TYPE	KIND	POW.	ACC.	PP	RANGE
TR00	Swords Dance	Normal	Status	—	—	20	Self
TR01	Body Slam	Normal	Physical	85	100	15	Normal
TR08	Thunderbolt	Electric	Special	90	100	15	Normal
TR09	Thunder	Electric	Special	110	70	10	Normal
TR20	Substitute	Normal	Status	—	—	10	Self
TR24	Outrage	Dragon	Physical	120	100	10	1 Random
TR26	Endure	Normal	Status	—	—	10	Self
TR27	Sleep Talk	Normal	Status	—	—	10	Self
TR46	Iron Defense	Steel	Status	—	—	15	Self
TR47	Dragon Claw	Dragon	Physical	80	100	15	Normal
TR52	Gyro Ball	Steel	Physical	—	100	5	Normal
TR58	Dark Pulse	Dark	Special	80	100	15	Normal
TR62	Dragon Pulse	Dragon	Special	85	100	10	Normal
TR70	Flash Cannon	Steel	Special	80	100	10	Normal
TR74	Iron Head	Steel	Physical	80	100	15	Normal
TR75	Stone Edge	Rock	Physical	100	80	5	Normal
TR76	Stealth Rock	Rock	Status	—	—	20	Other Side
TR79	Heavy Slam	Steel	Physical	—	100	10	Normal
TR81	Foul Play	Dark	Physical	95	100	15	Normal
TR99	Body Press	Fighting	Physical	80	100	10	Normal

Duraludon
p. 148

ABILITY
Light Metal
Heavy Metal

HIDDEN ABILITY
Stalwart

SPECIES STRENGTHS

HP	
ATTACK	
DEFENSE	
SP. ATK	
SP. DEF	
SPEED	

DAMAGE TAKEN IN BATTLE

×0.5 | ×2 | ×0.5
×1 | ×0 | ×1
×0.5 | ×2 | ×1
×0.25 | ×0.5 | ×1
×0.5 | ×0.5 | ×0.5
×1 | ×0.5 | ×1

MINERAL
DRAGON

372 Rotom

p. 148

ABILITY
Levitate
—

HIDDEN ABILITY
—

SPECIES STRENGTHS

HP
ATTACK
DEFENSE
SP. ATK
SP. DEF
SPEED

DAMAGE TAKEN IN BATTLE

×0 ×0 ×1
×1 ×0.5 ×2
×1 ×2 ×1
×1 ×0.5 ×2
×0.5 ×1 ×0.5
×1 ×0.5 ×1

AMORPHOUS

LEVEL-UP MOVES

LV.	NAME	TYPE	KIND	POW.	ACC.	PP	RANGE
1	Astonish	Ghost	Physical	30	100	15	Normal
1	Double Team	Normal	Status	—	—	15	Self
5	Thunder Shock	Electric	Special	40	100	30	Normal
10	Confuse Ray	Ghost	Status	—	100	10	Normal
15	Charge	Electric	Status	—	—	20	Self
20	Electro Ball	Electric	Special	—	100	10	Normal
25	Thunder Wave	Electric	Status	—	90	20	Normal
30	Shock Wave	Electric	Special	60	—	20	Normal
35	Hex	Ghost	Special	65	100	10	Normal
40	Substitute	Normal	Status	—	—	10	Self
45	Trick	Psychic	Status	—	100	10	Normal
50	Discharge	Electric	Special	80	100	15	All Others
55	Uproar	Normal	Special	90	100	10	1 Random
*	Air Slash	Flying	Special	75	95	15	Normal
*	Blizzard	Ice	Special	110	70	5	Many Others
*	Hydro Pump	Water	Special	110	80	5	Normal
*	Leaf Storm	Grass	Special	130	90	5	Normal
*	Overheat	Fire	Special	130	90	5	Normal

TUTOR MOVES

NAME	TYPE	KIND	POW.	ACC.	PP	RANGE

TM MOVES

NO.	NAME	TYPE	KIND	POW.	ACC.	PP	RANGE
TM14	Thunder Wave	Electric	Status	—	90	20	Normal
TM17	Light Screen	Psychic	Status	—	—	30	Your Side
TM18	Reflect	Psychic	Status	—	—	20	Your Side
TM21	Rest	Psychic	Status	—	—	10	Self
TM23	Thief	Dark	Physical	60	100	25	Normal
TM24	Snore	Normal	Special	50	100	15	Normal
TM25	Protect	Normal	Status	—	—	10	Self
TM33	Rain Dance	Water	Status	—	—	5	Both Sides
TM34	Sunny Day	Fire	Status	—	—	5	Both Sides
TM38	Will-O-Wisp	Fire	Status	—	85	15	Normal
TM39	Facade	Normal	Physical	70	100	20	Normal
TM40	Swift	Normal	Special	60	—	20	Many Others
TM41	Helping Hand	Normal	Status	—	—	20	1 Ally
TM76	Round	Normal	Special	60	100	15	Normal
TM77	Hex	Ghost	Special	65	100	10	Normal
TM80	Volt Switch	Electric	Special	70	100	20	Normal
TM82	Electroweb	Electric	Special	55	95	15	Many Others
TM90	Electric Terrain	Electric	Status	—	—	10	Both Sides
TM93	Eerie Impulse	Electric	Status	—	100	15	Normal

EVOLUTION MOVES

NAME	TYPE	KIND	POW.	ACC.	PP	RANGE

EGG MOVES

NAME	TYPE	KIND	POW.	ACC.	PP	RANGE

TR MOVES

NAME	TYPE	KIND	POW.	ACC.	PP	RANGE
TR08 Thunderbolt	Electric	Special	90	100	15	Normal
TR09 Thunder	Electric	Special	110	70	10	Normal
TR20 Substitute	Normal	Status	—	—	10	Self
TR26 Endure	Normal	Status	—	—	10	Self
TR27 Sleep Talk	Normal	Status	—	—	10	Self
TR33 Shadow Ball	Ghost	Special	80	100	15	Normal
TR35 Uproar	Normal	Special	90	100	10	1 Random
TR38 Trick	Psychic	Status	—	100	10	Normal
TR42 Hyper Voice	Normal	Special	90	100	10	Many Others
TR58 Dark Pulse	Dark	Special	80	100	15	Normal
TR68 Nasty Plot	Dark	Status	—	—	20	Self
TR80 Electro Ball	Electric	Special	—	100	10	Normal
TR81 Foul Play	Dark	Physical	95	100	15	Normal
TR82 Stored Power	Psychic	Special	20	100	10	Normal
TR83 Ally Switch	Psychic	Status	—	—	15	Self

*Rotom learns a different move when it changes forms. (Air Slash: Fan Rotom. Blizzard: Frost Rotom. Hydro Pump: Wash Rotom. Leaf Storm: Mow Rotom. Overheat: Heat Rotom.) If it returns to its default form, it forgets this move.

373 Ditto

p. 149

ABILITY
Limber
—

HIDDEN ABILITY
Imposter

SPECIES STRENGTHS

HP
ATTACK
DEFENSE
SP. ATK
SP. DEF
SPEED

DAMAGE TAKEN IN BATTLE

×1 ×2 ×1
×1 ×1 ×0
×1 ×1 ×1
×1 ×1 ×1
×1 ×1 ×1
×1 ×1 ×1

DITTO

LEVEL-UP MOVES

LV.	NAME	TYPE	KIND	POW.	ACC.	PP	RANGE
1	Transform	Normal	Status	—	—	10	Normal

TUTOR MOVES

NAME	TYPE	KIND	POW.	ACC.	PP	RANGE

TM MOVES

NO.	NAME	TYPE	KIND	POW.	ACC.	PP	RANGE

EVOLUTION MOVES

NAME	TYPE	KIND	POW.	ACC.	PP	RANGE

EGG MOVES

NAME	TYPE	KIND	POW.	ACC.	PP	RANGE

TR MOVES

NAME	TYPE	KIND	POW.	ACC.	PP	RANGE

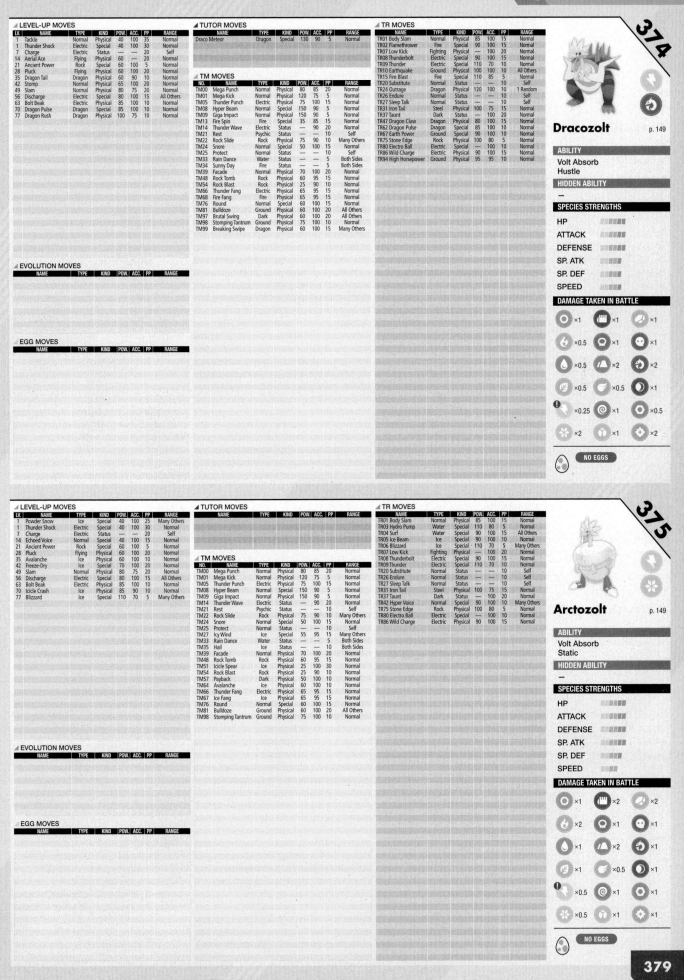

374 — Dracozolt (p. 149)

LEVEL-UP MOVES

LV.	NAME	TYPE	KIND	POW.	ACC.	PP	RANGE
1	Tackle	Normal	Physical	40	100	35	Normal
1	Thunder Shock	Electric	Special	40	100	30	Normal
7	Charge	Electric	Status	—	—	20	Self
14	Aerial Ace	Flying	Physical	60	—	20	Normal
21	Ancient Power	Rock	Special	60	100	5	Normal
28	Pluck	Flying	Physical	60	100	20	Normal
35	Dragon Tail	Dragon	Physical	60	90	10	Normal
42	Stomp	Normal	Physical	65	100	20	Normal
49	Slam	Normal	Physical	80	75	20	Normal
56	Discharge	Electric	Special	80	100	15	All Others
63	Bolt Beak	Electric	Physical	85	100	10	Normal
70	Dragon Pulse	Dragon	Special	85	100	10	Normal
77	Dragon Rush	Dragon	Physical	100	75	10	Normal

EVOLUTION MOVES

NAME	TYPE	KIND	POW.	ACC.	PP	RANGE

EGG MOVES

NAME	TYPE	KIND	POW.	ACC.	PP	RANGE

TUTOR MOVES

NAME	TYPE	KIND	POW.	ACC.	PP	RANGE
Draco Meteor	Dragon	Special	130	90	5	Normal

TM MOVES

NO.	NAME	TYPE	KIND	POW.	ACC.	PP	RANGE
TM00	Mega Punch	Normal	Physical	80	85	20	Normal
TM01	Mega Kick	Normal	Physical	120	75	5	Normal
TM05	Thunder Punch	Electric	Physical	75	100	15	Normal
TM08	Hyper Beam	Normal	Special	150	90	5	Normal
TM09	Giga Impact	Normal	Physical	150	90	5	Normal
TM13	Fire Spin	Fire	Special	35	85	15	Normal
TM14	Thunder Wave	Electric	Status	—	90	20	Normal
TM21	Rest	Psychic	Status	—	—	10	Self
TM22	Rock Slide	Rock	Physical	75	90	10	Many Others
TM24	Snore	Normal	Special	50	100	15	Normal
TM25	Protect	Normal	Status	—	—	10	Self
TM33	Rain Dance	Water	Status	—	—	5	Both Sides
TM34	Sunny Day	Fire	Status	—	—	5	Both Sides
TM39	Facade	Normal	Physical	70	100	20	Normal
TM48	Rock Tomb	Rock	Physical	60	95	15	Normal
TM54	Rock Blast	Rock	Physical	25	90	10	Normal
TM66	Thunder Fang	Electric	Physical	65	95	15	Normal
TM68	Fire Fang	Fire	Physical	65	95	15	Normal
TM76	Round	Normal	Special	60	100	15	Normal
TM81	Bulldoze	Ground	Physical	60	100	20	All Others
TM97	Brutal Swing	Dark	Physical	60	100	20	All Others
TM98	Stomping Tantrum	Ground	Physical	75	100	10	Normal
TM99	Breaking Swipe	Dragon	Physical	60	100	15	Many Others

TR MOVES

NO.	NAME	TYPE	KIND	POW.	ACC.	PP	RANGE
TR01	Body Slam	Normal	Physical	85	100	15	Normal
TR02	Flamethrower	Fire	Special	90	100	15	Normal
TR07	Low Kick	Fighting	Physical	—	100	20	Normal
TR08	Thunderbolt	Electric	Special	90	100	15	Normal
TR09	Thunder	Electric	Special	110	70	10	Normal
TR10	Earthquake	Ground	Physical	100	100	10	All Others
TR15	Fire Blast	Fire	Special	110	85	5	Normal
TR20	Substitute	Normal	Status	—	—	10	Self
TR24	Outrage	Dragon	Physical	120	100	10	1 Random
TR26	Endure	Normal	Status	—	—	10	Self
TR27	Sleep Talk	Normal	Status	—	—	10	Self
TR31	Iron Tail	Steel	Physical	100	75	15	Normal
TR37	Taunt	Dark	Status	—	—	20	Normal
TR47	Dragon Claw	Dragon	Physical	80	100	15	Normal
TR62	Dragon Pulse	Dragon	Special	85	100	10	Normal
TR67	Earth Power	Ground	Special	90	100	10	Normal
TR75	Stone Edge	Rock	Physical	100	80	5	Normal
TR80	Electro Ball	Electric	Special	—	100	10	Normal
TR86	Wild Charge	Electric	Physical	90	100	15	Normal
TR94	High Horsepower	Ground	Physical	95	95	10	Normal

ABILITY
Volt Absorb
Hustle

HIDDEN ABILITY
—

SPECIES STRENGTHS
HP
ATTACK
DEFENSE
SP. ATK
SP. DEF
SPEED

DAMAGE TAKEN IN BATTLE
×1 ×1 ×1
×0.5 ×1 ×1
×0.5 ×2 ×2
×0.5 ×0.5 ×1
×0.25 ×1 ×0.5
×2 ×1 ×2

NO EGGS

375 — Arctozolt (p. 149)

LEVEL-UP MOVES

LV.	NAME	TYPE	KIND	POW.	ACC.	PP	RANGE
1	Powder Snow	Ice	Special	40	100	25	Many Others
1	Thunder Shock	Electric	Special	40	100	30	Normal
7	Charge	Electric	Status	—	—	20	Self
14	Echoed Voice	Normal	Special	40	100	15	Normal
21	Ancient Power	Rock	Special	60	100	5	Normal
28	Pluck	Flying	Physical	60	100	20	Normal
35	Avalanche	Ice	Physical	60	100	10	Normal
42	Freeze-Dry	Ice	Special	70	100	20	Normal
49	Slam	Normal	Physical	80	75	20	Normal
56	Discharge	Electric	Special	80	100	15	All Others
63	Bolt Beak	Electric	Physical	85	100	10	Normal
70	Icicle Crash	Ice	Physical	85	90	10	Normal
77	Blizzard	Ice	Special	110	70	5	Many Others

EVOLUTION MOVES

NAME	TYPE	KIND	POW.	ACC.	PP	RANGE

EGG MOVES

NAME	TYPE	KIND	POW.	ACC.	PP	RANGE

TUTOR MOVES

NAME	TYPE	KIND	POW.	ACC.	PP	RANGE

TM MOVES

NO.	NAME	TYPE	KIND	POW.	ACC.	PP	RANGE
TM00	Mega Punch	Normal	Physical	80	85	20	Normal
TM01	Mega Kick	Normal	Physical	120	75	5	Normal
TM05	Thunder Punch	Electric	Physical	75	100	15	Normal
TM08	Hyper Beam	Normal	Special	150	90	5	Normal
TM09	Giga Impact	Normal	Physical	150	90	5	Normal
TM14	Thunder Wave	Electric	Status	—	90	20	Normal
TM21	Rest	Psychic	Status	—	—	10	Self
TM22	Rock Slide	Rock	Physical	75	90	10	Many Others
TM24	Snore	Normal	Special	50	100	15	Normal
TM25	Protect	Normal	Status	—	—	10	Self
TM27	Icy Wind	Ice	Special	55	95	15	Many Others
TM33	Rain Dance	Water	Status	—	—	5	Both Sides
TM35	Hail	Ice	Status	—	—	10	Both Sides
TM39	Facade	Normal	Physical	70	100	20	Normal
TM48	Rock Tomb	Rock	Physical	60	95	15	Normal
TM51	Icicle Spear	Ice	Physical	25	100	30	Normal
TM54	Rock Blast	Rock	Physical	25	90	10	Normal
TM57	Payback	Dark	Physical	50	100	10	Normal
TM64	Avalanche	Ice	Physical	60	100	10	Normal
TM66	Thunder Fang	Electric	Physical	65	95	15	Normal
TM67	Ice Fang	Ice	Physical	65	95	15	Normal
TM76	Round	Normal	Special	60	100	15	Normal
TM81	Bulldoze	Ground	Physical	60	100	20	All Others
TM98	Stomping Tantrum	Ground	Physical	75	100	10	Normal

TR MOVES

NO.	NAME	TYPE	KIND	POW.	ACC.	PP	RANGE
TR01	Body Slam	Normal	Physical	85	100	15	Normal
TR03	Hydro Pump	Water	Special	110	80	5	Normal
TR04	Surf	Water	Special	90	100	15	All Others
TR05	Ice Beam	Ice	Special	90	100	10	Normal
TR06	Blizzard	Ice	Special	110	70	5	Many Others
TR07	Low Kick	Fighting	Physical	—	100	20	Normal
TR08	Thunderbolt	Electric	Special	90	100	15	Normal
TR09	Thunder	Electric	Special	110	70	10	Normal
TR20	Substitute	Normal	Status	—	—	10	Self
TR26	Endure	Normal	Status	—	—	10	Self
TR27	Sleep Talk	Normal	Status	—	—	10	Self
TR31	Iron Tail	Steel	Physical	100	75	15	Normal
TR37	Taunt	Dark	Status	—	—	20	Normal
TR42	Hyper Voice	Normal	Special	90	100	10	Many Others
TR75	Stone Edge	Rock	Physical	100	80	5	Normal
TR80	Electro Ball	Electric	Special	—	100	10	Normal
TR86	Wild Charge	Electric	Physical	90	100	15	Normal

ABILITY
Volt Absorb
Static

HIDDEN ABILITY
—

SPECIES STRENGTHS
HP
ATTACK
DEFENSE
SP. ATK
SP. DEF
SPEED

DAMAGE TAKEN IN BATTLE
×1 ×2 ×2
×2 ×1 ×1
×1 ×2 ×1
×1 ×0.5 ×1
×0.5 ×1 ×1
×0.5 ×1 ×1

NO EGGS

376 Dracovish p. 150

TYPE: Water / Dragon

ABILITY
Water Absorb
Strong Jaw

HIDDEN ABILITY
—

SPECIES STRENGTHS
HP · ATTACK · DEFENSE · SP. ATK · SP. DEF · SPEED

DAMAGE TAKEN IN BATTLE

×1	×1	×1
×0.25	×1	×1
×0.25	×1	×2
×1	×1	×1
×1	×1	×0.5
×1	×1	×2

NO EGGS

LEVEL-UP MOVES

LV.	NAME	TYPE	KIND	POW.	ACC.	PP	RANGE
1	Tackle	Normal	Physical	40	100	35	Normal
1	Water Gun	Water	Special	40	100	25	Normal
7	Protect	Normal	Status	—	—	10	Self
14	Brutal Swing	Dark	Physical	60	100	20	All Others
21	Ancient Power	Rock	Special	60	100	5	Normal
28	Bite	Dark	Physical	60	100	25	Normal
35	Dragon Breath	Dragon	Special	60	100	20	Normal
42	Stomp	Normal	Physical	65	100	20	Normal
49	Super Fang	Normal	Physical	—	90	10	Normal
56	Crunch	Dark	Physical	80	100	15	Normal
63	Fishious Rend	Water	Physical	85	100	10	Normal
70	Dragon Pulse	Dragon	Special	85	100	10	Normal
77	Dragon Rush	Dragon	Physical	100	75	10	Normal

TUTOR MOVES

NAME	TYPE	KIND	POW.	ACC.	PP	RANGE
Draco Meteor	Dragon	Special	130	90	5	Normal

TM MOVES

NO.	NAME	TYPE	KIND	POW.	ACC.	PP	RANGE
TM01	Mega Kick	Normal	Physical	120	75	5	Normal
TM08	Hyper Beam	Normal	Special	150	90	5	Normal
TM09	Giga Impact	Normal	Physical	150	90	5	Normal
TM21	Rest	Psychic	Status	—	—	10	Self
TM22	Rock Slide	Rock	Physical	75	90	10	Many Others
TM24	Snore	Normal	Physical	50	100	15	Normal
TM25	Protect	Normal	Status	—	—	10	Self
TM33	Rain Dance	Water	Status	—	—	5	Both Sides
TM36	Whirlpool	Water	Special	35	85	15	Normal
TM39	Facade	Normal	Physical	70	100	20	Normal
TM45	Dive	Water	Physical	80	100	10	Normal
TM48	Rock Tomb	Rock	Physical	60	95	15	Normal
TM54	Rock Blast	Rock	Physical	25	90	10	Normal
TM55	Brine	Water	Special	65	100	10	Normal
TM67	Ice Fang	Ice	Physical	65	95	15	Normal
TM76	Round	Normal	Special	60	100	15	Normal
TM81	Bulldoze	Ground	Physical	60	100	20	All Others
TM97	Brutal Swing	Dark	Physical	60	100	20	All Others
TM98	Stomping Tantrum	Ground	Physical	75	100	10	Normal

TR MOVES

NO.	NAME	TYPE	KIND	POW.	ACC.	PP	RANGE
TR01	Body Slam	Normal	Physical	85	100	15	Normal
TR03	Hydro Pump	Water	Special	110	80	5	Normal
TR04	Surf	Water	Special	90	100	15	All Others
TR07	Low Kick	Fighting	Physical	—	100	20	Normal
TR10	Earthquake	Ground	Physical	100	100	10	All Others
TR16	Waterfall	Water	Physical	80	100	15	Normal
TR18	Leech Life	Bug	Physical	80	100	10	Normal
TR20	Substitute	Normal	Status	—	—	10	Self
TR24	Outrage	Dragon	Physical	120	100	10	1 Random
TR26	Endure	Normal	Status	—	—	10	Self
TR27	Sleep Talk	Normal	Status	—	—	10	Self
TR32	Crunch	Dark	Physical	80	100	15	Normal
TR62	Dragon Pulse	Dragon	Special	85	100	10	Normal
TR67	Earth Power	Ground	Special	90	100	10	Normal
TR69	Zen Headbutt	Psychic	Physical	80	90	15	Normal
TR74	Iron Head	Steel	Physical	80	100	15	Normal
TR75	Stone Edge	Rock	Physical	100	80	5	Normal
TR84	Scald	Water	Special	80	100	15	Normal
TR97	Psychic Fangs	Psychic	Physical	85	100	10	Normal
TR98	Liquidation	Water	Physical	85	100	10	Normal

EVOLUTION MOVES

NAME	TYPE	KIND	POW.	ACC.	PP	RANGE

EGG MOVES

NAME	TYPE	KIND	POW.	ACC.	PP	RANGE

---

377 Arctovish p. 150

TYPE: Water / Ice

ABILITY
Water Absorb
Ice Body

HIDDEN ABILITY
—

SPECIES STRENGTHS
HP · ATTACK · DEFENSE · SP. ATK · SP. DEF · SPEED

DAMAGE TAKEN IN BATTLE

×1	×2	×2
×1	×1	×1
×0.5	×1	×1
×2	×1	×1
×2	×1	×1
×0.25	×1	×1

NO EGGS

LEVEL-UP MOVES

LV.	NAME	TYPE	KIND	POW.	ACC.	PP	RANGE
1	Powder Snow	Ice	Special	40	100	25	Many Others
1	Water Gun	Water	Special	40	100	25	Normal
7	Protect	Normal	Status	—	—	10	Self
14	Icy Wind	Ice	Special	55	95	15	Many Others
21	Ancient Power	Rock	Special	60	100	5	Normal
28	Bite	Dark	Physical	60	100	25	Normal
35	Aurora Veil	Ice	Status	—	—	20	Your Side
42	Freeze-Dry	Ice	Special	70	100	20	Normal
49	Super Fang	Normal	Physical	—	90	10	Normal
56	Crunch	Dark	Physical	80	100	15	Normal
63	Fishious Rend	Water	Physical	85	100	10	Normal
70	Icicle Crash	Ice	Physical	85	90	10	Normal
77	Blizzard	Ice	Special	110	70	5	Many Others

TUTOR MOVES

NAME	TYPE	KIND	POW.	ACC.	PP	RANGE

TM MOVES

NO.	NAME	TYPE	KIND	POW.	ACC.	PP	RANGE
TM08	Hyper Beam	Normal	Special	150	90	5	Normal
TM09	Giga Impact	Normal	Physical	150	90	5	Normal
TM21	Rest	Psychic	Status	—	—	10	Self
TM22	Rock Slide	Rock	Physical	75	90	10	Many Others
TM24	Snore	Normal	Physical	50	100	15	Normal
TM25	Protect	Normal	Status	—	—	10	Self
TM27	Icy Wind	Ice	Special	55	95	15	Many Others
TM33	Rain Dance	Water	Status	—	—	5	Both Sides
TM35	Hail	Ice	Status	—	—	10	Both Sides
TM36	Whirlpool	Water	Special	35	85	15	Normal
TM39	Facade	Normal	Physical	70	100	20	Normal
TM45	Dive	Water	Physical	80	100	10	Normal
TM48	Rock Tomb	Rock	Physical	60	95	15	Normal
TM51	Icicle Spear	Ice	Physical	25	100	30	Normal
TM54	Rock Blast	Rock	Physical	25	90	10	Normal
TM55	Brine	Water	Special	65	100	10	Normal
TM64	Avalanche	Ice	Physical	60	100	10	Normal
TM67	Ice Fang	Ice	Physical	65	95	15	Normal
TM76	Round	Normal	Special	60	100	15	Normal

TR MOVES

NO.	NAME	TYPE	KIND	POW.	ACC.	PP	RANGE
TR01	Body Slam	Normal	Physical	85	100	15	Normal
TR03	Hydro Pump	Water	Special	110	80	5	Normal
TR04	Surf	Water	Special	90	100	15	All Others
TR05	Ice Beam	Ice	Special	90	100	10	Normal
TR06	Blizzard	Ice	Special	110	70	5	Many Others
TR16	Waterfall	Water	Physical	80	100	15	Normal
TR20	Substitute	Normal	Status	—	—	10	Self
TR26	Endure	Normal	Status	—	—	10	Self
TR27	Sleep Talk	Normal	Status	—	—	10	Self
TR46	Iron Defense	Steel	Status	—	—	15	Self
TR32	Crunch	Dark	Physical	80	100	15	Normal
TR69	Zen Headbutt	Psychic	Physical	80	90	15	Normal
TR74	Iron Head	Steel	Physical	80	100	15	Normal
TR75	Stone Edge	Rock	Physical	100	80	5	Normal
TR97	Psychic Fangs	Psychic	Physical	85	100	10	Normal
TR98	Liquidation	Water	Physical	85	100	10	Normal

EVOLUTION MOVES

NAME	TYPE	KIND	POW.	ACC.	PP	RANGE

EGG MOVES

NAME	TYPE	KIND	POW.	ACC.	PP	RANGE

378 — Charmander

LEVEL-UP MOVES

LV.	NAME	TYPE	KIND	POW.	ACC.	PP	RANGE
1	Growl	Normal	Status	—	100	40	Many Others
1	Scratch	Normal	Physical	40	100	35	Normal
4	Ember	Fire	Special	40	100	25	Normal
8	Smokescreen	Normal	Status	—	100	20	Normal
12	Dragon Breath	Dragon	Special	60	100	20	Normal
17	Fire Fang	Fire	Physical	65	95	15	Normal
20	Slash	Normal	Physical	70	100	20	Normal
24	Flamethrower	Fire	Special	90	100	15	Normal
28	Scary Face	Normal	Status	—	100	10	Normal
32	Fire Spin	Fire	Special	35	85	15	Normal
36	Inferno	Fire	Special	100	50	5	Normal
40	Flare Blitz	Fire	Physical	120	100	15	Normal

TUTOR MOVES

NAME	TYPE	KIND	POW.	ACC.	PP	RANGE
Fire Pledge	Fire	Special	80	100	10	Normal

TM MOVES

NO.	NAME	TYPE	KIND	POW.	ACC.	PP	RANGE
TM00	Mega Punch	Normal	Physical	80	85	20	Normal
TM01	Mega Kick	Normal	Physical	120	75	5	Normal
TM03	Fire Punch	Fire	Physical	75	100	15	Normal
TM05	Thunder Punch	Electric	Physical	75	100	15	Normal
TM13	Fire Spin	Fire	Special	35	85	15	Normal
TM15	Dig	Ground	Physical	80	100	10	Normal
TM21	Rest	Psychic	Status	—	—	10	Self
TM22	Rock Slide	Rock	Physical	75	90	10	Many Others
TM24	Snore	Normal	Special	50	100	15	Normal
TM25	Protect	Normal	Status	—	—	10	Self
TM26	Scary Face	Normal	Status	—	100	10	Normal
TM31	Attract	Normal	Status	—	100	15	Normal
TM34	Sunny Day	Fire	Status	—	—	5	Both Sides
TM37	Beat Up	Dark	Physical	—	100	10	Normal
TM38	Will-O-Wisp	Fire	Status	—	85	15	Normal
TM39	Facade	Normal	Physical	70	100	20	Normal
TM40	Swift	Normal	Special	60	—	20	Many Others
TM41	Helping Hand	Normal	Status	—	—	20	1 Ally
TM43	Brick Break	Fighting	Physical	75	100	15	Normal
TM46	Weather Ball*	Normal	Special	50	100	10	Normal
TM48	Rock Tomb	Rock	Physical	60	95	15	Normal
TM59	Fling	Dark	Physical	—	100	10	Normal
TM65	Shadow Claw	Ghost	Physical	70	100	15	Normal
TM68	Fire Fang	Fire	Physical	65	95	15	Normal
TM76	Round	Normal	Special	60	100	15	Normal
TM78	Acrobatics	Flying	Physical	55	100	15	Normal
TM94	False Swipe	Normal	Physical	40	100	40	Normal

TR MOVES

NO.	NAME	TYPE	KIND	POW.	ACC.	PP	RANGE
TR00	Swords Dance	Normal	Status	—	—	20	Self
TR01	Body Slam	Normal	Physical	85	100	15	Normal
TR02	Flamethrower	Fire	Special	90	100	15	Normal
TR15	Fire Blast	Fire	Special	110	85	5	Normal
TR20	Substitute	Normal	Status	—	—	10	Self
TR24	Outrage	Dragon	Physical	120	100	10	1 Random
TR26	Endure	Normal	Status	—	—	10	Self
TR27	Sleep Talk	Normal	Status	—	—	10	Self
TR31	Iron Tail	Steel	Physical	100	75	15	Normal
TR32	Crunch	Dark	Physical	80	100	15	Normal
TR36	Heat Wave	Fire	Special	95	90	10	Many Others
TR43	Overheat	Fire	Special	130	90	5	Normal
TR47	Dragon Claw	Dragon	Physical	80	100	15	Normal
TR51	Dragon Dance	Dragon	Status	—	—	20	Self
TR55	Flare Blitz	Fire	Physical	120	100	15	Normal
TR62	Dragon Pulse	Dragon	Special	85	100	10	Normal
TR85	Work Up	Normal	Status	—	—	30	Self

EVOLUTION MOVES

NAME	TYPE	KIND	POW.	ACC.	PP	RANGE

EGG MOVES

NAME	TYPE	KIND	POW.	ACC.	PP	RANGE
Ancient Power	Rock	Special	60	100	5	Normal
Belly Drum	Normal	Status	—	—	10	Self
Bite	Dark	Physical	60	100	25	Normal
Counter	Fighting	Physical	—	100	20	Varies
Dragon Rush	Dragon	Physical	100	75	10	Normal
Dragon Tail	Dragon	Physical	60	90	10	Normal
Metal Claw	Steel	Physical	50	95	35	Normal
Wing Attack	Flying	Physical	60	100	35	Normal

Charmander p. 151

ABILITY
Blaze

HIDDEN ABILITY
Solar Power

SPECIES STRENGTHS
HP
ATTACK
DEFENSE
SP. ATK
SP. DEF
SPEED

DAMAGE TAKEN IN BATTLE
×1 ×1 ×2 ×0.5 ×1 ×1 ×2 ×2 ×1 ×0.5 ×1 ×1 ×1 ×1 ×0.5 ×0.5 ×0.5 ×0.5

MONSTER
DRAGON

---

379 — Charmeleon

LEVEL-UP MOVES

LV.	NAME	TYPE	KIND	POW.	ACC.	PP	RANGE
1	Ember	Fire	Special	40	100	25	Normal
1	Growl	Normal	Status	—	100	40	Many Others
1	Scratch	Normal	Physical	40	100	35	Normal
1	Smokescreen	Normal	Status	—	100	20	Normal
12	Dragon Breath	Dragon	Special	60	100	20	Normal
19	Fire Fang	Fire	Physical	65	95	15	Normal
24	Slash	Normal	Physical	70	100	20	Normal
30	Flamethrower	Fire	Special	90	100	15	Normal
37	Scary Face	Normal	Status	—	100	10	Normal
42	Fire Spin	Fire	Special	35	85	15	Normal
48	Inferno	Fire	Special	100	50	5	Normal
54	Flare Blitz	Fire	Physical	120	100	15	Normal

TUTOR MOVES

NAME	TYPE	KIND	POW.	ACC.	PP	RANGE
Fire Pledge	Fire	Special	80	100	10	Normal

TM MOVES

NO.	NAME	TYPE	KIND	POW.	ACC.	PP	RANGE
TM00	Mega Punch	Normal	Physical	80	85	20	Normal
TM01	Mega Kick	Normal	Physical	120	75	5	Normal
TM03	Fire Punch	Fire	Physical	75	100	15	Normal
TM05	Thunder Punch	Electric	Physical	75	100	15	Normal
TM13	Fire Spin	Fire	Special	35	85	15	Normal
TM15	Dig	Ground	Physical	80	100	10	Normal
TM21	Rest	Psychic	Status	—	—	10	Self
TM22	Rock Slide	Rock	Physical	75	90	10	Many Others
TM24	Snore	Normal	Special	50	100	15	Normal
TM25	Protect	Normal	Status	—	—	10	Self
TM26	Scary Face	Normal	Status	—	100	10	Normal
TM31	Attract	Normal	Status	—	100	15	Normal
TM34	Sunny Day	Fire	Status	—	—	5	Both Sides
TM37	Beat Up	Dark	Physical	—	100	10	Normal
TM38	Will-O-Wisp	Fire	Status	—	85	15	Normal
TM39	Facade	Normal	Physical	70	100	20	Normal
TM40	Swift	Normal	Special	60	—	20	Many Others
TM41	Helping Hand	Normal	Status	—	—	20	1 Ally
TM43	Brick Break	Fighting	Physical	75	100	15	Normal
TM46	Weather Ball*	Normal	Special	50	100	10	Normal
TM48	Rock Tomb	Rock	Physical	60	95	15	Normal
TM59	Fling	Dark	Physical	—	100	10	Normal
TM65	Shadow Claw	Ghost	Physical	70	100	15	Normal
TM68	Fire Fang	Fire	Physical	65	95	15	Normal
TM76	Round	Normal	Special	60	100	15	Normal
TM78	Acrobatics	Flying	Physical	55	100	15	Normal
TM94	False Swipe	Normal	Physical	40	100	40	Normal

TR MOVES

NO.	NAME	TYPE	KIND	POW.	ACC.	PP	RANGE
TR00	Swords Dance	Normal	Status	—	—	20	Self
TR01	Body Slam	Normal	Physical	85	100	15	Normal
TR02	Flamethrower	Fire	Special	90	100	15	Normal
TR15	Fire Blast	Fire	Special	110	85	5	Normal
TR20	Substitute	Normal	Status	—	—	10	Self
TR24	Outrage	Dragon	Physical	120	100	10	1 Random
TR26	Endure	Normal	Status	—	—	10	Self
TR27	Sleep Talk	Normal	Status	—	—	10	Self
TR31	Iron Tail	Steel	Physical	100	75	15	Normal
TR32	Crunch	Dark	Physical	80	100	15	Normal
TR36	Heat Wave	Fire	Special	95	90	10	Many Others
TR43	Overheat	Fire	Special	130	90	5	Normal
TR47	Dragon Claw	Dragon	Physical	80	100	15	Normal
TR51	Dragon Dance	Dragon	Status	—	—	20	Self
TR55	Flare Blitz	Fire	Physical	120	100	15	Normal
TR62	Dragon Pulse	Dragon	Special	85	100	10	Normal
TR85	Work Up	Normal	Status	—	—	30	Self

EVOLUTION MOVES

NAME	TYPE	KIND	POW.	ACC.	PP	RANGE

EGG MOVES

NAME	TYPE	KIND	POW.	ACC.	PP	RANGE

Charmeleon p. 151

ABILITY
Blaze
—

HIDDEN ABILITY
Solar Power

SPECIES STRENGTHS
HP
ATTACK
DEFENSE
SP. ATK
SP. DEF
SPEED

DAMAGE TAKEN IN BATTLE
×1 ×1 ×2 ×0.5 ×1 ×1 ×2 ×2 ×1 ×0.5 ×1 ×1 ×1 ×1 ×0.5 ×0.5 ×0.5 ×0.5

MONSTER
DRAGON

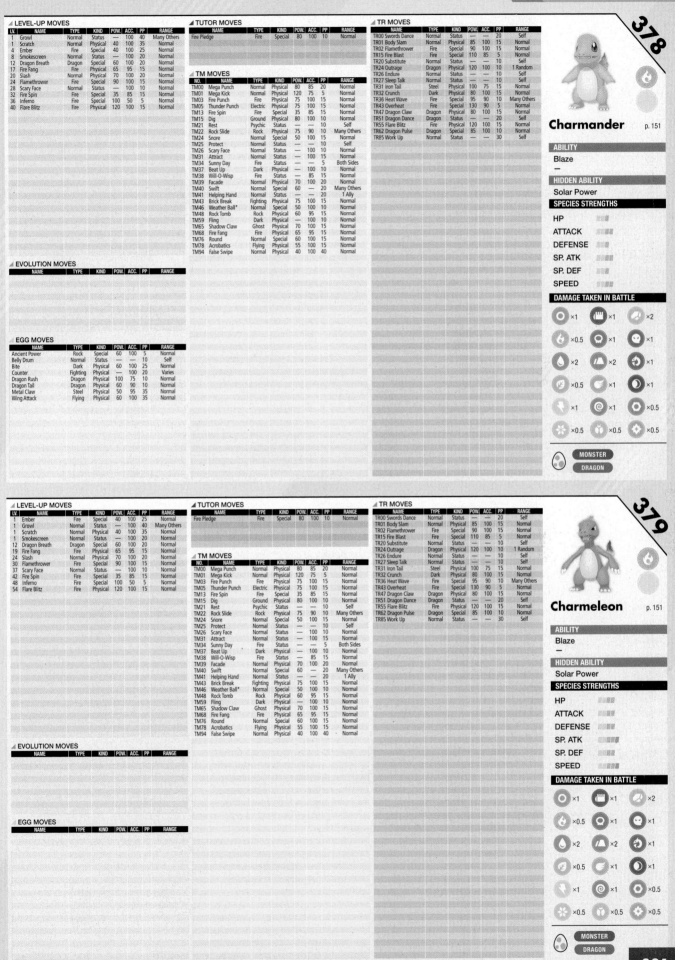

*Weather Ball changes type depending on weather condition. (Harsh sunlight: Fire type. Rain: Water type. Hail: Ice type. Sandstorm: Rock type.)

380 Charizard p. 151

ABILITY
Blaze
—

HIDDEN ABILITY
Solar Power

SPECIES STRENGTHS

HP	
ATTACK	
DEFENSE	
SP. ATK	
SP. DEF	
SPEED	

DAMAGE TAKEN IN BATTLE

×1	×0.5	×4
×0.5	×1	×1
×2	×0	×1
×0.25	×1	×1
×2	×1	×0.5
×1	×0.25	×0.5

MONSTER / DRAGON

LEVEL-UP MOVES

LV.	NAME	TYPE	KIND	POW.	ACC.	PP	RANGE
1	Air Slash	Flying	Special	75	95	15	Normal
1	Dragon Claw	Dragon	Physical	80	100	15	Normal
1	Ember	Fire	Special	40	100	25	Normal
1	Growl	Normal	Status	—	100	40	Many Others
1	Heat Wave	Fire	Special	95	90	10	Many Others
1	Scratch	Normal	Physical	40	100	35	Normal
1	Smokescreen	Normal	Status	—	100	20	Normal
12	Dragon Breath	Dragon	Special	60	100	20	Normal
19	Fire Fang	Fire	Physical	65	95	15	Normal
24	Slash	Normal	Physical	70	100	20	Normal
30	Flamethrower	Fire	Special	90	100	15	Normal
39	Scary Face	Normal	Status	—	100	10	Normal
46	Fire Spin	Fire	Special	35	85	15	Normal
54	Inferno	Fire	Special	100	50	5	Normal
62	Flare Blitz	Fire	Physical	120	100	15	Normal

EVOLUTION MOVES

NAME	TYPE	KIND	POW.	ACC.	PP	RANGE
Air Slash	Flying	Special	75	95	15	Normal

EGG MOVES

NAME	TYPE	KIND	POW.	ACC.	PP	RANGE

TUTOR MOVES

NAME	TYPE	KIND	POW.	ACC.	PP	RANGE
Blast Burn	Fire	Special	150	90	5	Normal
Fire Pledge	Fire	Special	80	100	10	Normal

TM MOVES

NO.	NAME	TYPE	KIND	POW.	ACC.	PP	RANGE
TM00	Mega Punch	Normal	Physical	80	85	20	Normal
TM01	Mega Kick	Normal	Physical	120	75	5	Normal
TM03	Fire Punch	Fire	Physical	75	100	15	Normal
TM05	Thunder Punch	Electric	Physical	75	100	15	Normal
TM06	Fly	Flying	Physical	90	95	15	Normal
TM08	Hyper Beam	Normal	Special	150	90	5	Normal
TM09	Giga Impact	Normal	Physical	150	90	5	Normal
TM11	Solar Beam	Grass	Special	120	100	10	Normal
TM13	Fire Spin	Fire	Special	35	85	15	Normal
TM15	Dig	Ground	Physical	80	100	10	Normal
TM21	Rest	Psychic	Status	—	—	10	Self
TM22	Rock Slide	Rock	Physical	75	90	10	Many Others
TM24	Snore	Normal	Special	50	100	15	Normal
TM25	Protect	Normal	Status	—	—	10	Self
TM26	Scary Face	Normal	Status	—	100	10	Normal
TM30	Steel Wing	Steel	Physical	70	90	25	Normal
TM31	Attract	Normal	Status	—	100	15	Normal
TM34	Sunny Day	Fire	Status	—	—	5	Both Sides
TM37	Beat Up	Dark	Physical	—	100	10	Normal
TM38	Will-O-Wisp	Fire	Status	—	85	15	Normal
TM39	Facade	Normal	Physical	70	100	20	Normal
TM40	Swift	Normal	Special	60	—	20	Many Others
TM41	Helping Hand	Normal	Status	—	—	20	1 Ally
TM43	Brick Break	Fighting	Physical	75	100	15	Normal
TM46	Weather Ball*	Normal	Special	50	100	10	Normal
TM48	Rock Tomb	Rock	Physical	60	95	15	Normal
TM59	Fling	Dark	Physical	—	100	10	Normal
TM65	Shadow Claw	Ghost	Physical	70	100	15	Normal
TM68	Fire Fang	Fire	Physical	65	95	15	Normal
TM76	Round	Normal	Special	60	100	15	Normal
TM78	Acrobatics	Flying	Physical	55	100	15	Normal
TM81	Bulldoze	Ground	Physical	60	100	20	All Others
TM92	Mystical Fire	Fire	Special	75	100	10	Normal
TM94	False Swipe	Normal	Physical	40	100	40	Normal
TM95	Air Slash	Flying	Special	75	95	15	Normal
TM97	Brutal Swing	Dark	Physical	60	100	20	All Others
TM99	Breaking Swipe	Dragon	Physical	60	100	15	Many Others

TR MOVES

NO.	NAME	TYPE	KIND	POW.	ACC.	PP	RANGE
TR00	Swords Dance	Normal	Status	—	—	20	Self
TR01	Body Slam	Normal	Physical	85	100	15	Normal
TR02	Flamethrower	Fire	Special	90	100	15	Normal
TR10	Earthquake	Ground	Physical	100	100	10	All Others
TR15	Fire Blast	Fire	Special	110	85	5	Normal
TR20	Substitute	Normal	Status	—	—	10	Self
TR24	Outrage	Dragon	Physical	120	100	10	1 Random
TR26	Endure	Normal	Status	—	—	10	Self
TR27	Sleep Talk	Normal	Status	—	—	10	Self
TR31	Iron Tail	Steel	Physical	100	75	15	Normal
TR32	Crunch	Dark	Physical	80	100	15	Normal
TR36	Heat Wave	Fire	Special	95	90	10	Many Others
TR41	Blaze Kick	Fire	Physical	85	90	10	Normal
TR43	Overheat	Fire	Special	130	90	5	Normal
TR47	Dragon Claw	Dragon	Physical	80	100	15	Normal
TR51	Dragon Dance	Dragon	Status	—	—	20	Self
TR55	Flare Blitz	Fire	Physical	120	100	15	Normal
TR62	Dragon Pulse	Dragon	Special	85	100	10	Normal
TR64	Focus Blast	Fighting	Special	120	70	5	Normal
TR85	Work Up	Normal	Status	—	—	30	Self
TR88	Heat Crash	Fire	Physical	—	100	10	Normal
TR89	Hurricane	Flying	Special	110	70	10	Normal

*Weather Ball changes type depending on weather condition. (Harsh sunlight: Fire type. Rain: Water type. Hail: Ice type. Sandstorm: Rock type.)

---

381 Type: Null p. 152

ABILITY
Battle Armor
—

HIDDEN ABILITY
—

SPECIES STRENGTHS

HP	
ATTACK	
DEFENSE	
SP. ATK	
SP. DEF	
SPEED	

DAMAGE TAKEN IN BATTLE

×1	×2	×1
×1	×1	×0
×1	×1	×1
×1	×1	×1
×1	×1	×1
×1	×1	×1

NO EGGS

LEVEL-UP MOVES

LV.	NAME	TYPE	KIND	POW.	ACC.	PP	RANGE
1	Imprison	Psychic	Status	—	—	10	Self
1	Tackle	Normal	Physical	40	100	35	Normal
5	Aerial Ace	Flying	Physical	60	—	20	Normal
9	Scary Face	Normal	Status	—	100	10	Normal
15	Double Hit	Normal	Physical	35	90	10	Normal
20	Metal Sound	Steel	Status	—	85	40	Normal
25	Crush Claw	Normal	Physical	75	95	10	Normal
30	Air Slash	Flying	Special	75	95	15	Normal
35	Tri Attack	Normal	Special	80	100	10	Normal
40	X-Scissor	Bug	Physical	80	100	15	Normal
45	Iron Head	Steel	Physical	80	100	15	Normal
50	Take Down	Normal	Physical	90	85	20	Normal
55	Double-Edge	Normal	Physical	120	100	15	Normal

EVOLUTION MOVES

NAME	TYPE	KIND	POW.	ACC.	PP	RANGE

EGG MOVES

NAME	TYPE	KIND	POW.	ACC.	PP	RANGE

TUTOR MOVES

NAME	TYPE	KIND	POW.	ACC.	PP	RANGE

TM MOVES

NO.	NAME	TYPE	KIND	POW.	ACC.	PP	RANGE
TM08	Hyper Beam	Normal	Special	150	90	5	Normal
TM09	Giga Impact	Normal	Physical	150	90	5	Normal
TM14	Thunder Wave	Electric	Status	—	90	20	Normal
TM21	Rest	Psychic	Status	—	—	10	Self
TM22	Rock Slide	Rock	Physical	75	90	10	Many Others
TM24	Snore	Normal	Special	50	100	15	Normal
TM25	Protect	Normal	Status	—	—	10	Self
TM26	Scary Face	Normal	Status	—	100	10	Normal
TM27	Icy Wind	Ice	Special	55	95	15	Many Others
TM32	Sandstorm	Rock	Status	—	—	10	Both Sides
TM33	Rain Dance	Water	Status	—	—	5	Both Sides
TM34	Sunny Day	Fire	Status	—	—	5	Both Sides
TM35	Hail	Ice	Status	—	—	10	Both Sides
TM39	Facade	Normal	Physical	70	100	20	Normal
TM40	Swift	Normal	Special	60	—	20	Many Others
TM44	Imprison	Psychic	Status	—	—	10	Self
TM56	U-turn	Bug	Physical	70	100	20	Normal
TM57	Payback	Dark	Physical	50	100	10	Normal
TM65	Shadow Claw	Ghost	Physical	70	100	15	Normal
TM76	Round	Normal	Special	60	100	15	Normal
TM95	Air Slash	Flying	Special	75	95	15	Normal

TR MOVES

NO.	NAME	TYPE	KIND	POW.	ACC.	PP	RANGE
TR00	Swords Dance	Normal	Status	—	—	20	Self
TR19	Tri Attack	Normal	Special	80	100	10	Normal
TR20	Substitute	Normal	Status	—	—	10	Self
TR26	Endure	Normal	Status	—	—	10	Self
TR27	Sleep Talk	Normal	Status	—	—	10	Self
TR46	Iron Defense	Steel	Status	—	—	15	Self
TR47	Dragon Claw	Dragon	Physical	80	100	15	Normal
TR60	X-Scissor	Bug	Physical	80	100	15	Normal
TR74	Iron Head	Steel	Physical	80	100	15	Normal
TR85	Work Up	Normal	Status	—	—	30	Self

382

LEVEL-UP MOVES

LV.	NAME	TYPE	KIND	POW.	ACC.	PP	RANGE
1	Aerial Ace	Flying	Physical	60	—	20	Normal
1	Bite	Dark	Physical	60	100	25	Normal
1	Explosion	Normal	Physical	250	100	5	All Others
1	Fire Fang	Fire	Physical	65	95	15	Normal
1	Ice Fang	Ice	Physical	65	95	15	Normal
1	Imprison	Psychic	Status	—	—	10	Self
1	Iron Head	Steel	Physical	80	100	15	Normal
1	Multi-Attack*	Normal	Physical	120	100	10	Normal
1	Poison Fang	Poison	Physical	50	100	15	Normal
1	Scary Face	Normal	Status	—	100	10	Normal
1	Tackle	Normal	Physical	40	100	35	Normal
1	Thunder Fang	Electric	Physical	65	95	15	Normal
10	Double Hit	Normal	Physical	35	90	10	Normal
20	Metal Sound	Steel	Status	—	85	40	Normal
25	Crush Claw	Normal	Physical	75	95	10	Normal
30	Air Slash	Flying	Special	75	95	15	Normal
35	Tri Attack	Normal	Special	80	100	10	Normal
40	X-Scissor	Bug	Physical	80	100	15	Normal
45	Crunch	Dark	Physical	80	100	15	Normal
50	Take Down	Normal	Physical	90	85	20	Normal
55	Double-Edge	Normal	Physical	120	100	15	Normal
60	Parting Shot	Dark	Status	—	100	20	Normal

EVOLUTION MOVES

NAME	TYPE	KIND	POW.	ACC.	PP	RANGE
Multi-Attack*	Normal	Physical	120	100	10	Normal

EGG MOVES

NAME	TYPE	KIND	POW.	ACC.	PP	RANGE

TUTOR MOVES

NAME	TYPE	KIND	POW.	ACC.	PP	RANGE
Draco Meteor	Dragon	Special	130	90	5	Normal
Fire Pledge	Fire	Special	80	100	10	Normal
Grass Pledge	Grass	Special	80	100	10	Normal
Steel Beam	Steel	Special	140	95	5	Normal
Water Pledge	Water	Special	80	100	10	Normal

TM MOVES

NO.	NAME	TYPE	KIND	POW.	ACC.	PP	RANGE
TM08	Hyper Beam	Normal	Special	150	90	5	Normal
TM09	Giga Impact	Normal	Physical	150	90	5	Normal
TM14	Thunder Wave	Electric	Status	—	90	20	Normal
TM20	Self-Destruct	Normal	Physical	200	100	5	All Others
TM21	Rest	Psychic	Status	—	—	10	Self
TM22	Rock Slide	Rock	Physical	75	90	10	Many Others
TM24	Snore	Normal	Special	50	100	15	Normal
TM25	Protect	Normal	Status	—	—	10	Self
TM26	Scary Face	Normal	Status	—	100	10	Normal
TM27	Icy Wind	Ice	Special	55	95	15	Many Others
TM30	Steel Wing	Steel	Physical	70	90	25	Normal
TM32	Sandstorm	Rock	Status	—	—	10	Both Sides
TM33	Rain Dance	Water	Status	—	—	5	Both Sides
TM34	Sunny Day	Fire	Status	—	—	5	Both Sides
TM35	Hail	Ice	Status	—	—	10	Both Sides
TM39	Facade	Normal	Physical	70	100	20	Normal
TM40	Swift	Normal	Special	60	—	20	Many Others
TM44	Imprison	Psychic	Status	—	—	10	Self
TM56	U-turn	Bug	Physical	70	100	20	Normal
TM57	Payback	Dark	Physical	50	100	10	Normal
TM65	Shadow Claw	Ghost	Physical	70	100	15	Normal
TM66	Thunder Fang	Electric	Physical	65	95	15	Normal
TM67	Ice Fang	Ice	Physical	65	95	15	Normal
TM68	Fire Fang	Fire	Physical	65	95	15	Normal
TM76	Round	Normal	Special	60	100	15	Normal
TM85	Snarl	Dark	Special	55	95	15	Many Others
TM95	Air Slash	Flying	Special	75	95	15	Normal

TR MOVES

NO.	NAME	TYPE	KIND	POW.	ACC.	PP	RANGE
TR00	Swords Dance	Normal	Status	—	—	20	Self
TR02	Flamethrower	Fire	Special	90	100	15	Normal
TR04	Surf	Water	Special	90	100	15	All Others
TR05	Ice Beam	Ice	Special	90	100	10	Normal
TR08	Thunderbolt	Electric	Special	90	100	15	Normal
TR19	Tri Attack	Normal	Special	80	100	10	Normal
TR20	Substitute	Normal	Status	—	—	10	Self
TR21	Reversal	Fighting	Physical	—	100	15	Normal
TR24	Outrage	Dragon	Physical	120	100	10	1 Random
TR26	Endure	Normal	Status	—	—	10	Self
TR27	Sleep Talk	Normal	Status	—	—	10	Self
TR32	Crunch	Dark	Physical	80	100	15	Normal
TR33	Shadow Ball	Ghost	Special	80	100	15	Normal
TR36	Heat Wave	Fire	Special	95	90	10	Many Others
TR42	Hyper Voice	Normal	Special	90	100	10	Many Others
TR46	Iron Defense	Steel	Status	—	—	15	Self
TR47	Dragon Claw	Dragon	Physical	80	100	15	Normal
TR60	X-Scissor	Bug	Physical	80	100	15	Normal
TR69	Zen Headbutt	Psychic	Physical	80	90	15	Normal
TR70	Flash Cannon	Steel	Special	80	100	10	Normal
TR74	Iron Head	Steel	Physical	80	100	15	Normal
TR85	Work Up	Normal	Status	—	—	30	Self
TR97	Psychic Fangs	Psychic	Physical	85	100	10	Normal

Silvally

p. 152

ABILITY
RKS System
—

HIDDEN ABILITY
—

SPECIES STRENGTHS
HP
ATTACK
DEFENSE
SP. ATK
SP. DEF
SPEED

DAMAGE TAKEN IN BATTLE
×1 ×2 ×1
×1 ×1 ×0
×1 ×1 ×1
×1 ×1 ×1
×1 ×1 ×1

NO EGGS

*Multi-Attack's type changes depending on what memory disc is held by the user.

383

LEVEL-UP MOVES

LV.	NAME	TYPE	KIND	POW.	ACC.	PP	RANGE
1	Leer	Normal	Status	—	100	30	Many Others
1	Tackle	Normal	Physical	40	100	35	Normal
3	Rock Throw	Rock	Physical	50	90	15	Normal
6	Payback	Dark	Physical	50	100	10	Normal
9	Bite	Dark	Physical	60	100	25	Normal
12	Scary Face	Normal	Status	—	100	10	Normal
15	Rock Slide	Rock	Physical	75	90	10	Many Others
18	Stomping Tantrum	Ground	Physical	75	100	10	Normal
21	Screech	Normal	Status	—	85	40	Normal
24	Dark Pulse	Dark	Special	80	100	15	Normal
27	Crunch	Dark	Physical	80	100	15	Normal
31	Earthquake	Ground	Physical	100	100	10	All Others
33	Stone Edge	Rock	Physical	100	80	5	Normal
36	Thrash	Normal	Physical	120	100	10	1 Random
39	Sandstorm	Rock	Status	—	—	10	Both Sides
42	Hyper Beam	Normal	Special	150	90	5	Normal

EVOLUTION MOVES

NAME	TYPE	KIND	POW.	ACC.	PP	RANGE

EGG MOVES

NAME	TYPE	KIND	POW.	ACC.	PP	RANGE
Ancient Power	Rock	Special	60	100	5	Normal
Curse	Ghost	Status	—	—	10	Varies
Stomp	Normal	Physical	65	100	20	Normal

TUTOR MOVES

NAME	TYPE	KIND	POW.	ACC.	PP	RANGE

TM MOVES

NO.	NAME	TYPE	KIND	POW.	ACC.	PP	RANGE
TM08	Hyper Beam	Normal	Special	150	90	5	Normal
TM15	Dig	Ground	Physical	80	100	10	Normal
TM16	Screech	Normal	Status	—	85	40	Normal
TM21	Rest	Psychic	Status	—	—	10	Self
TM22	Rock Slide	Rock	Physical	75	90	10	Many Others
TM24	Snore	Normal	Special	50	100	15	Normal
TM25	Protect	Normal	Status	—	—	10	Self
TM26	Scary Face	Normal	Status	—	100	10	Normal
TM31	Attract	Normal	Status	—	100	15	Normal
TM32	Sandstorm	Rock	Status	—	—	10	Both Sides
TM33	Rain Dance	Water	Status	—	—	5	Both Sides
TM34	Sunny Day	Fire	Status	—	—	5	Both Sides
TM39	Facade	Normal	Physical	70	100	20	Normal
TM43	Brick Break	Fighting	Physical	75	100	15	Normal
TM48	Rock Tomb	Rock	Physical	60	95	15	Normal
TM49	Sand Tomb	Ground	Physical	35	85	15	Normal
TM57	Payback	Dark	Physical	50	100	10	Normal
TM58	Assurance	Dark	Physical	60	100	10	Normal
TM76	Round	Normal	Special	60	100	15	Normal
TM79	Retaliate	Normal	Physical	70	100	5	Normal
TM81	Bulldoze	Ground	Physical	60	100	20	All Others
TM85	Snarl	Dark	Special	55	95	15	Many Others
TM98	Stomping Tantrum	Ground	Physical	75	100	10	Normal

TR MOVES

NO.	NAME	TYPE	KIND	POW.	ACC.	PP	RANGE
TR01	Body Slam	Normal	Physical	85	100	15	Normal
TR10	Earthquake	Ground	Physical	100	100	10	All Others
TR13	Focus Energy	Normal	Status	—	—	30	Self
TR20	Substitute	Normal	Status	—	—	10	Self
TR24	Outrage	Dragon	Physical	120	100	10	1 Random
TR26	Endure	Normal	Status	—	—	10	Self
TR27	Sleep Talk	Normal	Status	—	—	10	Self
TR31	Iron Tail	Steel	Physical	100	75	15	Normal
TR32	Crunch	Dark	Physical	80	100	15	Normal
TR35	Uproar	Normal	Special	90	100	10	1 Random
TR37	Taunt	Dark	Status	—	100	20	Normal
TR39	Superpower	Fighting	Physical	120	100	5	Normal
TR45	Muddy Water	Water	Special	90	85	10	Many Others
TR46	Iron Defense	Steel	Status	—	—	15	Self
TR51	Dragon Dance	Dragon	Status	—	—	20	Self
TR58	Dark Pulse	Dark	Special	80	100	15	Normal
TR67	Earth Power	Ground	Special	90	100	10	Normal
TR74	Iron Head	Steel	Physical	80	100	15	Normal
TR75	Stone Edge	Rock	Physical	100	80	5	Normal
TR76	Stealth Rock	Rock	Status	—	—	20	Other Side

Larvitar

p. 153

ABILITY
Guts
—

HIDDEN ABILITY
Sand Veil

SPECIES STRENGTHS
HP
ATTACK
DEFENSE
SP. ATK
SP. DEF
SPEED

DAMAGE TAKEN IN BATTLE
×0.5 ×2 ×0.5
×0.5 ×0.25 ×1
×4 ×2 ×1
×4 ×0.5 ×1
×0 ×1 ×2
×2 ×1 ×1

MONSTER

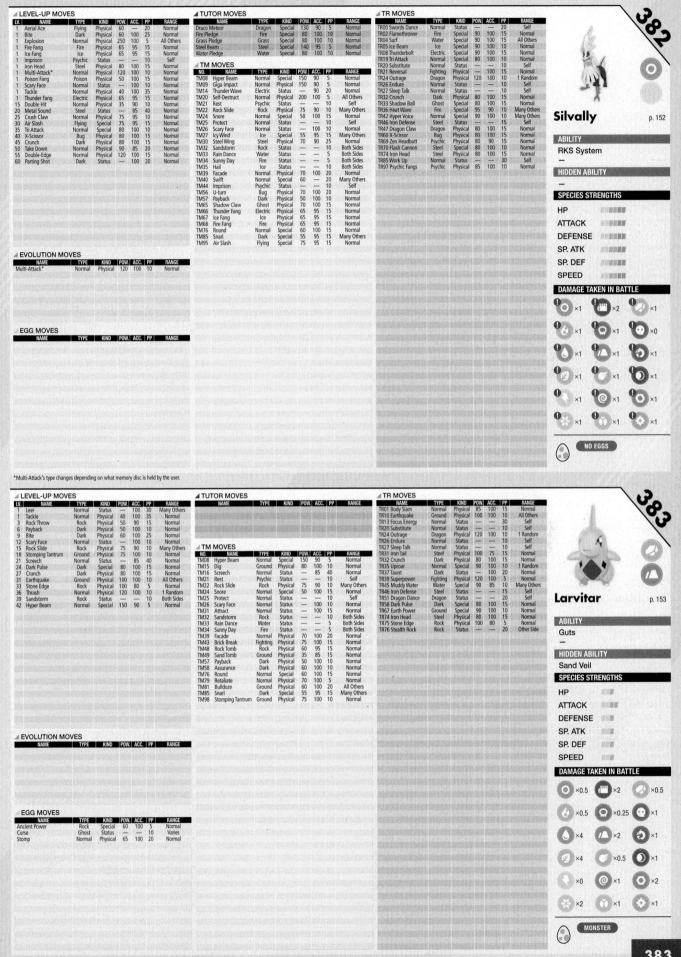

384 Pupitar

p. 153

ABILITY
Shed Skin
—

HIDDEN ABILITY
—

SPECIES STRENGTHS

HP	
ATTACK	
DEFENSE	
SP. ATK	
SP. DEF	
SPEED	

DAMAGE TAKEN IN BATTLE

×0.5	×2	×0.5
×0.5	×0.25	×1
×4	×2	×1
×4	×0.5	×1
×0	×1	×2
×2	×1	×1

MONSTER

LEVEL-UP MOVES

LV.	NAME	TYPE	KIND	POW.	ACC.	PP	RANGE
1	Iron Defense	Steel	Status	—	—	15	Self
1	Leer	Normal	Status	—	100	30	Many Others
1	Payback	Dark	Physical	50	100	10	Normal
1	Rock Throw	Rock	Physical	50	90	15	Normal
1	Tackle	Normal	Physical	40	100	35	Normal
9	Bite	Dark	Physical	60	100	25	Normal
12	Scary Face	Normal	Status	—	100	10	Normal
15	Rock Slide	Rock	Physical	75	90	10	Many Others
18	Stomping Tantrum	Ground	Physical	75	100	10	Normal
21	Screech	Normal	Status	—	85	40	Normal
24	Dark Pulse	Dark	Special	80	100	15	Normal
27	Crunch	Dark	Physical	80	100	15	Normal
33	Earthquake	Ground	Physical	100	100	10	All Others
37	Stone Edge	Rock	Physical	100	80	5	Normal
42	Thrash	Normal	Physical	120	100	10	1 Random
47	Sandstorm	Rock	Status	—	—	10	Both Sides
52	Hyper Beam	Normal	Special	150	90	5	Normal

EVOLUTION MOVES

NAME	TYPE	KIND	POW.	ACC.	PP	RANGE
Iron Defense	Steel	Status	—	—	15	Self

EGG MOVES

NAME	TYPE	KIND	POW.	ACC.	PP	RANGE

TUTOR MOVES

NAME	TYPE	KIND	POW.	ACC.	PP	RANGE

TM MOVES

NO.	NAME	TYPE	KIND	POW.	ACC.	PP	RANGE
TM08	Hyper Beam	Normal	Special	150	90	5	Normal
TM15	Dig	Ground	Physical	80	100	10	Normal
TM16	Screech	Normal	Status	—	85	40	Normal
TM21	Rest	Psychic	Status	—	—	10	Self
TM22	Rock Slide	Rock	Physical	75	90	10	Many Others
TM24	Snore	Normal	Special	50	100	15	Normal
TM25	Protect	Normal	Status	—	—	10	Self
TM26	Scary Face	Normal	Status	—	100	10	Normal
TM31	Attract	Normal	Status	—	100	15	Normal
TM32	Sandstorm	Rock	Status	—	—	10	Both Sides
TM33	Rain Dance	Water	Status	—	—	5	Both Sides
TM34	Sunny Day	Fire	Status	—	—	5	Both Sides
TM39	Facade	Normal	Physical	70	100	20	Normal
TM43	Brick Break	Fighting	Physical	75	100	15	Normal
TM48	Rock Tomb	Rock	Physical	60	95	15	Normal
TM49	Sand Tomb	Ground	Physical	35	85	15	Normal
TM57	Payback	Dark	Physical	50	100	10	Normal
TM58	Assurance	Dark	Physical	60	100	10	Normal
TM76	Round	Normal	Special	60	100	15	Normal
TM79	Retaliate	Normal	Physical	70	100	5	Normal
TM81	Bulldoze	Ground	Physical	60	100	20	All Others
TM85	Snarl	Dark	Special	55	95	15	Many Others
TM98	Stomping Tantrum	Ground	Physical	75	100	10	Normal

TR MOVES

NO.	NAME	TYPE	KIND	POW.	ACC.	PP	RANGE
TR01	Body Slam	Normal	Physical	85	100	15	Normal
TR10	Earthquake	Ground	Physical	100	100	10	All Others
TR13	Focus Energy	Normal	Status	—	—	30	Self
TR20	Substitute	Normal	Status	—	—	10	Self
TR24	Outrage	Dragon	Physical	120	100	10	1 Random
TR26	Endure	Normal	Status	—	—	10	Self
TR27	Sleep Talk	Normal	Status	—	—	10	Self
TR31	Iron Tail	Steel	Physical	100	75	15	Normal
TR32	Crunch	Dark	Physical	80	100	15	Normal
TR35	Uproar	Normal	Special	90	100	10	1 Random
TR37	Taunt	Dark	Status	—	100	20	Normal
TR39	Superpower	Fighting	Physical	120	100	5	Normal
TR45	Muddy Water	Water	Special	90	85	10	Many Others
TR46	Iron Defense	Steel	Status	—	—	15	Self
TR51	Dragon Dance	Dragon	Status	—	—	20	Self
TR58	Dark Pulse	Dark	Special	80	100	15	Normal
TR67	Earth Power	Ground	Special	90	100	10	Normal
TR74	Iron Head	Steel	Physical	80	100	15	Normal
TR75	Stone Edge	Rock	Physical	100	80	5	Normal
TR76	Stealth Rock	Rock	Status	—	—	20	Other Side

---

385 Tyranitar

p. 153

ABILITY
Sand Stream
—

HIDDEN ABILITY
Unnerve

SPECIES STRENGTHS

HP	
ATTACK	
DEFENSE	
SP. ATK	
SP. DEF	
SPEED	

DAMAGE TAKEN IN BATTLE

×0.5	×4	×1
×0.5	×0.5	×0.5
×2	×2	×1
×1	×0.5	×0.5
×1	×0	×2
×2	×2	×2

MONSTER

LEVEL-UP MOVES

LV.	NAME	TYPE	KIND	POW.	ACC.	PP	RANGE
1	Fire Fang	Fire	Physical	65	95	15	Normal
1	Ice Fang	Ice	Physical	65	95	15	Normal
1	Iron Defense	Steel	Status	—	—	15	Self
1	Leer	Normal	Status	—	100	30	Many Others
1	Payback	Dark	Physical	50	100	10	Normal
1	Rock Throw	Rock	Physical	50	90	15	Normal
1	Tackle	Normal	Physical	40	100	35	Normal
1	Thunder Fang	Electric	Physical	65	95	15	Normal
9	Bite	Dark	Physical	60	100	25	Normal
12	Scary Face	Normal	Status	—	100	10	Normal
15	Rock Slide	Rock	Physical	75	90	10	Many Others
18	Stomping Tantrum	Ground	Physical	75	100	10	Normal
21	Screech	Normal	Status	—	85	40	Normal
24	Dark Pulse	Dark	Special	80	100	15	Normal
27	Crunch	Dark	Physical	80	100	15	Normal
33	Earthquake	Ground	Physical	100	100	10	All Others
37	Stone Edge	Rock	Physical	100	80	5	Normal
42	Thrash	Normal	Physical	120	100	10	1 Random
47	Sandstorm	Rock	Status	—	—	10	Both Sides
52	Hyper Beam	Normal	Special	150	90	5	Normal
59	Giga Impact	Normal	Physical	150	90	5	Normal

EVOLUTION MOVES

NAME	TYPE	KIND	POW.	ACC.	PP	RANGE

EGG MOVES

NAME	TYPE	KIND	POW.	ACC.	PP	RANGE

TUTOR MOVES

NAME	TYPE	KIND	POW.	ACC.	PP	RANGE

TM MOVES

NO.	NAME	TYPE	KIND	POW.	ACC.	PP	RANGE
TM00	Mega Punch	Normal	Physical	80	85	20	Normal
TM01	Mega Kick	Normal	Physical	120	75	5	Normal
TM03	Fire Punch	Fire	Physical	75	100	15	Normal
TM04	Ice Punch	Ice	Physical	75	100	15	Normal
TM05	Thunder Punch	Electric	Physical	75	100	15	Normal
TM08	Hyper Beam	Normal	Special	150	90	5	Normal
TM09	Giga Impact	Normal	Physical	150	90	5	Normal
TM14	Thunder Wave	Electric	Status	—	90	20	Normal
TM15	Dig	Ground	Physical	80	100	10	Normal
TM16	Screech	Normal	Status	—	85	40	Normal
TM21	Rest	Psychic	Status	—	—	10	Self
TM22	Rock Slide	Rock	Physical	75	90	10	Many Others
TM24	Snore	Normal	Special	50	100	15	Normal
TM25	Protect	Normal	Status	—	—	10	Self
TM26	Scary Face	Normal	Status	—	100	10	Normal
TM31	Attract	Normal	Status	—	100	15	Normal
TM32	Sandstorm	Rock	Status	—	—	10	Both Sides
TM33	Rain Dance	Water	Status	—	—	5	Both Sides
TM34	Sunny Day	Fire	Status	—	—	5	Both Sides
TM36	Whirlpool	Water	Special	35	85	15	Normal
TM39	Facade	Normal	Physical	70	100	20	Normal
TM42	Revenge	Fighting	Physical	60	100	10	Normal
TM43	Brick Break	Fighting	Physical	75	100	15	Normal
TM48	Rock Tomb	Rock	Physical	60	95	15	Normal
TM49	Sand Tomb	Ground	Physical	35	85	15	Normal
TM54	Rock Blast	Rock	Physical	25	90	10	Normal
TM57	Payback	Dark	Physical	50	100	10	Normal
TM58	Assurance	Dark	Physical	60	100	10	Normal
TM59	Fling	Dark	Physical	—	100	10	Normal
TM64	Avalanche	Ice	Physical	60	100	10	Normal
TM65	Shadow Claw	Ghost	Physical	70	100	15	Normal
TM66	Thunder Fang	Electric	Physical	65	95	15	Normal
TM67	Ice Fang	Ice	Physical	65	95	15	Normal
TM68	Fire Fang	Fire	Physical	65	95	15	Normal
TM76	Round	Normal	Special	60	100	15	Normal
TM79	Retaliate	Normal	Physical	70	100	5	Normal
TM81	Bulldoze	Ground	Physical	60	100	20	All Others
TM85	Snarl	Dark	Special	55	95	15	Many Others
TM97	Brutal Swing	Dark	Physical	60	100	20	All Others
TM98	Stomping Tantrum	Ground	Physical	75	100	10	Normal
TM99	Breaking Swipe	Dragon	Physical	60	100	15	Many Others

TR MOVES

NO.	NAME	TYPE	KIND	POW.	ACC.	PP	RANGE
TR01	Body Slam	Normal	Physical	85	100	15	Normal
TR02	Flamethrower	Fire	Special	90	100	15	Normal
TR03	Hydro Pump	Water	Special	110	80	5	Normal
TR04	Surf	Water	Special	90	100	15	All Others
TR05	Ice Beam	Ice	Special	90	100	10	Normal
TR06	Blizzard	Ice	Special	110	70	5	Many Others
TR07	Low Kick	Fighting	Physical	—	100	20	Normal
TR08	Thunderbolt	Electric	Special	90	100	15	Normal
TR09	Thunder	Electric	Special	110	70	10	Normal
TR10	Earthquake	Ground	Physical	100	100	10	All Others
TR13	Focus Energy	Normal	Status	—	—	30	Self
TR15	Fire Blast	Fire	Special	110	85	5	Normal
TR20	Substitute	Normal	Status	—	—	10	Self
TR24	Outrage	Dragon	Physical	120	100	10	1 Random
TR26	Endure	Normal	Status	—	—	10	Self
TR27	Sleep Talk	Normal	Status	—	—	10	Self
TR31	Iron Tail	Steel	Physical	100	75	15	Normal
TR32	Crunch	Dark	Physical	80	100	15	Normal
TR35	Uproar	Normal	Special	90	100	10	1 Random
TR37	Taunt	Dark	Status	—	100	20	Normal
TR39	Superpower	Fighting	Physical	120	100	5	Normal
TR45	Muddy Water	Water	Special	90	85	10	Many Others
TR46	Iron Defense	Steel	Status	—	—	15	Self
TR47	Dragon Claw	Dragon	Physical	80	100	15	Normal
TR51	Dragon Dance	Dragon	Status	—	—	20	Self
TR58	Dark Pulse	Dark	Special	80	100	15	Normal
TR62	Dragon Pulse	Dragon	Special	85	100	10	Normal
TR64	Focus Blast	Fighting	Special	120	70	5	Normal
TR67	Earth Power	Ground	Special	90	100	10	Normal
TR74	Iron Head	Steel	Physical	80	100	15	Normal
TR75	Stone Edge	Rock	Physical	100	80	5	Normal
TR76	Stealth Rock	Rock	Status	—	—	20	Other Side
TR79	Heavy Slam	Steel	Physical	—	100	10	Normal
TR81	Foul Play	Dark	Physical	95	100	15	Normal
TR94	High Horsepower	Ground	Physical	95	95	10	Normal
TR99	Body Press	Fighting	Physical	80	100	10	Normal

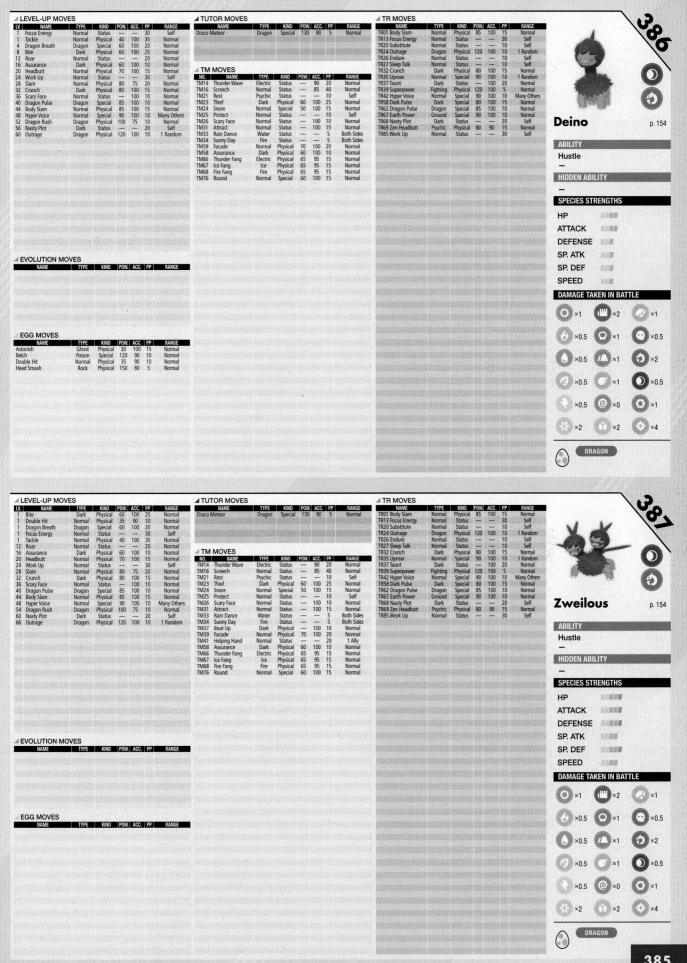

386 — Deino

LEVEL-UP MOVES

LV	NAME	TYPE	KIND	POW.	ACC.	PP	RANGE
1	Focus Energy	Normal	Status	—	—	30	Self
1	Tackle	Normal	Physical	40	100	25	Normal
4	Dragon Breath	Dragon	Special	60	100	20	Normal
8	Bite	Dark	Physical	60	100	25	Normal
12	Roar	Normal	Status	—	—	20	Normal
16	Assurance	Dark	Physical	60	100	10	Normal
20	Headbutt	Normal	Physical	70	100	15	Normal
24	Work Up	Normal	Status	—	—	30	Self
28	Slam	Normal	Physical	80	75	20	Normal
32	Crunch	Dark	Physical	80	100	15	Normal
36	Scary Face	Normal	Status	—	100	10	Normal
40	Dragon Pulse	Dragon	Special	85	100	10	Normal
44	Hyper Voice	Normal	Special	90	100	10	Many Others
52	Dragon Rush	Dragon	Physical	100	75	10	Normal
56	Nasty Plot	Dark	Status	—	—	20	Self
60	Outrage	Dragon	Physical	120	100	10	1 Random

EVOLUTION MOVES

NAME	TYPE	KIND	POW.	ACC.	PP	RANGE

EGG MOVES

NAME	TYPE	KIND	POW.	ACC.	PP	RANGE
Astonish	Ghost	Physical	30	100	15	Normal
Belch	Poison	Special	120	90	10	Normal
Double Hit	Normal	Physical	35	90	10	Normal
Head Smash	Rock	Physical	150	80	5	Normal

TUTOR MOVES

NAME	TYPE	KIND	POW.	ACC.	PP	RANGE
Draco Meteor	Dragon	Special	130	90	5	Normal

TM MOVES

NO.	NAME	TYPE	KIND	POW.	ACC.	PP	RANGE
TM14	Thunder Wave	Electric	Status	—	90	20	Normal
TM16	Screech	Normal	Status	—	85	40	Normal
TM21	Rest	Psychic	Status	—	—	10	Self
TM23	Thief	Dark	Physical	60	100	25	Normal
TM24	Snore	Normal	Special	50	100	15	Normal
TM25	Protect	Normal	Status	—	—	10	Self
TM26	Scary Face	Normal	Status	—	100	10	Normal
TM31	Attract	Normal	Status	—	100	15	Normal
TM33	Rain Dance	Water	Status	—	—	5	Both Sides
TM34	Sunny Day	Fire	Status	—	—	5	Both Sides
TM39	Facade	Normal	Physical	70	100	20	Normal
TM58	Assurance	Dark	Physical	60	100	10	Normal
TM66	Thunder Fang	Electric	Physical	65	95	15	Normal
TM67	Ice Fang	Ice	Physical	65	95	15	Normal
TM68	Fire Fang	Fire	Physical	65	95	15	Normal
TM76	Round	Normal	Special	60	100	15	Normal

TR MOVES

NO.	NAME	TYPE	KIND	POW.	ACC.	PP	RANGE
TR01	Body Slam	Normal	Physical	85	100	15	Normal
TR13	Focus Energy	Normal	Status	—	—	30	Self
TR20	Substitute	Normal	Status	—	—	10	Self
TR24	Outrage	Dragon	Physical	120	100	10	1 Random
TR26	Endure	Normal	Status	—	—	10	Self
TR27	Sleep Talk	Normal	Status	—	—	10	Self
TR32	Crunch	Dark	Physical	80	100	15	Normal
TR35	Uproar	Normal	Special	90	100	10	1 Random
TR37	Taunt	Dark	Status	—	100	20	Normal
TR39	Superpower	Fighting	Physical	120	100	5	Normal
TR42	Hyper Voice	Normal	Special	90	100	10	Many Others
TR58	Dark Pulse	Dark	Special	80	100	15	Normal
TR62	Dragon Pulse	Dragon	Special	85	100	10	Normal
TR67	Earth Power	Ground	Special	90	100	10	Normal
TR68	Nasty Plot	Dark	Status	—	—	20	Self
TR69	Zen Headbutt	Psychic	Physical	80	90	15	Normal
TR85	Work Up	Normal	Status	—	—	30	Self

Deino — p. 154

ABILITY
Hustle

HIDDEN ABILITY
—

SPECIES STRENGTHS
- HP
- ATTACK
- DEFENSE
- SP. ATK
- SP. DEF
- SPEED

DAMAGE TAKEN IN BATTLE

×1	×2	×1
×0.5	×1	×0.5
×0.5	×1	×2
×0.5	×1	×0.5
×0.5	×0	×1
×2	×2	×4

DRAGON

---

387 — Zweilous

LEVEL-UP MOVES

LV	NAME	TYPE	KIND	POW.	ACC.	PP	RANGE
1	Bite	Dark	Physical	60	100	25	Normal
1	Double Hit	Normal	Physical	35	90	10	Normal
1	Dragon Breath	Dragon	Special	60	100	20	Normal
1	Focus Energy	Normal	Status	—	—	30	Self
1	Tackle	Normal	Physical	40	100	35	Normal
12	Roar	Normal	Status	—	—	20	Normal
16	Assurance	Dark	Physical	60	100	10	Normal
20	Headbutt	Normal	Physical	70	100	15	Normal
24	Work Up	Normal	Status	—	—	30	Self
28	Slam	Normal	Physical	80	75	20	Normal
32	Crunch	Dark	Physical	80	100	15	Normal
36	Scary Face	Normal	Status	—	100	10	Normal
40	Dragon Pulse	Dragon	Special	85	100	10	Normal
44	Body Slam	Normal	Physical	85	100	15	Normal
48	Hyper Voice	Normal	Special	90	100	10	Many Others
54	Dragon Rush	Dragon	Physical	100	75	10	Normal
60	Nasty Plot	Dark	Status	—	—	20	Self
66	Outrage	Dragon	Physical	120	100	10	1 Random

EVOLUTION MOVES

NAME	TYPE	KIND	POW.	ACC.	PP	RANGE

EGG MOVES

NAME	TYPE	KIND	POW.	ACC.	PP	RANGE

TUTOR MOVES

NAME	TYPE	KIND	POW.	ACC.	PP	RANGE
Draco Meteor	Dragon	Special	130	90	5	Normal

TM MOVES

NO.	NAME	TYPE	KIND	POW.	ACC.	PP	RANGE
TM14	Thunder Wave	Electric	Status	—	90	20	Normal
TM16	Screech	Normal	Status	—	85	40	Normal
TM21	Rest	Psychic	Status	—	—	10	Self
TM23	Thief	Dark	Physical	60	100	25	Normal
TM24	Snore	Normal	Special	50	100	15	Normal
TM25	Protect	Normal	Status	—	—	10	Self
TM26	Scary Face	Normal	Status	—	100	10	Normal
TM31	Attract	Normal	Status	—	100	15	Normal
TM33	Rain Dance	Water	Status	—	—	5	Both Sides
TM34	Sunny Day	Fire	Status	—	—	5	Both Sides
TM37	Beat Up	Dark	Physical	—	100	10	Normal
TM39	Facade	Normal	Physical	70	100	20	Normal
TM41	Helping Hand	Normal	Status	—	—	20	1 Ally
TM58	Assurance	Dark	Physical	60	100	10	Normal
TM66	Thunder Fang	Electric	Physical	65	95	15	Normal
TM67	Ice Fang	Ice	Physical	65	95	15	Normal
TM68	Fire Fang	Fire	Physical	65	95	15	Normal
TM76	Round	Normal	Special	60	100	15	Normal

TR MOVES

NO.	NAME	TYPE	KIND	POW.	ACC.	PP	RANGE
TR01	Body Slam	Normal	Physical	85	100	15	Normal
TR13	Focus Energy	Normal	Status	—	—	30	Self
TR20	Substitute	Normal	Status	—	—	10	Self
TR24	Outrage	Dragon	Physical	120	100	10	1 Random
TR26	Endure	Normal	Status	—	—	10	Self
TR27	Sleep Talk	Normal	Status	—	—	10	Self
TR32	Crunch	Dark	Physical	80	100	15	Normal
TR35	Uproar	Normal	Special	90	100	10	1 Random
TR37	Taunt	Dark	Status	—	100	20	Normal
TR39	Superpower	Fighting	Physical	120	100	5	Normal
TR42	Hyper Voice	Normal	Special	90	100	10	Many Others
TR58	Dark Pulse	Dark	Special	80	100	15	Normal
TR62	Dragon Pulse	Dragon	Special	85	100	10	Normal
TR67	Earth Power	Ground	Special	90	100	10	Normal
TR68	Nasty Plot	Dark	Status	—	—	20	Self
TR69	Zen Headbutt	Psychic	Physical	80	90	15	Normal
TR85	Work Up	Normal	Status	—	—	30	Self

Zweilous — p. 154

ABILITY
Hustle

HIDDEN ABILITY
—

SPECIES STRENGTHS
- HP
- ATTACK
- DEFENSE
- SP. ATK
- SP. DEF
- SPEED

DAMAGE TAKEN IN BATTLE

×1	×2	×1
×0.5	×1	×0.5
×0.5	×1	×2
×0.5	×1	×0.5
×0.5	×0	×1
×2	×2	×4

DRAGON

388 Hydreigon — p. 154

ABILITY
Levitate
—

HIDDEN ABILITY
—

SPECIES STRENGTHS
HP
ATTACK
DEFENSE
SP. ATK
SP. DEF
SPEED

LEVEL-UP MOVES

LV.	NAME	TYPE	KIND	POW.	ACC.	PP	RANGE
1	Bite	Dark	Physical	60	100	25	Normal
1	Double Hit	Normal	Physical	35	90	10	Normal
1	Dragon Breath	Dragon	Special	60	100	20	Normal
1	Focus Energy	Normal	Status	—	—	30	Self
1	Tackle	Normal	Physical	40	100	35	Normal
1	Tri Attack	Normal	Special	80	100	10	Normal
12	Roar	Normal	Status	—	—	20	Normal
16	Assurance	Dark	Physical	60	100	10	Normal
20	Headbutt	Normal	Physical	70	100	15	Normal
24	Work Up	Normal	Status	—	—	30	Self
28	Slam	Normal	Physical	80	75	20	Normal
32	Crunch	Dark	Physical	80	100	15	Normal
36	Scary Face	Normal	Status	—	100	10	Normal
40	Dragon Pulse	Dragon	Special	85	100	10	Normal
44	Body Slam	Normal	Physical	85	100	15	Normal
48	Hyper Voice	Normal	Special	90	100	10	Many Others
54	Dragon Rush	Dragon	Physical	100	75	10	Normal
60	Nasty Plot	Dark	Status	—	—	20	Self
68	Outrage	Dragon	Physical	120	100	10	1 Random
76	Hyper Beam	Normal	Special	150	90	5	Normal

EVOLUTION MOVES

NAME	TYPE	KIND	POW.	ACC.	PP	RANGE

EGG MOVES

NAME	TYPE	KIND	POW.	ACC.	PP	RANGE

TUTOR MOVES

NAME	TYPE	KIND	POW.	ACC.	PP	RANGE
Draco Meteor	Dragon	Special	130	90	5	Normal

TM MOVES

NO.	NAME	TYPE	KIND	POW.	ACC.	PP	RANGE
TM06	Fly	Flying	Physical	90	95	15	Normal
TM08	Hyper Beam	Normal	Special	150	90	5	Normal
TM09	Giga Impact	Normal	Physical	150	90	5	Normal
TM13	Fire Spin	Fire	Special	35	85	15	Normal
TM14	Thunder Wave	Electric	Status	—	90	20	Normal
TM16	Screech	Normal	Status	—	85	40	Normal
TM18	Reflect	Psychic	Status	—	—	20	Your Side
TM21	Rest	Psychic	Status	—	—	10	Self
TM22	Rock Slide	Rock	Physical	75	90	10	Many Others
TM24	Snore	Normal	Special	50	100	15	Normal
TM25	Protect	Normal	Status	—	—	10	Self
TM26	Scary Face	Normal	Status	—	100	10	Normal
TM30	Steel Wing	Steel	Physical	70	90	25	Normal
TM31	Attract	Normal	Status	—	100	15	Normal
TM33	Rain Dance	Water	Status	—	—	5	Both Sides
TM34	Sunny Day	Fire	Status	—	—	5	Both Sides
TM37	Beat Up	Dark	Physical	—	100	10	Normal
TM39	Facade	Normal	Physical	70	100	20	Normal
TM41	Helping Hand	Normal	Status	—	—	20	1 Ally
TM48	Rock Tomb	Rock	Physical	60	95	15	Normal
TM56	U-turn	Bug	Physical	70	100	20	Normal
TM57	Payback	Dark	Physical	50	100	10	Normal
TM58	Assurance	Dark	Physical	60	100	10	Normal
TM66	Thunder Fang	Electric	Physical	65	95	15	Normal
TM67	Ice Fang	Ice	Physical	65	95	15	Normal
TM68	Fire Fang	Fire	Physical	65	95	15	Normal
TM76	Round	Normal	Special	60	100	15	Normal
TM78	Acrobatics	Flying	Physical	55	100	15	Normal
TM81	Bulldoze	Ground	Physical	60	100	20	All Others
TM85	Snarl	Dark	Special	55	95	15	Many Others
TM97	Brutal Swing	Dark	Physical	60	100	20	All Others
TM99	Breaking Swipe	Dragon	Physical	60	100	15	Many Others

TR MOVES

NO.	NAME	TYPE	KIND	POW.	ACC.	PP	RANGE
TR01	Body Slam	Normal	Physical	85	100	15	Normal
TR02	Flamethrower	Fire	Special	90	100	15	Normal
TR03	Hydro Pump	Water	Special	110	80	5	Normal
TR04	Surf	Water	Special	90	100	15	All Others
TR10	Earthquake	Ground	Physical	100	100	10	All Others
TR13	Focus Energy	Normal	Status	—	—	30	Self
TR19	Tri Attack	Normal	Special	80	100	10	Normal
TR20	Substitute	Normal	Status	—	—	10	Self
TR24	Outrage	Dragon	Physical	120	100	10	1 Random
TR26	Endure	Normal	Status	—	—	10	Self
TR27	Sleep Talk	Normal	Status	—	—	10	Self
TR31	Iron Tail	Steel	Physical	100	75	15	Normal
TR32	Crunch	Dark	Physical	80	100	15	Normal
TR35	Uproar	Normal	Special	90	100	10	1 Random
TR36	Heat Wave	Fire	Special	95	90	10	Many Others
TR37	Taunt	Dark	Status	—	100	20	Normal
TR39	Superpower	Fighting	Physical	120	100	5	Normal
TR42	Hyper Voice	Normal	Special	90	100	10	Many Others
TR51	Dragon Dance	Dragon	Status	—	—	20	Self
TR58	Dark Pulse	Dark	Special	80	100	15	Normal
TR62	Dragon Pulse	Dragon	Special	85	100	10	Normal
TR64	Focus Blast	Fighting	Special	120	70	5	Normal
TR67	Earth Power	Ground	Special	90	100	10	Normal
TR68	Nasty Plot	Dark	Status	—	—	20	Self
TR69	Zen Headbutt	Psychic	Physical	80	90	15	Normal
TR70	Flash Cannon	Steel	Special	80	100	10	Normal
TR75	Stone Edge	Rock	Physical	100	80	5	Normal
TR85	Work Up	Normal	Status	—	—	30	Self
TR95	Throat Chop	Dark	Physical	80	100	15	Normal

DAMAGE TAKEN IN BATTLE

×1	×2	×1
×0.5	×1	×0.5
×0.5	×1	×2
×0.5	×1	×0.5
×0.5	×0	×1
×2	×2	×4

DRAGON

---

389 Goomy — p. 155

ABILITY
Sap Sipper
Hydration

HIDDEN ABILITY
Gooey

SPECIES STRENGTHS
HP
ATTACK
DEFENSE
SP. ATK
SP. DEF
SPEED

LEVEL-UP MOVES

LV.	NAME	TYPE	KIND	POW.	ACC.	PP	RANGE
1	Absorb	Grass	Special	20	100	25	Normal
1	Tackle	Normal	Physical	40	100	35	Normal
5	Water Gun	Water	Special	40	100	25	Normal
10	Dragon Breath	Dragon	Special	60	100	20	Normal
15	Protect	Normal	Status	—	—	10	Self
20	Flail	Normal	Physical	—	100	15	Normal
25	Water Pulse	Water	Special	60	100	20	Normal
30	Rain Dance	Water	Status	—	—	5	Both Sides
35	Dragon Pulse	Dragon	Special	85	100	10	Normal
41	Curse	Ghost	Status	—	—	10	Varies
45	Body Slam	Normal	Physical	85	100	15	Normal
50	Muddy Water	Water	Special	90	85	10	Many Others

EVOLUTION MOVES

NAME	TYPE	KIND	POW.	ACC.	PP	RANGE

EGG MOVES

NAME	TYPE	KIND	POW.	ACC.	PP	RANGE
Counter	Fighting	Physical	—	100	20	Varies
Life Dew	Water	Status	—	—	10	Your Side

TUTOR MOVES

NAME	TYPE	KIND	POW.	ACC.	PP	RANGE
Draco Meteor	Dragon	Special	130	90	5	Normal

TM MOVES

NO.	NAME	TYPE	KIND	POW.	ACC.	PP	RANGE
TM21	Rest	Psychic	Status	—	—	10	Self
TM22	Rock Slide	Rock	Physical	75	90	10	Many Others
TM24	Snore	Normal	Special	50	100	15	Normal
TM25	Protect	Normal	Status	—	—	10	Self
TM31	Attract	Normal	Status	—	100	15	Normal
TM33	Rain Dance	Water	Status	—	—	5	Both Sides
TM34	Sunny Day	Fire	Status	—	—	5	Both Sides
TM39	Facade	Normal	Physical	70	100	20	Normal
TM53	Mud Shot	Ground	Special	55	95	15	Normal
TM76	Round	Normal	Special	60	100	15	Normal

TR MOVES

NO.	NAME	TYPE	KIND	POW.	ACC.	PP	RANGE
TR01	Body Slam	Normal	Physical	85	100	15	Normal
TR08	Thunderbolt	Electric	Special	90	100	15	Normal
TR20	Substitute	Normal	Status	—	—	10	Self
TR22	Sludge Bomb	Poison	Special	90	100	10	Normal
TR24	Outrage	Dragon	Physical	120	100	10	1 Random
TR26	Endure	Normal	Status	—	—	10	Self
TR27	Sleep Talk	Normal	Status	—	—	10	Self
TR31	Iron Tail	Steel	Physical	100	75	15	Normal
TR45	Muddy Water	Water	Special	90	85	10	Many Others
TR62	Dragon Pulse	Dragon	Special	85	100	10	Normal
TR78	Sludge Wave	Poison	Special	95	100	10	All Others

DAMAGE TAKEN IN BATTLE

×1	×1	×1
×0.5	×1	×1
×0.5	×1	×2
×0.5	×1	×1
×0.5	×1	×2
×2	×1	×2

DRAGON

390

Sliggoo — p. 155

LEVEL-UP MOVES

LV.	NAME	TYPE	KIND	POW.	ACC.	PP	RANGE
1	Absorb	Grass	Special	20	100	25	Normal
1	Acid Spray	Poison	Special	40	100	20	Normal
1	Dragon Breath	Dragon	Special	60	100	20	Normal
1	Tackle	Normal	Physical	40	100	35	Normal
1	Water Gun	Water	Special	40	100	25	Normal
15	Protect	Normal	Status	—	—	10	Self
20	Flail	Normal	Physical	—	100	15	Normal
25	Water Pulse	Water	Special	60	100	20	Normal
30	Rain Dance	Water	Status	—	—	5	Both Sides
35	Dragon Pulse	Dragon	Special	85	100	10	Normal
43	Curse	Ghost	Status	—	—	10	Varies
49	Body Slam	Normal	Physical	85	100	15	Normal
56	Muddy Water	Water	Special	90	85	10	Many Others

TUTOR MOVES

NAME	TYPE	KIND	POW.	ACC.	PP	RANGE
Draco Meteor	Dragon	Special	130	90	5	Normal

TM MOVES

NO.	NAME	TYPE	KIND	POW.	ACC.	PP	RANGE
TM21	Rest	Psychic	Status	—	—	10	Self
TM22	Rock Slide	Rock	Physical	75	90	10	Many Others
TM24	Snore	Normal	Special	50	100	15	Normal
TM25	Protect	Normal	Status	—	—	10	Self
TM31	Attract	Normal	Status	—	100	15	Normal
TM33	Rain Dance	Water	Status	—	—	5	Both Sides
TM34	Sunny Day	Fire	Status	—	—	5	Both Sides
TM39	Facade	Normal	Physical	70	100	20	Normal
TM53	Mud Shot	Ground	Special	55	95	15	Normal
TM76	Round	Normal	Special	60	100	15	Normal

TR MOVES

NAME	TYPE	KIND	POW.	ACC.	PP	RANGE
TR01 Body Slam	Normal	Physical	85	100	15	Normal
TR05 Ice Beam	Ice	Special	90	100	10	Normal
TR06 Blizzard	Ice	Special	110	70	5	Many Others
TR08 Thunderbolt	Electric	Special	90	100	15	Normal
TR20 Substitute	Normal	Status	—	—	10	Self
TR22 Sludge Bomb	Poison	Special	90	100	10	Normal
TR24 Outrage	Dragon	Physical	120	100	10	1 Random
TR26 Endure	Normal	Status	—	—	10	Self
TR27 Sleep Talk	Normal	Status	—	—	10	Self
TR31 Iron Tail	Steel	Physical	100	75	15	Normal
TR45 Muddy Water	Water	Special	90	85	10	Many Others
TR62 Dragon Pulse	Dragon	Special	85	100	10	Normal
TR78 Sludge Wave	Poison	Special	95	100	10	All Others

EVOLUTION MOVES

NAME	TYPE	KIND	POW.	ACC.	PP	RANGE
Acid Spray	Poison	Special	40	100	20	Normal

EGG MOVES

NAME	TYPE	KIND	POW.	ACC.	PP	RANGE

ABILITY
Sap Sipper
Hydration

HIDDEN ABILITY
Gooey

SPECIES STRENGTHS
HP, ATTACK, DEFENSE, SP. ATK, SP. DEF, SPEED

DAMAGE TAKEN IN BATTLE
×1, ×1, ×1, ×0.5, ×1, ×1, ×0.5, ×1, ×2, ×0.5, ×1, ×1, ×0.5, ×1, ×1, ×2, ×1, ×2

DRAGON

391

Goodra — p. 155

LEVEL-UP MOVES

LV.	NAME	TYPE	KIND	POW.	ACC.	PP	RANGE
1	Absorb	Grass	Special	20	100	25	Normal
1	Acid Spray	Poison	Special	40	100	20	Normal
1	Aqua Tail	Water	Physical	90	90	10	Normal
1	Dragon Breath	Dragon	Special	60	100	20	Normal
1	Feint	Normal	Physical	30	100	10	Normal
1	Poison Tail	Poison	Physical	50	100	25	Normal
1	Tackle	Normal	Physical	40	100	35	Normal
1	Tearful Look	Normal	Status	—	—	20	Normal
1	Water Gun	Water	Special	40	100	25	Normal
15	Protect	Normal	Status	—	—	10	Self
20	Flail	Normal	Physical	—	100	15	Normal
25	Water Pulse	Water	Special	60	100	20	Normal
30	Rain Dance	Water	Status	—	—	5	Both Sides
35	Dragon Pulse	Dragon	Special	85	100	10	Normal
43	Curse	Ghost	Status	—	—	10	Varies
49	Body Slam	Normal	Physical	85	100	15	Normal
58	Muddy Water	Water	Special	90	85	10	Many Others
67	Power Whip	Grass	Physical	120	85	10	Normal

TUTOR MOVES

NAME	TYPE	KIND	POW.	ACC.	PP	RANGE
Draco Meteor	Dragon	Special	130	90	5	Normal

TM MOVES

NO.	NAME	TYPE	KIND	POW.	ACC.	PP	RANGE
TM00	Mega Punch	Normal	Physical	80	85	20	Normal
TM01	Mega Kick	Normal	Physical	120	75	5	Normal
TM03	Fire Punch	Fire	Physical	75	100	15	Normal
TM05	Thunder Punch	Electric	Physical	75	100	15	Normal
TM08	Hyper Beam	Normal	Special	150	90	5	Normal
TM09	Giga Impact	Normal	Physical	150	90	5	Normal
TM21	Rest	Psychic	Status	—	—	10	Self
TM22	Rock Slide	Rock	Physical	75	90	10	Many Others
TM24	Snore	Normal	Special	50	100	15	Normal
TM25	Protect	Normal	Status	—	—	10	Self
TM31	Attract	Normal	Status	—	100	15	Normal
TM33	Rain Dance	Water	Status	—	—	5	Both Sides
TM34	Sunny Day	Fire	Status	—	—	5	Both Sides
TM35	Hail	Ice	Status	—	—	10	Both Sides
TM39	Facade	Normal	Physical	70	100	20	Normal
TM46	Weather Ball*	Normal	Special	50	100	10	Normal
TM53	Mud Shot	Ground	Special	55	95	15	Normal
TM58	Assurance	Dark	Physical	60	100	10	Normal
TM76	Round	Normal	Special	60	100	15	Normal
TM81	Bulldoze	Ground	Physical	60	100	20	All Others
TM97	Brutal Swing	Dark	Physical	60	100	20	All Others
TM98	Stomping Tantrum	Ground	Physical	75	100	10	Normal
TM99	Breaking Swipe	Dragon	Physical	60	100	15	Many Others

TR MOVES

NAME	TYPE	KIND	POW.	ACC.	PP	RANGE
TR01 Body Slam	Normal	Physical	85	100	15	Normal
TR02 Flamethrower	Fire	Special	90	100	15	Normal
TR03 Hydro Pump	Water	Special	110	80	5	All Others
TR04 Surf	Water	Special	90	100	15	All Others
TR05 Ice Beam	Ice	Special	90	100	10	Normal
TR06 Blizzard	Ice	Special	110	70	5	Many Others
TR08 Thunderbolt	Electric	Special	90	100	15	Normal
TR09 Thunder	Electric	Special	110	70	10	Normal
TR10 Earthquake	Ground	Physical	100	100	10	All Others
TR15 Fire Blast	Fire	Special	110	85	5	Normal
TR20 Substitute	Normal	Status	—	—	10	Self
TR22 Sludge Bomb	Poison	Special	90	100	10	Normal
TR24 Outrage	Dragon	Physical	120	100	10	1 Random
TR26 Endure	Normal	Status	—	—	10	Self
TR27 Sleep Talk	Normal	Status	—	—	10	Self
TR31 Iron Tail	Steel	Physical	100	75	15	Normal
TR39 Superpower	Fighting	Physical	120	100	5	Normal
TR45 Muddy Water	Water	Special	90	85	10	Many Others
TR62 Dragon Pulse	Dragon	Special	85	100	10	Normal
TR64 Focus Blast	Fighting	Special	120	70	5	Normal
TR72 Power Whip	Grass	Physical	120	85	10	Normal
TR78 Sludge Wave	Poison	Special	95	100	10	All Others
TR99 Body Press	Fighting	Physical	80	100	10	Normal

EVOLUTION MOVES

NAME	TYPE	KIND	POW.	ACC.	PP	RANGE
Aqua Tail	Water	Physical	90	90	10	Normal

EGG MOVES

NAME	TYPE	KIND	POW.	ACC.	PP	RANGE

ABILITY
Sap Sipper
Hydration

HIDDEN ABILITY
Gooey

SPECIES STRENGTHS
HP, ATTACK, DEFENSE, SP. ATK, SP. DEF, SPEED

DAMAGE TAKEN IN BATTLE
×1, ×1, ×1, ×0.5, ×1, ×1, ×0.5, ×1, ×2, ×0.5, ×1, ×1, ×0.5, ×1, ×1, ×2, ×1, ×2

DRAGON

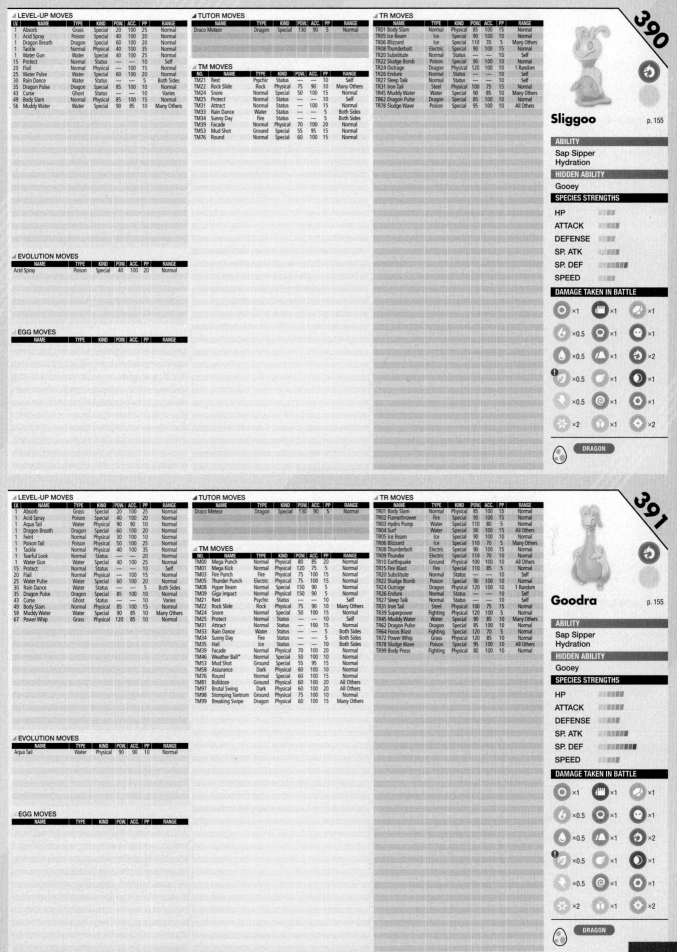

*Weather Ball changes type depending on weather condition. (Harsh sunlight: Fire type. Rain: Water type. Hail: Ice type. Sandstorm: Rock type.)

392 Jangmo-o   p. 156

ABILITY
Bulletproof
Soundproof

HIDDEN ABILITY
Overcoat

SPECIES STRENGTHS
HP
ATTACK
DEFENSE
SP. ATK
SP. DEF
SPEED

DAMAGE TAKEN IN BATTLE

×1 · ×1 · ×1
×0.5 · ×1 · ×2
×0.5 · ×1 · ×2
×0.5 · ×1 · ×1
×0.5 · ×1 · ×1
×2 · ×1 · ×2

DRAGON

LEVEL-UP MOVES

LV.	NAME	TYPE	KIND	POW.	ACC.	PP	RANGE
1	Leer	Normal	Status	—	100	30	Many Others
1	Tackle	Normal	Physical	40	100	35	Normal
4	Protect	Normal	Status	—	—	10	Self
8	Dragon Tail	Dragon	Physical	60	90	10	Normal
12	Scary Face	Normal	Status	—	100	10	Normal
16	Headbutt	Normal	Physical	70	100	15	Normal
20	Work Up	Normal	Status	—	—	30	Self
24	Screech	Normal	Status	—	85	40	Normal
28	Iron Defense	Steel	Status	—	—	15	Self
32	Dragon Claw	Dragon	Physical	80	100	15	Normal
36	Noble Roar	Normal	Status	—	100	30	Normal
40	Dragon Dance	Dragon	Status	—	—	20	Self
44	Outrage	Dragon	Physical	120	100	10	1 Random

EVOLUTION MOVES

NAME	TYPE	KIND	POW.	ACC.	PP	RANGE

EGG MOVES

NAME	TYPE	KIND	POW.	ACC.	PP	RANGE
Counter	Fighting	Physical	—	100	20	Varies
Dragon Breath	Dragon	Special	60	100	20	Normal
Focus Punch	Fighting	Physical	150	100	20	Normal

TUTOR MOVES

NAME	TYPE	KIND	POW.	ACC.	PP	RANGE
Draco Meteor	Dragon	Special	130	90	5	Normal

TM MOVES

NO.	NAME	TYPE	KIND	POW.	ACC.	PP	RANGE
TM16	Screech	Normal	Status	—	85	40	Normal
TM19	Safeguard	Normal	Status	—	—	25	Your Side
TM21	Rest	Psychic	Status	—	—	10	Self
TM22	Rock Slide	Rock	Physical	75	90	10	Many Others
TM24	Snore	Normal	Special	50	100	15	Normal
TM25	Protect	Normal	Status	—	—	10	Self
TM26	Scary Face	Normal	Status	—	100	10	Normal
TM31	Attract	Normal	Status	—	100	15	Normal
TM32	Sandstorm	Rock	Status	—	—	10	Both Sides
TM39	Facade	Normal	Physical	70	100	20	Normal
TM43	Brick Break	Fighting	Physical	75	100	15	Normal
TM48	Rock Tomb	Rock	Physical	60	95	15	Normal
TM57	Payback	Dark	Physical	50	100	10	Normal
TM59	Fling	Dark	Physical	—	100	10	Normal
TM65	Shadow Claw	Ghost	Physical	70	100	15	Normal
TM76	Round	Normal	Special	60	100	15	Normal
TM81	Bulldoze	Ground	Physical	60	100	20	All Others
TM94	False Swipe	Normal	Physical	40	100	40	Normal

TR MOVES

NAME	TYPE	KIND	POW.	ACC.	PP	RANGE
TR00 Swords Dance	Normal	Status	—	—	20	Self
TR07 Low Kick	Fighting	Physical	—	100	20	Normal
TR10 Earthquake	Ground	Physical	100	100	10	All Others
TR20 Substitute	Normal	Status	—	—	10	Self
TR21 Reversal	Fighting	Physical	—	100	15	Normal
TR24 Outrage	Dragon	Physical	120	100	10	1 Random
TR26 Endure	Normal	Status	—	—	10	Self
TR27 Sleep Talk	Normal	Status	—	—	10	Self
TR31 Iron Tail	Steel	Physical	100	75	15	Normal
TR35 Uproar	Normal	Special	90	100	10	1 Random
TR37 Taunt	Dark	Status	—	100	20	Normal
TR46 Iron Defense	Steel	Status	—	—	15	Self
TR47 Dragon Claw	Dragon	Physical	80	100	15	Normal
TR48 Bulk Up	Fighting	Status	—	—	20	Self
TR51 Dragon Dance	Dragon	Status	—	—	20	Self
TR60 X-Scissor	Bug	Physical	80	100	15	Normal
TR62 Dragon Pulse	Dragon	Special	85	100	10	Normal
TR64 Focus Blast	Fighting	Special	120	70	5	Normal
TR74 Iron Head	Steel	Physical	80	100	15	Normal
TR85 Work Up	Normal	Status	—	—	30	Self

---

393 Hakamo-o   p. 156

ABILITY
Bulletproof
Soundproof

HIDDEN ABILITY
Overcoat

SPECIES STRENGTHS
HP
ATTACK
DEFENSE
SP. ATK
SP. DEF
SPEED

DAMAGE TAKEN IN BATTLE

×1 · ×1 · ×0.5
×0.5 · ×1 · ×1
×0.5 · ×1 · ×2
×0.5 · ×2 · ×0.5
×0.5 · ×2 · ×1
×2 · ×0.5 · ×4

DRAGON

LEVEL-UP MOVES

LV.	NAME	TYPE	KIND	POW.	ACC.	PP	RANGE
1	Autotomize	Steel	Status	—	—	15	Self
1	Dragon Tail	Dragon	Physical	60	90	10	Normal
1	Leer	Normal	Status	—	100	30	Many Others
1	Protect	Normal	Status	—	—	10	Self
1	Tackle	Normal	Physical	40	100	35	Normal
12	Scary Face	Normal	Status	—	100	10	Normal
16	Headbutt	Normal	Physical	70	100	15	Normal
20	Work Up	Normal	Status	—	—	30	Self
24	Screech	Normal	Status	—	85	40	Normal
28	Iron Defense	Steel	Status	—	—	15	Self
32	Dragon Claw	Dragon	Physical	80	100	15	Normal
38	Noble Roar	Normal	Status	—	100	30	Normal
44	Dragon Dance	Dragon	Status	—	—	20	Self
50	Outrage	Dragon	Physical	120	100	10	1 Random
56	Close Combat	Fighting	Physical	120	100	5	Normal

EVOLUTION MOVES

NAME	TYPE	KIND	POW.	ACC.	PP	RANGE

EGG MOVES

NAME	TYPE	KIND	POW.	ACC.	PP	RANGE

TUTOR MOVES

NAME	TYPE	KIND	POW.	ACC.	PP	RANGE
Draco Meteor	Dragon	Special	130	90	5	Normal

TM MOVES

NO.	NAME	TYPE	KIND	POW.	ACC.	PP	RANGE
TM00	Mega Punch	Normal	Physical	80	85	20	Normal
TM01	Mega Kick	Normal	Physical	120	75	5	Normal
TM16	Screech	Normal	Status	—	85	40	Normal
TM19	Safeguard	Normal	Status	—	—	25	Your Side
TM21	Rest	Psychic	Status	—	—	10	Self
TM22	Rock Slide	Rock	Physical	75	90	10	Many Others
TM24	Snore	Normal	Special	50	100	15	Self
TM25	Protect	Normal	Status	—	—	10	Self
TM26	Scary Face	Normal	Status	—	100	10	Normal
TM31	Attract	Normal	Status	—	100	15	Normal
TM32	Sandstorm	Rock	Status	—	—	10	Both Sides
TM39	Facade	Normal	Physical	70	100	20	Normal
TM43	Brick Break	Fighting	Physical	75	100	15	Normal
TM48	Rock Tomb	Rock	Physical	60	95	15	Normal
TM57	Payback	Dark	Physical	50	100	10	Normal
TM59	Fling	Dark	Physical	—	100	10	Normal
TM63	Drain Punch	Fighting	Physical	75	100	10	Normal
TM65	Shadow Claw	Ghost	Physical	70	100	15	Normal
TM76	Round	Normal	Special	60	100	15	Normal
TM81	Bulldoze	Ground	Physical	60	100	20	All Others
TM94	False Swipe	Normal	Physical	40	100	40	Normal
TM97	Brutal Swing	Dark	Physical	60	100	20	All Others

TR MOVES

NAME	TYPE	KIND	POW.	ACC.	PP	RANGE
TR00 Swords Dance	Normal	Status	—	—	20	Self
TR07 Low Kick	Fighting	Physical	—	100	20	Normal
TR10 Earthquake	Ground	Physical	100	100	10	All Others
TR20 Substitute	Normal	Status	—	—	10	Self
TR21 Reversal	Fighting	Physical	—	100	15	Normal
TR24 Outrage	Dragon	Physical	120	100	10	1 Random
TR26 Endure	Normal	Status	—	—	10	Self
TR27 Sleep Talk	Normal	Status	—	—	10	Self
TR31 Iron Tail	Steel	Physical	100	75	15	Normal
TR35 Uproar	Normal	Special	90	100	10	1 Random
TR37 Taunt	Dark	Status	—	100	20	Normal
TR46 Iron Defense	Steel	Status	—	—	15	Self
TR47 Dragon Claw	Dragon	Physical	80	100	15	Normal
TR48 Bulk Up	Fighting	Status	—	—	20	Self
TR51 Dragon Dance	Dragon	Status	—	—	20	Self
TR53 Close Combat	Fighting	Physical	120	100	5	Normal
TR60 X-Scissor	Bug	Physical	80	100	15	Normal
TR62 Dragon Pulse	Dragon	Special	85	100	10	Normal
TR64 Focus Blast	Fighting	Special	120	70	5	Normal
TR74 Iron Head	Steel	Physical	80	100	15	Normal
TR85 Work Up	Normal	Status	—	—	30	Self

394 Kommo-o

LEVEL-UP MOVES

LV.	NAME	TYPE	KIND	POW.	ACC.	PP	RANGE
1	Autotomize	Steel	Status	—	—	15	Self
1	Belly Drum	Normal	Status	—	—	10	Self
1	Clanging Scales	Dragon	Special	110	100	5	Many Others
1	Dragon Tail	Dragon	Physical	60	90	10	Normal
1	Leer	Normal	Status	—	100	30	Many Others
1	Protect	Normal	Status	—	—	10	Self
1	Tackle	Normal	Physical	40	100	35	Normal
12	Scary Face	Normal	Status	—	100	10	Normal
16	Headbutt	Normal	Physical	70	100	15	Normal
20	Work Up	Normal	Status	—	—	30	Self
24	Screech	Normal	Status	—	85	40	Normal
28	Iron Defense	Steel	Status	—	—	15	Self
32	Dragon Claw	Dragon	Physical	80	100	15	Normal
38	Noble Roar	Normal	Status	—	100	30	Normal
44	Dragon Dance	Dragon	Status	—	—	20	Self
52	Outrage	Dragon	Physical	120	100	10	1 Random
60	Close Combat	Fighting	Physical	120	100	5	Normal
68	Clangorous Soul	Dragon	Status	—	100	5	Self
76	Boomburst	Normal	Special	140	100	10	All Others

EVOLUTION MOVES

NAME	TYPE	KIND	POW.	ACC.	PP	RANGE
Clanging Scales	Dragon	Special	110	100	5	Many Others

EGG MOVES

NAME	TYPE	KIND	POW.	ACC.	PP	RANGE

TUTOR MOVES

NAME	TYPE	KIND	POW.	ACC.	PP	RANGE
Draco Meteor	Dragon	Special	130	90	5	Normal

TM MOVES

NO.	NAME	TYPE	KIND	POW.	ACC.	PP	RANGE
TM00	Mega Punch	Normal	Physical	80	85	20	Normal
TM01	Mega Kick	Normal	Physical	120	75	5	Normal
TM03	Fire Punch	Fire	Physical	75	100	15	Normal
TM04	Ice Punch	Ice	Physical	75	100	15	Normal
TM05	Thunder Punch	Electric	Physical	75	100	15	Normal
TM08	Hyper Beam	Normal	Special	150	90	5	Normal
TM09	Giga Impact	Normal	Physical	150	90	5	Normal
TM16	Screech	Normal	Status	—	85	40	Normal
TM19	Safeguard	Normal	Status	—	—	25	Your Side
TM21	Rest	Psychic	Status	—	—	10	Self
TM22	Rock Slide	Rock	Physical	75	90	10	Many Others
TM24	Snore	Normal	Special	50	100	15	Normal
TM25	Protect	Normal	Status	—	—	10	Self
TM26	Scary Face	Normal	Status	—	100	10	Normal
TM31	Attract	Normal	Status	—	100	15	Normal
TM32	Sandstorm	Rock	Status	—	—	10	Both Sides
TM39	Facade	Normal	Physical	70	100	20	Normal
TM42	Revenge	Fighting	Physical	60	100	10	Normal
TM43	Brick Break	Fighting	Physical	75	100	15	Normal
TM48	Rock Tomb	Rock	Physical	60	95	15	Normal
TM57	Payback	Dark	Physical	50	100	10	Normal
TM59	Fling	Dark	Physical	—	100	10	Normal
TM63	Drain Punch	Fighting	Physical	75	100	10	Normal
TM65	Shadow Claw	Ghost	Physical	70	100	15	Normal
TM76	Round	Normal	Special	60	100	15	Normal
TM81	Bulldoze	Ground	Physical	60	100	20	All Others
TM94	False Swipe	Normal	Physical	40	100	40	Normal
TM97	Brutal Swing	Dark	Physical	60	100	20	All Others
TM98	Stomping Tantrum	Ground	Physical	75	100	10	Normal
TM99	Breaking Swipe	Dragon	Physical	60	100	15	Many Others

TR MOVES

NO.	NAME	TYPE	KIND	POW.	ACC.	PP	RANGE
TR00	Swords Dance	Normal	Status	—	—	20	Self
TR02	Flamethrower	Fire	Special	90	100	15	Normal
TR07	Low Kick	Fighting	Physical	—	100	20	Normal
TR10	Earthquake	Ground	Physical	100	100	10	All Others
TR20	Substitute	Normal	Status	—	—	10	Self
TR21	Reversal	Fighting	Physical	—	100	15	Normal
TR24	Outrage	Dragon	Physical	120	100	10	1 Random
TR26	Endure	Normal	Status	—	—	10	Self
TR27	Sleep Talk	Normal	Status	—	—	10	Self
TR31	Iron Tail	Steel	Physical	100	75	15	Normal
TR35	Uproar	Normal	Special	90	100	10	1 Random
TR37	Taunt	Dark	Status	—	100	20	Normal
TR39	Superpower	Fighting	Physical	120	100	5	Normal
TR42	Hyper Voice	Normal	Special	90	100	10	Many Others
TR46	Iron Defense	Steel	Status	—	—	15	Self
TR47	Dragon Claw	Dragon	Physical	80	100	15	Normal
TR48	Bulk Up	Fighting	Status	—	—	20	Self
TR51	Dragon Dance	Dragon	Status	—	—	20	Self
TR53	Close Combat	Fighting	Physical	120	100	5	Normal
TR56	Aura Sphere	Fighting	Special	80	—	20	Normal
TR57	Poison Jab	Poison	Physical	80	100	20	Normal
TR60	X-Scissor	Bug	Physical	80	100	15	Normal
TR62	Dragon Pulse	Dragon	Special	85	100	10	Normal
TR64	Focus Blast	Fighting	Special	120	70	5	Normal
TR70	Flash Cannon	Steel	Special	80	100	10	Normal
TR74	Iron Head	Steel	Physical	80	100	15	Normal
TR76	Stealth Rock	Rock	Status	—	—	20	Other Side
TR85	Work Up	Normal	Status	—	—	30	Self
TR99	Body Press	Fighting	Physical	80	100	10	Normal

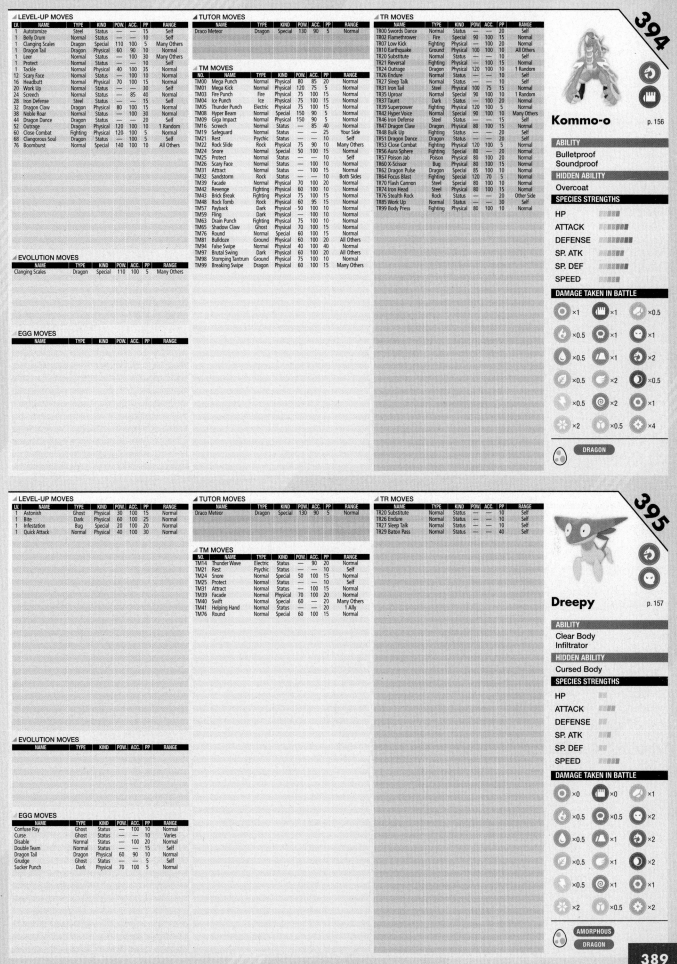

Kommo-o p. 156

ABILITY
Bulletproof
Soundproof

HIDDEN ABILITY
Overcoat

SPECIES STRENGTHS
HP
ATTACK
DEFENSE
SP. ATK
SP. DEF
SPEED

DAMAGE TAKEN IN BATTLE
×1 | ×1 | ×0.5
×0.5 | ×1 | ×1
×0.5 | ×1 | ×2
×0.5 | ×2 | ×0.5
×0.5 | ×2 | ×1
×2 | ×0.5 | ×4

DRAGON

---

395 Dreepy

LEVEL-UP MOVES

LV.	NAME	TYPE	KIND	POW.	ACC.	PP	RANGE
1	Astonish	Ghost	Physical	30	100	15	Normal
1	Bite	Dark	Physical	60	100	25	Normal
1	Infestation	Bug	Special	20	100	20	Normal
1	Quick Attack	Normal	Physical	40	100	30	Normal

EVOLUTION MOVES

NAME	TYPE	KIND	POW.	ACC.	PP	RANGE

EGG MOVES

NAME	TYPE	KIND	POW.	ACC.	PP	RANGE
Confuse Ray	Ghost	Status	—	100	10	Normal
Curse	Ghost	Status	—	—	10	Varies
Disable	Normal	Status	—	100	20	Normal
Double Team	Normal	Status	—	—	15	Self
Dragon Tail	Dragon	Physical	60	90	10	Normal
Grudge	Ghost	Status	—	—	5	Self
Sucker Punch	Dark	Physical	70	100	5	Normal

TUTOR MOVES

NAME	TYPE	KIND	POW.	ACC.	PP	RANGE
Draco Meteor	Dragon	Special	130	90	5	Normal

TM MOVES

NO.	NAME	TYPE	KIND	POW.	ACC.	PP	RANGE
TM14	Thunder Wave	Electric	Status	—	90	20	Normal
TM21	Rest	Psychic	Status	—	—	10	Self
TM24	Snore	Normal	Special	50	100	15	Normal
TM25	Protect	Normal	Status	—	—	10	Self
TM31	Attract	Normal	Status	—	100	15	Normal
TM39	Facade	Normal	Physical	70	100	20	Normal
TM40	Swift	Normal	Special	60	—	20	Many Others
TM41	Helping Hand	Normal	Status	—	—	20	1 Ally
TM76	Round	Normal	Special	60	100	15	Normal

TR MOVES

NO.	NAME	TYPE	KIND	POW.	ACC.	PP	RANGE
TR20	Substitute	Normal	Status	—	—	10	Self
TR26	Endure	Normal	Status	—	—	10	Self
TR27	Sleep Talk	Normal	Status	—	—	10	Self
TR29	Baton Pass	Normal	Status	—	—	40	Self

Dreepy p. 157

ABILITY
Clear Body
Infiltrator

HIDDEN ABILITY
Cursed Body

SPECIES STRENGTHS
HP
ATTACK
DEFENSE
SP. ATK
SP. DEF
SPEED

DAMAGE TAKEN IN BATTLE
×0 | ×0 | ×1
×0.5 | ×0.5 | ×2
×0.5 | ×1 | ×2
×0.5 | ×1 | ×2
×0.5 | ×1 | ×1
×2 | ×0.5 | ×2

AMORPHOUS
DRAGON

396 Drakloak

p. 157

ABILITY
Clear Body
Infiltrator

HIDDEN ABILITY
Cursed Body

SPECIES STRENGTHS
HP
ATTACK
DEFENSE
SP. ATK
SP. DEF
SPEED

DAMAGE TAKEN IN BATTLE

×0	×0	×1
×0.5	×0.5	×2
×0.5	×1	×2
×0.5	×1	×2
×0.5	×1	×1
×2	×0.5	×2

AMORPHOUS
DRAGON

LEVEL-UP MOVES

LV.	NAME	TYPE	KIND	POW.	ACC.	PP	RANGE
1	Astonish	Ghost	Physical	30	100	15	Normal
1	Bite	Dark	Physical	60	100	25	Normal
1	Dragon Pulse	Dragon	Special	85	100	10	Normal
1	Infestation	Bug	Special	20	100	20	Normal
1	Quick Attack	Normal	Physical	40	100	30	Normal
6	Lock-On	Normal	Status	—	—	5	Normal
12	Assurance	Dark	Physical	60	100	10	Normal
18	Hex	Ghost	Special	65	100	10	Normal
24	Agility	Psychic	Status	—	—	30	Self
30	Double Hit	Normal	Physical	35	90	10	Normal
36	U-turn	Bug	Physical	70	100	20	Normal
42	Dragon Dance	Dragon	Status	—	—	20	Self
48	Phantom Force	Ghost	Physical	90	100	10	Normal
54	Take Down	Normal	Physical	90	85	20	Normal
61	Dragon Rush	Dragon	Physical	100	75	10	Normal
66	Double-Edge	Normal	Physical	120	100	15	Normal
72	Last Resort	Normal	Physical	140	100	5	Normal

EVOLUTION MOVES

NAME	TYPE	KIND	POW.	ACC.	PP	RANGE
Dragon Pulse	Dragon	Special	85	100	10	Normal

EGG MOVES

NAME	TYPE	KIND	POW.	ACC.	PP	RANGE

TUTOR MOVES

NAME	TYPE	KIND	POW.	ACC.	PP	RANGE
Draco Meteor	Dragon	Special	130	90	5	Normal

TM MOVES

NO.	NAME	TYPE	KIND	POW.	ACC.	PP	RANGE
TM14	Thunder Wave	Electric	Status	—	90	20	Normal
TM21	Rest	Psychic	Status	—	—	10	Self
TM23	Thief	Dark	Physical	60	100	25	Normal
TM24	Snore	Normal	Special	50	100	15	Normal
TM25	Protect	Normal	Status	—	—	10	Self
TM30	Steel Wing	Steel	Physical	70	90	25	Normal
TM31	Attract	Normal	Status	—	100	15	Normal
TM37	Beat Up	Dark	Physical	—	100	10	Normal
TM38	Will-O-Wisp	Fire	Status	—	85	15	Normal
TM39	Facade	Normal	Physical	70	100	20	Normal
TM40	Swift	Normal	Special	60	—	20	Many Others
TM41	Helping Hand	Normal	Status	—	—	20	1 Ally
TM45	Dive	Water	Physical	80	100	10	Normal
TM55	Brine	Water	Special	65	100	10	Normal
TM56	U-turn	Bug	Physical	70	100	20	Normal
TM58	Assurance	Dark	Physical	60	100	10	Normal
TM76	Round	Normal	Special	60	100	15	Normal
TM77	Hex	Ghost	Special	65	100	10	Normal
TM78	Acrobatics	Flying	Physical	55	100	15	Normal
TM86	Phantom Force	Ghost	Physical	90	100	10	Normal
TM99	Breaking Swipe	Dragon	Physical	60	100	15	Many Others

TR MOVES

NO.	NAME	TYPE	KIND	POW.	ACC.	PP	RANGE
TR02	Flamethrower	Fire	Special	90	100	15	Normal
TR03	Hydro Pump	Water	Special	110	80	5	Normal
TR04	Surf	Water	Special	90	100	15	All Others
TR08	Thunderbolt	Electric	Special	90	100	15	Normal
TR09	Thunder	Electric	Special	110	70	10	Normal
TR12	Agility	Psychic	Status	—	—	30	Self
TR15	Fire Blast	Fire	Special	110	85	5	Normal
TR20	Substitute	Normal	Status	—	—	10	Self
TR24	Outrage	Dragon	Physical	120	100	10	1 Random
TR26	Endure	Normal	Status	—	—	10	Self
TR27	Sleep Talk	Normal	Status	—	—	10	Self
TR29	Baton Pass	Normal	Status	—	—	40	Self
TR33	Shadow Ball	Ghost	Special	80	100	15	Normal
TR51	Dragon Dance	Dragon	Status	—	—	20	Self
TR62	Dragon Pulse	Dragon	Special	85	100	10	Normal
TR83	Ally Switch	Psychic	Status	—	—	15	Self
TR84	Scald	Water	Special	80	100	15	Normal
TR97	Psychic Fangs	Psychic	Physical	85	100	10	Normal

---

397 Dragapult

p. 157

ABILITY
Clear Body
Infiltrator

HIDDEN ABILITY
Cursed Body

SPECIES STRENGTHS
HP
ATTACK
DEFENSE
SP. ATK
SP. DEF
SPEED

DAMAGE TAKEN IN BATTLE

×0	×0	×1
×0.5	×0.5	×2
×0.5	×1	×2
×0.5	×1	×2
×0.5	×1	×1
×2	×0.5	×2

AMORPHOUS
DRAGON

LEVEL-UP MOVES

LV.	NAME	TYPE	KIND	POW.	ACC.	PP	RANGE
1	Astonish	Ghost	Physical	30	100	15	Normal
1	Bite	Dark	Physical	60	100	25	Normal
1	Dragon Breath	Dragon	Special	60	100	20	Normal
1	Dragon Darts	Dragon	Physical	50	100	10	Normal
1	Infestation	Bug	Special	20	100	20	Normal
1	Quick Attack	Normal	Physical	40	100	30	Normal
1	Sucker Punch	Dark	Physical	70	100	5	Normal
6	Lock-On	Normal	Status	—	—	5	Normal
12	Assurance	Dark	Physical	60	100	10	Normal
18	Hex	Ghost	Special	65	100	10	Normal
24	Agility	Psychic	Status	—	—	30	Self
30	Double Hit	Normal	Physical	35	90	10	Normal
36	U-turn	Bug	Physical	70	100	20	Normal
42	Dragon Dance	Dragon	Status	—	—	20	Self
48	Phantom Force	Ghost	Physical	90	100	10	Normal
54	Take Down	Normal	Physical	90	85	20	Normal
61	Dragon Rush	Dragon	Physical	100	75	10	Normal
70	Double-Edge	Normal	Physical	120	100	15	Normal
78	Last Resort	Normal	Physical	140	100	5	Normal

EVOLUTION MOVES

NAME	TYPE	KIND	POW.	ACC.	PP	RANGE
Dragon Darts	Dragon	Physical	50	100	10	Normal

EGG MOVES

NAME	TYPE	KIND	POW.	ACC.	PP	RANGE

TUTOR MOVES

NAME	TYPE	KIND	POW.	ACC.	PP	RANGE
Draco Meteor	Dragon	Special	130	90	5	Normal

TM MOVES

NO.	NAME	TYPE	KIND	POW.	ACC.	PP	RANGE
TM06	Fly	Flying	Physical	90	95	15	Normal
TM08	Hyper Beam	Normal	Special	150	90	5	Normal
TM09	Giga Impact	Normal	Physical	150	90	5	Normal
TM11	Solar Beam	Grass	Special	120	100	10	Normal
TM14	Thunder Wave	Electric	Status	—	90	20	Normal
TM17	Light Screen	Psychic	Status	—	—	30	Your Side
TM18	Reflect	Psychic	Status	—	—	20	Your Side
TM21	Rest	Psychic	Status	—	—	10	Self
TM23	Thief	Dark	Physical	60	100	25	Normal
TM24	Snore	Normal	Special	50	100	15	Normal
TM25	Protect	Normal	Status	—	—	10	Self
TM30	Steel Wing	Steel	Physical	70	90	25	Normal
TM31	Attract	Normal	Status	—	100	15	Normal
TM37	Beat Up	Dark	Physical	—	100	10	Normal
TM38	Will-O-Wisp	Fire	Status	—	85	15	Normal
TM39	Facade	Normal	Physical	70	100	20	Normal
TM40	Swift	Normal	Special	60	—	20	Many Others
TM41	Helping Hand	Normal	Status	—	—	20	1 Ally
TM45	Dive	Water	Physical	80	100	10	Normal
TM55	Brine	Water	Special	65	100	10	Normal
TM56	U-turn	Bug	Physical	70	100	20	Normal
TM58	Assurance	Dark	Physical	60	100	10	Normal
TM76	Round	Normal	Special	60	100	15	Normal
TM77	Hex	Ghost	Special	65	100	10	Normal
TM78	Acrobatics	Flying	Physical	55	100	15	Normal
TM86	Phantom Force	Ghost	Physical	90	100	10	Normal
TM99	Breaking Swipe	Dragon	Physical	60	100	15	Many Others

TR MOVES

NO.	NAME	TYPE	KIND	POW.	ACC.	PP	RANGE
TR01	Body Slam	Normal	Physical	85	100	15	Normal
TR02	Flamethrower	Fire	Special	90	100	15	Normal
TR03	Hydro Pump	Water	Special	110	80	5	Normal
TR04	Surf	Water	Special	90	100	15	All Others
TR08	Thunderbolt	Electric	Special	90	100	15	Normal
TR09	Thunder	Electric	Special	110	70	10	Normal
TR12	Agility	Psychic	Status	—	—	30	Self
TR15	Fire Blast	Fire	Special	110	85	5	Normal
TR19	Tri Attack	Normal	Special	80	100	10	Normal
TR20	Substitute	Normal	Status	—	—	10	Self
TR24	Outrage	Dragon	Physical	120	100	10	1 Random
TR26	Endure	Normal	Status	—	—	10	Self
TR27	Sleep Talk	Normal	Status	—	—	10	Self
TR29	Baton Pass	Normal	Status	—	—	40	Self
TR33	Shadow Ball	Ghost	Special	80	100	15	Normal
TR51	Dragon Dance	Dragon	Status	—	—	20	Self
TR62	Dragon Pulse	Dragon	Special	85	100	10	Normal
TR83	Ally Switch	Psychic	Status	—	—	15	Self
TR84	Scald	Water	Special	80	100	15	Normal
TR97	Psychic Fangs	Psychic	Physical	85	100	10	Normal

398

Zacian — p. 158

LEVEL-UP MOVES

LV.	NAME	TYPE	KIND	POW.	ACC.	PP	RANGE
1	Bite	Dark	Physical	60	100	25	Normal
1	Howl	Normal	Status	—	—	40	Your Side
1	Metal Claw	Steel	Physical	50	95	35	Normal
1	Quick Attack	Normal	Physical	40	100	30	Normal
1	Quick Guard	Fighting	Status	—	—	15	Your Side
1	Sacred Sword	Fighting	Physical	90	100	15	Normal
11	Slash	Normal	Physical	70	100	20	Normal
22	Swords Dance	Normal	Status	—	—	20	Self
33	Iron Head	Steel	Physical	80	100	15	Normal
44	Laser Focus	Normal	Status	—	—	30	Self
55	Crunch	Dark	Physical	80	100	15	Normal
66	Moonblast	Fairy	Special	95	100	15	Normal
77	Close Combat	Fighting	Physical	120	100	5	Normal
88	Giga Impact	Normal	Physical	150	90	5	Normal
*	Behemoth Blade*	Steel	Physical	100	100	5	Normal

EVOLUTION MOVES

NAME	TYPE	KIND	POW.	ACC.	PP	RANGE

EGG MOVES

NAME	TYPE	KIND	POW.	ACC.	PP	RANGE

TUTOR MOVES

NAME	TYPE	KIND	POW.	ACC.	PP	RANGE
Steel Beam	Steel	Special	140	95	5	Normal

TM MOVES

NO.	NAME	TYPE	KIND	POW.	ACC.	PP	RANGE
TM08	Hyper Beam	Normal	Special	150	90	5	Normal
TM09	Giga Impact	Normal	Physical	150	90	5	Normal
TM12	Solar Blade	Grass	Physical	125	100	10	Normal
TM15	Dig	Ground	Physical	80	100	10	Normal
TM21	Rest	Psychic	Status	—	—	10	Self
TM24	Snore	Normal	Special	50	100	15	Normal
TM25	Protect	Normal	Status	—	—	10	Self
TM26	Scary Face	Normal	Status	—	100	10	Normal
TM39	Facade	Normal	Physical	70	100	20	Normal
TM40	Swift	Normal	Special	60	—	20	Many Others
TM41	Helping Hand	Normal	Status	—	—	20	1 Ally
TM42	Revenge	Fighting	Physical	60	100	10	Normal
TM43	Brick Break	Fighting	Physical	75	100	15	Normal
TM44	Imprison	Psychic	Status	—	—	10	Self
TM58	Assurance	Dark	Physical	60	100	10	Normal
TM66	Thunder Fang	Electric	Physical	65	95	15	Normal
TM67	Ice Fang	Ice	Physical	65	95	15	Normal
TM68	Fire Fang	Fire	Physical	65	95	15	Normal
TM69	Psycho Cut	Psychic	Physical	70	100	20	Normal
TM76	Round	Normal	Special	60	100	15	Normal
TM79	Retaliate	Normal	Physical	70	100	5	Normal
TM84	Tail Slap	Normal	Physical	25	85	10	Normal
TM85	Snarl	Dark	Special	55	95	15	Many Others
TM94	False Swipe	Normal	Physical	40	100	40	Normal
TM95	Air Slash	Flying	Special	75	95	15	Normal
TM97	Brutal Swing	Dark	Physical	60	100	20	All Others

TR MOVES

NO.	NAME	TYPE	KIND	POW.	ACC.	PP	RANGE
TR00	Swords Dance	Normal	Status	—	—	20	Self
TR12	Agility	Psychic	Status	—	—	30	Self
TR13	Focus Energy	Normal	Status	—	—	30	Self
TR20	Substitute	Normal	Status	—	—	10	Self
TR21	Reversal	Fighting	Physical	—	100	15	Normal
TR26	Endure	Normal	Status	—	—	10	Self
TR27	Sleep Talk	Normal	Status	—	—	10	Self
TR31	Iron Tail	Steel	Physical	100	75	15	Normal
TR32	Crunch	Dark	Physical	80	100	15	Normal
TR42	Hyper Voice	Normal	Special	90	100	10	Many Others
TR53	Close Combat	Fighting	Physical	120	100	5	Normal
TR64	Focus Blast	Fighting	Special	120	70	5	Normal
TR74	Iron Head	Steel	Physical	80	100	15	Normal
TR85	Work Up	Normal	Status	—	—	30	Self
TR86	Wild Charge	Electric	Physical	90	100	15	Normal
TR90	Play Rough	Fairy	Physical	90	90	10	Normal
TR97	Psychic Fangs	Psychic	Physical	85	100	10	Normal

ABILITY
Intrepid Sword
—

HIDDEN ABILITY
—

SPECIES STRENGTHS
- HP
- ATTACK
- DEFENSE
- SP. ATK
- SP. DEF
- SPEED

DAMAGE TAKEN IN BATTLE
×1, ×0.5, ×1, ×1, ×2, ×1, ×1, ×1, ×0, ×1, ×1, ×0.5, ×2, ×0.5, ×1

NO EGGS

*If Zacian knows the move Iron Head when it changes form to its Crowned Sword form, Iron Head will be replaced with Behemoth Blade. When Zacian returns to its Hero of Many Battles form, Behemoth Blade will revert back to Iron Head.

399

Zamazenta — p. 159

LEVEL-UP MOVES

LV.	NAME	TYPE	KIND	POW.	ACC.	PP	RANGE
1	Bite	Dark	Physical	60	100	25	Normal
1	Howl	Normal	Status	—	—	40	Your Side
1	Metal Burst	Steel	Physical	—	100	10	Varies
1	Metal Claw	Steel	Physical	50	95	35	Normal
1	Quick Attack	Normal	Physical	40	100	30	Normal
1	Wide Guard	Rock	Status	—	—	10	Your Side
11	Slash	Normal	Physical	70	100	20	Normal
22	Iron Defense	Steel	Status	—	—	15	Self
33	Iron Head	Steel	Physical	80	100	15	Normal
44	Laser Focus	Normal	Status	—	—	30	Self
55	Crunch	Dark	Physical	80	100	15	Normal
66	Moonblast	Fairy	Special	95	100	15	Normal
77	Close Combat	Fighting	Physical	120	100	5	Normal
88	Giga Impact	Normal	Physical	150	90	5	Normal
*	Behemoth Bash*	Steel	Physical	100	100	5	Normal

EVOLUTION MOVES

NAME	TYPE	KIND	POW.	ACC.	PP	RANGE

EGG MOVES

NAME	TYPE	KIND	POW.	ACC.	PP	RANGE

TUTOR MOVES

NAME	TYPE	KIND	POW.	ACC.	PP	RANGE
Steel Beam	Steel	Special	140	95	5	Normal

TM MOVES

NO.	NAME	TYPE	KIND	POW.	ACC.	PP	RANGE
TM08	Hyper Beam	Normal	Special	150	90	5	Normal
TM09	Giga Impact	Normal	Physical	150	90	5	Normal
TM11	Solar Beam	Grass	Special	120	100	10	Normal
TM15	Dig	Ground	Physical	80	100	10	Normal
TM17	Light Screen	Psychic	Status	—	—	30	Your Side
TM18	Reflect	Psychic	Status	—	—	20	Your Side
TM19	Safeguard	Normal	Status	—	—	25	Your Side
TM21	Rest	Psychic	Status	—	—	10	Self
TM24	Snore	Normal	Special	50	100	15	Normal
TM25	Protect	Normal	Status	—	—	10	Self
TM26	Scary Face	Normal	Status	—	100	10	Normal
TM39	Facade	Normal	Physical	70	100	20	Normal
TM40	Swift	Normal	Special	60	—	20	Many Others
TM41	Helping Hand	Normal	Status	—	—	20	1 Ally
TM42	Revenge	Fighting	Physical	60	100	10	Normal
TM44	Imprison	Psychic	Status	—	—	10	Self
TM57	Payback	Dark	Physical	50	100	10	Normal
TM60	Power Swap	Psychic	Status	—	—	10	Normal
TM61	Guard Swap	Psychic	Status	—	—	10	Normal
TM66	Thunder Fang	Electric	Physical	65	95	15	Normal
TM67	Ice Fang	Ice	Physical	65	95	15	Normal
TM68	Fire Fang	Fire	Physical	65	95	15	Normal
TM76	Round	Normal	Special	60	100	15	Normal
TM79	Retaliate	Normal	Physical	70	100	5	Normal
TM84	Tail Slap	Normal	Physical	25	85	10	Normal
TM85	Snarl	Dark	Special	55	95	15	Many Others

TR MOVES

NO.	NAME	TYPE	KIND	POW.	ACC.	PP	RANGE
TR12	Agility	Psychic	Status	—	—	30	Self
TR13	Focus Energy	Normal	Status	—	—	30	Self
TR20	Substitute	Normal	Status	—	—	10	Self
TR21	Reversal	Fighting	Physical	—	100	15	Normal
TR26	Endure	Normal	Status	—	—	10	Self
TR27	Sleep Talk	Normal	Status	—	—	10	Self
TR31	Iron Tail	Steel	Physical	100	75	15	Normal
TR32	Crunch	Dark	Physical	80	100	15	Normal
TR42	Hyper Voice	Normal	Special	90	100	10	Many Others
TR46	Iron Defense	Steel	Status	—	—	15	Self
TR53	Close Combat	Fighting	Physical	120	100	5	Normal
TR64	Focus Blast	Fighting	Special	120	70	5	Normal
TR70	Flash Cannon	Steel	Special	80	100	10	Normal
TR74	Iron Head	Steel	Physical	80	100	15	Normal
TR85	Work Up	Normal	Status	—	—	30	Self
TR86	Wild Charge	Electric	Physical	90	100	15	Normal
TR90	Play Rough	Fairy	Physical	90	90	10	Normal
TR92	Dazzling Gleam	Fairy	Special	80	100	10	Many Others
TR97	Psychic Fangs	Psychic	Physical	85	100	10	Normal

ABILITY
Dauntless Shield
—

HIDDEN ABILITY
—

SPECIES STRENGTHS
- HP
- ATTACK
- DEFENSE
- SP. ATK
- SP. DEF
- SPEED

DAMAGE TAKEN IN BATTLE
×1, ×1, ×0.5, ×1, ×1, ×1, ×1, ×1, ×1, ×2, ×0.5, ×1, ×2, ×1, ×0.5, ×2

NO EGGS

*If Zamazenta knows the move Iron Head when it changes form to its Crowned Shield form, Iron Head will be replaced with Behemoth Bash. When Zamazenta returns to its Hero of Many Battles form, Behemoth Bash will revert back to Iron Head.

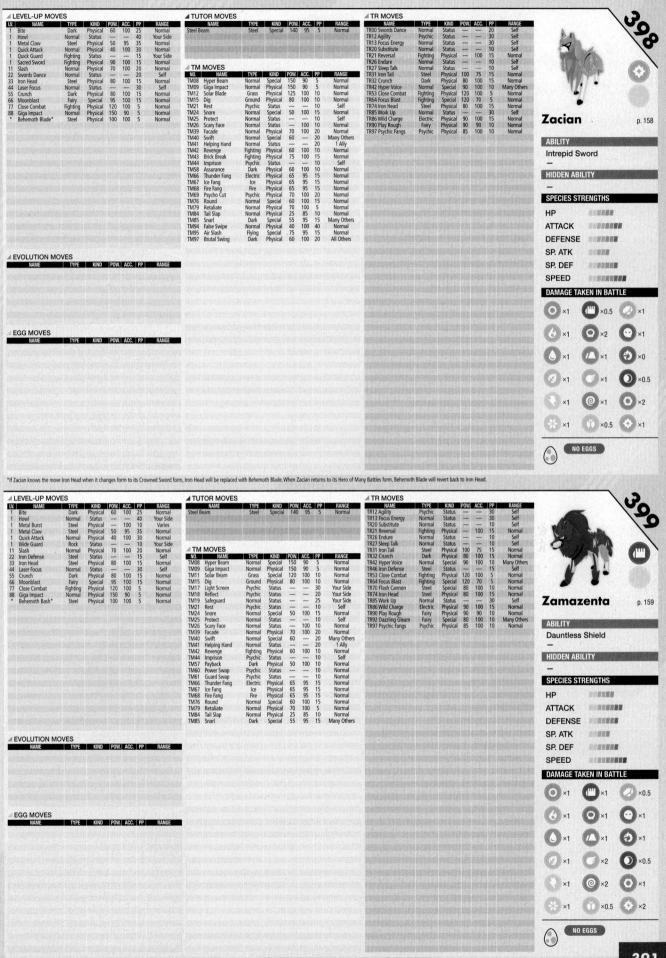

400

Eternatus
p. 160

ABILITY
Pressure
—

HIDDEN ABILITY
—

SPECIES STRENGTHS

HP	
ATTACK	
DEFENSE	
SP. ATK	
SP. DEF	
SPEED	

DAMAGE TAKEN IN BATTLE

⬤ ×1	🔨 ×0.5	🗡 ×1			
🔥 ×0.5	💬 ×0.5	👊 ×1			
💧 ×0.5	🔺 ×2	🔄 ×2			
🌿 ×0.25	🪶 ×1	🌙 ×1			
⚡ ×0.5	◎ ×2	⬤ ×1			
❄ ×2	🕷 ×0.5	◆ ×1			

NO EGGS

LEVEL-UP MOVES

LV.	NAME	TYPE	KIND	POW.	ACC.	PP	RANGE
1	Agility	Psychic	Status	—	—	30	Self
1	Confuse Ray	Ghost	Status	—	100	10	Normal
1	Dragon Tail	Dragon	Physical	60	90	10	Normal
1	Poison Tail	Poison	Physical	50	100	25	Normal
8	Toxic	Poison	Status	—	90	10	Normal
16	Venoshock	Poison	Special	65	100	10	Normal
24	Dragon Dance	Dragon	Status	—	—	20	Self
32	Cross Poison	Poison	Physical	70	100	20	Normal
40	Dragon Pulse	Dragon	Special	85	100	10	Normal
48	Flamethrower	Fire	Special	90	100	15	Normal
56	Dynamax Cannon	Dragon	Special	100	100	5	Normal
64	Cosmic Power	Psychic	Status	—	—	20	Self
72	Recover	Normal	Status	—	—	10	Self
80	Hyper Beam	Normal	Special	150	90	5	Normal
88	Eternabeam	Dragon	Special	160	90	5	Normal

EVOLUTION MOVES

NAME	TYPE	KIND	POW.	ACC.	PP	RANGE

EGG MOVES

NAME	TYPE	KIND	POW.	ACC.	PP	RANGE

TUTOR MOVES

NAME	TYPE	KIND	POW.	ACC.	PP	RANGE
Draco Meteor	Dragon	Special	130	90	5	Normal

TM MOVES

NO.	NAME	TYPE	KIND	POW.	ACC.	PP	RANGE
TM06	Fly	Flying	Physical	90	95	15	Normal
TM08	Hyper Beam	Normal	Special	150	90	5	Normal
TM09	Giga Impact	Normal	Physical	150	90	5	Normal
TM11	Solar Beam	Grass	Special	120	100	10	Normal
TM16	Screech	Normal	Status	—	85	40	Normal
TM17	Light Screen	Psychic	Status	—	—	30	Your Side
TM18	Reflect	Psychic	Status	—	—	20	Your Side
TM21	Rest	Psychic	Status	—	—	10	Self
TM24	Snore	Normal	Special	50	100	15	Normal
TM25	Protect	Normal	Status	—	—	10	Self
TM26	Scary Face	Normal	Status	—	100	10	Normal
TM39	Facade	Normal	Physical	70	100	20	Normal
TM57	Payback	Dark	Physical	50	100	10	Normal
TM58	Assurance	Dark	Physical	60	100	10	Normal
TM73	Cross Poison	Poison	Physical	70	100	20	Normal
TM74	Venoshock	Poison	Special	65	100	10	Normal
TM76	Round	Normal	Special	60	100	15	Normal
TM92	Mystical Fire	Fire	Special	75	100	10	Normal
TM97	Brutal Swing	Dark	Physical	60	100	20	All Others

TR MOVES

NO.	NAME	TYPE	KIND	POW.	ACC.	PP	RANGE
TR02	Flamethrower	Fire	Special	90	100	15	Normal
TR12	Agility	Psychic	Status	—	—	30	Self
TR20	Substitute	Normal	Status	—	—	10	Self
TR22	Sludge Bomb	Poison	Special	90	100	10	Normal
TR26	Endure	Normal	Status	—	—	10	Self
TR27	Sleep Talk	Normal	Status	—	—	10	Self
TR33	Shadow Ball	Ghost	Special	80	100	15	Normal
TR44	Cosmic Power	Psychic	Status	—	—	20	Self
TR51	Dragon Dance	Dragon	Status	—	—	20	Self
TR54	Toxic Spikes	Poison	Status	—	—	20	Other Side
TR57	Poison Jab	Poison	Physical	80	100	20	Normal
TR62	Dragon Pulse	Dragon	Special	85	100	10	Normal
TR70	Flash Cannon	Steel	Special	80	100	10	Normal
TR78	Sludge Wave	Poison	Special	95	100	10	All Others
TR91	Venom Drench	Poison	Status	—	100	20	Many Others

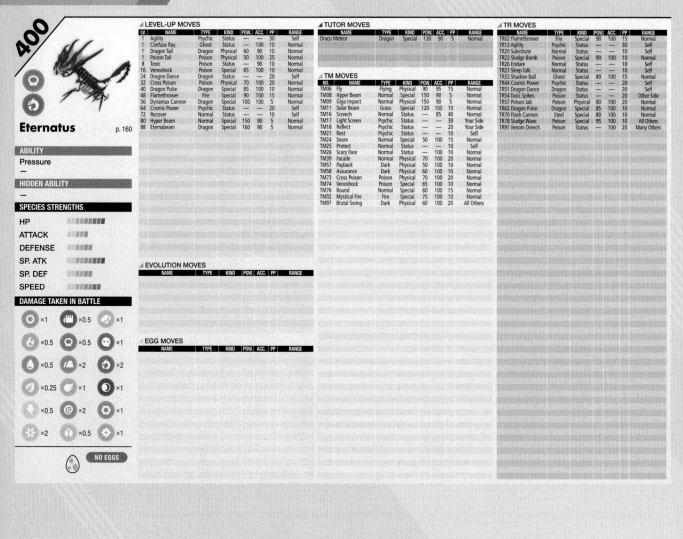

ADVENTURE DATA

Moves

The following pages list the moves that you might face or use during your adventure in the Galar region. Refer to the keys below to understand what each column tells you. There are some universal rules to keep in mind, too, as you get familiar with all the intricacies of Pokémon battle!

Keep in mind these move universals

- Types can affect what moves do! Turn to the type matchup chart on page 479 to check how
- Priority overrules your Pokémon's Speed stat, so check the priority table on page 410 to learn more
- Moves and status conditions can interact, such as frozen Pokémon being thawed out if they're hit by a Fire-type move
- Moves can become less powerful when targeting multiple Pokémon in Double Battles
- Sound-based moves, like Boomburst or Growl, and certain status moves can bypass Substitute

Different rules for Dynamax Pokémon

- Dynamax Pokémon never flinch because of a move, and they can't be forced to flee or swap out of battle
- They're immune to any move that references a Pokémon's weight (such as Grass Knot, Heat Crash, Heavy Slam, and Low Kick)
- Moves, items, or Abilities that reference how much HP a Pokémon has generally use the Pokémon's pre-Dynamax HP
- Moves that automatically KO an opponent (such as Fissure or Destiny Bond) won't work on Dynamax Pokémon!

Understanding Move Tables

Move	The move's name.
Type	The move's type.
Kind	Whether the move is a physical, special, or status move.
	Physical moves deal damage. They do more damage the higher the user's Attack stat is. They do less damage the higher the target's Defense stat is.
	Special moves deal damage. They do more damage the higher the user's Sp. Atk stat is. They do less damage the higher the target's Sp. Def stat is.
	Status moves affect stats or inflict status conditions—or have various other effects.
Pow.	The move's power. If there is a number here, this move deals damage. If you see a dash (—), the move is either a status move or deals varying amounts of damage. Read the Notes to find out which is the case!
Acc.	The move's accuracy out of a max of 100. If you see a dash (—), the move never misses!
PP	How many times the move can be used before the Pokémon must have its PP restored with an item or at a Pokémon Center.
Range	The number and range of targets the move can affect. Each range is explained in the next key.
DA	A circle means the move's user makes direct contact with the target or targets when the move is used.
Max Move Pow.	The power this move will have when transformed into a Max Move.
Notes	If a move does more than simple damage, any additional effects or other details are listed here!

Range Guide

Normal	The move affects a selected target. If the move is used by a Pokémon during a Double Battle or Max Raid Battle, the move can target any of the other Pokémon (including allies).
Self	The move targets the user.
Self/Ally	The move can target the user or an ally in a Double Battle or Max Raid Battle.
1 Ally	The move affects an ally Pokémon during a Double Battle or Max Raid Battle. It has no effect in a Single Battle.
1 Random	The move affects one of the opposing Pokémon at random in a Double Battle. It affects the opposing Pokémon in a Single Battle or Max Raid Battle.
Many Others	If the move is used during a Double Battle, it will affect both opposing Pokémon. Otherwise, it affects the opposing Pokémon in a Single Battle or Max Raid Battle.
All Others	The move affects all surrounding Pokémon at the same time. If the move is used by a Pokémon during a Double Battle or Max Raid Battle, the move will affect all the other Pokémon (including your ally or allies) simultaneously.
Your Side	The move affects your side of the battlefield. In a Double Battle or a Max Raid Battle, these effects will be felt by the user and any ally Pokémon. Some of these moves affect the battlefield, meaning the move's effects continue even if Pokémon are switched out.
Other Side	The move affects the opponent's side of the battlefield. In a Double Battle, these effects will be felt by both opposing Pokémon. Some of these moves affect the battlefield, meaning the move's effects continue even if Pokémon are switched out.
Both Sides	The move affects the entire battlefield and all Pokémon on it. Since the move affects the battlefield, the move's effects continue even if Pokémon are switched out.
All	The move affects all Pokémon on the battlefield at the time the move is used.
Varies	The move is influenced by things such as the opposing Pokémon using a move, so the effect and range are not fixed.
Your Party	The move affects your entire party, including Pokémon that aren't currently on the battlefield, as well as your allies.

Move	Type	Kind	Pow.	Acc.	PP	Range	DA	Max Move Pow.	Notes
Absorb	Grass	Special	20	100	25	Normal	—	90	Restores the user's HP by an amount equal to 1/2 of the damage dealt to the target.
Acid	Poison	Special	40	100	30	Many Others	—	70	Has a 10% chance of lowering the targets' Sp. Def by 1 stage.
Acid Armor	Poison	Status	—	—	20	Self	—	—	Raises the user's Defense by 2 stages.
Acid Spray	Poison	Special	40	100	20	Normal	—	70	Lowers the target's Sp. Def by 2 stages.
Acrobatics	Flying	Physical	55	100	15	Normal	○	110	This move's power is doubled if the user isn't holding an item.
Acupressure	Normal	Status	—	—	30	Self/Ally	—	—	Raises a random stat by 2 stages. Stats that were already boosted to the max will not be selected.
Aerial Ace	Flying	Physical	60	—	20	Normal	○	110	
After You	Normal	Status	—	—	15	Normal	—	—	Forces the target to use its move immediately after this move is used, regardless of the target's Speed. This move fails if the user doesn't act before the target or if the target was going to use its move right after anyway.
Agility	Psychic	Status	—	—	30	Self	—	—	Raises the user's Speed by 2 stages.
Air Cutter	Flying	Special	60	95	25	Many Others	—	110	This move is more likely than average to deliver a critical hit.
Air Slash	Flying	Special	75	95	15	Normal	—	130	Has a 30% chance of making the target flinch (unable to use moves on that turn).
Ally Switch	Psychic	Status	—	—	15	Self	—	—	A high-priority move. The user switches places with an ally in a Double Battle. This move fails if used in a Single Battle or a Max Raid Battle.
Amnesia	Psychic	Status	—	—	20	Self	—	—	Raises the user's Sp. Def by 2 stages.
Anchor Shot	Steel	Physical	80	100	20	Normal	○	130	The target becomes unable to flee or be switched out of battle.
Ancient Power	Rock	Special	60	100	5	Normal	—	110	Has a 10% chance of raising the user's Attack, Defense, Sp. Atk, Sp. Def, and Speed by 1 stage each.
Apple Acid	Grass	Special	80	100	10	Normal	—	130	Lowers the target's Sp. Def by 1 stage.
Aqua Jet	Water	Physical	40	100	20	Normal	○	90	A high-priority move.
Aqua Ring	Water	Status	—	—	20	Self	—	—	Restores 1/16 of the user's max HP at the end of each turn.
Aqua Tail	Water	Physical	90	90	10	Normal	○	130	
Arm Thrust	Fighting	Physical	15	100	20	Normal	○	70	Attacks 2–5 times in a row in a single turn.
Aromatherapy	Grass	Status	—	—	5	Your Party	—	—	Heals the status conditions of all Pokémon in your party.
Aromatic Mist	Fairy	Status	—	—	20	1 Ally	—	—	Raises one ally's Sp. Def by 1 stage.
Assurance	Dark	Physical	60	100	10	Normal	○	110	This move's power is doubled if the target has already taken some damage on the same turn.
Astonish	Ghost	Physical	30	100	15	Normal	○	90	Has a 30% chance of making the target flinch (unable to use moves on that turn).
Attack Order	Bug	Physical	90	100	15	Normal	—	130	This move is more likely than average to deliver a critical hit.
Attract	Normal	Status	—	100	15	Normal	—	—	Leaves the target unable to attack 50% of the time. This move only works if the user and the target are of different genders.
Aura Sphere	Fighting	Special	80	—	20	Normal	—	90	
Aura Wheel	Electric	Physical	110	100	10	Normal	—	140	This move's type changes depending on the user's form.
Aurora Beam	Ice	Special	65	100	20	Normal	—	120	Has a 10% chance of lowering the target's Attack by 1 stage.
Aurora Veil	Ice	Status	—	—	20	Your Side	—	—	Halves the damage taken by the Pokémon on your side from physical or special moves for 5 turns. This move can only be used when the weather condition is hail. Effects continue even if the user switches out.
Autotomize	Steel	Status	—	—	15	Self	—	—	Raises the user's Speed by 2 stages and lowers its weight by 220 lbs.
Avalanche	Ice	Physical	60	100	10	Normal	○	110	A low-priority move. This move's power is doubled if the user has taken damage from the target on the same turn.
Baby-Doll Eyes	Fairy	Status	—	100	30	Normal	—	—	A high-priority move. Lowers the target's Attack by 1 stage.
Baneful Bunker	Poison	Status	—	—	10	Self	—	—	A high-priority move. The user protects itself from all damage-dealing moves and most status moves on the same turn. If an opposing Pokémon hits the user with a move that makes direct contact, the attacker will be inflicted with the poisoned status condition. This move becomes more likely to fail if used repeatedly. When used against a Max Move, this move will prevent 3/4 of the damage.
Baton Pass	Normal	Status	—	—	40	Self	—	—	The user switches out with another Pokémon in the party and passes along any stat changes.
Beat Up	Dark	Physical	—	100	10	Normal	—	100	Attacks once for each Pokémon in your party, including the user. Does not count Pokémon that have fainted or have status conditions.
Behemoth Bash	Steel	Physical	100	100	5	Normal	○	130	Deals twice the damage if the target is Dynamaxed.
Behemoth Blade	Steel	Physical	100	100	5	Normal	○	130	Deals twice the damage if the target is Dynamaxed.
Belch	Poison	Special	120	90	10	Normal	—	95	This move cannot be selected unless the user has already eaten a held Berry during the current battle.
Belly Drum	Normal	Status	—	—	10	Self	—	—	The user loses 1/2 of its max HP but raises its Attack to the maximum.
Bind	Normal	Physical	15	85	20	Normal	○	90	Inflicts damage equal to 1/8 of the target's max HP at the end of each turn for 4–5 turns. The target cannot flee or be switched out of battle during that time.

Move	Type	Kind	Pow.	Acc.	PP	Range	DA	Max Move Pow.	Notes
Bite	Dark	Physical	60	100	25	Normal	○	110	Has a 30% chance of making the target flinch (unable to use moves on that turn).
Blast Burn	Fire	Special	150	90	5	Normal	—	150	The user cannot act, be switched out, or have items used on it during the next turn.
Blaze Kick	Fire	Physical	85	90	10	Normal	○	130	Has a 10% chance of inflicting the burned status condition on the target. This move is more likely than average to deliver a critical hit.
Blizzard	Ice	Special	110	70	5	Many Others	—	140	Has a 10% chance of inflicting the frozen status condition on the targets. This move is 100% accurate in the hail weather condition.
Block	Normal	Status	—	—	5	Normal	—	—	The target becomes unable to flee or be switched out of battle.
Body Press	Fighting	Physical	80	100	10	Normal	○	90	The user's defenses become its strength. Damage dealt by this move is calculated using the user's Defense rather than the user's Attack.
Body Slam	Normal	Physical	85	100	15	Normal	○	130	Has a 30% chance of inflicting the paralysis status condition on the target. If the target has used Minimize, this move will be a sure hit and its power will be doubled.
Bolt Beak	Electric	Physical	85	100	10	Normal	○	130	This move's power is doubled if the target has not yet used a move on the same turn.
Bone Rush	Ground	Physical	25	90	10	Normal	—	130	Attacks 2–5 times in a row in a single turn.
Boomburst	Normal	Special	140	100	10	All Others	—	140	
Bounce	Flying	Physical	85	85	5	Normal	○	130	This move takes 2 turns. The user flies into the air on the first turn and attacks on the second. Has a 30% chance of inflicting the paralysis status condition on the target.
Branch Poke	Grass	Physical	40	100	40	Normal	○	90	
Brave Bird	Flying	Physical	120	100	15	Normal	○	140	The user also takes 1/3 of the damage dealt to the target.
Breaking Swipe	Dragon	Physical	60	100	15	Many Others	○	110	Lowers opposing Pokémon's Attack by 1 stage.
Brick Break	Fighting	Physical	75	100	15	Normal	○	90	This move is not affected by Aurora Veil or Reflect. It removes the effects of Aurora Veil, Light Screen, and Reflect.
Brine	Water	Special	65	100	10	Normal	—	120	This move's power is doubled if the target's HP is at 1/2 or below.
Brutal Swing	Dark	Physical	60	100	20	All Others	○	110	
Bubble Beam	Water	Special	65	100	20	Normal	—	120	Has a 10% chance of lowering the target's Speed by 1 stage.
Bug Bite	Bug	Physical	60	100	20	Normal	○	110	If the target is holding a Berry, the user eats that Berry and uses its battle effect if it has one.
Bug Buzz	Bug	Special	90	100	10	Normal	—	130	Has a 10% chance of lowering the target's Sp. Def by 1 stage.
Bulk Up	Fighting	Status	—	—	20	Self	—	—	Raises the user's Attack and Defense by 1 stage each.
Bulldoze	Ground	Physical	60	100	20	All Others	—	110	Lowers the targets' Speed by 1 stage.
Bullet Punch	Steel	Physical	40	100	30	Normal	○	90	A high-priority move.
Bullet Seed	Grass	Physical	25	100	30	Normal	—	130	Attacks 2–5 times in a row in a single turn.
Burn Up	Fire	Special	130	100	5	Normal	—	140	After attacking, the user is no longer Fire type.
Calm Mind	Psychic	Status	—	—	20	Self	—	—	Raises the user's Sp. Atk and Sp. Def by 1 stage each.
Charge	Electric	Status	—	—	20	Self	—	—	Doubles the power of an Electric-type move used by the same user on the next turn. Raises the user's Sp. Def by 1 stage.
Charge Beam	Electric	Special	50	90	10	Normal	—	100	Has a 70% chance of raising the user's Sp. Atk by 1 stage.
Charm	Fairy	Status	—	100	20	Normal	—	—	Lowers the target's Attack by 2 stages.
Circle Throw	Fighting	Physical	60	90	10	Normal	○	80	A low-priority move. Ends battles against wild Pokémon if the target's level is lower than the user's. Forces the target to swap out in a Trainer battle, unless there are no other Pokémon available to battle.
Clanging Scales	Dragon	Special	110	100	5	Many Others	—	140	Lowers the user's Defense by 1 stage.
Clangorous Soul	Dragon	Status	—	100	5	Self	—	—	Raises all of the user's stats by 1 stage but reduces the user's HP by 1/3 of its maximum. If the user's HP is at 1/3 of its maximum or lower, this move fails.
Clear Smog	Poison	Special	50	—	15	Normal	—	75	Eliminates every stat change affecting the target.
Close Combat	Fighting	Physical	120	100	5	Normal	○	95	Lowers the user's Defense and Sp. Def by 1 stage each.
Coil	Poison	Status	—	—	20	Self	—	—	Raises the user's Attack, Defense, and accuracy by 1 stage each.
Confide	Normal	Status	—	—	20	Normal	—	—	Lowers the target's Sp. Atk by 1 stage.
Confuse Ray	Ghost	Status	—	100	10	Normal	—	—	Makes the target confused.
Confusion	Psychic	Special	50	100	25	Normal	—	100	Has a 10% chance of making the target confused.
Copycat	Normal	Status	—	—	20	Self	—	—	The user repeats the last move used in the battle. If the opponent chooses a Max Move, this move will copy the normal version of that move. (For example, if the opponent chooses Max Flare that was formerly Flamethrower, this move will copy Flamethrower.)
Cosmic Power	Psychic	Status	—	—	20	Self	—	—	Raises the user's Defense and Sp. Def by 1 stage each.
Cotton Guard	Grass	Status	—	—	10	Self	—	—	Raises the user's Defense by 3 stages.
Cotton Spore	Grass	Status	—	100	40	Many Others	—	—	Lowers the targets' Speed by 2 stages.

Move	Type	Kind	Pow.	Acc.	PP	Range	DA	Max Move Pow.	Notes
Counter	Fighting	Physical	—	100	20	Varies	○	75	A low-priority move. If the user is hit with a physical move during the same turn, this move inflicts twice the damage taken by the user onto the attacker.
Court Change	Normal	Status	—	100	10	Both Sides	—	—	Swaps the battle effects affecting each side of the battlefield. This includes the effects of moves such as Reflect, Spikes, Tailwind, and others.
Covet	Normal	Physical	60	100	25	Normal	○	110	When the target is holding an item and the user is not, the user can steal that item. When the target is not holding an item, this move will function as a simple damage-dealing move.
Crabhammer	Water	Physical	100	90	10	Normal	○	130	This move is more likely than average to deliver a critical hit.
Crafty Shield	Fairy	Status	—	—	10	Your Side	—	—	A high-priority move. Protects your side from status moves used on the same turn. Does not protect against damage-dealing moves.
Cross Chop	Fighting	Physical	100	80	5	Normal	○	90	This move is more likely than average to deliver a critical hit.
Cross Poison	Poison	Physical	70	100	20	Normal	○	85	Has a 10% chance of inflicting the poisoned status condition on the target. This move is more likely than average to deliver a critical hit.
Crunch	Dark	Physical	80	100	15	Normal	○	130	Has a 20% chance of lowering the target's Defense by 1 stage.
Crush Claw	Normal	Physical	75	95	10	Normal	○	130	Has a 50% chance of lowering the target's Defense by 1 stage.
Curse	Ghost	Status	—	—	10	Varies	—	—	If used by a non-Ghost-type Pokémon, this move lowers the user's Speed by 1 stage and raises its Attack and Defense by 1 stage each. If used by a Ghost-type Pokémon, this move causes the user to lose 1/2 of its max HP but the move lowers the target's HP by 1/4 of its maximum each turn.
Dark Pulse	Dark	Special	80	100	15	Normal	—	130	Has a 20% chance of making the target flinch (unable to use moves on that turn).
Darkest Lariat	Dark	Physical	85	100	10	Normal	○	130	Ignores the stat changes of the target when dealing damage.
Dazzling Gleam	Fairy	Special	80	100	10	Many Others	—	130	
Decorate	Fairy	Status	—	—	15	Normal	—	—	Raises the target's Attack and Sp. Atk by 2 stages each.
Defend Order	Bug	Status	—	—	10	Self	—	—	Raises the user's Defense and Sp. Def by 1 stage each.
Defense Curl	Normal	Status	—	—	40	Self	—	—	Raises the user's Defense by 1 stage.
Defog	Flying	Status	—	—	15	Normal	—	—	Lowers the target's evasiveness by 1 stage. Nullifies Aurora Veil, Light Screen, Mist, Reflect, and Safeguard on the opponents' side. Nullifies Spikes, Stealth Rock, Sticky Web, and Toxic Spikes on both sides. When the target has a substitute, only the effect that lowers evasiveness will fail.
Destiny Bond	Ghost	Status	—	—	5	Self	—	—	If the user faints due to damage caused by an opposing Pokémon, that Pokémon faints as well. This effect lasts until the user's next turn. This move fails if used repeatedly.
Detect	Fighting	Status	—	—	5	Self	—	—	A high-priority move. The user evades all damage-dealing moves and most status moves on the same turn. This move becomes more likely to fail if used repeatedly. When used against a Max Move, this move will prevent 3/4 of the damage.
Dig	Ground	Physical	80	100	10	Normal	○	130	This move takes 2 turns. The user burrows underground on the first turn and attacks on the second.
Disable	Normal	Status	—	100	20	Normal	—	—	Makes the target unable to use its last-used move for 4 turns. This move has no effect against Max Moves.
Disarming Voice	Fairy	Special	40	—	15	Many Others	—	90	
Discharge	Electric	Special	80	100	15	All Others	—	130	Has a 30% chance of inflicting the paralysis status condition on the targets.
Dive	Water	Physical	80	100	10	Normal	○	130	This move takes 2 turns. The user dives deep on the first turn and attacks on the second.
Double Hit	Normal	Physical	35	90	10	Normal	○	120	Attacks twice in a row in a single turn.
Double Kick	Fighting	Physical	30	100	30	Normal	○	80	Attacks twice in a row in a single turn.
Double Team	Normal	Status	—	—	15	Self	—	—	Raises the user's evasiveness by 1 stage.
Double-Edge	Normal	Physical	120	100	15	Normal	○	140	The user also takes 1/3 of the damage dealt to the target.
Draco Meteor	Dragon	Special	130	90	5	Normal	—	140	Lowers the user's Sp. Atk by 2 stages.
Dragon Breath	Dragon	Special	60	100	20	Normal	—	110	Has a 30% chance of inflicting the paralysis status condition on the target.
Dragon Claw	Dragon	Physical	80	100	15	Normal	○	130	
Dragon Dance	Dragon	Status	—	—	20	Self	—	—	Raises the user's Attack and Speed by 1 stage each.
Dragon Darts	Dragon	Physical	50	100	10	Normal	—	130	Attacks twice in a row in a single turn. If there are two opponents, each will be struck once.
Dragon Pulse	Dragon	Special	85	100	10	Normal	—	130	
Dragon Rush	Dragon	Physical	100	75	10	Normal	○	130	Has a 20% chance of making the target flinch (unable to use moves on that turn). If the target has used Minimize, this move will be a sure hit and its power will be doubled.
Dragon Tail	Dragon	Physical	60	90	10	Normal	○	110	A low-priority move. Ends battles against wild Pokémon if the target's level is lower than the user's. Forces the target to swap out in a Trainer battle, unless there are no other Pokémon available to battle.
Drain Punch	Fighting	Physical	75	100	10	Normal	○	90	Restores the user's HP by an amount equal to 1/2 of the damage dealt to the target.
Draining Kiss	Fairy	Special	50	100	10	Normal	○	100	Restores the user's HP by an amount equal to 3/4 of the damage dealt to the target.

Move	Type	Kind	Pow.	Acc.	PP	Range	DA	Max Move Pow.	Notes
Dream Eater	Psychic	Special	100	100	15	Normal	—	130	This move only works when the target is asleep. Restores the user's HP by an amount equal to 1/2 of the damage dealt to the target. This move has no effect against mysterious barriers protecting Dynamax Pokémon.
Drill Peck	Flying	Physical	80	100	20	Normal	○	130	
Drill Run	Ground	Physical	80	95	10	Normal	○	130	This move is more likely than average to deliver a critical hit.
Drum Beating	Grass	Physical	80	100	10	Normal	—	130	Lowers the target's Speed by 1 stage.
Dual Chop	Dragon	Physical	40	90	15	Normal	○	130	Attacks twice in a row in a single turn.
Dynamax Cannon	Dragon	Special	120	100	1	Normal	—	140	Deals twice the damage if the target is Dynamaxed.
Dynamic Punch	Fighting	Physical	100	50	5	Normal	○	90	Makes the target confused.
Earth Power	Ground	Special	90	100	10	Normal	—	130	Has a 10% chance of lowering the target's Sp. Def by 1 stage.
Earthquake	Ground	Physical	100	100	10	All Others	—	130	This move hits targets that are underground due to using Dig and has doubled power against them.
Echoed Voice	Normal	Special	40	100	15	Normal	—	90	This move's power increases every turn that it is used (max power of 200), no matter which Pokémon uses it. Power returns to normal if no Pokémon uses it in a turn.
Eerie Impulse	Electric	Status	—	100	15	Normal	—	—	Lowers the target's Sp. Atk by 2 stages.
Electric Terrain	Electric	Status	—	—	10	Both Sides	—	—	Electrifies the battlefield for 5 turns. During that time, Pokémon on the ground will be able to do 30% more damage with Electric-type moves and cannot fall asleep.
Electrify	Electric	Status	—	—	20	Normal	—	—	Changes any move used by the target on the same turn into an Electric-type move. This move will have the same effect on Max Moves.
Electro Ball	Electric	Special	—	100	10	Normal	—	130	This move's power becomes greater (max power of 150) the faster the user is compared to the target.
Electroweb	Electric	Special	55	95	15	Many Others	—	110	Lowers the targets' Speed by 1 stage.
Ember	Fire	Special	40	100	25	Normal	—	90	Has a 10% chance of inflicting the burned status condition on the target.
Encore	Normal	Status	—	100	5	Normal	—	—	The target is forced to keep using the last move it used. This effect lasts 3 turns. This move will fail when used against a Dynamax Pokémon. Even if the target was affected by this move before Dynamaxing, the effect will be nullified once it Dynamaxes.
Endeavor	Normal	Physical	—	100	5	Normal	○	130	The target's HP is cut to equal the user's HP. If the target's HP is already lower than the user's, this move will do nothing.
Endure	Normal	Status	—	—	10	Self	—	—	A high-priority move. Leaves the user with 1 HP when hit by a move that would normally knock it out. This move becomes more likely to fail if used repeatedly.
Energy Ball	Grass	Special	90	100	10	Normal	—	130	Has a 10% chance of lowering the target's Sp. Def by 1 stage.
Entrainment	Normal	Status	—	100	15	Normal	—	—	Makes the target's Ability the same as the user's. Fails with certain Abilities, however.
Eruption	Fire	Special	150	100	5	Many Others	—	150	The lower the user's HP, the lower this move's power becomes.
Eternabeam	Dragon	Physical	150	100	5	Normal	—	150	The user cannot act, be switched out, or have items used on it during the next turn.
Explosion	Normal	Physical	250	100	5	All Others	—	150	The user faints after using this move.
Extrasensory	Psychic	Special	80	100	20	Normal	—	130	Has a 10% chance of making the target flinch (unable to use moves on that turn).
Extreme Speed	Normal	Physical	80	100	5	Normal	○	130	A high-priority move.
Facade	Normal	Physical	70	100	20	Normal	○	120	This move's power is doubled if the user has the paralyzed, poisoned, or burned status condition.
Fairy Wind	Fairy	Special	40	100	30	Normal	—	90	
Fake Out	Normal	Physical	40	100	10	Normal	○	90	A high-priority move. Makes the target flinch (unable to use moves on that turn). This move only works if used on the first turn after the user is sent out.
Fake Tears	Dark	Status	—	100	20	Normal	—	—	Lowers the target's Sp. Def by 2 stages.
False Surrender	Dark	Physical	80	—	10	Normal	○	130	
False Swipe	Normal	Physical	40	100	40	Normal	○	90	Always leaves the target with at least 1 HP, even if the damage would have normally made the target faint.
Feather Dance	Flying	Status	—	100	15	Normal	—	—	Lowers the target's Attack by 2 stages.
Feint	Normal	Physical	30	100	10	Normal	—	90	A high-priority move. Strikes even if the target has used a protection move, and removes the protection move's effect.
Fell Stinger	Bug	Physical	50	100	25	Normal	○	100	If the user knocks out an opponent with this move, its Attack is raised by 3 stages.
Final Gambit	Fighting	Special	—	100	5	Normal	—	100	The user faints, and the target takes damage equal to the HP lost by the user. If the move misses or otherwise fails, the user will not faint.
Fire Blast	Fire	Special	110	85	5	Normal	—	140	Has a 10% chance of inflicting the burned status condition on the target.
Fire Fang	Fire	Physical	65	95	15	Normal	○	120	Has a 10% chance of inflicting the burned status condition on the target and a 10% chance of making the target flinch (unable to use moves on that turn).
Fire Lash	Fire	Physical	80	100	15	Normal	○	130	Lowers the target's Defense by 1 stage.

Move	Type	Kind	Pow.	Acc.	PP	Range	DA	Max Move Pow.	Notes
Fire Pledge	Fire	Special	80	100	10	Normal	—	130	When this is combined with Grass Pledge or Water Pledge, the power and effect change. If this is combined with Grass Pledge, the power of this move becomes 150 and it remains a Fire-type move. It will also inflict damage equal to 1/8 of the opposing Pokémon's max HP at the end of each turn for 4 turns, unless they are Fire types. If this is combined with Water Pledge, the power of this move becomes 150 and it becomes a Water-type move. It will also make it more likely that your team's moves will trigger any additional effects they might have for 4 turns.
Fire Punch	Fire	Physical	75	100	15	Normal	○	130	Has a 10% chance of inflicting the burned status condition on the target.
Fire Spin	Fire	Special	35	85	15	Normal	—	90	Inflicts damage equal to 1/8 of the target's max HP at the end of each turn for 4–5 turns. The target cannot flee or be switched out of battle during that time.
First Impression	Bug	Physical	90	100	10	Normal	○	130	A high-priority move. This move only works if used on the first turn after the user is sent out.
Fishious Rend	Water	Physical	85	100	10	Normal	○	130	This move's power is doubled if the target has not yet used a move on the same turn.
Fissure	Ground	Physical	—	30	5	Normal	—	130	The target faints with one hit. The higher the user's level is compared to the target's, the more accurate the move is. If the target's level is higher than the user's, this move fails. If this move hits a Dynamax Pokémon, this move will destroy 2 segments of the mysterious barrier's meter.
Flail	Normal	Physical	—	100	15	Normal	○	130	This move's power becomes greater (max power of 200) the lower the user's HP is.
Flame Charge	Fire	Physical	50	100	20	Normal	○	100	Raises the user's Speed by 1 stage.
Flame Wheel	Fire	Physical	60	100	25	Normal	○	110	Has a 10% chance of inflicting the burned status condition on the target. This move can be used even if the user is frozen and will thaw the user.
Flamethrower	Fire	Special	90	100	15	Normal	—	130	Has a 10% chance of inflicting the burned status condition on the target.
Flare Blitz	Fire	Physical	120	100	15	Normal	○	140	The user also takes 1/3 of the damage dealt to the target. Has a 10% chance of inflicting the burned status condition on the target. This move can be used even if the user is frozen and will thaw the user.
Flash Cannon	Steel	Special	80	100	10	Normal	—	130	Has a 10% chance of lowering the target's Sp. Def by 1 stage.
Flatter	Dark	Status	—	100	15	Normal	—	—	Makes the target confused but also raises its Sp. Atk by 1 stage.
Fling	Dark	Physical	—	100	10	Normal	—	100	The user attacks by throwing its held item at the target. The move's power varies depending on the item. The following items can be thrown to inflict additional effects. Flame Orb: Burned status condition. King's Rock / Razor Fang: Flinching. Light Ball: Paralysis status condition. Mental Herb: Removes Cursed Body, Disable, Encore, infatuation, Taunt, and Torment. Poison Barb: Poisoned status condition. Toxic Orb: Badly poisoned status condition. White Herb: Resets lowered stats.
Flower Shield	Fairy	Status	—	—	10	All	—	—	Raises the Defense of any Grass-type Pokémon on the battlefield by 1 stage.
Fly	Flying	Physical	90	95	15	Normal	○	130	This move takes 2 turns. The user flies into the air on the first turn and attacks on the second.
Flying Press	Fighting	Physical	100	95	10	Normal	○	90	This move is both Fighting type and Flying type. If the target has used Minimize, this move will be a sure hit and its power will be doubled. This move will become Max Knuckle when used by a Dynamax Pokémon.
Focus Blast	Fighting	Special	120	70	5	Normal	—	95	Has a 10% chance of lowering the target's Sp. Def by 1 stage.
Focus Energy	Normal	Status	—	—	30	Self	—	—	Makes the user's future moves more likely than average to deliver critical hits.
Focus Punch	Fighting	Physical	150	100	20	Normal	○	100	A low-priority move. This move fails if the user is hit before this move lands.
Follow Me	Normal	Status	—	—	20	Self	—	—	A high-priority move. Opposing Pokémon aim only at the user for the rest of the turn in which this move is used. This move will cause Dynamax Pokémon to aim only at the user. However, the additional effects of Max Moves will occur as usual.
Force Palm	Fighting	Physical	60	100	10	Normal	○	80	Has a 30% chance of inflicting the paralysis status condition on the target.
Forest's Curse	Grass	Status	—	100	20	Normal	—	—	Gives the target the Grass type in addition to its original type(s).
Foul Play	Dark	Physical	95	100	15	Normal	○	130	The user turns the target's strength against it. Damage dealt by this move is calculated using the target's Attack rather than the user's Attack.
Freeze-Dry	Ice	Special	70	100	20	Normal	—	120	Super effective against Water-type Pokémon. Has a 10% chance of inflicting the frozen status condition on the target.
Frenzy Plant	Grass	Special	150	90	5	Normal	—	150	The user cannot act, be switched out, or have items used on it during the next turn.
Frost Breath	Ice	Special	60	90	10	Normal	—	110	Always delivers a critical hit.
Fury Attack	Normal	Physical	15	85	20	Normal	○	90	Attacks 2–5 times in a row in a single turn.
Fury Cutter	Bug	Physical	40	95	20	Normal	○	90	This move's power is doubled with every successful hit (max power of 320). Power returns to normal once it misses or if another move is selected.
Fury Swipes	Normal	Physical	18	80	15	Normal	○	100	Attacks 2–5 times in a row in a single turn.
Future Sight	Psychic	Special	120	100	10	Normal	—	140	Damage is dealt to the target 2 turns after this move is used.
Gastro Acid	Poison	Status	—	100	10	Normal	—	—	Disables the target's Ability. Fails with certain Abilities, however.
Gear Grind	Steel	Physical	50	85	15	Normal	○	130	Attacks twice in a row in a single turn.

Move	Type	Kind	Pow.	Acc.	PP	Range	DA	Max Move Pow.	Notes
Gear Up	Steel	Status	—	—	20	Your Side	—	—	Raises Attack and Sp. Atk by 1 stage each for any Pokémon on your side with the Plus Ability or Minus Ability.
Giga Drain	Grass	Special	75	100	10	Normal	—	130	Restores the user's HP by an amount equal to 1/2 of the damage dealt to the target.
Giga Impact	Normal	Physical	150	90	5	Normal	○	150	The user cannot act, be switched out, or have items used on it during the next turn.
Glare	Normal	Status	—	100	30	Normal	—	—	Inflicts the paralysis status condition on the target.
Grass Knot	Grass	Special	—	100	20	Normal	○	130	This move's power becomes greater (max power of 120) the heavier the target is. This move has no effect against Dynamax Pokémon.
Grass Pledge	Grass	Special	80	100	10	Normal	—	130	When this is combined with Water Pledge or Fire Pledge, the power and effect change. If this is combined with Water Pledge, the power of this move becomes 150 and it remains a Grass-type move. It will also lower the Speed of opposing Pokémon for 4 turns. If this is combined with Fire Pledge, the power of this move becomes 150 and it becomes a Fire-type move. It will also inflict damage equal to 1/8 of the opposing Pokémon's max HP at the end of each turn for 4 turns, unless they are Fire types.
Grassy Terrain	Grass	Status	—	—	10	Both Sides	—	—	Covers the battlefield with grass for 5 turns. During that time, Pokémon on the ground will be able to do 30% more damage with Grass-type moves and will recover 1/16 of their max HP at the end of each turn. Damage done to Pokémon on the ground by Bulldoze or Earthquake is also halved during this time.
Grav Apple	Grass	Physical	80	100	10	Normal	—	130	Lowers the target's Defense by 1 stage. This move will do 50% more damage when used while the effects of Gravity are present.
Gravity	Psychic	Status	—	—	5	Both Sides	—	—	Airborne Pokémon are grounded. Ground-type moves will now hit Pokémon normally immune to them. Prevents the use of Bounce, Fly, Flying Press, High Jump Kick, Magnet Rise, and Splash. Raises the accuracy of all Pokémon in battle. Lasts 5 turns. Moves that normally would be prevented can still be used as Max Moves by Dynamax Pokémon.
Growl	Normal	Status	—	100	40	Many Others	—	—	Lowers the targets' Attack by 1 stage.
Growth	Normal	Status	—	—	20	Self	—	—	Raises the user's Attack and Sp. Atk by 1 stage each. Raises them by 2 stages when the weather condition is harsh sunlight.
Grudge	Ghost	Status	—	—	5	Self	—	—	Any move that causes the user to faint will have its PP reduced to 0. This move will fail when used against Max Moves.
Guard Split	Psychic	Status	—	—	10	Normal	—	—	The user's and the target's Defense and Sp. Def are each added, then divided equally between them.
Guard Swap	Psychic	Status	—	—	10	Normal	—	—	Swaps the user's and target's stat changes for both Defense and Sp. Def.
Guillotine	Normal	Physical	—	30	5	Normal	○	130	The target faints with one hit. The higher the user's level is compared to the target's, the more accurate the move is. If the target's level is higher than the user's, this move fails. If this move hits a Dynamax Pokémon, this move will destroy 2 segments of the mysterious barrier's meter.
Gunk Shot	Poison	Physical	120	80	5	Normal	—	95	Has a 30% chance of inflicting the poisoned status condition on the target.
Gust	Flying	Special	40	100	35	Normal	—	90	This move hits targets that are in the sky due to using moves such as Bounce or Fly and has doubled power against them.
Gyro Ball	Steel	Physical	—	100	5	Normal	○	130	This move's power becomes greater (max power of 150) the slower the user is compared to the target.
Hail	Ice	Status	—	—	10	Both Sides	—	—	Changes the weather condition to hail for 5 turns. All Pokémon other than Ice types take damage at the end of each turn equal to 1/16 of their max HP.
Hammer Arm	Fighting	Physical	100	90	10	Normal	○	90	Lowers the user's Speed by 1 stage.
Harden	Normal	Status	—	—	30	Self	—	—	Raises the user's Defense by 1 stage.
Haze	Ice	Status	—	—	30	Both Sides	—	—	Eliminates stat changes of all Pokémon in battle.
Head Smash	Rock	Physical	150	80	5	Normal	○	150	The user also takes 1/2 of the damage dealt to the target.
Headbutt	Normal	Physical	70	100	15	Normal	○	120	Has a 30% chance of making the target flinch (unable to use moves on that turn).
Heal Pulse	Psychic	Status	—	—	10	Normal	—	—	Restores 1/2 of the target's max HP.
Healing Wish	Psychic	Status	—	—	10	Self	—	—	The user faints, but the next Pokémon to be switched in will have its HP fully restored and status conditions healed.
Heat Crash	Fire	Physical	—	100	10	Normal	○	130	This move's power becomes greater (max power of 120) the heavier the user is compared to the target. If the target has used Minimize, this move will be a sure hit and its power will be doubled. This move has no effect against Dynamax Pokémon.
Heat Wave	Fire	Special	95	90	10	Many Others	—	130	Has a 10% chance of inflicting the burned status condition on the targets.
Heavy Slam	Steel	Physical	—	100	10	Normal	○	130	This move's power becomes greater (max power of 120) the heavier the user is compared to the target. If the target has used Minimize, this move will be a sure hit and its power will be doubled. This move has no effect against Dynamax Pokémon.
Helping Hand	Normal	Status	—	—	20	1 Ally	—	—	Acts before all other moves on the same turn. Boosts the power of whichever move an ally chooses to use next by 50%.
Hex	Ghost	Special	65	100	10	Normal	—	120	This move's power is doubled if the target has a status condition.
High Horsepower	Ground	Physical	95	95	10	Normal	○	130	

Move	Type	Kind	Pow.	Acc.	PP	Range	DA	Max Move Pow.	Notes
High Jump Kick	Fighting	Physical	130	90	10	Normal	○	95	If this move misses or otherwise fails, the user loses 1/2 of its max HP.
Hone Claws	Dark	Status	—	—	15	Self	—	—	Raises the user's Attack and accuracy by 1 stage each.
Horn Attack	Normal	Physical	65	100	25	Normal	○	120	
Horn Drill	Normal	Physical	—	30	5	Normal	○	130	The target faints with one hit. The higher the user's level is compared to the target's, the more accurate the move is. If the target's level is higher than the user's, this move fails. If this move hits a Dynamax Pokémon, this move will destroy 2 segments of the mysterious barrier's meter.
Horn Leech	Grass	Physical	75	100	10	Normal	○	130	Restores the user's HP by an amount equal to 1/2 of the damage dealt to the target.
Howl	Normal	Status	—	—	40	Your Side	—	—	Raises the user's and ally Pokémon's Attack by 1 stage.
Hurricane	Flying	Special	110	70	10	Normal	—	140	Has a 30% chance of making the target confused. Is 100% accurate in the rain weather condition and 50% accurate in the harsh sunlight weather condition. This move hits targets that are in the sky due to moves such as Bounce or Fly.
Hydro Cannon	Water	Special	150	90	5	Normal	—	150	The user cannot act, be switched out, or have items used on it during the next turn.
Hydro Pump	Water	Special	110	80	5	Normal	—	140	
Hyper Beam	Normal	Special	150	90	5	Normal	—	150	The user cannot act, be switched out, or have items used on it during the next turn.
Hyper Voice	Normal	Special	90	100	10	Many Others	—	130	
Hypnosis	Psychic	Status	—	60	20	Normal	—	—	Inflicts the asleep status condition on the target.
Ice Beam	Ice	Special	90	100	10	Normal	—	130	Has a 10% chance of inflicting the frozen status condition on the target.
Ice Fang	Ice	Physical	65	95	15	Normal	○	120	Has a 10% chance of inflicting the frozen status condition on the target or making the target flinch (unable to use moves on that turn).
Ice Punch	Ice	Physical	75	100	15	Normal	○	130	Has a 10% chance of inflicting the frozen status condition on the target.
Ice Shard	Ice	Physical	40	100	30	Normal	—	90	A high-priority move.
Icicle Crash	Ice	Physical	85	90	10	Normal	—	130	Has a 30% chance of making the target flinch (unable to use moves on that turn).
Icicle Spear	Ice	Physical	25	100	30	Normal	—	130	Attacks 2–5 times in a row in a single turn.
Icy Wind	Ice	Special	55	95	15	Many Others	—	110	Lowers the targets' Speed by 1 stage.
Imprison	Psychic	Status	—	—	10	Self	—	—	Opposing Pokémon are prevented from using any moves that the user also knows. This move will have no effect against Max Moves. Even if the target was affected by this move before Dynamaxing, the effect will be nullified once it Dynamaxes.
Incinerate	Fire	Special	60	100	15	Many Others	—	110	Burns up any Berries being held by the targets, which makes them unusable.
Inferno	Fire	Special	100	50	5	Normal	—	130	Inflicts the burned status condition on the target.
Infestation	Bug	Special	20	100	20	Normal	○	90	Inflicts damage equal to 1/8 of the target's max HP at the end of each turn for 4–5 turns. The target cannot flee or be switched out of battle during that time.
Ingrain	Grass	Status	—	—	20	Self	—	—	Restores 1/16 of the user's max HP at the end of each turn. The user cannot be switched out after using this move. Ground-type moves can now hit the user even if it is normally immune to them.
Instruct	Psychic	Status	—	—	15	Normal	—	—	The target is forced to use the same move it just used. This move fails if the target move is a Max Move.
Iron Defense	Steel	Status	—	—	15	Self	—	—	Raises the user's Defense by 2 stages.
Iron Head	Steel	Physical	80	100	15	Normal	○	130	Has a 30% chance of making the target flinch (unable to use moves on that turn).
Iron Tail	Steel	Physical	100	75	15	Normal	○	130	Has a 30% chance of lowering the target's Defense by 1 stage.
Jaw Lock	Dark	Physical	80	100	10	Normal	○	130	Both the user and target become unable to flee or be switched out of battle.
King's Shield	Steel	Status	—	—	10	Self	—	—	A high-priority move. The user protects itself from all damage-dealing moves used on the same turn. If an opposing Pokémon uses a move that makes direct contact, its Attack will be lowered by 1 stage. This move becomes more likely to fail if used repeatedly. When used against a Max Move, this move will prevent 3/4 of the damage.
Knock Off	Dark	Physical	65	100	20	Normal	○	120	This move's power is increased by 50% if the target is holding an item. The target is forced to drop its held item, but it gets the item back after the battle.
Laser Focus	Normal	Status	—	—	30	Self	—	—	The user's next move will be a critical hit.
Last Resort	Normal	Physical	140	100	5	Normal	○	140	This move fails unless the user has already used each of its other moves at least once.
Lava Plume	Fire	Special	80	100	15	All Others	—	130	Has a 30% chance of inflicting the burned status condition on the targets.
Leaf Blade	Grass	Physical	90	100	15	Normal	○	130	This move is more likely than average to deliver a critical hit.
Leaf Storm	Grass	Special	130	90	5	Normal	—	140	Lowers the user's Sp. Atk by 2 stages.
Leaf Tornado	Grass	Special	65	90	10	Normal	—	120	Has a 50% chance of lowering the target's accuracy by 1 stage.
Leafage	Grass	Physical	40	100	40	Normal	—	90	

401

Move	Type	Kind	Pow.	Acc.	PP	Range	DA	Max Move Pow.	Notes
Leech Life	Bug	Physical	80	100	10	Normal	○	130	Restores the user's HP by an amount equal to 1/2 of the damage dealt to the target.
Leech Seed	Grass	Status	—	90	10	Normal	—	—	Steals 1/8 of the target's max HP each turn and absorbs it to heal the user. Effects continue even if the user faints or is switched out, with the healing passing to the Pokémon that is switched in.
Leer	Normal	Status	—	100	30	Many Others	—	—	Lowers the targets' Defense by 1 stage.
Lick	Ghost	Physical	30	100	30	Normal	○	90	Has a 30% chance of inflicting the paralysis status condition on the target.
Life Dew	Water	Status	—	100	10	Your Side	—	—	Restores 1/4 of max HP to the user and its ally Pokémon in the battle.
Light Screen	Psychic	Status	—	—	30	Your Side	—	—	Halves the damage Pokémon on your side take from special moves for 5 turns. Effects continue even if the user faints or is switched out.
Liquidation	Water	Physical	85	100	10	Normal	○	130	Has a 20% chance of lowering the target's Defense by 1 stage.
Lock-On	Normal	Status	—	—	5	Normal	—	—	The user's next move against the target will be a sure hit.
Low Kick	Fighting	Physical	—	100	20	Normal	○	100	This move's power becomes greater (max power of 120) the heavier the target is. This move has no effect against Dynamax Pokémon.
Low Sweep	Fighting	Physical	65	100	20	Normal	○	85	Lowers the target's Speed by 1 stage.
Lunge	Bug	Physical	80	100	15	Normal	○	130	Lowers the target's Attack by 1 stage.
Mach Punch	Fighting	Physical	40	100	30	Normal	○	70	A high-priority move.
Magic Coat	Psychic	Status	—	—	15	Self	—	—	A high-priority move. Reflects back moves that attempt to lower the user's stats or inflict status conditions, as well as the effects of moves like Stealth Rock or Taunt.
Magic Powder	Psychic	Status	—	100	20	Normal	—	—	Changes the target's type to Psychic.
Magic Room	Psychic	Status	—	—	10	Both Sides	—	—	No held items will have any effect for 5 turns. Fling cannot be used to throw items while Magic Room is in effect. If Magic Room is used again before its effects end, Magic Room's effects are canceled.
Magical Leaf	Grass	Special	60	—	20	Normal	—	110	
Magnet Rise	Electric	Status	—	—	10	Self	—	—	Makes the user immune to Ground-type moves for 5 turns.
Magnetic Flux	Electric	Status	—	—	20	Your Side	—	—	Raises Defense and Sp. Def by 1 stage each for any Pokémon on your side with the Plus Ability or Minus Ability.
Mean Look	Normal	Status	—	—	5	Normal	—	—	The target becomes unable to flee or be switched out of battle.
Mega Drain	Grass	Special	40	100	15	Normal	—	90	Restores the user's HP by an amount equal to 1/2 of the damage dealt to the target.
Mega Kick	Normal	Physical	120	75	5	Normal	○	140	
Mega Punch	Normal	Physical	80	85	20	Normal	○	130	
Megahorn	Bug	Physical	120	85	10	Normal	○	140	
Memento	Dark	Status	—	100	10	Normal	—	—	The user faints, but the target's Attack and Sp. Atk are lowered by 2 stages each.
Metal Burst	Steel	Physical	—	100	10	Varies	—	100	Targets the opponent that most recently damaged the user with a move. Inflicts 150% of the damage taken.
Metal Claw	Steel	Physical	50	95	35	Normal	○	100	Has a 10% chance of raising the user's Attack by 1 stage.
Metal Sound	Steel	Status	—	85	40	Normal	—	—	Lowers the target's Sp. Def by 2 stages.
Meteor Assault	Fighting	Physical	150	100	5	Normal	—	100	The user cannot act, be switched out, or have items used on it during the next turn.
Meteor Mash	Steel	Physical	90	90	10	Normal	○	130	Has a 20% chance of raising the user's Attack by 1 stage.
Metronome	Normal	Status	—	—	10	Self	—	—	Uses one move randomly chosen from nearly all moves Pokémon can learn.
Mimic	Normal	Status	—	—	10	Normal	—	—	Copies the move the target used on that turn. The copy has the original's max PP and will be retained until the battle ends or the user is switched out. This move fails if the user acts before the target or if it tries to copy Metronome, Struggle, a move that the user already knows, or a Max Move.
Mind Reader	Normal	Status	—	—	5	Normal	—	—	The user's next move against the target will be a sure hit.
Minimize	Normal	Status	—	—	10	Self	—	—	Raises the user's evasiveness by 2 stages. The user will take twice the usual damage, however, if hit by Body Slam, Dragon Rush, Flying Press, Heat Crash, Heavy Slam, or Stomp.
Mirror Coat	Psychic	Special	—	100	20	Varies	—	100	A low-priority move. If the user is hit with a special move during the same turn, this move inflicts twice the damage taken by the user onto the attacker.
Mist	Ice	Status	—	—	30	Your Side	—	—	Protects your side from stat-lowering moves and additional effects for 5 turns.
Misty Terrain	Fairy	Status	—	—	10	Both Sides	—	—	Covers the battlefield with mist for 5 turns. During that time, Pokémon on the ground cannot be afflicted with new status conditions or confusion. Damage done to Pokémon on the ground by Dragon-type moves is also halved during this time.
Moonblast	Fairy	Special	95	100	15	Normal	—	130	Has a 30% chance of lowering the target's Sp. Atk by 1 stage.
Moonlight	Fairy	Status	—	—	5	Self	—	—	Restores 1/2 of the user's max HP in normal weather conditions. Restores 2/3 of the user's max HP in the harsh sunlight weather condition. Restores 1/4 of the user's max HP in the rain/sandstorm/hail weather conditions.

Move	Type	Kind	Pow.	Acc.	PP	Range	DA	Max Move Pow.	Notes
Morning Sun	Normal	Status	—	—	5	Self	—	—	Restores 1/2 of the user's max HP in normal weather conditions. Restores 2/3 of the user's max HP in the harsh sunlight weather condition. Restores 1/4 of the user's max HP in the rain/sandstorm/hail weather conditions.
Mud Shot	Ground	Special	55	95	15	Normal	—	110	Lowers the target's Speed by 1 stage.
Muddy Water	Water	Special	90	85	10	Many Others	—	130	Has a 30% chance of lowering the targets' accuracy by 1 stage.
Mud-Slap	Ground	Special	20	100	10	Normal	—	90	Lowers the target's accuracy by 1 stage.
Multi-Attack	Normal	Physical	120	100	10	Normal	◯	95	This move's type changes according to the memory disc that Silvally is holding. This move will become a different Max Move depending on what memory disc is held by the user.
Mystical Fire	Fire	Special	75	100	10	Normal	—	130	Lowers the target's Sp. Atk by 1 stage.
Nasty Plot	Dark	Status	—	—	20	Self	—	—	Raises the user's Sp. Atk by 2 stages.
Nature Power	Normal	Status	—	—	20	Normal	—	—	Turns into a different move depending on the environment. Cave: Power Gem. Dirt/Sand: Earth Power. Grass / Grassy Terrain: Energy Ball. Electric Terrain: Thunderbolt. Indoors / Link Battle: Tri Attack. Misty Terrain: Moonblast. Psychic Terrain: Psychic. Snow/Ice: Ice Beam. Water surface: Hydro Pump. This move will become Max Guard when used by a Dynamax Pokémon.
Night Shade	Ghost	Special	—	100	15	Normal	—	100	Deals a fixed amount of damage equal to the user's level.
Night Slash	Dark	Physical	70	100	15	Normal	◯	120	This move is more likely than average to deliver a critical hit.
No Retreat	Fighting	Status	—	—	5	Self	—	—	Raises all of the user's stats by 1 stage but makes it unable to flee or be switched out of battle.
Noble Roar	Normal	Status	—	100	30	Normal	—	—	Lowers the target's Attack and Sp. Atk by 1 stage each.
Nuzzle	Electric	Physical	20	100	20	Normal	◯	90	Inflicts the paralysis status condition on the target.
Obstruct	Dark	Status	—	100	10	Self	—	—	A high-priority move. The user protects itself from all damage-dealing moves used on the same turn. If an opposing Pokémon uses a move that makes direct contact, its Defense will be lowered by 2 stages. This move becomes more likely to fail if used repeatedly.
Octazooka	Water	Special	65	85	10	Normal	—	120	Has a 50% chance of lowering the target's accuracy by 1 stage.
Octolock	Fighting	Status	—	100	15	Normal	—	—	Lowers the target's Defense and Sp. Def by 1 stage each turn. The target becomes unable to flee or be switched out of battle. The effect ends if the user leaves the battlefield.
Outrage	Dragon	Physical	120	100	10	1 Random	◯	140	Attacks consecutively over 2–3 turns. The user cannot choose other moves during this time, and it becomes confused afterward.
Overdrive	Electric	Special	80	100	10	Many Others	—	130	The sound of the move differs in Amped Form and Low Key Form.
Overheat	Fire	Special	130	90	5	Normal	—	140	Lowers the user's Sp. Atk by 2 stages.
Pain Split	Normal	Status	—	—	20	Normal	—	—	The user's and target's HP are added, then divided equally between them.
Parabolic Charge	Electric	Special	65	100	20	All Others	—	120	Restores the user's HP by an amount equal to 1/2 of the damage dealt to the targets.
Parting Shot	Dark	Status	—	100	20	Normal	—	—	Lowers the target's Attack and Sp. Atk by 1 stage each. After attacking, the user is switched out and another Pokémon from the party is sent onto the battlefield.
Pay Day	Normal	Physical	40	100	20	Normal	—	90	Pays out money after battle. The amount depends on the user's level and the number of times the move was used (₽5 × user's level × times used).
Payback	Dark	Physical	50	100	10	Normal	◯	100	This move's power is doubled if the user strikes after the target uses a move or has an item used on it.
Peck	Flying	Physical	35	100	35	Normal	◯	90	
Perish Song	Normal	Status	—	—	5	All	—	—	All Pokémon on the battlefield when this move is used will faint after 3 turns unless switched out.
Petal Blizzard	Grass	Physical	90	100	15	All Others	—	130	
Petal Dance	Grass	Special	120	100	10	1 Random	◯	140	Attacks consecutively over 2–3 turns. The user cannot choose other moves during this time, and it becomes confused afterward.
Phantom Force	Ghost	Physical	90	100	10	Normal	◯	130	This move takes 2 turns. The user disappears on the first turn and attacks on the second. Strikes even if the target has used a protection move and removes the protection move's effect.
Pin Missile	Bug	Physical	25	95	20	Normal	—	130	Attacks 2–5 times in a row in a single turn.
Play Nice	Normal	Status	—	—	20	Normal	—	—	Lowers the target's Attack by 1 stage.
Play Rough	Fairy	Physical	90	90	10	Normal	◯	130	Has a 10% chance of lowering the target's Attack by 1 stage.
Pluck	Flying	Physical	60	100	20	Normal	◯	110	If the target is holding a Berry, the user eats that Berry and uses its battle effect if it has one.
Poison Fang	Poison	Physical	50	100	15	Normal	◯	75	Has a 50% chance of inflicting the badly poisoned status condition on the target.
Poison Gas	Poison	Status	—	90	40	Many Others	—	—	Inflicts the adoisoned status condition on the targets.
Poison Jab	Poison	Physical	80	100	20	Normal	◯	90	Has a 30% chance of inflicting the poisoned status condition on the target.
Poison Powder	Poison	Status	—	75	35	Normal	—	—	Inflicts the poisoned status condition on the target.
Poison Sting	Poison	Physical	15	100	35	Normal	—	70	Has a 30% chance of inflicting the poisoned status condition on the target.

403

Move	Type	Kind	Pow.	Acc.	PP	Range	DA	Max Move Pow.	Notes
Poison Tail	Poison	Physical	50	100	25	Normal	○	75	Has a 10% chance of inflicting the poisoned status condition on the target. This move is more likely than average to deliver a critical hit.
Pollen Puff	Bug	Special	90	100	15	Normal	—	130	When targeting an ally, this move restores 1/2 of the ally's max HP. This move becomes a damaging move when transformed into a Max Move.
Pound	Normal	Physical	40	100	35	Normal	○	90	
Powder Snow	Ice	Special	40	100	25	Many Others	—	90	Has a 10% chance of inflicting the frozen status condition on the targets.
Power Gem	Rock	Special	80	100	20	Normal	—	130	
Power Split	Psychic	Status	—	—	10	Normal	—	—	The user's and the target's Attack and Sp. Atk are each added, then divided equally between them.
Power Swap	Psychic	Status	—	—	10	Normal	—	—	Swaps the user's and target's stat changes to both their Attack and Sp. Atk.
Power Trick	Psychic	Status	—	—	10	Self	—	—	Swaps the user's original Attack and Defense stats. (Does not swap stat changes.)
Power Trip	Dark	Physical	20	100	10	Normal	○	130	This move's power increases by 20 (max power of 860) for each stage the user's stats have been boosted.
Power Whip	Grass	Physical	120	85	10	Normal	○	140	
Power-Up Punch	Fighting	Physical	40	100	20	Normal	○	70	Raises the user's Attack by 1 stage.
Present	Normal	Physical	—	90	15	Normal	—	100	This move's power varies between 40 (40% chance), 80 (30% chance), and 120 (10% chance). It also has a 20% chance of restoring 1/4 of the target's max HP. When the healing effect occurs against a Dynamax Pokémon, it won't reduce its mysterious barrier's meter.
Protect	Normal	Status	—	—	10	Self	—	—	A high-priority move. The user protects itself from all damage-dealing moves and most status moves on the same turn. This move becomes more likely to fail if used repeatedly. When used against a Max Move, this move will prevent 3/4 of the damage.
Psybeam	Psychic	Special	65	100	20	Normal	—	120	Has a 10% chance of making the target confused.
Psych Up	Normal	Status	—	—	10	Normal	—	—	Copies the target's stat changes over to the user.
Psychic	Psychic	Special	90	100	10	Normal	—	130	Has a 10% chance of lowering the target's Sp. Def by 1 stage.
Psychic Fangs	Psychic	Physical	85	100	10	Normal	○	130	This move is not affected by Aurora Veil or Reflect. It removes the effects of Aurora Veil, Light Screen, and Reflect.
Psychic Terrain	Psychic	Status	—	—	10	Both Sides	—	—	Covers the battlefield with psychic energy for 5 turns. During that time, Pokémon on the ground will be able to do 30% more damage with Psychic-type moves and will evade high-priority moves.
Psycho Cut	Psychic	Physical	70	100	20	Normal	—	120	This move is more likely than average to deliver a critical hit.
Psycho Shift	Psychic	Status	—	100	10	Normal	—	—	Shifts the user's status condition (paralysis, poisoned, badly poisoned, burned, or asleep) to the target, removing it from the user.
Psyshock	Psychic	Special	80	100	10	Normal	—	130	Damage dealt by this move is calculated using the target's Defense rather than the target's Sp. Def.
Purify	Poison	Status	—	—	20	Normal	—	—	Heals the target's status condition, then restores 1/2 of the user's max HP. This move fails if the target does not have a status condition.
Pyro Ball	Fire	Physical	130	95	10	Normal	—	140	Has a 10% chance of inflicting the burned status condition on the target.
Quash	Dark	Status	—	100	15	Normal	—	—	This move makes the target act last during the current turn. This move fails if the user doesn't act before the target.
Quick Attack	Normal	Physical	40	100	30	Normal	○	90	A high-priority move.
Quick Guard	Fighting	Status	—	—	15	Your Side	—	—	A high-priority move. Protects your side from other high-priority moves used on the same turn.
Quiver Dance	Bug	Status	—	—	20	Self	—	—	Raises the user's Sp. Atk, Sp. Def, and Speed by 1 stage each.
Rage Powder	Bug	Status	—	—	20	Self	—	—	A high-priority move. Opposing Pokémon aim only at the user for the rest of the turn in which this move is used. This move will cause Dynamax Pokémon to aim only at the user. However, the additional effects of Max Moves will occur as usual.
Rain Dance	Water	Status	—	—	5	Both Sides	—	—	Changes the weather condition to rain for 5 turns, boosting the power of Water-type moves by 50% and reducing the power of Fire-type moves by 50%.
Rapid Spin	Normal	Physical	50	100	40	Normal	○	100	Releases the user from moves such as Bind, Leech Seed, and Wrap and removes the effects of moves such as Spikes from the user's side of the battlefield. Also raises the user's Speed by 1 stage.
Razor Leaf	Grass	Physical	55	95	25	Many Others	—	110	This move is more likely than average to deliver a critical hit.
Razor Shell	Water	Physical	75	95	10	Normal	○	130	Has a 50% chance of lowering the target's Defense by 1 stage.
Recover	Normal	Status	—	—	10	Self	—	—	Restores 1/2 of the user's max HP.
Recycle	Normal	Status	—	—	10	Self	—	—	Allows the user to regain a held item it had already used during the battle.
Reflect	Psychic	Status	—	—	20	Your Side	—	—	Halves the damage Pokémon on your side take from physical moves for 5 turns. Effects continue even if the user faints or is switched out.
Reflect Type	Normal	Status	—	—	15	Normal	—	—	The user becomes the same type as the target.
Rest	Psychic	Status	—	—	10	Self	—	—	Fully restores HP and heals status conditions of the user but makes the user sleep for 2 turns.
Retaliate	Normal	Physical	70	100	5	Normal	○	120	This move's power is doubled if an ally fainted during the previous turn.

Move	Type	Kind	Pow.	Acc.	PP	Range	DA	Max Move Pow.	Notes
Revenge	Fighting	Physical	60	100	10	Normal	○	80	A low-priority move. This move's power is doubled if the user has taken damage from the target on the same turn.
Reversal	Fighting	Physical	—	100	15	Normal	○	100	This move's power becomes greater (max power of 200) the lower the user's HP is.
Roar	Normal	Status	—	—	20	Normal	—	—	A low-priority move. Ends battles against wild Pokémon if the target's level is lower than the user's. Forces the target to swap out in a Trainer battle, unless there are no other Pokémon available to battle. This move has no effect against Dynamax Pokémon.
Rock Blast	Rock	Physical	25	90	10	Normal	—	130	Attacks 2–5 times in a row in a single turn.
Rock Polish	Rock	Status	—	—	20	Self	—	—	Raises the user's Speed by 2 stages.
Rock Slide	Rock	Physical	75	90	10	Many Others	—	130	Has a 30% chance of making the targets flinch (unable to use moves on that turn).
Rock Smash	Fighting	Physical	40	100	15	Normal	○	70	Has a 50% chance of lowering the target's Defense by 1 stage.
Rock Throw	Rock	Physical	50	90	15	Normal	—	100	
Rock Tomb	Rock	Physical	60	95	15	Normal	—	110	Lowers the target's Speed by 1 stage.
Rock Wrecker	Rock	Physical	150	90	5	Normal	—	150	The user cannot act, be switched out, or have items used on it during the next turn.
Role Play	Psychic	Status	—	—	10	Normal	—	—	Copies the target's Ability. Fails with certain Abilities, however.
Rollout	Rock	Physical	30	90	20	Normal	○	90	Attacks consecutively over 5 turns or until it misses. The user cannot choose other moves during this time. This move's power is doubled (max power of 480) with every successful hit. This move's power is further doubled if the user has also used Defense Curl.
Roost	Flying	Status	—	—	10	Self	—	—	Restores 1/2 of the user's max HP but takes away the Flying type from the user for that turn.
Round	Normal	Special	60	100	15	Normal	—	110	When multiple Pokémon select this move in a turn, the first one to use it is followed immediately by any allies and the power is doubled for those allies.
Sacred Sword	Fighting	Physical	90	100	15	Normal	○	90	Ignores the stat changes of the target when dealing damage.
Safeguard	Normal	Status	—	—	25	Your Side	—	—	Protects your side from status conditions and confusion for 5 turns. Effects continue even if the user faints or is switched out.
Sand Attack	Ground	Status	—	100	15	Normal	—	—	Lowers the target's accuracy by 1 stage.
Sand Tomb	Ground	Physical	35	85	15	Normal	—	90	Inflicts damage equal to 1/8 of the target's max HP at the end of each turn for 4–5 turns. The target cannot flee or be switched out of battle during that time.
Sandstorm	Rock	Status	—	—	10	Both Sides	—	—	Changes the weather condition to sandstorm for 5 turns, boosting the Sp. Def of Rock-type Pokémon by 50%. All Pokémon other than Ground, Rock, and Steel types take damage at the end of each turn equal to 1/16 of their max HP.
Scald	Water	Special	80	100	15	Normal	—	130	Has a 30% chance of inflicting the burned status condition on the target. This move can be used even if the user is frozen and will thaw the user. This move will also thaw out a frozen target.
Scary Face	Normal	Status	—	100	10	Normal	—	—	Lowers the target's Speed by 2 stages.
Scratch	Normal	Physical	40	100	35	Normal	○	90	
Screech	Normal	Status	—	85	40	Normal	—	—	Lowers the target's Defense by 2 stages.
Seed Bomb	Grass	Physical	80	100	15	Normal	—	130	
Seismic Toss	Fighting	Physical	—	100	20	Normal	○	75	Deals a fixed amount of damage equal to the user's level.
Self-Destruct	Normal	Physical	200	100	5	All Others	—	150	The user faints after using this move.
Shadow Ball	Ghost	Special	80	100	15	Normal	—	130	Has a 20% chance of lowering the target's Sp. Def by 1 stage.
Shadow Claw	Ghost	Physical	70	100	15	Normal	○	120	This move is more likely than average to deliver a critical hit.
Shadow Punch	Ghost	Physical	60	—	20	Normal	○	110	
Shadow Sneak	Ghost	Physical	40	100	30	Normal	○	90	A high-priority move.
Sheer Cold	Ice	Special	—	30	5	Normal	—	130	The target faints with one hit. The higher the user's level is compared to the target's, the more accurate the move is. If the target's level is higher than the user's, this move fails. Accuracy is also lowered when a Pokémon that is not an Ice type uses it. Does not hit Ice-type Pokémon. If this move hits a Dynamax Pokémon, this move will destroy 2 segments of the mysterious barrier's meter.
Shell Smash	Normal	Status	—	—	15	Self	—	—	Lowers the user's Defense and Sp. Def by 1 stage each and raises the user's Attack, Sp. Atk, and Speed by 2 stages each.
Shell Trap	Fire	Special	150	100	5	Many Others	—	150	A low-priority move. Sets a trap at the start of the turn. If the user is hit by a physical move during the same turn, the trap explodes and deals damage.
Shift Gear	Steel	Status	—	—	10	Self	—	—	Raises the user's Speed by 2 stages and Attack by 1 stage.
Shock Wave	Electric	Special	60	—	20	Normal	—	110	
Simple Beam	Normal	Status	—	100	15	Normal	—	—	Changes the target's Ability to Simple. Fails with certain Abilities, however.
Sing	Normal	Status	—	55	15	Normal	—	—	Inflicts the asleep status condition on the target.
Skill Swap	Psychic	Status	—	—	10	Normal	—	—	Swaps the user's and the target's Abilities. Fails with certain Abilities and on Dynamax Pokémon, however.

Move	Type	Kind	Pow.	Acc.	PP	Range	DA	Max Move Pow.	Notes
Skull Bash	Normal	Physical	130	100	10	Normal	○	140	This move takes 2 turns. The user raises its Defense by 1 stage on the first turn and attacks on the second.
Sky Attack	Flying	Physical	140	90	5	Normal	—	140	This move takes 2 turns. The user builds power on the first turn and attacks on the second. Has a 30% chance of making the target flinch (unable to use moves on that turn). This move is more likely than average to deliver a critical hit.
Slack Off	Normal	Status	—	—	10	Self	—	—	Restores 1/2 of the user's max HP.
Slam	Normal	Physical	80	75	20	Normal	○	130	
Slash	Normal	Physical	70	100	20	Normal	○	120	This move is more likely than average to deliver a critical hit.
Sleep Powder	Grass	Status	—	75	15	Normal	—	—	Inflicts the asleep status condition on the target.
Sleep Talk	Normal	Status	—	—	10	Self	—	—	This move only works when the user is asleep. Randomly uses one of the user's other moves.
Sludge	Poison	Special	65	100	20	Normal	—	85	Has a 30% chance of inflicting the poisoned status condition on the target.
Sludge Bomb	Poison	Special	90	100	10	Normal	—	90	Has a 30% chance of inflicting the poisoned status condition on the target.
Sludge Wave	Poison	Special	95	100	10	All Others	—	90	Has a 10% chance of inflicting the poisoned status condition on the targets.
Smack Down	Rock	Physical	50	100	15	Normal	—	100	Makes Ground-type moves able to hit the target even if it is normally immune to them. This move will also bring down Pokémon that are in the sky due to moves such as Bounce or Fly, causing those moves to fail.
Smart Strike	Steel	Physical	70	—	10	Normal	○	120	
Smog	Poison	Special	30	70	20	Normal	—	70	Has a 40% chance of inflicting the poisoned status condition on the target.
Smokescreen	Normal	Status	—	100	20	Normal	—	—	Lowers the target's accuracy by 1 stage.
Snap Trap	Grass	Physical	35	100	15	Normal	○	90	Inflicts damage equal to 1/8 of the target's max HP at the end of each turn for 4–5 turns. The target cannot flee or be switched out of battle during that time.
Snarl	Dark	Special	55	95	15	Many Others	—	110	Lowers the targets' Sp. Atk by 1 stage.
Snipe Shot	Water	Special	80	100	15	Normal	—	130	The user can select a target freely, ignoring the effects of the Ability Storm Drain or the moves Ally Switch, Follow Me, and Rage Powder.
Snore	Normal	Special	50	100	15	Normal	—	100	This move only works when the user is asleep. Has a 30% chance of making the target flinch (unable to use moves on that turn).
Soak	Water	Status	—	100	20	Normal	—	—	Changes the target's type to Water.
Solar Beam	Grass	Special	120	100	10	Normal	—	140	This move takes 2 turns. The user builds power on the first turn and attacks on the second. In the harsh sunlight weather condition, this move only takes 1 turn. In the rain/sandstorm/hail weather conditions, this move's power is halved.
Solar Blade	Grass	Physical	125	100	10	Normal	○	140	This move takes 2 turns. The user builds power on the first turn and attacks on the second. In the harsh sunlight weather condition, this move only takes 1 turn. In the rain/sandstorm/hail weather conditions, this move's power is halved.
Spark	Electric	Physical	65	100	20	Normal	○	120	Has a 30% chance of inflicting the paralysis status condition on the target.
Sparkling Aria	Water	Special	90	100	10	All Others	—	130	Heals targets of the burned status condition.
Speed Swap	Psychic	Status	—	—	10	Normal	—	—	Swaps the user's and the target's Speeds.
Spikes	Ground	Status	—	—	20	Other Side	—	—	Damages Pokémon as they are sent out on the opposing side. Can be used up to 2 more times to increase damage. Inflicts damage equal to 1/8 of max HP on first use, 1/6 of max HP on second use, and 1/4 of max HP on third use.
Spiky Shield	Grass	Status	—	—	10	Self	—	—	A high-priority move. The user protects itself from all damage-dealing moves and most status moves on the same turn. If an opposing Pokémon uses a move that makes direct contact, the attacker will be damaged for 1/8 of its max HP. This move becomes more likely to fail if used repeatedly. When used against a Max Move, this move will prevent 3/4 of the damage.
Spirit Break	Fairy	Physical	75	100	15	Normal	○	130	Lowers the target's Sp. Atk by 1 stage.
Spit Up	Normal	Special	—	100	10	Normal	—	100	This move's power becomes greater (max power of 300) the more times the user has used Stockpile. This move fails if the user has not used Stockpile first. If the user's Defense and Sp. Def have been boosted by Stockpile, those boosts are reset.
Spite	Ghost	Status	—	100	10	Normal	—	—	Deducts 4 PP from the last move the target used.
Splash	Normal	Status	—	—	40	Self	—	—	Has no effect.
Spore	Grass	Status	—	100	15	Normal	—	—	Inflicts the asleep status condition on the target.
Stealth Rock	Rock	Status	—	—	20	Other Side	—	—	Damages Pokémon as they are sent out on the opposing side. This damage is Rock type and subject to type matchups.
Steel Beam	Steel	Special	140	95	5	Normal	—	140	The user loses 1/2 of its max HP to deal damage to the target.
Steel Wing	Steel	Physical	70	90	25	Normal	○	120	Has a 10% chance of raising the user's Defense by 1 stage.
Sticky Web	Bug	Status	—	—	20	Other Side	—	—	Lowers the Speed of any Pokémon sent out on the opposing side by 1 stage.
Stockpile	Normal	Status	—	—	20	Self	—	—	Raises the user's Defense and Sp. Def by 1 stage each. Its effect stacks up to three times.

Move	Type	Kind	Pow.	Acc.	PP	Range	DA	Max Move Pow.	Notes
Stomp	Normal	Physical	65	100	20	Normal	○	120	Has a 30% chance of making the target flinch (unable to use moves on that turn). If the target has used Minimize, this move will be a sure hit and its power will be doubled.
Stomping Tantrum	Ground	Physical	75	100	10	Normal	○	130	This move's power is doubled if the user's move missed or otherwise failed during the previous turn.
Stone Edge	Rock	Physical	100	80	5	Normal	—	130	This move is more likely than average to deliver a critical hit.
Stored Power	Psychic	Special	20	100	10	Normal	—	130	This move's power increases by 20 (max power of 860) for each stage the user's stats have been boosted.
Storm Throw	Fighting	Physical	60	100	10	Normal	○	80	Always delivers a critical hit.
Strange Steam	Fairy	Special	90	95	10	Normal	—	130	Has a 20% chance of making the target confused.
Strength	Normal	Physical	80	100	15	Normal	○	130	
Strength Sap	Grass	Status	—	100	10	Normal	—	—	Restores the user's HP by an amount equal to the target's Attack, then lowers the target's Attack by 1 stage.
String Shot	Bug	Status	—	95	40	Many Others	—	—	Lowers the targets' Speed by 2 stages.
Struggle	Normal	Physical	50	—	1	1 Random	○	—	This move becomes available when all other moves are out of PP, and it inflicts damage to the target regardless of type matchup. The user also takes damage equal to 1/4 of its max HP when it uses this move. If a Dynamax Pokémon runs out of PP, it will use Struggle. Struggle will not become a Max Move.
Struggle Bug	Bug	Special	50	100	20	Many Others	—	100	Lowers the targets' Sp. Atk by 1 stage.
Stuff Cheeks	Normal	Status	—	—	10	Self	—	—	If the user is holding a Berry, it eats that Berry and uses its battle effect if it has one. This also raises the user's Defense by 2 stages.
Stun Spore	Grass	Status	—	75	30	Normal	—	—	Inflicts the paralysis status condition on the target.
Submission	Fighting	Physical	80	80	20	Normal	○	90	The user also takes 1/4 of the damage dealt to the target.
Substitute	Normal	Status	—	—	10	Self	—	—	Depletes 1/4 of the user's max HP to create a substitute for the user that protects it from moves that lower stats or inflict status conditions. The substitute also takes damage in the user's place until the substitute runs out of HP. The substitute will disappear if the user Dynamaxes while the substitute is still active.
Sucker Punch	Dark	Physical	70	100	5	Normal	○	120	A high-priority move. Deals damage only if the target's chosen move is a damage-dealing move.
Sunny Day	Fire	Status	—	—	5	Both Sides	—	—	Changes the weather condition to harsh sunlight for 5 turns, boosting the power of Fire-type moves by 50% and reducing the power of Water-type moves by 50%.
Super Fang	Normal	Physical	—	90	10	Normal	○	100	Halves the target's HP.
Superpower	Fighting	Physical	120	100	5	Normal	○	95	Lowers the user's Attack and Defense by 1 stage each.
Supersonic	Normal	Status	—	55	20	Normal	—	—	Makes the target confused.
Surf	Water	Special	90	100	15	All Others	—	130	This move hits and has doubled power against targets that are underwater due to using Dive.
Swagger	Normal	Status	—	85	15	Normal	—	—	Makes the target confused but also raises its Attack by 2 stages.
Swallow	Normal	Status	—	—	10	Self	—	—	Restores the user's HP based on how many times the user has used Stockpile. This move fails if the user has not used Stockpile first. If the user's Defense and Sp. Def have been boosted by Stockpile, those boosts are reset.
Sweet Kiss	Fairy	Status	—	75	10	Normal	—	—	Makes the target confused.
Sweet Scent	Normal	Status	—	100	20	Many Others	—	—	Lowers the targets' evasiveness by 2 stages.
Swift	Normal	Special	60	—	20	Many Others	—	110	
Switcheroo	Dark	Status	—	100	10	Normal	—	—	Swaps the user's and the target's held items.
Swords Dance	Normal	Status	—	—	20	Self	—	—	Raises the user's Attack by 2 stages.
Synthesis	Grass	Status	—	—	5	Self	—	—	Restores 1/2 of the user's max HP in normal weather conditions. Restores 2/3 of the user's max HP in the harsh sunlight weather condition. Restores 1/4 of the user's max HP in the rain/sandstorm/hail weather conditions.
Tackle	Normal	Physical	40	100	35	Normal	○	90	
Tail Slap	Normal	Physical	25	85	10	Normal	○	130	Attacks 2–5 times in a row in a single turn.
Tail Whip	Normal	Status	—	100	30	Many Others	—	—	Lowers the targets' Defense by 1 stage.
Tailwind	Flying	Status	—	—	15	Your Side	—	—	Doubles the Speed of the Pokémon on your side for 4 turns.
Take Down	Normal	Physical	90	85	20	Normal	○	130	The user also takes 1/4 of the damage dealt to the target.
Tar Shot	Rock	Status	—	100	15	Normal	—	—	Lowers the target's Speed by 1 stage and makes it weaker to Fire-type moves, doubling the damage it takes from them.
Taunt	Dark	Status	—	100	20	Normal	—	—	Prevents the target from using status moves for 3 turns.
Tearful Look	Normal	Status	—	—	20	Normal	—	—	Lowers the target's Attack and Sp. Atk by 1 stage each.
Teatime	Normal	Status	—	—	10	All	—	—	Forces all the Pokémon on the battlefield to eat their Berry if they are holding one.
Teeter Dance	Normal	Status	—	100	20	All Others	—	—	Makes all Pokémon on the battlefield confused, except for the user.

407

Move	Type	Kind	Pow.	Acc.	PP	Range	DA	Max Move Pow.	Notes
Teleport	Psychic	Status	—	—	20	Self	—	—	A low-priority move. This move ends wild Pokémon battles. In a Trainer battle, the user teleports out and another Pokémon from the party is sent onto the battlefield. This move fails if there are no other Pokémon available to battle.
Thief	Dark	Physical	60	100	25	Normal	○	110	When the target is holding an item and the user is not, the user can steal that item. When the target is not holding an item, this move will function as a simple damage-dealing move.
Thrash	Normal	Physical	120	100	10	1 Random	○	140	Attacks consecutively over 2–3 turns. The user cannot choose other moves during this time and becomes confused afterward.
Throat Chop	Dark	Physical	80	100	15	Normal	○	130	The target will not be able to use sound-based moves for 2 turns. Moves that normally would be prevented can still be used as Max Moves by Dynamax Pokémon.
Thunder	Electric	Special	110	70	10	Normal	—	140	Has a 30% chance of inflicting the paralysis status condition on the target. Is 100% accurate in the rain weather condition and 50% accurate in the harsh sunlight weather condition. This move hits targets that are in the sky due to moves such as Bounce or Fly.
Thunder Fang	Electric	Physical	65	95	15	Normal	○	120	Has a 10% chance of inflicting the paralysis status condition on the target or making the target flinch (unable to use moves on that turn).
Thunder Punch	Electric	Physical	75	100	15	Normal	○	130	Has a 10% chance of inflicting the paralysis status condition on the target.
Thunder Shock	Electric	Special	40	100	30	Normal	—	90	Has a 10% chance of inflicting the paralysis status condition on the target.
Thunder Wave	Electric	Status	—	90	20	Normal	—	—	Inflicts the paralysis status condition on the target.
Thunderbolt	Electric	Special	90	100	15	Normal	—	130	Has a 10% chance of inflicting the paralysis status condition on the target.
Tickle	Normal	Status	—	100	20	Normal	—	—	Lowers the target's Attack and Defense by 1 stage each.
Topsy-Turvy	Dark	Status	—	—	20	Normal	—	—	Inverts the effects of any stat changes affecting the target.
Torment	Dark	Status	—	100	15	Normal	—	—	Makes the target unable to use the same move twice in a row. This move will fail when used against a Dynamax Pokémon. Even if the target was affected by this move before Dynamaxing, the effect will be nullified once it Dynamaxes.
Toxic	Poison	Status	—	90	10	Normal	—	—	Inflicts the badly poisoned status condition on the target. This move never misses if used by a Poison-type Pokémon.
Toxic Spikes	Poison	Status	—	—	20	Other Side	—	—	Lays a trap of poison spikes on the opposing side that inflicts the poisoned status condition on Pokémon that switch into battle. Using Toxic Spikes twice inflicts the badly poisoned status condition. This move's effects end if a Poison-type Pokémon switches into battle on the opposing side.
Transform	Normal	Status	—	—	10	Normal	—	—	The user transforms into a copy of the target. The user has the same moves and Ability as the target (all moves have 5 PP).
Tri Attack	Normal	Special	80	100	10	Normal	—	130	Has a 20% chance of inflicting the paralysis, burned, or frozen status condition on the target.
Trick	Psychic	Status	—	100	10	Normal	—	—	Swaps the user's and the target's held items.
Trick Room	Psychic	Status	—	—	5	Both Sides	—	—	Acts after all other moves on the same turn. For 5 turns, Pokémon with lower Speed go first. High-priority moves still go first. If Trick Room is used again before its effects end, Trick Room's effects are canceled.
Trick-or-Treat	Ghost	Status	—	100	20	Normal	—	—	Gives the target the Ghost type in addition to its original type(s).
Triple Kick	Fighting	Physical	10	90	10	Normal	○	80	Attacks 3 times in a row in a single turn. Power increases (max power of 30) each time it hits.
Trop Kick	Grass	Physical	70	100	15	Normal	○	120	Lowers the target's Attack by 1 stage.
Twister	Dragon	Special	40	100	20	Many Others	—	90	Has a 20% chance of making the targets flinch (unable to use moves on that turn). This move hits targets that are in the sky due to moves such as Bounce or Fly and has doubled power against them.
Uproar	Normal	Special	90	100	10	1 Random	—	130	The user makes an uproar for 3 turns. During that time, no Pokémon can fall asleep.
U-turn	Bug	Physical	70	100	20	Normal	○	120	After attacking, the user switches out with another Pokémon in the party.
Vacuum Wave	Fighting	Special	40	100	30	Normal	—	70	A high-priority move.
Venom Drench	Poison	Status	—	100	20	Many Others	—	—	Lowers the Attack, Sp. Atk, and Speed of opposing Pokémon afflicted with the poisoned or badly poisoned status conditions by 1 stage each.
Venoshock	Poison	Special	65	100	10	Normal	—	85	This move's power is doubled if the target has the poisoned or badly poisoned status condition.
Vise Grip	Normal	Physical	55	100	30	Normal	○	110	
Vital Throw	Fighting	Physical	70	—	10	Normal	○	85	A low-priority move.
Volt Switch	Electric	Special	70	100	20	Normal	—	120	After attacking, the user switches out with another Pokémon in the party.
Volt Tackle	Electric	Physical	120	100	15	Normal	○	140	The user also takes 1/3 of the damage dealt to the target. Has a 10% chance of inflicting the paralysis status condition on the target.
Water Gun	Water	Special	40	100	25	Normal	—	90	

Move	Type	Kind	Pow.	Acc.	PP	Range	DA	Max Move Pow.	Notes
Water Pledge	Water	Special	80	100	10	Normal	—	130	When this is combined with Fire Pledge or Grass Pledge, the power and effect change. If this is combined with Fire Pledge, the power of this move becomes 150 and it remains a Water-type move. It will also make it more likely that your team's moves will trigger any additional effects they might have for 4 turns. If this is combined with Grass Pledge, the power of this move becomes 150 and it becomes a Grass-type move. It will also lower the Speed of opposing Pokémon for 4 turns.
Water Pulse	Water	Special	60	100	20	Normal	—	110	Has a 20% chance of making the target confused.
Water Shuriken	Water	Special	15	100	20	Normal	—	90	A high-priority move. Attacks 2–5 times in a row in a single turn.
Water Spout	Water	Special	150	100	5	Many Others	—	150	The lower the user's HP, the lower this move's power becomes.
Waterfall	Water	Physical	80	100	15	Normal	◯	130	Has a 20% chance of making the target flinch (unable to use moves on that turn).
Weather Ball	Normal	Special	50	100	10	Normal	—	130	In special weather conditions, this move's type changes and its power is doubled. Harsh sunlight weather condition: Fire type. Rain weather condition: Water type. Hail weather condition: Ice type. Sandstorm weather condition: Rock type. The Max Move this move becomes is determined by the weather condition at the time the move is used.
Whirlpool	Water	Special	35	85	15	Normal	—	90	Inflicts damage equal to 1/8 of the target's max HP at the end of each turn for 4–5 turns. The target cannot flee or be switched out of battle during that time. This move hits and has doubled power against targets that are underwater due to using Dive.
Whirlwind	Normal	Status	—	—	20	Normal	—	—	A low-priority move. Ends battles against wild Pokémon if the target's level is lower than the user's. Forces the target to swap out in a Trainer battle, unless there are no other Pokémon available to battle.
Wide Guard	Rock	Status	—	—	10	Your Side	—	—	A high-priority move. Protects your side from the effects of any moves used on the same turn that target multiple Pokémon.
Wild Charge	Electric	Physical	90	100	15	Normal	◯	130	The user also takes 1/4 of the damage dealt to the target.
Will-O-Wisp	Fire	Status	—	85	15	Normal	—	—	Inflicts the burned status condition on the target.
Wing Attack	Flying	Physical	60	100	35	Normal	◯	110	
Wish	Normal	Status	—	—	10	Self	—	—	Restores 1/2 of the user's max HP at the end of the next turn. If the user is switched out, the Pokémon that takes its place will be healed instead.
Withdraw	Water	Status	—	—	40	Self	—	—	Raises the user's Defense by 1 stage.
Wonder Room	Psychic	Status	—	—	10	Both Sides	—	—	Each Pokémon has its Defense and Sp. Def stats swapped for 5 turns. If Wonder Room is used again before its effects end, Wonder Room's effects are canceled.
Wood Hammer	Grass	Physical	120	100	15	Normal	◯	140	The user also takes 1/3 of the damage dealt to the target.
Work Up	Normal	Status	—	—	30	Self	—	—	Raises the user's Attack and Sp. Atk by 1 stage each.
Worry Seed	Grass	Status	—	100	10	Normal	—	—	Changes the target's Ability to Insomnia. Fails with certain Abilities, however.
Wrap	Normal	Physical	15	90	20	Normal	◯	90	Inflicts damage equal to 1/8 of the target's max HP at the end of each turn for 4–5 turns. The target cannot flee or be switched out of battle during that time.
X-Scissor	Bug	Physical	80	100	15	Normal	◯	130	
Yawn	Normal	Status	—	—	10	Normal	—	—	Inflicts the asleep status condition on the target at the end of the next turn unless the target switches out.
Zap Cannon	Electric	Special	120	50	5	Normal	—	140	Inflicts the paralysis status condition on the target.
Zen Headbutt	Psychic	Physical	80	90	15	Normal	◯	130	Has a 20% chance of making the target flinch (unable to use moves on that turn).
Zing Zap	Electric	Physical	80	100	10	Normal	◯	130	Has a 30% chance of making the target flinch (unable to use moves on that turn).

Priority Moves

In addition to all the other factors that affect how moves deal damage, such as their range and their power, there is also priority. Most moves have no priority. That means that for those moves, it is only the Speed stat of the Pokémon in the battle that will decide which move is used first in a turn. If your Pokémon has a higher Speed stat than any other Pokémon on the battlefield, then it'll get to use its move first.

But priority overrules the Speed stat. If a move has higher priority, it will be used first in a turn—no matter how high or low a Pokémon's Speed might be! On the other hand, moves with low priority will be used later in a turn, even if the Pokémon using them would usually be very speedy.

In the table below, you can see how moves fall on these scales of high and low priority. As you move up and down through the rows, you can see how different groups of moves have ever higher or lower priority. For example, if two Pokémon used Extreme Speed and Aqua Jet, the one using Extreme Speed would go first and Aqua Jet second—no matter their Speed. But if the Pokémon used Extreme Speed and Fake Out, then Fake Out would go first, because it's higher in the priority tiers. Study the table below if you want to become a pro at using priority moves!

❗ There are other ways to play with priority and Speed, like using the move Trick Room. Experienced Trainers may use these strategies on you, so be prepared for anything!

	Moves
High Priority ↑	Helping Hand
	Baneful Bunker, Detect, Endure, King's Shield, Magic Coat, Max Guard, Obstruct, Protect, Spiky Shield
	Crafty Shield, Fake Out, Quick Guard, Wide Guard
	Ally Switch, Extreme Speed, Feint, First Impression, Follow Me, Rage Powder
	Aqua Jet, Baby-Doll Eyes, Bullet Punch, Ice Shard, Mach Punch, Quick Attack, Shadow Sneak, Sucker Punch, Vacuum Wave, Water Shuriken
	All moves that are not listed here have standard priority
	Vital Throw
	Focus Punch, Shell Trap
	Avalanche, Revenge
	Counter, Mirror Coat
	Circle Throw, Dragon Tail, Roar, Teleport, Whirlwind
Low Priority ↓	Trick Room

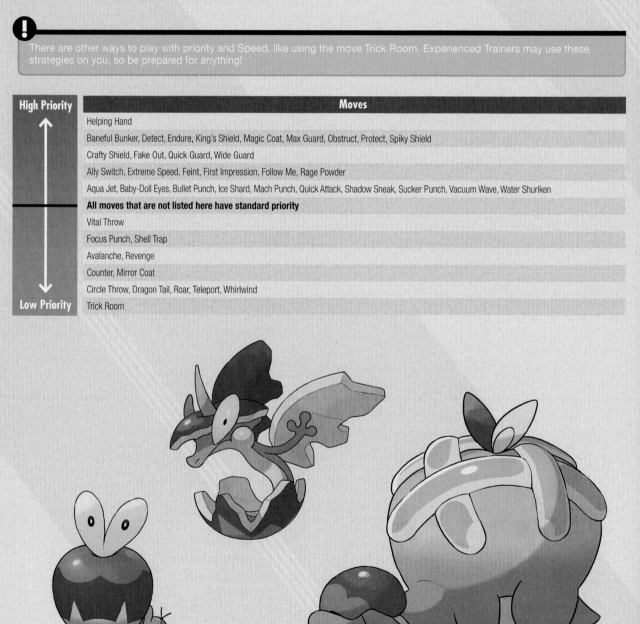

Max Moves and G-Max Moves

Max Moves

When a Pokémon has Dynamaxed, its moves will all be transformed into awesome Max Moves! The Max Move that each move becomes will be based on two things—the original move's type and its category. Any damage-dealing move will be changed to the Max Move that corresponds to its type. Any status move, regardless of type, will be changed into Max Guard when a Pokémon is Dynamaxed.

> ❗ The power of a Max Move also varies depending on the original move it is based on. So check the Max Move Pow. column in the regular move tables to see how powerful each move can become when it turns into a Max Move!

Move	Type	Kind	Range	DA	Notes
Max Airstream	Flying	Physical/Special	Normal	—	Any damage-dealing Flying-type move will turn into this move when used by a Dynamax Pokémon. Raises the user's and ally Pokémon's Speed by 1 stage.
Max Darkness	Dark	Physical/Special	Normal	—	Any damage-dealing Dark-type move will turn into this move when used by a Dynamax Pokémon. Lowers opposing Pokémon's Sp. Def by 1 stage.
Max Flare	Fire	Physical/Special	Normal	—	Any damage-dealing Fire-type move will turn into this move when used by a Dynamax Pokémon. Changes the weather condition to harsh sunlight for 5 turns, boosting the power of Fire-type moves by 50% and reducing the power of Water-type moves by 50%.
Max Flutterby	Bug	Physical/Special	Normal	—	Any damage-dealing Bug-type move will turn into this move when used by a Dynamax Pokémon. Lowers opposing Pokémon's Sp. Atk by 1 stage.
Max Geyser	Water	Physical/Special	Normal	—	Any damage-dealing Water-type move will turn into this move when used by a Dynamax Pokémon. Changes the weather condition to rain for 5 turns, boosting the power of Water-type moves by 50% and reducing the power of Fire-type moves by 50%.
Max Guard	Normal	Status	Self	—	Any status move will turn into this move when used by a Dynamax Pokémon. The user protects itself from all moves used on the same turn. This move becomes more likely to fail if used repeatedly.
Max Hailstorm	Ice	Physical/Special	Normal	—	Any damage-dealing Ice-type move will turn into this move when used by a Dynamax Pokémon. Changes the weather condition to hail for 5 turns. All Pokémon other than Ice types take damage at the end of each turn equal to 1/16 of their max HP.
Max Knuckle	Fighting	Physical/Special	Normal	—	Any damage-dealing Fighting-type move will turn into this move when used by a Dynamax Pokémon. Raises the user's and ally Pokémon's Attack by 1 stage.
Max Lightning	Electric	Physical/Special	Normal	—	Any damage-dealing Electric-type move will turn into this move when used by a Dynamax Pokémon. Electrifies the battlefield for 5 turns. During that time, Pokémon on the ground will be able to do 50% more damage with Electric-type moves and cannot fall asleep.
Max Mindstorm	Psychic	Physical/Special	Normal	—	Any damage-dealing Psychic-type move will turn into this move when used by a Dynamax Pokémon. Covers the battlefield with psychic energy for 5 turns. During that time, Pokémon on the ground will be able to do 50% more damage with Psychic-type moves and will evade high-priority moves.
Max Ooze	Poison	Physical/Special	Normal	—	Any damage-dealing Poison-type move will turn into this move when used by a Dynamax Pokémon. Raises the user's and ally Pokémon's Sp. Atk by 1 stage.
Max Overgrowth	Grass	Physical/Special	Normal	—	Any damage-dealing Grass-type move will turn into this move when used by a Dynamax Pokémon. Covers the battlefield with grass for 5 turns. During that time, Pokémon on the ground will be able to do 50% more damage with Grass-type moves and will recover 1/16 of their max HP at the end of each turn. Damage done to Pokémon on the ground by Bulldoze or Earthquake is also halved during this time.
Max Phantasm	Ghost	Physical/Special	Normal	—	Any damage-dealing Ghost-type move will turn into this move when used by a Dynamax Pokémon. Lowers opposing Pokémon's Defense by 1 stage.
Max Quake	Ground	Physical/Special	Normal	—	Any damage-dealing Ground-type move will turn into this move when used by a Dynamax Pokémon. Raises the user's and ally Pokémon's Sp. Def by 1 stage.
Max Rockfall	Rock	Physical/Special	Normal	—	Any damage-dealing Rock-type move will turn into this move when used by a Dynamax Pokémon. Changes the weather condition to sandstorm for 5 turns, boosting the Sp. Def of Rock-type Pokémon by 50%. All Pokémon other than Ground, Rock, and Steel types take damage at the end of each turn equal to 1/16 of their max HP.
Max Starfall	Fairy	Physical/Special	Normal	—	Any damage-dealing Fairy-type move will turn into this move when used by a Dynamax Pokémon. Covers the battlefield with mist for 5 turns. During that time, Pokémon on the ground cannot be afflicted with new status conditions or confusion. Damage done to Pokémon on the ground by Dragon-type moves is also halved during this time.
Max Steelspike	Steel	Physical/Special	Normal	—	Any damage-dealing Steel-type move will turn into this move when used by a Dynamax Pokémon. Raises the user's and ally Pokémon's Defense by 1 stage.
Max Strike	Normal	Physical/Special	Normal	—	Any damage-dealing Normal-type move will turn into this move when used by a Dynamax Pokémon. Lowers opposing Pokémon's Speed by 1 stage.
Max Wyrmwind	Dragon	Physical/Special	Normal	—	Any damage-dealing Dragon-type move will turn into this move when used by a Dynamax Pokémon. Lowers opposing Pokémon's Attack by 1 stage.

G-Max Moves

Remember that even within the Dynamax phenomenon, there is an even rarer phenomenon—Gigantamaxing! If a Pokémon can Gigantamax, it has access to a unique powered-up version of one of the Max Moves! Each of these G-Max Moves has different additional effects than the Max Move it's based on, and these effects only occur for these rare Gigantamax Pokémon.

Move	Pokémon that can use it	Type	Additional effects
G-Max Befuddle	Gigantamax Butterfree	Bug	Inflicts the poison, paralysis, or asleep status condition on all opposing Pokémon.
G-Max Centiferno	Gigantamax Centiskorch	Fire	Inflicts damage equal to 1/8 of max HP to all opponents at the end of each turn for 4–5 turns. Opponents cannot flee or be switched out of battle during that time.
G-Max Chi Strike	Gigantamax Machamp	Fighting	Increases critical hit rates of all ally Pokémon by 2 stages.
G-Max Cuddle	Gigantamax Eevee	Normal	Makes all opposing Pokémon become infatuated, which causes moves to fail 50% of the time.
G-Max Depletion	Gigantamax Duraludon	Dragon	Reduces the PP of the moves used by all opposing Pokémon by 2.
G-Max Finale	Gigantamax Alcremie	Fairy	Restores 1/6 of all ally Pokémon's max HP.
G-Max Foam Burst	Gigantamax Kingler	Water	Decreases the Speed stats of all opposing Pokémon by 2 stages.
G-Max Gold Rush	Gigantamax Meowth	Normal	Pays out money after battle. The amount depends on the user's level and the number of times the move was used. First use: ₽100 × user's level. Second use: ₽300 × user's level. Third use: ₽600 × user's level. Also makes all opposing Pokémon confused.
G-Max Gravitas	Gigantamax Orbeetle	Psychic	Airborne Pokémon are grounded. Ground-type moves will now hit Pokémon normally immune to them. Prevents the use of Bounce, Fly, Flying Press, High Jump Kick, Magnet Rise, and Splash. Raises the accuracy of all Pokémon in battle. Lasts 5 turns.
G-Max Malodor	Gigantamax Garbodor	Poison	Inflicts the poison status condition on all opposing Pokémon.
G-Max Replenish	Gigantamax Snorlax	Normal	Recycles the Berries held by all ally Pokémon.
G-Max Resonance	Gigantamax Lapras	Ice	Reduces damage from physical and special moves for 5 turns.
G-Max Sandblast	Gigantamax Sandaconda	Ground	Inflicts damage equal to 1/8 of max HP to all opponents at the end of each turn for 4–5 turns. Opponents cannot flee or be switched out of battle during that time.
G-Max Smite	Gigantamax Hatterene	Fairy	Makes all opposing Pokémon confused.
G-Max Snooze	Gigantamax Grimmsnarl	Dark	Inflicts the asleep status condition on the target at the end of the next turn unless the target switches out.
G-Max Steelsurge	Gigantamax Copperajah	Steel	Damages Pokémon as they are sent out to the opposing side. This damage is Steel type and subject to type matchups.
G-Max Stonesurge	Gigantamax Drednaw	Water	Damages Pokémon as they are sent out to the opposing side. This damage is Rock type and subject to type matchups.
G-Max Sweetness	Gigantamax Appletun	Grass	Heals the status conditions of all ally Pokémon in battle.
G-Max Tartness	Gigantamax Flapple	Grass	Decreases the evasiveness of all opposing Pokémon by 1 stage.
G-Max Terror	Gigantamax Gengar	Ghost	Prevents all opposing Pokémon from fleeing or being switched out while this Pokémon is in battle.
G-Max Volcalith	Gigantamax Coalossal	Rock	Inflicts damage equal to 1/6 of max HP to all non-Rock-type opponents for 4 turns.
G-Max Volt Crash	Gigantamax Pikachu	Electric	Inflicts the paralysis status condition on all opposing Pokémon.
G-Max Wildfire	Gigantamax Charizard	Fire	Inflicts damage equal to 1/6 of max HP to all non-Fire-type opponents for 4 turns.
G-Max Wind Rage	Gigantamax Corviknight	Flying	Nullifies Aurora Veil, Light Screen, Mist, Reflect, and Safeguard on the opponents' side. Nullifies Spikes, Stealth Rock, Sticky Web, and Toxic Spikes on both sides.

Move Tutors

Pokémon learn many moves by leveling up, evolving, or having TMs or TRs used on them. But sometimes Pokémon can also learn certain moves with the help of a Move Tutor. These special people can teach Pokémon moves they generally wouldn't be able to learn otherwise, so check out the table below if you need help finding a particular tutor!

❗ There may be other Pokémon that can learn these moves once you are able to send them over from Pokémon HOME, available in 2020.

Location	Where to find them	Move	Pokémon that can learn it	Special conditions
Hammerlocke	Down the stairs near the exit to Route 6	Grass Pledge	Grookey, Thwackey, Rillaboom, Silvally	
Hammerlocke	Down the stairs near the exit to Route 6	Fire Pledge	Scorbunny, Raboot, Cinderace, Charmander, Charmeleon, Charizard, Silvally	
Hammerlocke	Down the stairs near the exit to Route 6	Water Pledge	Sobble, Drizzile, Inteleon, Silvally	
Circhester	At the Hero's Bath, on the west side of the pool	Draco Meteor	Any Dragon-type Pokémon, Silvally	
Wyndon	Near the court in the park	Frenzy Plant	Rillaboom	
Wyndon	Near the court in the park	Blast Burn	Cinderace, Charizard	
Wyndon	Near the court in the park	Hydro Cannon	Inteleon	
Motostoke	Near the canals, all the way down the stairs near the east lift	Steel Beam	Any Steel-type Pokémon, Silvally, Zacian, Zamazenta	Become the Champion

How to Obtain TMs

TMs are a great way to teach Pokémon moves, since they can be used over and over for as many different Pokémon as you like! All you have to do is track them down, which can be a bit tricky. Some are available in shops, but many can only be found by talking to particular people around the region, meeting certain conditions, or simply finding them lying about in Galar's nooks and crannies!

TM No.	Move	Type	How to obtain	Price
TM00	Mega Punch	Normal	Purchase from a Poké Mart in Hammerlocke (east), which becomes available after you defeat the Fairy-type Gym Leader, Opal	₽10,000
TM01	Mega Kick	Normal	Purchase from a Poké Mart in Hammerlocke (east), which becomes available after you defeat the Fairy-type Gym Leader, Opal	₽40,000
TM02	Pay Day	Normal	Find in Motostoke	—
TM03	Fire Punch	Fire	Purchase from a Poké Mart in Wyndon (stadium front)	₽50,000
TM04	Ice Punch	Ice	Purchase from a Poké Mart in Wyndon (stadium front)	₽50,000
TM05	Thunder Punch	Electric	Purchase from a Poké Mart in Wyndon (stadium front)	₽50,000
TM06	Fly	Flying	Receive from a Flying Taxi driver in the house by the stairs that lead to Stow-on-Side Stadium in Stow-on-Side	—
TM07	Pin Missile	Bug	Find on Route 4	—
TM08	Hyper Beam	Normal	Purchase from a Poké Mart in Wyndon (stadium front)	₽50,000
TM09	Giga Impact	Normal	Purchase from a Poké Mart in Wyndon (stadium front)	₽50,000
TM10	Magical Leaf	Grass	Receive after defeating the Grass-type Gym Leader, Milo	—
TM11	Solar Beam	Grass	Find in Turffield (must have Water Mode for the Rotom Bike)	—
TM12	Solar Blade	Grass	Purchase from a Poké Mart in Wyndon (stadium front)	₽50,000
TM13	Fire Spin	Fire	Purchase from a Poké Mart in Hammerlocke (west)	₽10,000
TM14	Thunder Wave	Electric	Receive after completing a Rotom Rally course for the first time in the Wild Area	—
TM15	Dig	Ground	Find on Route 6	—
TM16	Screech	Normal	Receive from a hiker found upstairs in the eastern building of Circhester's Hotel Ionia (first room to the right of the elevator)	—
TM17	Light Screen	Psychic	Purchase from a Poké Mart in Motostoke (upper level)	₽10,000
TM18	Reflect	Psychic	Purchase from a Poké Mart in Motostoke (upper level)	₽10,000
TM19	Safeguard	Normal	Purchase from a Poké Mart in Motostoke (upper level)	₽10,000
TM20	Self-Destruct	Normal	Purchase from a Pokémon League staff member selling TMs in the Battle Tower (after becoming Champion)	₽100,000
TM21	Rest	Psychic	Find in Ballonlea	—
TM22	Rock Slide	Rock	Find on Route 9	—
TM23	Thief	Dark	Purchase from a Poké Mart in Hammerlocke (west)	₽10,000
TM24	Snore	Normal	Find in Glimwood Tangle	—
TM25	Protect	Normal	Purchase from a Poké Mart in Motostoke (upper level)	₽10,000
TM26	Scary Face	Normal	Find in Galar Mine	—
TM27	Icy Wind	Ice	Receive from a young man in Circhester ♠ / Receive after defeating the Ice-type Gym Leader, Melony ♣	—
TM28	Giga Drain	Grass	Purchase from a Pokémon League staff member selling TMs in the Battle Tower (after becoming Champion)	₽100,000
TM29	Charm	Fairy	Find in Hammerlocke	—
TM30	Steel Wing	Steel	Find on Route 6	—
TM31	Attract	Normal	Find on Route 5	—
TM32	Sandstorm	Rock	Purchase from a Poké Mart in Hammerlocke (west)	₽10,000
TM33	Rain Dance	Water	Purchase from a Poké Mart in Hammerlocke (west)	₽10,000
TM34	Sunny Day	Fire	Purchase from a Poké Mart in Hammerlocke (west)	₽10,000
TM35	Hail	Ice	Purchase from a Poké Mart in Hammerlocke (west)	₽10,000
TM36	Whirlpool	Water	Receive after defeating the Water-type Gym Leader, Nessa	—
TM37	Beat Up	Dark	Find on Route 3	—
TM38	Will-O-Wisp	Fire	Receive after defeating the Fire-type Gym Leader, Kabu	—
TM39	Facade	Normal	Find behind one of the pipes on the Motostoke Riverbank in the Wild Area	—
TM40	Swift	Normal	Receive from Hop in front of Wedgehurst Station during the main story	—
TM41	Helping Hand	Normal	Purchase from a Poké Mart in Motostoke (upper level)	₽10,000
TM42	Revenge	Fighting	Receive after defeating the Fighting-type Gym Leader, Bea ♠ / Receive from an old lady in Ballonlea ♣	—
TM43	Brick Break	Fighting	Find on Route 8	—
TM44	Imprison	Psychic	Purchase from a Pokémon League staff member selling TMs in the Battle Tower (after becoming Champion)	₽100,000
TM45	Dive	Water	Receive from a female swimmer on the secret beach on Route 9 (Circhester Bay)	—
TM46	Weather Ball	Normal	Purchase from a Poké Mart in Hammerlocke (east), which becomes available after you defeat the Fairy-type Gym Leader, Opal	₽30,000
TM47	Fake Tears	Dark	Receive from a musician found upstairs in the eastern building of Circhester's Hotel Ionia (second hotel room to the right of the elevator)	—

TM No.	Move	Type	How to obtain	Price
TM48	Rock Tomb	Rock	Receive after defeating the Rock-type Gym Leader, Gordie † / Receive from a young man in Circhester ♣	—
TM49	Sand Tomb	Ground	Find in Galar Mine No. 2	—
TM50	Bullet Seed	Grass	Purchase from a Poké Mart in Hammerlocke (west)	₽10,000
TM51	Icicle Spear	Ice	Find in Circhester near the Hero's Bath	—
TM52	Bounce	Flying	Purchase from a Pokémon League staff member selling TMs in the Battle Tower (after becoming Champion)	₽100,000
TM53	Mud Shot	Ground	Find in Galar Mine No. 2 (must have Water Mode for the Rotom Bike)	—
TM54	Rock Blast	Rock	Find on Route 3	—
TM55	Brine	Water	Purchase from a Poké Mart in Hammerlocke (west)	₽10,000
TM56	U-turn	Bug	Find in Glimwood Tangle	—
TM57	Payback	Dark	Find on Route 2 behind Professor Magnolia's house	—
TM58	Assurance	Dark	Find on Route 7 near the campsite	—
TM59	Fling	Dark	Purchase from a Pokémon League staff member selling TMs in the Battle Tower (after becoming Champion)	₽100,000
TM60	Power Swap	Psychic	Purchase from a Poké Mart in Wyndon (stadium front)	₽30,000
TM61	Guard Swap	Psychic	Purchase from a Poké Mart in Wyndon (stadium front)	₽30,000
TM62	Speed Swap	Psychic	Purchase from a Poké Mart in Wyndon (stadium front)	₽30,000
TM63	Drain Punch	Fighting	Purchase from a Poké Mart in Wyndon (stadium front)	₽50,000
TM64	Avalanche	Ice	Find on Route 9	—
TM65	Shadow Claw	Ghost	Find across the Lake of Outrage in the Wild Area (must have Water Mode for the Rotom Bike)	—
TM66	Thunder Fang	Electric	Purchase from a Poké Mart in Hammerlocke (east), which becomes available after you defeat the Fairy-type Gym Leader, Opal	₽30,000
TM67	Ice Fang	Ice	Purchase from a Poké Mart in Hammerlocke (east), which becomes available after you defeat the Fairy-type Gym Leader, Opal	₽30,000
TM68	Fire Fang	Fire	Purchase from a Poké Mart in Hammerlocke (east), which becomes available after you defeat the Fairy-type Gym Leader, Opal	₽30,000
TM69	Psycho Cut	Psychic	Find on Route 2 (must have Water Mode for the Rotom Bike)	—
TM70	Trick Room	Psychic	Purchase from a Pokémon League staff member selling TMs in the Battle Tower (after becoming Champion)	₽50,000
TM71	Wonder Room	Psychic	Purchase from a Pokémon League staff member selling TMs in the Battle Tower (after becoming Champion)	₽50,000
TM72	Magic Room	Psychic	Purchase from a Pokémon League staff member selling TMs in the Battle Tower (after becoming Champion)	₽50,000
TM73	Cross Poison	Poison	Find in the Dusty Bowl in the Wild Area (must have Water Mode for the Rotom Bike)	—
TM74	Venoshock	Poison	Find in Stow-on-Side	—
TM75	Low Sweep	Fighting	Find in the Bridge Field in the Wild Area (must have Water Mode for the Rotom Bike)	—
TM76	Round	Normal	Purchase from a Poké Mart in Motostoke (upper level)	₽10,000
TM77	Hex	Ghost	Receive from an old lady in Ballonlea † / Receive after defeating the Ghost-type Gym Leader, Allister ♣	—
TM78	Acrobatics	Flying	Receive from an artist in Ballonlea who wants to become a Pokémon (show him a Fire-type Tracksuit Jacket)	—
TM79	Retaliate	Normal	Receive from Sonia in the seafood restaurant in Hulbury during the main story	—
TM80	Volt Switch	Electric	Receive by achieving a very high score in the Rotom Rally in the Wild Area	—
TM81	Bulldoze	Ground	Find near the Giant's Seat in the Wild Area	—
TM82	Electroweb	Electric	Find in Hulbury	—
TM83	Razor Shell	Water	Purchase from a Pokémon League staff member selling TMs in the Battle Tower (after becoming Champion)	₽100,000
TM84	Tail Slap	Normal	Find in a fallen tree on the east side of the Rolling Fields in the Wild Area	—
TM85	Snarl	Dark	Receive after defeating the Dark-type Gym Leader, Piers	—
TM86	Phantom Force	Ghost	Find in the Slumbering Weald when you revisit it	—
TM87	Draining Kiss	Fairy	Receive after defeating the Fairy-type Gym Leader, Opal	—
TM88	Grassy Terrain	Grass	Purchase from a Poké Mart in Hammerlocke (east), which becomes available after you defeat the Fairy-type Gym Leader, Opal	₽20,000
TM89	Misty Terrain	Fairy	Purchase from a Poké Mart in Hammerlocke (east), which becomes available after you defeat the Fairy-type Gym Leader, Opal	₽20,000
TM90	Electric Terrain	Electric	Purchase from a Poké Mart in Hammerlocke (east), which becomes available after you defeat the Fairy-type Gym Leader, Opal	₽20,000
TM91	Psychic Terrain	Psychic	Purchase from a Poké Mart in Hammerlocke (east), which becomes available after you defeat the Fairy-type Gym Leader, Opal	₽20,000
TM92	Mystical Fire	Fire	Purchase from a Pokémon League staff member selling TMs in the Battle Tower (after becoming Champion)	₽100,000
TM93	Eerie Impulse	Electric	Find in Wyndon	—
TM94	False Swipe	Normal	Purchase from a Poké Mart in Motostoke (upper level)	₽10,000
TM95	Air Slash	Flying	Find on Axew's Eye, an island in the Wild Area (must have Water Mode for the Rotom Bike)	—
TM96	Smart Strike	Steel	Find on Route 8	—
TM97	Brutal Swing	Dark	Find in Turffield	—
TM98	Stomping Tantrum	Ground	Find on Route 10 on a side path just over the hill heading toward Wyndon	—
TM99	Breaking Swipe	Dragon	Receive after defeating the Dragon-type Gym Leader, Raihan	—

How to Obtain TRs

There are a couple of ways you can obtain TRs during your adventure. You can receive them as rewards for participating in Max Raid Battles, or you can purchase them from the Watt Trader service offered by the Rotom Rallyists hanging out in the Wild Area. Each Rotom Rallyist offers a different selection of TRs, and their inventories change every day. Visit them all in turn, and if you still can't find a TR you want, just check back with each of them again the next day! The table below shows you all the TRs you can find in the Galar region—plus how many Watts they cost if you want to purchase them.

TR No.	Move	Type	Price	TR No.	Move	Type	Price	TR No.	Move	Type	Price
TR00	Swords Dance	Normal	2,000 W	TR43	Overheat	Fire	8,000 W	TR86	Wild Charge	Electric	5,000 W
TR01	Body Slam	Normal	3,000 W	TR44	Cosmic Power	Psychic	2,000 W	TR87	Drill Run	Ground	3,000 W
TR02	Flamethrower	Fire	5,000 W	TR45	Muddy Water	Water	5,000 W	TR88	Heat Crash	Fire	3,000 W
TR03	Hydro Pump	Water	8,000 W	TR46	Iron Defense	Steel	2,000 W	TR89	Hurricane	Flying	8,000 W
TR04	Surf	Water	5,000 W	TR47	Dragon Claw	Dragon	3,000 W	TR90	Play Rough	Fairy	5,000 W
TR05	Ice Beam	Ice	5,000 W	TR48	Bulk Up	Fighting	2,000 W	TR91	Venom Drench	Poison	2,000 W
TR06	Blizzard	Ice	8,000 W	TR49	Calm Mind	Psychic	2,000 W	TR92	Dazzling Gleam	Fairy	3,000 W
TR07	Low Kick	Fighting	3,000 W	TR50	Leaf Blade	Grass	5,000 W	TR93	Darkest Lariat	Dark	5,000 W
TR08	Thunderbolt	Electric	5,000 W	TR51	Dragon Dance	Dragon	2,000 W	TR94	High Horsepower	Ground	5,000 W
TR09	Thunder	Electric	8,000 W	TR52	Gyro Ball	Steel	3,000 W	TR95	Throat Chop	Dark	3,000 W
TR10	Earthquake	Ground	8,000 W	TR53	Close Combat	Fighting	8,000 W	TR96	Pollen Puff	Bug	5,000 W
TR11	Psychic	Psychic	5,000 W	TR54	Toxic Spikes	Poison	2,000 W	TR97	Psychic Fangs	Psychic	5,000 W
TR12	Agility	Psychic	2,000 W	TR55	Flare Blitz	Fire	8,000 W	TR98	Liquidation	Water	3,000 W
TR13	Focus Energy	Normal	1,000 W	TR56	Aura Sphere	Fighting	3,000 W	TR99	Body Press	Fighting	3,000 W
TR14	Metronome	Normal	1,000 W	TR57	Poison Jab	Poison	3,000 W				
TR15	Fire Blast	Fire	8,000 W	TR58	Dark Pulse	Dark	3,000 W				
TR16	Waterfall	Water	3,000 W	TR59	Seed Bomb	Grass	3,000 W				
TR17	Amnesia	Psychic	2,000 W	TR60	X-Scissor	Bug	3,000 W				
TR18	Leech Life	Bug	3,000 W	TR61	Bug Buzz	Bug	5,000 W				
TR19	Tri Attack	Normal	2,000 W	TR62	Dragon Pulse	Dragon	3,000 W				
TR20	Substitute	Normal	3,000 W	TR63	Power Gem	Rock	3,000 W				
TR21	Reversal	Fighting	2,000 W	TR64	Focus Blast	Fighting	8,000 W				
TR22	Sludge Bomb	Poison	5,000 W	TR65	Energy Ball	Grass	5,000 W				
TR23	Spikes	Ground	2,000 W	TR66	Brave Bird	Flying	8,000 W				
TR24	Outrage	Dragon	8,000 W	TR67	Earth Power	Ground	5,000 W				
TR25	Psyshock	Psychic	3,000 W	TR68	Nasty Plot	Dark	2,000 W				
TR26	Endure	Normal	1,000 W	TR69	Zen Headbutt	Psychic	3,000 W				
TR27	Sleep Talk	Normal	2,000 W	TR70	Flash Cannon	Steel	5,000 W				
TR28	Megahorn	Bug	8,000 W	TR71	Leaf Storm	Grass	8,000 W				
TR29	Baton Pass	Normal	2,000 W	TR72	Power Whip	Grass	8,000 W				
TR30	Encore	Normal	2,000 W	TR73	Gunk Shot	Poison	8,000 W				
TR31	Iron Tail	Steel	5,000 W	TR74	Iron Head	Steel	5,000 W				
TR32	Crunch	Dark	3,000 W	TR75	Stone Edge	Rock	8,000 W				
TR33	Shadow Ball	Ghost	3,000 W	TR76	Stealth Rock	Rock	3,000 W				
TR34	Future Sight	Psychic	3,000 W	TR77	Grass Knot	Grass	3,000 W				
TR35	Uproar	Normal	3,000 W	TR78	Sludge Wave	Poison	5,000 W				
TR36	Heat Wave	Fire	5,000 W	TR79	Heavy Slam	Steel	3,000 W				
TR37	Taunt	Dark	2,000 W	TR80	Electro Ball	Electric	3,000 W				
TR38	Trick	Psychic	2,000 W	TR81	Foul Play	Dark	3,000 W				
TR39	Superpower	Fighting	8,000 W	TR82	Stored Power	Psychic	2,000 W				
TR40	Skill Swap	Psychic	1,000 W	TR83	Ally Switch	Psychic	2,000 W				
TR41	Blaze Kick	Fire	3,000 W	TR84	Scald	Water	3,000 W				
TR42	Hyper Voice	Normal	5,000 W	TR85	Work Up	Normal	1,000 W				

Pokémon Moves Reverse Lookup

If you found a move listed in the move tables that you can't wait to use in battle, then the following pages will help you check exactly which species can learn it. Moves are listed in alphabetical order, and under each move, you'll find a list of the Pokémon in *Pokémon Sword* and *Pokémon Shield* that can learn it. Use the Pokémon's Pokédex numbers to turn back to their entries in the data pages starting on page 188 if you want to find out exactly how a species learns a particular move—such as by leveling up, from a TM or TR, or maybe even by hatching with it as an Egg Move! And don't forget that some Pokémon can have multiple forms. Forms may not necessarily all learn the same moves, so review their move tables to decide which form you need for your strategy.

Absorb
276 Accelgor
058 Bellossom
059 Budew
262 Cottonee
187 Cutiefly
360 Dhelmise
305 Frillish
065 Galvantula
056 Gloom
391 Goodra
389 Goomy
306 Jellicent
064 Joltik
037 Lombre
036 Lotad
038 Ludicolo
296 Maractus
340 Morelull
104 Nincada
105 Ninjask
176 Noibat
177 Noivern
040 Nuzleaf
055 Oddish
188 Ribombee
060 Roselia
061 Roserade
039 Seedot
106 Shedinja
275 Shelmet
041 Shiftry
341 Shiinotic
390 Sliggoo
057 Vileplume
263 Whimsicott

Acid
276 Accelgor
058 Bellossom
056 Gloom
055 Oddish
133 Palpitoad
134 Seismitoad
275 Shelmet
227 Shuckle
310 Toxel
311 Toxtricity
132 Tympole
057 Vileplume

Acid Armor
276 Accelgor
186 Alcremie
305 Frillish
306 Jellicent
287 Litwick
185 Milcery
230 Shellos
275 Shelmet
270 Solosis

073 Vanillish
072 Vanillite
074 Vanilluxe
197 Vaporeon

Acid Spray
276 Accelgor
274 Escavalier
189 Ferroseed
206 Flapple
158 Garbodor
391 Goodra
273 Karrablast
304 Qwilfish
148 Remoraid
224 Scraggy
131 Skuntank
390 Sliggoo
130 Stunky
311 Toxtricity
157 Trubbish
100 Wooper

Acrobatics (TM78)
015 Butterfree
380 Charizard
017 Charjabug
378 Charmander
379 Charmeleon
006 Cinderace
187 Cutiefly
397 Dragapult
396 Drakloak
125 Drifblim
124 Drifloon
206 Flapple
350 Frosmoth
001 Grookey
016 Grubbin
320 Hawlucha
388 Hydreigon
009 Inteleon
362 Lunatone
355 Mantine
354 Mantyke
105 Ninjask
176 Noibat
177 Noivern
343 Passimian
005 Raboot
188 Ribombee
003 Rillaboom
245 Salazzle
004 Scorbunny
363 Solrock
175 Swoobat
030 Thievul
002 Thwackey
054 Tsareena
117 Vespiquen
018 Vikavolt

174 Woobat

Acupressure
180 Arrokuda
052 Bounsweet
286 Drapion
146 Goldeen
290 Inkay
296 Maractus
353 Pincurchin
304 Qwilfish
227 Shuckle
285 Skorupi

Aerial Ace
332 Aegislash
282 Braviary
309 Cramorant
331 Doublade
374 Dracozolt
123 Gallade
320 Hawlucha
330 Honedge
105 Ninjask
281 Rufflet
382 Silvally
257 Togepi
381 Type: Null
062 Wingull

After You
051 Cinccino
256 Clefable
255 Clefairy
241 Hatenna
337 Indeedee
296 Maractus
050 Minccino
366 Mr. Rime
055 Oddish
342 Oranguru
012 Orbeetle
212 Spritzee
210 Swirlix
259 Togekiss
257 Togepi
258 Togetic
100 Wooper

Agility (TR12)
276 Accelgor
071 Arcanine
180 Arrokuda
181 Barraskewda
154 Basculin
278 Beheeyem
047 Boltund
282 Braviary
048 Bunnelby
220 Chinchou
006 Cinderace
023 Corviknight
022 Corvisquire

309 Cramorant
078 Delibird
049 Diggersby
164 Diglett
397 Dragapult
396 Drakloak
286 Drapion
035 Dubwool
165 Dugtrio
316 Durant
370 Eiscue
066 Electrike
277 Elgyem
274 Escavalier
400 Eternatus
345 Falinks
065 Galvantula
146 Goldeen
070 Growlithe
320 Hawlucha
319 Heliolisk
318 Helioptile
109 Hitmonchan
110 Hitmontop
019 Hoothoot
009 Inteleon
198 Jolteon
064 Joltik
099 Kingler
098 Krabby
221 Lanturn
299 Lucario
067 Manectric
355 Mantine
354 Mantyke
344 Morpeko
029 Nickit
069 Ninetales
105 Ninjask
020 Noctowl
176 Noibat
177 Noivern
012 Orbeetle
063 Pelipper
026 Pidove
194 Pikachu
333 Ponyta
005 Raboot
195 Raichu
334 Rapidash
298 Riolu
021 Rookidee
281 Rufflet
004 Scorbunny
147 Seaking
106 Shedinja
285 Skorupi
292 Sneasel
030 Thievul

348 Togedemaru
027 Tranquill
028 Unfezant
018 Vikavolt
068 Vulpix
293 Weavile
062 Wingull
034 Wooloo
398 Zacian
399 Zamazenta

Air Cutter
176 Noibat
177 Noivern
040 Nuzleaf
026 Pidove
041 Shiftry
297 Sigilyph
175 Swoobat
027 Tranquill
028 Unfezant
062 Wingull
174 Woobat

Air Slash (TM95)
332 Aegislash
247 Bisharp
282 Braviary
015 Butterfree
380 Charizard
023 Corviknight
022 Corvisquire
309 Cramorant
206 Flapple
323 Flygon
350 Frosmoth
123 Gallade
019 Hoothoot
009 Inteleon
284 Mandibuzz
355 Mantine
354 Mantyke
092 Natu
105 Ninjask
020 Noctowl
176 Noibat
177 Noivern
063 Pelipper
026 Pidove
021 Rookidee
372 Rotom
281 Rufflet
041 Shiftry
382 Silvally
175 Swoobat
259 Togekiss
027 Tranquill
381 Type: Null
028 Unfezant
117 Vespiquen

322 Vibrava
018 Vikavolt
283 Vullaby
062 Wingull
174 Woobat
093 Xatu
398 Zacian

Ally Switch (TR83)
213 Aromatisse
082 Baltoy
278 Beheeyem
119 Bronzong
118 Bronzor
289 Chandelure
006 Cinderace
083 Claydol
256 Clefable
255 Clefairy
329 Cofagrigus
187 Cutiefly
360 Dhelmise
164 Diglett
011 Dottler
397 Dragapult
396 Drakloak
125 Drifblim
124 Drifloon
165 Dugtrio
271 Duosion
136 Dusclops
137 Dusknoir
135 Duskull
277 Elgyem
200 Espeon
208 Espurr
081 Froslass
123 Gallade
122 Gardevoir
141 Gastly
143 Gengar
088 Golett
089 Golurk
267 Gothita
269 Gothitelle
268 Gothorita
192 Gourgeist
142 Haunter
320 Hawlucha
319 Heliolisk
318 Helioptile
337 Indeedee
290 Inkay
099 Kingler
121 Kirlia
114 Klang
115 Klinklang
098 Krabby
288 Lampent

287 Litwick
362 Lunatone
291 Malamar
209 Meowstic
364 Mime Jr.
365 Mr. Mime
366 Mr. Rime
090 Munna
091 Musharna
092 Natu
342 Oranguru
012 Orbeetle
338 Phantump
336 Polteageist
333 Ponyta
191 Pumpkaboo
005 Raboot
120 Ralts
334 Rapidash
272 Reuniclus
188 Ribombee
372 Rotom
328 Runerigus
294 Sableye
004 Scorbunny
106 Shedinja
335 Sinistea
270 Solosis
363 Solrock
212 Spritzee
175 Swoobat
259 Togekiss
339 Trevenant
073 Vanillish
072 Vanillite
074 Vanilluxe
174 Woobat
093 Xatu
327 Yamask

Amnesia (TR17)
207 Appletun
228 Barboach
220 Chinchou
256 Clefable
255 Clefairy
254 Cleffa
236 Corsola
309 Cramorant
237 Cursola
346 Drampa
125 Drifblim
124 Drifloon
370 Eiscue
158 Garbodor
231 Gastrodon
025 Greedent
317 Heatmor
314 Hippopotas
315 Hippowdon

019 Hoothoot
099 Kingler
098 Krabby
221 Lanturn
038 Ludicolo
077 Mamoswine
355 Mantine
354 Mantyke
182 Meowth
340 Morelull
260 Munchlax
090 Munna
091 Musharna
020 Noctowl
040 Nuzleaf
183 Perrserker
184 Persian
076 Piloswine
101 Quagsire
328 Runerigus
225 Scrafty
224 Scraggy
039 Seedot
230 Shellos
041 Shiftry
341 Shiinotic
024 Skwovet
211 Slurpuff
261 Snorlax
075 Swinub
210 Swirlix
175 Swoobat
259 Togekiss
300 Torkoal
157 Trubbish
356 Wailmer
357 Wailord
229 Whiscash
217 Wobbuffet
174 Woobat
100 Wooper
216 Wynaut

Anchor Shot
360 Dhelmise

Ancient Power
377 Arctovish
375 Arctozolt
082 Baltoy
235 Barbaracle
234 Binacle
162 Carkol
378 Charmander
083 Claydol
163 Coalossal
102 Corphish
236 Corsola
237 Cursola
164 Diglett
376 Dracovish
374 Dracozolt
231 Gastrodon
098 Krabby
361 Lapras
383 Larvitar
077 Mamoswine
295 Mawile
076 Piloswine
161 Rolycoly
230 Shellos
297 Sigilyph
369 Stonjourner
075 Swinub
259 Togekiss

257 Togepi
258 Togetic
300 Torkoal
100 Wooper

Apple Acid
207 Appletun

Aqua Jet
180 Arrokuda
181 Barraskewda
154 Basculin
280 Beartic
102 Corphish
304 Qwilfish
007 Sobble
232 Wimpod

Aqua Ring
215 Araquanid
220 Chinchou
309 Cramorant
214 Dewpider
370 Eiscue
146 Goldeen
221 Lanturn
355 Mantine
354 Mantyke
153 Milotic
133 Palpitoad
147 Seaking
134 Seismitoad
150 Shellder
007 Sobble
132 Tympole
197 Vaporeon
356 Wailmer
062 Wingull
155 Wishiwashi

Aqua Tail
228 Barboach
154 Basculin
146 Goldeen
391 Goodra
145 Gyarados
153 Milotic
050 Minccino
101 Quagsire
304 Qwilfish
229 Whiscash
155 Wishiwashi
100 Wooper

Arm Thrust
111 Pancham
112 Pangoro

Aromatherapy
186 Alcremie
213 Aromatisse
052 Bounsweet
128 Cherubi
254 Cleffa
187 Cutiefly
127 Eldegoss
126 Gossifleur
241 Hatenna
243 Hatterene
242 Hattrem
337 Indeedee
185 Milcery
336 Polteageist
188 Ribombee
060 Roselia
061 Roserade
335 Sinistea
211 Slurpuff
212 Spritzee

053 Steenee
210 Swirlix
054 Tsareena
117 Vespiquen
057 Vileplume
251 Weezing

Aromatic Mist
186 Alcremie
213 Aromatisse
052 Bounsweet
187 Cutiefly
241 Hatenna
185 Milcery
336 Polteageist
335 Sinistea
053 Steenee
054 Tsareena
117 Vespiquen
251 Weezing

Assurance (TM58)
180 Arrokuda
324 Axew
235 Barbaracle
181 Barraskewda
154 Basculin
280 Beartic
234 Binacle
247 Bisharp
282 Braviary
042 Chewtle
006 Cinderace
023 Corviknight
022 Corvisquire
309 Cramorant
222 Croagunk
279 Cubchoo
386 Deino
078 Delibird
360 Dhelmise
164 Diglett
397 Dragapult
396 Drakloak
286 Drapion
043 Drednaw
165 Dugtrio
400 Eternatus
345 Falinks
218 Farfetch'd
189 Ferroseed
190 Ferrothorn
325 Fraxure
233 Golisopod
391 Goodra
025 Greedent
240 Grimmsnarl
001 Grookey
320 Hawlucha
326 Haxorus
388 Hydreigon
238 Impidimp
114 Klang
113 Klink
115 Klinklang
250 Koffing
383 Larvitar
045 Liepard
032 Linoone
140 Machamp
284 Mandibuzz
355 Mantine
296 Maractus
295 Mawile
182 Meowth

239 Morgrem
344 Morpeko
029 Nickit
040 Nuzleaf
033 Obstagoon
149 Octillery
343 Passimian
246 Pawniard
183 Perrserker
184 Persian
353 Pincurchin
384 Pupitar
044 Purrloin
304 Qwilfish
005 Raboot
148 Remoraid
003 Rillaboom
021 Rookidee
281 Rufflet
004 Scorbunny
225 Scrafty
224 Scraggy
041 Shiftry
219 Sirfetch'd
285 Skorupi
131 Skuntank
024 Skwovet
369 Stonjourner
130 Stunky
175 Swoobat
030 Thievul
002 Thwackey
348 Togedemaru
223 Toxicroak
385 Tyranitar
201 Umbreon
117 Vespiquen
283 Vullaby
293 Weavile
251 Weezing
232 Wimpod
174 Woobat
398 Zacian
031 Zigzagoon
387 Zweilous

Astonish
207 Appletun
205 Applin
289 Chandelure
329 Cofagrigus
236 Corsola
222 Croagunk
237 Cursola
386 Deino
360 Dhelmise
164 Diglett
397 Dragapult
396 Drakloak
395 Dreepy
125 Drifblim
124 Drifloon
165 Dugtrio
136 Dusclops
137 Dusknoir
135 Duskull
277 Elgyem
206 Flapple
323 Flygon
081 Froslass
141 Gastly
080 Glalie
088 Golett
089 Golurk

192 Gourgeist
288 Lampent
287 Litwick
037 Lombre
036 Lotad
038 Ludicolo
295 Mawile
301 Mimikyu
340 Morelull
040 Nuzleaf
338 Phantump
336 Polteageist
191 Pumpkaboo
304 Qwilfish
372 Rotom
328 Runerigus
294 Sableye
039 Seedot
041 Shiftry
341 Shiinotic
335 Sinistea
079 Snorunt
270 Solosis
226 Stunfisk
130 Stunky
223 Toxicroak
321 Trapinch
339 Trevenant
073 Vanillish
072 Vanillite
074 Vanilluxe
322 Vibrava
356 Wailmer
357 Wailord
327 Yamask

Attack Order
117 Vespiquen

Attract (TM31)
097 Abomasnow
276 Accelgor
332 Aegislash
186 Alcremie
207 Appletun
205 Applin
215 Araquanid
071 Arcanine
213 Aromatisse
180 Arrokuda
359 Avalugg
324 Axew
235 Barbaracle
228 Barboach
181 Barraskewda
154 Basculin
280 Beartic
278 Beheeyem
058 Bellossom
358 Bergmite
095 Bewear
234 Binacle
247 Bisharp
169 Boldore
047 Boltund
252 Bonsly
052 Bounsweet
282 Braviary
059 Budew
048 Bunnelby
015 Butterfree
162 Carkol
160 Centiskorch
289 Chandelure
380 Charizard

017 Charjabug
378 Charmander
379 Charmeleon
129 Cherrim
128 Cherubi
042 Chewtle
220 Chinchou
051 Cinccino
006 Cinderace
256 Clefable
255 Clefairy
254 Cleffa
351 Clobbopus
151 Cloyster
163 Coalossal
329 Cofagrigus
173 Conkeldurr
303 Copperajah
102 Corphish
236 Corsola
023 Corviknight
022 Corvisquire
262 Cottonee
309 Cramorant
103 Crawdaunt
222 Croagunk
087 Crustle
279 Cubchoo
302 Cufant
237 Cursola
187 Cutiefly
368 Darmanitan
367 Darumaka
386 Deino
078 Delibird
214 Dewpider
049 Diggersby
164 Diglett
011 Dottler
331 Doublade
397 Dragapult
396 Drakloak
346 Drampa
286 Drapion
043 Drednaw
395 Dreepy
125 Drifblim
124 Drifloon
166 Drilbur
008 Drizzile
035 Dubwool
165 Dugtrio
271 Duosion
371 Duraludon
316 Durant
136 Dusclops
137 Dusknoir
135 Duskull
086 Dwebble
196 Eevee
370 Eiscue
127 Eldegoss
066 Electrike
277 Elgyem
274 Escavalier
200 Espeon
208 Espurr
167 Excadrill
218 Farfetch'd
152 Feebas
189 Ferroseed
190 Ferrothorn
206 Flapple

199 Flareon
323 Flygon
325 Fraxure
305 Frillish
081 Froslass
350 Frosmoth
123 Gallade
065 Galvantula
158 Garbodor
122 Gardevoir
141 Gastly
231 Gastrodon
143 Gengar
170 Gigalith
203 Glaceon
080 Glalie
056 Gloom
146 Goldeen
233 Golisopod
391 Goodra
389 Goomy
126 Gossifleur
267 Gothita
269 Gothitelle
268 Gothorita
192 Gourgeist
352 Grapploct
025 Greedent
240 Grimmsnarl
001 Grookey
070 Growlithe
016 Grubbin
172 Gurdurr
145 Gyarados
393 Hakamo-o
241 Hatenna
243 Hatterene
242 Hattrem
142 Haunter
320 Hawlucha
326 Haxorus
317 Heatmor
319 Heliolisk
318 Helioptile
314 Hippopotas
315 Hippowdon
109 Hitmonchan
108 Hitmonlee
110 Hitmontop
330 Honedge
019 Hoothoot
388 Hydreigon
238 Impidimp
337 Indeedee
290 Inkay
009 Inteleon
392 Jangmo-o
306 Jellicent
198 Jolteon
064 Joltik
273 Karrablast
099 Kingler
121 Kirlia
250 Koffing
394 Kommo-o
098 Krabby
288 Lampent
221 Lanturn
361 Lapras
383 Larvitar
202 Leafeon
045 Liepard
032 Linoone

287 Litwick
037 Lombre
036 Lotad
299 Lucario
038 Ludicolo
140 Machamp
139 Machoke
138 Machop
291 Malamar
077 Mamoswine
284 Mandibuzz
067 Manectric
355 Mantine
354 Mantyke
296 Maractus
307 Mareanie
295 Mawile
209 Meowstic
182 Meowth
185 Milcery
153 Milotic
364 Mime Jr.
301 Mimikyu
050 Minccino
340 Morelull
239 Morgrem
344 Morpeko
365 Mr. Mime
366 Mr. Rime
084 Mudbray
085 Mudsdale
260 Munchlax
090 Munna
091 Musharna
092 Natu
029 Nickit
069 Ninetales
020 Noctowl
176 Noibat
177 Noivern
040 Nuzleaf
033 Obstagoon
149 Octillery
055 Oddish
178 Onix
342 Oranguru
012 Orbeetle
133 Palpitoad
111 Pancham
112 Pangoro
343 Passimian
246 Pawniard
063 Pelipper
183 Perrserker
184 Persian
338 Phantump
193 Pichu
026 Pidove
194 Pikachu
076 Piloswine
353 Pincurchin
333 Ponyta
191 Pumpkaboo
384 Pupitar
044 Purrloin
156 Pyukumuku
101 Quagsire
304 Qwilfish
005 Raboot
195 Raichu
120 Ralts
334 Rapidash
148 Remoraid

272 Reuniclus
265 Rhydon
264 Rhyhorn
266 Rhyperior
188 Ribombee
003 Rillaboom
298 Riolu
168 Roggenrola
161 Rolycoly
021 Rookidee
060 Roselia
061 Roserade
281 Rufflet
328 Runerigus
294 Sableye
244 Salandit
245 Salazzle
313 Sandaconda
249 Sawk
004 Scorbunny
225 Scrafty
224 Scraggy
147 Seaking
039 Seedot
134 Seismitoad
150 Shellder
230 Shellos
275 Shelmet
041 Shiftry
341 Shiinotic
227 Shuckle
297 Sigilyph
312 Silicobra
219 Sirfetch'd
159 Sizzlipede
285 Skorupi
131 Skuntank
024 Skwovet
390 Sliggoo
211 Slurpuff
292 Sneasel
349 Snom
261 Snorlax
079 Snorunt
096 Snover
007 Sobble
270 Solosis
212 Spritzee
179 Steelix
053 Steenee
369 Stonjourner
094 Stufful
226 Stunfisk
130 Stunky
253 Sudowoodo
075 Swinub
210 Swirlix
175 Swoobat
204 Sylveon
030 Thievul
248 Throh
002 Thwackey
171 Timburr
348 Togedemaru
259 Togekiss
257 Togepi
258 Togetic
300 Torkoal
308 Toxapex
310 Toxel
223 Toxicroak
311 Toxtricity
027 Tranquill

321 Trapinch
339 Trevenant
157 Trubbish
054 Tsareena
347 Turtonator
132 Tympole
385 Tyranitar
107 Tyrogue
201 Umbreon
028 Unfezant
073 Vanillish
072 Vanillite
074 Vanilluxe
197 Vaporeon
117 Vespiquen
322 Vibrava
018 Vikavolt
057 Vileplume
283 Vullaby
068 Vulpix
356 Wailmer
357 Wailord
293 Weavile
251 Weezing
263 Whimsicott
229 Whiscash
232 Wimpod
062 Wingull
155 Wishiwashi
174 Woobat
034 Wooloo
100 Wooper
093 Xatu
327 Yamask
046 Yamper
031 Zigzagoon
387 Zweilous

Aura Sphere (TR56)
123 Gallade
109 Hitmonchan
108 Hitmonlee
394 Kommo-o
299 Lucario
259 Togekiss

Aura Wheel
344 Morpeko

Aurora Beam
151 Cloyster
078 Delibird
350 Frosmoth
149 Octillery
148 Remoraid
150 Shellder
197 Vaporeon

Aurora Veil
097 Abomasnow
377 Arctovish
358 Bergmite
078 Delibird
370 Eiscue
081 Froslass
350 Frosmoth
072 Vanillite

Autotomize
332 Aegislash
331 Doublade
393 Hakamo-o
330 Honedge
114 Klang
113 Klink
115 Klinklang
394 Kommo-o

168 Roggenrola
179 Steelix
157 Trubbish
072 Vanillite

Avalanche (TM64)
097 Abomasnow
377 Arctovish
375 Arctozolt
359 Avalugg
280 Beartic
358 Bergmite
151 Cloyster
103 Crawdaunt
279 Cubchoo
368 Darmanitan
367 Darumaka
078 Delibird
370 Eiscue
081 Froslass
350 Frosmoth
203 Glaceon
080 Glalie
145 Gyarados
361 Lapras
077 Mamoswine
153 Milotic
365 Mr. Mime
366 Mr. Rime
076 Piloswine
265 Rhydon
266 Rhyperior
150 Shellder
292 Sneasel
079 Snorunt
096 Snover
075 Swinub
385 Tyranitar
073 Vanillish
072 Vanillite
074 Vanilluxe
356 Wailmer
357 Wailord
293 Weavile

Baby-Doll Eyes
095 Bewear
051 Cinccino
196 Eevee
200 Espeon
199 Flareon
203 Glaceon
198 Jolteon
202 Leafeon
032 Linoone
185 Milcery
301 Mimikyu
050 Minccino
033 Obstagoon
094 Stufful
204 Sylveon
201 Umbreon
197 Vaporeon
068 Vulpix
031 Zigzagoon

Baneful Bunker
308 Toxapex

Baton Pass (TR29)
276 Accelgor
058 Bellossom
015 Butterfree
006 Cinderace
256 Clefable

255 Clefairy
222 Croagunk
187 Cutiefly
078 Delibird
397 Dragapult
396 Drakloak
395 Dreepy
125 Drifblim
124 Drifloon
008 Drizzile
035 Dubwool
316 Durant
196 Eevee
200 Espeon
199 Flareon
203 Glaceon
241 Hatenna
243 Hatterene
242 Hattrem
320 Hawlucha
337 Indeedee
290 Inkay
009 Inteleon
198 Jolteon
202 Leafeon
045 Liepard
362 Lunatone
291 Malamar
295 Mawile
364 Mime Jr.
365 Mr. Mime
366 Mr. Rime
092 Natu
029 Nickit
105 Ninjask
012 Orbeetle
183 Perrserker
336 Polteageist
044 Purrloin
156 Pyukumuku
005 Raboot
334 Rapidash
188 Ribombee
004 Scorbunny
275 Shelmet
335 Sinistea
007 Sobble
363 Solrock
175 Swoobat
204 Sylveon
030 Thievul
259 Togekiss
257 Togepi
258 Togetic
223 Toxicroak
201 Umbreon
197 Vaporeon
174 Woobat
093 Xatu

Beat Up (TM37)
235 Barbaracle
234 Binacle
247 Bisharp
380 Charizard
378 Charmander
379 Charmeleon
262 Cottonee
164 Diglett
397 Dragapult
396 Drakloak
165 Dugtrio
316 Durant
345 Falinks

388 Hydreigon
301 Mimikyu
029 Nickit
040 Nuzleaf
112 Pangoro
343 Passimian
246 Pawniard
244 Salandit
245 Salazzle
225 Scrafty
224 Scraggy
039 Seedot
041 Shiftry
292 Sneasel
030 Thievul
074 Vanilluxe
117 Vespiquen
293 Weavile
263 Whimsicott
155 Wishiwashi
387 Zweilous

Behemoth Bash
399 Zamazenta

Behemoth Blade
398 Zacian

Belch
309 Cramorant
222 Croagunk
302 Cufant
386 Deino
158 Garbodor
025 Greedent
317 Heatmor
250 Koffing
260 Munchlax
092 Natu
029 Nickit
312 Silicobra
131 Skuntank
024 Skwovet
261 Snorlax
130 Stunky
310 Toxel
223 Toxicroak
311 Toxtricity
157 Trubbish
251 Weezing
229 Whiscash

Belly Drum
378 Charmander
368 Darmanitan
367 Darumaka
370 Eiscue
394 Kommo-o
260 Munchlax
024 Skwovet
261 Snorlax

Bind
095 Bewear
351 Clobbopus
008 Drizzile
136 Dusclops
137 Dusknoir
352 Grapploct
317 Heatmor
009 Inteleon
114 Klang
113 Klink
115 Klinklang
178 Onix
007 Sobble
179 Steelix
226 Stunfisk
248 Throh

Bite
215 Araquanid
071 Arcanine
377 Arctovish
180 Arrokuda
359 Avalugg
324 Axew
181 Barraskewda
154 Basculin
358 Bergmite
047 Boltund
160 Centiskorch
017 Charjabug
378 Charmander
042 Chewtle
368 Darmanitan
367 Darumaka
386 Deino
214 Dewpider
376 Dracovish
397 Dragapult
396 Drakloak
286 Drapion
043 Drednaw
395 Dreepy
316 Durant
196 Eevee
066 Electrike
200 Espeon
199 Flareon
323 Flygon
325 Fraxure
081 Froslass
203 Glaceon
080 Glalie
025 Greedent
240 Grimmsnarl
070 Growlithe
016 Grubbin
145 Gyarados
326 Haxorus
314 Hippopotas
315 Hippowdon
388 Hydreigon
238 Impidimp
198 Jolteon
383 Larvitar
202 Leafeon
067 Manectric
307 Mareanie
295 Mawile
182 Meowth
239 Morgrem
344 Morpeko
260 Munchlax
176 Noibat
177 Noivern
184 Persian
384 Pupitar
298 Riolu
382 Silvally
159 Sizzlipede
285 Skorupi
131 Skuntank
024 Skwovet
292 Sneasel
261 Snorlax
079 Snorunt
130 Stunky
075 Swinub
204 Sylveon
308 Toxapex
321 Trapinch

385 Tyranitar
201 Umbreon
197 Vaporeon
322 Vibrava
018 Vikavolt
046 Yamper
398 Zacian
399 Zamazenta
387 Zweilous

Blast Burn
380 Charizard
006 Cinderace

Blaze Kick (TR41)
380 Charizard
006 Cinderace
108 Hitmonlee
299 Lucario
005 Raboot
298 Riolu
004 Scorbunny

Blizzard (TR06)
097 Abomasnow
215 Araquanid
377 Arctovish
375 Arctozolt
359 Avalugg
235 Barbaracle
228 Barboach
280 Beartic
358 Bergmite
234 Binacle
220 Chinchou
256 Clefable
255 Clefairy
151 Cloyster
102 Corphish
236 Corsola
309 Cramorant
103 Crawdaunt
279 Cubchoo
237 Cursola
368 Darmanitan
367 Darumaka
078 Delibird
214 Dewpider
346 Drampa
043 Drednaw
136 Dusclops
137 Dusknoir
135 Duskull
370 Eiscue
152 Feebas
305 Frillish
081 Froslass
350 Frosmoth
231 Gastrodon
203 Glaceon
080 Glalie
146 Goldeen
233 Golisopod
391 Goodra
145 Gyarados
009 Inteleon
306 Jellicent
099 Kingler
098 Krabby
221 Lanturn
361 Lapras
032 Linoone
037 Lombre
036 Lotad
038 Ludicolo
362 Lunatone

077 Mamoswine
355 Mantine
354 Mantyke
307 Mareanie
153 Milotic
365 Mr. Mime
366 Mr. Rime
260 Munchlax
033 Obstagoon
149 Octillery
063 Pelipper
076 Piloswine
101 Quagsire
304 Qwilfish
148 Remoraid
265 Rhydon
264 Rhyhorn
266 Rhyperior
372 Rotom
147 Seaking
150 Shellder
230 Shellos
390 Sliggoo
292 Sneasel
261 Snorlax
079 Snorunt
096 Snover
075 Swinub
308 Toxapex
385 Tyranitar
073 Vanillish
072 Vanillite
074 Vanilluxe
197 Vaporeon
356 Wailmer
357 Wailord
293 Weavile
229 Whiscash
062 Wingull
100 Wooper
031 Zigzagoon

Block
252 Bonsly
119 Bronzong
086 Dwebble
330 Honedge
366 Mr. Rime
178 Onix
161 Rolycoly
261 Snorlax
079 Snorunt
369 Stonjourner
253 Sudowoodo

Body Press (TR99)
207 Appletun
359 Avalugg
280 Beartic
095 Bewear
169 Boldore
119 Bronzong
162 Carkol
083 Claydol
163 Coalossal
329 Cofagrigus
303 Copperajah
023 Corviknight
087 Crustle
302 Cufant
368 Darmanitan
360 Dhelmise
011 Dottler
043 Drednaw

035 Dubwool
371 Duraludon
190 Ferrothorn
158 Garbodor
170 Gigalith
089 Golurk
391 Goodra
025 Greedent
240 Grimmsnarl
320 Hawlucha
315 Hippowdon
394 Kommo-o
361 Lapras
032 Linoone
077 Mamoswine
355 Mantine
085 Mudsdale
033 Obstagoon
178 Onix
012 Orbeetle
265 Rhydon
266 Rhyperior
003 Rillaboom
168 Roggenrola
328 Runerigus
313 Sandaconda
261 Snorlax
179 Steelix
369 Stonjourner
253 Sudowoodo
300 Torkoal
347 Turtonator
385 Tyranitar
356 Wailmer
357 Wailord

Body Slam (TR01)
276 Accelgor
207 Appletun
071 Arcanine
377 Arctovish
375 Arctozolt
359 Avalugg
095 Bewear
380 Charizard
378 Charmander
379 Charmeleon
042 Chewtle
256 Clefable
255 Clefairy
254 Cleffa
351 Clobbopus
163 Coalossal
303 Copperajah
102 Corphish
236 Corsola
023 Corviknight
103 Crawdaunt
302 Cufant
237 Cursola
368 Darmanitan
386 Deino
078 Delibird
049 Diggersby
164 Diglett
376 Dracovish
374 Dracozolt
397 Dragapult
043 Drednaw
125 Drifblim
124 Drifloon
035 Dubwool
165 Dugtrio
371 Duraludon

136 Dusclops
137 Dusknoir
135 Duskull
196 Eevee
066 Electrike
200 Espeon
218 Farfetch'd
199 Flareon
323 Flygon
081 Froslass
123 Gallade
158 Garbodor
122 Gardevoir
231 Gastrodon
143 Gengar
203 Glaceon
080 Glalie
146 Goldeen
089 Golurk
391 Goodra
389 Goomy
352 Grapploct
025 Greedent
240 Grimmsnarl
070 Growlithe
145 Gyarados
317 Heatmor
314 Hippopotas
315 Hippowdon
109 Hitmonchan
108 Hitmonlee
110 Hitmontop
388 Hydreigon
198 Jolteon
099 Kingler
121 Kirlia
098 Krabby
361 Lapras
383 Larvitar
202 Leafeon
032 Linoone
037 Lombre
036 Lotad
038 Ludicolo
362 Lunatone
140 Machamp
139 Machoke
138 Machop
077 Mamoswine
067 Manectric
355 Mantine
295 Mawile
182 Meowth
153 Milotic
365 Mr. Mime
366 Mr. Rime
084 Mudbray
085 Mudsdale
260 Munchlax
069 Ninetales
040 Nuzleaf
033 Obstagoon
178 Onix
111 Pancham
112 Pangoro
183 Perrserker
184 Persian
193 Pichu
194 Pikachu
076 Piloswine
333 Ponyta
384 Pupitar
101 Quagsire

195 Raichu
120 Ralts
334 Rapidash
265 Rhydon
264 Rhyhorn
266 Rhyperior
003 Rillaboom
060 Roselia
061 Roserade
294 Sableye
147 Seaking
039 Seedot
230 Shellos
275 Shelmet
041 Shiftry
227 Shuckle
219 Sirfetch'd
024 Skwovet
390 Sliggoo
261 Snorlax
079 Snorunt
363 Solrock
179 Steelix
369 Stonjourner
253 Sudowoodo
075 Swinub
204 Sylveon
248 Throh
259 Togekiss
257 Togepi
258 Togetic
300 Torkoal
321 Trapinch
347 Turtonator
385 Tyranitar
107 Tyrogue
201 Umbreon
197 Vaporeon
322 Vibrava
057 Vileplume
068 Vulpix
356 Wailmer
357 Wailord
100 Wooper
031 Zigzagoon
387 Zweilous

Bolt Beak
375 Arctozolt
374 Dracozolt

Bone Rush
299 Lucario
284 Mandibuzz

Boomburst
323 Flygon
394 Kommo-o
177 Noivern
003 Rillaboom
311 Toxtricity
322 Vibrava

Bounce (TM52)
180 Arrokuda
228 Barboach
181 Barraskewda
154 Basculin
052 Bounsweet
048 Bunnelby
220 Chinchou
006 Cinderace
256 Clefable
255 Clefairy
222 Croagunk
078 Delibird
049 Diggersby

008 Drizzile
035 Dubwool
065 Galvantula
146 Goldeen
145 Gyarados
320 Hawlucha
108 Hitmonlee
009 Inteleon
064 Joltik
221 Lanturn
144 Magikarp
355 Mantine
354 Mantyke
296 Maractus
149 Octillery
133 Palpitoad
333 Ponyta
304 Qwilfish
005 Raboot
334 Rapidash
148 Remoraid
004 Scorbunny
147 Seaking
041 Shiftry
007 Sobble
053 Steenee
226 Stunfisk
348 Togedemaru
223 Toxicroak
054 Tsareena
132 Tympole
356 Wailmer
357 Wailord
229 Whiscash

Branch Poke
001 Grookey
338 Phantump
003 Rillaboom
002 Thwackey
339 Trevenant

Brave Bird (TR66)
282 Braviary
023 Corviknight
022 Corvisquire
309 Cramorant
078 Delibird
218 Farfetch'd
320 Hawlucha
284 Mandibuzz
063 Pelipper
021 Rookidee
281 Rufflet
219 Sirfetch'd
028 Unfezant
283 Vullaby

Breaking Swipe (TM99)
324 Axew
380 Charizard
374 Dracozolt
397 Dragapult
396 Drakloak
346 Drampa
371 Duraludon
323 Flygon
325 Fraxure
391 Goodra
326 Haxorus
319 Heliolisk
388 Hydreigon
009 Inteleon
394 Kommo-o

153 Milotic
178 Onix
265 Rhydon
266 Rhyperior
245 Salazzle
179 Steelix
385 Tyranitar

Brick Break (TM43)
097 Abomasnow
332 Aegislash
180 Arrokuda
235 Barbaracle
181 Barraskewda
280 Beartic
095 Bewear
234 Binacle
247 Bisharp
252 Bonsly
048 Bunnelby
380 Charizard
378 Charmander
379 Charmeleon
256 Clefable
255 Clefairy
351 Clobbopus
173 Conkeldurr
303 Copperajah
102 Corphish
103 Crawdaunt
222 Croagunk
302 Cufant
368 Darmanitan
367 Darumaka
078 Delibird
360 Dhelmise
049 Diggersby
331 Doublade
286 Drapion
166 Drilbur
371 Duraludon
136 Dusclops
137 Dusknoir
167 Excadrill
345 Falinks
218 Farfetch'd
123 Gallade
143 Gengar
088 Golett
233 Golisopod
089 Golurk
269 Gothitelle
352 Grapploct
240 Grimmsnarl
172 Gurdurr
393 Hakamo-o
320 Hawlucha
326 Haxorus
109 Hitmonchan
108 Hitmonlee
110 Hitmontop
330 Honedge
392 Jangmo-o
099 Kingler
394 Kommo-o
098 Krabby
383 Larvitar
037 Lombre
299 Lucario
038 Ludicolo
140 Machamp
139 Machoke
138 Machop
295 Mawile

419

364 Mime Jr.
344 Morpeko
365 Mr. Mime
366 Mr. Rime
260 Munchlax
176 Noibat
177 Noivern
040 Nuzleaf
033 Obstagoon
342 Oranguru
111 Pancham
112 Pangoro
343 Passimian
246 Pawniard
194 Pikachu
384 Pupitar
101 Quagsire
195 Raichu
265 Rhydon
266 Rhyperior
003 Rillaboom
298 Riolu
294 Sableye
249 Sawk
225 Scrafty
224 Scraggy
134 Seismitoad
041 Shiftry
219 Sirfetch'd
285 Skorupi
292 Sneasel
261 Snorlax
094 Stufful
253 Sudowoodo
248 Throh
171 Timburr
259 Togekiss
258 Togetic
223 Toxicroak
385 Tyranitar
107 Tyrogue
293 Weavile
398 Zacian

Brine (TM55)
377 Arctovish
154 Basculin
280 Beartic
220 Chinchou
351 Clobbopus
151 Cloyster
236 Corsola
279 Cubchoo
237 Cursola
360 Dhelmise
376 Dracovish
397 Dragapult
396 Drakloak
370 Eiscue
152 Feebas
305 Frillish
231 Gastrodon
352 Grapploct
145 Gyarados
306 Jellicent
099 Kingler
098 Krabby
221 Lanturn
361 Lapras
355 Mantine
307 Mareanie
153 Milotic
149 Octillery
063 Pelipper

353 Pincurchin
304 Qwilfish
148 Remoraid
150 Shellder
230 Shellos
308 Toxapex
197 Vaporeon
356 Wailmer
357 Wailord
062 Wingull
155 Wishiwashi

Brutal Swing (TM97)
332 Aegislash
235 Barbaracle
095 Bewear
160 Centiskorch
380 Charizard
173 Conkeldurr
303 Copperajah
302 Cufant
078 Delibird
360 Dhelmise
049 Diggersby
331 Doublade
376 Dracovish
374 Dracozolt
286 Drapion
125 Drifblim
124 Drifloon
274 Escavalier
400 Eternatus
167 Excadrill
218 Farfetch'd
190 Ferrothorn
323 Flygon
391 Goodra
192 Gourgeist
352 Grapploct
025 Greedent
172 Gurdurr
145 Gyarados
393 Hakamo-o
243 Hatterene
242 Hattrem
326 Haxorus
317 Heatmor
319 Heliolisk
110 Hitmontop
330 Honedge
388 Hydreigon
099 Kingler
394 Kommo-o
291 Malamar
295 Mawile
153 Milotic
178 Onix
342 Oranguru
343 Passimian
195 Raichu
265 Rhydon
266 Rhyperior
003 Rillaboom
328 Runerigus
313 Sandaconda
041 Shiftry
312 Silicobra
219 Sirfetch'd
159 Sizzlipede
024 Skwovet
179 Steelix
369 Stonjourner
094 Stufful

171 Timburr
339 Trevenant
347 Turtonator
385 Tyranitar
251 Weezing
327 Yamask
398 Zacian

Bubble Beam
215 Araquanid
154 Basculin
220 Chinchou
102 Corphish
103 Crawdaunt
214 Dewpider
305 Frillish
099 Kingler
098 Krabby
221 Lanturn
037 Lombre
036 Lotad
038 Ludicolo
355 Mantine
354 Mantyke
149 Octillery
133 Palpitoad
353 Pincurchin
304 Qwilfish
148 Remoraid
134 Seismitoad
150 Shellder
132 Tympole

Bug Bite
215 Araquanid
015 Butterfree
013 Caterpie
160 Centiskorch
017 Charjabug
116 Combee
087 Crustle
214 Dewpider
286 Drapion
316 Durant
086 Dwebble
065 Galvantula
233 Golisopod
016 Grubbin
317 Heatmor
064 Joltik
273 Karrablast
104 Nincada
105 Ninjask
227 Shuckle
159 Sizzlipede
285 Skorupi
349 Snom
321 Trapinch
117 Vespiquen
018 Vikavolt

Bug Buzz (TR61)
276 Accelgor
215 Araquanid
015 Butterfree
160 Centiskorch
116 Combee
187 Cutiefly
214 Dewpider
011 Dottler
286 Drapion
274 Escavalier
323 Flygon
350 Frosmoth
065 Galvantula
233 Golisopod

064 Joltik
273 Karrablast
104 Nincada
105 Ninjask
012 Orbeetle
188 Ribombee
106 Shedinja
275 Shelmet
159 Sizzlipede
285 Skorupi
349 Snom
117 Vespiquen
322 Vibrava
018 Vikavolt
232 Wimpod

Bulk Up (TR48)
235 Barbaracle
280 Beartic
095 Bewear
047 Boltund
282 Braviary
048 Bunnelby
006 Cinderace
351 Clobbopus
173 Conkeldurr
023 Corviknight
222 Croagunk
368 Darmanitan
049 Diggersby
345 Falinks
123 Gallade
233 Golisopod
352 Grapploct
240 Grimmsnarl
172 Gurdurr
393 Hakamo-o
320 Hawlucha
109 Hitmonchan
108 Hitmonlee
110 Hitmontop
392 Jangmo-o
394 Kommo-o
299 Lucario
140 Machamp
139 Machoke
138 Machop
301 Mimikyu
033 Obstagoon
111 Pancham
112 Pangoro
343 Passimian
005 Raboot
003 Rillaboom
298 Riolu
281 Rufflet
249 Sawk
225 Scrafty
224 Scraggy
094 Stufful
248 Throh
171 Timburr
223 Toxicroak
347 Turtonator
107 Tyrogue

Bulldoze (TM81)
097 Abomasnow
207 Appletun
071 Arcanine
375 Arctozolt
359 Avalugg
082 Baltoy
235 Barbaracle
228 Barboach

280 Beartic
095 Bewear
234 Binacle
169 Boldore
119 Bronzong
118 Bronzor
048 Bunnelby
380 Charizard
083 Claydol
163 Coalossal
173 Conkeldurr
303 Copperajah
236 Corsola
222 Croagunk
087 Crustle
302 Cufant
237 Cursola
368 Darmanitan
360 Dhelmise
049 Diggersby
164 Diglett
376 Dracovish
374 Dracozolt
346 Drampa
286 Drapion
043 Drednaw
166 Drilbur
165 Dugtrio
136 Dusclops
137 Dusknoir
086 Dwebble
167 Excadrill
190 Ferrothorn
323 Flygon
123 Gallade
231 Gastrodon
170 Gigalith
080 Glalie
088 Golett
089 Golurk
391 Goodra
145 Gyarados
393 Hakamo-o
326 Haxorus
319 Heliolisk
318 Helioptile
314 Hippopotas
315 Hippowdon
109 Hitmonchan
108 Hitmonlee
110 Hitmontop
388 Hydreigon
392 Jangmo-o
394 Kommo-o
361 Lapras
383 Larvitar
299 Lucario
362 Lunatone
140 Machamp
139 Machoke
138 Machop
077 Mamoswine
355 Mantine
354 Mantyke
153 Milotic
084 Mudbray
085 Mudsdale
260 Munchlax
178 Onix
342 Oranguru
133 Palpitoad
111 Pancham
112 Pangoro

343 Passimian
338 Phantump
076 Piloswine
384 Pupitar
101 Quagsire
265 Rhydon
264 Rhyhorn
266 Rhyperior
003 Rillaboom
298 Riolu
168 Roggenrola
328 Runerigus
313 Sandaconda
249 Sawk
134 Seismitoad
227 Shuckle
312 Silicobra
261 Snorlax
363 Solrock
179 Steelix
369 Stonjourner
094 Stufful
226 Stunfisk
253 Sudowoodo
075 Swinub
248 Throh
300 Torkoal
223 Toxicroak
321 Trapinch
339 Trevenant
347 Turtonator
385 Tyranitar
107 Tyrogue
322 Vibrava
356 Wailmer
357 Wailord
229 Whiscash
155 Wishiwashi
100 Wooper

Bullet Punch
222 Croagunk
109 Hitmonchan
138 Machop
112 Pangoro
298 Riolu
107 Tyrogue

Bullet Seed (TM50)
097 Abomasnow
207 Appletun
058 Bellossom
059 Budew
129 Cherrim
128 Cherubi
051 Cinccino
127 Eldegoss
189 Ferroseed
190 Ferrothorn
206 Flapple
056 Gloom
126 Gossifleur
192 Gourgeist
025 Greedent
202 Leafeon
037 Lombre
036 Lotad
038 Ludicolo
355 Mantine
296 Maractus
344 Morpeko
040 Nuzleaf
149 Octillery
055 Oddish

191 Pumpkaboo
148 Remoraid
003 Rillaboom
060 Roselia
061 Roserade
039 Seedot
041 Shiftry
024 Skwovet
096 Snover
057 Vileplume

Burn Up
071 Arcanine
162 Carkol
160 Centiskorch
163 Coalossal
159 Sizzlipede

Calm Mind (TR49)
186 Alcremie
213 Aromatisse
082 Baltoy
278 Beheeyem
252 Bonsly
119 Bronzong
118 Bronzor
289 Chandelure
051 Cinccino
083 Claydol
256 Clefable
255 Clefairy
329 Cofagrigus
236 Corsola
237 Cursola
187 Cutiefly
011 Dottler
346 Drampa
125 Drifblim
124 Drifloon
271 Duosion
136 Dusclops
137 Dusknoir
135 Duskull
277 Elgyem
200 Espeon
208 Espurr
350 Frosmoth
123 Gallade
122 Gardevoir
267 Gothita
269 Gothitelle
268 Gothorita
241 Hatenna
243 Hatterene
242 Hattrem
019 Hoothoot
337 Indeedee
290 Inkay
121 Kirlia
288 Lampent
287 Litwick
299 Lucario
362 Lunatone
291 Malamar
209 Meowstic
364 Mime Jr.
050 Minccino
365 Mr. Mime
366 Mr. Rime
090 Munna
091 Musharna
092 Natu
069 Ninetales
020 Noctowl
342 Oranguru

012 Orbeetle
333 Ponyta
120 Ralts
334 Rapidash
272 Reuniclus
188 Ribombee
328 Runerigus
294 Sableye
297 Sigilyph
211 Slurpuff
292 Sneasel
270 Solosis
363 Solrock
212 Spritzee
253 Sudowoodo
210 Swirlix
175 Swoobat
204 Sylveon
339 Trevenant
293 Weavile
174 Woobat
093 Xatu
327 Yamask

Charge
375 Arctozolt
047 Boltund
017 Charjabug
220 Chinchou
374 Dracozolt
066 Electrike
319 Heliolisk
318 Helioptile
114 Klang
113 Klink
115 Klinklang
221 Lanturn
067 Manectric
344 Morpeko
193 Pichu
353 Pincurchin
372 Rotom
348 Togedemaru
311 Toxtricity
018 Vikavolt
046 Yamper

Charge Beam
114 Klang
113 Klink
115 Klinklang
209 Meowstic

Charm (TM29)
186 Alcremie
213 Aromatisse
280 Beartic
058 Bellossom
095 Bewear
047 Boltund
052 Bounsweet
051 Cinccino
256 Clefable
255 Clefairy
254 Cleffa
262 Cottonee
279 Cubchoo
187 Cutiefly
271 Duosion
196 Eevee
127 Eldegoss
200 Espeon
199 Flareon
081 Froslass
123 Gallade
122 Gardevoir
203 Glaceon
056 Gloom
126 Gossifleur
267 Gothita
269 Gothitelle
268 Gothorita
241 Hatenna
243 Hatterene
242 Hattrem
198 Jolteon
121 Kirlia
361 Lapras
202 Leafeon
045 Liepard
209 Meowstic
182 Meowth
185 Milcery
364 Mime Jr.
301 Mimikyu
050 Minccino
365 Mr. Mime
366 Mr. Rime
260 Munchlax
055 Oddish
184 Persian
193 Pichu
194 Pikachu
333 Ponyta
044 Purrloin
195 Raichu
120 Ralts
334 Rapidash
272 Reuniclus
188 Ribombee
211 Slurpuff
261 Snorlax
270 Solosis
212 Spritzee
053 Steenee
094 Stufful
210 Swirlix
175 Swoobat
204 Sylveon
259 Togekiss
257 Togepi
258 Togetic
054 Tsareena
201 Umbreon
197 Vaporeon
057 Vileplume
263 Whimsicott
217 Wobbuffet
174 Woobat
216 Wynaut
046 Yamper

Circle Throw
351 Clobbopus
111 Pancham
112 Pangoro
298 Riolu
248 Throh

Clanging Scales
394 Kommo-o

Clangorous Soul
394 Kommo-o

Clear Smog
124 Drifloon
158 Garbodor
141 Gastly
250 Koffing
287 Litwick
230 Shellos
300 Torkoal
157 Trubbish
251 Weezing

Close Combat (TR53)
332 Aegislash
071 Arcanine
180 Arrokuda
181 Barraskewda
095 Bewear
282 Braviary
351 Clobbopus
173 Conkeldurr
103 Crawdaunt
331 Doublade
274 Escavalier
345 Falinks
218 Farfetch'd
123 Gallade
233 Golisopod
089 Golurk
352 Grapploct
070 Growlithe
172 Gurdurr
393 Hakamo-o
320 Hawlucha
326 Haxorus
109 Hitmonchan
108 Hitmonlee
110 Hitmontop
330 Honedge
394 Kommo-o
299 Lucario
140 Machamp
139 Machoke
138 Machop
084 Mudbray
085 Mudsdale
033 Obstagoon
112 Pangoro
343 Passimian
183 Perrserker
281 Rufflet
249 Sawk
225 Scrafty
219 Sirfetch'd
398 Zacian
399 Zamazenta

Coil
160 Centiskorch
153 Milotic
313 Sandaconda
312 Silicobra
159 Sizzlipede

Confide
240 Grimmsnarl
238 Impidimp
239 Morgrem

Confuse Ray
119 Bronzong
118 Bronzor
289 Chandelure
220 Chinchou
236 Corsola
395 Dreepy
136 Dusclops
137 Dusknoir
135 Duskull
400 Eternatus
152 Feebas
305 Frillish
081 Froslass
141 Gastly
143 Gengar
192 Gourgeist
142 Haunter
288 Lampent
221 Lanturn
361 Lapras
287 Litwick
355 Mantine
354 Mantyke
364 Mime Jr.
340 Morelull
365 Mr. Mime
092 Natu
069 Ninetales
012 Orbeetle
338 Phantump
191 Pumpkaboo
120 Ralts
372 Rotom
294 Sableye
106 Shedinja
341 Shiinotic
285 Skorupi
270 Solosis
339 Trevenant
201 Umbreon
117 Vespiquen
068 Vulpix
093 Xatu

Confusion
082 Baltoy
278 Beheeyem
119 Bronzong
118 Bronzor
015 Butterfree
083 Claydol
011 Dottler
271 Duosion
277 Elgyem
200 Espeon
208 Espurr
123 Gallade
122 Gardevoir
267 Gothita
269 Gothitelle
268 Gothorita
241 Hatenna
243 Hatterene
242 Hattrem
019 Hoothoot
121 Kirlia
362 Lunatone
209 Meowstic
364 Mime Jr.
365 Mr. Mime
366 Mr. Rime
020 Noctowl
342 Oranguru
012 Orbeetle
333 Ponyta
120 Ralts
334 Rapidash
272 Reuniclus
297 Sigilyph
270 Solosis
363 Solrock
175 Swoobat
174 Woobat

Copycat
252 Bonsly
256 Clefable
255 Clefairy
254 Cleffa
035 Dubwool
196 Eevee
200 Espeon
199 Flareon
203 Glaceon
198 Jolteon
202 Leafeon
299 Lucario
364 Mime Jr.
301 Mimikyu
365 Mr. Mime
366 Mr. Rime
044 Purrloin
298 Riolu
253 Sudowoodo
210 Swirlix
204 Sylveon
201 Umbreon
197 Vaporeon
034 Wooloo

Cosmic Power (TR44)
082 Baltoy
278 Beheeyem
083 Claydol
256 Clefable
255 Clefairy
277 Elgyem
400 Eternatus
269 Gothitelle
362 Lunatone
092 Natu
297 Sigilyph
363 Solrock
093 Xatu

Cotton Guard
262 Cottonee
035 Dubwool
127 Eldegoss
296 Maractus
211 Slurpuff
210 Swirlix
263 Whimsicott
034 Wooloo

Cotton Spore
059 Budew
262 Cottonee
127 Eldegoss
296 Maractus
060 Roselia
211 Slurpuff
210 Swirlix
263 Whimsicott

Counter
324 Axew
252 Bonsly
378 Charmander
042 Chewtle
006 Cinderace
222 Croagunk
078 Delibird
043 Drednaw
086 Dwebble
345 Falinks
218 Farfetch'd
389 Goomy
025 Greedent
109 Hitmonchan
110 Hitmontop
392 Jangmo-o
273 Karrablast
032 Linoone
036 Lotad
299 Lucario
138 Machop
084 Mudbray
085 Mudsdale
260 Munchlax
033 Obstagoon
343 Passimian
156 Pyukumuku
005 Raboot
264 Rhyhorn
298 Riolu
249 Sawk
004 Scorbunny
224 Scraggy
230 Shellos
024 Skwovet
292 Sneasel
261 Snorlax
226 Stunfisk
253 Sudowoodo
171 Timburr
107 Tyrogue
217 Wobbuffet
034 Wooloo
100 Wooper
216 Wynaut
031 Zigzagoon

Court Change
006 Cinderace

Covet
196 Eevee
200 Espeon
208 Espurr
218 Farfetch'd
199 Flareon
203 Glaceon
025 Greedent
070 Growlithe
198 Jolteon
202 Leafeon
209 Meowstic
182 Meowth
260 Munchlax
044 Purrloin
188 Ribombee
227 Shuckle
261 Snorlax
204 Sylveon
201 Umbreon
197 Vaporeon

Crabhammer
102 Corphish
103 Crawdaunt
099 Kingler
098 Krabby

Crafty Shield
329 Cofagrigus
328 Runerigus
327 Yamask

Cross Chop
235 Barbaracle
234 Binacle
222 Croagunk
320 Hawlucha
140 Machamp
139 Machoke
138 Machop
033 Obstagoon
298 Riolu

Cross Poison (TM73)
286 Drapion
400 Eternatus
065 Galvantula
158 Garbodor
064 Joltik
140 Machamp
033 Obstagoon
245 Salazzle
285 Skorupi
308 Toxapex
223 Toxicroak
117 Vespiquen

Crunch (TR32)
215 Araquanid
071 Arcanine
377 Arctovish
180 Arrokuda
359 Avalugg
324 Axew
181 Barraskewda
154 Basculin
358 Bergmite
047 Boltund
160 Centiskorch
380 Charizard
017 Charjabug
378 Charmander
379 Charmeleon
102 Corphish
103 Crawdaunt
386 Deino
214 Dewpider
376 Dracovish
286 Drapion
043 Drednaw
316 Durant
066 Electrike
323 Flygon
325 Fraxure
081 Froslass
080 Glalie
025 Greedent
240 Grimmsnarl
070 Growlithe
016 Grubbin
145 Gyarados
326 Haxorus
314 Hippopotas
315 Hippowdon
388 Hydreigon
383 Larvitar
299 Lucario
067 Manectric
295 Mawile
182 Meowth
344 Morpeko
111 Pancham
112 Pangoro
183 Perrserker
384 Pupitar
265 Rhydon
264 Rhyhorn
266 Rhyperior
298 Riolu
225 Scrafty
224 Scraggy
382 Silvally
159 Sizzlipede
285 Skorupi
131 Skuntank
024 Skwovet
261 Snorlax
079 Snorunt
179 Steelix
226 Stunfisk
130 Stunky

030 Thievul
321 Trapinch
385 Tyranitar
201 Umbreon
322 Vibrava
018 Vikavolt
046 Yamper
398 Zacian
399 Zamazenta
387 Zweilous

Crush Claw
282 Braviary
166 Drilbur
167 Excadrill
281 Rufflet
382 Silvally
381 Type: Null

Curse
276 Accelgor
207 Appletun
359 Avalugg
358 Bergmite
252 Bonsly
289 Chandelure
329 Cofagrigus
236 Corsola
302 Cufant
237 Cursola
395 Dreepy
136 Dusclops
137 Dusknoir
135 Duskull
086 Dwebble
196 Eevee
066 Electrike
218 Farfetch'd
189 Ferroseed
190 Ferrothorn
141 Gastly
143 Gengar
088 Golett
089 Golurk
391 Goodra
389 Goomy
142 Haunter
317 Heatmor
314 Hippopotas
250 Koffing
288 Lampent
361 Lapras
383 Larvitar
287 Litwick
182 Meowth
301 Mimikyu
260 Munchlax
090 Munna
178 Onix
338 Phantump
353 Pincurchin
336 Polteageist
191 Pumpkaboo
156 Pyukumuku
264 Rhyhorn
168 Roggenrola
328 Runerigus
230 Shellos
275 Shelmet
390 Sliggoo
261 Snorlax
179 Steelix
369 Stonjourner
226 Stunfisk
253 Sudowoodo

075 Swinub
300 Torkoal
339 Trevenant
157 Trubbish
347 Turtonator
356 Wailmer
100 Wooper
327 Yamask

Dark Pulse (TR58)
278 Beheeyem
247 Bisharp
289 Chandelure
329 Cofagrigus
103 Crawdaunt
222 Croagunk
386 Deino
286 Drapion
371 Duraludon
136 Dusclops
137 Dusknoir
135 Duskull
277 Elgyem
208 Espurr
305 Frillish
158 Garbodor
141 Gastly
143 Gengar
080 Glalie
233 Golisopod
267 Gothita
269 Gothitelle
268 Gothorita
192 Gourgeist
240 Grimmsnarl
145 Gyarados
241 Hatenna
243 Hatterene
242 Hattrem
142 Haunter
319 Heliolisk
318 Helioptile
388 Hydreigon
238 Impidimp
290 Inkay
009 Inteleon
306 Jellicent
250 Koffing
288 Lampent
383 Larvitar
045 Liepard
287 Litwick
299 Lucario
291 Malamar
284 Mandibuzz
295 Mawile
209 Meowstic
182 Meowth
301 Mimikyu
239 Morgrem
344 Morpeko
069 Ninetales
176 Noibat
177 Noivern
040 Nuzleaf
111 Pancham
112 Pangoro
246 Pawniard
183 Perrserker
184 Persian
338 Phantump
336 Polteageist
191 Pumpkaboo

384 Pupitar
044 Purrloin
372 Rotom
328 Runerigus
294 Sableye
225 Scrafty
224 Scraggy
041 Shiftry
297 Sigilyph
335 Sinistea
285 Skorupi
292 Sneasel
179 Steelix
130 Stunky
030 Thievul
223 Toxicroak
339 Trevenant
157 Trubbish
385 Tyranitar
201 Umbreon
283 Vullaby
068 Vulpix
293 Weavile
251 Weezing
327 Yamask
387 Zweilous

Darkest Lariat (TR93)
095 Bewear
137 Dusknoir
089 Golurk
240 Grimmsnarl
140 Machamp
112 Pangoro
003 Rillaboom
261 Snorlax

Dazzling Gleam (TR92)
186 Alcremie
213 Aromatisse
082 Baltoy
058 Bellossom
052 Bounsweet
059 Budew
129 Cherrim
128 Cherubi
220 Chinchou
051 Cinccino
083 Claydol
256 Clefable
255 Clefairy
262 Cottonee
187 Cutiefly
200 Espeon
305 Frillish
350 Frosmoth
123 Gallade
122 Gardevoir
141 Gastly
143 Gengar
056 Gloom
240 Grimmsnarl
241 Hatenna
243 Hatterene
242 Hattrem
238 Impidimp
337 Indeedee
306 Jellicent
121 Kirlia
221 Lanturn
185 Milcery

364 Mime Jr.
301 Mimikyu
050 Minccino
340 Morelull
239 Morgrem
365 Mr. Mime
366 Mr. Rime
090 Munna
091 Musharna
092 Natu
055 Oddish
333 Ponyta
120 Ralts
334 Rapidash
188 Ribombee
060 Roselia
061 Roserade
294 Sableye
341 Shiinotic
297 Sigilyph
211 Slurpuff
212 Spritzee
053 Steenee
210 Swirlix
204 Sylveon
259 Togekiss
257 Togepi
258 Togetic
054 Tsareena
057 Vileplume
251 Weezing
263 Whimsicott
093 Xatu
399 Zamazenta

Decorate
186 Alcremie

Defend Order
117 Vespiquen

Defense Curl
205 Applin
252 Bonsly
048 Bunnelby
128 Cherubi
256 Clefable
255 Clefairy
302 Cufant
035 Dubwool
088 Golett
233 Golisopod
089 Golurk
260 Munchlax
090 Munna
091 Musharna
178 Onix
227 Shuckle
159 Sizzlipede
024 Skwovet
261 Snorlax
094 Stufful
253 Sudowoodo
348 Togedemaru
356 Wailmer
232 Wimpod
034 Wooloo

Defog
282 Braviary
309 Cramorant
124 Drifloon
218 Farfetch'd
350 Frosmoth
320 Hawlucha
019 Hoothoot
284 Mandibuzz

176 Noibat
026 Pidove
021 Rookidee
281 Rufflet
039 Seedot
219 Sirfetch'd
171 Timburr
283 Vullaby
251 Weezing

Destiny Bond
329 Cofagrigus
236 Corsola
078 Delibird
125 Drifblim
124 Drifloon
137 Dusknoir
277 Elgyem
305 Frillish
081 Froslass
141 Gastly
143 Gengar
142 Haunter
330 Honedge
290 Inkay
306 Jellicent
250 Koffing
301 Mimikyu
338 Phantump
191 Pumpkaboo
304 Qwilfish
120 Ralts
328 Runerigus
339 Trevenant
117 Vespiquen
251 Weezing
217 Wobbuffet
216 Wynaut
327 Yamask

Detect
351 Clobbopus
196 Eevee
218 Farfetch'd
352 Grapploct
320 Hawlucha
109 Hitmonchan
110 Hitmontop
299 Lucario
026 Pidove
298 Riolu
294 Sableye
224 Scrafty
219 Sirfetch'd
171 Timburr
027 Tranquill
028 Unfezant

Dig (TM15)
071 Arcanine
324 Axew
082 Baltoy
235 Barbaracle
280 Beartic
234 Binacle
247 Bisharp
047 Boltund
252 Bonsly
048 Bunnelby
162 Carkol
380 Charizard
017 Charjabug
378 Charmander
379 Charmeleon
051 Cinccino
083 Claydol

256 Clefable
255 Clefairy
254 Cleffa
163 Coalossal
173 Conkeldurr
303 Copperajah
102 Corphish
236 Corsola
103 Crawdaunt
222 Croagunk
087 Crustle
279 Cubchoo
302 Cufant
237 Cursola
368 Darmanitan
367 Darumaka
049 Diggersby
164 Diglett
286 Drapion
043 Drednaw
166 Drilbur
165 Dugtrio
316 Durant
086 Dwebble
196 Eevee
200 Espeon
167 Excadrill
199 Flareon
323 Flygon
325 Fraxure
231 Gastrodon
203 Glaceon
088 Golett
089 Golurk
352 Grapploct
025 Greedent
070 Growlithe
016 Grubbin
172 Gurdurr
320 Hawlucha
326 Haxorus
317 Heatmor
319 Heliolisk
318 Helioptile
314 Hippopotas
315 Hippowdon
110 Hitmontop
198 Jolteon
099 Kingler
098 Krabby
383 Larvitar
202 Leafeon
032 Linoone
299 Lucario
140 Machamp
139 Machoke
138 Machop
077 Mamoswine
209 Meowstic
182 Meowth
050 Minccino
029 Nickit
104 Nincada
069 Ninetales
105 Ninjask
040 Nuzleaf
033 Obstagoon
178 Onix
111 Pancham
112 Pangoro
246 Pawniard
183 Perrserker
184 Persian

338 Phantump
194 Pikachu
076 Piloswine
384 Pupitar
101 Quagsire
195 Raichu
265 Rhydon
264 Rhyhorn
266 Rhyperior
298 Riolu
161 Rolycoly
294 Sableye
313 Sandaconda
249 Sawk
225 Scrafty
224 Scraggy
039 Seedot
134 Seismitoad
106 Shedinja
041 Shiftry
227 Shuckle
312 Silicobra
285 Skorupi
131 Skuntank
024 Skwovet
292 Sneasel
179 Steelix
226 Stunfisk
130 Stunky
253 Sudowoodo
075 Swinub
204 Sylveon
030 Thievul
248 Throh
171 Timburr
223 Toxicroak
321 Trapinch
339 Trevenant
385 Tyranitar
201 Umbreon
197 Vaporeon
322 Vibrava
018 Vikavolt
068 Vulpix
293 Weavile
100 Wooper
046 Yamper
398 Zacian
399 Zamazenta
031 Zigzagoon

Disable
329 Cofagrigus
236 Corsola
237 Cursola
395 Dreepy
124 Drifloon
136 Dusclops
137 Dusknoir
135 Duskull
277 Elgyem
141 Gastly
290 Inkay
069 Ninetales
338 Phantump
191 Pumpkaboo
120 Ralts
328 Runerigus
294 Sableye
245 Salazzle
079 Snorunt
212 Spritzee
068 Vulpix
327 Yamask

Disarming Voice

213 Aromatisse
256 Clefable
255 Clefairy
254 Cleffa
208 Espurr
123 Gallade
122 Gardevoir
241 Hatenna
243 Hatterene
242 Hattrem
337 Indeedee
121 Kirlia
209 Meowstic
153 Milotic
193 Pichu
120 Ralts
204 Sylveon
348 Togedemaru

Discharge

375 Arctozolt
017 Charjabug
220 Chinchou
374 Dracozolt
066 Electrike
065 Galvantula
016 Grubbin
319 Heliolisk
198 Jolteon
064 Joltik
114 Klang
113 Klink
115 Klinklang
221 Lanturn
067 Manectric
194 Pikachu
353 Pincurchin
195 Raichu
372 Rotom
348 Togedemaru
311 Toxtricity
018 Vikavolt
046 Yamper

Dive (TM45)

215 Araquanid
377 Arctovish
180 Arrokuda
235 Barbaracle
228 Barboach
181 Barraskewda
154 Basculin
280 Beartic
042 Chewtle
220 Chinchou
351 Clobbopus
151 Cloyster
309 Cramorant
103 Crawdaunt
376 Dracovish
397 Dragapult
396 Drakloak
043 Drednaw
008 Drizzile
370 Eiscue
152 Feebas
305 Frillish
231 Gastrodon
146 Goldeen
233 Golisopod
352 Grapploct
145 Gyarados
009 Inteleon
306 Jellicent

099 Kingler
098 Krabby
221 Lanturn
361 Lapras
037 Lombre
038 Ludicolo
355 Mantine
354 Mantyke
153 Milotic
149 Octillery
101 Quagsire
304 Qwilfish
148 Remoraid
147 Seaking
134 Seismitoad
150 Shellder
230 Shellos
007 Sobble
197 Vaporeon
356 Wailmer
357 Wailord
229 Whiscash
155 Wishiwashi
100 Wooper

Double Hit

102 Corphish
103 Crawdaunt
386 Deino
397 Dragapult
396 Drakloak
388 Hydreigon
077 Mamoswine
003 Rillaboom
382 Silvally
292 Sneasel
002 Thwackey
381 Type: Null
251 Weezing
387 Zweilous

Double Kick

048 Bunnelby
006 Cinderace
049 Diggersby
035 Dubwool
196 Eevee
070 Growlithe
108 Hitmonlee
198 Jolteon
365 Mr. Mime
366 Mr. Rime
084 Mudbray
085 Mudsdale
333 Ponyta
005 Raboot
249 Sawk
004 Scorbunny
034 Wooloo
100 Wooper

Double Team

276 Accelgor
395 Dreepy
081 Froslass
123 Gallade
122 Gardevoir
080 Glalie
064 Joltik
121 Kirlia
301 Mimikyu
105 Ninjask
176 Noibat
177 Noivern
194 Pikachu
044 Purrloin

195 Raichu
120 Ralts
372 Rotom
079 Snorunt
007 Sobble

Double-Edge

180 Arrokuda
359 Avalugg
181 Barraskewda
154 Basculin
358 Bergmite
095 Bewear
252 Bonsly
006 Cinderace
102 Corphish
302 Cufant
397 Dragapult
396 Drakloak
035 Dubwool
196 Eevee
370 Eiscue
274 Escavalier
200 Espeon
218 Farfetch'd
199 Flareon
203 Glaceon
070 Growlithe
314 Hippopotas
315 Hippowdon
198 Jolteon
273 Karrablast
202 Leafeon
032 Linoone
140 Machamp
139 Machoke
138 Machop
182 Meowth
084 Mudbray
260 Munchlax
033 Obstagoon
178 Onix
343 Passimian
333 Ponyta
005 Raboot
004 Scorbunny
275 Shelmet
382 Silvally
261 Snorlax
096 Snover
179 Steelix
094 Stufful
130 Stunky
253 Sudowoodo
075 Swinub
204 Sylveon
259 Togekiss
257 Togepi
258 Togetic
381 Type: Null
201 Umbreon
197 Vaporeon
356 Wailmer
155 Wishiwashi
034 Wooloo
046 Yamper
031 Zigzagoon

Draco Meteor

207 Appletun
205 Applin
324 Axew
386 Deino
376 Dracovish
374 Dracozolt

397 Dragapult
396 Drakloak
346 Drampa
395 Dreepy
371 Duraludon
400 Eternatus
206 Flapple
323 Flygon
325 Fraxure
391 Goodra
389 Goomy
393 Hakamo-o
326 Haxorus
388 Hydreigon
392 Jangmo-o
394 Kommo-o
176 Noibat
177 Noivern
382 Silvally
390 Sliggoo
347 Turtonator
322 Vibrava
387 Zweilous

Dragon Breath

380 Charizard
378 Charmander
379 Charmeleon
386 Deino
376 Dracovish
397 Dragapult
346 Drampa
152 Feebas
206 Flapple
323 Flygon
391 Goodra
389 Goomy
388 Hydreigon
392 Jangmo-o
178 Onix
390 Sliggoo
179 Steelix
322 Vibrava
387 Zweilous

Dragon Claw (TR47)

324 Axew
235 Barbaracle
095 Bewear
380 Charizard
378 Charmander
379 Charmeleon
374 Dracozolt
397 Dragapult
346 Drampa
371 Duraludon
323 Flygon
325 Fraxure
393 Hakamo-o
326 Haxorus
392 Jangmo-o
394 Kommo-o
177 Noivern
112 Pangoro
244 Salandit
245 Salazzle
225 Scrafty
224 Scraggy
382 Silvally
347 Turtonator
381 Type: Null
385 Tyranitar

Dragon Dance (TR51)

324 Axew
228 Barboach
380 Charizard
378 Charmander
379 Charmeleon
102 Corphish
103 Crawdaunt
397 Dragapult
396 Drakloak
346 Drampa
400 Eternatus
206 Flapple
323 Flygon
325 Fraxure
145 Gyarados
393 Hakamo-o
326 Haxorus
388 Hydreigon
392 Jangmo-o
394 Kommo-o
361 Lapras
383 Larvitar
153 Milotic
177 Noivern
178 Onix
384 Pupitar
245 Salazzle
225 Scrafty
224 Scraggy
179 Steelix
385 Tyranitar
229 Whiscash

Dragon Darts

397 Dragapult

Dragon Pulse (TR62)

207 Appletun
071 Arcanine
324 Axew
380 Charizard
378 Charmander
379 Charmeleon
386 Deino
376 Dracovish
374 Dracozolt
397 Dragapult
396 Drakloak
346 Drampa
371 Duraludon
400 Eternatus
152 Feebas
206 Flapple
323 Flygon
325 Fraxure
391 Goodra
389 Goomy
145 Gyarados
393 Hakamo-o
326 Haxorus
319 Heliolisk
388 Hydreigon
392 Jangmo-o
394 Kommo-o
361 Lapras
299 Lucario
153 Milotic
176 Noibat
177 Noivern
178 Onix
265 Rhydon
264 Rhyhorn

266 Rhyperior
328 Runerigus
244 Salandit
245 Salazzle
225 Scrafty
224 Scraggy
390 Sliggoo
179 Steelix
347 Turtonator
385 Tyranitar
322 Vibrava
387 Zweilous

Dragon Rush

378 Charmander
386 Deino
376 Dracovish
374 Dracozolt
397 Dragapult
396 Drakloak
346 Drampa
206 Flapple
323 Flygon
318 Helioptile
388 Hydreigon
176 Noibat
264 Rhyhorn
312 Silicobra
322 Vibrava
387 Zweilous

Dragon Tail

378 Charmander
042 Chewtle
374 Dracozolt
395 Dreepy
371 Duraludon
400 Eternatus
323 Flygon
393 Hakamo-o
318 Helioptile
392 Jangmo-o
394 Kommo-o
153 Milotic
178 Onix
322 Vibrava

Drain Punch (TM63)

276 Accelgor
186 Alcremie
213 Aromatisse
058 Bellossom
095 Bewear
256 Clefable
255 Clefairy
173 Conkeldurr
222 Croagunk
123 Gallade
158 Garbodor
143 Gengar
056 Gloom
088 Golett
089 Golurk
352 Grapploct
240 Grimmsnarl
001 Grookey
172 Gurdurr
393 Hakamo-o
320 Hawlucha
317 Heatmor
109 Hitmonchan
238 Impidimp
337 Indeedee
394 Kommo-o
037 Lombre

299 Lucario
038 Ludicolo
296 Maractus
364 Mime Jr.
301 Mimikyu
239 Morgrem
365 Mr. Mime
366 Mr. Rime
111 Pancham
112 Pangoro
343 Passimian
272 Reuniclus
003 Rillaboom
298 Riolu
294 Sableye
225 Scrafty
224 Scraggy
134 Seismitoad
341 Shiinotic
211 Slurpuff
002 Thwackey
171 Timburr
259 Togekiss
258 Togetic
223 Toxicroak
311 Toxtricity
339 Trevenant
157 Trubbish
057 Vileplume

Draining Kiss (TM87)

186 Alcremie
213 Aromatisse
052 Bounsweet
015 Butterfree
129 Cherrim
128 Cherubi
256 Clefable
255 Clefairy
254 Cleffa
187 Cutiefly
081 Froslass
123 Gallade
122 Gardevoir
240 Grimmsnarl
241 Hatenna
243 Hatterene
242 Hattrem
238 Impidimp
337 Indeedee
121 Kirlia
295 Mawile
185 Milcery
301 Mimikyu
340 Morelull
239 Morgrem
194 Pikachu
195 Raichu
120 Ralts
188 Ribombee
341 Shiinotic
211 Slurpuff
212 Spritzee
053 Steenee
210 Swirlix
204 Sylveon
259 Togekiss
257 Togepi
258 Togetic
054 Tsareena

Dream Eater

123 Gallade
122 Gardevoir

141 Gastly
143 Gengar
142 Haunter
019 Hoothoot
121 Kirlia
340 Morelull
090 Munna
091 Musharna
020 Noctowl
342 Oranguru
120 Ralts
341 Shiinotic

Drill Peck
023 Corviknight
022 Corvisquire
309 Cramorant
078 Delibird
092 Natu
021 Rookidee

Drill Run (TR87)
180 Arrokuda
082 Baltoy
181 Barraskewda
083 Claydol
078 Delibird
166 Drilbur
274 Escavalier
167 Excadrill
146 Goldeen
233 Golisopod
110 Hitmontop
273 Karrablast
361 Lapras
178 Onix
334 Rapidash
265 Rhydon
264 Rhyhorn
266 Rhyperior
313 Sandaconda
147 Seaking
312 Silicobra
179 Steelix

Drum Beating
003 Rillaboom

Dual Chop
324 Axew
325 Fraxure
326 Haxorus
140 Machamp
139 Machoke
138 Machop

Dynamax Cannon
400 Eternatus

Dynamic Punch
173 Conkeldurr
222 Croagunk
088 Golett
089 Golurk
172 Gurdurr
140 Machamp
139 Machoke
138 Machop
171 Timburr

Earth Power (TR67)
097 Abomasnow
082 Baltoy
235 Barbaracle
228 Barboach
169 Boldore
252 Bonsly
083 Claydol
163 Coalossal

303 Copperajah
236 Corsola
302 Cufant
237 Cursola
386 Deino
049 Diggersby
164 Diglett
376 Dracovish
374 Dracozolt
043 Drednaw
166 Drilbur
165 Dugtrio
167 Excadrill
323 Flygon
231 Gastrodon
170 Gigalith
088 Golett
089 Golurk
314 Hippopotas
315 Hippowdon
388 Hydreigon
383 Larvitar
362 Lunatone
077 Mamoswine
084 Mudbray
085 Mudsdale
178 Onix
133 Palpitoad
076 Piloswine
384 Pupitar
101 Quagsire
265 Rhydon
264 Rhyhorn
266 Rhyperior
003 Rillaboom
168 Roggenrola
328 Runerigus
313 Sandaconda
134 Seismitoad
230 Shellos
227 Shuckle
312 Silicobra
363 Solrock
179 Steelix
369 Stonjourner
226 Stunfisk
253 Sudowoodo
075 Swinub
300 Torkoal
321 Trapinch
132 Tympole
385 Tyranitar
322 Vibrava
229 Whiscash
100 Wooper
327 Yamask
387 Zweilous

Earthquake (TR10)
097 Abomasnow
207 Appletun
359 Avalugg
082 Baltoy
235 Barbaracle
228 Barboach
095 Bewear
234 Binacle
169 Boldore
119 Bronzong
118 Bronzor
048 Bunnelby
380 Charizard
083 Claydol

163 Coalossal
173 Conkeldurr
303 Copperajah
236 Corsola
222 Croagunk
087 Crustle
237 Cursola
368 Darmanitan
360 Dhelmise
049 Diggersby
164 Diglett
376 Dracovish
374 Dracozolt
346 Drampa
286 Drapion
043 Drednaw
166 Drilbur
165 Dugtrio
136 Dusclops
137 Dusknoir
086 Dwebble
167 Excadrill
323 Flygon
123 Gallade
231 Gastrodon
170 Gigalith
080 Glalie
088 Golett
089 Golurk
391 Goodra
025 Greedent
145 Gyarados
393 Hakamo-o
326 Haxorus
314 Hippopotas
315 Hippowdon
109 Hitmonchan
108 Hitmonlee
110 Hitmontop
388 Hydreigon
392 Jangmo-o
394 Kommo-o
383 Larvitar
299 Lucario
362 Lunatone
140 Machamp
139 Machoke
138 Machop
077 Mamoswine
355 Mantine
354 Mantyke
084 Mudbray
085 Mudsdale
260 Munchlax
178 Onix
342 Oranguru
112 Pangoro
343 Passimian
076 Piloswine
384 Pupitar
101 Quagsire
265 Rhydon
264 Rhyhorn
266 Rhyperior
003 Rillaboom
298 Riolu
168 Roggenrola
328 Runerigus
313 Sandaconda
249 Sawk
134 Seismitoad
227 Shuckle
312 Silicobra

261 Snorlax
363 Solrock
179 Steelix
369 Stonjourner
094 Stufful
226 Stunfisk
253 Sudowoodo
075 Swinub
248 Throh
300 Torkoal
223 Toxicroak
321 Trapinch
339 Trevenant
347 Turtonator
385 Tyranitar
107 Tyrogue
322 Vibrava
356 Wailmer
357 Wailord
229 Whiscash
155 Wishiwashi
100 Wooper
327 Yamask

Echoed Voice
375 Arctozolt
213 Aromatisse
051 Cinccino
346 Drampa
019 Hoothoot
050 Minccino
020 Noctowl
133 Palpitoad
134 Seismitoad
212 Spritzee
132 Tympole

Eerie Impulse (TM93)
082 Baltoy
047 Boltund
017 Charjabug
083 Claydol
066 Electrike
319 Heliolisk
221 Lanturn
067 Manectric
101 Quagsire
195 Raichu
372 Rotom
348 Togedemaru
018 Vikavolt
100 Wooper

Electric Terrain (TM90)
047 Boltund
319 Heliolisk
318 Helioptile
115 Klinklang
067 Manectric
344 Morpeko
193 Pichu
194 Pikachu
353 Pincurchin
195 Raichu
372 Rotom
348 Togedemaru

Electrify
047 Boltund
319 Heliolisk
318 Helioptile

Electro Ball (TR80)
375 Arctozolt
047 Boltund

017 Charjabug
220 Chinchou
006 Cinderace
374 Dracozolt
035 Dubwool
066 Electrike
065 Galvantula
319 Heliolisk
318 Helioptile
198 Jolteon
064 Joltik
221 Lanturn
067 Manectric
344 Morpeko
194 Pikachu
005 Raboot
195 Raichu
372 Rotom
004 Scorbunny
348 Togedemaru
311 Toxtricity
018 Vikavolt
034 Wooloo
046 Yamper

Electroweb (TM82)
015 Butterfree
013 Caterpie
017 Charjabug
065 Galvantula
016 Grubbin
319 Heliolisk
318 Helioptile
064 Joltik
014 Metapod
344 Morpeko
343 Passimian
193 Pichu
194 Pikachu
195 Raichu
372 Rotom
348 Togedemaru
018 Vikavolt

Ember
071 Arcanine
160 Centiskorch
289 Chandelure
380 Charizard
378 Charmander
379 Charmeleon
006 Cinderace
199 Flareon
070 Growlithe
288 Lampent
287 Litwick
069 Ninetales
005 Raboot
244 Salandit
245 Salazzle
004 Scorbunny
159 Sizzlipede
300 Torkoal
347 Turtonator
068 Vulpix

Encore (TR30)
276 Accelgor
186 Alcremie
213 Aromatisse
280 Beartic
051 Cinccino
256 Clefable
255 Clefairy
254 Cleffa
262 Cottonee

222 Croagunk
279 Cubchoo
368 Darmanitan
367 Darumaka
271 Duosion
274 Escavalier
123 Gallade
122 Gardevoir
143 Gengar
142 Haunter
320 Hawlucha
337 Indeedee
273 Karrablast
121 Kirlia
045 Liepard
037 Lombre
038 Ludicolo
140 Machamp
139 Machoke
138 Machop
364 Mime Jr.
050 Minccino
365 Mr. Mime
366 Mr. Rime
260 Munchlax
069 Ninetales
342 Oranguru
193 Pichu
194 Pikachu
044 Purrloin
101 Quagsire
195 Raichu
120 Ralts
272 Reuniclus
294 Sableye
245 Salazzle
275 Shelmet
227 Shuckle
261 Snorlax
270 Solosis
212 Spritzee
348 Togedemaru
259 Togekiss
257 Togepi
258 Togetic
310 Toxel
223 Toxicroak
311 Toxtricity
068 Vulpix
263 Whimsicott
217 Wobbuffet
100 Wooper
216 Wynaut

Endeavor
324 Axew
154 Basculin
052 Bounsweet
102 Corphish
262 Cottonee
103 Crawdaunt
271 Duosion
001 Grookey
320 Hawlucha
110 Hitmontop
272 Reuniclus
003 Rillaboom
244 Salandit
245 Salazzle
211 Slurpuff
270 Solosis
210 Swirlix
175 Swoobat
002 Thwackey

310 Toxel
263 Whimsicott
155 Wishiwashi
174 Woobat

Endure (TR26)
097 Abomasnow
276 Accelgor
332 Aegislash
186 Alcremie
207 Appletun
215 Araquanid
071 Arcanine
377 Arctovish
375 Arctozolt
213 Aromatisse
180 Arrokuda
359 Avalugg
324 Axew
082 Baltoy
235 Barbaracle
228 Barboach
181 Barraskewda
154 Basculin
280 Beartic
278 Beheeyem
058 Bellossom
358 Bergmite
095 Bewear
234 Binacle
247 Bisharp
169 Boldore
047 Boltund
252 Bonsly
052 Bounsweet
282 Braviary
119 Bronzong
118 Bronzor
059 Budew
048 Bunnelby
015 Butterfree
162 Carkol
160 Centiskorch
289 Chandelure
380 Charizard
017 Charjabug
378 Charmander
379 Charmeleon
129 Cherrim
128 Cherubi
042 Chewtle
220 Chinchou
051 Cinccino
006 Cinderace
083 Claydol
256 Clefable
255 Clefairy
254 Cleffa
351 Clobbopus
151 Cloyster
163 Coalossal
329 Cofagrigus
173 Conkeldurr
303 Copperajah
102 Corphish
236 Corsola
023 Corviknight
022 Corvisquire
262 Cottonee
309 Cramorant
103 Crawdaunt
222 Croagunk
087 Crustle
279 Cubchoo

302 Cufant
237 Cursola
187 Cutiefly
368 Darmanitan
367 Darumaka
386 Deino
078 Delibird
214 Dewpider
360 Dhelmise
049 Diggersby
164 Diglett
011 Dottler
331 Doublade
376 Dracovish
374 Dracozolt
397 Dragapult
396 Drakloak
346 Drampa
286 Drapion
043 Drednaw
395 Dreepy
125 Drifblim
124 Drifloon
166 Drilbur
008 Drizzile
035 Dubwool
165 Dugtrio
271 Duosion
371 Duraludon
316 Durant
136 Dusclops
137 Dusknoir
135 Duskull
086 Dwebble
196 Eevee
370 Eiscue
127 Eldegoss
066 Electrike
277 Elgyem
274 Escavalier
200 Espeon
208 Espurr
400 Eternatus
167 Excadrill
345 Falinks
218 Farfetch'd
152 Feebas
189 Ferroseed
190 Ferrothorn
206 Flapple
199 Flareon
323 Flygon
325 Fraxure
305 Frillish
081 Froslass
350 Frosmoth
123 Gallade
065 Galvantula
158 Garbodor
122 Gardevoir
141 Gastly
231 Gastrodon
143 Gengar
170 Gigalith
203 Glaceon
080 Glalie
056 Gloom
146 Goldeen
088 Golett
233 Golisopod
089 Golurk
391 Goodra
389 Goomy

126 Gossifleur
267 Gothita
269 Gothitelle
268 Gothorita
192 Gourgeist
352 Grapploct
025 Greedent
240 Grimmsnarl
001 Grookey
070 Growlithe
016 Grubbin
172 Gurdurr
145 Gyarados
393 Hakamo-o
241 Hatenna
243 Hatterene
242 Hattrem
142 Haunter
320 Hawlucha
326 Haxorus
317 Heatmor
319 Heliolisk
318 Helioptile
314 Hippopotas
315 Hippowdon
109 Hitmonchan
108 Hitmonlee
110 Hitmontop
330 Honedge
019 Hoothoot
388 Hydreigon
238 Impidimp
337 Indeedee
290 Inkay
009 Inteleon
392 Jangmo-o
306 Jellicent
198 Jolteon
064 Joltik
273 Karrablast
099 Kingler
121 Kirlia
114 Klang
113 Klink
115 Klinklang
250 Koffing
394 Kommo-o
098 Krabby
288 Lampent
221 Lanturn
361 Lapras
383 Larvitar
202 Leafeon
045 Liepard
032 Linoone
287 Litwick
037 Lombre
036 Lotad
299 Lucario
038 Ludicolo
362 Lunatone
140 Machamp
139 Machoke
138 Machop
291 Malamar
077 Mamoswine
284 Mandibuzz
067 Manectric
355 Mantine
354 Mantyke
296 Maractus
307 Mareanie
295 Mawile

209 Meowstic
182 Meowth
185 Milcery
153 Milotic
364 Mime Jr.
301 Mimikyu
050 Minccino
340 Morelull
239 Morgrem
344 Morpeko
365 Mr. Mime
366 Mr. Rime
084 Mudbray
085 Mudsdale
260 Munchlax
090 Munna
091 Musharna
092 Natu
029 Nickit
104 Nincada
069 Ninetales
105 Ninjask
020 Noctowl
176 Noibat
177 Noivern
040 Nuzleaf
033 Obstagoon
149 Octillery
055 Oddish
178 Onix
342 Oranguru
012 Orbeetle
133 Palpitoad
111 Pancham
112 Pangoro
343 Passimian
246 Pawniard
063 Pelipper
183 Perrserker
184 Persian
338 Phantump
193 Pichu
026 Pidove
194 Pikachu
076 Piloswine
353 Pincurchin
336 Polteageist
333 Ponyta
191 Pumpkaboo
384 Pupitar
044 Purrloin
156 Pyukumuku
101 Quagsire
304 Qwilfish
005 Raboot
195 Raichu
120 Ralts
334 Rapidash
148 Remoraid
272 Reuniclus
265 Rhydon
264 Rhyhorn
266 Rhyperior
188 Ribombee
003 Rillaboom
298 Riolu
168 Roggenrola
161 Rolycoly
021 Rookidee
060 Roselia
061 Roserade
372 Rotom
281 Rufflet

328 Runerigus
294 Sableye
244 Salandit
245 Salazzle
313 Sandaconda
249 Sawk
004 Scorbunny
225 Scrafty
224 Scraggy
147 Seaking
039 Seedot
134 Seismitoad
106 Shedinja
150 Shellder
230 Shellos
275 Shelmet
041 Shiftry
341 Shiinotic
227 Shuckle
297 Sigilyph
312 Silicobra
382 Silvally
335 Sinistea
219 Sirfetch'd
159 Sizzlipede
285 Skorupi
131 Skuntank
024 Skwovet
390 Sliggoo
211 Slurpuff
292 Sneasel
349 Snom
261 Snorlax
079 Snorunt
096 Snover
007 Sobble
270 Solosis
363 Solrock
212 Spritzee
179 Steelix
053 Steenee
369 Stonjourner
094 Stufful
226 Stunfisk
130 Stunky
253 Sudowoodo
075 Swinub
210 Swirlix
175 Swoobat
204 Sylveon
030 Thievul
248 Throh
002 Thwackey
171 Timburr
348 Togedemaru
259 Togekiss
257 Togepi
258 Togetic
300 Torkoal
308 Toxapex
310 Toxel
223 Toxicroak
311 Toxtricity
027 Tranquill
321 Trapinch
339 Trevenant
157 Trubbish
054 Tsareena
347 Turtonator
132 Tympole
381 Type: Null
385 Tyranitar
107 Tyrogue

201 Umbreon
028 Unfezant
073 Vanillish
072 Vanillite
074 Vanilluxe
197 Vaporeon
117 Vespiquen
322 Vibrava
018 Vikavolt
057 Vileplume
283 Vullaby
068 Vulpix
356 Wailmer
357 Wailord
293 Weavile
251 Weezing
263 Whimsicott
229 Whiscash
232 Wimpod
062 Wingull
155 Wishiwashi
174 Woobat
034 Wooloo
100 Wooper
093 Xatu
327 Yamask
046 Yamper
398 Zacian
399 Zamazenta
031 Zigzagoon
387 Zweilous

Energy Ball (TR65)

097 Abomasnow
276 Accelgor
186 Alcremie
207 Appletun
213 Aromatisse
278 Beheeyem
058 Bellossom
052 Bounsweet
059 Budew
015 Butterfree
289 Chandelure
129 Cherrim
128 Cherubi
329 Cofagrigus
262 Cottonee
187 Cutiefly
360 Dhelmise
011 Dottler
271 Duosion
316 Durant
127 Eldegoss
277 Elgyem
274 Escavalier
208 Espurr
189 Ferroseed
190 Ferrothorn
206 Flapple
305 Frillish
123 Gallade
065 Galvantula
122 Gardevoir
141 Gastly
143 Gengar
056 Gloom
126 Gossifleur
267 Gothita
269 Gothitelle
268 Gothorita
192 Gourgeist
001 Grookey

142 Haunter
337 Indeedee
306 Jellicent
064 Joltik
273 Karrablast
288 Lampent
202 Leafeon
287 Litwick
037 Lombre
036 Lotad
038 Ludicolo
296 Maractus
209 Meowstic
340 Morelull
365 Mr. Mime
366 Mr. Rime
090 Munna
091 Musharna
069 Ninetales
040 Nuzleaf
149 Octillery
055 Oddish
342 Oranguru
012 Orbeetle
343 Passimian
338 Phantump
191 Pumpkaboo
272 Reuniclus
188 Ribombee
003 Rillaboom
060 Roselia
061 Roserade
328 Runerigus
039 Seedot
275 Shelmet
041 Shiftry
341 Shiinotic
297 Sigilyph
211 Slurpuff
096 Snover
270 Solosis
212 Spritzee
053 Steenee
210 Swirlix
175 Swoobat
002 Thwackey
339 Trevenant
054 Tsareena
018 Vikavolt
057 Vileplume
068 Vulpix
263 Whimsicott
174 Woobat
327 Yamask

Entrainment

186 Alcremie
215 Araquanid
214 Dewpider
316 Durant
320 Hawlucha
185 Milcery
111 Pancham
112 Pangoro

Eruption

300 Torkoal

Eternabeam

400 Eternatus

Explosion

082 Baltoy
169 Boldore
083 Claydol
125 Drifblim
124 Drifloon

189 Ferroseed
190 Ferrothorn
158 Garbodor
170 Gigalith
192 Gourgeist
250 Koffing
362 Lunatone
040 Nuzleaf
168 Roggenrola
161 Rolycoly
039 Seedot
041 Shiftry
382 Silvally
131 Skuntank
363 Solrock
130 Stunky
157 Trubbish
347 Turtonator
072 Vanillite
251 Weezing

Extrasensory

082 Baltoy
119 Bronzong
118 Bronzor
059 Budew
083 Claydol
346 Drampa
019 Hoothoot
337 Indeedee
209 Meowstic
069 Ninetales
020 Noctowl
040 Nuzleaf
342 Oranguru
060 Roselia
041 Shiftry
257 Togepi
068 Vulpix

Extreme Speed

071 Arcanine
299 Lucario
259 Togekiss

Facade (TM39)

097 Abomasnow
276 Accelgor
332 Aegislash
186 Alcremie
207 Appletun
215 Araquanid
071 Arcanine
377 Arctovish
375 Arctozolt
213 Aromatisse
180 Arrokuda
359 Avalugg
324 Axew
082 Baltoy
235 Barbaracle
228 Barboach
181 Barraskewda
154 Basculin
280 Beartic
278 Beheeyem
058 Bellossom
358 Bergmite
095 Bewear
234 Binacle
247 Bisharp
169 Boldore
047 Boltund
252 Bonsly
052 Bounsweet
282 Braviary

119 Bronzong
118 Bronzor
059 Budew
048 Bunnelby
015 Butterfree
162 Carkol
160 Centiskorch
289 Chandelure
380 Charizard
017 Charjabug
378 Charmander
379 Charmeleon
129 Cherrim
128 Cherubi
042 Chewtle
220 Chinchou
051 Cinccino
006 Cinderace
083 Claydol
256 Clefable
255 Clefairy
254 Cleffa
351 Clobbopus
151 Cloyster
163 Coalossal
329 Cofagrigus
173 Conkeldurr
303 Copperajah
102 Corphish
236 Corsola
023 Corviknight
022 Corvisquire
262 Cottonee
309 Cramorant
103 Crawdaunt
222 Croagunk
087 Crustle
279 Cubchoo
302 Cufant
237 Cursola
187 Cutiefly
368 Darmanitan
367 Darumaka
386 Deino
078 Delibird
214 Dewpider
360 Dhelmise
049 Diggersby
164 Diglett
011 Dottler
331 Doublade
376 Dracovish
374 Dracozolt
397 Dragapult
396 Drakloak
346 Drampa
286 Drapion
043 Drednaw
395 Dreepy
125 Drifblim
124 Drifloon
166 Drilbur
008 Drizzile
035 Dubwool
165 Dugtrio
271 Duosion
371 Duraludon
316 Durant
136 Dusclops
137 Dusknoir
135 Duskull
086 Dwebble
196 Eevee

370 Eiscue
127 Eldegoss
066 Electrike
277 Elgyem
274 Escavalier
200 Espeon
208 Espurr
400 Eternatus
167 Excadrill
345 Falinks
218 Farfetch'd
152 Feebas
189 Ferroseed
190 Ferrothorn
206 Flapple
199 Flareon
323 Flygon
325 Fraxure
305 Frillish
081 Froslass
350 Frosmoth
123 Gallade
065 Galvantula
158 Garbodor
122 Gardevoir
141 Gastly
231 Gastrodon
143 Gengar
170 Gigalith
203 Glaceon
080 Glalie
056 Gloom
146 Goldeen
088 Golett
233 Golisopod
089 Golurk
391 Goodra
389 Goomy
126 Gossifleur
267 Gothita
269 Gothitelle
268 Gothorita
192 Gourgeist
025 Greedent
240 Grimmsnarl
001 Grookey
070 Growlithe
016 Grubbin
172 Gurdurr
145 Gyarados
393 Hakamo-o
241 Hatenna
243 Hatterene
242 Hattrem
142 Haunter
320 Hawlucha
326 Haxorus
317 Heatmor
319 Heliolisk
318 Helioptile
314 Hippopotas
315 Hippowdon
109 Hitmonchan
108 Hitmonlee
110 Hitmontop
330 Honedge
019 Hoothoot
388 Hydreigon
238 Impidimp
337 Indeedee
290 Inkay
009 Inteleon

392 Jangmo-o
306 Jellicent
198 Jolteon
064 Joltik
273 Karrablast
099 Kingler
121 Kirlia
114 Klang
113 Klink
115 Klinklang
250 Koffing
394 Kommo-o
098 Krabby
288 Lampent
221 Lanturn
361 Lapras
383 Larvitar
202 Leafeon
045 Liepard
032 Linoone
287 Litwick
037 Lombre
036 Lotad
299 Lucario
038 Ludicolo
362 Lunatone
140 Machamp
139 Machoke
138 Machop
291 Malamar
077 Mamoswine
284 Mandibuzz
067 Manectric
355 Mantine
354 Mantyke
296 Maractus
307 Mareanie
295 Mawile
209 Meowstic
182 Meowth
185 Milcery
153 Milotic
364 Mime Jr.
301 Mimikyu
050 Minccino
340 Morelull
239 Morgrem
344 Morpeko
365 Mr. Mime
366 Mr. Rime
084 Mudbray
085 Mudsdale
260 Munchlax
090 Munna
091 Musharna
092 Natu
029 Nickit
104 Nincada
069 Ninetales
105 Ninjask
020 Noctowl
176 Noibat
177 Noivern
040 Nuzleaf
033 Obstagoon
149 Octillery
055 Oddish
178 Onix
342 Oranguru
012 Orbeetle
133 Palpitoad
111 Pancham
112 Pangoro

343 Passimian
246 Pawniard
063 Pelipper
183 Perrserker
184 Persian
338 Phantump
193 Pichu
026 Pidove
194 Pikachu
076 Piloswine
353 Pincurchin
336 Polteageist
333 Ponyta
191 Pumpkaboo
384 Pupitar
044 Purrloin
101 Quagsire
304 Qwilfish
005 Raboot
195 Raichu
120 Ralts
334 Rapidash
148 Remoraid
272 Reuniclus
265 Rhydon
264 Rhyhorn
266 Rhyperior
188 Ribombee
003 Rillaboom
298 Riolu
168 Roggenrola
161 Rolycoly
021 Rookidee
060 Roselia
061 Roserade
372 Rotom
281 Rufflet
328 Runerigus
294 Sableye
244 Salandit
245 Salazzle
313 Sandaconda
249 Sawk
004 Scorbunny
225 Scrafty
224 Scraggy
147 Seaking
039 Seedot
134 Seismitoad
106 Shedinja
150 Shellder
230 Shellos
275 Shelmet
041 Shiftry
341 Shiinotic
227 Shuckle
297 Sigilyph
312 Silicobra
382 Silvally
335 Sinistea
219 Sirfetch'd
159 Sizzlipede
285 Skorupi
131 Skuntank
024 Skwovet
390 Sliggoo
211 Slurpuff
292 Sneasel
349 Snom
261 Snorlax
079 Snorunt
096 Snover
007 Sobble

270 Solosis
363 Solrock
212 Spritzee
179 Steelix
053 Steenee
369 Stonjourner
094 Stufful
226 Stunfisk
130 Stunky
253 Sudowoodo
075 Swinub
210 Swirlix
175 Swoobat
204 Sylveon
030 Thievul
248 Throh
002 Thwackey
171 Timburr
348 Togedemaru
259 Togekiss
257 Togepi
258 Togetic
300 Torkoal
308 Toxapex
310 Toxel
223 Toxicroak
311 Toxtricity
027 Tranquill
321 Trapinch
339 Trevenant
157 Trubbish
054 Tsareena
347 Turtonator
132 Tympole
381 Type: Null
385 Tyranitar
107 Tyrogue
201 Umbreon
028 Unfezant
073 Vanillish
072 Vanillite
074 Vanilluxe
197 Vaporeon
117 Vespiquen
322 Vibrava
018 Vikavolt
057 Vileplume
283 Vullaby
068 Vulpix
356 Wailmer
357 Wailord
293 Weavile
251 Weezing
263 Whimsicott
229 Whiscash
232 Wimpod
062 Wingull
155 Wishiwashi
174 Woobat
034 Wooloo
100 Wooper
093 Xatu
327 Yamask
046 Yamper
398 Zacian
399 Zamazenta
031 Zigzagoon
387 Zweilous

Fairy Wind
213 Aromatisse
262 Cottonee
187 Cutiefly
295 Mawile

333 Ponyta
334 Rapidash
188 Ribombee
211 Slurpuff
349 Snom
212 Spritzee
210 Swirlix
259 Togekiss
258 Togetic
251 Weezing
263 Whimsicott

Fake Out
222 Croagunk
078 Delibird
208 Espurr
267 Gothita
240 Grimmsnarl
001 Grookey
109 Hitmonchan
108 Hitmonlee
110 Hitmontop
238 Impidimp
337 Indeedee
045 Liepard
037 Lombre
038 Ludicolo
209 Meowstic
182 Meowth
364 Mime Jr.
239 Morgrem
344 Morpeko
365 Mr. Mime
040 Nuzleaf
183 Perrserker
184 Persian
193 Pichu
044 Purrloin
294 Sableye
244 Salandit
224 Scraggy
041 Shiftry
292 Sneasel
348 Togedemaru
107 Tyrogue

Fake Tears (TM47)
186 Alcremie
213 Aromatisse
252 Bonsly
051 Cinccino
256 Clefable
255 Clefairy
254 Cleffa
329 Cofagrigus
023 Corviknight
022 Corvisquire
262 Cottonee
187 Cutiefly
196 Eevee
200 Espeon
208 Espurr
199 Flareon
081 Froslass
203 Glaceon
080 Glalie
267 Gothita
269 Gothitelle
268 Gothorita
240 Grimmsnarl
238 Impidimp
290 Inkay
198 Jolteon
202 Leafeon

045 Liepard
032 Linoone
291 Malamar
284 Mandibuzz
295 Mawile
209 Meowstic
050 Minccino
239 Morgrem
344 Morpeko
366 Mr. Rime
029 Nickit
069 Ninetales
033 Obstagoon
044 Purrloin
188 Ribombee
021 Rookidee
328 Runerigus
245 Salazzle
225 Scrafty
224 Scraggy
211 Slurpuff
292 Sneasel
212 Spritzee
253 Sudowoodo
210 Swirlix
175 Swoobat
204 Sylveon
030 Thievul
201 Umbreon
197 Vaporeon
283 Vullaby
293 Weavile
263 Whimsicott
174 Woobat
327 Yamask
031 Zigzagoon

False Surrender
240 Grimmsnarl
239 Morgrem

False Swipe (TM94)
332 Aegislash
324 Axew
235 Barbaracle
234 Binacle
247 Bisharp
380 Charizard
378 Charmander
379 Charmeleon
102 Corphish
103 Crawdaunt
331 Doublade
286 Drapion
043 Drednaw
274 Escavalier
345 Falinks
325 Fraxure
123 Gallade
233 Golisopod
001 Grookey
393 Hakamo-o
320 Hawlucha
326 Haxorus
330 Honedge
392 Jangmo-o
273 Karrablast
099 Kingler
394 Kommo-o
098 Krabby
295 Mawile
104 Nincada
105 Ninjask

040 Nuzleaf	380 Charizard	295 Mawile	266 Rhyperior	300 Torkoal	160 Centiskorch
111 Pancham	378 Charmander	344 Morpeko	294 Sableye	**Flamethrower**	380 Charizard
112 Pangoro	379 Charmeleon	005 Raboot	249 Sawk	**(TR02)**	378 Charmander
246 Pawniard	006 Cinderace	265 Rhydon	225 Scrafty	071 Arcanine	379 Charmeleon
003 Rillaboom	256 Clefable	264 Rhyhorn	224 Scraggy	162 Carkol	006 Cinderace
039 Seedot	255 Clefairy	266 Rhyperior	261 Snorlax	160 Centiskorch	163 Coalossal
106 Shedinja	254 Cleffa	313 Sandaconda	253 Sudowoodo	289 Chandelure	368 Darmanitan
041 Shiftry	163 Coalossal	004 Scorbunny	248 Throh	380 Charizard	367 Darumaka
285 Skorupi	368 Darmanitan	382 Silvally	171 Timburr	378 Charmander	199 Flareon
292 Sneasel	367 Darumaka	179 Steelix	311 Toxtricity	379 Charmeleon	070 Growlithe
002 Thwackey	374 Dracozolt	030 Thievul	385 Tyranitar	006 Cinderace	317 Heatmor
293 Weavile	397 Dragapult	385 Tyranitar	**Fire Spin (TM13)**	256 Clefable	069 Ninetales
398 Zacian	396 Drakloak	046 Yamper	071 Arcanine	255 Clefairy	005 Raboot
Feather Dance	346 Drampa	398 Zacian	162 Carkol	254 Cleffa	245 Salazzle
309 Cramorant	199 Flareon	399 Zamazenta	160 Centiskorch	163 Coalossal	363 Solrock
350 Frosmoth	323 Flygon	387 Zweilous	289 Chandelure	368 Darmanitan	068 Vulpix
320 Hawlucha	391 Goodra	**Fire Lash**	380 Charizard	367 Darumaka	**Flash Cannon**
019 Hoothoot	192 Gourgeist	160 Centiskorch	378 Charmander	374 Dracozolt	**(TR70)**
092 Natu	070 Growlithe	317 Heatmor	379 Charmeleon	397 Dragapult	332 Aegislash
026 Pidove	145 Gyarados	245 Salazzle	006 Cinderace	396 Drakloak	213 Aromatisse
027 Tranquill	317 Heatmor	159 Sizzlipede	163 Coalossal	346 Drampa	359 Avalugg
028 Unfezant	388 Hydreigon	**Fire Pledge**	368 Darmanitan	066 Electrike	278 Beheeyem
Feint	250 Koffing	380 Charizard	367 Darumaka	400 Eternatus	358 Bergmite
006 Cinderace	288 Lampent	378 Charmander	374 Dracozolt	199 Flareon	169 Boldore
351 Clobbopus	287 Litwick	379 Charmeleon	199 Flareon	323 Flygon	119 Bronzong
222 Croagunk	140 Machamp	006 Cinderace	323 Flygon	391 Goodra	118 Bronzor
218 Farfetch'd	139 Machoke	005 Raboot	070 Growlithe	192 Gourgeist	303 Copperajah
323 Flygon	138 Machop	004 Scorbunny	317 Heatmor	070 Growlithe	023 Corviknight
123 Gallade	295 Mawile	382 Silvally	388 Hydreigon	145 Gyarados	360 Dhelmise
391 Goodra	260 Munchlax	**Fire Punch (TM03)**	288 Lampent	317 Heatmor	331 Doublade
352 Grapploct	069 Ninetales	380 Charizard	287 Litwick	388 Hydreigon	271 Duosion
320 Hawlucha	149 Octillery	378 Charmander	069 Ninetales	290 Inkay	371 Duraludon
109 Hitmonchan	191 Pumpkaboo	379 Charmeleon	159 Sizzlipede	250 Koffing	316 Durant
108 Hitmonlee	005 Raboot	006 Cinderace	131 Skuntank	394 Kommo-o	400 Eternatus
110 Hitmontop	148 Remoraid	256 Clefable	363 Solrock	288 Lampent	189 Ferroseed
299 Lucario	265 Rhydon	255 Clefairy	300 Torkoal	287 Litwick	190 Ferrothorn
182 Meowth	264 Rhyhorn	163 Coalossal	347 Turtonator	140 Machamp	170 Gigalith
343 Passimian	266 Rhyperior	173 Conkeldurr	068 Vulpix	139 Machoke	089 Golurk
184 Persian	244 Salandit	368 Darmanitan	**First Impression**	138 Machop	330 Honedge
194 Pikachu	245 Salazzle	367 Darumaka	324 Axew	291 Malamar	388 Hydreigon
195 Raichu	004 Scorbunny	049 Diggersby	316 Durant	067 Manectric	114 Klang
298 Riolu	131 Skuntank	136 Dusclops	345 Falinks	295 Mawile	113 Klink
294 Sableye	261 Snorlax	137 Dusknoir	233 Golisopod	260 Munchlax	115 Klinklang
275 Shelmet	363 Solrock	323 Flygon	219 Sirfetch'd	069 Ninetales	394 Kommo-o
131 Skuntank	130 Stunky	123 Gallade	321 Trapinch	177 Noivern	299 Lucario
292 Sneasel	259 Togekiss	122 Gardevoir	**Fishious Rend**	149 Octillery	295 Mawile
130 Stunky	257 Togepi	141 Gastly	377 Arctovish	191 Pumpkaboo	149 Octillery
321 Trapinch	258 Togetic	143 Gengar	376 Dracovish	005 Raboot	178 Onix
107 Tyrogue	300 Torkoal	088 Golett	**Fissure**	148 Remoraid	272 Reuniclus
Fell Stinger	347 Turtonator	089 Golurk	228 Barboach	265 Rhydon	266 Rhyperior
286 Drapion	385 Tyranitar	391 Goodra	302 Cufant	264 Rhyhorn	168 Roggenrola
274 Escavalier	068 Vulpix	240 Grimmsnarl	164 Diglett	266 Rhyperior	297 Sigilyph
304 Qwilfish	251 Weezing	172 Gurdurr	166 Drilbur	244 Salandit	382 Silvally
285 Skorupi	**Fire Fang (TM68)**	142 Haunter	165 Dugtrio	245 Salazzle	270 Solosis
007 Sobble	071 Arcanine	320 Hawlucha	167 Excadrill	004 Scorbunny	212 Spritzee
348 Togedemaru	047 Boltund	317 Heatmor	323 Flygon	382 Silvally	179 Steelix
117 Vespiquen	160 Centiskorch	319 Heliolisk	314 Hippopotas	131 Skuntank	226 Stunfisk
Final Gambit	380 Charizard	109 Hitmonchan	315 Hippowdon	211 Slurpuff	347 Turtonator
276 Accelgor	378 Charmander	121 Kirlia	361 Lapras	261 Snorlax	073 Vanillish
154 Basculin	379 Charmeleon	394 Kommo-o	084 Mudbray	363 Solrock	072 Vanillite
164 Diglett	006 Cinderace	037 Lombre	260 Munchlax	130 Stunky	074 Vanilluxe
218 Farfetch'd	368 Darmanitan	038 Ludicolo	261 Snorlax	210 Swirlix	018 Vikavolt
299 Lucario	367 Darumaka	140 Machamp	226 Stunfisk	259 Togekiss	399 Zamazenta
104 Nincada	386 Deino	139 Machoke	075 Swinub	257 Togepi	**Flatter**
298 Riolu	374 Dracozolt	138 Machop	300 Torkoal	258 Togetic	222 Croagunk
275 Shelmet	286 Drapion	365 Mr. Mime	321 Trapinch	300 Torkoal	267 Gothita
227 Shuckle	066 Electrike	260 Munchlax	322 Vibrava	347 Turtonator	269 Gothitelle
219 Sirfetch'd	199 Flareon	033 Obstagoon	356 Wailmer	385 Tyranitar	268 Gothorita
Fire Blast (TR15)	025 Greedent	111 Pancham	229 Whiscash	068 Vulpix	240 Grimmsnarl
071 Arcanine	070 Growlithe	112 Pangoro	**Flail**	251 Weezing	238 Impidimp
162 Carkol	315 Hippowdon	120 Ralts	213 Aromatisse	**Flare Blitz (TR55)**	284 Mandibuzz
160 Centiskorch	388 Hydreigon	272 Reuniclus	228 Barboach	071 Arcanine	239 Morgrem
289 Chandelure	067 Manectric	265 Rhydon	154 Basculin	162 Carkol	344 Morpeko

294 Sableye
223 Toxicroak
283 Vullaby
174 Woobat

Fling (TM59)
097 Abomasnow
186 Alcremie
324 Axew
235 Barbaracle
280 Beartic
058 Bellossom
095 Bewear
234 Binacle
247 Bisharp
048 Bunnelby
380 Charizard
378 Charmander
379 Charmeleon
051 Cinccino
256 Clefable
255 Clefairy
254 Cleffa
173 Conkeldurr
303 Copperajah
102 Corphish
103 Crawdaunt
222 Croagunk
279 Cubchoo
302 Cufant
368 Darmanitan
367 Darumaka
078 Delibird
049 Diggersby
346 Drampa
286 Drapion
166 Drilbur
008 Drizzile
136 Dusclops
137 Dusknoir
135 Duskull
167 Excadrill
325 Fraxure
081 Froslass
123 Gallade
158 Garbodor
122 Gardevoir
143 Gengar
056 Gloom
088 Golett
233 Golisopod
089 Golurk
267 Gothita
269 Gothitelle
268 Gothorita
025 Greedent
001 Grookey
172 Gurdurr
393 Hakamo-o
142 Haunter
320 Hawlucha
326 Haxorus
317 Heatmor
109 Hitmonchan
108 Hitmonlee
290 Inkay
009 Inteleon
392 Jangmo-o
099 Kingler
121 Kirlia
394 Kommo-o
098 Krabby
032 Linoone
037 Lombre

299 Lucario
038 Ludicolo
140 Machamp
139 Machoke
138 Machop
291 Malamar
295 Mawile
185 Milcery
364 Mime Jr.
301 Mimikyu
050 Minccino
344 Morpeko
365 Mr. Mime
366 Mr. Rime
260 Munchlax
040 Nuzleaf
033 Obstagoon
342 Oranguru
111 Pancham
112 Pangoro
343 Passimian
246 Pawniard
063 Pelipper
183 Perrserker
193 Pichu
194 Pikachu
101 Quagsire
195 Raichu
120 Ralts
272 Reuniclus
265 Rhydon
266 Rhyperior
003 Rillaboom
298 Riolu
294 Sableye
244 Salandit
245 Salazzle
249 Sawk
225 Scrafty
224 Scraggy
134 Seismitoad
041 Shiftry
285 Skorupi
024 Skwovet
292 Sneasel
261 Snorlax
053 Steenee
094 Stufful
253 Sudowoodo
248 Throh
002 Thwackey
171 Timburr
348 Togedemaru
259 Togekiss
257 Togepi
258 Togetic
223 Toxicroak
311 Toxtricity
054 Tsareena
347 Turtonator
385 Tyranitar
117 Vespiquen
057 Vileplume
293 Weavile
263 Whimsicott
031 Zigzagoon

Flower Shield
129 Cherrim
128 Cherubi

Fly (TM06)
282 Braviary
380 Charizard
023 Corviknight

022 Corvisquire
309 Cramorant
078 Delibird
397 Dragapult
346 Drampa
125 Drifblim
400 Eternatus
206 Flapple
323 Flygon
089 Golurk
320 Hawlucha
019 Hoothoot
388 Hydreigon
284 Mandibuzz
020 Noctowl
176 Noibat
177 Noivern
063 Pelipper
026 Pidove
021 Rookidee
281 Rufflet
297 Sigilyph
175 Swoobat
259 Togekiss
258 Togetic
027 Tranquill
028 Unfezant
322 Vibrava
018 Vikavolt
283 Vullaby
062 Wingull
174 Woobat
093 Xatu

Flying Press
320 Hawlucha

Focus Blast (TR64)
097 Abomasnow
276 Accelgor
235 Barbaracle
280 Beartic
095 Bewear
247 Bisharp
380 Charizard
051 Cinccino
006 Cinderace
256 Clefable
351 Clobbopus
173 Conkeldurr
222 Croagunk
368 Darmanitan
346 Drampa
137 Dusknoir
274 Escavalier
167 Excadrill
345 Falinks
123 Gallade
158 Garbodor
122 Gardevoir
143 Gengar
088 Golett
233 Golisopod
089 Golurk
192 Gourgeist
352 Grapploct
240 Grimmsnarl
172 Gurdurr
393 Hakamo-o
320 Hawlucha
326 Haxorus
317 Heatmor
319 Heliolisk
109 Hitmonchan

108 Hitmonlee
110 Hitmontop
388 Hydreigon
392 Jangmo-o
394 Kommo-o
299 Lucario
038 Ludicolo
140 Machamp
139 Machoke
138 Machop
295 Mawile
365 Mr. Mime
366 Mr. Rime
085 Mudsdale
177 Noivern
342 Oranguru
112 Pangoro
343 Passimian
101 Quagsire
195 Raichu
272 Reuniclus
265 Rhydon
266 Rhyperior
003 Rillaboom
298 Riolu
249 Sawk
225 Scrafty
224 Scraggy
134 Seismitoad
041 Shiftry
261 Snorlax
094 Stufful
248 Throh
171 Timburr
223 Toxicroak
339 Trevenant
347 Turtonator
385 Tyranitar
293 Weavile
398 Zacian
399 Zamazenta
387 Zweilous

Focus Energy (TR13)
180 Arrokuda
324 Axew
181 Barraskewda
047 Boltund
006 Cinderace
173 Conkeldurr
023 Corviknight
022 Corvisquire
368 Darmanitan
367 Darumaka
386 Deino
125 Drifblim
124 Drifloon
196 Eevee
200 Espeon
345 Falinks
218 Farfetch'd
206 Flapple
199 Flareon
323 Flygon
325 Fraxure
203 Glaceon
240 Grimmsnarl
001 Grookey
172 Gurdurr
393 Hakamo-o
320 Hawlucha
326 Haxorus
317 Heatmor
109 Hitmonchan
108 Hitmonlee
110 Hitmontop
388 Hydreigon

009 Inteleon
198 Jolteon
383 Larvitar
202 Leafeon
299 Lucario
140 Machamp
139 Machoke
138 Machop
033 Obstagoon
149 Octillery
112 Pangoro
343 Passimian
026 Pidove
384 Pupitar
005 Raboot
148 Remoraid
003 Rillaboom
021 Rookidee
249 Sawk
004 Scorbunny
219 Sirfetch'd
131 Skuntank
130 Stunky
204 Sylveon
248 Throh
002 Thwackey
171 Timburr
027 Tranquill
107 Tyrogue
201 Umbreon
028 Unfezant
197 Vaporeon
322 Vibrava
398 Zacian
399 Zamazenta
387 Zweilous

Focus Punch
173 Conkeldurr
279 Cubchoo
367 Darumaka
089 Golurk
172 Gurdurr
109 Hitmonchan
392 Jangmo-o
225 Scrafty
224 Scraggy
171 Timburr

Follow Me
256 Clefable
255 Clefairy
337 Indeedee
259 Togekiss
257 Togepi
258 Togetic

Force Palm
299 Lucario
298 Riolu
094 Stufful

Forest's Curse
338 Phantump
339 Trevenant

Foul Play (TR81)
247 Bisharp
252 Bonsly
222 Croagunk
049 Diggersby
371 Duraludon
141 Gastly
143 Gengar
267 Gothita
269 Gothitelle

268 Gothorita
192 Gourgeist
240 Grimmsnarl
142 Haunter
238 Impidimp
290 Inkay
045 Liepard
291 Malamar
284 Mandibuzz
295 Mawile
182 Meowth
239 Morgrem
344 Morpeko
365 Mr. Mime
366 Mr. Rime
029 Nickit
069 Ninetales
040 Nuzleaf
342 Oranguru
111 Pancham
112 Pangoro
246 Pawniard
183 Perrserker
184 Persian
338 Phantump
336 Polteageist
191 Pumpkaboo
044 Purrloin
372 Rotom
294 Sableye
244 Salandit
245 Salazzle
225 Scrafty
224 Scraggy
039 Seedot
041 Shiftry
335 Sinistea
131 Skuntank
292 Sneasel
226 Stunfisk
130 Stunky
253 Sudowoodo
030 Thievul
223 Toxicroak
339 Trevenant
385 Tyranitar
201 Umbreon
283 Vullaby
068 Vulpix
293 Weavile
093 Xatu

Freeze-Dry
377 Arctovish
375 Arctozolt
367 Darumaka
078 Delibird
370 Eiscue
203 Glaceon
080 Glalie
361 Lapras
365 Mr. Mime
366 Mr. Rime
075 Swinub
074 Vanilluxe

Frenzy Plant
003 Rillaboom

Frost Breath
280 Beartic
279 Cubchoo
081 Froslass
080 Glalie
079 Snorunt

Fury Attack
180 Arrokuda
181 Barraskewda
023 Corviknight
022 Corvisquire
309 Cramorant
353 Pincurchin
021 Rookidee

Fury Cutter
332 Aegislash
235 Barbaracle
234 Binacle
247 Bisharp
087 Crustle
331 Doublade
316 Durant
086 Dwebble
274 Escavalier
218 Farfetch'd
123 Gallade
065 Galvantula
233 Golisopod
330 Honedge
064 Joltik
273 Karrablast
105 Ninjask
246 Pawniard
219 Sirfetch'd
321 Trapinch
117 Vespiquen

Fury Swipes
235 Barbaracle
280 Beartic
234 Binacle
279 Cubchoo
166 Drilbur
167 Excadrill
317 Heatmor
045 Liepard
032 Linoone
037 Lombre
038 Ludicolo
182 Meowth
104 Nincada
105 Ninjask
033 Obstagoon
183 Perrserker
184 Persian
044 Purrloin
294 Sableye
106 Shedinja
131 Skuntank
292 Sneasel
130 Stunky
117 Vespiquen
293 Weavile

Future Sight (TR34)
228 Barboach
278 Beheeyem
119 Bronzong
118 Bronzor
083 Claydol
078 Delibird
011 Dottler
271 Duosion
136 Dusclops
137 Dusknoir
135 Duskull
200 Espeon
123 Gallade
122 Gardevoir
267 Gothita

269 Gothitelle	141 Gastly	282 Braviary	315 Hippowdon	030 Thievul	267 Gothita	002 Thwackey
268 Gothorita	143 Gengar	119 Bronzong	388 Hydreigon	248 Throh	269 Gothitelle	**Grassy Terrain (TM88)**
243 Hatterene	056 Gloom	015 Butterfree	009 Inteleon	348 Togedemaru	268 Gothorita	058 Bellossom
337 Indeedee	126 Gossifleur	160 Centiskorch	306 Jellicent	259 Togekiss	192 Gourgeist	129 Cherrim
290 Inkay	192 Gourgeist	289 Chandelure	198 Jolteon	258 Togetic	001 Grookey	128 Cherubi
121 Kirlia	001 Grookey	380 Charizard	099 Kingler	300 Torkoal	172 Gurdurr	262 Cottonee
361 Lapras	241 Hatenna	129 Cherrim	115 Klinklang	223 Toxicroak	320 Hawlucha	127 Eldegoss
362 Lunatone	243 Hatterene	051 Cinccino	394 Kommo-o	311 Toxtricity	326 Haxorus	056 Gloom
291 Malamar	242 Hattrem	006 Cinderace	221 Lanturn	339 Trevenant	319 Heliolisk	126 Gossifleur
209 Meowstic	142 Haunter	083 Claydol	361 Lapras	054 Tsareena	318 Helioptile	296 Maractus
364 Mime Jr.	317 Heatmor	256 Clefable	202 Leafeon	347 Turtonator	121 Kirlia	040 Nuzleaf
365 Mr. Mime	306 Jellicent	151 Cloyster	045 Liepard	381 Type: Null	202 Leafeon	055 Oddish
366 Mr. Rime	064 Joltik	163 Coalossal	032 Linoone	385 Tyranitar	045 Liepard	003 Rillaboom
090 Munna	273 Karrablast	329 Cofagrigus	299 Lucario	201 Umbreon	032 Linoone	061 Roserade
091 Musharna	202 Leafeon	173 Conkeldurr	038 Ludicolo	028 Unfezant	037 Lombre	039 Seedot
092 Natu	037 Lombre	303 Copperajah	362 Lunatone	074 Vanilluxe	036 Lotad	041 Shiftry
020 Noctowl	036 Lotad	023 Corviknight	140 Machamp	197 Vaporeon	038 Ludicolo	057 Vileplume
342 Oranguru	038 Ludicolo	309 Cramorant	291 Malamar	117 Vespiquen	362 Lunatone	263 Whimsicott
012 Orbeetle	296 Maractus	103 Crawdaunt	077 Mamoswine	018 Vikavolt	296 Maractus	**Grav Apple**
333 Ponyta	301 Mimikyu	087 Crustle	284 Mandibuzz	057 Vileplume	295 Mawile	206 Flapple
120 Ralts	340 Morelull	237 Cursola	067 Manectric	357 Wailord	364 Mime Jr.	**Gravity**
334 Rapidash	092 Natu	368 Darmanitan	355 Mantine	293 Weavile	050 Minccino	256 Clefable
272 Reuniclus	104 Nincada	360 Dhelmise	295 Mawile	251 Weezing	340 Morelull	255 Clefairy
297 Sigilyph	105 Ninjask	049 Diggersby	209 Meowstic	263 Whimsicott	365 Mr. Mime	136 Dusclops
270 Solosis	040 Nuzleaf	376 Dracovish	153 Milotic	229 Whiscash	366 Mr. Rime	137 Dusknoir
175 Swoobat	055 Oddish	374 Dracozolt	301 Mimikyu	093 Xatu	092 Natu	189 Ferroseed
259 Togekiss	012 Orbeetle	397 Dragapult	365 Mr. Mime	398 Zacian	040 Nuzleaf	168 Roggenrola
257 Togepi	338 Phantump	346 Drampa	366 Mr. Rime	399 Zamazenta	033 Obstagoon	297 Sigilyph
258 Togetic	336 Polteageist	286 Drapion	085 Mudsdale	**Glare**	055 Oddish	369 Stonjourner
229 Whiscash	191 Pumpkaboo	043 Drednaw	091 Musharna	346 Drampa	111 Pancham	**Growl**
174 Woobat	003 Rillaboom	125 Drifblim	069 Ninetales	318 Helioptile	112 Pangoro	280 Beartic
093 Xatu	060 Roselia	035 Dubwool	105 Ninjask	313 Sandaconda	343 Passimian	278 Beheeyem
Gastro Acid	061 Roserade	165 Dugtrio	020 Noctowl	312 Silicobra	246 Pawniard	380 Charizard
042 Chewtle	039 Seedot	371 Duraludon	177 Noivern	**Grass Knot (TR77)**	338 Phantump	378 Charmander
065 Galvantula	106 Shedinja	316 Durant	033 Obstagoon	097 Abomasnow	193 Pichu	379 Charmeleon
064 Joltik	275 Shelmet	136 Dusclops	149 Octillery	207 Appletun	194 Pikachu	006 Cinderace
156 Pyukumuku	041 Shiftry	137 Dusknoir	342 Oranguru	082 Baltoy	191 Pumpkaboo	256 Clefable
134 Seismitoad	341 Shiinotic	127 Eldegoss	012 Orbeetle	235 Barbaracle	044 Purrloin	255 Clefairy
227 Shuckle	335 Sinistea	274 Escavalier	112 Pangoro	234 Binacle	195 Raichu	303 Copperajah
261 Snorlax	096 Snover	200 Espeon	343 Passimian	247 Bisharp	120 Ralts	279 Cubchoo
Gear Grind	053 Steenee	400 Eternatus	063 Pelipper	052 Bounsweet	272 Reuniclus	302 Cufant
114 Klang	175 Swoobat	167 Excadrill	183 Perrserker	119 Bronzong	003 Rillaboom	164 Diglett
113 Klink	002 Thwackey	345 Falinks	184 Persian	118 Bronzor	060 Roselia	008 Drizzile
115 Klinklang	321 Trapinch	190 Ferrothorn	076 Piloswine	059 Budew	061 Roserade	035 Dubwool
Gear Up	339 Trevenant	206 Flapple	336 Polteageist	048 Bunnelby	328 Runerigus	165 Dugtrio
115 Klinklang	157 Trubbish	199 Flareon	101 Quagsire	129 Cherrim	249 Sawk	196 Eevee
Giga Drain (TM28)	054 Tsareena	323 Flygon	195 Raichu	128 Cherubi	225 Scrafty	277 Elgyem
097 Abomasnow	322 Vibrava	325 Fraxure	334 Rapidash	051 Cinccino	224 Scraggy	200 Espeon
276 Accelgor	057 Vileplume	081 Froslass	272 Reuniclus	083 Claydol	039 Seedot	199 Flareon
186 Alcremie	263 Whimsicott	350 Frosmoth	265 Rhydon	256 Clefable	134 Seismitoad	123 Gallade
207 Appletun	174 Woobat	123 Gallade	266 Rhyperior	255 Clefairy	041 Shiftry	122 Gardevoir
215 Araquanid	093 Xatu	065 Galvantula	188 Ribombee	254 Cleffa	341 Shiinotic	203 Glaceon
058 Bellossom	**Giga Impact (TM09)**	158 Garbodor	003 Rillaboom	329 Cofagrigus	096 Snover	001 Grookey
052 Bounsweet	097 Abomasnow	122 Gardevoir	061 Roserade	173 Conkeldurr	363 Solrock	019 Hoothoot
059 Budew	276 Accelgor	231 Gastrodon	328 Runerigus	262 Cottonee	053 Steenee	009 Inteleon
015 Butterfree	332 Aegislash	143 Gengar	249 Sawk	279 Cubchoo	030 Thievul	198 Jolteon
129 Cherrim	186 Alcremie	170 Gigalith	225 Scrafty	368 Darmanitan	248 Throh	121 Kirlia
128 Cherubi	207 Appletun	203 Glaceon	147 Seaking	367 Darumaka	002 Thwackey	361 Lapras
236 Corsola	071 Arcanine	080 Glalie	134 Seismitoad	360 Dhelmise	171 Timburr	202 Leafeon
262 Cottonee	377 Arctovish	233 Golisopod	106 Shedinja	049 Diggersby	348 Togedemaru	045 Liepard
237 Cursola	375 Arctozolt	089 Golurk	041 Shiftry	346 Drampa	259 Togekiss	037 Lombre
214 Dewpider	213 Aromatisse	391 Goodra	341 Shiinotic	127 Eldegoss	257 Togepi	036 Lotad
360 Dhelmise	359 Avalugg	269 Gothitelle	297 Sigilyph	200 Espeon	258 Togetic	038 Ludicolo
127 Eldegoss	324 Axew	192 Gourgeist	382 Silvally	190 Ferrothorn	339 Trevenant	295 Mawile
274 Escavalier	235 Barbaracle	352 Grapploct	131 Skuntank	206 Flapple	054 Tsareena	182 Meowth
189 Ferroseed	181 Barraskewda	025 Greedent	211 Slurpuff	123 Gallade	057 Vileplume	020 Noctowl
190 Ferrothorn	280 Beartic	240 Grimmsnarl	261 Snorlax	122 Gardevoir	263 Whimsicott	133 Palpitoad
206 Flapple	278 Beheeyem	145 Gyarados	363 Solrock	031 Zigzagoon	093 Xatu	063 Pelipper
323 Flygon	058 Bellossom	243 Hatterene	179 Steelix	056 Gloom	031 Zigzagoon	183 Perrserker
305 Frillish	095 Bewear	320 Hawlucha	369 Stonjourner	088 Golett	**Grass Pledge**	184 Persian
350 Frosmoth	247 Bisharp	326 Haxorus	175 Swoobat	089 Golurk	001 Grookey	026 Pidove
065 Galvantula	047 Boltund	317 Heatmor	204 Sylveon	126 Gossifleur	003 Rillaboom	194 Pikachu
158 Garbodor		319 Heliolisk			382 Silvally	

333 Ponyta
044 Purrloin
005 Raboot
195 Raichu
120 Ralts
334 Rapidash
003 Rillaboom
004 Scorbunny
134 Seismitoad
007 Sobble
204 Sylveon
002 Thwackey
259 Togekiss
257 Togepi
258 Togetic
310 Toxel
311 Toxtricity
027 Tranquill
132 Tympole
201 Umbreon
028 Unfezant
197 Vaporeon
356 Wailmer
357 Wailord
062 Wingull
155 Wishiwashi
034 Wooloo

Growth
207 Appletun
058 Bellossom
059 Budew
129 Cherrim
128 Cherubi
262 Cottonee
360 Dhelmise
206 Flapple
056 Gloom
126 Gossifleur
001 Grookey
296 Maractus
340 Morelull
040 Nuzleaf
055 Oddish
338 Phantump
060 Roselia
061 Roserade
039 Seedot
041 Shiftry
096 Snover
339 Trevenant
057 Vileplume
263 Whimsicott

Grudge
329 Cofagrigus
236 Corsola
237 Cursola
395 Dreepy
135 Duskull
141 Gastly
250 Koffing
301 Mimikyu
069 Ninetales
338 Phantump
120 Ralts
106 Shedinja
068 Vulpix
327 Yamask

Guard Split
082 Baltoy
278 Beheeyem
083 Claydol
329 Cofagrigus
035 Dubwool
277 Elgyem
337 Indeedee
264 Rhyhorn
328 Runerigus
275 Shelmet
227 Shuckle
034 Wooloo
327 Yamask

Guard Swap (TM61)
276 Accelgor
082 Baltoy
278 Beheeyem
119 Bronzong
118 Bronzor
083 Claydol
329 Cofagrigus
011 Dottler
035 Dubwool
271 Duosion
277 Elgyem
122 Gardevoir
267 Gothita
269 Gothitelle
268 Gothorita
243 Hatterene
337 Indeedee
290 Inkay
291 Malamar
295 Mawile
365 Mr. Mime
366 Mr. Rime
090 Munna
091 Musharna
092 Natu
012 Orbeetle
101 Quagsire
272 Reuniclus
328 Runerigus
275 Shelmet
270 Solosis
201 Umbreon
034 Wooloo
100 Wooper
093 Xatu
399 Zamazenta

Guillotine
324 Axew
247 Bisharp
102 Corphish
103 Crawdaunt
316 Durant
325 Fraxure
326 Haxorus
099 Kingler
098 Krabby
246 Pawniard
018 Vikavolt

Gunk Shot (TR73)
051 Cinccino
006 Cinderace
222 Croagunk
078 Delibird
049 Diggersby
158 Garbodor
045 Liepard
032 Linoone
355 Mantine
307 Mareanie
182 Meowth
050 Minccino
260 Munchlax
033 Obstagoon
149 Octillery
111 Pancham
112 Pangoro
343 Passimian
063 Pelipper
183 Perrserker
184 Persian
044 Purrloin
005 Raboot
148 Remoraid
244 Salandit
245 Salazzle
004 Scorbunny
261 Snorlax
308 Toxapex
223 Toxicroak
311 Toxtricity
157 Trubbish
031 Zigzagoon

Gust
015 Butterfree
116 Combee
125 Drifblim
124 Drifloon
284 Mandibuzz
104 Nincada
176 Noibat
177 Noivern
026 Pidove
297 Sigilyph
175 Swoobat
027 Tranquill
028 Unfezant
117 Vespiquen
283 Vullaby
263 Whimsicott
062 Wingull
174 Woobat

Gyro Ball (TR52)
332 Aegislash
207 Appletun
213 Aromatisse
359 Avalugg
082 Baltoy
358 Bergmite
119 Bronzong
118 Bronzor
162 Carkol
083 Claydol
163 Coalossal
368 Darmanitan
367 Darumaka
360 Dhelmise
331 Doublade
125 Drifblim
124 Drifloon
271 Duosion
371 Duraludon
189 Ferroseed
190 Ferrothorn
080 Golett
088 Golett
089 Golurk
192 Gourgeist
025 Greedent
110 Hitmontop
330 Honedge
250 Koffing
362 Lunatone
182 Meowth
090 Munna
091 Musharna

178 Onix
343 Passimian
183 Perrserker
191 Pumpkaboo
304 Qwilfish
272 Reuniclus
161 Rolycoly
294 Sableye
227 Shuckle
024 Skwovet
270 Solosis
363 Solrock
212 Spritzee
179 Steelix
175 Swoobat
348 Togedemaru
300 Torkoal
251 Weezing
174 Woobat

Hail (TM35)
097 Abomasnow
377 Arctovish
375 Arctozolt
359 Avalugg
228 Barboach
154 Basculin
280 Beartic
358 Bergmite
220 Chinchou
151 Cloyster
102 Corphish
236 Corsola
103 Crawdaunt
279 Cubchoo
237 Cursola
078 Delibird
370 Eiscue
152 Feebas
305 Frillish
081 Froslass
350 Frosmoth
231 Gastrodon
203 Glaceon
080 Glalie
146 Goldeen
233 Golisopod
391 Goodra
145 Gyarados
306 Jellicent
099 Kingler
098 Krabby
221 Lanturn
361 Lapras
037 Lombre
036 Lotad
038 Ludicolo
362 Lunatone
077 Mamoswine
355 Mantine
354 Mantyke
307 Mareanie
153 Milotic
365 Mr. Mime
366 Mr. Rime
133 Palpitoad
063 Pelipper
076 Piloswine
156 Pyukumuku
101 Quagsire
304 Qwilfish
147 Seaking
134 Seismitoad
150 Shellder

230 Shellos
382 Silvally
292 Sneasel
079 Snorunt
096 Snover
075 Swinub
308 Toxapex
132 Tympole
381 Type: Null
073 Vanillish
072 Vanillite
074 Vanilluxe
197 Vaporeon
356 Wailmer
357 Wailord
293 Weavile
229 Whiscash
232 Wimpod
062 Wingull
155 Wishiwashi
100 Wooper

Hammer Arm
095 Bewear
173 Conkeldurr
367 Darumaka
049 Diggersby
088 Golett
089 Golurk
240 Grimmsnarl
001 Grookey
172 Gurdurr
099 Kingler
098 Krabby
112 Pangoro
272 Reuniclus
265 Rhydon
266 Rhyperior
261 Snorlax
094 Stufful
253 Sudowoodo
171 Timburr

Harden
359 Avalugg
324 Axew
082 Baltoy
358 Bergmite
169 Boldore
252 Bonsly
015 Butterfree
083 Claydol
102 Corphish
236 Corsola
103 Crawdaunt
237 Cursola
189 Ferroseed
190 Ferrothorn
231 Gastrodon
170 Gigalith
016 Grubbin
099 Kingler
098 Krabby
362 Lunatone
014 Metapod
104 Nincada
105 Ninjask
040 Nuzleaf
178 Onix
156 Pyukumuku
304 Qwilfish
168 Roggenrola
039 Seedot
106 Shedinja
230 Shellos

041 Shiftry
363 Solrock
179 Steelix
253 Sudowoodo
073 Vanillish
072 Vanillite
074 Vanilluxe
232 Wimpod

Haze
329 Cofagrigus
236 Corsola
124 Drifloon
135 Duskull
152 Feebas
141 Gastly
146 Goldeen
250 Koffing
287 Litwick
355 Mantine
354 Mantyke
307 Mareanie
101 Quagsire
304 Qwilfish
148 Remoraid
328 Runerigus
007 Sobble
130 Stunky
157 Trubbish
197 Vaporeon
251 Weezing
100 Wooper
327 Yamask

Head Smash
332 Aegislash
154 Basculin
236 Corsola
386 Deino
043 Drednaw
370 Eiscue
178 Onix
225 Scrafty
224 Scraggy
253 Sudowoodo
347 Turtonator

Headbutt
207 Appletun
215 Araquanid
154 Basculin
278 Beheeyem
169 Boldore
252 Bonsly
042 Chewtle
006 Cinderace
222 Croagunk
368 Darmanitan
367 Darumaka
386 Deino
214 Dewpider
164 Diglett
043 Drednaw
035 Dubwool
370 Eiscue
066 Electrike
277 Elgyem
274 Escavalier
345 Falinks
081 Froslass
170 Gigalith
080 Glalie
393 Hakamo-o
388 Hydreigon
392 Jangmo-o
273 Karrablast

394 Kommo-o
032 Linoone
355 Mantine
354 Mantyke
033 Obstagoon
246 Pawniard
005 Raboot
168 Roggenrola
313 Sandaconda
004 Scorbunny
225 Scrafty
224 Scraggy
312 Silicobra
079 Snorunt
253 Sudowoodo
034 Wooloo
031 Zigzagoon
387 Zweilous

Heal Pulse
213 Aromatisse
128 Cherubi
254 Cleffa
123 Gallade
122 Gardevoir
267 Gothita
241 Hatenna
243 Hatterene
242 Hattrem
337 Indeedee
121 Kirlia
299 Lucario
333 Ponyta
120 Ralts
334 Rapidash

Healing Wish
128 Cherubi
256 Clefable
255 Clefairy
122 Gardevoir
241 Hatenna
243 Hatterene
242 Hattrem
337 Indeedee
090 Munna
333 Ponyta
334 Rapidash

Heat Crash (TR88)
162 Carkol
160 Centiskorch
380 Charizard
163 Coalossal
303 Copperajah
089 Golurk
265 Rhydon
266 Rhyperior
161 Rolycoly
159 Sizzlipede
261 Snorlax
369 Stonjourner
300 Torkoal
347 Turtonator

Heat Wave (TR36)
071 Arcanine
282 Braviary
162 Carkol
160 Centiskorch
289 Chandelure
380 Charizard
378 Charmander
379 Charmeleon
006 Cinderace
163 Coalossal
368 Darmanitan

367 Darumaka	369 Stonjourner	202 Leafeon	119 Bronzong	333 Ponyta	046 Yamper	353 Pincurchin
346 Drampa	347 Turtonator	032 Linoone	118 Bronzor	101 Quagsire	398 Zacian	101 Quagsire
199 Flareon	385 Tyranitar	299 Lucario	289 Chandelure	334 Rapidash	399 Zamazenta	304 Qwilfish
323 Flygon	356 Wailmer	362 Lunatone	083 Claydol	265 Rhydon	**Hurricane (TR89)**	148 Remoraid
070 Growlithe	357 Wailord	140 Machamp	329 Cofagrigus	264 Rhyhorn	282 Braviary	265 Rhydon
317 Heatmor	**Helping Hand (TM41)**	139 Machoke	236 Corsola	266 Rhyperior	015 Butterfree	266 Rhyperior
019 Hoothoot	186 Alcremie	138 Machop	237 Cursola	003 Rillaboom	380 Charizard	372 Rotom
388 Hydreigon	071 Arcanine	355 Mantine	360 Dhelmise	313 Sandaconda	023 Corviknight	147 Seaking
288 Lampent	213 Aromatisse	354 Mantyke	397 Dragapult	261 Snorlax	309 Cramorant	134 Seismitoad
287 Litwick	235 Barbaracle	296 Maractus	396 Drakloak	179 Steelix	346 Drampa	150 Shellder
284 Mandibuzz	058 Bellossom	295 Mawile	125 Drifblim	385 Tyranitar	350 Frosmoth	230 Shellos
092 Natu	234 Binacle	209 Meowstic	124 Drifloon	**High Jump Kick**	145 Gyarados	261 Snorlax
069 Ninetales	047 Boltund	185 Milcery	136 Dusclops	320 Hawlucha	019 Hoothoot	308 Toxapex
020 Noctowl	252 Bonsly	153 Milotic	137 Dusknoir	108 Hitmonlee	020 Noctowl	132 Tympole
176 Noibat	052 Bounsweet	364 Mime Jr.	135 Duskull	298 Riolu	176 Noibat	385 Tyranitar
177 Noivern	380 Charizard	050 Minccino	305 Frillish	004 Scorbunny	177 Noivern	197 Vaporeon
026 Pidove	378 Charmander	365 Mr. Mime	081 Froslass	225 Scrafty	063 Pelipper	356 Wailmer
005 Raboot	379 Charmeleon	366 Mr. Rime	141 Gastly	224 Scraggy	281 Rufflet	357 Wailord
281 Rufflet	129 Cherrim	090 Munna	143 Gengar	054 Tsareena	313 Sandaconda	229 Whiscash
244 Salandit	128 Cherubi	091 Musharna	080 Glalie	107 Tyrogue	041 Shiftry	155 Wishiwashi
245 Salazzle	051 Cinccino	033 Obstagoon	192 Gourgeist	**Hone Claws**	028 Unfezant	100 Wooper
004 Scorbunny	006 Cinderace	149 Octillery	142 Haunter	235 Barbaracle	263 Whimsicott	**Hyper Beam (TM08)**
041 Shiftry	256 Clefable	012 Orbeetle	306 Jellicent	234 Binacle	062 Wingull	097 Abomasnow
297 Sigilyph	255 Clefairy	111 Pancham	288 Lampent	282 Braviary	**Hydro Cannon**	276 Accelgor
382 Silvally	254 Cleffa	112 Pangoro	287 Litwick	023 Corviknight	009 Inteleon	332 Aegislash
159 Sizzlipede	173 Conkeldurr	193 Pichu	301 Mimikyu	022 Corvisquire	**Hydro Pump (TR03)**	186 Alcremie
363 Solrock	262 Cottonee	194 Pikachu	069 Ninetales	164 Diglett	215 Araquanid	207 Appletun
175 Swoobat	222 Croagunk	156 Pyukumuku	338 Phantump	286 Drapion	377 Arctovish	071 Arcanine
259 Togekiss	187 Cutiefly	195 Raichu	353 Pincurchin	166 Drilbur	375 Arctozolt	377 Arctovish
258 Togetic	078 Delibird	120 Ralts	336 Polteageist	371 Duraludon	359 Avalugg	375 Arctozolt
300 Torkoal	360 Dhelmise	148 Remoraid	191 Pumpkaboo	167 Excadrill	228 Barboach	213 Aromatisse
027 Tranquill	011 Dottler	272 Reuniclus	304 Qwilfish	320 Hawlucha	181 Barraskewda	359 Avalugg
347 Turtonator	397 Dragapult	265 Rhydon	372 Rotom	317 Heatmor	154 Basculin	235 Barbaracle
028 Unfezant	396 Drakloak	266 Rhyperior	328 Runerigus	045 Liepard	042 Chewtle	181 Barraskewda
322 Vibrava	346 Drampa	188 Ribombee	294 Sableye	032 Linoone	220 Chinchou	280 Beartic
283 Vullaby	395 Dreepy	298 Riolu	106 Shedinja	182 Meowth	151 Cloyster	278 Beheeyem
068 Vulpix	271 Duosion	372 Rotom	335 Sinistea	301 Mimikyu	102 Corphish	058 Bellossom
251 Weezing	316 Durant	294 Sableye	131 Skuntank	029 Nickit	236 Corsola	095 Bewear
174 Woobat	136 Dusclops	244 Salandit	079 Snorunt	033 Obstagoon	309 Cramorant	247 Bisharp
093 Xatu	137 Dusknoir	245 Salazzle	130 Stunky	183 Perrserker	103 Crawdaunt	047 Boltund
Heavy Slam (TR79)	135 Duskull	249 Sawk	308 Toxapex	044 Purrloin	237 Cursola	282 Braviary
207 Appletun	196 Eevee	227 Shuckle	311 Toxtricity	021 Rookidee	360 Dhelmise	119 Bronzong
359 Avalugg	127 Eldegoss	219 Sirfetch'd	339 Trevenant	281 Rufflet	376 Dracovish	015 Butterfree
280 Beartic	200 Espeon	211 Slurpuff	117 Vespiquen	285 Skorupi	397 Dragapult	160 Centiskorch
169 Boldore	208 Espurr	270 Solosis	068 Vulpix	292 Sneasel	396 Drakloak	289 Chandelure
119 Bronzong	345 Falinks	363 Solrock	327 Yamask	030 Thievul	346 Drampa	380 Charizard
118 Bronzor	218 Farfetch'd	212 Spritzee	**High Horsepower (TR94)**	293 Weavile	043 Drednaw	129 Cherrim
162 Carkol	199 Flareon	053 Steenee	207 Appletun	**Horn Attack**	370 Eiscue	051 Cinccino
163 Coalossal	350 Frosmoth	253 Sudowoodo	359 Avalugg	146 Goldeen	305 Frillish	006 Cinderace
303 Copperajah	123 Gallade	210 Swirlix	095 Bewear	265 Rhydon	231 Gastrodon	083 Claydol
023 Corviknight	122 Gardevoir	175 Swoobat	162 Carkol	264 Rhyhorn	146 Goldeen	256 Clefable
087 Crustle	203 Glaceon	204 Sylveon	163 Coalossal	266 Rhyperior	391 Goodra	151 Cloyster
360 Dhelmise	088 Golett	248 Throh	173 Conkeldurr	147 Seaking	352 Grapploct	163 Coalossal
371 Duraludon	089 Golurk	171 Timburr	303 Copperajah	**Horn Drill**	145 Gyarados	329 Cofagrigus
190 Ferrothorn	126 Gossifleur	348 Togedemaru	302 Cufant	167 Excadrill	388 Hydreigon	173 Conkeldurr
206 Flapple	267 Gothita	259 Togekiss	049 Diggersby	146 Goldeen	009 Inteleon	303 Copperajah
170 Gigalith	269 Gothitelle	257 Togepi	374 Dracozolt	361 Lapras	306 Jellicent	023 Corviknight
088 Golett	268 Gothorita	258 Togetic	043 Drednaw	333 Ponyta	099 Kingler	309 Cramorant
089 Golurk	070 Growlithe	223 Toxicroak	166 Drilbur	265 Rhydon	221 Lanturn	103 Crawdaunt
315 Hippowdon	172 Gurdurr	054 Tsareena	165 Dugtrio	264 Rhyhorn	361 Lapras	087 Crustle
140 Machamp	241 Hatenna	107 Tyrogue	167 Excadrill	266 Rhyperior	037 Lombre	237 Cursola
139 Machoke	243 Hatterene	201 Umbreon	089 Golurk	147 Seaking	038 Ludicolo	368 Darmanitan
138 Machop	242 Hattrem	197 Vaporeon	172 Gurdurr	**Horn Leech**	144 Magikarp	360 Dhelmise
077 Mamoswine	320 Hawlucha	263 Whimsicott	314 Hippopotas	338 Phantump	355 Mantine	049 Diggersby
084 Mudbray	109 Hitmonchan	155 Wishiwashi	315 Hippowdon	339 Trevenant	354 Mantyke	376 Dracovish
085 Mudsdale	108 Hitmonlee	174 Woobat	099 Kingler	**Howl**	307 Mareanie	374 Dracozolt
178 Onix	110 Hitmontop	046 Yamper	140 Machamp	071 Arcanine	153 Milotic	397 Dragapult
183 Perrserker	388 Hydreigon	398 Zacian	077 Mamoswine	066 Electrike	260 Munchlax	346 Drampa
265 Rhydon	337 Indeedee	399 Zamazenta	084 Mudbray	070 Growlithe	149 Octillery	286 Drapion
266 Rhyperior	198 Jolteon	031 Zigzagoon	085 Mudsdale	067 Manectric	133 Palpitoad	043 Drednaw
168 Roggenrola	121 Kirlia	387 Zweilous	178 Onix	029 Nickit	063 Pelipper	125 Drifblim
261 Snorlax	361 Lapras	**Hex (TM77)**	076 Piloswine	298 Riolu		035 Dubwool
179 Steelix		082 Baltoy		068 Vulpix		

165 Dugtrio	177 Noivern	375 Arctozolt	124 Drifloon	089 Golurk	286 Drapion	272 Reuniclus
371 Duraludon	040 Nuzleaf	047 Boltund	152 Feebas	391 Goodra	043 Drednaw	265 Rhydon
136 Dusclops	033 Obstagoon	051 Cinccino	123 Gallade	145 Gyarados	066 Electrike	266 Rhyperior
137 Dusknoir	149 Octillery	256 Clefable	122 Gardevoir	009 Inteleon	081 Froslass	298 Riolu
127 Eldegoss	342 Oranguru	255 Clefairy	141 Gastly	306 Jellicent	203 Glaceon	294 Sableye
274 Escavalier	012 Orbeetle	254 Cleffa	143 Gengar	099 Kingler	080 Glalie	249 Sawk
200 Espeon	112 Pangoro	386 Deino	267 Gothita	098 Krabby	025 Greedent	225 Scrafty
400 Eternatus	343 Passimian	346 Drampa	269 Gothitelle	221 Lanturn	145 Gyarados	224 Scraggy
167 Excadrill	063 Pelipper	196 Eevee	268 Gothorita	361 Lapras	315 Hippowdon	134 Seismitoad
345 Falinks	183 Perrserker	127 Eldegoss	142 Haunter	032 Linoone	388 Hydreigon	292 Sneasel
190 Ferrothorn	184 Persian	200 Espeon	019 Hoothoot	037 Lombre	077 Mamoswine	261 Snorlax
206 Flapple	076 Piloswine	199 Flareon	290 Inkay	036 Lotad	067 Manectric	096 Snover
199 Flareon	336 Polteageist	123 Gallade	121 Kirlia	038 Ludicolo	295 Mawile	094 Stufful
323 Flygon	384 Pupitar	122 Gardevoir	362 Lunatone	362 Lunatone	344 Morpeko	253 Sudowoodo
081 Froslass	101 Quagsire	203 Glaceon	291 Malamar	077 Mamoswine	076 Piloswine	248 Throh
350 Frosmoth	195 Raichu	126 Gossifleur	182 Meowth	355 Mantine	265 Rhydon	171 Timburr
123 Gallade	334 Rapidash	025 Greedent	364 Mime Jr.	354 Mantyke	264 Rhyhorn	223 Toxicroak
065 Galvantula	148 Remoraid	319 Heliolisk	365 Mr. Mime	307 Mareanie	266 Rhyperior	385 Tyranitar
158 Garbodor	272 Reuniclus	019 Hoothoot	366 Mr. Rime	295 Mawile	382 Silvally	293 Weavile
122 Gardevoir	265 Rhydon	388 Hydreigon	090 Munna	153 Milotic	079 Snorunt	100 Wooper
231 Gastrodon	266 Rhyperior	337 Indeedee	091 Musharna	365 Mr. Mime	179 Steelix	**Ice Shard**
143 Gengar	188 Ribombee	198 Jolteon	020 Noctowl	366 Mr. Rime	226 Stunfisk	097 Abomasnow
170 Gigalith	003 Rillaboom	121 Kirlia	012 Orbeetle	260 Munchlax	030 Thievul	151 Cloyster
203 Glaceon	061 Roserade	394 Kommo-o	026 Pidove	033 Obstagoon	385 Tyranitar	078 Delibird
080 Glalie	328 Runerigus	361 Lapras	333 Ponyta	149 Octillery	398 Zacian	081 Froslass
233 Golisopod	313 Sandaconda	202 Leafeon	120 Ralts	063 Pelipper	399 Zamazenta	203 Glaceon
089 Golurk	225 Scrafty	045 Liepard	297 Sigilyph	076 Piloswine	387 Zweilous	080 Glalie
391 Goodra	147 Seaking	032 Linoone	363 Solrock	101 Quagsire	**Ice Punch (TM04)**	361 Lapras
269 Gothitelle	134 Seismitoad	037 Lombre	068 Vulpix	304 Qwilfish	097 Abomasnow	077 Mamoswine
192 Gourgeist	106 Shedinja	038 Ludicolo	**Ice Beam (TR05)**	148 Remoraid	280 Beartic	365 Mr. Mime
352 Grapploct	041 Shiftry	067 Manectric	097 Abomasnow	265 Rhydon	095 Bewear	366 Mr. Rime
025 Greedent	341 Shiinotic	296 Maractus	215 Araquanid	264 Rhyhorn	256 Clefable	076 Piloswine
240 Grimmsnarl	297 Sigilyph	182 Meowth	377 Arctovish	266 Rhyperior	255 Clefairy	150 Shellder
145 Gyarados	382 Silvally	050 Minccino	375 Arctozolt	147 Seaking	351 Clobbopus	292 Sneasel
243 Hatterene	131 Skuntank	260 Munchlax	359 Avalugg	150 Shellder	173 Conkeldurr	079 Snorunt
326 Haxorus	211 Slurpuff	020 Noctowl	082 Baltoy	230 Shellos	222 Croagunk	096 Snover
319 Heliolisk	261 Snorlax	176 Noibat	235 Barbaracle	297 Sigilyph	279 Cubchoo	007 Sobble
315 Hippowdon	363 Solrock	177 Noivern	228 Barboach	382 Silvally	368 Darmanitan	075 Swinub
388 Hydreigon	179 Steelix	033 Obstagoon	154 Basculin	390 Sliggoo	367 Darumaka	072 Vanillite
009 Inteleon	369 Stonjourner	133 Palpitoad	280 Beartic	292 Sneasel	078 Delibird	293 Weavile
306 Jellicent	175 Swoobat	111 Pancham	358 Bergmite	261 Snorlax	049 Diggersby	**Icicle Crash**
198 Jolteon	204 Sylveon	112 Pangoro	234 Binacle	079 Snorunt	136 Dusclops	377 Arctovish
099 Kingler	030 Thievul	183 Perrserker	220 Chinchou	096 Snover	137 Dusknoir	375 Arctozolt
114 Klang	348 Togedemaru	184 Persian	083 Claydol	075 Swinub	370 Eiscue	280 Beartic
113 Klink	259 Togekiss	044 Purrloin	256 Clefable	308 Toxapex	081 Froslass	151 Cloyster
115 Klinklang	258 Togetic	120 Ralts	255 Clefairy	385 Tyranitar	123 Gallade	368 Darmanitan
394 Kommo-o	300 Torkoal	003 Rillaboom	151 Cloyster	073 Vanillish	122 Gardevoir	370 Eiscue
221 Lanturn	223 Toxicroak	372 Rotom	102 Corphish	072 Vanillite	141 Gastly	292 Sneasel
361 Lapras	311 Toxtricity	134 Seismitoad	236 Corsola	074 Vanilluxe	143 Gengar	079 Snorunt
383 Larvitar	321 Trapinch	382 Silvally	309 Cramorant	197 Vaporeon	088 Golett	075 Swinub
202 Leafeon	339 Trevenant	024 Skwovet	103 Crawdaunt	356 Wailmer	089 Golurk	072 Vanillite
045 Liepard	054 Tsareena	261 Snorlax	279 Cubchoo	357 Wailord	352 Grapploct	074 Vanilluxe
032 Linoone	347 Turtonator	204 Sylveon	237 Cursola	293 Weavile	240 Grimmsnarl	**Icicle Spear (TM51)**
299 Lucario	381 Type: Null	259 Togekiss	368 Darmanitan	229 Whiscash	172 Gurdurr	097 Abomasnow
038 Ludicolo	385 Tyranitar	257 Togepi	367 Darumaka	062 Wingull	142 Haunter	377 Arctovish
362 Lunatone	201 Umbreon	258 Togetic	078 Delibird	155 Wishiwashi	109 Hitmonchan	375 Arctozolt
140 Machamp	028 Unfezant	311 Toxtricity	214 Dewpider	100 Wooper	121 Kirlia	359 Avalugg
291 Malamar	074 Vanilluxe	347 Turtonator	346 Drampa	031 Zigzagoon	394 Kommo-o	280 Beartic
077 Mamoswine	197 Vaporeon	132 Tympole	043 Drednaw	**Ice Fang (TM67)**	037 Lombre	358 Bergmite
284 Mandibuzz	117 Vespiquen	201 Umbreon	136 Dusclops	377 Arctovish	299 Lucario	151 Cloyster
067 Manectric	322 Vibrava	073 Vanillish	137 Dusknoir	375 Arctozolt	038 Ludicolo	236 Corsola
355 Mantine	018 Vikavolt	072 Vanillite	135 Duskull	180 Arrokuda	140 Machamp	237 Cursola
295 Mawile	057 Vileplume	074 Vanilluxe	370 Eiscue	359 Avalugg	139 Machoke	078 Delibird
209 Meowstic	357 Wailord	197 Vaporeon	152 Feebas	181 Barraskewda	138 Machop	370 Eiscue
153 Milotic	293 Weavile	356 Wailmer	305 Frillish	154 Basculin	295 Mawile	081 Froslass
301 Mimikyu	251 Weezing	357 Wailord	081 Froslass	280 Beartic	365 Mr. Mime	350 Frosmoth
365 Mr. Mime	263 Whimsicott	398 Zacian	350 Frosmoth	358 Bergmite	366 Mr. Rime	203 Glaceon
366 Mr. Rime	229 Whiscash	399 Zamazenta	231 Gastrodon	042 Chewtle	260 Munchlax	080 Glalie
085 Mudsdale	093 Xatu	031 Zigzagoon	203 Glaceon	279 Cubchoo	033 Obstagoon	009 Inteleon
091 Musharna	398 Zacian	387 Zweilous	080 Glalie	368 Darmanitan	111 Pancham	077 Mamoswine
069 Ninetales	399 Zamazenta	**Hypnosis**	146 Goldeen	367 Darumaka	112 Pangoro	365 Mr. Mime
105 Ninjask	**Hyper Voice (TR42)**	119 Bronzong	088 Golett	386 Deino	101 Quagsire	366 Mr. Rime
020 Noctowl	071 Arcanine	118 Bronzor	233 Golisopod	376 Dracovish	120 Ralts	
			376 Dracovish			

076 Piloswine	307 Mareanie	122 Gardevoir	069 Ninetales	167 Excadrill	247 Bisharp	380 Charizard
150 Shellder	295 Mawile	143 Gengar	300 Torkoal	345 Falinks	282 Braviary	378 Charmander
349 Snom	182 Meowth	088 Golett	068 Vulpix	189 Ferroseed	119 Bronzong	379 Charmeleon
075 Swinub	153 Milotic	089 Golurk	**Infestation**	190 Ferrothorn	048 Bunnelby	051 Cinccino
073 Vanillish	364 Mime Jr.	269 Gothitelle	215 Araquanid	206 Flapple	162 Carkol	256 Clefable
072 Vanillite	365 Mr. Mime	192 Gourgeist	010 Blipbug	170 Gigalith	006 Cinderace	255 Clefairy
074 Vanilluxe	366 Mr. Rime	241 Hatenna	214 Dewpider	088 Golett	163 Coalossal	254 Cleffa
293 Weavile	260 Munchlax	243 Hatterene	397 Dragapult	233 Golisopod	303 Copperajah	049 Diggersby
Icy Wind (TM27)	033 Obstagoon	242 Hattrem	396 Drakloak	089 Golurk	023 Corviknight	374 Dracozolt
097 Abomasnow	149 Octillery	019 Hoothoot	395 Dreepy	393 Hakamo-o	302 Cufant	286 Drapion
215 Araquanid	133 Palpitoad	337 Indeedee	316 Durant	330 Honedge	368 Darmanitan	043 Drednaw
377 Arctovish	063 Pelipper	306 Jellicent	350 Frosmoth	392 Jangmo-o	360 Dhelmise	196 Eevee
375 Arctozolt	184 Persian	121 Kirlia	064 Joltik	273 Karrablast	049 Diggersby	066 Electrike
359 Avalugg	076 Piloswine	288 Lampent	307 Mareanie	099 Kingler	331 Doublade	200 Espeon
235 Barbaracle	101 Quagsire	287 Litwick	227 Shuckle	114 Klang	376 Dracovish	208 Espurr
228 Barboach	304 Qwilfish	209 Meowstic	**Ingrain**	113 Klink	371 Duraludon	152 Feebas
154 Basculin	120 Ralts	153 Milotic	097 Abomasnow	115 Klinklang	316 Durant	199 Flareon
280 Beartic	148 Remoraid	090 Munna	189 Ferroseed	394 Kommo-o	370 Eiscue	323 Flygon
358 Bergmite	265 Rhydon	091 Musharna	190 Ferrothorn	098 Krabby	274 Escavalier	325 Fraxure
234 Binacle	264 Rhyhorn	092 Natu	296 Maractus	383 Larvitar	167 Excadrill	203 Glaceon
220 Chinchou	266 Rhyperior	069 Ninetales	340 Morelull	299 Lucario	345 Falinks	391 Goodra
256 Clefable	294 Sableye	020 Noctowl	055 Oddish	284 Mandibuzz	189 Ferroseed	389 Goomy
255 Clefairy	147 Seaking	342 Oranguru	338 Phantump	307 Mareanie	190 Ferrothorn	025 Greedent
254 Cleffa	134 Seismitoad	012 Orbeetle	060 Roselia	295 Mawile	170 Gigalith	070 Growlithe
151 Cloyster	150 Shellder	338 Phantump	061 Roserade	182 Meowth	080 Glalie	145 Gyarados
102 Corphish	230 Shellos	336 Polteageist	341 Shiinotic	014 Metapod	233 Golisopod	393 Hakamo-o
236 Corsola	041 Shiftry	333 Ponyta	096 Snover	365 Mr. Mime	145 Gyarados	326 Haxorus
309 Cramorant	297 Sigilyph	191 Pumpkaboo	339 Trevenant	366 Mr. Rime	393 Hakamo-o	319 Heliolisk
103 Crawdaunt	382 Silvally	120 Ralts	**Instruct**	084 Mudbray	320 Hawlucha	318 Helioptile
222 Croagunk	292 Sneasel	334 Rapidash	342 Oranguru	085 Mudsdale	315 Hippowdon	314 Hippopotas
279 Cubchoo	349 Snom	272 Reuniclus	**Iron Defense**	033 Obstagoon	330 Honedge	315 Hippowdon
237 Cursola	261 Snorlax	188 Ribombee	**(TR46)**	012 Orbeetle	392 Jangmo-o	388 Hydreigon
078 Delibird	079 Snorunt	328 Runerigus	332 Aegislash	246 Pawniard	394 Kommo-o	392 Jangmo-o
214 Dewpider	096 Snover	294 Sableye	207 Appletun	183 Perrserker	361 Lapras	198 Jolteon
346 Drampa	075 Swinub	297 Sigilyph	215 Araquanid	384 Pupitar	383 Larvitar	394 Kommo-o
125 Drifblim	308 Toxapex	382 Silvally	377 Arctovish	272 Reuniclus	362 Lunatone	361 Lapras
124 Drifloon	223 Toxicroak	335 Sinistea	359 Avalugg	265 Rhydon	077 Mamoswine	383 Larvitar
136 Dusclops	132 Tympole	270 Solosis	235 Barbaracle	266 Rhyperior	355 Mantine	202 Leafeon
137 Dusknoir	381 Type: Null	369 Stonjourner	358 Bergmite	298 Riolu	295 Mawile	045 Liepard
135 Duskull	073 Vanillish	175 Swoobat	234 Binacle	168 Roggenrola	182 Meowth	032 Linoone
370 Eiscue	072 Vanillite	259 Togekiss	247 Bisharp	161 Rolycoly	153 Milotic	299 Lucario
152 Feebas	074 Vanilluxe	258 Togetic	169 Boldore	328 Runerigus	084 Mudbray	067 Manectric
305 Frillish	197 Vaporeon	339 Trevenant	119 Bronzong	313 Sandaconda	085 Mudsdale	209 Meowstic
081 Froslass	356 Wailmer	381 Type: Null	118 Bronzor	225 Scrafty	178 Onix	182 Meowth
350 Frosmoth	357 Wailord	073 Vanillish	015 Butterfree	224 Scraggy	111 Pancham	153 Milotic
123 Gallade	293 Weavile	072 Vanillite	162 Carkol	227 Shuckle	112 Pangoro	050 Minccino
122 Gardevoir	229 Whiscash	074 Vanilluxe	017 Charjabug	382 Silvally	343 Passimian	069 Ninetales
141 Gastly	062 Wingull	068 Vulpix	083 Claydol	219 Sirfetch'd	246 Pawniard	176 Noibat
231 Gastrodon	100 Wooper	174 Woobat	151 Cloyster	270 Solosis	183 Perrserker	177 Noivern
143 Gengar	031 Zigzagoon	093 Xatu	163 Coalossal	363 Solrock	384 Pupitar	033 Obstagoon
203 Glaceon	**Imprison (TM44)**	327 Yamask	329 Cofagrigus	179 Steelix	266 Rhyperior	178 Onix
080 Glalie	186 Alcremie	398 Zacian	303 Copperajah	226 Stunfisk	161 Rolycoly	343 Passimian
146 Goldeen	082 Baltoy	399 Zamazenta	102 Corphish	253 Sudowoodo	313 Sandaconda	183 Perrserker
088 Golett	278 Beheeyem	**Incinerate**	236 Corsola	300 Torkoal	225 Scrafty	184 Persian
233 Golisopod	119 Bronzong	162 Carkol	023 Corviknight	308 Toxapex	224 Scraggy	193 Pichu
089 Golurk	118 Bronzor	163 Coalossal	103 Crawdaunt	347 Turtonator	382 Silvally	194 Pikachu
145 Gyarados	289 Chandelure	367 Darumaka	087 Crustle	381 Type: Null	261 Snorlax	333 Ponyta
142 Haunter	083 Claydol	317 Heatmor	302 Cufant	385 Tyranitar	363 Solrock	384 Pupitar
009 Inteleon	256 Clefable	069 Ninetales	237 Cursola	073 Vanillish	179 Steelix	044 Purrloin
306 Jellicent	255 Clefairy	161 Rolycoly	368 Darmanitan	072 Vanillite	094 Stufful	101 Quagsire
099 Kingler	329 Cofagrigus	244 Salandit	214 Dewpider	074 Vanilluxe	348 Togedemaru	195 Raichu
121 Kirlia	187 Cutiefly	245 Salazzle	360 Dhelmise	018 Vikavolt	347 Turtonator	334 Rapidash
098 Krabby	011 Dottler	347 Turtonator	011 Dottler	283 Vullaby	381 Type: Null	265 Rhydon
221 Lanturn	125 Drifblim	068 Vulpix	331 Doublade	327 Yamask	385 Tyranitar	264 Rhyhorn
361 Lapras	271 Duosion	**Inferno**	286 Drapion	399 Zamazenta	357 Wailord	266 Rhyperior
032 Linoone	136 Dusclops	160 Centiskorch	043 Drednaw	**Iron Head (TR74)**	398 Zacian	298 Riolu
037 Lombre	137 Dusknoir	289 Chandelure	166 Drilbur	332 Aegislash	399 Zamazenta	244 Salandit
036 Lotad	135 Duskull	380 Charizard	271 Duosion	071 Arcanine	**Iron Tail (TR31)**	245 Salazzle
038 Ludicolo	277 Elgyem	378 Charmander	371 Duraludon	377 Arctovish	097 Abomasnow	225 Scrafty
362 Lunatone	305 Frillish	379 Charmeleon	316 Durant	359 Avalugg	071 Arcanine	224 Scraggy
077 Mamoswine	081 Froslass	317 Heatmor	086 Dwebble	095 Bewear	375 Arctozolt	285 Skorupi
355 Mantine	350 Frosmoth	288 Lampent	370 Eiscue		324 Axew	131 Skuntank
354 Mantyke	123 Gallade	287 Litwick	274 Escavalier		048 Bunnelby	024 Skwovet

390 Sliggoo
292 Sneasel
096 Snover
179 Steelix
130 Stunky
204 Sylveon
348 Togedemaru
300 Torkoal
347 Turtonator
385 Tyranitar
201 Umbreon
197 Vaporeon
068 Vulpix
293 Weavile
155 Wishiwashi
100 Wooper
398 Zacian
399 Zamazenta
031 Zigzagoon

Jaw Lock
042 Chewtle
043 Drednaw

King's Shield
332 Aegislash

Knock Off
102 Corphish
103 Crawdaunt
286 Drapion
086 Dwebble
218 Farfetch'd
189 Ferroseed
001 Grookey
273 Karrablast
098 Krabby
037 Lombre
038 Ludicolo
140 Machamp
139 Machoke
138 Machop
284 Mandibuzz
050 Minccino
029 Nickit
343 Passimian
120 Ralts
003 Rillaboom
294 Sableye
245 Salazzle
227 Shuckle
219 Sirfetch'd
159 Sizzlipede
285 Skorupi
002 Thwackey
283 Vullaby
062 Wingull
174 Woobat
031 Zigzagoon

Laser Focus
180 Arrokuda
324 Axew
181 Barraskewda
247 Bisharp
048 Bunnelby
049 Diggersby
371 Duraludon
323 Flygon
325 Fraxure
326 Haxorus
299 Lucario
246 Pawniard
321 Trapinch
322 Vibrava
398 Zacian
399 Zamazenta

Last Resort
051 Cinccino
397 Dragapult
396 Drakloak
035 Dubwool
196 Eevee
200 Espeon
199 Flareon
203 Glaceon
337 Indeedee
198 Jolteon
202 Leafeon
182 Meowth
185 Milcery
050 Minccino
260 Munchlax
342 Oranguru
312 Silicobra
024 Skwovet
261 Snorlax
204 Sylveon
259 Togekiss
257 Togepi
258 Togetic
201 Umbreon
197 Vaporeon

Lava Plume
199 Flareon
300 Torkoal

Leaf Blade (TR50)
058 Bellossom
218 Farfetch'd
123 Gallade
202 Leafeon
040 Nuzleaf
041 Shiftry
219 Sirfetch'd

Leaf Storm (TR71)
097 Abomasnow
058 Bellossom
059 Budew
127 Eldegoss
126 Gossifleur
202 Leafeon
038 Ludicolo
296 Maractus
003 Rillaboom
060 Roselia
061 Roserade
372 Rotom
041 Shiftry
053 Steenee
339 Trevenant
054 Tsareena

Leaf Tornado
127 Eldegoss
126 Gossifleur
041 Shiftry

Leafage
097 Abomasnow
129 Cherrim
128 Cherubi
127 Eldegoss
126 Gossifleur
096 Snover

Leech Life (TR18)
276 Accelgor
215 Araquanid
160 Centiskorch
237 Cursola
187 Cutiefly
214 Dewpider
011 Dottler
376 Dracovish
286 Drapion
350 Frosmoth
065 Gurdurr
233 Golisopod
240 Grimmsnarl
238 Impidimp
064 Joltik
301 Mimikyu
239 Morgrem
104 Nincada
105 Ninjask
176 Noibat
177 Noivern
012 Orbeetle
188 Ribombee
244 Salandit
245 Salazzle
106 Shedinja
275 Shelmet
159 Sizzlipede
232 Wimpod

Leech Seed
207 Appletun
129 Cherrim
128 Cherubi
262 Cottonee
189 Ferroseed
206 Flapple
126 Gossifleur
192 Gourgeist
001 Grookey
202 Leafeon
036 Lotad
296 Maractus
340 Morelull
055 Oddish
338 Phantump
191 Pumpkaboo
060 Roselia
061 Roserade
039 Seedot
096 Snover
339 Trevenant
263 Whimsicott

Leer
097 Abomasnow
071 Arcanine
324 Axew
095 Bewear
247 Bisharp
282 Braviary
048 Bunnelby
351 Clobbopus
151 Cloyster
173 Conkeldurr
102 Corphish
023 Corviknight
022 Corvisquire
103 Crawdaunt
049 Diggersby
286 Drapion
371 Duraludon
136 Dusclops
137 Dusknoir
135 Duskull
066 Electrike
274 Escavalier
208 Espurr
218 Farfetch'd
325 Fraxure
081 Froslass
123 Gallade
080 Glalie
352 Grapploct
070 Growlithe
172 Gurdurr
145 Gyarados
393 Hakamo-o
326 Haxorus
392 Jangmo-o
273 Karrablast
099 Kingler
394 Kommo-o
098 Krabby
383 Larvitar
032 Linoone
140 Machamp
139 Machoke
138 Machop
284 Mandibuzz
067 Manectric
209 Meowstic
344 Morpeko
092 Natu
033 Obstagoon
111 Pancham
112 Pangoro
343 Passimian
246 Pawniard
026 Pidove
384 Pupitar
021 Rookidee
281 Rufflet
294 Sableye
249 Sawk
225 Scrafty
224 Scraggy
150 Shellder
219 Sirfetch'd
285 Skorupi
292 Sneasel
079 Snorunt
096 Snover
007 Sobble
270 Solosis
363 Solrock
212 Spritzee
053 Steenee
075 Swinub
210 Swirlix
175 Swoobat
204 Sylveon
259 Togekiss
257 Togepi
258 Togetic
308 Toxapex
054 Tsareena
073 Vanillish
072 Vanillite
074 Vanilluxe
018 Vikavolt
263 Whimsicott
174 Woobat
093 Xatu
031 Zigzagoon

Lick
141 Gastly
143 Gengar
142 Haunter
317 Heatmor
032 Linoone
260 Munchlax
033 Obstagoon
261 Snorlax
031 Zigzagoon

Life Dew
059 Budew
256 Clefable
255 Clefairy
123 Gallade
122 Gardevoir
389 Goomy
241 Hatenna
243 Hatterene
242 Hattrem

121 Kirlia
361 Lapras
299 Lucario
153 Milotic
120 Ralts
060 Roselia
150 Shellder
259 Togekiss
257 Togepi
258 Togetic

Light Screen (TM17)
097 Abomasnow
186 Alcremie
207 Appletun
213 Aromatisse
082 Baltoy
278 Beheeyem
052 Bounsweet
119 Bronzong
118 Bronzor
017 Charjabug
051 Cinccino
083 Claydol
256 Clefable
255 Clefairy
254 Cleffa
151 Cloyster
236 Corsola
023 Corviknight
237 Cursola
187 Cutiefly
011 Dottler
397 Dragapult
346 Drampa
008 Drizzile
271 Duosion
371 Duraludon
127 Eldegoss
066 Electrike
277 Elgyem
200 Espeon
208 Espurr
400 Eternatus
152 Feebas
081 Froslass
350 Frosmoth
123 Gallade
065 Galvantula
122 Gardevoir
080 Glalie
126 Gossifleur
267 Gothita
269 Gothitelle
268 Gothorita
192 Gourgeist
240 Grimmsnarl
016 Grubbin
241 Hatenna
243 Hatterene
242 Hattrem
319 Heliolisk
318 Helioptile
337 Indeedee
290 Inkay
009 Inteleon
198 Jolteon
064 Joltik
121 Kirlia
362 Lunatone
140 Machamp
139 Machoke
138 Machop

291 Malamar
077 Mamoswine
067 Manectric
209 Meowstic
153 Milotic
364 Mime Jr.
301 Mimikyu
340 Morelull
239 Morgrem
365 Mr. Mime
366 Mr. Rime
090 Munna
091 Musharna
092 Natu
342 Oranguru
012 Orbeetle
193 Pichu
194 Pikachu
076 Piloswine
336 Polteageist
191 Pumpkaboo
156 Pyukumuku
195 Raichu
120 Ralts
272 Reuniclus
188 Ribombee
372 Rotom
341 Shiinotic
297 Sigilyph
211 Slurpuff
079 Snorunt
096 Snover
007 Sobble
270 Solosis
363 Solrock
212 Spritzee
053 Steenee
075 Swinub
210 Swirlix
175 Swoobat
204 Sylveon
259 Togekiss
257 Togepi
258 Togetic
308 Toxapex
054 Tsareena
073 Vanillish
072 Vanillite
074 Vanilluxe
018 Vikavolt
263 Whimsicott
174 Woobat
093 Xatu
399 Zamazenta

Liquidation (TR98)
215 Araquanid
377 Arctovish
180 Arrokuda
235 Barbaracle
181 Barraskewda
154 Basculin
280 Beartic
234 Binacle
042 Chewtle
351 Clobbopus
151 Cloyster
236 Corsola
309 Cramorant
103 Crawdaunt
237 Cursola
214 Dewpider
360 Dhelmise
376 Dracovish

043 Drednaw
008 Drizzile
370 Eiscue
233 Golisopod
352 Grapploct
290 Inkay
009 Inteleon
099 Kingler
098 Krabby
361 Lapras
291 Malamar
355 Mantine
307 Mareanie
149 Octillery
063 Pelipper
353 Pincurchin
101 Quagsire
304 Qwilfish
134 Seismitoad
150 Shellder
007 Sobble
308 Toxapex
197 Vaporeon
357 Wailord
229 Whiscash
062 Wingull
155 Wishiwashi

Lock-On
397 Dragapult
396 Drakloak
114 Klang
113 Klink
115 Klinklang
149 Octillery
148 Remoraid

Low Kick (TR07)
375 Arctozolt
235 Barbaracle
280 Beartic
095 Bewear
247 Bisharp
252 Bonsly
006 Cinderace
173 Conkeldurr
222 Croagunk
279 Cubchoo
049 Diggersby
376 Dracovish
374 Dracozolt
325 Fraxure
123 Gallade
088 Golett
089 Golurk
240 Grimmsnarl
001 Grookey
172 Gurdurr
393 Hakamo-o
320 Hawlucha
326 Haxorus
317 Heatmor
319 Heliolisk
109 Hitmonchan
108 Hitmonlee
110 Hitmontop
238 Impidimp
392 Jangmo-o
394 Kommo-o
299 Lucario
140 Machamp
139 Machoke
138 Machop
239 Morgrem
084 Mudbray

085 Mudsdale
040 Nuzleaf
033 Obstagoon
111 Pancham
112 Pangoro
246 Pawniard
333 Ponyta
005 Raboot
334 Rapidash
003 Rillaboom
298 Riolu
294 Sableye
249 Sawk
004 Scorbunny
225 Scrafty
224 Scraggy
134 Seismitoad
041 Shiftry
292 Sneasel
253 Sudowoodo
248 Throh
002 Thwackey
171 Timburr
223 Toxicroak
054 Tsareena
385 Tyranitar
107 Tyrogue
293 Weavile

Low Sweep (TM75)
095 Bewear
247 Bisharp
006 Cinderace
173 Conkeldurr
222 Croagunk
123 Gallade
088 Golett
089 Golurk
269 Gothitelle
240 Grimmsnarl
172 Gurdurr
320 Hawlucha
319 Heliolisk
318 Helioptile
109 Hitmonchan
108 Hitmonlee
110 Hitmontop
299 Lucario
140 Machamp
139 Machoke
138 Machop
084 Mudbray
085 Mudsdale
040 Nuzleaf
111 Pancham
112 Pangoro
343 Passimian
246 Pawniard
005 Raboot
298 Riolu
294 Sableye
249 Sawk
004 Scorbunny
225 Scrafty
224 Scraggy
041 Shiftry
292 Sneasel
053 Steenee
094 Stufful
248 Throh
171 Timburr
223 Toxicroak
054 Tsareena
107 Tyrogue
293 Weavile

Lunge
215 Araquanid
160 Centiskorch
214 Dewpider
064 Joltik
159 Sizzlipede

Mach Punch
109 Hitmonchan
171 Timburr
107 Tyrogue

Magic Coat
090 Munna
091 Musharna
012 Orbeetle

Magic Powder
243 Hatterene

Magic Room (TM72)
186 Alcremie
215 Araquanid
187 Cutiefly
214 Dewpider
011 Dottler
200 Espeon
208 Espurr
123 Gallade
122 Gardevoir
267 Gothita
269 Gothitelle
268 Gothorita
243 Hatterene
337 Indeedee
121 Kirlia
362 Lunatone
209 Meowstic
364 Mime Jr.
301 Mimikyu
340 Morelull
365 Mr. Mime
366 Mr. Rime
092 Natu
342 Oranguru
012 Orbeetle
120 Ralts
334 Rapidash
188 Ribombee
341 Shiinotic
297 Sigilyph
093 Xatu

Magical Leaf (TM10)
097 Abomasnow
186 Alcremie
058 Bellossom
052 Bounsweet
129 Cherrim
128 Cherubi
256 Clefable
255 Clefairy
254 Cleffa
127 Eldegoss
123 Gallade
122 Gardevoir
126 Gossifleur
001 Grookey
241 Hatenna
243 Hatterene
242 Hattrem
337 Indeedee
121 Kirlia
202 Leafeon
209 Meowstic
365 Mr. Mime
338 Phantump
120 Ralts
188 Ribombee
003 Rillaboom
060 Roselia
061 Roserade
096 Snover
053 Steenee
204 Sylveon
002 Thwackey
259 Togekiss
258 Togetic
339 Trevenant
054 Tsareena

Magnet Rise
179 Steelix
348 Togedemaru
072 Vanillite

Magnetic Flux
115 Klinklang
311 Toxtricity

Mean Look
329 Cofagrigus
136 Dusclops
137 Dusknoir
135 Duskull
141 Gastly
143 Gengar
267 Gothita
142 Haunter
320 Hawlucha
209 Meowstic
246 Pawniard
120 Ralts
328 Runerigus
294 Sableye
201 Umbreon
283 Vullaby
327 Yamask

Mega Drain
276 Accelgor
058 Bellossom
262 Cottonee
360 Dhelmise
056 Gloom
037 Lombre
036 Lotad
038 Ludicolo
296 Maractus
340 Morelull
040 Nuzleaf
055 Oddish
336 Polteageist
060 Roselia
061 Roserade
039 Seedot
275 Shelmet
041 Shiftry
341 Shiinotic
335 Sinistea
057 Vileplume
263 Whimsicott

Mega Kick (TM01)
097 Abomasnow
375 Arctozolt
280 Beartic
095 Bewear
380 Charizard
378 Charmander
379 Charmeleon
006 Cinderace
256 Clefable
255 Clefairy
254 Cleffa
163 Coalossal
173 Conkeldurr
303 Copperajah
222 Croagunk
279 Cubchoo
302 Cufant
368 Darmanitan
367 Darumaka
078 Delibird
049 Diggersby
376 Dracovish
374 Dracozolt
035 Dubwool
136 Dusclops
137 Dusknoir
323 Flygon
123 Gallade
122 Gardevoir
143 Gengar
088 Golett
089 Golurk
391 Goodra
240 Grimmsnarl
001 Grookey
172 Gurdurr
393 Hakamo-o
320 Hawlucha
319 Heliolisk
109 Hitmonchan
108 Hitmonlee
110 Hitmontop
238 Impidimp
121 Kirlia
394 Kommo-o
037 Lombre
299 Lucario
038 Ludicolo
140 Machamp
139 Machoke
138 Machop
295 Mawile
239 Morgrem
365 Mr. Mime
366 Mr. Rime
084 Mudbray
085 Mudsdale
260 Munchlax
040 Nuzleaf
033 Obstagoon
342 Oranguru
111 Pancham
112 Pangoro
343 Passimian
193 Pichu
194 Pikachu
101 Quagsire
195 Raichu
120 Ralts
265 Rhydon
266 Rhyperior
003 Rillaboom
298 Riolu
294 Sableye
249 Sawk
004 Scorbunny
225 Scrafty
224 Scraggy
134 Seismitoad
041 Shiftry
292 Sneasel
261 Snorlax
369 Stonjourner
094 Stufful
253 Sudowoodo
248 Throh
002 Thwackey
171 Timburr
259 Togekiss
257 Togepi
258 Togetic
223 Toxicroak
311 Toxtricity
054 Tsareena
347 Turtonator
385 Tyranitar
107 Tyrogue
293 Weavile

Mega Punch (TM00)
097 Abomasnow
375 Arctozolt
280 Beartic
095 Bewear
380 Charizard
378 Charmander
379 Charmeleon
256 Clefable
255 Clefairy
254 Cleffa
351 Clobbopus
163 Coalossal
173 Conkeldurr
222 Croagunk
279 Cubchoo
368 Darmanitan
367 Darumaka
078 Delibird
049 Diggersby
374 Dracozolt
136 Dusclops
137 Dusknoir
323 Flygon
123 Gallade
122 Gardevoir
143 Gengar
088 Golett
089 Golurk
391 Goodra
352 Grapploct
240 Grimmsnarl
001 Grookey
172 Gurdurr
393 Hakamo-o
320 Hawlucha
319 Heliolisk
109 Hitmonchan
108 Hitmonlee
110 Hitmontop
238 Impidimp
121 Kirlia
394 Kommo-o
037 Lombre
299 Lucario
038 Ludicolo
140 Machamp
139 Machoke
138 Machop
295 Mawile
239 Morgrem
365 Mr. Mime
366 Mr. Rime
260 Munchlax
033 Obstagoon
342 Oranguru
111 Pancham
112 Pangoro
343 Passimian
193 Pichu
194 Pikachu
101 Quagsire
195 Raichu
120 Ralts
272 Reuniclus
265 Rhydon
266 Rhyperior
003 Rillaboom
298 Riolu
294 Sableye
249 Sawk
225 Scrafty
224 Scraggy
134 Seismitoad
292 Sneasel
261 Snorlax
096 Snover
094 Stufful
253 Sudowoodo
248 Throh
002 Thwackey
171 Timburr
259 Togekiss
257 Togepi
258 Togetic
223 Toxicroak
311 Toxtricity
347 Turtonator
385 Tyranitar
107 Tyrogue
293 Weavile

Megahorn (TR28)
043 Drednaw
274 Escavalier
345 Falinks
146 Goldeen
273 Karrablast
361 Lapras
334 Rapidash
265 Rhydon
264 Rhyhorn
266 Rhyperior
147 Seaking

Memento
289 Chandelure
262 Cottonee
078 Delibird
164 Diglett
124 Drifloon
135 Duskull
231 Gastrodon
250 Koffing
288 Lampent
287 Litwick
353 Pincurchin
336 Polteageist
156 Pyukumuku
120 Ralts
230 Shellos
335 Sinistea
131 Skuntank
130 Stunky
068 Vulpix
251 Weezing
263 Whimsicott
327 Yamask

Metal Burst
247 Bisharp
371 Duraludon
316 Durant
274 Escavalier
183 Perrserker
264 Rhyhorn
294 Sableye
399 Zamazenta

Metal Claw
247 Bisharp
378 Charmander
102 Corphish
166 Drilbur
371 Duraludon
316 Durant
167 Excadrill
189 Ferroseed
190 Ferrothorn
158 Garbodor
099 Kingler
098 Krabby
299 Lucario
182 Meowth
104 Nincada
105 Ninjask
246 Pawniard
183 Perrserker
298 Riolu
106 Shedinja
292 Sneasel
226 Stunfisk
293 Weavile
232 Wimpod
398 Zacian
399 Zamazenta

Metal Sound
332 Aegislash
247 Bisharp
119 Bronzong
118 Bronzor
023 Corviknight
360 Dhelmise
331 Doublade
166 Drilbur
371 Duraludon
316 Durant
330 Honedge
114 Klang
113 Klink
115 Klinklang
299 Lucario
182 Meowth
246 Pawniard
183 Perrserker
382 Silvally
226 Stunfisk
310 Toxel
381 Type: Null

Meteor Assault
219 Sirfetch'd

Meteor Mash
256 Clefable
255 Clefairy
299 Lucario

Metronome (TR14)
186 Alcremie
213 Aromatisse
256 Clefable
255 Clefairy
254 Cleffa
136 Dusclops

137 Dusknoir
143 Gengar
240 Grimmsnarl
109 Hitmonchan
108 Hitmonlee
238 Impidimp
337 Indeedee
009 Inteleon
038 Ludicolo
140 Machamp
139 Machoke
138 Machop
239 Morgrem
365 Mr. Mime
366 Mr. Rime
260 Munchlax
336 Polteageist
294 Sableye
335 Sinistea
211 Slurpuff
261 Snorlax
259 Togekiss
257 Togepi
258 Togetic

Mimic

252 Bonsly
364 Mime Jr.
301 Mimikyu
365 Mr. Mime
366 Mr. Rime
253 Sudowoodo

Mind Reader

108 Hitmonlee
104 Nincada
105 Ninjask
298 Riolu
106 Shedinja
275 Shelmet
107 Tyrogue

Minimize

289 Chandelure
256 Clefable
255 Clefairy
125 Drifblim
124 Drifloon
288 Lampent
287 Litwick
304 Qwilfish
313 Sandaconda
312 Silicobra

Mirror Coat

215 Araquanid
358 Bergmite
236 Corsola
237 Cursola
214 Dewpider
371 Duraludon
152 Feebas
203 Glaceon
267 Gothita
355 Mantine
354 Mantyke
365 Mr. Mime
366 Mr. Rime
012 Orbeetle
156 Pyukumuku
230 Shellos
349 Snom
073 Vanillish
072 Vanillite
074 Vanilluxe
217 Wobbuffet
216 Wynaut

Mist

097 Abomasnow
358 Bergmite
220 Chinchou
346 Drampa
370 Eiscue
152 Feebas
305 Frillish
350 Frosmoth
361 Lapras
037 Lombre
036 Lotad
038 Ludicolo
077 Mamoswine
063 Pelipper
076 Piloswine
101 Quagsire
230 Shellos
096 Snover
007 Sobble
075 Swinub
132 Tympole
073 Vanillish
072 Vanillite
074 Vanilluxe
356 Wailmer
357 Wailord
062 Wingull
155 Wishiwashi
100 Wooper

Misty Terrain (TM89)

186 Alcremie
213 Aromatisse
256 Clefable
255 Clefairy
254 Cleffa
262 Cottonee
123 Gallade
122 Gardevoir
121 Kirlia
295 Mawile
209 Meowstic
185 Milcery
364 Mime Jr.
365 Mr. Mime
366 Mr. Rime
120 Ralts
334 Rapidash
212 Spritzee
204 Sylveon
251 Weezing
263 Whimsicott

Moonblast

213 Aromatisse
058 Bellossom
256 Clefable
255 Clefairy
187 Cutiefly
122 Gardevoir
056 Gloom
192 Gourgeist
019 Hoothoot
362 Lunatone
340 Morelull
090 Munna
091 Musharna
020 Noctowl
055 Oddish
341 Shiinotic
212 Spritzee
204 Sylveon
057 Vileplume

Moonlight

058 Bellossom
256 Clefable
255 Clefairy
056 Gloom
362 Lunatone
340 Morelull
090 Munna
091 Musharna
177 Noivern
055 Oddish
341 Shiinotic
201 Umbreon
057 Vileplume

Morning Sun

129 Cherrim
128 Cherubi
200 Espeon
070 Growlithe
026 Pidove
333 Ponyta
363 Solrock
257 Togepi

Mud Shot (TM53)

276 Accelgor
235 Barbaracle
228 Barboach
154 Basculin
234 Binacle
048 Bunnelby
017 Charjabug
042 Chewtle
006 Cinderace
351 Clobbopus
151 Cloyster
303 Copperajah
102 Corphish
103 Crawdaunt
302 Cufant
049 Diggersby
043 Drednaw
166 Drilbur
008 Drizzile
167 Excadrill
152 Feebas
323 Flygon
231 Gastrodon
146 Goldeen
233 Golisopod
391 Goodra
389 Goomy
352 Grapploct
145 Gyarados
314 Hippopotas
315 Hippowdon
009 Inteleon
306 Jellicent
025 Greedent
016 Grubbin
099 Kingler
098 Krabby
032 Linoone
037 Lombre
038 Ludicolo
077 Mamoswine
307 Mareanie
153 Milotic
085 Mudsdale
029 Nickit
033 Obstagoon
149 Octillery

133 Palpitoad
076 Piloswine
101 Quagsire
005 Raboot
148 Remoraid
265 Rhydon
264 Rhyhorn
266 Rhyperior
003 Rillaboom
313 Sandaconda
004 Scorbunny
147 Seaking
134 Seismitoad
150 Shellder
230 Shellos
275 Shelmet
227 Shuckle
312 Silicobra
024 Skwovet
390 Sliggoo
007 Sobble
226 Stunfisk
075 Swinub
030 Thievul
308 Toxapex
321 Trapinch
132 Tympole
322 Vibrava
018 Vikavolt
229 Whiscash
232 Wimpod
155 Wishiwashi
100 Wooper
031 Zigzagoon

Muddy Water (TR45)

235 Barbaracle
228 Barboach
154 Basculin
351 Clobbopus
102 Corphish
103 Crawdaunt
360 Dhelmise
043 Drednaw
008 Drizzile
152 Feebas
231 Gastrodon
146 Goldeen
233 Golisopod
391 Goodra
389 Goomy
352 Grapploct
145 Gyarados
314 Hippopotas
315 Hippowdon
009 Inteleon
306 Jellicent
383 Larvitar
037 Lombre
038 Ludicolo
307 Mareanie
153 Milotic
133 Palpitoad
353 Pincurchin
384 Pupitar
101 Quagsire
147 Seaking
134 Seismitoad
230 Shellos
390 Sliggoo
007 Sobble
226 Stunfisk
308 Toxapex

132 Tympole
385 Tyranitar
197 Vaporeon
229 Whiscash
155 Wishiwashi
100 Wooper

Mud-Slap

082 Baltoy
235 Barbaracle
228 Barboach
234 Binacle
169 Boldore
048 Bunnelby
017 Charjabug
083 Claydol
222 Croagunk
049 Diggersby
164 Diglett
166 Drilbur
165 Dugtrio
196 Eevee
167 Excadrill
323 Flygon
231 Gastrodon
170 Gigalith
146 Goldeen
088 Golett
089 Golurk
016 Grubbin
319 Heliolisk
318 Helioptile
077 Mamoswine
084 Mudbray
085 Mudsdale
104 Nincada
105 Ninjask
076 Piloswine
168 Roggenrola
161 Rolycoly
244 Salandit
106 Shedinja
230 Shellos
312 Silicobra
226 Stunfisk
075 Swinub
223 Toxicroak
321 Trapinch
132 Tympole
322 Vibrava
018 Vikavolt
229 Whiscash

Multi-Attack

382 Silvally

Mystical Fire (TM92)

186 Alcremie
160 Centiskorch
289 Chandelure
380 Charizard
256 Clefable
255 Clefairy
307 Mareanie
153 Milotic
133 Palpitoad
199 Flareon
122 Gardevoir
192 Gourgeist
241 Hatenna
243 Hatterene
242 Hattrem
337 Indeedee
288 Lampent
287 Litwick
365 Mr. Mime
069 Ninetales

333 Ponyta
191 Pumpkaboo
334 Rapidash
204 Sylveon
259 Togekiss
257 Togepi
258 Togetic
068 Vulpix

Nasty Plot (TR68)

213 Aromatisse
278 Beheeyem
083 Claydol
329 Cofagrigus
023 Corviknight
022 Corvisquire
103 Crawdaunt
222 Croagunk
386 Deino
277 Elgyem
208 Espurr
143 Gengar
267 Gothita
269 Gothitelle
268 Gothorita
192 Gourgeist
240 Grimmsnarl
019 Hoothoot
388 Hydreigon
238 Impidimp
290 Inkay
045 Liepard
299 Lucario
362 Lunatone
291 Malamar
284 Mandibuzz
209 Meowstic
182 Meowth
364 Mime Jr.
239 Morgrem
344 Morpeko
365 Mr. Mime
366 Mr. Rime
029 Nickit
069 Ninetales
020 Noctowl
040 Nuzleaf
342 Oranguru
183 Perrserker
184 Persian
193 Pichu
194 Pikachu
336 Polteageist
044 Purrloin
195 Raichu
298 Riolu
021 Rookidee
372 Rotom
328 Runerigus
294 Sableye
244 Salandit
245 Salazzle
039 Seedot
041 Shiftry
335 Sinistea
131 Skuntank
212 Spritzee
130 Stunky
175 Swoobat
030 Thievul
259 Togekiss
257 Togepi
258 Togetic
223 Toxicroak

283 Vullaby
293 Weavile
174 Woobat
327 Yamask
387 Zweilous

Nature Power

128 Cherubi
236 Corsola
262 Cottonee
001 Grookey
037 Lombre
036 Lotad
038 Ludicolo
040 Nuzleaf
055 Oddish
039 Seedot
041 Shiftry

Night Shade

289 Chandelure
329 Cofagrigus
236 Corsola
237 Cursola
136 Dusclops
137 Dusknoir
135 Duskull
305 Frillish
141 Gastly
143 Gengar
088 Golett
089 Golurk
142 Haunter
019 Hoothoot
306 Jellicent
288 Lampent
287 Litwick
092 Natu
328 Runerigus
294 Sableye
093 Xatu
327 Yamask

Night Slash

332 Aegislash
180 Arrokuda
324 Axew
234 Binacle
247 Bisharp
102 Corphish
103 Crawdaunt
279 Cubchoo
331 Doublade
286 Drapion
165 Dugtrio
371 Duraludon
086 Dwebble
218 Farfetch'd
123 Gallade
317 Heatmor
330 Honedge
290 Inkay
273 Karrablast
098 Krabby
045 Liepard
032 Linoone
291 Malamar
182 Meowth
029 Nickit
104 Nincada
033 Obstagoon
112 Pangoro
246 Pawniard
026 Pidove
044 Purrloin
039 Seedot

285 Skorupi
131 Skuntank
130 Stunky
030 Thievul
293 Weavile

No Retreat
345 Falinks

Noble Roar
393 Hakamo-o
392 Jangmo-o
394 Kommo-o
003 Rillaboom
311 Toxtricity
357 Wailord

Nuzzle
047 Boltund
241 Hatenna
193 Pichu
194 Pikachu
195 Raichu
348 Togedemaru
310 Toxel
311 Toxtricity
046 Yamper

Obstruct
033 Obstagoon

Octazooka
352 Grapploct
149 Octillery
148 Remoraid

Octolock
352 Grapploct

Outrage (TR24)
097 Abomasnow
207 Appletun
071 Arcanine
324 Axew
380 Charizard
378 Charmander
379 Charmeleon
303 Copperajah
386 Deino
376 Dracovish
374 Dracozolt
397 Dragapult
396 Drakloak
346 Drampa
371 Duraludon
206 Flapple
323 Flygon
325 Fraxure
391 Goodra
389 Goomy
070 Growlithe
145 Gyarados
393 Hakamo-o
326 Haxorus
388 Hydreigon
392 Jangmo-o
394 Kommo-o
361 Lapras
383 Larvitar
344 Morpeko
176 Noibat
177 Noivern
112 Pangoro
384 Pupitar
265 Rhydon
266 Rhyperior
313 Sandaconda
225 Scrafty
382 Silvally
390 Sliggoo

261 Snorlax
347 Turtonator
385 Tyranitar
322 Vibrava
387 Zweilous

Overdrive
311 Toxtricity

Overheat (TR43)
071 Arcanine
162 Carkol
160 Centiskorch
289 Chandelure
380 Charizard
378 Charmander
379 Charmeleon
006 Cinderace
163 Coalossal
368 Darmanitan
367 Darumaka
199 Flareon
070 Growlithe
317 Heatmor
288 Lampent
287 Litwick
067 Manectric
069 Ninetales
005 Raboot
372 Rotom
244 Salandit
245 Salazzle
004 Scorbunny
363 Solrock
300 Torkoal
347 Turtonator
068 Vulpix
251 Weezing

Pain Split
095 Bewear
289 Chandelure
351 Clobbopus
271 Duosion
135 Duskull
305 Frillish
158 Garbodor
192 Gourgeist
250 Koffing
288 Lampent
287 Litwick
301 Mimikyu
191 Pumpkaboo
156 Pyukumuku
272 Reuniclus
270 Solosis
094 Stufful
226 Stunfisk
157 Trubbish

Parabolic Charge
319 Heliolisk
318 Helioptile

Parting Shot
344 Morpeko
111 Pancham
112 Pangoro
382 Silvally
030 Thievul
031 Zigzagoon

Pay Day (TM02)
196 Eevee
200 Espeon
208 Espurr
199 Flareon
203 Glaceon
337 Indeedee

198 Jolteon
202 Leafeon
045 Liepard
209 Meowstic
182 Meowth
260 Munchlax
183 Perrserker
184 Persian
194 Pikachu
044 Purrloin
195 Raichu
334 Rapidash
265 Rhydon
266 Rhyperior
261 Snorlax
204 Sylveon
201 Umbreon
197 Vaporeon

Payback (TM57)
207 Appletun
375 Arctozolt
324 Axew
235 Barbaracle
095 Bewear
234 Binacle
247 Bisharp
119 Bronzong
118 Bronzor
048 Bunnelby
289 Chandelure
042 Chewtle
351 Clobbopus
151 Cloyster
329 Cofagrigus
173 Conkeldurr
303 Copperajah
102 Corphish
023 Corviknight
022 Corvisquire
103 Crawdaunt
222 Croagunk
368 Darmanitan
360 Dhelmise
049 Diggersby
011 Dottler
286 Drapion
043 Drednaw
125 Drifblim
124 Drifloon
035 Dubwool
136 Dusclops
137 Dusknoir
135 Duskull
208 Espurr
400 Eternatus
345 Falinks
189 Ferroseed
190 Ferrothorn
325 Fraxure
081 Froslass
158 Garbodor
141 Gastly
143 Gengar
080 Glalie
233 Golisopod
267 Gothita
269 Gothitelle
268 Gothorita
352 Grapploct
025 Greedent
172 Gurdurr
145 Gyarados
393 Hakamo-o

142 Haunter
320 Hawlucha
326 Haxorus
388 Hydreigon
290 Inkay
392 Jangmo-o
250 Koffing
394 Kommo-o
288 Lampent
383 Larvitar
045 Liepard
032 Linoone
287 Litwick
299 Lucario
140 Machamp
139 Machoke
138 Machop
291 Malamar
284 Mandibuzz
307 Mareanie
295 Mawile
209 Meowstic
182 Meowth
301 Mimikyu
344 Morpeko
365 Mr. Mime
366 Mr. Rime
084 Mudbray
085 Mudsdale
069 Ninetales
040 Nuzleaf
033 Obstagoon
149 Octillery
178 Onix
342 Oranguru
012 Orbeetle
111 Pancham
112 Pangoro
343 Passimian
246 Pawniard
063 Pelipper
183 Perrserker
184 Persian
353 Pincurchin
336 Polteageist
384 Pupitar
044 Purrloin
304 Qwilfish
265 Rhydon
264 Rhyhorn
266 Rhyperior
298 Riolu
021 Rookidee
328 Runerigus
294 Sableye
244 Salandit
245 Salazzle
249 Sawk
225 Scrafty
224 Scraggy
039 Seedot
134 Seismitoad
150 Shellder
041 Shiftry
382 Silvally
335 Sinistea
285 Skorupi
131 Skuntank
024 Skwovet
292 Sneasel
179 Steelix
053 Steenee
094 Stufful

226 Stunfisk
130 Stunky
248 Throh
171 Timburr
348 Togedemaru
308 Toxapex
223 Toxicroak
311 Toxtricity
157 Trubbish
054 Tsareena
347 Turtonator
381 Type: Null
385 Tyranitar
201 Umbreon
283 Vullaby
068 Vulpix
293 Weavile
251 Weezing
034 Wooloo
327 Yamask
399 Zamazenta
031 Zigzagoon

Peck
180 Arrokuda
181 Barraskewda
282 Braviary
023 Corviknight
022 Corvisquire
309 Cramorant
274 Escavalier
218 Farfetch'd
146 Goldeen
019 Hoothoot
290 Inkay
273 Karrablast
291 Malamar
296 Maractus
307 Mareanie
092 Natu
020 Noctowl
353 Pincurchin
021 Rookidee
281 Rufflet
147 Seaking
219 Sirfetch'd
257 Togepi
308 Toxapex
093 Xatu

Perish Song
237 Cursola
141 Gastly
143 Gengar
361 Lapras

Petal Blizzard
058 Bellossom
129 Cherrim
128 Cherubi
296 Maractus
060 Roselia
061 Roserade
057 Vileplume

Petal Dance
058 Bellossom
129 Cherrim
056 Gloom
055 Oddish
060 Roselia
061 Roserade
057 Vileplume

Phantom Force (TM86)
329 Cofagrigus

360 Dhelmise
397 Dragapult
396 Drakloak
125 Drifblim
143 Gengar
088 Golett
089 Golurk
192 Gourgeist
301 Mimikyu
338 Phantump
336 Polteageist
328 Runerigus
106 Shedinja
335 Sinistea
339 Trevenant

Pin Missile (TM07)
059 Budew
151 Cloyster
237 Cursola
286 Drapion
189 Ferroseed
190 Ferrothorn
065 Galvantula
233 Golisopod
198 Jolteon
064 Joltik
032 Linoone
296 Maractus
307 Mareanie
033 Obstagoon
353 Pincurchin
304 Qwilfish
060 Roselia
061 Roserade
285 Skorupi
348 Togedemaru
308 Toxapex
117 Vespiquen
031 Zigzagoon

Play Nice
280 Beartic
052 Bounsweet
279 Cubchoo
346 Drampa
267 Gothita
269 Gothitelle
268 Gothorita
241 Hatenna
243 Hatterene
242 Hattrem
337 Indeedee
193 Pichu
194 Pikachu
195 Raichu
211 Slurpuff
053 Steenee
210 Swirlix
054 Tsareena

Play Rough (TR90)
186 Alcremie
071 Arcanine
280 Beartic
058 Bellossom
047 Boltund
052 Bounsweet
129 Cherrim
051 Cinccino
256 Clefable
255 Clefairy
254 Cleffa
303 Copperajah
279 Cubchoo

302 Cufant
187 Cutiefly
346 Drampa
208 Espurr
350 Frosmoth
240 Grimmsnarl
070 Growlithe
241 Hatenna
243 Hatterene
242 Hattrem
238 Impidimp
337 Indeedee
045 Liepard
295 Mawile
209 Meowstic
182 Meowth
301 Mimikyu
050 Minccino
239 Morgrem
029 Nickit
183 Perrserker
184 Persian
193 Pichu
194 Pikachu
333 Ponyta
044 Purrloin
195 Raichu
334 Rapidash
188 Ribombee
131 Skuntank
211 Slurpuff
053 Steenee
130 Stunky
210 Swirlix
204 Sylveon
030 Thievul
259 Togekiss
257 Togepi
258 Togetic
054 Tsareena
251 Weezing
263 Whimsicott
046 Yamper
398 Zacian
399 Zamazenta

Pluck
375 Arctozolt
023 Corviknight
022 Corvisquire
309 Cramorant
374 Dracozolt
290 Inkay
291 Malamar
284 Mandibuzz
021 Rookidee
283 Vullaby

Poison Fang
286 Drapion
244 Salandit
245 Salazzle
382 Silvally
285 Skorupi

Poison Gas
158 Garbodor
250 Koffing
244 Salandit
245 Salazzle
131 Skuntank
130 Stunky
157 Trubbish
251 Weezing

Poison Jab (TR57)
215 Araquanid

180 Arrokuda	311 Toxtricity	375 Arctozolt	041 Shiftry	154 Basculin	124 Drifloon	318 Helioptile
324 Axew	339 Trevenant	359 Avalugg	297 Sigilyph	280 Beartic	166 Drilbur	314 Hippopotas
235 Barbaracle	018 Vikavolt	280 Beartic	270 Solosis	278 Beheeyem	008 Drizzile	315 Hippowdon
181 Barraskewda	293 Weavile	358 Bergmite	363 Solrock	058 Bellossom	035 Dubwool	109 Hitmonchan
234 Binacle	**Poison Powder**	279 Cubchoo	068 Vulpix	358 Bergmite	165 Dugtrio	108 Hitmonlee
247 Bisharp	058 Bellossom	368 Darmanitan	093 Xatu	095 Bewear	271 Duosion	110 Hitmontop
017 Charjabug	015 Butterfree	367 Darumaka	399 Zamazenta	234 Binacle	371 Duraludon	330 Honedge
151 Cloyster	262 Cottonee	370 Eiscue	**Power Trick**	247 Bisharp	316 Durant	019 Hoothoot
173 Conkeldurr	056 Gloom	081 Froslass	332 Aegislash	169 Boldore	136 Dusclops	388 Hydreigon
222 Croagunk	126 Gossifleur	350 Frosmoth	082 Baltoy	047 Boltund	137 Dusknoir	238 Impidimp
087 Crustle	340 Morelull	080 Glalie	083 Claydol	252 Bonsly	135 Duskull	337 Indeedee
214 Dewpider	055 Oddish	077 Mamoswine	331 Doublade	052 Bounsweet	086 Dwebble	290 Inkay
286 Drapion	057 Vileplume	076 Piloswine	330 Honedge	282 Braviary	196 Eevee	009 Inteleon
043 Drednaw	263 Whimsicott	349 Snom	227 Shuckle	119 Bronzong	370 Eiscue	392 Jangmo-o
166 Drilbur	**Poison Sting**	079 Snorunt	**Power Trip**	118 Bronzor	127 Eldegoss	306 Jellicent
086 Dwebble	222 Croagunk	096 Snover	023 Corviknight	059 Budew	066 Electrike	198 Jolteon
274 Escavalier	286 Drapion	075 Swinub	022 Corvisquire	048 Bunnelby	277 Elgyem	064 Joltik
400 Eternatus	305 Frillish	**Power Gem (TR63)**	344 Morpeko	015 Butterfree	274 Escavalier	273 Karrablast
167 Excadrill	306 Jellicent	169 Boldore	111 Pancham	162 Carkol	200 Espeon	099 Kingler
345 Falinks	064 Joltik	236 Corsola	021 Rookidee	160 Centiskorch	208 Espurr	121 Kirlia
218 Farfetch'd	307 Mareanie	237 Cursola	**Power Whip (TR72)**	289 Chandelure	400 Eternatus	114 Klang
189 Ferroseed	304 Qwilfish	170 Gigalith	160 Centiskorch	380 Charizard	167 Excadrill	113 Klink
190 Ferrothorn	060 Roselia	114 Klang	303 Copperajah	378 Charmander	345 Falinks	115 Klinklang
325 Fraxure	061 Roserade	113 Klink	302 Cufant	379 Charmeleon	218 Farfetch'd	250 Koffing
123 Gallade	285 Skorupi	115 Klinklang	360 Dhelmise	129 Cherrim	152 Feebas	394 Kommo-o
065 Galvantula	308 Toxapex	362 Lunatone	190 Ferrothorn	128 Cherubi	189 Ferroseed	098 Krabby
141 Gastly	223 Toxicroak	184 Persian	391 Goodra	042 Chewtle	190 Ferrothorn	288 Lampent
143 Gengar	117 Vespiquen	294 Sableye	192 Gourgeist	220 Chinchou	206 Flapple	221 Lanturn
146 Goldeen	**Poison Tail**	117 Vespiquen	240 Grimmsnarl	051 Cinccino	199 Flareon	361 Lapras
233 Golisopod	400 Eternatus	**Power Split**	145 Gyarados	006 Cinderace	323 Flygon	383 Larvitar
016 Grubbin	391 Goodra	082 Baltoy	243 Hatterene	083 Claydol	325 Fraxure	202 Leafeon
172 Gurdurr	312 Silicobra	278 Beheeyem	133 Palpitoad	256 Clefable	305 Frillish	045 Liepard
142 Haunter	**Pollen Puff (TR96)**	083 Claydol	060 Roselia	255 Clefairy	081 Froslass	032 Linoone
320 Hawlucha	015 Butterfree	329 Cofagrigus	061 Roserade	254 Cleffa	350 Frosmoth	287 Litwick
326 Haxorus	129 Cherrim	214 Dewpider	134 Seismitoad	351 Clobbopus	123 Gallade	037 Lombre
108 Hitmonlee	128 Cherubi	277 Elgyem	159 Sizzlipede	151 Cloyster	065 Galvantula	036 Lotad
064 Joltik	127 Eldegoss	337 Indeedee	054 Tsareena	163 Coalossal	158 Garbodor	299 Lucario
273 Karrablast	126 Gossifleur	287 Litwick	**Power-Up Punch**	329 Cofagrigus	122 Gardevoir	038 Ludicolo
394 Kommo-o	340 Morelull	364 Mime Jr.	351 Clobbopus	173 Conkeldurr	141 Gastly	362 Lunatone
299 Lucario	188 Ribombee	365 Mr. Mime	367 Darumaka	303 Copperajah	231 Gastrodon	140 Machamp
140 Machamp	341 Shiinotic	328 Runerigus	240 Grimmsnarl	102 Corphish	143 Gengar	139 Machoke
139 Machoke	057 Vileplume	227 Shuckle	109 Hitmonchan	236 Corsola	170 Gigalith	138 Machop
138 Machop	**Pound**	327 Yamask	299 Lucario	023 Corviknight	203 Glaceon	291 Malamar
296 Maractus	051 Cinccino	**Power Swap (TM60)**	295 Mawile	022 Corvisquire	080 Glalie	077 Mamoswine
307 Mareanie	256 Clefable	276 Accelgor	224 Scraggy	262 Cottonee	056 Gloom	284 Mandibuzz
112 Pangoro	255 Clefairy	082 Baltoy	171 Timburr	309 Cramorant	146 Goldeen	067 Manectric
246 Pawniard	254 Cleffa	278 Beheeyem	310 Toxel	103 Crawdaunt	088 Golett	355 Mantine
338 Phantump	173 Conkeldurr	119 Bronzong	100 Wooper	222 Croagunk	233 Golisopod	354 Mantyke
353 Pincurchin	008 Drizzile	118 Bronzor	**Present**	087 Crustle	089 Golurk	296 Maractus
304 Qwilfish	158 Garbodor	083 Claydol	254 Cleffa	279 Cubchoo	391 Goodra	307 Mareanie
265 Rhydon	088 Golett	329 Cofagrigus	078 Delibird	302 Cufant	389 Goomy	295 Mawile
264 Rhyhorn	089 Golurk	011 Dottler	193 Pichu	237 Cursola	126 Gossifleur	209 Meowstic
266 Rhyperior	267 Gothita	271 Duosion	348 Togedemaru	187 Cutiefly	267 Gothita	182 Meowth
298 Riolu	269 Gothitelle	277 Elgyem	257 Togepi	368 Darmanitan	269 Gothitelle	185 Milcery
060 Roselia	268 Gothorita	200 Espeon	**Protect (TM25)**	367 Darumaka	268 Gothorita	153 Milotic
061 Roserade	172 Gurdurr	122 Gardevoir	097 Abomasnow	386 Deino	192 Gourgeist	364 Mime Jr.
294 Sableye	319 Heliolisk	240 Grimmsnarl	276 Accelgor	078 Delibird	352 Grapploct	301 Mimikyu
244 Salandit	318 Helioptile	243 Hatterene	332 Aegislash	214 Dewpider	025 Greedent	050 Minccino
245 Salazzle	009 Inteleon	337 Indeedee	186 Alcremie	360 Dhelmise	001 Grookey	340 Morelull
249 Sawk	364 Mime Jr.	362 Lunatone	207 Appletun	049 Diggersby	070 Growlithe	239 Morgrem
225 Scrafty	050 Minccino	365 Mr. Mime	215 Araquanid	164 Diglett	016 Grubbin	344 Morpeko
224 Scraggy	365 Mr. Mime	366 Mr. Rime	071 Arcanine	011 Dottler	172 Gurdurr	365 Mr. Mime
147 Seaking	366 Mr. Rime	090 Munna	377 Arctovish	331 Doublade	145 Gyarados	366 Mr. Rime
134 Seismitoad	245 Salazzle	091 Musharna	375 Arctozolt	376 Dracovish	393 Hakamo-o	084 Mudbray
219 Sirfetch'd	007 Sobble	092 Natu	213 Aromatisse	374 Dracozolt	241 Hatenna	085 Mudsdale
285 Skorupi	171 Timburr	069 Ninetales	180 Arrokuda	397 Dragapult	243 Hatterene	260 Munchlax
131 Skuntank	259 Togekiss	040 Nuzleaf	359 Avalugg	396 Drakloak	242 Hattrem	090 Munna
292 Sneasel	257 Togepi	012 Orbeetle	324 Axew	346 Drampa	142 Haunter	091 Musharna
248 Throh	258 Togetic	272 Reuniclus	082 Baltoy	286 Drapion	320 Hawlucha	092 Natu
171 Timburr	157 Trubbish	328 Runerigus	235 Barbaracle	043 Drednaw	326 Haxorus	029 Nickit
348 Togedemaru	**Powder Snow**	039 Seedot	228 Barboach	395 Dreepy	317 Heatmor	104 Nincada
308 Toxapex	097 Abomasnow		181 Barraskewda	125 Drifblim	319 Heliolisk	069 Ninetales
223 Toxicroak	377 Arctovish					105 Ninjask

020 Noctowl
176 Noibat
177 Noivern
040 Nuzleaf
033 Obstagoon
149 Octillery
055 Oddish
178 Onix
342 Oranguru
012 Orbeetle
133 Palpitoad
111 Pancham
112 Pangoro
343 Passimian
246 Pawniard
063 Pelipper
183 Perrserker
184 Persian
338 Phantump
193 Pichu
026 Pidove
194 Pikachu
076 Piloswine
353 Pincurchin
336 Polteageist
333 Ponyta
191 Pumpkaboo
384 Pupitar
044 Purrloin
156 Pyukumuku
101 Quagsire
304 Qwilfish
005 Raboot
195 Raichu
120 Ralts
334 Rapidash
148 Remoraid
272 Reuniclus
265 Rhydon
264 Rhyhorn
266 Rhyperior
188 Ribombee
003 Rillaboom
298 Riolu
168 Roggenrola
161 Rolycoly
021 Rookidee
060 Roselia
061 Roserade
372 Rotom
281 Rufflet
328 Runerigus
294 Sableye
244 Salandit
245 Salazzle
313 Sandaconda
249 Sawk
004 Scorbunny
225 Scrafty
224 Scraggy
147 Seaking
039 Seedot
134 Seismitoad
106 Shedinja
150 Shellder
230 Shellos
275 Shelmet
041 Shiftry
341 Shiinotic
227 Shuckle
297 Sigilyph
312 Silicobra
382 Silvally
335 Sinistea
219 Sirfetch'd
159 Sizzlipede
285 Skorupi
131 Skuntank
024 Skwovet
390 Sliggoo
211 Slurpuff
292 Sneasel
349 Snom
261 Snorlax
079 Snorunt
096 Snover
007 Sobble
270 Solosis
363 Solrock
212 Spritzee
179 Steelix
053 Steenee
369 Stonjourner
094 Stufful
226 Stunfisk
130 Stunky
253 Sudowoodo
075 Swinub
210 Swirlix
175 Swoobat
204 Sylveon
030 Thievul
248 Throh
002 Thwackey
171 Timburr
348 Togedemaru
259 Togekiss
257 Togepi
258 Togetic
300 Torkoal
308 Toxapex
310 Toxel
223 Toxicroak
311 Toxtricity
027 Tranquill
321 Trapinch
339 Trevenant
157 Trubbish
054 Tsareena
347 Turtonator
132 Tympole
381 Type: Null
385 Tyranitar
107 Tyrogue
201 Umbreon
028 Unfezant
073 Vanillish
072 Vanillite
074 Vanilluxe
197 Vaporeon
117 Vespiquen
322 Vibrava
018 Vikavolt
057 Vileplume
283 Vullaby
068 Vulpix
356 Wailmer
357 Wailord
293 Weavile
251 Weezing
263 Whimsicott
229 Whiscash
232 Wimpod
062 Wingull
155 Wishiwashi
174 Woobat
034 Wooloo
100 Wooper
093 Xatu
327 Yamask
046 Yamper
398 Zacian
399 Zamazenta
031 Zigzagoon
387 Zweilous

Psybeam
082 Baltoy
278 Beheeyem
015 Butterfree
220 Chinchou
083 Claydol
271 Duosion
277 Elgyem
200 Espeon
208 Espurr
123 Gallade
122 Gardevoir
146 Goldeen
267 Gothita
269 Gothitelle
268 Gothorita
241 Hatenna
243 Hatterene
242 Hattrem
337 Indeedee
290 Inkay
121 Kirlia
250 Koffing
291 Malamar
355 Mantine
209 Meowstic
364 Mime Jr.
365 Mr. Mime
366 Mr. Rime
090 Munna
091 Musharna
149 Octillery
012 Orbeetle
333 Ponyta
120 Ralts
334 Rapidash
148 Remoraid
272 Reuniclus
297 Sigilyph
270 Solosis

Psych Up
213 Aromatisse
277 Elgyem
200 Espeon
267 Gothita
269 Gothitelle
268 Gothorita
337 Indeedee
342 Oranguru
204 Sylveon

Psychic (TR11)
186 Alcremie
213 Aromatisse
082 Baltoy
278 Beheeyem
119 Bronzong
118 Bronzor
015 Butterfree
289 Chandelure
083 Claydol
256 Clefable
255 Clefairy
254 Cleffa
329 Cofagrigus
236 Corsola
237 Cursola
187 Cutiefly
368 Darmanitan
011 Dottler
125 Drifblim
124 Drifloon
271 Duosion
136 Dusclops
137 Dusknoir
135 Duskull
277 Elgyem
200 Espeon
208 Espurr
305 Frillish
081 Froslass
123 Gallade
158 Garbodor
122 Gardevoir
141 Gastly
143 Gengar
088 Golett
089 Golurk
267 Gothita
269 Gothitelle
268 Gothorita
192 Gourgeist
241 Hatenna
243 Hatterene
242 Hattrem
142 Haunter
019 Hoothoot
337 Indeedee
290 Inkay
306 Jellicent
121 Kirlia
288 Lampent
361 Lapras
287 Litwick
299 Lucario
362 Lunatone
291 Malamar
209 Meowstic
364 Mime Jr.
301 Mimikyu
365 Mr. Mime
366 Mr. Rime
260 Munchlax
090 Munna
091 Musharna
092 Natu
020 Noctowl
176 Noibat
177 Noivern
149 Octillery
342 Oranguru
012 Orbeetle
338 Phantump
336 Polteageist
333 Ponyta
191 Pumpkaboo
120 Ralts
334 Rapidash
148 Remoraid
272 Reuniclus
188 Ribombee
328 Runerigus
294 Sableye
297 Sigilyph
335 Sinistea
211 Slurpuff
261 Snorlax
270 Solosis
363 Solrock
212 Spritzee
210 Swirlix
175 Swoobat
030 Thievul
259 Togekiss
257 Togepi
258 Togetic
339 Trevenant
201 Umbreon
263 Whimsicott
174 Woobat
093 Xatu
327 Yamask

Psychic Fangs (TR97)
071 Arcanine
377 Arctovish
180 Arrokuda
181 Barraskewda
154 Basculin
047 Boltund
376 Dracovish
397 Dragapult
396 Drakloak
066 Electrike
200 Espeon
025 Greedent
070 Growlithe
067 Manectric
295 Mawile
344 Morpeko
382 Silvally
179 Steelix
175 Swoobat
398 Zacian
399 Zamazenta

Psychic Terrain (TM91)
082 Baltoy
278 Beheeyem
119 Bronzong
083 Claydol
011 Dottler
271 Duosion
122 Gardevoir
337 Indeedee
362 Lunatone
209 Meowstic
364 Mime Jr.
365 Mr. Mime
366 Mr. Rime
091 Musharna
342 Oranguru
012 Orbeetle
334 Rapidash
272 Reuniclus
270 Solosis
363 Solrock

Psycho Cut (TM69)
332 Aegislash
247 Bisharp
331 Doublade
123 Gallade
243 Hatterene
326 Haxorus
330 Honedge
290 Inkay
045 Liepard
291 Malamar
012 Orbeetle
246 Pawniard
334 Rapidash
297 Sigilyph
292 Sneasel
175 Swoobat
293 Weavile
174 Woobat
398 Zacian

Psycho Shift
019 Hoothoot
337 Indeedee
092 Natu
020 Noctowl
297 Sigilyph
257 Togepi
174 Woobat
093 Xatu

Psyshock (TR25)
186 Alcremie
213 Aromatisse
082 Baltoy
278 Beheeyem
119 Bronzong
118 Bronzor
083 Claydol
256 Clefable
255 Clefairy
254 Cleffa
011 Dottler
271 Duosion
277 Elgyem
200 Espeon
208 Espurr
123 Gallade
122 Gardevoir
267 Gothita
269 Gothitelle
268 Gothorita
241 Hatenna
243 Hatterene
242 Hattrem
337 Indeedee
121 Kirlia
362 Lunatone
291 Malamar
209 Meowstic
364 Mime Jr.
365 Mr. Mime
366 Mr. Rime
090 Munna
091 Musharna
092 Natu
069 Ninetales
342 Oranguru
012 Orbeetle
336 Polteageist
120 Ralts
272 Reuniclus
297 Sigilyph
335 Sinistea
270 Solosis
363 Solrock
175 Swoobat
204 Sylveon
259 Togekiss
257 Togepi
258 Togetic
174 Woobat
093 Xatu

Purify
156 Pyukumuku

Pyro Ball
006 Cinderace

Quash
241 Hatenna
344 Morpeko
342 Oranguru
111 Pancham
294 Sableye

Quick Attack
276 Accelgor
048 Bunnelby
006 Cinderace
078 Delibird
049 Diggersby
397 Dragapult
396 Drakloak
395 Dreepy
196 Eevee
066 Electrike
200 Espeon
218 Farfetch'd
199 Flareon
203 Glaceon
319 Heliolisk
318 Helioptile
110 Hitmontop
198 Jolteon
202 Leafeon
299 Lucario
067 Manectric
344 Morpeko
092 Natu
029 Nickit
069 Ninetales
343 Passimian
063 Pelipper
026 Pidove
194 Pikachu
044 Purrloin
005 Raboot
195 Raichu
334 Rapidash
298 Riolu
004 Scorbunny
039 Seedot
292 Sneasel
204 Sylveon
030 Thievul
027 Tranquill
321 Trapinch
201 Umbreon
028 Unfezant
197 Vaporeon
068 Vulpix
293 Weavile
062 Wingull
398 Zacian
399 Zamazenta

Quick Guard
222 Croagunk
274 Escavalier
218 Farfetch'd
123 Gallade
320 Hawlucha
109 Hitmonchan
110 Hitmontop
299 Lucario
138 Machop
209 Meowstic
365 Mr. Mime
029 Nickit
111 Pancham
343 Passimian
246 Pawniard
298 Riolu

249 Sawk
224 Scraggy
398 Zacian
031 Zigzagoon

Quiver Dance
058 Bellossom
015 Butterfree
187 Cutiefly
350 Frosmoth
188 Ribombee

Rage Powder
015 Butterfree

Rain Dance (TM33)
097 Abomasnow
276 Accelgor
332 Aegislash
215 Araquanid
377 Arctovish
375 Arctozolt
213 Aromatisse
180 Arrokuda
359 Avalugg
324 Axew
082 Baltoy
235 Barbaracle
228 Barboach
181 Barraskewda
154 Basculin
280 Beartic
278 Beheeyem
358 Bergmite
234 Binacle
247 Bisharp
282 Braviary
119 Bronzong
118 Bronzor
059 Budew
015 Butterfree
017 Charjabug
042 Chewtle
220 Chinchou
051 Cinccino
083 Claydol
256 Clefable
255 Clefairy
254 Cleffa
151 Cloyster
329 Cofagrigus
173 Conkeldurr
102 Corphish
236 Corsola
309 Cramorant
103 Crawdaunt
222 Croagunk
279 Cubchoo
237 Cursola
386 Deino
078 Delibird
214 Dewpider
360 Dhelmise
331 Doublade
376 Dracovish
374 Dracozolt
346 Drampa
286 Drapion
043 Drednaw
125 Drifblim
124 Drifloon
008 Drizzile
271 Duosion
136 Dusclops
137 Dusknoir
135 Duskull
196 Eevee
066 Electrike
277 Elgyem
274 Escavalier
200 Espeon
208 Espurr
152 Feebas
199 Flareon
325 Fraxure
305 Frillish
081 Froslass
123 Gallade
065 Galvantula
158 Garbodor
122 Gardevoir
141 Gastly
231 Gastrodon
143 Gengar
203 Glaceon
080 Glalie
146 Goldeen
088 Golett
233 Golisopod
089 Golurk
391 Goodra
389 Goomy
267 Gothita
269 Gothitelle
268 Gothorita
016 Grubbin
172 Gurdurr
145 Gyarados
142 Haunter
320 Hawlucha
326 Haxorus
317 Heatmor
319 Heliolisk
318 Helioptile
109 Hitmonchan
108 Hitmonlee
110 Hitmontop
330 Honedge
019 Hoothoot
388 Hydreigon
290 Inkay
009 Inteleon
306 Jellicent
198 Jolteon
064 Joltik
273 Karrablast
099 Kingler
121 Kirlia
250 Koffing
098 Krabby
221 Lanturn
361 Lapras
383 Larvitar
202 Leafeon
045 Liepard
032 Linoone
037 Lombre
036 Lotad
299 Lucario
038 Ludicolo
362 Lunatone
140 Machamp
139 Machoke
138 Machop
291 Malamar
077 Mamoswine
284 Mandibuzz
067 Manectric
355 Mantine
354 Mantyke
296 Maractus
307 Mareanie
295 Mawile
209 Meowstic
182 Meowth
153 Milotic
364 Mime Jr.
050 Minccino
365 Mr. Mime
366 Mr. Rime
260 Munchlax
090 Munna
091 Musharna
092 Natu
020 Noctowl
033 Obstagoon
149 Octillery
342 Oranguru
133 Palpitoad
111 Pancham
112 Pangoro
343 Passimian
246 Pawniard
063 Pelipper
183 Perrserker
184 Persian
193 Pichu
026 Pidove
194 Pikachu
076 Piloswine
353 Pincurchin
384 Pupitar
044 Purrloin
156 Pyukumuku
101 Quagsire
304 Qwilfish
195 Raichu
120 Ralts
148 Remoraid
272 Reuniclus
265 Rhydon
264 Rhyhorn
266 Rhyperior
298 Riolu
060 Roselia
061 Roserade
372 Rotom
281 Rufflet
328 Runerigus
294 Sableye
249 Sawk
225 Scrafty
224 Scraggy
147 Seaking
134 Seismitoad
150 Shellder
230 Shellos
275 Shelmet
341 Shiinotic
297 Sigilyph
382 Silvally
285 Skorupi
131 Skuntank
390 Sliggoo
211 Slurpuff
292 Sneasel
261 Snorlax
079 Snorunt
096 Snover
007 Sobble
270 Solosis
363 Solrock
212 Spritzee
226 Stunfisk
130 Stunky
075 Swinub
210 Swirlix
175 Swoobat
204 Sylveon
248 Throh
171 Timburr
259 Togekiss
257 Togepi
258 Togetic
308 Toxapex
223 Toxicroak
027 Tranquill
157 Trubbish
132 Tympole
381 Type: Null
385 Tyranitar
107 Tyrogue
201 Umbreon
028 Unfezant
073 Vanillish
072 Vanillite
074 Vanilluxe
197 Vaporeon
117 Vespiquen
018 Vikavolt
283 Vullaby
356 Wailmer
357 Wailord
293 Weavile
251 Weezing
229 Whiscash
232 Wimpod
062 Wingull
155 Wishiwashi
174 Woobat
100 Wooper
093 Xatu
327 Yamask
031 Zigzagoon
387 Zweilous

Razor Leaf
097 Abomasnow
052 Bounsweet
059 Budew
128 Cherubi
262 Cottonee
127 Eldegoss
126 Gossifleur
192 Gourgeist
001 Grookey
202 Leafeon
036 Lotad
040 Nuzleaf
055 Oddish
191 Pumpkaboo
003 Rillaboom
060 Roselia
041 Shiftry
096 Snover
053 Steenee
002 Thwackey
054 Tsareena
263 Whimsicott

Razor Shell (TM83)
235 Barbaracle
234 Binacle
151 Cloyster
102 Corphish
103 Crawdaunt
043 Drednaw
274 Escavalier
233 Golisopod
099 Kingler
098 Krabby
150 Shellder

Recover
276 Accelgor
186 Alcremie
207 Appletun
359 Avalugg
278 Beheeyem
358 Bergmite
010 Blipbug
271 Duosion
277 Elgyem
400 Eternatus
305 Frillish
231 Gastrodon
306 Jellicent
307 Mareanie
185 Milcery
153 Milotic
353 Pincurchin
156 Pyukumuku
272 Reuniclus
294 Sableye
230 Shellos
275 Shelmet
270 Solosis
308 Toxapex
100 Wooper

Recycle
207 Appletun
205 Applin
206 Flapple
158 Garbodor
364 Mime Jr.
365 Mr. Mime
366 Mr. Rime
260 Munchlax
261 Snorlax
157 Trubbish

Reflect (TM18)
332 Aegislash
207 Appletun
215 Araquanid
213 Aromatisse
082 Baltoy
278 Beheeyem
052 Bounsweet
119 Bronzong
118 Bronzor
162 Carkol
083 Claydol
256 Clefable
255 Clefairy
254 Cleffa
163 Coalossal
236 Corsola
023 Corviknight
237 Cursola
187 Cutiefly
011 Dottler
331 Doublade
397 Dragapult
008 Drizzile
271 Duosion
371 Duraludon
370 Eiscue
277 Elgyem
200 Espeon
208 Espurr
400 Eternatus
081 Froslass
350 Frosmoth
123 Gallade
122 Gardevoir
267 Gothita
269 Gothitelle
268 Gothorita
240 Grimmsnarl
330 Honedge
019 Hoothoot
388 Hydreigon
337 Indeedee
290 Inkay
009 Inteleon
121 Kirlia
362 Lunatone
291 Malamar
077 Mamoswine
209 Meowstic
364 Mime Jr.
239 Morgrem
365 Mr. Mime
366 Mr. Rime
090 Munna
091 Musharna
092 Natu
020 Noctowl
342 Oranguru
012 Orbeetle
338 Phantump
193 Pichu
194 Pikachu
076 Piloswine
336 Polteageist
156 Pyukumuku
195 Raichu
120 Ralts
272 Reuniclus
188 Ribombee
161 Rolycoly
372 Rotom
297 Sigilyph
292 Sneasel
007 Sobble
270 Solosis
363 Solrock
212 Spritzee
053 Steenee

Reflect Type
141 Gastly
143 Gengar
226 Stunfisk

Rest (TM21)
097 Abomasnow
276 Accelgor
332 Aegislash
186 Alcremie
207 Appletun
215 Araquanid
071 Arcanine
377 Arctovish
375 Arctozolt
213 Aromatisse
180 Arrokuda
359 Avalugg
324 Axew
082 Baltoy
235 Barbaracle
228 Barboach
181 Barraskewda
154 Basculin
280 Beartic
278 Beheeyem
058 Bellossom
358 Bergmite
095 Bewear
234 Binacle
247 Bisharp
169 Boldore
047 Boltund
252 Bonsly
052 Bounsweet
282 Braviary
119 Bronzong
118 Bronzor
059 Budew
048 Bunnelby
015 Butterfree
162 Carkol
160 Centiskorch
289 Chandelure
380 Charizard
017 Charjabug
378 Charmander
379 Charmeleon
129 Cherrim
128 Cherubi
042 Chewtle
220 Chinchou
051 Cinccino
006 Cinderace
083 Claydol
256 Clefable
255 Clefairy
254 Cleffa
351 Clobbopus
151 Cloyster
163 Coalossal

329 Cofagrigus
173 Conkeldurr
303 Copperajah
102 Corphish
236 Corsola
023 Corviknight
022 Corvisquire
262 Cottonee
309 Cramorant
103 Crawdaunt
222 Croagunk
087 Crustle
279 Cubchoo
302 Cufant
237 Cursola
187 Cutiefly
368 Darmanitan
367 Darumaka
386 Deino
078 Delibird
214 Dewpider
360 Dhelmise
049 Diggersby
164 Diglett
011 Dottler
331 Doublade
376 Dracovish
374 Dracozolt
397 Dragapult
396 Drakloak
346 Drampa
286 Drapion
043 Drednaw
395 Dreepy
125 Drifblim
124 Drifloon
166 Drilbur
008 Drizzile
035 Dubwool
165 Dugtrio
271 Duosion
371 Duraludon
316 Durant
136 Dusclops
137 Dusknoir
135 Duskull
086 Dwebble
196 Eevee
370 Eiscue
127 Eldegoss
066 Electrike
277 Elgyem
274 Escavalier
200 Espeon
208 Espurr
400 Eternatus
167 Excadrill
345 Falinks
218 Farfetch'd
152 Feebas
189 Ferroseed
190 Ferrothorn
206 Flapple
199 Flareon
323 Flygon
325 Fraxure
305 Frillish
081 Froslass
350 Frosmoth
123 Gallade
065 Galvantula
158 Garbodor
122 Gardevoir

141 Gastly
231 Gastrodon
143 Gengar
170 Gigalith
203 Glaceon
080 Glalie
056 Gloom
146 Goldeen
088 Golett
233 Golisopod
089 Golurk
391 Goodra
389 Goomy
126 Gossifleur
267 Gothita
269 Gothitelle
268 Gothorita
192 Gourgeist
352 Grapploct
025 Greedent
240 Grimmsnarl
001 Grookey
070 Growlithe
016 Grubbin
172 Gurdurr
145 Gyarados
393 Hakamo-o
241 Hatenna
243 Hatterene
242 Hattrem
142 Haunter
320 Hawlucha
326 Haxorus
317 Heatmor
319 Heliolisk
318 Helioptile
314 Hippopotas
315 Hippowdon
109 Hitmonchan
108 Hitmonlee
110 Hitmontop
330 Honedge
019 Hoothoot
388 Hydreigon
238 Impidimp
337 Indeedee
290 Inkay
009 Inteleon
392 Jangmo-o
306 Jellicent
198 Jolteon
064 Joltik
273 Karrablast
099 Kingler
121 Kirlia
114 Klang
113 Klink
115 Klinklang
250 Koffing
394 Kommo-o
098 Krabby
288 Lampent
221 Lanturn
361 Lapras
383 Larvitar
202 Leafeon
045 Liepard
032 Linoone
287 Litwick
037 Lombre
036 Lotad
299 Lucario
038 Ludicolo

362 Lunatone
140 Machamp
139 Machoke
138 Machop
291 Malamar
077 Mamoswine
284 Mandibuzz
067 Manectric
355 Mantine
354 Mantyke
296 Maractus
307 Mareanie
295 Mawile
182 Meowth
185 Milcery
153 Milotic
364 Mime Jr.
301 Mimikyu
050 Minccino
340 Morelull
239 Morgrem
344 Morpeko
365 Mr. Mime
366 Mr. Rime
084 Mudbray
085 Mudsdale
260 Munchlax
090 Munna
091 Musharna
092 Natu
029 Nickit
104 Nincada
069 Ninetales
105 Ninjask
020 Noctowl
176 Noibat
177 Noivern
040 Nuzleaf
033 Obstagoon
149 Octillery
055 Oddish
178 Onix
342 Oranguru
012 Orbeetle
133 Palpitoad
111 Pancham
112 Pangoro
343 Passimian
246 Pawniard
063 Pelipper
183 Perrserker
184 Persian
338 Phantump
193 Pichu
026 Pidove
194 Pikachu
076 Piloswine
353 Pincurchin
336 Polteageist
333 Ponyta
191 Pumpkaboo
384 Pupitar
044 Purrloin
156 Pyukumuku
101 Quagsire
304 Qwilfish
005 Raboot
195 Raichu
120 Ralts
334 Rapidash
148 Remoraid
272 Reuniclus

265 Rhydon
264 Rhyhorn
266 Rhyperior
188 Ribombee
003 Rillaboom
298 Riolu
168 Roggenrola
161 Rolycoly
021 Rookidee
060 Roselia
061 Roserade
372 Rotom
281 Rufflet
328 Runerigus
294 Sableye
244 Salandit
245 Salazzle
313 Sandaconda
249 Sawk
004 Scorbunny
225 Scrafty
224 Scraggy
147 Seaking
039 Seedot
134 Seismitoad
106 Shedinja
150 Shellder
230 Shellos
275 Shelmet
041 Shiftry
341 Shiinotic
227 Shuckle
297 Sigilyph
312 Silicobra
382 Silvally
335 Sinistea
219 Sirfetch'd
159 Sizzlipede
285 Skorupi
131 Skuntank
024 Skwovet
390 Sliggoo
211 Slurpuff
292 Sneasel
349 Snom
261 Snorlax
079 Snorunt
096 Snover
007 Sobble
270 Solosis
363 Solrock
212 Spritzee
179 Steelix
053 Steenee
369 Stonjourner
094 Stufful
226 Stunfisk
130 Stunky
253 Sudowoodo
075 Swinub
210 Swirlix
175 Swoobat
204 Sylveon
030 Thievul
248 Throh
002 Thwackey
171 Timburr
348 Togedemaru
259 Togekiss
257 Togepi
258 Togetic
300 Torkoal
308 Toxapex

310 Toxel
223 Toxicroak
311 Toxtricity
027 Tranquill
321 Trapinch
339 Trevenant
157 Trubbish
054 Tsareena
347 Turtonator
132 Tympole
381 Type: Null
385 Tyranitar
107 Tyrogue
201 Umbreon
028 Unfezant
073 Vanillish
072 Vanillite
074 Vanilluxe
197 Vaporeon
117 Vespiquen
322 Vibrava
018 Vikavolt
057 Vileplume
283 Vullaby
068 Vulpix
356 Wailmer
357 Wailord
293 Weavile
251 Weezing
263 Whimsicott
229 Whiscash
232 Wimpod
062 Wingull
155 Wishiwashi
174 Woobat
034 Wooloo
100 Wooper
093 Xatu
327 Yamask
046 Yamper
398 Zacian
399 Zamazenta
031 Zigzagoon
387 Zweilous

Retaliate (TM79)
332 Aegislash
071 Arcanine
247 Bisharp
282 Braviary
051 Cinccino
256 Clefable
255 Clefairy
351 Clobbopus
173 Conkeldurr
023 Corviknight
022 Corvisquire
103 Crawdaunt
222 Croagunk
331 Doublade
286 Drapion
035 Dubwool
316 Durant
196 Eevee
200 Espeon
345 Falinks
218 Farfetch'd
199 Flareon
123 Gallade
203 Glaceon
352 Grapploct
240 Grimmsnarl
070 Growlithe
172 Gurdurr

320 Hawlucha
109 Hitmonchan
108 Hitmonlee
110 Hitmontop
330 Honedge
238 Impidimp
290 Inkay
198 Jolteon
383 Larvitar
202 Leafeon
032 Linoone
299 Lucario
140 Machamp
139 Machoke
138 Machop
291 Malamar
284 Mandibuzz
182 Meowth
050 Minccino
239 Morgrem
260 Munchlax
040 Nuzleaf
033 Obstagoon
111 Pancham
112 Pangoro
343 Passimian
246 Pawniard
183 Perrserker
184 Persian
384 Pupitar
298 Riolu
021 Rookidee
281 Rufflet
294 Sableye
249 Sawk
225 Scrafty
224 Scraggy
039 Seedot
041 Shiftry
219 Sirfetch'd
292 Sneasel
261 Snorlax
204 Sylveon
248 Throh
171 Timburr
259 Togekiss
258 Togetic
223 Toxicroak
385 Tyranitar
107 Tyrogue
201 Umbreon
197 Vaporeon
283 Vullaby
293 Weavile
398 Zacian
399 Zamazenta
031 Zigzagoon

Revenge (TM42)
154 Basculin
095 Bewear
247 Bisharp
042 Chewtle
006 Cinderace
351 Clobbopus
329 Cofagrigus
173 Conkeldurr
303 Copperajah
023 Corviknight
022 Corvisquire
103 Crawdaunt
222 Croagunk
237 Cursola
043 Drednaw

136 Dusclops
137 Dusknoir
135 Duskull
274 Escavalier
345 Falinks
218 Farfetch'd
189 Ferroseed
190 Ferrothorn
123 Gallade
352 Grapploct
240 Grimmsnarl
172 Gurdurr
320 Hawlucha
314 Hippopotas
315 Hippowdon
109 Hitmonchan
108 Hitmonlee
110 Hitmontop
238 Impidimp
394 Kommo-o
299 Lucario
140 Machamp
139 Machoke
138 Machop
239 Morgrem
344 Morpeko
085 Mudsdale
033 Obstagoon
112 Pangoro
343 Passimian
246 Pawniard
304 Qwilfish
298 Riolu
021 Rookidee
328 Runerigus
249 Sawk
225 Scrafty
224 Scraggy
041 Shiftry
219 Sirfetch'd
226 Stunfisk
248 Throh
171 Timburr
223 Toxicroak
347 Turtonator
385 Tyranitar
117 Vespiquen
293 Weavile
398 Zacian
399 Zamazenta

Reversal (TR21)
276 Accelgor
332 Aegislash
071 Arcanine
324 Axew
154 Basculin
095 Bewear
006 Cinderace
351 Clobbopus
173 Conkeldurr
023 Corviknight
022 Corvisquire
309 Cramorant
368 Darmanitan
164 Diglett
331 Doublade
035 Dubwool
165 Dugtrio
370 Eiscue
274 Escavalier
345 Falinks
325 Fraxure
123 Gallade

352 Grapploct	043 Drednaw	236 Corsola	090 Munna	383 Larvitar	088 Golett	248 Throh
070 Growlithe	086 Dwebble	103 Crawdaunt	091 Musharna	362 Lunatone	233 Golisopod	171 Timburr
172 Gurdurr	167 Excadrill	222 Croagunk	040 Nuzleaf	178 Onix	089 Golurk	300 Torkoal
393 Hakamo-o	158 Garbodor	087 Crustle	178 Onix	384 Pupitar	267 Gothita	223 Toxicroak
320 Hawlucha	170 Gigalith	302 Cufant	342 Oranguru	227 Shuckle	269 Gothitelle	321 Trapinch
326 Haxorus	362 Lunatone	237 Cursola	111 Pancham	363 Solrock	268 Gothorita	347 Turtonator
108 Hitmonlee	140 Machamp	368 Darmanitan	112 Pangoro	179 Steelix	172 Gurdurr	385 Tyranitar
330 Honedge	077 Mamoswine	367 Darumaka	343 Passimian	369 Stonjourner	393 Hakamo-o	322 Vibrava
392 Jangmo-o	355 Mantine	360 Dhelmise	338 Phantump	253 Sudowoodo	320 Hawlucha	283 Vullaby
394 Kommo-o	149 Octillery	049 Diggersby	076 Piloswine	171 Timburr	326 Haxorus	356 Wailmer
299 Lucario	178 Onix	164 Diglett	191 Pumpkaboo	385 Tyranitar	317 Heatmor	357 Wailord
140 Machamp	148 Remoraid	331 Doublade	384 Pupitar	**Rock Tomb**	319 Heliolisk	229 Whiscash
139 Machoke	265 Rhydon	376 Dracovish	101 Quagsire	**(TM48)**	318 Helioptile	327 Yamask
138 Machop	264 Rhyhorn	374 Dracozolt	272 Reuniclus	097 Abomasnow	314 Hippopotas	**Rock Wrecker**
291 Malamar	266 Rhyperior	346 Drampa	265 Rhydon	377 Arctovish	315 Hippowdon	087 Crustle
033 Obstagoon	168 Roggenrola	286 Drapion	264 Rhyhorn	375 Arctozolt	109 Hitmonchan	086 Dwebble
112 Pangoro	161 Rolycoly	043 Drednaw	266 Rhyperior	359 Avalugg	108 Hitmonlee	266 Rhyperior
343 Passimian	328 Runerigus	166 Drilbur	298 Riolu	324 Axew	388 Hydreigon	**Role Play**
193 Pichu	313 Sandaconda	165 Dugtrio	168 Roggenrola	082 Baltoy	392 Jangmo-o	209 Meowstic
194 Pikachu	150 Shellder	271 Duosion	161 Rolycoly	235 Barbaracle	099 Kingler	364 Mime Jr.
353 Pincurchin	227 Shuckle	371 Duraludon	281 Rufflet	228 Barboach	394 Kommo-o	365 Mr. Mime
304 Qwilfish	363 Solrock	316 Durant	328 Runerigus	280 Beartic	098 Krabby	366 Mr. Rime
005 Raboot	179 Steelix	136 Dusclops	313 Sandaconda	278 Beheeyem	383 Larvitar	**Rollout**
195 Raichu	369 Stonjourner	137 Dusknoir	249 Sawk	358 Bergmite	299 Lucario	205 Applin
265 Rhydon	253 Sudowoodo	086 Dwebble	225 Scrafty	095 Bewear	362 Lunatone	252 Bonsly
264 Rhyhorn	157 Trubbish	277 Elgyem	224 Scraggy	234 Binacle	140 Machamp	048 Bunnelby
266 Rhyperior	385 Tyranitar	167 Excadrill	134 Seismitoad	247 Bisharp	139 Machoke	128 Cherubi
298 Riolu	**Rock Polish**	345 Falinks	041 Shiftry	169 Boldore	138 Machop	303 Copperajah
021 Rookidee	235 Barbaracle	323 Flygon	227 Shuckle	252 Bonsly	077 Mamoswine	302 Cufant
249 Sawk	234 Binacle	123 Gallade	382 Silvally	282 Braviary	284 Mandibuzz	040 Nuzleaf
004 Scorbunny	252 Bonsly	231 Gastrodon	390 Sliggoo	119 Bronzong	355 Mantine	178 Onix
227 Shuckle	162 Carkol	170 Gigalith	261 Snorlax	118 Bronzor	295 Mawile	039 Seedot
382 Silvally	163 Coalossal	088 Golett	270 Solosis	048 Bunnelby	084 Mudbray	041 Shiftry
248 Throh	087 Crustle	233 Golisopod	363 Solrock	162 Carkol	085 Mudsdale	227 Shuckle
171 Timburr	043 Drednaw	089 Golurk	179 Steelix	380 Charizard	260 Munchlax	159 Sizzlipede
348 Togedemaru	086 Dwebble	391 Goodra	369 Stonjourner	378 Charmander	090 Munna	024 Skwovet
117 Vespiquen	362 Lunatone	389 Goomy	094 Stufful	379 Charmeleon	091 Musharna	079 Snorunt
034 Wooloo	178 Onix	267 Gothita	226 Stunfisk	083 Claydol	040 Nuzleaf	094 Stufful
398 Zacian	264 Rhyhorn	269 Gothitelle	253 Sudowoodo	163 Coalossal	178 Onix	253 Sudowoodo
399 Zamazenta	161 Rolycoly	268 Gothorita	075 Swinub	173 Conkeldurr	111 Pancham	157 Trubbish
Roar	363 Solrock	192 Gourgeist	248 Throh	303 Copperajah	112 Pangoro	356 Wailmer
071 Arcanine	179 Steelix	172 Gurdurr	171 Timburr	102 Corphish	343 Passimian	232 Wimpod
047 Boltund	369 Stonjourner	393 Hakamo-o	300 Torkoal	236 Corsola	246 Pawniard	**Roost**
386 Deino	253 Sudowoodo	320 Hawlucha	223 Toxicroak	103 Crawdaunt	076 Piloswine	309 Cramorant
066 Electrike	**Rock Slide**	326 Haxorus	321 Trapinch	222 Croagunk	384 Pupitar	320 Hawlucha
070 Growlithe	**(TM22)**	319 Heliolisk	339 Trevenant	087 Crustle	101 Quagsire	019 Hoothoot
314 Hippopotas	097 Abomasnow	318 Helioptile	381 Type: Null	279 Cubchoo	272 Reuniclus	355 Mantine
315 Hippowdon	332 Aegislash	314 Hippopotas	385 Tyranitar	302 Cufant	265 Rhydon	092 Natu
388 Hydreigon	377 Arctovish	315 Hippowdon	107 Tyrogue	237 Cursola	264 Rhyhorn	020 Noctowl
067 Manectric	375 Arctozolt	109 Hitmonchan	322 Vibrava	368 Darmanitan	266 Rhyperior	176 Noibat
084 Mudbray	359 Avalugg	108 Hitmonlee	229 Whiscash	367 Darumaka	298 Riolu	177 Noivern
068 Vulpix	082 Baltoy	110 Hitmontop	327 Yamask	049 Diggersby	168 Roggenrola	063 Pelipper
046 Yamper	235 Barbaracle	330 Honedge	**Rock Smash**	164 Diglett	161 Rolycoly	026 Pidove
387 Zweilous	280 Beartic	388 Hydreigon	351 Clobbopus	376 Dracovish	281 Rufflet	021 Rookidee
Rock Blast	278 Beheeyem	290 Inkay	303 Copperajah	374 Dracozolt	328 Runerigus	297 Sigilyph
(TM54)	358 Bergmite	392 Jangmo-o	302 Cufant	286 Drapion	294 Sableye	027 Tranquill
377 Arctovish	095 Bewear	099 Kingler	371 Duraludon	043 Drednaw	313 Sandaconda	028 Unfezant
375 Arctozolt	234 Binacle	394 Kommo-o	345 Falinks	166 Drilbur	249 Sawk	283 Vullaby
235 Barbaracle	169 Boldore	098 Krabby	218 Farfetch'd	165 Dugtrio	225 Scrafty	062 Wingull
234 Binacle	252 Bonsly	383 Larvitar	233 Golisopod	271 Duosion	224 Scraggy	174 Woobat
169 Boldore	282 Braviary	299 Lucario	352 Grapploct	371 Duraludon	134 Seismitoad	**Round (TM76)**
162 Carkol	119 Bronzong	362 Lunatone	299 Lucario	316 Durant	041 Shiftry	097 Abomasnow
051 Cinccino	118 Bronzor	140 Machamp	362 Lunatone	136 Dusclops	227 Shuckle	276 Accelgor
151 Cloyster	048 Bunnelby	139 Machoke	140 Machamp	137 Dusknoir	285 Skorupi	332 Aegislash
163 Coalossal	162 Carkol	138 Machop	139 Machoke	086 Dwebble	261 Snorlax	186 Alcremie
173 Conkeldurr	380 Charizard	291 Malamar	138 Machop	277 Elgyem	270 Solosis	207 Appletun
303 Copperajah	378 Charmander	077 Mamoswine	291 Malamar	167 Excadrill	363 Solrock	215 Araquanid
236 Corsola	379 Charmeleon	355 Mantine	077 Mamoswine	345 Falinks	179 Steelix	071 Arcanine
087 Crustle	083 Claydol	354 Mantyke	355 Mantine	323 Flygon	369 Stonjourner	377 Arctovish
302 Cufant	163 Coalossal	295 Mawile	354 Mantyke	325 Fraxure	094 Stufful	375 Arctozolt
237 Cursola	173 Conkeldurr	084 Mudbray	295 Mawile	123 Gallade	226 Stunfisk	213 Aromatisse
376 Dracovish	303 Copperajah	085 Mudsdale	084 Mudbray	231 Gastrodon	253 Sudowoodo	180 Arrokuda
374 Dracozolt	102 Corphish	260 Munchlax	085 Mudsdale	170 Gigalith	075 Swinub	359 Avalugg
			343 Passimian			
			298 Riolu			
			021 Rookidee			
			249 Sawk			
			219 Sirfetch'd			
			Rock Throw			
			252 Bonsly			
			173 Conkeldurr			
			172 Gurdurr			
			170 Gigalith			

324 Axew
082 Baltoy
235 Barbaracle
228 Barboach
181 Barraskewda
154 Basculin
280 Beartic
278 Beheeyem
058 Bellossom
358 Bergmite
095 Bewear
234 Binacle
247 Bisharp
169 Boldore
047 Boltund
252 Bonsly
052 Bounsweet
282 Braviary
119 Bronzong
118 Bronzor
059 Budew
048 Bunnelby
015 Butterfree
162 Carkol
160 Centiskorch
289 Chandelure
380 Charizard
017 Charjabug
378 Charmander
379 Charmeleon
129 Cherrim
128 Cherubi
042 Chewtle
220 Chinchou
051 Cinccino
006 Cinderace
083 Claydol
256 Clefable
255 Clefairy
254 Cleffa
351 Clobbopus
151 Cloyster
163 Coalossal
329 Cofagrigus
173 Conkeldurr
303 Copperajah
102 Corphish
236 Corsola
023 Corviknight
022 Corvisquire
262 Cottonee
309 Cramorant
103 Crawdaunt
222 Croagunk
087 Crustle
279 Cubchoo
302 Cufant
237 Cursola
187 Cutiefly
368 Darmanitan
367 Darumaka
386 Deino
078 Delibird
214 Dewpider
360 Dhelmise
049 Diggersby
164 Diglett
011 Dottler
331 Doublade
376 Dracovish
374 Dracozolt
397 Dragapult
396 Drakloak

346 Drampa
286 Drapion
043 Drednaw
395 Dreepy
125 Drifblim
124 Drifloon
166 Drilbur
008 Drizzile
035 Dubwool
165 Dugtrio
271 Duosion
371 Duraludon
316 Durant
136 Dusclops
137 Dusknoir
135 Duskull
086 Dwebble
196 Eevee
370 Eiscue
127 Eldegoss
066 Electrike
277 Elgyem
274 Escavalier
200 Espeon
208 Espurr
400 Eternatus
167 Excadrill
345 Falinks
218 Farfetch'd
152 Feebas
189 Ferroseed
190 Ferrothorn
206 Flapple
199 Flareon
323 Flygon
325 Fraxure
305 Frillish
081 Froslass
350 Frosmoth
123 Gallade
065 Galvantula
158 Garbodor
122 Gardevoir
141 Gastly
231 Gastrodon
143 Gengar
170 Gigalith
203 Glaceon
080 Glalie
056 Gloom
146 Goldeen
088 Golett
233 Golisopod
089 Golurk
391 Goodra
389 Goomy
126 Gossifleur
267 Gothita
269 Gothitelle
268 Gothorita
192 Gourgeist
025 Greedent
240 Grimmsnarl
001 Grookey
070 Growlithe
016 Grubbin
172 Gurdurr
145 Gyarados
393 Hakamo-o
241 Hatenna
243 Hatterene
242 Hattrem

142 Haunter
320 Hawlucha
326 Haxorus
317 Heatmor
319 Heliolisk
318 Helioptile
314 Hippopotas
315 Hippowdon
109 Hitmonchan
108 Hitmonlee
110 Hitmontop
330 Honedge
019 Hoothoot
388 Hydreigon
238 Impidimp
337 Indeedee
290 Inkay
009 Inteleon
392 Jangmo-o
306 Jellicent
198 Jolteon
064 Joltik
273 Karrablast
099 Kingler
121 Kirlia
114 Klang
113 Klink
115 Klinklang
250 Koffing
394 Kommo-o
098 Krabby
288 Lampent
221 Lanturn
361 Lapras
383 Larvitar
202 Leafeon
045 Liepard
032 Linoone
287 Litwick
037 Lombre
036 Lotad
299 Lucario
038 Ludicolo
362 Lunatone
140 Machamp
139 Machoke
138 Machop
291 Malamar
077 Mamoswine
284 Mandibuzz
067 Manectric
355 Mantine
354 Mantyke
296 Maractus
307 Mareanie
295 Mawile
209 Meowstic
182 Meowth
185 Milcery
153 Milotic
364 Mime Jr.
301 Mimikyu
050 Minccino
340 Morelull
239 Morgrem
344 Morpeko
365 Mr. Mime
366 Mr. Rime
084 Mudbray
085 Mudsdale
260 Munchlax
090 Munna
091 Musharna

092 Natu
029 Nickit
104 Nincada
069 Ninetales
105 Ninjask
020 Noctowl
176 Noibat
177 Noivern
040 Nuzleaf
033 Obstagoon
149 Octillery
055 Oddish
178 Onix
342 Oranguru
012 Orbeetle
133 Palpitoad
111 Pancham
112 Pangoro
343 Passimian
246 Pawniard
063 Pelipper
183 Perrserker
184 Persian
338 Phantump
193 Pichu
026 Pidove
194 Pikachu
076 Piloswine
353 Pincurchin
336 Polteageist
333 Ponyta
191 Pumpkaboo
384 Pupitar
044 Purrloin
101 Quagsire
304 Qwilfish
005 Raboot
195 Raichu
120 Ralts
334 Rapidash
148 Remoraid
272 Reuniclus
265 Rhydon
264 Rhyhorn
266 Rhyperior
188 Ribombee
003 Rillaboom
298 Riolu
168 Roggenrola
161 Rolycoly
021 Rookidee
060 Roselia
061 Roserade
372 Rotom
281 Rufflet
328 Runerigus
294 Sableye
244 Salandit
245 Salazzle
313 Sandaconda
249 Sawk
004 Scorbunny
225 Scrafty
224 Scraggy
147 Seaking
039 Seedot
134 Seismitoad
106 Shedinja
150 Shellder
230 Shellos
275 Shelmet
041 Shiftry
341 Shiinotic

227 Shuckle
297 Sigilyph
312 Silicobra
382 Silvally
335 Sinistea
219 Sirfetch'd
159 Sizzlipede
285 Skorupi
131 Skuntank
024 Skwovet
390 Sliggoo
211 Slurpuff
292 Sneasel
349 Snom
261 Snorlax
079 Snorunt
096 Snover
007 Sobble
270 Solosis
363 Solrock
212 Spritzee
179 Steelix
053 Steenee
369 Stonjourner
094 Stufful
226 Stunfisk
130 Stunky
253 Sudowoodo
075 Swinub
210 Swirlix
175 Swoobat
204 Sylveon
030 Thievul
248 Throh
002 Thwackey
171 Timburr
348 Togedemaru
259 Togekiss
257 Togepi
258 Togetic
300 Torkoal
308 Toxapex
310 Toxel
223 Toxicroak
311 Toxtricity
027 Tranquill
321 Trapinch
339 Trevenant
157 Trubbish
054 Tsareena
347 Turtonator
132 Tympole
381 Type: Null
385 Tyranitar
107 Tyrogue
201 Umbreon
028 Unfezant
073 Vanillish
072 Vanillite
074 Vanilluxe
197 Vaporeon
117 Vespiquen
322 Vibrava
018 Vikavolt
057 Vileplume
283 Vullaby
068 Vulpix
356 Wailmer
357 Wailord
293 Weavile
251 Weezing
263 Whimsicott
229 Whiscash

232 Wimpod
062 Wingull
155 Wishiwashi
174 Woobat
034 Wooloo
100 Wooper
093 Xatu
327 Yamask
046 Yamper
398 Zacian
399 Zamazenta
031 Zigzagoon
387 Zweilous

Sacred Sword
332 Aegislash
331 Doublade
330 Honedge
398 Zacian

Safeguard (TM19)
097 Abomasnow
186 Alcremie
207 Appletun
215 Araquanid
071 Arcanine
359 Avalugg
082 Baltoy
235 Barbaracle
278 Beheeyem
058 Bellossom
358 Bergmite
234 Binacle
052 Bounsweet
119 Bronzong
118 Bronzor
015 Butterfree
289 Chandelure
129 Cherrim
128 Cherubi
051 Cinccino
083 Claydol
256 Clefable
255 Clefairy
254 Cleffa
329 Cofagrigus
236 Corsola
262 Cottonee
237 Cursola
187 Cutiefly
011 Dottler
346 Drampa
008 Drizzile
271 Duosion
277 Elgyem
208 Espurr
305 Frillish
081 Froslass
350 Frosmoth
123 Gallade
122 Gardevoir
080 Glalie
088 Golett
089 Golurk
267 Gothita
269 Gothitelle
268 Gothorita
192 Gourgeist
070 Growlithe
393 Hakamo-o
241 Hatenna
243 Hatterene
242 Hattrem
337 Indeedee
009 Inteleon

392 Jangmo-o
306 Jellicent
121 Kirlia
394 Kommo-o
288 Lampent
361 Lapras
287 Litwick
362 Lunatone
296 Maractus
307 Mareanie
209 Meowstic
153 Milotic
364 Mime Jr.
301 Mimikyu
050 Minccino
340 Morelull
365 Mr. Mime
366 Mr. Rime
090 Munna
091 Musharna
069 Ninetales
342 Oranguru
012 Orbeetle
338 Phantump
191 Pumpkaboo
156 Pyukumuku
101 Quagsire
195 Raichu
120 Ralts
272 Reuniclus
188 Ribombee
328 Runerigus
341 Shiinotic
227 Shuckle
297 Sigilyph
211 Slurpuff
079 Snorunt
096 Snover
007 Sobble
270 Solosis
363 Solrock
053 Steenee
369 Stonjourner
210 Swirlix
175 Swoobat
204 Sylveon
259 Togekiss
257 Togepi
258 Togetic
308 Toxapex
339 Trevenant
054 Tsareena
057 Vileplume
068 Vulpix
263 Whimsicott
217 Wobbuffet
174 Woobat
100 Wooper
216 Wynaut
327 Yamask
399 Zamazenta

Sand Attack
234 Binacle
169 Boldore
087 Crustle
164 Diglett
165 Dugtrio
316 Durant
086 Dwebble
196 Eevee
200 Espeon
218 Farfetch'd
199 Flareon

323 Flygon	
170 Gigalith	
203 Glaceon	
233 Golisopod	
314 Hippopotas	
315 Hippowdon	
198 Jolteon	
202 Leafeon	
045 Liepard	
032 Linoone	
104 Nincada	
105 Ninjask	
033 Obstagoon	
044 Purrloin	
168 Roggenrola	
021 Rookidee	
244 Salandit	
313 Sandaconda	
004 Scorbunny	
225 Scrafty	
224 Scraggy	
106 Shedinja	
312 Silicobra	
219 Sirfetch'd	
285 Skorupi	
204 Sylveon	
321 Trapinch	
157 Trubbish	
201 Umbreon	
197 Vaporeon	
322 Vibrava	
232 Wimpod	
046 Yamper	
031 Zigzagoon	

Sand Tomb (TM49)

082 Baltoy
169 Boldore
252 Bonsly
162 Carkol
083 Claydol
163 Coalossal
087 Crustle
049 Diggersby
286 Drapion
043 Drednaw
166 Drilbur
165 Dugtrio
086 Dwebble
167 Excadrill
323 Flygon
231 Gastrodon
170 Gigalith
314 Hippopotas
315 Hippowdon
383 Larvitar
362 Lunatone
077 Mamoswine
084 Mudbray
085 Mudsdale
178 Onix
076 Piloswine
384 Pupitar
168 Roggenrola
161 Rolycoly
328 Runerigus
313 Sandaconda
227 Shuckle
312 Silicobra
363 Solrock
179 Steelix
369 Stonjourner
253 Sudowoodo
075 Swinub

321 Trapinch
385 Tyranitar
322 Vibrava
229 Whiscash

Sandstorm (TM32)

276 Accelgor
082 Baltoy
235 Barbaracle
228 Barboach
234 Binacle
247 Bisharp
169 Boldore
252 Bonsly
119 Bronzong
118 Bronzor
048 Bunnelby
162 Carkol
083 Claydol
163 Coalossal
236 Corsola
087 Crustle
237 Cursola
049 Diggersby
164 Diglett
043 Drednaw
166 Drilbur
165 Dugtrio
316 Durant
086 Dwebble
167 Excadrill
190 Ferrothorn
323 Flygon
231 Gastrodon
170 Gigalith
145 Gyarados
393 Hakamo-o
319 Heliolisk
318 Helioptile
314 Hippopotas
315 Hippowdon
110 Hitmontop
392 Jangmo-o
114 Klang
113 Klink
115 Klinklang
394 Kommo-o
383 Larvitar
362 Lunatone
077 Mamoswine
295 Mawile
084 Mudbray
085 Mudsdale
260 Munchlax
104 Nincada
105 Ninjask
178 Onix
246 Pawniard
076 Piloswine
384 Pupitar
101 Quagsire
265 Rhydon
264 Rhyhorn
266 Rhyperior
168 Roggenrola
161 Rolycoly
328 Runerigus
313 Sandaconda
106 Shedinja
227 Shuckle
312 Silicobra
382 Silvally
261 Snorlax

363 Solrock
179 Steelix
369 Stonjourner
226 Stunfisk
253 Sudowoodo
075 Swinub
321 Trapinch
381 Type: Null
385 Tyranitar
322 Vibrava
229 Whiscash
100 Wooper
327 Yamask

Scald (TR84)

215 Araquanid
180 Arrokuda
235 Barbaracle
228 Barboach
181 Barraskewda
154 Basculin
234 Binacle
162 Carkol
160 Centiskorch
220 Chinchou
163 Coalossal
236 Corsola
309 Cramorant
103 Crawdaunt
237 Cursola
214 Dewpider
376 Dracovish
397 Dragapult
396 Drakloak
043 Drednaw
152 Feebas
305 Frillish
231 Gastrodon
146 Goldeen
233 Golisopod
145 Gyarados
009 Inteleon
306 Jellicent
099 Kingler
098 Krabby
221 Lanturn
037 Lombre
036 Lotad
038 Ludicolo
355 Mantine
354 Mantyke
307 Mareanie
153 Milotic
149 Octillery
133 Palpitoad
063 Pelipper
353 Pincurchin
101 Quagsire
304 Qwilfish
148 Remoraid
147 Seaking
134 Seismitoad
230 Shellos
159 Sizzlipede
226 Stunfisk
308 Toxapex
132 Tympole
197 Vaporeon
356 Wailmer
357 Wailord
229 Whiscash
232 Wimpod
062 Wingull

155 Wishiwashi
100 Wooper

Scary Face (TM26)

071 Arcanine
324 Axew
181 Barraskewda
154 Basculin
280 Beartic
247 Bisharp
282 Braviary
380 Charizard
378 Charmander
379 Charmeleon
329 Cofagrigus
173 Conkeldurr
303 Copperajah
023 Corviknight
022 Corvisquire
386 Deino
286 Drapion
043 Drednaw
371 Duraludon
274 Escavalier
400 Eternatus
206 Flapple
199 Flareon
325 Fraxure
141 Gastly
143 Gengar
080 Glalie
192 Gourgeist
352 Grapploct
240 Grimmsnarl
172 Gurdurr
145 Gyarados
393 Hakamo-o
142 Haunter
326 Haxorus
388 Hydreigon
392 Jangmo-o
273 Karrablast
394 Kommo-o
383 Larvitar
032 Linoone
299 Lucario
140 Machamp
139 Machoke
138 Machop
291 Malamar
077 Mamoswine
284 Mandibuzz
067 Manectric
344 Morpeko
085 Mudsdale
033 Obstagoon
178 Onix
112 Pangoro
343 Passimian
246 Pawniard
076 Piloswine
191 Pumpkaboo
384 Pupitar
304 Qwilfish
265 Rhydon
264 Rhyhorn
266 Rhyperior
003 Rillaboom
021 Rookidee
281 Rufflet
328 Runerigus
249 Sawk
225 Scrafty

224 Scraggy
382 Silvally
285 Skorupi
131 Skuntank
179 Steelix
130 Stunky
075 Swinub
248 Throh
171 Timburr
311 Toxtricity
381 Type: Null
385 Tyranitar
283 Vullaby
398 Zacian
399 Zamazenta
031 Zigzagoon
387 Zweilous

Scratch

324 Axew
235 Barbaracle
234 Binacle
247 Bisharp
380 Charizard
378 Charmander
379 Charmeleon
164 Diglett
166 Drilbur
165 Dugtrio
208 Espurr
167 Excadrill
325 Fraxure
001 Grookey
326 Haxorus
045 Liepard
209 Meowstic
182 Meowth
301 Mimikyu
104 Nincada
105 Ninjask
246 Pawniard
183 Perrserker
184 Persian
044 Purrloin
003 Rillaboom
294 Sableye
244 Salandit
245 Salazzle
106 Shedinja
131 Skuntank
292 Sneasel
130 Stunky
002 Thwackey
293 Weavile

Screech (TM16)

332 Aegislash
235 Barbaracle
278 Beheeyem
234 Binacle
247 Bisharp
017 Charjabug
220 Chinchou
151 Cloyster
303 Copperajah
236 Corsola
023 Corviknight
222 Croagunk
302 Cufant
237 Cursola
386 Deino
164 Diglett
331 Doublade
286 Drapion
165 Dugtrio

371 Duraludon
316 Durant
277 Elgyem
274 Escavalier
400 Eternatus
345 Falinks
323 Flygon
065 Galvantula
158 Garbodor
233 Golisopod
001 Grookey
016 Grubbin
393 Hakamo-o
330 Honedge
019 Hoothoot
388 Hydreigon
392 Jangmo-o
064 Joltik
273 Karrablast
114 Klang
113 Klink
115 Klinklang
250 Koffing
394 Kommo-o
221 Lanturn
383 Larvitar
045 Liepard
032 Linoone
299 Lucario
296 Maractus
182 Meowth
301 Mimikyu
365 Mr. Mime
366 Mr. Rime
260 Munchlax
029 Nickit
020 Noctowl
176 Noibat
177 Noivern
033 Obstagoon
149 Octillery
178 Onix
133 Palpitoad
246 Pawniard
183 Perrserker
184 Persian
384 Pupitar
044 Purrloin
156 Pyukumuku
148 Remoraid
003 Rillaboom
298 Riolu
313 Sandaconda
134 Seismitoad
150 Shellder
041 Shiftry
312 Silicobra
285 Skorupi
131 Skuntank
292 Sneasel
261 Snorlax
179 Steelix
226 Stunfisk
130 Stunky
030 Thievul
002 Thwackey
223 Toxicroak
311 Toxtricity
132 Tympole
385 Tyranitar
201 Umbreon
117 Vespiquen

322 Vibrava
018 Vikavolt
293 Weavile
251 Weezing
232 Wimpod
031 Zigzagoon
387 Zweilous

Seed Bomb (TR59)

097 Abomasnow
207 Appletun
058 Bellossom
052 Bounsweet
059 Budew
129 Cherrim
128 Cherubi
051 Cinccino
262 Cottonee
078 Delibird
127 Eldegoss
189 Ferroseed
190 Ferrothorn
206 Flapple
158 Garbodor
056 Gloom
192 Gourgeist
025 Greedent
202 Leafeon
045 Liepard
032 Linoone
037 Lombre
036 Lotad
038 Ludicolo
355 Mantine
296 Maractus
182 Meowth
050 Minccino
340 Morelull
344 Morpeko
260 Munchlax
040 Nuzleaf
033 Obstagoon
149 Octillery
055 Oddish
343 Passimian
063 Pelipper
183 Perrserker
184 Persian
338 Phantump
191 Pumpkaboo
044 Purrloin
148 Remoraid
060 Roselia
061 Roserade
039 Seedot
041 Shiftry
341 Shiinotic
024 Skwovet
261 Snorlax
096 Snover
053 Steenee
339 Trevenant
157 Trubbish
054 Tsareena
057 Vileplume
263 Whimsicott
031 Zigzagoon

Seismic Toss

351 Clobbopus
140 Machamp
139 Machoke
138 Machop
295 Mawile

111 Pancham
343 Passimian
248 Throh

Self-Destruct (TM20)

082 Baltoy
252 Bonsly
162 Carkol
083 Claydol
151 Cloyster
163 Coalossal
236 Corsola
237 Cursola
125 Drifblim
124 Drifloon
189 Ferroseed
190 Ferrothorn
158 Garbodor
141 Gastly
143 Gengar
170 Gigalith
080 Glalie
088 Golett
089 Golurk
142 Haunter
250 Koffing
362 Lunatone
260 Munchlax
040 Nuzleaf
178 Onix
353 Pincurchin
336 Polteageist
304 Qwilfish
161 Rolycoly
039 Seedot
150 Shellder
041 Shiftry
382 Silvally
261 Snorlax
363 Solrock
179 Steelix
369 Stonjourner
253 Sudowoodo
300 Torkoal
157 Trubbish
073 Vanillish
072 Vanillite
074 Vanilluxe
356 Wailmer
357 Wailord
251 Weezing

Shadow Ball (TR33)

097 Abomasnow
332 Aegislash
082 Baltoy
278 Beheeyem
119 Bronzong
118 Bronzor
059 Budew
015 Butterfree
289 Chandelure
006 Cinderace
083 Claydol
256 Clefable
255 Clefairy
254 Cleffa
329 Cofagrigus
236 Corsola
222 Croagunk
237 Cursola
360 Dhelmise
011 Dottler

397 Dragapult
396 Drakloak
346 Drampa
286 Drapion
125 Drifblim
124 Drifloon
271 Duosion
136 Dusclops
137 Dusknoir
135 Duskull
196 Eevee
277 Elgyem
200 Espeon
400 Eternatus
199 Flareon
305 Frillish
081 Froslass
123 Gallade
122 Gardevoir
141 Gastly
143 Gengar
203 Glaceon
080 Glalie
088 Golett
089 Golurk
267 Gothita
269 Gothitelle
268 Gothorita
192 Gourgeist
243 Hatterene
142 Haunter
019 Hoothoot
337 Indeedee
009 Inteleon
306 Jellicent
198 Jolteon
121 Kirlia
250 Koffing
288 Lampent
202 Leafeon
045 Liepard
032 Linoone
287 Litwick
299 Lucario
362 Lunatone
284 Mandibuzz
295 Mawile
209 Meowstic
182 Meowth
364 Mime Jr.
301 Mimikyu
365 Mr. Mime
366 Mr. Rime
260 Munchlax
090 Munna
091 Musharna
092 Natu
104 Nincada
069 Ninetales
105 Ninjask
020 Noctowl
176 Noibat
177 Noivern
040 Nuzleaf
033 Obstagoon
342 Oranguru
012 Orbeetle
343 Passimian
183 Perrserker
184 Persian
338 Phantump
336 Polteageist
191 Pumpkaboo

044 Purrloin
304 Qwilfish
120 Ralts
272 Reuniclus
060 Roselia
061 Roserade
372 Rotom
328 Runerigus
294 Sableye
039 Seedot
106 Shedinja
041 Shiftry
297 Sigilyph
382 Silvally
335 Sinistea
285 Skorupi
131 Skuntank
292 Sneasel
261 Snorlax
079 Snorunt
096 Snover
270 Solosis
363 Solrock
130 Stunky
175 Swoobat
204 Sylveon
030 Thievul
259 Togekiss
257 Togepi
258 Togetic
223 Toxicroak
339 Trevenant
201 Umbreon
197 Vaporeon
283 Vullaby
293 Weavile
251 Weezing
263 Whimsicott
174 Woobat
093 Xatu
327 Yamask
031 Zigzagoon

Shadow Claw (TM65)

332 Aegislash
235 Barbaracle
280 Beartic
095 Bewear
234 Binacle
247 Bisharp
282 Braviary
380 Charizard
378 Charmander
379 Charmeleon
329 Cofagrigus
087 Crustle
279 Cubchoo
360 Dhelmise
164 Diglett
331 Doublade
346 Drampa
166 Drilbur
165 Dugtrio
316 Durant
086 Dwebble
167 Excadrill
190 Ferrothorn
325 Fraxure
143 Gengar
233 Golisopod
240 Grimmsnarl
393 Hakamo-o
243 Hatterene

142 Haunter
326 Haxorus
317 Heatmor
330 Honedge
392 Jangmo-o
394 Kommo-o
045 Liepard
032 Linoone
299 Lucario
182 Meowth
301 Mimikyu
239 Morgrem
176 Noibat
177 Noivern
033 Obstagoon
111 Pancham
112 Pangoro
246 Pawniard
183 Perrserker
184 Persian
338 Phantump
044 Purrloin
265 Rhydon
266 Rhyperior
298 Riolu
281 Rufflet
328 Runerigus
294 Sableye
244 Salandit
245 Salazzle
106 Shedinja
382 Silvally
131 Skuntank
292 Sneasel
130 Stunky
030 Thievul
339 Trevenant
381 Type: Null
385 Tyranitar
293 Weavile

Shadow Punch

136 Dusclops
137 Dusknoir
143 Gengar
088 Golett
089 Golurk
142 Haunter

Shadow Sneak

332 Aegislash
331 Doublade
136 Dusclops
137 Dusknoir
135 Duskull
192 Gourgeist
330 Honedge
301 Mimikyu
191 Pumpkaboo
120 Ralts
294 Sableye
106 Shedinja

Sheer Cold

097 Abomasnow
280 Beartic
279 Cubchoo
080 Glalie
361 Lapras
096 Snover
073 Vanillish
072 Vanillite
074 Vanilluxe

Shell Smash

235 Barbaracle
234 Binacle

151 Cloyster
087 Crustle
086 Dwebble
336 Polteageist
150 Shellder
227 Shuckle
335 Sinistea
300 Torkoal
347 Turtonator

Shell Trap

347 Turtonator

Shift Gear

114 Klang
113 Klink
115 Klinklang
311 Toxtricity

Shock Wave

066 Electrike
067 Manectric
372 Rotom
311 Toxtricity

Simple Beam

218 Farfetch'd
092 Natu
175 Swoobat
174 Woobat

Sing

051 Cinccino
256 Clefable
255 Clefairy
254 Cleffa
127 Eldegoss
126 Gossifleur
361 Lapras
050 Minccino

Skill Swap (TR40)

213 Aromatisse
082 Baltoy
278 Beheeyem
119 Bronzong
118 Bronzor
015 Butterfree
083 Claydol
329 Cofagrigus
187 Cutiefly
011 Dottler
125 Drifblim
124 Drifloon
271 Duosion
136 Dusclops
137 Dusknoir
135 Duskull
277 Elgyem
200 Espeon
208 Espurr
123 Gallade
122 Gardevoir
141 Gastly
143 Gengar
267 Gothita
269 Gothitelle
268 Gothorita
192 Gourgeist
241 Hatenna
243 Hatterene
242 Hattrem
142 Haunter
121 Kirlia
362 Lunatone
209 Meowstic
364 Mime Jr.
365 Mr. Mime
366 Mr. Rime

090 Munna
091 Musharna
092 Natu
012 Orbeetle
338 Phantump
191 Pumpkaboo
120 Ralts
272 Reuniclus
188 Ribombee
328 Runerigus
297 Sigilyph
270 Solosis
363 Solrock
212 Spritzee
175 Swoobat
204 Sylveon
339 Trevenant
174 Woobat
093 Xatu
327 Yamask

Skull Bash

359 Avalugg
235 Barbaracle
042 Chewtle
264 Rhyhorn
313 Sandaconda
096 Snover
300 Torkoal

Sky Attack

282 Braviary
218 Farfetch'd
320 Hawlucha
284 Mandibuzz
020 Noctowl
026 Pidove
021 Rookidee
297 Sigilyph
259 Togekiss
027 Tranquill
028 Unfezant

Slack Off

314 Hippopotas
315 Hippowdon
366 Mr. Rime

Slam

375 Arctozolt
160 Centiskorch
051 Cinccino
173 Conkeldurr
302 Cufant
386 Deino
360 Dhelmise
374 Dracozolt
218 Farfetch'd
001 Grookey
172 Gurdurr
388 Hydreigon
099 Kingler
098 Krabby
355 Mantine
354 Mantyke
295 Mawile
050 Minccino
178 Onix
194 Pikachu
101 Quagsire
195 Raichu
003 Rillaboom
328 Runerigus
313 Sandaconda
312 Silicobra
219 Sirfetch'd
159 Sizzlipede

179 Steelix
253 Sudowoodo
002 Thwackey
171 Timburr
100 Wooper
327 Yamask
387 Zweilous

Slash

332 Aegislash
180 Arrokuda
324 Axew
235 Barbaracle
280 Beartic
234 Binacle
247 Bisharp
282 Braviary
380 Charizard
378 Charmander
379 Charmeleon
102 Corphish
087 Crustle
279 Cubchoo
164 Diglett
331 Doublade
166 Drilbur
165 Dugtrio
371 Duraludon
086 Dwebble
325 Fraxure
123 Gallade
065 Galvantula
233 Golisopod
326 Haxorus
317 Heatmor
330 Honedge
290 Inkay
064 Joltik
273 Karrablast
098 Krabby
291 Malamar
182 Meowth
301 Mimikyu
105 Ninjask
111 Pancham
112 Pangoro
246 Pawniard
183 Perrserker
184 Persian
044 Purrloin
281 Rufflet
285 Skorupi
292 Sneasel
130 Stunky
117 Vespiquen
293 Weavile
398 Zacian
399 Zamazenta

Sleep Powder

058 Bellossom
059 Budew
015 Butterfree
056 Gloom
126 Gossifleur
340 Morelull
055 Oddish
060 Roselia
341 Shiinotic
057 Vileplume

Sleep Talk (TR27)

097 Abomasnow
276 Accelgor
332 Aegislash

186 Alcremie
207 Appletun
215 Araquanid
071 Arcanine
377 Arctovish
375 Arctozolt
213 Aromatisse
180 Arrokuda
359 Avalugg
324 Axew
082 Baltoy
235 Barbaracle
228 Barboach
181 Barraskewda
154 Basculin
280 Beartic
278 Beheeyem
058 Bellossom
358 Bergmite
095 Bewear
234 Binacle
247 Bisharp
169 Boldore
047 Boltund
252 Bonsly
052 Bounsweet
282 Braviary
119 Bronzong
118 Bronzor
059 Budew
048 Bunnelby
015 Butterfree
162 Carkol
160 Centiskorch
289 Chandelure
380 Charizard
017 Charjabug
378 Charmander
379 Charmeleon
129 Cherrim
128 Cherubi
042 Chewtle
220 Chinchou
051 Cinccino
006 Cinderace
083 Claydol
256 Clefable
255 Clefairy
254 Cleffa
351 Clobbopus
151 Cloyster
163 Coalossal
329 Cofagrigus
173 Conkeldurr
303 Copperajah
102 Corphish
236 Corsola
023 Corviknight
022 Corvisquire
262 Cottonee
309 Cramorant
103 Crawdaunt
222 Croagunk
087 Crustle
279 Cubchoo
302 Cufant
237 Cursola
187 Cutiefly
368 Darmanitan
367 Darumaka
386 Deino
078 Delibird
214 Dewpider

360 Dhelmise
049 Diggersby
164 Diglett
011 Dottler
331 Doublade
376 Dracovish
374 Dracozolt
397 Dragapult
396 Drakloak
346 Drampa
286 Drapion
043 Drednaw
395 Dreepy
125 Drifblim
124 Drifloon
166 Drilbur
008 Drizzile
035 Dubwool
165 Dugtrio
271 Duosion
371 Duraludon
316 Durant
136 Dusclops
137 Dusknoir
135 Duskull
086 Dwebble
196 Eevee
370 Eiscue
127 Eldegoss
066 Electrike
277 Elgyem
274 Escavalier
200 Espeon
208 Espurr
400 Eternatus
167 Excadrill
345 Falinks
218 Farfetch'd
152 Feebas
189 Ferroseed
190 Ferrothorn
206 Flapple
199 Flareon
323 Flygon
325 Fraxure
305 Frillish
081 Froslass
350 Frosmoth
123 Gallade
065 Galvantula
158 Garbodor
122 Gardevoir
141 Gastly
231 Gastrodon
143 Gengar
170 Gigalith
203 Glaceon
080 Glalie
056 Gloom
146 Goldeen
088 Golett
233 Golisopod
089 Golurk
391 Goodra
389 Goomy
126 Gossifleur
267 Gothita
269 Gothitelle
268 Gothorita
192 Gourgeist
352 Grapploct
025 Greedent
240 Grimmsnarl

001 Grookey
070 Growlithe
016 Grubbin
172 Gurdurr
145 Gyarados
393 Hakamo-o
241 Hatenna
243 Hatterene
242 Hattrem
142 Haunter
320 Hawlucha
326 Haxorus
317 Heatmor
319 Heliolisk
318 Helioptile
314 Hippopotas
315 Hippowdon
109 Hitmonchan
108 Hitmonlee
110 Hitmontop
330 Honedge
019 Hoothoot
388 Hydreigon
238 Impidimp
337 Indeedee
290 Inkay
009 Inteleon
392 Jangmo-o
306 Jellicent
198 Jolteon
064 Joltik
273 Karrablast
099 Kingler
121 Kirlia
114 Klang
113 Klink
115 Klinklang
250 Koffing
394 Kommo-o
098 Krabby
288 Lampent
221 Lanturn
361 Lapras
383 Larvitar
202 Leafeon
045 Liepard
032 Linoone
287 Litwick
037 Lombre
036 Lotad
299 Lucario
038 Ludicolo
362 Lunatone
140 Machamp
139 Machoke
138 Machop
291 Malamar
077 Mamoswine
284 Mandibuzz
067 Manectric
355 Mantine
354 Mantyke
296 Maractus
307 Mareanie
295 Mawile
209 Meowstic
182 Meowth
185 Milcery
153 Milotic
364 Mime Jr.
301 Mimikyu
050 Minccino
340 Morelull

239 Morgrem
344 Morpeko
365 Mr. Mime
366 Mr. Rime
084 Mudbray
085 Mudsdale
260 Munchlax
090 Munna
091 Musharna
092 Natu
029 Nickit
104 Nincada
069 Ninetales
105 Ninjask
020 Noctowl
176 Noibat
177 Noivern
040 Nuzleaf
033 Obstagoon
149 Octillery
055 Oddish
178 Onix
342 Oranguru
012 Orbeetle
133 Palpitoad
111 Pancham
112 Pangoro
343 Passimian
246 Pawniard
063 Pelipper
183 Perrserker
184 Persian
338 Phantump
193 Pichu
026 Pidove
194 Pikachu
076 Piloswine
353 Pincurchin
336 Polteageist
333 Ponyta
191 Pumpkaboo
384 Pupitar
044 Purrloin
156 Pyukumuku
101 Quagsire
304 Qwilfish
005 Raboot
195 Raichu
120 Ralts
334 Rapidash
148 Remoraid
272 Reuniclus
265 Rhydon
264 Rhyhorn
266 Rhyperior
188 Ribombee
003 Rillaboom
298 Riolu
168 Roggenrola
161 Rolycoly
021 Rookidee
060 Roselia
061 Roserade
372 Rotom
281 Rufflet
328 Runerigus
294 Sableye
244 Salandit
245 Salazzle
313 Sandaconda
249 Sawk
004 Scorbunny
225 Scrafty

224 Scraggy
147 Seaking
039 Seedot
134 Seismitoad
106 Shedinja
150 Shellder
230 Shellos
275 Shelmet
041 Shiftry
341 Shiinotic
227 Shuckle
297 Sigilyph
312 Silicobra
382 Silvally
335 Sinistea
219 Sirfetch'd
159 Sizzlipede
285 Skorupi
131 Skuntank
024 Skwovet
390 Sliggoo
211 Slurpuff
292 Sneasel
349 Snom
261 Snorlax
079 Snorunt
096 Snover
007 Sobble
270 Solosis
363 Solrock
212 Spritzee
179 Steelix
053 Steenee
369 Stonjourner
094 Stufful
226 Stunfisk
130 Stunky
253 Sudowoodo
075 Swinub
210 Swirlix
175 Swoobat
204 Sylveon
030 Thievul
248 Throh
002 Thwackey
171 Timburr
348 Togedemaru
259 Togekiss
257 Togepi
258 Togetic
300 Torkoal
308 Toxapex
310 Toxel
223 Toxicroak
311 Toxtricity
027 Tranquill
321 Trapinch
339 Trevenant
157 Trubbish
054 Tsareena
347 Turtonator
132 Tympole
381 Type: Null
385 Tyranitar
107 Tyrogue
201 Umbreon
028 Unfezant
073 Vanillish
072 Vanillite
074 Vanilluxe
197 Vaporeon
117 Vespiquen
322 Vibrava

018 Vikavolt
057 Vileplume
283 Vullaby
068 Vulpix
356 Wailmer
357 Wailord
293 Weavile
251 Weezing
263 Whimsicott
229 Whiscash
232 Wimpod
062 Wingull
155 Wishiwashi
174 Woobat
034 Wooloo
100 Wooper
093 Xatu
327 Yamask
046 Yamper
398 Zacian
399 Zamazenta
031 Zigzagoon
387 Zweilous

Sludge

158 Garbodor
250 Koffing
230 Shellos
157 Trubbish
251 Weezing

Sludge Bomb (TR22)

276 Accelgor
235 Barbaracle
058 Bellossom
234 Binacle
059 Budew
048 Bunnelby
102 Corphish
103 Crawdaunt
222 Croagunk
049 Diggersby
164 Diglett
286 Drapion
166 Drilbur
165 Dugtrio
400 Eternatus
167 Excadrill
305 Frillish
158 Garbodor
141 Gastly
231 Gastrodon
143 Gengar
056 Gloom
233 Golisopod
391 Goodra
389 Goomy
192 Gourgeist
142 Haunter
306 Jellicent
250 Koffing
307 Mareanie
295 Mawile
340 Morelull
149 Octillery
055 Oddish
133 Palpitoad
111 Pancham
112 Pangoro
191 Pumpkaboo
101 Quagsire
304 Qwilfish
060 Roselia
061 Roserade

244 Salandit
245 Salazzle
225 Scrafty
224 Scraggy
134 Seismitoad
275 Shelmet
341 Shiinotic
227 Shuckle
285 Skorupi
131 Skuntank
390 Sliggoo
226 Stunfisk
130 Stunky
300 Torkoal
308 Toxapex
223 Toxicroak
311 Toxtricity
157 Trubbish
132 Tympole
117 Vespiquen
057 Vileplume
251 Weezing
100 Wooper

Sludge Wave (TR78)

235 Barbaracle
234 Binacle
103 Crawdaunt
222 Croagunk
360 Dhelmise
165 Dugtrio
400 Eternatus
305 Frillish
158 Garbodor
141 Gastly
231 Gastrodon
143 Gengar
233 Golisopod
391 Goodra
389 Goomy
142 Haunter
306 Jellicent
250 Koffing
307 Mareanie
149 Octillery
133 Palpitoad
101 Quagsire
304 Qwilfish
244 Salandit
245 Salazzle
134 Seismitoad
227 Shuckle
390 Sliggoo
226 Stunfisk
308 Toxapex
223 Toxicroak
311 Toxtricity
157 Trubbish
132 Tympole
057 Vileplume
251 Weezing
100 Wooper

Smack Down

169 Boldore
162 Carkol
163 Coalossal
087 Crustle
086 Dwebble
170 Gigalith
084 Mudbray
178 Onix
265 Rhydon
264 Rhyhorn

266 Rhyperior
168 Roggenrola
161 Rolycoly
179 Steelix

Smart Strike (TM96)

151 Cloyster
043 Drednaw
274 Escavalier
167 Excadrill
345 Falinks
146 Goldeen
361 Lapras
334 Rapidash
265 Rhydon
264 Rhyhorn
266 Rhyperior
147 Seaking
259 Togekiss
258 Togetic

Smog

289 Chandelure
199 Flareon
141 Gastly
250 Koffing
288 Lampent
287 Litwick
244 Salandit
245 Salazzle
130 Stunky
300 Torkoal
347 Turtonator
251 Weezing

Smokescreen

162 Carkol
160 Centiskorch
380 Charizard
378 Charmander
379 Charmeleon
163 Coalossal
250 Koffing
161 Rolycoly
159 Sizzlipede
131 Skuntank
130 Stunky
300 Torkoal
251 Weezing

Snap Trap

226 Stunfisk

Snarl (TM85)

071 Arcanine
247 Bisharp
047 Boltund
006 Cinderace
303 Copperajah
103 Crawdaunt
346 Drampa
286 Drapion
371 Duraludon
066 Electrike
233 Golisopod
070 Growlithe
326 Haxorus
388 Hydreigon
383 Larvitar
045 Liepard
032 Linoone
284 Mandibuzz
067 Manectric
344 Morpeko
029 Nickit
040 Nuzleaf
033 Obstagoon
112 Pangoro
246 Pawniard
384 Pupitar
044 Purrloin
003 Rillaboom
294 Sableye
225 Scrafty
224 Scraggy
041 Shiftry
382 Silvally
131 Skuntank
292 Sneasel
130 Stunky
030 Thievul
311 Toxtricity
385 Tyranitar
201 Umbreon
283 Vullaby
293 Weavile
046 Yamper
398 Zacian
399 Zamazenta
031 Zigzagoon

Snipe Shot

009 Inteleon

Snore (TM24)

097 Abomasnow
276 Accelgor
332 Aegislash
186 Alcremie
207 Appletun
215 Araquanid
071 Arcanine
377 Arctovish
375 Arctozolt
213 Aromatisse
180 Arrokuda
359 Avalugg
324 Axew
082 Baltoy
235 Barbaracle
228 Barboach
181 Barraskewda
154 Basculin
280 Beartic
278 Beheeyem
058 Bellossom
358 Bergmite
095 Bewear
234 Binacle
247 Bisharp
169 Boldore
047 Boltund
252 Bonsly
052 Bounsweet
282 Braviary
119 Bronzong
118 Bronzor
059 Budew
048 Bunnelby
015 Butterfree
162 Carkol
160 Centiskorch
289 Chandelure
380 Charizard
017 Charjabug
378 Charmander
379 Charmeleon
129 Cherrim
128 Cherubi
042 Chewtle
220 Chinchou
051 Cinccino
006 Cinderace
083 Claydol
256 Clefable
255 Clefairy
254 Cleffa
351 Clobbopus
151 Cloyster
163 Coalossal
329 Cofagrigus
116 Combee
173 Conkeldurr
303 Copperajah
102 Corphish
236 Corsola
023 Corviknight
022 Corvisquire
262 Cottonee
309 Cramorant
103 Crawdaunt
222 Croagunk
087 Crustle
279 Cubchoo
302 Cufant
237 Cursola
187 Cutiefly
368 Darmanitan
367 Darumaka
386 Deino
078 Delibird
360 Dhelmise
049 Diggersby
164 Diglett
011 Dottler
331 Doublade
376 Dracovish
374 Dracozolt
397 Dragapult
396 Drakloak
346 Drampa
286 Drapion
043 Drednaw
395 Dreepy
125 Drifblim
124 Drifloon
166 Drilbur
008 Drizzile
035 Dubwool
165 Dugtrio
271 Duosion
371 Duraludon
316 Durant
136 Dusclops
137 Dusknoir
135 Duskull
086 Dwebble
196 Eevee
370 Eiscue
127 Eldegoss
066 Electrike
277 Elgyem
274 Escavalier
200 Espeon
208 Espurr
400 Eternatus
167 Excadrill
345 Falinks
218 Farfetch'd
152 Feebas
189 Ferroseed
190 Ferrothorn
206 Flapple
199 Flareon
323 Flygon
325 Fraxure
305 Frillish
081 Froslass
350 Frosmoth
123 Gallade
065 Galvantula
158 Garbodor
122 Gardevoir
141 Gastly
231 Gastrodon
143 Gengar
170 Gigalith
203 Glaceon
080 Glalie
056 Gloom
146 Goldeen
088 Golett
233 Golisopod
089 Golurk
391 Goodra
389 Goomy
126 Gossifleur
267 Gothita
269 Gothitelle
268 Gothorita
192 Gourgeist
352 Grapploct
025 Greedent
240 Grimmsnarl
001 Grookey
070 Growlithe
016 Grubbin
172 Gurdurr
145 Gyarados
393 Hakamo-o
241 Hatenna
243 Hatterene
242 Hattrem
142 Haunter
320 Hawlucha
326 Haxorus
317 Heatmor
319 Heliolisk
318 Helioptile
314 Hippopotas
315 Hippowdon
109 Hitmonchan
108 Hitmonlee
110 Hitmontop
330 Honedge
019 Hoothoot
388 Hydreigon
238 Impidimp
337 Indeedee
290 Inkay
009 Inteleon
392 Jangmo-o
306 Jellicent
198 Jolteon
064 Joltik
273 Karrablast
099 Kingler
121 Kirlia
114 Klang
113 Klink
115 Klinklang
250 Koffing
394 Kommo-o
098 Krabby
288 Lampent
221 Lanturn
361 Lapras
383 Larvitar
202 Leafeon
045 Liepard
032 Linoone
287 Litwick
037 Lombre
036 Lotad
299 Lucario
038 Ludicolo
362 Lunatone
140 Machamp
139 Machoke
138 Machop
291 Malamar
077 Mamoswine
284 Mandibuzz
067 Manectric
355 Mantine
354 Mantyke
296 Maractus
307 Mareanie
295 Mawile
209 Meowstic
182 Meowth
185 Milcery
153 Milotic
364 Mime Jr.
301 Mimikyu
050 Minccino
340 Morelull
239 Morgrem
344 Morpeko
365 Mr. Mime
366 Mr. Rime
084 Mudbray
085 Mudsdale
260 Munchlax
090 Munna
091 Musharna
092 Natu
029 Nickit
104 Nincada
069 Ninetales
105 Ninjask
020 Noctowl
176 Noibat
177 Noivern
040 Nuzleaf
033 Obstagoon
149 Octillery
055 Oddish
178 Onix
342 Oranguru
012 Orbeetle
133 Palpitoad
111 Pancham
112 Pangoro
343 Passimian
246 Pawniard
063 Pelipper
183 Perrserker
184 Persian
338 Phantump
193 Pichu
026 Pidove
194 Pikachu
076 Piloswine
353 Pincurchin
336 Polteageist
333 Ponyta
191 Pumpkaboo
384 Pupitar
044 Purrloin
101 Quagsire
304 Qwilfish
005 Raboot
195 Raichu
120 Ralts
334 Rapidash
148 Remoraid
272 Reuniclus
265 Rhydon
264 Rhyhorn
266 Rhyperior
188 Ribombee
003 Rillaboom
298 Riolu
168 Roggenrola
161 Rolycoly
021 Rookidee
060 Roselia
061 Roserade
372 Rotom
281 Rufflet
328 Runerigus
294 Sableye
244 Salandit
245 Salazzle
313 Sandaconda
249 Sawk
004 Scorbunny
225 Scrafty
224 Scraggy
147 Seaking
039 Seedot
134 Seismitoad
106 Shedinja
150 Shellder
230 Shellos
275 Shelmet
041 Shiftry
341 Shiinotic
227 Shuckle
297 Sigilyph
312 Silicobra
382 Silvally
335 Sinistea
219 Sirfetch'd
159 Sizzlipede
285 Skorupi
131 Skuntank
024 Skwovet
390 Sliggoo
211 Slurpuff
292 Sneasel
349 Snom
261 Snorlax
079 Snorunt
096 Snover
007 Sobble
270 Solosis
363 Solrock
212 Spritzee
179 Steelix
053 Steenee
369 Stonjourner
094 Stufful
226 Stunfisk
130 Stunky
253 Sudowoodo
075 Swinub
210 Swirlix
175 Swoobat
204 Sylveon
030 Thievul
248 Throh
002 Thwackey
171 Timburr
348 Togedemaru
259 Togekiss
257 Togepi
258 Togetic
300 Torkoal
308 Toxapex
310 Toxel
223 Toxicroak
311 Toxtricity
027 Tranquill
321 Trapinch
339 Trevenant
157 Trubbish
054 Tsareena
347 Turtonator
132 Tympole
381 Type: Null
385 Tyranitar
107 Tyrogue
201 Umbreon
028 Unfezant
073 Vanillish
072 Vanillite
074 Vanilluxe
197 Vaporeon
117 Vespiquen
322 Vibrava
018 Vikavolt
057 Vileplume
283 Vullaby
068 Vulpix
356 Wailmer
357 Wailord
293 Weavile
251 Weezing
263 Whimsicott
229 Whiscash
232 Wimpod
062 Wingull
155 Wishiwashi
174 Woobat
034 Wooloo
100 Wooper
093 Xatu
327 Yamask
046 Yamper
398 Zacian
399 Zamazenta
031 Zigzagoon
387 Zweilous

Soak

215 Araquanid
154 Basculin
220 Chinchou
351 Clobbopus
214 Dewpider
008 Drizzile
370 Eiscue
146 Goldeen
009 Inteleon
149 Octillery
063 Pelipper
156 Pyukumuku
148 Remoraid
147 Seaking
007 Sobble
356 Wailmer
357 Wailord
062 Wingull
155 Wishiwashi

Solar Beam (TM11)
097 Abomasnow
186 Alcremie
207 Appletun
071 Arcanine
082 Baltoy
058 Bellossom
052 Bounsweet
119 Bronzong
118 Bronzor
059 Budew
015 Butterfree
160 Centiskorch
289 Chandelure
380 Charizard
129 Cherrim
128 Cherubi
083 Claydol
256 Clefable
255 Clefairy
254 Cleffa
163 Coalossal
262 Cottonee
087 Crustle
368 Darmanitan
367 Darumaka
360 Dhelmise
011 Dottler
397 Dragapult
346 Drampa
371 Duraludon
086 Dwebble
127 Eldegoss
400 Eternatus
189 Ferroseed
190 Ferrothorn
206 Flapple
323 Flygon
158 Garbodor
170 Gigalith
056 Gloom
089 Golurk
126 Gossifleur
192 Gourgeist
001 Grookey
317 Heatmor
319 Heliolisk
288 Lampent
202 Leafeon
287 Litwick
037 Lombre
036 Lotad
038 Ludicolo
296 Maractus
295 Mawile
364 Mime Jr.
340 Morelull
365 Mr. Mime
366 Mr. Rime
260 Munchlax
092 Natu
104 Nincada
069 Ninetales
105 Ninjask
176 Noibat
177 Noivern
040 Nuzleaf
055 Oddish
012 Orbeetle
338 Phantump
191 Pumpkaboo
188 Ribombee

003 Rillaboom
060 Roselia
061 Roserade
039 Seedot
106 Shedinja
041 Shiftry
341 Shiinotic
297 Sigilyph
261 Snorlax
096 Snover
363 Solrock
053 Steenee
002 Thwackey
259 Togekiss
257 Togepi
258 Togetic
300 Torkoal
321 Trapinch
339 Trevenant
054 Tsareena
347 Turtonator
322 Vibrava
018 Vikavolt
057 Vileplume
263 Whimsicott
093 Xatu
399 Zamazenta

Solar Blade (TM12)
332 Aegislash
129 Cherrim
087 Crustle
360 Dhelmise
331 Doublade
218 Farfetch'd
123 Gallade
001 Grookey
330 Honedge
202 Leafeon
040 Nuzleaf
003 Rillaboom
041 Shiftry
219 Sirfetch'd
002 Thwackey
054 Tsareena
398 Zacian

Spark
228 Barboach
047 Boltund
017 Charjabug
220 Chinchou
066 Electrike
016 Grubbin
221 Lanturn
344 Morpeko
194 Pikachu
353 Pincurchin
195 Raichu
348 Togedemaru
311 Toxtricity
018 Vikavolt
046 Yamper

Sparkling Aria
361 Lapras

Speed Swap (TM62)
119 Bronzong
118 Bronzor
187 Cutiefly
065 Galvantula
064 Joltik
195 Raichu
188 Ribombee

297 Sigilyph
175 Swoobat
174 Woobat

Spikes (TR23)
276 Accelgor
059 Budew
048 Bunnelby
162 Carkol
151 Cloyster
163 Coalossal
087 Crustle
078 Delibird
049 Diggersby
086 Dwebble
189 Ferroseed
190 Ferrothorn
081 Froslass
158 Garbodor
080 Glalie
233 Golisopod
296 Maractus
353 Pincurchin
304 Qwilfish
161 Rolycoly
060 Roselia
061 Roserade
275 Shelmet
079 Snorunt
157 Trubbish
232 Wimpod

Spiky Shield
296 Maractus
348 Togedemaru

Spirit Break
240 Grimmsnarl

Spit Up
309 Cramorant
214 Dewpider
125 Drifblim
124 Drifloon
025 Greedent
317 Heatmor
314 Hippopotas
250 Koffing
221 Lanturn
307 Mareanie
295 Mawile
063 Pelipper
304 Qwilfish
230 Shellos
024 Skwovet
100 Wooper

Spite
236 Corsola
237 Cursola
141 Gastly
143 Gengar
233 Golisopod
142 Haunter
250 Koffing
182 Meowth
069 Ninetales
156 Pyukumuku
021 Rookidee
106 Shedinja
292 Sneasel
226 Stunfisk
068 Vulpix

Splash
052 Bounsweet
256 Clefable
255 Clefairy
254 Cleffa

078 Delibird
152 Feebas
145 Gyarados
144 Magikarp
355 Mantine
354 Mantyke
153 Milotic
301 Mimikyu
053 Steenee
054 Tsareena
356 Wailmer
357 Wailord
217 Wobbuffet
216 Wynaut

Spore
340 Morelull
341 Shiinotic

Stealth Rock (TR76)
082 Baltoy
235 Barbaracle
234 Binacle
247 Bisharp
169 Boldore
252 Bonsly
119 Bronzong
118 Bronzor
162 Carkol
083 Claydol
256 Clefable
255 Clefairy
163 Coalossal
303 Copperajah
236 Corsola
087 Crustle
302 Cufant
237 Cursola
164 Diglett
043 Drednaw
166 Drilbur
165 Dugtrio
371 Duraludon
086 Dwebble
167 Excadrill
189 Ferroseed
190 Ferrothorn
170 Gigalith
088 Golett
089 Golurk
314 Hippopotas
315 Hippowdon
394 Kommo-o
383 Larvitar
362 Lunatone
077 Mamoswine
295 Mawile
084 Mudbray
085 Mudsdale
178 Onix
133 Palpitoad
246 Pawniard
076 Piloswine
384 Pupitar
265 Rhydon
264 Rhyhorn
266 Rhyperior
168 Roggenrola
161 Rolycoly
328 Runerigus
313 Sandaconda
134 Seismitoad
227 Shuckle
363 Solrock

179 Steelix
369 Stonjourner
226 Stunfisk
253 Sudowoodo
075 Swinub
300 Torkoal
385 Tyranitar

Steel Beam
332 Aegislash
247 Bisharp
119 Bronzong
118 Bronzor
303 Copperajah
023 Corviknight
302 Cufant
331 Doublade
371 Duraludon
316 Durant
274 Escavalier
167 Excadrill
189 Ferroseed
190 Ferrothorn
330 Honedge
114 Klang
113 Klink
115 Klinklang
299 Lucario
295 Mawile
182 Meowth
246 Pawniard
183 Perrserker
382 Silvally
179 Steelix
226 Stunfisk
348 Togedemaru
398 Zacian
399 Zamazenta

Steel Wing (TM30)
278 Beheeyem
282 Braviary
380 Charizard
023 Corviknight
309 Cramorant
078 Delibird
397 Dragapult
396 Drakloak
346 Drampa
277 Elgyem
218 Farfetch'd
323 Flygon
320 Hawlucha
019 Hoothoot
388 Hydreigon
284 Mandibuzz
092 Natu
020 Noctowl
176 Noibat
177 Noivern
063 Pelipper
026 Pidove
281 Rufflet
297 Sigilyph
382 Silvally
219 Sirfetch'd
175 Swoobat
259 Togekiss
258 Togetic
027 Tranquill
028 Unfezant
322 Vibrava
283 Vullaby
062 Wingull

174 Woobat
093 Xatu

Sticky Web
010 Blipbug
017 Charjabug
187 Cutiefly
214 Dewpider
065 Galvantula
016 Grubbin
227 Shuckle
211 Slurpuff
210 Swirlix
018 Vikavolt

Stockpile
309 Cramorant
214 Dewpider
125 Drifblim
124 Drifloon
158 Garbodor
025 Greedent
317 Heatmor
314 Hippopotas
250 Koffing
221 Lanturn
307 Mareanie
295 Mawile
260 Munchlax
063 Pelipper
304 Qwilfish
230 Shellos
024 Skwovet
261 Snorlax
157 Trubbish
100 Wooper

Stomp
207 Appletun
303 Copperajah
302 Cufant
376 Dracovish
374 Dracozolt
099 Kingler
098 Krabby
383 Larvitar
084 Mudbray
085 Mudsdale
333 Ponyta
334 Rapidash
265 Rhydon
264 Rhyhorn
266 Rhyperior
096 Snover
053 Steenee
369 Stonjourner
094 Stufful
054 Tsareena
034 Wooloo

Stomping Tantrum (TM98)
097 Abomasnow
375 Arctozolt
359 Avalugg
095 Bewear
169 Boldore
252 Bonsly
173 Conkeldurr
303 Copperajah
236 Corsola
087 Crustle
302 Cufant
237 Cursola
049 Diggersby
164 Diglett
376 Dracovish

374 Dracozolt
346 Drampa
286 Drapion
043 Drednaw
165 Dugtrio
371 Duraludon
316 Durant
167 Excadrill
325 Fraxure
158 Garbodor
231 Gastrodon
170 Gigalith
088 Golett
089 Golurk
391 Goodra
352 Grapploct
025 Greedent
240 Grimmsnarl
326 Haxorus
317 Heatmor
314 Hippopotas
315 Hippowdon
108 Hitmonlee
099 Kingler
394 Kommo-o
383 Larvitar
032 Linoone
362 Lunatone
140 Machamp
139 Machoke
077 Mamoswine
344 Morpeko
365 Mr. Mime
366 Mr. Rime
084 Mudbray
085 Mudsdale
260 Munchlax
033 Obstagoon
178 Onix
112 Pangoro
076 Piloswine
384 Pupitar
101 Quagsire
265 Rhydon
264 Rhyhorn
266 Rhyperior
003 Rillaboom
134 Seismitoad
261 Snorlax
363 Solrock
179 Steelix
369 Stonjourner
094 Stufful
226 Stunfisk
253 Sudowoodo
248 Throh
300 Torkoal
347 Turtonator
385 Tyranitar
229 Whiscash
100 Wooper

Stone Edge (TR75)
377 Arctovish
375 Arctozolt
359 Avalugg
235 Barbaracle
280 Beartic
358 Bergmite
234 Binacle
247 Bisharp
169 Boldore
048 Bunnelby

162 Carkol	011 Dottler	237 Cursola	359 Avalugg	396 Drakloak	242 Hattrem	091 Musharna
083 Claydol	271 Duosion	125 Drifblim	324 Axew	346 Drampa	142 Haunter	092 Natu
163 Coalossal	196 Eevee	305 Frillish	082 Baltoy	286 Drapion	320 Hawlucha	029 Nickit
173 Conkeldurr	277 Elgyem	340 Morelull	235 Barbaracle	043 Drednaw	326 Haxorus	104 Nincada
303 Copperajah	200 Espeon	055 Oddish	228 Barboach	395 Dreepy	317 Heatmor	069 Ninetales
236 Corsola	199 Flareon	336 Polteageist	181 Barraskewda	125 Drifblim	319 Heliolisk	105 Ninjask
087 Crustle	123 Gallade	341 Shiinotic	154 Basculin	124 Drifloon	318 Helioptile	020 Noctowl
237 Cursola	122 Gardevoir	**String Shot**	280 Beartic	166 Drilbur	314 Hippopotas	176 Noibat
368 Darmanitan	203 Glaceon	015 Butterfree	278 Beheeyem	008 Drizzile	315 Hippowdon	177 Noivern
049 Diggersby	267 Gothita	013 Caterpie	058 Bellossom	035 Dubwool	109 Hitmonchan	040 Nuzleaf
376 Dracovish	269 Gothitelle	017 Charjabug	358 Bergmite	165 Dugtrio	108 Hitmonlee	033 Obstagoon
374 Dracozolt	268 Gothorita	065 Galvantula	095 Bewear	271 Duosion	110 Hitmontop	149 Octillery
043 Drednaw	241 Hatenna	016 Grubbin	234 Binacle	371 Duraludon	330 Honedge	055 Oddish
165 Dugtrio	243 Hatterene	064 Joltik	247 Bisharp	316 Durant	019 Hoothoot	178 Onix
371 Duraludon	242 Hattrem	211 Slurpuff	169 Boldore	136 Dusclops	388 Hydreigon	342 Oranguru
316 Durant	019 Hoothoot	210 Swirlix	047 Boltund	137 Dusknoir	238 Impidimp	012 Orbeetle
086 Dwebble	337 Indeedee	018 Vikavolt	252 Bonsly	135 Duskull	337 Indeedee	133 Palpitoad
323 Flygon	290 Inkay	**Struggle Bug**	052 Bounsweet	086 Dwebble	290 Inkay	111 Pancham
123 Gallade	198 Jolteon	276 Accelgor	282 Braviary	196 Eevee	009 Inteleon	112 Pangoro
231 Gastrodon	121 Kirlia	010 Blipbug	119 Bronzong	370 Eiscue	392 Jangmo-o	343 Passimian
170 Gigalith	202 Leafeon	116 Combee	118 Bronzor	127 Eldegoss	306 Jellicent	246 Pawniard
089 Golurk	362 Lunatone	187 Cutiefly	059 Budew	066 Electrike	198 Jolteon	063 Pelipper
172 Gurdurr	291 Malamar	011 Dottler	048 Bunnelby	277 Elgyem	064 Joltik	183 Perrserker
145 Gyarados	209 Meowstic	316 Durant	015 Butterfree	274 Escavalier	273 Karrablast	184 Persian
320 Hawlucha	185 Milcery	350 Frosmoth	162 Carkol	200 Espeon	099 Kingler	338 Phantump
315 Hippowdon	364 Mime Jr.	233 Golisopod	160 Centiskorch	208 Espurr	121 Kirlia	193 Pichu
109 Hitmonchan	365 Mr. Mime	064 Joltik	289 Chandelure	400 Eternatus	114 Klang	026 Pidove
108 Hitmonlee	366 Mr. Rime	012 Orbeetle	380 Charizard	167 Excadrill	113 Klink	194 Pikachu
110 Hitmontop	090 Munna	188 Ribombee	017 Charjabug	345 Falinks	115 Klinklang	076 Piloswine
388 Hydreigon	091 Musharna	275 Shelmet	378 Charmander	218 Farfetch'd	250 Koffing	353 Pincurchin
383 Larvitar	092 Natu	227 Shuckle	379 Charmeleon	152 Feebas	394 Kommo-o	336 Polteageist
299 Lucario	069 Ninetales	159 Sizzlipede	129 Cherrim	189 Ferroseed	098 Krabby	333 Ponyta
362 Lunatone	020 Noctowl	349 Snom	128 Cherubi	190 Ferrothorn	288 Lampent	191 Pumpkaboo
140 Machamp	342 Oranguru	117 Vespiquen	042 Chewtle	206 Flapple	221 Lanturn	384 Pupitar
077 Mamoswine	012 Orbeetle	232 Wimpod	220 Chinchou	199 Flareon	361 Lapras	044 Purrloin
295 Mawile	336 Polteageist	**Stuff Cheeks**	051 Cinccino	323 Flygon	383 Larvitar	156 Pyukumuku
178 Onix	333 Ponyta	025 Greedent	006 Cinderace	325 Fraxure	202 Leafeon	101 Quagsire
111 Pancham	120 Ralts	024 Skwovet	083 Claydol	305 Frillish	045 Liepard	304 Qwilfish
112 Pangoro	334 Rapidash	**Stun Spore**	256 Clefable	081 Froslass	032 Linoone	005 Raboot
076 Piloswine	272 Reuniclus	058 Bellossom	255 Clefairy	350 Frosmoth	287 Litwick	195 Raichu
384 Pupitar	372 Rotom	059 Budew	254 Cleffa	123 Gallade	037 Lombre	120 Ralts
101 Quagsire	297 Sigilyph	015 Butterfree	351 Clobbopus	065 Galvantula	036 Lotad	334 Rapidash
265 Rhydon	335 Sinistea	262 Cottonee	151 Cloyster	158 Garbodor	299 Lucario	148 Remoraid
264 Rhyhorn	270 Solosis	187 Cutiefly	163 Coalossal	122 Gardevoir	038 Ludicolo	272 Reuniclus
266 Rhyperior	363 Solrock	350 Frosmoth	329 Cofagrigus	141 Gastly	362 Lunatone	265 Rhydon
168 Roggenrola	175 Swoobat	056 Gloom	173 Conkeldurr	231 Gastrodon	140 Machamp	264 Rhyhorn
161 Rolycoly	204 Sylveon	126 Gossifleur	303 Copperajah	143 Gengar	139 Machoke	266 Rhyperior
328 Runerigus	259 Togekiss	340 Morelull	102 Corphish	170 Gigalith	138 Machop	188 Ribombee
313 Sandaconda	257 Togepi	055 Oddish	236 Corsola	203 Glaceon	291 Malamar	003 Rillaboom
249 Sawk	258 Togetic	188 Ribombee	023 Corviknight	080 Glalie	077 Mamoswine	298 Riolu
225 Scrafty	311 Toxtricity	060 Roselia	022 Corvisquire	056 Gloom	284 Mandibuzz	168 Roggenrola
224 Scraggy	201 Umbreon	061 Roserade	262 Cottonee	146 Goldeen	067 Manectric	161 Rolycoly
227 Shuckle	197 Vaporeon	057 Vileplume	309 Cramorant	088 Golett	355 Mantine	021 Rookidee
363 Solrock	174 Woobat	263 Whimsicott	103 Crawdaunt	233 Golisopod	354 Mantyke	060 Roselia
179 Steelix	093 Xatu	**Submission**	222 Croagunk	089 Golurk	296 Maractus	061 Roserade
369 Stonjourner	**Storm Throw**	351 Clobbopus	087 Crustle	391 Goodra	307 Mareanie	372 Rotom
226 Stunfisk	111 Pancham	166 Drilbur	279 Cubchoo	389 Goomy	295 Mawile	281 Rufflet
253 Sudowoodo	248 Throh	352 Grapploct	302 Cufant	126 Gossifleur	209 Meowstic	328 Runerigus
248 Throh	**Strange Steam**	320 Hawlucha	237 Cursola	267 Gothita	182 Meowth	294 Sableye
171 Timburr	251 Weezing	138 Machop	187 Cutiefly	269 Gothitelle	185 Milcery	244 Salandit
300 Torkoal	**Strength**	033 Obstagoon	368 Darmanitan	268 Gothorita	153 Milotic	245 Salazzle
223 Toxicroak	095 Bewear	**Substitute (TR20)**	367 Darumaka	192 Gourgeist	364 Mime Jr.	313 Sandaconda
347 Turtonator	303 Copperajah	097 Abomasnow	386 Deino	352 Grapploct	301 Mimikyu	249 Sawk
385 Tyranitar	302 Cufant	276 Accelgor	078 Delibird	025 Greedent	050 Minccino	004 Scorbunny
229 Whiscash	001 Grookey	332 Aegislash	214 Dewpider	240 Grimmsnarl	340 Morelull	225 Scrafty
Stored Power (TR82)	140 Machamp	186 Alcremie	360 Dhelmise	001 Grookey	365 Mr. Mime	224 Scraggy
186 Alcremie	139 Machoke	207 Appletun	049 Diggersby	070 Growlithe	366 Mr. Rime	147 Seaking
278 Beheeyem	138 Machop	215 Araquanid	164 Diglett	016 Grubbin	084 Mudbray	039 Seedot
083 Claydol	084 Mudbray	071 Arcanine	011 Dottler	172 Gurdurr	085 Mudsdale	134 Seismitoad
256 Clefable	085 Mudsdale	377 Arctovish	331 Doublade	145 Gyarados	260 Munchlax	106 Shedinja
255 Clefairy	094 Stufful	375 Arctozolt	376 Dracovish	393 Hakamo-o	090 Munna	150 Shellder
254 Cleffa	**Strength Sap**	213 Aromatisse	374 Dracozolt	241 Hatenna		230 Shellos
	236 Corsola	180 Arrokuda	397 Dragapult	243 Hatterene		275 Shelmet

041 Shiftry
341 Shiinotic
227 Shuckle
297 Sigilyph
312 Silicobra
382 Silvally
335 Sinistea
219 Sirfetch'd
159 Sizzlipede
285 Skorupi
131 Skuntank
024 Skwovet
390 Sliggoo
211 Slurpuff
292 Sneasel
349 Snom
261 Snorlax
079 Snorunt
096 Snover
007 Sobble
270 Solosis
363 Solrock
212 Spritzee
179 Steelix
053 Steenee
369 Stonjourner
094 Stufful
226 Stunfisk
130 Stunky
253 Sudowoodo
075 Swinub
210 Swirlix
175 Swoobat
204 Sylveon
030 Thievul
248 Throh
002 Thwackey
171 Timburr
348 Togedemaru
259 Togekiss
257 Togepi
258 Togetic
300 Torkoal
308 Toxapex
310 Toxel
223 Toxicroak
311 Toxtricity
027 Tranquill
321 Trapinch
339 Trevenant
157 Trubbish
054 Tsareena
347 Turtonator
132 Tympole
381 Type: Null
385 Tyranitar
107 Tyrogue
201 Umbreon
028 Unfezant
073 Vanillish
072 Vanillite
074 Vanilluxe
197 Vaporeon
117 Vespiquen
322 Vibrava
018 Vikavolt
057 Vileplume
283 Vullaby
068 Vulpix
356 Wailmer
357 Wailord
293 Weavile
251 Weezing

263 Whimsicott
229 Whiscash
232 Wimpod
062 Wingull
155 Wishiwashi
174 Woobat
034 Wooloo
100 Wooper
093 Xatu
327 Yamask
046 Yamper
398 Zacian
399 Zamazenta
031 Zigzagoon
387 Zweilous

Sucker Punch
205 Applin
252 Bonsly
351 Clobbopus
222 Croagunk
164 Diglett
397 Dragapult
395 Dreepy
008 Drizzile
165 Dugtrio
065 Galvantula
141 Gastly
143 Gengar
233 Golisopod
240 Grimmsnarl
142 Haunter
317 Heatmor
110 Hitmontop
238 Impidimp
009 Inteleon
064 Joltik
045 Liepard
296 Maractus
295 Mawile
209 Meowstic
364 Mime Jr.
239 Morgrem
365 Mr. Mime
366 Mr. Rime
092 Natu
029 Nickit
040 Nuzleaf
246 Pawniard
338 Phantump
353 Pincurchin
336 Polteageist
044 Purrloin
294 Sableye
004 Scorbunny
039 Seedot
041 Shiftry
335 Sinistea
131 Skuntank
007 Sobble
226 Stunfisk
130 Stunky
253 Sudowoodo
030 Thievul
223 Toxicroak

Sunny Day (TM34)
332 Aegislash
207 Appletun
071 Arcanine
213 Aromatisse
324 Axew
082 Baltoy
058 Bellossom
252 Bonsly

052 Bounsweet
282 Braviary
119 Bronzong
118 Bronzor
059 Budew
015 Butterfree
160 Centiskorch
289 Chandelure
380 Charizard
378 Charmander
379 Charmeleon
129 Cherrim
128 Cherubi
051 Cinccino
006 Cinderace
083 Claydol
256 Clefable
255 Clefairy
254 Cleffa
173 Conkeldurr
236 Corsola
262 Cottonee
222 Croagunk
237 Cursola
187 Cutiefly
368 Darmanitan
367 Darumaka
386 Deino
360 Dhelmise
164 Diglett
374 Dracozolt
346 Drampa
286 Drapion
125 Drifblim
124 Drifloon
165 Dugtrio
136 Dusclops
137 Dusknoir
135 Duskull
196 Eevee
127 Eldegoss
200 Espeon
208 Espurr
218 Farfetch'd
189 Ferroseed
190 Ferrothorn
206 Flapple
199 Flareon
323 Flygon
325 Fraxure
123 Gallade
158 Garbodor
122 Gardevoir
141 Gastly
143 Gengar
203 Glaceon
056 Gloom
391 Goodra
389 Goomy
126 Gossifleur
192 Gourgeist
001 Grookey
070 Growlithe
172 Gurdurr
142 Haunter
320 Hawlucha
326 Haxorus
317 Heatmor
319 Heliolisk
314 Hippopotas
315 Hippowdon
109 Hitmonchan
108 Hitmonlee

110 Hitmontop
019 Hoothoot
388 Hydreigon
290 Inkay
198 Jolteon
121 Kirlia
250 Koffing
288 Lampent
383 Larvitar
202 Leafeon
045 Liepard
032 Linoone
287 Litwick
037 Lombre
036 Lotad
299 Lucario
038 Ludicolo
140 Machamp
139 Machoke
138 Machop
291 Malamar
284 Mandibuzz
296 Maractus
295 Mawile
209 Meowstic
182 Meowth
364 Mime Jr.
050 Minccino
340 Morelull
365 Mr. Mime
366 Mr. Rime
260 Munchlax
092 Natu
104 Nincada
069 Ninetales
105 Ninjask
020 Noctowl
176 Noibat
177 Noivern
040 Nuzleaf
033 Obstagoon
149 Octillery
055 Oddish
178 Onix
342 Oranguru
111 Pancham
112 Pangoro
343 Passimian
183 Perrserker
184 Persian
338 Phantump
026 Pidove
191 Pumpkaboo
384 Pupitar
044 Purrloin
005 Raboot
120 Ralts
148 Remoraid
265 Rhydon
264 Rhyhorn
266 Rhyperior
188 Ribombee
003 Rillaboom
298 Riolu
060 Roselia
061 Roserade
372 Rotom
281 Rufflet
294 Sableye
249 Sawk
004 Scorbunny
225 Scrafty
224 Scraggy

039 Seedot
106 Shedinja
041 Shiftry
341 Shiinotic
227 Shuckle
382 Silvally
219 Sirfetch'd
159 Sizzlipede
285 Skorupi
131 Skuntank
390 Sliggoo
211 Slurpuff
292 Sneasel
261 Snorlax
363 Solrock
212 Spritzee
179 Steelix
053 Steenee
130 Stunky
253 Sudowoodo
210 Swirlix
204 Sylveon
248 Throh
002 Thwackey
171 Timburr
259 Togekiss
257 Togepi
258 Togetic
300 Torkoal
223 Toxicroak
027 Tranquill
321 Trapinch
339 Trevenant
157 Trubbish
054 Tsareena
347 Turtonator
381 Type: Null
385 Tyranitar
107 Tyrogue
201 Umbreon
028 Unfezant
197 Vaporeon
117 Vespiquen
322 Vibrava
057 Vileplume
283 Vullaby
068 Vulpix
293 Weavile
251 Weezing
263 Whimsicott
093 Xatu
031 Zigzagoon
387 Zweilous

Super Fang
377 Arctovish
048 Bunnelby
049 Diggersby
376 Dracovish
025 Greedent
344 Morpeko
176 Noibat
177 Noivern
004 Scorbunny
024 Skwovet

Superpower (TR39)
207 Appletun
359 Avalugg
324 Axew
235 Barbaracle
154 Basculin
280 Beartic
095 Bewear

282 Braviary
351 Clobbopus
173 Conkeldurr
303 Copperajah
102 Corphish
309 Cramorant
103 Crawdaunt
279 Cubchoo
302 Cufant
368 Darmanitan
367 Darumaka
386 Deino
049 Diggersby
346 Drampa
043 Drednaw
316 Durant
345 Falinks
218 Farfetch'd
199 Flareon
323 Flygon
325 Fraxure
170 Gigalith
088 Golett
089 Golurk
391 Goodra
352 Grapploct
025 Greedent
240 Grimmsnarl
172 Gurdurr
320 Hawlucha
326 Haxorus
317 Heatmor
314 Hippopotas
315 Hippowdon
108 Hitmonlee
388 Hydreigon
290 Inkay
099 Kingler
394 Kommo-o
098 Krabby
383 Larvitar
140 Machamp
139 Machoke
138 Machop
291 Malamar
077 Mamoswine
084 Mudbray
085 Mudsdale
260 Munchlax
111 Pancham
112 Pangoro
343 Passimian
076 Piloswine
384 Pupitar
272 Reuniclus
265 Rhydon
264 Rhyhorn
266 Rhyperior
003 Rillaboom
281 Rufflet
249 Sawk
219 Sirfetch'd
261 Snorlax
369 Stonjourner
094 Stufful
075 Swinub
248 Throh
171 Timburr
300 Torkoal
321 Trapinch
385 Tyranitar
322 Vibrava
387 Zweilous

Supersonic
010 Blipbug
015 Butterfree
220 Chinchou
151 Cloyster
323 Flygon
146 Goldeen
019 Hoothoot
221 Lanturn
355 Mantine
354 Mantyke
176 Noibat
177 Noivern
133 Palpitoad
063 Pelipper
304 Qwilfish
148 Remoraid
147 Seaking
134 Seismitoad
150 Shellder
132 Tympole
322 Vibrava
062 Wingull
174 Woobat

Surf (TR04)
215 Araquanid
377 Arctovish
375 Arctozolt
359 Avalugg
235 Barbaracle
228 Barboach
181 Barraskewda
154 Basculin
280 Beartic
358 Bergmite
234 Binacle
048 Bunnelby
042 Chewtle
220 Chinchou
151 Cloyster
102 Corphish
236 Corsola
309 Cramorant
103 Crawdaunt
279 Cubchoo
237 Cursola
214 Dewpider
360 Dhelmise
049 Diggersby
376 Dracovish
397 Dragapult
396 Drakloak
346 Drampa
043 Drednaw
008 Drizzile
370 Eiscue
152 Feebas
305 Frillish
231 Gastrodon
146 Goldeen
233 Golisopod
391 Goodra
352 Grapploct
145 Gyarados
326 Haxorus
319 Heliolisk
318 Helioptile
388 Hydreigon
009 Inteleon
306 Jellicent
099 Kingler
098 Krabby
221 Lanturn

361 Lapras
032 Linoone
037 Lombre
036 Lotad
038 Ludicolo
355 Mantine
354 Mantyke
307 Mareanie
153 Milotic
260 Munchlax
033 Obstagoon
149 Octillery
133 Palpitoad
111 Pancham
112 Pangoro
063 Pelipper
193 Pichu
194 Pikachu
353 Pincurchin
101 Quagsire
304 Qwilfish
195 Raichu
148 Remoraid
265 Rhydon
266 Rhyperior
147 Seaking
134 Seismitoad
150 Shellder
230 Shellos
382 Silvally
211 Slurpuff
292 Sneasel
261 Snorlax
007 Sobble
226 Stunfisk
210 Swirlix
308 Toxapex
132 Tympole
385 Tyranitar
197 Vaporeon
356 Wailmer
357 Wailord
293 Weavile
229 Whiscash
232 Wimpod
155 Wishiwashi
100 Wooper
031 Zigzagoon

Swagger
097 Abomasnow
280 Beartic
023 Corviknight
022 Corvisquire
222 Croagunk
302 Cufant
240 Grimmsnarl
238 Impidimp
290 Inkay
291 Malamar
182 Meowth
239 Morgrem
344 Morpeko
040 Nuzleaf
183 Perrserker
026 Pidove
156 Pyukumuku
021 Rookidee
245 Salazzle
225 Scrafty
224 Scraggy
041 Shiftry
096 Snover
223 Toxicroak

311 Toxtricity
027 Tranquill
054 Tsareena
028 Unfezant
117 Vespiquen
034 Wooloo

Swallow
309 Cramorant
125 Drifblim
124 Drifloon
158 Garbodor
025 Greedent
317 Heatmor
314 Hippopotas
250 Koffing
221 Lanturn
307 Mareanie
295 Mawile
260 Munchlax
063 Pelipper
230 Shellos
024 Skwovet
261 Snorlax
157 Trubbish
100 Wooper

Sweet Kiss
186 Alcremie
213 Aromatisse
256 Clefable
255 Clefairy
254 Cleffa
185 Milcery
193 Pichu
194 Pikachu
195 Raichu
212 Spritzee
259 Togekiss
257 Togepi
258 Togetic

Sweet Scent
186 Alcremie
207 Appletun
213 Aromatisse
058 Bellossom
052 Bounsweet
128 Cherubi
116 Combee
187 Cutiefly
127 Eldegoss
056 Gloom
126 Gossifleur
036 Lotad
296 Maractus
295 Mawile
185 Milcery
055 Oddish
188 Ribombee
060 Roselia
061 Roserade
244 Salandit
245 Salazzle
227 Shuckle
211 Slurpuff
212 Spritzee
053 Steenee
210 Swirlix
054 Tsareena
117 Vespiquen
057 Vileplume

Swift (TM40)
276 Accelgor
071 Arcanine
180 Arrokuda
029 Nickit

324 Axew
181 Barraskewda
154 Basculin
047 Boltund
282 Braviary
059 Budew
015 Butterfree
380 Charizard
378 Charmander
379 Charmeleon
051 Cinccino
006 Cinderace
151 Cloyster
023 Corviknight
022 Corvisquire
262 Cottonee
103 Crawdaunt
187 Cutiefly
078 Delibird
397 Dragapult
396 Drakloak
346 Drampa
395 Dreepy
125 Drifblim
124 Drifloon
008 Drizzile
196 Eevee
066 Electrike
200 Espeon
208 Espurr
152 Feebas
199 Flareon
323 Flygon
325 Fraxure
123 Gallade
065 Galvantula
122 Gardevoir
203 Glaceon
146 Goldeen
233 Golisopod
001 Grookey
070 Growlithe
320 Hawlucha
326 Haxorus
319 Heliolisk
318 Helioptile
109 Hitmonchan
108 Hitmonlee
110 Hitmontop
019 Hoothoot
337 Indeedee
009 Inteleon
198 Jolteon
064 Joltik
121 Kirlia
202 Leafeon
045 Liepard
032 Linoone
299 Lucario
362 Lunatone
284 Mandibuzz
067 Manectric
355 Mantine
354 Mantyke
209 Meowstic
182 Meowth
153 Milotic
050 Minccino
344 Morpeko
090 Munna
091 Musharna
092 Natu
029 Nickit

069 Ninetales
105 Ninjask
020 Noctowl
176 Noibat
177 Noivern
040 Nuzleaf
033 Obstagoon
149 Octillery
063 Pelipper
184 Persian
193 Pichu
026 Pidove
194 Pikachu
333 Ponyta
044 Purrloin
304 Qwilfish
005 Raboot
195 Raichu
120 Ralts
334 Rapidash
148 Remoraid
188 Ribombee
003 Rillaboom
298 Riolu
021 Rookidee
060 Roselia
061 Roserade
372 Rotom
281 Rufflet
244 Salandit
245 Salazzle
004 Scorbunny
147 Seaking
150 Shellder
041 Shiftry
297 Sigilyph
382 Silvally
131 Skuntank
292 Sneasel
007 Sobble
363 Solrock
130 Stunky
175 Swoobat
204 Sylveon
030 Thievul
002 Thwackey
348 Togedemaru
259 Togekiss
257 Togepi
258 Togetic
311 Toxtricity
027 Tranquill
381 Type: Null
107 Tyrogue
201 Umbreon
028 Unfezant
197 Vaporeon
117 Vespiquen
322 Vibrava
283 Vullaby
068 Vulpix
293 Weavile
263 Whimsicott
232 Wimpod
062 Wingull
174 Woobat
093 Xatu
046 Yamper
398 Zacian
399 Zamazenta
031 Zigzagoon

Switcheroo
234 Binacle

102 Corphish
262 Cottonee
187 Cutiefly
360 Dhelmise
066 Electrike
290 Inkay
032 Linoone
033 Obstagoon
184 Persian
188 Ribombee
079 Snorunt

Swords Dance (TR00)
097 Abomasnow
332 Aegislash
324 Axew
235 Barbaracle
280 Beartic
058 Bellossom
095 Bewear
234 Binacle
247 Bisharp
059 Budew
048 Bunnelby
380 Charizard
378 Charmander
379 Charmeleon
129 Cherrim
128 Cherubi
102 Corphish
103 Crawdaunt
087 Crustle
360 Dhelmise
049 Diggersby
331 Doublade
286 Drapion
043 Drednaw
166 Drilbur
035 Dubwool
371 Duraludon
086 Dwebble
274 Escavalier
167 Excadrill
345 Falinks
218 Farfetch'd
190 Ferrothorn
325 Fraxure
123 Gallade
056 Gloom
146 Goldeen
233 Golisopod
025 Greedent
001 Grookey
393 Hakamo-o
243 Hatterene
320 Hawlucha
326 Haxorus
330 Honedge
009 Inteleon
392 Jangmo-o
273 Karrablast
099 Kingler
394 Kommo-o
098 Krabby
202 Leafeon
037 Lombre
036 Lotad
038 Ludicolo
295 Mawile
182 Meowth
301 Mimikyu

105 Ninjask
040 Nuzleaf
055 Oddish
111 Pancham
112 Pangoro
246 Pawniard
183 Perrserker
304 Qwilfish
334 Rapidash
265 Rhydon
264 Rhyhorn
266 Rhyperior
003 Rillaboom
298 Riolu
060 Roselia
061 Roserade
147 Seaking
039 Seedot
041 Shiftry
382 Silvally
219 Sirfetch'd
285 Skorupi
292 Sneasel
096 Snover
363 Solrock
094 Stufful
002 Thwackey
223 Toxicroak
381 Type: Null
057 Vileplume
293 Weavile
398 Zacian

Synthesis
052 Bounsweet
059 Budew
127 Eldegoss
126 Gossifleur
202 Leafeon
036 Lotad
296 Maractus
040 Nuzleaf
055 Oddish
060 Roselia
061 Roserade
039 Seedot
041 Shiftry

Tackle
332 Aegislash
186 Alcremie
359 Avalugg
154 Basculin
358 Bergmite
095 Bewear
169 Boldore
047 Boltund
119 Bronzong
118 Bronzor
048 Bunnelby
015 Butterfree
162 Carkol
013 Caterpie
129 Cherrim
128 Cherubi
006 Cinderace
151 Cloyster
163 Coalossal
303 Copperajah
236 Corsola
302 Cufant
237 Cursola
368 Darmanitan
367 Darumaka

386 Deino
049 Diggersby
331 Doublade
376 Dracovish
374 Dracozolt
043 Drednaw
035 Dubwool
196 Eevee
370 Eiscue
066 Electrike
200 Espeon
345 Falinks
152 Feebas
189 Ferroseed
190 Ferrothorn
199 Flareon
170 Gigalith
203 Glaceon
391 Goodra
389 Goomy
025 Greedent
145 Gyarados
393 Hakamo-o
320 Hawlucha
317 Heatmor
314 Hippopotas
315 Hippowdon
109 Hitmonchan
108 Hitmonlee
110 Hitmontop
330 Honedge
019 Hoothoot
388 Hydreigon
290 Inkay
392 Jangmo-o
198 Jolteon
250 Koffing
394 Kommo-o
383 Larvitar
202 Leafeon
032 Linoone
362 Lunatone
144 Magikarp
291 Malamar
077 Mamoswine
067 Manectric
355 Mantine
354 Mantyke
185 Milcery
153 Milotic
260 Munchlax
020 Noctowl
176 Noibat
177 Noivern
040 Nuzleaf
033 Obstagoon
178 Onix
111 Pancham
112 Pangoro
343 Passimian
338 Phantump
076 Piloswine
333 Ponyta
384 Pupitar
304 Qwilfish
005 Raboot
334 Rapidash
265 Rhydon
264 Rhyhorn
266 Rhyperior
168 Roggenrola
161 Rolycoly
004 Scorbunny

039 Seedot
150 Shellder
041 Shiftry
382 Silvally
024 Skwovet
390 Sliggoo
211 Slurpuff
261 Snorlax
363 Solrock
179 Steelix
094 Stufful
226 Stunfisk
075 Swinub
210 Swirlix
204 Sylveon
348 Togedemaru
339 Trevenant
347 Turtonator
381 Type: Null
385 Tyranitar
107 Tyrogue
201 Umbreon
197 Vaporeon
251 Weezing
034 Wooloo
046 Yamper
031 Zigzagoon
387 Zweilous

Tail Slap (TM84)
051 Cinccino
025 Greedent
209 Meowstic
050 Minccino
029 Nickit
069 Ninetales
131 Skuntank
024 Skwovet
130 Stunky
030 Thievul
068 Vulpix
398 Zacian
399 Zamazenta

Tail Whip
154 Basculin
047 Boltund
196 Eevee
200 Espeon
199 Flareon
203 Glaceon
146 Goldeen
025 Greedent
319 Heliolisk
318 Helioptile
198 Jolteon
202 Leafeon
182 Meowth
050 Minccino
344 Morpeko
029 Nickit
069 Ninetales
193 Pichu
194 Pikachu
333 Ponyta
101 Quagsire
195 Raichu
334 Rapidash
265 Rhydon
264 Rhyhorn
266 Rhyperior
147 Seaking
024 Skwovet
204 Sylveon
030 Thievul

201 Umbreon
197 Vaporeon
068 Vulpix
100 Wooper
046 Yamper

Tailwind
282 Braviary
015 Butterfree
125 Drifblim
124 Drifloon
350 Frosmoth
284 Mandibuzz
355 Mantine
354 Mantyke
176 Noibat
177 Noivern
063 Pelipper
026 Pidove
021 Rookidee
281 Rufflet
297 Sigilyph
027 Tranquill
028 Unfezant
283 Vullaby
263 Whimsicott
093 Xatu

Take Down
071 Arcanine
359 Avalugg
228 Barboach
154 Basculin
358 Bergmite
095 Bewear
048 Bunnelby
129 Cherrim
128 Cherubi
220 Chinchou
367 Darumaka
049 Diggersby
397 Dragapult
396 Drakloak
035 Dubwool
196 Eevee
274 Escavalier
200 Espeon
199 Flareon
158 Garbodor
203 Glaceon
070 Growlithe
314 Hippopotas
315 Hippowdon
019 Hoothoot
198 Jolteon
273 Karrablast
221 Lanturn
202 Leafeon
032 Linoone
077 Mamoswine
355 Mantine
354 Mantyke
020 Noctowl
033 Obstagoon
343 Passimian
076 Piloswine
333 Ponyta
304 Qwilfish
334 Rapidash
265 Rhydon
264 Rhyhorn
266 Rhyperior
168 Roggenrola
039 Seedot
382 Silvally

094 Stufful
075 Swinub
204 Sylveon
157 Trubbish
291 Malamar
381 Type: Null
201 Umbreon
197 Vaporeon
155 Wishiwashi
034 Wooloo
031 Zigzagoon

Tar Shot
163 Coalossal

Taunt (TR37)
375 Arctozolt
324 Axew
235 Barbaracle
154 Basculin
280 Beartic
095 Bewear
234 Binacle
247 Bisharp
289 Chandelure
006 Cinderace
351 Clobbopus
173 Conkeldurr
303 Copperajah
102 Corphish
023 Corviknight
022 Corvisquire
262 Cottonee
103 Crawdaunt
222 Croagunk
368 Darmanitan
367 Darumaka
386 Deino
374 Dracozolt
286 Drapion
136 Dusclops
137 Dusknoir
135 Duskull
274 Escavalier
325 Fraxure
305 Frillish
081 Froslass
123 Gallade
122 Gardevoir
141 Gastly
143 Gengar
080 Glalie
233 Golisopod
267 Gothita
269 Gothitelle
268 Gothorita
352 Grapploct
240 Grimmsnarl
001 Grookey
172 Gurdurr
145 Gyarados
393 Hakamo-o
142 Haunter
320 Hawlucha
326 Haxorus
317 Heatmor
388 Hydreigon
238 Impidimp
290 Inkay
392 Jangmo-o
306 Jellicent
121 Kirlia
250 Koffing
394 Kommo-o
288 Lampent
383 Larvitar

045 Liepard
032 Linoone
287 Litwick
291 Malamar
284 Mandibuzz
295 Mawile
182 Meowth
364 Mime Jr.
301 Mimikyu
239 Morgrem
344 Morpeko
365 Mr. Mime
366 Mr. Rime
029 Nickit
176 Noibat
177 Noivern
033 Obstagoon
178 Onix
342 Oranguru
111 Pancham
112 Pangoro
343 Passimian
246 Pawniard
183 Perrserker
184 Persian
026 Pidove
384 Pupitar
044 Purrloin
156 Pyukumuku
304 Qwilfish
005 Raboot
120 Ralts
003 Rillaboom
021 Rookidee
328 Runerigus
294 Sableye
244 Salandit
245 Salazzle
249 Sawk
004 Scorbunny
225 Scrafty
224 Scraggy
285 Skorupi
131 Skuntank
292 Sneasel
179 Steelix
094 Stufful
130 Stunky
253 Sudowoodo
175 Swoobat
030 Thievul
248 Throh
002 Thwackey
171 Timburr
223 Toxicroak
311 Toxtricity
027 Tranquill
054 Tsareena
347 Turtonator
385 Tyranitar
201 Umbreon
028 Unfezant
073 Vanillish
072 Vanillite
074 Vanilluxe
283 Vullaby
293 Weavile
251 Weezing
263 Whimsicott
232 Wimpod
174 Woobat
031 Zigzagoon
387 Zweilous

Tearful Look
252 Bonsly
008 Drizzile
391 Goodra
009 Inteleon
007 Sobble
253 Sudowoodo
310 Toxel
311 Toxtricity
155 Wishiwashi

Teatime
336 Polteageist

Teeter Dance
052 Bounsweet
037 Lombre
036 Lotad
038 Ludicolo
364 Mime Jr.
365 Mr. Mime
366 Mr. Rime
055 Oddish
053 Steenee
054 Tsareena

Teleport
278 Beheeyem
083 Claydol
277 Elgyem
123 Gallade
122 Gardevoir
121 Kirlia
092 Natu
120 Ralts
093 Xatu

Thief (TM23)
071 Arcanine
235 Barbaracle
278 Beheeyem
234 Binacle
247 Bisharp
252 Bonsly
048 Bunnelby
015 Butterfree
289 Chandelure
051 Cinccino
329 Cofagrigus
023 Corviknight
022 Corvisquire
309 Cramorant
222 Croagunk
187 Cutiefly
368 Darmanitan
367 Darumaka
386 Deino
078 Delibird
360 Dhelmise
049 Diggersby
164 Diglett
397 Dragapult
396 Drakloak
286 Drapion
125 Drifblim
124 Drifloon
165 Dugtrio
136 Dusclops
137 Dusknoir
135 Duskull
066 Electrike
277 Elgyem
123 Gallade
065 Galvantula
158 Garbodor
122 Gardevoir
141 Gastly

143 Gengar
088 Golett
089 Golurk
267 Gothita
269 Gothitelle
268 Gothorita
192 Gourgeist
025 Greedent
240 Grimmsnarl
070 Growlithe
142 Haunter
317 Heatmor
109 Hitmonchan
108 Hitmonlee
110 Hitmontop
019 Hoothoot
388 Hydreigon
238 Impidimp
290 Inkay
064 Joltik
099 Kingler
121 Kirlia
250 Koffing
098 Krabby
288 Lampent
045 Liepard
032 Linoone
287 Litwick
037 Lombre
036 Lotad
038 Ludicolo
140 Machamp
139 Machoke
138 Machop
291 Malamar
284 Mandibuzz
067 Manectric
182 Meowth
364 Mime Jr.
301 Mimikyu
050 Minccino
239 Morgrem
344 Morpeko
365 Mr. Mime
366 Mr. Rime
092 Natu
029 Nickit
105 Ninjask
020 Noctowl
176 Noibat
177 Noivern
040 Nuzleaf
033 Obstagoon
149 Octillery
112 Pangoro
343 Passimian
246 Pawniard
063 Pelipper
183 Perrserker
184 Persian
338 Phantump
194 Pikachu
191 Pumpkaboo
044 Purrloin
101 Quagsire
195 Raichu
120 Ralts
066 Electrike
277 Elgyem
148 Remoraid
265 Rhydon
264 Rhyhorn
266 Rhyperior
188 Ribombee
021 Rookidee

372 Rotom
328 Runerigus
294 Sableye
244 Salandit
245 Salazzle
225 Scrafty
224 Scraggy
106 Shedinja
041 Shiftry
297 Sigilyph
285 Skorupi
131 Skuntank
024 Skwovet
211 Slurpuff
292 Sneasel
130 Stunky
253 Sudowoodo
210 Swirlix
175 Swoobat
030 Thievul
348 Togedemaru
223 Toxicroak
339 Trevenant
157 Trubbish
107 Tyrogue
201 Umbreon
117 Vespiquen
283 Vullaby
293 Weavile
251 Weezing
263 Whimsicott
062 Wingull
174 Woobat
093 Xatu
327 Yamask
031 Zigzagoon
387 Zweilous

Thrash
180 Arrokuda
228 Barboach
154 Basculin
280 Beartic
095 Bewear
282 Braviary
309 Cramorant
279 Cubchoo
368 Darmanitan
367 Darumaka
070 Growlithe
145 Gyarados
383 Larvitar
077 Mamoswine
182 Meowth
344 Morpeko
343 Passimian
183 Perrserker
076 Piloswine
333 Ponyta
384 Pupitar
281 Rufflet
094 Stufful
385 Tyranitar
356 Wailmer
229 Whiscash

Throat Chop (TR95)
180 Arrokuda
181 Barraskewda
280 Beartic
247 Bisharp
236 Corsola
309 Cramorant
237 Cursola

286 Drapion
043 Drednaw
345 Falinks
218 Farfetch'd
323 Flygon
123 Gallade
065 Galvantula
170 Gigalith
146 Goldeen
233 Golisopod
240 Grimmsnarl
320 Hawlucha
317 Heatmor
109 Hitmonchan
108 Hitmonlee
388 Hydreigon
045 Liepard
032 Linoone
140 Machamp
291 Malamar
296 Maractus
182 Meowth
239 Morgrem
033 Obstagoon
112 Pangoro
183 Perrserker
184 Persian
353 Pincurchin
304 Qwilfish
334 Rapidash
249 Sawk
225 Scrafty
147 Seaking
041 Shiftry
219 Sirfetch'd
131 Skuntank
292 Sneasel
130 Stunky
223 Toxicroak
311 Toxtricity
201 Umbreon
322 Vibrava
293 Weavile

Thunder (TR09)
375 Arctozolt
213 Aromatisse
047 Boltund
220 Chinchou
051 Cinccino
256 Clefable
255 Clefairy
374 Dracozolt
397 Dragapult
396 Drakloak
346 Drampa
125 Drifblim
124 Drifloon
271 Duosion
371 Duraludon
066 Electrike
190 Ferrothorn
081 Froslass
065 Galvantula
143 Gengar
391 Goodra
145 Gyarados
319 Heliolisk
318 Helioptile
198 Jolteon
115 Klinklang
250 Koffing
221 Lanturn
361 Lapras
032 Linoone
067 Manectric
182 Meowth
364 Mime Jr.
301 Mimikyu
344 Morpeko
365 Mr. Mime
366 Mr. Rime
260 Munchlax
033 Obstagoon
342 Oranguru
183 Perrserker
184 Persian
193 Pichu
194 Pikachu
353 Pincurchin
195 Raichu
272 Reuniclus
265 Rhydon
264 Rhyhorn
266 Rhyperior
372 Rotom
211 Slurpuff
261 Snorlax
270 Solosis
348 Togedemaru
311 Toxtricity
385 Tyranitar
018 Vikavolt
251 Weezing
046 Yamper
031 Zigzagoon

Thunder Fang (TM66)
071 Arcanine
375 Arctozolt
047 Boltund
160 Centiskorch
386 Deino
374 Dracozolt
286 Drapion
316 Durant
066 Electrike
025 Greedent
315 Hippowdon
388 Hydreigon
198 Jolteon
067 Manectric
295 Mawile
344 Morpeko
265 Rhydon
264 Rhyhorn
266 Rhyperior
382 Silvally
179 Steelix
030 Thievul
385 Tyranitar
046 Yamper
398 Zacian
399 Zamazenta
387 Zweilous

Thunder Punch (TM05)
375 Arctozolt
095 Bewear
380 Charizard
378 Charmander
379 Charmeleon
256 Clefable
255 Clefairy
173 Conkeldurr
222 Croagunk
049 Diggersby
374 Dracozolt
136 Dusclops
137 Dusknoir
323 Flygon
123 Gallade
122 Gardevoir
141 Gastly
143 Gengar
088 Golett
089 Golurk
391 Goodra
240 Grimmsnarl
172 Gurdurr
142 Haunter
320 Hawlucha
317 Heatmor
319 Heliolisk
109 Hitmonchan
121 Kirlia
394 Kommo-o
037 Lombre
299 Lucario
038 Ludicolo
140 Machamp
139 Machoke
138 Machop
295 Mawile
344 Morpeko
365 Mr. Mime
260 Munchlax
033 Obstagoon
111 Pancham
112 Pangoro
193 Pichu
194 Pikachu
195 Raichu
120 Ralts
272 Reuniclus
265 Rhydon
266 Rhyperior
298 Riolu
294 Sableye
249 Sawk
225 Scrafty
224 Scraggy
261 Snorlax
094 Stufful
253 Sudowoodo
248 Throh
171 Timburr
223 Toxicroak
311 Toxtricity
385 Tyranitar

Thunder Shock
375 Arctozolt
374 Dracozolt
319 Heliolisk
318 Helioptile
198 Jolteon
114 Klang
113 Klink
115 Klinklang
344 Morpeko
193 Pichu
194 Pikachu
353 Pincurchin
195 Raichu
372 Rotom
348 Togedemaru
311 Toxtricity

Thunder Wave (TM14)
375 Arctozolt
278 Beheeyem
247 Bisharp
047 Boltund
017 Charjabug
220 Chinchou
051 Cinccino
256 Clefable
255 Clefairy
254 Cleffa
386 Deino
374 Dracozolt
397 Dragapult
396 Drakloak
346 Drampa
395 Dreepy
125 Drifblim
124 Drifloon
035 Dubwool
271 Duosion
371 Duraludon
316 Durant
066 Electrike
277 Elgyem
208 Espurr
189 Ferroseed
190 Ferrothorn
081 Froslass
123 Gallade
065 Galvantula
122 Gardevoir
267 Gothita
269 Gothitelle
268 Gothorita
240 Grimmsnarl
016 Grubbin
145 Gyarados
241 Hatenna
243 Hatterene
242 Hattrem
319 Heliolisk
318 Helioptile
388 Hydreigon
238 Impidimp
198 Jolteon
064 Joltik
121 Kirlia
114 Klang
113 Klink
115 Klinklang
221 Lanturn
045 Liepard
032 Linoone
067 Manectric
209 Meowstic
364 Mime Jr.
301 Mimikyu
050 Minccino
340 Morelull
239 Morgrem
344 Morpeko
365 Mr. Mime
366 Mr. Rime
090 Munna
091 Musharna
092 Natu
033 Obstagoon
149 Octillery
246 Pawniard
193 Pichu
194 Pikachu
353 Pincurchin
044 Purrloin
304 Qwilfish
195 Raichu
120 Ralts
148 Remoraid
272 Reuniclus
372 Rotom
244 Salandit
245 Salazzle
341 Shiinotic
297 Sigilyph
382 Silvally
270 Solosis
226 Stunfisk
175 Swoobat
348 Togedemaru
259 Togekiss
257 Togepi
258 Togetic
311 Toxtricity
381 Type: Null
385 Tyranitar
018 Vikavolt
174 Woobat
034 Wooloo
093 Xatu
046 Yamper
031 Zigzagoon
387 Zweilous

Thunderbolt (TR08)
375 Arctozolt
213 Aromatisse
278 Beheeyem
047 Boltund
017 Charjabug
220 Chinchou
051 Cinccino
256 Clefable
255 Clefairy
374 Dracozolt
397 Dragapult
396 Drakloak
346 Drampa
125 Drifblim
124 Drifloon
371 Duraludon
066 Electrike
277 Elgyem
208 Espurr
189 Ferroseed
190 Ferrothorn
081 Froslass
123 Gallade
065 Galvantula
158 Garbodor
122 Gardevoir
141 Gastly
143 Gengar
089 Golurk
391 Goodra
389 Goomy
267 Gothita
269 Gothitelle
268 Gothorita
016 Grubbin
145 Gyarados
142 Haunter
319 Heliolisk
318 Helioptile
290 Inkay
198 Jolteon
064 Joltik
121 Kirlia
114 Klang
113 Klink
115 Klinklang
250 Koffing
221 Lanturn
361 Lapras
032 Linoone
291 Malamar
067 Manectric
209 Meowstic
182 Meowth
364 Mime Jr.
301 Mimikyu
050 Minccino
344 Morpeko
365 Mr. Mime
366 Mr. Rime
260 Munchlax
033 Obstagoon
342 Oranguru
183 Perrserker
184 Persian
193 Pichu
194 Pikachu
353 Pincurchin
195 Raichu
120 Ralts
265 Rhydon
264 Rhyhorn
266 Rhyperior
372 Rotom
382 Silvally
390 Sliggoo
211 Slurpuff
261 Snorlax
212 Spritzee
210 Swirlix
348 Togedemaru
311 Toxtricity
385 Tyranitar
018 Vikavolt
251 Weezing
046 Yamper
031 Zigzagoon

Tickle
128 Cherubi
051 Cinccino
254 Cleffa
262 Cottonee
346 Drampa
196 Eevee
208 Espurr
152 Feebas
267 Gothita
269 Gothitelle
268 Gothorita
317 Heatmor
361 Lapras
036 Lotad
138 Machop
295 Mawile
364 Mime Jr.
050 Minccino
344 Morpeko
365 Mr. Mime
055 Oddish
193 Pichu
156 Pyukumuku
348 Togedemaru
356 Wailmer
229 Whiscash

Topsy-Turvy
352 Grapploct
290 Inkay
291 Malamar

Torment
247 Bisharp
267 Gothita
240 Grimmsnarl
238 Impidimp
045 Liepard
239 Morgrem
344 Morpeko
029 Nickit
040 Nuzleaf
246 Pawniard
044 Purrloin
294 Sableye
245 Salazzle
041 Shiftry

Toxic
276 Accelgor
058 Bellossom
222 Croagunk
286 Drapion
400 Eternatus
189 Ferroseed
158 Garbodor
141 Gastly
056 Gloom
250 Koffing
284 Mandibuzz
307 Mareanie
055 Oddish
156 Pyukumuku
101 Quagsire
304 Qwilfish
060 Roselia
061 Roserade
244 Salandit
245 Salazzle
227 Shuckle
285 Skorupi
131 Skuntank
130 Stunky
308 Toxapex
223 Toxicroak
311 Toxtricity
157 Trubbish
132 Tympole
117 Vespiquen
057 Vileplume
283 Vullaby
251 Weezing
100 Wooper

Toxic Spikes (TR54)
276 Accelgor
151 Cloyster
329 Cofagrigus
286 Drapion
400 Eternatus
158 Garbodor
250 Koffing
307 Mareanie
353 Pincurchin
304 Qwilfish
060 Roselia
061 Roserade
328 Runerigus
275 Shelmet
285 Skorupi
308 Toxapex
157 Trubbish
117 Vespiquen
251 Weezing
327 Yamask

Transform
373 Ditto

Tri Attack (TR19)
186 Alcremie
278 Beheeyem
256 Clefable
255 Clefairy
151 Cloyster
397 Dragapult
165 Dugtrio
388 Hydreigon
337 Indeedee
150 Shellder
382 Silvally
259 Togekiss
257 Togepi
258 Togetic
381 Type: Null

Trick (TR38)
082 Baltoy
278 Beheeyem
119 Bronzong
118 Bronzor
289 Chandelure
083 Claydol
256 Clefable
255 Clefairy
254 Cleffa
329 Cofagrigus
187 Cutiefly
011 Dottler
125 Drifblim
124 Drifloon
271 Duosion
136 Dusclops
137 Dusknoir
135 Duskull
277 Elgyem
200 Espeon
208 Espurr
305 Frillish
081 Froslass
123 Gallade
122 Gardevoir
141 Gastly
143 Gengar
089 Golurk
267 Gothita
269 Gothitelle
268 Gothorita
192 Gourgeist
240 Grimmsnarl
142 Haunter
238 Impidimp
337 Indeedee
306 Jellicent
121 Kirlia
288 Lampent
045 Liepard
032 Linoone
287 Litwick
209 Meowstic
364 Mime Jr.
301 Mimikyu
239 Morgrem
365 Mr. Mime
366 Mr. Rime
090 Munna
091 Musharna
092 Natu
033 Obstagoon
342 Oranguru

012 Orbeetle
338 Phantump
336 Polteageist
191 Pumpkaboo
044 Purrloin
120 Ralts
272 Reuniclus
188 Ribombee
372 Rotom
328 Runerigus
294 Sableye
106 Shedinja
297 Sigilyph
335 Sinistea
270 Solosis
175 Swoobat
259 Togekiss
257 Togepi
258 Togetic
339 Trevenant
174 Woobat
093 Xatu
327 Yamask
031 Zigzagoon

Trick Room (TM70)
213 Aromatisse
082 Baltoy
278 Beheeyem
119 Bronzong
118 Bronzor
289 Chandelure
083 Claydol
329 Cofagrigus
011 Dottler
271 Duosion
136 Dusclops
137 Dusknoir
135 Duskull
277 Elgyem
200 Espeon
208 Espurr
305 Frillish
123 Gallade
122 Gardevoir
141 Gastly
143 Gengar
267 Gothita
269 Gothitelle
268 Gothorita
192 Gourgeist
243 Hatterene
142 Haunter
337 Indeedee
290 Inkay
306 Jellicent
121 Kirlia
115 Klinklang
288 Lampent
287 Litwick
362 Lunatone
291 Malamar
209 Meowstic
364 Mime Jr.
301 Mimikyu
365 Mr. Mime
366 Mr. Rime
090 Munna
091 Musharna
092 Natu
342 Oranguru
012 Orbeetle

338 Phantump
191 Pumpkaboo
120 Ralts
334 Rapidash
272 Reuniclus
328 Runerigus
297 Sigilyph
270 Solosis
363 Solrock
212 Spritzee
175 Swoobat
339 Trevenant
263 Whimsicott
174 Woobat
093 Xatu
327 Yamask

Trick-or-Treat
192 Gourgeist
191 Pumpkaboo

Triple Kick
110 Hitmontop

Trop Kick
054 Tsareena

Twister
346 Drampa
206 Flapple
145 Gyarados
355 Mantine
354 Mantyke
153 Milotic
062 Wingull

Uproar (TR35)
235 Barbaracle
154 Basculin
278 Beheeyem
058 Bellossom
234 Binacle
047 Boltund
252 Bonsly
059 Budew
051 Cinccino
256 Clefable
255 Clefairy
254 Cleffa
309 Cramorant
368 Darmanitan
367 Darumaka
386 Deino
049 Diggersby
164 Diglett
346 Drampa
165 Dugtrio
066 Electrike
277 Elgyem
323 Flygon
141 Gastly
143 Gengar
267 Gothita
269 Gothitelle
268 Gothorita
025 Greedent
240 Grimmsnarl
001 Grookey
145 Gyarados
393 Hakamo-o
142 Haunter
109 Hitmonchan
108 Hitmonlee
110 Hitmontop
019 Hoothoot
388 Hydreigon
238 Impidimp
387 Zweilous

392 Jangmo-o
114 Klang
113 Klink
115 Klinklang
250 Koffing
394 Kommo-o
383 Larvitar
037 Lombre
036 Lotad
038 Ludicolo
067 Manectric
296 Maractus
182 Meowth
364 Mime Jr.
050 Minccino
239 Morgrem
344 Morpeko
365 Mr. Mime
366 Mr. Rime
260 Munchlax
105 Ninjask
020 Noctowl
176 Noibat
177 Noivern
133 Palpitoad
111 Pancham
112 Pangoro
343 Passimian
063 Pelipper
183 Perrserker
184 Persian
193 Pichu
026 Pidove
194 Pikachu
384 Pupitar
195 Raichu
265 Rhydon
264 Rhyhorn
266 Rhyperior
003 Rillaboom
060 Roselia
061 Roserade
372 Rotom
134 Seismitoad
024 Skwovet
261 Snorlax
226 Stunfisk
253 Sudowoodo
175 Swoobat
002 Thwackey
259 Togekiss
257 Togepi
258 Togetic
311 Toxtricity
027 Tranquill
347 Turtonator
132 Tympole
385 Tyranitar
107 Tyrogue
028 Unfezant
073 Vanillish
072 Vanillite
074 Vanilluxe
117 Vespiquen
322 Vibrava
251 Weezing
229 Whiscash
062 Wingull
155 Wishiwashi
174 Woobat
046 Yamper
387 Zweilous

U-turn (TM56)
276 Accelgor
282 Braviary
048 Bunnelby
015 Butterfree
051 Cinccino
006 Cinderace
023 Corviknight
022 Corvisquire
187 Cutiefly
368 Darmanitan
367 Darumaka
049 Diggersby
397 Dragapult
396 Drakloak
008 Drizzile
206 Flapple
323 Flygon
350 Frosmoth
001 Grookey
320 Hawlucha
319 Heliolisk
318 Helioptile
388 Hydreigon
009 Inteleon
045 Liepard
284 Mandibuzz
182 Meowth
050 Minccino
092 Natu
105 Ninjask
176 Noibat
177 Noivern
012 Orbeetle
343 Passimian
063 Pelipper
183 Perrserker
184 Persian
026 Pidove
044 Purrloin
005 Raboot
188 Ribombee
003 Rillaboom
021 Rookidee
281 Rufflet
004 Scorbunny
382 Silvally
007 Sobble
175 Swoobat
030 Thievul
002 Thwackey
348 Togedemaru
027 Tranquill
054 Tsareena
381 Type: Null
028 Unfezant
117 Vespiquen
322 Vibrava
283 Vullaby
263 Whimsicott
062 Wingull
155 Wishiwashi
174 Woobat
093 Xatu

Vacuum Wave
222 Croagunk
109 Hitmonchan
298 Riolu
107 Tyrogue

Venom Drench (TR91)
276 Accelgor

222 Croagunk
286 Drapion
400 Eternatus
158 Garbodor
250 Koffing
307 Mareanie
133 Palpitoad
338 Phantump
353 Pincurchin
156 Pyukumuku
304 Qwilfish
061 Roserade
244 Salandit
245 Salazzle
134 Seismitoad
131 Skuntank
130 Stunky
175 Swoobat
308 Toxapex
223 Toxicroak
311 Toxtricity
339 Trevenant
157 Trubbish
132 Tympole
251 Weezing
174 Woobat

Venoshock (TM74)
276 Accelgor
058 Bellossom
059 Budew
015 Butterfree
160 Centiskorch
222 Croagunk
286 Drapion
400 Eternatus
158 Garbodor
141 Gastly
143 Gengar
056 Gloom
233 Golisopod
142 Haunter
250 Koffing
307 Mareanie
055 Oddish
353 Pincurchin
304 Qwilfish
060 Roselia
061 Roserade
244 Salandit
245 Salazzle
134 Seismitoad
275 Shelmet
227 Shuckle
159 Sizzlipede
285 Skorupi
131 Skuntank
130 Stunky
308 Toxapex
223 Toxicroak
311 Toxtricity
157 Trubbish
347 Turtonator
117 Vespiquen
057 Vileplume
251 Weezing

Vise Grip
017 Charjabug
316 Durant
016 Grubbin
114 Klang
113 Klink
115 Klinklang

018 Vikavolt

Vital Throw
140 Machamp
139 Machoke
138 Machop
111 Pancham
112 Pangoro
343 Passimian
248 Throh

Volt Switch (TM80)
047 Boltund
017 Charjabug
220 Chinchou
066 Electrike
065 Galvantula
016 Grubbin
319 Heliolisk
318 Helioptile
198 Jolteon
064 Joltik
114 Klang
113 Klink
115 Klinklang
221 Lanturn
067 Manectric
344 Morpeko
193 Pichu
194 Pikachu
195 Raichu
372 Rotom
348 Togedemaru
311 Toxtricity
018 Vikavolt
046 Yamper

Volt Tackle
193 Pichu*

Water Gun
215 Araquanid
377 Arctovish
235 Barbaracle
228 Barboach
154 Basculin
234 Binacle
042 Chewtle
220 Chinchou
151 Cloyster
102 Corphish
309 Cramorant
103 Crawdaunt
214 Dewpider
376 Dracovish
043 Drednaw
008 Drizzile
305 Frillish
231 Gastrodon
391 Goodra
389 Goomy
009 Inteleon
306 Jellicent
099 Kingler
098 Krabby
221 Lanturn
361 Lapras
037 Lombre
036 Lotad
038 Ludicolo
355 Mantine
354 Mantyke
153 Milotic
149 Octillery
063 Pelipper

*Leave Pikachu or Raichu at the Pokémon Nursery with a compatible partner. One of the two Pokémon left at the Nursery must be holding a Light Ball if you hope to find an Egg that will hatch into a Pichu that knows Volt Tackle.

353 Pincurchin
101 Quagsire
304 Qwilfish
148 Remoraid
150 Shellder
230 Shellos
390 Sliggoo
007 Sobble
226 Stunfisk
197 Vaporeon
356 Wailmer
357 Wailord
229 Whiscash
062 Wingull
155 Wishiwashi
100 Wooper

Water Pledge
008 Drizzile
009 Inteleon
382 Silvally
007 Sobble

Water Pulse
228 Barboach
220 Chinchou
236 Corsola
008 Drizzile
305 Frillish
231 Gastrodon
146 Goldeen
391 Goodra
389 Goomy
009 Inteleon
306 Jellicent
361 Lapras
355 Mantine
354 Mantyke
153 Milotic
149 Octillery
063 Pelipper
304 Qwilfish
148 Remoraid
147 Seaking
150 Shellder
230 Shellos
390 Sliggoo
007 Sobble
132 Tympole
197 Vaporeon
356 Wailmer
357 Wailord
229 Whiscash
062 Wingull
155 Wishiwashi

Water Shuriken
276 Accelgor

Water Spout
305 Frillish
306 Jellicent
148 Remoraid
356 Wailmer
357 Wailord

Waterfall (TR16)
215 Araquanid
377 Arctovish
180 Arrokuda
228 Barboach
181 Barraskewda
154 Basculin
220 Chinchou
351 Clobbopus
102 Corphish
103 Crawdaunt
214 Dewpider

376 Dracovish
043 Drednaw
370 Eiscue
152 Feebas
305 Frillish
231 Gastrodon
146 Goldeen
233 Golisopod
352 Grapploct
145 Gyarados
009 Inteleon
306 Jellicent
221 Lanturn
361 Lapras
037 Lombre
038 Ludicolo
355 Mantine
354 Mantyke
153 Milotic
149 Octillery
101 Quagsire
304 Qwilfish
148 Remoraid
147 Seaking
197 Vaporeon
356 Wailmer
357 Wailord
229 Whiscash
232 Wimpod
155 Wishiwashi
100 Wooper

Weather Ball (TM46)
097 Abomasnow
119 Bronzong
059 Budew
380 Charizard
378 Charmander
379 Charmeleon
129 Cherrim
128 Cherubi
151 Cloyster
309 Cramorant
078 Delibird
125 Drifblim
124 Drifloon
008 Drizzile
196 Eevee
370 Eiscue
127 Eldegoss
200 Espeon
199 Flareon
081 Froslass
350 Frosmoth
231 Gastrodon
170 Gigalith
203 Glaceon
080 Glalie
391 Goodra
319 Heliolisk
314 Hippopotas
315 Hippowdon
009 Inteleon
198 Jolteon
361 Lapras
202 Leafeon
038 Ludicolo
362 Lunatone
296 Maractus
153 Milotic
069 Ninetales
133 Palpitoad
063 Pelipper

060 Roselia
061 Roserade
134 Seismitoad
341 Shiinotic
079 Snorunt
096 Snover
007 Sobble
363 Solrock
204 Sylveon
300 Torkoal
132 Tympole
201 Umbreon
074 Vanilluxe
197 Vaporeon
068 Vulpix
356 Wailmer
357 Wailord
229 Whiscash

Whirlpool (TM36)
377 Arctovish
180 Arrokuda
235 Barbaracle
228 Barboach
181 Barraskewda
154 Basculin
042 Chewtle
220 Chinchou
151 Cloyster
102 Corphish
236 Corsola
309 Cramorant
103 Crawdaunt
237 Cursola
360 Dhelmise
376 Dracovish
043 Drednaw
008 Drizzile
370 Eiscue
152 Feebas
305 Frillish
231 Gastrodon
146 Goldeen
352 Grapploct
145 Gyarados
009 Inteleon
306 Jellicent
099 Kingler
098 Krabby
221 Lanturn
361 Lapras
032 Linoone
037 Lombre
036 Lotad
038 Ludicolo
355 Mantine
354 Mantyke
153 Milotic
260 Munchlax
033 Obstagoon
149 Octillery
063 Pelipper
101 Quagsire
304 Qwilfish
148 Remoraid
265 Rhydon
266 Rhyperior
147 Seaking
150 Shellder
230 Shellos
292 Sneasel
261 Snorlax
007 Sobble
385 Tyranitar

197 Vaporeon
356 Wailmer
357 Wailord
293 Weavile
229 Whiscash
155 Wishiwashi
100 Wooper
031 Zigzagoon

Whirlwind
282 Braviary
015 Butterfree
302 Cufant
314 Hippopotas
019 Hoothoot
284 Mandibuzz
176 Noibat
177 Noivern
281 Rufflet
041 Shiftry
297 Sigilyph
285 Skorupi
283 Vullaby

Wide Guard
215 Araquanid
359 Avalugg
086 Dwebble
350 Frosmoth
123 Gallade
108 Hitmonlee
110 Hitmontop
330 Honedge
099 Kingler
140 Machamp
355 Mantine
354 Mantyke
307 Mareanie
365 Mr. Mime
178 Onix
168 Roggenrola
369 Stonjourner
248 Throh
171 Timburr
308 Toxapex
347 Turtonator
232 Wimpod
062 Wingull
399 Zamazenta

Wild Charge (TR86)
071 Arcanine
375 Arctozolt
047 Boltund
048 Bunnelby
017 Charjabug
220 Chinchou
049 Diggersby
374 Dracozolt
035 Dubwool
066 Electrike
065 Galvantula
025 Greedent
070 Growlithe
016 Grubbin
319 Heliolisk
318 Helioptile
198 Jolteon
064 Joltik
114 Klang
113 Klink
115 Klinklang
221 Lanturn
067 Manectric
344 Morpeko

176 Noibat
177 Noivern
193 Pichu
194 Pikachu
333 Ponyta
195 Raichu
334 Rapidash
261 Snorlax
348 Togedemaru
311 Toxtricity
018 Vikavolt
034 Wooloo
046 Yamper
398 Zacian
399 Zamazenta

Wil-O-Wisp (TM38)
071 Arcanine
162 Carkol
160 Centiskorch
289 Chandelure
380 Charizard
378 Charmander
379 Charmeleon
163 Coalossal
329 Cofagrigus
236 Corsola
237 Cursola
368 Darmanitan
367 Darumaka
397 Dragapult
396 Drakloak
125 Drifblim
124 Drifloon
136 Dusclops
137 Dusknoir
135 Duskull
199 Flareon
305 Frillish
081 Froslass
123 Gallade
122 Gardevoir
141 Gastly
143 Gengar
192 Gourgeist
070 Growlithe
142 Haunter
317 Heatmor
306 Jellicent
121 Kirlia
250 Koffing
288 Lampent
287 Litwick
301 Mimikyu
069 Ninetales
338 Phantump
336 Polteageist
191 Pumpkaboo
120 Ralts
161 Rolycoly
372 Rotom
328 Runerigus
294 Sableye
244 Salandit
245 Salazzle
106 Shedinja
335 Sinistea
363 Solrock
300 Torkoal
339 Trevenant
347 Turtonator
068 Vulpix
251 Weezing

327 Yamask

Wing Attack
282 Braviary
378 Charmander
206 Flapple
320 Hawlucha
019 Hoothoot
355 Mantine
354 Mantyke
176 Noibat
177 Noivern
063 Pelipper
281 Rufflet
062 Wingull

Wish
254 Cleffa
196 Eevee
122 Gardevoir
092 Natu
193 Pichu
026 Pidove
211 Slurpuff
212 Spritzee
210 Swirlix
348 Togedemaru
259 Togekiss
257 Togepi
258 Togetic
093 Xatu

Withdraw
207 Appletun
205 Applin
235 Barbaracle
234 Binacle
151 Cloyster
087 Crustle
086 Dwebble
206 Flapple
336 Polteageist
150 Shellder
227 Shuckle
335 Sinistea
300 Torkoal

Wonder Room (TM71)
186 Alcremie
215 Araquanid
082 Baltoy
278 Beheeyem
119 Bronzong
118 Bronzor
083 Claydol
256 Clefable
255 Clefairy
254 Cleffa
329 Cofagrigus
187 Cutiefly
214 Dewpider
011 Dottler
271 Duosion
136 Dusclops
137 Dusknoir
135 Duskull
277 Elgyem
208 Espurr
123 Gallade
122 Gardevoir
141 Gastly
143 Gengar
240 Grimmsnarl
243 Hatterene
142 Haunter
337 Indeedee

121 Kirlia
209 Meowstic
364 Mime Jr.
340 Morelull
365 Mr. Mime
366 Mr. Rime
090 Munna
091 Musharna
342 Oranguru
012 Orbeetle
336 Polteageist
120 Ralts
334 Rapidash
272 Reuniclus
188 Ribombee
328 Runerigus
294 Sableye
341 Shiinotic
335 Sinistea
270 Solosis
363 Solrock
369 Stonjourner
201 Umbreon
251 Weezing
327 Yamask

Wood Hammer
097 Abomasnow
001 Grookey
296 Maractus
301 Mimikyu
338 Phantump
003 Rillaboom
096 Snover
253 Sudowoodo
002 Thwackey
339 Trevenant

Work Up (TR85)
095 Bewear
282 Braviary
048 Bunnelby
380 Charizard
378 Charmander
379 Charmeleon
051 Cinccino
006 Cinderace
256 Clefable
255 Clefairy
254 Cleffa
351 Clobbopus
173 Conkeldurr
303 Copperajah
023 Corviknight
022 Corvisquire
222 Croagunk
302 Cufant
368 Darmanitan
367 Darumaka
386 Deino
049 Diggersby
164 Diglett
346 Drampa
008 Drizzile
165 Dugtrio
196 Eevee
200 Espeon
208 Espurr
218 Farfetch'd
199 Flareon
123 Gallade
203 Glaceon
352 Grapploct
001 Grookey
172 Gurdurr

393 Hakamo-o	224 Scraggy	**Wrap**	064 Joltik	275 Shelmet	370 Eiscue	298 Riolu
320 Hawlucha	382 Silvally	160 Centiskorch	273 Karrablast	261 Snorlax	277 Elgyem	281 Rufflet
109 Hitmonchan	219 Sirfetch'd	360 Dhelmise	099 Kingler	226 Stunfisk	200 Espeon	328 Runerigus
108 Hitmonlee	261 Snorlax	290 Inkay	394 Kommo-o	210 Swirlix	208 Espurr	294 Sableye
110 Hitmontop	007 Sobble	291 Malamar	098 Krabby	259 Togekiss	345 Falinks	313 Sandaconda
019 Hoothoot	094 Stufful	153 Milotic	202 Leafeon	257 Togepi	123 Gallade	249 Sawk
388 Hydreigon	204 Sylveon	149 Octillery	301 Mimikyu	258 Togetic	122 Gardevoir	225 Scrafty
009 Inteleon	248 Throh	313 Sandaconda	104 Nincada	300 Torkoal	089 Golurk	224 Scraggy
392 Jangmo-o	002 Thwackey	227 Shuckle	105 Ninjask	100 Wooper	267 Gothita	297 Sigilyph
198 Jolteon	171 Timburr	312 Silicobra	176 Noibat	**Zap Cannon**	269 Gothitelle	382 Silvally
394 Kommo-o	348 Togedemaru	159 Sizzlipede	177 Noivern	114 Klang	268 Gothorita	261 Snorlax
202 Leafeon	259 Togekiss	**X-Scissor (TR60)**	033 Obstagoon	113 Klink	320 Hawlucha	270 Solosis
032 Linoone	257 Togepi	215 Araquanid	112 Pangoro	115 Klinklang	019 Hoothoot	363 Solrock
299 Lucario	258 Togetic	324 Axew	246 Pawniard	018 Vikavolt	388 Hydreigon	053 Steenee
140 Machamp	223 Toxicroak	235 Barbaracle	106 Shedinja	**Zen Headbutt (TR69)**	337 Indeedee	094 Stufful
139 Machoke	027 Tranquill	234 Binacle	041 Shiftry	377 Arctovish	121 Kirlia	175 Swoobat
138 Machop	347 Turtonator	247 Bisharp	382 Silvally	082 Baltoy	361 Lapras	248 Throh
209 Meowstic	381 Type: Null	160 Centiskorch	285 Skorupi	154 Basculin	037 Lombre	348 Togedemaru
182 Meowth	107 Tyrogue	017 Charjabug	292 Sneasel	278 Beheeyem	036 Lotad	259 Togekiss
301 Mimikyu	201 Umbreon	102 Corphish	223 Toxicroak	095 Bewear	299 Lucario	257 Togepi
050 Minccino	028 Unfezant	103 Crawdaunt	339 Trevenant	052 Bounsweet	038 Ludicolo	258 Togetic
260 Munchlax	197 Vaporeon	222 Croagunk	381 Type: Null	282 Braviary	362 Lunatone	054 Tsareena
020 Noctowl	398 Zacian	087 Crustle	117 Vespiquen	119 Bronzong	209 Meowstic	068 Vulpix
033 Obstagoon	399 Zamazenta	214 Dewpider	018 Vikavolt	006 Cinderace	365 Mr. Mime	356 Wailmer
342 Oranguru	031 Zigzagoon	286 Drapion	293 Weavile	083 Claydol	366 Mr. Rime	357 Wailord
111 Pancham	387 Zweilous	166 Drilbur	**Yawn**	256 Clefable	260 Munchlax	229 Whiscash
112 Pangoro	**Worry Seed**	316 Durant	276 Accelgor	255 Clefairy	090 Munna	174 Woobat
343 Passimian	059 Budew	086 Dwebble	279 Cubchoo	254 Cleffa	091 Musharna	093 Xatu
183 Perrserker	129 Cherrim	274 Escavalier	367 Darumaka	329 Cofagrigus	092 Natu	327 Yamask
184 Persian	128 Cherubi	167 Excadrill	196 Eevee	303 Copperajah	069 Ninetales	387 Zweilous
026 Pidove	262 Cottonee	325 Fraxure	208 Espurr	302 Cufant	020 Noctowl	**Zing Zap**
005 Raboot	126 Gossifleur	123 Gallade	314 Hippopotas	368 Darmanitan	342 Oranguru	353 Pincurchin
003 Rillaboom	192 Gourgeist	065 Galvantula	315 Hippowdon	367 Darumaka	012 Orbeetle	348 Togedemaru
298 Riolu	001 Grookey	233 Golisopod	090 Munna	386 Deino	111 Pancham	
021 Rookidee	296 Maractus	016 Grubbin	091 Musharna	011 Dottler	112 Pangoro	
281 Rufflet	191 Pumpkaboo	393 Hakamo-o	342 Oranguru	376 Dracovish	333 Ponyta	
249 Sawk	060 Roselia	320 Hawlucha	044 Purrloin	035 Dubwool	120 Ralts	
004 Scorbunny	061 Roserade	326 Haxorus	101 Quagsire	271 Duosion	334 Rapidash	
225 Scrafty	039 Seedot	392 Jangmo-o	230 Shellos		272 Reuniclus	

Abilities

Every Pokémon has an Ability, and the table below will help you understand the varied effects Abilities can have! The column titled **Effects in battle** lists how each Ability affects the Pokémon that has it—and sometimes also allies, opponents, or even the entire battlefield! The **Effects outside of battle** column lists the effects that a few Abilities exert on either your party Pokémon or your encounters with wild Pokémon when you're out exploring.

Ability	Effects in battle	Effects outside of battle
Adaptability	Increases the same-type attack bonus from the usual 50% boost in power to 100%.	—
Aftermath	Causes damage to an attacker equal to 1/4 of its max HP if the attacker knocks the Pokémon out using a move that makes direct contact.	—
Analytic	Boosts the power of the Pokémon's moves by 30% if the Pokémon goes last during a turn.	—
Anticipation	Provides a warning if an opposing Pokémon has supereffective moves or one-hit knockout moves. This warning occurs when the Pokémon with this Ability enters the battlefield.	—
Arena Trap	Prevents opposing Pokémon from fleeing or being switched out. Has no effect against Flying- or Ghost-type Pokémon and Pokémon with the Levitate Ability. Pokémon with the Run Away Ability can flee from a Pokémon with Arena Trap, but they will be prevented from switching out.	Makes it more likely you will encounter wild Pokémon if your lead Pokémon has this Ability.
Aroma Veil	Protects the Pokémon's side of the battlefield from the effects of Disable, Encore, Taunt, and Torment. Also protects from infatuation and the effect of the Cursed Body Ability.	—
Ball Fetch	Allows the Pokémon to retrieve a Poké Ball that was used in a battle but failed to catch a wild Pokémon. This effect will only apply to the first Poké Ball used. If the Pokémon is already holding an item, nothing happens.	—
Battery	Boosts the power of special moves used by the Pokémon's allies by 30%.	—
Battle Armor	Prevents opponents' damage-dealing moves from ever delivering a critical hit to the Pokémon.	—
Berserk	Raises the Pokémon's Sp. Atk by 1 stage when the Pokémon takes a hit that causes its HP to drop to 1/2 or less.	—
Big Pecks	Protects the Pokémon from having its Defense lowered by the moves or Abilities of other Pokémon.	—
Blaze	Boosts the power of the Pokémon's Fire-type moves by 50% when the Pokémon's HP drops to 1/3 or less.	—

Ability	Effects in battle	Effects outside of battle
Bulletproof	Protects the Pokémon from Acid Spray, Aura Sphere, Bullet Seed, Electro Ball, Energy Ball, Focus Blast, Gyro Ball, Octazooka, Pollen Puff, Pyro Ball, Rock Blast, Rock Wrecker, Seed Bomb, Shadow Ball, Sludge Bomb, Weather Ball, and Zap Cannon.	—
Cheek Pouch	Restores 1/3 of the Pokémon's max HP when the Pokémon eats a Berry (in addition to the Berry's usual benefits).	—
Chlorophyll	Doubles the Pokémon's Speed in the harsh sunlight weather condition.	—
Clear Body	Protects the Pokémon from having its stats lowered by the moves or Abilities of other Pokémon.	—
Cloud Nine	Negates the effects of weather conditions for all Pokémon on the battlefield.	—
Competitive	Raises the Pokémon's Sp. Atk by 2 stages whenever any of the Pokémon's stats are lowered due to an opponent's move or Ability.	—
Compound Eyes	Raises the Pokémon's accuracy by 30%.	Makes it more likely that the wild Pokémon you encounter will be holding items if your lead Pokémon has this Ability.
Contrary	Inverts the Pokémon's stat changes to have the opposite effect (lowered stats are instead raised and vice versa).	—
Corrosion	Allows the Pokémon to inflict the poisoned or badly poisoned status condition on Poison types and Steel types.	—
Cotton Down	Scatters cotton fluff around the Pokémon when the Pokémon is hit by a damage-dealing move. This lowers the Speed of all other Pokémon on the battlefield.	—
Cursed Body	Provides a 30% chance of disabling damage-dealing moves used against the Pokémon. Moves disabled this way cannot be used for 4 turns.	—
Cute Charm	Provides a 30% chance of inflicting infatuation on an attacker if the attacker hits the Pokémon with a move that makes direct contact. Gender-unknown Pokémon and Pokémon of the same gender are immune to this effect.	Makes it more likely you will encounter wild Pokémon of the opposite gender if your lead Pokémon has this Ability.
Damp	Prevents all Pokémon on the battlefield from using Explosion or Self-Destruct and nullifies the Aftermath Ability.	—
Dauntless Shield	Raises the Pokémon's Defense by 1 stage when the Pokémon enters the battlefield.	
Defiant	Raises the Pokémon's Attack by 2 stages whenever any of the Pokémon's stats are lowered due to an opponent's move or Ability.	—
Disguise	Protects the Pokémon from most damage the first time it is hit by a damage-dealing move. Then the Pokémon changes to its Busted Form.	—
Drizzle	Triggers the rain weather condition when the Pokémon enters the battlefield. This weather condition lasts for 5 turns.	—
Drought	Triggers the harsh sunlight weather condition when the Pokémon enters the battlefield. This weather condition lasts for 5 turns.	—
Dry Skin	Absorbs Water-type moves, making the Pokémon immune to their damage and effects. Instead, such moves restore 1/4 of the Pokémon's max HP. Restores 1/8 of the Pokémon's max HP at the end of each turn in the rain weather condition. However, this Ability also increases the damage the Pokémon takes from Fire-type moves by 25% and reduces its HP by 1/8 of its maximum at the end of each turn in the harsh sunlight weather condition.	—
Early Bird	Allows the Pokémon to wake more quickly when afflicted with the asleep status condition.	—
Effect Spore	Provides a 30% chance of inflicting the poisoned, paralysis, or asleep status condition on an attacker if the attacker hits the Pokémon with a move that makes direct contact. Grass-type Pokémon are immune to this effect.	—
Electric Surge	Triggers Electric Terrain when the Pokémon enters the battlefield. This terrain lasts for 5 turns.	—
Emergency Exit	Causes the Pokémon to automatically switch out of battle when its HP drops to 1/2 or less during a Trainer battle. During a battle with a wild Pokémon, the Pokémon flees when its HP drops to 1/2 or less. This Ability still triggers for Dynamax Pokémon but uses their Dynamax HP as the starting number instead. Does not trigger in Max Raid Battles.	—
Filter	Reduces the damage the Pokémon takes from supereffective moves by 25%.	—
Flame Body	Provides a 30% chance of inflicting the burned status condition on an attacker if the attacker hits the Pokémon with a move that makes direct contact.	Halves the time it takes for Pokémon Eggs to hatch if a Pokémon in your party has this Ability. This effect is not increased by also having other Pokémon with Flame Body or Steam Engine in your party.
Flare Boost	Boosts the power of the Pokémon's special moves by 50% when the Pokémon has the burned status condition.	—
Flash Fire	Absorbs Fire-type moves, making the Pokémon immune to their damage and effects. Also boosts the power of the Pokémon's Fire-type moves by 50% the first time this is triggered in battle.	Makes it more likely you will encounter wild Fire-type Pokémon if your lead Pokémon has this Ability.
Flower Gift	Raises the Pokémon's and the Pokémon's allies' Attack and Sp. Def by 50% each in the harsh sunlight weather condition. Causes Cherrim to change to its Sunshine Form in the harsh sunlight weather condition.	—
Fluffy	Halves the damage the Pokémon takes from moves that make direct contact. Doubles the damage the Pokémon takes from Fire-type moves.	
Forewarn	Reveals a move an opponent knows when the Pokémon with this Ability enters the battlefield. Damage-dealing moves with high power are prioritized.	—
Friend Guard	Reduces the damage taken by the Pokémon's allies by 25%.	—
Frisk	Identifies opponents' held items when the Pokémon with this Ability enters the battlefield.	—
Gluttony	Held Berries that are normally eaten at very low HP will instead be eaten when the Pokémon's HP drops to 1/2 or less.	—
Gooey	Lowers the Speed of an attacker by 1 stage if the attacker hits the Pokémon with a move that makes direct contact.	—
Gorilla Tactics	Raises the Pokémon's Attack by 1 stage, but the Pokémon can only use the first move it chooses when it enters the battlefield.	—

Ability	Effects in battle	Effects outside of battle
Gulp Missile	Allows the Pokémon to gulp up prey and change forms when it uses Surf or Dive. If the Pokémon's HP is more than 1/2 of its maximum, the Pokémon will catch an Arrokuda. If the Pokémon's HP is 1/2 of its maximum or below, the Pokémon will catch a Pikachu. When the Pokémon takes damage from an opponent, it will spit out its prey to damage the opponent and also trigger additional effects (Arrokuda: lowers opponent's Defense by 1 stage; Pikachu: inflicts paralysis status condition on the opponent).	—
Guts	Raises the Pokémon's Attack by 50% when the Pokémon is affected by a status condition. Although the burned status condition would usually lower the Pokémon's Attack, the Guts Ability prevents this.	—
Harvest	Provides a 50% chance of restoring one of the Pokémon's used Berries at the end of each turn. This becomes guaranteed in the harsh sunlight weather condition.	Makes it more likely you will encounter wild Grass-type Pokémon if your lead Pokémon has this Ability.
Healer	Provides a 30% chance that an ally Pokémon's status condition will be healed at the end of each turn.	—
Heatproof	Halves the damage the Pokémon takes from Fire-type moves and from the burned status condition.	—
Heavy Metal	Doubles the Pokémon's weight.	—
Honey Gather	Has no effect.	If the Pokémon has no held item, it sometimes finds a jar of Honey after a battle (even if it didn't participate). The chance of finding Honey increases with the Pokémon's level.
Huge Power	Doubles the Pokémon's Attack.	—
Hunger Switch	Causes the Pokémon to change form at the end of each turn, rotating between Full Belly Mode and Hangry Mode.	—
Hustle	Raises the Pokémon's Attack by 50% but lowers the accuracy of the Pokémon's physical moves by 20%.	—
Hydration	Heals the Pokémon's status conditions at the end of each turn in the rain weather condition.	—
Hyper Cutter	Protects the Pokémon from having its Attack lowered by the moves or Abilities of other Pokémon.	—
Ice Body	Restores 1/16 of the Pokémon's max HP at the end of each turn in the hail weather condition. Hail does not damage a Pokémon with this Ability.	—
Ice Face	Protects the Pokémon from damage the first time the Pokémon is hit by a physical move. Then the Pokémon's form changes from Ice Face to Noice Face. Does not protect from special moves. The Pokémon can return to its Ice Face form if the weather condition becomes hail, if it's sent out into battle during hail, or when the battle ends, allowing this Ability to be triggered again.	—
Ice Scales	Halves the damage the Pokémon takes from special moves.	—
Illuminate	Has no effect.	Makes it more likely you will encounter wild Pokémon if your lead Pokémon has this Ability.
Immunity	Protects the Pokémon from the poisoned and badly poisoned status conditions.	—
Imposter	Transforms the Pokémon into a copy of the opponent it is directly facing when it enters the battlefield.	—
Infiltrator	Allows the Pokémon's moves to hit despite Mist, Safeguard, or Substitute. Also prevents damage from being reduced by Aurora Veil, Light Screen, or Reflect.	Makes it less likely you will encounter wild Pokémon if your lead Pokémon has this Ability.
Innards Out	Causes damage to an attacker if the Pokémon with this Ability is knocked out. The attacker's HP is reduced by the same amount of HP as the attacked Pokémon had left before it was knocked out.	—
Inner Focus	Prevents the Pokémon from flinching and protects it from the effects of the Intimidate Ability.	—
Insomnia	Protects the Pokémon from the asleep status condition.	—
Intimidate	Lowers opponents' Attack by 1 stage when the Pokémon with this Ability enters the battlefield.	—
Intrepid Sword	Raises the Pokémon's Attack by 1 stage when the Pokémon enters the battlefield.	—
Iron Barbs	Causes damage to an attacker equal to 1/8 of its max HP if the attacker hits the Pokémon with a move that makes direct contact.	—
Iron Fist	Boosts the power of the Pokémon's punching moves by 20%. This affects Bullet Punch, Drain Punch, Dynamic Punch, Fire Punch, Focus Punch, Hammer Arm, Ice Punch, Mach Punch, Mega Punch, Meteor Mash, Power-Up Punch, Shadow Punch, and Thunder Punch.	—
Justified	Raises the Pokémon's Attack by 1 stage when the Pokémon is hit by a damage-dealing Dark-type move.	—
Keen Eye	Protects the Pokémon from having its accuracy lowered by opponents' moves. Ignores the effects of opponents' evasiveness-raising moves as well.	—
Klutz	The Pokémon can't use held items in battle, even if it is given an item to hold.	—
Leaf Guard	Protects the Pokémon from status conditions in the harsh sunlight weather condition.	—
Levitate	Gives the Pokémon immunity to damage-dealing Ground-type moves, as well as the effects of Spikes, Sticky Web, Toxic Spikes, and terrains.	—
Light Metal	Halves the Pokémon's weight.	—
Lightning Rod	Draws all Electric-type moves to the Pokémon. Absorbs Electric-type moves, making the Pokémon immune to their damage and effects. Instead, such moves raise the Pokémon's Sp. Atk by 1 stage.	Makes it more likely you will encounter wild Electric-type Pokémon if your lead Pokémon has this Ability.
Limber	Protects the Pokémon from the paralysis status condition.	—
Magic Bounce	Reflects back moves that attempt to lower the Pokémon's stats or inflict status conditions, as well as the effects of moves like Stealth Rock or Taunt.	—
Magic Guard	Protects the Pokémon from any damage not directly dealt by a move. This nullifies the damage from Abilities, weather conditions, status conditions, items, and ongoing move effects (such as Bind or Spikes).	—
Marvel Scale	Raises the Pokémon's Defense by 50% when the Pokémon has a status condition.	—

Ability	Effects in battle	Effects outside of battle
Merciless	Guarantees that the Pokémon's moves will deliver critical hits as long as the target has the poisoned or badly poisoned status condition.	—
Mimicry	Changes the Pokémon's type depending on the terrain. Electric Terrain: Changes to Electric type. Grassy Terrain: Changes to Grass type. Misty Terrain: Changes to Fairy type. Psychic Terrain: Changes to Psychic type. If the terrain returns to normal, the Pokémon also returns to its regular type.	—
Minus	Raises the Pokémon's Sp. Atk by 50% if an ally has either the Plus or Minus Ability.	—
Mirror Armor	Reflects back any attempt to lower the Pokémon's stats. This does not prevent damage from moves, but additional effects from moves like Breaking Swipe, Mud-Slap, or Psychic are applied to the move's user instead.	—
Misty Surge	Triggers Misty Terrain when the Pokémon enters the battlefield. This terrain lasts for 5 turns.	—
Mold Breaker	Makes the Pokémon's moves ignore the effects of Abilities. For example, Earthquake will hit even Pokémon with the Levitate Ability. Does not nullify Abilities that have effects after a move lands.	—
Moody	Raises one stat by 2 stages and lowers another by 1 stage at the end of each turn. When selecting a stat to raise, this Ability will not select a stat that cannot be raised any higher. The same applies when selecting a stat to lower.	—
Moxie	Raises the Pokémon's Attack by 1 stage when the Pokémon uses a move that knocks out another Pokémon.	—
Mummy	Changes an attacker's Ability if the attacker hits the Pokémon with a move that makes direct contact. That attacker's Ability becomes Mummy. Fails with certain Abilities, however.	—
Natural Cure	Heals the Pokémon's status conditions when the Pokémon is switched out of battle.	—
Neutralizing Gas	Nullifies the Abilities of all other Pokémon on the battlefield and prevents them from being activated. Fails with certain Abilities, however.	—
No Guard	Moves used by or against the Pokémon don't miss.	Makes it more likely you will encounter wild Pokémon if your lead Pokémon has this Ability.
Oblivious	Protects the Pokémon from infatuation, as well as the effects of Taunt and the Intimidate Ability.	—
Overcoat	Protects the Pokémon from taking damage in the hail and sandstorm weather conditions. Also protects it from Cotton Spore, Magic Powder, Poison Powder, Rage Powder, Sleep Powder, Spore, and Stun Spore, as well as the Effect Spore Ability.	—
Overgrow	Boosts the power of the Pokémon's Grass-type moves by 50% when the Pokémon's HP drops to 1/3 or less.	—
Own Tempo	Protects the Pokémon from confusion and from the effects of the Intimidate Ability.	—
Pastel Veil	Protects the Pokémon's side of the battlefield from the poisoned and badly poisoned status conditions.	—
Perish Body	If the Pokémon is hit by a move that makes direct contact, both the Pokémon and the attacker will faint after 3 turns unless switched out.	—
Pickpocket	Allows the Pokémon to steal an attacker's held item if the attacker hits the Pokémon with a move that makes direct contact. If the Pokémon is already holding an item, nothing happens.	—
Pickup	Allows the Pokémon to pick up a held item that an opposing Pokémon used in the same turn. If the Pokémon with this Ability is already holding an item, nothing happens.	If the Pokémon has no held item, it sometimes picks one up after a battle (even if it didn't participate). It picks up different items depending on its level.
Pixilate	Changes the Pokémon's Normal-type moves to Fairy type and boosts their power by 20%. This effect also applies to Max Moves. (Max Strike will become the Fairy-type Max Move, Max Starfall.)	—
Plus	Raises the Pokémon's Sp. Atk by 50% if an ally has either the Plus or Minus Ability.	—
Poison Point	Provides a 30% chance of inflicting the poisoned status condition on an attacker if the attacker hits the Pokémon with a move that makes direct contact.	—
Poison Touch	Provides a 30% chance of inflicting the poisoned status condition on a target if the Pokémon with this Ability hits the target with a move that makes direct contact.	—
Power Spot	Boosts the power of moves used by the adjacent Pokémon by 30%.	—
Prankster	Gives higher priority to the Pokémon's status moves. A move affected by this Ability will fail if the target is a Dark-type Pokémon.	—
Pressure	When the Pokémon is targeted by an opponent's move, this Ability causes that move to lose an extra point from its PP.	—
Propeller Tail	Allows the Pokémon to ignore the effects of the Lightning Rod and Storm Drain Abilities, as well as the Ally Switch, Follow Me, and Rage Powder moves.	—
Psychic Surge	Triggers Psychic Terrain when the Pokémon enters the battlefield. This terrain lasts for 5 turns.	—
Punk Rock	Boosts the power of the Pokémon's sound-based moves, such as Boomburst and Overdrive, by 30%. Also halves the damage the Pokémon takes from sound-based moves.	—
Queenly Majesty	Prevents opposing Pokémon from using damage-dealing moves that have high priority.	—
Quick Feet	Raises the Pokémon's Speed by 50% when the Pokémon has a status condition. Although the paralysis status condition would usually lower the Pokémon's Speed, the Quick Feet Ability prevents this.	Makes it less likely you will encounter wild Pokémon if your lead Pokémon has this Ability.
Rain Dish	Restores 1/16 of the Pokémon's max HP at the end of each turn in the rain weather condition.	—
Rattled	Raises the Pokémon's Speed by 1 stage when the Pokémon is hit by a damage-dealing Bug-, Ghost-, or Dark-type move or affected by the Intimidate Ability.	—
Receiver	Copies the Ability of a defeated ally over to the Pokémon, replacing Receiver with that Ability. Fails with certain Abilities, however.	—
Reckless	Boosts the power of any of the Pokémon's moves by 20% if those moves cause recoil damage.	—
Regenerator	Restores 1/3 of the Pokémon's max HP when the Pokémon is switched out of battle.	—
Ripen	Doubles the effect of Berries eaten by the Pokémon. Doubles healing effects, damage reduction, stat changes, friendship gains, and damage dealt to an opponent. Has no effect on Berries that heal status conditions.	—

Ability	Effects in battle	Effects outside of battle
Rivalry	Boosts the power of the Pokémon's moves by 25% if they are used against a target of the same gender as the Pokémon. If a target is of the opposite gender, moves' power goes down by 25%. No effect when the target's gender is unknown.	—
RKS System	Causes the Pokémon to change its type according to the memory disc it is holding.	—
Rock Head	Protects the Pokémon from recoil damage from moves like Double-Edge and Take Down.	—
Run Away	Allows the Pokémon to always escape from a battle with a wild Pokémon.	—
Sand Force	Boosts the power of the Pokémon's Ground-, Rock-, and Steel-type moves by 30% in the sandstorm weather condition. Sandstorms do not damage a Pokémon with this Ability.	—
Sand Rush	Doubles the Pokémon's Speed in the sandstorm weather condition. Sandstorms do not damage a Pokémon with this Ability.	—
Sand Spit	Triggers the sandstorm weather condition when the Pokémon takes damage. This weather condition lasts for 5 turns.	—
Sand Stream	Triggers the sandstorm weather condition when the Pokémon enters the battlefield. This weather condition lasts for 5 turns.	—
Sand Veil	Lowers the accuracy of moves used on the Pokémon by 20% in the sandstorm weather condition. Sandstorms do not damage a Pokémon with this Ability.	—
Sap Sipper	Absorbs Grass-type moves, making the Pokémon immune to their damage and effects. Instead, such moves raise the Pokémon's Attack by 1 stage.	—
Schooling	Causes the Pokémon to change to its School Form if its level is 20 or greater. It changes back to its Solo Form when its HP drops to 1/4 or less.	—
Scrappy	Allows the Pokémon to hit Ghost-type Pokémon with Normal- and Fighting-type moves. Also protects the Pokémon from the effects of the Intimidate Ability.	—
Screen Cleaner	Nullifies the effects of Aurora Veil, Light Screen, and Reflect for both sides of the battlefield when the Pokémon enters the battlefield.	—
Serene Grace	Doubles the chances of the Pokémon's moves inflicting additional effects.	—
Shadow Tag	Prevents opposing Pokémon from fleeing or switching out. This effect is canceled if an opposing Pokémon also has this Ability.	—
Shed Skin	Provides a 33% chance of healing the Pokémon's status conditions at the end of each turn.	—
Sheer Force	Boosts the power of the Pokémon's moves by 30% if they can have additional effects. However, the additional effects do not trigger.	—
Shell Armor	Prevents opponents' damage-dealing moves from ever delivering a critical hit to the Pokémon.	—
Shield Dust	Protects the Pokémon from the additional effects of moves. However, the Pokémon is still affected by additional effects generated by Max Moves.	—
Simple	Doubles any stat changes affecting the Pokémon.	—
Skill Link	Ensures that the Pokémon's multihit moves always hit the maximum number of times. (Moves that can hit 2–5 times always hit 5 times.)	—
Slush Rush	Doubles the Pokémon's Speed in the hail weather condition. Hail does not damage a Pokémon with this Ability.	—
Sniper	Boosts the power of the Pokémon's critical hits. Power increases by 125% rather than the usual 50%.	—
Snow Cloak	Lowers the accuracy of moves used on the Pokémon by 20% in the hail weather condition. Hail does not damage a Pokémon with this Ability.	—
Snow Warning	Triggers the hail weather condition when the Pokémon enters the battlefield. This weather condition lasts for 5 turns.	—
Solar Power	Raises the Pokémon's Sp. Atk by 50% in the harsh sunlight weather condition. But the Pokémon also loses 1/8 of its max HP at the end of each turn as long as that weather condition continues.	—
Solid Rock	Reduces the damage the Pokémon takes from supereffective moves by 25%.	—
Soundproof	Protects the Pokémon from sound-based moves, such as Clanging Scales and Parting Shot.	—
Speed Boost	Raises the Pokémon's Speed by 1 stage at the end of each turn.	—
Stall	Causes the Pokémon to move last each turn.	—
Stalwart	Allows the Pokémon to ignore the effects of the Lightning Rod and Storm Drain Abilities, as well as the Ally Switch, Follow Me, and Rage Powder moves.	—
Stamina	Raises the Pokémon's Defense by 1 stage every time the Pokémon takes damage from a move.	—
Stance Change	Causes the Pokémon to change from its Shield Forme to its Blade Forme when using a damage-dealing move. The Pokémon changes back to Shield Forme if King's Shield is used.	—
Static	Provides a 30% chance of inflicting the paralysis status condition on an attacker if the attacker hits the Pokémon with a move that makes direct contact.	Makes it more likely you will encounter wild Electric-type Pokémon if your lead Pokémon has this Ability.
Steadfast	Raises the Pokémon's Speed by 1 stage every time the Pokémon flinches.	—
Steam Engine	Raises the Pokémon's Speed to the max if the Pokémon is hit by a Fire- or Water-type move.	Halves the time it takes for Pokémon Eggs to hatch if a Pokémon in your party has this Ability. This effect is not increased by also having other Pokémon with Flame Body or Steam Engine in your party.
Steelworker	Boosts the power of the Pokémon's Steel-type moves by 50%.	—
Steely Spirit	Boosts the power of Steel-type moves for the Pokémon and its allies by 50%.	—
Stench	Provides a 10% chance of making targets flinch when the Pokémon hits them with a damage-dealing move.	Makes it less likely you will encounter wild Pokémon if your lead Pokémon has this Ability.
Sticky Hold	Prevents the Pokémon's held item from being removed by other Pokémon's moves or Abilities.	—

Ability	Effects in battle	Effects outside of battle
Storm Drain	Draws all Water-type moves to the Pokémon. Absorbs Water-type moves, making the Pokémon immune to their damage and effects. Instead, such moves raise the Pokémon's Sp. Atk by 1 stage.	Makes it more likely you will encounter wild Water-type Pokémon if your lead Pokémon has this Ability.
Strong Jaw	Boosts the power of Bite, Crunch, Fire Fang, Fishious Rend, Ice Fang, Jaw Lock, Poison Fang, Psychic Fangs, and Thunder Fang by 50%.	—
Sturdy	Protects the Pokémon from one-hit knockout moves, like Horn Drill and Sheer Cold. If the Pokémon's HP is full, this Ability also leaves the Pokémon with 1 HP if the Pokémon is hit by a move that would normally knock it out.	—
Suction Cups	Protects the Pokémon from being switched out by moves like Dragon Tail, Roar, and Whirlwind and items like Red Card.	—
Super Luck	Makes the Pokémon's moves more likely to deliver a critical hit.	Makes it more likely that the wild Pokémon you encounter will be holding items if your lead Pokémon has this Ability.
Swarm	Boosts the power of the Pokémon's Bug-type moves by 50% when the Pokémon's HP drops to 1/3 or less.	—
Sweet Veil	Protects the Pokémon's side of the battlefield from the asleep status condition.	—
Swift Swim	Doubles the Pokémon's Speed in the rain weather condition.	—
Symbiosis	Causes the Pokémon to give its held item to an ally if that ally uses its own held item.	—
Synchronize	Shares the Pokémon's status conditions. If the Pokémon is inflicted with the poisoned, badly poisoned, paralysis, or burned status condition, the Pokémon that caused the status condition is also afflicted with it.	Guarantees that the wild Pokémon you encounter will have the same Nature as your lead Pokémon if your lead Pokémon has this Ability.
Tangled Feet	Lowers the accuracy of moves used on the Pokémon by 50% if the Pokémon with this Ability is confused.	—
Technician	Boosts the power of the Pokémon's moves by 50% if their power is 60 or less. This effect is triggered for moves of variable power or moves affected by other factors as long as an individual move's power ends up being 60 or less.	—
Telepathy	Prevents the Pokémon from taking damage from allies.	—
Thick Fat	Halves the damage the Pokémon takes from Fire- and Ice-type moves.	—
Tinted Lens	Makes the Pokémon's moves more effective against Pokémon that have a type advantage. (Half damage turns into regular damage, and 1/4 damage turns into half damage.)	—
Torrent	Boosts the power of the Pokémon's Water-type moves by 50% when the Pokémon's HP drops to 1/3 or less.	—
Tough Claws	Boosts the power of the Pokémon's moves by 30% if those moves make direct contact.	—
Trace	Makes the Pokémon's Ability the same as the opponent's. Fails with certain Abilities, however. When the Pokémon is faced with multiple opponents, the Ability of one is chosen at random.	—
Truant	Causes the Pokémon to slack off, making its moves fail every other turn.	—
Unaware	When the Pokémon uses or is the target of a damage-dealing move, the move ignores changes to all opponents' stats except Speed.	—
Unburden	Doubles the Pokémon's Speed if the Pokémon loses or consumes a held item. Its Speed returns to normal if the Pokémon gains a held item again. This Ability has no effect if the Pokémon has no held item throughout the battle.	—
Unnerve	Prevents opposing Pokémon from eating Berries they hold.	—
Vital Spirit	Protects the Pokémon from the asleep status condition.	—
Volt Absorb	Absorbs Electric-type moves, making the Pokémon immune to their damage and effects. Instead, such moves restore 1/4 of the Pokémon's max HP.	—
Wandering Spirit	Exchanges the Pokémon's Ability with an attacker's if the attacker hits the Pokémon with a move that makes direct contact. Fails with certain Abilities, however.	—
Water Absorb	Absorbs Water-type moves, making the Pokémon immune to their damage and effects. Instead, such moves restore 1/4 of the Pokémon's max HP.	—
Water Bubble	Halves the damage the Pokémon takes from Fire-type moves and protects the Pokémon from the burned status condition.	—
Water Veil	Protects the Pokémon from the burned status condition.	—
Weak Armor	Lowers the Pokémon's Defense by 1 stage when the Pokémon is hit by a physical move but also raises the Pokémon's Speed by 2 stages.	—
White Smoke	Protects the Pokémon from having its stats lowered by the moves or Abilities of other Pokémon.	Makes it less likely you will encounter wild Pokémon if your lead Pokémon has this Ability.
Wimp Out	Causes the Pokémon to automatically switch out of battle when its HP drops to 1/2 or less during a Trainer battle. During a battle with a wild Pokémon, the Pokémon flees when its HP drops to 1/2 or less. This Ability still triggers for Dynamax Pokémon but uses their Dynamax HP as the starting number instead. Does not trigger in Max Raid Battles.	—
Wonder Guard	Protects the Pokémon from all moves except supereffective ones.	—
Wonder Skin	Makes status moves more likely to miss the Pokémon.	—
Zen Mode	Causes the Pokémon to change to its Zen Mode form when its HP drops to 1/2 or less.	—

Pokémon Abilities Reverse Lookup

Every species of Pokémon typically has one or two common Abilities. You can even switch which one your Pokémon has with the Ability Capsule item, which you can get at the BP Shop in the Battle Tower (p. 478) after becoming Champion. But if you're hoping to build your battle strategy around a certain Ability, how do you know which Pokémon have that Ability? The following pages will help with that! They list the species of Pokémon that can have a given Ability as one of their common Abilities or as a rare Hidden Ability. Hidden Abilities are unusual Abilities that a Pokémon might have if you catch it in a Max Raid Battle (p. 18). Keep in mind that some Hidden Abilities may not have been discovered yet! A Pokémon with different forms may also have different Abilities depending on the form it's in. Check out the specifics of which Ability each form can have and whether each Ability is a common Ability or a Hidden Ability by turning back to the data pages starting on page 189.

Adaptability
154 Basculin
102 Corphish
103 Crawdaunt
196 Eevee
152 Feebas

Aftermath
125 Drifblim
124 Drifloon
158 Garbodor
131 Skuntank
130 Stunky
157 Trubbish

Analytic
278 Beheeyem
277 Elgyem

Anticipation
228 Barboach
222 Croagunk
196 Eevee
190 Ferrothorn
241 Hatenna
243 Hatterene
242 Hattrem
333 Ponyta
334 Rapidash
223 Toxicroak
229 Whiscash

Arena Trap
164 Diglett
165 Dugtrio
321 Trapinch

Aroma Veil
186 Alcremie
213 Aromatisse
185 Milcery
212 Spritzee

Ball Fetch
046 Yamper

Battery
017 Charjabug

Battle Armor
286 Drapion
345 Falinks
183 Perrserker
285 Skorupi
381 Type: Null

Berserk
346 Drampa

Big Pecks
022 Corvisquire
284 Mandibuzz
026 Pidove
021 Rookidee
027 Tranquill
028 Unfezant
283 Vullaby

Blaze
380 Charizard
378 Charmander
379 Charmeleon
006 Cinderace
005 Raboot
004 Scorbunny

Bulletproof
205 Applin
393 Hakamo-o
392 Jangmo-o
394 Kommo-o

Cheek Pouch
048 Bunnelby
049 Diggersby
025 Greedent
024 Skwovet

Chlorophyll
058 Bellossom
128 Cherubi
262 Cottonee
056 Gloom
202 Leafeon
296 Maractus
040 Nuzleaf
055 Oddish
039 Seedot
041 Shiftry
057 Vileplume
263 Whimsicott

Clear Body
397 Dragapult
396 Drakloak
395 Dreepy
114 Klang
113 Klink
115 Klinklang

Cloud Nine
346 Drampa

Competitive
267 Gothita
269 Gothitelle
268 Gothorita
209 Meowstic
153 Milotic

Compound Eyes
010 Blipbug
015 Butterfree
011 Dottler
065 Galvantula
064 Joltik
104 Nincada

Contrary
290 Inkay
291 Malamar
227 Shuckle

Corrosion
244 Salandit
245 Salazzle

Cotton Down
127 Eldegoss
126 Gossifleur

Cursed Body
236 Corsola
397 Dragapult
396 Drakloak
395 Dreepy
305 Frillish
081 Froslass
143 Gengar
306 Jellicent
336 Polteageist
335 Sinistea

Cute Charm
051 Cinccino
256 Clefable
255 Clefairy
254 Cleffa
153 Milotic
050 Minccino
094 Stufful
204 Sylveon

Damp
305 Frillish
306 Jellicent
101 Quagsire
100 Wooper

Dauntless Shield
399 Zamazenta

Defiant
247 Bisharp
282 Braviary
345 Falinks
033 Obstagoon
343 Passimian
246 Pawniard

Disguise
301 Mimikyu

Drizzle
063 Pelipper
153 Milotic

Drought
069 Ninetales
300 Torkoal
068 Vulpix

Dry Skin
222 Croagunk
319 Heliolisk
318 Helioptile
223 Toxicroak

Early Bird
092 Natu
040 Nuzleaf
039 Seedot

Frisk
136 Dusclops
137 Dusknoir

041 Shiftry
093 Xatu

Effect Spore
127 Eldegoss
126 Gossifleur
340 Morelull
341 Shiinotic
057 Vileplume

Electric Surge
353 Pincurchin

Emergency Exit
233 Golisopod

Filter
364 Mime Jr.
365 Mr. Mime

Flame Body
162 Carkol
160 Centiskorch
289 Chandelure
163 Coalossal
288 Lampent
287 Litwick
159 Sizzlipede

Flare Boost
125 Drifblim
124 Drifloon

Flash Fire
071 Arcanine
162 Carkol
160 Centiskorch
289 Chandelure
163 Coalossal
199 Flareon
070 Growlithe
317 Heatmor
288 Lampent
287 Litwick
069 Ninetales
161 Rolycoly
159 Sizzlipede
068 Vulpix

Flower Gift
129 Cherrim

Fluffy
095 Bewear
035 Dubwool
094 Stufful
034 Wooloo

Forewarn
090 Munna
091 Musharna

Friend Guard
255 Clefairy
254 Cleffa

Heatproof
119 Bronzong
118 Bronzor

135 Duskull
267 Gothita
269 Gothitelle
268 Gothorita
192 Gourgeist
240 Grimmsnarl
238 Impidimp
239 Morgrem
176 Noibat
177 Noivern
012 Orbeetle
338 Phantump
191 Pumpkaboo
339 Trevenant

Gluttony
207 Appletun
205 Applin
206 Flapple
317 Heatmor
032 Linoone
260 Munchlax
227 Shuckle
261 Snorlax
031 Zigzagoon

Gooey
391 Goodra
389 Goomy
390 Sliggoo

Gorilla Tactics
368 Darmanitan

Gulp Missile
309 Cramorant

Guts
173 Conkeldurr
199 Flareon
172 Gurdurr
383 Larvitar
140 Machamp
139 Machoke
138 Machop
033 Obstagoon
161 Rolycoly
159 Sizzlipede
068 Vulpix
248 Throh
171 Timburr
107 Tyrogue

Harvest
338 Phantump
339 Trevenant

Healer
213 Aromatisse
058 Bellossom
241 Hatenna
243 Hatterene
242 Hattrem
212 Spritzee

Ice Body
377 Arctovish
359 Avalugg
358 Bergmite
203 Glaceon
080 Glalie
365 Mr. Mime

161 Rolycoly

Heavy Metal
119 Bronzong
118 Bronzor
303 Copperajah
302 Cufant
371 Duraludon

Honey Gather
116 Combee
187 Cutiefly
188 Ribombee

Huge Power
048 Bunnelby
049 Diggersby

Hunger Switch
344 Morpeko

Hustle
116 Combee
317 Heatmor
367 Darumaka
386 Deino
078 Delibird
374 Dracozolt
316 Durant
206 Flapple
148 Remoraid
281 Rufflet
259 Togekiss
257 Togepi
258 Togetic
387 Zweilous

Hydration
276 Accelgor
228 Barboach
391 Goodra
389 Goomy
361 Lapras
133 Palpitoad
275 Shelmet
390 Sliggoo
132 Tympole
197 Vaporeon
229 Whiscash
062 Wingull

Hyper Cutter
102 Corphish
103 Crawdaunt
099 Kingler
098 Krabby
295 Mawile
321 Trapinch

366 Mr. Rime
079 Snorunt
073 Vanillish
072 Vanillite
074 Vanilluxe

Ice Face
370 Eiscue

Ice Scales
350 Frosmoth
349 Snom

Illuminate
220 Chinchou
221 Lanturn
340 Morelull
341 Shiinotic

Immunity
261 Snorlax

Imposter
373 Ditto

Infiltrator
289 Chandelure
262 Cottonee
397 Dragapult
396 Drakloak
395 Dreepy
208 Espurr
290 Inkay
288 Lampent
287 Litwick
291 Malamar
209 Meowstic
105 Ninjask
176 Noibat
177 Noivern
263 Whimsicott

Innards Out
156 Pyukumuku

Inner Focus
247 Bisharp
367 Darumaka
080 Glalie
109 Hitmonchan
337 Indeedee
299 Lucario
084 Mudbray
085 Mudsdale
342 Oranguru
246 Pawniard
298 Riolu
249 Sawk
292 Sneasel
079 Snorunt
248 Throh
201 Umbreon

Insomnia
078 Delibird
192 Gourgeist
019 Hoothoot
020 Noctowl
191 Pumpkaboo

Intimidate
071 Arcanine
070 Growlithe
145 Gyarados
110 Hitmontop
295 Mawile
304 Qwilfish
225 Scrafty
224 Scraggy

Intrepid Sword
398 Zacian

Iron Barbs
189 Ferroseed
190 Ferrothorn
348 Togedemaru

Iron Fist
173 Conkeldurr
088 Golett
089 Golurk
172 Gurdurr
109 Hitmonchan
111 Pancham
112 Pangoro
171 Timburr

Justified
071 Arcanine
123 Gallade
070 Growlithe
299 Lucario

Keen Eye
282 Braviary
022 Corvisquire
286 Drapion
208 Espurr
109 Hitmonchan
019 Hoothoot
209 Meowstic
020 Noctowl
063 Pelipper
021 Rookidee
281 Rufflet
294 Sableye
285 Skorupi
131 Skuntank
292 Sneasel
130 Stunky
062 Wingull

Klutz
095 Bewear
088 Golett
089 Golurk
094 Stufful
175 Swoobat
310 Toxel
174 Woobat

Leaf Guard
052 Bounsweet
059 Budew
202 Leafeon
060 Roselia
053 Steenee
054 Tsareena

Levitate
082 Baltoy
119 Bronzong
118 Bronzor
083 Claydol
135 Duskull
323 Flygon
141 Gastly
142 Haunter
388 Hydreigon
250 Koffing
362 Lunatone
372 Rotom
363 Solrock
322 Vibrava
018 Vikavolt
251 Weezing

Light Metal
371 Duraludon

Lightning Rod
066 Electrike
067 Manectric
146 Goldeen
147 Seaking
193 Pichu
194 Pikachu
353 Pincurchin
195 Raichu
265 Rhydon
264 Rhyhorn
266 Rhyperior
348 Togedemaru

Limber
351 Clobbopus
373 Ditto
352 Grapploct
320 Hawlucha
108 Hitmonlee
045 Liepard
307 Mareanie
184 Persian
044 Purrloin
308 Toxapex

Magic Bounce
200 Espeon
241 Hatenna
243 Hatterene
242 Hattrem
092 Natu
093 Xatu

Magic Guard
256 Clefable
255 Clefairy
254 Cleffa
271 Duosion
272 Reuniclus
297 Sigilyph
270 Solosis

Marvel Scale
153 Milotic

Merciless
307 Mareanie
308 Toxapex

Mimicry
226 Stunfisk

Minus
066 Electrike
114 Klang
113 Klink
115 Klinklang
067 Manectric
311 Toxtricity

Mirror Armor
023 Corviknight

Misty Surge
251 Weezing

Mold Breaker
324 Axew
154 Basculin
166 Drilbur
167 Excadrill
325 Fraxure
320 Hawlucha
326 Haxorus
111 Pancham
112 Pangoro
249 Sawk
248 Throh

Moody
080 Glalie
149 Octillery
148 Remoraid
079 Snorunt

Moxie
145 Gyarados
225 Scrafty
224 Scraggy

Mummy
329 Cofagrigus
327 Yamask

Natural Cure
059 Budew
338 Phantump
060 Roselia
061 Roserade
339 Trevenant

Neutralizing Gas
250 Koffing
251 Weezing

No Guard
331 Doublade
088 Golett
089 Golurk
330 Honedge
273 Karrablast
140 Machamp
139 Machoke
138 Machop

Oblivious
228 Barboach
052 Bounsweet
152 Feebas
077 Mamoswine
076 Piloswine
244 Salandit
245 Salazzle
053 Steenee
075 Swinub
356 Wailmer
357 Wailord
229 Whiscash

Overcoat
151 Cloyster
271 Duosion
274 Escavalier
393 Hakamo-o
392 Jangmo-o
394 Kommo-o
284 Mandibuzz
272 Reuniclus
150 Shellder
275 Shelmet
270 Solosis
283 Vullaby

Overgrow
001 Grookey
003 Rillaboom
002 Thwackey

Own Tempo
359 Avalugg
358 Bergmite
208 Espurr
337 Indeedee
037 Lombre
036 Lotad
038 Ludicolo
084 Mudbray
085 Mudsdale

Pastel Veil
333 Ponyta
334 Rapidash

Perish Body
237 Cursola

Pickpocket
235 Barbaracle
234 Binacle
240 Grimmsnarl
238 Impidimp
239 Morgrem
040 Nuzleaf
039 Seedot
041 Shiftry
292 Sneasel
293 Weavile

Pickup
048 Bunnelby
049 Diggersby
192 Gourgeist
032 Linoone
182 Meowth
260 Munchlax
191 Pumpkaboo
031 Zigzagoon

Pixilate
204 Sylveon

Plus
114 Klang
113 Klink
115 Klinklang
311 Toxtricity

Poison Point
059 Budew
304 Qwilfish
060 Roselia
061 Roserade

Poison Touch
222 Croagunk
134 Seismitoad
223 Toxicroak

Power Spot
369 Stonjourner

Prankster
262 Cottonee
240 Grimmsnarl
238 Impidimp
045 Liepard
209 Meowstic
239 Morgrem
044 Purrloin
298 Riolu
294 Sableye
263 Whimsicott

Pressure
247 Bisharp
023 Corvikight
136 Dusclops
137 Dusknoir
400 Eternatus
246 Pawniard
117 Vespiquen
356 Wailmer
357 Wailord
293 Weavile

Propeller Tail
180 Arrokuda
181 Barraskewda

Psychic Surge
337 Indeedee

Punk Rock
311 Toxtricity

Queenly Majesty
054 Tsareena

Quick Feet
198 Jolteon
032 Linoone
031 Zigzagoon

Rain Dish
037 Lombre
036 Lotad
038 Ludicolo
340 Morelull
063 Pelipper
341 Shiinotic
062 Wingull

Rattled
252 Bonsly
279 Cubchoo
144 Magikarp
253 Sudowoodo
310 Toxel

Receiver
343 Passimian

Reckless
154 Basculin
108 Hitmonlee
033 Obstagoon
265 Rhydon
264 Rhyhorn
266 Rhyperior

Regenerator
271 Duosion
127 Eldegoss
126 Gossifleur
307 Mareanie
272 Reuniclus
270 Solosis
308 Toxapex

Ripen
207 Appletun
205 Applin
206 Flapple

Rivalry
324 Axew
325 Fraxure
326 Haxorus
026 Pidove
027 Tranquill
028 Unfezant

RKS System
382 Silvally

Rock Head
154 Basculin
252 Bonsly
178 Onix
265 Rhydon
264 Rhyhorn
253 Sudowoodo

Run Away
013 Caterpie
196 Eevee
029 Nickit
104 Nincada
055 Oddish
333 Ponyta
334 Rapidash
030 Thievul
034 Wooloo

Sand Force
169 Boldore
164 Diglett
166 Drilbur
165 Dugtrio
167 Excadrill
231 Gastrodon
170 Gigalith
314 Hippopotas
315 Hippowdon
168 Roggenrola
230 Shellos

Sand Rush
166 Drilbur
167 Excadrill

Sand Spit
313 Sandaconda
312 Silicobra

Sand Stream
170 Gigalith
314 Hippopotas
315 Hippowdon
385 Tyranitar

Sand Veil
164 Diglett
165 Dugtrio
319 Heliolisk
318 Helioptile
383 Larvitar
313 Sandaconda
312 Silicobra

Sap Sipper
346 Drampa
391 Goodra
389 Goomy
390 Sliggoo

Schooling
155 Wishiwashi

Scrappy
218 Farfetch'd
111 Pancham
112 Pangoro
219 Sirfetch'd

Screen Cleaner
365 Mr. Mime
366 Mr. Rime

Serene Grace
259 Togekiss
257 Togepi
258 Togetic

Shadow Tag
267 Gothita
269 Gothitelle
268 Gothorita
217 Wobbuffet
216 Wynaut

Shed Skin
273 Karrablast
014 Metapod
384 Pupitar
313 Sandaconda
225 Scrafty
224 Scraggy
312 Silicobra

Sheer Force
282 Braviary
173 Conkeldurr
303 Copperajah
302 Cufant
172 Gurdurr
099 Kingler
098 Krabby
295 Mawile
281 Rufflet
179 Steelix
171 Timburr
321 Trapinch

Shell Armor
042 Chewtle
151 Cloyster
102 Corphish
103 Crawdaunt
087 Crustle
043 Drednaw
086 Dwebble
274 Escavalier
099 Kingler
098 Krabby
361 Lapras
150 Shellder
275 Shelmet
300 Torkoal
347 Turtonator

Shield Dust
013 Caterpie
187 Cutiefly
350 Frosmoth
188 Ribombee
349 Snom

Simple
175 Swoobat
174 Woobat

Skill Link
051 Cinccino
151 Cloyster
050 Minccino
150 Shellder

Slush Rush
280 Beartic
279 Cubchoo

Sniper
235 Barbaracle
234 Binacle
286 Drapion
149 Octillery
148 Remoraid
285 Skorupi

Snow Cloak
280 Beartic
279 Cubchoo
081 Froslass
203 Glaceon
077 Mamoswine
076 Piloswine
075 Swinub
073 Vanillish
072 Vanillite

Snow Warning
097 Abomasnow
096 Snover
074 Vanilluxe

Solar Power
380 Charizard
378 Charmander
379 Charmeleon
319 Heliolisk
318 Helioptile

Solid Rock
266 Rhyperior

Soundproof
097 Abomasnow
393 Hakamo-o
392 Jangmo-o
394 Kommo-o

364 Mime Jr.
365 Mr. Mime
096 Snover

Speed Boost
105 Ninjask

Stall
294 Sableye

Stalwart
371 Duraludon

Stamina
084 Mudbray
085 Mudsdale

Stance Change
332 Aegislash

Static
375 Arctozolt
066 Electrike
067 Manectric
193 Pichu
194 Pikachu
195 Raichu
310 Toxel

Steadfast
035 Dubwool
218 Farfetch'd
123 Gallade
110 Hitmontop
299 Lucario
140 Machamp
139 Machoke
138 Machop
298 Riolu
219 Sirfetch'd
107 Tyrogue

Steam Engine
162 Carkol
163 Coalossal
161 Rolycoly

Steelworker
360 Dhelmise

Steely Spirit
183 Perrserker

Stench
158 Garbodor

056 Gloom
250 Koffing
131 Skuntank
130 Stunky
157 Trubbish

Sticky Hold
276 Accelgor
231 Gastrodon
230 Shellos
157 Trubbish

Storm Drain
231 Gastrodon
296 Maractus
230 Shellos

Strong Jaw
047 Boltund
042 Chewtle
376 Dracovish
043 Drednaw

Sturdy
359 Avalugg
358 Bergmite
169 Boldore
252 Bonsly
087 Crustle
086 Dwebble
170 Gigalith
178 Onix
168 Roggenrola
249 Sawk
227 Shuckle
179 Steelix
253 Sudowoodo
348 Togedemaru

Suction Cups
290 Inkay
291 Malamar
149 Octillery

Super Luck
026 Pidove
259 Togekiss
257 Togepi
258 Togetic
027 Tranquill

028 Unfezant

Swarm
010 Blipbug
011 Dottler
316 Durant
274 Escavalier
065 Galvantula
016 Grubbin
064 Joltik
273 Karrablast
012 Orbeetle

Sweet Veil
186 Alcremie
052 Bounsweet
187 Cutiefly
185 Milcery
188 Ribombee
211 Slurpuff
053 Steenee
210 Swirlix
054 Tsareena

Swift Swim
180 Arrokuda
181 Barraskewda
280 Beartic
042 Chewtle
043 Drednaw
152 Feebas
146 Goldeen
037 Lombre
036 Lotad
038 Ludicolo
144 Magikarp
355 Mantine
354 Mantyke
133 Palpitoad
304 Qwilfish
147 Seaking
134 Seismitoad
132 Tympole

Symbiosis
342 Oranguru

Synchronize
278 Beheeyem

277 Elgyem
200 Espeon
122 Gardevoir
337 Indeedee
121 Kirlia
090 Munna
091 Musharna
092 Natu
120 Ralts
201 Umbreon
093 Xatu

Tangled Feet
366 Mr. Rime

Technician
051 Cinccino
351 Clobbopus
352 Grapploct
110 Hitmontop
182 Meowth
364 Mime Jr.
050 Minccino
365 Mr. Mime
184 Persian
061 Roserade
311 Toxtricity

Telepathy
278 Beheeyem
010 Blipbug
011 Dottler
277 Elgyem
122 Gardevoir
121 Kirlia
090 Munna
091 Musharna
176 Noibat
177 Noivern
342 Oranguru
012 Orbeetle
120 Ralts
217 Wobbuffet
216 Wynaut

Thick Fat
207 Appletun
077 Mamoswine

260 Munchlax
076 Piloswine
261 Snorlax
075 Swinub

Tinted Lens
015 Butterfree
019 Hoothoot
020 Noctowl
297 Sigilyph

Torrent
008 Drizzile
009 Inteleon
007 Sobble

Tough Claws
235 Barbaracle
234 Binacle
182 Meowth
183 Perrserker

Trace
122 Gardevoir
121 Kirlia
120 Ralts

Truant
316 Durant

Unaware
256 Clefable
156 Pyukumuku
101 Quagsire
175 Swoobat
174 Woobat
100 Wooper

Unburden
276 Accelgor
125 Drifblim
124 Drifloon
320 Hawlucha
108 Hitmonlee
045 Liepard
029 Nickit
044 Purrloin
211 Slurpuff
210 Swirlix
030 Thievul

Unnerve
324 Axew
095 Bewear
023 Corviknight
022 Corvisquire
325 Fraxure
065 Galvantula
326 Haxorus
064 Joltik
182 Meowth
184 Persian
021 Rookidee
385 Tyranitar
117 Vespiquen

Vital Spirit
078 Delibird
365 Mr. Mime
107 Tyrogue

Volt Absorb
375 Arctozolt
220 Chinchou
374 Dracozolt
198 Jolteon
221 Lanturn

Wandering Spirit
328 Runerigus
327 Yamask

Water Absorb
215 Araquanid
377 Arctovish
220 Chinchou
214 Dewpider
376 Dracovish
305 Frillish
306 Jellicent
221 Lanturn
361 Lapras
355 Mantine
354 Mantyke
296 Maractus
133 Palpitoad
101 Quagsire
134 Seismitoad
132 Tympole

197 Vaporeon
100 Wooper

Water Bubble
215 Araquanid
214 Dewpider

Water Veil
146 Goldeen
355 Mantine
354 Mantyke
147 Seaking
356 Wailmer
357 Wailord

Weak Armor
169 Boldore
236 Corsola
087 Crustle
237 Cursola
086 Dwebble
158 Garbodor
284 Mandibuzz
178 Onix
336 Polteageist
168 Roggenrola
335 Sinistea
073 Vanillish
072 Vanillite
074 Vanilluxe
283 Vullaby

White Smoke
160 Centiskorch
317 Heatmor
159 Sizzlipede
300 Torkoal

Wimp Out
232 Wimpod

Wonder Guard
106 Shedinja

Wonder Skin
297 Sigilyph

Zen Mode
368 Darmanitan

Natures

Every Pokémon has an innate Nature, which affects how it will react to certain things. This Nature generally makes one of its stats grow more quickly than usual, while another stat will grow slower than usual. You can see which stats are affected by each Nature in the table below.

!

If the Nature your Pokémon started out with isn't helping your Pokémon grow strong in a stat you want, you can help by using a special mint item, like a Jolly Mint or a Modest Mint. You can get these sprigs of mint at the Battle Tower, and they'll change which of your Pokémon's stats get boosted or reduced, just as if your Pokémon had the Nature in that mint's name all along!

Natures can also affect which of the five flavors—Spicy, Dry, Sweet, Bitter, and Sour—are liked and disliked by each Pokémon. When consumed during battle, some healing Berries can confuse Pokémon that don't like their flavor, so this is well worth keeping in mind! Study up on Berry flavors and take note of your Pokémon's Nature when giving them one of these Berries to use.

Nature	Increased stat	Decreased stat	Disliked flavor
Adamant	Attack	Sp. Atk	Dry
Bashful	—	—	—
Bold	Defense	Attack	Spicy
Brave	Attack	Speed	Sweet
Calm	Sp. Def	Attack	Spicy
Careful	Sp. Def	Sp. Atk	Dry
Docile	—	—	—
Gentle	Sp. Def	Defense	Sour
Hardy	—	—	—
Hasty	Speed	Defense	Sour
Impish	Defense	Sp. Atk	Dry
Jolly	Speed	Sp. Atk	Dry
Lax	Defense	Sp. Def	Bitter

Nature	Increased stat	Decreased stat	Disliked flavor
Lonely	Attack	Defense	Sour
Mild	Sp. Atk	Defense	Sour
Modest	Sp. Atk	Attack	Spicy
Naive	Speed	Sp. Def	Bitter
Naughty	Attack	Sp. Def	Bitter
Quiet	Sp. Atk	Speed	Sweet
Quirky	—	—	—
Rash	Sp. Atk	Sp. Def	Bitter
Relaxed	Defense	Speed	Sweet
Sassy	Sp. Def	Speed	Sweet
Serious	—	—	—
Timid	Speed	Attack	Spicy

Characteristics

Each Pokémon also has a characteristic that you can see when you check its summary. Unlike Natures, these characteristics don't have a direct impact on your Pokémon's stats. Instead, they simply give you a clue as to which of your Pokémon's stats might have the highest individual strength. See the table below to get a better idea what each might be telling you!

Stat that grows easily	Characteristic				
HP	Likes to relax	Loves to eat	Nods off a lot	Scatters things often	Takes plenty of siestas
Attack	A little quick tempered	Likes to fight	Likes to thrash about	Proud of its power	Quick tempered
Defense	Capable of taking hits	Good endurance	Good perseverance	Highly persistent	Sturdy body
Sp. Atk	Highly curious	Mischievous	Often lost in thought	Thoroughly cunning	Very finicky
Sp. Def	Hates to lose	Somewhat stubborn	Somewhat vain	Strong willed	Strongly defiant
Speed	Alert to sounds	Impetuous and silly	Likes to run	Quick to flee	Somewhat of a clown

Items

There are many types of items you can collect and use in the Galar region. They tend to fall in certain categories, as you'll find when you open your Bag. On the following pages, items are divided up by the same categories as in your Bag, so you can find the type of item you're looking for based on what you want to do.

Medicine

Name	Description	Main way to obtain
Antidote	A consumable item. If used on a Pokémon, this item will heal the poisoned and badly poisoned status conditions.	Buy at any Poké Mart
Awakening	A consumable item. If used on a Pokémon, this item will heal the asleep status condition.	Buy at any Poké Mart
Berry Juice	A consumable item. If a Pokémon holds this item, it can drink the juice to restore 20 HP during battle when its HP drops to 1/2 of its maximum or lower.	Get as a reward at a Battle Café
Big Malasada	A consumable item. This famous fried bread from the Alola region can be used to heal a Pokémon of any status condition or confusion.	Get as a reward at a Battle Café
Burn Heal	A consumable item. If used on a Pokémon, this item will heal the burned status condition.	Buy at any Poké Mart
Casteliacone	A consumable item. This famous ice cream from Castelia City can be used to heal a Pokémon of any status condition or confusion.	Get as a reward at a Battle Café
Elixir	A consumable item. If used on a Pokémon, this item will restore the PP of all its moves by 10 points each.	Find as a hidden item on Route 8 / Pickup Ability
Energy Powder	A consumable item. If used on a Pokémon, this item will restore the Pokémon's HP by 60 points. However, the very bitter taste will make the Pokémon less friendly.	Buy from the Herb Shop in Hulbury
Energy Root	A consumable item. If used on a Pokémon, this item will restore the Pokémon's HP by 120 points. However, the very bitter taste will make the Pokémon less friendly.	Buy from the Herb Shop in Hulbury
Ether	A consumable item. If used on a Pokémon, this item will restore the PP of one of its moves by 10 points.	Find as a hidden item in Galar Mine or on Route 4 / Pickup Ability
Fresh Water	A consumable item. If used on a Pokémon, this item will restore the Pokémon's HP by 30 points.	Buy from a vending machine in a train station
Full Heal	A consumable item. If used on a Pokémon, this item will heal any status condition or confusion.	Buy at any Poké Mart once you have 6 Gym Badges
Full Restore	A consumable item. If used on a Pokémon, this item will fully restore the Pokémon's HP and cure any status condition or confusion.	Buy at any Poké Mart once you have 8 Gym Badges
Heal Powder	A consumable item. If used on a Pokémon, this item will heal the Pokémon of any status condition or confusion. However, the very bitter taste will make the Pokémon less friendly.	Buy from the Herb Shop in Hulbury
Hyper Potion	A consumable item. If used on a Pokémon, this item will restore the Pokémon's HP by 120 points.	Buy at any Poké Mart once you have 4 Gym Badges
Ice Heal	A consumable item. If used on a Pokémon, this item will heal the frozen status condition.	Buy at any Poké Mart
Lava Cookie	A consumable item. This famous treat from Lavaridge Town can be used to heal a Pokémon of any status condition or confusion.	Get as a reward at a Battle Café
Lemonade	A consumable item. If used on a Pokémon, this item will restore the Pokémon's HP by 70 points.	Buy from a vending machine in a train station
Lumiose Galette	A consumable item. This popular pastry from Lumiose City can be used to heal a Pokémon of any status condition or confusion.	Get as a reward at a Battle Café
Max Elixir	A consumable item. If used on a Pokémon, this item will restore the PP of all its moves completely.	Find as a hidden item on Route 9 / Pickup Ability
Max Ether	A consumable item. If used on a Pokémon, this item will restore the PP of one of its moves completely.	Find as a hidden item on Route 2 / Pickup Ability
Max Potion	A consumable item. If used on a Pokémon, this item will fully restore the Pokémon's HP.	Buy at any Poké Mart once you have 7 Gym Badges
Max Revive	A consumable item. If used on a fainted Pokémon, this item will revive the Pokémon and fully restore its HP.	Find in the Watchtower Ruins in the Wild Area, on Routes 8, 9, or 10, or in Spikemuth / Pickup Ability
Moomoo Milk	A consumable item. If used on a Pokémon, this item will restore the Pokémon's HP by 100 points.	Get as a reward at a Battle Café
Old Gateau	A consumable item. This secret specialty of the Old Chateau can be used to heal a Pokémon of any status condition or confusion.	Get as a reward at a Battle Café
Paralyze Heal	A consumable item. If used on a Pokémon, this item will heal the paralysis status condition.	Buy at any Poké Mart
Pewter Crunchies	A consumable item. This famous snack from Pewter City can be used to heal a Pokémon of any status condition or confusion.	Get as a reward at a Battle Café
Potion	A consumable item. If used on a Pokémon, this item will restore the Pokémon's HP by 20 points.	Buy at any Poké Mart
Rage Candy Bar	A consumable item. This famous snack from Mahogany Town can be used to heal a Pokémon of any status condition or confusion.	Get as a reward at a Battle Café
Revival Herb	A consumable item. It can be used to revive a Pokémon that has fainted. However, the very bitter taste will make the Pokémon less friendly.	Buy from the Herb Shop in Hulbury
Revive	A consumable item. If used on a fainted Pokémon, this item will revive the Pokémon and restore half of its max HP.	Buy at any Poké Mart
Shalour Sable	A consumable item. This famous shortbread from Shalour City can be used to heal a Pokémon of any status condition or confusion.	Get as a reward at a Battle Café
Soda Pop	A consumable item. If used on a Pokémon, this item will restore the Pokémon's HP by 50 points.	Buy from a vending machine in a train station
Super Potion	A consumable item. If used on a Pokémon, this item will restore the Pokémon's HP by 60 points.	Buy at any Poké Mart once you have 1 Gym Badge
Sweet Heart	A consumable item. If used on a Pokémon, this item will restore the Pokémon's HP by 20 points.	Get as a reward at a Battle Café

Poké Balls

Name	Description	Main way to obtain
Beast Ball	A type of Poké Ball. It is most effective for catching Ultra Beasts that appear in other regions. It's not very effective at catching regular Pokémon.	Get one from the bargain stall in Stow-on-Side after becoming Champion
Dive Ball	A type of Poké Ball. It is most effective for catching Pokémon that live in the water or that are encountered on the water's surface.	Get from a Rotom Rallyist in the Wild Area / Buy in Hammerlocke's central Pokémon Center
Dream Ball	A type of Poké Ball. It is most effective for catching Pokémon when they are asleep.	Get one from the Ball Guy in Wyndon
Dusk Ball	A type of Poké Ball. It is most effective for catching Pokémon at night or in dark places such as caves.	Get from a Rotom Rallyist in the Wild Area / Buy in Hammerlocke's central Pokémon Center
Fast Ball	A type of Poké Ball. It is most effective for catching Pokémon that have a high Speed stat.	Get one as a reward after completing a Rotom Rally course for the eleventh time.
Friend Ball	A type of Poké Ball. It will immediately make a Pokémon caught with it more friendly toward you.	Get one from the Ball Guy in Turffield
Great Ball	A type of Poké Ball. It is more likely to successfully catch a Pokémon than a basic Poké Ball.	Buy at any Poké Mart once you have 1 Gym Badge
Heal Ball	A type of Poké Ball. It will fully restore the HP and PP of the Pokémon caught with it and heal any status conditions.	Get from a Rotom Rallyist in the Wild Area / Buy in Motostoke's lower Pokémon Center
Heavy Ball	A type of Poké Ball. It is most effective for catching Pokémon that weigh a lot.	Get one from the Ball Guy in Stow-on-Side
Level Ball	A type of Poké Ball. It is most effective for catching Pokémon that are lower in level than your own.	Get one from the Ball Guy in Hammerlocke
Love Ball	A type of Poké Ball. It is most effective for catching Pokémon that are the same species as and the opposite gender to your active Pokémon.	Get one from the Ball Guy in Ballonlea
Lure Ball	A type of Poké Ball. It is most effective for catching Pokémon that have been fished up with a fishing rod.	Get one from the Ball Guy in Hulbury
Luxury Ball	A type of Poké Ball. It makes a Pokémon caught with it quickly become more friendly toward you.	Get from a Rotom Rallyist in the Wild Area / Buy in Wyndon's southern Pokémon Center
Master Ball	A very rare type of Poké Ball. It is guaranteed to catch any wild Pokémon.	Get one from Professor Magnolia after becoming Champion / Win one in the Loto-ID if you're very lucky
Moon Ball	A type of Poké Ball. It is most effective for catching Pokémon that can be evolved using a Moon Stone.	Get one from the Ball Guy in Circhester
Nest Ball	A type of Poké Ball. It is most effective for catching Pokémon of lower levels.	Get from a Rotom Rallyist in the Wild Area / Buy in Motostoke's lower Pokémon Center
Net Ball	A type of Poké Ball. It is most effective for catching Water- or Bug-type Pokémon.	Get from a Rotom Rallyist in the Wild Area / Buy in Motostoke's lower Pokémon Center
Poké Ball	A type of Poké Ball. It is the most basic model and is decently successful at catching wild Pokémon.	Buy at any Poké Mart after you meet up with Leon on Route 2
Premier Ball	A type of Poké Ball made to celebrate a special event of some sort. It is as effective as a basic Poké Ball.	Get one each time you buy 10 Poké Balls at a Poké Mart
Quick Ball	A type of Poké Ball. It is most effective for catching Pokémon on the first turn in battle.	Get from a Rotom Rallyist in the Wild Area / Buy in Wyndon's southern Pokémon Center
Repeat Ball	A type of Poké Ball. It is most effective for catching a species of Pokémon that you've caught at least once before.	Get from a Rotom Rallyist in the Wild Area / Buy in Wyndon's southern Pokémon Center
Timer Ball	A type of Poké Ball. It is most effective for catching Pokémon after many turns have passed in a battle.	Get from a Rotom Rallyist in the Wild Area / Buy in Hammerlocke's central Pokémon Center
Ultra Ball	A type of Poké Ball. It is more likely to successfully catch a Pokémon than even a Great Ball.	Buy at any Poké Mart once you have 5 Gym Badges

See the list of TMs and TRs and how to obtain them all on pages 413 and 415.

Battle Items

Name	Description	Main way to obtain
Dire Hit	A consumable item. If used on a Pokémon, it becomes much more likely the Pokémon will deliver critical hits.	Buy in Hammerlocke's central Pokémon Center
Guard Spec.	A consumable item. If used during battle, this item will prevent stat reduction among the Trainer's party Pokémon for 5 turns. Cannot be used again until the effect wears off.	Buy in Hammerlocke's central Pokémon Center
Poké Doll	A consumable item. If used in a battle against a wild Pokémon, this item ends the battle instantly.	Buy at any Poké Mart once you have 1 Gym Badge
X Accuracy	A consumable item. If used on a Pokémon during battle, this item will raise the accuracy of the Pokémon by 2 stages.	Buy in Hammerlocke's central Pokémon Center
X Attack	A consumable item. If used on a Pokémon during battle, this item will raise the Attack of the Pokémon by 2 stages.	Buy in Motostoke's lower Pokémon Center
X Defense	A consumable item. If used on a Pokémon during battle, this item will raise the Defense of the Pokémon by 2 stages.	Buy in Motostoke's lower Pokémon Center
X Sp. Atk	A consumable item. If used on a Pokémon during battle, this item will raise the Sp. Atk of the Pokémon by 2 stages.	Buy in Motostoke's lower Pokémon Center
X Sp. Def	A consumable item. If used on a Pokémon during battle, this item will raise the Sp. Def of the Pokémon by 2 stages.	Buy in Motostoke's lower Pokémon Center
X Speed	A consumable item. If used on a Pokémon during battle, this item will raise the Speed of the Pokémon by 2 stages.	Buy in Hammerlocke's central Pokémon Center

Berries

Name	Description	Main way to obtain
Aguav Berry	A consumable item. If a Pokémon holds one, it can eat this Berry to restore some HP when its HP drops to 1/4 of its maximum or lower. It restores 1/3 of max HP but also confuses Pokémon that don't like bitter flavors.	Collect from the Berry tree on Route 9 (Circhester Bay)
Apicot Berry	A consumable item. If a Pokémon holds one, it can eat this Berry to raise its Sp. Def by 1 stage when its HP drops to 1/4 of its maximum or lower.	Collect from the Berry tree at the Lake of Outrage in the Wild Area
Aspear Berry	A consumable item. If a Pokémon holds one, it can eat this Berry to cure itself of the frozen status condition during battle. Using this Berry on a Pokémon directly can also cure the frozen status condition.	Collect from the Berry tree on Route 7 (north side)
Babiri Berry	A consumable item. If a Pokémon holds one, it can eat this Berry to halve the damage taken from one supereffective Steel-type move.	Collect from the Berry tree in the area surrounded by the lake in the Bridge Field in the Wild Area
Charti Berry	A consumable item. If a Pokémon holds one, it can eat this Berry to halve the damage taken from one supereffective Rock-type move.	Collect from the Berry tree at the Lake of Outrage in the Wild Area
Cheri Berry	A consumable item. If a Pokémon holds one, it can eat this Berry to cure itself of the paralysis status condition during battle. Using this Berry on a Pokémon directly can also cure the paralysis status condition.	Buy at Wedgehurst Berry Grocer / Collect from the Berry trees in the Rolling Fields in the Wild Area
Chesto Berry	A consumable item. If a Pokémon holds one, it can eat this Berry to cure itself of the asleep status condition during battle. Using this Berry on a Pokémon directly can also cure the asleep status condition.	Collect from the Berry tree on Route 5
Chilan Berry	A consumable item. If a Pokémon holds one, it can eat this Berry to halve the damage taken from one Normal-type move.	Collect from the Berry trees near West Lake Axewell in the Dappled Grove in the Wild Area
Chople Berry	A consumable item. If a Pokémon holds one, it can eat this Berry to halve the damage taken from one supereffective Fighting-type move.	Collect from the Berry tree on Route 9 (Outer Spikemuth)
Coba Berry	A consumable item. If a Pokémon holds one, it can eat this Berry to halve the damage taken from one supereffective Flying-type move.	Collect from the Berry tree by the river at the Motostoke Riverbank in the Wild Area
Colbur Berry	A consumable item. If a Pokémon holds one, it can eat this Berry to halve the damage taken from one supereffective Dark-type move.	Collect from the Berry tree on Axew's Eye in the Wild Area
Figy Berry	A consumable item. If a Pokémon holds one, it can eat this Berry to restore some HP when its HP drops to 1/4 of its maximum or lower. It restores 1/3 of max HP but also confuses Pokémon that don't like spicy flavors.	Collect from the Berry tree on Route 7 (north side)
Ganlon Berry	A consumable item. If a Pokémon holds one, it can eat this Berry to raise its Defense by 1 stage when its HP drops to 1/4 of its maximum or lower.	Collect from the Berry tree in the area surrounded by the lake in the Bridge Field in the Wild Area
Grepa Berry	A consumable item. If used on a Pokémon, this Berry will make that Pokémon more friendly, but it will also take away base points from its Sp. Def stat.	Collect from the left Berry tree under the bridge in the Bridge Field in the Wild Area
Haban Berry	A consumable item. If a Pokémon holds one, it can eat this Berry to halve the damage taken from one supereffective Dragon-type move.	Collect from the Berry tree at the Lake of Outrage in the Wild Area
Hondew Berry	A consumable item. If used on a Pokémon, this Berry will make that Pokémon more friendly, but it will also take away base points from its Sp. Atk stat.	Collect from the left Berry tree under the bridge in the Bridge Field in the Wild Area
Iapapa Berry	A consumable item. If a Pokémon holds one, it can eat this Berry to restore some HP when its HP drops to 1/4 of its maximum or lower. It restores 1/3 of max HP but also confuses Pokémon that don't like sour flavors.	Collect from the Berry tree on Route 9 (Circhester Bay)
Kasib Berry	A consumable item. If a Pokémon holds one, it can eat this Berry to halve the damage taken from one supereffective Ghost-type move.	Collect from the Berry tree in the area surrounded by the lake in the Bridge Field in the Wild Area
Kebia Berry	A consumable item. If a Pokémon holds one, it can eat this Berry to halve the damage taken from one supereffective Poison-type move.	Collect from the Berry tree on Axew's Eye in the Wild Area
Kee Berry	A consumable item. If a Pokémon holds one, it can eat this Berry to raise its Defense by 1 stage when hit with a physical move.	Collect from the Berry tree on Axew's Eye in the Wild Area
Kelpsy Berry	A consumable item. If used on a Pokémon, this Berry will make that Pokémon more friendly, but it will also take away base points from its Attack stat.	Collect from the right Berry tree under the bridge in the Bridge Field in the Wild Area

Name	Description	Main way to obtain
Lansat Berry	A consumable item. If a Pokémon holds one, it can eat this Berry to make itself more likely to deliver critical hits when its HP drops to 1/4 of its maximum or lower.	Get as a reward at the Battle Tower
Leppa Berry	A consumable item. If a Pokémon holds one, it can eat this Berry to restore 10 points to the PP of one of its moves.	Collect from the Berry tree near the Lake of Outrage on the Hammerlocke Hills in the Wild Area
Liechi Berry	A consumable item. If a Pokémon holds one, it can eat this Berry to raise its Attack by 1 stage when its HP drops to 1/4 of its maximum or lower.	Collect from the Berry tree in the area surrounded by the lake in the Bridge Field in the Wild Area
Lum Berry	A consumable item. If a Pokémon holds one, it can eat this Berry to cure itself of any status condition or confusion during battle. Using this Berry on a Pokémon directly can also cure any status condition or confusion.	Collect from the Berry tree on Route 9 (Outer Spikemuth)
Mago Berry	A consumable item. If a Pokémon holds one, it can eat this Berry to restore some HP when its HP drops to 1/4 of its maximum or lower. It restores 1/3 of max HP but also confuses Pokémon that don't like sweet flavors.	Collect from the Berry tree on Route 7 (north side)
Maranga Berry	A consumable item. If a Pokémon holds one, it can eat this Berry to raise its Sp. Def by 1 stage when hit with a special move.	Collect from the Berry tree on Axew's Eye in the Wild Area
Occa Berry	A consumable item. If a Pokémon holds one, it can eat this Berry to halve the damage taken from one supereffective Fire-type move.	Collect from the center Berry tree under the bridge in the Bridge Field in the Wild Area
Oran Berry	A consumable item. If a Pokémon holds one, it can eat this Berry to restore 10 HP when its HP drops to 1/2 of its maximum or lower.	Buy at Wedgehurst Berry Grocer / Collect from the Berry trees in the Rolling Fields in the Wild Area
Passho Berry	A consumable item. If a Pokémon holds one, it can eat this Berry to halve the damage taken from one supereffective Water-type move.	Collect from the right Berry tree in the Bridge Field in the Wild Area
Payapa Berry	A consumable item. If a Pokémon holds one, it can eat this Berry to halve the damage taken from one supereffective Psychic-type move.	Collect from the Berry tree near the Lake of Outrage on the Hammerlocke Hills in the Wild Area
Pecha Berry	A consumable item. If a Pokémon holds one, it can eat this Berry to cure itself of the poisoned or badly poisoned status condition during battle. Using this Berry on a Pokémon directly can also cure the poisoned status condition.	Buy at Wedgehurst Berry Grocer / Collect from the Berry tree near the Meetup Spot in the Rolling Fields in the Wild Area
Persim Berry	A consumable item. If a Pokémon holds one, it can eat this Berry to cure itself of confusion during battle. Using this Berry on a Pokémon directly can also cure confusion.	Collect from the Berry tree at North Lake Miloch in the Wild Area
Petaya Berry	A consumable item. If a Pokémon holds one, it can eat this Berry to raise its Sp. Atk by 1 stage when its HP drops to 1/4 of its maximum or lower.	Collect from the Berry tree at the Lake of Outrage in the Wild Area
Pomeg Berry	A consumable item. If used on a Pokémon, this Berry will make that Pokémon more friendly, but it will also take away base points from its HP stat.	Collect from the center Berry tree under the bridge in the Bridge Field in the Wild Area
Qualot Berry	A consumable item. If used on a Pokémon, this Berry will make that Pokémon more friendly, but it will also take away base points from its Defense stat.	Collect from the right Berry tree under the bridge in the Bridge Field in the Wild Area
Rawst Berry	A consumable item. If a Pokémon holds one, it can eat this Berry to cure itself of the burned status condition during battle. Using this Berry on a Pokémon directly can also cure the burned status condition.	Collect from the Berry tree at North Lake Miloch in the Wild Area
Rindo Berry	A consumable item. If a Pokémon holds one, it can eat this Berry to halve the damage taken from one supereffective Grass-type move.	Collect from the left Berry tree under the bridge in the Bridge Field in the Wild Area
Roseli Berry	A consumable item. If a Pokémon holds one, it can eat this Berry to halve the damage taken from one supereffective Fairy-type move.	Collect from the Berry tree on Route 9 (Outer Spikemuth)
Salac Berry	A consumable item. If a Pokémon holds one, it can eat this Berry to raise its Speed by 1 stage when its HP drops to 1/4 of its maximum or lower.	Collect from the Berry tree on Axew's Eye in the Wild Area
Shuca Berry	A consumable item. If a Pokémon holds one, it can eat this Berry to halve the damage taken from one supereffective Ground-type move.	Collect from the Berry tree at the Lake of Outrage in the Wild Area
Sitrus Berry	A consumable item. If a Pokémon holds one, it can eat this Berry to restore 1/2 of its max HP when its HP drops to 1/4 of its maximum or lower.	Collect from the Berry tree by the river at the Motostoke Riverbank in the Wild Area
Starf Berry	A consumable item. If a Pokémon holds one, it can eat this Berry to raise one of its stats by 2 stages when its HP drops to 1/4 of its maximum or lower. The stat is selected at random.	Get as a reward at the Battle Tower
Tamato Berry	A consumable item. If used on a Pokémon, this Berry will make that Pokémon more friendly, but it will also take away base points from its Speed stat.	Collect from the center Berry tree under the bridge in the Bridge Field in the Wild Area
Tanga Berry	A consumable item. If a Pokémon holds one, it can eat this Berry to halve the damage taken from one supereffective Bug-type move.	Collect from the Berry tree on Route 9 (Outer Spikemuth)
Wacan Berry	A consumable item. If a Pokémon holds one, it can eat this Berry to halve the damage taken from one supereffective Electric-type move.	Collect from the Berry tree near the Lake of Outrage on the Hammerlocke Hills in the Wild Area
Wiki Berry	A consumable item. If a Pokémon holds one, it can eat this Berry to restore some HP when its HP drops to 1/4 of its maximum or lower. It restores 1/3 of max HP but also confuses Pokémon that don't like dry flavors.	Collect from the Berry tree on Route 9 (Circhester Bay)
Yache Berry	A consumable item. If a Pokémon holds one, it can eat this Berry to halve the damage taken from one supereffective Ice-type move.	Collect from the Berry tree at the Lake of Outrage in the Wild Area

Other Items

Items that can be used to help your Pokémon grow

Name	Description	Main way to obtain
Ability Capsule	A consumable item. Allows a Pokémon of a species that has two possible Abilities (excluding Hidden Abilities) to change its Ability to the one it currently does not have.	Get from the right-hand clerk at the Battle Tower's BP Shop after becoming Champion
Adamant Mint	A consumable item. If used on a Pokémon, this item will cause the Pokémon's Attack to grow more easily while its Sp. Atk will grow more slowly.	Get from the left-hand clerk at the Battle Tower's BP Shop after becoming Champion
Bold Mint	A consumable item. If used on a Pokémon, this item will cause the Pokémon's Defense to grow more easily while its Attack will grow more slowly.	Get from the left-hand clerk at the Battle Tower's BP Shop after becoming Champion
Brave Mint	A consumable item. If used on a Pokémon, this item will cause the Pokémon's Attack to grow more easily while its Speed will grow more slowly.	Get from the left-hand clerk at the Battle Tower's BP Shop after becoming Champion
Calcium	A consumable item. If used on a Pokémon, this item will add base points to the Pokémon's Sp. Atk stat.	Buy in Wyndon's southern Pokémon Center
Calm Mint	A consumable item. If used on a Pokémon, this item will cause the Pokémon's Sp. Def to grow more easily while its Attack will grow more slowly.	Get from the left-hand clerk at the Battle Tower's BP Shop after becoming Champion
Carbos	A consumable item. If used on a Pokémon, this item will add base points to the Pokémon's Speed stat.	Buy in Wyndon's southern Pokémon Center
Careful Mint	A consumable item. If used on a Pokémon, this item will cause the Pokémon's Sp. Def to grow more easily while its Sp. Atk will grow more slowly.	Get from the left-hand clerk at the Battle Tower's BP Shop after becoming Champion
Clever Feather	A consumable item. If used on a Pokémon, this item will add a small number of base points to the Pokémon's Sp. Def stat. It can be used until base points for that stat have been maxed.	Find as a hidden item on the bridge on Route 5 or the bridge in the Motostoke Outskirts
Dynamax Candy	A consumable item. If used on a Pokémon, this item will raise the Pokémon's Dynamax Level by 1.	Find after a Max Raid Battle
Exp. Candy L	A consumable item. If used on a Pokémon, it will award a large amount of Exp. Points.	Find after a Max Raid Battle
Exp. Candy M	A consumable item. If used on a Pokémon, it will award a moderate amount of Exp. Points.	Find after a Max Raid Battle
Exp. Candy S	A consumable item. If used on a Pokémon, it will award a small amount of Exp. Points.	Find after a Max Raid Battle
Exp. Candy XL	A consumable item. If used on a Pokémon, it will award a very large amount of Exp. Points.	Find after a Max Raid Battle
Exp. Candy XS	A consumable item. If used on a Pokémon, it will award a very small amount of Exp. Points.	Find after a Max Raid Battle
Genius Feather	A consumable item. If used on a Pokémon, this item will add a small number of base points to the Pokémon's Sp. Atk stat. It can be used until base points for that stat have been maxed.	Find as a hidden item on the bridge on Route 5 or the bridge in the Motostoke Outskirts
Gentle Mint	A consumable item. If used on a Pokémon, this item will cause the Pokémon's Sp. Def to grow more easily while its Defense will grow more slowly.	Get from the left-hand clerk at the Battle Tower's BP Shop after becoming Champion
Hasty Mint	A consumable item. If used on a Pokémon, this item will cause the Pokémon's Speed to grow more easily while its Defense will grow more slowly.	Get from the left-hand clerk at the Battle Tower's BP Shop after becoming Champion
Health Feather	A consumable item. If used on a Pokémon, this item will add a small number of base points to the Pokémon's HP. It can be used until base points for that stat have been maxed.	Find as a hidden item on the bridge on Route 5 or the bridge in the Motostoke Outskirts
HP Up	A consumable item. If used on a Pokémon, this item will add base points to the Pokémon's HP stat.	Buy in Wyndon's southern Pokémon Center
Impish Mint	A consumable item. If used on a Pokémon, this item will cause the Pokémon's Defense to grow more easily while its Sp. Atk will grow more slowly.	Get from the left-hand clerk at the Battle Tower's BP Shop after becoming Champion
Iron	A consumable item. If used on a Pokémon, this item will add base points to the Pokémon's Defense stat.	Buy in Wyndon's southern Pokémon Center
Jolly Mint	A consumable item. If used on a Pokémon, this item will cause the Pokémon's Speed to grow more easily while its Sp. Atk will grow more slowly.	Get from the left-hand clerk at the Battle Tower's BP Shop after becoming Champion
Lax Mint	A consumable item. If used on a Pokémon, this item will cause the Pokémon's Defense to grow more easily while its Sp. Def will grow more slowly.	Get from the left-hand clerk at the Battle Tower's BP Shop after becoming Champion
Lonely Mint	A consumable item. If used on a Pokémon, this item will cause the Pokémon's Attack to grow more easily while its Defense will grow more slowly.	Get from the left-hand clerk at the Battle Tower's BP Shop after becoming Champion
Macho Brace	A nonconsumable item. If held by a Pokémon, this item will halve the holder's Speed but increase the rate at which it gains base points.	Get from the BP Shop in Hammerlocke's central Pokémon Center
Mild Mint	A consumable item. If used on a Pokémon, this item will cause the Pokémon's Sp. Atk to grow more easily while its Defense will grow more slowly.	Get from the left-hand clerk at the Battle Tower's BP Shop after becoming Champion
Modest Mint	A consumable item. If used on a Pokémon, this item will cause the Pokémon's Sp. Atk to grow more easily while its Attack will grow more slowly.	Get from the left-hand clerk at the Battle Tower's BP Shop after becoming Champion
Muscle Feather	A consumable item. If used on a Pokémon, this item will add a small number of base points to the Pokémon's Attack stat. It can be used until base points for that stat have been maxed.	Find as a hidden item on the bridge on Route 5 or the bridge in the Motostoke Outskirts
Naive Mint	A consumable item. If used on a Pokémon, this item will cause the Pokémon's Speed to grow more easily while its Sp. Def will grow more slowly.	Get from the left-hand clerk at the Battle Tower's BP Shop after becoming Champion
Naughty Mint	A consumable item. If used on a Pokémon, this item will cause the Pokémon's Attack to grow more easily while its Sp. Def will grow more slowly.	Get from the left-hand clerk at the Battle Tower's BP Shop after becoming Champion
Power Anklet	A nonconsumable item. If held by a Pokémon, this item will halve the holder's Speed but increase the rate at which it gains base points for its Speed stat.	Get from the BP Shop in Hammerlocke's central Pokémon Center
Power Band	A nonconsumable item. If held by a Pokémon, this item will halve the holder's Speed but increase the rate at which it gains base points for its Sp. Def stat.	Get from the BP Shop in Hammerlocke's central Pokémon Center
Power Belt	A nonconsumable item. If held by a Pokémon, this item will halve the holder's Speed but increase the rate at which it gains base points for its Defense stat.	Get from the BP Shop in Hammerlocke's central Pokémon Center
Power Bracer	A nonconsumable item. If held by a Pokémon, this item will halve the holder's Speed but increase the rate at which it gains base points for its Attack stat.	Get from the BP Shop in Hammerlocke's central Pokémon Center
Power Lens	A nonconsumable item. If held by a Pokémon, this item will halve the holder's Speed but increase the rate at which it gains base points for its Sp. Atk stat.	Get from the BP Shop in Hammerlocke's central Pokémon Center
Power Weight	A nonconsumable item. If held by a Pokémon, this item will halve the holder's Speed but increase the rate at which it gains base points for its HP stat.	Get from the BP Shop in Hammerlocke's central Pokémon Center
PP Max	A consumable item. If used on a Pokémon, this item can increase the max PP of one of the Pokémon's moves as high as it will go.	Find on Route 2 / Get as a reward at the Battle Tower

Name	Description	Main way to obtain
PP Up	A consumable item. If used on a Pokémon, this item can increase the max PP of one of the Pokémon's moves by a small amount.	Find as a hidden item in the Motostoke Outskirts, on Route 7, or elsewhere
Protein	A consumable item. If used on a Pokémon, this item will add base points to the Pokémon's Attack stat.	Get from the BP Shop in Hammerlocke's central Pokémon Center
Quiet Mint	A consumable item. If used on a Pokémon, this item will cause the Pokémon's Sp. Atk to grow more easily while its Speed will grow more slowly.	Get from the left-hand clerk at the Battle Tower's BP Shop after becoming Champion
Rare Candy	A consumable item. If used on a Pokémon, this item will raise the Pokémon's level by 1.	Get from the BP Shop in Hammerlocke's central Pokémon Center / Get as a reward at a Battle Café
Rash Mint	A consumable item. If used on a Pokémon, this item will cause the Pokémon's Sp. Atk to grow more easily while its Sp. Def will grow more slowly.	Get from the left-hand clerk at the Battle Tower's BP Shop after becoming Champion
Relaxed Mint	A consumable item. If used on a Pokémon, this item will cause the Pokémon's Defense to grow more easily while its Speed will grow more slowly.	Get from the left-hand clerk at the Battle Tower's BP Shop after becoming Champion
Resist Feather	A consumable item. If used on a Pokémon, this item will add a small number of base points to the Pokémon's Defense stat. It can be used until base points for that stat have been maxed.	Find as a hidden item on the bridge on Route 5 or the bridge in the Motostoke Outskirts
Sassy Mint	A consumable item. If used on a Pokémon, this item will cause the Pokémon's Sp. Def to grow more easily while its Speed will grow more slowly.	Get from the left-hand clerk at the Battle Tower's BP Shop after becoming Champion
Serious Mint	A consumable item. If used on a Pokémon, this item will cause the Pokémon's stats to grow at an equal rate.	Get from the left-hand clerk at the Battle Tower's BP Shop after becoming Champion
Swift Feather	A consumable item. If used on a Pokémon, this item will add a small number of base points to the Pokémon's Speed stat. It can be used until base points for that stat have been maxed.	Find as a hidden item on the bridge on Route 5 or the bridge in the Motostoke Outskirts
Timid Mint	A consumable item. If used on a Pokémon, this item will cause the Pokémon's Speed to grow more easily while its Attack will grow more slowly.	Get from the left-hand clerk at the Battle Tower's BP Shop after becoming Champion
Zinc	A consumable item. If used on a Pokémon, this item will add base points to the Pokémon's Sp. Def stat.	Get at Hammerlocke's BP Shop

Items that can be used to influence Pokémon's forms or Evolutions

Name	Description	Main way to obtain
Berry Sweet	A consumable item. It can be used to help Milcery evolve.	Get as a reward at a Battle Café
Bug Memory	A nonconsumable item. If held by Silvally, this item will change Silvally's type to Bug type.	Get Type: Null and all of Silvally's memory discs at the Battle Tower after becoming Champion
Chipped Pot	A consumable item. It can be used to help certain Sinistea evolve.	Buy at the bargain stall in Stow-on-Side
Clover Sweet	A consumable item. It can be used to help Milcery evolve.	Get as a reward at a Battle Café
Cracked Pot	A consumable item. It can be used to help certain Sinistea evolve.	Find in Stow-on-Side / Buy at the bargain stall in Stow-on-Side
Dark Memory	A nonconsumable item. If held by Silvally, this item will change Silvally's type to Dark type.	Get Type: Null and all of Silvally's memory discs at the Battle Tower after becoming Champion
Dawn Stone	A consumable item. It can be used to help Kirlia or Snorunt evolve.	Find as a hidden item at the Lake of Outrage in the Wild Area
Dragon Memory	A nonconsumable item. If held by Silvally, this item will change Silvally's type to Dragon type.	Get Type: Null and all of Silvally's memory discs at the Battle Tower after becoming Champion
Dusk Stone	A consumable item. It can be used to help Lampent or Doublade evolve.	Find as a hidden item at the Lake of Outrage in the Wild Area
Electric Memory	A nonconsumable item. If held by Silvally, this item will change Silvally's type to Electric type.	Get Type: Null and all of Silvally's memory discs at the Battle Tower after becoming Champion
Everstone	A nonconsumable item. If held by a Pokémon, this item will prevent the holder from evolving.	Find as a hidden item in Turffield
Fairy Memory	A nonconsumable item. If held by Silvally, this item will change Silvally's type to Fairy type.	Get Type: Null and all of Silvally's memory discs at the Battle Tower after becoming Champion
Fighting Memory	A nonconsumable item. If held by Silvally, this item will change Silvally's type to Fighting type.	Get Type: Null and all of Silvally's memory discs at the Battle Tower after becoming Champion
Fire Memory	A nonconsumable item. If held by Silvally, this item will change Silvally's type to Fire type.	Get Type: Null and all of Silvally's memory discs at the Battle Tower after becoming Champion
Fire Stone	A consumable item. It can be used to help Vulpix, Growlithe, or Eevee evolve.	Find as a hidden item at the Lake of Outrage in the Wild Area
Flower Sweet	A consumable item. It can be used to help Milcery evolve.	Get as a reward at a Battle Café
Flying Memory	A nonconsumable item. If held by Silvally, this item will change Silvally's type to Flying type.	Get Type: Null and all of Silvally's memory discs at the Battle Tower after becoming Champion
Ghost Memory	A nonconsumable item. If held by Silvally, this item will change Silvally's type to Ghost type.	Get Type: Null and all of Silvally's memory discs at the Battle Tower after becoming Champion
Grass Memory	A nonconsumable item. If held by Silvally, this item will change Silvally's type to Grass type.	Get Type: Null and all of Silvally's memory discs at the Battle Tower after becoming Champion
Ground Memory	A nonconsumable item. If held by Silvally, this item will change Silvally's type to Ground type.	Get Type: Null and all of Silvally's memory discs at the Battle Tower after becoming Champion
Ice Memory	A nonconsumable item. If held by Silvally, this item will change Silvally's type to Ice type.	Get Type: Null and all of Silvally's memory discs at the Battle Tower after becoming Champion
Ice Stone	A consumable item. It can be used to help Eevee evolve.	Find as a hidden item at the Lake of Outrage in the Wild Area
Leaf Stone	A consumable item. It can be used to help Gloom, Eevee, or Nuzleaf evolve.	Find as a hidden item at the Lake of Outrage in the Wild Area
Love Sweet	A consumable item. It can be used to help Milcery evolve.	Get as a reward at a Battle Café
Metal Coat	An item with different uses. It can be used to help Onix evolve. When used in this way, the item will be consumed.	Find as a hidden item in Stow-on-Side

Name	Description	Main way to obtain
Moon Stone	A consumable item. It can be used to help Clefairy or Munna evolve.	Find in the Dusty Bowl in the Wild Area
Poison Memory	A nonconsumable item. If held by Silvally, this item will change Silvally's type to Poison type.	Get Type: Null and all of Silvally's memory discs at the Battle Tower after becoming Champion
Prism Scale	A consumable item. It can be used to help Feebas evolve.	Find as a hidden item on Route 2
Protector	A consumable item. It can be used to help Rhydon evolve.	Find on Route 9 (Circhester Bay)
Psychic Memory	A nonconsumable item. If held by Silvally, this item will change Silvally's type to Psychic type.	Get Type: Null and all of Silvally's memory discs at the Battle Tower after becoming Champion
Razor Claw	An item with different uses. It can be used to help Sneasel evolve. When used in this way, the item will be consumed.	Find as a hidden item in the Dusty Bowl in the Wild Area
Reaper Cloth	A consumable item. It can be used to help Dusclops evolve.	Get by helping deliver an Old Letter for a little girl in Hammerlocke
Ribbon Sweet	A consumable item. It can be used to help Milcery evolve.	Get as a reward at a Battle Café
Rock Memory	A nonconsumable item. If held by Silvally, this item will change Silvally's type to Rock type.	Get Type: Null and all of Silvally's memory discs at the Battle Tower after becoming Champion
Rusted Shield	A nonconsumable item. If held by Zamazenta, this item will change it to its Crowned Shield form.	Obtain during your main adventure ⬛
Rusted Sword	A nonconsumable item. If held by Zacian, this item will change it to its Crowned Sword form.	Obtain during your main adventure ✝
Sachet	A consumable item. It can be used to help Spritzee evolve.	Get from the BP Shop in Hammerlocke's central Pokémon Center
Shiny Stone	A consumable item. It can be used to help Togetic, Roselia, and Minccino evolve.	Find as a hidden item at the Lake of Outrage in the Wild Area
Star Sweet	A consumable item. It can be used to help Milcery evolve.	Get as a reward at a Battle Café
Steel Memory	A nonconsumable item. If held by Silvally, this item will change Silvally's type to Steel type.	Get Type: Null and all of Silvally's memory discs at the Battle Tower after becoming Champion
Strawberry Sweet	A consumable item. It can be used to help Milcery evolve.	Find in Hammerlocke / Get as a reward at a Battle Café
Sun Stone	A consumable item. It can be used to help Gloom, Cottonee, or Helioptile evolve.	Find in the Dusty Bowl in the Wild Area
Sweet Apple	A consumable item. It can be used to help Applin evolve.	Get from a guy in Hammerlocke by helping him ⬛ / Find as a hidden item on Axew's Eye in the Wild Area ⬛
Tart Apple	A consumable item. It can be used to help Applin evolve.	Get from a guy in Hammerlocke by helping him ✝ / Find as a hidden item on Axew's Eye in the Wild Area ✝
Thunder Stone	A consumable item. It can be used to help Pikachu or Eevee evolve.	Find as a hidden item at the Lake of Outrage in the Wild Area
Water Memory	A nonconsumable item. If held by Silvally, this item will change Silvally's type to Water type.	Get Type: Null and all of Silvally's memory discs at the Battle Tower after becoming Champion
Water Stone	A consumable item. It can be used to help Shellder, Eevee, and Lombre evolve.	Find as a hidden item at the Lake of Outrage in the Wild Area
Whipped Dream	A consumable item. It can be used to help Swirlix evolve.	Get from the BP Shop in Hammerlocke's central Pokémon Center

Items that affect battles and encounters

Name	Description	Main way to obtain
Absorb Bulb	A consumable item. If held by a Pokémon, this item will raise the holder's Sp. Atk by 1 stage if it is hit with a damage-dealing Water-type move.	Find as a hidden item on Route 5
Adrenaline Orb	A consumable item. If held by a Pokémon, this item will boost the holder's Speed when affected by Intimidate.	Get from the right-hand clerk at the Battle Tower's BP Shop after becoming Champion
Air Balloon	A consumable item. If held by a Pokémon, this item will grant immunity to all Ground-type moves until the holder is hit by a damage-dealing move.	Find in Wyndon
Amulet Coin	A nonconsumable item. If a Pokémon holding it appears in battle, this item will double the prize money received from that battle.	Find in the Motostoke Outskirts
Assault Vest	A nonconsumable item. If held by a Pokémon, this item will boost the holder's Sp. Def by 50% but prevent the Pokémon from using status moves.	Find at the Lake of Outrage in the Wild Area
Big Root	A nonconsumable item. If held by a Pokémon, this item will increase the amount of HP restored to the holder by HP-draining moves by 30%.	Find in the Glimwood Tangle
Binding Band	A nonconsumable item. If held by a Pokémon, this item will boost the effectiveness of the holder's binding moves. They will damage the target for 1/6 of its max HP each turn, instead of the regular 1/8.	Buy at the bargain stall in Stow-on-Side
Black Belt	A nonconsumable item. If held by a Pokémon, this item will boost the power of the holder's Fighting-type moves by 20%.	Find as a hidden item on Route 9 (Circhester Bay)
Black Glasses	A nonconsumable item. If held by a Pokémon, this item will boost the power of the holder's Dark-type moves by 20%.	Find in Motostoke
Black Sludge	A nonconsumable item. If held by a Poison-type Pokémon, this item will restore 1/16 of the holder's max HP each turn. If held by any other type, it will cause the holder to lose 1/8 of its max HP each turn.	Find as a hidden item in Wyndon
Blunder Policy	A consumable item. If held by a Pokémon, this item will raise the holder's Speed by 2 stages if one of its moves misses due to low accuracy.	Get from the right-hand clerk at the Battle Tower's BP Shop after becoming Champion
Bright Powder	A nonconsumable item. If held by a Pokémon, this item will lower the accuracy of moves that target the holder.	Find in Glimwood Tangle
Cell Battery	A consumable item. If held by a Pokémon, this item will raise the holder's Attack by 1 stage if it is hit with a damage-dealing Electric-type move.	Find in Wyndon

Name	Description	Main way to obtain
Charcoal	A nonconsumable item. If held by a Pokémon, this item will boost the power of the holder's Fire-type moves by 20%.	Receive from Leon in Motostoke if you chose Scorbunny / Buy at the bargain stall in Stow-on-Side
Choice Band	A nonconsumable item. If held by a Pokémon, this item will boost the holder's Attack by 50%. However, the holder will become unable to use any move but the first move it chooses when it enters the battlefield.	Find on Route 2
Choice Scarf	A nonconsumable item. If held by a Pokémon, this item will boost the holder's Speed by 50%. However, the holder will become unable to use any move but the first move it chooses when it enters the battlefield.	Get by helping deliver an Old Letter for a little girl in Hammerlocke
Choice Specs	A nonconsumable item. If held by a Pokémon, this item will boost the holder's Sp. Atk by 50%. However, the holder will become unable to use any move but the first move it chooses when it enters the battlefield.	Find in Spikemuth
Cleanse Tag	A nonconsumable item. If held by the lead Pokémon in your party, this item will reduce wild Pokémon encounters.	Find on Route 4
Damp Rock	A nonconsumable item. If a Pokémon holding this item causes the weather condition to change to rain, the rain will last 8 turns instead of 5.	Get from a gentleman in a house in Hammerlocke
Destiny Knot	A nonconsumable item. If a Pokémon holding this item is afflicted with infatuation, the Pokémon that caused it will also become infatuated.	Get from the BP Shop in Hammerlocke's central Pokémon Center
Dragon Fang	A nonconsumable item. If held by a Pokémon, this item will boost the power of the holder's Dragon-type moves by 20%.	Buy at the bargain stall in Stow-on-Side
Eject Button	A consumable item. If held by a Pokémon, this item will force the holder to switch out of battle if it is hit by a damage-dealing move.	Get from the right-hand clerk at the Battle Tower's BP Shop after becoming Champion
Eject Pack	A consumable item. If held by a Pokémon, this item will force the holder to switch out of battle if any of its stats are lowered.	Get from the right-hand clerk at the Battle Tower's BP Shop after becoming Champion
Electric Seed	A consumable item. If held by a Pokémon, this item will boost the holder's Defense by 1 stage on Electric Terrain.	Find in Wyndon / Sometimes held by wild Togedemaru
Eviolite	A nonconsumable item. If held by a Pokémon, this item will boost the Defense and Sp. Def of the holder by 50% each as long as that Pokémon is still capable of evolving.	Get from a Breeder in a house in Ballonlea
Expert Belt	A nonconsumable item. If held by a Pokémon, this item will boost the power of the holder's supereffective moves by 20%.	Find by solving a riddle in Turffield
Flame Orb	A nonconsumable item. If held by a Pokémon, this item will inflict the burned status condition on the holder.	Get as a reward in a Champion tournament after becoming Champion
Float Stone	A nonconsumable item. If held by a Pokémon, this item will halve the holder's weight.	Get from the Digging Duo in the Wild Area
Focus Band	A nonconsumable item. If held by a Pokémon, this item will give the holder a 10% chance of surviving with 1 HP when it receives damage that would normally cause it to faint.	Sometimes held by wild Machop, Machoke, and Machamp
Focus Sash	A consumable item. If held by a Pokémon with full HP, this item will allow the holder to survive with 1 HP when it receives damage that would normally cause it to faint.	Find at the Lake of Outrage in the Wild Area
Full Incense	A nonconsumable item. If held by a Pokémon, this item will make the holder move later in the turn. It can also be used to help find Pokémon Eggs that hatch into certain species.	Buy from the Incense Merchant in Hulbury
Grassy Seed	A consumable item. If held by a Pokémon, this item will boost the holder's Defense by 1 stage on Grassy Terrain.	Find in Wyndon
Grip Claw	A nonconsumable item. If held by a Pokémon, this item will extend the duration of the holder's moves like Bind and Wrap to 7 turns.	Find in Galar Mine No. 2
Hard Stone	A nonconsumable item. If held by a Pokémon, this item will boost the power of the holder's Rock-type moves by 20%.	Find it as a hidden item in Galar Mine
Heat Rock	A nonconsumable item. If a Pokémon holding this item causes the weather condition to change to harsh sunlight, the harsh sunlight will last 8 turns instead of 5.	Get from a gentleman in a house in Hammerlocke
Heavy-Duty Boots	A nonconsumable item. If held by a Pokémon, this item will protect the holder from the effects of Spikes, Stealth Rock, Sticky Web, and Toxic Spikes.	Find in Galar Mine
Icy Rock	A nonconsumable item. If a Pokémon holding this item causes the weather condition to change to hail, the hail will last 8 turns instead of 5.	Get from a gentleman in a house in Hammerlocke
Iron Ball	A nonconsumable item. If held by a Pokémon, this item will reduce the holder's Speed stat by 50%. If the holder is a Flying-type Pokémon or has the Levitate Ability, it will also lose its immunity to Ground-type moves.	Get from the Digging Duo in the Wild Area
King's Rock	A nonconsumable item. If held by a Pokémon, the holder may cause targets to flinch when dealing damage.	Find on Route 8 / Sometimes held by wild Hawlucha
Lagging Tail	A nonconsumable item. If held by a Pokémon, this item will cause the holder to move later.	Get from the Digging Duo in the Wild Area / Sometimes held by wild Cufant and Copperajah
Lax Incense	A nonconsumable item. If held by a Pokémon, this item will boost the holder's evasiveness. It can also be used to help find Pokémon Eggs that hatch into certain species.	Buy from the Incense Merchant in Hulbury
Leek	A nonconsumable item. If held by a Farfetch'd, this item will make the Farfetch'd much more likely to deliver critical hits.	Sometimes held by wild Farfetch'd
Leftovers	A nonconsumable item. If held by a Pokémon, this item will restore 1/16 of the holder's max HP each turn.	Find at the Giant's Seat in the Wild Area / Get from a Berry tree in the Wild Area
Life Orb	A nonconsumable item. If held by a Pokémon, the holder will lose HP each time it attacks, but the power of its moves will be boosted by 30%.	Find in the Slumbering Weald
Light Ball	A nonconsumable item. If held by a Pikachu, this item will double the Pikachu's Attack and Sp. Atk.	Sometimes held by wild Pikachu
Light Clay	A nonconsumable item. If held by a Pokémon, this item will extend the duration of the moves Aurora Veil, Light Screen, and Reflect by 3 turns.	Find on Route 6
Luck Incense	A nonconsumable item. If a Pokémon holding it appears in battle, this item will double the prize money received from that battle.	Buy from the Incense Merchant in Hulbury
Lucky Egg	A nonconsumable item. If held by a Pokémon, the holder will gain 50% more Exp. Points from battle.	Get from a chef by helping him in Hulbury
Luminous Moss	A consumable item. If held by a Pokémon, this item will raise the holder's Sp. Def by 1 stage if it is hit with a damage-dealing Water-type move.	Find in Glimwood Tangle
Macho Brace	A nonconsumable item. If held by a Pokémon, this item will halve the holder's Speed but increase the rate at which it gains base points.	Get from the BP Shop in Hammerlocke's central Pokémon Center
Magnet	A nonconsumable item. If held by a Pokémon, this item will boost the power of the holder's Electric-type moves by 20%.	Find in Hulbury

Name	Description	Main way to obtain
Max Repel	A consumable item. If you use it, this item will prevent you from encountering lower-level Pokémon in the wild. The effect lasts longer than a Super Repel.	Buy at any Poké Mart once you have 7 Gym Badges
Mental Herb	A consumable item. If held by a Pokémon, the holder will instantly shake off the effects of Attract, Disable, Encore, Taunt, and Torment, as well as Abilities that inflict similar effects.	Find in the Slumbering Weald
Metal Coat	An item with different uses. If held by a Pokémon, this item will boost the power of the holder's Steel-type moves by 20%.	Find as a hidden item in Stow-on-Side
Metal Powder	A nonconsumable item. If held by a Ditto, this item will double the Ditto's Defense.	Sometimes held by wild Ditto
Metronome	A nonconsumable item. If held by a Pokémon, this item will boost the power of a move used consecutively by the holder. The power increases with each use until it reaches the max of 200%.	Buy at the bargain stall in Stow-on-Side
Miracle Seed	A nonconsumable item. If held by a Pokémon, this item will boost the power of the holder's Grass-type moves by 20%.	Receive from Leon in Motostoke if you chose Grookey / Buy at the bargain stall in Stow-on-Side
Misty Seed	A consumable item. If held by a Pokémon, this item will boost the holder's Sp. Def by 1 stage on Misty Terrain.	Find in the Slumbering Weald
Muscle Band	A nonconsumable item. If held by a Pokémon, this item will boost the power of the holder's physical moves by 10%.	Find in Hammerlocke
Mystic Water	A nonconsumable item. If held by a Pokémon, this item will boost the power of the holder's Water-type moves by 20%.	Receive from Leon in Motostoke if you chose Sobble / Buy at the bargain stall in Stow-on-Side
Never-Melt Ice	A nonconsumable item. If held by a Pokémon, this item will boost the power of the holder's Ice-type moves by 20%.	Find as a hidden item on Route 9 (Circhester Bay)
Normal Gem	A consumable item. If held by a Pokémon, this item will boost the power of a Normal-type move used by the holder by 30%.	Find as a hidden item on Route 9 (Circhester Bay)
Odd Incense	A nonconsumable item. If held by a Pokémon, this item will boost the power of the holder's Psychic-type moves by 20%. It can also be used to help find Pokémon Eggs that hatch into certain species.	Buy from the Incense Merchant in Hulbury
Poison Barb	A nonconsumable item. If held by a Pokémon, this item will boost the power of the holder's Poison-type moves by 20%.	Buy at the bargain stall in Stow-on-Side
Power Anklet	A nonconsumable item. If held by a Pokémon, this item will halve the holder's Speed but increase the rate at which it gains base points for its Speed stat.	Get from the BP Shop in Hammerlocke's central Pokémon Center
Power Band	A nonconsumable item. If held by a Pokémon, this item will halve the holder's Speed but increase the rate at which it gains base points for its Sp. Def stat.	Get from the BP Shop in Hammerlocke's central Pokémon Center
Power Belt	A nonconsumable item. If held by a Pokémon, this item will halve the holder's Speed but increase the rate at which it gains base points for its Defense stat.	Get from the BP Shop in Hammerlocke's central Pokémon Center
Power Bracer	A nonconsumable item. If held by a Pokémon, this item will halve the holder's Speed but increase the rate at which it gains base points for its Attack stat.	Get from the BP Shop in Hammerlocke's central Pokémon Center
Power Herb	A consumable item. If held by a Pokémon, the holder will be able to immediately use a move that would normally require one turn to charge.	Get from the right-hand clerk at the Battle Tower's BP Shop after becoming Champion
Power Lens	A nonconsumable item. If held by a Pokémon, this item will halve the holder's Speed but increase the rate at which it gains base points for its Sp. Atk stat.	Get from the BP Shop in Hammerlocke's central Pokémon Center
Power Weight	A nonconsumable item. If held by a Pokémon, this item will halve the holder's Speed but increase the rate at which it gains base points for its HP stat.	Get from the BP Shop in Hammerlocke's central Pokémon Center
Protective Pads	A nonconsumable item. If held by a Pokémon, this item will protect the holder from effects caused by making direct contact with a target.	Buy at the bargain stall in Stow-on-Side
Psychic Seed	A consumable item. If held by a Pokémon, this item will boost the holder's Sp. Def by 1 stage on Psychic Terrain.	Find on Route 2
Pure Incense	A nonconsumable item. If held by the lead Pokémon in your party, this item will reduce wild Pokémon encounters.	Buy from the Incense Merchant in Hulbury
Quick Claw	A nonconsumable item. If held by a Pokémon, this item will occasionally allow the holder to strike with high priority.	Buy at the bargain stall in Stow-on-Side
Quick Powder	A nonconsumable item. If held by a Ditto, this item will double the Ditto's Speed.	Sometimes held by wild Ditto
Razor Claw	An item with different uses. If held by a Pokémon, the holder will become much more likely to deliver critical hits.	Find as a hidden item in the Dusty Bowl in the Wild Area
Red Card	A consumable item. If held by a Pokémon, any other Pokémon that hits the holder with a damage-dealing move will be forced to switch out.	Get from the right-hand clerk at the Battle Tower's BP Shop after becoming Champion
Repel	A consumable item. If you use it, this item will prevent you from encountering lower-level Pokémon in the wild.	Buy at any Poké Mart once you have 3 Gym Badges
Ring Target	A nonconsumable item. If held by a Pokémon, moves that would usually deal no damage to the holder due to type matchups will instead deal regular damage.	Buy at the bargain stall in Stow-on-Side
Rock Incense	A nonconsumable item. If held by a Pokémon, this item will boost the power of the holder's Rock-type moves by 20%. It can also be used to help find Pokémon Eggs that hatch into certain species.	Buy from the Incense Merchant in Hulbury
Rocky Helmet	A nonconsumable item. If held by a Pokémon, any other Pokémon that uses a move that makes direct contact with the holder will lose 1/6 of its max HP.	Find in Stow-on-Side
Room Service	A consumable item. If held by a Pokémon, this item will lower the holder's Speed by 1 stage if Trick Room is used.	Get from the right-hand clerk at the Battle Tower's BP Shop after becoming Champion
Rose Incense	A nonconsumable item. If held by a Pokémon, this item will boost the power of the holder's Grass-type moves by 20%. It can also be used to help find Pokémon Eggs that hatch into certain species.	Buy from the Incense Merchant in Hulbury
Safety Goggles	A nonconsumable item. If held by a Pokémon, the holder will be protected from weather-related damage, certain moves (Cotton Spore, Magic Powder, Poison Powder, Rage Powder, Sleep Powder, Spore, and Stun Spore), and from the Effect Spore Ability.	Find on Route 7
Scope Lens	A nonconsumable item. If held by a Pokémon, it becomes much more likely the holder will deliver critical hits.	Find on Route 9 (Outer Spikemuth)
Sea Incense	A nonconsumable item. If held by a Pokémon, this item will boost the power of the holder's Water-type moves by 20%. It can also be used to help find Pokémon Eggs that hatch into certain species.	Buy from the Incense Merchant in Hulbury
Sharp Beak	A nonconsumable item. If held by a Pokémon, this item will boost the power of the holder's Flying-type moves by 20%.	Find on Route 4
Shed Shell	A nonconsumable item. If held by a Pokémon, this item will allow the holder to switch out even when trapped by the effects of moves or Abilities.	Find on Route 5
Shell Bell	A nonconsumable item. If held by a Pokémon, this item will restore the holder's HP when it hits another Pokémon with a damage-dealing move. The holder will regain HP equal to 1/8 of the damage dealt.	Find in Hulbury

Name	Description	Main way to obtain
Silk Scarf	A nonconsumable item. If held by a Pokémon, this item will boost the power of the holder's Normal-type moves by 20%.	Find in Motostoke
Silver Powder	A nonconsumable item. If held by a Pokémon, this item will boost the power of the holder's Bug-type moves by 20%.	Find on Route 4
Smoke Ball	A nonconsumable item. If held by a Pokémon, this item will allow the holder to run away from wild Pokémon even when trapped by the effects of moves or Abilities.	Find in the Slumbering Weald
Smooth Rock	A nonconsumable item. If a Pokémon holding this item causes the weather condition to change to sandstorm, the sandstorm will last 8 turns instead of 5.	Get from a gentleman in a house in Hammerlocke
Snowball	A consumable item. If held by a Pokémon, this item will raise the holder's Attack by 1 stage if it is hit with a damage-dealing Ice-type move.	Find in Circhester
Soft Sand	A nonconsumable item. If held by a Pokémon, this item will boost the power of the holder's Ground-type moves by 20%.	Find as a hidden item in Galar Mine No. 2
Soothe Bell	A nonconsumable item. If held by a Pokémon, the holder will become friendly more quickly.	Get from a girl in a house in Motostoke
Spell Tag	A nonconsumable item. If held by a Pokémon, this item will boost the power of the holder's Ghost-type moves by 20%.	Buy at the bargain stall in Stow-on-Side
Sticky Barb	A nonconsumable item. If held by a Pokémon, this item will cause the holder to lose 1/8 of its max HP each turn. If another Pokémon uses a move that makes direct contact with the holder, this item will pass to the attacker.	Get from the Digging Duo in the Wild Area
Super Repel	A consumable item. If you use it, this item will prevent you from encountering lower-level Pokémon in the wild. The effect lasts longer than a basic Repel.	Buy at any Poké Mart once you have 5 Gym Badges
Terrain Extender	A nonconsumable item. If held by a Pokémon, any terrain triggered by the holder's moves or Ability will last 8 turns instead of 5.	Find on Route 8
Throat Spray	A consumable item. If held by a Pokémon, this item will raise the holder's Sp. Atk by 1 stage if it uses a sound-based move in battle.	Get from a boy by finding his Minccino in Motostoke
Toxic Orb	A nonconsumable item. If held by a Pokémon, this item will inflict the badly poisoned status condition on the holder during battle.	Get as a reward in a Champion tournament after becoming Champion
Twisted Spoon	A nonconsumable item. If held by a Pokémon, this item will boost the power of the holder's Psychic-type moves by 20%.	Buy at the bargain stall in Stow-on-Side
Utility Umbrella	A nonconsumable item. If held by a Pokémon, this item will negate the effects of both the rain and harsh sunlight weather conditions.	Get from a gentleman in a house in Hammerlocke
Wave Incense	A nonconsumable item. If held by a Pokémon, this item will boost the power of the holder's Water-type moves by 20%. It can also be used to help find Pokémon Eggs that hatch into certain species.	Buy from the Incense Merchant in Hulbury
Weakness Policy	A consumable item. If held by a Pokémon, this item will increase the holder's Attack and Sp. Atk by 2 stages each if the holder is hit with a supereffective move.	Get from the right-hand clerk at the Battle Tower's BP Shop after becoming Champion
White Herb	A consumable item. If held by a Pokémon, this item will restore any lowered stats one time.	Find at the Watchtower Ruins in the Wild Area
Wide Lens	A nonconsumable item. If held by a Pokémon, this item will boost the holder's accuracy by 10%.	Get from Howses by solving a mystery in Circhester's Hotel Ionia
Wise Glasses	A nonconsumable item. If held by a Pokémon, this item will boost the power of the holder's special moves by 10%.	Find in Hammerlocke
Wishing Piece	A consumable item. If you use one at a Pokémon Den, it may attract a wild Dynamax Pokémon.	Get from a Rotom Rallyist in the Wild Area
Zoom Lens	A nonconsumable item. If held by a Pokémon, this item will boost the holder's accuracy by 20% if its targets have already moved that turn.	Find on Route 9 (Circhester Bay)

Items that can be used to help find particular kinds of Pokémon Eggs

Name	Description	Main way to obtain
Destiny Knot	A nonconsumable item. It can be used to help ensure that Pokémon Eggs you find inherit five individual strengths from the Pokémon you leave at the Nursery.	Get from the BP Shop in Hammerlocke's central Pokémon Center
Everstone	A nonconsumable item. It can be used to help ensure that Pokémon Eggs you find inherit regional forms or Natures from the Pokémon you leave at the Nursery.	Find as a hidden item in Turffield
Full Incense	A nonconsumable item. It can be used to help you find a Pokémon Egg that will hatch into a Munchlax.	Buy from the Incense Merchant in Hulbury
Lax Incense	A nonconsumable item. It can be used to help you find a Pokémon Egg that will hatch into a Wynaut.	Buy from the Incense Merchant in Hulbury
Light Ball	A nonconsumable item. It can be used to help you find a Pokémon Egg that will hatch into a Pichu that knows the move Volt Tackle.	Sometimes held by wild Pikachu
Odd Incense	A nonconsumable item. It can be used to help you find a Pokémon Egg that will hatch into a Mime Jr.	Buy from the Incense Merchant in Hulbury
Power Anklet	A nonconsumable item. It can be used to help ensure that Pokémon Eggs you find inherit the Speed individual strength from the Pokémon you leave at the Nursery.	Get from the BP Shop in Hammerlocke's central Pokémon Center
Power Band	A nonconsumable item. It can be used to help ensure that Pokémon Eggs you find inherit the Sp. Def individual strength from the Pokémon you leave at the Nursery.	Get from the BP Shop in Hammerlocke's central Pokémon Center
Power Belt	A nonconsumable item. It can be used to help ensure that Pokémon Eggs you find inherit the Defense individual strength from the Pokémon you leave at the Nursery.	Get from the BP Shop in Hammerlocke's central Pokémon Center
Power Bracer	A nonconsumable item. It can be used to help ensure that Pokémon Eggs you find inherit the Attack individual strength from the Pokémon you leave at the Nursery.	Get from the BP Shop in Hammerlocke's central Pokémon Center
Power Lens	A nonconsumable item. It can be used to help ensure that Pokémon Eggs you find inherit the Sp. Atk individual strength from the Pokémon you leave at the Nursery.	Get from the BP Shop in Hammerlocke's central Pokémon Center
Power Weight	A nonconsumable item. It can be used to help ensure that Pokémon Eggs you find inherit the HP individual strength from the Pokémon you leave at the Nursery.	Get from the BP Shop in Hammerlocke's central Pokémon Center
Rock Incense	A nonconsumable item. It can be used to help you find a Pokémon Egg that will hatch into a Bonsly.	Buy from the Incense Merchant in Hulbury
Rose Incense	A nonconsumable item. It can be used to help you find a Pokémon Egg that will hatch into a Budew.	Buy from the Incense Merchant in Hulbury
Wave Incense	A nonconsumable item. It can be used to help you find a Pokémon Egg that will hatch into a Mantyke.	Buy from the Incense Merchant in Hulbury

Treasures

Name	Description	Main way to obtain
Balm Mushroom	A fragrant mushroom. It can be sold at shops for profit.	Find as a hidden item near trees in the Wild Area
Big Mushroom	A big mushroom. It can be sold at shops for profit.	Find as a hidden item near trees in the Wild Area
Big Nugget	A big nugget of pure gold. It can be sold at shops for profit.	Find on Route 8 or in Wyndon
Big Pearl	A big pearl. It can be sold at shops for profit.	Find as a hidden item near or on the lakes in the Wild Area
Bottle Cap	A beautiful bottle cap that gives off a silver gleam. Use one to have a Lv. 100 Pokémon train up one stat via Hyper Training.	Get from the right-hand clerk at the Battle Tower's BP Shop after becoming Champion
Comet Shard	A shard that fell to the ground when a comet passed by. It can be sold at shops for profit.	Find as a hidden item in the North Wild Area
Fossilized Bird	The fossil of an ancient Pokémon that once soared through the sky. It can be restored, together with another fossil, to obtain certain Pokémon.	Find as a hidden item in the Dusty Bowl in the Wild Area ⬆ / Get from the Digging Duo in the Wild Area
Fossilized Dino	The fossil of an ancient Pokémon that once lived in the sea. It can be restored, together with another fossil, to obtain certain Pokémon.	Find as a hidden item in the Dusty Bowl in the Wild Area ⬆ / Get from the Digging Duo in the Wild Area
Fossilized Drake	The fossil of an ancient Pokémon that once roamed the land. It can be restored, together with another fossil, to obtain certain Pokémon.	Find as a hidden item in the Dusty Bowl in the Wild Area ● / Get from the Digging Duo in the Wild Area
Fossilized Fish	The fossil of an ancient Pokémon that once lived in the sea. It can be restored, together with another fossil, to obtain certain Pokémon.	Find as a hidden item in the Dusty Bowl in the Wild Area ● / Get from the Digging Duo in the Wild Area
Gold Bottle Cap	A beautiful bottle cap that gives off a golden gleam. Use one to have a Lv. 100 Pokémon train up all six stats via Hyper Training.	Receive as a prize at the Battle Tower
Honey	A sweet honey collected by wild Pokémon. It can be sold at shops for profit.	Find as a hidden item in flower patches in the Wild Area
Nugget	A nugget of pure gold. It can be sold at shops for profit.	Find as a hidden item in Motostoke, Hammerlocke, or elsewhere
Pearl	A pretty pearl. It can be sold at shops for profit.	Find as a hidden item near or on the lakes in the Wild Area
Pearl String	A string of large pearls with a silvery sheen. It can be sold at shops for profit.	Find as a hidden item near or on the lakes in the Wild Area
Pretty Feather	A beautiful feather. It can be sold at shops for profit.	Find as a hidden item on the bridge on Route 5 or the bridge in the Motostoke Outskirts
Rare Bone	A rare bone. It can be sold at shops for profit.	Find as a hidden item in the Dusty Bowl or at the Giant's Mirror in the Wild Area
Star Piece	A sparkling red gem. It can be sold at shops for profit.	Find as a hidden item in the North Wild Area
Stardust	Lovely, red-colored sand. It can be sold at shops for profit.	Find as a hidden item in the North Wild Area
Tiny Mushroom	A tiny mushroom. It can be sold at shops for profit.	Find as a hidden item near trees in the Wild Area

Key Items

Name	Description	Main way to obtain
Adventure Guide	A device that automatically collects and records advice during your adventure.	You'll obtain it automatically during your main adventure
Camping Gear	A set of camping gear, including the equipment you need to cook at camp.	You'll obtain it automatically during your main adventure
Catching Charm	A curious charm said to increase the likelihood of catching Pokémon as a critical catch in the wild. Simply possessing one awards a Trainer with its effects.	Get from the game director in Circhester's Hotel Ionia
Dynamax Band	A wristband that allows a Trainer to Dynamax their Pokémon at a Power Spot.	You'll obtain it automatically during your main adventure
Endorsement	A letter you need in order to participate in the Gym Challenge.	You'll obtain it automatically during your main adventure
Escape Rope	A rope that can be used over and over to help you escape from locations like caves or dungeons.	You'll obtain it automatically during your main adventure
Fishing Rod	A fishing rod that allows you to fish up Pokémon living in the water.	You'll obtain it automatically during your main adventure
Hi-tech Earbuds	Strange earbuds that allow you to adjust the volume of various sounds in the Options.	Talk to a man on the street near the eastern record shop in Motostoke
Oval Charm	An oval charm said to increase the chance of Pokémon Eggs being found at the Nursery. Simply possessing one awards a Trainer with its effects.	Get from Morimoto if you defeat him in a battle at Circhester's Hotel Ionia after becoming Champion
Pokémon Box Link	A device that allows you to access your Boxes in the Pokémon storage system even when you're out and about.	You'll obtain it automatically during your main adventure
Rotom Bike	A bike that has been powered up by the Pokémon Rotom. With the right parts, it can run over water as well as on land.	You'll obtain it automatically during your main adventure
Rotom Catalog	A catalog of devices that Rotom like. It can be used to have a Rotom change form.	Get from a Rotom user in Wyndon
Shiny Charm	A shiny charm said to increase the chances of encountering Shiny Pokémon in the wild. Simply possessing one awards a Trainer with its effects.	Get from the game director in Circhester's Hotel Ionia if you complete your Pokédex
Sonia's Book	Professor Sonia's published writings about the Galar region's legends.	Meet Sonia in the Slumbering Weald after becoming Champion
Wishing Star	A stone with a mysterious power. It's said your dreams come true if you find one.	You'll obtain it automatically during your main adventure

Shop Lists

There are many shops to visit around the Galar region, which means plenty of different shopping destinations to keep straight. If you're looking for a particular item, use the tables below to help track down where you can buy it!

> **!**
>
> Don't forget to check out these other shops and ways to obtain items in the Galar region!
>
> - Rotom Rallyists around the Wild Area who also serve as Watt Traders
> - The Ingredients Sellers in the Wild Area, along with their daily lineup of ingredients
> - The Digging Duo who may dig up some finds for you in the Wild Area
> - The various Trainers wandering about the Wild Area who may offer you their finds for Watts
> - The fellow selling bargains at the Street Market in Stow-on-Side
> - Boutiques in Wedgehurst, Motostoke, Hammerlocke, Circhester, and Wyndon, as well as uniform shops in most stadiums!

Poké Mart	
Items that are always available	
From the start	
Antidote	₽200
Awakening	₽200
Burn Heal	₽200
Ice Heal	₽200
Paralyze Heal	₽200
Poké Ball*	₽200
Potion	₽200
Revive	₽2,000
After earning 1 Gym Badge	
Great Ball	₽600
Super Potion	₽700
After earning 2 Gym Badges	
Poké Doll	₽300
After earning 3 Gym Badges	
Repel	₽400
After earning 4 Gym Badges	
Hyper Potion	₽1,500
After earning 5 Gym Badges	
Super Repel	₽700
Ultra Ball	₽800
After earning 6 Gym Badges	
Full Heal	₽400
After earning 7 Gym Badges	
Max Potion	₽2,500
Max Repel	₽900
After earning 8 Gym Badges	
Full Restore	₽3,000

*Poké Balls become available after you meet Leon on Route 2.

Poké Mart	
Specialty offerings	
Motostoke (lower level)	
Heal Ball	₽300
Nest Ball	₽1,000
Net Ball	₽1,000
X Attack	₽1,000
X Defense	₽2,000
X Sp. Atk	₽1,000
X Sp. Def	₽2,000
Motostoke (upper level)	
TM17 Light Screen	₽10,000
TM18 Reflect	₽10,000
TM19 Safeguard	₽10,000
TM25 Protect	₽10,000
TM41 Helping Hand	₽10,000
TM76 Round	₽10,000
TM94 False Swipe	₽10,000
Hammerlocke (west)	
TM13 Fire Spin	₽10,000
TM23 Thief	₽10,000
TM32 Sandstorm	₽10,000
TM33 Rain Dance	₽10,000
TM34 Sunny Day	₽10,000
TM35 Hail	₽10,000
TM50 Bullet Seed	₽10,000
TM55 Brine	₽10,000
Hammerlocke (central)	
Dire Hit	₽1,000
Dive Ball	₽1,000
Dusk Ball	₽1,000
Guard Spec.	₽1,500
Timer Ball	₽1,000
X Accuracy	₽1,000
X Speed	₽1,000

Poké Mart	
Hammerlocke (east)	
TM00 Mega Punch	₽10,000
TM01 Mega Kick	₽40,000
TM46 Weather Ball	₽30,000
TM66 Thunder Fang	₽30,000
TM67 Ice Fang	₽30,000
TM68 Fire Fang	₽30,000
TM88 Grassy Terrain	₽20,000
TM89 Misty Terrain	₽20,000
TM90 Electric Terrain	₽20,000
TM91 Psychic Terrain	₽20,000
Wyndon (south)	
Calcium	₽10,000
Carbos	₽10,000
HP Up	₽10,000
Iron	₽10,000
Luxury Ball	₽3,000
Protein	₽10,000
Quick Ball	₽1,000
Repeat Ball	₽1,000
Zinc	₽10,000
Wyndon (stadium front)	
TM03 Fire Punch	₽50,000
TM04 Ice Punch	₽50,000
TM05 Thunder Punch	₽50,000
TM08 Hyper Beam	₽50,000
TM09 Giga Impact	₽50,000
TM12 Solar Blade	₽50,000
TM60 Power Swap	₽30,000
TM61 Guard Swap	₽30,000
TM62 Speed Swap	₽30,000
TM63 Drain Punch	₽50,000

BP Shops

Hammerlocke (central Pokémon Center)

Calcium	2 BP
Carbos	2 BP
Destiny Knot	10 BP
HP Up	2 BP
Iron	2 BP
Macho Brace	10 BP
Power Anklet	10 BP
Power Band	10 BP
Power Belt	10 BP
Power Bracer	10 BP
Power Lens	10 BP
Power Weight	10 BP
PP Up	10 BP
Protector	10 BP
Protein	2 BP
Rare Candy	20 BP
Razor Claw	10 BP
Reaper Cloth	10 BP
Sachet	10 BP
Whipped Dream	10 BP
Zinc	2 BP

Battle Tower counter (left)

Adamant Mint	50 BP
Bold Mint	50 BP
Brave Mint	50 BP
Calm Mint	50 BP
Careful Mint	50 BP
Gentle Mint	50 BP
Hasty Mint	50 BP
Impish Mint	50 BP
Jolly Mint	50 BP
Lax Mint	50 BP
Lonely Mint	50 BP
Mild Mint	50 BP
Modest Mint	50 BP
Naive Mint	50 BP
Naughty Mint	50 BP
Quiet Mint	50 BP
Rash Mint	50 BP
Relaxed Mint	50 BP
Sassy Mint	50 BP
Serious Mint	50 BP
Timid Mint	50 BP

BP Shops

Battle Tower counter (right)

Ability Capsule	50 BP
Absorb Bulb	10 BP
Adrenaline Orb	10 BP
Air Balloon	15 BP
Assault Vest	25 BP
Blunder Policy	20 BP
Bottle Cap	25 BP
Cell Battery	10 BP
Choice Band	25 BP
Choice Scarf	25 BP
Choice Specs	25 BP
Eject Button	20 BP
Eject Pack	20 BP
Focus Sash	15 BP
Life Orb	25 BP
Light Clay	15 BP
Luminous Moss	10 BP
Mental Herb	15 BP
Power Herb	15 BP
Red Card	20 BP
Room Service	15 BP
Snowball	10 BP
Terrain Extender	15 BP
Throat Spray	10 BP
Weakness Policy	20 BP
White Herb	15 BP

Other Shops

Wedgehurst Berry Grocer

Cheri Berry	₽80
Oran Berry	₽80
Pecha Berry	₽80

Hulbury Incense Merchant

Full Incense	₽5,000
Lax Incense	₽5,000
Luck Incense	₽11,000
Odd Incense	₽2,000
Pure Incense	₽6,000
Rock Incense	₽2,000
Rose Incense	₽2,000
Sea Incense	₽2,000
Wave Incense	₽2,000

Hulbury Herb Shop

Energy Powder	₽500
Energy Root	₽1,200
Heal Powder	₽300
Revival Herb	₽2,800

Battle Tower TM seller

TM20 Self-Destruct	₽100,000
TM28 Giga Drain	₽100,000
TM44 Imprison	₽100,000
TM52 Bounce	₽100,000
TM59 Fling	₽100,000
TM70 Trick Room	₽50,000
TM71 Wonder Room	₽50,000
TM72 Magic Room	₽50,000
TM83 Razor Shell	₽100,000
TM92 Mystical Fire	₽100,000

Vending Machines

Found in train stations

Fresh Water	₽200
Lemonade	₽350
Soda Pop	₽300

Type Matchup Chart

Remember that all Pokémon—and their moves—have types. Each type has its own strengths and weaknesses, as well as types it will simply deal regular damage to. Damage will be calculated using the Pokémon's stats and the move's power, plus any multiplier caused by the type matchups.

You'll quickly notice that some Pokémon have two types. If a Pokémon has two types, the strengths and weaknesses of the types are both taken into account. They might multiply the damage the Pokémon takes, or they might cancel each other out.

Type	Effect
NORMAL	• Immune to damage-dealing Ghost-type moves.
FIRE	• Cannot be burned.
GRASS	• Immune to Leech Seed. • Immune to powder and spore moves.
ELECTRIC	• Cannot be paralyzed.
ICE	• Cannot be frozen. • Take no damage from hail. • Immune to Sheer Cold.
POISON	• Cannot be poisoned or badly poisoned.* • Nullify Toxic Spikes on their side of the battlefield so no other Pokémon will be poisoned when switching in. (If the Poison-type Pokémon is also a Flying type, has the Levitate Ability, or holds an Air Balloon, this nullifying effect will not occur.)
GROUND	• Immune to Electric-type moves (including nondamaging moves, such as Thunder Wave). • Take no damage from sandstorms.
FLYING	• Immune to Ground-type moves (including nondamaging moves, such as Sand Attack).* • Cannot be damaged or otherwise affected by the effects of moves like Spikes or Sticky Web when switching in.* • Not affected by any terrains.*
ROCK	• Take no damage from sandstorms. • Sp. Def goes up in a sandstorm.
GHOST	• Immune to Fighting-type moves (including nondamaging moves, such as Octolock) and damage-dealing Normal-type moves.* • Cannot be prevented from fleeing or switching out of battle.
DARK	• Immune to damage-dealing Psychic-type moves. • Immune to the effects of status moves used by Pokémon with the Prankster Ability.
STEEL	• Immune to damage-dealing Poison-type moves. • Cannot be poisoned or badly poisoned.* • Take no damage from sandstorms.
FAIRY	• Immune to damage-dealing Dragon-type moves.

Defending Pokémon's Type

Attacking Pokémon's Move Type

	NORMAL	FIRE	WATER	GRASS	ELECTRIC	ICE	FIGHTING	POISON	GROUND	FLYING	PSYCHIC	BUG	ROCK	GHOST	DRAGON	DARK	STEEL	FAIRY
NORMAL													△	×			△	
FIRE		△	△	◎		◎						◎	△		△		◎	
WATER		◎	△	△					◎				◎		△			
GRASS		△	◎	△				△	◎	△		△	◎		△		△	
ELECTRIC			◎	△	△				×	◎					△			
ICE		△	△	◎		△			◎	◎					◎		△	
FIGHTING	◎					◎		△		△	△	△	◎	×		◎	◎	△
POISON				◎				△	△				△	△			×	◎
GROUND		◎		△	◎			◎		×		△	◎				◎	
FLYING				◎	△		◎					◎	△				△	
PSYCHIC							◎	◎			△					×	△	
BUG		△		◎			△	△		△	◎			△		◎	△	△
ROCK		◎				◎	△		△	◎		◎					△	
GHOST	×										◎			◎		△		
DRAGON															◎		△	×
DARK							△				◎			◎		△		△
STEEL		△	△		△	◎							◎				△	◎
FAIRY		△					◎	△							◎	◎	△	

⊙ NORMAL	⌀ FLYING
⌀ FIRE	⌀ PSYCHIC
⌀ WATER	⌀ BUG
⌀ GRASS	⌀ ROCK
⌀ ELECTRIC	⌀ GHOST
⌀ ICE	⌀ DRAGON
⌀ FIGHTING	⌀ DARK
⌀ POISON	⌀ STEEL
⌀ GROUND	⌀ FAIRY

Key

Super effective
Moves will do 2× damage. ◎

No weakness or resistance
Moves will do the regular amount of damage. No icon

Not very effective
Moves will do ½ damage. △

No effect
Moves will do no damage. ✕

*Some immunities can be negated by moves, Abilities, or items. For example, the Corrosion Ability allows even Poison- or Steel-type Pokémon to be poisoned. Likewise, moves like Smack Down cause Flying-type Pokémon to be grounded, taking away their immunity to Ground-type moves.

Credits

Content & Writing
Jillian Nonaka
Sayuri Munday
Jordan Blanco
Shawn Williams-Brown

Editing Lead
Rei Nakazawa

Editing Support
Kellyn Ballard
Julia Ryer

Additional Research & Fact Checking
Bryson Clark
Isaac Nickerson
Stephan Kim
Irene Mascaró Genestar
Matthieu Béthencourt

Screenshots
Jeff Hines
Robert Colling
Marvin Andrews
Peter Bagley
Steve Stratton (AltaSource Group)

Design Direction & Management
Chris Franc
Kevin Lalli

Lead Designers
Hiromi Kimura
Elisabeth Lariviere
Mark Pedini

Design Support
Justin Gonyea
Dan Stephens

Project Management
Terry Mihashi
Yohei Sugiyama
Hannah Vassallo

Acknowledgments
Heather Dalgleish
Debra Kempker (Piggyback)
Anja Weinbach
Mikiko Ryu
Blaise Selby
Hisato Yamamori
Mayu Todo
Elena Nardo
Kaori Aoki
Bertrand Lecocq
Cyril Schultz
Diego Figaredo
Owen Preece
Pierre Gauthier
Daniel Anscomb

Special Thanks
GAME FREAK inc.
The Pokémon Company

POKÉMON SWORD & POKÉMON SHIELD
THE OFFICIAL GALAR REGION POKÉDEX

©2019 The Pokémon Company International

ISBN: 978-1-6043820-51
Published in the United States by

The Pokémon Company International
10400 NE 4th Street, Suite 2800
Bellevue, WA 98004 USA

3rd Floor Building 10, Chiswick Park
566 Chiswick High Road
London, W4 5XS United Kingdom

Printed in the United States of America.

The Pokémon Company
INTERNATIONAL